Crosscurrents *of* Children's Literature

Crosscurrents *of* Children's Literature

AN ANTHOLOGY OF TEXTS AND CRITICISM

J. D. Stahl
Virginia Tech

Tina L. Hanlon
Ferrum College

Elizabeth Lennox Keyser
Hollins University

New York   Oxford
OXFORD UNIVERSITY PRESS
2007

Oxford University Press, Inc., publishes works that further Oxford University's
objective of excellence in research, scholarship, and education.

Oxford   New York
Auckland   Cape Town   Dar es Salaam   Hong Kong   Karachi
Kuala Lumpur   Madrid   Melbourne   Mexico City   Nairobi
New Delhi   Shanghai   Taipei   Toronto

With offices in
Argentina   Austria   Brazil   Chile   Czech Republic   France   Greece
Guatemala   Hungary   Italy   Japan   Poland   Portugal   Singapore
South Korea   Switzerland   Thailand   Turkey   Ukraine   Vietnam

Copyright © 2007 by Oxford University Press, Inc.

Published by Oxford University Press, Inc.
198 Madison Avenue, New York 10016
http://www.oup.com

Oxford is a registered trademark of Oxford University Press

Library of Congress Cataloging-in-Publication Data

Crosscurrents of children's literature : an anthology of texts and criticism / [edited by] J. D. Stahl, Tina L. Hanlon,
Elizabeth Lennox Keyser.
   p. cm.
   This volume combines a wide variety of primary texts with critical readings, examines the texts within the context
of critical debates, explores the ways in which children's literature combines instruction and entertainment, oral and
written traditions, words and pictures, fantasy and realism, classics and adaptations, and perspectives on childhood
and adult life. It spans a wide range of literary periods, genres, and cultural traditions, and examines how these
overlapping forms and genres, diverse influences, and evolving values and attitudes towards children and childhood
have shaped the body of literature written for young adults and children.
   Includes bibliographical references and index.
   ISBN-13: 978-0-19-513493-3 (pbk. : acid-free paper)
                      1. Children's literature, English. 2. Children's literature,
American. 3. Children's literature. 4. Children's literature, English—History and criticism. 5. Children's literature,
American—History and criticism. 6. Children's literature—History and criticism. 7. Children—Books and reading. I.
Stahl, J. D. (John Daniel) II. Hanlon, Tina L. III. Keyser, Elizabeth Lennox, 1942–
   PR1111.C52C76 2007

                            2006024446

Printed in the United States of America
on acid-free paper

For Sarah, Daniel, and Hans
—J.D.S.

For my colleagues at Ferrum College and Hollins University
—T.L.H.

For our graduate students at Hollins University
—E.L.K.

CONTENTS

PART 2   SUBJECTION OF THE CHILD OR SUBVERSION OF ADULT AUTHORITY?   127

PART 3   ORAL AND WRITTEN LITERARY TRADITIONS   209

PART 4 REALISM AND FANTASY   411

PART 5 BOYS' BOOKS AND GIRLS' BOOKS: GENDER ISSUES

PART 7   SATIRES AND SPIN-OFFS: REWORKING CLASSIC CHILDREN'S LITERATURE   767

PART 8   VALUES AND CENSORSHIP   853

ALTERNATE TABLE OF CONTENTS BY GENRE

CRITICISM

DRAMA

FICTION

ILLUSTRATIONS

Nonfiction

Poetry

TALES FROM THE ORAL TRADITION

PREFACE

Each era has produced what can be described as a public literature for its children;
that is, a model of what society desired for them. . . . This literature came in horizontal waves from 1700 to 1900, but always cutting across it vertically was the literature of delight, the literature of mankind.

Sheila Egoff

Our epigraph from Sheila Egoff's essay "Precepts, Pleasures, and Portents," first published in
1980 and reprinted as the second selection in Part 1, suggests our aspirations for this volume.
We have certainly wanted to give readers a sense of the historical development of children's literature, including the "public" or edifying texts that each era has produced, following these horizontal waves into the twenty-first century. We have also wanted to introduce readers to the various genres of children's literature, some of which, like fantasy, have been associated with
Egoff's vertical dimension of pleasure and delight. This book is different from other textbooks
on children's literature, however, in that the crosscurrents of literary history and genre are presented in relation to critical debates that distinguish the modern study of children's literature.
We want to convey the complexities of our subject and to encourage readers to challenge common assumptions about childhood, children, and the books that are produced for them. One
such assumption is that didactic or "public" literature prevailed until the middle of the nineteenth century, at which point the Victorians ushered in a Golden Age of sumptuous stories and
illustrations, an emphasis on enjoyment that has dominated the publishing industry, especially
in books for younger children, right into the twenty-first century.

But Egoff's word *always* anticipates our view, and that of a growing number of children's literature teachers and scholars, that the public and private, the socializing and the entertaining,
currents of children's literature have intermingled from its inception. Perhaps even more important, Egoff equates the "literature of delight" for children with the "literature of mankind,"
or, as we would probably phrase it now, the "literature of humanity." She could, of course, be re-
iterating the timeworn association of children with the childhood of the human race, but we prefer to believe that she is instead complicating a central issue of children's literature—just what
it is and how it differs, if it does at all, from literature for men and women. Has not literature
for children, like the larger history of literature for adults, always blended "instruction and
delight"?

To accomplish our various purposes (perhaps even cross-purposes) in this textbook, we have designed it to resemble Egoff's conception of children's literature. In other words, the selections, many of which have played a crucial role in the chronological development of children's literature, are arranged in thematic sections (Parts 1–8) that contain several critical essays about a particular topic, question, problem, or issue. As the Table of Contents reveals, most of these topics are phrased as dichotomies or seeming opposites, such as oral and written literature, realism and fantasy, words and pictures. There are few sharp contrasts within these topics, however, since most of them involve many complex crosscurrents of overlapping forms, evolving traditions, and diverse influences. Much of the magic of children's literature lies in the various ways it combines oral and written traditions, words and pictures, fantasy and realism, classics and adaptations, perspectives on childhood and adult life. Moreover, there are many crosscurrents among the topics of the eight sections, and most of the reading selections have relevance to sections other than the one in which they appear.

Part 1 deals with the crosscurrents implied in our epigraph from Egoff: the impulse for adult writers to instruct, inform, or influence children and the often-contrary desire to amuse, entertain, or divert them. And we introduce the section with three essays (by C. S. Lewis, Egoff, and John Rowe Townsend) that clearly instruct or inform more than they amuse or entertain, although we hope that students will find them stimulating, rather than stuffy. The selections that follow (with the exception of Sarah Trimmer's diatribe on fairy tales, which, we trust, modern readers will find amusing) represent the shifting tides of children's literature from the cautionary tales of the eighteenth century to a mock cautionary tale of the late twentieth century (R. L. Stine's *Be Careful What You Wish For*).

Part 2 focuses on a related pair of ideas that we refer to as subjection of the child and subversion of adult authority. Do adult efforts, however well-meaning, to indoctrinate children rob them of a precious innocence and freedom, thereby actually corrupting them? Or does the very idea of childhood innocence, and the related notion that children have the power to regenerate adults or serve as models for them, do the young a disservice? Again, we begin with two essays (by Alison Lurie and Marina Warner) that explore these ideas and two short selections (by John Huddlestone Wynne and William Wordsworth) that epitomize them. The selections for children that follow, like many of those in Part 1, portray young people both succumbing to and defying or confounding adult authority. But, as our introductions to this and other sections suggest, children in the older selections are allowed a surprising degree of resilience and even defiance. Maria Edgeworth in "The Purple Jar," in Part 1, often cited as the quintessential didactic story, permits her heroine, Rosamond, what we today call agency; Rosamond has a distinctive voice and an irrepressible spirit. The heroines of several historical novels discussed in Part 2 resist, rail against, but ultimately cannot control their fates. As several essays in the 2002 volume of the annual *Children's Literature* imply, Victorian era authors, such as Nathaniel Hawthorne, whose retelling of the Pandora story is included in Part 1, frequently granted their child characters, as well as their child readers, more freedom vis-à-vis adults than so-called postmodern authors, such as Robert Cormier.

The critical essay by Nina Mikkelsen asks who can tell an authentic story about children within a specific culture or ethnic group. Is it legitimate for a non-Jewish German author to imagine what it was like to be a Jewish girl being deported to an extermination camp in World War II, as Gudrun Pausewang does in *The Final Journey?* Can a Norwegian author like Mette Newth, in *The Abduction*, accurately represent what it meant to be an Inuit girl of centuries ago, abducted, raped, and abused by her European captors? Can European Americans write authentically about African American experience? Although Mikkelsen explicitly addresses only the last question, her essay provides some general principles for arriving at answers that apply to the other questions as well.

Subsequent sections deal with more specific tensions or seeming polarities in different genres of children's literature. The final selection in Part 2, the contemporary Australian story "Up Taree Way," dramatizes the power of an aboriginal storyteller to transform the life of a young listener and thereby her mother. Part 3 then celebrates the power of traditional stories—myths, legends, folktales, fables, and ballads, as well as their more familiar descendants from the oral tradition—nursery rhymes and fairy tales. The significance of these traditional forms and their continuing evolution are discussed in essays by psychoanalyst Bruno Bettelheim, storyteller Anne Pellowski, and writers who combine, in various ways, the perspectives of folklorist, storyteller, literary scholar, and editor or creative writer (Kay F. Stone, Maria Tatar, John Langstaff, Diane Wolkstein, and Jane Yolen). Selections in this part illustrate many crosscurrents and overlappings in the forms of literature derived from the oral tradition, allowing for comparisons of regional traditions (with a number of selections from the southern Appalachian region of the United States) and international variations on universal themes. For example, the adventures of the mistreated or underestimated younger sibling who achieves heroic status in the end is represented in variations on the Cinderella story and related tales in this section and others. Part 3's selections also range across the oral-written spectrum, from transcribed oral rhymes and tales to literary creations by individual writers. Two contemporary adaptations of traditional tales, Jane Yolen's literary fairy tale "Dove Isabeau" and R. Rex Stephenson's story theater script "Mutsmag," are juxtaposed with antecedents of these same stories transcribed directly from the oral tradition. Of course, we encourage readers to listen to live storytellers and children or, at least, audio or video recordings of live performances for greater appreciation of past and present oral traditions.

In Part 4 the genres of realism and fantasy are defined by Elizabeth Segel and C. W. Sullivan III, respectively. But on reading the selections that follow, students will soon see that generic waters are rarely clear. Realistic novels, such as Katherine Paterson's *Bridge to Terabithia,* often pay homage to the power of fantasy, whereas many fantasies, such as Madeline L'Engle's *A Wrinkle in Time,* are solidly grounded in the real world of school and family life. Subcategories of fantasy, such as domestic fantasy, toy fantasy, time travel, and high fantasy, contain different combinations of realistic elements and the fantastic. The phenomenal popularity of J. K. Rowling's Harry Potter series can perhaps be ascribed to its blend of sorcery and a recognizable school setting in contemporary Britain. Highly popular fantasies also tend to incur the disapproval of some moralists and realists, a problem addressed in essays by Ursula K. Le Guin and Perry Nodelman. Selections throughout this volume occupy different positions along a continuum from fantasy to realistic fiction and nonfiction, as well as different approaches to the relationship between reality and fantasy. For example, at the end of Part 1, a short biography of Langston Hughes and the African American poems following it demonstrate the blend of personal and social history, memory, dreams, and imagination in the work of Hughes and several contemporary writers.

The Harry Potter series has also succeeded, as few books have done, in appealing equally to boys and girls (and perhaps to both children and adults). Part 5 opens with an essay that traces the history of how girls' books diverged from boys' books. A second essay presents the now-familiar view that one of the earliest genres of children's literature, the fairy tale, conditioned girl readers to accept a passive and submissive role. Selections from early realistic fiction, such as *Little Women* and *Tom Sawyer,* epitomize the constraints placed on middle-class girls and the comparative freedom of boys. The strikingly similar formulas employed by the writers of the original Hardy Boys and Nancy Drew series fail to disguise such significant differences as the boys' professional ambitions and Nancy's gifted amateurism. Revelations about revisions of older Nancy Drew books and recent reissues of the original versions add new twists to popular images of one of America's favorite heroines. Readers are encouraged to question whether more recent books, written in the wake of the modern feminist movement, or books with both male and female protagonists deal more progressively with gender.

Gender representations, as well as the relationship between fantasy and realism, are also important issues in picture books and book illustration. Part 6 presents essays by a leading theorist on children's picture books, Perry Nodelman, and by perhaps the most famous illustrator of our time, Maurice Sendak. We also include a selection of images to represent some landmarks and trends in the history of children's book illustration and the crosscurrents of words and pictures in books. Since illustrations are not reproduced in color in this volume, we focused primarily on selecting examples of black-and-white illustrations from the past several centuries. The earliest illustrators of printed books had very few choices with regard to medium or color, while several of our examples, in Part 6 as well as in other sections, come from books that were designed to alternate between color and black-and-white pictures. Moreover, some modern masters of illustration, such as Arthur Rackham, Tom Feelings, and Chris Van Allsburg, have chosen to exploit the artistic potential of black-and-white illustration through a variety of innovative techniques. Students will want, however, to read the books from which these images come, as well as other books by these and different author/illustrators. With picture books even more than longer illustrated books, the interdependence of words and pictures cannot be appreciated fully without examining the colors and format of the original works.

Part 7 continues to explore the relationship between words and visual images, as well as the crosscurrents of classic literature and popular culture, in the ways that old and new narratives for children are adapted in a variety of media. Jon Stott's essay discusses the teaching of satire to middle-grade children, while the satiric selections in Part 7 range from lighthearted dragon poems for young children to sophisticated short stories for young adults that twist the conventions of traditional fairy tales in many different directions. Essays by Julaine Gillispie, Joe Winston, Marina Warner, and Ellen Seiter revisit the issue of gender, as do a number of the satires and "spin-offs" in this section, including contemporary stories such as Francesca Lia Block's "Weetzie Wants a Baby" from *Weetzie Bat* and Bruce Coville's "Am I Blue?" These selections, with their frank treatments of sexuality, lead into our final section, "Values and Censorship," on the role of ideology in children's literature.

Essays such as Mark I. West's "Teaching Banned Children's Books" and Herbert R. Kohl's "Should We Burn *Babar?*" provide no easy answer to the question of how we should handle works for children that we find, in their entirety or in part, offensive. This problem cuts across the currents of history, for teaching *Huckleberry Finn* is every bit as problematic as assigning Judy Blume. Students are encouraged to arrive at their own conclusions by reading the "Indian" chapters from *Little House on the Prairie,* as well as Michael Dorris's critique and Louise Erdrich's expansion of "frontier" experience from a Native American perspective in *The Birchbark House,* or by reading Hans Christian Andersen's "Little Mermaid," as well as A. Waller Hastings's indictment of the Disney film version, with which many students are doubtless more familiar. Paula Fox's *The Slave Dancer* and Mark Twain's story of Huck Finn's friendship with Jim both represent controversial fictional portrayals of African American characters and experiences—controversial in part because of what they do not show: individualized, named black characters in *The Slave Dancer,* anger, bitterness, and open rebellion in the case of Jim. The selections by African American and Native American authors support the idea that one answer to deficient portrayals of particular ethnic or cultural groups is to widen the reading horizon of children and young adults, not narrow it.

Part 8 in a sense brings us full circle, for the urge to censor, limit access to, or direct the reading of works that make us cringe constitutes what John Rowe Townsend in Part 1 calls "Didacticism in Modern Dress" and indicates that the "horizontal waves" of what Egoff calls "public literature" continue to break upon the postmodern shore. But we trust that we have provided plenty of selections that will delight as well as inspire our readers, selections that may well take their place, if they have not already, among the "literature of mankind." The study of children's literature, once treated as a minor subject by literary scholars in the past, has become an exciting and rapidly growing field of research since the 1960s. The essays in this anthology represent a range of critical approaches developed since that time (as well as some samples of older commentary), from historical overviews of literary trends and genres to sharp critiques that provoke us to think about children and their literature in new ways. (Notice how many titles of critical selections take the form of questions.) Whether their interests center on critical theory, pedagogical approaches, or studies of childhood and popular culture, we encourage both teachers and students to explore the larger body of criticism and other resources available to them, as challenging new studies of children's literature will continue to appear in an expanding array of journals, books, and web sites.

In each section we have strived for a balance between primary texts (literature) and critical commentary, among early, modern, and contemporary literature, between whole texts and excerpts, and between literature for older and younger children. On this last point, perhaps a few more words are in order. At some colleges, we know, a separate course is taught in Young Adult Literature. Sometimes children's literature is offered through the English department and young adult literature through the education department, while in other schools both courses are offered by the education department. As our Table of Contents indicates, we have included much that may be considered young adult literature. One reason we have done so is that the distinction is a fairly recent one. In the nineteenth century, a book like *Little Women,* for example, was considered a children's book even though Alcott followed the little women into adulthood. Similarly, L. M. Montgomery's heroines, Anne Shirley and Emily Starr, become mature women by the conclusions of the series in which they appear. It was not until the 1940s that adolescent or young adult literature began to emerge as a distinct category of children's literature, and perhaps this would be the strongest rationale for including it in an anthology or course in children's literature—it is just that, a category.

Interestingly, early exemplars of the genre, such as Maureen Daly's *Seventeenth Summer* (1942) and S. E. Hinton's *The Outsiders* (1967), were written by young authors, whose protagonists did not go on to become mature adults (see Timeline). To muddy the waters still further, the postwar period also produced a number of popular books for adults that featured adolescents, which have since become staples of the middle school or high school curriculum (for example, *Lord of the Flies* by William Golding, *Catcher in the Rye* by J. D. Salinger, and *A Separate Peace* by John Knowles). Typically, young adult novels deal with adolescents in crisis, and although most bookstores place them in a special section of the children's department, additional copies can often be found on the children's shelves—and, depending on the author, on adult shelves as well. Recently bookstores and libraries have tried different strategies for labeling and locating books so that teenage and preteen readers will be attracted to them without being put off by the proximity of "baby books." Readers of young adult fiction are frequently preadolescents; many adolescents move directly from children's to adult literature or, unfortunately, abandon pleasure reading altogether. Finally, although many young adult books deal with mature or adult (i.e., sexual) themes, their style is often less demanding than that of chapter books for younger readers, and usually far less demanding than that of earlier children's books. For all these reasons, then, we include young adult fiction in our anthology, and we encourage students and teachers to grapple with the problem of its distinctive nature.

Many works of literature are most profitably read in their entirety, rather than in excerpts. We expect that teachers—and students—will have their own preferences for books that they will want to study in conjunction with this anthology. At the conclusion of each section, we provide brief introductions to works that we recommend reading in addition to the selections in this anthology, titled Further Recommended Reading. We urge you to consider selecting the works that best supplement your own approach to the study of children's literature, and hope that our recommendations will prove useful to you.

If teachers want to devise a special unit on young adult fiction or other topics, they can readily group together selections from several different sections. Such a unit could begin with precursors, such as *Little Women* and *The Adventures of Tom Sawyer,* and progress to selections by Gary Paulsen, Katherine Paterson, Monica Hughes, Isabelle Holland, Gudrun Pausewang, Mette Newth, Phyllis Naylor, and Francesca Lia Block. By the same token, teachers may want to devise a unit on fairy tales, examples of which appear in several sections. Students and teachers who are especially interested in studying gender in children's literature need not restrict themselves to the section on girls' and boys' books, for fascinating juxtapositions and pairings appear in almost every section. For example, Harriet's confrontation with the psychiatrist (in *Harriet the Spy* in Further Recommended Reading) and Wil Neuton's with the reporter (in *The Island* in Part 1) provide the opportunity to compare and contrast children's and young adult fiction as well as gender roles. If teachers prefer a chronological approach, the timeline will help them group the early selections in each section together, then the later, and so forth. Or if they prefer to subordinate our thematic concerns to genre, they can group together the fantasy, realistic fiction, poetry, fairy tales, and tales from the oral tradition (see the Alternate Table of Contents by Genre). In general, our selections are arranged chronologically within sections, except in a number of cases where thematic considerations have led us to group interrelated selections by topic or genre.

Crosscurrents in Children's Literature is thus designed to meet the traditional needs of the undergraduate children's literature course: an introduction to literary history and genres; exposure to a wide range of writings (and illustrations) by classic and contemporary, including multicultural, authors (and artists); and suggestions for further reading (and viewing). In addition, however, it is designed to encourage critical thinking—the kind of thinking that most teachers desire from students but that students are often surprised to find necessary in dealing with literature for children. We editors of *Crosscurrents* have among us over fifty years of experience teaching children's literature in the undergraduate college classroom, as well as over twenty-five years of teaching graduate students in children's literature. *Crosscurrents,* which has been in the planning stages for a number of years, is a distillation of all that we have learned—from children's books, from colleagues, from students, and from children themselves—and of all that we continue to ponder. With the publication of *Crosscurrents,* we invite other students and their teachers to join us on a voyage of discovery.

ACKNOWLEDGMENTS

The making of this anthology has been a long process of collaboration. Over meals, via letters, phone calls, and email, the three of us, J. D. Stahl, Tina Hanlon, and Elizabeth Keyser, have selected our materials, developed our ideas, and written and edited our contributions to this anthology, as well as deepened and extended our friendships.

We are indebted to all our capable Oxford University Press editors and staff members: D. Anthony English, Jan Beatty, Talia Krohn, Christine D'Antonio, Jackie Ardam, and Marta Peimer, who piloted us through revisions and negotiations.

Without the administrative support of our department chairs, we could not have accomplished this. We wish to thank Hilbert Campbell, Johann Norstedt, and Lucinda Roy at Virginia Tech, and John Bruton and Peter Crow at Ferrum College.

Tina Hanlon would like to thank the faculty and staff of Ferrum College for their support. For many insights into the pleasures of reading children's books, she is indebted to her students and the children of her family and friends.

J. D. Stahl also would like to thank Sarah Windes for her patience and support. He is also grateful to Harry McCoy, M.D., and Dr. Dianne Jones-Freeman.

Thanks are also due to the College of Liberal Arts and Sciences at Virginia Tech for a Research/Study Leave and a Travel Grant for J. D. Stahl, and to the Center for Programs in the Humanities at Virginia Tech for a summer stipend for J. D. Stahl to work on this anthology. We are grateful also to Nancy Metz, Dan Mosser, Len Hatfield, and other faculty members and staff of the English Department at Virginia Tech for gracious and generous support. Thanks to Michelle Vincent, Lana Whited, and Katherine Grimes at Ferrum and to Erin Blackman, Lynn Robinson, Sara Thorne-Thomsen, and Aranda Vance at Virginia Tech for their diligent work. The Center for Applied Technologies in the Humanities (CATH) supplied crucial technical aid.

We received indispensable assistance from the staffs of the Newberry Library, Chicago; Dan Meyer, at the University of Chicago Library; the Donnell Children's Library, New York; and the Library of Congress. We also wish to thank the librarians at Virginia Tech, Hollins University, and Ferrum College, who provided so much help.

We thank Laureen Tedesco, Naomi Wood, and other reviewers for their thoughtful and constructive suggestions. The Children's Literature Association has, over the years, provided much of the scholarly framework that has made an anthology such as this possible. We also owe a debt of gratitude to the Hollins Faculty Writing Workshop, among them Barbara Bowen in particular, for suggestions and constructive criticism. We wish to express our appreciation to the many scholars and writers who worked with us on revisions of their work or on permissions questions. Our colleagues in children's literature studies, among them Kathryn V. Graham, Frieda Bostian, Mark Armstrong, Julie Pfeiffer, Amanda Cockrell, Mark West, Roberta Herrin, Judy Teaford, and many others, have given us stimulating and provocative ideas that have entered into the writing and editing of this anthology.

BOOK

Dear Friend,
    Dear Reader,
Look at the book
you have just opened.
    What is it
you hold in your hand?

A BOOK is a HOUSE
that is all windows and doors.

Some walls are slick
with the zing of ink,
some old and cloth-soft,
smelling of dust.

Walk in.
Find your way.
Light falls
through the windows of words.

Learn the secret
    passages.
            Turn
pages, corners,
    holding your breath.

A BOOK is a CHEST
that keeps the heart's treasure.
Lift the plain lid
and look in.

You may find a castle,
a cave,
a wild pony,

or a child
in a farmhouse,
opening a chest.

A BOOK is a FARM,
its fields sown with words.

Reader, you are its weather:
your tears, your eyes shining.
The writer, working these words,
cried and laughed, too.

Now you meet
as the gate of the book
    swings wide.

A BOOK is full of LEAVES
that feed the tree of life,
each page
bound on one edge,
free on three.

BOOK   BOON COMPANION

    Field
        Home
            Treasure

May it hold you.
May it set you free.

George Ella Lyon

TO TEACH OR TO ENTERTAIN?

To Master John the English maid
A Horn-book gives of Ginger-bread:
And that the Child may learn the better,
As he can name, he eats the Letter:
Proceeding thus with vast Delight,
He spells, and gnaws, from left to right.

Matthew Prior, *Alma*, 1718

For centuries, the first "book" a child read was a sheet of paper mounted on a paddle, called a "hornbook." Usually the paddle was made of wood, sometimes leather or other material. In this poem, it is edible. Hornbooks were, in fact, sometimes made of ginger-bread.[1] Matthew Prior's humorous description of a gingerbread hornbook reveals that pondering the interaction between instruction and enjoyment in the education of young children was a concern of cooks and social critics as early as the first few decades of the eighteenth century.

The study of children's literature is central to the study of literature and culture partly because the historical record of how children's literature has changed is the record of evolving values and attitudes toward children and childhood. Since children represent the future in any society, the approach that a culture takes to its children often epitomizes what that culture considers to be of central and enduring value. The iconic significance of children's books helps to explain why they are both immensely popular and often controversial in our society. Children's literature is an arena in which conflicting ideas about values and practices confront each other, often in swirling crosscurrents.

For centuries, the main purpose of literature offered to children in Western societies was religious instruction, although the literature was presented not to children only, but to a mixed audience of adults, young people, and children. School books were licensed by church authorities and reflected the basic tenets of Christian belief. In fact, many books that were used in schools were either catechisms (list of church teachings, to be memorized and recited in response to set questions), prayer books, or versions of biblical stories and doctrines. This was true in Europe during the Middle Ages and well through the Renaissance, and it was also the case in the colonies of North America settled by Puritans and other Dissenters who came to America in search of religious freedom.

However, not all instructional writing for children was purely religious. A tradition of ratio-nalist writing in education coexisted with religious instruction, dating back many centuries and rooted, in Western culture, in ancient Greek philosophy. This approach to teaching emphasized learners' ability to think and discern for themselves. The renowned abbot Aelfric, in his *Collo-quy* written around the year 1000, not only invented dramatic roles for his pupils to enact, but encouraged them to observe the natural and social worlds and to develop ideas about what they saw and heard. Much closer to our time, about 1800, Maria Edgeworth, a popular Irish novelist, wrote stories that captured how children think and respond. Her purpose was to teach practical ideas about proper behavior, but it is important to see in her stories, such as "The Purple Jar" and "The Birthday Present," in this section, that she expected children to be able to acquire the tools to make judgments themselves, once they had developed certain cognitive skills.

Long before any of these writings existed, in oral traditions around the world, the distinction between teaching and entertaining was often blurred, as it is again in media such as television and popular films today. Tales of Coyote the trickster in the American Southwest or of Anansi the Spider in West Africa combined instruction in the mores and worldview of their tellers with delight in stories full of suspense, humor, and insight into human characters. Although some of the writers who are represented in this section opposed the publication of fairy tales for chil-dren, as Sarah Trimmer's early nineteenth-century reviews demonstrate, the popularity of tales that originated in oral traditions has never waned, including the ones by Charles Perrault in this section and other traditional tales throughout this volume (especially in Part 3). "The Paradise of Children," from Nathaniel Hawthorne's *A Wonder Book,* reflects the great American novel-ist's view in the mid-nineteenth century that children would naturally enjoy and benefit from adaptations of classical myths. Langston Hughes's twentieth-century poem "Aunt Sue's Sto-ries" depicts a child's enjoyment at learning about the past through a loving aunt's oral stories.

At the beginning of written children's literature in the West, adults were unquestionably in control, despite signs in some of our selections that grown-ups had to exert their authority in or-der to maintain control when children were unruly or disobedient. In the earliest forms of liter-ature that addressed children, teaching often meant discipline, including corporal discipline, such as beatings or whippings, which were common in the medieval classroom. Aelfric's pupils' statement that "We would rather be beaten for the sake of learning than be ignorant" sounds implausible to our ears—a version of the child as the adult wants him or her to be. But such statements expressed the expectations that teachers had of their pupils in classrooms on the basis of the instructors' authority, which was backed by the authority of the church and of a so-ciety that was based on ideas of hierarchy and obedience.

Historians and critics of children's literature in the twentieth century often date the begin-nings of a genuine "literature for children" to the middle of the eighteenth century. This view is based on the idea that publishers such as John Newbery, who, in a famous phrase, sought to unite "instruction with delight," were the first to acknowledge that children needed to be enter-tained and pleased by their reading material. This is an assumption that we more or less take for granted today, but it was certainly not held by most writers of books of instruction before the eighteenth century. Because Newbery, in books like his renowned *A Little Pretty Pocket-Book,* published in London in 1744, stated that his purpose was the "Instruction and Amusement" of his readers and emphasized the legitimacy of pleasure and play, together with learning proper morals and behavior, his publications were seen as the fountainhead of a new kind of literature that was specifically addressed to the needs of children.

Whereas earlier critics tended to claim that children's literature was invented when pleasure became an explicit goal of writing for children, recent critics have recognized as literary works the stories and texts that were aimed at teaching children, particularly by appealing to children's innate capacity to reason and comprehend. Later in the eighteenth century, Rational Moralists like Maria Edgeworth were no less alert to the needs of children as readers, although they placed great faith in the reasoning abilities of children and did not put the goal of entertaining their readers first. As critic Mitzi Myers and others have shown, Edgeworth and other writers who were concerned with children's moral, social, and intellectual development showed a shrewd understanding of children's psychology, thought patterns, and motivations, and they created engaging literary works in the process as well.[2]

In any case, the history of texts for children, whether "didactic" or "literary" or both, is a history of tension between the desire to teach children and the desire to please them. Sometimes, the approach taken is to teach children by pleasing them, but for many centuries the main goal was to teach, regardless of whether the process involved pain or pleasure, and pain was often thought to be the more effective inducement to learning. Teaching takes many forms; as Peter Hollindale and others have argued, all children's literature is indoctrination, even when it does not appear to be.[3] Whether we recognize it or not, children's literature is one of the most powerful ways in which adults indoctrinate children into thinking and behaving the way adults want them to. This is, of course, most clearly visible to us in children's literature that is most alien to our own ways of thinking, as in the moralistic literature that was prevalent in the eighteenth and nineteenth centuries (and well into the twentieth)—stories and poems that often strike us as manipulative, cruel, or heavy-handed, like Jane Taylor's bloody cautionary poem, "The Little Fisherman," in this section. Stories for children can be purposefully used to teach political, religious, and social values, as the Nazis showed when they used children's literature to glorify obedience, blind patriotism, and racism in the Third Reich. However, it may be more difficult for us to see that our own children's literature is ideological because we are not conscious of it. As theorists such as Fredric Jameson have made clear, ideology consists precisely of those values and ideas that we cannot recognize as such because we take them for granted.[4]

How do we respond to this realization? Some adults mourn their loss of innocence when they realize that children's literature is not a territory free of social values and ideological content. Can't we just read children's books without thinking about problems such as racism or sexism, and political, ethical, and religious issues? Children often do, these adults argue, and why should we spoil their innocent enjoyment? The problem is that if we read without analyzing the values that are inherent in children's books (or in books in general), we are more likely to accept the values being taught or to encourage the acceptance of those values without recognizing that we are doing so. A number of essays in this volume, such as those by Herbert R. Kohl, A. Waller Hastings, and Michael Dorris in Part 8, reveal the presence of values that these critics find objectionable in popular books and films for children. On the other hand, John Rowe Townsend's 1967 essay in this section cautions modern critics that if they overemphasize their search for desirable values and social issues in contemporary books, new forms of didacticism may impede children's enjoyment of reading, as well as the freedom of authors to produce high-quality, aesthetically pleasing literature. Critics at the dawn of the twenty-first century often debate whether adults' faith in literature as good therapy for emotional and social problems is another variation on the centuries-old impulse to provide books that will improve children's lives, when perhaps children need more freedom to choose literature in which they find escape, inspiration, instruction, emotional outlet, or comic relief according to their own needs at different times.

With few exceptions, literature for children is written by adults, and even when children write books, adults select, edit, and publish them. To some, this seems like a contradiction or, at least, an interesting paradox: a body of literature that represents the world ostensibly from the point of view of children and certainly intended in most cases for children to read is created by adults, who have different perspectives and interests. Some critics see this distance between the readers and the authors of children's books as natural and unproblematic. Why shouldn't adults, who have mastered literacy, write for children, either to teach them what can be learned through reading or to give them pleasure? Other critics, such as Jacqueline Rose, have argued that children's literature is conceptually an impossibility because adults can only pretend to know what and how children think.[5] Still others, such as Perry Nodelman, see the tension between the writer's dual consciousness (adult and child ways of thinking mingled) and the readers' blend of innocence and experience as the main source of the pleasure offered by children's books.[6] Some of the best writers of children's books seem not to have been writing for "children" in general at all, but rather, as C. S. Lewis argues in his essay in this section, for a specific child to whom they wanted to tell stories or for something or someone within themselves that remained childlike. Lewis Carroll wrote his landmark fantasies for children, the *Alice in Wonderland* books, after making up stories to entertain Alice Liddell and her sisters. Louisa May Alcott and Mark Twain drew on and transformed their own childhood experiences to create the different views of American childhood that are represented by the domestic lives of Alcott's adolescent New England sisters in *Little Women* and the adventures of Tom Sawyer's gang along the banks of the Mississippi River in Twain's novels.

There is no doubt that writers of children's books have often written for children as they imagined them to be, and we may find these implied readers (or the characters that represent the children of these authors' imaginations) artificial, false, or problematic. On the other hand, who is to say what "real" children are? Our ideas about this question are different from those of people in other cultures and periods. It may be that children's books give us as adults pleasure to the degree that they confirm what we think about children and what we like about what we remember or imagine is "childhood."

In short, children almost certainly often find in children's books guidance about what they, as children, are expected to be and to become. Thus, viewed from one perspective, children reading books are engaged in the always-continuing process of responding to (or reacting against) the process of socialization that leads from infancy to adulthood. Whenever children choose the books they enjoy and want to read, they are expressing a preference about the kinds of ideas and values that they want to incorporate into their imaginative lives. It is also often true that children take the elements of stories that they like and enhance and develop them in their imaginations to suit their needs. It may be a mistake, therefore, to assume that because adults write children's books and children's interests are sometimes different from those of adults, adults are the primary ones to determine what children's books mean to children.

The Rational Moralists (from the mid-1700s to the mid-1800s) disguised the authority of their adult figures by calling parents, teachers, and adults "friends," emphasizing that grownups were simply trying to help children accept reasonable rules and principles. While this approach was certainly more attractive than the punitive one to be found in much religious moralism for children, it was also a bit euphemistic; it glossed over the fact that, when push came to shove, adults still held the power to decide. We may find the euphemism of calling authority figures "friends" appealing for a different reason today; in our time, the generations are often thought of as innately hostile and opposed to each other. We may yearn for a society in which children and adults (and all the young people at transitional stages in between—adolescents, young adults, or Generation X and Y) can talk to each other without hostility or alienation.

In the middle decades of the twentieth century, children's writers evaded the problem of intergenerational conflict by establishing a common theme in children's books, depicting the lives of children free from the interference of adults. Writers such as Elizabeth Enright, in the Gone-Away Lake novels, and C. S. Lewis, in his Narnia Chronicles, envisioned realms in which children had a measure of autonomy. (Series such as Arthur Ransome's Swallows and Amazons and the American Hardy Boys books were another expression of this trend.) What many authors in this period imagined was a world in which adult society was so stable and in control that it could become invisible in children's books. Enright's Melendy children, in the episode from *The Saturdays* in this section, could explore New York City on their own and return home safely. The children in these stories could live secure and independent lives precisely because grown-ups were dependably on call when needed but relegated to the margins of these stories.

This situation changed in the 1960s, however, when social problems of all kinds, such as divorce, racial tensions, sexuality, and conflict between the generations, became (with much initial resistance) standard themes of a new breed of writers such as Louise Fitzhugh. In works such as *Harriet the Spy,* adults are as important to the young protagonists as are their peers. Children's books, as a result, became more self-conscious, often more satirical and critical; they were no longer just the megaphones of adult values, but sometimes the mirrors held up to adults, in which both children and adults could see the flaws and faults of grown-ups. In other words, children's books became tools of self-criticism and social criticism for adult authors. Although some earlier children's books also criticized adult failings, the center of moral authority shifted during the twentieth century: as a society, we are unsure whether adults ought to be in charge, which earlier generations never doubted. Instead, we wonder whether it isn't the proper business of the younger generation to challenge the authority of adults, as an abundance of novels for older children and young adults has been suggesting. By the end of the century, some novelists were showing how children and teenagers could survive the most horrifying problems that families and communities can face, without demonizing the adults or destroying all family ties. For example, Virginia Hamilton depicted an abusive mother with a carefully balanced measure of sympathy in *Sweet Whispers, Brother Rush* (1982), and Julius Lester wrote of children learning to cope with their mother's murder in *When Dad Killed Mom* (2001).

However, nonfiction books for children, such as the biography of Langston Hughes by Floyd Cooper reprinted here, continue to offer the experience of previous generations as instruction for the young. Furthermore, as the poems by Hughes himself and by Lucille Clifton at the end of this section show, the hard-won life experience of elders can be a source of wisdom and determination to the next generation as well. These African American authors recognize that children who are threatened by racism and economic hardship need strong role models and hope, but their twentieth-century writings differ from older didactic literature in that the theme of dreams, expressed so eloquently by Hughes early in the twentieth century, encourages individuals to develop their own ideals and abilities in a world where adult society is sometimes oppressive or indifferent and sometimes supportive.

As this overview shows, children's books can engage their readers in many different ways. How important is a child's pleasure in reading a story? How important is it that a child learn the "lesson" or "lessons" that the adult writer intends the child to learn? Why and how did earlier writers who included children among their readers ignore or perhaps subtly acknowledge the interests and demands of their child readers? What does it teach children to assume that "entertainment" is the highest value a child can derive from a story? These are some of the questions that we hope the following selections will help you to reflect upon.

NOTES

1. See *Children's Literature: An Illustrated History,* ed. Peter Hunt, for pictures of gingerbread molds shaped like hornbooks (Oxford: Oxford UP, 1995) 38.
2. Mitzi Myers, "Portrait of the Female Artist as a Young Robin: Maria Edgeworth's Telltale Tailpiece," *The Lion and the Unicorn: A Critical Journal of Children's Literature* 20:2 (1996): 230–63.
3. Peter Hollindale, "Ideology and the Children's Book," *Signal* 55 (1988): 3–22, *Literature for Children: Contemporary Criticism,* ed. Peter Hunt (London: Routledge, 1992).
4. Fredric Jameson, *The Political Unconscious: Narrative as a Socially Symbolic Act* (Ithaca, NY: Cornell UP, 1981).
5. Jacqueline Rose, *The Case of Peter Pan, or The Impossibility of Children's Fiction* (1984; Philadelphia: U of Pennsylvania P, 1993).
6. Perry Nodelman, *The Pleasures of Children's Literature,* 2nd ed. (White Plains, NY: Longman, 1996).

C. S. Lewis (1898–1963)

Clive Staples Lewis is famous for his Narnia series of fantasies for children, of which the best-known work is *The Lion, the Witch and the Wardrobe* (1950). A scholar at Oxford and then Cambridge University, he also wrote a number of theological and academic books. In this well-known 1952 essay, he defines three ways of writing for children. Two of these ways depend upon the relationship of the writer to the child. The first, which he condemns, invents an imaginary child (or imaginary children) as the audience for children's books and caters to the presumed desires of that audience. The second, which he supports, is writing for a specific child whom the author knows and frequently tells the story to in person. The third way, which he professes to use himself, is to write in the genre of the children's book because that happens to be the most suitable form for the ideas the author wishes to express. Lewis claims to have written as much for the child within himself as for any other audience. But the essay is also a vigorous defense of fantasy and the imagination in children's books. Lewis believes that maturity does not consist of shedding our child nature but adding to it, and thinks that conflict and heroism are the natural subjects of children's literature. His essay is a lively attack on condescending modern attitudes toward children and childhood. See also the discussion of C. S. Lewis's Narnia series in Further Recommended Reading.

On Three Ways of Writing for Children

I think there are three ways in which those who write for children may approach their work; two good ways and one that is generally a bad way.

I came to know of the bad way quite recently and from two unconscious witnesses. One was a lady who sent me the MS of a story she had written in which a fairy placed at a child's disposal a wonderful gadget. I say "gadget" because it was not a magic ring or hat or cloak or any such traditional matter. It was a machine, a thing of taps and handles and buttons you could press. You could press one and get an ice cream, another and get a live puppy, and so forth. I had to tell the author honestly that I didn't much care for that sort of thing. She replied, "No more do I, it bores me to distraction. But it is what the modern child wants." My other bit of evidence was this. In my own first story I had described at length what I thought a rather fine high tea given by a hospitable faun to the little girl who was my heroine. A man, who has children of his own, said, "Ah, I see how you got to that. If you want to please grown-up readers you give them sex, so you thought to yourself, 'That won't do for children, what shall I give them instead? I know! The little blighters like plenty of good eating.'" In reality, however, I myself like eating and drinking. I put in what I would have liked to read when I was a child and what I still like reading now that I am in my fifties.

The lady in my first example, and the married man in my second, both conceived writing for children as a special department of "giving the public what it wants." Children are, of course, a special public and you find out what they want and give them that, however little you like it yourself.

The next way may seem at first to be very much the same, but I think the resemblance is superficial. This is the way of Lewis Carroll, Kenneth Grahame, and Tolkien. The printed story grows out of a story told to a particular child with the living voice and perhaps *ex tempore*. It resembles the first way because you are certainly trying to give that child what it wants. But then you are dealing with a concrete person, this child who, of course, differs from all other children. There is no question of "children" conceived as a strange species whose habits you have "made up" like an anthropologist or a commercial traveller. Nor, I suspect, would it be possible, thus face to face, to regale the child with things calculated to please it but regarded by yourself with indifference or contempt. The child, I am certain, would see through that. In any personal relation the two participants modify each other. You would become slightly different because you were talking to a child and the child would become slightly different because it was being talked to by an adult. A

community, a composite personality, is created and out of that the story grows.

The third way, which is the only one I could ever use myself, consists in writing a children's story because a children's story is the best art-form for something you have to say: just as a composer might write a Dead March not because there was a public funeral in view but because certain musical ideas that had occurred to him went best into that form. This method could apply to other kinds of children's literature besides stories. I have been told that Arthur Mee never met a child and never wished to: it was, from his point of view, a bit of luck that boys liked reading what he liked writing. This anecdote may be untrue in fact but it illustrates my meaning.

Within the species "children's story" the subspecies which happened to suit me is the fantasy or (in a loose sense of that word) the fairy tale. There are, of course, other sub-species. E. Nesbit's trilogy about the Bastable family is a very good specimen of another kind. It is a "children's story" in the sense that children can and do read it: but it is also the only form in which E. Nesbit could have given us so much of the humours of childhood. It is true that the Bastable children appear, successfully treated from the adult point of view, in one of her grown-up novels, but they appear only for a moment. I do not think she would have kept it up. Sentimentality is so apt to creep in if we write at length about children as seen by their elders. And the reality of childhood, as we all experienced it, creeps out. For we all remember that our childhood, as lived, was immeasurably different from what our elders saw. Hence Sir Michael Sadler, when I asked his opinion about a certain new experimental school, replied, "I never give an opinion on any of those experiments till the children have grown up and can tell us *what really happened*." Thus the Bastable trilogy, however improbable many of its episodes may be, provides even adults, in one sense, with more realistic reading about children than they could find in most books addressed to adults. But also, conversely, it enables the children who read it to do something much more mature than they realize. For the whole book is a character study of Oswald, an unconsciously satiric self-portrait, which every intelligent child can fully appreciate: but no child would sit down to read a character study in any other form. There is another way in which children's stories mediate this psychological interest, but I will reserve that for later treatment.

In this short glance at the Bastable trilogy I think we have stumbled on a principle. Where the children's story is simply the right form for what the author has to say, then of course readers who want to hear that, will read the story or re-read it, at any age. I never met *The Wind in the Willows* or the Bastable books till I was in my late twenties, and I do not think I have enjoyed them any the less on that account. I am almost inclined to set it up as a canon that a children's story which is enjoyed only by children is a bad children's story. The good ones last. A waltz which you can like only when you are waltzing is a bad waltz.

This canon seems to me most obviously true of that particular type of children's story which is dearest to my own taste, the fantasy or fairy tale. Now the modern critical world uses "adult" as a term of approval. It is hostile to what it calls "nostalgia" and contemptuous of what it calls "Peter Pantheism." Hence a man who admits that dwarfs and giants and talking beasts and witches are still dear to him in his fifty-third year is now less likely to be praised for his perennial youth than scorned and pitied for arrested development. If I spend some little time defending myself against these charges, this is not so much because it matters greatly whether I am scorned and pitied as because the defence is germane to my whole view of the fairy tale and even of literature in general. My defence consists of three propositions.

1. I reply with a *tu quoque*. Critics who treat *adult* as a term of approval, instead of as a merely descriptive term, cannot be adult themselves. To be concerned about being grown up, to admire the grown up because it is grown up, to blush at the suspicion of being childish; these things are the marks of childhood and adolescence. And in childhood and adolescence they are, in moderation, healthy symptoms. Young things ought to want to grow. But to carry on into middle life or even into early manhood this concern about being adult is a mark of really arrested development. When I was ten, I read fairy tales in secret and would have been ashamed if I had been found doing so. Now that I am fifty I read them openly. When I became a man I put away childish things, including the fear of childishness and the desire to be very grown up.

2. The modern view seems to me to involve a false conception of growth. They accuse us of arrested de-velopment because we have not lost a taste we had in childhood. But surely arrested development consists not in refusing to lose old things but in failing to add new things? I now like hock, which I am sure I should not have liked as a child. But I still like lemon-squash. I call this growth or development because I have been enriched: where I formerly had only one pleasure, I now have two. But if I had to lose the taste for lemon-squash before I acquired the taste for hock, that would not be growth but simple change. I now enjoy Tolstoy and Jane Austen and Trollope as well as fairy tales and I call that growth: if I had had to lose the fairy tales in order to acquire the novelists, I would not say that I had grown but only that I had changed. A tree grows because it adds rings: a train doesn't grow by leaving one station behind and puffing on to the next. In reality, the case is stronger and more complicated than this. I think my growth is just as apparent when I now read the fairy tales as when I read the novelists, for I now enjoy the fairy tales better than I did in childhood: being now able to put more in, of course I get more out. But I do not here stress that point. Even if it were merely a taste for grown-up literature added to an unchanged taste for children's literature, addition would still be entitled to the name "growth," and the process of merely dropping one parcel when you pick up another would not. It is, of course, true that the process of growing does, incidentally and unfortunately, involve some more losses. But that is not the essence of growth, certainly not what makes growth admirable or desirable. If it were, if to drop parcels and to leave stations behind were the essence and virtue of growth, why should we stop at the adult? Why should not *senile* be equally a term of approval? Why are we not to be congratulated on losing our teeth and hair? Some critics seem to confuse growth with the cost of growth and also to wish to make that cost far higher than, in nature, it need be.

3. The whole association of fairy tale and fantasy with childhood is local and accidental. I hope everyone has read Tolkien's essay on Fairy Tales, which is perhaps the most important contribution to the subject that anyone has yet made. If so, you will know already that, in most places and times, the fairy tale has not been specially made for, nor exclusively enjoyed by, children. It has gravitated to the nursery when it became unfashionable in literary circles, just as unfashionable furniture gravitated to the nursery in Victorian

houses. In fact, many children do not like this kind of book, just as many children do not like horsehair sofas: and many adults do like it, just as many adults like rocking chairs. And those who do like it, whether young or old, probably like it for the same reason. And none of us can say with any certainty what that reason is. The two theories which are most often in my mind are those of Tolkien and of Jung.

According to Tolkien[1] the appeal of the fairy story lies in the fact that man there most fully exercises his function as a 'subcreator'; not, as they love to say now, making a "comment upon life" but making, so far as possible, a subordinate world of his own. Since, in Tolkien's view, this is one of man's proper functions, delight naturally arises whenever it is successfully performed. For Jung, fairy tale liberates Archetypes which dwell in the collective unconscious, and when we read a good fairy tale we are obeying the old precept "Know thyself." I would venture to add to this my own theory, not indeed of the Kind as a whole, but of one feature in it: I mean, the presence of beings other than human which yet behave, in varying degrees, humanly: the giants and dwarfs and talking beasts. I believe these to be at least (for they may have many other sources of power and beauty) an admirable hieroglyphic which conveys psychology, types of character, more briefly than novelistic presentation and to readers whom novelistic presentation could not yet reach. Consider Mr. Badger in *The Wind in the Willows*—that extraordinary amalgam of high rank, coarse manners, gruffness, shyness, and goodness. The child who has once met Mr. Badger has ever afterwards, in its bones, a knowledge of humanity and of English social history which it could not get in any other way.

Of course as all children's literature is not fantastic, so all fantastic books need not be children's books. It is still possible, even in an age so ferociously anti-romantic as our own, to write fantastic stories for adults: though you will usually need to have made a name in some more fashionable kind of literature before anyone will publish them. But there may be an author who at a particular moment finds not only fantasy but fantasy-for-children the exactly right form for what he wants to say. The distinction is a fine one. His fantasies for children and his fantasies for adults will have very much more in common with one another than either has with the ordinary novel or with what is sometimes called "the novel of child life." Indeed

the same readers will probably read both his fantastic "juveniles" and his fantastic stories for adults. For I need not remind such an audience as this that the neat sorting-out of books into age-groups, so dear to publishers, has only a very sketchy relation with the habits of any real readers. Those of us who are blamed when old for reading childish books were blamed when children for reading books too old for us. No reader worth his salt trots along in obedience to a time-table. The distinction, then, is a fine one: and I am not quite sure what made me, in a particular year of my life, feel that not only a fairy tale, but a fairy tale addressed to children, was exactly what I must write—or burst. Partly, I think, that this form permits, or compels you to leave out things I wanted to leave out. It compels you to throw all the force of the book into what was done and said. It checks what a kind, but discerning critic called "the expository demon" in me. It also imposes certain very fruitful necessities about length.

If I have allowed the fantastic type of children's story to run away with this discussion, that is because it is the kind I know and love best, not because I wish to condemn any other. But the patrons of the other kinds very frequently want to condemn it. About once every hundred years some wiseacre gets up and tries to banish the fairy tale. Perhaps I had better say a few words in its defence, as reading for children.

It is accused of giving children a false impression of the world they live in. But I think no literature that children could read gives them less of a false impression. I think what profess to be realistic stories for children are far more likely to deceive them. I never expected the real world to be like the fairy tales. I think that I did expect school to be like the school stories. The fantasies did not deceive me: the school stories did. All stories in which children have adventures and successes which are possible, in the sense that they do not break the laws of nature, but almost infinitely improbable, are in more danger than the fairy tales of raising false expectations.

Almost the same answer serves for the popular charge of escapism, though here the question is not so simple. Do fairy tales teach children to retreat into a world of wish-fulfilment—"fantasy" in the technical psychological sense of the word—instead of facing the problems of the real world? Now it is here that the problem becomes subtle. Let us again lay the fairy tale side by side with the school story or any other story which is labelled a "Boy's Book" or a "Girl's Book," as distinct from a "Children's Book." There is no doubt that both arouse, and imaginatively satisfy, wishes. We long to go through the looking glass, to reach fairy land. We also long to be the immensely popular and successful schoolboy or schoolgirl, or the lucky boy or girl who discovers the spy's plot or rides the horse that none of the cowboys can manage. But the two longings are very different. The second, especially when directed on something so close as school life, is ravenous and deadly serious. Its fulfilment on the level of imagination is in very truth compensatory: we run to it from the disappointments and humiliations of the real world: it sends us back to the real world undivinely discontented. For it is all flattery to the ego. The pleasure consists in picturing oneself the object of admiration. The other longing, that for fairy land, is very different. In a sense a child does not long for fairy land as a boy longs to be the hero of the first eleven. Does anyone suppose that he really and prosaically longs for all the dangers and discomforts of a fairy tale?—really wants dragons in contemporary England? It is not so. It would be much truer to say that fairy land arouses a longing for he knows not what. It stirs and troubles him (to his life-long enrichment) with the dim sense of something beyond his reach and, far from dulling or emptying the actual world, gives it a new dimension of depth. He does not despise real woods because he has read of enchanted woods: the reading makes all real woods a little enchanted. This is a special kind of longing. The boy reading the school story of the type I have in mind desires success and is unhappy (once the book is over) because he can't get it: the boy reading the fairy tale desires and is happy in the very fact of desiring. For his mind has not been concentrated on himself, as it often is in the more realistic story.

I do not mean that school stories for boys and girls ought not to be written. I am only saying that they are far more liable to become "fantasies" in the clinical sense than fantastic stories are. And this distinction holds for adult reading too. The dangerous fantasy is always superficially realistic. The real victim of wishful reverie does not batten on the *Odyssey, The Tempest,* or *The Worm Ouroboros:* he (or she) prefers stories about millionaires, irresistible beauties, posh hotels, palm beaches and bedroom scenes—things that really might happen, that ought to happen, that would have happened if the reader had had a fair chance. For,

as I say, there are two kinds of longing. The one is an *askesis,* a spiritual exercise, and the other is a disease.

A far more serious attack on the fairy tale as children's literature comes from those who do not wish children to be frightened. I suffered too much from night-fears myself in childhood to undervalue this objection. I would not wish to heat the fires of that private hell for any child. On the other hand, none of my fears came from fairy tales. Giant insects were my specialty, with ghosts a bad second. I suppose the ghosts came directly or indirectly from stories, though certainly not from fairy stories, but I don't think the insects did. I don't know anything my parents could have done or left undone which would have saved me from the pincers, mandibles, and eyes of those many-legged abominations. And that, as so many people have pointed out, is the difficulty. We do not know what will or will not frighten a child in this particular way. I say "in this particular way" for we must here make a distinction. Those who say that children must not be frightened may mean two things. They may mean (1) that we must not do anything likely to give the child those haunting, disabling, pathological fears against which ordinary courage is helpless: in fact, *phobias.* His mind must, if possible, be kept clear of things he can't bear to think of. Or they may mean (2) that we must try to keep out of his mind the knowledge that he is born into a world of death, violence, wounds, adventure, heroism and cowardice, good and evil. If they mean the first I agree with them: but not if they mean the second. The second would indeed be to give children a false impression and feed them on escapism in the bad sense. There is something ludicrous in the idea of so educating a generation which is born to the Ogpu and the atomic bomb. Since it is so likely that they will meet cruel enemies, let them at least have heard of brave knights and heroic courage. Otherwise you are making their destiny not brighter but darker. Nor do most of us find that violence and bloodshed, in a story, produce any haunting dread in the minds of children. As far as that goes, I side impenitently with the human race against the modern reformer. Let there be wicked kings and beheadings, battles and dungeons, giants and dragons, and let villains be soundly killed at the end of the book. Nothing will persuade me that this causes an ordinary child any kind or degree of fear beyond what it wants, and needs, to feel. For, of course, it wants to be a little frightened.

The other fears—the phobias—are a different matter. I do not believe one can control them by literary means. We seem to bring them into the world with us ready made. No doubt the particular image on which the child's terror is fixed can sometimes be traced to a book. But is that the source, or only the occasion, of the fear? If he had been spared that image, would not some other, quite unpredictable by you, have had the same effect? Chesterton has told us of a boy who was more afraid of the Albert Memorial than anything else in the world. I know a man whose great childhood terror was the India paper edition of the *Encyclopaedia Britannica*—for a reason I defy you to guess. And I think it possible that by confining your child to blameless stories of child life in which nothing at all alarming ever happens, you would fail to banish the terrors, and would succeed in banishing all that can ennoble them or make them endurable. For in the fairy tales, side by side with the terrible figures, we find the immemorial comforters and protectors, the radiant ones; and the terrible figures are not merely terrible, but sublime. It would be nice if no little boy in bed, hearing, or thinking he hears, a sound, were ever at all frightened. But if he is going to be frightened, I think it better that he should think of giants and dragons than merely of burglars. And I think St. George, or any bright champion in armour, is a better comfort than the idea of the police.

I will even go further. If I could have escaped all my own night-fears at the price of never having known "faerie," would I now be the gainer by that bargain? I am not speaking carelessly. The fears were very bad. But I think the price would have been too high.

But I have strayed far from my theme. This has been inevitable for, of the three methods, I know by experience only the third. I hope my title did not lead anyone to think that I was conceited enough to give you advice on how to write a story for children. There were two very good reasons for not doing that. One is that many people have written very much better stories than I, and I would rather learn about the art than set up to teach it. The other is that, in a certain sense, I have never exactly "made" a story. With me the process is much more like bird-watching than like either talking or building. I see pictures. Some of these pictures have a common flavour, almost a common smell, which groups them together. Keep quiet and watch and they will begin joining themselves up. If you were very lucky (I have never been as lucky as all that) a whole set might join themselves so consistently that there you had a complete story: without doing anything yourself. But more often (in my experience always) there are gaps. Then at last you have to do some deliberate inventing, have to contrive reasons why these characters should be in these various places doing these various things. I have no idea whether this is the usual way of writing stories, still less whether it is the best. It is the only one I know: images always come first.

Before closing, I would like to return to what I said at the beginning. I rejected any approach which begins with the question "What do modern children like?" I might be asked, "Do you equally reject the approach which begins with the question 'What do modern children need?'—in other words, with the moral or didactic approach?" I think the answer is Yes. Not because I don't like stories to have a moral: certainly not because I think children dislike a moral. Rather because I feel sure that the question "What do modern children need?" will not lead you to a good moral. If we ask that question we are assuming too superior an attitude. It would be better to ask "What moral do I need?" for I think we can be sure that what does not concern us deeply will not deeply interest our readers, whatever their age. But it is better not to ask the question at all. Let the pictures tell you their own moral. For the moral inherent in them will rise from whatever spiritual roots you have succeeded in striking during the whole course of your life. But if they don't show you any moral, don't put one in. For the moral you put in is likely to be a platitude, or even a falsehood, skimmed from the surface of your consciousness. It is impertinent to offer the children that. For we have been told on high authority that in the moral sphere they are probably at least as wise as we. Anyone who *can* write a children's story without a moral, had better do so: that is, if he is going to write children's stories at all. The only moral that is of any value is that which arises inevitably from the whole cast of the author's mind.

Indeed everything in the story should arise from the whole cast of the author's mind. We must write for children out of those elements in our own imagination which we share with children: differing from our child readers not by any less, or less serious, interest in the things we handle, but by the fact that we have other interests which children would not share with us. The matter of our story should be a part of the habitual furniture of our minds. This, I fancy, has been so with all great writers for children, but it is not generally understood. A critic not long ago said in praise of a very serious fairy tale that the author's tongue "never once got into his cheek." But why on earth should it?—unless he had been eating a seed-cake. Nothing seems to me more fatal, for this art, than an idea that whatever we share with children is, in the privative sense, "childish" and that whatever is childish is somehow comic. We must meet children as equals in that area of our nature where we are their equals. Our superiority consists partly in commanding other areas, and partly (which is more relevant) in the fact that we are better at telling stories than they are. The child as reader is neither to be patronized nor idolized: we talk to him as man to man. But the worst attitude of all would be the professional attitude which regards children in the lump as a sort of raw material which we have to handle. We must of course try to do them no harm: we may, under the Omnipotence, sometimes dare to hope that we may do them good. But only such good as involves treating them with respect. We must not imagine that we are Providence or Destiny. I will not say that a good story for children could never be written by someone in the Ministry of Education, for all things are possible. But I should lay very long odds against it.

Once in a hotel dining-room I said, rather too loudly, "I loathe prunes." "So do I," came an unexpected six-year-old voice from another table. Sympathy was instantaneous. Neither of us thought it funny. We both knew that prunes are far too nasty to be funny. That is the proper meeting between man and child as independent personalities. Of the far higher and more difficult relations between child and parent or child and teacher, I say nothing. An author, as a mere author, is outside all that. He is not even an uncle. He is a freeman and an equal, like the postman, the butcher, and the dog next door.

NOTE

1. J. R. R. Tolkien, "On Fairy-Stories," *Essays Presented to Charles Williams* (1947), p. 66 ff.

Sheila Egoff (1918–2005)

Sheila Egoff's "Precepts, Pleasures, and Portents" is part of a longer essay, which appeared in the second edition of Egoff's *Only Connect: Readings on Children's Literature* (1980). Egoff, a Canadian literary critic and librarian, is best known for her book *The Republic of Childhood: A Critical Guide to Canadian Children's Books* (1967) and for her seminal essay on the problem novel of the 1960s and 1970s, which also appears in *Only Connect.* In the excerpt that follows, Egoff clearly and concisely outlines the history of children's literature from its beginnings to the mid-nineteenth century.

Precepts, Pleasures, and Portents

Changing Emphases in Children's Literature

When Caxton began printing in England in 1476, the child was still looked upon as a miniature adult and was merged into the adult world. With the gradual realization that the child's natural carefree ways were a barrier between adult and child, adults hastened to teach the child "manners," and the first books for children were books of manners and "courtesie." What more palatable candy coating for the traditional morals of mankind than Aesop's *Fables?* Here was an ideal way to present acceptable actions to the child— by means of talking animals. Caxton printed the first English edition in 1484 and the work rapidly became part of the schoolroom tradition.

The Puritan concept of sin that took hold in the seventeenth century led to a change in the accepted view of children: they were still thought of as miniature adults but they now had to be specially trained. And so a separate stream of children's books began. "Children are not too young to die," said the Puritans, "they are not too little to go to hell," and a great spate of writing and publishing supported this view. What was described by later generations as the "brand of hell" school of writing reached its peak in 1671 with James Janeway's *A Token For Children: Being an Exact Account of the Conversion, Holy and Exemplary Lives and Joyful Deaths of several Young Children.* The Puritans contended that books of this kind gave the highest pleasure to children, "that of studying and enjoying the Will of God." What emerges from an overall look at the children's books of this period is a picture of a society that was narrow and intolerant, that saw children as separate from adults even while it brought the full force of adult values to bear upon them. It also reveals a remarkably consistent viewpoint. This society knew exactly what it wanted for its children: happiness in the next world.

Although the tone of religious ferocity was to abate in children's books until they became only mildly moralistic, the spirit of fear engendered by the Puritan era lingered in them for about a hundred and fifty years. Few books were free of religious overtones. The title of a spelling book of 1705 reads: *A Help to True Spelling and Reading . . . Here are also the Chief Principles of Religion laid down in a plain and easie Metre.* In Dr. Aikin's and Mrs. Barbauld's *Evenings at Home* (1792), a kind of junior encyclopaedia, with suggestions for keeping children out of mischief, a section on geography reads:

> Asia lies east of Europe; it is about 4,800 miles long, and 4,300 broad; bounded on the North by the Frozen Ocean, by the Pacific on the East, by the Red Sea on the West, and the Indian Sea on the South. This,

though the second, is the principal quarter of the globe; for here our first parents were created, and placed in the garden of Eden . . .

A somewhat less grim view of pleasure in the Puritan sense was offered by a seventeenth-century philosopher. In *Some Thoughts Concerning Education* (1690) John Locke urged that children should be brought to pleasure in reading, but through animal stories accompanied by pictures. Although his choice of books was very narrow—Aesop's *Fables* and *Reynard the Fox* were his strongest recommendations—he enunciated the first great principle about children and reading. "Children do not like to be constrained to read," he warned, "any more than adults."

John Locke was not listened to in his day and it would appear that he had only one disciple, in the person of John Newbery who, in 1744, set up his bookshop for children in St Paul's churchyard. Newbery intended to please children, but his break with tradition came in the way he approached them rather than in the contents of the books he published for them: he provided stories with the obvious morals of the time but in a gayer, more childlike way than his contemporaries. He covered his books with "flowery and gilt" Dutch paper; he added woodcuts that illustrated the text, though they were crude in execution; with his bookshop he provided a place children could call their own and he supplemented his stock of books with baubles to delight a child—tops, pincushions, and games. Newbery has been called the "commercial dynamo" of his time in the field of publishing. As a publisher his activities included much of what is good and bad in publishing for children today. He commissioned writers (it is supposed that Oliver Goldsmith was the author of Newbery's *Goody Two Shoes*); he saw the market for children's books as well as the need; and he had other ventures associated with his publishing (in *Goody Two Shoes* it is noted that little Marjory's father died from a want of Dr. James's fever powder—a patent medicine sold by Newbery).

The overall influence of John Newbery was slight and fleeting—although the marketing lesson remained. The deliberate motives of both writers and critics throughout the eighteenth century and well into the nineteenth were the constraint and edification of children through books written for them. The emphasis continued to be on children and what was thought to be their needs rather than on literature, and children's books became tools for the educational process. The chief influence on English children's books came from France with the publication of Rousseau's *Emile* (1762) and its translation into English in 1762. Rousseau's idea of bringing up a child in a natural state, far from the corrupting influences of civilization but with an adult always at hand to teach and explain, was seized upon by writers for children. A flood of books was unleashed that portrayed children as constantly and of necessity under the surveillance of adults, who turned even a glance at a butterfly into a lesson on entomology or a sermon on the brevity of life. Hence Thomas Day in *Sandford and Merton* (1795–8) shows a minister, Mr. Barlow, undertaking the complete education of two boys (obviously at the expense of his clerical duties) and turning the rich, bad child into a duplicate of the good farmer's son. Mrs. Sherwood in *The History of the Fairchild Family* (1818–47) shows a father and mother devoting all their time to their children, who get into trouble whenever they are freed from parental supervision. Who in the 1960s would not expect such children to get into trouble the moment parental supervision was relaxed? For Rousseau's disciples the solution to this problem was not to encourage children to develop moral responsibility of their own from an early age; it was to make the external application of a moral code yet more stringent. The naughty Fairchild children are taken to visit a gibbet to see the body of a criminal who "had hung there some years."

Time brought modifications. The grip on children's books shifted from the French master (much misinterpreted by his English followers) to a group of English women and clergymen of Established, Unitarian, Evangelical, and Quaker persuasion. This included Dr. Aikin, Mrs. Barbauld, Mrs. Trimmer, Mrs. Sherwood, Maria Edgeworth, Mary Belson, Mary Elliott, Dorothy Kilner, and many others. Their motives were best expressed by Mrs. Trimmer in her magazine *The Guardian of Education* (1802): "to contribute to the preservation of the young and innocent from the dangers which threaten them in the form of infantine literature." Their vehicles were the Moral Tale and the Matter-of-Fact Tale, which were devoted to telling children how to behave, extolling missionary work among the heathen, and cramming the children with elementary information that was little more than religious didacticism. A geography book of 1818 contains this passage:

Q. What do the I-tal-i-ans wor-ship?

A. They wor-ship i-dols and a piece of bread.

Q. Would not God be ang-ry that I-tal-ians wor-ship i-dols and a piece of bread?

A. God is ang-ry.

The literature of the "moral" school mixed a liberal dose of menace in with its precepts. If children do not obey adults they will be punished and the punishment will be carried out. The heroine of Maria Edgeworth's *Rosamond* is told not to buy a purple jar. She does so and has to go shoeless and misses out on a treat. In much of the writing, death, the ultimate threat, is introduced. Moreover, God will see to it that death is the outcome of wrongdoing. In a little book of 1801 called *Pleasant Tales, to improve the mind and correct the morals of youth* (no irony is intended in the word "pleasant"), we meet Patty's cousin who was haughty and arrogant and who, having the misjudgement to marry her father's valet, was thrust out into the snow in true *East Lynne* style. The book ends thus:

> Patty put her poor Cousin to bed, where she lingered a few hours, and then expired, saying—"had I been GOOD, I should have been HAPPY; the GUILTY and the UNFEELING can never taste of PEACE." Patty lived long and happily, a striking example to the world, that HONESTY, FILIAL DUTY, and RELIGION, are well-pleasing in the sight of the Almighty who is the punisher of VICE, and the liberal rewarder of VIRTUE.

Charles Lamb in a famous letter to Coleridge commented on the effects of this type of book rather than on its spirit: "Mrs. Barbauld's stuff has banished all the old classics of the nursery. . . . Think what you would have been now, if instead of being fed with tales and old wives' fables in childhood, you had been fed with geography and natural history." The old classics of the nursery were not specifically designed for children but were literature they had taken for themselves—myth, faerie and folklore, romances, nonsense rhymes, and such adult books as *Pilgrim's Progress* (1678), *Robinson Crusoe* (1719), and *Gulliver's Travels* (1726). These classics existed in a kind of underground movement, however—they were not dead.

Each era has produced what can be described as a public literature for its children; that is, a model of what society desired for them. Leonard de Vries's

Flowers of Delight (1965), which gives a sampling of what was available for children from 1765–1830, shows how prominent this public literature was. Here is the round of *Easy Lessons, The Parental Instructor,* and stories containing "caution and instruction for children." Mr. de Vries has included a few folktales and nonsense rhymes that tend only to heighten the dreariness of the writing considered "good" for children. This literature came in horizontal waves from 1700 to 1900, but always cutting across it vertically was the literature of delight, the literature of mankind. As Paul Hazard has put it, children have simply refused to be oppressed and have taken what they wanted, be it Malory's *Le Morte d'Arthur* or Blake's *Songs of Innocence.* They had in addition the hundreds of little chapbooks that flooded England in the eighteenth century through the chapmen who sold them for a penny along with ribbons and needles and pins and thread. In these crude little books was stuff to make the sky turn round—*The Babes in the Wood, Valentine and Orson,* and *The Death and Burial of Cock Robin.*

Since "Up with didacticism!" was the battle cry of the guardians of public morality, the fairies were in retreat. Denigrations of imagination, pleasure, and faerie were not new of course. Plato in *The Republic* condemned the Homeric epics for portraying the passions of men in the form of gods. In 1554 Hugh Rhodes, a gentleman of the king's chapel, urged parents in his *Book of Nurture* to keep their children from "reading of feigned fables, vain fantasies, and wanton stories, and songs of love, which bring much mischief to youth." About the same time, Roger Ascham, the otherwise enlightened tutor of Queen Elizabeth I, was exclaiming against *King Arthur* for the young. The Puritans almost succeeded in driving out imagination and pleasure by the sheer numbers of their own kind of book, but nothing exceeded the attempts of the writers of the moral tale in the late eighteenth and early nineteenth century for either ferocity or length of attack on imaginative literature. And when George Cruikshank in his *Fairy Library* rewrote the old tales such as "Puss in Boots" and "Cinderella" as temperance tracts, it

seemed as if fear and didacticism in children's books were to last forever. Even Charles Dickens's now-famous article, "Frauds on the Fairies"—a spirited attack on Cruikshank's emasculated moralizing versions of the old tales—was seemingly an insufficient counterthrust. Time, however, was on the side of the underground movement.

Yet the authors of the moral tale meant so well. Their concern for the good of children is obvious: they were the first to pay attention to the children of the poor through the Sunday School movement. As writers they often used the English language with power and precision; they wrote with a passionate conviction that most modern writers for children should envy; and their plots were skilfully contrived to give concrete support for abstract ideas. In *Simple Susan* (1796) Maria Edgeworth uses a disagreement between a farmer and a lawyer to make her point:

> "Then why so stiff about it, Price? All I want of you is to say—"
>
> "To say that black is white, which I won't do, Mr. Case; the ground is a thing not worth talking of, but it's neither yours nor mine; in my memory, since the new lane was made, it has always been open to the parish, and no man shall enclose it with my good will.—Truth is truth, and must be spoken; justice is justice, and should be done, Mr. Attorney."
>
> "And law is law, Mr Farmer, and shall have its course, to your cost," cried the attorney, exasperated by the dauntless spirit of this village Hampden.

In retrospect it can be seen that until about 1850 the books deliberately intended for children were judged on their extraliterary qualities. They were used to preach, teach, exhort, and reprimand. However, their captive audience, children, resisted literature that was didactic and explicitly moral in favour of literature that was pleasurable—and *implicitly* moral. They were helped by the indestructible qualities of literature itself and by a few defenders such as Charles Lamb and Charles Dickens. As a result the underground movement held its own sufficiently to provide the inspiration for the flowering of children's literature that was to come.

John Rowe Townsend (b.1922)

John Rowe Townsend is a British novelist and critic whose history of children's literature, *Written for Children,* first published in 1965, has gone through six editions. "Didacticism in Modern Dress" first appeared in *The Horn Book Magazine* in 1967. Townsend calls for a reexamination of the assumption that modern books for children are not didactic as literature of earlier centuries was. In observations that also have bearing on the discussion of censorship and values in Part 8 of this anthology, he warns that too much emphasis on values and social issues in the criticism and selection of children's books can have detrimental effects on the reading habits of children, the attitudes of their teachers, and the creative work of writers. It is interesting to consider whether the didacticism that Townsend identifies has persisted or even intensified during the past several decades.

Didacticism in Modern Dress

During most of the nineteenth century it was taken for granted that children's books had a didactic aim. The emphasis could be mainly instructional, as in the Peter Parley series or Jacob Abbott's Rollo books. It could be moral, as in Mary Butt Sherwood's alarming *Fairchild Family* or the tearful saga of Elsie Dinsmore or the novels-for-young-ladies of the impeccable Charlotte M. Yonge. It could serve other ideals: that of Empire in the boys' stories of Englishman George Alfred Henty or of self-help in the rags-to-riches novelettes of Horatio Alger. But simply giving children pleasure would have seemed too frivolous an aim to most nineteenth-century writers.

Most; not all. Didacticism began to break down with the Alice books, with *Treasure Island,* which seemed to its author to be "as original as sin," with *The Adventures of Tom Sawyer* and *The Adventures of Huckleberry Finn,* in which, as Mark Twain said, "persons attempting to find a moral . . . will be banished." And today nearly all the old didactic books are dead; the survivors are those that rejected didacticism, with the addition of a few such as *Little Women* that transcended it.

Is the didactic spirit extinct in children's literature today? We tend to talk and write as though it were. It is contrary to our view of the happy, relaxed, and more-or-less-equal relationship between the generations which we now regard as ideal. Yet the urge to instruct the young is deeply built into human nature. And if one looks at the "quality" children's books of today, and still more at what is written about them, it is hard to avoid the conclusion that didacticism is still very much alive and that, by an engaging intellectual frailty, we are able to reject the concept while accepting the reality. We can accommodate this contradiction because of another of our frailties: we cannot extend any historical sense we may possess in order to look objectively at our own time. Years ago we threw the old didacticism (dowdy morality) out of the window; it has come back in at the door wearing modern dress (smart values) and we do not even recognize it.

The standards of those concerned with the assessment and selection of children's books are more often implicit than explicit; but in situations where these standards are being passed on they can be found stated plainly in print. Here are a few instances; I do not quote them with disapproval but only to make my point. May Hill Arbuthnot's *Children and Books* is the basic text for a great many teachers' courses, and the following passages are among a number of similar ones.

> . . . such books as *Little Women* and the Wilder stories, without referring to specific religious practices or creeds, leave children with the conviction that decent, kindly people can maintain an inner serenity even as they struggle with and master the evils that threaten them.
>
> . . . they [children] need books that, in the course of a good story, help to develop clear standards of right and wrong.
>
> Above all, to balance the speed and confusions of our modern world, we need to find books which build strength and steadfastness in the child, books which develop his faith in the essential decency and nobility of life, books which give him a feeling for the wonder and the goodness of the universe.

These views are not confined to one commentator. Charlotte S. Huck and Doris Young state in *Children's Literature in the Elementary School:*

> Through reading and guided discussion of their reading experiences children may gain understanding of self and others. They may come to realize that all behavior is caused and results from individual needs. Children may gain insight into their own behavior and the process of growth by identifying with individuals or families in good literature.

Dr. Bernice Cooper wrote, in an article on Laura Ingalls Wilder in a recent number of *Elementary English:*

> . . . the value of the "Little House" books is enhanced for boys and girls because Laura Ingalls Wilder's philosophy of life, without didacticism, permeates the series. That philosophy is expressed in the letter from Mrs. Wilder which the sixth grade received in response to their letters to her. She wrote, "But remember it is not the things you have that make you happy. It is love and kindness, helping each other and just plain being good."

The use of the phrase "without didacticism" seems to me to be a mere genuflection toward the accepted view that didacticism is out of fashion.

And here are two extracts from the excellent children's-book-selection policy of The Free Library of Philadelphia:

> In the field of purely recreational reading, stress is laid upon those books which develop the imagina-

tive faculties, promote understanding, and cultivate worthwhile ideals and values.

> Recreational books of all kinds, whether story or fact, are purchased with a view towards giving pleasure in reading and developing healthy attitudes towards the family, the community, the nation, and the world.

The views of the critics and selectors of children's books are of importance because these people are so largely the ones who decide whether a children's book will be published and whether, if published, it will succeed. It is a platitude to say that when we talk of quality children's books today we are not talking about something that children buy for themselves. There is a relationship between a child's pocket money and the price of an ice cream or a root beer or a candy bar or a comic; there is no relationship between a child's pocket money and the price of a book. The child himself hardly enters into the process by which quality children's books are assessed and distributed. They are written by adults, they are read by adults for adult publishers, they are reviewed by adults, they are bought by adults. This is inevitable. But the result is that a children's book can go far on the road to success before a single child has seen it.

The expensive, approved children's book costing $3.95 or $5.50 will do well if the libraries take it and not too well if they do not. A small number of parents with taste and money will buy it too; like the librarians they will almost certainly be serious, well-meaning, conscientious people. Quality publishing for children is governed by a complex social-institutional-economic equation which replaces the law of supply and demand; and as a result the adults are uniquely able to procure on the child's behalf not so much the thing he wants as the thing they feel he ought to have.

And what the child ought to have is apt to be something that fits in with the image of our society as serious, well-meaning, conscientious people feel it ought to be. We see our ideal society as one in which everybody is thoughtful, gentle, compassionate, withal humorous and fun loving; in which everyone is integrated but nevertheless individual. We expect, consciously or otherwise, that writers for children will provide us with instruments for bringing this society into being. And if our hands are on the levers, we cannot merely expect this; we can practically insist upon it. Now is the time to recognize just what we are doing and consider the dangers we run.

The first danger is an obvious one: the child opts out of the whole procedure and reads comics or nothing. He has, after all, the ultimate veto; however much adults approve of a book, no power on earth can make him read it if he does not want to. Indeed, teachers may also opt out of the whole procedure. I have met some—more in England than in the United States—who are utterly cynical. They say in effect: "It's no good trying to wish all this highbrow stuff on us. You just spend a day with the underprivileged kids I have in my class, and you'll see it's a blessed miracle if you can get them to read *any* kind of rubbish." Even the child who is a natural reader is no longer, as in the nineteenth century, virtually a captive audience. There is no dearth of other reading matter or of other things that an intelligent child can do with his time.

The existence of approved books that children will not read is a sizeable danger, though somewhat diminished by the fact that librarians cannot afford to give space to shelf-sitters. If the reviewers like a certain author but the children do not, the news soon gets around. The book that no child will read cannot survive—at least as a children's book—nor does it deserve to. Authors have to write books that the child can and will read, and the effect has been to concentrate their minds wonderfully. Even so, the danger of undercutting by the comics or formula stories is there. The writer or publisher with an eye on the main chance has a long start over the one who is practising or encouraging an art.

The second danger is the effect upon authorship. Writers are human and have to eat. With a few dogged exceptions, they will not write the kind of books that are going to be unacceptable. The people who pay the piper can call the tune. In an article in the spring 1966 *Author,* Philippa Pearce describes the demand for values as insidious. If a writer has moral standards, she says, "they will appear explicitly or implicitly in his books; or at least their corrupting contrary will not appear. He should not need to bother about values; his job is imaginative writing." Arthur Ransome, author of *Swallows and Amazons,* would not have it that the author is responsible to anybody but himself: "You write not for children but for yourself," he says, "and if by good fortune children enjoy what you enjoy, why then, you are a writer of children's books . . . no spe-

cial credit to you, but simply thumping good luck." But if you write for yourself and the result is dismissed as flippant or unwholesome, you will not feel like congratulating yourself on your luck.

The danger that the author is silenced, or more probably redirected toward producing acceptable work, must of course be seen in perspective. Plenty of good writers exist to whom the desired values are as natural as air. Ransome himself is an example. While there is no preaching in his books, they form in a sense a course for children, a powerful influence on them to look at life in a certain way—and a way that serious, well-meaning adults are likely to approve of. His children are truthful, loyal, straightforward; the things they do are sensible, constructive, character-building. And Philippa Pearce's *Tom's Midnight Garden* and *A Dog So Small* are just as firmly rooted in civilized values. Excellent authors may be found whose moral sense comes out still more explicitly in their books. One of many possible examples is Madeleine L'Engle, whose prize-winning *A Wrinkle in Time* describes a cosmic war of good against evil—evil here is the reduction of people to a mindless mass, while good is individuality, art, and love. Miss L'Engle finds it quite natural to bring in the great, and greatest, names on "our" side:

"Who have our fighters been?" Calvin asked. . . .

"Jesus!" Charles Wallace said. "Why, of course, Jesus!"

"Of course!" Mrs Whatsit said. "Go on, Charles, love. There were others. All your great artists. They've been lights for us to see by."

"Leonardo da Vinci?" Calvin suggested tentatively. "And Michelangelo?"

"And Shakespeare," Charles Wallace called out, "and Bach! And Pasteur and Madame Curie and Einstein!"

Now Calvin's voice rang with confidence. "And Schweitzer and Gandhi and Buddha and Beethoven and Rembrandt and St Francis!"

Miss L'Engle's was openly and joyfully a moral theme. I take not the slightest exception to her approach. But neither morality nor magnificent invocations will make a work of art live if the breath of life is not in it. And a moral posture assumed by an author in deference to current requirements could result in nauseating and disastrous work. A British literary editor suggested to me last year that I ought to write a children's novel "against racial prejudice"; he was as much puzzled as disappointed when I politely declined. But it seems to me that an author will do best to write only the books that come naturally to him. Anything else is done at the peril of his soul.

A third danger, which follows closely from the second, is the evaluation of books by the wrong standards. We are, I think, getting onto critically shaky ground when books like Louisa Shotwell's *Roosevelt Grady*, which deals with the life of a Negro family of migrant workers, and Dorothy Sterling's *Mary Jane*, telling of the ordeal of a Negro girl who goes to a newly integrated junior high school, and even Ezra Jack Keats' *The Snowy Day*, a bright, cheerful picture book about a little coloured boy's day in the snow, are discussed not on their literary merits but only as representations of racial problems. It is natural if you feel as strongly as most decent people do about racial discrimination to welcome books that give it short shrift; but to assess books on their racial attitude rather than their literary value, and still more to look on books as ammunition in the battle, is to take a further and still more dangerous step from literature-as-morality to literature-as-propaganda—a move toward conditions in which, hitherto, literary art has signally failed to thrive.

I should emphasize again that I am not in general opposed to the system or standards by which children's books are chosen; it is hard to see a practical alternative, other than a lapse into commercialism with the mass production of titles aimed at the lowest common denominator. And we in the United States and Great Britain can congratulate ourselves that at least there is no official children's literature, no crude plugging of a national or party line. Authors, publishers, critics, teachers, and librarians would unite—thank heaven—in horror at the very idea. All I am suggesting is that we should see our standards as they really are and should recognize that our emphasis on quality and on values exposes us to certain risks—which may be worth running but which we should be aware of. Let me sum them up, briefly. One is that if we are not careful the ordinary, unliterary child loses interest in books; for this problem the United States, through first-class work for children in the schools and libraries, is doing much better than England. Another is that we expect from authors what it is not right or wise to expect from them, and thus possibly stultify their creative impulse. And a third is that we judge books by the wrong standards. It is not irrelevant that a book may contribute to moral perception or social adjustment or the advancement of a minority group or the Great Society in general; but in writing there is no substitute for the creative imagination, and in criticism there is no criterion except literary merit.

Aelfric (c.955–c.1010)

This dialogue was written in Latin for use in a monastic classroom. Scholars have called it "the earliest document that communicates directly with children rather than adults."[1] It is exceptional for its time in that it is a kind of verbal drama: each of the pupils is asked, in turn, to assume a different role and to interact with the master. This dramatic premise enlivens what might otherwise have been (and probably usually was) a dull undertaking: studying Latin, the language of the Church and of the educated across the Holy Roman Empire. Aelfric was a Benedictine monk with greater than ordinary talents for writing sermons and instructional materials. In the *Colloquy*, he gives us a catalogue of something we rarely glimpse: the lives of ordinary folk in the Middle Ages. Aelfric reveals himself as a kindly, if stern, teacher, and his pupils, though idealized versions of what the real ones probably were like, still show us hints of what boys might have been like in a classroom a thousand years ago. A later monk wrote an interlinear gloss (a commentary between the lines) in Anglo-Saxon, the language of ordinary people in England at that time. This gloss suggests that the *Colloquy* was useful, among other things, for teaching translation from the language of the Church to the speech of everyday pursuits.

NOTE

1. Patricia Demers and Gordon Moyles, ed., *From Instruction to Delight: An Anthology of Children's Literature to 1850* (Toronto: Oxford UP, 1982) 2.

Carius est nobis flagellari pro doctrina quam nescire

AELFRIC'S COLLOQUY

PUPILS. *Nos pueri rogamus te, magister, ut doceas nos loqui latialiter recte, quia idiote sumus et corrupte loquimur.*

We children ask you, oh master, that you will teach us to speak Latin correctly, because we are ignorant and speak brokenly.

MASTER. *Quid vultis loqui?*

What do you want to speak about?

PUPILS. *Quid curamus quid loquamur, nisi recta loentio sit et utilis, non anilis aut turpis.*

We are not concerned with what we talk about, except that it be correct and useful conversation, and not superstitious or foul.

MASTER. *Vultis flagellari in discendo?*

Are you willing to be flogged while learning?

PUPILS. *Carious est nobis flagellari pro doctrina quam nescire. Sed scimus te mansuetum esse et nolle inferre plagas nobis, nisi cogaris a nobis.*

It is dearer to us to be beaten for the sake of learning than not to know. But we know that you are gentle and unwilling to inflict blows on us unless we force you to.

MASTER. *Interrogo te, quid mihi loqueris? Quid habes operis?* I ask you, what do you say to me? What sort of work do you do?

PUPIL "MONK". *Professus sum monachus, et psallam omni die septem sinaxes cum fratribus, et occupatus sum lectionibus et cantu, sed tamen vellem interim discere sermocinari latina langua.*

I am a professed monk, and I sing every day seven times with the brothers, and I am busy with reading and singing, but for all that I want in the meantime to learn to converse in the Latin language.

MASTER. *Quid sciunt isti tui socii?*

What do your comrades do?

PUPIL "MONK". *Alii sunt aratores, alii opiliones, quidam bubulci, quidam etiam venatores, alii piscatores, alii aucupes, quidam mercatores, quidam sutores, quidam salinatores, quidam pistores, coci.*

Some are ploughmen, others are shepherds, some oxherds, some again huntsmen, some fishermen, others fowlers, some merchants, some cobblers, some salters, some bakers, cooks.

MASTER. *Quid dicis tu, arator? Quomodo exerces opus tuum?*

What do you say, ploughman? How do you perform your work?

PUPIL "PLOUGHMAN". *O, mi domine, nimium laboro. Exeo diluculo minando boves ad campum, et iungo los ad aratrum; non est tam aspera hiems ut audeam latere domi pro timore domini mei, sed iunctis bobus, et confirmato vomere et cultro aratro, omni die debeo arare integrum agrum aut plus.*

Oh, my Lord, I work a great deal. I go out at dawn driving the oxen to the plain, and yoke them to the plough; there is not so severe a winter that I would dare conceal myself at home for fear of my master, but having yoked the oxen and fastened the share and coulter to the plough, every day I must plough a whole acre or more. (The Pupils describe the occupations of the Shepherd, Oxherd, Huntsman, Fowler, Merchant, Shoemaker, Salter, Baker, and Cook.)

MASTER. *Quid dicis tu, sapiens? Que ars tibi videtur inter istas prior esse?*
What do you say, wise one? Which skill seems to you among all these to be of first importance?

PUPIL "COUNSELLOR." *Dico tibi, mihi videtur servitium Dei inter istas artes primatum tenere, sicut legitur in evangelio: "Primum querite regnum Dei et iustitiam eius, et haec omnia adicientur vobis."*
I tell you, it seems to me that the service of God among these skills holds the first place, just as it reads in the gospel: "Seek first the kingdom of God and his justice and all things will be added to you."

MASTER. *Et qualis tibi videtur inter artes seculares retinere primatum?*
And which among the secular crafts seems to you to hold the first place?

PUPIL "COUNSELLOR." *Agricultura, quia arator omnes pascit.*
Agriculture, because the ploughman feeds everybody.

PUPIL "SMITH." *Ferrarius dicit: unde aratori vomer aut culter, qui nec stimulum habet nisi ex arte mea? Unde piscatori hamus, aut sutori subula sive sartori acus? Nonne ex meo opere?*
The blacksmith says: where does the ploughman get the ploughshare or coulter or even goad except through my skill? Where does the fisherman get his hook, or the cobbler his awl or the tailor his needle? Is it not from my work?

PUPIL "COUNSELLOR." *Consilarius respondit: Verum quidem dicis, sed omnibus nobis carius est hospitari apud te aratorem quam apud te, quia arator dat nobis panem et potum; tu, quid das nobis in officina tua nisi ferreas scintillas et sonitus tundentium malleorum et flantium follium?*
The Counsellor says: What you say is true, but it would be more esteemed by all of us to live near you, ploughman, than to live near to you, because the ploughman gives us bread and drink; you, what do you give us in your workshop except iron sparks and the noise of hammers beating and bellows blowing?

PUPIL "CARPENTER." *Lignarius dicit: quis vestrum non utitur arte mea, cum domos et diversa vasa et naves omnibus fabrico?*
The carpenter says: Which of you does not use my skill, when I make houses and different utensils and boats for everyone?

PUPIL "SMITH." *Ferrarius respondit: O, lignare, cur sic loqueris, cum nec saltem unum foramen sine arte mea vales facere?*
The blacksmith says: Oh, carpenter, why do you speak thus, when without my skill you could not pierce even one hole?

PUPIL "COUNSELLOR." *Consilarius dicit: O, socii et boni operarii, dissolvamus citius has contentiones, et sit pax et concordia inter vos, et prosit unusquisque alteri arte sua, et conveniamus semper apud aratorem, ubi victum nobis et pabula equis nostris habemus. Et hoc consilium do omnibus operariis, ut unusquisque artem suam diligenter exerceat, quia qui artem suam dimiserit, ipse dimittatur ab arte. Sive sis sacerdos, sive monachus, seu laicus, seu miles, exerce temet ipsum in hoc, et esto quod es; quia magnum dampnum et verecundia est homini nolle esse quod est et quod esse debet.*
The counsellor says: Oh, comrades and good workmen, let us break up these arguments quickly, let peace and concord be between us, and let each one help the others by his skill, and let us always be in harmony with the ploughman from whom we have food for ourselves and fodder for our horses. And I give this counsel to all workmen, that each one perform his craft diligently, since the man who abandons his craft will be abandoned by his craft. Whoever you be, whether priest or monk, whether laymen or soldier, exercise yourself in this and be what you are; because it is a great injury and shame for a man not to want to be what he is and what he ought to be.

MASTER. *O, pueri, quomodo vobis placet ista locutio?*
Oh, boys, how does this speech please you?

PUPIL. *Bene quidem placet nobis, sed valde profunde loqueris et ultra etatem nostram protrahis sermonem: sed loquere nobis uixta nostrum intellectum, ut possimus intelligere que loqueris.*

It pleases us well, but you certainly talk profoundly and use discourse beyond our ability; but talk to us according to our perception, so that we can understand what you say.

MASTER. *Interrogo vos cur tam diligenter discitis?*
I ask you, why are you learning so diligently?

PUPIL. *Quia nolumus esse sicut bruta animalia, que nihil sciunt, nisi herbam et aquam.*
Because we do not wish to be as stupid animals, who know nothing except grass and water.

MASTER. *Et quid vultis vos?*
And what do you want?

PUPIL. *Volumus esse sapientes.*
We wish to be prudent.

MASTER. *Qua sapientia? Vultis esse versipelles aut milleformes in mendaciis, astuti in loquelis, astuti, versuti, bene loquentes et male cogitantes, dulcibus verbis dediti, dolum intus alentes, sicut sepulchrum depicto mausoleo, intus plenum fetore?*
What sort of prudence? Do you want to be sly or cunning in lies, adroit in speech, clever, wily, speaking well and thinking evil, given to agreeable words, feeding anguish within, just like a sepulchre, painted like a splendid monument, and full of a stink inside?

PUPIL. *Nolumus sic esse sapientes, quia non est sapiens, qui simulatione semet ipsum decipit.*
We do not want to be clever in that way, because he is not clever who deceives himself with false show.

MASTER. *Sed quomodo vultis?*
But how do you want to be?

PUPIL. *Volumus esse simplices sine hipochrisi, et sapientes ut declinemus a malo et faciamus bona. Adhunc tamen profundius nobiscum disputas, quam etas nostra capere possit; sed loquere nobis nostro more, non tam profunde.*
We want to be upright without hypocrisy, and wise so that we avoid evil and do good. However, you are still debating with us more deeply than our years can take; therefore, speak to us in our own way, not so deeply.

MASTER. *Et ego faciam sicut rogatis. Tu, puer, quid fecisti hodie?*
And I will do as you ask. You, boy, what did you do today?

PUPIL. *Multas res feci. Hac nocte, quando signum audivi, surrexi de lectulo et exiui ad ecclesiam, et cantavi nocturnam cum fratribus; deinde cantavimus de omnibus sanctis et matutinales laudes; post haec primam et VII psalmos cum letaniis et primam missam; deinde tertiam, et fecimus missam de die; post haec cantavimus sextam, et manducavimus et bibimus et dormivimus, et iterum surreximus et cantavimus nonam; et modo sumus hic coram te, parati audire quid nobis dixeris.*
I did many things. Last night, when I heard the bell, I got up from bed and went to church and sang matins with the brothers; then we sang of all the holy ones and the morning praises; after this the six o'clock service and the seven psalms with the litanies and the first mass; then the nine o'clock service, and we celebrated the mass of the day; after this we sang the noon service, and ate and drank and slept, and we got up a second time and sang the three o'clock service; and now we are here in your presence, ready to hear what you will say to us.

MASTER. *O, probi pueri et venusti mathites, vos hortatur vester eruditor ut pareatis divinis disciplinis et observetis vosmet eleganter ubique locorum. Inceditis morigerate cum auscultaveritis ecclesie campanas, et ingredimini in orationem, et inclinate suppliciter ad almas aras, et state disciplinabiliter, et concinite unanimiter, et intervenite pro vestris erratibus, et egredimini sine scurrilitate in claustrum vel in gimnasium.*
O, good boys and charming students, your teacher encourages you to obey the divine commandments and to conduct yourselves with taste in every situation. Proceed in a reverent fashion when you hear the church bells, and enter in prayer, and bow humbly towards the dear altars, and stand as you have been instructed, and sing all together, and pray for your wrongdoings and go out either into the cloister or school without any buffoonery.

Charles Perrault (1628–1703)

Charles Perrault, a French bureaucrat during the regime of Louis XIV, championed the role of folklore in creating a modern literature distinct from classical Greek and Roman models. Although he was not the first European to produce a volume of folk or fairy tales, he proved among the most influential. His *Histories ou contes du temps passé* (*Stories or Tales of Times Past,* 1697) included some of our best-known fairy tales, such as "Sleeping Beauty," "Little Red Riding-Hood," "Blue Beard," "Cinderella," and "Puss in Boots." These tales, first translated into English in 1729, were not originally intended solely, or even mainly, for children, but despite the opposition of those like Sarah Trimmer, they had, by the mid-nineteenth century, become a beloved part of the children's literature canon. Ironically, toward the end of the twentieth century, their appropriateness for children was again being challenged. Perrault's versions of "Little Red Riding-Hood" and "Blue Beard" are cautionary tales, warning young female readers against trusting predatory men. In his "Little Red Riding-Hood," the story startlingly ends with the girl being swallowed by the wolf, instead of being rescued, as in the Grimm Brothers' version. Blue Beard's wife, however, has a narrow escape and is allowed to use the money and social position she has gained to secure her siblings' futures. "Puss in Boots" is a "clothes makes the man" story. It pointedly demonstrates how power and social position can be gained through illusion, manipulation, and intimidation: a cynical, "courtly" moral. The cat in dashing boots (who is an enchanted female in older versions of the tale) is one of the most flamboyant animal helpers in European fairy tales. Perrault concluded each tale with a sophisticated, ironic moral or two reflecting his aristocratic values, but these are often not reprinted in modern editions of children's literature (see also Perrault's "Cinderella" in Part 5).

Little Red Riding-Hood

Once upon a time there lived in a certain village a little country girl, the prettiest creature that ever was seen. Her mother was very fond of her, and her grandmother loved her still more. This good woman made for her a little red riding-hood, which became the girl so well that everybody called her Little Red Riding-hood.

One day her mother, having made some custards, said to her:—

"Go, my dear, and see how your grandmother does, for I hear she has been very ill; carry her a custard and this little pot of butter."

Little Red Riding-hood set out immediately to go to her grandmother's, who lived in another village.

As she was going through the wood, she met Gaffer* Wolf, who had a very great mind to eat her up; but he dared not, because of some fagotmakers† hard by in the forest. He asked her whither she was going. The poor child, who did not know that it was dangerous to stay and hear a wolf talk, said to him:—

"I am going to see my grandmother, and carry her a custard and a little pot of butter from my mamma."

"Does she live far off?" said the Wolf.

---

* godfather, "old man."

† wood cutters.

Gustave Dorè, a nineteenth-century French artist, produced high-quality engravings that became classic images of "Little Red Riding Hood" and other tales.

"Oh, yes," answered Little Red Riding-hood; "it is beyond that mill you see there, the first house you come to in the village."

"Well," said the Wolf, "and I'll go and see her, too. I'll go this way, and you go that, and we shall see who will be there first."

The Wolf began to run as fast as he could, taking the shortest way, and the little girl went by the longest way, amusing herself by gathering nuts, running after butterflies, and making nosegays of such little flowers as she met with. The Wolf was not long before he reached the old woman's house. He knocked at the door—tap, tap, tap.

"Who's there?" called the grandmother.

"Your grandchild, Little Red Riding-hood," replied the Wolf, imitating her voice, "who has brought a custard and a little pot of butter sent to you by mamma."

The good grandmother, who was in bed, because she was somewhat ill, cried out:—

"Pull the bobbin, and the latch will go up."

The Wolf pulled the bobbin, and the door opened. He fell upon the good woman and ate her up in no time, for he had not eaten anything for more than three days. He then shut the door, went into the grandmother's bed, and waited for Little Red Riding-hood, who came sometime afterward and knocked at the door—tap, tap, tap.

"Who's there?" called the Wolf.

Little Red Riding-hood, hearing the big voice of the Wolf, was at first afraid; but thinking her grandmother had a cold, answered:—

"'Tis your grandchild, Little Red Riding-hood, who has brought you a custard and a little pot of butter sent to you by mamma."

The Wolf cried out to her, softening his voice a little:—

"Pull the bobbin, and the latch will go up."

Little Red Riding-hood pulled the bobbin, and the door opened.

The Wolf, seeing her come in, said to her, hiding himself under the bedclothes:—

"Put the custard and the little pot of butter upon the stool, and come and lie down with me."

Little Red Riding-hood undressed herself and went into bed, where she was much surprised to see how grandmother looked in her nightclothes.

She said to her:—

"Grandmamma, what great arms you have got!"

"That is the better to hug thee, my dear."

"Grandmamma, what great legs you have got!"

"That is to run the better, my child."

"Grandmamma, what great ears you have got!"

"That is to hear the better, my child."

"Grandmamma, what great eyes you have got!"

"It is to see the better, my child."

"Grandmamma, what great teeth you have got!"

"That is to eat thee up."

And, saying these words, this wicked Wolf fell upon Little Red Riding-hood, and ate her all up.

The Master Cat, or Puss in Boots

Once upon a time there was a miller who left no more riches to the three sons he had than his mill, his ass, and his cat. The division was soon made. Neither the lawyer nor the attorney was sent for. They would soon have eaten up all the poor property. The eldest had the mill, the second the ass, and the youngest nothing but the cat.

The youngest, as we can understand, was quite unhappy at having so poor a share.

"My brothers," said he, "may get their living handsomely enough by joining their stocks together; but, for my part, when I have eaten up my cat, and made me a muff of his skin, I must die of hunger."

The Cat, who heard all this, without appearing to take any notice, said to him with a grave and serious air:—

"Do not thus afflict yourself, my master; you have nothing else to do but to give me a bag, and get a pair of boots made for me, that I may scamper through the brambles, and you shall see that you have not so poor a portion in me as you think."

Though the Cat's master did not think much of what he said, he had seen him play such cunning tricks to catch rats and mice— hanging himself by the heels, or hiding himself in the meal, to make believe he was dead—that he did not altogether despair of his helping him in his misery. When the Cat had what he asked for, he booted himself very gallantly, and putting his bag about his neck, he held the strings of it in his two forepaws, and went into a warren where was a great number of rabbits. He put bran and sow-thistle into his bag, and, stretching out at length, as if he were dead, he waited for some young rabbits, not yet acquainted with the deceits of the world, to come and rummage his bag for what he had put into it.

Scarcely was he settled but he had what he wanted. A rash and foolish young rabbit jumped into his bag, and Monsieur Puss, immediately drawing close the strings, took him and killed him at once. Proud of his prey, he went with it to the palace, and asked to speak with the King. He was shown upstairs into his Majesty's apartment, and, making a low bow to the King, he said:—

"I have brought you, sire, a rabbit which my noble Lord, the Marquis of Carabas" (for that was the title which Puss was pleased to give his master) "has commanded me to present to your Majesty from him."

"Tell thy master," said the King, "that I thank him, and that I am pleased with his gift."

Another time he went and hid himself among some standing corn, still holding his bag open; and when a brace of partridges ran into it, he drew the strings, and

so caught them both. He then went and made a present of these to the King, as he had done before of the rabbit which he took in the warren. The King, in like manner, received the partridges with great pleasure, and ordered his servants to reward him.

The Cat continued for two or three months thus to carry his Majesty, from time to time, some of his master's game. One day when he knew that the King was to take the air along the riverside, with his daughter, the most beautiful princess in the world, he said to his master:—

"If you will follow my advice, your fortune is made. You have nothing else to do but go and bathe in the river, just at the spot I shall show you, and leave the rest to me."

The Marquis of Carabas did what the Cat advised him to, without knowing what could be the use of doing it. While he was bathing, the King passed by, and the Cat cried out with all his might:—

"Help! help! My Lord the Marquis of Carabas is drowning!"

At this noise the King put his head out of the coach window, and seeing the Cat who had so often brought him game, he commanded his guards to run immediately to the assistance of his Lordship the Marquis of Carabas.

While they were drawing the poor Marquis out of the river, the Cat came up to the coach and told the King that, while his master was bathing, there came by some rogues, who ran off with his clothes, though he had cried out, "Thieves! thieves!" several times, as loud as he could. The cunning Cat had hidden the clothes under a great stone. The King immediately commanded the officers of his wardrobe to run and fetch one of his best suits for the Lord Marquis of Carabas.

The King was extremely polite to him, and as the fine clothes he had given him set off his good looks (for he was well made and handsome), the King's daughter found him very much to her liking, and the Marquis of Carabas had no sooner cast two or three respectful and somewhat tender glances than she fell in love with him to distraction. The King would have him come into the coach and take part in the airing. The Cat, overjoyed to see his plan begin to succeed, marched on before, and, meeting with some countrymen, who were mowing a meadow, he said to them:—

"Good people, you who are mowing, if you do not tell the King that the meadow you mow belongs to my

Lord Marquis of Carabas, you shall be chopped as small as herbs for the pot."

The King did not fail to ask the mowers to whom the meadow they were mowing belonged.

"To my Lord Marquis of Carabas," answered they all together, for the Cat's threat had made them afraid.

"You have a good property there," said the King of the Marquis of Carabas.

"You see, sire," said the Marquis, "this is a meadow which never fails to yield a plentiful harvest every year."

The Master Cat, who went still on before, met with some reapers, and said to them:—

"Good people, you who are reaping, if you do not say that all this corn belongs to the Marquis of Carabas, you shall be chopped as small as herbs for the pot."

The King, who passed by a moment after, wished to know to whom belonged all that corn, which he then saw.

"To my Lord Marquis of Carabas," replied the reapers, and the King was very well pleased with it, as well as the Marquis, whom he congratulated thereupon. The Master Cat, who went always before, said the same thing to all he met, and the King was astonished at the vast estates of my Lord Marquis of Carabas.

Monsieur Puss came at last to a stately castle, the master of which was an Ogre, the richest ever known; for all the lands which the King had then passed through belonged to this castle. The Cat, who had taken care to inform himself who this Ogre was and what he could do, asked to speak with him, saying he could not pass so near his castle without having the honor of paying his respects to him.

The Ogre received him as civilly as an Ogre could do, and made him sit down.

"I have been assured," said the Cat, "that you have the gift of being able to change yourself into all sorts of creatures you have a mind to; that you can, for example, transform yourself into a lion, or elephant, and the like."

"That is true," answered the Ogre, roughly; "and to convince you, you shall see me now become a lion."

Puss was so terrified at the sight of a lion so near him that he immediately climbed into the gutter, not without much trouble and danger, because of his boots, which were of no use at all to him for walking upon the tiles. A little while after, when Puss saw that the Ogre had resumed his natural form, he came down, and owned he had been very much frightened.

"I have, moreover, been informed," said the Cat, "but I know not how to believe it, that you have also the power to take on you the shape of the smallest animal; for example, to change yourself into a rat or a mouse, but I must own to you I take this to be impossible."

"Impossible!" cried the Ogre; "you shall see." And at the same time he changed himself into a mouse, and began to run about the floor. Puss no sooner perceived this than he fell upon him and ate him up.

Meanwhile, the King, who saw, as he passed, this fine castle of the Ogre's, had a mind to go into it. Puss, who heard the noise of his Majesty's coach coming over the drawbridge, ran out, and said to the King, "Your Majesty is welcome to this castle of my Lord Marquis of Carabas."

"What! my Lord Marquis," cried the King, "and does this castle also belong to you? There can be nothing finer than this courtyard and all the stately buildings which surround it; let us see the interior, if you please."

The Marquis gave his hand to the young Princess, and followed the King, who went first. They passed into the great hall, where they found a magnificent collation, which the Ogre had prepared for his friends, who were that very day to visit him, but dared not to enter, knowing the King was there. His Majesty, charmed with the good qualities of my Lord of Carabas, as was also his daughter, who had fallen violently in love with him, and seeing the vast estate he possessed, said to him:—

"It will be owing to yourself only, my Lord Marquis, if you are not my son-in-law."

The Marquis, with low bows, accepted the honor which his Majesty conferred upon him, and forthwith that very same day married the Princess.

Puss became a great lord, and never ran after mice any more except for his diversion.

Blue Beard

Once upon a time there was a man who had fine houses, both in town and country, a deal of silver and gold plate, carved furniture, and coaches gilded all over. But unhappily this man had a blue beard, which made him so ugly and so terrible that all the women and girls ran away from him.

One of his neighbors, a lady of quality, had two daughters who were perfect beauties. He asked for one of them in marriage, leaving to her the choice of which she would bestow on him. They would neither of them have him, and they sent him backward and forward from one to the other, neither being able to make up her mind to marry a man who had a blue beard. Another thing which made them averse to him was that he had already married several wives, and nobody knew what had become of them.

Blue Beard, to become better acquainted, took them, with their mother and three or four of their best friends, with some young people of the neighborhood to one of his country seats, where they stayed a whole week.

There was nothing going on but pleasure parties, hunting, fishing, dancing, mirth, and feasting. Nobody went to bed, but all passed the night in playing pranks on each other. In short, everything succeeded so well that the youngest daughter began to think that the beard of the master of the house was not so very blue, and that he was a very civil gentleman. So as soon as they returned home, the marriage was concluded.

About a month afterward Blue Beard told his wife that he was obliged to take a country journey for six weeks at least, upon business of great importance. He desired her to amuse herself well in his absence, to send for her friends, to take them into the country, if she pleased, and to live well wherever she was.

"Here," said he, "are the keys of the two great warehouses wherein I have my best furniture: these are of the room where I keep my silver and gold plate, which is not in everyday use; these open my safes, which hold my money, both gold and silver; these my caskets of jewels; and this is the master-key to all my apartments. But as for this little key, it is the key of the closet at the end of the great gallery on the ground floor. Open them all; go everywhere; but as for that lit-tle closet, I forbid you to enter it, and I promise you surely that, if you open it, there's nothing that you may not expect from my anger."

She promised to obey exactly all his orders; and he, after having embraced her, got into his coach and proceeded on his journey.

Her neighbors and good friends did not stay to be sent for by the new-married lady, so great was their impatience to see all the riches of her house, not daring to come while her husband was there, because of his blue beard, which frightened them. They at once ran through all the rooms, closets, and wardrobes, which were so fine and rich, and each seemed to surpass all others. They went up into the warehouses, where was the best and richest furniture; and they could not sufficiently admire the number and beauty of the tapestry, beds, couches, cabinets, stands, tables, and looking-glasses, in which you might see yourself from head to foot. Some of them were framed with glass, others with silver, plain and gilded, the most beautiful and the most magnificent ever seen.

They ceased not to praise and envy the happiness of their friend, who, in the meantime, was not at all amused by looking upon all these rich things, because of her impatience to go and open the closet on the ground floor. Her curiosity was so great that, without considering how uncivil it was to leave her guests, she went down a little back staircase, with such excessive haste that twice or thrice she came near breaking her neck. Having reached the closet-door, she stood still for some time, thinking of her husband's orders, and considering that unhappiness might attend her if she was disobedient; but the temptation was so strong she could not overcome it. She then took the little key, and opened the door, trembling. At first she could not see anything plainly, because the windows were shut. After some moments she began to perceive that several dead women were scattered about the floor. (These were all the wives whom Blue Beard had married and murdered, one after the other, because they did not obey his orders about the closet on the ground floor.) She thought she surely would die for fear, and the key, which she pulled out of the lock, fell out of her hand.

After having somewhat recovered from the shock, she picked up the key, locked the door, and went upstairs into her chamber to compose herself; but she could not rest, so much was she frightened.

Having observed that the key of the closet was stained, she tried two or three times to wipe off the stain, but the stain would not come out. In vain did she wash it, and even rub it with soap and sand. The stain still remained, for the key was a magic key, and she could never make it quite clean; when the stain was gone off from one side, it came again on the other.

Blue Beard returned from his journey that same evening, and said he had received letters upon the road, informing him that the business which called him away was ended to his advantage. His wife did all she could to convince him she was delighted at his speedy return.

Next morning he asked for the keys, which she gave him, but with such a trembling hand that he easily guessed what had happened.

"How is it," said he, "that the key of my closet is not among the rest?"

"I must certainly," said she, "have left it upstairs upon the table."

"Do not fail," said Blue Beard, "to bring it to me presently."

After having put off doing it several times, she was forced to bring him the key. Blue Beard, having examined it, said to his wife:—

"How comes this stain upon the key?"

"I do not know," cried the poor woman, paler than death.

"You do not know!" replied Blue Beard. "I very well know. You wished to go into the cabinet? Very well, madam; you shall go in, and take your place among the ladies you saw there."

She threw herself weeping at her husband's feet, and begged his pardon with all the signs of a true repentance for her disobedience. She would have melted a rock, so beautiful and sorrowful was she; but Blue Beard had a heart harder than any stone.

"You must die, madam," said he, "and that at once."

"Since I must die," answered she, looking upon him with her eyes all bathed in tears, "give me some little time to say my prayers."

"I give you," replied Blue Beard, "half a quarter of an hour, but not one moment more."

When she was alone she called out to her sister, and said to her:—

"Sister Anne"—for that was her name—"go up, I beg you, to the top of the tower and look if my brothers are not coming; they promised me they would come to-day, and if you see them, give them a sign to make haste."

Her sister Anne went up to the top of the tower, and the poor afflicted wife cried out from time to time:—

"Anne, sister Anne, do you see any one coming?"

And sister Anne said:—

"I see nothing but the sun, which makes a dust, and the grass, which looks green."

In the meanwhile Blue Beard, holding a great sabre in his hand, cried to his wife as loud as he could:—

"Come down instantly, or I shall come up to you."

"One moment longer, if you please," said his wife; and then she cried out very softly, "Anne, sister Anne, dost thou see anybody coming?"

And sister Anne answered:—

"I see nothing but the sun, which makes a dust, and the grass, which is green."

"Come down quickly," cried Blue Beard, "or I will come up to you."

"I am coming," answered his wife; and then she cried, "Anne, sister Anne, dost thou not see any one coming?"

"I see," replied sister Anne, "a great dust, which comes from this side."

"Are they my brothers?"

"Alas! no, my sister, I see a flock of sheep."

"Will you not come down?" cried Blue Beard.

"One moment longer," said his wife, and then she cried out, "Anne, sister Anne, dost thou see anybody coming?"

"I see," said she, "two horsemen, but they are yet a great way off."

"God be praised," replied the poor wife, joyfully; "they are my brothers; I will make them a sign, as well as I can, for them to make haste."

Then Blue Beard bawled out so loud that he made the whole house tremble. The distressed wife came down, and threw herself at his feet, all in tears, with her hair about her shoulders.

"All this is of no help to you," says Blue Beard; "you must die"; then, taking hold of her hair with one hand, and lifting up his sword in the air with the other, he was about to take off her head. The poor lady, turning about to him, and looking at him with dying eyes, desired him to afford her one little moment to her thoughts.

"No, no," said he, "commend thyself to God," and again lifting his arm—

At this moment there was such a loud knocking at the gate that Blue Beard stopped suddenly. The gate was opened, and presently entered two horsemen, who, with sword in hand, ran directly to Blue Beard. He knew them to be his wife's brothers, one a dragoon, the other a musketeer. He ran away immediately, but the two brothers pursued him so closely that they overtook him before he could get to the steps of the porch. There they ran their swords through his body, and left him dead. The poor wife was almost as dead as her husband, and had not strength enough to arise and welcome her brothers.

Blue Beard had no heirs, and so his wife became mistress of all his estate. She made use of one portion of it to marry her sister Anne to a young gentleman who had loved her for a long while; another portion to buy captains' commissions for her brothers; and the rest to marry herself to a very worthy gentleman, who made her forget the sorry time she had passed with Blue Beard.

Sarah Trimmer (1741–1810)

The aptly named Sarah Trimmer, Sunday school educator, writer, and editor of *Guardian of Education* (1802–06), is notorious for her watchdog attitude toward children's literature. "On the Care Which Is Requisite" and the two reviews that follow all appeared in the *Guardian of Education,* the first periodical to review children's books on a regular basis. In these essays and elsewhere, Trimmer represented the views of educators who believed that popular stories, such as Defoe's *Robinson Crusoe* and Perrault's fairy tales, were too immoral and terrifying for children. Among her own exemplary works is *The History of the Robins,* an outgrowth of the lessons she gave her own twelve children. *The History of the Robins* is the moralistic story of a family of robins, interwoven with the story of a family of humans. In her introduction to the book, Trimmer was careful to say that, although "the sentiments and affections of a good father and mother, and a family of children, are supposed to be possessed by a nest of Redbreasts," young readers should be "taught to consider them, not as containing the real conversations of birds (for that it is impossible we should ever understand), but as a series of FABLES." In the essays reprinted here, she seeks to make careful distinctions about what is proper for children of different ages to learn and what is not.

On the Care Which Is Requisite in the Choice of Books for Children

Formerly children's reading, whether for instruction or amusement, was confined to a very small number of volumes; of late years they have multiplied to an astonishing and alarming degree, and much mischief lies hid in many of them. The utmost circumspection is therefore requisite in making a proper selection; and children should not be permitted to make their own choice, or to read any books that may accidentally be thrown in their way, or offered to their perusal; but should be taught to consider it as a *duty,* to consult their parents in this momentous concern.

Between the ages of *eight* and *twelve years* children of both sexes may lay in a considerable stock of literary knowledge, if their school exercises are so managed as to prevent the encroachments of ornamental accomplishments at the hours which should be devoted to better purposes. Whilst the course of religious instruction, before recommended, is going on by means of the *Selection from the Scriptures,* together with the *partial reading of the Bible,* Rollin's Ancient History may be read, and some well-chosen modern Histories of England, France, &c. &c. The study of *Natural History,* that never-failing source of instruction and delight, may also be extended, by means of Books, and Museums, or private collections of natural curiosities; but in the choice of the former, particular care should be taken to provide those which are free from the general objection to books of this kind, of relating circumstances unfit for young people to be acquainted with: the occasional view of the *natural objects* which these books represent, will answer the double purpose of amusement and information. Books which treat in a general way of *Arts* and *Sciences* may also be put into the hands of children in this stage of their education; not as a regular study, but by way of assisting their ingenuity, should they discover a natural turn for simple mechanical experiments, or for any works of taste and ingenuity. But books of *Chemistry* or *Electricity,* and all that might lead them prematurely to making philosophical experiments, we would still keep from them. To the *Gardener's Dictionary* and *Calendar* they may be allowed free access, in order to instruct them to manage their little gardens, which in a family where there are boys and girls, should be the joint concern of brothers and sisters; as some parts of gardening are unfit for girls to perform.

The study of *Botany,* we would still reserve for a more advanced age. Poetry may be read and committed to memory; and select pieces in prose, such as are to be found in various collections, calculated at the same time to improve them in useful knowledge and in the art of reading aloud. Fables are also very proper for children of this age, and they are usually much delighted with them, and enter into the morals of them with surprising facility, when they relate to the common affairs of life. Some of Gay's Fables, though it is a favourite book, are too political for children. Works of fancy highly wrought, such as the Tales of the Genii, the Arabian Nights Entertainment, and the like, we would not put into the hands of young people till their religious principles are fixed, and their judgment sufficiently strong to restrain the imagination within due bounds, whilst it is led to expatiate in the regions of fiction and romance.

Novels certainly, however abridged, and however excellent, should not be read by young persons, till they are in some measure acquainted with real life; but under this denomination we do not mean to include those exemplary tales which inculcate the duties of *childhood* and *youth* without working too powerfully upon the feelings of the mind, or giving false pictures of life and manners.

Before we quit the subject of Books for Children, we must not omit to give a caution respecting those which go under the general name of *School Books,* viz. *Grammars, Dictionaries, Spelling Books, Exercise Books,* and *Books of Geography,* &c. &c. into some of which the leaven of false philosophy has found its way. In short, there is not a species of Books for Children and Youth, any more than for those of maturer years, which has not been made in some way or other an engine of mischief; nay, even well-intentioned authors have, under a mistaken idea that it is necessary to conform to the taste of the times, contributed to encrease the evil. However, there are in the mixed multitude, books of all sorts that are truly estimable; and others that might be rendered so with a little trouble in revising them; a task which we assure ourselves, the respective authors of these last-mentioned books will chearfully undertake, for *new Editions,* if they consider the infinite importance it is of, to be correct in principle, and cautious in expression, when they are writing for the young and ignorant, upon whose minds new ideas frequently make very strong impressions.

The remarks we have now made upon the different kinds of books for children, . . . will, we trust, be sufficient to guide the inexperienced mother in her choice for children under twelve years of age. . . .

An objection may probably be made to the course of reading we have recommended, as too *desultory,* but let it be remembered, that it is designed for children, who at this period of their lives are engaged in studies which require thought and application; and that, besides their stated tasks and exercises, they have the science of Religious Wisdom to call forth the exer-tion of their mental faculties. Young as they still are, they may look forward to a time of more leisure for the study of the Belles Lettres; therefore, it will be suffi-cient if a love of reading is excited.

Review of *The History of Little Goody Two Shoes*

This Book is a great favourite with us on account of the simplicity of style in which it is written, yet we could wish some parts to be altered, or omitted. It was the practice of Mr. Newbery's writers, to convey les-sons to those whom they sometimes facetiously called *Children of six feet high,* through the medium of Children's Books; and this has been done in the lit-tle volume we are examining. But in these times, when such pains are taken to prejudice the poor against the higher orders, and to set them against parish officers, we could wish to have a veil thrown over the faults of oppressive 'squires and hard-hearted overseers. Margaret and her brother might have been represented as helpless orphans, without imputing their distress to crimes of which young readers can form no accurate judgment; and should these readers be of the *lowest class,* such a narration as this might tend to prejudice their minds during life, against those whose favour it may be their future in-terest to conciliate, and who may be provoked by their insolence (the fruits of this prejudice) to treat them with harshness instead of kindness. We have also a very great objection to the Story of *Lady Duck-lington's Ghost* (though extremely well told, and as well applied) for reasons we have repeatedly given. The observations upon animals are not quite correct; and if nothing had been introduced about witchcraft, the Book would in our opinion have been more com-plete. However, with all its faults, we wish to see this Book continue in circulation, as some of these faults *a pair of scissors* can rectify, and the ill effect of oth-ers may be remedied by proper explanation from the parent. But amongst the numerous writers for chil-dren of the present day, who knows but some one may take in hand to give an edition of this little Work with the *proper emendations?*

Review of *Nursery Tales*

These Tales are announced to the public as *new trans-lations,* but in what respect this term applies we are at a loss to say, for, on the perusal of them we recognized the identical *Mother Goose's Tales,* with all their *vul-garities of expression,* which were in circulation when those who are now grandmothers, were themselves children, and we doubt not but that many besides our-selves can recollect, their horrors of imagination on reading that of *Blue Beard,* and the terrific impressions it left upon their minds. This is certainly a very im-proper tale for children. *Cinderella* and *Little Red Rid-ing Hood* are perhaps merely absurd. But it is not on account of their subjects and language only that these Tales, (Blue Beard at least) are exceptionable, another objection to them arises from the nature of their em-bellishments, consisting of coloured prints, in which the most striking incidents in the stories are placed be-fore the eyes of the little readers in glaring colours, representations we believe of play-house scenes, (for the figures are in theatrical dresses). In Blue Beard for instance, the second plate represents the opening of the *forbidden closet,* in which appears, not what the story describes, (which surely is *terrific enough!*) "*a floor clotted with blood, in which the bodies of several women were lying (the wives whom Blue Beard had married and murdered,")* but, *the flames of Hell* with *Devils* in frightful shapes, threatening the unhappy lady who had given way to her curiosity! The concluding print is, *Blue Beard* holding his terrified wife by the hair, and lifting up his sabre to cut off her head. We expected in Little Red Riding Hood, to have found a picture of the wolf tearing the poor innocent dutiful child to pieces, but happily the number of prints was complete without it. A moment's consideration will surely be sufficient to convince people of the least reflection, of the danger, as well as the impropriety, of putting such books as these into the hands of little children, whose minds are susceptible of every impression; and who from the liveliness of their imaginations are apt to convert into realities whatever forcibly strikes their fancy.

Isaac Watts (1674–1748)

Isaac Watts was a Nonconformist minister and author of hymns (many of which are still being sung today). "Against Idleness and Mischief" first appeared in *Divine Songs Attempted in Easy Language for the Use of Children* (1715). Like many Puritan writers, Watts drew upon the life of animals (in this case insects) to illustrate moral examples. (A noteworthy successor in this genre is Sarah Trimmer.) The speaker of the poem is a child. Most remarkable is Watts's implied affirmation of the validity of play as a legitimate childhood activity, although, of course, it is joined with study and work. "Obedience to Parents" was published in the same volume of songs, while "The Sluggard" was one of seven "Moral Songs" added to the 1740 edition. Both contain cautions about the dire consequences of disobedience and laziness. It is interesting to note that the horrifying image of ravens pecking out the eyes of disobedient children is similar to harsh punishments found in some traditional fairy tales (for example, in "Ashputtle" by the Grimm Brothers, in Part 5, the doves that help the heroine peck out the eyes of the "wicked and false" stepsisters in the end). Lewis Carroll paid tribute to Watts's famous poems, "Against Idleness and Mischief" and "The Sluggard," by parodying them in *Alice's Adventures in Wonderland* (see "How doth the little crocodile" in chapter 2 and "Tis the voice of the Lobster" in chapter 10, reprinted later in this section).

Against Idleness and Mischief

HOW doth the little busy bee
Improve each shining hour,
And gather honey all the day
From every opening flower!

How skillfully she builds her cell!
How neat she spreads the wax!
And labours hard to store it well
With the sweet food she makes.

In works of labour or of skill,
I would be busy too;
For Satan finds some mischief still
For idle hands to do.

In books, or work, or healthful play,
Let my first years be passed,
That I may give for every day
Some good account at last.

The Sluggard

'Tis the voice of the sluggard; I heard him
      complain,
"You have wak'd me too soon, I must slumber
      again."
As the door on its hinges, so he on his bed,
Turns his sides and his shoulders and his heavy
      head.

"A little more sleep, and a little more slumber;"
Thus he wastes half his days, and his hours
      without number,
And when he gets up, he sits folding his hands,
Or walks about sauntering, or trifling he stands.

I pass'd by his garden, and saw the wild brier,
The thorn and the thistle grow broader and higher;
The clothes that hang on him are turning to rags;

And his money still wastes till he starves or he
      begs.

I made him a visit, still hoping to find
That he took better care for improving his mind:
He told me his dreams, talked of eating and
      drinking;
But scarce reads his Bible, and never loves
      thinking.

Said I then to my heart, "Here's a lesson for me,"
This man's but a picture of what I might be:
But thanks to my friends for their care in my
      breeding,
Who taught me betimes to love working and
      reading.

Obedience to Parents

Let children that would fear the Lord
Hear what their teachers say;
With reverence meet their parents' word,
And with delight obey.

Have you not heard what dreadful plagues
Are threaten'd by the Lord,
To him that breaks a father's law,
Or mocks his mother's word?

What heavy guilt upon him lies!
How cursed is his name!
The ravens shall pick out his eyes,
And eagles eat the same.

But those who worship God, and give
Their parents honour due,
Here on this earth they long shall live,
And live hereafter too.

Robert Southey (1744–1843)

Robert Southey served as Poet Laureate of England from 1813 until his death. He was mocked
by Lord Byron as being the author of "blank verse and blanker prose."[1] A number of his works
were considered suitable for children, however, and appeared in anthologies for the young. One

of his most famous poems, "The Old Man's Comforts" (1799), is straight-forwardly pious and moralistic: the lesson is clear and sober. This poem would have been well known to many children of Lewis Carroll's day; in fact, many are likely to have memorized it. Its platitudes presented Carroll with an easy target, but Carroll did not merely parody it; he gave his version unforgettable wit, energy, and irreverence (see chapter 5, "Advice from a Caterpillar," in *Alice's Adventures in Wonderland,* presented later in this section). Today, Southey is notorious for his admonition to Charlotte Brontë, who wrote to him when she was twenty, seeking advice about writing. He wrote, "Literature cannot be the business of a woman's life, and it ought not to be. The more she is engaged in her proper duties, the less leisure will she have for it, even as an accomplishment and a recreation."[2] In the field of children's literature, Southey has been most famous for publishing "The Three Bears" in 1837, although earlier versions of the popular tale were found later, and the irresponsible old woman in Southey's version has evolved into the young girl Goldilocks.

NOTES

1. George Gordon, Lord Byron, Stanza XCVIII, *The Vision of Judgement* (London: John Hunt, 1822).
2. Robert Southey quoted in Cuthbert Southey, *The Life and Correspondence of Robert Southey,* vol. VI (London: Longman, Brown, Green, and Longmans, 1849–50) 327.

The Old Man's Comforts and How He Gained Them

"You are old, father William," the young man
   cried,
"The few locks which are left you are grey;
You are hale, father William, a hearty old man;
Now tell me the reason, I pray."

"In the days of my youth," father William replied,
"I remember'd that youth would fly fast,
And abus'd not my health and my vigour at first,
That I never might need them at last."

"You are old, father William," the young man
   cried,
"And pleasures with youth pass away.
And yet you lament not the days that are gone;
Now tell me the reason, I pray."

"In the days of my youth," father William replied,
"I rememberd that youth could not last;
I thought of the future, whatever I did,
That I never might grieve for the past."

"You are old, father William," the young man
   cried,
"And life must be hast'ning away;
You are cheerful and love to converse upon death;
Now tell me the reason, I pray."

"I am cheerful, young man," father William
   replied,
"Let the cause thy attention engage;
In the days of my youth I remember'd my God!
And He hath not forgotten my age."

Maria Edgeworth (1767–1849)

A popular Irish novelist and a skillful storyteller, Maria Edgeworth was one of the Rational Moralists who believed in principles of reason and practicality in the rearing of children. She herself helped to raise a large family of siblings, and with her educator father, she wrote *Practical Education* (1798), a manual of rational child rearing. While Edgeworth had strong objections to fantasy and fairy tales, she believed in making stories dramatic to instill moral values in children. Although the mother in "The Purple Jar" and the father in "The Birthday Present" may seem harsh and inflexible to some modern readers, they (like Edgeworth herself) believe that Rosamond, the impetuous girl, can learn from her experiences and discover better ways to make decisions. Whether we agree with the methods of child rearing that Rosamond's parents use or not, we can enjoy the lively and plausible Rosamond, who reflects Edgeworth's knowledge of real children, how they act and how they talk. Edgeworth, a contemporary of Jane Austen, was an acclaimed novelist for adults as well.

The Purple Jar

Rosamond, a little girl about seven years old, was walking with her mother in the streets of London. As she passed along she looked in at the windows of several shops, and saw a great variety of different sorts of things, of which she did not know the use, or even the names. She wished to stop to look at them, but there was a great number of people in the streets, and a great many carts, carriages and wheelbarrows, and she was afraid to let go her mother's hand.

"Oh, mother, how happy I should be," she said, as she passed a toy-shop, "if I had all these pretty things!"

"What, all! Do you wish for them all, Rosamond?"

"Yes, mamma, all."

As she spoke they came to a milliner's shop, the windows of which were decorated with ribands and lace, and festoons of artificial flowers.

"Oh, mamma, what beautiful roses! Won't you buy some of them?"

"No, my dear."

"Why?"

"Because I don't want them, my dear."

They went a little further, and came to another shop, which caught Rosamond's eye. It was a jeweller's shop, and in it were a great many pretty baubles, ranged in drawers behind glass.

"Mamma, will you buy some of these?"

"Which of them, Rosamond?"

"Which? I don't know which; any of them will do, for they are all pretty."

"Yes, they are all pretty; but of what use would they be to me?"

"Use! Oh, I am sure you could find some use or other for them if you would only buy them first."

"But I would rather find out the use first."

"Well, then, mamma, there are buckles; you know that buckles are useful things, very useful things."

"I have a pair of buckles; I don't want another pair," said her mother, and walked on.

Rosamond was very sorry that her mother wanted nothing. Presently, however, they came to a shop, which appeared to her far more beautiful than the rest. It was a chemist's shop, but she did not know that.

"Oh, mother, oh!" cried she, pulling her mother's hand, "look, look! blue, green, red, yellow, and purple!

Oh, mamma, what beautiful things! Won't you buy some of these?"

Still her mother answered as before, "Of what use would they be to me, Rosamond?"

"You might put flowers in them, mamma, and they would look so pretty on the chimney-piece. I wish I had one of them."

"You have a flower-pot," said her mother, "and that is not a flower pot."

"But I could use it for a flower-pot, mamma, you know."

"Perhaps if you were to see it nearer, if you were to examine it, you might be disappointed."

"No, indeed, I'm sure I should not; I should like it exceedingly."

Rosamond kept her head turned to look at the purple vase, till she could see it no longer.

"Then, mother," said she, after a pause, "perhaps you have no money."

"Yes, I have."

"Dear me, if I had money I would buy roses, and boxes and buckles, and purple flower-pots, and everything." Rosamond was obliged to pause in the midst of her speech.

"Oh, mamma, would you stop a minute for me? I have got a stone in my shoe; it hurts me very much."

"How came there to be a stone in your shoe?"

"Because of this great hole, mamma—it comes in there; my shoes are quite worn out. I wish you would be so very good as to give me another pair."

"Nay, Rosamond, but I have not money enough to buy shoes, and flower-pots, and buckles, and boxes, and everything."

Rosamond thought that was a great pity. But now her foot, which had been hurt by the stone, began to give her so much pain that she was obliged to hop every other step, and she could think of nothing else. They came to a shoemaker's shop soon afterwards.

"There, there! mamma, there are shoes; there are little shoes that would just fit me, and you know shoes would be really of use to me."

"Yes, so they would, Rosamond. Come in."

She followed her mother into the shop.

Mr. Sole the shoemaker, had a great many customers, and this shop was full, so they were obliged to wait.

"Well, Rosamond," said her mother, "you don't think this shop so pretty as the rest?"

"No, not nearly; it is black and dark, and there are nothing but shoes all round; and, besides, there's a very disagreeable smell."

"That smell is the smell of new leather."

"Is it? Oh!" said Rosamond, looking round, "there is a pair of little shoes; they'll just fit me, I'm sure."

"Perhaps they might; but you cannot be sure till you have tried them on, any more than you can be quite sure that you should like the purple vase exceedingly, till you have examined it more attentively."

"Why, I don't know about the shoes, certainly, till I have tried; but, mamma, I am quite sure that I should like the flower-pot."

"Well, which would you rather have, a jar or a pair of shoes? I will buy either for you."

"Dear mamma, thank you—but if you could buy both?"

"No, not both."

"Then the jar, if you please."

"But I should tell you, that in that case I shall not give you another pair of shoes this month."

"This month! that's a very long time indeed! You can't think how these hurt me; I believe I'd better have the new shoes. Yet, that purple flower-pot. Oh, indeed, mamma, these shoes are not so very, very bad! I think I might wear them a little longer, and the month will soon be over. I can make them last till the end of the month, can't I? Don't you think so, mamma?"

"Nay, my dear, I want you to think for yourself; you will have time enough to consider the matter, whilst I speak to Mr. Sole about my clogs."

Mr. Sole was by this time at leisure, and whilst her mother was speaking to him, Rosamond stood in profound meditation, with one shoe on, and the other in her hand.

"Well, my dear, have you decided?"

"Mama!—yes,—I believe I have. If you please, I should like to have the flower-pot; that is, if you won't think me very silly, mamma."

"Why, as to that, I can't promise you, Rosamond; but, when you have to judge for yourself you should choose what would make you happy, and then it would not signify who thought you silly."

"Then, mama, if that's all, I'm sure the flower-pot would make me happy," said she, putting on her old shoe again; "so I choose the flower-pot."

"Very well, you shall have it; clasp your shoe and come home."

Rosamond clasped her shoe and ran after her mother. It was not long before the shoe came down at the heel, and many times she was obliged to stop to take the stones out of it, and she often limped with pain! but still the thoughts of the purple flower-pot prevailed, and she persisted in her choice.

When they came to the shop with the large window, Rosamond felt much pleasure upon hearing her mother desire the servant, who was with them, to buy the purple jar, and bring it home. He had other commissions, so he did not return with them. Rosamond, as soon as she got in ran to gather all her own flowers, which she kept in a corner of her mother's garden.

"I am afraid they'll be dead before the flower-pot comes, Rosamond," said her mother to her, as she came in with the flowers in her lap.

"No, indeed, mamma, it will come home very soon, I dare say. I shall be very happy putting them into the purple flower-pot."

"I hope so, my dear."

The servant was much longer returning home than Rosamond had expected; but at length he came, and brought with him the long-wished-for jar. The moment it was set down upon the table, Rosamond ran up to it with an exclamation of joy: "I may have it now, mamma?"

"Yes, my dear, it is yours."

Rosamond poured the flowers from her lap upon the carpet, and seized the purple flower-pot.

"Oh, dear, mother!" cried she, as soon as she had taken off the top, "but there's something dark in it which smells very disagreeably. What is it? I didn't want this black stuff."

"Nor I, my dear."

"But what shall I do with it, mamma?"

"That I cannot tell."

"It will be of no use to me, mamma."

"That I cannot help."

"But I must pour it out, and fill the flower-pot with water."

"As you please, my dear."

"Will you lend me a bowl to pour it into, mamma?"

"That was more than I promised you, my dear; but I will lend you a bowl."

The bowl was produced, and Rosamond proceeded to empty the purple vase. But she experienced much surprise and disappointment, on finding, when it was entirely empty, that it was no longer a purple vase. It was a plain white glass jar, which had appeared to have that beautiful colour merely from the liquor with which it had been filled.

Little Rosamond burst into tears.

"Why should you cry, my dear?" said her mother; "it will be of as much use to you now as ever, for a flower-pot."

"But it won't look so pretty on the chimney-piece. I am sure, if I had known that it was not really purple, I should not have wished to have it so much."

"But didn't I tell you that you had not examined it; and that perhaps you would be disappointed?"

"And so I am disappointed, indeed. I wish I had believed you at once. Now I had much rather have the shoes, for I shall not be able to walk all this month; even walking home that little way hurt me exceedingly. Mamma, I will give you the flower-pot back again, and that purple stuff and all, if you'll only give me the shoes."

"No, Rosamond; you must abide by your own choice; and now the best thing you can possibly do is to bear your disappointment with good humour."

"I will bear it as well as I can," said Rosamond, wiping her eyes, and she began slowly and sorrowfully to fill the vase with flowers.

But Rosamond's disappointment did not end here. Many were the difficulties and distresses into which her imprudent choice brought her, before the end of the month.

Every day her shoes grew worse and worse, till at last she could neither run, dance, jump, or walk in them.

Whenever Rosamond was called to see anything she was detained pulling her shoes up at the heels, and was sure to be too late.

Whenever her mother was going out to walk, she could not take Rosamond with her, for Rosamond had no soles to her shoes; and at length, on the very last day of the month, it happened that her father proposed to take her with her brother to a glasshouse, which she had long wished to see. She was very happy; but, when she was quite ready, had her hat and gloves on, and was making haste downstairs to her brother and father, who was waiting for her at the hall door, the shoe dropped off. She put it on again in a great hurry, but, as she was going across the hall, her father turned round.

"Why are you walking slip-shod? no one must walk slip-shod with me; why, Rosamond," said he, looking at her shoes with disgust, "I thought that you were always neat; go, I cannot take you with me."

Rosamond coloured and retired.

"Oh, mamma," said she, as she took off her hat, "how I wish that I had chosen the shoes! They would have been of so much more use to me than that jar: however, I am sure, no, not quite sure, but I hope I shall be wiser another time."

The Birthday Present

"Mamma," said Rosamond, after a long silence, "do you know what I have been thinking of all this time?" "No, my dear—What?" "Why, mamma, about my cousin Bell's birthday; do you know what day it is?" "No, I don't remember." "Dear mother! don't you remember it's the 22nd of December; and her birthday is the day after to-morrow? Don't you recollect now? But you never remember about birthdays, mamma. That was just what I was thinking of, that you never remember my sister Laura's birthday, or—or—or *mine,* mamma."

"What do you mean, my dear? I remember your birthday perfectly well." "Indeed! but you never *keep* it, though." "What do you mean by keeping your birthday?" "Oh, mamma, you know very well—as Bell's birthday is kept. In the first place, there is a great dinner." "And can Bell eat more upon her birthday than upon any other day?" "No; nor I should not mind about the dinner, except the mince-pies. But Bell has a great many nice things—I don't mean nice eatable things, but nice new playthings, given to her always on her birthday; and everybody drinks her health, and she's so happy."

"But stay, Rosamond, how you jumble things together! Is it everybody's drinking her health that makes her so happy? or the new playthings, or the nice mince-pies? I can easily believe that she is happy whilst she is eating a mince-pie, or whilst she is playing; but how does everybody's drinking her health at dinner make her happy?"

Rosamond paused, and then said she did not know. "But," added she, "the *nice new* playthings, mother!" "But why the nice new playthings? Do you like them only because they are *new?*" "Not *only*—I do not like playthings *only* because they are new: but Bell *does,* I believe—for that puts me in mind—Do you know, mother, she had a great drawer full of *old* playthings that she never used, and she said that they were good for nothing, because they were *old;* but I thought many of them were good for a great deal more than the new ones. Now you shall be judge, mamma; I'll tell you all that was in the drawer."

"Nay, Rosamond, thank you, not just now; I have not time to listen to you."

"Well then, mamma, the day after to-morrow I can show you the drawer. I want you to judge very much, because I am sure I was in the right. And, mother," added Rosamond, stopping her as she was going out of the room, "will you—not now, but when you've time—will you tell me why you never keep my birthday—why you never make any difference between that day and any other day?" "And will you, Rosamond—not now, but when you have time to think about it—tell me why I should make any difference between your birthday and any other day?"

Rosamond thought, but she could not find out any reason; besides, she suddenly recollected that she had not time to think any longer; for there was a certain work-basket to be finished, which she was making for her cousin Bell, as a present upon her birthday. The work was at a stand for want of some filigree-paper, and, as her mother was going out, she asked her to take her with her, that she might buy some. Her sister Laura went with them.

"Sister," said Rosamond, as they were walking along, "what have you done with your half-guinea?" "I have it in my pocket." "Dear! you will keep it for ever in your pocket. You know, my godmother when she gave it to you said you would keep it longer than I should keep mine; and I know what she thought by her look at the time. I heard her say something to my mother." "Yes," said Laura, smiling; "she whispered so loud that I could not help hearing her too. She said I was a little miser." "But did not you hear her say that I was very *generous?* and she'll see that she was not mistaken. I hope she'll be by when I give my basket to Bell—won't it be beautiful? There is to be a wreath of myrtle, you know, round the handle, and a frost ground, and then the medallions—"

"Stay," interrupted her sister, for Rosamond, anticipating the glories of her work-basket, talked and walked so fast that she had passed, without perceiving it, the shop where the filigree-paper was to be bought. They turned back. Now it happened that the shop was the corner house of a street, and one of the windows looked out into a narrow lane. A coach full of ladies stopped at the door, just before they went in, so that no one had time immediately to think of Rosamond and her filigree-paper, and she went to the window where she saw her sister Laura looking earnestly at something that was passing in the lane.

Opposite to the window, at the door of a poor-looking house, there was sitting a little girl weaving lace. Her bobbins moved as quick as lightning, and she never once looked up from her work. "Is not she very industrious?" said Laura; "and very honest, too?" added she in a minute afterwards; for just then a baker with a basket of rolls on his head passed, and by accident one of the rolls fell close to the little girl. She took it up eagerly, looked at it as if she was very hungry, then put aside her work, and ran after the baker to return it to him. Whilst she was gone, a footman in a livery laced with silver, who belonged to the coach that stood at the shop door, as he was lounging with one of his companions, chanced to spy the weaving pillow, which she had left upon a stone before the door. To divert himself (for idle people do mischief often to divert themselves) he took up the pillow, and entangled all the bobbins. The little girl came back out of breath to her work; but what was her surprise and sorrow to find it spoiled. She twisted and untwisted, placed and replaced, the bobbins, while the footman stood laughing at her distress. She got up gently, and was retiring into the house, when the silver-laced footman stopped her, saying, insolently, "Sit still, child." "I must go to my mother, sir," said the child; "besides, you have spoiled all my lace. I can't stay." "Can't you?" said the brutal footman, snatching her weaving-pillow again, "I'll teach you to complain of me." And he broke off, one after another, all the bobbins, put them into his pocket, rolled her weaving-pillow down the dirty lane, then jumped up

behind his mistress's coach, and was out of sight in an instant.

"Poor girl!" exclaimed Rosamond, no longer able to restrain her indignation at this injustice; "poor little girl!"

At this instant her mother said to Rosamond— "Come, now, my dear, if you want this filigree-paper, buy it." "Yes, madam," said Rosamond; and the idea of what her godmother and her cousin Bell would think of her generosity rushed again upon her imagination. All her feelings of pity were immediately suppressed. Satisfied with bestowing another exclamation upon the "*poor little girl!*" she went to spend her half-guinea upon her filigree basket. In the meantime, she that was called the "*little miser*" beckoned to the poor girl, and, opening the window, said, pointing to the cushion, "Is it quite spoiled?" "Quite! quite spoiled! and I can't, nor mother neither, buy another; and I can't do anything else for my bread." A few, but very few, tears fell as she said this.

"How much would another cost?" said Laura. "Oh, a great—*great* deal." "More than that?" said Laura, holding up her half-guinea. "Oh no." "Then you can buy another with that," said Laura, dropping the half-guinea into her hand; and she shut the window before the child could find words to thank her, but not before she saw a look of joy and gratitude, which gave Laura more pleasure probably than all the praise which could have been bestowed upon her generosity.

Late on the morning of her cousin's birthday, Rosamond finished her work-basket. The carriage was at the door—Laura came running to call her; her father's voice was heard at the same instant; so she was obliged to go down with her basket but half wrapped up in silver paper—a circumstance at which she was a good deal disconcerted; for the pleasure of surprising Bell would be utterly lost if one bit of the filigree should peep out before the proper time. As the carriage went on, Rosamond pulled the paper to one side and to the other, and by each of the four corners.

"It will never do, my dear," said her father, who had been watching her operations. "I am afraid you will never make a sheet of paper cover a box which is twice as large as itself."

"It is not a box, father," said Rosamond, a little peevishly; "it's a basket."

"Let us look at this basket," said he, taking it out of her unwilling hands, for she knew of what frail materials it was made, and she dreaded its coming to pieces under her father's examination. He took hold of the handle rather roughly; when, starting off the coach seat, she cried, "Oh, sir! father! sir! you will spoil it indeed!" said she, with increased vehemence, when, after drawing aside the veil of silver paper, she saw him grasp the myrtle-wreathed handle. "Indeed, sir, you will spoil the poor handle."

"But what is the use of *the poor handle*," said her father, "if we are not to take hold of it? And pray," continued he, turning the basket round with his finger and thumb, rather in a disrespectful manner, "pray, is this the thing you have been about all this week? I have seen you all this week dabbling with paste and rags; I could not conceive what you were about. Is this the thing?" "Yes, sir. You think, then, that I have wasted my time, because the basket is of no use; but then it is for a present for my cousin Bell." "Your cousin Bell will be very much obliged to you for a present that is of no use. You had better have given her the purple jar."

"Oh, father! I thought you had forgotten that—it was two years ago; I'm not so silly now. But Bell will like the basket, I know, though it is of no use."

"Then you think Bell is sillier *now* than you were two years ago,—well, perhaps that is true; but how comes it, Rosamond, now that you are so wise, that you are fond of such a silly person?" "*I*, father?" said Rosamond, hesitating; "I don't think I am *very* fond of her." "I did not say *very* fond." "Well, but I don't think I am at all fond of her." "But you have spent a whole week in making this thing for her." "Yes, and all my half-guinea besides."

"Yet you think her silly, and you are not fond of her at all; and you say you know this thing will be of no use to her."

"But it is her birthday, sir; and I am sure she will *expect* something, and everybody else will give her something."

"Then your reason for giving is because she expects you to give her something. And will you, or can you, or should you, always give, merely because others *expect*, or because somebody else gives?" "Always?—no, not always." "Oh, only on birthdays."

Rosamond, laughing: "Now you are making a joke of me, papa, I see; but I thought you liked that people should be generous,—my godmother said that she did." "So do I, full as well as your godmother; but we have not yet quite settled what it is to be generous." "Why, is it not generous to make presents?" said Rosamond. "That is the question which it would take up a great deal of time to answer. But, for instance, to make a present of a thing that you know can be of no use to a person you neither love nor esteem, because it is her birthday, and because everybody gives her something, and because she expects something, and because your godmother says she likes that people should be generous, seems to me, my dear Rosamond, to be, since I must say it, rather more like folly than generosity."

Rosamond looked down upon the basket, and was silent. "Then I am a fool, am I?" said she, looking up at last. "Because you have made *one* mistake? No. If you have sense enough to see your own mistakes, and can afterwards avoid them, you will never be a fool."

Here the carriage stopped, and Rosamond recollected that the basket was uncovered.

Now we must observe that Rosamond's father had not been too severe upon Bell when he called her a silly girl. From her infancy she had been humoured; and at eight years old she had the misfortune to be a spoiled child. She was idle, fretful, and selfish; so that nothing could make her happy. On her birthday she expected, however, to be perfectly happy. Everybody in the house tried to please her, and they succeeded so well that between breakfast and dinner she had only six fits of crying. The cause of five of these fits no one could discover: but the last, and most lamentable, was occasioned by a disappointment about a worked muslin frock; and accordingly, at dressing time, her maid brought it to her, exclaiming, "See here, miss, what your mamma has sent you on your birthday. Here's a frock fit for a queen—if it had but lace round the cuffs." "And why has not it lace around the cuffs? mamma said it should." "Yes, but mistress was disappointed about the lace; it is not come home." "Not come home, indeed! and didn't they know it was my birthday? But then I say I won't wear it without the lace—I can't wear it without the lace, and I won't."

The lace, however, could not be had; and Bell at length submitted to let the frock be put on. "Come, Miss Bell, dry your eyes," said the maid who *educated* her; "dry your eyes, and I'll tell you something that will please you."

"What, then?" said the child, pouting and sobbing. "Why—but you must not tell that I told you." "No,— but if I am asked?" "Why, if you are asked, you must tell the truth, to be sure. So I'll hold my tongue, miss." "Nay, tell me, though, and I'll never tell—if I *am* asked." "Well, then," said the maid, "your cousin Rosamond is come, and has brought you the most *beautifullest* thing you ever saw in your life; but you are not to know anything about it till after dinner, because she wants to surprise you; and mistress has put it into her wardrobe till after dinner." "Till after dinner!" repeated Bell impatiently; "I can't wait till then; I must see it this minute." The maid refused her several times, till Bell burst into another fit of crying, and the maid, fearing that her mistress would be angry with *her,* if Bell's eyes were red at dinner time, consented to show her the basket.

"How pretty!—but let me have it in my own hands," said Bell, as the maid held the basket up out of her reach. "Oh, no, you must not touch it; for if you should spoil it, what would become of me?" "Become of you, indeed!" exclaimed the spoiled child, who never considered anything but her own immediate gratification—"Become of *you,* indeed! what signifies that?—I shan't spoil it; and I will have it in my own hands. If you don't hold it down for me directly, I'll tell that you showed it to me." "Then you won't snatch it?" "No, no, I won't indeed," said Bell; but she had learned from her maid a total disregard of truth. She snatched the basket the moment it was within her reach. A struggle ensued, in which the handle and lid were torn off, and one of the medallions crushed inwards, before the little fury returned to her senses.

Calmed at this sight, the next question was, how she should conceal the mischief which she had done. After many attempts, the handle and lid were replaced; the basket was put exactly in the same spot in which it had stood before, and the maid charged the child "*to look as if nothing was the matter.*"

We hope that both children and parents will here pause for a moment to reflect. The habits of tyranny, meanness, and falsehood, which children acquire from living with bad servants, are scarcely ever conquered in the whole course of their future lives.

After shutting up the basket they left the room, and in the adjoining passage they found a poor girl waiting with a small parcel in her hand. "What's your business?" said the maid. "I have brought home the lace, madam, that was bespoke for the young lady." "Oh, you have, have you, at last?" said Bell; "and pray why

didn't you bring it sooner?" The girl was going to answer, but the maid interrupted her, saying, "Come, come, none of your excuses; you are a little idle, good-for-nothing thing, to disappoint Miss Bell upon her birthday. But now you have brought it, let us look at it!"

The little girl gave the lace without reply, and the maid desired her to go about her business, and not to expect to be paid; for that her mistress could not see anybody, *because* she was in a room full of company.

"May I call again, madam, this afternoon?" said the child, timidly.

"Lord bless my stars!" replied the maid, "what makes people so poor, I *wonders!* I wish mistress would buy her lace at the warehouse, as I told her, and not of these folks. Call again! yes, to be sure. I believe you'd call, call, call twenty times for twopence."

However ungraciously the permission to call again was granted, it was received with gratitude. The little girl departed with a cheerful countenance, and Bell teased her maid till she got her to sew the long-wished-for lace upon her cuffs.

Unfortunate Bell!—All dinner time passed, and people were so hungry, so busy, or so stupid, that not an eye observed her favourite piece of finery. Till at length she was no longer able to conceal her impatience, and turning to Laura, who sat next to her, she said, "You have no lace upon your cuffs. Look how beautiful mine is!—is not it? Don't you wish your mamma could afford to give some like it? But you can't get any if she would, for this was made on purpose for me on my birthday, and nobody can get a bit more anywhere, if they would give the world for it" "But cannot the person who made it," said Laura, "make any more like it?" "No, no, no!" cried Bell; for she had already learned, either from her maid or her mother, the mean pride which values things not for being really pretty or useful, but for being such as nobody else can procure. "Nobody can get any like it, I say," repeated Bell; "nobody in all London can make it but one person, and that person will never make a bit for anybody but me, I am sure. Mamma won't let her, if I ask her not." "Very well," said Laura coolly, "I do not want any of it; you need not be so violent: I assure you that I don't want any of it." "Yes, but you do, though," said Bell, more angrily. "No, indeed," said Laura, smiling. "You do, in the bottom of your heart; but you say you don't to plague me, I know," cried Bell, swelling with disappointed vanity. "It is pretty for all that, and it cost a great deal of money too, and nobody shall have any like it, if they cried their eyes out."

Laura received this declaration in silence—Rosamond smiled; and at her smile the ill-suppressed rage of the spoiled child burst forth into the seventh and loudest fit of crying which had yet been heard on her birthday.

"What's the matter, my pet?" cried her mother; "come to me and tell me what's the matter." Bell ran roaring to her mother; but no otherwise explained the cause of her sorrow than by tearing the fine lace with frantic gestures from her cuffs, and throwing the fragments into her mother's lap. "Oh! the lace, child!—are you mad?" said her mother, catching hold of both her hands. "Your beautiful lace, my dear love—do you know how much it cost?" "I don't care how much it cost—it is not beautiful, and I'll have none of it," replied Bell, sobbing; "for it is not beautiful." "But it is beautiful," retorted her mother; "I chose the pattern myself. Who has put it into your head, child, to dislike it? Was it Nancy?" "No, not Nancy, but *them,* mamma," said Bell, pointing to Laura and Rosamond. "Oh, fie! don't *point,*" said her mother, putting down her stubborn finger; "nor say *them,* like Nancy; I am sure you misunderstood. Miss Laura, I am sure, did not mean any such thing." "No, madam; and I did not say any such thing, that I recollect," said Laura, gently. "Oh no, indeed!" cried Rosamond, warmly, rising in her sister's defence.

No defence or explanation, however, was to be heard, for everybody had now gathered round Bell, to dry her tears, and to comfort her for the mischief she had done to her own cuffs. They succeeded so well, that in about a quarter of an hour the young lady's eyes and the reddened arches over her eyebrows came to their natural colour; and the business being thus happily hushed up, the mother, as a reward to her daughter for her good humour, begged that Rosamond would now be so good as to produce her "charming present."

Rosamond, followed by all the company, amongst whom, to her great joy, was her godmother, proceeded to the dressing-room. "Now I am sure," thought she, "Bell will be surprised, and my godmother will see she was right about my generosity."

The doors of the wardrobe were opened with due ceremony, and the filigree basket appeared in all its glory. "Well, this is a charming present, indeed!" said

the godmother, who was one of the company; "*my* Rosamond knows how to make presents." And as she spoke, she took hold of the basket, to lift it down to the admiring audience. Scarcely had she touched it, when, lo! the basket fell to the ground, and only the handle remained in her hand. All eyes were fixed upon the wreck. Exclamations of sorrow were heard in various tones; and "Who can have done this?" was all that Rosamond could say. Bell stood in sullen silence, which she obstinately preserved in the midst of the inquiries that were made about the disaster.

At length the servants were summoned, and amongst them Nancy, Miss Bell's maid and governess. She affected much surprise when she saw what had befallen the basket, and declared that she knew nothing of the matter, but that she had seen her mistress in the morning put it quite safe into the wardrobe; and that, for her part, she had never touched it, or thought of touching it, in her born days. "Nor Miss Bell, neither, ma'am,—I can answer for her; for she never knew of its being there, because I never so much as mentioned it to her, that there was such a thing in the house, because I knew Miss Rosamond wanted to surprise her with the secret; so I never mentioned a sentence of it—did I, Miss Bell?"

Bell, putting on the deceitful look which her maid had taught her, answered boldly, "*No*"; but she had hold of Rosamond's hand, and at the instant she uttered this falsehood she squeezed it terribly. "Why do you squeeze my hand so?" said Rosamond, in a low voice; "what are you afraid of?" "Afraid of!" cried Bell, turning angrily; "I'm not afraid of anything—I've nothing to be afraid about." "Nay, I did not say you had," whispered Rosamond; "but only if you did by accident—you know what I mean—I should not be angry if you did—only say so." "I say I did not!" cried Bell furiously. "Mamma, mamma! Nancy! my cousin Rosamond won't believe me! That's very hard. It's very rude, and I won't bear it—I won't." "Don't be angry, love. Don't," said the maid. "Nobody suspects you, darling," said her mother; "but she has too much sensibility. Don't cry, love; nobody suspected you." "But you know," continued she, turning to the maid, "somebody must have done this, and I must know how it was done. Miss Rosamond's charming present must not be spoiled in this way, in my house, without my taking proper notice of it. I assure you I am very angry about it, Rosamond."

Rosamond did not rejoice in her anger, and had nearly made a sad mistake by speaking aloud her thoughts—"*I was very foolish*—" she began and stopped.

"Ma'am," cried the maid, suddenly, "I'll venture to say I know who did it." "Who?" said every one, eagerly. "Who?" said Bell, trembling. "Why, miss, don't you recollect that little girl with the lace, that we saw peeping about in the passage? I'm sure she must have done it; for here she was by herself half an hour or more, and not another creature has been in mistress's dressing-room, to my certain knowledge, since morning. Those sort of people have so much curiosity. I'm sure she must have been meddling with it," added the maid.

"Oh yes, that's the thing," said the mistress, decidedly. "Well, Miss Rosamond, for your comfort she shall never come into my house again." "Oh, that would not comfort me at all," said Rosamond; "besides, we are not sure that she did it, and if—" A single knock at the door was heard at this instant. It was the little girl, who came to be paid for her lace. "Call her in," said the lady of the house; "let us see her directly."

The maid, who was afraid that the girl's innocence would appear if she were produced, hesitated; but upon her mistress repeating her commands, she was forced to obey. The girl came in with a look of simplicity; but when she saw a room full of company she was a little abashed. Rosamond and Laura looked at her and one another with surprise, for it was the same little girl whom they had seen weaving lace. "Is not it she?" whispered Rosamond to her sister. "Yes, it is; but hush," said Laura, "she does not know us. Don't say a word, let us hear what she will say."

Laura got behind the rest of the company as she spoke, so that the little girl could not see her.

"Vastly well!" said Bell's mother; "I am waiting to see how long you will have the assurance to stand there with that innocent look. Did you ever see that basket before?" "Yes, ma'am," said the girl. "*Yes, ma'am!*" cried the maid; "and what else do you know about it? You had better confess it at once, and mistress, perhaps, will say no more about it." "Yes, do confess it," added Bell, earnestly. "Confess what, madam?" said the little girl; "I never touched the basket, madam." "You never *touched* it; but you confess," interrupted Bell's mother, "that you *did see* it before. And, pray, how came you to see it? You must have

opened my wardrobe." "No, indeed, ma'am," said the little girl; "but I was waiting in the passage, ma'am, and this door was partly open; and looking at the maid, you know, I could not help seeing it." "Why, how could you see through the doors of my wardrobe?" rejoined the lady.

The maid, frightened, pulled the little girl by the sleeve.

"Answer me," said the lady, "where did you see this basket?" Another stronger pull. "I saw it, madam, in her hands," looking at the maid; "and—" "Well, and what became of it afterwards?" "Ma'am"—hesitating—"miss pulled, and by accident—I believe, I saw, ma'am—miss, you know what I saw." "I do not know—I do not know; and if I did, you had no business there; and mamma won't believe you, I am sure." Everybody else, however, did believe; and their eyes were fixed upon Bell in a manner which made her feel rather ashamed. "What do you all look at me so for? Why do you all look so? And am I to be put to shame on my birthday?" cried she, bursting into a roar of passion; "and all for this nasty thing!" added she, pushing away the remains of the basket, and looking angrily at Rosamond. "Bell! Bell! oh, fie! fie!—Now I *am* ashamed of you; that's quite rude to your cousin," said her mother, who was more shocked at her daughter's want of politeness than at her falsehood. "Take her away, Nancy, till she has done crying," added she to the maid, who accordingly carried off her pupil.

Rosamond, during this scene, especially at the moment when her present was pushed away with such disdain, had been making reflections upon the nature of true generosity. A smile from her father, who stood by, a silent spectator of the catastrophe of the filigree basket, gave rise to these reflections; nor were they entirely dissipated by the condolence of the rest of the company, nor even by the praises of her godmother, who, for the purpose of condoling with her, said, "Well, my dear Rosamond, I admire your generous spirit. You know I prophesied that your half-guinea would be gone the soonest. Did I not, Laura?" said she, appealing, in a sarcastic tone, to where she thought Laura was. "Where is Laura? I don't see her." Laura came forward. "You are too *prudent* to throw away your money like your sister. Your half-guinea, I'll answer for it, is snug in your pocket—is it not?" "No, madam," answered she, in a low voice.

But low as the voice of Laura was, the poor little lace-girl heard it; and now, for the first time, fixing her eyes upon Laura, recollected her benefactress. "Oh, that's the young lady!" she exclaimed, in a tone of joyful gratitude, "the good, good young lady who gave me the half-guinea, and would not stay to be thanked for it; but I *will* thank her now."

"The half-guinea, Laura!" said her godmother. "What is all this?" "I'll tell you, madam, if you please," said the little girl.

It was not in expectation of being praised for it that Laura had been generous, and therefore everybody was really touched with the history of the weaving-pillow; and whilst they praised, felt a certain degree of respect, which is not always felt by those who pour forth eulogiums. *Respect* is not an improper word, even applied to a child of Laura's age; for let the age or situation of the person be what it may, they command respect who deserve it.

"Ah, madam!" said Rosamond to her godmother, "now you see—you see she is *not* a little miser. I'm sure that's better than wasting half a guinea upon a filigree basket; is it not, ma'am?" said she, with an eagerness which showed that she had forgotten all her own misfortunes in sympathy with her sister. "This is being *really generous,* father, is it not?"

"Yes, Rosamond," said her father, and he kissed her; "this *is* being really generous. It is not only by giving away money that we can show generosity; it is by giving up to others anything that we like ourselves; and therefore," added he, smiling, "it is really generous of you to give your sister the thing you like best of all others."

"The thing I like the best of all others, father," said Rosamond, half pleased, half vexed. "What is that, I wonder? You don't mean *praise,* do you, sir?" "Nay, you must decide that yourself, Rosamond." "Why, sir," said she, ingenuously, "perhaps it *was* ONCE the thing I liked best; but the pleasure I have just felt makes me like something else much better."

Jane Taylor (1783–1824)

The theme of cruelty to animals was a common one in moralistic children's literature, and the pantry was frequently the place of reckoning, as it is in Jane Taylor's poem about a young fisherman. What distinguishes this poem from many other similar tales, however, is its emphasis on two standards: one for adults who need to kill animals to provide food and one for children who might "do the same in play." In this "awful warning" poem, the retribution horrifyingly resembles the injury inflicted by the boy. Recent critics have observed that nineteenth-century children's literature encouraging appreciation for nature and opposing cruelty to animals helped launch the twentieth-century environmental movement. See the selection after "The Little Fisherman" for more information on Jane Taylor, her sister Ann, and their still-popular poem "The Star."

The Little Fisherman

There was a little fellow once,
And Harry was his name,

And many a naughty trick had he—
I tell it to his shame.

He minded not his friends' advice,
But followed his own wishes;
And one most cruel trick of his,
Was that of catching fishes.

His father had a little pond,
Where often Harry went;
And there in this unfeeling sport,
He many an evening spent.

One day he took his hook and bait
And hurried to the pond
And there began the cruel game,
Of which he was so fond.

And many a little fish he caught,
And pleased was he to look,
To see them writhe in agony,
And struggle on the hook.

At last, when having caught enough,
And also tired himself,
He hastened home, intending there
To put them on a shelf.

But as he jumped to reach a dish,
To put his fishes in,
A large meat-hook, that hung close by,
Did catch him by the chin.

Poor Harry kick'd, and call'd aloud,
And scream'd, and cried, and roar'd,

While from his wound the crimson blood
In dreadful torrents pour'd.

The maids came running, frighten'd much,
To see him hanging there,
And soon they took him from the hook,
And set him in a chair.

The surgeon came and stopped the blood,
And bound his aching head;
And then they carried him up-stairs,
And laid him on his bed.

Conviction darted on his mind,
As groaning there he lay,
And with compunction then he thought
About his cruel play.

"And oh!" said he "poor little fish,
What tortures they have borne:
While I, well pleased, have stood to see
Their tender bodies torn!

"Though fishermen must earn their bread,
And butchers too must slay,
That can be no excuse for me,
Who do the same in play.

"And now I feel how great the smart,
How terrible the pain!
I think, while I can feel myself,
I will not fish again."

Jane Taylor (1783–1824) and
Ann Taylor Gilbert (1782–1866)

The Taylor sisters, who lived in Colchester, England, were prolific writers of lively poems and hymns for children that remained popular through most of the nineteenth century. Their father and brother and another poet contributed to their 1804–05 collection *Original Poems for Infant Minds* (see "The Little Fisherman"). "The Star" was published in *Rhymes for the Nursery* in 1806. We do not know for certain which sister is more responsible for this poem, but it is most likely the work of Jane Taylor. "The Star" is their most famous work, although most people to-day know it through the oral tradition as "Twinkle, Twinkle, Little Star" and learn only the first verse. Like other popular nursery rhymes, it has been often parodied, most famously by Lewis Carroll in chapter 7 of *Alice's Adventures in Wonderland,* when the Mad Hatter recites at the tea party, "Twinkle, twinkle, little bat! / How I wonder where you're at! / . . . Up above the world you fly, / Like a tea-tray in the sky."

The Star

Twinkle, twinkle, little star,
How I wonder what you are!
Up above the world so high,
Like a diamond in the sky.
Twinkle, twinkle, little star,
How I wonder what you are!

When the blazing sun is gone,
When he nothing shines upon,
Then you show your little light,
Twinkle, twinkle, all the night.
Twinkle, twinkle, little star,
How I wonder what you are!

Then the trav'ler in the dark
Thanks you for your tiny spark;
How could he see where to go,

If you did not twinkle so?
Twinkle, twinkle, little star,
How I wonder what you are!

In the dark blue sky you keep, and
Through my curtains often peep,
For you never shut your eyes,
Till the morning sun does rise.
Twinkle, twinkle, little star,
How I wonder what you are!

As your bright and tiny spark
Lights the trav'ler in the dark,
Though I know not what you are,
Twinkle on, please, little star.
Twinkle, twinkle, little star,
How I wonder what you are!

Mary Botham Howitt (1799–1888)

With undertones of seduction, this little history of flattery and the disastrous consequences of listening to it draws a negative lesson from nature. Howitt alerts her child readers to the dangers of listening to cunning flattery, but she herself woos the reader with an alluring tale of sly invitation. A prolific English writer, Mary Botham Howitt was a Quaker who was tutored at home and married another writer for children, William Howitt. She was a reformer and an early translator of the works of Hans Christian Andersen. This poem, her most famous, was first published in 1829 and then appeared in her collection of poems about insects and animals, *Sketches of Natural History* (1834). Lewis Carroll parodies this poem in chapter 10 of *Alice's Adventures in Wonderland.*

The Spider and the Fly

An Apologue
A New Version of an Old Story

"Will you walk into my parlour?" said the Spider
    to the Fly,
"'Tis the prettiest little parlour that ever you did
    spy;
The way into my parlour is up a winding stair,
And I've a many curious thing to shew when you
    are there."
"Oh no, no," said the little Fly, "to ask me is in
    vain,
For who goes up your winding stair can ne'er
    come down again."

"I'm sure you must be weary, dear, with soaring up
    so high;
Will you rest upon my little bed?" said the Spider
    to the Fly.
"There are pretty curtains drawn around; the sheets
    are fine and thin,
And if you like to rest awhile, I'll snugly tuck you
    in!"
"Oh no, no," said the little Fly, "for I've often
    heard it said,
They never, never wake again, who sleep upon
    your bed!"

Said the cunning Spider to the Fly, "Dear friend
    what can I do,
To prove the warm affection I've always felt for
    you?
I have within my pantry, good store of all that's
    nice;
I'm sure you're very welcome—will you please to
    take a slice?"
"Oh no, no," said the little Fly, "kind sir, that
    cannot be,
I've heard what's in your pantry, and I do not wish
    to see!"

"Sweet creature!" said the Spider, "you're witty
    and you're wise,

How handsome are your gauzy wings, how
    brilliant are your eyes!
I've a little looking-glass upon my parlour
    shelf,
If you'll step in one moment, dear, you shall
    behold yourself."
"I thank you, gentle sir," she said, "for what you're
    pleased to say,
And bidding you good morning now, I'll call
    another day."

The Spider turned him round about, and went into
    his den,
For well he knew the silly Fly would soon come
    back again:
So he wove a subtle web, in a little corner sly,
And set his table ready, to dine upon the Fly.
Then he came out to his door again, and merrily
    did sing,
"Come hither, hither, pretty Fly, with the pearl and
    silver wing;
Your robes are green and purple—there's a crest
    upon your head;
Your eyes are like the diamond bright, but mine
    are dull as lead!"

Alas, alas! how very soon this silly little Fly,
Hearing his wily, flattering words, came slowly
    flitting by;
With buzzing wings she hung aloft, then near and
    nearer drew,
Thinking only of her brilliant eyes, and green and
    purple hue—
Thinking only of her crested head—poor foolish
    thing! At last,
Up jumped the cunning Spider, and fiercely held
    her fast.
He dragged her up his winding stair, into his
    dismal den,

Within his little parlour—but she ne'er came out
again!

And now dear little children, who may this story
read,
To idle, silly flattering words, I pray you ne'er give
heed:

Unto an evil counsellor, close heart and ear and
eye,
And take a lesson from this tale, of the Spider and
the Fly.

Peter Parley (Samuel Griswold Goodrich, 1793–1860)

Born in Ridgefield, Connecticut, Samuel Griswold Goodrich was a prolific writer of cheerful, factual stories for children. Peter Parley, a doddering but talkative old man, was the character through whom he dispensed much of his popular wisdom and information. He opposed fantasy and believed in the value of energy and perseverance, emphasizing a practical morality of hard work, prudence, and obedience to parents and other authorities. His stories in periodicals, such as *Parley's Magazine,* and collections, such as *Make the Best of It* (1843), were extremely popular in Britain and America. In "The Pleasure Boat," some children learn the value of obedience and truthfulness through a terrifying experience, helped by their wise and forgiving parents. An editorial persona similar to Peter Parley appeared in another educational children's periodical founded by Griswold in 1841, *Robert Merry's Museum.* It was later called *Merry's Museum* and was edited by Louisa May Alcott and others until 1872. The name Peter Parley was adopted by several other writers of factual books and became a derogatory term used by those who defended literature of the imagination.

The Pleasure Boat: or, The Broken Promise

A Gentleman, who lived in a fine house upon the banks of a beautiful lake, had five children, the two youngest of whom were twins—a boy and girl: these were four years old; while the others, a brother and two sisters, were much older.

The father of this family had a very pretty boat, and it was one of the greatest pleasures that the children could enjoy, to sail in it upon the lake. It was delightful to glide over the blue water; to see the fishes playing down deep in its bosom; to see the birds shooting over its surface, and often dipping their wings in the wave; and above all—it was delightful to visit a little island in the lake, upon which a pair of swans had hatched a brood of young ones, and which were now able to swim with their parents over the water.

One fine summer day these children begged their

parents to let them go to the lake, and sail upon it in the boat; but the parents were afraid that they would get drowned, and refused their consent. The children then requested permission to go and walk along the border of the lake, saying that they would not go out in the boat. Upon this promise, the parents consented to the request, and accordingly the children started for their ramble.

They strolled along the edge of the water for some time, picking flowers upon the banks, or gathering shells and pebbles on the beach. By and by they saw the swans near the island, at a little distance, and they looked so quiet, beautiful and happy, that the children longed to get into the boat, and go out and see them. At last Thomas, the eldest of the group, proposed that they should do so, saying that the water was so smooth, no doubt their parents would be willing to let them go.

Now as Thomas was the eldest, he had influence over the others, and as he promised to be very careful, they consented. Having all got into the boat, Thomas took the paddle, placed it at the stern, and shoved the little vessel briskly through the water.

Directing its course at the same time that he urged it forward, he took the party from place to place, and at last they came to the island of the swans. Close by its margin they found the flock, consisting of the two parent birds, and their three young ones.

The swans were well acquainted with the children, and seemed to regard them as friends; so that when the boat approached, they arched their long necks, and came up close to it. The old ones even put their heads forward and ate some corn out of the hands of the twins, which they had brought for the purpose. The young ones ate the pieces of bread which were given to them in the water, and dived down to seize the grains of corn that were thrown out.

The twins, who were named Frank and Fanny, were greatly charmed with all this, but they seemed to enjoy it in different ways. Fanny was mild and gentle in her feelings, and her happiness seemed to partake of her general character. She regarded the swans with a pleased but tranquil look, and spoke to them in soft and tender tones.

But Frank was more ardent in his temper. He could not conduct himself with much order. He threw up his arms, and clapped his hands, and shouted till the borders of the lake echoed with his merry cries. Nor was all this enough. He was very anxious to take hold of one of the little swans. His sisters both warned him against this, and told him that in stooping over as he had done several times, he was in danger of falling into the water.

But most children are thoughtless, and seldom fear danger, till they have had some experience of evil. So it was with our joyous little boy of the boat. He heeded not the caution of his sisters, but continued his pranks, and at last, reaching forward to seize one of the young swans, fell headlong into the water!

There was a wild shriek from all the children as their little brother plunged into the lake and disappeared beneath the water. In a few seconds the poor boy came to the surface, and being very near the boat, the two sisters reached suddenly forward to take hold of him; this turned the boat on its side, and in an instant it was upset and all the party were thrown into the water.

Fortunately the water at this place was not deep, and Thomas soon succeeded in getting his sisters, including little Fanny, to the island, which was close at hand. But Frank, who was the cause of the accident, was still in the water, and had disappeared beneath its surface.

I cannot tell you with what agony Thomas searched about in the water for his dear little brother. I cannot tell you how his older sisters, standing on the shore, wrung their hands in anxiety and grief. I cannot tell you how little Fanny too cried out to Thomas to bring brother Frank out of the water.

Already Frank had been two or three minutes in the lake, and Thomas knew that if he was not very soon taken out he would never breathe again. It was, therefore, with a degree of distress which I cannot describe, that he plunged into the water, and searched along the bottom for his little brother. At last he felt something upon the sand, and, laying hold of it, he drew it forth, and lo! it was little Frank. Thomas brought him to the land, but how pale and deathlike was the face of the child!

One of the sisters took him in her arms, and held him to her bosom, seeking to bring back the colour and warmth to his cold cheek. She sat down with him in her lap, and they all knelt around, and while they wept they took his little cold hands in theirs, and with streaming eyes kissed him over and over again.

It was heart-rending to see little Fanny, looking into his face with terror at seeing it so white and so still. It seemed to her like sleep, but oh, how fearful seemed that strange, cold sleep, in one, but a few minutes before, the very image and impress of love and life and joy.

With timid and trembling fingers, Fanny at length took the hand of her brother, and lifting it to her lips, kissed it tenderly; and then she kissed his cheek; and then she spoke gently to him, saying, "Dear Frank, do you not know little Fanny? will you not speak to Fanny? will you not open your eyes, and look at me?" There was no answer, and the child burst into a gush of tears. But at this moment there was a slight movement in the little boy's frame, and he opened his eyes.

These signs of life gave inexpressible joy to the children. They even sobbed aloud, and clapped their hands, and wept, and jumped up and down, all in the same moment. After some minutes, and symptoms of great distress, Frank recovered, and looking round, seemed to know his sisters, and to become conscious of his situation. Soon after this, Thomas swam to the boat, and having pushed it to the shore and baled out the water, the little party returned towards their home.

Now these children loved their parents very much, but they were afraid to meet them, and really did not wish to go home. The reason was that they were conscious of their error, and saw that their disobedience had put to risk the life of their little brother. It was proposed by one of the unhappy party to conceal the fact, and account for the condition of Frank by saying that he had slipped into the water while walking along the bank. Thus it is that one fault begets another. Disobedience brings about accident, and this leads to falsehood: nay, it makes children, who before loved father and mother, dread their presence, seek to avoid them, and at last to deceive them.

But I am glad to say, that in this instance the little party did not act thus: they went straight to their mother, told the truth, confessed their faults, and begged forgiveness. This was granted, and then the father knelt down, and they all knelt with him, and they thanked God that the life of the little boy had been saved, and prayed that the erring boys and girls might be kept from further disobedience.

Nathaniel Hawthorne (1804–64)

Nathaniel Hawthorne is, of course, best known for such classic American novels as *The Scarlet Letter* (1850) and *The House of the Seven Gables* (1851). But throughout the most productive period of his career, he was also writing for young people. Some of this early writing was hackwork, such as the *Universal History* (1837) that he and his sister collaborated on for Samuel Griswold Goodrich's Peter Parley series. More characteristic are *The Whole History of Grandfather's Chair* (1851), originally published as a series, and *Biographical Stories* (1842). Perhaps his best juvenile works, however, the ones still read today, are *A Wonder Book* (1851) and *Tanglewood Tales* (1852), written after he had fathered three children of his own. They were the first books to adapt classical myths in English for children. Hawthorne's 1851 Preface emphasizes the timelessness of "these immortal fables" for all ages, although he notes that his adaptations "may have lost much of their classical aspect . . . and have, perhaps, assumed a Gothic or romantic guise." The Preface also observes that Hawthorne believed it is unnecessary to write down to children, since they "possess an unestimated sensibility to whatever is deep or high, in imagination or feeling."[1]

In *A Wonder Book,* which includes "The Paradise of Children," a frame story depicts a group of young relatives and friends, identified by pastoral names, such as Primrose and Cowslip, in an idyllic New England setting. Eustace Bright, a college student who is good at telling stories, supervises the children. Despite its source and intended audience, the adaptation of the myth of Pandora in "The Paradise of Children" reveals many of Hawthorne's adult preoccupations, such as the origin and nature of sin and the possibility of redemption. His narrator, Eustace, toys with his child listeners much as Hawthorne teases the readers of his adult fiction. (See Part 3 for more on classical mythology, including a retelling of "Daedalus and Icarus.")

NOTE

1. Nathaniel Hawthorne, Preface, *A Wonder Book* (1851; New York: Quality Paperback Book Club, 2000).

From *A Wonder Book for Boys and Girls*

TANGLEWOOD PLAY-ROOM

Introductory to "The Paradise of Children"

The golden days of October passed away, as so many other Octobers have, and brown November likewise, and the greater part of chill December, too. At last came merry Christmas, and Eustace Bright along with it, making it all the merrier by his presence. And, the day after his arrival from college, there came a mighty snowstorm. Up to this time, the winter had held back, and had given us a good many mild days, which were like smiles upon its wrinkled visage. The grass had kept itself green, in sheltered places, such as the nooks of southern hill-slopes, and along the lee of the stone-fences. It was but a week or two ago, and since the beginning of the month, that the children had found a dandelion in bloom, on the margin of Shadow Brook, where it glides out of the dell.

But no more green grass and dandelions, now! This was such a snow-storm! Twenty miles of it might have been visible at once, between the windows of Tangle-wood and the Dome of Taconic, had it been possible to see so far, among the eddying drifts that whitened all the atmosphere. It seemed as if the hills were giants, and were flinging monstrous handfulls of snow at one another, in their enormous sport. So thick were the fluttering snow-flakes, that even the trees, mid-way down the valley, were hidden by them, the greater part of the time. Sometimes, it is true, the little prisoners of Tanglewood could discern a dim outline of Monument Mountain, and the smooth whiteness of the frozen lake at its base, and the black or gray tracts of woodland, in the nearer landscape. But these were merely peeps through the tempest.

Nevertheless, the children rejoiced greatly in the snowstorm. They had already made acquaintance with it, by tumbling heels over head into its highest drifts, and flinging snow at one another, as we have just fancied the Berkshire mountains to be doing. And now they had come back to their spacious play-room, which was as big as the great drawing-room, and was lumbered with all sorts of playthings, large and small. The biggest was a rocking-horse, that looked like a real pony; and there was a whole family of wooden, waxen, plaster and china-dolls, besides rag-babies; and blocks enough to build Bunker-hill monument, and nine-pins, and balls, and humming-tops, and battledoors, and grace-sticks, and skipping-ropes, and more of such valuable property than I could tell of, in a printed page. But the children liked the snow-storm better than them all. It suggested so many brisk enjoyments for tomorrow, and all the remainder of the winter! The sleigh-ride; the slides down-hill into the valley; the snow-images that were to be shaped out; the snow-fortresses that were to be built, and the snow-balling to be carried on!

So the little folks blessed the snow-storm, and were glad to see it come thicker and thicker, and watched hopefully the long drift that was piling itself up in the avenue, and was already higher than any of their heads.

"Why, we shall be blocked up till spring!" cried they, with the hugest delight. "What a pity, that the house is too high to be quite covered up! The little red house, down yonder, will be buried up to its eaves."

"You silly children, what do you want of more snow?" asked Eustace, who, tired of some novel that he was skimming through, had strolled into the play-room. "It has done mischief enough already, by spoiling the only skating that I could hope for, through the winter. We shall see nothing more of the lake, till April; and this was to have been my first day upon it! Don't you pity me, Primrose?"

"Oh, to be sure!" answered Primrose, laughing. "But, for your comfort, we will listen to another of your old stories, such as you told us under the porch, and down in the hollow, by Shadow Brook. Perhaps I shall like them better now, when there is nothing to do, than while there were nuts to be gathered, and beautiful weather to enjoy."

Hereupon, Periwinkle, Clover, Sweet Fern, and as many others of the little fraternity and cousinhood as were still at Tanglewood, gathered about Eustace, and earnestly besought him for a story. The student yawned, stretched himself, and then, to the vast admiration of the small people, skipped three times back and forth over the top of a chair, in order, as he explained to them, to set his wits in motion.

"Well, well, children," said he, after these preliminaries, "since you insist, and Primrose has set her heart upon it, I will see what can be done for you. And, that you may know what happy days there were, before snow-storms came into fashion, I will tell you a story of the oldest of all old times, when the world was as new as Sweet Fern's bran-new humming-top. There was then but one season in the year, and that was the delightful summer; and but one age for mortals—and that was childhood."

"I never heard of that before," said Primrose.

"Of course, you never did," answered Eustace. "It shall be a story of what nobody but myself ever dreamed of—a Paradise of Children—and how, by the naughtiness of just such a little imp as Primrose here, it all came to nothing."

So Eustace Bright sat down in the chair which he had just been skipping over, took Cowslip upon his knee, ordered silence throughout the auditory, and be-

gan a story about a sad naughty child, whose name was Pandora, and about her playfellow Epimetheus. You may read it, word for word, in the pages that come next.

THE PARADISE OF CHILDREN

Long, long ago, when this old world was in its tender infancy, there was a child, named Epimetheus, who never had either father or mother; and that he might not be lonely, another child, fatherless and motherless like himself, was sent from a far country, to live with him, and be his playfellow and helpmate. Her name was Pandora.

The first thing that Pandora saw, when she entered the cottage where Epimetheus dwelt, was a great box. And almost the first question which she put to him, after crossing the threshold, was this:—

"Epimetheus, what have you in that box?"

"My dear little Pandora," answered Epimetheus, "that is a secret; and you must be kind enough not to ask any questions about it. The box was left here to be kept safely, and I do not myself know what it contains."

"But who gave it to you?" asked Pandora. "And where did it come from?"

"That is a secret too," replied Epimetheus.

"How provoking!" exclaimed Pandora, pouting her lip. "I wish the great ugly box were out of the way!"

"Oh, come, don't think of it any more!" cried Epimetheus. "Let us run out of doors, and have some nice play with the other children!"

It is thousands of years since Epimetheus and Pandora were alive; and the world, now-a-days, is a very different sort of thing from what it was in their time. Then, everybody was a child. There needed no fathers and mothers, to take care of the children; because there was no danger, nor trouble of any kind, and no clothes to be mended, and there was always plenty to eat and drink. Whenever a child wanted his dinner, he found it growing on a tree; and, if he looked at the tree in the morning, he could see the expanding blossom of that night's supper; or, at eventide, he saw the tender bud of tomorrow's breakfast. It was a very pleasant life indeed. No labor to be done, no tasks to be studied; nothing but sports and dances, and sweet voices of children talking, or carolling like birds, or gushing out in merry laughter, throughout the live-long day.

What was most wonderful of all, the children never quarrelled among themselves; neither had they any crying-fits; nor, since time first began, had a single one of these little mortals ever gone apart into a corner, and sulked! Oh, what a good time was that, to be alive in! The truth is, those ugly little winged monsters, called Troubles, which are now almost as numerous as mosquitoes, had never yet been seen on the earth. It is probable that the very greatest disquietude, which a child had ever experienced, was Pandora's vexation at not being able to discover the secret of the mysterious box.

This was at first only the faint shadow of a Trouble; but, every day, it grew more and more substantial; until, before a great while, the cottage of Epimetheus and Pandora was less sunshiny than those of the other children.

"Whence can the box have come!" Pandora continually kept saying to herself and to Epimetheus. "And what in the world can be inside of it!"

"Always talking about this box!" said Epimetheus, at last; for he had grown extremely tired of the subject. "I wish, dear Pandora, you would try to talk of something else. Come; let us go and gather some ripe figs, and eat them under the trees, for our supper! And I know a vine that has the sweetest and juiciest grapes you ever tasted!"

"Always talking about grapes and figs!" cried Pandora, pettishly.

"Well then," said Epimetheus, who was a very good-tempered child, like a multitude of children, in those days, "let us run out and have a merry time with our playmates!"

"I am tired of merry times, and don't care if I never have any more," answered our pettish little Pandora. "And, besides, I never do have any! This ugly box! I am so taken up with thinking about it, all the time! I insist upon your telling me what is inside of it."

"As I have already said, fifty times over, I do not know!" replied Epimetheus, getting a little vexed. "How, then, can I tell you what is inside?"

"You might open it," said Pandora, looking sideways at Epimetheus, "and then we could see for ourselves."

"Pandora, what are you thinking of!" exclaimed Epimetheus.

And his face expressed so much horror at the idea of looking into a box, which had been confided to him on the condition of his never opening it, that Pandora thought it best not to suggest it any more. Still, however, she could not help thinking and talking about the box.

"At least," said she, "you can tell me how it came here."

"It was left at the door," replied Epimetheus, "just before you came, by a person who looked very smiling and intelligent, and who could hardly forbear laughing, as he put it down. He was dressed in an odd kind of a cloak, and had on a cap that seemed to be made partly of feathers, so that it looked almost as if it had wings."

"What sort of a staff had he?" asked Pandora.

"Oh, the most curious staff you ever saw!" cried Epimetheus. "It was like two serpents twisting around a stick, and was carved so naturally, that I at first thought the serpents were alive."

"I know him," said Pandora, thoughtfully. "Nobody else has such a staff. It was Quicksilver; and he brought me hither, as well as the box. No doubt, he intended it for me; and, most probably, it contains pretty dresses for me to wear, or toys for you and me to play with, or something very nice for us both to eat!"

"Perhaps so," answered Epimetheus, turning away. "But, until Quicksilver comes back and tells us so, we have neither of us any right to lift the lid of the box!"

"What a dull boy he is!" muttered Pandora, as Epimetheus left the cottage. "I do wish he had a little more enterprise!"

For the first time since her arrival, Epimetheus had gone out, without asking Pandora to accompany him. He went to gather figs and grapes by himself, or to seek whatever amusement he could find, in other society than his little playfellow's. He was tired to death of hearing about the box, and heartily wished that Quicksilver, or whatever was the messenger's name, had left it at some other child's door, where Pandora would never have set eyes on it. So perseveringly as she did babble about this one thing! The box; the box; and nothing but the box! It seemed as if the box were bewitched, and as if the cottage were not big enough to hold it, without Pandora's continually stumbling over it, and making Epimetheus stumble over it likewise, and bruising all four of their shins.

Well; it was really hard that poor Epimetheus should have a box in his ears, from morning till night; especially as the little people of the earth were so unaccustomed to vexations, in those happy days, that they knew not how to deal with them. Thus, a small vexation made as much disturbance, then, as a far bigger one would, in our own times.

After Epimetheus was gone, Pandora stood gazing at the box. She had called it ugly, above a hundred times; but, in spite of all that she had said against it, it was positively a very handsome article of furniture, and would have been quite an ornament to any room in which it should be placed. It was made of a beautiful kind of wood, with dark and rich veins spreading over its surface, which was so highly polished that little Pandora could see her face in it. As the child had no other looking-glass, it is odd that she did not value the box, merely on this account.

The edges and corners of the box were carved with most wonderful skill. Around the margin there were figures of graceful men and women, and the prettiest children ever seen, reclining or sporting amid a profusion of flowers and foliage; and these various objects were so exquisitely represented, and were wrought together in such harmony, that flowers, foliage and human beings, seemed to combine into a wreath of mingled beauty. But, here and there, peeping forth from behind the carved foliage, Pandora once or twice fancied that she saw a face not so lovely, or something or other that was disagreeable, and which stole the beauty out of all the rest. Nevertheless, on looking more closely, and touching the spot with her finger, she could discover nothing of the kind. Some face, that was really beautiful, had been made to look ugly by her catching a sideway glimpse at it.

The most beautiful face of all was done, in what is called high relief, in the centre of the lid. There was nothing else, save the dark, smooth richness of the polished wood, and this one face, in the centre, with a garland of flowers about its brow. Pandora had looked at this face, a great many times, and imagined that the mouth could smile if it liked, or be graver, when it chose, the same as any living mouth. The features, indeed, all wore a very lively and rather mischievous expression, which looked almost as if it needs must burst out of the carved lips, and utter itself in words.

Had the mouth spoken, it would probably have been something like this:—

"Do not be afraid, Pandora! What harm can there be in opening the box? Never mind that poor, simple Epimetheus! You are wiser than he, and have ten times as much spirit. Open the box, and see if you do not find something very pretty!"

The box, I had almost forgotten to say, was fastened; not by a lock, nor by any other such contrivance, but by a very intricate knot of gold cord. There appeared to be no end to this knot, and no beginning. Never was a knot so cunningly twisted, nor with so many ins and outs, which roguishly defied the skilfullest fingers to disentangle them. And yet, by the very difficulty that there was in it, Pandora was the more tempted to examine the knot, and just see how it was made. Two or three times, already, she had stooped over the box, and taken the knot between her thumb and forefinger, but without positively trying to undo it.

"I really believe," said she to herself, "that I begin to see how it was done. Nay, perhaps I could tie it up again, after undoing it. There would be no harm in that, surely! Even Epimetheus would not blame me for that. I need not open the box, and should not, of course, without the foolish boy's consent, even if the knot were untied!"

It might have been better for Pandora if she had had a little work to do, or anything to employ her mind upon, so as not to be so constantly thinking of this one subject. But children led so easy a life, before any Troubles came into the world, that they had really a great deal too much leisure. They could not be forever playing at hide-and-seek among the flower-shrubs, or at blindman's buff with garlands over their eyes, or at whatever other games had been found out, while Mother Earth was in her babyhood. When life is all sport, toil is the real play. There was absolutely nothing to do. A little sweeping and dusting about the cottage, I suppose, and the gathering of fresh flowers, (which were only too abundant, everywhere,) and arranging them in vases;—and poor little Pandora's day's work was over! And then, for the rest of the day, there was the box!

After all, I am not quite so sure that the box was not a blessing to her, in its way. It supplied her with such a variety of ideas to think of, and to talk about, whenever she had anybody to listen! When she was in good humor, she could admire the bright polish of its sides, and the rich border of beautiful faces and foliage that ran all around it. Or, if she chanced to be ill-tempered, she could give it a push, or kick it with her naughty little foot. And many a kick did the box—(but it was a mischievous box, as we shall see, and deserved all it got)—many a kick did it receive! But, certain it is, if it had not been for the box, our active-minded little Pandora would not have known half so well how to spend her time, as she now did.

For it was really an endless employment to guess what was inside. What could it be, indeed? Just imagine, my little hearers, how busy your wits would be, if there were a great box in the house, which, as you might have reason to suppose, contained something new and pretty for your Christmas or New Year's gifts! Do you think that you should be less curious than Pandora? If you were left alone with the box, might you not feel a little tempted to lift the lid? But you would not do it! Oh, fie! No, no! Only, if you thought there were toys in it, it would be so very hard to let slip an opportunity of taking just one peep! I know not whether Pandora expected any toys; for none had yet begun to be made, probably, in those days, when the world itself was one great plaything for the children that dwelt upon it. But Pandora was convinced that there was something very beautiful and valuable in the box; and therefore she felt just as anxious to take a peep, as any of these little girls, here around me, would have felt. And, possibly, a little more so;—but of that, I am not quite so certain.

On this particular day, however, which we have so long been talking about, her curiosity grew so much greater than it usually was, that, at last, she approached the box. She was more than half determined to open it, if she could. Ah, naughty Pandora!

First, however, she tried to lift it. It was heavy; quite too heavy for the slender strength of a child, like Pandora. She raised one end of the box a few inches from the floor, and let it fall again, with a pretty loud thump. A moment afterwards, she almost fancied that she heard something stir, inside of the box. She applied her ear as closely as possible, and listened. Positively, there did seem to be a kind of stifled murmur, within! Or was it merely the singing in Pandora's ears? Or could it be the beating of her heart? The child could not quite satisfy herself whether she had heard anything or no. But, at all events, her curiosity was stronger than ever.

As she drew back her head, her eyes fell upon the knot of gold cord.

"It must have been a very ingenious person who tied this knot," said Pandora to herself. "But I think I could untie it, nevertheless! I am resolved, at least, to find the two ends of the cord."

So she took the golden knot in her fingers, and pryed into its intricacies as sharply as she could. Almost without intending it, or quite knowing what she was about, she was soon busily engaged in attempting to undo it. Meanwhile, the bright sunshine came through the open window; as did likewise the merry voices of the children, playing at a distance, and perhaps the voice of Epimetheus among them. Pandora stopt to listen. What a beautiful day it was! Would it not be wiser, if she were to let the troublesome knot alone, and think no more about the box, but run and join her little playfellows, and be happy?

All this time, however, her fingers were half unconsciously busy with the knot; and happening to glance at the flower-wreathed face, on the lid of the enchanted box, she seemed to perceive it slily grinning at her.

"That face looks very mischievous," thought Pandora. "I wonder whether it smiles because I am doing wrong! I have the greatest mind in the world to run away!"

But, just then, by the merest accident, she gave the knot a kind of a twist, which produced a wonderful result. The gold cord untwined itself, as if by magic, and left the box without a fastening.

"This is the strangest thing I ever knew!" said Pandora. "What will Epimetheus say? And how can I possibly tie it up again?"

She made one or two attempts to restore the knot, but soon found it quite beyond her skill. It had disentangled itself so suddenly, that she could not in the least remember how the strings had been doubled into one another; and when she tried to recollect the shape and appearance of the knot, it seemed to have gone entirely out of her mind. Nothing was to be done, therefore, but to let the box remain as it was, until Epimetheus should come in.

"But," said Pandora, "when he finds the knot untied, he will know that I have done it. How shall I make him believe that I have not looked into the box?"

And then the thought came into her naughty little heart, that, since she would be suspected of having looked into the box, she might just as well do so, at once. Oh, very naughty, and very foolish Pandora! You should have thought only of doing what was right, and of leaving undone what was wrong, and not of what your playfellow Epimetheus would have said or believed. And so perhaps she might, if the enchanted face, on the lid of the box, had not looked so bewitchingly persuasive at her, and if she had not seemed to hear, more distinctly than before, the murmur of small voices within. She could not tell whether it was fancy or no; but there was quite a little tumult of whispers in her ear—or else it was her curiosity that whispered,

"Let us out, dear Pandora, pray let us out! We will be such nice pretty playfellows for you! Only let us out!"

"What can it be?" thought Pandora. "Is there something alive in the box? Well!—yes!—I am resolved to take just one peep! Only one peep; and then the lid shall be shut down as safely as ever! There cannot possibly be any harm in just one little peep!"

But it is now time for us to see what Epimetheus was doing.

This was the first time, since his little playmate had come to dwell with him, that he had attempted to enjoy any pleasure in which she did not partake. But nothing went right; nor was he nearly so happy as on other days. He could not find a sweet grape or a ripe fig, (if Epimetheus had a fault, it was a little too much fondness for figs,) or, if ripe at all, they were over-ripe, and so sweet as to be cloying. There was no mirth in his heart, such as usually made his voice gush out, of its own accord, and swell the merriment of his companions. In short, he grew so uneasy and discontented, that the other children could not imagine what was the matter with Epimetheus. Neither did he himself know what ailed him, any better than they did. For you must recollect, that, at the time we are speaking of, it was everybody's nature, and constant habit, to be happy. The world had not yet learned to be otherwise. Not a single soul or body, since these children were first sent to enjoy themselves on the beautiful earth, had ever been sick or out of sorts.

At length, discovering that, somehow or other, he put a stop to all the play, Epimetheus judged it best to go back to Pandora, who was in a humor better suited to his own. But, with a hope of giving her pleasure, he gathered some flowers and made them into a wreath, which he meant to put upon her head. The flowers were very lovely—roses, and lilies, and orange-blossoms, and a great many more, which left a trail of fragrance behind, as Epimetheus carried them along;—and the wreath was put together with as much skill as could reasonably be expected of a boy. The fingers of little girls, it has always appeared to me, are the fittest to twine flower-wreaths; but boys could do it, in those days, rather better than they can now.

And here I must mention, that a great black cloud had been gathering in the sky, for some time past, although it had not yet overspread the sun. But, just as Epimetheus reached the cottage-door, this cloud began to intercept the sunshine, and thus to make a sudden and sad obscurity.

He entered softly; for he meant, if possible, to steal behind Pandora, and fling the wreath of flowers over her head, before she should be aware of his approach. But, as it happened, there was no need of his treading so very lightly. He might have trod as heavily as he pleased—as heavily as a grown man—as heavily, I was going to say, as an elephant—without much probability of Pandora's hearing his footsteps. She was too intent upon her purpose. At the moment of his entering the cottage, the naughty child had put her hand to the lid, and was on the point of opening the mysterious box. Epimetheus beheld her. If he had cried out, Pandora would probably have withdrawn her hand, and the fatal mystery of the box might never have been known.

But Epimetheus himself, although he said very little about it, had his own share of curiosity to know what was inside. Perceiving that Pandora was resolved to find out the secret, he determined that his playfellow should not be the only wise person in the cottage. And if there were anything pretty or valuable in the box, he meant to take half of it to himself. Thus, after all his sage speeches to Pandora about restraining her curiosity, Epimetheus turned out to be quite as foolish, and nearly as much in fault, as she. So, whenever we blame Pandora for what happened, we must not forget to shake our heads at Epimetheus likewise.

As Pandora raised the lid, the cottage grew very dark and dismal; for the black cloud had now swept quite over the sun, and seemed to have buried it alive. There had, for a little while past, been a low growling and muttering, which all at once broke into a heavy peal of thunder. But Pandora, heeding nothing of all this, lifted the lid nearly upright, and looked inside. It seemed as if a sudden swarm of winged creatures brushed past her, taking flight out of the box; while, at the same instant, she heard the voice of Epimetheus, with a lamentable tone, as if he were in pain.

"Oh, I am stung!" cried he. "I am stung! Naughty Pandora! Why have you opened this wicked box?"

Pandora let fall the lid, and starting up, looked about her, to see what had befallen Epimetheus. The thunder-cloud had so darkened the room, that she could not very clearly discern what was in it. But she heard a disagreeable buzzing, as if a great many huge flies, or gigantic musquitoes, or those insects which we call dor-bugs and pinching-dogs, were darting about. And, as her eyes grew more accustomed to the imperfect light, she saw a crowd of ugly little shapes, with bats' wings, looking abominably spiteful, and armed with terribly long stings in their tails. It was one of these that had stung Epimetheus. Nor was it a great while, before Pandora herself began to scream, in no less pain and affright than her playfellow, and making a vast deal more hubbub about it. An odious little monster had settled on her forehead, and would have stung her I know not how deeply, if Epimetheus had not run and brushed it away.

Now, if you wish to know what these ugly things might be, which had made their escape out of the box, I must tell you that they were the whole family of earthly Troubles. There were evil Passions; there were a great many species of Cares; there were more than a hundred and fifty Sorrows; there were Diseases, in a vast number of miserable and painful shapes; there were more kinds of Naughtiness, than it would be of any use to talk about. In short, everything, that has since afflicted the souls and bodies of mankind, had been shut up in the mysterious box, and given to Epimetheus and Pandora to be kept safely, in order that the happy children of the world might never be molested by them. Had they been faithful to their trust, all would have gone well. No grown person would ever have been sad, nor any child have had cause to shed a single tear, from that hour until this moment.

But—and you may see by this how a wrong act of any one mortal is a calamity to the whole world—by Pandora's lifting the lid of that miserable box, and by the fault of Epimetheus, too, in not preventing her, these Troubles have obtained a foothold among us, and do not seem very likely to be driven away in a hurry. For it was impossible, as you will easily guess, that the two children should keep the ugly swarm in their own little cottage. On the contrary, the first thing that they did was to fling open the doors and windows, in hopes of getting rid of them; and sure enough, away flew the winged Troubles all abroad, and so pestered and tormented the small people, everywhere about, that none of them so much as smiled for many days afterwards. And what was very singular, all the flowers and dewy blossoms on earth, not one of which had hitherto faded, now began to droop and shed their leaves, after a day or two. The children, moreover, who before seemed immortal in their childhood, now grew older, day by day, and came soon to be youths and maidens, and men and women by-and-by, and aged people, before they dreamed of such a thing.

Meanwhile, the naughty Pandora, and hardly less naughty Epimetheus, remained in their cottage. Both of them had been grievously stung, and were in a good deal of pain, which seemed the more intolerable to them, because it was the very first pain that had ever been felt since the world began. Of course, they were entirely unaccustomed to it, and could have no idea what it meant. Besides all this, they were in exceedingly bad humor, both with themselves and with one another. In order to indulge it to the utmost, Epimetheus sat down sullenly in a corner, with his back towards Pandora; while Pandora flung herself upon the floor, and rested her head on the fatal and abominable box. She was crying bitterly, and sobbing as if her heart would break.

Suddenly, there was a gentle little tap, on the inside of the lid.

"What can that be?" cried Pandora, lifting her head.

But either Epimetheus had not heard the tap, or was too much out of humor to notice it. At any rate, he made no answer.

"You are very unkind," said Pandora, sobbing anew, "not to speak to me!"

Again, the tap! It sounded like the tiny knuckles of a fairy's hand, knocking lightly and playfully on the inside of the box.

"Who are you?" asked Pandora, with a little of her former curiosity. "Who are you, inside of this naughty box?"

A sweet little voice spoke from within,

"Only lift the lid, and you shall see!"

"No, no," answered Pandora, again beginning to sob, "I have had enough of lifting the lid! You are inside of the box, naughty creature, and there you shall stay! There are plenty of your ugly brothers and sisters, already flying about the world. You need never think that I shall be so foolish as to let you out!"

She looked towards Epimetheus, as she spoke, perhaps expecting that he would commend her for her wisdom. But the sullen boy only muttered, that she was wise a little too late.

"Ah," said the sweet little voice again, "you had much better let me out! I am not like those naughty creatures that have stings in their tails. They are no brothers and sisters of mine, as you would see at once, if you were only to get a glimpse of me. Come, come, my pretty Pandora! I am sure you will let me out!"

And, indeed, there was a kind of cheerful witchery in the tone, that made it almost impossible to refuse anything which this little voice asked. Pandora's heart had insensibly grown lighter, at every word that came from within the box. Epimetheus, too, though still in the corner, had turned half round, and seemed to be in rather better spirits than before.

"My dear Epimetheus," cried Pandora, "have you heard this little voice?"

"Yes; to be sure I have!" answered he, but in no very good humor, as yet. "And what of it?"

"Shall I lift the lid again?" asked Pandora.

"Just as you please!" said Epimetheus. "You have done so much mischief already, that perhaps you may as well do a little more. One other Trouble, in such a swarm as you have set adrift about the world, can make no very great difference!"

"You might speak a little more kindly!" murmured Pandora, wiping her eyes.

"Ah, naughty boy!" cried the little voice within the box, in an arch and laughing tone. "He knows he is longing to see me! Come, my dear Pandora, lift up the lid! I am in a great hurry to comfort you. Only let me have some fresh air, and you shall soon see that matters are not quite so dismal as you think them!"

"Epimetheus," exclaimed Pandora, "come what may, I am resolved to open the box!"

"And, as the lid seems very heavy," cried Epimetheus, running across the room, "I will help you!"

So, with one consent, the two children again lifted the lid. Out flew a sunny and smiling little personage, and hovered about the room, throwing a light wherever she went. Have you never made the sunshine dance into dark corners, by reflecting it from a bit of looking-glass? Well; so looked the winged cheerfulness of this fairylike stranger, amid the gloom of the cottage. She flew to Epimetheus, and laid the least touch of her finger on the inflamed spot where the Trouble had stung him; and immediately the anguish of it was gone. Then, she kissed Pandora on the forehead; and her hurt was cured likewise.

After performing these good offices, the bright stranger fluttered sportively over the children's heads, and looked so sweetly at them, that they both began to think it not so very much amiss to have opened the box; since, otherwise, their cheery guest must have been kept a prisoner, among those naughty imps with stings in their tails.

"Pray, who are you, beautiful creature?" inquired Pandora.

"I am to be called Hope!" answered the sunshiny figure. "And because I am such a cheery little body, I was packed into the box, to make amends to the human race for that swarm of ugly Troubles, which was destined to be let loose among them. Never fear! we shall do pretty well, in spite of them all."

"Your wings are colored like the rainbow!" exclaimed Pandora. "How very beautiful!"

"Yes; they are like the rainbow," said Hope, "because, glad as my nature is, I am partly made of tears as well as smiles!"

"And will you stay with us," asked Epimetheus, "forever and ever?"

"As long as you need me," said Hope, with her pleasant smile—"and that will be as long as you live in the world—I promise never to desert you! There may come times and seasons, now and then, when you will think that I have utterly vanished. But again, and again, and again, when perhaps you least dream of it, you shall see the glimmer of my wings on the ceiling of your cottage. Yes, my dear children; and I know something very good and beautiful that is to be given you, hereafter!"

"Oh, tell us," they exclaimed, "tell us what it is!"

"Do not ask me," replied Hope, putting her finger on her rosy mouth. "But do not despair, even if it should never happen while you live on this earth. Trust in my promise; for it is true!"

"We do trust you!" cried Epimetheus and Pandora, both in one breath.

And so they did; and not only they, but so has everybody trusted Hope, that has since been alive. And, to tell you the truth, I cannot help being glad—(though, to be sure, it was an uncommonly naughty thing for her to do)—but I cannot help being glad that our foolish Pandora peeped into the box. No doubt—no doubt—the Troubles are still flying about the world, and have increased in multitude, rather than lessened, and are a very ugly set of imps, and carry most venomous stings in their tails. I have felt them already, and expect to feel them more, as I grow older. But then that lovely and lightsome little figure of Hope! What in the world could we do without her? Hope spiritualizes the earth; Hope makes it always new; and, even in the earth's best and brightest aspect, Hope shows it to be only the shadow of an infinite bliss, hereafter!

TANGLEWOOD PLAY-ROOM

AFTER THE STORY

"Primrose," asked Eustace, pinching her ear, "how do you like my little Pandora? Don't you think her the exact picture of yourself? But you would not have hesitated half so long about opening the box."

"Then I should have been well punished for my naughtiness," retorted Primrose smartly; "for the first thing to pop out, after the lid was lifted, would have been Mr. Eustace Bright, in the shape of a Trouble!"

"Cousin Eustace," said Sweet Fern, "did the box hold all the trouble that has ever come into the world?"

"Every mite of it!" answered Eustace. "This very snowstorm, which has spoilt my skating, was packed up there."

"And how big was the box?" asked Sweet Fern.

"Why, perhaps three feet long," said Eustace, "two feet wide, and two feet and a half high."

"Ah," said the child, "you are making fun of me, Cousin Eustace! I know there is not trouble enough in the world to fill such a great box as that. As for the snow-storm, it is no trouble at all, but a pleasure; so it could not have been in the box."

"Hear the child!" cried Primrose, with an air of superiority. "How little he knows about the troubles of this world! Poor fellow! He will be wiser when he has seen as much of life as I have."

So saying, she began to skip the rope.

Meantime, the day was drawing towards its close. Out of doors the scene certainly looked dreary. There was a gray drift, far and wide, through the gathering twilight;—the earth was as pathless as the air;—and the bank of snow, over the steps of the porch, proved that nobody had entered or gone out, for a good many hours past. Had there been only one child at the window of Tanglewood, gazing at this wintry prospect, it would perhaps have made him sad. But half-a-dozen children together, though they cannot quite turn the world into a paradise, may defy old Winter and all his storms to put them out of spirits. Eustace Bright, moreover, on the spur of the moment, invented several new kinds of play, which kept them all in a roar of merriment till bedtime, and served for the next stormy day besides.

Jacob Abbott (1803–79)

A New England teacher and minister, Jacob Abbott wrote a popular series of books featuring the boy Rollo, whose life is documented from early childhood to his travels abroad at age twelve. Though often factually inaccurate, Abbott's children's stories featured a clear style and a gentle, thoughtful approach to children. In these excerpts from the first series of 1835, both the instructions for parents and the stories show that Abbott had a good grasp of children's psychology and methods of motivating young children to become actively engaged in learning; he recommends combining oral and written instruction, as well as using both words and pictures. Abbott also founded a Massachusetts girls' school and wrote scores of other stories, biographies, and books of instruction.

Notice to Parents

These little talks about pictures are mainly intended to be read by a mother, or by one of the older children, to a little one who is learning to talk. Their design is to interest and amuse the child, and at the same time to teach it the use of language and the meaning of words. To the reader, I have three directions to give.

1. Act out all the motions described. For instance, begin the first story when the child is away at play, and let the first sentence be the summons to you. Point at all the parts of the picture which are described; and, in fine, in every case suit the action to the word.

2. Read distinctly and with all the natural tones, and in the manner of conversation. Do this so completely that the child cannot tell whether you are reading or talking. Read *"No indeed,"* and *"Oh no,"* and *"Come, quick, quick,"* &c., with the ardor of emphasis which is natural to childhood. In a word, talk it off to them, with inflexions and tones exceedingly varied and emphatic.

A great many words are introduced which the child cannot be supposed to understand; but the connection explains them. To teach language thus, is one great object of the book. These words are generally in italics. They should be read very distinctly and emphatically, and sometimes paused upon, so that the child may ask questions upon them if he pleases. You will be amused at hearing him introduce them into his own conversation often, if he once understands them in the lesson.

3. Do not confine yourself to what is written. Wait patiently for an answer to all the questions; make additional remarks yourselves; when the child is interested, let him look at the picture *as long as he will.* He will ask you a question sometimes, after a long pause, which will be exceedingly interesting. Let your object

be to arouse and concentrate his powers, to awaken his curiosity, and to fix his attention. Let him in fact lead and guide the exercise.

The above directions are all that are necessary in regard to the reading of the lessons. A word as to the general use of the book.

It is bound in a substantial manner, so that it may be given to the child sometimes when nobody is at leisure to attend to him. With a little effort you can teach him to use it as gently and as carefully as you would yourself. Watch him a moment, and, if he begins to use it roughly, take it immediately away, and do not let him have it again for some hours. Never mind his crying. A few firm, decided experiments of this kind will teach him such habits as will make the book as safe in his hands as it would be in yours. It will be a great source of amusement and occupation to him to turn over the leaves and tell the stories to himself.

Do not let him have it too often, however, so as to lead him to treat it with contempt; and, above all, never let him have it for crying,—nor for *stopping crying.* The regular way in which some children get their wishes is to begin to cry, and then have their parents tell them they cannot have what they want *until they are pleasant.* They cry for the express purpose of getting an opportunity to stop.

A child of three or four years old can easily be taught to explain the pictures, or as he will call it, tell the stories, in his own way, from memory, to a younger child. In this way his intellect, his imagination, his memory will be cultivated, but more than this, he will be taught to be kind to his little brother or sister,—he will secure a practical lesson in the happiness of doing good.

From *Rollo Learning to Talk*

William, William,*—come run here—I have got some pictures to show you. Come and sit up in my lap, and I will show them all to you. Do you not see what an excellent book it is? It has got some good strong covers, and is full of pictures. I shall show them all to you, but not all to-day. Perhaps I shall let you take the book sometimes. If I do, you must be very careful of it.

FEEDING THE CHICKENS

Here is a picture of a little girl feeding the chickens. Little girl!† Little girl, did you know that you had left the gate open? Little girl, I say, *little girl,* did you know that you had left the gate open? She does not know what I say, she does not hear me; she is nothing but a picture of a girl. She has come out to feed her chickens. I can see the house she lives in. Do you see it? Where is it? Touch it with your finger. It stands back among the trees. I should like to go into that little gate, and walk along under the trees, and go into that house. Who do you think lives there? I think it must be that little girl's father and mother.

She took a little wooden bowl with a handle, and has come out to feed the chickens; and the hens too. There are some large hens. One is running very fast to get some of the corn. I rather think that is corn she is feeding the hens and chickens with. Run, Biddy, run, run, run fast, or you will lose all your corn.

Don't you see the little chickens? How many are there? You may count the chickens. Now you may count the hens. They are all picking up the corn. And there stands the *rooster,* too, opening his mouth to crow. He says, cock-a-doodle-doo, cock-a-doodle-doo!

Do you know why they call him *a roost-er?* It is because he roosts. When it is night do you suppose those hens go to bed, and lie down and cover themselves up with clothes and go to sleep? No indeed; they do not do that. If you should put one of them into a bed in that way, she would jump out and run away as fast as she could. What do you think the hens do when they want to go to sleep? Why, they get up on a long pole and cling to it with their long, sharp claws, and sleep there on a high pole. And that is roosting. So they call the great cock a roost-er. Do you think you could sleep on a high pole?

I can see a beautiful little house in the picture, and that is on a high pole. It is for little birds to live in. The birds are flying all about it. How many birds can you see? What kind of birds do you think they are? They are martins. Martins live in houses like that on the end of a pole.

THE DOG IN THE WATER

Do you see that little girl on the next page who has fallen into the water? You may touch her with your finger. Poor little girl! She was playing on the bank and fell in. Don't you see that large black dog? He is in the water too. Don't you see? His legs are down under the water. His back is out of the water. His legs look *faint.* His back looks *distinct.* The reason why his legs looks faint is because they are under the water, and we cannot see them very plain. Do you know why he is in the water? He jumped in to pull out that little girl. He is biting hold of her clothes to pull her out. He will not bite the little girl. Oh no, he will be careful and not bite the little girl. He loves the little girl, and wants to pull her out of the water. He is a kind dog. He is a good, kind, black dog. You must not be afraid of a dog when you see one. He will not bite you. No indeed. Perhaps he will pull you out of the water if you fall in. I think if you should see a dog, and if you should have some bread and butter, you had better give him a little piece. Dogs like bread.

See the little girl's mother. She is very much frightened because her little girl has fallen in.

I see three little birds in the picture. Can you see them?

---

*Note to the Mother. In reading this, use the name of your own child, and so in all similar cases.

†Call "Little girl!" in the tone you would use if you really expected an answer, and pause a moment for a reply. So in all similar cases.

THE GREAT BLACK BEAR

Shall I tell you about the next picture? Do you see this great bear? He is a great black bear. What do you think that string is, on his nose? It is a muzzle. Do you know what it is for? It is to keep his mouth shut, so that he cannot bite. Should you think he could bite with a muzzle round his mouth? It is tied on with a string, so that it cannot slip off, and while it is on he cannot bite. Bears live in the woods. They go growling about in the woods a great many hundred miles from here.

They caught this bear in the woods and tamed him. Do you see that thing on his back? What is it? It is a monkey. He is dressed up like a man to make him look droll.

Do you see that boy and girl looking out of the gate? Perhaps the tall one is meant for a lady. It may be the little girl's mother. Do you think it is a lady or boy? Why?

That little girl's name is Lucy. Lucy, don't be afraid. The bear and the monkey cannot hurt you. Don't you see the man has the bear's mouth tied with a string?

What has that man on his back? That great thing. It is an organ. I see the handle. When he puts it down,

The instructions for understanding this picture of a tamed bear and monkey show how Jacob Abbot combined texts and illustrations for parents to use while teaching children practical skills and values.

and turns the handle, it makes beautiful music. He is going to the town which is away beyond the trees, to show the children there the bear and the monkey, and to let them hear the music.

Lewis Carroll (1832–98)

Lewis Carroll's real name was Charles L. Dodgson. He was a mathematics tutor at Oxford and a shy and reclusive man—except with little girls, such as Alice Liddell, to whom he first told the story of Alice in Wonderland (an example of what C. S. Lewis regards as one of the important ways of writing for children: telling a story to an actual child—see Lewis's essay at the beginning of this section). Carroll's most famous work is framed by sentimental tributes to the Victorians' romantic conception of childhood: "where Childhood's dreams are twined / In Memory's mystic band," and the "simple sorrows" and "simple joys" of "child-life." But the fantasy novels, *Alice's Adventures in Wonderland* (1965) and the sequel *Through the Looking Glass* (1871), are actually a complicated and (to some readers) distressing mixture of aggression, anxiety, humor, and satire. Carroll derides the familiar moralism of Victorian children's literature and portrays adult authority figures with sarcasm and irony. Alice herself is a contradictory, confused, and at times cruel child—not an idealized innocent.

Carroll collaborated with illustrator John Tenniel, who created the famous drawings that remain firmly and fondly associated with both books, although many other prominent artists have produced fascinating interpretations of Alice's Wonderland adventures. The influence of Carroll's imaginative satire and nonsense humor has been far reaching; his word-play and memorable phrases have pervaded British and American culture. By sending his heroine into a world full of altered images from his own society and from older oral traditions, such as talking animals and objects, magical transformations, and details from nursery rhymes, Carroll established a pattern followed by generations of fantasy writers. Stories in which characters enter another world through a portal (a nursery window in James Barrie's *Peter Pan,* an old wardrobe in C. S. Lewis's Narnia Chronicles) are sometimes called "looking glass" fantasies in honor of Alice's second adventure. The chapters reprinted here show how thoroughly chaotic and unpredictable Carroll's fantasy world is and how much it pokes fun at the proprieties of Victorian rules of behavior. The poems in these chapters are satiric versions of familiar moralistic poetry, including the poems by Isaac Watts, Robert Southey, and Mary Howitt reprinted in this section.

From *Alice's Adventures in Wonderland*

All in the golden afternoon
Full leisurely we glide;
For both our oars, with little skill,
By little arms are plied,
While little hands make vain pretence
Our wanderings to guide.

Ah, cruel Three! In such an hour,
Beneath such dreamy weather,
To beg a tale of breath too weak
To stir the tiniest feather!
Yet what can one poor voice avail
Against three tongues together?

Imperious Prima flashes forth
Her edict "to begin it"—
In gentler tone Secunda hopes
"There will be nonsense in it!"—
While Tertia interrupts the tale
Not *more* than once a minute.

Anon, to sudden silence won,
In fancy they pursue
The dream-child moving through a land
Of wonders wild and new,
In friendly chat with bird or beast—
And half believe it true.

And ever, as the story drained
The wells of fancy dry,

And faintly strove that weary one
To put the subject by,
"The rest next time—" "It *is* next time!"
The happy voices cry.

Thus grew the tale of Wonderland:
Thus slowly, one by one,
Its quaint events were hammered out—
And now the tale is done,
And home we steer, a merry crew,
Beneath the setting sun.

Alice! a childish story take,
And with a gentle hand
Lay it where Childhood's dreams are twined
In Memory's mystic band,
Like pilgrim's wither'd wreath of flowers
Pluck'd in a far-off land.

CHAPTER 1. DOWN THE RABBIT-HOLE

Alice was beginning to get very tired of sitting by her sister on the bank, and of having nothing to do: once or twice she had peeped into the book her sister was reading, but it had no pictures or conversations in it, "and what is the use of a book," thought Alice, "without pictures or conversation?"

So she was considering in her own mind (as well as

John Tenniel's famous drawing of the White Rabbit, a parody of a gentleman obsessed with punctuality, just before he leads Alice "Down the Rabbit-Hole."

she could, for the hot day made her feel very sleepy and stupid), whether the pleasure of making a daisy-chain would be worth the trouble of getting up and picking the daisies, when suddenly a White Rabbit with pink eyes ran close by her.

There was nothing so *very* remarkable in that; nor did Alice think it so *very* much out of the way to hear the Rabbit say to itself, "Oh dear! Oh dear! I shall be too late!" (when she thought it over afterwards, it occurred to her that she ought to have wondered at this, but at the time it all seemed quite natural); but when the Rabbit actually *took a watch out of its waistcoat-pocket,* and looked at it, and then hurried on, Alice started to her feet, for it flashed across her mind that she had never before seen a rabbit with either a waistcoat-pocket, or a watch to take out of it, and burning with curiosity, she ran across the field after it, and fortunately was just in time to see it pop down a large rabbit-hole under the hedge.

In another moment down went Alice after it, never once considering how in the world she was to get out again.

The rabbit-hole went straight on like a tunnel for some way, and then dipped suddenly down, so suddenly that Alice had not a moment to think about stopping herself before she found herself falling down what seemed to be a very deep well.

Either the well was very deep, or she fell very slowly, for she had plenty of time as she went down to look about her, and to wonder what was going to happen next. First, she tried to look down and make out what she was coming to, but it was too dark to see anything; then she looked at the sides of the well, and noticed that they were filled with cupboards and book-shelves: here and there she saw maps and pictures hung upon pegs. She took down a jar from one of the shelves as she passed; it was labelled "ORANGE MARMALADE," but to her great disappointment it was empty: she did not like to drop the jar for fear of killing somebody, so managed to put it into one of the cupboards as she fell past it.

"Well!" Thought Alice to herself, "after such a fall as this, I shall think nothing of tumbling down stairs! How brave they'll all think me at home! Why, I wouldn't say anything about it, even if I fell off the top of the house!" (Which was very likely true.)

Down, down, down. Would the fall *never* come to an end! "I wonder how many miles I've fallen by this time?" she said aloud. "I must be getting somewhere near the centre of the earth. Let me see: that would be four thousand miles down, I think—" (for, you see, Alice had learnt several things of this sort in her lessons in the schoolroom, and though this was not a *very* good opportunity for showing off her knowledge, as there was no one to listen to her, still it was good practice to say it over) "—yes, that's about the right distance—but then I wonder what Latitude or Longitude I've got to?" (Alice had no idea what Latitude was, or Longitude either, but thought they were nice grand words to say.)

Presently she began again. "I wonder if I shall fall right *through* the earth! How funny it'll seem to come out among the people that walk with their heads downwards! The Antipathies, I think—" (she was rather glad there *was* no one listening, this time, as it didn't sound at all the right word) "—but I shall have to ask them what the name of the country is, you know.

Please, Ma'am, is this New Zealand or Australia?" (and she tried to curtsey as she spoke—fancy *curtseying* as you're falling through the air! Do you think you could manage it!) "And what an ignorant little girl she'll think me for asking! No, it'll never do to ask: perhaps I shall see it written up somewhere."

Down, down, down. There was nothing else to do, so Alice soon began talking again. "Dinah'll miss me very much to-night, I should think!" (Dinah was the cat.) "I hope they'll remember her saucer of milk at tea-time. Dinah, my dear! I wish you were down here with me! There are no mice in the air, I'm afraid, but you might catch a bat, and that's very like a mouse, you know. But do cats eat bats, I wonder?" And here Alice began to get rather sleepy, and went on saying to herself, in a dreamy sort of way, "Do cats eat bats? Do cats eat bats?" and sometimes, "Do bats eat cats?" for, you see, as she couldn't answer either question, it didn't much matter which way she put it. She felt that she was dozing off, and had just begun to dream that she was walking hand in hand with Dinah, and saying to her very earnestly, "Now, Dinah, tell me the truth: did you ever eat a bat?" when suddenly, thump! thump! down she came upon a heap of sticks and dry leaves, and the fall was over.

Alice was not a bit hurt, and she jumped up on to her feet in a moment: she looked up, but it was all dark overhead; before her was another long passage, and the White Rabbit was still in sight, hurrying down it. There was not a moment to be lost: away went Alice like the wind, and was just in time to hear it say, as it turned a corner, "Oh my ears and whiskers, how late it's getting!" She was close behind it when she turned the corner, but the Rabbit was no longer to be seen: she found herself in a long, low hall, which was lit up by a row of lamps hanging from the roof.

There were doors all round the hall, but they were all locked; and when Alice had been all the way down one side and up the other, trying every door, she walked sadly down the middle, wondering how she was ever to get out again.

Suddenly she came upon a little three-legged table, all made of solid glass; there was nothing on it except a tiny golden key, and Alice's first thought was that it might belong to one of the doors of the hall; but, alas! either the locks were too large, or the key was too small, but at any rate it would not open any of them. However, on the second time round, she came upon a low curtain she had not noticed before, and behind it was a little door about fifteen inches high: she tried the little golden key in the lock, and to her great delight it fitted!

Alice opened the door and found that it led into a small passage, not much larger than a rat-hole: she knelt down and looked along the passage into the loveliest garden you ever saw. How she longed to get out of that dark hall, and wander about among those beds of bright flowers and those cool fountains, but she could not even get her head through the doorway; "and even if my head would go through," thought poor Alice, "it would be of very little use without my shoulders. Oh, how I wish I could shut up like a telescope! I think I could, if I only knew how to begin." For, you see, so many out-of-the-way things had happened lately, that Alice had begun to think that very few things indeed were really impossible.

There seemed to be no use in waiting by the little door, so she went back to the table, half hoping she might find another key on it, or at any rate a book of rules for shutting people up like telescopes: this time she found a little bottle on it, ("which certainly was not here before," said Alice,) and round the neck of the bottle was a paper label, with the words "DRINK ME" beautifully printed on it in large letters.

It was all very well to say "Drink me," but the wise little Alice was not going to do *that* in a hurry. "No, I'll look first," she said, "and see whether it's marked '*poison*' or not"; for she had read several nice little histories about children who had got burnt, and eaten up by wild beasts and other unpleasant things, all because they *would* not remember the simple rules their friends had taught them: such as, that a red-hot poker will burn you if you hold it too long; and that if you cut your finger *very* deeply with a knife, it usually bleeds; and she had never forgotten that, if you drink much from a bottle marked "poison," it is almost certain to disagree with you, sooner or later.

However, this bottle was *not* marked "poison," so Alice ventured to taste it, and finding it very nice, (it had, in fact, a sort of mixed flavour of cherry-tart, custard, pine-apple, roast turkey, toffee, and hot buttered toast,) she very soon finished it off.

    *   *   *   *

       *   *   *

    *   *   *   *

"What a curious feeling!" said Alice; "I must be shutting up like a telescope."

And so it was indeed: she was now only ten inches high, and her face brightened up at the thought that she was now the right size for going through the little door into that lovely garden. First, however, she waited for a few minutes to see if she was going to shrink any further: she felt a little nervous about this; "for it might end, you know," said Alice to herself, "in my going out altogether, like a candle. I wonder what I should be like then?" And she tried to fancy what the flame of a candle is like after the candle is blown out, for she could not remember ever having seen such a thing.

After a while, finding that nothing more happened, she decided on going into the garden at once; but, alas for poor Alice! when she got to the door, she found she had forgotten the little golden key, and when she went back to the table for it, she found she could not possibly reach it: she could see it quite plainly through the glass, and she tried her best to climb up one of the legs of the table, but it was too slippery; and when she had tired herself out with trying, the poor little thing sat down and cried.

"Come, there's no use in crying like that!" said Alice to herself, rather sharply; "I advise you to leave off this minute!" She generally gave herself very good advice, (though she very seldom followed it), and sometimes she scolded herself so severely as to bring tears into her eyes; and once she remembered trying to box her own ears for having cheated herself in a game of croquet she was playing against herself, for this curious child was very fond of pretending to be two people. "But it's no use now," thought poor Alice, "to pretend to be two people! Why, there's hardly enough of me left to make *one* respectable person!"

Soon her eye fell on a little glass box that was lying under the table: she opened it, and found in it a very small cake, on which the words "EAT ME" were beautifully marked in currants. "Well, I'll eat it," said Alice, "and if it makes me grow larger, I can reach the key; and if it makes me grow smaller, I can creep under the door; so either way I'll get into the garden, and I don't care which happens!"

She ate a little bit, and said anxiously to herself, "Which way? Which way?" holding her hand on the top of her head to feel which way it was growing, and she was quite surprised to find that she remained the same size: to be sure, this generally happens when one eats cake, but Alice had got so much into the way of expecting nothing but out-of-the-way things to happen, that it seemed quite dull and stupid for life to go on in the common way.

So she set to work, and very soon finished off the cake.

CHAPTER 2. THE POOL OF TEARS

"Curiouser and curiouser!" cried Alice (she was so much surprised, that for the moment she quite forgot how to speak good English); "now I'm opening out like the largest telescope that ever was! Good-bye, feet!" (for when she looked down at her feet, they seemed to be almost out of sight, they were getting so far off). "Oh, my poor little feet, I wonder who will put on your shoes and stockings for you now, dears? I'm sure *I* shan't be able! I shall be a great deal too far off to trouble myself about you: you must manage the best way you can;—but I must be kind to them," thought Alice, "or perhaps they won't walk the way I want to go! Let me see: I'll give them a new pair of boots every Christmas."

And she went on planning to herself how she would manage it. "They must go by the carrier," she thought;

"Curiouser and Curiouser." John Tenniel captured the grotesque effects of Alice's bewildering changes in size.

"and how funny it'll seem, sending presents to one's own feet! And how odd the directions will look!

Alice's Right Foot, Esq.
　　Hearthrug,
　　　　near the Fender,
　　　　　　(with Alice's love).

Oh dear, what nonsense I'm talking!"

Just then her head struck against the roof of the hall: in fact she was now more than nine feet high, and she at once took up the little golden key and hurried off to the garden door.

Poor Alice! It was as much as she could do, lying down on one side, to look through into the garden with one eye; but to get through was more hopeless than ever: she sat down and began to cry again.

"You ought to be ashamed of yourself," said Alice, "a great girl like you," (she might well say this), "to go on crying in this way! Stop this moment, I tell you!" But she went on all the same, shedding gallons of tears, until there was a large pool all round her, about four inches deep and reaching half down the hall.

After a time she heard a little pattering of feet in the distance, and she hastily dried her eyes to see what was coming. It was the White Rabbit returning, splendidly dressed, with a pair of white kid gloves in one hand and a large fan in the other: he came trotting along in a great hurry, muttering to himself as he came, "Oh! the Duchess, the Duchess! Oh! won't she be savage if I've kept her waiting!" Alice felt so desperate that she was ready to ask help of any one; so, when the Rabbit came near her, she began, in a low, timid voice, "If you please, sir—" The Rabbit started violently, dropped the white kid gloves and the fan, and skurried away into the darkness as hard as he could go.

Alice took up the fan and gloves, and, as the hall was very hot, she kept fanning herself all the time she went on talking: "Dear, dear! How queer everything is to-day! And yesterday things went on just as usual. I wonder if I've been changed in the night? Let me think: was I the same when I got up this morning? I almost think I can remember feeling a little different. But if I'm not the same, the next question is, Who in the world am I? Ah, *that's* the great puzzle!" And she began thinking over all the children she knew that were of the same age as herself, to see if she could have been changed for any of them.

"I'm sure I'm not Ada," she said, "for her hair goes in such long ringlets, and mine doesn't go in ringlets at all; and I'm sure I can't be Mabel, for I know all sorts of things, and she, oh! she knows such a very little! Besides, *she's* she, and *I'm* I, and—oh dear, how puzzling it all is! I'll try if I know all the things I used to know. Let me see: four times five is twelve, and four times six is thirteen, and four times seven is—oh dear! I shall never get to twenty at that rate! However, the Multiplication Table doesn't signify: let's try Geography. London is the capital of Paris, and Paris is the capital of Rome, and Rome—no, *that's* all wrong, I'm certain! I must have been changed for Mabel! I'll try and say '*How doth the little—*'" and she crossed her hands on her lap as if she were saying lessons, and began to repeat it, but her voice sounded hoarse and strange, and the words did not come the same as they used to do:—

"How doth the little crocodile
Improve his shining tail,
And pour the waters of the Nile
On every golden scale!

"How cheerfully he seems to grin,
How neatly spread his claws,
And welcome little fishes in
With gently smiling jaws!"

"I'm sure those are not the right words," said poor Alice, and her eyes filled with tears again as she went on, "I must be Mabel after all, and I shall have to go and live in that poky little house, and have next to no toys to play with, and oh! ever so many lessons to learn! No, I've made up my mind about it; if I'm Mabel, I'll stay down here! It'll be no use their putting their heads down and saying 'Come up again, dear!' I shall only look up and say 'Who am I then? Tell me that first, and then, if I like being that person, I'll come up: if not, I'll stay down here till I'm somebody else'—but, oh dear!" cried Alice, with a sudden burst of tears, "I do wish they *would* put their heads down! I am so *very* tired of being all alone here!"

As she said this she looked down at her hands, and was surprised to see that she had put on one of the Rabbit's little white kid gloves while she was talking. "How *can* I have done that?" she thought. "I must be growing small again." She got up and went to the table to measure herself by it, and found that, as nearly as she could guess, she was now about two feet high, and was going on shrinking rapidly: she soon found out that the cause of this was the fan she was holding, and she dropped it hastily, just in time to avoid shrinking away altogether.

"That *was* a narrow escape!" said Alice, a good deal frightened at the sudden change, but very glad to find herself still in existence; "and now for the garden!" and she ran with all speed back to the little door: but, alas! the little door was shut again, and the little golden key was lying on the glass table as before, "and things are worse than ever," thought the poor child, "for I never was so small as this before, never! And I declare it's too bad, that it is!"

As she said these words her foot slipped, and in another moment, splash! she was up to her chin in salt water. Her first idea was that she had somehow fallen into the sea, "and in that case I can go back by railway," she said to herself. (Alice had been to the seaside once in her life, and had come to the general conclusion, that wherever you go to on the English coast you find a number of bathing machines in the sea, some children digging in the sand with wooden spades, then a row of lodging houses, and behind them a railway station.) However, she soon made out that she was in the pool of tears which she had wept when she was nine feet high.

"I wish I hadn't cried so much!" said Alice, as she swam about, trying to find her way out. "I shall be punished for it now, I suppose, by being drowned in my own tears! That *will* be a queer thing, to be sure! However, everything is queer to-day."

Just then she heard something splashing about in the pool a little way off, and she swam nearer to make out what it was: at first she thought it must be a walrus or hippopotamus, but then she remembered how small she was now, and she soon made out that it was only a mouse that had slipped in like herself.

"Would it be of any use, now," thought Alice, "to speak to this mouse? Everything is so out-of-the-way down here, that I should think very likely it can talk: at any rate, there's no harm in trying." So she began: "O Mouse, do you know the way out of this pool? I am very tired of swimming about here, O Mouse!" (Alice thought this must be the right way of speaking to a mouse: she had never done such a thing before, but she remembered having seen in her brother's Latin Grammar, "A mouse—of a mouse—to a mouse—a mouse—O mouse!" The Mouse looked at her rather inquisitively, and seemed to her to wink with one of its little eyes, but it said nothing.

"Perhaps it doesn't understand English," thought Alice; "I daresay it's a French mouse, come over with William the Conqueror." (For, with all her knowledge of history, Alice had no very clear notion how long ago anything had happened.) So she began again: "Où est ma chatte?" which was the first sentence in her French lesson-book. The Mouse gave a sudden leap out of the

"The Pool of Tears." John Tenniel's realistic treatment of Alice swimming in her tears intensifies the fantastic nature of the tale.

water, and seemed to quiver all over with fright. "Oh, I beg your pardon!" cried Alice hastily, afraid that she had hurt the poor animal's feelings. "I quite forgot you didn't like cats."

"Not like cats!" cried the Mouse, in a shrill, passionate voice. "Would *you* like cats if you were me?"

"Well, perhaps not," said Alice in a soothing tone: "don't be angry about it. And yet I wish I could show you our cat Dinah: I think you'd take a fancy to cats if you could only see her. She is such a dear quiet thing," Alice went on, half to herself, as she swam lazily about in the pool, "and she sits purring so nicely by the fire, licking her paws and washing her face—and she is such a nice soft thing to nurse—and she's such a capital one for catching mice—oh, I beg your pardon!" cried Alice again, for this time the Mouse was bristling all over, and she felt certain it must be really offended. "We won't talk about her any more if you'd rather not."

"We, indeed!" cried the Mouse, who was trembling down to the end of his tail. "As if *I* would talk on such a subject! Our family always *hated* cats: nasty, low, vulgar things! Don't let me hear the name again!"

"I won't indeed!" said Alice, in a great hurry to change the subject of conversation. "Are you—are you fond—of—of dogs?" The Mouse did not answer, so Alice went on eagerly: "There is such a nice little dog near our house I should like to show you! A little bright-eyed terrier, you know, with oh, such long curly brown hair! And it'll fetch things when you throw them, and it'll sit up and beg for its dinner, and all sorts of things—I can't remember half of them—and it belongs to a farmer, you know, and he says it's so useful, it's worth a hundred pounds! He says it kills all the rats and—oh dear!" cried Alice in a sorrowful tone, "I'm afraid I've offended it again!" For the Mouse was swimming away from her as hard as it could go, and making quite a commotion in the pool as it went.

So she called softly after it, "Mouse dear! Do come back again, and we won't talk about cats or dogs either, if you don't like them!" When the Mouse heard this, it turned round and swam slowly back to her: its face was quite pale (with passion, Alice thought), and it said in a low trembling voice, "Let us get to the shore, and then I'll tell you my history, and you'll understand why it is I hate cats and dogs."

It was high time to go, for the pool was getting quite crowded with the birds and animals that had fallen into it: there were a Duck and a Dodo, a Lory and an Eaglet, and several other curious creatures. Alice led the way, and the whole party swam to the shore.

CHAPTER 5. ADVICE FROM A CATERPILLAR

The Caterpillar and Alice looked at each other for some time in silence: at last the Caterpillar took the hookah out of its mouth, and addressed her in a languid, sleepy voice.

"Who are *you?*" said the Caterpillar.

This was not an encouraging opening for a conversation. Alice replied, rather shyly, "I-I hardly know, sir, just at present—at least I know who I *was* when I got up this morning, but I think I must have been changed several times since then."

"What do you mean by that?" said the Caterpillar sternly. "Explain yourself!"

"I can't explain *myself,* I'm afraid, sir," said Alice, "because I'm not myself, you see."

"I don't see," said the Caterpillar.

"Advice from a Caterpillar." John Tenniel depicts the shrunken Alice's continuing confusion as she finds herself the right size to converse with a caterpillar.

"I'm afraid I can't put it more clearly," Alice replied very politely, "for I can't understand it myself to begin with; and being so many different sizes in a day is very confusing."

"It isn't," said the Caterpillar.

"Well, perhaps you haven't found it so yet," said Alice; "but when you have to turn into a chrysalis—you will some day, you know—and then after that into a butterfly, I should think you'll feel it a little queer, won't you?"

"Not a bit," said the Caterpillar.

"Well, perhaps your feelings may be different," said Alice; "all I know is, it would feel very queer to *me*."

"You!" said the Caterpillar contemptuously. "Who are *you?*"

Which brought them back again to the beginning of the conversation. Alice felt a little irritated at the Caterpillar's making such *very* short remarks, and she drew herself up and said, very gravely, "I think you ought to tell me who *you* are, first."

"Why?" said the Caterpillar.

Here was another puzzling question; and as Alice could not think of any good reason, and as the Caterpillar seemed to be in a *very* unpleasant state of mind, she turned away.

"Come back!" the Caterpillar called after her. "I've something important to say!"

This sounded promising, certainly: Alice turned and came back again.

"Keep your temper," said the Caterpillar.

"Is that all?" said Alice, swallowing down her anger as well as she could.

"No," said the Caterpillar.

Alice thought she might as well wait, as she had nothing else to do, and perhaps after all it might tell her something worth hearing. For some minutes it puffed away without speaking, but at last it unfolded its arms, took the hookah out of its mouth again, and said, "So you think you're changed, do you?"

"I'm afraid I am, sir," said Alice; "I can't remember things as I used—and I don't keep the same size for ten minutes together!"

"Can't remember *what* things?" said the Caterpillar.

"Well, I've tried to say '*How doth the little busy bee,*' but it all came different!" Alice replied in a very melancholy voice.

"Repeat, '*You are old, Father William,*'" said the Caterpillar.

Alice folded her hands, and began:—

"You are old, Father William," the young man said,
"And your hair has become very white;
And yet you incessantly stand on your head—
Do you think, at your age, it is right?"

"In my youth," Father William replied to his son,
"I feared it might injure the brain;
But, now that I'm perfectly sure I have none,
Why, I do it again and again."

"You are old," said the youth, "as I mentioned before,
And have grown most uncommonly fat;
Yet you turned a back-somersault in at the door—
Pray, what is the reason of that?"

"In my youth," said the sage, as he shook his grey locks,
"I kept all my limbs very supple
By the use of this ointment—one shilling the box—
Allow me to sell you a couple?"

"You are old," said the youth, "and your jaws are too weak
For anything tougher than suet;
Yet you finished the goose, with the bones and the beak—
Pray how did you manage to do it?"

"In my youth," said his father, "I took to the law,
And argued each case with my wife;
And the muscular strength, which it gave to my jaw,
Has lasted the rest of my life."

"You are old," said the youth, "one would hardly suppose
That your eye was as steady as ever;
Yet you balanced an eel on the end of your nose—
What made you so awfully clever?"

"I have answered three questions, and that is enough,"
Said his father; "don't give yourself airs!
Do you think I can listen all day to such stuff?
Be off, or I'll kick you down stairs!"

"That is not said right," said the Caterpillar.

"Not *quite* right, I'm afraid," said Alice, timidly; "some of the words have got altered."

"It is wrong from beginning to end," said the Cat-

Two panels from John Tenniel's four drawings for the parody in chapter 5 of Southey's poem "You are Old, Father William." The combination of charming art, humorous prose, and musical lyrics make the novel a classic of fantasy for children.

erpillar decidedly, and there was silence for some minutes.

The Caterpillar was the first to speak.

"What size do you want to be?" it asked.

"Oh, I'm not particular as to size," Alice hastily replied; "only one doesn't like changing so often, you know."

"I *don't* know," said the Caterpillar.

Alice said nothing: she had never been so much contradicted in all her life before, and she felt that she was losing her temper.

"Are you content now?" said the Caterpillar.

"Well, I should like to be a *little* larger, sir, if you wouldn't mind," said Alice: "three inches is such a wretched height to be."

"It is a very good height indeed!" said the Caterpillar angrily, rearing itself upright as it spoke (it was exactly three inches high).

"But I'm not used to it!" pleaded poor Alice in a piteous tone. And she thought to herself, "I wish the creatures wouldn't be so easily offended!"

"You'll get used to it in time," said the Caterpillar; and it put the hookah into its mouth and began smoking again.

This time Alice waited patiently until it chose to speak again. In a minute or two the Caterpillar took the hookah out of its mouth and yawned once or twice, and shook itself. Then it got down off the mushroom, and crawled away into the grass, merely remarking as

it went, "One side will make you grow taller, and the other side will make you grow shorter."

"One side of *what*? The other side of *what*?" thought Alice to herself.

"Of the mushroom," said the Caterpillar, just as if she had asked it aloud; and in another moment it was out of sight.

Alice remained looking thoughtfully at the mushroom for a minute, trying to make out which were the two sides of it; and as it was perfectly round, she found this a very difficult question. However, at last she stretched her arms round it as far as they would go, and broke off a bit of the edge with each hand.

"And now which is which?" she said to herself, and nibbled a little of the right-hand bit to try the effect: the next moment she felt a violent blow underneath her chin: it had struck her foot!

She was a good deal frightened by this very sudden change, but she felt that there was no time to be lost, as she was shrinking rapidly; so she set to work at once to eat some of the other bit. Her chin was pressed so closely against her foot, that there was hardly room to open her mouth; but she did it at last, and managed to swallow a morsel of the left-hand bit.

 *　　　*　　　*　　　*　　　*
 　*　　　*　　　*　　　*
 *　　　*　　　*　　　*　　　*

"Come, my head's free at last!" said Alice in a tone of delight, which changed into alarm in another moment, when she found that her shoulders were nowhere to be found: all she could see, when she looked down, was an immense length of neck, which seemed to rise like a stalk out of a sea of green leaves that lay far below her.

"What *can* all that green stuff be?" said Alice. 'And where *have* my shoulders got to? And oh, my poor hands, how is it I can't see you?' She was moving them about as she spoke, but no result seemed to follow, except a little shaking among the distant green leaves.

As there seemed to be no chance of getting her hands up to her head, she tried to get her head down to them, and was delighted to find that her neck would bend about easily in any direction, like a serpent. She had just succeeded in curving it down into a graceful zigzag, and was going to dive in among the leaves, which she found to be nothing but the tops of the trees under which she had been wandering, when a sharp hiss made her draw back in a hurry: a large pigeon had flown into her face, and was beating her violently with its wings.

"Serpent!" screamed the Pigeon.

"I'm *not* a serpent!" said Alice indignantly. "Let me alone!"

"Serpent, I say again!" repeated the Pigeon, but in a more subdued tone, and added with a kind of sob, "I've tried every way, and nothing seems to suit them!"

"I haven't the least idea what you're talking about," said Alice.

"I've tried the roots of trees, and I've tried banks, and I've tried hedges," the Pigeon went on, without attending to her; "but those serpents! There's no pleasing them!"

Alice was more and more puzzled, but she thought there was no use in saying anything more till the Pigeon had finished.

"As if it wasn't trouble enough hatching the eggs," said the Pigeon; "but I must be on the look-out for serpents night and day! Why, I haven't had a wink of sleep these three weeks!"

"I'm very sorry you've been annoyed," said Alice, who was beginning to see its meaning.

"And just as I'd taken the highest tree in the wood," continued the Pigeon, raising its voice to a shriek, "and just as I was thinking I should be free of them at last, they must needs come wriggling down from the sky! Ugh, Serpent!"

"But I'm *not* a serpent, I tell you!" said Alice. "I'm a—I'm a—"

"Well, *What* are you?" said the Pigeon. "I can see you're trying to invent something!"

"I—I'm a little girl," said Alice, rather doubtfully, as she remembered the number of changes she had gone through that day.

"A likely story indeed!" said the Pigeon in a tone of the deepest contempt. "I've seen a good many little girls in my time, but never *one* with such a neck as that! No, no! You're a serpent; and there's no use denying it. I suppose you'll be telling me next that you never tasted an egg!"

"I *have* tasted eggs, certainly," said Alice, who was a very truthful child; "but little girls eat eggs quite as much as serpents do, you know."

"I don't believe it," said the Pigeon; "but if they do, why then they're a kind of serpent, that's all I can say."

This was such a new idea to Alice, that she was quite silent for a minute or two, which gave the Pigeon the opportunity of adding, "You're looking for eggs, I know *that* well enough; and what does it matter to me whether you're a little girl or a serpent?"

"It matters a good deal to *me*," said Alice hastily; "but I'm not looking for eggs, as it happens; and if I was, I shouldn't want *yours:* I don't like them raw."

"Well, be off, then!" said the Pigeon in a sulky tone, as it settled down again into its nest. Alice crouched down among the trees as well as she could, for her neck kept getting entangled among the branches, and every now and then she had to stop and untwist it. After a while she remembered that she still held the pieces of mushroom in her hands, and she set to work very carefully, nibbling first at one and then at the other, and growing sometimes taller and sometimes shorter, until she had succeeded in bringing herself down to her usual height.

It was so long since she had been anything near the right size, that it felt quite strange at first; but she got used to it in a few minutes, and began talking to herself, as usual. "Come, there's half my plan done now! How puzzling all these changes are! I'm never sure what I'm going to be, from one minute to another! However, I've got back to my right size: the next thing is, to get into that beautiful garden—how *is* that to be done, I wonder?" As she said this, she came suddenly upon an open place, with a little house in it about four feet high. "Whoever lives there," thought Alice, "it'll never do to come upon them *this* size: why, I should frighten them out of their wits!" So she began nibbling at the right-hand bit again, and did not venture to go near the house till she had brought herself down to nine inches high.

CHAPTER 10. THE LOBSTER QUADRILLE

The Mock Turtle sighed deeply, and drew the back of one flapper across his eyes. He looked at Alice, and tried to speak, but for a minute or two sobs choked his voice. "Same as if he had a bone in his throat," said the Gryphon: and it set to work shaking him and punching him in the back. At last the Mock Turtle recovered his voice, and, with tears running down his cheeks, he went on again:—

"You may not have lived much under the sea—" ("I haven't," said Alice)—"and perhaps you were never even introduced to a lobster—" (Alice began to say "I once tasted—" but checked herself hastily, and said "No, never") "—so you can have no idea what a delightful thing a Lobster Quadrille is!"

"No, indeed," said Alice. "What sort of a dance is it?"

"Why," said the Gryphon, "you first form into a line along the sea-shore—"

"Two lines!" cried the Mock Turtle. "Seals, turtles, salmon, and so on; then, when you've cleared all the jelly-fish out of the way—"

"*That* generally takes some time," interrupted the Gryphon.

"—you advance twice—"

"Each with a lobster as a partner!" cried the Gryphon.

"Of course," the Mock Turtle said: "advance twice, set to partners—"

"—change lobsters, and retire in same order," continued the Gryphon.

"Then, you know," the Mock Turtle went on, "you throw the—"

"The lobsters!" shouted the Gryphon, with a bound into the air.

"—as far out to sea as you can—"

"Swim after them!" screamed the Gryphon.

"Turn a somersault in the sea!" cried the Mock Turtle, capering wildly about.

"Change lobsters again!" yelled the Gryphon.

"The Lobster-Quadrille." John Tenniel shows the weeping Mock Turtle standing on a rock as if delivering a lecture while he tells his absurd history to Alice and the Gryphon.

"Back to land again, and that's all the first figure," said the Mock Turtle, suddenly dropping his voice; and the two creatures, who had been jumping about like mad things all this time, sat down again very sadly and quietly, and looked at Alice.

"It must be a very pretty dance," said Alice timidly.

"Would you like to see a little of it?" said the Mock Turtle.

"Very much indeed," said Alice.

"Come, let's try the first figure!" said the Mock Turtle to the Gryphon. "We can do without lobsters, you know. Which shall sing?"

"Oh, *you* sing," said the Gryphon. "I've forgotten the words."

So they began solemnly dancing round and round Alice, every now and then treading on her toes when they passed too close, and waving their forepaws to mark the time, while the Mock Turtle sang this, very slowly and sadly:—

> "'Will you walk a little faster?' said a whiting to a
>   snail.
> 'There's a porpoise close behind us, and he's tread-
>   ing on my tail.
> See how eagerly the lobsters and the turtles all
>   advance!

They are waiting on the shingle—will you come and
   join the dance?
Will you, won't you, will you, won't you, will you
   join the dance?
Will you, won't you, will you, won't you, won't you
   join the dance?

"You can really have no notion how delightful it will
   be
When they take us up and throw us, with the lobsters,
   out to sea!'
But the snail replied 'Too far, too far!' and gave a
   look askance—
Said he thanked the whiting kindly, but he would not
   join the dance.
Would not, could not, would not, could not, would
   not join the dance.
Would not, could not, would not, could not, could not
   join the dance.

"'What matters it how far we go?' his scaly friend
   replied.
'There is another shore, you know, upon the other
   side.
The further off from England the nearer is to
   France—
Then turn not pale, beloved snail, but come and join
   the dance.
Will you, won't you, will you, won't you, will you
   join the dance?
Will you, won't you, will you, won't you, won't you
   join the dance?'"

"Thank you, it's a very interesting dance to watch,"
said Alice, feeling very glad that it was over at last:
"and I do so like that curious song about the whiting!"

"Oh, as to the whiting," said the Mock Turtle,
"they—you've seen them, of course?"

"Yes," said Alice, "I've often seen them at dinn—"
she checked herself hastily.

"I don't know where Dinn may be," said the Mock
Turtle, "but if you've seen them so often, of course
you know what they're like."

"I believe so," Alice replied thoughtfully. "They
have their tails in their mouths—and they're all over
crumbs."

"You're wrong about the crumbs," said the Mock
Turtle: "crumbs would all wash off in the sea. But they
have their tails in their mouths; and the reason is—"
here the Mock Turtle yawned and shut his eyes.—
"Tell her about the reason and all that," he said to the
Gryphon.

"The reason is," said the Gryphon, "that they *would*
go with the lobsters to the dance. So they got thrown
out to sea. So they had to fall a long way. So they got
their tails fast in their mouths. So they couldn't get
them out again. That's all."

"Thank you," said Alice, "it's very interesting. I
never knew so much about a whiting before."

"I can tell you more than that, if you like," said the
Gryphon. "Do you know why it's called a whiting?"

"I never thought about it," said Alice. "Why?"

"*It does the boots and shoes,*" the Gryphon replied
very solemnly.

Alice was thoroughly puzzled. "Does the boots and
shoes!" she repeated in a wondering tone.

"Why, what are *your* shoes done with?" said the
Gryphon. "I mean what makes them so shiny?"

Alice looked down at them, and considered a little
before she gave her answer. "They're done with blacking, I believe."

"Boots and shoes under the sea," the Gryphon went
on in a deep voice, "are done with whiting. Now you
know."

"And what are they made of?" Alice asked in a tone
of great curiosity.

"Soles and eels, of course," the Gryphon replied
rather impatiently: "any shrimp could have told you
that."

"If I'd been the whiting," said Alice, whose
thoughts were still running on the song, "I'd have said
to the porpoise, 'Keep back, please: we don't want *you*
with us!'"

"They were obliged to have him with them," the
Mock Turtle said: "no wise fish would go anywhere
without a porpoise."

"Wouldn't it really?" said Alice in a tone of great
surprise.

"Of course not," said the Mock Turtle: "why, if a
fish came to *me,* and told me he was going a journey, I
should say 'With what porpoise?'"

"Don't you mean 'purpose?'" said Alice.

"I mean what I say," the Mock Turtle replied in an
offended tone. And the Gryphon added "Come, let's
hear some of *your* adventures."

"I could tell you my adventures—beginning from
this morning," said Alice a little timidly: "but it's no
use going back to yesterday, because I was a different
person then."

"Explain all that," said the Mock Turtle.

"No, no! The adventures first," said the Gryphon in an impatient tone: "explanations take such a dreadful time."

So Alice began telling them her adventures from the time when she first saw the White Rabbit. She was a little nervous about it just at first, the two creatures got so close to her, one on each side, and opened their eyes and mouths so *very* wide, but she gained courage as she went on. Her listeners were perfectly quiet till she got to the part about her repeating "*You are old, Father William,*" to the Caterpillar, and the words all coming different, and then the Mock Turtle drew a long breath, and said "That's very curious."

"It's all about as curious as it can be," said the Gryphon.

"It all came different!" the Mock Turtle repeated thoughtfully. "I should like to hear her try and repeat something now. Tell her to begin." He looked at the Gryphon as if he thought it had some kind of authority over Alice.

"Stand up and repeat "'*Tis the voice of the sluggard,*'" said the Gryphon.

"How the creatures order one about, and make one repeat lessons!" thought Alice; "I might as well be at school at once." However, she got up, and began to repeat it, but her head was so full of the Lobster Quadrille, that she hardly knew what she was saying, and the words came very queer indeed:—

'Tis the voice of the Lobster; I heard him declare,
'You have baked me too brown, I must sugar my
    hair.'
As a duck with its eyelids, so he with his nose
Trims his belt and his buttons, and turns out his toes."

"That's different from what *I* used to say when I was a child," said the Gryphon.

"Well, I never heard it before," said the Mock Turtle; "but it sounds uncommon nonsense."

Alice said nothing; she had sat down with her face in her hands, wondering if anything would *ever* happen in a natural way again.

"I should like to have it explained," said the Mock Turtle.

"She can't explain it," said the Gryphon hastily. "Go on with the next verse."

"But about his toes?" the Mock Turtle persisted. "How *could* he turn them out with his nose, you know?"

"It's the first position in dancing," Alice said; but was dreadfully puzzled by the whole thing, and longed to change the subject.

"Go on with the next verse," the Gryphon repeated impatiently: "it begins '*I passed by his garden.*'"

Alice did not dare to disobey, though she felt sure it would all come wrong, and she went on in a trembling voice:—

"I passed by his garden, and marked, with one eye,
How the Owl and the Panther were sharing a pie—"

"What *is* the use of repeating all that stuff," the Mock Turtle interrupted, "if you don't explain it as you go on? It's by far the most confusing thing *I* ever heard!"

"Yes, I think you'd better leave off," said the Gryphon: and Alice was only too glad to do so.

"Shall we try another figure of the Lobster Quadrille?" the Gryphon went on. "Or would you like the Mock Turtle to sing you a song?"

"Oh, a song, please, if the Mock Turtle would be so kind," Alice replied, so eagerly that the Gryphon said, in a rather offended tone, "Hm! No accounting for tastes! Sing her '*Turtle Soup,*' will you, old fellow?"

The Mock Turtle sighed deeply, and began, in a voice sometimes choked with sobs, to sing this:—

"Beautiful Soup, so rich and green,
Waiting in a hot tureen!
Who for such dainties would not stoop?
Soup of the evening, beautiful Soup!
Soup of the evening, beautiful Soup!
Beau—ootiful Soo—oop!
Beau—ootiful Soo—oop!
Soo—oop of the e—e—evening,
Beautiful, beautiful Soup!

"Beautiful Soup! Who cares for fish,
Game, or any other dish?
Who would not give all else for two p
ennyworth only of beautiful Soup?
Pennyworth only of beautiful Soup?
Beau—ootiful Soo—oop!
Beau—ootiful Soo—oop!
Soo—oop of the e—e—evening,
Beautiful, beauti—FUL SOUP!"

"Chorus again!" cried the Gryphon, and the Mock Turtle had just begun to repeat it, when a cry of "The trial's beginning!" was heard in the distance.

"Come on!" cried the Gryphon, and, taking Alice by the hand, it hurried off, without waiting for the end of the song.

"What trial is it?" Alice panted as she ran; but the Gryphon only answered "Come on!" and ran the faster, while more and more faintly came, carried on the breeze that followed them, the melancholy words:—

"Soo—oop of the e—e—evening,
Beautiful, beautiful Soup!"

From CHAPTER 12. ALICE'S EVIDENCE

. . . "Wake up, Alice dear!" said her sister; "Why, what a long sleep you've had!"

"Oh, I've had such a curious dream!" said Alice, and she told her sister, as well as she could remember them, all these strange Adventures of hers that you have just been reading about; and when she had finished, her sister kissed her, and said, "It *was* a curious dream, dear, certainly: but now run in to your tea; it's getting late." So Alice got up and ran off, thinking while she ran, as well she might, what a wonderful dream it had been.

But her sister sat still just as she left her, leaning her head on her hand, watching the setting sun, and thinking of little Alice and all her wonderful Adventures, till she too began dreaming after a fashion, and this was her dream:—

First, she dreamed of little Alice herself, and once again the tiny hands were clasped upon her knee, and the bright eager eyes were looking up into hers—she could hear the very tones of her voice, and see that queer little toss of her head to keep back the wander-

ing hair that *would* always get into her eyes—and still as she listened, or seemed to listen, the whole place around her became alive with the strange creatures of her little sister's dream.

The long grass rustled at her feet as the White Rabbit hurried by—the frightened Mouse splashed his way through the neighbouring pool—she could hear the rattle of the teacups as the March Hare and his friends shared their never-ending meal, and the shrill voice of the Queen ordering off her unfortunate guests to execution—once more the pig-baby was sneezing on the Duchess's knee, while plates and dishes crashed around it—once more the shriek of the Gryphon, the squeaking of the Lizard's slate-pencil, and the choking of the suppressed guinea-pigs, filled the air, mixed up with the distant sobs of the miserable Mock Turtle.

So she sat on, with closed eyes, and half believed herself in Wonderland, though she knew she had but to open them again, and all would change to dull reality—the grass would be only rustling in the wind, and the pool rippling to the waving of the reeds—the rattling teacups would change to tinkling sheep-bells, and the Queen's shrill cries to the voice of the shepherd boy—and the sneeze of the baby, the shriek of the Gryphon, and all the other queer noises, would change (she knew) to the confused clamour of the busy farm-yard—while the lowing of the cattle in the distance would take the place of the Mock Turtle's heavy sobs.

Lastly, she pictured to herself how this same little sister of hers would, in the after-time, be herself a grown woman; and how she would keep, through all her riper years, the simple and loving heart of her childhood: and how she would gather about her other little children, and make *their* eyes bright and eager with many a strange tale, perhaps even with the dream of Wonderland of long ago: and how she would feel with all their simple sorrows, and find a pleasure in all their simple joys, remembering her own child-life, and the happy summer days.

From *Through the Looking-Glass*

CHAPTER 4. TWEEDLEDUM AND TWEEDLEDEE

They were standing under a tree, each with an arm round the other's neck, and Alice knew which was which in a moment, because one of them had "DUM" embroidered on his collar, and the other "DEE." "I suppose they've each got "TWEEDLE" round at the back of the collar," she said to herself.

They stood so still that she quite forgot they were alive, and she was just going round to see if the word "TWEEDLE" was written at the back of each collar, when she was startled by a voice coming from the one marked "DUM."

"If you think we're wax-works," he said, "you ought to pay, you know. Wax-works weren't made to be looked at for nothing. Nohow!"

"Contrariwise," added the one marked "DEE," "if you think we're alive, you ought to speak."

"I'm sure I'm very sorry," was all Alice could say; for the words of the old song kept ringing through her head like the ticking of a clock, and she could hardly help saying them out loud:—

"Tweedledum and Tweedledee
Agreed to have a battle;
For Tweedledum said Tweedledee
Had spoiled his nice new rattle.

Just then flew down a monstrous crow,
As black as a tar-barrel;
Which frightened both the heroes so,
They quite forgot their quarrel."

"I know what you're thinking about," said Tweedledum; "but it isn't so, nohow."

"Contrariwise," continued Tweedledee, "if it was so, it might be; and if it were so, it would be; but as it isn't, it ain't. That's logic."

"I was thinking," Alice said politely, "which is the best way out of this wood: it's getting so dark. Would you tell me, please?"

But the fat little men only looked at each other and grinned.

They looked so exactly like a couple of great schoolboys, that Alice couldn't help pointing her finger at Tweedledum, and saying "First Boy!"

"Nohow!" Tweedledum cried out briskly, and shut his mouth up again with a snap.

"Next Boy!" said Alice, passing on to Tweedledee, though she felt quite certain he would only shout out "Contrariwise!" and so he did.

"You've begun wrong!" cried Tweedledum. "The first thing in a visit is to say 'How d'ye do?' and shake hands!" And here the two brothers gave each other a hug, and then they held out the two hands that were free, to shake hands with her.

Alice did not like shaking hands with either of them first, for fear of hurting the other one's feelings; so, as the best way out of the difficulty, she took hold of both hands at once: the next moment they were dancing round in a ring. This seemed quite natural (she remembered afterwards), and she was not even surprised to hear music playing: it seemed to come from the tree under which they were dancing, and it was done (as well as she could make it out) by the branches rubbing one across the other, like fiddles and fiddle-sticks.

"But it certainly *was* funny," (Alice said afterwards, when she was telling her sister the history of all this,) "to find myself singing '*Here we go round the mulberry bush.*' I don't know when I began it, but somehow I felt as if I'd been singing it a long long time!"

The other two dancers were fat, and very soon out of breath. "Four times round is enough for one dance," Tweedledum panted out, and they left off dancing as suddenly as they had begun: the music stopped at the same moment.

Then they let go of Alice's hands, and stood looking at her for a minute: there was a rather awkward pause, as Alice didn't know how to begin a conversation with people she had just been dancing with. "It would never do to say 'How d'ye do?' *now*," she said to herself: "we seem to have got beyond that, somehow!"

"I hope you're not much tired?" she said at last.

"Nohow. And thank you very much for asking," said Tweedledum.

"So *much* obliged!" added Tweedledee. "You like poetry?"

"Ye-es, pretty well—*some* poetry," Alice said doubtfully. "Would you tell me which road leads out of the wood?"

"What shall I repeat to her?" said Tweedledee, looking round at Tweedledum with great solemn eyes, and not noticing Alice's question.

"'*The Walrus and the Carpenter*' is the longest," Tweedledum replied, giving his brother an affectionate hug.

Tweedledee began instantly:

"The sun was shining—"

Here Alice ventured to interrupt him. "If it's *very* long," she said, as politely as she could, "would you please tell me first which road—"

Tweedledee smiled gently, and began again:

"The sun was shining on the sea,
Shining with all his might:
He did his very best to make
The billows smooth and bright—
And this was odd, because it was
The middle of the night.

The moon was shining sulkily,
Because she thought the sun
Had got no business to be there
After the day was done—
'It's very rude of him,' she said,
'To come and spoil the fun!'

The sea was wet as wet could be,
The sands were dry as dry.
You could not see a cloud, because
No cloud was in the sky:
No birds were flying overhead—
There were no birds to fly.

The Walrus and the Carpenter
Were walking close at hand:
They wept like anything to see
Such quantities of sand:
'If this were only cleared away,'
They said, 'it would be grand!'

'If seven maids with seven mops
Swept it for half a year,
Do you suppose,' the Walrus said,
'That they could get it clear?'
'I doubt it,' said the Carpenter,
And shed a bitter tear.

'O Oysters, come and walk with us!'
The Walrus did beseech.
'A pleasant walk, a pleasant talk,
Along the briny beach:
We cannot do with more than four,
To give a hand to each.'

The eldest Oyster looked at him,
But never a word he said:
The eldest Oyster winked his eye,
And shook his heavy head—
Meaning to say he did not choose
To leave the oyster-bed.

But four young Oysters hurried up,
All eager for the treat:
Their coats were brushed, their faces washed,
Their shoes were clean and neat—
And this was odd, because, you know,
They hadn't any feet.

Four other Oysters followed them,
And yet another four;
And thick and fast they came at last,
And more, and more, and more—
All hopping through the frothy waves,
And scrambling to the shore.

The Walrus and the Carpenter
Walked on a mile or so,
And then they rested on a rock
Conveniently low:
And all the little Oysters stood
And waited in a row.

'The time has come,' the Walrus said,
'To talk of many things:
Of shoes—and ships—and sealing wax—
Of cabbages—and kings—
And why the sea is boiling hot—
And whether pigs have wings.'

'But wait a bit,' the Oysters cried,
'Before we have our chat;
For some of us are out of breath,
And all of us are fat!'
'No hurry!' said the Carpenter.
They thanked him much for that.

'A loaf of bread,' the Walrus said,
'Is what we chiefly need:
Pepper and vinegar besides
Are very good indeed—
Now, if you're ready, Oysters dear,
We can begin to feed.'

"The Walrus and the Carpenter." John Tenniel depicts the devious walrus and carpenter devouring the oysters they had just befriended.

'But not on us!' the Oysters cried,
Turning a little blue.
'After such kindness, that would be
A dismal thing to do!'
'The night is fine,' the Walrus said.
'Do you admire the view?

'It was so kind of you to come!
And you are very nice!'
The Carpenter said nothing but
'Cut us another slice.
I wish you were not quite so deaf—
I've had to ask you twice!'

'It seems a shame,' the Walrus said,
'To play them such a trick,
After we've brought them out so far,
And made them trot so quick!'
The Carpenter said nothing but
'The butter's spread too thick!'

'I weep for you,' the Walrus said:
'I deeply sympathize.'
With sobs and tears he sorted out
Those of the largest size,
Holding his pocket-handkerchief
Before his streaming eyes.

'O Oysters,' said the Carpenter,
'You've had a pleasant run!
Shall we be trotting home again?'

But answer came there none—
And this was scarcely odd, because
They'd eaten every one."

"I like the Walrus best," said Alice: "because he was a *little* sorry for the poor oysters."

"He ate more than the Carpenter, though," said Tweedledee. "You see he held his handkerchief in front, so that the Carpenter couldn't count how many he took: contrariwise."

"That was mean!" Alice said indignantly. "Then I like the Carpenter best—if he didn't eat so many as the Walrus."

"But he ate as many as he could get," said Tweedledum.

This was a puzzler. After a pause, Alice began, "Well! They were *both* very unpleasant characters—" Here she checked herself in some alarm, at hearing something that sounded to her like the puffing of a large steam-engine in the wood near them, though she feared it was more likely to be a wild beast. "Are there any lions or tigers about here?" she asked timidly.

"It's only the Red King snoring," said Tweedledee.

"Come and look at him!" the brothers cried, and they each took one of Alice's hands, and led her up to where the King was sleeping.

"Isn't he a *lovely* sight?" said Tweedledum.

Alice couldn't say honestly that he was. He had a tall red night-cap on, with a tassel, and he was lying crumpled up into a sort of untidy heap, and snoring loud—"fit to snore his head off!" as Tweedledum remarked.

"I'm afraid he'll catch cold with lying on the damp grass," said Alice, who was a very thoughtful little girl.

"He's dreaming now," said Tweedledee: "and what do you think he's dreaming about?"

Alice said "Nobody can guess that."

"Why, about *you!*" Tweedledee exclaimed, clapping his hands triumphantly. "And if he left off dreaming about you, where do you suppose you'd be?"

"Where I am now, of course," said Alice.

"Not you!" Tweedledee retorted contemptuously. "You'd be nowhere. Why, you're only a sort of thing in his dream!"

"'If that there King was to wake," added Tweedledum, "you'd go out—bang!—just like a candle!"

"I shouldn't!" Alice exclaimed indignantly. "Besides, if *I'm* only a sort of thing in his dream, what are *you,* I should like to know?"

"Ditto," said Tweedledum.

"Ditto, ditto!" cried Tweedledee.

He shouted this so loud that Alice couldn't help saying "Hush! You'll be waking him, I'm afraid, if you make so much noise."

"Well, it's no use *your* talking about waking him," said Tweedledum, "when you're only one of the things in his dream. You know very well you're not real."

"I *am* real!" said Alice, and began to cry.

"You won't make yourself a bit realler by crying," Tweedledee remarked: "there's nothing to cry about."

"If I wasn't real," Alice said—half laughing through her tears, it all seemed so ridiculous—"I shouldn't be able to cry."

"I hope you don't suppose those are *real* tears?" Tweedledum interrupted in a tone of great contempt.

"I know they're talking nonsense," Alice thought to herself: "and it's foolish to cry about it." So she brushed away her tears, and went on, as cheerfully as she could, "At any rate I'd better be getting out of the wood, for really it's coming on very dark. Do you think it's going to rain?"

Tweedledum spread a large umbrella over himself and his brother, and looked up into it. "No, I don't think it is," he said: "at least—not under *here.* Nohow."

"But it may rain *outside?*"

"It may—if it chooses," said Tweedledee: "we've no objection. Contrariwise."

"Selfish things!" thought Alice, and she was just going to say "Good-night" and leave them, when Tweedledum sprang out from under the umbrella, and seized her by the wrist.

"Do you see *that?*" he said, in a voice choking with passion, and his eyes grew large and yellow all in a moment, as he pointed with a trembling finger at a small white thing lying under the tree.

"It's only a rattle," Alice said, after a careful examination of the little white thing. "Not a rattle-*snake,* you know," she added hastily, thinking that he was frightened: "only an old rattle—quite old and broken."

"I knew it was!" cried Tweedledum, beginning to stamp about wildly and tear his hair. "It's spoilt, of course!" Here he looked at Tweedledee, who immediately sat down on the ground, and tried to hide himself under the umbrella.

Alice laid her hand upon his arm, and said, in a soothing tone, "You needn't be so angry about an old rattle."

"But it *isn't* old!" Tweedledum cried, in a greater fury than ever. "It's *new,* I tell you—I bought it yesterday—my nice new RATTLE!" and his voice rose to a perfect scream.

All this time Tweedledee was trying his best to fold up the umbrella, with himself in it: which was such an extraordinary thing to do, that it quite took off Alice's attention from the angry brother. But he couldn't quite succeed, and it ended in his rolling over, bundled up in the umbrella, with only his head out: and there he lay, opening and shutting his mouth and his large eyes—"looking more like a fish than anything else," Alice thought.

"Of course you agree to have a battle?" Tweedledum said in a calmer tone.

"I suppose so," the other sulkily replied, as he crawled out of the umbrella: "only *she* must help us to dress up, you know."

So the two brothers went off hand-in-hand into the wood, and returned in a minute with their arms full of things—such as bolsters, blankets, hearth-rugs, table-cloths, dish-covers, and coal-scuttles. "I hope you're a good hand at pinning and tying strings?" Tweedledum remarked. "Every one of these things has got to go on, somehow or other."

John Tenniel's detailed drawing shows the absurdity of the mock battle as Tweedledum and Tweedledee prepare to fight.

Alice said afterwards she had never seen such a fuss made about anything in all her life—the way those two bustled about—and the quantity of things they put on—and the trouble they gave her in tying strings and fastening buttons—"Really they'll be more like bundles of old clothes than anything else, by the time they're ready!" she said to herself, as she arranged a bolster round the neck of Tweedledee, "to keep his head from being cut off," as he said.

"You know," he added very gravely, "it's one of the most serious things that can possibly happen to one in a battle—to get one's head cut off."

Alice laughed loud: but she managed to turn it into a cough, for fear of hurting his feelings.

"Do I look very pale?" said Tweedledum, coming up to have his helmet tied on. (He *called* it a helmet, though it certainly looked much more like a saucepan.)

"Well—yes—a *little,*" Alice replied gently.

"I'm very brave, generally," he went on in a low voice: "only to-day I happen to have a headache."

"And *I've* got a toothache!" said Tweedledee, who had overheard the remark. "I'm far worse than you!"

"Then you'd better not fight to-day," said Alice, thinking it a good opportunity to make peace.

"We *must* have a bit of a fight, but I don't care about going on long," said Tweedledum. "What's the time now?"

Tweedledee looked at his watch, and said "Half-past four."

"Let's fight till six, and then have dinner," said Tweedledum.

"Very well," the other said, rather sadly: "and *she* can watch us—only you'd better not come *very* close," he added: "I generally hit every thing I can see—when I get really excited."

"And *I* hit every thing within reach," cried Tweedledum, "whether I can see it or not!"

Alice laughed. "You must hit the *trees* pretty often, I should think," she said.

Tweedledum looked round him with a satisfied smile. "I don't suppose," he said, "there'll be a tree left standing, for ever so far round, by the time we've finished!"

"And all about a rattle!" said Alice, still hoping to make them a *little* ashamed of fighting for such a trifle.

"I shouldn't have minded it so much," said Tweedledum, "if it hadn't been a new one."

"I wish the monstrous crow would come!" thought Alice.

"There's only one sword, you know," Tweedledum said to his brother: "but *you* can have the umbrella—it's quite as sharp. Only we must begin quick. It's getting as dark as it can."

"And darker," said Tweedledee.

It was getting dark so suddenly that Alice thought there must be a thunderstorm coming on. "What a thick black cloud that is!" she said. "And how fast it comes! Why, I do believe it's got wings!"

"It's the crow!" Tweedledum cried out in a shrill voice of alarm; and the two brothers took to their heels and were out of sight in a moment.

Alice ran a little way into the wood, and stopped under a large tree. "It can never get at me *here*," she thought: "it's far too large to squeeze itself in among the trees. But I wish it wouldn't flap its wings so—it makes quite a hurricane in the wood—here's somebody's shawl being blown away!"

Louisa May Alcott (1832–88)

Louisa May Alcott, the daughter of American Transcendentalist philosopher Bronson Alcott and the neighbor in Concord, Massachusetts, of Ralph Waldo Emerson, Nathaniel Hawthorne, and Henry David Thoreau, created a classic work of realistic fiction for girls in *Little Women* (1868–69). Prior to *Little Women,* Alcott experimented with a variety of genres, including the sensational fiction that she published under a pseudonym, and edited the children's periodical *Merry's Museum.* She first won recognition for *Hospital Sketches* (1862), a narrative based on her Civil War nursing experience. Like *Hospital Sketches, Little Women* is autobiographical, but although Alcott later claimed that "we really lived most of it," she took considerable liberty with her material, softening what had actually been a life of emotional conflict and economic hardship. After the success of *Little Women,* Alcott went on to write two sequels, *Little Men* (1871) and *Jo's Boys* (1886), as well as many other novels and collections of stories for young people. Generations of readers have identified with Jo March, the second sister in a family of four girls, who rebels against the proprieties of female life in New England in the 1860s and devotes herself passionately to her writing. During the past twenty-five years, feminist critics have enhanced Alcott's reputation as a writer for both adults and children by examining closely such scenes as that between Marmee and Jo in Chapter 8 of *Little Women.* (Several other chapters are reprinted in Part 5.)

From *Little Women*

CHAPTER 8. JO MEETS APOLLYON

"Girls, where are you going?" asked Amy, coming into their room one Saturday afternoon, and finding them getting ready to go out, with an air of secrecy which excited her curiosity.

"Never mind; little girls shouldn't ask questions," returned Jo, sharply.

Now if there *is* anything mortifying to our feelings, when we are young, it is to be told that; and to be bidden to "run away, dear," is still more trying to us. Amy bridled up at this insult, and determined to find out the secret, if she teased for an hour. Turning to Meg, who never refused her anything very long, she said, coaxingly, "Do tell me! I should think you might let me go, too; for Beth is fussing over her dolls, and I haven't got anything to do, and am *so* lonely."

"I can't, dear, because you aren't invited," began Meg; but Jo broke in impatiently, "Now, Meg, be quiet, or you will spoil it all. You can't go, Amy; so don't be a baby, and whine about it."

"You are going somewhere with Laurie, I know you are; you were whispering and laughing together, on the sofa, last night, and you stopped when I came in. Aren't you going with him?"

"Yes, we are; now do be still, and stop bothering."

Amy held her tongue, but used her eyes, and saw Meg slip a fan into her pocket.

"I know! I know! you're going to the theatre to see the 'Seven Castles!'" she cried; adding, resolutely, "and I *shall* go, for mother said I might see it; and I've got my rag-money, and it was mean not to tell me in time."

"Just listen to me a minute, and be a good child," said Meg, soothingly. "Mother doesn't wish you to go this week, because your eyes are not well enough yet to bear the light of this fairy piece. Next week you can go with Beth and Hannah, and have a nice time."

"I don't like that half as well as going with you and Laurie. Please let me; I've been sick with this cold so long, and shut up, I'm dying for some fun. Do, Meg! I'll be ever so good," pleaded Amy, looking as pathetic as she could.

"Suppose we take her. I don't believe mother would mind, if we bundle her up well," began Meg.

"If *she* goes *I* shan't; and if I don't, Laurie won't like it; and it will be very rude, after he invited only us, to go and drag in Amy. I should think she'd hate to poke herself where she isn't wanted," said Jo, crossly, for she disliked the trouble of overseeing a fidgety child, when she wanted to enjoy herself.

Her tone and manner angered Amy, who began to put her boots on, saying, in her most aggravating way, "I *shall* go; Meg says I may; and if I pay for myself, Laurie hasn't anything to do with it."

"You can't sit with us, for our seats are reserved, and you mustn't sit alone; so Laurie will give you his place, and that will spoil our pleasure; or he'll get another seat for you, and that isn't proper, when you weren't asked. You shan't stir a step; so you may just stay where you are," scolded Jo, crosser than ever, having just pricked her finger in her hurry.

Sitting on the floor, with one boot on, Amy began to cry, and Meg to reason with her, when Laurie called from below, and the two girls hurried down, leaving their sister wailing; for now and then she forgot her grown-up ways, and acted like a spoilt child. Just as the party was setting out, Amy called over the banisters, in a threatening tone, "You'll be sorry for this, Jo March! see if you ain't."

"Fiddlesticks!" returned Jo, slamming the door.

They had a charming time, for "The Seven Castles of the Diamond Lake" was as brilliant and wonderful as heart could wish. But, in spite of the comical red imps, sparkling elves, and gorgeous princes and princesses, Jo's pleasure had a drop of bitterness in it; the fairy queen's yellow curls reminded her of Amy; and between the acts she amused herself with wondering what her sister would do to make her "sorry for it." She and Amy had had many lively skirmishes in the course of their lives, for both had quick tempers, and were apt to be violent when fairly roused. Amy teased Jo, and Jo irritated Amy, and semi-occasional explosions occurred, of which both were much ashamed afterward. Although the oldest, Jo had the least self-control, and had hard times trying to curb the fiery spirit which was continually getting her into trouble; her anger never lasted long, and, having humbly confessed her fault, she sincerely repented, and tried to do better. Her sisters used to say, that they rather liked to get Jo into a fury, because she was such an angel afterward. Poor Jo tried desperately to be good, but her bosom enemy was always ready to flame up and defeat her; and it took years of patient effort to subdue it.

When they got home, they found Amy reading in the parlor. She assumed an injured air as they came in; never lifted her eyes from her book, or asked a single question. Perhaps curiosity might have conquered resentment, if Beth had not been there to inquire, and receive a glowing description of the play. On going up to put away her best hat, Jo's first look was toward the bureau; for, in their last quarrel, Amy had soothed her feelings by turning Jo's top drawer upside down, on the floor. Everything was in its place, however; and after a hasty glance into her various closets, bags and boxes, Jo decided that Amy had forgiven and forgotten her wrongs.

There Jo was mistaken; for next day she made a discovery which produced a tempest. Meg, Beth and Amy were sitting together, late in the afternoon, when

Jo burst into the room, looking excited, and demand-ing, breathlessly, "Has any one taken my story?"

Meg and Beth said "No," at once, and looked sur-prised; Amy poked the fire, and said nothing. Jo saw her color rise, and was down upon her in a minute.

"Amy, you've got it!"

"No, I haven't."

"You know where it is, then!"

"No, I don't."

"That's a fib!" cried Jo, taking her by the shoulders, and looking fierce enough to frighten a much braver child than Amy.

"It isn't. I haven't got it, don't know where it is now, and don't care."

"You know something about it, and you'd better tell at once, or I'll make you," and Jo gave her a slight shake.

"Scold as much as you like, you'll never get your silly old story again," cried Amy, getting excited in her turn.

"Why not?"

"I burnt it up."

"What! my little book I was so fond of, and worked over, and meant to finish before father got home? Have you really burnt it?" said Jo, turning very pale, while her eyes kindled and her hands clutched Amy nervously.

"Yes, I did! I told you I'd make you pay for being so cross yesterday, and I have, so—"

Amy got no farther, for Jo's hot temper mastered her, and she shook Amy till her teeth chattered in her head; crying, in a passion of grief and anger,—

"You wicked, wicked girl! I never can write it again, and I'll never forgive you as long as I live."

Meg flew to rescue Amy, and Beth to pacify Jo, but Jo was quite beside herself; and, with a parting box on her sister's ear, she rushed out of the room up to the old sofa in the garret, and finished her fight alone.

The storm cleared up below, for Mrs. March came home, and, having heard the story, soon brought Amy to a sense of the wrong she had done her sister. Jo's book was the pride of her heart, and was regarded by her family as a literary sprout of great promise. It was only half a dozen little fairy tales, but Jo had worked over them patiently, putting her whole heart into her work, hoping to make something good enough to print. She had just copied them with great care, and had destroyed the old manuscript, so that Amy's bon-

fire had consumed the loving work of several years. It seemed a small loss to others, but to Jo it was a dreadful calamity, and she felt that it never could be made up to her. Beth mourned as for a departed kitten, and Meg refused to defend her pet; Mrs. March looked grave and grieved, and Amy felt that no one would love her till she had asked pardon for the act which she now regretted more than any of them.

When the tea-bell rung, Jo appeared, looking so grim and unapproachable, that it took all Amy's courage to say, meekly,—

"Please forgive me, Jo; I'm very, very sorry."

"I never shall forgive you," was Jo's stern answer; and, from that moment, she ignored Amy entirely.

No one spoke of the great trouble,—not even Mrs. March,—for all had learned by experience that when Jo was in that mood words were wasted; and the wis-est course was to wait till some little accident, or her own generous nature, softened Jo's resentment, and healed the breach. It was not a happy evening; for, though they sewed as usual, while their mother read aloud from Bremer, Scott, or Edgeworth, something was wanting, and the sweet home-peace was dis-turbed. They felt this most when singing-time came; for Beth could only play, Jo stood dumb as a stone, and Amy broke down, so Meg and mother sang alone. But in spite of their efforts to be as cheery as larks, the flute-like voices did not seem to chord as well as usual, and all felt out of tune.

As Jo received her good-night kiss, Mrs. March whispered, gently,—

"My dear, don't let the sun go down upon your anger; forgive each other, help each other, and begin again to-morrow."

Jo wanted to lay her head down on that motherly bosom, and cry her grief and anger all away, but tears were an unmanly weakness, and she felt so deeply in-jured that she really *couldn't* quite forgive yet. So she winked hard, shook her head, and said, gruffly, be-cause Amy was listening,—

"It was an abominable thing, and she don't deserve to be forgiven."

With that she marched off to bed, and there was no merry or confidential gossip that night.

Amy was much offended that her overtures of peace had been repulsed, and began to wish she had not humbled herself, to feel more injured than ever, and to plume herself on her superior virtue in a way which was particularly exasperating. Jo still looked like a thunder-cloud, and nothing went well all day. It was bitter cold in the morning; she dropped her precious turn-over in the gutter, Aunt March had an attack of fidgets, Meg was pensive, Beth *would* look grieved and wistful when she got home, and Amy kept making remarks about people who were always talking about being good, and yet wouldn't try, when other people set them a virtuous example.

"Everybody is so hateful, I'll ask Laurie to go skating. He is always kind and jolly, and will put me to rights, I know," said Jo to herself, and off she went.

Amy heard the clash of skates, and looked out with an impatient exclamation,—

"There! she promised I should go next time, for this is the last ice we shall have. But it's no use to ask such a cross patch to take me."

"Don't say that; you *were* very naughty, and it *is* hard to forgive the loss of her precious little book; but I think she might do it now, and I guess she will, if you try her at the right minute," said Meg. "Go after them; don't say anything till Jo has got good-natured with Laurie, then take a quiet minute, and just kiss her, or do some kind thing, and I'm sure she'll be friends again, with all her heart."

"I'll try," said Amy, for the advice suited her; and, after a flurry to get ready, she ran after the friends, who were just disappearing over the hill.

It was not far to the river, but both were ready before Amy reached them. Jo saw her coming, and turned her back; Laurie did not see, for he was carefully skating along the shore, sounding the ice, for a warm spell had preceded the cold snap.

"I'll go on to the first bend, and see if it's all right, before we begin to race," Amy heard him say, as he shot away, looking like a young Russian, in his fur-trimmed coat and cap.

Jo heard Amy panting after her run, stamping her feet, and blowing her fingers, as she tried to put her skates on; but Jo never turned, and went slowly zig-zagging down the river, taking a bitter, unhappy sort of satisfaction in her sister's troubles. She had cherished her anger till it grew strong, and took possession of her, as evil thoughts and feelings always do, unless cast out at once. As Laurie turned the bend, he shouted back,—

"Keep near the shore; it isn't safe in the middle."

Jo heard, but Amy was just struggling to her feet, and did not catch a word. Jo glanced over her shoulder, and the little demon she was harboring said in her ear,—

"No matter whether she heard or not, let her take care of herself."

Laurie had vanished round the bend; Jo was just at the turn, and Amy, far behind, striking out toward the smoother ice in the middle of the river. For a minute Jo stood still, with a strange feeling at her heart; then she resolved to go on, but something held and turned her round, just in time to see Amy throw up her hands and go down, with a sudden crash of rotten ice, the splash of water, and a cry that made Jo's heart stand still with fear. She tried to call Laurie, but her voice was gone; she tried to rush forward, but her feet seemed to have no strength in them; and, for a second, she could only stand motionless, staring, with a terror-stricken face, at the little blue hood above the black water. Something rushed swiftly by her, and Laurie's voice cried out,—

"Bring a rail; quick, quick!"

How she did it, she never knew; but for the next few minutes she worked as if possessed, blindly obeying Laurie, who was quite self-possessed; and, lying flat, held Amy up by his arm and hockey, till Jo dragged a rail from the fence, and together they got the child out, more frightened than hurt.

"Now then, we must walk her home as fast as we can; pile our things on her, while I get off these confounded skates," cried Laurie, wrapping his coat round Amy, and tugging away at the straps, which never seemed so intricate before.

Shivering, dripping, and crying, they got Amy home; and, after an exciting time of it, she fell asleep, rolled in blankets, before a hot fire. During the bustle Jo had scarcely spoken; but flown about, looking pale and wild, with her things half off, her dress torn, and her hands cut and bruised by ice and rails, and refractory buckles. When Amy was comfortably asleep, the house quiet, and Mrs. March sitting by the bed, she called Jo to her, and began to bind up the hurt hands.

"Are you sure she is safe?" whispered Jo, looking remorsefully at the golden head, which might have been swept away from her sight forever, under the treacherous ice.

"Quite safe, dear; she is not hurt, and won't even take cold, I think, you were so sensible in covering her and getting her home quickly," replied her mother, cheerfully.

"Laurie did it all; I only let her go. Mother, if she *should* die, it would be my fault"; and Jo dropped down beside the bed, in a passion of penitent tears, telling all that had happened, bitterly condemning her hardness of heart, and sobbing out her gratitude for being spared the heavy punishment which might have come upon her.

"It's my dreadful temper! I try to cure it; I think I have, and then it breaks out worse than ever. Oh, mother! what shall I do! what shall I do?" cried poor Jo, in despair.

"Watch and pray, dear; never get tired of trying; and never think it is impossible to conquer your fault," said Mrs. March, drawing the blowzy head to her shoulder, and kissing the wet cheek so tenderly, that Jo cried harder than ever.

"You don't know, and you can't guess how bad it is! It seems as if I could do anything when I'm in a passion; I get so savage, I could hurt any one, and enjoy it. I'm afraid I *shall* do something dreadful some day, and spoil my life, and make everybody hate me. Oh, mother! help me, do help me!"

"I will, my child; I will. Don't cry so bitterly, but remember this day, and resolve, with all your soul, that you will never know another like it. Jo, dear, we all have our temptations, some far greater than yours, and it often takes us all our lives to conquer them. You think your temper is the worst in the world; but mine used to be just like it."

"Yours, mother? Why, you are never angry!" and, for the moment, Jo forgot remorse in surprise.

"I've been trying to cure it for forty years, and have only succeeded in controlling it. I am angry nearly every day of my life, Jo; but I have learned not to show it; and I still hope to learn not to feel it, though it may take me another forty years to do so."

The patience and the humility of the face she loved so well, was a better lesson to Jo than the wisest lecture, the sharpest reproof. She felt comforted at once by the sympathy and confidence given her; the knowledge that her mother had a fault like hers, and tried to mend it, made her own easier to bear, and strengthened her resolution to cure it; though forty years seemed rather a long time to watch and pray, to a girl of fifteen.

"Mother, are you angry when you fold your lips tight together, and go out of the room sometimes, when Aunt March scolds, or people worry you?" asked Jo, feeling nearer and dearer to her mother than ever before.

"Yes, I've learned to check the hasty words that rise to my lips; and when I feel that they mean to break out against my will, I just go away a minute, and give myself a little shake, for being so weak and wicked," answered Mrs. March, with a sigh and a smile, as she smoothed and fastened up Jo's dishevelled hair.

"How did you learn to keep still? That is what troubles me—for the sharp words fly out before I know what I'm about; and the more I say the worse I get, till it's a pleasure to hurt people's feelings, and say dreadful things. Tell me how you do it, Marmee dear."

"My good mother used to help me—"

"As you do us—" interrupted Jo, with a grateful kiss.

"But I lost her when I was a little older than you are, and for years had to struggle on alone, for I was too proud to confess my weakness to any one else. I had a hard time, Jo, and shed a good many bitter tears over my failures; for, in spite of my efforts, I never seemed to get on. Then your father came, and I was so happy that I found it easy to be good. But by and by, when I had four little daughters round me, and we were poor, then the old trouble began again; for I am not patient by nature, and it tried me very much to see my children wanting anything."

"Poor mother! what helped you then?"

"Your father, Jo. He never loses patience,—never doubts or complains,—but always hopes, and works, and waits so cheerfully, that one is ashamed to do otherwise before him. He helped and comforted me, and showed me that I must try to practise all the virtues I would have my little girls possess, for I was their example. It was easier to try for your sakes than for my own; a startled or surprised look from one of you, when I spoke, sharply rebuked me more than any words could have done; and the love, respect, and confidence of my children was the sweetest reward I could receive for my efforts to be the woman I would have them copy."

"Oh, mother! if I'm ever half as good as you, I shall be satisfied," cried Jo, much touched.

"I hope you will be a great deal better, dear; but you must keep watch over your 'bosom enemy,' as father calls it, or it may sadden, if not spoil your life. You have had a warning; remember it, and try with heart and soul to master this quick temper, before it brings you greater sorrow and regret than you have known to-day."

"I will try, mother: I truly will. But you must help me, remind me, and keep me from flying out. I used to see father sometimes put his finger on his lips, and look at you with a very kind, but sober face; and you always folded your lips tight, or went away; was he reminding you then?" asked Jo, softly.

"Yes; I asked him to help me so, and he never forgot it, but saved me from many a sharp word by that little gesture and kind look."

Jo saw that her mother's eyes filled, and her lips trembled, as she spoke; and, fearing that she had said too much, she whispered anxiously, "Was it wrong to watch you, and to speak of it? I didn't mean to be rude, but it's so comfortable to say all I think to you, and feel so safe and happy here."

"My Jo, you may say anything to your mother, for it is my greatest happiness and pride to feel that my girls confide in me, and know how much I love them."

"I thought I'd grieved you."

"No, dear; but speaking of father reminded me how much I miss him, how much I owe him, and how faithfully I should watch and work to keep his little daughters safe and good for him."

"Yet you told him to go, mother, and didn't cry when he went, and never complain now, or seem as if you needed any help," said Jo, wondering.

"I gave my best to the country I love, and kept my tears till he was gone. Why should I complain, when we both have merely done our duty, and will surely be the happier for it in the end? If I don't seem to need help, it is because I have a better friend, even than father, to comfort and sustain me. My child, the troubles and temptations of your life are beginning, and may be many; but you can overcome and outlive them all, if you learn to feel the strength and tenderness of your Heavenly Father as you do that of your earthly one. The more you love and trust Him, the nearer you will feel to Him, and the less you will depend on human power and wisdom. His love and care never tire or change, can never be taken from you, but may become the source of life-long peace, happiness, and strength. Believe this heartily, and go to God with all your little cares, and hopes, and sins, and sorrows, as freely and confidingly as you come to your mother."

Jo's only answer was to hold her mother close, and, in the silence which followed, the sincerest prayer she had ever prayed left her heart, without words; for in that sad, yet happy hour, she had learned not only the bitterness of remorse and despair, but the sweetness of self-denial and self-control; and, led by her mother's hand, she had drawn nearer to the Friend who welcomes every child with a love stronger than that of any father, tenderer than that of any mother.

Amy stirred, and sighed in her sleep; and, as if eager to begin at once to mend her fault, Jo looked up with an expression on her face which it had never worn before.

"I let the sun go down on my anger; I wouldn't forgive her, and to-day, if it hadn't been for Laurie, it might have been too late! How could I be so wicked?" said Jo, half aloud, as she leaned over her sister, softly stroking the wet hair scattered on the pillow.

As if she heard, Amy opened her eyes, and held out her arms, with a smile that went straight to Jo's heart. Neither said a word, but they hugged one another close, in spite of the blankets, and everything was forgiven and forgotten in one hearty kiss.

Mark Twain (1835–1910)

Mark Twain was the pen name of Samuel Langhorne Clemens, a self-educated printer and river pilot who wrote his way into American literary history and popular culture with his stories of humor and frontier adventure. He despised the conventional children's stories of his day and satirized them vigorously in his "Story of the Bad Little Boy Who Didn't Come to Grief"

(1865) and "Story of the Good Little Boy Who Did Not Prosper" (1870). Although at first he was not consciously writing for a child audience, he was persuaded by his friend William Dean Howells, the distinguished editor and novelist, that in *The Adventures of Tom Sawyer* (1876), he had written a book for boys, and he is now considered to have authored two of the greatest American novels for and about children, the other being *Adventures of Huckleberry Finn* (1884). Twain's versions of American boyhood, which developed from his own experiences growing up in Hannibal, Missouri, have shaped our consciousness of what it was like to be young in nineteenth-century America. Both novels demonstrate, however, that many nineteenth-century authors did not differentiate as greatly between their child and adult reading audiences. Within the novels, relations between children and adults as modern authors do alternate between antagonism and affection, especially in Tom's relationship with his guardian, Aunt Polly. In this selection from *Tom Sawyer*, Twain satirizes the way in which adults readily assume that they have the right to make children suffer—for their own good, of course—in ways they might think twice about imposing on animals. (See other excerpts from *Tom Sawyer* in Part 5 and from *Huckleberry Finn* in Part 8.)

From *The Adventures of Tom Sawyer*

CHAPTER 12. TOM SHOWS HIS GENEROSITY

One of the reasons why Tom's mind had drifted away from its secret troubles was, that it had found a new and weighty matter to interest itself about. Becky Thatcher had stopped coming to school. Tom had struggled with his pride a few days, and tried to "whistle her down the wind," but failed. He began to find himself hanging around her father's house, nights, and feeling very miserable. She was ill. What if she should die! There was distraction in the thought. He no longer took an interest in war, nor even in piracy. The charm of life was gone; there was nothing but dreariness left. He put his hoop away, and his bat; there was no joy in them any more. His aunt was concerned. She began to try all manner of remedies on him. She was one of those people who are infatuated with patent medicines and all new-fangled methods of producing health or mending it. She was an inveterate experimenter in these things. When something fresh in this line came out she was in a fever, right away, to try it; not on herself, for she was never ailing, but on anybody else that came handy. She was a subscriber for all the "Health" periodicals and phrenological frauds; and the solemn ignorance they were inflated with was breath to her

nostrils. All the "rot" they contained about ventilation, and how to go to bed, and how to get up, and what to eat, and what to drink, and how much exercise to take, and what frame of mind to keep one's self in, and what sort of clothing to wear, was all gospel to her, and she never observed that her health-journals of the current month customarily upset everything they had recommended the month before. She was as simple-hearted and honest as the day was long, and so she was an easy victim. She gathered together her quack periodicals and her quack medicines, and thus armed with death, went about on her pale horse, metaphorically speaking, with "hell following after." But she never suspected that she was not an angel of healing and the balm of Gilead in disguise, to the suffering neighbors.

The water treatment was new, now, and Tom's low condition was a windfall to her. She had him out at daylight every morning, stood him up in the woodshed and drowned him with a deluge of cold water; then she scrubbed him down with a towel like a file, and so brought him to; then she rolled him up in a wet sheet and put him away under blankets till she sweated his soul clean and "the yellow stains of it came through his pores"—as Tom said.

Yet notwithstanding all this, the boy grew more and more melancholy and pale and dejected. She added hot baths, sitz baths, shower baths and plunges. The boy remained as dismal as a hearse. She began to assist the water with a slim oatmeal diet and blister plasters. She calculated his capacity as she would a jug's, and filled him up every day with quack cure-alls.

Tom had become indifferent to persecution, by this time. This phase filled the old lady's heart with consternation. This indifference must be broken up at any cost. Now she heard of Pain-Killer for the first time. She ordered a lot at once. She tasted it and was filled with gratitude. It was simply fire in a liquid form. She dropped the water treatment and everything else, and pinned her faith to Pain-Killer. She gave Tom a teaspoonful and watched with the deepest anxiety for the result. Her troubles were instantly at rest, her soul at peace again; for the "indifference" was broken up. The boy could not have shown a wilder, heartier interest, if she had built a fire under him.

Tom felt that it was time to wake up; this sort of life might be romantic enough, in his blighted condition, but it was getting to have too little sentiment and too much distracting variety about it. So he thought over various plans for relief, and finally hit upon that of professing to be fond of Pain-Killer. He asked for it so often that he became a nuisance, and his aunt ended by telling him to help himself and quit bothering her. If it had been Sid, she would have had no misgivings to alloy her delight; but since it was Tom, she watched the bottle clandestinely. She found that the medicine did really diminish, but it did not occur to her that the boy was mending the health of a crack in the sitting-room floor with it.

One day Tom was in the act of dosing the crack when his aunt's yellow cat came along, purring, eyeing the tea-spoon avariciously, and begging for a taste. Tom said:

"Don't ask for it unless you want it, Peter."

But Peter signified that he did want it.

"You better make sure."

Peter was sure.

"Now you've asked for it, and I'll give it to you, because there ain't anything mean about *me;* but if you find you don't like it, you mustn't blame anybody but your own self."

Peter was agreeable. So Tom pried his mouth open and poured down the Pain-Killer. Peter sprang a couple of yards into the air, and then delivered a war-whoop and set off round and round the room, banging against furniture, upsetting flower pots and making general havoc. Next he rose on his hind feet and pranced around, in a frenzy of enjoyment, with his head over his shoulder and his voice proclaiming his unappeasable happiness. Then he went tearing around the house again spreading chaos and destruction in his path. Aunt Polly entered in time to see him throw a few double summersets, deliver a final mighty hurrah, and sail through the open window, carrying the rest of the flower-pots with him. The old lady stood petrified with astonishment, peering over her glasses; Tom lay on the floor expiring with laughter.

"Tom, what on earth ails that cat?"

"*I* don't know, aunt," gasped the boy.

"Why I never see anything like it. What *did* make him act so?"

"Deed I don't know aunt Polly; cats always act so when they're having a good time."

"They do, do they?" There was something in the tone that made Tom apprehensive.

"Yes'm. That is, I believe they do."

"You *do?*"

"Yes'm."

The old lady was bending down, Tom watching, with interest emphasized by anxiety. Too late he divined her "drift." The handle of the tell-tale tea-spoon was visible under the bed-valance. Aunt Polly took it, held it up. Tom winced, and dropped his eyes. Aunt Polly raised him by the usual handle—his ear—and cracked his head soundly with her thimble.

"Now, sir, what did you want to treat that poor dumb beast so, for?"

"I done it out of pity for him—because he hadn't any aunt."

"Hadn't any aunt!—you numscull. What has that got to do with it?"

"Heaps. Because if he'd a had one she'd a burnt him out herself! She'd a roasted his bowels out of him 'thout any more feeling than if he was a human!"

Aunt Polly felt a sudden pang of remorse. This was putting the thing in a new light; what was cruelty to a cat *might* be cruelty to a boy, too. She began to soften; she felt sorry. Her eyes watered a little, and she put her hand on Tom's head and said gently:

"I was meaning for the best, Tom. And Tom, it *did* do you good."

Tom looked up in her face with just a perceptible twinkle peeping through his gravity:

"I know you was meaning for the best, aunty, and so was I with Peter. It done *him* good, too. I never seen him get around so since—"

"O, go 'long with you, Tom, before you aggravate me again. And you try and see if you can't be a good boy, for once, and you needn't take any more medicine."

Tom reached school ahead of time. It was noticed that this strange thing had been occurring every day latterly. And now, as usual of late, he hung about the gate of the school yard instead of playing with his comrades. He was sick, he said; and he looked it. He tried to seem to be looking everywhere but whither he really was looking—down the road. Presently Jeff Thatcher hove in sight, and Tom's face lighted; he gazed a moment, and then turned sorrowfully away. When Jeff arrived, Tom accosted him, and "led up" warily to opportunities for remark about Becky, but the giddy lad never could see the bait. Tom watched and watched, hoping whenever a frisking frock came in sight, and hating the owner of it as soon as he saw she was not the right one. At last frocks ceased to appear, and he dropped hopelessly into the dumps; he entered the empty school house and sat down to suffer. Then one more frock passed in at the gate, and Tom's heart gave a great bound. The next instant he was out, and "going on" like an Indian; yelling, laughing, chasing boys, jumping over the fence at risk of life and limb, throwing hand-springs, standing on his head—doing all the heroic things he could conceive of, and keeping a furtive eye out, all the while, to see if Becky Thatcher was noticing. But she seemed to be unconscious of it all; she never looked. Could it be possible that she was not aware that he was there? He carried his exploits to her immediate vicinity; came war-whooping around, snatched a boy's cap, hurled it to the roof of the schoolhouse, broke through a group of boys, tumbling them in every direction, and fell sprawling, himself, under Becky's nose, almost upsetting her—and she turned, with her nose in the air, and he heard her say, "Mf! some people think they're mighty smart—always showing off!"

Tom's cheeks burned. He gathered himself up and sneaked off, crushed and crestfallen.

Elizabeth Enright (1909–68)

Elizabeth Enright was an American author of many finely observed and elegantly written novels for young readers, including *Thimble Summer* (1938), which won a Newbery medal. She is best known for two sets of fictional children, the group in the Gone-Away Lake books (1957 and 1961) and the Melendy family. In *The Saturdays* (1941), the Melendy children are living in New York City during World War II. Their story continues with several more books, including *Spiderweb for Two* (1951), perhaps the best of the series. While most of Enright's novels are set in the country, *The Saturdays* shows that many twentieth-century child characters also had adventures in the city (see also *Harriet the Spy* in Further Recommended Reading and Ruth Sawyer's 1936 novel *Roller Skates*). Despite the war, the city seems a remarkably safe place in *The Saturdays*. Each Saturday, one of the children ventures into the streets for an adventure of his or her own, supplied from the shared treasury of the Independent Saturday Afternoon Adventure Club (ISAAC), a club they've formed for this express purpose. Enright has a sharp eye for the telling and vivid detail, and a keen ear for how children really talk (or, more accurately, how they talked at the time she was writing).

From *The Saturdays*

SATURDAY TWO

Of course Father said yes. But he had certain conditions which they already knew by heart. They were the same ones he had imposed when they started going to school by themselves.

"Don't get run over," he said. "That's the first and most important rule. Look where you're going, and watch the lights when you cross the street. This applies to Randy in particular who believes too often that she's walking in another world: a safer, better one. It's the people who make the safety on this earth as well as the trouble, unfortunately." Father glared at the newspaper that lay on the floor beside him. "Sometimes I think the Golden Age must have been the Age of Reptiles. Well, anyway, let me see what was I saying—? Oh, yes. Randy and the lights. And another thing. If you get lost or in trouble of any kind *always* look for a policeman. Sooner or later you'll find one and he'll know what to do; and don't hesitate to ask him even if he's the traffic cop at Forty-second and Fifth with busses breathing fire on every side. Let's see, what clse?"

"Don't talk to strangers," Randy prompted him.

"Yes, that's right, don't talk to strangers. Unless you know by looking at them that they're kind people, and even then think twice. Be home no later than quarter to six, and Randy had better make it five." He picked up his newspaper and flapped it open. "That's about all. Oh, one last thing— See that you do something you really want; something you'll always remember. Don't waste your Saturdays on unimportant things."

"Yes, that's one of the rules," Mona told him.

"Is it? Good. Then go with my blessings."

Then they went to Cuffy who naturally said yes too, but not as if she cared for the idea.

"Well, I hope it's all right, I'm sure. Seems to me like you're pretty young to be kiting all over a big city by yourselves. And one at a time, too, not even together. Don't you get run over now!" They couldn't help laughing at that: all grownups had learned the same set of precautions apparently.

"And it's nothing to giggle about, neither," said Cuffy severely. "I don't want nobody run over, nor nobody lost so's we have to get the police out after 'em. I suppose I can't keep you from getting a little lost once in a while. It'd be against nature. But not so lost that we have to get the police out after you."

Good old Cuffy. It was that sort of thing that made them love her so much.

"If you do get lost," she continued, "you can always go up and ask—"

"A *policeman!*" shouted Mona and Randy and Rush in unison.

"Do you think it's polite to take the words right out of people's mouths?" inquired Cuffy, pretending to be offended. "And another thing—"

"DON'T TALK TO STRANGERS!" they cried.

"Well," said Cuffy, giving up. "I can't say much for your manners but I'm glad to see you've got the right ideas at least."

"What about strange policemen?" said Rush, looking innocent.

"Oh, go on with you! Out of my kitchen, the whole tribe of you!" Cuffy made sweeping gestures with the broom. "My patience is worn about's thin as the sole of my shoe."

But that wasn't true, and they knew it. Cuffy's patience was as deep as the earth itself.

After a brief discussion it was decided that Randy as founder of the Club should have the privilege of the first Saturday. For the next five days she worked feverishly in her school craft shop whenever she got a chance, and by Friday evening she was able to distribute four small pins cut out of copper, and each bearing the mysterious name Isaac.

"Swear on your sacred word of honor *never* to tell anyone what this pin means," Randy said to the Club members. And they all swore, even Oliver. It was a solemn moment.

Saturday dawned much the same as any other day, maybe even a little greyer than most, but when Randy woke up she had the same feeling in her stomach that she always had on Christmas Day. A wonderful morning smell of coffee and bacon drifted up the stair well from the kitchen, and she could hear a familiar clattering spasm deep in the house: Willy Sloper shaking down the furnace. Mona was still asleep, a mound entirely covered up except for one long trailing pigtail that looked as if it were awake all by itself.

Randy lay staring absently at the wall beside her bed where pictures hung at haphazard intervals. She had painted all the pictures herself and there was a reason for their strange arrangement: the wallpaper was old and the pictures served to cover up peeled and faded places. They were all drawings of enigmatic-faced princesses and sorceresses. Each had mysterious, slanted eyes, a complicated headdress and elaborate jewels; each was posed against a background of palaces, rocks and dashing waves, or forests with unicorns. "Don't you ever get tired of drawing Lucrezia Borgia all the time?" Rush had once asked her.

For a while Randy lay still just being happy; then she stretched. S-t-r-e-t-ch-ed way up and way down. During it she probably grew half an inch. After that she got out of bed, stepping over her bedroom slippers as usual.

"Ow! Is it cold!" Randy complained happily, and closed the window with a crash that drew protesting grumbles from the little mountain range that was Mona.

The morning finally went by with Randy pushing it every second. It was awful to sit at the lunch table while Cuffy calmly insisted that she must eat everything on her plate. Everything.

"Oh, Cuffy, even my *beets?*"

"*All* your beets," replied Cuffy inexorably. "And *all* your squash."

Randy looked witheringly at the food on her plate.

"Beets are so boring," she said. "The most boring vegetable in the whole world next to squash."

"Not so boring as spinach," said Rush. "Spinach is like eating a wet mop."

"That will be enough of that!" commanded Cuffy in the voice that meant no nonsense.

At last it was over, even the tapioca, and Randy just stopped herself in time from remarking that she considered tapioca the most boring dessert in the world next to stewed rhubarb.

Mona came into their room while Randy was changing her dress.

"How'd you like to borrow my ambers?" she asked.

"Oh, Mona!" Randy was overcome. "Do you mean you'd let me? Honestly? Oh, I'd be so careful of them, I promise I would."

She felt like a princess in her brown velveteen dress with the amber necklace that had belonged to Mother. "It's like big lumps of honey," she said, staring into the mirror.

"Well, don't you lose it now," admonished Mona, not quite regretting her generosity. "Have a good time, Ran, and don't forget you have to be back by five."

"I won't," promised Randy, giving her sister a hug. "Good-bye, you're swell to let me wear the ambers."

She said good-bye to everyone just as though she were going away for a long voyage. Cuffy gazed at her thoughtfully.

"You look awful little to be going off by yourself like this," she said. "Now remember, don't you get run over and don't—"

"I won't, I won't!" cried Randy, quickly running down the steps and waving her blue leather pocketbook in which the dollar and sixty cents rattled wealthily.

My, it's a nice day, she thought. Nobody else would have thought so. The sky was full of low clouds and the air had a damp, deep feeling in it that meant rain after a while. But being by yourself, all by yourself, in a big city for the first time is like the first time you find you can ride a bicycle or do the dog paddle. The sense of independence is intoxicating. Randy skipped halfway up the block, a leisurely lighthearted skip, and then she walked the rest of the way, stepping over each crack in the pavement. It was very dangerous, she had to be careful, because if she did step on a crack she would be turned into stone forevermore.

In Fifth Avenue the big green busses rattled by like dinosaurs. I'm going to walk though, Randy decided. I'm going to walk all the way and look in all the windows. So that's what she did. The shop windows were wonderful: Woolworth's dime store was just as wonderful as Tiffany's jewelry store, and she reached Fifty-seventh Street in either a very long or a very short time, she wasn't sure which, because the walk had been so interesting.

It was just beginning to rain when she came to the art gallery where the French pictures were being shown for the benefit of war relief. It cost seventy-five cents to go in, so Randy planned to stay a long time and gave her coat to the doorman.

The gallery was hushed and dim after the bright, sharp street. The soft rugs on the floor, the soft neutral color of the walls, with each picture glowing beneath its own special light, made her feel as if she had walked into a jewel case.

"Catalogue, miss?" said a man at a little desk. His eyeglasses flashed in the dimness.

"Thank you," Randy said, and took one of the little folders he offered; then, almost on tiptoe, she stepped into the main room of the gallery. There were a lot of people looking at the pictures and talking to each other as if they were in church, low-voiced and serious. One of the people she knew, and at sight of her Randy's heart sank. It was old Mrs. Oliphant ("the Elephant," Rush called her behind her back) who really was old because she had known Father's father way back in the last century. She was a big, tall old lady with a lot of furs that smelled of camphor, and a great many chains around her neck that got caught on each other. Now and then she came to the Melendys', and once they had all been taken to Sunday dinner at her house when it was raining and everybody ate too much and Oliver got sick on the bus going home. She was nice, Randy supposed, but so far away in her oldness and dignity. She hoped Mrs. Oliphant wouldn't notice her.

Pretty soon she forgot about everything but the pictures. There was a nice one of a girl in an old-fashioned dress playing the piano. She had a snub nose and a long yellow braid sort of like Mona (only of course it was probably a French girl). If she looked at a picture long enough, without being interrupted, Randy could make it come alive sometimes; and now she could almost hear the music the girl in the picture was playing: quite hard music, probably, but played very stiffly, with a lot of mistakes, the way Mona played.

"Marvelous substance," murmured a hushed voice behind her, and another hushed voice replied, "Unbelievable resilience in the flesh tones!"

Gee whiz, thought Randy, are they talking about the picture? And she moved on to the next one; a field all burning yellow in the sunshine. You could tell it was twelve o'clock noon on a summer day; probably July. Randy could nearly smell the heat, and hear the locusts in the trees sounding exactly like Father's electric razor in the mornings. She was having a good time. She looked at all the pictures: fat ladies bathing in a brook, a girl with opera glasses, apples and pears on a blue plate, a man in a boat, two dead rabbits, and then all of a sudden she came to the picture that was hers, her very own one.

Randy was always finding things that belonged to her in a special way, though ownership had nothing to do with it. Now she had found the picture. The catalogue told her that the picture was called The Princess, that it had been painted by someone named Jules Clairon in the year 1881. In the picture a girl about Randy's age was sitting on a garden wall and looking out over an enormous city. She had a solemn little face: her long hair hung to the sash of her old-fashioned dress, and her high-heeled boots were buttoned almost to the knee. Among the potted chrysanthemums at her feet sat a black poodle with a red bow on top of his head. On either side the clipped plane trees were almost bare, and in the distance the huge city was spread in a dusky web of blue and grey.

It was easy to make this picture alive. Randy stared at it fixedly, hardly breathing, hardly thinking, and pretty soon she thought she could smell the mixture of damp earth and burning leaves and smoke from distant chimney pots; she thought she could hear the hum of the city and the clear voices of children somewhere out of sight. A day had come and gone, years ago, and still it was alive. I wish I'd known that girl, Randy thought.

She felt a touch on her shoulder that brought her back to her own world with a start. On her shoulder she saw a knuckly black glove, and against her cheek she felt the prickling of camphory fur. The Elephant, darn it, thought Randy crossly. Just when I was getting right into that picture, too.

"Well, well! Why, Mona dear! What are you doing here?" inquired Mrs. Oliphant in her deep cavernous voice with its faint foreign accent. "Or is it little Miranda?"

"Miranda," replied Randy politely, with a smile that was nothing but stretching the corners of her mouth.

"Of course, of course. Mona is the one with the hair," said Mrs. Oliphant, whacking Randy's shoulder absent-mindedly. "You seem very interested in this picture, Miranda."

"I think it's beautiful," Randy said, sloping her shoulder out from under Mrs. Oliphant's hand as tactfully as she could.

"It isn't so beautiful as I remembered it," observed Mrs. Oliphant, regarding it with a frown. "But then I haven't seen it for sixty years. Not since I was eleven years old."

"Eleven years old!" repeated Randy. It was impossible that Mrs. Oliphant had ever been eleven. "Not since the day it was finished," the old lady explained. "You see, I was the girl in the picture."

"You!" cried Randy, amazed. Her mouth dropped open half an inch.

"That's I at the age of eleven," said Mrs. Oliphant, very pleased at Randy's surprise. "Not much to look at, was I?"

"I think you looked nice," Randy considered the girl in the picture. "Interesting and, well, nice. I was just wishing I'd known that girl."

"And how she would have loved knowing you. Sometimes she was very lonely," said Mrs. Oliphant. "Unfortunately she disappeared long, long ago."

Randy looked up at her companion's face. What she said was true. The face was so old, crossed with a thousand lines, and the dark, fiery eyes were overhung by such severe black brows that every trace of the little girl she had once been had vanished with the past.

"What was that big city in the distance?"

"It was Paris," said the old lady, with a sigh.

"Who was the dog?"

"Tartuffe, we called him. He was a selfish old beast, and very dull company." Mrs. Oliphant shook her head and laughed, remembering. Then she looked about her questioningly. "Who is with you, Miranda? I don't see any of your family."

"I'm all alone," Randy told her.

"*Alone?* How old are you, child?"

"Ten," said Randy.

Mrs. Oliphant shook her head again. "When I was your age such a thing was unheard of. My aunts would have fainted dead away at the suggestion. What a lucky girl you are!"

Randy agreed. Really, I am lucky, she thought.

"Well, since we are both alone," suggested the old lady, "why don't you come with me and have a cup of tea, or an ice-cream soda, or a chocolate marshmallow walnut sundae, or whatever you prefer?"

Randy was beginning to like Mrs. Oliphant very much. "I'd love to," she said.

Surrounded by an aura of camphor and eau de Cologne, and with all her chains jingling, the old lady swept splendidly from the gallery. Randy followed in her wake, like a dinghy behind a large launch.

Outside the moist air had become moister. A fine mist was driving down. Mrs. Oliphant disentangled an umbrella from her handbag and the tail of one of her furs. When it was opened the umbrella proved to be extremely large and deep. They walked under it, close together, as under a small pavilion. "I've had it for twenty-five years," Mrs. Oliphant told Randy. "It's been lost once on a bus, twice on railway trains, and once at the London Zoo. But I always get it back. I call it the Albatross."

After they had walked a block or two, they came to a large hotel which they entered, and the old lady, having checked the Albatross, led Randy to a large room full of little tables, gilt chairs, mirrors, and palms in fancy pots. At one end of the room on a raised platform there was a three-piece orchestra: piano, violin, and cello. All the musicians looked about fifty years old.

A waiter who looked old enough to be the father of any one of the musicians led Mrs. Oliphant and Randy to a table by a long window. After a period of deliberation, it was decided that the old lady would have tea and toast, and Randy would have vanilla ice cream with chocolate sauce.

"And, François, bring some petits fours, also."

"Parfaitement, madame," said François, creaking agedly away in the direction of the kitchen. Randy did not know what "petits fours" meant, but she did not like to ask.

"Ah, yes," said Mrs. Oliphant when she had uncoiled from her layers of furs, taken off her gloves, untied her scarf, and arranged her necklaces. "My childhood was a very different thing from yours."

"Tell me about it," said Randy. Then "please," as an afterthought.

"Would you like to hear the whole story?"

"Yes, yes, please, the whole story," begged Randy, giving an involuntary bounce on the hard chair. She loved to be told stories.

"Well, it's a long time ago," said the old lady. "Before you were born, even before your father was born, imagine it! The garden in the picture was the garden of my father's house in Saint-Germain near Paris. It was an old house even then, tall and narrow and grey, with patches of ivy. The inside of it was stuffy and dark and full of furniture. When house cleaning was going on, all the windows were opened; never any other time, and I can remember the smell of it to this day: the mixed odors of cloth and cough medicine and age. I was the only young thing in the house, even Tartuffe, the dog, was older than I. My mother had died when I was born and my father's business kept him in Paris all day, so I was brought up by my aunts and an English governess. They gave me my lessons too, I was never allowed to go to school. The aunts were all maiden ladies years older than my father. They always wore black, took pills with their meals, worried about drafts, and spoke in quiet polite voices except when shouting at Tante Amélie, the deaf aunt, who carried a great curved ear trumpet like the tusk of an elephant. Ah, here is the tea."

François arranged the feast before them. Petits fours turned out to be the most wonderful little cakes in frilled paper collars: pink, and pale yellow, and chocolate, with silver peppermint buttons on top. Randy's eyes glittered with such enthusiasm that the old lady was delighted. "You shall have some to take home to the other children. François, please bring us a boxful of petits fours to take home."

"That will be wonderful," Randy said, not quite with her mouth full, but almost. "Please tell me some more."

"Very well," said her friend. "The English governess was also a spinster, also elderly. Her name was Miss Buff-Towers and she was related in some way to an earl, a fact she was very proud of and never forgot. She had long front teeth, the color of old piano keys, and a huge coiled arrangement of braided hair on top of her head like an orderly eagle's nest. She was a kindhearted creature but she knew as much about raising children as I know about raising coati-mundis. (I'm not even sure what they are.)

"You can see that my life was far from exciting. I knew no children, rarely left my own home at all. If it hadn't been for the garden I might have gone mad from boredom.

"This garden was very large, enclosed by a high wall, and shaded by old chestnut trees that bloomed every spring in great cornucopias of popcorn. There was a tiny bamboo jungle, and a summerhouse with a wasp's nest, and a little lead fountain, and two enormous mossy statues: one of Diana, and one of Apollo. At the end of the garden the wall was low enough to permit seeing the magnificent view of the city. In the distance the whole of Paris lay spread out like a map:

golden in the morning, blue in the dusk, shining like a thousand fires at night.

"I spent all the time I could in the garden. I had a swing there, and many hiding places for myself, my dolls, and Tartuffe. I used to take my lessons to the wall at the end, looking up from my dull books every other minute to see the city far beyond. I never tired of looking at it and wondering about it.

"One September evening when I was eleven years old I had gone into the garden, and was sitting in my usual place on the wall looking at the city and hoping dinner would be ready soon. I heard steps on the little gravel path behind me and, turning, saw my father and another gentleman, a friend whom he had brought home for dinner. I stood up respectfully and was introduced to Monsieur Clairon. He was a tall man with a brown beard and pleasant eyes. I had a feeling, looking at him, that he was more alive than most people.

"'Your daughter makes me think of the princess in a fairy tale who looks out of her tower at the world,' he told my father. 'Someday I would like to paint her just as she was: sitting on that wall.'

"I was flattered and self-conscious, but only for a moment.

"'We mustn't make her vain, Jules,' said my father in a stately voice. 'That plain little face was never meant for Art.' Dinner, for once, was fun. Monsieur Clairon told jokes and stories, everybody laughed, and each story was repeated in loud brays for Tante Amélie with the greatest good will.

"'I've been making sketches at the carnival down the street,' he told me. 'I can never resist carnivals. This one has a camel and a dancing bear as well as the usual carrousel and fortunetellers. It makes good pictures. You've seen it, I suppose, mademoiselle?' He turned to me.

"'No, monsieur,' I said sadly. I knew there was a carnival somewhere in the town. Bursts of music had been drifting over the wall all day.

"'But you must see it!' Monsieur Clairon insisted. 'It leaves at midnight. I should be happy to take you this evening—'

"'Heaven forbid, Jules,' said my father, with a distressed smile. 'Gabrielle would come home with smallpox or whooping cough or measles or all three.'

"'And so *dreadfully dirty!*' added Miss Buff-Towers.

"'Someone might even kidnap her!' said my Tante Marthe, who always expected the worst.

"'It's out of the question,' stated my father firmly.

"For the first time since I was a tiny child I dared to defy the collective opinion of my aunts, father, and governess.

"'But I want to go!' said I, laying down my fork. 'I want to go *terribly!* Why can't I? I'll wear gloves and not touch anything, I promise. When I come home I'll gargle. Please let me go, please please please!'

"My father stared at me. Even his eyebrows and mustache looked annoyed.

"'That will be enough, Gabrielle,' he said.

"'You never let me go anywhere!' I persisted. 'I've never seen a carnival. Or a real live camel. Or a dancing bear. I'd like to *see something* besides just this old house all the time!'

"My father's face was dark as the wine in his glass.

"'Go!' he roared. 'Upstairs, immediately! Without dessert!'

"And up I went, crying into my sleeve and hearing above my sobs the turmoil in the dining room: Monsieur Clairon interceding for me, my father expostulating, and above that the loud, toneless voice of Tante Amélie saying, 'What's the matter? Why is Gabrielle crying? Why doesn't someone tell me something?' And Tante Marthe bellowing into the ear trumpet: 'GABRIELLE HAS BEEN A VERY NAUGHTY GIRL!'

"After I had gone to bed and Miss Buff-Towers had heard my prayers, and wept a few embarrassing tears over my disobedience, I lay in bed very still and straight and angry. Through the closed window I could hear rowdy strains of music.

"At last I got out of bed and opened the window which looked out over the garden and the distant lighted city spread like a jeweled fabric. For the first time I was sorry that my room was not at the front of the house since then I might have glimpsed the carnival. The music sounded gayer than ever, and I could hear bursts of laughter above the noise. Slowly my anger turned to curiosity and active rebellion. An adventurous flame sprang to life within me. Quickly in the dark I dressed in my oldest dress. Quickly I stuffed the bolster under the blankets just in case someone should look in. But money! I wanted to ride on the carrousel and to see the dancing bear. There were only twenty centimes in my pocketbook, and then I remem-

bered the gold piece! My father had given it to me on my last birthday; at the time I had been disappointed, but now I was glad. I took it out of its box, put it in my pocket with the twenty centimes, and cautiously opened the door to the hall.

"The fat bronze goddess on the upstairs landing was brandishing the gas lamp like a hand grenade. Downstairs I heard my father shout, 'Why don't you move your queen?' and knew that he was playing chess with Tante Amélie. I turned back to my room and closed the door behind me. Nothing was going to stop me now. I went over to the window and opened it again. Aged ivy covered the walls at either side, and, scared to death, in my clumsy old-fashioned clothes, I reached out among the leaves till I felt a strong stem like a cable, stepped over the iron grille in front of the window, and with a breathless prayer, began my descent. Very awkward it was, too. I made a lot of noise, and all the sparrows in the ivy woke up and flew chattering away. About six feet above the ground the ivy ripped away from the wall, and down I went with a crash into a fuchsia bush. I sat there listening to my heart and waiting for the entire household to come out with lanterns.

"But nothing happened! After an eternity I got up and stole out of the garden. Both the knees had been torn out of my stockings, I was dirty, and my hair was full of ivy twigs, but it didn't matter.

"In less than five minutes I had arrived at the carnival! It was even better than I had hoped: full of crowds and bright lights and noise. The carrousel with its whirling painted horses and its music was like nothing I had ever seen before. I rode on it twice and when I screamed with excitement nobody paid any attention because they were all doing the same thing. After that I bought a ride on a camel. That took some courage, as I had never seen a camel before and did not know that they possessed such sarcastic faces. Have you ever ridden on one?"

"Never," said Randy.

"You must try it sometime. It made me a little seasick but I enjoyed it. Then I went and watched the dancing bear softly rocking to and fro on his hind paws like a tipsy old man in bedroom slippers. There was too much to see; I was dazzled, and just walked about staring blissfully.

"I was fascinated by the fortuneteller's booth. It was really a large wagon with a hooped roof which you entered by a pair of wooden steps. On one side there was a large placard bearing the words: 'Zenaïda, world-renowned seeress and soothsayer! Advice and prophecy on affairs of business, or the heart. Palmistry, cards, or crystal as preferred.' On the other side there was a life-sized picture of a dark, beautiful woman gazing into a crystal globe. I hesitated only a moment, then I mounted the steps, parted the flaps of the tent, and entered. Inside the tent was draped with shabby shawls of many colors; overhead a red glass lantern cast a murky light, and at a small table sat a gypsy woman glittering and jingling with earrings, clattering bracelets and necklaces. She looked almost nothing like the picture outside. She was older, and her fingernails were dirty. I was dreadfully disappointed.

"'What do you want, kid?' she said. Her voice was hoarse and rough as though she had spent her whole life shouting.

"'To-to-have my fortune told,' I stammered.

"'Got any money?' asked the woman doubtfully, looking at my torn stockings and dirty dress.

"'Yes,' I said.

"'Let me see it,' she demanded.

"'I brought the gold piece out of my pocket. The gypsy examined it craftily; then she smiled a wide, delighted smile. One of her teeth was black.

"'You must have found that in a well-lined pocket,' said she.

"At first I did not understand what she meant. Then I was angry.

"'I never stole anything in my life!' I told her. 'My father gave it to me for a present.'

"'Your father? He is a rich man?'

"'I suppose he is,' I said. 'I don't know. I never thought about it. Anyway I don't think I want you to tell my fortune after all.'

"Quick as a cat the gypsy sprang from her chair and barred the entrance.

"'Forgive me, mademoiselle,' she wheedled. 'I didn't realize—Your clothes are torn and you have such a dirty face. Come and sit down; I'll tell you a fortune you'll never forget: splendid, wonderful things are going to happen to you. I see luck shining all around you!'

"Well, who could resist that? In spite of myself, I was soon seated opposite Zenaïda, my dirty hand in her dirtier one. Before she began to read my palm she called out in her harsh gypsy voice, 'Bastien!'

"A young man's face appeared at the entrance, and Zenaïda said something to him in a strange language. The young man nodded, looked at me, and burst out laughing. Then he disappeared.

"The gypsy lived up to her word. Never was such a fortune told to a human being! Jewels, lovers, fame, travels into far countries, all were promised to me, and I sat there like a half-wit believing every word.

"'I must go,' I said at last. 'Please take what I owe you out of this.' I gave her the gold piece trustingly. And that, of course, was the last I ever saw of it.

"'We will drive you home in the wagon,' said Zenaïda, smiling. I could hear Bastien hitching up the horses outside.

"'No, thank you,' said I. 'It's not far, only a little way. If you will give me what you owe me I will go.' I realized that the music had stopped, and a sound of hammering and clattering had taken its place. The carnival was being dismantled. I had been in the wagon for a long time.

"'We will take you home,' Zenaïda insisted. 'It's almost midnight and we must be on our way anyhow. Where do you live, and what is your father's name?'

"Like a fool I told her.

"Bastien called to the horses, and the wagon began to move; the red lantern swinging in a slow circle overhead.

"I was so busy thinking of my glittering future that it was some time before I realized that we must have left my house far behind. When I began asking frightened questions the gypsy came close to me and grabbed my arm. She told me that I was not going home, but far away, till my father was ready to pay a price to get me back. When I cried and struggled she called Bastien and they bound my wrists and ankles and tied a rag over my mouth. All night I lay on the floor in the dark feeling the wagon lurch and sway, and hearing Zenaïda's snores and Bastien's voice swearing at the horses. I was sick with terror.

"I remained with the gypsies for three weeks. The first day Zenaïda unbraided my hair, took away my shoes and stockings, and dressed me in gaudy rags. She pierced my ears for brass earrings, and, stooping down, picked up a handful of earth and rubbed it across my face. 'There!' she said. 'Now even a gypsy would think you were a gypsy!'

"In spite of her, and in spite of the letter I was forced to write my father during the second week, telling him where to leave the ransom money if he wished to see me again, I enjoyed many things about those three weeks. The wagon and the travel and the going barefoot! The sound of rain on canvas overhead; the noise and smell of the carnival: a noise of bells and talk and music; a smell of garlic and tobacco and people and that camel! But the bad things more than overshadowed the good. Zenaïda was cruel, and so was Bastien when he got drunk, which was often.

"One fine day we came to a small town in the Loire district. There was a big cathedral on the square, I remember, that looked huge and disapproving beyond the carnival's tawdry, jingling whirl of light and music.

"When Zenaïda was telling fortunes in the wagon Bastien was supposed to keep an eye on me. I had to stay near the wagon, or run the risk of a bad whipping. But on this particular evening, Bastien, a little tipsier than usual, went to sleep under the wagon with his head on his hat. I saw my chance and wandered away. I had no thought of escape. I was too dirty and dispirited, and I had no money; my sheltered life had taught me nothing of fending for myself or what to do in an emergency. However, for the moment I enjoyed myself watching the familiar sights of the carnival and the many unfamiliar faces.

"Suddenly I saw something that made me gasp!

"Standing under a gas lamp at the outskirts of the crowd was a tall man with a beard. In his hands were a small sketchbook and a pencil. It was Monsieur Jules Clairon who never could resist a carnival!

"I ran to him bleating like a lost sheep. 'Oh, Monsieur Clairon, save me, save me, and take me away from here!'

"Poor man, he looked horrified, and who can blame him? I had accumulated the dirt of three weeks.

"'I don't know any gypsies!' said he. 'How do you know my name?'

"'But I'm the *princess,* don't you remember?' I cried idiotically. And then I explained.

"'Good Lord!' he said, horrified. 'I knew nothing about your disappearance. I left Saint-Germain early the next morning on a walking tour.'

"He took me back to the house where he was staying, and the landlady scrubbed me and gave me clean clothes, while he got the police and went back to the carnival. But Zenaïda must have found out what had

happened, for the gypsy wagon had disappeared. Nobody ever saw it again.

"As for me, I was rushed home by train the next day. I was embraced by my haggard father, who was relieved on two accounts: first because of my safe return, and second because the ransom money had never been collected. All my aunts wept over me wetly, and I had to have my hair washed every day for two weeks, but in spite of everything I was glad to be home.

"When my father begged Monsieur Clairon to tell him how he could reward him, Monsieur Clairon replied, 'Allow me to paint the portrait of your daughter.' So that is how it came about. Later on it was he who persuaded my family to send me to school in England. I went to a convent there for seven years which, though it would have seemed dreadfully strict to you, was heaven itself as far as I was concerned."

Mrs. Oliphant opened a pocketbook like a giant clam, extracted some money to pay the bill, and clapped it shut again. "That's all," she said.

Randy rose slowly to the surface and emerged from the story dreamily.

"It was wonderful," she said. "Things like that never happen to us. We lead a humdrum life when I think about it. It's funny how it doesn't seem humdrum."

"That's because you have 'eyes the better to see with, my dear' and 'ears the better to hear with.' Nobody who has them and uses them is likely to find life humdrum very often. Even when they have to use bifocal lenses, like me."

It was dark when they came out. The rain had stopped but the streets were still wet; crisscrossed with reflected light. The shop windows were lighted too. In one bright rectangle floated a mannequin in a dress of green spangles, exactly like a captured mermaid in an aquarium.

"I go up and you go down town," said Mrs. Oliphant when they came to Fifth Avenue. She held out her hand. "Thank you for coming to tea."

"Oh, thank you very much for inviting me," said Randy. "Could I—would you let me come to see you someday?"

The old lady looked pleased. "Do come, child. Come by all means, and I'll show you the brass earrings Zenaïda made me wear. I kept them for luck. I have a lot of interesting things: Javanese puppets, and a poison ring, and a beetle carved out of an emerald, and the tooth of a czarina—"

"The tooth of a czarina!" cried Randy, stopping dead.

"That's another story, my dear," said the old lady exasperatingly. A big Brontosaurus of a bus clattered to a pause. "This is mine," said Mrs. Oliphant, climbing on it and waving her hand. "Good-bye, Miranda!"

Randy crossed the street and boarded a big Stegosaurus going the other way.

At home she went straight to Rush's room. He was having a peaceful half hour before dinner reading, with his feet on the radiator and the radio going full blast. A voice that made all the furniture tremble was describing the excellence of a certain kind of hair tonic.

"Are you worried by the possibility of premature baldness?" inquired the voice in intimately confidential tones that could be heard a block away. "Does it trouble you to see your once luxuriant hair thinning out—"

Randy snapped off the radio. "You don't have to worry about that yet awhile," she said.

Rush looked up from his book. "Huh? Oh, hello. Have a good time?"

"Wonderful. Guess who I met?"

"Mickey Rooney," said Rush.

"No, silly. The Elephant. Only I'm never going to call her that again."

"Oh, just the Elephant." Rush was disappointed.

"Not just the Elephant. She's swell, she's a friend of mine now, and I'm going to see her. She was kidnaped by gypsies and lived with them for weeks."

"Recently?" inquired Rush, startled.

"No, no. Years ago when she was a little girl in France. I'll tell you about it after dinner. And look, she sent you these. All of you I mean."

"What are they?" said Rush, taking a bite.

"Pitty foors," said Randy. "I think it's French. For cakes, probably."

"Pitty foors," repeated Rush mellowly, through chocolate custard. "Not bad, not bad at all. So she was kidnaped by gypsies, was she? Do you think the El— Mrs. Oliphant would care to have me come along with you when you go calling on her?"

"I know she would," said Randy. "And, Rush, let's go soon and often."

Beverly Cleary (b.1916)

Beverly Cleary became a librarian after she earned B.A. degrees at the University of California, Berkeley, and the University of Washington. As a child, she loved books; her mother established the first lending library in the town of McMinnville, Oregon, where Beverly was born. However, Beverly had difficulty learning to read at school, where she was asked to read books about "wealthy English children who had nannies and pony carts or books about poor children whose problems were solved by a long-lost rich relative turning up in the last chapter," instead of books about American children like herself.[1] When Cleary began to write for children, her goal was to write humorous stories about the sort of children she knew, surrounded by their families, friends, neighbors, teachers, and librarians. The result was the popular characters of Henry Huggins and Ramona Quimby, whom she portrays with affection and insight. At the request of Cleary's readers, Ramona moved from the minor role of a friend's annoying little sister in early Henry Huggins stories to a more prominent position alongside her sister in *Beezus and Ramona* (1955) and into the spotlight in the Ramona series (1968–99). *Ramona the Pest* begins the series with Ramona's high expectations and problems as she prepares to start school. Cleary has a particular talent for writing in a clear, funny, yet wise way about the foibles and misadventures of childhood, creating believable and appealing characters through deft dialogue.

NOTE

1. Beverly Cleary, "The Laughter of Children," *The Horn Book* 58.5 (1982): 555–564.

From *Ramona the Pest*

CHAPTER 1. RAMONA'S GREAT DAY

"I am *not* a pest," Ramona Quimby told her big sister Beezus.

"Then stop acting like a pest," said Beezus, whose real name was Beatrice. She was standing by the front window waiting for her friend Mary Jane to walk to school with her.

"I'm not acting like a pest. I'm singing and skipping," said Ramona, who had only recently learned to skip with both feet. Ramona did not think she was a pest. No matter what others said, she never thought she was a pest. The people who called her a pest were always bigger and so they could be unfair.

Ramona went on with her singing and skipping. "This is a great day, a great day, a great day!" she sang, and to Ramona, who was feeling grown-up in a dress instead of play clothes, this was a great day, the greatest day of her whole life. No longer would she have to sit on her tricycle watching Beezus and Henry Huggins and the rest of the boys and girls in the neighborhood go off to school. Today she was going to school, too. Today she was going to learn to read and write and do all the things that would help her catch up with Beezus.

"Come *on,* Mama!" urged Ramona, pausing in her singing and skipping. "We don't want to be late for school."

"Don't pester, Ramona," said Mrs. Quimby. "I'll get you there in plenty of time."

"I'm *not* pestering," protested Ramona, who never meant to pester. She was not a slow-poke grownup. She was a girl who could not wait. Life was so interesting she had to find out what happened next.

Then Mary Jane arrived. "Mrs. Quimby, would it be all right if Beezus and I take Ramona to kindergarten?" she asked.

"No!" said Ramona instantly. Mary Jane was one of those girls who always wanted to pretend she was a mother and who always wanted Ramona to be the baby. Nobody was going to catch Ramona being a baby on her first day of school.

"Why not?" Mrs. Quimby asked Ramona. "You could walk to school with Beezus and Mary Jane just like a big girl."

Louis Darling's drawings of Ramona capture the exuberance of a delightful American child.

"No, I couldn't." Ramona was not fooled for an instant. Mary Jane would talk in that silly voice she used when she was being a mother and take her by the hand and help her across the street, and everyone would think she really was a baby.

"Please, Ramona," coaxed Beezus. "It would be lots of fun to take you in and introduce you to the kindergarten teacher."

"No!" said Ramona, and stamped her foot. Beezus and Mary Jane might have fun, but she wouldn't. Nobody but a genuine grownup was going to take her to school. If she had to, she would make a great big noisy fuss, and when Ramona made a great big noisy fuss, she usually got her own way. Great big noisy fusses were often necessary when a girl was the youngest member of the family and the youngest person on her block.

"All right, Ramona," said Mrs. Quimby. "Don't make a great big noisy fuss. If that's the way you feel about it, you don't have to walk with the girls. I'll take you."

"Hurry, Mama," said Ramona happily, as she watched Beezus and Mary Jane go out the door. But when Ramona finally got her mother out of the house, she was disappointed to see one of her mother's friends, Mrs. Kemp, approaching with her son Howie and his little sister Willa Jean, who was riding in a stroller. "Hurry, Mama," urged Ramona, not wanting to wait for the Kemps. Because their mothers were friends, she and Howie were expected to get along with one another.

"Hi, there!" Mrs. Kemp called out, so of course Ramona's mother had to wait.

Howie stared at Ramona. He did not like having to get along with her any more than she liked having to get along with him.

Ramona stared back. Howie was a solid-looking boy with curly blond hair. ("Such a waste on a boy," his mother often remarked.) The legs of his new jeans were turned up, and he was wearing a new shirt with long sleeves. He did not look the least bit excited about starting kindergarten. That was the trouble with Howie, Ramona felt. He never got excited. Straight-haired Willa Jean, who was interesting to Ramona because she was so sloppy, blew out a mouthful of wet zwieback crumbs and laughed at her cleverness.

"Today my baby leaves me," remarked Mrs.

Quimby with a smile, as the little group proceeded down Klickitat Street toward Glenwood School.

Ramona, who enjoyed being her mother's baby, did not enjoy being called her mother's baby, especially in front of Howie.

"They grow up quickly," observed Mrs. Kemp.

Ramona could not understand why grownups always talked about how quickly children grew up. Ramona thought growing up was the slowest thing there was, slower even than waiting for Christmas to come. She had been waiting years just to get to kindergarten, and the last half hour was the slowest part of all.

When the group reached the intersection nearest Glenwood School, Ramona was pleased to see that Beezus's friend Henry Huggins was the traffic boy in charge of that particular corner. After Henry had led them across the street, Ramona ran off toward the kindergarten, which was a temporary wooden building with its own playground. Mothers and children were already entering the open door. Some of the children looked frightened, and one girl was crying.

"We're late!" cried Ramona. "Hurry!"

Howie was not a boy to be hurried. "I don't see any tricycles," he said critically. "I don't see any dirt to dig in."

Ramona was scornful. "This isn't nursery school. Tricycles and dirt are for nursery school." Her own tricycle was hidden in the garage, because it was too babyish for her now that she was going to school.

Some big first-grade boys ran past yelling, "Kindergarten babies! Kindergarten babies!"

"We are *not* babies!" Ramona yelled back, as she led her mother into the kindergarten. Once inside she stayed close to her. Everything was so strange, and there was so much to see: the little tables and chairs; the row of cupboards, each with a different picture on the door; the play stove; and the wooden blocks big enough to stand on.

The teacher, who was new to Glenwood School, turned out to be so young and pretty she could not have been a grownup very long. It was rumored she had never taught school before. "Hello, Ramona. My name is Miss Binney," she said, speaking each syllable distinctly as she pinned Ramona's name to her dress. "I am so glad you have come to kindergarten." Then she took Ramona by the hand and led her to one of the little tables and chairs. "Sit here for the present," she said with a smile.

A present! thought Ramona, and knew at once she was going to like Miss Binney.

"Good-by, Ramona," said Mrs. Quimby. "Be a good girl."

As she watched her mother walk out the door, Ramona decided school was going to be even better than she had hoped. Nobody had told her she was going to get a present the very first day. What kind of present could it be, she wondered, trying to remember if Beezus had ever been given a present by her teacher.

Ramona listened carefully while Miss Binney showed Howie to a table, but all her teacher said was, "Howie, I would like you to sit here." Well! thought Ramona. Not everyone is going to get a present so Miss Binney must like me best. Ramona watched and listened as the other boys and girls arrived, but Miss Binney did not tell anyone else he was going to get a present if he sat in a certain chair. Ramona wondered if her present would be wrapped in fancy paper and tied with a ribbon like a birthday present. She hoped so.

As Ramona sat waiting for her present she watched the other children being introduced to Miss Binney by their mothers. She found two members of the morning kindergarten especially interesting. One was a boy named Davy, who was small, thin, and eager. He was the only boy in the class in short pants, and Ramona liked him at once. She liked him so much she decided she would like to kiss him.

The other interesting person was a big girl named Susan. Susan's hair looked like the hair on the girls in the pictures of the old-fashioned stories Beezus liked to read. It was reddish-brown and hung in curls like springs that touched her shoulders and bounced as she walked. Ramona had never seen such curls before. All the curly-haired girls she knew wore their hair short. Ramona put her hand to her own short straight hair, which was an ordinary brown, and longed to touch that bright springy hair. She longed to stretch one of those curls and watch it spring back. *Boing!* thought Ramona, making a mental noise like a spring of a television cartoon and wishing for thick, springy *boing-boing* hair like Susan's.

Howie interrupted Ramona's admiration of Susan's hair. "How soon do you think we get to go out and play?" he asked.

"Maybe after Miss Binney gives me the present," Ramona answered. "She said she was going to give me one."

"How come she's going to give you a present?" Howie wanted to know. "She didn't say anything about giving me a present."

"Maybe she likes me best," said Ramona.

This news did not make Howie happy. He turned to the next boy, and said, "*She's* going to get a present."

Ramona wondered how long she would have to sit there to get the present. If only Miss Binney understood how hard waiting was for her! When the last child had been welcomed and the last tearful mother had departed, Miss Binney gave a little talk about the rules of the kindergarten and showed the class the door that led to the bathroom. Next she assigned each person a little cupboard. Ramona's cupboard had a picture of a yellow duck on the door, and Howie's had a green frog. Miss Binney explained that their hooks in the cloakroom were marked with the same pictures. Then she asked the class to follow her quietly into the cloakroom to find their hooks.

Difficult though waiting was for her, Ramona did not budge. Miss Binney had not told her to get up and go into the cloakroom for her present. She had told her to sit for the present, and Ramona was going to sit until she got it. She would sit as if she were glued to the chair.

Howie scowled at Ramona as he returned from the cloakroom, and said to another boy, "The teacher is going to give *her* a present."

Naturally the boy wanted to know why. "I don't know," admitted Ramona. "She told me that if I sat here I would get a present. I guess she likes me best."

By the time Miss Binney returned from the cloakroom, word had spread around the classroom that Ramona was going to get a present.

Next Miss Binney taught the class the words of a puzzling song about "the dawnzer lee light," which Ramona did not understand because she did not know what a dawnzer was. "Oh, say, can you see by the dawnzer lee light," sang Miss Binney, and Ramona decided that a dawnzer was another word for a lamp.

When Miss Binney had gone over the song several times, she asked the class to stand and sing it with her. Ramona did not budge. Neither did Howie and some of the others, and Ramona knew they were hoping for a present, too. Copycats, she thought.

"Stand up straight like good Americans," said Miss Binney so firmly that Howie and the others reluctantly stood up.

Ramona decided she would have to be a good American sitting down.

"Ramona," said Miss Binney, "aren't you going to stand with the rest of us?"

Ramona thought quickly. Maybe the question was some kind of test, like a test in a fairy tale. Maybe Miss Binney was testing her to see if she could get her out of her seat. If she failed the test, she would not get the present.

"I can't," said Ramona.

Miss Binney looked puzzled, but she did not insist that Ramona stand while she led the class through the dawnzer song. Ramona sang along with the others and hoped that her present came next, but when the song ended, Miss Binney made no mention of the present. Instead she picked up a book. Ramona decided that at last the time had come to learn to read.

Miss Binney stood in front of her class and began to read aloud from *Mike Mulligan and His Steam Shovel,* a book that was a favorite of Ramona's because, unlike so many books for her age, it was neither quiet and sleepy nor sweet and pretty. Ramona, pretending she was glued to her chair, enjoyed hearing the story again and listened quietly with the rest of the kindergarten to the story of Mike Mulligan's old-fashioned steam shovel, which proved its worth by digging the basement for the new town hall of Poppersville in a single day beginning at dawn and ending as the sun went down.

As Ramona listened a question came into her mind, a question that had often puzzled her about the books that were read to her. Somehow books always left out one of the most important things anyone would want to know. Now that Ramona was in school, and school was a place for learning, perhaps Miss Binney could answer the question. Ramona waited quietly until her teacher had finished the story, and then she raised her hand the way Miss Binney had told the class they should raise their hands when they wanted to speak in school.

Joey, who did not remember to raise his hand, spoke out. "That's a good book."

Miss Binney smiled at Ramona, and said, "I like the way Ramona remembers to raise her hand when she has something to say. Yes, Ramona?"

Ramona's hopes soared. Her teacher had smiled at her. "Miss Binney, I want to know—how did Mike Mulligan go to the bathroom when he was digging the basement of the town hall?"

Miss Binney's smile seemed to last longer than smiles usually last. Ramona glanced uneasily around and saw that others were waiting with interest for the answer. Everybody wanted to know how Mike Mulligan went to the bathroom.

"Well—" said Miss Binney at last. "I don't really know, Ramona. The book doesn't tell us."

"I always wanted to know, too," said Howie, without raising his hand, and others murmured in agreement. The whole class, it seemed, had been wondering how Mike Mulligan went to the bathroom.

"Maybe he stopped the steam shovel and climbed out of the hole he was digging and went to a service station," suggested a boy named Eric.

"He couldn't. The book says he had to work as fast as he could all day," Howie pointed out. "It doesn't say he stopped."

Miss Binney faced the twenty-nine earnest members of the kindergarten, all of whom wanted to know how Mike Mulligan went to the bathroom.

"Boys and girls," she began, and spoke in her clear, distinct way. "The reason the book does not tell us how Mike Mulligan went to the bathroom is that it is not an important part of the story. The story is about digging the basement of the town hall, and that is what the book tells us."

Miss Binney spoke as if this explanation ended the matter, but the kindergarten was not convinced. Ramona knew and the rest of the class knew that knowing how to go to the bathroom *was* important. They were surprised that Miss Binney did not understand, because she had showed them the bathroom the very first thing. Ramona could see there were some things she was not going to learn in school, and along with the rest of the class she stared reproachfully at Miss Binney.

The teacher looked embarrassed, as if she knew she had disappointed her kindergarten. She recovered quickly, closed the book, and told the class that if they would walk quietly out to the playground she would teach them a game called Gray Duck.

Ramona did not budge. She watched the rest of the class leave the room and admired Susan's *boing-boing* curls as they bounced about her shoulders, but she did not stir from her seat. Only Miss Binney could unstick the imaginary glue that held her there.

"Don't you want to learn to play Gray Duck, Ramona?" Miss Binney asked.

Ramona nodded. "Yes, but I can't."

"Why not?" asked Miss Binney.

"I can't leave my seat," said Ramona. When Miss Binney looked blank, she added, "Because of the present."

"What present?" Miss Binney seemed so genuinely puzzled that Ramona became uneasy. The teacher sat down in the little chair next to Ramona's, and said, "Tell me why you can't play Gray Duck."

Ramona squirmed, worn out with waiting. She had an uneasy feeling that something had gone wrong someplace. "I want to play Gray Duck, but you—" she stopped, feeling that she might be about to say the wrong thing.

"But I what?" asked Miss Binney.

"Well . . . uh . . . you said if I sat here I would get a present," said Ramona at last, "but you didn't say how long I had to sit here."

If Miss Binney had looked puzzled before, she now looked baffled. "Ramona, I don't understand—" she began.

"Yes, you did," said Ramona, nodding. "You told me to sit here for the present, and I have been sitting here ever since school started and you haven't given me a present."

Miss Binney's face turned red and she looked so embarrassed that Ramona felt completely confused. Teachers were not supposed to look that way.

Miss Binney spoke gently. "Ramona, I'm afraid we've had a misunderstanding."

Ramona was blunt. "You mean I don't get a present?"

"I'm afraid not," admitted Miss Binney. "You see 'for the present' means for now. I meant that I wanted you to sit here for now, because later I may have the children sit at different desks."

"Oh." Ramona was so disappointed she had nothing to say. Words were so puzzling. *Present* should mean a present just as *attack* should mean to stick tacks in people.

By now all the children were crowding around the door to see what had happened to their teacher. "I'm so sorry," said Miss Binney. "It's all my fault. I should have used different words."

"That's all right," said Ramona, ashamed to have the class see that she was not going to get a present after all.

"All right, class," said Miss Binney briskly. "Let's go outside and play Gray Duck. You, too, Ramona."

Gray Duck turned out to be an easy game, and Ramona's spirits recovered quickly from her disappointment. The class formed a circle, and the person who was "it" tagged someone who had to chase him around the circle. If "it" was caught before he got back to the empty space in the circle, he had to go into the center of the circle, which was called the mush pot, and the person who caught him became "it."

Ramona tried to stand next to the girl with the springy curls, but instead she found herself beside Howie. "I thought you were going to get a present," gloated Howie.

Ramona merely scowled and made a face at Howie, who was "it," but quickly landed in the mush pot because his new jeans were so stiff they slowed him down. "Look at Howie in the mush pot!" crowed Ramona.

Howie looked as if he were about to cry, which Ramona thought was silly of him. Only a baby would cry in the mush pot. Me, me, somebody tag me, thought Ramona, jumping up and down. She longed for a turn to run around the circle. Susan was jumping up and down, too, and her curls bobbed enticingly.

At last Ramona felt a tap on her shoulder. Her turn had come to run around the circle! She ran as fast as she could to catch up with the sneakers pounding on the asphalt ahead of her. The *boing-boing* curls were on the other side of the circle. Ramona was coming closer to them. She put out her hand. She took hold of a curl, a thick, springy curl—

"*Yow!*" screamed the owner of the curls.

Startled, Ramona let go. She was so surprised by the scream that she forgot to watch Susan's curl spring back.

Susan clutched her curls with one hand and pointed at Ramona with the other. "That girl pulled my hair! That girl pulled my hair! Ow-ow-ow." Ramona felt that Susan did not have to be so touchy. She had not meant to hurt her. She only wanted to touch that beautiful, springy hair that was so different from her own straight brown hair.

"Ow-ow-ow!" shrieked Susan, the center of everyone's attention.

"Baby," said Ramona.

"Ramona," said Miss Binney, "in our kindergarten we do not pull hair."

"Susan doesn't have to be such a baby," said Ramona.

"You may go sit on the bench outside the door while the rest of us play our game," Miss Binney told Ramona.

Ramona did not want to sit on any bench. She wanted to play Gray Duck with the rest of the class. "No," said Ramona, preparing to make a great big noisy fuss. "I won't."

Susan stopped shrieking. A terrible silence fell over the playground. Everyone stared at Ramona in such a way that she almost felt as if she were beginning to shrink. Nothing like this had ever happened to her before.

"Ramona," said Miss Binney quietly. "Go sit on the bench."

Without another word Ramona walked across the playground and sat down on the bench by the door of the kindergarten. The game of Gray Duck continued without her, but the class had not forgotten her. Howie grinned in her direction. Susan continued to look injured. Some laughed and pointed at Ramona. Others, particularly Davy, looked worried, as if they had not known such a terrible punishment could be given in kindergarten.

Ramona swung her feet and pretended to be watching some workmen who were building a new market across the street. In spite of the misunderstanding about the present, she wanted so much to be loved by her pretty new teacher. Tears came into Ramona's eyes, but she would not cry. Nobody was going to call Ramona Quimby a crybaby. Never.

Next door to the kindergarten two little girls, about two and four years old, peered solemnly through the fence at Ramona. "See that girl," said the older girl to her little sister. "She's sitting there because she's been bad." The two-year-old looked awed to be in the presence of such wickedness. Ramona stared at the ground, she felt so ashamed.

When the game ended, the class filed past Ramona into the kindergarten. "You may come in now, Ramona," said Miss Binney pleasantly.

Ramona slid off the bench and followed the others. Even though she was not loved, she was forgiven, and that helped. She hoped that learning to read and write came next.

Inside Miss Binney announced that the time had come to rest. This news was another disappointment to Ramona, who felt that anyone who went to kindergarten was too old to rest. Miss Binney gave each child a mat on which there was a picture that matched the picture on his cupboard door and told him where to spread his mat on the floor. When all twenty-nine children were lying down they did not rest. They popped up to see what others were doing. They wiggled. They whispered. They coughed. They asked, "How much longer do we have to rest?"

"Sh-h," said Miss Binney in a soft, quiet, sleepy voice. "The person who rests most quietly will get to be the wake-up fairy."

"What's the wake-up fairy?" demanded Howie, bobbing up.

"Sh-h," whispered Miss Binney. "The wake-up fairy tiptoes around and wakes up the class with a magic wand. Whoever is the fairy wakes up the quietest resters first."

Ramona made up her mind that she would get to be the wake-up fairy, and then Miss Binney would know she was not so bad after all. She lay flat on her back with her hands tight to her sides. The mat was thin and the floor was hard, but Ramona did not wiggle. She was sure she must be the best rester in the class, because she could hear others squirming around on their mats. Just to show Miss Binney she really and truly was resting she gave one little snore, not a loud snore but a delicate snore, to prove what a good rester she was.

A scatter of giggles rose from the class, followed by several snores, less delicate than Ramona's. They led to more and more, less and less delicate snores until everyone was snoring except the few who did not know how to snore. They were giggling.

Miss Binney clapped her hands and spoke in a voice that was no longer soft, quiet, and sleepy. "All right, boys and girls!" she said. "This is enough! We do not snore or giggle during rest time."

"Ramona started it," said Howie.

Ramona sat up and scowled at Howie. "Tattletale," she said in a voice of scorn. Across Howie she saw that Susan was lying quietly with her beautiful curls spread out on her mat and her eyes screwed tight shut.

"Well, you did," said Howie.

"Children!" Miss Binney's voice was sharp. "We must rest so that we will not be tired when our mothers come to take us home."

"Is your mother coming to take you home?" Howie asked Miss Binney. Ramona had been wondering the same thing.

"That's enough, Howie!" Miss Binney spoke the way mothers sometimes speak just before dinnertime. In a moment she was back to her soft, sleepy voice. "I like the way Susan is resting so quietly," she said. "Susan, you may be the wake-up fairy and tap the boys and girls with this wand to wake them up."

The magic wand turned out to be nothing but an everyday yardstick. Ramona lay quietly, but her efforts were of no use. Susan with her curls bouncing about her shoulders tapped Ramona last. It's not fair, Ramona thought. She was not the worst rester in the class. Howie was much worse.

The rest of the morning went quickly. The class was allowed to explore the paints and the toys, and those who wanted to were allowed to draw with their new crayons. They did not, however, learn to read and write, but Ramona cheered up when Miss Binney explained that anyone who had anything to share with the class could bring it to school the next day for Show and Tell. Ramona was glad when the bell finally rang and she saw her mother waiting for her outside the fence. Mrs. Kemp and Willa Jean were waiting for Howie, too, and the five started home together.

Right away Howie said, "Ramona got benched, and she's the worst rester in the class."

After all that had happened that morning, Ramona found this too much. "Why don't you shut up?" she yelled at Howie just before she hit him.

Mrs. Quimby seized Ramona by the hand and dragged her away from Howie. "Now Ramona," she said, and her voice was firm, "this is no way to behave on your first day of school."

"Poor little girl," said Mrs. Kemp. "She's worn out."

Nothing infuriated Ramona more than having a grownup say, as if she could not hear, that she was worn out. "I'm *not* worn out!" she shrieked.

"She got plenty of rest while she was benched," said Howie.

"Now Howie, you stay out of this," said Mrs. Kemp. Then to change the subject, she asked her son, "How do you like kindergarten?"

"Oh—I guess it's all right," said Howie without enthusiasm. "They don't have any dirt to dig in or tricycles to ride."

"And what about you, Ramona?" asked Mrs. Quimby. "Did you like kindergarten?"

Ramona considered. Kindergarten had not turned out as she had expected. Still, even though she had not been given a present and Miss Binney did not love her, she had liked being with boys and girls her own age. She liked singing the song about the dawnzer and having her own little cupboard. "I didn't like it as much as I thought I would," she answered honestly, "but maybe it will get better when we have Show and Tell."

Gary Paulsen (b. 1939)

Gary Paulsen, a Minnesota writer, is best known for his young adult novels of adventure and survival in natural settings. *Hatchet* (1987) and its sequels show how a boy who has been stranded by a plane crash learns to live alone in a Canadian wilderness. *The Island* (1988) is also typical of the Robinsonnade tradition (stories modeled after Daniel Defoe's classic eighteenth-century novel, *Robinson Crusoe*) in that a young man spends time on an island alone.

But Paulsen revises the tradition, since Wil goes to the island voluntarily after his family moves to a new home nearby and there develops his artistic sensibilities. Paulsen also subverts the conventional morality of earlier Robinsonnades. Defoe's novel served as a vehicle for his Puritan values: the seagoing rebel develops practical skills as a castaway, turns to the Bible, and converts the childlike "savage" he names Friday. In the best-known nineteenth-century Robinsonnade, *The Swiss Family Robinson,* a wise and pious father sets out to colonize the tropics with a family of boys who are improved by his continual teachings and discipline. These roles are reversed in many twentieth-century novels, as Paulsen's portrayal of an inept psychologist shows. Fictional castaways often have visitors who prove to be friends or foes. In *The Island,* the unneeded psychologist sent by Wil's parents contrasts with an earlier visitor, a frank, open-minded reporter. The reporter's comments at the end of their talk sum up the symbolic significance and immense popularity of island adventures: "we all want to find an island and learn all we can about all we are."

From *The Island*

19

One day about four of us were sitting during the lunch hour outside—we bring lunches because the cafeteria food is not believable and what do they put in those "nuggets" anyway?—and we decided to figure out what made a dirty word dirty. We threw a few of them back and forth, the way you do, and said them to each other, but they didn't seem dirty. After a while we decided that no word is dirty if you don't want it to be and the best way to stop it from being bad is to stand alone somewhere and say the dirtiest word you know aloud over and over—maybe for fifteen or twenty minutes. By the time you said a dirty word that many times alone, to yourself, it wouldn't be dirty any longer. It would just be boring. But Frank Kline said he wasn't going to do it because the dirtiest word he knew was actually two words and he wasn't going to stand for twenty minutes saying "greasy salve" over and over. Turns out he had a skin condition when he was a kid, and they kept rubbing this greasy salve on him, and he still thinks it's the dirtiest thing there is. Greasy salve. How could you look at somebody and say, "Oh, go to greasy salve." Dirt is definitely in the eye of the beholder. Or as Frank said, there are dirters and dirtees, and it isn't dirty unless the dirtee says it is.

—Wil Neuton

"Hello." The voice came from the beach just as Wil was thinking about getting up. He had finally dozed just before dawn, and the sun hitting the boat had awakened him. "Anybody home?"

Woman's voice, he thought. *Strange woman. Probably the shrink. That was sure fast.* He thought it would take at least a couple of days for his mom and dad to find a psychiatrist out here in the sticks. *Ahh, well, why not?*

"I'll be right out," he said from beneath the boat, pulling on his pants, "as soon as I get dressed." *I feel like a troll,* he thought, *living under this boat.* He had a mental image of a wiry little man with a peaked cap and a beard living under old boats, wearing old leather clothes. *Some kind of hobbit. A troll.*

He crawled out from under the boat and thought that this was an awkward way to meet a psychiatrist. Crawling at her feet. *No, I'm not crazy, and I live under this boat and crawl around on the beach.* He stood up, brushed the sand off his knees and smiled. "Overslept. I had a late night. I didn't figure you'd come for at least another day."

"You didn't?" She was tall, with brown hair and long arms that were graceful-looking. He couldn't tell age on adults, but maybe thirty or forty or so. Older woman. But she had a nice smile and a tanned face. In back of her, pulled up on the sand, was a sixteen-foot canoe with a paddle across the front seat. The woman was wearing jeans and a T-shirt and a cap that had a picture of a bass jumping on it. She had a shoulder-pack, which she took off and put down on the sand.

"You were expecting me?" She looked puzzled. "How strange. I didn't know myself I was coming until last night. . . ."

"My folks said they were going to get you—or get someone. I just thought it would take more time. I didn't know they could get a doctor on such short notice."

"Doctor?" She laughed. "Not likely. You've got me confused with somebody else. Although I would like to know why you need a doctor—for that mess on your face?" She stepped forward and held out her hand. "My name is Anne Kelliher. I'm kind of a reporter, and I'm here to interview you and find out what this is all about."

"A reporter?"

"Well, sort of. I work for the Pinewood *Caller*—I didn't name the paper. I do advertising selling, writing, editing—most of it. But I also do stories, which appear in a whole series of small northern newspapers, along with the *Caller*. And that's why I'm here. I heard about you and thought you might make a good story."

"Heard what?"

"Nothing detailed. Just about the boy who wouldn't leave the island and then a little about the problem you had with Ray Bunner."

"You know about Ray Bunner?"

"Everybody knows about Ray Bunner. Although I hear he's settled a bit since he came out here. You must have put the fear into him."

"No. I didn't mean to, anyway. It's just something that . . . happened. That's all. Not a big thing."

"Would you mind if we did an interview? And if I took some pictures?" She held up her bag. "There's a camera and tape recorder in here."

Wil thought about it, rubbed the back of his neck. On the one hand he seemed to be getting a lot of people involved in something he was trying to do alone. It started alone, but now there were Susan and his parents and Ray and, of all things, a reporter. "I don't know. . . ."

She smiled, open and genuine. "I won't push it if you don't think it would be right. But maybe if we talk, just talk, and you explain to me what you're doing out here, we can see if it's going to be a story or not. Sometimes things that seem interesting for stories

don't pan out, and sometimes they seem wrong and come out right."

"I know. I tried to do the loon song and it didn't come out right for me, and when I tried to write the song it didn't work. . . ." He stopped. She was watching him with interest, her face slightly puzzled, but not pushing. Perhaps if he talked it over with her, just talked, he could understand more of what was happening with his mind.

"Maybe that would be best. I mean what we have here, on the face of it, is a perfectly normal fifteen-year-old boy who has always been pretty level suddenly going whacko and trying to learn things on an island."

"I don't think you're whacko. Not at all. But let me start my recorder first. Then if we don't like it, I'll leave the tape with you and that's the end of it. On the other hand, if it works out I'll have it. All right?"

He nodded. She turned on the recorder and brought out an omnidirectional mike, and they sat in the sand. "Just let it come," she said. "I might ask a question now and then, but you talk about anything you want."

Again he nodded but was silent. The mike stopped him for a moment. "I can't think how to start. . . ."

"Just begin with the first time you came out here. Start with that and let it come. What brought you to the island?"

Wil frowned, thinking. A fly came in close, and he waved it away. "Well, let's see. I was riding my bike and I came on this lake and there was the boat, an old minnow boat, and I saw the island sitting out there alone, this island, so I got the boat going and took the old oars. . . ."

And he was into it and gone and talking. He couldn't stop. It seemed the more he told her, the more he wanted to tell her and the more he wanted to find out. Things came to him as he talked, things he didn't know he knew; they flowed out of him, flowed out of him as if he were writing or painting or moving to learn. Before he knew what or why, he had taken out the notebook and paintings and showed them to the reporter, showed them all except the paintings of Susan when she'd been swimming, and Anne took pictures of them, pictures of the notebook, of the watercolors. At one point he went to the rock and moved, did the dance of the heron, did his exercises and she took pictures of all of it.

All of it.

When at last he was done, tired, sitting again on the sand and done, he had told her not just about the island but about his life, about what he was, what his parents were, his grandmother. He had told her all that he was, all that he knew, and when he stopped it happened just that way. He stopped. He was talking about Ray Bunner coming out, and he didn't know how that happened, so he stopped.

Anne Kelliher sat across from him, by the dead fire, the recorder still going, her mouth half open. Stunned.

"So . . ." Wil smiled. He was hoarse from talking and run-out in his mind. "So. Am I whacko?"

She said nothing, still staring at him, her forehead wrinkled in a frown. At last she shook her head. Slightly at first, then with more emphasis. "No. No. No. I don't . . . I don't know what to say. This is astounding . . . something. I don't know what has happened to you, but I know you're not crazy. You're doing, you're doing, you're doing something . . . I don't know. I don't know what to say."

"Is there a story there?"

"Story? Is there a story there? Listen, this . . . what's happened to you is special, is wonderful and special. I think it's really something, somehow it's something we all want to do—we all want to find an island and learn all we can about all we are. It's more than a story. You've found something . . . I don't know. But I do know it's a story. The pictures, what you said, the writing, all of it. It might be a great story, and I hope you let me do it."

And he did. Without thinking he told her to go ahead and do it, and she nodded and turned to leave, slid her canoe out. Just as she jumped in, she turned to him. "Listen. Don't worry about the doctor. Just tell him what you told me and you'll be all right."

She was gone, gliding across the bay with smooth strokes of the paddle. He watched her until the canoe silently disappeared around the corner of the island; then he found wood and started a fire. Night was coming and the mosquitoes, and he wanted to write more of what he had learned while talking to her, more on the grandmother piece, and he felt serene and happy.

There was not a single indication of the storm he'd just unleashed.

R. L. Stine (b. 1943)

Robert Lawrence Stine grew up in a suburb of Columbus, Ohio. He had an active imagination from a young age; his writing career began at age nine, when he typed stories and jokes that were modeled on comic books and distributed them at school. He graduated with a B.A. in education from The Ohio State University in 1965 and then moved to New York. Stine has written under the pseudonyms Eric Affabee, Zachary Blue, and Jovial Bob Stine. His books have been enormously popular with children and young adults, but have been received with disdain or skepticism by many, yet not all, adult critics. Promotional materials often note the presence of "age-appropriate chills" in Stine's thrillers. Gross and scary things happen, but no one ever dies in Goosebumps novels for grade-schoolers. However, more graphic horror prevails in the Fear Street series for teenagers. A significant part of the appeal of the extensive Goosebumps series, which was collected avidly by children in the 1990s, is the sense of community it tends to create among its readers, who swap notes on stories they have read or compete to see who has acquired and read the most (and the scariest). Number 12 in the series, *Be Careful What You Wish For . . .*, was published in 1993. Stine's writing represents the opposite of the moralistic, didactic tradition endorsed by early children's literature critics, such as Sarah Trimmer; his stories are full of fantasy, chaos, and unpredictable, amoral frightfulness.

From *Be Careful What You Wish For . . .*

1

Judith Bellwood deliberately tripped me in math class.

I saw her white sneaker shoot out into the aisle. Too late.

I was carrying my notebook up to the chalkboard to put a problem on the board. My eyes were on the scrawls in my notebook. I'm not the neatest writer in the world.

And before I could stop, I saw the white sneaker shoot out. I tripped over it and went sprawling to the floor, landing hard on my elbows and knees. Of course all the papers flew out of my notebook and scattered everywhere.

And the whole class thought it was a riot. Everyone was laughing and cheering as I struggled to pull myself up. Judith and her pal, Anna Frost, laughed hardest of all.

I landed on my funny bone, and the pain vibrated up and down my whole body. As I climbed to my feet and then bent to pick up my notebook papers, I knew my face was as red as a tomato.

"Nice move, Sam!" Anna called, a big grin on her face.

"Instant replay!" someone else shouted.

I glanced up to see a triumphant glow in Judith's green eyes.

I'm the tallest girl in my seventh-grade class. No. Correct that. I'm the tallest *kid* in my seventh-grade class. I'm at least two inches taller than my friend, Cory Blinn, and he's the tallest guy.

I'm also the biggest klutz who ever stumbled over the face of the earth. I mean, just because I'm tall and slender doesn't mean I have to be graceful. And believe me, I'm not.

But why is it such a riot when I stumble over a wastebasket or drop my tray in the lunchroom or trip over someone's foot in math class?

Judith and Anna are just cruel, that's all.

I know they both call me "Stork" behind my back. Cory told me they do.

And Judith is always making fun of my name, which is Byrd. Samantha Byrd. *"Why don't you fly away, Byrd!"* That's what she's always saying to me.

Then she and Anna laugh as if that's the funniest joke they've ever heard.

"Why don't you fly away, Byrd!"

Ha-ha. Big joke.

Cory says that Judith is just jealous of me. But that's stupid. I mean, why should Judith be jealous? She's not nine feet tall. She's about five-two, perfect for a twelve-year-old. She's graceful. She's athletic. And she's really pretty, with pale, creamy skin, big green eyes, and wavy, copper-colored hair down to her shoulders.

So what's to be jealous about?

I think Cory is just trying to make me feel better—and doing a *lousy* job of it.

Anyway, I gathered all my papers together and shoved them back into the notebook. Sharon asked if I was okay. (Sharon is my teacher. We call all the teachers by their first names here at Montrose Middle School.)

I muttered that I was fine, even though my elbow was throbbing like crazy. And I copied the problem onto the board.

The chalk squeaked, and everyone groaned and complained. I can't help it. I've never been able to write on the board without squeaking the chalk.

It isn't *such* a big deal—*is* it?

I heard Judith whisper some crack about me to Anna, but I couldn't hear what it was. I glanced up from the problem to see the two of them snickering and smirking at me.

And wouldn't you know it—I couldn't solve the problem. I had something wrong with the equation, and I couldn't figure out what.

Sharon stepped up behind me, her skinny arms crossed over her ugly chartreuse sweater. She moved her lips as she read what I had written, trying to see where I had gone wrong.

And of course Judith raised her hand and called out, "I see the problem, Sharon. Byrd can't add. Four and two is six, not five."

I could feel myself blushing again.

Where would I be without Judith to point out my mistakes to the whole class?

Everyone was laughing again. Even Sharon thought it was funny.

And I had to stand there and take it. Good old Samantha, the class klutz. The class idiot.

My hand was shaking as I erased my stupid mistake and wrote in the right numbers.

I was *so angry*. At Judith. And at myself.

But I kept it together as I walked—carefully—back to my seat. I didn't even glance at Judith as I walked past her.

I kept it together until Home Ec. class that afternoon.

Then it got ugly.

2

Daphne is our teacher in Home Ec. I like Daphne. She is a big, jolly woman with several chins and a great sense of humor.

The rumor is that Daphne always makes us bake cakes and pies and brownies so that she can eat them all after we leave the class.

That's kind of mean, I think. But it's probably a little bit true.

We have Home Ec. right after lunch, so we're never very hungry. Most of what we make wouldn't make good *dog food*, anyway. So it mostly gets left in the Home Ec. room.

I always look forward to the class. Partly because Daphne is a fun teacher. And partly because it's the one class where there's no homework.

The only bad thing about Home Ec. class is that Judith is in it, too.

Judith and I had a little run-in in the lunchroom. I sat down at the far end of the table, as far away from her as I could get. But I still heard her telling a couple of eighth-graders, "Byrd tried to fly in math class."

Everyone laughed and stared at me.

"You tripped me, Judith!" I shouted angrily. My mouth was full of egg salad, which dribbled down my chin when I shouted.

And everyone laughed at me again.

Judith said something, which I couldn't hear over all the noise in the lunchroom. She smirked at me and tossed her red hair behind her shoulders.

I started to get up and go over to her. I don't know *what* I was thinking of doing. But I was so angry, I wasn't thinking too clearly.

Luckily, Cory appeared across the table. He dropped his lunch down on the table, turned the chair around backwards the way he always does, and sat down.

"What's four plus two?" he teased.

"Forty-two," I replied, rolling my eyes. "Do you *believe* Judith?" I asked bitterly.

"Of course I believe Judith," he said, pulling open his brown lunchbag. "Judith is Judith."

"What's that supposed to mean?" I snapped.

He shrugged. A grin broke out across his face. "I don't know."

Cory is kind of cute. He has dark brown eyes that sort of crinkle up in the corners, a nose that's a little too long, and a funny, crooked smile.

He has great hair, but he never brushes it. So he never takes off his cap. It's an Orlando Magic cap, even though he doesn't know or care about the team. He just likes the cap.

He peeked into his lunchbag and made a face.

"Again?" I asked, wiping egg salad off the front of my T-shirt with a napkin.

"Yeah. Again," he replied glumly. He pulled out the same lunch his father packed for him every single morning. A grilled cheese sandwich and an orange. "Yuck!"

"Why does your dad give you grilled cheese every day?" I asked. "Didn't you tell him it gets cold and slimy by lunchtime?"

"I told him," Cory groaned, picking up one half of the sandwich in one hand and examining it as if it were some sort of science lab specimen. "He said it's good protein."

"How can it be good protein if you throw it in the trash every day?" I asked.

Cory grinned his crooked grin. "I didn't tell him that I throw it in the trash every day." He shoved the rubbery sandwich back into the bag and started to peel the orange.

"It's a good thing you came by," I said, swallowing the last bite of my egg salad sandwich. "I was about to get up and go murder Judith over there."

We both glanced down the table. Judith and the two eighth-graders had their chairs tilted back and were laughing about something. One of the eighth-graders had a magazine, *People* magazine, I think, and she was showing a picture in it to the others.

"Don't murder Judith," Cory advised, still peeling the orange. "You'll get into trouble."

I laughed, scornful laughter. "You kidding? I'd get an award."

"If you murder Judith, your basketball team will never win another game," Cory said, concentrating on the orange.

"Ooh, that's cruel!" I exclaimed. I tossed my balled-up aluminum foil at him. It bounced off his chest and dropped to the floor.

He was right, of course. Judith was the best player on our team, the Montrose Mustangs. She was the *only* good player. She could dribble really well without getting the ball tangled up in her legs. And she had a great shooting eye.

I, of course, was the *worst* player on the team.

I admit it. I'm a total klutz, as I've said, which doesn't get you very far on the basketball court.

I really hadn't wanted to be on the Mustangs. I knew I'd stink.

But Ellen insisted. Ellen is the girls' basketball coach. Ellen insisted I be on the team.

"Sam, you're so tall!" she told me. "You've *got* to play basketball. You're a natural!"

Sure, I'm a natural. A natural klutz.

I can't shoot at all, not even foul shots. *Especially* not foul shots.

And I can't run without tripping over my own Reeboks. And my hands are small, even though the rest of me isn't, so I'm not too good at passing or catching the ball.

I think Ellen has learned her lesson: *Tall ain't all.*

But now she's too embarrassed to take me off the team. And I keep at it. I work hard at practice. I mean, I keep thinking I'll get better. I couldn't get any worse.

If only Judith wasn't such a hotshot.

And if only she was nicer to me.

But, as Cory put it, "Judith is Judith." She's always yelling at me during practice, and making fun of me, and making me feel two feet tall (which I sometimes wish I were)!

"Byrd, why don't you give us a break and fly away!"

If she says that one more time, I'll punch out her lights. I really will.

"What are you thinking about, Sam?" Cory's voice broke into my bitter thoughts.

"About Judith, of course," I muttered. "Miss Perfect."

"Hey, stop," he said, pulling apart the orange sections. "You have good qualities, too, you know."

"Oh, really?" I snapped. "What are my good qualities? That I'm tall?"

"No." He finally popped an orange section into his mouth. I never saw anyone take so long to eat an orange! "You're also smart," he said. "And you're funny."

"Thanks a bunch," I replied, frowning.

"And you're very generous," he added. "You're so generous, you're going to give me that bag of potato chips, right?" He pounced on it before I could grab it away from him.

I knew there was a reason for his compliments.

I watched Cory stuff down my potato chips. He didn't even offer me one.

Then the bell rang, and I hurried to Home Ec.

Where I totally lost it.

What happened was this: We were making tapioca pudding. And it was really messy.

We all had big orange mixing bowls, and the ingredients were spread out on the long table next to the stove.

I was busily stirring mine. It was nice and gloppy, and it made this great *glop glop* sound as I stirred it with a long wooden spoon.

My hands were sticky for some reason. I had probably spilled some of the pudding on them. So I stopped to wipe them on my apron.

I was being pretty neat—for me. There were only a few yellow puddles of pudding on my table. Most of it was actually in the mixing bowl.

I finished stirring and, when I looked up, there was Judith.

I was a little surprised because she had been working on the other side of the room by the windows. We generally keep as far apart from each other as possible.

Judith had this odd smile on her face. And as she approached me, she pretended to trip.

I *swear* she only pretended to trip!

And she spilled her whole mixing bowl of tapioca onto my shoes.

My brand-new blue Doc Martens.

"Oops!" she said.

That's all. Just "Oops."

I looked down at my brand-new shoes covered in gloppy yellow pudding.

And that's when I lost it.

I uttered an angry roar and went for Judith's throat.

I didn't plan it or anything. I think it was temporary insanity.

I just reached out both hands and grabbed Judith by the throat, and began to strangle her.

I mean, they were *brand-new shoes!*

Judith started struggling and tried to scream. She pulled my hair and tried to scratch me.

But I held onto her throat and roared some more, like an angry tiger.

And Daphne had to pull us apart.

She pulled me away by the shoulders, then thrust her wide body between us, blocking our view of each other.

I was panting loudly. My chest was heaving up and down.

"Samantha! Samantha! What were you *doing?*" I *think* that's what Daphne was screaming.

I couldn't really hear her. I had this roaring in my ears, loud as a waterfall. I think it was just my anger.

Before I knew it, I had pushed myself away from the table and was running out of the room. I ran out into the empty hall—and stopped.

I didn't know what to do next. I was *so* angry.

If I had three wishes, I told myself, I know what they would be: Destroy Judith! Destroy Judith! Destroy Judith!

Little did I know that I would soon get my wish.

All three of them.

3

Daphne made Judith and me shake hands and apologize to each other after she dragged me back into the classroom. I had to do it. It was either that or be tossed out of school.

"It really was an accident," Judith muttered under her breath. "What's your problem, Byrd?"

Not much of an apology, if you ask me.

But I shook hands with her. I didn't need my parents being called to school because their daughter had tried to strangle a classmate.

And I showed up—reluctantly—for basketball practice after school. I knew if I didn't show, Judith would tell everyone that she had scared me away.

I showed up because I knew Judith didn't want me to. Which I think is as good a reason as any.

Also, I needed the exercise. I needed to run back

and forth across the court a few hundred times to get the anger out. I needed to sweat out the frustration from not being able to finish strangling Judith.

"Let's do some fast laps," Ellen suggested.

Some of the other girls groaned, but I didn't. I started running before Ellen even blew her whistle.

We were all in shorts and sleeveless T-shirts. Ellen wore gray sweats that were baggy in all the wrong places. She had frizzy red hair, and she was so straight and skinny, she looked sort of like a kitchen match.

Ellen wasn't very athletic. She told us she coached girls' basketball because they paid her extra, and she needed the money.

After running our laps around the gym, practice went pretty much as usual.

Judith and Anna passed the ball to each other a lot. And they both took a lot of shots—jump shots, lay-ups, even hook shots.

The others tried to keep up with them.

I tried not to be noticed.

I was still simmering about the tapioca pudding disaster and wanted as little contact with Judith—or *any-one*—as possible. I mean, I was really feeling glum.

And watching Judith sink a twenty-foot jumper, catch her own rebound, and scoop a perfect two-handed shovel pass to Anna wasn't helping to cheer me up one bit.

Of course, things got worse.

Anna actually passed the ball to me. I muffed it. It bounced off my hands, hit me in the forehead, and rolled away.

"Heads up, Byrd!" I heard Ellen cry.

I kept running. I tried not to look upset that I had blown my first opportunity of the practice.

A few minutes later, I saw the ball flying toward me again, and I heard Judith shout, "Get this one, Stork!"

I was so startled that she had called me "Stork" to my face that I *caught* the ball. I started to dribble to the basket—and Anna reached a hand in and easily stole the ball. She spun around and sent an arching shot to the basket, which nearly went in.

"Nice steal, Anna!" Ellen cried.

Breathing hard, I turned angrily to Judith. "What did you call me?"

Judith pretended she didn't hear me.

Ellen blew the whistle. "Fast breaks!" she shouted.

We practiced fast breaks three at a time. Dribbling fast, we'd pass the ball back and forth. Then the one under the hoop with the ball was supposed to take the shot.

I need to practice *slow* breaks! I thought to myself.

I had no trouble keeping up with the others. I mean, I had the longest legs, after all. I could run fast enough. I just couldn't do anything else while I was running.

As Judith, Anna, and I came roaring down the court, I prayed I wouldn't make a total fool of myself. Sweat poured down my forehead. My heart was racing.

I took a short pass from Anna, dribbled under the basket, and took a shot. The ball flew straight up in the air, then bounced back to the floor. It didn't even come close to the backboard.

I could hear girls laughing on the sidelines. Judith and Anna had their usual superior smirks on their faces. "Good eye!" Judith called, and everyone laughed some more.

After twenty minutes of fast-break torture, Ellen blew her whistle. "Scrimmage," she called out. That was the signal for us to divide into two teams and play each other.

I sighed, wiping perspiration off my forehead with the back of my hand. I tried to get into the game. I concentrated hard, mainly on not messing up. But I was pretty discouraged.

Then, a few minutes into the game, Judith and I both dove for the ball at the same time.

Somehow, as I dove, my arms outstretched, Judith's knee came up hard—and plunged like a knife into my chest.

The pain shot through my entire body.

I tried to cry out. But I couldn't make a sound.

I uttered a weird, gasping noise, sort of like the honk of a sick seal—and realized I couldn't breathe.

Everything turned red. Bright, shimmering red.

Then black.

I knew I was going to die.

4

Having your breath knocked out has to be the worst feeling in the world. It's just so scary. You try to breathe, and you can't. And the pain just keeps swelling, like a balloon being blown up right inside your chest.

I really thought I was dead meat.

Of course I was perfectly okay a few minutes later. I still felt a little shaky, a little dizzy. But I was basically okay.

Ellen insisted that one of the girls walk me to the locker room. Naturally, Judith volunteered. As we walked, she apologized. She said it had been an accident. Totally an accident.

I didn't say anything. I didn't want her to apologize. I didn't want to talk to her at all. I just wanted to strangle her again.

This time for good.

I mean, how much can one girl take in a day? Judith had tripped me in math class, dumped her disgusting tapioca pudding all over my new Doc Martens in Home Ec., and kicked me unconscious in basketball practice.

Did I really have to smile and accept her apology now?

No way! No way in a million years.

I trudged silently to the locker room, my head bent, my eyes on the floor.

When she saw that I wasn't going to buy her cheap apology, Judith got angry. *Do you believe that?* She shoves her knee through my chest—then *she* gets angry!

"Why don't you just fly away, Byrd!" she muttered. Then she went trotting back to the gym floor.

I got changed without showering. Then I collected my stuff, and slunk out of the building, and got my bike.

That's really the last straw, I thought, walking my bike across the parking lot in back of school.

It was about half an hour later. The late afternoon sky was gray and overcast. I felt a few light drops of rain on my head.

The last straw, I repeated to myself.

I live two blocks from the school, but I didn't feel like going home. I felt like riding and riding and riding. I felt like just going straight and never turning back.

I was angry and upset and shaky. But mainly angry.

Ignoring the raindrops, I climbed onto my bike and began pedaling in the direction away from my house. Front yards and houses went by in a whir. I didn't see them. I didn't see anything.

I pedaled harder and harder. It felt so good to get away from school. To get away from Judith.

The rain started to come down a little harder. I didn't mind. I raised my face to the sky as I pedaled. The raindrops felt cold and refreshing on my hot skin.

When I looked down, I saw that I had reached Jeffers' Woods, a long stretch of trees that divides my neighborhood from the next.

A narrow bike path twisted through the tall, old trees, which were winter bare and looked sort of sad and lonely without their leaves. Sometimes I took the path, seeing how fast I could ride over its curves and bumps.

But the sky was darkening, the black clouds hovering lower. And I saw a glimmering streak of lightning in the sky over the trees.

I decided I'd better turn around and ride home.

But as I turned, someone stepped in front of me.

A woman!

I gasped, startled to see someone on this empty road by the woods.

I squinted at her as the rain began to fall harder, pattering on the pavement around me. She wasn't young, and she wasn't old. She had dark eyes, like two black coals, on a pale, white face. Her thick, black hair flowed loosely behind her.

Her clothing was sort of old-fashioned. She had a bright red, heavy woolen shawl pulled around her shoulders. She wore a long black skirt down to her ankles.

Her dark eyes seemed to light up as she met my stare.

She looked confused.

I should have run.

I should have pedaled away from her as fast as I could.

If only I had known . . .

But I didn't flee. I didn't escape.

Instead, I smiled at her. "Can I help you?" I asked.

5

The woman's eyes narrowed. I could see she was checking me out.

I lowered my feet to the ground, balancing the bike between my legs. The rain pattered on the pavement, big cold drops.

I suddenly remembered I had a hood on my windbreaker. So I reached up behind my head and slipped it over my hair.

The sky darkened to an eerie olive color. The bare trees in the woods shivered in a swirling breeze.

The woman took a few steps closer. She was so pale, I thought. Almost ghostlike, except for the deep, dark eyes that were staring so hard at me.

"I—I seem to have lost my way," she said. To my surprise, she had an old woman's voice, sort of shaky and frail.

I squinted at her from under my hood. The rain was matting her thick, black hair to her head. It was impossible to tell how old she was. She could have been twenty or sixty!

"This is Montrose Avenue," I told her, speaking loudly because of the drumming of the raindrops. "Actually, Montrose ends here. At the woods."

She nodded thoughtfully, pursing her pale lips. "I am trying to get to Madison," she said. " I think I have completely lost my direction."

"You're pretty far from Madison," I said. "It's way over there." I pointed.

She chewed at her lower lip. "I'm usually pretty good at directions," she said fretfully in her shaky voice. She adjusted the heavy red shawl over her slender shoulders.

"Madison is way over on the east side," I said with a shiver. The rain was cold. I was eager to go home and get into some dry clothes.

"Can you take me there?" the woman asked. She grabbed my wrist.

I almost gasped out loud. Her hand was as cold as ice!

"Can you take me there?" she repeated, bringing her face close to mine. "I would be ever so grateful."

She had taken her hand away. But I could still feel the icy grip on my wrist.

Why didn't I run away?

Why didn't I raise my feet to the pedals and ride out of there as fast as I could?

"Sure. I'll show you where it is," I said.

"Thank you, dear." She smiled. She had a dimple in one cheek when she smiled. I realized she was kind of pretty, in an old-fashioned way.

I climbed off my bike and, holding onto the handlebars, began to walk it. The woman stepped beside me, adjusting her shawl. She walked in the middle of the street, her eyes trained on me.

The rain continued to come down. I saw another jagged bolt of lightning far away in the olive sky. The swirling wind made my windbreaker flap against my legs.

"Am I going too fast?" I asked.

"No, dear. I can keep up," she replied with a smile. She had a small purple bag slung over her shoulder. She protected the bag by tucking it under her arm.

She wore black boots under the long skirt. The boots, I saw, had tiny buttons running up the sides. The boots clicked on the wet pavement as we walked.

"I am sorry to be so much trouble," the woman said, again pursing her lips fretfully.

"No trouble," I replied. My good deed for the day, I thought, brushing a drop of rain off my nose.

"I love the rain," she said, raising her hands to it, letting the raindrops splash her open palms. "Without the rain, what would wash the evil away?"

That's a weird thing to say, I thought. I muttered a reply. I wondered what evil she was talking about.

Her long, black hair was completely soaked, but she didn't seem to mind. She walked quickly with long, steady strides, swinging one hand as she walked, protecting the purple bag under the other arm.

A few blocks later, the handlebars slipped out of my hands. My bike toppled over, and the pedal scraped my knee as I tried to grab the bike before it fell.

What a klutz!

I pulled the bike up and began walking it again. My knee throbbed. I shivered. The wind blew the rain into my face.

What am I doing out here? I asked myself.

The woman kept walking quickly, a thoughtful expression on her face. "It's quite a rain," she said, gazing up at the dark clouds. "This is so nice of you, dear."

"It isn't too far out of my way," I said politely. *Just eight or ten blocks!*

"I don't know how I could have gone so far astray," she said, shaking her head. "I was sure I was headed in the right direction. Then when I came to those woods . . ."

"We're almost there," I said.

"What is your name?" she asked suddenly.

"Samantha," I told her. "But everyone calls me Sam."

"My name is Clarissa," she offered. "I'm the Crystal Woman."

I wasn't sure I'd heard that last part correctly. I puzzled over it, then let it slip from my mind.

It was late, I realized. Mom and Dad might already be home from work. Even if they weren't, my brother, Ron, was probably home, wondering where I was.

A station wagon rolled toward us, its headlights on. I shielded my eyes from the bright lights and nearly dropped my bike again.

The woman was still walking in the center of the street. I moved toward the curb so she could move out of the station wagon's path. But she didn't seem to care about it. She kept walking straight, her expression not changing, even though the bright headlights were in her face.

"Look out!" I cried.

I don't know if she heard me.

The station wagon swerved to avoid her and honked its horn as it rolled by.

She smiled warmly at me as we kept walking. "So good of you to care about a total stranger," she said.

The streetlights flashed on suddenly. They made the wet street glow. The bushes and hedges, the grass, the sidewalks—everything seemed to glow. It all looked unreal.

"Here we are. This is Madison," I said, pointing to the street sign. *Finally!* I thought.

I just wanted to say good-bye to this strange woman and pedal home as fast as I could.

Lightning flickered. Closer this time.

What a dreary day, I thought with a sigh.

Then I remembered Judith.

The whole miserable day suddenly rolled through my mind again. I felt a wave of anger sweep over me.

"Which way is east?" the woman asked, her shaky voice breaking into my bitter thoughts.

"East?" I gazed both ways on Madison, trying to clear Judith from my mind. I pointed.

The wind picked up suddenly, blowing a sheet of rain against me. I tightened my grip on the handlebars.

"You are so kind," the woman said, wrapping the shawl around her. Her dark eyes stared hard into mine. "So kind. Most young people aren't kind like you."

"Thank you," I replied awkwardly. The cold made me shiver again. "Well . . . good-bye." I started to climb onto my bike.

"No. Wait," she pleaded. "I want to repay you."

"Huh?" I uttered. "No. Really. You don't have to."

"I want to repay you," the woman insisted. She grabbed my wrist again. And again I felt a shock of cold.

"You've been so kind," the woman repeated. "So kind to a total stranger."

I tried to free my wrist, but her grip was surprisingly tight. "You don't have to thank me," I said.

"I want to repay you," she replied, bringing her face close to mine, still holding onto my wrist. "Tell you what. I'll grant you three wishes."

6

She's crazy, I realized.

I stared into those coal black eyes. Rainwater trickled from her hair, down the sides of her pale face. I could feel the coldness of her hand, even through the sleeve of my windbreaker.

The woman is *crazy,* I thought.

I've been walking through the pouring rain for twenty minutes with a crazy person.

"Three wishes," the woman repeated, lowering her voice as if not wanting to be overheard by anyone.

"No. Thanks. I've really got to get home," I said. I tugged my wrist from her grasp and turned to my bike.

"I'll grant you three wishes," the woman repeated. "Anything you wish shall come true." She moved the purple bag in front of her and carefully pulled something from it. It was a glass ball, bright red, the size of a large grapefruit. It sparkled despite the darkness around us.

"That's nice of you," I said, wiping water off the bike seat with my hand. "But I don't really have any wishes right now."

"Please—let me repay you for your kindness," the woman insisted. She raised the gleaming red ball in one hand. Her hand was small and as pale as her face, the fingers bony. "I really do want to repay you."

"My—uh—mom will be worried," I said, glancing up and down the street.

No one in sight.

No one to protect me from this lunatic if she turned dangerous.

Just how crazy was she? I wondered. Could she be dangerous? Was I making her angry by not playing along, by not making a wish?

"It isn't a joke," the woman said, reading the doubt in my eyes. "Your wishes will come true. I promise you." She narrowed her gaze. The red ball suddenly glowed brighter. "Make your first wish, Samantha."

I stared back at her, thinking hard. I was cold and wet and hungry—and a little frightened. I just wanted to get home and get dry.

What if she won't let me go?

What if I can't get rid of her? What if she follows me home?

Again, I searched up and down the block. Most of the houses had lights on. I could probably run to the nearest one and get help if I needed it.

But, I decided, it might be easier just to play along with the crazy woman and make a wish.

Maybe that would satisfy her, and she'd go on her way and let me go home.

"What is your wish, Samantha?" she demanded. Her black eyes glowed red, the same color as the gleaming ball in her hand.

She suddenly looked very old. Ancient. Her skin was so pale and tight, I thought I could see her skull underneath.

I froze.

I couldn't think of a wish.

And then I blurted out, "My wish is . . . to be the strongest player on my basketball team!"

I don't know why I said that. I guess I was just nervous. And I had Judith on my mind and all that had happened that day, ending up with the *disaster* at basketball practice.

And so that was my wish. Of course I immediately felt like a total jerk. I mean, of all the things to wish for in the world, why would anyone pick that?

But the woman didn't seem at all surprised.

She nodded, closing her eyes for a moment. The red ball glowed brighter, brighter, until the fiery red radiated around me. Then it quickly faded.

Clarissa thanked me again, turned, tucked the glass ball back in the purple bag, and began walking quickly away.

I breathed a sigh of relief. I was so glad she was gone!

I jumped on my bike, turned it around, and began pedaling furiously toward home.

A perfect end to a perfect day, I thought bitterly.

Trapped in the rain with a crazy woman.

And the wish?

I knew it was totally stupid.

I knew I'd never have to think about it again.

Floyd Cooper (b. 1956)

Floyd Cooper, a native of Tulsa, studied fine art the University of Oklahoma and worked as a commercial artist before beginning his career as a book illustrator in Manhattan in 1988. He has illustrated books for children by a wide variety of writers, including many books based on the daily lives and history of Africans and African Americans. His oil wash-on-board technique, using erasers to remove paint from an illustration board in a "subtractive process," produces a soft texture and warm glow in his paintings, which often focus eloquently on the expressive faces and active bodies of people he depicts. *Coming Home: From the Life of Langston Hughes* (1994) was the first book that Cooper wrote himself. Later he wrote and illustrated *Mandela: From the Life of the South African Statesman* (1996) and *Jump! The Life of Michael Jordan* (2004). *Coming Home* is one of innumerable books from the late twentieth century that teach children about history, biography, and other nonfiction subjects through appealing texts and illustrations, with a focus on the child's point of view. Cooper depicts the early life of the great poet Langston Hughes. The accomplishments of his ancestors of different races form a historical backdrop for Hughes's own varied personal and cultural experiences in early twentieth-century America and Mexico. Although Hughes was sometimes lonely and was uprooted from different homes in childhood, Cooper develops a theme that is consistent with the belief in hope and dreams found in Hughes's poems, as the story builds toward the idea that Hughes could form his own concept of home within himself. In an "Author's Note," Cooper writes, "I have always thought of Langston Hughes as a beacon for all dreamers. For me, dreams spawn hope, and from hope springs life . . . he left his stories and poems living on as an example to all."

Coming Home

From the Life of Langston Hughes

HOPE

Sometimes when I'm lonely,
Don't know why,
Keep thinkin' I won't be lonely,
By and by.

Langston Hughes

James Langston Hughes was a dreamer, there in Lawrence, Kansas, where he lived alone with his Granma Mary Langston. Langston was a dreamer in the fields behind the two-room house he shared with her. Or on the porch.

His grandma didn't much like him playing with the neighborhood kids, so he'd hear kids playing ball or riding bikes, but he'd stay put.

Mostly in his early years, James Langston Hughes was alone.

Unless the distant faint familiar sound of a freight train pressed against his ears. Then Langston would bolt off the porch, hit the ground running, chickens aflutter. Quick! past the woodshed. Swoop! around the pump for drawing water.

He'd hurry across the vacant lot and through the wheat field. He'd run and run until between breaths, he could see the big freighter pulling its load around the curve of tracks, whistle blowing sweet, as it screeched and clanked: clackedy, clackedy, clackedy. The old rusty cars talking, talking.

The old iron snake'd tell him its stories about the places it'd been. Langston would talk back. Dream back. He'd dream of riding the train to Mexico where his pa, James Nathaniel Hughes, went to live after they wouldn't let him be a lawyer in Oklahoma because he was a black man. He'd dream of riding to where his ma, Carrie Hughes, was trying to be an actress on stage. He loved going to the theater with her those times he'd had the chance to be with her.

Mostly, he dreamed of the three of them together, of having a home with his ma and pa. A home he would never have to leave.

But each time the train would trail off, getting quieter and quieter, and quieter still, engine smoke barely clinging to the blue sky before it disappeared; Langston's dreams disappeared, too.

Living with Granma wasn't easy. She was poor. Dinner was often dandelion greens and whatever the neighbors passed over the backyard fence. Sometimes the neighbors passed clothes, too, their used dresses, worn shirts, and old shoes.

Once Langston had to wear a woman's shoes, because his grandma couldn't buy him new ones.

But Granma believed a boy needed heroes, and one day she took Langston all the way to Topeka to hear Booker T. Washington speak. Booker T. Washington in person!

And she would read to young Langston—and storytell. Sometimes she'd read from the Bible. Other times it would be a beautiful tale from the Brothers Grimm.

Almost always, his grandma told stories of heroes. Heroes who were black, just like Langston.

His grandma's first husband, Lewis Sheridan Leary, had ridden with John Brown and was killed in the struggle to free slaves. She still wore his torn, bullet-riddled shawl.

Even on warm summer evenings she'd pull the shawl over Langston and tell him stories of her first husband, and of two uncles who were Buffalo soldiers, named that by the Indians because of their curly hair, and called the "bravest of the brave." And about Langston's uncle, John Mercer Langston, the first black American to hold office. He was a lawyer and later elected to Congress.

His grandma herself had worked on the Underground Railroad, helping slaves flee north to freedom, and she told him those stories.

Langston would hear these stories over and over. Wrapped in the torn shawl—and wrapped in family stories of pride and glory—he'd listen and dream.

Sometimes Langston's dreams about having a family came true. Like the time he, his ma, and grandma really did go to Mexico to see his father. Maybe, finally, Langston would have a home of his own.

But on April 14, 1907, the ground in Mexico began to tremble. Everything shook, including the building they were in. Langston's pa, carrying Langston, led everyone out into the street.

Everywhere walls of buildings cracked and split open. Giant tarantula spiders scurried out of the cracks. That was enough for his mama. As soon as the trains were running again, she and his grandma and Langston climbed back on the train and rode back to Kansas. Langston whispered a goodbye to Mexico, his father, and to having a home of his own.

Sometimes Langston's ma would send for him. He'd ride the train to the Kansas City Bottoms where she'd meet him and off they'd go. They'd see plays, the opera, and visit the library, where Langston was fascinated by the big, bright, silent reading room, the long smooth tables, and librarians who would so kindly get books for him.

Sometimes, when she was busy, his mother would leave him at his uncle Des's barbershop. He liked it there, right in the center of the black district. He'd go and wander the nearby streets. Speak to folks passing by. A nod here. A hat-tip there.

But mostly Langston would listen.

He'd ride his ears around the city. Through Market Street where everyone sang the song of haggle. Down side streets filled with kids who ran and played forever. Up the block where clubs and dance halls played jazzy old blues music that drifted down the alleys and tickled his soul. Langston felt the rhythms.

Other times Langston's ma would come to Lawrence. Once it wasn't the best of times for her. Money was scarce. She snapped at Langston and it hurt.

Later that evening they went to St. Luke's Church where Langston's ma was giving a performance. She told him that she had a wonderful surprise for him. That he was going to be on the stage with her. That he was going to be a star, just like she was going to be.

Langston didn't like the surprise. That evening he was the one with the surprise. As his ma introduced him, behind her back Langston made faces: He crossed his eyes, stretched his mouth, and imitated her. Everyone burst out laughing. The more people laughed, the more faces he made.

Embarrassed, his mother rushed off stage.

As Langston's grandma got on in years, she grew more and more silent. Then the time came when she hardly spoke at all. The little home where he had lived so long was quiet and lonely, with Granma rocking silent in her rocking chair.

A real home seemed less than ever like something Langston would ever have.

Then he went to live with friends of the family across town, Auntie and Uncle Reed, he called them.

When Langston first saw the dinner table at the Reeds' he had never seen so much food in his life. After the blessing, Uncle Reed smiled and told Langston to eat up. He didn't have to tell Langston twice. Then Auntie, in a voice as sweet as dessert, said there was more out in the kitchen.

Langston soon learned that there would always be "more" from Auntie and Uncle Reed. More food, and more hugs and love.

On Sundays Auntie Reed would take Langston to church. He'd never gone before. Auntie Reed's church was all right, but in time Langston preferred the Baptist church down the street. The singing and preaching felt so familiar—like the rhythms of the streets in Kansas City. The words seemed to roll out of the preacher's mouth like jazzy old blues.

He had trouble understanding what everyone was feeling when they felt God, but he liked being there.

It grew clearer to Langston in those days what home really was. Life with his grandma had never been exactly like home. Life with his ma and pa never had been home, as much as he wanted it to be. Life with his Auntie and Uncle Reed felt like home, it smelled like home and looked like home. And home was all of the things the Reeds' home was.

But home was something more for him.

For him, home was a blues song sung in the pale evening night on a Kansas City street corner. Home was the theater where his ma performed, the library where he sat quiet, reading the books he loved. Home was the church, alive with music, where everybody was "brother" and "sister."

By now, Langston had grown popular at school, was thought of as "smart," and chosen class poet. He had begun writing poetry and sharing it. One of his first poems was "When Sue Wears Red," about a girl he admired in school. And then he wrote "Just Because I Loves You" and "The Negro Speaks of Rivers."

Now after school, he'd run and play with friends. Sometimes afterward they'd gather around Langston on the Reeds' front porch. There in the dark shadows of a summer night, Langston would tell stories.

Of the time he stood ten feet from Booker T. Washington, of his two uncles who were Buffalo soldiers, the "bravest of the brave." Of John Mercer Langston, the U.S. congressman. About his grandma's first husband who was killed with John Brown trying to free the slaves, and of Granma herself who used to work on the Underground Railroad.

Stories of real heroes who were black, just like Langston.

As he grew older, Langston Hughes wrote more and more. About everyday people, common folk. He wrote about dancers and children, troubled people and people in love; Walt Whitman and the black Pierrot; all kinds of people. And he traveled all over the world, to Russia and France, and to Africa, experiencing the stories and rhythms of yet other people.

He lived in many cities in America, like Cleveland and Los Angeles, but Harlem, New York, where all kinds of black artists gathered—writers, painters, musicians—became the place where he stayed longest and that he knew best.

It seemed Langston Hughes had finally found a home.

But the truth is, Langston never had a home like most people. Home was in him. And it was about his black family that he wrote in words that reached his own people, and all kinds of people of different races and different countries, all over the world.

Langston Hughes (1902–67)

The 1994 biography by Floyd Cooper tells of Langston Hughes's childhood, of his mixed-blood ancestors and their accomplishments, of his many travels to live with different relatives and friends, and of the youthful development of his talents as a poet and storyteller. Born in Joplin, Missouri, Hughes traveled around the continent and abroad, but he is best known as an acclaimed author of the Harlem Renaissance, writing poetry, fiction, plays, and essays. His leading role in the remarkable artistic and political movements of African American culture in the 1920s and 1930s, centered in Harlem, New York, established his position as one of the most influential American writers of the twentieth century. In the period leading up to the civil rights era of the 1960s, Hughes wrote a number of historical, biographical, and informational books for children, but his most enduring legacy lies in his lyrical poems enjoyed by children and adults. Generations of readers have been inspired by his compelling belief that each individual must "hold fast to dreams."

The Brownies' Book, a magazine for African American children published by the National Association for the Advancement of Colored People in 1920–21, printed a poem that Hughes wrote at age seventeen, "Winter Sweetness," which describes "a maple-sugar child" peeping out of a house covered with snow. The poem later appeared with fifty-eight other poems in *The Dream Keeper* (1932), the only book of verse Hughes wrote for young people. A new edition was published in 1994 with seven additional poems and artwork done in scratchboard (black ink scratched off a white board) by Brian Pinkney (b. 1961). Augusta Baker, a famous New York children's librarian and storyteller, wrote in 1986 that Hughes "had great pride in his race, and he often said that he wished to give black boys and girls the same pride which he had."[1] She noted that "Mother to Son" was always a favorite with children. The mother in the poem uses a series of realistic images that are associated with a stairway to warn her son about the difficulties of life while urging him to keep climbing higher as she does. "Aunt Sue's Stories" affirms the value for the young child of learning about the past, even when it involves the sorrows of slavery, in the loving arms of a family member whose head is full of "real stories" from her own life. This poem pays tribute to the most meaningful method available—one that so many adults use instinctively—to combine teaching and enjoyment in the nurturing of children.

NOTE

1. Augusta Baker, "A Personal Note," *The Dream Keeper and Other Poems,* by Langston Hughes, illus. Brian Pinkney (New York: Knopf, 1994) 82.

Aunt Sue's Stories

Aunt Sue has a head full of stories.
Aunt Sue has a whole heart full of stories.
Summer nights on the front porch
Aunt Sue cuddles a brown-faced child to her
   bosom
And tells him stories.

Black slaves
Working in the hot sun,
And black slaves
Walking in the dewy night,
And black slaves
Singing sorrow songs on the banks of a mighty
   river
Mingle themselves softly
In the flow of old Aunt Sue's voice,
Mingle themselves softly
In the dark shadows that cross and recross
Aunt Sue's stories.

And the dark-faced child, listening,
Knows that Aunt Sue's stories are real stories.
He knows that Aunt Sue
Never got her stories out of any book at all,
But that they came
Right out of her own life.

And the dark-faced child is quiet
Of a summer night
Listening to Aunt Sue's stories.

The flowing, expressive rhythms of Brian Pinkney's scratch-board illustration complement the description of family love in Langston Hughes's 1932 poem "Aunt Sue's Stories."

Mother to Son

Well, son, I'll tell you:
Life for me ain't been no crystal stair.
It's had tacks in it,
And splinters,
And boards torn up,
And places with no carpet on the floor—
Bare.
But all the time
I'se been a-climbin' on,
And reachin' landin's,
And turnin' corners,
And sometimes goin' in the dark
Where there ain't been no light.
So, boy, don't you turn back.
Don't you set down on the steps
'Cause you finds it kinder hard.
Don't you fall now—
For I'se still goin', honey,
I'se still climbin',
And life for me ain't been no crystal stair.

Lucille Clifton (b.1936)

Lucille Clifton, a distinguished poet and educator, grew up near Buffalo, New York. She attended Howard University and the State University of New York at Fredonia, where she studied drama. After working in government jobs until 1971, Clifton became a writer in residence at Coppin State College in Baltimore, Maryland. The publication of her first book of poems, *Good Times,* in 1969, brought her wide recognition. She has said, "I am a black woman poet, and I sound like one."[1] Clifton has been Poet Laureate of Maryland and has taught at a number of colleges and universities. While she was raising six children, her poetry for adults often dealt with the concerns of African American mothers in a racist society. In more than twenty books for children, including a series of picture books about Everett Anderson, who is six or seven years old, Clifton upholds the strengths that young people need to survive. Scholars have observed that "Clifton's books for young people reflect the same themes, views, and landscapes as her poetry. Clifton addresses the fears, joys, and pain of children, reassures them, teaches them self-reliance, self-acceptance, and the assumption of responsibility for their actions. Her writing for children is honest and lacks condescension."[2]

The poems that are included here illustrate this honesty and connectedness, revealing both empathic poignancy (in "Elevator") and a sense of continuity between generations ("Under the Rainbow"). Clifton donated "Elevator" for a 1992 anthology called *Home,* edited by Michael J. Rosen as a fund-raising project for organizations that assist the homeless. Like the image of stairs in Langston Hughes's "Mother to Son" (presented earlier), the elevator where a child takes refuge in the projects represents her hope for "moving up," along with the book that helps her wait for the elevator to move and conditions to improve. "Under the Rainbow" appeared in a 1993 book of African American poetry compiled and illustrated by Tom Feelings, who wrote, "The artists who came together to create *Soul Looks Back in Wonder* understand that one way to project our positive hopes for the future is for young people to see their own beauty reflected in our eyes, through our work." (See also the poem by Maya Angelou in Part 4 and an illustration by Tom Feelings in Part 6.)

NOTES

1. "(Thelma) Lucille Clifton," *Contemporary Poets,* 7th ed. (Detroit: St. James Press, 2001), *Biography Resource Center,* Thomson Gale, 2005, 18 Apr. 2005 <http://galenet.galegroup.com/servlet/BioRC>.
2. *The Oxford Companion to Women's Writing in the United States,* ed. Cathy N. Davidson and Linda Wagner-Martin, et al. (New York: Oxford UP, 1995).

Elevator

down
in the corner
my book and i
traveling
over the project
walls
so the world
is more than this
elevator

stuck between
floors again
and home
is a corner
where i crouch
safe
reading waiting
to start moving
up

Under the Rainbow

I close my eyes
and slide along the arc
to home where my long grandmothers
sleep, dreaming of me,

dreaming of how dark
and beautiful we are together
under the bright
rainbow of our nights.

FURTHER RECOMMENDED READING

C. S. LEWIS (1898–1963)

THE LION, THE WITCH AND THE WARDROBE

C. S. Lewis began his series of seven Narnia novels in 1950 with *The Lion, the Witch and the Wardrobe.* When the four Pevensie children first enter Narnia through an old wardrobe in an English country house, they learn of the magic world's ancient history and prophecies about their own roles in battles between good and evil forces, which are led by Aslan, a Christ-like lion, and Jadis, an evil witch. Other books in the Narnia Chronicles deal with Narnia's earlier and later history. Since the siblings in the first book have been sent away from the city during World War II to live in a big house with an unmarried professor, they are like displaced protagonists in other fantasy novels, such as Dorothy in *The Wonderful Wizard* of Oz by L. Frank Baum and Tom in *Tom's Midnight Garden* by Philippa Pearce. They must decide whom to trust and learn how to cope with unfamiliar and dangerous situations when fantastic adventures interrupt their tedious everyday lives.

Conflicts among the siblings arise early in the novel because their unfamiliarity with magic and Edmund's dishonesty make the others doubt the word of Lucy, the youngest and the first to see Narnia. An unexpected mediator between the ordinary world and the world beyond appears when Peter and Susan consult the kindly Professor, who, it turns out later, has been to Narnia himself and is able to support Lucy's claims of having visited a world on the other side of the wardrobe with several arguments that have to do with truth, character, and the nature of reality. Lewis was a neo-Platonist Christian who wrote the Narnia books to imagine what it would be like if someone like Jesus were to visit a world like Narnia. Though Lewis was careful to point out that his children's books were not allegories in the sense that *Pilgrim's Progress* is an allegory (each character and event has a specific, intended meaning), the Narnia stories clearly embody many of Lewis's religious ideas and beliefs in symbolic form. Unlike many fundamentalist Christians, Lewis saw the events and symbols of pagan mythology, many of which he incorporated into his fantasy, not as contradicting of, but as pointing to the message of Christianity. Boosted in popularity by film adaptations, the Narnia books join other twentieth-century fantasy cycles such as *The Lord of the Rings* that interpret the world through heroic and mythic dimensions. See Lewis's essay about writing for children in this section.

LOUISE FITZHUGH (1928–74)

HARRIET THE SPY

With *Harriet the Spy* (1964), Louise Fitzhugh inaugurated New Realism in children's books. Not content, as many children's authors had been, to exclude realistic problems and social criticism from children's stories, Fitzhugh created a memorable and distinctive heroine: independent and eccentric Harriet, a writer-in-training, who observes the world with a sharp and often merciless eye. Harriet lives with her affluent parents in New York City, where Fitzhugh had settled after an unhappy childhood with her wealthy divorced father in the South. Harriet's rebellion against dancing

Louise Fitzhugh's own drawing of her heroine shows Harriet as an isolated figure absorbed in her secret notebook.

school foreshadows a feminist revolution in consciousness, and the open-ended conclusion of the book signals Fitzhugh's rejection of the literary convention of resolving protagonists' difficulties. In chapter 6, Ole Golly, Harriet's nursemaid and mentor, takes Harriet on an unauthorized excursion to the movies with her boyfriend, Mr. Waldenstein— a venture that has distressing consequences. Harriet and Ole Golly recite their favorite nonsense poem from Lewis Carroll's *Through the Looking-Glass,* an affirmation of the bond between them. In chapter 14, Harriet's habit of observing and writing down what she sees is comically mirrored and parodied in the psychiatrist's parallel habit. Harriet still has a way to go before she recognizes her own behavior as others see it. Fitzhugh, who was an artist as well as an author, illustrated the novel with her own drawings. (See also the selection from Fitzhugh's *Nobody's Family Is Going to Change* in Part 8.)

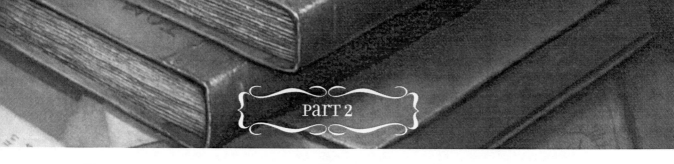

{ Part 2 }

SUBJECTION OF THE CHILD OR SUBVERSION OF ADULT AUTHORITY?

Children, I confess, are not born in this full state of equality, though they are born to it. Their parents have a sort of rule and jurisdiction over them when they come into the world, and for some time after, but it is but a temporary one. The bonds of this subjection are like the swaddling clothes they are wrapt up in and supported by in the weakness of their infancy. Age and reason as they grow up loosen them, till at length they drop quite off, and leave a man at his own free disposal.

John Locke, "An Essay Concerning the True Original, Extent and End of Civil Government" (1690)

In the twentieth century, children's literature evolved from reinforcing adults' right to determine their children's actions to encouraging children to think for themselves and act independently: behavior that, two centuries earlier, was taboo. The seeds of this gradual revolution lie in the eighteenth-century Enlightenment, which attributed rationality to children, and in nineteenth-century Romanticism, which elevated the child's innocence to the status of the nearly sacred. Both views are a far cry from the Puritan concept of the child as "conceived in sin, born in sin, and growing up in sin."[1] The Puritans valued literacy highly because reading the Bible was their hope for salvation. As alien as their harsh condemnation of children's innate sin may seem to us, we need to recognize that their emphasis on universal literacy laid the groundwork for a society in which everyone is expected to learn to read. A new emphasis on rationality and the positive potential of the child, very different from the Puritan belief in inherent evil, emerges in the eighteenth-century Enlightenment.

The English philosopher John Locke outlined a new approach to the child that emphasized that the mind begins as a "tabula rasa," a blank slate. He still endorsed the authority of adults, as when he wrote, in his influential essay *Some Thoughts Concerning Education* (1693), "I imagine every one will judge it reasonable, that their children, when little, should look upon their parents as their lords, their absolute governors, and as such stand in awe of them; and that when they come to riper years, they should look on them as their best, as their only sure friends, and as such love and reverence them." However, he also urged a more moderate and restrained use of physical punishment than most of his predecessors, and believing that children learn best when their interest is engaged in what they are learning, he suggested techniques for stimulating curiosity and thought. The French philosopher Jean Jacques Rousseau wrote in his *Émile, or On Education* (1762), "We know nothing of childhood, and with our mistaken notions the further we advance the further we go astray." Furthermore, he asserted, "All wickedness comes from weakness. The child is only wicked because he is weak; make him strong and he will be good." Rousseau imagined a boy's ideal education as life in the country, far from the influence of the corrupt court or city, exploring the world with only the guidance of a kindly mentor and no books until the one he recommended: Daniel Defoe's *Robinson Crusoe*—itself a story of solitary adventure, far from society. Rousseau and Locke both emphasized the potential inherent in childhood. They laid the groundwork for generations of writers for children (authors of school books or of fictional works) by making the ideas of learning and of development central to their definitions of childhood. The English poet William Wordsworth (1770–1850) experienced his childhood as illuminated by "a celestial light / The glory and freshness of a dream." (See the poem "Ode: Intimations of Immortality from Recollections of Early Childhood" in this section.) For him, as for many Romantic poets, childhood was a time of innocence and closeness to nature, while growing up meant increasing imprisonment: "Shades of the prison-house begin to close / Upon the growing Boy."

The modern view of childhood as a series of developmental stages, accompanied by formal education that is conducted in classes with one's peers of the same age, is a product of the Enlightenment. Formal education was also made possible by the affluence that accompanied industrial society, which provided a sufficient surplus of wealth to enable parents to release their children from the labor that, until fairly recently, had been necessary for the survival of working-class and even many middle-class families. We now think of childhood as a period of relative leisure (or, at least, freedom from the need to work for a living), although work has been replaced by the busyness of recreation and education. Our media portray children of different ages, such as preteens, teens, and "young adults," as having various tastes and styles, even distinct languages. Some form of rebellion has virtually been institutionalized: independent-minded if not positively unruly children are the most common kind of heroes and heroines in children's and young adult books—think of L. M. Montgomery's Anne of Green Gables, Jim Hawkins in Robert Louis Stevenson's *Treasure Island,* Astrid Lindgren's Pippi Longstocking, Mark Twain's Tom Sawyer and Huckleberry Finn, or Louise Fitzhugh's Harriet the Spy, not to mention Holden Caulfield in J. D. Salinger's *Catcher in the Rye* or Jerry Renault in Robert Cormier's *The Chocolate War.* Yet in daily life, children are required to adhere to schedules, to complete homework assignments, to conform in class or on the school bus, and to cooperate with parents and teachers—or else face disciplinary action or, in an increasing number of cases, compulsory medication. Thus, one could argue, contemporary children's literature sends messages that contradict the actual experience of modern children's lives. Books (and films and video games, too) urge children to determine their own course and defy adults; authority figures urge obedience and cooperation, if not conformity.

For centuries, children's books were primarily tools to educate and train children into submission and acceptance of adult standards. The moralistic children's literature of earlier eras not only taught the rules of proper behavior, it frequently showed children the disastrous consequences of disobedience and misbehavior. In these books, disrespectful children were beaten, poisoned, drowned, hacked to death, or otherwise discomfited because they would not listen to their adult "advisers." Sometimes, as in the German author and illustrator Heinrich Hoffmann's

Struwwelpeter stories, the purpose was both to amuse children with exaggerated consequences (the thumb-sucking boy in Hoffmann's Struwwelpeter collection has his thumbs cut off by a tailor with a pair of giant shears) and to warn children not to disobey certain rules (such as not to play with matches). "Good" children were rewarded, often in the most blatant material fashion, according to their virtues and good deeds. Of course, we do not know what actual children of those eras thought about the propaganda they were fed; many of them probably saw it for exactly what it was and discounted it, although many probably were also shaped and tamed by it.

Alison Lurie, in her essay "A Child's Garden of Subversion," tells how, even as a child, she knew the difference between books that were urging her to do what grown-ups wanted her to do and ones that offered adventure and risk. Marina Warner's essay in this section points out some of the subtle ways in which grown-ups today, whether they do so consciously or not, try to keep children innocent, while foisting cynical or even exploitative values upon them. Books, it sometimes appears, are part of the battle between children and adults about who is in control. The ironic, unequal part of this equation is that grown-ups write the books that children read. Yet, in recent decades, children's books have increasingly represented children's points of view—or, more accurately, what adults, often persuasively, imagine them to be. Such a book is Louise Fitzhugh's *Nobody's Family Is Going to Change,* which suggests its message in its title. Fitzhugh's radicalism in advocating the child's interests—she imagines a Children's Liberation Army that prepares to take action against abusive parents or teachers—is tempered by her recognition that children, too, engage in power struggles and exhibit prejudice and cruelty. (See Part 8.)

Sometimes modern children's literature offers a critique of society, contrasting the implicit rights of children with the wrongs done to them. Mildred Taylor's story of Cassie Logan in *Roll of Thunder, Hear My Cry* exposes racial prejudice and its ugly consequences. Abduction and rape are the results of racial arrogance, greed, and exploitation in Mette Newth's *The Abduction,* a story of seventeenth-century northern European ventures into the Arctic regions of the Inuit. Libby Hathorn's Australian story "Up Taree Way" illustrates the dangers of internalizing prejudicial racial attitudes. And Gudrun Pausewang tells an unsparing story of degradation and desperation in her novel *The Final Journey,* the account of a Jewish girl who has been protected from all knowledge of the impending Holocaust in Germany, traveling with her grandfather in a cattle car toward the death camps. These stories make massive accusations: the adults who have created and control the worlds in which these children live are responsible for terrible distortions of the human spirit. Yet, as Pausewang angrily implies, trying to keep children innocent is not the answer.

Still, the idea of childhood innocence has not lost its power. As controversies over censorship show, debate continues to rage about what kinds of knowledge and experience children should be sheltered from. Is the protection of children from certain areas of life, such as violence or sexuality, a fundamental right, or is the sheltering of children a form of adult control over children's lives that deprives them of the ability to form their own beliefs, values, and responses? Is reading about brutality or sex or social injustice an invitation to depravity and despair or preparation for the reality of life in the world at large? Of course, the answer is likely to vary, depending on the age of the reader; what we consider suitable for a fourteen-year-old may well not be suitable for a seven-year-old, and individual children of the same age differ in their needs, desires, and levels of understanding. But even taking such age differences into account, there remains a fundamental question about the role of literature in shaping the lives of children: does literature about violence, sexuality, or despair function more like an addictive drug (inducing certain kinds of behaviors that are beyond the control of the drug taker), or more like a vaccination, preventing worse diseases by allowing the recipient to experience a mild and ultimately protective version of the illness? The answers we give depend, in part, on the fundamental assumptions that we make about human nature: are children basically inexperienced versions of ourselves at our best, humane and rational, able to make wise decisions and to experience life fully when permitted to confront genuine choices? Or are children—actually or potentially—little monsters, inclined toward mischief and trouble, perhaps even evil, by their very nature and thus in need of adult supervision and control, including control over what they read? The selections in this section imply and express a variety of views about these questions.

NOTE

1. For one source of this Puritan concept, see Psalm 51: 5: "Behold, I was shapen in iniquity; and in sin did my mother conceive me" (King James Bible).

Alison Lurie (b.1926)

Alison Lurie is a professor of English at Cornell University and a prolific and distinguished novelist, as well as a critic of children's literature. She has written about the need to rediscover folktales with strong heroines and has edited a feminist collection, *Clever Gretchen and Other Forgotten Folktales* (1980). The ideas of the present essay are developed at length in her 1990 book *Don't Tell the Grown-ups: Subversive Children's Literature.* Lurie tells how, when she was a child, she discovered that there were two kinds of children's books: the kind that sought to teach her lessons and the other kind: the subversive books, which she calls "sacred texts" of childhood, such as *Tom Sawyer* and *The Wonderful Wizard of Oz.*[1]

NOTE

1. Alison Lurie, *Clever Gretchen and Other Forgotten Folktales* (New York: HarperCollins, 1980).

A Child's Garden of Subversion

There exists in our world an unusual, partly savage tribe, ancient and widely distributed, yet until recently little studied by anthropologists or historians. All of us were at one time members of this tribe: we knew its customs, manners and rituals, its folklore and sacred texts. I refer, of course, to childhood.

The sacred texts of childhood, however, are not always the ones adults recommend, as I discovered very early. Soon after I began going to the library, I realized that there were two sorts of books on its shelves. The first kind, the great majority, told me what grown-ups had decided I ought to know or believe about the world. Many of these books were practical: they wanted me to understand how the automobile worked, or who George Washington was. Also, and not just incidentally, they wanted me to admire both automobiles and the Father of Our Country; you didn't hear much about the mothers of our country in those days.

Along with these improving books there were also some that hoped to teach me manners or morals or both. These books had no Dewey decimal numbers on their spines, and their lessons came disguised as stories. They were about children or bunny rabbits or little engines who had problems or faults and got into difficult situations, sometimes comic and sometimes serious. But in the end they were always saved by some wise, helpful older person or rabbit or engine. The protagonists of these books, that is, learned to depend on authority for help and advice. They also learned to be hardworking, responsible and practical; to stay on the track and be content with their lot in life. They learned, in other words, to be more like respectable grown-ups. It was the same message I and my friends heard every day: Sit up straight, dear. Don't go too far into the woods. Say thank you to Aunt Etta. Come along, stop daydreaming and fill in your workbook. Now, darling, you mustn't make up stories.

But there was another sort of children's literature, I discovered. Some of these books, like "Tom Sawyer," "Little Women," "Peter Pan" and "Alice's Adventures in Wonderland," were on the shelves of the library; others, like "The Wizard of Oz" and the Nancy Drew series, had been judged unworthy and had to be bought in shops or borrowed from friends. These were the sacred texts of childhood, whose authors had not forgotten what it was like to be a child. To read them was to feel a shock of recognition, a rush of liberating energy.

These books, and others like them, recommended—even celebrated—daydreaming, disobedience, answering back, running away from home and concealing one's private thoughts and feelings from unsympathetic grown-ups. They overturned adult pretensions and made fun of adult institutions, including school and family. In a word, they were subversive, just like many of the rhymes and jokes and games I learned on the school playground.

It is a long while since I was a child, but I don't think the situation has changed very much. In every era, including the present one, run-of-the-mill children's literature tends to support the status quo. The books that win prizes for stylistic or artistic excellence often—though not always—belong to this category; and when they do, they are at best only politely tolerated by children.

I am sometimes asked why anyone who is not a teacher or a librarian or the parent of little children should concern herself with children's books and folklore. I know the standard answers: that many famous writers have written for children and that the great children's books are also great literature; that these books and tales are an important source of archetype and symbol and that they can help us to understand the structure and functions of the novel.

All this is true. But I think we should also take children's literature seriously because it is sometimes subversive: because its values are not always those of the conventional adult world. Of course in a sense much great literature is subversive, since its very existence implies that what matters is art, imagination and truth. In what we call the real world, on the other hand, what usually counts is money, power and fame.

The great subversive works of children's literature suggest that there are other views of human life besides those of the shopping mall and the corporation. They mock current assumptions and express the imaginative, unconventional, noncommercial view of the world in its simplest and purest form. They appeal to the imaginative, questioning, rebellious child within all of us, renew our instinctive energy and act as a force for change. This is why such literature is worthy of our attention and will endure long after more conventional tales have been forgotten.

An interesting question I sometimes hear is: what—besides intention—makes a particular story a "children's book"? With the exception of picture books for toddlers, juvenile classics are not necessarily shorter or simpler than so-called adult fiction, and they are surely not less well written. The heroes and heroines of these tales, it is true, are often children: but then so are the protagonists of "What Maisie Knew" by Henry James and "The Bluest Eye" by Toni Morrison. Yet the barrier between children's books and adult fiction remains: editors, critics and readers seem to have little trouble in assigning a given work to one category or the other.

In classic children's fiction a pastoral convention is maintained. It is assumed that the world of childhood is simpler and more natural than that of adults, and that children, though they may have faults, are essentially good or at least capable of becoming so. The transformation of selfish, whiny, disagreeable Mary and hysterical, demanding Colin in Frances Hodgson Burnett's "Secret Garden" is a paradigm. Of course, there are often unpleasant minor juvenile characters who give the protagonist a lot of trouble and are defeated or evaded rather than re-educated. But on occasion even the angry bully and the lying sneak can be reformed and forgiven. Richard Hughes's "High Wind in Jamaica," though most of its characters are children, never appears on lists of recommended juvenile fiction; not so much because of the elaborations of its diction (which is no more complex than that of, say, "Treasure Island"), but because in it children are irretrievably damaged and corrupted.

Adults in most children's books, on the other hand, are usually stuck with their characters and incapable of alteration or growth. If they are really unpleasant, the only thing that can rescue them is the natural goodness of a child. Here again Mrs. Burnett provides the classic example, in "Little Lord Fauntleroy." (Scrooge's somewhat similar change of heart in "A Christmas Carol," however, is due mainly to regret for his past and terror of the future. This is one of the things that make the book a family rather than a juvenile romance; another is the helpless passivity of the principal child character, Tiny Tim.)

Of the three principal preoccupations of adult fiction—sex, money and death—the first is absent from classic children's literature and the other two either absent or much muted. Love in these stories may be intense, but it is romantic rather than sensual, at least overtly. Peter Pan passionately desires Wendy, but what he wants is for her to be his mother.

Money is a motive in children's literature, in the sense that many stories deal with a search for treasure of some sort. These quests, unlike real-life ones, are almost always successful, though occasionally what is found in the end is some form of family happiness, which is declared by the author and the characters to be a "real treasure." Simple economic survival, however, is almost never the problem; what is sought, rather, is a magical (sometimes literally) surplus of wealth.

Death, which was a common theme in 19th-century fiction for children, was almost banished during the first half of this century. Since then it has begun to reappear; the breakthrough book was E. B. White's "Charlotte's Web." Today not only animals but people die, notably in the sort of books that get awards and are recommended by librarians and psychologists for children who have lost a relative. But even today the characters who die tend to be of another generation; the protagonist and his or her friends survive.

Though there are some interesting exceptions, even the most subversive of contemporary children's books usually follow these conventions. They portray an ideal world of perfectible beings, free of the necessity for survival and reproduction: not only a pastoral but a paradisal universe—for without sex and death, humans may become as angels. The romantic child, trailing clouds of glory, is not as far off as we might think.

Marina Warner (b.1946)

Anglo-Italian novelist and critic Marina Warner's series of lectures on myths about childhood in the contemporary world for the BBC (the Reith Lectures) formed the basis of her book *Six Myths of Our Time* (1994). Warner also authored a feminist critique of fairy tales, *From the Beast to the Blonde: On Fairy Tales and Their Tellers* (1994). She has a keen eye for how marketing and media create our modern expectations of children, as well as an erudite knowledge of the history of Western society and the evolution of childhood as a social construct within it. She writes with clarity and incisiveness about the paradoxes of our ideas about children's innocence—and our promotion of their tendencies toward violence and mayhem. (See also the essay by Warner in Part 7.)

Little Angels, Little Monsters

Keeping Childhood Innocent

In 1828, a young man was found in the market square of Nuremberg; he could write his name, Caspar Hauser, but he couldn't speak, except for a single sentence, "I want to be a rider like my father." He had been kept all his life in a cellar alone in the dark until his unexplained release that day. Though he was in his teens when he suddenly appeared, he seemed a symbolic child, a stranger to society, a tabula rasa in whom ignorance and innocence perfectly coincided. In his wild state, Caspar Hauser offered his new minders and teachers a blueprint of human nature—untouched. And in his case, his character fulfilled the most idealised image of original innocence.

He was sick when given meat to eat, passed out when given beer, and showed so little aggression and cruelty that he picked off his fleas without crushing them to set them free through the bars of his cell. His story attracted myth-making in his own time, and has continued to inspire writers and filmmakers. The most recent work, a book-length narrative poem by David Constantine, opens with the apparition of Caspar Hauser out of nowhere:

He stood there swaying on his sticky feet,

His head was bowed, the light hurt his eyes,
The pigeons ran between his feet like toys
And he was mithered by the scissoring swifts . . .
       Even an embryo
Raises its little paws against the din
But Caspar stood there sucking it all in

Dowsing for more of it on the square's navel,
Arms stiff like compasses, at the end of one
He held his letter of introduction

'To whom it may concern' and at the end
Of the other a wide-awake hat,
Both very tightly. There he remained . . .

        until the windows
Folded their wooden lids back and in rows . . .

From all the openings of their ordinary lives
The people stared . . .

They inched, already aghast
At all the questions he would make them ask.

Caspar Hauser was an enigma, and after his mysterious return to the world, his life was never free from strange, turbulent incident: he was suspected of fabrication, he was assaulted and wounded by an unknown assailant, and later, was thought to be the usurped heir to the throne of Baden. His innate gentle goodness couldn't save him: he was attacked, seduced, betrayed, and abandoned by his would-be adoptive father, the Englishman Lord Stanhope. And finally he was murdered, in still unsolved circumstances, in 1833.

There'd been other wild children who'd inspired scientific experiments into human development, but Caspar Hauser more than any other foreshadows this century's struggle with the question of the child's natural character. And his fate still offers a timely parable about the nostalgic worship of childhood innocence, which is more marked today than it ever has been: the difference of the child from the adult has become a dominant theme in contemporary mythology. In literature this has produced two remarkable dream figures living in voluntary exile from grown-up society—Kipling's unforgettably vivid Mowgli, and J. M. Barrie's cocky hero, the boy who wouldn't grow up, Peter Pan. Both reveal the depth of adult investment in a utopian childhood state. This can lead to disillusion, often punitive and callous, with the young as people. The shock of James Bulger's death was deepened by his murderers' ages, yet their trial revealed a brutal absence of pity for them as children.* It was conducted as if they were adults not because they had behaved with adult consciousness, but because they had betrayed an abstract myth about children's proper childlikeness.

The belief that there's a proper childlike way for children to be has deep roots. In his novel about Caspar Hauser written in 1908, the German writer Jacob Wassermann put his finger on the dreams the boy stirred:

> This creature reeling helplessly in an alien world, his gaze cumbered with sleep, his gestures curbed by fear, his noble brow enthroned above a somewhat wasted face, the peace and purity of heart that appear in that brow: to my mind, they are incontestable signs. If my suspicions prove correct, if I can lay bare the

roots of this life and make its branches blossom, I shall hold up a mirror of immaculate humanity to our dull insensitive world, and people will see that there are valid proofs of the existence of the soul—which the idolaters of our times deny with so squalid a vehemence.

In this ringing declaration we catch the full expression of a belief which still has purchase today, seventy years on: that the child and the soul are somehow interchangeable, and that consequently children are the keepers and the guarantors of humanity's reputation. This has inspired a wonderfully rich culture of childhood, one of the most remarkable phenomena of modern society—from an unsurpassed imaginative literature for children today to deep psychoanalytical speculation on the thinking processes and even language of the foetus. But it also has social consequences for children themselves that are not all benign.

Childhood, placed at a tangent to adulthood, perceived as special and magical, precious and dangerous at once, has turned into some volatile stuff—hydrogen, or mercury, which has to be contained. The separate condition of the child has never been so bounded by thinking, so established in law as it is today. This mythology is not fallacious, or merely repressive—myths are not only delusions—chimaeras—but also tell stories which can give shape and substance to practical, social measures. How we treat children really tests who we are, fundamentally conveys who we hope to be.

The separate sphere of childhood has grown—as a social concept, as a market possibility, as an area of research, as a problem: children are no longer chattels, any more than women, and new legal measures like the Children's Act give them voice in choices and decision-making about their legal situation. Incest, molestation and even rape in families have always taken place, but never have more attempts been made—often with appalling clumsiness—to save children from their violators.

Fiction and reportage also focus on the child as so radically different that he or she stands in an oblique relation to human society, not entirely part of it, not yet incorporated into history. Charities in hard-pressed competition for funds resort to more and more explicit images of maimed, starving, diseased, orphaned, and doomed infants and children in order to raise money for schemes which are frequently intended to help

---

*James Bulger was a toddler who was abducted and killed by two ten-year-old boys in Britain in 1993.

everyone—like cancer research, water purification. The children in the photographs provide a solution to what could be called "the Oxfam syndrome": how to portray the need and poverty of others without making it look like their endemic, perennial hopelessness. Images of children, who are vulnerable and dependent in every society, whatever its circumstances, help to evade that implicit condescension.

The injured child has become today's icon of humanity. It's no accident that the Victorian melodrama *Les Misérables* inspired one of the contemporary theatre's greatest successes, that the saucer-eyed, starveling waif staring from the posters drew thousands to the musical. The phantom face of James Bulger has become the most haunting image of present horrors and social failure—his innocence an appeal and an accusation.

Some historians, like Philippe Ariès, have suggested—rather influentially—that the comparative offhandedness towards children in the past denotes indifference and that the kind of love we expect and know today is a comparatively modern phenomenon, a bourgeois luxury. Certainly hardly any examples of children's own writings or paintings survive, and few records of their behaviour have come down, until parents—in seventeenth-century Holland, for instance—began keeping diaries. But this doesn't necessarily mean parents didn't care. The testimony of graves yields another story: from Roman epitaphs to memorials in Westminster Abbey, the accents of grief sound across the centuries. On a tomb in the Etruscan necropolis of Cerveteri, near Rome, a father had these verses written for his daughter Asiatica:

> Here lies the lifeless body of my beloved little girl, who has been plunged into a bitter death by the Fates—her unlucky life had lasted less than ten years. Cruel fates, who have saddened my old age! For I shall always seek, little Asiatica, to see your face again, shaping its features in my mind to find some consolation. My only solace will be to see you again, as soon as ever possible, when, my life over, our two shades will be united.

Not only tombs, but stories too convey the intense attachment felt for children. In tragedy, the murders of offspring provide the believable motive for the most terrible revenges: Clytemnestra never forgets that Agamemnon allowed her daughter Iphigenia to be sacrificed to get a fair wind for Troy. For this, in Euripides's play, she makes the first literal bloodbath of him.

It seems to me that children have always been cherished. But the present cult of the child loves them for a new and different reason. It insists on children's intimate connection, above all, to a wonderful, free-floating world of the imagination. Their observable, active fantasy life, their fluid make-believe play seem to give them access to a world of wisdom, and this in turn brings them close to myth and fairy tale. These ideas were grown in the ground of Romanticism: for Wordsworth, heaven lay about us in our infancy and the child was father to the man. He was influenced by the idealism of German metaphysics at the time. The mystical poet Novalis stressed the importance of becoming childlike to gain wisdom: writing about fairy tales, a form he believed held huge possibilities of truth-telling, Novalis noted in his journals, "A true fairy tale must . . . be a prophetic account of things— an ideal account . . . [the] confessions . . . of an ideal child. A child is a good deal cleverer and wiser than an adult—but the child must be an ironic child."

Novalis can be heard, in mid-sentence, realising that the claim of childlikeness in a genre like the fairy tale is always ironical—you or I, when we long to be as little children, can only masquerade as such, we can only perform childlikeness as far as we can observe it or recall it. We are doomed to an ironic innocence.

But it is also difficult to grasp how innocence would show itself without adults to influence it—this was the miracle of Caspar Hauser. Novalis's journal entry immediately adds that a child's games are "imitation[s] of grown-ups." Mummies and Daddies, Doctors and Nurses, Pirates and Soldiers, Cowboys and Indians, Cops and Robbers. How would a child play if there were no grown-ups to imitate? In what games would a child's untouched imagination be different?

The Romantic thirst to recover childlikeness had a huge influence on the growth of interest in children and the activities of their minds. Anthologies with titles like *Myths of the Greeks and Romans; Tanglewood Tales; Tales of the Norse Gods and Heroes,* all treating myth and legend, began to be produced as children's literature in the last century. The childhood of the species—the era of myth and legend—seemed appropriate for the young. And the heroes of wonder narratives of all kinds gradually became younger, to invite the young listener's or reader's identification. This change had certain, serious consequences. The tale of Cupid and Psyche, for instance, which later inspired *Beauty and the Beast,* first appears in the second century, in the ribald, metaphysical novel by Apuleius, *The Golden Ass:* there, it's an adult romance and Cupid and Psyche have been lovers for some time when Psyche breaks the spell by looking at Cupid in bed with her. The Neoplatonists in the Renaissance allegorised the tale as the spiritual quest of the Soul for love—still no hint of child protagonists or a child audience. But by the eighteenth century, the romance itself is transformed into a fairy tale, *Beauty and the Beast.* Filtered through the eyes of a well-meaning governess, it turns into a moral lesson in love, directed at her young charges to prepare them for tricky moments lying ahead: Beauty is certainly not going to bed with the Beast, but deciding whether or not they should get engaged.

At the beginning of the nineteenth century, the Grimm brothers collected the material for their famous collection of German fairy tales. They relied on a heterogeneous group of sources—members of their own family, servants, a tailor's wife, several landed aristocratic friends—all of them adults who had continued to pass on the stories in mixed company of men and women, old and young. The Grimms' full title, *Children's and Household Tales,* retained the hint of a universal audience, but there's no doubt that their pioneering work nourished the concept that such tales belonged in a special way to children. However, the brothers quickly realised that if the tales were to become children's fare, their previous adult entertainment value, their sadism, eroticism, cruelty, and immoral distribution of just and unjust deserts, had to be either censored or explained. This led to clipping and tucking and letting in here and letting out there. On the whole, sex was out and violence was in, and lots of it, especially in the form of gleeful retributive justice. The wicked stepmother in *Snow White* could dance to death in her red-hot shoes, but the Sleeping Beauty—who had borne twins to the prince in earlier versions—could now only be kissed.

The difficulty is that by angling such material at children in particular, the pleasure they took in it marked out bloodthirstiness, fearlessness, and even callousness as childish—rather than universally hu-

man—characteristics. By making children the heroes and heroines of such fairy tales, the erotic discoveries and ordeals many of them describe had to be disinfected—leaving sexuality latent in violent symbols and gory plots.

In the postwar period, psychoanalytic thinkers, like Bruno Bettelheim in his influential study *The Uses of Enchantment,* deepened the association of fairy tale with children, and of cruel fantasy with the childish imagination. Bettelheim affirmed the therapeutic value of struggle and horror for the growing child, arguing that as a small, vulnerable creature suffering from adults' tyranny, it was very helpful to read about other small vulnerable creatures, like Cinderella or Tom Thumb, who survived—or better still, won through against all adversity. From this perspective, nothing in fantasy was perceived as too foul or too violent. Brightly coloured picture books of Cinderella now include the bloody chopping of one sister's toes and the lopping of the other's heel, and climax with the putting out of the ugly sisters' eyes.

The theory that children need to compensate for their own hapless dependence by imagining themselves huge and powerful and cruel has also normalised all manner of frightening playacting, equating children with monsters, childhood with a savage state. Stephen Jay Gould, the biologist, has pointed out that kids don't have an innate kinship with dinosaurs, but that it has been fostered by intensive marketing; the relationship seems based in some idea of shared primitiveness—and future extinction. Lots of toys appeal to the idea of children's savagery: from huge furry, clawed slippers for tiny tots to wear to bed to warn off any other beasts in the night, to dinosaur lunchboxes and watches. As a gift catalogue describes, "At the touch of a button, the fearsome tyrannosaurus rex emits a blood-curdling little roar."

In the very midst of consecrating innocence, the modern mythology of childhood ascribes to children a specially rampant natural appetite for all kinds of transgressive pleasures, including above all the sado-masochistic thrills of fear. And these child heroes—and heroines—now enjoy a monopoly on all kinds of unruly passions which adults later have to learn to control in themselves.

Child protagonists have become so commonplace that the convention has become invisible. In books written for children, from the great Victorian originals, like *The Water Babies* and the two Alice stories, to the Billy Bunter and Angela Brazil series, the Famous Five and the Secret Seven, as well as books by rather more original and inspired contemporaries of ours like Sue Townsend and Joan Aiken, with their vivid protagonists Adrian Mole and Dido Twite, it's become axiomatic that the child reader enjoys identifying with a child. Films reaching—successfully—for the family audience also place children centre stage: in almost all Spielberg vehicles and offshoots, from *E.T.* to *Back to the Future,* children outsmart adults; in *Jurassic Park,* the two kids take the conventional place of the blonde in more adult movies, as victims of the predators on the rampage, until the obligatory ending, when the girl works the computer and saves the day, Enid Blyton–style. Characters like Dorothy in *The Wizard of Oz,* or now Aladdin in the new Disney cartoon, have grown younger and younger as the cinema as a medium grows older.

The tendency isn't limited to the growing market in children's entertainment; the child's-eye view has become one of the most adopted and fertile narrative positions in all media: Henry James explored its dense and poignant ironies in his novel *What Maisie Knew,* still the greatest study of divorce and what the papers call a tug-of-love baby. It's interesting to glance at a list of really successful novels and see just how many adopt a child's eye: from *The Catcher in the Rye* to *Empire of the Sun,* and more recently, Ben Okri's *The Famished Road* and Roddy Doyle's *Paddy Clarke, Ha Ha Ha.* In the cinema, the device gives the camera itself a role: what the child sees, the lens follows, claiming equal impartiality, of ignorance or innocence. Again, a list includes highly successful films destined for an adult audience: the big-budget *Witness,* the arthouse masterpiece *The Spirit of the Beehive,* or Ingmar Bergman's lyrical and tender memoir, *Fanny and Alexander* use the central perspective of a child to draw the spectator into a different angle of vision, to make us accept the camera's pristine truthfulness, to intensify the pathos and the drama. By making us as little children, we are helped to shed cynicism and resistance to the material on view, and to mind more because more is at stake—the image of a child always opens up the horizon to a possible future, and so when the clouds lower, it feels darker.

The nagging, yearning desire to work back to a pristine state of goodness, an Eden of lost innocence, has focussed on children. On the map of contemporary imaginative pathways, J. M. Barrie stands as firmly as the statue of Peter Pan gives West London children their bearings in the park. He truly became a founding father of today's cult of children when in his famous play of 1904, he made the audience responsible for the continued existence of fairyland: the fairy Tinkerbell drinks poison and Peter Pan cries out to the audience, "Do you believe in fairies? Say quick that you believe! If you believe, clap your hands!" Barry was so anxious that nobody would clap in reply that he paid a claque to do so in the first performances, but then found that it was unnecessary.

Adults applaud their loyalty to the world of pretend and children follow. The statement of faith in fairies signals collusion with Peter Pan, the boy who never grew up—it affirms the connection of the adult with that childhood Eden in which the Lost Boys are still living; it defies the death of the child within. But at this point, a double bind catches us in its toils: for the defiance of itself admits the impossibility of Peter Pan and the Lost Boys' state. Grown-ups want them to stay like that for their sakes, not the children's, and they want children to be simple enough to believe in fairies too, again, for humanity's sake on the whole, to prove something against the evidence.

Contemporary child mythology enshrines children to meet adult desires and dreams, including Romantic and Surrealist yearnings to live through the imagination, with unfettered, unrepressed fantasy; in turn, this presupposes that the child has access to a form of desirable wisdom, of potent innocence which cannot tell pretend from real, and sex from sexlessness, a kind of supernatural irrationality. But perhaps only a Caspar Hauser, raised in total isolation, could ever meet these demands.

The Spielberg school of filmmaking flatters the child audience with a picture of their superiority: not only the computer nerd who saves the show in *Jurassic Park,* but E.T.'s friends, and, above all, the hero of *Back to the Future* who time travels into the past and finds he has to save his own parents there from making a complete mess of their lives. This admiration for children appeals to them, as box office, of course, as all images of heroism do; but it's ambivalent in its effect, since it exaggerates kids' know-how and contributes to the prevailing myth of their apartness, their difference, their unreachability.

Yet, even as I speak, I can hear objections flying thick and fast: for every dozen wonderful innocents in literature or popular culture, there are unsettling figures of youthful untruth and perversity: children today, far from holding up the lit lamp of hope like the little girl in Picasso's "Guernica," have become the focus of even greater anxiety and horror than their mothers, than even their single mothers. Michael Jackson was once a child performer of exactly that adorable cuddly cuteness that makes grown-ups purr and coo. Now a boy sprite who won't grow up, he epitomises the intense, risky, paradoxical allure of the Peter Pan myth. He leaps and dances and sings "I'm Bad," gives his estate the name Neverland, draws the passionate worship of millions of children, and then finds himself charged with child abuse.

We call children "little devils," "little monsters," "little beasts"—with the full ambiguous force of the terms, all the complications of love and longing, repulsion and fear. Jesus said "Suffer the little children to come unto me," and Christianity worships its god as a baby in a manger, but the Christian moral tradition has also held, simultaneously, the inherent sinfulness of children.

Original Sin holds up the spectre of innate human wickedness: whatever glosses theologians put on it, Christian children have been raised to believe that without divine help the species is bound for hell. Grimly, parents and carers confronted child wickedness: in New England, Cotton Mather used to beat his daughter to drive the demons of sin from her, and recommended the practice to his fellow Americans; in 1844, a German pastor [sic.—see p. 156] wrote the terrifyingly punitive *Struwwelpeter,* with its scissor man and other bogeys for making little boys and girls be good. It's one of the major ironies in the history of children's literature that Heinrich Hoffmann wrote *Struwwelpeter* for his son, to poke fun, Belloc-style, at the moralising tone of current schoolbooks. But the humour of his effort has largely gone missing, and *Struwwelpeter* has joined the shelf of finger-wagging volumes to become one of the nastiest texts ever used to scare the naughtiness out of naughty children.

But the Child has never been seen as such a menacing enemy as today. Never before have children been so saturated with all the power of projected monstrousness to excite repulsion—and even terror. Henry James, in his peculiar, brilliant and troubling ghost story of 1894, *The Turn of the Screw,* defined the unease of the modern dilemma, that even the most beautiful and shining examples may be counterfeit.

When the governess looks at Flora and Miles, she can't conquer her fears that they're indeed possessed by some evil:

> To gaze into the depths of blue of the child's eyes and pronounce their loveliness a trick of premature cunning was to be guilty of cynicism in preference to which I naturally preferred to abjure my judgement and, so far as might be, my agitation . . . with our small friends' voices in the air, their pressure on one's heart and their fragrant faces against one's cheek, everything fell to the ground but their incapacity and their beauty.

Every knotted phrase of this protestation passes through the teller's continuing, helpless suspicion that the children may look like angels and still be devils underneath.

Today, such doubts match widespread fears, and public grief focusses obsessively on the loss of an ideal of children, of their playfulness, their innocence, their tenderness, their beauty. The child holds up an image of origin, but origins are compounded of good and evil together, battling it out; this conflict spreads rings of disquiet all around. Children are perceived as innocent because they're outside society, pre-historical, pre-social, instinctual, creatures of unreason, primitive, kin to unspoiled nature. Whether this is seen as good or evil often reflects the self-image of the society. Surveillance cameras register the walk of young killers on their way to acts of unimaginable violence; special seats have to be made to raise these child murderers above the level of the dock; my local paper wails, "Terror Tots Attack Frail Victim"; the most notorious of video nasties is called *Child's Play.*

Bad children—a symptom of modernity—surface again and again in some of the most powerful contemporary fiction, like Golding's classic *Lord of the Flies*—a book to bury in any time capsule seeking to convey the flavour of this half of the century. In Richard Hughes's *High Wind in Jamaica,* in Rumer Godden's *The Greengage Summer,* and of course Nabokov's *Lolita,* children collude erotically with adults, and even betray them; in Doris Lessing's *The Fifth Child,* the evil baby actually wrecks a stable family. Popular satanist entertainment, including *Rosemary's Baby, The Exorcist, Poltergeist,* build on Christian theories of demonic possession to dramatise the full-blown development of evil in seeming cherubim. Gone are the cheerful catapults and squashed toffees and fallen socks of a scallywag like Just William, the devilry of Dennis the Menace. Horror has spread into teenage fiction, too, with titles like *The Babysitter, The Burning Baby,* and *Dance of the Scalpel.*

Although the cultural and social investment in childhood innocence is constantly tested by experience, and assailed by doubts, it's still continued to grow. As psychoanalytical understanding of children's sexuality has deepened, so have attempts to contain it. The duration of the age of expected innocence has been greatly extended since Victorian times, for instance: a good thing, if it can prevent exploiting child labour and adult molestation but perhaps not, in other cases.

Most teenagers will have broken at least one of the many laws that forbid them adult behaviour—like smoking, drinking, clubbing, watching X-rated films or having sex—thus placing them willy-nilly outside the law, and helping to reconfirm their identity as intrinsically delinquent anyway (something they don't find entirely uncongenial, of course).

At the same time, the notion of child sexuality is encoded in upbringing at a much younger age than before. The modern emphasis on sex difference, on learning masculinity and femininity, begins with the clothing of the infants, and has developed markedly since the end of the First World War. A boy who was dressed in pink ribbons by his father today would very likely be taken away from his care. Yet Robert Louis Stevenson, whose character was hardly disturbed, appears in a daguerreotype around the age of three dressed in fur-trimmed cape, full skirts, hair slide and spit curls; a photograph album in the Victoria and Albert Museum from the beginning of the century shows a boy child on his birthday every year—ringletted from curling papers, full-skirted, with button boots. The portraits of the French or English aristocracy and gentry showing children clothed as adults, with jewels and powdered wigs and crinolines and farthingales, were displaying the status of their families; but the little girl in the little black dress, patent pumps, lipstick and earrings who was brought out in the finale of a recent Chanel collection was showing off her body, and looked like a travesty of the sex-free youth children are supposed to enjoy.

Yet even if children today aren't titillatingly dressed, they can still be looked at salaciously. It's we who have lost innocent eyes, we who can only be ironical children. Lewis Carroll's friends were undisturbed by his photographs of their children, while some pederasts today, it seems, are kept very happy by Mothercare catalogues.

Pornography clusters to the sacred and the forbidden like wasps' nests in chimneys: and children have in many ways replaced women. The very term child abuse, of recent, highly symptomatic coinage, implies that there's a proper use for children, and it is not sexual. Yet at the same time, there circulates more disguised kiddie porn than at any other period in history, and more speculation about their internal lives of fantasy and desire. The nineteenth century used femmes fatales with bedroom eyes and trailing tresses, wetlook drapery and floating chiffon on their official buildings and advertisements, but the late twentieth century has seen children emerge as the principal incitements to desire: the nymph or the vamp has yielded pride of place to the nymphet, the urchin and the toddler.

There's probably no way out of this maze of mirrors, at least on this side of eternity, unless, like Islam, we were to ban graven images—especially of children as objects of desire. The consecration of childhood raises the real-life examples of children to an ideal which they must fail, modestly by simply being ordinary kids, or horrendously by becoming victims or criminals. But childhood doesn't occupy some sealed Eden or Neverland set apart from the grown-up world: our children can't be better than we are.

Children have never been so visible as points of identification, as warrants of virtue, as markers of humanity. Yet the quality of their lives has been deteriorating for a good fifteen years in this and many other Western countries; in England and the United States, one of the fastest-growing groups living in poverty are children and their mothers. The same ministers who sneer about babies on benefit, and trumpet a return to basic values cannot see that our social survival as a civilised community depends on stopping this spiralling impoverishment of children's lives. In the UK alone, the Child Poverty Action Group estimates that a third of all children are suffering from an unacceptably low standard of living. Of the million jobs to be created in this country, between now and the year 2000, 90 percent—yes, 90 percent—will be for women, according to one official forecast. And yet there's publicly funded child care for only 2 per cent of under-threes. Meanwhile, the government's proposed to allocate £100 million to creating prisons for eleven- to thirteen-year old offenders.

To add to the difficulties, economic individualism has brought us the ultimate nightmare—not just the child as commodity, but the child consumer. Plenty of dinosaur lunchboxes at school, not many books in the library. The wicked, greedy, knowing child grows in the same ground as the industry around childhood innocence: children are expensive to raise, anyway, but all the products made for them unashamedly appeal to their pester power—as consumers of films, hamburgers, the right brand of sneakers, video games. The child, as a focus of worship, has been privatised as an economic unit, has become a link in the circulation of money and desire.

That very vitality of imagination so envied in children needs to be tended—and not only by expensive theme parks. Yet the BBC uproots the tradition of children's radio at a stroke, citing falling ratings. And in the same playgrounds where Peter and Iona Opie collected the skipping songs and hopscotch rhymes of generations, children apparently now hang around, having forgotten how to play. Local, oral traditions are dropping away just like larks and hedges. I'm not turning into a reactionary Little England ruralist—but children's songs flourish in context, in conditions when children can play together in groups in safety. At present, playgrounds and other school facilities—among the only safe spaces for children—are routinely left idle after school hours, at weekends and during holidays for want of funds to staff them.

Fallow playgrounds are a tiny aspect of the disgrace: the hours that British men work are longer than almost all of their counterparts in Europe. And yet the cry goes up about children with only mothers to look after them. Children with fathers who live with them aren't looked after by them either, even when they would like to, since employment is still structured to consider childcare the mother's task. And measures which would grant fathers paternity and sickness leave on behalf of their children are rejected because they might jeopardise profits.

Many of these problems result from the concept that childhood and adult life are separate when they are in effect inextricably intertwined. Children aren't separate from adults, and unlike Mowgli or Peter Pan, can't be kept separate; they can't live innocent lives on behalf of adults, like medieval hermits maintained at court by libertine kings to pray for them, or the best china kept in tissue in the cupboard. Nor can individuals who happen to be young act as the living embodiments of adults' inner goodness, however much adults may wish it. Without paying attention to adults and their circumstances, children cannot begin to meet the hopes and expectations of our torn dreams about what a child and childhood should be. Children are our copy, in little: in Pol Pot's Cambodia they'll denounce their own families; in affluent cities of the West, they'll wail for expensive sneakers with the right label like their friend's. The one thing that can be said for absolute certain about children is that they're very quick to learn.

We know by now that the man is father to the child; we fear that children will grow up to be even more like us than they already are. Caspar Hauser the innocent was murdered; now we're scared that if such a wild child were to appear today he might kill us.

John Huddlestone Wynne (1743–88)

The title of Wynne's 1788 book for children, *Choice Emblems, natural, historical, fabulous, moral, and divine; for the improvement and pastime of youth; displaying the beauties and morals of the ancient fabulists: the whole calculated to convey the golden lessons of instruction under a new and more delightful dress. For the use of schools. Written for the amusement of a young nobleman,* is characteristically wordy, as was the preference of many eighteenth-century authors. Wynne was working within the then-widespread emblem tradition, which also influenced John Newbery and other eighteenth-century children's book authors. As Karl Josef Höltgen wrote, "The emblem is a mixed form that typically combines a motto, a symbolic picture and an epigram. An emblem was meant to convey knowledge and truth in a brief and compelling form that would persuade the reader and imprint itself on memory."[1] Wynne seeks to persuade his young readers that the example of the boy who steals honey from the hive teaches a universal lesson—a perfect example of the kind of lesson that Alison Lurie encountered as a child—and despised.

NOTE

1. Karl Josef Höltgen, "William Blake and the Emblem Tradition," *Erfurt Electronic Studies in English* (2002), Niedersächsische Staats-und Universitätsbibliothek, Göttingen, 11 May 2005 <http://webdoc .sub.gwdg.de/edoc/ia/eese/artic22/hoeltgen/2_2002.html>.

Of the Danger of Pleasure

Behold the Boy, forbidden sweets to prove,
With luckless hand the *honied Hive* remove:
Strait with an angry hum that sounds to arms,
Forth rush the winged tribe in all their swarms;
Too late, alas! they make th' offender find,
That Pleasure's Honey leaves a sting behind.

MORAL

Learn hence, ye heedless train, who gaily glide
In youth's trim bark, down life's uncertain tide,
That death oft lurks beneath some gilded toy,
And poison mingles in the cup of joy.

EMBLEM III.

Of the Danger of Pleasure.

The thoughtless child overturns the Hive, in order to get at the Honey; he knows the Bees have Sweets, but he forgets that they have also Stings. When he has done the mischief, he perceives it too late; for the industrious people show him that they will not be disturbed with impunity; and he finds it impossible to get the Honey, unless he were able to destroy those who guard it.

Amazed at the consequence of his action, he flies with precipitation, but is overtaken by the insects, who settling upon him, leave behind them their stings, the anguish of which may serve as a perpetual memorial of his rashness, and warn him how he attempts stolen sweets for the future.

APPLICATION

In many people of a more mature age, we see the Emblem verified; and though common experience might prevent the evil, yet so careless are some, that they will make use of no experience but their own, which is always dearly bought, and often comes too late to have the effect desired by every rational and thinking person.

The wild and unthinking always imagine forbidden pleasures to be sweet; and, proceeding on this maxim, often plunge themselves into the most ruinous circumstances, and repent only when it is too late to amend them.

But they will overturn the Hive; they must have the Honey, while they little expect the Sting:—when they feel it (like the Boy in the Emblem) surprize is added to their affliction, and their distress is doubled, by their being no ways provided to sustain the accident.

If you would be wise, take not the Honey while the Hive is swarming; let not your Pleasures be mixed with Guilt; and then you may rest secure that they will leave no Sting behind them.

William Wordsworth (1770–1850)

In this famous poem, published in 1807, William Wordsworth expresses a central Romantic idea about childhood: that children are closer to nature and to God than are adults. Wordsworth was influenced by the classical Greek philosopher Plato in the view that the soul exists before birth, as well as after death, and to Wordsworth it was the blissful recollection of heaven that gave young children an instinctive and joyful kinship with the natural world. This mystical idea (and ideal) has influenced writers for children for 200 years and has shaped part of the modern concept of childhood. Ironically, few of the Romantic authors wrote directly for children, although many of their poems have been anthologized for children, but their idealizations of childhood resulted, frequently in debased form, in the sentimental notions about childhood that were prevalent in the Victorian era. The seeds of rebellion against adult authority are sown, however, in Wordsworth's and other Romantic writers' portrayal of the institutions of adult society as oppressive. For Wordsworth, adulthood was a kind of "prison-house" looming over childhood and adolescence. Throughout the Golden Age of children's literature, many stories depict children who escape the detrimental influences of adults and benefit from the healing powers of nature, from *Heidi* by Joanna Spyri (1881) to *The Secret Garden* by Frances Hodgson Burnett (1911) and beyond. (See excerpts from *The Secret Garden* in Part 5.)

Ode

Intimations of Immortality from Recollections of Early Childhood

The Child is father of the Man;
And I could wish my days to be
Bound each to each by natural piety.

I

THERE was a time when meadow, grove, and
    stream,
The earth, and every common sight,
To me did seem
Apparelled in celestial light,
The glory and the freshness of a dream.   5
It is not now as it hath been of yore;—
Turn wheresoe'er I may,
By night or day,
The things which I have seen I now can see no
    more.

II

The Rainbow comes and goes,   10
And lovely is the Rose,
The Moon doth with delight
Look round her when the heavens are bare;
Waters on a starry night
Are beautiful and fair;   15
The sunshine is a glorious birth;
But yet I know, where'er I go,
That there hath past away a glory from the
    earth.

III

Now, while the birds thus sing a joyous song,
And while the young lambs bound   20
As to the tabor's sound,
To me alone there came a thought of grief:
A timely utterance gave that thought relief,
And I again am strong:
The cataracts blow their trumpets from the
    steep;   25

No more shall grief of mine the season wrong;
I hear the Echoes through the mountains throng,
The Winds come to me from the fields of sleep,
And all the earth is gay;
Land and sea   30
Give themselves up to jollity,
And with the heart of May
Doth every Beast keep holiday;—
Thou Child of Joy,
Shout round me, let me hear thy shouts, thou
    happy Shepherd-boy!   35

IV

Ye blessèd Creatures, I have heard the call
Ye to each other make; I see
The heavens laugh with you in your jubilee;
My heart is at your festival,
My head hath its coronal,   40
The fulness of your bliss, I feel—I feel it all.
Oh evil day! if I were sullen
While Earth herself is adorning,
This sweet May-morning,
And the Children are culling   45
On every side,
In a thousand valleys far and wide,
Fresh flowers; while the sun shines warm,
And the Babe leaps up on his Mother's arm:—
I hear, I hear, with joy I hear!   50
—But there's a Tree, of many, one,
A single Field which I have looked upon,
Both of them speak of something that is gone:
The Pansy at my feet
Doth the same tale repeat: 55
Whither is fled the visionary gleam?
Where is it now, the glory and the dream?

V

Our birth is but a sleep and a forgetting:
The Soul that rises with us, our life's Star,

Hath had elsewhere its setting,   60
And cometh from afar:
Not in entire forgetfulness,
And not in utter nakedness,
But trailing clouds of glory do we come
From God, who is our home: 65
Heaven lies about us in our infancy!
Shades of the prison-house begin to close
Upon the growing Boy,
But He
Beholds the light, and whence it flows,   70
He sees it in his joy;
The Youth, who daily farther from the east
Must travel, still is Nature's Priest,
And by the vision splendid
Is on his way attended;   75
At length the Man perceives it die away,
And fade into the light of common day.

VI

Earth fills her lap with pleasures of her own;
Yearnings she hath in her own natural kind,
And, even with something of a Mother's
  mind,   80
And no unworthy aim,
The homely Nurse doth all she can
To make her Foster-child, her Inmate Man,
Forget the glories he hath known,
And that imperial palace whence he came.   85

VII

Behold the Child among his new-born blisses,
A six years' Darling of a pigmy size!
See, where 'mid work of his own hand he lies,
Fretted by sallies of his mother's kisses,
With light upon him from his father's eyes!   90
See, at his feet, some little plan or chart,
Some fragment from his dream of human life,
Shaped by himself with newly-learned art;
A wedding or a festival,
A mourning or a funeral;   95
And this hath now his heart,
And unto this he frames his song:
Then will he fit his tongue
To dialogues of business, love, or strife;

But it will not be long   100
Ere this be thrown aside,
And with new joy and pride
The little Actor cons another part;
Filling from time to time his "humorous stage"
With all the Persons, down to palsied Age,   105
That Life brings with her in her equipage;
As if his whole vocation
Were endless imitation.

VIII

Thou, whose exterior semblance doth belie
Thy Soul's immensity;   110
Thou best Philosopher, who yet dost keep
Thy heritage, thou Eye among the blind,
That, deaf and silent, read'st the eternal deep,
Haunted for ever by the eternal mind,—
Mighty Prophet! Seer blest!   115
On whom those truths do rest,
Which we are toiling all our lives to find,
In darkness lost, the darkness of the grave;
Thou, over whom thy Immortality
Broods like the Day, a Master o'er a Slave,   120
A Presence which is not to be put by;
Thou little Child, yet glorious in the might
Of heaven-born freedom on thy being's height,
Why with such earnest pains dost thou provoke
The years to bring the inevitable yoke,   125
Thus blindly with thy blessedness at strife?
Full soon thy Soul shall have her earthly freight,
And custom lie upon thee with a weight,
Heavy as frost, and deep almost as life!

IX

O joy! that in our embers   130
Is something that doth live,
That nature yet remembers
What was so fugitive!
The thought of our past years in me doth breed
Perpetual benediction: not indeed   135
For that which is most worthy to be blest;
Delight and liberty, the simple creed
Of Childhood, whether busy or at rest,
With new-fledged hope still fluttering in his
  breast:—

Not for these I raise   140
The song of thanks and praise;
But for those obstinate questionings
Of sense and outward things,
Fallings from us, vanishings;
Blank misgivings of a Creature   145
Moving about in worlds not realised,
High instincts before which our mortal Nature
Did tremble like a guilty Thing surprised:
But for those first affections,
Those shadowy recollections,   150
Which, be they what they may,
Are yet the fountain light of all our day,
Are yet a master light of all our seeing;
Uphold us, cherish, and have power to make
Our noisy years seem moments in the being   155
Of the eternal Silence: truths that wake,
To perish never;
Which neither listlessness, nor mad endeavour,
Nor Man nor Boy,
Nor all that is at enmity with joy,   160
Can utterly abolish or destroy!
Hence in a season of calm weather
Though inland far we be,
Our Souls have sight of that immortal sea
Which brought us hither,   165
Can in a moment travel thither,
And see the Children sport upon the shore,
And hear the mighty waters rolling evermore.

X

Then sing, ye Birds, sing, sing a joyous song!
And let the young Lambs bound   170
As to the tabor's sound!
We in thought will join your throng,
Ye that pipe and ye that play,

Ye that through your hearts to-day
Feel the gladness of the May!   175
What though the radiance which was once so
   bright
Be now for ever taken from my sight,
Though nothing can bring back the hour
Of splendour in the grass, of glory in the flower;
We will grieve not, rather find   180
Strength in what remains behind;
In the primal sympathy
Which having been must ever be;
In the soothing thoughts that spring
Out of human suffering;   185
In the faith that looks through death,
In years that bring the philosophic mind.

XI

And O, ye Fountains, Meadows, Hills, and
   Groves,
Forebode not any severing of our loves!
Yet in my heart of hearts I feel your might;   190
I only have relinquished one delight
To live beneath your more habitual sway.
I love the Brooks which down their channels fret,
Even more than when I tripped lightly as they;
The innocent brightness of a new-born Day   195
Is lovely yet;
The Clouds that gather round the setting sun
Do take a sober colouring from an eye
That hath kept watch o'er man's mortality;
Another race hath been, and other palms are
   won.   200
Thanks to the human heart by which we live,
Thanks to its tenderness, its joys, and fears,
To me the meanest flower that blows can give
Thoughts that do often lie too deep for tears.

Jacob Grimm (1785–1863) and Wilhelm Grimm (1786–1859)

The Grimm Brothers are world famous for their collection of German folktales. Seeking to preserve the legacy of German culture, these brothers, who were learned philologists (both also studied law at the University of Marburg), collected tales from a range of tellers, many of whom were middle class and well educated, male and female. Ironically, although the Grimm Brothers thought of the tales they collected as quintessentially German, some of the tales they recorded had been told by the French aristocrat Charles Perrault more than a century earlier in his *Histoires ou contes du temps passé* (*Stories or Tales of Times Past,* see Part 1). The Grimm Brothers' tales were translated into English and widely read in England after their publication in 1823, with illustrations by the famous George Cruikshank. In successive versions, the Grimm Brothers edited the tales to de-emphasize sexuality and increase their violence, adapting the stories to their ideas of what was best suited to the education of children. Their collections of stories, entitled *Kinder und Hausmärchen* (*Children's and Household Tales,* 1812–14) did a great deal to overcome the objections of moralists, such as Sarah Trimmer, who thought that fantasy and folktales were not appropriate materials for children. The history of the Grimm Brothers' tales illustrates how stories can pass back and forth between the oral and the written traditions.

These examples show that European folktales often depict the lower classes of poor peasants—a rural family who cannot feed their children in "Hansel and Gretel" and, as in "The Frog King," the highest classes of aristocrats and royals. They also dramatize some of the deepest fears and fantasies of children and adolescents. Hansel and Gretel survive abandonment by their parents, and then (similar to the spunky orphan Mutsmag in Part 3), they use trickery and quick action to defeat the cannibalistic witch. The witch's house, made of sweet things, entices hungry children deep in the woods, but for young children, returning to a safe home and loving parent is the greatest desire. Many other tales depict the marriage choices of young adults. In "The Frog King," a strong-willed princess encounters a persistent frog who undergoes a magical transformation that reveals his eligibility as a bridegroom. Lore Segal's and Randall Jarrell's beautiful translation of these tales in *The Juniper Tree* (1973) reflects the simple, poetic language of the German originals. In "Mother Holle," a modest and obedient stepdaughter proves her virtue by responding to the pleas of various objects for help. Her service to Mother Holle brings her ample rewards, but her lazy sister is punished according to her faults, as are many folktale siblings who behave badly. Mother Holle is an embodiment of nature, suggesting that nature punishes and rewards vices and virtues according to their deserts. This representation of duty and service reinforces obedience to adult authority. Ralph Manheim's clear and readable translation of "Mother Holle" comes from what is often considered the standard modern translation of the collection (*Grimms' Tales for Young and Old: The Complete Stories,* 1977). (See other tales collected by the Grimms in Parts 3 and 5.)

The Frog King, or Iron Henry

In the old days, when wishing still helped, there lived a king and all his daughters were beautiful, but the youngest was so beautiful that even the sun, which has seen so much, marveled every time it shone into her face. Near the king's castle lay a great, dark forest and in the forest, under an old linden tree, there stood a well. Now on the days when it was very hot the princess would go out into the forest and sit at the edge of the cool well and if time hung heavy on her hands she took a golden ball, threw it in the air, and caught it, and it was her favorite plaything.

It happened once that the princess's golden ball did not fall into her outstretched hand but slipped past, struck the ground, made straight for the water, and rolled in. The princess followed it with her eyes but the ball disappeared, and the well was deep, so deep that you couldn't see the bottom, and she began to cry and kept crying louder and louder and could not stop. And as she sat wailing, someone called, "What's the matter, Princess? The way you howl would melt the heart of a stone!" The princess looked around to see who it could be and saw a frog sticking his thick, ugly head out of the water. "Oh, it's you, you old puddle-splasher," said she. "I'm crying because my golden ball has fallen into the well." "Well, don't cry any more," answered the frog, "I can help you. What will you give me if I bring back your toy?" "Anything you want, dear frog," said she, "my dresses, my pearls and all my jewels, and the gold crown on my head as well." "I don't care anything about your dresses, your pearls and jewels, or your golden crown, but if you will promise to love me best and play with me, and let me be your dearest friend, and sit beside you at the table, eat off your golden plate, drink from your cup, and sleep in your bed with you, I will climb down and bring back your golden ball." "Yes, yes, I promise everything, only bring me my ball," said she, thinking, The silly frog! What nonsense he does talk; he sits here in the water with his own kind and croaks, and can never be friends with real people.

When the frog had obtained her promise, he put his head in the water, sank down, and after a little while came paddling back up with the ball in his mouth and threw it on the grass. The princess was overjoyed to see her pretty toy, picked it up, and ran away. "Wait for me, wait for me," cried the frog. "Take me with you, I can't run so fast," but what was the good of his croaking after her as loud as he could? She would not hear him but hurried home and soon forgot the poor frog, who had to climb back into his well.

The next day, as she was sitting at the table with the king and all the court, and was eating from her golden plate, there came something crawling, splash, splash, up the marble stair. When it arrived at the top, it knocked and cried, "Princess, youngest princess, open the door." She ran to see who it was, but when she opened the door, there sat the frog. She quickly slammed the door, came back, and sat down, but she was in a great fright. The king could see how her heart was beating, and said, "Why are you afraid, my child? Is there a giant at the door maybe, come to carry you away?" "Oh, no," she answered, "it's not a giant, only a nasty frog." "What does the frog want with you?" "Ah, dear Father, in the forest yesterday I was sitting by the well, playing, and my golden ball fell in the water. And because I was crying so hard, the frog went and fetched it up for me, and made me promise that he could be my best friend, but I never, never thought he'd get out of his water, and now he's here and wants to come inside with me." At that moment there was more knocking and a voice cried:

"Princess, youngest princess,
open the door,
don't you know what you
said to me yesterday
by the cool well-water?
Princess, youngest princess,
open the door."

Then the king said, "If you made a promise, you must keep it. Go, open the door for him." The princess went and opened the door and the frog hopped in, following her every footstep right up to her chair, and sat there and cried, "Lift me up where you are." She hesitated until finally the king commanded it. When the frog was on her chair, he wanted to be up on the table, and when

"He came crawling and said, 'I'm tired, too.'" Maurice Sendak's drawing of a huge frog intruding on the startled princess's bed and body accentuates the strangeness of events in "The Frog King." See Part 6 for more on Sendak's illustrations for the Grimm Brothers' tales reprinted in *The Juniper Tree* (1973).

he sat on the table he said, "Now push your golden plate nearer, so we can eat together." She did, but one could tell she did not like it. The frog ate heartily, but as for her, every bite stuck in her throat. Finally he said, "I have eaten till I am full, and now I'm tired. Carry me to your room and make up your silken bed so we can lie down and go to sleep." The princess began to cry. She was afraid of the cold frog, whom she could not bear to touch and who wanted to sleep in her nice clean bed. But the king got angry and said, "If someone helps you in your need, you must not look down on him after-

wards." And so she took hold of the frog with two fingers, carried him upstairs, and set him in a corner, but when she was lying in bed he came crawling and said, "I'm tired too and want to sleep comfortably just like you. Lift me up, or I'll tell your father." Now this gets her really angry! She picked him up and she threw him against the wall as hard as she could: "Now will you be satisfied, you nasty frog!"

As he fell to the ground, however, he was no longer a frog but a prince with kind and beautiful eyes who, by her father's wishes, now became her friend and husband. And he told her how a wicked witch had put a spell on him and how nobody had been able to set him free from the well but she alone, and tomorrow they would go to his kingdom together. Then they went to sleep and next morning, when the sun woke them, a coach came driving up with eight white horses that had white ostrich feathers on their heads, all harnessed in golden chains, and in the back stood the young king's servant and it was his faithful Henry. Faithful Henry had been so grieved when his master was changed into a frog that he had three iron bands laid around his heart to keep it from bursting with pain and sorrow. And the coach had come to fetch the young king home to his kingdom. Faithful Henry set them both inside and went and stood in the back and was overjoyed that his master had been freed. And when they had gone a little way, the prince heard a cracking behind him as if something had broken in two. He turned and cried:

> "Henry, the carriage breaks apart."
> "No, sire, it's not the carriage breaking,
> it's the iron band around my heart—
> my heart that lay so sorely aching
> while you were a frog, while you sat in the well."

Again, and once again, as they drove along, came the cracking sound, and each time the prince thought the coach was breaking apart but it was only another band bursting from around the heart of his faithful Henry because his master was free and happy.

Hansel and Gretel

Once upon a time, on the edge of a great forest, there lived a poor woodcutter with his wife and his two children. The boy was named Hansel and the girl was named Gretel. The family had little enough to eat, and once when there was a great famine in the land the man could no longer even get them their daily bread. One night, lying in bed thinking, in his worry he kept tossing and turning, and sighed, and said to his wife: "What is going to become of us? How can we feed our poor children when we don't even have anything for ourselves?"

"You know what, husband?" answered the wife. "The first thing in the morning we'll take the children out into the forest, to the thickest part of all. There we'll make them a fire and give each of them a little piece of bread; then we'll go off to our work and leave them there alone. They won't be able to find their way back home, and we'll have got rid of them for good."

"No, wife," said the man, "I won't do it. How could I have the heart to leave my children alone in the forest—in no time the wild beasts would come and tear them to pieces."

"Oh, you fool!" said she. "Then all four of us will starve to death—you may as well start planing the planks for our coffins," and she gave him no peace until he agreed. "I do feel sorry for the poor children, though," said the man.

The two children hadn't been able to go to sleep either, they were so hungry, and they heard what their stepmother said to their father. Gretel cried as if her heart would break, and said to Hansel: "We're as good as dead." "Ssh! Gretel," said Hansel, "don't you worry, I'll find some way to help us." And as soon as the old folks had gone to sleep, he got up, put on his little coat, opened the bottom half of the door, and slipped out. The moon was shining bright as day, and the white pebbles that lay there in front of the house glittered like new silver coins. Hansel stooped over and put as many as he could into his coat pocket. Then he went back in again, and said to Gretel: "Don't you feel bad, dear little sister! You just go to sleep. God will take care of us." Then he lay down in his bed again.

The next morning, before the sun had risen, the woman came and woke the two children: "Get up, you lazy creatures, we're going to the forest and get wood." Then she gave each of them a little piece of bread and said: "There is something for your dinner, but don't you eat it before, because it's all you're going to get." Gretel put the bread in her apron, since Hansel had the pebbles in his pocket. Then they all started out together on the way to the forest. After they had been walking a little while Hansel stopped and looked back at the house, and did it again and again. His father said: "Hansel, what are you looking at? What are you hanging back there for? Watch out or you'll forget your legs."

"Oh, Father," said Hansel, "I'm looking at my little white pussycat that's sitting on the roof and wants to say goodbye to me."

The wife said: "Fool, that's not your pussycat, that's the morning sun shining on the chimney." But Hansel hadn't been looking back at the cat—every time he'd stopped he'd dropped onto the path one of the white pebbles from his pocket.

When they came to the middle of the forest the father said: "Now get together some wood, children! I'll light you a fire, so you won't be cold." Hansel and Gretel pulled together brushwood till it was as high as a little mountain. The wood was lighted, and when the flames were leaping high, the woman said: "Now lie down by the fire, children, and take a rest, we're going into the forest to cut wood. When we're finished we'll come back and get you."

Hansel and Gretel sat by the fire, and when noon came they each ate their little piece of bread. And since they heard the blows of the ax, they thought their father was near. But it wasn't the ax, it was a branch that he'd fastened to a dead tree so that the wind would blow it back and forth. And when they'd been sitting there a long time, they got so tired that their eyes closed, and they fell fast asleep. When at last they woke up, it was pitch black. Gretel began to cry, and said: "Now how will we ever get out of the forest?" But Hansel comforted her: "Just wait awhile till the moon comes up, then we'll be able to find our way." And when the full moon had risen, Hansel took his little sister by the hand and followed the pebbles, that glittered like new silver coins and showed them the way.

They walked the whole night through, and just as the day was breaking they came back to their father's house. They knocked on the door, and when the woman opened it and saw that it was Hansel and Gretel, she said: "You bad children, why did you sleep so long in the forest? We thought you weren't coming back at all." But the father was very glad, for it had almost broken his heart to leave them behind alone.

Not long afterwards there was again a famine throughout the land, and the children heard their mother saying to their father in bed one night: "Everything's eaten again. We've only a half a loaf left, and that will be the end of us. The children must go. We'll take them deeper into the forest, so that this time they won't find their way back; it's our only chance." The man's heart was heavy, and he thought: "It would be better for you to share the last bite of food with your children." But the woman wouldn't listen to what he had to say, but scolded him and reproached him. If you say "A" then you have to say "B" too, and since he had given in the first time, he had to give in the second time too.

But the children were still awake, and had heard what was said. As soon as the old folks were asleep, Hansel got up again to go out and pick up pebbles as he'd done the time before, but the woman had locked the door, and Hansel couldn't get out. He comforted his little sister, though, and said: "Don't cry, Gretel, but just go to sleep. The good Lord will surely take care of us."

Early in the morning the woman came and got the children out of their beds. She gave them their little piece of bread, but this time it was even smaller than the time before. On the way to the forest Hansel broke up the bread in his pocket, and often would stop and scatter the crumbs on the ground. "Hansel, what are you stopping and looking back for?" said the father. "Come on!"

"I'm looking at my little pigeon that's sitting on the roof and wants to say goodbye to me," answered Hansel.

"Fool," said the woman, "that isn't your pigeon, that's the morning sun shining on the chimney." But Hansel, little by little, scattered all the crumbs on the path.

The woman led the children still deeper into the forest, where they'd never been before in all their lives. Then there was again a great fire made, and the mother said: "Just sit there, children, and if you get tired you can take a nap. We're going into the forest to cut wood, and this evening when we're finished we'll come and get you."

When it was noon, Gretel shared her bread with Hansel, who'd scattered his along the way. Then they fell asleep, and the afternoon went by, but no one came to the poor children. They didn't wake until it was pitch black, and Hansel comforted his little sister, and said: "Just wait till the moon comes up, Gretel, then we'll see the bread crumbs I scattered. They'll show us the way home." When the moon rose they started out, but they didn't find any crumbs, for the many thousands of birds that fly about in the fields and in the forest had picked them all up. Hansel said to Gretel: "Surely we'll find the way." But they didn't find it. They walked all that night and all the next day, from morning to evening, but they never did get out of the forest. And they were so hungry, for they'd had nothing to eat but a few berries they found on the ground. And when they got so tired that their legs wouldn't hold them up any longer, they lay down under a tree and fell asleep.

By now it was already the third morning since they'd left their father's house. They started to go on again, but they kept getting deeper and deeper into the forest, and unless help came soon they must die of hunger. When it was noon, they saw a beautiful snow-white bird, sitting on a bough, who sang so beautifully that they stood still and listened to him. As soon as he had finished he spread his wings and flew off ahead of them, and they followed him till they came to a little house. The bird perched on the roof of it, and when they got up close to it they saw that the little house was made of bread and the roof was made of cake; the windows, though, were made out of transparent sugar-candy.

"We'll get to work on that," said Hansel, "and have a real feast. I'll eat a piece of the roof. Gretel, you can eat some of the window—that will taste sweet!" Hansel reached up and broke off a little of the roof, to see how it tasted, and Gretel went up to the window-pane and nibbled at it. Then a shrill voice called out from inside the house:

"Nibble, nibble, little mouse,
Who is gnawing at my house?"

The children answered:

"It is not I, it is not I—
It is the wind, the child of the sky,"

and they went on eating without stopping. The roof tasted awfully good to Hansel, so he tore off a great big piece of it, and Gretel pushed out a whole round windowpane, and sat down and really enjoyed it.

All at once the door opened, and a woman as old as the hills, leaning on crutches, came creeping out. Hansel and Gretel were so frightened that they dropped what they had in their hands. But the old woman just nodded her head and said: "My, my, you dear children, who has brought you here? Come right in and stay with me. No harm will befall you." She took both of them by the hand and led them into her little house. Then she set nice food before them—milk and pancakes with sugar, apples and nuts. After that she made up two beautiful white beds for them, and Hansel and Gretel lay down in them and thought they were in heaven.

But the old woman had only pretended to be so friendly; really she was a wicked witch who lay in wait for children, and had built the house of bread just to lure them inside. When one came into her power she would kill it, cook it, and eat it, and that would be a real feast for her. Witches have red eyes and can't see far, but they have a keen sense of smell, like animals, so that they can tell whenever human beings get near. As Hansel and Gretel had got close the witch had given a wicked laugh, and had said mockingly: "Now I've got them. This time they won't get away."

Early in the morning, before the children were awake, she was already up, and when she saw both of them fast asleep and looking so darling, with their rosy fat cheeks, she muttered to herself: "That will be a nice bite!" Then she seized Hansel with her shriveled hands and shut him up in a little cage with a grating in the lid, and locked it; and scream as he would, it didn't help him any. Then she went to Gretel, shook her till she woke up, and cried: "Get up, you lazy creature, fetch some water and cook your brother something good. He has to stay in the cage and get fat. As soon as he's fat I'll eat him." Gretel began to cry as if her heart would break, but it was all no use. She had to do what the wicked witch told her to do.

Now the finest food was cooked for poor Hansel, but Gretel got nothing but crab shells. Every morning the old woman would creep out to the cage and cry:

"Hansel, put your finger out so I can feel whether you are getting fat." But Hansel would put out a bone, and the old woman's eyes were so bad that she couldn't tell that, but thought it was Hansel's finger, and she just couldn't understand why he didn't get fat.

When four weeks had gone by and Hansel still was as thin as ever, she completely lost patience, and was willing to wait no longer. "Come on, Gretel, hurry up and get some water! Whether he's fat or whether he's thin, tomorrow I'll kill Hansel and cook him."

Oh, how the poor little sister did grieve as she had to get the water, and how the tears ran down her cheeks! "Dear Lord, help us now!" she cried out. "If only the wild beasts in the forest had eaten us, then at least we'd have died together."

"Stop making all that noise," said the old woman. "It won't help you one bit."

Early the next morning Gretel had to go out and fill the kettle with water and light the fire. "First we'll bake," said the old woman. "I've already heated the oven and kneaded the dough." She pushed poor Gretel up to the oven, out of which the flames were already shooting up fiercely. "Crawl in," said the witch, "and see whether it's got hot enough for us to put the bread in." And when Gretel was in, she'd close the oven and Gretel would be baked, and then she'd eat her too. But Gretel saw what she was up to, and said: "I don't know how to. How do I get inside?"

"Goose, goose!" cried the witch, "the oven is big enough—why, look, I can even get in myself," and she scrambled up and stuck her head in the oven. Then Gretel gave her a push, so that she fell right in, and Gretel shut the door and fastened the bolt. Oh, then she began to howl in the most dreadful way imaginable, but Gretel ran away, and the wicked witch burned to death miserably.

But Gretel ran to Hansel as fast as she could, opened the cage, and cried: "Hansel, we are saved! The old witch is dead!" Hansel sprang out like a bird from its cage when the door was opened. How they did rejoice, and throw their arms around each other's necks, and dance around and kiss each other! And since there wasn't anything to fear, now, they went into the witch's house, and in every corner of it stood chests of pearls and precious stones. "These are even better than pebbles," said Hansel, and stuck into his pocket as many as he could; and Gretel said, "I'll take some home too," and filled her apron full.

"Now it's time for us to go. We must get out of this enchanted forest," said Hansel. But when they'd walked for a couple of hours they came to a wide lake. "We can't get across," said Hansel. "There isn't a plank or a bridge anywhere."

"There isn't a boat either," answered Gretel, "but there's a little white duck swimming over there—if I ask her to, she will help us over." Then she cried:

"They haven't a bridge and they haven't a plank,
Hansel and Gretel are out of luck.
Please take us across to the other bank
And we'll thank you so, you little white duck!"

The duck did come over to them, and Hansel sat down on her back and told his sister to sit behind him. "No," answered Gretel, "it would be too heavy for the little duck. She can take us over one at a time."

The good little bird did that, and when they were happily on the other side, and had gone on for a little while, they came to a wood that kept looking more and more familiar, and at last, in the distance, they saw their father's house. Then they started to run, burst into the living room, and threw themselves on their father's neck. Since he had left the children in the forest he had not had a single happy hour. His wife, though, had died. Gretel shook out her apron, and pearls and precious stones rolled all over the room, and Hansel threw down out of his pocket one handful after another. All their troubles were at an end and they lived together in perfect happiness. My tale is done, there is no more, but there's a mouse upon the floor—the first of you that catches her can make a great big cap from her fur.

Mother Holle

A widow had two daughters, the one beautiful and hard-working, the other ugly and lazy. But she was much fonder of the ugly, lazy one, because she was her own daughter, and the other was the household drudge who had to do all the work. Every day the poor girl had to sit near a well by the roadside and spin until her fingers bled. Now it so happened that once when her spindle was covered with blood she bent over the well and dipped it in the water to wash it off. But the spindle slipped from her hands and fell to the bottom. She burst into tears, ran home to her stepmother, and told her what had happened. The stepmother scolded her unmercifully. "You let it fall in,"she cried. "So you can just get it out again." The poor girl went back to the well and she didn't know what to do. In the end she was so frightened that she jumped into the well in the hope of retrieving the spindle. Then she lost consciousness, and when she awoke she was in a beautiful meadow. The sun was shining and there were thousands of lovely flowers.

She started walking across the meadow, and after a while she came to a baker's oven. It was full of bread, and the bread cried out: "Oh, take me out, take me out, or I'll burn; I was done long ago." So the girl found a baker's shovel and took all the loaves out, one by one. Then she went on and came to a tree that was full of apples and it cried to her: "Oh, shake me, shake me; all of us apples are ripe." She shook the tree, the apples fell like rain, until none were left on the tree, and after piling them up she went on.

Finally she came to a little house. An old woman was looking out of the window, and she had such big teeth that the girl was afraid and started to run away. But the old woman called out to her: "What are you afraid of, dear child? Stay with me; if you do my housework and do it properly, you won't regret it. Just so you take care to make my bed nicely and shake it till the feathers fly, for then it will snow on earth. I'm Mother Holle."* The old woman spoke so kindly that the girl took heart and agreed to work for her. And she did her work to Mother Holle's satisfaction, and always shook the bed so hard that the feathers flew about like snowflakes. In return she had a good life, never a harsh word, and every day there was boiled meat or roast meat. But after she had been with Mother Holle for

_____

* When it snows in Hessen, the people say: "Mother Holle is making her bed."

some time she grew sad. At first she herself didn't know what was wrong, but then she knew it was homesickness. Though she was a thousand times better off than she had ever been at home, she longed to be back. In the end she said to Mother Holle: "I'm homesick. I know how well off I am down here, but I can't stay any longer, I must go back to my family." Mother Holle said: "It pleases me that you should long for home, and because you've served me so faithfully I'll take you back myself." So she took her by the hand and led her to a big door. The door opened, and just as the girl was going through, gold came raining down from above and clung to her, so that she was soon covered with gold from head to toe. "That's your reward for working so hard," said Mother Holle. And then she gave the girl the spindle that had fallen into the well. The door closed and the girl was up in the world again, not far from her mother's house. When she went into the yard, the rooster was standing on the rim of the well, and he crowed:

"Cock-a-doodle-doo,
Our golden girl is home anew."

Then she went into the house, and her mother and sister made a great fuss over her because she was covered with gold.

She told them everything that had happened, and when the mother heard how she had come by her great riches, she wanted the same good fortune for her ugly, lazy daughter, so she told her to sit by the well and spin. To make her spindle bloody, she pricked her fingers and put her hand in a bramblebush, and then she threw the spindle in the well and jumped in after it. She woke up on the same beautiful meadow as her sister, and walked the same way. When she got to the oven, the bread cried out again: "Oh, take me out, take me out, or I'll burn. I was done long ago." But the lazy girl answered: "Do you think I want to get all dirty?" and went on. Soon she came to the apple tree, which cried: "Oh, shake me, shake me, all of us apples are ripe." But she answered: "Wouldn't you like that! Suppose one of you fell on my head!" And she went on. When she got to Mother Holle's house, she wasn't afraid, because she had heard about her big teeth, and she agreed right away to work for her. The first day she forced herself to work hard and do as Mother Holle told her, for she was thinking of all the money she would give her. But the second day she began to take it easy, and on the third day it was even worse, for she didn't even want to get up in the morning. And she didn't make Mother Holle's bed properly, and didn't shake it till the feathers flew. Mother Holle soon had enough of her slovenly ways and dismissed her. The lazy girl was glad because now, she thought, it was time for the golden rain. And true enough, Mother Holle took her to the door, but as she was passing through, it wasn't gold that poured down on her, but a big caldron full of pitch. "That's your reward for your services," said Mother Holle, and closed the door. So then the lazy girl went home, but she was all covered with pitch and when the rooster on the rim of the well saw her he crowed:

"Cock-a-doodle-doo,
Our dirty girl is home anew."

And the pitch refused to come off, and it stuck to her as long as she lived.

Hans Christian Andersen (1805–75)

Born in Odense, Denmark, in 1805, Hans Christian Andersen was a poor child, ambitious but a social outcast, who grew up to know firsthand both the lowest and the highest strata of society. First published in English in 1846, his allegorical literary fairy tales skewer social pretensions, but some, like "The Ugly Duckling," are also full of unfulfilled yearning and sometimes a world-weary bitterness. In this famous and more upbeat story, the child is the only one who tells the truth about the emperor; the tale dramatizes how the force of social opinion coerces everyone else (i.e., the adults) into pretending that what is not there is, in fact, there. Andersen illustrates the idea that Alison Lurie advances, that adults and children have opposing views of reality, and children are more honest about what they see. (See also the Andersen story "The Little Mermaid" in Part 8.)

The Emperor's New Clothes

Many years ago there lived an Emperor who was so uncommonly fond of gay new clothes that he spent all his money on finery. He cared nothing for his soldiers; nor did he care about going to the theatre or riding in the woods, except for one thing—it gave him a chance to show off his new clothes. He had a different suit for every hour of the day, and since he spent so much time changing, instead of saying, as one does of a king, "He is in his Council Chamber," they said, "The Emperor is in his Wardrobe."

Life was very entertaining in the big city where he had his court. Strangers arrived every day, and one day there appeared two rogues who spread the story that they were weavers who had mastered the art of weaving the most beautiful cloth you can imagine. Not only were the colours and patterns outstandingly lovely, but the clothes made from the cloth had the wonderful property of remaining invisible to anyone who was not fit for his job or who was particularly stupid.

"They would indeed be fine clothes to have!" thought the Emperor. "With those on, I could find out what men in my kingdom are unfit for the jobs they have. And I should be able to tell the wise men from the fools! Yes, I must have some of that cloth made up for me at once!" And he handed over a large sum of money to the two rogues to enable them to begin the work.

So they set their two looms up and looked as if they were hard at work, but there was nothing at all on the looms. They boldly demanded the finest silk and gold thread, which they put in their haversacks, and went on pretending to work at the empty looms until far into the night.

"I should like to know how far they've got with my cloth," thought the Emperor. But when he remembered that no one who was stupid or unfit for his job could see it, he felt somewhat hesitant about going to

see for himself. Now, of course, he was quite certain that, as far as he was concerned, there were no grounds for fear, but nevertheless he felt he would rather send someone else first to see how they were getting on. Everybody in the city knew what wonderful powers the cloth had, and they were all very anxious to see how incompetent and stupid their neighbours were.

"I'll send my honest old minister to the weavers," thought the Emperor. "He's the best one to see how the cloth's coming on, for he's sense enough, and no one's fitter for his job than he is."

So the good-natured old minister entered the room where the two rogues sat pretending to work at the empty looms. "God help us!" thought the old minister, his eyes wide open, "I can't see a thing!" But, of course, he was careful not to say so out loud.

Both rogues requested him very politely to take a step nearer, and asked him whether he didn't think the pattern beautiful and the colours charming. As they pointed to the empty loom, the poor old minister stared and stared, but he still could not see anything, for the simple reason that there was nothing to see. "Heavens above," he thought, "surely I am not a stupid person! I must say such an idea has never occurred to me, and it must not occur to anyone else either! Am I really unfit for my job? No, it certainly won't do for me to say I can't see the cloth!"

"Well, you don't say anything," said the one who was still weaving. "Don't you like it?"

"Oh, er—it's delightful, quite the finest thing I've ever seen!" said the old minister, peering through his glasses. "The design and the colours—oh, yes, I shall tell the Emperor they please me immensely!"

"Well, it's very kind of you to say so!" said the two weavers, and they went on to describe the colours and the unusual nature of the pattern. The old minister listened very carefully so that he could say the same thing when he returned to the Emperor. And that is just what he did.

The rogues now demanded a further supply of money, silk, and gold, which they said they must have for their work. But they put it all in their own pockets, and not a single thread ever appeared on the loom. However, they continued, as before, to weave away at the empty loom.

Soon afterwards the Emperor sent another unsuspecting official to see how the weaving was going on and whether the cloth would soon be finished. The same thing happened to him that happened to the minister: he stared and stared, but as there was nothing but the empty loom, he could not see a thing.

"Yes, it's a lovely piece of stuff, isn't it?" said the two rogues. And they showed him the cloth, and explained the charming pattern that was not there.

"Stupid I most certainly am not!" thought the official. "Then the answer must be that I am not fit for my job, I suppose. That would be a very odd thing, and I really can't believe it. I shall have to see that no one else suspects it." And then he praised the cloth he could not see, and assured them how happy he was with the beautiful colours and the charming pattern. "Yes," he told the Emperor, "It's quite the finest thing I've ever seen!"

The story of the magnificent cloth was now on everybody's lips.

And now the Emperor wanted to see it himself while it was still on the loom.

With a large number of carefully chosen courtiers—among them the two good old men who had been there before—he paid a visit to the two crafty rogues, who were weaving away with all their might, but with neither weft nor warp.

"Isn't it really magnificent?" asked the two officials. "Will Your Majesty be pleased to examine it? What a pattern! What colours!" And they pointed to the empty loom, fully believing that the others could undoubtedly see the cloth.

"What's this!" thought the Emperor. "I don't see a thing! This is really awful! Am I stupid? Am I not fit to be Emperor? That would be the most shocking thing that could happen to me!—Oh, it's very beautiful," he said aloud. "It has my very highest approval." He nodded in a satisfied manner, and looked at the empty loom: on no account would he tell anyone that he could not see anything. All the courtiers who had come with

him stared and stared, but none of them could make out any more than the others. But they all repeated after the Emperor, "Oh, it's very beautiful!" And they advised him to have a suit made of the wonderful new cloth so that he could wear it for the first time for the great procession that had been arranged. "It's magnificent! Delightful, excellent!" was repeated from mouth to mouth, and they all appeared to be deeply impressed and delighted with it. The Emperor gave each of the rogues an Order of Knighthood to hang in his buttonhole and the title of Knight of the Loom.

The two rogues sat up the whole night before the morning when the procession was to take place, and they had sixteen candles burning. Everyone could see that they had a job on to get the Emperor's new clothes ready in time. They pretended to take the cloth off the loom, they cut out large pieces of air with their big tailor's scissors, they sewed away with needles that had no thread in them, and at last they said. "Look, the clothes are ready!"

The Emperor with the most distinguished of his gentlemen came to see for himself, and the rogues both held one arm up as if they were holding something, and they said, "Look, here are the trousers. Here's the jacket. This is the cap." And so on and so on. "They are as light as gossamer! You'd think you'd nothing on your body, and that, of course, is the whole point of it!"

"Yes," said all the gentlemen, but they couldn't see anything, because there was nothing there.

"Will Your Imperial Majesty most graciously be pleased to take your clothes off?" said the rogues. "Then we shall put the new ones on Your Majesty over here in front of the big mirror."

The Emperor laid aside all his clothes, and the two rogues pretended to hand him his new clothes, one at a time. They put their arms round his waist, and appeared to fasten something that was obviously his train, and the Emperor turned himself round in front of the mirror.

"My, how well it suits His Majesty! What a perfect fit!" they all said. "What a pattern! What colours! It must be worth a fortune!"

"The canopy which is to be borne over Your Majesty in the procession is waiting outside," said the Chief Master of Ceremonies.

"Right," said the Emperor, "I'm quite ready. Doesn't it fit well?" And he turned round once more in front of the mirror and pretended to take a good look at his fine suit.

The Gentlemen of the Chamber, whose job it was to bear the train, fumbled on the floor with their hands as if they were picking it up, and then they held their hands up in the air. They dared not let anyone notice that they couldn't see anything.

And so the Emperor walked in the procession under his fine canopy, and everybody in the streets and at their windows said, "My, look at the Emperor's new clothes! There's never been anything like them! Look at the beautiful train he has to his coat! Doesn't it hang marvellously!" No one would let anyone else see that he couldn't see anything, for if he did, they would have thought that he was not fit for his job, or else that he was very stupid. None of the Emperor's clothes had ever had such a success before.

"But, Daddy, he's got nothing on!" piped up a small child.

"Heavens, listen to the voice of innocence!" said his father. And what the child had said was whispered from one to another.

"He's nothing on! A little child said so. He's nothing on!"

At last, everybody who was there was shouting, "He's nothing on!" And it gradually dawned upon the

Arthur Rackham's artistic skill with finely detailed silhouettes enabled him to depict the strutting body of the vain Emperor amid the frills of a courtly parade, even though the Emperor is wearing no clothes.

Emperor that they were probably right. But he thought to himself, "I must carry on, or I shall ruin the procession." And so he held himself up even more proudly than before, and the Gentlemen of the Chamber walked along carrying a train that was most definitely not there.

Heinrich Hoffmann (1809–94)

Heinrich Hoffmann was a German physician living in Frankfurt who noticed that his child patients and his own son responded well to comical drawings and verses depicting the horrible fates of disobedient children in humorous language. Some of his *Struwwelpeter* or *Slovenly Peter* stories have been controversial at times because they are (at least potentially) frightening— the most notorious is the story of the boy who sucks his thumb in spite of his mother's prohibition against thumb-sucking, and who has his thumbs cut off by a tailor with a giant pair of shears. Nonetheless, the tales remain popular in Germany and have been frequently imitated and parodied. Mark Twain sought to capitalize on their popularity when he was living in Berlin in 1891 by translating Hoffmann's 1845 cautionary tales for an English-speaking audience, but the slim volume was not published until after Twain's death. Recently, London and New York productions of *Shockheaded Peter* adapted the Hoffmann stories for adults by making them "ghoulishly comic" instead of cautionary. For a more contemporary satire of this tradition of cautionary tales, see Shel Silverstein's poem "Sarah Cynthia Sylvia Stout Would Not Take the Garbage Out," in Part 3.

The Sad Tale of the Match-Box

TRANSLATED BY MARK TWAIN

Paulinchen was alone at home,
The parents they down-town did roam.
As she now through the room did spring,
All light of heart and soul a-wing,
She saw where sudden burst on sight
The things wherewith one strikes a light.
"Oho," says she, "my hopes awake;
Ah, what a plaything these will make!
I'll take them on the wall, h'hoo!
As oft I've seen my Mother do."
And Mintz and Mountz, the catties,
Lift up their little patties,
They threaten with their pawses:
"It is against the lawses!
Me-yow! Me-yo! Me-yow! Me-yo!
You'll burn yourself to ashes, O!"

Paulinchen heard the catties not,
The match did burn both bright and hot,
It crackled gaily, sputtered free,
As you it in the picture see.
Paulinchen waltzed and whirled and spun,
Near mad with joy for what she'd done.
Still Mintz and Mountz, the catties,
Lift up their little patties,
They threaten with their pawses:
"It is against the lawses!
Me-yow! Me-yo! Me-yow! Me-yo!
Drop it or you are ashes, O!"

But ah, the flame it caught her clothes,
Her apron, too; and higher rose;
Her hand is burnt, her hair's afire,
Consumed is that child entire.
And Mintz and Mountz wild crying,
The while the child was frying,
"Come quick!" they said, "O Sire,
Your darling child's afire!
Me-yow! Me-yo! Me-yow! Me-yo!
She's cinders, soot, and ashes, O!"

Consumed is all, so sweet and fair,
The total child, both flesh and hair,
A pile of ashes, two small shoes,
Is all that's left, and they're no use.
And Mintz and Mountz sit sighing,
With breaking hearts and crying,
"Me-yow! Me-yo! Me-yow! Me-yo!
How could we let the parents know!"
While round that ash-pile glowing
In brooks their tears keep flowing.

Heinrich Hoffmann depicted cause and effect in words and pictures, as Paulinchen's grieving cats in "The Sad Tale of the Match-Box" fail to persuade the disobedient girl that playing with matches will lead to a horrific end: "You'll burn yourself to ashes!"

Thomas Bailey Aldrich (1836–1907)

Aldrich was a poet, novelist, short-story writer, and editor from New Hampshire; he edited *The Atlantic Monthly* in the 1880s. His best-known book, which influenced Mark Twain's writing of *Tom Sawyer,* was *The Story of a Bad Boy* (1870). It is based on his own childhood, and it portrays not so much a bad boy as a mischievous one with exuberant spirits, up to pranks and high jinks, such as setting an old stagecoach on fire or firing a pistol on the Fourth of July. The protagonist of the story is solidly middle class; Huck Finn is a lower-class outcast, but it is noteworthy that, like Huck in his novel, this boy tells his story himself.

From *The Story of a Bad Boy*

CHAPTER 7. ONE MEMORABLE NIGHT

Two months had elapsed since my arrival at Rivermouth, when the approach of an important celebration produced the greatest excitement among the juvenile population of the town.

There was very little hard study done in the Temple Grammar School the week preceding the Fourth of July. For my part, my heart and brain were so full of firecrackers, Roman candles, rockets, pin wheels, squibs, and gunpowder in various seductive forms, that I wonder I didn't explode under Mr. Grimshaw's very nose. I couldn't tell, for love or money, whether Tallahassee was the capital of Tennessee or of Florida; the present and the pluperfect tenses were inextricably mixed in my memory, and I didn't know a verb from an adjective when I met one. This was not alone my condition, but that of every boy in the school.

Mr. Grimshaw considerately made allowances for our temporary distraction, and sought to fix our interest on the lessons by connecting them directly or indirectly with the coming events. The class in arithmetic, for instance, was requested to state how many boxes of firecrackers, each box measuring sixteen inches square, could be stored in a room of such and such dimensions. He gave us the Declaration of Independence for a parsing exercise, and in geography confined his questions almost exclusively to localities rendered famous in the Revolutionary War.

"What did the people of Boston do with the tea on board the English vessel?" asked our wily instructor.

"Threw it into the river!" shrieked the smaller boys, with an impetuosity that made Mr. Grimshaw smile in spite of himself. One luckless urchin said, "Chucked it," for which happy expression he was kept in at recess.

Notwithstanding these clever stratagems, there was not much solid work done by anybody. The trail of the serpent (an inexpensive but dangerous fire toy) was over us all. We went round deformed by quantities of Chinese crackers artlessly concealed in our trousers pockets; and if a boy whipped out his handerkchief without proper precaution, he was sure to let off two or three torpedoes.

Even Mr. Grimshaw was made a sort of accessory to the universal demoralization. In calling the school to order, he always rapped on the table with a heavy ruler. Under the green baize tablecloth, on the exact spot where he usually struck, a certain boy, whose name I withhold, placed a fat torpedo. The result was a loud explosion, which caused Mr. Grimshaw to look queer. Charley Marden was at the water pail, at the time, and directed general attention to himself by strangling for several seconds and then squirting a slender thread of water over the blackboard.

Mr. Grimshaw fixed his eyes reproachfully on Charley, but said nothing. The real culprit (it wasn't Charley Marden, but the boy whose name I withhold) instantly regretted his badness, and after school confessed the whole thing to Mr. Grimshaw, who heaped coals of fire upon the nameless boy's head by giving him five cents for the Fourth of July. If Mr. Grimshaw had caned this unknown youth, the punishment would not have been half so severe.

On the last day of June the Captain received a letter from my father, enclosing five dollars "for my son Tom," which enabled that young gentleman to make regal preparations for the celebration of our national independence. A portion of this money, two dollars, I hastened to invest in fireworks; the balance I put by for contingencies. In placing the fund in my possession, the Captain imposed one condition that dampened my ardor considerably—I was to buy no gunpowder. I might have all the snapping crackers and torpedoes I wanted; but gunpowder was out of the question.

I thought this rather hard, for all my young friends were provided with pistols of various sizes. Pepper Whitcomb had a horse pistol nearly as large as himself; and Jack Harris, though he, to be sure, was a big boy, was going to have a real old-fashioned flintlock musket. However, I didn't mean to let this drawback destroy my happiness. I had one charge of powder stowed away in the little brass pistol which I brought from New Orleans, and was bound to make a noise in the world once, if I never did again.

It was a custom observed from time immemorial for the townsboys to have a bonfire on the Square on the midnight before the Fourth. I didn't ask the Captain's leave to attend this ceremony, for I had a general idea that he wouldn't give it. If the Captain, I reasoned, doesn't forbid me, I break no orders by going. Now this was a specious line of argument, and the mishaps that befell me in consequence of adopting it were richly deserved.

On the evening of the third I retired to bed very early, in order to disarm suspicion. I didn't sleep a wink, waiting for eleven o'clock to come round; and I thought it never would come round, as I lay counting from time to time the slow strokes of the ponderous bell in the steeple of the Old North Church. At length

the laggard hour arrived. While the clock was striking I jumped out of bed and began dressing.

My grandfather and Miss Abigail were heavy sleepers, and I might have stolen downstairs and out at the front door undetected; but such a commonplace proceeding did not suit my adventurous disposition. I fastened one end of a rope (it was a few yards nearest the window) and cautiously climbed out on the wide pediment over the hall door. I had neglected to knot the rope; the result was, that, the moment I swung clear of the pediment, I descended like a flash of lightning and warmed both my hands smartly. The rope, moreover, was four or five feet too short; so I got a fall that would have proved serious, had I not tumbled into the middle of one of the big rosebushes growing on either side of the steps.

I scrambled out of that without delay and was congratulating myself on my good luck, when I saw by the light of the setting moon the form of a man leaning over the garden gate. It was one of the town watch, who had probably been observing my operations with curiosity. Seeing no chance of escape, I put a bold face on the matter and walked directly up to him.

"What on airth air you a doin'?" asked the man, grasping the collar of my jacket.

"I live here, sir, if you please," I replied, "and am going to the bonfire. I didn't want to wake up the old folks, that's all."

The man cocked his eyes at me in the most amiable manner, and released his hold.

"Boys is boys," he muttered. He didn't attempt to stop me as I slipped through the gate.

Once beyond his clutches, I took to my heels and soon reached the Square, where I found forty or fifty fellows assembled, engaged in building a pyramid of tar barrels. The palms of my hands still tingled so that I couldn't join in the sport. I stood in the doorway of the Nautilus Bank, watching the workers, among whom I recognized lots of my schoolmates. They looked like a legion of imps, coming and going in the twilight, busy in raising some infernal edifice. What a Babel of voices it was, everybody directing everybody else, and everybody doing everything wrong!

When all was prepared, someone applied a match to the somber pile. A fiery tongue thrust itself out here and there, then suddenly the whole fabric burst into flames, blazing and crackling beautifully. This was a signal for the boys to join hands and dance around the burning barrels, which they did shouting like mad creatures. When the fire had burned down a little, fresh staves were brought and heaped on the pyre. In the excitement of the moment I forgot my tingling palms, and found myself in the thick of the carousal.

Before we were half ready, our combustible material was expended and a disheartening kind of darkness settled down upon us. The boys collected together here and there in knots, consulting as to what should be done. It yet lacked four or five hours of daybreak, and none of us were in the humor to return to bed. I approached one of the groups standing near the town pump, and discovered in the uncertain light of the dying brands the figures of Jack Harris, Phil Adams, Harry Blake, and Pepper Whitcomb, their faces streaked with perspiration and tar, and their whole appearance suggestive of New Zealand chiefs.

"Hullo! here's Tom Bailey!" shouted Pepper Whitcomb, "he'll join in!"

Of course he would. The sting had gone out of my hands, and I was ripe for anything—none the less ripe for not knowing what was on the tapis. After whispering together for a moment, the boys motioned me to follow them.

We glided out from the crowd and silently wended our way through a neighboring alley, at the head of which stood a tumble-down old barn, owned by one Ezra Wingate. In former days this was the stable of the mail coach that ran between Rivermouth and Boston. When the railroad superseded that primitive mode of travel, the lumbering vehicle was rolled into the barn, and there it stayed. The stage driver, after prophesying the immediate downfall of the nation, died of grief and apoplexy, and the old coach followed in his wake as fast as it could by quietly dropping to pieces. The barn had the reputation of being haunted, and I think we all kept very close together when we found ourselves standing in the black shadow cast by the tall gable. Here, in a low voice, Jack Harris laid bare his plan, which was to burn the ancient stagecoach.

"The old trundle-cart isn't worth twenty-five cents," said Jack Harris, "and Ezra Wingate ought to thank us for getting the rubbish out of the way. But if any fellow here doesn't want to have a hand in it, let him cut and run, and keep a quiet tongue in his head ever after."

With this he pulled out the staples that held the rusty padlock, and the big barn door swung slowly open. The interior of the stable was pitch-dark, of course. As we made a movement to enter, a sudden scrambling, and the sound of heavy bodies leaping in all directions, caused us to start back in terror.

"Rats!" cried Phil Adams.

"Bats!" exclaimed Harry Blake.

"Cats!" suggested Jack Harris. "Who's afraid?"

Well, the truth is, we were all afraid; and if the pole of the stage had not been lying close to the threshold, I don't believe anything on earth would have induced us to cross it. We seized hold of the pole straps and succeeded with great trouble in dragging the coach out. The two fore wheels had rusted to the axletree, and refused to revolve. It was the merest skeleton of a coach. The cushions had long since been removed, and the leather hangings, where they had not crumbled away, dangled in shreds from the worm-eaten frame. A load of ghosts and a span of phantom horses to drag them would have made the ghastly thing complete.

Luckily for our undertaking, the stable stood at the top of a very steep hill. With three boys to push behind, and two in front to steer, we started the old coach on its last trip with little or no difficulty. Our speed increased every moment, and, the fore wheels becoming unlocked as we arrived at the foot of the declivity, we charged upon the crowd like a regiment of cavalry, scattering the people right and left. Before reaching the bonfire, to which someone had added several bushels of shavings, Jack Harris and Phil Adams, who were steering, dropped on the ground and allowed the vehicle to pass over them, which it did without injuring them; but the boys who were clinging for dear life to the trunk rack behind fell over the prostrate steersmen, and there we all lay in a heap, two or three of us quite picturesque with nosebleed.

The coach, with an intuitive perception of what was expected of it, plunged into the center of the kindling shavings, and stopped. The flames sprung up and clung to the rotten woodwork, which burned like tinder. At this moment a figure was seen leaping wildly from the inside of the blazing coach. The figure made three bounds toward us, and tripped over Harry Blake. It was Pepper Whitcomb, with his hair somewhat singed and his eyebrows completely scorched off!

Pepper had slyly ensconced himself on the back seat before we started, intending to have a neat little

"At this moment a figure was seen leaping wildly from the inside of the blazing coach." Illustration by Edwin John Prittie from a 1927 edition of *The Story of a Bad Boy* by Thomas Bailey Aldrich.

ride downhill, and a laugh at us afterwards. But the laugh, as it happened, was on our side, or would have been, if half a dozen watchmen had not suddenly pounced down upon us, as we lay scrambling on the ground, weak with mirth over Pepper's misfortune. We were collared and marched off before we well knew what had happened.

The abrupt transition from the noise and light of the Square to the silent, gloomy brick room in the rear of the Meat Market, seemed like the work of enchantment. We stared at each other aghast.

"Well," remarked Jack Harris, with a sickly smile, "this is a go!"

"No go, I should say," whimpered Harry Blake, glancing at the bare brick walls and the heavy iron-plated door.

"Never say die," muttered Phil Adams, dolefully.

The bridewell was a small low-studded chamber built up against the rear end of the Meat Market, and approached from the Square by a narrow passageway. A portion of the room was partitioned off into eight cells, numbered, each capable of holding two persons. The cells were full at the time, as we presently discovered by seeing several hideous faces leering out at us through the gratings of the doors.

A smoky oil lamp in a lantern suspended from the ceiling threw a flickering light over the apartment, which contained no furniture excepting a couple of stout wooden benches. It was a dismal place by night, and only little less dismal by day, for the tall houses surrounding "the lockup" prevented the faintest ray of sunshine from penetrating the ventilator over the door—a long, narrow window opening inward and propped up by a piece of lath.

As we seated ourselves in a row on one of the benches, I imagine that our aspect was anything but cheerful. Adams and Harris looked very anxious, and Harry Blake, whose nose had just stopped bleeding, was mournfully carving his name, by sheer force of habit, on the prison bench. I don't think I ever saw a more "wrecked" expression on any human countenance than Pepper Whitcomb's presented. His look of natural astonishment at finding himself incarcerated in a jail was considerably heightened by his lack of eyebrows.

As for me, it was only by thinking how the late Baron Trenck would have conducted himself under similar circumstances that I was able to restrain my tears.

None of us were inclined to conversation. A deep silence, broken now and then by a startling snore from the cells, reigned throughout the chamber. By and by Pepper Whitcomb glanced nervously toward Phil Adams and said, "Phil, do you think they will hang us?"

"Hang your grandmother!" returned Adams, impatiently, "what I'm afraid of is that they'll keep us locked up until the Fourth is over."

"You ain't smart ef they do!" cried a voice from one of the cells. It was a deep bass voice that sent a chill through me.

"Who are you?" said Jack Harris, addressing the cells in general; for the echoing qualities of the room made it difficult to locate the voice.

"That don't matter," replied the speaker, putting his

face close up to the gratings of No. 3, "but ef I was a youngster like you, free an' easy outside ther, this spot wouldn't hold me long."

"That's so!" chimed several of the prison birds, wagging their heads behind the iron lattices.

"Hush!" whispered Jack Harris, rising from his seat and walking on tiptoe to the door of cell No. 3. "What would you do?"

"Do? Why, I'd pile them 'ere benches up agin that 'ere door, an' crawl out of that 'ere winder in no time. That's my advice."

"And werry good adwice it is, Jim," said the occupant of No. 5, approvingly.

Jack Harris seemed to be of the same opinion, for he hastily placed the benches one on the top of another under the ventilator, and, climbing up on the highest bench, peeped out into the passageway.

"If any gent happens to have a ninepence about him," said the man in cell No. 3, "there's a sufferin' family here as could make use of it. Smallest favors gratefully received, an' no questions axed."

This appeal touched a new silver quarter of a dollar in my trousers pocket; I fished out the coin from a mass of fireworks, and gave it to the prisoner. He appeared to be so good-natured a fellow that I ventured to ask what he had done to get into jail.

"Intirely innocent. I was clapped in here by a rascally nevew as wishes to enjoy my wealth afore I'm dead."

"Your name, sir?" I inquired, with a view of reporting the outrage to my grandfather and having the injured person reinstated in society.

"Git out, you insolent young reptyle!" shouted the man, in a passion.

I retreated precipitately, amid a roar of laughter from the other cells.

"Can't you keep still?" exclaimed Harris, withdrawing his head from the window.

A portly watchman usually sat on a stool outside the door day and night; but on this particular occasion, his services being required elsewhere, the bridewell had been left to guard itself.

"All clear," whispered Jack Harris, as he vanished through the aperture and dropped softly on the ground outside. We all followed him expeditiously—Pepper Whitcomb and myself getting stuck in the window for a moment in our frantic efforts not to be last.

"Now, boys, everybody for himself!"

CHAPTER 8. THE ADVENTURES OF A FOURTH

The sun cast a broad column of quivering gold across the river at the foot of our street, just as I reached the doorstep of the Nutter House. Kitty Collins, with her dress tucked about her so that she looked as if she had on a pair of calico trousers, was washing off the sidewalk.

"Arrah, you bad boy!" cried Kitty, leaning on the mop handle, "the Capen has jist been askin' for you. He's gone up town, now. It's a nate thing you done with my clothes line, and it's me you may thank for gettin' it out of the way before the Capen come down."

The kind creature had hauled in the rope, and my escapade had not been discovered by the family; but I knew very well that the burning of the stagecoach, and the arrest of the boys concerned in the mischief, were sure to reach my grandfather's ears sooner or later.

"Well, Thomas," said the old gentleman, an hour or so afterwards, beaming upon me benevolently across the breakfast table, "you didn't wait to be called this morning."

"No, sir," I replied, growing very warm, "I took a little run up town to see what was going on."

I didn't say anything about the little run I took home again!

"They had quite a time on the Square last night," remarked Captain Nutter, looking up from the Rivermouth Barnacle, which was always placed beside his coffee cup at breakfast.

I felt that my hair was preparing to stand on end.

"Quite a time," continued my grandfather. "Some boys broke into Ezra Wingate's barn and carried off the old stagecoach. The young rascals! I do believe they'd burn up the whole town if they had their way."

With this he resumed the paper. After a long silence he exclaimed, "Hullo!"—upon which I nearly fell off the chair.

"'Miscreants unknown,'" read my grandfather, following the paragraph with his forefinger; "'escaped from the bridewell, leaving no clue to their identity except the letter "H" cut on one of the benches. Five dollars reward offered for the apprehension of the perpetrators.' Sho! I hope Wingate will catch them."

I don't see how I continued to live, for on hearing this the breath went entirely out of my body. I beat a retreat from the room as soon as I could, and flew to the stable with a misty intention of mounting Gypsy and escaping from the place. I was pondering what steps to take, when Jack Harris and Charley Marden entered the yard.

"I say," said Harris, as blithe as a lark, "has old Wingate been here?"

"Been here?" I cried, "I should hope not!"

"The whole thing's out, you know," said Harris, pulling Gypsy's forelock over her eyes and blowing playfully into her nostrils.

"You don't mean it!" I gasped.

"Yes, I do, and we are to pay Wingate three dollars apiece. He'll make rather a good spec out of it."

"But how did he discover that we were the—the miscreants?" I asked, quoting mechanically from the Rivermouth Barnacle.

"Why, he saw us take the old ark, confound him! He's been trying to sell it any time these ten years. Now he has sold it to us. When he found that we had slipped out of the Meat Market, he went right off and wrote the advertisement offering five dollars reward; though he knew well enough who had taken the coach, for he came round to my father's house before the paper was printed to talk the matter over. Wasn't the governor mad, though! But it's all settled, I tell you. We're to pay Wingate fifteen dollars for the old gocart, which he wanted to sell the other day for seventy-five cents, and couldn't. It's a downright swindle. But the funny part of it is to come."

"Oh, there's a funny part to it, is there?" I remarked bitterly.

"Yes. The moment Billy Conway saw the advertisement, he knew it was Harry Blake who cut that letter "H" on the bench; so off he rushes up to Wingate—kind of him, wasn't it?—and claims the reward. 'Too late, young man,' says old Wingate, 'the culprits have been discovered.' You see Sly-boots hadn't any intention of paying that five dollars."

Jack Harris's statement lifted a weight from my bosom. The article in the Rivermouth Barnacle had placed the affair before me in a new light. I had thoughtlessly committed a grave offense. Though the property in question was valueless, we were clearly wrong in destroying it. At the same time Mr. Wingate *had* tacitly sanctioned the act by not preventing it when he might easily have done so. He had allowed his property to be destroyed in order that he might realize a large profit.

Without waiting to hear more I went straight to Captain Nutter, and, laying my remaining three dollars on his knee, confessed my share in the previous night's transaction.

The Captain heard me through in profound silence, pocketed the bank notes, and walked off without speaking a word. He had punished me in his own whimsical fashion at the breakfast table, for, at the very moment he was harrowing up my soul by reading the extracts from the Rivermouth Barnacle, he not only knew all about the bonfire, but had paid Ezra Wingate his three dollars. Such was the duplicity of that aged impostor!

I think Captain Nutter was justified in retaining my pocket money, as additional punishment, though the possession of it later in the day would have got me out of a difficult position, as the reader will see further on.

I returned with a light heart and a large piece of punk to my friends in the stable yard, where we celebrated the termination of our trouble by setting off two packs of firecrackers in an empty wine cask. They made a prodigious racket, but failed somehow fully to express my feelings. The little brass pistol in my bedroom suddenly occurred to me. It had been loaded I don't know how many months, long before I left New Orleans, and now was the time, if ever, to fire it off. Muskets, blunderbusses, and pistols were banging away lively all over town, and the smell of gunpowder, floating on the air, set me wild to add something respectable to the universal din.

When the pistol was produced, Jack Harris examined the rusty cap and prophesized that it would not explode.

"Never mind," said I, "let's try it."

I had fired the pistol once, secretly, in New Orleans; and, remembering the noise it gave birth to on that occasion, I shut both eyes tight as I pulled the trigger. The hammer clicked on the cap with a dull, dead sound. Then Harris tried it; then Charley Marden; then I took it again, and after three or four trials was on the point of giving it up as a bad job, when the obstinate thing went off with a tremendous explosion, nearly jerking my arm from the socket. The smoke cleared away, and there I stood with the stock of the pistol clutched convulsively in my hand—the barrel, lock, trigger, and ramrod having vanished into thin air.

"Are you hurt?" cried the boys, in one breath.

"N-no," I replied, dubiously, for the concussion had bewildered me a little.

When I realized the nature of the calamity, my grief was excessive. I can't imagine what led me to do so ridiculous a thing, but I gravely buried the remains of my beloved pistol in our back garden, and erected over the mound a slate tablet to the effect that "Mr. Barker, formerly of new orleans, was Killed accidentally on the Fourth of july, 18—in the second year of his Age." Binny Wallace, arriving on the spot just after the disaster, and Charley Marden (who enjoyed the obsequies immensely), acted with me as chief mourners. I, for my part, was a very sincere one.

As I turned away in a disconsolate mood from the garden, Charley Marden remarked that he shouldn't be surprised if the pistol butt took root and grew into a mahogany tree or something. He said he once planted an old musket stock, and shortly afterwards a lot of shoots sprung up! Jack Harris laughed; but neither I nor Binny Wallace saw Charley's wicked joke.

We were now joined by Pepper Whitcomb, Fred Langdon, and several other desperate characters, on their way to the Square, which was always a busy place when public festivities were going on. Feeling that I was still in disgrace with the Captain, I thought it politic to ask his consent before accompanying the boys.

He gave it with some hesitation, advising me to be careful not to get in front of the firearms. Once he put his fingers mechanically into his vest pocket and half drew forth some dollar bills, then slowly thrust them back again as his sense of justice overcame his genial disposition. I guess it cut the old gentleman to the heart to be obliged to keep me out of my pocket money. I know it did me. However, as I was passing through the hall, Miss Abigail, with a very severe cast of countenance, slipped a brand new quarter into my hand. We had silver currency in those days, thank Heaven!

Great were the bustle and confusion on the Square. By the way, I don't know why they called this large open space a square, unless because it was an oval—an oval formed by the confluence of half a dozen streets, now thronged by crowds of smartly dressed townspeople and country folks; for Rivermouth on the Fourth was the center of attraction to the inhabitants of the neighboring villages.

On one side of the Square were twenty or thirty booths arranged in a semicircle, gay with the little flags and seductive with lemonade, ginger beer, and seed cakes. Here and there were tables at which could be purchased the smaller sort of fireworks, such as pin wheels, serpents, double headers, and punk warranted not to go out. Many of the adjacent houses made a pretty display of bunting, and across each of the streets opening on the Square was an arch of spruce and evergreen, blossoming all over with patriotic mottoes and paper roses.

It was a noisy, merry, bewildering scene as we came upon the ground. The incessant rattle of small arms, the booming of the twelve pounder firing on the Mill Dam, and the silvery clangor of the church bells ringing simultaneously—not to mention an ambitious brass band that was blowing itself to pieces on a balcony—was enough to drive one distracted. We amused ourselves for an hour or two, darting in and out among the crowd and setting off our crackers. At one o'clock the Hon. Hezekiah Elkins mounted a platform in the middle of the Square and delivered an oration, to which his "feller citizens" didn't pay much attention, having all they could do to dodge the squibs that were set loose upon them by mischievous boys stationed on the surrounding housetops.

Our little party which had picked up recruits here and there, not being swayed by eloquence, withdrew to a booth on the outskirts of the crowd, where we regaled ourselves with root beer at two cents a glass. I recollect being much struck by the placard surmounting this tent:

ROOT BEER
SOLD HERE

It seemed to me the perfection of pith and poetry. What could be more terse? Not a word to spare, and yet everything fully expressed. Rime and rhythm faultless. It was a delightful poet who made those verses. As for the beer itself—that, I think, must have been made from the root of all evil! A single glass of it insured an uninterrupted pain for twenty-four hours.

The influence of my liberality working on Charley Marden—for it was I who paid for the beer—he presently invited us all to take an ice cream with him at Pettingil's saloon. Pettingil was the Delmonico of Rivermouth. He furnished ices and confectionery for aristocratic balls and parties, and didn't disdain to officiate as leader of the orchestra at the same; for Pettingil played on the violin, as Pepper Whitcomb described it, "like Old Scratch."

Pettingil's confectionery store was on the corner of Willow and High Streets. The saloon, separated from the shop by a flight of three steps leading to a door hung with faded red drapery, had about it an air of mystery and seclusion quite delightful. Four windows, also draped, faced the side street, affording an unobstructed view of Marm Hatch's back yard, where a number of inexplicable garments on a clothes line were always to be seen careening in the wind.

There was a lull just then in the ice-cream business, it being dinner time, and we found the saloon unoccupied. When we had seated ourselves around the largest marble-topped table, Charley Marden in a manly voice ordered twelve sixpenny ice creams, "strawberry and verneller mixed."

It was a magnificent sight, those twelve chilly glasses entering the room on a waiter, the red and white custard rising from each glass like a church steeple, and the spoon handle shooting up from the apex like a spire. I doubt if a person of the nicest palate could have distinguished, with his eyes shut, which was the vanilla and which the strawberry; but if I could at this moment obtain a cream tasting as that did, I would give five dollars for a very small quantity.

We fell to with a will, and so evenly balanced were our capabilities that we finished our creams together, the spoons clinking in the glasses like one spoon.

"Let's have some more!" cried Charley Marden, with the air of Aladdin ordering up a fresh hogshead of pearls and rubies. "Tom Bailey, tell Pettingil to send in another round."

Could I credit my ears? I looked at him to see if he were in earnest. He meant it. In a moment more I was leaning over the counter giving directions for a second supply. Thinking it would make no difference to such a gorgeous young sybarite as Marden, I took the liberty of ordering ninepenny creams this time.

On returning to the saloon, what was my horror at finding it empty!

There were twelve cloudy glasses, standing in a circle on the sticky marble slab, and not a boy to be seen.

A pair of hands letting go their hold on the window sill outside explained matters. I had been made a victim.

I couldn't stay and face Pettingil, whose peppery temper was well known among the boys. I hadn't a cent in the world to appease him. What should I do? I heard the clink of approaching glasses—the ninepenny creams. I rushed to the nearest window. It was only five feet to the ground. I threw myself out as if I had been an old hat.

Landing on my feet, I fled breathlessly down High Street, through Willow, and was turning into Brierwood Place when the sound of several voices, calling to me in distress, stopped my progress.

"Look out, you fool! the mine! the mine!" yelled the warning voices.

Several men and boys were standing at the head of the street, making insane gestures to me to avoid something. But I saw no mine, only in the middle of the road in front of me was a common flour barrel, which, as I gazed at it, suddenly rose into the air with a terrific explosion. I felt myself thrown violently off my feet. I remember nothing else, excepting that, as I went up, I caught a momentary glimpse of Ezra Wingate leering through his shop window like an avenging spirit.

The mine that had wrought me woe was not properly a mine at all, but merely a few ounces of powder placed under an empty keg or barrel and fired with a slow match. Boys who didn't happen to have pistols or cannon generally burned their powder in this fashion.

For an account of what followed I am indebted to hearsay, for I was insensible when the people picked me up and carried me home on a shutter borrowed from the proprietor of Pettingil's saloon. I was supposed to be killed, but happily (happily for me at least) I was merely stunned. I lay in a semi-unconscious state until eight o'clock that night, when I attempted to speak. Miss Abigail who watched by the bedside, put her ear down to my lips and was saluted with these remarkable words:

"Strawberry and verneller mixed!"

"Mercy on us! what is the boy saying?" cried Miss Abigail.

"ROOTBEERSOLDHERE!"

L. M. Montgomery (1874–1942)

L. M. Montgomery's best-known novel is not only a classic in the genre of orphan novels, which are remarkably prevalent in children's literature, but the novel and its sequels present a vivid evocation of a place and a community as well: Prince Edward Island, Nova Scotia, Canada. *Anne of Green Gables* (1908) is arguably the classic Canadian children's book; Prince Edward Island is a tourist attraction for fans from as far away as Japan, and the novel was filmed in an excellent adaptation with Megan Follows as Anne, Colleen Dewhurst as Marilla, and Richard Farnsworth as Matthew Cuthbert. Montgomery also wrote the fine *Emily of New Moon* series about another talented orphan. Both Anne and Emily have strong autobiographical elements. Montgomery grew up in a farming community on Prince Edward Island with her grandparents after her mother died. She became a teacher and later gave up her job to care for her grandmother. Anne is a self-inventing personality: she uses her imagination to survive hardship and loneliness, and she creates an identity for herself that transcends her narrow circumstances. She keeps making mistakes, but she never makes the same mistake twice, which suggests that she is constantly learning, but also that she has a great deal more to learn. In the chapter excerpted here, Anne's continued stay at Green Gables depends on her apologizing for her rudeness to the proper Mrs. Lynde, who insulted her looks and the color of her hair. Anne at first refuses, but then manages to transform an act of contrition into a dramatic triumph. (See also the excerpts from the *Emily* stories in Part 5.)

From *Anne of Green Gables*

CHAPTER 10. ANNE'S APOLOGY

Marilla said nothing to Matthew about the affair that evening; but when Anne proved still refractory the next morning an explanation had to be made to account for her absence from the breakfast-table. Marilla told Matthew the whole story, taking pains to impress him with a due sense of the enormity of Anne's behaviour.

"It's a good thing Rachel Lynde got a calling down; she's a meddlesome old gossip," was Matthew's consolatory rejoinder.

"Matthew Cuthbert, I'm astonished at you. You know that Anne's behaviour was dreadful, and yet you take her part! I suppose you'll be saying next thing that she oughtn't to be punished at all."

"Well now—no—not exactly," said Matthew uneasily. "I reckon she ought to be punished a little. But don't be too hard on her, Marilla. Recollect she hasn't ever had any one to teach her right. You're—you're going to give her something to eat, aren't you?"

"When did you ever hear of me starving people into good behaviour?" demanded Marilla indignantly. "She'll have her meals regular, and I'll carry them up to her myself. But she'll stay up there until she's willing to apologize to Mrs. Lynde, and that's final, Matthew."

Breakfast, dinner, and supper were very silent meals—for Anne still remained obdurate. After each meal Marilla carried a well-filled tray to the east gable and brought it down later on not noticeably depleted. Matthew eyed its last descent with a troubled eye. Had Anne eaten anything at all?

When Marilla went out that evening to bring the cows from the back pasture, Matthew, who had been hanging about the barns and watching, slipped into the house with the air of a burglar and crept upstairs. As a general thing Matthew gravitated between the kitchen and the little bedroom off the hall where he slept; once in a while he ventured uncomfortably into the parlour or sitting-room when the minister came to tea. But he had never been upstairs in his own house since the spring he helped Marilla paper the spare bedroom, and that was four years ago.

He tiptoed along the hall and stood for several minutes outside the door of the east gable before he summoned courage to tap on it with his fingers and then open the door to peep in.

Anne was sitting on the yellow chair by the window, gazing mournfully out into the garden. Very small and unhappy she looked, and Matthew's heart smote him. He softly closed the door and tiptoed over to her.

"Anne," he whispered, as if afraid of being overheard, "how are you making it, Anne?"

Anne smiled wanly.

"Pretty well. I imagine a good deal, and that helps to pass the time. Of course, it's rather lonesome. But then, I may as well get used to that."

Anne smiled again, bravely facing the long years of solitary imprisonment before her.

Matthew recollected that he must say what he had come to say without loss of time, lest Marilla return prematurely.

"Well now, Anne, don't you think you'd better do it and have it over with?" he whispered. "It'll have to be done sooner or later, you know, for Marilla's a dreadful determined woman—dreadful determined, Anne. Do it right off, I say, and have it over."

"Do you mean apologize to Mrs. Lynde?"

"Yes—apologize—that's the very word," said Matthew eagerly. "Just smooth it over so to speak. That's what I was trying to get at."

"I suppose I could do it to oblige you," said Anne thoughtfully. "It would be true enough to say I am sorry, because I *am* sorry now. I wasn't a bit sorry last night. I was mad clear through, and I stayed mad all night. I know I did because I woke up three times and I was just furious every time. But this morning it was all over. I wasn't in a temper any more—and it left a dreadful sort of goneness, too. I felt so ashamed of myself. But I just couldn't think of going and telling Mrs. Lynde so. It would be so humiliating. I made up my mind I'd stay shut up here for ever rather than do that. But still—I'd do anything for you—if you really want me to—"

"Well now, of course I do. It's terrible lonesome down-stairs without you. Just go and smooth it over—that's a good girl."

"Very well," said Anne resignedly. "I'll tell Marilla as soon as she comes in that I've repented."

"That's right—that's right, Anne. But don't tell Marilla I said anything about it. She might think I was putting my oar in and I promised not to do that."

"Wild horses won't drag the secret from me," promised Anne solemnly. "How would wild horses drag a secret from a person anyhow?"

But Matthew was gone, scared at his own success. He fled hastily to the remotest corner of the horse pasture lest Marilla should suspect what he had been up to. Marilla herself, upon her return to the house, was agreeably surprised to hear a plaintive voice calling, "Marilla," over the banisters.

"Well?" she said, going into the hall.

"I'm sorry I lost my temper and said rude things, and I'm willing to go and tell Mrs. Lynde so."

"Very well." Marilla's crispness gave no sign of her relief. She had been wondering what under the canopy she should do if Anne did not give in. "I'll take you down after milking."

Accordingly, after milking, behold Marilla and Anne walking down the lane, the former erect and triumphant, the latter drooping and dejected. But half-way down Anne's dejection vanished as if by enchantment. She lifted her head and stepped lightly along, her eyes fixed on the sunset sky and an air of subdued exhilaration about her. Marilla beheld the change disapprovingly. This was no meek penitent such as it behooved her to take into the presence of the offended Mrs. Lynde.

"What are you thinking of, Anne?" she asked sharply.

"I'm imagining out what I must say to Mrs. Lynde," answered Anne dreamily.

This was satisfactory—or should have been so. But Marilla could not rid herself of the notion that something in her scheme of punishment was going askew. Anne had no business to look so rapt and radiant.

Rapt and radiant Anne continued until they were in the very presence of Mrs. Lynde, who was sitting knitting by her kitchen window. Then the radiance vanished. Mournful penitence appeared on every feature. Before a word was spoken Anne suddenly went down on her knees before the astonished Mrs. Rachel and held out her hands beseechingly.

"Oh, Mrs. Lynde, I am so extremely sorry," she said with a quiver in her voice. "I could never express all my sorrow, no, not if I used up a whole dictionary. You must just imagine it. I behaved terribly to you—and I've disgraced the dear friends, Matthew and Marilla, who have let me stay at Green Gables although I'm not a boy. I'm a dreadfully wicked and ungrateful girl, and I deserve to be punished and cast out by respectable people for ever. It was very wicked of me to fly into a temper because you told me the truth. It *was* the truth; every word you said was true. My hair is red and I'm freckled and skinny and ugly. What I said to you was true, too, but I shouldn't have said it. Oh, Mrs. Lynde, please, please, forgive me. If you refuse it will be a life-long sorrow to me. You wouldn't like to inflict a life-long sorrow on a poor little orphan girl, would you, even if she had a dreadful temper? Oh, I am sure you wouldn't. Please say you forgive me, Mrs. Lynde."

Anne clasped her hands together, bowed her head, and waited for the word of judgment.

There was no mistaking her sincerity—it breathed in every tone of her voice. Both Marilla and Mrs. Lynde recognized its unmistakable ring. But the former understood in dismay that Anne was actually enjoying her valley of humiliation—was revelling in the thoroughness of her abasement. Where was the wholesome punishment upon which she, Marilla, had plumed herself? Anne had turned it into a species of positive pleasure.

Good Mrs. Lynde, not being overburdened with perception, did not see this. She only perceived that Anne had made a very thorough apology and all resentment vanished from her kindly, if somewhat officious heart.

"There, there, get up, child," she said heartily. "Of course I forgive you. I guess I was a little too hard on you, anyway. But I'm such an outspoken person. You just mustn't mind me, that's what. It can't be denied your hair is terrible red; but I knew a girl once—went to school with her, in fact—whose hair was every mite as red as yours when she was young, but when she grew up it darkened to a real handsome auburn. I wouldn't be a mite surprised if yours did, too—not a mite."

"Oh, Mrs. Lynde!" Anne drew a long breath as she rose to her feet. "You have given me a hope. I shall always feel that you are a benefactor. Oh, I could endure anything if I only thought my hair would be a handsome auburn when I grew up. It would be so much easier to be good if one's hair was a handsome auburn, don't you think? And now may I go out into your garden and sit on that bench under the apple-trees while you and Marilla are talking? There is so much more scope for imagination out there."

"Laws, yes, run along, child. And you can pick a bouquet of them white June lilies over in the corner if you like."

As the door closed behind Anne Mrs. Lynde got briskly up to light a lamp.

"She's a real odd little thing. Take this chair, Marilla; it's easier than the one you've got; I just keep that for the hired boy to sit on. Yes, she certainly is an odd child, but there is something kind of taking about her after all. I don't feel so surprised at you and Matthew keeping her as I did—nor so sorry for you, either. She may turn out all right. Of course, she has a queer way of expressing herself—a little too—well, too kind of forcible, you know; but she'll likely get over that now that she's come to live among civilized folks. And then, her temper's pretty quick, I guess; but there's one comfort, a child that has a quick temper, just blaze up and cool down, ain't never likely to be sly or deceitful. Preserve me from a sly child, that's what. On the whole, Marilla, I kind of like her."

When Marilla went home Anne came out of the fragrant twilight of the orchard with a sheaf of white narcissi in her hands.

"I apologized pretty well, didn't I?" she said proudly as they went down the lane. "I thought since I had to do it I might as well do it thoroughly."

"You did it thoroughly, all right enough," was Marilla's comment. Marilla was dismayed at finding herself inclined to laugh over the recollection. She had also an uneasy feeling that she ought to scold Anne for apologizing so well; but then, that was ridiculous! She compromised with her conscience by saying severely:

"I hope you won't have occasion to make many more such apologies. I hope you'll try to control your temper now, Anne."

"That wouldn't be so hard if people wouldn't twit me about my looks," said Anne with a sigh. "I don't get cross about other things; but I'm *so* tired of being twitted about my hair and it just makes me boil right over. Do you suppose my hair will really be a handsome auburn when I grow up?"

"You shouldn't think so much about your looks, Anne. I'm afraid you are a very vain little girl."

"How can I be vain when I know I'm homely?" protested Anne. "I love pretty things; and I hate to look in the glass and see something that isn't pretty. It makes me feel so sorrowful—just as I feel when I look at any ugly thing. I pity it because it isn't beautiful."

"Handsome is as handsome does," quoted Marilla.

"I've had that said to me before, but I have my doubts about it," remarked sceptical Anne, sniffing at her narcissi. "Oh, aren't these flowers sweet! It was lovely of Mrs. Lynde to give them to me. I have no hard feelings against Mrs. Lynde now. It gives you a lovely, comfortable feeling to apologize and be forgiven, doesn't it? Aren't the stars bright to-night? If you could live in a star, which one would you pick? I'd like that lovely clear big one away over there above that dark hill."

"Anne, do hold your tongue," said Marilla, thoroughly worn out trying to follow the gyrations of Anne's thoughts.

Anne said no more until they turned into their own lane. A little gypsy wind came down it to meet them, laden with the spicy perfume of young dew-wet ferns. Far up in the shadows a cheerful light gleamed out through the trees from the kitchen at Green Gables. Anne suddenly came close to Marilla and slipped her hand into the older woman's hard palm.

"It's lovely to be going home and know it's home," she said. "I love Green Gables already, and I never loved any place before. No place ever seemed like home. Oh, Marilla, I'm so happy. I could pray right now and not find it a bit hard."

Something warm and pleasant welled up in Marilla's heart at touch of that thin little hand in her own—a throb of the maternity she had missed perhaps. Its very unaccustomedness and sweetness disturbed her. She hastened to restore her sensations to their normal calm by inculcating a moral.

"If you'll be a good girl you'll always be happy, Anne. And you should never find it hard to say your prayers."

"Saying one's prayers isn't exactly the same thing as praying," said Anne meditatively. "But I'm going to imagine that I'm the wind that is blowing up there in those tree-tops. When I get tired of the trees I'll imagine I'm gently waving down here in the ferns—and then I'll fly over to Mrs. Lynde's garden and set the flowers dancing—and then I'll go with one great swoop over the clover field—and then I'll blow over the Lake of Shining Waters and ripple it all up into little sparkling waves. Oh, there's so much scope for imagination in a wind! So I'll not talk any more just now, Marilla."

"Thanks be to goodness for that," breathed Marilla in devout relief.

Astrid Lindgren (1907–2002)

The world-famous Swedish author of many children's fantasy and adventure books, Astrid Lindgren began telling the story of Pippi Longstocking in response to her daughter's request when her daughter was sick with pneumonia. Her daughter made up Pippi's name, and the wild and original story took off from there. Pippi, who appears in a series of books, beginning with *Pippi Longstocking* (1945), has a string of adventures that do not so much form a plot as express a way of experiencing the world. Pippi is an orphan: her mother died and her father, a pirate captain, was swept overboard in a storm. Pippi is startlingly different from the well-behaved, obedient children of most of previous Swedish children's literature. She is independent, irreverent, and unconventional. She breaks taboos and violates expectations—without disastrous consequences. She is a kind of supergirl—she has powers no ordinary child possesses, but she also has something refreshingly real and familiar about her. This mixture of fantasy and realism amounts to a kind of magic realism.

From *Pippi Longstocking*

CHAPTER 3. PIPPI PLAYS TAG WITH SOME POLICEMEN

It soon became known throughout the little town that a nine-year-old girl was living all by herself in Villa Villekulla, and all the ladies and gentlemen in the town thought this would never do. All children must have someone to advise them, and all children must go to school to learn the multiplication tables. So the ladies and gentlemen decided that the little girl in Villa Villekulla must immediately be placed in a children's home.

One lovely afternoon Pippi had invited Tommy and Annika over for afternoon coffee and *pepparkakor.* She had spread the party out on the front steps. It was so sunny and beautiful there, and the air was filled with the fragrance of the flowers in Pippi's garden. Mr. Nilsson climbed around on the porch railing, and every now and then the horse stuck out his head so that he'd be invited to have a cooky.

"Oh, isn't it glorious to be alive?" said Pippi, stretching out her legs as far as she could reach.

Just at that moment two police officers in full uniform came in through the gate.

"Hurray," said Pippi, "this must be my lucky day too! Policemen are the very best things I know. Next to rhubarb pudding." And with her face beaming she went to meet them.

"Is this the girl who has moved into Villa Villekulla?" asked one of the policemen.

"Quite the contrary," said Pippi. "This is a tiny little auntie who lives on the third floor at the other end of the town."

She said that only because she wanted to have a little fun with the policemen, but they didn't think it was funny at all.

They said she shouldn't be such a smarty. And then they went on to tell her that some nice people in the town were arranging for her to get into a children's home.

"I already have a place in a children's home," said Pippi.

"What?" asked one of the policemen. "Has it been arranged already then? What children's home?"

"This one," said Pippi haughtily. "I am a child and this is my home; therefore it is a children's home, and I have room enough here, plenty of room."

"Dear child," said the policeman, smiling, "you don't understand. You must get into a real children's home and have someone look after you."

"Is one allowed to bring horses to your children's home?" asked Pippi.

"No, of course not," said the policeman.

"That's what I thought," said Pippi sadly. "Well, what about monkeys?"

"Of course not. You ought to realize that."

"Well then," said Pippi, "you'll have to get kids for your children's home somewhere else. I certainly don't intend to move there."

"But don't you understand that you must go to school?"

"Why?"

"To learn things, of course."

"What sort of things?" asked Pippi.

"All sorts," said the policeman. "Lots of useful things—the multiplication tables, for instance."

"I have got along fine without any pluttifikation tables for nine years," said Pippi, "and I guess I'll get along without it from now on, too."

"Yes, but just think how embarrassing it will be for you to be so ignorant. Imagine when you grow up and somebody asks you what the capital of Portugal is, and you can't answer!"

"Oh, I can answer all right," said Pippi. "I'll answer like this: 'If you are so bound and determined to find out what the capital of Portugal is, then, for goodness' sakes, write directly to Portugal and ask.'"

"Yes, but don't you think that you would be sorry not to know it yourself?"

"Oh, probably," said Pippi. "No doubt I should lie awake nights and wonder and wonder, 'What in the world is the capital of Portugal?' But one can't be having fun all the time," she continued, bending over and standing on her hands for a change. "For that matter, I've been in Lisbon with my papa," she added, still standing upside down, for she could talk that way too.

But then one of the policemen said that Pippi certainly didn't need to think she could do just as she pleased. She must come to the children's home, and immediately. He went up to her and took hold of her arm, but Pippi freed herself quickly, touched him lightly, and said, "Tag!" Before he could wink an eye she had climbed up on the porch railing and from there onto the balcony above the porch. The policemen couldn't quite see themselves getting up the same way, and so they rushed into the house and up the stairs, but by the time they had reached the balcony Pippi was halfway up the roof. She climbed up the shingles almost as if she were a little monkey herself. In a moment she was up on the ridgepole and from there jumped easily to the chimney. Down on the balcony stood the two policemen, scratching their heads, and on the lawn stood Tommy and Annika, staring at Pippi.

"Isn't it fun to play tag?" cried Pippi. "And weren't you nice to come over. It certainly *is* my lucky day today too."

When the policemen had stood there a while wondering what to do, they went and got a ladder, leaned it against one of the gables of the house and then climbed up, first one policeman and then the other, to get Pippi down. They looked a little scared when they climbed out on the ridgepole and, carefully balancing themselves, went step by step, toward Pippi.

"Don't be scared," cried Pippi. "There's nothing to be afraid of. It's just fun."

When the policemen were a few steps away from Pippi, down she jumped from the chimney and, screeching and laughing, ran along the ridgepole to the opposite gable. A few feet from the house stood a tree.

"Now I'm going to dive," she cried and jumped right down into the green crown of the tree, caught fast hold of a branch, swung back and forth a while, and then let herself fall to the ground. Quick as a wink she dashed around to the other side of the house and took away the ladder.

"Pippi Plays Tag with Some Policemen." Louis Glanzman's cartoon-like drawing captures the humor of Pippi's mythic powers as she proves that she doesn't need the police to take her off to a children's home.

The policemen had looked a little foolish when Pippi jumped, but they looked even more so when they had balanced themselves backward along the ridgepole and were about to climb down the ladder. At first they were very angry at Pippi, who stood on the ground looking up at them, and they told her in no uncertain terms to get the ladder and be quick about it, or she would soon get something she wasn't looking for.

"Why are you so cross at me?" asked Pippi reproachfully. "We're just playing tag, aren't we?"

The policemen thought a while, and at last one of them said, "Oh, come on, won't you be a good girl and put the ladder back so that we can get down?"

"Of course I will," said Pippi and put the ladder back instantly. "And when you get down we can all drink coffee and have a happy time."

But the policemen were certainly tricky, because the minute they were down on the ground again they pounced on Pippi and cried, "Now you'll get it, you little brat!"

"Oh, no, I'm sorry. I haven't time to play any longer," said Pippi. "But it was fun."

Then she took hold of the policemen by their belts and carried them down the garden path, out through the gate, and onto the street. There she set them down, and it was quite some time before they were ready to get up again.

"Wait a minute," she cried and ran into the kitchen and came back with two cooky hearts. "Would you like a taste?" she asked. "It doesn't matter that they are a little burned, does it?"

Then she went back to Tommy and Annika, who stood there wide-eyed and just couldn't get over what they had seen. And the policemen hurried back to the town and told all the ladies and gentlemen that Pippi wasn't quite fit for an orphanage. (They didn't tell that they had been up on the roof.) And the ladies and gentlemen decided that it would be best after all to let Pippi remain in Villa Villekulla, and if she wanted to go to school she could make the arrangements herself.

But Pippi and Tommy and Annika had a very pleasant afternoon. They went back to their interrupted coffee party. Pippi stuffed herself with fourteen cookies and then she said, "They weren't what I mean by real policemen. No sirree! Altogether too much talk about children's homes and pluttifikation and Lisbon."

Afterward she lifted the horse down on the ground and they rode on him, all three. At first Annika was afraid and didn't want to, but when she saw what fun Tommy and Pippi were having, she let Pippi lift her up on the horse's back. The horse trotted round and round in the garden, and Tommy sang, "Here come the Swedes with a clang and a bang."

When Tommy and Annika had gone to bed that night Tommy said, "Annika, don't you think it's good that Pippi moved here?"

"Oh, *yes*," said Annika.

"I don't even remember what we used to play before she came, do you?"

"Oh, sure, we played croquet and things like that," said Annika. "But it's lots more fun with Pippi around, I think. And with horses and things."

Nina Mikkelsen (b. 1942)

Nina Mikkelsen has written widely in the field of children's literature. She is the author of a book about the distinguished African American author Virginia Hamilton (1994) and another about the fantasy writer Susan Cooper (1998). She has also published *Words and Pictures: Lessons in Children's Literature and Literacies* (2000) and *Powerful Magic: Learning from Children's Responses to Fantasy Literature* (2005). She has a Ph.D. in English from Florida State University and has taught at universities in Florida, North Carolina, and Pennsylvania. Her 1998 essay, reprinted here, was first published in a special issue of *African American Review* on children's and young adult literature. In this essay, she thoughtfully probes the question of what "authentic" means in the representation of different cultures. Although there may not be one single "authentic" way of telling a story, she argues, it does matter who tells the story and, above all, how.

Insiders, Outsiders, and the Question of Authenticity

Who Shall Write for African American Children?

"Let the Portmans go to Ireland, but as you know nothing of the Manners there, you had better not go with them. You will be in danger of giving false impressions. Stick to Bath & the Foresters. There you will be quite at home."

> Jane Austen, from a letter to Austen's niece, who had sent her the manuscript of a novel (qtd. in Mercer 307)

This romance was sketched out during a residence of considerable length in Italy, and has been rewritten and prepared for the press in England. The author proposed to himself merely to write a fanciful story, evolving a thoughtful moral, and did not purpose attempting a portraiture of Italian manners and character. He has lived too long abroad not to be aware that a foreigner seldom acquires that knowledge of a country, at once flexible and profound, which may justify him in endeavoring to idealize its traits. Italy, as the site of his romance, was chiefly valuable to him as affording a sort of poetic or fairy precinct.

> Nathaniel Hawthorne (Preface to *The Marble Faun* vi)

My themes are universal. And because the black people are the people I know, and the part of the group that I am, that is my center, so to speak, so my characters are black. Most of the time. . . . But it's very difficult when you're a black writer to write outside of the black experience. People don't allow it; critics won't allow it. If I would do a book that didn't have blacks, people would say, "Oh, what is Virginia Hamilton doing?" Yet a white writer can write about anything.

> Virginia Hamilton (qtd. in Rochman 1021)

This is a popular Japanese folktale and tells the story of a devoted pair of wild ducks. The illustrations in this beautiful book are subtle and suggestive but also an education in the dress, hairstyles, hierarchical levels of society, homes, customs and, not least, in eighteenth-century Japanese art. (I have been told that there are "inaccuracies" in the representations; the cummerbunds of the ladies are the wrong width and the upper-class ladies sport the hair styles of courtesans. And the Japanese never wear shoes in the house. This doesn't lessen my bonding with this book and, indeed, makes me want to find out more.)

> Judith Graham (commenting on *The Tale of the Mandarin Ducks* [retold by Katherine Paterson and illustrated by Leo and Diane Dillon], 24)

One central concern of scholars, literary historians, and critics these days is the matter of authenticity, especially the authenticity of cross-cultural and multicultural stories, and the ensuing conflict or question, Who will produce the literature of parallel cultures? An author of the character's own particular culture—or anyone? And for those who feel it doesn't matter (that anyone who can tell a good story should do so), we must ask, What makes a story good? Replicating reality to the fullest? Getting the facts and feelings *right?* Suppressing or distorting reality to make us think and feel differently? (Giving us new images to think with—and about?) But good for whom? Writers who want or need freedom of expression? Publishers who want the story to sell? Readers who want to find themselves in a book? Readers who want to find others in a book?

And which readers? Those closest to the author's own reality? Or those with different background experiences? Can a story really be *good* if it does not derive its material from the traditions (the memories, beliefs, preoccupations, and concerns) of an author whose cultural origins are shared by those of the story's characters? Jane Austen, with her concern for social realism, did not think so. And the remark she made about "the little bit (two inches wide) of ivory on which I work with so fine a brush" (qtd. in Tanner 1) has now become legendary. Nathaniel Hawthorne agreed in principle, and that is why he decided to make his story *The Marble Faun,* set in Italy, a fantasy and why he took great pains to sidestep a realistic portrait of his Italian characters. Virginia Hamilton protests the fact that she does not have the liberty of white authors, who either ignore Austen's advice or follow Hawthorne's example.

The question then arises, should Austen's advice be followed? What is the worst that can happen if it is not? Could the belief system of Austen's English niece have seeped into the words, thoughts, and behaviors of her Irish characters, usurping the traditions of the Irish culture being depicted? Could her story have been a really *good* one if this had happened? Judith Graham says yes, if readers become bonded with the book.

But what about the insiders of the culture being inaccurately presented who are made to feel demeaned, especially when these insiders are children just coming to grips with issues of identity, heritage, and self-esteem? Do we really want children—insiders or outsiders—bonding with inauthentic books? And what happens when they are left to do so? Consider Alice Walker, who tells how she felt about the Disney film in which Uncle Remus "saw fit largely to ignore his own children and grandchildren in order to pass on our heritage—indeed, our birthright—to patronizing white children" (31).

And what about children who are outsiders of the culture being mistakenly presented and are misled to feel that all belief systems are identical to their own; that all people's feelings, perceptions, propensities are the same as theirs—or that theirs is the one that counts? Consider the many adults who have read and loved Frances Hodgson Burnett's *The Secret Garden* (1911), but never noticed that Mary calls Martha "the daughter of a pig" because Martha had expected Mary to be a *native* of India, rather than "respectable white people." Then consider the main character of Mitali Perkins's *The Sunita Experiment* (1993), who does notice, as Perkins herself, growing up Indian-American in California, apparently did.

At times, when inclusion is the point of the story, as with *Amazing Grace* (London: Frances Lincoln, 1991, and New York: Dial, 1991), an amazingly popular children's book these days, it may seem that little if any harm is done if an outsider like Mary Hoffman, a London writer and journalist, according to my dustjacket, and white, according to my research, has produced the story. (Grace wants to dance the role of Peter Pan in her school play, but she cannot, her classmates tell her. She is black and she is a girl. She is also the best dancer, as she finally shows everyone, so she wins the role.)

On the other hand, if such books, or what we might call the literature of cultural pluralism, crowd out or replace books by insiders that may be more difficult for outsiders to understand but are particularly important for their growing, *multicultural* needs, then we may need to reassess our priorities. Or we at least need to ask ourselves, If schools and libraries cannot afford to purchase every book that is published, which books should be sacrificed—the ones that explore ethnic differences or those that highlight commonalities among members of different cultures?

Studies by Alan Purves have found that many students want only literature about people with whom they feel they have much in common; otherwise the students are not responsive (see Ostrowski). The idea of *multicultural* literature (that in which the idea of *different* world views or cultural references are built into the texture of the book itself—its focus, its emphasis, its subject matter) is a challenging one for readers who are not insiders of the culture being depicted. It necessitates, according to Reed Dasenbrock, that readers become "inscribed" into the text in various ways (17).

The usual way is for readers to undergo an initiation into a different world view: that of a character in a particular cultural group—related to ethnic, religious, or national ties—in a particular era. And in the area of children's or young adult literature, the initiation occurs as the character is *growing up* African American, Native American, Jewish American, Italian American, Indian American, and so on, although quite often these days we consider multicultural literature to be that written about members of under-represented cultures, which in America usually means Asian, African, Native, and Hispanic American. How the writer goes about initiating the character, however, is a particularly individual thing. Thus, there is no one way to create a multicultural book, certainly no one "right" way, since no two cultural experiences, even of the "same" ethnicity, are ever the same. (Even siblings might tell the supposedly "same" story differently.)

To incorporate readers into the tale, author Faith Ringgold places them into the situations of African American children, often those of earlier times (or the time of her own childhood). Modern readers might find themselves stepping into the "shoes" of barefoot Cassie, eight years old in 1939, in *Tar Beach* (Crown, 1991), who flies over the scenes of her family's history, telling her own story of growing up African American in New York City. Ringgold thus inscribes readers into Cassie's family's contemporary history by creating a children's picture book from an African American quilt on which was printed across the top and bottom borders the tiny text of her flying-child story. A wandering viewpoint causes readers to travel with Cassie through the pages. Often the viewpoint looks down on the scene, in order to elevate the importance of the characters, as when readers look up to see Cassie flying overhead as the story opens. Then, in the next scene, she is seen flying over her brother, who is lying down on the apartment building roof, across from the other family members who sit talking. Cassie's power (her ability to fly) is therefore a female power, also; she, not her brother, is the one overhead.

Readers, then, view Cassie sleeping below, and *they* are the important ones, sorting out the fact that Cassie is dreaming and journeying through a past time of family history. Later, readers are positioned above the scene, but at the same time they are alongside Cassie, who is flying over the scene in her dream/wish/memory visions; so they and Cassie look down together to see Cassie's mother sleeping under a vibrant red, green, and yellow African quilt pattern. Thus, child character and child reader assume adult importance: They are watching over the sleeping mother. Most of the time, however, readers are standing *alongside* Cassie, but outside the "picture": Cassie is no longer visible; she is projecting this story on a picture

book "screen" for readers who, alongside her, are viewing it. Flying, says Cassie, takes you somewhere "you can't get to another way." It also means claiming something as your own that is beautiful and has ties to you through family history.

Another and even more challenging way for readers to undergo cultural initiation is for the characters themselves to explore or become inscribed into a different world view *alongside* the reader throughout the story (character and reader are initiated together every step of the way). This approach is particularly important when the time and place are very different from those of the modern child. In Ringgold's *Aunt Harriet's Underground Railroad in the Sky* (Crown, 1992), Cassie encounters Harriet Tubman in one of her dream flights and is taken back into slavery days to learn more about her cultural history.

In Virginia Hamilton's *The Magical Adventures of Pretty Pearl* (Harper, 1983), Pearl, a goddess on Mount Kenya, looks across the ocean and sees the American slaves, and her strong empathy for them enables her to fly to them, transformed (or disguised) as a bird that rests atop a slavery ship (a bird of passage for the Middle Passage). Later, in America, she becomes a human child, one of the freed slaves who is attempting to find a way to live in the antebellum South during the reconstruction era when many black Americans suddenly found themselves facing man-made obstacles of bigotry and greed.

Readers of both books are being inscribed not only into the historical era but also into the narrative structures, strategies, and movements that the authors have chosen to complement their subjects, in this case genre blending (time-slip historical fantasy) and magic realism (imagined visions or dreamlike sequences sometimes involving levitating figures that represent a character's response to cataclysmic or traumatic events).

Where Ringgold and Hamilton use written text along with illustrations, Tom Feelings places readers and historical characters into the same situation the characters faced in their own day in a remarkable pictures-only book, *The Middle Passage: White Ships/Black Cargo* (Dial, 1995).

Readers are, as a result, inscribed into the slavery condition, just as the slaves are, at the exact moment of their passage. Feelings's intention is to align reader and character, one *inside* the other, in order to achieve a total emotional response to this painful human experience: "I want readers to participate in this," says Feelings, "to bring something to it" (qtd. in Ingalls B7). He carries out his intention through a combination of visual and critical strategies that may supersede any picture book artist's inventive conception for historical visualization.

Using the "colors" black and white for power and symbolism and imaginative evocation, a design of abstraction for graphic energy, and realism for reader identification, Feelings begins with the cover picture of the chained slaves aboard a boat on their way to the large "white" slave ship waiting farther out in the water, which is designed intentionally to draw reader and character together—to fuse them as one as they step into the larger "picture" of the story:

> The figures in the boat you can't see so clearly. . . . They're very dark. You have to look into the dark to see. When you look, you realize there are human beings, drawn realistically, who are chained. And then you realize you are in the boat with them, and the chains are connected to you. I wanted to make the thing . . . seductive. So that even if you couldn't take it at a certain point and [you] put the book down and closed it, the images will pull you back and you'll open it again. (qtd. in Ingalls B7)

Feelings says he wanted to create a book he "could hand to the people in Guyana, in Puerto Rico, in Cuba, in all the places that Africans were taken, and they would understand it." Who was the book made for? "For black people, of course . . . [and] for whoever opens it and can feel the human feelings" (qtd. in Ingalls B7). So the question of audience enters into any attempt to define the term *multicultural literature*. The primary audience, from Feelings's perspective, is the cultural group being represented. But readers of all groups are also important potential participants of the human experience that affects us all.

What counts is being an author with experiential understanding, gained usually through heritage (growing up in a particular ethnicity) and, if the time span is historical, through extensive reading and imaginative bonding with the people of the era, which produces strong commitment to helping others into and through the same emotional "passage." For twenty years Feelings worked on this book, reading all the materials he could find (journals, history books, fiction, ships' logs), reworking the book six times in order to, in his words, "reach that spot" in his

readers (the book is marketed for both children and adults) "that is open to the truth" (qtd. in Ingalls B6). Such perseverance does not rule out an outsider with strong empathetic feelings about a project; it is perhaps more often seen, however, when there is an inherited cultural imperative.

The multicultural book, then, is one that is thoroughly researched, in the case of historical genres or those involving realistic dimensions, and, at the very least, authentic in the sense of freedom from stereotypes and inaccurate details. An English children's book like *Amazing Grace* can be seen as multicultural in the broadest sense, in that it focuses on children of different color and background learning to live together or learning to respect one another's ways of thinking, living, or being. With such a large immigrant population (Indian, African, African Caribbean), English multicultural books often emphasize this broader conception of the term (with outsiders writing many of these books and educators, critics, and reviewers of the dominant English culture, like Judith Graham in the epigraph above, finding no fault with it). But for American children, the stereotypical (racist, sexist) thinking the book strives to overturn may be outdated. (Why couldn't Grace play Peter Pan? they ask. Sandy Duncan did. Diana Ross could.)

For English children, it might be otherwise. In fact a subtle "message" of the book may be that both the indigenous Anglo-female and the anti-feminist Indian male hold back the African Caribbean female, since in Grace's English classroom, it is blonde Natalie who tells Grace that she can't be Peter Pan ("'He isn't black'") and Indian Raj who tells her she can't be Peter ("'That's a boy's name'"). In the play, as it turns out, Natalie gets the part of Wendy, and Raj plays Captain Hook. So the names and casting choices may be the author's way to give each of these children a way to play the role he or she "fits" (an Indian boy gets to be a sexist villain of some importance; Natalie gets to be the confident big sister; Grace gets the lead). The question arises, however, is this type-casting or stereotyping?

What has been especially problematic about American multicultural books (and the same appears to be true in England) is the marketing tactic of coupling issues, which results in painting the multicultural child with a very broad brush. In *Amazing Grace* you get two "isms" for the price of one. And in the sequel to this book, *Boundless Grace* (Dial, 1995), as the book is entitled in America, and *Grace and Family* (Frances Lincoln, 1995), as it is called in England, Hoffman piles issue upon issue, none of which, in a picture book format, can be treated with the depth it deserves. First of all, Grace is a member of a bi-cultural family, African and African Caribbean; then her African father, she discovers, has a second family in Gambia, and this ultimately involves cross-cultural travel to Gambia for Grace and her African Caribbean grandmother, who lives with her and her mother. In addition there are the identity conflicts of two homes and two families, and a child's home culture where, in her school books, there are no stories about families like Grace's that don't live together—black, single-parent families, it is implied—and as a last issue, there is a child making her own "story" as she accepts her two families as they are.

Of equal concern, Grace is, in the second book, said to be from America in the American edition and from England in the English edition: "The children thought it was wonderful to have a big sister all the way from America [England]." And information about Mary Hoffman and the illustrator Caroline Binch, as Londoners, is dropped from the American book jacket, which also shows no pictures of them as *white* Londoners. But what is the rationale (except perhaps a wider market) for "dubbing in" a different national identity for Grace, especially since nothing in either book reflects an African American ethnicity? There is one sentence in the first book that attempts to reproduce an authentic speech pattern of the insider culture. The Caribbean grandmother, in the last sentence of the book says, "'If Grace put her mind to it, she can do anything she want.'" But can this one speech pattern produce an authentic portrait of the black child in England, much less an *African American* child in the American edition? (And is this particular speech pattern really an accurate one, or does the outsider author simply imagine that all black children, in all places, at all times, speak the same so-called "Black English"?)

Can we be satisfied with a jacket blurb that says "the author traveled to Gambia to ensure the accuracy of every background detail" and that "this commitment to authenticity brings the book vividly to life"? At least one group of American teacher-reviewers do seem to be buying, quite readily, into the advertising assertions:

> Caroline Binch's beautiful, painted illustrations are carefully researched. The artist visited Africa and her photographs became the source of the book's illustrations. Mary Hoffman also traveled to Gambia in Africa to make sure that every detail of her text was accurate. The students appreciated how much legwork is required in professional writers' and artists' lives. (Backer 64)

Publishers these days seem to have decided that traveling to a place can substitute for cultural affiliation or long-term interest and research in a culture. But do *professional* writers really operate in the manner that these writing teachers assume? Did Jane Austen advise her niece to imagine a story about Ireland and then make a brief visit to check out the facts? (Or did she tell her to stay at home where she was most at home?) Did Tom Feelings spend a few weeks in Uganda and then produce the pictures for *Moja Means One* (Dial, 1971)? Or did he live, work, travel, and study the culture there for several years beforehand?

So we come to the difference between deep and surface structures of multicultural literature and what ultimately produces greater concern for critics when outsiders attempt to write for other ethnicities: that writers will attend to surface features (observable details, facts, and idioms) but miss the bigger picture—the values, beliefs, and world view of the insider that can so easily be subsumed, usurped, or crowded out entirely by an outsider's pervasive thinking. What is especially strange in both *Boundless Grace* and *Grace and Family* is that Grace, with her African Caribbean grandmother (whom she calls Nana), doesn't seem to have been affected to any extent by the Caribbean oral tradition, as Virginia Hamilton's Junius was so strongly affected by his Caribbean grandfather's tellings in *Junius Over Far* (Harper, 1985).

Instead the text reads, "Grace knew lots of stories about wicked stepmothers—Cinderella, Snow White, Hansel and Gretel"—and "she wanted a father like Beauty's." When she arrives in Africa, she tells her stepbrothers and stepsisters "all the stories she knew—Beauty and the Beast, Rapunzel, Rumpelstiltskin"—and she finds it "amazing how many stories were about fathers who gave their daughters away." Hoffman does give a passing nod to the African storytelling tradition, when at one point Grace's father shows her the place in his Gambian village where his grandmother told him stories. And Grace replies that her Nana tells her stories, too. But there is no follow up to this comment.

Wouldn't the stories told to her by a Caribbean grandmother have been a bigger part of Grace's literary repertoire than they are here? Might they even have been so much a part of her cultural heritage that they gave her some kind of sustenance for the conflicts she faced? What stories might she have heard from her grandmother? How might they have differed from European stories? And how might their differences have been woven into this story—or even changed it significantly? Do African, African Caribbean, or African American folktales have wicked stepmothers? Do they show fathers giving their daughters away? Maybe they don't; in John Steptoe's Cinderella variant *Mufaro's Beautiful Daughters* (Lothrop, 1987), the father doesn't give his daughters away, at least not until they are of marriageable age—and then he accompanies them to the marriage place himself, along with a wedding party from his village.

Not every African American child reader would be familiar with Steptoe's picture book nor the African tale Steptoe draws upon for his story (G. M. Theal's *Kaffir Folk-lore,* 1896); thus, neither might Grace. The question is whether or not outsider authors are familiar with insider materials when they begin writing such a book and whether editors should consider the problems they face in changing a child's national identity for the American edition of a book. Not only does it insult members of an insider culture to treat them in such a generic manner, but it also produces a weaker book in literary terms (plot, conflict, depth of characterization, and most of all thematic "texture").

Perhaps Steptoe's book or a Caribbean grandmother's stories would have given Grace a different picture of her father—or has he become so Europeanized that he has become a Beauty-and-the-Beast father of European tradition, and no longer the father of Gambian traditions? Was he trying to get back to African traditions—and that's why he is there now and why he has invited Grace to Gambia? Is Grace's con-

flict rooted in the fact that she does read so many European fairy tales (that she has become Europeanized in England, despite a Caribbean grandmother)? None of this gets sorted out in the book, nor can it be, since the publisher has turned Grace into a generic child whose identity changes whenever the book crosses a national border. The problem is also one of focus (too many issues for a picture book); therefore another problem may be genre. There are seeds of a novel here, not a genre that an outsider author can tackle easily, or complete sufficiently, through travel research.

When outsider books succeed (*The Horn Book* gave *Boundless Grace* a glowing review), they seem to do so because of, rather than in spite of, the author's outsider status. (No one has to be inscribed into anything.) In fact *Boundless Grace,* says the reviewer, "transcends social, cultural, and geographic boundaries" (Burns 451), which means that the book is not really about what multicultural books are about: growing up in a parallel culture, or in this case growing up African American. Grace is growing up; she is said to be from America—in the American edition at least. But even though it is the author's purpose to picture a child who represents a world that is culturally diverse (a great deal is made of Gambian clothing, at any rate), we see only a surface texture of Gambian ways of life and nothing that can really be defined as American or African American. Have cultural boundaries been *transcended* here, or merely overlooked? What does Grace (or the reader) really learn about the deep structure of her ancestral heritage? Actually not much beyond what the illustrations show of a Gambian open market or Gambian dress styles.

A second-grade, Anglo-American teacher told me recently, "My students love Grace! She's strong and determined. Nothing stops her!" And when I described some of my concerns about authenticity, she replied very much like the English educator, Judith Graham, that none of those things bothered her. They didn't get in the way of the story for her and the fact that the book was *good* for children. They saw a strong female, she said, and that gave them hope that they could be strong too—not just the girls, but the boys, too. *Amazing Grace,* she said, was a color-blind and a gender-blind book. Like Graham, she had bonded with the story—and so nothing else mattered. Should it? Books like this might be described as literature of cultural pluralism, since they "forge a communal identity," in

Henry Louis Gates's words, that "may not yet have been achieved" (xiv). And that may be why white mainstream readers like them. They produce a good feeling that children like Grace, whom a reviewer describes as "one of the most engaging protagonists in contemporary picture books" (Burns 450–51), are out there dancing the lead or discovering crocodiles, fathers, and beautiful clothes in Gambia—and all's right with the world.

The general consensus of so-called mainstream thinking has always been that literature of cultural pluralism, at its best, helps children form empathetic bonds with fictional characters, and if these characters portray underrepresented cultural groups, children of the dominant culture bond with those of parallel cultures. "If we all could see each other exactly as the other is," Ezra Keats once said, "this would be a different world. But first I think we have to begin to see each other" (qtd. in Silvey 363).

In the 1960s, outsiders to African American culture produced books about a child finding a place of his own (Elizabeth Starr Hill's *Evan's Corner* [Holt, 1967]), a child's adventure with snow (Ezra Jack Keats's *A Snowy Day* [Viking, 1962]), a child learning to whistle (Keats's *Whistle for Willie* [Viking, 1964]), a child learning to live with a new sibling (Keats's *Peter's Chair* [Viking, 1967]), and a child who finds the perfect teddy bear (Don Freeman's *Corduroy* [Viking, 1968]).

In the decades since, we have seen a child who loves drawing everywhere and all the time (Rachael Isadora's *Willaby* [Macmillan, 1977]); a child who gets into trouble with his little brother, loses a tooth, and finds a new friend (Ann Cameron's *The Stories Julian Tells* [Knopf, 1981]); a child who plays detective (Cameron's *Julian, Secret Agent* [Random, 1988]); and a child imagining what it would be like to grow up in Africa (Virginia Kroll's *Masai and I* [Macmillan, 1992]). And because the children in all these books happen to be black (and the world view truly a *world* view), the black child became a world "player." None of the children in literature of cultural pluralism are necessarily American children; therefore, they are neither African American nor African in any specific way. Thus, like Grace, they are less ethnic, in core identity, than generic (the broad-brush approach) in their behavior, actions, and supposed feelings.

At other times white writers have given us books about white children finding a place of their own with black friends and black families in books like Lois Lowry's *Autumn Street* (Houghton, 1980) and Jerry Spinelli's *Maniac Magee* (Little, 1992). And even though the black characters in these books *are* necessarily American (Lowry's story is set in Boston, Spinelli's in Pennsylvania), because the emphasis is so strongly one of commonalities rather than differences, they fit easily the category as it is currently defined: the literature of cultural pluralism. Like the stories about Grace, the story is written from a white point of view (the outsider author's own "world" view). And readers of the same view can bond easily with the book and the characters because they feel so comfortable with that view (despite the fact that the black characters might never, in reality, share or possess that view).

What books like these seem to provide, more than anything else, are cathartic, "feel-good" experiences for white readers. In the case of *Autumn Street,* the black cook, Tatie, helps Elizabeth to see another side of her rigid, proper grandmother, by telling her the story of the grandmother attending a black child's funeral (that of Tatie's grandson) and not caring "right then" what color she or the black child's grandmother was. In the case of *Maniac Magee,* the white child continues to expose his black friend, Mars Bar, to various degrees of white bigotry in the hope of teaching the overt message: "Do not judge people by their color." The lesson never gets taught, however—and this is the *big* lesson of the book—even though the black child sacrifices his own life to save the child of the worst of these bigots, who learn the "lesson" and then quickly forget it. In either case, the black character is used as an instrument for the white reader's "feel-good" experience (there but for the grace of God go I as a bigot), and the books are showered with accolades and awards. (*Maniac McGee* actually won the Newbery Award in 1991).

"Feel-good" books do not necessarily present *authentic* experiences, even in Newbery winners, unless outsider authors are *exploring* or *representing* differences at the same time that they are attempting to *bridge* them. And bridging differences becomes something of a double bind for the outsider, who cannot really explore the insider culture *from the inside*—s/he has not *lived* the insider's experience. Lowry doesn't show us anything of Tatie's own grief for her grandson; her feelings must be subordinated entirely to serving the white child's feelings. We are left to assume that the hearts of the black church members were just as touched by the white grandmother's "liberated" gesture in entering a black church as readers are expected to feel. Spinelli tells rather than shows us differences between the white and black families (the McNabs and the Beales) depicted here in order to emphasize Maniac's color-blind condition in a racist world. Either family could be labeled any possible ethnicity, and the focus would simply change to classism or prejudice generally.

Arnold Adoff has been more successful in creating what might be described as an *authentic* literature of cultural pluralism, as a special category of multicultural literature. (Here the clauses—and emphasis—of the Keats quote would be reversed: If we all could begin to see each other, this would be a different world. But *first* we have to begin to see each other more clearly, or more completely.) In Adoff's story-poem picture books, he depicts children growing up in bicultural families (*Black is brown is tan* [Harper, 1973]), a girl who loves to run (*I am the running girl* [Harper, 1979]), and a girl reflecting on her bi-cultural identity (*All the Colors of the Race* [Lothrop, 1982]). Adoff is the father of bi-cultural children from his marriage to Virginia Hamilton, and he has incorporated authentic experiences of his own family life in these books.

In *Black is brown is tan,* he shows these experiences rising out of both European American and African American traditions important to the lives of both "branches" of the children's family. Hearing idioms and familiar expressions of the different family members and hearing about their foods, ways of preparing them, their music, songs, musical instruments, and storytelling activities—all of this helps to inscribe readers into what it means to be growing up *between* two particular ethnicities. The children are like all children in all families engaged in activities at mealtime, bedtime, a family-together time, but we see them depicted here as related specifically to the different ethnic backgrounds of the two parents. Cultural backgrounds are bridged by the concept of one family, but they also count as important for the story (they are explored).

Much of the same is true of *All the Colors of the Race,* which is probably Adoff's best poem-storybook, due to the imagery, language patterns, thought-provoking ideas, and humor. But here, since the intended reader is a slightly older child, Adoff can explore in greater detail the backgrounds of extended family members and the child's experiences at school (playing Harriet Tubman in the play) and at home (discovering different hair styles), as well as the child's inner feelings about race, prejudice, being different, being loved. A companion piece occurs in *I am the running girl.* Dedicated to the Adoffs' own "running girl Leigh," the book seems to be simply about running; however, the way Adoff plays with the word *race* produces for readers a deeper look at multicultural relationships, so that the text is particularly effective for showing all the different strands of cultural heritage in all of these girls who run—and running *through* Rhonda/Leigh. The illustrations by Ronald Himler support well this textual purpose.

In the novel form of this category, *authentic literature of cultural pluralism,* there is Sharon Dennis Wyeth's *The World of Daughter McGuire* (Delacorte, 1994), in which eleven-year-old Daughter (African-Italian-Irish-Jewish-Russian-American) explores her multi-faceted heritage (sorted out very nicely for readers in the cover art of Jerry Pinkney) in and out of her classroom, when her absentee father returns home and helps her to deal with the everyday problems of growing up. In her case, these problems include the more specific conflicts of identity she faces as a poly-ethnic child, conflicts she eventually can transcend, thereby realizing that she is a citizen of the *world.*

Unlike the books about Grace, Wyeth's main character is learning that families of fragmented ethnicity make traditions of their own that can nourish the need for family history at those times when stories are lost, forgotten, or thinly textured. Grace is making a story where there supposedly isn't one, but we see neither new traditions nor old stories here, simply messages: Families are what you make of them; stories are what you make of them. But what is Grace supposed to make of "Beauty and the Beast"? That it can have a different ending for her, if she wants to accept things as they are and has a great vacation?

What counts for the reviewer of *Amazing Grace,* we have seen, is that the book "transcends social, cultural, and geographic boundaries." But this "transcending" in so many examples of the "literature of cultural pluralism" occurs without the protagonist learning about the actual cultures being transcended (without readers being *inscribed* into them, as Adoff and Wyeth manage to do). And this is the real problem with simplistic thinking about American society, according to Gates: ". . . it's only when we're free to explore the complexities of our hyphenated American culture that we can discover what a genuinely common American culture might actually look like" (175–76). In other words, what gets to count as "universal" is an illusion, with an "Anglo-American regional culture" masking itself as "our common culture" (175).

Perhaps it all begins, this appropriation by the outsider of an insider culture, when writers like Hawthorne find themselves in foreign (or "foreign") places, because there is no way to write a new or different story at home (or the writer has run out of ideas for doing so). Hawthorne began borrowing Italian materials for the shadow, the mystery, the antiquity in them, in the same way that Americans at home began borrowing African American materials for the imaginative spirit in them. And just as Hawthorne, in 1859, was producing romance or fanciful realism in Italy because their "actualities" did not need to be so "terribly insisted upon" (vi), a young boy named Joel Chandler Harris, three years later, in 1862, was listening to the slaves on a Georgia plantation telling animal tales that he would retell for audiences around the world. The genre of folktale had the same effect for Harris that leaving America had for Hawthorne: He did not have to struggle with producing realistic portraits of African American manners and characters. Each writer succeeded because each divorced himself from what he really didn't know—the deep structure of an intriguing foreign (or "foreign") culture not his own.

Fortunately, Harris's work today, except as literary and cultural history, is not indispensable. Even without his collections, the stories would have come down the line orally, and African American tellers today would still be producing collections like Hamilton's *The People Could Fly* (Knopf, 1985) and *Her Stories* (Scholastic, 1995), filled with humor and rich, ca-

denced language to rival any other telling. And when storytellers tie the stories in their collections or picture books to the African or African American teller who inspired their own telling, as Lester does in the Afterword to *Black Folktales* (Richard Baron, 1969; illustrations by Tom Feelings) and Steptoe does in his Forward to *Mufaro's Beautiful Daughters,* they bring to light older and often neglected books. (Hurston's *Mules and Men* might have been out of print in 1969 when Lester's book was published, but that is certainly no longer the case.) They also inform American readers about African tales published or told in other countries, as does Lester's reference to the English edition (1968) of Bakare Gbadamosi and Ulli Beier's Yoruba stories and Steptoe's reference to G. M. Theal's collection of Kaffir tales. They situate modern readers in the social setting of the time when the stories were originally (or continually) told. Perhaps of greatest importance, however, they add more African and African American materials to the world caldron of stories: Divulging a source of a folktale (usually another collection of folktales) gives us all a look, as Lester says, at "many more good stories" (158).

Examining so many stories for possible use, African American story collectors and storytellers (oral, written, visual, editorial) ultimately become the ones with critical expertise in choosing the best stories to retell, recast, or create anew. They are also the ones with the need, as Gates says, to "arrive at theories of criticism indigenous" to the "black tradition" (67). He notes several ways African American writers for adults have explored their own materials through the years, and we can see these same "ways" filtering through African American literature for children and young adults as well.

In the beginning were the slave narratives: told, retold, remembered, later written down, published, read, reread, and then even later recast, recreated, transformed. Then there was the Harlem Renaissance of the 1920s and an interest by black editors like James Weldon Johnson in refuting stereotypes and promoting a theme of struggle shared by many African American writers through the production of black art, as a "self-defense against racist literary conventions" (Gates 29). African American literature and visual art forms were to come from black, rather than white, models in order to provide insight into the social realism of this group. The children's magazine founded by W. E. B. Du Bois, *The Brownies' Book* (1920–21), reflected this same goal.

In the 1930s, after Du Bois had set the standard and issued the call for books and illustrations modeled on and developed for African American children, two prominent members of the Harlem literary establishment, Langston Hughes and Arna Bontemps, discovered in *Popo and Fifina: Children of Haiti* (Macmillan, 1932), a way to wed adult aims for African American art and children's literature. Hughes's poetic language effectively complemented Bontemps's understanding of both childhood playfulness and parental concerns. "Langston had the story and . . . I had the children," Bontemps, a father of six, later said (qtd. in Hopkins 49). Bontemps went on without Hughes to produce more books about the black child, at the same time searching for a more realistic way to depict the child's speech. From a total use of standard English in *Popo and Fifina,* he reverted to moderate use of regional Alabama dialect in *You Can't Pet a Possum* (Morrow, 1934), finally producing in *Sad Faced Boy* (Houghton, 1937) an early version of Black English, as he moved from reproducing phonemic levels of speech to the replication of syntactic levels. Bontemps's books are perhaps even more important, however, for their authenticity. Here, for the first time, black children could read books written by a black adult who had observed the segregated worlds of both rural Alabama and urban Harlem.

A new emphasis emerged in the 1960s, Gates explains, when Amiri Baraka and Larry Neal published an anthology called *Black Fire* (1968), producing a black canon defined by the black vernacular and "the urge toward black liberation, toward `freedom now' with an up-against-the-wall subtext" (31). Virginia Hamilton's biographies of the early 1970s focused on two prominent African Americans who were often up against the wall: *W. E. B. Du Bois* (Crowell, 1972) and *Paul Robeson* (Harper, 1974). And two of her novels from these same years utilized this metaphor as the centerpiece of the books and her discussion of them.

Going through the "wall" is essentially what *The Planet of Junior Brown* (Macmillan, 1972) is about: emotional, physical, and mental survival in the modern, urban world. "When you find yourself up against the wall long enough," said Hamilton in 1972, "you begin to calculate your endurance against the wall. You begin to know how strong you are" ("Thoughts" 63). Building a wall to avert human disaster (the "burial" of home, heritage, and identity) is what *M. C. Higgins the Great,* written two years later (Macmillan, 1972), focused upon. Warren Miller's *The Cool World* (1959) reproduced both naturalistic setting and language in this novel about black urban street life—and the "wall." The book became an important "nugget" of one of Hamilton's later novels, *Sweet Whispers, Brother Rush* (1982).

To create works of authentic cultural representation, Hamilton begins most often with a character and some question, problem, or premise about the character. Although characters of the Hamilton canon have been African American, Amerind, African Caribbean, African, Black Indian, mixed (black/white, black/Amerind, African American/Caribbean), and white, her protagonists have usually been African American, except in the case of *Arilla Sun Down* (Morrow, 1976), in which the main character is part Native American, as was Hamilton's grandmother. What Hamilton brings to the Amerind character then is "sensitivity" and cultural memories (her mother often talked about her Amerind ancestry), she notes, rather than a "cultural imperative" (qtd. in Mikkelsen, "Virginia" 71), plus imagination and knowledge gained from research about Black Indians: "I write from the black experience for an audience as free and as large as I can find," says Hamilton ("Hagi" 90). That audience is generally young adults of approximately twelve or thirteen years old. The problem is one common to young adults generally in contemporary America (an absentee parent, a coming-of-age identity crisis, a new home in a new town, a visit to an uncle's home in the country one summer, a sibling rivalry or conflict), although it may also have a strong multicultural focus. For the writing of *Arilla Sun Down,* Hamilton says she wondered "what would happen in a strong black identity family [a bi-cultural family] if the Indian identity became very strong" (qtd. in Mikkelsen, "Virginia" 71).

Hamilton weaves into this "universal" situation a richly textured picture of African voices, traditions, values, beliefs, idioms, concerns, people, and stories that helps to inscribe the reader (of whatever ethnicity) into her own particular parallel culture—that of the Midwestern, rural African American. (The term *parallel culture* is one generated by Hamilton to designate "polyethnic, culturally diverse communities of present-day America," or communities other than those of the dominant culture: equal yet diverse ("Toiler" 6). At least seven interwoven threads produce the cultural fabric of Virginia Hamilton's books, or seven ways she has of inscribing readers into her own view of her own ethnicity:

1. Storytelling is a cultural way of knowing for the characters who tell stories, one to another (often an older character tells a younger one stories to teach about the heritage and history of a family or the entire cultural group), and to themselves, in order to amplify and comment on the story as a whole.

2. Ethnic feminist values permeate the books (women, especially mothers and foremothers of female children, tell stories for the transmission of culture). In fact, females appear in a range of situations, particularly those in which the supernatural exerts a magical and mystical power.

3. Mysteries of all kinds run through Hamilton's work, and stories may end with or without the mystery being solved (there is often an unresolved ending in order to keep a mystery alive).

4. The happy ending is often an elusive one also: Bad could follow good, as African Americans knew well. But Hamilton's world view rests on what she calls "the black American hopescape" ("Everything" 370), so the ending is at the same time always upbeat.

5. There is a preoccupation with freedom, equality, respect, and privacy for the individual and with the way members of the cultural community care for and bestow importance on the individual, particularly the growing child (it takes a village . . .).

6. Multiple perspectives about characters provide a sleight of hand for this author who is continually testing reader assumptions (subtleties of characterization—such as the use of color to heighten fictional mysteries, overturn conventions, and reverse stereotypical thinking—produce complex and complicated humans, never entirely good nor bad).

7. An important subject is the relationship of humans and animals (ecology is a natural part of the African American world, since the slavery condition caused black people, like Native Americans, to value the land and those dependent on nature as they were).

The values Du Bois emphasized (equality, justice, and self-esteem) produced for Hamilton "the moral sense of things" that she would later bring to her books as a "black American hopescape" ("Everything" 370). So there has been a direct line from Du Bois (1920) to children's literature today. We see this stream of Johnson and Du Bois operating most clearly in Hamilton's early novels, *Zeely* (Macmillan, 1967) and *The House of Dies Drear* (Macmillan, 1968), in which children learn to take pride in native materials and forms out of which family members carve, whittle, and create (oak tables, pine sculptures, dramas, histories, and stories). This "line" is alive and well at the present moment with the recently published collection *The Best of The Brownies' Book* (Oxford UP, 1996), edited by Dianne Johnson-Feelings, so that children today can not only learn about their cultural history; they can participate in it anew.

Another writer who has contributed to literary theory and African American traditions, especially in relation to children's and young adult books, is Walter Dean Myers. In 1994, interviewer Roger Sutton asked Myers, "Do you think it's possible to write a story about kids who *just happen* to be black?" Myers replied: "Absolutely. You can. You can write a story like this, but the question is, are you writing this story from a black point of view . . . not from any conscious deliberation, but because it's what you remember. It's your cultural fabric" (178). What Myers was really advocating was, at the very least, authentic literature of cultural pluralism. So we are back to our original question: Who should write for the black child? The outsider who sidesteps the insider point of view by placing a black child outside any particular cultural fabric? The insider who often resents this sidestepping? We have only to remember the Keats-Steptoe controversy that arose as Keats completed his seventh book about Peter, of *A Snowy Day* fame, in the early 1970s and drew a blistering attack from black critic Ray Shepard.

Keats was not telling the *real* story of a black child, said Shepard. The color of his characters was never relevant to the story. If white writers saw equality only in terms of similarity, his theory went, they could never really tell the black child's story. Thus the black child needed black writers, like John Steptoe, who could expose a reader to different ethnic experience and show that children could be equal and still be different. The notion that the black child might have separate feelings because of separate experiences was a new one to white writers, who for so long had followed the credo of the '40s—that all people have similar basic emotions, a fact more significant than differences in heritage, environment, or training.

And once Shepard's idea caught on with publishers, the doors opened wider for black writers and artists like Carole Byard, Lucille Clifton, Tom Feelings, Muriel Feelings, Leo Dillon, Nikki Giovanni, Eloise Greenfield, Sharon Bell Mathis, Mildred Taylor, and Camille Yarbrough in the 1970s, and more recently for Jeannette Caines, Pat Cummings, Valerie Flournoy, Vanessa Flournoy, Joyce Hansen, Angela Johnson, Patricia McKissack, Walter Dean Myers, Jerry Pinkney, Eleanora Tate, and Joyce Carol Thomas in the 1980s, and for Floyd Cooper, Donald Crews, Christopher Paul Curtis, Carol Fenner, Deborah Hopkins, Elizabeth Howard, Gloria Pinkney, Brian Pinkney, James Ransome, Faith Ringgold, and Jacqueline Woodson in the 1990s.

White writers and illustrators have continued to publish books featuring black characters: Arnold Adoff, Lloyd Alexander, William Armstrong, Marcia Brown, Louise Fitzhugh, Betty Greene, Ann Grifalconi, Trina Hyman, Rachael Isadora, Elaine Konigsberg, Jill Krementz, Mercer Mayer, Jerry Spinelli, and Margaret Zemach. But since these writers did not actually grow up African American or African, they have not, for the most part, been able to call up the necessary cultural memories required to present the most authentic black point of view.

Granted Jill Krementz's *A Black Girl Growing Up in the Rural South* (Harcourt, 1969), a photographic picture book featuring a nine-year-old living in a large, single-parent family in Montgomery, Alabama, and still, in the late '60s, attending a segregated school, is a rare achievement and an important historical document. Rachael Isadora's *Ben's Trumpet* (Greenwillow,

1979) is an outstanding work of art. There are the eloquent picture storybooks of Ann Grifalconi and Arnold Adoff that go far beyond surface multiculturalism. And the artwork of Diane Dillon, in collaboration with Leo Dillon, is always vibrant and exciting.

On the other hand, there have been disturbing examples of stereotypes (Brown, Konigsberg, and Meyer), caricatured artwork (Hyman), cultural inaccuracies in pictorial details (Zemach), unconvincing narrative voice (Brooks, Fitzhugh, and Greene), unconvincing setting (Alexander), artwork filled with implied negatives (Brown), condescending and superficial treatment of the ethnicity portrayed (Armstrong, Lowry, and Spinelli), and no distinguishing ethnic traits whatsoever for a black protagonist (Greene).

A defensive and largely white "industry" of publishers, editors, critics, and reviewers often seems unwilling or unable to see that children of *all* ethnicities deserve literature of artistic merit presented authentically—or well-told stories. Far too often critics leave out the factor of authenticity when they proclaim a story "well-told." But a *good* story is an *authentic* story, as Jane Austen explained centuries ago and as Hawthorne acknowledged by producing a romance about Italians since he knew he didn't really have enough experience with the social realism of Donatello's world to produce an authentic picture. For the last century, African American writers have been asking nothing less than to tell their own stories. Who can imagine any Anglo-American writer (for that matter any writer of any number of ethnicities) having to make such a plea? Who can imagine any Irish, Jewish, Greek, or Yoruba child having to learn about her ancestral heritage as told by an outsider to her culture—and by outsiders often too arrogant or too indifferent to do the necessary research?

Writers, no matter what their ethnicity, seem to see it a little differently. "You need to grow as an artist," Myers told Sutton, "and you can't do that when you're forced into an ethnic kind of role" (180). He recalls writing on subjects as various as bullfighting, kickboxing, and men's adventure stories when he "wasn't thinking only of writing about 'the problem'" (179). Myers's complaint comes down on the side of experience, realism, the actual, the representative, the real, or a sense of social realism, in that he knows about a great many things and feels that the narrative "voice" of these subjects transcends ethnicity or speaks to a larger world than that of his own ethnic background.

Hamilton also argues for a way out of ethnic roles: "Imaginative use of language and ideas illuminates for us a human condition, and we are reminded again to care who we Americans are" ("Hagi" 91). And her writing process is the best lesson in everything-you-ever-wanted-to-know-about-creating-authentic-fiction of the human condition: "I create characters and the characters create the society in which they live. Once the characters are defined, they have brought their world with them, and so I have uncovered that world. . . . it's like a painting. You fill in all this around the person—the history, the time, the place . . . the way somebody moves or what they say or how they act" (qtd. in Mikkelsen, "Virginia" 75).

Myers has through the years enlarged his experiential "canvas" far beyond the two-inch African American square with which he began; he wants to be able to paint on his own entire canvas. In *Shadow of the Red Moon* (Scholastic, 1995), he produces two races of fantasy children struggling for survival; thus he finds a way to expand far beyond his own ethnic "picture." Hamilton's large canvas is overflowing with many larger-than-life figures. For Hamilton, imagination involves risk, but it also manages to rescue her each time from difficulties, limits, and impediments. "I'm always running up against" limitations, says Hamilton, "and knocking it down in different ways, whichever way I can" (qtd. in Rochman 1021). She asks only for equity. If others are allowed to paint on her canvas, she wants the same privilege: to paint on theirs. Who presents the best case?

Is is it down with the barricades—*all* barricades for *all* writers—and on with the show? No. Those who have lived the black experience, in any of its myriad dimensions (region, nation, ethnicity, social group, economic status, gender), can still do the job better. This is not to say that an outsider's story should be censored or suppressed; it is too important for showing how we have seen and depicted insider cultures through the

years. Let Helen Bannerman's *Little Black Sambo* (Frederick Stokes, 1900) remain on the shelves beside Julius Lester's *Sam and the Tigers* (Dial, 1996) and Fred Marcellino's *The Story of Little Babaji* (Harper, 1996) to teach us all more about the American past. Let *Amazing Grace* remain on the shelves beside Joyce Carol Thomas's *Brown Honey in Broomwheat Tea* (Harper, 1993) and *Gingerbread Days* (Harper, 1995) to teach us more about the American present and to remind us that, if the social consciousness of children is shaped by outsider writers, the result will be a homogenized culture and synthetic rather than *real* literature, whether or not it is produced with the eloquence of William Armstrong's *Sounder* (Harper, 1969) or the mediocrity of *Amazing Grace*.

We need to see the widest spectrum of insider voices—old and young, female and male, urban and rural, North and South, Midwest and Far West, upper-class and under-class—and ethnicities of the most diverse blendings—monocultural, bi-cultural, cross-cultural, multicultural. And the more of these poly-ethnic voices the better. The question is no longer whether we will have white authors or black authors, since race is a social construct and we are all, in some way, "mixed"; nor is it whether we will have authentic or inauthentic authors, since cultural memories (experiential understandings) will nearly always produce greater authenticity than research alone can provide. It is instead a question of whether we will have diversity *within* authenticity. And we are more likely to have such nuances, such distinctions, such subtleties, such *realism,* whatever the genre, if insiders tell their own stories. Ultimately it's not the size of the canvas but the type of brush strokes that matters. Austen painted with the tiniest of brushes for her grand designs.

Writers like Hamilton (and Julius Lester, Patricia McKissack, and John Steptoe, among others), who have made a lifetime choice of listening to, collecting, and transmitting the stories of their own culture, reveal that it *does* matter who tells the stories. They are the ones who know the tales firsthand from their own family and community storytelling traditions. They are the ones who have heard and internalized the language patterns in the cultural transmissions. They are also the ones who often spend long hours searching out the long-hidden or forgotten African American and African sources for new tellings. They are the ones with the cultural imperative to do the telling, and to get it *right.*

WORKS CITED

Austen-Leigh, J. E. *A Memoir of Jane Austen.* Ed. R. W. Chapman. London: Oxford UP, 1926.

Backer, Joan, et al. "Weaving Literature into the School Community." *New Advocate* 9 (Winter 1996): 61–74.

Burns, Mary. Rev. of *Boundless Grace. Horn Book* 72 (July/Aug. 1996): 450–51.

Dasenbrock, Reed. "Intelligibility and Meaningfulness in Multicultural Literature in English." *PMLA* 102 (Jan. 1987): 10–19.

Gates, Henry Louis. *Loose Canons: Notes on the Culture Wars.* New York: Oxford UP, 1992.

Graham, Judith. "Using Illustration as a Bridge Between Fact and Fiction." *English in Education* 30 (Spring 1996): 18–25.

Hamilton, Virginia. "Everything of Value: Moral Realism in Literature for Children." *Journal of Youth Services in Libraries* 6 (Summer 1993): 363–77.

———. "Hagi, Mose, and Drylongso." *The Zena Sutherland Lectures, 1983–1991.* Ed. Betsy Hearne. New York: Clarion, 1992. 75–91.

———. "Thoughts on Children's Books, Reading and Ethnic America." *Reading, Children's Books, and Our Pluralistic Society.* Ed. Harold Tanyzer and Jean Karl. Newark: International Reading Association, 1972. 61–64.

———. "A Toiler, A Teller." *Many Faces, Many Voices: Multicultural Literary Experiences for Youth; The Virginia Hamilton Conference.* Ed. Anthony Manna and Carolyn Brodie. Fort Atkinson: Highsmith P, 1992. 6.

Hawthorne, Nathaniel. "Preface." *The Marble Faun.* New York: NAL, 1961. v–vii.

Hopkins, Lee Bennett. *More Books By More People.* New York: Citation P, 1974.

Ingalls, Zoe. "Images of Slavery." *Chronicle of Higher Education* 15 Feb. 1996: B6–B7.

Mercer, Caroline. "Afterword." *Sense and Sensibility,* by Jane Austen. New York: NAL, 1980. 307–14.

Mikkelsen, Nina. *Virginia Hamilton.* New York: Twayne, 1994.

———. "Virginia Hamilton: Continuing the Conversation." *New Advocate* 8 (Spring 1995): 67–82.

Ostrowski, Steven. "Literature and Multiculturalism: The Challenge of Teaching and Learning About the Literature of Diverse Cultures." *National Research Center on Literature Teaching and Learning Literature Update* Fall 1994: 1–2, 4.

Rochman, Hazel. "The Booklist Interview." *Booklist* 1 Feb. 1992: 1020–21.

Shepard, Ray. "Adventures in Blackland with Keats and Steptoe." *Interracial Books for Children* 3 (Autumn 1971): 2–3.

Silvey, Anita, ed. *Children's Books and Their Creators.* Boston: Houghton, 1995.

Sutton, Roger. "Interview" [with Walter Dean Myers]. *School Library Journal* 40 (June 1994): 24–28.

Tanner, Tony. *Jane Austen.* Cambridge: Harvard UP, 1986.

Theal, George. *Kaffir Folk-lore.* 1896. Westport: Greenwood, 1970.

Walker, Alice. *Living By the Word.* New York: Harcourt, 1989.

Mette Newth (b.1942)

Norwegian author Mette Newth's *The Abduction* (1989) is told from two different perspectives—that of Osuqo, an Inuit girl who is brutally abducted, with her intended husband, Poq, from her native Greenland in the seventeenth century, and that of Christine, the Norwegian servant girl who is assigned the task of tending to Osuqo and Poq. Earlier in the story, Osuqo is raped on board the ship on which she is a captive, and the traumatized young people are transported to a society where they are regarded as barely human or worse. Christine's father, a member of the expedition that "captures" Osuqo and Poq, is killed in a freak accident aboard the ship, and Osuqo is blamed for his death. Yet, as this excerpt shows, Christine finds herself strangely drawn to these aliens. The book is a powerful indictment of the greed and arrogance of European explorers and traders, and it seeks to re-create, as in the excerpted passage, something of the worldview as well as the experiences of the Inuit whose lives were disrupted by them. Newth is seeking to recuperate the experiences of the Inuit, who were killed and enslaved by her ancestors, European traders and explorers. Thus, she is writing as an outsider in the portions of the book portraying the Inuit perspective—a dilemma that she is acutely conscious of. Newth reflects on the suppressed history of European exploitation and abuse of the people of the North. She had to dig deep into the historical record to uncover the shameful evidence of this history. Her essay "On Writing *The Abduction*" addresses the question of what responsibility and what consequences the knowledge of this history bring with it. Related issues are addressed in Nina Mikkelsen's essay, "Insiders, Outsiders, and the Question of Authenticity."

From *The Abduction*

"I will."

"You can't."

"I will anyway," he said stubbornly.

Osuqo couldn't see his eyes, only his shiny black forelock, which was just as obstinate as he was.

"Mother and Father have said no. You know that."

Chubby arms were suddenly clasped around her neck. Black eyes stared into hers. Black with glints of gold and laughter.

"Osuqo! You're my best friend."

"You still can't do it."

They were sitting silently in the heather. Little Brother's hand gently brushed over the tiny glowing flowers, part of the brilliant bounty that nature had given the land.

The summer was almost over. The journey back to the winter settlement was about to begin.

"They want me to go with them," he said suddenly.

"You? Little Brother. You're too young!"

"Grandfather and Grandmother want me to go. Grandfather has something to give me when we get there. I *want* to go, Osuqo. Can't you ask Father and Mother for me again?"

"Oh, Little Brother!" Her tears were close at hand now.

She had dreaded this all summer long. Now Little Brother was making it more difficult, but he didn't understand that.

Home at the winter settlement, when they had started out on the long journey to the summer encampment, Osuqo had realized that it would be Grandmother's last journey.

Grandmother had never recovered from the long famine the previous winter when the storms had raged day after day and the hunters couldn't go out on the ice after seals. Without fresh meat, their supply of dried meat and fish had diminished very quickly. Trapped inside the longhouses, the families had to ration their food. But Grandmother had refused to accept even the few scraps that everyone got each day. "It is the young who need energy, let them have it. My strength will soon be gone anyway." Osuqo had seen her give Little Brother most of the small amount she accepted. He had managed better than most during the long famine, but Grandmother had grown thin and weak. When the time came for the summer journey, Father had looked at her anxiously. "I'll manage the journey to the summer encampment," she had said calmly, "but you know it will be my last one." Father had nodded silently, and Osuqo realized with sorrow that her grandmother would choose a different path when summer was over and the deadly winter cold approached.

Osuqo knew very well that the nomadic people had lived with this law of life from time immemorial. She understood that when sickness or age turned the body into a painful burden, the soul had to be set free. Many old people before her grandmother had chosen the narrow path up to the top of the mountain where it split into a jagged cliff that cut right down to the inland lake in the summer land. Her grandmother, too, would choose the leap from the mountain rather than the pain and shame of being a burden to her family.

This was so easy for Osuqo to understand when it concerned other people, but now it was *her* grandmother and she ached with sorrow.

Now her stubborn little brother wanted to accompany them to the ancestral place.

He's too young! she thought, and knew at once that that was a lie. His body was still small, but his thoughts, his mind, and his love were big enough.

Hadn't she herself seen the wonderful friendship that had developed between him and his grandparents that summer? He had grown closer to them, just as she had.

It was as if she saw the old people clearly for the first time when she realized that Grandmother was going to leave them.

Suddenly it was more important than anything else to get to know Grandmother. Hear what she thought and felt, and listen to the tales of her life. Osuqo was near her, gathering, gathering—words, gestures, actions, gathering images that would always be *her* grandmother.

house until spring, and then her grandmother wouldn't be among them anymore . . .

"I will never leave you," said her grandmother gently. "You will receive my magic words before I go, remember that. One day you may need them. Then I will be there with you."

Osuqo bowed her head and let the words sink in.

Suddenly Little Brother was there. Pushed past her and put the young swan in Grandmother's lap.

"It won't eat," he said sadly.

It had grown big, had lost its downy feathers. The young swan was beautiful and helpless.

"That's not so strange," said Grandmother dryly. "You feed it too often."

"But it has to eat to grow big and strong so it can fly and be free!"

"Then you must teach it freedom and independence," she said sternly. "Teach it to catch food itself, don't catch food for it."

"But it can't do it alone. It's too young," said Little Brother. "I can."

Grandmother laughed and took his head in her hands. "Stubborn little goat! How would you like it if your father didn't let you manage on your own? Just imagine!"

"I'd be mad!" he exclaimed.

"Exactly. Go to your grandfather, he knows everything about the way swans catch food themselves. Then you can teach the bird freedom!"

Grandmother had shrunk that summer. She had become dried up and small. Her hands were still beautiful, even though they were ominously thin.

Like delicate brown butterfly wings, thought Osuqo as her grandmother worked with a pair of fine skin pants. No one did such beautiful skin embroidery as she did.

"The pants are for you, my dear one." She smiled. "For your marriage, for it won't be long now, will it?"

Osuqo blushed deeply and felt the tears burning in her eyes. How did she know? Had she seen the looks between her and Poq? Probably. Nothing escaped her sharp gaze. But Poq wouldn't come for her in the long-

It was a strange summer. Like all the others Osuqo could remember, with the same long walks to find puffins, which they stuffed into the skins of newly slaughtered seals and put aside to cure, the same aching back after gathering berries, the same stiff fingers after flensing, tanning, drying, and hanging. The summer days ran on like a peaceful stream, just as warm, just as fine, and utterly different.

The difference was the tension.

That summer was like a taut bow. An arrow quivering at the bowstring, ready for release. There was no way back. Everyone knew it, and it made them extra-sensitive.

Osuqo's mother also changed that summer. Her stern, reserved mother dissolved in sudden tears and laughter.

The most beautiful thing was seeing her grandparents grow together, their roots intertwining like two plants.

Her grandfather still went out with the hunters, for he was hardy and strong, and the hand that threw the spear was as steady as ever.

But as soon as they returned from the hunt, he would go to Grandmother. They talked very little to each other; they had never talked much. But they would look at each other, and Osuqo knew that they did not see the same things she did. Grandfather had always told many stories, but that summer there were many more. Beautiful, exciting, frightening songs and tales. The family listened and remembered. They knew that he was giving them their inheritance.

Osuqo's father grew uneasy, but Grandfather stopped him. "I know what you want to say, that I'm still strong and could endure many more winters. But you know that I must decide for myself when it's time, and now it has come, my son. She must not go alone."

That was when Little Brother decided to go with them.

Father and Mother said no, but he would not give in.

Soon afterwards Grandfather decided not to go out with the other hunters.

"I have more important things to do," he just said when the hunters tried to persuade him.

The thing that was more important than going with the hunters was building a kayak for Little Brother and teaching him all the secrets of the hunt.

Osuqo watched them, with envy and sorrow.

They had such a good time together, the three of them. Grandmother stitched the kayak while Grandfather made the hunting implements and showed Little Brother how they should be used.

They resembled each other, in a way, young and old at the same time, equally absorbed in one another and in the joy of what they were sharing.

She would see them from far away whenever she returned from her walks in the mountains, see her little brother striving earnestly to throw the hunting line the way his grandfather did. She would hear their laughter when her brother amused them with the polar-bear dance he had made up himself. She knew that she was not the only one who would feel the emptiness when they were gone.

Osuqo had often witnessed sudden death. It was brutal and painful, but this long waiting for the inevitable was even more cruel. As the time for separation approached, their bonds to their grandparents grew stronger. She wished for things to be different, but deep down inside she knew that it couldn't have been any other way.

"Are you sleeping, Osuqo?" The voice of her little brother was reproachful.

"No, I'm not sleeping. I'm just thinking," she whispered, raising her head.

"About what you're going to say to Mother and Father?" he said hopefully. "Oh, do it for me, Osuqo! Do it!"

She nodded faintly. It wouldn't do any good to say no. And besides, it was the right thing to do. She never found out what made her parents change their minds. She didn't have to talk very long with them before they agreed. They had probably also realized how wrong it would be to refuse him the right to go with his grandparents on their last journey. But they wanted Osuqo to go, too, so that they could be sure he would come back safely from the mountain.

They were ready for the journey.

Both of them had dressed up. The large bun on top of Grandmother's head was tight and smooth, decorated with many rows of tiny white shells.

It was chilly in the evening sunshine, and the farewell was brief.

Everything had already been said that summer.

Her grandparents walked ahead, with Little Brother between them. Osuqo hung back. She tried to stretch out the time, put off the irrevocable for a little longer.

Grandmother walked slowly. She could manage only a few steps before she had to catch her breath.

"It's a beautiful evening," said Grandfather calmly. "We have all the time in the world. When you can't go any farther, I will carry you."

Little Brother chattered endlessly, asking question after question about everything between heaven and earth: Why do puffins fly so strangely? What do flies eat? Where does the Moon God really live?

And Grandfather answered, gently and patiently. But his eyes followed Grandmother. Ready to carry her when the journey grew too painful.

They had made it halfway up the steep slope when she remained sitting and could not muster the strength to stand up again. Silently he lifted her and held her close like a little child.

Grief burned inside Osuqo. She wanted to scream: Stop! Don't do it! I love you, and you must not leave me!

But she clenched her teeth and continued on the difficult journey. It was their lives and their choice, and she loved them for that, too.

The sun hung night-red on the horizon when they reached the top of the mountain.

In front of them lay the glittering white expanse of stone, striped with blood-red granite.

It was a short way to the precipice.

This is where the journey ends, thought Osuqo.

Grandfather turned toward them, tall and erect against the evening sky.

"Put me down," whispered Grandmother. "Before we part, you must have our magic words, children."

Grandfather carefully put her down on the stones, and Osuqo put her head in her lap. Grandmother's thin fingers gently stroked her as she gave Osuqo her most secret power. Osuqo opened herself and let the words take hold like seeds. She knew that they would grow within her to a unique power.

"But you will always be with me," she said softly, touching the weary face.

Little Brother was sitting close to Grandfather. His round face was listening gravely.

"You have received my magic words and my best songs," said Grandfather. "Go now, and grow up to be a brave hunter, little bird."

"Now we must part," said Grandmother. "Go now. The last moment is ours alone."

Osuqo took Little Brother's hand. They stood for a moment with bowed heads before they turned and walked away from the precipice, without looking back. On the edge of the steep slope down to the valley and the summer encampment, they stopped, listening anxiously. Everything was quiet behind them.

"Wait, Osuqo, I'll show you something wonderful," said Little Brother.

He lifted the young swan up in his arms, high over his head. Then he opened his hands and the beautiful bird, which had been helpless for so long, spread its wings, fluttered tentatively several times, and suddenly took off.

Like an arrow it shot toward the sky, circled around them, and gave a cry of joy that almost drowned out the sound of something falling into the water far below them.

"I won't!"

"You have to, Osuqo! I can't do it without you. We are one."

"It's wrong! Shameful!"

"It's our only chance. You know what they're planning. You know what they think about us."

"They're evil . . . insane. Nothing we say or do will change their opinion of us! They will only steal even more from us!"

"Not all of them are like that," said Poq. "Henrik and Christine are trying to help."

"Two weak sparrows against hungry ravens!" snapped Osuqo bitterly. "They want to help us—to do what? Do you see anything but hopelessness ahead of you?"

"I see freedom," said Poq with longing. "We must seek all paths to freedom before it's too late."

"Oh, Poq," she said simply.

She would follow him, of course. No matter what it cost.

This was not the first time they sat like this, close together with a wall of hopelessness between them.

That's the way it had been since that long day in the room with the black-clad men. The ones who reminded Osuqo of carrion birds waiting for their prey.

After that day came new carrion birds, often. They were no longer allowed to be in peace in the dark dungeon where they dreamed—together and alone—about a different world.

Every day they were dragged into a naked room where the light had the same color as the ocean. Three foreigners were waiting for them. Two behind a table covered with papers. One of them stern and pale, the other gentle, with a friendly voice. The third man was disgustingly fat, with a red face and bulging eyes. It was the first two who questioned and probed and stripped them of everything. The third man sat motionless. But his hands had a life of their own, sliding slowly across his fat thighs.

Henrik was always there as interpreter. Christine was there, too, like a pale shadow in the cold light.

The questions were always the same—about their country, their people, their family, about animals, hunting, food, about their language, their songs, their games.

They had both answered in the beginning. Poq spoke eagerly and with ease, but Osuqo grew more and more silent.

Then the day came when Osuqo withdrew completely from the foreigners. The guards arrived as usual, dragged them into the cold room. The three were already waiting for them. The man with the gentle voice ordered the guards to remove their chains.

The sudden freedom from the heavy chains rekindled hope in them, which was abruptly extinguished at the next command. Two guards held Poq and her while the other two stripped the clothes off them.

The surprise paralyzed them, and they never managed to resist. Suddenly they were standing there, naked and humiliated. The guards put on the chains again. Osuqo saw Poq shut his eyes in despair and bow his head.

For the first time the foreigners had broken his pride. It made her forget her own degradation for a moment.

Then suddenly she remembered the terror, the blood, and the pain, and she pleaded with her eyes: It must not happen again! Never! Never!

But Henrik turned his face away, ashen, unrecognizable. The pale girl put her hands over her face. Osuqo could see that her shoulders were shaking.

The stern man's face was as if hewn from stone, while the man with the gentle voice quietly circled them. Lifted their arms and legs, touched their hair, peered into their mouths and ears, pinched, looked, and mumbled. Never had she felt so helpless and humiliated.

What did he want? Her terror grew as she felt the foreigner's hands and eyes on her and watched him making strange marks and lines on paper.

Then she heard the sound. At first far away, like an echo of a hideous dream, then close by. The dry rustling of outspread wings and burning eyes engulfed her. Fat body waiting as his fingers danced impatiently on his thighs. Stinging breath as the bird opened his sharp, filthy yellow beak, and she screamed: "No! Please don't! No, no . . . not . . ." The words were lost in a moan.

The gentle foreigner stopped, looked with astonishment at her desperate attempt to cover herself with her chained hands. Laughing, he turned to the others. They nodded. The guards removed the chains and threw their clothes to them again.

"They . . . they robbed us of our bodies!" she stammered.

She and Poq were alone in the darkness again.

He didn't answer.

"Poq! Did you see the drawings they made of our

bodies? Disgusting figures covered with strange symbols—perhaps evil, magic words! What are they going to do with the symbols? Make *tupilaqs,* evil beasts that kill? What if they capture our souls the way they've captured our bodies! Poq!"

He gasped: "I don't know, Osuqo. I don't understand either, but I'm just as scared as you are. The foreigners aren't like us. They think and believe and act in a totally different way."

He was silent for a while.

"Their drawings are outrageous, it's true. But I don't believe that they're dangerous. I fear that there is even greater evil in store for us at the hands of the foreigners."

"Are you sure of that?!" she whispered, frightened. She had only his staccato breathing in reply.

It began with new questions—incomprehensible, meaningless words flung at them like accusations by the foreigner with the stone face.

The small, cold room with its cool green light had changed, hot and brilliantly lit by thin white smoking candles.

His voice thundered in the hot room.

Osuqo felt faint, infinitely tired. What did he want them to understand? She looked at Poq. He was stiff and motionless, as if he had removed himself, off on a journey of his own.

She looked at Henrik. His mouth was tightly closed, his eyes firmly shut, as if he were seeking help in a place where she couldn't reach him.

All she knew was that the foreigner with the stone face was some kind of shaman and he was bellowing at them about the foreigners' gods.

Henrik had tried to explain to Poq and her about the god among the stars and his son. They were goodness. Under the sea dwelled Satan. He was evil. These forces fought for people's souls and eternal life, she understood. But why should it concern her? She and Poq had their own gods.

"Thou shalt have no other gods than me . . . the Almighty God our Father . . . Jesus Christ . . . sin . . . heaven . . . hell . . . Satan and all his works . . ."

The foreign words, the hate-filled voice hammered into Osuqo, day after day. She didn't have strength enough to reply. Finally she no longer lifted her eyes from the floor.

Poq tried to reach her, wanted them to attempt to understand what the foreigner wanted, but she shook her head.

"They say that we have sinned," she said. "But I don't understand . . . don't understand . . . don't want to . . ." She turned away from him in the dark. "Leave me alone, I will find strength in my dreams."

"Don't forsake me!" She knew he spoke from a despair that was deeper than her own.

Their fingers sought each other.

But the hate-filled voice continued, thundered at them the way waves thunder against cliffs, and little by little Osuqo felt a deep shame and guilt. She didn't know why. She only knew that Poq felt the same way. As waves wear down cliffs, the stern voice wore down their confidence and resistance. Soon they were like bewildered children, meek and voiceless among adults.

As their confusion grew, the foreigner with the stone face became more stern, his eyes more filled with contempt.

Poq begged Henrik for an explanation, but he turned away and said: "Do everything he wants. He holds your lives in his hands!"

Osuqo suddenly saw that his eyes were glistening with tears. He was betraying them and felt ashamed. But he bowed to the power.

The guards came to get them earlier than usual.

The room was full of foreigners. Osuqo recognized the black-clad men, but there were others, too. Foreigners with eyes that shone in the glow of the numerous candles burning in the room. It was suffocatingly hot. A singed smell filled the room. Osuqo felt her body trembling as if from fever. Suddenly she knew that the greatest evil was about to happen.

She and Poq were thrown to their knees in front of the foreigner with the face of stone. He towered over them. In one hand he held the shining stick with the little figure on it. Osuqo recognized the suffering in his face as her own. "The Holy Cross," Henrik had called the stick. She knew that it was the foreigners' strongest amulet.

In his other hand the foreigner held many papers covered with tiny, peculiar symbols. "The Holy Scriptures," Henrik called them. Osuqo stared at them as if bewitched. She knew that the foreigners' strongest magic words were hidden in the symbols.

They were the same symbols that the foreigners had used to capture Poq's and her stories about the land of the People, about their own lives and beliefs. Now they had lost everything to the foreigners' amulets.

Poq had told the foreigners that in the land of the People there were no papers or symbols that would capture words forever. In the land of the People, all songs and tales were preserved by the elders, who passed them on to the young and the children. The young took care of the tales until they grew old themselves, then they were passed on to new children. In this way the stories and songs lived on forever in the land of the People.

The foreigners had listened as Poq spoke, but Osuqo had noticed that the face of stone had grown even harsher.

The foreigner with the gentle voice had shown them how their own language could be captured by the little symbols, and they had watched with astonishment. They had given him many poems and songs; many days later he could repeat the poems to them—with no mistakes. They had thought it was a terrifying and wondrous magic.

Now it was just terrifying.

The cross flashed, the holy symbols gleamed toward her. It was as if they were alive, crawling toward her from the white paper, wanting to force their way into her. She was numb with terror.

The foreigner's voice had changed, from the thunder that hammered inside her head to a keening, high-pitched tone that made the black-clad men bow their heads and fold their hands.

The evil was approaching, she knew it. It was approaching!

She felt Poq tremble. He, too, knew that it was approaching, that they lay helplessly bound, on their knees in front of the foreigners' god and terrible magic.

"What does it mean? What are they doing to us?" whispered Poq to Henrik. His voice was weak with fear.

"Just do what he tells you!" hissed Henrik. The sweat was running down his pale face.

"What are you doing to us?" Poq barely managed to utter the words.

"Satan and all his works are being driven out of you! All false gods are being chased away! You have renounced heathenism and witchcraft! You will receive the sacrament and be baptized in God's name and find eternal life in His kingdom! Don't you understand yet? It's the only way you can be saved from burning at the stake!" Henrik snapped like a terrified dog.

"What are you doing to us!"

Osuqo realized the awful truth, and she screamed out in horror. The foreigners had robbed her father and her brother of their lives, they had destroyed her life and Poq's, they had tortured them and had captured their stories and lives forever with their magic symbols. Now they were going to force the foreign god on them, a god who did not know mercy or compassion for them.

"No!!" she howled, and saw the flashing cross approaching, inexorably.

They were not going to shut out the Mother of the Sea and the Father of the Moon from Osuqo with their evil magic. Her entire life was dedicated to the mother and father of life and death, just as Poq's life was dedicated to the eternal search for paths to the Realm of the Dead. They knew no other gods! They wished for no other gods!

"We can't!" shouted Poq. His voice was steady, but he was quivering with rage. "Never!"

To touch the amulets of the foreigners would mean eternal imprisonment and perdition. They would forever lose the way to the only freedom they desired—the way to the Realm of the Dead.

The foreigners murmured, filled with horror and revulsion. The man with the face of stone gave orders to the guards. They forced Osuqo's and Poq's heads up, held them in painful grips while the foreigner performed his rituals.

They fought against him, but his power was too great.

Terrified, she felt foreign fingers, hard warmth. Felt the cross, flashing coldness. Felt something dry, soft against her lips. Saw the symbols crawl off the white paper and into her mouth. Then she fainted. She didn't hear the shouts, didn't see the confusion, didn't notice that she was dragged away.

Everything was drowned in the deafening chaos when the irrevocable happened and she became un-clean—forever imprisoned like a fly in a spider's web.

The chaos lasted a long time.

She was drawn into a whirlwind of terror and ha-tred where she could not see, hear, or grasp anything familiar. Only one thing approached her repeatedly—a vague shape that grabbed at her with big, hairy hands before it vanished in a foaming sea like the chaos within her. Was this the punishment? She received no answer, for the chaos overpowered her, and her body remained motionless on the filthy straw in the dungeon while her eyes stared wide open into the darkness.

No one could help her now.

She didn't want them to.

She was far removed from Henrik and the others who shook her, the man with the gentle voice who forced food and drink into her.

She let it happen. Threw up immediately, anyway.

They spoke with concern about her and Poq. The voices came from another world.

They feared that they would die. Why? Didn't they realize that they had robbed them of everything, everything that was worth living for, even death?

Her body cringed with loathing when the slimy leeches sucked at her neck, her arms, and her thighs, sucked out her blood. The gentle voice spoke calmly to her, but waves of nausea forced up bile in painful thrusts until she fainted again.

It was dark inside and out, but in the darkness was Poq.

She knew his thoughts, his body, his hands, his breathing.

They sought out each other, like half people who don't have a whole life until the gap between them is closed.

"Poq."

"Little Sister. I could not reach you in the chaos."

His fingers stroked her long hair, once soft as down, now stiff and tangled with vomit and sweat.

"You've been wandering." Her voice was hopeful.

His fingers pressed lightly against her cheek.

"Have you . . . do you know . . ." She didn't have the strength to finish her question.

"We are not lost, Osuqo," he said softly. "But I am tired. It was a more difficult journey than I thought was possible. We must get away from here before it's too late."

She knew that he was right. They didn't have much time.

Suddenly the hatred burned inside her again, just as strong and alive.

"They've stolen everything! Everything!" she said. "Our thoughts, our gods, our past. They've captured us with their magic symbols and changed us. Don't you see that we are empty shells?"

"Yes. I finally understand what the foreigners' in-tentions are. They want to shape us in their own image. They cannot bear that we are different from them. They have to steal, crush, destroy. Do you know that they have also taken away our names and adorned us with their own? You are no longer called Osuqo but Maria. And they call me Peder."

They were silent while their hands and skin spoke.

"A new humiliation awaits us," said Poq suddenly. "Henrik gave me the order from the foreign carrion birds. We will be displayed for people's amusement, like peculiar animals. Henrik begged us to do it volun-tarily. It would save our lives, he said."

"No!" she screamed. "Don't you think our lives have cost enough?!"

"Osuqo," he said quietly. "We must escape. It's our only chance."

On Writing *The Abduction*

In my novel, I attempted to portray a 13-year-old Inuit girl living in Greenland in the seventeenth century. My incentive was the recorded abduction of Inuits from Greenland to Norway, Denmark, Holland, and England during the sixteenth and seventeenth centuries. I found records of at least 150 to 200 abductions from Greenland alone, but it was obvious that many more were *not* recorded by the abductors. This "trade" continued for as long as Inuits and other natives who were taken from Chuchi, the Aleutian Islands, and other parts of the Amerindian continent made exotic gifts to kings or provided entertainment in European marketplaces.

I had visited Greenland many times before I came across any historical references to the abductions, and they came as a total surprise. Had *my* forefathers really been involved in this? Why did I not know? The answer was painfully simple. Norway boasts of a keen interest in the medieval history of Greenland, due to the fact that the Vikings sailed from Bergen in Norway around A.D. 800, populated Iceland and Greenland, and later, around A.D. 1000, sailed to America. Yet the abductions were never mentioned by Norwegian historians, probably because they were not regarded as important.

I spent two years searching for facts, reading the diaries and log books of the captains of the exploration ships and other contemporary accounts. I found that Queen Elizabeth I of England probably was the first documented abductor, clearly aware of her intentions, as her instructions to Captain Frobisher (1577) reveal: "Wee doe not thinke it good you should bring hither above the number of 8 or tenne at the most of the people of that countrie. Whereof some to be oulde and the other younge whome we mynd shall not return agayne thither."

There exist a number of brief accounts of the fate of the unfortunates; how they tried to flee home to Greenland in their fragile kayaks, how they died of alien sickness—the common cold, alcohol poisoning—or, simply, of grief. But not once did I come across any account of what the victims thought and felt. Finally, I realized that I had uncovered a blank space in history, or, more precisely, *another* blank space; like the unheard voices of the Amerindians that witnessed the exploitation and theft of their lands, or the innumerable slaves captured in Africa, and the Sami (the indigenous people of northern Scandinavia), who have only begun to be heard in recent times.

This silence of the victims presented me with a major problem; how could I truly relate what it felt like for a 13-year-old girl of an arctic country and a non-Christian culture to be captured, raped, and then imprisoned by terrifying strangers? What would the concept of a city be to someone from an ancient arctic culture? Or the wheeled cart, obviously useless in Greenland? What would be the point of books to the nomadic Inuits, who entrusted all their knowledge and history to memory? Or the concept of one Almighty God, to the Inuits who worshipped guardian spirits and the mother of the sea—Sedna.

All this became crucial as the writing began. And the terrible feeling of loss increased—of being a witness to the consequences of centuries of suppression of people and their invaluable information. I came to a bitter understanding of the real crimes our culture had committed in its superior ignorance.

The task I faced was to write convincingly from outside of a culture alien to me. I was forced to view my own culture's interpretation of history with great skepticism. It was painful, but enlightening, like removing a pair of sunglasses.

To attempt to reconstruct the thoughts and feelings of a young girl imprisoned in an alien world, to depict her joy and excitement, her fears and beliefs, her understanding of life and death, her pride and love, I turned to the only sources I felt I could trust. These were the oral literature, the poetry and songs, visual images and symbols of the arctic peoples, that somehow survived through centuries of misinterpretation.

Writing from the outside gives the feeling of actually being an excavator, attempting to dig through layers of languages foreign to the cultures they interpreted. It is a sad contradiction that our wonderful tool—the written language—also is a powerful instrument of obliteration. What is still hidden underneath, we do not know. We may never know.

Realizing all this—I believe—is what makes writing from the outside important today. My book *The Abduction* must not be regarded as an homage to cultures lost, but as an urgent attempt to enlighten my own culture to the possibilities of survival.

Gudrun Pausewang (b.1928)

The German writer Gudrun Pausewang has tackled unusually difficult and controversial subjects in her children's books. In *Die Wolke* (*The Cloud,* 1987) she imagines what happens to children in the event of a major nuclear accident. In *The Final Journey* (German, 1992; English, 1996), she envisions a sheltered Jewish girl taking a train ride with her grandfather, without knowing that they are headed for a concentration camp and death. The novel assumes that her parents and grandparents have decided to protect her from all knowledge about the hatred and destruction closing in on them—which makes her gradual discoveries of the horrors of the journey all the more poignant and disturbing, even if the premise of a family attempting (and succeeding at) such total deception of a child is unconvincing.

With the publisher's permission, American expressions have been substituted for British ones in cases where the British words may be confusing to American readers. In the last chapter, not reprinted here, Alice and the group she is with enter the gas chamber, expecting it to be a shower room. The book ends with a brief historical note.

From *The Final Journey*

23

Alice started. Had she nodded off again? Even the two Maibaum daughters seemed to be asleep. It was still quite quiet in the railway car.

She stood up and looked around at the sleepers. She was the only one on her feet, the only one awake, and yet it was morning. A reddish shaft of light fell through the opposite grating: sunrise, another brilliant August day.

Then she heard the sound of brakes which by now she knew so well. Her whole body listened, and at last the sleepers were also woken up by the hissing of the brakes.

Questions tumbled over one another: "Where are we?" "Are we there?" Samuel jumped up and peered through his grating, Isolde crowding against him.

"Nothing to be seen," he announced, "only a couple of sheds and brick buildings."

Then Samuel said, "The place is called Auschwitz."

Auschwitz? Alice looked across at Mr. Blum, who pulled down the corners of his mouth and shrugged his shoulders.

How different the men looked now: unshaven, uncombed, with crumpled shirt collars and creased, stained trousers. And the women were no better: their clothes dirty and wrinkled, their hair tousled. Only the two Maibaum daughters and Isolde stood out, with their red lips, powdered cheeks and eyeshadow. Ilse and Ida cried. They wanted to look beautiful too; they had never been allowed to use make-up.

The railway car was becoming very noisy. The children complained; Ernstl started crying and would not be silenced. The trench-coat woman cursed when she discovered that her case was standing in the muck. The two Cohns wailed softly.

Suddenly there was a lot to do. The luggage was organized at high speed.

"Pack up, Alice!" cried Ruth. "Get ready quickly, Ruben, David!"

"Yes, Ida, of course there will be a washroom in the camp."

"Be quiet, Walter. We're there now and we'll get a drink."

The train rumbled across some points, slowing down all the time. The men crowded to the gratings.

Mrs. Maibaum gave one of her boys a resounding box on the ear, but Alice never knew why. Mr. Ehrlich dusted his hat while the Trench-coats were busy trying to clean their cases. The red-cheeked woman beside Alice was on her feet, packing her rucksack, and Alice saw for the first time that she had a club foot.

"Listen, Alice," called out the blonde woman, an undertone of desperation in her voice, "you've got your backpack for your things. Couldn't you leave me the heavy holdall—for my Lotti?"

Alice nodded, stooped and began to pull the remaining bits and pieces out of the holdall.

"Looks as if we're going through an archway," said Samuel.

"Thanks, my girl," said the blonde woman distractedly. "Give it here, quick. We'll be there in a minute."

Alice tipped the holdall upside-down. Everything left inside now fell on Paul's body. But something flat, large and unwieldy was stuck at the bottom of the bag: the family tree. Grandfather had packed it.

"Come on!" cried the blonde woman, panicking.

Alice handed the bag over to her, opened her backpack and stuffed all her things in it: washing things, some underwear, socks, a nightdress, a second dress, a pair of gym shoes, the torch, all kinds of bits and pieces. And suddenly Mummy's jewel case was in her hand. Oh, Grandfather. He must have managed to stuff it in the bag at the last moment, because she had been playing with the necklaces and bracelets only the day before. She pushed the jewel case hastily into her coat pocket.

The train was stopping, with a horribly shrill, metallic screech. There was a rattling already at the opposite sliding-door, which was pushed open. Light flooded in, making the people in the railway car blink.

Then there was utter confusion. Suddenly everything was happening at breathtaking speed.

Men in striped clothing appeared in the door opening and roared something at the people in the car. They lifted down the old Cohns, who did not know what was happening to them. Outside a loudspeaker boomed.

"Get out! Everyone out!" shouted the men in stripes.

"These belong to us, of course," said Mrs Maibaum, giving her daughters a bucket each to hold. "Or has anyone any objection? Buckets are always useful. Get out? Gladly! Whatever you say . . ."

The car emptied. Suddenly there was so much room. Alice was astonished to see how much of the floor the muck had not reached. A striped man climbed in, lifted Sarah Wormser and passed her over to another standing below. Then he helped the Maibaum grandparents out of the car.

"What about Grandfather and Paul!" cried Alice, pointing desperately at the dead bodies.

"They will be taken care of, child," said the striped man.

Rebekka, David and Ruben were already on the platform, calling her. Ruth was in a hurry. A second striped man climbed into the railway car.

"But I want to know where they will be buried," sobbed Alice.

"You'll find out all about it, and today," said the striped man solemnly. "So now, out with you, girl."

He took her under the armpits and handed her down to Ruth.

"You don't even know my name," she cried in panic fear. "How are you going to find me among all these people?"

"That's right," said the striped man, who was already pulling Paul towards the opening. "I had almost forgotten that. What is your name?"

"Alice Dubsky," she said. "Eleven years old, nearly twelve."

"Alice in Wonderland," said the striped man. "That's easy to see. So, we'll tell you all about it, today. You can depend on it."

Alice took a deep breath. That was arranged, then. The loudspeaker was still booming and, once outside, Alice could understand what it was saying: "Leave all luggage. Women on one side! Men on the other!"

She stared back into the open rail car, saw her grandfather lying there and could not bear to be parted from him. This was the last time she would see him. Next time she would be able to see only his grave.

"Come on!" urged Ruth, pulling Alice away.

All the luggage was lined up in front of the train cars, only Mrs. Silbermann was clinging to her backpack. "My pills," she clamoured. "If Ilse gets an attack of asthma and we haven't got the luggage with us—"

"We can't simply leave our cases here," Alice heard the trench-coat woman protesting. She turned round, ran a few steps back and looked into the car again. Inside, the striped man was just pulling Grandfather towards the door opening. Alice burst into tears. Ruth tried to pull her away, but Alice resisted.

"He's dead, child," said the striped man. "He doesn't feel anything now. He's all right, believe me. Better than the rest of us."

"Bury them side-by-side," pleaded Alice. "At least they know each other. They won't be so alone—"

"Shall be done, Alice," said the striped man. "Word of honour."

"Women and children who cannot walk," boomed the voice from the loudspeaker repeatedly, "go to the vehicles waiting for them!"

Rebekka, Ruben and David had already gone ahead in the direction everyone was taking. People seemed to be gathering at the front, in an open space beside the train.

Ruth took Alice's backpack and added it to her own luggage.

"Come on!" called Rebekka, beckoning impatiently.

Alice walked along the train, looking into each car she passed. All of them stank; some of them were dripping brown mush. Dead bodies lay outside three cars. She turned her head and looked the other way. There were three covered trucks. The blonde woman went straight over to one of them, the holdall in one hand, the curly-haired child holding the other, her backpack on her back. What of the baby? It must be in the holdall. Behind her the old Cohns limped along, and in the truck Alice recognized Mr. Wormser with the little carrying bag in which the new-born baby lay. He spoke to one of the striped men, then disappeared inside the truck, in which his wife was probably waiting. It was good that she could be driven; she was still too weak to walk without help.

A few metres away from the railway cars stood uni-formed men with dogs. Somebody screamed. Alice looked this way and that. There was so much happening, all at the same time, she simply did not know where to look first. It was a child that was screaming, a little girl from another train car, wearing a bright blue dress. "Mum! Mum!" she screamed, stumbling along beside the train. A striped man took her by the hand and led her to one of the trucks.

24

The loudspeaker was silent now. Alice turned. The people who had been travelling in the train at the back had formed a long procession, blocking her view. She could not see if the striped men had already taken Paul and Grandfather out of the train car, but the men had promised to let her know today where they were buried. So it must be quite possible here to find one particular person among so many. And, it seemed, it must be possible to get all those many pieces of luggage, whether they had names on or not, back to their owners. Many things seemed to be possible here!

She kept on looking about her. Yes, Samuel had been right: the train had run under a great archway. It spanned the lines in the background, gleaming in the morning sun.

"Don't hang about like that," said Ruth. "We might miss something because of you . . ."

So many men in uniform. So many dogs. Why were they there? One man in stripes was standing in the opening of a train car. "Where are we going now?" asked a woman with a child in her arms, walking ahead of Alice.

"To shower," he said. "And afterwards, to start with, hot coffee."

Shower! Of course, that was more than necessary for all of them.

When they reached the open square they saw two groups, which were visibly growing: women and children on one side, men on the other. Alice saw a uni-formed man cross over to the men's group and beckon to Aaron. "That one's still a child," he shouted.

"But I'm a widower," she heard Mr. Ehrlich call back. "My boy won't have anyone to take care of him over there."

"You'll be seeing each other in no time," shouted the uniformed man, and Alice was surprised that his voice was quite friendly. He even clapped Aaron on the shoulder, said something to him and then pushed him towards the mothers and children.

"Come in with us," Ruth called to him. He nodded with relief and came over.

"What did that man say to you?" asked Rebekka.

The words seemed to have stuck in Aaron's mind: "You're not so small that you still need to hold Daddy's hand, boy . . ."

Now they were wedged into the huge crowd made up of women and children. Ruth tried to stay on the outside so that Aaron did not lose sight of his father and brother. Next to them were the Silbermanns without Mr. Silbermann, and Mrs. Grün and her two girls were close by—Mrs. Grün, who had thrown all those letters from the train.

"If only I knew how they think they're going to arrange for the luggage later on," said Mrs. Silbermann.

A man in stripes pushed past them to a group walking a little ahead. Surely those were the hats of the three Herschel sisters and between them Ernstl, easy to see in his peaked cap. Why were they pressing round him so closely? Did they want to make him invisible? Were they trying to hide him from somebody? At that moment the man in stripes took him by the arm and tried to pull him out of the little press of women—probably because he should have been on the other side.

But Ernstl was struggling. "No!" cried the sisters, "he needs us!" And, "He's just like a child!"

The other women squeezed quickly past the group, and two more uniformed men came up and pushed the sisters away. They boxed Ernstl's ears, seized him by the arms and dragged him over to the men's side. Ernstl shouted desperately, "Lina! Selma! Edith!" The men stepped back, startled, from the uniformed men and Ernstl, who vanished in the crowd. Alice heard Ernstl give one last screech, before the sisters' shrill, lamenting cries drowned all other sounds: "Ernstl! Ernstl!"

"Move on," a man in stripes shouted at Ruth and the children.

The procession was in order again, the gap closed.

"What will they do with him now, Ruth?" asked David, very upset.

"I don't know, David," said Ruth quietly.

"Where are they taking him?"

"I don't know, I don't know—"

Alice's head thudded. There was a rushing in her ears and her knees grew weak. And this pain in her stomach!

They were approaching a group of uniformed men, visible between the shoulders of the people walking in front of them. Among them was an older man in civilian clothes, wearing a long, dark coat. It was like Grandfather's—double-breasted, with slanting pockets.

A thought shot through Alice's mind. "The coat is still in the traincar!" she cried. "Grandfather's coat, the one Mrs. Wormser was lying on."

She let go of Ruth and tried to push her way back through the crowd that was building up behind them, but Ruth held on to her. "Forget it," she said. "It's covered with blood, and they certainly won't let you go back to the train."

Between them and the group of uniformed men there were now only the Maibaums, the trench-coat woman, the singer and the red-cheeked woman with the club foot. The central figure was a tall, slim man, with braid and piping on his uniform—an officer. He flicked a casual, elegant hand: the trench-coat woman to the right, the red-cheeked woman and the singer to the left, the Maibaum daughters to the right, Mrs. Maibaum with her little boy, the grandmother and the youngest, in her arms, to the left.

And now it was their turn—Ruth with the boys and Rebekka, together with Aaron and herself, all to the left. When Alice looked round, she saw that Mrs. Grün with her two little girls was following them. After that there was a brief hold-up, because Ida had been waved to the left and Isolde, Ilse and their mother to the right. But Mrs. Silbermann clutched Ida and would not be parted from her. The officer smiled, as though he understood, and sent all four of them to the left.

"Come on, Alice," Ruth commanded. "We've got no time to stand here staring."

"Thank you," Alice heard Mrs. Silbermann's relieved voice.

Alice too felt relieved. Soon they would be under the shower—clean at last, free to drink. The world turned black before her eyes and she felt her knees give way.

25

When she came to she was immediately struck by the long rows of clothes' hooks. Then she became aware of the numbers beside the hooks. Each hook had a large, clear number.

"There," said Ruth, patting her cheeks gently, "there you are again. You got a bit too heavy for me, my dear, from out there to in here. If Rebekka and Aaron had not helped me . . ."

"No wonder she collapsed," said the singer, stroking Alice's hair. Then she hung her coat up on a hook. There were Rebekka, David and Ruben too, beside Ruth, and Aaron behind Ruben. They were all smiling at her.

"Your color will soon come back," said the red-cheeked woman, who had also hung up her coat.

"Undress, undress," came a voice. "There's a lot more to go through today!"

Alice understood. So this was a cloakroom, and probably the shower-room was next door.

"*If* I hurry," said the singer, "it's only for the sake of the hot coffee."

"Coffee?" said the red-cheeked woman. "Are you sure?"

"Get undressed, children," said Ruth, pulling her blouse over her head.

"In front of the children?" said the singer, giving Aaron an angry look.

"Let's look forward to the water," said Ruth calmly. "We all need it. It's only a shame that we can't wash our clothes at the same time. Once we're clean we shall have to get back into this filthy stuff again."

The singer rolled down her stockings, the red-cheeked woman stepped out of her dress, and somewhere in the next row Alice heard the Silbermann girls whispering and giggling. A baby was crying. "Come here, Benni!" came the blonde woman's voice.

Alice was still dazed. Slowly she pulled off her shoes, still crusted with muck. How they stank! She hung up her coat on one of the hooks that was still free. One hundred and seventy-three. One, seven, three. It would be too silly if afterwards she had to wander about naked among all these naked people, looking for her clothes

"Tie your shoes together," said Ruth, pointing to the wall, where the instruction was written up

in large letters. It also said that the clothes were to be arranged tidily—and it actually said so in several languages!

"They have thought of everything," Alice heard Mrs. Silbermann say.

Ruth was already naked, and now Alice also dared to pull off her dress. She would not be the first naked person in the room. How difficult it was, in front of so many people . . . Never, not since she could remember, had she been naked in front of anyone but her parents and grandparents.

She glanced sideways at Rebekka, who was also naked and had arranged her clothes tidily. Now Rebekka was undoing her plaits. That was a good idea: their hair was in great need of a wash. Alice pulled the ends of wool out of her plaits and put them in her shoes. Her plaits were springing loose on their own, but she helped them along with nervous fingers.

The singer beside her was also completely undressed. How creased her legs were, and how slack her breasts. Alice scarcely dared to look, but now she had to, for out of her bag the singer took a tiny bottle, opened it and dabbed herself behind both ears and between her breasts.

"Why don't you put it off until afterwards?" asked a strange woman. "The water will wash it all away."

"You feel less naked with it on," said the singer. She handed Alice the bottle and said, "Here, you cover yourself in lilac too."

Alice dabbed, and a wonderful scent of lilac floated round them. Suddenly it no longer seemed so very bad having to undress in front of other people. Zip-zip, everything off, folded up—done. Now only the locket was left. The singer was also wearing a locket round her neck.

"They evidently don't think we need a mirror," she said, opening her handbag, which was hanging on the hook. She took out a hand-mirror and looked at herself. "Unrecognizable," she sighed. "After the shower I shall need a long time for my toilette." She tugged at her chain and her golden earrings.

"Hurry up, Ruben," said Ruth, helping David to take off his shoes. He had knotted his shoelaces and Alice could see that Ruth's fingers were trembling.

The room was beginning to empty. One woman after another, many with children, some without, disappeared into the shower-room through a big door in the background.

Alice suddenly remembered the jewel case. She tugged it out of her coat pocket, opened it hastily and looked inside. Yes, there they were, the beautiful chains and collars, the bracelets and earrings which had trickled through her fingers so many times—and which she had so often put on and admired in the basement bathroom mirror.

"*Oh, là là!*" said the singer, her voice hushed. "Have you any idea what you've got there, child? They belonged to your mother, didn't they?"

Alice nodded.

The singer looked anxiously round. "I would not leave those here while we're in the shower," she whispered. "You never know if the supervisors can be trusted." Her gold tooth flashed.

"But what shall I do with them?" asked Alice.

'Put them all on,' whispered the singer. 'If you're wearing them, they can't get lost.'

She was already putting one necklace after another round Alice's neck, holding out the open bracelets to her, closing the fastenings and slipping on the rings. They were too big, so she pushed them on to Alice's thumb.

"Some people do have problems." said Ruth indignantly.

One necklace of shining green beads reached almost to Alice's knees, dangling uncomfortably against her thighs, so the singer arranged the necklace in a fourfold crown and pressed it down on her hair.

"Look" she said, handing her the glass.

Alice saw a bright, smiling face, a good face. And the green necklace shimmering on her forehead looked beautiful.

"Leave all that frippery," urged Ruth. "We are almost the last."

There was no time left for the earrings. Alice dropped them back in the jewel case and put it in her coat pocket.

Libby Hathorn (b.1943)

Australian author Libby Hathorn addresses the stigma that has poisoned white attitudes toward Aboriginal peoples in Australia. She tells the story of a girl who discovers her living connection to the stories of the Dreamtime, the mythic Aboriginal space and time. Her mother, however, wants nothing to do with these stories, having experienced the prejudice and ostracism that may result from being identified as Aboriginal. Only when she accepts her kinship to the storyteller does the mother experience catharsis and a kind of liberation. This 1989 story presents an example of a child leading the way toward recovery of identity and tradition.

Up Taree Way

The idiots at the back of the hall were quiet once Neil Symon started speaking. Even the smartarse Leandra Evans was quiet and Shane Winter forgot to cough like he usually did when there were talks on. The old man's voice, rich and deep, was important. It rang through the darkened room and made everyone feel shivery.

In the Dreamtime, a long ago, a far off time, there was a big darkness all over the land. They came, those An-

cestral Beings then, the good spirits. They carved the beautiful land, shaping it this way and that as they went, making the beautiful animals too—the kangaroo, the possum and the lyrebird . . . His hand moved swiftly through the air, making big sweeping shapes as he talked, as if he was conducting . . . *the goanna, the snake and the kookaburra. They left their paths all over this land, the Ancestral Beings. They made the hills and the gullies. They made the rocks and the trees and the rivers . . . and they made the first people in the Dreamtime long ago.*

They listened so quietly you could hear a pin drop. There was something magic about that voice.

Milly listened nervously to the words of the old man with the soft brown eyes. Sometimes he spoke as if he was almost singing, she thought. She was glad when he picked up the guitar and he did sing. All the kids clapped along with him then, but she sat still thinking. His voice had somehow worried her. It was good and bad at the same time. It made her remember things. Things she didn't want to remember. It was good—and yet it was full of something deep and painful that she was trying to forget.

"Some old guy Miss Kirby dredged up from the local pub to tell stories. Just so's she can get out of work, I'll bet," Maureen had said scornfully in the playground. Their English teacher had announced a story session for their class in the hall every morning for a whole week. "And I s'pose we'll have to answer questions for homework," she sighed.

"Who is he anyway?" Pete asked.

"Neil Symon, an Aboriginal storyteller," Nerida said, glancing down at the crumpled notice in her hand. She started reading in Miss Kirby's precise clipped voice. "He's over 70, boahs and girhls, and he travels round the countrahside telling stories. He's come for a week of stories and workshops at ouah school. And to take part in ouah History Australia Day."

Pete laughed. "Sounds okay to me," but Maureen frowned. "Hmmm. Well it's going to mean a load more work, I bet."

"We'll get off some work, you idiot," Pete insisted, taking the notice from Nerida. "See there's the History Day on Friday. Miss Kirby says we're having a sausage sizzle and dances and things."

"I s'pose they'll ask my dad to donate the sausages again," Nerida said darkly.

"And if there's one thing I hate," Maureen said, "it's sausages!"

"Neil Symon. Sounds like a singer or something," Pete said, and then, "Hey Milly, he's got the same name as you. Look—Symon spelt the same way. With the 'y.'"

Milly's stomach clenched into a tight knot. "So what?" she asked.

"Just thought he might be a relation or something," Pete said.

Maureen was incensed. "But Milly's Italian, not *Aboriginal*, you dag."

Mum had told her not to say that they were Aboriginal and not to say they came from up Taree way. "Don't say anything about Taree or Forster Beach or Seal Rocks or anything unless they ask," she'd said in such a worried voice. Milly didn't know who *they* were that her mother feared so much. Maureen, Nerida and Pete, her best friends at Coogee High School maybe?

"You've been to Brisbane once," Mum said, "so say you came from there and your dad is Italian. That's if anyone asks. And don't say anything to Bob."

Bob was Mum's boyfriend. Maureen had seen Mum with him in a pale green sporty-looking car once. "Gees, your Mum's boyfriend's a spunk, isn't he?"

Milly didn't say she didn't like Bob much at all. Bob hardly spoke to her when he came to their flat. And she didn't like to speak to him in case she said something Mum had told her not to. And she hated the long evenings by herself when they went out.

She was glad Pete lived in the red brick block right next door, or some nights she might go mad with the loneliness. Pete wasn't a spunk but he was a good friend. Sometimes they did homework together. She liked helping him with English and Maths. Pete wasn't all that good at schoolwork but he was funny and friendly. She never worried too much about what she said to Pete. But like Mum had said, she didn't ever tell their secret. Not to anyone. It seemed important to Mum.

But now, out of the blue, Neil Symon had turned up and she felt all mixed up. She lay awake wondering again, "Who am I? Who am I not allowed to be? Milly Symon from up Taree way? Not from Brisbane with an Italian father?"

For years now since she was a little girl and they'd left Grandma Pearl and old Bill and all of them up north and come to live in the city by themselves, she'd wondered about herself like this. She'd had a burning dreadful secret and quite often if Mum went on about it, it turned into a burning pain inside her.

"Where did you say your school was when you were little?" Nerida had asked one day when the new boy arrived from Brisbane.

The terrible secret again. She swallowed, "In Brisbane."

"Banana land, eh?" Pete had said.

"Well, this is Glen and he's from Brisbane too," Nerida had said.

"Whereabouts did you live?" Glen asked.

Mum had drilled her well. "Uh, Holland Park," she said.

"Hey, what about that place you used to go with your uncle? Round the headland with the cave and the secret rock pool? Glen might know that place," Pete said enthusiastically.

They had all heard Milly's stories about the beaches she had loved as a little girl. And the adventures she had had with her cousins there.

"No beaches in Brisbane but," Glen said in a puzzled way. "None near Holland Park, that's for sure. Must've been down the coast?"

"Yeah," Milly said uneasily, "it was down the coast where we went on holidays and things." She fell silent then.

Down, down the coast to Taree, the lovely country town. And then further on to the beautiful beaches, all the way along to the splendid Seal Rocks where she had lived for a while as a very young child. Near the cool beaches and the green forests. Not in hot old Brisbane.

"Hey Milly, tell Glen your cave story. Boy, is it spooky!"

The kids liked listening to Milly's stories. The real ones and the ones she liked to make up. Even the ones she wrote for Miss Kirby.

"Milly's writing a soapie, you know, and she'll send it into Channel 5. It's better than Dynasty, no kidding."

But Milly didn't want to talk to Glen anymore.

"I'm going to the canteen," she said, even though the burning feeling in her stomach meant she wouldn't be able to eat.

"There's a note from school," Milly said. She never bothered Mum with notes usually. Mum was always so tired. But this one, about the Aboriginal storyteller called Neil Symon, spelt with a "y," she wanted to show her.

"Oh?" Mum dried her hands on the old apron behind the door, the one she never wore. She took the note from Milly and held it at a distance because Mum needed glasses now to read any small print. Milly shot into the lounge room and switched on the TV. She was going to hurt her mother with that note. She was sure of it.

A replay of *The Addams Family* was on and she hunched up in her chair, hardly watching. She was kind of listening to the sprinkles of canned laughter from the TV and the silence from the kitchen.

It wasn't till dinner that Milly said to Mum, "You read the note from school?"

"Yes," Mum said, "about the storytelling and all." She sounded bored. "Seems okay."

"Aboriginal stories, Mum." She looked up. "And the storyteller who's come to our school for the whole week—well, his name's Symon. Neil Symon. Spelt the same way as ours. Maybe you know him?"

"Never heard of him," Mum said, but something in the way she said it, so sharply and loudly, gave her away. Mum attacked her chop then as if she was angry.

She knew Neil Symon all right, Milly was sure of it.

"I know you know him," she wanted to call out at her mother, but all she said was, "He's nice."

"Mmmm."

"Will you come to the History Day on Friday? Anyone can come. He's telling stories at two o'clock. There's going to be a barbeque." She knew Mum finished early on Fridays.

"No," Mum said, "I can't. I don't have the time. It's a real busy time at work. Belle's going to be away and I'm doing an extra shift this week." Her voice was loud. "I just can't come, Milly."

"Okay. Okay. Don't go on, Mum. I just asked. That's all." Milly didn't stay at the table and talk to Mum. She went straight to her bedroom.

That night as she lay in her bed wide awake, she thought about Neil's Dreamtime story.

I am the land and the land goes on and on, he had said. She could see the great formless expanse, humped and carved and pressed and pushed into shapes of canyons and gullies and caves and creek-beds and mountains and beaches by the Ancestor Spirits. Even the land under her suburb here at Coogee. Not that you could see much of the land with all the shops and houses. Only at the edge where cliffs and beaches met the sea.

But you could see it and smell it, she remembered suddenly and vividly, in the timber forests or the secret caves or the deep gushing rock pools where she had once lived. And in the strange shaped mountains near home that the highway wove through. She remembered the highway through the mountains, that took them away from everybody she knew and loved. "It's going to be much better for us in the city where we're going," Mum had said over and over. But Mum had cried too, when they left.

Some of that countryside they'd left behind was just like it must have been in Neil's Dreamtime, Milly thought with a start. In *her* Dreamtime. But Neil's Dreamtime had turned into her nightmare. She wanted to ask Neil about Taree and Seal Rocks. About Grandma Pearl and Bill. He must know them. She wanted to tell Neil about Mum and herself but she couldn't. When Neil had spoken again today, her heart had spurted with pain just like it had when their little cat had gone. Only difference was she felt as if something she'd lost had been found. But she couldn't have it anyway.

Next day at the story session the kids really liked the way Neil let them act out the stories he told. They laughed like anything when he made Leandra the crow

and Shane the dingo in one of the stories about a chase across the land. Shane had been chasing Leandra the whole year.

"He could go on the telly, you know, that old guy," Pete said. "He's pretty good."

"Yeah, he's not as bad as I thought," Nerida yawned on the third morning.

"And so far no homework from Kirby," Maureen enthused. "Hey, didn't Shane look funny though when he jumped into the waterhole? Gees I laughed."

But on the fourth morning of Neil's stories, when he mentioned some names of places that Milly found she remembered, her heart froze again. The secret cave around from Blackhead Beach, the rainforest near Buledelah Mountain. Purfleet out of Taree where they had friends. And Seal Rocks. He described places that she'd been to—oh, so long ago—when she was little. And now in his magic sing-song voice he told about those places. And she could remember them all, clear as day.

Oh, it was awful. She shouldn't remember this stuff. Mum'd be so mad about it. She felt the burning feeling again in her stomach and in her chest. But she did remember it all now. So clearly too.

A great blue expanse of sea. Humped rocks gouging out into the blueness. Kids on their surfboards taking the waves at the corner. An old weatherboard house and Grandma Pearl taking her hand. Tumbling down onto the beach to pick up shells or to swim at the edge where the frothy lace of foam drenched you. Running back to take Pearl's hand, to show Bill the treasure shells.

"Oh yes, Neil Symon, I know you. I know you," she rejoiced "and I know the places that you know—the place you come from. It's my place as well as yours. And I know it."

"Mum, Neil Symon says he lives near Seal Rocks."

"So?" Mum said tersely. She was tired. They were both sitting in front of the TV but Milly's thoughts were not on *Young Talent Time.* Her head was full of Neil's stories.

"So . . ." Milly's stomach had the old familiar burning sensation, "so you might know him, Mum. That's all. I thought he looked a bit, well, a bit familiar. And I thought he might know Grandma, you know, with his name being Symon and all . . ."

Mum turned to her, her eyes blazing. "I said I don't know him! I wish you'd stop harping on about it. I told you, Milly, to forget all that. Forget those places. That's the past, Milly. It's dead. We live here now. We're new people now."

"We're the same," Milly said stubbornly. "I reckon I am anyway."

Her mother jumped to her feet, "What is this, Milly? Do you want to spoil everything for us. Is that it? I told you to forget the past. Now I don't want to hear another word about Neil Symon or Seal Rocks or anything else."

Mum walked away from her in angry clipping footsteps across the room.

Milly felt tears of anger in her eyes. What was Mum so frightened of? Who were the *they* who would spoil everything for them? And how? It must be Mum's boyfriend, Bob, and his friends. Mum was frightened of Bob knowing. But Bob loves Mum, that's easy to see, and if he really cares, then . . .

Milly lay in the dark that night staring out through the slice of window that the blind did not cover. The old question tormented her. "Who am I?" she asked herself again and again. "Who is it that I'm not allowed to be?" She tossed in her bed hot and uncomfortable. She'd upset Mum now and she was angry with herself.

"Well I'm not going to let it get to me. I'll forget it. Like Mum says, I'll forget the past. Why should I worry? I won't think about it anymore. And I won't go to any more of Neil's stories. I won't think about him or them anymore. I won't remember Grandma Pearl and Bill and . . ." She breathed deeply, closing her eyes, willing Neil's voice away. It was peaceful and quiet for a moment.

And then, *I am the land and the land goes on and on* . . . It seemed to be inside the room, inside her head.

She sat up suddenly, angrily, and said out loud, "All right, Neil Symon, you win! I'm Milly Symon from up Taree way and I bet you're our family. Tomorrow I'm going to ask you. I am! I'm asking about Grandma Pearl and Bill from Seal Rocks and all of the others too. And tomorrow I'm going to tell the kids at school that I'm Milly Symon from up Taree way." She felt glad when she said this but when she lay back she thought of Mum's angry blazing eyes. Please, Mum, don't be angry with me. Don't get that hard, cold closed-up look you get every time we talk about this. But I've got to know.

The alarm buzzed in her ear. It was Mum's early shift and she'd already gone. Milly pulled up the blind and waved across the side alley of the flats where she could see Pete at his window. He always made faces and mouthed goodmorning to her through the glass. She pushed up the window this morning and motioned him to do the same, "Pete," she called across the dampish space between them. "I reckon that Neil Symon man, you know the storyteller, *is* related to us," she called. "I'm going to ask him today."

"Yeah?" Pete was yawning, "You do that. Hey Milly, did you do your Maths homework?"

"Yeah, did you?"

"W-e-ell. I went to footy training and then I watched that late movie and Bovis is still down on me about the test." He yawned again.

"I'll give you mine," she said. "You can copy it at the bus stop."

At school before the story session in the library she told the others that Neil Symon might be her uncle. Nerida said, "Just because you like telling stories and acting and things and his name's the same spelling . . . you're getting a bit carried away, aren't you?"

"Anyway he's Abo!" Maureen said.

"So?" Milly said.

"Well that means that you'd have to be."

"I guess it does," Milly said quietly, with her heart thumping.

"So?" Pete said.

"Gees," was all Maureen said and looked away.

They went into the big auditorium for the concert. There was a bush dance display and the band played folksongs, and then a hush went over the crowd as Neil Symon took the middle of the stage.

"You kids want to know how the sun got in the sky?" he asked.

"Yes," they all called out together.

"Well then I'm gonna tell you." He took up his guitar and strummed. He half-sang, half-told the amazing story of how Bralagah the Crane threw an emu egg into the sky where it hit a pile of wood and burst into flames and how a good spirit saw how beautiful the earth was all lit up. And how Gurgurgaga the Kookaburra was chosen by the good spirit to call out each morning so that the sun-fire is lit every day. Then he picked up his guitar and sang a song and the kids clapped, too.

And then when it was finished he put down the guitar and he talked to them again. That was when Milly felt shivery. He told them about the first time *he* had heard the story. It was when he was a small boy away in the middle of the forest.

"We were camping out in the bush—Buledelah way. My father said he reckoned we'd have a visitor that night. Someone we knew and wanted to see very much would come to our campfire that very night. And sure enough, someone did come. My grandfather. We hadn't seen him in months. But he arrived at our camp in the middle of the bush. And late into the night he told the old stories. Just like I'm telling you. And just like his mum and dad told him."

"You know, it's a funny thing," the old man continued in a quiet voice that nevertheless seemed to fill the hall, "but my people are so close to the land and so close to each other, we know things sometimes before they happen. Like my father did at the campfire."

"I reckon if any of you were coming to visit me in my house up the coast a way, something would kind of tell me you were coming. Like something's telling me right now that someone here today, right here in this hall, is kind of special to me."

Pete dug Milly in the ribs.

"Sucked in," Nerida said admiringly.

Neil picked up the guitar and began another song and the spell of his voice was broken.

Milly's heart was beating fast and gladly. So Neil knew that she was here. Knew that Milly Symon, who was part of the big Symon family, had been sitting and listening, so scared and so delighted every day of the week. He knew she was here, just like that. Even without her saying it. She sat in the hall, not watching and not listening to anything else. She was waiting for the end when everyone would go.

"See you outside then," Pete had said as he and the others trailed outside. Now, now she would walk down towards him where he'd finished talking to the small knot of kids round him. And she would say, "Here I am, Milly Symon from up Taree way." And she would ask about Grandma Pearl and Bill and all of them.

But when the kids finally moved away, Neil stared past Milly and right to the back of the hall. He wasn't smiling now. There was such a strange look in his eyes that Milly didn't know if he was sad or glad. But his voice, even though it was a bit chokey, came out very glad. Very, very glad, Milly thought. "I knew you were coming today," Neil said. "I just knew you'd come today."

Milly turned around in surprise. Who was there that Neil knew so well? Who was it he had just known would come today? And then she saw who it was all right. She gave such a start.

It was her mother. She was sitting alone at the very back row. It looked as if Mum had been crying but she had a kind of soft look on her face when Neil spoke to her.

"Uncle," Mum said very quietly.

Then Mum got to her feet and slowly walked down the aisle towards the old man as if she was in a bit of a dream.

"Mum," Milly said anxiously as she reached her seat, "Mum, I'm here too." And then Mum had looked at her, not hard and angry and closed up. Not at all. Mum had put out her hand and Milly took it and squeezed it hard.

Then together they walked towards the old man who stood waiting. He put out both his arms to welcome them.

FURTHER RECOMMENDED READING

MILDRED TAYLOR (b. 1943)

ROLL OF THUNDER, HEAR MY CRY

Born in Jackson, Mississippi, but raised in Toledo, Ohio, Mildred Taylor drew on her family's stories of survival in the racist atmosphere of the South. She recalls that when her own family traveled South for visits, her parents sheltered her from experiencing some of the indignities of racism, by taking their own food instead of trying to stop at restaurants, for example. Taylor's series of novels about the Logan family begins with *Song of the Trees* (1975) and continues with *Roll of Thunder, Hear My Cry* (1976) and further sequels and prequels. Presenting a vivid picture of Cassie Logan and her family and community in Depression-era Mississippi, *Roll of Thunder* tells the story of survival and determination in the face of racism and oppression. As landowners, the Logans have a proud, deep-rooted heritage to protect, but they also face many threats from whites who want them to fail and lose the land. Cassie, the novel's narrator, is smart, quick-witted, and wryly funny. She has been somewhat sheltered by her parents, as her brothers have also, in order to preserve her dignity and self-respect; thus, when brutal events force her Ma and Big Mama to teach her about the realities of the society they live in, she has to do some painful growing up. (See also the discussion of Taylor's 1990 book *The Road to Memphis* in Part 5.)

PART 3

ORAL AND WRITTEN LITERARY TRADITIONS

Tell us a thing to make our hearts all glad.

Geoffrey Chaucer, Prologue to "The Nun's Priest's Tale"

"There was something magic about that voice." Part 2 ends with Libby Hathorn's modern Australian story of an old Aboriginal storyteller who combines words and music to tell urban students about the creation of land, sun, and people in the ancient Dreamtime, inspiring a young girl and her mother to remember their physical and spiritual kinship with him and their native culture. Hathorn is one of many writers demonstrating that attempts to separate children from the oral tradition linking one generation to the next deny them their birthright, restricting their psychosocial development, rather than enriching their moral, spiritual, or practical lives. Just as Hans Christian Andersen's child in "The Emperor's New Clothes" (in Part 2) is the only one who does not hesitate to speak the truth about the literal reality that everyone sees, children also respond instinctively to the magical poetry and underlying truths of traditional literature. Adults have tried for centuries to shelter children from its stark realities or its magical metaphors for a variety of reasons, but they cannot stop the powerful crosscurrents of rhymes and tales that touch us most deeply and irresistibly with echoes of our ancestors' voices. Geoffrey Chaucer, writing in the century before printing was invented, demonstrated the pleasures of oral storytelling on the pages of one of the world's most celebrated literary works. His fourteenth-century pilgrims in *The Canterbury Tales* knew that telling stories during their long journey would make their "hearts all glad" by amusing them as well as giving them ideas to ponder and debate.

Like Hathorn, Andersen, and Chaucer, the storytellers, editors, writers, and scholars who are represented in this section explore the relationships between the ageless oral tradition and written literature tied to particular times and authors or editors. Some of them have multiple roles within these traditions, with careers that combine oral storytelling, collecting folklore, writing, and drama. As their work crosses varied cultural landscapes in different parts of the world, it recreates the timeless rhythms and patterns of old forms with new variations in each generation. The selections in this section show how traditional poems and tales change over time, how they spread from place to place, how they combine prose and verse, and how ancient oral traditions continue to influence individual writers and artists. Since there is no precise date of origin for most works that are derived from oral traditions, and modern readers have been interested in the ways in which structural or archetypal similarities in the traditional literature of the world intersect with historical developments and cultural differences, this section is arranged by grouping together related types of folk literature and, in some cases, examples from related cultural traditions. The critical essays also show how the fields of folklore, literature, social history, and psychology overlap as teachers and scholars study the importance of oral traditions in the lives of children and in society. Because many texts from oral traditions are so deeply rooted in cultural traditions that are older than writing, schools, or mass media, but their appropriation for education, entertainment, and mass marketing has widespread influence, modern approaches to presenting them to children involve complex questions about evaluating the authenticity of folklore and legends that are retold outside their original cultural context, and deciding what is suitable for children of different ages to hear or read.

Although we still enjoy reading about the oral tales of Chaucer's pilgrims, adults in Western cultures have increasingly privileged written literature over oral storytelling, especially in the past few centuries as literacy and education have spread to all classes of society. It is ironic that so many modern adults think of fairy tales as stories only for children and trivialize the tales and rhymes of childhood, when their own culture is full of allusions to fairy tales and nursery rhymes, from automobile ads featuring Little Red Riding Hood to political commentary about big bad wolves and murder mysteries with clues based on "Simple Simon." When asked, most adults enjoy describing their powerful memories of rhymes they recited in childhood and stories and poems that were read or told to them by family members and teachers. We all started out as preliterate infants absorbing the sights and sounds around us, and psychologists now understand that we do our most profound learning in the first few years of life. There is a natural magic in the universal oral skills that human children develop, and then there is the artificial magic we can learn when we are taught to use the invention of writing, but writing retains more prestige in our society. In *The World of Storytelling,* Anne Pellowski discusses the irony in adult characterizations of storytelling as childish. Her overview of storytelling, from ancient times to twentieth-century storytelling revivals, compares the efforts of folklorists, professional storytellers, and "folk storytellers." Pellowski builds on the work of theorists such as Walter Ong, who compared preliterate and literate cultures to observe their differences and argued that the spoken word and written literature could not be separated in a literate culture.

Long before scholars such as Pellowski and Ong theorized about the history of storytelling, oral storytellers developed their own fascinating accounts of how their stories began. Thus, this section begins with a *pourquoi* (or "why") tale from the oral tradition about how stories came to earth. "How Spider Obtained the Sky-God's Stories," an Ashanti tale from West Africa, is one of many tales around the world that are built on the premise that stories have divine origins. The fairies and animal characters in this tale and others throughout this anthology show how oral stories often blend human, natural, and supernatural elements in ways that disappeared from most Western literature and art after the Renaissance. Because oral tellings spread and change through so many unrecorded variations, the original religious, political, and symbolic meanings of some words and images in folk stories may be lost to audiences in other times or places; Virginia Hamilton comments on this phenomenon in her African American collection *The People Could Fly.* She retells "A Wolf and Little Daughter," for example, with African song fragments that Little Daughter uses to entrance a threatening wolf. While modern thinkers debate whether the universal or the culturally specific values of mythology and folklore are more important, the rhymes and stories continue to flow from generation to generation and place to place through the oral traditions of childhood and folklife. At the end of *The People Could Fly,* Hamilton pays tribute to the slaves "who had only their imaginations to set them free." She writes that descendants of slaves told their children about the magic of those who flew to freedom. "And now, me, I have told it to you." When Hamilton reads these lines on an audiotape purchased by thousands of strangers, the relationship between teller and listener is not bound to specific landscapes, not intensely personal as it is for Hathorn's Australian storyteller and his displaced nieces or for Anansi when he offers his mother in exchange for stories—not even as intimate as it would be at a live performance by a professional storyteller. But hearing this sentence in Hamilton's own voice reminds listeners of the historic importance of receiving the old stories from tellers in our time, even when they rely on modern technologies, such as printing and audio recording, to retell traditional tales.

The rhythmic language of these folktales and the remnants of old rhymes, incantations, and songs they contain illustrate the crosscurrents of verse and prose in the oral transmission of folklore and childhood amusements. The selections in verse in this section represent the most popular forms from the oral traditions and some common overlaps in lyric and narrative categories of poetry. Traditional rhymes with content ranging from obvious and practical observations to utter nonsense are called nursery rhymes when we associate them with our earliest memories of hearing, reciting, or singing verses that stay with us forever. Nursery rhymes actually encompass a number of traditional forms. They also contain remnants of ancient superstitions, historical facts, or political satire, and a few have known written sources, such as American Sarah Hale's 1830 poem "Mary had a little lamb." But it is their rhythms and word play more than their meanings that children delight in and remember. The nursery rhymes that were collected in England by the distinguished scholars Iona and Peter Opie, and in the southern Appalachian Mountains of the United States by a beloved regional author, James Still, show how the transplanted oral tradition of European immigrants adds new twists to the silly rhymes of the Old World. As Still's Preface points out, children themselves often make these changes and create new rhymes. While Still reminisces about one-room rural schools where children memorized and refashioned traditional rhymes, John Langstaff, another American writer working with both oral and written media, set out to find the oral tradition in urban America. His essay "The Oral Tradition: Alive, Alive-oh" records examples of contemporary street rhymes recited by children. The recent popularity of oral performances in poetry slams and rap lyrics (which often allude to nursery rhymes and classic stories) confirms Langstaff's conclusion that the oral tradition is alive and well.

Many nursery rhymes are well known in both spoken and musical renditions, such as "London Bridge," "Jack and Jill," and "Mary Had a Little Lamb." "A Frog Went A-Courting" has a dual history as a comic ballad and a poem written in nursery rhyme books since the eighteenth century. (And Maurice Sendak praises the illustrated version by a prominent Victorian artist in his essay on Randolph Caldecott, in Part 6.) It is fondly remembered as a favorite song for parents and grandparents to sing to young children, and playwright R. Rex Stephenson spoofs that family oral tradition when he depicts the folk heroine Mutsmag using the familiar song to keep her undeserving sisters awake at night in order to save them from a giant. "A Frog Went A-Courting," "The Tree in the Wood," and "John Henry" show that folk songs shared by children and adults encompass a wide variety of subjects, from comical animal fantasy to more lyrical celebrations of nature and heroic legends or tall tales. "John Henry" is also associated with the oral tradition of work songs or hammer songs because it is not only the most famous American legend about a hardworking man trying to compete with a machine, but it exemplifies the strong rhythms and refrains of songs that, in the past, accompanied grueling physical labor, such as driving steel to build the railroads.

As ballads, "A Frog Went A-Courting," "John Henry," and "Kemp Owyne" belong to the tradition of narrative folk songs that tell fantastical or sensational stories in extended sequences of short stanzas. Their endings are sometimes tragic (or perhaps tragicomical with "A Frog Went

A-Courting") but as with most folktales, the story is told dispassionately. The listener's emotions are aroused by the unadorned but gripping outlines of their narratives—the life-or-death struggle of the superhuman worker John Henry and the rescue from a dragon transformation in "Kemp Owyne"—as well as the rhythms and repetitions of their phrasing and the vocal qualities supplied by the singer or storyteller. "Kemp Owyne" is one of many ancient tales retold in both ballads and prose tales with numerous variations in names, plot, and setting, a tradition that Jane Yolen continued in her literary fairy tale "Dove Isabeau." "John Henry" has also been retold in prose in recent times, in numerous collections of American tall tales and in picture books by prominent writers such as Ezra Jack Keats and Julius Lester.

Traditions of oral and written poetry also overlap in several ways in the narrative and lyric poems by Victorian and modern poets in this anthology. Edward Lear's "The Owl and the Pussycat," a classic of mid-Victorian nonsense verse, is reminiscent of the animal fantasies and mock romances of "A Frog Went A-Courting" or "Hey Diddle Diddle," with absurdities such as traveling with "money wrapped up in a five-pound note," eating with "a runcible spoon," and borrowing a pig's nose ring for an interspecies marriage. However, while it has been reprinted, memorized, and set to music countless times, it would be unimaginable to alter Lear's carefully crafted words. We may also think that the exact phrasing of a favorite nursery rhyme or folk song is timeless after growing attached to a particular version in childhood, but someone else next door or across the world is no doubt reciting it differently. The samples of illustrated short poems by Kate Greenaway in Part 6 also show the influence of nursery rhymes on Victorian writers of original poems. Like Greenaway, contemporary poet Grace Nichols has reprinted nursery rhymes in addition to writing her own poems, some of which include images and themes from the folklore she grew up with in Guyana. "I Like to Stay Up" is a particularly interesting depiction of "orality and literacy" (to use Walter Ong's phrase),[1] since the child in Nichols's postcolonial "tropical garden" can enjoy both the security of reading in bed and the fun of being scared by her grandmother's oral ghost stories. Several other poems in this section illustrate the oral tradition's influence on contemporary poets and the combination of oral and visual effects in written poetry, including the tributes to family storytelling by Navajo poet Shonto Begay and the animal fantasies and wordplay in poems by Shel Silverstein and Jeanne Steig. "Toads" by Jane Yolen, reprinted in her essay "The Brothers Grimm and Sister Jane," has more in common with the satires of traditional literature and spin-offs with contemporary twists discussed in Part 7.

Myths and fables from the classical literature of the ancient Greek and Roman empires, which have also been retold through the centuries in both prose and poetry, provide additional perspectives on the crosscurrents of oral and written traditions through history. They were so highly revered in ancient times, and especially in post-Renaissance Europe, that their long history as written literature is relatively well documented. However, in spite of legendary accounts of a Greek poet named Homer and a talented storyteller who was a Greek slave named Aesop, fragmentary written records from the ancient world provide little evidence that particular authors are responsible for the fables and myths associated with their names. Stories such as "Daedalus and Icarus" were centuries old when the Roman poet Ovid compiled traditional myths and legends to retell them in his own style in *Metamorphoses* (8 C.E.). *Aesop's Fables* was among the first books published after printing was introduced in fifteenth-century England. Its compact combinations of short narratives and explicit conclusions about human behavior were especially appealing to Neoclassical Europeans who were eager to provide moral instruction in succinct, palatable forms. Thus, fables naturally became a staple of children's literature, easy for readers of any age to comprehend and easy to retell orally to children even before the eighteenth century, when editions of fables that were designed especially for children began to appear. Although gods appear in some fables as the voices of wisdom, most fables use human and nonhuman characters to focus on lessons for people of all ages and classes to apply to everyday life: cautions against greed, deceit, pride, and laziness; praise for loyalty, ingenuity, moderation, and self-reliance.

Critics have more difficulty explaining how mythology fits into the history of children's literature because it deals with larger issues of creation and conflict, struggles between good and evil on international and cosmic levels, intense and tragic relationships among humans and divine beings, and disastrous human errors, such as Pandora's release of troubles into the world. Young adults discuss these themes when they study mythology, but the psychoanalyst Bruno Bettelheim argued in "Reflections: The Uses of Enchantment" that both myths and fables are too pessimistic for young children, who need the optimistic symbolic patterns of traditional fairy tales. Nathaniel Hawthorne, on the other hand, wrote in his 1851 Preface to *A Wonder Book* that he believed that "many of the classical myths were capable of being rendered into very capital reading for children." Their antiquity convinced him that "by their indestructibility itself, they are legitimate subjects for every age to clothe with its own garniture of manners and sentiment, and to imbue with its own morality," but he vowed that he would not write down to children, since they "possess an unestimated sensibility to whatever is deep or high, in imagination or feeling." Hawthorne's "The Paradise of Children" in Part 1 shows how he recast the Pandora myth, in the manner of his own Romantic sensibility, into a story about childhood innocence and mischief. His Pandora is not a seductive Eve figure, but a naughty child.

Rolfe Humphries's "Daedalus and Icarus," in this section, is a twentieth-century verse translation of Ovid, not an adaptation like Hawthorne's myths. This one always has been a myth about a child and his father, comparable, perhaps, to stern cautionary tales for children of earlier centuries, and now it seems to support Bettelheim's modern view of myths because the young son's disobedience and carelessness lead to his death. Jane Yolen's 1991 prose retelling in the picture book *Wings* is also faithful to Ovid and earlier Greek sources. Yolen emphasizes throughout, without softening the moral, that Daedalus is a man punished for pride. The only consolation offered is the beauty of Dennis Nolan's illustrations and Yolen's language, particularly in the assurance that "the gods wept bitterly for the child." Whatever adults may think of various styles of retelling myths, there is no denying that many children are fascinated by the stories of suspense and adventure, transgression and heroism, love and loss. As Yolen points out in *Touch Magic,* a book defending fantasy literature, many childhood heroes of popular culture and literature are modeled on characters from ancient mythology and history.[2] Comic book superheroes who have shouted the acronym "SHAZAM" since at least 1940 are conjuring up "Solomon's wisdom, Hercules' strength, Atlas' stamina, Zeus' power, Achilles' courage, and Mercury's speed."[3]

While Bettelheim's observation about pessimistic endings does apply to many myths and fables, there are mythological stories of creation, heroism, and love with more positive conclusions, while fables such as "The Crow and the Pitcher," "The North Wind and the Sun," and "The Lion and the Mouse" have optimistic morals about solving problems with ingenuity, persuasion, and kindness. Moreover, mythologies, the complex networks of stories that dramatize the belief systems of world cultures, overlap in the oral tradition with stories called fable, legend, and folktale. Many folk and fairy tales contain echoes and remnants of older myths. "Beauty and the Beast," for example, is often compared to Apuleius' second-century Roman story about Cupid and Psyche, from older Greco-Roman mythology. In the Russian fairy tale "Vasilissa the Fair," the horsemen representing morning, day, and night are reminiscent of ancient myths and fables with personified elements of nature. Because the word *myth* has been used to label supernatural stories as untrue from the perspective of those outside a particular belief system or to refer to any kind of fiction or misconception, that term is often avoided when referring to the Bible or sacred legends from any culture. James Mooney's nineteenth-century collection from the Cherokee oral tradition is entitled *Myths of the Cherokee,* but contemporary retellings of the same stories are usually called legends or tales. The two Cherokee tales in this section, "The Story of the Milky Way" and "Dancing Drum," contain mythological themes involving the origins of natural phenomena, natural cycles of weather and fertility, and relationships between the human and divine. In "Dancing Drum," an attempt to retrieve the Sun's daughter from the land of the dead is similar to the Greek myths of Orpheus and Demeter.

These Cherokee stories do not have a long history in writing like Greek and Roman myths and fables or India's ancient written fables from *The Panchatantra* and *The Jataka Tales,* since Native American languages (like most other languages of the world) have had no writing systems, or none until modern times. As Native American cultures continue to emerge from several centuries of oppression, contemporary storytellers, such as Gayle Ross and Joseph Bruchac, now attract national audiences with their oral and written retellings of Native tales. These storytellers and their forebears have seen the stories move back and forth between the oral tradition and written records, since Ross's family, for example, preserved their Cherokee tales orally and through written copies from James Mooney's collection, which was published in English.

The late twentieth-century revival of interest in storytelling and multicultural folklore, which Kay Stone discusses in "Oral Narration in Contemporary North America," produced innumerable retellings in children's books, as well as oral recordings and performances of traditional stories from around the world with similar histories. In *Spiderman Anancy,* James Berry thanks Mother Africa, ancestors who brought their folktales to Jamaica, folklorists who recorded them, and his Jamaican family for passing down the stories retold in his 1988 book. His comment illustrates how complex questions of origin and authenticity can be when dealing with traditional materials and cultural history—questions also discussed in the essays by Nina Mikkelsen in Part 2 and Jon Stott in Part 8. Recent oral and written retellings of traditional tales often include some historical background, source notes, and samples of the story's language of origin, as in the Cherokee story of the *Gil'liutsun stanun'yi* or Milky Way. While Native Americans and storytelling colleagues with whom they share their tales often express their reverence for the traditional wisdom of their people and individuals who pass on the stories, "Dancing Drum" and "The Story of the Milky Way" also show how they adapt them for young audiences, adding or emphasizing child characters in both of these retellings.

These Cherokee tales and countless other Native American stories also represent the tradition of *pourquoi* tales, along with the Anansi tales in this section and the Pandora myth in Part 1. Judith V. Lechner observes that "pourquoi or 'why' tales are a blend of myths, legends and fables." *Pourquoi* tales often convey a lighter tone than more serious mythic creation stories like the ones in Genesis because they tell the origin of particular creatures, natural phenomena, and human customs, such as speech and stories.[4] They may include divine immortals, as in "How Spider Obtained the Sky-God's Stories," or the new creation or characteristic may result from earthly actions without apparent divine intervention. Their unscientific accounts of natural features, from a mountain range to a possum's bare tail or a bat's wings, convey cultural values, for like fables, they often depict animals or inanimate objects that represent admirable or unwise human behaviors. In "The Story of the Milky Way," a constellation is formed to honor the hero who stops the terrible crime of stealing food from elderly people. The culture hero Anansi's evolution through the oral traditions of West Africa and the Caribbean includes a range of traits from the godlike wisdom and powers of a creator to clever and subversive trickery to the selfish and scandalous foolishness of the spider-man. The numerous tales around the world about how tortoises got cracked shells also illustrate the overlap between fable and the *pourquoi* tale, since the one reprinted here from *Aesop's Fables* shows Tortoise being punished for pride, while the Tortoise in the Nigerian tale from Chinua Achebe's *Things Fall Apart* is like Anancy, using clever talk to survive trouble of his own making.

These *pourquoi* tales are primarily a subcategory of folktale, not only as part of the broad tradition of tales told orally by folk around the world, but because they typically deal with life and nature on a human scale. They usually describe individual features of animals or plants, yet even when they dramatize the origin of winter and summer or the acquisition of fire, these global phenomena are explained in terms of conflicts or competitions among individuals or groups. In "The First Fire," for example, Grandmother Spider, a central figure in Cherokee culture, is the only animal that is able to carry fire across water or across the world because she has a bowl or basket on her back. Although the cannibalistic giants, deadly dragons, beautiful mermaids, and magical transformations in many tales may derive from ancient myths that share the same motifs, folk and fairy tales focus on the life-altering adventures of individual people, whether they are poor peasants like Hansel and Gretel or Jack the giantkiller; rich girls, such as Cinderella or Beauty; or princes and princesses in Japan or Germany.

Many tales in this section, along with "Puss in Boots" in Part 1, show that animals sometimes represent typical human behavior, functioning as helpers for human protagonists (the fox in "Munsmeg" and the doves in "Ashputtle") or antagonists (the wolf in "Little Red Riding Hood" and Virginia Hamilton's "A Wolf and Little Daughter"). Animal transformations symbolize struggles with identity and relationships; in animal bridegroom tales around the world, such as "Beauty and the Beast" and "The Frog King" (in Part 2), women endure various kinds of ordeals before the enchanted beasts who are destined to become their husbands are restored to human form. "Kemp Owyne" and Yolen's "Dove Isabeau" are related to animal bride tales in which the woman suffers a horrible transformation as a frog; a snake; or even, as in these stories, a dragon. Hans Christian Andersen adapted folklore about half-human sea creatures coming on land, transforming into humans, and marrying men, although his little mermaid never fulfills her dream of love (in "The Little Mermaid" in Part 8). While many folktales do not include magic—for example, there is only the pretense of magic in oral tales that inspired Andersen's "The Emperor's New Clothes," these magical tales have remained most popular in the history of children's literature, continuing to evolve in the crosscurrents of stories called fairy tales (*conte de fees* in French, märchen in German). Since they seldom contain fairies, but represent the "world of faery," tales of magic from the oral tradition are also called wonder tales by contemporary scholars and storytellers.

Even a pancake can be enchanted in the fantastical world of folktales, where the most primal fears of humans and animal characters often involve being eaten or having nothing to eat. "The Pancake" also represents the tradition of cumulative tales, with its humorous accumulations of repeated names and actions (like "The House that Jack Built" and "The Tree in the Wood" in verse). Repetition is common throughout world folklore because it aids memory, structuring narratives and sound patterns in sequences that are rhythmic and captivating—easy to tell, to hear, and to repeat. Children and adults know that "Fee fie fo fum/I smell the blood of an Englishman" signals each entrance of the giant in "Jack and the Beanstalk." Again, prose and verse are combined as rhymes or songs are inserted and repeated in many folktales to signal intense moments of warning, escape, desire, and triumph. Events occur in predictable but endlessly varying patterns, often in groups of three. Three siblings may attempt the same task in turn, as in "The Water of Life," or a hero completes a series of three tasks, faces three obstacles, or accepts three types of magic help. Cinderella goes to three royal balls, and Snow White's evil stepmother in disguise tricks her three times with deadly gifts (in spite of help from dwarfs in a group of seven—another magical number in folklore and mythology). Oral storytellers sometimes engage the audience in repeating a verse or refrain, as Diane Wolkstein indicates by providing music for the song about the false stepmother in "The Magic Orange Tree." Many story-tellers also use formulaic lines to move their audiences in and out of the magic, communal world of the story, as illustrated also in Wolkstein's book and in the quaint lines about making a fur hat out of a mouse at the end of the Grimm Brothers' "Hansel and Gretel" (in Part 2).

When folktales are written down, they may be based closely on oral tellings or heavily edited and embellished. In *Favorite Folktales from Around the World,* Jane Yolen writes, "Basically there are three kinds of folk stories: the oral, the transcribed, and the literary or art tale."[5] Diane Wolkstein's introduction and tales from *The Magic Orange Tree* in this section show how she moved from close observation of master storytellers in Haiti to editing transcribed tales, discovering the differences between entertaining oral performances and tales that ring true in print. Wolkstein followed the recent trend of folklorists who describe the style of the teller, the story-telling community, and the occasion of the tale's telling, as well as reprinting the text. In *Touch Magic,* Yolen describes the ear and eye as different listeners when stories are told or written.[6] Most creators of successful folktale books that are meant to be read to or with children, from the Grimm Brothers, who continued to revise their tales for decades in the nineteenth century, to Richard Chase and Virginia Hamilton in the twentieth century, occupy a middle ground between the folklorist and the literary artist, collecting tales from a variety of sources and retelling them with carefully selected details and phrasing. These modern authors have also participated in creating audio recordings and encouraging oral readings or retellings of their tales. Literary fairy tales blend motifs from older stories with more freedom and originality than most retellings of particular traditional tales, often including more elaborate details than oral tales. Examples from earlier centuries include Andersen's Danish fairy tales (see Parts 2 and 8) and the genteel French "Beauty and the Beast" by Madame de Beaumont.

One of Yolen's many literary fairy tales, "Dove Isabeau," appears in this section with her essay on the influence of her lifelong reading of Grimms' fairy tales and with "Kemp Owyne," a transcribed ballad from the oral tradition that tells one older version of this story about a dovelike heroine who is transformed into a loathsome dragon and rescued by her knight or kemp. While other literary fairy tales in Part 7 represent various types of adaptations or spin-offs and satires of classic literature, the two contemporary adaptations at the end of this section, "Dove Isabeau" and "Mutsmag," are paired with sources directly from the oral tradition. "Mutsmag," dramatized by R. Rex Stephenson in 2000, is based on "Munsmeg," which Richard Chase collected from oral storytellers in southern Appalachia in the first half of the twentieth century. Like "Dove Isabeau," this tale has roots in ancient Celtic folklore; "Mutsmag" is similar to the British tale "Molly Whuppie" and was no doubt brought to the Appalachian Mountains by Scots-Irish immigrants. "Molly Whuppie" has a longer history in print, appearing in Joseph Jacobs's nineteenth-century *English Fairy Tales,* for example, and it is often reprinted in contemporary feminist anthologies. Jacobs's version of "Jack and the Beanstalk" helps to show that Mutsmag, like Molly, a poor girl who acquires wealth by tricking a giant, also has much in common with the more famous folk hero Jack, who overcomes giants, witches, and other obstacles in dozens of British and North American Jack tales. In the 1970s, when Stephenson began dramatizing Jack tales, he found a treasure trove of forgotten folktale variants transcribed from oral sources and stored in southwestern Virginia archives. Tales from the oral tradition have been a major source of inspiration for dramatists since commercial theater for children began in the late nineteenth century, and Stephenson's Jack Tale Players have used the story theatre method of dramatizing regional folktales since 1975. His script for "Mutsmag" illustrates this approach to adaptation that combines the traditional methods of the oral storyteller and the dramatist.

Thus, although we need to attend a performance, listen to a recording, or tell a story to experience the oral tradition, the traditional tales and rhymes that are reprinted in this anthology represent a variety of forms, methods of retelling, and cultural traditions from the crosscurrents of the world's oral folklore and mythology. The West African-Caribbean Anansi tales, British American Jack tales, and African American Brer Rabbit tales (such as Virginia Hamilton's group of animal tales in *The People Could Fly*) illustrate the phenomenon of cycles of tales revolving around a recurring hero and sometimes traveling with storytellers from an old homeland to a chosen or forced new land. This section also contains a variety of selections from different cultural groups within the same American region—the European American, African American, and Cherokee rhymes, songs, and tales from southern Appalachia, along with some parallels from different parts of the world. And the Russian "Vasilissa the Fair," Haitian "Magic Orange Tree," and Japanese "Princess Who Wore a Hachi," along with the French, German, and Native American tales in other sections, show how widespread the "Cinderella" archetype is.

But how do we move farther away from the bias inherent in the tendency to refer to Cinderella or Little Red Riding Hood as the archetype when discussing similar tales from non-European traditions? By the beginning of the twentieth century, scholars were cataloging the structural similarities, recurring motifs, and archetypes that united traditional stories from different places, and editors such as Joseph Jacobs and Andrew Lang were publishing collections of tales from around the world retold in English. By the end of the century, there was much debate about the authenticity of traditional materials removed from their original cultural context and edited for performance or publication. Oral traditions have always spread and changed as peoples migrated and mingled, but critics such as Maria Tatar and Jack Zipes have analyzed the widespread effects of cultural biases that determined which tales were canonized in print and, in the twentieth century, in film, as rhymes and tales from the oral tradition were increasingly treated as literature specifically for the entertainment and instruction of children.[7]

Thus, texts that are derived from oral traditions or show the influence of traditional literature appear in every part of this anthology because tales with the most enduring appeal not only evolve into new styles of literature, but they also reflect our most difficult problems in relation to age, race, gender, class, and commerce. Even though varied waves of preachers, moralists, and social critics in different generations have questioned the effects on children of folk literature that embodies the values of the past, the powerful symbols, captivating language, and underlying truths of rhymes and tales from oral traditions make them irresistible. In Part 1, Langston Hughes's poem "Aunt Sue's Stories" and the biography of Hughes by Floyd Cooper provide examples of one early-twentieth-century child benefiting from oral storytelling, learning about the joys and sorrows and diverse influences in his own cultural history from the loving arms of family members. It remains to be seen how methods of analyzing traditional literature and presenting it to children will change in the future, as more stories and verses are retold from previously ignored cultural traditions, with greater recognition of the oral tradition's vital role in everyone's cultural background, regardless of age or heritage. Because it is inherent in oral traditions for stories and poems to change with each retelling, they appeal simultaneously to our desire for the familiar and the new as we pass on the familiar forms of folk literature while making it new for each generation of children.

NOTES

1. Walter Ong, *Orality and Literacy: The Technologizing of the World* (New York: Methuen, 1982).
2. Jane Yolen, "How Basic Is Shazam?" *Touch Magic: Fantasy, Faerie, and Folklore in the Literature of Childhood,* 2nd ed. (Little Rock, AR: August House, 2000) 13–19.

3. "Shazam." *The Oxford English Dictionary,* 2nd ed. (Oxford: Oxford UP, 1989), The Electronic Text Center, University of Virginia Library 30 Apr. 2005 <http://etext.virginia.edu/oed.html>.
4. Judith V. Lechner, *Allyn & Bacon Anthology of Traditional Literature* (Boston: Pearson, 2004) 156.
5. Jane Yolen, Introduction, *Favorite Folktales from Around the World* (New York: Pantheon, 1986) 4.
6. Jane Yolen, "The Eye and the Ear," *Touch Magic,* 2nd ed. (Little Rock, AR: August House, 2000) 37–42.
7. Jack Zipes, *Breaking the Magic Spell: Radical Theories of Folk and Fairy Tales,* 2nd ed. (Lexington: UP of Kentucky, 2002).

Ashanti Tribe (Africa)

Many folktales around the world explain how language and stories were obtained from the gods and spread among people. This tale from the Ashanti people's ancient oral tradition in Ghana, West Africa, gives the culture hero Anansi credit for acquiring all the African lore known as spider-stories. One of the most famous trickster heroes in the world, Anansi is identified explicitly in this tale as both man and spider. Boastful and devious, he takes advantage of the weaknesses of other animals and a fairy to obtain what the sky-god requires in exchange for stories. Anansi's use of a doll covered with sticky fluid to trap the fairy is similar to the tricks with tar figures in African American and Native American folklore (such as the Tar Baby story by Virginia Hamilton in *The People Could Fly*). Although Anansi may seem ruthless in trapping these creatures to get what he wants and then voluntarily offering his mother to the sky-god to seal the bargain, actions that please the gods are not questioned in the story. In other tales, Anansi himself is outsmarted, he is shamed publicly and punished for greed (see the Anancy story by James Berry in this section), or he even gets himself killed, but in this one, he shows how a mere man can achieve greatness, receiving the blessing of the sky-god with his eternal reward of stories. Gail E. Haley's Caldecott-award-winning picture book (*A Story, A Story*), based on the same Anansi (or Ananse) tale, records an African storyteller's reminder that accepting the magic and transience of each oral story should be our first priority: "We do not really mean, we do not really mean that what we are about to say is true. A story, a story; let it come, let it go."[1]

NOTE

1. Gail E. Haley, *A Story, A Story* (New York: Aladdin/Macmillan, 1970).

How Spider Obtained the Sky-God's Stories

Translated by R. S. Rattray

Kwaku Anansi, the spider, once went to Nyankonpon, the sky-god, in order to buy the sky-god's stories. The sky-god said, "What makes you think *you* can buy them?" The spider answered and said, "I know I shall be able." Thereupon the sky-god said, "Great and powerful towns like Kokofu, Bekwai, Asumengya, have come, but they were unable to purchase them, and yet you who are but a mere masterless man, you say you will be able?"

The spider said, "What is the price of the stories?" The sky-god said, "They cannot be bought for anything except Onini, the python; Osebo, the leopard; Mmoatia, the fairy; and Mmoboro, the hornets." The spider said, "I will bring some of all these things, and, what is more, I'll add my old mother, Nsia, the sixth child, to the lot."

The sky-god said, "Go and bring them then." The spider came back, and told his mother all about it, saying, "I wish to buy the stories of the sky-god, and the sky-god says I must bring Onini, the python; Osebo, the leopard; Mmoatia, the fairy, and Mmoboro, the hornets; and I said I would add you to the lot and give you to the sky-god." Now the spider consulted his wife, Aso, saying, "What is to be done that we may get Onini, the python?" Aso said to him, "You go off and cut a branch of a palm tree, and cut some string-creeper as well, and bring them." And the spider came back with them. And Aso said, "Take them to the stream." So Anansi took them; and, as he was going along, he said, "It's longer than he is, it's not so long as he; you lie, it's longer than he."

The spider said, "There he is, lying yonder." The python, who had overheard this imaginary conversation, then asked, "What's this all about?" To which the spider replied, "Is it not my wife, Aso, who is arguing with me that this palm branch is longer than you, and I say she is a liar." And Onini, the python, said, "Bring it, and come and measure me." Anansi took the palm branch and laid it along the python's body. Then he said, "Stretch yourself out." And the python stretched himself out, and Anansi took the rope-creeper and wound it and the sound of the tying was *nwenene! nwenene! nwenene!* until he came to the head.

Anansi, the spider, said, "Fool, I shall take you to the sky-god and receive the sky-god's tales in exchange." So Anansi took him off to Nyame, the sky-god. The sky-god then said, "My hand has touched it, there remains what still remains." The spider returned and came and told his wife what had happened, saying, "There remain the hornets." His wife said, "Look for a gourd, and fill it with water and go off with it." The spider went along through the bush, when he saw a swarm of hornets hanging there, and he poured out some of the water and sprinkled it on them. He then poured the remainder upon himself and cut a leaf of plantain and covered his head with it. And now he addressed the hornets, saying, "As the rain has come, had you not better come and enter this, my gourd, so that the rain will not beat you; don't you see that I have taken a plantain leaf to cover myself?" Then the hornets said, "We thank you, Aku, we thank you, Aku." All the hornets flew, disappearing into the gourd, *fom!* Father Spider covered the mouth, and exclaimed, "Fools, I have got you, and I am taking you to receive the tales of the sky-god in exchange."

And he took the hornets to the sky-god. The sky-god said, "My hand has touched it; what remains still remains."

The spider came back once more, and told his wife, and said, "There remains Osebo, the leopard." Aso said, "Go and dig a hole." Anansi said, "That's enough, I understand." Then the spider went off to look for the leopard's tracks, and, having found them, he dug a very deep pit, covered it over, and came back home. Very early next day, when objects began to be visible, the spider said he would go off, and when he went, lo, a leopard was lying in the pit. Anansi said, "Little father's child, little mother's child, I have told you not to get drunk, and now, just as one would expect of you, you have become intoxicated, and that's why you have fallen into the pit. If I were to say I would get you out, next day, if you saw me, or likewise any of my children, you would go and catch me and them." The leopard said, "O! I could not do such a thing."

Anansi then went and cut two sticks, put one here, and one there, and said, "Put one of your paws here, and one also of your paws here." And the leopard placed them where he was told. As he was about to climb up, Anansi lifted up his knife, and in a flash it descended on his head, *gao!* was the sound it made. The pit received the leopard and *fom!* was the sound of the falling. Anansi got a ladder to descend into the pit to go and get the leopard out. He got the leopard out and came back with it, exclaiming, "Fool, I am taking you to exchange for the stories of the sky-god." He lifted up the leopard to go and give to Nyame, the sky-god. The sky-god said, "My hands have touched it; what remains still remains."

Then the spider came back, carved an Akua's child, a black flat-faced wooden doll, tapped some sticky fluid from a tree and plastered the doll's body with it. Then he made *eto,* pounded yams, and put some in the doll's hand. Again he pounded some more and placed it in a brass basin; he tied string round the doll's waist, and went with it and placed it at the foot of the odum tree, the place where the fairies come to play. And a fairy came along. She said, "Akua, may I eat a little of this mash?" Anansi tugged at the string, and the doll nodded her head. The fairy turned to one of the sisters, saying, "She says I may eat some." She said, "Eat some, then." And she finished eating, and thanked her. But when she thanked her, the doll did not answer. And the fairy said to her sister, "When I thank her, she does not reply." The sister of the first fairy said, "Slap her crying-place." And she slapped it, *pa!* And her hand stuck there. She said to her sister, "My hand has stuck there." She said, "Take the one that remains and slap her crying-place again." And she took it and slapped her, *pa!* and this one, too, stuck fast. And the fairy told her sister, saying, "My two hands have stuck fast." She said, "Push it with your stomach." She pushed it and her stomach stuck to it. And Anansi came and tied her up, and he said, "Fool, I have got you, I shall take you to the sky-god in exchange for his stories." And he went off home with her.

Now Anansi spoke to his mother, Ya Nsia, the sixth child, saying, "Rise up, let us go, for I am taking you along with the fairy to go and give you to the sky-god in exchange for his stories." He lifted them up, and went off there to where the sky-god was. Arrived there he said, "Sky-god, here is a fairy and my old woman whom I spoke about, here she is, too." Now the sky-god called his elders, the Kontire and Akwam chiefs, the Adonten, the Gyase, the Oyoko, Ankobea, and Kyidom. And he put the matter before them, saying, "Very great kings have come, and were not able to buy the sky-god's stories, but Kwaku Anansi, the spider, has been able to pay the price: I have received from him Osebo, the leopard; I have received from him Onini, the python; and of his own accord, Anansi has added his mother to the lot; all these things lie here." He said, "Sing his praise." "*Eee!*" they shouted. The sky-god said, "Kwaku Anansi, from today and going on forever, I take my sky-god's stories and I present them to you, *kose! kose! kose!* my blessing, blessing, blessing! No more shall we call them the stories of the sky-god, but we shall call them spider-stories."

This, my story, which I have related, if it be sweet, or if it be not sweet, take some elsewhere, and let some come back to me.

Anne Pellowski (b. 1933)

Anne Pellowski is an American writer, educator, and librarian who has extensive international experience with storytelling and children's literature and culture. *Four Farms* is a series of novels based on her family's history as Polish immigrant farmers in the Midwest. *The World of Storytelling* (1978), which grew out of her work at the New York Public Library and abroad, introduces a broad interdisciplinary audience to the history and methods of oral storytelling around the world. Pellowski provides valuable comparisons of the goals and methods of folklorists, professional storytellers, and "folk storytellers" in different cultures, using observations from within a culture as much as possible to avoid misinterpretation of tales and traditions.

These chapters from the revised 1990 edition of the book begin by summarizing evidence of ancient storytelling practices, both religious and secular. Pellowski traces the history of storytelling through the influence of the German Grimm Brothers on the institutionalized storytelling that was established by the 1920s in the United States and then spread elsewhere, using both oral and written sources for children's story hours in libraries and recreational centers. Chapter 4, "Folk Storytelling," is one of six chapters on "Types of Storytelling: Past and Present." It discusses the irony in characterizations of storytelling throughout history as childish and less important than other types of literature of history, when there is ample evidence that leaders in every field of endeavor have been influenced by stories they were told in their childhood homes and communities. The second half of the book discusses the format, style, and training of storytellers in different cultures. While the title of chapter 15, "Visuality, Orality, Literacy," sounds theoretical and technical, and each chapter is supported by extensive documentation, Pellowski maintains throughout a practical and accessible approach to considering questions that have been raised by all types of storytellers and theorists. Her synthesis in this chapter encourages readers to acknowledge the cultural sources of stories and to consider carefully how best to combine oral and written sources when working with children in our literate culture.

From *The World of Storytelling*

CHAPTER 1. HISTORY AND DEFINITION OF STORYTELLING

Most modern dictionaries define a storyteller, first, as one who tells or writes stories and, second, as one who tells fibs or falsehoods. This order is relatively recent. Until well into the nineteenth century, the more frequent use of the word was in the latter sense. The first definition generally was reserved for describing storytellers in non-English-speaking areas of the world.

The earliest use of the English term "storyteller" that is cited in the Oxford English Dictionary occurred in 1709, by Steele in the *Tatler*, but it is likely that the word was used widely long before that date. The same dictionary, under the entry for "story," cites a line from William Dunbar's *Poems* (c. 1500–1520 C.E.): "Sum singis, sum dancis, sum tellis storeis." Whether or not the terms "story" and "storytelling" were in use, in English or in other language equivalents, the telling of tales was commonly recognized as a form of entertainment from ancient times up to the present.

There are a number of early examples of stories or story fragments in texts from ancient Babylonian,

Canaanite, Hittite, Sumerian, Egyptian, Chinese, and Sanskrit. However, many of these contain no indication as to who told the stories, to whom they were told, and how or why. Some artifacts indicate that storytelling was an early entertainment. The beautiful lyre that was made at Ur more than 5,000 years ago has an inlay showing animals acting like men. Frankfort speculates that this type of illustration must have had something to do with the reciting or recording of myths or fables.[1] The first written description of an action that at least vaguely resembles storytelling appears to be in the Egyptian papyrus known as the Westcar Papyrus, recorded sometime between the twelfth and eighteenth dynasties (2000–1300 B.C.E.). It describes an encounter between Khufu (Cheops) and his sons:

> "Know ye a man who can tell me tales of the deeds of magicians?" Then the royal son Khafra stood forth and said, "I will tell thy Majesty a tale of the days of thy forefather Nebka. . . ."[2]

After Khafra has told his tale, another son, Baiufra, tells one from the time of Seneferu (father of Cheops) and the third son, Herutatef, concludes with a contemporary tale.

Another papyrus of approximately the same date, known as the Golenischeff Papyrus and now in the Hermitage in Leningrad, gives an account of the conversation between a nobleman and a sailor. The nobleman has returned from an unsuccessful mission and is reluctant to report to the ruling powers. The sailor, to convince the nobleman that he should not be afraid, then narrates his adventures as a kind of "proof" that such things can befall anyone! This has come to be known as the story of "The Shipwrecked Sailor."[3]

The Bible has, as Ranke puts it, "most of the forms of folktales in some shape or other, complete or incomplete."[4] But in the Old Testament there are few descriptions of actual storytelling occasions. The most striking one is in Judges 9:7, where Jotham tells a tale to convince the people of Shechem of the terrible deeds done by Abimelech, their ruler. The Chadwicks believe that this and other passages (Deut. 11:29, and Josh.: 8:33, among others) reflect a custom followed by Hebrew prophets or orators on public occasions. Their general conclusion is that "we cannot recall any recitation for the sake of entertainment" in early Hebrew literature.[5]

Sanskrit scripture, on the other hand, does have a number of passages that indicate storytelling was practiced for religious and secular reasons. In the *Kaushitaki Brahmana Upanishad,* Part III (c. 500 B.C.E.), at the end of a story about Soma (a Hindu god), the narrator remarks that "it is thus told us by those versed in legend *(âkhyânavidah)."*[6] Later, in several of the *Grihya-Sûtras,* or *Rules of Vedic Domestic Ceremonies* (c. 200 B.C.E.), appropriate times are mentioned for telling tales. Two examples are:

> They who have lost a Guru by death, or are afflicted by other misfortune, should perform on the new-moon day an expiatory ceremony.... Keeping that (fire) burning, they sit till the silence of the night, repeating the tales of the aged, and getting stories of auspicious contents, Itihasas and Puranas, told to them.
> *Âsvalâyana-Grihya Sûtra,* IV Adhyâya 6 Kândikâ
> 1,6, trans. by Hermann Oldenburg[7]

> [In preparation for a festival] therefore (husband and wife) should eat fast-day food which is pleasant to them. Let them sleep that night on the ground. They should spend that night so as to alternate their sleep with waking, entertaining themselves with tales or with other discourse.
> *Grihya-Sûtra of Gobhila,* I Prapâthaka 6 Kândikâ
> 4,5,6, trans. by Hermann Oldenburg[8]

There is also fairly good evidence that some early forms of storytelling in India were accompanied by pictures. A number of scholars conclude that brief descriptions in the *Sûtras* of Panini (sixth or fifth century B.C.E.), in the *Mahabhasya* of Patanjali (160–140 B.C.E.) and in numerous other texts are probably referring to the recitation of tales while showing individual pictures or a sequence of pictures on a scroll or cloth.[9]

Buddhist teaching, from early times to the present day, makes use of stories. The *Tripitaka,* part of the sacred scriptures of Buddhism, contains many passages in which some storytelling device is used to make a point. The part known as the fift *Nikaya,* which contains fifteen books, is full of dialogues, lives of sages and saints, fables, the birth stories (Jatakas), and numerous tales of all types. The recitation of these stories was looked on with favor by the Buddhist authorities, and continued to be so regarded throughout the later centuries of Buddhist expansion and development. In a work that probably dates to around 300–400 C.E., *The Questions of King Milinda,* the sage Nagasena reassures the king that the recitations are a good practice.[10]

Taoism and Confucianism did not have quite this richness of oral narrative, but they, too, probably used story to spread or reinforce belief. The *Tao-te-Ching* (c. 300 B.C.E.) contains little in the way of narrative, but the writings of Chuang-Tze (c. 100 B.C.E.) are full of parables, narratives, and short tales of all kinds. Chuang-Tze's work cannot be taken as literal history, since it describes encounters and confrontations between Confucius, Lao-Tze, and a host of other sages, heroes, and characters that could not possibly have taken place. However, it is quite possible, and even likely, that Chuang-Tze did not invent the parables and tales he wrote down, but simply recorded many from the oral tradition extant in his time. In describing how he believes Lao-Tze and Confucius told their parables and proverbs, Chuang-tze was probably recording some of the ways he had heard tales told by members of the two philosophical systems.

Early Greek writing makes frequent reference to the art of telling stories, either through implication or by actually describing when and by whom it was done. Euripides, in the play *Heracles* (c. 423 B.C.E.), puts such a description in the mouth of Amphitryon. Advising his daughter-in-law Megara on how to spend the time waiting for her husband's return, Amphitryon says:

Be calm;
dry the living springs of tears that fill
your children's eyes. Console them with stories,
those sweet thieves of wretched make-believe.

Heracles, lines 97–103,
trans. by Gilbert Murray[11]

Aristophanes also refers to storytelling in his plays. In *Lysistrata* (c. 411 B.C.E.) the chorus of old men says:

I want to tell you a fable they used to relate to me when I was a little boy.

Lysistrata, line 718, trans. unknown[12]

The old men proceed to tell the story of Atalanta and how she fled from marriage to Melanion, except that they reverse the action of the characters to make their point with the women.

In an amusing scene in *The Wasps* (c. 422 B.C.E.), Bdelycleon is trying to instruct Philocleon as to how to behave and talk in polite society. Philocleon then announces that he will tell the legend of Lamia, whereupon the following exchange takes place:

Bdel.: Come, no fabulous tales, pray! talk of realities, of domestic facts, as is usually done.
    Phil.: Ah! I know something that is indeed most domestic. Once upon a time there was a rat and a cat. . . .

The Wasps, lines 1178–1180, trans. unknown[13]

Earlier in the same play (line 566) is the statement: "Others tell us anecdotes or some comic story from Aesop [to get on their good side]."

In *The Republic* (c. 400 B.C.E.) Plato writes:

. . . we begin by telling children stories which though not wholly destitute of truth, are in the main fictitious; and these stories are told them when they are not of an age to learn gymnastics. . . .the beginning is the most important part of any work, especially in the case of a young and tender thing; for that is the time at which the character is being formed and the desired impression is more readily taken.

The Republic, Book 2,
trans. by Benjamin Jowett[14]

Aristotle, in his *Politics*, Book 7, Part 1336 (c. 322 B.C.E.), mentions that "educational directors, as they are called, should be careful what tales, fact or fiction, children hear." Two centuries later the Greek writer Dio Chrysostom imagines the following dialogue to have taken place between Alexander and Diogenes:

Have you not heard the Libyan myth? And the king replied that he had not. Then Diogenes told it to him with zest and charm, because he wanted to put him in a good humour, just as nurses, after giving the children a whipping, tell them a story to comfort and please them.

Discourse, 4, 74, trans. by J. W. Cohoon[15]

Ovid's *Metamorphoses* (c. 7 C.E.) depicts a scene of storytelling that would be seen later throughout Europe and the British Isles, namely that of women sewing or spinning and telling tales to make the work move more swiftly. He is here describing the daughters of Minyas, who do not wish to go out and celebrate the feast of Bacchus:

Then one of them . . . says: While the other women are deserting their tasks and thronging this so-called festival, let us also, who keep Pallas, a truer goddess, lighten with various talk the serviceable work of our hands, and to beguile the tedious hours, let us take turns in telling stories, while all the others listen. The sisters agree and bid her be first to speak. She mused awhile which she should tell of many tales, for very many she knew.

Metamorphoses, Book 4, 36–44,
trans. by F. J. Miller[16]

The historian Strabo in his *Geography* (c. 7 B.C.E.–18 C.E.) does not depict one particular storytelling scene, but in several places implies that tale telling was a common human experience:

Man is eager to learn and his fondness for tales is a prelude to this quality. It is fondness for tales, then, that induces children to give their attention to narratives and more and more to take part in them. The reason for this is that myth is a new language to them—a language that tells them, not of things as they are, but of a different set of things. And what is new is pleasing, and so is what one did not know before, and it is just this that makes men eager to learn. But if you add to this the marvellous and the portentous, you thereby increase the pleasure, and pleasure acts as a charm to

incite to learning. At the beginning we must needs
make use of such bait for children. . . .

Geography, Book 1, Part 2, 8,
trans. by Horace L. Jones[17]

Even pre-Christian Latin literature includes a few
brief mentions of storytelling occasions. In one of Cicero's works (c. 45 B.C.E.) we find one of the earliest
denigrations of the fairy tale:

. . . as for your school's account of the matter, it is the
merest fairy-story, hardly worthy of old wives at work
by lamplight.

De natura Deorum, I, 34, trans. by H. Rackham[18]

Cicero does not say so directly, but he certainly implies that one of the things done by "old wives at work
by lamplight" is storytelling, probably to make the
task go faster.

Horace, in one of his satires (c. 30 B.C.E.), is much
more specific in describing a storytelling scene:

O evenings, and suppers fit for the gods! with which I
and my friends regale ourselves in the presence of my
household gods. . . .Then conversation arises, not
concerning other people's villas and houses, nor
whether Lepos dances well or not; but we debate on
what is more to our purpose, and what it is pernicious
not to know. . . . Meanwhile, my neighbor Cervius
prates away old stories relative to the subject.

Satires, Book II, 6, trans. by Christopher Smart[19]

One of the stories that Cervius "prates away" is "The
Country Mouse and the City Mouse." This entire passage gives a vivid picture of one type of entertaining
storytelling among well-to-do Romans.

The above examples would suggest that folktales
and legends and myths were clearly perceived as entertainment (and sometimes education) to be enjoyed
by adults and children. They were told by anyone who
felt so inclined and in a variety of situations.

But what about the professional storytellers and re-
citers—the bards, minstrels and *rhapsodes*—also described in some detail in early literature, especially
Greek? The *Odyssey* (seventh or sixth century B.C.E.)
has numerous references to bards, the occasions on
which they perform, and the content of their stories.
These examples are from Book 1:

Now when the wooers had put from them the desire of
meat and drink, they minded them of other things,
even of the song and dance, for these are the crown of

the feast. And a henchman placed a beauteous lyre in
the hands of Phemius, who was minstrel to the wooers
despite his will. . . .

Phemius starts to sing of the return of the Achaeans.
Penelope hears him, enters and says to him:

"Phemius, since thou knowest many other charms for
mortals, deeds of men and gods, which bards rehearse, some of these do thou sing. . . ."

Later, Telemachus answers:

". . . men always prize that song the most, which
rings newest in their ears."

Odyssey, trans. by S. H. Butcher
and Andrew Lang[20]

Pindar, in one of his *Nemean Odes* (c. 485 B.C.E.)
gives a picture of one of the ways in which the bard
found narrative subjects for his tales in song:

Even as the sons of Homer, those singers of deftly
woven lays, begin most often with Zeus for their prelude; even so hath our hero laid a first foundation for a
tale of achievements in the sacred games by receiving
a crown in the sacred grove of Nemean Zeus.

Odes, II, 1–5, trans. by Sir John Sandys[21]

Plato's *Ion* (c. 400 B.C.E.) gives an excellent picture of the *rhapsode* (the reciter-type bard) and his
position in society. Although it is colored by Plato's
irony and his poking fun at the pretensions of some
rhapsodes, it can still tell us much about this type of
storyteller:

I often envy the profession of a *rhapsode,* Ion, for you
have always to wear fine clothes, and to look as beautiful as you can is a part of your art. . . . you are
obliged to be continually in the company of many
good poets.

Trans. by Benjamin Jowett[22]

A form of bardic storytelling is probably being
referred to in this passage from the *Śatapatha-
Brāhmaṇa,* part of Sanskrit scriptures (c. 500 B.C.E.):

And on the following day, he goes out to the house of
the *Sûta* (court minstrel and chronicler), and prepares
a barley pap for Varuna; for the *Sûta* is a spiriter. . . .
And he, the *Sûta,* assuredly is one of his jewels: it is
for him that he is thereby consecrated; and him he
makes his own faithful [follower].

V Kanda 3, Adhyâya, 1 Brāhmana 5,
trans. by Julius Eggeling[23]

There are even very early descriptions of the bard's position among the Gauls. Diodorus of Sicily, writing in Greek (c. 50 B.C.E.), comments:

The Gauls are terrifying in their aspect and their voices are deep and altogether harsh; when they meet together they converse with few words and in riddles, hinting darkly at things for the most part and using one word when they mean another. . . . Among them are also to be found lyric poets whom they call Bards. These men sing to the accompaniment of instruments which are like lyres, and their song may be either of praise or of obloquy.

Library of History, V, 31,
trans. by C. H. Oldfather[24]

The question has often been asked: Did these bards, minstrels, *rhapsodes,* and the like precede or follow the telling of tales by persons not looked on as professionals? Did this special career develop as a secularization of originally priestly or religious functions? Or were the first storytellers merely the best from those who entertained their particular social group informally, then realized their special talents and power, and gradually sought to protect their status by devising systems regulating training, practice, and performance?

Going back to Strabo, we find that he has this to say:

. . . the fact that the ancients used the verb "sing" instead of the verb "tell" bears witness to this very thing, namely, that poetry was the source and origin of style. . . . For when poetry was recited, it employed the assistance of song. . . . Therefore since "tell" was first used in reference to poetic "style" and since among the ancients the poetic style was accompanied by song, the term "sing" was to them equivalent to the term "tell."

Geography, Book 1, Part 2, 6,
trans. by Horace L. Jones[25]

The modern philosopher Johan Huizinga would agree with this. In *Homo Ludens: A Study of the Play Element in Culture,* he begins:

Play is older than culture, for culture, however inadequately defined, always presupposes society, and animals have not waited for man to teach them their playing.[26]

Later he writes:

Poetry everywhere precedes prose. . . . All poetry is born of play. . . . Gradually the poet-seer splits up into the figures of the prophet, the priest, the soothsayer,

the mystagogue and the poet as we know him; even the philosopher, the legislator, the orator, the demagogue, the sophist and the rhetor spring from that primordial composite type, the *vates.* The early Greek poets all show traces of their common progenitor. Their function is eminently a social one; they speak as the educators and monitors of the people. They are the nation's leaders. . . .[27]

In light of these passages and others, Huizinga might well have answered the question like this: Storytelling was first practiced by ordinary persons gifted in poetic speech, which had been discovered in their play; gradually this playful aspect of poetic tale telling was grafted onto religious rituals, historical recitations, epic compositions, educational functions, and the like.

The Chadwicks, scholars in the history of literature, divided oral literature into five types. They were unwilling to state definitely that Type D (oral literature of celebration, including religious ritual) followed or preceded Type A (narrative poetry or saga designed for entertainment). They found too many instances in which the order apparently could have evolved in either direction. However, they imply that narration for entertainment preceded other types in quite a number of other cultures. They do not speculate on whether the professional bard preceded the popular, nonprofessional poet-reciter.[28]

Arthur Ransome, in his chapter on the origins of storytelling, states unequivocally:

At first there would be no professional storytellers. But it would not be long before . . . there would be found some one whose adventures were always the pleasantest to hear, whose deeds were the most marvelous, whose realistic details the most varied.[29]

A. B. Lord and his mentor and predecessor Milman Parry, both important scholars of oral epic narrative, analyzed the performances of Serbo-Croatian oral epic singers. They developed a system whereby texts could be examined for repeated phraseologies and parallelisms, similar to those they had found in readings of the Homeric epics. This led them to speculate that the twentieth century oral epic performers were following language patterns close to those of ancient Greek performers, and also using music and poetic rhythm in the same way. They do not theorize about whether this bardic type preceded or followed folk storytelling, although they do firmly state their belief that written literature supplanted the oral but did not grow out of it directly.[30]

G. S. Kirk, in *The Songs of Homer*, came up with the premise that Greek oral epic performers were "corrupted" once they began to rely on written texts. That is, he believed that no true bards or minstrels could be called by those names if they were once exposed to writing and reading. The *Iliad* and the *Odyssey*, he contended, were oral epics, written down, and virtually all that came after them was no longer truly oral-based. But Kirk also left out of his discussion the possible role and influence folk storytellers might have had on oral epic performers, and vice versa. Nor did he comment much on the ability of folk tellers to maintain extensive repertoires that used the special language of orality, even after they had been exposed to literacy.

In the past two decades, the discussions about orality and literacy have been greatly expanded by the work of many thinkers and scholars. Eric A. Havelock summed up his life-long preoccupation with this theme in his book *The Muse Learns to Write*. His basic conclusion was that the unique quality of the Greek alphabet (which he believed to be the only true ancient alphabet), changed not only the basic means of communication, but also the shape of Greek consciousness, and European consciousness when that area of the world came to adapt and use the Greek alphabet for its languages. It was not only the story crafters and tellers whose lives were dramatically changed by the appearance of a system that enabled human speech to be recorded in an accurate and easy manner, capable of being learned even by children; all levels of society were affected by this revolutionary device, and they began thinking and acting in different ways because they no longer had to keep in memory everything they knew.

Havelock implied that this had as dramatic an effect as the discovery of human speech. The brain was freed from the heavy responsibility of memorization and could expand in creative, new directions. Furthermore, the Greek alphabet, he believed, brought about what is commonly called "logical" and "categorical" modes of thinking. Storytelling was forever changed, even for those who themselves did not become literate, because the surrounding society had been transformed. But he did not imply that this was necessarily a superior way of thinking or that oral-based civilizations of an equally complex character did not exist. On

the contrary, he stated that "Not creativity, whatever that may mean, but recall and recollection pose the key to our civilized existence."[31]

Walter J. Ong is another scholar who has explored this question extensively. He defined orality in a number of ways, and described "primary orality" as being the means of communication in societies that are totally nonliterate; but this orality is as much a shaper of complex social consciousness as is literacy. It is simply different. In his view, there can be no such thing as "oral literature" because it is a contradiction in terms. There is literature which is sometimes recited or interpreted by speaking it aloud, and there is the oral performance and passing down of narrative, history, laws, customs, and other communications that have never been written down.[32]

Other scholars in this century (anthropologists, archeologists, folklorists, philologists, semioticians, and others who study linguistics and literature), have attempted to find evidence for one theory or another by studying peoples not yet touched by written cultures, especially those using linear alphabets; or they examine still further the earliest examples of pictures, signs, writing, memory aids and artifacts from ancient and even more recent civilizations. Out of this research has come much speculation about the ways in which humans have told stories in the past, their reasons for doing so, and how this changed with the gradual spread of composition in writing.

The best one can say about the earliest origins of storytelling is that there is evidence to support many theories:

[handwritten marginalia: Twins of story telling]

1. That it grew out of playful, self-entertainment needs of humans.
2. That it satisfied the need to explain the surrounding physical world.
3. That it came about because of an intrinsic religious need in humans to honor or propitiate the supernatural force(s) believed to be present in the world.
4. That it evolved from the human need to communicate experience to other humans.
5. That it fulfilled an aesthetic need for beauty, regularity, and form through expressive language and music and body movement.
6. That it stemmed from the desire to record the actions or qualities of one's ancestors or lead-

ers, in the hope that this would give them a kind of immortality.

7. That it encoded and preserved the norms of social interaction that a given society lived by.

Documentation for the same kinds of storytelling, such as those cited above, continues up to the time of printing by movable type. It can be found in Sanskrit, Chinese, Parthian, Greek, Latin, Anglo-Saxon, Old German, Icelandic, Old Slavonic, and probably in many of the other written languages in use during that period. For example, depictions of bardic storytelling (see definition, page 21) are to be found in Lucan's *Pharsalia* (c. 60 C.E.), Athenaeus' *Deipnosophistae* (c. 200 C.E.), in *Beowulf* (c. 700 C.E.), in Bede's *Ecclesiastical History of the English People* (c. 700 C.E.), in Asser's *Life of King Alfred* (c. 970 C.E.), and in the narrative poem *Deor* (c. 1000 C.E.), describing an Old Teutonic minstrel. These are, of course, different types of bards, and some suffered a decline in legal or social position before the arrival of mass printing. However, it appears as though all of them used narratives with a heroic/poetic content, and a formal style of presentation seems to have been common to all of them.

As for the professional storytellers in civilizations for which there is little or no written record, such as the Incan and some of the early African kingdoms, we must base our suppositions on other surviving artifacts. Scholars and researchers are now only in the beginning stages of examining the impact of primary orality on these cultures. Also, there must be much more intensive study of the performances of tellers who were recorded shortly after they came into contact with persons from literate cultures.

Descriptions of folk storytelling in the home, work place, street or other public venue are encountered in numerous sources, as will be noted in Chapter 4. The occasions remained essentially the same as those in classical times. Storytelling as a means of educating and socializing the child continued to be mentioned, just as it had been in the works of Plato and Aristotle. Quintillian (C.E. 35–100)wrote:

> Their pupils should learn to paraphrase Aesop's fables, the natural successors of the fairy-stories of the nursery, in simple and restrained language and subsequently to set down this paraphrase in writing with the same simplicity of style.
>
> *Institutio Oratorio,* Book 1, ch. 9, pt. 2,
> trans. by H. E. Butler[33]

In the opening part of the *Panchatantra* (c. 400 C.E.), compiled for the education and enlightenment of the royal children of India, there is this "guarantee" of the efficacy of storytelling, with the use of tales from that collection:

> Whoever learns the work by heart,
> Or through the storyteller's art
> Becomes acquainted;
> His life by sad defeat—although
> The king of heaven be his foe—
> Is never tainted.
>
> Trans. by Arthur W. Ryder[34]

Strabo mentioned that Parthian teachers rehearsed their pupils "both with song and without song" in narratives about their gods and noble men.[35]

Only in what shall be called religious storytelling in this book (see definition, page 44) are there documented changes in the approach to storytelling style that can be called dramatic. The sacred scriptures of the Judaic, Christian, and Islamic religions are obviously based on much that was orally passed down, and included narratives that can be said to have entertaining as well as moral or didactic power. However, shortly after these texts became fairly fixed, there appears to have been a change in attitude to storytelling. It was frowned upon by the orthodox religious authorities because it resulted in versions or interpretations of the sacred texts that were not "true." Priests, monks, rabbis, imams and other recognized teachers of these religions were expected to read or recite word for word, or at least paraphrase closely the original text. Of course, this did not prevent some of them, or members of the laity, from passing down orally their own versions of their religious experiences, and their own interpretations of stories in the scriptures.

Hindu and Buddhist religious authorities, on the other hand, seemed to tolerate and even encourage the use of storytelling. The belief in the superiority of the spoken word over the written word has always been very strong in India, and survives to this day.[36] However, there is evidence that in some sects in these religions, too, a certain inflexibility set in, once certain sacred story texts were regarded as fixed.

In any case, long before the advent of mass printing and distribution, there was a gradual secularization of both the style and content of many stories from all of these religions. Storytellers were telling them in public, for purely entertaining purposes, and they probably changed a bit with each telling, while the scriptural versions stayed pretty much the same.

Mass distribution of printed stories and tales began in Asia and Europe at approximately the same time: the late fifteenth and the beginning of the sixteenth century. Print did not so much usurp the place of the storyteller as use the devices of storytelling to advertise. Bardic performances did suffer a decline in those areas saturated by print where a sizable number of the populace learned to read, or had occasions to hear things read aloud. Their place was partly taken up by street and marketplace storytelling, usually promoting the sale of narrative ballads or news sheets or cheaply printed chapbooks. Sometimes these street performers tried to evoke the same kinds of heroic and high-minded feelings as had the bards, but they usually succeeded in appealing more to the curiosity of the folk. And they certainly never attained the professionalism and social position that bards, and even wandering minstrels, had enjoyed in earlier centuries.

The market storytellers in the Arabic-speaking world continued to relate the elaborate tales-within-frameworks that had entered their oral repertoires from India via Persia, but they also added other elements that had evolved from Islamic tradition. In the Hindu- and Buddhist-influenced areas of Asia, the differences among Vedic, classical, and folk myths and tales had always been difficult to perceive. With the spread of Buddhism under Aśoka and, later, the increasing influence of the Moghul Empire, trade and travel increased so much that peoples in all parts of Asia began to hear stories that once had been confined to a relatively fixed area. It became virtually impossible to sort out all of the origins of Hindu- and Buddhist-inspired tales.

There is little doubt that many of these stories passed rapidly into China and East Asia, and later into Europe via Persia and through the Arabs living in North Africa and Spain.[37] Many scholars agree that certain elements now present in folktales throughout Europe entered during some period of trade with or conquest by Asian peoples. Some claimed that Manichaeism was the strongest force in the movement of Hindu-Buddhist story elements from Asia to the Middle East and Europe.[38] The method of entry may have been oral, but the stories were quickly converted into print. What is still widely debated, however, is whether there was a reverse flow, and to what extent European stories influenced those in Asia in the periods prior to the nineteenth century.

Europe was also enriched by the firsthand, tale-bearing accounts of exploration and colonization coming from Africa and the Americas. Unfortunately, most of the manuscripts and many of the other records extant among the Aztecs, the Maya, the Incas, and other Native American groups were destroyed by the colonizing powers. The only documentation one can find for storytelling is in some artifacts, and in those records that were re-created from memory decades or even hundreds of years after the destruction of the originals. Accounts of some of the more sympathetic explorers and missionaries also contain descriptions of myth, ritual, and legends, as well as information about how and when they were told. A good example of the latter is in Fray Diego Durán's *The Ancient Calendar* (1579 C.E.), describing the ceremony after the birth of the Aztec child, subsequent to the use of prophetic pictures by the astrologer:

> The parents or kinsmen were told about these many things, having first listened to assurances and then to long, flowery speeches. After this the soothsayers told two dozen lies and fables.
>
> Trans. by Fernando Horcasitas and
> Doris Heyden[39]

One must take into account, of course, that it is a foreign missionary who calls the tales told "lies and fables." It may well be that the stories were embedded with important beliefs that were not apparent to the outsider.

The *Popol Vuh* of the Maya was also written down again shortly after the conquest, from the memories of those who had preserved it, probably through continued oral recitation. It is replete with myths, parables, and tales, but no actual storytelling occasions are depicted.

In Africa, storytelling obviously had been commonly practiced in many areas. There do not appear to be any written descriptions prior to the arrival of Arabic and European traders, but oral tradition speaks of the practice as being an ancient one. Ben-Amos finds at least tentative evidence of storytelling in the appearance of the *akpata* players in two of the Benin bronzes from the seventeenth century. He theorizes that it is as likely as not that these performers accompanying the

Oba (ruler) did praise singing and ritual-narrative singing. The *akpata* has lost most of its ceremonial meaning and use but it is still employed by professional storytellers in present-day Nigeria.[40]

Whether or not this form of storytelling was practiced in the seventeenth century kingdom of Benin, there is evidence from the works of Leo Africanus (c. 1600 C.E.) and from a number of European travelers and traders that both heroic/poetic and folk stories were recited on occasion in different parts of Africa. Such accounts, together with those coming from the Americas and those that had already come from Asia, enriched the possibilities of fantasy and imaginative speculation for the European storyteller. As the folklorist Linda Dégh has pointed out, the storyteller is generally experienced and widely traveled, knowledgeable, and well-versed in the ways of the world. The storyteller attracts new narrative material "like a magnet."[41]

People tend to clarify their own identities in learning how others differ from them. It is no wonder then that, following their fascination with other parts of the world during the preceding centuries, the Europeans of the nineteenth century began to look more closely at their own traditions. The French critic of children's literature Isabelle Jan states that "there is a time in the evolution of every nation when it will seek to assert its specific identity by means of folklore."[42] For many of the European nations, this time was the nineteenth century.

Among the educated and highly literate classes, oral narration as a form of entertainment for adults had died out by the late eighteenth century. True, the same kinds of tales that delighted the listening audience among the folk were appreciated by the reading audience, but in polished form, as in Perrault or in the elegant versions of the Arabian Nights. For children, it was another matter. Folktales, legends, and myths were still commonly being told to them orally, more for didactic than for entertainment purposes. Paraphrasing Lucretius, Francis Bacon wrote:

Men fear death, as children fear to go in the dark; and as that natural fear in children is increased with tales, so is the other.

Essays 2, "Of Death"[43]

In one of his plays, Schiller is probably transfering his own childhood feelings to the character of idealis-

tic young Max Piccolomini. Max reassures Thekla, daughter of Wallenstein, and says that her father's fascination with the supernatural is common to many people. He tells her:

Not only human pride fills the air
With ghosts, with secret forces;
Also for a loving heart is this ordinary
World too narrow, and deeper meaning
Lies in the fairy tales of my childhood
Than in the truths that life has taught.

Die Piccolomini, III, 4[44]

It was the appearance of the Grimm Brothers' *Kinder- und Hausmärchen* (1812–1815) that excited the educated and involved the literate adult population once again with oral tradition. After the erudite Jakob Grimm and the poetic Wilhelm Grimm had published their versions of the tales, complete with notes and comments, they made such "collecting" acceptable as an academic discipline. The tales became the rage of scholar and dilettante alike. It was probably fashionable to visit one's childhood nurse, listen to her tales, and report on them to one's intellectual and social peers at the next gathering. For the traveler, it became *de rigeur* to report on storytelling "among the natives." The only trouble was that all too often the stories and the manner of telling them were recorded and presented in such a refined and literary language that the flavor and style of the oral originals was practically gone. By 1891 Hartland was writing:

To sum up it would appear that national differences in the manner of storytelling are for the most part superficial.[45]

Nothing could have been further from the truth. There were and still are enormous differences in the manner of telling tales.

Modern scholars agree that most folktale or storytelling research of the nineteenth or early twentieth century is not valid in terms of present-day standards. The tales taken down in this period by missionaries, travelers, anthropologists, philologists, social scientists, psychologists, and folklorists are still studied and compared with later versions recorded under more stringent controls and with greater care for the entire context. But they are rarely accepted now as the authoritative versions, as was often the case formerly.

Nevertheless, in spite of their disfavor among some

scholars, the Grimm Brothers' tales must be considered as the single most important group of folktales that affected storytelling for children. Their widespread appeal and their contemporaneous legitimacy helped educated European parents to believe it was important to continue telling such stories to children, even though, in many cases, there was opposition from formal educational authorities. In the United States, with the public library just beginning to expand its work with children, the first children's librarians looked to such collections, and many later ones inspired by or modeled on that of the Grimm Brothers, to justify the need for the story hour as a part of the regular work of every children's library. It is doubtful that this could have happened without the apparent mantle of scholarship and prestige spread over the folktale collections of the Brothers Grimm, and later of Afanas'ev, Asbjørnsen and Moe, and others.

It did not take long for this institutionalized type of storytelling to take hold. By 1927 it was an established part of most public library programs. Furthermore, it had also spread to municipal recreation departments. When these institutions inspired the establishment of similar ones in Canada, England, Denmark, Sweden, Norway, Australia, and other countries, it was quite natural that the storytelling component would be carried along.

Storytellers in such cases were usually trained during in-service seminars and learned their stories from books more often than from oral sources. Not one of the more than fifty storytelling manuals published in the United States from 1900–1975 suggests that the novice storyteller learn stories only (or principally) from oral sources. In fact, most of them have lists of suggested books from which it is good to learn stories.

Toward a Definition of Storytelling

For whatever reasons—training, limitations of time and opportunity, or their own frame of reference—librarian-storytellers tended to focus on already published stories as sources of story hour material. They saw storytelling, for the most part, as an introduction to books and a means of encouraging children to read. A definition of storytelling widely used in library courses and workshops was the following:

> Storytelling as an art means recreating literature—taking the printed words in a book and giving them life.[46]

However, there are recent indications that librarians and other institutional storytellers are beginning to regard oral storytelling as a medium in its own right, and do not restrict it to the retelling of written literature.

Among literature specialists, Mia Gerhardt, in her masterful study of The Thousand and One Nights, uses the term storyteller to encompass "those who created the stories, and those who repeated them, the narrators who worked them over, the redactors who wrote them down, the compilers who collected them, and the translators who made them accessible in other languages."[47]

The literary critic Walter Benjamin defined storytelling by contrasting it to the sharing of information. Information has value only for the moment it is new, but storytelling is capable of releasing information even when the story is very old. He concluded that:

> . . . nothing . . . commends a story to memory more effectively than that chaste compactness which precludes psychological analysis. And the more natural the process by which the storyteller forgoes psychological shading, the greater becomes the story's claim to a place in the memory of the listener. . . .[48]

But Benjamin then goes on to equate this essentially oral craft with the craft of the writer, and makes little distinction between the two very different processes of composing stories orally and in written form.

The above definitions are not acceptable to folklorists, ethnologists, anthropologists, philologists, and others who are interested mostly in orally learned and transmitted stories. They use definitions developed in their own frame of reference. Axel Olrik, the folklorist who coined the phrase "epic laws of folk literature," believed that the folk narrator was one who told tales by unconsciously obeying such epic laws as the "law of opening and closing," the "law of repetition," and others.[49] William Jansen, on the other hand, wrote that the folk storytelling performance may be "at various times and for various reasons, an art, a craft, a common skill, or a universal and general capability."[50] Harold Scheub, a folklorist with extensive field experience in Africa, defines the type of storytelling he observed as "the creation of a dramatic narrative whose conflict and resolution are derived from . . . remembered core cliches and shaped into a plot during performance."[51]

Dell Hymes[52] and Robert Georges[53] both describe at length the "communicative event," a culturally defined social event that is appropriate for certain forms of communication. Georges draws up a set of postulates that are contained in his definition of a "storytelling event," and one of these postulates is that the storyteller is an "encoder" who uses linguistic, paralinguistic, and kinesic codes to formulate, encode, and transmit the message of the story.[54] Linda Dégh believes that the teller is the bearer of tradition (or the communal contribution of past bearers of tradition) to the storytelling community of which she or he is a part.[55]

Dennis Tedlock emphasizes the totality of the storytelling experience and finds it important to distinguish orally composed texts from those composed in written form. The teller, he contends, learned language structure and meaning, plot structure and characterization, the art of telling, and everything else that comprises the storytelling act, as a totality, not in bits and pieces as the modern student tends to learn about written literature. He believes the orally told story is not a genre, but "a complex ceremony in miniature."[56] He has devised his own method for writing down oral performances.

Those who use storytelling for religious reasons today would probably formulate still another set of definitions, as would those who have developed an elaborate style of theatrical storytelling.

Since all of these kinds of storytelling are still going on in different parts of the world, it was necessary to draft a new definition that would embrace the institutional and theatrical storyteller's conception of storytelling, as well as that of the folklorist, the ethnographer, the semiotician, and the linguistics scholar.

There is not only much disagreement about the words "tell," "teller," and "telling" and their use to describe both oral and written processes; the term "story" is also the subject of much discussion. In recent years, so much research has focused on the meaning of story, the process through which humans learn to use story, and the various forms of story, that it would take a book longer than this one to summarize all the theories and examples. In this book, the term "story" will refer to any connected narrative, in prose or poetry or a mixture of the two, that has one or more characters involved in a plot with some action and at least a partial resolution. It may or may not have fictional aspects.

The definition of storytelling used here is: the entire context of a moment when oral narration of stories in verse and/or prose, is performed or led by one person before a live audience; the narration may be spoken, chanted, or sung, with or without musical, pictorial, and/or other accompaniment, and may be learned from oral, printed or mechanically recorded sources; one of its purposes must be that of entertainment or delight and it must have at least a small element of spontaneity in the performance.

NOTES

1. H. Frankfort, *The Art and Architecture of the Ancient Orient,* pp. 35–36.
2. "Tales of the Magicians," in *Egyptian Literature,* ed. and tr. by Epiphanius Wilson, pp. 159–169.
3. Ibid., pp. 173–176.
4. K. Ranke. "Volkserzählung," in *Die Religion in Geschichte und Gegenwart,* 3rd ed., vol. 6, p. 1451.
5. H. M. and N. K. Chadwick, *The Growth of Literature,* vol. 2, p. 753.
6. *The Sacred Books of the East* (S.B.E.), vol. 12, p. xxiv.
7. S.B.E., vol. 29, pp. 246–248.
8. S.B.E. vol. 30, p. 29.
9. V. Mair, *Painting and Performance,* pp. 17–37.
10. S.B.E., vol. 36, book 4, chap. 7, 1–7, pp. 92–96.
11. Euripides, *Complete Greek Tragedies,* vol. 5. New York: Modern Library, n.d., p. 132.
12. Aristophanes, *The Eleven Comedies,* vol. 1, New York: Liveright, 1943, p. 267.
13. Ibid., vol. 2, pp. 61–62.
14. W. C. Greene, ed., *The Dialogues of Plato,* New York. Liveright, 1927, p. 295.
15. Loeb Classical Library (L.C.L.), no. 257, 1932, p. 203.
16. L.C.L., no. 42, 1916, p. 181.
17. L.C.L., no. 49, 1917, pp. 67–69.
18. L.C.L., no. 268, 1933, p. 93.
19. New York: Everyman's Library, 1911, pp. 206–207.
20. New York: Modern Library, 1950, pp. 5ff.
21. L.C.L., no. 56, 1915, p. 329.
22. W. C. Greene, *The Dialogues of Plato,* p. 123.
23. S.B.E., vol. 41, p. 60.
24. L.C.L., no. 340, 1939, pp. 177–179.
25. L.C.L., no. 49, 1917, p. 65.
26. J. Huizinga, *Homo Ludens,* p. 1.
27. Ibid., p. 129.
28. H. M. and N. K. Chadwick, *Growth of Literature,* vol. 3, pp. 706ff.
29. A. Ransome, *A History of Storytelling,* pp. 6–7.
30. A. B. Lord, *The Singer of Tales,* pp. 137–138.
31. E. Havelock, *The Muse Learns to Write,* p. 70.
32. W. J. Ong, *Orality and Literacy,* p. 8.
33. L.C.L., 1920, p. 157.
34. *Panchatantra,* p. 16.
35. *Geography,* xv, 3, 18, L.C.L., 8, p. 179.

36. J. P. Losty, *The Art of the Book in India,* p. 14.

37. For a map describing some of the possible ways that one type of storytelling may have spread in these directions, see the endpapers in Victor Mair's *Painting and Performance.*

38. W. Bang, "Manichäische Erzähler."

39. D. Durán, *Book of the Gods and Rites* and *The Ancient Calendar,* pp. 398–399.

40. D. Ben-Amos, *Sweet Words,* pp. 30–31.

41. L. Dégh, *Folktales and Society,* pp. 79, 171.

42. I. Jan, *On Children's Literature,* p. 32.

43. F. Bacon, *The Essays,* p. 64.

44. F. Schiller, *Werke,* Vol. 4, p. 107.

45. E. S. Hartland, *The Science of Fairy Tales,* pp. 18–21.

46. E. Greene, "Storytelling," *World Book Encyclopedia,* vol. 18 (1976 edition), p. 718.

47. M. Gerhardt, *The Art of Storytelling,* p. 41.

48. W. Benjamin, *Illuminations,* p. 91.

49. A. Olrik, "Epic Laws of Folk Narrative," first published in 1908.

50. W. H. Jansen, "Classifying Performance in the Study of Verbal Folklore," pp. 110–118.

51. H. Scheub, "The Art of Nongenile Mazithathu Zenani," p. 115.

52. D. Hymes, "Models of the Interaction of Language and Social Life," pp. 35–71.

53. R. A. Georges, "Towards an Understanding of Storytelling Events," p. 313.

54. Ibid., p. 317.

55. L. Dégh, *Folktales and Society,* pp. 50–52.

56. D. Tedlock, *The Spoken Word,* p. 3.

CHAPTER 4. FOLK STORYTELLING

In the first chapter of this book a number of quotations from ancient sources were cited to indicate that there is written evidence that storytelling took place in homes, during communal or group work, at religious and social gatherings, and in streets or marketplaces. The persons who told the stories to adults and children were generally not trained in that art, except through practice and imitation; they did not seem to be restricted to any particular educational level or social class. Folk storytelling, for purposes of this book, will be comprised of most of the qualities listed above.

Some early commentaries did seem to regard this kind of story with disdain, as though it were somehow less important than heroic literature or history. The Emperor Julian (C.E. 331–363), for example, wrote:

But I am bound to say something in defense of those who originally invented myths; I think they wrote them for childish souls: and I liken them to nurses who hang leathern toys to the hands of children when they are irritated and teething . . . So those mythologists wrote for the feeble soul whose wings are just beginning to sprout, and who, though still incapable of being taught the truth, is yearning for further knowledge . . .

Orations VII, 206 D.,
trans. by Wilmer C. Wright[1]

This is an attitude that is carried over, to a certain extent, to modern times. As recently as 1935, the eminent anthropologist Ruth Benedict could find great interest in myths as socio-religious expressions of a culture when they were performed or transmitted in a serious manner or in what we would call bardic form; but as soon as the stories served as children's amusements they were, in her view, not worth studying.[2] Delargy also slighted the stories told for and by women and children. In his opinion they were obviously not as worthy of merit as those told by men at their gatherings.[3]

This disposition on the part of some folklorists and anthropologists appears strange in view of the fact that numerous testimonies to the power of the folktale stress that it was those heard during childhood that seemed to have the most profound and lasting effect. They might well appear in retrospect to have little artistic or literary merit. And yet, writers, artists, inventors, scientists, politicians, and a host of others have testified in memoirs and autobiographies that it was the stories they heard when they were very young that most profoundly affected them. T. S. Eliot was speaking of written literature when he wrote:

I incline to come to the alarming conclusion that it is just the literature that we read for "amusement" or "purely for pleasure" that may have the greatest and least suspected influence upon us.[4]

His conclusion might well have applied also to stories that were heard and seen, much like those referred to by Goethe.

This will be one of the premises on which this chapter and parts of subsequent chapters are based: that the stories told to children or overheard by them by accident or through guile are indeed very important; and storytelling sessions involving children have as much cultural validity as those involving mostly adults.

Storytelling in the Home

Linda Dégh is one folklorist who would agree to the importance of storytelling to children. In her opinion, it is the vital link that provides the means for transmission of the folktale tradition.

> It does not matter whether the children's stories are told well or badly or whether they are read. They constitute the first real encounter with the folktale, and it quite often happens that it is decided then and there who will become, sometimes after many decades, a good storyteller.[5]

This is what must be kept in mind when reading the accounts of folk storytelling in many parts of the world. Some of the sessions might appear to have very little to do with children. Yet it is likely that even those meant strictly and exclusively for adult audiences had their secret child listeners who were deeply moved by the things they heard, and remembered them all the better for having heard them illicitly.

Fortunately, children do not have to get all their exposure to stories by secretive means. Storytelling in the home is one of the most universal of human experiences. Here we shall discuss only those accounts that specifically mention the importance of this activity for children.

Among many African peoples, there is still a high priority assigned to family storytelling. Béart quotes this maxim from the Ivory Coast:

> "The *gouros* gods only give children to those who can tell at least a hundred tales."[6]

Children of the Ewe people of Ghana are simply not considered educated unless they have heard many times the *gliwo,* animal stories that are intended to teach basic lessons in obedience, kindness, courage, honesty, and other virtues through indirect example.[7]

According to Mbiti, children have to be present when a story is being told to the Akamba of Kenya. If one child has to go to another house to fetch something, the narrator will wait until he or she returns.[8] The Shinqiti of Mauritania have a cycle of folktales especially for children that consist of episodes in the life of an imaginary woman, each one of which implies a moral or a virtue that is supposed to be absorbed by the young in entertaining fashion.[9]

Some groups in Africa have special names to describe the storytelling events within the family circle.

For the Edo of Benin, Nigeria, such a gathering is called an *ibota.* It includes the children, youths, wives, and the head of household in one compound. It usually takes place in the largest room and it can celebrate anything from the successful sale of a crop to the visit of a relative, or just being in a good mood. Anyone can tell stories or make riddles or sing songs at the ibota, except the head of the household who is always the listener.[10] The *okpobhie,* in contrast, is a storytelling event also held in the family compound, but performed only by professional storytellers who play the *akpata* or *asologun.*

For Xhosa and Zulu children it is assumed that an accepted part of their social life will be not only listening to narratives, but also learning to perform them adequately, so that when they in turn are parents and grandparents, they will be able to tell them regularly to their offspring. The performance of the *ntsomi* among the Xhosa and the *nganekwane* among the Zulu is almost exclusively a family compound affair. This does not prevent it from being an art form that achieves a high degree of aesthetic harmony. The children in such situations are often just as demanding an audience as the adults, because they have had training in listening and narrating beginning at an early age. They are well aware of those performances that reach a peak of perfection and those that don't. Often they will join in the calls for bringing to a close a poor performance.[11]

In the Bahamas, where folk stories are nominally directed toward children, it is usually they who begin the storytelling sessions, either by a direct appeal, or by referring to the "Cric-crac" opening.[12]

Native Americans also perceive the narration of stories to children as being of the greatest significance. "If my children hear the stories, they will grow up to be good people; if they don't hear them, they will turn out to be bad," opined Yellowman, a Navajo informant.[13] This is substantiated by the fact that virtually all collections of Native American tales that describe the storytelling occasions and audience mention the fact that children were present and were expected to listen carefully and attentively.

And yet, as Hymes points out, the stories were entertainment, too. "Scholars are sometimes the last to understand that these stories were told and told again, not simply to reflect or express or maintain social structure, interpersonal tensions, or something similar, but because they were great stories, great fun."[14]

Some families not only had sessions for education and fun, but needed and wanted to perform regularly the tales considered as the sacred property of the family. This is commonly reported in the Pacific and borders on religious storytelling. These stories were sometimes told in a special language and had to be told exactly, but their sacredness did not prevent them from being enjoyed as entertainment as well.[15]

The same situation is reported among the Australian aborigines. The telling of their myths was—and still is—"the most common form of aboriginal entertainment, one which included the women and children, so they, too, might learn some of the great stories."[16] A favorite style for many of the women to tell these myths is by accompanying their dramatic narrations with equally dramatic designs drawn in the sand.

In some societies, wealthy homes had a man or woman among the servants whose special task was to tell stories for both the adults and children. Sometimes there was a different teller for each age group. This was frequently encountered in India and Russia in the nineteenth century and in the early years of the twentieth.

In the Hungarian community of the Szeklers, folk storytelling took place both within the family and at other social gatherings or occasions. The home-based telling was principally for the benefit of the children, but there does not seem to be any indication that the tales used were different ones, except that the average woman who did the home storytelling rarely used her creative talent consciously, as did the best storytellers (women and men) who told for the village at large. There were exceptions, like Zsuzsánna Palkó, who put the same feeling into the versions of tales she told her grandchildren at home that she did when narrating at a more special, public occasion.[17]

The Romansh tellers in Switzerland described by Uffer also told a great deal in the home.[18] One of them, Ursula Bisaz, reported a reaction common to children in many parts of the world, that is, their dislike of change once they find something they like. Bisaz, who was a gifted storyteller, would occasionally like to alter or change the words and even some of the events of the stories she told, but if she did, her grandchildren would invariably say with disappointment: "Granny, last time you didn't tell it that way."[19]

It must be mentioned that there are a few instances reported where recreational storytelling was not considered appropriate for children. For example, Ammar writes:

> There is hardly any adult . . . who admits he tells stories to his children. Stories . . . are considered to be demonic, and of no particular value.[20]

Nevertheless, children in the village in Egypt where this was noted managed to tell eleven tales, so they must have heard them somewhere. Furthermore, two folklorists working just a bit further south on the Nile were able to observe any number of occasions when grandmothers told to groups of children, generally from ages six to nine.[21]

The only reference to storytelling practices in Africa south of the Sahara that could be interpreted as restrictive for children in any way is the description Raum gives for the Chagga people of Tanzania. According to that account children are told a few very simple animal stories with a moral, for didactic purposes, but they are restricted in their permission to listen to the stories adults tell each other for entertainment.[22]

Gorer reported that the Lepchas of Sikkim also did not consider their tales, with the exception of one or two animal fables, as appropriate for children.[23] It is likely that had he asked some of the children to recount them, he would have heard at least the bare outlines of the stories told by the adults.

In an early study related to child life in what was called "primitive" society, Miller implied that children heard stories only for purely didactic reasons,[24] but this flies in the face of much evidence to the contrary.

The reason for the lack of storytelling opportunities for children is much more likely to be a lack of time or interest on the part of the parents, rather than a desire to protect children from hearing stories. This trend can be noticed dramatically in immigrant groups or in those that are changing swiftly from rural to industrialized societies. Bianco reported, for example, that almost all the informants among the Italian Americans she interviewed had heard stories from their parents. Those parents were in most cases born in Italy. But the younger age group, especially those under thirty, rarely told stories to their children or among themselves.[25]

Contrasted with this were the *veglia,* or storytelling evenings in homes in the Tuscan part of Italy. Falassi describes the manner in which the first part invariably concentrated on *märchen* and other types of folktales most appealing to the children. Following this was a period of "riddles, catches, lullabies and folk prayers." The children then went to bed, often protestingly, and there were then narratives and folk songs about courtship and marriage.[26]

Because there has been a lessening of such family telling, grandmothers or older storytellers will frequently voice complaints that the younger generation is too lazy or too preoccupied to carry it out. This is not a new complaint as is evident from the words of Anna Liberata de Souza, as reported by Mary Frere in 1881:

> When I was young, old people used to be very fond of telling stories; but instead of that, it seems to me that now the old people are fond of nothing but making money.[27]

The fact remains that there are parents and grandparents and other adults still telling stories to their children, and not only in so-called "traditional" societies, or among economically poor classes who have little access to other entertainment. To cite just two relatively recent examples: the children's book writer Jane Yolen has described in some detail the manner in which she writes and tells stories for children as a professional, and how she has done so for her own children in the privacy of her own home.[28] The late Nobel-Prize-winning scientist Richard Feynman, in a NOVA television interview, went on at some length about the different methods of storytelling he used with his son and his daughter, not because of their sex differences, but because of their different personalities.[29] The pages of past issues of *The National Storytelling Journal* (now *Storytelling Magazine*) are full of descriptions of current family storytelling of an informal nature.

Seasons and Times for Storytelling

Some families have storytelling activities only for short, fixed periods of the year. In rural Korea, this is during the month of October, or harvest time. At this time, the myths that usually are only performed during rituals will often be recited in the family.[30]

Many African groups also selected the time just after the rice or millet or other main crop was ripe as the most appropriate for telling tales, and the sessions were invariably in the evenings, for it was believed that it was unlucky to tell in the daytime. This was probably because the tribal authorities wanted to be sure the necessary work in the fields was not delayed by the fun of storytelling. An Igbo proverb says: "A lazy person listens to tales in the morning."[31]

There is ample evidence that, even if supposedly prohibited, storytelling was and is done in the daytime in Africa. For example, children among the Masai knot grass as a kind of "crossing one's fingers" method to ward off any misfortune that might come to them when they feel they simply must tell stories in the daytime.[32] Obviously, some of these methods got carried by Africans to the Americas, because in Surinam, if a narrator absolutely must tell in the daytime, he or she plucks a hair from the eyelid before beginning.[33]

Among the Dinka of Sudan the session would last as long as there were people awake. The last storyteller was often the last person awake.[34] In Rwanda, the telling might take place during the day, if it were particularly dark and rainy and no work could go on.[35]

For Native American groups, telling was invariably done in the winter. Children were required to listen to the myths as part of their training, and sometimes, if they fell asleep, had to jump into an ice cold lake or river for a short swim.[36]

Cammann describes such a warm and intimate picture of the "*märchen* evening" in a West Prussian village home at the turn of the century that one can only envy the children and adults lucky enough to have been present.[37] The usual time for starting was on winter evenings at four o'clock in the afternoon. A favorite request of the children, then as now, was for something scary or creepy.

One woman, Anna Spurgarth, remembered eight straight winters, from 1900 to 1908, of frequent storytelling in her home, at which most of her school friends from the village were also present. Some adults were always on hand as well, for Anna's father was well known as a good and entertaining storyteller. Whoever fell asleep had to put a fifty-penny piece in a saucer on the table. Smaller children might be sent to bed when something of an adult nature, not considered appropriate for children, was being told. Most of the stories were told by Anna's father, Karl Restin, but other adults sometimes contributed a story. Birthdays, anniversaries, and other special days always called for a story evening.[38]

The Italian *veglia* in Tuscany was also held in the evenings, during the period after fall sowing and the beginning of Lent, generally on Thursday, Saturday, and Sunday.[39]

Peninnah Schram and James S. Goodman are two storytellers who point out that for many Jewish families, the Sabbath, especially in holiday time, is the most frequent time for shared stories that entertain and teach. For Schram, the stories she heard on such occasions in childhood "transmitted concrete as well as moral meanings, emotions, attitudes, and interpretations of Jewish values."[40]

COMMUNITY SITES FOR FOLK STORYTELLING

In some countries, storytelling took place in a home, but not in the home of the narrator. Such occasions often had special names, and they cannot be treated as family storytelling because there were usually members of an entire village present. Typical of this kind of event is the Irish *céilidhe*. Delargy called a house where such an event took place a *toigh áirneáil*. The storytelling "season" usually opened near Halloween (October 31) and ended near St. Patrick's Day (March 17). The audience did not pay, but they were responsible for bringing in turf for the fire, and plenty of water for the home owner.[41] Carmichael's description of a *céilidh* in the Scottish Hebrides is a bit different, in that women and children seemed to be accepted members of the audience. He speaks of the women as knitting, sewing, spinning, carding, or embroidering in the background. The children squeeze in wherever they will fit, even in the rafters. "Occasionally a moment of excitement occurs when heat and sleep overpower a boy and he tumbles down among the people below, to be trounced out and sent home."[42]

The *céilidhe* has changed format only slightly in some communities, and can still be encountered if one has patience and spends time in certain villages in rural Ireland. Henry Glassie found that in Ballymenone, it is now called a *ceili,* and the tales told there can be historical, but more often now they are based on present-day events, serious or humorous. Everyone who lives there is aware of which homes are "*ceili* homes." Sometimes a gathering results only in pleasant talk and exchange of news, but other times it is lifted out of the ordinary into a performance.[43]

In a recent summary of how the folk traditions are living on and being recorded in Wales, Gwyndaf mentions the types of village centers that still operate for the Welsh equivalent of the *céilidhe*.[44]

There were and are other traditions of public gatherings for folk storytelling, not in homes, but in village "gathering houses" or in tea or coffee houses. The latter were often the setting for professional tellers to perform. . . . But there were some instances when groups of villagers gathered in a tea or coffee house to hear one of their members entertain them with stories. The setting was chosen because it was convenient and convivial and had the requisite amount of space. In Persian, such an occasion was called a *ma'rika* and is a custom dating back to at least the sixteenth century. Modern variations of it still take place in coffeehouses.[45] Both folk and bardic storytelling are practiced at such times.

This has a modern parallel in North America and parts of Europe as well—storytelling in the local bar or tavern. Many of Richard Dorson's informants were located in such locales.[46] Taggart also noted that Nahuat men frequently told stories while drinking in bars, as have any number of other modern folklorists searching for storytelling in the present day.[47]

And storytelling is as likely to take place in urban work and play environments of today as it is in small town or rural areas. Jan Brunvand, a folklorist who has made a specialty of collecting such tales, calls them "urban folklore."[48] Schwartzman found that spontaneous stories were extremely important in the daily work life of staff and patients at a community mental health center.[49]

Adams gives an excellent picture of a village folk storyteller who usually performed for groups of children in the candy shop she managed. Tsune Watanabe told chiefly *mukashi-banashi,* the equivalent of *märchen.* It was interesting to note that although Watanabe perceived her role of storyteller as having been greatly diminished in recent years, she was still held in esteem by the young people of the village. She claimed that the children and young people no longer had an interest in her stories, and yet it was a young man who led Adams to her, pointing out that she was the best storyteller around.[50]

During the winter months, the gathering place for families in northern Italy was the stable, because there was more warmth there from the animals. Clementina Todesco, who grew up in Faller, learned most of her stories from her next-door neighbor, an elderly man who spent most of his evenings with Clementina's family.[51]

Sherzer tells about the gathering house of the Kuna, of the San Blas Islands of Panama:

> The "gathering house" is the nerve center of a Kuna village. It serves to bring people together on a regular basis. It is a place to see and be seen, to learn the latest news, often as it is happening. . . . [It is] a talking house, a performing house, a listening house. Here, through language and speech, the Kuna learn about proper ways of behaving, learn about the past and present world around them, solve their problems, joke, enjoy words, and relax.[52]

Storytelling During Work

The tedium of work was often relieved by a background of tale telling. Sometimes the very rhythm of work became part of the rhythm of the story, or vice versa. Linda Dégh found that several members of the famous Hungarian Szekler storytelling family, the Zaiczes, told quite regularly in the fields of sugar beets. They were foremen and entertained the other workers as they hacked away. According to one worker: "everybody was glad to work under a foreman who could tell good stories."[53] Other work during which storytelling was practiced by this group of people included carting wood from the forest, fishing, and cobbling.[54]

Brinkmann mentioned that a favorite time for storytelling in a rural German village was during weeding or during harvesting of potatoes. He also observed it among a group of workers in a sand pit, and in a place where a building was going up.[55]

Gorer remarked that one of the occasions for storytelling for the Lepchas of Sikkim was while weeding. Often one skilled teller would be selected to tell short stories all day, while the others worked. That person would get special tidbits of food at the evening meal as a kind of pay.[56]

The work that seemed best suited for storytelling was that associated with cotton or wool. Persons sifting, carding, spinning, and weaving were so well suited to listening to stories, without breaking the concentration of their work, that this is reported wherever such work was done. East mentioned this as a favorite pastime of the spinners of cotton among the Tiv of northern Nigeria.

As soon as it was dark they lit a fire in the middle of the village, and the children, the older men and the women all gathered round it to spin cotton and tell hare-stories.[57]

A similar custom was noted among the Jula of Burkina Faso, formerly Upper Volta, where the women had to clean, card and spin the cotton grown each year.[58]

Hoogasian-Villa found among her older Armenian informants in Detroit quite a number who had learned stories while listening and sifting the seeds out of cotton, back in their Armenian childhood.[59]

Delargy mentioned that at the Irish *airneán* a women's gathering to spin and card wool, storytelling was the expected accompaniment for at least a part of the working time.[60] Sometimes one of the women would tell, but at other times a shanachie would be invited in and even paid a bit to tell his tales. A gypsy teller in Romania mentioned to the folklorist Bela Gunda that he, too, had frequently been paid to come in and tell tales to women as they spun.[61]

The Szekler ethnic group from Hungary had a very strong tradition of telling tales in the spinning rooms of the village. This was true in the period when they lived in Bucovina, Romania, and also after they were repatriated to the area around Kakasd in southern Hungary. Spinning took place during part of the day, from Monday through Thursday, and on most winter evenings. For the day spinning, the women found tellers among themselves. In the evenings the men often gathered with their wives, and then some of the best tellers, usually men, would narrate, often until one or two in the morning.[62]

This writer remembers family storytelling in Polish-American families in Wisconsin that took place during the evenings of Advent and Lent, when goose feathers were stripped from their tiny quills. Also, women often told stories while quilting together at large frames. If the stories were a bit vulgar or bawdy, they were told in a Polish full of Kashubian expressions, so that the children could not understand.

The Nahuat of Mexico, who frequently come north as migrant laborers, sometimes use the brief time while resting in the evening for storytelling.[63]

Some folklorists report that after long working days it is rare to find a storytelling occasion because people are too tired. But a community work project, in which all have shared the tasks equally, usually resulted in the shared good feelings necessary for a communal storytelling atmosphere. Such an occasion was called a *mingaco* in Chile. It has apparently died out.[64]

OTHER OCCASIONS FOR FOLK STORYTELLING

Personal celebrations and feasts on the occasion of a wedding or child naming are often the time to tell stories. Babalola reported that the *ijála* chanters of the Yoruba, who used to recite only for hunters' groups, now are commonly asked by other persons in the community to perform on those two occasions, regardless of whether they are members of the hunters' groups or not.[65] Cejpek mentioned that weddings and births were also times for storytelling in Iran.[66] The Lepchas had a long story lasting from two to three hours that was a part of every marriage ceremony.[67] The Suk, from the Sudan, also used the marriage feast as one of their favorite periods for a good long story session.[68]

Stories at wakes for the dead were common in Ireland and Europe and can also be found in India and some parts of Africa. For the Szeklers of Hungary, this kind of storytelling had tremendous social importance. The order of narration was an indispensable part of the ritual of the wakes, which lasted forty-eight hours. The wake served as the single most important social occasion for the married and the elderly. A beautifully arranged wake would be discussed for years after the event, and all who had been present would remember the stories told. The storytelling alternated with singing and the saying of prayers. The stories told were usually short anecdotes and long, involved *märchen*.[69]

Although the above are comparatively recent examples, the custom of storytelling at wakes is very ancient. As cited in Chapter 1, it is mentioned in a number of the *Rules of Vedic Domestic Ceremonies,* compiled about 200 B.C.E. in India. The sūtra already cited referred to the death of a guru. In a later sūtra there is another mention of storytelling at what might be called wakes for ordinary persons:

> Now the water libations [which are performed for deceased persons] . . .
> When they have come out [of the water] and have sat down on a pure spot that is covered with grass, those who are versed in ancient tales should entertain them [by telling tales].
> *Páraskara-Grihya-Sútra,* III Kanda, 10 Kândikâ, 1, 22, trans. by Hermann Oldenburg[70]

In some Catholic countries, storytelling followed after special services during Lent. A Canadian informant remarks:

> At this time, young boys and girls in the region would set out from home after the daily family prayer and gather at his house to hear one or two folktales each evening.[71]

Delargy mentioned that after the stations of the cross each week in Lent, it was customary to gather for a folktale session.[72]

Storytelling among soldiers has also been mentioned since ancient times. In Israel, a particular kind of storytelling session, called a *kumsitz,* developed among the Palmakhnik. This was a kind of paramilitary or underground group organized during the fight for independence and existence as a separate state. The men and women would usually get together for an evening of self-entertainment. The stories they told were known as *ha-chizbat,* derived from an Arabic word meaning "to lie." The stories could be fanciful, exaggerated, humorous, and even preposterous, but they had to be based on a kernel of truth. Sometimes the *kumsitz* was used as a device to recruit youths from the high schools.[73]

An intriguing use of persuasive storytelling for a better legal outcome occurred in medieval times in Europe. When a person who had been judged guilty of some crime applied for a pardon, he or she often told an account of the crime and the reasons for asking for the pardon in the form of a long story. Many of these "tales" were written down and at least one scholar has suggested that from the evidence, one can tell that the best storytellers were often the most successful in getting pardons.[74]

The folklorist Richard Bauman focused on another amusing and unusual occasion for storytelling, most often of the highly exaggerative type. He studied the tale telling and other verbal exchanges that go on in the small town of Canton, Texas, on the Sunday preceding the first Monday every month, when there is a session of coon dog trading or selling.[75]

Ed Bell, who has appeared at a number of storytelling festivals and can also be seen on videotape, originally began his storytelling at a bait camp for sport fishermen, in Indianola, Texas.[76]

Some persons have such an urge to share their tales, they need no special occasion in order to be persuaded to tell them. Delia Poirier, a storyteller of French Canada, baldly confessed:

> One winter, I visited in turn every house in the entire village to tell my tales. I went out three nights a week. I would have gone more often, but I didn't want people to think I was a gadabout.[77]

She was reported to be well liked in the community, so her "gadding about" obviously was not a nuisance.

STREET AND MARKETPLACE STORYTELLERS

The most visible of folk storytellers have been the street and marketplace narrators of the past and present. India may well be the source and inspiration for many of them. As was discussed in greater detail in Chapter 3, the religious storytellers gradually absorbed a rather secular style and content. The "picture showmen," as the Indian scholar Coomaraswamy called them, took to the streets and public places. By the time this custom was spread by Buddhists to China, Java, the other parts of western, eastern and southern Asia, it began to have more and more secular content and appeal. Traders probably carried the public manner of telling stories to Persia, Greece, and toward Europe and the Middle East. Whether or not they were influenced by these accounts from the East, minstrels and bards in Europe were undergoing much of the same process of change, from sacred and/or heroic performances to many that were secular and popular in appeal.

Unfortunately, there is as yet no complete history of storytelling in India, at least none readily available to the Western reader. From Sanskrit scriptures and other early works, it is evident that tales of an entertaining nature were told (see Chapter 1). How street storytelling could spring up from the traditions of family, religious and folk storytelling or from the courtly minstrel tradition in India is not totally clear, any more than it is in Europe. The only point on which scholars agree is that it is still impossible to entirely separate the folktales from the myths, the secular from the religious, the popular from the classical. They are inextricably intertwined in our old stories. Since this is so, one can turn to modern storytellers in an attempt to find out what they might have been like in the past. There is not likely to have been dramatic change in their storytelling style and content over the last few centuries.

In present-day India, in rural villages, small towns, and even some of the bigger towns and cities, one can still encounter itinerant storytellers. Those that perform in a more elaborate style, using large picture cloths and scrolls, have been mentioned . . . as being of the bardic type, mostly because the content of their stories is heroic. It must be admitted that this is rather arbitrary, since the *Ramayana* and other epics can be perceived by the average Indian as heroic, homey and folklike, or religious, and sometimes all of that in the same performance.

Others that fall somewhere between bardic, folk, and religious in their style include the type that can be represented here by the *burrakatha* performers and the *Dasarulu,* both found in Andhra Pradesh. The former are believed to have developed from a type of storytelling that was done only by women, beginning in about the fifteenth century, C.E. Now, however, the majority of performers are male. They go about in groups of three, a teller and two musician-responders. One of the responders is expected to add or insert comments on contemporary social and political problems as they might fit into the story; the other responder-musician is expected to add comic relief whenever needed. They perform either in front of a building where they expect to attract attention, or in the courtyard of a home, if they arc invited to perform there for a special gathering or occasion. There are full-time professional performers, as well as those who do it only part-time. Their repertoire consists of historical tales and myths, episodes from the *Ramayana* or *Mahabharata,* local folklore, and even stories borrowed from Christian scriptures.[78]

The *Dasarulu* sometimes make their appeals in the street, but they generally are invited into a home to perform. They go about in pairs, approach houses in the village likely to be able to pay in grain or cash for their entertainment, and sing samples of their work, accompanying themselves on lute and drum. They only perform during the off-season, when there is no planting or harvesting to be done. Their style is a lively and rapid prosimetric mixture, and their repertoires range from the Indian epics, to *puranas,* fairy tales, pilgrimage tales, historical events, local events and personal experience tales.[79]

In her study of the Thousand and One Nights as a genre, Gerhardt states that time-gaining frame stories are apparently of Indian origin, but they were adapted and taken over by Persians fairly early, probably in the late Sassanian period (224–651 C.E.). The Arabic versions appeared a bit later. Virtually all of these collections of stories, she finds, have "highly ingenious devices to introduce, to justify, to authenticate the telling of a story, to set it off, to make it serve a purpose. Stories are fitted one into the other like Chinese boxes."[80]

Boyce believed that the kernel for the *Thousand and One Nights* came from *Hazar Afsan,* an early Persian work, although many of the stories were obviously Indian in origin.[81]

These frame stories were probably performed orally at inns and in caravanserai in a manner similar to that described by a nineteenth century traveler:

> . . . they had lighted a fire in front of their tent, and were squatting around it. . . . One of the camel-drivers was engaged in telling stories to a rapt audience. . . .With a clear, unhesitating voice, which he raised or lowered as occasion required, he pursued his tale, pausing only when he had made a point and expected the applause of his hearers.[82]

After the Middle Ages, the time-gaining frame stories were written down in more and more versions. They could be found in manuscripts in Persian, Arabic, and a number of European languages.

However, public telling of these same stories survived in the marketplace and in the teahouses and coffeehouses in the Middle East and North Africa. It is really because of the colorful and dramatic presence of these narrators that we find the word "storyteller" began to be used to describe an oral teller of tales, rather than a person who told fibs. English travelers of the nineteenth century describing such public storytelling sessions were the first to use the term consistently in their written and printed accounts, as in the following example:

> In a Persian town they are to be met with in every street. In open sites, such as are often found near market-places, great sheds are erected, open on all sides and furnished with rows of steps capable of seating three to four hundred persons squatting on their heels. In front of the audience is a platform from whence a succession of storytellers repeat their stories to a succession of listeners from morning to night.[83]

This might almost be considered theatrical storytelling, except that in most cases there was no fixed entrance fee for these performances.

One of the most colorful scenes still frequently encountered in present-day North African marketplaces is the animated storyteller, surrounded by a wide variety of listeners. The audience can be a mixture of young and old, in modern or traditional dress. This writer has seen a number of such performances in Morocco and Tunisia. In Tunisia this itinerant type of teller is called *fdawi*. His performance is geared to building suspense until the climax of the story. With the audience waiting with bated breath, he stops to collect whatever coins he can, and only then finishes his tale. An impressive aerial photographic view of one such teller and his large audience in Marrakech, Morocco can be seen in the *National Geographic* for March 1932.[84]

When the tales of India moved in the other direction, to China and Southeast Asia, it was Buddhism that carried along this richness of narrative. After becoming secularized, the tales were added to and narrated by all types of tellers. The professional performers who told in teahouses and in special theaters are described in Chapter 5. There were also amateur storytellers who went from town to town and village to village, presenting their tales at marketplaces and on street corners. A number of the picture-telling performers were itinerant tellers who told purely secular tales. Examples of these could be found recently among the *patua* of Bengal.[85]

Other street storytellers would try to attract attention by clapping together two small pieces of wood. Or they might play a two-stringed instrument. Some of them were blind or physically handicapped. Many of these latter were accompanied by other family members.[86]

Chinese marketplaces were often in temple courtyards. As recently as 1950–1954 the *T'ien-ch'iao,* Beijing's Heavenly Bridge, was a place where one could encounter outdoor performers of all types. The storyteller sat at a small table, and the listeners were on benches in a semi-circle around it. Fees were not fixed. Contributions were collected in the middle of the story or just before the climax, as in Persia and Turkey. The narrator had to hope for the best and tried his utmost to perform well. Although these street storytellers were usually very poor and of the lowest social classes, they had a certain pride that lent them dignity.[87]

Japan had street and itinerant storytellers in the past, but it is much more difficult to locate precise information on how and where they performed and what their social position was. There was, for example, a secular *etoki hoshi,* a man who recited stories to pictures, using a pheasant feather on a stick to point out the various scenes as he narrated. The stories may well have been bardic in character, rather than folkloric. The female equivalent, the *Kumano bikuni* also became secular, itinerant performers, and Barbara Ruch speculates that many of the narratives they used were changed by their personal experiences. Essentially, however, they remained in the public consciousness as religious performers, regardless of how they changed.[88]

For the modern types of Japanese public storytellers, there is more documentation. One of the more extensively practiced forms was *kamishibai.* The term means "paper drama" or "theater of paper." It had its roots in earlier forms of picture storytelling, in *kabuki* theater, and in shadow-puppet plays. Satoshi Kako and Koji Kata have documented the gradual adaptation of earlier indoor theater forms into the outdoor form of storytelling with pictures known as *kamishibai.* Koji Kata was himself a *kamishibai* performer, and his autobiography was a bestseller in Japan when it came out in 1977.[89]

In its modern, most popular form, *kamishibai* began around 1930. This was a time of economic depression, and *kamishibai* was used by many unemployed workers as a means of making a little money. The performers were exclusively men, and they were looked down on by middle-class parents because they were identified with the racketeers who had dominated earlier groups of outdoor performers. Also, many of the stories they told were considered to be vulgar and in bad taste, and the candies they sold were believed by many mothers to be unsanitary.[90]

It was the children who began to enjoy the *kamishibai,* especially the children of the urban poor and working classes. There were performers in most of the major cities. They usually went about on bicycles for greater mobility. Each had a repertoire of three or four stories which he carried with him in the wooden frame that also served as a means of presenting the picture cards during the telling of the tales. . . .

During the Second World War and immediately after, *kamishibai* was virtually the only entertainment regularly available to children. There were about 25,000 performers around 1950. Kako estimates as many as 7.5 million children could have seen a perfor-

mance on any given day when they were all performing, since the performers usually repeated their programs about ten times in different places during each day and had an average audience of thirty children each time.[91]

Educators tried to prohibit *kamishibai,* but in vain. Later they attempted to adapt it to an educational format, with stories that were considered more "suitable" or proper. In this way, many of the favorite folk tales were eventually printed in *kamishibai* format.

A contemporary writer, Morio Kita, has given a memorable picture (semiautobiographical) of one child's reaction to the *kamishibai.*

> The fact was this. Lately Shuji, all by himself, went out more frequently than before and was absorbed in *kamishibai,* which visited the neighborhood at twilight time. In comparison to other children, he could be described as unhappy. The reason for this unhappiness was that he had not a single *sen.* At the beating of the clatters, a mass of children ran to the *kamishibai* player, each trying to be the first to give the tightly grasped one-*sen* piece to him. The player gave a candy, dyed red and white, in exchange for the one *sen.* Nibbling their candies, the children intently watched the illustrations painted on coarse papers, listening to the narrative given by the player in a husky voice. Shuji, however, had no capital to procure candies. Stationing himself, mostly by luck, in the front row, he was roughly thrust aside by the *kamishibai* player.
>
> "Those who don't buy candies go behind the others!"
>
> Shuji, stealing occasional, envious glances at the candies possessed by the other children, stretched himself from behind to catch glimpses of a monstrous figure of a man with the mask of a skull, long ominous fingernails and a flying red cape.
>
> "Here comes the man of justice! His name is no other than the Golden Bat!" At this point the player thundered a little drum.
>
> After several such experiences, even the little head of Shuji began to realize the importance and necessity of money.
>
> *Nireke no Hitobito (The Nine Families),*
> trans. by Kiyoko Toyama.[92]

In Europe, the street storytellers usually did not relate long, complex tales of the *märchen* type. Their stories were more likely to be based on news events of the most sensational type, often put into ballad form. Or they were short anecdotes strung together. Like the storytellers of India and China, some of them probably had their roots in the religious storytelling of wandering monks. Others were probably the remnants of organized troupes of bards and minstrels that had once been common in courts, and at all public gatherings of any size. Wherever they came from, they quickly seized on the medium of print as an adjunct to their oral talents rather than viewing it as a totally competitive medium.

According to Coupe, the publisher-vendors first appeared in the sixteenth century. At that time, the engraver, publisher, and printer was generally the same person. They went to all the fairs and sold their wares to anyone who would buy.[93] Hans Fehr, who has also written on the mass printing media of the sixteenth century, states that the printers directed three types of printed matter toward three kinds of readers. The book was aimed at the learned and scholarly; the *flugschrift* (chapbook or pamphlet), at the educated, that is, those who could read; and the *flugblatt* (picture sheet or broadsheet), at the mostly nonliterate folk.[94]

Booksellers, hawkers, peddlers, itinerant street singers, and others would buy the materials in quantity. The street singers were a motley crowd, looked down upon as the dregs of society. This contempt may well have been political or religious in origin because the authorities feared the growing awareness of the masses. And there was no question that the masses listened to the street singer with all of his or her gory details. They then often bought the cheap broadsheets or chapbooks in hopes of finding still more detail than had been given in the performance, or to be able to repeat part of it to their families or neighbors.[95]

The street performer was often called a *bänkel-sänger* in German because he or she stood on a bench in order to be seen better. Some of the other names for this performer were: *krámařský zpěvák* (Czech); *liedjeszanger* (Flemish or Dutch); *chanteur en foire* or *crieur de journeaux* (French); *cantambanco* or *cantas-torie* (Italian); *ploshchadnoi pevetz* (Russian); *cantor da feria* (Spanish); *pevci* (South Slavic); *marknadsån-gere* (Swedish).

The *bänkelsänger* usually had a long pointed stick, which was used to point to the pictures that showed all the lurid details of the most melodramatic events in the story. Most of the pictures were woodcut prints, painted in by illuminators. After the story had been sung, the singer, or members of the singer's family, passed through the crowd; they either collected coins outright for the performance, or they sold individual broadsheets or pamphlets that contained the story ballads or news events written up in exaggerated style. There is no concrete evidence for the prices at which the broadsheets were sold, nor is it known in what numbers they were issued, or how many the average performer might have sold.

The broadsheets of the seventeenth century were the most artistic of all. The printers used copperplate engravings and woodcuts. During this period, the picture story played an important part in the imaginative life of all classes. This was true for much of Europe, for the peddlers and performers penetrated into all parts of the continent.[96]

The quality of the picture sheets, the broadsheets, and the chapbooks began to decline in the eighteenth and nineteenth centuries, and with the exception of a few publishing efforts, such as the *Münchener Bilder-bogen,* they were designed for the poor and non-literate masses only. The middle classes thought it proper to purchase regular books and newspapers. There are few contemporary descriptions of that time to tell us how the singer might have changed performance techniques or how extensive the individual repertoires were. The best one can do is to speculate, based on some of the statements of the few surviving performers of this kind, from the twentieth century. Dominik Rolsch was one who inherited from his father the profession of itinerant street singer. He remembered that his father had told him that shortly after his marriage he owned a wagon in which to live, two dozen new *schilder,* and a music wagon with a built-in organ.[97]

Curiously, in northeastern Brazil there is a surviving form of this tradition, the *literatura de cordel.* The name comes from the custom of hanging out *folhetos,* cheap publications with woodblock illustrations, on a clothesline type of string, from tree to tree, usually in an open marketplace. The poets there, for the most part, now sing or recite by reading aloud from their printed works in some public hall, or even on recordings or television or radio. However, there are those poets who still perform outdoors, extemporaneously, and from comments by some in the audience, it is apparent that they prefer this style. In her book examining this tradition Slater quotes one of the listeners:

> I grew up in the countryside, and we learned a lot of *folhetos* by heart just listening to them over and over again when there was nothing else to do. Those old

stories remind me of all those long hot mornings with a deep blue sky above us, and so, I like to hear them because they remind me of where I was born.[98]

Itinerant street storytellers were obviously popular in parts of Africa, at least at the turn of the century and on into the 1950s.

NOTES

1. Julian, *Works,* L.C.L., p. 79.
2. R. Benedict, *Zuni Mythology.* vol. 1, p. xii.
3. J. H. Delargy, *The Gaelic Storyteller,* p. 19.
4. T. S. Eliot, "Religion and Literature," p. 105.
5. L. Dégh, *Folktales and Society,* p. 104.
6. C. Béart, *Jeux et Jouets de l'Ouest Africain,* vol. 2, p. 767.
7. E. Y. Egblewogbe, *Games and Songs as Education Media,* p. 47.
8. J. Mbiti, *Akamba Stories,* pp. 23–24.
9. H. T. Norris, *Shinqiti Folk Literature and Song,* p. 118.
10. D. Ben-Amos, *Sweet Words,* pp. 23–24.
11. H. Scheub, *The Xhosa Ntsomi,* pp. 12–13.
12. D. J. Crowley, *I Could Talk Old-Story Good,* p. 12.
13. B. Toelken, "The 'Pretty Languages' of Yellowman," p. 155.
14. D. Hymes, *"In Vain I Tried to Tell You,"* p. 22.
15. R. E. Mitchell, "A Study of . . . Two Trukese Informants," pp. 169–170.
16. L. A. Allen, *Time Before Morning,* p. 23.
17. L. Dégh, *Folktales and Society,* p. 118.
18. L. Uffer, *Rätoromanische Märchen,* p. 63.
19. Ibid., p. 73.
20. H. Ammar, *Growing Up in an Egyptian Village,* p. 161.
21. A. Al-Shahi, and F. C. T. Moore, *Wisdom from the Nile.*
22. O. F. Raum, *Chaga Childhood,* pp. 217–218.
23. G. Gorer, *Himalayan Village,* p. 266.
24. N. Miller, *The Child in Primitive Society,* pp. 167–172.
25. C. Bianco, "The Two Rosetos," pp. 127–137.
26. A Falassi, *Folklore by the Fireside,* p. xviii.
27. M. Frere, *Hindoo Fairy Legends,* p. xxvii.
28. J. Yolen, *Touch Magic,* pp. 48–49.
29. NOVA Program No. 1002, WGBH, Boston; this is transcribed in A. Pellowski, *The Family Storytelling Handbook,* pp. 40–41.
30. D. Chang, *Folk Treasury of Korea,* pp. 10–11.
31. R. N. Umeasiegbu, *Words Are Sweet,* p. 9.
32. N. Kipury, *Oral Literature of the Maasai,* p. 11.
33. A. P. and T. E. Penard, "Surinam Folk-tales," pp. 242–243.
34. F. M. Deng, *Dinka Folktales,* p. 30.
35. P. Smith, *Le récit populaire,* p. 15.
36. D. Hymes, *"In Vain I Tried to Tell You,"* p. 21.
37. A. Cammann, *Westpreussische Märchen,* p. 63.
38. Ibid., p. 19.
39. A. Falassi, *Folklore by the Fireside,* p. 4.
40. J. S. Goodman, "My Grandpa's Name Was Avraham"; P. Schram, *Jewish Stories: One Generation Tells Another.*
41. J. H. Delargy, *The Gaelic Storyteller,* pp. 9ff.
42. A. Carmichael, *Carmina Gadelica,* p. xxiii.
43. H. Glassie, *Passing the Time in Ballymenone,* pp. 40–42.
44. R. Gwyndaf, "The Welsh Folk Narrative Tradition."
45. J. Cejpek, "Iranian Folk Literature," p. 653.
46. R. Dorson, "Oral Styles of American Folk Narrators."
47. J. M. Taggart, *Nahuat Myth and Social Structure,* p. 1.
48. See, for example, his books *The Vanishing Hitchhiker* and *The Choking Doberman and Other Urban Folktales.*
49. H. B. Schwartzman, "Stories at Work," pp. 80–93.
50. R. J. Adams, "Social Identity of a Japanese Storyteller," pp. 6ff.
51. E. Mathias and R. Raspa, *Italian Folktales in America,* pp. 37–45.
52. J. Sherzer, *Kuna Ways of Speaking,* p. 108.
53. L. Dégh, *Folktales and Society,* pp. 95–96.
54. Ibid., pp. 102–103.
55. O. Brinkmann, *Das Erzählen in einer Dorfgemeinschaft,* p. 9.
56. G. Gorer, *Himalayan Village,* p. 266.
57. R. East, *Akiga's Story,* pp. 308–309.
58. M. Nebie, "Et si on disait un conte?" p. 43.
59. S. Hoogasian-Villa, *100 Armenian Tales,* pp. 26–40.
60. J. H. Delargy, *The Gaelic Storyteller,* p. 18.
61. B. Gunda, "Die Funktion des Märchens," p. 101.
62. L. Dégh, *Folktales and Society,* pp. 97–98.
63. J. M. Taggart, *Nahuat Myth and Social Structure,* p. 1.
64. Y. Pino-Saavedra, *Folktales of Chile,* p. xliii.
65. S. A. Babalola, *The Content and Form of Yoruba Ijala,* p. 18.
66. J. Cejpek, "Iranian Folk Literature," p. 653.
67. G. Gorer, *Himalayan Village,* p. 265.
68. M. W. H. Beech, *The Suk,* p. 38.
69. L. Dégh, *Folktales and Society,* pp. 105–110.
70. S.B.E., vol. 29, pp. 355–357.
71. L. Lacourcière, "Canada," p. 450.
72. J. H. Delargy, *The Gaelic Storyteller,* p. 20.
73. E. Oring, "Ha-Chizbat," pp. 35ff.
74. N. Z. Davis, *Fiction in the Archives,* pp. 7–35.
75. R. Bauman, *Story, Performance and Event,* p. 12.

76. P. B. Mullen, "A Traditional Storyteller," p. 22.
77. L. Lacourcière, "Canada," p. 448.
78. K. K. Das, *Burrakatha,* pp. 4–10.
79. G. H. Roghair, *The Epic of Palnādu,* p. 35.
80. M. I. Gerhardt, *The Art of Storytelling,* pp. 382ff.
81. M. Boyce, "The Parthian Gosan and the Iranian Minstrel Tradition," p. 34.
82. A. H. Sayce, "Storytelling in the East," pp. 176–80.
83. R. Heath, "Storytelling in All Ages," pp. 199ff.
84. V. C. S. O'Connor, "Beyond the Great Atlas," vol. 61, 1932, p. 285.
85. S. Sen Gupta, *The Patas and the Patuas of Bengal,* p. 53.
86. V. Hrdličková, "The Chinese Storytellers," p. 99.
87. Ibid., p. 100.
88. B. Ruch, "Medieval Jongleurs," pp. 301–302.
89. S. Kako, "Kamishibai," pp. 6–7; K. Kata, *Machi no jijyoden (Autobiography of a Street-Person).*
90. S. Kako, "Kamishibai," p. 7.
91. Ibid.
92. M. Kita, *Nireke no Hitobito,* p. 231. New English translation by Dennis Keene, *The House of Nire.* Tokyo: Kodansha, 1984.
93. W. A. Coupe, *The German Illustrated Broadsheet,* vol. 1, pp. 13–17.
94. H. Fehr, *Massenkunst,* p. 3.
95. Same as note 88.
96. Ibid.
97. E. Janda and F. Nötzoldt, *Die Moritat vom Bänkelsang,* p. 9.
98. C. Slater, *Stories on a String,* p. 191.

CHAPTER 15. VISUALITY, ORALITY, LITERACY: THEIR MEANING IN RELATION TO STORYTELLING FOR ENTERTAINMENT, EDUCATION, AND HEALTH

In the past two decades there has been an explosion of research about the meaning and use of story, about orality, literacy, and "visual" literacy. Educators, psychologists, philosophers, folklorists, ethnologists, semioticians and many other specialists have attempted to explore such questions as:

Is the use of story (narrative) a universal human phenomenon?

Are those uses different in each culture? If so, how?

Can different genres of stories be classified on a universal basis or is the very concept of genre a western idea?

Is there a difference (in story itself, story giver, and receiver) when stories are told orally or read aloud or privately?

What differences exist between orally composed and written stories?

Is there a difference when story writing is alphabetic and phonetic?

Is there a difference when story writing is partly pictorial?

What is the effect of story when it is presented orally and visually, but by a live storyteller?

What is the effect of story when it is presented orally and visually in a medium such as film or television?

How much does the context (i.e., where and why a story is heard, read, seen, experienced) affect perception of the content of story?

Does a person have to learn the concept of "reading" pictures or symbols before learning to read?

Does the very fact of knowing how to read and write change a person's attitude to story?

These questions, and many related ones, have been explored not only for their own sake, but also because some of the answers might prove useful in the process of educating and socializing children and adults. It would be impossible in the limited space here to mention even briefly all the persons who have contributed to the research examining those questions. Here it will simply be accepted that all of the questions have some merit.

The previous chapters have shown that from earliest recorded history to the present, most cultures have used story for a variety of purposes and in a variety of ways. Whether the purposes were considered "good" or "bad" by the different authorities in each era, the average human obviously found something compelling, satisfying, validating, entertaining, informative or uplifting in any given encounter with story. To this very present time, one can find affirmations of the power of story (told or read or seen) made by all types of people. Cited here are just a few of these recent statements:

When young people were asked "What would happen if there were no stories in the world?" they answered with replies like these—

"People would die of seriousness."

"When you went to bed at night it would be boring, because your head would be blank."

"There wouldn't be a world, because stories made the world."

Reported by Ellin Greene and Laura Simms,
Chicago Journal, May 26, 1982.

I think of that mountain called "white rocks lie above in a compact cluster" as if it were my maternal grandmother. I recall stories of how it once was at that mountain. The stories told to me were like arrows. Elsewhere, hearing that mountain's name, I see it. Its name is like a picture. Stories go to work on you like arrows. Stories make you live right. Stories make you replace yourself.

Mr. Benson Lewis, Age 64, Western Apache,
Cibecue, Arizona 1979[1]

For the little ones who frolic in the moonlight, my tale is a fantastic story. For the cotton spinners during the long nights of the cold season, my tale is a delightful time passer. For the hairy chins and uneven heels, it's a genuine revelation. I am therefore all at the same time frivolous, useful and instructive.

Peul (West African) storyteller[2]

Their stories, yours, mine—it's what we all carry with us on this trip we take, and we owe it to each other to respect our stories and learn from them.

William Carlos Williams, quoted by
Robert Coles, psychiatrist[3]

Despite the numerous indications that story is a very important factor in the development of the healthy human personality, there are very few books or articles that discuss, in an integrated way, the comparative effectiveness of told stories, read-aloud stories, silently read stories, visual stories (in all formats) and stories presented in a combination of media. Where such studies exist, they invariably concentrate only on western (or westernized) stories in western contexts. Further, there has been even less published research and discussion about the use of story from one culture being adapted for use in a different context in another culture, and the changes that occur in the story itself and the different responses of its listeners or readers or viewers.

Since there are now many countries with heterogenous populations, often because of the arrival of groups of recent immigrants, there has been a renewed interest in using story to better understand the cultures of the different groups. More often than not, however, stories from non-European cultures have been put into formats that are western, and they are generally used in totally western contexts, rather than in the manner they might be used in their country or area of origin.

The average librarian, teacher, psychologist or other professional then asks:

1. What do I need to know about storytelling in the contexts that it is usually encountered in my own culture?
2. What are the other contexts of storytelling I need to know about, based on the different groups of people I work with?
3. What kinds of stories (and in what formats) are available to me?
4. When and where and how should I use storytelling?

There are no final or fixed answers to these questions, of course, but the information in this chapter and the other chapters of this book might help to point the way to partial answers.

Before getting into a discussion of various theories of visuality, orality, and literacy, and how they affect storytelling, we must first define these terms as they are being used here. They are defined specifically as they relate to story, although there are other forms of verbal and visual expression that they relate to as well. Those other forms are not under consideration here.

Primary visuality will mean here the ability to appreciate, interpret, and understand a local narrative depicted in two-dimensional pictures; it will also refer to the ability to draw, sketch, or paint such a narrative well enough for another person to be able to appreciate, interpret, and understand it. Secondary visuality will refer to the ability to appreciate, interpret, and understand a local narrative on television, film, filmstrip, or video.

Primary orality will mean the ability to appreciate, interpret, and understand a local narrative told by a live person to an audience listening in real time, and the ability to narrate well enough for that same audience to appreciate, interpret and understand most of a local narrative. Secondary orality will refer to the ability to do the above by means of listening or telling via telephone, radio, disc, cassette, video (but only showing the narrator), or some other mechanical means.

Primary literacy will mean the ability to read and write a local narrative in one's native language well enough to appreciate, interpret, and understand the major part of its generally accepted local meaning.

Local narrative refers to a story that is generally known by the people of a given locality.

There are some who believe that primary visuality was the first human method of experiencing story. Certainly, a number of narrative cave paintings predate by far the first written narrative records. But did these pictures tell a story to the people who painted them? And if they did, were such picture stories in existence before the first oral or pantomimed narratives?

It has been interesting for this writer to note that in informal questioning of numerous groups of schoolchildren around the world (usually prior to an oral storytelling session) the responses are roughly thus:

How did the earliest human beings first pass on their stories? Which of these came first?

> They painted pictures of stories. (close to 50 percent)
> They told them in human speech and gesture. (30 percent)
> They sang and/or danced them. (20 percent)

There are hardly ever any respondents indicating early humans wrote them down. Children seem to sense, even though they may not know it as a historical fact, that scripts are a relatively recent part of human history.

Does their obvious preference for primary visuality indicate that children view the making of sequential pictures as a necessary prelude to alphabetic or phonetic writing? There are some who would be delighted with the perspicacity of these children in coming to a conclusion that has taken scholars enormous effort and time to reach, and then only tentatively.

There is still much disagreement about the early alphabets, and their impact on the human mind and consciousness. DeFrancis, for example, finds that there is an "essential oneness" in all full writing systems. He rejects the arguments of those who believe that logical and empirical modes of thought came about because of the uniqueness of the Greek alphabet, with its consonant plus vowel script, which was so easily learned and came so close to representing the totality of speech. On the contrary, he insists that the difficulty of script does not inhibit innovative thought, which is initiated by individuals, not society as a whole.[4]

DeFrancis and most other philologists and linguists do seem to agree that in the early stages of attempts to put speech into writing, virtually all societies used some type of pictographs. But there is almost no discussion of the possibility that pictures and pictographs came first and the words of human speech followed. Were the shapes, sounds, and structures of words for common objects invented to match the pictures of those objects? Did individual words of human speech first get put into narrative form because there were sequential pictures on a cave wall that some early human wanted to "interpret" for other humans? Could this possibility account for the preference among some societies for visual accompaniments to oral speech?

As mentioned in Chapter 12, among certain groups of aborigines in Australia and Eskimo in Alaska, it was and is common for virtually all narrative to be characterized by primary visuality as well as primary orality. When adults grow up in such a society, they often cannot carry out an ordinary conversation without making pictorial signs in the air with their fingers and hands.

In India, primary visuality has been as important as primary orality in conveying certain key myths, from the earliest recorded times to the present. Does this explain the equally strong development of secondary visuality there, where film production and film viewings are among the highest per capita in the world? And does this mean these myths could have evolved first from images, to which words were added only later?

On the other hand, there are societies where primary orality is extremely rich, but primary visuality is almost non-existent. Is this really because the ear is a better predictor of danger than the eye, as a number of scholars have suggested, and therefore humans developed and refined this sense first? Or is it because, as Walter Ong and others have stated so frequently, the human voice is the most effective way for one person to reveal interior thoughts and feelings to another, and also the best way for the listener to respond in kind?

Sometimes this primary orality is combined with music and dance, so that one could say primary motility is equally important among those groups. Is it the sound of this music (its aural quality) or its tendency to lead the human body into dance or motion that is most important in conveying narrative?[5] The few prehistoric records in those societies, as in most others, exist chiefly in pictorial form. There remains the question: did these societies have primary visuality and then lose it? If so, when and why?

Did primary literacy, especially that brought about by the Greek alphabet, really change human thought (and eventually the physiology of the brain) as much as Havelock and others suggest? Can this fact really explain the different ways of thinking that exist among peoples? Or is it, as DeFrancis insists, simply too facile an answer to suggest that differences in language and writing have created the enormously complicated problems regarding communication among societies. If, as he and others argue, discourse (and presumably story) can be carried out equally effectively in any language, then the problem is not one of mere translation, but of understanding the personal, moral and world views of the writer or teller and the context in which the words are written, sung, or spoken. Assuming an ideal and complete understanding of these views, we could then presumably have an exact translation of the words, gestures, music, and pictures, irrespective of language.

Yet we know there have been many difficulties caused by poor translation. And there have been many differences noted between societies that essentially use primary literacy for communication and those in which a majority use primary orality. Few studies have compared the variations that exist between societies that use primary orality and primary visuality (such as parts of rural India, for example, or certain Australian aborigine groups) and similar societies that use primary orality *and* primary literacy, so we know much less about those contrasts.

In the societies penetrated by primary literacy, there often remain large segments of the population who continue to use primary and secondary visuality and orality as their chief media of communication. The usual reason given for this is that the means to acquiring and maintaining the skills of primary literacy are hard to come by. This reason does not hold up too well in places like the United States. Could it be that some of the present population actually *prefers* primary and secondary orality and visuality, and not primary literacy?

Or does this occur because children are raised and educated with such conflicting advice and modeling? It is known that many parents and teachers will stress the importance of reading and writing to the children under their charge, but they themselves model chiefly primary and secondary visuality and orality. As Shirley Brice Heath has so convincingly pointed out in *Ways with Words,* the school and the formal education system, even when it uses teachers from the community, can have norms and expectations very different from those in the home.[6]

Is it for the above reasons that so many children today grow up without developing fluency and skill in *any* form of communication: speaking, writing, reading, or drawing? Or is it perhaps that they are educated and entertained chiefly by secondary visuality and orality?

These are some of the points professionals may wish to consider when evaluating the different ways of producing and using story:

1. There are children who grow up in an almost complete absence of primary visuality and primary literacy. Primary orality might be a better method to use with them for the first stages of their formal schooling, especially primary orality that gradually introduces primary visuality. But this should be a genuine primary orality that is also well-modeled by the teachers and encourages children to work at and perfect their oral storytelling skills. In other words, such teachers would have to be very good storytellers.

2. Teachers and children who have developed fairly good skills in both primary orality and primary literacy might be encouraged to do more comparing of the ways in which those skills differ, and learn to value each of them for the specific needs they seem to answer in human communication.

3. In those formal and informal educational systems relying almost totally on literacy and secondary orality and visuality, some consideration might be given to incorporating primary orality and primary visuality, both on the part of teachers and those taught.

4. The current attempts at primary visuality (that is, the heavy use of picture books or picture sequences with young children, often without words) might be expanded to include the skill that was once probably a part of general human communication in many parts of the world: the ability to sketch or draw a story in pictures. This

skill could then be combined with primary orality or primary literacy.

5. There is probably no single ideal mix of primary visuality, orality and literacy that could result in maximum educational effect everywhere, but it would seem useful to experiment more with all three formats, among children in schools in many different places, to determine whether there are combinations that are more effective than others; this might be especially helpful in places where children coming from widely differing cultural groups are placed in the same learning environment.

RECOGNIZING AND ACKNOWLEDGING THE CONTEXTS OF STORY

The experience of hearing stories told is universal. The contexts of that experience are not. It is difficult, if not impossible, to describe or recreate something one has not seen, heard, or felt. To attempt to tell stories "in an African style" or "in an Indian style" after reading only this book would be problematic. The intent of the author is not to be a substitute for the opportunity to see and hear stories told firsthand by the many individuals and groups mentioned in this book.

In virtually all school systems in the United States and Canada, and certainly in many other countries as well, there are textbooks, story books, films, filmstrips and videos that identify all or part of their contents as coming from a particular country or cultural group. There are also live storytellers who present their stories in that way, even though the sources of the stories might well be many times removed from the groups identified as the originators of the stories.

Is there any validity in telling a story from another culture, when one does not know that culture first hand? Of course, storytellers and writers have always picked up stories from whatever sources they could find. Throughout the ages, they either introduced the tales intact or changed them to suit their own personal tastes, most often not identifying where the tale came from. This is one of the reasons why we have such difficulty in tracing the origins of some of the old stories.

But this is not the kind of cross-cultural story exchange referred to here. The aspect that has changed about this process is the subtle but conscious addition of a pedagogical message. When a publisher prints, essentially for use in schools and libraries, an Ananse story from the Ashanti people of Ghana, and identifies it as such, the implication to the reader or audience is: here in this story you can learn something about the Ashanti people. The same is true when a storyteller announces to an audience of school children that "this is a story from the Ashanti of Ghana." In reality, the story might have had its entire context and meaning changed by the editor and storyteller, making it an American story with characters that have Ashanti names.

It is probably too much to expect that the habits built up over many years in the publishing industry and the educational purchaser institutions will change in the near future. The institutional teller can, however, learn enough to become skilled at recognizing authenticity in stories, especially those taken from printed collections. Let us say, for example, that a book of tales from Sierra Leone is being reviewed. It consists of long stories that have themes similar to European *märchen,* couched in very poetic language, but definitely set in West Africa and using personal and place names from the various groups in that country. There are no rhymes or songs included in the tales, and there is little use of onomatopoeia. The compiler has given no source for the stories, except that they were written down in the last century. A check through the appropriate sections of this book will show that there have been a number of excellent studies of folktales in Sierra Leone, and a literary *märchen* style does not appear to be common to any of them, nor indeed in any West African folktales, as recorded by folklorists and anthropologists. It would be wise to review the collection as an original work, pointing out that the contents did not represent the traditional patterns of Sierra Leone folktales.

Let us further assume that in the collection are a few stories that strongly and immediately appeal to the teller. When telling stories such as those, it is better to introduce them by a general statement such as this: "Here are some stories I like; the author has set them in West Africa; she (he) has imagined what they would be like if they happened there." This allows the teller to use stories that are appealing, even though they are not "authentic" in the sense that they do not represent the oral traditions of the people with whom the editor or author has identified them. When feasible, of course, the best solution is to consult someone who has recorded and studied such stories first-hand, but this is seldom possible. If the text appears to be completely changed from the oral traditions with which it is identified by name, it is better to remove all place names and treat the story as an invented fiction.

For the stories that do appear to have authenticity, it is still challenging to create a storytelling event that might suggest some of the ambiance of the sessions in which the stories were recorded. This is especially the case if one has not been present at such a session. In such a situation the teller might try to describe briefly the atmosphere and occasions that might surround such a tale if it were being told in its place of origin. Many such descriptions can be culled from this book, and from items listed in the bibliography. And fortunately, there are now more and more folklorists who record the tales in such a way that it is easier to tell them in a manner that is at least similar to the original. An excellent example of such a book is Peter Seitel's *See So that We May See*. At a 1989 preconference of the American Library Association, the storyteller Margaret Read MacDonald told one of the stories in that book and was able to bring about, in an audience of librarians sitting in a modern hotel meeting room, a reaction that seemed not unlike that of a group of Haya villagers in Tanzania.

The storyteller presenting tales in an educational setting has a greater responsibility than one telling for sheer entertainment in a private situation. Learning about stories and the peoples from whom they were collected should be part of the preparation expected of any professional teller performing in institutions. Such tellers should be evaluated not only for their talent in keeping the audience involved and attentive, but also for their knowledge about story sources and contexts and the ways in which they convey this to the audience.

A good opening for those who have doubts about how closely they can recreate both the text and context of a story from another culture is to say something like this: "I cannot tell you the story in the way you would hear it from _____ or in _____. But I like the story so much I want to tell it for you in my own way." Some specific examples of story types when this teller has used such an opening include:

> Stories from many different parts of Africa for which accompaniment to the musical segments should be an *mbira, sanza* or other instrument. One can show the instrument and pluck out a few sounds, but it would take years of practice to be a master player; yet the very showing of the instrument indicates there is more to the tale than just the words.

> Stories in which the audience is expected to respond with words, phrases, or musical chants; teaching even a few words in the original language of the story is an enhancement.

> Coyote tales and other Native American stories that should be told only in winter.

> Stories from the *Ramayana, Mahabharata,* and other Hindu and Buddhist tradition, which have a rich visual counterpart in story cloths, scrolls, palm leaf books, and the like.

> Picture-drawing stories from different cultures; learning and showing a few of the basic designs can give a hint of the complexity and richness of such unusual methods of telling.

Publishing Folktales

Much as we might like to see more stories passed on through primary orality, it is not likely that a great number will reach the next generation in that manner, at least not in the United States. The majority will certainly be inherited, directly or indirectly, through some recorded form.

On the whole folktales that have been edited and published for popular, commercial sale have not been accorded the individual respect that is routinely given to stories with known authors. Rare is the folktale collection, or the individual picture-book folktale, that mentions the name of the original teller, even when it is known, or the original context of the tale as first recorded. This is partly the result of selecting stories from out-of-print nineteenth-century compilations, but mostly out of fear that if a source is cited, the copyright cannot be claimed by the reteller or the current publisher.

This situation could be remedied if editors and publishers insisted that every modern reteller or compiler provide at least a brief paragraph listing the specific source or sources. Some indication would also have to be given as to whether the tales have been modified or changed extensively, and how. There is nothing intrinsically wrong about taking a story and making it one's own through retelling. This is part and parcel of the storytelling process. What is dishonest, professionally if not legally, is to pretend that the story is close to the original recorded version. The reteller claims authenticity, but leaves out mention of the original source or sources, so there is no way to check whether the story does represent the genuine folklore of the people with whom it is identified.

Such a phrase as "Loosely based on a tale found in . . . or heard from . . ." can go a long way to helping the reader and user identify how much of the story is newly invented and how much is traditional. It should also be made clear when the illustrations are fantasy and when they are based on actual artistic motifs coming from the same culture as the story.

Universality of Storytelling

It is not possible to claim for storytelling, as DeFrancis does for writing systems, an essential oneness. There is simply too much diversity of form, content, and purpose. But there is universality of storytelling, in that it continues to be used as a form of human expression in virtually all parts of the world. And the most common purpose, even though it might appear in varying degrees, is that of entertainment, especially entertainment that creates a sense of well-being. If this book can assist tellers and listeners to enjoy story more, it will have achieved its purpose.

NOTES

1. Quoted by K. H. Basso, "Stalking with Stories," p. 21.
2. A. H. Bá, *Kaydara*, p. 17.
3. R. Coles, *The Call of Stories*, p. 13.
4. J. DeFrancis, *Visible Speech*, pp. 244–247.
5. For an interesting extended discussion of these questions see K. B. Maxwell, *Bemba Myth and Ritual*, pp. 1–3 and W. J. Ong, *Orality and Literacy*.
6. S. B. Heath, *Ways with Words*, pp. 157–189.

REFERENCES

Adams, Robert J. "Social Identity of a Japanese Storyteller." Ph.D. dissertation, Indiana University, 1972.

Al-Shahi, Ahmed, and Moore, F. C. T. *Wisdom from the Nile; A Collection of Folk-Stories from Northern and Central Sudan*. New York: Clarendon Press, 1978.

Allen, Louise A. *Time Before Morning: Art and Myth of the Australian Aborigines*. New York: Thomas Y. Crowell, 1975.

Ammar, Hamed. *Growing Up in an Egyptian Village: Silwa, Province of Aswan*. New York: Octagon, 1966.

Bá, Amadou Hampaté. *Kaydara*. Abidjan and Dakar: Nouvelles Editions Africaines, 1978.

Babalola, S. A. *The Content and Form of Yoruba Ijála*. Oxford Univ. Pr., 1966.

Bacon, Francis. *The Essays*, ed. by John Pitcher. New York: Penguin, 1986.

Bang, W. "Manichäische Erzähler." *Le Museon* 44 (1931): 1–36.

Basso, Keith H. "Stalking with Stories: Names, Places, and Moral Narratives among the Western Apache." In *Text, Play, and Story: The Construction and Reconstruction of Self and Society*, ed. by Edward M. Bruner. Proceedings, 1983. Washington, D.C.: American Ethnological Society, 1984.

Bauman, Richard. *Story, Performance, and Event*. Cambridge Univ. Pr., 1986.

Béart, Charles. *Jeux et Jouets de l'Ouest Africain*. 2 vols. Dakar: IFAN, 1955.

Beech, Mervyn W. H. *The Suk*. New York: Negro Universities Press, 1966. (Originally pub. 1911 by Clarendon Press.)

Ben-Amos, Dan. *Sweet Words: Storytelling Events in Benin*. Philadelphia: Institute for the Study of Human Issues, 1975.

Benedict, Ruth. *Zuni Mythology*. 2 vols. Contributions to Anthropology, 21. New York: Columbia Univ. Pr., 1935.

Benjamin, Walter, and Arendt, Hannah. *Illuminations*. Tr. by H. Zorn. New York: Harcourt, Brace, 1968.

Bianco, Carla. "The Two Rosetos: The Folklore of an Italian-American Community in Northeastern Pennsylvania." Ph.D. dissertation, Indiana University, 1972.

Boyce, Mary. "The Parthian Gosan and the Iranian Minstrel Tradition." *Journal of the Royal Asiatic Society* (1957): 10–45.

Brinkmann, Otto. *Das Erzahlen in einer Dorfgemeinschaft*. Veröffentlichungen der Volkskundlichen Kommission des Provinzialinstituts für Westfälische Landes- und Volkskunde. Erste Reihe, Heft 4. Münster: Aschendorffschen Verlagsbuchhandlung, 1931.

Brunvand, Jan Harold. *The Choking Doberman and Other Urban Folktales*. New York: W. W. Norton, 1984.

———. *The Vanishing Hitchhiker*. New York: W. W. Norton, 1981.

Cammann, Alfred. *Westpreussische Märchen. Fabula*. Supplement Series. Reihe A, Band 3. Berlin: W. de Gruyter, 1961.

Carmichael, Alexander. *Carmina Gadelica*, 2nd ed. Edinburgh and London: Oliver and Boyd, 1928.

Cejpek, Jiří. "Iranian Folk Literature." In *History of Iranian Literature*, ed. by Jan Rypka. Dordrecht, Holland: D. Reidel Pub. Co., 1956.

Chadwick, H. Munro, and Chadwick, Nora Kershaw. *The Growth of Literature.* 3 vols. Cambridge Univ. Pr., 1932–1940.

Chang, Duk-soon. *The Folk Treasury of Korea: Sources in Myth, Legend and Folktale.* Seoul: Society of Korean Oral Literature, 1970.

Coles, Robert. *The Call of Stories.* Boston: Houghton Mifflin, 1989.

Coupe, William A. *The German Illustrated Broadsheet in the Seventeenth Century.* Bibliotheca Bibliographica Aureliana, 17. Baden-Baden: Heitz, 1966–1967.

Crowley, Daniel J. *I Could Talk Old-Story Good: Creativity in Bahamian Folklore.* Publications in Folklore Studies, 17. Berkeley: Univ. of California Pr., 1966.

Das, Kajal Kumar. *Burrakatha of Andhra Pradesh.* New Delhi: IIMC, 1980.

Davis, Natalie Zemon. *Fiction in the Archives.* Palo Alto: Stanford Univ. Press, 1987.

DeFrancis, John. *Visible Speech: The Diverse Oneness of Writing Systems.* Honolulu: Univ. of Hawaii Pr., 1989.

Dégh Linda. *Folktales and Society: Storytelling in a Hungarian Peasant Community.* Tr. from the German by Emily M. Schlossberger. Bloomington: Indiana Univ. Pr., 1969.

Delargy, James H. *The Gaelic Storyteller.* Rhys Memorial Lecture for 1945. *Proceedings of the British Academy,* 31. London: The Academy, 1945.

Deng, Francis Mading. *Dinka Folktales; African Stories from the Sudan.* New York: Africana Pub. Co., 1974.

Dorson, Richard. "Oral Styles of American Folk Narrators." In his *Folklore: Selected Essays,* pp. 99–146. Bloomington: Indiana Univ. Pr., 1972.

Durán, Fray Diego. *Book of the Gods and Rites* and *The Ancient Calendar.* Tr. and ed. by Fernando Horcasitas and Doris Heyden. Norman: Univ. of Oklahoma Pr., 1971.

East, Rupert. *Akiga's Story; the Tiv Tribe As Seen By One of Its Members.* Oxford Univ. Pr., 1965. (First pub. 1939.)

Egblewogbe, E. Y. *Games and Songs as Education Media: A Case Study among the Ewes of Ghana.* Accra: Ghana Pub. Corp., 1975.

Egyptian Literature. Tr. and ed by Epiphanas Wilson. London: Colonial Pr., 1901.

Eliot, T. S. "Religion and Literature." In his *Essays, Ancient and Modern.* London: Faber and Faber, 1936.

Falassi, Alessandro. *Folklore by the Fireside: Text and Context of the Tuscan Veglia.* Austin: Univ. of Texas Pr., 1980.

Fehr, Hans. *Massenkunst im 16. Jahrhundert.* Denkmale der Volkskunst, vol. 1. Berlin: Herbert Stubenrauch, 1924.

Feynman, Richard P. "The Pleasure of Finding Things Out." Transcript, Program No. 1002, NOVA. Boston: WGBH, 1982.

Frankfort, Henri. *The Art and Architecture of the Ancient Orient.* Baltimore: Penguin Books, 1969.

Frere, Mary. *Hindoo Fairy Legends (Old Deccan Days).* New York: Dover, 1967. (First pub. 1881.)

Georges, Robert A. "Toward an Understanding of Storytelling Events." *Journal of American Folklore* 82 (1969): 313–328.

Gerhardt, Mia I. *The Art of Storytelling.* Leiden: E. J. Brill, 1963.

Glassie, Henry. *Passing the Time in Ballymenone; Culture and History of an Ulster Community.* Philadelphia: Univ. of Pennsylvania Pr., 1982.

Goodman, James S. "My Grandpa's Name is Avraham." *National Storytelling Journal* 2, 4 (Fall 1985): 12.

Gorer, Geoffrey. *Himalayan Village: An Account of the Lepchas of Sikkim.* 2nd ed. New York: Basic Books, 1967. (First pub. 1938.)

Gunda, Bela. "Die Funktion des Märchens in der Gemeinschaft der Zigeuner." *Fabula* [Berlin] 6 (1964): 95–107.

Gwyndaf, Robin. "The Welsh Folk Narrative Tradition; Continuity and Adaptation." *Folk Life* [Leeds] 26 (1987–1988): 78–100.

Hartland, Edwin Sidney. *The Science of Fairy Tales.* New York: Fred A. Stokes, [c.1891].

Havelock, Eric A. *The Muse Learns to Write.* New Haven: Yale Univ. Pr., 1986.

Heath, R. "Storytelling in All Ages." *Leisure Hour* 34 (1885): 199ff; 273ff.

Heath, Shirley Brice. *Ways with Words; Language, Life, and Work in Communities and Classrooms.* Cambridge Univ. Pr., 1983.

Hoogasian-Villa, Susie, ed. *100 Armenian Tales and Their Folkloristic Relevance.* Detroit: Wayne State Univ. Pr., 1966.

Hrdličková, Věna. "The Chinese Storytellers and Singers of Ballads: Their Performances and Storytelling Techniques." Asiatic Society of Japan, *Transactions,* 3rd ser., vol. 10, pp. 97–115. Tokyo: The Society, 1968.

Huizinga, Johan. *Homo Ludens.* Boston: Beacon Pr., 1955.

Hymes, Dell. *"In Vain I Tried to Tell You": Essays in Native American Ethnopoetics.* Philadelphia: Univ. of Pennsylvania Pr., 1981.

———. "Models of the Interaction of Language and Social Life." In *Directions in Sociolinguistics,* ed. by J. J. Gumperz and Dell Hymes, pp. 35–71. New York: Holt, Rinehart and Winston, 1972.

Jan, Isabelle. *On Children's Literature.* New York: Schocken, 1974.

Janda, Elsbeth, and Nötzoldt, Fritz. *Die Moritat vom Bänkelsang: oder das Lied der Strasse.* Munich: Ehrenwirth Verlag, 1959.

Jansen, William Hugh. "Classifying Performance in the

Study of Verbal Folklore." In *Studies in Folklore,* ed. by W. Edson Richmond, pp. 110–118. Bloomington: Indiana Univ. Pr., 1957.

Kako, Satoshi. "Kamishibai—the Unique Cultural Property of Japan." Tokyo Book Development Centre, *Newsletter* 8, 2 (September 1976): 6–7.

Kata, Koji. *Machi no jijyoden (Autobiography of a Street-Person).* Tokyo: Bansei-sha, 1977.

Kipury, Naomi. *Oral Literature of the Maasai.* Nairobi: Heinemann Educational Books, 1983.

Kita, Morio. *Nireke no Hitobito (The Nine Families).* Tokyo: Shinchosha, 1964.

Lacourcière, Luc. "Canada." In *Folktales Told around the World,* ed. by Richard Dorson, pp. 429–467. Univ. of Chicago Pr., 1975.

Loeb Classical Library. Founded by James Loeb. Vol. 1–. Cambridge: Harvard University Pr., 1912–.

Lord, Albert B. *The Singer of Tales.* Harvard Studies in Comparative Literature, 24 Cambridge: Harvard Univ. Pr., 1960.

Losty, Jeremiah P. *The Art of the Book in India.* London: British Library, 1982.

Mair, Victor. *Painting and Performance; Chinese Picture Recitation and its Indian Genesis.* Honolulu: Univ. of Hawaii Pr., 1988.

Mathias, Elizabeth, and Raspa, Richard. *Italian Folktales in America: the Verbal Art of an Immigrant Woman.* Detroit: Wayne State Univ. Pr., 1985.

Maxwell, Kevin B. *Bemba Myth and Ritual; the Impact of Literacy on an Oral Culture.* American Univ. Studies, series 11, vol. 2. Frankfurt/Main: Peter Lang, 1983.

Mbiti, John S. *Akamba Stories.* Oxford Library of African Literature. Oxford Univ. Pr., 1966.

Miller, Nathan. *The Child in Primitive Society.* New York: Brentano's, 1928.

Mitchell, Roger E. "A Study of the Cultural, Historical and Acculturative Factors Influencing the Repertoires of Two Trukese Informants." Ph.D. dissertation, University of Indiana, 1967.

Mullen, Patrick B. "A Traditional Storyteller in Changing Contexts." *National Storytelling Journal,* 4, 2 (Spring 1987): 22–27.

Nebie, Marc. "Et si on disart un conte?" *Cahiers de Litterature Orale* 16 (1984): 35–58.

Norris, H. T. *Shinqiti Folk Literature and Song.* Oxford Library of African Literature. Oxford Univ. Pr., 1968.

O'Connor, V. C. Scott. "Beyond the Grand Atlas." *National Geographic* 61 (March 1932): 261–320.

Olrik, Axel. "Epic Laws of Folk Narrative." In *The Study of Folklore,* ed. by Alan Dundes, pp. 129–141. New York: Prentice-Hall, 1965.

Ong, Walter J. *Orality and Literacy: The Technologizing of the Word.* New York: Methuen, 1982.

Oring, Elliott. "Ha-Chizbat: The Content and Structure of Israeli Oral Tradition." Ph.D. dissertation, Indiana University, 1974.

Penard, A. P., and Penard, T. E. "Surinam Folk-tales." *Journal of American Folklore* 30 (1917): 239–250.

Pino-Saavedra, Yolando. *Folktales of Chile.* Tr. by Rockwell Gray. Univ. of Chicago Pr., 1967.

Ranke, Kurt. "Volkserzählung." In *Die Religion in Geschichte und Gegenwart,* 3rd ed., vol. 6. Tübingen: J. C. B. Mohr, 1965.

Ransome, Arthur. *A History of Storytelling: Studies in the Development of Narrative.* London: T. C. & E. C. Jack, 1909.

Raum, O. F. *Chaga Childhood: A Description of Indigenous Education in an East African Tribe.* Oxford Univ. Pr., 1940.

Roghair, Gene H. *The Epic of Palnādu: A Study and Translation of "Palnāti Virula Kātha," a Telugu Oral Tradition from Andhra Pradesh, India.* Oxford Univ. Pr., 1982.

Ruch, Barbara. "Medieval Jongleurs and the Making of a National Literature." In *Japan in the Muromachi Age,* ed. by John W. Hall and Toyoda Takeshi, pp. 279–309. Berkeley: Univ. of California Pr., 1977.

Sayce, A. H. "Storytelling in the East." *Living Age,* 5th series, 64 (Oct. 20, 1888): 176–180.

Scheub, Harold. "The Art of Nongenile Mazithathu Zenani, a Gcaleka *Ntsomi* Performer." In *African Folklore,* ed. by Richard Dorson, pp. 115–142. Bloomington: Indiana Univ. Pr., 1972.

———. *The Xhosa Ntsomi.* Oxford Library of African Literature. Oxford Univ. Pr., 1975.

Schiller, Friedrich von. *Werke,* vol. 4. Berlin & Weimar: Aufbau Verlag, 1967.

Schwartzman, Helen B. "Stories at Work: Play in an Organizational Context." In *Text, Play and Story: The Construction and Reconstruction of Self and Society,* ed. by Edward M. Bruner, pp. 80–93. Proceedings 1983. Washington, D.C.: American Ethnological Society, 1984.

Seitel, Peter. *See So That We May See: Performances and Interpretations of Traditional Tales from Tanzania.* Bloomington: Indiana Univ. Pr., 1980.

Sen Gupta, Sankar. *The Patas and the Patuas of Bengal.* Foreword by Niharranjan Ray. Calcutta: Indian Publications, 1973.

Sherzer, Joel. *Kuna Ways of Speaking: An Ethnographic Perspective.* Austin: Univ. of Texas Pr., 1983.

Slater, Candace. *Stories on a String: The Brazilian "Literatura de Cordel."* Berkeley: Univ. of California Pr., 1982.

Smith, Pierre. *Le récit populaire au Rwanda.* Classiques africains, 17. Paris: Armand Colin, 1975.

Taggart, James M. *Nahuat Myth and Social Structure.* Austin: Univ. of Texas Pr., 1983.

Tedlock, Dennis. *The Spoken Word and the Work of Interpretation.* Philadelphia: Univ. of Pennsylvania Pr., 1983.

Toelken, Barre. "The 'Pretty Languages' of Yellowman: Genre, Mode and Texture in Navajo Coyote Narratives." In *Folklore Genres,* ed. by Dan Ben-Amos, pp. 93–123. Austin: Univ. of Texas Pr., 1976.

Uffer, Leza. *Rätoromanische Märchen und ihre Erzähler.* Schriften, Band 29. Basel: Schweizerische Gesellschaft für Volkskunde, 1945.

Umeasiegbu, Rems Nna. *Words Are Sweet; Igbo Stories and Storytelling.* Leiden: F. J. Brill, 1982.

Yolen, Jane. *Touch Magic.* New York: Philomel, 1981.

Kay F. Stone (b.1939)

Kay F. Stone, a professor of folklore at the University of Winnipeg, has written widely and insightfully about oral storytelling traditions and feminist interpretations of folktales. Her 1998 book *Burning Brightly: New Light on Old Tales Told Today* analyzes different types of storytelling communities; individual oral storytellers, including herself; and tales they told in the previous two decades. "Oral Narration in Contemporary North America," published in 1986, describes earlier stages of the late twentieth-century storytelling revival. While Anne Pellowski's chapters provide a more global survey, Stone gives a helpful overview of three types of storytelling in modern North America. The Appalachian storytellers she discusses are part of the same southern mountain folk traditions that produced the versions of "Mutsmag" in this section. Stone's own writing helps bridge the gap she describes between folklorists, with their emphasis on oral performance, and fairy tale scholars focusing on written texts.

Oral Narration in Contemporary North America

Fairy tales, for both scholars and general readers alike, most often mean printed texts in books. Folklorists are aware that behind each printed text are hundreds of unrecorded tales by hundreds of traditional artists, with no single telling capturing the full potential of any story. Nonfolklorists, however, place far too much weight on a single text or at best a handful of variants, without giving much attention to the dynamics of oral context. Traditional tales were meant to be heard, not read, and exist in specific geographical, historical, and cultural settings. No traditional tale can be fully comprehended without some understanding of its vitality in these settings.

For the past few decades folklorists have examined traditional tales and tellers within specific tale-telling societies and have contributed greatly to our understanding of narrative traditions.[1] However, scholarly attention has focused totally on traditional tales, tellers, and listeners. It is my intent here to expand this perspective to include what has been described popularly as "the storytelling revival," a phenomenon of the past two decades. To provide a context for this "revival" I will briefly examine traditional narration in English only as it continues to exist in some rural areas of North America, as well as the nontraditional urban storytelling that preceded and continues to exist along with revivalist storytelling. This is unexplored territory, a new continent whose coastline can only begin to be described here. My hope is that other scholars, folklorists and nonfolklorists, will see the value in including contemporary tale-telling in their various examinations of the *Märchen.*

I will concentrate here on the process of narration rather than on the *Märchen* as a unique genre, but I emphasize that *Märchen* continue to exist alongside other narrative forms favored by traditional and non-traditional tellers. I am constantly surprised at the resistance I receive from students, listeners, and other scholars when I insist that *Märchen* are still very much alive (along with the other oral forms) beyond the printed page. I insist that anyone who studies *Märchen* with serious intent should be aware of their continuing oral vitality within known geographical and historical settings. I intend this essay, then, to provide a useful framework for anyone attempting an examination of *Märchen* or of oral tale-telling.

To clarify the literary and verbal artistry of traditional tales and tellers, I will briefly examine four key folkloric studies offering complementary approaches. The earliest of these is Max Lüthi's literary and philosophic work, *The European Folktale: Form and Nature,* which explores the traditional *Märchen* as a unique form of human expression. Lüthi challenges folklorists by insisting that the full power of the *Märchen* lies in the text itself, without reference to either individual narrators or specific storytelling communities:

> Although in many ways, like everything human, the folktale is to be interpreted historically, I have preferred to search for its lasting truths. Today more than ever I am convinced that, despite increased interest in the functions of tales and in what has been called folktale biology, the tales themselves merit the greatest attention, just as always. Even though much is clarified by their context, the texts themselves take on an ever new life with the passage of time. They speak to all kinds of people and to widely separated generations; they speak in terms that sometimes differ and yet in many ways remain the same. Only a small part of the secret and the fascination of folktales can be grasped by research into the present-day context of their performance in days past. The secret of the folktale resides essentially in its message, structure and style.[2]

Lüthi's careful examination of oral tales in print explains the continuing vitality of old tales in today's world of written literature.

Linda Dégh's study of Hungarian peasant narrators presents traditional tales in their oral and social contexts.[3] In another article on this contextual approach, termed "the biology of storytelling" by folklorists, Dégh insists on the necessity of looking at tales as they actually live for the people who tell and listen.

> "Biology" indicates a significant switch of focus in scholarship, from text to context. The term signals a change in concentration from the static view of artificially constructed and isolated oral narrative sequences, to the dynamics of telling and transmitting stories from person to person and from people to people, through means of direct contact, interaction, and resulting processes responsible for the formation and continual recreation of narratives.[4]

Another classic study of oral material in context, Albert Lord's *The Singer of Tales,* examines the ways in which traditional narratives are learned, practiced, performed, and received.[5] Based on the Yugoslav heroic epic, his observations are nonetheless relevant to other narrative forms, particularly the complex *Märchen.* Like Dégh, Lord concentrates on the actual existence of oral narratives in specific communities, and like Lüthi he is interested in the artistic and historic merits of specific texts. He is also aware of the misunderstandings literate societies impose on oral creativity.

> A culture based upon the printed book, which has prevailed from the Renaissance until lately, has bequeathed to us—along with its immeasurable riches—snobberies which ought to be cast aside. We ought to take a fresh look at tradition, considered not as the inert acceptance of a fossilized corpus of themes and conventions, but as an organic habit of recreating what has been received and is handed on. It may be that we ought to re-examine the concept of originality, which is relatively modern as a shibboleth of criticism; there may be other and better ways of being original than that concern for the writer's own individuality which characterizes so much of our self-conscious fiction.[6]

Taken together, these three works are indispensable to a full understanding of traditional narratives as forms of artistic, social, and personal expression. A fourth and more recent work, Richard Bauman's *Verbal Art as Performance,* is even more immediately relevant to the subject of oral narration.[7] Bauman emphasizes the necessity of viewing verbal arts in actual performance as well as in broad social contexts. He defines performance flexibly enough to cover the various aspects of verbal creativity addressed here, and I will refer to it throughout this essay.

Fundamentally, performance as a mode of spoken verbal communication consists in the assumption of responsibility to an audience for a display of communicative competence. This competence rests on the knowledge and ability to speak in socially appropriate ways.[8]

While in a broad sense his definition could also be applied to nontraditional arts such as drama or opera, he expands on the essential quality of verbal material as ever-changing rather than static, as in dramatic scripts or literary texts.

The emergent quality of performance resides in the interplay between communicative resources, individual competence, and the goals of the participants, within the contexts of particular situations. We consider as resources all those aspects of the communication system available to the members of a community for the conduct of performance.[9]

Bauman includes with his theoretical statements texts and textual analysis by folklorists and anthropologists working in many world cultures. Thus he combines the considerations expressed by Lüthi, Dégh, and Lord. These works and others are familiar to traditional narrative scholars but are generally not so familiar either to those studying texts alone (as in literary and psychological studies) or to those writing about nontraditional storytelling.[10] Folklorists, in devoting their attention to traditional narration alone, have not considered other forms of nontraditional storytelling found today in schools and libraries and at concerts and festivals.[11]

Oral narration of both traditional and nontraditional stories is carried on in three broad public contexts in North America today:[12] among traditional storytellers in predominantly rural communities such as the maritime provinces of Canada and the mountains of the southern United States, among nontraditional storytellers in predominantly urban school classrooms and libraries, and among "neo-traditional" storytellers in concerts and festivals in both urban and rural areas. Traditional storytellers (excluding native Americans) were active from the beginnings of European settlement here, nontraditional urban storytellers since about the 1870s, and neo-traditional storytellers since the late 1960s. The term *neo-traditional* is deliberately paradoxical since these storytellers, despite their recent emergence, blend old and new in challenging ways.

Within each of these contexts storytellers learn and perform their tales differently, and the listeners receive them differently. I am more interested in the connections than the differences and will illustrate how storytellers, tales, and performances interweave in North America today.

TRADITIONAL ORAL NARRATION

Folklore scholarship reveals that oral tales are the products of chains of individual, though usually anonymous, narrators. In the sense that each verbal artist contributes to any single tale, this literature can be regarded as a communally created product. We should remember that this communal creativity is not superorganic, not some mystical concept suspended above human culture, but can only come into being when actual people retell actual tales. The first people to retell tales on this continent were native Americans, for whom tale-telling continues to provide a body of oral literature. Other ethnic and racial groups, notably black Americans, also continue the active recreation of their traditional literature. Much of this literature—native American, ethnic, black American—has been gathered in published collections available for use by storytellers from any background.[13] In fact, these traditions are extensive enough to deserve complete attention, and the scope of this essay is too narrow to do them justice here. Hence most of my remarks are relevant to tales and tale-telling adapted to this continent from the traditions of the British Isles.[14]

Much popular and scholarly attention centers on storytelling in the southern mountains. In two compilations of reworked tales from North Carolina by Richard Chase, for example, we meet storytellers whose tales can be traced to ancestors alive in the 1700s.[15] The descendents of one such family, Ray Hicks, Stanley Hicks, and Hattie Presnell, are still performing today. Another contribution, Marie Campbell's descriptions of tellers, tales, and community, was inspired by her years as a school teacher in the Kentucky mountains.[16]

Within tale-telling communities such as these, tellers learn tales in the same way that they learn language, as part of a holistic complex of cultural expression. Tale texts are not isolated, consciously memorized, and formally performed. Instead they are gradually learned and absorbed through watching, listening, and imitating. Traditional tellers with the opportunity of hearing a variety of tellers and tales over long periods develop a flexible concept of verbal creativity quite different from our perceptions of a story as a fixed text. They also learn, by observing many different narrative styles and techniques, to balance between the traditional limitations of old tales and their own individuality in reinterpreting them. As Parry and Lord have emphasized, such creativity is never static and is capable of recreating not only old stories but also new tales based on traditional models.[17] It is precisely this flexibility that allowed traditional European tales to find new roots in North America.

Unlike in other parts of the world where tale-telling was sometimes limited to specific times of the day or the year, in North America storytelling could take place any time, at any place, for anyone, and for any length of time.[18] Teller and listeners tacitly determined what, for that moment, was socially appropriate. The precise wording and length of any given tale was in a constant state of emergence through performance in differing contexts. Within the intimate family or small gatherings of friends, women were active narrators, but in larger and more public settings, male narrators predominated.[19] For example, it is the male members of the Hicks family of North Carolina who continue to tell tales at large folk festivals.[20] Women tend to be seen (and often see themselves) as preservers rather than as creators of expressive forms, and thus they assume the role of passing on material to others, notably children, rather than taking on the role of public performer.[21]

In summary, oral traditional tales are learned and performed as part of the wider cultural milieu and are regarded by both tellers and listeners as an important literary expression. They are passed on both horizontally (intragenerationally within peer groups) and vertically (intergenerationally within family groups), with men performing primarily for adults and women primarily for children.

NONTRADITIONAL URBAN STORYTELLING

With the rise of liberal and universal education in the late 1800s storytelling came to be regarded as an important pedagogic tool. A lengthy study by Richard Alvey details the development of storytelling in schools, libraries, and churches and on playgrounds from the 1870s to the 1970s.[22] Initially inspired by the innovative kindergarten programs modeled on the concepts of Friedrich Froebel, storytelling spread quickly to libraries and other institutions as a more flexible method of teaching. At one of its developmental peaks in the early part of this century, storytelling was even extolled as the primary means of education, along with other aspects of "folk" culture. A statement from the National Story Tellers' League, founded by and for teachers in 1903, makes a strong statement along these lines: "We believe folk-culture is better than book-culture. By folk-culture we mean a rich social life in the home—folksongs, games, stories and the folk dance; one touch of folk-lore would make the whole civilized world kin."[23]

This sentimental misconception of "folk-culture" inspired the League to encourage storytelling among teachers at every level of public education. As the popularity of storytelling increased, however, so did the controversies over its proper functions. Some insisted that it was a wasted activity unless it offered only tales with clear pedagogical value, while others felt that stories and storytelling were valuable in and of themselves and should not be altered to suit narrow interests.[24]

Librarians, too, were increasingly involved in storytelling and in debates over its value as either a means of leading children to books or as "art for art's sake." While librarians did not form a separate storytelling organization as had the teachers, their national organization, the American Library Association (founded in 1876), and its publications firmly supported storytelling activities.

In addition to concerns about the uses of enchantment, teachers and librarians debated standards for proper storytelling: What could be considered "good" style in storytelling? How were storytellers to be adequately trained? Many books on these topics appeared and various methods of training and teaching aspiring storytellers were proposed and tried. Despite an abundance of organized storytelling on this continent, little agreement has been reached either on the value of storytelling or on acceptable standards for training and performance. The debate continues in the publications of the National Association for the Preservation and Perpetuation of Storytelling (NAPPS), and these issues continue to affect the many ways in which stories are told today in organized urban settings.

Modern urban storytellers, lacking a natural storytelling community in which to learn and perform their stories, must find their own methods of preparing themselves as performers. Many attend workshops that last anywhere from one hour to two days. They typically perform individually in a classroom or library room before ten to thirty children. Here the great majority of performers are—and have been from the early days of organized storytelling—women, since women have long dominated children's activities in schools and libraries. The school classroom and the library "story hour" restrict these tellers both in physical setting and in time. Most performances last no more than one hour, and the times are carefully scheduled in advance. Modern urban tellers, then, have far less flexibility than do traditional tellers, since their storytelling is scheduled rather than spontaneous.

The public at large no longer regards storytelling as a significant literary expression. The *Märchen* in particular is seen at best as child's play, and at worst as inappropriate even for young ears.[25] Thus urban storytellers cannot rely on a knowledgeable audience of peers to judge their "communicative competency." Often tales are not *told* at all but are read or recited from memory, with none of what Bauman calls "emergent quality." Nontraditional urban storytelling often resembles cooking from a recipe rather than recreating dishes learned from watching other cooks.

Few urban tellers have been aware of the dynamics of oral telling beyond nostalgically sentimental notions of quaint old peasants sitting beside glowing fires enchanting rapt listeners with their tales of wonder.

Yet despite their great distance from traditional storytelling, these urban nontraditionalists have kept the remnants of storytelling alive and thus have provided the basis for neo-traditional tale-tellers.

In summary, urban nontraditional storytelling has not been regarded as a significant literary expression for the public at large. It has been consciously learned and performed in a restricted milieu such as a classroom or library and primarily for children. Women, who have predominated as teachers and librarians, have most often been the narrators. The dissemination of tales has been mainly from books and has been nei-ther horizontal nor vertical, but individual. Listeners have not been expected to pass tales on to others.

NEO-TRADITIONAL TALE-TELLING

The spontaneous appearance of a more dynamic style of storytelling in the early 1970s is directly traceable to the earlier urban pattern. Many of the first performers were teachers and librarians who had given up their stable jobs for the risky life of the performer. Tale-telling began to move closer to traditional models as more tellers became full-time professionals who traveled the folk-festival circuit, learning tales and techniques from other performers rather than from printed sources. They began to create and perform in their own words rather than reciting fixed texts and to adapt old tales to the new urban milieu. Gradually such tellers began to attract audiences of adults who reevaluated the potential of old tales, and of new tales formed on old models.

Since this phenomenon has not been formally studied, its precise origins can only be guessed at. Certainly the rich soil of the counter-cultural movement of the 1960s nourished many revived craft and art forms. However nostalgic such revivals were initially, many have now become firmly established as artistic expressions. The concerts and festivals of folksong revival of earlier decades also provided models for professional performances. One teller describes his beginning as a storyteller in Berkeley in the 1960s.

> I was too old to be mistaken for a "Hippie," but as a "Beat" poet who identified with the new movement I was accepted by that generation ["Hippies"] and moved easily within it. Pete Seeger and Joan Baez were (and still are) very important to me, and folk music festivals were deeply moving. The performance *skills* and *personal warmth* of Pete and Joan (among others), won me over. That's when I began storytelling. I'm not a singer, so I started telling stories, and that filled a vacuum I so keenly felt in what I was doing at the time.[26]

As storytelling grew, tellers began to experiment with a variety of creative oral styles, using many narrative models. Some, following the well-established model of the stand-up comedian, favored brief humorous anecdotes strung together as personal-experience stories. Increasingly, performers turned to the wonder tale as a more challenging medium for their messages. Such tellers viewed their performances as a deeper form of communication beyond entertainment. One well-known teller, a former priest and social activist, saw his storytelling as a balance between entertainment and enlightenment: "I think stories should always be entertaining. It's the basic responsibility of the storyteller. But I think the kinds of stories I like are stories that disturb too—that raise questions."[27]

Other tellers spoke of involving, provoking, and challenging listeners, of engaging them more fully in the creative process. To this end some favored traditional *Märchen* and sacred tales of all sorts, while others created their own tales of serious fantasy. Even the most individualistic of these performers, however, emphasized originality far less than did literary writers. The teller quoted above, for example, comments:

> I call myself a storymaker as well as a storyteller. So almost all the stories I tell never existed before, until I created them inside of me. That's true in one sense but there's also a sense that they probably pre-existed in some form I wasn't aware of—I just happened to be a vessel for that form and it became me.[28]

Such tellers bridged the gap between oral and written composition, using both written and oral sources for their tales, first writing them, then performing them orally, not reciting them as fixed texts.[29]

The connection between teller and tale remained philosophical and psychological rather than sociocultural, and the emphasis was on a dramatic performance separating teller and audience more clearly than in traditional oral narration. Thus the teller as an individualistic performer often became more important than the tale. Concerts and festivals aimed at adult audiences encouraged the further development of storytelling on a theatrical model more appropriate to a public familiar with mass entertainment rather than traditional storytelling.

Storytelling settings for festival and concert performances today are even more circumscribed than those of school and library contexts. Not only are stories told in specific places at specific, pre-announced times, but they are most often told from a raised stage with a microphone, special lighting, and occasionally other stage props. Audiences, mainly adult, range in size from fifty to two hundred or more. In a concert setting two or more performers entertain listeners in turn, one

following the other with a full performance of several tales. In a festival setting, several performers share the stage and take turns telling one or two stories each. In both settings tellers have to contend with increased distances between themselves and their audiences. The continuing popularity of seminars and workshops devoted to the development of individual style and technique has further encouraged storytelling as a theatrical performance.

In a narrow sense, a storytelling community of tellers and listeners has emerged in many urban areas. The establishment of a noncommercial national storytelling center, NAPPS, has encouraged the development of such "communities" throughout the continent.[30] This national center is situated in a tiny town in Tennessee rather than in a major urban center, and its annual storytelling festival has always featured traditional narrators along with urban tellers. Among traditional tellers regularly featured at the festival are members of the Hicks family, one of whom, Ray, inspired the first storytelling festival.[31] NAPPS now sponsors year-round workshops in addition to its major festival in the fall, publishes a newsletter and a journal, and serves as a central resource and a model for hundreds of regional organizations.[32]

It is impossible to say how long-lived these artificial storytelling "communities" might be, since they are less stable than traditional communities. Also, tale-dissemination tends to be horizontal rather than vertical: certain tales and styles are periodically in fashion before they are replaced by other tales and styles. Neo-traditional storytelling has continued to grow steadily since the early 1970s, attracting performers with widely varied backgrounds, interests, and narrative styles. *Märchen,* both traditional and newly created, are central in the neo-traditional movement.

With the reevaluation of *Märchen* as adult entertainment, men have reentered the scene as important performers. This does not mean that women have stepped back. They continue to retain their centuries-old position as storytellers and are experimenting with new tales and techniques. In North America today both women and men perform at large public gatherings such as the tenth-anniversary NAPPS-sponsored festival in 1983 in Tennessee, at which 22 women and 26 men performed.[33] Of the ten performers from traditional backgrounds, only three were women, a clear reflection of the pattern in traditional tale-telling communities. This festival continues to offer a variety of traditional narration. In 1985, for example, performers from Bengal, Ethiopia, and Acoma Pueblo were featured.

Neo-traditional storytelling blends the old with the new: the flexibility of true oral composition with the rigidity of self-consciously created individual performances; the gradual absorption of tales learned orally from other performers with the memorization of printed texts; the individualistic position of the isolated modern professional performer with the old ties with a quasi-communal storytelling "society." If verbal creativity is at the heart of folklore scholarship, this new form of verbal expression deserves attention not only from folklorists but also from other observers of contemporary society and culture.

In summary, neo-traditional tale-telling has regained some significance as a literary expression for adults as well as for children. Both women and men are recognized public performers in concerts, festivals, and workshops. Stories are learned both from books and from other tellers. Tales are spread both horizontally, with peers as listeners and fellow narrators, and vertically, within family groups. The interaction between neo-traditional, nontraditional, and traditional artists continues to blur the boundaries between all contemporary tale-tellers.

Contemporary tale-telling in North America is a complex phenomenon. I will describe three storytellers whose verbal artistry illustrates both the differences and the connections in the three broad categories discussed here: Donald Davis, Laura Simms, and Jay O'Callahan.[34] They all appear regularly at concerts, festivals, and workshops, and they all have written about their storytelling.[35]

Donald Davis is the only one of the three with a background of traditional tale-telling. His family has lived in Haywood County, North Carolina, since the late 1700s and has kept alive a rich body of old tales. Davis's primary narrative models were his grandmother, who told wonder tales, and his uncle, who preferred humorous tales. Davis did not set them apart as

"storytellers," however, nor did he think of storytelling as a special activity:

> On days like that, storytelling was going on, but we didn't know it. There was no formal time set aside as "storytime" or any real separation of story from the total fabric of conversation. Story was the language of normal communication and the natural result of talking, much as going somewhere is the result of walking.[36]

His casual view of tales and tale-telling almost caused their demise in his own life, since he at first rejected them when he began university studies. When he read the stories of Chaucer and Shakespeare, however, he began to reexamine his narrative heritage and to retell some of the stories he remembered. "I recognized some of my stories there, and I also recognized that mine were better."[37] He had never thought of tale-telling as a special activity for children.

> In the storytelling of my childhood, there was no distinction between stories for children and stories for adults. A story was told because it was to be told, not to entertain or hold an audience. As we grew up we absorbed stories so often that the deeper and deeper levels of meaning emerged as we heard the same stories at a different age.[38]

Now a minister in Charlotte, North Carolina, Davis still performs and teaches traditional tales though he does not regard himself as a full-time professional.

> People are always asking me when I am going to become a "full time" storyteller. I guess I've been a full time storyteller all my life, but I just can't see myself making storytelling the end of what I do rather than the means by which I am who I am. Storytelling is not what I do for a living, but instead it is how I do all I do while I am living.[39]

For Davis, stories are no more separate from his life than is language itself.

In contrast, Laura Simms began as a library storyteller in the nontraditional urban milieu, learning exotic tales from books and consciously performing them for children. Without oral models on which to draw for tales and techniques, she has had to develop her own way of finding, learning, and performing stories. For her, research and rehearsal are critical in preparing a story for performance, and she has become a major performer in less than a decade. She now performs for adults as often as for children, has founded a storytelling center in Oneonta, New York (an urban "storytelling community"), and has developed an effective workshop program for formally teaching her techniques.

Because her learning experiences, unlike those of Donald Davis, were of necessity formal and conscious, Simms's connections with her tales are philosophical and personal rather than cultural and familial, and thus she often expresses herself more abstractly.

> Storytelling is the direct and shared communication of something true about being alive. It is not only the story, but a combination of a living storyteller, situation, sound and rhythm of voice, silence, gesture, facial expressions, and response of listeners that makes it potent.[40]

Her own performance experiences have taught her what Davis learned by observing others as he grew up. But unlike him, Simms views storytelling as a separate, specialized form of literature. She considers herself a full-time professional carrying on an ancient art.

> We have lost touch with the time when an entire village hung on story; when every aspect of life was presented, questioned and given meaning by story, music, dance, art, architecture and metaphor. But we still possess that common bond of existence whose continuous story we share with everyone. This is the source and the power of the revival in storytelling today.[41]

In her own way Simms has come to understand that story and society are intimately connected, yesterday and today.

Yet another perspective is offered by Jay O'Callahan, a writer who performs his own stories and traditional wonder tales. O'Callahan was a writer by profession but a storyteller at heart and has found a new voice in combining the two.

> In four years as a writer I earned $40, but I developed a hobby of entertaining children at a library by telling stories. One day a group offered me several hundred dollars to do the same thing, and soon after the school system of Brookline [Massachusetts] paid me $2,500 to tell stories to the upper grades and in the high school. It had never occurred to me that I could be a professional storyteller, but suddenly I had become one.[42]

Like Simms, O'Callahan lacks Davis's traditional background and came to his understanding about stories and storytelling—as opposed to story writing—through his own experiences as a live performer. He describes storytelling today as "the liveliest, most probing art in America" touching drama, dance, healing, history, mime, music, poetry, politics—and all with a powerful intimacy."[43] While he usually performs his own compositions, he also uses traditional materials.

O'Callahan has performed nationally and internationally for large audiences of adults but has not lost sight of the storyteller's advantage of immediacy and intimacy. He expresses this not only in the stories he tells but in the classes and workshops on storytelling he offers. Perhaps more important in understanding the intricacies of tales and society, he functions within a small but vibrant community of urban tale-tellers in the Boston area and rehearses his stories orally with them. The potential impersonality of urban existence has made him acutely aware of the importance of storytelling as an art form capable of touching modern audiences in the same way that listeners have always been touched by a well-told tale: "Nothing has a chance to touch us very deeply these days. We need an opportunity to get away from other people's images and finally learn what is inside us."[44]

Although he performs his own written compositions rather than traditional tales, O'Callahan senses the creative possibilities offered by interaction with a participating audience. Thus his stories remain flexible and "emergent," in Bauman's terms.

The fundamental difference between traditional tellers and neo- and nontraditional tellers is the relationship between teller and community. To return to Bauman's definition of performance, all tellers discussed here assume "responsibility to an audience for a display of communicative competence" each time they perform. However, the "ability to speak in socially appropriate ways"—that is, to understand and react immediately to one's live audience—is perceived differently by both tellers and audiences in all three oral contexts. In a traditional setting where stories may more easily arise spontaneously, the teller determines social appropriateness by judging the responses of the listeners. In the more restrictive and less spontaneous setting of classroom, library, and concert hall, tellers more often present a predetermined program with less immediate responses to listeners. The fact that the listeners do not form a true storytelling community, since they represent only a very small and age-specific part of the community at large, also encourages tellers to dominate rather than to exchange.

In general, traditional and nontraditional tellers are at opposite ends of a continuum in the relationship between teller and community. Between them are the neo-traditionalists, who attempt to respond to their audiences in socially appropriate ways, to create an interplay between themselves and their listeners that provides their narrative performances with "emergent quality." Those who reject dramatic models of mass entertainment in favor of developing this emergent quality manage to overcome the lack of a stable storytelling community and emerge as full oral performers.[45]

In a recent article Donald Davis suggests an alternative for the theatrical stage as a model for storytellers—the courtroom.

> As a storyteller I do not work with a behaving audience but with an unpredictable jury. If it is clear the jury is not following my argument, I must respond to their challenge with a new approach. The evidence, the facts (the real story) don't change; but my approach, my presentation, my clothing of the facts (the words) must be retailored to suit this jury.[46]

Davis's words illustrate the dynamic tensions between traditional stability ("the real story") and individual innovation (his presentation of it) that is at the heart of storytelling.

The only connection most revivalist tellers have with the traditional "oral medium" is the printed page on which they find a story. However, with the increased contacts between traditional and revivalist tellers at contemporary festivals, concerts, and workshops, storytelling as a full expression in the oral medium is coming into bloom. As I noted earlier, the relationship between written and oral literature has always been synchronic rather than diachronic, and this increasing synchronicity is well illustrated by the three tellers Davis, Simms, and O'Callahan. Revivalist tellers have begun to free themselves from the printed page and the scripted dramatic performance while continuing to use traditional tales as an important source for their performing events. Still, some see themselves as inheritors of the ancient tradition of storytelling, failing to understand the absence of diachronic relations between traditional and revivalist narration. One writer warns against such a nostalgic view of modern telling: "As literate persons, raised in a literate society, there is no way we can carry on oral tradition. We never belonged to it in the first place, and we cannot reenter it like an astronaut coming back into earth's gravitational field."[47]

I am intrigued by the willingness of many contemporary performers to understand and to review their position as inheritors of an ancient form of human expression. Neo-traditional performers in particular maintain a tenuous position between the full oral creativity of traditional narration and the literate traditions to which they belong, and in which they attempt to practice their art. Many insist that their art is, despite their literate backgrounds, a truly oral accomplishment. As storyteller Ruth Stotter observes, for example:

> The tradition has changed. Folklore is, by definition, dynamic. I feel I am a teller in the oral *tradition*. I feel comfortable calling myself a storyteller in the oral tradition because part of that tradition is people sitting down and listening to new and old tales. It is not the material alone that makes the tradition, it is the experience.[48]

Many folklorists might insist that such narrators are not "in the oral tradition" no matter how they might view themselves, since they are not historically or culturally connected with long-standing narrative communities. I find it more useful to admit that while revivalist tellers might not be the legitimate heirs of a full oral tradition, they are its stepchildren who demand recognition in their own right. Every *Märchen* reader will recognize the powerful claims of the stepchild.

I have no intention of claiming that revivalist narrators fully parallel or succeed or even replace traditional narrators. They learn, present, and view their stories and listeners differently than do traditional narrators. They do, however, function as verbal artists in a rich variety of ways. In contemporary settings we can view artists from all backgrounds and see how they diverge and converge: some, like Donald Davis, draw their tales from a vibrant oral tradition; others, like Laura Simms, bring new oral life to traditional tales in print; still others, like Jay O'Callahan, create new tales on old models. All offer us new perspective on *Märchen* as verbal art, as an expression of the people. They provide us with the timeless literary artistry of the wonder tale as examined by Max Lüthi, as well as with more immediate social and artistic connections as suggested by Albert Lord, Linda Dégh, and Richard Bauman. The *Märchen* continues its emergent quality in contemporary performances.

NOTES

1. As it is impossible to list all of even the most significant contributions here in this limited space, I can only suggest a beginning. See Dan Ben-Amos, *Sweet Words: Storytelling Events in Benin* (Philadelphia: Institute for the Study of Human Issues, 1975); Daniel J. Crowley, *I Could Talk Old Story Good: Creativity in Bahamian Folklore,* Publications in Folklore Studies, no. 17 (Berkeley: University of California Press, 1966); Diane Wolkstein, *The Golden Orange Tree and Other Haitian Folktales* (New York: Alfred A. Knopf, 1978).
2. Max Lüthi, *The European Folktale: Form and Nature* (Philadelphia: Institute for the Study of Human Issues, 1982), p. xv.
3. Linda Dégh, *Folktales and Society: Story-Telling in a Hungarian Peasant Community* (Bloomington: Indiana University Press, 1969).
4. Dégh, "Biology of Storytelling," *Folklore Preprint Series* 7 (March 1979): 1.
5. Albert Lord, *The Singer of Tales* (New York: Atheneum, 1970); see also Milman Parry and Albert Lord, *Serbocroatian Heroic Songs,* vol. I (Cambridge, MA: Harvard University Press, 1954).
6. Lord, *The Singer of Tales,* p. i.
7. Richard Bauman, *Verbal Art as Performance* (Prospect Heights, IL: Waveland Press, 1984).
8. Ibid., p. 11.
9. Ibid., p. 38.
10. In the oft-quoted *Uses of Enchantment* (New York: Alfred A. Knopf, 1976), for example, Bruno Bettelheim offers lip-service to tale variants and to the importance of hearing the stories, but he shows little comprehension of the nature of oral creativity.
11. European scholars have been more attentive. See, for example: Johannes Merkel and Michael Nagel, eds., *Erzählen* (Reinbek bei Hamburg: Rowohlt, 1982) and Klaus Doderer, ed., *Über Märchen für Kinder von heute* (Weinheim: Beltz, 1983).
12. In determining these contexts I have employed the concept of "organized storytelling" developed by Richard Alvey in his study of the history of storytelling on this continent. See n.22, below. Obviously a great deal of oral creativity takes place outside organized contexts—joke-telling at parties, for example—but I could not possibly examine all forms of verbal art for all groups in North America. Thus I am confining myself to organized storytelling in English.
13. For black American material, begin with various studies by Roger Abrahams, *Deep Down in the Jungle,* rev. ed. (Chicago: Aldine Press, 1974); for native material, begin with Dennis Tedlock, *Finding the Center: Narrative Poetry of the Zuni Indians* (New York: Dial, 1972). (Tedlock includes an excellent bibliography for further reading.) Particularly relevant for contemporary storytelling is a master's thesis by Ruth Stotter, "Interpretive Performance of Traditional Native American Narratives," Sonoma State University, 1984.
14. Marie Campbell, *Tales from the Cloud-Walking Country* (Bloomington, Ind.: Indiana University Press, 1958. repr. Westport, CT: Greenwood Press, 1976); Richard Chase, *The Jack Tales* (Cambridge: Houghton Mifflin, 1943) and *Grandfather Tales* (Boston: Houghton Mifflin, 1948); Arthur Huff Fauset, *Folklore from Nova Scotia* (New York: American Folklore Society Memoire 24, 1931); Emelyn Gardner, *Folklore from the Schoharie Hills, New York* (Ann Arbor: University of Michigan, 1937); Vance Randolph, *The Devil's Pretty Daughter* (New York: Columbia University Press, 1955), *Sticks in the Knapsack* (New York: Columbia University Press, 1958), *The Talking Turtle* (New York: Columbia University Press, 1957), and *Who Blowed Up the Church House?* (New York: Columbia University Press, 1952); Leonard Roberts, *South from Hellfer-sartin* (Lexington, Ky.: University of Kentucky, 1964), *Old Greasybeard* (Detroit: Folklore Associates, 1969), *Sang Branch Settlers* (Austin, Tex.: University of Texas, 1974); Carol Spray, *Will o'the Wisp: Folktales and Legends of New Brunswick* (Fredericton, New Brunswick: Brunswick Press, 1979). These collections include only Anglo-American materials. The wealth of tales from other groups can hardly be covered here.

15. These tales appear in Richard Chase's two books listed above. For a recent scholarly study see: W. F. Nicolaisen, "AT 1535 in Beech Mountain, North Carolina," *Scandinavian Yearbook of Folklore* 36 (1980): 99–106.

16. Campbell's description of the Kentucky community in which she taught is found in *Cloud-Walking*. All narrators mentioned in her tale collections are described in *Cloud-Walking*. (Bloomington: Indiana University Press, 1960).

17. A fine example of original composition based on traditional models is found in Lord, *The Singer of Tales,* pp. 272–75. Here epic singer Milovan Vojičić composes an epic poem dedicated to Milman Parry.

18. In many tale-telling communities this is not true: Certain kinds of narratives can only be told at certain times by certain individuals. For example, Ojibwa sacred versions of the culture-hero Nanabush are properly told by religious specialists during initiation rites for the Midewiwin, or Great Medicine Society.

19. See, for example, Dégh, *Folktales and Society,* esp. pp. 92–93 and 99–102. The dominance of male narrators can also be seen in the Anglo-American collections mentioned in n. 14, above. Folklorist Margaret Mills, who has conducted field research in Afghanistan, commented to me in a personal communication: "Women (in traditional societies) are left in the cultural-educational backwaters, holding the bag of traditional culture. Dialectologists treat it as a truism that if you want to study archaism in dialects, women often predominante as subjects, because their opportunity to travel and to learn to talk to outsiders are limited compared to men's. So their lore tends to be more local or regional—in modern times and, perhaps, always. Men tend to have the floor, but women have the lore!"

20. Ray Hicks and Stanley Hicks have appeared at several of the national festivals in Jonesborough, Tennessee. This information was gathered from NAPPS festival programs for the past ten years. See n. 30, below.

21. Dégh, *Folktales and Society;* also Nicolaisen, "AT 1535 in Beech Mountain."

22. Richard Alvey, "The Historical Development of Organized Story-Telling to Children in the United States." Ph.D. dissertation, University of Pennsylvania, 1974.

23. Ibid., p. 36.

24. See, for example: Sara Cone Bryant, *How to Tell Stories to Children* (New York: Houghton Mifflin, 1924); Ruth Sawyer, *The Way of the Storyteller* (New York: Viking Press, 1942; repr. 1962). Both of these early classics warn against forcing tales into narrow pedagogic channels.

25. The *Märchen* has excited controversy since its first appearances in print. See Kay Stone, "*Märchen* to Fairytale: An Unmagical Transformation." *Western Folklore* 40, no. 3 (July 1981): 232–44; and Michael C. Kotzin, *Dickens and The Fairy Tale* (Bowling Green, Ohio: Bowling Green University Popular Press, 1972).

26. John Harrell, letter to the author, 5 November 1984.

27. David Holt, "An Interview with Ken Feit,"*The Yarnspinner* 6 (March 1982): 3.

28. Ibid., p. 2.

29. Canadian children's writer Robert Munsch, for example, composes his stories orally in school performances before writing them down. "It may take me as long as three years of telling to get a story ready for print" (CBC radio interview, 16 November 1984). American writer Jane Yolen, on the other hand, writes her stories and then performs them orally—not reciting or reading them (conversation with the author, 20 March 1984).

30. The National Association for the Preservation and Perpetuation of Storytelling offered its first annual festival in October 1973, in Jonesborough, Tennessee.

31. From a conversation with Doc McConnell, a founding member of NAPPS, in Jonesborough, July 1983.

32. *The Yarnspinner,* formerly a monthly newsletter, is now a bimonthly supplement alternating with the bimonthly *National Storytelling Journal,* the first issue of which was published in January 1984.

33. As described in the 1982 National Storytelling Festival program.

34. Comments are based on conversations with these performers in 1982–83 and on material by and about them in NAPPS publications.

35. Many pieces have appeared over the past several years in *The Yarnspinner* and *The National Storytelling Journal.*

36. Kay Stone and Donald D. Davis, "To Ease the Heart: Traditional Storytelling," *The National Storytelling Journal* 1. no. 1 (Winter 1984): 3.

37. Conversation at the John C. Campbell Folk School in Brasstown, North Carolina, December 1982.

38. Stone and Davis, "To Ease the Heart," p. 5.

39. Ibid., pp. 4–5.

40. Laura Simms, "Storytelling, Children and Imagination," *The Yarnspinner* 6 (June 1982): 2.

41. Laura Simms, "The Lamplighter: Storytelling in the Modern World," *The National Storytelling Journal* 1 (1984): 8.

42. "Profile: Jay O'Callahan," *The Yarnspinner* 6 (January 1982): 3.

43. Ibid., p. 2.

44. Ibid.

45. Storyteller Ruth Stotter, for example, writes: "Another thought triggered by your paper was a reappraisal of

what happened at my Bookseller Cafe evenings. The same people (basically) attended twice a month for $3^{1}/_{2}$ years ... mostly singles, a few couples, a few families. They would stay and talk afterwards, almost as if sharing the stories (time?) created a bond. There was a sense of community. Whenever I do regular storytelling programs like this it is an entirely different experience than a one-time performance for entertainment." (Letter to the author, 20 November 1984).

46. Donald D. Davis, "Inside the Oral Medium." *National Storytelling Journal* 1, no. 3 (Summer 1984): 7.
47. John Harrell, *Origins and Early Traditions of Storytelling* (Kensington, Calif.: York House, 1983), p. 63.
48. Ruth Stotter, letter to the author, 20 November 1984.

BIBLIOGRAPHY

Alvey, Richard. *The Historical Development of Organized Storytelling to Children in the United States.* Ph.D. dissertation, University of Pennsylvania, 1974. A very detailed description of storytelling in schools, libraries, churches, and playgrounds.

Bauman, Richard. *Verbal Art as Performance.* Prospect Heights, IL: Waveland Press, 1984. Bauman's theoretical statements on the nature of oral performance, supported by articles by other anthropologists and folklorists.

Ben-Amos, Dan. *Sweet Words: Storytelling Events in Benin.* Philadelphia: Institute for the Study of Human Issues, 1975. A study of tellers and performances in Nigeria.

Crowley, Daniel J. *I Could Talk Old Story Good: Creativity in Bahamian Folklore.* Publications in Folklore Studies, no. 17. Berkeley: University of California Press, 1966. A description of several tellers and their stories, including full texts of the tales.

Dégh, Linda. *Folktales and Society: Storytelling in a Hungarian Peasant Community.* Bloomington: Indiana University Press, 1969. A careful examination of traditional narrators, the society in which they function, and occasions for tale-telling. Some story texts are included.

Lord, Albert. *The Singer of Tales.* New York: Atheneum, 1970. This study of how Yugoslav epic singers learn and practice their art employs the Parry-Lord formulaic theory, a model for verbal creativity relevant to the *Märchen* as a complex verbal expression.

Lüthi, Max. *The European Folktale: Form and Nature.* Philadelphia: Institute for the Study of Human Issues, 1982. Originally published in 1947 as *Das Europäische Volksmärchen: Form Und Wesen.* A careful study of the folktale as a literary form, heavily reliant on the Grimm collections and other important gatherings of German tales.

Stone, Kay. "I Won't Tell These Stories to My Kids." *Canadian Ethnic Studies* 7, no. 2 (1975): 33–41. A brief description of a young Polish Canadian and the texts of two folktales.

———. "*Märchen* to Fairy Tale: An Unmagical Transformation." *Western Folklore* 40, no. 3 (July 1981): 232–44.

———. "Der Goldene Schlüssel." *Erzählen,* ed. J. Merkel and Michael Nagel. Hamburg: Rowohlt Taschenbuch Verlag, 1983.

Stone, Kay, and Donald D. Davis. "To Ease the Heart: Traditional Storytelling." *The National Storytelling Journal* 1, no. 1 (Winter 1984): 3–7.

Bruno Bettelheim (1903–90)

Bruno Bettelheim was born in Vienna and studied psychology with Sigmund Freud there. After his release from a Nazi concentration camp in 1939, he became a distinguished and controversial child psychologist in the United States, writing many books about child development and the Holocaust throughout his long career. This 1975 *New Yorker* article presents ideas that were developed more fully in his 1976 book *The Uses of Enchantment: The Meaning and Importance of Fairy Tales.* Although there have been many different psychological studies of fairy tales before and after Bettelheim, his book is the most famous and influential defense of the tales based on their power to help children cope with unconscious anxieties and desires. Writing at a time when many adults feared that traditional fairy tales were too unrealistic or violent for children,

Bettelheim argues that they provide essential outlets for irrational and destructive tendencies. Freud himself had been interested in the relationships between fairy tales and dreams, since both represent human problems and desires symbolically. Bettelheim maintains that fables, myths, and realistic stories do not help children learn to solve problems as effectively as traditional fairy tales; their symbolic, optimistic patterns show that small and weak folk can survive injustice or abuse at home, become independent, triumph over monsters that represent external and internal evils, develop mature relationships, and rise to high positions in the world.

Psychoanalysts such as Bettelheim have been criticized by folklorists and literary critics like Jack Zipes and Maria Tatar (see Tatar's "Reading Fairy Tales" in this section) for ignoring the historical basis and variations of individual tales, for using outdated premises about gender and Freudian theories of child development, and for dogmatic interpretations of particular tales. James W. Heisig's 1977 review in the journal *Children's Literature* includes some of these criticisms but also praises the subtlety of Bettelheim's detailed readings of individual tales, noting that his book "probably does more for the respectability of the fairy tale as an interpretative tool than has anyone before him."[1] Bettelheim simplifies fairy tale history by assuming there are original versions of classic tales that children need to hear, yet this article also stresses that oral storytelling is best, that adult tellers will alter their stories to suit their interaction with the child who is listening. The article provides samples of Bettelheim's interpretations of a number of European fairy tales found in this anthology.

NOTE

1. James W. Heisig, "Bruno Bettelheim and the Fairy Tales," *Children's Literature* 6 (1977): 93–114.

Reflections

The Uses of Enchantment

If we do not live just from moment to moment but try to be conscious of our existence, then our greatest need and most difficult achievement is to find meaning in life. It is well known that many people lose the will to live because such meaning evades them. An understanding of the meaning of life is not suddenly acquired at the age of chronological maturity, or at any particular age. On the contrary, gaining this understanding is what constitutes having attained psychological maturity. This achievement is the result of a long development; wisdom is built up, small step by small step, from most irrational beginnings. Unfortunately, too many parents want their children's minds to function as their own do—as if a child's understanding of himself and the world did not have to develop as slowly as his body does. To find meaning in life, the child must become able to transcend the confines of a self-centered existence and believe that he will make a significant contribution—if not right now, then at some future time. This belief is necessary if he is to be satisfied with himself and with what he is doing; only hope for the future can sustain us in the adversities we unavoidably encounter.

As an educator and therapist, I have had as my main task giving meaning to the lives of severely disturbed children. This work has made it obvious to me that if children are reared so that their lives are meaningful to them they will not need special help. I have been confronted with the problem of deducing what experiences are suitable to promote a child's ability to find meaning in his own life and thereby endow life in general with more meaning. Of the first importance in providing such experiences is the impact of parents and others who take care of the child; second is our cultural heritage, if it is transmitted to the child in the right manner. Because it quickly became apparent to me that when the child is young this heritage reaches him best through literature, I grew deeply dissatisfied with much of the literature intended to develop the child's mind and personality, finding that it fails to stimulate and nurture those resources he needs most in order to cope with his difficult inner problems. The pre-primers and primers from which he learns to read in school are designed to teach merely that skill, irrespective of the meaning of what is read. The overwhelming majority of the rest of the so-called "children's books" currently available attempt to entertain or inform, or both, but are so shallow that little of significance can be gained from them. The idea that by learning to read one may be able later to enrich one's life is experienced as an empty promise when the stories that the child listens to or reads are vacuous. For a story to truly hold the child's attention, it must entertain him and arouse his curiosity. But for a story to enrich his life it must stimulate his imagination, help him to develop his intellect and to clarify his emotions, be attuned to his anxieties and aspirations, give full recognition to his difficulties, suggest solutions to the problems that perturb him, and promote confidence in himself and his future.

In all these respects and many others, nothing in the entire range of "children's literature"—with rare exceptions—can be as enriching and satisfying to child and adult alike as the folk fairy tale. True, fairy tales teach little overtly about the specific conditions of life in modern mass society; these tales were created long before modern society came into being. But from them a child can learn more about the inner problems of man, and about solutions to his own (and our) predicaments in any society, than he can from any other type of story within his comprehension. Since the child is exposed at every moment to the society in which he lives, he will learn to cope with its conditions—provided, that is, that his inner resources permit him to do so. The child must therefore be helped to bring order into the turmoil of his feelings. He needs—and the

point hardly requires emphasis at this moment in our history—a moral education that subtly, by implication only, conveys to him the advantages of moral behavior, not through abstract ethical concepts but through that which seems tangibly right and therefore has meaning for him. The child can find meaning through fairy tales. Like so many other modern psychological insights, this one was anticipated long ago by poets. The German poet Schiller wrote, "Deeper meaning resides in the fairy tales told to me in my childhood than in the truth that is taught by life." Through the centuries (if not millennia) during which fairy tales, in their retelling, became ever more refined, they came to convey overt and covert meanings at the same time; came to speak simultaneously to all levels of the human personality, communicating in a manner that reaches the uneducated mind of the child as well as the sophisticated mind of the adult. In terms of the psychoanalytic model of the human personality, fairy tales carry important messages to the conscious, the preconscious, and the unconscious mind, on whatever level these are functioning. By dealing with universal human problems, and especially with those that preoccupy the child's mind, these stories speak to his budding ego and encourage its development, and at the same time relieve preconscious and unconscious pressures. As the stories unfold, they give conscious credence and body to id pressures and show how to satisfy these in ways that are in line with ego and superego requirements.

But my interest in fairy tales is not a result of such technical analysis of their merits. It is, on the contrary, a consequence of my asking myself why, in my experience, children—normal and abnormal alike, and at every level of intelligence—have found folk fairy tales more satisfying than all other children's stories. The more I tried to understand why these stories are so successful in enriching the inner life of the child, the clearer it became to me that, in a much deeper sense than any other reading material, they start where the child really is in his psychological and emotional being. They speak about his severe inner pressures in a way that the child unconsciously understands and, without belittling the serious inner struggles that growing up entails, offer examples of both temporary and permanent solutions to acute psychological difficulties.

In order to master the psychological problems of growing up—overcoming narcissistic disappointments, oedipal dilemmas, sibling rivalries, becoming able to relinquish childhood dependencies, gaining a feeling of selfhood and self-worth and a sense of moral obligation—a child needs to be able to cope with what goes on in his unconscious. He can achieve this ability not by attaining rational comprehension of the nature and content of his unconscious but by becoming familiar with it through spinning out daydreams—ruminating on, rearranging, and fantasizing about suitable story elements in response to unconscious pressures. By doing this, the child fits into conscious fantasies matter from his unconscious, which he is then able to deal with. Here fairy tales have an unequalled value, because they offer new dimensions to the child's imagination, suggesting to him images with which he can structure his daydreams.

In child or adult, the unconscious is a powerful determinant of behavior. When the unconscious is repressed and its content denied entrance into awareness, the person's conscious mind will eventually become partly overwhelmed by derivatives of these unconscious elements, or else he will be forced to keep such rigid, compulsive control over them that his personality may be severely crippled. But when unconscious material is to some degree permitted to come to awareness and to be worked through in imagination, its propensity to cause harm—to him or others—is much reduced; indeed, some of its forces can be made to serve positive purposes. However, the prevalent parental belief is that a child must be diverted from what troubles him most: his formless, nameless anxieties and his chaotic, angry, and even violent fantasies. Many parents believe that only conscious reality or pleasant and wish-fulfilling images should be presented to the child—that he should be exposed only to the sunny side of things. But such one-sided fare nourishes the mind only in a one-sided way, and real life is not all sunny. There is a widespread disinclination to let children know that the source of much that goes wrong in life is due to our own natures—the propensity of all men to act aggressively, asocially, selfishly, out of anger and anxiety. Instead, we want our children to believe that all men are inherently good. But every child knows that *he* is not always good, and that even when he is he would often prefer not to be. This contradicts what he is told by his parents, and therefore makes the child a monster in his own eyes.

Psychoanalysis was created to enable man to accept life's problematic nature without being defeated or giving in to escapism. Freud's prescription is that only by struggling courageously against what seem like overwhelming odds can man succeed in wringing meaning out of human existence. This is exactly the message that fairy tales get across to the child in manifold form: that a struggle against severe difficulties in life is unavoidable—is part of the human condition—but that if, instead of shying away, one steadfastly meets unexpected and often unjust hardships, one masters all obstacles in the end and emerges victorious. Modern stories written for young children mainly avoid these existential problems, which are such crucial issues for all of us. The child needs most particularly to be given suggestions in symbolic form about how he may deal with these issues and grow successfully to maturity. "Safe" stories mention neither death nor aging, neither the limits to our existence nor the wish for eternal life. The fairy tale, by contrast, confronts the child squarely with the basic human predicaments. For example, many fairy tales begin with the death of a mother or father; in these tales the death of a parent creates the most agonizing problems, as it (or the fear of it) does in real life. Other fairy tales tell about an aging parent who has decided that the time has come to let the new generation take over. But before this can happen, the successor has to prove himself capable and worthy. The Brothers Grimm's story "The Three Feathers" begins, "There was once upon a time a king who had three sons. . . . When the king had become old and weak, and was thinking of his end, he did not know which of his sons should inherit the kingdom after him." In order to decide, the king sets all his sons a number of difficult tasks; the son who meets them best "shall be king after my death." It is characteristic of fairy tales to state an existential dilemma briefly and pointedly. This permits the child to come to grips with the problem in its most essential form; a more complex plot would merely confuse matters for him. The fairy tale simplifies all situations. Its figures are clearly drawn, and details, unless they are very important, are eliminated. All characters are typical rather than unique.

Unlike many modern stories for children, fairy tales present evil as being no less omnipresent than virtue. In practically every fairy tale, both good and evil are given body in the form of figures and their actions, as both good and evil are omnipresent in life and the propensities for both are present in every man. It is this duality that poses the moral problem and requires the struggle to solve it. Evil is not without its attractions—symbolized by the might of the giant or dragon, the power of the witch, the cunning of the queen in "Snow White"—and often it is temporarily in the ascendancy. In many fairy tales, a usurper succeeds for a time in seizing the place that rightfully belongs to the hero—as the wicked stepsisters do in "Cinderella." It is not so much that the evildoer is punished at the story's end which makes immersing oneself in fairy tales an experience in moral education, although this is part of it. In fairy tales, as in life, punishment or fear of it is a limited deterrent to crime. The conviction that crime does not pay is much more effective as a deterrent, and in fairy tales the bad person always loses out. However, it is not even the fact that virtue wins in the end that promotes morality but that the hero is the most attractive figure to the child, who thus identifies with the hero in all his struggles and triumphs with him when virtue is victorious. The child makes such identifications on his own, and the inner and outer struggles of the hero imprint morality on him.

The figures in fairy tales are not good and bad at the same time, as we all are in reality. But polarization dominates the child's mind, and that is another reason he is so receptive to fairy tales. In the tales, a person is either good or bad—not both, and nothing in between. One brother is stupid, the other is clever. One sister is virtuous and industrious, the others are vile and lazy; one is beautiful, the others are ugly. One parent is all good, the other evil. But opposite characters are not juxtaposed merely for the purpose of stressing right behavior, as in cautionary tales. (There are some amoral fairy tales, in which goodness and badness, beauty and ugliness play no role at all.) Rather, the polarities simply exist as the basis for the tale that is to be told. Being presented with the polarities of character in this way permits the child to comprehend easily the difference between the two, which he could not do if the figures were drawn more true to life, with all the complexities that characterize real people. Ambiguities must wait until a relatively firm personality has been established, on the basis of positive identifications—until the child comes to understand that there are great differences between people, and that there-

fore one has to make choices about the kind of person one wants to be. This fundamental decision, on which all later personality development will build, is facilitated by the polarizations of the fairy tale.

Amoral fairy tales, which show no polarization or juxtaposition of good and bad persons, serve an entirely different purpose. Puss in Boots, who arranges for the hero's success through trickery, and Jack, in "Jack and the Beanstalk," who steals the giant's treasure, both answer needs very different from those answered by the good heroes. These amoral stories or motifs build character not by promoting choices between good and bad but by giving the child the hope that even the lowliest can succeed in life. After all, what's the use of choosing to become a good person when you feel so insignificant that you fear you will never amount to anything? In these tales, the issue is not morality but assurance that one can succeed. Whether one meets life with a belief in the possibility of mastering its difficulties or with the expectation of certain defeat is also, of course, a very important existential problem.

The child is subject to desperate feelings of loneliness and isolation, and often experiences mortal anxiety. More often than not, he is unable to express these feelings in words, or can do so only by indirection: by claiming fear of the dark or of some animal, for instance. Since it creates discomfort in parents to recognize negative emotions in their child, the parents tend to overlook them, or they belittle the spoken fears out of their own anxiety, believing that such a response will allay the child's fears. The fairy tale, by contrast, takes these existential anxieties and dilemmas very seriously and addresses itself directly to them: to the need to be loved and the fear that one is thought worthless; to the love of life and the fear of death. Further, the fairy tale offers solutions on the child's level of understanding. For example, fairy tales recognize the dilemma of wishing to live eternally by occasionally concluding, "If they have not died, they are living still." As for the ending "And they lived happily ever after," it does not for a moment fool the child into believing that eternal life is possible. Instead, it indicates that which alone can take the sting out of recognition of the narrow limits of our time on this earth: forming a truly satisfying bond to another. The tales teach that when one has done this, one has reached the ultimate in emotional security and permanency of relation available to man, and that this alone can dissipate the fear of death. If one has found true adult love, the fairy tale makes plain, one doesn't need to wish for eternal life. This is also suggested by another ending found in fairy tales: "They lived for a long time afterward, happy and contented."

An uninformed view of fairy tales sees in this type of ending an unrealistic wish fulfillment, and misses completely the important message that it conveys to the child. These stories tell him that by forming a true interpersonal relation one escapes separation anxiety, which haunts the child—and which sets the stage for many fairy tales but is always resolved at the story's ending. Furthermore, these stories indicate that this desirable condition is not to be achieved by holding on to Mother eternally, as the child wishes and believes. If we try to escape anxiety about separation and death by desperately keeping our grasp on our parents, we will be cruelly forced out, like Hansel and Gretel. Only by going out into the world can the fairy-tale hero (child) find himself there; and as he does, he will also find the other with whom he will be able to live happily ever after—that is, without ever again having to experience separation anxiety. The fairy tale is future-oriented and guides the child—in terms he can understand in both his conscious and his unconscious mind—to relinquish his infantile wishes for dependency and achieve an independent existence, which the fairy tale helps him to perceive as more satisfying. Children no longer grow up within the security of an extended family or of a well-integrated community. Therefore, it is even more important than it was when fairy tales were invented that the child be provided with images of heroes who have to go out into the world by themselves and, although they are originally ignorant of the ultimate things, find themselves secure places by following the way that is right for them with deep inner confidence.

In most cultures, there is no clear line separating fairy tales from myths; together, the two forms constitute the literature of pre-literate societies. Myths and fairy tales alike attain a definite form only when they are committed to writing, for then they are no longer sub-

ject to continuous change. Up to that point, these stories would be sometimes condensed, sometimes vastly elaborated in their retelling over the centuries. Some stories would merge with others. All would be modified by what the teller thought was of greatest interest to his listeners, by his concerns of the moment, and by the special problems of his era.

Myths and fairy tales have much in common. Both speak to us in the language of symbols representing certain aspects of the unconscious. The appeal of both is simultaneously to the conscious and the unconscious, to all three of the mind's aspects—id, ego, and superego. But there are also inherent differences between myths and fairy tales. Although the same exemplary figures and situations are found in the two forms, and equally miraculous events occur in the two, these are not communicated in the same way. Put simply, the dominant feeling that a myth conveys is: this is unique; it could not have happened to any other creature, or in any other setting; such events are grandiose, awe-inspiring, and could never be duplicated in the lives of ordinary mortals like you and me. The reason is not so much that what takes place is miraculous as that it is described as such. By contrast, although the events that occur in fairy tales are often unusual and most improbable, they are always presented as quite ordinary—as something that could happen to you or me or the person next door while taking a walk in the woods.

An even more significant difference in these two kinds of stories concerns the ending. The myth is pessimistic, while the fairy tale, no matter how terrifyingly serious some of its features may be, is optimistic. Whether the happy outcome is due to the virtues of the hero, to chance, or to the intervention of supernatural figures, it sets the fairy tale apart from all other stories in which fantastic events occur. Because the fairy tale, with its promise of a happy ending, reassures by giving hope for the future, Lewis Carroll called it a love gift—a term hardly applicable to a myth. Obviously, not every story contained in a collection called "Fairy Tales" necessarily meets these criteria. For example, Hans Christian Andersen's "The Little Match Girl" and "The Steadfast Tin Soldier" are beautiful but extremely sad; they do not convey the feeling of consolation so characteristic of fairy tales. But Andersen's "The Snow Queen" comes quite close to being a true fairy tale. Many of the stories in fairy-tale collections may be simply diversions, fables, cautionary tales. If they are fables, they tell by means of words, actions, or events—implausible though these may be—what one ought to do. Cautionary tales demand and threaten—they are moralistic—and the diversions just entertain. Not a bad way of deciding whether a story is a fairy tale or something else might be to consider whether it could rightly be called a love gift to a child.

The child asks himself, "Who am I? Where did I come from? How did the world come into being? Who created man and all the animals? What is the purpose of life?" True, he ponders these vital questions not in the abstract but mainly as they pertain to him. He worries not about whether there is justice for individual man but about whether *he* will be treated justly. He wonders who or what brings adversity upon him, and what can protect him against it. Are there benevolent powers in addition to his parents? *Are* his parents benevolent powers? How should he form himself, and why? Is there hope for him, though he may have done wrong? Why did all this happen to him? What will it mean for his future? Fairy tales provide answers to these questions—questions that, pressing though they are, the child may become aware of only as he follows the stories.

From an adult point of view and in terms of modern science, the answers that fairy tales offer are fantastic rather than true. As a matter of fact, these answers seem so wrong to many adults, who have become estranged from the ways in which young people experience the world, that they object to having children exposed to such "false" information. However, a realistic explanation is usually incomprehensible to children, because they lack the abstract understanding required to make sense of it. While scientifically correct answers make an adult think that he has clarified things for the child, they leave the child confused, overpowered, intellectually defeated. A child can derive security only from the conviction that he understands now what baffled him before; being given facts that create *new* uncertainties simply makes everything seem more precarious. As the child accepts such a factual answer, he comes to doubt whether he has asked the right question. Since the explanation fails to make sense to him, it must apply to some unknown problem, not the one he asked about.

To tell a child that the earth floats in space, attracted by gravity into circling around the sun, but that the earth doesn't fall to the sun, as the child falls to the ground, is very confusing to him. The child knows from his experience that everything has to rest on something or be held up by something. Only an explanation based on that knowledge can make him feel that he understands better about the earth in space. What is more important, in order for the child to feel secure on earth he needs to believe that this world is held firmly in place. Therefore, a more satisfactory explanation for him will be a myth that tells him that the earth rests on a turtle or is held up by a giant. Considerable intellectual maturity is needed to believe that there can be stability to one's life when the ground one walks on (the firmest thing around, on which everything rests) rotates with incredible speed on an invisible axis, that in addition it revolves around the sun, and furthermore that the entire solar system is itself hurtling through space. I have seldom encountered a child under ten who could comprehend all these combined movements, although I have known many who could repeat the information. A child will parrot explanations that according to his own experience of the world are lies, feeling that he must believe them to be true because some adult has said so. The consequence is that the child comes to distrust his own experience, and therefore himself and what his mind can do for him.

In trying to get a child to accept scientifically correct explanations, parents all too frequently discount scientific findings of how a child's mind works. Research on the child's mental processes—most notably by Piaget—convincingly demonstrates that the young child is not able to comprehend two vital abstract concepts: the conservation of quantity, and reversibility; for instance, that the same quantity of water rises high in a narrow receptacle and falls low in a wide one, and that subtraction reverses the process of addition. Until the child can understand abstract concepts such as these, he can experience the world only subjectively.

I have known many young people who, particularly in late adolescence, come to a belief in magic, to compensate for their having been deprived of it prematurely in childhood. It is as if such young people felt that now was their last chance to make up for a severe deficiency in their life experience—that without having had a period of belief in magic they would be unable to meet the rigors of adult life. Many of the young people who today suddenly seek escape in drug-induced dreams, apprentice themselves to a guru, believe in astrology, practice "black magic," or in some other fashion escape from reality into daydreams about magic experiences were prematurely pressed to view reality as adults view it. Trying to evade reality by the methods these adolescents adopt has its ultimate cause in early experiences that prevented the development of the conviction that life can be mastered in realistic ways. It is apparently desirable for the individual to repeat in his life span the process involved historically in the genesis of scientific thought. For a good part of human history, men used emotional projections (such as gods) born of their immature hopes and anxieties to explain man, his society, and the universe; these explanations gave men a feeling of security. Then, slowly, by their own social, scientific, and technological progress, men freed themselves of the constant fear for their very existence. Feeling more secure in the world, and also within themselves, they could now begin to question the validity of the images they had used in the past as explanatory tools. From there, men's "childish" projections dissolved and more rational explanations took their place.

"True" stories about the "real" world may provide children with some interesting and often useful information. But the way such stories unfold is as alien to the way the child's mind functions as the supernatural events of the fairy tale are to the way the mature intellect comprehends the world. Strictly realistic stories run counter to the child's inner experiences; he will listen to them and maybe get something out of them, but he cannot extract from them much personal meaning that transcends their obvious content. These stories inform without enriching, and the same thing is unfortunately true of much learning in school. Factual knowledge profits the total personality only when it is turned into personal knowledge. Outlawing realistic stories for children would be as foolish as banning fairy tales; there is an important place in the life of the child for each. Yet a fare of nothing but realistic stories is barren. When realistic stories are combined with ample and psychologically sound exposure to fairy tales, the child receives information that speaks to both parts of his budding personality—the rational and the emotional.

The child who is familiar with fairy tales understands that they speak to him in the language of symbols, not that of everyday reality. The fairy tale conveys from its first words, throughout its plot, and by its ending that the things he is being told about are not tangible facts or real persons and places. "Once upon a time," "In a certain country," "A thousand years ago, or longer," "At a time when animals still talked," "There was once an old castle in the midst of a large and dense forest"—such beginnings suggest that what follows does not pertain to the here and now that we know. This deliberate vagueness in the beginnings of fairy tales symbolizes a departure from the concrete world of ordinary reality. The old castles, the dark caves, the locked rooms one is forbidden to enter, the impenetrable woods all suggest that something normally hidden will be revealed, and the "long ago" implies that we are going to learn about the most archaic events. The Brothers Grimm could not have begun their collection of fairy tales with a more telling sentence than the one that introduces their first story, "The Frog King": "In olden times when wishing still helped, there lived a king whose daughters were all beautiful, but the youngest was so beautiful that the sun itself, which has seen so much, was astonished whenever it shone in her face." This beginning very clearly locates the story in a unique fairy-tale time: the archaic period when we all believed that our wishes could, if not move mountains, change our fate, and when, in our animistic view of the world, the sun took notice of us and reacted to events. After the age of approximately five—the age when fairy tales really begin to have meaning—no normal child takes these stories as true to external reality. Much as the little girl wishes to imagine that she is a princess living in a castle and spins elaborate fantasies that she is, when her mother calls her to dinner she knows that she is not. And while a grove in a park may be experienced at times as a deep, dark forest full of hidden secrets, the little boy knows what it really is, just as the little girl knows that her doll is not really her baby, even though she calls it that and treats it as such.

There is a right time for certain growth experiences, and childhood is the time to learn how to bridge the immense gap between inner experiences and the real world. Fairy tales may seem senseless, fantastic, scary, and totally unbelievable to the adult who was deprived of fairy-tale fantasy in his own childhood or has repressed the memory of it. An adult who has not achieved a satisfactory integration of the two worlds of reality and imagination is put off by such tales. But an adult who in his own life is able to integrate rational order with the illogic of his unconscious will be responsive to the manner in which fairy tales help the child with this integration. To the child, and to the adult who, like Socrates, knows that there is still a child in the wisest of us, fairy tales reveal truths about mankind and about himself.

In "Little Red Riding Hood," the kindly grandmother undergoes a sudden replacement by the rapacious wolf, who threatens to destroy the child. How silly a transformation it is when it is viewed objectively, and how frightening! We might think that transformation unnecessarily scary, contrary to all possible reality. But when it is viewed from a child's way of experiencing, is it really any more scary than the sudden transformation that his own kindly grandma undergoes, into a figure who threatens his very sense of self, when she humiliates him for a pants-wetting accident? To the child, Grandma is no longer the same person she was just a moment ago; she has become an ogre. How can someone who was so very kind, who brought presents and was more understanding and tolerant and uncritical than even his own mother, suddenly act in such a radically different fashion? Unable to see any congruence between the different manifestations, the child truly experiences Grandma as two separate entities—the loving and the threatening. She is indeed Grandma *and* the wolf. By dividing her up, so to speak, the child can preserve his image of the good grandmother. If she changes into a wolf—well, that's certainly scary, but he need not compromise his vision of Grandma's benevolence. And, in any case, as the story tells him, the wolf is a passing manifestation; Grandma will return triumphant. Similarly, although Mother is most often the all giving protector, she can also change into the cruel stepmother if she is so evil as to deny the child something he wants.

Far from being a device used only by fairy tales, such a splitting up of one person into two to keep the good image uncontaminated occurs to many children as a solution to a relationship too difficult to manage or comprehend. While all young children sometimes need to split the image of a parent into its benevolent and threatening aspects in order to feel fully sheltered by the first, most children cannot do it consciously. Most cannot find their own solution to the impasse of Mother's suddenly changing into a look-alike impostor. Fairy tales, which contain good fairies suddenly appearing to help the child find happiness despite this "impostor" or "stepmother," permit the child not to be destroyed by the "impostor." Fairy tales indicate that somewhere hidden the good fairy godmother watches over the child's fate, ready to assert her power when it is critically needed. The fairy tale tells the child, "Although there are witches, don't ever forget that there are also the good fairies, who are much more powerful." The very name of the stories stresses this fact; they might have been called witches' tales. The same tales assure that the ferocious giant can always be outwitted by the clever little man—somebody seemingly as powerless as the child feels himself to be.

When the child experiences the emotional need to do so, he not only splits a parent into two figures but may also split himself into two people, who, he wishes to believe, have nothing in common. I have known a young child who was dry during the day but wet his bed at night and then, on waking up, would move with disgust to a corner and say with conviction, "Somebody has wet my bed." He did not do this, as his parents may have thought, to put the blame on somebody else, knowing that it was really he himself who had urinated in the bed. The "somebody" who did it was that part of himself with which he had parted company; this aspect of his personality had become a stranger to him. To insist that the child recognize that it was he who wet the bed would have been to make a premature attempt to impose on him the concept of the integrity of the human personality, and such insistence actually retards its development. In order to develop a secure feeling of his self, the child needs to constrict it for a time to only what he fully approves and desires. After he has thus achieved a self of which he can be unambivalently proud, he can slowly accept the possibility that it may also contain aspects of a more dubious nature.

The fairy-tale literature does not fail to consider the problematic nature of sometimes seeing Mother as an evil stepmother; in its own way the fairy tale warns against being swept away too far and too fast by angry feelings. A child easily gives in to his annoyance with a person dear to him, or to his impatience when he is kept waiting; he tends to harbor angry feelings, and to make furious wishes with little thought of the consequences if the wishes should come true. Many fairy tales depict the tragic outcome of such rash wishes, engaged in because one desires something too much or is unable to wait until things come about in their good time. Both mental states are typical of the child. Two stories of the Brothers Grimm may illustrate. In "Hans the Hedge-hog," a man becomes angry when his great desire for children of his own is frustrated by his wife's inability to have any. Finally, he gets carried away and exclaims, "I will have a child, even if it be a hedgehog!" His wish is granted: his wife gives birth to a child who is a hedgehog on top, while the lower part of his body is that of a boy. In "The Seven Ravens," a newborn daughter so preoccupies a father's emotions that he turns his anger against his older children—seven sons. The father sends one of the sons to fetch baptismal water for the christening of the infant daughter, and the son is joined on his errand by his six brothers. The father, angered at being kept waiting, shouts, "I wish the boys were all turned into ravens!"—which instantly happens.

If these fairy tales in which angry wishes come true ended there, they would be merely cautionary tales, warning us not to permit ourselves to be carried away by our negative emotions—something that the child is unable to avoid. But the fairy tale knows better than to expect the impossible of the child and to make him anxious about having angry wishes that he cannot help having. While the fairy tale realistically warns the child that being carried away by anger or impatience leads to trouble, it reassures him that the consequences are only temporary ones, and that good will or a good deed can undo the harm done by bad wishing. Hans the Hedge-hog helps a king lost in the forest to return home safely. The king promises beforehand to give Hans as a reward the first thing he encounters on his return home, which happens to be the king's only daughter. Despite Hans's appearance, the princess marries him. After the marriage, in the marital bed, Hans changes into completely human form, and he inherits the kingdom. In "The Seven Ravens," the sister who was the innocent cause of her brothers' being turned into ravens travels to the end of the world and makes a great sacrifice to undo the spell put on them. The ravens all regain their human form, and happiness is restored.

Before and well into the oedipal period (roughly, the ages between three and six or seven), the child's experience of the world is chaotic—but only as seen from an adult point of view, for chaos implies an awareness of this state of affairs. If this "chaotic" fashion of experiencing the world is all that one knows, then it is accepted as the way the world is. During and because of the oedipal struggles, the outside world comes to hold more meaning for the child, and he begins to try to make some sense of it. He no longer takes it for granted that the confused way in which he sees the world is the only possible one.

As a child listens to a fairy tale, he gets ideas about how he may create order out of the chaos that is his inner life. The fairy tale suggests isolating and separating the disparate and confusing aspects of the child's experience and projecting them onto different figures. Even Freud found no better way to help make sense out of the incredible mixture of contradictions that coexist in the human mind and inner life than by creating symbols for isolated aspects of the personality. He named these id, ego, and superego. If we, as adults, must have recourse to the creation of separate entities to bring some sensible order into the chaos of our inner experiences, how much greater is the child's need for this! Unfortunately, in using these symbols we have lost something that is inherent in the fairy tale: the realization that these externalizations are fictions, useful only for sorting out and comprehending mental processes.

When the hero of a fairy tale is the youngest child, or is specifically called "the dummy" or Simpleton at the start of the story, this is the fairy tale's rendering of the original debilitated state of the ego as it begins its struggle to cope with the inner world of drives and with the difficult problems that the outer world presents. Not unlike psychoanalysis, the fairy tale frequently depicts the id in the form of some animal, standing for our animal nature. Fairy-tale animals come in two forms: dangerous and destructive animals (the wolf in "Little Red Riding Hood") and wise and helpful animals, which guide and rescue the hero (the animals that revive the dead hero and gain him his just reward in "The Two Brothers"). Both the dangerous and the helpful animals stand for our animal nature, our instinctual drives. The dangerous ones symbolize the untamed id in all its dangerous energy, not yet subjected to ego and superego control. The helpful animals also represent our id, but now made to serve the best interests of the total personality. There are also some animals—usually white birds, like doves—that symbolize the superego.

No single fairy tale does justice to the richness of all the images that give external body to the most complex inner processes, but a little-known story called "The Queen Bee," reported by the Brothers Grimm, may illustrate the symbolic struggle of personality integration against chaotic disintegration. (A bee is a particularly apt image for the two opposite aspects of our nature, since the child knows that the bee produces honey but can also sting painfully. He knows, too, that the bee works hard, collecting the nectar out of which it produces the honey.) In "The Queen Bee," the two older sons of a king go out to seek adventure, and live such wild, dissolute lives that they never return home. In short, they live an id-dominated existence, without any regard for the requirements of reality or the justified demands and criticisms of the superego. The youngest son, called Simpleton, sets out to find them, and, through persistence, succeeds. But they mock him for thinking that he, in his simplicity, could get through life better than they, who are supposedly so much more clever. On the surface, the two brothers are right; as the story unfolds, Simpleton would be just as incapable as they are of mastering life, represented by difficult tasks that all three are asked to perform, if he were not able to call for help on his inner resources, represented by the helpful animals.

As the three brothers travel through the world, they come to an anthill. The two older brothers want to destroy it, just to enjoy the ants' terror. Simpleton does not permit this. He says, "Leave the creatures in peace. I will not allow you to disturb them." Next, they come to a lake where ducks are swimming. The older brothers, considering nothing but their pleasure and oral cravings, want to catch some ducks and roast them. Simpleton prevents this, too. They proceed, and come

to a bees' nest; the two brothers now want to make a fire beneath the tree holding the nest, to suffocate the bees and get at the honey. Simpleton again interferes, insisting that the creatures must be neither killed nor disturbed. The three brothers finally arrive at a castle, where everything has been turned to stone or is in a deathlike sleep, with the exception of a little gray man who lets them in, feeds them, and beds them down for the night. The next morning, the little man presents the oldest brother with three tasks, each of which must be accomplished within a day, to undo the spell over the castle and its inhabitants. The first task is to gather a thousand pearls that are spread and hidden in the moss of the forest. But, the brother is warned, if he fails in this task he will be turned to stone. He tries and fails, and the same thing happens to the second brother. When Simpleton's turn comes, he finds that he is also not up to the task. Feeling defeated, he sits down and cries. At this point, the five thousand ants that he saved come to his help, and gather the pearls for him. The second task is to fetch from the depths of a lake the key to the king's daughter's bedchamber. This time, the ducks that Simpleton protected come, dive into the lake, and give him the key. The final task is to select from among three sleeping princesses who look exactly alike the youngest and most lovable. The queen of the beehive that Simpleton saved now comes to his help; she settles on the lips of the princess whom Simpleton must choose. With the three tasks fulfilled, the spell is broken and the enchantment is at its end. All who were asleep or were turned to stone—including Simpleton's two brothers—come to life. Simpleton marries the youngest princess and eventually inherits the kingdom.

The two brothers who were unresponsive to the requirements of personality integration failed to meet the demands of reality. Insensitive to everything but the proddings of the id, they were turned into stone. As in many other fairy tales, this state symbolizes not death but a lack of true humanity, an inability to respond to higher values; the person who suffers this lack, being dead to what life is all about in the best sense, might as well be made of stone. Simpleton (standing for the ego), despite his obvious virtues, and despite his obedience to the commands of his superego, which tells him that it is wrong to disturb or kill wantonly, is by himself unequal to the demands of reality (symbolized by the three tasks to be performed), just as his brothers were.

Only when animal nature has been befriended and recognized as important—brought into accord with ego and superego—do we have the power of an integrated personality. Thereafter, our accomplishments seem like miracles. Far from suggesting that we subjugate our animal nature to our ego or superego, the fairy tale shows that each element must be given its due; if Simpleton had not followed his inner goodness (read superego) and protected the animals, these id representations would never have come to his aid. The three animals, incidentally, represent different elements: the ants stand for earth, the ducks for the water in which they swim, and the bees for the air in which they fly. Again, only the coöperation of all three different elements, or aspects of our nature, permits true success. Not until Simpleton has achieved his full integration, symbolically expressed by his having mastered the three tasks, does he become master of his fate, which in fairy-tale fashion is expressed by his becoming king.

The fairy-tale motif of the child abused and rejected by older siblings is well known all through history, especially in the form of "Cinderella." But the stories centering on a stupid child, of which "The Three Languages" and "The Three Feathers" are examples, tell a different tale. The unhappiness of the "dumb" child, whom the rest of the family holds in such low esteem, is not mentioned. His being considered stupid is stated as a fact of life, and one that does not seem to concern him much. Sometimes one gets the feeling that the "simpleton" does not mind this condition, because as a result of it others expect nothing of him. Such stories begin to unfold when the simpleton's uneventful life is interrupted by some demand.

A small child, bright though he may be, feels himself stupid and inadequate when he is confronted with the complexity of the world that surrounds him. Everybody else seems to know so much more than he, and to be so much more capable. In the same way, many fairy tales begin with the hero's being depreciated and considered stupid. These are the child's feelings about himself, which are projected not so much onto the world at large as onto his parents and older

brothers and sisters. Even when in some fairy stories, like "Cinderella," we are told that the child lived in bliss before the advent of misfortune, the happy time is not described as one during which the child was competent. The child was so happy because nothing was expected of him; everything was provided for him. A young child's inadequacy, which makes him fear that he is stupid, is not his fault, and so the fairy tale that never explains why the child is considered stupid is psychologically sound.

As far as a child's consciousness is concerned, nothing happened during his first years, because in the normal course of events the child remembers no inner conflicts before parents began making specific demands that ran counter to his desires. It is in part because of these demands that the child experiences conflicts with the world, and internalization of these demands contributes to the establishment of the superego and the awareness of inner conflicts. Hence, these few first years are remembered as conflict-free and blissful, but empty. This situation is represented in the fairy tale by an absence of events in the child's life before he awakens to the conflicts between him and his parents and, with those, to the conflicts within himself. Being "dumb" suggests an undifferentiated stage of existence, which precedes the struggles between the id, the ego, and the superego of the complex personality.

On the simplest and most direct level, fairy tales in which the hero is the youngest and most inept offer the child consolation and hope for the future. Though the child thinks little of himself—a view he projects onto others' views of him—and fears he will never amount to anything, the story shows that he has already started on the process of realizing his potential. As the son learns the language of dogs and later those of birds and frogs in "The Three Languages," the father sees in this only a clear indication of the boy's stupidity, while the boy has actually taken very important steps toward selfhood. The outcome of these stories tells the child that he who regarded himself, or was viewed by others, as the least able nonetheless surpasses all.

Such a message can best carry conviction through repeated telling of the story. Upon first being told a story with a "dumb" hero, a child may not be able to identify with him, stupid though the child feels himself to be. That would be too threatening, too contrary to his self-love. Only when the child feels completely assured of the hero's superiority, through repeated hearings, can he afford to identify with the hero from the beginning. And only on the basis of such identification can the story encourage the child to believe that his depreciated view of himself is erroneous. Before such identification occurs, the story means little to the child as a person. But as the child comes to identify with the stupid or degraded hero of the fairy tale, who he knows will eventually show his superiority, the child himself is started on the process of realizing his potential.

Hans Christian Andersen's "The Ugly Duckling" is the story of a bird that is thought little of as a fledgling but in the end proves its superiority to all those who had scoffed at it and mocked it. This story, too, contains the element of the hero's being the youngest and the last born, since all the other ducklings pecked their way out of their eggs and into the world sooner. As is true of most Andersen stories, this one, charming as it is, is much more a story for adults. Though children enjoy it, too, it is not helpful to them, because it misdirects their fantasy. The child who feels misunderstood and unappreciated may wish to be of a different breed, but he knows he is not. His chance for success in life is *not* to grow into a creature of a different nature, as the duckling grows into a swan, but, while being of the same nature as his parents and brothers and sisters, to acquire better qualities and to do better than others expect. In folk fairy tales, we find that no matter how many transformations the hero undergoes, including being turned into an animal, or even to stone, in the end he is always a human being, as he started out. To encourage a child to believe that he is of a different breed, much as he may like the thought, can lead him in the opposite direction from the one that folk fairy tales point to: that he must do something to achieve his superiority. No need to accomplish something is expressed in "The Ugly Duckling;" things are simply fated and unfold accordingly, whether or not the hero takes any action. In the folk fairy tale, it is the hero's doing that changes his life. That one's fate is inexorable—a depressive world view—is as clear in "The Ugly Duckling," with its favorable outcome, as it is in the sad ending of Andersen's "The Little Match Girl," a story that is deeply moving but hardly suitable for identification. The child, in his misery, may indeed identify with this heroine, but if he does, the identification leads only to utter pessimism and defeatism. "The Little Match Girl" is a moralistic tale about the cruelty of the world; it arouses compassion for the downtrodden. But what the child who feels downtrodden needs is not compassion for others who are in the same predicament but the conviction that he can escape this fate.

The first steps toward achieving a well-integrated personality are made as the child begins to struggle with his deep and ambivalent attachments to his parents—that is, during his oedipal conflicts. In regard to these, too, fairy tales help the child to comprehend the nature of his difficulties and offer him hope for their successful resolution. In the throes of oedipal conflict, a young boy resents his father for standing in the way of his receiving Mother's exclusive attention. The boy wants Mother to admire *him* as the greatest hero of all; that means that somehow he has to get Father out of the way. This idea creates anxiety in the child, though, because without Father to protect them, what will happen to the family? And what if Father were to find out that the little boy wanted him out of the way? Might he not take a most terrible revenge?

One can tell a small boy many times—without avail—that someday he will grow up, marry, and be like his father. Such realistic advice provides no relief from the pressures that the child feels right now. But the fairy tale tells the child how he can live with his conflicts: it suggests fantasies he could never invent for himself. For example, the fairy tale offers the story of the little unnoticed boy who goes out into the world and makes a great success of life. Details may differ, but the basic plot is always the same: the unlikely hero proves himself through slaying dragons, solving riddles, and living by his wits and his goodness until eventually he frees the beautiful princess, marries her, and lives happily ever after. No little boy has ever failed to see himself in this starring role. The story implies: It's not Father whose jealousy prevents you from having Mother all to yourself; it's an evil dragon. What you really have in mind is to slay an evil dragon. Further, the story gives veracity to the boy's feeling that the most desirable female is kept in captivity by an evil figure, while implying that it is not Mother whom the child wants for himself but a marvellous and wonderful woman he hasn't met yet but certainly will meet. The story tells more of what the boy wants to hear and believe: that it is not of her own free will that this wonderful female (Mother) abides with this bad male figure. On the contrary, if she just could, she would much prefer to be with a young hero (the child). The dragon slayer always has to be young, like the child, and innocent. The innocence of the hero with whom the child identifies proves by proxy the child's innocence; thus, far from having to feel guilty about these fantasies, the child can feel himself to be the hero.

The oedipal problems of a girl are different from those of a boy, and so the fairy tales that help her to cope with her oedipal situation are of a different character. What blocks the oedipal girl's uninterrupted blissful existence with Father is an older, ill-intentioned female (Mother). But since the little girl wants very much to continue enjoying Mother's loving care, there is also a benevolent female in the past or in the background of the fairy tale the happy memory of whom is kept intact, although she has become inoperative. A little girl wishes to see herself as a young and beautiful maiden—a princess or the like—who is kept captive, and hence unavailable to the male lover, by the selfish, evil female figure. The captive princess's real father is depicted as benevolent but helpless to come to the rescue of his lovely girl. In "Rapunzel," it is a vow that stymies him. In "Cinderella" and "Snow White," he seems unable to hold his own against the all-powerful stepmother. The mother is split into two figures: the pre-oedipal wonderful, good mother, and the oedipal evil stepmother. (Sometimes there are bad stepmothers in fairy tales about boys, but such tales deal with problems other than oedipal ones.) The good mother, so the fantasy goes, would never have been jealous of her daughter or have prevented the prince (Father) and the girl from living happily together. So for the oedipal girl belief and trust in the goodness of the pre-oedipal mother, and deep loyalty to her, tend to reduce the guilt about what the girl wishes would happen to the (step)-mother who stands in her way.

Thus, thanks to the fairy tale, both oedipal girls and boys can have the best of two worlds: they can fully enjoy oedipal satisfactions in fantasy and can keep good relations with both parents in reality. For the oedipal boy, if Mother disappoints him there is the fairy princess in the back of his mind—that wonderful woman of the future who will compensate for all his present hardships, and so makes it much easier to bear

up under them. If Father is less attentive to his little girl than she desires, she can endure such adversity, because a prince will arrive who will prefer her to all competitors. Since everything takes place in never-never land, the child need not feel guilty or anxious about casting Father in the role of the dragon or evil giant, or Mother in the role of a miserable stepmother or witch.

If one would believe in a grand design to human life, one could admire the wisdom with which it is arranged that a wide variety of psychological events coincide to reinforce each other and propel the young human being out of infancy into childhood. Because of the child's growing ability to cope, he can have more contact with people outside the family, and with wider aspects of the world. Also, because the child is able to do more, his parents feel that the time has come to expect more of him, and they become less ready to do for him. This change in their relations is an enormous disappointment of the child's hope that he will always receive endlessly; it is the most severe disillusionment of his young life, made infinitely worse because it is inflicted by those who he believes owe him unlimited care. Because of his new experiences with the outside world, however, the child can afford to become aware of the "limitations" of his parents—that is, their shortcomings as seen in the light of his unrealistic expectations of them. In consequence, the child grows so disgusted with his parents that he ventures to seek satisfaction elsewhere. When this comes about, so overwhelming are the new challenges presented to the child by his enlarging experiences, and so very small is his ability to meet them, that he needs fantasy satisfactions in order not to give up in despair. Considerable as the child's real achievements are, they all seem to vanish into insignificance whenever he fails in any respect—if only because he has no comprehension of what is actually possible. This disillusionment may lead to such severe disappointment in himself that he gives up all effort and withdraws into himself completely, unless fantasy comes to his rescue. If any one of the various steps the child is taking in growing up could be viewed in isolation, it might be said that the ability to spin fantasies beyond the present is the new achievement that makes all others possible—because it makes bearable the frustrations experienced in reality.

If only we could recall how we felt when we were small, or could imagine how utterly defeated a young child feels when his playmates or older brothers and sisters temporarily reject him or when adults—worst of all, his parents—seem to make fun of him or belittle him, then we would know why the child often feels like an outcast, a "simpleton." How enormous the frustration and despair of the child are at moments of unrelieved defeat can be seen from his temper tantrums, which are the visible expression of the conviction that he can do nothing to improve the "unbearable" conditions of his life. As soon as a child is able to imagine (that is, to fantasize) a favorable solution to his present predicament, temper tantrums disappear; the hope for the future makes the present difficulty no longer insufferable. Random physical discharge through kicking and screaming is then replaced by thought or activity designed to reach a desired goal, either now or at some future date.

If a child is for some reason unable to imagine his future optimistically, arrest of development sets in. The extreme example of this can be found in the behavior of the child suffering from infantile autism. He does nothing or he intermittently breaks out into severe temper tantrums, but in either case he insists that nothing must be altered in his environment and the conditions of his life. All this is the consequence of his complete inability to imagine any change for the better. When one such child, after prolonged therapy, finally emerged from her total autistic withdrawal and reflected on what characterizes good parents, she said, "They hope for you." The implication was that her parents had been bad parents, because they had failed both to feel hope for her and to give her hope for herself and her future.

We know that the more deeply unhappy and despairing we are, the more we need to be able to engage in optimistic fantasies. But these are not available to us at such periods. Then, more than at any other time, we need others to uplift us with their hope for us and our future. No fairy tale all by itself will do this for the child; as the autistic girl reminded us, first we need our parents to instill hope in us. Once we have this—are aware of the positive ways in which our parents view us and our future—we can go ahead and build castles in the air, half recognizing that they are just that but gaining deep reassurance from them nonetheless. While the fantasy is unreal, the good feelings it gives us about ourselves and our future are real, and these good real feelings are what we need to sustain us. Every parent responsive to his child's feeling down and out tells the child that things will take a turn for the better. But the child's despair is all-encompassing (he feels either in darkest Hell or gloriously happy, because he does not know gradations) and therefore nothing but perfect and everlasting bliss can at that moment combat his fear of total devastation. No reasonable parent can promise his child that perfect bliss is available to him. But by telling his child fairy tales the parent can encourage him to borrow for his private use fantastic hopes for the future, while not misleading him by suggesting that there is reality in such imaginings.

Feeling acutely the disappointments that come with being dominated by adults while also being dispossessed of the small child's kingdom, where no demands were made on him and it seemed that all his wishes were satisfied by his parents, every child is bound to wish for a new kingdom, of the sort promised by fairy tales. What is this kingdom that many fairy-tale heroes gain at the story's end? Its main characteristic is that we are never told anything about it—not even what the king or queen does. There is no purpose in being king or queen of this kingdom other than being a ruler instead of being ruled. To have become king or queen at the conclusion of the story symbolizes a state of true independence, in which the hero feels as secure, satisfied, and happy as the infant felt in his most dependent state, when he was well taken care of in the kingdom of his cradle. The hero has become an autocrat in the best sense of the word: a self-ruler, a truly autonomous person—not a person who rules over others. The child understands this very well. No child believes that one day he will become a ruler over any kingdom other than the realm of his own life. The fairy tale assures him that this kingdom can be his someday, but not without struggle. How the child specifically imagines the "kingdom" depends on his age and state of development, but he never takes it literally. To the younger child, it may simply mean that nobody will order him around and that all his wishes will be fulfilled. For the older child, it will also include the obligation to rule—that is, to live and act wisely. But at any age a child interprets becoming king or queen as having gained maturity.

Many fairy tales center on solving a riddle, which leads to marriage and the gaining of the kingdom. For example, in the Brothers Grimm's story "The Cunning Little Tailor" only the hero is able to guess correctly the two colors of the princess's hair, and he wins the princess. Similarly, the story of Princess Turandot tells that she can be won only by the man who gives the correct answers to her three riddles. Solving the riddle posed by a particular woman stands for solving the riddle of woman in general, and since marriage usually follows the right solution, it does not seem far-fetched to conclude that the riddle to be solved is a sexual one: whoever understands the secret that the other sex presents has gained his maturity. In the myth of Oedipus, the figure who correctly answers the riddle destroys himself and marital tragedy follows, but in fairy tales the discovery of the secret leads to the happiness of both the person who solved the riddle and the one who posed it. Oedipus marries a woman who is his mother, so obviously she is much older than he. The fairy-tale hero, whether male or female, marries a partner of about the same age. That is, whatever oedipal attachment the fairy-tale hero may have had to his parent he has successfully transferred to a suitable non-oedipal partner. Again and again in fairy tales, an unsatisfactory relation to a parent, like Cinderella's link to a weak and ineffective father, is replaced by a happy relation to the rescuing marital partner.

The parent in such fairy tales, far from resenting the child's transcending his oedipal attachment, is delighted that he does, and is often instrumental in arranging it. For example, in "Hans the Hedgehog" and in "Beauty and the Beast," the father (willingly or unwillingly) causes his daughter to marry; relinquishing his oedipal attachment to his daughter, and inducing her to give up hers to him, leads to a happy solution for both. Never in a fairy tale does a son take his father's kingdom away from him. If a father gives it up, it is always because of old age. Even then, the son has to earn it, by finding the most desirable wife for himself, as in "The Three Feathers." This story makes it quite clear that gaining the kingdom is tantamount to having reached moral and sexual maturity. The hero is given a task that he must fulfill in order to inherit the kingdom. When he succeeds, this turns out not to be sufficient. The same thing happens the second time round. And then there is a third task: to find and bring home the right bride. When the hero manages to do this, the kingdom is finally his. Thus, far from showing the son as being jealous of his father, or the father as resenting his son's sexual endeavors, the fairy tale shows the opposite: when the child has reached the right age and degree of maturity, the parent wants him to come into his own sexu-

ally; in fact, the parent will accept the son as a worthy successor only after he has done so. Gaining his kingdom through being united in love and marriage with the most appropriate and desirable partner—a union that the parents thoroughly approve and that leads to the happiness of everybody but the villains—symbolizes the perfect resolution of oedipal difficulties as well as the gaining of true independence and complete personality integration. Is it so unrealistic to speak of this high achievement as coming into one's own kingdom?

Fairy tales underwent severe criticism when the new discoveries of psychoanalysis and child psychology revealed just how violent, anxious, destructive, and even sadistic a child's imagination is. For example, a young child not only loves his parents with an incredible intensity but at times also hates them. With this knowledge, it should have been easy to recognize that fairy tales speak to the inner mental life of the child. Instead, doubters claimed that these stories created, or at least greatly encouraged these upsetting feelings. Those who outlawed traditional folk fairy tales decided that if there was a monster in a story told to children, it must be a friendly one. They missed the monster a child knows best and is most concerned with: the monster he feels or fears himself to be, which also sometimes persecutes him. When this monster within the child remains unspoken of, and hidden in his unconscious, the child is prevented from spinning fantasies around it in the image of the fairy tales he knows. Without such fantasies, the child fails to get to know his monster better, and is given no suggestions as to how he may gain mastery over it. As a result, the child remains helpless with his worst anxieties—much more so than if he had been told fairy tales, which give these anxieties form and body and then show ways to overcome them. If our fear of being devoured takes the tangible form of a witch, it can be got rid of—by burning her in the oven! But these considerations did not occur to those who outlawed fairy tales.

It was a strangely one-sided picture of adults and life which many children were expected to accept as the only correct one. Starving the imagination of the child was expected to extinguish the giants and ogres of the fairy tale—that is, the dark monsters residing in the unconscious—so that they would not obstruct the development of the child's rational mind. The rational ego was expected to reign supreme from babyhood on. This was not to be achieved by the ego's conquering the dark forces of the id but by adults' preventing the child from paying attention to his unconscious or hearing stories that would speak to it. In short, the child would supposedly repress his unpleasant fantasies and have only pleasant ones.

The rationalizations for continuing to forbid fairy tales, despite what psychoanalysis revealed about the unconscious—particularly that of children—took many forms. When it could no longer be denied that the child is beset by deep conflicts, anxieties, and violent desires and helplessly tossed about by all kinds of irrational processes, it was concluded that because the child is already afraid of so many things anything else that looks fearful should be kept from him. A particular story may indeed make some children anxious, but once they become better acquainted with fairy tales, the fearful aspects seem to disappear and the reassuring features become ever more dominant. The original displeasure of anxiety then turns into the great pleasure of anxiety successfully faced and mastered. Parents who wish to deny that their child has murderous wishes and wants to tear things, and even people, to pieces believe that their child must be prevented from engaging in such thoughts (as if this were possible). Denied access to stories implying that others have the same fantasies, the child is left to feel that he is the only one who imagines such things. This makes his fantasies really scary. On the other hand, learning that others have the same or similar fantasies makes us feel that we are a part of humanity, and allays our fear that having such destructive ideas has put us outside the common pale.

The shortcomings of the realistic stories with which many parents have replaced fairy tales is suggested by a comparison of two such stories—"The Little Engine That Could" and "The Swiss Family Robinson"—with the fairy tale of "Rapunzel." "The Little Engine That Could" encourages the child to believe that if he tries hard and does not give up, he will finally succeed. A young adult has recalled how much impressed she was at the age of seven when her mother read her this story. She became convinced that one's attitude indeed af-

fects one's achievements—that if she would now approach a task with the conviction that she could conquer it, she would succeed. A few days later, this child encountered in first grade a challenging situation: she was trying to make a house out of paper, gluing various sheets together. But her house continually collapsed. Frustrated, she began to seriously doubt whether her idea of building such a paper house could be realized. But then the story of "The Little Engine That Could" came to her mind; twenty years later, she recalled how at that moment she began to sing to herself the magic formula "I think I can, I think I can, I think I can . . ." So she continued to work on her paper house, and it continued to collapse. The project ended in complete defeat, with this little girl convinced that she had failed where anybody else could have succeeded, as the Little Engine had. Since "The Little Engine That Could" was a story set in the present, using such common props as engines that pulled trains, this girl had tried to apply its lesson directly in her daily life, without any fantasy elaboration, and had experienced a defeat that still rankled twenty years later.

Very different was the impact of "The Swiss Family Robinson" on another little girl. The story tells how a shipwrecked family manages to live an adventurous, idyllic, and constructive, and pleasurable life—a life very different from this child's own existence. Her father had to be away from home a great deal, and her mother was mentally ill and spent protracted periods in institutions. So the girl was shuttled from her home to that of an aunt, then to that of a grandmother, and back home again, as the need arose. During these years, the girl read over and over again the story of this happy family who lived on a desert island, where no member could be away from the rest of the family. Many years later, she recalled what a warm, cozy feeling she had when, propped up by a few large pillows, she forgot all about her present predicament as she read this story. As soon as she had finished it, she started to read it over again. The happy hours she spent with the Family Robinson in that fantasy land permitted her not to be defeated by the difficulties that reality presented to her. She was able to counteract the impact of harsh reality by imaginary gratifications. But since the story was not a fairy tale, it merely gave her a temporary escape from her problems; it did not hold out any promise to her that her life would take a turn for the better.

Consider the effect that "Rapunzel" had on a third

girl. This girl's mother had died in a car accident. The girl's father, deeply upset by what had happened to his wife (he had been driving the car), withdrew entirely into himself and handed the care of his daughter over to a nursemaid, who was little interested in the girl and gave her complete freedom to do as she liked. When the girl was seven, her father remarried, and, as she recalled it, it was around that time that "Rapunzel" became so important to her. Her stepmother was clearly the witch of the story, and she was the girl locked away in the tower. The girl recalled that she felt akin to Rapunzel because the witch had "forcibly" taken possession of her, as her stepmother had forcibly worked her way into the girl's life. The girl felt imprisoned in her new home, in contrast to her life of freedom with the nursemaid. She felt as victimized as Rapunzel, who, in her tower, had so little control over her life. Rapunzel's long hair was the key to the story. The girl wanted her hair to grow long, but her stepmother cut it short; long hair in itself became the symbol of freedom and happiness to her. The story convinced her that a prince (her father) would come someday and rescue her, and this conviction sustained her. If life became too difficult, all she needed was to imagine herself as Rapunzel, her hair grown long, and the prince loving and rescuing her.

"Rapunzel" suggests why fairy tales can offer more to the child than even such a very nice children's story as "The Swiss Family Robinson." In "The Swiss Family Robinson," there is no witch against whom the child can discharge her anger in fantasy and on whom she can blame the father's lack of interest. "The Swiss Family Robinson" offers escape fantasies, and it did help the girl who read it over and over to forget temporarily how difficult life was for her. But it offered no specific hope for the future. "Rapunzel," on the other hand, offered the girl a chance to see the witch of the story as so evil that by comparison even the "witch" stepmother at home was not really so bad. "Rapunzel" also promised the girl that her rescue would be effected by her own body, when her hair grew long. Most important of all, it promised that the "prince" was only temporarily blinded—that he would regain his sight and rescue his princess. This fantasy continued to sustain the girl, though to a less intense degree, until she fell in love and married, and then she no longer needed it. We can understand why at first glance the stepmother, if she had known the meaning of "Rapunzel" to her stepdaughter, would have felt that fairy tales are bad for children. What she would not have known was that unless the stepdaughter had been able to find that fantasy satisfaction through "Rapunzel," she would have tried to break up her father's marriage, and that without the hope for the future which the story gave her she might have gone badly astray in life.

It seems quite understandable that when children are asked to name their favorite fairy tales, hardly any modern tales are among their choices. Many of the new tales have sad endings, which fail to provide the escape and consolation that the fearsome events in the fairy tale require if the child is to be strengthened for meeting the vagaries of his life. Without such encouraging conclusions, the child, after listening to the story, feels that there is indeed no hope for extricating himself from his despairs. In the traditional fairy tale, the hero is rewarded and the evil person meets his well deserved fate, thus satisfying the child's deep need for justice to prevail. How else can a child hope that justice will be done to him, who so often feels unfairly treated? And how else can he convince himself that he must act correctly, when he is so sorely tempted to give in to the asocial proddings of his desires? Chesterton once remarked that some children with whom he saw Maeterlinck's play "The Blue Bird" were dissatisfied, "because it did not end with a Day of Judgment, and it was not revealed to the hero and the heroine that the Dog had been faithful and the Cat faithless." He added, "For children are innocent and love justice, while most of us are wicked and naturally prefer mercy."

One may rightly question Chesterton's belief in the innocence of children, but he is absolutely correct in observing that the appreciation of mercy for the unjust, while characteristic of a mature mind, baffles the child. It seems particularly appropriate to a child that exactly what the evildoer wishes to inflict on the hero should be the bad person's fate—as in the case of the witch in "Hansel and Gretel," who wants to cook children in the oven and is pushed into it and burned to death, or of the usurper in "The Goose Girl," who names her own punishment and suffers it. Consolation requires that the right order of the world be restored, and this means punishment of the evildoer.

Prettified or bowdlerized fairy tales are rightly rejected by any child who has heard them in their original form. It does not seem fitting to the child that Cinderella's evil stepsisters should go scot-free, or actually be elevated by Cinderella. Such magnanimity does not impress the child favorably, nor will he learn it from a parent who bowdlerizes the story so that the just and the wicked are both rewarded. The child knows better what he needs to be told. When a seven-year-old was read the story of Snow White, an adult, anxious not to disturb the child's mind, ended the story with Snow White's wedding. The child, who knew the story, immediately demanded, "What about the red-hot shoes that killed the wicked queen?" The child feels that all's well with the world, and he can be secure in it, only if the wicked are punished in the end.

Perhaps the greatest consolation offered to the child by fairy tales, however, is not the promise that justice will be done but the promise that he will never be deserted. There is no greater threat in life than that we will he left all alone. Psychoanalysis has given this—man's greatest fear—the name separation anxiety; and the younger we are, the more excruciating is our anxiety when we feel deserted, for the young child actually perishes when he is not adequately protected and taken care of. There is a cycle of Turkish fairy tales in which the heroes again and again find themselves in the most impossible situations but succeed in evading or overcoming the danger as soon as they have gained a friend. For example, in one famous tale, the hero, Iskender, arouses the enmity of his mother, who forces his father to put Iskender into a casket and set him adrift on the ocean. Iskender's helper is a green bird, which rescues him from this danger, and later from innumerable others, each more threatening than the preceding one. The bird reassures Iskender each time with the words "Know that you are never deserted." This, then, is the ultimate consolation—the one that is implied in the common fairy-tale ending "And they lived happily ever after."

For a fairy tale to attain to the full its consoling propensities, all its symbolic meanings, and, most of all, its interpersonal meanings, it should be told rather than read. If it is read, it ought to be read with emotional involvement in the story, with emotional concern for the child, with empathy for what the story may mean to him. Telling is preferable to reading because it permits greater flexibility. The folk fairy tale, as distinct from more recently invented fairy tales, is the result of a story's being shaped and reshaped through being told millions of times, by different adults, to all kinds of other adults and to all kinds of children. As each narrator told the story, he dropped and added elements to give it more meaning for himself and for the listeners, whom he knew well. When the adult was talking to a child, he responded to what he surmised from the child's reactions. Thus, the narrator let his unconscious understanding of what the story told be influenced by the child's own understanding of it. Successive narrators adapted the story according to the questions that children asked, the delight and fear they either expressed openly or indicated by the way they snuggled up against the adults. Slavishly sticking to the way a fairy story is printed robs it of much of its value. The telling of the story to the child, to be most effective, has to be an interpersonal event, shaped by those who participate in it.

There is no getting around the possibility that this approach contains some pitfalls. A parent who is not attuned to his child or is too beholden to what goes on in his own unconscious may choose to tell fairy tales on the basis of *his* needs rather than those of the child. But even if he does, all is not lost. The child will better understand what moves his parent, and such understanding is of great interest and value to him in comprehending the motives of those most important in his life. Fortunately, children not only know how to deal with such parental distortions of fairy tales but also have their own ways of dealing with story elements that run counter to their emotional needs. They do this by changing the story around and remembering it differently from its original version, or by adding details to it. The fantastic ways in which the stories unfold encourage spontaneous changes; stories that deny the irrational in us do not so easily permit such variations. It is fascinating to view the changes that even the most widely known stories undergo in the minds of children. One boy reversed the story of Hansel and Gretel, so that it was Gretel who was put in the cage and Hansel who pushed the witch into the oven, thereby freeing Gretel. To add some female distortions of fairy tales which made them conform to individual needs: a girl remembered "Hansel and Gretel" with the change that it was the father who insisted that the children had to be cast out, despite his wife's entreaties not to do it, and that the father did his evil deed behind his wife's back. A young woman remembered "Hansel and Gretel" mainly as a story depicting Gretel's dependency on her older brother, and objected to its "male chauvinistic" character. As far as her recollection of the story went—and she claimed to remember it vividly—it was Hansel who managed to escape by his own wits, and who pushed the witch into the oven and thus rescued Gretel. On rereading the story, she was much surprised by the way her memory had distorted it; she realized that all through her childhood she had relished her dependency on a somewhat older brother, and, as she put it, "I have been unwilling to accept my own strength and the responsibilities that go along with that awareness." Then, in her early adolescence, something happened that strongly reinforced this distortion. While her brother was abroad, her mother had died and she had had to make the arrangements for the cremation. Therefore, even on rereading the fairy tale as an adult she felt revulsion at the idea that it was Gretel who was responsible for the witch's being burned to death; it reminded her too painfully of the cremation of her mother. Unconsciously, she had understood the story well—especially the degree to which the witch represented the bad mother about whom we all harbor negative feelings.

Goethe wrote that he gained from his mother his pleasure in spinning fantasies, and with it his cheerful outlook on life. It all had begun in his childhood with his mother's telling him fairy tales. And his mother recounted in her old age, "Air, fire, water, and earth I presented to him as beautiful princesses, and everything in all nature took on a deeper meaning. We invented roads between stars, and what great minds we would encounter. . . . He devoured me with his eyes; and if the fate of one of his favorites did not go as he wished, this I could see from the anger in his face, or his efforts not to break out in tears. Occasionally he interfered by saying, 'Mother, the princess will *not* marry the miserable tailor, even if he slays the giant,' at which I stopped and postponed the catastrophe until the next evening. So my imagination was often re-

placed by his; and when the following morning I arranged fate according to his suggestions and said, 'You guessed it, that's how it came out,' he was all excited, and one could see his heart beating." Not every parent can invent stories as well as Goethe's mother, who during her lifetime was known as a great teller of fairy tales. She told the stories in line with her listeners' inner feelings of how things should proceed in the tale, and this was considered the right way. Unfortunately, many modern parents have never known how it felt to be told fairy tales. Having been deprived as children of realizing how enjoyable fairy tales are, and how much they enrich the inner life of the child, even the best of parents cannot be spontaneous in providing his child with such experiences. In such cases, an intellectual understanding of how significant a fairy tale can be for a child, and why, must replace direct empathy based on recollections of one's own childhood.

When we speak of an intellectual understanding of the meaning of a fairy tale, it should be emphasized that it will not do to approach the telling of fairy tales with didactic intentions. When I say that a fairy tale helps the child to understand himself, guides him to find solutions to the problems that beset him, and so on, I always mean it metaphorically. The purpose in telling a fairy tale ought to be that of Goethe's mother—a shared experience of enjoying the story, even though what makes for this enjoyment may be quite different for child and adult. While the child enjoys the fantasy, the adult may well derive his pleasure from the child's enjoyment; while the child may be elated because he now understands something about himself better, the adult's delight in telling the story may derive from the child's experiencing a sudden shock of recognition. Telling a fairy tale with a purpose other than that of enriching the child's experience turns it into a cautionary tale, a fable, or some other didactic experience. One must never "explain" to the child the meanings of fairy tales. If the parent tells his child fairy tales in the right spirit—that is, with a feeling for the meaning that the story had for him when he was a child, and for its different present meaning to him, and with sensitivity to the reasons why his child may derive some personal meaning from hearing the tale—then the child feels understood in his most tender longings, his most ardent wishes, his most severe anxieties and feelings of misery. The child feels that he is not alone in his fantasy life—that it is shared by the person he needs and loves most. Under such favorable conditions, fairy tales communicate to the child an intuitive, subconscious understanding of his own nature and of what his future may hold if he develops his potential. He senses that to be a human being means having to accept difficult challenges, but also means encountering the most wondrous adventures.

Maria Tatar (b. 1945)

Maria Tatar has translated and edited collections of classic fairy tales, in addition to writing books of criticism with titles such as *Off with Their Heads! Fairy Tales and the Culture of Childhood* (1992) and *The Hard Facts of the Grimms' Fairy Tales* (1987, revised in 2004). Tatar is Dean for the Humanities at Harvard and a professor of Germanic languages and literatures. This 1992 essay (revised in 2005) summarizes the history of fairy tales as stories for both adults and children, the relationship between oral and written versions of folktales, and the multitude of critical approaches that have developed since the nineteenth century. While providing a critique of some of the conflicting interpretations proposed by both historians and psychoanalytical critics, such as Bruno Bettelheim, Tatar acknowledges that the tales have multiple meanings and allow for an endless variety of interpretations. She is most interested in the ways in which they reflect the values of their place and time, exploring the ironies of how they are used to socialize children even though they contain brutal violence; harsh punishment; and many weak, greedy, or underhanded characters who are not exactly positive role models.

Reading Fairy Tales

Those who write about fairy tales are often accused of casting evil spells on the world of fantasy or, worse yet, of breaking magic spells. We are entitled to search for the hidden meanings of literary texts, but fairy tales count as sacred stories meant to enchant rather than to signify. Analysis at its best leads to demystification, and who would want to remove the magic from a fairy tale, especially since there may be nothing left once the magic is banished? It is easy to take a cynical view and adopt the position taken by the King of Hearts in *Alice in Wonderland*. "If there's no meaning in it," he asserts, "that saves a world of trouble, you know, as we needn't try to find any" (Carroll 94). Most critics, however, have favored the position embraced by the Duchess: "Everything's got a moral, if only you can find it" (67). There is something to be said for the view that fairy tales have no stable meaning (they lack definitive formulations and delight in the absurd) as well as for the view that they are charged with meaning (they set up oppositions that lend themselves to allegorical readings). But there are numerous other positions and possibilities between these two extremes, and I propose to explore them by looking at the evolution of these cultural stories and their interpretive history.

Tolkien tells us that fairy tales did not always belong to children and that they were retired only relatively recently to the nursery, just as "shabby or old-fashioned furniture is relegated to the play-room, primarily because the adults do not want it" (34). For centuries, folktales served the cause of adult entertainment. At fireside gatherings, around the kiln, in the spinning room, or in workrooms, tales were told to while away a long winter evening or to shorten the hours devoted to domestic and agricultural chores. Peasants told many of the tales, but aristocrats also found them amusing and depended on them, sometimes to relieve boredom, at times to induce sleep (Ariès 95–98). Oral storytelling traditions survive today in pockets of culture—folk raconteurs still entertain with their tales of mystery and magic, librarians improvise on Saturday mornings for local children, and urban storytellers like Brother Blue in Boston create curbside performances for tourists and shoppers (Dégh 163–64).

The precise historical juncture at which folktales, in particular fairy tales, transformed themselves from adult entertainment into children's literature is difficult to identify. The frame story of Giambattista Basile's *Pentamerone* (1634–37) describes the Neapolitan narratives in that collection as "those tales that old women tell to amuse children" (1:9). Yet the stories in the *Pentamerone* must have been aimed primarily at adults: it is hard to believe that a tale (I cite only one of many possible examples) in which a boy calls an old woman "a blood-sucking witch, baby-smotherer, lump of filth, fart-face" was really intended as bedtime reading for children. Charles Perrault's *Tales of Mother Goose (Histoires; ou, Contes du temps passé)*, published in 1697, is often seen as pivotal with respect to the question of audience. As Robert Samber, its first English translator, observed, "not only Children, but those of Maturity" would find in the tales "uncommon Pleasure and Delight." Perrault offered "morals" right along with entertainment, and they were often framed with both adult and child in mind. Consider, for example, the double lesson of "Bluebeard." I present each "moral" in abbreviated form:

Curiosity in spite of its charms
Often brings with it many regrets . . .

and for "those of Maturity":

The time of strict husbands has passed,
And none will demand the impossible,
Even if plagued by jealousy and doubt.
He whispers sweet things in his wife's ear;

And no matter what color his beard may be,
It is not hard to tell who is the master.
                    (*Contes* 128–29; my trans.)

The story is clearly directed at two audiences. The first of its two morals teaches children a lesson about a vice that can be an endless source of aggravation to parents. The second is not really a moral but a witticism designed to capture the attention of adults through its pointed engagement with gender politics.

Perrault's collection straddles almost perfectly the line between adult entertainment and children's literature. Later collectors may initially have conceived their volumes of folktales, legends, and folk songs for the amusement and edification of adults, but they found themselves, whether intentionally or not, increasingly responding to a growing demand for children's books. Fairy tales, always notoriously elastic, began to expand their commitment to moral lessons and to moderate their enthusiasm for earthy realism. The Grimms' *Children's Stories and Household Tales* (1812/1815), for example, began as a scholarly project that was to serve as a contribution to the "history of poetry" for the entire nation, but it turned into an anthology of tales directed almost exclusively at children—the Grimms even came to refer to a volume that had once contained bawdy material inappropriate for children's ears as a "manual of manners." The same holds true for many of the other great nineteenth-century collections, a large number of which were inspired by the Grimms' pioneering work in the field of folklore (Afanasev; Jacobs; Asbjørnsen and Moe).

Not all folktales became a part of the culture of childhood. Adults bequeathed to children specific types of stories, primarily magical tales that placed heroes and heroines on the road to high adventure. "Hansel and Gretel," "Little Red Riding Hood," "Jack the Giant Killer," "Cinderella," and "Tom Thumb," which have all become classics of children's literature, pit the weak against witches, ogres, giants, and other menacing supernatural presences. No matter how helpless the victims seem at the start of these tales, they nearly always succeed in triumphing over their wicked adversaries. That these tales would prove especially satisfying to children, who perceive themselves without the requisite strength or power to challenge the adult world, is a point well made by the psychologist Bruno Bettelheim in his *Uses of Enchantment*.

Many of the magical tales cited above have also been turned into cautionary tales. "Little Red Riding Hood," for example, which started out as a bawdy folktale with a heroine who performs a striptease for the wolf, was turned by Perrault, the Grimms, and others into a stern lesson on the importance of obedience. Some versions of the tale show Red Riding Hood escaping from the wolf by telling him that she must go outdoors to relieve herself. When she tarries too long, the wolf wants to know exactly what she is up to: "Are you making a load out there? Are you making a load?" (Delarue). As folktales moved from workrooms and fireside gatherings into the nursery, they generally lost much of their humor (both bawdy and scatological) even as they retained and sometimes strengthened their exposition of violence. Neither Perrault nor the brothers Grimm show us the protagonist of "Little Red Riding Hood" stripping before the wolf or relieving herself, but both work hard to build tension in the scene that unfolds in the bedroom right before the wolf pounces on his victim. And both turn the story into a cautionary tale, the one warning about the dangers of listening to strangers (Perrault), the other about the perils of straying from the proper path (Grimms). Magical tales, which show the heroes and heroines defeating ogres and outwitting giants, generally follow the pattern of victimization and revenge. Cautionary tales, by contrast, defeat the protagonists by staging a transgression and its punishment (with a rescue scene often appended to soften the blow). These stories, with their strong disciplinary edge, have a certain undeniable appeal to parents who seek to teach lessons as they tell stories (Tatar 179–92).

The term *fairy tale* has gained the widest currency for designating the two (overlapping) types of stories described above. Although the term is misleading (there are very few fairies in most such tales) and is used in a notoriously imprecise fashion (to designate everything from rough-hewn traditional tales to stylized literary texts), I will use it here to identify those folktales that have, by common consensus and convention, become children's literature.

The avenues for approaching fairy tales and for understanding the complexities of their seeming simplicity are legion. The history of folklore scholarship began, however, not with the interpretation of tales but with the task of defining, collecting, and classifying them. Let us start with the most basic question: Just what is a folktale? Purists might insist that the genre exists only as part of an oral tradition passed on from one generation to the next—preferably by rugged peasant narrators seated around the fire husking corn and mending scythes on chilling autumn nights. In this case, the experts actually know better. The folktale is a notoriously elastic genre, accommodating all manner of prose narratives, both written and oral. Stith Thompson reminds us of the folktale's most salient feature: "The teller of a folktale," he observes, "is proud of his ability to hand on that which he has received" (*Folktale* 4). Rather than priding themselves on their creative genius and inventive spirit, folk raconteurs bank heavily on traditional materials (themes worked and reworked over a period of centuries) to shape their stories. For this reason, the tales they tell are often referred to as *traditional tales* or *traditional literature*. Recording an oral narrative does not necessarily deprive it of its status as a folktale. The recorded version may fall flat; it may be retold nearly beyond recognition of the original; and it may fail to capture the interpretive elements (facial movements, gestures, changes in intonation) that often accompany an oral narrative. Still it remains a folktale, even if it moves from the realm of folklore into the area of what Richard Dorson and Alan Dundes have defined as "fakelore."

Unlike the literary text, the folktale knows no stable form. For nearly every tale, we have hundreds, and in some cases thousands, of extant forms. Each text could be called a corrupt version of the original (if it ever existed at all), but it could also be seen as one of an infinite number of legitimate variant forms. Soon after the term *folktale* was coined by William Thoms and the field became established as a scholarly discipline, folklorists set themselves the task of collecting and classifying the vast array of materials that constituted their domain. *The Types of the Folktale (Verzeichnis der Märchentypen)*, a landmark study of 1910 by the Finnish scholar Antti Aarne, set up a classification system of tale types that, despite criticism from various quarters, today still provides the basic point of reference for the study of folktales. In its final form Aarne's catalog, which was translated and enlarged by Thompson, contains 2,499 tale types divided into five categories: animal tales, ordinary folktales, jokes and anecdotes, formula tales, and unclassified tales. For each type, Aarne and Thompson provide a summary of the tale, a breakdown of the chief motifs (the smallest possible narrative units) and bibliographical references. The tale-type index is supplemented by Thompson's *Motif-Index of Folk-Literature,* a six-volume reference work classifying the basic elements that constitute the plots of traditional literature from around the world.

The work of Aarne and Thompson laid the foundation for folktale scholarship and made clear the importance of comparative analysis. Henceforth it would be impossible—or at least methodologically unsound—to study a tale in isolation. It may have seemed astonishing that Aarne and Thompson could reduce the countless numbers of extant folktales to only 2,499 tale types, but by contrast with the calculations of their Russian colleague Vladimir Propp, that number seemed downright astronomical. In *The Morphology of the Folktale,* published in 1928, Propp declared that "all fairy tales are of one type in regard to their structure." Rather than classify tales by themes (a "dangerous" mistake made by Aarne), the Russian folklorist preferred to show how the building blocks (he identifies thirty-one-functions and seven spheres of action) of all fairy tales remain constant and help us understand the predictability of fairy-tale plots.

In recent years, folklorists have heeded the call of Alan Dundes not to abdicate the important work of analysis to those unschooled in their discipline ("Study of Folklore"). They too have begun to produce readings that, along with those of anthropologists, feminists, theologians, psychologists, historians, literary critics, and others, have enriched and deepened our understanding of the tales. Dundes himself, an avowed Freudian, has urged his colleagues to focus on the family conflicts dramatized in fairy tales ("Psychoanalytic Study of Folklore"). Incest, child abandonment, sexual jealousy, sibling rivalry, mutilation, murder, and cannibalism: these are just a few of the preferred themes of fairy tales. In many instances, especially when studying unbowdlerized tales, it makes no sense to search for latent meanings, because the tales in fact conceal so little. They openly dramatize the kinds of events that are ordinarily suppressed in children's literature: erotic intrigue, physical suffering, violent deaths, and grim acts of revenge. Freud's description of myth as "psychology projected onto the external world" (6:258) could be said to hold true for folktales as well. Fairy tales, in particular, give us ex-

aggerated and distorted (one might even say uncensored) forms of internal conflicts played out in the context of family life.

Although psychoanalysis remains one of the best optics we have for looking at the dynamics of family life in fairy tales, psychoanalytic criticism seems to raise a red flag wherever it goes—not entirely without reason. In the name of psychoanalysis, red caps have been turned into symbols of menstruation, houses made of gingerbread into the bodies of mothers, and golden eggs into anal ideas of possession. Our faith in psychoanalytic reading of fairy tales is quickly undermined once we begin comparing the interpretations and discover how different they are, even when they have all emerged from the same school. It is not only the larger contours of the tale's plot that generate disagreement, but even the fine points of detail. Let us look at the case of the dwarfs in "Snow White." For Bettelheim, these seven hardworking fellows represent the days of the week, and also the seven metals. In addition, these little men, "with their stunted bodies and their mining occupation—they skillfully penetrate into dark holes—all suggest phallic connotations" (210). Bettelheim's obvious discomfort with these creatures (since he cannot find one satisfactory explanation for their existence, he reaches for several) will be shared by anyone who reviews various assessments of the dwarfs' role in the tale. One critic sees the seven men as siblings of the heroine, another finds that they represent Snow White's unconscious mind, while a third views them as homosexuals who have set up housekeeping (Spörk 176–78). When we turn to another analysis and discover that the dwarfs symbolize Snow White's genitals, it becomes difficult not to flinch in disbelief (Gmelin 41).

While even the most astute psychoanalytic critics can go wrong when it comes to details, less restrained interpreters are perfectly capable of doing violence to an entire text. Consider the following recent observations on "Rumpelstiltskin":

> The miller's boasting of his daughter's gold-spinning ability conveys as well as conceals the threat of a son's powerful rivalry toward his father (the King). Thus, on a preoedipal level of understanding, the miller cedes his great power (gold-feces) to his father, a manic-restitutive defense conveyed verbally by his boastfulness. On an oedipal level of understanding, he thereby also denies his incestuous wish to impreg-

nate his own daughter, to have a baby by her. Also inherent in his offer are the elements of a covert *menage-à-trois,* a sharing of one female between two males which, together with the anal aspects of the miller's offer, point toward his self-abnegatory homosexual desire toward his King-father.

(Rinsley and Bergmann 7)

When we further hear that Rumpelstiltskin's stomping is "symbolic of masturbation" and learn that his gold-spinning suggests "a child playing with his own feces, a masturbatory precursor," it becomes difficult to suspend disbelief. These are the kinds of uncontrolled interpretations that give psychoanalytic criticism of both folktales and literary texts a bad name.

These documented cases of overinterpretation or misinterpretation would be enough to discourage most people from adopting psychoanalysis as a tool for analyzing fairy tales. More serious, however, are the undocumented cases of misguided psychoanalytic discourse. These virtually all begin in the same way: "Psychoanalytic critics would say. . . ." That opening phrase, or a variant of it, is followed by a preposterous statement equating one character, motif, or object in a tale with an anatomical part or a psychoanalytic concept. The very ring of the phrase "psychoanalytic critics would say" is now a negative one, and few fail to cringe in anticipation of the far-fetched statements that inevitably follow. Two examples must suffice. In an analysis of "The Juniper Tree," Lutz Röhrich observes that "psychoanalytic critics would see in the motif of dismemberment a symbol of castration or castration anxiety" (194; my trans.). The child psychologist Carl-Heinz Mallet notes, with regard to the male hero of "The Juniper Tree," that "psychoanalytic critics would immediately see the boy as the phallus of the husband" (216). These hypothetical psychoanalytic critics lead a strange, ghostly double life in the literature on fairy tales: they serve as both straw men and as whipping boys for other critics. Anyone who accepts the label "psychoanalytic critic" has to take on the burden of all the actual errors made by such critics along with all the potential mistakes attributed to them.

Psychoanalytic critics can be dogmatic; they can misread the details of a text; and they can even get an entire text wrong. But their errors are no graver than those found in sociohistorical readings, in feminist interpretations, and even in folkloristic analyses. At the same time, psychoanalysis can put us on the right track

for understanding a number of prominent fairy tale themes. In stories ranging from "The Juniper Tree" through "Tom Thumb" to "Sleeping Beauty," for example, cannibalism figures as a significant motif. A woman chops up the corpse of her stepson and serves him up to her husband in a stew; an ogre relishes the thought of eating seven brothers for dinner; a woman develops an appetite for her grandchildren. It would not be terribly useful in any of these cases to consult handbooks on the actual practice of cannibalism. Here, psychoanalysis, with its attempt to investigate such matters as the fear of being devoured and oral fixation, can be far more useful than the study of historically documented incidents of cannibalism (*Destins du cannibalisme;* Fenichal).

Because the fairy tale privileges descriptions of family life, it lends itself eminently well to psychoanalysis. But fairy tales also operate like magnets, picking up bits and pieces of everyday reality so that they come to be littered with cultural debris. As Italo Calvino has put it, "The folktale, regardless of its origin, tends to absorb something of the place where it is narrated—a landscape, a custom, a moral outlook, or else merely a very faint accent or flavor of the locality" (xxi). In an Italian version of "The Three Spinners," for example, the heroine downs endless amounts of lasagna in order to take the edge off her nervousness about spinning endless quantities of flax. Such culturally determined details can be found in any folkloric item, though it is not always as easy as in this case to assign a place to them.

To state that fairy tales give us psychological drama set in culturally determined scenes is to make an almost trivial point. But even our best interpreters of fairy tales have a way of choosing up sides in the debate over the degree to which fairy tales reflect psychic or cultural realities. We have seen how psychoanalytic critics can take tales and treat them as if they were "flattened out, like patients on a couch, in a timeless contemporaneity" (Darnton 13). But historians slide with ease to the opposite extreme when they argue, as Eugen Weber does, that these tales may be about "real people" and then proceed to treat these literary tales as if they were historical documents (96). To be sure, most historians take a more measured view and study fairy tales in search of clues about the facts of everyday life in past ages and about the *mentalité* of a specific culture. But even if one assumes that history was "immobile" at the village level during the age in which these tales flourished in oral form and just before they were recorded in the large collections of the nineteenth century, it becomes difficult to sort out fact from fantasy and to determine exactly which details can be seen as timeless universals and which can be read as specific to a culture.

The battle between psychoanalysis and history on the terrain of folklore should not divert our attention completely from various skirmishes of less central methodological importance. It is astonishing to observe how scholars from virtually every discipline and of every methodological persuasion have a contribution to make when it comes to fairy tales. "Little Red Riding Hood" has been read by historians as a realistic text based on accounts of werewolves attacking and devouring children. Psychiatrists have found in the story an exposition of "human passions, oral greediness, aggression, and pubertal desires" (Bettelheim 182). But there are also studies of the tale by legal experts (who offer disquisitions on the wolf's punishment) and by solar mythologists (who liken Little Red Riding Hood to the sun, which is engulfed by darkness at the end of its journey). Ideologues of the Third Reich hailed Red Riding Hood as a symbol of the German people, terrorized but finally liberated from the clutches of a Jewish wolf, and feminists have found in the story a parable of rape that teaches young women about ferocious male beasts. Once we decide to move from a literal reading to a symbolic interpretation, we perform an operation that frees us to substitute virtually any power perceived as predatory for the wolf and any entity perceived as innocent for Red Riding Hood. Each fairy tale text has a certain polysemic quality to it, rendering it capable of generating an almost endless number of interpretations (Turner 41–42).

Readings of Perrault's "Bluebeard" tell us something about the hazards of moving too swiftly from the literal to the symbolic plane. When the key that Bluebeard's wife used to open the door forbidden to her becomes stained with the blood of Bluebeard's dead wives, it is not Bluebeard who comes under fire as a serial murderer, but his wife as an adulteress. The bloodied key has been read as a sign of "marital infidelity"; it marks the heroine's "irreversible loss of her virginity"; it stands as a sign of "defloration." For one critic, the forbidden chamber is "clearly the vaginal area," while the bloody key is a "symbol of the loss of chastity" (Dundes, "Psychoanalytic Study of the Grimms' Tales" 56). If one recalls that the bloody chamber is strewn with the corpses of Bluebeard's previous wives, this reading becomes more than odd. And it is difficult to understand exactly why the heroine's opening of a door should be equated with sexual betrayal (Tatar 156–70).

The proper interpretation of fairy tales remains a hotly debated subject. Just as controversial has been the question of the pedagogical value of these tales. Bettelheim's claim that listening to fairy tales can provide children with powerful therapeutic benefits has been challenged by many critics, but that has not prevented it from becoming dogma in many circles. The graphic descriptions of cruel and unusual punishments in many fairy-tale anthologies may in fact not provide children with the best possible nighttime fare. In Italian tales, witches are regularly coated with pitch and burned to death; German tales show them being rolled down hills in barrels studded with nails; in Russian tales they freeze to death. Fairy-tale heroes and heroines also do not always serve as ideal models for children. When faced with a crisis, they typically respond by sitting down and having a good cry. Rather than rely on their own resources, they often depend on magical means and supernatural helpers to gain their ends. Lying, cheating, and stealing also become perfectly acceptable, so long as such practices enable them to move further down the road to wealth and social promotion through a good marriage.

Jack Zipes has argued persuasively that fairy tales play an influential role in socializing children. Most of the tale collections canonized by our culture, however, fail his test of the right values. Perrault, for example, shows us women who demonstrate "reserve and patience," who remain passive until "the right man comes along." For the male figures alone, Perrault reserves "remarkable minds, courage, and deft manners." The "ideal types" fashioned by Perrault were used to reinforce "the standards of the civilizing process set by upper-class French society" (25–26). Zipes concedes that "it would be foolish to reject the entire classical canon as socially useless or aesthetically outmoded" and advocates reappropriation of the tales by more liberal and enlightened minds. His concerns are shared by feminist critics in particular, for so many fairy-tale heroines suffer silently until released from a humble state by a male figure (Stone; Bottigheimer).

Heroes are not always as courageous and dashing as some would have us believe—but they generally take a more active role than their female counterparts in shaping their destinies.

Fairy tales have left a mark on nearly every childhood. Scholars in pursuit of their deeper meanings and their hidden messages may risk breaking their magic spell, but they also help us understand something about the values and assumptions embedded in a story. There is nothing sacred about any specific fairy tale. Each is of value as a document true to its time and place. But since we may not necessarily want a child to hear how the Grimms' wicked queen demands Snow White's lungs and liver or to witness the thrill that Walt Disney's Snow White gets from housekeeping, there is nothing wrong with preserving the old versions as historical documents and creating new ones for the entertainment of children. Keeping the storytelling tradition alive requires changes in words and variations in detail.

Children may have appropriated fairy tales, turning the childhood of fiction into the fiction of childhood, but they did not leave adults entirely empty-handed. George Dasent, a renowned scholar of Old Norse, congratulated the brothers Grimm in particular on elevating "what had come to be looked on as mere nursery fictions and old wives' fables—to a study fit for the energies of grown men, and to all the dignity of a science" (xix). Now, one hundred years after these observations, the need to legitimize the study of fairy tales is no longer so urgent. It has become both an art and a science—for young and for old, for male and for female.

WORKS CITED

Aarne, Antti. *The Types of the Folktale: A Classification and Bibliography*. Trans, and enlarged by Stith Thompson. 2nd ed. Helsinki: Academic Scientiarum Fennica, 1981.

———. *Verzeichnis der Märchentypen*. Helsinki: Academia Scientiarum Fennica, 1910.

Afanasev, Alexander Nikolaevitch. *Russian Folktales*. 1855–64. New York: Pantheon, 1945.

Ariès, Philippe. *Centuries of Childhood: A Social History of Family Life*. Trans. Robert Baldick. New York: Vintage-Random, 1962.

Asbjørnsen, Peter Christen, and Jørgen Moe. *Norwegian Folk Tales*. 1845. Trans. Pat Shaw and Carl Norman. New York: Pantheon, 1960.

Basile, Giambattista. *The Pentamerone*. Trans. Benedetto Croce. Ed. N. M. Penzer. 2 vols. London: Bodley, 1932.

Bettelheim, Bruno. *The Uses of Enchantment: The Meaning and Importance of Fairy Tales*. New York: Vintage-Random, 1977.

Bottigheimer, Ruth B. *Grimms' Bad Girls and Bold Boys: The Moral and Social Vision of the Tales*. New Haven: Yale UP, 1987.

Calvino, Italo. Introduction. *Italian Folktales*. Selected and retold by Italo Calvino. Trans. George Martin. New York: Pantheon, 1980.

Carroll, Lewis. *Alice's Adventures in Wonderland* and *Through the Looking-Glass*. New York: Bantam, 1981.

Darnton, Robert. "Peasants Tell Tales: The Meaning of Mother Goose." *The Great Cat Massacre and Other Episodes in French Cultural History*. New York: Basic, 1984. 8–72.

Dasent, George. Introduction. *Popular Tales from the Norse*. New York: Putnam's, 1888.

Dégh, Linda. *Märchen, Erzähler und Erzählgemeinschaft*. East Berlin: Akademie, 1962.

Delarue, Paul, ed. "Le Petit Chaperon Rouge." *Le Conte populaire français*. Vol. 1. Paris: Maisonneuve, 1967. 373–74.

Destins du cannibalisme. Spec. issue of *Nouvelle Revue de Psychanalyse* 6 (1972).

Dorson, Richard M. "Fakelore." *Zeitschrift für Volkskunde* 65 (1969): 56–64.

Dundes, Alan. "Nationalistic Inferiority Complexes and the Fabrication of Fakelore: A Reconsideration of Ossian, the *Kinder- und Hausmärchen*, the *Kalevala*, and Paul Bunyan." *Journal of Folklore Research* 22 (1985): 5–18.

———. "The Psychoanalytic Study of Folklore." *Annals of Scholarship* 3 (1985): 1–42.

———. "The Psychoanalytic Study of the Grimms' Tales with Special Reference to 'The Maiden without Hands' (AT 706)." *Germanic Review* 62 (1987): 50–65.

———. "The Study of Folklore in Literature and Culture: Identification and Interpretation." *Journal of American Folklore* 78 (1965): 136–42.

Fenichal, Otto. "The Dread of Being Eaten." *Collected Papers*. New York: Norton, 1953. 158–59.

Freud, Sigmund. *The Psychopathology of Everyday Life*. Vol. 6 of *The Standard Edition of the Complete Psychological Works*. Trans. James Strachey. London: Hogarth, 1960.

Gmelin, Otto F. *Böses kommt aus Kinderbüchern: Die verpassten Möglichkeiten kindlicher Bewusstseinsbildung*. Munich: Kindler, 1972.

Jacobs, Joseph. *English Fairy Tales*. 1890. London: Bodley, 1968.

Mallet, Carl-Heinz. *Kopf ab! Gewalt im Märchen*. Hamburg: Rasch, 1985.

Perrault, Charles. *Histoires; ou, Contes du temps passé.* Ed. Gilbert Rouger. Paris: Garnier, 1967.

Propp, Vladimir. *The Morphology of the Folktale.* 1928. Trans. Laurence Scott. 2nd ed. Austin: U of Texas P, 1968.

Rinsley, Donald B., and Elizabeth Bergmann. "Enchantment and Alchemy: The Story of Rumpelstiltskin." *Bulletin of the Menninger Clinic* 47 (1984): 1–14.

Röhrich, Lutz. "Die Grausamkeit im deutschen Märchen." *Rheinisches Jahrbuch für Volkskunde.* Bonn: Dümmler, 1955. 176–224.

Samber, Robert. Dedication. *Histories or Tales of Past Times.* By M. Perrault. Trans. Robert Samber. London: Pote, 1729. Rpt. in *The Authentic Mother Goose Fairy Tales and Nursery Rhymes.* Ed. Jacques Barchilon and Henry Pettit. Denver: Swallow, 1960.

Spörk, Ingrid. *Studien zu ausgewählten Märchen der Brüder Grimm: Frauenproblematik, Struktur, Rollentheorie, Psychoanalyse, Überlieferung, Rezeption.* Königstein: Hain, 1985.

Stone, Kay F. "Feminist Approaches to the Interpretation of Fairy Tales." *Fairy Tales and Society: Illusion, Allusion, and Paradigm.* Ed. Ruth B. Bottigheimer. Philadelphia: U of Pennsylvania P, 1986. 229–36.

Tatar, Maria. *The Hard Facts of the Grimms' Fairy Tales.* Princeton: Princeton UP, 1987.

Thompson, Stith. *The Folktale.* 1946. Berkeley: U of California P, 1977.

———. *The Motif-Index of Folk-Literature.* Rev. ed. 6 vols. Bloomington: Indiana UP, 1955–58.

Thoms, William. "Folklore." *The Study of Folklore.* Ed. Alan Dundes. Englewood Cliffs: Prentice, 1965. 4–6.

Tolkien, J. R. R. "On Fairy-Stories." *The Tolkien Reader.* New York: Ballantine, 1966. 3–84.

Turner, Victor W. *The Ritual Process: Structure and Anti-Structure.* New York: Aldine, 1969.

Weber, Eugen. "Fairies and Hard Facts: The Reality of Folktales." *Journal of the History of Ideas* 42 (1981): 93–113.

Zipes, Jack. *Fairy Tales and the Art of Subversion: The Classical Genre for Children and the Process of Civilization.* New York: Wildman, 1983.

John Langstaff (1920–2005)

John Langstaff, like many authors for children, worked with both oral and written media. Much of his long career as a musician, storyteller, and writer of children's books involved adapting and performing traditional literature. His picture book *Frog Went A-Courtin',* illustrated by Feodor Rojankovsky, won the Caldecott Medal in 1956. In 1957, Langstaff created a program called *The Revels,* a combination of drama, song, and dance intended to provide American children with communal rituals celebrating the seasons. He eventually became director of Revels, a Massachusetts company that still produces these popular programs every year in various locations. "The Oral Tradition: Alive, Alive-oh" was published in a 1987 book, *Innocence & Experience,* based on programs at Simmons College Center for the Study of Children's Literature, where Langstaff served as a faculty member in the 1970s and 1980s. The essay offers interesting insights on relations between oral traditions and written literature at the end of the twentieth century, with enthusiastic recognition of the vigorous oral tradition that is alive among American children with a wide variety of cultural backgrounds. The examples of street rhymes that Langstaff and others collected from city children complement the selections of nursery rhymes and folk songs reprinted in this section, and the other examples in this volume of spin-offs and satires based on older verses.

The Oral Tradition

Alive, Alive-oh

Ballads are among the most ancient forms of traditional music. Many of our ballads are rich narratives as well. Over the years many of these—all of the Robin Hood ballads and many of the great epic ballads—have been retold as stories in prose, and they are still being put into books today.

I remember hearing as a young boy some of the traditional singers, like Horton Barker, *sing* some of these ballads. Jean Ritchie, from Kentucky, is still singing them today, but the tradition is dying out; unfortunately, the oral tradition of ballad singing is not being passed on. The same thing happened to storytelling, which died out for a long time; but now it has been revived, and people are going back to telling stories. We'll go on singing the ballads, but we'll sing them as we learn them from books.

So what is going to happen to the oral tradition? Where do we find the oral tradition today? Is there such a tradition anymore, and—because everything is now available in print and in other media—will there continue to be one?

Of course, there are always jokes, superstitions, and riddles. You probably know Alvin Schwartz; he is marvelous, and he's doing a lot of very interesting work, talking to people who are eighty and ninety years old and gathering material from them. It's a fascinating development, for us and for children, to go and talk with older people and learn from them.

I, too, have found some sources of a living oral tradition. When I was a teacher, the parents of my young students would sometimes say that my music teaching wasn't always about *music*. Sometimes I would use material that wasn't strictly musical. Poetry, of course, is very much a part of song, and I always used it; but what about the nonsense rhymes that can be such an integral part of childhood? Like this:

Rain, rain, come down dashing,
Put my mother in a passion.
Rain, rain, go away,
Come again on washing day.

Or this:

Ahem, ahem, my mother's gone to church,
She told me not to play with you because you're in the dirt,
It isn't because you're dirty, it isn't because you're clean,
It's because you have the whooping cough from eating margarine.

Or:

Paddy on the railway, picking up stones,
Along came an engine and broke Paddy's nose,
Oh, says Paddy, that's not fair,
Oh, says the engine, I don't care.

Now, what kind of doggerel is that? It's for jumping rope or bouncing a ball, something functional. I was curious about the fact that a lot of parents said, "Well, 'London Bridge' and all those things, that's sort of old-fashioned—that's all from the past and not really relevant to children today."

So we went out, my daughter and I, to collect street rhymes. She had just become a student in the Boston area, so she did the legwork of collecting in the streets, playing with children all over Boston and Cambridge. I even got her to go down to New York and try to find street chants among some of the American Indian people; I thought they might be in New York, having come to work on the skyscrapers. She went with a photographer and played games with the children, teaching them games that she knew until they began to include her in their games. There were Portuguese, Armenian, Italian, Black, Irish—children from all kinds of background. She found street rhymes still very much alive, tremendously alive, an oral tradition being carried on—by children.

It's an incredible phenomenon because adults have no connection with it at all. Neither parents nor teachers are teaching the children these chants; in fact, we wondered, frankly, whether we should publish them in a book. For example, since I put "Frog Went A-Courtin'" into a book, children have thought it is *the* "Frog Went A-Courtin'." That's so wrong. I have to keep explaining that to children all the time. I say that there are many of singing "Frog Went A-Courtin'" and that their great-grandfathers and great-grandmothers might have known it very differently. There's no right way. I simply collect variants of traditional material.

I can't remember who wrote these words, but I have them in my notes: "For the children of big cities, the city sidewalk is where the action is and from the secret society of city children come these songs, rhymes, and games with their primitive vitality. In them lives the American city child's world. Their origins stretch all over the world of Europe, Africa, and Asia. Some are very old, and some strictly contemporary." Whooping cough? Children hardly know what it is today. "You have the whooping cough from eating margarine"; but in the North End of Boston you have it "because you kissed the boy behind the magazines"— or something like that.

We found a little six-year-old singing:

Ringo, Ringo, Ringo Starr,
How I wonder what you are.
Underneath that mop of hair,
Ringo, are you really there?
Ringo, Ringo, Ringo Starr,
How I wonder what you are.

I said to this child, "Do you know who Ringo Starr is?" He had never heard of Ringo Starr. Maybe a fourteen-year-old brother or sister would have known, but the child didn't know who Ringo Starr was; the name just had a wonderful sound. In years to come it's going to be fascinating when people, reading a book by collectors like the Opies, may say, "Hmmm, what is this about? 'Underneath that mop of hair'?" Perhaps in 1999 everybody will be wearing crew cuts again. People may say, "That's an interesting thing; way back in the seventies men had long hair."

We found that there were a lot of things going on in the street among these children, aged five to ten. You talk about people handing on the traditional ballads from generation to generation, but what is a generation? To a grown-up, twenty-five or fifty years, but to children, five to ten years. And these children were learning chants in the way the oral tradition has always been passed along, the way I've seen the American Indians learn their long dances: the older men in the front, the strong young men in the middle, and then at the very back the tiny children trying to get the feel of it. They're not being taught anything;

they're just trying to get the step, and eventually they're going to move up toward the front. And that's what I think happens to the little city children. They don't learn a thing from anybody except by hanging around and listening.

They pick up name-calling:

Eddie Spaghetti with meatball eyes,
Put in the oven and make French fries.

And all kinds of strange nonsense:

Sam, Sam, the dirty man,
Washed his face in a frying pan,
Combed his hair with the back of a chair,
And danced with a toothache in the air.

Now, that's interesting; I wonder, do they know "Old Dan Tucker"? Those lines are straight out of "Old Dan Tucker." And this one, with an adult overtone:

Mary made a dumpling, she made it so sweet,
She cut it up in pieces and gave us all a treat,
Saying, "Take this, take this, and don't be slow,
For tomorrow is my wedding day and I must go!"

And for ball-bouncing:

Down by the river where the green grass grows,
Where little Mary washes her clothes.
She sang, she sang, she sang so sweet,
That she sang Patrick across the street.

What a great line: "That she sang Patrick across the street."

And then near Boston we came across some children singing the identical tune to these words:

Down in the valley where the green grass grows,
There sits Kennedy as sweet as a rose,
Along came Nixon and kissed him on the cheek,
How many kisses did he receive?
One, two, three, four, five. . . .

These children didn't know who Kennedy and Nixon were, not at that age.

In Boston we came upon a group of Black children playing a very interesting game with a lot of pantomime in it, on the four corners of a sidewalk. We took notes and taped what they said, but I couldn't make anything out of it, I couldn't understand what the words were. The photographer said, "Oh, that's a Chuck Berry tune the kids have picked up, and if you know the Chuck Berry tune, you know what those words are." Yet there was something about those words we couldn't understand, so we went back and saw the Black children and said to them, "Where did this game come from?" And they told us they had learned it from the Chinese children over in Chinatown. They had learned it just as they heard it! Here was the oral tradition being passed on without any knowledge of its significance.

We found a lovely tune in Harlem in New York City. The children were all sitting around in a circle singing something that sounded like "Duck, Duck, Goose, Goose." One child got up and walked around and tapped three children, and then those three children got up and moved around; later on, a few more children got up and moved around, till they were all moving around. Then all of them bowed to the king of the mountain while they sang, "And we'll all sing glory to the mountain, and we'll all bow to the mountain." I said in my unguarded, foolish way, "Oh, what is that tune you're singing; do you know what tune it is?" It was, of course, "Go Tell It on the Mountain," note for note. But the children in their wonderful way said, "No, no, it's not 'Go Tell It on the Mountain'; it's 'Glory to the Mountain.'" It was different to them.

One tune was a carol, and one was a game, and they didn't want me telling them that both tunes were the same. They were right. This was their game. It was different, and that's right; the innocence of the child is quite vast and wonderful.

About counting rhymes: I don't know how you count off with children but there are many rhymes besides "eeny, meeny, miney-mo." Here is one of them:

My mother and your mother live across the bay,
Every time they have a fight, this is what they say:
"Ichabocka, ichabocka, ichabocka boo,
Ichabocka soda cracker, out goes you!"

And that means *you;* that means you're *it;* but for what? A game of tag? Or was it something else far, far back in ancient times when people needed to choose a victim? This sort of ritual comes from adults, somewhere back in the distant past.

And there are other wonderful counting rhymes; one rather lyrical one begins, "Intree, mintree, cutree corn." This rhyme is from New England, with lots of apples and pears in it, not just McIntosh and Delicious apples but the really old ones.

It is good to bring these traditional folk rhymes into the lives of modern children.

Iona Opie (b. 1923)
and Peter Opie (1918–92)

Nursery rhymes have appeared in countless children's books, illustrated in a wide variety of appealing styles by artists over the past three centuries, like other forms of literature derived from oral traditions. But more than any other type of literature, nursery rhymes or Mother Goose rhymes are derived from a jumbled array of oral and written sources and represent our most primal experiences with language in early childhood. Among the most basic functions of parents or caretakers is to hold children, comfort them, talk, sing, and play—and in the course of these actions, they instinctively transmit the traditional rhymes of their culture. No matter what language or nonsense syllables are uttered, the strong cadences of the rhymes complement the rhythms of the human body, enhance interactions between speakers and children in the process of acquiring language, and express the unfettered joys and perversions of the human imagination.

The nursery rhymes reprinted here have long remained familiar in print and speech, owing, in part, to the work of Peter and Iona Opie. The English husband and wife team, avid collectors of rare children's books and folklore, made invaluable contributions to the history and preservation of rhymes and stories by and for children, editing collections of traditional literature for children, and extensively documented volumes for adults. *I Saw Esau,* a 1947 book of verses reprinted in 1992 with comic illustrations by Maurice Sendak, is one of their collections of folklore based on fieldwork with British schoolchildren, focusing on rhymes that children chant among themselves when they think they have become too old for nursery rhymes. *The Classic Fairy Tales* (1974) and *The Oxford Dictionary of Nursery Rhymes* (1951) give detailed background on standard works of folk literature in English. Their interesting notes on nursery rhymes, often critiquing legends about historical origins and possible symbolic meanings, update the writings of James O. Halliwell, who produced the first scholarly collections of nursery rhymes in the 1840s but was not accurate about all his sources.

The examples presented here represent a number of nursery rhyme types, with excerpts from the Opies' notes. Some reflect stages of child development and some are just nonsense. Their sound patterns and the fun of playing with their language are more important than their meanings, which in many cases were lost in the long histories of the folklore, rituals, jingles, literature, and satires from which they evolved. "Pat-a-Cake" is usually part of a hand-clapping game with a baby, and "London Bridge" is often a song or a game for a group of children. "One, Two, Buckle My Shoe" is a counting verse with silly but memorable rhymes, while "Thirty Days Hath September" taught many of us how to remember the months of the year. "The House that Jack Built" is a cumulative rhyme that challenges the memory with a chain of interrelated actions. "Humpty Dumpty" and "In Marble Halls" are riddles, one of the oldest known forms of literature, while "As I Was Going to St. Ives" is a more complex type of riddle or trick with a deceptively simple answer. "Ladybird, Ladybird" refers to lost superstitions about the insect associated with the Virgin Mary (perhaps related to the practice of burning vines where the insects would live). "I See the Moon" seems like a simple blessing now, although it could be based on ancient fears of lunacy and spells against it. The wife in "Three Blind Mice" and the old woman who lived in a shoe seem shockingly violent by today's standards, although violence is common in nursery rhymes. Other verses attributed to Mother Goose may express straightforward wishes ("Rain, rain go away") or practical wisdom ("All work and no play/Makes Jack a dull boy").

London Bridge (which has been rebuilt throughout history) and St. Ives (in Cornwall) are real places, while most nursery rhymes have unknown settings and histories. "Little Boy Blue," "Little Jack Horner," and "Mary, Mary, Quite Contrary" are based on scenes of everyday life, like some of the poems about childhood by Robert Louis Stevenson and Grace Nichols in this volume. "Mary Had a Little Lamb" (by Boston poet Sara Josepha Hale), "Little Miss Muffet," and "Jack and Jill" narrate miniature dramatic adventures that begin with everyday actions. The English village of Kilmersdon, which contains an unusual well on a hill, began capitalizing in the 1990s on its claim that Jack and Jill lived there, since historical records show that a Jill died in childbirth after Jack's accidental death. In a more fantastical vein, "Sing a Song of Sixpence" is one of many nursery rhymes referring to royalty and magic, while "Hey Diddle Diddle" is a romantic fantasy even stranger than "Froggie Went A Courtin'" or Edward Lear's nonsense poem "The Owl and the Pussy-cat." There is no way of knowing whether it is an allegory featuring Queen Elizabeth I or a royal or noble Cat(herine) of the past. As the Opies wrote, "Probably the best-known nonsense verse in the language, a considerable amount of nonsense has been written about it" (p. 203).

Just as nursery rhymes change through the vagaries of the oral tradition and lose their ties with older literature of high or low repute, they continue to weave their way through popular culture and literary traditions. "Mistress Mary, Quite Contrary" forms a theme early in *The Se-*

cret Garden (see Part 5), when Mary Lennox, a neglected orphan, is teased by other children for being so contrary. Humpty Dumpty is a pompous, demanding character who confronts Alice in Lewis Carroll's Alice in Wonderland books. "Wee Willie Winkie," an allegory of nightfall and bedtime that moved into the oral tradition from the first stanza of William Miller's Scottish poem of the 1840s, became the title of a Rudyard Kipling story by the end of the century, about a mischievous six-year-old boy in colonial India who spies on adults and saves a young woman. In 1937, Kipling's boy became a precocious girl with golden curls, and Willie became the name of an Indian spy in one of Shirley Temple's best movies, *Wee Willie Winkie*. Contemporary spin-offs of enigmatic old nursery rhymes include Ruth Brown's visually striking English picture book about a factory polluting the countryside, *The World That Jack Built* (1991), and Maurice Sendak's treatment of urban poverty and wish fulfillment in *We Are All in the Dumps with Jack and Guy* (1993).

From *The Oxford Dictionary of Nursery Rhymes*

Pat-a-cake, pat-a-cake, baker's man,
Bake me a cake as fast as you can;
Pat it and prick it, and mark it with B,
Put it in the oven for baby and me.

This was portrayed as an infants' ditty as early as 1698. In D'Urfey's comedy *The Campaigners* the "affected tattling nurse" murmurs endearments as she suckles her charge:

> "Ah Doddy blesse dat pitty face of myn Sylds, and his pitty, pitty hands, and his pitty, pitty foots, and all his pitty things, and pat a cake, pat a cake Bakers man, so I will master as I can, and prick it, and prick it, and prick it, and prick it, and prick it, and throw't into the Oven."

The verse often accompanies a game. Mrs. Child, in the nineteenth century, instructed, "Clap the hands together, saying 'Pat a cake, pat a cake, baker's man; that I will, master, as fast as I can'; then rub the hands together, saying, 'Roll it, and roll it'; then peck the palm of the left hand with the forefinger of the right, saying, 'Prick it, and prick it'; then throw up both hands saying, 'Toss it in the oven and bake it.'" More usually today the words punctuate the excellent hand-warming exercise also associated with "Pease porridge hot."

Parody by James Robinson Planché on the publication of *The Nursery Rhymes of England*, 1842, by his friend Halli-

well, "Halliwell-Halliwell, My pretty man, Make me a book as fast as you can; Write it and print it, And mark it with P., And send it by Parcels Deliverye."

One, two,
Buckle my shoe;
Three, four,
Knock at the door;
Five, six,
Pick up sticks;
Seven, eight,
Lay them straight;
Nine, ten,
A big fat hen;
Eleven, twelve,
Dig and delve;
Thirteen, fourteen,
Maids a-courting;
Fifteen, sixteen,
Maids in the kitchen;
Seventeen, eighteen,
Maids in waiting;
Nineteen, twenty,
My plate's empty.

Bolton quotes a version which originally, he believed, went up to thirty, "make a kerchy"; "Eleven, twelve, bake it well; Thirteen, fourteen, go a courtin'; Fifteen, sixteen, go to milkin'; Seventeen, eighteen, do the bakin'; Nineteen, twenty, the mill is empty; Twenty-one, charge the gun; Twenty-two, the partridge flew; Twenty-three, she lit on a tree; Twenty-four she lit down lower," and "Twenty-nine, the game is mine." This was said to be "Used in Wrentham, Massachusetts, as early as 1786." The form of the rhyme is common in Germany, France, Holland, and Turkey.

Thirty days hath September
April, June, and November;
All the rest have thirty-one,
Excepting February alone,
And that has twenty-eight days clear
And twenty-nine in each leap year.

The best-known mnemonic rhyme in the language—probably through its inclusion in the canons of the nursery. It appears in most nursery rhyme books subsequent to 1825. Versions of this "rule to knowe how many dayes euery moneth in the yere hath" are cited by several Elizabethan writers.

Hey diddle diddle,
The cat and the fiddle,
The cow jumped over the moon;
The little dog laughed
To see such sport,
And the dish ran away with the spoon.

Probably the best-known nonsense verse in the language, a considerable amount of nonsense has been written about it. One of the few statements which can be authenticated is that it appeared in print *c.* 1765. A quotation which may possibly refer to it is in *A lamentable tragedy mixed ful of pleasant mirth, conteyning the life of Cambises King of Percia,* by Thomas Preston, printed 1569,

They be at hand Sir with stick and fidle;
They can play a new dance called hey-diddle-didle.

Another is in *The Cherry and the Slae* by Alexander Montgomerie, 1597,

But since ye think't an easy thing
To mount above the moon,
Of your own fidle take a spring
And dance when ye have done.

Mary, Mary, quite contrary,
How does your garden grow?
With silver bells and cockle shells,
And pretty maids all in a row.

Sing a song of sixpence,
A pocket full of rye;
Four and twenty blackbirds,
Baked in a pie.

When the pie was opened,
The birds began to sing;
Was not that a dainty dish,
To set before the king?

The king was in his counting-house,
Counting out his money;
The queen was in the parlour,
Eating bread and honey.

The maid was in the garden,
Hanging out the clothes,
There came a little blackbird,
And snapped off her nose.

When Henry James Pye was appointed Poet Laureate in 1790 his first ode, a very poor one, was in honour of the king's birthday and was full of allusions to the "vocal groves and the feathered choir." George Steevens immediately punned, "And when the PYE was opened the birds began to sing; Was not that a dainty dish to set before the king?" The story became well known

(Lamb recounted it to Mary's nurse), and in consequence the rhyme has (as in *DNB*) been attributed to Steevens. This possibility is precluded by the rhyme's prior appearance in toy book literature. Other stories, giving the rhyme allegorical significance, are not so easy to disprove. Theories upon which too much ink has been expended are [numerous].

Jack and Jill went up the hill
To fetch a pail of water;
Jack fell down and broke his crown,
And Jill came tumbling after.

Up Jack got, and home did trot,
As fast as he could caper,
To old Dame Dob, who patched his nob
With vinegar and brown paper.

This nursery rhyme, on account of its romantic possibilities, has vied with the fairy tales as a favourite for pantomime performances, e.g., *Harlequin Jack and Jill; or Mother Goose at Home Once More* at the Adelphi, 1855; *Jack and Jill* at His Majesty's, 1942. From the beginning of the nineteenth century it formed one of the chapbook series, the story being extended to fifteen verses. The second verse, above, is probably a legacy of this extension and not so old as the first which alone appears in the eighteenth-century recordings. The rhyming of water with after (*wahter* and *ahter*) in the first verse may be an indication that it dates from the first half of the seventeenth century. Claims that traces of antiquity and mystery may be seen in the rhyme have received undue notice.

Ladybird, ladybird,
Fly away home,
Your house is on fire
And your children all gone;
All except one
And that's little Ann

And she has crept under
The warming pan.

Child's warning to the ladybird. Traditionally the insect is set on a finger before being addressed. This is what the present writers used to do, and what a woodcut of the reign of George II depicts. When the warning has been recited (and the ladybird blown upon once), it nearly always happens that the seemingly earthbound little beetle produces wings and flies away. The names by which it is popularly known in this and other countries show that it has always had sacred associations: "Ladybird" (from Our Lady's bird), "Marygold," "God's Little Cow," "Bishop that burneth"; the German "Marienkäfer" and "Himmelsküchlichen," the Swedish "Marias Nyckelpiga," the Russian "Bózhia koróvka," the French "Bête à bon Dieu," the Spanish "Vaquilla de Dios," and the Hindu "Indragôpa." The rhyme is undoubtedly a relic of something once possessed of an awful significance. It is closely matched by incantations known in France, Germany, Switzerland, Denmark, and Sweden, sometimes even to the detail of the name Ann.

London Bridge is broken down,
Broken down, broken down,
London Bridge is broken down,
My fair lady.

Build it up with wood and clay,
Wood and clay, wood and clay,
Build it up with wood and clay,
My fair lady.

Wood and clay will wash away,
Wash away, wash away,
Wood and clay will wash away,
My fair lady.

Build it up with bricks and mortar,
Bricks and mortar, bricks and mortar,
Build it up with bricks and mortar,
My fair lady.

Bricks and mortar will not stay,
Will not stay, will not stay,

Bricks and mortar will not stay,
My fair lady.

Build it up with iron and steel,
Iron and steel, iron and steel,
Build it up with iron and steel,
My fair lady.

Iron and steel will bend and bow,
Bend and bow, bend and bow,
Iron and steel will bend and bow,
My fair lady.

Build it up with silver and gold,
Silver and gold, silver and gold,
Build it up with silver and gold,
My fair lady.

Silver and gold will be stolen away,
Stolen away, stolen away,
Silver and gold will be stolen away,
My fair lady.

Set a man to watch all night,
Watch all night, watch all night,
Set a man to watch all night,
My fair lady.

Suppose the man should fall asleep,
Fall asleep, fall asleep,
Suppose the man should fall asleep?
My fair lady.

Give him a pipe to smoke all night,
Smoke all night, smoke all night,
Give him a pipe to smoke all night,
My fair lady.

Few songs stir the imagination more deeply, evoking pictures both of a mysterious bridge which must ceaselessly be rebuilt, and of children singing light-heartedly as they play a game upon which there still rests an element of fear. The words, however, are now often separated from the play, and are known to even the smallest in the nursery; "London Bridge is falling down" has become a popular nursery recitation. It is one of the few, perhaps the only one, in which there is justification for suggesting that it preserves the memory of a dark and terrible rite of past times; and the [extensive] literary history of the song does not frustrate the idea of its antiquity. London Bridge itself is not without a tainted reputation, for there is in the cap-

ital a tradition that the stones of this great bridge, too, were once bespattered with the blood of little children.

Mary had a little lamb,
Its fleece was white as snow;
And everywhere that Mary went
The lamb was sure to go.

It followed her to school one day,
That was against the rule;
It made the children laugh and play
To see a lamb at school.

And so the teacher turned it out,
But still it lingered near,
And waited patiently about
Till Mary did appear.

Why does the lamb love Mary so?
The eager children cry;
Why, Mary loves the lamb, you know,
The teacher did reply.

E. V. Lucas came to the conclusion that these were the best known four-line verses in the English language. They were written by Mrs. Sarah Josepha Hale (1788–1879) of Boston, "early in the year 1830" about an incident which was "partly true." They were published in September 1830 over her initials in the *Juvenile Miscellany,* a periodical of which she was the editor, and later in the year appeared in a volume of her work, *Poems for Our Children.* The verses have been claimed for several other authors including her son, Horatio Hale, Jane Burls, and for John Roulstone by a Mrs. Tyler.

There was an old woman who lived in a shoe,
She had so many children she didn't know what to
    do;
She gave them some broth without any bread;
She whipped them all soundly and put them to
    bed.

The celebrated inhabitant of a shoe has been identified with several ladies for little reason other than the size of their families, e.g. Caroline, wife of George II, who had eight children, and Elizabeth Vergoose of Boston who had six of her own, and ten stepchildren. If the rhyme is very old, it may be wondered whether it has folk-lore significance. The shoe has long been symbolic of what is personal to a woman until marriage. Casting a shoe after the bride when she goes off on her honeymoon is possibly a relic of this, symbolizing the wish that the union shall be fruitful. This is consistent with the many children belonging to a woman who actually lived in a shoe.

Three blind mice, see how they run!
They all ran after the farmer's wife,
Who cut off their tails with a carving knife,
Did you ever see such a thing in your life,
    As three blind mice?

Arthur Rackham, a leading Edwardian illustrator, filled a page in *Mother Goose Rhymes* (1913) with the expressive, energetic lines of his drawing for "Three Blind Mice."

Little Jack Horner
Sat in the corner,
Eating a Christmas pie;
He put in his thumb,
And pulled out a plum,
And said, What a good boy am I!

The legend which has gained currency during the past century is that the original Jack Horner was steward to Richard Whiting, last of the abbots of Glastonbury. The story goes that at the time of the Dissolution the abbot, perhaps hoping to appease Henry VIII, sent his steward to London with a Christmas gift: a pie in which were hidden the title deeds of twelve manors. On the journey Jack Horner is said to have opened the pie and extracted the deeds of the Manor of Mells. However this may be, it is a fact that one Thomas Horner took up residence at Mells soon after the Dissolution and his descendants live there to this day. What the Horner family say is that their ancestor bought the manor (together with several other manors and neighbouring farms) for £1,831. 9*s*. 1³/₄d.

The *History of Jack Horner* formed one of the favourite productions of the chapbook printers in the latter half of the eighteenth century, the earliest dated copy found being issued in 1764.

Little Boy Blue,
    Come blow your horn,
The sheep's in the meadow,
    The cow's in the corn;
But where is the boy
    Who looks after the sheep?
He's under a haycock,
    Fast asleep.
Will you wake him?
    No, not I,
For if I do,
    He's sure to cry.

It has been asserted that Little Boy Blue was intended to represent Cardinal Wolsey. It is pointed out that Wolsey was the son of an Ipswich butcher and, as a boy, undoubtedly looked after his father's livestock. As proof, the second couplet of the rhyme has been quoted as being incorporated in *The Tragedy of Cardinal Wolsey* (1587) by Thomas Churchyard; a careful search of the original edition, however, has failed to produce anything more resembling the rhyme than,

> O fie on wolves, that march in masking-clothes,
> For to devour the lambs, when shepherd sleeps.

A more likely allusion occurs in *King Lear* (III. vi), when Edgar, talking in his character of mad Tom, in a confusion of rhyme, cries:

> Sleepest or wakest thou, jolly shepheard?
> Thy sheepe bee in the corne;
> And for one blast of thy minikin mouth
> Thy sheepe shall take no harme.

> I see the moon,
> And the moon sees me;
> God bless the moon,
> And God bless me.

The English nursery is on friendly terms with the moon. Little children bow to it when it is new, see a man in it when it is eight days old, and cry when they can't have it. Yorkshire nurses say: "Moon penny bright as silver, come and play with little childer." The lads and lassies of Lancashire say: "I see the moon, and the moon sees me; God bless the priest that christened me." And when the moon shines into the bedrooms of trawlermen's children, they say: "I see the moon, and the moon sees me, God bless the sailors on the sea."

> This is the house that Jack built.

> This is the malt
> That lay in the house that Jack built.

> This is the rat,
> That ate the malt
> That lay in the house that Jack built.

> This is the cat,
> That killed the rat,
> That ate the malt
> That lay in the house that Jack built.

> This is the dog,
> That worried the cat,
> That killed the rat,
> That ate the malt
> That lay in the house that Jack built.

> This is the cow with the crumpled horn,
> That tossed the dog,
> That worried the cat,
> That killed the rat,
> That ate the malt
> That lay in the house that Jack built.

> This is the maiden all forlorn,
> That milked the cow with the crumpled horn,
> That tossed the dog,
> That worried the cat,
> That killed the rat,
> That ate the malt
> That lay in the house that Jack built.

> This is the man all tattered and torn,
> That kissed the maiden all forlorn,
> That milked the cow with the crumpled horn,
> That tossed the dog,
> That worried the cat,
> That killed the rat,
> That ate the malt
> That lay in the house that Jack built.

> This is the priest all shaven and shorn,
> That married the man all tattered and torn,
> That kissed the maiden all forlorn,
> That milked the cow with the crumpled horn,
> That tossed the dog,
> That worried the cat,
> That killed the rat,
> That ate the malt
> That lay in the house that Jack built.

> This is the cock that crowed in the morn,
> That waked the priest all shaven and shorn,

That married the man all tattered and torn,
That kissed the maiden all forlorn,
That milked the cow with the crumpled horn,
That tossed the dog,
That worried the cat,
That killed the rat,
That ate the malt
That lay in the house that Jack built.

This is the farmer sowing his corn,
That kept the cock that crowed in the morn,
That waked the priest all shaven and shorn,
That married the man all tattered and torn,
That kissed the maiden all forlorn,
That milked the cow with the crumpled horn,
That tossed the dog,
That worried the cat,
That killed the rat,
That ate the malt
That lay in the house that Jack built.

An accumulative rhyme which has had immense popularity during the past 150 years, and has probably been more parodied than any other nursery story, e.g. William Hone's *The Political House that Jack Built,* published 1819, illustrated by Cruikshank, which went into fifty-four editions; *The House that Austin Reed Built,* advertisement displayed in London Undergrounds in 1946. The rhyme has attracted the attention of both scholars and cranks, and at least two whole publications have been devoted to its significance. Facts to go on, however, are meagre.

Humpty Dumpty sat on a wall,
Humpty Dumpty had a great fall.
    All the king's horses,
    And all the king's men,
Couldn't put Humpty together again.

Humpty Dumpty has become so popular a nursery figure and is pictured so frequently that few people today think of the verse as containing a riddle. The reason the king's men could not put him together again is known to everyone. "It's very provoking to be called an egg—very," as Humpty admits in *Through the*

Charles Folkard combined the formal lines and patterns of a medieval scene with melodramatic details at the climactic moment when the king's men can't save Humpty Dumpty.

Looking-Glass, but such common knowledge cannot be gainsaid. What is not so certain is for how long the riddle has been known. It does not appear in early riddle books, but this may be because it was already too well-known. Students of linguistics believe that it is one of those pieces the antiquity of which "is to be measured in thousands of years, or rather it is so great that it cannot be measured at all" (Bett). Humpty Dumpty of England is elsewhere known as "Boule, boule" (France), "Thille Lille" (Sweden), "Lille-Trille" (Denmark), "Hillerin-Lillerin" (Finland), "Annebadadeli" (Switzerland), and "Trille Trölle," "Etje-Papetje," "Wirgele-Wargele," "Gigele-Gagele," "Rüntzelken-Püntzelken," and "Hümpelken-Pümpelken" (different parts of Germany). The riddles have the same form and motif, and it seems undeniable that they are connected with the English rhyme.

In marble halls as white as milk,
Lined with a skin as soft as silk,
Within a fountain crystal-clear,
A golden apple doth appear.
No doors there are to this stronghold,
Yet thieves break in and steal the gold.

RIDDLE. *Solution:* an egg.

MS collection "Riddles, Jokes, and Charades," c. 1810, begins with the more literal "In marble walls as white as milk" (Opie collection).

Little Miss Muffet
Sat on a tuffet,
Eating her curds and whey;
There came a big spider,
Who sat down beside her
And frightened Miss Muffet away.

Arthur Rackham's delicate watercolor (1913) exaggerates the frightening implications of "Little Miss Muffet" as his elegant young lady sits unaware of the gigantic gentleman spider approaching her.

This rhyme provides entertaining material for speculation. The suggestion has been put forward that Miss Muffet was Patience, the daughter of the entomologist Dr. Thomas Muffet (*d.* 1604) a man "whose admiration for spiders has never been surpassed." Since Dr. Muffet (or Moffett or Moufet) was the author of *The Silkwormes and their flies* "lively described in verse," it may be seen how easily the rhyme can be attributed to him. But as only Dr. Muffet could describe his verse as "lively," and no record of the epigram has been found earlier than 1805, any estimation must be cautious. Also it subsequently appears with material variations. "Little Mary Ester sat upon a tester" (1812), and "Little Miss Mopsey, Sat in the shopsey" (1842). It has, however, noticeable similarity to "Little Polly Flinders," "Little Poll Parrot," "Little Tommy Tacket," "Little General Monk," and "Little Jack Horner" (qq.v.). The last-named jingle is known to have been current in 1720, and is probably earlier, as also the lampoon "Little General Monk." Eckenstein compares these verses with the singing game "Little Polly Sanders" or "Little Alice Sander" who "sat upon a cinder" (recorded by Gomme), hence with the Cushion Dance called "Joan Saunderson" (described in 1686) which may be a variation of "Sally Waters." The Cush-

ion Dance is said to preserve "the association with weddings and with the May-Day festival which at one time was the occasion for mating and marriage." The inference is that the *form* of the rhyme, a person sitting and waiting and something important arriving, dates to heathen times. It is possible that most of these rhymes are parodies of whichever is the earliest of them. An analysis of the children's books published in 1945–6 showed that of all the nursery verses "Miss Muffet" figures the most frequently, perhaps because the subject lends itself to illustration. Millais painted the picture "Little Miss Muffet" in 1884.

***Miss Muffet probably sat on a grassy hillock, though *tuffet* has also been described as a "three-legged-stool." When she sits on a *buffet* she is certainly on a stool, and may come from the north country. Whether Mary Ester perched on a sixpence, a bed canopy, or a piece of armour for the head is a moot point.

As I was going to St. Ives,
I met a man with seven wives,
Each wife had seven sacks,
Each sack had seven cats,
Each cat had seven kits:
Kits, cats, sacks, and wives,
How many were there going to St. Ives?

Catch. The solution is "one" or "none" according to how the question is read. If the question is as plainly put as it was by a writer 200 years ago, "Qu: How many Wives, Sacs, Cats and Kittens went to St. Ives?" the answer is clearly "none."

Wee Willie Winkie runs through the town,
Upstairs and downstairs in his night-gown,
Rapping at the window, crying through the
    lock,
Are the children all in bed, for now it's eight
    o'clock?

The author of this "hamely clinky" personifying sleep was William Miller (1810–72), "the Laureate of the Nursery." It appears above his name in *Whistle-Binkie; a Collection of Songs for the Social Circle,* published by David Robertson in 1841, and is the first of five verses.

L. Leslie Brooke, called "a spiritual descendant of Caldecott" by Maurice Sendak, turned short nursery rhymes into energetic multi-page dramas with his whimsical series of detailed drawings. Brooke's Wee Willie Winkie puts himself to bed in a later scene, after his sprightly run through the town.

Kate Greenaway (1846–1901)

One of the best-known old alphabet jingles, "A Apple Pie" was mentioned in print as "A Apple-pasty" in the seventeenth century and was published from the eighteenth century on with various names, such as "The Tragical Death of A, Apple-Pye." A picture-alphabet based on sounds made by animals appeared in one of the oldest illustrated books for children, *Orbis Sensualium Pictus* by Johan Comenius (1658, see Part 6), while "A Apple Pie" uses action verbs to make the alphabet humorous and memorable. Kate Greenaway's *A Apple Pie* (1886) is one of the most popular picture book versions, with a lively illustration for each line of the verse. In spite of their fashionable frilly clothing, it is noteworthy that in the illustration for T, girls have active roles as both the taker of the pie and her pursuers. See the headnote on Kate Greenaway in Part 6, with two of her original poems and illustrations, as well as illustrations from another alphabet book by Chris Van Allsburg in that section.

A Apple Pie

A Apple Pie
B Bit It
C Cut It
D Dealt It
E Eat It
F Fought for It
G Got It
H Had It
I Inspected It
J Jumped for It
K Knelt for It
L Longed for It
M Mourned for It
N Nodded for It
O Opened It
P Peeped in It
Q Quartered It
R Ran for It
S Sang for It
T Took It

UVWXYZ All Had A Large Slice And Went Off
 To Bed

Kate Greenaway's bold capital letters and groups of energetic boys and girls set a new standard for alphabet books when she illustrated an ancient rhyme in *A Apple Pie,* engraved and printed by Edmund Evans (1886).

Folk Song

"The Tree in the Wood" is best known as a popular folk song in England and America, recorded from the oral tradition in many collections of children's songs and camp songs, as well as adult audio recordings. Some variations are called an echo song when different singers repeat the lines of each new verse. Like other cumulative tales (such as "The Pancake") and rhymes (such as "The House that Jack Built"), it accumulates a series of repetitive lines. In contrast to the silly nonsense of so many nursery rhymes, its cyclical structure eloquently follows the life cycles of a tree, the birds it shelters, and a human who plants a new tree, making it appealing to contemporary readers and singers who promote environmental awareness through the arts. This version, from S. Baring-Gould's *A Book of Nursery Songs and Rhymes* (1895), was adapted by Christopher Manson in a picture book with beautiful painted woodcuts in an Arts and Crafts style (1993).

The Tree in the Wood

All in a wood there grew a fine tree,
The finest tree that ever you did see,
And the green grass grew around, around, around,
And the green grass grew around.

And on this tree there grew a fine bough,
The finest bough that ever you did see,
And the bough on the tree, and the tree in the wood,
And the green leaves flourished thereon, thereon,
    thereon,
And the green leaves flourished thereon.

And on this bough there grew a fine twig,
The finest twig that ever you did see,
And the twig on the bough, and the bough on the
    tree, and the tree in the wood,
And the green leaves flourished thereon, etc.

And on this twig there stood a fine nest,
The finest nest that ever you did see,
And the nest on the twig, and the twig on the
    bough, etc.

And in this nest there sat a fine bird,
The finest bird, etc.

And on this bird there grew a fine feather,
The finest feather, etc.

And of this feather was made a fine bed,
The finest bed, etc.

And on this bed was laid a fine mother,
The finest mother, etc.

In the arms of this mother was laid a fine babe,
The finest babe, etc.

And the babe he grew up and became a fine
    boy,
The finest boy, etc.

And boy put an acorn all into the earth,
The finest acorn, etc.

And out of this acorn there grew a fine tree,
The finest tree, etc.

James Still (1906–2001)

James Still was best known for writing poetry and prose for adults, but he said when he was over seventy, "I'd rather light up a child's eyes than earn a grunt of approval from a dozen of their elders."[1] Spending most of his life in eastern Kentucky's Cumberland Plateau, Still served as a librarian at Hindman Settlement School in the 1930s, and always strove to improve the lives of children in the region. Rural children looked forward to regular visits from "the book boy," as they called him when he carried books on foot to the country schools near Hindman, to provide them with a varied selection of good literature to read. As a writer, he earned acclaim for his eloquent poetry and realistic fiction about ordinary Appalachian people, especially *River of Earth* (1940). *Sporty Creek,* a sequel that is also narrated by a young boy living through the Great Depression, was published as a children's novel in 1977. Still's strong interest in childhood, folklore, and dialect is evident in many other works besides these novels, including *Jack and the Wonder Beans* (an Appalachian "Jack and the Beanstalk") and two books of riddles with other lore and poetry. He was over ninety years old when novelist Lee Smith persuaded him to publish *An Appalachian Mother Goose* (1998), after Still showed her some verses he had written down for fun.

Comparing the nursery rhymes Still collected and older versions published by the Opies shows how oral traditions evolve, as new silly rhymes build on and parody the old nonsense rhymes. Many Scots-Irish, English, and German immigrants brought their folk cultures to Appalachia, where tales, poems, and songs developed interesting blends of Old World and New World language and images. Hazard (a Kentucky town) replaces Norwich, England, in a funny rhyme about a blizzard, while regional "victuals" such as stack cakes and turnip greens appear elsewhere. Some of the fantasy disappeared from these familiar rhymes, replaced by down-to-earth humor about Jack Be Nimble scorching his pants and the dog laughing at the musical cow and cat in "Hey Diddle Diddle." The old woman in a shoe is more resourceful and humane than her European ancestor. The king's men are gone from "Humpty Dumpty," which is no longer a riddle as the speaker explicitly longs for the lost egg for breakfast. Picture book artist Paul Brett Johnson, a native of the Kentucky mountains and former student of Still's, illustrated the book with black-and-white drawings that enhance the rhymes' blend of homey charm and silly humor. Johnson's cow posed daintily on two back legs singing ballads is more amusing than most of her predecessors as they have been depicted jumping over moons in "Hey Diddle Diddle" by generations of nursery rhyme illustrators.

NOTE

1. "An Interview with James Still," *Appalachian Journal* 6 (Winter 1979): 124.

From *An Appalachian Mother Goose*

PREFACE

There was a time not so long ago when the hills and hollows of Appalachia abounded in creekbed roads, and travel was by horseback, mountain sled, or shank's-mare (walking). The one-room schools were taught by masters of limited learning, and the custom was to recite lessons in a chorus of voices. Thus they were called Blab Schools. Among verses of renown, students got "by heart" the Mother Goose rhymes and often changed them to match their time and place and understanding. And sometimes they created their own.

> Do not take us for a dunce
> Reciting lessons all at once.

> Pat-a-cake, pat-a-cake, baker's man,
> Mix me a stack-cake, bake it in a pan;
> A slice for Mary Belle, a slice for Lum,
> A slice for Sally, and save me some.

> Humpty Dumpty sat on a wall,
> And if he'd managed not to fall,
> Teeter or totter, clung to the last,
> We'd had an egg to break our fast.

> Hey diddle diddle,
> The cat played the fiddle,

Paul Brett Johnson's pencil drawing of a soulful cow who sings ballads instead of jumping over the moon in James Still's Appalachian version of "Hey Diddle Diddle."

> The cow sang ballads to the moon;
> The little dog laughed,
> He thought them daft,
> And the dish banged away with the spoon.

Jack and Jill went up the hill
To fetch a bucket of water:
Jack fell down and cracked his crown,
And Jill died of laughter.

Jill came to life, became Jack's wife,
And soon they had a daughter;
Jack spent his days in several ways,
The womenfolk fetched the water.

The man in the moon came down too soon
To inquire the way to Hazard;
The man from the sun arrived too late
And got himself caught in a blizzard.

The Appalachian mountains of Kentucky make an appropriate setting for the well up high in "Jack and Jill," especially when James Still's verses and Paul Brett Johnson's drawing show that Jill pays for laughing at Jack's injury through years of lugging water downhill for a lazy husband.

Folk Song

"A Frog Went A-Courting" is one of the most popular folk songs in history. People all around the English-speaking world have fond memories of parents singing it to them in early childhood, and it appears in numerous nursery rhyme books with pictures by prominent illustrators, such as Randolph Caldecott and Feodor Rojankovsky (winner of the 1956 Caldecott medal for illustrating a version by John Langstaff, whose article on oral traditions appears above). Perhaps the fable "The Mouse, the Frog, and the Hawk" is an ancient antecedent, since an unlucky Mouse "formed an intimate acquaintance with a Frog" (see *Aesop's Fables,* later in this section). A 1580 entry for the ballad "A Moste Strange Weddinge of the Frogge and the Mouse," in the register of the London Company of Stationers, indicates that people have enjoyed nonsense tales about romance between different species for a long time, as Edward Lear confirmed when he wrote "The Owl and the Pussy-cat." Beatrix Potter, influenced by Caldecott's *A Frog He Would a Wooing Go,* used part of the rhyme in her privately printed edition of *A Tailor of Gloucester* (1902) and in a booklet of sketches called "A Frog He Would A-Fishing Go." A century later, dramatist R. Rex Stephenson put the song in the mouth of the Appalachian folktale heroine Mutsmag in a humorous and suspenseful bedtime scene (see "Mutsmag" in this section).

"Froggie Went A'Courtin' " was recorded in the twentieth century by prominent folk singers, such as Bob Dylan, who sang a well-known American version ending with a verse about cornbread. Many variants have different nonsense refrains, such as "With a rowley powley, gammon and spinach, / Heigho, says Anthony Rowley!" or "Siminik-a-bominik-laddy-bone-a-rigdum / Rigdum-laddy-bone-a-kimo." American versions often follow each line with a simple "Umph—humph," which some view as the place to imitate the frog's croaking. With many variations on the cast of different animals and exact sequence of events, the plot that begins as a mock romance is like many other old nursery rhymes and tales when it ends with the sudden and brutal deaths of characters who fall victim to natural predators like a snake, a bird, or a duck. In other versions, the married couple survive and even have children. This one leaves us wondering about the fate of the mouse who goes to live in a deep well with her frog husband. A Kentucky girl sang it in 1917 for the English folklorist Cecil Sharp, who recorded a number of American variants on this song while collecting ballads in the southern mountains (published in *English Folk Songs from the Southern Appalachians,* 1932).

A Frog Went A-Courting

A frog went a-courting and he did ride, Ha . . . ha,
A frog went a-courting and he did ride,
A sword and pistol by his side, Ha . . . ha.

Frog rode up to Lady Mouse's den,
Says: Lady Mouse, will you let me in?

Took Lady Mouse on his knee,
Said: Lady Mouse, will you marry me?

Without the rat's consent,
I'll not marry the President.

Uncle Rat's gone to town
To buy his niece a wedding-gown.

What will be the wedding-gown?
A piece of hair of an old greyhound.

What will the wedding-dinner be?
Two soup beans and a black-eyed pea.

Where will the wedding-dinner be?
Away down yonder in the hollow tree.

First come in was a little old fly,
He ate up all the wedding-pie.

Next came in was a little old chick,
Ate so much it made him sick.

Next came in was a bumble-bee,
Fiddle and a bow all on his knee.

The Lady Mouse down to dwell,
Down in the bottom of an old deep well.

Piece of cold bread laying on the shelf.
If you want any more you must sing it
    yourself.

"Pray, Miss MOUSE, will you give us some beer?" *Heigho, says* ROWLEY! "For Froggy and I are fond of good cheer." After this scene of merry-making in Randolph Caldecott's 1883 version of the traditional rhyme, Frog sees his friends attacked by cats and then a duck gobbles him up. See Part 6 for more on Caldecott's influential Victorian picture books such as *A Frog He Would A-Wooing Go* (1883).

Edward Lear (1812—88)

Edward Lear, an artist and writer of travel books, became, along with his fellow Victorian Lewis Carroll, an unrivaled master of nonsense verse. Raised primarily by much older sisters in a huge London family that lost its money, Lear was ill, depressed, and insecure throughout much of his life. He found relief in entertaining children, sharing their love of activity, friendship, fun, and wordplay. In the 1830s he began writing for the children of his patron. *A Book of Nonsense* (1846) eventually established the literary fame of Lear and the comical new poetic form of the limerick. The great Victorian art critic John Ruskin said his "idle self" was grateful for "surely the most beneficent and innocent of all books yet produced . . . inimitable and refreshing, and perfect in rhythm."[1] *Nonsense Songs, Stories, Botany and Alphabets* (1871) contains Lear's best narrative poems, including "The Jumblies" (those fantasy creatures who went to sea in a sieve) and the two poems reprinted here. Musically talented, Lear liked to sing nursery rhymes to friends, and his own silly rhymes and songs are literary descendants of the old oral nursery rhymes—lyrical, memorable, illogical, and fantastical. He also illustrated them with humorous drawings. Many of the limericks are miniature melodramas, like the Man of Bohemia's daughter running away with a thief, or descriptions of people with absurd problems or accomplishments related to fantastical physical features or superhuman abilities. "The Broom, the Shovel, the Poker, and the Tongs" is a fantasy with inanimate objects as the characters, like the dish running away with the spoon in "Hey Diddle Diddle." It would be an ordinary romance without the silly rhymes and discussion of physical features of household implements. "The Owl and the Pussy-cat," the romantic story of an unlikely elopement (with the lady making the proposal!), contains one of the few really happy endings in the lonely poet's books. Beatrix Potter, a later Victorian writer of animal fantasy, was so intrigued with the pig that lived "in the land where the Bong tree grows" that she wrote her longest story about him, *Little Pig Robinson* (1930).

NOTE

1. John Ruskin quoted in *A Book of Nonsense* by Edward Lear (1861; London: Routledge, 2002).

The Owl and the Pussy-cat

The Owl and the Pussy-cat went to sea
  In a beautiful pea-green boat,
They took some honey, and plenty of
    money,
  Wrapped up in a five-pound note.
The Owl looked up to the stars above,

  And sang to a small guitar,
"O lovely Pussy! O Pussy, my love,
  What a beautiful Pussy you are,
    You are,
    You are!
  What a beautiful Pussy you are!"

Pussy said to the Owl, "You elegant fowl!
  How charmingly sweet you sing!
O let us be married! too long we have tarried:
  But what shall we do for a ring?"
They sailed away, for a year and a day,
  To the land where the Bong-tree grows,
And there in a wood a Piggy-wig stood
  With a ring at the end of his nose,
    His nose,
    His nose,
  With a ring at the end of his nose.

"Dear Pig, are you willing to sell for one shilling
  Your ring?" Said the Piggy, "I will."
So they took it away, and were married next day
  By the turkey who lives on the hill.
They dined on mince, and slices of quince,
  Which they ate with a runcible spoon;

And hand in hand, on the edge of the sand,
  They danced by the light of the moon,
    The moon,
    The moon,
  They danced by the light of the moon.

Edward Lear was an artist who created fanciful line drawings for his own nonsense poems.

The Broom, the Shovel, the Poker, and the Tongs

I

The Broom and the Shovel, the Poker and Tongs,
  They all took a drive in the Park,
And they each sang a song, Ding-a-dong, Ding-a-
    dong,
  Before they went back in the dark.
Mr. Poker he sate quite upright in the coach,
  Mr. Tongs made a clatter and clash,
Miss Shovel was dressed all in black (with a
    brooch),
  Mrs. Broom was in blue (with a sash).
    Ding-a-dong! Ding-a-dong!
    And they all sang a song!

II

"O Shovely so lovely!" the Poker he sang,
  "You have perfectly conquered my heart!
Ding-a-dong! Ding-a-dong! If you're pleased with
    my song,

I will feed you with cold apple tart!
When you scrape up the coals with a delicate
    sound,
  You enrapture my life with delight!
Your nose is so shiny! your head is so round!
  And your shape is so slender and bright!
    Ding-a-dong! Ding-a-dong!
    Ain't you pleased with my song?"

Like owls and pussy-cats, household implements get to travel in style in Edward Lear's fantastical poems.

III

"Alas! Mrs. Broom!" sighed the Tongs in his song,
  "O is it because I'm so thin,
And my legs are so long—Ding-a-dong! Ding-a-
    dong!
  That you don't care about me a pin?
Ah! fairest of creatures, when sweeping the room,
  Ah! why don't you heed my complaint!
Must you needs be so cruel, you beautiful Broom,
  Because you are covered with paint?
      Ding-a-dong! Ding-a-dong!
      You are certainly wrong!"

IV

Mrs. Broom and Miss Shovel together they sang,
  "What nonsense you're singing to-day!"
Said the Shovel, "I'll certainly hit you a bang!"
  Said the Broom, "And I'll sweep you away!"
So the Coachman drove homeward as fast as he
    could,
  Perceiving their anger with pain;
But they put on the kettle, and little by little,
  They all became happy again.
      Ding-a-dong! Ding-a-dong!
      There's an end of my song!

There Was an Old Man with a Beard

There was an Old Man with a beard, who said, "It
    is just as I feared!—
Two Owls and a Hen, four Larks and a Wren,
Have all built their nests in my beard!"

Edward Lear's own drawing of the unfortunate man with
birds nesting in his beard.

There Was an Old Man of Bohemia

There was an old Man of Bohemia, whose
    daughter was christened Euphemia;
Till one day, to his grief, she married a thief,
Which grieved that old Man of Bohemia.

Edward Lear created a family melodrama within a few lines
of limerick and this drawing of the wayward couple fleeing,
apparently, with the family silver.

There Was a Young Lady Whose Nose

There was a Young Lady whose nose, was so long
   that it reached to her toes;
So she hired an Old Lady, whose conduct was
   steady,
To carry that wonderful nose.

Fantastically long noses appear in several of Edward Lear's limericks.

Shel Silverstein (1932–99)

Shel Silverstein was the most popular American poet for children in the second half of the twentieth century. A native of Chicago, he worked as a cartoonist and playwright for adults, and also wrote and performed songs. When picture book artist Tomi Ungerer introduced him to the influential editor Ursula Nordstrom, they persuaded him to begin writing for children in 1963. His picture book *The Giving Tree,* which established his fame in 1964, continues to spark debate between readers who love it as a sentimental tribute to motherhood or a religious parable about altruism and those who see in it a cautionary tale about human selfishness, since a boy who grows into a man repeatedly takes everything a motherly tree offers until there is no tree left. Like Edward Lear, Silverstein illustrated volumes of poetry with his own humorous, eccentric line drawings. But he focused more intently than Lear on the child's point of view, revealing the dark moments, as well as the joy and fun of childhood experiences. *Where the Sidewalk Ends* (1974) opens by alluding to the oral traditions of storytelling and folktales, inviting anyone who is "a dreamer, a wisher, a liar, / A hope-er, a pray-er, a magic bean buyer . . . a pretender" to "come sit by my fire / For we have some flax-golden tales to spin." Many of these poetic tales are about contemporary problems of everyday life, like Sarah Cynthia Silvia Stout's refusal to take the garbage out. Silverstein mocks old cautionary tales (see Hoffmann's *Struwwelpeter* poem in Part 2), with exaggerated descriptions of Sarah's garbage and the narrator's reluctance to reveal her "awful fate." Silverstein's other poetry collections include *A Light in the Attic* (1981) and *Falling Up* (1996). Critic Morag Styles observes that "his nonsense is difficult to describe, but a kind of crazy, contorted, irrepressible energy seems to spring from Silverstein's pen," as well as "a feeling for the 'underdog' and those who are weak, troubled, or eccentric."[1] The boy in "Zebra Question" is a little like Lewis Carroll's Alice in Wonderland, bewildered by the barrage of questions thrown back at him by an indignant zebra—questions that extend his own naive inquiry about zebra stripes incessantly, but make the reader think about the combination of dark and light in each life. As Silverstein's poem "New World" says, "it's nice to see / The world—from a different angle."

NOTE

1. Morag Styles, *From the Garden to the Street: An Introduction to Three Hundred Years of Poetry for Children* (London: Cassell, 1998) 118.

Sarah Cynthia Sylvia Stout Would Not Take the Garbage Out

Sarah Cynthia Sylvia Stout
Would not take the garbage out!
She'd scour the pots and scrape the pans,
Candy the yams and spice the hams,
And though her daddy would scream and shout,
She simply would not take the garbage out.
And so it piled up to the ceilings:
Coffee grounds, potato peelings,
Brown bananas, rotten peas,
Chunks of sour cottage cheese.
It filled the can, it covered the floor,
It cracked the window and blocked the door
With bacon rinds and chicken bones,
Drippy ends of ice cream cones,
Prune pits, peach pits, orange peel,
Gloppy glumps of cold oatmeal,
Pizza crusts and withered greens,
Soggy beans and tangerines,
Crusts of black burned buttered toast,
Gristly bits of beefy roasts . . .
The garbage rolled on down the hall,
It raised the roof, it broke the wall . . .
Greasy napkins, cookie crumbs,
Globs of gooey bubble gum,

Cellophane from green baloney,
Rubbery blubbery macaroni,
Peanut butter, caked and dry,
Curdled milk and crusts of pie,
Moldy melons, dried-up mustard,
Eggshells mixed with lemon custard,
Cold french fries and rancid meat,
Yellow lumps of Cream of Wheat.
At last the garbage reached so high
That finally it touched the sky.
And all the neighbors moved away,
And none of her friends would come to play.
And finally Sarah Cynthia Stout said,
"OK, I'll take the garbage out!"
But then, of course, it was too late . . .
The garbage reached across the state,
From New York to the Golden Gate.
And there, in the garbage she did hate,
Poor Sarah met an awful fate,
That I cannot right now relate
Because the hour is much too late.
But children, remember Sarah Stout
And always take the garbage out!

Zebra Question

I asked the zebra,
Are you black with white stripes?
Or white with black stripes?
And the zebra asked me,
Are you good with bad habits?
Or are you bad with good habits?
Are you noisy with quiet times?
Or are you quiet with noisy times?
Are you happy with some sad days?
Or are you sad with some happy days?
Are you neat with some sloppy ways?
Or are you sloppy with some neat ways?
And on and on and on and on
And on and on he went.
I'll never ask a zebra
About stripes
Again.

Shel Silverstein's drawing for his poem "Zebra Question" captures the fury of boy and zebra when they ask each other annoying questions.

Jeanne Steig (b.1930) and William Steig (1907–2003)

Alpha Beta Chowder is one of Jeanne Steig's books of humorous poems and tales illustrated by her famous husband in his later years. William Steig, who had been a successful cartoonist for *The New Yorker* since 1930, began a second career as a writer and illustrator of children's books at age 61. Among the early successes that he wrote himself were *CDB!* (1968), a little book of letter puzzles and wordplay, and *Roland, The Minstrel Pig* (1968). He is best known for animal fantasies that combine archetypal adventures with modem details and wry humor, such as *Sylvester and the Magic Pebble* (1969) and *Doctor De Soto* (1982). *Abel's Island* (1976), one of his longer stories, is an illustrated chapter book about a spoiled, elitist mouse who is stranded on an island for a year without his wife. When Steig died in 2003, the films based on his picture book *Shrek!* (1993) were immensely popular, but they altered the image of Steig's irredeemably mean, ugly monster who finds a wife just like himself. Jeanne Steig, who is also an artist, collaborated with William on lighthearted collections of fairy tales, myths, and verses based on the Bible (*The Old Testament Made Easy,* 1990). *Alpha Beta Chowder* (1992) is in the tradition of alphabet books with a poem for each letter. It is full of witty, alliterative caricatures, such as Deplorable Dora ("drab and dreary"), Gruesome Gilbert ("a greedy glutton"), Noisome Naomi, and Toby "tweaking tiny Tina," The offbeat stories range from medieval quest and interplanetary romance to mundane slices of ordinary life, such as the warthogs' nostalgia for younger days and determination to get the husband on a diet. The poems, which have been compared to the comic verses of Ogden Nash, weave big words into tongue twisters with relentless rhythms that make some adults reluctant to read them to children, but children love hearing the humorous sounds of the exuberant wordplay.

Worrywart

"Whatever happened to your waist!"
The warthog's wife exclaimed.
"How weirdly wide you have become!
Why aren't you ashamed?"

"Ah, woe is me," the warthog wailed,
"My wardrobe doesn't fit.
I've gained such wobbly wads of weight,
My woolen pants are split.

"I waddle wildly when I walk,
And weep to contemplate
How winningly I used to waltz.
My polka was first-rate."

"When we," his wife went on, "were wed,
You were a winsome lad,
While now you are a wheezing wreck!
It's worrisome and sad."

The warthog wrung his heavy hooves.
"Dear Wife, I'm mortified.
I'll whittle down this wretched flesh—
I give my word," he cried.

"I'll live on watercress and weeds
Till I am willow thin.
And you and I shall waltz once more.
Next Wednesday I begin!"

William Steig continued the old tradition of mocking human behavior through animal fantasy in his colorful images of animals in clothing and furnished houses. Here the aging but well-dressed warthog in Jeanne Steig's poem "Worrywart" considers his wife's advice about dieting.

Grace Nichols (b.1950)

Grace Nichols, who grew up in Guyana, has lived in Britain since 1977, writing poetry and prose for children and adults. These poems are from her first collection for children, *Come On into My Tropical Garden* (1988). Since then, she has written and edited a number of other award-winning books, including collections of new and traditional nursery rhymes. Like the poems of Robert Louis Stevenson a century earlier (in Part 4), Nichols's verses capture the perspective of a young child while also revealing elements of adult awareness. Both poets celebrate the child's love of nature, small details of everyday life, and the active, playful world of the child's imagination. Both personify elements of nature, although Nichols adds a late twentieth-century note of concern about the fate of the environment in poems such as "For Forest." Both book titles refer to the garden as an archetypal setting of childhood, but Stevenson's child persona is a privileged white child of the nineteenth-century British Empire, one who imagines "foreign lands" as vague, distant fairy places or thinks of "foreign children" as exotic but less fortunate than himself. Nichols invites readers into a "tropical garden" where we might kiss a chimpanzee while reveling in the tastes, sights, sounds, and feel of life in a former British colony in South America. Like James Berry and other British-Caribbean writers who rose to prominence in the 1980s, Nichols believes that children need to see their own environment and experiences celebrated in their literature, as well as to learn about the history and folklife of different cultures. She uses regional dialect and folklore along with standard English and universal images of sea and sky, childhood fun, and adult labor. Her compelling poems are admired for their strong and lively yet controlled rhythms. Some of the poems reprinted here imitate the silly fun of nursery rhymes, while others have the feel of ritualistic chants celebrating nature and family. The interplay of oral tradition and literacy in the child's world comes to the forefront in "I Like to Stay Up," when the child loves the thrill of listening to old ghost stories, called "jumbie stories," but gets so frightened that she longs for the security of reading a book in bed.

From *Come On into My Tropical Garden*

POOR GRANDMA

Why this child
so spin-spin spin-spin
Why this child can't keep still

Why this child
so turn-round
turn-round

Why this child
can't settle down

Why this child
can't eat without getting
up to look through window
Why this child must behave so
I want to know
Why this child

so spin-spin spin-spin
Why this child
can't keep still

RIDDLE

Me-riddle me-riddle me-ree
Me father got a tree
Tell me what you see
hanging from this tree

You can boil it
you can bake it
you can roast it
you can fry it
it goes lovely in a dish
with flying fish

It's big
it's rough
it's green
it came with old Captain
Bligh
from way across the sea

Still can't guess?
well, it's a breadfruit
Me-riddle me-riddle me-ree

WHA ME MUDDER DO

Mek me tell you wha me mudder do
wha me mudder do
wha me mudder do

Me mudder pound plaintain mek fufu
Me mudder catch crab mek calaloo stew

Mek me tell you wha me mudder do
wha me mudder do
wha me mudder do

Me mudder beat hammer
Me mudder turn screw
she paint chair red
then she paint it blue

Mek me tell you wha me mudder do
wha me mudder do
wha me mudder do

Me mudder chase bad-cow
with one "Shoo"
she paddle down river
in she own canoe
Ain't have nothing
dat me mudder can't do
Ain't have nothing
dat me mudder can't do

Mek me tell you

I LIKE TO STAY UP

I like to stay up
and listen
when big people talking
jumbie stories

I does feel
so tingly and excited
inside me

But when my mother say
"Girl, time for bed"

Then is when
I does feel a dread

Then is when
I does jump into me bed

Then is when
I does cover up
from me feet to me head

Then is when
I does wish I didn't listen
to no stupid jumbie story

Then is when I does wish I did read
me book instead

("Jumbie" is a Guyanese word for "ghost")

MOON-GAZER

On moonlight night
when moon is bright
Beware, Beware—

Moon-Gazer man
with his throw-back head
and his open legs
gazing, gazing
up at the moon

Moon-Gazer man
with his seal-skin hair
and his round-eye stare
staring, staring
up at the moon

Moon-Gazer man
standing tall,
lamp-post tall,
just gazing up
at moon eye-ball

But never try to pass
between those open legs
cause Moon-Gazer man
will close them with a snap—
you'll be trapped

Moon-Gazer man
will crush you flat.
Yes, with just one shake
suddenly you'll be—
a human pancake,

On moonlight night
when moon is bright
for goodness' sake
stay home—
and pull your window-curtain tight.

("Moon-Gazer" is a supernatural folk-figure, extremely tall,
who could be seen mostly straddling roadways on moonlit
nights, gazing up at the moon. It is best to avoid passing between his legs.)

THE SUN

The sun is a glowing spider
that crawls out
from under the earth
to make her way across the sky
warming and weaving

with her bright old fingers
of light

THEY WERE MY PEOPLE

They were those who cut cane
to the rhythm of the sunbeat

They were those who carried cane
to the rhythm of the sunbeat

They were those who crushed cane
to the rhythm of the sunbeat

They were women weeding, carrying babies
to the rhythm of the sunbeat

They were my people working so hard
to the rhythm of the sunbeat

They were my people, working so hard
to the rhythm of the sunbeat—long ago
to the rhythm of the sunbeat

SKY

Tall and blue
true and open

So open my arms have room
for all the world
for sun and moon
        for birds and stars

Yet how I wish I had the chance
to come drifting down to earth—
        a simple bed sheet
covering some little girl or boy
just for a night
        but I am Sky
        that's why

I AM THE RAIN

I am the rain
I like to play games
like sometimes
        I pretend

I'm going
        to fall
Man, that's the time
I don't come at all

Like sometimes
I get these laughing stitches
up my sides
        rushing people in
and out
        with the clothesline
I just love drip
        dropping
down collars
        and spines
Maybe it's a shame
but it's the only way
I get some fame

FOR FOREST

Forest could keep secrets
Forest could keep secrets

Forest tune in every day
to watersound and birdsound
Forest letting her hair down
to the teeming creeping of her forest-ground

But Forest don't broadcast her business
no Forest cover her business down
from sky and fast-eye sun
and when night come
and darkness wrap her like a gown
Forest is a bad dream woman

Forest dreaming about mountain
and when earth was young

Forest dreaming of the caress of gold
Forest rootsing with mysterious Eldorado

and when howler monkey
wake her up with howl
Forest just stretch and stir
to a new day of sound

but coming back to secrets
Forest could keep secrets
Forest could keep secrets

And we must keep Forest

SEA TIMELESS SONG

Hurricane come
and hurricane go
but sea—sea timeless
sea timeless
sea timeless
sea timeless
sea timeless

Hibiscus bloom
then dry wither so
but sea—sea timeless
sea timeless
sea timeless
sea timeless
sea timeless

Tourist come
and tourist go
but sea—sea timeless
sea timeless
sea timeless
sea timeless
sea timeless

Shonto Begay (b.1954)

Shonto Begay, born on the reservation near Shonto, Arizona, is a Navajo (Diné) children's book illustrator and author. As a boy, he was removed from his hogan home and forced to attend a government boarding school, like many twentieth-century Native American children in the United States. He studied art at the Institute of American Indian Arts, Santa Fe, New Mexico, and the California College of Arts and Crafts in Oakland, California. He has illustrated Native American picture books such as *The Mud Pony: A Traditional Skidi Pawnee Tale* (1988). He represents Native American life in his work with realism and respect. In the illustrations for *Navajo Visions and Voices Across the Mesa,* one finds affection for the traditional Diné way of life and a clear-eyed vision of contemporary realities. His poems in this collection recall his childhood—the hardships as well as the celebrations and the mysteries of the natural environment. Begay pays tribute to his grandparents for teaching him creation stories and cultural traditions, while he describes his mother in her kitchen in relation to his more personal memories and "childhood dreams." In an interview, Begay said, "I learned to savor the beauty and to feel at home among the red mesas, piñon, and juniper. My world was the circular line of the horizon. This was the place that harbored ancient Gods and animal beings that were so alive in the stories of my people. The teachings of my elders make it very clear that this land is sacred and we belong to it; it does not belong to us. I learned that Nature was more than just what I saw—that she is life and therefore gives and maintains life. She commands respect."[1]

NOTE

1. Shonto Begay, "The Author Page," *The Internet Public Library* 31 Mar. 1997, School of Information and Library Studies, University of Michigan, 22 Apr. 2005 <http://www.ipl.org/div/kidspace/askauthor/begay.html>.

From *Navajo Visions and Voices Across the Mesa*

CREATION

Many winter nights,
my father sat up and told us stories—
stories that came alive through voice and gesture.
Shadows from an old oil drum stove
danced on the hogan wall.
The stove pipe rattled every once in a while
as the snow and wind whined outside.

Tiny drifts of snow sifted through
the cracks in the door.
The story hogan was warm,
the storytelling voice soothing.
He told us stories of creation, of the journey
through four worlds to get to the present one.

First World was the dark world.
Insects lived in the cold.
Unhappiness drove them into the Second World,

the blue world. Birds lived there.
Jealousy ruled and the beings
of the Second World emerged into the Third.
The Third World was inhabited
by larger mammal beings,
Bear, Deer, Coyote, and Wolf,
and all of their cousins.
Life was good in the Third World for many years,
until slowly these beings began to argue
and fight among themselves.
Coyote stole Water-Being's baby
and the Third World was flooded.
The beings moved up to the Fourth World
through a reed.
Locust came up first. Turkey came up last.

First Man and First Woman were created
on the rim of the Fourth World.
The hero twins, Born-for-Water and Monster
    Slayer,
were born of their mother, Changing Woman,
and their father, the sun.
They were born for a purpose.
Monsters of great size and power roamed the land,
making life miserable for the first people.
The hero twins were to save the people
and the land from these monsters.
In a great battle, mountain ranges fell,
lakes dried up, and the earth trembled.
One by one, the great giants were felled.
These scars and places where Monster fell can still
be seen as mountains, volcanic plugs, and gorges.
After the people of the Fourth World were saved,
they were instructed to rule wisely.
They were placed in charge of maintaining
    harmony.
They were given the four sacred mountains
as guardians of our holy land, *Diné tah*.

The younger ones are usually asleep by now.
My father ends his story for the night.
There will be many more nights
this winter for stories. The fire in the stove roars,
and shadows on the wall continue their dance.

GRANDMOTHER

Grandmother was strong, like a distant mesa.
From her sprang many stories of days long ago.

From her gentle manners
lessons were learned
not easily forgotten.
She told us time and again
that the earth is our mother,
our holy mother.

"Always greet the coming day
by greeting your grandparents,
Yá' át' ééh Shi cheii (Hello, My Grandfather)
to the young juniper tree.
Yá' át' ééh Shi másání (Hello, My Grandmother)
to the young piñon tree."

The lines in her face were marks of honor,
countless winters gazing into the blizzard,
many summers in the hot cornfield.
Her strong brown hands, once smooth,
carried many generations,
gestured many stories,
wiped away many tears.
The whiteness of her windblown hair,
a halo against the setting sun.

My grandmother was called Asdzán Alts'íísí,
Small Woman. Wife of Little Hat,
mother of generations of Bitter Water Clan,
she lived 113 years.

IN MY MOTHER'S KITCHEN

Fragrance of fresh tortillas and corn stew
Fills my mother's kitchen
Sparsely furnished
Crowded with warmth
Soot-grayed walls, secretive and blank
She moves gently in and out of light
Like a dream just out of reach

The morning light gives her a halo
That plays upon her crown of dark hair
Strong brown hands caress soft mounds of dough
She gazes out into the warming day
Past sagebrush hills, out towards the foot of Black
    Mesa
How far would she let the goats wander today
Before it rains

Childhood dreams and warmth
Tight in my throat, tears in my eyes

The radio softly tuned to a local AM station
News of ceremonies and chapter meetings
And funerals
Flows into the peaceful kitchen
Lines upon her face, features carved of hard times
Lines around her eyes, creases of happy times
Bittersweet tears and ringing silvery laughter
I ache in my heart

My mother's gentle movements light up dark corners
Her gentle smiles recall childhood dreams still so
alive
My mother moves in and out of light
Like clouds on days of promising rain

Joseph Bruchac (b.1942) and Gayle Ross (b.1951)

Joseph Bruchac and Gayle Ross are two of America's most popular Native American storytellers. Their oral performances and books show reverence for the traditional wisdom of their people and for individual storytellers who share their stories, as their notes on this tale in "The Origin of the Story" illustrate. Bruchac, who is also a poet and a member of the Abenaki nation from upstate New York, has written and edited dozens of books for children based on Native American folklore and culture. He and Michael Caduto produced the Keepers of the Earth series, combining Native tales with environmental activities for students. Ross, a Cherokee from Texas, is a direct descendant of John Ross, Principal Chief of the Cherokee nation during the Trail of Tears, the forced removal of Cherokees from southern Appalachia to Oklahoma in 1838. Bruchac and Ross also collaborated on a collection of Native American tales about women and girls, *The Girl Who Married the Moon* (1994). Like many other Native American legends, *The Story of the Milky Way* is a *pourquoi* or "why" tale, explaining a phenomenon of nature in relation to a particular event, often some foolish behavior by people or animal characters. Ross's collection *How Rabbit Tricked Otter and Other Cherokee Trickster Stories* (1994) contains many *pourquoi* incidents in tales about the perpetually mischievous Cherokee trickster hero Rabbit, telling why rabbits have short tails and chew underbrush, why otters live in water, and so on. This version of the Milky Way story also teaches a lesson about stealing from the elderly.

The Story of the Milky Way

A Cherokee Tale

THE ORIGIN OF THE STORY

Numerous Cherokee friends have shared this story with me over the years, including Robert Conley, a Cherokee novelist, and Jean Starr, a Cherokee poet, both of whom have included versions of the tale in their writing. Other versions of the story can be found in many published collections. One of the earliest is James Mooney's *Myths of the Cherokee* (1900).

—Joseph Bruchac

I first learned this story when I was a child, to share with my friends on a weekend camp-out. It appeared in a little booklet that had belonged to my grandmother, Anne Ross Piburn—which, I later learned, had been reprinted from the James Mooney collection. I also had a typed transcript of the story as Grandmother Anne, a Cherokee storyteller, had told it. In her version the emphasis was on the old couple and the anger felt by the people for anyone who would steal from the elderly. That is the way I have always told the story.

Joe Bruchac and I felt it was important to identify the elder who provides the solution to the riddle of the theft; the Beloved Woman would be the most honored of the elders among the Cherokee. We felt that not enough is known about the powerful women figures who are part of Cherokee tradition. We added the character of the grandson to our version to represent the love children everywhere feel for their grandparents.

—Gayle Ross

This is what the old people told me when I was a child.

Long ago when the world was new, there were not many stars in the sky.

In those days the people depended on corn for their food.

They would grind it and keep it in bins behind their homes. Bread made from the cornmeal often kept them from starving during the long winter months.

One morning an old man and an old woman went to their bin for some cornmeal. What they found there upset them very much. The lid was off the bin, the level inside had dropped by a handspan, and there was cornmeal scattered over the ground. Surely no one in the village would steal from the elders! Who could the thief be?

Now, the old couple had a young grandson who loved them very much. When he heard about the stolen cornmeal, he decided he would be the one to catch the thief.

That evening when Grandmother Sun had gone to her rest and Elder Brother Moon was not yet in the sky, the boy went to his grandparents' home. He hid near the bin of cornmeal and waited.

Late that night the boy saw an eerie light coming across the fields. When it was closer, he saw it was in the shape of a great dog. The dog nosed the lid off the bin and began to eat. When it had eaten its fill of the cornmeal, the dog turned and ran through the woods into the night.

The boy lay in his hiding place, not quite believing what his eyes had seen.

But in the morning, in the cornmeal scattered around the bin, he saw the tracks of a giant dog.

When the boy told the people what he had seen, no one knew what to do. So they decided to go to the Beloved Woman, a leader among the people. She was old and wise and understood many things.

When the Beloved Woman looked at the tracks, she said, "These are the tracks of a creature like no dog on this earth. It is a spirit dog and may have great power. We must be very careful."

The Beloved Woman instructed the people to gather all their drums and turtleshell rattles.

"We will hide near the cornmeal bin and wait," she said. "When the giant dog comes, we will make a great noise. That will frighten it so badly, it will never return."

The people hurried to get their drums and rattles.

Then they hid near the old couple's cornmeal bin. It grew dark and the few stars sparkled in the sky. Soon they saw the shining form of the great spirit dog coming across the fields.

It was so big that many of the people were frightened and wanted to run, but the wise old woman whispered, "Do not be afraid. Only wait for my signal."

The great dog came to the bin and began to eat, filling its big mouth with the white cornmeal.

"NOW!" the Beloved Woman shouted.

Then all the people rose up, beating their drums and shaking their rattles:

THUM-THUM THUM-THUM
SHISSH SHISSH SHISSH SHISSH

The noise was as loud as the Thunderer when he speaks. The great dog leaped in fear and began to run, but the people chased it, still beating their drums and shaking their rattles.

On and on the great dog ran, white cornmeal spilling from its mouth.

It ran till it came to the top of a hill and then it leaped . . . up into the sky!

It ran across the sky until the people could see it no longer. But the cornmeal that had spilled from its mouth remained behind as a great band of light across the night sky. Each grain of cornmeal that fell became a star.

Just as the Beloved Woman had said, the great dog never returned to bother the people. But where it ran across the sky was left that pattern of stars the Cherokee call *Gil'liutsun stanun'yi* (Gil-LEE-oot-soon stan-UNH-yee), "the place where the dog ran." That is how the Milky Way came to be.

Terri Cohlene (b.1950)

"Dancing Drum" is one of the tales that poet and editor Terri Cohlene retold for the Native American Legends series of picture books. This story's culturally specific details and motifs are found in a number of traditional Cherokee tales. References to "the People of the Mountain" are reminders of the Cherokees' ancient history in the Smoky Mountains, and the "swiftest stickball players" represent the game played on a large scale in Cherokee communities, an important traditional activity for men. The main characters are instructed by their chief and the Shaman, their spiritual leader, as well as mythological "little men," one of several types of small people or spirits associated with nature who cause mischief or provide help for people in Cherokee tales. The conflict between the personified Sun and Moon is similar to the contest in "The Wind and the Sun" from Aesop's fables. When an attempt is made to recover the Sun's daughter from the land of the dead, the tale is comparable to ancient Greek myths about Orpheus and his dead wife Eurydice and especially the ones about Demeter, the earth goddess who makes the land fruitful during part of the year when her daughter Persephone is allowed to return from the underworld. Both traditions link the weather and fertility of the earth with the bonds between mother and daughter. But death becomes irreversible in this tale. Although human disobedience has severe permanent consequences, the boy hero in this adaptation of the tale for children leads the way in learning to use human skills and emotional appeals to convince Grandmother Sun to smile on her people again.

Dancing Drum

A Cherokee Legend

One day long ago, when souls could still return from the Land of the Spirits, the Sun looked down upon the Earth. "The People of the Mountain do not like me," she said to her brother, the Moon. "See how they twist up their faces when they look to the sky."

"Ah, but they love me," replied the Moon. "They smile when they see me, and they make music and dance and send me songs." This did not please the Sun, for she thought she was more important than her brother, and more deserving.

That night, as she always did, the Sun visited her daughter for the evening meal. "How can The People love my brother and not me?" she asked. "I will show them it is unwise to offend me!" And the next morning, followed by the next and the next, she sent scorching heat onto the land.

During this time of the angry Sun, there lived in a small Cherokee village, a boy named Dancing Drum. He saw the suffering of his people. The crops no longer flourished, the children no longer laughed, the old women no longer gossiped, and the river, Long Man, was drying up. Soon, there would be no water even for drinking.

Dancing Drum went to the Shaman, and asked, "Why is Grandmother Sun burning the land and The People? How can we make her stop?"

The Shaman drank the last drop of water from her drinking gourd. "I do not know," she said. "But in a dream, a woodpecker came to me and told me to go to the little men in the wood. Alas, I have grown too weak to travel. You are young and strong. It is up to you to go."

Honored to be chosen for such an important mission, Dancing Drum followed the Shaman's directions and soon found the little men in the wood. "How can we make Grandmother Sun stop burning The People?" he asked them.

"You must go to the Land of the Sky People and kill the Sun before she destroys us all," they said. "First, take these snake rattles and tie them onto your moccasins."

As soon as he did this, Dancing Drum felt a strange tingling flow from his heels to his head. Suddenly, he could not move his arms, and when he tried to move his legs, he only heard the shaking of the rattles. He called for help. "Hsssssss!" was all he could say, for he had become a snake!

"Do not worry," said the leader of the little men. "You will be yourself again when your task is complete." He pointed to a small opening in the underbrush. "Now follow this path to the house of the Sun's daughter. In the morning, when the Sun comes out, bite her quickly."

Soon, Dancing Drum became used to the sidewinding movements of his new body. He slithered along the path into the woods, up the tallest mountain, and through the mist to the clouds themselves. At last, he came upon a large domed house made of mud and cane. It was the house of the Sun's daughter.

Since it was near dawn, Dancing Drum hid behind the clay pots stacked outside the door. I'll catch the Sun as she comes out, he thought. But when the door opened, she rushed by him so quickly, he didn't even have time to strike.

He would have to be more alert next time. He slept throughout the day, and as twilight approached, Dancing Drum was ready. This time, when the Sun drew near, he tensed to spring at her. But at the last instant, he turned away, blinded for a moment by her brilliance.

I must try again, he vowed, and this time, I will not miss. Through the night he waited. As soon as he heard stirrings from inside the house, he slithered to the door and closed his eyes.

"Forgive me, Grandmother Sun," he hissed. A moment later, the door opened and Dancing Drum struck. He felt his fangs sink deep into her ankle. But when he looked, he saw that it was not the Sun, but her daughter who lay dead on the ground.

Just then, Dancing Drum shed his scaly skin. He was a boy once more. With the Sun's wail filling the air, he ran from the Land of the Sky People. Over the clouds he went, through the mist, and down the tallest mountain. After many days, he reached his village.

There, the chief was holding counsel. "At last, we have relief from Grandmother Sun's burning heat," he said. "But, in her sadness over the death of her daughter, she no longer leaves her house." He pulled his robe tighter around his shoulders. "Now, The People are cold and in darkness."

Stepping into the chief's circle, Dancing Drum announced, "I am the cause of this darkness. I stopped the heat, but our suffering grows worse. I will go to the Land of the Spirits and bring back the Daughter of the Sun. Then our grandmother will once again smile upon The People."

Once more, Dancing Drum consulted the Shaman. "Take six others with you," she advised, "and a large basket. You will find the Daughter of the Sun dancing with the ghosts in Tsusgina'i. Each of you must touch her with a sourwood rod. When she falls to the ground, put her into the basket and secure the lid. Then bring her back here."

"This we shall do," answered Dancing Drum. He chose six of the swiftest stickball players in the village.

They were about to leave for the Darkening-land when the Shaman cautioned, "Once you have her in the basket, do not lift the lid."

For days, the runners followed the path to the Land of the Spirits. At the end of the seventh day, they heard drums and chanting, then they saw the ghosts, circling around a low fire. The Daughter of the Sun danced in the outer ring, heel-toe, heel-toe.

From their hiding place in the shrubs, Dancing Drum and his companions took turns reaching out with their sourwood rods. Each time the Daughter of the Sun passed, one of them touched her. Dancing Drum's rod was the seventh. As it brushed her, she collapsed. The ghosts seemed not to notice, so the boys hastily picked her up, put her into their basket, and secured the lid tightly.

After a time, the Daughter of the Sun started moving around in the basket. "Let me out!" she called to the runners. "I must eat!" At first, the seven ignored her. Then she called, "Let me out! I must have water!" Again, her plea went unanswered.

When they were almost to the village, the basket started to shake. "Let me out," called the Daughter of the Sun. This time, her voice sounded strangled. "I cannot breathe!" she croaked. Dancing Drum was afraid she might die again, so he opened the lid a tiny crack.

Suddenly, a flapping sound came from inside the basket, and a flash of red flew past, followed by the "Kwish, kwish, kwish!" cry of a redbird. Not sure what had happened, Dancing Drum quickly refastened the lid and hurried with his companions back to the village.

Once there, the Shaman opened the basket. It was empty! The Daughter of the Sun had been transformed into the redbird. "You disobeyed," the Shaman said to Dancing Drum. "For this, souls can no longer be returned from the Land of the Spirits."

Dancing Drum hung his head, and Grandmother Sun, watching from the Sky World, began to weep. She cried so hard, her tears filled Long Man to overflowing, threatening a great flood over the land.

"What shall we do?" The People cried.

"We shall sing!" declared Dancing Drum. So The People put on their most beautiful clothes of embroidered buckskins. They wore necklaces of deer and panther teeth, and painted their faces white. They lifted their faces to the sky and chanted for Grandmother Sun. They drummed, and kept rhythm with their gourd rattles. But still Grandmother Sun grieved.

Finally, Dancing Drum left the singing and went to his lodge for his own drum. It had been a special gift from his grandfather. He filled the hollow log with water and dampened the groundhog skin. At last he was ready. Returning to the group of singers, he sat and began playing his own song.

From the Land of the Sky People, Grandmother Sun heard the new music. She stopped crying and looked down to see her beautiful people smiling up at her. She saw them offering their special dances, and she heard their special song.

Dancing Drum lifted his face to the sky as he played from his heart for his ancestors, for his people, and for his land. And as he played, Grandmother Sun came out of her house to once again smile down on her Children of the Mountain.

Ovid (43 B.C.E.–17 or 18 C.E.)

Although not many of the best-known classical myths are about childhood, parent-child relationships are important in the human and divine realms of mythology. In the story of the earth goddess Demeter or Ceres, for example, when her daughter Persephone was abducted by Hades to be his bride, Demeter left the earth barren until Zeus ordered that Persephone could spend most of the year above ground, so that Demeter would make the earth fertile from spring to fall. "Daedalus and Icarus" captures the curiosity of a younger child setting off on a new adventure and the poignant fears of the father who knows their journey is dangerous. As a cautionary tale, its lessons are typical of ancient Greek literature (including the myth of Pandora, retold by Nathaniel Hawthorne in Part 1, and Aesop's fables), as well as children's literature of more recent centuries; it shows the disastrous consequences of disobedience and the wisdom of taking "a middle course." This retelling of the ancient story is from a 1955 translation of Ovid's *Metamorphoses* by American poet (George) Rolfe Humphries. It is a translation long admired for capturing the energy and tone of the Roman poet Ovid, one of the writers from the classical Greek and Roman era who retold this story and many other myths and legends that remain well known in modern times. The storytelling skill of these writers is evident in the way this episode focuses on the interactions and emotions of father and son within the historical context of an ancient tale about how the Icarian Sea got its name. There is heartbreaking irony in small details such as the boy's "fooling around" with the feathers and wax while his father works, "[n]ot knowing he was dealing with his downfall." Daedalus was an Athenian prince, inventor, and master craftsman who created a number of wonders in other stories, including the labyrinth in which the monstrous Minotaur was captured. To escape from exile and imprisonment in Crete, he uses his ingenuity to achieve the eternal human dream of flying, but he pays a tragic price when his "fatal art" defies the laws of nature and allows him to imitate the gods in the sky.

The Story of Daedalus and Icarus

TRANSLATED BY ROLFE HUMPHRIES

Homesick for homeland, Daedalus hated Crete
And his long exile there, but the sea held him.
"Though Minos blocks escape by land or water,"
Daedalus said, "surely the sky is open,
5   And that's the way we'll go. Minos' dominion
Does not include the air." He turned his thinking
Toward unknown arts, changing the laws of
        nature.

He laid out feathers in order, first the smallest,
A little larger next to it, and so continued,
10 The way that panpipes rise in gradual sequence.
He fastened them with twine and wax, at middle,
At bottom, so, and bent them, gently curving,
So that they looked like wings of birds, most
        surely.
And Icarus, his son, stood by and watched him,
15 Not knowing he was dealing with his downfall,
Stood by and watched and raised his shiny face
To let a feather, light as down, fall on it,

330

Or stuck his thumb in the yellow wax,
Fooling around, the way a boy will, always,
20 Whenever a father tries to get some work done.
Still, it was done at last, and the father hovered,
Poised, in the moving air, and taught his son:
"I warn you, Icarus, fly a middle course:
Don't go too low, or water will weigh the wings
      down;
25 Don't go too high, or the sun's fire will burn them.
Keep to the middle way. And one more thing,
No fancy steering by star or constellation,
Follow my lead!" That was the flying lesson.
And now to fit the wings to the boy's shoulders.
30 Between the work and warning the father found
His cheeks were wet with tears, and his hands
      trembled.
He kissed his son (Good-bye, if he had known it),
Rose on his wings, flew on ahead, as fearful
As any bird launching the little nestlings
35 Out of high nest into thin air. Keep on,
Keep on, he signals, follow me! He guides him
In flight—O fatal art!—and the wings move
And the father looks back to see the son's wings
      moving.
Far off, far down, some fisherman is watching
40 As the rod dips and trembles over the water,
Some shepherd rests his weight upon his crook,
Some plowman on the handles of the plowshare,
And all look up, in absolute amazement,
At those airborne above. They must be gods!
45 They were over Samos, Juno's sacred island,
Delos and Paros toward the left, Lebinthus
Visible to the right, and another island,
Calymne, rich in honey. And the boy
Thought This is wonderful! And left his father,
50 Soared higher, higher, drawn to the vast heaven,
Nearer the sun, and the wax that held the wings
Melted in that fierce heat, and the bare arms
Beat up and down in air, and lacking oarage
Took hold of nothing. Father! he cried, and
      Father!
55 Until the blue sea hushed him, the dark water
Men call the Icarian now. And Daedalus,
Father no more, called "Icarus, where are you!

Where are you Icarus? Tell me where to find
      you!"
And saw the wings on the waves and cursed his
      talents,
60 Buried the body in a tomb, and the land
Was named for Icarus.

Charles Stanley Reinhart's romantic 1896 illustration for "Daedalus and Icarus" juxtaposes the ingenious father's dramatic success at flying and the more distant image of Icarus's fall from above as his wings melt.

Aesop's Fables

Aesop's fables are as familiar to most children in the Western world as are nursery rhymes and classic fairy tales, such as "Little Red Riding Hood" or "Cinderella." We may not remember when we first learned of that famous race in "The Tortoise and the Hare" or the fox who started the spiteful habit of labeling things out of reach as sour grapes, but if we lied about something dangerous as a child, we might have heard admonitions about "The Boy Who Cried Wolf." The hundreds of fables associated with the name of Aesop are very short memorable tales, usually about talking animals who represent distinct human traits and behaviors, such as greed, pride, cunning, or resourcefulness. Some include characters who are humans; gods; inanimate objects, such as a reed and an oak tree; or forces of nature, such as the wind and the sun. They most often focus on one central action and do not invite multiple interpretations as fairy tales do with their rich symbolic meanings. The moral at the end is often stated explicitly, but even if it is not, the message is clear cut: the sun that makes a man so hot that he will remove his cloak proves most effectively that persuasion is better than force, and the ingenious thirsty crow trying to get water out of a tall pitcher demonstrates that "necessity is the mother of invention." The supernatural intervention and love plot in "The Cat and Venus" are more often found in traditional fairy tales with animal transformations, but the fable's dispassionate observation that people cannot always change to suit their spouses does not encourage a belief in happy romantic endings. "The Lion and the Mouse," on the other hand, presents a heartwarming lesson for children, because it shows how big and small creatures of goodwill can help each other in unexpected ways.

Although evidence for the existence of the legendary Aesop is scant, Aesop may have been a slave in sixth-century Greece who won favor and freedom with his talent for storytelling. Some say that he was later put to death for speaking out too freely against injustice. Important classical writers, such as Plato and Plutarch, referred to him, and the Latin poet Phaedrus recorded his fables in the first century C.E. Recent critics see similarities in Aesop's shrewd observations on power relationships and the tales later told by African American slaves, who used the trickster Brer Rabbit and other animal characters to represent struggles between the underdog and the powerful. Jack Zipes stresses that Aesop's "sober and revelatory" fables are primarily about "survival of the fittest," showing the limits of freedom for the less powerful and promoting "freedom from oppression" without "promis[ing] a better world or ideal justice."[1] The Greek myth "Daedalus and Icarus" also dramatizes the desire for freedom and disaster for the innocent if they do not follow a cautious course. Fables like these existed thousands of years before the era of Aesop, and they have parallels in other cultural traditions of folktales and wisdom literature. For example, a careless man in "The Poor Man and the Flask of Oil," from the Buddhist *Jataka Tales,* spills his precious oil while distracting himself with visions of future prosperity, exactly like Aesop's milkmaid who counts her chickens before they hatch.

Aesop's Fables was one of the first books printed in England on William Caxton's fifteenth-century printing press, and the crude but energetic woodcuts that Caxton used encouraged others to continue publishing illustrated editions of fables and other stories for children. Fables were especially popular as succinct expressions of rational thought and satires of human folly in the Age of Reason, but they were increasingly relegated to the nursery, rather than to the adult library, beginning in the eighteenth century. The fables reprinted here come from a large, influential nineteenth-century collection translated by George Fyler Townsend, who ended each one with a concise moral. From the multitude of fables that have been rewritten and imitated in prose and verse through the centuries, writers for children obviously choose the ones that best fit their views of human nature and the moral, social, and intellectual development of the young. There may be little disagreement about teaching children that honesty is the best policy or that they should look before they leap, but adults in each generation disagree about when and how to warn children about the harsh realities that are revealed in some of the fables, where plans and friends are not always reliable and where, in general, humans often behave foolishly.

NOTE

1. Jack Zipes, ed., Afterword, *Aesop's Fables* (New York: Signet, 1992) 276, 280.

The Bear and the Two Travelers

Two men were traveling together, when a Bear suddenly met them on their path. One of them climbed up quickly into a tree and concealed himself in the branches. The other, seeing that he must be attacked, fell flat on the ground, and when the Bear came up and felt him with his snout, and smelt him all over, he held his breath, and feigned the appearance of death as much as he could. The Bear soon left him, for it is said he will not touch a dead body. When he was quite gone, the other Traveler descended from the tree, and jocularly inquired of his friend what it was the Bear had whispered in his ear. "He gave me this advice," his companion replied. "Never travel with a friend who deserts you at the approach of danger."

Misfortune tests the sincerity of friends.

The Cat and Venus

A Cat fell in love with a handsome young man, and entreated Venus to change her into the form of a woman. Venus consented to her request and transformed her into a beautiful damsel, so that the youth saw her and loved her, and took her home as his bride. While the two were reclining in their chamber, Venus wishing to discover if the Cat in her change of shape had also altered her habits of life, let down a mouse in the middle of the room. The Cat, quite forgetting her present condition, started up from the couch and pursued the mouse, wishing to eat it. Venus was much disappointed and again caused her to return to her former shape.

Nature exceeds nurture.

The Crow and the Pitcher

A Crow perishing with thirst saw a pitcher, and hoping to find water, flew to it with delight. When he reached it, he discovered to his grief that it contained so little water that he could not possibly get at it. He tried everything he could think of to reach the water, but all his efforts were in vain. At last he collected as many stones as he could carry and dropped them one by one with his beak into the pitcher, until he brought the water within his reach and thus saved his life.

Necessity is the mother of invention.

Thomas Bewick's innovations in wood engraving set a new standard for illustrated editions of fables and other books. "The Crow and the Pitcher" (1818) shows Bewick's lifelong love of rural scenery.

The Fox and the Goat

A Fox one day fell into a deep well and could find no means of escape. A Goat, overcome with thirst, came to the same well, and seeing the Fox, inquired if the water was good. Concealing his sad plight under a merry guise, the Fox indulged in a lavish praise of the water, saying it was excellent beyond measure, and encouraging him to descend. The Goat, mindful only of his thirst, thoughtlessly jumped down, but just as he drank, the Fox informed him of the difficulty they were both in and suggested a scheme for their common escape. "If," said he, "you will place your forefeet upon the wall and bend your head, I will run up your back and escape, and will help you out afterwards." The Goat readily assented and the Fox leaped upon his back. Steadying himself with the Goat's horns, he safely reached the mouth of the well and made off as fast as he could. When the Goat upbraided him for breaking his promise, he turned around and cried out, "You foolish old fellow! If you had as many brains in your head as you have hairs in your beard, you would never have gone down before you had inspected the way up, nor have exposed yourself to dangers from which you had no means of escape."

Look before you leap.

The Fox and the Grapes

A Famished Fox saw some clusters of ripe black grapes hanging from a trellised vine. She resorted to all her tricks to get at them, but wearied herself in vain, for she could not reach them. At last she turned away, hiding her disappointment and saying: "The Grapes are sour, and not ripe as I thought."

In "The Fox and the Grapes," Thomas Bewick combined formal design elements with images of vegetation that is ironically abundant, yet the fox can't reach the grapes.

The Hare and the Tortoise

A Hare one day ridiculed the short feet and slow pace of the Tortoise, who replied, laughing: "Though you be swift as the wind, I will beat you in a race." The Hare, believing her assertion to be simply impossible, assented to the proposal; and they agreed that the Fox should choose the course and fix the goal. On the day appointed for the race the two started together. The Tortoise never for a moment stopped, but went on with a slow but steady pace straight to the end of the course. The Hare, lying down by the wayside, fell fast asleep. At last waking up, and moving as fast as he could, he saw the Tortoise had reached the goal, and was comfortably dozing after her fatigue.

Slow but steady wins the race.

The Hen and the Golden Eggs

A cottager and his wife had a Hen that laid a golden egg every day. They supposed that the Hen must contain a great lump of gold in its inside, and in order to get the gold they killed it. Having done so, they found to their surprise that the Hen differed in no respect from their other hens. The foolish pair, thus hoping to become rich all at once, deprived themselves of the gain of which they were assured day by day.

Hercules and the Wagoner

A carter was driving a wagon along a country lane, when the wheels sank down deep into a rut. The rustic driver, stupefied and aghast, stood looking at the wagon, and did nothing but utter loud cries to Hercules to come and help him. Hercules, it is said, appeared and thus addressed him: "Put your shoulders to the wheels, my man. Goad on your bullocks, and never more pray to me for help, until you have done your best to help yourself, or depend upon it you will henceforth pray in vain."

Self-help is the best help.

Thomas Bewick's detailed wood engraving for "Hercules and the Carter" highlights the predicament of a man learning the hard lesson that the gods want him to help himself.

The Lion and the Mouse

A Lion was awakened from sleep by a Mouse running over his face. Rising up angrily, he caught him and was about to kill him, when the Mouse piteously entreated, saying: "If you would only spare my life, I would be sure to repay your kindness." The Lion laughed and let him go. It happened shortly after this that the Lion was caught by some hunters, who bound him by strong ropes to the ground. The Mouse, recognizing his roar, came and gnawed the rope with his teeth, and set him free, exclaiming: "You ridiculed the idea of my ever being able to help you, not expecting to receive from me any repayment of your favor; now you know that it is possible for even a Mouse to confer benefits on a Lion."

Mercury and the Workmen

A Workman, felling wood by the side of a river, let his axe drop—by accident into a deep pool. Being thus deprived of the means of his livelihood, he sat down on the bank and lamented his hard fate. Mercury appeared and demanded the cause of his tears. After he told him his misfortune, Mercury plunged into the stream, and, bringing up a golden axe, inquired if that were the one he had lost. On his saying that it was not his, Mercury disappeared beneath the water a second time, returned with a silver axe in his hand, and again asked the Workman if it were his. When the Workman said it was not, he dived into the pool for the third time and brought up the axe that had been lost. The Workman claimed it and expressed his joy at its recovery. Mercury, pleased with his honesty, gave him the golden and silver axes in addition to his own. The Workman, on his return to his house, related to his companions all that had happened. One of them at once resolved to try and secure the same good fortune for himself. He ran to the river and threw his axe on purpose into the pool at the same place, and sat down on the bank to weep. Mercury appeared to him just as he hoped he would; and having learned the cause of his grief, plunged into the stream and brought up a golden axe, inquiring if he had lost it. The Workman seized it greedily, and declared that truly it was the very same axe that he had lost. Mercury, displeased at his knavery, not only took away the golden axe, but refused to recover for him the axe he had thrown into the pool.

(Honesty is the best policy.)

The Milk-Woman and Her Pail

A Farmer's daughter was carrying her Pail of milk from the field to the farmhouse, when she fell a-musing. "The money for which this milk will be sold, will buy at least three hundred eggs. The eggs, allowing for all mishaps, will produce two hundred and fifty chickens. The chickens will become ready for the market when poultry will fetch the highest price, so that by the end of the year I shall have money enough from my share to buy a new gown. In this dress I will go to the Christmas parties, where all the young fellows will propose to me, but I will toss my head and refuse them every one." At this moment she tossed her head in unison with her thoughts, when down fell the milk pail to the ground, and all her imaginary schemes perished in a moment.

(Don't count your chickens before they are hatched.)

The Mouse, the Frog, and the Hawk

A Mouse who always lived on the land, by an unlucky chance formed an intimate acquaintance with a Frog, who lived for the most part in the water. The Frog, one day intent on mischief, bound the foot of the Mouse tightly to his own. Thus joined together, the Frog first of all led his friend the Mouse to the meadow where they were accustomed to find their food. After this, he gradually led him towards the pool in which he lived, until reaching the very brink, he suddenly jumped in, dragging the Mouse with him. The Frog enjoyed the water amazingly, and swam croaking about, as if he had done a good deed. The unhappy Mouse was soon suffocated by the water, and his dead body floated about on the surface, tied to the foot of the Frog. A Hawk observed it, and, pouncing upon it with his talons, carried it aloft. The Frog, being still fastened to the leg of the Mouse, was also carried off a prisoner, and was eaten by the Hawk.

Harm hatch, harm catch.

The North Wind and the Sun

The North Wind and the Sun disputed as to which was the most powerful, and agreed that he should be declared the victor who could first strip a wayfaring man of his clothes. The North Wind first tried his power and blew with all his might, but the keener his blasts, the closer the Traveler wrapped his cloak around him, until at last, resigning all hope of victory, the Wind called upon the Sun to see what he could do. The Sun suddenly shone out with all his warmth. The Traveler no sooner felt his genial rays than he took off one garment after another, and at last, fairly overcome with heat, undressed and bathed in a stream that lay in his path.

Persuasion is better than Force.

"The Wind and the Sun." Victorian artist Walter Crane advocated the development of artistic, unified designs for picture books. His 1887 fables blend hand-lettered verses with flowing classical images surrounding them.

[handwritten marginalia: Story tellers would go to towns a day and advance to make sure their stories would have an effect on that town.]

The Oak and the Reeds

A very large Oak was uprooted by the wind and thrown across a stream. It fell among some Reeds, which it thus addressed: "I wonder how you, who are so light and weak, are not entirely crushed by these strong winds." They replied, "You fight and contend with the wind, and consequently you are destroyed; while we on the contrary bend before the least breath of air, and therefore remain unbroken, and escape."

Stoop to conquer.

The Shepherd's Boy and the Wolf

A Shepherd-boy, who watched a flock of sheep near a village, brought out the villagers three or four times by crying out, "Wolf! Wolf!" and when his neighbors came to help him, laughed at them for their pains. The Wolf, however, did truly come at last. The Shepherd-boy, now really alarmed, shouted in an agony of terror: "Pray, do come and help me; the Wolf is killing the sheep"; but no one paid any heed to his cries, nor rendered any assistance. The Wolf, having no cause of fear, at his leisure lacerated or destroyed the whole flock.

There is no believing a liar, even when he speaks the truth.

The Tortoise and the Eagle

depressing

The master promises the slave more so they do what they want out there *Warning to the dangers out there*

A Tortoise, lazily basking in the sun, complained to the sea-birds of her hard fate, that no one would teach her to fly. An Eagle, hovering near, heard her lamentation and demanded what reward she would give him if he would take her aloft and float her in the air. "I will give you," she said, "all the riches of the Red Sea." "I will teach you to fly then," said the Eagle; and taking her up in his talons he carried her almost to the clouds; suddenly he let her go, and she fell on a lofty mountain, dashing her shell to pieces. The Tortoise exclaimed in the moment of death: "I have deserved my present fate; for what had I to do with wings and clouds, who can with difficulty move about on the earth?"

If men had all they wished, they would be often ruined.

Be smart

Careful who you trust.

The Town Mouse and the Country Mouse

A Country Mouse invited a Town Mouse, an intimate friend, to pay him a visit and partake of his country fare. As they were on the bare plowlands, eating there wheat-stocks and roots pulled up from the hedgerow, the Town Mouse said to his friend, "You live here the life of the ants, while in my house is the horn of

[Handwritten margin notes: "Convince you that your life is great as it is"; "And story also undercuts the slavery time"; "Easy life better than the Hectic"; "(Slaves were lucky to be so 'introduced')"; "obvious moral"]

plenty. I am surrounded by every luxury, and if you will come with me, as I wish you would, you shall have an ample share of my dainties." The Country Mouse was easily persuaded, and returned to town with his friend. On his arrival, the Town Mouse placed before him bread, barley, beans, dried figs, honey, raisins, and, last of all, brought a dainty piece of cheese from a basket. The Country Mouse, being much delighted at the sight of such good cheer, expressed his satisfaction in warm terms and lamented his own hard fate. Just as they were beginning to eat, someone opened the door, and they both ran off squeaking, as fast as they could, to a hole so narrow that two could only find room in it by squeezing. They had scarcely begun their repast again when someone else entered to take something out of a cupboard, whereupon the two Mice, more frightened than before, ran away and hid themselves. At last the Country Mouse, almost famished, said to his friend: "Although you have prepared for me so dainty a feast, I must leave you to enjoy it by yourself. It is surrounded by too many dangers to please me. I prefer my bare plowlands and roots from the hedgerow, where I can live in safety, and without fear."

The Wolf in Sheep's Clothing

Once upon a time a Wolf resolved to disguise his appearance in order to secure food more easily. Encased in the skin of a sheep, he pastured with the flock deceiving the shepherd by his costume. In the evening he was shut up by the shepherd in the fold; the gate was closed, and the entrance made thoroughly secure.

But the shepherd, returning to the fold during the night to obtain meat for the next day, mistakenly caught up the Wolf instead of a sheep, and killed him instantly.

Harm seek, harm find.

Chinua Achebe (b.1930)

Chinua Achebe, an internationally acclaimed writer of fiction, poetry, and essays, is credited with leading a literary renaissance that provides authentic views of his native Nigerian culture. He has written and edited several works for and about children, but this tale about Tortoise appears in the middle of the novel *Things Fall Apart* (1958), when a late nineteenth-century mother and daughter are engaged in a typical evening of telling each other folk stories. The passage illustrates Achebe's stylistic mastery of English as he adopted the language of European colonizers to depict the everyday lives of villagers and the cultural values embedded in the Ibo oral traditions.

One of the most popular themes in *pourquoi* tales around the world involves different explanations for the cracked appearance of tortoise shells. This detailed story about Tortoise's behavior shows that folktales about the origins of things are not just prescientific or "primitive" explanations of natural phenomena but served to pass on social norms to children. In Aesop's fable "The Tortoise and the Eagle," the tortoise is punished for pride when the eagle that is persuaded to teach him to fly drops him to his death. Achebe's Tortoise is punished for trickery and greed when he takes everyone's food and wine in a time of famine. But the fate of this Tortoise is not like that of the ill-fated transgressor of the stern Aesop fables or the taciturn tragic hero of Achebe's novel. Unlike Okonkwo (the father of the girl listening to this tale), Tortoise uses conversational skills and a trick with wordplay to get what he wants in a place where he does not belong; then he survives his punishment, as trickster heroes usually do in folktales.

How Tortoise Cracked His Shell

[Handwritten marginalia: Tricksters are loved by audience. Oral stories were always accompanied by song. Easier to remember.]

Low voices, broken now and again by singing, reached Okonkwo from his wives' huts as each woman and her children told folk stories. Ekwefi and her daughter, Ezinma, sat on a mat on the floor. It was Ekwefi's turn to tell a story.

"Once upon a time," she began, "all the birds were invited to a feast in the sky. They were very happy and began to prepare themselves for the great day. They painted their bodies with red cam wood and drew beautiful patterns on them with *uli*.

"Tortoise saw all these preparations and soon discovered what it all meant. Nothing that happened in the world of the animals ever escaped his notice; he was full of cunning. As soon as he heard of the great feast in the sky his throat began to itch at the very thought. There was a famine in those days and Tortoise had not eaten a good meal for two moons. His body rattled like a piece of dry stick in his empty shell. So he began to plan how he would go to the sky."

[Handwritten marginalia: Once that audience interrupts, since of oral story]

"But he had no wings," said Ezinma.

"Be patient," replied her mother. "That is the story. Tortoise had no wings, but he went to the birds and asked to be allowed to go with them.

"'We know you too well,' said the birds when they had heard him. 'You are full of cunning and you are ungrateful. If we allow you to come with us you will soon begin your mischief.'

"'You do not know me,' said Tortoise. 'I am a changed man. I have learned that a man who makes trouble for others is also making it for himself.'

"Tortoise had a sweet tongue, and within a short time all the birds agreed that he was a changed man, and they each gave him a feather, with which he made two wings.

"At last the great day came and Tortoise was the first to arrive at the meeting place. When all the birds

[Handwritten marginalia: His smooth shell could be like the mark of cain?]

had gathered together, they set off in a body. Tortoise was very happy and voluble as he flew among the birds, and he was soon chosen as the man to speak for the party because he was a great orator.

"'There is one important thing which we must not forget,' he said as they flew on their way. 'When people are invited to a great feast like this, they take new names for the occasion. Our hosts in the sky will expect us to honor this age-old custom.'

"None of the birds had heard of this custom but they knew that Tortoise, in spite of his failings in other directions, was a widely-traveled man who knew the customs of different peoples. And so they each took a new name. When they had all taken, Tortoise also took one. He was to be called *All of you*.

[Handwritten marginalia: This tortoise is a plotter.]

"At last the party arrived in the sky and their hosts were very happy to see them. Tortoise stood up in his many-colored plumage and thanked them for their invitation. His speech was so eloquent that all the birds were glad they had brought him, and nodded their heads in approval of all he said. Their hosts took him as the king of the birds, especially as he looked somewhat different from the others.

[Handwritten marginalia: More entertainment story.]

"After kola nuts had been presented and eaten, the people of the sky set before their guests the most delectable dishes Tortoise had even seen or dreamed of. The soup was brought out hot from the fire and in the very pot in which it had been cooked. It was full of meat and fish. Tortoise began to sniff aloud. There was pounded yam and also yam pottage cooked with palm-oil and fresh fish. There were also pots of palm-wine. When everything had been set before the guests, one of the people of the sky came forward and tasted a little from each pot. He then invited the birds to eat. But Tortoise jumped to his feet and asked: 'For whom have you prepared this feast?'

"'For all of you,' replied the man.

[Handwritten marginalia: Children stories always need explinations & questions]

[Handwritten marginalia: Give up one feather means the community support to him. & they can also tear him down.]

"Tortoise turned to the birds and said: 'You remember that my name is *All of you*. The custom here is to serve the spokesman first and the others later. They will serve you when I have eaten.'

"He began to eat and the birds grumbled angrily. The people of the sky thought it must be their custom to leave all the food for their king. And so Tortoise ate the best part of the food and then drank two pots of palm-wine, so that he was full of food and drink and his body filled out in his shell.

"The birds gathered round to eat what was left, and to peck at the bones he had thrown all about the floor. Some of them were too angry to eat. They chose to fly home on an empty stomach. But before they left each took back the feather he had lent to Tortoise. And there he stood in his hard shell full of food and wine but without any wings to fly home. He asked the birds to take a message for his wife, but they all refused. In the end Parrot, who had felt more angry than the others, suddenly changed his mind and agreed to take the message.

"'Tell my wife,' said Tortoise, 'to bring out all the soft things in my house and cover the compound with them so that I can jump down from the sky without very great danger.'

"Parrot promised to deliver the message, and then flew away. But when he reached Tortoise's house he told his wife to bring out all the hard things in the house. And so she brought out her husband's hoes, machetes, spears, guns and even his cannon. Tortoise looked down from the sky and saw his wife bringing things out, but it was too far to see what they were. When all seemed ready he let himself go. He fell and fell and fell until he began to fear that he would never stop falling. And then like the sound of his cannon he crashed on the compound."

"Did he die?" asked Ezinma.

"No," replied Ekwefi. "His shell broke into pieces. But there was a great medicine man in the neighborhood. Tortoise's wife sent for him and he gathered all the bits of shell and stuck them together. That is why Tortoise's shell is not smooth."

"There is no song in the story," Ezinma pointed out.

"No," said Ekwefi. "I shall think of another one with a song. But it is your turn now."

Peter Christen Asbjørnsen (1812–85)

This version of the cumulative nursery tale about a fleeing pancake comes from the extensive collections of Norse folktales by Peter Christen Asbjørnsen and Jørgen Moe. After meeting as students, Asbjørnsen and Moe decided to do for Norse folktales what the Grimm Brothers had done for the German, publishing their first volume, *Norwegian Folktales,* in 1841. They were more interested than the Grimm Brothers in retaining the vernacular language of their many informants. Like other cumulative tales and rhymes, such as the nursery rhyme "The House that Jack Built," this tale contains an expanding collection of repeated phrases, in this case the list of characters from whom the pancake escapes. In the original Norse and in English translations, such as this one by H. L. Brækstad, the rhyming names of people and animals are amusing to repeat with young children, like the character names in another type of nursery tale about running and predators, "Henny-Penny" or "Chicken Little." In other countries, the runaway food may be a cake; a kolobok (Russian bun); a johnny cake; or, most famously in America, a gingerbread man. Usually, the runaway falls prey to a tricky pig or a fox after getting smug about escaping from so many hungry pursuers. There is a German version in which "the thick, fat pancake" escapes from Oink-Oink Sow but then lets itself be eaten by three hungry orphans. Contemporary spin-offs include regional and humorous tales about runaway tortillas, rice cakes, and pickles. A man made of cheese that is so stinky that no one wants to chase him is featured in the zany picture-book satire by Jon Scieszka and Lane Smith, *The Stinky Cheese Man and Other Fairly Stupid Tales* (1992).

The Pancake

Once upon a time there was a good housewife, who had seven hungry children. One day she was busy frying pancakes for them, and this time she had used new milk in the making of them. One was lying in the pan, frizzling away—ah! so beautiful and thick—it was a pleasure to look at it. The children were standing round the fire, and the husband sat in the corner and looked on.

"Oh, give me a bit of pancake, mother, I am so hungry!" said one child.

"Ah, do! dear mother," said the second.

"Ah, do! dear, good mother," said the third.

"Ah, do! dear, good, kind mother," said the fourth.

"Ah, do! dear, good, kind, nice mother," said the fifth.

"Ah, do! dear, good, kind, nice, sweet mother," said the sixth.

"Ah, do! dear, good, kind, nice, sweet, darling mother," said the seventh. And thus they were all begging for pancakes, the one more prettily than the other, because they were so hungry, and such good little children.

"Yes, children dear, wait a bit until it turns itself," she answered—she ought to have said "until I turn it"—"and then you shall all have pancakes, beautiful pancakes, made of new milk—only look how thick and happy it lies there."

When the pancake heard this, it got frightened, and all of a sudden, it turned itself and wanted to get out of the pan, but it fell down in it again on the other side, and when it had been fried a little on that side too, it felt a little stronger in the back, jumped out on the floor, and rolled away, like a wheel, right through the door and down the road.

John D. Batten used different styles to suit the varied moods and settings of folktales collected by Joseph Jacobs (1890). This amusing line drawing of the chase in "Johnny-Cake" illustrates an American variant of "The Pancake."

"Halloo!" cried the good wife, and away she ran after it, with the frying pan in one hand and the ladle in the other, as fast as she could, and the children behind her, while the husband came limping after, last of all.

"Halloo, won't you stop? Catch it, stop it. Halloo there!" they all screamed, the one louder than the other, trying to catch it on the run, but the pancake rolled and rolled, and before long, it was so far ahead, that they could not see it, for the pancake was much smarter on its legs than any of them.

When it had rolled a time, it met a man.

"Good day, pancake!" said the man.

"Well met, Manny Panny," said the pancake.

"Dear pancake," said the man, "don't roll so fast, but wait a bit and let me eat you."

"When I have run away from Goody Poody and the husband and seven squalling children, I must run away from you too, Manny Panny," said the pancake, and rolled on and on, until it met a hen.

"Good day, pancake," said the hen.

"Good day, Henny Penny," said the pancake.

"My dear pancake, don't roll so fast, but wait a bit and let me eat you," said the hen.

"When I have run away from Goody Poody and the husband and seven squalling children, and from Manny Panny, I must run away from you too, Henny Penny," said the pancake, and rolled on like a wheel down the road. Then it met a cock.

"Good day, pancake," said the cock.

"Good day, Cocky Locky," said the pancake.

"My dear pancake, don't roll so fast, but wait a bit and let me eat you," said the cock.

"When I have run away from Goody Poody and the husband and seven squalling children, from Manny Panny, and Henny Penny, I must run away from you too, Cocky Locky," said the pancake, and rolled and rolled on as fast as it could. When it had rolled a long time, it met a duck.

"Good day, pancake," said the duck.

"Good day, Ducky Lucky," said the pancake.

"My dear pancake, don't roll so fast, but wait a bit and let me eat you," said the duck.

"When I have run away from Goody Poody and the husband and seven squalling children, from Manny Panny, and Henny Penny, and Cocky Locky, I must run away from you too, Ducky Lucky," said the pancake, and with that it fell to rolling and rolling as fast as ever it could. When it had rolled a long, long time, it met a goose.

"Good day, pancake," said the goose.

"Good day, Goosey Poosey," said the pancake.

"My dear pancake, don't roll so fast, but wait a bit and let me eat you," said the goose.

"When I have run away from Goody Poody and the husband and seven squalling children, from Manny Panny, and Henny Penny, and Cocky Locky, and Ducky Lucky, I must run away from you too, Goosey Poosey," said the pancake, and away it rolled. So when it had rolled a long, very long time, it met a gander.

"Good day, pancake," said the gander.

"Good day, Gander Pander," said the pancake.

"My dear pancake, don't roll so fast, but wait a bit and let me eat you," said the gander.

"When I have run away from Goody Poody and the husband and seven squalling children, from Manny Panny, and Henny Penny, and Cocky Locky, and Ducky Lucky, and Goosey Poosey, I must run away from you too, Gander Pander," said the pancake, and rolled and rolled as fast as it could. When it had rolled on a long, long time, it met a pig.

"Good day, pancake," said the pig.

"Good day, Piggy Wiggy," said the pancake, and began to roll on faster than ever.

"Nay, wait a bit," said the pig, "you needn't be in such a hurry-scurry; we two can walk quietly together and keep each other company through the wood, because they say it isn't very safe there."

The pancake thought there might be something in that, and so they walked together through the wood; but when they had gone some distance, they came to a brook.

The pig was so fat it wasn't much trouble for him to swim across, but the pancake couldn't get over.

"Sit on my snout," said the pig, "and I will ferry you over."

The pancake did so.

"Ouf, ouf," grunted the pig, and swallowed the pancake in one gulp, and as the pancake couldn't get any farther—well, you see we can't go on with this story any farther, either.

African American Ballad

America's most popular folk song tells the story of an African American man's heroic contest with a steel-driving machine. John Henry is tall-tale hero, a gigantic man with superhuman strength like Paul Bunyan, Pecos Bill and others. Like tall tales about Davy Crockett (who definitely was a frontiersman and congressman in real life), the John Henry stories are also examples of legends, associated with real places and events. Some of these legends tell about an African American baby who wielded a hammer and moved from Tennessee to West Virginia, where he helped build the Big Bend railway tunnel in Summers County in the late nineteenth century. (There is a monument to John Henry at Marlington, West Virginia.) The contest that kills John Henry is a noble attempt to show that the coming of stronger machines would not displace human workers. Since the 1920s, both white and black musicians have remembered "John Henry" as one of the first and best songs they learned. From traditional ballads and hammer songs or work songs to contemporary picture books, innumerable books and recordings present different versions of the story. John Henry has also been portrayed as a white man, sometimes a worker on docks instead of a railroad, sometimes almost a saint and sometimes a gambling, womanizing trickster, or both. In the version presented here, he is a family man with a wife who can also drive steel. In the novel *The Magical Adventures of Pretty Pearl* (1983), Virginia Hamilton reimagined him as an African god who chose mortality in post–Civil War America, a trickster and brother to another African American folk hero, John de Conquer.

John Henry

When John Henry was a little baby boy, sitting on
   his papa's knee
Well he picked up a hammer and little piece of
   steel
Said Hammer's gonna be the death of me, lord,
   lord
Hammer's gonna be the death of mine

The captain said to John Henry
I'm gonna bring that steam drill around
I'm gonna bring that steam drill out on the job
I'm gonna whup that steel on down

John Henry told his captain
Lord a man ain't nothing but a man
But before I'd let your steam drill beat me down
I'd die with a hammer in my hand

John Henry said to his shaker
Shaker why don't you sing
Because I'm swinging thirty pounds from my hips
   on down
Just listen to that cold steel ring

Now the captain said to John Henry
I believe that mountain's caving in
John Henry said right back to the captain
Ain't nothing but my hammer sucking wind

Now the man that invented the steam drill
He thought he was mighty fine
But John Henry drove fifteen feet
The steam drill only made nine

John Henry hammered in the mountains
His hammer was striking fire

But he worked so hard, it broke his poor heart
And he laid down his hammer and he died

Now John Henry had a little woman
Her name was Polly Anne
John Henry took sick and had to go to bed
Polly Anne drove steel like a man

John Henry had a little baby
You could hold him in the palm of your hand

And the last words I heard that poor boy say
My daddy was a steel driving man

So every Monday morning
When the blue birds begin to sing
You can hear John Henry a mile or more
You can hear John Henry's hammer ring

James Berry (b.1926)

James Berry is a distinguished author of poetry, short stories, and novels. He grew up in Jamaica hearing some of the oral stories he has retold, but has been living in Britain since 1948. He writes in a poetic mixture of Jamaican dialect and literary English. His collection of short stories entitled *A Thief in the Village and Other Stories* (1988) won the prestigious British Smarties Award. In this book, he tells the absorbing stories of various boys and girls in rural Jamaica, describing the growth and yearnings of characters who discover important insights about themselves and their community. His novel *Ajeemah and His Son* (1991) describes the horrific journey that a West African father and son make when they are captured, enslaved, and transported to Jamaica to work on the sugar cane plantations. In his Anancy story collection, Berry seasons West African and Caribbean stories about the trickster spider god Anancy with a spice of wit and humor. He describes his Anancy (spelled the old Jamaican way rather than the African "Anansi") as "the African Anancy showing his new Caribbean roots," surrounded by "familiar Caribbean characters" such as Dog and Puss. Anancy is part human, part spider, and part god: a hero with flaws. (For an African Anansi tale, see "How Spider Obtained the Sky-God's Stories" at the beginning of Part 3.) Berry also explains that he "deepened, clarified, and expanded the stories" because readers of a book will not all bring to it the shared cultural values of a native audience and oral storyteller. Berry's version of this Anancy story weaves subtle commentary about political campaigns, human nature, and women's rights into the tale.

Anancy and the Making of the Bro Title

At the time, nobody is called Bro.

Anancy gets everybody to spread news that something special is ready to happen. It's ready to happen because everybody is ready for it. Come to the meeting in the village square. The big new happening will be revealed.

Anancy is pleased-pleased. A big crowd surrounds him in the early night. Anancy feels good and ready to make a sweetmouth speech.

"Friends," he starts, "you know and I know, everybody is a good-good person. But every person uses only a little goodness and a little bigness. People give teeny bits of gifts, a sprinkle of kind words, a pinch of this and a pinch of that. Friends, just think now of all the big extras that can come from making goodness work bigger and better."

"Hear, hear!" somebody says.

"Thank you, Dog," Anancy says.

"Friends," Anancy goes on, "make bigness work, and your fields are always full of harvest, your cupboards are always full of food."

"How can goodness make things happen just like that?" Rabbit asks.

"By becoming a Bro, which means Brother," Anancy says. "He who holds the title of Bro accepts everybody as brother. A Bro is building a little house; a Bro from every house comes and helps the building of a big house. A Bro is planting a little field; a Bro from every house comes and helps the planting of a big field. Drought is on; every Bro becomes rainmaker. It's hurricane; every Bro together clears up disaster. It's eating and drinking and dancing; every Bro and kinfolks are together in big merriment."

"Hear, hear!" Dog says.

"The title of Bro is good, but why no title of Sis for sister?" Anancy's wife says.

"Dear wife, thank you. But 'Bro' stands for 'Sis' as well."

"Dear husband, you well-well know Bro doesn't stand for Sis."

"Yes, dear wife, it stands for Sis, till one day, one day."

"Till one day, one day, what?"

"One day when you get your Sis title."

"Will we work on it together?"

"Yes," Anancy says. "We'll work on it together."

"And this is a good-good promise?"

"Yes, dear wife. This is a good-good promise, because everybody's ready to have their bigness, have their abundantness, their beautifulness, their wonderfulness!"

"Hear, hear!" Dog says.

"Friends," Anancy goes on, "take on the title of Bro in front of your name and you have a mummah and a puppah in every house. No bad-mouth will hurt you and loved ones. No bad-mind will work on you and loved ones. No bad spell, no curse, no enemy will get you and loved ones. You are to be killed and everybody saves you. You are to be hungry and every family feeds you. You are sick and every family worries about you, gets you balm and heals you. Everybody is brother, everybody is friend. No enemies anywhere."

"Hear, hear!" Dog says. "Hip, hip, hooray!"

"Hip, hip, hooray!" the crowd say. "Hip, hip, hooray! Hip, hip, hooray!"

Anancy breaks into song:

"You, me, all a Bro—
A Bro, a Bro, a Bro—
Every head is friend.
Clothes, food, fire will never ever end
Like full barrel and full barrel and full barrel.

I gi' you, you gi' me.
I gi' you, you gi' me.
Every head is friend.
Clothes, food, fire will never ever end
Like full barrel and full barrel and full barrel.

You, me, all, a Bro—
A Bro, a Bro, a Bro—
Make chain of full baskets,
Make chain of full baskets
Long-long, longer than day,
Long-long, longer than day,
Longer than day, O,
Longer than day, O!"

In noises and cheering, people rush forward. People want to be called Bro. Anancy puts his arm around Monkey. Anancy raises his other arm to the crowd and says, "Friends, I am your Bro Nancy. This is your Bro Monkey!" The crowd cheer them. Anancy gives Bro Monkey a big bag of corn. Rabbit becomes a Bro and gets two good cuts of cedar board from Anancy. Dog becomes a Bro and gets a shining necklace. Nearly everybody comes forward and becomes a Bro.

Next day early-early Anancy is ready to travel into everybody's country to spread the news about becoming a Bro.

In Anancy's yard, Bro Jackass stands there in the shaft of a cart. A garland of flowers is around the neck of Bro Jackass. Others with musical instruments sit in the cart. Bro Monkey has a drum, Bro Dog a banjo, Bro Rabbit a flute and Bro Puss a tambourine. Everybody is decorated with a garland of flowers or leaves. Peacock and Turkey have no instruments. Three other people are without instruments too; they are One-Eye Pig, Broken-Wing John Crow and Dropped-Leg Goat.

Though Jackass knows his way, Bro Nancy sits in the cart in front looking like the driver.

Bro Nancy picks up his sawn-off cowhorn and begins to blow it like a foghorn. That tells everybody something eventful is happening. In the sound of the horn, Anancy and his party start out with music and singing:

"You, me, all a Bro—
A Bro, a Bro, a Bro—
Every head is friend . . ."

With groups of people following them sometimes, Anancy and his band of people travel till they come into Blackbird country.

Anancy begins to blow his cowhorn at great lengths to arouse the bird-people to the event of his arrival. And he and his band come to a road lined with Blackbird KlingKling-people cheering them and singing and clapping and dancing for them. In the sounds of the cowhorn and their music, they go on to a big square and find Chiefman Blackbird in official colours waiting for them.

As the crowd of Blackbird-people surround them, Anancy and his party play on and on and sing:

"You, me, all a Bro—
A Bro, a Bro, a Bro—
Every head is friend . . ."

As the music and singing end, Bro Turkey says, "Gobble gobble gobble gobble gobble!" Bro Peacock opens out his tail and spins. One-Eye Pig stares bright-bright, smiling. Broken-Wing John Crow and Dropped-Leg Goat flap and hop about in a little dance.

Anancy stands up in the cart and makes his speech about becoming a Bro.

In loud cheering Anancy steps down from his cart and embraces Chiefman Blackbird KlingKling. He declares Chiefman Blackbird and his people all a Bro.

Anancy hands out gifts, gets gifts himself and moves off again blowing his cowhorn, with his band, playing and singing, "You, me, all a Bro."

In the same way as before, Anancy and his party travel on and stop in Yellow-Snake country, in Mon-key, Patoo, Rabbit, Hawk, John Crow and Ratbat countries, and then go on to Tiger country.

Here, in Tiger country, Anancy is to find more than usual resistance.

A great crowd of Tiger-people stand around Anancy and his party.

As usual, Bro Monkey bangs his drum, Bro Dog strums his banjo, Bro Rabbit plays his flute, Bro Puss shakes his tambourine. At the end of the music and singing, Bro Turkey says, "Gobble gobble gobble gobble gobble!" Bro Peacock opens out his tail and spins. One-Eye Pig stares bright-bright, smiling. Broken-Wing John Crow and Dropped-Leg Goat flap and hop about in their little dance. The Tiger-people clap and cheer.

Anancy gets going with his sweetmouth speech. The Tiger-people listen and listen keen-keen. Then sudden-sudden Chiefman Tiger stops Anancy, saying, "Anancy, I can defend myself. My people can defend themselves, in a group or as individuals. Why do we need this Bro business? I myself, I don't want to go and sit about with other people one bit. And you talk about getting hungry. We may get hungry, but certainly not for long. You talk about giving and getting. Why should I want to be given anything when I can take as I like?"

"Because as a Bro other Bro people won't be frightened of you," Anancy says.

"But I like other people to be frightened of me," Chiefman Tiger says. "I like people to hide when I walk past. It's great."

"Would it be the same," Anancy says, "if people didn't hide? If different people talked to you? And cheered you openly for your honour and your beauty and you knew that people talked about your good temper and the beautiful gentleman you are? Would it all be the same?"

Chiefman Tiger thinks, then in surprise he says, "Me a beautiful gentleman? Me having some honour?"

"Yes," Anancy says.

"Nobody has ever said that. How else am I beautiful?"

"Well," Anancy says, "your coat—the coat of all Tiger-people—is a blessing. Your handsome head and strong-strong shoulders are all a blessing. The Bro title comes to you and all Tiger-people as a much later blessing."

"Is this true? Is all this true?"

"It's true. Bro title gives you a new status. With it you become Bro Chiefman Tiger. And once you're a Bro you can go on to become Mister."

"Me become Mister?"

"Yes," Anancy says. "You can even go on from Mister to Sir and on to Honourable."

"What will I become then?" Chiefman Tiger asks.

"You'll be Honourable Sir Mister Bro Chiefman Tiger."

"Wow!" Chiefman Tiger says. "With all the weight of that honour, I couldn't walk. I'd have to be carried."

A great laughter and cheering goes up.

"Tell me how I'll actually get all that honour," Chiefman Tiger says. "How I'll know I've got it. And everybody'll know I've got it. And tell me more about the good things about me I don't know and about all I'll get if I become a Bro."

"Well," Anancy says, "if you treat, say, Bro Monkey or Bro Rabbit or Bro Dog—all other people—like they are your own Tiger-people, the news will come back to me. And I'll see you get your honour in front of everybody."

Chiefman Tiger goes silent, then says, "But I don't want to be good to everybody. I want to be very bad to some people. I have a lot of badness I must use. Can I start being good to some people who aren't Tiger people and go on being very bad to others?"

"Chiefman, Chiefman Tiger," Anancy says, "to be a Bro means everybody makes their own country a place of Bro, and so, at the same time, everybody makes all the countries one big place of Bro."

"Wow!" Chiefman Tiger says. "All this is new! Very new!"

"Yes," Anancy says. "Very new. But everybody is ready for it."

"I like the honour I'll get," Chiefman Tiger says. "I like the honour very much. But there is a spot of bother, I must admit. You see, as it is now, I can walk through anybody's country, and, apart from Lion, nobody, nobody can stop me. Or even challenge me. I have that safeguard already."

"Yes," Anancy says, "that's really so, Chiefman Tiger. But mightn't you get some news from Monkey-people or Rabbit-people, if when you walk through their country you were able to stop and have a chat, and have some refreshments they give you?"

"Hear, hear!" the Tiger-people say. "Hear, hear!"

Chiefman Tiger goes silent for a little while. Then he looks up and says, "Anancy, I'll join."

"Hear, hear!" the Tiger-people say. "Hear, hear!"

Bro Nancy comes and puts his arms around Chiefman Tiger. The Tiger-people become Bro. Anancy gives the people gifts. In turn, the Tiger-people pile on their gifts in Anancy's cart.

Anancy and his cart-band of people leave Tiger country in an uproar of cheering, cowhorn blowing and music and singing.

At home again, Anancy finds he has come into a new and difficult problem. How should he share out the cartload of gifts? Anancy tells his cart-band of people that silence has overtaken him.

"Silence has come upon me, friends," Anancy tells them. "It is like a night a man must sleep in. Welcome in different countries make a man happy and sad. Unbrothers have become brothers. It calls for silence and fasting. I must have silence and fasting for seven days and seven nights."

Everybody is struck by Anancy's new mood. All agree to help Bro Nancy and leave him alone. "Let Bro Nancy deal with his deep mind," they say.

Anancy will have nothing to do with the gifts. Anancy lets his cart-band of people unload the cart and carry the bags of rabbits and birds, box of dried fish, barrel of crabs, barrels of different corned meat, bags of corn and dry beans, bags of yams, spices, bottles of rum and baskets of fruit and puddings and bread, and stack them in his kitchen.

The moment Anancy sees that everyone is really gone—and everywhere is quiet-quiet—Anancy leaps up and begins to dance and sing around the pile of gifts:

"Bro Nancy O, Bro Nancy—
    Eat, O eat.
Donkeys come load up—
    Eat, O eat.
Carts come load up—
    Eat, O eat.
Plenty-plenty is abundance, O—
    Eat, O eat.
Abundance O—
    Eat, O eat.
O Bro Nancy—
    Eat, O eat.
Bro Nancy, O Bro Nancy!"

Anancy drinks rum and sings and dances. He begins to season and pickle different meats for keeping. At the same time, he cooks a sample of every kind of the meat and of everything else. And the more the kitchen gets stronger with the smell of cooking and spices and seasoning the more Anancy sips his drink, takes a taste of things and sings and dances.

Almost bursting with food and drink, Anancy falls asleep.

Anancy wakes up in his long furry gown. Anancy sings and dances round the gifts, and drinks, cooks, eats and falls asleep again.

Not caring whether it is day or night, Anancy drinks, dances and sings, cooks and eats and falls asleep for three days.

Worried about her husband, Mrs Anancy arrives at the kitchen doorway. She cannot really believe what she sees. Her husband is a round and fat Anancy singing and dancing round a smaller pile of gifts.

Mrs Anancy steps inside, looks round and is shocked. She asks Anancy, "What's the meaning of all this?"

"Wife," Anancy says, "sit down and join your husband. Lots of meals are ready. There's drink. Come, sit down."

"I'll have none of it. None of it," she says. "The gifts were never yours to have alone. Everybody will have to know about this."

"Shall I promote your title of Sis or not?" Anancy says with a threat.

"Not," Mrs Anancy says crossly. "Promoting a Sis title is bigger than you. Much bigger than you."

"Wife," Anancy says, "you are wife and I am husband. We don't let each other down."

Disappointed and angry but feeling trapped, Mrs Anancy gives a loud sigh and sits down heavily.

Somewhere, loud-loud, unexpectedly, Blackbird Kling-Kling begins to sing this little song:

"People, O people,
Come and see Bro Nancy.
People, O people,
Come and see Bro Nancy.
Come and see Bro Nancy, O!
Come and see Bro Nancy, O!. . ."

Other Blackbird-people begin to sing this same song, passing the news round the whole village.

Sudden-sudden, the yard is full of people.

Anancy's cart-band of people are the first to arrive. Immediately, Anancy says, "Oh, Bro Dog, Bro Monkey, Bro Jackass, and everybody, so pleased you've come! So, so glad-glad you heard the KlingKling call! Come. We'll put out long tables and benches. We'll put out the cooked meats with everything cooked. We'll cook more meat and everything else. We'll have all the drinks and get some more. We'll strike up the music. And Bro and Bro and Bro and everybody, when the merriment is on, and you see Anancy dancing, know that Anancy dances away his badness. With all his heart, Anancy dances away his badness."

That whole day and night, Anancy's yard becomes a place of great feasting and merriment.

From that time, leaders always try to cover up the lion-share of things they take for themselves.

Diane Wolkstein (b. 1942)

Diane Wolkstein has been a leader of the storytelling revival in North America since the 1960s, publishing a number of picture book adaptations and collections of tales from different parts of the world. She studied drama, pantomime, and education before she decided to concentrate on storytelling in her native New York City, where she started a radio show and persuaded the city's parks department to hire her as one of the nation's first professional storytellers. She has also traveled widely for storytelling festivals and research. Wolkstein collected folktales during several visits to Haiti, recording, editing, and retelling the stories she listened to in group settings where audience participation is as important as the identity of the teller. In *The Magic Orange Tree* (first published in 1978), she describes the personalities and storytelling techniques of the tellers vividly and perceptively, providing valuable insights into some of the differences between oral and written storytelling. The Haitian stories, many of which have parallels among other folktale traditions, are lively and witty. "The Magic Orange Tree" is a pared-down version of "Cinderella" (see Part 5), and "Mother of the Waters" corresponds in some ways to the Grimm Brothers tale "Mother Holle" (in Part 2). But these stories, told in Creole (a language related to French) have a character all their own.

From *The Magic Orange Tree*

INTRODUCTION

"*Cric?*" the Haitian storyteller calls out when she or he has a story to tell. "*Crac!*" the audience responds *if* they want that storyteller to begin. If they do not respond with *crac!*, the storyteller cannot begin. "*Cric?*" another storyteller calls out, hoping for the welcoming "*crac!*"*

It is not that the audience is rude in refusing one storyteller and choosing another; rather, they are giving their pledge. For if the listeners cry *crac!* they are expected to, and do, give their full support to the storyteller. They listen to hear that the story is told correctly. Embellishments are accepted, confusion or losses of memory are not. The listeners comment on the events and characters of the stories. They comment on the storyteller's talents. And as soon as a song begins within a story, the audience joins in. I have heard groups joyously sing the chorus ten and twenty times.

Communal storytelling in Haiti takes place outside the capital city of Port-au-Prince, in the plains, mountains, and countryside. In these rural areas the men work in the fields and the women take care of the household. Once a week the women sell the family produce in the marketplace. The houses are small thatched-roof huts, without electricity. In the evenings the families create their own entertainment. When the adults are not too tired, and especially when the moon is full or on a Saturday evening, they gather outside on their steps and talk and gossip. Soon a story may be thought of. *Cric?*

In moments a group might gather: friends, neighbors, teen-agers, children, and toddlers. With many ready to tell, the storytellers must compete for a chance. If a storyteller tells well, he will call out *cric?* just as he is finishing his last sentence, but perhaps someone else has already called out *cric?* Then the general sentiment of the crowd decides who will be the one to unwind the magic thread.

Children of seven or eight mouth the words as the storytellers speak, for most of the stories are already well-known. But if the children are too noisy, they will be reprimanded and sent away. Sometimes they will gather at a distance and form their own group, telling stories and imitating the gestures and intonations of the adults.

Though the stories involve set gestures and expressions, what is most exciting is the variety and inventiveness of the individual storyteller. The best storyteller takes a story known to all and creates his or her own story. Everyone knows the tale, but this time what will the storyteller give? in entertainment? in imagery? in wisdom?

Many of the tales I recognized at once because of their European or African counterparts. "Mother of the Waters" is a version of the German "Mother Holle"

Cric is pronounced "creek." *Crac* is pronounced "crack." *Cric?-Crac!* an introductory phrase to French stories, is said to have been brought to Haiti by the *Breton* sailors in the seventeenth century.

Since there is still controversy in Haiti concerning the phonetic spellings of Creole words, I have chosen the gallicized spellings. The Frenchified system also permits a certain access to the Creole words to the English- and French-speaking reader.

collected by the Grimm brothers. "Bye-Bye" resembles the Basotho tale "Tortoise and Dove" collected by Minnie Postma. Other stories, such as "The Two Donkeys," "Owl," and "The Last Tiger in Haiti," were new to me. Yet even those stories I had known were different. It was like eating fruit such as apples and pears all your life and suddenly tasting mangoes and papayas and guavas.

Odette Menesson Rigaud and Milo Rigaud, who have lived in Haiti for the past forty years and are profoundly involved in Voodoo, the religious life of the peasants, were the ones who introduced me to the fruits of the Haitian night. It was Odette who, in 1971, wrote a letter of introduction to Jean-Baptiste Romain, director of the Faculté d'Ethnologie of the State University of Haiti. He in turn introduced me to the remarkable Jeanne Philippe, a practicing psychoanalyst, country doctor, lover of stories, and child of a Carib Indian mother and Haitian father. Many evenings I sat on the porch of Dr. Philippe's house and listened with Jeanne and her parents to the peasants in the neighborhood tell stories, which the family knew well but loved to hear again. Jeanne's neighbor, Willy, often accompanied me to hear stories in Carrefour-Dufort, a country village fifteen miles southwest of Port-au-Prince. And Odette took me to visit her friends at Croix-des-Missions, Diquini, Planton-Café, and Masson.

Before I left for Haiti, I had read of the tradition of the professional storytellers *(maître conte),* who were not paid but offered food and lodging in exchange for their talents. In the eighteenth century, they traveled from one plantation to another and were most often called upon to perform at festivals and wakes. If a child died, they would tell simple stories; if an important man died, long romances. But in the 1920s, most of the master storytellers left Haiti with the other farmers because there was work available cutting sugar cane in Cuba.

On the chance that a few master storytellers might still be in Haiti, I would ask at each storytelling evening if anyone knew a *maître conte.* Almost everyone knew or had known of one who lived in this or that village, always one village or one night away. I began to wonder if the master storyteller was not mythic. Then one evening in Carrefour-Dufort two villagers rushed up to me and whispered: "Delaba has just returned from Port-au-Prince." (For weeks I had heard that Delaba, a goatherd, was also a great *maître conte.*)

"Where is he?" I whispered. "He's coming," they announced.

When Delaba arrived, the whole atmosphere changed. A group of teen-agers, children, and adults surrounded him, laughing and talking animatedly. He was tall, dark in color, and he had a charismatic presence. The storyteller who was speaking quickly finished, for all attention was on Delaba.

Delaba nodded to me, walked to the place the other storyteller had occupied, and began: "*Cric?*"

"*Crac!*" the others responded.

Delaba shook his head in disgust. He raised his voice: "*Cric?*"

And this time a resounding "*CRAC!*" answered him.

He smiled at his audience, pleased. It was this contact with his audience that differentiated Delaba from the other storytellers. Delaba not only created his own story, but he also played with the audience. If they sang loudly, he would raise his hand and admonish them. "Sweetly," he would say, or at other points in the story, "More, louder, stronger." And the audience complied.

He was an excellent entertainer. He varied his voice from contralto to falsetto, from loud to soft. He impersonated animals with gesture and voice. He sang and danced. When he danced, he not only turned in a circle clapping (as did Edouard, the narrator of "Bouki Dances the Kokioko"), but he also invented steps and gestures. He danced slowly, he danced fast. The audience loved him. They sang louder and louder. Again he admonished them, this time with a twinkle in his eye and a tilt of his head.

After each storytelling event, I would return with the *cric* on my Sony battery tape recorder. But the words of the story were not enough, for what was told and how and why was often affected by the *crac,* by the presence and reactions of the audience. By my second trip to Haiti, I began to take notes, either during the stories or after I had returned to my hotel.

Yet, when I began to compare the notes concerning the different storytellers with the quality of the stories that were told, I was surprised to find that there was often very little correspondence. Although Delaba was the best entertainer, none of his stories appear in this collection. The words of his stories did not have sufficient substance, beauty, or humor. And while Edouard was among the worst performers—his speech was often inaudible and garbled, his movements awkward—his story "Bouki Dances the Kokioko" is included. In a printed collection, words alone had to determine which of the storytellers' stories would be included. Yet who can measure the joy and delight that Delaba gave to others?

I thought about the brothers Grimm, Joseph Jacobs, and Harold Courlander, and about all the stories they had *not* included in their collections. I began to realize that story collectors, unlike folklorists, who make statistical samplings of all the stories they have gathered, choose in the end those stories they believe in.

Stories about the trickster team, Bouki and Malice, abound in Haiti. The history of Haiti has long been one of oppression, deprivation, and suffering. Twenty-five years after Columbus landed in Haiti, only a handful of the native Indian population remained. The Spanish brought slaves from Africa to work their sugar-cane and cotton plantations. When the French took control of the western part of the island in 1697, they continued to import slaves. Although Haiti has been independently governed since 1804, the majority of the people today still do not have enough to eat. Farmers are taxed on their produce to and from market. Infractions of governmental regulations are met with by severe punishments. People fix evil spells on their relatives and neighbors. This harsh reality of Haitian survival is reflected in a multitude of stories dealing with beatings, killings, shame, and dishonor. Clever little Malice triumphs; and big, stupid Bouki is fooled once again.

And the difficulties continue. In the 1970s, two thousand people inhabit each square mile of tillable soil, and over eighty-five percent of the populace cannot read or write. Education became free in 1816, but for more than a century only the rich could afford to pay for the supplies and books needed for schooling. The supplies have been free since 1946, but half the teachers have had no formal training and the books are in French. Since the peasant children grow up speaking Creole, which sounds similar to French but is structurally a different language, the illiteracy rate has not changed significantly. The farmers continue to be tied to the land, and the land is eroded and insufficient to provide for the children.

Yet, despite the inconsistencies, irrationalities, and intense problems of survival there *is* an order, a sense of life, and a richness of understanding among the Haitian peasants that goes beyond the daily poverty and difficulties and emerges in certain of their songs, proverbs, and stories.

In almost every story in this collection the background of hunger and survival exists, but there is also the humor ("I'm Tipingee, She's Tipingee, We're Tipingee, Too"), the silliness ("Cat Baptism"), the psychological insight ("The One Who Wouldn't Listen to His Own Dream"), the political acumen ("Horse and Toad"), the poetic imagery ("Papa God Sends Turtle Doves"), the wisdom, ("The Forbidden Apple"), and the will to live ("The Magic Orange Tree") of a people who have not only survived but have done so with a creativity in art, song, dance, and story to rival Papa God.

If there is an abundance of stories with songs, *contes chantés,* that is because I am a storyteller and delighted in the participation of the audience in the story and with the storyteller. This enthusiastic communal participation is undoubtedly related to the religious experience of the people. The Voodoo priest or priestess does not speak to a passive, subdued congregation. On the contrary, it is the beat of the drum that announces the entrance of the spirits, and any member (regardless of age, status, or sex) of the singing, dancing congregation who is sufficiently immersed in the ceremony may be chosen by the spirits and possessed.

It is my hope that when you, my reader, turn the page and bite into the strange fruit of the Haitian night, your present world will dissolve and you will for the moment be possessed by the mysterious world of the spirit: the story.

Cric?

THE MAGIC ORANGE TREE

About the Story: When a child is born in the countryside, the umbilical cord may be saved and dried and planted in the earth, with a pit from a fruit tree placed on top of the cord. The tree that grows then belongs to the child. And when the tree gives fruit in five or six years, that fruit is considered the property of the child, who can barter or sell it. (Young children in Haiti very quickly become economically active.) Trees in Haiti are thus thought to protect children and are sometimes referred to as the guardian angel of the child. However, if the tree should die or grow in a deformed manner, that would be considered an evil omen for the child who owned the tree.

Artist Elsa Henriquez used a folk art style with bold shapes to illustrate a scene of domestic conflict between stepmother and child in the Haitian folktale "The Magic Orange Tree."

The song of the orange tree is often sung by the storyteller after the *cric?*, before the beginning of the story. Each storyteller may offer a slightly different melodic version of the song. Therefore, the storyteller's decision to sing before the story not only teaches the audience the storyteller's specific melody but also warms up the audience, for singing gets the blood flowing and the heart's juices jumping.

Cric? crac! There was once a girl whose mother died when she was born. Her father waited for some time to remarry, but when he did, he married a woman who was both mean and cruel. She was so mean there were some days she would not give the girl anything at all to eat. The girl was often hungry.

One day the girl came from school and saw on the table three round ripe oranges. *Hmmmm.* They smelled good. The girl looked around her. No one was there. She took one orange, peeled it, and ate it. *Hmmm-mmm.* It was good. She took a second orange and ate it. She ate the third orange. Oh-oh, she was happy. But soon her stepmother came home.

"Who has taken the oranges I left on the table?" she said. "Whoever has done so had better say their prayers now, for they will not be able to say them later."

The girl was so frightened she ran from the house. She ran through the woods until she came to her own mother's grave. All night she cried and prayed to her mother to help her. Finally she fell asleep.

In the morning the sun woke her, and as she rose to her feet something dropped from her skirt onto the ground. What was it? It was an orange pit. And the moment it entered the earth a green leaf sprouted from it. The girl watched, amazed. She knelt down and sang:

> Orange tree,
> Grow and grow and grow.
> Orange tree, orange tree.
> Grow and grow and grow,
> Orange tree.
> Stepmother is not real mother,
> Orange tree.

The orange tree grew. It grew to the size of the girl. The girl sang:

> Orange tree,
> Branch and branch and branch.
> Orange tree, orange tree,
> Branch and branch and branch,
> Orange tree.
> Stepmother is not real mother,
> Orange tree.

And many twisting, turning, curving branches appeared on the tree. Then the girl sang:

> Orange tree,
> Flower and flower and flower.
> Orange tree, orange tree,
> Flower and flower and flower,
> Orange tree.
> Stepmother is not real mother,
> Orange tree.

Beautiful white blossoms covered the tree. After a time they began to fade, and small green buds appeared where the flowers had been. The girl sang:

Orange tree,
Ripen and ripen and ripen.
Orange tree, orange tree,
Ripen and ripen and ripen,
Orange tree.
Stepmother is not real mother.
Orange tree.

The oranges ripened, and the whole tree was filled with golden oranges. The girl was so delighted she danced around and around the tree, singing:

Orange tree,
Grow and grow and grow.
Orange tree, orange tree,
Grow and grow and grow,
Orange tree.
Stepmother is not real mother,
Orange tree.

But then when she looked, she saw the orange tree had grown up to the sky, far beyond her reach. What was she to do? Oh she was a clever girl. She sang:

Orange tree,
Lower and lower and lower.
Orange tree, orange tree,
Lower and lower and lower,
Orange tree.
Stepmother is not real mother,
Orange tree.

When the orange tree came down to her height, she filled her arms with oranges and returned home.

The moment the stepmother saw the gold oranges in the girl's arms, she seized them and began to eat them. Soon she had finished them all.

"Tell me, my sweet," she said to the girl, "where have you found such delicious oranges?"

The girl hesitated. She did not want to tell. The stepmother seized the girl's wrist and began to twist it.

"Tell me!" she ordered.

The girl led her stepmother through the woods to the orange tree. You remember the girl was very clever? Well, as soon as the girl came to the tree, she sang:

Orange tree,
Grow and grow and grow.
Orange tree, orange tree,
Grow and grow and grow,
Orange tree.
Stepmother is not real mother,
Orange tree.

And the orange tree grew up to the sky. What was the stepmother to do then? She began to plead and beg.

"Please," she said. "You shall be my own dear child. You may always have as much as you want to eat. Tell the tree to come down and *you* shall pick the oranges for me." So the girl quietly sang:

Orange tree,
Lower and lower and lower.
Orange tree, orange tree,
Lower and lower and lower,
Orange tree.
Stepmother is not real mother,
Orange tree.

The tree began to lower. When it came to the height of the stepmother, she leapt on it and began to climb so quickly you might have thought she was the daughter of an ape. And as she climbed from branch to branch, she ate every orange. The girl saw that there would soon be no oranges left. What would happen to her then? The girl sang:

Orange tree,
Grow and grow and grow.
Orange tree, orange tree,
Grow and grow and grow,
Orange tree.
Stepmother is not real mother,
Orange tree.

The orange tree grew and grew and grew and grew. "Help!" cried the stepmother as she rose into the sky. "H-E-E-lp. . . ."

The girl cried: *Break! Orange tree, Break!*

The orange tree broke into a thousand pieces . . . and the stepmother as well.

Then the girl searched among the branches until she found . . . a tiny orange pit. She carefully planted it in the earth. Softly she sang:

Orange tree,
Grow and grow and grow.
Orange tree, orange tree,
Grow and grow and grow,
Orange tree.
Stepmother is not real mother,
Orange tree.

The orange tree grew to the height of the girl. She picked some oranges and took them to market to sell. They were so sweet the people bought all her oranges.

Every Saturday she is at the marketplace selling her oranges. Last Saturday, I went to see her and asked her if she would give me a free orange. "What?" she cried. "After all I've been through!" And she gave me such a kick in the pants that that's how I got here today, to tell you the story—"The Magic Orange Tree."

MOTHER OF THE WATERS

About the Story: Whenever I have told this story I have been questioned as to whether this is an authentic folktale. Listeners are puzzled by the idea of a young girl disobeying the magic figure of the Mother of the Waters. It is rather daring for an inexperienced person to go against the magic of a spirit.

Though the act of disobedience is unusual in folktales, this particular story was recorded by Suzanne Comhaire-Sylvain in Haiti, and the version she published in 1937 is nearly identical to the one I recorded in Haiti in 1973. In her version, the girl articulates her thoughts and says, "I can not obey the old woman, that cat is hungry."

It may be that Comhaire-Sylvain was also intrigued by the question of disobedience, for she chose to write the first part of her doctoral thesis *(Les Contes Haitiens)* at the Sorbonne on just this story. In her thesis, Comhaire-Sylvain describes over one hundred parallel versions of "Mother of the Waters." The ones that most closely resemble the Haitian one are from the Caribbean (they contain the search for water, the old woman with sores, the cooking, the large and small eggs, and the beating of the cat) and from Africa (the same images, but no beating of the cat). The images of fertility are different in both the American Indian (Spiderwoman, large and small pottery jugs) and the European (the oven, the cow, the feather bed, the apple tree). But in all these versions there are only six in which there is any act of disobedience.

A young seamstress told this story one evening after work as she was sitting with her co-workers in a tiny dress shop in Pétionville. She was timid and correct in her behavior toward her boss, but once she began the story, she was in her own world. She spoke quietly and intently, as if she were seeing each image as she spoke it.

There was once a young girl whose mother and father were both dead. As she had no way to get anything to eat, she had to hire herself out as a servant. She worked for a woman who lived by the river. But even though the woman had a daughter the same age as the servant girl, she showed no kindness to her. She beat her and spoke roughly to her and gave her only scraps to eat.

One day, the woman sent the servant girl to the river to wash the silverware. As the girl was washing the silver, a tiny silver teaspoon slipped through her fingers and was carried away by the water. The servant girl reached for the teaspoon, but the current was moving too swiftly. She went back to the house and told her mistress what had happened.

"Find my teaspoon," the woman screamed, "or never return to my house."

The servant girl returned to the river and followed the stream, She walked all day without finding the teaspoon, and as the sun began to set in the sky, she started crying.

An old woman sitting on a stone near the river's edge asked her why she was crying.

"I have dropped my mistress's silver teaspoon in the river. She says if I do not find it, I may not return. I will have no work. How will I eat?"

The old woman did not answer. Instead, she asked, "Will you wash my back?"

"Of course," the girl answered.

She soaped and scrubbed the old woman's back, but the woman's back was rough and hard and covered with sores and thistles, and the girl's hands were soon bleeding.

"What is it?" the woman asked.

"It is nothing," the girl answered.

"Let me see your hands," the old woman said.

The girl held them out. The old woman spit on them. The cuts closed up and the girl's hands were as they were before.

"Come home with me," the old woman said, "and I will give you dinner."

She led the girl to her home in the mountains and gave her banana pudding. Then they went to sleep.

The next day, after the girl had swept the yard, the woman gave her a bone, a grain of rice, and one bean and told her to make dinner.

"Grandmother," the girl said respectfully, "please forgive me, but I do not know how to make dinner with these."

"It is simple," the old woman said. "Place them in a pot of boiling water and dinner will soon be ready."

The girl followed the woman's directions, and by noon a delicious-smelling casserole of rice, beans, and meat was steaming inside the pot.

As they ate the old woman told the girl: "I will be going out. In a few hours a wild cat will come and beg for food. Do not give it any food. Beat it with my stick."

A few hours after the old woman left, the girl heard a mewing outside the door. *Me-ow. Me-ow. Me-ow.* The cat was so thin and hungry the girl did not have the heart to hit it. She brought it a saucer of milk and watched it eat. After a while the cat went away.

A short time later the old woman returned. She was pleased with the girl. So the servant girl stayed on with the old woman. The girl helped her, and the old woman always gave her enough to eat.

Then, after several months, the old woman told her it was time for her to return to her mistress.

"Yes," said the girl. "But how can I go back without the silver teaspoon?"

"Walk down the road," the old woman said. "When you come to the first crossroads you will see a pile of eggs lying on some straw. The larger ones will call out: *Take me, take me!* Take one of the smaller eggs and break it open at the next crossroads."

The servant girl thanked the old woman and set out.

At the first crossroads she saw the pile of eggs. The larger ones cried: *Take me, take me!* The girl chose the smallest egg and when she cracked it open at the next crossroads, out came a tiny box, which grew and grew until it filled her arms. The girl opened it and inside were forks and knives and spoons—all made of silver.

The woman and her daughter were so jealous when they saw the servant girl's box of silverware that they made her tell the story of how she had gotten it three times. Then the very next morning, the mother sent her own daughter down to the river to wash the silverware.

The girl didn't even bother to wash the silverware. She simply threw the small coffee teaspoon into the river and went home.

"I have lost the coffee spoon," the girl declared.

"Then go and find it," the mother said knowingly, "and do not come home until you do."

The daughter walked alongside the river all day. Then, toward evening, she saw the old woman sitting on a stone. Immediately she began to cry.

"Why are you crying?" the woman asked.

"Oh-oh. I have lost my mother's silver spoon. She says I may not go home unless I find it. What shall I do?"

"Will you wash my back?" the woman asked.

The girl took the soap and began to wash the woman's back when the thistles on the woman's back cut her hands.

"Oh-oh!" she cried.

"What is it?" asked the woman.

"It's your filthy rotting back. It cut my hands and they are bleeding."

The old woman took the girl's hands and spit on them and they were healed. Then she brought her to her home in the mountains and fed her supper.

The next morning, the old woman gave the girl a bone, a grain of rice, and one bean and told her to make dinner.

"With this garbage?" said the girl.

"What a sorry tongue you have," the woman answered. "I only hope you are not as nasty as your words. Place what I have given you in a pot of boiling water and dinner will soon be ready."

At noon the pot was filled with rice and beans and meat. They ate their meal and the old woman said:

"I am going out. In a few hours a wild cat will come and beg for food. Do not give it any food. Beat it with my stick."

Some time after the old woman left, the girl heard a mewing outside. *Me-ow. Me-ow. Me-ow.* She grabbed the old woman's stick and rushed for the cat. She hit it and hit it and hit it and hit it until she broke one of its legs.

Much later that evening, the old woman returned. She was leaning on a cane and limping, for one of her legs was broken. The next morning she told the girl: "You must leave my house today. You will not learn and I cannot help you anymore."

"But I will not go home without my silverware," the girl insisted.

"Then I shall give you one last bit of advice. At the next crossroads you will find a pile of eggs lying on some straw. The larger ones will call out: *Take me, take me!* Choose one of the smaller eggs and break it open at the next crossroads."

The girl ran out of the house and down the road. When she came to the first crossroads the larger eggs called out: *Take me, take me!*

"I am not foolish," said the girl. "If an egg speaks to me, I will listen. If it is a large one, all the better!"

She chose the largest egg and broke it open at the next crossroads. Out came all kinds of lizards, goblins, demons, and devils and ate the girl up.

Angela Carter (1940–92)

This version of one of Russia's most popular fairy tales was reprinted in the last book by English writer Angela Carter, *Strange Things Sometimes Still Happen: Fairy Tales from Around the World* (1993). Carter experimented with fairy tale motifs and fantasy in her feminist fiction for adults, while her collections of fairy tales emphasize the problems and powers of girls and women in both classic and lesser-known tales. In an Introduction to this volume, Marina Warner praises one of Carter's "original and effective strategies, snatching out of the jaws of misogyny itself, 'useful stories' for women."[1] Vasilissa the Fair, like Ashputtle, Mutsmag, and Dove Isabeau, treasures and uses wisely objects, such as a magic doll, that represent the spirit of her good mother and help her triumph through dangerous adventures. Vasilissa is similar to Hansel and Gretel (see Part 2), as well as to Cinderella (in Part 5), in surviving ordeals at home and in the witch Baba-Yaga's house. Encounters with mysterious horsemen representing the dawn, daylight, and night appear to be remnants of ancient myths in which cosmic and natural phenomena are personified. Carter noted that since stern Baba-Yaga possesses fire and skulls as well as control over morning, day, and night, and her mortar and pestle are associated with food production, "the Baba-Yaga's origins are probably in the Mother goddess of various mythologies."[2] Baba-Yaga is an even more ambiguous antagonist than the cruel stepmothers in many tales, the witch in "Rapunzel," or the false father in "The Enchanter's Daughter" by Antonia Barber (in Part 7). She threatens to eat Vasilissa but ultimately helps her learn how to ask questions and destroy her enemies. It is also interesting that although the heroine's beauty is emphasized in relation to her stepfamily's jealousy, it is her incredible skill in sewing that attracts the attention of the tsar and leads to her marriage into royalty.

NOTES

1. Marina Warner, Introduction, *Strange Things Sometimes Still Happen,* ed. Angela Carter (Boston: Faber and Faber, 1992) x.
2. Angela Carter, ed., Notes, *Strange Things Sometimes Still Happen* (Boston: Faber and Faber, 1992) 216–17.

Vasilissa the Fair

A merchant and his wife living in a certain country had an only daughter, the beautiful Vasilissa. When the child was eight years old the mother was seized with a fatal illness, but before she died she called Vasilissa to her side and, giving her a little doll, said. "Listen, dear daughter! remember my last words. I am dying, and bequeath to you now, together with a parent's blessing, this doll. Keep it always beside you, but show it to nobody; if at any time you are in trouble, give the doll some food and ask its advice." Then the mother kissed her daughter, sighed deeply and died.

After his wife's death the merchant grieved for a long time, and next began to think whether he should not wed again. He was handsome and would have no difficulty in finding a bride; moreover, he was especially pleased with a certain little widow, no longer young, who possessed two daughters of about the same age as Vasilissa.

The widow was famous as both a good house-keeper and a good mother to her daughters, but when the merchant married her he quickly found she was unkind to his daughter. Vasilissa, being the chief beauty in the village, was on that account envied by her stepmother and stepsisters. They found fault with her on every occasion, and tormented her with impossible tasks; thus, the poor girl suffered from the severity of her work and grew dark from exposure to wind and sun. Vasilissa endured all and became every day more beautiful; but the stepmother and her daughters who sat idle with folded hands, grew thin and almost lost their minds from spite. What supported Vasilissa? This. She received assistance from her doll; otherwise she could not have surmounted her daily difficulties.

Vasilissa, as a rule, kept a dainty morsel for her doll, and in the evening when everyone had gone to bed she would steal to her closet and regale her doll and say, "Now, dear, eat and listen to my grief! Though I am living in my father's house, my life is joyless; a wicked stepmother makes me wretched; please direct my life and tell me what to do."

The doll tasted the food, and gave advice to the sorrowing child, and in the morning performed her work, so that Vasilissa could rest in the shade or pluck flowers; already the beds had been weeded, and the cab-bages watered, and the water carried, and the stove heated. It was nice for Vasilissa to live with her doll.

Several years passed. Vasilissa grew up, and the young men in the town sought her hand in marriage; but they never looked at the stepsisters. Growing more angry than ever, the stepmother answered Vasilissa's suitors thus: "I will not let you have my youngest daughter before her sisters." She dismissed the suitors and vented her spite on Vasilissa with harsh words and blows.

But it happened that the merchant was obliged to visit a neighbouring country, where he had business; and in the meanwhile the stepmother went to live in a house situated close to a thick forest. In the forest was a glade, in which stood a cottage, and in the cottage

Ivan Bilibin was one of the masters in a rich tradition of Russian fairy tale art. This 1900 illustration of Vasilissa combines Russian folk designs with haunting supernatural images and the brave, beautiful figure of the heroine.

lived Baba-Yaga, who admitted nobody to her cottage, and devoured people as if they were chickens. Having moved to the new house, the merchant's wife continually, on some pretext or other, sent the hated Vasilissa into the forest, but the girl always returned home safe and unharmed, because the doll directed her and took care she did not enter Baba-Yaga's cottage.

Spring arrived, and the stepmother assigned to each of the three girls an evening task; thus, she set one to make lace, a second to knit stockings, and Vasilissa to spin. One evening, having extinguished all the lights in the house except one candle in the room where the girls sat at work, the stepmother went to bed. In a little while the candle needed attention, and one of the stepmother's daughters took the snuffers and, beginning to cut the wick, as if by accident, put out the light.

"What are we to do now?" said the girls. "There is no light in the whole house, and our tasks are unfinished; someone must run for a light to Baba-Yaga."

"I can see my pins," said the daughter who was making lace. "I shall not go."

"Neither shall I," said the daughter who was knitting stockings; "my needles are bright."

"You must run for a light. Go to Baba-Yaga's," they both cried, pushing Vasilissa from the room.

Vasilissa went to her closet, placed some supper ready for the doll, and said, "Now, little doll, have something to eat and hear my trouble. They have sent me to Baba-Yaga's for a light, and she will eat me."

"Do not be afraid!" answered the doll. "Go on your errand, but take me with you. No harm will befall you while I am present." Vasilissa placed the doll in her pocket, crossed herself and entered the thick forest, but she trembled.

Suddenly a horseman galloped past; he was white and dressed in white, his steed was white and had a white saddle and bridle. The morning light was appearing.

The girl went further and another horseman rode past; he was red and dressed in red and his steed was red. The sun rose.

Vasilissa walked all night and all day, but on the following evening she came out in a glade, where stood Baba-Yaga's cottage. The fence around the cottage was made of human bones, and on the fence there were fixed human skulls with eyes. Instead of doorposts at the gates there were human legs; instead of bolts there were hands, instead of a lock there was

a mouth with sharp teeth. Vasilissa grew pale from terror and stood as if transfixed. Suddenly another horseman rode up; he was black and dressed in black and upon a black horse; he sprang through Baba-Yaga's gates and vanished, as if he had been hurled into the earth. Night came on. But the darkness did not last long; the eyes in all the skulls on the fence lighted up, and at once it became as light throughout the glade as if it were midday. Vasilissa trembled from fear, and not knowing whither to run, she remained motionless.

Suddenly she heard a terrible noise. The trees cracked, the dry leaves rustled, and out of the forest Baba-Yaga appeared, riding in a mortar which she drove with a pestle, while she swept away traces of her progress with a broom. She came up to the gates and stopped; then sniffing about her, cried, "Phoo, phoo, I smell a Russian! Who is here?"

Vasilissa approached the old woman timidly and gave her a low bow; then she said, "It is I, granny! My stepsisters have sent me to you for a light."

"Very well," said Baba-Yaga, "I know them. If you first of all live with me and do some work, then I will give you a light. If you refuse, I will eat you." Then she turned to the gates and exclaimed, "Strong bolts, unlock; wide gates, open!" The gates opened, and Baba-Yaga went out whistling. Vasilissa followed, and all again closed.

Having entered the room, the witch stretched herself and said to Vasilissa, "Hand me everything in the oven; I am hungry." Vasilissa lit a torch from the skulls upon the fence and, drawing the food from the oven, handed it to the witch. The meal would have been sufficient for ten men. Moreover, Vasilissa brought up from the cellar kvass, and honey, and beer and wine. The old woman ate and drank almost everything. She left nothing for Vasilissa but some fragments, endcrusts of bread and tiny morsels of sucking pig. Baba-Yaga lay down to sleep and said, "When I go away tomorrow, take care that you clean the yard, sweep out the cottage, cook the dinner and get ready the linen. Then go to the cornbin, take a quarter of the wheat and cleanse it from impurities. See that all is done! otherwise I shall eat you."

After giving these injunctions Baba-Yaga began to snore. But Vasilissa placed the remains of the old woman's meal before her doll and, bursting into tears, said, "Now, little doll, take some food and hear my grief. Baba-Yaga has set me a terrible task, and has threatened to eat me if I fail in any way; help me!"

The doll answered, "Have no fear, beautiful Vasilissa! Eat your supper, say your prayers and lie down to sleep; morning is wiser than evening."

It was early when Vasilissa woke, but Baba-Yaga, who had already risen, was looking out of the window. Suddenly the light from the eyes in the skulls was extinguished; then a pale horseman flashed by, and it was altogether daylight. Baba-Yaga went out and whistled; a mortar appeared before her with a pestle and a hearth broom. A red horseman flashed by, and the sun rose. Then Baba-Yaga took her place in the mortar and went forth, driving herself with the pestle and sweeping away traces of her progress with the broom.

Vasilissa remained alone and, eyeing Baba-Yaga's house, wondered at her wealth. The girl did not know which task to begin with. But when she looked she found that the work was already done: the doll had separated from the wheat the last grains of impurity.

"Oh, my dear liberator," said Vasilissa to the doll, "you have rescued me from misfortune!"

"You have only to cook the dinner," said the doll, climbing into Vasilissa's pocket. "God help you to prepare it; then rest in peace!"

Towards evening Vasilissa laid the table and awaited Baba-Yaga's return. It became dusk, and a black horseman flashed by the gates; it had grown altogether dark. But the eyes in the skulls shone and the trees cracked and the leaves rustled. Baba-Yaga came. Vasilissa met her. "Is all done?" asked the witch. "Look for yourself, granny!"

Baba-Yaga examined everything and, vexed that she had no cause for anger, said, "My true servants, my bosom friends, grind my wheat!" Three pairs of hands appeared, seized the wheat and bore it from sight.

Baba-Yaga ate to repletion, prepared for sleep, and again gave an order to Vasilissa. "Tomorrow repeat your task of today; in addition remove the poppies from the cornbin and cleanse them from earth, seed by seed: you see, someone has maliciously mixed earth with them!" Having spoken, the old woman turned to the wall and snored.

Vasilissa began to feed her doll, who said, as on the previous day, "Pray to God and go to sleep; morning is wiser than evening; all will be done, dear Vasilissa!"

In the morning Baba-Yaga departed again in her mortar, and immediately Vasilissa and the doll set to work at their tasks. The old woman returned, observed everything and cried out, "My faithful servants, my close friends, squeeze the oil from the poppies!" Three pairs of hands seized the poppies and bore them from sight. Baba-Yaga sat down to dine, and Vasilissa stood silent.

"Why do you say nothing?" remarked the witch. "You stand as if you were dumb."

Timidly Vasilissa replied, "If you would permit me, I should like to ask you a question."

"Ask, but remember, not every question leads to good. You will learn much; you will soon grow old."

"I only wish to ask you," said the girl, "about what I have seen. When I came to you a pale horseman dressed in white on a white horse overtook me. Who was he?"

"He is my clear day," answered Baba-Yaga.

"Then another horseman, who was red and dressed in red, and who rode a red horse, overtook me. Who was he?"

"He was my little red sun!" was the answer.

"But who was the black horseman who passed me at the gate, granny?"

"He was my dark night; all three are my faithful servants."

Vasilissa recalled the three pairs of hands, but was silent. "Have you nothing more to ask?" said Baba-Yaga.

"I have, but you said, granny, that I shall learn much as I grow older."

"It is well" answered the witch, "that you have enquired only about things outside and not about anything here! I do not like my rubbish to be carried away, and I eat over-inquisitive people! Now I will ask you something. How did you succeed in performing the tasks which I set you?"

"My mother's blessing assisted me," answered Vasilissa.

"Depart, favoured daughter! I do not require people who have been blessed." Baba-Yaga dragged Vasilissa out of the room and pushed her beyond the gate, took down from the fence a skull with burning eyes and, putting it on a stick, gave it to the girl and said, "Take this light to your stepsisters; they sent you here for it."

Vasilissa ran off, the skull giving her light, which only went out in the morning; and at last, on the evening of the second day, she reached home. As she approached the gates, she was on the point of throwing away the skull, for she thought that there would no longer be any need for a light at home. Then suddenly a hollow voice from the skull was heard to say, "Do not cast me aside, but carry me to your stepmother." Glancing at the house, and not seeing a light in any of the windows, she decided to enter with the skull.

At first her stepmother and stepsisters met her with caresses, telling her that they had been without a light from the moment of her departure; they could not strike a light in any way, and if anybody brought one from the neighbours, it went out directly it was carried into the room. "Perhaps your light will last," said the stepmother. When they carried the skull into the room its eyes shone brightly and looked continually at the stepmother and her daughters. All their efforts to hide themselves were vain; wherever they rushed they were ceaselessly pursued by the eyes, and before dawn had been burnt to ashes, though Vasilissa was unharmed.

In the morning the girl buried the skull in the ground, locked up the house and visited the town, where she asked admission into the home of a certain old woman who was without kindred. Here she lived quietly and awaited her father. But one day she said to the old woman, "It tires me to sit idle, granny! Go off and buy me some of the best flax; I will busy myself with spinning."

The old woman purchased the flax and Vasilissa sat down to spin. The work proceeded rapidly, and the thread when spun was as smooth and fine as a small hair. The thread lay in heaps, and it was time to begin weaving, but a weaver's comb could not be found to suit Vasilissa's thread, and nobody would undertake to make one. Then the girl had recourse to her doll, who said, "Bring me an old comb that has belonged to a weaver, and an old shuttle, and a horse's mane, and I will do everything for you." Vasilissa obtained everything necessary, and lay down to sleep. The doll, in a single night, made a first-rate loom. Towards the end of winter linen had been woven of so fine a texture that it could be drawn through the needle where the thread should pass.

In spring the linen was bleached, and Vasilissa said to the old woman, "Sell this linen, granny, and keep the money for yourself."

The old woman glanced at the work and said with a sigh, "Ah! my child, nobody but a tsar would wear such linen. I will take it to the palace."

She went to the royal dwelling, and walked up and down in front of the windows. When the tsar saw her he said, "What do you desire, old woman?"

"Your Majesty," she answered, "I have brought some wonderful material, and will show it to nobody but yourself."

The tsar ordered that she should be admitted, and marvelled when he saw the linen. "How much do you ask for it?" he enquired.

"It is not for sale, Tsar and Father! I have brought it as a gift." The tsar thanked her, and sent her away with some presents.

Some shirts for the tsar were cut out from this linen, but a seamstress could nowhere be found to complete them. At last the tsar summoned the old woman and said to her, "You were able to spin and weave this linen, so you will be able to sew together some shirts from it."

"Tsar, it was not I who spun and wove the linen; it is the work of a beautiful maiden."

"Well, let her sew them!"

The old woman returned home and related everything to Vasilissa. The girl said in reply, "I knew that this work would not pass out of my hands." She shut herself in her room and began the undertaking; soon without resting her hands, she had completed a dozen shirts.

The old woman bore them to the tsar, while Vasilissa washed herself and combed her hair, dressed and then took a seat at the window, and there awaited events. She saw a royal servant come to the old woman's house. He entered the room and said, "The Tsar-Emperor desires to see the skilful worker who made his shirts, and to reward her out of his royal hands."

Vasilissa presented herself before the tsar. So much did she please him that he said, "I cannot bear to separate from you; become my wife!" The tsar took her by her white hands, placed her beside himself, and the wedding was celebrated.

Vasilissa's father quickly returned to rejoice at his daughter's good fortune and to live with her. Vasilissa took the old woman into the palace, and never separated from the little doll, which she kept in her pocket.

Rieko Okuhara (b. 1974)

Rieko Okuhara, who lives in Tokyo, has studied literature and clinical psychology in Japan and in the United States. "Hachi-kazuki-hime: The Princess Who Wore a Hachi" is one of the ancient Japanese tales she has retold for Western readers. Her translation of it was published in an article in *The Lion and the Unicorn* in 2000, with her analysis of its combination of Japanese and European elements. The otogi-zoshi tales were illustrated Japanese stories to be enjoyed by adults and children alike. These tales, of which about 400 survive, were popular from the Muromachi period to the early Edo period (from the late sixteenth to the early eighteenth centuries), and were written mostly by anonymous authors. Like "Cinderella" and many another Western tale, this story features an abused girl whose stepmother treats her cruelly. However, this tale has several distinctively Japanese features. For example, a childless couple's desire for a child makes the opening similar to European tales such as "Snow White" and "Rapunzel," but it also shows the influence of Buddhism in the role played by Kannon, a Japanese Buddhist goddess, in the birth and life of the daughter. The heroine rescues a single rich man from *mujo,* a pessimistic loss of hope for the future caused by wartime devastation at the time the otogi-zoshi tales became popular. A *hachi* is a big wooden bowl. It is not normally worn as a hat.

Hachi-kazuki-hime

The Princess Who Wore a Hachi

A long time ago there was a man called Bicchunokami Sanetaka in Kawachi, the middle part of Japan. Sanetaka was rich and had lots of gold and precious gems, but he was a very kind lord. He also liked to make songs and play music. His wife was a clever and wise woman. She loved to memorize classic literature and watch the moon. They were happy, but they had no children, even though they wanted some very much. The couple walked all the way to Hase Temple, far away from their place, and prayed and prayed to *Kannon* the Merciful for a baby. She was a Buddhist goddess who protected children, and it was a custom for people to go to her when they wanted a baby and couldn't have one.

After a while they had a beautiful daughter and they were very happy. The baby grew into a fine child, and her mother taught her everything she knew. The child was clever like her mother. She soon learned how to dance, how to make songs, and how to play musical instruments, and she even memorized Buddhist texts.

When the girl was thirteen years old, her mother became sick. One day the mother got worse and everyone thought that the mother would surely die. Then she called her daughter to her bed.

"If you were seventeen or eighteen, I could find some good man for you and die happily. It is supposed to be the mother's job to find a good husband for her daughter."

After the mother said this, she tied a heavy box on the girl's head and put a big wooden bowl over it. The *hachi* was big enough to cover her whole head, and its edge reached her shoulders.

The mother cried, "Please, *Kannon sama,* protect my daughter!" And then she died.

The father was very sad about his wife's death, since he loved her dearly. But when he saw his daughter after the funeral, he was shocked and stopped crying. "What happened to you, my child?" he said.

Weeping, the girl answered, "Mother put this *hachi* over my head before she died, and I cannot take it off how hard I try."

The father put his hands on the hachi and tried to pull it carefully, but it didn't come off. The father called his strong servants to try and take the *hachi* off by force, but it didn't even move. The girl kept crying because of the terrible pain.

"Oh, it hurts! Please stop, Father! My neck will be torn apart!"

The father stopped his servants and grew sorrowful because he loved his lovely child very much.

"It's terrible enough that her mother died so soon, but, even worse, she is a monster now," the father said and cried.

After this, worried about his daughter, Sanetaka always took great care of his child. She still wore the *hachi* and she was sad all the time. He couldn't tell how she could see, because she didn't talk much now, but she seemed to be able to see somehow. But the girl often stayed in her room alone, missing and thinking of her mother. But it was scary for anyone to see the girl who wore a *hachi* in a dark room. The servants who used to be friendly with her began to look at her as if she were a monster and stopped talking to her. And everyone started calling her *Hachi-kazuki,* the one who wears a *hachi.*

When *Hachi-kazuki* was fifteen years old, the father took himself another wife. His relatives believed it best for both the father and his daughter. But the stepmother thought that the maiden was ugly and hated her and treated her in a mean way. The stepmother even said mean things to her when the father was not at home.

"It's unbelievable how ugly you look. I can't imagine how you can live, looking as you do!"

When the stepmother got pregnant, she began to hate the maiden even more and started saying all kinds of evil things to her. She was so cruel that the maiden went to her mother's grave and cried.

"I can't blame my new mother for hating me because I look so ugly. Father will want to get rid of me after he has a new child. There is no one who can help

me now. If I have to live in this form, I would rather die and go to you, Mother!"

As soon as the stepmother found out that *Hachi-kazuki* had gone to her mother's grave, she said to her husband, "I know she is trying to put a curse on us."

The father became angry. The maiden tried to explain, but he took away her beautiful *kimono* and kicked her out in a torn, dirty one.

Hachi-kazuki did not know where to go, and she cried and cried. She couldn't understand why her mother put the *hachi* on her head and made her live so miserably.

The maiden walked and walked. When she saw a big river in front of her, she decided to end her wretched life and jumped into the river. But the *hachi* didn't sink. She got stuck in a fish net and fishermen pulled her out of the river. The fishermen were very surprised and scared when they saw her in the net and let her go without questioning her.

The maiden didn't know where she was going, but she still walked and walked. Everyone looked at her and screamed. Some pointed at her and laughed, and others threw stones.

One day *Hachi-kazuki* passed a gorgeous, big house. The master of this house, Sanmi-no-chujo of Yamakage, was in the garden and saw her through the hedge. He called the maiden and asked her why she was wearing a *hachi.* She told all about what had happened to her after her mother died. Sanmi-no-chujo was a kind man, and, when he heard her story, he felt very sorry for her. He made his servants try to pull the *hachi* from her head, but it still didn't come off. The master decided to let her stay at his house and work as a servant.

The maiden was very glad to have a place to stay. Her job was to make fires for the bath. Covered with ashes, she blew the bamboo stick and made fires all day. The master and his wife were very kind to her, and she was happy.

The master had four sons, and three were already married. Only the youngest son had no wife, and he was the handsomest, the kindest, and the most clever of the four. Sanimi-no-chujo loved this son best of all.

One day, when the youngest son was taking a bath, *Hachi-kazuki* came to the door. Because it was one of her jobs, she asked him, "Would you like me to wash your back?"

"Come in," the young son said.

When the maiden was washing his back, he saw her hands and legs. They were usually covered with ashes, but now he could see how beautiful and white they were. He thought that she was not an ordinary maiden from a poor family. She was also very kind, and he fell in love with her.

The youngest son said to the maiden, "Living is in vain when we are born into such a changing world as this. Now I am twenty years old, and my parents want me to find a wife. But I was always thinking only about my life and never met anyone I wanted to marry . . . until I met you. We must have something between us because I feel so close to you."

The youngest son decided to marry the maiden and began to visit her room every night, as it was the traditional custom before marriage. The rumor went to his parents. People said, "Your youngest son goes to *Hachi-kazuki* every night. It's a shameful thing. Men always like women, no matter who they are or what they are, but he doesn't need to go to a monster!"

The father called his son at once. When the youngest son went to the room, the father glanced at him grimly, and the mother sent an anxious look to her son. The father said, "I know how kind you always are, but you cannot stay with *Hachi-kazuki*. Imagine what people would say! If you marry her, I won't give you any land or money and we won't be family any more."

But the youngest son did not change his mind. Without hesitating, he said to his father and mother, "I can't leave her. If you make her leave this place, I'll go with her and stay with her wherever she goes. I love her. If I can live with her, I don't need any land or money. I don't care even if you won't be my parents any more."

The parents were very troubled by his decision. After the son left the room, the mother said to the father, "*Hachi-kazuki* must have seduced our son, like a witch or something of that sort. We can invite all the maidens around here and all the wives of our three sons and have a competition. If our youngest son sees that woman among all the beautiful ones, he will feel ashamed of her."

The mother knew that *Hachi-kazuki* was very ashamed of her appearance, so she thought that the girl would leave the house if she heard that she had to show her skills in front of many people.

Hachi-kazuki heard what happened between the youngest son and his father. But she believed that he was planning to marry her only because he felt sorry for her ugly looks, and she didn't want to trouble him anymore.

When the youngest son came to her room that night, he asked her to marry him. But she quietly said no. She continued, "I cannot trouble you anymore. I will leave the house tonight."

But he said to her with a grave smile, "I will not let you go alone. If you are leaving, I will go with you."

When *Hachi-kazuki* heard this, she realized that she had found a man who truly loved her. She accepted his love, and the couple decided to leave the house together that night.

Hachi-kazuki and the youngest son were at the gate when something happened. Suddenly the *hachi* dropped from the maiden's head and the most beautiful face under the sun appeared. The youngest son exclaimed, "You are as beautiful as the moon! Nobody can be as lovely as you!" In the box under the *hachi* were gold, silver, precious gems, many *kimono* fabrics, and all kinds of things a maiden needs for marriage.

Hachi-kazuki appeared at the competition in her beautiful *kimono*. No one recognized her without the *hachi,* and everyone whispered to each other, "Who is that beautiful woman? She must be a *hime sama* of a country nearby!"

Hachi-kazuki danced beautifully, played all the musical instruments very well, and made lovely songs. She knew classical poems by heart and could recite Buddhist texts as well. No other woman did as well as she did, and no one was as lovely as she was.

When Sanmi-no-chujo and his wife asked their son who the beautiful *hime* was, he proudly told them that the princess was *Hachi-kazuki*. They were amazed, but they were very happy about the marriage of *Hachi-kazuki* and the youngest son now because they liked her and were only worried about their son's future. The father decided right there that the youngest son would have the house after the master's death, even though he was not the eldest son who usually took the house.

Soon afterwards, *Hachi-kazuki* and the youngest son married and started their happy life together. Sanmi-no-chujo and his old wife loved their new daughter dearly, and they were very happy.

One day, when the young wife went to Hase Temple with her husband, she saw an old man in a shabby *kimono* standing in front of *Kannon*. Suddenly she recognized the man, and it was her father. He was very glad to see his daughter again. He told the couple that the stepmother had been so mean that all the servants left the house and eventually the family had become poor. He regretted that he had kicked out his daughter because of the bad things the stepmother had said about her. He left the house soon afterwards and he had been looking for her ever since.

When the father finished his story, his daughter said to him, "*Kannon sama* protected me until I found a man who truly loves me. I think that she had led us here in her mercy to meet and start over again. Please, Father, come to our house and live with us."

The father gladly accepted this offer. The couple took the father back to their house and they all lived together happily ever after.

Marie Le Prince de Beaumont (1711–80)

"Beauty and the Beast" is one of the most widely loved European fairy tales, yet scholars and students disagree about whether it is an inspiring love story demonstrating the value of virtue over appearance or an acknowledgment that beautiful and humble women inevitably sacrifice themselves for the sake of marriage and family. The popularity of this tale, "The Frog King" (in Part 2), and a multitude of other "animal bridegroom" stories in world folklore surely reflects the reality that, throughout history, women have been compelled to marry men they did not know well, often men who were older and unappealing, and have entered into marriage with great trepidation. Perhaps it is this ambiguity that gives this tale its lasting appeal, since it explores the tensions between attraction and repulsion, friendship and romantic love, economic hardship and wealth, family loyalty and bonds formed in the outside world as a young person matures.

This version of the tale by Marie Le Prince de Beaumont is the best-known text and the first one written for the edification and enjoyment of children. Among the multitude of this tale's predecessors are the classical myth "Cupid and Psyche," recorded in Latin by Lucius Apuleius in the second century, and the extremely long "Beauty and the Beast" of 1740 by Madame Gabrielle de Gallon de Villeneuve, who dwelt more explicitly on the beast's repulsiveness and sexual relationship with Beauty. Mme. de Beaumont went to live in London, where "Beauty and the Beast" appeared in her 1757 collection of tales and essays called *Le Magasin des Enfans,* or *The Young Misses' Magazine.* It is obvious that her retelling of the tale about modest, loyal Beauty is intended to instill genteel virtues in young women. Much has been made of the fact that the popular animated film adaptation by the Disney Company in 1991 depicts Beauty as a spunky bookworm, but the eighteenth-century French heroine is a well-rounded young woman who enjoys reading and speaks her mind honestly. Both versions stress in the end that "a true heart" and marriage are more important than brains. Today feminist editors and critics prefer other animal bridegroom tales, such as variants of the Norse "East of the Sun and West of the Moon," in which a fearless young woman in circumstances similar to Beauty's undertakes a heroic quest alone to rescue her husband from bestial enchantment.

Beauty and the Beast

There was once a very rich merchant, who had six children, three boys and three girls. As he was himself a man of great sense, he spared no expense for their education. The three daughters were all handsome, but particularly the youngest; indeed, she was so very beautiful, that in her childhood everyone called her the Little Beauty; and being equally lovely when she was grown up, nobody called her by any other name, which made her sisters very jealous of her. This youngest daughter was not only more handsome than her sisters, but also was better tempered. The two eldest were vain of their wealth and position. They gave themselves a thousand airs, and refused to visit other merchants' daughters; nor would they condescend to be seen except with persons of quality.

They went every day to balls, plays, and public walks, and always made game of their youngest sister for spending her time in reading or other useful employments. As it was well known that these young ladies would have large fortunes, many great merchants wished to get them for wives; but the two eldest always answered, that, for their parts, they had no thoughts of marrying anyone below a duke or an earl at least. Beauty had quite as many offers as her sisters, but she always answered, with the greatest civility, that though she was obliged to her lovers, she would rather live some years longer with her father, as she thought herself too young to marry.

It happened that, by some unlucky accident, the merchant suddenly lost all his fortune, and had nothing left but a small cottage in the country. Upon this he said to his daughters, while the tears ran down his cheeks, "My children, we must now go and dwell in the cottage, and try to get a living by labor, for we have no other means of support." The two eldest replied that they did not know how to work, and would not leave town; for they had lovers enough who would be glad to marry them, though they had no longer any fortune. But in this they were mistaken; for when the lovers heard what had happened, they said: "The girls were so proud and ill-tempered, that all we wanted was their fortune; we are not sorry at all to see their pride brought down; let them show off their airs to their

cows and sheep." But everybody pitied poor Beauty, because she was so sweet-tempered and kind to all, and several gentlemen offered to marry her, though she had not a penny; but Beauty still refused, and said she could not think of leaving her poor father in this trouble. At first Beauty could not help sometimes crying in secret for the hardships she was now obliged to suffer; but in a very short time she said to herself, "All the crying in the world will do me no good, so I will try to be happy without a fortune."

When they had removed to their cottage, the merchant and his three sons employed themselves in plowing and sowing the fields, and working in the garden. Beauty also did her part, for she rose by four o'clock every morning, lighted the fires, cleaned the house, and got ready the breakfast for the whole family. At first she found all this very hard; but she soon grew quite used to it, and thought it no hardship; indeed, the work greatly benefited her health. When she had done, she used to amuse herself with reading, playing her music, or singing while she spun. But her two sisters were at a loss what to do to pass the time away; they had their breakfast in bed, and did not rise till ten o'clock. Then they commonly walked out, but always found themselves very soon tired; when they would often sit down under a shady tree, and grieve for the loss of their carriage and fine clothes, and say to each other, "What a mean-spirited, poor stupid creature our young sister is, to be so content with this low way of life!" But their father thought differently; and loved and admired his youngest child more than ever.

After they had lived in this manner about a year the merchant received a letter, which informed him that one of his richest ships, which he thought was lost, had just come into port. This news made the two eldest sisters almost mad with joy; for they thought they should now leave the cottage, and have all their finery again. When they found that their father must take a journey to the ship, the two eldest begged he would not fail to bring them back some new gowns, caps, rings, and all sorts of trinkets. But Beauty asked for nothing; for she thought in herself that all the ship was worth would hardly buy everything her sisters wished for. "Beauty," said the merchant, "you ask for nothing: what can I bring you, my child?"

"Since you are so kind as to think of me, dear father," she answered, "I should be glad if you would bring me a rose, for we have none in our garden." Now Beauty did not indeed wish for a rose, nor anything else, but she only said this that she might not affront her sisters; otherwise they would have said she wanted her father to praise her for desiring nothing. The merchant took his leave of them, and set out on his journey; but when he got to the ship, some persons went to law with him about the cargo, and after a deal of trouble he came back to his cottage as poor as he had left it. When he was within thirty miles of his home, and thinking of the joy of again meeting his children, he lost his way in the midst of a dense forest. It rained and snowed very hard, and besides, the wind was so high as to throw him twice from his horse. Night came on, and he feared he should die of cold and hunger, or be torn to pieces by the wolves that he heard howling around him. All at once, he cast his eyes toward a long avenue, and saw at the end a light, but it seemed a great way off. He made the best of his way toward it, and found that it came from a splendid palace, the windows of which were all blazing with light. It had great bronze gates, standing wide open, and fine courtyards, through which the merchant passed; but not a living soul was to be seen. There were stables, too, which his poor, starved horse, less scrupulous than himself, entered at once, and took a good meal of oats and hay. His master then tied him up, and walked toward the entrance hall, but still without seeing a single creature. He went on to a large dining parlor, where he found a good fire, and a table covered with some very nice dishes, but only one plate with a knife and fork. As the snow and rain had wetted him to the skin, he went up to the fire to dry himself. "I hope," said he, "the master of the house or his servants will excuse me, for it surely will not be long now before I see them." He waited some time, but still nobody came: at last the clock struck eleven, and the merchant, being quite faint for the want of food, helped himself to a chicken, and to a few glasses of wine, yet all the time trembling with fear. He sat till the clock struck twelve, and then, taking courage, began to think he might as well look about him: so he opened a door at the end of the hall, and went through it into a very grand room, in which

there was a fine bed; and as he was feeling very weary, he shut the door, took off his clothes, and got into it.

It was ten o'clock in the morning before he awoke, when he was amazed to see a handsome new suit of clothes laid ready for him, instead of his own, which were all torn and spoiled. "To be sure," said he to himself, "this place belongs to some good fairy, who has taken pity on my ill luck." He looked out of the window, and instead of the snow-covered wood, where he had lost himself the previous night, he saw the most charming arbors covered with all kinds of flowers. Returning to the hall where he had supper, he found a breakfast table, ready prepared. "Indeed, my good fairy," said the merchant aloud, "I am vastly obliged to you for your kind care of me." He then made a hearty breakfast, took his hat, and was going to the stable to pay his horse a visit; but as he passed under one of the arbors, which was loaded with roses, he thought of what Beauty had asked him to bring back to her, and so he took a bunch of roses to carry home. At the same moment he heard a loud noise, and saw coming toward him a beast, so frightful to look at that he was ready to faint with fear. "Ungrateful man!" said the beast in a terrible voice. "I have saved your life by admitting you into my palace, and in return you steal my roses, which I value more than anything I possess. But you shall atone for your fault—die in a quarter of an hour."

The merchant fell on his knees, and clasping his hands, said, "Sir, I humbly beg your pardon: I did not think it would offend you to gather a rose for one of my daughters, who had entreated me to bring her one home. Do not kill me, my lord!"

"I am not a lord, but a beast," replied the monster. "I hate false compliments: so do not fancy that you can coax me by any such ways. You tell me that you have daughters; now I will suffer you to escape, if one of them will come and die in your stead. If not, promise you will yourself return in three months, to be dealt with as I may choose."

The tender-hearted merchant had no thoughts of letting any one of his daughters die for his sake; but he knew that if he seemed to accept the beast's terms, he should at least have the pleasure of seeing them once again. So he gave his promise, and was told that he might then set off as soon as he liked. "But," said the beast, "I do not wish you to go back empty-handed. Go to the room you slept in, and you will find a chest there; fill it with whatsoever you like best, and I will have it taken to your own house for you."

When the beast said this, he went away. The good merchant, left to himself, began to consider that, as he must die—for he had no thought of breaking a promise, made even to a beast—he might as well have the comfort of leaving his children provided for. He returned to the room he had slept in, and found there heaps of gold pieces lying about. He filled the chest with them to the very brim, locked it, and, mounting his horse, left the palace as sorrowful as he had been glad when he first beheld it. The horse took a path across the forest of his own accord, and in a few hours they reached the merchant's house. His children came running round him, but, instead of kissing them with joy, he could not help weeping as he looked at them. He held in his hand the bunch of roses, which he gave to Beauty, saying, "Take these roses, Beauty; but little do you think how dear they have cost your poor father"; and then he gave them an account of all that he had seen or heard in the palace of the beast.

The two eldest sisters now began to shed tears, and to lay the blame upon Beauty, who, they said, would be cause of her father's death. "See," said they, "what happens from the pride of the little wretch; why did not she ask for such things as we did? But, to be sure, Miss must not be like other people; and though she will be the cause of her father's death, yet she does not shed a tear."

"It would be useless," replied Beauty, "for my father shall not die. As the beast will accept one of his daughters, I will give myself up, and be only too happy to prove my love for the best of fathers."

"No, sister," said the three brothers with one voice, "that cannot be; we will go in search of this monster, and either he or we will perish."

"Do not hope to kill him," said the merchant, "his power is far too great. But Beauty's young life shall not be sacrificed; I am old, and cannot expect to live much longer; so I shall but give up a few years of my life, and shall only grieve for the sake of my children."

"Never, father," cried Beauty; "if you go back to the palace, you cannot hinder my going after you! Though young, I am not over-fond of life; and I would much rather be eaten up by the monster, than die of grief for your loss."

The merchant in vain tried to reason with Beauty who still obstinately kept to her purpose; which, in truth, made her two sisters glad, for they were jealous of her, because everybody loved her.

The merchant was so grieved at the thought of losing his child, that he never once thought of the chest filled with gold, but at night, to his great surprise, he found it standing by his bedside. He said nothing about his riches to his eldest daughters, for he knew very well it would at once make them want to return to town; but he told Beauty his secret, and she then said, that while he was away, two gentlemen had been on a visit at her cottage, who had fallen in love with her two sisters. She entreated her father to marry them without delay, for she was so sweet-natured she only wished them to be happy.

Three months went by, only too fast, and then the merchant and Beauty got ready to set out for the palace of the beast. Upon this, the two sisters rubbed their eyes with an onion, to make believe they were crying; both the merchant and his sons cried in earnest. Only Beauty shed no tears. They reached the palace in a very few hours, and the horse, without bidding, went into the stable as before. The merchant and Beauty walked toward the large hall, where they found a table covered with every dainty and two plates laid already. The merchant had very little appetite; but Beauty, that she might the better hide her grief, placed herself at the table, and helped her father; she then began to eat herself, and thought all the time that, to be sure, the beast had a mind to fatten her before he ate her up, since he had provided such good cheer for her. When they had done their supper, they heard a great noise, and the good old man began to bid his poor child farewell, for he knew that it was the beast coming to them. When Beauty first saw that frightful form, she was very much terrified, but tried to hide her fear. The creature walked up to her, and eyed her all over—then asked her in a dreadful voice if she had come quite of her own accord.

"Yes," said Beauty.

"Then you are a good girl, and I am very much obliged to you."

This was such an astonishingly civil answer that Beauty's courage rose: but it sank again when the beast, addressing the merchant, desired him to leave the palace next morning, and never return to it again. "And so good night, merchant. And good night, Beauty."

"Good night, beast," she answered, as the monster shuffled out.

"Ah! my dear child," said the merchant, kissing his daughter, "I am half dead already, at the thought of leaving you with this dreadful beast; you shall go back and let me stay in your place."

"No," said Beauty, boldly, "I will never agree to that; you must go home tomorrow morning."

They then wished each other good night, and went to bed, both of them thinking they should not be able to close their eyes; but as soon as ever they had lain down, they fell in to a deep sleep, and did not awake till morning. Beauty dreamed that a lady came up to her, who said, "I am very much pleased, Beauty, with the goodness you have shown, in being willing to give your life to save that of your father. Do not be afraid of anything; you shall not go without a reward."

As soon as Beauty awoke she told her father this dream; but though it gave him some comfort, he was a long time before he could be persuaded to leave the palace. At last Beauty succeeded in getting him safely away.

When her father was out of sight, poor Beauty began to weep sorely; still, having naturally a courageous spirit, she soon resolved not to make her sad case still worse by sorrow, which she knew was vain, but to wait and be patient. She walked about to take a view of all the palace, and the elegance of every part of it much charmed her.

But what was her surprise, when she came to a door on which was written, BEAUTY'S ROOM! She opened it in haste, and her eyes were dazzled by the splendor and taste of the apartment. What made her wonder more than all the rest, was a large library filled with books, a harpsichord, and many pieces of music. "The beast surely does not mean to eat me up immediately," said she, "since he takes care I shall not be at loss how to amuse myself." She opened the library and saw these verses written in letters of gold in the back of one of the books:

"Beauteous lady, dry your tears,
Here's no cause for sighs or fears.
Command as freely as you may,
For you command and I obey."

"Alas!" said she, sighing: "I wish I could only command a sight of my poor father, and to know what he is doing at this moment." Just then, by chance, she cast her eyes upon a looking-glass that stood near her, and in it she saw a picture of her old home, and her father

Victorian artist Eleanor Vere Boyle imagined Beast as a dark animal with long tusks, a form far removed from human shape, in contrast to Beauty's elegant medieval attire and lovely face.

riding mournfully up to the door. Her sisters came out to meet him, and although they tried to look sorry, it was easy to see that in their hearts they were very glad. In a short time all this picture disappeared, but it caused Beauty to think that the beast, besides being very powerful, was also very kind. About the middle of the day she found a table laid ready for her, and a sweet concert of music played all the time she was dining, without her seeing anybody. But at supper, when she was going to seat herself at table, she heard the noise of the beast, and could not help trembling with fear.

"Beauty," said he, "will you give me leave to see you sup?"

"That is as you please," answered she, very much afraid.

"Not in the least," said the beast. "You alone command in this place. If you should not like my company, you need only say so, and I will leave you that moment. But tell me, Beauty, do you not think me very ugly?"

"Why, yes," said she, "for I cannot tell a falsehood; but then I think you are very good."

"Am I?" sadly replied the beast. "Yet, besides being ugly, I am also very stupid; I know well enough that I am but a beast."

"Stupid people," said Beauty, "are never aware of it themselves."

At which kindly speech the beast looked pleased, and replied, not without an awkward sort of politeness: "Pray do not let me detain you from supper, and be sure that you are well served. All you see is your own, and I should be deeply grieved if you wanted for anything."

"You are very kind—so kind that I almost forgot you are so ugly," said Beauty, earnestly.

"Ah! yes," answered the beast, with a great sigh; "I hope I am good-tempered, but still I am only a monster."

"There is many a monster who wears the form of a man; it is better of the two to have the heart of a man and the form of a monster."

"I would thank you, Beauty, for this speech, but I am too senseless to say anything that would please you," returned the beast in a melancholy voice; and altogether he seemed so gentle and so unhappy that Beauty, who had the tenderest heart in the world, felt her fear of him gradually vanish.

She ate her supper with a good appetite, and conversed in her own sensible and charming way, till at last, when the beast rose to depart, he terrified her more than ever by saying abruptly, in his gruff voice, "Beauty, will you marry me?"

Now Beauty, frightened as she was, would speak only the exact truth; besides her father had told her that the beast liked only to have the truth spoken to him. So she answered, in a very firm tone, "No, beast."

He did not get into a passion, but sighed deeply and departed.

When Beauty found herself alone, she began to feel pity for the poor beast. "Oh," she said, "what a sad thing it is that he should be so very frightful, since he is so good-tempered!"

Beauty lived three months in this palace very well pleased. The beast came to see her every night, and talked with her while she supped; and though what he

said was not very clever, yet, as she saw in him every day some new goodness, instead of dreading the time of his coming, she soon began continually looking at her watch, to see if it were nine o'clock; for that was the hour when he never failed to visit her. One thing only vexed her, which was that every night before he went away, he always made it a rule to ask her if she would be his wife, and seemed very much grieved at her steadfastly replying "No." At last, one night, she said to him, "You wound me greatly, beast, by forcing me to refuse you so often; I wish I could take such a liking to you as to agree to marry you; but I must tell you plainly that I do not think it will ever happen. I shall always be your friend; so try to let that content you."

"I must," sighed the beast, "for I know well enough how frightful I am; but I love you better than myself. Yet I think I am very lucky in your being pleased to stay with me; now promise, Beauty, that you will never leave me."

Beauty would almost have agreed to this, so sorry was she for him, but she had that day seen in her magic glass, which she looked at constantly, that her father was dying of grief for her sake.

"Alas!" she said. "I long so much to see my father, that if you do not give me leave to visit him, I shall break my heart."

"I would rather break mine, Beauty," answered the beast; "I will send you to your father's cottage: you shall stay there, and your poor beast shall die of sorrow."

"No," said Beauty, crying, "I love you too well to be the cause of your death; I promise to return in a week. You have shown me that my sisters are married, and my brothers are gone for soldiers, so that my father is left all alone. Let me stay a week with him."

"You shall find yourself with him tomorrow morning," replied the beast; "but mind, do not forget your promise. When you wish to return, you have nothing to do but to put your ring on a table when you go to bed. Good-bye, Beauty!" The beast sighed as he said these words, and Beauty went to bed very sorry to see him so much grieved. When she awoke in the morning, she found herself in her father's cottage. She rang a bell that was at her bedside, and a servant entered; but as soon as she saw Beauty, the woman gave a loud shriek; upon which the merchant ran upstairs, and when he beheld his daughter he ran to her, and kissed her a hundred times. At last Beauty began to remember that she had brought no clothes with her to put on; but the servant told her she had just found in the next room a large chest full of dresses, trimmed all over with gold, and adorned with pearls and diamonds.

Beauty, in her own mind, thanked the beast for his kindness, and put on the plainest gown she could find among them all. She then desired the servant to lay the rest aside, for she intended to give them to her sisters; but, as soon as she had spoken these words, the chest was gone out of sight in a moment. Her father then suggested, perhaps the beast chose for her to keep them all for herself: and as soon as he had said this, they saw the chest standing again in the same place. While Beauty was dressing herself, a servant brought word to her that her sisters were come with their husbands to pay her a visit. They both lived unhappily with the gentlemen they had married. The husband of the eldest was very handsome, but was so proud of this that he thought of nothing else from morning till night, and did not care a pin for the beauty of his wife. The second had married a man of great learning; but he made no use of it, except to torment and affront all his friends, and his wife more than any of them. The two sisters were ready to burst with spite when they saw Beauty dressed like a princess, and looking so very charming. All the kindness that she showed them was of no use; for they were vexed more than ever when she told them how happy she lived at the palace of the beast. The spiteful creatures went by themselves into the garden, where they cried to think of her good fortune.

"Why should the little wretch be better off than we?" said they. "We are much handsomer than she is."

"Sister," said the eldest, "a thought has just come into my head; let us try to keep her here longer than the week for which the beast gave her leave; and then he will be so angry that perhaps when she goes back to him he will eat her up in a moment."

"That is well thought of," answered the other, "but to do this, we must pretend to be very kind."

They then went to join her in the cottage, where they showed her so much false love that Beauty could not help crying for joy.

When the week was ended, the two sisters began to pretend such grief at the thought of her leaving them that she agreed to stay a week more; but all that time Beauty could not help fretting for the sorrow that she knew her absence would give her poor beast; for she tenderly loved him, and much wished for his company again. Among all the grand and clever people she saw, she found nobody who was half so sensible, so affectionate, so thoughtful, or so kind. The tenth night of her being at the cottage, she dreamed she was in the garden of the palace, that the beast lay dying on a grass plot, and with his last breath put her in mind of her promise, and laid his death to her forsaking him. Beauty awoke in a great fright, and she burst into tears. "Am not I wicked," said she, "to behave so ill to a beast who has shown me so much kindness? Why will I not marry him? I am sure I should be more happy with him than my sisters are with their husbands. He shall not be wretched any longer on my account; for I should do nothing but blame myself all the rest of my life."

She then rose, put her ring on the table, got into bed again, and soon fell asleep. In the morning she with joy found herself in the palace of the beast. She dressed herself very carefully, that she might please him the better, and thought she had never known a day pass away so slowly. At last the clock struck nine, but the beast did not come. Beauty, dreading lest she might truly have caused his death, ran from room to room, calling out: "Beast, dear beast"; but there was no answer. At last she remembered her dream, rushed to the grass plot, and there saw him lying apparently dead beside the fountain. Forgetting all his ugliness, she threw herself upon his body, and finding his heart still beating, she fetched some water and sprinkled it over him, weeping and sobbing the while.

The beast opened his eyes. "You forgot your promise, Beauty, and so I determined to die; for I could not live without you. I have starved myself to death, but I shall die content since I have seen your face once more."

"No, dear beast," cried Beauty, passionately, "you shall not die; you shall live to be my husband. I thought it was only friendship I felt for you, but now I know it was love."

The moment Beauty had spoken these words, the palace was suddenly lighted up, and all kinds of rejoicings were heard around them, none of which she noticed, but hung over her dear beast with the utmost tenderness. At last, unable to restrain herself, she dropped her head over her hands, covered her eyes, and cried for joy; and, when she looked up again, the beast was gone. In his stead she saw at her feet a handsome, graceful young prince, who thanked her with the tenderest expressions for having freed him from enchantment.

"But where is my poor beast? I only want him and nobody else," sobbed Beauty.

"I am he," replied the prince. "A wicked fairy condemned me to this form, and forbade me to show that I had any wit or sense, till a beautiful lady should consent to marry me. You alone, dearest Beauty, judged me neither by my looks nor by my talents, but by my heart alone. Take it then, and all that I have besides, for all is yours."

Beauty, full of surprise, but very happy, suffered the prince to lead her to his palace, where she found her father and sisters, who had been brought there by the fairy lady whom she had seen in a dream the first night she came.

"Beauty," said the fairy, "you have chosen well, and you have your reward, for a true heart is better than either good looks or clever brains. As for you, ladies," and she turned to the two elder sisters, "I know all your ill deeds, but I have no worse punishment for you than to see your sister happy. You shall stand as statues at the door of her palace, and when you repent of and have amended your faults, you shall become women again. But, to tell you the truth, I very much fear you will remain statues forever."

Jacob Grimm (1785–1863) and Wilhelm Grimm (1786–1859)

Snow-White and Rapunzel are two of the most popular fairy tale heroines in history, along with Cinderella, the Beauty who marries the Beast, and a few others. These tales show that the magical effects of fairy tales are rooted in powerful physical symbols: a pregnant wife's intense craving that compels her husband to bargain with his child's life for a specific herb, the isolated tower where that child grows up with no knowledge of the world or men, a talking mirror reflecting the vanity of an evil queen, a poison apple that represents fallen innocence, the glass coffin in which the princess is neither alive nor dead while magically growing to maturity, and, of course, Rapunzel's fine golden hair stretching down her tower. Although Bruno Bettelheim (in his article reprinted in this section) interprets the hair as a hopeful symbol that the heroine can save herself with her own body, other modern readers respond differently to the emphasis on the female body and beauty in classic fairy tales, especially Rapunzel's fantastically exaggerated version of a most sensuous feminine symbol. Rapunzel and Snow-White are both victimized by a false or evil mother and separated from the world during their coming-of-age adventures, dependent on dwarfs and men to rescue them, while male heroes who start out as the underdogs, like the son in "The Water of Life," prove themselves worthy to become leaders in the world.

While the Grimms' most famous versions of these tales exemplify the cultural biases of past collectors and editors of fairy tales, scholars continue to ponder their undying fascination by exploring different interpretations and variants that came before and after the Grimm Brothers. Paul O. Zelinsky examined German, French, and Italian versions for his Caldecott Award winning *Rapunzel* (1997), with his stunning illustrations in Italian Renaissance style. The Grimm Brothers themselves had sources influenced by oral and written versions from other countries. Their "Rapunzel" also shows how they revised some tales to make their later editions more suitable for children and families. Earlier versions contain more explicit references to Rapunzel's pregnancy but no marriage within the tower to legitimize her children. Although Snow-White's name emphasizes her purity, the most famous modern adaptation of her tale highlights the sexual themes that are more subtle in the Grimms' text. In the first feature-length animated film ever made (1937), Snow White is a young woman before she meets the dwarfs (not a child of seven) and is revived with a kiss by the prince. But Walt Disney borrowed the kiss from another classic tale about a comatose princess who marries a prince after she awakes, "Sleeping Beauty."

"The Water of Life" is not as well known as the other Grimm tales in this anthology, but the search for magic water that will restore health or life is a recurring legend in world folklore. Jane Yolen discusses this tale briefly in "The Brothers Grimm and Sister Jane" in this section. A sequence of quests pursued by three siblings, in turn, occurs in Jack tales and many other fairy tales of European origin. Usually, the older siblings fail because they behave inappropriately and do not recognize or obtain magic help. In this tale, their getting stuck in mountain gorges, their plot to destroy their brother, and their interest in the golden road obviously represent their immaturity and greed. The youngest son, courteous and willing to follow instructions, has a sibling rivalry problem like so many other folk heroes, and like Mutsmag, he even rescues his undeserving siblings. He is also saved by a servant more compassionate than his brothers, a huntsman like the one in "Snow-White" who cannot follow his order to kill the princess. The wish fulfillment in this fairly complicated tale has an especially extensive scope, in that the hero's rewards range from the personal gratification of saving his father and finding a bride in another land to showing that he can use his gifts to feed the hungry, control armies, and lead a kingdom. For more background on the Grimm Brothers and other tales, see Parts 2 and 5. Illustrations for "Snow-White" and "Rapunzel" are discussed in Part 6.

Snow-White and the Seven Dwarfs

Once it was the middle of winter, and the snowflakes fell from the sky like feathers. At a window with a frame of ebony a queen sat and sewed. And as she sewed and looked out at the snow, she pricked her finger with the needle, and three drops of blood fell in the snow. And in the white snow the red looked so beautiful that she thought to herself: "If only I had a child as white as snow, as red as blood, and as black as the wood in the window frame!" And after a while she had a little daughter as white as snow, as red as blood, and with hair as black as ebony, and because of that she was called Snow-White. And when the child was born, the queen died.

After a year the king took himself another wife. She was a beautiful woman, but she was proud and haughty and could not bear that anyone should be more beautiful than she. She had a wonderful mirror, and when she stood in front of it and looked in it and said:

"Mirror, mirror on the wall,
Who is fairest of us all?"

then the mirror would answer:

"Queen, thou art the fairest of us all!"

Then she was satisfied, because she knew that the mirror spoke the truth.

But Snow-White kept growing, and kept growing more beautiful, and when she was seven years old, she was as beautiful as the bright day, and more beautiful than the Queen herself. Once when she asked her mirror:

"Mirror, mirror on the wall,
Who is fairest of us all?"

it answered:

"Queen, thou art the fairest in this hall,
But Snow-White's fairer than us all."

Then the Queen was horrified, and grew yellow and green with envy. From that hour on, whenever she saw Snow-White the heart in her body would turn over, she hated the girl so. And envy and pride, like weeds, kept growing higher and higher in her heart, so that day and night she had no peace. Then she called a huntsman and said: "Take the child out into the forest, I don't want to lay eyes on her again. You kill her, and bring me her lung and liver as a token."

The hunter obeyed, and took her out, and when he had drawn his hunting knife and was about to pierce Snow-White's innocent heart, she began to weep and said: "Oh, dear huntsman, spare my life! I'll run off into the wild forest and never come home again." And because she was so beautiful, the huntsman pitied her and said: "Run away then, you poor child."

"Soon the wild beasts will have eaten you," he thought, and yet it was as if a stone had been lifted from his heart not to have to kill her. And as a young boar just then came running by, he killed it, cut out its lung and liver, and brought them to the Queen as a token. The cook had to cook them in salt, and the wicked woman ate them up and thought that she had eaten Snow-White's lung and liver.

Now the poor child was all, all alone in the great forest, and so terrified that she stared at all the leaves on the trees and didn't know what to do. She began to run, and ran over the sharp stones and through the thorns, and the wild beasts sprang past her, but they did her no harm. She ran on till her feet wouldn't go any farther, and when it was almost evening she saw a little house and went inside to rest. Inside the house everything was small, but cleaner and neater than words will say. In the middle there stood a little table with a white tablecloth, and on it were seven little plates, each plate with its own spoon, and besides that, seven little knives and forks and seven little mugs. Against the wall were seven little beds, all in a row, spread with snow-white sheets. Because she was so hungry and thirsty, Snow-White ate a little of the vegetables and bread from each of the little plates, and drank a drop of wine from each little mug, since she didn't want to take all of anybody's. After that, because she was so tired, she lay down in a bed, but not a one would fit; this one was too long, the other was too short, and so on, until finally the seventh was just right, and she lay down in it, said her prayers, and went to sleep.

As soon as it had got all dark, the owners of the house came back. These were seven dwarfs who dug and delved for ore in the mountains. They lighted their seven little candles, and as soon as it got light in their little house, they saw that someone had been inside, because everything wasn't the way they'd left it.

The first said: "Who's been sitting in my little chair?"

The second said: "Who's been eating out of my little plate?"

The third said: "Who's been taking some of my bread?"

The fourth said: "Who's been eating my vegetables?"

The fifth said: "Who's been using my little fork?"

The sixth said: "Who's been cutting with my little knife?"

The seventh said: "Who's been drinking out of my little mug?"

Then the first looked around and saw that his bed was a little mussed, so he said: "Who's been lying on my little bed?" The others came running and cried out: "Someone's been lying in mine too." But the seventh, when he looked in his bed, saw Snow-White, who was lying in it fast asleep.

He called the others, who came running up and shouted in astonishment, holding up their little candles so that the light shone on Snow-White. "Oh my goodness gracious! Oh my goodness gracious!" cried they, "how beautiful the child is!" And they were so happy that they didn't wake her, but let her go on sleeping in the little bed. The seventh dwarf, though, slept with the others, an hour with each, till the night was over.

When it was morning Snow-White awoke, and when she saw the seven dwarfs she was frightened. They were friendly, though, and asked: "What's your name?"

"I'm named Snow-White," she answered.

"How did you get to our house?" went on the dwarfs. Then she told them that her stepmother had tried to have her killed, but that the huntsman had spared her life, and that she'd run the whole day and at last had found their house.

The dwarfs said: "If you'll look after our house for us, cook, make the beds, wash, sew, and knit, and if you'll keep everything clean and neat, then you can stay with us, and you shall lack for nothing."

"Yes," said Snow-White, "with all my heart," and stayed with them. She kept their house in order: in the morning the dwarfs went to the mountains and looked for gold and ores, in the evening they came back, and then their food had to be ready for them. In the daytime the little girl was alone, so the good dwarfs warned her and said: "Watch out for your stepmother. Soon she'll know you're here; be sure not to let anybody inside."

But the Queen, since she thought she had eaten Snow-White's lung and liver, was sure that she was the fairest of all. But one day she stood before her mirror and said:

"Mirror, mirror on the wall,
Who is fairest of us all?"

Then the mirror answered:

"Queen, thou art the fairest that I see,
But over the hills, where the seven dwarfs dwell,
Snow-White is still alive and well,
And there is none so fair as she."

This horrified her, because she knew that the mirror never told a lie; and she saw that the hunter had betrayed her, and that Snow-White was still alive. And she thought and thought about how to kill her, for as long as she wasn't the fairest in all the land, her envy gave her no rest. And when at last she thought of something, she painted her face and dressed herself like an old peddler woman, and nobody could have recognized her. In this disguise she went over the seven mountains to the seven dwarfs' house, knocked at the door, and called: "Lovely things for sale! Lovely things for sale!"

Snow-White looked out of the window and called: "Good day, dear lady, what have you to sell?"

"Good things, lovely things," she answered, "bodice laces of all colors," and she pulled out one that was woven of many-colored silk.

"It will be all right to let in the good old woman," thought Snow-White, unbolted the door, and bought herself some pretty laces.

"Child," said the old woman, "how it does become you! Come, I'll lace you up properly." Snow-White hadn't the least suspicion, and let the old woman lace her up with the new laces. But she laced so tight and laced so fast that it took Snow-White's breath away,

and she fell down as if she were dead. "Now you're the most beautiful again," said the Queen to herself, and hurried away.

Not long after, at evening, the seven dwarfs came home, but how shocked they were to see their dear Snow-White lying on the ground; and she didn't move and she didn't stir, as if she were dead. They lifted her up, and when they saw how tightly she was laced, they cut the laces in two; then she began to breathe a little, and little by little returned to consciousness. When the dwarfs heard what had happened, they said: "The old peddler woman was no one else but that wicked Queen; be careful, don't ever let another soul inside when we're not with you."

But the wicked Queen, as soon as she'd got home, stood in front of the mirror and asked:

"Mirror, mirror on the wall,
Who is fairest of us all?"

It answered the same as ever:

"Queen, thou art the fairest that I see,
But over the hills, where the seven dwarfs dwell,
Snow-White is still alive and well,
And there is none so fair as she."

When she heard this all the blood rushed to her heart, she was so horrified, for she saw plainly that Snow-White was alive again. "But now," said she, "I'll think of something that really will put an end to you," and with the help of witchcraft, which she understood, she made a poisoned comb. Then she dressed herself up and took the shape of another old woman. So she went over the seven mountains to the seven dwarfs' house, knocked on the door, and called: "Lovely things for sale! Lovely things for sale!"

Snow-White looked out and said: "You may as well go on, I'm not allowed to let anybody in."

"But surely you're allowed to look," said the old woman, and she took out the poisoned comb and held it up. It looked so nice to the child that she let herself be fooled, and opened the door. When they'd agreed on the price the old woman said: "Now, for once, I'll comb your hair properly." Poor Snow-White didn't suspect anything, and let the old woman do as she pleased. But hardly had she put the comb in Snow-White's hair than the poison in it began to work, and the girl fell down unconscious. "You paragon of beauty," cried the wicked woman, "now you're done for," and went away.

By good luck, though, it was almost evening, when the seven dwarfs came home. When they saw Snow-White lying on the ground as if she were dead, right away they suspected the stepmother and looked and found the poisoned comb. Hardly had they drawn it out than Snow-White returned to consciousness, and told them what had happened. Then they warned her all over again to stay in the house and open the door to no one.

At home the Queen stood in front of the mirror and said:

"Mirror, mirror on the wall,
Who is fairest of us all?"

It answered the same as ever:

"Queen, thou art the fairest that I see,
But over the hills, where the seven dwarfs dwell,
Snow-White is still alive and well,
And there is none so fair as she."

When she heard the mirror say that, she shook with rage. "Snow-White shall die," cried she, "even if it costs me my own life!" Then she went to a very secret, lonely room that no one ever came to, and there she made a poisoned apple. On the outside it was beautiful, white with red cheeks, so that anyone who saw it wanted it; but whoever ate even the least bite of it would die. When the apple was ready she painted her face and disguised herself as a farmer's wife, and then went over the seven mountains to the seven dwarfs' house. She knocked, and Snow-White put her head out of the window and said: "I'm not allowed to let anybody in, the seven dwarfs told me not to."

"That's all right with me," answered the farmer's wife. "I'll get rid of my apples without any trouble. Here, I'll give you one."

"No," said Snow-White, "I'm afraid to take it."

"Are you afraid of poison?" said the old woman. "Look, I'll cut the apple in two halves; you eat the red cheek and I'll eat the white." But the apple was so cunningly made that only the red part was poisoned. Snow-White longed for the lovely apple, and when she saw that the old woman was eating it, she couldn't resist it any longer, put out her hand, and took the poisoned half. But hardly had she a bite of it in her mouth than she fell down on the ground dead. Then the Queen gave her a dreadful look, laughed aloud, and cried: "White as snow, red as blood, black as ebony! This time the dwarfs can't wake you!"

And when, at home, she asked the mirror:

"Mirror, mirror on the wall,
Who is fairest of us all?"

at last it answered:

"Queen, thou art the fairest of us all."

Then her envious heart had rest, as far as an envious heart can have rest.

When they came home at evening, the dwarfs found Snow-White lying on the ground. No breath came from her mouth, and she was dead. They lifted

"Snow-White and the Seven Dwarfs." See Part 6 for discussion of Walter Crane's elaborately designed illustrations for his sister Lucy Crane's fairy tale translations.

her up, looked to see if they could find anything poisonous, unlaced her, combed her hair, washed her with water and wine, but nothing helped; the dear child was dead and stayed dead. They laid her on a bier, and all seven of them sat down and wept for her, and wept for three whole days. Then they were going to bury her, but she still looked as fresh as though she were alive, and still had her beautiful red cheeks. They said: "We can't bury her in the black ground," and had made for her a coffin all of glass, into which one could see from every side, laid her in it, and wrote her name on it in golden letters, and that she was a king's daughter. Then they set the coffin out on the mountainside, and one of them always stayed by it and guarded it. And the animals, too, came and wept over Snow-White—first an owl, then a raven, and last of all a dove.

Now Snow-White lay in the coffin for a long, long time, and her body didn't decay. She looked as if she were sleeping, for she was still as white as snow, as red as blood, and her hair was as black as ebony. But a king's son happened to come into the forest and went to the dwarfs' house to spend the night. He saw the coffin on the mountain, and the beautiful Snow-White inside, and read what was written on it in golden letters. Then he said to the dwarfs: "Let me have the coffin. I'll give you anything that you want for it."

But the dwarfs answered: "We wouldn't give it up for all the gold in the world."

Then he said: "Give it to me then, for I can't live without seeing Snow-White. I'll honor and prize her as my own beloved." When he spoke so, the good dwarfs took pity on him and gave him the coffin.

Now the king's son had his servants carry it away on their shoulders. They happened to stumble over a bush, and with the shock the poisoned piece of apple that Snow-White had bitten off came out of her throat. And in a little while she opened her eyes, lifted the lid of the coffin, sat up, and was alive again. "Oh, heavens, where am I?" cried she.

The king's son, full of joy, said: "You're with me," and told her what had happened, and said: "I love you more than anything in all the world. Come with me to my father's palace; you shall be my wife." And Snow-White loved him and went with him, and her wedding was celebrated with great pomp and splendor.

But Snow-White's wicked stepmother was invited to the feast. When she had put on her beautiful clothes, she stepped in front of the mirror and said:

"Mirror, mirror on the wall,
Who is fairest of us all?"

The mirror answered:

"Queen, thou art the fairest in this hall,
But the young queen's fairer than us all."

Then the wicked woman cursed and was so terrified and miserable, so completely miserable, that she didn't know what to do. At first she didn't want to go to the wedding at all, but it gave her no peace; she had to go and see the young queen. And as she went in she recognized Snow-White and, what with rage and terror, she stood there and couldn't move. But they had already put iron slippers over a fire of coals, and they brought them in with tongs and set them before her. Then she had to put on the red-hot slippers and dance till she dropped down dead.

Rapunzel

Once upon a time there was a man and wife who had long wished for a child. Finally the woman was filled with hope and expected God would grant her wish. The couple had a little window in back of their house and you could look down into a magnificent garden full of the loveliest flowers and herbs. But the garden was surrounded by a high wall and nobody dared go in because it belonged to a great and powerful witch who was feared by all the world. One day the woman was standing by the window looking into the garden and saw a bed planted with the most beautiful lettuce, of the kind they call Rapunzel. It looked so fresh and green that she began to crave it and longed fiercely to taste the lettuce. Each day her longing grew and because she knew she could not have it, she began to pine and look pale and miserable. Her husband got frightened and said, "Dear wife, are you ill?" "Ah," said she, "if I cannot have some lettuce from the garden behind our house, I will die." The husband loved her very much, and said to himself, You can't let your wife die; fetch her some lettuce, whatever the cost may be. In the evening, therefore, at twilight, he clambered over the wall into the witch's garden, hurriedly dug up a handful of lettuce, and brought it home to his wife, and she made herself a salad right away and ate it ravenously. It tasted good, oh so good that the next day she craved it three times as much. If she was to have any peace, her husband must climb into the garden once again. And so at twilight he went back, but when he got down the other side of the wall he stood horrified, for there, standing right in front of him, was the witch. "How dare you come climbing into my garden, stealing my lettuce like a thief?" said she, and her eyes were angry. "You shall pay for this!" "Ah, no, please," cried the man. "Let justice be tempered with mercy! Only my despair made me do what I did. My wife saw your lettuce out of our window and felt such a craving that she had to have some, or die." And so the witch's anger began to cool and she said, "If that is so, I will allow you to take as much lettuce as you want on one condition: You must give me the child your wife brings into the world. It shall be well cared for. I will look after it like a mother." In his terror the man agreed to everything and no sooner had the wife been brought to bed than the witch appeared. She named the child Rapunzel and took it away with her.

Rapunzel grew into the most beautiful child under the sun. When she was twelve years old, the witch locked her up in a tower that stood in the forest and had neither stair nor door, only way at the top there was a little window. If the witch wanted to get inside, she came and stood at the bottom and called:

"Rapunzel, Rapunzel,
Let down your hair."

Rapunzel had magnificent long hair, fine as spun gold. Now when she heard the voice of the witch, she unfastened her braids, wound them around a hook on the window, and let the hair fall twenty feet to the ground below, and the witch climbed up.

After some years it happened that the king's son rode through the forest, past the tower, and heard singing so lovely he stood still and listened. It was Rapunzel in her loneliness, who made the time pass by letting her sweet voice ring through the forest. The prince wanted to climb up the tower and looked for the door but could not find one. So he rode home, but the singing had so moved his heart he came back to the forest day after day and listened. Once, when he was standing there behind a tree, he saw how a witch came along and heard her calling:

"Rapunzel, Rapunzel,
Let down your hair."

And then Rapunzel let her braids down and the witch climbed up. "If that's the ladder one takes to the top, I'll try my luck too." Next day, when it began to get dark, he went to the tower and called:

"Rapunzel, Rapunzel,
Let down your hair."

And the hair was let down and the prince climbed up.

At first Rapunzel was very much frightened when a man stepped in, because her eyes had never seen anything like him before, but the prince spoke very kindly to her and told her how his heart had been so moved by her singing he had wanted to see her. And so Rapunzel lost her fear, and when he asked her if she would take him for her husband and she saw how young and beautiful he was, she thought, He will love me better than my old godmother, and said, "Yes," and put her hand in his hand. She said, "I would like to go with you but I don't know how to get down from here. Every time you come, bring a skein of silk with you. I will braid a ladder and when the ladder is finished I will climb down and you will take me on your horse." Until that time the prince was to come to her every evening, for by day came the old woman. The witch knew nothing about all this until one day Rapunzel opened her mouth and said, "Tell me, Godmother, why is it you are so much harder to pull up than the young prince? He's with me in the twinkling of an eye." "Oh, wicked child!" cried the witch. "What is this! I thought I had kept you from all the world and still you deceive me," and in her fury she grasped Rapunzel's lovely hair, wound it a number of times around her left hand, and with her right hand seized a pair of scissors and snip snap, the beautiful braids lay on the floor. And so pitiless was she that she took poor Rapunzel into a wilderness and left her there to live in great misery and need.

On the evening of the day on which she had banished Rapunzel, the witch tied the severed braids to the hook at the window, and when the prince came and called:

> "Rapunzel, Rapunzel,
> Let down your hair,"

she let the hair down. The prince climbed up and found not his dearest Rapunzel but the witch looking at him with her wicked, venomous eyes. "Ah, ha," cried she mockingly, "you come to fetch your ladylove, but the pretty bird has flown the nest and stopped singing. The cat's got it and will scratch out your eyes too. You have lost Rapunzel and will never see her again." The prince was beside himself with grief and in his despair jumped out of the tower. His life was saved but he had fallen into thorns that pierced his eyes. And so he stumbled blindly about the forest, living on roots and berries, and did nothing but wail and weep for the loss of his dearest wife. And so for years he wandered in misery; finally he came into the wilderness where Rapunzel lived meagerly with her twin children, a boy and a girl, whom she had brought into the world. He heard her voice and it sounded so familiar to him. He walked toward it and Rapunzel recognized him and fell around his neck and cried. Two of her tears moistened his eyes and they regained their light and he could see as well as ever. He took her to his kingdom, where he was received with joy, and they lived happily and cheerfully for many years to come.

The Water of Life

There was once a king who was sick, and no one thought he would live. His three sons were very sad. They went down into the palace garden and wept, and there they met an old man, who asked them what the trouble was. They told him their father was very sick and would surely die, for nothing seemed to do him any good. The old man said: "I know of a remedy: the Water of Life. If he drinks of it, he will get well, but it's hard to find." "I'll find it," said the eldest, and he went to the sick king and asked him for leave to search for the Water of Life, since that alone could cure him. "No," said the king, "the danger is too great. I would rather die." But the son begged and pleaded until the king finally consented. The prince thought in his heart: "If I bring him the Water of Life, my father will love me the best, and I shall inherit the kingdom."

So he started out and when he had ridden awhile, a dwarf, who was standing on the road, called out to him: "Where are you going so fast?" "You stupid runt," said the prince haughtily, "what business is it of yours?" And he rode on. The dwarf was furious and cursed him. The prince soon came to a ravine. The farther he rode the closer the mountains came together, and in the end the path was so narrow that his horse couldn't take another step. The prince could neither turn his horse around nor dismount, and all he could do was sit there, wedged tight in his saddle. The sick king waited in vain for his eldest son to return, and then one day the second son said: "Father, let me go and look for the Water." He thought to himself: "If my brother is dead, the kingdom will fall to me." At first the king didn't want to let him go, but in the end he gave in. So the prince set out, taking the same road as his brother, and he too met the dwarf, who stopped him and asked where he was going so fast. "You little runt," said the prince, "what business is it of yours?" And he rode on without so much as looking around. Whereupon the dwarf cursed him, and like his brother he rode deep into a ravine until he got wedged in and was unable to go forward or backward. That's what happens to haughty people.

When the second son also failed to return, the youngest son asked leave to search for the Water, and the king finally had to let him go. When he met the dwarf and the dwarf asked him where he was going in such a hurry, he stopped and answered him: "I'm looking for the Water of Life, because my father is deathly sick." "Do you know where to find it?" "No," said the prince. "Since you've spoken kindly and haven't been haughty like your two wicked brothers, I'll tell you where the Water of Life is and how to get there. It springs from a fountain in the courtyard of an enchanted castle, but you'll never get in unless I give you an iron wand and two loaves of bread. Strike the castle gate three times with the wand and it will open. Inside, there will be two lions with gaping jaws, but if you throw a loaf to each of them, they will calm down. Then you must hurry and take the Water of Life before the clock strikes twelve, because otherwise the gate will close and you will be locked in." The prince thanked him, took the wand and the bread, and went his way. When he reached the castle, everything was just as the dwarf had said. The gate opened at the third stroke of the wand, and when he had calmed the lions with the bread, he went into the castle and came to a big, beautiful hall, full of enchanted princes. He drew the rings from their fingers and also took a sword and a loaf of bread that he found in the great hall. Farther on he came to a room, where a beautiful maiden was standing. She was overjoyed to see him, kissed him and told him he had set her free. "My whole kingdom will be yours," she said. "If you come back in a year's time we shall celebrate our wedding." Then she told him where to find the fountain with the Water of Life and bade him hurry and draw the water before the clock struck twelve. He went on and came at last to a room with a beautiful, freshly made bed in it. As he was tired, he thought he would rest awhile. He lay down and fell asleep, and when he awoke the clock was striking a quarter to twelve. He jumped up in a fright, ran to the fountain, drew the water in a cup that he found nearby, and hurried away. Just as he was passing through the iron gate, the clock struck twelve, and the gate slammed with such force that it took off a piece of his heel.

All the same, he was glad to have found the Water of Life, and started for home. On the way he came to the dwarf and when the dwarf saw the sword and the loaf, he said: "Those are great treasures you've come by. With that sword you can defeat whole armies, and that loaf will always be the same size no matter how much is eaten from it." But the prince didn't want to go home to his father without his brothers, and he said: "Dear dwarf, could you tell me where my two brothers are? They set out in search of the Water of Life before I did, and they never came back." "They're wedged in between mountains," said the dwarf. "I wished them there because they were haughty." The prince pleaded and at length the dwarf released them, though he warned him, saying: "Don't trust them. They have wicked hearts."

When his brothers appeared, he was glad to see them. He told them of his adventures, how he had found the Water of Life and brought back a cupful of it, and how he had saved a beautiful princess, who was going to wait a year for him and then they were going to be married and he would be king over a great kingdom. The brothers rode on together and came to a country where war and famine were raging and the misery was so great that the king of the country thought he would perish. The prince went to the king and gave him the loaf, whereupon the king fed all his people, and stilled their hunger. Next the prince gave the king his sword, the king destroyed the enemy armies, and after that he was able to live in peace. Then the prince took back his loaf and his sword, and the three brothers rode on. They passed through two more countries where war and famine were raging, and in both the prince lent the kings his loaf and his sword, so, all in all, he saved three kingdoms. Then they boarded a ship and sailed across the sea. During the voyage the two elder brothers went aside and said: "Our young brother has found the Water of Life and we haven't found anything. Our father will reward him by giving him the kingdom, which should properly be ours, and he will rob us of our birthright." They longed for revenge and decided on a way to destroy him. They waited until he was fast asleep, and then they poured the Water of Life out of his cup, took it away, and filled the cup with bitter sea water.

When they got home, the youngest brother brought the sick king his cup, expecting him to drink and be cured. But the king had barely tasted the bitter sea water when he became sicker than ever. As he was lamenting, his two elder sons came in and accused the youngest of wanting to poison him. Then they brought in the real Water of Life and handed it to him. The moment he drank of it he felt his sickness leaving him, and was as strong and healthy as in the days of his youth. The two deceivers went to the youngest brother and jeered at him: "Oh yes," they said, "you found the Water of Life, but much good it has done you. Yours the hardship and ours the reward. You should have been smarter and kept your eyes open. We took it away from you on the ship, while you were sleeping, and a year from now one of us will go and claim the beautiful princess. But whatever you do, don't tell our father about this. He wouldn't believe you, and if you say so much as a single word you will die, but if you keep silent your life will be spared."

The old king was very angry, for he thought his youngest had wanted to kill him. He summoned his council and had them sentence the boy to be secretly shot. One day the prince, who suspected no evil, went hunting, and the king's huntsman rode along with him. When they were all alone in the forest, the huntsman looked so sad that the prince asked him: "Dear huntsman, what's the matter?" "I can't tell you," said the huntsman, "and yet I should." "Speak up," said the prince. "Whatever it is, I'll forgive you." "Well," said the huntsman, "I'm supposed to kill you. The king ordered me to." The prince was aghast. "Dear huntsman," he said, "let me live! I'll give you my royal garments. Give me your lowly ones in exchange." "Gladly," said the hunter. "I wouldn't have been able to shoot you in any case." Whereupon they changed clothes. Then the huntsman went home and the prince went deeper into the forest.

Some time later three wagonloads of gold and precious stones came to the king for his youngest son. They had been sent in token of gratitude by the three kings who had destroyed their enemies with the prince's sword and fed their people with his loaf. The old king thought to himself: "Can my son have been innocent?" And he said aloud: "If only he were alive! I can't forgive myself for having him killed." At that the huntsman spoke up: "He is alive. I couldn't bring myself to carry out your order." And then he told the king what had happened. A weight fell from the king's heart and he had it proclaimed in all the kingdoms that his son was free to come home and would be welcomed with open arms.

Meanwhile the princess had a golden road built leading to her castle, and said to her guards: "The man who comes riding straight up to me in the middle of the road will be the right one and you must let him in. If anyone rides alongside the road, he will not be the right man, and you are not to let him in." When the year had almost passed, the eldest son thought he would hurry to the princess and pass himself off as her savior. He fully expected to win her as his wife and become master over her kingdom as well. He started out, and when he came to the castle and saw the beautiful golden road, he thought: "It would be a pity to ride on such a beautiful road." So he veered off and went on to the right of it. When he reached the gate, the guards said to him: "You are not the right man. Go away." A little later the second prince started out, and when he came to the golden road and his horse had only set one foot on it, he thought: "It would be a pity. What if the hoofbeats should crack it!" So he veered off and went on to the left of the road. When he reached the gate, the guards said: "You are not the right man. Go away." When the year had wholly passed, the third prince decided to leave his forest, ride away to his beloved, and forget his sorrows with her. Throughout his journey he thought of her and wished he were already with her, so when he got to the golden road he didn't even see it. His horse galloped right up the middle of it, and when he reached the gate it was opened. The princess welcomed him joyfully and said: "You are my savior and the lord of my kingdom." The marriage was celebrated with great rejoicing, and when it was over she told him that his father had sent for him and had forgiven him. Thereupon he rode home and told his father how his brothers had cheated him and how he had kept silent. The king wanted to punish them, but they had boarded a ship and sailed away, and they never came back as long as they lived.

Ballad

This version of "Kemp Owyne" is one of several hundred ballads collected by Francis James Child (1825–96), an American scholar whose most famous work is his five volumes of *English and Scottish Popular Ballads* (1882–98). Most ballads, like folktales, have many variants differing in large or small details, and sometimes ancient narratives in song are retold in prose as well. "Tam Lin," another Scottish ballad that has become popular recently because it has a strong heroine who rescues her lover, has also been adapted in prose by Jane Yolen and others. "The Laidly Worm of Spindleston Heugh," a story similar to "Kemp Owyne," has appeared in folktale collections for young readers since the nineteenth century; it is the subject of a painting by the great Victorian illustrator Walter Crane, and the print shown here, by John D. Batten (from Joseph Jacobs' *English Fairy Tales*, 1890).

The heroine's brother or lover in the ballad rescues her by kissing the monster, and some versions go on to tell how they get revenge by turning the wicked stepmother into a toad that is destined to live forever in a cave below Bamburgh Castle (which still stands on the Northumbrian coast, near the Scottish border). The story is related to Icelandic sagas and Scandinavian legends about women who are transformed into loathsome or laidly creatures and are "borrowed," "unspelled," or disenchanted by brave heroes like Kemp (or Knight) Owyne or Owain. Various types of monstrous serpents and snakes appear in ancient legends, where a dragon may be called "worm" or "wyrm." As in so many other traditional ballads, the short stanzas, repeated lines, and musical rhythms help the ballad singer remember the story, which proceeds with few other embellishments through a plot focusing on a single sensational event involving love, mystery, and the supernatural. Even though Jane Yolen's contemporary "Dove Isabeau" devotes more attention to the power of the heroine, the gifts and instructions that dove Isabel gives in the ballad to protect her rescuer—a ring, a royal belt, and a brand or sword, remind us that in many old tales, women were in possession of the wisdom and powerful magic that enabled men to help them escape from evil.

Kemp Owyne (The Laidly Worm)

Her mother died when she was young,
Which gave her cause to make great moan;
Her father married the warst woman
That ever lived in Christendom.

She served her with foot and hand,
In every thing that she could dee,
Till once, in an unlucky time,
She threw her in ower Craigy's sea.

Says, "Lie you there, dove Isabel,
And all my sorrows lie with thee;
Till Kemp Owyne come ower the sea,
And borrow you with kisses three,
Let all the warld do what they will,
Oh borrowed shall you never be!"

Her breath grew strang, her hair grew lang,
And twisted thrice about the tree,
And all the people, far and near,
Thought that a savage beast was she.

These news did come to Kemp Owyne,
Where he lived, far beyond the sea;
He hasted him to Craigy's sea,
And on the savage beast lookd he.

Her breath was strang, her hair was lang,
And twisted was about the tree,
And with a swing she came about:
"Come to Craigy's sea, and kiss with me.

"Here is a royal belt," she cried,
"That I have found in the green sea;
And while your body it is on,
Drawn shall your blood never be;
But if you touch me, tail or fin,
I vow my belt your death shall be."

He stepped in, gave her a kiss,
The royal belt he brought him wi;
Her breath was strang, her hair was lang,
And twisted twice about the tree,

And with a swing she came about:
"Come to Craigy's sea, and kiss with me.

"Here is a royal ring," she said,
"That I have found in the green sea;
And while your finger it is on,
Drawn shall your blood never be;
But if you touch me, tail or fin,
I swear my ring your death shall be."

He stepped in, gave her a kiss,
The royal ring he brought him wi;
Her breath was strang, her hair was lang,
And twisted ance about the tree,
And with a swing she came about:
"Come to Craigy's sea, and kiss with me.

"Here is a royal brand," she said,
"That I have found in the green sea;
And while your body it is on,
Drawn shall your blood never be;
But if you touch me, tail or fin,
I swear my brand your death shall be."

He stepped in, gave her a kiss,
The royal brand he brought him wi;
Her breath was sweet, her hair grew short,
And twisted nane about the tree,
And smilingly she came about,
As fair a woman as fair could be.

Childe·Wynd·thrice·kifses·the
Laidly·Worm·&·refcues·his·Sifter
the·Princefs·Margaret·

Like other Victorian artists, John D. Batten imitated the lavish beauty of medieval design and hand lettering in his illustration for the ancient legend "The Laidly Worm of Spindleston Heugh" (a tale similar to "Kemp Owyne").

Jane Yolen (b. 1939)

Jane Yolen is an American writer of over 200 books for children and young adults, as well as fiction and poetry for adults. While many of her picture books, poems, and novels deal with realistic subjects, she is best known as a writer of fairy tales and fantasy. She says that her literary or art fairy tales "use the elements of old stories—the cadences, the magical settings or objects—but concern themselves with modern themes." *Touch Magic* (1981) contains some of Yolen's many essays that eloquently affirm the enduring value of fantasy and fairy tales in children's literature, as Ursula K. Le Guin does in "Why Are Americans Afraid of Dragons?" (in Part 4). For Yolen, the psychological power of old fairy tales is so deep that in her novel *Briar Rose* (1992), a Holocaust survivor can talk of the horrors of Nazi persecution only by burying her story of near-death and resuscitation in a haunting version of "Sleeping Beauty" that she retells obsessively until her death (see Further Recommended Reading, Part 7). Yolen has also written and edited collections of tales and poems with many traditional and modern themes, including *Favorite Folktales from Around the World* (1986). She is especially interested in Arthurian legends; dragon tales; and, as the essay reprinted here discusses, our rich heritage of folktales. "The Brothers Grimm and Sister Jane" provides insights into the influence of old tales, including "The Water of Life," on a gifted writer from childhood to adult life. "Toads," a poem reprinted within the article, puts a humorous contemporary spin on an old folk motif, like some of the poems and stories in Part 7.

"Dove Isabeau," like "The Enchanter's Daughter" by Antonia Barber in Part 7, shows how a contemporary master of the literary fairy tale uses the influences that Yolen describes in her essay, weaving together traditional motifs to create a new tale of magic and wonder. When Dove Isabeau loses her mother and becomes subservient to a wicked stepmother/witch, she seems similar to Snow White or Cinderella. But Isabeau's transformation into a bloodthirsty red dragon is a dramatic departure from familiar tales in which adolescent girls must be rescued from fierce dragons or put to sleep until their prince arrives. Yolen's prince and princess are both incapacitated by the evil enemy but they rescue each other. While this tale echoes ancient British legends of Kemp Owain or Childe Wynde of Northumberland, Yolen's Isabeau has a more powerful role than the heroine in the ballad "Kemp Owyne." Images of the dragon weeping while it devours young men and ironic symbols of Isabeau's loss and recapturing of innocence suggest that the dragon transformation represents destructive as well as redemptive powers within a strong woman as she comes of age.

A positive theme that is also found in older folktales is the legacy of wisdom and magic healing that Isabeau's dying mother leaves behind. Like the hazel tree and doves in "Ashputtle" (in Part 5), the white cat is associated with the spirit of the good mother, and as in "Puss in Boots" (in Part 1), the cat can talk to the young man who is smart enough to follow its advice. Yolen's ending is more traditional than most of the fairy tale revisions and satires in Part 7 because the heroine's tears, like Rapunzel's, help to heal her lover and there is a romantic reunion. But Dove Isabeau's shocking red gown and her depiction as the "glorious dragon queen" ensure that both Kemp Owain and the reader admire her power from beginning to end and expect the couple to rule the kingdom equally. As Yolen wrote, "Both hero and dragon have to take on male and female aspects before they are ready to become man and wife."[1] There are many twentieth-century dragon tales featuring strong heroines, including E. Nesbit's "The Last of the Dragons" (in Part 7), but this one shows that the power of the dragon does not have to be weakened or caricatured for an enchanted maiden to achieve heroic status. *Dove Isabeau* was published as a picture book with striking realistic illustrations by Dennis Nolan in 1989.

NOTE

1. Jane Yolen, *"Dove Isabeau," The Book on Jane Yolen,* 2000, 29 April 2005 <http://www.janeyolen .com/pictbooks.html>.

The Brothers Grimm and Sister Jane

My first taste of fairy tales was in the collected color fairy books of Andrew Lang. Bowdlerized and tarted up as they were, the stories in those books still mesmerized me. Though I was a New York City child, I rode across the steppes of Russia, swam in the cold Scandinavian rivers, ran down African forest paths, hunted in the haunted Celtic woods with the heroes of the stories I read. I became in turn the girl on the back of a great white bear riding east of the sun and west of the moon, the Hoodie-crow's lovely wife, the farmer's woman stolen away by the fairies.

Like an addict, I went from the Lang samplers to the stronger stuff. The local librarians got used to me pulling out dusty collections from the shelves: the Afanas'ev Russian stories, Asbjørnsen and Moe's Norwegian tales, Yeats's Irish fairy lore, the *Thousand and One Nights*. (It was years before I learned it was the expurgated version.) And—of course—the Brothers Grimm.

By the time I was ten, a tomboy by day and a reader by night under the covers, I had devoured whole cultures. To the outsider, I must have seemed omniverous in my reading, catholic in my taste. But there were three stories in the Grimm collection that were my favorites. Though I could not have known it at the time, they were *life myths* to me. As it says in one of the early Gnostic gospels, *The Gospel According to Thomas:* "Whoever drinks from my mouth shall become as I am and I myself will become he, and the hidden things shall be revealed to him." If *that* is not a fairy-tale transformative curse—or blessing—I have misspent my youth! In loving these three particular stories, I became them. They were my meat and I theirs, a literary eucharist.

The three were: "Faithful John" (No. 6), "Brother and Sister" (No. 11), and "The Three Little Men in the Woods" (No. 13).

It is an odd trio I adopted. They are certainly not the most popular stories in the Grimm canon. Disney has not touched them. Nor are they found in picture-book format for the youngest readers. One must search them out within the body of the Grimm tales, a task for the true child bibliophile. Yet though these were not the popular and often reprinted stories, each spoke to me in a way that knifed clear to the soul. Like Yeats's description of the class of people who loved the folk tales, the peasants who "have steeped everything in the heart; to whom everything was a symbol" (xii), I was a breather-in of stories. Those three tales, though I did not understand it at the time, were to be accurate forecasters of my adult concerns.

The first of the trio, "Faithful John," is the story of a servant to the king who promises the dying monarch that he will be equally faithful to the prince "even if it should cost me my life" (43). And of course, as such stories go, John is forced to be as good as his word. He accompanies his young master on his bridal trip and overhears three ravens prophesying what dire things await the bridal pair. Furthermore, the ravens state that anyone foolish enough to explain it to the king would immediately be turned to stone. Naturally, Faithful John saves the royal couple three times and, when ordered to explain his actions, does so and becomes stone. Only when the king and queen willingly sacrifice their own children and use the innocents' blood to return the stone to life does the tale end happily. Happily for the children, too, for they are magically restored as well.

The story is full of magic, sacrifice, and reward, all the wonderful accoutrements of a fairy tale. It is satisfyingly rounded, wasting little time between the opening, in which the dying king accepts Faithful John's pledge, to the conclusion in which "They dwelt together in much happiness until their death" (51). An economical tale between two dyings, a critic might carp. But oh, as a child, how I loved that tale.

The faithful servant—tale type 516—was well known for centuries before the Grimms' particular version was recorded, travelling from India both orally and in the eleventh-century *Ocean of Story* collection. Some scholars point out a connection as well with the French romance *Amis and Amiloun*, which contains both the stone and the disenchantment by means of innocent children's blood. (For a fuller discussion of this see Stith Thompson's *The Folktale* 111–12.) But all that mattered to me as a child was the driving force behind that story: that faithfulness, even unto a quasi-death, would be rewarded in the end.

By the time I was an adult, only vaguely remembering the outlines of the story, I had become a peace marcher, a stander-on-line for causes. I was—in essence—a Faithful John, willing to go to jail or even to be turned to stone as the possible consequence of my actions. My stories, too, had more than a casual reference to the old tale. *Dove Isabeau* is a picture-book fairy tale about a prince who is turned to stone because of his willingness to save his own true love. He does what must be done—knowing full well that stone is his doom, that he will, quite literally, become his own monument. He is saved in the very end by a drop of blood from an innocent girl. *Friend,* a biography of my hero, that great stander-up-to-power George Fox, the first Quaker, was another offshoot of the "Faithful John" story. And "The Hundredth Dove" is a fairy tale about a faithful servant to his king who even wears the motto "Servo"—*I serve*—over his breast until he is forced to serve his king in an ignoble and terrible fashion. That was a story fueled by the Watergate hearings, but its antecedent is, unquestionably, Grimm story No. 6.

The second tale that imprinted itself on my consciousness was "Brother and Sister," an odd tale in the Grimm collection because it has always seemed unfinished to me, or strangely conglomerate, as if two stories had been badly or inappropriately stitched together.

A brother and sister who are abused by their stepmother "go forth together into the wide world" (67) and become lost in a forest whose very brooks have been bewitched by their sorcerous foe. Dying of thirst, they go from one stream to another, not daring to drink, for the first two announce, "Who drinks of me will be a tiger" and "Who drinks of me will be a wolf" (68). (Does this sound remarkably like the *Gospel According to Thomas* quotation with which I began this essay?) At last, the brother cannot stand it any longer and drinks from a stream that promises he will become a deer. His sister ties her golden garter around his neck and leads him even further into the woods where they discover an empty cottage. There they live until a king comes upon them, falls in love with the girl, and brings them both back to the palace. Of course the wicked stepmother substitutes her own ugly daughter for the queen at the moment of childbirth, and the story finishes with the rightful queen restored, the false queen torn to pieces by wild beasts in the very

woods her mother had enchanted, and the witch burnt at the stake. The deer—at last—is turned back into a man.

It was the relationship between the brother and sister that first compelled me. As an older sister to an adored younger brother, I considered myself a twin to the heroine of the tale. As she is not named in the story, I named her—Jane.

Tale type 450, called after the story "Little Brother, Little Sister," it is the prototype story of family loyalty that has been found in many different cultures. Family loyalty was prized in our house.

When I became a writer, I used the tale very consciously in my own story "Brother Hart," though that particular tale is more a romance than a fairy story, with a bittersweet ending. It is a story of jealousy and possessiveness, created at the height of feminist rage and the ongoing discussions about a woman's place in a loving relationship. Not just a recasting of an old, familiar story, it is a tale that could only have been written in the mid-twentieth century. I also used the transformation motif in a variety of other stories, all harkening back to "Brother and Sister." "The Promise," in which a boy transformed into a fish by a sorcerer is saved by his own true love; "The Cat-bride," in which a cat becomes a human girl in order to be married; "The White Seal Maid," in which a seal becomes a woman and bears seven sons to a fisherman to revive her dying tribe; and the transfigured brother and sister in the "Wild Goose and Gander" section of my fairy-tale novel *The Magic Three of Solatia* are just a few of them.

The third—and in some ways the oddest—of my life stories was the relatively unknown "The Three Little Men in the Woods." It begins with a widow and widower marrying and the stepmother offering preferment to her own ugly daughter. The beautiful stepdaughter is sent out into the woods in the middle of winter in a paper frock to gather strawberries, a traditional "impossible task." Since she is as good as she is beautiful, she treats the three little men she meets in the woods politely and shares her meagre dinner—a piece of hard bread—with them, thus winning their approval. They wish that she grow more beautiful every day, that whenever she speaks gold should fall from her lips, and that she marry a king. When she returns home with strawberries found miraculously in the snow, speaking a fortune at every utterance, the stepmother packs her own daughter off for the same trip. Of course she is swathed in furs and carries along a bread-and-butter cake which she neglects to share with the little men, whom she snubs. Naturally she is cursed: that she grow uglier every day, that toads spring from her mouth, and that she die a miserable death. As the adventure proceeds, both the blessings and the curses come true.

Similar to the more popular Grimms' "Frau Holle" or "Mother Holle" (No. 24), the tale at its core contains the well-known motif "Kind and unkind" daughter (Q2). Other Grimm stories also revolve around Q2: "Bearskin" (No. 101) and "The Water of Life" (No. 97; unkind sons in this case). But it was the idea of the gold pouring out of the good girl's mouth, the toads from the bad's, that riveted me. It was—though I did not know it at the time—a metaphor for the life I was to choose.

I was to use that toad image in *Sleeping Ugly,* a parody of several fairy tales, in which the nasty Princess Miserella is cursed, for a moment, to speak in toads until the homely but goodhearted Plain Jane asks for a reprieve. I also used the image in the following poem, part of a series of fairy-tale poems I wrote in the mid and late 1980s:

TOADS

Sure, I called her *stupid cow*
and *witch,*
but only under my breath.
And I took an extra long lunch
last Friday,
and quit right at five
every day this week,
slapping my desk top down
with a noise
like the snap of gum.
She could've fired me right then.
Or docked my check.
Or put a pink slip
in my envelope
with that happy face
she draws on all her notes.
But not her.
Witch!
This morning
at the coffee shop,
when I went to order
a Danish and a decaf to go,

instead of words,
this great gray toad
the size of a bran muffin
dropped out between my lips
onto the formica.
It looked up at me,
its dark eyes sorrowful,
its back marked
with Revlon's Lady Love
the shape of my kiss.
Tell me,
do you think
I should apologize?
Do you think I should let
the shop steward know?

I also used the idea of something unnatural coming from a girl's mouth in the story "Silent Bianca." Bianca speaks in slivers of ice, and anyone who wants to know what she is saying has to gather the slivers and warm them by the hearthfire until the slivers melt and the room is filled with the sounds of Bianca's voice.

Every author hopes that the words pouring from the pen—or typewriter, word processor, or number 2 pencil, all mouth substitutes—are golden, indeed. Golden means the words are precious, important, powerful. Golden means that the author can make a good living. Golden suggests permanence and worth. However, I—and most writers I know—suspect that when we open our mouths we usually spit out toads, as big as bran muffins, onto the plates of our eager readers. For that nightmare—for that metaphor—we have the Brothers Grimm to thank.

WORKS CITED

Grimm, Brothers. *The Complete Grimm's Fairy Tales.* Trans. Margaret Hunt. Rev. James Stern. 1944. New York: Pantheon Books, 1972.

Thompson, Stith. *The Folktale.* 1946. Berkeley: U of California P, 1977.

Yeats, William Butler. *Irish Fairy and Folk Tales.* New York: Random, n.d.

Yolen, Jane. "Brother Hart." *Dream Weaver* 10–20.

———. "The Catbride." *Dream Weaver* 43–47.

———. *Dove Isabeau.* San Diego: Harcourt, 1989.

———. *Dream Weaver.* 1979. New York: Philomel Books, 1989.

———. *Friend: The Story of George Fox and the Quakers.* New York: Seabury Press, 1972.

———. *The Hundredth Dove and Other Tales.* New York: Crowell, 1977.

———. "The Hundredth Dove." *Hundredth Dove* 1–9.

———. *The Magic Three of Solatia.* New York: Crowell, 1974.

———. "The Promise." *Hundredth Dove* 39–50.

———. "Silent Bianca." *The Girl Who Cried Flowers and Other Tales.* New York: Crowell, 1974. 45–55.

———. *Sleeping Ugly.* New York: Coward, 1981.

———. "Toads." *Isaac Asimov's Science Fiction Magazine* June 1989: 145.

———. "The White Seal Maid." *Hundredth Dove* 29–37.

Dove Isabeau

In the cold northern shore of Craig's Cove, where the trees bear leaves only three months of the year, there stood a great stone castle with three towers. In the central tower lived a girl named Isabeau, and she was fair.

Her hair was the color of the tops of waves when the sun lights them from above, and her eyes were as dark blue as the sea. Her figure was slender, her hands gentle, her fingers slim and fine. She spoke with a voice that was clear and low. And because she always dressed in gray or white, the color of a dove, she was known as Dove Isabeau.

All the young men in the kingdom loved her, gardener and guardsman alike. They loved her for her gentle nature, her lovely face, and her fine form. But no one loved her more than the king's son, Kemp Owain. He had been sent beyond the sea for several years to get learning and to study the great magicks. All his boyhood he had loved Dove Isabeau; he had always looked beyond her face and gentle form, loving her for her spirit and for the fire that lay beneath the skin.

One hard winter, when Isabeau was fourteen, her mother took sick, an illness that turned her own considerable beauty to sores and scales and brought her great suffering. All that was left her was her voice, sweet and pure. Isabeau and her father, Lord Darnton, tended her day and night, and Lady Darnton's little white cat especially never left her side. But Isabeau's mother died at last, when winter had a hold on both the land and their hearts.

Lord Darnton married again in the summer, all too hastily, because he needed to believe in life again. The woman he wed had eyes the green of May but a heart as bleak as February. Unknown to Isabeau and her father, the woman was a witch. Her magic was as deep as the waters of the Craig. She was jealous of youth; she was jealous of beauty; she was jealous of Dove Isabeau.

She disguised her coldness behind soft slow smiles, but the servants were not fooled. They heard her talking aloud in her tower room when she thought none of them were about:

> Silver glass, my only friend,
> Show me how Dove's life shall end.
> Great and great my hate does grow
> For the lovely Isabeau.

A hanging ball of glass twisted in the window, turning first black, then white. She waited to see what picture the ball would show her, a picture that would spell out the fate she asked of it. But it showed her only the landscape of her own heart, as hard and unyielding as the tumbled rocks of the cove.

Dove Isabeau missed her own mother dreadfully. She had terrible dreams at night. So she tried to please her father's new wife, giving all to her that she wished she could still give to her mother. She served the woman breakfast each morning in the great curtained bed. She washed her stepmother's undergarments in the cold streams with her own hands.

But nothing Isabeau did pleased the woman, and, at last, the stepmother barred Isabeau and the white cat from her room with one of those soft smiles that disguised her true heart.

Isabeau, with the cat in her arms, descended the tower stairs feeling as if she had, indeed, buried her mother and her own life in the same box.

Silently, the cat licked Isabeau's hand.

But the witch did not mind the hurt she had given. Just as she did every night, she consulted the hanging glass ball, speaking to it in the hushed tones of a conspirator. But because she did not see an answer in the glass, the witch left Isabeau alone.

One night, when the full moon shone through the window of the witch's tower room, a small frightened lizard climbed down the chain and across the face of the glass ball. In the room of shadows, he seemed a part of the picture in the glass. The witch read the message there—for magic has its own strange alphabet— and she laughed aloud.

"Oh, Isabeau, I have you now. No longer dove, no longer loved, you shall be as cold and hard as the rocks of Craig's Cove, even as I am." She took the little lizard by the tail and flung it out the window onto the stones below.

Then, guided by moonlight, she made her way down the cliffs. There she gathered sea polyps from the water and dark moss that clung to the rocks. Inland she picked pennyroyal, henbane, chervil, and rue. It was late into the night when she made her way back to the house, her apron filled with the herbs of devilry.

All the servants and Lord Darnton were fast asleep. But Isabeau, troubled by dreams, was downstairs, awake. She opened the castle door to the witch.

"My dear new mother!" cried Isabeau in alarm. "Your gown is wet and trailing mud. Your eyes are red and worn. Is anything the matter?"

The witch smiled coldly. "Come up to my room, child, and I will show you what I have here in my apron."

They were the first kind words she had spoken, and Isabeau was grateful.

"I will be up at once," she said. "Though first I must bar the door."

"Bar the door," the witch said, still smiling. Turning away she added under her breath, "For all the good it will do."

But Isabeau did not hear that, and she gladly pushed the wooden bolt home. A sliver pricked her finger, and her cry brought the little white cat, who came up and licked the wound clean. It healed as if by magic.

They went upstairs together, the stepmother in the lead, and all the house quiet about them. The white cat followed, careful not to be seen. Its fur was all rumpled and full of dirt, for it had been trailing the stepmother all night long.

In the tower room, Dove Isabeau looked about in surprise. It was no longer the bright, cheery room her mother had loved, with its tapestries of dancing maidens, the spinning wheel and embroidery frames, the baskets filled with skeins of wool. Now it was a place of dark magicks: the great wooden table held beakers, bowls, and books; herbs dried from hooks in the wooden beams; and, though it was midsummer's eve, a fire blazed in the hearth, with a black cauldron at the boil.

"Stand there, child," the witch said, pointing to a rug on the floor emblazoned with a great red star. "Stand there that I may better see your lovely face."

Unsuspecting, Isabeau did as her stepmother asked, stepping into the very center of the star. She turned her face from the window, where the last lines of night were just stretching into dawn.

The witch waved her hands three times in Isabeau's direction before the girl could protest. And then it was too late. Isabeau could no longer move at all.

Flinging the herbs into Isabeau's face, the witch cried out:

Herbs of evil, herbs of woe,
Change the shape of Isabeau.

A river of fire suddenly ran through Isabeau's veins. Her breath grew strong; her nails grew long. Her hair lengthened into a tangled mane. A reddish scale grew over her face and arms and legs. From between her shoulders, bursting the careful stitches of her gown, great pinioned wings began to sprout. And stretching behind her was a sinuous, twisting tail.

"Go, Wyrm!" the witch cried triumphantly. "Wind yourself around the rocks upon which this castle stands. What man will look at you now, my dove? What heart will love you? When you were innocent and fair to behold, you held every man's affection. But in this twisted, scaly form you will command no kisses—only curses and the point of a sword. Even your father will despise you. When all the young men have died beneath your claws, and even the king's son, Kemp Owain, is killed, then I shall claim first this castle and then this kingdom for my own."

The witch began to laugh and spin around the room. She danced with shadows and bowed to the waning moon. As she did so, the great red dragon that had been Dove Isabeau began to move. She climbed clumsily out the window and coasted down on untried wings to settle on the cold stones.

And the little white cat crept away down the stairs, careful not to be seen.

Morning came, a pale sun rising, shrouded by clouds. But even more shrouded were the stones of the castle around which the great red dragon wrapped itself.

Inside, Lord Darnton and all the servants felt their blood thin out; their bones grow brittle; their heartbeats slow. They grew weaker with each passing hour as if the dragon were draining them of all life.

That day, when the young men of the kingdom came, one by one, to court Isabeau, the sight of the dragon—with its fierce red jaws, its mighty pinions, and its cruel, slashing claws—sent each of them galloping home afraid.

But later, shamed, one by one they returned with weapons to slay the wyrm and rescue Isabeau and her father from the dragon's grasp.

On the high road to the great stone castle, each suitor was met by the little white cat, who mewed piteously and tried to bar the way. One by one the young men drove it off with blows and curses, eager to kill the giant wyrm.

But however they tried to slay it, by spear or by stake, by sword or by bow, the young men died as young men will: foolishly, carelessly, bravely, and well. No one was left to watch the red beast weep as it gnawed upon their bones.

Under the dragon's shadow, Lord Darnton's castle and the entire kingdom seemed doomed.

At last Kemp Owain was summoned by his frightened father. He returned from across the sea.

"Oh, my son," the king said, "a great, hideous dragon circles the place where Lord Darnton and Isabeau dwell. There is a terrible dark sorcery there. None of the young men of the kingdom has succeeded in slaying the wyrm. Nine and ninety have gone out. Not one has returned."

Kemp Owain nodded. "Dark sorcery indeed," he said. He saddled his good gray horse and put a sword and dagger at his waist. "Father, if I, who know the good magicks, do not return, let no one else come. For it will mean that I, and Isabeau, and all her house are dead."

Then he kissed his mother and father good-bye,

mounted his horse, and rode off toward the north shore of the Craig.

As he turned onto the high road, the little white cat crossed before him. The horse shied, and it was all Kemp Owain could do to keep his seat. But instead of striking at the cat or cursing it, he calmed the horse and dismounted, for he recognized the cat as Lady Darnton's.

"Little catkin," he said, picking it up and stroking its fur, "you must run away and quickly. If that dragon can devour grown men, surely you would be but a single *snick-snack* in its giant maw."

Much to his surprise, the cat began to speak in Lady Darnton's sweet, pure voice.

> If the sword bites tail or fin,
> Isabeau you will not win.
> If the sword bites wing or tail,
> Isabeau you'll surely fail.
> But give the red wyrm kisses three,
> And Isabeau you shall set free.

Now, as Kemp Owain knew sorcery, he was sure that that verse was not all there was to the spell.

"What more, catkin?" he asked.

Giving a soft miaou, the cat leaped from his hands. Looking back over its shoulder, it spoke again.

> Give the red wyrm kisses three,
> Turned to stone you'll surely be.

Then it ran off down the road toward the castle.

Kemp Owain rode after the cat. As he got closer, he could see the dragon's bright red scales flashing in the sun. Without thinking, he rode straight for the front gate. But catching the dragon's smell, his horse reared suddenly, and Kemp Owain was thrown to the ground. He got to his feet, threw off his cape, and drew his sword. The dragon unwrapped itself from the rocky face of the middle tower and launched its giant body into the air.

As the wyrm hovered above him, Kemp Owain saw that whenever he raised his sword, the dragon advanced. But when he lowered it, the dragon retreated.

Then the white cat's words came back to him:

> If the sword bites tail or fin,
> Isabeau you will not win.
> If the sword bites wing or tail,
> Isabeau you'll surely fail.

Once more he raised his sword. Roaring fire and smoke, the dragon plunged down toward him.

Kemp Owain drew a great breath. He knew what he had to do. Using more courage than he thought he had, he threw the sword away. The dragon banked suddenly and flew off.

Staring through the smoke, Kemp Owain thought he saw only dragon, all talons and tail and teeth. Then, remembering his lessons in sorcery, he squinted his eyes and looked *beneath* the wyrm form. There he saw the faint outline of a slim, fair girl. She was weeping tears of blood.

"Dove Isabeau," he whispered. And slowly, so as not to alarm the dragon, he took the knife from his waist and threw it away as well.

"Come, wyrm or dove," he called, his voice shaking. "I would give you a token of my love." Then he opened his arms to his death.

The dragon dove straight for him, pulling up only at the last to backwing frantically and settle down by his side, When it landed, it shook the earth. Its head was as high as the rooftree of a house, its middle he could not have spanned. Its jaws were large enough to roast an entire ox. In its burnished scales, Kemp Owain could read his own face a hundred times.

He closed his eyes and was bending over to kiss the great beast on the mouth when he suddenly remembered the other words the little cat had said:

Give the red wyrm kisses three,
Turned to stone you'll surely be.

But it was already too late to change his mind. His lips touched the dragon's lips. And though he had expected the thin, cold mouth of a serpent, the touch was as warm and soft as a girl's. Not knowing what to expect, he opened his eyes. The dragon was still there before him, but a coldness was spreading up from his feet. When he looked down, he saw that he had turned to stone from his toes to his waist.

What had he done? The dragon was unchanged, but *he* was surely lost. Still, what did his own life matter? It was Isabeau he must free and the kingdom he must save. He stared through the haze of dragon smoke and scale to the weeping girl beneath and kissed the dragon a second time.

The dragon's mouth was warmer still, but Kemp Owain felt the coldness spreading throughout his body, turning it to stone from waist to neck. Yet he could feel the beating of his own steady heart beneath the stone.

The dragon turned its sad, dark, weeping eyes on him.

"Do not mourn for me, wyrm," Kemp Owain cried. "I only do what must be done."

Then, for the third time, he closed his eyes and readied himself for the dragon's kiss.

Since he could no longer move, the dragon came to him, its massive head gentle against his own. And this kiss was the sweetest kiss of all, for it was the last thing Kemp Owain knew.

No sooner did their lips meet for the third time than the dragon's scales began to drop away. The dragon form peeled open, and from its center stepped Isabeau. She wrapped herself in Kemp Owain's cape.

Her hair was as light as the tops of waves, but her eyes were as dark as the sea. She touched Kemp Owain gently on his stone cheek and felt a tear beneath her fingers.

"I shall avenge you, Kemp Owain," she whispered to his stone ears. Picking up his dagger and sword, she marched into the house.

Isabeau mounted the steps two at a time till she came to the tower room. The witch was standing by the window, staring into her crystal globe. When Isabeau came through the door, a thousand tiny cracks jetted around the glass ball.

Looking up, the witch laughed, "So, Isabeau, you are to be my death. The glass did not tell me, but I can read it in your eyes. You could not have done it before. You had not the right fire for it, nor the blood. But what runs in your veins now is the legacy of all those rash young men you devoured. Yet know this— whatever you do, Kemp Owain is lost. Only the blood of the innocent young girl you once were can bring him back." She laughed and laughed until the walls of the tower room rang with the sound.

Isabeau gave an awful cry, part dragon's curse, part maiden's prayer. She flung the dagger as hard as she could. It hit the witch in the shoulder with such force she staggered back, tumbled through the open window, and fell to the rocks below.

Though Isabeau could not bear to look down, she hurled the sword after.

For a long moment she waited for the sound of sword on stone. When it did not come, she smiled the dragon's smile and went back down the stairs. Opening the front doors, she walked to the statue of Kemp Owain and stared at it for a long, long time.

She was still standing there when Lord Darnton found her. With him were all the members of his household. Isabeau was weeping as if her tears might wash away the stone.

Just then the little white cat rubbed against her ankles. She picked it up and stroked its silken head. Remembering how it had once licked the blood from her hand when the wooden sliver had pricked her, Isabeau cried: "Alas, catkin, that was the last bit of innocent blood I will ever shed! If only I could have it back. I would give it all, every drop, to have Kemp Owain alive and whole."

"The wish is the deed," purred the cat in a familiar voice, both sweet and pure. "And so breaks the spell."

The white cat leaped from Isabeau's hands and ran to the statue, where it began licking the feet. The cat licked and licked until it had worn away the outer stone, revealing to them what lay beneath. There stood Kemp Owain, alive and only slightly dazed, remembering nothing after the dragon's final kiss.

What feasting and celebration occurred then, for seven days and seven nights, until they were all thoroughly tired of it. And when Kemp Owain and Dove Isabeau were married, the cat was the happiest celebrant of them all, with its own silver bowl of cream and a dozen small sprats caught fresh from the cove. And never a word more did it speak but *miaou*.

Much to the surprise of all the guests, Isabeau wore neither white nor gray for the wedding. Instead she dressed in a grown of red. And after, though others still called her Dove Isabeau, remembering her innocent past, Kemp Owain did not. Delighting in her spirit and fire, which he had always known was hidden beneath her gentle form, he called her his fierce guardian, his mighty warrior, and his glorious dragon queen for all the long, happy years they ruled the kingdom together.

Joseph Jacobs (1854-1916)

"Jack and the Beanstalk" is the world's most popular Jack tale, retold in hundreds of picture books, folktale collections, plays, and films. An ordinary young man named Jack in English and Celtic folklore (or John, Jake, Jock, Hans, and Jean in various cultures) has fantastic adventures in many different folktales. He typically begins as a lowly peasant, often a quite foolish one, and rises to prosperity through a combination of luck, magical help, and trickery. As with many other folk heroes, including Odysseus outwitting the giant Polyphemus in *The Odyssey* and young David killing Goliath in the Bible, his success provides wish fulfillment for ordinary people. Children, who must negotiate the world of larger, more powerful beings every day, enjoy stories about little people who go up against giants. Famous twentieth-century storytellers from old families in the Appalachian mountains, who told Americanized tales, such as "Jack and the Bean Tree," said that they identified closely with Jack, or they would like to name all their children Jack because he was so lucky. Since there is so little evidence of more ancient oral sources, scholars debate whether this story and Jack's second most popular group of tales, "Jack the Giant Killer," came from oral traditions or written sources, such as Renaissance poems and chapbooks. Most likely, oral and written versions blended over the centuries.

This version is one of six tales about characters named Jack in *English Fairy Tales* (3rd ed., 1898), one of Joseph Jacobs's influential collections of Anglo-Celtic folktales. Jacobs, an Australian historian and folklorist who moved to England and later America, provided notes on his sources, but changed their dialect or literary diction to more accessible language for reading aloud, striving to capture "the colloquial-romantic tone . . . which English children will listen to."[1] He heard this tale as a child in Australia, about 1860. He consulted an old chapbook but rejected its inclusion of a fairy explaining that the giant had stolen Jack's father's wealth. Jacobs did not expect the story to encourage children to steal, but expressed "greater confidence in my young friends." Debates continue about whether Jack is an amoral trickster, who naturally steals from a cannibalistic giant, or whether he is morally justified in reclaiming his father's wealth, like more virtuous fairy tale heroes. The giant beanstalk has been compared to symbolic trees of life or trees to heaven in ancient mythology and to Jacob's ladder in the Bible. The wife (or mother or daughter) who helps the hero is a common figure in folktales about encounters with giants, devils, or dragons in unearthly places. Although Jack does marry a princess in many tales, Jacobs's ending seems tacked on, while in other versions, Jack simply takes riches home to his mother. For a related tale with a more independent girl as the giant killer, see "Mutsmag" in this section.

NOTE

1. Joseph Jacobs, Preface, *English Fairy Tales* (3rd ed., 1898; New York: Dover, 1967) viii. See also comments on "Jack and the Beanstalk" variants in Jacobs' Notes and References, 238.

Jack and the Beanstalk

There was once upon a time a poor widow who had an only son named Jack, and a cow named Milky-white. And all they had to live on was the milk the cow gave every morning which they carried to the market and sold. But one morning Milky-white gave no milk and they didn't know what to do.

"What shall we do, what shall we do ?" said the widow, wringing her hands.

"Cheer up, mother, I'll go and get work somewhere," said Jack.

"We've tried that before, and nobody would take you," said his mother; "we must sell Milky-white and with the money start shop, or something."

"All right, mother," says Jack ; "it's market-day today, and I'll soon sell Milky-white, and then we'll see what we can do."

So he took the cow's halter in his hand, and off he started. He hadn't gone far when he met a funny-looking old man who said to him: "Good morning, Jack."

"Good morning to you," said Jack, and wondered how he knew his name.

"Well, Jack, and where are you off to?" said the man.

"I'm going to market to sell our cow here."

"Oh, you look the proper sort of chap to sell cows," said the man; "I wonder if you know how many beans make five."

"Two in each hand and one in your mouth," says Jack, as sharp as a needle.

"Right you are," says the man, "and here they are, the very beans themselves," he went on, pulling out of his pocket a number of strange-looking beans. "As you are so sharp," says he, "I don't mind doing a swop with you—your cow for these beans."

"Go along," says Jack; "wouldn't you like it?"

"Ah! you don't know what these beans are," said the man; "if you plant them over-night, by morning they grow right up to the sky."

"Really?" says Jack; "you don't say so."

"Yes, that is so, and if it doesn't turn out to be true you can have your cow back."

"Right," says Jack, and hands him over Milky-white's halter and pockets the beans.

Back goes Jack home, and as he hadn't gone very far it wasn't dusk by the time he got to his door.

"Back already, Jack?" said his mother; "I see you haven't got Milky-white, so you've sold her. How much did you get for her?"

"You'll never guess, mother," says Jack.

"No, you don't say so. Good boy! Five pounds, ten, fifteen, no, it can't be twenty."

"I told you you couldn't guess, what do you say to these beans; they're magical, plant them over-night and——"

"What!" says Jack's mother, "have you been such a fool, such a dolt, such an idiot, as to give away my Milky-white, the best milker in the parish, and prime beef to boot, for a set of paltry beans. Take that! Take that! Take that! And as for your precious beans here they go out of the window. And now off with you to bed. Not a sup shall you drink, and not a bit shall you swallow this very night"

So Jack went upstairs to his little room in the attic, and sad and sorry he was, to be sure, as much for his mother's sake, as for the loss of his supper.

At last he dropped off to sleep.

When he woke up, the room looked so funny. The sun was shining into part of it, and yet all the rest was quite dark and shady. So Jack jumped up and dressed himself and went to the window. And what do you think he saw? why, the beans his mother had thrown out of the window into the garden, had sprung up into a big beanstalk which went up and up and up till it reached the sky. So the man spoke truth after all.

The beanstalk grew up quite close past Jack's window, so all he had to do was to open it and give a jump on to the beanstalk which ran up just like a big ladder. So Jack climbed, and he climbed and he climbed and he climbed and he climbed and he climbed and he climbed and he climbed till at last he reached the sky. And when he got there he found a long broad road going as straight as a dart. So he walked along and he walked along and he walked along till he came to a great big tall house, and on the doorstep there was a great big tall woman.

"Good morning, mum," says Jack, quite polite-like. "Could you be so kind as to give me some breakfast?" For he hadn't had anything to eat, you know, the night before and was as hungry as a hunter.

"It's breakfast you want, is it?" says the great big tall woman, "it's breakfast you'll be if you don't move off from here. My man is an ogre and there's nothing he likes better than boys broiled on toast. You'd better be moving on or he'll soon be coming."

"Oh! please mum, do give me something to eat, mum. I've had nothing to eat since yesterday morning, really and truly, mum," says Jack, "I may as well be broiled as die of hunger."

Well, the ogre's wife was not half so bad after all. So she took Jack into the kitchen, and gave him a junk of bread and cheese and a jug of milk. But Jack hadn't half finished these when thump! thump! thump! the whole house began to tremble with the noise of some one coming.

"Goodness gracious me! It's my old man," said the ogre's wife, "what on earth shall I do? Come along quick and jump in here." And she bundled Jack into the oven just as the ogre came in.

He was a big one, to be sure. At his belt he had three calves strung up by the heels, and he unhooked them and threw them down on the table and said: "Here, wife, broil me a couple of these for breakfast. Ah! what's this I smell?

Fee-fi-fo-fum,
I smell the blood of an Englishman,
Be he alive, or be he dead
I'll have his bones to grind my bread."

"Nonsense, dear," said his wife, "you're dreaming. Or perhaps you smell the scraps of that little boy you liked so much for yesterday's dinner. Here, you go and have a wash and tidy up, and by the time you come back your breakfast'll be ready for you."

So off the ogre went, and Jack was just going to jump out of the oven and run away when the woman told him not. "Wait till he's asleep," says she; "he always has a doze after breakfast"

Well, the ogre had his breakfast; and after that he goes to a big chest and takes out of it a couple of bags of gold, and down he sits and counts till at last his head began to nod and he began to snore till the whole house shook again.

Then Jack crept out on tiptoe from his oven, and as he was passing the ogre he took one of the bags of gold under his arm, and off he pelters till he came to the beanstalk, and then he threw down the bag of gold, which of course fell in to his mother's garden, and then he climbed down and climbed down till at last he got home and told his mother and showed her the gold and said: "Well, mother, wasn't I right about the beans. They are really magical, you see."

So they lived on the bag of gold for some time, but at last they came to the end of it, and Jack made up his mind to try his luck once more up at the top of the beanstalk. So one fine morning he rose up early, and got on to the beanstalk, and he climbed and he climbed and he climbed and he climbed and he climbed and he climbed till at last he came out on to the road again and up to the great big tall house he had been to before. There, sure enough, was the great big tall woman a-standing on the door-step.

"Good morning, mum," says Jack, as bold as brass, "could you be so good as to give me something to eat?"

"Go away, my boy," said the big tall woman, "or else my man will eat you up for breakfast. But aren't you the youngster who came here once before? Do you know, that very day, my man missed one of his bags of gold."

"That's strange, mum," says Jack, "I dare say I could tell you something about that, but I'm so hungry I can't speak till I've had something to eat"

Well the big tall woman was so curious that she took him in and gave him something to eat. But he had scarcely begun munching it as slowly as he could when thump! thump! thump! they heard the giant's footstep, and his wife hid Jack away in the oven.

All happened as it did before. In came the ogre as he did before, said: "Fee-fi-fo-fum," and had his breakfast off three broiled oxen. Then he said: "Wife, bring me the hen that lays the golden eggs." So she brought it, and the ogre said: "Lay," and it laid an egg all of gold. And then the ogre began to nod his head, and to snore till the house shook.

Then Jack crept out of the oven on tiptoe and caught hold of the golden hen, and was off before you could say "Jack Robinson." But this time the hen gave a cackle which woke the ogre, and just as Jack got out of the house he heard him calling: "Wife, wife, what have you done with my golden hen?"

And the wife said: "Why, my dear?"

But that was all Jack heard, for he rushed off to the beanstalk and climbed down like a house on fire. And when he got home he showed his mother the wonderful hen and said "Lay," to it; and it laid a golden egg every time he said "Lay."

Well, Jack was not content, and it wasn't very long before he determined to have another try at his luck up there at the top of the beanstalk. So one fine morning, he rose up early, and got on to the beanstalk, and he climbed and he climbed and he climbed and he climbed till he got to the top. But this time he knew better than to

go straight to the ogre's house. And when he got near it he waited behind a bush till he saw the ogre's wife come out with a pail to get some water, and then he crept into the house and got into the copper. He hadn't been there long when he heard thump! thump! thump! as before, and in come the ogre and his wife.

"Fee-fi-fo-fum, I smell the blood of an Englishman," cried out the ogre; "I smell him, wife, I smell him."

"Do you, my dearie?" says the ogre's wife. "Then if it's that little rogue that stole your gold and the hen that laid the golden eggs he's sure to have got into the

The Fairies tie the Giant up in the Bean-Stalk

George Cruikshank, best known for illustrating Charles Dickens and the first English edition of the Grimm Brothers' tales, also produced a group of controversial tales that were marred by his excessive moralizing. In one of these, *The History of Jack & the Bean-Stalk* (1854), he contrasts the rugged fury of the doomed giant descending from his kingdom in the sky with the airy freedom of the fairies who help Jack.

oven." And they both rushed to the oven. But Jack wasn't there, luckily, and the ogre's wife said: "There you are again with your fee-fi-fo-fum. Why of course it's the boy you caught last night that I've just broiled for your breakfast. How forgetful I am, and how careless you are not to know the difference between live and dead after all these years."

So the ogre sat down to the breakfast and ate it, but every now and then he would mutter: "Well, I could have sworn—" and he'd get up and search the larder and the cupboards, and everything, only luckily he didn't think of the copper.

After breakfast was over, the ogre called out: "Wife, wife, bring me my golden harp." So she brought it and put it on the table before him. Then he said: "Sing!" and the golden harp sang most beautifully. And it went on singing till the ogre fell asleep, and commenced to snore like thunder.

Then Jack lifted up the copper-lid very quietly and got down like a mouse and crept on hands and knees till he came to the table when up he crawled, caught hold of the golden harp and dashed with it towards the door. But the harp called out quite loud: "Master! Master!" and the ogre woke up just in time to see Jack running off with his harp.

Jack ran as fast as he could, and the ogre came rushing after, and would soon have caught him only Jack had a start and dodged him a bit and knew where he was going. When he got to the beanstalk the ogre was not more than twenty yards away when suddenly he saw Jack disappear like, and when he came to the end of the road he saw Jack underneath climbing down for dear life. Well, the ogre didn't like trusting himself to such a ladder, and he stood and waited, so Jack got another start. But just then the harp cried out: "Master! master!" and the ogre swung himself down on to the beanstalk which shook with his weight. Down climbs Jack, and after him climbed the ogre. By this time Jack had climbed down and climbed down and climbed down till he was very nearly home. So he called out: "Mother! mother! bring me an axe, bring me an axe." And his mother came rushing out with the axe in her hand, but when she came to the beanstalk she stood stock still with fright for there she saw the ogre with his legs just through the clouds.

But Jack jumped down and got hold of the axe and gave a chop at the beanstalk which cut it half in two. The ogre felt the beanstalk shake and quiver so he stopped to see what was the matter. Then Jack gave another chop with the axe, and the beanstalk was cut in two and began to topple over. Then the ogre fell down and broke his crown, and the beanstalk came toppling after.

Then Jack showed his mother his golden harp, and what with showing that and selling the golden eggs, Jack and his mother became very rich, and he married a great princess, and they lived happy ever after.

Appalachian Folktale

Richard Chase (1904–88) a native of northern Alabama, devoted his life to collecting, performing, and preserving British American folklore. As he combined and revised tales from rural storytellers in North Carolina, Kentucky, and Virginia, he acknowledged that he had "taken a free hand in the re-telling,"[1] using his own storytelling experience when preparing tales to publish. His best-known books, *The Jack Tales* (1943), *Grandfather Tales* (1948), and *American Folk Tales and Songs* (1956), are still among the most popular folktale collections in America. Chase and James Taylor Adams (1892–1954), of Wise County, Virginia, both worked for the federal Works Progress Administration in the 1930s and 1940s. The folklore archives in southwestern Virginia of the James Taylor Adams Collection contain many hundreds of items that they collected and typed, most of which have never been published.

This version of "Munsmeg," labeled with Richard Chase's name and no date, is similar to "Mutsmag" in *Grandfather Tales*. There Chase lists a number of oral sources, including Adams and Cratis D. Williams, a prominent scholar and storyteller in Boone, North Carolina, whose great-grandmother had told the tale in early nineteenth-century Virginia.[2] Williams's writings about the difficult lives of his grandmothers help us imagine how satisfying Mutsmag's triumph would have seemed to them. Virginia novelist Lee Smith also heard "Mutsmag" told in her childhood, and her protagonist Ivy Rowe is influenced by an unusual version of the tale she hears as a child, in the compelling 1988 novel for adults, *Fair and Tender Ladies*. This tale is still told orally by regional storytellers, and it was adapted in the live-action film *Mutzmag* by Virginia filmmaker Tom Davenport in 1992, as well as the script by R. Rex Stephenson reprinted here.

In the text below, where the faded typed manuscript is illegible, uncertain words are enclosed in square brackets. Only a few editorial changes have been made to correct obvious typographical errors. Spellings that reflect the regional dialect of the storyteller have not been altered.

NOTES

1. Richard Chase, Preface, *Grandfather Tales* (Boston: Houghton Mifflin, 1948) vii.
2. Cratis D. Williams, "Mutts Mag," *Tales from Sacred Wind: Coming of Age in Appalachia,* eds. David Cratis Williams and Patricia D. Beaver. (Jefferson, NC: McFarland, 2003) 72–83.

Munsmeg

COLLECTED BY RICHARD CHASE

One time there was an old woman who had three girls, Poll and Betz and Munsmeg. Munsmeg was the youngest and they treated her mean. She wasn't pretty like her sisters, and they called her Roughface.

Well, the old woman died and about all she had was a cabbage patch and a big old knife. She left the cabbage to Poll and Betz and left Munsmeg nothing but that ol' knife. Poll and Betz started in eatin' that cabbage, didn't let Munsmeg have any of it, made her eat mush and ashcakes. Then directly they'd eat up all the cabbage so Poll and Betz decided they'd make some journey-cakes and pack up and go a great journey to seek their fortune. Munsmeg wanted to go with 'em but they told her she couldn't So Munsmeg begged and begged and finally they told her, said,

"All right, old Roughface, but you'll have to fix your own johhnycakes. Here, go get you some water in this."

And they handed her a riddle. (That's an old-time sifter—a thing all full of holes.)

So Munsmeg took the riddle and ran down to the spring and she'd dig up water and it 'uld all run out, dip it up, it 'uld all run out, dip it up, it 'uld all run out. Then a little bluebird lit on a limb and sang out,

> "Stop it with moss and stick it with clay,
> You can pack your riddle of water away."

Then Munsmeg daubed it with moss and smeared it with clay and brought the riddle back full of water. So her sisters *had* to let her go. But when they got everything fixed up and were about to start, they snatched Munsmeg's sack of journeycakes away from her and grabbed her and fastened her up in an old ash house, and went on and left her behind.

Munsmeg tried every way to get out of that ash-house but her sisters had pulled the latch string out, and finally she set in to hollerin' for somebody to come let her out. An old fox heard her and he came to the ash-house door, says,

"Who's in there, and what d'ye want?"

"It's me, Munsmeg, and I want out."

"Pull the latch string."

"Ain't none. You push the latch up."

"What'll you give me?"

"I'll take ye to a fine flock of geese."

Then the old fox pushed the latch up and Munsmeg got out. She took the old fox over to the place where the geese were and he thanked her, and she went on and caught up with Poll and Betz.

So they went on and went on and it [got dark and the] next house they came to they called and asked to stay all night. An old woman came to the door and told 'em to come on in. She had three girls there. So they all ate supper and the old woman told Poll and Betz and Munsmeg they could go up in the loft and be with her girls. Poll and Betz went on to sleep but Munsmeg stayed awake and watched the old woman through a knot hole in the floor.

Now they didn't know it but that old woman was a witch and her old man was a giant. And directly he came in home with a lot of people under his arm. He throwed 'em down in the floor for the old woman to cook up for him, hung up his hat on the peg, and sat down by the fire. Then he throwed up his head and got to smellin' this way and that, says,

"FEE, FO, FUM!
I SMELL THE BLOOD OF AN IRISHMAN!"

"Hush up! You'll wake up these three fine fat pullets I've got for your supper."

So she told him about the three girls asleep in the loft, and he asked her how he'd know 'em from the other girls.

"My girls have got lockets on their necks. You can feel of 'em and tell that way."

So Munsmeg slipped over quick to where the girls were and changed the lockets to her neck and her sisters! Then she laid down and went to snorin'. The old giant came and felt for the lockets. He grabbed the old woman's girls and slit their throats, and threw 'em down the scuttle hole to the old woman. Then he got down the ladder and there stood the old woman mad as a hornet.

"Just look now!" she says to him, "You've gone and killed the wrong ones."

And she lit in to beatin' the old giant with the poker. So while all that was goin' on Munsmeg took her old knife and cut up the sheets and tied 'em together. Then she knocked a hole in the shingles and cut the sheet rope out and she and her sisters got away.

They came to the King's house, and the King invited 'em in, asked 'em to eat supper and stay the night. He got to askin' 'em who they were and where they came from and where they were travellin' to and Munsmeg told him about what all happened at the old giant's house. So the King told Munsmeg, says,

"I'd like mighty well to get shet of him and his old woman. They've killed a sight of folks around here. I'll pay anybody two bushels of gold for him and another bushel for the old woman, to go down there and kill either one of 'em, or both."

So Munsmeg went back to the old giant's house that night and cloomb up on the chimney with a poke of salt. The old woman had a pot of meat on the fire a-cookin' and Munsmeg sprinkled ever' bit of that salt down in it.

The old giant started in eatin'.

"OLD WOMAN, THE MEAT'S TOO SALTY."

"Why, I never put in but one pinch."

"I CAN'T HELP THAT. [FETCH ME] SOME WATER [HERE]."

"There ain't a bit of water up."

"GO TO [THE] SPRING AND DIP US SOME."

"Hit's too dark."

"GET OUT YOUR LIGHT-BALL."

So the old woman threw out her light-ball towards the spring, but about the time she got a good piece from the house Munsmeg had stuck her old knife into that light-ball and run with it and squinched it in the spring water, and the old woman stumped her toe in the dark and fell head foremost right in the spring and drownded.

Then Munsmeg went back to the King and he paid her that bushel of gold.

Then the King says to her, says, "Now he's got a fine horse down there, the old giant has, and if you bring me that horse I'll pay you another bushel of gold. And if you should happen to kill that giant, that'll make three bushels for ye."

Munsmeg went back to the giant's place and looked in the stable. She saw that the old giant had his horse belled. Well, she hadn't figured out how to kill the old giant yet, so she thought she'd try gettin' his horse. She threw some barley in the trough, and the horse threw up his head. The bell went—

"Tingle! Tingle!"

and the old giant came runnin' out. Munsmeg hid under the trough. The giant looked around, went on back. The horse ate that barley up 'fore Munsmeg could untie the halter rope, so she threw in another handful of barley. The horse went for it.

"Tingle! Tingle!"

And here came the old giant. Munsmeg hid behind the stable door. The giant came in the stable that time but he didn't notice anything and went on back. Munsmeg worked at that knot hard as she could but the horse got the barley eat up and started rar'in' at the halter rope so Munsmeg had to throw in some more barley to make him stand.

"Tingle! Tingle."

And the old giant came so fast Munsmeg had to hide under the bresh of the horse's tail. But that time the giant had him a lantern lit and he started lookin' all around and directly he ran his hand under the horse's belly, felt of his hind legs, says,

"YOU GOT TOO MANY LEGS BACK HERE, OLD HORSE."

And just about that time the horse switched his tail and there was Munsmeg. She made for the door but the old giant grabbed her, says,

"NOW I'VE GOT YE."

"What you goin' to do with me."

"I DON'T KNOW YET. HAIN'T MADE UP MY MIND."

"Please don't feed me on honey and butter. I just can't stand the taste of honey and butter."

"HONEY AND BUTTER IS ALL YOU'LL GIT."

So he kept her about two weeks and made her eat all the honey and butter she could hold. Munsmeg just loved honey and butter. Then one day he told her, says,

"I'M GOIN' TO KILL YE TODAY."

"How you goin' to kill me?" she asked him.

"DON'T KNOW," he says, "HAIN'T MADE UP MY MIND."

"Please don't tie me up in a sack and beat me to death," she told him. "It 'uld make me howl like a dog and squall like cats, and my bones 'uld rattle like pewter dishes, and my blood 'uld drip like honey."

The old giant got him a big pole.

"I'M GOIN' TO PUT YOU [RIGHT] IN THIS VERY SACK," he says, "AND BEAT YOU TO DEATH." And he put her in and hung her up on the kitchen wall and took up his club.

"Wait a minute," says Munsmeg.

"WHAT FOR?" he asked her.

"I want to pray for my sins. You go out and tend to your horse so I can have time to pray for forgiveness for all the meanness I've done."

The old giant went out to the stable to feed and water his horse. And soon as he was gone Munsmeg took her old knife and cut out of the sack. Then she caught the old giant's dog and his cats and got all his dishes and a big pot of honey and put all that in the poke, and sewed it up and tied it back just like it was. Then she hid behind the door.

The old giant came back in and got his club and drawed back—hit one lick. His dog howled.

"OH YES, I'LL MAKE YOU HOWL LIKE A DOG."

Then he hit another lick. Them cats just squalled. The giant grinned.

"OH, I'LL MAKE YE SQUALL LIKE CATS."

Then he hit it several licks and broke all his dishes. He grinned again.

"OH, I'LL MAKE YOUR BONES RATTLE LIKE PEWTER DISHES."

This time he drawed way back and hit it an awful hard lick. That pot honey broke and it started drippin' out. That nearly tickled him to death.

"OH, YES," he says, "I'LL MAKE YOUR BLOOD RUN AND DRIP LIKE HONEY."

Then he throwed down his club and untied the sack. There was his dog and all his cats killed and his pewter dishes all broken up, and his big pot of honey broke. He was so mad he nearly busted.

And while he had been a-doin' all that Munsmeg had run to the stable and saddled and bridled his horse and started ridin' off. The old giant took out after her. He trailed the horse till he came to a big river, and there was Munsmeg on the other side, sittin on a millstone with the halter rope around her neck.

"HOW'D YOU GET OVER THERE?"

"I pecked a hole in this rock and tied a rope around my neck and floated across."

So the old giant he started pickin' a hole in a rock and when he got through it he got a rope and tied one end in the hole and the other end to his neck and took that rock up and threw it in the river. The rope jerked him after the rock and carried him right to the bottom. And that was the last of the old giant.

So Munsmeg went on back to the King's house and got her three bushels of gold and she was well off the rest of her life. And Poll and Betz got so mad about Munsmeg gettin' all that money they went on back home and raised 'em some more cabbage, and died old maids.

R. Rex Stephenson (b. 1943)

"Mutsmag" and "Munsmeg" provide a final illustration in this section of the relationship between stories that are taken directly from oral traditions and adaptations by contemporary writers, in this case a playwright. As several selections in this section demonstrate, the oral tradition behind this drama is one of the richest in America, for "Mutsmag" is one of many folktales that were brought to the southern Appalachian Mountains by Scots-Irish immigrants and other European settlers from the eighteenth to the twentieth centuries. Retold by generations of mountain storytellers, the tales blend Old World folktale motifs with elements of regional American culture and dialect.

R. Rex Stephenson, professor of drama at Ferrum College, has written many plays that are based on folklore, history, and classic works of children's literature, such as *Treasure Island, The Jungle Book,* and *Alice in Wonderland.* In 1975, after his daughter brought home a copy of *The Jack Tales* by Richard Chase, Stephenson began to dramatize Appalachian folktales using the story theatre method, a style that lies between storytelling and an acted-out play. A narrator makes some sound effects, and the actors use few costumes or props as they portray human characters, animals, and objects. Stephenson consulted with Chase and obtained unpublished versions of folktales from archives and oral storytellers. Since 1975, the Jack Tale Players, a group of student and professional actors directed by Stephenson, have performed regularly for audiences of all ages in southern Virginia and have traveled to other states and England.

"Ashpet" (related to "Ashputtle" and "Cinderella"), "Mutsmag," and "The Three Old Women's Bet" are Appalachian tales adapted by Stephenson in 1998–2001 that focus on female protagonists instead of the folk hero Jack. As storytellers often do, Stephenson changed some details, and he blended motifs from related folktales more in "Mutsmag" than he had in earlier adaptations. Using the oral tale "Munsmeg" as his primary source, he expanded the traits that make Mutsmag, like other Appalachian heroes and contemporary heroines, less dependent on magic help than her European counterparts and more reliant on her own wits and resourcefulness, as well as gifts inherited from her dying mother. This tale is related to "Molly Whuppie," a tale of English and Celtic origins about a poor but brave girl who defeats a cannibalistic giant and his wife. Molly is comparable to Jack the giant killer in many British and American folktales, while boys named Nippy and Merrywise have similar adventures in other American tales. Stephenson's ending is a compromise between variants of this tale with the traditional conclusion of marriage to a prince and those with monetary rewards but no marriage. In 2002,

Stephenson adapted his "Mutsmag" script as a story published on the web site *AppLit,* with illustrations drawn by Virginia schoolchildren. In 2004 it was published in *Grandmother Tales,* a longer play retelling "Ashpet" and "Mutsmag" within a frame story.

Stephenson said that he likes to dramatize folktales about girls because "a father of girls is always interested in strong female characters. You hope all your kids would turn out like Mutsmag, would stand up to people and make right decisions based on what they want out of life rather than what is expected of them" (October 1, 2001).

Mutsmag

STAGING AND SCENE IDEAS

No set is required, although a painted drop of the Blue Ridge Mountains creates a nice background. Almost no furniture and few props are required; it is basically up to the actors to create objects, setting, and place with the use of their bodies.

While the script calls for at least 27 different characters and objects, three actors can play 19 of these roles. Thus, only three actors portray "the house," "the cabbage patch buyers," "the trees," "the doorway," "the One-Eyed Gang," "the Three Ugly Sisters," etc. By clever use of a minimum of costumes, several wigs, and the actor's voice and body, this repetitive use of only three actors not only surprises but also fascinates an audience. The key here is a presentational style of acting in which the actor selects one element of the character or object and makes it so recognizable that the audience visualizes the tree or the fireplace as well as the Ugly Sisters.

Two actors create the two-headed giant, one on the other's shoulders. Both actors speak the lines in unison and their movements and facial expressions should be in sync. (See photograph.)

Costumes should be minimal. If the actors all wear simple outfits such as blue jeans and checked shirts, Mutsmag's Mother can simply add an apron to create her character, The One-Eyed Gang should add a patch over one eye, and the Three Ugly Sisters add ugly wigs and maybe grossly tacky skirts.

CAST

Narrator
Mother
Mutsmag
Poll
Betts
Old Woman
Giant

Undertaker, One-Eyed Gang, trees, Three Ugly Sisters, King, Prince, etc. all can be played by three actors.

NARRATOR: This is a story about a girl named Mutsmag. *(She enters.)* Some people call her Muncimeg, and back over in England they called her Molly Whuppie, but it is all the same girl. Now she had two sisters, Poll and Betts. *(They enter.)* They were older than she was and they didn't like Mutsmag a lick. *(The two sisters pantomime trying to hit Mutsmag. She ducks and they hit each other. Sound effect: cowbell. They fall; Mutsmag rises and smiles.)* Now these three girls lived with their mother *(Mother enters.)* in a little house that had a cabbage patch. Our story begins when their mother is about ready to die.

MOTHER: Girls, I think I am going to die.

MUTSMAG: Oh, mother, please don't die. I don't know what I would do without you.

(Poll crosses to Mother. She is not the least concerned with her poor health.)

The Jack Tale Players of Ferrum College use two actors talking in unison to create a two-headed giant, here plotting with his mean old wife while Mutsmag and her sisters sleep behind them.

POLL: When you die, what do we get? What do I get?

MOTHER: I guess, Poll, you can have my house. And, if you take care of it, it will take care of you.

(Betts approaches, afraid she will get cheated.)

BETTS: Then what will I get?

MOTHER: I guess you can have my cabbage patch, Betts. If you take care of it, it will take care of you.

POLL: So if I get the house and Betts gets the cabbage patch, that leaves nothin' for Mutsmag.

BETTS: Good, I don't like her anyway. Mother, do you think you will be dead before sundown? If you can do that for me, then I can sell the cabbage patch and be off to seek my fortune.

POLL: And I can sell the house and go with you to seek my fortune. And Mutsmag will have nothin' so she can't go with us. Do you think you are going to die in the next hour or so? Could you hurry it up?

MOTHER: *(She crosses to Mutsmag.)* Mutsmag, I am sorry. I have nothin' for you but this old rusty knife.

(She hands Mutsmag the knife.) If you take care of it, it will take care of you.

NARRATOR: And then she died.

(Mother staggers around a little bit and Betts goes off for help.)

MOTHER: Children, I am dead.

(Betts has brought back help: this is an undertaker for Mother, who carries her off.)

NARRATOR: And they no more buried her when the girls sold the house and the cabbage patch. *(Enter two buyers and they pantomime purchasing the property from the two girls; they exchange money.)*

BETTS: Let's be off, sister.

MUTSMAG: What about me? I got no place to live and no money. I got nothin' but this old knife.

POLL: That's right, you got nothin'. *(Poll and Betts start walking away from Mutsmag.)*

MUTSMAG: *(To the audience.)* I'll just follow.

(She goes behind them and actors appear as forest and bushes.)

NARRATOR: And that is exactly what Mutsmag did. But she didn't get too close 'cause she knew how mean her sisters were. *(Mutsmag sneezes.)*

POLL: Did you hear something?

(They look around.)

BETTS: Sounded like something was behind us.

(Mutsmag hides behind tree.)

POLL: Must have been our imagination. Let's go on.

(All walk a step or two; Mutsmag stumbles.)

POLL: Did you hear something?

BETTS: *(Mutsmag becomes part of a tree.)* Sounded like something was behind us.

(They look, but are fooled by her using her body as part of the tree.)

POLL: Must have been our imagination. *(And they walk on; Mutsmag follows.)* I know there is someone following us.

BETTS: Me too. Quick, hide behind this bush and we will catch them.

(Poll and Betts hide behind bush, then jump out when Mutsmag walks by.)

POLL: We told you not to follow us, Mutsmag.

BETTS: You got no money, nothin'. And besides, we never liked you anyway.

MUTSMAG: Please? Please, let me go with you.

POLL: Nope. That's final. Nope.

MUTSMAG: I'll just keep following you and there is nothin' you can do about it, so there.

POLL: Mutsmag, I oughta punch you right in the nose.

(The forest turns into a doorway; two actors create the doorframe and the other uses his body to make the door.)

BETTS: *(After seeing the doorway, Betts gets an idea.)* Why can't she go with us? *(She crosses the doorway.)* I've always sort of liked her. She was always good to do our laundry, wash the dishes, and tend the cabbage patch.

POLL: Are you serious? *(She doesn't know that Betts has a plan.)*

MUTSMAG: Oh, thank you, Betts. *(Coming to her.)* Thank you.

BETTS: Let's rest here and make some cabbage sandwiches. Mutsmag, you go in this little house that only has *one door* and *no windows* and use your knife to fix us somethin' to eat.

(Poll has finally caught on.)

POLL: Yes, Mutsmag, why don't you go in this cabin that has only *one door, no windows, and a great big lock* and fix us somethin' to eat.

MUTSMAG: Oh, I would love to. You two are the best sisters in the whole wide world.

BETTS: Quick, lock the door.

(Poll locks door.)

POLL: Now Mutsmag, you are trapped and we can go on our way without you.

MUTSMAG: *(From behind the doorway.)* But what is going to happen to me? I am all alone with no food or water, locked in this cabin.

POLL: I don't know and I don't care!

BETTS: Maybe you will die. *(Betts and Poll laugh and then exit.)*

NARRATOR: Now Mutsmag just sat down on the floor of that cabin and commenced to cry and cry. But do you know whose cabin that was? Why, it belonged to a whole band of ornery robbers. *(Cabin turns into the robbers. Robbers swing around. They have a patch over one eye; one has a gun, or a sword.)* And they were called "The One-Eyed Gang."

ROBBER 1: What are you doing in our cabin?

MUTSMAG: My sisters locked me in.

ROBBER 2: Well, we best kill her and be done with it.

ROBBER 3: Unless she has something to buy her freedom with.

MUTSMAG: I got nothin' but this rusty old knife. Which is the total inheritance from my dear departed Ma.

ROBBER 1: That ain't worth nothin'. I am sorry about this, but you are going to have to die.

(They are really sad about it, but a robber must do what is expected of him.)

ROBBER 2: You understand, don't you?

ROBBER 3: We'll bury you with your knife if that makes you feel any better.

MUTSMAG: *(Robbers start toward her.)* Wait! Wait! What if I can tell you where you can get some cash money?

ROBBER 2: Then we might not kill you.

ROBBER 1: No, then we wouldn't have to kill ya! We *could,* but we wouldn't have to!

ROBBER 3: We would, however, have to vote on it. We are often called the "Democratic One-Eyed Gang."

ROBBER 1: All in favor of not killing Mutsmag if she tells where we can get some cash money, say "Aye."

ALL: Aye *(Including Mutsmag.)*

ROBBER 1: All those in favor of killing her say "Aye."

ROBBER 2: Aye.

MUTSMAG: He voted twice. *(Pointing to Robber 2.)*

ROBBER 1: Did you vote twice?

ROBBER 2: I am sorry. I just get so excited. You know how I love to vote.

MUTSMAG: It doesn't make any difference. The vote was 4 to 1. *(Robbers look around and count themselves.)* I voted.

ALL: Oh . . . *(Now they understand.)*

MUTSMAG: Now here's where to get the money. My sisters, that locked me in this cabin, they sold my ma's house and cabbage patch for cash money and they are walkin' down this here road.

ROBBER 1: I know a short cut. Let's be off ta get that cash money. *(They start to exit.)*

MUTSMAG: Wait! First, you've got to promise me not to kill them. Not that they shouldn't be killed, but they are my sisters. All the kin I got in the world.

ROBBER 1: Well, I don't know about that.

ROBBER 2: No. We don't know about that.

ROBBER 3: We have to vote on it.

MUTSMAG: I will tell you their names, which will make it much easier for you to rob them. They won't be suspicious, you see, just curious.

ROBBER 1: Let's vote. Do it by a show of hands this time. All in favor of not killin' the mean sisters even though they ought to be killed, raise your hand. *(All raise their right hand.)* All in favor of killing the means sisters 'cause they ought to be killed raise your hand.

(Robber 2 raises left hand. Everyone looks at him.)

ROBBER 2: Well, this hand didn't get to vote this first time. *(He slowly lowers his hand.)*

ROBBER 1: So we don't kill them. Let's go rob them.

MUTSMAG: You could do me one favor, though. After you rob them and swear that you're not going to kill them, could you tie them up to a tree?

(The robbers nod and are off.)

NARRATOR: Now the robbers knew a shortcut and they stole all the sisters' money *(They pantomime action described by Narrator.)* and they tied them up to a tree. *(One of the robbers becomes the tree.)* After they had been out there in the hot sun for two or three hours, along came Mutsmag.

MUTSMAG: Hello, sisters. *(Trying to act surprised.)* Fancy meetin' you here.

BETTS: Mutsmag, we were robbed.

POLL: And tied to this here tree.

BETTS: And left out in the boiling sun.

MUTSMAG: *(Walking around tree.)* Well, I wondered about that. I would think bein' tied to a tree would be right uncomfortable.

BETTS: Get us loose!

POLL: Yes, get us loose . . .

MUTSMAG: *(Interrupting.)* Then you don't like bein' tied to that tree.

BETTS: No, you idiot. Now, get us loose.

MUTSMAG: *(She pulls out her knife.)* Ask nicely.

POLL & BETTS: *(In mean voice; they cannot be nice to her.)* Sister cut us loose. Please!

MUTSMAG: That didn't sound very nice to me. I would think that unless you two wanted to spend forever tied to this tree, you could be nicer to your baby sister.

BETTS: Never! Never! Never!

MUTSMAG: Then I'll be on my way. *(She starts off.)*

POLL & BETTS: *(Nicely this time.)* Please cut us loose, Sister.

POLL: Pretty please . . .

MUTSMAG: One more thing. You gotta promise I can go with you.

POLL & BETTS: *(Nicely.)* We promise. *(Meanly.)* Cut us free!

(She frees them from the tree.)

NARRATOR: Off the three girls walked. And when it started to get dark they came upon a house. *(They pantomime the action described by Narrator.)* When they knocked on the door, *(Old Woman enters with a lantern or a candle.)* this ugly Old Woman invited them in.

OLD WOMAN: Step into the light. Step out of the dark. *(Sound effect: creaky door opening.)* You sure are three pretty young and tender things.

POLL: Will you feed us?

BETTS: Yes, we are right hungry.

OLD WOMAN: Feed you? That's what you want. I don't know; my man's not home. A fragile, defenseless woman like me ought to be careful 'bout who she lets in.

POLL: We're trustworthy. We just want shelter from the dark and food for our stomachs.

OLD WOMAN: Yes. Yes, I see. But to cook for the three of you?

POLL: No. No. This is our servant girl, Mutsmag. She would be happy to cook all the food, wash all the dishes, and clean your entire house.

MUTSMAG: Servant girl? Me?

BETTS: And a mighty fine servant girl she be, too.

OLD WOMAN: Good. I could use some help. Girls! *(She calls out.)* Girls! *(The Ugly Sisters enter; they are even uglier than the Old Woman.)* These are my three lovely daughters. They can cook just fine, but what they fix is usually awful.

SISTER 1: It's her fault she uses too much salt.

SISTER 2: No, it's her fault she uses too much pepper.

SISTER 3: It's not my fault if they don't like salt and pepper.

OLD WOMAN: Come Mutsmag, I will show you to the kitchen. And you girls stay here and entertain each other. *(Secretly to her daughters.)* And see if you can discover any important information about these three girls that seem all alone in the mountains. *(She and Mutsmag exit.)*

SISTER 1: *(To Betts.)* Got any family?

BETTS: Nope.

SISTER 2: Then no one would miss you, if you sort of . . . uh, disappeared.

POLL: Not a soul.

SISTER 3: Have you talked to anybody along the way?

POLL: Only some robbers that stole our money.

SISTER 1: All alone and poor.

BETTS: I have a question for you. Do you have a pa?

SISTERS: Yes. *(They cackle knowingly.)*

POLL: When do we meet him?

SISTER 2: Sooner than you would like.

SISTER 1 & 3: Yes, yes. *(They cackle as before.)*

NARRATOR: Meanwhile, Mutsmag had made them all a fine dinner and they ate their fill. And just before they went up to the loft to go to sleep, the Old Woman gave each of her three daughters something.

OLD WOMAN: All of you will go to sleep in the loft and I want to give my three pretties these lockets to wear tonight. *(She hands them lockets.)*

SISTER 1: Why do we have to wear lockets to bed?

OLD WOMAN: Because I want you to! I am your mother. Don't argue with me.

SISTER 2: They will get all tangled up around our necks and I won't be able to get my beauty sleep.

SISTER 3: *(She holds locket up.)* It will probably make me choke.

OLD WOMAN: Believe me, these lockets will keep you three safe.

3 SISTERS: Keep us three safe?

OLD WOMAN: Now to the loft and good night.

(Old Woman exits; all girls either lie down or stand up stage right. A quilt could help to suggest a bed. They stand behind it in the medieval fashion of a comic bed.)

NARRATOR: It weren't long till five of those six girls were fast asleep. *(Five of the girls snore.)* However, Mutsmag had found something curious.

MUTSMAG: *(She is talking to herself.)* "Lockets keep you *three* safe." Does that mean that if we don't have lockets, we won't be safe? I don't trust that old woman. *(Mutsmag is trying to figure out a way to get the lockets. She starts singing "Froggy Went a Courtin'" in hopes of waking up her sisters. At first they join her even though they are still asleep. Finally Mutsmag almost shouts the song to wake them up. All the girls wake up.)*

BETTS: What are you doing?

MUTSMAG: I can't sleep

POLL: Try somethin' else.

BETTS: Count sheep.

ALL SISTERS: Yes. Count sheep!

MUTSMAG: *(Mutsmag becomes a sheep. She jumps over an imaginary fence and "Baas.")* That's one. *(She keeps this up, trying to wake up her sisters by getting louder each time, until . . .)*

EVERYONE: *(They sit up.)* What are you doin'?

MUTSMAG: I was counting sheep.

POLL: We can't sleep with you jumping and baaing.

MUTSMAG: *(She is putting her plan into action, but in a very coy manner.)* Maybe, if I had one of those pretty lockets, that would help me sleep.

SISTER 3: She can have mine; it tangles around my neck anyway.

MUTSMAG: *(She gets the locket.)* Thank you, thank you. *(All lie back down to go to sleep.)* One more problem.

EVERYONE: *(All jump up.)* What now?

MUTSMAG: Since I am their "servant girl," it wouldn't be right for me to have a locket and for them *(Meaning her sisters.)* not to have a locket.

POLL: She's right!

BETTS: For once she's absolutely right. We want a locket, too!

SISTER 1: Here, take my locket.

SISTER 2: And mine, too. It was interfering with my beauty sleep.

SISTER 3: Daddy will be home shortly. *(All three evil sisters laugh knowingly.)* We all need to be asleep. *(They laugh again.)*

NARRATOR: Five of the girls slept and one pretended. Of course, you know the one pretending; that was Mutsmag. And you probably already figured out that that old Woman was plannin' somethin ornery. And those of you that thought that are right on the money.

(Enter the Giant.)

OLD WOMAN: All right, husband Giant, there's three orphan girls up in the loft. They are mighty tender and will make mighty good eatin'.

GIANT: I like good eatin'. Yup. Good eatin'.

OLD WOMAN: So you go up in the loft, tie 'em up, and put 'em in the shed. And we will have them for Sunday dinner.

GIANT: *(Scratching his head.)* Well, now. How will I know the difference between our three *beautiful* girls and these three girls that are ready for eatin'? 'Cause you know, it's mighty dark up there.

OLD WOMAN: I got that all figgered out. Our beautiful girls are all wearin' lockets.

(Giant crosses to sleeping sisters, who snore loudly. They are still asleep. Old Woman exits.)

NARRATOR: *(Giant action is pantomimed.)* That old Giant felt around until he found those three lockets. *(He is behind Mutsmag and her sisters.)*

GIANT: These are my beautiful daughters. *(Crossing downstage.)*

NARRATOR: And he felt around some more and he said . . .

(Giant crosses back to Ugly Sisters.)

GIANT: And these aren't.

NARRATOR: And so he grabbed them by their hair. *(Ugly Sisters and Giant exit.)* And he took them off to the shed. Tied them up, and left them. Meanwhile . . .

MUTSMAG: Wake up, sisters. There is a giant here that is goin' to kill us and that old woman is going to cook us for Sunday dinner. We have gotta get outta here. Now!

NARRATOR: Believe it or not, for once Poll and Betts followed their sister's advice, which probably saved their life. *(Exit girls.)* Those girls walked and walked until they ended up at the palace of the king. Now the King of Virginia was a mighty nice fella. *(Enter King followed by son. Girls enter and pantomime the story escaping from the Giant.)* Not like those kings you hear about over in Spain or Italy or France or any of those other countries where they don't speak English. And then those girls told him all about their adventures with the Giant and the mean Old Woman. Naturally, though, Poll and Betts took all the credit. The King invited them to stay a spell.

KING: Girls, I have a plan. Now Poll, Betts and Mutsmag, you have been here a week or so and I have been thinking. The way the two of you outsmarted that old Giant and that Old Woman, I wonder if there was a ways you could figure out how to kill them. You know they terrorize my kingdom something fierce.

POLL: No, I don't think, we . . . uh . . . would want to do that.

KING: It would be worth a basket of gold or you could marry my son here, the Prince.

BETTS: Would that mean that someday I could be a Queen?

POLL: I don't think. . . . Uh . . . We want . . . uh . . . To tackle that Giant . . . again. Besides, we need to stay here and take care of our little sister, Mutsmag.

KING: But since the two of you did so well the first time, I am sure you could make short work of him and I would like to keep Mutsmag here to help me with my kingdom. You know she is a pretty bright girl. (*Betts bursts forth with great enthusiasm.*)

BETTS: We'll do it. We will do it!

POLL: (*Taking Betts to side.*) Are you crazy, sister? Take on that Giant?

BETTS: (*Ignoring her sister.*) We need to be off. But we need Mutsmag to carry some supplies for us, if we are to rid your kingdom of that giant.

KING: Go take what you want, Mutsmag. I'll tell you, Mutsmag, I'm sure going to miss you.

PRINCE: (*Smiling.*) Me too!

NARRATOR: (*Mutsmag pantomimes action described by Narrator.*) Now Mutsmag went into the storage shed and she got herself a whole bag full of salt and another bag full of pepper. And off the three of them went towards that Giant's house. (*They exit.*)

KING: Son, I think we should just follow along. Just to see how those two girls kill that Giant and his Old Woman.

PRINCE: Yes, Pa, (*Realizing he is being too informal.*) I mean your Kingship. (*They exit.*)

NARRATOR: Meanwhile, and I bet most of you have already figured this out, Betts and Poll had no intentions of trying to kill that Giant or his Old Woman.

POLL: (*The sisters and Mutsmag enter.*) Mutsmag, we are going to wait here. Now you go off and kill that Giant. Naturally we can't go. We have to make ourselves beautiful, because one of us is going to marry the Prince.

BETTS: So be off, Mutsmag. Kill them nice and tidy like. And be quick about it too!

MUTSMAG: You two are going to stay here?

NARRATOR: Believe me, Mutsmag figured that the killing would fall to her, and she had a plan. It was near suppertime (*Old Woman enters.*) and that Old Woman was fixing' a big pot of stew. (*An actor portrays the pot.*) And Mutsmag took her knife and threw it across the room.

OLD WOMAN: What is that noise? Maybe it is a rat! I can put that in my stew!

(*When she crosses, Mutsmag goes to the pot and holds up the bag of salt.*)

MUTSMAG: I will dump this whole bag of this salt in this stew.

OLD WOMAN: (*She finds knife.*) No rat, just a knife. (*Mutsmag scampers back to her hiding place. Old Woman throws knife in pot.*) I will throw it in the stew anyway. Now to taste it.

NARRATOR: (*Old Woman pantomimes the action.*) Well, when that Old Woman tasted that stew, with all that salt in it, it plum doubled her over. And it got her to coughin' and wheezin', to the point where she thought she was going to die.

OLD WOMAN: I'm dyin'! I'm nearly about to die.

MUTSMAG: (*She crosses to Old Woman.*) I can save ye.

OLD WOMAN: You're that Mutsmag girl that tricked me.

MUTSMAG: That's because my powers are greater than yours and I can save ye.

OLD WOMAN: How? How? I'm dying! I'm dying!

MUTSMAG: This is what you have to do. You need to drink gallons and gallons of a special water that only I know about.

OLD WOMAN: Where? Where is it?

MUTSMAG: You ever heard of the Atlantic Ocean?

OLD WOMAN: No, no, tell me where it is.

MUTSMAG: Believe me, I was countin' on that. You run due east until you come to the biggest body of water you ever seen. It is called the Atlantic Ocean. And you must drink it dry.

OLD WOMAN: I will, I will. (*She exits running through house.*)

NARRATOR: Well believe it or not, that Old Woman ran all the way to the Atlantic Ocean, and darn if she didn't try to drink it all dry. And no one has ever seen her again. Now to be honest, there are some stories that folks have seen her in France, but I don't put much stock in that. Anyway, it was at that moment that the Giant walked into the house.

GIANT: Mutsmag, what you doin' here?

MUTSMAG: I come here to save you from your Old Woman.

GIANT: My Old Woman don't mean me any harm. Besides, I'm bigger than she is.

MUTSMAG: Taste that stew. Hit's got enough salt in it to kill ya.

GIANT: *(Tastes stew.)* Nah, that don't prove nothin'; she never knew how to salt a stew.

MUTSMAG: Look again in that stew. There is an old rusty knife in there. She's plannin' on you swallowin' it and cuttin' up your innards till you died.

GIANT: *(Sees knife, picks it up.)* That could even kill a giant. Where is she now? I'll kill my Old Woman. *(Throws the knife down; Mutsmag picks it up.)*

MUTSMAG: Oh, you can't do that. 'Cause I got her hidden. Oh, wait, hold everything. I am losin' my magical powers. *(She pretends to be weakening. Runs over, picks up pepper, pretends to inhale lots of pepper.)* My powers is comin' back again. I was worried fer a minute.

GIANT: What is that, *(Pointing to the pepper.)* magic powder?

MUTSMAG: Ya see, Giant, the reason I escaped from you before, and the way I sent your old woman packin' off, is 'cause this here powder gives me mystical powers.

GIANT: Give me some of that. I want to try it myself.

MUTSMAG: I couldn't. I just have enough for myself. And besides, a fella as big as you with magical powers would be right dangerous.

GIANT: Let me have it! Let me have it! *(Runs over, takes pepper, starts sniffing; then he begins to sneeze.)*

NARRATOR: You know that old pepper made that Giant sneeze. He sneezed and he sneezed until he sneezed himself in two. *(Two actors making Giant split and roll across the stage: Giant is dead.)* And it was then that the two sisters showed up with the King and the Prince right behind them. *(King, Prince, Poll, and Betts enter from opposite sides of the stage. The King is carrying a basket of gold.)*

KING: Mutsmag, I had a feelin' it was you that was the bright one and not these two sisters of yours. So the choice is yours. Do you want this basket of gold? Or do you want to marry my son the Prince?

MUTSMAG: No offense, King, and none meant to you, Prince, but I am not ready to settle down yet. So I am going to take the basket of gold and seek my fortune over there in the Blue Ridge Mountains.

(Mutsmag exits.)

POLL: Well, if Mutsmag doesn't want you, I sure do.

BETTS: Me too. I would be a good lovin' wife.

(Both kneel and take his hand.)

POLL & BETTS: Will you marry me?

(Prince looking back and forth, then pantomimes the action described by Narrator.)

NARRATOR: You know the Prince never could make up his mind. Finally he decided he didn't want to marry either one of them 'cause they was too mean and too ornery. *(He crosses away from them and to the King.)* I will tell you the truth and, I ain't told this to many folks, but that Prince had a soft spot in his heart for Mutsmag and he hoped some day, if she ever returned, why, she might agree to become his Queen. And that is the story of a spunky girl named Mutsmag.

FURTHER RECOMMENDED READING

VIRGINIA HAMILTON (1936–2002)

THE PEOPLE COULD FLY: AMERICAN BLACK FOLKTALES

Virginia Hamilton was named Virginia because her great-grandmother fled from slavery in Virginia, crossed the Ohio River on the Underground Railroad in the 1850s, and then disappeared. Her son often retold this story to his descendants on the family farmland in central Ohio. His granddaughter Virginia, who spent most of her life there, inherited his gift of storytelling, becoming one of the most influential writers for children in the second half of the twentieth century. The first African American writer to win the American Newbery Medal and the international Hans Christian Andersen award, Hamilton wrote nearly forty books for children and young adults, using innovative combinations of realism, biography, history, science fiction, magic realism, and fantasy. She spoke eloquently about the need to create a "hopescape" for children who are coping with troubled histories and to celebrate parallel cultures (not minority and majority cultures) in our society.[1] Hamilton's folklore collections, beautifully illustrated by prominent artists, made valuable contributions to the growing body of multicultural books that were available by the end of the twentieth century.

A variety of tales in *The People Could Fly: American Black Folktales* (1985) represent African American oral traditions. Believing that the tales should be read out loud to all ages, Hamilton said she told them in her own voice, using "a reasonably colloquial language or dialect" (pp. xi–xii). Among the multitude of animal trickster tales told by African Americans and Native Americans, the Tar Baby story is the most popular, with a rabbit trickster hero who uses reverse psychology to escape a sticky trap. "Tappin, the Land Turtle" is one of many *pourquoi* tales about why turtles or tortoises appear to have cracked shells (see the African version by Chinua Achebe in this section). "The Peculiar Such

Thing" is a scary story also known as "Tailypo." "Little Eight John" is a cautionary tale about the fate of disobedient children. In "A Wolf and Little Daughter," a child faces danger as a result of disobeying, but she uses the magical, mythic power of music to protect herself, providing a refreshing alternative to traditional girl versus wolf tales such as "Little Red Riding Hood" (see Charles Perrault in Part 1 and Roald Dahl in Part 7).

"Papa John's Tall Tale," unlike the type of tall tales with heroes of superhuman size and physical power (such as "John Henry"), depicts ordinary people in a plot with nonsensical exaggeration about an impossibly fast horse and gigantic vegetables. Several other tales with heroes named John or Jack, including John de Conquer, resemble European American Jack tales and other world folktales in which the hero outwits the devil or overcomes other obstacles. "The People Could Fly" is a most painful and beautiful tale of magic and wish fulfillment about slaves and their longings for freedom and home. As in the myth "Daedalus and Icarus," a secret knowledge of flying is used for escape, but this legend and others in the final section of Hamilton's book are associated with the historical period of the African slave trade. Her Introduction notes "that these folktales were once a creative way for an oppressed people to express their fears and hopes to one another." They "were created out of sorrow," but they "belong to all of us," and "we must look on the tales as a celebration of the human spirit" (p. xii).

NOTE

1. Virginia Hamilton, "Ah, Sweet Rememory!" *The Horn Book* (1981), *Innocence and Experience: Essays and Conversations on Children's Literature,* ed. Barbara Harrison and Gregory Maguire (New York: Lothrop, Lee & Shepard, 1987) 6–12.

PART 4

REALISM AND FANTASY

Shams and delusions are esteemed for soundest truths, while reality is fabulous. If men would steadfastly observe realities only, and not allow themselves to be deluded, life, to compare it with such things as we know, would be like a fairy tale and the Arabian Nights' Entertainments.

Henry David Thoreau, *Walden*

Henry David Thoreau, like his British predecessor William Wordsworth, recognized that the most common everyday experiences and objects are imbued with a magical quality and that "children, who play life, discern its true law and relations more clearly than men." Wordsworth believed that children, because they came into the world "trailing clouds of glory" from heaven, "from God, who is our home," are either peculiarly susceptible to this magic or project something of their own radiance onto their surroundings (see "Ode: Intimations of Immortality" in Part 2). Wordsworth's conception of the child as a visionary, prophet, or seer, while extreme, anticipated the view that came to prevail in the nineteenth century—that not only could children be trusted to read fairy tales and fantasy stories, but such fare was uniquely suited to their stage in life. Furthermore, many educators and writers came to believe that if children were denied access to the realm of the imagination, they would confuse such "shams and delusions" as material progress and scientific advancement with the "soundest truths" and find that indeed a glory had departed from the earth. Writers of the Victorian and Edwardian periods, commonly regarded as the Golden Age of children's literature, recognized, as Bruno Bettelheim was to do several generations later, the power of fantasy to convey the deepest psychological and spiritual truths and to dramatize the most profound psychological and ethical dilemmas.

The four critical essays in this section explain why adults have not always approved of fantasy in books for children—or of genuine realism, either, before or after the Golden Age. As Elizabeth Segel points out in "Realism and Children's Literature," writers of pre–Golden Age "nonfantasy fiction" did not want children to form their own judgments about right and wrong through exposure to psychological realism or learn about cultural diversity or social problems as contemporary children do, except within the limits of the conventional morality that their literature was designed to instill. Segel provides a useful short history of realism as it developed in literature for adults and eventually in literature for children. The essay by C. W. Sullivan III similarly provides a brief overview of the history of fantasy. The selections by Ursula K. LeGuin and Perry Nodelman offer additional insights into adults' resistance to fantasy in modern culture, particularly in North America.

The literature selections throughout this anthology represent wide-ranging variations along the continuum that Sullivan recommends as a way of conceptualizing the terms *fantasy* and *realism* or *mimesis* (imitations of nature or life). For example, Part 1 includes *Little Women* (1868) and *Tom Sawyer* (1876), often considered the first great realistic novels for children, while *Alice in Wonderland* (1865) is a landmark in the development of fantasy fiction for children in English. Gary Paulsen's *The Island* (1988), with less adventure or romance than countless other novels about island isolation that have descended from Daniel Defoe's eighteenth-century *Robinson Crusoe,* is a distinctly realistic and contemplative book about a teenage boy making an unconventional choice to explore nature, art, and self-knowledge on an island near his home. Most of the selections in Part 5, on boys' books and girls' books, are also realistic, although some contain strong elements of adventure or romance. Poems throughout this anthology range from animal fantasies and absurd nonsense verse to realistic subjects from the child's world of home and books, with a "coloring of the imagination" thrown over "ordinary things."[1] Fiction by Katherine Paterson, Louise Erdrich, Christopher Paul Curtis, and others illustrates Segel's observations about the growth of realism in modern children's literature, in their depictions of specific regional settings, psychological complexity, race, gender, class, and other social issues.

Other selections also show how, since the development of New Realism in the late twentieth century, contemporary writers for children deal with subjects that were formerly considered taboo, such as sexuality, genocide, and colonial exploitation. Several of the texts excerpted or recommended in this section are by masters of realism, such as Charles Dickens (who often added comic exaggeration and satire to realistic subjects) and Katherine Paterson. Their stories demonstrate how vital the world of the imagination is to children. But most of the texts in this section (which are arranged chronologically) show how prominent modern authors rely on elements of realism to bring their fantasies to life and use fantasy to represent the realities of human experience. As Sullivan writes, "All literature, then, is part mimetic and part fantastic."

What is fantasy? Sullivan's essay "Fantasy" defines the genre by identifying two essential characteristics: an element of the impossible and the presence of what J. R. R. Tolkien called a "secondary world." According to Sullivan's definition, the tales from ancient oral traditions, including the fairy tales that occupy such a prominent place in children's literature, while fantastic to modern readers, would fall outside the genre because, as with poems such as *Beowulf* or *Sir Gawain and the Green Knight,* "we have no way of knowing exactly how the original composers of or audience for those poems felt about them." In other words, what we take to be a secondary world, a land of enchantment, may have been much closer to a primary world for pre-Renaissance cultures that did not separate the supernatural from the natural. Nonetheless, the publication of folk fairy tales by the Grimm Brothers in the early nineteenth century encouraged the development of fantasy as we know it today. And some writers, such as psychoanalyst Bruno Bettelheim and author-critic Jane Yolen (both in Part 3), would argue that as literature for children, the folk fairy tale has hardly been surpassed. John Goldthwaite's widely praised 1996 book, *The Natural History of Make-Believe,* theorizes that the nursery rhyme "descended" into modern nonsense verse, the fable evolved into literary animal fantasies, and the fairy tale inspired fantasy novels and picture books, from Lewis Carroll's Alice books to Maurice Sendak's *Where the Wild Things Are.* Of these three "parent classes of make-believe," fairy tales maintained the strongest position in the world of children's literature through the end of the twentieth century, alongside but not superseded by many varieties of modern fantasy in different media.[2] Could this be the case because they evoke a primal longing for the world of our ancestors where belief in the supernatural was taken for granted as part of everyday life? After all, as Wordsworth's "Ode" suggests, we are born without the post-Renaissance education and socialization that teach us to separate magic and reality. P. L. Travers even claimed in *Mary Poppins* that infants could understand the language of the birds and wind and that only Mary Poppins herself retained this ability after the age of one. In her book *About the Sleeping Beauty,* Travers wrote, "Perhaps we are born knowing the tales, for our grandmothers and all their ancestral kin continually run in our blood repeating them endlessly, and the shock they give us when we first hear them is not of surprise but of recognition."[3]

Writers of both literary fairy tales and fantasy fiction use a variety of literary techniques to create secondary worlds for readers to believe in. For example, Hans Christian Andersen's "The Little Mermaid" (in Part 8) is set in a fully imagined, logically consistent secondary world, where the undersea mer-kingdom is described with more elaborate detail than the human world on land. Fairy tale and fantasy illustrators most often use a realistic style to depict unrealistic scenes and creatures, inspired by Renaissance art or pre-Raphaelite painting (see, for example, Maurice Sendak's illustrations for "The Frog King," in Part 2, and "Hans My Hedgehog," in Part 6). Psychological realism is another key to the success of most fantasies, even when characters are somewhat idealized, sentimental, or satiric, whether it is the restlessness and lovesickness of Andersen's Little Mermaid; the camaraderie of talking animals in *The Wind in the Willows* and *Charlotte's Web* or talking toys in *Pinocchio* and *Winnie the Pooh;* or the human emotions and weaknesses with which fantasy creatures are endowed in E. Nesbit's dragon tales (see Part 7), *The Keeper of the Isis Light* by Monica Hughes, or L. Frank Baum's Oz books. Most of these examples are set in the real world, in familiar forests or farms or towns, but fantastical beings appear in these realistic settings, or animals and toys start talking, just as ancient cultures such as the Cherokee believed that people and animals could talk to each other in prehistoric times.

High fantasies and speculative fiction set entirely within a secondary world challenge our rational minds to view the universe and human experience in new ways; they thrill our imaginations with the wonders that authors create, but to succeed as literature, they must have realistic elements from the reader's existing frames of reference, such as familiar landscapes, or technological innovations that we can imagine developing in the future. The kingdoms of J. R. R. Tolkien's Middle Earth and Ursula K. Le Guin's Earthsea look much like ancient Britain at times. The opening of *The Giver* by Lois Lowry seems to depict an ordinary modern scene with citizens and bicycles, aircraft flying overhead, a little sister in after-school child care. We gradually read of rules and rituals revealing that this is a futuristic society different from our own and designed to make us think differently about our own. Lowry shows how scientific advances and stable social structures could be used to give everyone types of comfort and equality that many of us already have in some measure or hope we will have in the future. But the more the young hero Jonas learns about his world, the more we reflect along with him on the value and costs of deeper human experiences and individual freedoms that have been sacrificed to provide all members of his community with comfortable, secure lives.

The Wonderful Wizard of Oz, C. S. Lewis's Narnia Chronicles, and the more recent Harry Potter series by J. K. Rowling are also set in secondary worlds, although they open, like many fantasy stories, in the primary world. Sometimes called "looking glass" fantasies, stories with this structure contain portals into the secondary world or objects that facilitate movement from one world to another: a rabbit hole and a looking glass in Carroll's two Alice books (see Part 1), the nursery window in J. M. Barrie's *Peter Pan,* a drab Kansas farmhouse displaced by a cyclone in

The Wonderful Wizard of Oz, the magic barrier at the real King's Cross Railway Station in London and the Hogwarts Express train in *Harry Potter,* and an old clock and garden door in Philippa Pearce's *Tom's Midnight Garden.* The makers of the classic MGM film *The Wizard of Oz* (1939) chose to make Dorothy's journey into Oz a dream, revealing at the end that she has been ill since the cyclone and that her three companions in Oz are really farmhands from her home in Kansas. Alice's Wonderland adventures are also depicted in Carroll's frame stories as wondrous dreams that only a child could have. The use of a dream vision that for some readers seems to take back or deny the truth of the fantasy adventure gives Carroll's books a more ambiguous position in the history of fantasy literature than their reputation as landmarks of fantasy for children may suggest. But in Baum's original 1900 Oz novel and many other looking-glass fantasies, the relationships among dreams, daily life, and fantasy worlds are not revealed so explicitly; readers develop their own level of awareness of connections between the primary and secondary worlds. As in any work of fiction, thematic, symbolic, and intertextual links make our reading experiences in a newly imagined world relevant to our previous knowledge of life and literature and our personal beliefs. In the first Narnia book, *The Lion, the Witch, and the Wardrobe,* Lucy and her siblings enter Narnia through a wardrobe in a realistic English country house and find themselves in a fantastic world that, for many readers, is grounded in New Testament reality. Like many works of fantasy, the book itself opposes inspired truth to literal-mindedness and deception or delusion. Aslan, the Christlike lion, intimates that, through his sacrifice, "all names will soon be restored to their proper owners," or, in other words, everything will be revealed for what it really is when the witch loses her power to "make things look like they weren't."

Madeleine L'Engle's *A Wrinkle in Time* and its sequels, like the Narnia Chronicles, are also works of high fantasy steeped in Christian tradition. *Wrinkle* also belongs to an important subgenre of modern fantasy or speculative fiction, science fiction, and in its portrayal of the secondary world of Camazotz, it participates, like Lowry's *The Giver,* in the subgenre of dystopian fantasy as well (that is, they depict bad societies, the opposite of the ideal worlds portrayed in utopias). Interestingly, *Wrinkle* begins, as does the Harry Potter series, like a realistic story about a misfit, although Meg Murry is a misfit at school, rather than at home. In fact, *Wrinkle* also begins as a family story: an absent father; a scientist mother; and four siblings, including the extraordinarily gifted child, Charles Wallace. And, finally, Meg's developing friendship with another misfit, Calvin O'Keefe, suggests a realistic teenage romance. Only gradually do we become aware that supernatural forces are involved. Since the book's first publication in 1962, this blending of genres has become common in speculative fiction for young adults. The secondary world in *Wrinkle* is much stranger than in *The Giver* or even *Harry Potter,* so that it relies more on challenging readers with the unfamiliar than on exploiting our sense of the familiar, yet Camazotz bears more than a passing resemblance to the stultifying environment of Meg's school.

As in *Wrinkle,* the secondary world of fantasy tends to critique the primary world: if utopian, the secondary world implies a contrast; if dystopian, it holds up a mirror to flaws and dangers in the primary world. Thus, to those who support the status quo, fantasy constitutes a threat, a threat discussed by Ursula K. Le Guin in "Why Are Americans Afraid of Dragons?" Over a hundred years earlier, Charles Dickens and Louisa May Alcott, novelists who are associated more with the development of realistic fiction than with fantasy, recognized the threat that fantasy posed to the prevailing ideologies of capitalism, industrialism, and male privilege. The opening chapters of Dickens's novel *Hard Times* (1854) depict the way in which schoolchildren were discouraged, indeed forbidden, from exercising their imaginations. The rest of the book depicts the disastrous consequences of such repression for Tom and Louisa Gradgrind, who finally owe their salvation, if such it can be called, to the previously scorned denizens of the circus. Their father, Thomas Gradgrind, in his insistence on facts as the "one thing necessary," eerily anticipates Meg Murry's principal in *Wrinkle,* who implores her to face, like Dickens's Sissy Jupe, the "fact" of her father's desertion. Louisa May Alcott, in both her realistic novels and allegorical fantasy stories, such as "Fancy's Friend," expressed her belief that a sound up-bringing and education included healthy exposure to nature and the imagination, while overly strict discipline and the close study of facts stunted the growth of children.

Like Alcott's Fancy, who creates an imaginary mermaid Lorelei, the child protagonist of Robert Louis Stevenson's *A Child's Garden of Verses* is a solitary child, who lives in his imagination and the fantasy world he enters through books. He, like Fancy, finds in solitude an imaginary friend and even creates an entire imaginary kingdom. So powerful is the influence of "story-books" that he can imagine himself a hunter and explorer while in the same room as his parents. Poems about everyday life and nature alternate with poems about the world of the imagination in Stevenson's classic collection. His recollections of his childhood double life as an intrepid adventurer, on the one hand, and a nursery inmate, on the other hand, may well have contributed to the creation of his fantastic adult story, *Dr. Jekyll and Mr. Hyde.*

Philippa Pearce, in *Tom's Midnight Garden,* also deals with the child's double life and ability to construct a fantasy world. She, too, makes use of a garden setting, but *Tom's Midnight Garden* represents another subgenre of fantasy, time travel, or time-slip fantasy. Time travel is depicted as a scientific method of getting characters to distant planets in *A Wrinkle in Time,* but in novels like Pearce's, Lucy M. Boston's Green Knowe series, some of E. Nesbit's stories, or Mark Twain's *A Connecticut Yankee in King Arthur's Court,* the time slip is a magical device for juxta-posing people from different historical eras. Learning to compare cultures or understand histori-cal differences is of greater or lesser importance in different or time-slip fantasies. In *The Devil's Arithmetic,* for example, the use of time travel is controversial because of Jane Yolen's treatment of reality in a children's novel; it places a late twentieth-century Jewish girl in a World War II concentration camp, although the novel is consistent with its literary tradition in returning her safely to her American home in the end, where no time has passed in the present since she slipped into the past early in the novel. It is most important for twelve-year-old Hannah to learn to appre-ciate her older relatives' memories and cultural traditions because of what they suffered during the Holocaust. Yolen believes that even when historical reality seems mind numbing and impos-sible to imagine, "a storyteller," through both fantasy and realistic fiction, "can attempt to tell the human tale, can make a galaxy out of the chaos."[4] In *Tom's Midnight Garden,* Tom's search for historical facts plays a more minor role in his psychological journey when he becomes preoccu-pied with trying to understand and control his time-slip experiences. A mid-twentieth-century child, he is unaware at first that he is visiting the nineteenth century when he becomes friends with little Hatty on her turf and in her time, without his unimaginative aunt and uncle becoming any the wiser. His time slip is a refuge from present loneliness for him and Hatty more than a les-son of historical significance. In the end, the secondary or Victorian world merges with the pri-mary or modern world when Tom discovers that Hatty is part of his present time as well; as in Yolen's novel, the main characters from different generations really could be alive at the same time in the present. The magic that allows Tom and Hatty to spend parts of their childhood to-gether helps both of them get through difficult times in their lives.

Katherine Paterson's realistic *Bridge to Terabithia* (see Further Recommended Reading) fea-tures a similar friendship between a rather prosaic boy and a more imaginative girl. Just as Hatty creates a kingdom for Tom, so Leslie creates an imaginary kingdom, Terabithia, for Jess. Ter-abithia, an invented place that is based partly on Leslie's reading of Lewis's Narnia series, attests to the powerful influence of imaginative literature on the minds of young readers. So powerful is this influence that it even survives the death of Leslie and enables Jess to cope with her loss. A fantastic experience also consoles Lizzie, a girl who is mourning the death of her father, in

Gillian Rubenstein's otherwise realistic story "Dolphin Dreaming." Like Alcott's Fancy, who conjures her friend Lorelei by outlining the figure of a mermaid on the sand, Lizzie seems to summon the mysterious "dolphin man" by arranging her treasures on the beach. Ted Hughes also believed in the power of fantasy to alleviate present troubles. In his stories *The Iron Man* and *The Iron Woman,* Hughes placed science fiction characters, a giant mechanical man and woman, in realistic English settings to create late twentieth-century fables in which children help solve environmental problems. As Bettelheim, Le Guin, and Hughes argue, fantasy has the power to heal.

Dr. Dorian, E. B. White's character in one of the two chapters reprinted here from *Charlotte's Web,* would agree with Le Guin that "all the best faculties of a mature human being exist in a child" and that fantasy "isn't factual, but it is true." When Mrs. Arable consults him about her daughter, Fern, who insists that the animals in her uncle's barn can talk, Dr. Dorian treats the idea with respect. To him, Charlotte the spider's ability to weave a web is as miraculous as her ability to tell a story. For Dr. Dorian, like Thoreau, the most mundane reality is fabulous. And unlike Dickens's Gradgrind or Alcott's Uncle Fact, he does not believe that every phenomenon must yield to rational explanation. Neither does he believe that a solitary child is an unhappy or unhealthy one. He realizes that all too soon the child, "with [her] blessedness at strife," as Wordsworth put it, will voluntarily surrender her fantasy life, as Fern does when she meets Henry Fussy at the fair and as Hatty does when, in *Tom's Midnight Garden,* she becomes interested in an ordinary young man. White's talking-animal fantasy can also be viewed as a realistic depiction of the way in which children acquire language and literacy. On the one hand, Charlotte teaches both the human and the animal child the pleasure—and sometimes the crucial importance—of the well-chosen word as well as the power of story; on the other, Charlotte, in her laborious efforts to create the words in her web, is like a child herself, for whom the formation of even single letters is a challenge—and a miracle. In *Charlotte's Web,* as in all the literature selected for this section, fantasy and realism are so inextricably intertwined as to pay tribute to "the wonder of everything."

NOTES

1. William Wordsworth, "Preface to *Lyrical Ballads*" (1802).
2. John Goldthwaite, *The Natural History of Make-Believe: A Guide to the Principal Works of Britain, Europe, and America* (Oxford: Oxford UP, 1996) 8–12.
3. P. L. Travers, Afterword, *About the Sleeping Beauty* (New York: McGraw-Hill, 1975) 50.
4. Jane Yolen, "What Is True about This Book," *The Devil's Arithmetic* (New York: Penguin Puffin, 1988) 169–70.

Elizabeth Segel (b. 1938)

Reading expert Elizabeth Segel is a coauthor of *For Reading Out Loud! A Guide to Sharing Books with Children* (1983). While teaching at the University of Pittsburgh, she also founded Beginning with Books, a successful family literacy program in southwestern Pennsylvania that has had nationwide influence. This 1980 essay provides valuable insights into adults' attitudes that limited the types of realistic content in children's books long after the rise of realism in literature for adults, led by Daniel Defoe in the eighteenth century and the great realists of nineteenth-century fiction. Selections in Part 1 of this anthology by writers such as Maria Edgeworth, Peter Parley, and Jacob Abbot illustrate Segel's observations that early writers of juvenile literature simplified reality in order to fulfill their didactic purposes of instilling morality and shaping the character of children. Observations in Segel's useful overview of the types of realism that have been introduced into children's books in the past century and a half apply to many selections throughout this anthology, from Mark Twain and Louisa May Alcott to Katherine Paterson and Victor Martinez. (See also Segel's essay on boys' books and girls' books in Part 5.)

Realism and Children's Literature

Notes from a Historical Perspective

Realism in the sense of verisimilitude, or a faithful mirroring of actual experience, has been present in works of many periods and genres. In the *Iliad*'s scene of Hector's leavetaking from his wife and infant son (Book VI), for instance, the image of the child clinging to his nurse, fearful of his father's plumed helmet, stands out from the poem's supernatural events and heroic texture in its close fidelity to observed experience.

Realism in a narrower sense refers, however, to a literary movement that began to take shape with Defoe's fictions in the early eighteenth century and came into full flower in the English and French novels of the 1850's. This movement consisted of (1) a set of attitudes concerning the proper subject-matter and aims of the novel and (2) particular methods for achieving these aims.

The practitioners of realism rejected the conventional plots and stereotyped characters of romance in favor of a form that would reflect more accurately the random and inconclusive nature of actual events and the complex individuality of actual people. In place of the romantic-idealist philosophy that art should limit itself to depicting the beautiful, realism adopted the premise that the novel should be "a full and authentic report of human experience," in Ian Watt's phrase.[1]

This conception of the novel determined its characteristic subject-matter: everyday events, particularized settings, and characters from all ranks of life. The distinctive techniques of realism included a predominantly plain narrative style and the use of detail to particularize time, place and character.

In assessing the impact of the realistic movement on children's literature one is first struck by the absolute incompatibility between the aims of most writers for children and the aims of the realistic school. Juvenile authors saw their mission as shaping the young reader's character and believed in the efficacy of presenting ideal types of vice and virtue to that end; the result was a far cry from "a full and authentic report of human experience." Yet, adult purposes notwithstanding, realism has been a shaping force in children's literature ever since young readers appropriated for themselves that ground-breaking realistic fiction, *Robinson Crusoe*. This is no doubt because certain of the distinctive qualities of formal realism are very much in tune with the child's perception of the world and therefore with his/her aesthetic preferences.

The dismissal of fantasy as frivolous and immoral by educators of all persuasions prior to the mid-nineteenth century meant that in those years most books written specifically for children took as their subject everyday events in contemporary settings. Yet they are certainly not examples of realism. Speaking of U.S. children's books, Anne Scott MacLeod writes: "According to its creators, the fiction written for children before 1860 was realistic . . . In fact, of course, the realism in juvenile books was always subordinated to didacticism. Both consciously and unconsciously, the authors edited reality in order to teach morality. . . ."[2] MacLeod uses the term "nonfantasy fiction" to describe this literature rather than the misleading "realistic fiction."

This view that children's books were instruments for shaping child character dictated that instead of the realists' psychological complexity in characterization, one had schematized simplicity: lazy vs. industrious apprentices, Sanford vs. Merton. Since obedience to authority was the chief virtue juvenile authors sought to drum into little heads, adult characters in authority tended to be drawn as paragons of wisdom and virtue.

Consequently, few if any children's books before the twentieth century stand as thorough-going instances of formal realism. Yet many outstanding children's books of the past 150 years benefited from the example of the realists, and the character of children's books today owes a great deal to the realistic movement.

From Daniel Defoe to Laura Ingalls Wilder, for example, the realists' method of establishing authenticity through an accumulation of detail has resulted in books of profound appeal to children. (Mary Norton's *Borrowers* series owes a great debt to this realist technique also, as do many other fantasies.) The concrete and literal nature of the young child's mind coupled with the drive to master skills and acquire information account in part for this appeal. Isabelle Jan points out, too, that such a reliance on detail achieves a strong visual impact that is "particularly attractive to children.

. . ." She views the *Little House* series as "the masterpiece of realistic literature for children."[3] It is interesting that in Defoe and Wilder, the methods of realism were coupled with an idealism and didacticism that earned them adult approval from the start.

Realism departed from the romance in substituting a distinctive, particularized setting for the typical vague backdrop of romance. Twain, whose work bridged the chasm between the novel and the children's book, advanced this feature of realism in his rich portraits of the river towns of his boyhood and his skillful rendering of the nuances of actual speech. In American children's books, the influence of Twain and other regionalists extends through Wilder and Lenski to the Cleavers and Betsy Byars. In England, Arthur Ransome's novels captured a distinctive sense of place which then operated "as if it were an actor in his stories," to quote Marcus Crouch.[4] The novels of John Rowe Townsend, Jill Paton Walsh, and Jane Gardam have brought this legacy of the realistic tradition to new heights in recent years.

The most striking effect of realist practice on children's books, however, was in characterization. From the one-dimensional walking object-lessons that had passed for characters in so many early children's books, characters of psychological complexity capable of growth and change began to appear in the domestic stories of Charlotte Yonge, Louisa May Alcott, Mrs. Molesworth, and Juliana Ewing (even though their stories often contained idealized characters as well). Novelists successfully challenged the edict that only model children could be treated sympathetically in children's books, and the lively tradition of the appealing bad boy and the spunky rebellious girl was initiated. In some versions these figures were so sentimentalized as to bear no more resemblance to real children than did Giles Gingerbread. Yet the potential of psychological realism to deepen characterization is handsomely realized in such protagonists as Tom Bailey, Jo March, Tom Sawyer, Katy Carr, and Oswald Bastable. Here, too, the advances of realism benefited those working in other genres as the characterizations of Peter Rabbit, Alice, and Long John Silver testify.

In the 1920's, out of the movement in American education which emphasized the role of experience in learning came an extension of realism to books for very young children. Lucy Sprague Mitchell advocated realistic stories for the very young as a supplement to the traditional nursery tales. Since these stories were too brief to accommodate the physical and psychological detail on which the realistic novel depended, sometimes the results were mundane. But in the best efforts of Mitchell and her followers (who include Margaret Wise Brown and Ruth Krauss) distinction of form and language enhanced portrayals of the little child's daily experiences, and the picture book was greatly enriched thereby.[5]

Perhaps the best-known innovation of realism was its depiction of "low" subjects. Nowhere is realism's impetus to widen the territory of acceptable subject-matter for fiction more evident than in children's books over the last century. The selective, idealized version of life has steadily given way to one that reflects the world more fully and accurately. In fact, this aspect of the realist tradition, which has typically been allied with a concern for social justice, is responsible for the increasing number of books in recent years which depict minority experience and non-stereotyped gender roles.

Often the extension of subject-matter meant breaking explicit taboos. The taboo against depicting a disobedient child in a positive light was broken, as we have seen, in the nineteenth century. But the full force of realism's impact in this area has been felt in the last quarter of a century. Bad parents, poverty, war, death, and sex in all its manifestations have become accepted subjects in books for older children. (Poverty, war, and, of course, death had long been depicted in juvenile fiction but in sentimentalized, softened versions.)

Inasmuch as the push to extend the limits of appropriate subject-matter has characterized realism since Balzac, the application of the term "New Realism" to the flood of books in recent years treating formerly taboo subjects is apt. Unfortunately, in the minds of all too many critics and teachers of children's literature, realism is today equated with this New Realism, and the sophisticated achievements and complex influences of realism are boiled down to the latest shocker on the young adult shelf. Nina Bawden, in a recent article on "Emotional Realism in Books for Young People," suggests that realism has come to mean "writing about the unpleasant side of life . . . because the realistic approach to fiction, which should mean a faithful account of the human condition without resort to easy generalities, is more striking when it is applied to un-

pleasant subjects."[6] This misapprehension is particularly damaging because many examples of the New Realism fail to employ traditional realism's careful observation and skillful accumulation of detail. As a consequence, they lack the vivid settings, the complexity of character, and the resonance of theme that have marked the best realistic fiction for adults and for children.

And what of the future of realism in children's books? Many mainstream novelists beginning with Proust, Woolf, and Joyce have found the methods of realism inadequate and have explored other techniques in their attempt to convey the essence of human experience. Their technical innovations have enriched the possibilities for writers of children's novels. And yet the methods and aims of realism will without doubt retain their usefulness to those who write for the young and inexperienced reader. For one thing, as Watt points out, the conventions of realism "make much smaller demands on the audience than do most literary conventions."[7] In addition, the young child's concreteness of perception will always respond to the detailed density of the realist's account of experience, and the older child's acute need to know what the world is like out there will always engender appreciation for the realist's attempt to faithfully mirror physical and psychological reality.

NOTES

1. Ian Watt, *The Rise of the Novel* (Berkeley: University of California Press, 1957), p. 32.
2. Anne Scott MacLeod, *A Moral Tale: Children's Fiction and American Culture, 1820–1860* (Hamden, CT: Archon Books, 1975), p. 41.
3. Isabelle Jan, *On Children's Literature,* ed. Catherine Storr (New York: Schocken Books, 1974), p. 119.
4. Marcus Crouch, *The Nesbit Tradition: The Children's Novel in England 1945–1970* (Totowa, NJ: Rowman and Littlefield, 1972), p. 18.
5. For a fuller account, see Joan W. Blos, "Form and Content in Children's Books: A Critical Tribute to Lucy Sprague Mitchell," *Children's Literature in Education,* VIII (Spring 1977), pp. 40–41.
6. Nina Bawden, *The Horn Book Magazine,* LVI (February 1980), pp. 32–33.
7. Watt, p. 32.

C. W. Sullivan III (b. 1944)

A history of the relationship between realism and fantasy is outlined in this essay by C. W. Sullivan III. An American critic, editor, and educator at East Carolina University, Sullivan is an expert on fantasy and children's literature whose work does not segregate children's literature from adults' literature as much modern criticism has done. This introduction to fantasy appeared in *Stories and Society: Children's Literature in Its Social Context* (Dennis Butts, ed., 1992). Surveying the views of many important critics and writers of fantasy, Sullivan clarifies fundamental differences between fantasy writing of the past few centuries and stories before the modern age of science and rationality, when the preternatural was not considered "the impossible" but was encompassed within the prevailing worldview. Like Sullivan's book *Welsh Celtic Myth in Modern Fantasy* (1989), this essay also explains the relationship between fantasy fiction and the myths, epics, and folklore of older oral traditions. After discussing four novels of the nineteenth century that influenced the development of twentieth-century fantasy and science fiction, Sullivan surveys the types of fantasy that were popular in the twentieth century, ending with an insightful introduction to the genre of high fantasy.

Fantasy

In a great many respects, fantasy literature is a nineteenth- and twentieth-century concept and creation. To some extent, publishers and booksellers have made it a category so that readers can go directly to the fantasy section of W. H. Smith's or Waldenbooks' shelves and make their selections. But fantasy literature, as an international genre, developed in response to realistic fiction, a genre only a century or so older than fantasy and itself a development of the seventeenth-century's interest in non-fiction prose—journalism, essay, history, and biography. Before the consciously realistic fiction of the eighteenth century, the *Beowulf* poet, the *Gawain* poet, Shakespeare, and Spenser (to name but the most prominent) could use what we would now call elements of the fantastic without anyone's remarking on them as such.

Lin Carter's argument, in *Imaginary Worlds,* that fantasy has been around since epic, saga, and myth suggests either a desperate attempt to provide a noble heritage for modern fantasy or a sincere misunderstanding of what modern fantasy actually is.[1] Certainly, some of the elements of epic, saga, and myth—as well as legend and folktale—appear in modern fantasies, but the contemporary fantasy writer's borrowing of materials from medieval and ancient literatures for his modern text automatically makes those older narratives no more fantasy than it makes them modern. While we as modern readers might consider *Beowulf* or *Sir Gawain and the Green Knight* pieces of fantastic literature, we have no way of knowing exactly how the original composers of or audiences for those poems felt about them.

Reality and fantasy are terms which we use today without much analytical thought, perhaps because, when we apply them to literature, we use them as labels more often than we use them as critical tools. Moreover, we have set them up as opposites when, following Kathryn Hume's lead in *Fantasy and Mimesis,* we might better see them as separate ends of a continuum. Hume suggests that:

literature is the product of two impulses. These are *mimesis,* felt as the desire to imitate, to describe events, people, and objects with such verisimilitude that others can share your experience; and *fantasy,* the desire to change givens and alter reality—out of boredom, play, vision, longing for something lacking, or need for metaphoric images that will bypass the audience's verbal defenses.[2]

All literature, then, is part mimetic and part fantastic, with what we call realistic fiction toward one end of the spectrum and what we call fantasy fiction at the other.

"*Fantasy,*" Hume continues, "*is any departure from consensus reality*" (italics in original).[3] Consensus reality includes that which most of the population of a culture group believes to be or will accept as real.

Moreover, since the Renaissance and especially since the seventeenth century in England, which saw the promulgation of Francis Bacon's scientific method and the founding of the Royal Society, the real and the not-real (or fantastic) have been mutually exclusive terms, and western Europeans and Americans have been led to believe that they can know what is real and what is not. Therefore, fantasy must contain a large element of what is not real; fantasy must deal with the impossible.

In fact, "impossible" is a word which appears in a good many twentieth-century definitions of fantasy. In *An Experiment in Criticism,* C. S. Lewis defines fantasy as "any narrative that deals with impossibles and preternaturals."[4] S. C. Fredericks calls fantasy "the literature of the impossible" in "Problems of Fantasy."[5] Colin Manlove, in *Modern Fantasy: Five Studies,* suggests that "a substantial and irreducible element of supernatural or impossible worlds, beings, or objects" is essential to fantasy; and he explains "supernatural or impossible" as "of another order of reality from that in which we exist and form our notions of possibility."[6] And in *The Fantastic in Literature,* Eric Rabkin says of fantasy that "its polar opposite is Reality."[7] These definitions, and others, have led Gary K. Wolfe, in "The Encounter with Fantasy," to assert that the "criterion of the impossible . . . may indeed be the first principle generally agreed upon for the study of fantasy."[8]

The writer cannot merely toss a few "impossible" characters, creatures, items, or events into a narrative and call it a fantasy, however; he or she must create a place in which the impossible can exist. J. R. R. Tolkien said it best in "On Fairy-Stories":

What really happens is that the story-maker proves a successful "sub-creator." He makes a Secondary World which your mind can enter. Inside it, what he relates is "true": it accords with the laws of that world. You therefore believe it, while you are, as it were, inside. The moment disbelief arises, the spell is broken; the magic, or rather art, has failed. You are then out in the Primary World again, looking at the little abortive Secondary World from outside.[9]

Others have since made similar comments about the Secondary World. In *Touch Magic,* Jane Yolen remarks that the "amazing thing about fantasy is its absolute consistency."[10] Lloyd Alexander, in "Flat-Heeled Muse," says that the muse of fantasy writers wears "very sensible shoes" and bothers writers with questions about consistency.[11] In *The Green and Burning Tree,* Eleanor Cameron says, "It is required of [the author] that he create an inner logic for his story and that he draw boundary lines outside of which his fantasy may not wander."[12] And Brian Attebury asserts that fantasy "needs consistency" in *The Fantasy Tradition in America from Irving to LeGuin.*[13] In light of such remarks, it might be argued (as I have in *Welsh Celtic Myth and Modern Fantasy*) that the logically-created Secondary World is the second principle generally agreed upon for the study of fantasy.[14]

An important aspect of these two principles is that they are reader-oriented and, ultimately, dependent for their meanings upon readers who can distinguish between the possible and the impossible, the Primary World and the Secondary World. The audiences of *Beowulf* and *Sir Gawain and the Green Knight* lived in cultures whose worldview included a large component of the preternatural; their world was one of vast wilderness tracts in which anything might exist. Their world was one of magic and mystery. Modern western European/American readers live in a culture with a very small preternatural component; their world is largely explored, mapped and settled, with only a few spots in which a Bigfoot, Abominable Snowman, or Loch Ness Monster might exist. And contemporary consensus reality may, in fact, not include them either; the modern Western world is one of science and rationality.

For the modern reader, then, reality and fantasy have meanings which would not have been understood by the audience for *Beowulf* or *Sir Gawain and the Green Knight.* Although we cannot know how they might have reacted, it is doubtful that the people listening to the Beowulf poet would have said "Impossible!" the way modern readers of those poems would. The modern reader makes categorical distinctions between the possible (real) and the impossible (not-real) and between the Primary World and the Secondary World (and is quite comfortable doing so). Thus fantasy literature, which by these definitions and limitations is fiction set in a Secondary World where the fantastic (departures from consensus reality) occurs in believable ways, is a product of the nineteenth and twentieth centuries and should be approached as such.

It has become a commonplace among social and literary historians that the Western cultural attitude toward or view of children and childhood changed early in the nineteenth century. Immediately prior to the Romantic movement, children were thought of as miniature adults, and their literature was, to a large extent, instructive without being particularly entertaining; but as the Romantic movement took hold and an emphasis on imagination, naturalness, and innocence developed, children, who were thought to possess these qualities in greater quantity and purer form than did adults, were assigned their own existence which, while still leading to adulthood, was significantly different from it.

Wordsworth's "Intimations of Immortality from Recollections of Early Childhood" separates and, at the same time, attempts to reconcile the two states of being, the child having a higher state of spiritual perception and the adult a greater capacity to know and appreciate. This focus on children as innocently and naturally perceptive has led a number of critics, especially Stephen Prickett in *Victorian Fantasy* and Humphrey Carpenter in *Secret Gardens,* to discuss fantasy in such a way as to emphasise its connection with children (and all of their literature) and de-emphasise fantasy's connection with adult literature.

Prickett concentrates on Lewis Carroll, Charles Dickens, Charles Kingsley, Rudyard Kipling, George MacDonald, and E. Nesbit. Carpenter looks closely at Charles Kingsley, Lewis Carroll, George MacDonald, and Louisa Alcott in the first section of his book and at

Richard Jeffries, Kenneth Grahame, E. Nesbit, Beatrix Potter, J. M. Barrie, and A. A. Milne in the second. All of the writers and many of their books are important in the development of fantasy, and Prickett and Carpenter mention a number of others in passing; but they also leave out some important books which, if not written specifically for children, had an important formative effect on all fantasy, including children's fantasy. Four of these works, two discussed by both Prickett and Carpenter and two virtually ignored by them, are signposts in the development of fantasy in the nineteenth century.

The first is Mary Shelley's *Frankenstein.* In part, Shelley's book belongs to the horror literature tradition, and her immediate predecessors were the Gothic writers—Matthew "Monk" Lewis, Horace Walpole, Ann Radcliffe, William Beckford, and many others— of the late eighteenth and early nineteenth centuries. Like most of them, Shelley portrayed her contemporary world with something menacing added to it. In the Gothics, the menace was often, but not always, connected to the satanic or to ancient, non-Christian powers. *Frankenstein,* however, was also, if not primarily, a scientific fantasy or, more accurately, a scientific extrapolation. In his *Billion Year Spree,* Brian Aldiss credits Mary Shelley's *Frankenstein* as the first science fiction novel.[15]

Instead of rejecting the emerging technological world, Shelley extrapolated on it. Dr Frankenstein uses the latest in medical skill and technology to create his monster, and Shelley used her extrapolation to suggest that technological capabilities were advancing more rapidly than the moral, ethical, or philosophical perceptions needed to interpret and control them. Her horror is not based on otherworldly or satanic powers using humans for evil, but on humans using their own powers with horrific results.

Rejected by his maker, the creature turns on Frankenstein and destroys everything, especially his family and his new bride, that he holds dear.

Mary Shelley's *Frankenstein* may have been the formative influence on the sub-generic category of fantasy called science fiction, but that influence was not felt in force until the twentieth century's increased interest in science and technology made science fiction a popular literature. The world may not have been quite ready for science fiction when Shelley wrote her novel, but in just half a century, her first great successor, Jules Verne, began publishing scientifically-based extrapolations featuring technological marvels, many of which actually came into being in the next century. Three decades later, H. G. Wells would begin publishing his five "scientific romances," novels which, more so than Verne's, used science fiction as a vehicle for social criticism. Ironically, Wells, like Shelley, is remembered much more for his monsters than his social criticism.

The next two books are closer to what one generally considers fantasy, and both are discussed by Prickett and Carpenter. The first is Charles Kingsley's *The Water Babies*. The main character, Tom, escapes both from and to in this book. He escapes from the horrible life of a mid-nineteenth century child chimney-sweep, which Kingsley seems to have drawn in rather mimetically, and escapes into the river to become a water baby who, living in the river, discovers an essential kinship with the other river creatures. Prickett calls *The Water Babies* a "theological allegory"[16] and Carpenter remarks that it was "full . . . of his personal convictions, his destructive hatred of the wrong-headedness of children's authors, and his obsession with maternal-sexual female figures and the purifying, regenerative power of cold water."[17] It is that, and more.

The Water Babies is a serious escape novel. According to Prickett, Kingsley, like many other Victorian fantasy writers, "makes use of 'another world,' but his underwater is essentially a part of this one and is ready-created for him."[18] It was this particular creation of another world that makes Kingsley's novel important here, for as Carpenter notes, Kingsley "was the first writer in England, perhaps the first in the world with the exception of Hans Andersen, to discover that a children's book can be the perfect vehicle for an adult's most personal and private concerns."[19] Explained another way, Kingsley synthesises the *story* component of literature for entertainment with the *thematic* content of the literature for instruction, successfully bringing the separate strands of late eighteenth- and early nineteenth-century children's literature together in a single novel.

The next book, George MacDonald's *The Princess and the Goblin*, is also a synthesis and, perhaps, a religious allegory. Prickett certainly thinks this way; he discusses MacDonald and Kingsley in the same chapter, "Adults in Allegory Land."[20] And while that inter-

pretation has merit, Carpenter is more to the point in saying that *The Princess and the Goblin* "was in fact the first British children's book to make an utterly confident, fresh use of such traditional materials as an old fairy spinning in a tower, and a race of wicked dwarfs beneath a mountain—or, rather, beneath the castle itself."[21] MacDonald discovered that one can do more with the old tales than merely retell them; they can be a fresh source of materials with which to tell a story.

MacDonald's "confident use of traditional materials" opened the way for all manner of stories about elves, dwarfs, goblins, fairies, and the like; and it did more. It set both the *pattern* and the *style* for the fantasy novel. The pattern is that of the märchen, or magic tale, in which an ordinary mortal (who is to be the hero) is drawn into a magical adventure during which he or she is challenged and tested, through which he or she matures, and after which he or she returns "home" to dispense justice, marry, and live happily ever after.[22] Curdie and the Princess do all of this, even though they have children to carry on after they die. The style MacDonald sets is the serious and sometimes almost medieval prose style of High Fantasy which never makes fun of itself or in any way suggests that what happens in the novel is fanciful or inconsequential; it is a style appropriate to actions upon which the fate of the world may depend.

The nineteenth-century novel in which the full potential of High Fantasy was first realised was William Morris's *The Wood Beyond the World*. Prickett and Carpenter mention Morris only in passing, and that seems unfortunate. Morris's effect on fantasy was profound. *The Wood Beyond the World* synthesises the best of what Kingsley and MacDonald contributed to the fantasy genre: style, theme, pattern, traditional materials, and the invented world. In fact, Lin Carter calls Morris's novel "the first great masterpiece of the imaginary-world tradition."[23] And it is the invented world that makes the difference.

When Golden Walter leaves Langton on Holm, he leaves the ordinary world for an imaginary Medieval world, an impossible Secondary World of the sort Tolkien would not define for another four decades. Walking on the docks one day, Walter sees a ship that seems to beckon him, and he decides to sail wherever she is going. More by instinct than plan, Walter arrives in a new land and becomes entangled with three persons he had seen several times before: a Maid, a hideous Dwarf who mistreats her, and an astoundingly beautiful woman called the Mistress who seems to control the other two. In the end, of course, Walter and the Maid marry, but the traditional adventures of the plot are carried out in a medieval world populated by characters from folktale and legend as well as from medieval history.

The Wood Beyond the World is also important as a part of many nineteenth-century authors' reaction to the new emphasis on science and technology that was central to the Industrial Revolution. That reaction was founded, to some extent, by the Romantic poets, beginning with Blake's "dark Satanic mills" and continuing with the emphasis on nature and ruralness found in the poetry of Wordsworth *et al.* Even Shelley's *Frankenstein,* with its dire warnings about the possible dangers of misusing the "new knowledge," was a part of this concern. But where Shelley used the context and constructs of the new technology as a part of her fiction, Morris used the Secondary World of High Fantasy to pose an alternative, almost atechnological worldview.

These four nineteenth-century novels—*Frankenstein, The Water Babies, The Princess and the Goblin,* and *The Wood Beyond the World*—are important because they set the standards for the two major branches of fantasy popular in the twentieth century: science fiction and High Fantasy. The science fiction of Robert Heinlein, Isaac Asimov, and Arthur C. Clarke is descended directly from Mary Shelley's novel; and the fantasies of Lord Dunsany, T. H. White, C. S. Lewis, and J. R. R. Tolkien are descended from the novels of Kingsley, MacDonald and Morris. These novels establish the subject matters and the styles, the patterns and the themes, of the fantasy that is read today; and while there are more sub-genres of fantasy than the two mentioned here, they, too, have been affected by what these four authors created.

As the century turned, advances in book production were combining with advances in literacy to expand significantly the number of books and magazines available to an ever-increasing market. This market included not only a lot more books, but an even greater number of new magazines and, soon, a new kind of book, a book of smaller size, softer cover, and lower price—the paperback. Even though most children's fantasy continued to be published first (and often only) in hardback volumes, fantasy in general found its greater and more profitable home first in the magazines and later in the paperbacks.

This expanded fantasy audience has helped make children's fantasy more popular and, therefore, more possible. It has also increased the amount of fantasy being published so that there are now categories within which to discuss fantasy literature in the twentieth century. The following categories, and most of the books mentioned therein, are from Ruth Nadelman Lynn's *Fantasy Literature for Children and Young Adults: An Annotated Bibliography,* a most useful volume which not only categorises and annotates but also cross references (as many fantasy books could legitimately be placed in more than one category) hundreds of fantasy books.[24]

Several of Lynn's categories are relatively self-explanatory. "Allegorical Fantasy and Literary Fairy Tales" includes such examples as C. S. Lewis's Narnia books and all of Hans Christian Andersen's stories respectively. "Animal Fantasy" is split into two categories: "Beast Tales," serious and often didactic stories about animals trying to escape human evils as in Richard Adams's *The Plague Dogs* or Robert O'Brien's *Mrs Frisby and the Rats of NIMH,* and "Talking Animal Fantasy," lighter and anthropomorphic stories like Michael Bond's Paddington series or E. B. White's *Charlotte's Web.* "Magic Adventure Fantasy" includes those stories of lighter tone such as P. L. Travers's *Mary Poppins,* E. Nesbit's *The Five Children* (trilogy), and Chris Van Allsberg's *Jumanji* in which ordinary people gain special powers or otherwise come into contact with magical beings, objects, or events. A lighter tone is also present in the category of "Humorous Fantasy," examples of which are Joan Aiken's *The Wolves of Willoughby Chase* (and its sequels), Russell Hoban's *How Tom Beat Captain Najork and His Hired Sportsmen,* and Daniel Pinkwater's *The Frankenbagel Monster.*

"Ghost Fantasy" includes Lucy Boston's Green Knowe books and Eleanor Cameron's *The Court of the Stone Children;* but Lynn saves the scarier stories for the "Witchcraft and Sorcery" category and includes John Bellairs's *The Face in the Frost,* Ray Bradbury's

Something Wicked This Way Comes, and Diana Wynne Jones's *Fire and Hemlock* therein. "Time Travel Fantasy," which owes its greatest debt to H. G. Wells's *The Time Machine,* includes Janet Lynn's *The Root Cellar,* Jill Paton Walsh's *A Chance Child,* and Phillipa Pearce's *Tom's Midnight Garden.* "Toy Fantasy," as the name implies, focuses on fantasies whose main characters are toys (regardless, almost, of whatever else the fantasy contains) and include Margery Bianco's *The Velveteen Rabbit,* Carlo Collodi's *The Adventures of Pinocchio,* E. T. A. Hoffman's *The Nutcraker,* and A.A. Milne's *Winnie-the-Pooh.*

I mention these categories here to suggest the current scope of that which we call fantasy literature, literature which includes an element or elements of the impossible and which takes place in a Secondary World (which may only be this world with the added impossible). There is one other category in Lynn's book, indeed the largest category in the book by far, which includes those works which spring most readily to mind when one thinks of fantasy literature—works such as Ursula LeGuin's Earthsea trilogy, Lloyd Alexander's Prydain novels, Susan Cooper's "Dark is Rising" series, T. H. White's *The Once and Future King,* L. Frank Baum's *The Wizard of Oz,* Lewis Carroll's Alice books, J. M. Barrie's *Peter Pan,* and perhaps the best and the brightest of all, J. R. R. Tolkien's *The Hobbit* and *The Lord of the Rings.* That category is High Fantasy.

Lynn uses the term High Fantasy for this category, and although she subdivides it into "Alternate Worlds/ Histories," "Myth Fantasy," and "Travel to Other Worlds," she does not really define High Fantasy other than to say that such books "involve worlds other than our own."[25] In his generally excellent *Critical Terms for Fantasy and Science Fiction,* Gary Wolfe does little better, defining High Fantasy as "Fantasy set in a fully imagined Secondary World . . . as opposed to Low Fantasy which concerns supernatural intrusions into the 'real' world."[26] These definitions may point in the right direction, but they are too broad to be of much use to someone who is not already familiar with the field of fantasy. For example, these definitions could allow a newcomer to include science fiction (travel to other worlds) in this category, even though more experienced readers and critics "know" that science fiction is quite another matter.

Lynn and Wolfe define only the location of the story; neither says anything about the style or subject matter. Dainis Bisenieks comments, "There is no pretending, as in some modern novels, that inconsequence is the rule of life; tales of Faërie are of those who walk with destiny and must be careful what they are about."[27] As Ursula LeGuin has said:

> I think "High Fantasy" a beautiful phrase. It summarises, for me, what I value most in an imaginative work: the fact that the author takes absolutely seriously the world and the people which he has created, as seriously as Homer took the Trojan War, and Odysseus; that he plays his game with all his skill, and all his art, and all his heart. When he does that, the fantasy game becomes one of the High Games men play. Otherwise, you might as well play Monopoly.[28]

The first and perhaps most obvious indication of this seriousness lies in the writer's style. LeGuin argues, "The style is, of course, the book. . . . If you remove the style, all you have left is a synopsis of the plot."[29] Style is especially important in fantasy, LeGuin continues, because to "create what Tolkien calls a 'secondary universe' is to make a new world. A world where no voice has ever spoken before; where the act of speech is the act of creation. The only voice that speaks there is the creator's voice. And every word counts."[30]

The subject matter also makes the best High Fantasy a literature of consequence and places it in the company of the epic. As I have said elsewhere, High Fantasy implies a number of concepts which make it a particular type of fantasy: "seriousness of tone, importance of theme, characters of noble birth or lineage (secondary if not primary characters), emphasis on magic and mystery (and an almost total lack of technology and machinery as effective devices in the action), and a generally clear presentation of good and evil, right and wrong."[31] And although it may be true of all High Fantasy, the High Fantasy written for children and young adults is, as Lloyd Alexander suggests, "about growing up,"[32] even if it does not feature a main character who ages chronologically.

More generally, High Fantasy derives much of its form and content from older literatures. The noble knights and ladies, the magicians, the quests, the raw youth who is tested throughout before he becomes hero and king, the young girl (sometimes a princess) who will become the queen, the true companions of the hero, the villains and monsters (especially the dragons), the elves and dwarfs and goblins, the castles and caverns, and the noble ideals can be traced back through Medieval Romance, and especially the Arthurian romances, to the origins of western literature in myth, legend, and folktale. Lloyd Alexander, Alan Garner, and Kenneth Morris draw on the *Mabinogi;* Rosemary Sutcliff sets much of her fiction in very realistic ancient or Roman Britain; T. H. White bases his novel on Malory's rendition of the Arthurian materials; Mary Renault rewrites the Mediterranean stories; C. S. Lewis draws on Christian, Greek, and Norse materials for the Narnia stories; and there are many more. Even those who create their own worlds—LeGuin's Earthsea, Norton's Witch World, Tolkien's Middle Earth, and others—use characters, ideas, and constructs from myth, legend, and folktales to add depth and texture to their narratives.

Tolkien is, perhaps, the ultimate example. *The Hobbit* and, more to the point, *The Lord of the Rings* are novels in which the author creates a fully-imagined Secondary World, a world which Tolkien takes as seriously as Homer took the Trojan War, and a world in which the characters walk with destiny. The story of Frodo's attempt to return the One Ring to Mount Doom and destroy it is more than just the story of one Hobbit's quest: it is the account of a period of Middle Earth's history during which an evil power was thwarted, and the true king returned to his throne, and the fate of the known world decided for generations to come. External indications of the seriousness with which Tolkien took his narratives include the appendices to *The Lord of the Rings* as well as the whole mythology behind it later published as *The Silmarillion.* As material published since his death has shown, there was a creation of even larger than epic proportions from which *The Lord of the Rings* sprang. In many ways, Middle Earth was his life's work.

The creation of Middle Earth certainly drew heavily on Tolkien's academic life. The names of the Dwarfs in *The Hobbit* and *The Lord of the Rings* come from the Norse Eddas as do the Trolls and the Elves. Gandalf's name, from the same source, can be translated as "Sorcerer-Elf."[33] Beorn, the shape-changer, is a character from Scandinavian legend. Smaug, the dragon, is very similar to the dragon in *Beowulf*—right down to knowing his treasure hoard so well that he can tell when a cup is missing. Aragorn and Galadriel come from Arthurian romance. As Gandalf becomes more of a guide and a wizard, he grows to resemble Merlin. The idea of Hobbits living in caves inside hills may have come from Tolkien's knowledge of the Celtic *sidhe* dwellers. Tolkien's style, too, comes from these traditional narratives; it is the plain and direct language of the Greek epics, the Norse sagas, the *Mabinogi,* and the *Song of Roland,* valuable especially for its clarity and its flexibility.[34]

Tolkien once intimated that *The Lord of the Rings* "contains, in the way of presentation that I find most natural, much of what I have personally received from the study of things Celtic."[35] That "way of presentation" and the borrowings I have already cited (a few of the many) have, unfortunately, left Tolkien, and the other High Fantasy writers who draw on older materials, open to the charge of being derivative. Such a charge might be true if Tolkien, or any other High Fantasy author, were trying to write a modern novel, but such is not the case. I believe that Tolkien was trying to write, in so far as such might be possible in the twentieth century, a Heroic Age narrative, perhaps an epic; and in doing so, he was following in an ancient and honourable tradition.[36] As Gerhard Herm states in *The Celts,* one of the areas of learning which the druids were to master included "all of the old stories circulating that the public invariably wished to hear again and again, in the same traditional form."[37] The ancient tellers were valued less for their creation of new stories than for their ability to tell an old story well. And judged by his performance, Tolkien is a pre-eminent storyteller.

In addition to its subject matter and style, High Fantasy also derives much of its power from the older materials it incorporates. The characters and archetypes from myth, legend, and folktale resonate with a power of their own.[38] Tolkien, one example among many, uses Light to represent good and order and uses Dark to represent evil and chaos, and in doing so, he employs archetypes traceable to many ancient mythologies. But such materials must be used in ways consistent with their traditional intent or value. When the reader picks up an Arthurian fantasy, he or she has a number of expectations about what the narrative will contain. If the expectations are met, the whole narrative will be enhanced by the Arthurian inclusion; if the expectations are violated (should Arthur be cast as an evil character, for example), the reader may, re-acting negatively to this use of the Arthurian materi-als, reject the whole book. The well-integrated narra-tive, then, has not only the power of the fantastic, but also the power of the traditional materials included therein.

The power of High Fantasy, Stephen Donaldson suggests, is the power to portray internal conflicts. "Put simply, fantasy is a form of fiction in which the internal crises or conflicts or processes of the charac-ters are dramatised as if they were external individuals or events."[39] Ursula LeGuin says that fantasy "is a journey into the subconscious mind, just as psycho-analysis is. Like psychoanalysis, it can be dangerous; and *it will change you*" (italics in original).[40] And Lloyd Alexander asserts, "If the creator of fantasy has done his work well, we should be a little bit different at the end of the journey than we were at the beginning. Maybe just for the moment, maybe for a long while."[41] While these statements are true of much fantasy, they are especially true of High Fantasy; and if we under-stand the darker aspects of our own personalities bet-ter after Frodo's confrontation with Gollum in *The Lord of the Rings* or Ged's integration of his conscious Self with his Shadow in *A Wizard of Earthsea*, it is the result of the writer's ability to create High Fantasy and High Fantasy's power to tell us something about ourselves.

Regarded thus, fantasy is certainly not an escape liter-ature. As Alexander notes, these fantasies "are written by adults living in an adult world, trying to cope with it and understand it, subjected to and responding to all the pressures and problems of real life. If the writer of fantasy is a serious creator, his work is going to reflect this."[42] *The Lord of the Rings* may, indeed, have been influenced by Tolkien's experiences in World War I, however well he kept them hidden; and Grahame's *The Wind in the Willows* may, on one level, reflect a "Victorian paranoia about the mob."[43] If so, those nov-els are reflecting "the pressures and problems" with which Tolkien and Grahame had to deal. In this way, too, modern fantasy is a creation of the modern world.

NOTES

1. L. Carter, *Imaginary Worlds* (New York: Ballantine, 1973), p. 5.
2. K. Hume, *Fantasy and Mimesis* (New York: Methuen, 1984), p. 20.
3. K. Hume, *Fantasy and Mimesis*, p. 21.
4. C. S. Lewis, *An Experiment in Criticism* (Cambridge: Cambridge University Press, 1965), p. 50.
5. S. C. Fredericks, "Problems of Fantasy," *Science Fiction Studies* 5 (March 1978), p. 37.
6. C. N. Manlove, *Modern Fantasy: Five Studies* (Cambridge: Cambridge University Press, 1975), p. 3.
7. E. Rabkin, *The Fantastic in Literature* (Princeton: Princeton University Press, 1976), p. 15.
8. G. K. Wolfe, "The Encounter With Fantasy," in Roger C. Schlobin (ed.), *The Aesthetics of Fantasy Literature and Art* (Notre Dame: Notre Dame University Press, 1982), pp. 1–2.
9. J. R. R. Tolkien, "On Fairy-Stories," in *The Tol-kien Reader* (1947, New York: Ballantine, 1966), p. 37.
10. J. Yolen, *Touch Magic* (New York: Philomel, 1981), p. 77.
11. L. Alexander, "Flat-Heeled Muse," *Hornbook* 41 (1965), pp. 141–6.
12. E. Cameron, *The Green and Burning Tree* (Boston: Lit-tle, Brown, 1962), p. 17.
13. B. Attebury, *The Fantasy Tradition in America from Irv-ing to LeGuin* (Bloomington: Indiana University Press, 1980), p. 2.
14. C. W. Sullivan III, *Welsh Celtic Myth in Modern Fan-tasy* (Westport: Greenwood Press, 1989), pp. 94–6.
15. B. Aldiss, *Billion Year Spree* (New York: Schocken Books, 1974), pp. 20–37.
16. S. Prickett, *Victorian Fantasy* (Hassocks: Harvester Press, 1979), p. 151.
17. H. Carpenter, *Secret Gardens* (Boston: Houghton Mif-flin, 1985), p. 41.
18. S. Prickett, *Victorian Fantasy*, p. 156.
19. H. Carpenter, *Secret Gardens*, p. 37.
20. S. Prickett, *Victorian Fantasy*, pp. 150–97.
21. H. Carpenter, *Secret Gardens*, p. 83.
22. L. Dégh, "Folk Narrative," in R. Dorson (ed.), *Folklore and Folklife* (Chicago: University of Chicago Press, 1972), p. 63.
23. L. Carter, *Imaginary Worlds*, p. 25.
24. R. N. Lynn, *Fantasy Literature for Children and Young Adults: An Annotated Bibliography*, 3rd ed. (New York: Bowker, 1989), p. 155.
25. Ibid.

26. G. K. Wolfe, *Critical Terms for Fantasy and Science Fiction* (Westport: Greenwood Press, 1986), p. 52.

27. D. Bisenieks, "Tales from the 'Perilous Realm': Good News for the Modern Child," *Christian Century* 91 (1974), p. 617.

28. U. K. LeGuin quoted in E. Cameron, "High Fantasy: *A Wizard of Earthsea,*" *Hornbook* 47 (1971), p. 130.

29. U. K. LeGuin, "From Elfland to Poughkeepsie," in S. Wood (ed.), *The Language of the Night* (New York: Berkley Books, 1982), p. 84.

30. U. K. LeGuin, "From Elfland to Poughkeepsie," p. 85.

31. C. W. Sullivan III, *Welsh Celtic Myth in Modern Fantasy,* p. 106.

32. L. Alexander, "Substance and Fantasy," *Library Journal* 91 (1966), p. 6158.

33. S. Sturluson, *The Prose Edda,* trans J. Young (Berkeley: University of California Press, 1966), p. 41.

34. U. K. LeGuin, "From Elfland to Poughkeepsie," p. 83.

35. J. R. R. Tolkien, "English and Welsh," in *Angles and Britons* (Cardiff: University of Wales Press, 1963), p. 1.

36. C. W. Sullivan III, "Name and Lineage Patterns: Aragorn and Beowulf," *Extrapolation* 25 (1984), pp. 244–5.

37. G. Herm, *The Celts* (New York: St. Martin's Press, 1976), p. 239.

38. K. Hume, *Fantasy and Mimesis,* p. 88.

39. S. Donaldson, *Epic Fantasy in the Modern World* (Kent: Kent State University Libraries, 1986), pp. 3–4.

40. U. K. LeGuin, "From Elfland to Poughkeepsie," p. 84.

41. L. Alexander, "Truth About Fantasy," *Top of the News* 24 (1968), p. 174.

42. L. Alexander, "Truth About Fantasy," p. 170.

43. H. Brogan, "Tolkien's Great War," in G. Avery and J. Briggs (eds.), *Children and Their Books* (Oxford: Clarendon Press, 1989), p. 353; and N. Philip, "*The Wind in the Willows:* the Vitality of a Classic," in G. Avery and J. Briggs (eds), *Children and Their Books* (Oxford: Clarendon Press, 1989), p. 313.

Ursula K. Le Guin (b. 1929)

Ursula K. Le Guin is one of America's leading writers of fantasy and science fiction. She has written many stories for children and adults, while her best-known series of high fantasy novels and stories, the Earthsea books (published from 1968 on), is popular with young adult readers. "Why Are Americans Afraid of Dragons?" was first written in 1974 and then published in a collection of her talks and essays, *The Language of the Night: Essays on Fantasy and Science Fiction* (1979). Le Guin writes frankly about how her fiction and nonfiction changed along with political and social developments over the years, and about her frustrations with biases against fantasy writing in twentieth-century society and literary circles. Like other thinkers and writers from Albert Einstein to Jane Yolen, Le Guin eloquently defends good fantasy writing for the profound and challenging truths that are inherent in it, which children instinctively recognize and adults often denigrate because they fear perceptions that threaten the status quo. She values what she calls "the uses of the imagination, especially in fiction, and most especially in fairy tale, legend, fantasy, science fiction and the rest of the lunatic fringe." That last phrase reflects the biting tone in her indictment of historical and social developments that have fostered "moral disapproval of fantasy."

Why Are Americans Afraid of Dragons?

This was to be a talk about fantasy. But I have not been feeling very fanciful lately, and could not decide what to say; so I have been going about picking people's brains for ideas. "What about fantasy? Tell me something about fantasy." And one friend of mine said, "All right, I'll tell you something fantastic. Ten years ago, I went to the children's room of the library of such-and-such a city, and asked for *The Hobbit;* and the librarian told me, 'Oh, we keep that only in the adult collection; we don't feel that escapism is good for children.'"

My friend and I had a good laugh and shudder over that, and we agreed that things have changed a great deal in these past ten years. That kind of moralistic censorship of works of fantasy is very uncommon now, in the children's libraries. But the fact that the children's libraries have become oases in the desert doesn't mean that there isn't still a desert. The point of view from which that librarian spoke still exists. She was merely reflecting, in perfect good faith, something that goes very deep in the American character: a moral disapproval of fantasy, a disapproval so intense, and often so aggressive, that I cannot help but see it as arising, fundamentally, from fear.

So: Why are Americans afraid of dragons?

Before I try to answer my question, let me say that it isn't only Americans who are afraid of dragons. I suspect that almost all very highly technological peoples are more or less antifantasy. There are several national literatures which, like ours, have had no tradition of adult fantasy for the past several hundred years: the French, for instance. But then you have the Germans, who have a good deal; and the English, who have it, and love it, and do it better than anyone else. So this fear of dragons is not merely a Western, or a technological, phenomenon. But I do not want to get into these vast historical questions; I will speak of modern Americans, the only people I know well enough to talk about.

In wondering why Americans are afraid of dragons, I began to realize that a great many Americans are not only antifantasy, but altogether antifiction. We tend, as a people, to look upon all works of the imagination either as suspect or as contemptible.

"My wife reads novels. I haven't got the time."

"I used to read that science fiction stuff when I was a teenager, but of course I don't now."

"Fairy stories are for kids. I live in the real world."

Who speaks so? Who is it that dismisses *War and Peace, The Time Machine* and *A Midsummer Night's Dream* with this perfect self-assurance? It is, I fear, the man in the street—the hard-working, over-thirty American male—the men who run this country.

Such a rejection of the entire art of fiction is related to several American characteristics: our Puritanism, our work ethic, our profit-mindedness, and even our sexual mores.

To read *War and Peace* or *The Lord of the Rings* plainly is not "work"—you do it for pleasure. And if it cannot be justified as "educational" or as "self-improvement," then, in the Puritan value system, it can only be self-indulgence or escapism. For pleasure is not a value, to the Puritan; on the contrary, it is a sin.

Equally, in the businessman's value system, if an act does not bring in an immediate, tangible profit, it has no justification at all. Thus the only person who has an excuse to read Tolstoy or Tolkien is the English teacher, who gets paid for it. But our businessman might allow himself to read a best-seller now and then: not because it is a good book, but because it is a best-seller—it is a success, it has made money. To the strangely mystical mind of the money-changer, this justifies its existence; and by reading it he may participate, a little, in the power and mana of its success. If this is not magic, by the way, I don't know what it is.

The last element, the sexual one, is more complex. I hope I will not be understood as being sexist if I say that, within our culture, I believe that this antifiction attitude is basically a male one. The American boy and man is very commonly forced to define his maleness by rejecting certain traits, certain human gifts and potentialities, which our culture defines as "womanish" or "childish." And one of these traits or potentialities is, in cold sober fact, the absolutely essential human faculty of imagination.

Having got this far, I went quickly to the dictionary.

The *Shorter Oxford Dictionary* says: "Imagination. 1. The action of imagining, or forming a mental concept of what is not actually present to the senses; 2. The mental consideration of actions or events not yet in existence."

Very well; I certainly can let "absolutely essential human faculty" stand. But I must narrow the definition to fit our present subject. By "imagination," then, I personally mean the free play of the mind, both intellectual and sensory. By "play" I mean recreation, re-creation, the recombination of what is known into what is new. By "free" I mean that the action is done without an immediate object of profit—spontaneously. That does not mean, however, that there may not be a purpose behind the free play of the mind, a goal; and the goal may be a very serious object indeed. Children's imaginative play is clearly a practicing at the acts and emotions of adulthood; a child who did not play would not become mature. As for the free play of an adult mind, its result may be *War and Peace,* or the theory of relativity.

To be free, after all, is not to be undisciplined. I should say that the discipline of the imagination may in fact be the essential method or technique of both art and science. It is our Puritanism, insisting that discipline means repression or punishment, which confuses the subject. To discipline something, in the proper sense of the word, does not mean to repress it, but to train it—to encourage it to grow, and act, and be fruitful, whether it is a peach tree or a human mind.

I think that a great many American men have been taught just the opposite. They have learned to repress their imagination, to reject it as something childish or effeminate, unprofitable, and probably sinful.

They have learned to fear it. But they have never learned to discipline it at all.

Now, I doubt that the imagination can be suppressed. If you truly eradicated it in a child, that child would grow up to be an eggplant. Like all our evil propensities, the imagination will out. But if it is rejected and despised, it will grow into wild and weedy shapes; it will be deformed. At its best, it will be mere ego-centered daydreaming; at its worst, it will be wishful thinking, which is a very dangerous occupation when it is taken seriously. Where literature is concerned, in the old, truly Puritan days, the only permitted reading was the Bible. Nowadays, with our secular Puritanism, the man who refuses to read novels because it's unmanly to do so, or because they aren't true, will most likely end up watching bloody detective thrillers on the television, or reading hack Westerns or sports stories, or going in for pornography, from *Playboy* on down. It is his starved imagination, craving nourishment, that forces him to do so. But he can rationalize such entertainment by saying that it is realistic—after all, sex exists, and there are criminals, and there are baseball players, and there used to be cowboys—and also by saying that it is virile, by which he means that it doesn't interest most women.

That all these genres are sterile, hopelessly sterile, is a reassurance to him, rather than a defect. If they were genuinely realistic, which is to say genuinely imagined and imaginative, he would be afraid of them. Fake realism is the escapist literature of our time. And probably the ultimate escapist reading is that masterpiece of total unreality, the daily stock market report.

Now what about our man's wife? She probably wasn't required to squelch her private imagination in order to play her expected role in life, but she hasn't been trained to discipline it either. She is allowed to read novels, and even fantasies. But, lacking training and encouragement, her fancy is likely to glom on to very sickly fodder, such things as soap operas, and "true romances," and nursy novels, and historico-sentimental novels, and all the rest of the baloney ground out to replace genuine imaginative works by the artistic sweatshops of a society that is profoundly distrustful of the uses of the imagination.

What, then, are the uses of imagination?

You see, I think we have a terrible thing here: a hardworking, upright, responsible citizen, a full-grown, educated person, who is afraid of dragons, and afraid of hobbits, and scared to death of fairies. It's funny, but it's also terrible. Something has gone very wrong. I don't know what to do about it but to try and give an honest answer to that person's question, even though he often asks it in an aggressive and contemptuous tone of voice. "What's the good of it all?" he says. "Dragons and hobbits and little green men— what's the *use* of it?"

The truest answer, unfortunately, he won't even listen to. He won't hear it. The truest answer is, "The use of it is to give you pleasure and delight."

"I haven't got the time," he snaps, swallowing a Maalox pill for his ulcer and rushing off to the golf course.

So we try the next-to-truest answer. It probably won't go down much better, but it must be said: "The use of imaginative fiction is to deepen your understanding of your world, and your fellow men, and your own feelings, and your destiny."

To which I fear he will retort, "Look, I got a raise last year, and I'm giving my family the best of everything, we've got two cars and a color TV. I understand enough of the world!"

And he is right, unanswerably right, if that is what he wants, and all he wants.

The kind of thing you learn from reading about the problems of a hobbit who is trying to drop a magic ring into an imaginary volcano has very little to do with your social status, or material success, or income. Indeed, if there is any relationship, it is a negative one. There is an inverse correlation between fantasy and money. That is a law, known to economists as Le Guin's Law. If you want a striking example of Le Guin's Law, just give a lift to one of those people along the roads who own nothing but a backpack, a guitar, a fine head of hair, a smile and a thumb. Time and again, you will find that these waifs have read *The Lord of the Rings*—some of them can practically recite it. But now take Aristotle Onassis or J. Paul Getty: could you believe that those men ever had anything to do, at any age, under any circumstances, with a hobbit?

But, to carry my example a little further, and out of the realm of economics, did you ever notice how very gloomy Mr. Onassis and Mr. Getty and all those billionaires look in their photographs? They have this strange, pinched look, as if they were hungry. As if they were hungry for something, as if they had lost something and were trying to think where it could be, or perhaps what it could be, what it was they've lost.

Could it be their childhood?

So I arrive at my personal defense of the uses of the imagination, especially in fiction, and most especially in fairy tale, legend, fantasy, science fiction and the rest of the lunatic fringe. I believe that maturity is not an outgrowing, but a growing up: that an adult is not a dead child, but a child who survived. I believe that all the best faculties of a mature human being exist in the child, and that if these faculties are encouraged in youth they will act well and wisely in the adult, but if they are repressed and denied in the child they will stunt and cripple the adult personality. And finally, I believe that one of the most deeply human, and humane, of these faculties is the power of imagination: so that it is our pleasant duty, as librarians, or teachers, or parents, or writers, or simply as grownups, to encourage that faculty of imagination in our children, to encourage it to grow freely, to flourish like the green bay tree, by giving it the best, absolutely the best and purest, nourishment that it can absorb. And never, under any circumstances, to squelch it, or sneer at it, or imply that it is childish, or unmanly, or untrue.

For fantasy is true, of course. It isn't factual, but it is true. Children know that. Adults know it too, and that is precisely why many of them are afraid of fantasy. They know that its truth challenges, even threatens, all that is false, all that is phony, unnecessary, and trivial in the life they have let themselves be forced into living. They are afraid of dragons, because they are afraid of freedom.

So I believe that we should trust our children. Normal children do not confuse reality and fantasy—they confuse them much less often than we adults do (as a certain great fantasist pointed out in a story called "The Emperor's New Clothes"). Children know perfectly well that unicorns aren't real, but they also know that books about unicorns, if they are good books, are true books. All too often, that's more than Mummy and Daddy know; for, in denying their childhood, the adults have denied half their knowledge, and are left with the sad, sterile little fact: "Unicorns aren't real." And that fact is one that never got anybody anywhere (except in the story "The Unicorn in the Garden," by another great fantasist, in which it is shown that a devotion to the unreality of unicorns may get you straight into the loony bin). It is by such statements as, "Once upon a time there was a dragon," or "In a hole in the ground there lived a hobbit"—it is by such beautiful non-facts that we fantastic human beings may arrive, in our peculiar fashion, at the truth.

Perry Nodelman (b. 1945)

Perry Nodelman is a writer for children and young adults and one of the most distinguished critics of children's literature. He teaches at the University of Winnipeg and has written about a wide range of topics, from picture books (see the selection from *Words About Pictures* in Part 6) to criticism (*The Pleasures of Children's Literature,* 1992). His analyses are incisive and often provocative. In this 1997 statement from an on-line discussion, he suggests that fantasy may be offensive to some readers because it is too realistic.

Liking and Not Liking Fantasy

I've noticed something that interests me in the discussion of liking and not liking fantasy. Some people say they like it because it ISN'T real (it's an escape, etc.), and on the other hand, some people say they like it because it IS real (along the lines of Le Guin's idea that a fantasy setting allows a writer the freedom to explore real concerns with some honesty). Meanwhile, people who say they don't like fantasy have focussed on its lack of realism, their inability to identify with it or see its relevance to their own existences, etc. What interests me is that so far, no one has expressed the fourth term of this pair of opposites—the position that they don't like fantasy because it's too realistic.

If there's any validity in the Le Guin theory—and I personally think there is—then might that also be a possibility? Perhaps the fiction we can easily identify as being realistic is the fiction that most satisfies what we already like to believe or pretend to believe to be true about reality—and is therefore comforting to us, an escape into complacency; whereas fantasy might well be asking us to acknowledge aspects of our actual reality, present as or allowed by fantasy elements, that we don't particularly want to recognize or accept as being real?

I happily acknowledge the existence of huge numbers of fantasies for children and adults that are anything but unsettling, and that merely represent tired versions of desperately overused pseudo-medieval or other antiquated fantasy conventions. Even so, good fantasies can and often do manage to move past the conventional, and do tend to be dangerous.

Consider, for instance, stories for young children about talking animals. The danger in them becomes clear if you imagine for an instant that the characters are human beings and not animals. Would E. B. White get away with describing how a boy named Wilbur is incarcerated and threatened with death by a group of cannibals? Would Beatrix Potter seem so charming if Peter Human was an accomplished thief and was threatened with instant death by the property owner McGregor? Putting an animal or some other fantasy character in the position a child might occupy—and that a child reader is most often invited to identify with—allows a writer to explore a whole range of emotional and sexual and intellectual and religious concerns that would be forbidden or at least very surprising in a story about human children. For that matter, the very idea of animals who talk functions as an interesting (and unsettling) metaphor for human lives and specifically for the relationship of human minds to human bodies and bodily functions—a subject generally considered controversial in books for children about human children.

My own experience as a writer of fiction is that I can get away with what I see as a far more honest depiction of childhood life and thought far more easily in

432

the context of fantasy. When my character Johnny Nesbit confronted weird fairies and changelings and Cowalkers in *The Same Place But Different* and *A Completely Different Place,* he could have all sorts of thoughts about death and violence and about his own bodily functions and desires. But my new book, *Behaving Bradley* (coming out next spring), is a realistic book, i.e., with no fantasy elements, and intended for a slightly older and more sophisticated audience than the fantasies—and I found that friends who read the drafts were often distressed by exactly the same kinds of ideas or emotions that they accepted without comment in the fantasies. As much as I enjoyed writing *Bradley* (and did, despite some friendly advice to the contrary, keep it as honest and dangerous as I'd first conceived it), I've decided I much prefer doing fantasy, exactly because it allows me to be more easily and acceptably honest and realistic.

Unfortunately, however, I may not get the chance. Fantasy for older children and young adults is less marketable than it once was, exactly for the reason that has come up more than once in this thread—the conviction of the adults who deal with children's books that older children and young adults no longer much like to read fantasy, so there's little point in producing much of it or buying much of it for libraries. If it's actually true that they don't like fantasy—and I hope it isn't—then it worries me a lot, because it seems to me to mean that we've managed to produce a generation of children who are much too committed to one limited view of what reality is and much too afraid of new ideas and dangerous possibilities in themselves and their world.

Charles Dickens (1812–70)

The great English novelist Charles Dickens had an intuitive and deeply sympathetic understanding of childhood—especially of poor and exploited children. He had been one himself, working in a London blacking factory as a boy and visiting his family while they lived in a debtors' prison. Although he wrote only a few stories specifically for children, depictions of children from all social classes and their complex relationships with adults play prominent roles in many of Dickens's novels, especially *David Copperfield, Great Expectations,* and *Dombey and Son.* And who can forget poor Oliver Twist begging for more gruel in a workhouse for orphans or the lame child Tiny Tim asking for God's blessing on the struggling Cratchit family in *A Christmas Carol?* The death of the homeless poor child Little Nell in *The Old Curiosity Shop* (1841), now considered excessively sentimental, was one of the most popular literary episodes in its day, anxiously anticipated by crowds of readers on both sides of the Atlantic when the novel first appeared as a magazine serial. In *Hard Times* (1854), a novel exposing the dehumanizing effects of Utilitarian attitudes during the Industrial Revolution, Dickens portrays a Victorian schoolmaster, Mr. Gradgrind, whose unimaginative and harsh approach to teaching is, like his voice, "inflexible, dry, and dictatorial." Dickens satirizes the attitude that only fact, never fancy, should be the foundation of education—and of life.

From *Hard Times*

CHAPTER 1. THE ONE THING NEEDFUL

"Now, what I want is, Facts. Teach these boys and girls nothing but Facts. Facts alone are wanted in life. Plant nothing else, and root out everything else. You can only form the minds of reasoning animals upon Facts: nothing else will ever be of any service to them. This is the principle on which I bring up my own children, and this is the principle on which I bring up these children. Stick to Facts, sir!"

The scene was a plain, bare, monotonous vault of a schoolroom, and the speaker's square forefinger emphasised his observations by underscoring every sentence with a line on the schoolmaster's sleeve. The emphasis was helped by the speaker's square wall of a forehead, which had his eyebrows for its base, while his eyes found commodious cellarage in two dark caves, overshadowed by the wall. The emphasis was helped by the speaker's mouth, which was wide, thin, and hard set. The emphasis was helped by the speaker's voice, which was inflexible, dry, and dictatorial. The emphasis was helped by the speaker's hair, which bristled on the skirts of his bald head, a plantation of firs to keep the wind from its shining surface, all covered with knobs, like the crust of a plum pie, as if the head had scarcely warehouse-room for the hard facts stored inside. The speaker's obstinate carriage, square coat, square legs, square shoulders,—nay, his very neckcloth, trained to take him by the throat with an unaccommodating grasp, like a stubborn fact, as it was,—all helped the emphasis.

"In this life, we want nothing but Facts, sir; nothing but Facts!"

The speaker, and the schoolmaster, and the third grown person present, all backed a little, and swept with their eyes the inclined plane of little vessels then and there arranged in order, ready to have imperial gallons of facts poured into them until they were full to the brim.

CHAPTER 2. MURDERING THE INNOCENTS

Thomas Gradgrind, sir. A man of realities. A man of facts and calculations. A man who proceeds upon the principle that two and two are four, and nothing over, and who is not to be talked into allowing for anything over. Thomas Gradgrind, sir—peremptorily Thomas—Thomas Gradgrind. With a rule and a pair of scales, and the multiplication table always in his pocket, sir, ready to weigh and measure any parcel of human nature, and tell you exactly what it comes to. It is a mere question of figures, a case of simple arithmetic. You might hope to get some other nonsensical belief into the head of George Gradgrind, or Augustus Gradgrind, or John Gradgrind, or Joseph Gradgrind (all supposititious, nonexistent persons), but into the head of Thomas Gradgrind—no, sir!

In such terms Mr. Gradgrind always mentally introduced himself, whether to his private circle of acquaintance, or to the public in general. In such terms, no doubt, substituting the words "boys and girls," for "sir," Thomas Gradgrind now presented Thomas Gradgrind to the little pitchers before him, who were to be filled so full of facts.

Indeed, as he eagerly sparkled at them from the cellarage before mentioned, he seemed a kind of cannon loaded to the muzzle with facts, and prepared to blow them clean out of the regions of childhood at one discharge. He seemed a galvanizing apparatus, too, charged with a grim mechanical substitute for the tender young imaginations that were to be stormed away.

"Girl number twenty," said Mr. Gradgrind, squarely pointing with his square forefinger, "I don't know that girl. Who is that girl?"

"Sissy Jupe, sir," explained number twenty, blushing, standing up, and curtseying.

"Sissy is not a name," said Mr. Gradgrind. "Don't call yourself Sissy. Call yourself Cecilia."

"It's father as calls me Sissy, sir," returned the young girl in a trembling voice, and with another curtsey.

"Then he has no business to do it," said Mr. Gradgrind. "Tell him he mustn't. Cecilia Jupe. Let me see. What is your father?"

"He belongs to the horse-riding, if you please, sir."

Mr. Gradgrind frowned, and waved off the objectionable calling with his hand.

"We don't want to know anything about that, here.

You mustn't tell us about that, here. Your father breaks horses, don't he?"

"If you please, sir, when they can get any to break, they do break horses in the ring, sir."

"You mustn't tell us about the ring, here. Very well, then. Describe your father as a horsebreaker. He doctors sick horses, I dare say?"

"Oh yes, sir."

"Very well, then. He is a veterinary surgeon, a farrier, and horsebreaker. Give me your definition of a horse."

(Sissy Jupe thrown into the greatest alarm by this demand.)

"Girl number twenty unable to define a horse!" said Mr. Gradgrind, for the general behoof of all the little pitchers. "Girl number twenty possessed of no facts, in reference to one of the commonest of animals! Some boy's definition of a horse. Bitzer, yours."

The square finger, moving here and there, lighted suddenly on Bitzer, perhaps because he chanced to sit in the same ray of sunlight which, darting in at one of the bare windows of the intensely whitewashed room, irradiated Sissy. For, the boys and girls sat on the face of the inclined plane in two compact bodies, divided up the centre by a narrow interval; and Sissy, being at the corner of a row on the sunny side, came in for the beginning of a sunbeam, of which Bitzer, being at the corner of a row on the other side, a few rows in advance, caught the end. But, whereas the girl was so dark-eyed and dark-haired, that she seemed to receive a deeper and more lustrous colour from the sun, when it shone upon her, the boy was so light-eyed and light-haired that the self-same rays appeared to draw out of him what little colour he ever possessed. His cold eyes would hardly have been eyes, but for the short ends of lashes which, by bringing them into immediate contrast with something paler than themselves, expressed their form. His short-cropped hair might have been a mere continuation of the sandy freckles on his forehead and face. His skin was so unwholesomely deficient in the natural tinge, that he looked as though, if he were cut, he would bleed white.

"Bitzer," said Thomas Gradgrind. "Your definition of a horse."

"Quadruped. Graminivorous. Forty teeth, namely twenty-four grinders, four eye-teeth, and twelve incisive. Sheds coat in the spring; in marshy countries, sheds hoofs, too. Hoofs hard, but requiring to be shod with iron. Age known by marks in mouth." Thus (and much more) Bitzer.

"Now girl number twenty," said Mr. Gradgrind. "You know what a horse is."

She curtseyed again, and would have blushed deeper, if she could have blushed deeper than she had blushed all this time. Bitzer, after rapidly blinking at Thomas Gradgrind with both eyes at once, and so catching the light upon his quivering ends of lashes that they looked like the antennæ of busy insects, put his knuckles to his freckled forehead, and sat down again.

ALWAYS IN TRAINING

The third gentleman now stepped forth. A mighty man at cutting and drying, he was; a government officer; in his way (and in most other people's too), a professed pugilist; always in training, always with a system to force down the general throat like a bolus, always to be heard of at the bar of his little Public-office, ready to fight all England. To continue in fistic phraseology, he had a genius for coming up to the scratch, wherever and whatever it was, and proving himself an ugly customer. He would go in and damage any subject whatever with his right, follow up with his left, stop, exchange, counter, bore his opponent (he always fought All England) to the ropes, and fall upon him neatly. He was certain to knock the wind out of common sense, and render that unlucky adversary deaf to the call of time. And he had it in charge from high authority to bring about the great public-office Millennium, when Commissioners should reign upon earth.

"Very well," said this gentleman, briskly smiling, and folding his arms. "That's a horse. Now, let me ask you girls and boys, Would you paper a room with representations of horses?"

After a pause, one half of the children cried in chorus, "Yes, sir!" Upon which the other half, seeing in the gentleman's face that Yes was wrong, cried out in chorus, "No, sir!"—as the custom is, in these examinations.

"Of course, No. Why wouldn't you?"

A pause. One corpulent slow boy, with a wheezy manner of breathing, ventured the answer, Because he wouldn't paper a room at all, but would paint it.

"You *must* paper it," said the gentleman, rather warmly.

"You must paper it," said Thomas Gradgrind, "whether you like it or not. Don't tell *us* you wouldn't paper it. What do you mean, boy?"

"I'll explain to you, then," said the gentleman, after another and a dismal pause, "why you wouldn't paper a room with representations of horses. Do you ever see horses walking up and down the sides of rooms in reality—in fact? Do you?"

"Yes, sir!" from one half. "No, sir!" from the other.

"Of course, No," said the gentleman, with an indignant look at the wrong half. "Why, then, you are not to see anywhere, what you don't see in fact; you are not to have anywhere, what you don't have in fact. What is called Taste, is only another name for Fact."

Thomas Gradgrind nodded his approbation.

"This is a new principle, a discovery, a great discovery," said the gentleman. "Now, I'll try you again. Suppose you were going to carpet a room. Would you use a carpet having a representation of flowers upon it?"

There being a general conviction by this time that "No, sir!" was always the right answer to this gentleman, the chorus of No was very strong. Only a few feeble stragglers said Yes: among them Sissy Jupe.

"Girl number twenty," said the gentleman, smiling in the calm strength of knowledge.

Sissy blushed, and stood up.

"So you would carpet your room—or your husband's room, if you were a grown woman, and had a husband—with representations of flowers, would you?" said the gentleman. "Why would you?"

"If you please, sir, I am very fond of flowers," returned the girl.

"And is that why you would put tables and chairs upon them, and have people walking over them with heavy boots?"

"It wouldn't hurt them, sir. They wouldn't crush and wither, if you please, sir. They would be the pictures of what was very pretty and pleasant, and I would fancy—"

"Ay, ay, ay! But you mustn't fancy," cried the gentleman, quite elated by coming so happily to his point. "That's it! You are never to fancy."

"You are not, Cecilia Jupe," Thomas Gradgrind solemnly repeated, "to do anything of that kind."

MATTERS OF FACT

"Fact, fact, fact!" said the gentleman. And "Fact, fact, fact!" repeated Thomas Gradgrind.

"You are to be in all things regulated and governed," said the gentleman, "by fact. We hope to have, before long, a board of fact, composed of commissioners of fact, who will force the people to be a people of fact, and of nothing but fact. You must discard the word Fancy altogether. You have nothing to do with it. You are not to have, in any object of use or ornament, what would be a contradiction in fact. You don't walk upon flowers in fact; you cannot be allowed to walk upon flowers in carpets. You don't find that foreign birds and butterflies come and perch upon your crockery; you cannot be permitted to paint foreign birds and butterflies upon your crockery. You never meet with quadrupeds going up and down walls; you must not have quadrupeds represented upon walls. You must use," said the gentleman, "for all these purposes, combinations and modifications (in primary colours) of mathematical figures which are susceptible of proof and demonstration. This is the new discovery. This is fact. This is taste."

The girl curtseyed, and sat down. She was very young, and she looked as if she were frightened by the matter of fact prospect the world afforded.

"Now, if Mr. M'Choakumchild," said the gentleman, "will proceed to give his first lesson here, Mr. Gradgrind, I shall be happy, at your request, to observe his mode of procedure."

Mr. Gradgrind was much obliged. "Mr. M'Choakumchild, we only wait for you."

So, Mr. M'Choakumchild began in his best manner. He and some one hundred and forty other schoolmasters, had been lately turned at the same time, in the same factory, on the same principles, like so many pianoforte legs. He had been put through an immense variety of paces, and had answered volumes of headbreaking questions. Orthography, etymology, syntax, and prosody, biography, astronomy, geography, and general cosmography, the sciences of compound proportion, algebra, land-surveying and levelling, vocal music, and drawing from models, were all at the ends of his ten chilled fingers. He had worked his stony way into Her Majesty's most Honourable Privy Council's Schedule B, and had taken the bloom off the higher branches of mathematics and physical science, French, German, Latin, and Greek. He knew all about all the Water Sheds of all the world (whatever they are), and all the histories of all the peoples, and all the names of all the rivers and mountains, and all the productions, manners, and customs of all the countries, and all their boundaries and bearings on the two and thirty points of the compass. Ah, rather overdone, M'Choakumchild. If he had only learnt a little less, how infinitely better he might have taught much more!

He went to work in this preparatory lesson, not unlike Morgiana in the Forty Thieves: looking into all the vessels ranged before him, one after another, to see what they contained. Say, good M'Choakumchild. When from thy boiling store, thou shalt fill each jar brim full by-and-by, dost thou think that thou wilt always kill outright the robber Fancy lurking within—or sometimes only maim him and distort him!

CHAPTER 3. A LOOPHOLE

Mr. Gradgrind walked homeward from the school, in a state of considerable satisfaction. It was his school, and he intended it to be a model. He intended every child in it to be a model—just as the young Gradgrinds were all models.

There were five young Gradgrinds, and they were models every one. They had been lectured at, from their tenderest years; coursed, like little hares. Almost as soon as they could run alone, they had been made to run to the lecture-room. The first object with which they had an association, or of which they had a remembrance, was a large black board with a dry Ogre chalking ghastly white figures on it.

Not that they knew, by name or nature, anything about an Ogre. Fact forbid! I only use the word to express a monster in a lecturing castle, with Heaven knows how many heads manipulated into one, taking childhood captive, and dragging it into gloomy statistical dens by the hair.

No little Gradgrind had ever seen a face in the moon; it was up in the moon before it could speak distinctly. No little Gradgrind had ever learnt the silly jingle, Twinkle, twinkle, little star; how I wonder what you are! No little Gradgrind had ever known wonder on the subject, each little Gradgrind having at five years old dissected the Great Bear like a Professor Owen, and driven Charles's Wain like a locomotive engine-driver. No little Gradgrind had ever associated a cow in a field with that famous cow with the crumpled horn who tossed the dog who worried the cat who killed the rat who ate the malt, or with that yet more fa-

mous cow who swallowed Tom Thumb: it had never heard of those celebrities, and had only been introduced to a cow as a graminivorous ruminating quadruped with several stomachs.

To his matter of fact home, which was called Stone Lodge, Mr. Gradgrind directed his steps. He had virtually retired from the wholesale hardware trade before he built Stone Lodge, and was now looking about for a suitable opportunity of making an arithmetical figure in Parliament. Stone Lodge was situated on a moor within a mile or two of a great town—called Coketown in the present faithful guide-book.

A very regular feature on the face of the country, Stone Lodge was. Not the least disguise toned down or shaded off that uncompromising fact in the landscape. A great square house, with a heavy portico darkening the principal windows, as its master's heavy brows overshadowed his eyes. A calculated, cast up, balanced, and proved house. Six windows on this side of the door, six on that side; a total of twelve in this wing, a total of twelve in the other wing; four and twenty carried over to the back wings. A lawn and garden and an infant avenue, all ruled straight like a botanical account-book. Gas and ventilation, drainage and water-service, all of the primest quality. Iron clamps and girders, fireproof from top to bottom; mechanical lifts for the housemaids, with all their brushes and brooms; everything that heart could desire.

Everything? Well, I suppose so. The little Gradgrinds had cabinets in various departments of science too. They had a little conchological cabinet, and a little metallurgical cabinet, and a little mineralogical cabinet; and the specimens were all arranged and labelled, and the bits of stone and ore looked as though they might have been broken from the parent substances by those tremendously hard instruments their own names. And, to paraphrase the idle legend of Peter Piper, who had never found his way into their nursery, if the greedy little Gradgrinds grasped at more than this, what was it for good gracious goodness' sake, that the greedy little Gradgrinds grasped at!

Their father walked on in a hopeful and satisfied frame of mind. He was an affectionate father, after his manner; but he would probably have described himself (if he had been put, like Sissy Jupe, upon a definition) as "an eminently practical" father. He had a particular pride in the phrase eminently practical, which was considered to have a special application to him.

"Thomas Gradgrind Apprehends His Children Louisa and Tom at the Circus." Harry French's illustration draws attention to the imposing black figure of the stern father who disapproves of amusements and imagination.

Whatsoever the public meeting held in Coketown, and whatsoever the subject of such meeting, some Coketowner was sure to seize the occasion of alluding to his eminently practical friend Gradgrind. This always pleased the eminently practical friend. He knew it to be his due, but his due was acceptable.

He had reached the neutral ground upon the outskirts of the town, which was neither town nor country, and yet was either spoiled, when his ears were invaded by the sound of music. The clashing and banging band attached to the horse-riding establishment which had there set up its rest in a wooden pavilion was in full bray. A flag, floating from the summit of the temple, proclaimed to mankind that it was "Sleary's Horse-riding" which claimed their suffrages. Sleary himself, a stout modern statue with a money-box at its elbow, in an ecclesiastical niche of early Gothic architecture, took the money. Miss Josephine Sleary, as some very long and very narrow strips of

printed bill announced, was then inaugurating the entertainments with her graceful equestrian Tyrolean Flower-Act. Among the other pleasing but always strictly moral wonders which must be seen to be believed, Signor Jupe was that afternoon to "elucidate the diverting accomplishments of his highly trained performing dog Merrylegs." He was also to exhibit "his astounding feat of throwing seventy-five hundred-weight in rapid succession backhanded over his head, thus forming a fountain of solid iron in mid-air, a feat never before attempted in this or any other country, and which having elicited such rapturous plaudits from enthusiastic throngs it cannot be withdrawn." The same Signor Jupe was to "enliven the varied performances at frequent intervals with his chaste Shakespearean quips and retorts." Lastly, he was to wind them up by appearing in his favourite character of Mr. William Button, of Tooley Street, in "the highly novel and laughable hippo-comedietta of The Tailor's Journey to Brentford."

THE TOUCH OF NATURE

Thomas Gradgrind took no heed of these trivialities of course, but passed on as a practical man ought to pass on, either brushing the noisy insects from his thoughts, or consigning them to the House of Correction. But, the turning of the road took him by the back of the booth, and at the back of the booth a number of children were congregated in a number of stealthy attitudes, striving to peep in at the hidden glories of the place.

This brought him to a stop. "Now, to think of these vagabonds," said he, "attracting the young rabble from a model school."

A space of stunted grass and dry rubbish being between him and the young rabble, he took his eyeglass out of his waistcoat to look for any child he knew by name, and might order off. Phenomenon almost incredible though distinctly seen, what did he then behold but his own metallurgical Louisa, peeping with all her might through a hole in a deal board, and his own mathematical Thomas abasing himself on the ground to catch but a hoof of the graceful equestrian Tyrolean Flower-Act!

Dumb with amazement, Mr. Gradgrind crossed to the spot where his family was thus disgraced, laid his hand upon each erring child, and said:

"Louisa! ! Thomas! !"

Both rose, red and disconcerted. But, Louisa looked at her father with more boldness than Thomas did. Indeed, Thomas did not look at him, but gave himself up to be taken home like a machine.

"In the name of wonder, idleness, and folly!" said Mr. Gradgrind, leading each away by a hand; "what do you do here?"

"Wanted to see what it was like," returned Louisa, shortly.

"What it was like?"

"Yes, father."

There was an air of jaded sullenness in them both, and particularly in the girl: yet, struggling through the dissatisfaction of her face, there was a light with nothing to rest upon, a fire with nothing to burn, a starved imagination keeping life in itself somehow, which brightened its expression. Not with the brightness natural to cheerful youth, but with uncertain, eager, doubtful flashes, which had something painful in them, analogous to the changes on a blind face groping its way.

She was a child now, of fifteen or sixteen; but at no distant day would seem to become a woman all at once. Her father thought so as he looked at her. She was pretty. Would have been self-willed (he thought in his eminently practical way) but for her bringing-up.

"Thomas, though I have the fact before me, I find it difficult to believe that you, with your education and resources, should have brought your sister to a scene like this."

"I brought *him,* father," said Louisa quickly. "I asked him to come."

"I am sorry to hear it. I am very sorry indeed to hear it. It makes Thomas no better, and it makes you worse, Louisa."

She looked at her father again, but no tear fell down her cheek.

"You! Thomas and you, to whom the circle of the sciences is open; Thomas and you, who may be said to be replete with facts; Thomas and you, who have been trained to mathematical exactness; Thomas and you, here!" cried Mr. Gradgrind. "In this degraded position! I am amazed."

"I was tired, father. I have been tired a long time," said Louisa.

"Tired? Of what?" asked the astonished father.

"I don't know of what—of everything, I think."

"Say not another word," returned Mr. Gradgrind. "You are childish. I will hear no more." He did not speak again until they had walked some half-a-mile in silence, when he gravely broke out with: "What would your best friends say, Louisa? Do you attach no value to their good opinion? What would Mr. Bounderby say?"

At the mention of this name, his daughter stole a look at him, remarkable for its intense and searching character. He saw nothing of it, for before he looked at her, she had again cast down her eyes.

"What," he repeated presently, "would Mr. Bounderby say?" All the way to Stone Lodge, as with grave indignation he led the two delinquents home, he repeated at intervals "What would Mr. Bounderby say!"—as if Mr. Bounderby had been Mrs. Grundy.

Carlo Lorenzini (Carlo Collodi) (1826–90)

Pinocchio is famous as the puppet-boy whose nose grows whenever he tells a lie. He was created by the Italian writer Carlo Lorenzini, a journalist and educator who founded a journal called *Il Lampione* (*The Lantern*) and fought in two wars for Italian independence from Austria. Lorenzini took his pen name, Collodi, from the village in Tuscany where his mother was born. He first wrote the story of Pinocchio (which literally translated means "little pine nut") for the children's section of a newspaper in Rome, where it appeared in serialized form. The most beloved children's book ever written in Italy, it is much more raucous, witty, and lively than the 1940 Disney film that was based upon it. It reflects the harsh conditions of working-class life in nineteenth-century Italy. Pinocchio is a juvenile delinquent who keeps making unwise choices, such as selling the schoolbook his "father," the wood carver, sacrificed his precious jacket for, in order to gain admission to a fair. Yet most readers cannot dislike the incorrigible puppet-boy; his liveliness and sauciness make him irresistible. In chapter 3, this toy fantasy about a boy carved from a talking block of wood, brought to life through a strange combination of nature, magic, and human effort, shows that some children are born wild. Even before his puppet body is fully formed, Pinocchio begins his cycle of injuring his father, tearfully regretting his mischief, and running off to cause more trouble in public. Although the narrator is often moralistic about Pinocchio's misdeeds, the story conveys a mixed message of admiration and condemnation.

From *The Adventures of Pinocchio*

TRANSLATED BY NICHOLAS J. PERELLA

CHAPTER 3

After returning home, Geppetto begins at once to make his puppet and names him Pinocchio. The first pranks of the puppet.

Geppetto's home was a small room on the ground floor that got its light from the areaway under a staircase. The furnishings couldn't have been more modest: a rickety chair, a broken-down bed and a battered table. At the back wall you could see a fireplace with a fire burning; but it was a painted fire, and along with the fire there was painted a kettle that boiled merrily and sent up a cloud of steam that really looked like steam.

Once inside, Geppetto immediately got his tools and began to carve and shape his puppet.

"What name shall I give him?" he said to himself. "I'll call him Pinocchio. The name will bring him good luck. I once knew a whole family of Pinocchios: the father was a Pinocchio, the mother was a Pinocchia, and the children were Pinocchios. And they all did well for themselves. The richest one of them begged for a living."

Having found a name for his puppet, he then began to work in earnest, and quickly made his hair, then his forehead, and then his eyes.

When the eyes were done, just imagine his astonishment when he realized that those eyes moved and that they were staring him straight in the face.

Seeing himself looked at by those two eyes of wood, Geppetto took a little offense and said in an irritated tone:

"Spiteful wooden eyes, why are you looking at me?"

Nobody answered.

Then, after the eyes he made him a nose. But as soon as the nose was made, it began to grow; and it grew and grew and grew so that in a few minutes it became an endless nose.

Poor Geppetto kept struggling to cut it back; but the more he cut and shortened it, the longer that impudent nose became.

After the nose he made him a mouth.

The mouth wasn't even done when it quickly began to laugh and mock him.

"Stop laughing!" said Geppetto out of sorts; but it was like talking to the wall.

"Stop laughing, I repeat!" he roared in a threatening voice.

The mouth stopped laughing then; but it stuck its tongue out all the way.

So as not to spoil what he was doing, Geppetto pretended not to notice this and went on working. After the mouth, he made his chin, then his neck, then his shoulders, his trunk, his arms and his hands.

As soon as the hands were finished, Geppetto felt his wig being snatched from his head. He looked up, and what did he see? He saw his yellow wig in the puppet's hands.

"Pinocchio! . . . give me back my wig at once."

"As soon as he gets home, Geppetto fashions the Marionette and calls it Pinocchio." Enrico Mazzanti's drawing shows Gepetto's amazement at his own creation when his puppet starts behaving rudely before its limbs are all formed.

But instead of giving back the wig, Pinocchio put it on his own head, nearly suffocating underneath it.

At that insolent and mocking behavior, Geppetto became sadder and more dejected than he had ever been in his life; and turning to Pinocchio, he said:

"Scamp of a child, you aren't even finished and you're already beginning to lack respect for your father! That's bad, my boy, bad!"

And he wiped away a tear.

The legs and feet still remained to be done.

When Geppetto finished making him feet, he felt a kick land on the tip of his nose.

"I deserve it!" he said to himself then. "I should have thought of it before; now it's too late."

Then he took the puppet under his arms and put him down on the floor of the room in order to make him walk.

Pinocchio's legs were stiff, and he didn't know how to move; so Geppetto led him by the hand, teaching him how to take one step after the other.

When his legs were limbered, Pinocchio began to walk on his own and then to run around the room; and then, having rushed out the door, he jumped into the street and set off on the run.

And there was poor Geppetto running after him without being able to catch up, because that imp of a Pinocchio bounded along like a hare; and as his wooden feet struck the pavement, he made a clatter like twenty pairs of peasants' clogs.

"Catch him! Catch him!" shouted Geppetto; but the passersby, seeing a wooden puppet running like a racehorse, just stood still in amazement to watch him, and laughed and laughed and laughed beyond belief.

At last, by a lucky chance, a carabiniere happened along. Hearing all that racket and thinking it was a colt running wildly out of control, he set himself bravely with legs wide apart in the middle of the street, determined to stop it and prevent anything worse from happening.

But when Pinocchio, from a distance, noticed that the carabiniere was blocking the whole street, he planned to surprise him by passing between his legs; but he botched it.

Without budging at all, the carabiniere snatched him neatly by the nose (it was an enormously long nose that seemed made expressly to be seized by carabinieri) and handed him over to Geppetto who, for the sake of discipline, immediately wanted to box his ears. But just imagine how he felt when, looking for his ears, he wasn't able to find them. And do you know why? Because in his haste to carve him, he had forgotten to make them.

So he took him by the scruff of the neck and as he led him back, he said, shaking his head threateningly:

"Let's go straight home. And when we're home, you can be sure that we'll settle our accounts!"

Hearing this tune, Pinocchio threw himself to the ground and refused to walk any further. Meanwhile the curious and the idlers began to stop and gather around them in a group.

Some said one thing; some said another.

"Poor puppet," some said, "he's right not to want to go home. Who knows how that awful Geppetto would beat him!"

And the others added maliciously:

"That Geppetto looks like a good man, but he's a real tyrant with children. If they leave that poor puppet in his hands, he's more than capable of hacking him to pieces."

In short, they made such a hue and cry that the carabiniere set Pinocchio free again and marched poor old Geppetto off to prison. And he, not finding words to defend himself just then, cried like a calf; and on the way to jail he stammered amid his sobbing:

"Wicked child! And to think that I worked so hard to make him into a nice puppet! But it serves me right. I should have known better."

What happened afterward is so strange a story that it is hardly to be believed; but I will tell you about it in the following chapters.

Robert Louis Stevenson (1850–94)

The Scottish writer Robert Louis Stevenson produced some of the most beloved literature of the nineteenth century, including *A Child's Garden of Verses* (1885), his only volume of poetry. While some of the poems in this famous collection sound pious and conventional today ("It is very nice to think / The world is full of meat and drink, / With little children saying grace / In every Christian kind of place"), many are still regarded as classics, imprinted on the memory of generations of readers. The secret of their enduring quality lies in Stevenson's ability to re-create not only the voice but the perspective of a child seeing the world afresh, with delight, and a sense of the awe and mystery inherent in the ordinary. So, for example, in one poem the speaker imagines his shadow as a constant companion. In another, the ill child's bed becomes a "land of counterpane" and the child himself a giant. Stevenson is able to evoke a sense of the magic and the vastness of what, to adults, has often become mundane, as in his short poem "Rain": "The rain is falling all around, / It falls on field and tree, / It rains on the umbrellas here, / And on the ships at sea." As both his poems and novels show (see the excerpt from *Treasure Island* in Part 5), Stevenson was, like Kenneth Grahame and his animal characters in *The Wind in the Willows,* alternating between the lure of adventure in the "wide world," or, at least, the world of the imagination, and nostalgia for the simple comforts of home and childhood. Stevenson traveled more widely than Grahame, seeking stories and relief from ill health around the world. The writings of both authors reflect the elitist attitudes of gentlemen of the British Empire; Stevenson's poem "Foreign Children" may seem smug and condescending in its attitude toward non-Western cultures, yet his affection for home, play, and the naive child's point of view remain amusing and endearing. Many parents today would love for their children to think like the child in "The Dumb Soldier," who is not playing war but imagining the tales his toy soldier could tell after spending time underground watching the "fairy things" of nature. To compare poems by a postcolonial writer from Guyana who combines realism and fantasy in her depictions of childhood, see the selections from Grace Nichols' *Come On into My Tropical Garden* in Part 3.

From *A Child's Garden of Verses*

THE LAND OF COUNTERPANE

When I was sick and lay a-bed,
I had two pillows at my head,
And all my toys beside me lay
To keep me happy all the day.

And sometimes for an hour or so
I watched my leaden soldiers go,
With different uniforms and drills,
Among the bed-clothes, through the hills;

And sometimes sent my ships in fleets
All up and down among the sheets;
Or brought my trees and houses out,
And planted cities all about.

I was the giant great and still
That sits upon the pillow-hill,
And sees before him, dale and plain,
The pleasant land of counterpane.

MY SHADOW

I have a little shadow that goes in and out with me,
And what can be the use of him is more than I can
    see.
He is very, very like me from the heels up to the
    head;
And I see him jump before me, when I jump into
    my bed.

The funniest thing about him is the way he likes to
    grow—
Not at all like proper children, which is always
    very slow;
For he sometimes shoots up taller like an india-
    rubber ball,
And he sometimes gets so little that there's none of
    him at all.

He hasn't got a notion of how children ought to
    play,
And can only make a fool of me in every sort of
    way.

"My Shadow." After studying with Thomas Eakins and Howard Pyle, American artist Jessie Willcox Smith achieved success with her realistic drawings of charming children in many classic children's books.

He stays so close beside me, he's a coward you can
    see;
I'd think shame to stick to nursie as that shadow
    sticks to me!

One morning, very early, before the sun was up,
I rose and found the shining dew on every
    buttercup;
But my lazy little shadow, like an arrant sleepy-
    head,
Had stayed at home behind me and was fast asleep
    in bed.

FOREIGN CHILDREN

Little Indian, Sioux or Crow,
Little frosty Eskimo,
Little Turk or Japanee,
Oh! don't you wish that you were me?

You have seen the scarlet trees
And the lions over seas;
You have eaten ostrich eggs,
And turned the turtles off their legs.

Such a life is very fine,
But it's not so nice as mine:

You must often, as you trod,
Have wearied *not* to be abroad.

You have curious things to eat,
I am fed on proper meat;
You must dwell beyond the foam,
But I am safe and live at home.
   Little Indian, Sioux or Crow,
   Little frosty Eskimo,
   Little Turk or Japanee,
Oh! don't you wish that you were me?

FOREIGN LANDS

Up into the cherry tree
Who should climb but little me?
I held the trunk with both my hands
And looked abroad on foreign lands.

I saw the next door garden lie,
Adorned with flowers, before my eye,
And many pleasant places more
That I had never seen before.

I saw the dimpling river pass
And be the sky's blue looking-glass;
The dusty roads go up and down
With people tramping in to town.

If I could find a higher tree
Farther and farther I should see,
To where the grown-up river slips
Into the sea among the ships,

To where the roads on either hand
Lead onward into fairy land,
Where all the children dine at five,
And all the playthings come alive.

THE UNSEEN PLAYMATE

When children are playing alone on the green,
In comes the playmate that never was seen.
When children are happy and lonely and good,
The Friend of the Children comes out of the wood.

Nobody heard him and nobody saw,
His is a picture you never could draw,
But he's sure to be present, abroad or at home,
When children are happy and playing alone.

He lies in the laurels, he runs on the grass,
He sings when you tinkle the musical glass;
Whene'er you are happy and cannot tell why,
The Friend of the Children is sure to be by!

He loves to be little, he hates to be big,
'Tis he that inhabits the caves that you dig;
'Tis he when you play with your soldiers of tin
That sides with the Frenchmen and never can win.

'Tis he, when at night you go off to your bed,
Bids you go to your sleep and not trouble your
   head;
For wherever they're lying, in cupboard or shelf,
'Tis he will take care of your playthings himself!

MY KINGDOM

Down by a shining water well
I found a very little dell,
   No higher than my head.
The heather and the gorse about
In summer bloom were coming out,
   Some yellow and some red.

I called the little pool a sea;
The little hills were big to me;
   For I am very small.
I made a boat, I made a town,
I searched the caverns up and down,
   And named them one and all.

And all about was mine, I said,
The little sparrows overhead,
   The little minnows too.
This was the world and I was king;
For me the bees came by to sing,
   For me the swallows flew.

I played there were no deeper seas,
Nor any wider plains than these,
   Nor other kings than me.
At last I heard my mother call
Out from the house at evenfall,
   To call me home to tea.

And I must rise and leave my dell,
And leave my dimpled water well,
   And leave my heather blooms.
Alas! and as my home I neared,

How very big my nurse appeared.
How great and cool the rooms!

THE LAND OF STORY-BOOKS

At evening when the lamp is lit,
Around the fire my parents sit;
They sit at home and talk and sing,
And do not play at anything.

Now, with my little gun, I crawl
All in the dark along the wall,
And follow round the forest track
Away behind the sofa back.

There, in the night, where none can spy,
All in my hunter's camp I lie,
And play at books that I have read
Till it is time to go to bed.

These are the hills, these are the woods,
These are my starry solitudes;
And there the river by whose brink
The roaring lions come to drink.

I see the others far away
As if in firelit camp they lay,
And I, like to an Indian scout,
Around their party prowled about.

So, when my nurse comes in for me,
Home I return across the sea,
And go to bed with backward looks
At my dear land of Story-books.

THE FLOWERS

All the names I know from nurse:
Gardener's garters, Shepherd's purse,
Bachelor's buttons, Lady's smock,
And the Lady Hollyhock.

Fairy places, fairy things,
Fairy woods where the wild bee wings,
Tiny trees for tiny dames—
These must all be fairy names!

Tiny woods below whose boughs
Shady fairies weave a house;
Tiny tree-tops, rose or thyme,
Where the braver fairies climb!

Fair are grown-up people's trees,
But the fairest woods are these;
Where, if I were not so tall,
I should live for good and all.

THE DUMB SOLDIER

When the grass was closely mown,
Walking on the lawn alone,
In the turf a hole I found,
And hid a soldier underground.

Spring and daisies came apace;
Grasses hide my hiding place;
Grasses run like a green sea
O'er the lawn up to my knee.

Under grass alone he lies,
Looking up with leaden eyes,
Scarlet coat and pointed gun,
To the stars and to the sun.

When the grass is ripe like grain,
When the scythe is stoned again,
When the lawn is shaven clear,
Then my hole shall reappear.

I shall find him, never fear,
I shall find my grenadier;
But for all that's gone and come,
I shall find my soldier dumb.

He has lived, a little thing,
In the grassy woods of spring;
Done, if he could tell me true,
Just as I should like to do.

He has seen the starry hours
And the springing of the flowers;
And the fairy things that pass
In the forests of the grass.

In the silence he has heard
Talking bee and ladybird,
And the butterfly has flown
O'er him as he lay alone.

Not a word will he disclose,
Not a word of all he knows.
I must lay him on the shelf,
And make up the tale myself.

L. Frank Baum (1856–1919) and W. W. Denslow (1856–1915)

The publication of *The Wonderful Wizard of Oz* in 1900 was a turning point in American children's literature, the first full-length book of original fantasy for children in the United States, just as *Alice in Wonderland* (1865) broke new ground in British fiction for children. Lyman Frank Baum responded to attacks on fairy tales by moralists such as Sarah Trimmer and Samuel Goodrich and to the call for new, genuinely American literature at the end of the nineteenth century, especially literature representing the West (he had moved from New York State to South Dakota and Chicago). As Baum's Introduction indicates, he sought to entertain children with "a modernized fairy tale," without the "horrible and blood-curdling" elements that drove home the morals in older folk stories. Ironically, even though Baum included good witches as well as bad witches and avoided other "stereotyped" creatures that had frightened him as a child reading old fairy tales, some children are terrified by the deaths of his bad witches and scenes such as the Tin Woodman's grisly story about his past in the episode reprinted here. Moreover, adults subject each detail of his whimsical, entertaining story to every type of interpretation, including debates about whether he symbolized or satirized aspects of American culture and politics at the turn of the century, such as conflicts between East and West. Although no one allegorical interpretation works with any consistency, there are intriguing symbolic possibilities in images such as the Tin Woodman's struggle to pursue love while a witch from the East turns his own tool against him and his body is dehumanized, replaced by a collection of manufactured parts.

Baum, like Mark Twain, lived in different parts of the country and worked in a variety of fields throughout his life, including acting, business, journalism, and the film industry. In the 1890s he began publishing stories that he had made up for his children and collaborating with illustrator W. W. Denslow. Denslow was influenced by the Victorian Arts and Crafts movement and, in particular, the toy books by artist Walter Crane and others, printed by Edmund Evans, which were popular in England but had not caught on in America. Working closely together to combine Baum's original nursery verses with Denslow's carefully crafted illustrations in a beautifully designed book, the partners produced *Father Goose, His Book,* which became an immediate best-seller in 1899. As the two pages presented here illustrate, the book celebrates the exciting traditions of fantasy literature, with dragons and giant slayers and, on other pages, sailors and pirates; the "civilized" boy in ruffled shirt does not seem to be as far removed from heroic adventures in the pictures as the words suggest.

The next year, *The Wonderful Wizard of Oz* was received so enthusiastically that Baum and Denslow worked together on a musical stage adaptation in 1902, although their partnership ended in discord after that, and both men suffered from financial and personal problems before they died. Baum wrote a number of sequels illustrated by others, as well as less successful fantasies and films. Other authors continued to write Oz books after his death. While readers of all ages and some critics praised Denslow's illustrations for the first Oz book and Baum's story, for decades many librarians kept Baum's books out of libraries because of their supposed literary inferiority. All the sequels and various stage and film adaptations are eclipsed by the enduring popularity of the 1939 MGM musical film starring Judy Garland.

In the third chapter of the first Oz book, Dorothy is still in the farmhouse, blown into Oz by a cyclone. Like many plucky, resourceful frontier women before her, she prepares for a journey in a strange new world. The Munchkins and benevolent Witch of the North have advised her to follow a yellow brick road to the City of Emeralds to ask the great wizard how to get home. The colorful, prosperous country of the Munchkins contrasts with the gray bleakness of her prairie home in Kansas. Chapters 3 and 5 introduce two of the three loyal companions who join her quest. After she rescues the Scarecrow and rusted Tin Woodman from their immobile conditions in the field and woods, their comments about needing a brain and a heart, respectively, are poignant, humorous, and ironic, since they both obviously think and feel but need greater self-awareness and confidence, just as the lion they meet later needs to believe in his own courage. Their debate about whether a heart or a brain is more important raises interesting philosophical questions about Romanticism and Rationalism, but Dorothy's more practical focus on her need for food and home keeps the story's momentum going as they travel on together.

From *Father Goose, His Book*

Pray, what can a civilized
        boy do now,
When the Dragons all
        are dead,
And the Giants stout,
        that we read about,
Have never a one a head?

Writer L. Frank Baum and illustrator W. W. Denslow worked together to integrate verses into appealing visual designs, combining medieval images with modern touches on these pages from *Father Goose, His Book* (1899).

From *The Wonderful Wizard of Oz*

INTRODUCTION

Folk lore, legends, myths and fairy tales have followed childhood through the ages, for every healthy youngster has a wholesome and instinctive love for stories fantastic, marvelous and manifestly unreal. The winged fairies of Grimm and Andersen have brought more happiness to childish hearts than all other human creations.

Yet the old-time fairy tale, having served for generations, may now be classed as "historical" in the children's library; for the time has come for a series of newer "wonder tales" in which the stereotyped genie, dwarf and fairy are eliminated, together with all the horrible and blood-curdling incident devised by their authors to point a fearsome moral to each tale. Modern education includes morality; therefore the modern child seeks only entertainment in its wonder-tales and gladly dispenses with all disagreeable incident.

Having this thought in mind, the story of "The Wonderful Wizard of Oz" was written solely to pleasure children of today. It aspires to being a modernized fairy tale, in which the wonderment and joy are retained and the heart-aches and nightmares are left out.

L. FRANK BAUM.
CHICAGO, APRIL, 1900

CHAPTER 3. HOW DOROTHY SAVED THE SCARECROW

When Dorothy was left alone she began to feel hungry. So she went to the cupboard and cut herself some bread, which she spread with butter. She gave some to Toto, and taking a pail from the shelf she carried it down to the little brook and filled it with clear, sparkling water. Toto ran over to the trees and began to bark at the birds sitting there. Dorothy went to get him, and saw such delicious fruit hanging from the branches that she gathered some of it, finding it just what she wanted to help out her breakfast.

Then she went back to the house, and having helped herself and Toto to a good drink of the cool, clear water, she set about making ready for the journey to the City of Emeralds.

Dorothy had only one other dress, but that happened to be clean and was hanging on a peg beside her bed. It was gingham, with checks of white and blue; and although the blue was somewhat faded with many washings, it was still a pretty frock. The girl washed herself carefully, dressed herself in the clean gingham, and tied her pink sunbonnet on her head. She took a little basket and filled it with bread from the cupboard, laying a white cloth over the top. Then she looked down at her feet and noticed how old and worn her shoes were.

"They surely will never do for a long journey, Toto," she said. And Toto looked up into her face with his little black eyes and wagged his tail to show he knew what she meant.

At that moment Dorothy saw lying on the table the silver shoes that had belonged to the Witch of the East.

"I wonder if they will fit me," she said to Toto. "They would be just the thing to take a long walk in, for they could not wear out."

She took off her old leather shoes and tried on the silver ones, which fitted her as well as if they had been made for her.

Finally she picked up her basket.

"Come along, Toto," she said, "we will go to the Emerald City and ask the great Oz how to get back to Kansas again."

She closed the door, locked it, and put the key carefully in the pocket of her dress. And so, with Toto trotting along soberly behind her, she started on her journey.

There were several roads near by, but it did not take her long to find the one paved with yellow brick. Within a short time she was walking briskly toward the Emerald City, her silver shoes tinkling merrily on the hard, yellow roadbed. The sun shone bright and the birds sang sweet and Dorothy did not feel nearly as bad as you might think a little girl would who had been suddenly whisked away from her own country and set down in the midst of a strange land.

She was surprised, as she walked along, to see how pretty the country was about her. There were neat fences at the sides of the road, painted a dainty blue color, and beyond them were fields of grain and vegetables in abundance. Evidently the Munchkins were good farmers and able to raise large crops. Once in a while she would pass a house, and the people came out to look at her and bow low as she went by; for everyone knew she had been the means of destroying the wicked witch and setting them free from bondage. The houses of the Munchkins were odd looking dwellings, for each was round, with a big dome for a roof. All were painted blue, for in this country of the East blue was the favorite color.

Towards evening, when Dorothy was tired with her long walk and began to wonder where she should pass the night, she came to a house rather larger than the rest. On the green lawn before it many men and women were dancing. Five little fiddlers played as loudly as possible and the people were laughing and singing, while a big table near by was loaded with delicious fruits and nuts, pies and cakes, and many other good things to eat.

The people greeted Dorothy kindly, and invited her to supper and to pass the night with them; for this was the home of one of the richest Munchkins in the land, and his friends were gathered with him to celebrate their freedom from the bondage of the wicked witch.

Dorothy ate a hearty supper and was waited upon by the rich Munchkin himself, whose name was Boq. Then she sat down upon a settee and watched the people dance.

When Boq saw her silver shoes he said,

"You must be a great sorceress."

"Why?" asked the girl.

"Because you wear silver shoes and have killed the wicked witch. Besides, you have white in your frock, and only witches and sorceresses wear white."

"My dress is blue and white checked," said Dorothy, smoothing out the wrinkles in it.

"It is kind of you to wear that," said Boq. "Blue is the color of the Munchkins, and white is the witch color; so we know you are a friendly witch."

Dorothy did not know what to say to this, for all the people seemed to think her a witch, and she knew very well she was only an ordinary little girl who had come by the chance of a cyclone into a strange land.

When she had tired watching the dancing, Boq led her into the house, where he gave her a room with a pretty bed in it. The sheets were made of blue cloth, and Dorothy slept soundly in them till morning, with Toto curled up on the blue rug beside her.

She ate a hearty breakfast, and watched a wee Munchkin baby, who played with Toto and pulled his tail and crowed and laughed in a way that greatly amused Dorothy. Toto was a fine curiosity to all the people, for they had never seen a dog before.

"How far is it to the Emerald City?" the girl asked.

"I do not know," answered Boq, gravely, "for I have never been there. It is better for people to keep away from Oz, unless they have business with him. But it is a long way to the Emerald City, and it will take you many days. The country here is rich and pleasant, but you must pass through rough and dangerous places before you reach the end of your journey."

This worried Dorothy a little, but she knew that only the great Oz could help her get to Kansas again, so she bravely resolved not to turn back.

She bade her friends good-bye, and again started along the road of yellow brick. When she had gone several miles she thought she would stop to rest, and so climbed to the top of the fence beside the road and sat down. There was a great cornfield beyond the fence, and and not far away she saw a Scarecrow, placed high on a pole to keep the birds from the ripe corn.

Dorothy leaned her chin upon her hand and gazed thoughtfully at the Scarecrow. Its head was a small sack stuffed with straw, with eyes, nose and mouth painted on it to represent a face. An old, pointed blue hat, that had belonged to some Munchkin, was perched on this head, and the rest of the figure was a blue suit of clothes, worn and faded, which had also been stuffed with straw. On the feet were some old boots with blue tops, such as every man wore in this country, and the figure was raised above the stalks of corn by means of the pole stuck up its back.

While Dorothy was looking earnestly into the queer, painted face of the Scarecrow, she was surprised to see one of the eyes slowly wink at her. She thought she must have been mistaken, at first, for none of the scarecrows in Kansas ever wink; but presently the figure nodded its head to her in a friendly way. Then she climbed down from the fence and walked up to it, while Toto ran around the pole and barked.

"Good day," said the Scarecrow, in a rather husky voice.

"Did you speak?" asked the girl, in wonder.

"Certainly," answered the Scarecrow; "how do you do?"

"I'm pretty well, thank you," replied Dorothy, politely; "how do you do?"

"I'm not feeling well," said the Scarecrow, with a smile, "for it is very tedious being perched up here night and day to scare away crows."

"Can't you get down?" asked Dorothy.

"No, for this pole is stuck up my back. If you will please take away the pole I shall be greatly obliged to you."

Dorothy reached up both arms and lifted the figure off the pole; for, being stuffed with straw, it was quite light.

"Thank you very much," said the Scarecrow, when he had been set down on the ground. "I feel like a new man."

Dorothy was puzzled at this, for it sounded queer to hear a stuffed man speak, and to see him bow and walk along beside her.

"Who are you?" asked the Scarecrow, when he had stretched himself and yawned, "and where are you going?"

"My name is Dorothy," said the girl, "and I am going to the Emerald City, to ask the great Oz to send me back to Kansas."

"Where is the Emerald City?" he enquired; "and who is Oz?"

"Why, don't you know?" she returned, in surprise.

"No, indeed; I don't know anything. You see I am stuffed, so I have no brains at all" he answered, sadly.

"Oh," said Dorothy; "I'm awfully sorry for you."

"Do you think," he asked, "If I go to the Emerald City with you, that the great Oz would give me some brains?"

"I cannot tell," she returned; "but you may come with me, if you like. If Oz will not give you any brains you will be no worse off than you are now."

"That is true," said the Scarecrow. "You see," he continued, confidentially, "I don't mind my legs and arms and body being stuffed, because I cannot get hurt. If anyone treads on my toes or sticks a pin into me, it doesn't matter, for I can't feel it. But I do not want people to call me a fool, and if my head stays stuffed with straw instead of with brains, as yours is, how am I ever to know anything?"

"I understand how you feel," said the little girl, who was truly sorry for him. "If you will come with me I'll ask Oz to do all he can for you."

"Thank you," he answered, gratefully.

They walked back to the road, Dorothy helped him over the fence, and they started along the path of yellow brick for the Emerald City.

Toto did not like this addition to the party, at first. He smelled around the stuffed man as if he suspected there might be a nest of rats in the straw, and he often growled in an unfriendly way at the Scarecrow.

"Don't mind Toto," said Dorothy, to her new friend; "he never bites."

"Oh, I'm not afraid," replied the Scarecrow, "he can't hurt the straw. Do let me carry that basket for you. I shall not mind it, for I can't get tired. I'll tell you a secret," he continued, as he walked along; "there is only one thing in the world I am afraid of."

"What is that?" asked Dorothy; "the Munchkin farmer who made you?"

"No," answered the Scarecrow; "it's a lighted match."

CHAPTER 5. THE RESCUE OF THE TIN WOODMAN

When Dorothy awoke the sun was shining through the trees and Toto had long been out chasing birds and squirrels. She sat up and looked around her. There was the Scarecrow, still standing patiently in his corner, waiting for her.

"We must go and search for water," she said to him.

"Why do you want water?" he asked.

"To wash my face clean after the dust of the road, and to drink, so the dry bread will not stick in my throat."

"It must be inconvenient to be made of flesh," said the Scarecrow, thoughtfully; "for you must sleep, and eat and drink. However, you have brains, and it is worth a lot of bother to be able to think properly."

They left the cottage and walked through the trees until they found a little spring of clear water, where Dorothy drank and bathed and ate her breakfast. She saw there was not much bread left in the basket, and the girl was thankful the Scarecrow did not have to eat anything, for there was scarcely enough for herself and Toto for the day.

When she had finished her meal, and was about to go back to the road of yellow brick, she was startled to hear a deep groan near by.

"What was that?" she asked, timidly.

"I cannot imagine," replied the Scarecrow; "but we can go and see."

Just then another groan reached their ears, and the sound seemed to come from behind them. They turned and walked through the forest a few steps, when Dorothy discovered something shining in a ray of sunshine that fell between the trees. She ran to the place, and then stopped short, with a cry of surprise.

One of the big trees had been partly chopped through, and standing beside it, with an uplifted axe in his hands, was a man made entirely of tin. His head and arms and legs were jointed upon his body, but he stood perfectly motionless, as if he could not stir at all.

Dorothy looked at him in amazement, and so did the Scarecrow, while Toto barked sharply and made a snap at the tin legs, which hurt his teeth.

W. W. Denslow's whimsical illustrations for the original edition of L. Frank Baum's classic fantasy include smaller drawings within a wide variety of page designs, and full-page plates with bold outlines along the stages of Dorothy's travels through Oz. Here she and the Scarecrow learn the Tin Woodman's history.

"Did you groan?" asked Dorothy.

"Yes," answered the tin man; "I did. I've been groaning for more than a year, and no one has ever heard me before or come to help me."

"What can I do for you?" she enquired, softly, for she was moved by the sad voice in which the man spoke.

"Get an oil-can and oil my joints," he answered. "They are rusted so badly that I cannot move them at all; if I am well oiled I shall soon be all right again. You will find an oil-can on a shelf in my cottage."

Dorothy at once ran back to the cottage and found the oil-can, and then she returned and asked, anxiously, "Where are your joints?"

"Oil my neck, first," replied the Tin Woodman; So she oiled it, and as it was quite badly rusted the Scarecrow took hold of the tin head and moved it gently from side to side until it worked freely, and then the man could turn it himself.

"Now oil the joints in my arms," he said. And Dorothy oiled them and the Scarecrow bent them carefully until they were quite free from rust and as good as new.

The Tin Woodman gave a sigh of satisfaction and lowered his axe, which he leaned against the tree.

"This is a great comfort," he said. "I have been holding that axe in the air ever since I rusted, and I'm glad to be able to put it down at last. Now, if you will oil the joints of my legs, I shall be all right once more."

So they oiled his legs until he could move them freely; and he thanked them again and again for his release, for he seemed a very polite creature, and very grateful.

"I might have stood there always if you had not come along," he said; "so you have certainly saved my life. How did you happen to be here?"

"We are on our way to the Emerald City, to see the great Oz," she answered, "and we stopped at your cottage to pass the night."

"Why do you wish to see Oz?" he asked.

"I want him to send me back to Kansas; and the Scarecrow wants him to put a few brains into his head," she replied.

The Tin Woodman appeared to think deeply for a moment. Then he said:

"Do you suppose Oz could give me a heart?"

"Why, I guess so," Dorothy answered; "it would be as easy as to give the Scarecrow brains."

"True," the Tin Woodman returned. "So, if you will allow me to join your party, I will also go to the Emerald City and ask Oz to help me."

"Come along," said the Scarecrow, heartily; and Dorothy added that she would be pleased to have his company. So the Tin Woodman shouldered his axe and they all passed through the forest until they came to the road that was paved with yellow brick.

The Tin Woodman had asked Dorothy to put the oil-can in her basket. "For," he said, "if I should get caught in the rain, and rust again, I would need the oil-can badly."

It was a bit of good luck to have their new comrade join the party, for soon after they had begun their journey again they came to a place where the trees and branches grew so thick over the road that the travellers could not pass. But the Tin Woodman set to work with his axe and chopped so well that soon he cleared a passage for the entire party.

Dorothy was thinking so earnestly as they walked along that she did not notice when the Scarecrow stumbled into a hole and rolled over to the side of the road. Indeed, he was obliged to call to her to help him up again.

"Why didn't you walk around the hole?" asked the Tin Woodman.

"I don't know enough," replied the Scarecrow, cheerfully. "My head is stuffed with straw, you know, and that is why I am going to Oz to ask him for some brains."

"Oh, I see;" said the Tin Woodman. "But, after all, brains are not the best things in the world."

"Have you any?" enquired the Scarecrow.

"No, my head is quite empty," answered the Woodman; "but once I had brains, and a heart also; so, having tried them both, I should much rather have a heart."

"And why is that?" asked the Scarecrow.

"I will tell you my story, and then you will know."

So, while they were walking through the forest, the Tin Woodman told the following story:

"I was born the son of a woodman who chopped down trees in the forest and sold the wood for a living. When I grew up I too became a wood-chopper, and after my father died I took care of my old mother as long as she lived. Then I made up my mind that instead of living alone I would marry, so that I might not become lonely.

"There was one of the Munchkin girls who was so beautiful that I soon grew to love her with all my heart. She, on her part, promised to marry me as soon as I could earn enough money to build a better house for her; so I set to work harder than ever. But the girl lived with an old woman who did not want her to marry anyone, for she was so lazy she wished the girl to remain with her and do the cooking and the housework. So the old woman went to the wicked Witch of the East, and promised her two sheep and a cow if she would prevent the marriage. Thereupon the wicked Witch enchanted my axe, and when I was chopping away at my best one day, for I was anxious to get the new house and my wife as soon as possible, the axe slipped all at once and cut off my left leg.

"This at first seemed a great misfortune, for I knew a one-legged man could not do very well as a wood-chopper. So I went to a tin-smith and had him make me a new leg out of tin. The leg worked very well, once I was used to it; but my action angered the wicked Witch of the East, for she had promised the old woman I should not marry the pretty Munchkin girl. When I began chopping again my axe slipped and cut off my right leg. Again I went to the tinner, and again he made me a leg out of tin. After this the enchanted axe cut off my arms, one after the other; but, nothing daunted, I had them replaced with tin ones. The wicked Witch then made the axe slip and cut off my head, and at first I thought that was the end of me. But the tinner happened to come along, and he made me a new head out of tin.

"I thought I had beaten the wicked Witch then, and I worked harder than ever; but I little knew how cruel my enemy could be. She thought of a new way to kill my love for the beautiful Munchkin maiden, and made my axe slip again, so that it cut right through my body, splitting me into two halves. Once more the tinner came to my help and made me a body of tin, fastening my tin arms and legs and head to it, by means of joints, so that I could move around as well as ever. But, alas! I had now no heart, so that I lost all my love for the Munchkin girl, and did not care whether I married her or not. I suppose she is still living with the old woman, waiting for me to come after her.

"My body shone so brightly in the sun that I felt very proud of it and it did not matter now if my axe slipped, for it could not cut me. There was only one danger—that my joints would rust; but I kept an oil-can in my cottage and took care to oil myself when-

W. W. Denslow's full-page scenes have neat borders that are occasionally interrupted by the energetic lines of overlapping shapes, such as the Scarecrow in this dramatic scene introducing the Lion, who reveals that he is cowardly rather than dangerous.

ever I needed it. However, there came a day when I forgot to do this, and, being caught in a rainstorm, before I thought of the danger my joints had rusted, and I was left to stand in the woods until you came to help me. It was a terrible thing to undergo, but during the year I stood there I had time to think that the greatest loss I had known was the loss of my heart. While I was in love I was the happiest man on earth; but no one can love who has not a heart, and so I am resolved to ask Oz to give me one. If he does, I will go back to the Munchkin maiden and marry her."

Both Dorothy and the Scarecrow had been greatly interested in the story of the Tin Woodman, and now they knew why he was so anxious to get a new heart.

"All the same," said the Scarecrow, "I shall ask for brains instead of a heart; for a fool would not know what to do with a heart if he had one."

"I shall take the heart," returned the Tin Woodman; "for brains do not make one happy, and happiness is the best thing in the world."

Dorothy did not say anything, for she was puzzled to know which of her two friends was right, and she decided if she could only get back to Kansas and Aunt Em it did not matter so much whether the Woodman had no brains and the Scarecrow no heart, or each got what he wanted.

What worried her most was that the bread was nearly gone, and another meal for herself and Toto would empty the basket. To be sure neither the Woodman nor the Scarecrow ever ate anything, but she was not made of tin nor straw, and could not live unless she was fed.

Kenneth Grahame (1859–1932)

The Wind in the Willows (1908), by Kenneth Grahame, shows how the beast fable from ancient times evolved into the full-length animal fantasy in the Golden Age of children's literature. It also illustrates the romantic lure of the natural world as a continuing theme in twentieth-century children's literature. Grahame described English landscape and animals with affectionate detail, but, like E. B. White in America and Beatrix Potter, he also endowed the animals with speech, strong friendships, and other human traits. In A. A. Milne's *Winnie the Pooh,* the animal friends are toys who join the child Christopher Robin (named after Milne's son) on make-believe adventures in the English countryside near his home. Grahame's book, like Milne's, began as stories he told to his son Alistair at bedtime and in letters, but most of his animal characters are very much like human adults, and the book's tone of nostalgia for freedom and enjoyment in an idyllic pastoral setting is like many other classic children's books that reflect the adult's longing for the idealized pleasures of childhood more than a child's perspective.

This dual point of view is reflected in Grahame's description of this novel as "a book of youth, and so perhaps chiefly *for* youth and those who still keep the spirit of youth alive in them."[1] Grahame, who retired as a banker just before this book was published, enjoyed watching nature near the Thames River as a child and, as a man, escaping from the world of women and everyday realities during weekends in the country with male friends. His fascination with the dreamy preindustrial world of mythology and imagination is also reflected in the titles of his previous books of essays and stories about childhood: *Pagan Papers, The Golden Age* and *Dream Days* (which contains the story "The Reluctant Dragon"). "The Piper at the Gates of Dawn" is the mystical middle chapter in which Mole and Rat have a vision of the nature god Pan protecting a lost baby otter in *The Wind in the Willows.*

The chapters called "The Open Road" and "Dulce Domum" illustrate two contrasting moods in *The Wind and the Willows:* the impulse to wander and have adventures is tempered with an even stronger attachment to the comforts of home. Toad is the focus of the novel's energetic mock-heroic escapades. He is wealthy enough and amiable enough to get away with plunging impetuously into one new pastime after another, letting his friends and servants take care of practical details while he causes trouble in a series of comical episodes. His infatuation with motor cars parodies the dilettante's thoughtless fascination with inventions that bring noise and disruption to the peaceful countryside. Mole is the youth who begins the novel with a celebration of spring as he ventures away from his underground home to discover the blissful life of the riverbank. Rat, the poetic man of leisure, makes friends by taking him on his first boat ride with a bountiful picnic lunch. Characters in children's books are often preoccupied with food, whether it is plentiful, inadequate, or terrifying (when characters are eaten by predators or enticed by witches with sweets), and this picnic is most famous for Rat's modest explanation that his picnic basket contains "coldtonguecoldhamcoldbeefpickledgherkinssaladfrenchrollscress-sandwichespottedmeatgingerbeerlemonadesodawater—." Mole is thrilled to have new experiences with Rat and other animal friends, but their love of "home sweet home" is epitomized in the return to Mole's snug little home at Christmas time in "Dulce Domum." Although Grahame's pastoral paradise along the river is an exclusive club for gentlemanly animals—a refuge from the lower class, hostile animals in the Wild Wood and the fearful unknown beyond in the Wide World—the generosity, hospitality, and loyalty of these animal friends have warmed the hearts of generations of readers.

NOTE

1. Kenneth Grahame quoted in Preface by Margaret Hodges, *The Wind in the Willows* by Kenneth Grahame (1908; New York: Scribner's, 1983) v–vi.

From *The Wind in the Willows*

CHAPTER 2. THE OPEN ROAD

"Ratty," said the Mole suddenly, one bright summer morning, "if you please, I want to ask you a favour."

The Rat was sitting on the river bank, singing a little song. He had just composed it himself, so he was very taken up with it, and would not pay proper attention to Mole or anything else. Since early morning he had been swimming in the river in company with his friends the ducks. And when the ducks stood on their heads suddenly, as ducks will, he would dive down and tickle their necks just under where their chins would be if ducks had chins, till they were forced to come to the surface again in a hurry, spluttering and angry and shaking their feathers at him, for it is impossible to say quite *all* you feel when your head is under water. At last they implored him to go away and attend to his own affairs and leave them to mind theirs. So the Rat went away, and sat on the river bank in the sun, and made up a song about them, which he called

"DUCKS' DITTY"

> All along the backwater,
> Through the rushes tall,
> Ducks are a-dabbling,
> Up tails all!
>
> Ducks' tails, drakes' tails,
> Yellow feet a-quiver,
> Yellow bills all out of sight
> Busy in the river!
>
> Slushy green undergrowth
> Where the roach swim—
> Here we keep our larder,
> Cool and full and dim.
>
> Every one for what he likes!
> *We* like to be
> Heads down, tails up,
> Dabbling free!
>
> High in the blue above
> Swifts whirl and call—
> *We* are down a-dabbling
> Up tails all!

"I don't know that I think so *very* much of that little song, Rat," observed the Mole cautiously. He was no poet himself and didn't care who knew it; and he had a candid nature.

"Nor don't the ducks neither," replied the Rat cheerfully. "They say, *Why* can't fellows be allowed to do what they like *when* they like and *as* they like, instead of other fellows sitting on banks and watching them all the time and making remarks and poetry and things about them? What *nonsense* it all is! That's what the ducks say."

"So it is, so it is," said the Mole, with great heartiness.

"No, it isn't!" cried the Rat indignantly.

"Well then, it isn't, it isn't," replied the Mole soothingly. "But what I wanted to ask you was, won't you take me to call on Mr. Toad? I've heard so much about him, and I do so want to make his acquaintance."

"Why, certainly," said the good-natured Rat, jumping to his feet and dismissing poetry from his mind for the day. "Get the boat out, and we'll paddle up there at once. It's never the wrong time to call on Toad. Early or late he's always the same fellow. Always good-tempered, always glad to see you, always sorry when you go!"

"He must be a very nice animal," observed the Mole, as he got into the boat and took the sculls, while the Rat settled himself comfortably in the stern.

"He is indeed the best of animals," replied Rat. "So simple, so good-natured, and so affectionate. Perhaps he's not very clever—we can't all be geniuses; and it may be that he is both boastful and conceited. But he has got some great qualities, has Toady."

Rounding a bend in the river, they came in sight of a handsome, dignified old house of mellowed red brick, with well-kept lawns reaching down to the water's edge.

"There's Toad Hall," said the Rat; "and that creek on the left, where the notice-board says, 'Private. No landing allowed,' leads to his boathouse, where we'll leave the boat. The stables are over there to the right, That's the banqueting-hall you're looking at now— very old, that is. Toad is rather rich, you know, and this is really one of the nicest houses in these parts, though we never admit as much to Toad."

They glided up the creek, and the Mole shipped his sculls as they passed into the shadow of a large boat-house. Here they saw many handsome boats, slung from the cross-beams or hauled up on a slip, but none in the water; and the place had an unused and a deserted air.

The Rat looked around him. "I understand," said he. "Boating is played out. He's tired of it, and done with it. I wonder what new fad he has taken up now? Come along and let's look him up. We shall hear all about it quite soon enough."

They disembarked, and strolled across the gay flower-decked lawns in search of Toad, whom they presently happened upon resting in a wicker garden-chair, with a preoccupied expression of face, and a large map spread out on his knees.

"Hooray!" he cried, jumping up on seeing them, "this is splendid!" He shook the paws of both of them warmly, never waiting for an introduction to the Mole. "How *kind* of you!" he went on, dancing round them. "I was just going to send a boat down the river for you, Ratty, with strict orders that you were to be fetched up here at once, whatever you were doing. I want you badly—both of you. Now what will you take? Come inside and have something! You don't know how lucky it is, your turning up just now!"

"Let's sit quiet a bit, Toady!" said the Rat, throwing himself into an easy chair, while the Mole took another by the side of him and made some civil remark about Toad's "delightful residence."

"Finest house on the whole river," cried Toad boisterously. "Or anywhere else, for that matter," he could not help adding.

Here the Rat nudged the Mole. Unfortunately the Toad saw him do it, and turned very red. There was a moment's painful silence. Then Toad burst out laughing. "All right, Ratty," he said. "It's only my way, you know. And it's not such a very bad house, is it? You know you rather like it yourself. Now, look here. Let's be sensible. You are the very animals I wanted. You've got to help me. It's most important!"

"It's about your rowing, I suppose," said the Rat, with an innocent air. "You're getting on fairly well, though you splash a good bit still. With a great deal of patience, and any quantity of coaching, you may—"

"O, pooh! boating!" interrupted the Toad, in great disgust. "Silly boyish amusement. I've given that up *long* ago. Sheer waste of time, that's what it is. It makes me downright sorry to see you fellows, who ought to know better, spending all your energies in that aimless manner. No, I've discovered the real thing, the only genuine occupation for a lifetime. I propose to devote the remainder of mine to it, and can only regret the wasted years, that lie behind me, squandered in trivialities. Come with me, dear Ratty, and your amiable friend also, if he will be so very good, just as far as the stableyard, and you shall see what you shall see!"

He led the way to the stable-yard accordingly, the Rat following with a most mistrustful expression; and there, drawn out of the coach-house into the open, they saw a gipsy caravan, shining with newness, painted a canary-yellow picked out with green, and red wheels.

"There you are!" cried the Toad, straddling and expanding himself. "There's real life for you, embodied in that little cart. The open road, the dusty highway, the heath, the common, the hedgerows, the rolling downs! Camps, villages, towns, cities! Here today, up and off to somewhere else to-morrow! Travel, change, interest, excitement! The whole world before you, and a horizon that's always changing! And mind, this is the very finest cart of its sort that was ever built, without any exception. Come inside and look at the arrangements. Planned 'em all myself, I did!"

The Mole was tremendously interested and excited, and followed him eagerly up the steps and into the interiors of the caravan. The Rat only snorted and thrust his hands deep into his pockets, remaining where he was.

It was indeed very compact and comfortable. Little sleeping-bunks—a little table that folded up against the wall—a cooking-stove, lockers, bookshelves, a bird-cage with a bird in it; and pots, pans, jugs and kettles of every size and variety.

"All complete!" said the Toad triumphantly, pulling open a locker. "You see—biscuits, potted lobster, sardines—everything you can possibly want. Soda-water here—baccy there—letter-paper, bacon, jam, cards and dominoes—you'll find," he continued, as they descended the steps again, "you'll find that nothing whatever has been forgotten, when we make our start this afternoon."

"I beg your pardon," said the Rat slowly, as he chewed a straw, "but did I overhear you say something about '*we,*' and '*start,*' and '*this afternoon?*'"

"Now, you dear good old Ratty," said Toad imploringly, "don't begin talking in that stiff and sniffy sort of way, because you know you've *got* to come. I can't possibly manage without you, so please consider it settled, and don't argue—it's the one thing I can't stand. You surely don't mean to stick to your dull fusty old river all your life, and just live in a hole in a bank, and *boat?* I want to show you the world! I'm going to make an *animal* of you, my boy!"

"I don't care," said the Rat doggedly. "I'm not coming, and that's flat. And I *am* going to stick to my old river, *and* live in a hole, *and* boat, as I've always done. And what's more, Mole's going to stick to me and do as I do, aren't you, Mole?"

"Of course I am," said the Mole loyally. "I'll always stick to you, Rat, and what you say is to be—has got to be. All the same, it sounds as if it might have been—well, rather fun, you know!" he added wistfully. Poor Mole! The Life Adventurous was so new a thing to him, and so thrilling; and this fresh aspect of it was so tempting; and he had fallen in love at first sight with the canary-coloured cart and all its little fitments.

The Rat saw what was passing in his mind, and wavered. He hated disappointing people, and he was fond of the Mole, and would do almost anything to oblige him. Toad was watching both of them closely.

"Come along in and have some lunch," he said diplomatically, "and we'll talk it over. We needn't decide anything in a hurry. Of course, I don't really care. I only want to give pleasure to you fellows. 'Live for others!' That's my motto in life."

During luncheon—which was excellent, of course, as everything at Toad Hall always was—the Toad simply let himself go. Disregarding the Rat, he proceeded to play upon the inexperienced Mole as on a harp. Naturally a voluble animal, and always mastered by his imagination, he painted the prospects of the trip and the joys of the open life and the roadside in such glowing colours that the Mole could hardly sit in his chair for excitement. Somehow, it soon seemed taken for granted by all three of them that the trip was a settled thing; and the Rat, though still unconvinced in his mind, allowed his good nature to override his personal objections. He could not bear to disappoint his two friends, who were already deep in schemes and anticipations, planning out each day's separate occupation for several weeks ahead.

When they were quite ready, the now triumphant Toad led his companions to the paddock and set them to capture the old grey horse, who, without having been consulted, and to his own extreme annoyance, had been told off by Toad for the dustiest job in this dusty expedition. He frankly preferred the paddock, and took a deal of catching. Meantime Toad packed the lockers still tighter with necessaries, and hung nose-bags, nets of onions, bundles of hay, and baskets from the bottom of the cart. At last the horse was caught and harnessed, and they set off, all talking at once, each animal either trudging by the side of the cart or sitting on the shaft, as the humour took him. It was a golden afternoon. The smell of the dust they kicked up was rich and satisfying; out of thick orchards on either side the road, birds called and whistled to them cheerily; good-natured wayfarers, passing them gave them "Good day," or stopped to say nice things about their beautiful cart; and rabbits, sitting at their front doors in the hedgerows, held up their forepaws, and said, "O my! O my! O my!"

Late in the evening, tired and happy and miles from home, they drew up on a remote common far from habitations, turned the horse loose to graze, and ate their simple supper sitting on the grass by the side of the cart. Toad talked big about all he was going to do in the days to come, while stars grew fuller and larger all around them, and a yellow moon, appearing suddenly and silently from nowhere in particular, came to keep them company and listen to their talk. At last they turned into their little bunks in the cart; and Toad, kicking out his legs, sleepily said, "Well, good night, you fellows! This is the real life for a gentleman! Talk about your old river!"

"I *don't* talk about my river," replied the patient Rat. "You *know* I don't, Toad. But I *think* about it," he added pathetically, in a lower tone: "I think about it—all the time!"

The Mole reached out from under his blanket, felt for the Rat's paw in the darkness, and gave it a squeeze. "I'll do whatever you like, Ratty," he whispered. "Shall we run away tomorrow morning, quite early—*very* early—and go back to our dear old hole on the river?"

"No, no, we'll see it out," whispered back the Rat. "Thanks awfully, but I ought to stick by Toad till this trip is ended. It wouldn't be safe for him to be left to himself. It won't take very long. His fads never do. Good night!"

The end was indeed nearer than even the Rat suspected.

After so much open air and excitement the Toad slept very soundly, and no amount of shaking could rouse him out of bed next morning. So the Mole and Rat turned to, quietly and manfully, and while the Rat saw to the horse, and lit a fire, and cleaned last night's cups and platters, and got things ready for breakfast, the Mole trudged off to the nearest village, a long way off, for milk and eggs and various necessaries the Toad had, of course, forgotten to provide. The hard work had all been done, and the two animals were resting, thoroughly exhausted, by the time Toad appeared on the scene, fresh and gay, remarking what a pleasant easy life it was they were all leading now, after the cares and worries and fatigues of housekeeping at home.

They had a pleasant ramble that day over grassy downs and along narrow by-lanes, and camped, as before, on a common, only this time the two guests took care that Toad should do his fair share of work. In consequence, when the time came for starting next morning, Toad was by no means so rapturous about the simplicity of the primitive life, and indeed attempted to resume his place in his bunk, whence he was hauled by force. Their way lay, as before, across country by narrow lanes, and it was not till the afternoon that they came out on the high road, their first high road; and there disaster, fleet and unforeseen, sprang out on them—disaster momentous indeed to their expedition, but simply overwhelming in its effect on the after-career of Toad.

They were strolling along the high road easily, the Mole by the horse's head, talking to him, since the horse had complained that he was being frightfully left out of it, and nobody considered him in the least; the Toad and the Water Rat walking behind the cart talking together—at least Toad was talking, and Rat was saying at intervals, "Yes, precisely; and what did *you* say to *him?*"—and thinking all the time of something very different, when far behind them they heard a faint warning hum, like the drone of a distant bee. Glancing back, they saw a small cloud of dust, with a dark centre of energy, advancing on them at incredible speed, while from out the dust a faint "Poop-poop!" wailed like an uneasy animal in pain. Hardly regarding it, they turned to resume their conversation, when in an instant (as it seemed) the peaceful scene was changed, and with a blast of wind and a whirl of sound that made them jump for the nearest ditch, it was on them! The "poop-poop" rang with a brazen shout in their ears, they had a moment's glimpse of an interior of glittering plate-glass and rich morocco, and the magnificent motor-car immense, breath-snatching, passionate, with its pilot tense and hugging his wheel, possessed all earth and air for the fraction of a second, flung an enveloping cloud of dust that blinded and enwrapped them utterly, and then dwindled to a speck in the far distance, changed back into a droning bee once more.

The old grey horse, dreaming, as he plodded along, of his quiet paddock, in a new raw situation such as this simply abandoned himself to his natural emotions. Rearing, plunging, backing steadily, in spite of all the Mole's efforts at his head, and all the Mole's lively language directed at his better feelings, he drove the cart backwards towards the deep ditch at the side of the road. It wavered an instant—then there was a heart-rending crash—and the canary-coloured cart, their pride and their joy, lay on its side in the ditch, an irredeemable wreck.

The Rat danced up and down in the road, simply transported with passion. "You villains!" he shouted, shaking both fists, "You scoundrels, you highwaymen, you—you—road-hogs!—I'll have the law of you! I'll report you! I'll take you through all the Courts!" His home-sickness had quite slipped away from him, and for the moment he was the skipper of the canary-coloured vessel driven on a shoal by the reckless jockeying of rival mariners, and he was trying to recollect all the fine and biting things he used to say to masters of steam-launches when their wash, as they drove too near the bank, used to flood his parlour carpet at home.

Toad sat straight down in the middle of the dusty road, his legs stretched out before him, and stared fixedly in the direction of the disappearing motor-car. He breathed short, his face wore a placid, satisfied expression, and at intervals he faintly murmured "Poop-poop!"

The Mole was busy trying to quiet the horse, which he succeeded in doing after a time. Then he went to look at the cart, on its side in the ditch. It was indeed a sorry sight. Panels and windows smashed, axles hopelessly bent, one wheel off, sardine-tins scattered over the wide world, and the bird in the bird-cage sobbing pitifully and calling to be let out.

The Rat came to help him, but their united efforts were not sufficient to right the cart. "Hi! Toad!" they cried. "Come and bear a hand, can't you!"

The Toad never answered a word, or budged from his seat in the road; so they went to see what was the matter with him. They found him in a sort of trance, a happy smile on his face, his eyes still fixed on the dusty wake of their destroyer. At intervals he was still heard to murmur "Poop-poop!"

The Rat shook him by the shoulder. "Are you coming to help us, Toad?" he demanded sternly.

"Glorious, stirring sight!" murmured Toad, never offering to move. "The poetry of motion! The *real* way to travel! The *only* way to travel! Here today—in next week tomorrow! Villages skipped, towns and cities jumped—always somebody else's horizon! O bliss! O poop-poop! O my! O my!"

"O *stop* being an ass, Toad!" cried the Mole despairingly.

"And to think I never *knew!*" went on the Toad in a dreamy monotone. "All those wasted years that lie behind me, I never knew, never even *dreamt!* But *now*—but now that I know, now that I fully realize! O what a flowery track lies spread before me, henceforth! What dust-clouds shall spring up behind me as I speed on my reckless way! What carts I shall fling carelessly into the ditch in the wake of my magnificent onset! Horrid little carts—common carts—canary-coloured carts!"

"What are we to do with him?" asked the Mole of the Water Rat.

"Nothing at all," replied the Rat firmly. "Because there is really nothing to be done. You see, I know him from old. He is now possessed. He has got a new craze, and it always takes him that way, in its first stage. He'll continue like that for days now, like an animal walking in a happy dream, quite useless for all practical purposes. Never mind him. Let's go and see what there is to be done about the cart."

A careful inspection showed them that, even if they succeeded in righting it by themselves, the cart would travel no longer. The axles were in a hopeless state, and the missing wheel was shattered into pieces.

The Rat knotted the horse's reins over his back and took him by the head, carrying the bird-cage and its hysterical occupant in the other hand. "Come on!" he said grimly to the Mole. "It's five or six miles to the nearest town, and we shall just have to walk it. The sooner we make a start the better."

"But what about Toad?" asked the Mole anxiously, as they set off together. "We can't leave him here, sitting in the middle of the road by himself, in the distracted state he's in! It's not safe. Supposing another Thing were to come along?"

"O, *bother* Toad," said the Rat savagely; "I've done with him!"

They had not proceeded very far on their way, however, when there was a pattering of feet behind them, and Toad caught them up and thrust a paw inside the elbow of each of them; still breathing short and staring into vacancy.

"Now, look here, Toad!" said the Rat sharply: "as soon as we get to the town, you'll have to go straight to the police-station, and see if they know anything about that motor-car and who it belongs to, and lodge a complaint against it. And then you'll have to go to a blacksmith's or a wheelwright's and arrange for the cart to be fetched and mended and put to rights. It'll take time, but it's not quite a hopeless smash. Meanwhile, the Mole and I will go to an inn and find comfortable rooms where we can stay till the cart's ready, and till your nerves have recovered their shock."

E. H. Shepard's engaging small drawings enhance the camaraderie of Mole, Toad, and Rat, a band of small animals with very human personalities and pastimes.

"Police-station! Complaint!" murmured Toad dreamily. "Me *complain* of that beautiful, that heavenly vision that has been vouchsafed me! *Mend* the *cart!* I've done with carts for ever. I never want to see the cart, or to hear of it, again. O, Ratty! You can't think how obliged I am to you for consenting to come on this trip! I wouldn't have gone without you, and then I might never have seen that—that swan, that sunbeam, that thunderbolt! I might never have heard that entrancing sound, or smelt that bewitching smell! I owe it all to you, my best of friends!"

The Rat turned from him in despair. "You see what it is?" he said to the Mole, addressing him across Toad's head: "He's quite hopeless. I give it up—when we get to the town we'll go to the railway-station, and with luck we may pick up a train there that'll get us back to River Bank tonight. And if ever you catch me going a-pleasuring with this provoking animal again!"—He snorted, and during the rest of that weary trudge addressed his remarks exclusively to Mole.

E. H. Shepard provides glimpses of Toad's aristocratic country manor as Toad saunters down the stairs, putting on the air of debonair adventurer.

On reaching the town they went straight to the station and deposited Toad in the second-class waiting-room, giving a porter twopence to keep a strict eye on him. They then left the horse at an inn stable, and gave what directions they could about the cart and its contents. Eventually, a slow train having landed them at a station not very far from Toad Hall, they escorted the spell-bound, sleep-walking Toad to his door, put him inside it, and instructed his housekeeper to feed him, undress him, and put him to bed. Then they got out their boat from the boat-house, sculled down the river home and at a very late hour sat down to supper in their own cosy riverside parlour, to the Rat's great joy and contentment.

The following evening the Mole, who had risen late and taken things very easy all day, was sitting on the bank fishing, when the Rat, who had been looking up his friends and gossiping, came strolling along to find him. "Heard the news?" he said. "There's nothing else being talked about, all along the river bank. Toad went up to Town by an early train this morning. And he has ordered a large and very expensive motor-car."

CHAPTER 5. DULCE DOMUM

The sheep ran huddling together against the hurdles, blowing out thin nostrils and stamping with delicate fore-feet, their heads thrown back and a light steam rising from the crowded sheep-pen into the frosty air, as the two animals hastened by in high spirits, with much chatter and laughter. They were returning across country after a long day's outing with Otter, hunting and exploring on the wide uplands where certain streams tributary to their own River had their first small beginnings; and the shades of the short winter day were closing in on them, and they had still some distance to go. Plodding at random across the plough, they had heard the sheep and had made for them; and now, leading from the sheep-pen, they found a beaten track that made walking a lighter business, and responded, moreover, to that small inquiring something which all animals carry inside them, saying unmistakably, "Yes, quite right; *this* leads home!"

"It looks as if we were coming to a village," said the Mole somewhat dubiously, slackening his pace, as the track, that had in time become a path and then had developed into a lane, now handed them over to the charge of a well-metalled road. The animals did not hold with villages, and their own highways, thickly frequented as they were, took an independent course, regardless of church, post office, or public-house.

"Oh, never mind!" said the Rat. "At this season of the year they're all safe indoors by this time, sitting round the fire; men, women, and children, dogs and cats and all. We shall slip through all right, without any bother or unpleasantness, and we can have a look at them through their windows if you like, and see what they're doing."

The rapid nightfall of mid-December had quite beset the little village as they approached it on soft feet over a first thin fall of powdery snow. Little was visible but squares of a dusky orange-red on either side of the street, where the firelight or lamplight of each cottage overflowed through the casements into the dark world without. Most of the low latticed windows were innocent of blinds, and to the lookers-in from outside, the inmates, gathered round the tea-table, absorbed in handiwork, or talking with laughter and gesture, had each that happy grace which is the last thing the skilled actor shall capture—the natural grace which goes with perfect unconsciousness of observation. Moving at will from one theatre to another, the two spectators, so far from home themselves, had something of wistfulness in their eyes as they watched a cat being stroked, a sleepy child picked up and huddled off to bed, or a tired man stretch and knock out his pipe on the end of a smouldering log.

But it was from one little window, with its blind drawn down, a mere blank transparency on the night, that the sense of home and the little curtained world within walls—the larger stressful world of outside Nature shut out and forgotten—most pulsated. Close against the white blind hung a bird-cage, clearly silhouetted, every wire, perch, and appurtenance distinct and recognisable, even to yesterday's dull-edged lump of sugar. On the middle perch the fluffy occupant, head tucked well into feathers, seemed so near to them as to be easily stroked, had they tried; even the delicate tips of his plumped-out plumage pencilled plainly on the illuminated screen. As they looked, the sleepy little fellow stirred uneasily, woke, shook himself, and raised his head. They could see the gape of his tiny beak as he yawned in a bored sort of way, looked round, and then settled his head into his back again, while the ruffled feathers gradually subsided into per-

fect stillness. Then a gust of bitter wind took them in the back of the neck, a small sting of frozen sleet on the skin woke them as from a dream, and they knew their toes to be cold and their legs tired, and their own home distant a weary way.

Once beyond the village, where the cottages ceased abruptly, on either side of the road they could smell through the darkness the friendly fields again; and they braced themselves for the last long stretch, the home stretch, the stretch that we know is bound to end, some time, in the rattle of the door-latch, the sudden firelight, and the sight of familiar things greeting us as long-absent travellers from far oversea. They plodded along steadily and silently, each of them thinking his own thoughts. The Mole's ran a good deal on supper, as it was pitch-dark, and it was all a strange country for him as far as he knew, and he was following obediently in the wake of the Rat, leaving the guidance entirely to him. As for the Rat, he was walking a little way ahead, as his habit was, his shoulders humped, his eyes fixed on the straight grey road in front of him; so he did not notice poor Mole when suddenly the summons reached him, and took him like an electric shock.

We others, who have long lost the more subtle of the physical senses, have not even proper terms to express an animal's inter-communications with his surroundings, living or otherwise, and have only the word "smell," for instance, to include the whole range of delicate thrills which murmur in the nose of the animal night and day, summoning, warning, inciting, repelling. It was one of these mysterious fairy calls from out the void that suddenly reached Mole in the darkness, making him tingle through and through with its very familiar appeal, even while yet he could not clearly remember what it was. He stopped dead in his tracks, his nose searching hither and thither in its efforts to recapture the fine filament, the telegraphic current, that had so strongly moved him. A moment, and he had caught it again; and with it this time came recollection in fullest flood.

Home! That was what they meant, those caressing appeals, those soft touches wafted through the air, those invisible little hands pulling and tugging, all one way! Why, it must be quite close by him at that moment, his old home that he had hurriedly forsaken and never sought again, that day when he first found the river! And now it was sending out its scouts and its messengers to capture him and bring him in. Since his escape on that bright morning he had hardly given it a thought, so absorbed had he been in his new life, in all its pleasures, its surprises, its fresh and captivating experiences. Now, with a rush of old memories, how clearly it stood up before him, in the darkness! Shabby indeed, and small and poorly furnished, and yet his, the home he had made for himself, the home he had been so happy to get back to after his day's work. And the home had been happy with him, too, evidently, and was missing him, and wanted him back, and was telling him so, through his nose, sorrowfully, reproachfully, but with no bitterness or anger; only with plaintive reminder that it was there, and wanted him.

The call was clear, the summons was plain. He must obey it instantly, and go. "Ratty!" he called, full of joyful excitement, "hold on! Come back! I want you, quick!"

"Oh, *come* along, Mole, do!" replied the Rat cheerfully, still plodding along.

"*Please* stop, Ratty!" pleaded the poor Mole, in anguish of heart. "You don't understand! It's my home, my old home! I've just come across the smell of it, and it's close by here, really quite close. And I *must* go to it, I must, I must! Oh, come back, Ratty! Please, please come back!"

The Rat was by this time very far ahead, too far to hear clearly what the Mole was calling, too far to catch the sharp note of painful appeal in his voice. And he was much taken up with the weather, for he too could smell something—something suspiciously like approaching snow.

"Mole, we mustn't stop now, really!" he called back. "We'll come for it to-morrow, whatever it is you've found. But I daren't stop now—it's late, and the snow's coming on again, and I'm not sure of the way! And I want your nose, Mole, so come on quick, there's a good fellow!" And the Rat pressed forward on his way without waiting for an answer.

Poor Mole stood alone in the road, his heart torn asunder, and a big sob gathering, gathering, somewhere low down inside him, to leap up to the surface presently, he knew, in passionate escape. But even under such a test as this his loyalty to his friend stood firm. Never for a moment did he dream of abandoning him. Meanwhile, the wafts from his old home pleaded, whispered, conjured, and finally claimed him imperiously. He dared not tarry longer within their magic cir-

cle. With a wrench that tore his very heartstrings he set his face down the road and followed submissively in the track of the Rat, while faint, thin little smells, still dogging his retreating nose, reproached him for his new friendship and his callous forgetfulness.

With an effort he caught up to the unsuspecting Rat, who began chattering cheerfully about what they would do when they got back, and how jolly a fire of logs in the parlour would be, and what a supper he meant to eat; never noticing his companion's silence and distressful state of mind. At last, however, when they had gone some considerable way further, and were passing some tree-stumps at the edge of a copse that bordered the road, he stopped and said kindly, "Look here, Mole old chap, you seem dead tired. No talk left in you, and your feet dragging like lead. We'll sit down here for a minute and rest. The snow has held off so far, and the best part of our journey is over."

The Mole subsided forlornly on a tree-stump and tried to control himself, for he felt it surely coming. The sob he had fought with so long refused to be beaten. Up and up, it forced its way to the air, and then another, and another, and others thick and fast; till poor Mole at last gave up the struggle, and cried freely and helplessly and openly, now that he knew it was all over and he had lost what he could hardly be said to have found.

The Rat, astonished and dismayed at the violence of Mole's paroxysm of grief, did not dare to speak for a while. At last he said, very quietly and sympathetically, "What is it, old fellow? Whatever can be the matter? Tell us your trouble, and let me see what I can do."

Poor Mole found it difficult to get any words out between the upheavals of his chest that followed one upon another so quickly and held back speech and choked it as it came. "I know it's a—shabby, dingy little place," he sobbed forth at last, brokenly: "not like—your cosy quarters—or Toad's beautiful hall—or Badger's great house—but it was my own little home—and I was fond of it—and I went away and forgot all about it—and then I smelt it suddenly—on the road, when I called and you wouldn't listen, Rat—and everything came back to me with a rush—and I *wanted* it!—O dear, O dear!—and when you *wouldn't* turn back, Ratty—and I had to leave it, though I was smelling it all the time—I thought my heart would break.—We might have just gone and had one look at it, Ratty—only one look—it was close by—but you wouldn't turn back, Ratty, you wouldn't turn back! O dear, O dear!"

Recollection brought fresh waves of sorrow, and sobs again took full charge of him, preventing further speech.

The Rat stared straight in front of him, saying nothing, only patting Mole gently on the shoulder. After a time he muttered gloomily, "I see it all now! What a *pig* I have been! A pig—that's me! Just a pig—a plain pig!"

He waited till Mole's sobs became gradually less stormy and more rhythmical; he waited till at last sniffs were frequent and sobs only intermittent. Then he rose from his seat, and, remarking carelessly, "Well, now we'd really better be getting on, old chap!" set off up the road again, over the toilsome way they had come.

"Wherever are you (hic) going to (hic), Ratty?" cried the tearful Mole, looking up in alarm.

"We're going to find that home of yours, old fellow," replied the Rat pleasantly; "so you had better come along, for it will take some finding, and we shall want your nose."

"Oh, come back, Ratty, do!" cried the Mole, getting up and hurrying after him. "It's no good, I tell you! It's too late, and too dark, and the place is too far off, and the snow's coming! And—and I never meant to let you know I was feeling that way about it—it was all an accident and a mistake! And think of River Bank, and your supper!"

"Hang River Bank, and supper too!" said the Rat heartily, "I tell you, I'm going to find this place now, if I stay out all night. So cheer up, old chap, and take my arm, and we'll very soon be back there again."

Still snuffling, pleading, and reluctant, Mole suffered himself to be dragged back along the road by his imperious companion, who by a flow of cheerful talk and anecdote endeavoured to beguile his spirits back and make the weary way seem shorter. When at last it seemed to the Rat that they must be nearing that part of the road where the Mole had been "held up," he said, "Now, no more talking. Business! Use your nose, and give your mind to it."

They moved on in silence for some little way, when suddenly the Rat was conscious, through his arm that was linked in Mole's, of a faint sort of electric thrill that was passing down that animal's body. Instantly he disengaged himself, fell back a pace, and waited, all attention.

The signals were coming through!

Mole stood a moment rigid, while his uplifted nose, quivering slightly, felt the air.

Then a short, quick run forward—a fault—a check—a try back; and then a slow, steady, confident advance.

The Rat, much excited, kept close to his heels as the Mole, with something of the air of a sleep-walker, crossed a dry ditch, scrambled through a hedge, and nosed his way over a field open and trackless and bare in the faint starlight.

Suddenly, without giving warning, he dived; but the Rat was on the alert, and promptly followed him down the tunnel to which his unerring nose had faithfully led him.

It was close and airless, and the earthy smell was strong, and it seemed a long time to Rat ere the passage ended and he could stand erect and stretch and shake himself. The Mole struck a match, and by its light the Rat saw that they were standing in an open space, neatly swept and sanded underfoot, and directly facing them was Mole's little front door, with "Mole End" painted, in Gothic lettering, over the bell-pull at the side.

Mole reached down a lantern from a nail on the wall and lit it, and the Rat, looking round him, saw that they were in a sort of fore-court. A garden-seat stood on one side of the door, and on the other a roller; for the Mole, who was a tidy animal when at home, could not stand having his ground kicked up by other animals into little runs that ended in earth-heaps. On the walls hung wire baskets with ferns in them, alternating with brackets carrying plaster statuary—Garibaldi, and the infant Samuel, and Queen Victoria, and other heroes of modern Italy. Down on one side of the fore-court ran a skittle-alley, with benches along it and little wooden tables marked with rings that hinted at beer-mugs. In the middle was a small round pond containing gold-fish and surrounded by a cockle-shell border. Out of the centre of the pond rose a fanciful erection clothed in more cockle-shells and topped by a large silvered glass ball that reflected everything all wrong and had a very pleasing effect.

Mole's face beamed at the sight of all these objects so dear to him, and he hurried Rat through the door, lit a lamp in the hall, and took one glance round his old home. He saw the dust lying thick on everything, saw the cheerless, deserted look of the long-neglected house, and its narrow, meagre dimensions, its worn and shabby contents—and collapsed again on a hall-chair, his nose to his paws. "O Ratty!" he cried dismally, "why ever did I do it? Why did I bring you to this poor, cold little place, on a night like this, when you might have been at River Bank by this time, toasting your toes before a blazing fire, with all your own nice things about you!"

The Rat paid no heed to his doleful self-reproaches. He was running here and there, opening doors, inspecting rooms and cupboards, and lighting lamps and candles and sticking them up everywhere. "What a capital little house this is!" he called out cheerily. "So compact! So well planned! Everything here and everything in its place! We'll make a jolly night of it. The first thing we want is a good fire; I'll see to that—I always know where to find things. So this is the parlour? Splendid! Your own idea, those little sleeping-bunks in the wall? Capital! Now, I'll fetch the wood and the coals, and you get a duster, Mole—you'll find one in the drawer of the kitchen table—and try and smarten things up a bit. Bustle about, old chap!"

Encouraged by his inspiriting companion, the Mole roused himself and dusted and polished with energy and heartiness, while the Rat, running to and fro with armfuls of fuel, soon had a cheerful blaze roaring up the chimney. He hailed the Mole to come and warm himself; but Mole promptly had another fit of the blues, dropping down on a couch in dark despair and burying his face in his duster. "Rat," he moaned, "how about your supper, you poor, cold, hungry, weary animal? I've nothing to give you—nothing—not a crumb!"

"What a fellow you are for giving in!" said the Rat reproachfully. "Why, only just now I saw a sardine-opener on the kitchen dresser, quite distinctly; and everybody knows that means there are sardines about somewhere in the neighbourhood. Rouse yourself! pull yourself together, and come with me and forage."

They went and foraged accordingly, hunting through every cupboard and turning out every drawer. The result was not so very depressing after all, though of course it might have been better; a tin of sardines—a box of captain's biscuits, nearly full—and a German sausage encased in silver paper.

"There's a banquet for you!" observed the Rat, as he arranged the table. "I know some animals who would give their ears to be sitting down to supper with us to-night!"

"No bread!" groaned the Mole dolorously "no butter, no——"

"No *pâté de foie gras*, no champagne!" continued the Rat, grinning. "And that reminds me—what's that little door at the end of the passage? Your cellar, of course! Every luxury in this house! Just you wait a minute."

He made for the cellar-door, and presently reappeared, somewhat dusty, with a bottle of beer in each paw and another under each arm. "Self-indulgent beggar you seem to be, Mole," he observed. "Deny yourself nothing. This is really the jolliest little place I ever was in. Now, wherever did you pick up those prints? Make the place look so home-like, they do. No wonder you're so fond of it, Mole. Tell us all about it, and how you came to make it what it is."

Then, while the Rat busied himself fetching plates, and knives and forks, and mustard which he mixed in an egg-cup, the Mole, his bosom still heaving with the stress of his recent emotion, related—somewhat shyly at first, but with more freedom as he warmed to his subject—how this was planned, and how that was thought out, and how this was got through a windfall from an aunt, and that was a wonderful find and a bargain, and this other thing was bought out of laborious savings and a certain amount of "going without." His spirits finally quite restored, he must needs go and caress his possessions, and take a lamp and show off their points to his visitor and expatiate on them, quite forgetful of the supper they both so much needed; Rat, who was desperately hungry but strove to conceal it, nodding seriously, examining with a puckered brow, and saying, "wonderful," and "most remarkable," at intervals, when the chance for an observation was given him.

At last the Rat succeeded in decoying him to the table, and had just got seriously to work with the sardine-opener when sounds were heard from the forecourt without—sounds like the scuffling of small feet in the gravel and a confused murmur of tiny voices, while broken sentences reached them—"Now, all in a line—hold the lantern up a bit, Tommy—clear your throats first—no coughing after I say one, two, three.—Where's young Bill?—Here, come on, do, we're all a-waiting——"

"What's up?" inquired the Rat, pausing in his labours.

"I think it must be the field-mice," replied the

Mole, with a touch of pride in his manner. "They go round carol-singing regularly at this time of the year. They're quite an institution in these parts. And they never pass me over—they come to Mole End last of all; and I used to give them hot drinks, and supper too sometimes, when I could afford it. It will be like old times to hear them again."

"Let's have a look at them!" cried the Rat, jumping up and running to the door.

It was a pretty sight, and a seasonable one, that met their eyes when they flung the door open. In the fore-court, lit by the dim rays of a horn lantern, some eight or ten little field-mice stood in a semicircle, red worsted comforters round their throats, their fore-paws thrust deep into their pockets, their feet jigging for warmth. With bright beady eyes they glanced shyly at each other, sniggering a little, sniffing and applying coat-sleeves a good deal. As the door opened, one of the elder ones that carried the lantern was just say-ing, "Now then, one, two, three!" and forthwith their shrill little voices uprose on the air, singing one of the old-time carols that their forefathers composed in fields that were fallow and held by frost, or when snow-bound in chimney corners, and handed down to be sung in the miry street to lamp-lit windows at Yule-time.

CAROL

Villagers all, this frosty tide,
Let your doors swing open wide,
Though wind may follow, and snow beside,
Yet draw us in by your fire to bide;
    Joy shall be yours as the morning!

Here we stand in the cold and the sleet,
Blowing fingers and stamping feet,
Come from far away you to greet—
You by the fire and we in this street—
    Bidding you joy in the morning!

For ere one half of the night was gone,
Sudden a star has led us on,
Raining bliss and benison—
Bliss to-morrow and more anon,
    Joy for every morning!

Goodman Joseph toiled through the snow—
Saw the star o'er a stable low;
Mary she might not further go—

Welcome thatch, and litter below!
    Joy was hers in the morning!

And then they heard the angels tell
"Who were the first to cry Nowell?
Animals all, as it befell,
In the stable where they did dwell!
    Joy shall be theirs in the morning!"

The voices ceased, the singers, bashful but smiling, exchanged sidelong glances, and silence succeeded—but for a moment only. Then, from up above and far away, down the tunnel they had so lately travelled was borne to their ears in a faint musical hum the sound of distant bells ringing a joyful and clangorous peal.

"Very well sung, boys!" cried the Rat heartily. "And now come along in, all of you, and warm your-selves by the fire, and have something hot!"

"Yes, come along, field-mice," cried the Mole ea-gerly. "This is quite like old times! Shut the door af-ter you. Pull up that settle to the fire. Now, you just wait a minute, while we—O, Ratty!" he cried in de-spair, plumping down on a seat, with tears impend-ing. "Whatever are we doing? We've nothing to give them!"

"You leave all that to me," said the masterful Rat. "Here, you with the lantern! Come over this way. I want to talk to you. Now, tell me, are there any shops open at this hour of the night?"

"Why, certainly, sir," replied the field-mouse re-spectfully. "At this time of the year our shops keep open to all sorts of hours."

"Then look here!" said the Rat. "You go off at once, you and your lantern, and you get me——"

Here much muttered conversation ensued, and the Mole only heard bits of it, such as—"Fresh, mind!—no, a pound of that will do—see you get Buggins's, for I won't have any other—no, only the best—if you can't get it there, try somewhere else—yes, of course, home-made, no tinned stuff—well then, do the best you can!" Finally, there was a chink of coin passing from paw to paw, the field-mouse was provided with an ample basket for his purchases, and off he hurried, he and his lantern.

The rest of the field-mice, perched in a row on the settle, their small legs swinging, gave themselves up to enjoyment of the fire, and toasted their chilblains till they tingled; while the Mole, failing to draw them into easy conversation, plunged into family history and made each of them recite the names of his numerous brothers, who were too young, it appeared, to be allowed to go out a-carolling this year, but looked forward very shortly to winning the parental consent.

The Rat, meanwhile, was busy examining the label on one of the beer-bottles. "I perceive this to be Old Burton," he remarked approvingly. "*Sensible* Mole! The very thing! Now we shall be able to mull some ale! Get the things ready, Mole, while I draw the corks."

It did not take long to prepare the brew and thrust the tin heater well into the red heart of the fire; and soon every field-mouse was sipping and coughing and choking (for a little mulled ale goes a long way) and wiping his eyes and laughing and forgetting he had ever been cold in all his life.

"They act plays too, these fellows," the Mole explained to the Rat. "Make them up all by themselves, and act them afterwards. And very well they do it, too! They gave us a capital one last year, about a field-mouse who was captured at sea by a Barbary corsair, and made to row in a galley; and when he escaped and got home again, his lady-love had gone into a convent. Here, *you!* You were in it, I remember. Get up and recite a bit."

The field-mouse addressed got up on his legs, giggled shyly, looked round the room, and remained absolutely tongue-tied. His comrades cheered him on, Mole coaxed and encouraged him, and the Rat went so far as to take him by the shoulders and shake him; but nothing could overcome his stage-fright. They were all busily engaged on him like watermen applying the Royal Humane Society's regulations to a case of long submersion, when the latch clicked, the door opened, and the field-mouse with the lantern reappeared, staggering under the weight of his basket.

There was no more talk of play-acting once the very real and solid contents of the basket had been tumbled out on the table. Under the generalship of Rat, everybody was set to do something or to fetch something. In a very few minutes supper was ready, and Mole, as he took the head of the table in a sort of a dream, saw a lately barren board set thick with savoury comforts; saw his little friends' faces brighten and beam as they fell to without delay; and then let himself loose—for he was famished indeed—on the provender so magically provided, thinking what a happy home-coming this had turned out, after all. As they ate, they talked of old times, and the field-mice gave him the local gossip up to date, and answered as well as they could the hundred questions he had to ask them. The Rat said little or nothing, only taking care that each guest had what he wanted, and plenty of it, and that Mole had no trouble or anxiety about anything.

They clattered off at last, very grateful and showering wishes of the season, with their jacket pockets stuffed with remembrances for the small brothers and sisters at home. When the door had closed on the last of them and the chink of the lanterns had died away, Mole and Rat kicked the fire up, drew their chairs in, brewed themselves a last nightcap of mulled ale, and discussed the events of the long day. At last the Rat, with a tremendous yawn, said, "Mole, old chap, I'm ready to drop. Sleepy is simply not the word. That your own bunk over on that side? Very well, then, I'll take this. What a ripping little house this is! Everything so handy!"

He clambered into his bunk and rolled himself well up in the blankets, and slumber gathered him forthwith, as a swathe of barley is folded into the arms of the reaping-machine.

The weary Mole also was glad to turn in without delay, and soon had his head on his pillow, in great joy and contentment. But ere he closed his eyes he let them wander round his old room, mellow in the glow of the firelight that played or rested on familiar and friendly things which had long been unconsciously a part of him, and now smilingly received him back, without rancour. He was now in just the frame of mind that the tactful Rat had quietly worked to bring about in him. He saw clearly how plain and simple—how narrow, even—it all was; but clearly, too, how much it all meant to him, and the special value of some such anchorage in one's existence. He did not at all want to abandon the new life and its splendid spaces, to turn his back on sun and air and all they offered him and creep home and stay there; the upper world was all too strong, it called to him still, even down there, and he knew he must return to the larger stage. But it was good to think he had this to come back to, this place which was all his own, these things which were so glad to see him again and could always be counted upon for the same simple welcome.

E. B. White (1889–1985)

E. B. White called himself "a man who has frittered away the best years of his life writing." Millions of readers believe it was time well spent, since *Charlotte's Web* (1952), which is in one sense a fantasy about writing, is one of America's most beloved children's books. Its stylistic beauty is a testament to White's skills as one of the most popular essayists of the twentieth century and coauthor of an enduring short handbook for writers, Strunk and White's *Elements of Style*. White's other well-known children's novels are *Stuart Little* (1945), about a mouse child born into a human family, and *The Trumpet of the Swan* (1970), in which a swan without a voice goes to school with a boy to learn to read and write. *Charlotte's Web* is also a domestic fantasy, set in realistic New England farms where the animals talk to each other and a spider writes words in her web to help save Wilbur the pig from the butcher's knife. Chapter 13 shows how White, like Beatrix Potter with her realistic depictions of animal characters, draws the reader in with close observation of details from nature, such as the spider's method of web spinning, while convincing us at the same time that if we had been present we would have heard her talking to herself like a person concentrating on an arduous task. Charlotte, with the habits and life cycle of a real spider, is also a storyteller, a motherly singer of lullabies, a sister to the mythological Fates spinning the threads of life, and a writer looking for just the right word. That she sends a grouchy rat to the trash dump to hunt for words in the refuse of the humans' consumer culture is at once comical, resourceful, and a wonderfully symbolic joke about writers creating beauty out of unpleasant reality.

Chapter 14 focuses on the human protagonist Fern, the child who opens the novel by rebelling against the violent practicalities of farming, thereby saving the life of the runt pig. She moves with ease between her parents' world of human reality and the animal fantasy realm of the barnyard. Like many parents in modern children's stories, her mother represents the biases of conventional adults of her time, worrying about a girl who could be so preoccupied with animals and believe so firmly in an adventure story told by a spider. The doctor, however, is the hero of this chapter. Unlike the unimaginative psychiatrist in Gary Paulsen's *The Island* (see Part 1), Dr. Dorian represents the wise man of science who appreciates the mysteries and miracles of both the natural world and the growing child. The novel later ends with elegies for lost friends and the passing of childhood, with celebrations of renewed life and new friends, and with the ultimate wish-fulfillment fantasy symbolized by Charlotte's web—the belief that writing something wonderful can make it so.

From *Charlotte's Web*

CHAPTER 13. GOOD PROGRESS

Far into the night, while the other creatures slept, Charlotte worked on her web. First she ripped out a few of the orb lines near the center. She left the radial lines alone, as they were needed for support. As she worked, her eight legs were a great help to her. So were her teeth. She loved to weave and she was an expert at it. When she was finished ripping things out, her web looked something like this:

A spider can produce several kinds of thread. She uses a dry, tough thread for foundation lines, and she uses a sticky thread for snare lines—the ones that catch and hold insects. Charlotte decided to use her dry thread for writing the new message.

"If I write the word 'Terrific' with sticky thread," she thought, "every bug that comes along will get stuck in it and spoil the effect."

"Now let's see, the first letter is T."

Charlotte climbed to a point at the top of the left hand side of the web. Swinging her spinnerets into position, she attached her thread and then dropped down. As she dropped, her spinning tubes went into action and she let out thread. At the bottom, she attached the thread. This formed the upright part of the letter T. Charlotte was not satisfied, however. She climbed up and made another attachment, right next to the first. Then she carried the line down, so that she had a double line instead of a single line. "It will show up better if I make the whole thing with double lines."

She climbed back up, moved over about an inch to the left, touched her spinnerets to the web, and then carried a line across to the right, forming the top of the T. She repeated this, making it double. Her eight legs were very busy helping.

"Now for the E!"

Charlotte got so interested in her work, she began to talk to herself, as though to cheer herself on. If you had been sitting quietly in the barn cellar that evening, you would have heard something like this:

"Now for the R! Up we go! Attach! Descend! Pay out line! Whoa! Attach! Good! Up you go! Repeat! Attach! Descend! Pay out line. Whoa, girl! Steady now!

Attach! Climb! Attach! Over to the right! Pay out line! Attach! Now right and down and swing that loop and around and around! Now in to the left! Attach! Climb! Repeat! O.K.! Easy, keep those lines together! Now, then, out and down for the leg of the R! Pay out line! Whoa! Attach! Ascend! Repeat! Good girl!"

And so, talking to herself, the spider worked at her difficult task. When it was completed, she felt hungry. She ate a small bug that she had been saving. Then she slept.

Next morning, Wilbur arose and stood beneath the web. He breathed the morning air into his lungs. Drops of dew, catching the sun, made the web stand out clearly. When Lurvy arrived with breakfast, there was

E. B. White advised illustrator Garth Williams to depict Charlotte as a realistic spider, but this classic scene also displays her magical ability to transform Wilbur's life and self-image by writing words in her web.

the handsome pig, and over him, woven neatly in block letters, was the word TERRIFIC. Another miracle.

Lurvy rushed and called Mr. Zuckerman. Mr. Zuckerman rushed and called Mrs. Zuckerman. Mrs. Zuckerman ran to the phone and called the Arables. The Arables climbed into their truck and hurried over. Everybody stood at the pigpen and stared at the web and read the word, over and over, while Wilbur, who really *felt* terrific, stood quietly swelling out his chest and swinging his snout from side to side.

"Terrific!" breathed Zuckerman, in joyful admiration. "Edith, you better phone the reporter on the *Weekly Chronicle* and tell him what has happened. He will want to know about this. He may want to bring a photographer. There isn't a pig in the whole state that is as terrific as our pig."

The news spread. People who had journeyed to see Wilbur when he was "some pig" came back again to see him now that he was "terrific."

That afternoon, when Mr. Zuckerman went to milk the cows and clean out the tie-ups, he was still thinking about what a wondrous pig he owned.

"Lurvy!" he called. "There is to be no more cow manure thrown down into that pigpen. I have a terrific pig. I want that pig to have clean, bright straw every day for his bedding. Understand?"

"Yes, sir," said Lurvy

"Furthermore," said Mr. Zuckerman, "I want you to start building a crate for Wilbur. I have decided to take the pig to the County Fair on September sixth. Make the crate large and paint it green with gold letters!"

"What will the letters say?" asked Lurvy.

"They should say *Zuckerman's Famous Pig.*"

Lurvy picked up a pitchfork and walked away to get some clean straw. Having such an important pig was going to mean plenty of extra work, he could see that.

Below the apple orchard, at the end of a path, was the dump where Mr. Zuckerman threw all sorts of trash and stuff that nobody wanted any more. Here, in a small clearing hidden by young alders and wild raspberry bushes, was an astonishing pile of old bottles and empty tin cans and dirty rags and bits of metal and broken bottles and broken hinges and broken springs and dead batteries and last month's magazines and old discarded dishmops and tattered overalls and rusty spikes and leaky pails and forgotten stoppers and useless junk of all kinds, including a wrong-size crank for a broken ice-cream freezer.

Templeton knew the dump and liked it. There were good hiding places there—excellent cover for a rat. And there was usually a tin can with food still clinging to the inside.

Templeton was down there now, rummaging around. When he returned to the barn, he carried in his mouth an advertisement he had torn from a crumpled magazine.

"How's this?" he asked, showing the ad to Charlotte. "It says 'Crunchy.' 'Crunchy' would be a good word to write in your web."

"Just the wrong idea," replied Charlotte. "Couldn't be worse. We don't want Zuckerman to think Wilbur is crunchy. He might start thinking about crisp, crunchy bacon and tasty ham. That would put ideas into his head. We must advertise Wilbur's noble qualities, not his tastiness. Go get another word, please, Templeton!"

The rat looked disgusted. But he sneaked away to the dump and was back in a while with a strip of cotton cloth. "How's this?" he asked. "It's a label off an old shirt."

Charlotte examined the label. It said PRE-SHRUNK.

"I'm sorry, Templeton," she said, "but 'Pre-shrunk' is out of the question. We want Zuckerman to think Wilbur is nicely filled out, not all shrunk up. I'll have to ask you to try again."

"What do you think I am, a messenger boy?" grumbled the rat. "I'm not going to spend all my time chasing down to the dump after advertising material."

"Just once more—please!" said Charlotte.

"I'll tell you what I'll do," said Templeton. "I know where there's a package of soap flakes in the woodshed. It has writing on it. I'll bring you a piece of the package."

He climbed the rope that hung on the wall and disappeared through a hole in the ceiling. When he came back he had a strip of blue-and-white cardboard in his teeth.

"There!" he said, triumphantly. "How's that?"

Charlotte read the words: "With New Radiant Action."

"What does it mean?" asked Charlotte, who had never used any soap flakes in her life.

"How should I know?" said Templeton. "You asked for words and I brought them. I suppose the next thing you'll want me to fetch is a dictionary."

Together they studied the soap ad. "'With new radiant action,'" repeated Charlotte, slowly. "Wilbur!" she called.

Wilbur, who was asleep in the straw, jumped up.

"Run around!" commanded Charlotte. "I want to see you in action, to see if you are radiant."

Wilbur raced to the end of his yard.

"Now back again, faster!" said Charlotte.

Wilbur galloped back. His skin shone. His tail had a fine, tight curl in it.

"Jump into the air!" cried Charlotte.

Wilbur jumped as high as he could.

"Keep your knees straight and touch the ground with your ears!" called Charlotte.

Wilbur obeyed.

"Do a back flip with a half twist in it!" cried Charlotte.

Wilbur went over backwards, writhing and twisting as he went.

"O.K., Wilbur," said Charlotte. "You can go back to sleep. O.K., Templeton, the soap ad will do, I guess. I'm not sure Wilbur's action is exactly radiant, but it's interesting."

"Actually," said Wilbur, "I *feel* radiant."

"Do you?" said Charlotte, looking at him with affection. "Well, you're a good little pig, and radiant you shall be. I'm in this thing pretty deep now—I might as well go the limit."

Tired from his romp, Wilbur lay down in the clean straw. He closed his eyes. The straw seemed scratchy—not as comfortable as the cow manure, which was always delightfully soft to lie in. So he pushed the straw to one side and stretched out in the manure. Wilbur sighed. It had been a busy day—his first day of being terrific. Dozens of people had visited his yard during the afternoon, and he had had to stand and pose, looking as terrific as he could. Now he was tired. Fern had arrived and seated herself quietly on her stool in the corner.

"Tell me a story, Charlotte!" said Wilbur, as he lay waiting for sleep to come. "Tell me a story!"

So Charlotte, although she, too, was tired, did what Wilbur wanted.

"Once upon a time," she began, "I had a beautiful cousin who managed to build her web across a small stream. One day a tiny fish leaped into the air and got tangled in the web. My cousin was very much surprised, of course. The fish was thrashing wildly. My cousin hardly dared tackle it. But she did. She swooped down and threw great masses of wrapping material around the fish and fought bravely to capture it."

"Did she succeed?" asked Wilbur.

"It was a never-to-be-forgotten battle," said Charlotte. "There was the fish, caught only by one fin, and its tail wildly thrashing and shining in the sun. There was the web, sagging dangerously under the weight of the fish."

"How much did the fish weigh?" asked Wilbur eagerly.

"I don't know," said Charlotte. "There was my cousin, slipping in, dodging out, beaten mercilessly over the head by the wildly thrashing fish, dancing in, dancing out, throwing her threads and fighting hard. First she threw a left around the tail. The fish lashed back. Then a left to the tail and a right to the midsection. The fish lashed back. Then she dodged to one side and threw a right, and another right to the fin. Then a hard left to the head, while the web swayed and stretched."

"Then what happened?" asked Wilbur.

"Nothing," said Charlotte. "The fish lost the fight. My cousin wrapped it up so tight it couldn't budge."

"Then what happened?" asked Wilbur.

"Nothing," said Charlotte. "My cousin kept the fish for a while, and then, when she got good and ready, she ate it."

"Tell me another story!" begged Wilbur.

So Charlotte told him about another cousin of hers who was an aeronaut.

"What is an aeronaut?" asked Wilbur.

"A balloonist," said Charlotte. "My cousin used to stand on her head and let out enough thread to form a balloon. Then she'd let go and be lifted into the air and carried upward on the warm wind."

"Is that true?" asked Wilbur. "Or are you just making it up?"

"It's true," replied Charlotte. "I have some very remarkable cousins. And now, Wilbur, it's time you went to sleep."

"Sing something!" begged Wilbur, closing his eyes.

So Charlotte sang a lullaby, while crickets chirped in the grass and the barn grew dark. This was the song she sang.

"Sleep, sleep, my love, my only,
Deep, deep, in the dung and the dark;
Be not afraid and be not lonely!
This is the hour when frogs and thrushes
Praise the world from the woods and the rushes.
Rest from care, my one and only,
Deep in the dung and the dark!"

But Wilbur was already asleep. When the song ended, Fern got up and went home.

CHAPTER 14. DR. DORIAN

The next day was Saturday. Fern stood at the kitchen sink drying the breakfast dishes as her mother washed them. Mrs. Arable worked silently. She hoped Fern would go out and play with other children, instead of heading for the Zuckermans' barn to sit and watch animals.

"Charlotte is the best storyteller I ever heard," said Fern, poking her dish towel into a cereal bowl.

"Fern," said her mother sternly, "you must not invent things. You know spiders don't tell stories. Spiders can't talk."

"Charlotte can," replied Fern. "She doesn't talk very loud, but she talks."

"What kind of story did she tell?" asked Mrs. Arable.

"Well," began Fern, "she told us about a cousin of hers who caught a fish in her web. Don't you think that's fascinating?"

"Fern, dear, how would a fish get in a spider's web?" said Mrs. Arable. "You know it couldn't happen. You're making this up."

"Oh, it happened all right," replied Fern. "Charlotte never fibs. This cousin of hers built a web across a stream. One day she was hanging around on the web and a tiny fish leaped into the air and got tangled in the web. The fish was caught by one fin, Mother; its tail was wildly thrashing and shining in the sun. Can't you just see the web, sagging dangerously under the weight of the fish? Charlotte's cousin kept slipping in, dodging out, and she was beaten mercilessly over the head by the wildly thrashing fish, dancing in, dancing out, throwing . . ."

"Fern!" snapped her mother. "Stop it! Stop inventing these wild tales!"

"I'm not inventing," said Fern. "I'm just telling you the facts."

"What finally happened?" asked her mother, whose curiosity began to get the better of her.

"Charlotte's cousin won. She wrapped the fish up, then she ate him when she got good and ready. Spiders have to eat, the same as the rest of us."

"Yes, I suppose they do," said Mrs. Arable, vaguely.

"Charlotte has another cousin who is a balloonist. She stands on her head, lets out a lot of line, and is carried aloft on the wind. Mother, wouldn't you simply love to do that?"

"Yes, I would, come to think of it," replied Mrs. Arable. "But Fern, darling, I wish you would play outdoors today instead of going to Uncle Homer's barn. Find some of your playmates and do something nice outdoors. You're spending too much time in that barn—it isn't good for you to be alone so much."

"Alone?" said Fern. "Alone? My best friends are in the barn cellar. It is a very sociable place. Not at all lonely."

Fern disappeared after a while, walking down the road toward Zuckermans'. Her mother dusted the sitting room. As she worked she kept thinking about Fern. It didn't seem natural for a little girl to be so interested in animals. Finally Mrs. Arable made up her mind she would pay a call on old Doctor Dorian and ask his advice. She got in the car and drove to his office in the village.

Dr. Dorian had a thick beard. He was glad to see Mrs. Arable and gave her a comfortable chair.

"It's about Fern," she explained. "Fern spends entirely too much time in the Zuckermans' barn. It doesn't seem normal. She sits on a milk stool in a corner of the barn cellar, near the pigpen, and watches animals, hour after hour. She just sits and listens."

Dr. Dorian leaned back and closed his eyes.

"How enchanting!" he said. "It must be real nice and quiet down there. Homer has some sheep, hasn't he?"

"Yes," said Mrs. Arable. "But it all started with that pig we let Fern raise on a bottle. She calls him Wilbur. Homer bought the pig, and ever since it left our place Fern has been going to her uncle's to be near it."

"I've been hearing things about that pig," said Dr. Dorian, opening his eyes. "They say he's quite a pig."

"Have you heard about the words that appeared in the spider's web?" asked Mrs. Arable nervously.

"Yes," replied the doctor.

"Well, do you understand it?" asked Mrs. Arable.

"Understand what?"

"Do you understand how there could be any writing in a spider's web?"

"Oh, no," said Dr. Dorian. "I don't understand it. But for that matter I don't understand how a spider learned to spin a web in the first place. When the words appeared, everyone said they were a miracle. But nobody pointed out that the web itself is a miracle."

"What's miraculous about a spider's web?" said Mrs. Arable. "I don't see why you say a web is a miracle—it's just a web."

"Ever try to spin one?" asked Dr. Dorian.

Mrs. Arable shifted uneasily in her chair. "No," she replied. "But I can crochet a doily and I can knit a sock."

"Sure," said the doctor. "But somebody taught you, didn't they?"

"My mother taught me."

"Well, who taught a spider? A young spider knows how to spin a web without any instructions from anybody. Don't you regard that as a miracle?"

"I suppose so," said Mrs. Arable. "I never looked at it that way before. Still, I don't understand how those words got into the web. I don't understand it, and I don't like what I can't understand."

"None of us do," said Dr. Dorian, sighing. "I'm a doctor. Doctors are supposed to understand everything. But I don't understand everything, and I don't intend to let it worry me."

Mrs. Arable fidgeted. "Fern says the animals talk to each other. Dr. Dorian, do you believe animals talk?"

"I never heard one say anything," he replied. "But that proves nothing. It is quite possible that an animal has spoken civilly to me and that I didn't catch the remark because I wasn't paying attention. Children pay better attention than grownups. If Fern says that the animals in Zuckerman's barn talk, I'm quite ready to believe her. Perhaps if people talked less, animals would talk more. People are incessant talkers—I can give you my word on that."

"Well, I feel better about Fern," said Mrs. Arable. "You don't think I need worry about her?"

"Does she look well?" asked the doctor.

"Oh, yes."

"Appetite good?"

"Oh, yes, she's always hungry."

"Sleep well at night?"

"Oh, yes."

"Then don't worry," said the doctor.

"Do you think she'll ever start thinking about something besides pigs and sheep and geese and spiders?"

"How old is Fern?"

"She's eight."

"Well," said Dr. Dorian, "I think she will always love animals. But I doubt that she spends her entire life in Homer Zuckerman's barn cellar. How about boys—does she know any boys?"

"She knows Henry Fussy," said Mrs. Arable brightly.

Dr. Dorian closed his eyes again and went into deep thought. "Henry Fussy," he mumbled. "Hmm. Remarkable. Well, I don't think you have anything to worry about. Let Fern associate with her friends in the barn if she wants to. I would say, offhand, that spiders and pigs were fully as interesting as Henry Fussy. Yet I predict that the day will come when even Henry will drop some chance remark that catches Fern's attention. It's amazing how children change from year to year. How's Avery?" he asked, opening his eyes wide.

"Oh, Avery," chuckled Mrs. Arable. "Avery is always fine. Of course, he gets into poison ivy and gets stung by wasps and bees and brings frogs and snakes home and breaks everything he lays his hands on. He's fine."

"Good!" said the doctor.

Mrs. Arable said good-bye and thanked Dr. Dorian very much for his advice. She felt greatly relieved.

Philippa Pearce (b. 1920)

In *Tom's Midnight Garden* (1958), the powerfully felt realism of setting and characterization make this masterpiece of twentieth-century fiction for children an especially compelling time-slip fantasy. Like many great English novelists, such as the Brontë sisters, George Eliot, and Thomas Hardy, Philippa Pearce builds her stories on strong memories of places from her own family background, in her case in southeastern England. In *Minnow on the Say* (1955), for example, two boys spend a summer hunting for a real hidden treasure along the banks of the River Say (Pearce's fictional name for the River Cam). *Tom's Midnight Garden* brings together a mid-twentieth-century boy and a Victorian girl, with echoes of Mary and Colin's experiences in Burnett's *The Secret Garden* (see Part 5). The children are displaced and neglected like so many protagonists in fantasy and adventure stories, badly in need of more fulfilling kinds of companionship and stimulation. Tom Long is away from his loving middle-class family, quarantined during his brother's illness in an apartment with dull relatives, missing his brother and garden at home. During restless nights, when the defective old grandfather clock in the hall strikes thirteen, he discovers a place that does not exist during the day, a garden outside the back door. Hatty is a lonely orphan living in the old house before it was divided into flats, when it was a mansion occupied by her widowed aunt and cousins who do not treat her kindly. As in the Golden Age classics *The Secret Garden* (1911) and Johanna Spyri's *Heidi* (1881), nature and friendship have healing power for troubled children.

Chapters 9 and 10 show Tom and Hatty getting acquainted, at the outset of Tom's intense quest to understand the nature of his midnight time travel. Although the novel's undercurrents of suspense, self-doubt, and sexual tension are present in these chapters, many physical and symbolic details show that Tom is irresistibly drawn to the little girl's "kingdom" of make-believe because, for young people like Tom with conflicting feelings about growing up, as for adult writers and readers, the garden is an idyllic place that fulfills our longing for escape and nostalgia for childhood innocence, imagination, and play.

From *Tom's Midnight Garden*

CHAPTER 9. HATTY

Tom only rarely saw the three boys in the garden. They would come strolling out with the air-gun, or for fruit. They came for apples on the second occasion of Tom's seeing them, which was only a few days after the first.

With a terrier at their heels, they sauntered out of the house and—apparently aimlessly—took the path by the greenhouse, and so came into the kitchen-garden. Then, suddenly, they bunched together and closed upon a young tree of early ripening apples.

"We were only told not to pick any," said Hubert. "Come on, lads! Shake the tree and make them fall!"

He and James set their hands to the tree-trunk and shook it to and fro. An apple dropped, and then several more. Edgar was gathering them up from the ground, when he paused, looked sharply across to the bushes, and cried: "Spying!" There stood the child, Hatty. She came out into the open, then, as concealment had become pointless.

"Give me an apple, please," she said.

"Or you'll tell, I suppose!" cried Edgar. "Spy and telltale!"

"Oh, give her an apple—she means no harm!" said James. As Edgar seemed unwilling, he himself threw one to her, and she caught it in the bottom of her pinafore held out in front of her. "Only don't leave the core on the lawn, Hatty, as you did last time, or you'll get yourself into trouble, and us too, perhaps."

She promised, and, eating her apple, drew nearer to the group. Each boy had an apple now, and they were eating them hurriedly, scuffling the earth with their feet as they came away from the tree, to confuse the tracks they had made.

Now they halted again—and it happened to be quite near Tom, but with their backs to him—while they finished their apples. The terrier snuffed his way round their legs and so came to Tom's side of the group. He was closer to Tom than he had ever been before, and became—in some degree—aware of him. So much was clear from the dog's behaviour: he faced Tom; his hackles rose; he growled again and again. Hubert said, "What is it, Pincher?" and turned; he looked at Tom, and never saw him.

Edgar had turned quickly, at the same time: he looked more searchingly, through and through Tom. Then James turned, and lastly even Hatty. They all four stared and stared through Tom, while the dog at their feet continued his growling.

It was very rude of them, Tom felt, and very stupid, too. Suddenly he lost patience with the lot of them. He felt the impulse to be rude back, and gave way to it—after all, no one could see him: he stuck out his tongue at them.

In retort, the girl Hatty darted out her tongue at Tom.

For a moment, Tom was so astounded that he almost believed he had imagined it; but he knew he had not. The girl had stuck out her tongue at him.

She could see him.

"What did you stick out your tongue for, Hatty?" asked Edgar, who must be able to see things even out of the corners of his eyes.

"My tongue was hot in my mouth," said Hatty, with a resourcefulness that took Tom by surprise. "It wanted to be cool—it wanted fresh air."

"Don't give pert, lying answers!"

"Let her be, Edgar," said James.

They lost interest in the dog's curious behaviour, and in Hatty's. They began to move back to the house. The dog skulked along nervously beside them, keeping them between himself and Tom, and still muttering to himself deep in his throat; the girl walked slightly ahead of them all.

Tom followed, seething with excitement, waiting his chance.

They went in single file by the narrow path between the greenhouse and the large box-bush. Hatty went first, then the three boys. Tom followed behind the four of them; but, when he emerged from the path and came on to the lawn, there were only the three boys ahead of him.

"Where's Hatty?" James was asking. He had been the last of the three.

"Slipped off somewhere among the trees," said Edgar, carelessly. The three boys continued upon their way back into the house.

Tom was left on the lawn, gazing about him in determination and anger. She thought she had slipped through his fingers, but she hadn't. He would find her. He would have this out with her.

He began his search. He looked everywhere that he could think of: among the bushes; up the trees; behind the heating-house; beyond the nut stubs; under the summerhouse arches; inside the gooseberry wire; beyond the bean-poles . . .

No . . . No . . . No . . . She was nowhere. At last, behind him, he heard her call, "Coo-eee!"

She was standing there, only a few yards from him, staring at him. There was a silence. Then Tom—not knowing whether he was indeed speaking to ears that could hear him—said: "I knew you were hiding from me and watching me, just now."

She might have meant to pretend not to hear him, as, earlier, she must have pretended not to see him; but her vanity could not resist this opening. "Just now!" she cried, scornfully. "Why, I've hidden and watched you, often and often, before this! I saw you when you ran along by the nut stubs and then used my secret hedge tunnel into the meadow! I saw you when Susan was dusting and you waved from the top of the yew-tree! I saw you when you went right through the orchard door!" She hesitated, as though the memory upset her a little; but then went on. "Oh, I've seen you often—and often—and often—when you never knew it!"

So that was the meaning of the footprints on the grass, on that first day; that was the meaning of the shadowy form and face at the back of the bedroom, across the lawn; that, in short, was the meaning of the queer feeling of being watched, which Tom had had in the garden so often, that, in the end, he had come to accept it without speculation.

A kind of respect for the girl crept into Tom's mind. "You don't hide badly, for a girl," he said. He saw at once that the remark angered her, so he hurried on to introduce himself: "I'm Tom Long," he said. She said nothing, but looked as if she had little opinion of that, as a name. "Well," said Tom, nettled, "I know your name: Hatty—Hatty Something." Into the saying he threw a careless disdain: it was only tit for tat.

The little girl, with only the slightest hesitation, drew herself up into a stiffness, and said: "Princess Hatty, if you please: I am a Princess."

CHAPTER 10. GAMES AND TALES

Tom was half-inclined to believe her, at first.

Her gaze was very bright and steady; and, with her red cheeks and long black hair and stiff little dignity, there was perhaps something regal about her—something of a picture-book queen. Immediately behind her was the dark-green background of a yew-tree. In one hand she held up a twig of yew she had broken off in nervousness, or to play with; in the other hand she held her half-eaten apple: she held the two things like a queen's sceptre and orb.

"You can kiss my hand," she said.

"I don't want to," said Tom. He added, "Thank you," as an afterthought, in case she really were a princess; but he had his suspicions. "If you're a Princess, your father and mother must be a King and Queen: where's their kingdom—where are they?"

"I'm not allowed to say."

"Why not?"

She hesitated, and then said: "I am held here a prisoner. I am a Princess in disguise. There is someone here who calls herself my aunt, but she isn't so: she is wicked and cruel to me. And those aren't my cousins, either, although I have to call them so. Now you know my whole secret. I will permit you to call me Princess."

She stretched out her hand towards him again, but Tom ignored it.

"And now," she said, "I will allow myself to play with you."

"I don't mind playing," said Tom, doggedly, "but I'm not used to playing silly girls' games."

"Come with me," said the girl.

She showed him the garden. Tom had thought that he knew it well already; but, now, with Hatty, he saw places and things he had not guessed at before. She showed him all her hiding-places: a leafy crevice between a wall and a tree-trunk, where a small human body could just wedge itself; a hollowed-out centre to a box-bush, and a run leading to it—like the run made in the hedge by the meadow; a wigwam shelter made by a re-arrangement of the bean-sticks that Abel had left leaning against the side of the heating-house; a series of hiding-holes behind the fronds of the great ferns that grew along the side of the greenhouse; a feathery green tunnel between the asparagus ridges. She showed Tom how to hide from a search simply by standing behind the trunk of the big fir-tree: you had to listen intently and move exactly—and noiselessly, of course—so a that the trunk was always between yourself and the searcher.

Hatty showed Tom many things he could not have seen for himself. When she was lifting the sacking over the rhubarb-tubs, to show him the sticks of rhubarb, Tom remembered something: "Did you once leave a written message here?"

"Did you once find one?" asked Hatty.

"Yes—a letter to fairies." Tom did not hide the disgust he had felt. "Fairies!"

"Whoever could have put it there?" Hatty wondered. "To fairies! Just fancy!" She pulled a grimace, but awkwardly; and she changed the subject quickly. "Come on, Tom! I'll show you more!"

She opened doors for him. She unlatched the door into the gooseberry wire, and they went in. Among the currant bushes at the end they found a blackbird that must have squeezed in by a less official entrance, attracted by the fruit. The bird beat its wings frantically against the wire at their approach, but they manoeuvred round it and then drove it before them down the gooseberry wire and out—in a glad rush—through the door they had left open. "It's lucky we found it," said Hatty. "I'm afraid that Abel . . ." She shook her head. "I really think he'd rather see birds *starving* than eating his fruit."

For Tom, she opened the orchard door from the

sundial path, and then the door into the potting-shed. Among the tools and seed-boxes and flower-pots and rolls of chicken-wire, they found a sack full of feathers—hen feathers and goose feathers. Hatty dug her fingers in and threw them up into the air in a brown-and-white storm so thick that even Tom thought he felt a tickling on his nose, and sneezed. Then Hatty crept over the floor, laughing, and picked up all the fallen feathers, and put them back, because otherwise Abel would be angry. Tom sat on the side of the wheelbarrow and swung his legs and pointed out any stray feathers still drifting down. He could not have helped Hatty: he knew that, with both hands and all his force, he could not have lifted even a feather's weight. Meanwhile Hatty, on her hands and knees, seemed to have forgotten that she was a Princess.

After that, they went to the little brick-built heating-house, at the end of the greenhouse, and Hatty set about opening that door for Tom. She was far too small to be able to reach the flat square of iron that latched the top of the door; but, standing on tiptoe and straining upward with her yew-twig, she was finally able to poke it aside. She opened the door, and they went down steps inside into darkness and the smell of rust and cold cinders—the weather was so warm that the stove for the greenhouse was not working. There was a small shelf with two or three books on it, that Hatty said belonged to Abel. The shelf was just out of reach, but they could see that the topmost book of the pile was a Bible. "Abel says the Bible must be above all the other books, like—like the Queen ruling over all England."

They went into the greenhouse, among the cacti and the creepers that swayed down from their roof-suspended cage-pots, and plants with strange flowers that could never be expected to live, like other plants, out of doors. Tom gasped for breath in the greenhouse, and wondered how they endured the stifling air. There was a Castor-oil Plant—Tom felt a little sick when Hatty named it. There was a Sensitive Plant, too, and Hatty showed Tom how, when she touched a leaf-tip, the whole, frond drooped and shrank from her by folding itself together. The plant's sensitivity was something quite out of the ordinary; it seemed to feel even Tom's touch. He was so delighted that he worked his fingers over the whole plant, and left it in one droop of nervous dejection.

Then they leant over the water-tank and tried to see the goldfish—and tried to catch them. Hatty bared her arm, to plunge it in; and Tom laid his arm along hers and behind it, with his open hand behind hers, finger to finger. So, as with one arm and one hand, they dipped into the water and hunted. Tom could have done nothing by himself; but when Hatty very nearly caught a fish, Tom's hand seemed one with hers in the catching.

Then Hatty led Tom back to the doorway of the greenhouse and showed him the coloured panes that bordered the glass panelling of the upper half. Through each colour of pane, you could see a different garden outside. Through the green pane, Tom saw a garden with green flowers under a green sky; even the geraniums were green-black. Through the red pane lay a garden as he might have seen it through the redness of shut eyelids. The purple glass filled the garden with thunderous shadow and with oncoming night. The yellow glass seemed to drench it in lemonade. At each of the four corners of this bordering was a colourless square of glass, engraved with a star.

"And if you look through this one . . ." said Hatty. They screwed up their eyes and looked through the engraved glass.

"You can't really see anything, through the star," said Tom disappointed.

"Sometimes I like that the best of all," said Hatty. "You look and see nothing, and you might think there wasn't a garden at all; but, all the time, of course, there is, waiting for you."

They went out into the garden again, and Hatty began to tell Tom about the yew-trees round the lawn. The one he had climbed and waved from was called the Matterhorn. Another tree was called the Look-out, and another the Steps of St Paul's. One tree was called Tricksy, because of the difficulty of climbing it: its main trunk was quite bare for some way up from the ground and could only be swarmed. Hubert and James and Edgar had all swarmed it in their time; Hatty could not swarm. (Tom felt superior—Princess or no Princess.)

Sometimes Hatty's information seemed doubtful to Tom. They paused by a bushy plant, to which Hatty drew attention. "This is the Burning Bush," she said. She plucked a leaf, rubbed it between her fingers, and then held them up to Tom's nose.

He sniffed the finger-tips; the smell was of the faintest to him. "Should it be a smell of scorching?" he asked doubtfully.

"No, James says the smell is of lemon-verbena."

"Why is it called Burning Bush, then?"

"They say that if you come out at midnight on Midsummer Eve, and set a flame to this, the whole plant will blaze up"

"How do you know—have you ever tried?"

"No, of course not. Because there's only one plant in the garden, and we don't want that burnt to ashes."

"Oh!" Tom supposed to himself that it might be true.

Hatty drew nearer to him. "Shall I tell you something—something secret?"

"If you like."

"This bush is grown from a slip of the real burning bush—the one that burnt when Moses was there."

"But that was long, long ago, and in the Bible!"

"I shan't tell you secrets again!" said Hatty, offendedly.

But she could never resist telling him. Not only on that first day of meeting, but on all the days following, her secrets and stories poured from her with haste and eagerness as though she were afraid that Tom's company would not be hers for long. When they were tired with playing in the garden, Hatty would lead the way to the summer-house. They went up the steps and Hatty opened the door for them. From the back of the summer-house she brought forward two twisted iron garden chairs, and put them in the doorway, for herself and Tom. There they used to sit, looking over the oblong pond, watching the fish rise, and Hatty talked.

Once Edgar found them. They were not aware that he had been standing staring and listening, until suddenly—from one side of their view down the garden—he called to Hatty: "What are you up to there, Hatty?"

"I am not 'up to' anything, Cousin Edgar."

"For the last five minutes you've been talking and nodding and smiling and listening, all by yourself."

"I am not by myself. I am talking to a friend of mine."

"Where is he?"

"On this other chair, of course."

Edgar burst out laughing, very unpleasantly. "Really, Cousin Hatty, people will think you're queer in the head—once it used to be fairies, which was just silliness; and now its somebody who isn't there!" He went off, laughing.

Hatty was trembling, when she turned back to Tom. "And now he'll go and tell the others, and they'll jeer at me, and Aunt Grace will say it shows how unfit I am to go anywhere with other children, outside, in the village."

"Well, then," said Tom, "why did you tell Edgar about me?"

She opened her eyes very wide at him: "But one must tell the truth, mustn't one?"

Often, from their seat, they could see Abel at work down the garden. He would sometimes stop and look in the direction of the summer-house, and Hatty would then wave to him, in a Princess-like manner.

"So sad about Abel," said Hatty, mysteriously.

"Sad?"

"The whole family is a sad one. But you must promise not to tell, if I tell you."

Tom said nothing, and Hatty went straight on.

"He had just one brother, and they were together in the fields one day—it was just before Abel became gardener here. His brother was very jealous of him, and one day, in the fields, they fought. Well, really, his brother just attacked Abel—with a weapon—murderously."

"Go on."

"He killed Abel—that is, of course, he very nearly killed him. There was a great deal of blood. It lay smoking on the ground of the field."

There was a horrified silence; and then Tom said suddenly, "What was Abel's brother's name?"

"Really, I don't remember," said Hatty, looking away from Tom at a bird in the sky.

"Was his brother's name Cain?" asked Tom. Hatty pretended not to have heard him. This was particularly irritating to Tom, as it was what he had to suffer from all the other people in the garden. "Because the story of Cain and Abel is in the Bible, and Cain really killed Abel. I don't believe this Abel who gardens here has anything to do with the Bible Abel—except that he was called after him. I don't believe this Abel ever had a brother who tried to murder him."

"Suppose I told you that Susan had told me— and Susan is Abel's sweetheart? Or suppose I told you that Abel himself told me, as a secret?"

"I'm not sure you don't tell fibs," said Tom; and

even then he knew that he was choosing a mild word, to be kind to Hatty. "I dare you to go to Abel now, and ask him whether he has a brother who tried to murder him!"

"I shan't ever—ever—tell you any more secrets—ever!" Hatty cried passionately; but Tom knew how much to fear that. Meanwhile, she did not take up his challenge to have the matter out with Abel, and Tom took this as permission to disbelieve her story. It was only a step from that to disbelieving that Hatty herself was the Princess she claimed to be.

Yet it was true that she had made this garden a kind of kingdom.

Madeleine L'Engle (b. 1918)

Madeleine L'Engle has written novels, plays, poetry, and nonfiction for children and adults. A native of New York City, she is best known for her "time-fantasy" novel *A Wrinkle in Time* (1962), which won the Newbery Medal and was followed by several sequels. L'Engle's father, who had been exposed to mustard gas in World War I, died when she was seventeen, and in *A Wrinkle in Time,* two of the Murry children go on an intergalactic search for their missing father. Basing her depiction of time travel and other wonders on particular scientific theories, L'Engle sends her characters to several distant planets by tessering, employing wrinkles in time and space. The children encounter extremely strange creatures and phenomena on other planets, including human citizens on Camazotz whose minds have been subsumed into an evil superbrain. Like many other highly successful novels, this one is difficult to categorize by genre, blending science fiction with twentieth-century realism and religious themes about cosmic struggles between good and evil. Characters quote the Bible, as well as a variety of other works of world literature. As Lois Lowry does in the second half of *The Giver,* L'Engle ultimately stresses the role of love in overcoming evil.

Both Murry parents are scientists who have worked on the theory of the tesseract, but the three strange characters called Mrs. Whatsit, Mrs. Who, and Mrs. Which are more familiar with tessering and other mysteries of the universe. They are similar to supernatural helpers in fairy tales and myths, appearing as eccentric old women in a haunted house in the woods, using images that are associated with stereotypical witches as jokes, appearing and disappearing unexpectedly in different forms, and providing just enough advice and seemingly magical help for the heroes to fight cosmic forces of evil by exercising their own courage, intelligence, faith, and loyalty. Although the three Mrs. Ws are the title characters of the first three chapters reprinted here, the novel opens with a focus on domestic realism. Like Alcott's *Little Women,* this is first a family romance, with a mother and four children coping with daily problems at home and school in a small American town, worrying about the father who is away on a dangerous mission. They make friends with a teenage boy from a troubled family who appears to the community as a popular success (a smart basketball star, not a rich heir like Laurie in *Little Women*), but he needs nurturing and becomes attracted to the awkward teenage daughter Meg. Unlike Alcott's gently unconventional March family, the extraordinary Murrys are destined to star in mythic adventures like the Pevensie children in C. S. Lewis's Narnia Chronicles. Not only are the parents scientific geniuses, but these early chapters begin to reveal that little Charles Wallace, whose silence and strange ways encourage rumors that he's "a moron," has uncanny intelligence, extrasensory perceptions, and other amazing gifts beyond human understanding.

From *A Wrinkle in Time*

CHAPTER 1. MRS. WHATSIT

It was a dark and stormy night.

In her attic bedroom Margaret Murry, wrapped in an old patchwork quilt, sat on the foot of her bed and watched the trees tossing in the frenzied lashing of the wind. Behind the trees clouds scudded frantically across the sky. Every few moments the moon ripped through them, creating wraithlike shadows that raced along the ground.

The house shook.

Wrapped in her quilt, Meg shook.

She wasn't usually afraid of weather. —It's not just the weather, she thought. —It's the weather on top of everything else. On top of me. On top of Meg Murry doing everything wrong.

School. School was all wrong. She'd been dropped down to the lowest section in her grade. That morning one of her teachers had said crossly, "Really, Meg, I don't understand how a child with parents as brilliant as yours are supposed to be can be such a poor student. If you don't manage to do a little better you'll have to stay back next year."

During lunch she'd rough-housed a little to try to make herself feel better, and one of the girls said scornfully, "After all, Meg, we aren't grammar-school kids any more. Why do you always act like such a baby?"

And on the way home from school, walking up the road with her arms full of books, one of the boys had said something about her "dumb baby brother." At this she'd thrown the books on the side of the road and tackled him with every ounce of strength she had, and arrived home with her blouse torn and a big bruise under one eye.

Sandy and Dennys, her ten-year-old twin brothers, who got home from school an hour earlier than she did, were disgusted. "Let *us* do the fighting when it's necessary," they told her.

—A delinquent, that's what I am, she thought grimly. —That's what they'll be saying next. Not Mother. But Them. Everybody Else. I wish Father—

But it was still not possible to think about her father without the danger of tears. Only her mother could talk about him in a natural way, saying, "When your father gets back—"

Gets back from where? And when? Surely her mother must know what people were saying, must be aware of the smugly vicious gossip. Surely it must hurt her as it did Meg. But if it did she gave no outward sign. Nothing ruffled the serenity of her expression.

—Why can't I hide it, too? Meg thought. Why do I always have to *show* everything?

The window rattled madly in the wind, and she pulled the quilt close about her. Curled up on one of her pillows a gray fluff of kitten yawned, showing its pink tongue, tucked its head under again, and went back to sleep.

Everybody was asleep. Everybody except Meg. Even Charles Wallace, the "dumb baby brother," who had an uncanny way of knowing when she was awake and unhappy, and who would come, so many nights, tiptoeing up the attic stairs to her—even Charles Wallace was asleep.

How could they sleep? All day on the radio there had been hurricane warnings. How could they leave her up in the attic in the rickety brass bed, knowing that the roof might be blown right off the house, and she tossed out into the wild night sky to land who knows where?

Her shivering grew uncontrollable.

—You asked to have the attic bedroom, she told herself savagely. —Mother let you have it because you're the oldest. It's a privilege, not a punishment.

"Not during a hurricane, it isn't a privilege," she said aloud. She tossed the quilt down on the foot of the bed, and stood up. The kitten stretched luxuriously, and looked up at her with huge, innocent eyes.

"Go back to sleep," Meg said. "Just be glad you're a kitten and not a monster like me." She looked at herself in the wardrobe mirror and made a horrible face, baring a mouthful of teeth covered with braces. Automatically she pushed her glasses into position, ran her fingers through her mouse-brown hair, so that it stood wildly on end, and let out a sigh almost as noisy as the wind.

The wide wooden floorboards were cold against her feet. Wind blew in the crevices about the window frame, in spite of the protection the storm sash was supposed to offer. She could hear wind howling in the chimneys. From all the way downstairs she could hear Fortinbras, the big black dog, starting to bark. He must be frightened, too. What was he barking at? Fortinbras never barked without reason.

Suddenly she remembered that when she had gone to the post office to pick up the mail she'd heard about a tramp who was supposed to have stolen twelve sheets from Mrs. Buncombe, the constable's wife. They hadn't caught him, and maybe he was heading for the Murry's house right now, isolated on a back road as it was; and this time maybe he'd be after more than sheets. Meg hadn't paid much attention to the talk about the tramp at the time, because the postmistress, with a sugary smile, had asked if she'd heard from her father lately.

She left her little room and made her way through the shadows of the main attic, bumping against the ping-pong table. —Now I'll have a bruise on my hip on top of everything else, she thought.

Next she walked into her old dolls' house, Charles Wallace's rocking horse, the twins' electric trains. "Why must everything happen to me?" She demanded of a large teddy bear.

At the foot of the attic stairs she stood still and listened. Not a sound from Charles Wallace's room on the right. On the left, in her parents' room, not a rustle from her mother sleeping alone in the great double bed. She tiptoed down the hall and into the twins' room, pushing again at her glasses as though they could help her to see better in the dark. Dennys was snoring. Sandy murmured something about baseball and subsided. The twins didn't have any problems. They weren't great students, but they weren't bad ones, either. They were perfectly content with a succession of B's and an occasional A or C. They were strong and fast runners and good at games, and when cracks were made about anybody in the Murry family, they weren't made about Sandy and Dennys.

She left the twins' room and went on downstairs, avoiding the creaking seventh step. Fortinbras had stopped barking. It wasn't the tramp this time, then. Fort would go on barking if anybody was around.

—But suppose the tramp *does* come? Suppose he has a knife? Nobody lives near enough to hear if we screamed and screamed and screamed. Nobody'd care, anyhow.

—I'll make myself some cocoa, she decided. —That'll cheer me up, and if the roof blows off at least I won't go off with it.

In the kitchen a light was already on, and Charles Wallace was sitting at the table drinking milk and eating bread and jam. He looked very small and vulnerable sitting there alone in the big old-fashioned kitchen, a blond little boy in faded blue Dr. Dentons, his feet swinging a good six inches above the floor.

"Hi," he said cheerfully. "I've been waiting for you."

From under the table where he was lying at Charles Wallace's feet, hoping for a crumb or two, Fortinbras raised his slender dark head in greeting to Meg, and his tail thumped against the floor. Fortinbras had arrived on their doorstep, a half-grown puppy, scrawny and abandoned, one winter night. He was, Meg's father had decided, part Llewellyn setter and part greyhound, and he had a slender, dark beauty that was all his own.

"Why didn't you come up to the attic?" Meg asked her brother, speaking as though he were at least her own age. "I've been scared stiff."

"Too windy up in that attic of yours," the little boy said. "I knew you'd be down. I put some milk on the stove for you. It ought to be hot by now."

How did Charles Wallace always know about her? How could he always tell? He never knew—or seemed to care—what Dennys or Sandy were thinking. It was his mother's mind, and Meg's, that he probed with frightening accuracy.

Was it because people were a little afraid of him that they whispered about the Murry's youngest child, who was rumored to be not quite bright? "I've heard that clever people often have subnormal children," Meg had once overheard. "The two boys seem to be nice, regular children, but that unattractive girl and the baby boy certainly aren't all there."

It was true that Charles Wallace seldom spoke when anybody was around, so that many people thought he'd never learned to talk. And it was true that he hadn't talked at all until he was almost four. Meg would turn white with fury when people looked at him and clucked, shaking their heads sadly.

"Don't worry about Charles Wallace, Meg," her father had once told her. Meg remembered it very clearly because it was shortly before he went away. "There's nothing the matter with his mind. He just does things in his own way and in his own time."

"I don't want him to grow up to be dumb like me," Meg had said.

"Oh, my darling, you're not dumb," her father answered. "You're like Charles Wallace. Your development has to go at its own pace. It just doesn't happen to be the usual pace."

"How do you *know?*" Meg had demanded. "How do you *know* I'm not dumb? Isn't it just because you love me?"

"I love you, but that's not what tells me. Mother and I've given you a number of tests, you know."

Yes, that was true. Meg had realized that some of the "games" her parents played with her were tests of some kind, and that there had been more for her and Charles Wallace than for the twins. "IQ tests, you mean?"

"Yes, some of them."

"Is my IQ okay?"

"More than okay."

"What is it?"

"That I'm not going to tell you. But it assures me that both you and Charles Wallace will be able to do pretty much whatever you like when you grow up to yourselves. You just wait till Charles Wallace starts to talk. You'll see."

How right he had been about that, though he himself had left before Charles Wallace began to speak, suddenly, with none of the usual baby preliminaries, using entire sentences. How proud he would have been!

"You'd better check the milk," Charles Wallace said to Meg now, his diction clearer and cleaner than that of most five-year-olds. "You know you don't like it when it gets a skin on top."

"You put in more than twice enough milk." Meg peered into the saucepan.

Charles Wallace nodded serenely. "I thought Mother might like some."

"I might like what?" a voice said, and there was their mother standing in the doorway.

"Cocoa," Charles Wallace said. "Would you like a liver-wurst-and-cream-cheese sandwich? I'll be happy to make you one."

"That would be lovely," Mrs. Murry said, "but I can make it myself if you're busy."

"No trouble at all." Charles Wallace slid down from his chair and trotted over to the refrigerator, his pajamaed feet padding softly as a kitten's. "How about you, Meg?" he asked. "Sandwich?"

"Yes, please," she said. "But not liverwurst. Do we have any tomatoes?"

Charles Wallace peered into the crisper. "One. All right if I use it on Meg, Mother?"

"To what better use could it be put?" Mrs Murry smiled. "But not so loud, please, Charles. That is, unless you want the twins downstairs, too."

"Let's be exclusive," Charles Wallace said. "That's my new word for the day. Impressive, isn't it?"

"Prodigious," Mrs. Murry said. "Meg, come let me look at that bruise."

Meg knelt at her mother's feet. The warmth and light of the kitchen had relaxed her so that her attic fears were gone. The cocoa steamed fragrantly in the saucepan; geraniums bloomed on the window sills and there was a bouquet of tiny yellow chrysanthemums in the center of the table. The curtains, red, with a blue and green geometrical pattern, were drawn, and seemed to reflect their cheerfulness throughout the room. The furnace purred like a great, sleepy animal; the lights glowed with steady radiance; outside, alone in the dark, the wind still battered against the house, but the angry power that had frightened Meg while she was alone in the attic was subdued by the familiar comfort of the kitchen. Underneath Mrs. Murry's chair Fortinbras let out a contented sigh.

Mrs. Murry gently touched Meg's bruised cheek. Meg looked up at her mother, half in loving admiration, half in sullen resentment. It was not an advantage to have a mother who was a scientist and a beauty as well. Mrs. Murry's flaming red hair, creamy skin, and violet eyes with long dark lashes, seemed even more spectacular in comparison with Meg's outrageous plainness. Meg's hair had been passable as long as she wore it tidily in braids. When she went into high school it was cut, and now she and her mother struggled with putting it up, but one side would come out curly and the other straight, so that she looked even plainer than before.

"You don't know the meaning of moderation, do you, my darling?" Mrs. Murry asked. "A happy medium is something I wonder if you'll ever learn. That's a nasty bruise the Henderson boy gave you. By the way, shortly after you'd gone to bed his mother called up to complain about how badly you'd hurt him. I told her that since he's a year older and at least twenty-five pounds heavier than you are, I thought I was the one who ought to be doing the complaining. But she seemed to think it was all your fault."

"I suppose that depends on how you look at it," Meg said. "Usually no matter what happens people think it's my fault, even if I have nothing to do with it at all. But I'm sorry I tried to fight him. It's just been an awful week. And I'm full of bad feeling."

Mrs. Murry stroked Meg's shaggy head. "Do you know why?"

"I *hate* being an oddball," Meg said. "It's hard on Sandy and Dennys too. I don't know if they're really like everybody else, or if they're just able to pretend they are. I try to pretend, but it isn't any help."

"You're much too straightforward to be able to pretend to be what you aren't," Mrs. Murry said. "I'm sorry, Meglet. Maybe if Father were here he could help you, but I don't think I can do anything till you've managed to plow through some more time. Then things will be easier for you. But that isn't much help right now, is it?"

"Maybe if I weren't so repulsive-looking—maybe if I were pretty like you—"

"Mother's not a bit pretty; she's beautiful," Charles Wallace announced, slicing liverwurst. "Therefore I bet she was awful at your age."

"How right you are," Mrs. Murry said. "Just give yourself time, Meg."

"Lettuce on your sandwich, Mother?" Charles Wallace asked.

"No, thanks."

He cut the sandwich into sections, put it on a plate, and set it in front of his mother. "Yours'll be along in just a minute, Meg. I think I'll talk to Mrs. Whatsit about you."

"Who's Mrs. Whatsit?" Meg asked.

"I think I want to be exclusive about her for a while," Charles Wallace said. "Onion salt?"

"Yes, please."

"What's Mrs. Whatsit stand for?" Mrs. Murry asked.

"That's her name," Charles Wallace answered. "You know the old shingled house back in the woods that the kids won't go near because they say it's haunted? That's where they live."

"They?"

"Mrs. Whatsit and her two friends. I was out with Fortinbras a couple of days ago—you and the twins were at school, Meg. We like to walk in the woods, and suddenly he took off after a squirrel and I took off

after him and we ended up by the haunted house, so I met them by accident, as you might say."

"But nobody lives there," Meg said.

"Mrs. Whatsit and her friends do. They're very enjoyable."

"Why didn't you tell me about it before?" Mrs. Murry asked. "And you know you're not supposed to go off our property without permission, Charles."

"I know," Charles said. "That's one reason I didn't tell you. I just rushed off after Fortinbras without thinking. And then I decided, well, I'd better save them for an emergency, anyhow."

A fresh gust of wind took the house and shook it, and suddenly the rain began to lash against the windows.

"I don't think I like this wind," Meg said nervously.

"We'll lose some shingles off the roof, that's certain," Mrs. Murry said. "But this house has stood for almost two hundred years and I think it will last a little longer, Meg. There's been many a high wind up on this hill."

"But this is a hurricane!" Meg wailed. "The radio kept saying it was a hurricane!"

"It's October," Mrs. Murry told her. "There've been storms in October before."

As Charles Wallace gave Meg her sandwich Fortinbras came out from under the table. He gave a long, low growl, and they could see the dark fur slowly rising on his back. Meg felt her own skin prickle.

"What's wrong?" she asked anxiously.

Fortinbras stared at the door that opened into Mrs. Murry's laboratory which was in the old stone dairy right off the kitchen. Beyond the lab a pantry led outdoors, though Mrs. Murry had done her best to train the family to come into the house through the garage door or the front door and not through her lab. But it was the lab door and not the garage door toward which Fortinbras was growling.

"You didn't leave any nasty-smelling chemicals cooking over a Bunsen burner, did you, Mother?" Charles Wallace asked.

Mrs. Murray stood up. "No. But I think I'd better go see what's upsetting Fort, anyhow."

"It's the tramp, I'm sure it's the tramp," Meg said nervously.

"What tramp?" Charles Wallace asked.

"They were saying at the post office this afternoon that a tramp stole all Mrs. Buncombe's sheets."

"We'd better sit on the pillow cases, then," Mrs. Murry said lightly. "I don't think even a tramp would be out on a night like this, Meg."

"But that's probably why he *is* out," Meg wailed, "trying to find a place *not* to be out."

"In which case I'll offer him the barn till morning." Mrs. Murry went briskly to the door.

"I'll go with you." Meg's voice was shrill.

"No, Meg, you stay with Charles and eat your sandwich."

"Eat!" Meg exclaimed as Mrs. Murry went out through the lab. "How does she expect me to eat?"

"Mother can take care of herself," Charles said. "Physically, that is." But he sat in his father's chair at the table and his legs kicked at the rungs; and Charles Wallace, unlike most small children, had the ability to sit still.

After a few moments that seemed like forever to Meg, Mrs. Murry came back in, holding the door open for—was it the tramp? It seemed small for Meg's idea of a tramp. The age or sex was impossible to tell, for it was completely bundled up in clothes. Several scarves of assorted colors were tied about the head, and a man's felt hat perched atop. A shocking pink stole was knotted about a rough overcoat, and black rubber boots covered the feet.

"Mrs. Whatsit," Charles said suspiciously, "what are you doing here? And at this time of night, too?"

"Now don't you be worried, my honey." A voice emerged from among turned-up coat collar, stole, scarves, and hat, a voice like an unoiled gate, but somehow not unpleasant.

"Mrs.—uh—Whatsit—says she lost her way," Mrs. Murry said. "Would you care for some hot chocolate, Mrs. Whatsit?"

"Charmed, I'm sure," Mrs. Whatsit answered, taking off the hat and the stole. "It isn't so much that I lost my way as that I got blown off course. And when I realized that I was at little Charles Wallace's house I thought I'd just come in and rest a bit before proceeding on my way."

"How did you know this was Charles Wallace's house?" Meg asked.

"By the smell." Mrs. Whatsit untied a blue and green paisley scarf, a red and yellow flowered print, a gold Liberty print, a red and black bandanna. Under all this a sparse quantity of grayish hair was tied in a small but tidy knot on top of her head. Her eyes were bright, her nose a round, soft blob, her mouth puckered like an autumn apple. "My, but it's lovely and warm in here," she said.

"Do sit down." Mrs. Murry indicated a chair. "Would you like a sandwich, Mrs. Whatsit? I've had liverwurst and cream cheese; Charles has had bread and jam; and Meg, lettuce and tomato."

"Now, let me see," Mrs. Whatsit pondered. "I'm passionately fond of Russian caviar."

"You peeked!" Charles cried indignantly. "We're saving that for Mother's birthday and you can't have any!"

Mrs. Whatsit gave a deep and pathetic sigh.

"No," Charles said. "Now, you mustn't give in to her, Mother, or I shall be very angry. How about tuna-fish salad?"

"All right," Mrs. Whatsit said meekly.

"I'll fix it," Meg offered, going to the pantry for a can of tuna fish.

—For crying out loud, she thought, —this old woman comes barging in on us in the middle of the night and Mother takes it as though there weren't anything peculiar about it at all. I'll bet she *is* the tramp. I'll bet she *did* steal those sheets. And she's certainly no one Charles Wallace ought to be friends with, especially when he won't even talk to ordinary people.

"I've only been in the neighborhood a short time," Mrs. Whatsit was saying as Meg switched off the pantry light and came back into the kitchen with the tuna fish, "and I didn't think I was going to like the neighbors at all until dear little Charles came over with his dog."

"Mrs. Whatsit," Charles Wallace demanded severely, "why did you take Mrs. Buncombe's sheets?"

"Well, I *needed* them, Charles dear."

"You must return them at once."

"But Charles, dear, I *can't.* I've *used* them."

"It was very wrong of you," Charles Wallace scolded. "If you needed sheets that badly you should have asked me."

Mrs. Whatsit shook her head and clucked. "You can't spare any sheets. Mrs. Buncombe can."

Meg cut up some celery and mixed it in with the tuna. After a moment's hesitation she opened the refrigerator door and brought out a jar of little sweet pickles.—Though why I'm doing it for her I don't know, she thought, as she cut them up. —I don't trust her one bit.

"Tell your sister I'm all right," Mrs. Whatsit said to Charles. "Tell her my intentions are good."

"The road to hell is paved with good intentions," Charles intoned.

"My, but isn't he cunning." Mrs. Whatsit beamed at him fondly. "It's lucky he has someone to understand him."

"But I'm afraid he doesn't," Mrs. Murry said. "None of us is quite up to Charles."

"But at least you aren't trying to squash him down." Mrs. Whatsit nodded her head vigorously. "You're letting him be himself."

"Here's your sandwich," Meg said, bringing it to Mrs. Whatsit.

"Do you mind if I take off my boots before I eat?" Mrs. Whatsit asked, picking up the sandwich nevertheless. "Listen." She moved her feet up and down in her boots, and they could hear water squelching. "My toes are ever so damp. The trouble is that these boots are a mite too tight for me, and I never can take them off by myself."

"I'll help you," Charles offered.

"Not you. You're not strong enough."

"I'll help." Mrs. Murry squatted at Mrs. Whatsit's feet, yanking on one slick boot. When the boot came off it came suddenly. Mrs. Murry sat down with a thump. Mrs. Whatsit went tumbling backward with the chair onto the floor, sandwich held high in one old claw. Water poured out of the boot and ran over the floor and the big braided rug.

"Oh, dearie me," Mrs. Whatsit said, lying on her back in the overturned chair, her feet in the air, one in a red and white striped sock, the other still booted.

Mrs. Murry got to her feet. "Are you all right, Mrs. Whatsit?"

"If you have some liniment I'll put it on my dignity," Mrs. Whatsit said, still supine. "I think it's sprained. A little oil of cloves mixed well with garlic is rather good." And she took a large bite of sandwich.

"Do please get up," Charles said. "I don't like to see you lying there that way. You're carrying things too far."

"Have you ever tried to get to your feet with a sprained dignity?" But Mrs. Whatsit scrambled up, righted the chair, and then sat back down on the floor,

the booted foot stuck out in front of her, and took another bite. She moved with great agility for such an old woman. At least Meg was reasonably sure that she was an old woman, and a very old woman at that.

Mrs. Whatsit, her mouth full, ordered Mrs. Murry, "Now pull while I'm already down."

Quite calmly, as though this old woman and her boots were nothing out of the ordinary, Mrs. Murry pulled until the second boot relinquished the foot. This foot was covered with a blue and gray Argyle sock, and Mrs. Whatsit sat there, wriggling her toes, contentedly finishing her sandwich before scrambling to her feet. "Ah," she said, "that's ever so much better," and took both boots and shook them out over the sink. "My stomach is full and I'm warm inside and out and it's time I went home."

"Don't you think you'd better stay till morning?" Mrs. Murry asked.

"Oh, thank you, dearie, but there's *so* much to do I just can't waste time sitting around frivoling."

"It's much too wild a night to travel in."

"Wild nights are my glory," Mrs. Whatsit said. "I just got caught in a down draft and blown off course."

"Well, at least till your socks are dry—"

"Wet socks don't bother me. I just didn't like the water squishing around in my boots. Now don't worry about me, lamb." (Lamb was not a word one would ordinarily think of calling Mrs. Murry.) "I shall just sit down for a moment and pop on my boots and then I'll be on my way. Speaking of ways, pet, by the way, there *is* such a thing as a tesseract."

Mrs. Murry went very white and with one hand reached backward and clutched at a chair for support. Her voice trembled. "What did you say?"

Mrs. Whatsit tugged at her second boot. "I said," she grunted, shoving her foot down in, "that there is"—shove—"such a thing"—shove—"as a tesseract." Her foot went down into the boot, and grabbing shawls, scarves, and hat, she hustled out the door. Mrs. Murry stayed very still, making no move to help the old woman. As the door opened, Fortinbras streaked in, panting, wet and shiny as a seal. He looked at Mrs. Murry and whined.

The door slammed.

"Mother, what's the matter!" Meg cried. "What did she say? What is it?"

"The tesseract—" Mrs. Murry whispered. "What did she mean? How could she have known?"

CHAPTER 2. MRS. WHO

When Meg woke to the jangling of her alarm clock the wind was still blowing but the sun was shining; the worst of the storm was over. She sat up in bed, shaking her head to clear it.

It must have been a dream. She'd been frightened by the storm and worried about the tramp so she'd just dreamed about going down to the kitchen and seeing Mrs. Whatsit and having her mother get all frightened and upset by that word—what was it? Tess—tess something.

She dressed hurriedly, picked up the kitten still curled up on the bed, and dumped it unceremoniously on the floor. The kitten yawned, stretched, gave a piteous miaow, trotted out of the attic and down the stairs. Meg made her bed and hurried after it. In the kitchen her mother was making French toast and the twins were already at the table. The kitten was lapping milk out of a saucer.

"Where's Charles?" Meg asked.

"Still asleep. We had rather an interrupted night, if you remember."

"I hoped it was a dream," Meg said.

Her mother carefully turned over four slices of French toast, then said in a steady voice, "No, Meg. Don't hope it was a dream. I don't understand it any more than you do, but one thing I've learned is that you don't have to understand things for them to *be*. I'm sorry I showed you I was upset. Your father and I used to have a joke about tesseract"

"What *is* a tesseract?" Meg asked.

"It's a concept." Mrs. Murry handed the twins the syrup. "I'll try to explain it to you later. There isn't time before school."

"I don't see why you didn't wake us up," Dennys said. "It's a gyp we missed out on all the fun."

"You'll be a lot more awake in school today than I will." Meg took her French toast to the table.

"Who cares," Sandy said. "If you're going to let old tramps come into the house in the middle of the night, Mother, you ought to have Den and me around to protect you."

"After all, Father would expect us to," Dennys added.

"We know you have a great mind and all, Mother," Sandy said, "but you don't have much *sense*. And certainly Meg and Charles don't."

"I know. We're morons." Meg was bitter.

"I wish you wouldn't be such a *dope,* Meg. Syrup, please." Sandy reached across the table. "You don't have to take everything so *personally*. Use a happy *medium,* for heaven's sake. You just goof around in school and look out the window and don't pay any attention."

"You just make things harder for yourself," Dennys said. "And Charles Wallace is going to have an awful time next year when he starts school. *We* know he's bright, but he's so funny when he's around other people, and they're so used to thinking he's dumb, I don't know what's going to happen to him. Sandy and I'll sock anybody who picks on him, but that's about all we can do."

"Let's not worry about next year till we get through this one," Mrs. Murry said. "More French toast, boys?"

At school Meg was tired and her eyelids sagged and her mind wandered. In social studies she was asked to name the principal imports and exports of Nicaragua, and though she had looked them up dutifully the evening before, now she could remember none of them. The teacher was sarcastic, the rest of the class laughed, and she flung herself down in her seat in a fury. "Who *cares* about the imports and exports of Nicaragua, anyhow?" she muttered.

"If you're going to be rude, Margaret, you may leave the room," the teacher said.

"Okay, I will." Meg flounced out.

During study hall the principal sent for her. "What seems to be the problem now, Meg?" he asked, pleasantly enough.

Meg looked sulkily down at the floor. "Nothing, Mr. Jenkins."

"Miss Porter tells me you were inexcusably rude."

Meg shrugged.

"Don't you realize that you just make everything harder for yourself by your attitude?" the principal asked. "Now, Meg, *I'm* convinced that you can do the work and keep up with your grade if you will apply yourself, but some of your teachers are not. You're going to have to do something about yourself. Nobody can do it for you." Meg was silent. "Well? What about it, Meg?"

"I don't know what to do," Meg said.

"You could do your homework, for one thing. Wouldn't your mother help you?"

"If I asked her to."

"Meg, is something troubling you? Are you unhappy at home?" Mr. Jenkins asked.

At last Meg looked at him, pushing at her glasses in a characteristic gesture. "Everything's *fine* at home."

"I'm glad to hear it. But I know it must be hard on you to have your father away."

Meg eyed the principal warily, and ran her tongue over the barbed line of her braces.

"Have you had any news from him lately?"

Meg was sure it was not only imagination that made her feel that behind Mr. Jenkins' surface concern was a gleam of avid curiosity. Wouldn't he like to know! she thought. And if I knew anything he's the last person I'd tell. Well, one of the last.

The postmistress must know that it was almost a year now since the last letter, and heaven knows how many people *she'd* told, or what unkind guesses she'd made about the reason for the long silence.

Mr. Jenkins waited for an answer, but Meg only shrugged.

"Just what was your father's line of business?" Mr. Jenkins asked. "Some kind of scientist, wasn't he?"

"He *is* a physicist." Meg bared her teeth to reveal the two ferocious lines of braces.

"Meg, don't you think you'd make a better adjustment to life if you faced facts?"

"I do face facts," Meg said. "They're lots easier to face than people, I can tell you."

"Then why don't you face facts about your father?"

"You leave my father out of it!" Meg shouted.

"Stop bellowing," Mr. Jenkins said sharply. "Do you want the entire school to hear you?"

"So what?" Meg demanded. "I'm not ashamed of anything I'm saying. Are you?"

Mr. Jenkins sighed. "Do you enjoy being the most belligerent, uncooperative child in school?"

Meg ignored this. She leaned over the desk toward the principal. "Mr. Jenkins, you've met my mother, haven't you? You can't accuse her of not facing facts, can you? She's a scientist. She has doctors' degrees in both biology and bacteriology. Her *business* is facts. When she tells me that my father isn't coming home,

I'll believe it. As long as she says Father *is* coming home, then I'll believe that."

Mr. Jenkins sighed again. "No doubt your mother wants to believe that your father is coming home, Meg. Very well, I can't do anything else with you. Go on back to study hall. Try to be a little less antagonistic. Maybe your work would improve if your general attitude were more tractable."

When Meg got home from school her mother was in the lab, the twins were at Little League, and Charles Wallace, the kitten, and Fortinbras were waiting for her. Fortinbras jumped up, put his front paws on her shoulders, and gave her a kiss, and the kitten rushed to his empty saucer and mewed loudly.

"Come on," Charles Wallace said. "Let's go."

"Where?" Meg asked. "I'm hungry, Charles. I don't want to go anywhere till I've had something to eat." She was still sore from the interview with Mr. Jenkins, and her voice sounded cross. Charles Wallace looked at her thoughtfully as she went to the refrigerator and gave the kitten some milk, then drank a mugful herself.

He handed her a paper bag. "Here's a sandwich and some cookies and an apple. I thought we'd better go see Mrs. Whatsit."

"Oh, golly," Meg said. "*Why,* Charles?"

"You're still uneasy about her, aren't you?" Charles asked.

"Well, yes."

"Don't be. She's all right. I promise you. She's on our side."

"How do you know?"

"*Meg,*" he said impatiently. "I *know.*"

"But why should we go see her now?"

"I want to find out more about that tesseract thing. Didn't you see how it upset Mother? You know when Mother can't control the way she feels, when she lets us see she's upset, then it's something big."

Meg thought for a moment. "Okay, let's go. But let's take Fortinbras with us."

"Well, of course. He needs the exercise."

They set off, Fortinbras rushing ahead, then doubling back to the two children, then leaping off again.

The Murrys lived about four miles out of the village. Behind the house was a pine woods and it was through this that Charles Wallace took Meg.

"Charles, you know she's going to get in awful trouble—Mrs. Whatsit, I mean—if they find out she's broken into the haunted house. And taking Mrs. Buncombe's sheets and everything. They could send her to jail."

"One of the reasons I want to go over this afternoon is to warn them."

"Them?"

"I told you she was there with her two friends. I'm not even sure it was Mrs. Whatsit herself who took the sheets, though I wouldn't put it past her."

"But what would she want all those sheets for?"

"I intend to ask her," Charles Wallace said, "and to tell them they'd better be more careful. I don't really think they'll let anybody find them, but I just thought we ought to mention the possibility. Sometimes during vacations some of the boys go out there looking for thrills, but I don't think anybody's apt to right now, what with basketball and everything."

They walked in silence for a moment through the fragrant woods, the rusty pine needles gentle under their feet. Up above them the wind made music in the branches. Charles Wallace slipped his hand confidingly in Meg's, and the sweet, little-boy gesture warmed her so that she felt the tense knot inside her begin to loosen. *Charles* loves me at any rate, she thought.

"School awful again today?" he asked after a while.

"Yes. I got sent to Mr. Jenkins. He made snide remarks about Father."

Charles Wallace nodded sagely. "I know."

"*How* do you know?"

Charles Wallace shook his head. "I can't quite explain. You tell me, that's all."

"But I never say anything. You just seem to know."

"Everything about you tells me," Charles said.

"How about the twins?" Meg asked. "Do you know about them, too?"

"I suppose I could if I wanted to. If they needed me. But it's sort of tiring, so I just concentrate on you and Mother."

"You mean you read our minds?"

Charles Wallace looked troubled. "I don't think it's that. It's being able to understand a sort of language, like sometimes if I concentrate very hard I can understand the wind talking with the trees. You tell me, you see, sort of inad—inadvertently. That's a good word, isn't it? I got Mother to look it up in the dictionary for me this morning. I really must learn to read, except I'm afraid it will make it awfully hard for me in school next year if I already know things. I think it will be better if people go on thinking I'm not very bright. They won't hate me quite so much."

Ahead of them Fortinbras started barking loudly, the warning bay that usually told them that a car was coming up the road or that someone was at the door.

"Somebody's here," Charles Wallace said sharply. "Somebody's hanging around the house. Come *on*." He started to run, his short legs straining. At the edge of the woods Fortinbras stood in front of a boy, barking furiously.

As they came panting up the boy said, "For crying out loud, call off your dog."

"Who is he?" Charles Wallace asked Meg.

"Calvin O'Keefe. He's in Regional, but he's older than I am. He's a big bug."

"It's all right, fella. I'm not going to hurt you," the boy said to Fortinbras.

"Sit, Fort," Charles Wallace commanded, and Fortinbras dropped to his haunches in front of the boy, a low growl still pulsing in his dark throat.

"Okay." Charles Wallace put his hands on his hips. "Now tell us what you're doing here."

"I might ask the same of you," the boy said with some indignation. "Aren't you two of the Murry kids? This isn't your property, is it?" He started to move, but Fortinbras' growl grew louder and he stopped.

"Tell me about him, Meg," Charles Wallace demanded.

"What would I know about him?" Meg asked. "He's a couple of grades above me, and he's on the basketball team."

"Just because I'm tall." Calvin sounded a little embarrassed. Tall he certainly was, and skinny. His bony wrists stuck out of the sleeves of his blue sweater; his worn corduroy trousers were three inches too short. He had orange hair that needed cutting and the appropriate freckles to go with it. His eyes were an oddly bright blue.

"Tell us what you're doing here," Charles Wallace said.

"What *is* this? The third degree? Aren't you the one who's supposed to be the moron?"

Meg flushed with rage, but Charles Wallace answered placidly, "That's right. If you want me to call my dog off you'd better give."

"Most peculiar moron I've ever met," Calvin said. "I just came to get away from my family."

Charles Wallace nodded. "What kind of family?"

"They all have runny noses. I'm third from the top of eleven kids. I'm a sport"

At that Charles Wallace grinned widely. "So 'm I."

"I don't mean like in baseball," Calvin said.

"Neither do I."

"I mean like in biology," Calvin said suspiciously.

"A change in gene," Charles Wallace quoted, *"resulting in the appearance in the offspring of a character which is not present in the parents but which is potentially transmissible to its offspring."*

"What gives around here?" Calvin asked. "I was told you couldn't talk."

"Thinking I'm a moron gives people something to feel smug about," Charles Wallace said. "Why should I disillusion them? How old are you, Cal?"

"Fourteen."

"What grade?"

"Junior. Eleventh. I'm bright. Listen, did anybody ask you to come here this afternoon?"

Charles Wallace, holding Fort by the collar, looked at Calvin suspiciously. "What do you mean, *asked?*"

Calvin shrugged. "You still don't trust me, do you?"

"I don't *dis*trust you," Charles Wallace said.

"Do you want to tell me why you're here, then?"

"Fort and Meg and I decided to go for a walk. We often do in the afternoon."

Calvin dug his hands down in his pockets. "You're holding out on me."

"So 're you," Charles Wallace said.

"Okay, old sport," Calvin said, "I'll tell you this much. Sometimes I get a feeling about things. You might call it a compulsion. Do you know what compulsion means?"

"Constraint. Obligation. Because one is compelled. Not a very good definition, but it's the Concise Oxford."

"Okay, okay," Calvin sighed. "I must remember I'm preconditioned in my concept of your mentality."

Meg sat down on the coarse grass at the edge of the woods. Fort gently twisted his collar out of Charles Wallace's hands and came over to Meg, lying down beside her and putting his head in her lap.

Calvin tried now politely to direct his words toward Meg as well as Charles Wallace. "When I get this feeling, this compulsion, I always do what it tells me. I can't explain where it comes from or how I get it, and it doesn't happen very often. But I obey it. And this afternoon I had a feeling that I must come over to the haunted house. That's all I know, kid. I'm not holding anything back. Maybe it's because I'm supposed to meet you. You tell *me.*"

Charles Wallace looked at Calvin probingly for a moment; then an almost glazed look came into his eyes, and he seemed to be thinking at him. Calvin stood very still, and waited.

At last Charles Wallace said. "Okay. I believe you. But I can't tell you. I think I'd like to trust you. Maybe you'd better come home with us and have dinner."

"Well, sure, but—what would your mother say to that?" Calvin asked.

"She'd be delighted. Mother's all right. She's not one of us. But she's all right."

"What about Meg?"

"Meg has it tough," Charles Wallace said. "She's not really one thing or the other."

"What do you mean, *one of us?*" Meg demanded. "What do you mean I'm not one thing or the other?"

"Not now, Meg," Charles Wallace said. "Slowly. I'll tell you about it later." He looked at Calvin, then seemed to make a quick decision. "Okay, let's take him to meet Mrs. Whatsit. If he's not okay she'll know." He started off on his short legs toward the dilapidated old house.

The haunted house was half in the shadows of the clump of elms in which it stood. The elms were almost bare, now, and the ground around the house was yellow with damp leaves. The late afternoon light had a greenish cast which the blank windows reflected in a sinister way. An unhinged shutter thumped. Something else creaked. Meg did not wonder that the house had a reputation for being haunted.

A board was nailed across the front door, but Charles Wallace led the way around to the back. The door there appeared to be nailed shut, too, but Charles Wallace knocked, and the door swung slowly outward, creaking on rusty hinges. Up in one of the elms an old black crow gave its raucous cry, and a woodpecker went into a wild ratatat-tat. A large gray rat scuttled around the corner of the house and Meg let out a stifled shriek.

"They get a lot of fun out of using all the typical props," Charles Wallace said in a reassuring voice. "Come on. Follow me."

Calvin put a strong hand to Meg's elbow, and Fort pressed against her leg. Happiness at their concern was so strong in her that her panic fled, and she followed Charles Wallace into the dark recesses of the house without fear.

They entered into a sort of kitchen. There was a huge fireplace with a big black pot hanging over a merry fire. Why had there been no smoke visible from the chimney? Something in the pot was bubbling, and it smelled more like one of Mrs. Murry's chemical messes than something to eat. In a dilapidated Boston rocker sat a plump little woman. She wasn't Mrs. Whatsit, so she must, Meg decided, be one of Mrs. Whatsit's two friends. She wore enormous spectacles, twice as thick and twice as large as Meg's, and she was sewing busily, with rapid jabbing stitches, on a sheet. Several other sheets lay on the dusty floor.

Charles Wallace went up to her. "I really don't think you ought to have taken Mrs. Buncombe's sheets without consulting me," he said, as cross and bossy as only a very small boy can be. "What on earth do you want them for?"

The plump little woman beamed at him. "Why, Charlsie, my pet! *Le coeur a ses raisons que la raison ne connait point.* French. Pascal. *The heart has its reasons, whereof reason knows nothing.*"

"But that's not appropriate at all," Charles said crossly.

"Your mother would find it so." A smile seemed to gleam through the roundness of spectacles.

"I'm not talking about my mother's feelings about my father," Charles Wallace scolded. "I'm talking about Mrs. Buncombe's sheets."

The little woman sighed. The enormous glasses caught the light again and shone like an owl's eyes. "In case we need ghosts, of course," she said. "I should think you'd have guessed. If we have to frighten anybody away Whatsit thought we ought to do it appropriately. That's why it's so much fun to stay in a haunted house. But we really didn't mean you to know about the sheets. *Auf frischer Tat ertappt.* German. *In fla-*

grante delicto. Latin. *Caught in the act.* English. As I was saying—"

But Charles Wallace held up his hand in a peremptory gesture. "Mrs. Who, do you know this boy?"

Calvin bowed. "Good afternoon, Ma'am. I didn't quite catch your name."

"Mrs. Who will do," the woman said. "He wasn't my idea, Charlsie, but I think he's a good one."

"Where's Mrs. Whatsit?" Charles asked.

"She's busy. It's getting near time, Charlsie, getting near time. *Ab honesto virum bonum nihil deterret.* Seneca. *Nothing deters a good man from doing what is honorable.* And he's a very good man, Charlsie, darling, but right now he needs our help."

"Who?" Meg demanded.

"And little Megsie! Lovely to meet you, sweetheart. Your father, of course. Now go home, loves. The time is not yet ripe. Don't worry, we won't go without you. Get plenty of food and rest. Feed Calvin up. Now, off with you! *Justitiae soror fides.* Latin again, of course. *Faith is the sister of justice.* Trust in us! Now, shoo!" And she fluttered up from her chair and pushed them out the door with surprising power.

"Charles," Meg said. "I don't understand."

Charles took her by the hand and dragged her away from the house. Fortinbras ran on ahead, and Calvin was close behind them. "No," he said, "I don't either, yet. Not quite. I'll tell you what I know as soon as I can. But you saw Fort, didn't you? Not a growl. Not a quiver. Just as though there weren't anything strange about it. So you know it's okay. Look, do me a favor, both of you. Let's not talk about it till we've had something to eat. I need fuel so I can sort things out and assimilate them properly."

"Lead on, moron," Calvin cried gaily. "I've never even seen your house, and I have the funniest feeling that for the first time in my life I'm going home!"

CHAPTER 3. MRS. WHICH

In the forest evening was already beginning to fall, and they walked in silence. Charles and Fortinbras gamboled on ahead. Calvin walked with Meg, his fingers barely touching her arm in a protective gesture.

This has been the most impossible, the most confusing afternoon of my life, she thought, yet I don't feel confused or upset anymore; I only feel happy. Why?

"Maybe we weren't meant to meet before this," Calvin said. "I mean, I knew who you were in school and everything, but I didn't know you. But I'm glad we've met now, Meg. We're going to be friends, you know."

"I'm glad, too," Meg whispered, and they were silent again.

When they got back to the house Mrs. Murry was still in the lab. She was watching a pale blue fluid move slowly through a tube from a beaker to a retort. Over a Bunsen burner bubbled a big, earthenware dish of stew. "Don't tell Sandy and Dennys I'm cooking out here," she said. "They're always suspicious that a few chemicals may get in with the meat, but I had an experiment I wanted to stay with."

"This is Calvin O'Keefe, Mother," Meg said. "Is there enough for him, too? It smells super."

"Hello, Calvin." Mrs. Murry shook hands with him. "Nice to meet you. We aren't having anything but stew tonight, but it's a good thick one."

"Sounds wonderful to me," Calvin said. "May I use your phone so my mother'll know where I am?"

"Of course. Show him where it is, will you, please, Meg? I won't ask you to use the one out here, if you don't mind. I'd like to finish up this experiment."

Meg led the way into the house. Charles Wallace and Fortinbras had gone off. Outdoors she could hear Sandy and Dennys hammering at the fort they were building up in one of the maples. "This way." Meg went through the kitchen and into the living room.

"I don't know why I call her when I don't come home," Calvin said, his voice bitter. "She wouldn't notice." He sighed and dialed. "Ma?" he said. "Oh, Hinky. Tell Ma I won't be home till late. Now don't forget. I don't want to be locked out again." He hung up, looked at Meg. "Do you know how lucky you are?"

She smiled rather wryly. "Not most of the time."

"A mother like that! A house like this! Gee, your mother's gorgeous! You should see my mother. She had all her upper teeth out and Pop got her a plate but she won't wear it, and most days she doesn't even comb her hair. Not that it makes much difference when she does." He clenched his fists. "But I love her. That's the funny part of it. I love them all, and they don't give a hoot about me. Maybe that's why I call when I'm not going to be home. Because I care. No-

body else does. You don't know how lucky you are to be loved."

Meg said in a startled way, "I guess I never thought of that. I guess I just took it for granted."

Calvin looked somber; then his enormous smile lit up his face again. "Things are going to happen, Meg! Good things! I feel it!" He began wandering, still slowly, around the pleasant, if shabby, living room. He stopped before a picture on the piano of a small group of men standing together on a beach. "Who's this?"

"Oh, a bunch of scientists."

"Where?"

Meg went over to the picture. "Cape Canaveral. This one's Father."

"Which?"

"Here."

"The one with glasses?"

"Yup. The one who needs a haircut." Meg giggled, forgetting her worries in her pleasure at showing Calvin the picture. "His hair's sort of the same color as mine, and he keeps forgetting to have it cut. Mother usually ends up doing it for him—she bought clippers and stuff—because he won't take the time to go to the barber."

Calvin studied the picture. "I like him," he announced judiciously. "Looks kind of like Charles Wallace, doesn't he?"

Meg laughed again. "When Charles was a baby he looked *exactly* like Father. It was really funny."

Calvin continued to look at the picture. "He's not handsome or anything. But I like him."

Meg was indignant. "He is too handsome."

Calvin shook his head. "Nah. He's tall and skinny like me."

"Well, I think you're handsome," Meg said. "Father's eyes are kind of like yours, too. You know. Really blue. Only you don't notice his as much because of the glasses."

"Where is he now?"

Meg stiffened. But she didn't have to answer because the door from lab to kitchen slammed, and Mrs. Murry came in, carrying a dish of stew. "Now," she called, "I'll finish this up properly on the stove. Have you done your homework, Meg?"

"Not quite," Meg said, going back into the kitchen.

"Then I'm sure Calvin won't mind if you finish before dinner."

"Sure, go ahead." Calvin fished in his pocket and pulled out a wad of folded paper. "As a matter of fact I have some junk of mine to finish up. Math. That's one thing I have a hard time keeping up in. I'm okay on anything to do with words, but I don't do as well with numbers."

Mrs. Murry smiled. "Why don't you get Meg to help you?"

"But, see, I'm several grades above Meg."

"Try asking her to help you with your math, anyhow," Mrs. Murry suggested.

"Well, sure," Calvin said. "Here. But it's pretty complicated."

Meg smoothed out the paper and studied it. "Do they care *how* you do it?" she asked. "I mean, can you work it out your own way?"

"Well, sure, as long as I understand and get the answers right."

"Well, *we* have to do it *their* way. Now look, Calvin, don't you see how much easier it would be if you did it *this* way?" Her pencil flew over the paper.

"Hey!" Calvin said. "Hey! I think I get it. Show me once more on another one."

Again Meg's pencil was busy. "All you have to remember is that every ordinary fraction can be converted into an infinite periodic decimal fraction. See? So 3/7 is 0.428571."

"This is the craziest family." Calvin grinned at her. "I suppose I should stop being surprised by now, but you're supposed to be dumb in school, always being called up on the carpet."

"Oh, I am."

"The trouble with Meg and math," Mrs. Murry said briskly, "is that Meg and her father used to play with numbers and Meg learned far too many short cuts. So when they want her to do problems the long way around at school she gets sullen and stubborn and sets up a fine mental block for herself."

"Are there any more morons like Meg and Charles around?" Calvin asked. "If so, I should meet more of them."

"It might also help if Meg's handwriting were legible," Mrs. Murry said. "With a good deal of difficulty I can usually decipher it, but I doubt very much if her teachers can, or are willing to take the time. I'm planning on giving her a typewriter for Christmas. That may be a help."

"If I get anything right nobody'll believe it's me," Meg said.

"What's a megaparsec?" Calvin asked.

"One of Father's nicknames for me," Meg said. "It's also 3.26 million light years."

"What's $E = mc^2$?"

"Einstein's equation."

"What's E stand for?"

"Energy."

"m?"

"Mass."

"c^2?"

"The square of the velocity of light in centimeters per second."

"By what countries is Peru bounded?"

"I haven't the faintest idea. I think it's in South America somewhere."

"What's the capital of New York?"

"Well, New York City, of course!"

"Who wrote Boswell's *Life of Johnson?*"

"Oh, Calvin, I'm not any good at English."

Calvin groaned and turned to Mrs. Murry. "I see what you mean. Her I wouldn't want to teach."

"She's a little one-sided, I grant you," Mrs. Murry said, "though I blame her father and myself for that. She still enjoys playing with her dolls' house, though."

"*Mother!*" Meg shrieked in agony.

"Oh, darling, I'm sorry," Mrs. Murry said swiftly. "But I'm sure Calvin understands what I mean."

With a sudden enthusiastic gesture Calvin flung his arms out wide, as though he were embracing Meg and her mother, the whole house. "How did all this happen? Isn't it wonderful? I feel as though I were just being born! I'm not alone any more! Do you realize what that means to me?"

"But you're good at basketball and things," Meg protested. "You're good in school. Everybody likes you."

"For all the most unimportant reasons," Calvin said. "There hasn't been anybody, anybody in the world I could talk to. Sure, I can function on the same level as everybody else, I can hold myself down, but it isn't me."

Meg took a batch of forks from the drawer and turned them over and over, looking at them. "I'm all confused again."

"Oh, so'm I," Calvin said gaily. "But now at least I know we're going somewhere."

Meg was pleased and a little surprised when the twins were excited at having Calvin for supper. They knew more about his athletic record and were far more impressed by it than she. Calvin ate five bowls of stew, three saucers of Jello, and a dozen cookies, and then Charles Wallace insisted that Calvin take him up to bed and read to him. The twins, who had finished their homework, were allowed to watch half an hour of TV. Meg helped her mother with the dishes and then sat at the table and struggled with her homework. But she could not concentrate.

"Mother, are you upset?" she asked suddenly.

Mrs. Murry looked up from a copy of an English scientific magazine through which she was leafing. For a moment she did not speak. Then, "Yes."

"Why?"

Again Mrs. Murry paused. She held her hands out and looked at them. They were long and strong and beautiful. She touched with the fingers of her right hand the broad gold band on the third finger of her left hand. "I'm still quite a young woman, you know," she said finally, "though I realize that that's difficult for you children to conceive. And I'm still very much in love with your father. I miss him quite dreadfully."

"And you think all this has something to do with Father?"

"I think it must have."

"But what?"

"That I don't know. But it seems the only explanation."

"Do you think things always have an explanation?"

"Yes. I believe that they do. But I think that with our human limitations we're not always able to understand the explanations. But you see, Meg, just because we don't understand doesn't mean that the explanation doesn't exist."

"I like to understand things," Meg said.

"We all do. But it isn't always possible."

"Charles Wallace understands more than the rest of us, doesn't he?"

"Yes."

"Why?"

"I suppose because he's—well, because he's different, Meg."

"Different how?"

"I'm not quite sure. You know yourself he's not like anybody else."

"No. And I wouldn't want him to be," Meg said defensively.

"Wanting doesn't have anything to do with it. Charles Wallace is what he is. Different. New."

"New?"

"Yes. That's what your father and I feel."

Meg twisted her pencil so hard that it broke. She laughed. "I'm sorry. I'm really not being destructive. I'm just trying to get things straight."

"I know."

"But Charles Wallace doesn't *look* different from anybody else."

"No, Meg, but people are more than just the way they look. Charles Wallace's difference isn't physical. It's in essence."

Meg sighed heavily, took off her glasses and twirled them, put them back on again. "Well, I know Charles Wallace is different, and I know he's something *more*. I guess I'll just have to accept it without understanding it."

Mrs. Murry smiled at her. "Maybe that's really the point I was trying to put across."

"Yah," Meg said dubiously.

Her mother smiled again. "Maybe that's why our visitor last night didn't surprise me. Maybe that's why I'm able to have a—a willing suspension of disbelief. Because of Charles Wallace."

"Are *you* like Charles?" Meg asked.

"I? Heavens no. I'm blessed with more brains and opportunities than many people, but there's nothing about me that breaks out of the ordinary mold."

"Your looks do," Meg said.

Mrs. Murry laughed. "You just haven't had enough basis for comparison, Meg. I'm very ordinary, really."

Calvin O'Keefe, coming in then, said, "Ha ha."

"Charles all settled?" Mrs. Murry asked.

"Yes."

"What did you read to him?"

"Genesis. His choice. By the way, what kind of an experiment were you working on this afternoon, Mrs. Murry?"

"Oh, something my husband and I were cooking up

together. I don't want to be *too* far behind him when he gets back."

"Mother," Meg pursued. "Charles says I'm not one thing or the other, not flesh nor fowl nor good red herring."

"Oh, for crying out loud," Calvin said, "you're *Meg,* aren't you? Come on and let's go for a walk."

But Meg was still not satisfied. "And what do you make of Calvin?" she demanded of her mother.

Mrs. Murry laughed. "I don't want to make anything of Calvin. I like him very much, and I'm delighted he's found his way here."

"Mother, you were going to tell me about a tesseract."

"Yes." A troubled look came into Mrs. Murry's eyes. "But not now, Meg. Not now. Go on out for that walk with Calvin. I'm going up to kiss Charles and then I have to see that the twins get to bed."

Outdoors the grass was wet with dew. The moon was halfway up and dimmed the stars for a great arc. Calvin reached out and took Meg's hand with a gesture as simple and friendly as Charles Wallace's. "Were you upsetting your mother?" he asked gently.

"I don't think *I* was. But she's upset"

"What about?"

"Father."

Calvin led Meg across the lawn. The shadows of the trees were long and twisted and there was a heavy, sweet, autumnal smell to the air. Meg stumbled as the land sloped suddenly downhill, but Calvin's strong hand steadied her. They walked carefully across the twins' vegetable garden, picking their way through rows of cabbages, beets, broccoli, pumpkins. Looming on their left were the tall stalks of corn. Ahead of them was a small apple orchard bounded by a stone wall, and beyond this the woods through which they had walked that afternoon. Calvin led the way to the wall, and then sat there, his red hair shining silver in the moonlight, his body dappled with patterns from the tangle of branches. He reached up, pulled an apple off a gnarled limb, and handed it to Meg, then picked one for himself. "Tell me about your father."

"He's a physicist"

"Sure, we all know that. And he's supposed to have left your mother and gone off with some dame."

Meg jerked up from the stone on which she was perched, but Calvin grabbed her by the wrist and pulled her back down. "Hold it, kid. I didn't say anything you hadn't heard already, did I?"

"No," Meg said, but continued to pull away. "Let me go."

"Come on, calm down. *You* know it isn't true, *I* know it isn't true. And how *any*body after one look at your mother could believe any man would leave her for another woman just shows how far jealousy will make people go. Right?"

"I guess so," Meg said, but her happiness had fled and she was back in a morass of anger and resentment.

"Look, dope." Calvin shook her gently. "I just want to get things straight, sort of sort out the fact from fiction. Your father's a physicist. That's a fact, yes?"

"Yes."

"He's a Ph.D. several times over."

"Yes."

"Most of the time he works alone but some of the time he was at the Institute for Higher Learning in Princeton. Correct?"

"Yes."

"Then he did some work for the government, didn't he?"

"Yes."

"You take it from there. That's all I know."

"That's about all I know, too," Meg said. "Maybe Mother knows more. I don't know. What he did was— well, it was what they call Classified."

"Top Secret, you mean?"

"That's right."

"And you don't even have any idea what it was about?"

Meg shook her head. "No. Not really. Just an idea because of where he was."

"Well, where?"

"Out in New Mexico for a while; we were with him there; and then he was in Florida at Cape Canaveral, and we were with him there, too. And then he was going to be traveling a lot, so we came here."

"You'd always had this house?"

"Yes. But we used to live in it just in the summer."

"And you don't know where your father was sent?"

"No. At first we got lots of letters. Mother and Father always wrote each other every day. I think Mother still writes him every night. Every once in a while the postmistress makes some kind of a crack about all her letters."

"I suppose they think she's pursuing him or something," Calvin said, rather bitterly. "They can't understand plain, ordinary love when they see it. Well, go on. What happened next?"

"Nothing happened," Meg said. "That's the trouble."

"Well, what about your father's letters?"

"They just stopped coming."

"You haven't heard anything at all?"

"No," Meg said. "Nothing." Her voice was heavy with misery.

Silence fell between them, as tangible as the dark tree shadows that fell across their laps and that now seemed to rest upon them as heavily as though they possessed a measurable weight of their own.

At last Calvin spoke in a dry, unemotional voice, not looking at Meg. "Do you think he could be dead?"

Again Meg leaped up, and again Calvin pulled her down. "No! They'd have told us if he were dead! There's always a telegram or something. They always tell you!"

"What *do* they tell you?"

Meg choked down a sob, managed to speak over it. "Oh, Calvin, Mother's tried and tried to find out. She's been down to Washington and everything. And all they'll say is that he's on a secret and dangerous mission, and she can be very proud of him, but he won't be able to—to communicate with us for a while. And they'll give us news as soon as they have it."

"Meg, don't get mad, but do you think maybe *they* don't know?"

A slow tear trickled down Meg's cheek. "That's what I'm afraid of."

"Why don't you cry?" Calvin asked gently. "You're just crazy about your father, aren't you? Go ahead and cry. It'll do you good."

Meg's voice came out trembling over tears. "I cry much too much. I should be like Mother. I should be able to control myself."

"Your mother's a completely different person and she's a lot older than you are."

"I wish I were a different person," Meg said shakily. "I hate myself."

Calvin reached over and took off her glasses. Then he pulled a handkerchief out of his pocket and wiped her tears. This gesture of tenderness undid her com-

pletely, and she put her head down on her knees and sobbed. Calvin sat quietly beside her, every once in a while patting her head. "I'm sorry," she sobbed finally. "I'm terribly sorry. Now you'll hate me."

"Oh, Meg, you *are* a moron," Calvin said. "Don't you know you're the nicest thing that's happened to me in a long time?"

Meg raised her head, and moonlight shone on her tear-stained face; without the glasses her eyes were unexpectedly beautiful. "If Charles Wallace is a sport, I think I'm a biological mistake." Moonlight flashed against her braces as she spoke.

Now she was waiting to be contradicted. But Calvin said, "Do you know that this is the first time I've seen you without your glasses?"

"I'm blind as a bat without them. I'm near-sighted, like Father."

"Well, you know what, you've got dream-boat eyes," Calvin said. "Listen, you go right on wearing your glasses. I don't think I want anybody else to see what gorgeous eyes you have."

Meg smiled with pleasure. She could feel herself blushing and she wondered if the blush would be visible in the moonlight.

"Okay, hold it, you two," came a voice out of the shadows. Charles Wallace stepped into the moonlight. "I wasn't spying on you," he said quickly, "and I hate to break things up, but this is it, kids, this is it!" His voice quivered with excitement.

"This is what?" Calvin asked.

"We're going."

"Going? Where?" Meg reached out and instinctively grabbed for Calvin's hand.

"I don't know exactly," Charles Wallace said. "But I think it's to find Father."

Suddenly two eyes seemed to spring at them out of the darkness; it was the moonlight striking on Mrs. Who's glasses. She was standing next to Charles Wallace, and how she had managed to appear where a moment ago there had been nothing but flickering shadows in the moonlight Meg had no idea. She heard a sound behind her and turned around. There was Mrs. Whatsit scrambling over the wall.

"My, but I wish there were no wind," Mrs. Whatsit said plaintively. "It's so *difficult* with all these clothes." She wore her outfit of the night before, rubber boots and all, with the addition of one of Mrs. Buncombe's sheets which she had draped over her. As she slid off the wall the sheet caught in a low branch and came off. The felt hat slipped over both eyes, and another branch plucked at the pink stole. "Oh, *dear,*" she sighed. "I shall *never* learn to manage."

Mrs. Who wafted over to her, tiny feet scarcely seeming to touch the ground, the lenses of her glasses glittering. "*Come t'è picciol fallo amaro morso!* Dante. *What grievous pain a little fault doth give thee!*" With a clawlike hand she pushed the hat up on Mrs. Whatsit's forehead, untangled the stole from the tree, and with a deft gesture took the sheet and folded it.

"Oh, *thank* you," Mrs. Whatsit said. "You're *so* clever!"

"*Un asno viejo sabe más que un potro. A. Perez. An old ass knows more than a young colt.*"

"Just because you're a paltry few billion years—" Mrs. Whatsit was starting indignantly, when a sharp, strange voice cut in.

"Alll rrightt, girrllss. Thiss iss nno ttime forr bbickkerring."

"It's Mrs. Which," Charles Wallace said.

There was a faint gust of wind, the leaves shivered in it, the patterns of moonlight shifted, and in a circle of silver something shimmered, quivered, and the voice said, "I ddo nott thinkk I willl matterrialize commpletely. I ffindd itt verry ttirinngg, andd wee hhave mmuch ttoo ddoo."

Nikki Giovanni (b. 1943)

Nikki Giovanni was born in Knoxville, and although her family moved to Cincinnati, Ohio, for most of her childhood, this 1968 poem celebrates her enjoyment of summers in Knoxville. A poet, essayist, editor, and lecturer, Giovanni also teaches English at Virginia Tech. Many of her early poems deal with civil rights and social revolution, but much of her work is more personal, dealing with childhood, family experiences, and love relationships, often with humor. Her volumes of poetry for children and young adults include *Spin a Soft Black Song* (1971), *ego tripping and other poems for young people* (1973), *Vacation Time* (1980), and *The Sun Is So Quiet* (1996). In 1994 "knoxville, tennessee" was published as a picture book with paintings by Larry Johnson. Since then, Giovanni has edited collections for young readers, and her writing has appeared in other picture books, including *Rosa* (2005), about the civil rights heroine Rosa Parks. In "knoxville, tennessee," the exuberant listing of realistic images contains a few culturally specific details from African American family life in the southern Appalachian region, but most of the images of the joys of summer in childhood have universal appeal.

knoxville, tennessee

I always like summer
best
you can eat fresh corn
from daddy's garden
and okra
and greens
and cabbage
and lots of

barbecue
and buttermilk
and homemade ice-cream
at the church picnic
and listen to
gospel music
outside
at the church

homecoming
and go to the mountains with
your grandmother
and go barefooted
and be warm
all the time
not only when you go to bed
and sleep

Gillian Rubinstein (b. 1942)

Born in England, Gillian Rubinstein moved to West Africa when she was fourteen. After working as an editor, journalist, and film critic, she moved to Australia in 1973, where she has become a prolific and recognized author, publishing over three dozen picture books and novels for children and young adults. In her science fiction and fantasy novels, such as *Space Demons* (1986) and *Beyond the Labyrinth* (1988), she experiments with language and genre, depicting children who face dangerous situations and adults who are unwilling or unable to help. She stresses that contemporary children want and need to face difficult truths to make them strong. In "Dolphin Dreaming," she writes about two girls and their mother who are grieving, in different ways, for their father and husband who was killed in a car crash. They go to the beach where they used to vacation with their father, but grief seems to be driving them apart from each other until they have a shared, mysterious experience that brings them back together and enables them to see beyond their grief. This story and others in *Dream Time,* a 1989 collection of Australian stories, show how contemporary authors often weave fantastic or supernatural themes into realistic stories about intense psychological experiences. (See also the stories by Libby Hathorn in Part 2 and Lee Harding in Part 8.)

Dolphin Dreaming

Lizzie hardly cried at all when her father died. Everyone said it would have been much better if she had. But she was only eight, and it was as though she couldn't grasp what had happened. She seemed to be more puzzled than anything, puzzled and rather angry, as though he had let her down by dying. She started waking at night and wandering into her mother's room and saying in a sharp questioning voice, "Daddy? Daddy?"

Her mother found this much more unnerving than tears. Lara, who was three years older, cried extravagantly, as she always did everything, and the weeping helped to lessen the dreadful pain of loss. But Lizzie did not cry; instead she became angry and fearful as well as pale and thin.

Once school ended for the summer, none of them could bear the thought of Christmas without Dad.

"I wish we could go to the Peninsula," Lara said one morning, looking wearily at her cereal. Lizzie was still sleeping, having woken them up several times in the night.

Mum was about to drink a mouthful of tea. Instead she stopped with the cup half-way to her lips, and gazed thoughtfully at Lara. "That's just what I was thinking last night! Would you really like to? I think it would be so good for us all to get away, but you know how much Dad loved it over there. I'm afraid it will bring back too many memories."

"Everything here brings back too many memories anyway," Lara pointed out, blinking hard. "At least there there'll be a bit more space around them."

Now she had started thinking about it she was filled with longing, as though the wide sweep of the bay, the white, empty dunes and the turquoise water held some power that would heal her. Perhaps Mum felt the same thing. She put down her tea, gave Lara a grin that was nearly as good as her old ones, and jumped up from the table.

"Come on, Lara. Let's get going. You get the camping list, and get the gear together. I'll organise the food."

Getting on the road was as exciting as ever, and Lara found that she could almost forget about her father for a little while. When they were away from home his death did not seem so final, more like he had gone on a trip, and would be back in a few days. Her grief lifted, and when they came to the end of the four-hour journey, and the Subaru nosed carefully but firmly onto the white sands of the bay, she gave a hoot of excitement.

They set up camp in the dunes, putting up the tent and the cooking annex, organising the Eskies, the stove and the water bottles. Lara had never realised how much work there was to do, and Mum was looking exhausted by the time it was all finished, especially since Lizzie was being no help at all. She seemed to be getting angrier and angrier, and she shouted at her sister when Lara asked her to hold a rope.

"What's the matter with you?" Lara said. "You've got to help a little bit, since Dad's not here."

"Where is he?" Lizzie shouted even louder. "I thought he was going to be here! I thought that was why we came!" Her face was red and angry, and her eyes were bright, but the tears were tears of rage, and anyway they remained unshed.

"Oh darling," Mum said. "Daddy's not here. He's dead. He died in the car accident."

When they unpacked the swimming gear something caught Lara's eye at the bottom of the bag.

"Look, Mum," she exclaimed, pulling it out. "It's Dad's shell necklace!"

It was a short string of white shells that her father had worn on the beach, telling the children it was his last souvenir of the days when he was a surfie. Lara gazed at it sadly. It brought back such strong memories of him, she could almost feel him next to her. It seemed so strange that the necklace should still be there while he was not. It was too precious a thing to put back in the bag, so she put it round her own neck, where it lay cool against the brown skin, just above her collar bones. Then she cried again, and so did Mum, and the unpacking had to be interrupted while they held each other. But Lizzie ran away up the beach and threw stones at rocks.

Finally everything was done. Mum boiled up a kettle of water on the gas stove and made a cup of tea. She and Lara looked proudly at the little camp. They both felt a strong satisfaction, and relief that they had done it on their own. They had taken another step without him. They were sad, but they were going to survive.

"We'll make a fire on the beach later," Mum said, "and cook sausages and beans on it. But why don't we have a swim now, while it's still warm?"

Lara and Lizzie ran down to the water with their face masks and snorkels. Lara dived straight in, but when she surfaced through the clear, sparkling water, Lizzie was still standing on the edge.

Mum came up to her and took her hand gently. "Come on, darling, we'll go in together." But Lizzie twisted away.

"I don't want to go in! There are too many crabs!"

When she was little she had been terrified of crabs. Dad used to carry her into the sea so she did not have to put her feet on the sand. Last summer she had walked in through the wavelets fearlessly. Now, however, the crabs seemed to have returned.

"Don't be such a sook, Lizzie," Lara called meanly. She was afraid Lizzie was going to spoil the holiday, and she hated seeing the sad, worried look that came into Mum's eyes every time Lizzie got difficult.

"Just stay on the edge, then," Mum said. "I must get in the water or I'll die!"

She and Lara swam together, following shoals of fish, across the clean, smooth sand into enchanted worlds of rocks and seaweed. When they looked up to check on Lizzie she was by the high water mark, strolling along, head down, eyes on the ground, stopping every few steps to crouch down and examine something on the beach.

"She's a strandlooper," Lara said, hoping to see Mum smile. It was their father's word, one that he had gleaned from some book or other and handed on to them: *strandlooper*, the strange ancient race that once lived on the South African coast and loved beautiful shells.

Mum did smile. "I hope she's finding some treasures to cheer her up."

When they came out of the water and ran back to the camp to wrap themselves in their towels, Lizzie had arranged her treasures in a little hollow in the dunes. Around the edge was a circle of pipi shells, bleached white and mauve streaked, broken up every now and then by a shiny grey oyster with craggy white edges. In the middle was a most unusual bone, like a cross or a four-pointed star. There were lines radiating out from the centre almost as though it had been carved, and when Lara picked it up to look at it more closely she could see that there were holes in it, as though it had once hung on a string around someone's neck.

"What is it, Mum?"

Mum took it from her. "I think it's some sort of vertebra—part of the backbone." She ran her hand down the knobbles on Lara's spine. "But I don't know what sort of animal it's from." She put it back carefully in the centre of the circle. "It's lovely, Lizzie. You were clever to find such a treasure!"

Lizzie smiled a little then. "It's mine," she said proudly. "I found it!"

"You are a clever little strandlooper," Lara told her. "Let's all go strandlooping after dinner, Mum. I bet I can find some treasures too!"

Mum found an old green bottle, and Lara found a little brown glass jar which they were thrilled with, and Lizzie found some more treasures to add to her collection: a seaurchin shell, unhusked by the sea, and a piece of driftwood that looked like a goanna. By the time they got back to the tent it was nearly dark. Mum lit the gas lamps and built up the fire. Lara made hot chocolate with marshmallows, and she and Mum sang "Botany Bay" and "The Lime Juice Tub," "The North Wind" and "The Colours of Christmas," but their voices sounded thin and high without Dad's deeper voice beneath them, and after a few songs everyone decided to go to sleep, rather than sit up with their memories under the stars.

All the same, Lara did not feel unhappy as she snuggled down inside her sleeping bag and in the night Lizzie only woke once to say "Daddy!"

Magpies woke Lara next morning, long before the sun was up over the land. She crawled out of the tent and went to look for her mother whom she found a little way inland, among the dunes, under a small tree. Two magpies were sitting above her, and from where Lara stood they looked as if they were talking to each other.

"What did the magpies say to you?" she asked curiously as the two of them walked back to the tent together.

Mum laughed. She had her country face on, quite different from her city one, and she looked as though someone had been sweeping out her spirit overnight. "It's funny," she said, "but I just love magpies. I feel as though they are my sisters. And, do you know, I have never, ever been attacked by one."

"If you were a Nungga they would be your totem," Lara said. She had learned about this at school.

"That's exactly what I think," Mum replied. "And when we are out here the land speaks to me so clearly, I could sit and listen to it forever."

Lara stopped and listened to the land. She could feel it stretching and changing as the sun warmed it. She could hear its myriad animal and plant voices, underpinned by the constant murmur of the sea, and by something else that spoke directly to her own spirit, that told her she was its child.

"Oh, I can hear it too," she cried, and she and Mum hugged each other.

Lizzie had come out to see where they were, and was staring at them almost jealously.

"Someone else is here!" she announced.

"Here?" Mum repeated in surprise, but what Lizzie meant was another family had set up camp in the night about 500 metres along the beach. A four-wheel drive vehicle was parked on the sand, with two bright coloured tents already erected behind it, and a trailer with a boat and outboard engine alongside it.

"I don't like them," Lizzie said crossly. "This is our own private place."

Lara felt the same, but Mum sighed and said, "They've got as much right to be here as we have."

Later they were glad the other camp was there, for none of them was able to open the bottle of gherkins to have with lunch. Lara and Lizzie walked along the beach with the bottle, and the father of the family took it in his brown, strong hands and turned the lid as easily as turning on a tap.

"There you go, love," he said to Lara, handing the bottle back to her. "No worries. You like fish? You come up in the morning, I'll have some fresh snapper or whiting, with luck."

There were two boys, Chris, who looked about the same age as Lara, and Alex who was a little bit younger than Lizzie. They both had black hair and golden brown skin and they wore brightly coloured board shorts. Chris was so thin his board shorts were in danger of falling down altogether, but Alex had a little roll of puppy fat above his, and his legs were chubby. They were very friendly and after giving the girls a can of coke and showing them their camp and their boat, they walked back with them to say hello to Mum.

Later the children swam together; at least, Chris and Lara swam while Alex jumped up and down on the edge, and Lizzie stayed far up by the high water mark.

"Come in, Alex!" his brother called to him, but the little boy shook his head, and when Chris went back to lead him in, Alex cried and struggled.

"He's frightened of the sea," Chris explained to Lara. "He thinks there are sharks."

"My sister thinks there are crabs!" Lara said, and then she wanted to stand up for Lizzie, so she added, "But it's only because she's little."

"I was never frightened of sharks or crabs even when I was little," Chris said rather disgustedly. "Alex is a sook about everything! He's a dead loss!"

By the end of the day Lara agreed thoroughly with this remark and she had almost decided Lizzie was a dead loss too. Alex cried about everything, and Lizzie got in rages. Finally Lara and Chris left them to it, and ran down to have an evening swim when the tide was at its fullest.

After the blazing day the sun was setting into a purple sea and turning the sky the colour of rock-melon. The water where they swam was dark, almost purple too, paling to green above the reef.

"Look!" Chris exclaimed, seizing Lara's arm. "Dolphins!"

She gazed entranced as the sleek black bodies surfaced through the water. They were close enough for the children to see their clever, merry eyes and their hard grey beaks.

The magic of the moment was broken by screams from the shore. Lara and Chris stared in astonishment as Alex came running through the dunes, pursued by a furious Lizzie. Mum appeared from behind the tent, and captured Lizzie as she dashed by. Alex went on running doggedly towards his own tent, and as he ran he scattered something behind him.

"Oh no!" Lara said. "I think he's got her treasures!" Taking a last reluctant look at the dolphins she galloped out of the water, and Chris followed her.

Lizzie was shrieking hysterically in Mum's arms. "He stole my things!" she yelled. "I showed him my treasures and he ran away with them."

"I'll get them back," Chris promised. "Don't cry, I'll make him give them back."

But Alex had scattered the treasures all over the sand, and though they found the driftwood goanna and the sea-urchin shell, and a lot of shells that might have been Lizzie's, search as they might they could not find the strange bone.

"It was my favourite," Lizzie said forlornly. "It was the best treasure I ever found."

Chris made Alex come back and say he was sorry, and Mum got out lemonade and chips for everyone while she boiled up the water for spaghetti. The dolphins came back and swam up and down through the darkening sea, but even they did not cheer Lizzie up.

Lara went to see if she could help Mum, and found her staring at the sea while the water bubbled and boiled onto the gas stove.

"I was looking at the dolphins," Mum said, rescuing the spaghetti. "And remembering how much Dad loved them. Sometimes I feel as if he's just gone for a walk down the beach, and when he comes back I can tell him about them."

In the middle of the night Lara woke up. The moon was bright on her face through the tent door, and the sleeping bag next to her was empty. She struggled out of her own bag, hot and thirsty, and went to get a drink of water from the icebox. As she was drinking, she saw a shadowy shape on the beach, half-way between the dunes and the sea.

"Lizzie?" she whispered, going towards it. It was Lizzie. She was walking to and fro, her eyes fixed on the sand.

"What are you doing out of bed?" Lara said gently, taking hold of her arm carefully, in case she was sleep-walking. But Lizzie was wide awake. "I'm looking for my bone," she said in a normal voice, making Lara jump. "I woke up and I couldn't get back to sleep and I thought I'd be able to find it 'cause the moon's so bright."

"I'll look too," Lara said. The beach at night was beautifully mysterious, with black shadows on the white sand, and the brilliant moon above. The waves hissed gently on the shore, and the endless sea stretched away into the night. Out towards the horizon little lights showed where people were fishing from boats. Chris and his dad were probably out there somewhere, Lara thought, and she wondered if the dolphins were there, too.

They searched the sand for a long time but they could not find the bone. Lara wanted to give up, but Lizzie grew more stubborn. Finally Lara suggested, more in desperation than anything else, "Let's sit down for a bit and listen to the spirit of the land. Perhaps it'll tell us where the bone went to."

Perhaps Lizzie was tired too; anyway, to Lara's relief she sat down rather grumpily on the dry sand above the high water mark. Lara sat down next to her. "Put your head on my shoulder and close your eyes," she said.

After a few moments Lizzie said sleepily, "I can't hear anything," and yawned.

"Listen a bit harder," Lara said, her eyes closed too, and then they suddenly both heard something at the same time, and they opened their eyes with a start.

Out in the sea, something was splashing. They could see the white spray against the black water.

"It must be the dolphins," Lara said softly. "Look, Lizzie, aren't they magic!"

The dark shapes glistened as they caught the moonlight. They were coming closer and closer to the shore.

Lizzie said incredulously, "They're carrying something!"

Between them the dolphins were shouldering a fragile, helpless burden, a figure that floated in the water, limbs trailing. The dolphins held up its head with their strong beaks and nudged it through the shallows until it lay on the sand, nose and mouth free of water, able to breathe air again.

"It's a man!" Lara exclaimed, and made to get up, but at that moment the scene faded, and they could see nothing. At first Lara thought the moon had gone behind a cloud but then she remembered that the night was cloudless and she realised that they were seeing something that happened a long, long time ago.

When the darkness cleared and they could see again the man was standing upright on the beach, facing out to sea. He was a wonderful looking man, like a god or a hero, Lara said later to her mother, with rippling, shining black skin, and thick, black hair that curled around his head and glistened under the moon like the dolphins. When he turned to face the land, the children could see his broad noble nose and his huge, dark, deepset eyes. His body was painted with glowing white marks and he wore decorations of shells around his neck and limbs.

As they watched he began to dance. He danced swimming far out at sea, and then he danced himself drowning and the dolphins rescuing him. He danced the dolphins bringing him into land, so accurately that the girls had to blink their eyes once or twice to check they were not seeing a dolphin dancing a man. Then the man raced towards the water and dived into the sea and the dolphins came and danced with him in the shallows until darkness fell again.

Lizzie shivered and Lara sighed deeply, but neither girl could move away. They peered expectantly through the dark, waiting to see what happened next.

When they could see again they both cried out. A dolphin lay stranded on the beach, and the man sat on his heels next to it, wailing with grief.

"Oh, the poor dolphin!" Lara wailed, and Lizzie said urgently, "What's happened to it? What's happened to it?"

"The dolphin is dead!" Lara said, and next to her Lizzie sobbed quietly, "The dolphin is dead!"

Then they both hid their faces and cried fresh tears like springwater, and when they looked again the man was sitting a few metres away from them, singing a low chant and holding something in his hand, something that hung around his neck on a string.

"Don't be afraid," Lara whispered to Lizzie. "I don't think he can see us."

"I'm not afraid of him," Lizzie replied simply. "He's a dolphin man, and look, he's wearing my bone!"

Still chanting the dolphin man rose and, stooping low, drew in the clean, sea-washed sand. He drew the shape of a dolphin, and then he took the bone from his neck and placed it at a certain point in its tail. Then he sang a high-pitched, clicking song, and danced his dolphin dance around the bone.

A splash in the shallows told the children the dolphins were there, watching.

Everything faded, and when the moon returned Lizzie's bone lay a few metres away from them in the sand.

"There it is!" Lara said in surprise. "However did we miss it before?"

"The dolphin man brought it back," Lizzie said sleepily. She picked it up, and as they staggered off to the tent and their sleeping bags she was clutching it firmly in her hand.

"Do you think it was a dream?" Lara asked Mum the next morning.

Mum smiled at her. There were tears in her eyes, but they were not really sad ones.

"You can cry, Mum!" Lizzie said generously, giving her a tissue. "But don't worry about Dad. He's like the dolphin man. He's dead, but he's still somewhere. Here, or somewhere else. Let's go swimming now."

"Here come Alex and Chris," Lara said. "I expect they've brought us some fish."

"You can come swimming with me, Alex," Lizzie announced. "I won't let anything get you. The dolphins look after me, 'cause I'm a dolphin girl!"

"What about the crabs?" Chris asked, teasingly.

"The crabs are just getting on with living, just like us," Lizzie said.

For the rest of the holiday they swam and explored the dunes with Chris and Alex, went out in their boat and went strandlooping along the shore. Every day the dolphins in the bay watched them. When it was time to go home, Lizzie grew quieter and quieter as they packed up the camp.

"Are you all right, darling?" Mum asked anxiously. "I suppose you don't want to leave."

Lizzie nodded and smiled, but she said nothing until they were in the car, and half-way down the dirt track leading away from the beach. Then she said in a sudden, small voice, "Mum, do you mind going back?"

"Whatever for?" Mum said in surprise.

"Well, I've got a horrible feeling about taking my bone away. I think it wants to stay here."

Mum stopped the car, very patiently turned it round, and drove slowly back to their camp site.

"Why does it want to stay here?" Lara questioned.

"This is where it belongs. This is where its dreams happen," Lizzie replied slowly.

"Where its dreams happen," Lara repeated to herself. As she followed Lizzie across the sand that was still wet from last night's tide, she undid the clasp of her father's necklace.

They stopped at a point half-way between the dunes and the sea, and Lizzie dug a hole and buried the bone. Then Lara dug a hole a little way from it and buried the necklace.

When they got to their feet, they saw the dolphins leap and dive through the turquoise water.

"Both home now," Lara said to herself. "Both dolphin men have come home."

Maya Angelou (b. 1928)

Maya Angelou, who teaches at Wake Forest University in North Carolina, was born Marguerite Johnson in St. Louis and grew up in Arkansas. She has been active in a variety of roles in the performing arts, literature, education and in civic life (especially the civil rights movement). The first volume in her series of autobiographies, *I Know Why the Caged Bird Sings* (1970), was a best-seller that deeply moved a wide variety of readers with its piercing and eloquent examination of an African American girl's troubled childhood and adolescence. Her youthful experiences involved struggles against racism; a period of five years in which she did not speak because her relatives killed her mother's boyfriend, who had raped her when she was less than eight years old; and later becoming a young single mother. An educated African American woman, Mrs. Flowers, encouraged her to speak again and develop her love of language and reading.

Angelou, who has traveled widely and lived abroad, has published several volumes of poetry for adults and a number of picture book texts about African communities, life experiences, and children in different nations. In *Now Sheba Sings the Song* (1987), a poem by Angelou accompanies eighty-four drawings of black women by Tom Feelings. "I Love the Look of Words" appeared in *Soul Looks Back in Wonder,* a 1993 book of African American poetry written to accompany artworks by Feelings, who wrote, "My soul looks back in wonder, at how African creativity has sustained us and how it still flows. . . . Our creativity, moving, circling, improvising within the restricted form of oppression, reminds us that we must remain responsible to each other." Angelou's poem uses a familiar image from everyday life, popcorn, to create an imaginative celebration of devouring a book. (See also the poem by Lucille Clifton in Part 1 and an illustration by Tom Feelings in Part 6.)

I Love the Look of Words

Popcorn leaps, popping from the floor
of a hot black skillet
and into my mouth.
Black words leap,
snapping from the white
page. Rushing into my eyes. Sliding
into my brain which gobbles them
the way my tongue and teeth
chomp the buttered popcorn.

When I have stopped reading,
ideas from the words stay stuck
in my mind, like the sweet
smell of butter perfuming my
fingers long after the popcorn
is finished.

I love the book and the look of words
the weight of ideas that popped into my mind
I love the tracks
of new thinking in my mind.

Further Recommended Reading

TED HUGHES (1930–98)

The Iron Giant

Ted Hughes, named Poet Laureate in 1984, was one of many British writers who have devoted their careers to writing for both children and adults. He is best known for nature poems that are unconventional, challenging, and unsentimental in their penetration of different realities about the animal world and its relations with humanity. His powerful story, first published in 1968 as *The Iron Man,* became a classic of twentieth-century English children's literature. The name of the creature called space-bat-angel-dragon sums up the way Hughes combined science fiction, horror story, fantasy, and hero myth to create a story that he considered a fable of healing. It begins in a familiar rural English setting, where the first attempt to destroy the Iron Giant made of mechanical parts shows that hiding a problem will not eliminate it, and landfills will not solve environmental troubles that are caused by modern farming's dependence on manufacturing. The Iron Giant represents modern problems of humanity and society more explicitly than the Tin Woodman in Baum's *Wonderful Wizard of Oz.* He is a descendent of Frankenstein, King Kong, and other monsters that symbolize humanity's flaws and vulnerabilities, civilization's dangers and potential.

As in many children's stories, from Hans Christian Andersen's "The Emperor's New Clothes" (see Part 2) to Dr. Seuss's environmental fantasy *The Lorax,* Hughes emphasizes the child's role in solving problems that are created by adults. The boy Hogarth is a more fully developed character than the child listener in Dr. Seuss's cautionary tale. Hogarth not only provides hope for the future, but proof that he can help save the world by learning from mistakes and developing new responses to growing problems. In the middle episode of the book, Hogarth realizes that recycling, not military action, will solve the difficulty of the Iron Giant. The third episode expands the fable on a global scale, when the invasion of a much more monstrous creature becomes an apocalyptic warning of the dangers of earthly warfare. At the boy's urging, the Iron Giant becomes the trickster hero, "the champion of the earth," rather than a threat himself. The story's fantastical ending dramatizes an optimistic belief that humans could use their ingenuity and faith to turn today's technological problems into tomorrow's hope for world peace. In 1993, Hughes published *The Iron Woman,* a longer story in which the same characters help a young girl and giant woman struggle with the horrors of pollution.

VIRGINIA HAMILTON (1936–2002)

Zeely

Virginia Hamilton was named Virginia because her great-grandmother fled from slavery in Virginia, crossed the Ohio River on the Underground Railroad in the 1850s, and then disappeared. Her son often retold this story to his descendants on the family farmland in central Ohio. His granddaughter Virginia, who spent most of her life there, inherited his gift of storytelling, becoming one of the most influential writers for children in the second half of the twentieth century. The first African American writer to win the American Newbery medal and the international Hans Christian Andersen award, Hamilton wrote nearly forty books for children and young adults, using innovative combinations of realism, biography, history, science fiction, magic realism, and fantasy. She spoke eloquently about the need to create a "hopescape" for children coping with troubled histories and to celebrate parallel cultures (not minority and majority cultures) in our society.[1]

Hamilton has said, "I write from the black experience for an audience as free and as large as I can find."[2] Her novels frequently explore the themes of coming of age and coming to understand oneself. In her early novel *Zeely* (1969), Elizabeth Perry is living on her uncle's farm for the summer with her brother John. She calls herself "Geeder" (the first part is pronounced like the command to a horse), and she has dubbed her brother "Toeboy" just for the summer. When Elizabeth/Geeder sees the tall, dignified Zeely Tayber, she begins to spin a fantasy identity about the young woman, whom she imagines to be an African queen. Although Zeely does not entirely fit Geeder's fantasy image of her, they do have a meaningful encounter that transforms Geeder's sense of herself. The novel illustrates both an African American girl's quest for an ennobling ancestry and her eager imagination. (See also the folktales by Hamilton recommended in Part 3.)

KATHERINE PATERSON (b. 1932)

Bridge to Terabithia

Katherine Paterson was born in Qing Jiang, Jiangsu, the daughter of American Christian missionaries. Since her family moved frequently in several southern states when they returned to America from China and Paterson often felt like an outsider during her childhood, many of her fictional characters struggle with the need for friendship and acceptance. She taught for a year in rural Virginia, where, she says, many of her sixth-grade students were like Jesse Aarons in *Bridge to Terabithia,* her first novel with a modern American setting. She has also written historical novels, set in Asia and America, as well as retold and original fairy tales. She has twice won the Newbery Award, for *Jacob Have I Loved* (1980) and for *Bridge to Terabithia* (1977). Paterson combines a vivid, at times painful, honesty about children's feelings and experiences with spiritual vision and a sense of hard-won hope. She has written that in *Bridge to Terabithia,* she came to terms, through fiction, with the sudden death of her son's best friend, Lisa Hill, and with her own mortality. Although "problem novels" of the late twentieth century have been criticized by Paterson and others for sometimes sacrificing literary quality and depth in order to provide moral messages or solutions to social problems, and Paterson has expressed reservations about being placed on "issues" lists (such as books to help children cope with death), she lives up to her own high standards by writing compelling stories that "don't give children ready-made answers, but invite them "to go within themselves to listen to the sounds of their own hearts."[3]

Like *The Secret Garden* by Frances Hodgson Burnett and *Tom's Midnight Garden* by Philippa Pearce, *Bridge to Terabithia* focuses on a girl and boy who help each other cope with problems in daily life by sharing imaginative play in a natural setting and forming strong bonds of friendship that most people around them cannot understand. Leslie struggles to fit in after moving to Jess's rural Virginia community from more affluent suburbs, while Jess feels overwhelmed and neglected in a house full of annoying sisters and overworked parents. Gender bias and cultural differences make life difficult for Leslie and Jess at school and in Jess's home.

Miss Edmunds, the unconventional music teacher, believes she is helping Jess by taking him to his first art gallery because she was the only one to take an interest in his artistic talent before he met Leslie and her parents. After this idyllic day ends in disaster, the chapters that conclude the novel illustrate typical stages of grief, including denial, anger, bargaining, depression, and acceptance. As Joel D. Chaston observes in "The Other Deaths in *Bridge to Terabithia,*" there are numerous images of death throughout the novel, in the Easter Sunday service and other biblical references, in stories that Leslie retells and works of art that Jess encounters, but Paterson ultimately shows that nothing can prepare us for an unexpected death, and she does not glorify death or idealize the reactions of her characters.[4] She does show at the end of the novel that grief can motivate people of all ages to strengthen other relationships and "find strength in what remains behind," as Wordsworth wrote in "Ode: In-

timations of Immortality" (see Wordsworth in Part 2 and selections by Paterson in Parts 5 and 8.)

MONICA HUGHES (1925–2003)

THE KEEPER OF THE ISIS LIGHT

Monica Hughes, who was born in England and settled in Canada in 1952, has won many awards for her speculative fiction. Her family background as the daughter of a mathematician, service in the Women's Royal Navy in World War II, work as a laboratory technician, and studies and reading while living in the British Isles, Africa, and Canada, enhanced her knowledge of science, technology, the arts, and different cultures, and these influences appear in her books. Hughes often addresses the question of what might happen if a technologically more sophisticated culture encountered a less sophisticated one. Her novels are distinguished by her well-developed characters and her willingness to explore dark and troubling psychological situations, as well as the scientific and cultural dimensions of her fantasy worlds.

Her Isis trilogy begins with *The Keeper of the Isis Light* (1980), which won the Children's Literature Association's Phoenix Award in 2000. Many of Hughes's characters experience isolation in vast landscapes, and it is evident at the beginning of the novel that Olwen Pendennis has been isolated on the planet Isis with her faithful robot Guardian because she is receiving her first letter and seeing her name written by a stranger for the first time. Since human beings have arrived on the planet from Earth, which is polluted and overpopulated, she encounters the human Mark, who is shocked and repelled when he discovers who Olwen really is. But does he truly know? Olwen has adapted to the planet on which she lives by becoming partly lizard, but this external reality repels Mark when we, as readers, know that, if anything, Olwen is more fully human than he is—but her isolation has made her vulnerable. The sequels to this novel are *The Guardian of the Isis* (1981) and *The Isis Pedlar* (1982).

LOIS LOWRY (b. 1937)

THE GIVER

After Lois Lowry began her career as an American journalist and photographer, in 1977 she began publishing realistic novels about young people dealing with problems such as death, war, and single parenthood. Two series of humorous and insightful novels depict American characters who became popular with young readers: Anastasia Krupnik, her brother Sam, Caroline Tate, and her brother J. P. Lowry also contributed a story called "Holding" to the anthology *Am I*

Blue? (see title story by Bruce Coville in Part 7). Lowry has won Newbery medals for both *Number the Stars* (1988), a novel about the Holocaust set in Denmark, and her first futuristic novel, *The Giver* (1993). Readers of all ages have debated whether the open-ended conclusion in *The Giver* is unsatisfying or intriguing, but Lowry has asserted that she wants readers to imagine endings that suit their own beliefs and to believe as she does that the novel is optimistic.[5] *Gathering Blue* (2002) and *Messenger* (2004) are loosely linked to *The Giver* through recurring characters and details; Lowry continued to develop stories about utopias gone bad, but the societies in these later novels do not have the advanced technologies that are depicted in *The Giver.*

Eleven-year-old Jonas seems like a typical modern middle-class boy at the beginning of *The Giver,* but his daily life is rigidly controlled by rules that are enforced by a committee of Elders and followed by everyone in their community. Generations earlier, leaders decided to use technology to achieve Sameness, eliminating pain, crime, war, and many aspects of individuality. Citizens are provided with comfortable, secure lives, with homes and meals each day, with gentle child care and eldercare. But the middle of the novel reveals that they have no knowledge of history, animals, the outside world with varied landscapes and climate change, art, music, books, extended families, or strong emotions. Jonas realizes late in the novel that their "orderly, disciplined," predictable life is "the life without color, pain or past" (p. 165). Lowry's fictional world is reminiscent of the most famous dystopias of the mid-twentieth century, *1984* by George Orwell and *Brave New World* by Aldous Huxley, since reproduction is controlled scientifically by the authorities, who also choose each person's training and career, and speakers are placed everywhere (never turned off) for listening to citizens and announcing rules. Adults who request a spouse and children are assessed for compatibility and assigned one boy and one girl to raise, so Jonas has one sister, Lily. Because Jonas's father works as a Nurturer with "newchildren" before they are assigned to a family, his family is allowed to care at night for the baby they call Gabriel, trying to calm his atypical restlessness.

At first, this society seems a little less impersonal or inhumane than those in Orwell's and Huxley's novels for adults or the horrific world with no individuality on the planet Camazotz in Madeleine L'Engle's *A Wrinkle in Time.*

For example, children get to choose the volunteer work they do after school, to assess their skills and interests before their Assignments to a permanent role. Instead of celebrating individual birthdays, children are promoted to each new age communally at a December Ceremony, where, for example, the Ones receive Naming and Placement with a family and the Nines are given bicycles. Just before his twelfth Ceremony, Jonas begins taking the daily pills that suppress sexual "Stirrings" throughout adult life. In his Ceremony of Twelves, after all Jonas's cohorts are assigned to begin training for careers they will be happy with, the surprising announcement is made that Jonas is selected to be the next Receiver of Memory, a role requiring intelligence, integrity, courage, the ability to develop wisdom, and the mysterious Capacity to See Beyond. He begins training each day after school with the Giver, an Elder who lives in isolation. Holding the memories of all human experiences and history that the community had given up, the Giver starts transmitting these memories to Jonas. He begins by transferring pleasurable new experiences, such as a sled ride down a snowy hill. It is only later that Jonas begins to understand why the Giver's job is so painful. What he learns raises fascinating questions about the joys and burdens of human experience, and the consequences of individual choice.

NOTES

1. Virginia Hamilton, "Ah, Sweet Rememory!" *The Horn Book* (1981), *Innocence and Experience: Essays & Conversations on Children's Literature,* ed. Barbara Harrison and Gregory Maguire (New York: Lothrop, Lee & Shepard, 1987) 6–12.

2. Virginia Hamilton, "Hagi, Mose, and Drylongso," *The Zena Sutherland Lectures, 1983–1991,* ed. Betsy Hearne (New York: Clarion, 1992) 90.

3. Katherine Paterson, *The Spying Heart* (New York: E. P. Dutton, 1989) 34–35.

4. Joel D. Chaston, "The Other Deaths in *Bridge to Terabithia,*" *Children's Literature Association Quarterly* 16 (1991): 238–41.

5. Lois Lowry, "A Conversation with Lois Lowry," *The Giver* (New York: Laurel-Leaf, 2002).

PART FIVE

Boys' Books and Girls' Books
Gender Issues

I always thought that the only reason that girls seem to read all kinds of books, even if the protagonists are boys, is simply that girls are more open-minded and all embracing, less gender-conscious or something. This morning, I suddenly had this terrible hunch, that there might be another reason why boys react to girls' books much less favorably than girls to boys' books—could it be that both girls and boys regard female as a "secondary" gender?

On-line posting by fairrosa, March 8, 1995

In recent decades, there has been vigorous debate about the contents and effects of children's books in terms of teaching about gender. What do girls learn from stories about their interests, potentials, and characteristics as girls and young women? What do boys absorb from children's books about how to behave, what to expect, and who to be as boys and young men? Just as with other areas of learning, the perceived messages of children's books vary widely in what they say about gender. A widespread fear in our time is that passive or submissive female role models in children's books will teach girls, in particular, that their place is always destined to be second to that of boys, a fear related to "fairrosa's" suspicion expressed in the comment in the epigraph. The corresponding hope is that, shown active role models of courageous and intelligent girls, female readers will be inspired to emulate their heroines and fulfill their human potential. Whether these fears and hopes are realistic or not, we seldom examine the assumption that girls will identify with girls (or young women) in books and that boys will identify with boys and men. It has become a truism of popular culture that girls will read about boys in books, but that boys are averse to reading about girls—an assumption that has the potential to do much damage to the development of a healthy sense of self in relation to gender identity and relationships.

In a 2004 book *Out of This World: Why Literature Matters to Girls,* Holly Blackford reveals that the girls she interviewed in depth about their reading do not read fiction to find positive role models, but "to experience something radically different from their everyday lives." Blackford began her study expecting to find that girls might be reading fiction in order to find female characters who "struggle for or achieve self, agency, power, or social and self-awareness."[1] Instead, she found that girls are reading in order to experience a multiplicity of perspectives, not identifying with admirable characters so much as examining the world and fictional forms from a variety of angles for the sake of exploring diverse possibilities of being and relationship. Thus, female readers are as likely to examine the world from the perspectives of characters that are alien to their own identity as from the position of identifying with characters much like themselves. One of the implications of Blackford's study is that we may be limiting our conception of literature if we reduce it to a source for admirable role models, role models that fit our conception of how girls (or boys, for that matter) should develop their potentials.

As Elizabeth Segel argues in her essay in this section, separate literatures for boys and for girls are fairly recent developments in the history of literacy. It was not until the Victorian era that the idea of "boys' books" and "girls' books" as different genres emerged fully, as one expression of the separate realms of masculinity and femininity that arose in England and America from Western industrial capitalism, which segregated men and women into the spheres of "work" and "domesticity" or "public life" and "private life." It is interesting to note, as Segel points out, that in John Newbery's influential and historic little books that were designed to appeal to the newly affluent middle class of eighteenth-century London, he did not make significant distinctions between the boys and girls in his reading audience, at least not in terms of what would interest them. We can certainly find gendered expectations of proper behavior in the literature of Newbery's era, but the idea of separate reading audiences was still in its infancy.

However, by the latter half of the nineteenth century, the idea had become entrenched that boys would naturally want to read about adventure, travel, war, and tests of bravery and strength, while girls would choose stories about romance, relationships, feelings, and domestic values and experiences. This idea separated the literary education of males and females according to their presumed social destinies. Because people assumed that boys and girls would prefer different reading material, writers, editors, teachers, and parents catered to these preconceived preferences and, in doing so, created and reinforced them: a kind of self-fulfilling prophecy.

By the period often called the Golden Age of children's literature, which produced such masterpieces as Lewis Carroll's *Alice's Adventures in Wonderland* (1865), Louisa May Alcott's *Little Women* (1868–69), and *The Adventures of Tom Sawyer* (1876) by Mark Twain, the idea of separate literatures for boys and girls was well established and had begun to dominate the production of contemporary children's fiction. Girls in the nineteenth century were generally given only domestic, not literary or scholarly, educations, although there were, of course, notable exceptions. This meant that girls as a reading audience were not getting as much attention as boys, although novels of romance and domestic life were tremendously popular. Adventure stories were standard fare, such as Robert Louis Stevenson's *Treasure Island* and R. M. Ballantyne's seafaring novels, such as *The Coral Island,* dealing with piracy, shipwrecks, and exploration (with all the prejudices of Empire involved). Except for *The Swiss Family Robinson,* by Johann David Wyss, in which an unnamed mother helps to domesticate their island while her husband and four sons go exploring and hunting, the survival and adventure story was an almost exclusively masculine tradition until well into the twentieth century.

As Part 3 explores, however, there was a parallel literature with much older roots than the novels for children then being produced: the folk and fairy tales, which had become newly popular with the collections published by Jacob and Wilhelm Grimm (*Kinder und Hausmärchen,* 1812–57). Their translation into English by Edgar Taylor (*Nursery and Household Tales,* 1823) was followed by Joseph Jacobs's lively English vernacular retellings of popular tales, *English Fairy Tales* (1890), which won over generations of readers. Jacobs's "Jack and the Beanstalk," reprinted in Part 3, is one of innumerable tales in which an ordinary young man acquires wealth by triumphing over powerful adversaries.

Are the folk and fairy tales full of oppressive gender stereotypes, as critics frequently charge? Much depends on which version you read (or, as is often the case with modern children, which version you see). This section contains three different versions of one of the most popular tales, "Cinderella," which show a range of interpretations of the role of the heroine. Louise Bernikow, in her personal essay on her experience growing up with the story of Cinderella, sees it as one of insidious female rivalry. But, interestingly, she finds the harsher Grimm Brothers' version more inspiring than either the saccharine Disney film or the elegant Perrault tale. Feminist critics, who have debated this issue of gender roles in fairy tales extensively since 1970, have accused the best-known fairy tales, such as "Sleeping Beauty," "Cinderella," and "Snow White and the Seven Dwarfs," of teaching the notion that beauty and passivity are the supreme female virtues, while courage and action are the distinguishing marks of the male heroes of the fairy tales. "Waiting for the prince" and "living happily ever after" have become clichés that describe the false expectations that fairy tales supposedly encourage.

However, tales of strong and smart heroines have existed for centuries in folk and fairy tales from oral traditions, although they were not the ones most frequently reprinted and illustrated before the late twentieth century. These tales include "The Maid of the North" from Scandinavia, "Molly Whuppie" in Britain, and Molly's Appalachian counterpart "Mutsmag" (see Part 3). Another consideration, as critic Maria Tatar has pointed out, is that many of the male folktale heroes are passive and not particularly brave or smart. One can, in fact, find almost any kind of role model for either sex in the world's folk and fairy tales, from trickster to dumbling. Moreover, a number of selections in Part 7 show that modern satires and spin-offs of classic tales often subvert the Cinderella archetype and other traditional characterizations of gender roles. The young adult fiction by Bruce Coville and Francesca Lia Block in that section borrows motifs from familiar fairy tales to develop stories that deal with sexual orientation, homophobia, and in Block's *Weetzie Bat,* the growth of an unconventional family created by a homosexual and a heterosexual couple.

Although American children's books of the nineteenth century, like their British counterparts, often tended to fall into the categories of "boys' books" and "girls' books," we should keep in mind that many books, such as Mark Twain's, appealed to both and that children's periodicals, such as *St. Nicholas Magazine,* which ran Louisa May Alcott stories in serial form, had wide readerships of both girls and boys. There is no doubt, though, that Twain represented boys as seeking to escape from female control, in the shape of the Widow Douglas and Aunt Polly, who are kindly but are represented as repressive and onerous, causing Huck Finn to want to escape to the territories before being captured and "civilized" by women, while Alcott cultivated the domestic virtues of setting a moral example within the home through her focus on family relationships in her series about the March family.

Jo March is the heroine most readers find most appealing in Alcott's *Little Women,* and it is noteworthy that Jo puts up a fight against the expectations of becoming "feminine." She considers herself the "man" of the family while her father is away, despises fancy dress, loves running and vigorous physical activity, and relishes many behaviors that are boyish or androgynous. Like Mary Lennox in *The Secret Garden,* Jo resists conventionally girlish behavior, and we like her all the better for doing so. This is true of a number of heroines of children's literature, including Astrid Lindgren's extraordinary superheroine Pippi Longstocking, both Anne of Green Gables and Emily Byrd Starr by L. M. Montgomery, and Louise Fitzhugh's redoubtable Harriet the Spy.

If many of the most memorable heroines of children's literature do battle against the constraints of conventional behavior expected of their sex, many of the heroes of children's books appear to be stuck in a frame of mind that causes them to repeat their inadequate ways of coping, over and over. This is true of the wooden puppet Pinocchio, in his original incarnation in the nineteenth-century novel by Carlo Collodi (see the excerpt in Part 4), who keeps repeating self-centered and stupid mistakes, and of both Huck and Tom, who, in different ways, exhibit obsessive behaviors. Huck finally, heroically, decides to disobey his conventional conscience and listen to his heart while helping Jim escape slavery, but Tom (in *Adventures of Huckleberry Finn*) tiresomely repeats his juvenile, self-glorifying pranks. The boys' stories suggest that there is something mechanical, perhaps even imprisoning, about the stereotypically masculine urge to disobey parental authority (especially motherly rules) and strike out on one's own.

Some male protagonists in the children's literature of the last half of the twentieth century struggle against the subtle and unspoken constraints and restrictions of masculinity (or of the expectations of what masculinity should entail). Jess in Katherine Paterson's *Bridge to Terabithia* (see Further Recommended Reading in Part 4) yearns for the kind of physical affection his younger sister can take for granted, but that he was considered too big for "since the day he was born." He has to hide his talent for drawing and art from his father, who considers such interests "sissy" or something he thinks of as worse. Jess finds in Leslie, a talented and urbane girl, a more sophisticated and open-minded reflection of himself: a true alter ego. Leslie herself faces prejudices about the things a girl should or should not do, as for example, when she joins in the boys' races at school. Thus *Bridge to Terabithia* is a sensitive study of the costs of gender constraints for both girls and boys in the late twentieth century, and Paterson's *Jacob Have I Loved* explores the options that were available to a girl in the midst of World War II.

A distinct pattern in recent children's books is a duo of hero and heroine, boy and girl protagonists. A good example is furnished by Lyra and Will in Philip Pullman's *His Dark Materials* trilogy. However, whether the boy-girl duos always represent an advance over the stereotyping of male and female characteristics in older books is debatable. Sometimes the duo is expanded to include peers or siblings, as in the trio of Harry, Ron, and Hermione in J. K. Rowling's Harry Potter series. Lemony Snicket's contemporary series of mock-Gothic adventure stories feature Violet, Klaus, and Sunny Baudelaire, three orphans who are always barely escaping (and sometimes not quite escaping) from impending disasters. Since the oldest, Violet, is a budding inventor, Klaus has the book smarts, and Sunny is a baby girl who bites everything, these books, labeled A Series of Unfortunate Events, avoid gender stereotypes in their young protagonists. In other books, there is a tendency for female characters to become "sidekicks" of or pale alter egos to the main male characters, and Harry Potter fans of all ages vary widely in their interpretations of whether this fate has befallen Hermione. Traditional patterns can be reversed in other ways. In Mildred Taylor's Logan family series, Cassie is the main character, but her relationships with her brothers, particularly Stacie, the oldest, are crucial to her development. Phyllis Reynolds Naylor gives us a thoughtful teenage boy (in *The Year of the Gopher*) who displays his concern for his brother and sister. His siblings are both, in different ways, victims of social expectations. Christopher Paul Curtis develops the theme of male friendship through his story of how Kenny Watson, in *The Watsons Go to Birmingham,* learns to respect the feelings of Rufus and Cody, his country neighbors who are poked fun at by most of his classmates.

These finely conceived characters contrast with the stereotypical and mechanical quality of Franklin W. Dixon's Hardy Boys, who are so much alike that it is hard even to think of them as separate characters. The popular girl sleuth Nancy Drew, on the other hand, as feminist critics such as Carolyn Heilbrun and Bobbie Ann Mason have argued, has been an inspiration to generations of female readers, some of whom have found in her a liberating role model for girls.[2] Ellen Seiter's essay "Toy-Based Videos for Girls" (in Part 7) points out that popular culture fads often reinforce traditional gender stereotypes, but some, such as My Little Pony toys and videos, at least offer girls choices that free them from relying on male-dominated values and role models.

Elizabeth Segel argues that boys and girls have much to learn about each other by reading stories about the experiences and perspectives of the opposite gender. Our notions of gender will continue to evolve as research in biology, psychology, and sociology advances our understanding and shapes our debates about the roles of nature and nurture in the construction of gender. Our interpretations of older works, as well as the creation of new ones, will be influenced by these continuing developments, as well as by the directions our society moves in. Whether or not we accept the notion that there ought not to be distinct literatures that appeal to girls or to boys, it is clear that boys and girls will benefit from being exposed to engaging male and female protagonists, characters who both reflect and expand the realms of possibility for the imagination of readers. A literature that failed to represent the struggles of girls and boys against prejudice and stereotyping would be incomplete. In this area, as in many others, we need to ask ourselves whether we want literature that reflects the world as we want it to be (in this case, an idealized world in which gender stereotyping does not exist) or something more complicated: the world as it is, but peopled with characters who question and challenge and sometimes overcome the limitations of convention and tradition.

NOTES

1. Holly Blackford, *Out of This World: Why Literature Matters to Girls* (New York: Teachers College P, 2004) 12.
2. Bobbie Anne Mason, *The Girl Sleuth* (Athens: U of GA P, 1995). See also Carolyn Heilbrun, "Nancy Drew: A Moment in Feminist History," *Rediscovering Nancy Drew,* ed. Carolyn Stewart Dyer and Nancy Tillman Romalov (Iowa City: U of Iowa P, 1995) 11–21.

Elizabeth Segel (b. 1938)

Where did the notion of books for boys and books for girls come from? Reading expert Elizabeth Segel, of the University of Pittsburgh, answers this question carefully, showing that early children's books did not feature any such division and that the notion of separate bodies of literature aimed at each gender emerged from the mid-nineteenth century separation of men's and women's roles into separate spheres of work and home. Even when the categories began to blur as children's literature moved into the twentieth century, Segel shows, studies claiming to demonstrate that girls will read books about boys but boys will not read books about girls influenced the kinds of reading material provided to both boys and girls, reinforcing girls' second-class status and depriving boys of important insights into the lives and imaginations of girls. (For another essay by Segel, see Part 4.)

"As the Twig Is Bent . . ."

Gender and Childhood Reading

One of the most obvious ways gender influences our experience as readers is when it determines what books are made available to us or are designated as appropriate or inappropriate for our reading. Nowhere is this fact so apparent or its implications so disturbing as in childhood reading. This is partly because the child does not have direct access to books, by and large, but receives them from adult hands. Adults decide what books are written, published, offered for sale, and, for the most part, purchased for children. And over the last century and a half, most adults have firmly believed that literary sauce for the goose is not at all sauce for the gander. The publisher commissioning paperback romances for girls and marketing science fiction for boys, as well as Aunt Lou selecting a fairy tale collection for Susie and a dinosaur book for Sam, are part of a powerful system that operates to channel books to or away from children according to their gender. Furthermore, because the individual's attitudes concerning appropriate gender-role behaviors are formed during the early years, the reader's choice of reading material may be governed by these early experiences long after she or he has theoretically gained direct access to books of all kinds.

To understand how gender operates on this level to condition the reading process, it is useful, first, to look at reading in childhood, ask how the reading lives of girls and of boys have typically differed, and seek out the origins of those differences.

Geoffrey Trease, distinguished British author of children's novels, tells us that in the early 1930s, when he began writing for children, "Books were labelled, as strictly as school lavatories, 'Books for Boys' or 'Books for Girls'."[1] This was also the situation in America, and it prevailed in the same rigid form at least until the 1960s, when the boundaries began to loosen a bit. 'Twas not ever thus, however.

In the few books intended for children's use that were published before the eighteenth century, no distinction seems to have been made between boy readers and girl readers. Manuals of conduct—the various volumes of "a father's counsel" or "a mother's legacy"—were apparently addressed in roughly equal numbers to sons or daughters, depending on the gender of the writer's own offspring. The Puritan tracts depicting godly children on their deathbeds which dominated seventeenth-century juvenile publishing seem to have dwelt with equal fervor on the uplifting spectacle of godly girls and godly boys going meekly to their reward.

The 1740s are generally viewed as marking the coming of age of children's books in England. In that decade, three London publisher-booksellers, Thomas Boreman, Mary Cooper, and John Newbery, began to provide children with books designed to delight as well as instruct them. Increasing middle-class literacy and prosperity set the stage for this development, along with the gradual popular dissemination of John Locke's educational philosophy, which advocated teaching children through play.

One of Newbery's most appealing early publications appears at first glance to herald the publishers' practice of dividing children's books into boys' books and girls' books. *A Little Pretty Pocket-Book* (1744), a miscellany of rhymes and fables in an elegant gilt and flowered binding, opens with two whimsical letters from Jack the Giant Killer to the child reader.[2] One is addressed to Master Tommy, and the other to Pretty Miss Polly. Furthermore, Newbery—canny merchandiser that he was—offered with the book for two pence additional a pincushion (for Pretty Miss Polly, of course) or a ball (for Master Tommy). On closer inspection, however, we see that the wording is exactly the same in each of the two letters, except that one speaks of being a good boy, the other a good girl; where one addresses "my dear Tommy," and the other speaks to "my dear Polly." Both letters praise the child for his or her "Nurse's report": you are, the letters say, "loving and kind to your Play-fellows, and obliging to every body; . . . you rise early in the Morning, keep yourself clean, and learn your Book;. . . when you have done a Fault you confess it, and are sorry for it." Including two letters instead of one was not, it would seem, a way of prescribing different conduct for girls and boys, but a way of personalizing the letter and the book itself in an engaging way.

The two letters also specify the use to which the ball and the pincushion are to be put, and our initial supposition—that Tommy will be gaily playing ball with his fellows while poor Polly sits laboring over her sampler—proves false. No, the objects are to serve the very same function, according to the Giant Killer. Both are red on one side and black on the other, and both come with ten pins. "For every good Action you do, a Pin shall be stuck on the Red Side, and for every bad Action a Pin shall be stuck on the Black Side." Jack rashly promises to send a penny when all the pins arrive on the red side, and a whipping should they all be found on the black. The virtues Newbery and his contemporaries were aiming to develop—obedience, industry, good temper—were evidently the same for both sexes. The reward for such virtues was the same, too, if we can judge from two of Newbery's most popular children's stories: both Goody Two-Shoes and Giles Gingerbread achieve by their goodness and application to studies "the love of all who know them" and the epitome of material success, a fine coach to ride in.

Neither the Puritan aim of saving the child's soul nor the characteristic Georgian aim of developing good character seemed to require a distinction between girl-child and boy-child. The domestic tales of the late eighteenth and early nineteenth centuries, such as Mrs. Trimmer's *The History of the Robins* (1786), the Edgeworths' *Harry and Lucy* stories (1801, 1825), and Mrs. Sherwood's *The Fairchild Family* (1818–1847), all featured children of both sexes as characters and were intended for readers of both sexes. All of these books clearly taught obedience, submission to authority, and selflessness as the cardinal virtues of both girls and boys. The few volumes produced solely for the child's entertainment in the early years of the nineteenth century, such as *The Comic Adventures of Old Mother Hubbard and Her Dog* (1805?) and *The Butterfly's Ball* (1807), also took no account of gender. The latter begins, "Come take up your Hats, and away let us haste / To the Butterfly's Ball, and the Grasshop-

per's feast," and the illustration shows both girls and boys among the fortunate children who are invited to the unusual party.

Early school stories were an exception. Because boarding schools were for boys or girls, not both, thinly disguised moral tracts with school settings were aimed at one sex or the other. Sarah Fielding's *The Governess; Or, Little Female Academy* specifies on the title page that it is "calculated for the entertainment and instruction of young ladies in their education."[3] Elizabeth Sandham wrote *The Boys' School; Or, Traits of Character in Early Life* (1800). Another of her productions was "an equally purposeful work about girls at school."[4] Mrs. Pilkington's two volumes, *Biography for Boys* (1805) and *Biography for Girls* (1806), suggest that then, as now, it was assumed that the child reader's emulation of the lives of the great would be more likely if girls read about famous women, boys about famous men.

While certain of the school stories and biographies for older children were targeted for boys or for girls, Samuel Pickering's study of eighteenth-century children's books bears out my conclusion that the first "significant differentiation made between books for little girls and for little boys" came with Mary Ann Kilner's *The Adventures of a Pincushion* (1783?) and *Memoirs of a Peg-Top* (1783).[5] These stories were among the best of the purported biographies of inanimate objects which were popular at the time. The pincushion and the peg-top both travel to boarding school and from one owner to another, in varying stations of life, all the while making improving comments on the scenes they observe. *The Adventures of a Pincushion* was "designed chiefly for the use of young ladies,"[6] *Memoirs of a Peg-Top* for boys. This distinction was apparently based on supposed different interests of girls and boys, rather than on different socializing aims for the two books—a specialization of vehicle rather than message. Indeed, Kilner asserted in her preface to *Memoirs of a Peg-Top* that "the laws of justice, probity, and truth" are "of *general* obligation." Her purpose in addressing the books to the "*different amusements* . . . in which each sex [was] more particularly concerned" was to make her books more interesting to children. It is worth noting that the chief difference between the companion volumes, besides the gender of the child characters, is that the peg-top book departs from the usual standard of gentility in approved children's fiction of the day. The top recounts an incident, for example, in which a blindfolded boy is fed a concoction of custard and cow dung.

Kilner's experiment seems to have had no imitators, and when Victoria came to the throne in 1837, the wholesale fencing off of children's books into books for boys and books for girls had not yet been effected. Elizabeth Rigby's very long article on children's books in the *Quarterly Review* (1844) makes no mention of boys' books or girls' books, either in her critical essay or in the annotations of recommended books which follow.[7] Even in discussing Marryat's *Masterman Ready* (1841), a book invariably referred to today as a boys' book, Rigby noted the danger that parents may "dispute with *their children*"—not with *their sons*—"the possession of it" (my italics).

Within a few years, however, the adventure fiction of Marryat, Ballantyne, Henty, and Kingston would be universally thought of as "boys' books," and domestic chronicles like Susan Warner's *The Wide, Wide World* (1850) and Charlotte Yonge's *The Daisy Chain* (1856) would set a transatlantic pattern for the "girls' book." By the last quarter of the century, articles like William Graham Sumner's "What Our Boys Are Reading"[8] and Edward G. Salmon's "What Girls Read"[9] had become commonplace on both sides of the Atlantic.

How to account for this extensive staking out of boys' and girls' claims on the previously common territory of children's books is the interesting question. Certainly a favorable economic climate was an important precondition. The market had to grow large before publishers would consider restricting sales by excluding potential readers. In 1808 Charles Lamb received a letter from his publisher, William Godwin, suggesting changes in his adaptation of Chapman's *Odyssey* for children, *The Adventures of Ulysses*. Godwin wrote:

> We live in squeamish days. Amid the beauties of your manuscript, of which no man can think more highly than I do, what will the squeamish say to . . . the giant's vomit, page 14, or to the minute & shocking description of the extinguishing the giant's eye, in the page following. You I dare say have no formed plan of excluding the female sex from among your readers, & I, as a bookseller, must consider that if you have, you exclude one half of the human species.[10]

Appropriate subject matter for boys might be judged too "strong" for girls, but for economic reasons pub-

lishers at this time preferred to dilute the material rather than limit the book's readers to one sex.

F. J. Harvey Darton, still the ultimate authority on the social history of English children's books, acknowledged the role of economics in making it possible to publish different types of books for boys and for girls by the mid-nineteenth century: "Mere numbers now made sub-division inevitable." Yet he went further, and suggested that this development was a positive step in the evolution of a true children's literature, one that hinged on "the discovery that *The Child* was *a* child, and, on top of that, that he was male and female, and was also different at five years of age and fourteen. . . . Hitherto the young readers had never been clearly defined. They were just 'children,' and that meant anything from a baby lisping the alphabet to a young Miss or Master growing like the elder generation."[11]

"The young Miss . . . growing like the elder generation" presented a ticklish problem to her Victorian elders which provided further impetus to develop a distinctive literature for girls. "Girls' literature performs one very useful function," according to Salmon's important 1886 essay. "It enables girls to read something above mere baby tales, and yet keeps them from the influence of novels of a sort which should be read only by persons capable of forming a discreet judgment. It is a long jump from Aesop to 'Ouida', and to place Miss Sarah Doudney or Miss Anne Beale between Aesop and 'Ouida' may at least prevent a disastrous moral fall."[12] Mary Louisa Molesworth, also writing in 1886, cited *Mrs. Overtheway's Remembrances* (1866), by Mrs. Ewing, as a book "more particularly written for girls, and well adapted for that indefinite age, the despair of mothers and governesses, when maidens begin to look down upon 'regular children's stories,' and novels are as yet forbidden."[13]

While this literature for older girls, clearly the forerunner of today's "junior novels" or young adult fiction, can legitimately be viewed as being responsive to children's needs (after all, children do need books that fall between Marguerite Henry and Margaret Drabble), Salmon's tone indicates that girls' literature "for that indefinite age" was part of a concerted effort to keep females pure and their imaginations unsullied by restricting their world, even within the home. "The chief end served by 'girls' literature' is that, whilst it advances beyond the nursery, it stops short of the full blaze of the drawing-room," Salmon concluded.[14] It was, by and large, a stopgap, watered-down fare, a part of the Victorians' Podsnappian attempt, so well described by Dickens, to proscribe whatever "would . . . bring a blush to the cheek of the young person."[15]

The evidence suggests that more than economic feasibility and increasing dominance of the middle-class made the middle class's definilishment [sic] to develop distinctive girls' and boys' books. It was, above all, the sharp differentiation of male and female roles, well underway by the mid-nineteenth century, which mandated separate books for girls and boys.

The polarization of gender roles which accompanied the advance of industrialization and colonization has been well described elsewhere;[16] only the most salient features need be cited here. As work moved out of the home and female leisure became a sign of material success, middle-class women less and less were productive workers, becoming instead consumers confined to the domestic world. At the same time, the increasing dominance of the middle class made the middle class's definition of the role of women society's ideal of womanhood. Man's duties, in contrast, took him into the sordid and fiercely competitive world of industry and commerce and to the four corners of the world—to earn, to fight, and to rule the benighted subjects of empire. The home, under the aegis of the wife as "the angel in the house," was to be the refuge of moral and spiritual values. In place of her former active role of helpmate, the wife was offered the noble mission of influencing husband and children toward the good. This delegation to women of the responsibility for inculcating moral and religious values in men and children, and the generally enthusiastic acceptance of this function (even by women like Louisa May Alcott and George Eliot, who chafed at the restrictions this definition of women's role placed on them), had a profound impact on child-rearing practices and on the relations between the sexes.[17]

Its impact on children's books is unmistakable. For one thing, the women who dominated the ranks of juvenile authors viewed writing for children as the exercise of feminine moral "influence." The content of children's books naturally reflected the doctrine. As Salmon declared:

Boys' literature of a sound kind ought to help to build up men. Girls' literature ought to help to build up women. If in choosing the books that boys shall read it is necessary to remember that we are choosing mental food for the future chiefs of a great race, it is equally important not to forget in choosing books for girls that we are choosing mental food for the future wives and mothers of that race. When Mr. Ruskin says that man's work is public and woman's private, he seems for the moment insensible to the public work of women as exercised through their influence on their husbands, brothers, and fathers. Woman's work in the ordering, beautifying, and elevating of the commonweal is hardly second to man's; and it is this which ought to be borne in mind in rearing girls.[18]

Before the boys' book appeared on the scene, fiction for children typically had been domestic in setting, heavily didactic, and morally or spiritually uplifting, and this kind of earnest family story remained the staple of younger children's fiction. The boys' book was, above all, an escape from domesticity and from the female domination of the domestic world. The adventures of Tom and Huck, of Jim Hawkins and many lesser heroes of boys' books are the epitome of freedom in part because they are an escape from women, the chief agents of socialization in the culture. Though most boys' books entailed a simple code of honor, earnest introspection and difficult moral choices were taboo; these were books of action and adventure. As Gillian Avery puts it, "Long before girls were allowed amusing books, boys had their Marryat and Ballantyne—books of high adventure with the occasional pious sentiment slipped in as an afterthought, but with no continuous moral message."[19]

The authors of *these* books were not pious female pedagogues, but men of action! Of the British boys' book authors, Frederick Marryat had entered the Royal Navy at fourteen and had taken part in fifty naval engagements before he settled down to write books twenty-four years later. R. M. Ballantyne emigrated to Canada, where he worked for the Hudson Bay Company, often at remote outposts in the Far North. Thomas Mayne Reid, born in Ireland, came to America as a young man and became a trader on the western frontier, living among the native Americans. He fought in the thick of the Mexican War before returning England to write boys' fiction. And G. A. Henty, chronicler of military history and celebrator of empire, was a war correspondent who had witnessed famous battles all over Europe and Africa for thirty years.

The liberation of nineteenth-century boys into the book worlds of sailors and pirates, forests and battles, left their sisters behind in the world of childhood—that is, the world of home and family. When publishers and writers saw the commercial possibilities of books for girls, it is interesting that they did not provide comparable escape reading for them (that came later, with the pulp series books), but instead developed books designed to persuade the young reader to accept the confinement and self-sacrifice inherent in the doctrine of feminine influence. This was accomplished by depicting the rewards of submission and the sacred joys of serving as "the angel in the house." Whereas in many boys' books, the happy ending is the adolescent "bad boy" successfully escaping socialization, holding out against the Widow Douglasses of the world, and thereby earning the admiration of all, in the girls' book, the protagonist who resists the dictates of genteel feminity must be "tamed," her will broken to accept a submissive and sedentary role. The so-called happy ending of such books is that she herself stops rebelling and chooses the approved role in order to gain or to retain the love and approval of those around her.[20]

The classic example of a girl who is "broken" to the conventional woman's role in a girls' book is the heroine of *What Katy Did,* by Susan Coolidge, which was published in 1872 and widely read in America and Britain for nearly a century.[21] It is a book that repays close attention for the illumination it sheds on the nature of the girls' book.

Katy Carr is the eldest of six motherless children in a well-to-do New England family. A lanky, impulsive, awkward, and passionate twelve year old, she darts from one scrape to another. As crabby Aunt Izzy rails about Katy's missing bonnet-string, torn dresses, and tardiness, the reader responds to Katy's generosity, creativity, and affectionate nature. Moved by the pleadings of her father and of the saintly invalid, Aunt Helen, Katy resolves to conquer her faults, but her resolutions are in vain. One particularly tempestuous day, she vents her frustrations by vigorously swinging, though Aunt Izzy has forbidden it. What Katy doesn't know is that the rope is not secure. Her punishment for this disobedience is a terrible fall and an injury to her back which keeps her in bed and in pain for four years.

In the first months she experiences a deep depression. Then Aunt Helen, beautiful and beloved by all (and an invalid herself, remember), talks to Katy about "God's school," the School of Pain, where the lessons are Patience, Hopefulness, and—believe it or not—Neatness.

The rest of the book chronicles how Katy grows in virtue and gains the love and approval of all. She learns to think of others, not herself, and to fill the place of the dead mother to the younger children. And, of course, being unable to walk for four years effectively cures her coltish exuberance.

The disturbing message that the ideal woman is an invalid is scarcely veiled. Aunt Helen tells Katy that after her own crippling accident she took pains to keep herself and her room looking attractive. It wasn't easy but, she says, "The pleasure it gave my dear father repaid for all. He had been proud of his active, healthy girl, but I think she was never such a comfort to him as his sick one, lying there in her bed" (p. 110). Katy is moved by this chilling vision to wish to "be nice and sweet and patient, and a comfort to people" (p. 111). She succeeds so well that the "happy ending" of the book is not so much the few tottering steps she manages in the last chapter as a compliment from Aunt Helen which ends the book: "You have won the place, which, you recollect, I once told you an invalid should try to gain, of being to everybody 'The Heart of the House'" (p. 166). Since this was the place to which all women were urged to aspire, we may well wonder what the book's effect was on young readers. The book's popularity with previous generations of girls may well be owing to the vivid embodiment in crippled, chastened Katy of the painful limitations that the all too familiar feminine role imposed on active, carefree children.

If one contrasts *What Katy Did* with a comparably popular and respected boys' book of the period—say, *Treasure Island*[22]—one is first struck by the difference in setting: the domestic confinement of one book as against the extended voyage to exotic lands in the other. Also notable is the solemn introspection and moral earnestness that the girls' book expects of its heroine and readers, in contrast to the carefree suspension of moral judgment allowed Jim Hawkins. Good and evil exist in *Treasure Island*, to be sure, but Jim never has to make difficult moral choices (he kills mutineer Israel Hands involuntarily; Long John Silver's escape means Jim doesn't have to turn him over to be executed, etc.). Another revealing contrast is the premium placed on obedience in *What Katy Did*—but not in *Treasure Island*.

Children's books until the mid-nineteenth century had without exception depicted obedience as the most important childhood virtue. Anne S. MacLeod's study of antebellum American juvenile fiction concluded that "no child character was seen to defy authority successfully."[23] There were fictional children who disobeyed, of course, but they were not approved of by their creators. Disobedient children reaping their just deserts abound in early children's fiction: consigned to hellfire, chased by bulls, run over by wagons, or merely left at home when others go on coveted excursions, they are a chastened lot.

The advent of the "good bad boy" in the evolving boys' book marked a radical change in what adults expected of children, or, put another way, in what adults defined as the ideal child—ideal boy-child, that is. Jim Hawkins, Tom Sawyer, and many other rascals disobey adults and get away with it. In fact, their defiance of adult authority constitutes a major part of their charm. Tom's resistance to Aunt Polly's civilizing efforts and his enjoyment of forbidden pleasures are what give him the edge in Aunt Polly's affections over the good boy, Sid. Jim Hawkins's defiance of actual or understood orders of the treasure expedition's adult leaders—going ashore with the mutineers, leaving the stockade, and so on—is what saves all their necks and brings the voyage to a triumphant end.

The reason for this cultural redefinition of the ideal boy is not difficult to deduce. When the man's role will take him into the great world to engage in fierce battles of commerce and empire, pluck and enterprise are the virtues to cultivate in male children, and those are precisely the qualities the boys' book heroes sport in abundance. Obedience was required of the child, but the young man was encouraged to leave that virtue behind him. Thus, we see that the boys' book was every bit as much a tool of socialization as the girls' book—albeit one with more child appeal.

The docile obedience required of adolescent girls in the girls' book stands in marked contrast to the autonomy of the boys' book protagonist. The warning figures of Pandora and Eve seem to shadow many of these stories. To be sure, the appeal of many favorite girls' book heroines rested on their resistance to the confines of the feminine role, but nearly all of them capitulate in the end.[24] In many of these girls' books, the interest derives from the tension between the heroine's drive to activity and autonomy, and the pressure exerted by society to thwart these drives and clip her wings, so to speak. The obedience, self-sacrifice, and docility expected of the young woman in this fiction are the virtues of a dependent. Since until late in the century nearly all women, married or single, were dependent on men, we can see that these books were in fact fulfilling their mission of preparing girls for womanhood (though we can hardly call it adulthood).

We have at bottom, then, not just a divergence of subject matter between boys' books and girls' books, but two forms of literature that were as polar as the ideal man and the ideal woman of the day were. The boys' book, even when entertaining and escapist, was essentially a Bildungsroman, a chronicle of growth to manhood. The approved girls' book depicted a curbing of autonomy in adolescence; while in form purporting to be a Bildungsroman, it is, in Annis Pratt's words, "a genre that pursues the opposite of its generic intent—it provides models for 'growing down' rather than for 'growing up'."[25]

The mass-marketed, syndicate-produced girls' series books that flourished in the late nineteenth and early twentieth centuries—from Elizabeth Champney Williams's Vassar Girls series (1883–1892), which emulated the popular travel adventure books for boys, to that perennial survivor, Nancy Drew—finally provided girls with an escape from domesticity and with active role models. Series titles like The Motor Girls, The Outdoor Girls, The Ranch Girls, The Moving Picture Girls, and The Khaki Girls indicate how far girls' series books had roamed by 1920 from Susan Coolidge's bailiwick. But they were shallow, formulaic stories, for the most part, and Mary Thwaite is right when she judges that "the careful separation of stories into series, which publishers and librarians could complacently label 'Boys' or 'Girls,' had in fact become a minor oppression of young readers in the later nineteenth century."[26]

This careful separation of books by gender did not affect children's reading as simply as the discussion thus far might suggest, however, for children's actual reading behavior could not be controlled as easily as the content of the books themselves.

For one thing, though girls when they reached "that certain age" could be prevented from joining boys' games and lively exploits, it was harder to keep them from accompanying their brothers on vicarious adventures through the reading of boys' books. And girls were avid readers of boys' books from the start. Amy Cruse, in her survey of reading in the Victorian era, mentioned numerous women, notable and unknown, who were brought up on Scott, the forerunner of the boys' book novelists (Mary Ann Evans began reading him at the age of seven!), Marryat and his cohorts.[27] Salmon quoted a female correspondent who confessed a childhood preference for Jules Verne and Ballantyne—along with *Little Women*.[28] Alice Jordan, writing on American children's reading, asserted that "girls read boys' books then [in the 1870s] as they do today [1947], and it was well that they did, for even when such books were poor they were more vigorous as a whole than stories for girls."[29] Laura Richards, accomplished and prolific writer of children's verse and girls' books, claimed that "all she knew of natural history she learned from Mayne Reid, whose dazzling heroes were her delight."[30] G. A. Henty reported that he received numerous letters from girl readers and that he valued them highly, "for where there is a girl in the same family the brothers' books are generally common stock, and are carefully read, appreciated, and judged. The author declares that girls write more intelligently and evince greater judgment in their criticism."[31]

Cruse suggested that the girl reading her brother's books "risked incurring a painful rebuke for her unladylike tastes,"[32] but Salmon's influential article on girls' reading was sympathetic:

> There are few girls who boast brothers who do not insist on reading every work of Ballantyne's or Kingston's or Henty's which may be brought into the house. . . . The explanation is that they can get in boys' books what they cannot get in the majority of their own—a stirring plot and lively movement. . . . Nor is this lik-

ing for heroes rather than heroines to be deprecated. It ought to impart a vigour and breadth to a girl's nature, and to give sisters a sympathetic knowledge of the scenes wherein their brothers live and work.[33]

While it was assumed from the beginning of gender-typed children's books that girls regularly raided their brothers' libraries, the universal opinion was that boys did not and would not read girls' books. This was certainly true of the tamer girls' stories, which were long on submission and short on action—Charlotte Yonge's domestic novels, for instance. As Edith Sichel wrote in 1901: "It is impossible to imagine many men reading Miss Yonge. There is an intemperate tameness about her—at once her charm and her defect—which forbids our associating mankind with her. It would be as if we dreamed of them taking high tea *in perpetuo*."[34] We must suppose that younger male readers would find Yonge even less appealing.

Yet, a few published reminiscences indicate that an occasional boy did cross the gulf from the male side to read a girls' book, and that he enjoyed it. (The confessions are made from the safe distance of adulthood and success.) Alexander Woollcott read *Little Women* and reported it one of the handful of books which retained their appeal in later life.[35] William Lyon Phelps, distinguished professor and critic, read *Little Women* as a boy and confided to his journal that, like many girls, "he thought the book spoiled by not having Jo marry Laurie."[36]

That boys ventured into the territory of girls' reading only with considerable trepidation is clear from their accounts of the particular circumstances. One boy who grew up in the 1870s described his acquaintance with the quintessential "girls' books" of Sophie May:

> It was a shameful thing for one who had recently enacted Deerslayer and the Young Engineer even to look at such books and I averted my eyes [from sets of Sophie May books at a neighbor's house]; but in the evening with home lessons done and time heavy I bribed my sister to go across the street and borrow *Little Prudy's Captain Horace*—the military title taking off something of the curse. And once drawn in I read the whole lot . . . and I fell for them all, the heroines I mean—sedate Susie and patient Prudy and dashing Dotty Dimple—my first love.[37]

In our own day a similar confession was made by the novelist and broadcaster Melvyn Bragg. He became "hooked" on Alcott after having picked up at a seaside bookshop *Jo's Boys* (the title of which might well have caught a young boy off guard). "I read it countless times," he remembered,

> and the pleasure I found in it must have been powerful, for it enabled me to hurdle the terrible barrier presented by *Little Women,* which I sought out at the library on the hunt for anything else by Louisa May Alcott. . . . For *Little Women,* Miss Alcott announced, firmly, on the title page was *A Story for Girls.* Yet I read it. And I think that this is a rare case of Miss Alcott being mistaken. As years went on I discovered that quite a few men had read it as boys—although most of them would qualify the admission by muttering on about sisters or cousins leaving it lying around . . . or the teacher "forcing" them to read it at school.[38]

Well, then, if most girls were devouring boys' books and a few brave boys were reading girls' books, the categorizing of books by gender in an attempt to enforce restrictive gender roles must have been a failure, right? Not necessarily. The crossing of the well-marked lines by child readers, unfortunately, did not render ineffective the messages of the books regarding the cult of manliness, the counsel of feminine subservence.

For one thing, the restrictiveness of the woman's role as prescribed by girls' books was also embodied in the female characters (when there were any) of boys' books. The docility and dependent tearfulness of Becky Thatcher or the selflessness of Tom Sawyer's Cousin Mary communicated cultural expectations as effectively as Katy Carr's reformation (maybe more effectively, since minor characters need not be as complex as successful protagonists). Furthermore, the restrictive fate of females which was spelled out in girls' books must have been sharpened and clarified by contrast with the plucky, cocky heroes of boys' wide-ranging fictional adventures.

The girl reader, no doubt, identified with these enviable heroes as she read, and, theoretically, she could have used them as role models in the dearth of fictional female alternatives to tamed tomboys and saintly sisters. Yet it seems likely that this would have entailed such a strong consciousness of inappropriateness that it would render boys' books little more than escapist fantasy for most girls, not much use in expanding the possibilities of their own lives.

Another ramification of the boys' books-girls' books division is that the phenomenon itself constituted a denigration of the female. The very fact that little onus was attached to girls reading boys' books, while boys reading girls' books was surreptitious and was experienced as somehow shameful, revealed to every child the existence of a hierarchy of value favoring the male. Every trespass onto masculine fictional terrain by girls must have reinforced the awareness of their own inferiority in society's view. As students of the still prevalent practice note, "Girls probably feel some internal pressure to adopt the male-typed choices on which society places such high value. One must assume that girls know the difference between first and second place, and have the same inherent desire for status boys have."[39]

Finally, the numbers of boys reading girls' books most likely has always been small. Salmon rejoiced that reading boys' books might "give sisters a sympathetic knowledge of the scenes wherein their brothers live and work." It appears that few boys over the years have gained a similar sympathetic knowledge of the scenes wherein their *sisters* live and work—a knowledge that fiction could have given them.

In recent years, publishers and librarians have been less likely to segregate books and label them "for boys" and "for girls" than the Victorians were, but the old assumptions about what constitutes appropriate reading for boys and for girls are still with us in the guise of attention paid to children's own reading interests. This would seem to be a step forward, since the many twentieth-century studies of children's reading interests appear to have as their goal ascertaining children's own preferences in reading material rather than using books as instruments to mold children to rigid gender-typed ideals.

And, indeed, an increase in sensitivity to children's reading experiences seems to have sparked the initial studies of children's reading interests in the 1920s. The most substantial study was conducted by George Norvell, an educator who collected data on the subject for over forty years, beginning in the early 1920s. His worthy objective was to promote voluntary reading by young people. To achieve this goal, he reasonably suggested that one needs to consider "(1) the reader's ability and interests and (2) the difficulty and attractiveness of the reading materials."[40]

In his attempt to discover what books students actually do enjoy, Norvell queried some fifty thousand subjects in grades seven through twelve concerning 4,993 selected titles. Students were asked to rate each selection they had read on a three-point scale: very interesting, fairly interesting, or uninteresting. Norvell's study admitted at the outset the questionable reliability of its design: "The plan chosen was to examine the reactions of boys and of girls toward a list of selections, each of which was dominated by a single factor, and to depend upon the minimizing of the potency of other factors through cancellation. Undoubtedly the method has pitfalls, since cancellation may not function as expected" (p. 48). In other words, the researcher may categorize a literary work by one characteristic, assuming that the reader's like or dislike of the work stems from that characteristic, when, in fact, the reader is responding to something quite different. For instance, a student may have rated *The Red Badge of Courage* as very interesting, not because its subject is war (as the researcher might assume) but because he was intrigued by Crane's use of symbol. Another student may have found it interesting only in comparison to other titles on the list and may have indicated a preference for it because it is a short novel.

Norvell's recognition of the method's pitfalls did not restrain him from using his accumulated data to draw sweeping conclusions about the dominance of sex as a determinant of young people's reading choices. "The data of this study indicate that sex is so dominant and ever-present a force in determining young people's reading choices that it must be carefully considered in planning any reading program for the schools" (p. 47). "If adolescents are to be provided with satisfactory materials, the reading interests of boys and of girls must receive separate consideration," and "for reading in common, only materials well liked by both boys and girls should be used" (p. 7). Since Norvell asserted elsewhere that "while boys will not tolerate books primarily about women, girls generally read books about men with satisfaction" (p. 51), this means that his recommendation was that no books about females be assigned or read aloud to mixed classes of girls and boys. It is not surprising that, when they were interviewed by a student of mine, a number of boys said that they had never read a book about a girl in their classes. And neither, of course, had their female classmates.

Yet this study, with all its faults, is one of the more sophisticated ones. Others have relied on forced-choice questionnaires, with questions like "Would you rather read a story about spacemen or one about elves?" One of the problems with this method is that the child has to select one, but might well never choose a book on either subject to read. Or the question might be "Which book do you like better, *Black Beauty* or *Alice in Wonderland?*" The researcher may assume that the child who picks the first prefers animal stories to fantasy, when the child actually enjoys books that make her cry.

Some researchers have described categories of books and asked children which of two types of books they prefer to read. But often the categories are arbitrarily defined. One study concluded that fantasy ranked significantly higher with fourth-grade girls than with their male classmates. Yet fantasy was described on the questionnaire as "a book that is a story of fairies, knights, or imaginary people."[41] This suggests the fairy tale and romance-oriented fantasy, but leaves out many other sorts of literary fantasy. The conclusion is, therefore, misleading.

Samuel Weintraub, whose critique of reading interest studies provides more detail than is possible here, noted that because categories change with each study or are used with different definitions, it has been impossible to synthesize the results of different studies.[42] He concluded:

> In general, the research into children's reading interests has suffered from, among other things, lack of clear definitions and lack of rigor in design, as well as from questionable data-gathering instruments. The instruments appear, for the most part, not to have been scrutinized for reliability or validity except in the most superficial manner. Through the years the techniques that have been developed seem to have become established by repetition rather than by any careful consideration of their merits or shortcomings.[43]

Weak as the foundation they rest on is, the conclusions of these studies have had a powerful influence on the books boys and girls actually read today. Since it is not possible within the compass of this article to explore all the ways in which this influence has operated, I will focus on the striking effect of the "boys won't read about girls" conclusion of reading-interests researchers.

The following passages are taken from teacher education textbooks published in the last ten years:

> If forced to choose between a book appealing primarily to boys and one to girls, choose the boys' book. Girls might identify with and enjoy *Durango Street, Tuned Out,* or *Swiftwater,* but equally good books appealing chiefly to girls just won't fare equally well with boys.[44]

> The other major factor in reading interest [after age] is sex. Although children may be content to read the same books or have them read aloud, somewhere around the fourth grade, it is made clear to boys that they need special materials appealing to them. Unfair or not, after that time boys are not likely to enjoy girls' books, but girls will usually read and enjoy boys' books. Practically, that means the English teacher must choose common reading that will appeal to boys, ignoring *Jane Eyre, Rebecca, Mrs. Mike,* or *Pride and Prejudice.* . . . Getting boys to relate to literature is often a major problem, but it can become insoluble if the literature presented is incorrectly oriented.[45]

> It has been found that boys will not read "girl books," whereas girls will read "boy books." . . . Therefore, the ratio of "boy books" should be about two to one in the classroom library collection.[46]

The assumption has become a truism, one to which most teachers and librarians active today subscribe.

One effect of the resulting male domination of the literary curriculum in the schools was, of course, to assert the second-class status of the females as clearly as the boys' book phenomenon had ever done. The message to publishers of studies like Norvell's was to look for even more stories with male protagonists; they sold better. Scott O'Dell has related how his publisher asked him to change the sex of his protagonist in *Island of the Blue Dolphins,* a children's book based on an actual event, the survival for many years of a young Indian girl abandoned on a small Pacific island.[47] (Fortunately, O'Dell stood firm, and the story of Karana has become perhaps the most popular of all the books ever awarded the American Library Association's Newbery Medal.) Textbooks and early-reader trade books were particularly male dominated in the 1960s, since it had been noted with alarm that Johnny rather than Janey was likely to have trouble learning to read, and thus it seemed particularly important to offer at this level stories that appealed to boys.

The consciousness-raising that was at the heart of the women's movement began to awaken sociologists, educators, and literary critics to the staggering imbalance in the male-female ratio in picture books, textbooks, and others.[48] They objected to this practice as restricting the reading options of both boys and girls and negatively influencing the self-esteem of girls. Their protest fell on sympathetic ears, and because it was backed by the willingness of librarians and parents to purchase more balanced books as they became available, change was rapid. In the past ten years many fine books have been published with female characters who are much more varied in temperament and role. As early as 1976 a study of current trade books for children counted approximately equal numbers of male and female protagonists and an equal distribution of positive attributes between the two sexes.[49]

Girls now have numerous and varied feminine role models in the books published for children. Real progress has been made, as we can see when we compare the range of books about girls available today as compared to the books of even twenty-five years ago. In historical novels, contemporary fiction, biography, and fantasy, engaging, active heroines abound. Fairy tales featuring spry old ladies, female Paul Bunyans, and capable young girls of perilous quests have been resurrected and published to balance the passive princesses and wicked old witches of the most familiar tales.[50]

Yet what good is this wealth if in 1980 a textbook was telling prospective elementary school teachers that "boys will not read 'girl books'"? And however much we rejoice at the expansion of our daughters' literary horizons, we must recognize that the progress does not benefit our sons if most of them are as reluctant to read girls' books (defined as any book with a female protagonist) as boys were a century ago.

Granted, the appeal of certain books about girls has been strong enough to motivate boys to defy the taboo. Examples include O'Dell's *Island of the Blue Dolphins* (1960), mentioned above; Louise Fitzhugh's *Harriet the Spy* (1964), a revolutionary book in its intrepid, eccentric heroine and its funny yet telling satire of adult mores; and *A Wrinkle in Time,* by Madeleine L'Engle (1962), a rare science-fiction novel for preadolescents in which the heroine's problem of being the homely, awkward daughter of a gorgeous, competent mother is entwined with her quest-mission through a hostile universe to rescue her father and save the world from the powers of darkness.

But the phenomenon of large numbers of boys reading these books is an exceptional event, much remarked on in library and publishing circles. It doesn't happen often, and most adults would never think of giving a boy a book about a girl. Parents often ask me to recommend books for family reading aloud. One of my suggestions, Laura Ingalls Wilder's *Little House* series, is greeted with surprise and skepticism by the parents of boys, though I assure them that my son and all his classmates, male and female, were enthralled by the adventures of Laura and Mary when a creative teacher defied expert opinion and chose it to read to her second-grade class. People who work with children can testify to the sad fact that reading a book about a girl is still cause for embarrassment for many young male readers. The student I mentioned earlier, who interviewed boys about their reading, asked one sixth grader: "Can you remember any books about girls that you enjoyed?" He replied, "No [pause], . . . except *A Wrinkle in Time*." Then he quickly added, "But she wasn't really the main character." But Meg *is* the main character, of course; furthermore, the same boy had earlier named *A Wrinkle in Time* as his favorite book.

This makes clear what has been true all along—that the boys' book-girls' book division, while it depreciated the female experience and so extracted a heavy cost in feminine self-esteem, was at the same time more restrictive of boys' options, of their freedom to read (all the exotic voyages and bold explorations notwithstanding), than of girls.' The fact that girls could roam over the entire territory of children's books while most boys felt confined to boys' books didn't matter much when girls' books were for the most part tame, socializing tools geared to perfecting and indoctrinating young ladies, and virtually all the "good books" from a child's point of view were accessible to boys. But now that many girls' books (whether girls' books are defined as family stories and fairy tales or as all books featuring female characters) are enthralling and enriching stories, boys are the losers. The greater pressure on boys to confine themselves to male-typed reading and behavior, though stemming from the higher status of males, is revealed to be at heart a limitation—one obviously related to all the constraints that preserving the tradi-

tional male role impose. We can only speculate about the ramifications of this fact. In a society where many men and women are alienated from members of the other sex, one wonders whether males might be more comfortable with and understanding of women's needs and perspectives if they had imaginatively shared female experience through books, beginning in childhood. At the least, we must deplore the fact that many boys are missing out on one of fiction's greatest gifts, the chance to experience life from a perspective other than the one we were born to—in this case, from the female vantage point.

Patrick Lee and Nancy Gropper, in their article "Sex-Role Culture and Educational Practice," note that because girls experience less pressure than boys to assume same-sex-typed preferences, they tend to be more *bicultural* than boys.[51] (They are referring here to sex-role culture; the term more commonly used is *androgynous*.) They conclude that this biculturalism or androgyny is desirable, and that "boys and girls should be free to approach resources which are currently demarcated along sex-role lines, entirely in accord with individual differences in interests and aptitudes."[52]

If we agree, then an understanding of the subtle influence that restrictive nineteenth-century views on appropriate reading for girls and for boys still exerts on children's reading can help us to identify and challenge its hold.[53] Otherwise, unexamined adult assumptions about divergent reading interests of girls and boys will continue to perpetuate gender-role constraints we thought we had left behind.

NOTES

1. Geoffrey Trease, "The Revolution in Children's Literature," in *The Thorny Paradise: Writers on Writing for Children,* ed. Edward Blishen (Harmondsworth, Middlesex: Kestrel, 1975), p. 14.
2. *A Little Pretty Pocket-Book* (London: John Newbery, 1744; 1767 ed. reprinted, London: Oxford University Press, 1966).
3. Sarah Fielding, *The Governess; Or, Little Female Academy,* 2d ed. (London: Millar, 1758).
4. Mary Thwaite, *From Primer to Pleasure in Reading,* 2d ed. (London: Library Association, 1972), p. 152.
5. Samuel F. Pickering, Jr., *John Locke and Children's Books in Eighteenth-Century England* (Knoxville: University of Tennessee Press, 1981), p. 244.

6. Mary Ann Kilner, *Memoirs of a Peg-Top* (London: John Marshall, 1783; reprinted, New York: Garland, 1976), p. vi.

7. [Elizabeth Rigby], *Quarterly Review* 74 (1844): 21. Excerpted in *Children and Literature,* ed. Virginia Haviland (Glenview, Ill.: Scott, Foresman, 1973), p. 15.

8. William Graham Sumner, "What Our Boys Are Reading," *Scribner's Monthly* 15 (1878): 681–85.

9. Edward G. Salmon, "What Girls Read," *Nineteenth Century* 20 (1886): 515–29.

10. Charles and Mary Anne Lamb, *The Letters of Charles and Mary Anne Lamb,* 3 vols., ed. Edwin W. Marrs, Jr. (Ithaca: Cornell University Press, 1976), 2: 278–79. Lamb responded: "Dear Godwin,—The Giant's vomit was perfectly nauseous, and I am glad that you pointed it out. I have removed the objection." But he declined to make other suggested changes (p. 279).

11. F. J. Harvey Darton, *Children's Books in England: Five Centuries of Social Life,* 3d ed., rev. Brian Alderson (Cambridge: Cambridge University Press, 1958), p. 217.

12. Salmon, "What Girls Read," p. 522. Sarah Doudney and Anne Beale wrote novels for girls which were noted for their piety and pathos. When Lucy Lyttelton's grandmother began reading aloud *Adam Bede,* "the new novel about which the world raves," it was "duly bowdlerized for our young minds," Lucy reported in her diary. She was eighteen at the time. "In most families George Eliot's works were absolutely forbidden to the young," according to Amy Cruse; those of Charlotte Yonge, on the other hand, were "always open to them" (*The Victorians and Their Reading* [Boston: Houghton Mifflin, 1936,], p. 63).

13. Mrs. [Mary Louisa] Molesworth, "Juliana Horatia Ewing," *Contemporary Review* 49 (1886): 675–86; reprinted in *A Peculiar Gift: Nineteenth-Century Writings on Books for Children,* ed. Lance Salway (Harmondsworth, Middlesex: Kestrel, 1976), p. 506.

14. Salmon, "What Girls Read," p. 523.

15. Charles Dickens, *Our Mutual Friend* (Oxford: Oxford University Press, 1952), p. 129.

16. See Walter E. Houghton, *The Victorian Frame of Mind* (New Haven: Yale University Press, 1957), chap. 13; Anne S. MacLeod, *A Moral Tale: Children's Fiction and American Culture, 1820–1860* (Hamden, Conn.: Archon Books, 1975), chap. 1; and Ann Douglas, *The Feminization of American Culture* (New York: Alfred A. Knopf, 1977), chaps. 2 and 3.

17. The doctrine of feminine influence was articulated and embraced in both Britain and the United States, though the social and legal conditions of a frontier society made for interesting complications in America. See Helen Waite Papashvily, *All the Happy Endings* (New York: Harper, 1956), chap. 2; and Elizabeth Segel, "Laura Ingalls Wilder's America: An Unflinching Assessment," *Children's Literature in Education* 8 (1977): 63–70.

18. Salmon, "What Girls Read," p. 526.

19. Gillian Avery, *Childhood's Pattern: A Study of the Heroes and Heroines of Children's Fiction, 1770–1950* (London: Hodder and Stoughton, 1975), p. 166.

20. Papashvily argues persuasively that in popular romances written by women at this time the happy ending is a kind of wish-fulfilling fantasy wherein the woman is recognized as a heroic and noble survivor and her tyrannical or unfaithful husband is reduced to penitent beggary (*All the Happy Endings,* chap. 8). Though adolescent girls no doubt read some of these books, I do not find this compensating fantasy worked out in the books written by women specifically for girls.

21. Susan Coolidge [Sarah Chauncey Woolsey, pseud.], *What Katy Did* (London: J. M. Dent, 1968). Subsequent references are cited parenthetically in the text.

22. Robert Louis Stevenson, *Treasure Island* (London: Cassell, 1883).

23. MacLeod, *Moral Tale,* p. 10.

24. Whether Jo March, in marrying Professor Bhaer and becoming a sort of Earth-mother, has capitulated is still being debated. My own opinion is that because the final image of Jo is of a strong and successful woman (and because readers, aware of the autobiographical element, consider that she grew up to be a famous writer), Alcott transcended the formula to a great extent, and it is for this reason that the book retained its popularity longer than other girls' books.

25. Annis Pratt, *Archetypal Patterns in Women's Fiction* (Bloomington: Indiana University Press, 1981), p. 14. Pratt notes that in the women's novels about adolescence, "at the same time that the authors . . . suggest psychic dwarfing as the inevitable destiny of young women in British and American society, they manage to introduce a considerable degree of protest into the genre through a vivid depiction of the feelings of its victims" (p. 35). Most girls' books of the nineteenth century, as we might expect, contain few traces of this protest. Women might hint at rebellious feelings to adult women readers, but the sacred duty of preparing girls to accept their assigned role apparently led them to suppress their reservations when writing for girls. The passage describes very well, however, several twentieth-century chronicles of girls' coming of age: Ruth Sawyer's *Roller Skates,* Carol Ryrie Brink's *Caddie Woodlawn,* and Laura Ingalls Wilder's *Little House* books.

26. Thwaite, *From Primer to Pleasure in Reading,* p. 171.

27. Cruse, *Victorians and Their Reading,* pp. 294–97.

28. Salmon, "What Girls Read," p. 524.
29. Alice M. Jordan, *From Rollo to Tom Sawyer and Other Papers* (Boston: Horn Book, 1948), p. 35.
30. Ibid., pp. 48–49.
31. G. Manville Fenn, *George Alfred Henry: The Story of an Active Life* (London: Blackie, 1907); reprinted in Salway, *Peculiar Gift,* p. 430.
32. Cruse, *Victorians and Their Reading,* p. 297.
33. Salmon, "What Girls Read," p. 524.
34. Edith Sichel, "Charlotte Yonge as a Chronicler," *Monthly Review* 3 (1901): 88–97; reprinted in Salway, *Peculiar Gift,* p. 488.
35. Ruth Hill Viguers, "Laura E. Richards, Joyous Companion," in *The Hewins Lectures 1947–1962,* ed. Siri Andrews (Boston: Horn Book, 1963), p. 188.
36. Jordan, *From Rollo to Tom Sawyer,* p. 38.
37. Ibid., p. 37.
38. Melvyn Bragg, "Little Women," *Children's Literature in Education* 9 (1978): 95.
39. Patrick C. Lee and Nancy B. Gropper, "Sex-Role Culture and Educational Practice," *Harvard Educational Review* 44 (1974): 398.
40. George Norvell, *The Reading Interests of Young People,* rev. ed. (Lansing: Michigan State University Press, 1973), p. 3. Subsequent references are cited parenthetically in the text.
41. Lian-Hwang Chiu, "Reading Preferences of Fourth-Grade Children Related to Sex and Reading Ability," *Journal of Educational Research* 66 (1973): 371.
42. Samuel Weintraub, "Two Significant Trends in Reading Research," in *Reading and Writing Instruction in the United States: Historical Trends,* ed. H. Alan Robinson (Urbana: IRA-ERIC, 1977), p. 61.
43. Ibid., p. 63.
44. Steven Dunning and Alan B. Howes, *Literature for Adolescents* (Glenview, Ill.: Scott, Foresman, 1975), p. 198.
45. Dwight L. Burton, et al., *Teaching English Today* (Boston: Houghton Mifflin, 1975), p. 173.
46. Dorothy Rubin, *Teaching Elementary Language Arts,* rev. ed. (New York: Holt, Rinehart, and Winston, 1980), p. 183.
47. Alleen Pace Nilsen, "Women in Children's Literature," *College English* 32 (1971), p. 918.
48. Elizabeth Fisher, "The Second Sex, Junior Division," *New York Times Book Review* (May 21, 1970), pp. 6–7; Nilsen, "Women in Children's Literature," pp. 918–26; Feminists on Children's Literature, "A Feminist Look at Children's Books," *School Library Journal* 17 (1971), pp. 19–24; and Lenore J. Weitzman et al., "Sex-Role Socialization in Picture Books for Preschool Children," *American Journal of Sociology* 77 (1972), pp. 1125–50.
49. Ruth M. Noyce, "Equality of the Sexes in New Children's Fiction," Report prepared at the University of Kansas, 1976. Educational Resources Information Center, ED no. 137–802.
50. Rosemary Minard, *Womenfolk and Fairy Tales* (Boston: Houghton Mifflin, 1975); Ethel Johnston Phelps, *Tatterhood and Other Tales* (Old Westbury, N.Y.: Feminist Press, 1978) and *The Maid of the North: Feminist Folk Tales from around the World* (New York: Holt, Rinehart and Winston, 1981); and Alison Lurie, *Clever Gretchen and Other Forgotten Folktales* (New York: Crowell, 1980).
51. Lee and Gropper, "Sex-Role Culture and Educational Practice," p. 398.
52. Ibid., p. 404.
53. See my article "Choices for Girls, for Boys: Keeping Options Open," *School Library Journal* 28 (1982), pp. 105–7, for practical suggestions for breaking down the gender-determined patterns of children's reading.

Louise Bernikow (b. 1940)

In this autobiographical essay, Louise Bernikow explores the meanings of the story of Cinderella to her as a girl and as a grown woman. She vividly re-creates the emotions and perceptions she experienced while watching Disney's *Cinderella* as a girl and traces their reverberations through her readings of other versions of the Cinderella story, including the more brutal and graphic version told by the Grimm Brothers, the ancient Chinese story that includes footbinding, and the French version by Charles Perrault that Disney adapted for the screen. Bernikow has a keen eye for social detail and psychological nuance, and she discovers different lessons for readers and viewers of the various versions of the story and, through the process of reflecting on the meanings of this phenomenally popular fairy tale, an even more important set of lessons for herself as a contemporary woman.

Cinderella

Saturday Afternoon at the Movies

No, Cinderella, said the stepmother,
you have no clothes and cannot dance.
That's the way with stepmothers.
Anne Sexton, "Cinderella"

Turn and peep, turn and peep,
No blood is in the shoe,
The shoe is not too small for her,
The true bride rides with you.
Grimm's Cinderella

I begin with a memory of movies and mother, a dark theatre and a Saturday afternoon. In a miasma of Walt Disney images, Bambi burning and Snow White asleep, the most memorable is "Cinderella." I carry her story with me for the rest of my life. It is a story about women alone together and they are each other's enemies. This is more powerful as a lesson than the ball, the Prince or the glass slipper. The echoes of "Cinderella" in other fairy tales, in myth and literature, are about how awful women are to each other. The girl onscreen, as I squirm in my seat, needs to be saved. A man will come and save her. Some day my Prince will come. Women will not save her; they will thwart her. There is a magical fairy godmother who does help her, but this, for me, has no relation to life, for the fairy is not real and the bad women are. The magical good fairy is a saccharine fluff.

There are two worlds in the Cinderella cartoon, one of women, one of men. The women are close by and hostile, the men distant and glittering. Stepsisters and stepmother are three in one, a female battalion allied against Cinderella. The daughters are just like their mother. All women are alike. Lines of connection, en-

ergy fields, attach sisters to mother, leaving Cinderella in exile from the female community at home.

Father is far off. On film, neither he nor the Prince has much character. Father is her only tie, her actual blood tie, but the connection does her no good. Daddy is King in this world; I cannot keep Daddy and King apart in my memory. My own father was as far off, as full of authority, as surrounded by heraldry, the trumpets of fantasy, to me, to my mother. King Daddy.

The Prince is rich and handsome. Rich matters more than handsome. The girl among the cinders, dressed in rags, will escape—I am on her side, I want her to escape, get away from the cinders and the awful women—because the Prince will lift her out. The world of the Prince is the world of the ball, music, fine clothes and good feeling. Were everything to be right at home, were the women to be good to one another and have fun together, it would not be sufficient. The object is the ball, the Prince, the big house, the servants. Class mobility is at stake. Aspiration is being titillated.

To win the Prince, to be saved, requires being pretty. All the women care about this. Being pretty is the ticket and because Cinderella is pretty, the stepmother and stepsisters want to keep her out of the running. There is no other enterprise. Cinderella does not turn up her nose and hide in a corner reading a book. Being pretty, getting to the ball, winning the Prince is the common ground among the women. What we have in common is what keeps us apart.

Cinderella must be lonely. Why, I wonder, doesn't she have a friend? Why doesn't she go to school? Why doesn't her father tell the awful women to stop? A hurt and lonely girl, with only a prince to provide another kind of feeling. Why doesn't she run away? Why can't the situation be changed? It is as though the house they live in is the only world, there is no other landscape. Women are always in the house, being awful to each other.

Magic. Cinderella has a fairy godmother who likes her and wants her to be happy. She gives the girl beautiful clothes. She doesn't have to instruct Cinderella or give her advice about how to waltz or how to lift her skirt or even give her directions to the palace. Only the clothes and the accoutrements—and a prohibition about coming home at midnight. A powerful woman who wants Cinderella to be pretty and successful in the social world. I know, at whatever age it is that I watch this story unfold, that the mother beside me is not the woman on the screen. Her feelings on such matters are, at best, mixed up. She is not so powerful.

I am stirred and confused by the contrast between bad and good women and the way it all seems to revolve around the issue of being pretty. Some women are hostile and thwarting, others enabling and powerful. The stepmother hates Cinderella's prettiness; the fairy godmother adorns it. I look sideways at my mother, trying to decide which kind of woman she is, where she stands on the business of pretty. Often, she braids my hair and settles me into polka dot, parades me before my beaming father. It is good to be pretty. Yet, onscreen, it is bad to be pretty—Cinderella is punished for it. In the enterprise of pretty, other women are your allies and your enemies. They are not disinterested. The heat around the issue of pretty, the urgency and intensity of it, is located among the women, not the men, at whom it is supposedly aimed. Luckily, we move on to the ball and the lost slipper.

This is one of the oldest and most often-told stories, varying significantly from one version to another, one country to another, one period to another. What appears on movie theatre screens or television on Saturday afternoons comes from as far away as China, as long ago as four hundred years. Each teller, each culture along the way, retained some archetypal patterns and transformed others, emphasized some parts of the story, eradicated others. Disney took his version of Cinderella from one written down by a Frenchman named Perrault in the seventeenth century. Perrault's is a "civilized" version, cleaned up, dressed up and given several pointed "lessons" on top of the original material.

Many of the details about fashionability that we now associate with the story come from Perrault. His has the atmosphere of Coco Chanel's dressing rooms, is modern and glamorous. He concocted a froufrou, aimed at an aristocratic audience and airily decorated with things French. He named one of the sisters Charlotte and set the action in a world of full-length looking glasses and inlaid floors. He invented a couturière called Mademoiselle de Poche to create costumes for the ball, linens and ruffles, velvet suits and headdresses. Disney dropped the French touches.

Perrault's story is set in a world of women with their eyes on men. Even before the King's ball is announced, the stepmother and stepsisters are preoccupied with how they look. They are obsessed with their mirrors, straining to see what men would see. Once the ball is on the horizon, they starve themselves for days so that their shapes shall be, when laced into Mademoiselle de Poche's creations, as extremely slender as those in our own fashion magazines. The ball—and the prospects it implies—intensifies the hostility toward Cinderella. They have been envious. Now, they must keep the pretty girl out of competition. Most of the action of Perrault's story is taken up with the business of the ball.

Cinderella is a sniveling, self-pitying girl. Forbidden to go to the ball, she does not object but, instead, dutifully helps her stepsisters adorn themselves. She has no will, initiates no action. Then, magically, the fairy godmother appears. She comes from nowhere, summoned, we suppose, by Cinderella's wishes. Unlike the fairy godmother in other versions of the story, Perrault's and Disney's character has no connection to anything real, has no meaning, except to enable Cinderella to overcome the opposition of the women in her home, wear beautiful clothes and get to the ball. Cinderella stammers, unable to say what she wants—for she is passive, suffering and good, which comes across as relatively unconscious. The fairy divines Cinderella's desire and equips her with pumpkin/coach, mice/horses, rats/coachmen, lizards/footmen, clothes and dancing shoes. She adds the famous prohibition that Cinderella return by midnight or everything will be undone.

These details of the fairy godmother's magic—the pumpkin, image of All Hallows' Eve; midnight, the witching hour; mice, rats and lizards originated with Perrault. They are specific reminders of an actual and ancient female magic, witchcraft. Since Perrault wrote his story in the seventeenth century, it is not surprising to find echoes of this magic, which was enormously real to Perrault's audience.

Thousands had been burned at the stake for practicing witchcraft, most of them women. A witch was a woman with enormous power, a woman who might change the natural world. She was "uncivilized" and in opposition to the world of the King, the court, polite society. She had to be controlled. Perrault's story attempts to control the elements of witchcraft just as various kings' governments had, in the not too recent past, controlled what they believed to be an epidemic of witchcraft. Perrault controls female power by trivializing it. The witchcraft in this story is innocent, ridiculous, silly and playful. It is meant to entertain children.

The prohibition that Cinderella return by midnight is also related to witchcraft. She must avoid the witching hour, with its overtones of sexual abandon. The fairy godmother acts in this capacity in a way that is familiar to mothers and daughters—she controls the girl, warns her against darkness, uses her authority to enforce restraint, prevent excess, particularly excess associated with the ball, the world of men, sexuality.

Cinderella's dancing shoes are glass slippers. Perrault mistranslated the fur slipper in the version that came to him, substituting *verre* for *vire* and coming up glass. No pedant came along to correct the mistake, for the glass slipper is immensely appropriate to the story in its modern form and the values it embodies. Call it dainty or fragile, the slipper is quintessentially the stereotype of femininity. I wonder how Cinderella danced in it.

The rags-to-riches moment holds people's imaginations long after the details of the story have disappeared. It appeals to everyone's desire for magic, for change that comes without effort, for speedy escape from a bad place—bad feelings. We all want to go to the ball, want life to be full of good feeling and feeling good. But Cinderella's transformation points to a particular and limited kind of good feeling—from ugly to beautiful, raggedy to glamorous. The object of her transformation is not actually pleasure (she does not

then walk around her house feeling better) but transportation to the ball with all the right equipment for captivating the Prince.

Transformed, Cinderella goes to the ball, which is the larger world, the kingdom ruled by kings and fathers. The stepmother has no power in that world and does not even appear. This part of the story focuses on men, who are good to Cinderella as forcefully as women have been bad to her. Perrault embellishes Cinderella's appearance in a way that would have been congenial to the French court. In fact, she seems to have gone to the French court. The story is suffused with perfume and "fashionability." The Prince is taken with Cinderella and gives her some candy—"citrons and oranges," according to the text. How French. She, forever good, shares the candy with her stepsisters, who do not, of course, know who she is.

Cinderella has a wonderful time. As readers, hearers, watchers, we have a wonderful time along with her. More than the music and the dancing, the aura of sensual pleasure, everyone's good time comes from the idea that Cinderella is a "knockout." This is exciting. Perrault's word for what happens is that the people are *étonnés,* which means stunned. Cinderella is a showstopper, so "dazzling" that "the King himself, old as he was, could not help watching her." He remarks on this to his Queen, whose reactions we are not told. Being "stunning" is being powerful. This is the way women have impact, the story tells us. This is female power in the world outside the home, in contrast to her former powerlessness, which was within the home, which was another country. This tells me why women spend so much time trying to turn themselves into knockouts—because, in "Cinderella" and in other stories, it *works*.

Presumably, Cinderella's giddiness over her own triumph at the ball makes her forget her godmother's command and almost miss her midnight deadline. Lest we lose the idea that all men adore Cinderella, Perrault adds a courtier at the end of the story, as the search for the missing Cinderella is carried out, and has him, too, say how attractive Cinderella is. She fulfills, then, the masculine idea of what is beautiful in a woman. She is the woman men want women to be.

Cinderella flees at midnight and loses her shoe. Perrault plays this part down, but Disney has a visual festival with the glinting glass slipper on the staircase and the trumpet-accompanied quest to find its owner. Perrault's Prince sends a messenger to find the shoe's owner, which puts the action at some distance, but Disney gives us a prince in all his splendor.

Cinderella is a heroine and in the world of fairy tales what the heroine wins is marriage to the Prince. Like any classic romance, wafted by perfume and fancy clothes, the young girl is lifted from a lowly powerless situation (from loneliness and depression, too) by a powerful man. He has no character, not even a handsome face, but simply represents the things that princes represent, the power of the kingdom.

Opposition to achieving this triumph comes from the women in the house; help comes from daydream and fantasy. The only proper activity for women to engage in is primping. What is expected of them is that they wait "in the right way" to be discovered. Cinderella obeys the rules. Her reward is to be claimed by the Prince. The lesson of Cinderella in these versions is that a girl who knows and keeps her place will be rewarded with male favor.

Like a saint, she shows neither anger nor resentment toward the women who treated her so badly. In fact, she takes her stepsisters along to the castle, where she marries each off to a nobleman. Now everyone will be happy. Now there will be no conflict, no envy, no degradation. If each woman has a prince or nobleman, she will be content and the soft humming of satisfaction will fill the air. Women otherwise cannot be alone together.

This is the sort of story that poisoned Madame Bovary's imagination. In Flaubert's novel, a woman married to a country doctor, with aspirations for a larger life, goes to a ball where a princely character pays her some attention. The ball and the Prince, seen by Emma Bovary as possibilities for changing everyday life, haunted her uneasy sleep. The ball was over. Wait as she might for its return, for a second invitation, all she got was a false prince—a lover who did not lift her from the ordinariness of her life—and then despair.

The romance depends on aspiration. The Prince must be able to give the heroine something she cannot get for herself or from other women. He must represent a valuable and scarce commodity, for the women must believe there is only one, not enough to go around, and must set themselves to keeping other women from getting it. In "Cinderella," like other fairy tales and other romances, the world of the Prince represents both actual and psychological riches.

Perrault's Cinderella is the daughter of a gentleman, turned into a peasant within the household. She has been declassed by female interlopers, reduced to the status of servant, for she belongs to her father's class only precariously. One of the ways women exercise their power, the story tells us, is by degrading other women. Cinderella will be saved from her female-inflicted degradation first by another female, the fairy godmother, who puts her on the road to her ultimate salvation. At the end of the story, she is restored to her class position, or, better, raised to an even higher position by the Prince.

Her fall from class is represented not only by her tattered clothes, but by the work she is forced to do. She is the household "drudge" and housework is the image of her degradation. Her work has no value in the story; it is the invisible, repetitious labor that keeps things going and makes it possible for the sisters and stepmother to devote themselves to *their* work, which is indolence on the one hand and trying to be beautiful for men on the other. Historically, indolence has been revered as the mark of a lady. What is "feminine" and "ladylike" is far removed from the world of work. Or the world of self-satisfying work. A man prides himself on having a wife who does not work; it increases his value in the eyes of other men; it means he provides well; it enforces conventional bourgeois "masculinity." A lady has long fingernails; neither the typewriter nor the kitchen floor has cracked them. She has porcelain skin; neither the rough outdoors nor perspiration has cracked that. Out of the same set of values comes the famous glass slipper.

The stepmother's class position is as precarious as Cinderella's is. The story does not tell, but we can imagine that whether she was married before to a poorer man or one equally a gentleman, her status and security are now tied to the man she has married and the ones she can arrange for her daughters. History, experience, and literature are full of landless property-less women trying to secure marriage to stand as a bulwark against poverty, displacement and exile, both actual and psychological. The actual situation bears emphasis. The economic reality behind the fairy tale and the competition among the women for the favor of the Prince is a world in which women have no financial lives of their own. They cannot own businesses or inherit property. The kingdom is not theirs. In order to survive, a woman must have a husband. It is in the interests of her daughters' future—and her own—that the stepmother works to prevent competition from Cinderella. She is not evil. Within the confines of her world and the value systems of that world, she is quite nice to her own daughters, only cruel to Cinderella.

Still, the stepmother is an archetypal figure in fairy tales, always a thwarter, often a destroyer of children. Psychologists, and Bruno Bettelheim in particular, have a psychological explanation for this. The "bad" stepmother, Bettelheim points out, usually coexists with the "good" mother, representing two aspects of a real mother as experienced by a child. The stepmother is shaped by the child's unacceptable anger against her own mother. But there are real facts of life at work in these stepmother stories, too, especially as they describe what can happen among women at home. To a man's second wife, the daughter of the first marriage is a constant reminder of the first wife. The second wife is continually confronted with that memory and with the understanding that wives are replaceable, as they frequently and actually *were* in a world where women died young in childbirth, and men remarried, moved on.

A woman marries a man who has a daughter and comes to his household, where the daughter's strongest connection is to her father; the stepmother's strongest connection is to the husband. The Eternal Triangle appears, husband/father at the center, mediating the relationship, stepmother and daughter as antagonists, competing for the husband/father's attention and whatever he may represent. Anxious, each in her own way and equally displaced, they face each other with enmity. The masculine imagination takes prideful pleasure in the story, placing, as it does, husband/father at center stage, making him King, arbiter of a world of women.

In the nineteenth century the Grimm brothers recorded a version of "Cinderella" that was, in fact, a very old folktale, full of the "barbaric" elements that character-

ized such tales. It is a more frightening story with a very different emphasis. The lesson in this version is not that a girl who knows and keeps her place will be rewarded with male favor. Instead, the actual and original and far more interesting conflict of the story stands at the center: a conflict between two female forces, one represented by the stepmother, the other by the fairy godmother, who, in this and other versions, is an incarnation of Cinderella's real mother. The connection between mother and daughter was buried by Perrault, by Disney. This connection balances the idea that women are always each other's enemies. It provides a glimpse of something else.

As told by the brothers Grimm, the tale is closer to folk sources, denser with ritual and symbolic action, far from the perfumed courts of the French King. This version retains archetypal elements obliterated by the "civilizing" hand of Perrault. It does not show the mind of a censor who deems certain things "unfit" for children and is, therefore, like primitive tales, violent, bestial and grotesque.

The tale is divided, classically, into a brief prologue, three parts of action and an epilogue. Cinderella's real mother is present in the prologue—she is shown dying, telling her daughter to be good—and present throughout the story, so that the magical force that transforms Cinderella belongs less to the world of make-believe and more to the psychologically and spiritually actual. The first "act" shows life among the women at home—Cinderella, stepmother, stepsisters together and the father far off. In fact, father leaves on a journey. The second "act" is about the ball, here called a "festival." The third is the climax, the "test" of the shoe and the moment of recognition. The epilogue tells how the stepsisters get their retribution. It is very unlike Perrault's resolved, conciliatory finale.

Throughout the Grimm version, Cinderella has a counter-life. She has one kind of existence indoors, dominated and degraded by her stepmother, another kind outdoors, beside her mother's grave. There she is active, plants a tree, nourishes it with her tears and encounters a white bird, which flies out of the tree, representing her mother's spirit and changing her life. The two mothers take on another kind of meaning. The relationship of Cinderella's original mother to the girl is enhancing. The second mother, present because of the father's actions and therefore tied to him, dramatically, is the woman who degrades the girl.

The presence of the first mother changes the story and suggests other ways of reading it. Not only do we have a good and bad mother, but two different ways of seeing connections between women, particularly between mothers and daughters. The first mother—the "real" one or the "good" one—embodies matriarchal values. She cherishes her daughter. She values the feminine. She is allied with the natural world, either as Nature's representative or as a force in sympathy with nature. These are elements of the myth of Demeter, who searched for her daughter, Persephone, also called Kore. Demeter caused the grain to cease growing in sympathy with her grief and her loss. The power of the matriarchal mother would allow her to perform the kind of "magic" that more conventional versions of "Cinderella" show the fairy godmother performing. She can rearrange the world. The patriarchal mother or the mother in a patriarchal world is herself degraded, robbed of her power. Like the stepmother in this story, her energies are directed to patriarchal institutions, to becoming skillful at manipulating within them (the court, the ball, the festival or the world of fashion) and the power she exerts can only be over other women.

Cinderella is not passive. She acts and her action is ritual action. She plants the twig on her mother's grave. Nourished by her tears of lamentation, it grows into a tree out of which comes the white bird that is her mother's spirit. Her tears are not only cathartic, but productive. Unlike the sniveling of Perrault's Cinderella, the Grimm story shows Cinderella engaged in meaningful action—profound mourning leading to regeneration. Three times a day, the story says, Cinderella goes to her mother's grave. Three times, she approaches the tree and is given the means with which to go to the ball and three times, in the denouement, the slipper is tried on a foot, once on each stepsister, then on Cinderella. Only on the third try is the "problem" resolved and the "quest" fulfilled.

In language and imagery, as well as action, the story evokes ancient sources. Cinderella is assigned the task of picking lentils from the cinders of the hearth. This separation of the grain connects her again to the myth of Demeter, emphasizing the mother-daughter relation. Cinderella stands for all the daughters; in terms of the Demeter myth, she is the "Kore," the maiden or virgin. The white bird is a conventional representation of the Spirit, in this case, her mother's spirit. The action is set around the hearth, with all its symbolic resonance.

Throughout its history, "Cinderella" has been associated with the hearth. The ash girl is not only dirtied by the hearth, but, far more profoundly, derives her identity from it. The hearth was the center of homelife and, as such, it, too, represents Cinderella's mother and, beyond her, the matriarchal principle. By staying close to the hearth, Cinderella enacts her attachment to her mother and her ritual mourning for her death. The hearth is the antithesis of the stepmother's world, the world of women with their eyes on men. Far from being a symbol of degradation, the hearth is, or would have been in its original meaning in the story, a place of honor.

The matriarchal hearth reappears often in literature and has particular meaning for girls and women. The journey of Odysseus may have been to see the smoke in his own chimney again, but it was Penelope's task to keep the smoke going, to tend the hearth. The world of *Little Women* is a world centered around the hearth; the extent to which the patriarchal world intrudes on it, pulls women away from it is the drama of that novel. The tension between staying and leaving the hearth is one way of seeing the tension in women's lives.

Two women are alone in a room. One is content to sit near the hearth, stirring the evening's meal. Perhaps she is not really content, only appears so. It is her assigned task to stir the evening's meal. The second woman is restless. She wants to do something else, go elsewhere, take up a bow and prowl the woods, ride a horse. What will happen depends on how closely each woman feels compelled to translate her own preferences into proscription to say *all* women should stay near the hearth, or *all* women should reject the hearth. Do these women grant or withhold approval for differences? Will one chain the other to the hearth?

The honor of the hearth is derived from classical myth where the goddess Hestia, refusing the courtship of Poseidon and Apollo, chose to remain a virgin. Zeus took this to mean that Hestia preserved peace on Olympus and rewarded the goddess by placing her at the center of the house, where, sitting, she received offerings. "Hestia" means "hearth." The Romans called Hestia Vesta and her altar was tended, in religious ceremony, by Vestal Virgins. Cinderella is guardian of the hearth; she is a Vestal Virgin.

"Virginity" in the ancient world meant belonging to oneself. Ovid said that a virgin "neither gives nor takes seeds, and she loves companions in her virginity." From a female point of view, this "virginity" is valuable because it points to a woman's primary relation being with herself, as opposed to lover, husband or children.

The value accorded female virginity in most cultures does not stem from so benevolent a source, nor is its intention pure nor its presence in our lives so helpful. The Christian cult of the Virgin gives us Virgin as mother in spite of Ovid; the Virgin Mary gives seeds anyway and does not love female companions in her virginity, surrounded, as she is, by father and son. Virginity is a good thing for girls in Western culture for other reasons, having little to do with a woman's self-development and much to do with the patriarchal structure of the world. It has always been economically and politically important for men to know that they are the fathers of their children. The passing on of property and title depended upon paternity. How was a man to know? Once the connection between copulation and issue was established, it became an urgent matter of state to ensure that the seed in the woman's womb was her husband's. Virginity meant some naive kind of assurance. If you "get" a woman for your wife who is virgin and enforce chastity in your married life, you, the patriarch, might have a chance at keeping social order, developing laws of inheritance and imagining that you have got some aspect of human life and history under control.

So Cinderella dwells beside the hearth in the world her stepmother rules. This part of her life appears to be an empty shell. Her stepmother's house is where her body lives, but not her soul, her spirit or her consciousness, all of which thrive in another place, beside her mother's grave, in the world of the tree and the spirit/bird. Cinderella's transformation, in this version, comes because of her own action. She addresses this other part of her life, asks the tree to provide for her. From her mother's spirit, then, she gets what she needs to journey into the outer world. The tree delivers the ability to cope; the clothing needed to make her way. This is a serious transformation, not the simple silliness of being fashionably garbed. Three times, Cinderella asks. Three times, she is transformed and goes to the ball. Each step in her transformation is an echo of another ancient magic— she is given silk and silver, then gold, a progression that is the basis of the art of alchemy, where base metals were transmuted into higher ones. The source of this magic, the spirit of Cinderella's mother, is as powerful as Merlin the Magician was.

At the ball, Cinderella is taken up by the Prince, who says "This is my partner," much the way the Song of Solomon says "this is my lover and my friend." Each time, Cinderella decides to leave before nightfall. She *decides* to leave; no fairy godmother controls her. And nightfall, not midnight. She wants to avoid whatever is constellated by festivity, dancing, men and darkness.

Since we know that Cinderella is a virgin, it is clearly fear of a male sexual advance that causes her to leave. There are many versions of the story earlier than this one in which Cinderella's primary antagonist is male. In some parts of Europe, the story is known as "Brother and Sister" and she flees her home because she refuses her brother's sexual proposals. In others, the daughter's antagonist is her father and his sexual desire for her.

In conformity with conventional psychoanalytic theory, the tension that causes her to flee belongs to the daughter. What is represented in the story, for an orthodox Freudian interpreter like Bruno Bettelheim, is the daughter's desire for her father. Freud, of course, in one of his most familiar interpretations—cited by Bettelheim at exactly this point in his discussion—did the same thing. The good doctor mused on his female patients' report of rape by their fathers and decided that what they were really telling him, these troubled and repressed women, were their most unconscious fantasies.

Not one to discount the unconscious, nor fantasy nor Oedipal craving, I am still troubled by the avoidance of certain facts of life in the thinking of both good doctors and troubled in a way that relates to Cinderella. In the actual world, now, in Freud's time, and before that, there is a great deal of aggression on the part of men toward little girls. Freud's patients might well have been reporting the emotional content of something that happened and happened frequently—not rape, but sexual aggression. I remember the pinches and pats of my father, grandfather and other male relatives, gestures never bestowed in the same way on my brother. Given the sexually proprietary nature of the way men touch women and the terrifying modern statistics of incest rape among fathers and daughters, the reality of that male sexual aggression does not seem farfetched.

Suppose that the original Cinderella stories in which the antagonist is male and the antagonism sexual actually reflect something of how it was in the world out of which the stories came. Why, then, would female hostility replace male? Why would Cinderella's antagonists become stepmother and stepsisters rather than father and brother? It must have to do with what is congenial to the mind that tells the story. This is not a scientific matter—transformations do not proceed in a linear fashion; there is no single moment in time when it occurs, but simply a pattern and a possibility. The intensity of female hostility toward women might, in the hands of male creator, mask male hostility. It is certainly more congenial to a masculine world view.

The presence of earlier masculine antagonists and the incest theme go a long way toward illuminating one of the more bizarre details in the Grimm story. The father, virtually absent from Perrault, appears in this tale just once before Cinderella goes to the ball. Then he leaves on a trip, asking the girls left at home what they would like him to bring them. The stepsisters ask for pearls and Cinderella requests the twig of the first tree that touches his hat on his return journey. The twig becomes the tree on her mother's grave. This is a helpful gesture on the father's part, "fertilizing" Cinderella's connection to her mother. Cinderella goes to the ball three times and decides each time to leave. The Prince follows, but she disappears, first into a dovecote or pigeon house, the second time into a pear tree. Her father appears, asks for an ax, and chops down the pigeon house, then the pear tree. Each time, Cinderella

escapes. Such violent phallic behavior is not peculiar in terms of the story's history. The echo of earlier Oedipal stories points toward the father's action as a symbolic representation of rape.

The third time Cinderella escapes, the Prince has laid a trap—cobbler's pitch on the staircase—and he retains her shoe. So we come back to the shoe, the best-known image in the story.

The motif of Cinderella's shoe appears first at the moment of her degradation. Cinderella is forced to wear wooden clogs, which are peasant shoes, sturdy, unyielding, meant to be labored in. If the foot on the ground is our relation to the earth, the wooden clog fixes that relation, keeps it rigid. When Cinderella asks her stepmother for permission to attend the feast, she is told that she has no clothes and cannot dance—she is a girl of wooden clogs. The stepmother seeks to tie her down, her mother seeks to free her. Her mother's spirit "transforms" Cinderella and sets her free: silk and satin slippers replace the clogs, then golden slippers.

I am writing an essay about Cinderella, spending mornings at the typewriter, afternoons in libraries, interpreting information on index cards of various colors and sheets of yellow paper. I discover something bizarre woven in the story as we now know it: that the story took root in ancient China. The remnants of that culture, especially of the ancient practice of footbinding, are in the story, in the value of the small foot, in the use of the shoe to represent the potential bride. I see, then, the historical truth behind the terrible moment at the end of "Cinderella."

The Prince brings the slipper to the house of Cinderella's father. First one stepsister, then the other attempts to slip her foot into it, but each foot is too large. The first stepsister's toe is too large. The stepmother hands her daughter a knife and says, "Cut off the toe. When you are Queen you won't have to walk anymore." The second stepsister's heel is too large and her mother repeats the gesture and the advice.

Mutilation. Blood in the shoe, blood on the knife, blood on the floor and unbearable pain, borne, covered, masked by the smile. It is too familiar, frightening in its familiarity. The mother tells the daughter to mutilate herself in the interests of winning the Prince. She will not have to walk. Again, indolence enshrined. As mothers, in fact, did in China until the twentieth century—among the upper classes as unquestioned custom and among peasants as great sacrifice and gamble.

It began when the girl was between five and seven years old. The bandages were so tight, the girl might scream. Her mother pulled them tighter and might have tried to soothe her. Tighter. At night, in agony, the girl loosens them. She is punished, her hands tied to a post to prevent unlacing. The bones crack. The pain is constant. Tighter. She cannot walk. Tighter. By her adolescence, the girl has learned to bind her feet herself and the pain has lessened. She has, as a reward, special shoes, embroidered and decorated, for her tiny feet.

I translate the actual foot-binding, the ritual interaction of mother and daughter, to metaphor. A black mother straightens her daughter's hair with a hot iron, singeing the scalp, pulling and tugging. The daughter screams. My mother buys me a girdle when I am fifteen years old because she doesn't like the jiggle. She slaps my face when I begin to menstruate, telling me later that it is an ancient Russian custom and she does not know its origin. I sleep with buttons taped to my cheeks to make dimples and with hard metallic curlers in my hair. Tighter I hold myself tighter, as my mother has taught me to do.

Is the impulse to cripple a girl peculiar to China between the eleventh and twentieth centuries? The lotus foot was the size of a doll's and the woman could not walk without support. Her foot was four inches long and two inches wide. A doll. A girl-child. Crippled, indolent and bound. This is what it meant to be beautiful. And desired. This women did and do to each other.

Pain in the foot is pain in every part of the body. A mother is about to bind her daughter's feet. She knows the pain in her own memory. She says: "A daughter's pretty legs are achieved through the shedding of tears."

This women did to each other.
This women do.
Or refuse to do.

What began in a movie theatre ends in an apartment. Our drama is still played indoors. It is thirty years later and I have come to share my work with Nancy and to see hers. We do this now every other week. This time, I bring notes and ideas about Cinderella, the making of this essay. Nancy's friend Ann is in town for a fellowship interview. Ann understands that Nancy and I need to do our work and withdraws into her nervousness. Unstated but very present is the enormous respect we three have for each other.

Later—I am not sure how it happens—in sympathy for Ann's nervousness, having come to a stopping point in our work or understanding that what happens to Ann at her interview involves us, Nancy and I turn our attention to her. Nancy has done much of this the night before—rehearsing Ann, imagining the questions, helping her present herself and her work in their most effective way. Now it becomes a three-way enterprise. We look over the wardrobe, choose a lavender blouse and skirt, a jacket lent by Nancy. I suppose we have agreed on the "strategy" of looking conventionally feminine at these things. Ann is urged to eat and manages an English muffin. She likes having our help, but neither demands it nor overwhelms us with her need for it.

We share what we know about the lurking interview and speculate whether there is an unstated quota for women. Our fates, Nancy's, mine and Ann's overlap in specific ways. What happens to the project Ann has in mind, whether she gets the money that will enable her to do it or not, is something we will draw a lesson from. We are neither saints nor martyrs. We know it to be in our own best interests to support Ann's progress in the world.

We are not the terrible stepsisters.
What we have in common is not what keeps us apart.
Cinderella goes to the ball and wins the fellowship.
This is a happy ending.
Somehow, we have come to this.

Charles Perrault (1628–1703)

Charles Perrault, a French bureaucrat during the regime of Louis XIV, championed the role of folklore in creating a modern literature distinct from classical Greek and Roman models. Although he was not the first European to produce a volume of folk or fairy tales, he proved among the most influential. His *Histoires ou contes du temps passé* (*Stories or Tales of Times Past,* 1697) included some of our best-known fairy tales, such as "Sleeping Beauty," "Little Red Riding Hood," "Blue Beard," "Cinderella," and "Puss in Boots." These tales, first translated into English in 1729, were not originally intended solely, or even mainly, for children, but despite the opposition of those like Sarah Trimmer, they had by the mid-nineteenth century become a beloved part of the children's literature canon. Perrault's courtly setting and many elegant details became most familiar in the twentieth century through the Disney animated film adaptation of "Cinderella." Ironically, toward the end of the twentieth century, the tales' appropriateness for children was again being challenged. Perrault concluded each tale with an ironic moral or two, but these are often not included in modern editions. At the end of "Cinderella," he praised "graciousness," which is more valuable than beauty, and other blessings bestowed by a godmother or godfather. (See also tales by Perrault and writings by Sarah Trimmer in Part 1.)

Cinderella, or the Little Glass Slipper

TRANSLATOR CHARLES WELSH

Once upon a time there was a gentleman who married, for his second wife, the proudest and most haughty woman that ever was seen. She had two daughters of her own, who were, indeed, exactly like her in all things. The gentleman had also a young daughter, of rare goodness and sweetness of temper, which she took from her mother, who was the best creature in the world.

The wedding was scarcely over, when the stepmother's bad temper began to show itself. She could not bear the goodness of this young girl, because it made her own daughters appear the more odious. The stepmother gave her the meanest work in the house to do; she had to scour the dishes, tables, etc., and to scrub the floors and clean out the bedrooms. The poor girl had to sleep in the garret, upon a wretched straw bed, while her sisters lay in fine rooms with inlaid floors, upon beds of the very newest fashion, and where they had looking-glasses so large that they might see themselves at their full length. The poor girl bore all patiently, and dared not complain to her father, who would have scolded her if she had done so, for his wife governed him entirely.

When she had done her work, she used to go into the chimney corner, and sit down among the cinders, hence she was called Cinderwench. The younger sister of the two, who was not so rude and uncivil as the elder, called her Cinderella. However, Cinderella, in spite of her mean apparel, was a hundred times more handsome than her sisters, though they were always richly dressed.

It happened that the King's son gave a ball, and invited to it all persons of fashion. Our young misses were also invited, for they cut a very grand figure among the people of the country-side. They were highly delighted with the invitation, and wonderfully busy in choosing the gowns, petticoats, and head-dresses which might best become them. This made Cinderella's lot still harder, for it was she who ironed her sisters' linen and plaited their ruffles. They talked all day of nothing but how they should be dressed.

"For my part," said the elder, "I will wear my red velvet suit with French trimmings."

"And I," said the younger, "shall wear my usual skirt; but then, to make amends for that I will put on my gold-flowered mantle, and my diamond stomacher, which is far from being the most ordinary one in the world." They sent for the best hairdressers they could get to make up their hair in fashionable styles, and bought patches for their cheeks. Cinderella was consulted in all these matters, for she had good taste. She advised them always for the best, and even offered her services to dress their hair, which they were very willing she should do.

As she was doing this, they said to her:—

"Cinderella, would you not be glad to go to the ball?"

"Young ladies," she said, "you only jeer at me; it is not for such as I am to go there."

"You are right," they replied; "people would laugh to see a Cinderwench at a ball."

Any one but Cinderella would have dressed their hair awry, but she was good-natured, and arranged it perfectly well. They were almost two days without eating, so much were they transported with joy. They broke above a dozen laces in trying to lace themselves tight, that they might have a fine, slender shape, and they were continually at their looking glass.

At last the happy day came; they went to Court, and Cinderella followed them with her eyes as long as she could, and when she had lost sight of them, she fell a-crying.

Her godmother, who saw her all in tears, asked her what was the matter.

"I wish I could—I wish I could—" but she could not finish her sobbing.

Her godmother, who was a fairy, said to her, "You wish you could go to the ball; is it not so?"

"Alas, yes," said Cinderella, sighing.

"Well," said her godmother, "be but a good girl, and I will see that you go." Then she took her into her chamber, and said to her, "Run into the garden, and bring me a pumpkin."

Cinderella went at once to gather the finest she could get, and brought it to her godmother, not being able to imagine how this pumpkin could help her to go to the ball. Her godmother scooped out all the inside of it, leaving nothing but the rind. Then she struck it with her wand, and the pumpkin was instantly turned into a fine gilded coach.

She then went to look into the mouse-trap, where she found six mice, all alive. She ordered Cinderella to lift the trap-door, when, giving each mouse, as it went out, a little tap with her wand, it was that moment turned into a fine horse, and the six mice made a fine set of six horses of a beautiful mouse-colored, dapple gray.

Being at a loss for a coachman, Cinderella said, "I will go and see if there is not a rat in the rat-trap—we may make a coachman of him."

"You are right," replied her godmother; "go and look."

Cinderella brought the rat-trap to her, and in it there were three huge rats. The fairy chose the one which had the largest beard, and, having touched him with her wand, he was turned into a fat coachman with the finest mustache and whiskers ever seen.

After that, she said to her:—

"Go into the garden, and you will find six lizards behind the water-pot; bring them to me."

She had no sooner done so than her godmother turned them into six footmen, who skipped up immediately behind the coach, with their liveries all trimmed with gold and silver, and they held on as if they had done nothing else their whole lives.

The fairy then said to Cinderella, "Well, you see here a carriage fit to go to the ball in; are you not pleased with it?"

"Oh, yes!" she cried; "but must I go as I am in these rags?"

Her godmother simply touched her with her wand, and, at the same moment, her clothes were turned into cloth of gold and silver, all decked with jewels. This done, she gave her a pair of the prettiest glass slippers in the whole world. Being thus attired, she got into the carriage, her godmother commanding her, above all things, not to stay till after midnight, and telling her, at the same time, that if she stayed one moment longer, the coach would be a pumpkin again, her horses mice, her coachman a rat, her footmen lizards, and her clothes would become just as they were before.

She promised her godmother she would not fail to leave the ball before midnight. She drove away, scarce able to contain herself for joy. The King's son, who was told that a great princess, whom nobody knew, was come, ran out to receive her. He gave her his hand as she alighted from the coach, and led her into the hall where the company were assembled. There was at once a profound silence; every one left off dancing, and the violins ceased to play, so attracted was every one by the singular beauties of the unknown newcomer. Nothing was then heard but a confused sound of voices saying:—

"Ha! how beautiful she is! Ha! how beautiful she is!"

The King himself, old as he was, could not keep his eyes off her, and he told the Queen under his breath that it was a long time since he had seen so beautiful and lovely a creature.

All the ladies were busy studying her clothes and head-dress, so that they might have theirs made next day after the same pattern, provided they could meet with such fine materials and able hands to make them.

The King's son conducted her to the seat of honor, and afterwards took her out to dance with him. She danced so very gracefully that they all admired her more and more. A fine collation was served, but the young Prince ate not a morsel, so intently was he occupied with her.

She went and sat down beside her sisters, showing them a thousand civilities, and giving them among other things part of the oranges and citrons with which the Prince had regaled her. This very much surprised them, for they had not been presented to her.

Cinderella heard the clock strike a quarter to twelve. She at once made her adieus to the company and hastened away as fast as she could.

As soon as she got home, she ran to find her godmother, and, after having thanked her, she said she much wished she might go to the ball the next day, because the King's son had asked her to do so. As she was eagerly telling her godmother all that happened at the ball, her two sisters knocked at the door; Cinderella opened it. "How long you have stayed!" said she, yawning, rubbing her eyes, and stretching herself as if she had been just awakened. She had not, however, had any desire to sleep since they went from home.

"If you had been at the ball," said one of her sisters, "you would not have been tired with it. There came thither the finest princess, the most beautiful ever was seen with mortal eyes. She showed us a thousand civilities, and gave us oranges and citrons."

Cinderella did not show any pleasure at this. Indeed, she asked them the name of the princess; but they told her they did not know it, and that the King's son was very much concerned, and would give all the world to know who she was. At this Cinderella, smiling, replied:—

"Was she then so very beautiful? How fortunate you have been! Could I not see her? Ah! dear Miss Charlotte, do lend me your yellow suit of clothes which you wear every day."

"Ay, to be sure!" cried Miss Charlotte; "lend my clothes to such a dirty Cinderwench as thou art! I should be out of my mind to do so."

Cinderella, indeed, expected such an answer and was very glad of the refusal; for she would have been sadly troubled if her sister had lent her what she jestingly asked for. The next day the two sisters went to the ball, and so did Cinderella, but dressed more magnificently than before. The King's son was always by her side, and his pretty speeches to her never ceased. These by no means annoyed the young lady. Indeed, she quite forgot her godmother's orders to her, so that she heard the clock begin to strike twelve when she thought it could not be more than eleven. She then rose up and fled, as nimble as a deer. The Prince followed, but could not overtake her. She left behind one of her glass slippers, which the Prince took up most carefully. She got home, but quite out of breath, without her carriage, and in her old clothes, having nothing left her of all her finery but one of the little slippers, fellow to the one she had dropped. The guards at the palace gate were asked if they had not seen a princess go out, and they replied they had seen nobody go out but a young girl, very meanly dressed, and who had more the air of a poor country girl than of a young lady.

When the two sisters returned from the ball, Cinderella asked them if they had had a pleasant time, and if the fine lady had been there. They told her, yes; but that she hurried away the moment it struck twelve, and with so much haste that she dropped one of her little glass slippers, the prettiest in the world, which the

Italian artist Roberto Innocenti, illustrating Charles Perrault's seventeenth-century fairy tale in a 1983 picture book, creates the illusion of viewing Cinderella's album of sepia photographs after her English wedding in the 1920s.

King's son had taken up. They said, further, that he had done nothing but look at her all the time, and that most certainly he was very much in love with the beautiful owner of the glass slipper.

What they said was true; for a few days after the King's son caused it to be proclaimed, by sound of trumpet, that he would marry her whose foot this slipper would fit exactly. They began to try it on the princesses, then on the duchesses, and then on all the ladies of the Court; but in vain. It was brought to the two sisters, who did all they possibly could to thrust a foot into the slipper, but they could not succeed. Cinderella, who saw this, and knew her slipper, said to them laughing:—

"Let me see if it will not fit me."

Her sisters burst out a-laughing, and began to banter her. The gentleman who was sent to try the slipper looked earnestly at Cinderella, and, finding her very handsome, said it was but just that she should try, and that he had orders to let every lady try it on.

He obliged Cinderella to sit down, and, putting the slipper to her little foot, he found it went on very easily, and fitted her as if it had been made of wax. The astonishment of her two sisters was great, but it was still greater when Cinderella pulled out of her pocket the other slipper and put it on her foot. Thereupon, in came her godmother, who, having touched Cinderella's clothes with her wand, made them more magnificent than those she had worn before.

And now her sisters found her to be that beautiful lady they had seen at the ball. They threw themselves at her feet to beg pardon for all their ill treatment of her. Cinderella took them up, and, as she embraced them, said that she forgave them with all her heart, and begged them to love her always.

She was conducted to the young Prince, dressed as she was. He thought her more charming than ever, and, a few days after, married her. Cinderella, who was as good as she was beautiful, gave her two sisters a home in the palace, and that very same day married them to two great lords of the Court.

Jacob Grimm (1785–1863) and Wilhelm Grimm (1786–1850)

The Grimm Brothers are world famous for their collection of German folk tales. Seeking to preserve the legacy of German culture, these brothers, who were learned philologists (both also studied law at the University of Marburg), collected tales from a range of tellers, many of whom were middle class and well educated, male and female. Ironically, some of the tales they recorded had been told by Charles Perrault in his *Histoires ou contes du temps passé* (*Stories or Tales of Times Past,* 1697) more than a century earlier. (See the Perrault tales in this section and in Part 1.) The Grimms' tales were translated into English and widely read in England after 1823, with illustrations by the famous George Cruikshank. In successive versions, the Grimm Brothers edited the tales to de-emphasize sexuality and to increase their violence, adapting the stories to their ideas of what was best suited to the education of children.

In this German version of the widespread tale best known in English as "Cinderella," there is no fairy godmother. Instead, the spirit of the abused Ashputtle's mother aids her from beyond the grave, and doves help her to complete various tasks. In the Grimms' editions of 1819 and later, the birds are also the instruments of punishment for the wicked stepsisters who torment Ashputtle: they peck out the eyes of the girls on their way to and from the church where Ashputtle marries the prince. As Louise Bernikow's essay discusses, the German tale has an earthiness that seems to place it closer to its folk sources than does the elegant, courtly Perrault telling. It includes such vivid details as the prince's spreading lime on the steps to capture her shoe—and the stepsisters' cutting off their heels and toes to make them fit the golden slipper.

Ashputtle

A rich man's wife fell sick and, feeling that her end was near, she called her only daughter to her bedside and said: "Dear child, be good and say your prayers; God will help you, and I shall look down on you from heaven and always be with you." With that she closed her eyes and died. Every day the little girl went out to her mother's grave and wept, and she went on being good and saying her prayers. When winter came, the snow spread a white cloth over the grave, and when spring took it off, the man remarried.

His new wife brought two daughters into the house. Their faces were beautiful and lily-white, but their hearts were ugly and black. That was the beginning of a bad time for the poor stepchild. "Why should this silly goose sit in the parlor with us?" they said. "People who want to eat bread must earn it. Get into the kitchen where you belong!" They took away her fine clothes and gave her an old gray dress and wooden shoes to wear. "Look at the haughty princess in her finery!" they cried and, laughing, led her to the kitchen. From then on she had to do all the work, getting up before daybreak, carrying water, lighting fires, cooking and washing. In addition the sisters did everything they could to plague her. They jeered at her and poured peas and lentils into the ashes, so that she had to sit there picking them out. At night, when she was tired out with work, she had no bed to sleep in but had to lie in the ashes by the hearth. And they took to calling her Ashputtle because she always looked dusty and dirty.

One day when her father was going to the fair, he asked his two stepdaughters what he should bring them. "Beautiful dresses," said one. "Diamonds and pearls," said the other. "And you, Ashputtle. What would you like?" "Father," she said, "break off the first branch that brushes against your hat on your way home, and bring it to me." So he bought beautiful dresses, diamonds and pearls for his two stepdaughters, and on the way home, as he was riding through a copse, a hazel branch brushed against him and knocked off his hat. So he broke off the branch and took it home with him. When he got home, he gave the stepdaughters what they had asked for, and gave Ashputtle the branch. After thanking him, she went to her mother's grave and planted the hazel sprig over it and cried so hard that her tears fell on the sprig and watered it. It grew and became a beautiful tree. Three times a day Ashputtle went and sat under it and wept and prayed. Each time a little white bird came and perched on the tree, and when Ashputtle made a wish the little bird threw down what she had wished for.

Now it so happened that the king arranged for a celebration. It was to go on for three days and all the beautiful girls in the kingdom were invited, in order that his son might choose a bride. When the two stepsisters heard they had been asked, they were delighted. They called Ashputtle and said: "Comb our hair, brush our shoes, and fasten our buckles. We're going to the wedding at the king's palace." Ashputtle obeyed, but she wept, for she too would have liked to go dancing, and she begged her stepmother to let her go. "You little sloven!" said the stepmother. "How can you go to a wedding when you're all dusty and dirty? How can you go dancing when you have neither dress nor shoes?" But when Ashputtle begged and begged, the stepmother finally said: "Here, I've dumped a bowlful of lentils in the ashes. If you can pick them out in two hours, you may go." The girl went out the back door to the garden and cried out: "O tame little doves, O turtledoves, and all the birds under heaven, come and help me put

> the good ones in the pot,
> the bad ones in your crop."

Two little white doves came flying through the kitchen window, and then came the turtledoves, and finally all the birds under heaven came flapping and fluttering and settled down by the ashes. The doves nodded their little heads and started in, peck peck peck peck, and all the others started in, peck peck peck peck, and they sorted out all the good lentils and put them in the bowl. Hardly an hour had passed before they finished and flew away. Then the girl brought the bowl to her stepmother, and she was happy, for she thought she'd be allowed to go to the wedding. But the stepmother said: "No, Ashputtle. You have nothing to wear and you don't know how to dance; the people would only laugh at you." When Ashputtle began to cry, the stepmother said: "If you can pick two bowlfuls of lentils out of the ashes in an hour, you may come." And she thought: "She'll never be able to do it." When she had dumped the two bowlfuls of lentils in the ashes, Ashputtle went out the back door to the garden and cried out: "O tame little doves, O turtledoves, and all the birds under heaven, come and help me put

> the good ones in the pot,
> the bad ones in your crop."

Then two little white doves came flying through the kitchen window, and then came the turtledoves, and finally all the birds under heaven came flapping and fluttering and settled down by the ashes. The doves nodded their little heads and started in, peck peck peck peck, and all the others started in, peck peck peck peck, and they sorted out all the good lentils and put them in the bowls. Before half an hour had passed, they had finished and they all flew away. Then the girl brought the bowls to her stepmother, and she was happy, for she thought she'd be allowed to go to the wedding. But her stepmother said: "It's no use. You can't come, because you have nothing to wear and you don't know how to dance. We'd only be ashamed of you." Then she turned her back and hurried away with her two proud daughters.

When they had all gone out, Ashputtle went to her mother's grave. She stood under the hazel tree and cried:

> "Shake your branches, little tree,
> Throw gold and silver down on me."

Whereupon the bird tossed down a gold and silver dress and slippers embroidered with silk and silver.

Ashputtle slipped into the dress as fast as she could and went to the wedding. Her sisters and stepmother didn't recognize her. She was so beautiful in her golden dress that they thought she must be the daughter of some foreign king. They never dreamed it could be Ashputtle, for they thought she was sitting at home in her filthy rags, picking lentils out of the ashes. The king's son came up to her, took her by the hand and danced with her. He wouldn't dance with anyone else and he never let go her hand. When someone else asked for a dance, he said: "She is my partner."

She danced until evening, and then she wanted to go home. The king's son said: "I'll go with you, I'll see you home," for he wanted to find out whom the beautiful girl belonged to. But she got away from him and slipped into the dovecote. The king's son waited until her father arrived, and told him the strange girl had slipped into the dovecote. The old man thought: "Could it be Ashputtle?" and he sent for an ax and a pick and broke into the dovecote, but there was no one inside. When they went indoors, Ashputtle was lying in the ashes in her filthy clothes and a dim oil lamp was burning on the chimney piece, for Ashputtle had slipped out the back end of the dovecote and run to the hazel tree. There she had taken off her fine clothes and put them on the grave, and the bird had taken them away. Then she had put her gray dress on again, crept into the kitchen and lain down in the ashes.

Next day when the festivities started in again and her parents and stepsisters had gone. Ashputtle went to the hazel tree and said:

"Snake your branches, little tree,
Throw gold and silver down on me."

Whereupon the bird threw down a dress that was even more dazzling than the first one. And when she appeared at the wedding, everyone marveled at her beauty. The king's son was waiting for her. He took her by the hand and danced with no one but her. When others came and asked her for a dance, he said: "She is my partner." When evening came, she said she was going home. The king's son followed her, wishing to see which house she went into, but she ran away and disappeared into the garden behind the house, where there was a big beautiful tree with the most wonderful pears growing on it. She climbed among the branches as nimbly as a squirrel and the king's son didn't know

what had become of her. He waited until her father arrived and said to him: "The strange girl has got away from me and I think she has climbed up in the pear tree." Her father thought: "Could it be Ashputtle?" He sent for an ax and chopped the tree down, but there was no one in it. When they went into the kitchen, Ashputtle was lying there in the ashes as usual, for she had jumped down on the other side of the tree, brought her fine clothes back to the bird in the hazel tree, and put on her filthy gray dress.

On the third day, after her parents and sisters had gone, Ashputtle went back to her mother's grave and said to the tree:

"Shake your branches, little tree,
Throw gold and silver down on me."

Whereupon the bird threw down a dress that was more radiant than either of the others, and the slippers were all gold. When she appeared at the wedding, the people were too amazed to speak. The king's son danced with no one but her, and when someone else asked her for a dance, he said: "She is my partner."

When evening came, Ashputtle wanted to go home, and the king's son said he'd go with her, but she slipped away so quickly that he couldn't follow. But he had thought up a trick. He had arranged to have the whole staircase brushed with pitch, and as she was running down it the pitch pulled her left slipper off. The king's son picked it up, and it was tiny and delicate and all gold. Next morning he went to the father and said: "No girl shall be my wife but the one this golden shoe fits." The sisters were overjoyed, for they had beautiful feet. The eldest took the shoe to her room to try it on and her mother went with her. But the shoe was too small and she couldn't get her big toe in. So her mother handed her a knife and said: "Cut your toe off. Once you're queen you won't have to walk any more." The girl cut her toe off, forced her foot into the shoe, gritted her teeth against the pain, and went out to the king's son. He accepted her as his bride-to-be, lifted her up on his horse, and rode away with her. But they had to pass the grave. The two doves were sitting in the hazel tree and they cried out:

"Roocoo, roocoo,
There's blood in the shoe.
The foot's too long, the foot's too wide,
That's not the proper bride."

He looked down at her foot and saw the blood spurting. At that he turned his horse around and took the false bride home again. "No," he said, "this isn't the right girl; let her sister try the shoe on." The sister went to her room and managed to get her toes into the shoe, but her heel was too big. So her mother handed her a knife and said: "Cut off a chunk of your heel. Once you're queen you won't have to walk any more." The girl cut off a chunk of her heel, forced her foot into the shoe, gritted her teeth against the pain, and went out to the king's son. He accepted her as his bride-to-be, lifted her up on his horse, and rode away with her. As they passed the hazel tree, the two doves were sitting there, and they cried out:

"Roocoo, roocoo,
There's blood in the shoe.
The foot's too long, the foot's too wide,
That's not the proper bride."

He looked down at her foot and saw that blood was spurting from her shoe and staining her white stocking all red. He turned his horse around and took the false bride home again. "This isn't the right girl, either," he said. "Haven't you got another daughter?" "No," said the man, "there's only a puny little kitchen drudge that my dead wife left me. She couldn't possibly be the bride." "Send her up," said the king's son, but the mother said: "Oh no, she's much too dirty to be seen." But he insisted and they had to call her. First she washed her face and hands, and when they were clean,

she went upstairs and curtseyed to the king's son. He handed her the golden slipper and sat down on a footstool, took her foot out of her heavy wooden shoe, and put it into the slipper. It fitted perfectly. And when she stood up and the king's son looked into her face, he recognized the beautiful girl he had danced with and cried out: "This is my true bride!" The stepmother and the two sisters went pale with fear and rage. But he lifted Ashputtle up on his horse and rode away with her. As they passed the hazel tree, the two white doves called out:

"Roocoo, roocoo,
No blood in the shoe.
Her foot is neither long nor wide,
This one is the proper bride."

Then they flew down and alighted on Ashputtle's shoulders, one on the right and one on the left, and there they sat.

On the day of Ashputtle's wedding, the two stepsisters came and tried to ingratiate themselves and share in her happiness. On the way to church the elder was on the right side of the bridal couple and the younger on the left. The doves came along and pecked out one of the elder sister's eyes and one of the younger sister's eyes. Afterward, on the way out, the elder was on the left side and the younger on the right, and the doves pecked out both the remaining eyes. So both sisters were punished with blindness to the end of their days for being so wicked and false.

Micmac (Native American)

"The Indian Cindrella" is a composite story, combining elements of the European folktale with facets of the story as it was told in the French and Native American Micmac community in which it was collected. It was retold by Cyrus MacMillan (1882–1953), a Harvard-educated professor of English at McGill University in Montreal, Canada. In this version of the world-famous story of the abused younger sister, sometimes also known as "Little Burnt Scar-Face," the man whom the sisters wish to marry is a god, Strong Wind. He also has a sister, who puts all his potential mates to a test: can they see him, since he has the power to make himself invisible? Like the less virtuous siblings in many folktales, the older sisters of Burnt Face lie in order to get what they want. But the virtue that matters most of all is honesty. The cruel sisters are punished by being transformed into aspen trees, which shake at the least wind. The youngest sister with the burned face and the patience of a saint is magically transformed by Strong Wind when she passes his test. The tale says much about the qualities that are desirable in a woman. Whether these virtues are an expression of the collectors' and retellers' ideas about womanhood or of the indigenous culture from which elements of the story come is a question worthy of research. It is hard to know because MacMillan's telling is a blend of European and Native American elements, and we do not know how the story might have been told before Native Americans had contact with Europeans—if indeed it was told prior to contact at all. It is interesting to note that in *The Book of Virtues,* William J. Bennett uses this story to illustrate the virtue of honesty.[1]

NOTE

1. William J. Bennett, *The Book of Virtues* (New York: Simon and Schuster, 1993).

The Indian Cinderella

RETOLD BY CYRUS MACMILLAN

On the shores of a wide bay on the Atlantic coast there dwelt in old times a great Indian warrior. It was said that he had been one of Glooskap's best helpers and friends, and that he had done for him many wonderful deeds. But that, no man knows. He had, however, a very wonderful and strange power; he could make himself invisible; he could thus mingle unseen with his enemies and listen to their plots. He was known among the people as Strong Wind, the Invisible. He dwelt with his sister in a tent near the sea, and his sister helped him greatly in his work. Many maidens would have been glad to marry him, and he was much sought after because of his mighty deeds; and it was known that Strong Wind would marry the first maiden who could see him as he came home at night. Many made the trial, but it was a long time before one succeeded.

Strong Wind used a clever trick to test the truthfulness of all who sought to win him. Each evening as the day went down, his sister walked on the beach with any girl who wished to make the trial. His sister could always see him, but no one else could see him. And as he came home from work in the twilight, his sister as she saw him drawing near would ask the girl who

sought him, "Do you see him?" And each girl would falsely answer "Yes." And his sister would ask, "With what does he draw his sled?" And each girl would answer, "With the hide of a moose," or "With a pole," or "With a great cord." And then his sister would know that they all had lied, for their answers were mere guesses. And many tried and lied and failed, for Strong Wind would not marry any who were untruthful.

There lived in the village a great chief who had three daughters. Their mother had long been dead. One of these was much younger than the others. She was very beautiful and gentle and well beloved by all, and for that reason her older sisters were very jealous of her charms and treated her very cruelly. They clothed her in rags that she might be ugly; and they cut off her long black hair; and they burned her face with coals from the fire that she might be scarred and disfigured. And they lied to their father, telling him that she had done these things herself. But the young girl was patient and kept her gentle heart and went gladly about her work.

Like other girls, the chief's two eldest daughters tried to win Strong Wind. One evening, as the day went down, they walked on the shore with Strong Wind's sister and waited for his coming. Soon he came home from his day's work, drawing his sled. And his sister asked as usual, "Do you see him?" And each one, lying, answered "Yes." And she asked, "Of what is his shoulder strap made?" And each, guessing, said "Of rawhide." Then they entered the tent where they hoped to see Strong Wind eating his supper; and when he took off his coat and his moccasins they could see them, but more than these they saw nothing. And Strong Wind knew that they had lied, and he kept himself from their sight, and they went home dismayed.

One day the chief's youngest daughter with her rags and her burned face resolved to seek Strong Wind. She patched her clothes with bits of birch bark from the trees, and put on the few little ornaments she possessed, and went forth to try to see the Invisible One as all the other girls of the village had done before. And her sisters laughed at her and called her "fool"; and as she passed along the road all the people laughed at her because of her tattered frock and her burned face, but silently she went her way.

Strong Wind's sister received the little girl kindly, and at twilight she took her to the beach. Soon Strong Wind came home drawing his sled. And his sister asked, "Do you see him?" And the girl answered "No," and his sister wondered greatly because she spoke the truth. And again she asked, "Do you see him now?" And the girl answered, "Yes, and he is very wonderful." And she asked, "With what does he draw his sled?" And the girl answered, "With the Rainbow," and she was much afraid. And she asked further, "Of what is his bowstring?" And the girl answered, "His bowstring is the Milky Way."

Then Strong Wind's sister knew that because the girl had spoken the truth at first her brother had made himself visible to her. And she said, "Truly, you have seen him." And she took her home and bathed her, and all the scars disappeared from her face and body; and her hair grew long and black again like the raven's wing; and she gave her fine clothes to wear and many rich ornaments. Then she bade her take the wife's seat in the tent. Soon Strong Wind entered and sat beside her, and called her his bride. The very next day she became his wife, and ever afterward she helped him to do great deeds. The girl's two elder sisters were very cross and they wondered greatly at what had taken place. But Strong Wind, who knew of their cruelty, resolved to punish them. Using his great power, he changed them both into aspen trees and rooted them in the earth. And since that day the leaves of the aspen have always trembled, and they shiver in fear at the approach of Strong Wind, it matters not how softly he comes, for they are still mindful of his great power and anger because of their lies and their cruelty to their sister long ago.

Thomas Hughes (1822–96)

Tom Brown's Schooldays (1857) is one of the earliest and most influential school stories. Hughes fictionalized his own experience at Rugby, a famous English public school, where Thomas Arnold, father of the poet Matthew Arnold, was headmaster. The Tom of the story is adventurous and combative, but not malicious or rebellious. He is, in fact, the representative of what came to be called "muscular Christianity," an influential Victorian conception of energetic boyhood and manhood. Tom belongs to a better class of boys than his village peers, and Hughes does not think highly of the "private school" Tom attends before he goes to Rugby. The narrator says, "The object of all schools is not to ram Latin and Greek into boys, but to make them good English boys, good future citizens; and by far the most important part of that work must be done, or not done, out of school hours." Games and fights serve this purpose well, to Hughes's way of thinking. In these chapters, Tom Brown arrives at Rugby and begins his process of initiation, which takes place through sports and hazing. Hughes's school story is echoed in later stories of initiation at fictional schools, such as Hogwarts School of Witchcraft and Wizardry in J. K. Rowling's Harry Potter series.

From *Tom Brown's Schooldays*

CHAPTER 5. RUGBY AND FOOTBALL

"Foot and eye opposed
In dubious strife."

—Scott.

"And so here's Rugby, sir, at last, and you'll be in plenty of time for dinner at the School-house, as I told you," said the old guard, pulling his horn out of its case and tootle-tooing away, while the coachman shook up his horses, and carried them along the side of the school close, round Dead-man's corner, past the school-gates, and down the High Street to the Spread Eagle, the wheelers in a spanking trot, and leaders cantering, in a style which would not have disgraced "Cherry Bob," "ramping, stamping, tearing, swearing Billy Harwood," or any other of the old coaching heroes.

Tom's heart beat quick as he passed the great schoolfield or close, with its noble elms, in which several games at football were going on, and tried to take in at once the long line of gray buildings, beginning with the chapel, and ending with the School-house, the residence of the head-master, where the great flag was lazily waving from the highest round tower. And he began already to be proud of being a Rugby boy, as he passed the schoolgates, with the oriel window above, and saw the boys standing there, looking as if the town belonged to them, and nodding in a familiar manner to the coachman, as if any one of them would be quite equal to getting on the box, and working the team down street as well as he.

One of the young heroes, however, ran out from the rest, and scrambled up behind: where, having righted himself, and nodded to the guard, with "How do, Jem?" he turned short round to Tom, and after looking him over for a minute, began,—

"I say, you fellow, is your name Brown?"

"Yes," said Tom, in considerable astonishment, glad, however, to have lighted on some one already who seemed to know him.

"Ah, I thought so. You know my old aunt, Miss East. She lives somewhere down your way in Berkshire. She wrote to me that you were coming to-day, and asked me to give you a lift."

Tom was somewhat inclined to resent the patronizing air of his new friend, a boy of just about his own height and age, but gifted with the most transcendent coolness and assurance, which Tom felt to be aggravating and hard to bear, but couldn't for the life of him help admiring and envying—especially when young my lord begins hectoring two or three long loafing fellows, half porter, half stableman, with a strong touch of the blackguard, and in the end arranges with one of them, nicknamed Cooey, to carry Tom's luggage up to the School-house for sixpence.

"And hark 'ee, Cooey; it must be up in ten minutes, or no more jobs from me. Come along, Brown." And away swaggers the young potentate, with his hands in his pockets, and Tom at his side.

"All right, sir," says Cooey, touching his hat, with a leer and a wink at his companions.

"Hullo though," says East, pulling up, and taking another look at Tom; "this'll never do. Haven't you got a hat? We never wear caps here. Only the louts wear caps. Bless you, if you were to go into the quadrangle with that thing on, I don't know what'd happen." The very idea was quite beyond young Master East, and he looked unutterable things.

Tom thought his cap a very knowing affair, but confessed that he had a hat in his hat-box; which was accordingly at once extracted from the hind-boot, and Tom equipped in his go-to-meeting roof, as his new friend called it. But this didn't quite suit his fastidious taste in another minute, being too shiny; so, as they walk up the town, they dive into Nixon's the hatter's, and Tom is arrayed, to his utter astonishment, and without paying for it, in a regulation cat-skin at seven-and-sixpence, Nixon undertaking to send the best hat up to the matron's room, School-house, in half an hour.

"You can send in a note for a tile on Monday, and make it all right, you know," said Mentor; "we're allowed two seven-and-sixers a half, besides what we bring from home."

Tom by this time began to be conscious of his new social position and dignities, and to luxuriate in the realized ambition of being a public school-boy at last, with a vested right of spoiling two seven-and-sixers in half a year.

"You see," said his friend, as they strolled towards the school-gates, in explanation of his conduct, "a great deal depends on how a fellow cuts up at first. If he's got nothing odd about him, and answers straightforward, and holds his head up, he gets on. Now, you'll do very well as to rig, all but that cap. You see I'm doing the handsome thing by you, because my father knows yours; besides, I want to please the old lady. She gave me half a sov. this half, and perhaps'll double it next, if I keep in her good books."

There's nothing for candour like a lower-school boy, and East was a genuine specimen—frank, hearty, and good-natured, well-satisfied with himself and his position, and choke-full of life and spirits, and all the Rugby prejudices and traditions which he had been able to get together in the long course of one half-year during which he had been at the School-house.

And Tom, notwithstanding his bumptiousness, felt friends with him at once, and began sucking in all his ways and prejudices, as fast as he could understand them.

East was great in the character of cicerone. He carried Tom through the great gates, where were only two or three boys. These satisfied themselves with the stock questions, "You fellow, what's your name? Where do you come from? How old are you? Where do you board?" and, "What form are you in?" And so they passed on through the quadrangle and a small courtyard, upon which looked down a lot of little windows (belonging, as his guide informed him, to some of the School-house studies), into the matron's room, where East introduced Tom to that dignitary; made him give up the key of his trunk, that the matron might unpack his linen, and told the story of the hat and of his own presence of mind: upon the relation whereof the matron laughingly scolded him for the coolest new boy in the house; and East, indignant at the accusation of newness, marched Tom off into the quadrangle, and began showing him the schools, and examining him as to his literary attainments; the result of which was a prophecy that they would be in the same form, and could do their lessons together.

"And now come in and see my study—we shall have just time before dinner; and afterwards, before calling over, we'll do the close."

Tom followed his guide through the School-house hall, which opens into the quadrangle. It is a great room, thirty feet long and eighteen high, or thereabouts, with two great tables running the whole length, and two large fireplaces at the side, with blazing fires in them, at one of which some dozen boys were standing and lounging, some of whom shouted to East to stop; but he shot through with his convoy, and landed him in the long, dark passages, with a large fire at the end of each, upon which the studies opened. Into one of these, in the bottom passage, East bolted with our hero, slamming and bolting the door behind them, in case of pursuit from the hall, and Tom was for the first time in a Rugby boy's citadel.

He hadn't been prepared for separate studies, and was not a little astonished and delighted with the palace in question.

It wasn't very large, certainly, being about six feet long by four broad. It couldn't be called light, as there were bars and a grating to the window; which little precautions were necessary in the studies on the ground-floor looking out into the close, to prevent the exit of small boys after locking up, and the entrance of contraband articles. But it was uncommonly comfortable to look at, Tom thought. The space under the window at the farther end was occupied by a square table covered with a reasonably clean and whole red and blue check tablecloth; a hard-seated sofa covered with red stuff occupied one side, running up to the end, and making a seat for one, or by sitting close, for two, at the table and a good stout wooden chair afforded a seat to another boy, so that three could sit and work together. The walls were wainscoted half-way up, the wainscot being covered with green baize, the remainder with a bright-patterned paper, on which hung three or four prints of dogs' heads; Grimaldi winning the Aylesbury steeplechase; Amy Robsart, the reigning Waverley beauty of the day; and Tom Crib, in a posture of defence, which did no credit to the science of that hero, if truly represented. Over the door were a row of hat-pegs, and on each side bookcases with cupboards at the bottom, shelves and cupboards being filled indiscriminately with school-books, a cup or two, a mouse-trap and candlesticks, leather straps, a fustian bag, and some curious-looking articles which puzzled Tom not a little, until his friend explained that they were climbing-irons, and showed their use. A cricket-bat and small fishing-rod stood up in one corner.

This was the residence of East and another boy in the same form, and had more interest for Tom than Windsor Castle, or any other residence in the British

Isles. For was he not about to become the joint owner of a similar home, the first place he could call his own? One's own! What a charm there is in the words! How long it takes boy and man to find out their worth! How fast most of us hold on to them—faster and more jealously, the nearer we are to that general home into which we can take nothing, but must go naked as we came into the world! When shall we learn that he who multiplieth possessions multiplieth troubles, and that the one single use of things which we call our own is that they may be his who hath need of them?

"And shall I have a study like this too?" said Tom.

"Yes, of course; you'll be chummed with some fellow on Monday, and you can sit here till then."

"What nice places!"

"They're well enough," answered East, patronizingly, "only uncommon cold at nights sometimes. Gower—that's my chum—and I make a fire with paper on the floor after supper generally, only that makes it so smoky."

"But there's a big fire out in the passage," said Tom.

"Precious little we get out of that, though," said East. "Jones the prepostor has the study at the fire end, and he has rigged up an iron rod and green baize curtain across the passage, which he draws at night, and sits there with his door open; so he gets all the fire, and hears if we come out of our studies after eight, or make a noise. However, he's taken to sitting in the fifth-form room lately, so we do get a bit of fire now sometimes; only to keep a sharp lookout that he don't catch you behind his curtain when he comes down—that's all."

A quarter past one now struck, and the bell began tolling for dinner; so they went into the hall and took their places, Tom at the very bottom of the second table, next to the prepostor (who sat at the end to keep order there), and East a few paces higher. And now Tom for the first time saw his future schoolfellows in a body. In they came, some hot and ruddy from football or long walks, some pale and chilly from hard reading in their studies, some from loitering over the fire at the pastrycook's, dainty mortals, bringing with them pickles and saucebottles to help them with their dinners. And a great big-bearded man, whom Tom took for a master, began calling over the names, while the great joints were being rapidly carved on the third table in the corner by the old verger and the housekeeper. Tom's turn came last, and meanwhile he was all eyes, looking first with awe at the great man, who sat close

to him, and was helped first, and who read a hard-looking book all the time he was eating; and when he got up and walked off to the fire, at the small boys round him, some of whom were reading, and the rest talking in whispers to one another, or stealing one another's bread, or shooting pellets, or digging their forks through the tablecloth. However, notwithstanding his curiosity, he managed to make a capital dinner by the time the big man called "Stand up!" and said grace.

As soon as dinner was over, and Tom had been questioned by such of his neighbours as were curious as to his birth, parentage, education, and other like matters, East, who evidently enjoyed his new dignity of patron and mentor, proposed having a look at the close, which Tom, athirst for knowledge, gladly assented to; and they went out through the quadrangle and past the big fives court, into the great playground.

"That's the chapel, you see," said East; "and there, just behind it, is the place for fights. You see it's most out of the way of the masters, who all live on the other side, and don't come by here after first lesson or callings-over. That's when the fights come off. And all this part where we are is the little-side ground, right up to the trees; and on the other side of the trees is the big-side ground, where the great matches are played. And there's the island in the farthest corner; you'll know that well enough next half, when there's island fagging. I say, it's horrid cold; let's have a run across." And away went East, Tom close behind him. East was evidently putting his best foot foremost; and Tom, who was mighty proud of his running, and not a little anxious to show his friend that, although a new boy, he was no milksop, laid himself down to work in his very best style. Right across the close they went, each doing all he knew, and there wasn't a yard between them when they pulled up at the island moat.

"I say," said East, as soon as he got his wind, looking with much increased respect at Tom, "you ain't a bad scud, not by no means. Well, I'm as warm as a toast now."

"But why do you wear white trousers in November?" said Tom. He had been struck by this peculiarity in the costume of almost all the School-house boys.

"Why, bless us, don't you know? No; I forgot. Why, to-day's the School-house match. Our house plays the whole of the School at football. And we all wear white trousers, to show 'em we don't care for hacks. You're in luck to come to-day. You just will see a match; and Brooke's going to let me play in quarters. That's more than he'll do for any other lower-school boy, except James, and he's fourteen."

"Who's Brooke?"

"Why, that big fellow who called over at dinner, to be sure. He's cock of the school, and head of the School-house side, and the best kick and charger in Rugby."

"Oh, but do show me where they play. And tell me about it. I love football so, and have played all my life. Won't Brooke let me play?"

"Not he," said East, with some indignation. "Why, you don't know the rules; you'll be a month learning them. And then it's no joke playing-up in a match, I can tell you—quite another thing from your private school games. Why, there's been two collar-bones broken this half, and a dozen fellows lamed. And last year a fellow had his leg broken."

Tom listened with the profoundest respect to this chapter of accidents, and followed East across the level ground till they came to a sort of gigantic gallows of two poles, eighteen feet high, fixed upright in the ground some fourteen feet apart, with a cross-bar running from one to the other at the height of ten feet or thereabouts.

"This is one of the goals," said East, "and you see the other, across there, right opposite, under the Doctor's wall. Well, the match is for the best of three goals; whichever side kicks two goals wins: and it won't do, you see, just to kick the ball through these posts—it must go over the cross-bar; any height'll do, so long as it's between the posts. You'll have to stay in goal to touch the ball when it rolls behind the posts, because if the other side touch it they have a try at goal. Then we fellows in quarters, we play just about in front of goal here, and have to turn the ball and kick it back before the big fellows on the other side can follow it up. And in front of us all the big fellows play, and that's where the scrummages are mostly."

Tom's respect increased as he struggled to make out his friend's technicalities, and the other set to work to explain the mysteries of "off your side," "drop-kicks," "punts," "places," and the other intricacies of the great science of football.

"But how do you keep the ball between the goals?" said he; "I can't see why it mightn't go right down to the chapel."

"Why; that's out of play," answered East. "You see this gravel-walk running down all along this side of the playing-ground, and the line of elms opposite on the other? Well, they're the bounds. As soon as the ball gets past them, it's in touch, and out of play. And then whoever first touches it has to knock it straight out amongst the players-up, who make two lines with a space between them, every fellow going on his own side. Ain't there just fine scrummages then! And the three trees you see there which come out into the play, that's a tremendous place when the ball hangs there, for you get thrown against the trees, and that's worse than any hack."

Tom wondered within himself, as they strolled back again towards the fives court, whether the matches were really such break-neck affairs as East represented, and whether, if they were, he should ever get to like them and play up well.

He hadn't long to wonder, however, for next minute East cried out, "Hurrah! here's the punt-about; come along and try your hand at a kick." The punt-about is the practice-ball, which is just brought out and kicked about anyhow from one boy to another before callings-over and dinner, and at other odd times. They joined the boys who had brought it out, all small School-house fellows, friends of East; and Tom had the pleasure of trying his skill, and performed very creditably, after first driving his foot three inches into the ground, and then nearly kicking his leg into the air, in vigorous efforts to accomplish a drop-kick after the manner of East.

Presently more boys and bigger came out, and boys from other houses on their way to calling-over, and more balls were sent for. The crowd thickened as three o'clock approached; and when the hour struck, one hundred and fifty boys were hard at work. Then the balls were held, the master of the week came down in cap and gown to calling-over, and the whole school of three hundred boys swept into the big school to answer to their names.

"I may come in, mayn't I?" said Tom, catching East by the arm, and longing to feel one of them.

"Yes, come along; nobody'll say anything. You won't be so eager to get into calling-over after a month," replied his friend; and they marched into the big school together, and up to the farther end, where that illustrious form, the lower fourth, which had the honour of East's patronage for the time being, stood.

The master mounted into the high desk by the door, and one of the prepostors of the week stood by him on the steps, the other three marching up and down the middle of the school with their canes, calling out, "Silence, silence!" The sixth form stood close by the door on the left, some thirty in number, mostly great big grown men, as Tom thought, surveying them from a distance with awe; the fifth form behind them, twice their number, and not quite so big. These on the left; and on the right the lower fifth, shell, and all the junior forms in order; while up the middle marched the three prepostors.

Then the prepostor who stands by the master calls out the names, beginning with the sixth form; and as he calls each boy answers "here" to his name, and walks out. Some of the sixth stop at the door to turn the whole string of boys into the close. It is a great match-day, and every boy in the school, will he, nill he, must be there. The rest of the sixth go forwards into the close, to see that no one escapes by any of the side gates.

To-day, however, being the School-house match, none of the School-house prepostors stay by the door to watch for truants of their side; there is carte blanche to the School-house fags to go where they like. "They trust to our honour," as East proudly informs Tom; "they know very well that no School-house boy would cut the match. If he did, we'd very soon cut him, I can tell you."

The master of the week being short-sighted, and the prepostors of the week small and not well up to their work, the lower-school boys employ the ten minutes which elapse before their names are called in pelting one another vigorously with acorns, which fly about in all directions. The small prepostors dash in every now and then, and generally chastise some quiet, timid boy who is equally afraid of acorns and canes, while the principal performers get dexterously out of the way. And so calling-over rolls on somehow, much like the big world, punishments lighting on wrong shoulders, and matters going generally in a queer, cross-grained way, but the end coming somehow, which is, after all, the great point. And now the master of the week has finished, and locked up the big school; and the prepostors of the week come out, sweeping the last remnant of the school fags, who had been loafing about the corners by the fives court, in hopes of a chance of bolting, before them into the close.

"Hold the punt-about!" "To the goals!" are the cries; and all stray balls are impounded by the authorities, and the whole mass of boys moves up towards the two goals, dividing as they go into three bodies. That little band on the left, consisting of from fifteen to twenty boys, Tom amongst them, who are making for the goal under the School-house wall, are the School-house boys who are not to play up, and have to stay in goal. The larger body moving to the island goal are the School boys in a like predicament. The great mass in the middle are the players-up, both sides mingled together; they are hanging their jackets (and all who mean real work), their hats, waistcoats, neck-handkerchiefs, and braces, on the railings round the small trees; and there they go by twos and threes up to their respective grounds. There is none of the colour and tastiness of get-up, you will perceive, which lends such a life to the present game at Rugby, making the dullest and worst-fought match a pretty sight. Now each house has its own uniform of cap and jersey, of some lively colour; but at the time we are speaking of plush caps have not yet come in, or uniforms of any sort, except the School-house white trousers, which are abominably cold to-day. Let us get to work, bare-headed, and girded with our plain leather straps. But we mean business, gentlemen.

And now that the two sides have fairly sundered, and each occupies its own ground, and we get a good look at them, what absurdity is this? You don't mean to say that those fifty or sixty boys in white trousers, many of them quite small, are going to play that huge mass opposite? Indeed I do, gentlemen. They're going to try, at any rate, and won't make such a bad fight of it either, mark my word; for hasn't old Brooke won the toss, with his lucky halfpenny, and got choice of goals and kick-off? The new ball you may see lie there quite by itself, in the middle, pointing towards the School or island goal; in another minute it will be well on its way there. Use that minute in remarking how the School-house side is drilled. You will see, in the first place, that the sixth-form boy, who has the charge of goal, has spread his force (the goalkeepers) so as to occupy the whole space behind the goal-posts, at distances of about five yards apart. A safe and well-kept goal is the foundation of all good play. Old Brooke is talking to the captain of quarters, and now he moves away. See how that youngster spreads his men (the light brigade) carefully over the ground, half-way between their own goal and the body of their own players-up (the heavy brigade). These again play in several bodies. There is young Brooke and the bull-dogs. Mark them well. They are the "fighting brigade," the "die-hards," larking about at leap-frog to keep themselves warm, and playing tricks on one another. And on each side of old Brooke, who is now standing in the middle of the ground and just going to kick off, you see a separate wing of players-up, each with a boy of acknowledged prowess to look to—here Warner, and there Hedge; but over all is old Brooke, absolute as he of Russia, but wisely and bravely ruling over willing and worshipping subjects, a true football king. His face is earnest and careful as he glances a last time over his array, but full of pluck and hope—the sort of look I hope to see in my general when I go out to fight.

The School side is not organized in the same way. The goalkeepers are all in lumps, anyhow and nohow; you can't distinguish between the players-up and the boys in quarters, and there is divided leadership. But with such odds in strength and weight it must take more than that to hinder them from winning; and so their leaders seem to think, for they let the players-up manage themselves.

But now look! there is a slight move forward of the School-house wings, a shout of "Are you ready?" and loud affirmative reply. Old Brooke takes half a dozen quick steps, and away goes the ball spinning towards the School goal, seventy yards before it touches ground, and at no point above twelve or fifteen feet high, a model kick-off; and the School-house cheer and rush on. The ball is returned, and they meet it and drive it back amongst the masses of the School already in motion. Then the two sides close, and you can see nothing for minutes but a swaying crowd of boys, at one point violently agitated. That is where the ball is, and there are the keen players to be met, and the glory and the hard knocks to be got. You hear the dull thud, thud of the ball, and the shouts of "Off your side," "Down with him," "Put him over," "Bravo." This is what we call "a scrummage," gentlemen, and the first scrummage in a School-house match was no joke in the consulship of Plancus.

But see! it has broken; the ball is driven out on the Schoolhouse side, and a rush of the School carries it past the School-house players-up. "Look out in quarters," Brooke's and twenty other voices ring out. No need to call, though: the Schoolhouse captain of quar-

ters has caught it on the bound, dodges the foremost School boys, who are heading the rush, and sends it back with a good drop-kick well into the enemy's country. And then follows rush upon rush, and scrummage upon scrummage, the ball now driven through into the School-house quarters, and now into the School goal; for the School-house have not lost the advantage which the kick-off and a slight wind gave them at the outset, and are slightly "penning" their adversaries. You say you don't see much in it all—nothing but a struggling mass of boys, and a leather ball which seems to excite them all to great fury, as a red rag does a bull. My dear sir, a battle would look much the same to you, except that the boys would be men, and the balls iron; but a battle would be worth your looking at for all that, and so is a football match. You can't be expected to appreciate the delicate strokes of play, the turns by which a game is lost and won—it takes an old player to do that; but the broad philosophy of football you can understand if you will. Come along with me a little nearer, and let us consider it together.

The ball has just fallen again where the two sides are thickest, and they close rapidly around it in a scrummage. It must be driven through now by force or skill, till it flies out on one side or the other. Look how differently the boys face it! Here come two of the bull-dogs, bursting through the outsiders; in they go, straight to the heart of the scrummage, bent on driving that ball out on the opposite side. That is what they mean to do. My sons, my sons! you are too hot; you have gone past the ball, and must struggle now right through the scrummage, and get round and back again to your own side, before you can be of any further use. Here comes young Brooke; he goes in as straight as you, but keeps his head, and backs and bends, holding himself still behind the ball, and driving it furiously when he gets the chance. Take a leaf out of his book, you young chargers. Here comes Speedicut, and Flashman the School-house bully, with shouts and great action. Won't you two come up to young Brooke, after locking-up, by the School-house fire, with "Old fellow, wasn't that just a splendid scrummage by the three trees?" But he knows you, and so do we. You don't really want to drive that ball through that scrummage, chancing all hurt for the glory of the School-house, but to make us think that's what you want—a vastly different thing; and fellows of your kidney will never go through more than the skirts of a scrummage, where it's all push and no kicking. We respect boys who keep out of it, and don't sham going in; but you—we had rather not say what we think of you.

Then the boys who are bending and watching on the outside, mark them: they are most useful players, the dodgers, who seize on the ball the moment it rolls out from amongst the chargers, and away with it across to the opposite goal. They seldom go into the scrummage, but must have more coolness than the chargers. As endless as are boys' characters, so are their ways of facing or not facing a scrummage at football.

Three-quarters of an hour are gone; first winds are failing, and weight and numbers beginning to tell. Yard by yard the School-house have been driven back, contesting every inch of ground. The bull-dogs are the colour of mother earth from shoulder to ankle, except young Brooke, who has a marvellous knack of keeping his legs. The School-house are being penned in their turn, and now the ball is behind their goal, under the Doctor's wall. The Doctor and some of his family are there looking on, and seem as anxious as any boy for the success of the School-house. We get a minute's breathing-time before old Brooke kicks out, and he gives the word to play strongly for touch, by the three trees. Away goes the ball, and the bull-dogs after it, and in another minute there is shout of "In touch!" "Our ball!" Now's your time, old Brooke, while your men are still fresh. He stands with the ball in his hand, while the two sides form in deep lines opposite one another; he must strike it straight out between them. The lines are thickest close to him, but young Brooke and two or three of his men are shifting up farther, where the opposite line is weak. Old Brooke strikes it out straight and strong, and it falls opposite his brother. Hurrah! that rush has taken it right through the School line, and away past the three trees, far into their quarters, and young Brooke and the bull-dogs are close upon it. The School leaders rush back, shouting, "Look out in goal!" and strain every nerve to catch him, but they are after the fleetest foot in Rugby. There they go straight for the School goal-posts, quarters scattering before them. One after another the bull-dogs go down, but young Brooke holds on. "He is down." No! a long stagger, but the danger is past. That was the shock of Crew, the most dangerous of dodgers. And now he is close to the School goal, the ball not three yards before him. There is a hurried rush of the School fags to the spot, but no one throws himself on the ball,

the only chance, and young Brooke has touched it right under the School goal-posts.

The School leaders come up furious, and administer toco to the wretched fags nearest at hand. They may well be angry, for it is all Lombard Street to a china orange that the School-house kick a goal with the ball touched in such a good place. Old Brooke, of course, will kick it out, but who shall catch and place it? Call Crab Jones. Here he comes, sauntering along with a straw in his mouth, the queerest, coolest fish in Rugby. If he were tumbled into the moon this minute, he would just pick himself up without taking his hands out of his pockets or turning a hair. But it is a moment when the boldest charger's heart beats quick. Old Brooke stands with the ball under his arm motioning the School back; he will not kick out till they are all in goal, behind the posts. They are all edging forwards, inch by inch, to get nearer for the rush at Crab Jones, who stands there in front of old Brooke to catch the ball. If they can reach and destroy him before he catches, the danger is over; and with one and the same rush they will carry it right away to the School-house goal. Fond hope! it is kicked out and caught beautifully. Crab strikes his heel into the ground, to mark the spot where the ball was caught, beyond which the school line may not advance; but there they stand, five deep, ready to rush the moment the ball touches the ground. Take plenty of room. Don't give the rush a chance of reaching you. Place it true and steady. Trust Crab Jones. He has made a small hole with his heel for the ball to lie on, by which he is resting on one knee, with his eye on old Brooke. "Now!" Crab places the ball at the word, old Brooke kicks, and it rises slowly and truly as the School rush forward.

Then a moment's pause, while both sides look up at the spinning ball. There it flies, straight between the two posts, some five feet above the cross-bar, an unquestioned goal; and a shout of real, genuine joy rings out from the School-house players-up, and a faint echo of it comes over the close from the goalkeepers under the Doctor's wall. A goal in the first hour—such a thing hasn't been done in the School-house match these five years.

"Over!" is the cry. The two sides change goals, and the School-house goal-keepers come threading their way across through the masses of the School, the most openly triumphant of them—amongst whom is Tom, a School-house boy of two hours' standing—getting their ears boxed in the transit. Tom indeed is excited beyond measure, and it is all the sixth-form boy, kindest and safest of goal-keepers, has been able to do, to keep him from rushing out whenever the ball has been near their goal. So he holds him by his side, and instructs him in the science of touching.

At this moment Griffith, the itinerant vender of oranges from Hill Morton, enters the close with his heavy baskets. There is a rush of small boys upon the little pale-faced man, the two sides mingling together, subdued by the great goddess Thirst, like the English and French by the streams in the Pyrenees. The leaders are past oranges and apples, but some of them visit their coats, and apply innocent-looking ginger-beer bottles to their mouths. It is no ginger-beer though, I fear, and will do you no good. One short mad rush, and then a stitch in the side, and no more honest play. That's what comes of those bottles.

But now Griffith's baskets are empty, the ball is placed again midway, and the School are going to kick off. Their leaders have sent their lumber into goal, and rated the rest soundly, and one hundred and twenty picked players-up are there, bent on retrieving the game. They are to keep the ball in front of the School-house goal, and then to drive it in by sheer strength and weight. They mean heavy play and no mistake, and so old Brooke sees, and places Crab Jones in quarters just before the goal, with four or five picked players who are to keep the ball away to the sides, where a try at goal, if obtained, will be less dangerous than in front. He himself, and Warner and Hedge, who have saved themselves till now, will lead the charges.

"Are you ready?" "Yes." And away comes the ball, kicked high in the air, to give the School time to rush on and catch it as it falls. And here they are amongst us. Meet them like Englishmen, you Schoolhouse boys, and charge them home. Now is the time to show what mettle is in you; and there shall be a warm seat by the hall fire, and honour, and lots of bottled beer tonight for him who does his duty in the next half-hour. And they are well met. Again and again the cloud of their players-up gathers before our goal, and comes threatening on, and Warner or Hedge, with young Brooke and the relics of the bull-dogs, break through and carry the ball back; and old Brooke ranges the field like Job's war-horse. The thickest scrummage parts asunder before his rush, like the waves before a clipper's bows; his cheery voice rings out over the field, and his eye is everywhere. And if these miss the ball, and it rolls dangerously in front of our goal, Crab Jones and his men have seized it and sent it away towards the sides with the unerring drop-kick. This is worth living for—the whole sum of schoolboy existence gathered up into one straining, struggling half-hour, a half-hour worth a year of common life.

The quarter to five has struck, and the play slackens for a minute before goal; but there is Crew, the artful dodger, driving the ball in behind our goal, on the island side, where our quarters are weakest. Is there no one to meet him? Yes; look at little East! The ball is just at equal distances between the two, and they rush together, the young man of seventeen and the boy of twelve, and kick it at the same moment. Crew passes on without a stagger; East is hurled forward by the shock, and plunges on his shoulder, as if he would bury himself in the ground; but the ball rises straight into the air, and falls behind Crew's back, while the "bravoes" of the School-house attest the pluckiest charge of all that hard-fought day. Warner picks East up lame and half stunned, and he hobbles back into goal, conscious of having played the man.

And now the last minutes are come, and the School gather for their last rush, every boy of the hundred and twenty who has a run left in him. Reckless of the defence of their own goal, on they come across the level big-side ground, the ball well down amongst them, straight for our goal, like the column of the Old Guard up the slope at Waterloo. All former charges have been child's play to this. Warner and Hedge have met them, but still on they come. The bull-dogs rush in for the last time; they are hurled over or carried back, striving hand, foot, and eyelids. Old Brooke comes sweeping round the skirts of the play, and turning short round, picks out the very heart of the scrummage, and plunges in. It wavers for a moment; he has the ball. No, it has passed him, and his voice rings out clear over the advancing tide, "Look out in goal!" Crab Jones catches it for a moment; but before he can kick, the rush is upon him and passes over him; and he picks himself up behind them with his straw in his mouth, a little dirtier, but as cool as ever.

The ball rolls slowly in behind the School-house goal, not three yards in front of a dozen of the biggest School players-up.

There stands the School-house prepostor, safest of goal-keepers, and Tom Brown by his side, who has learned his trade by this time. Now is your time, Tom. The blood of all the Browns is up, and the two rush in together, and throw themselves on the ball, under the very feet of the advancing column—the prepostor on his hands and knees, arching his back, and Tom all along on his face. Over them topple the leaders of the rush, shooting over the back of the prepostor, but falling flat on Tom, and knocking all the wind out of his small carcass. "Our ball," says the prepostor, rising with his prize; "but get up there; there's a little fellow under you." They are hauled and roll off him, and Tom is discovered, a motionless body.

Old Brooke picks him up. "Stand back, give him air," he says; and then feeling his limbs, adds, "No bones broken.—How do you feel, young un?"

"Hah-hah!" gasps Tom, as his wind comes back; "pretty well, thank you—all right."

"Who is he?" says Brooke.

"Oh, it's Brown; he's a new boy; I know him," says East, coming up.

"Well, he is a plucky youngster, and will make a player," says Brooke.

And five o'clock strikes. "No side" is called, and the first day of the School-house match is over.

CHAPTER 6. AFTER THE MATCH

"Some food we had."

—Shakespeare

As the boys scattered away from the ground, and East, leaning on Tom's arm, and limping along, was beginning to consider what luxury they should go and buy for tea to celebrate that glorious victory, the two Brookes came striding by. Old Brooke caught sight of East, and stopped; put his hand kindly on his shoulder, and said, "Bravo, youngster; you played famously. Not much the matter, I hope?"

"No, nothing at all," said East—"only a little twist from that charge."

"Well, mind and get all right for next Saturday." And the leader passed on, leaving East better for those few words than all the opodeldoc in England would have made him, and Tom ready to give one of his ears for as much notice. Ah! light words of those whom we love and honour, what a power ye are, and how carelessly wielded by those who can use you! Surely for these things also God will ask an account.

"Tea's directly after locking-up, you see," said East, hobbling along as fast as he could, "so you come along down to Sally Harrowell's; that's our School-house tuck-shop. She bakes such stunning murphies, we'll have a penn'orth each for tea. Come along, or they'll all be gone."

Tom's new purse and money burnt in his pocket; he wondered, as they toddled through the quadrangle and along the street, whether East would be insulted if he suggested further extravagance, as he had not sufficient faith in a pennyworth of potatoes. At last he blurted out,—

"I say, East, can't we get something else besides potatoes? I've got lots of money, you know."

"Bless us, yes; I forgot," said East, "you've only just come. You see all my tin's been gone this twelve weeks—it hardly ever lasts beyond the first fortnight; and our allowances were all stopped this morning for broken windows, so I haven't got a penny. I've got a tick at Sally's, of course; but then I hate running it high, you see, towards the end of the half, 'cause one has to shell out for it all directly one comes back, and that's a bore."

Tom didn't understand much of this talk, but seized on the fact that East had no money, and was denying himself some little pet luxury in consequence. "Well, what shall I buy?" said he, "I'm uncommon hungry."

"I say," said East, stopping to look at him and rest his leg, "you're a trump, Brown. I'll do the same by you next half. Let's have a pound of sausages then. That's the best grub for tea I know of."

"Very well," said Tom, as pleased as possible; "where do they sell them?"

"Oh, over here, just opposite." And they crossed the street and walked into the cleanest little front room of a small house, half parlour, half shop, and bought a pound of most particular sausages, East talking pleasantly to Mrs. Porter while she put them in paper, and Tom doing the paying part.

From Porter's they adjourned to Sally Harrowell's, where they found a lot of School-house boys waiting for the roast potatoes, and relating their own exploits in the day's match at the top of their voices. The street opened at once into Sally's kitchen, a low brick-floored room, with large recess for fire, and chimney-corner seats. Poor little Sally, the most good-natured and much-enduring of womankind, was bustling about, with a napkin in her hand, from her own oven to those of the neighbours' cottages up the yard at the back of the house. Stumps, her husband, a short, easy-going shoemaker, with a beery, humorous eye and ponderous calves, who lived mostly on his wife's earnings, stood in a corner of the room, exchanging shots of the roughest description of repartee with every boy in turn. "Stumps, you lout, you've had too much beer again to-day." "'Twasn't of your paying for, then." "Stumps's calves are running down into his ankles; they want to get to grass." "Better be doing that than gone altogether like yours," etc. Very poor stuff it was, but it served to make time pass; and every now and then Sally arrived in the middle with a smoking tin of potatoes, which was cleared off in a few seconds, each boy as he seized his lot running off to the house with "Put me down two-penn'orth, Sally;" "Put down three-penn'orth between me and Davis," etc. How she ever kept the accounts so straight as she did, in her head and on her slate, was a perfect wonder.

East and Tom got served at last, and started back for the School-house, just as the locking-up bell began to ring, East on the way recounting the life and adventures of Stumps, who was a character. Amongst his other small avocations, he was the hind carrier of a sedan-chair, the last of its race, in which the Rugby ladies still went out to tea, and in which, when he was fairly harnessed and carrying a load, it was the delight of small and mischievous boys to follow him and whip his calves. This was too much for the temper even of Stumps, and he would pursue his tormentors in a vindictive and apoplectic manner when released, but was easily pacified by twopence to buy beer with.

The lower-school boys of the School-house, some fifteen in number, had tea in the lower-fifth school, and were presided over by the old verger or head-porter. Each boy had a quarter of a loaf of bread and pat of butter, and as much tea as he pleased; and there was scarcely one who didn't add to this some further luxury, such as baked potatoes, a herring, sprats, or something of the sort. But few at this period of the half-year could live up to a pound of Porter's sausages, and East was in great magnificence upon the strength of theirs. He had produced a toasting-fork from his study, and set Tom to toast the sausages, while he mounted guard over their butter and potatoes. "'Cause," as he explained, "you're a new boy, and they'll play you some trick and get our butter; but you can toast just as well as I." So Tom, in the midst of three or four more

urchins similarly employed, toasted his face and the sausages at the same time before the huge fire, till the latter cracked; when East from his watch-tower shouted that they were done, and then the feast proceeded, and the festive cups of tea were filled and emptied, and Tom imparted of the sausages in small bits to many neighbours, and thought he had never tasted such good potatoes or seen such jolly boys. They on their parts waived all ceremony, and pegged away at the sausages and potatoes, and remembering Tom's performance in goal, voted East's new crony a brick. After tea, and while the things were being cleared away, they gathered round the fire, and the talk on the match still went on; and those who had them to show pulled up their trousers and showed the hacks they had received in the good cause.

They were soon, however, all turned out of the school; and East conducted Tom up to his bedroom, that he might get on clean things, and wash himself before singing.

"What's singing?" said Tom, taking his head out of his basin, where he had been plunging it in cold water.

"Well, you are jolly green," answered his friend, from a neighbouring basin. "Why, the last six Saturdays of every half we sing of course; and this is the first of them. No first lesson to do, you know, and lie in bed to-morrow morning."

"But who sings?"

"Why, everybody, of course; you'll see soon enough. We begin directly after supper, and sing till bed-time. It ain't such good fun now, though, as in the summer half; 'cause then we sing in the little fives court, under the library, you know. We take out tables, and the big boys sit round and drink beer—double allowance on Saturday nights; and we cut about the quadrangle between the songs, and it looks like a lot of robbers in a cave. And the louts come and pound at the great gates, and we pound back again, and shout at them. But this half we only sing in the hall. Come along down to my study."

Their principal employment in the study was to clear out East's table; removing the drawers and ornaments and tablecloth; for he lived in the bottom passage, and his table was in requisition for the singing.

Supper came in due course at seven o'clock, consisting of bread and cheese and beer, which was all saved for the singing; and directly afterwards the fags went to work to prepare the hall. The School-house hall, as has been said, is a great long high room, with two large fires on one side, and two large iron-bound tables, one running down the middle, and the other along the wall opposite the fireplaces. Around the upper fire the fags placed the tables in the form of a horse-shoe, and upon them the jugs with the Saturday night's allowance of beer. Then the big boys used to drop in and take their seats, bringing with them bottled beer and song books; for although they all knew the songs by heart, it was the thing to have an old manuscript book descended from some departed hero, in which they were all carefully written out.

The sixth-form boys had not yet appeared; so, to fill up the gap, an interesting and time-honoured ceremony was gone through. Each new boy was placed on the table in turn, and made to sing a solo, under the penalty of drinking a large mug of salt and water if he resisted or broke down. However, the new boys all sing like nightingales to-night, and the salt water is not in requisition—Tom, as his part, performing the old west-country song of "The Leather Bottel" with considerable applause. And at the half-hour down come the sixth and fifth form boys, and take their places at the tables, which are filled up by the next biggest boys, the rest, for whom there is no room at the table, standing round outside.

The glasses and mugs are filled, and then the fugleman strikes up the old sea-song,

"A wet sheet and a flowing sea,
And a wind that follows fast," etc.,

which is the invariable first song in the School-house; and all the seventy voices join in, not mindful of harmony, but bent on noise, which they attain decidedly, but the general effect isn't bad. And then follow "The British Grenadiers," "Billy Taylor," "The Siege of Seringapatam," "Three Jolly Postboys," and other vociferous songs in rapid succession, including "The Chesapeake and Shannon," a song lately introduced in honour of old Brooke; and when they come to the words,

"Brave Broke he waved his sword, crying, Now, my
lads, aboard,
And we'll stop their playing Yankee-doodle-dandy
oh!"

you expect the roof to come down. The sixth and fifth know that "brave Broke" of the Shannon was no sort

of relation to our old Brooke. The fourth form are uncertain in their belief, but for the most part hold that old Brooke was a midshipman then on board his uncle's ship. And the lower school never doubt for a moment that it was our old Brooke who led the boarders, in what capacity they care not a straw. During the pauses the bottled-beer corks fly rapidly, and the talk is fast and merry, and the big boys—at least all of them who have a fellow-feeling for dry throats—hand their mugs over their shoulders to be emptied by the small ones who stand round behind.

Then Warner, the head of the house, gets up and wants to speak; but he can't, for every boy knows what's coming. And the big boys who sit at the tables pound them and cheer; and the small boys who stand behind pound one another, and cheer, and rush about the hall cheering. Then silence being made, Warner reminds them of the old School-house custom of drinking the healths, on the first night of singing, of those who are going to leave at the end of the half. "He sees that they know what he is going to say already" (loud cheers), "and so won't keep them, but only ask them to treat the toast as it deserves. It is the head of the eleven, the head of big-side football, their leader on this glorious day—Pater Brooke!"

And away goes the pounding and cheering again, becoming deafening when old Brooke gets on his legs; till, a table having broken down, and a gallon or so of beer been upset, and all throats getting dry, silence ensues, and the hero speaks, leaning his hands on the table, and bending a little forwards. No action, no tricks of oratory—plain, strong, and straight, like his play.

"Gentlemen of the School-house! I am very proud of the way in which you have received my name, and I wish I could say all I should like in return. But I know I shan't. However, I'll do the best I can to say what seems to me ought to be said by a fellow who's just going to leave, and who has spent a good slice of his life here. Eight years it is, and eight such years as I can never hope to have again. So now I hope you'll all listen to me" (loud cheers of "That we will"), "for I'm going to talk seriously. You're bound to listen to me for what's the use of calling me 'pater,' and all that, if you don't mind what I say? And I'm going to talk seriously, because I feel so. It's a jolly time, too, getting to the end of the half, and a goal kicked by us first day" (tremendous applause), "after one of the hardest and fiercest day's play I can remember in eight years." (Frantic shoutings.) "The School played splendidly, too, I will say, and kept it up to the last. That last charge of theirs would have carried away a house. I never thought to see anything again of old Crab there, except little pieces, when I saw him tumbled over by it." (Laughter and shouting, and great slapping on the back of Jones by the boys nearest him.) "Well, but we beat 'em." (Cheers.) "Ay, but why did we beat 'em? Answer me that." (Shouts of "Your play.") "Nonsense! 'Twasn't the wind and kick-off either—that wouldn't do it. 'Twasn't because we've half a dozen of the best players in the school, as we have. I wouldn't change Warner, and Hedge, and Crab, and the young un, for any six on their side." (Violent cheers.) "But half a dozen fellows can't keep it up for two hours against two hundred. Why is it, then? I'll tell you what I think. It's because we've more reliance on one another, more of a house feeling, more fellowship than the School can have. Each of us knows and can depend on his next-hand man better. That's why we beat 'em to-day. We've union, they've division—there's the secret." (Cheers.) "But how's this to be kept up? How's it to be improved? That's the question. For I take it we're all in earnest about beating the School, whatever else we care about. I know I'd sooner win two School-house matches running than get the Balliol scholarship any day." (Frantic cheers.)

"Now, I'm as proud of the house as any one. I believe it's the best house in the school, out and out." (Cheers.) "But it's a long way from what I want to see it. First, there's a deal of bullying going on. I know it well. I don't pry about and interfere; that only makes it more underhand, and encourages the small boys to come to us with their fingers in their eyes telling tales, and so we should be worse off than ever. It's very little kindness for the sixth to meddle generally—you youngsters mind that. You'll be all the better football players for learning to stand it, and to take your own parts, and fight it through. But depend on it, there's nothing breaks up a house like bullying. Bullies are cowards, and one coward makes many; so good-bye to the School-house match if bullying gets ahead here." (Loud applause from the small boys, who look meaningly at Flashman and other boys at the tables.) "Then there's fuddling about in the public-house, and drinking bad spirits, and punch, and such rot-gut stuff. That won't make good dropkicks or chargers of you, take

my word for it. You get plenty of good beer here, and that's enough for you; and drinking isn't fine or manly, whatever some of you may think of it.

"One other thing I must have a word about. A lot of you think and say, for I've heard you, 'There's this new Doctor hasn't been here so long as some of us, and he's changing all the old customs. Rugby, and the Schoolhouse especially, are going to the dogs. Stand up for the good old ways, and down with the Doctor!' Now I'm as fond of old Rugby customs and ways as any of you, and I've been here longer than any of you, and I'll give you a word of advice in time, for I shouldn't like to see any of you getting sacked. 'Down with the Doctor's' easier said than done. You'll find him pretty tight on his perch, I take it, and an awkwardish customer to handle in that line. Besides now, what customs has he put down? There was the good old custom of taking the linchpins out of the farmers' and bagmen's gigs at the fairs, and a cowardly, blackguard custom it was. We all know what came of it, and no wonder the Doctor objected to it. But come now, any of you, name a custom that he has put down."

"The hounds," calls out a fifth-form boy, clad in a green cutaway with brass buttons and cord trousers, the leader of the sporting interest, and reputed a great rider and keen hand generally.

"Well, we had six or seven mangy harriers and beagles belonging to the house, I'll allow, and had had them for years, and that the Doctor put them down. But what good ever came of them? Only rows with all the keepers for ten miles round; and big-side hare-and-hounds is better fun ten times over. What else?"

No answer.

"Well, I won't go on. Think it over for yourselves. You'll find, I believe, that he don't meddle with any one that's worth keeping. And mind now, I say again, look out for squalls if you will go your own way, and that way ain't the Doctor's, for it'll lead to grief. You all know that I'm not the fellow to back a master through thick and thin. If I saw him stopping football, or cricket, or bathing, or sparring, I'd be as ready as any fellow to stand up about it. But he don't; he encourages them. Didn't you see him out to-day for half an hour watching us?" (loud cheers for the Doctor); "and he's a strong, true man, and a wise one too, and a public-school man too" (cheers), "and so let's stick to him, and talk no more rot, and drink his health as the head of the house." (Loud cheers.) "And now I've done blowing up, and very glad I am to have done. But it's a solemn thing to be thinking of leaving a place which one has lived in and loved for eight years; and if one can say a word for the good of the old house at such a time, why, it should be said, whether bitter or sweet. If I hadn't been proud of the house and you— ay, no one knows how proud—I shouldn't be blowing you up. And now let's get to singing. But before I sit down I must give you a toast to be drunk with three-times-three and all the honours. It's a toast which I hope every one of us, wherever he may go hereafter, will never fail to drink when he thinks of the brave, bright days of his boyhood. It's a toast which should bind us all together, and to those who've gone before and who'll come after us here. It is the dear old School-house—the best house of the best school in England!"

My dear boys, old and young, you who have belonged, or do belong, to other schools and other houses, don't begin throwing my poor little book about the room, and abusing me and it, and vowing you'll read no more when you get to this point. I allow you've provocation for it. But come now—would you, any of you, give a fig for a fellow who didn't believe in and stand up for his own house and his own school? You know you wouldn't. Then don't object to me cracking up the old School-house, Rugby. Haven't I a right to do it, when I'm taking all the trouble of writing this true history for all of your benefits? If you ain't satisfied, go and write the history of your own houses in your own times, and say all you know for your own schools and houses, provided it's true, and I'll read it without abusing you.

The last few words hit the audience in their weakest place. They had been not altogether enthusiastic at several parts of old Brooke's speech; but "the best house of the best school in England" was too much for them all, and carried even the sporting and drinking interests off their legs into rapturous applause, and (it is to be hoped) resolutions to lead a new life and remember old Brooke's words—which, however, they didn't altogether do, as will appear hereafter.

But it required all old Brooke's popularity to carry down parts of his speech—especially that relating to the Doctor. For there are no such bigoted holders by established forms and customs, be they never so foolish or meaningless, as English school-boys—at least, as the school-boys of our generation. We magnified into

heroes every boy who had left, and looked upon him with awe and reverence when he revisited the place a year or so afterwards, on his way to or from Oxford or Cambridge; and happy was the boy who remembered him, and sure of an audience as he expounded what he used to do and say, though it were sad enough stuff to make angels, not to say head-masters, weep.

We looked upon every trumpery little custom and habit which had obtained in the School as though it had been a law of the Medes and Persians, and regarded the infringement or variation of it as a sort of sacrilege. And the Doctor, than whom no man or boy had a stronger liking for old school customs which were good and sensible, had, as has already been hinted, come into most decided collision with several which were neither the one nor the other. And as old Brooke had said, when he came into collision with boys or customs, there was nothing for them but to give in or take themselves off; because what he said had to be done, and no mistake about it. And this was beginning to be pretty clearly understood. The boys felt that there was a strong man over them, who would have things his own way, and hadn't yet learnt that he was a wise and loving man also. His personal character and influence had not had time to make itself felt, except by a very few of the bigger boys with whom he came more directly into contact; and he was looked upon with great fear and dislike by the great majority even of his own house. For he had found School and School-house in a state of monstrous license and misrule, and was still employed in the necessary but unpopular work of setting up order with a strong hand.

However, as has been said, old Brooke triumphed, and the boys cheered him and then the Doctor. And then more songs came, and the healths of the other boys about to leave, who each made a speech, one flowery, another maudlin, a third prosy, and so on, which are not necessary to be here recorded.

Half-past nine struck in the middle of the performance of "Auld Lang Syne," a most obstreperous proceeding, during which there was an immense amount of standing with one foot on the table, knocking mugs together and shaking hands, without which accompaniments it seems impossible for the youths of Britain to take part in that famous old song. The under-porter of the School-house entered during the performance, bearing five or six long wooden candlesticks with lighted dips in them, which he proceeded to stick into their holes in such part of the great tables as he could get at; and then stood outside the ring till the end of the song, when he was hailed with shouts.

"Bill you old muff, the half-hour hasn't struck." "Here, Bill, drink some cocktail." "Sing us a song, old boy." "Don't you wish you may get the table?" Bill drank the proffered cocktail not unwillingly, and putting down the empty glass, remonstrated. "Now gentlemen, there's only ten minutes to prayers, and we must get the hall straight."

Shouts of "No, no!" and a violent effort to strike up "Billy Taylor" for the third time. Bill looked appealingly to old Brooke, who got up and stopped the noise. "Now then, lend a hand, you youngsters, and get the tables back; clear away the jugs and glasses. Bill's right. Open the windows, Warner." The boy addressed, who sat by the long ropes, proceeded to pull up the great windows, and let in a clear, fresh rush of night air, which made the candles flicker and gutter, and the fires roar. The circle broke up, each collaring his own jug, glass, and song-book; Bill pounced on the big table, and began to rattle it away to its place outside the buttery door. The lower-passage boys carried off their small tables, aided by their friends; while above all, standing on the great hall-table, a knot of untiring sons of harmony made night doleful by a prolonged performance of "God Save the King." His Majesty King William the Fourth then reigned over us, a monarch deservedly popular amongst the boys addicted to melody, to whom he was chiefly known from the beginning of that excellent if slightly vulgar song in which they much delighted,—

> "Come, neighbours all, both great and small,
> Perform your duties here,
> And loudly sing, 'Live Billy, our king,'
> For bating the tax upon beer."

Others of the more learned in songs also celebrated his praises in a sort of ballad, which I take to have been written by some Irish loyalist. I have forgotten all but the chorus, which ran,

> "God save our good King William, be his name for
> ever blest;
> He's the father of all his people, and the guardian of
> all the rest."

In troth we were loyal subjects in those days, in a rough way. I trust that our successors make as much of her

present Majesty, and, having regard to the greater refinement of the times, have adopted or written other songs equally hearty, but more civilized, in her honour.

Then the quarter to ten struck, and the prayer-bell rang. The sixth and fifth form boys ranged themselves in their school order along the wall, on either side of the great fires, the middle-fifth and upper-school boys round the long table in the middle of the hall, and the lower-school boys round the upper part of the second long table, which ran down the side of the hall farthest from the fires. Here Tom found himself at the bottom of all, in a state of mind and body not at all fit for prayers, as he thought; and so tried hard to make himself serious, but couldn't, for the life of him, do anything but repeat in his head the choruses of some of the songs, and stare at all the boys opposite, wondering at the brilliancy of their waistcoats, and speculating what sort of fellows they were. The steps of the head-porter are heard on the stairs, and a light gleams at the door. "Hush!" from the fifth-form boys who stand there, and then in strides the Doctor, cap on head, book in one hand, and gathering up his gown in the other. He walks up the middle, and takes his post by Warner, who begins calling over the names. The Doctor takes no notice of anything, but quietly turns over his book and finds the place, and then stands, cap in hand and finger in book, looking straight before his nose. He knows better than any one when to look, and when to see nothing. To-night is singing night, and there's been lots of noise and no harm done—nothing but beer drunk, and nobody the worse for it, though some of them do look hot and excited. So the Doctor sees nothing, but fascinates Tom in a horrible manner as he stands there, and reads out the psalm, in that deep, ringing, searching voice of his. Prayers are over, and Tom still stares open-mouthed after the Doctor's retiring figure, when he feels a pull at his sleeve, and turning round, sees East.

"I say, were you ever tossed in a blanket?"

"No," said Tom; "why?"

"'Cause there'll be tossing to-night, most likely, before the sixth come up to bed. So if you funk, you just come along and hide, or else they'll catch you and toss you."

"Were you ever tossed? Does it hurt?" inquired Tom.

"Oh yes, bless you, a dozen times," said East, as he hobbled along by Tom's side upstairs. "It don't hurt unless you fall on the floor. But most fellows don't like it."

They stopped at the fireplace in the top passage, where were a crowd of small boys whispering together, and evidently unwilling to go up into the bedrooms. In a minute, however, a study door opened, and a sixth-form boy came out, and off they all scuttled up the stairs, and then noiselessly dispersed to their different rooms. Tom's heart beat rather quick as he and East reached their room, but he had made up his mind. "I shan't hide, East," said he.

"Very well, old fellow," replied East, evidently pleased; "no more shall I. They'll be here for us directly."

The room was a great big one, with a dozen beds in it, but not a boy that Tom could see except East and himself. East pulled off his coat and waistcoat, and then sat on the bottom of his bed whistling and pulling off his boots. Tom followed his example.

A noise and steps are heard in the passage, the door opens, and in rush four or five great fifth-form boys, headed by Flashman in his glory.

Tom and East slept in the farther corner of the room, and were not seen at first.

"Gone to ground, eh?" roared Flashman. "Push 'em out then, boys; look under the beds." And he pulled up the little white curtain of the one nearest him. "Who-o-op!" he roared, pulling away at the leg of a small boy, who held on tight to the leg of the bed, and sang out lustily for mercy.

"Here, lend a hand, one of you, and help me pull out this young howling brute.—Hold your tongue, sir, or I'll kill you."

"Oh, please, Flashman, please, Walker, don't toss me! I'll fag for you—I'll do anything—only don't toss me."

"You be hanged," said Flashman, lugging the wretched boy along; "'twon't hurt you,—you!—Come along, boys; here he is."

"I say, Flashey," sang out another of the big boys; "drop that; you heard what old Pater Brooke said tonight. I'll be hanged if we'll toss any one against their will. No more bullying. Let him go, I say."

Flashman, with an oath and a kick, released his prey, who rushed headlong under his bed again, for fear they should change their minds, and crept along underneath the other beds, till he got under that of the sixth-form boy, which he knew they daren't disturb.

"There's plenty of youngsters don't care about it," said Walker. "Here, here's Scud East—you'll be tossed, won't you, young un?" Scud was East's nickname, or Black, as we called it, gained by his fleetness of foot.

"Yes," said East, "if you like, only mind my foot."

"And here's another who didn't hide. —Hullo! new boy; what's your name, sir?"

"Brown."

"Well, Whitey Brown, you don't mind being tossed?"

"No," said Tom, setting his teeth.

"Come along then, boys," sang out Walker; and away they all went, carrying along Tom and East, to the intense relief of four or five other small boys, who crept out from under the beds and behind them.

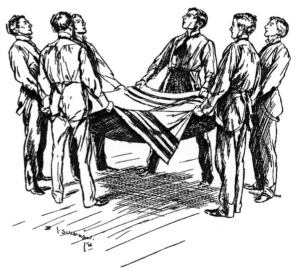

Arthur Hughes's wood engravings, with sharp black lines and artistic effects of light and dark, accompanied many Victorian children's stories.

"What a trump Scud is!" said one. "They won't come back here now."

"And that new boy, too; he must be a good-plucked one."

"Ah! wait till he has been tossed on to the floor; see how he'll like it then!"

Meantime the procession went down the passage to Number 7, the largest room, and the scene of the tossing, in the middle of which was a great open space. Here they joined other parties of the bigger boys, each with a captive or two, some willing to be tossed, some sullen, and some frightened to death. At Walker's suggestion all who were afraid were let off, in honour of Pater Brooke's speech.

Then a dozen big boys seized hold of a blanket, dragged from one of the beds. "In with Scud; quick! there's no time to lose." East was chucked into the blanket. "Once, twice, thrice, and away!" Up he went like a shuttlecock, but not quite up to the ceiling.

"Now, boys, with a will," cried Walker; "once, twice, thrice, and away!" This time he went clean up, and kept himself from touching the ceiling with his hand, and so again a third time, when he was turned out, and up went another boy. And then came Tom's turn. He lay quite still, by East's advice, and didn't dislike the "once, twice, thrice;" but the "away" wasn't so pleasant. They were in good wind now, and sent him slap up to the ceiling first time, against which his knees came rather sharply. But the moment's pause before descending was the rub—the feeling of utter helplessness and of leaving his whole inside behind him sticking to the ceiling. Tom was very near shouting to be set down when he found himself back in the blanket, but thought of East, and didn't; and so took his three tosses without a kick or a cry, and was called a young trump for his pains.

He and East, having earned it, stood now looking on. No catastrophe happened, as all the captives were cool hands, and didn't struggle. This didn't suit Flashman. What your real bully likes in tossing is when the boys kick and struggle, or hold on to one side of the blanket, and so get pitched bodily on to the floor; it's no fun to him when no one is hurt or frightened.

"Let's toss two of them together, Walker," suggested he.

"What a cursed bully you are, Flashey!" rejoined the other. "Up with another one."

And so now two boys were tossed together, the peculiar hardship of which is, that it's too much for human nature to lie still then and share troubles; and so the wretched pair of small boys struggle in the air which shall fall a-top in the descent, to the no small risk of both falling out of the blanket, and the huge delight of brutes like Flashman.

But now there's a cry that the prepostor of the room is coming; so the tossing stops, and all scatter to their different rooms; and Tom is left to turn in, with the first day's experience of a public school to meditate upon.

Louisa May Alcott (1832–88)

Louisa May Alcott, the daughter of American Transcendentalist philosopher Bronson Alcott and the neighbor, in Concord, Massachusetts, of Ralph Waldo Emerson, Nathaniel Hawthorne, and Henry David Thoreau, created an influential classic work of realistic fiction for girls in *Little Women* (1868–69). Prior to *Little Women*, Alcott experimented with a variety of genres, including the sensational fiction that she published under a pseudonym, and edited the children's periodical *Merry's Museum*. She first won recognition for *Hospital Sketches* (1862), a narrative based on her Civil War nursing experience. Like *Hospital Sketches, Little Women* is autobiographical, but although Alcott later claimed that "we really lived most of it," she took considerable liberty with her material, softening what had actually been a life of emotional conflict and economic hardship. After the success of *Little Women*, she went on to write two sequels, *Little*

Men (1871) and *Jo's Boys* (1886), as well as many other novels and collections of stories for young people. During the past several decades, feminist critics have enhanced Alcott's reputation as a writer for both adults and children by examining closely such scenes as that between Marmee and Jo in Chapter 8 of *Little Women* (see Part 1).

In the chapters from *Little Women* in this section, Alcott reveals her philosophy of education and of social values. As is the pattern throughout the novel, each chapter presents a girl's temptation and testing, and the resulting lesson. Some of the chapter titles allude to *Pilgrim's Progress* (1678), John Bunyan's Puritan allegory of Christian life. In Amy's case, the temptation is self-indulgence, symbolized by the pickled limes her teacher detests. Although Marmee makes it clear that she thinks Amy deserved some punishment for her transgression, she vehemently disapproves (as did Alcott) of physical punishment and takes Amy out of the school where Mr. Davis teaches. In Meg's chapter, the temptation is worldly sophistication. She flirts with fashionable society, but discovers that its values are incompatible with simplicity and integrity. In the chapter "Friend," Jo, encouraged by Professor Bhaer in New York, comes to feel that the "sensational" stories she has been writing are beneath her, and she resolves to stop writing them. These chapters emphasize that a woman's education and work are uniquely concerned with "manners, morals, feelings, and examples," unlike the rougher, mostly physical education and pursuits of boys, as reflected in the selections by Thomas Hughes and Mark Twain.

From *Little Women*

CHAPTER 7. AMY'S VALLEY OF HUMILIATION

"That boy is a perfect Cyclops, isn't he?" said Amy, one day, as Laurie clattered by on horse-back, with a flourish of his whip as he passed.

"How dare you say so, when he's got both his eyes? and very handsome ones they are, too"; cried Jo, who resented any slighting remarks about her friend.

"I didn't say anything about his eyes, and I don't see why you need fire up when I admire his riding."

"Oh, my goodness! that little goose means a centaur, and she called him a Cyclops," exclaimed Jo, with a burst of laughter.

"You needn't be so rude; it's only a 'lapse of lingy,' as Mr. Davis says," retorted Amy, finishing Jo with her Latin. "I just wish I had a little of the money Laurie spends on that horse," she added, as if to herself, yet hoping her sisters would hear.

"Why?" asked Meg, kindly, for Jo had gone off in another laugh at Amy's second blunder.

"I need it so much; I'm dreadfully in debt, and it won't be my turn to have the rag-money for a month."

"In debt, Amy; what do you mean?" and Meg looked sober.

"Why, I owe at least a dozen pickled limes, and I can't pay them, you know, till I have money, for Marmee forbid my having anything charged at the shop."

"Tell me all about it. Are limes the fashion now? It used to be pricking bits of rubber to make balls"; and Meg tried to keep her countenance, Amy looked so grave and important.

"Why, you see, the girls are always buying them, and unless you want to be thought mean, you must do it, too. It's nothing but limes now, for every one is sucking them in their desks in school-time, and trading them off for pencils, bead-rings, paper dolls, or something else, at recess. If one girl likes another, she gives her a lime; if she's mad with her, she eats one before her face, and don't offer even a suck. They treat by turns; and I've had ever so many, but haven't returned them, and I ought, for they are debts of honor, you know."

"How much will pay them off, and restore your credit?" asked Meg, taking out her purse.

"A quarter would more than do it, and leave a few cents over for a treat for you. Don't you like limes?"

"Not much; you may have my share. Here's the money,—make it last as long as you can, for it isn't very plenty, you know."

"Oh, thank you! it must be so nice to have pocket-money. I'll have a grand feast, for I haven't tasted a lime this week. I felt delicate about taking any, as I couldn't return them, and I'm actually suffering for one."

Next day Amy was rather late at school; but could not resist the temptation of displaying, with pardonable pride, a moist brown paper parcel, before she consigned it to the inmost recesses of her desk. During the next few minutes the rumour that Amy March had got twenty-four delicious limes (she ate one on the way), and was going to treat, circulated through her "set," and the attentions of her friends became quite overwhelming. Katy Brown invited her to her next party on the spot; Mary Kingsley insisted on lending her her watch till recess, and Jenny Snow, a satirical young lady who had basely twitted Amy upon her limeless state, promptly buried the hatchet, and offered to furnish answers to certain appalling sums. But Amy had not forgotten Miss Snow's cutting remarks about "some persons whose noses were not too flat to smell other people's limes, and stuck-up people, who were not too proud to ask for them"; and she instantly crushed "that Snow girl's" hopes by the withering telegram, "You needn't be so polite all of a sudden, for you won't get any."

A distinguished personage happened to visit the school that morning, and Amy's beautifully drawn maps received praise, which honor to her foe rankled in the soul of Miss Snow, and caused Miss March to assume the airs of a studious young peacock. But, alas, alas! pride goes before a fall, and the revengeful Snow turned the tables with disastrous success. No sooner had the guest paid the usual stale compliments, and bowed himself out, than Jenny, under pretence of asking an important question, informed Mr. Davis, the teacher, that Amy March had pickled limes in her desk.

Now Mr. Davis had declared limes a contraband article, and solemnly vowed to publicly ferule the first person who was found breaking the law. This much-enduring man had succeeded in banishing gum after a long and stormy war, had made a bonfire of the confiscated novels and newspapers, had suppressed a private post-office, had forbidden distortions of the face, nicknames, and caricatures, and done all that one man could do to keep half a hundred rebellious girls in order. Boys are trying enough to human patience, goodness knows! but girls are infinitely more so, especially to nervous gentlemen with tyrannical tempers, and no more talent for teaching than "Dr. Blimber." Mr. Davis knew any quantity of Greek, Latin, Algebra, and ologies of all sorts, so he was called a fine teacher; and manners, morals, feelings, and examples were not considered of any particular importance. It was a most unfortunate moment for denouncing Amy, and Jenny knew it. Mr. Davis had evidently taken his coffee too strong that morning; there was an east wind, which always affected his neuralgia; and his pupils had not done him the credit which he felt he deserved; therefore, to use the expressive, if not elegant, language of a schoolgirl, "he was as nervous as a witch and as cross as a bear." The word "limes" was like fire to powder; his yellow face flushed, and he rapped on his desk with an energy which made Jenny skip to her seat with unusual rapidity.

"Young ladies, attention, if you please!"

At the stern order the buzz ceased, and fifty pairs of blue, black, gray, and brown eyes were obediently fixed upon his awful countenance.

"Miss March, come to the desk."

Amy rose to comply, with outward composure, but a secret fear oppressed her, for the limes weighed upon her conscience.

"Bring with you the limes you have in your desk," was the unexpected command which arrested her before she got out of her seat.

"Don't take all," whispered her neighbor, a young lady of great presence of mind.

Amy hastily shook out half a dozen, and laid the rest down before Mr. Davis, feeling that any man possessing a human heart would relent when that delicious perfume met his nose. Unfortunately, Mr. Davis particularly detested the odor of the fashionable pickle, and disgust added to his wrath.

"Is that all?"

"Not quite," stammered Amy.

"Bring the rest, immediately."

With a despairing glance at her set she obeyed.

"You are sure there are no more?"

"I never lie, sir."

"So I see. Now take these disgusting things, two by two, and throw them out of the window."

There was a simultaneous sigh, which created quite a little gust as the last hope fled, and the treat was ravished from their longing lips. Scarlet with shame and anger, Amy went to and fro twelve mortal times; and as each doomed couple, looking, oh, so plump and juicy! fell from her reluctant hands, a shout from the street completed the anguish of the girls, for it told them that their feast was being exulted over by the little Irish children, who were their sworn foes. This— this was too much; all flashed indignant or appealing glances at the inexorable Davis, and one passionate lime-lover burst into tears.

As Amy returned from her last trip, Mr. Davis gave a portentous "hem," and said, in his most impressive manner,—

"Young ladies, you remember what I said to you a week ago. I am sorry this has happened; but I never allow my rules to be infringed, and I *never* break my word. Miss March, hold out your hand."

Amy started, and put both hands behind her, turning on him an imploring look, which pleaded for her better than the words she could not utter. She was rather a favorite with "old Davis," as, of course, he was called, and it's my private belief that he *would* have broken his word if the indignation of one irrepressible young lady had not found vent in a hiss. That hiss, faint as it was, irritated the irascible gentleman, and sealed the culprit's fate.

"Your hand, Miss March!" was the only answer her mute appeal received; and, too proud to cry or beseech, Amy set her teeth, threw back her head defiantly, and bore without flinching several tingling blows on her little palm. They were neither many nor heavy, but that made no difference to her. For the first time in her life she had been struck; and the disgrace, in her eyes, was as deep as if he had knocked her down.

"You will now stand on the platform till recess," said Mr. Davis, resolved to do the thing thoroughly, since he had begun.

That was dreadful; it would have been bad enough to go to her seat and see the pitying faces of her friends, or the satisfied ones of her few enemies; but to face the whole school, with that shame fresh upon her, seemed impossible, and for a second she felt as if she could only drop down where she stood, and break her heart with crying. A bitter sense of wrong, and the

thought of Jenny Snow, helped her to bear it; and, taking the ignominious place, she fixed her eyes on the stove-funnel above what now seemed a sea of faces, and stood there so motionless and white, that the girls found it very hard to study, with that pathetic figure before them.

During the fifteen minutes that followed, the proud and sensitive little girl suffered a shame and pain which she never forgot. To others it might seem a ludicrous or trivial affair, but to her it was a hard experience; for during the twelve years of her life she had been governed by love alone, and a blow of that sort had never touched her before. The smart of her hand, and the ache of her heart, were forgotten in the sting of the thought,—

"I shall have to tell at home, and they will be so disappointed in me!"

The fifteen minutes seemed an hour; but they came to an end at last, and the word "recess!" had never seemed so welcome to her before.

"You can go, Miss March," said Mr. Davis, looking, as he felt, uncomfortable.

He did not soon forget the reproachful look Amy gave him, as she went, without a word to any one, straight into the anteroom, snatched her things, and left the place "forever," as she passionately declared to herself. She was in a sad state when she got home; and when the older girls arrived, some time later, an indignation meeting was held at once. Mrs. March did not say much, but looked disturbed, and comforted her afflicted little daughter in her tenderest manner. Meg bathed the insulted hand with glycerine and tears; Beth felt that even her beloved kittens would fail as a balm for griefs like this, and Jo wrathfully proposed that Mr. Davis be arrested without delay, while Hannah shook her fist at the "villain," and pounded potatoes for dinner as if she had him under her pestle.

No notice was taken of Amy's flight, except by her mates; but the sharp-eyed demoiselles discovered that Mr. Davis was quite benignant in the afternoon, also unusually nervous. Just before school closed, Jo appeared, wearing a grim expression, as she stalked up to the desk, and delivered a letter from her mother; then collected Amy's property, and departed, carefully scraping the mud from her boots on the door-mat, as if she shook the dust of the place off her feet.

"Yes, you can have a vacation from school, but I want you to study a little every day, with Beth," said

Mrs. March, that evening. "I don't approve of corporal punishment, especially for girls. I dislike Mr. Davis' manner of teaching, and don't think the girls you associate with are doing you any good, so I shall ask your father's advice before I send you anywhere else."

"That's good! I wish all the girls would leave, and spoil his old school. It's perfectly maddening to think of those lovely limes," sighed Amy, with the air of a martyr.

"I am not sorry you lost them, for you broke the rules, and deserved some punishment for disobedience," was the severe reply, which rather disappointed the young lady, who expected nothing but sympathy.

"Do you mean you are glad I was disgraced before the whole school?" cried Amy.

"I should not have chosen that way of mending a fault," replied her mother; "but I'm not sure that it won't do you more good than a milder method. You are getting to be altogether too conceited and important, my dear, and it is quite time you set about correcting it. You have a good many little gifts and virtues, but there is no need of parading them, for conceit spoils the finest genius. There is not much danger that real talent or goodness will be overlooked long; even if it is, the consciousness of possessing and using it well should satisfy one, and the great charm of all power is modesty."

"So it is," cried Laurie, who was playing chess in a corner with Jo. "I knew a girl, once, who had a really remarkable talent for music, and she didn't know it; never guessed what sweet little things she composed when she was alone, and wouldn't have believed it if any one had told her."

"I wish I'd known that nice girl, maybe she would have helped me, I'm so stupid," said Beth, who stood beside him, listening eagerly.

"You do know her, and she helps you better than any one else could," answered Laurie, looking at her with such mischievous meaning in his merry black eyes, that Beth suddenly turned very red, and hid her face in the sofa-cushion, quite overcome by such an unexpected discovery.

Jo let Laurie win the game, to pay for that praise of her Beth, who could not be prevailed upon to play for them after her compliment. So Laurie did his best, and sung delightfully, being in a particularly lively humor, for to the Marches he seldom showed the moody side of his character. When he was gone, Amy, who had been pensive all the evening, said, suddenly, as if busy over some new idea,—

"Is Laurie an accomplished boy?"

"Yes; he has had an excellent education, and has much talent; he will make a fine man, if not spoilt by petting," replied her mother.

"And he isn't conceited, is he?" asked Amy.

"Not in the least; that is why he is so charming, and we all like him so much."

"I see; it's nice to have accomplishments, and be elegant; but not to show off, or get perked up," said Amy, thoughtfully.

"These things are always seen and felt in a person's manner and conversation, if modestly used; but it is not necessary to display them," said Mrs. March.

"Any more than it's proper to wear all your bonnets, and gowns, and ribbons, at once, that folks may know you've got 'em," added Jo; and the lecture ended in a laugh.

CHAPTER 9. MEG GOES TO VANITY FAIR

"I do think it was the most fortunate thing in the world, that those children should have the measles just now," said Meg, one April day, as she stood packing the "go abroady" trunk in her room, surrounded by her sisters.

"And so nice of Annie Moffat not to forget her promise. A whole fortnight of fun will be regularly splendid," replied Jo, looking like a windmill, as she folded skirts with her long arms.

"And such lovely weather; I'm so glad of that," added Beth, tidily sorting neck and hair ribbons in her best box, lent for the great occasion.

"I wish I was going to have a fine time, and wear all these nice things," said Amy, with her mouth full of pins, as she artistically replenished her sister's cushion.

"I wish you were all going; but, as you can't, I shall keep my adventures to tell you when I come back. I'm sure it's the least I can do, when you have been so kind, lending me things, and helping me get ready," said Meg, glancing round the room at the very simple outfit, which seemed nearly perfect in their eyes.

"What did mother give you out of the treasure-box?" asked Amy, who had not been present at the opening of a certain cedar chest, in which Mrs. March kept a few relics of past splendor, as gifts for her girls when the proper time came.

"A pair of silk stockings, that pretty carved fan, and a lovely blue sash. I wanted the violet silk; but there isn't time to make it over, so I must be contented with my old tarleton."

"It will look nicely over my new muslin skirt, and the sash will set it off beautifully. I wish I hadn't smashed my coral bracelet, for you might have had it," said Jo, who loved to give and lend, but whose possessions were usually too dilapidated to be of much use.

"There is a lovely old-fashioned pearl set in the treasure-box; but mother said real flowers were the prettiest ornament for a young girl, and Laurie promised to send me all I want," replied Meg. "Now, let me see; there's my new gray walking-suit,—just curl up the feather in my hat, Beth,—then my poplin, for Sunday, and the small party,—it looks heavy for spring, don't it? the violet silk would be so nice; oh, dear!"

"Never mind; you've got the tarleton for the big party, and you always look like an angel in white," said Amy, brooding over the little store of finery in which her soul delighted.

"It isn't low-necked, and it don't sweep enough, but it will have to do. My blue house-dress looks so well, turned and freshly trimmed, that I feel as if I'd got a new one. My silk sacque isn't a bit the fashion, and my bonnet don't look like Sallie's; I didn't like to say anything, but I was dreadfully disappointed in my umbrella. I told mother black, with a white handle, but she forgot, and bought a green one, with an ugly yellowish handle. It's strong and neat, so I ought not to complain, but I know I shall feel ashamed of it beside Annie's silk one, with a gold top," sighed Meg, surveying the little umbrella with great disfavor.

"Change it," advised Jo.

"I won't be so silly, or hurt Marmee's feelings, when she took so much pains to get my things. It's a nonsensical notion of mine, and I'm not going to give up to it. My silk stockings and two pairs of spandy gloves are my comfort. You are a dear, to lend me yours, Jo; I feel so rich, and sort of elegant, with two new pairs, and the old ones cleaned up for common"; and Meg took a refreshing peep at her glove-box.

"Annie Moffat has blue and pink bows on her night-caps; would you put some on mine?" she asked, as Beth brought up a pile of snowy muslins, fresh from Hannah's hands.

"No, I wouldn't; for the smart caps won't match the plain gowns, without any trimming on them. Poor folks shouldn't rig," said Jo, decidedly.

"I wonder if I shall *ever* be happy enough to have real lace on my clothes, and bows on my caps?" said Meg, impatiently.

"You said the other day that you'd be perfectly happy if you could only go to Annie Moffat's," observed Beth, in her quiet way.

"So I did! Well, I *am* happy, and I *won't* fret; but it does seem as if the more one gets the more one wants, don't it? There, now, the trays are ready, and everything in but my ball-dress, which I shall leave for mother," said Meg, cheering up, as she glanced from the half-filled trunk to the many-times pressed and mended white tarleton, which she called her "ball-dress," with an important air.

The next day was fine, and Meg departed, in style, for a fortnight of novelty and pleasure. Mrs. March had consented to the visit rather reluctantly, fearing that Margaret would come back more discontented than she went. But she had begged so hard, and Sallie had promised to take good care of her, and a little pleasure seemed so delightful after a winter of hard work, that the mother yielded, and the daughter went to take her first taste of fashionable life.

The Moffats *were* very fashionable, and simple Meg was rather daunted, at first, by the splendor of the house, and the elegance of its occupants. But they were kindly people, in spite of the frivolous life they led, and soon put their guest at her ease. Perhaps Meg felt, without understanding why, that they were not particularly cultivated or intelligent people, and that all their gilding could not quite conceal the ordinary material of which they were made. It certainly was agreeable to fare sumptuously, drive in a fine carriage, wear her best frock every day, and do nothing but enjoy herself. It suited her exactly; and soon she began to imitate the manners and conversation of those about her; to put on little airs and graces, use French phrases, crimp her hair, take in her dresses, and talk about the fashions, as well as she could. The more she saw of Annie Moffat's pretty things, the more she envied her, and sighed to be rich. Home now looked bare and dismal as she thought of it, work grew harder than ever, and she felt that she was a very destitute and much injured girl, in spite of the new gloves and silk stockings.

She had not much time for repining, however, for the three young girls were busily employed in "having a good time." They shopped, walked, rode, and called all day; went to theatres and operas, or frolicked at home in the evening; for Annie had many friends, and knew how to entertain them. Her older sisters were very fine young ladies, and one was engaged, which was extremely interesting and romantic, Meg thought. Mr. Moffat was a fat, jolly old gentleman, who knew her father; and Mrs. Moffat, a fat, jolly old lady, who took as great a fancy to Meg as her daughter had done. Every one petted her; and "Daisy," as they called her, was in a fair way to have her head turned.

When the evening for the "small party" came, she found that the poplin wouldn't do at all, for the other girls were putting on thin dresses, and making themselves very fine indeed; so out came the tarleton, looking older, limper, and shabbier than ever, beside Sallie's crisp new one. Meg saw the girls glance at it, and then at one another, and her cheeks began to burn; for, with all her gentleness, she was very proud. No one said a word about it, but Sallie offered to do her hair, and Annie to tie her sash, and Belle, the engaged sister, praised her white arms; but, in their kindness, Meg saw only pity for her poverty, and her heart felt very heavy as she stood by herself, while the others laughed and chattered, prinked, and flew about like gauzy butterflies. The hard, bitter feeling was getting pretty bad, when the maid brought in a box of flowers. Before she could speak, Annie had the cover off, and all were exclaiming at the lovely roses, heath, and fern within.

"It's for Belle, of course; George always sends her some, but these are altogether ravishing," cried Annie, with a great sniff.

"They are for Miss March," the man said. "And here's a note," put in the maid, holding it to Meg.

"What fun! Who are they from? Didn't know you had a lover," cried the girls, fluttering about Meg in a high state of curiosity and surprise.

"The note is from mother, and the flowers from Laurie," said Meg, simply, yet much gratified that he had not forgotten her.

"Oh, indeed!" said Annie, with a funny look, as Meg slipped the note in her pocket, as a sort of talisman against envy, vanity, and false pride; for the few loving words had done her good, and the flowers cheered her up by their beauty.

Feeling almost happy again, she laid by a few ferns and roses for herself, and quickly made up the rest in dainty bouquets for the breasts, hair, or skirts of her friends, offering them so prettily, that Clara, the elder sister, told her she was "the sweetest little thing she ever saw"; and they looked quite charmed with her small attention. Somehow the kind act finished her despondency; and, when all the rest went to show themselves to Mrs. Moffat, she saw a happy, bright-eyed face in the mirror, as she laid her ferns against her rippling hair, and fastened the roses in the dress that didn't strike her as so *very* shabby now.

She enjoyed herself very much that evening, for she danced to her heart's content; every one was very kind, and she had three compliments. Annie made her sing, and some one said she had a remarkably fine voice; Major Lincoln asked who "the fresh little girl, with the beautiful eyes, was"; and Mr. Moffat insisted on dancing with her, because she "didn't dawdle, but had some spring in her," as he gracefully expressed it. So, altogether, she had a very nice time, till she overheard a bit of a conversation, which disturbed her extremely. She was sitting just inside the conservatory, waiting for her partner to bring her an ice, when she heard a voice ask, on the other side of the flowery wall,—

"How old is he?"

"Sixteen or seventeen, I should say," replied another voice.

"It would be a grand thing for one of those girls, wouldn't it? Sallie says they are very intimate now, and the old man quite dotes on them."

"Mrs. M. has laid her plans, I dare say, and will play her cards well, early as it is. The girl evidently doesn't think of it yet," said Mrs. Moffat.

"She told that fib about her mamma, as if she did know, and colored up when the flowers came, quite prettily. Poor thing! she'd be so nice if she was only got up in style. Do you think she'd be offended if we offered to lend her a dress for Thursday?" asked another voice.

"She's proud, but I don't believe she'd mind, for that dowdy tarleton is all she has got. She may tear it to-night, and that will be a good excuse for offering a decent one."

"We'll see; I shall ask that Laurence, as a compliment to her, and we'll have fun about it afterward."

Here Meg's partner appeared, to find her looking much flushed, and rather agitated. She was proud, and her pride was useful just then, for it helped her hide her mortification, anger, and disgust, at what she had just heard; for, innocent and unsuspicious as she was, she could not help understanding the gossip of her friends. She tried to forget it, but could not, and kept repeating to herself, "Mrs. M. has her plans," "that fib about her mamma," and "dowdy tarleton," till she was ready to cry, and rush home to tell her troubles, and ask for advice. As that was impossible, she did her best to seem gay; and, being rather excited, she succeeded so well, that no one dreamed what an effort she was making. She was very glad when it was all over, and she was quiet in her bed, where she could think and wonder and fume till her head ached, and her hot cheeks were cooled by a few natural tears. Those foolish, yet well-meant words, had opened a new world to Meg, and much disturbed the peace of the old one, in which, till now, she had lived as happily as a child. Her innocent friendship with Laurie was spoilt by the silly speeches she had overheard; her faith in her mother was a little shaken by the worldly plans attributed to her by Mrs. Moffat, who judged others by herself; and the sensible resolution to be contented with the simple wardrobe which suited a poor man's daughter, was weakened by the unnecessary pity of girls, who thought a shabby dress one of the greatest calamities under heaven.

Poor Meg had a restless night, and got up heavy-eyed, unhappy, half resentful toward her friends, and half ashamed of herself for not speaking out frankly, and setting everything right. Everybody dawdled that morning, and it was noon before the girls found energy enough even to take up their worsted work. Something in the manner of her friends struck Meg at once; they treated her with more respect, she thought; took quite a tender interest in what she said, and looked at her with eyes that plainly betrayed curiosity. All this surprised and flattered her, though she did not understand it till Miss Belle looked up from her writing, and said, with a sentimental air,—

"Daisy, dear, I've sent an invitation to your friend, Mr. Laurence, for Thursday. We should like to know him, and it's only a proper compliment to you."

Meg colored, but a mischievous fancy to tease the girls made her reply, demurely,—

"You are very kind, but I'm afraid he won't come."

"Why not, *cherie*?" asked Miss Belle.

"He's too old."

"My child, what do you mean? What is his age, I beg to know!" cried Miss Clara.

"Nearly seventy, I believe," answered Meg, counting stitches, to hide the merriment in her eyes.

"You sly creature! of course, we meant the young man," exclaimed Miss Belle, laughing.

"There isn't any; Laurie is only a little boy," and Meg laughed also at the queer look which the sisters exchanged, as she thus described her supposed lover.

"About your age," Nan said.

"Nearer my sister Jo's; *I* am seventeen in August," returned Meg, tossing her head.

"It's very nice of him to send you flowers, isn't it?" said Annie looking wise about nothing.

"Yes, he often does, to all of us; for their house is full, and we are so fond of them. My mother and old Mr. Laurence are friends, you know, so it is quite natural that we children should play together"; and Meg hoped they would say no more.

"It's evident Daisy isn't out yet," said Miss Clara to Belle, with a nod.

"Quite a pastoral state of innocence all round," returned Miss Belle, with a shrug.

"I'm going out to get some little matters for my girls; can I do anything for you, young ladies?" asked Mrs. Moffat, lumbering in, like an elephant, in silk and lace.

"No, thank you, ma'am," replied Sallie. "I've got my new pink silk for Thursday, and don't want a thing."

"Nor I—" began Meg, but stopped, because it occurred to her that she *did* want several things, and could not have them.

"What shall you wear?" asked Sallie.

"My old white one again, if I can mend it fit to be seen; it got sadly torn last night," said Meg, trying to speak quite easily, but feeling very uncomfortable.

"Why don't you send home for another?" said Sallie, who was not an observing young lady.

"I haven't got any other." It cost Meg an effort to say that, but Sallie did not see it, and exclaimed, in amiable surprise,—

"Only that? how funny—." She did not finish her speech, for Belle shook her head at her, and broke in, saying, kindly,—

"Not at all; where is the use of having a lot of dresses when she isn't out? There's no need of sending home, Daisy, even if you had a dozen, for I've got a sweet blue silk laid away, which I've outgrown, and you shall wear it to please me; won't you, dear?"

"You are very kind, but I don't mind my old dress, if you don't; it does well enough for a little girl like me," said Meg.

"Now do let me please myself by dressing you up in style. I admire to do it, and you'd be a regular little beauty, with a touch here and there. I shan't let any one see you till you are done, and then we'll burst upon them like Cinderella and her godmother, going to the ball," said Belle, in her persuasive tone.

Meg couldn't refuse the offer so kindly made, for a desire to see if she would be "a little beauty" after touching up caused her to accept, and forget all her former uncomfortable feelings towards the Moffats.

On the Thursday evening, Belle shut herself up with her maid; and, between them, they turned Meg into a fine lady. They crimped and curled her hair, they polished her neck and arms with some fragrant powder, touched her lips with coralline salve, to make them redder, and Hortense would have added "a *soupçon* of rouge," if Meg had not rebelled. They laced her into a sky-blue dress, which was so tight she could hardly breathe, and so low in the neck that modest Meg blushed at herself in the mirror. A set of silver filagree was added, bracelets, necklace, brooch, and even ear-rings, for Hortense tied them on, with a bit of pink silk, which did not show. A cluster of tea rose-buds at the bosom, and a *ruche,* reconciled Meg to the display of her pretty white shoulders, and a pair of high-heeled blue silk boots satisfied the last wish of her heart. A laced handkerchief, a plumy fan, and a bouquet in a silver holder, finished her off; and Miss Belle surveyed her with the satisfaction of a little girl with a newly dressed doll.

"Mademoiselle is *charmante, très jolie,* is she not?" cried Hortense, clasping her hands in an affected rapture.

"Come and show yourself," said Miss Belle, leading the way to the room where the others were waiting.

As Meg went rustling after, with her long skirts trailing, her ear-rings tinkling, her curb waving, and her heart beating, she felt as if her "fun" had really begun at last, for the mirror had plainly told her that she *was* "a little beauty." Her friends repeated the pleasing phrase enthusiastically; and, for several minutes, she stood, like the jackdaw in the fable, enjoying her bor-

rowed plumes, while the rest chattered like a party of magpies.

"While I dress, do you drill her, Nan, in the management of her skirt, and those French heels, or she will trip herself up. Put your silver butterfly in the middle of that white barbe, and catch up that long curl on the left side of her head, Clara, and don't any of you disturb the charming work of my hands," said Belle, as she hurried away, looking well pleased with her success.

"I'm afraid to go down, I feel so queer and stiff, and half-dressed," said Meg to Sallie, as the bell rang, and Mrs. Moffat sent to ask the young ladies to appear at once.

"You don't look a bit like yourself, but you are very nice. I'm nowhere beside you, for Belle has heaps of taste, and you're quite French, I assure you. Let your flowers hang; don't be so careful of them, and be sure you don't trip," returned Sallie, trying not to care that Meg was prettier than herself.

Keeping that warning carefully in mind, Margaret got safely down stairs, and sailed into the drawing-rooms, where the Moffats and a few early guests were assembled. She very soon discovered that there is a charm about fine clothes which attracts a certain class of people, and secures their respect. Several young ladies, who had taken no notice of her before, were very affectionate all of a sudden; several young gentlemen, who had only stared at her at the other party, now not only stared, but asked to be introduced, and said all manner of foolish, but agreeable things to her; and several old ladies, who sat on sofas, and criticised the rest of the party, inquired who she was, with an air of interest. She heard Mrs. Moffat reply to one of them,—

"Daisy March—father a colonel in the army—one of our first families, but reverses of fortune, you know; intimate friends of the Laurences; sweet creature, I assure you; my Ned is quite wild about her."

"Dear me!" said the old lady, putting up her glass for another observation of Meg, who tried to look as if she had not heard, and been rather shocked at Mrs. Moffat's fibs.

The "queer feeling" did not pass away, but she imagined herself acting the new part of a fine lady, and so got on pretty well, though the tight dress gave her a side-ache, the train kept getting under her feet, and she was in constant fear lest her ear-rings should fly off and get lost or broken. She was flirting her fan, and laughing at the feeble jokes of a young gentleman who tried to be witty, when she suddenly stopped laughing, and looked confused; for, just opposite, she saw Laurie. He was staring at her with undisguised surprise, and disapproval also, she thought; for, though he bowed and smiled, yet something in his honest eyes made her blush, and wish she had her old dress on. To complete her confusion, she saw Belle nudge Annie, and both glance from her to Laurie, who, she was happy to see, looked unusually boyish and shy.

"Silly creatures, to put such thoughts into my head! I won't care for it, or let it change me a bit," thought Meg, and rustled across the room to shake hands with her friend.

"I'm glad you've come, I was afraid you wouldn't," she said, with her most grown-up air.

"Jo wanted me to come, and tell her how you looked, so I did"; answered Laurie, without turning his eyes upon her, though he half smiled at her maternal tone.

"What shall you tell her?" asked Meg, full of curiosity to know his opinion of her, yet feeling ill at ease with him, for the first time.

"I shall say I didn't know you; for you look so grown-up, and unlike yourself, I'm quite afraid of you," he said, fumbling at his glove-button.

"How absurd of you! the girls dressed me up for fun, and I rather like it. Wouldn't Jo stare if she saw me?" said Meg, bent on making him say whether he thought her improved or not.

"Yes, I think she would," returned Laurie, gravely.

"Don't you like me so?" asked Meg.

"No, I don't," was the blunt reply.

"Why not?" in an anxious tone.

He glanced at her frizzled head, bare shoulders, and fantastically trimmed dress, with an expression that abashed her more than his answer, which had not a particle of his usual politeness about it.

"I don't like fuss and feathers."

That was altogether too much from a lad younger than herself, and Meg walked away, saying, petulantly,—

"You are the rudest boy I ever saw."

Feeling very much ruffled, she went and stood at a quiet window, to cool her cheeks, for the tight dress gave her an uncomfortably brilliant color. As she stood there, Major Lincoln passed by; and, a minute after, she heard him saying to his mother,—

"They are making a fool of that little girl; I wanted you to see her, but they have spoilt her entirely; she's nothing but a doll, tonight."

"Oh dear!" sighed Meg; "I wish I'd been sensible, and worn my own things; then I should not have disgusted other people, or felt so uncomfortable and ashamed myself."

She leaned her forehead on the cool pane, and stood half hidden by the curtains, never minding that her favorite waltz had begun, till some one touched her; and, turning, she saw Laurie looking penitent, as he said, with his very best bow, and his hand out,—

"Please forgive my rudeness, and come and dance with me."

"I'm afraid it will be too disagreeable to you," said Meg, trying to look offended, and failing entirely.

"Not a bit of it; I'm dying to do it. Come, I'll be good; I don't like your gown, but I do think you are—just splendid"; and he waved his hands, as if words failed to express his admiration.

Meg smiled, and relented, and whispered, as they stood waiting to catch the time.

"Take care my skirt don't trip you up; it's the plague of my life, and I was a goose to wear it."

"Pin it round your neck, and then it will be useful," said Laurie, looking down at the little blue boots, which he evidently approved of.

Away they went, fleetly and gracefully; for, having practised at home, they were well matched, and the blithe young couple were a pleasant sight to see, as they twirled merrily round and round, feeling more friendly than ever after their small tiff.

"Laurie, I want you to do me a favor; will you?" said Meg, as he stood fanning her, when her breath gave out, which it did, very soon, though she would not own why.

"Won't I!" said Laurie, with alacrity.

"Please don't tell them at home about my dress tonight. They won't understand the joke, and it will worry mother."

"Then why did you do it?" said Laurie's eyes, so plainly, that Meg hastily added,—

"I shall tell them, myself, all about it and ' 'fess' to mother how silly I've been. But I'd rather do it myself; so you'll not tell, will you?"

"I give you my word I won't; only what shall I say when they ask me?"

"Just say I looked nice, and was having a good time."

"I'll say the first, with all my heart; but how about the other? You don't look as if you were having a good time; are you?" and Laurie looked at her with an expression which made her answer, in a whisper,—

"No; not just now. Don't think I'm horrid; I only wanted a little fun, but this sort don't pay, I find, and I'm getting tired of it."

"Here comes Ned Moffat; what does he want?" said Laurie, knitting his black brows, as if he did not regard his young host in the light of a pleasant addition to the party.

"He put his name down for three dances, and I suppose he's coming for them; what a bore!" said Meg, assuming a languid air, which amused Laurie immensely.

He did not speak to her again till supper-time, when he saw her drinking champagne with Ned, and his friend Fisher, who were behaving "like a pair of fools," as Laurie said to himself, for he felt a brotherly sort of right to watch over the Marches, and fight their battles, whenever a defender was needed.

"You'll have a splitting headache to-morrow, if you drink that stuff. I wouldn't, Meg; your mother don't like it, you know," he whispered, leaning over her chair, as Ned turned to refill her glass, and Fisher stooped to pick up her fan.

"I'm not Meg, to-night; I'm 'a doll,' who does all sorts of crazy things. To-morrow I shall put away my 'fuss and feathers,' and be desperately good again," she answered, with an affected little laugh.

"Wish to-morrow was here, then," muttered Laurie, walking off, ill-pleased at the change he saw in her.

Meg danced and flirted, chattered and giggled, as the other girls did; after supper she undertook the German, and blundered through it, nearly upsetting her partner with her long skirt, and romping in a way that scandalized Laurie, who looked on and meditated a lecture. But he got no chance to deliver it, for Meg kept away from him till he came to say good-night.

"Remember!" she said, trying to smile, for the splitting headache had already begun.

"*Silence à la mort,*" replied Laurie, with a melodramatic flourish, as he went away.

This little bit of by-play excited Annie's curiosity; but Meg was too tired for gossip, and went to bed, feeling as if she had been to a masquerade, and hadn't enjoyed herself as much as she expected. She was sick all the next day, and on Saturday went home, quite used up with her fortnight's fun, and feeling that she had sat in the lap of luxury long enough.

"It does seem pleasant to be quiet, and not have company manners on all the time. Home *is* a nice place, though it isn't splendid," said Meg, looking about her with a restful expression, as she sat with her mother and Jo on the Sunday evening.

"I'm glad to hear you say so, dear, for I was afraid home would seem dull and poor to you after your fine quarters," replied her mother, who had given her many anxious looks that day; for motherly eyes are quick to see any change in children's faces.

Meg had told her adventures gaily, and said over and over what a charming time she had had; but something still seemed to weigh upon her spirits, and, when the younger girls were gone to bed, she sat thoughtfully staring at the fire, saying little, and looking worried. As the clock struck nine, and Jo proposed bed, Meg suddenly left her chair, and, taking Beth's stool, leaned her elbows on her mother's knee, saying, bravely,—

"Marmee, I want to ''fess.'"

"I thought so; what is it, dear?"

"Shall I go away?" asked Jo, discreetly.

"Of course not; don't I always tell you everything? I was ashamed to speak of it before the children, but I want you to know all the dreadful things I did at the Moffats."

"We are prepared," said Mrs. March, smiling, but looking a little anxious.

"I told you they rigged me up, but I didn't tell you that they powdered, and squeezed, and frizzled, and made me look like a fashion-plate. Laurie thought I wasn't proper; I know he did, though he didn't say so, and one man called me 'a doll.' I knew it was silly, but they flattered me, and said I was a beauty, and quantities of nonsense, so I let them make a fool of me."

"Is that all?" asked Jo, as Mrs. March looked silently at the downcast face of her pretty daughter, and could not find it in her heart to blame her little follies.

"No; I drank champagne, and romped, and tried to flirt and was, altogether, abominable," said Meg, self-reproachfully.

"There is something more, I think"; and Mrs. March smoothed the soft cheek, which suddenly grew rosy, as Meg answered, slowly,—

"Yes; it's very silly, but I want to tell it, because I hate to have people say and think such things about us and Laurie."

Then she told the various bits of gossip she had heard at the Moffats'; and, as she spoke, Jo saw her mother fold her lips tightly, as if ill pleased that such ideas should be put into Meg's innocent mind.

"Well, if that isn't the greatest rubbish I ever heard," cried Jo, indignantly. "Why didn't you pop out and tell them so, on the spot?"

"I couldn't, it was so embarrassing for me. I couldn't help hearing, at first, and then I was so angry and ashamed, I didn't remember that I ought to go away."

"Just wait till *I* see Annie Moffat, and I'll show you how to settle such ridiculous stuff. The idea of having 'plans,' and being kind to Laurie, because he's rich, and may marry us by and by! Won't he shout, when I tell him what those silly things say about us poor children?" and Jo laughed, as if, on second thoughts, the thing struck her as a good joke.

"If you tell Laurie, I'll never forgive you! She mustn't, must she, mother?" said Meg, looking distressed.

"No; never repeat that foolish gossip, and forget it as soon as you can," said Mrs. March, gravely. "I was very unwise to let you go among people of whom I know so little; kind, I dare say, but worldly, ill-bred, and full of these vulgar ideas about young people. I am more sorry than I can express, for the mischief this visit may have done you, Meg."

"Don't be sorry, I won't let it hurt me; I'll forget all the bad, and remember only the good; for I did enjoy a great deal, and thank you very much for letting me go. I'll not be sentimental or dissatisfied, mother; I know I'm a silly little girl, and I'll stay with you till I'm fit to take care of myself. But it *is* nice to be praised and admired, and I can't help saying I like it," said Meg, looking half ashamed of the confession.

"That is perfectly natural, and quite harmless, if the liking does not become a passion, and lead one to do foolish or unmaidenly things. Learn to know and value the praise which is worth having, and to excite the admiration of excellent people, by being modest as well as pretty, Meg."

Margaret sat thinking a moment, while Jo stood with her hands behind her, looking both interested and a little perplexed; for it was a new thing to see Meg blushing and talking about admiration, lovers, and things of that sort, and Jo felt as if during that fortnight her sister had grown up amazingly, and was

drifting away from her into a world where she could not follow.

"Mother, do you have 'plans,' as Mrs. Moffat said?" asked Meg, bashfully.

"Yes, my dear, I have a great many; all mothers do, but mine differ somewhat from Mrs. Moffat's, I suspect. I will tell you some of them, for the time has come when a word may set this romantic little head and heart of yours right, on a very serious subject. You are young, Meg; but not too young to understand me, and mother's lips are the fittest to speak of such things to girls like you. Jo, your turn will come in time, perhaps, so listen to my 'plans,' and help me carry them out, if they are good."

Jo went and sat on one arm of the chair, looking as if she thought they were about to join in some very solemn affair. Holding a hand of each, and watching the two young faces wistfully, Mrs. March said, in her serious yet cheery way,—

"I want my daughters to be beautiful, accomplished, and good; to be admired, loved, and respected, to have a happy youth, to be well and wisely married, and to lead useful, pleasant lives, with as little care and sorrow to try them as God sees fit to send. To be loved and chosen by a good man is the best and sweetest thing which can happen to a woman; and I sincerely hope my girls may know this beautiful experience. It is natural to think of it, Meg; right to hope and wait for it, and wise to prepare for it; so that, when the happy time comes, you may feel ready for the duties, and worthy of the joy. My dear girls, I *am* ambitious for you, but not to have you make a dash in the world,—marry rich men merely because they are rich, or have splendid houses, which are not homes, because love is wanting. Money is a needful and precious thing,—and, when well used, a noble thing,—but I never want you to think it is the first or only prize to strive for. I'd rather see you poor men's wives, if you were happy, beloved, contented, than queens on thrones, without self-respect and peace."

"Poor girls don't stand any chance, Belle says, unless they put themselves forward," sighed Meg.

"Then we'll be old maids," said Jo, stoutly.

"Right, Jo; better be happy old maids than unhappy wives, or unmaidenly girls, running about to find husbands," said Mrs. March, decidedly. "Don't be troubled, Meg; poverty seldom daunts a sincere lover. Some of the best and most honored women I know were poor girls, but so love-worthy that they were not allowed to be old maids. Leave these things to time; make this home happy, so that you may be fit for homes of your own, if they are offered you, and contented here if they are not. One thing remember, my girls, mother is always ready to be your confidant, father to be your friend; and both of us trust and hope that our daughters, whether married or single, will be the pride and comfort of our lives."

"We will, Marmee, we will!" cried both, with all their hearts, as she bade them good-night.

CHAPTER 34. FRIEND

Though very happy in the social atmosphere about her, and very busy with the daily work that earned her bread, and made it sweeter for the effort, Jo still found time for literary labors. The purpose which now took possession of her was a natural one to a poor and ambitious girl; but the means she took to gain her end were not the best. She saw that money conferred power; money and power, therefore, she resolved to have; not to be used for herself alone, but for those whom she loved more than self. The dream of filling home with comforts, giving Beth everything she wanted, from strawberries in winter to an organ in her bedroom; going abroad herself, and always having *more* than enough, so that she might indulge in the luxury of charity, had been for years Jo's most cherished castle in the air.

The prize-story experience had seemed to open a way which might, after long travelling, and much uphill work, lead to this delightful *chateau en Espagne.* But the novel disaster quenched her courage for a time, for public opinion is a giant which has frightened stouter-hearted Jacks on bigger beanstalks than hers. Like that immortal hero, she reposed a while after the first attempt, which resulted in a tumble, and the least lovely of the giant's treasures, if I remember rightly. But the "up again and take another" spirit was as strong in Jo as in Jack; so she scrambled up on the shady side, this time, and got more booty, but nearly left behind her what was far more precious than the money-bags.

She took to writing sensation stories—for in those dark ages, even all-perfect America read rubbish. She told no one, but concocted a "thrilling tale," and boldly carried it herself to Mr. Dashwood, editor of the "Weekly Volcano." She had never read *Sartor Resartus,* But she had a womanly instinct that clothes possess an influence more powerful over many than the worth of character or the magic of manners. So she dressed herself in her best, and, trying to persuade herself that she was neither excited nor nervous, bravely climbed two pairs of dark and dirty stairs to find herself in a disorderly room, a cloud of cigar smoke, and the presence of three gentlemen sitting with their heels rather higher than their hats, which articles of dress none of them took the trouble to remove on her appearance. Somewhat daunted by this reception, Jo hesitated on the threshold, murmuring in much embarrassment,—

"Excuse me; I was looking for the 'Weekly Volcano' office; I wished to see Mr. Dashwood."

Down went the highest pair of heels, up rose the smokiest gentleman, and, carefully cherishing his cigar between his fingers, he advanced with a nod, and a countenance expressive of nothing but sleep. Feeling that she must get through with the matter somehow, Jo produced her manuscript, and, blushing redder and redder with each sentence, blundered out fragments of the little speech carefully prepared for the occasion.

"A friend of mine desired me to offer—a story— just as an experiment—would like your opinion—be glad to write more if this suits."

While she blushed and blundered, Mr. Dashwood had taken the manuscript, and was turning over the leaves with a pair of rather dirty fingers, and casting critical glances up and down the neat pages.

"Not a first attempt, I take it?" observing that the pages were numbered, covered only on one side, and *not* tied up with a ribbon—sure sign of a novice.

"No sir; she has had some experience, and got a prize for a tale in the 'Blarneystone Banner.'"

"Oh did she?" and Mr. Dashwood gave Jo a quick look, which seemed to take note of everything she had on, from the bow in her bonnet to the buttons on her boots. "Well, you can leave it, if you like; we've more of this sort of thing on hand than we know what to do with, at present; but I'll run my eye over it, and give you an answer next week."

Now Jo did *not* like to leave it, for Mr. Dashwood didn't suit her at all; but, under the circumstances, there was nothing for her to do but bow and walk away, looking particularly tall and dignified, as she was apt to do, when nettled or abashed. Just then she was both; for it was perfectly evident from the knowing glances exchanged among the gentlemen, that her little fiction of "my friend" was considered a good joke; and a laugh produced by some inaudible remark of the editor, as he closed the door, completed her discomfiture. Half resolving never to return, she went home, and worked off her irritation by stitching pinafores vigorously; and in an hour or two was cool enough to laugh over the scene, and long for next week.

When she went again, Mr. Dashwood was alone, whereat she rejoiced. Mr. Dashwood was much wider awake than before,—which was agreeable,—and Mr. Dashwood was not too deeply absorbed in a cigar to remember his manners,—so the second interview was much more comfortable than the first.

"We'll take this" (editors never say "I"), "if you don't object to a few alterations. It's too long,—but omitting the passages I've marked will make it just the right length," he said, in a businesslike tone.

Jo hardly knew her own MS. again, so. crumpled and underscored were its pages and paragraphs; but, feeling as a tender parent might on being asked to cut off her baby's legs in order that it might fit into a new cradle, she looked at the marked passages, and was surprised to find that all the moral reflections,—which she had carefully put in as ballast for much romance,—had all been stricken out.

"But, sir, I thought every story should have some sort of a moral, so I took care to have a few of my sinners repent."

Mr. Dashwood's editorial gravity relaxed into a smile, for Jo had forgotten her "friend," and spoken as only an author could.

"People want to be amused, not preached at, you know. Morals don't sell nowadays," which was not quite a correct statement, by the way.

"You think it would do with these alterations, then?"

"Yes, it's a new plot, and pretty well worked up—language good, and so on," was Mr. Dashwood's affable reply.

"What do you—that is, what compensation—" began Jo, not exactly knowing how to express herself.

"Oh, yes,—well, we give from twenty-five to thirty for things of this sort. Pay when it comes out," returned Mr Dashwood, as if that point had escaped him; such trifles often do escape the editorial mind, it is said.

"Very well; you can have it," said Jo, handing back the story, with a satisfied air; for, after the dollar-a-column work, even twenty-five seemed good pay.

"Shall I tell my friend you will take another if she has one better than this?" asked Jo, unconscious of her little slip of the tongue, and emboldened by her success.

"Well, we'll look at it; can't promise to take it; tell her to make it short and spicy, and never mind the moral. What name would your friend like to put to it?" in a careless tone.

"None at all, if you please; she doesn't wish her name to appear, and has no *nom de plume,*" said Jo, blushing in spite of herself.

"Just as she likes, of course. The tale win be out next week; will you call for the money, or shall I send it?" asked Mr. Dashwood, who felt a natural desire to know who his new contributor might be.

"I'll call; good morning sir."

As she departed, Mr. Dashwood put up his feet, with the graceful remark, "Poor and proud, as usual, but she'll do."

Following Mr. Dashwood's directions, and making Mrs. Northbury her model, Jo rashly took a plunge into the frothy sea of sensational literature; but, thanks to the life-preserver thrown her by a friend, she came up again, not much the worse for her ducking.

Like most young scribblers, she went abroad for her characters and scenery, and banditti, counts, gypsies, nuns, and duchesses appeared upon her stage, and played their parts with as much accuracy and spirit as could be expected. Her readers were not particular about such trifles as grammar, punctuation, and probability, and Mr. Dashwood graciously permitted her to fill his columns at the lowest prices, not thinking it necessary to tell her that the real cause of his hospitality was the fact that one of his hacks, on being offered higher wages, had basely left him in the lurch.

She soon became interested in her work,—for her emaciated purse grew stout, and the little hoard she was making to take Beth to the mountains next summer, grew slowly but surely, as the weeks passed. One thing disturbed her satisfaction, and that was that she did not tell them at home. She had a feeling that father and mother would not approve,—and preferred to have her own way first, and beg pardon afterward. It was easy to keep her secret, for no name appeared with her stories; Mr. Dashwood had, of course, found it out very soon, but promised to be dumb; and, for a wonder, kept his word.

She thought it would do her no harm, for she sincerely meant to write nothing of which she should be ashamed, and quieted all pricks of conscience by anticipations of the happy minute when she should show her earnings and laugh over her well-kept secret.

But Mr. Dashwood rejected any but thrilling tales; and, as thrills could not be produced except by harrowing up the souls of the readers, history and romance, land and sea, science and art, police records and lunatic asylums, had to be ransacked for the purpose. Jo soon found that her innocent experience had given her but few glimpses of the tragic world which underlies society; so, regarding it in a business light, she set about supplying her deficiencies with characteristic energy. Eager to find material for stories, and bent on making them original in plot, if not masterly in execution, she searched newspapers for accidents, incidents, and crimes; she excited the suspicions of public librarians by asking for works on poisons; she studied faces in the street,—and characters good, bad, and indifferent, all about her; she delved in the dust of ancient times, for facts or fictions so old that they were as good as new, and introduced herself to folly, sin, and misery, as well as her limited opportunities allowed. She thought she was prospering finely; but, unconsciously, she was beginning to desecrate some of the womanliest attributes of a woman's character. She was living in bad society; and, imaginary though it was, its influence affected her, for she was feeding heart and fancy on dangerous and unsubstantial food, and was fast brushing the innocent bloom from her nature by a premature acquaintance with the darker side of life, which comes soon enough to all of us.

She was beginning to feel rather than see this, for much describing of other people's passions and feelings set her to studying and speculating about her own,—a morbid amusement, in which healthy young minds do not voluntarily indulge. Wrong-doing always brings its own punishment; and, when Jo most needed hers, she got it.

I don't know whether the study of Shakespeare helped her to read character, or the natural instinct of a woman for what was honest, brave and strong; but while endowing her imaginary heroes with every perfection under the sun, Jo was discovering a live hero, who interested her in spite of many human imperfections. Mr. Bhaer, in one of their conversations, had advised her to study simple, true, and lovely characters, wherever she found them, as good training for a writer; Jo took him at his word,—for she coolly turned round and studied him,—a proceeding which would have much surprised him, had he known it,—for the worthy Professor was very humble in his own conceit.

Why everybody liked him was what puzzled Jo, at first. He was neither rich nor great, young nor handsome,—in no respect what is called fascinating, imposing, or brilliant; and yet he was as attractive as a genial fire, and people seemed to gather about him as naturally as about a warm hearth. He was poor, yet always appeared to be giving something away,—a stranger, yet every one was his friend; no longer young,—but as happy-hearted as a boy; plain and odd,—yet his face looked beautiful to many, and his oddities were freely forgiven for his sake. Jo often watched him, trying to discover the charm, and, at last, decided that it was benevolence which worked the miracle. If he had any sorrow "it sat with its head under its wing," and he turned only his sunny side to the world. There were lines upon his forehead, but Time seemed to have touched him gently, remembering how kind he was to others. The pleasant curves about his mouth were the memorials of many friendly words and cheery laughs, his eyes were never cold or hard, and his big hand had a warm, strong grasp that was more expressive than words.

His very clothes seemed to partake of the hospitable nature of the wearer. They looked as if they were at ease, and liked to make him comfortable; his capacious waistcoat was suggestive of a large heart underneath; his rusty coat had a social air, and the baggy pockets plainly proved that little hands often went in empty and came out full; his very boots were benevolent, and his collars never stiff and raspy like other people's.

"That's it!" said Jo to herself, when she at length discovered that genuine good-will toward one's fellow-men could beautify and dignify even a stout German teacher, who shovelled in his dinner, darned his own socks, and was burdened with the name of Bhaer.

Jo valued goodness highly, but she also possessed a most feminine respect for intellect, and a little discovery which she made about the Professor added much to her regard for him. He never spoke of himself, and no one ever knew that in his native city he had been a man much honored and esteemed for learning and integrity, till a countryman came to see him, and, in a conversation with Miss Norton, divulged the pleasing fact. From her Jo learned it,—and liked it all the better because Mr. Bhaer had never told it. She felt proud to know that he was an honored Professor in Berlin; though only a poor language-master in America, and his homely, hardworking life, was much beautified by the spice of romance which this discovery gave it.

Another and a better gift than intellect was shown her in a most unexpected manner. Miss Norton had the *entrée* into literary society, which Jo would have had no chance of seeing but for her. The solitary woman felt an interest in the ambitious girl, and kindly conferred many favors of this sort both on Jo and the Professor. She took them with her, one night, to a select symposium, held in honor of several celebrities.

Jo went prepared to bow down and adore the mighty ones whom she had worshipped with youthful enthusiasm afar off. But her reverence for genius received a severe shock that night, and it took her some time to recover from the discovery that the great creatures were only men and women, after all. Imagine her dismay, on stealing a glance of timid admiration at the poet whose lines suggested an ethereal being fed on "spirit, fire, and dew," to behold him devouring his supper with an ardor which flushed his intellectual countenance. Turning as from a fallen idol, she made other discoveries which rapidly dispelled her romantic illusions. The great novelist vibrated between two decanters with the regularity of a pendulum; the famous divine flirted openly with one of the Madame de Staëls of the age, who looked daggers at another Corinne, who was amiably satirizing her, after out-manœuvreing her in efforts to absorb the profound philosopher, who imbibed tea Johnsonianly and appeared to slumber,—the loquacity of the lady rendering speech impossible. The scientific celebrities, forgetting their mollusks and Glacial Periods, gossiped about art, while devoting themselves to oysters and ices with characteristic energy; the young musician, who was charming the city like a second Orpheus, talked horses; and the specimen of the British nobility present happened to be the most ordinary man of the party.

Before the evening was half over, Jo felt so completely *désillusionnée,* that she sat down in a corner, to recover herself. Mr. Bhaer soon joined her, looking rather out of his element, and presently several of the philosophers, each mounted on his hobby, came ambling up to hold an intellectual tournament in the recess. The conversation was miles beyond Jo's comprehension, but she enjoyed it, though Kant and Hegel were unknown gods, the Subjective and Objective unintelligible terms; and the only thing "revolved from her inner consciousness," was a bad headache after it was all over. It dawned upon her gradually, that the world was being picked to pieces, and put together on new, and, according to the talkers, on infinitely better principles than before; that religion was in a fair way to be reasoned into nothingness, and intellect was to be the only God. Jo knew nothing about philosophy or metaphysics of any sort, but a curious excitement, half pleasurable, half painful, came over her, as she listened with a sense of being turned adrift into time and space, like a young balloon out on a holiday.

She looked round to see how the Professor liked it, and found him looking at her with the grimmest expression she had ever seen him wear. He shook his head, and beckoned her to come away, but she was fascinated, just then, by the freedom of Speculative Philosophy, and kept her seat, trying to find out what the wise gentlemen intended to rely upon after they annihilated all the old beliefs.

Now Mr. Bhaer was a diffident man, and slow to offer his own opinions, not because they were unsettled, but too sincere and earnest to be lightly spoken. As he glanced from Jo to several other young people attracted by the brilliancy of the philosophic pyrotechnics, he knit his brows, and longed to speak, fearing that some inflammable young soul would be led astray by the rockets, to find, when the display was over, that they had only an empty stick, or a scorched hand.

He bore it as long as he could; but when he was appealed to for an opinion, he blazed up with honest indignation, and defended religion with all the eloquence of truth—an eloquence which made his broken English musical, and his plain face beautiful. He had a hard fight, for the wise men argued well; but he didn't know when he was beaten, and stood to his colors like a man. Somehow, as he talked, the world got right again to Jo; the old beliefs that had lasted so long, seemed better than the new. God was not a blind force, and immortality was not a pretty fable, but a blessed fact. She felt as if she had solid ground under her feet again; and when Mr. Bhaer paused, out-talked, but not one whit convinced, Jo wanted to clap her hands, and thank him.

She did neither; but she remembered this scene, and gave the Professor her heartiest respect, for she knew it cost him an effort to speak out then and there, because his conscience would not let him be silent. She began to see that character is a better possession than money, rank, intellect, or beauty; and to feel that if greatness is what a wise man has defined it to be,— "truth, reverence, and good will,"—then her friend Friedrich Bhaer was not only good, but great.

This belief strengthened daily. She valued his esteem, coveted his respect, she wanted to be worthy of his friendship; and, just when the wish was sincerest, she came near losing everything. It all grew out of a cocked-hat; for one evening the Professor came in to give Jo her lesson, with a paper soldier-cap on his head, which Tina had put there, and he had forgotten to take off.

"It's evident he doesn't prink at his glass before coming down," thought Jo, with a smile, as he said, "Goot efening," and sat soberly down, quite unconscious of the ludicrous contrast between his subject and his head-gear, for he was going to read her the "Death of Wallenstein."

She said nothing at first, for she liked to hear him laugh out his big, hearty laugh, when anything funny happened, so she left him to discover it for himself, and presently forgot all about it; for to hear a German read Schiller is rather an absorbing occupation. After the reading came the lesson, which was a lively one, for Jo was in a gay mood that night, and the cocked-hat kept her eyes dancing with merriment. The Professor didn't know what to make of her, and stopped, at last, to ask with an air of mild surprise that was irresistible,—

"Mees Marsch, for what do you laugh in your master's face? Haf you no respect for me, that you go on so bad?"

"How can I be respectful, sir, when you forget to take your hat off?" said Jo.

Lifting his hand to his head, the absent-minded Professor gravely felt and removed the little cocked-hat, looked at it a minute, and then threw back his head, and laughed like a merry bass-viol.

"Ah! I see him now; it is that imp Tina who makes me a fool with my cap. Well, it is nothing; but see you, if this lesson goes not well, you too shall wear him."

But the lesson did not go at all, for a few minutes, because Mr. Bhaer caught sight of a picture on the hat; and, unfolding it, said with an air of great disgust,—

"I wish these papers did not come in the house; they are not for children to see, nor young people to read. It is not well; and I haf no patience with those who make this harm."

Jo glanced at the sheet, and saw a pleasing illustration composed of a lunatic, a corpse, a villain, and a viper. She did not like it; but the impulse that made her turn it over was not one of displeasure, but fear, because, for a minute, she fancied the paper was the "Volcano." It was not, however, and her panic subsided as she remembered that, even if it had been, and one of her own tales in it, there would have been no name to betray her. She had betrayed herself, however, by a look and a blush; for, though an absent man, the Professor saw a good deal more than people fancied. He knew that Jo wrote, and had met her down among the newspaper offices more than once; but as she never spoke of it, he asked no questions, in spite of a strong desire to see her work. Now it occurred to him that she was doing what she was ashamed to own, and it troubled him. He did not say to himself, "It is none of my business; I've no right to say anything," as many people would have done; he only remembered that she was young and poor, a girl far away from mother's love and father's care; and he was moved to help her with an impulse as quick and natural as that which would prompt him to put out his hand to save a baby from a puddle. All this flashed through his mind in a minute, but not a trace of it appeared in his face; and by the time the paper was turned, and Jo's needle threaded, he was ready to say quite naturally, but very gravely,—

"Yes, you are right to put it from you. I do not like to think that good young girls should see such things. They are made pleasant to some, but I would more rather give my boys gunpowder to play with than this bad trash."

"All may not be bad—only silly, you know; and if there is a demand for it, I don't see any harm in supplying it. Many very respectable people make an honest living out of what are called sensation stories," said Jo, scratching gathers so energetically that a row of little slits followed her pin.

"There is a demand for whiskey, but I think you and I do not care to sell it. If the respectable people knew what harm they did, they would not feel that the living *was* honest. They haf no right to put poison in the sugarplum, and let the small ones eat it. No; they should think a little, and sweep mud in the street before they do this thing!"

Mr. Bhaer spoke warmly, and walked to the fire, crumpling the paper in his hands. Jo sat still, looking as if the fire had come to her; for her cheeks burned long after the cocked-hat had turned to smoke, and gone harmlessly up the chimney.

"I should like much to send all the rest after him," muttered the Professor, coming back with a relieved air.

Jo thought what a blaze her pile of papers, upstairs, would make, and her hard-earned money laid rather heavily on her conscience at that minute. Then she thought consolingly to herself, "Mine are not like that; they are only silly, never bad; so I won't be worried;" and, taking up her book, she said, with a studious face,—

"Shall we go on, sir? I'll be very good and proper now."

"I shall hope so," was all he said, but he meant more then she imagined; and the grave, kind look he gave her, made her feel as if the words "Weekly Volcano" were printed in large type, on her forehead.

As soon as she went to her room, she got out her papers, and carefully re-read every one of her stories. Being a little shortsighted, Mr. Bhaer sometimes used eye-glasses, and Jo had tried them once, smiling to see how they magnified the fine print of her book; now she seemed to have got on the Professor's mental or moral spectacles also, for the faults of these poor stories glared at her dreadfully, and filled her with dismay.

"They *are* trash, and will soon be worse than trash if I go on; for each is more sensational than the last I've gone blindly on, hurting myself and other people, for the sake of money;—I know it's so—for I can't read this stuff in sober earnest without being horribly ashamed of it; and *what should* I do if they were seen at home, or Mr. Bhaer got hold of them?"

Jo turned hot at the bare idea, and stuffed the whole bundle into her stove, nearly setting the chimney afire with the blaze.

"Yes, that's the best place for such inflammable nonsense; I'd better burn the house down, I suppose, than let other people blow themselves up with my gunpowder," she thought, as she watched the "Demon of the Jura" whisk away, a little black cinder with fiery eyes.

But when nothing remained of all her three months' work, except a heap of ashes, and the money in her lap, Jo looked sober, as she sat on the floor, wondering what she ought to do about her wages.

"I think I haven't done much harm *yet,* and may keep this to pay for my time," she said, after a long meditation, adding, impatiently, "I almost wish I hadn't any conscience, it's so inconvenient. If I didn't care about doing right, and didn't feel uncomfortable when doing wrong, I should get on capitally. I can't help wishing, sometimes, that father and mother hadn't been so dreadfully particular about such things."

Ah, Jo, instead of wishing that, thank God that "father and mother *were* particular," and pity from your heart those who have no such guardians to hedge them round with principles which may seem like prison walls to impatient youth, but which will prove sure foundations to build character upon in womanhood.

Jo wrote no more sensational stories, deciding that the money did not pay for her share of the sensation; but, going to the other extreme, as is the way with people of her stamp, she took a course of Mrs. Sherwood, Miss Edgeworth, and Hannah More, and then produced a tale which might have been more properly called an essay or a sermon, so intensely moral was it. She had her doubts about it from the beginning; for her lively fancy and girlish romance felt as ill at ease in the new style as she would have done masquerading in the stiff and cumbrous costume of the last century. She sent this didactic gem to several markets, but it found no purchaser; and she was inclined to agree with Mr. Dashwood, that morals didn't sell.

Then she tried a child's story, which she could easily have disposed of if she had not been mercenary enough to demand filthy lucre for it The only person who offered enough to make it worth her while to try juvenile literature, was a worthy gentleman who felt it his mission to convert all the world to his particular belief. But much as she liked to write for children, Jo could not consent to depict all her naughty boys as being eaten by bears, or tossed by mad bulls, because they did not go to a particular Sabbath-school, nor all the good infants who did go, of course, as rewarded by every kind of bliss, from gilded gingerbread to escorts of angels, when they departed this life, with psalms or sermons on their lisping tongues. So nothing came of these trials; and Jo corked up her inkstand, and said, in a fit of very wholesome humility,—

"I don't know anything; I'll wait till I do before I try again, and, meantime, 'sweep mud in the street,' if I can't do better—that's honest, any way;" which decision proved that her second tumble down the beanstalk had done her some good.

While these internal revolutions were going on, her external life had been as busy and uneventful as usual; and if she sometimes looked serious, or a little sad, no one observed it but Professor Bhaer. He did it so quietly, that Jo never knew he was watching to see if she would accept and profit by his reproof; but she stood the test, and he was satisfied; for, though no words passed between them, he knew that she had given up writing. Not only did he guess it by the fact that the second finger of her right hand was no longer inky, but she spent her evenings down stairs, now, was met no more among newspaper offices, and studied with a dogged patience, which assured him that she was bent on occupying her mind with something useful, if not pleasant.

He helped her in many ways, proving himself a true friend, and Jo was happy; for while her pen lay idle, she was learning other lessons beside German, and laying a foundation for the sensation story of her own life.

It was a pleasant winter and a long one, for she did not leave Mrs. Kirke till June. Every one seemed sorry when the time came; the children were inconsolable, and Mr. Bhaer's hair stuck straight up over his head—for he always rumpled it wildly when disturbed in mind.

"Going home! Ah, you are happy that you haf a home to go in," he said, when she told him, and sat silently pulling his beard, in the corner, while she held a little levee on that last evening.

She was going early, so she bade them all good-by over night; and when his turn came, she said, warmly—

"Now, sir, you won't forget to come and see us, if you ever travel our way, will you? I'll never forgive you, if you do, for I want them all to know my friend."

"Do you? Shall I come?" he asked, looking down at her with an eager expression, which she did not see.

"Yes, come next month; Laurie graduates then, and you'd enjoy Commencement as something new."

"That is your best friend, of whom you speak?" he said, in an altered tone.

"Yes, my boy Teddy; I'm very proud of him, and should like you to see him."

Jo looked up, then, quite unconscious of anything but her own pleasure, in the prospect of showing them to one another. Something in Mr. Bhaer's face suddenly recalled the fact that she might find Laurie more than a best friend, and simply because she particularly wished not to look as if anything was the matter, she involuntarily began to blush; and the more she tried not to, the redder she grew. If it had not been for Tina on her knee, she didn't know what would have become of her. Fortunately, the child was moved to hug her; so she managed to hide her face an instant, hoping the Professor did not see it. But he did, and his own changed again from that momentary anxiety to its usual expression, as he said, cordially,—

"I fear I shall not make the time for that, but I wish the friend much success, and you all happiness; Gott bless you!" and with that, he shook hands warmly, shouldered Tina, and went away.

But after the boys were abed, he sat long before his fire, with the tired look on his face, and the "*heimweh*," or homesickness lying heavy at his heart. Once when

English artist Shirley Hughes, illustrating *Little Women* in the 1990s, captured the individuality and the close relationships of the March sisters.

he remembered Jo, as she sat with the little child in her lap, and that new softness in her face, he leaned his head on his hands a minute, and then roamed about the room, as if in search of something he could not find.

"It is not for me; I must not hope it now," he said to himself, with a sigh that was almost a groan; then, as if reproaching himself for the longing that he could not repress, he went and kissed the two towzled heads upon the pillow, took down his seldom-used meerschaum, and opened his Plato.

He did his best, and did it manfully; but I don't think he found that a pair of rampant boys, a pipe, or even the divine Plato, were very satisfactory substitutes for wife and child, and home.

Early as it was, he was at the station, next morning, to see Jo off; and, thanks to him, she began her solitary journey with the pleasant memory of a familiar face smiling its farewell, a bunch of violets to keep her company, and, best of all, the happy thought,—

"Well, the winter's gone, and I've written no books—earned no fortune; but I've made a friend worth having and I'll try to keep him all my life."

Mark Twain (1835–1910)

Mark Twain was the pen name of Samuel Langhorne Clemens, a self-educated printer and river pilot from Missouri who wrote his way into American literary history and popular culture with his stories of humor and frontier adventure, most importantly *Adventures of Huckleberry Finn* (1884). His versions of American boyhood have shaped our consciousness of what it was like to be young in nineteenth-century America. In contrast to Alcott's version of the education of girls, which emphasizes increasing self-restraint and domestic relationships, Twain's stories of boys growing up feature rough-and-tumble outdoor adventures and narrow escapes. In the first of the two chapters from *Tom Sawyer* reprinted here, Tom reveals his love of superstitious lore and his admiration of "the romantic outcast," Huckleberry Finn. *The Adventures of Tom Sawyer* is a parody of romantic literature of various kinds: the story of romantic high adventure, as well as the conventional romance novel. Unlike Alcott, who rejected physical punishment (see the excerpts from *Little Women* in this section), Twain and his hero Tom take whippings for granted, whether at school or at home.

In Chapter 20, Tom has fallen in love with Becky Thatcher and carries on in what he considers heroic fashion to attract her attention and affection. Superstition, adventure, and pranks are always more interesting to Tom than school, which is portrayed as dull when it is not brutal. Tom envies Huck, the town "juvenile pariah," who has the freedom of dressing and acting as he wishes—at least from Tom's perspective. He aspires to the wild, romantic life of pirates and outlaws—but he also finds models for his adventures in the fiction he has been reading, and he revels in the admiration and approval of the townsfolk and, even more, his peers. (See other excerpts by Twain in Parts 1 and 8.)

From *The Adventures of Tom Sawyer*

CHAPTER 6

Self-Examination—Dentistry—The Midnight Charm—Witches and Devils—Cautious Approaches—Happy Hours

Monday morning found Tom Sawyer miserable. Monday morning always found him so—because it began another week's slow suffering in school. He generally began that day with wishing he had had no intervening holiday, it made the going into captivity and fetters again so much more odious.

Tom lay thinking. Presently it occurred to him that he wished he was sick; then he could stay home from school. Here was a vague possibility. He canvassed his system. No ailment was found, and he investigated again. This time he thought he could detect colicky symptoms, and he began to encourage them with considerable hope. But they soon grew feeble, and presently died wholly away. He reflected further. Suddenly he discovered something. One of his upper front teeth was loose. This was lucky; he was about to begin to groan, as a "starter," as he called it, when it occurred to him that if he came into court with that argument, his aunt would pull it out, and that would hurt. So he thought he would hold the tooth in reserve for the present, and seek further. Nothing offered for some little time, and then he remembered hearing the doctor tell about a certain thing that laid up a patient for two or three weeks and threatened to make him lose a finger. So the boy eagerly drew his sore toe from under the sheet and held it up for inspection. But now he did not know the necessary symptoms. However, it seemed well worth while to chance it, so he fell to groaning with considerable spirit.

But Sid slept on unconscious.

Tom groaned louder, and fancied that he began to feel pain in the toe.

No result from Sid.

Tom was panting with his exertions by this time. He took a rest and then swelled himself up and fetched a succession of admirable groans.

Sid snored on.

Tom was aggravated. He said, "Sid, Sid!" and shook him. This course worked well, and Tom began to groan again. Sid yawned, stretched, then brought himself up on his elbow with a snort, and began to stare at Tom. Tom went on groaning. Sid said:

"Tom! Say, Tom!" [No response.] "Here, Tom! *Tom!* What is the matter, Tom?" And he shook him, and looked in his face anxiously.

Tom moaned out:

"O don't, Sid. Don't joggle me."

"Why what's the matter, Tom? I must call auntie."

"No—never mind. It'll be over by and by, maybe. Don't call anybody."

"But I must! *Don't* groan so, Tom, it's awful. How long you been this way?"

"Hours. Ouch! O don't stir so, Sid, you'll kill me."

"Tom, why didn't you wake me sooner? O, Tom, *don't!* It makes my flesh crawl to hear you. Tom, what is the matter?"

"I forgive you everything, Sid. [Groan.] Everything you've ever done to me. When I'm gone—"

"Oh, Tom, you ain't dying, are you? Don't, Tom—O, don't. Maybe—"

"I forgive everybody, Sid. [Groan.] Tell 'em so, Sid. And Sid, you give my window-sash and my cat with one eye to that new girl that's come to town, and tell her—"

But Sid had snatched his clothes and gone. Tom was suffering in reality, now, so handsomely was his imagination working, and so his groans had gathered quite a genuine tone.

Sid flew down stairs and said:

"O, aunt Polly, come! Tom's dying!"

"Dying!"

"Yes'm. Don't wait—come quick!"

"Rubbage! I don't believe it!"

But she fled up stairs, nevertheless, with Sid and Mary at her heels. And her face grew white, too, and her lip trembled. When she reached the bedside she gasped out:

"You Tom! Tom, what's the matter with you!"

"O, auntie, I'm—"

"What's the matter with you—what *is* the matter with you, child!"

"O, auntie, my sore toe's mortified!"

The old lady sank down into a chair and laughed a little, then cried a little, then did both together. This restored her and she said:

"Tom, what a turn you did give me. Now you shut up that nonsense and climb out of this."

The groans ceased and the pain vanished from the toe. The boy felt a little foolish, and he said:

"Aunt Polly it *seemed* mortified, and it hurt so I never minded my tooth at all."

"Your tooth, indeed! What's the matter with your tooth?"

"One of them's loose, and it aches perfectly awful."

"There, there, now, don't begin that groaning again. Open your mouth. Well—your tooth *is* loose, but you're not going to die about that. Mary, get me a silk thread, and a chunk of fire out of the kitchen."

Tom said:

"O, please auntie, don't pull it out. It don't hurt any more. I wish I may never stir if it does. Please don't, auntie. I don't want to stay home from school."

"Oh, you don't, don't you? So all this row was because you thought you'd get to stay home from school and go a-fishing? Tom, Tom, I love you so, and you seem to try every way you can to break my old heart with your outrageousness."

By this time the dental instruments were ready. The old lady made one end of the silk thread fast to Tom's tooth with a loop and tied the other to the bedpost. Then she seized the chunk of fire and suddenly thrust it almost into the boy's face. The tooth hung dangling by the bedpost, now.

But all trials bring their compensations. As Tom wended to school after breakfast, he was the envy of every boy he met because the gap in his upper row of teeth enabled him to expectorate in a new and admirable way. He gathered quite a following of lads interested in the exhibition; and one that had cut his finger and had been a centre of fascination and homage up to this time, now found himself suddenly without an adherent, and shorn of his glory. His heart was heavy, and he said with a disdain which he did not feel, that it wasn't anything to spit like Tom Sawyer; but another boy said "Sour grapes!" and he wandered away a dismantled hero.

Shortly Tom came upon the juvenile pariah of the village, Huckleberry Finn, son of the town drunkard. Huckleberry was cordially hated and dreaded by all the mothers of the town, because he was idle, and law-less, and vulgar and bad—and because all their children admired him so, and delighted in his forbidden society, and wished they dared to be like him. Tom was like the rest of the respectable boys, in that he envied Huckleberry his gaudy outcast condition, and was under strict orders not to play with him. So he played with him every time he got a chance. Huckleberry was always dressed in the cast-off clothes of full-grown men, and they were in perennial bloom and fluttering with rags. His hat was a vast ruin with a wide crescent lopped out of its brim; his coat, when he wore one, hung nearly to his heels and had the rearward buttons far down the back; but one suspender supported his trousers; the seat of the trousers bagged low and contained nothing; the fringed legs dragged in the dirt when not rolled up.

Huckleberry came and went, at his own free will. He slept on doorsteps in fine weather and in empty hogsheads in wet; he did not have to go to school or to church, or call any being master or obey anybody; he could go fishing or swimming when and where he chose, and stay as long as it suited him; nobody forbade him to fight; he could sit up as late as he pleased; he was always the first boy that went barefoot in the spring and the last to resume leather in the fall; he never had to wash, nor put on clean clothes; he could swear wonderfully. In a word, everything that goes to make life precious, that boy had. So thought every harassed, hampered, respectable boy in St. Petersburg.

Tom hailed the romantic outcast:

"Hello, Huckleberry!"

"Hello yourself, and see how you like it."

"What's that you got?"

"Dead cat."

"Lemme see him, Huck. My, he's pretty stiff. Where'd you get him?"

"Bought him off'n a boy."

"What did you give?"

"I give a blue ticket and a bladder that I got at the slaughter house."

"Where'd you get the blue ticket?"

"Bought it off'n Ben Rogers two weeks ago for a hoop-stick."

"Say—what is dead cats good for, Huck?"

"Good for? Cure warts with."

"No! Is that so? I know something that's better."

"I bet you don't. What is it?"

"Why, spunk-water."

"Spunk-water! I wouldn't give a dern for spunk-water."

"You wouldn't, wouldn't you? D'you ever try it?"

"No, I hain't. But Bob Tanner did."

"Who told you so!"

"Why he told Jeff Thatcher, and Jeff told Johnny Baker, and Johnny told Jim Hollis, and Jim told Ben Rogers, and Ben told a nigger, and the nigger told me. There, now!"

"Well, what of it? They'll all lie. Leastways all but the nigger. I don't know *him*. But I never see a nigger that *wouldn't* lie. Shucks! Now you tell me how Bob Tanner done it, Huck."

"Why he took and dipped his hand in a rotten stump where the rain water was."

"In the daytime?"

"Cert'nly."

"With his face to the stump?"

"Yes. Least I reckon so."

"Did he *say* anything?"

"I don't reckon he did. I don't know."

"Aha! Talk about trying to cure warts with spunk-water such a blame fool way as that! Why that ain't a-going to do any good. You got to go all by yourself, to the middle of the woods, where you know there's a spunk-water stump, and just as it's midnight you back up against the stump and jam your hand in and say:

"Barley-corn, barley-corn, injun-meal shorts,
Spunk-water, spunk-water, swaller these warts;"

and then walk away quick, eleven steps, with your eyes shut, and then turn around three times and walk home without speaking to anybody. Because if you speak the charm's busted."

"Well that sounds like a good way; but that ain't the way Bob Tanner done."

"No, sir, you can bet he didn't; becuz he's the warti-est boy in this town; and he wouldn't have a wart on him if he'd knowed how to work spunk-water. I've took off thousands of warts off of my hands that way, Huck. I play with frogs so much that I've always got considerable many warts. Sometimes I take 'em off with a bean."

"Yes, bean's good. I've done that."

"Have you? What's your way?"

"You take and split the bean, and cut the wart so as to get some blood, and then you put the blood on one piece of the bean and take and dig a hole and bury it 'bout midnight at the cross-roads in the dark of the moon, and then you burn up the rest of the bean. You see that piece that's got the blood on it will keep draw-ing and drawing, trying to fetch the other piece to it, and so that helps the blood to draw the wart, and pretty soon off she comes."

"Yes, that's it, Huck—that's it; though when you're burying it, if you say 'Down bean; off, wart; come no more to bother me!' it's better. That's the way Joe Harper does, and he's ben nearly to Constantinople and most everywheres. But say—how do you cure 'em with dead cats?"

"Why you take your cat and go and get in the graveyard 'long about midnight when somebody that was wicked has been buried; and when it's mid-night a devil will come, or maybe two or three, but you can't see 'em, you can only hear something like the wind, or maybe hear 'em talk; and when they're taking that feller away, you heave your cat af-ter 'em and say 'Devil follow corpse, cat follow devil, warts follow cat, I'm done with ye!' That'll fetch *any* wart."

"Sounds right. D'you ever try it, Huck?"

"No, but old Mother Hopkins told me."

"Well I reckon it's so, then. Becuz they say she's a witch."

"Say! Why, Tom, I *know* she is. She witched pap. Pap says so his own self. He come along one day, and he see she was a-witching him, so he took up a rock, and if she hadn't dodged he'd a got her. Well that very night he rolled off'n a shed wher' he was a-layin' drunk, and broke his arm."

"Why that's awful. How did he know she was a-witching him."

"Lord, pap can tell, easy. Pap says when they keep looking at you right stiddy, they're a-witching you. Specially if they mumble. Becuz when they mumble they're a-saying the Lord's Prayer back'ards."

"Say, Huck, when you going to try the cat?"

"To-night. I reckon they'll come after old Hoss Williams to-night."

"But they buried him Saturday, Huck. Didn't they get him Saturday night?"

"Why how you talk! How could their charms work till midnight?—and *then* it's Sunday. Devils don't slosh around much of a Sunday, I don't reckon."

"I never thought of that. That's so. Lemme go with you?"

"Of course—if you ain't afeard."

"Afeard! 'Tain't likely. Will you meow?"

"Yes—and you meow back, if you get a chance. Last time, you kep' me a-meowing around till old Hays went to throwing rocks at me and says 'Dern that cat!' and so I hove a brick through his window—but don't you tell."

"I won't. I couldn't meow that night, becuz auntie was watching me, but I'll meow this time. Say, Huck, what's that?"

"Nothing but a tick."

"Where'd you get him?"

"Out in the woods."

"What'll you take for him?"

"I don't know. I don't want to sell him."

"All right. It's a mighty small tick, anyway."

"O, anybody can run a tick down that don't belong to them. I'm satisfied with it. It's a good enough tick for me."

"Sho, there's ticks a plenty. I could have a thousand of 'em if I wanted to."

"Well why don't you? Becuz you know mighty well you can't. This is a pretty early tick, I reckon. It's the first one I've seen this year."

"Say Huck—I'll give you my tooth for him."

"Less see it."

Tom got out a bit of paper and carefully unrolled it. Huckleberry viewed it wistfully. The temptation was very strong. At last he said:

"Is it genuwyne?"

Tom lifted his lip and showed the vacancy.

"Well, all right," said Huckleberry, "it's a trade."

Tom enclosed the tick in the percussion-cap box that had lately been the pinch-bug's prison, and the boys separated, each feeling wealthier than before.

When Tom reached the little isolated frame school-house, he strode in briskly, with the manner of one who had come with all honest speed. He hung his hat on a peg and flung himself into his seat with business-like alacrity. The master, throned on high in his great splint-bottom arm-chair, was dozing, lulled by the drowsy hum of study. The interruption roused him:

"Thomas Sawyer!"

Tom knew that when his name was pronounced in full, it meant trouble.

"Sir!"

"Come up here. Now sir, why are you late again, as usual?"

Tom was about to take refuge in a lie, when he saw two long tails of yellow hair hanging down a back that he recognized by the electric sympathy of love; and by that form was *the only vacant place* on the girl's side of the school-house. He instantly said:

"I stopped to talk with Huckleberry Finn!"

The master's pulse stood still, and he stared helplessly. The buzz of study ceased. The pupils wondered if this fool-hardy boy had lost his mind. The master said:

"You—you did what?"

"Stopped to talk with Huckleberry Finn."

There was no mistaking the words.

"Thomas Sawyer, this is the most astounding confession I have ever listened to. No mere ferule will answer for this offense. Take off your jacket."

The master's arm performed until it was tired and the stock of switches notably diminished. Then the order followed:

"Now sir, go and sit with the *girls!* And let this be a warning to you."

The titter that rippled around the room appeared to abash the boy, but in reality that result was caused rather more by his worshipful awe of his unknown idol and the dread pleasure that lay in his high good fortune. He sat down upon the end of the pine bench and the girl hitched herself away from him with a toss of her head. Nudges and winks and whispers traversed the room, but Tom sat still, with his arms upon the long, low desk before him, and seemed to study his book. By and by attention ceased from him, and the accustomed school murmur rose upon the dull air once more. Presently the boy began to steal furtive glances at the girl. She observed it, "made a mouth" at him and gave him the back of her head for the space of a minute. When she cautiously faced around again, a peach lay before her. She thrust it away. Tom gently put it back. She thrust it away, again, but with less animosity. Tom patiently returned it to its place. Then she let it remain. Tom scrawled on his slate, "Please take it—I got more." The girl glanced at the words, but made no sign. Now the boy began to draw something on the slate, hiding his work with his left hand. For a time the girl refused to notice; but her human curiosity presently began to manifest itself by hardly perceptible signs. The boy worked on, apparently unconscious. The girl made a sort of non-committal attempt to see, but the boy did not betray that he was aware of it. At last she gave in and hesitatingly whispered:

"Let me see it."

Tom partly uncovered a dismal caricature of a house with two gable ends to it and a cork-screw of smoke issuing from the chimney. Then the girl's interest began to fasten itself upon the work and she forgot everything else. When it was finished, she gazed a moment, then whispered:

"It's nice—make a man."

The artist erected a man in the front yard, that resembled a derrick. He could have stepped over the house; but the girl was not hypercritical; she was satisfied with the monster, and whispered:

"It's a beautiful man—now make me coming along."

Tom drew an hour-glass with a full moon and straw limbs to it and armed the spreading fingers with a portentous fan. The girl said:

"It's ever so nice—I wish I could draw."

"It's easy," whispered Tom, "I'll learn you."

"O, will you? When?"

"At noon. Do you go home to dinner?"

"I'll stay, if you will."

"Good,—that's a whack. What's your name?"

"Becky Thatcher. What's yours? Oh, I know. It's Thomas Sawyer."

"That's the name they lick me by. I'm Tom, when I'm good. You call me Tom, will you?"

"Yes."

Now Tom began to scrawl something on the slate, hiding the words from the girl. But she was not backward this time. She begged to see. Tom said:

"Oh it ain't anything."

"Yes it is."

"No it ain't. You don't want to see."

"Yes I do, indeed I do. Please let me."

"You'll tell."

"No I won't—deed and deed and double deed I won't."

"You won't tell anybody at all?—Ever, as long as you live?"

"No, I won't ever tell *any*body. Now let me."

"Oh, *you* don't want to see!"

"Now that you treat me so, I *will* see." And she put her small hand upon his and a little scuffle ensued, Tom pretending to resist in earnest but letting his hand slip by degrees till these words were revealed: *"I love you."*

"O, you bad thing!" And she hit his hand a smart rap, but reddened and looked pleased, nevertheless.

Just at this juncture the boy felt a slow, fateful grip closing on his ear, and a steady, lifting impulse. In that vise he was borne across the house and deposited in his own seat, under a peppering fire of giggles from the whole school. Then the master stood over him during a few awful moments, and finally moved away to his throne without saying a word. But although Tom's ear tingled, his heart was jubilant.

As the school quieted down Tom made an honest effort to study, but the turmoil within him was too great. In turn he took his place in the reading class and made a botch of it; then in the geography class and turned lakes into mountains, mountains into rivers, and rivers into continents, till chaos was come again; then in the spelling class, and got "turned down," by a succession of mere baby words till he brought up at the foot and yielded up the pewter medal which he had worn with ostentation for months.

CHAPTER 20

Becky in a Dilemma—Tom's Nobility Asserts Itself

There was something about aunt Polly's manner, when she kissed Tom, that swept away his low spirits and made him light-hearted and happy again. He started to school and had the luck of coming upon Becky Thatcher at the head of Meadow Lane. His mood always determined his manner. Without a moment's hesitation he ran to her and said:

"I acted mighty mean to-day, Becky, and I'm so sorry. I won't ever, ever do that way again, as long as ever I live—please make up, won't you?"

The girl stopped and looked him scornfully in the face:

"I'll thank you to keep yourself *to* yourself, Mr. Thomas Sawyer. I'll never speak to you again."

She tossed her head and passed on. Tom was so stunned that he had not even presence of mind enough to say "Who cares, Miss Smarty?" until the right time to say it had gone by. So he said nothing. But he was in a fine rage, nevertheless. He moped into the school-yard wishing she were a boy, and imagining how he would trounce her if she were. He presently encountered her and delivered a stinging remark as he passed. She hurled one in return, and the angry breach was complete. It seemed to Becky, in her hot resentment, that she could hardly wait for school to "take in," she was so impatient to see Tom flogged for the injured spelling-book. If she had had any lingering notion of exposing Alfred Temple, Tom's offensive fling had driven it entirely away.

Poor girl, she did not know how fast she was nearing trouble herself. The master, Mr. Dobbins, had reached middle age with an unsatisfied ambition. The darling of his desires was, to be a doctor, but poverty had decreed that he should be nothing higher than a village schoolmaster. Every day he took a mysterious book out of his desk and absorbed himself in it at times when no classes were reciting. He kept that book under lock and key. There was not an urchin in school but was perishing to have a glimpse of it, but the chance never came. Every boy and girl had a theory about the nature of that book; but no two theories were alike, and there was no way of getting at the facts in the case. Now, as Becky was passing by the desk, which stood near the door, she noticed that the key was in the lock! It was a precious moment. She glanced around; found herself alone, and the next instant she had the book in her hands. The title-page—Professor somebody's "Anatomy"—carried no information to her mind; so she began to turn the leaves. She came at once upon a handsomely engraved and colored frontispiece—a human figure, stark naked. At that moment a shadow fell on the page and Tom Sawyer stepped in at the door, and caught a glimpse of the picture. Becky snatched at the book to close it, and had the hard luck to tear the pictured page half down the middle. She thrust the volume into the desk, turned the key, and burst out crying with shame and vexation:

"Tom Sawyer, you are just as mean as you can be, to sneak up on a person and look at what they're looking at."

"How could *I* know you was looking at anything?"

"You ought to be ashamed of yourself Tom Sawyer; you know you're going to tell on me, and O, what shall I do, what shall I do! I'll be whipped, and I never was whipped in school."

Then she stamped her little foot and said:

"*Be* so mean if you want to! *I* know something that's going to happen. You just wait and you'll see! Hateful, hateful, hateful!"—and she flung out of the house with a new explosion of crying.

Tom stood still, rather flustered by this onslaught. Presently he said to himself:

"What a curious kind of a fool a girl is. Never been licked in school! Shucks, what's a licking! That's just like a girl—they're so thin-skinned and chicken-hearted. Well, of course *I* ain't going to tell old Dobbins on this little fool, because there's other ways of getting even on her, that ain't so mean; but what of it? Old Dobbins will ask who it was tore his book. Nobody'll answer. Then he'll do just the way he always does—ask first one and then t'other, and when he comes to the right girl he'll know it, without any telling. Girls' faces always tell on them. They ain't got any backbone. She'll get licked. Well, it's a kind of a tight place for Becky Thatcher, because there ain't any way out of it." Tom conned the thing a moment longer, and then added: "All right, though; she'd like to see me in just such a fix—let her sweat it out!"

Tom joined the mob of skylarking scholars outside. In a few moments the master arrived and school "took in." Tom did not feel a strong interest in his studies. Every time he stole a glance at the girls' side of the room Becky's face troubled him. Considering all things, he did not want to pity her, and yet it was all he could do to help it. He could get up no exultation that was really worthy the name. Presently the spelling-book discovery was made, and Tom's mind was entirely full of his own matters for a while after that. Becky roused up from her lethargy of distress and showed good interest in the proceedings. She did not expect that Tom could get out of his trouble by denying that he spilt the ink on the book himself; and she was right. The denial only seemed to make the thing worse for Tom. Becky supposed she would be glad of that, and she tried to believe she was glad of it, but she found she was not certain. When the worst came to the worst, she had an impulse to get up and tell on Alfred Temple, but she made an effort and forced herself to keep still—because, said she to herself, "he'll tell about me tearing the picture, sure—I wouldn't say a word, not to save his life!"

Tom took his whipping and went back to his seat not at all broken-hearted, for he thought it was possible that he had unknowingly upset the ink on the spelling-book himself, in some skylarking bout—he had denied it for form's sake and because it was custom, and had stuck to the denial from principle.

A whole hour drifted by; the master sat nodding in his throne, the air was drowsy with the hum of study. By and by, Mr. Dobbins straightened himself up, yawned, then unlocked his desk, and reached for his book, but seemed undecided whether to take it out or leave it. Most of the pupils glanced up languidly, but there were two among them that watched his movements with intent eyes. Mr. Dobbins fingered his book absently for a while, then took it out and settled himself in his chair to read! Tom shot a glance at Becky. He had seen a hunted and helpless rabbit look as she did, with a gun leveled at its head. Instantly he forgot his quarrel with her. Quick—something must be done!—done in a flash, too! But the very imminence of the emergency paralyzed his invention. Good!—he had an inspiration! He would run and snatch the book, spring through the door and fly! But his resolution shook for one little instant, and the chance was lost—the master opened the volume. If Tom only had the wasted opportunity back again! Too late; there was no help for Becky now, he said. The next moment the master faced the school. Every eye sunk under his gaze. There was that in it which smote even the innocent with fear. There was silence while one might count ten; the master was gathering his wrath. Then he spoke:

"Who tore this book?"

There was not a sound. One could have heard a pin drop. The stillness continued; the master searched face after face for signs of guilt.

"Benjamin Rogers, did you tear this book?"

A denial. Another pause.

"Joseph Harper, did you?"

Another denial. Tom's uneasiness grew more and more intense under the slow torture of these proceedings. The master scanned the ranks of boys—considered a while, then turned to the girls:

"Amy Lawrence?"

A shake of the head.

"Gracie Miller?"

The same sign.

"Susan Harper, did you do this?"

Another negative. The next girl was Becky Thatcher. Tom was trembling from head to foot with excitement and a sense of the hopelessness of the situation.

"Rebecca Thatcher," [Tom glanced at her face—it was white with terror,]—"did you tear—no, look me in the face"—[her hands rose in appeal]—"did you tear this book?"

A thought shot like lightning through Tom's brain. He sprang to his feet and shouted—

"*I* done it!"

The school stared in perplexity at this incredible folly. Tom stood a moment, to gather his dismembered faculties; and when he stepped forward to go to his punishment the surprise, the gratitude, the adoration that shone upon him out of poor Becky's eyes seemed pay enough for a hundred floggings. Inspired by the splendor of his own act, he took without an outcry the most merciless flaying that even Mr. Dobbins had ever administered; and also received with indifference the added cruelty of a command to remain two hours after school should be dismissed—for he knew who would wait for him outside till his captivity was done, and not count the tedious time as loss, either.

Tom went to bed that night planning vengeance against Alfred Temple; for with shame and repentance Becky had told him all, not forgetting her own treachery; but even the longing for vengeance had to give way, soon, to pleasanter musings, and he fell asleep at last with Becky's latest words lingering dreamily in his ear—

"Tom, how *could* you be so noble!"

William Dean Howells (1837–1920)

Author and editor William Dean Howells wrote this influential 1876 review of *The Adventures of Tom Sawyer* in the renowned literary magazine *The Atlantic Monthly*. He was a widely respected novelist, author of the acclaimed *A Hazard of New Fortunes* (1890), and an influential critic, sometimes called "the Dean of American letters." Howells praises Twain's vivid characters and setting, and he particularly singles out the portrayal of Tom as a boy who is cruel but not mean, mischievous but not vicious, and adventuresome but conventional in his thinking. To Howells, "The story is a wonderful study of the boy-mind, which inhabits a world quite distinct from that in which he is bodily present with his elders, and in this lies its great charm and its universality, for boy-nature, however human nature varies, is the same everywhere." It is precisely this assumption, that boy-nature is the same everywhere, that twentieth-century gender studies have challenged, asserting instead that how boys are raised largely determines how they think and act.

Review of *The Adventures of Tom Sawyer*

Mr. Aldrich has studied the life of *A Bad Boy* as the pleasant reprobate led it in a quiet old New England town twenty-five or thirty years ago, where in spite of the natural outlawry of boyhood he was more or less part of a settled order of things, and was hemmed in, to some measure, by the traditions of an established civilization. Mr. Clemens, on the contrary, has taken the boy of the Southwest for the hero of his new book, and has presented him with a fidelity to circumstance which loses no charm by being realistic in the highest degree, and which gives incomparably the best picture of life in that region as yet known to fiction. The town where Tom Sawyer was born and brought up is some such idle, shabby little Mississippi River town as Mr. Clemens has so well described in his piloting reminiscences, but Tom belongs to the better sort of people in it, and has been bred to fear God and dread the Sunday-school according to the strictest rite of the faiths that have characterized all the respectability of the West. His subjection in these respects does not so deeply affect his inherent tendencies but that he makes himself a beloved burden to the poor, tender-hearted old aunt who brings him up with his orphan brother and sister, and struggles vainly with his manifold sins, actual and imaginary. The limitations of his transgressions are nicely and artistically traced. He is mischievous, but not vicious; he is ready for almost any depredation that involves the danger and honor of adventure, but profanity he knows may provoke a thunderbolt upon the heart of the blasphemer, and he almost never swears; he resorts to any stratagem to keep out of school, but he is not a downright liar, except upon terms of after shame and remorse that make his falsehood bitter to him. He is

cruel, as all children are, but chiefly because he is ignorant; he is not mean, but there are very definite bounds to his generosity; and his courage is the Indian sort, full of prudence and mindful of retreat as one of the conditions of prolonged hostilities. In a word, he is a boy, and merely and exactly an ordinary boy on the moral side. What makes him delightful to the reader is that on the imaginative side he is very much more, and though every boy has wild and fantastic dreams, this boy cannot rest till he has somehow realized them. Till he has actually run off with two other boys in the character of buccaneer, and lived for a week on an island in the Mississippi, he has lived in vain; and this passage is but the prelude to more thrilling adventures, in which he finds hidden treasures, traces the bandits to their cave, and is himself lost in its recesses. The local material and the incidents with which his career is worked up are excellent, and throughout there is scrupulous regard for the boy's point of view in reference to his surroundings and himself, which shows how rapidly Mr. Clemens has grown as an artist. We do not remember anything in which this propriety is violated, and its preservation adds immensely to the grown-up reader's satisfaction in the amusing and exciting story. There is a boy's love-affair, but it is never treated otherwise than as a boy's love-affair. When the half-breed has murdered the young doctor, Tom and his friend, Huckleberry Finn, are really, in their boyish terror and superstition, going to let the poor old town-drunkard be hanged for the crime till the terror of that becomes unendurable. The story is a wonderful study of the boy-mind, which inhabits a world quite distinct from that in which he is bodily present with his elders, and in this lies its great charm and its universality, for boy nature, however human nature varies, is the same everywhere.

The tale is very dramatically wrought, and the subordinate characters are treated with the same graphic force that sets Tom alive before us. The worthless vagabond, Huck Finn, is entirely delightful throughout, and in his promised reform his identity is respected: he will lead a decent life in order that he may one day be thought worthy to become a member of that gang of robbers which Tom is to organize. Tom's aunt is excellent, with her kind heart's sorrow and secret pride in Tom; and so is his sister Mary, one of those good girls who are born to usefulness and charity and forbearance and unvarying rectitude. Many village people and local notables are introduced in well-conceived character; the whole little town lives in the reader's sense, with its religiousness, its lawlessness, its droll social distinctions, its civilization qualified by its slave-holding, and its traditions of the wilder West which has passed away. The picture will be instructive to those who have fancied the whole Southwest a sort of vast Pike County, and have not conceived of a sober and serious and orderly contrast to the sort of life that has come to represent the Southwest in literature. Mr. William M. Baker gives a notion of this in his stories, and Mr. Clemens has again enforced the fact here in a book full of entertaining character and of the greatest artistic sincerity.

Tom Brown and Tom Bailey are, among boys in books, alone deserving to be named with Tom Sawyer.

Robert Louis Stevenson (1850–94)

The novelist George Meredith called *Treasure Island* "the best of boys' books, and a book to make one feel a boy again," and generations of readers have agreed.[1] Jim, who like Huck Finn narrates his own experiences, is bright, courageous, sometimes foolhardy, loyal, and a straight arrow—but his story is not moralistic. Jim is horrified by the murders that Long John Silver commits and collaborates in, as we see in this excerpt, but there is also no doubt that Jim at times admires Silver's courage, intelligence, and leadership. There are virtually no women in this novel; Jim's mother makes a brief appearance at the beginning, notable for her insistence on having her due, no more, no less. But mostly, this is a novel about male society, and it can be read as Jim's quest for a surrogate father to take the place of his ineffectual father who dies at the beginning of the book. Jim's island adventure includes an encounter with Ben Gunn, who, like Robinson Crusoe, has developed his piety and survival skills while stranded alone on an island. Although Stevenson's life was cut short by ill health, this 1883 novel and his other stories of mystery, adventure, and history influenced a wide range of later writers, including J. M. Barrie, the creator of a most popular adventurer and seeker of eternal boyhood—Peter Pan. (For more information on Stevenson and his poems for children, see Part 4.)

NOTE

1. George Meredith, *Letters of George Meredith,* ed. C. L. Cline, vol. II (Oxford: Clarendon P, 1970) 730.

From *Treasure Island*

CHAPTER 13. HOW MY SHORE ADVENTURE BEGAN

The appearance of the island when I came on deck next morning was altogether changed. Although the breeze had now utterly ceased, we had made a great deal of way during the night, and were now lying becalmed about half a mile to the south-east of the low eastern coast. Grey-coloured woods covered a large part of the surface. This even tint was indeed broken up by streaks of yellow sandbreak in the lower lands, and by many tall trees of the pine family, out-topping the others—some singly, some in clumps; but the general colouring was uniform and sad. The hills ran up clear above the vegetation in spires of naked rock. All were strangely shaped, and the Spy-glass, which was by three or four hundred feet the tallest on the island, was likewise the strangest in configuration, running up sheer from almost every side, then suddenly cut off at the top like a pedestal to put a statue on.

The *Hispaniola* was rolling scuppers under in the ocean swell. The booms were tearing at the blocks, the rudder was banging to and fro, and the whole ship creaking, groaning, and jumping like a manufactory. I had to cling tight to the backstay, and the world turned giddily before my eyes; for though I was a good enough sailor when there was way on, this standing still and being rolled about like a bottle was a thing I never learned to stand without a qualm or so, above all in the morning, on an empty stomach.

Perhaps it was this—perhaps it was the look of the island, with its grey, melancholy woods, and wild stone spires, and the surf that we could both see and hear foaming and thundering on the steep beach—at least, although the sun shone bright and hot, and the shore birds were fishing and crying all around us, and you would have thought anyone would have been glad to get to land after being so long at sea, my heart sank, as the saying is, into my boots; and from that first look onward, I hated the very thought of Treasure Island.

We had a dreary morning's work before us, for there was no sign of any wind, and the boats had to be got out and manned, and the ship warped three or four miles round the corner of the island, and up the narrow passage to the haven behind Skeleton Island. I volunteered for one of the boats, where I had, of course, no business. The heat was sweltering, and the men grumbled fiercely over their work. Anderson was in command of my boat, and instead of keeping the crew in order, he grumbled as loud as the worst.

"Well," he said, with an oath, "it's not for ever."

I thought this was a very bad sign; for, up to that day, the men had gone briskly and willingly about their business; but the very sight of the island had relaxed the cords of discipline.

All the way in, Long John stood by the steersman and conned the ship. He knew the passage like the palm of his hand; and though the man in the chains got everywhere more water than was down in the chart, John never hesitated once.

"There's a strong scour with the ebb," he said. "and this here passage has been dug out, in a manner of speaking, with a spade."

We brought up just where the anchor was in the chart, about a third of a mile from each shore, the mainland on one side, and Skeleton Island on the other. The bottom was clean sand. The plunge of our anchor sent up clouds of birds wheeling and crying over the woods; but in less than a minute they were down again, and all was once more silent.

The place was entirely land-locked, buried in woods, the trees coming right down to high-water mark, the shores mostly flat, and the hill-tops standing round at a distance in a sort of amphitheatre, one here, one there. Two little rivers, or, rather, two swamps, emptied out into this pond, as you might call it; and the foliage round that part of the shore had a kind of poisonous brightness. From the ship, we could see nothing of the house or stockade, for they were quite buried among trees; and if it had not been for the chart on the companion, we might have been the first that had ever anchored there since the island arose out of the seas.

There was not a breath of air moving, nor a sound but that of the surf booming half a mile away along the beaches and against the rocks outside. A peculiar stagnant smell hung over the anchorage—a smell of sodden leaves and rotting tree trunks. I observed the doctor sniffing and sniffing, like someone tasting a bad egg.

"I don't know about treasure," he said, "but I'll stake my wig there's fever here."

If the conduct of the men had been alarming in the boat, it became truly threatening when they had come aboard. They lay about the deck growling together in talk. The slightest order was received with a black look, and grudgingly and carelessly obeyed. Even the honest hands must have caught the infection, for there was not one man aboard to mend another. Mutiny, it was plain, hung over us like a thunder-cloud.

And it was not only we of the cabin party who perceived the danger. Long John was hard at work going from group to group, spending himself in good advice, and as for example no man could have shown a better. He fairly outstripped himself in willingness and civility; he was all smiles to everyone. If an order were given, John would be on his crutch in an instant, with the cheeriest "Ay, ay, sir!" in the world; and when there was nothing else to do, he kept up one song after another, as if to conceal the discontent of the rest.

Of all the gloomy features of that gloomy afternoon, this obvious anxiety on the part of Long John appeared the worst.

We held a council in the cabin.

"Sir," said the captain, "if I risk another order, the whole ship'll come about our ears by the run. You see, sir, here it is. I get a rough answer, do I not? Well, if I speak back, pikes will be going in two shakes; if I don't, Silver will see there's something under that, and the game's up. Now, we've only one man to rely on."

"And who is that?" asked the squire.

"Silver, sir," returned the captain; "he's as anxious as you and I to smother things up. This is a tiff; he'd soon talk 'em out of it if he had the chance, and what I propose to do is to give him the chance. Let's allow the men an afternoon ashore. If they all go, why, we'll fight the ship. If they none of them go, well, then, we hold the cabin, and God defend the right. If some go, you mark my words, sir, Silver'll bring 'em aboard again as mild as lambs."

It was so decided; loaded pistols were served out to all the sure men; Hunter, Joyce, and Redruth were taken into our confidence, and received the news with less surprise and a better spirit than we had looked for, and then the captain went on deck and addressed the crew.

"My lads," said he, "we've had a hot day, and are all tired and out of sorts. A turn ashore'll hurt nobody—the boats are still in the water; you can take the gigs, and as many as please may go ashore for the afternoon. I'll fire a gun half an hour before sundown."

I believe the silly fellows must have thought they would break their shins over treasure as soon as they were landed; for they all came out of their sulks in a moment, and gave a cheer that started the echo in a faraway hill, and sent the birds once more flying and squalling round the anchorage.

The captain was too bright to be in the way. He whipped out of sight in a moment, leaving Silver to arrange the party; and I fancy it was as well he did so. Had he been on deck, he could no longer so much as have pretended not to understand the situation. It was as plain as day. Silver was the captain, and a mighty rebellious crew he had of it. The honest hands—and I was soon to see it proved that there were such on board—must have been stupid fellows. Or, rather, I suppose the truth was this, that all hands were disaffected by the example of the ringleaders—only some more, some less: and a few, being good fellows in the main, could neither be led nor driven any further. It is one thing to be idle and skulk, and quite another to take a ship and murder a number of innocent men.

At last, however, the party was made up. Six fellows were to stay on board, and the remaining thirteen, including Silver, began to embark.

Then it was that there came into my head the first of the mad notions that contributed so much to save our lives. If six men were left by Silver, it was plain our party could not take and fight the ship; and since only six were left, it was equally plain that the cabin party had no present need of my assistance. It occurred to me at once to go ashore. In a jiffy I had slipped over the side, and curled up in the fore-sheets of the nearest boat, and almost at the same moment she shoved off.

No one took notice of me, only the bow oar saying, "Is that you, Jim? Keep your head down." But Silver, from the other boat, looked sharply over and called out to know if that were me; and from that moment I began to regret what I had done.

The crews raced for the beach; but the boat I was in, having some start, and being at once the lighter and the better manned, shot far ahead of her consort, and the bow had struck among the shoreside trees, and I had caught a branch and swung myself out, and plunged into the nearest thicket, while Silver and the rest were still a hundred yards behind.

"Jim, Jim!" I heard him shouting.

But you may suppose I paid no heed; jumping, ducking, and breaking through, I ran straight before my nose, till I could run no longer.

CHAPTER 14. THE FIRST BLOW

I was so pleased at having given the slip to Long John, that I began to enjoy myself and look around me with some interest on the strange land that I was in.

I had crossed a marshy tract full of willows, bulrushes, and odd, outlandish, swampy trees; and I had now come out upon the skirts of an open piece of undulating, sandy country, about a mile long, dotted with a few pines, and a great number of contorted trees, not unlike the oak in growth, but pale in the foliage, like willows. On the far side of the open stood one of the hills, with two quaint, craggy peaks, shining vividly in the sun.

I now felt for the first time the joy of exploration. The isle was uninhabited; my shipmates I had left behind, and nothing lived in front of me but dumb brutes and fowls. I turned hither and thither among the trees. Here and there were flowering plants, unknown to me; here and there I saw snakes, and one raised his head from a ledge of rock and hissed at me with a noise not unlike the spinning of a top. Little did I suppose that he was a deadly enemy, and that the noise was the famous rattle.

Then I came to a long thicket of these oak-like trees—live, or evergreen, oaks, I heard afterwards they should be called—which grew low along the sand like brambles, the boughs curiously twisted, the foliage compact, like thatch. The thicket stretched down from the top of one of the sandy knolls, spreading and growing taller as it went, until it reached the margin of the broad, reedy fen, through which the nearest of the little rivers soaked its way into the anchorage. The marsh was steaming in the strong sun, and the outline of the Spy-glass trembled through the haze.

All at once there began to go a sort of bustle among the bulrushes; a wild duck flew up with a quack, another followed, and soon over the whole surface of the marsh a great cloud of birds hung screaming and circling in the air. I judged at once that some of my ship-

mates must be drawing near along the borders of the fen. Nor was I deceived; for soon I heard the very distant and low tones of a human voice, which, as I continued to give ear, grew steadily louder and nearer.

This put me in a great fear, and I crawled under cover of the nearest live-oak, and squatted there, hearkening, as silent as a mouse.

Another voice answered; and then the first voice, which I now recognised to be Silver's, once more took up the story, and ran on for a long while in a stream, only now and again interrupted by the other. By the sound they must have been talking earnestly, and almost fiercely; but no distinct word came to my hearing.

At last the speakers seemed to have paused, and perhaps to have sat down; for not only did they cease to draw any nearer, but the birds themselves began to grow more quiet, and to settle again to their places in the swamp.

And now I began to feel that I was neglecting my business; that since I had been so foolhardy as to come ashore with these desperadoes, the least I could do was to overhear them at their councils; and that my plain and obvious duty was to draw as close as I could manage, under the favourable ambush of the crouching trees.

I could tell the direction of the speakers pretty exactly, not only by the sound of their voices, but by the behaviour of the few birds that still hung in alarm above the heads of the intruders.

Crawling on all-fours, I made steadily but slowly towards them; till at last; raising my head to an aperture among the leaves, I could see clear down into a little green dell beside the marsh, and closely set about with trees, where Long John Silver and another of the crew stood face to face in conversation.

The sun beat full upon them. Silver had thrown his hat beside him on the ground, and his great, smooth, blond face, all shining with heat, was lifted to the other man's in a kind of appeal.

"Mate," he was saying, "it's because I thinks gold dust of you—gold dust, and you may lay to that! If I hadn't took to you like pitch, do you think I'd have been here a-warning of you? All's up—you can't make nor mend; it's to save your neck that I'm a-speaking, and if one of the wild 'uns knew it, where 'ud I be, Tom—now, tell me, where 'ud I be?"

"Silver," said the other man—and I observed he was not only red in the face, but spoke as hoarse as a crow, and his voice shook, too, like a taut rope—"Silver," says he, "you're old, and you're honest, or has the name for it; and you've money, too, which lots of poor sailors hasn't; and you're brave, or I'm mistook. And will you tell me you'll let yourself be led away with that kind of a mess of swabs? not you! As sure as God sees me, I'd sooner lose my hand. If I turn agin my dooty—"

And then all of a sudden he was interrupted by a noise. I had found one of the honest hands—well, here, at that same moment, came news of another. Far away out in the marsh there arose, all of a sudden, a sound like the cry of anger, then another on the back of it; and then one horrid, long-drawn scream. The rocks of the Spy-glass re-echoed it a score of times; the whole troop of marsh-birds rose again, darkening heaven, with a simultaneous whirr; and long after that death yell was still ringing in my brain, silence had re-established its empire, and only the rustle of the re-descending birds and the boom of the distant surges disturbed the languor of the afternoon.

Tom had leaped at the sound, like a horse at the spur; but Silver had not winked an eye. He stood where he was, resting lightly on his crutch, watching his companion like a snake about to spring.

"John!" said the sailor, stretching out his hand.

"Hands off!" cried Silver, leaping back a yard, as it seemed to me, with the speed and security of a trained gymnast.

"Hands off, if you like, John Silver," said the other. "It's a black conscience that can make you feared of me. But, in heaven's name, tell me what was that?"

"That?" returned Silver, smiling away, but warier than ever, his eye a mere pin-point in his big face, but gleaming like a crumb of glass. "That? Oh, I reckon that'll be Alan."

And at this poor Tom flashed out like a hero.

"Alan!" he cried. "Then rest his soul for a true seaman! And as for you, John Silver, long you've been a mate of mine, but you're mate of mine no more. If I die like a dog, I'll die in my dooty. You've killed Alan, have you? Kill me, too, if you can. But I defies you."

And with that, this brave fellow turned his back directly on the cook, and set off walking for the beach. But he was not destined to go far. With a cry, John seized the branch of a tree, whipped the crutch out of his armpit, and sent that uncouth missile hurtling through the air. It struck poor Tom, point foremost,

and with stunning violence, right between the shoulders in the middle of his back. His hands flew up, he gave a sort of gasp, and fell.

Whether he were injured much or little, none could ever tell. Like enough, to judge from the sound, his back was broken on the spot. But he had no time given him to recover. Silver, agile as a monkey, even without leg or crutch, was on the top of him next moment, and had twice buried his knife up to the hilt in that defenceless body. From my place of ambush, I could hear him pant aloud as he struck the blows.

I do not know what it rightly is to faint, but I do know that for the next little while the whole world swam away from before me in a whirling mist; Silver and the birds, and the tall Spy-glass hill-top, going round and round and topsy-turvy before my eyes, and all manner of bells ringing and distant voices shouting in my ear.

When I came again to myself, the monster had pulled himself together, his crutch under his arm, his hat upon his head. Just before him Tom lay motionless upon the sward; but the murderer minded him not a whit, cleansing his bloodstained knife the while upon a wisp of grass. Everything else was unchanged, the sun still shining mercilessly on the steaming marsh and the tall pinnacle of the mountain, and I could scarce persuade myself that murder had been actually done, and a human life cruelly cut short a moment since, before my eyes.

But now John put his hand into his pocket, brought out a whistle, and blew upon it several modulated blasts, that rang far across the heated air. I could not tell, of course, the meaning of the signal; but it instantly awoke my fears. More men would be coming. I might be discovered. They had already slain two of the honest people; after Tom and Alan, might not I come next?

Instantly I began to extricate myself and crawl back again, with what speed and silence I could manage, to the more open portion of the wood. As I did so, I could hear hails coming and going between the old buccaneer and his comrades, and this sound of danger lent me wings. As soon as I was clear of the thicket, I ran as I never ran before, scarce minding the direction of my flight, so long as it led me from the murderers; and as I ran, fear grew and grew upon me, until it turned into a kind of frenzy.

Indeed, could anyone be more entirely lost than I? When the gun fired, how should I dare to go down to the boats among those fiends, still smoking from their crime? Would not the first of them who saw me wring my neck like a snipe's? Would not my absence itself be an evidence to them of my alarm, and therefore of my fatal knowledge? It was all over, I thought. Good-bye to the *Hispaniola;* good-bye to the squire, the doctor, and the captain! There was nothing left for me but death by starvation, or death by the hands of the mutineers.

All this while, as I say, I was still running, and, without taking any notice, I had drawn near to the foot of the little hill with the two peaks, and had got into a part of the island where the live-oaks grew more widely apart, and seemed more like forest trees in their bearing and dimensions. Mingled with these were a few scattered pines, some fifty, some nearer seventy, feet high. The air, too, smelt more freshly than down beside the marsh.

And here a fresh alarm brought me to a standstill with a thumping heart.

CHAPTER 15. THE MAN OF THE ISLAND

From the side of the hill, which was here steep and stony, a spout of gravel was dislodged, and fell rattling and bounding through the trees. My eyes turned instinctively in that direction, and I saw a figure leap with great rapidity behind the trunk of a pine. What it was, whether bear or man or monkey, I could in no wise tell. It seemed dark and shaggy; more I knew not. But the terror of this new apparition brought me to a stand.

I was now, it seemed, cut off upon both sides; behind me the murderers, before me this lurking nondescript. And immediately I began to prefer the dangers that I knew to those I knew not. Silver himself appeared less terrible in contrast with this creature of the woods, and I turned on my heel, and, looking sharply behind me over my shoulder, began to retrace my steps in the direction of the boats.

Instantly the figure reappeared, and, making a wide circuit, began to head me off. I was tired, at any rate; but had I been as fresh as when I rose, I could see it was in vain for me to contend in speed with such an adversary. From trunk to trunk the creature flitted like a deer, running manlike on two legs, but unlike any man that I had ever seen, stooping almost double as it

ran. Yet a man it was, I could no longer be in doubt about that.

I began to recall what I had heard of cannibals. I was within an ace of calling for help. But the mere fact that he was a man, however wild, had somewhat reassured me, and my fear of Silver began to revive in proportion. I stood still, therefore, and cast about for some method of escape; and as I was so thinking, the recollection of my pistol flashed into my mind. As soon as I remembered I was not defenceless, courage glowed again in my heart; and I set my face resolutely for this man of the island, and walked briskly towards him.

He was concealed by this time, behind another tree trunk; but he must have been watching me closely, for as soon as I began to move in his direction he reappeared and took a step to meet me. Then he hesitated, drew back, came forward again, and at last, to my wonder and confusion, threw himself on his knees and held out his clasped hands in supplication.

At that I once more stopped.

"Who are you?" I asked.

"Ben Gunn," he answered, and his voice sounded hoarse and awkward, like a rusty lock. "I'm poor Ben Gunn, I am; and I haven't spoke with a Christian these three years."

I could now see that he was a white man like myself, and that his features were even pleasing. His skin, wherever it was exposed, was burnt by the sun; even his lips were black; and his fair eyes looked quite startling in so dark a face. Of all the beggar-men that I had seen or fancied, he was the chief for raggedness. He was clothed with tatters of old ship's canvas and old sea cloth; and this extraordinary patchwork was all held together by a system of the most various and incongruous fastenings, brass buttons, bits of stick, and loops of tarry gaskin. About his waist he wore an old brass-buckled leather belt, which was the one thing solid in his whole accoutrement.

"Three years!" I cried. "Were you shipwrecked?"

"Nay, mate," said he—"marooned."

I had heard the word, and I knew it stood for a horrible kind of punishment common enough among the buccaneers, in which the offender is put ashore with a little powder and shot, and left behind on some desolate and distant island.

"Marooned three years agone." he continued, "and lived on goats since then, and berries, and oysters. Wherever a man is, says I, a man can do for himself.

But, mate, my heart is sore for Christian diet. You mightn't happen to have a piece of cheese about you, now? No? Well, many's the long night I've dreamed of cheese—toasted, mostly—and woke up again, and here I were."

"If ever I can get aboard again," said I, "you shall have cheese by the stone."

All this time he had been feeling the stuff of my jacket, smoothing my hands, looking at my boots, and generally, in the intervals of his speech, showing a childish pleasure in the presence of a fellow-creature. But at my last words he perked up into a kind of startled slyness.

"If ever you can get aboard again, says you?" he repeated. "Why, now, who's to hinder you?"

"Not you, I know," was my reply.

"And right you was," he cried. "Now you—what do you call yourself, mate?"

"Jim," I told him.

"Jim, Jim," says he, quite pleased apparently. "Well, now, Jim, I've lived that rough as you'd be ashamed to hear of. Now, for instance, you wouldn't think I had had a pious mother—to look at me?" he asked.

"Why, no, not in particular," I answered.

"Ah, well," said he "but I had—remarkable pious. And I was a civil, pious boy, and could rattle off my catechism that fast, as you couldn't tell one word from another. And here's what it come to, Jim, and it begun with chuck-farthen on the blessed grave-stones! That's what it begun with, but it went further'n that; and so my mother told me, and predicked the whole, she did, the pious woman! But it were Providence that put me here. I've thought it all out in this here lonely island, and I'm back on piety. You don't catch me tasting rum so much; but just a thimbleful for luck, of course, the first chance I have. I'm bound I'll be good, and I see the way to. And, Jim"—looking all round him, and lowering his voice to a whisper—"I'm rich."

I now felt sure that the poor fellow had gone crazy in his solitude, and I suppose I must have shown the feeling in my face, for he repeated the statement hotly:—

"Rich! rich! I says. And I'll tell you what: I'll make a man of you, Jim. Ah, Jim, you'll bless your stars, you will, you was the first that found me!"

And at this there came suddenly a lowering shadow over his face; and he tightened his grasp upon my hand, and raised a forefinger threateningly before my eyes.

"Now, Jim, you tell me true: that ain't Flint's ship?" he asked.

At this I had a happy inspiration. I began to believe that I had found an ally, and I answered him at once.

"It's not Flint's ship, and Flint is dead; but I'll tell you true, as you ask me—there are some of Flint's hands aboard; worse luck for the rest of us."

"Not a man—with one—leg?" he gasped.

"Silver?" I asked.

"Ah, Silver!" says he; "that were his name."

"He's the cook; and the ringleader, too."

He was still holding me by the wrist, and at that he gave it quite a wring.

"If you was sent by Long John," he said, "I'm as good as pork, and I know it. But where was you, do you suppose?"

I had made my mind up in a moment, and by way of answer told him the whole story of our voyage, and the predicament in which we found ourselves. He heard me with the keenest interest, and when I had done he patted me on the head.

"You're a good lad, Jim," he said; "and you're all in a clove hitch, ain't you? Well, you just put your trust in Ben Gunn—Ben Gunn's the man to do it. Would you think it likely, now, that your squire would prove a liberal-minded one in case of help—him being in a clove hitch, as you remark?"

I told him the squire was the most liberal of men.

"Ay, but you see," returned Ben Gunn, "I didn't mean giving me a gate to keep, and a suit of livery clothes, and such; that's not my mark, Jim. What I mean is, would he be likely to come down to the toon of, say one thousand pounds out of money that's as good as a man's own already?"

"I am sure he would," said I. "As it was, all hands were to share."

"*And* a passage home?" he added, with a look of great shrewdness.

"Why," I cried, "the squire's a gentleman. And, besides, if we got rid of the others, we should want you to help work the vessel home."

"Ah," said he, "so you would." And he seemed very much relieved.

"Now, I'll tell you what." he went on. "So much I'll tell you, and no more. I were in Flint's ship when he buried the treasure; he and six along—six strong seamen. They were ashore nigh on a week, and us standing off and on in the old *Walrus*. One fine day up went the signal, and here come Flint by himself in a little boat, and his head done up in a blue scarf. The sun was getting up, and mortal white he looked about the cutwater. But, there he was, you mind, and the six all dead—dead and buried. How he done it, not a man aboard us could make out. It was battle, murder, and sudden death, leastways—him against six. Billy Bones was the mate; Long John, he was quartermaster; and they asked him where the treasure was. 'Ah,' says he, 'you can go ashore, if you like, and stay,' he says; 'but as for the ship, she'll beat up for more, by thunder!' That's what he said.

"Well, I was in another ship three years back, and we sighted this island. 'Boys,' said I, 'here's Flint's treasure; let's land and find it.' The cap'n was displeased at that; but my messmates were all of a mind, and landed. Twelve days they looked for it, and every day they had the worse word for me, until one fine morning all hands went aboard. 'As for you, Benjamin Gunn,' says they, 'here's a musket,' they says, 'and a spade, and pick-axe. You can stay here, and find Flint's money for yourself,' they says.

"Well, Jim, three years have I been here, and not a bite of Christian diet from that day to this. But now, you look here; look at me. Do I look like a man before the mast? No, says you. Nor I weren't, neither, I says."

And with that he winked and pinched me hard.

"Just you mention them words to your squire, Jim"—he went on: "Nor he weren't, neither—that's the words. Three years he were the man of this island, light and dark, fair and rain; and sometimes he would, maybe, think upon a prayer (says you), and sometimes he would, maybe, think of his old mother, so be as she's alive (you'll say); but the most part of Gunn's time (this is what you'll say)—the most part of his time was took up with another matter. And then you'll give him a nip, like I do."

And he pinched me again in the most confidential manner.

"Then," he continued—"then you'll up, and you'll say this:—Gunn is a good man (you'll say), and he puts a precious sight more confidence—a precious sight, mind that—in a gen'leman born than in these gen'lemen of fortune, having been one hisself."

"Well," I said, "I don't understand one word that you've been saying. But that's neither here nor there; for how am I to get on board?"

"Ah," said he, "that's the hitch, for sure. Well, there's my boat, that I made with my two hands. I keep her under the white rock. If the worst come to the worst, we might try that after dark. Hi!" he broke out, "what's that?"

For just then, although the sun had still an hour or two to run, all the echoes of the island awoke and bellowed to the thunder of a cannon.

"They have begun to fight!" I cried. "Follow me."

And I began to run towards the anchorage, my terrors all forgotten; while, close at my side, the marooned man in his goatskins trotted easily and lightly.

"Left, left," says he; "keep to your left hand, mate Jim! Under the trees with you! Theer's where I killed my first goat. They don't come down here now; they're all mast-headed on them mountings for the fear of Benjamin Gunn. Ah! and there's the cetemery"—cemetery, he must have meant. "You see the mounds? I come here and prayed, nows and thens, when I thought maybe a Sunday would be about doo. It weren't quite a chapel, but it seemed more solemn like; and then, says you, Ben Gunn was shorthanded—no chapling, nor so much as a Bible and a flag, you says."

So he kept talking as I ran, neither expecting nor receiving any answer.

The cannon-shot was followed, after a considerable interval, by a volley of small arms.

Another pause, and then, not a quarter of a mile in front of me, I beheld the Union Jack flutter in the air above a wood.

Frances Hodgson Burnett (1849–1924)

Frances Hodgson Burnett, who grew up in northern England, always viewed her childhood family garden as a Garden of Eden. After moving to the United States, she wrote novels for adults and children's stories, including classic novels such as *Little Lord Fauntleroy* (1886) and *A Little Princess* (1905). *The Secret Garden* (1911) is one of the most popular and enduring twentieth-century children's books. It has been dramatized and filmed in a number of versions (see Julaine Gillispie's essay on several film adaptations in Part 7). Burnett's heroine in this story, Mary Lennox, is not conventionally attractive. In fact, Burnett makes a point of telling us how disagreeable and self-absorbed Mary is. Nonetheless, most readers find her a sympathetic character, not merely because she rapidly becomes an orphan, but because she has a tough kernel of selfhood in the midst of adversity and an unfamiliar environment. She is capable of growth and tenderness, as she discovers while searching for and then nurturing a garden that has been locked away for years. The parallel between Mary's emergence from isolation and stunted selfhood to blossoming relationships and the development of the neglected garden provides one of the novel's central, abiding themes: the fertility and resilience of nature, including human nature, when properly tended. Burnett displays a romantic faith in the healing power of the psychosomatic connection between body and spirit. In the concluding chapter, Mary's cousin Colin has recovered from his crippling illness with the help of Mary, Dickon, and the "magic" of the garden. Then Dickon's mother, Susan Sowerby, the earth-mother figure who embodies love and wisdom in this novel, summons his father back from his distant travels to be reunited with his recovered son.

From *The Secret Garden*

CHAPTER 1. THERE IS NO ONE LEFT

When Mary Lennox was sent to Misselthwaite Manor to live with her uncle everybody said she was the most disagreeable-looking child ever seen. It was true, too. She had a little thin face and a little thin body, thin light hair and a sour expression. Her hair was yellow, and her face was yellow because she had been born in India and had always been ill in one way or another. Her father had held a position under the English Government and had always been busy and ill himself, and her mother had been a great beauty who cared only to go to parties and amuse herself with gay people. She had not wanted a little girl at all, and when Mary was born she handed her over to the care of an Ayah, who was made to understand that if she wished to please the Mem Sahib she must keep the child out of sight as much as possible. So when she was a sickly, fretful, ugly little baby she was kept out of the way, and when she became a sickly, fretful, toddling thing she was kept out of the way also. She never remembered seeing familiarly anything but the dark faces of her Ayah and the other native servants, and as they always obeyed her and gave her her own way in everything, because the Mem Sahib would be angry if she was disturbed by her crying, by the time she was six years old she was as tyrannical and selfish a little pig as ever lived. The young English governesses who came to teach her to read and write disliked her so much that she gave up her place in three months, and when other governesses came to try to fill it they always went away in a shorter time than the first one. So if Mary had not chosen to really want to know how to read books she would never have learned her letters at all.

One frightfully hot morning, when she was about nine years old, she awakened feeling very cross, and she became crosser still when she saw that the servant who stood by her bedside was not her Ayah.

"Why did you come?" she said to the strange woman. "I will not let you stay. Send my Ayah to me."

The woman looked frightened, but she only stammered that the Ayah could not come and when Mary threw herself into a passion and beat and kicked her, she looked only more frightened and repeated that it was not possible for the Ayah to come to Missie Sahib.

There was something mysterious in the air that morning. Nothing was done in its regular order and several of the native servants seemed missing, while those whom Mary saw slunk or hurried about with ashy and scared faces. But no one would tell her anything and her Ayah did not come. She was actually left alone as the morning went on, and at last she wandered out into the garden and began to play by herself under a tree near the veranda. She pretended that she was making a flower-bed, and she stuck big scarlet hibiscus blossoms into little heaps of earth, all the time growing more and more angry and muttering to herself the things she would say and the names she would call Saidie when she returned.

"Pig! Pig! Daughter of Pigs!" she said, because to call a native a pig is the worst insult of all.

She was grinding her teeth and saying this over and over again when she heard her mother come out on the veranda with some one. She was with a fair young man and they stood talking together in low strange voices. Mary knew the fair young man who looked like a boy. She had heard that he was a very young officer who had just come from England. The child stared at him, but she stared most at her mother. She always did this when she had a chance to see her, because the Mem Sahib—Mary used to call her that oftener than anything else—was such a tall, slim, pretty person and wore such lovely clothes. Her hair was like curly silk and she had a delicate little nose which seemed to be disdaining things, and she had large laughing eyes. All her clothes were thin and floating,

and Mary said they were "full of lace." They looked fuller of lace than ever this morning, but her eyes were not laughing at all. They were large and scared and lifted imploringly to the fair boy officer's face.

"Is it so very bad? Oh, is it?" Mary heard her say.

"Awfully," the young man answered in a trembling voice. "Awfully, Mrs. Lennox. You ought to have gone to the hills two weeks ago."

The Mem Sahib wrung her hands.

"Oh, I know I ought!" she cried. "I only stayed to go to that silly dinner party. What a fool I was!"

At that very moment such a loud sound of wailing broke out from the servants' quarters that she clutched the young man's arm, and Mary stood shivering from head to foot. The wailing grew wilder and wilder.

"What is it? What is it?" Mrs. Lennox gasped.

"Some one has died," answered the boy officer. "You did not say it had broken out among your servants."

"I did not know!" the Mem Sahib cried. "Come with me! Come with me!" and she turned and ran into the house.

After that, appalling things happened, and the mysteriousness of the morning was explained to Mary. The cholera had broken out in its most fatal form and people were dying like flies. The Ayah had been taken ill in the night, and it was because she had just died that the servants had wailed in the huts. Before the next day three other servants were dead and others had run away in terror. There was panic on every side, and dying people in all the bungalows.

During the confusion and bewilderment of the second day Mary hid herself in the nursery and was forgotten by everyone. (Nobody thought of her, nobody wanted her, and strange things happened of which she knew nothing. Mary alternately cried and slept through the hours) She only knew that people were ill and that she heard mysterious and frightening sounds. Once she crept into the dining-room and found it empty, though a partly finished meal was on the table and chairs and plates looked as if they had been hastily pushed back when the diners rose suddenly for some reason. The child ate some fruit and biscuits, and being thirsty she drank a glass of wine which stood nearly filled. It was sweet, and she did not know how strong it was. Very soon it made her intensely drowsy, and she went back to her nursery and shut herself in again, frightened by cries she heard in the huts and by the hurrying sound of feet. The wine made her so sleepy that she could scarcely keep her eyes open and she lay down on her bed and knew nothing more for a long time.

Many things happened during the hours in which she slept so heavily, but she was not disturbed by the wails and the sound of things being carried in and out of the bungalow.

When she awakened she lay and stared at the wall. The house was perfectly still. She had never known it to be so silent before. She heard neither voices nor footsteps, and wondered if everybody had got well of the cholera and all the trouble was over. She wondered also who would take care of her now her Ayah was dead. There would be a new Ayah, and perhaps she would know some new stories. Mary had been rather tired of the old ones. She did not cry because her nurse had died. She was not an affectionate child and had never cared much for any one. The noise and hurrying about and wailing over the cholera had frightened her, and she had been angry because no one seemed to remember that she was alive. Everyone was too panic-stricken to think of a little girl no one was fond of. When people had the cholera it seemed that they remembered nothing but themselves. But if everyone had got well again, surely some one would remember and come to look for her.

But no one came, and as she lay waiting the house seemed to grow more and more silent. She heard something rustling on the matting and when she looked down she saw a little snake gliding along and watching her with eyes like jewels. She was not frightened, because he was a harmless little thing who would not hurt her and he seemed in a hurry to get out of the room. He slipped under the door as she watched him.

"How queer and quiet it is," she said. "It sounds as if there were no one in the bungalow but me and the snake."

Almost the next minute she heard footsteps in the compound, and then on the veranda. They were men's footsteps, and the men entered the bungalow and talked in low voices. No one went to meet or speak to them and they seemed to open doors and look into rooms.

"What desolation!" she heard one voice say. "That pretty, pretty woman! I suppose the child, too. I heard there was a child, though no one ever saw her."

Mary was standing in the middle of the nursery when they opened the door a few minutes later. She looked an ugly, cross little thing and was frowning because she was beginning to be hungry and feel disgracefully neglected. The first man who came in was a large officer she had once seen talking to her father. He looked tired and troubled, but when he saw her he was so startled that he almost jumped back.

"Barney!" he cried out. "There is a child here! A child alone! In a place like this! Mercy on us, who is she!"

"I am Mary Lennox," the little girl said, drawing herself up stiffly. She thought the man was very rude to call her father's bungalow "A place like this!" "I fell asleep when everyone had the cholera and I have only just wakened up. Why does nobody come?"

"It is the child no one ever saw!" exclaimed the man, turning to his companions. "She has actually been forgotten!"

"Why was I forgotten?" Mary said, stamping her foot. "Why does nobody come?"

The young man whose name was Barney looked at her very sadly. Mary even thought she saw him wink his eyes as if to wink tears away.

"Poor little kid!" he said. "There is nobody left to come."

It was in that strange and sudden way that Mary found out that she had neither father nor mother left; that they had died and been carried away in the night, and that the few native servants who had not died also had left the house as quickly as they could get out of it, none of them even remembering that there was a Missie Sahib. That was why the place was so quiet. It was true that there was no one in the bungalow but herself and the little rustling snake.

CHAPTER 2. MISTRESS MARY QUITE CONTRARY

Mary had liked to look at her mother from a distance and she had thought her very pretty, but as she knew very little of her she could scarcely have been expected to love her or to miss her very much when she was gone. She did not miss her at all, in fact, and as she was a self-absorbed child she gave her entire thought to herself, as she had always done. If she had been older she would no doubt have been very anxious at being left alone in the world, but she was very young, and as she had always been taken care of, she supposed she always would be. What she thought was that she would like to know if she was going to nice people, who would be polite to her and give her her own way as her Ayah and the other native servants had done.

She knew that she was not going to stay at the English clergyman's house where she was taken at first. She did not want to stay. The English clergyman was poor and he had five children nearly all the same age and they wore shabby clothes and were always quarreling and snatching toys from each other. Mary hated their untidy bungalow and was so disagreeable to them that after the first day or two nobody would play with her. By the second day they had given her a nickname which made her furious.

It was Basil who thought of it first. Basil was a little boy with impudent blue eyes and a turned-up nose, and Mary hated him. She was playing by herself under a tree, just as she had been playing the day the cholera broke out. She was making heaps of earth and paths for a garden and Basil came and stood near to watch her. Presently he got rather interested and suddenly made a suggestion.

"Why don't you put a heap of stones there and pretend it is a rockery?" he said. "There in the middle," and he leaned over her to point.

"Go away!" cried Mary. "I don't want boys. Go away!"

For a moment Basil looked angry, and then he began to tease. He was always teasing his sisters. He danced round and round her and made faces and sang and laughed.

"Mistress Mary, quite contrary,
   How does your garden grow?
With silver bells, and cockle shells,
   And marigolds all in a row."

He sang it until the other children heard and laughed, too; and the crosser Mary got, the more they sang "Mistress Mary, quite contrary"; and after that as long as she stayed with them they called her "Mistress Mary Quite Contrary" when they spoke of her to each other, and often when they spoke to her.

"You are going to be sent home," Basil said to her, "at the end of the week. And we're glad of it."

"I am glad of it, too," answered Mary. "Where is home?"

"She doesn't know where home is!" said Basil, with seven-year-old scorn. "It's England, of course. Our grandmama lives there and our sister Mabel was sent to her last year. You are not going to your grandmama. You have none. You are going to your uncle. His name is Mr. Archibald Craven."

"I don't know anything about him," snapped Mary.

"I know you don't," Basil answered. "You don't know anything. Girls never do. I heard father and mother talking about him. He lives in a great, big, desolate old house in the country and no one goes near him. He's so cross he won't let them, and they wouldn't come if he would let them. He's a hunchback, and he's horrid."

"I don't believe you," said Mary; and she turned her back and stuck her fingers in her ears, because she would not listen any more.

But she thought over it a great deal afterward; and when Mrs. Crawford told her that night that she was going to sail away to England in a few days and go to her uncle, Mr. Archibald Craven, who lived at Misselthwaite Manor, she looked so stony and stubbornly uninterested that they did not know what to think about her. They tried to be kind to her, but she only turned her face away when Mrs. Crawford attempted to kiss her, and held herself stiffly when Mr. Crawford patted her shoulder.

"She is such a plain child," Mrs. Crawford said pityingly, afterward. "And her mother was such a pretty creature. She had a very pretty manner, too, and Mary has the most unattractive ways I ever saw in a child. The children call her 'Mistress Mary Quite Contrary,' and though it's naughty of them, one can't help understanding it."

"Perhaps if her mother had carried her pretty face and her pretty manners oftener into the nursery Mary might have learned some pretty ways too. It is very sad, now the poor beautiful thing is gone, to remember that many people never even knew that she had a child at all."

"I believe she scarcely ever looked at her," sighed Mrs. Crawford. "When her Ayah was dead there was no one to give a thought to the little thing. Think of the servants running away and leaving her all alone in that deserted bungalow. Colonel McGrew said he nearly jumped out of his skin when he opened the door and found her standing by herself in the middle of the room."

Mary made the long voyage to England under the care of an officer's wife, who was taking her children to leave them in a boarding-school. She was very much absorbed in her own little boy and girl, and was rather glad to hand the child over to the woman Mr. Archibald Craven sent to meet her, in London. The woman was his housekeeper at Misselthwaite Manor, and her name was Mrs. Medlock. She was a stout woman, with very red cheeks and sharp black eyes. She wore a very purple dress, a black silk mantle with jet fringe on it and a black bonnet with purple velvet flowers which stuck up and trembled when she moved her head. Mary did not like her at all, but as she very seldom liked people there was nothing remarkable in that; besides which it was very evident Mrs. Medlock did not think much of her.

"My word! she's a plain little piece of goods!" she said. "And we'd heard that her mother was a beauty. She hasn't handed much of it down, has she, ma'am?"

"Perhaps she will improve as she grows older," the officer's wife said good-naturedly. "If she were not so sallow and had a nicer expression . . . her features are rather good. Children alter so much."

"She'll have to alter a good deal," answered Mrs. Medlock. "And there's nothing likely to improve children at Misselthwaite—if you ask me!"

They thought Mary was not listening because she was standing a little apart from them at the window of the private hotel they had gone to. She was watching the passing buses and cabs and people, but she heard quite well and was made very curious about her uncle and the place he lived in. What sort of a place was it, and what would he be like? What was a hunchback? She had never seen one. Perhaps there were none in India.

Since she had been living in other people's houses and had had no Ayah, she had begun to feel lonely and to think queer thoughts which were new to her. She had begun to wonder why she had never seemed to belong to anyone even when her father and mother had been alive. Other children seemed to belong to their fathers and mothers, but she had never seemed to really be anyone's little girl. She had had servants, and food and clothes, but no one had taken any notice of her. She did not know that this was because she was a disagreeable child; but then, of course, she did not know she was disagreeable. She often thought that other people were, but she did not know that she was so herself.

She thought Mrs. Medlock the most disagreeable person she had ever seen, with her common, highly colored face and her common fine bonnet. When the next day they set out on their journey to Yorkshire, she walked through the station to the railway carriage with her head up and trying to keep as far away from her as she could, because she did not want to seem to belong to her. It would have made her very angry to think people imagined she was her little girl.

But Mrs. Medlock was not in the least disturbed by her and her thoughts. She was the kind of woman who would "stand no nonsense from young ones." At least, that is what she would have said if she had been asked. She had not wanted to go to London just when her sister Maria's daughter was going to be married, but she had a comfortable, well paid place as housekeeper at Misselthwaite Manor and the only way in which she could keep it was to do at once what Mr. Archibald Craven told her to do. She never dared even to ask a question.

"Captain Lennox and his wife died of the cholera," Mr. Craven had said in his short, cold way. "Captain Lennox was my wife's brother and I am their daughter's guardian. The child is to be brought here. You must go to London and bring her yourself."

So she packed her small trunk and made the journey.

Mary sat in her corner of the railway carriage and looked plain and fretful. She had nothing to read or to look at, and she had folded her thin little black-gloved hands in her lap. Her black dress made her look yellower than ever, and her limp light hair straggled from under her black crêpe hat.

"A more marred-looking young one I never saw in my life," Mrs. Medlock thought. (Marred is a Yorkshire word and means spoiled and pettish.) She had never seen a child who sat so still without doing anything; and at last she got tired of watching her and began to talk in a brisk, hard voice.

"I suppose I may as well tell you something about where you are going to," she said. "Do you know anything about your uncle?"

"No," said Mary.

"Never heard your father and mother talk about him?"

"No," said Mary frowning. She frowned because she remembered that her father and mother had never talked to her about anything in particular. Certainly they had never told her things.

"Humph," muttered Mrs. Medlock, staring at her queer, unresponsive little face. She did not say any more for a few moments and then she began again.

"I suppose you might as well be told something—to prepare you. You are going to a queer place."

Mary said nothing at all, and Mrs. Medlock looked rather discomfited by her apparent indifference, but, after taking a breath, she went on.

"Not but that it's a grand big place in a gloomy way, and Mr. Craven's proud of it in his way—and that's gloomy enough, too. The house is six hundred years old and it's on the edge of the moor, and there's near a hundred rooms in it, though most of them's shut up and locked. And there's pictures and fine old furniture and things that's been there for ages, and there's a big park round it and gardens and trees with branches trailing to the ground—some of them." She paused and took another breath. "But there's nothing else," she ended suddenly.

Mary had begun to listen in spite of herself. It all sounded so unlike India, and anything new rather attracted her. But she did not intend to look as if she were interested. That was one of her unhappy, disagreeable ways. So she sat still.

"Well," said Mrs. Medlock. "What do you think of it?"

"Nothing," she answered. "I know nothing about such places."

That made Mrs. Medlock laugh a short sort of laugh.

"Eh!" she said, "but you are like an old woman. Don't you care?"

"It doesn't matter," said Mary, "whether I care or not."

"You are right enough there," said Mrs. Medlock. "It doesn't. What you're to be kept at Misselthwaite Manor for I don't know, unless because it's the easiest way. *He's* not going to trouble himself about you, that's sure and certain. He never troubles himself about no one."

She stopped herself as if she had just remembered something in time.

"He's got a crooked back," she said. "That set him wrong. He was a sour young man and got no good of all his money and big place till he was married."

Mary's eyes turned toward her in spite of her intention not to seem to care. She had never thought of the hunchback's being married and she was a trifle surprised. Mrs. Medlock saw this, and as she was a talkative woman she continued with more interest. This was one way of passing some of the time, at any rate.

"She was a sweet, pretty thing and he'd have walked the world over to get her a blade o' grass she wanted. Nobody thought she'd marry him, but she did, and people said she married him for his money. But she didn't—she didn't," positively. "When she died—"

Mary gave a little involuntary jump.

"Oh! did she die!" she exclaimed, quite without meaning to. She had just remembered a French fairy story she had once read called "Riquet à la Houppe." It had been about a poor hunchback and a beautiful princess and it had made her suddenly sorry for Mr. Archibald Craven.

"Yes, she died," Mrs. Medlock answered. "And it made him queerer than ever. He cares about nobody. He won't see people. Most of the time he goes away, and when he is at Misselthwaite he shuts himself up in the West Wing and won't let any one but Pitcher see him. Pitcher's an old fellow, but he took care of him when he was a child and he knows his ways."

It sounded like something in a book and it did not make Mary feel cheerful. A house with a hundred rooms, nearly all shut up and with their doors locked—a house on the edge of a moor—whatsoever a moor was—sounded dreary. A man with a crooked back who shut himself up also! She stared out of the window with her lips pinched together, and it seemed quite natural that the rain should have begun to pour down in gray slanting lines and splash and stream down the windowpanes. If the pretty wife had been alive she might have made things cheerful by being something like her own mother and by running in and out and going to parties as she had done in frocks "full of lace." But she was not there any more.

"You needn't expect to see him, because ten to one you won't," said Mrs. Medlock. "And you mustn't expect that there will be people to talk to you. You'll have to play about and look after yourself. You'll be told what rooms you can go into and what rooms you're to keep out of. There's gardens enough. But when you're in the house don't go wandering and poking about. Mr. Craven won't have it."

"I shall not want to go poking about," said sour little Mary; and just as suddenly as she had begun to be rather sorry for Mr. Archibald Craven she began to cease to be sorry and to think he was unpleasant enough to deserve all that had happened to him.

And she turned her face toward the streaming panes of the window of the railway carriage and gazed out at the gray rainstorm which looked as if it would go on forever and ever. She watched it so long and steadily that the grayness grew heavier and heavier before her eyes and she fell asleep.

CHAPTER 3. ACROSS THE MOOR

She slept a long time, and when she awakened Mrs. Medlock had bought a lunchbasket at one of the stations and they had some chicken and cold beef and bread and butter and some hot tea. The rain seemed to be streaming down more heavily than ever and everybody in the station wore wet and glistening waterproofs. The guard lighted the lamps in the carriage, and Mrs. Medlock cheered up very much over her tea and chicken and beef. She ate a great deal and afterward fell asleep herself, and Mary sat and stared at her and watched her fine bonnet slip on one side until she herself fell asleep once more in the corner of the carriage, lulled by the splashing of the rain against the windows. It was quite dark when she awakened again. The train had stopped at a station and Mrs. Medlock was shaking her.

"You have had a sleep!" she said. "It's time to open your eyes! We're at Thwaite Station and we've got a long drive before us."

Mary stood up and tried to keep her eyes open while Mrs. Medlock collected her parcels. The little girl did not offer to help her, because in India native servants always picked up or carried things and it seemed quite proper that other people should wait on one.

The station was a small one and nobody but themselves seemed to be getting out of the train. The station-master spoke to Mrs. Medlock in a rough, good-natured way, pronouncing his words in a queer broad fashion which Mary found out afterward was Yorkshire.

"I see tha's got back," he said. "An' tha's browt th' young 'un with thee."

"Aye, that's her," answered Mrs. Medlock, speaking with a Yorkshire accent herself and jerking her head over her shoulder toward Mary. "How's thy Missus?"

"Well enow. Th' carriage is waitin' outside for thee."

A brougham stood on the road before the little outside platform. Mary saw that it was a smart carriage and that it was a smart footman who helped her in. His long waterproof coat and the waterproof covering of his hat were shining and dripping with rain as everything was, the burly station-master included.

When he shut the door, mounted the box with the coachman, and they drove off, the little girl found herself seated in a comfortably cushioned corner, but she was not inclined to go to sleep again. She sat and looked out of the window, curious to see something of the road over which she was being driven to the queer place Mrs. Medlock had spoken of. She was not at all a timid child and she was not exactly frightened, but she felt that there was no knowing what might happen in a house with a hundred rooms nearly all shut up—a house standing on the edge of a moor.

"What is a moor?" she said suddenly to Mrs. Medlock.

"Look out of the window in about ten minutes and you'll see," the woman answered. "We've got to drive five miles across Missel Moor before we get to the Manor. You won't see much because it's a dark night, but you can see something."

Mary asked no more questions but waited in the darkness of her corner, keeping her eyes on the window. The carriage lamps cast rays of light a little distance ahead of them and she caught glimpses of the things they passed. After they had left the station they had driven through a tiny village and she had seen whitewashed cottages and the lights of a public house. Then they had passed a church and a vicarage and a little shop-window or so in a cottage with toys and sweets and odd things set out for sale. Then they were on the highroad and she saw hedges and trees. After that there seemed nothing different for a long time—or at least it seemed a long time to her.

At last the horses began to go more slowly, as if they were climbing up-hill, and presently there seemed to be no more hedges and no more trees. She could see nothing, in fact, but a dense darkness on either side. She leaned forward and pressed her face against the window just as the carriage gave a big jolt.

"Eh! We're on the moor now sure enough," said Mrs. Medlock.

The carriage lamps shed a yellow light on a rough-looking road which seemed to be cut through bushes and low-growing things which ended in the great expanse of dark apparently spread out before and around them. A wind was rising and making a singular, wild, low, rushing sound.

"It's—it's not the sea, is it?" said Mary, looking round at her companion.

"No, not it," answered Mrs. Medlock. "Nor it isn't fields nor mountains, it's just miles and miles and miles of wild land that nothing grows on but heather and gorse and broom, and nothing lives on but wild ponies and sheep."

"I feel as if it might be the sea, if there were water on it," said Mary. "It sounds like the sea just now."

"That's the wind blowing through the bushes," Mrs. Medlock said. "It's a wild, dreary enough place to my mind, though there's plenty that likes it— particularly when the heather's in bloom."

On and on they drove through the darkness, and though the rain stopped, the wind rushed by and whistled and made strange sounds. The road went up and down, and several times the carriage passed over a little bridge beneath which water rushed very fast with a great deal of noise. Mary felt as if the drive would never come to an end and that the wide, bleak moor was a wide expanse of black ocean through which she was passing on a strip of dry land.

"I don't like it," she said to herself. "I don't like it," and she pinched her thin lips more tightly together.

The horses were climbing up a hilly piece of road when she first caught sight of a light. Mrs. Medlock saw it as soon as she did and drew a long sigh of relief.

"Eh, I am glad to see that bit o' light twinkling," she exclaimed. "It's the light in the lodge window. We shall get a good cup of tea after a bit, at all events."

It was "after a bit," as she said, for when the carriage passed through the park gates there was still two miles of avenue to drive through and the trees (which nearly met overhead) made it seem as if they were driving through a long dark vault.

They drove out of the vault into a clear space and stopped before an immensely long but lowbuilt house which seemed to ramble round a stone court. At first Mary thought that there were no lights at all in the windows, but as she got out of the carriage she saw that one room in a corner upstairs showed a dull glow.

The entrance door was a huge one made of massive, curiously shaped panels of oak studded with big iron nails and bound with great iron bars. It opened into an enormous hall, which was so dimly lighted that the faces in the portraits on the walls and the figures in the suits of armor made Mary feel that she did not want to look at them. As she stood on the stone floor she looked a very small, odd little black figure and she felt as small and lost and odd as she looked.

A neat, thin old man stood near the manservant who opened the door for them.

"You are to take her to her room," he said in a husky voice. "He doesn't want to see her. He's going to London in the morning."

"Very well, Mr. Pitcher," Mrs. Medlock answered. "So long as I know what's expected of me, I can manage."

"What's expected of you, Mrs. Medlock," Mr. Pitcher said, "is that you make sure that he's not disturbed and that he doesn't see what he doesn't want to see."

And then Mary Lennox was led up a broad staircase and lown a long corridor and up a short flight of steps and through another corridor and another, until a door opened in a wall and she found herself in a room with a fire in it and a supper on a table.

Mrs. Medlock said unceremoniously:

"Well, here you are! This room and the next are where you'll live—and you must keep to them. Don't you forget that!"

It was in this way Mistress Mary arrived at Misselthwaite Manor and she had perhaps never felt quite so contrary in all her life.

CHAPTER 4. MARTHA

When she opened her eyes in the morning it was because a young housemaid had come into her room to light the fire and was kneeling on the hearth-rug raking out the cinders noisily. Mary lay and watched her for a few moments and then began to look about the room. She had never seen a room at all like it and thought it curious and gloomy. The walls were covered with tapestry with a forest scene embroidered on it. There were fantastically dressed people under the trees and in the distance there was a glimpse of the turrets of a castle. There were hunters and horses and dogs and ladies. Mary felt as if she were in the forest with them. Out of a deep window she could see a great climbing stretch of land which seemed to have no trees on it, and to look rather like an endless, dull, purplish sea.

"What is that?" she said, pointing out of the window.

Martha, the young housemaid, who had just risen to her feet, looked and pointed also.

"That there?" she said.

"Yes."

"That's th' moor," with a good-natured grin. "Does tha' like it?"

"No," answered Mary. "I hate it."

"That's because tha'rt not used to it," Martha said, going back to her hearth. "Tha' thinks it's too big an' bare now. But tha' will like it."

"Do you?" inquired Mary.

"Aye, that I do," answered Martha, cheerfully polishing away at the grate. "I just love it. It's none bare. It's covered wi' growin' things as smells sweet. It's fair lovely in spring an' summer when th' gorse an' broom an' heather's in flower. It smells o' honey an' there's such a lot o' fresh air—an' th' sky looks so high an' th' bees an' skylarks makes such a nice noise hummin' an' singin'. Eh! I wouldn't live away from th' moor for anythin'."

Mary listened to her with a grave, puzzled expression. The native servants she had been used to in India were not in the least like this. They were obsequious and servile and did not presume to talk to their masters as if they were their equals. They made salaams and called them "protector of the poor" and names of that sort. Indian servants were commanded to do things, not asked. It was not the custom to say "please" and "thank you" and Mary had always slapped her Ayah in the face when she was angry. She wondered a little what this girl would do if one slapped her in the face. She was a round, rosy, good-natured looking creature, but she had a sturdy way which made Mistress Mary wonder if she might not even slap back—if the person who slapped her was only a little girl.

"You are a strange servant," she said from her pillows, rather haughtily.

Martha sat up on her heels, with her blackingbrush in her hand, and laughed, without seeming the least out of temper.

"Eh! I know that," she said. "If there was a grand Missus at Misselthwaite I should never have been even one of th' under housemaids. I might have been let to be scullery-maid but I'd never have been let upstairs. I'm too common an' I talk too much Yorkshire. But this is a funny house for all it's so grand. Seems like there's neither Master nor Mistress except Mr. Pitcher an' Mrs. Medlock. Mr. Craven, he won't be troubled about anythin' when he's here, an' he's nearly always away. Mrs. Medlock gave me th' place out o' kindness. She told me she could never have done it if Misselthwaite had been like other big houses."

"Are you going to be my servant?" Mary asked, still in her imperious little Indian way.

Martha began to rub her grate again.

"I'm Mrs. Medlock's servant," she said stoutly. "An' she's Mr. Craven's—but I'm to do the housemaid's work up here an' wait on you a bit. But you won't need much waitin' on."

"Who is going to dress me?" demanded Mary.

Martha sat up on her heels again and stared. She spoke in broad Yorkshire in her amazement.

"Canna' tha' dress thysen!" she said.

"What do you mean? I don't understand your language," said Mary.

"Eh! I forgot," Martha said. "Mrs. Medlock told me I'd have to be careful or you wouldn't know what I was sayin'. I mean can't you put on your own clothes?"

"No," answered Mary, quite indignantly. "I never did in my life. My Ayah dressed me, of course."

"Well," said Martha, evidently not in the least aware that she was impudent, "it's time tha' should learn. Tha' cannot begin younger. It'll do thee good to wait on thysen a bit. My mother always said she couldn't see why grand people's children didn't turn out fair fools—what with nurses an' bein' washed an' dressed an' took out to walk as if they was puppies!"

"It is different in India," said Mistress Mary disdainfully. She could scarcely stand this.

But Martha was not at all crushed.

"Eh! I can see it's different," she answered almost sympathetically. "I dare say it's because there's such a lot o' blacks there instead o' respectable white people. When I heard you was comin' from India I thought you was a black too."

Mary sat up in bed furious.

"What!" she said. "What! You thought I was a native. You—you daughter of a pig!"

Martha stared and looked hot.

"Who are you callin' names?" she said. "You needn't be so vexed. That's not th' way for a young lady to talk. I've nothin' against th' blacks. When you read about 'em in tracts they're always very religious. You always read as a black's a man an' a brother. I've never seen a black an' I was fair pleased to think I was goin' to see one close. When I come in to light your fire this mornin' I crep' up to your bed an' pulled th' cover back careful to look at you. An' there you was," disappointedly, "no more black than me—for all you're so yeller."

Mary did not even try to control her rage and humiliation.

"You thought I was a native! You dared! You don't know anything about natives! They are not people— they're servants who must salaam to you. You know nothing about India. You know nothing about anything!"

She was in such a rage and felt so helpless before the girl's simple stare, and somehow she suddenly felt so horribly lonely and far away from everything she understood and which understood her, that she threw herself face downward on the pillows and burst into passionate sobbing. She sobbed so unrestrainedly that good-natured Yorkshire Martha was a little frightened and quite sorry for her. She went to the bed and bent over her.

"Eh! you mustn't cry like that there!" she begged. "You mustn't for sure. I didn't know you'd be vexed. I don't know anythin' about anythin'—just like you said. I beg your pardon, Miss. Do stop cryin'."

There was something comforting and really friendly in her queer Yorkshire speech and sturdy way which had a good effect on Mary. She gradually ceased crying and became quiet. Martha looked relieved.

"It's time for thee to get up now," she said. "Mrs. Medlock said I was to carry tha' breakfast an' tea an' dinner into th' room next to this. It's been made into a nursery for thee. I'll help thee on with thy clothes if tha'll get out o' bed. If th' buttons are at th' back tha' cannot button them up tha'self."

When Mary at last decided to get up, the clothes Martha took from the wardrobe were not the ones she had worn when she arrived the night before with Mrs. Medlock.

"Those are not mine," she said. "Mine are black."

She looked the thick white wool coat and dress over, and added with cool approval:

"Those are nicer than mine."

"These are th' ones tha' must put on," Martha answered. "Mr. Craven ordered Mrs. Medlock to get 'em in London. He said 'I won't have a child dressed in black wanderin' about like a lost soul,' he said. 'It'd make the place sadder than it is. Put color on her.' Mother she said she knew what he meant. Mother always knows what a body means. She doesn't hold with black hersel'."

"I hate black things," said Mary.

The dressing process was one which taught them both something. Martha had "buttoned up" her little sisters and brothers but she had never seen a child who stood still and waited for another person to do things for her as if she had neither hands nor feet of her own.

"Why doesn't tha' put on tha' own shoes?" she said when Mary quietly held out her foot.

"My Ayah did it," answered Mary, staring. "It was the custom."

She said that very often—"It was the custom." The native servants were always saying it. If one told them to do a thing their ancestors had not done for a thousand years they gazed at one mildly and said, "It is not the custom" and one knew that was the end of the matter.

It had not been the custom that Mistress Mary should do anything but stand and allow herself to be dressed like a doll, but before she was ready for breakfast she began to suspect that her life at Misselthwaite Manor would end by teaching her a number of things quite new to her—things such as putting on her own shoes and stockings, and picking up things she let fall. If Martha had been a well-trained fine young lady's maid she would have been more subservient and respectful and would have known that it was her business to brush hair, and button boots, and pick things up and lay them away. She was, however, only an untrained Yorkshire rustic who had been brought up in a moorland cottage with a swarm of little brothers and sisters who had never dreamed of doing anything but waiting on themselves and on the younger ones who were either babies in arms or just learning to totter about and tumble over things.

If Mary Lennox had been a child who was ready to be amused she would perhaps have laughed at Martha's readiness to talk, but Mary only listened to her coldly and wondered at her freedom of manner. At first she was not at all interested, but gradually, as the girl rattled on in her good-tempered, homely way, Mary began to notice what she was saying.

"Eh! you should see 'em all," she said. "There's twelve of us an' my father only gets sixteen shilling a week. I can tell you my mother's put to it to get porridge for 'em all. They tumble about on th' moor an' play there all day an' mother says th' air of th' moor fattens 'em. She says she believes they' eat th' grass same as th' wild ponies do. Our Dickon, he's twelve years old and he's got a young pony he calls his own."

"Where did he get it?" asked Mary.

"He found it on th' moor with its mother when it was a little one an' he began to make friends with it an' give it bits o' bread an' pluck young grass for it. And it got to like him so it follows him about an' it lets him get on its back. Dickon's a kind lad an' animals likes him."

Mary had never possessed an animal pet of her own and had always thought she should like one. So she began to feel a slight interest in Dickon, and as she had never before been interested in any one but herself, it was the dawning of a healthy sentiment. When she went into the room which had been made into a nursery for her, she found that it was rather like the one she had slept in. It was not a child's room, but a grown-up person's room, with gloomy old pictures on the walls and heavy old oak chairs. A table in the center was set with a good substantial breakfast. But she had always had a very small appetite, and she looked with something more than indifference at the first plate Martha set before her.

"I don't want it," she said.

"Tha' doesn't want thy porridge!" Martha exclaimed incredulously.

"No."

"Tha' doesn't know how good it is. Put a bit o' treacle on it or a bit o' sugar."

"I don't want it," repeated Mary.

"Eh!" said Martha. "I can't abide to see good victuals go to waste. If our children was at this table they'd clean it bare in five minutes."

"Why?" said Mary coldly.

"Why!" echoed Martha. "Because they scarce ever had their stomachs full in their lives. They're as hungry as young hawks an' foxes."

"I don't know what it is to be hungry," said Mary, with the indifference of ignorance.

Martha looked indignant.

"Well, it would do thee good to try it. I can see that plain enough," she said outspokenly. "I've no patience with folk as sits an' just stares at good bread an' meat. My word! don't I wish Dickon and Phil an' Jane an' th' rest of 'em had what's here under their pinafores."

"Why don't you take it to them?" suggested Mary.

"It's not mine," answered Martha stoutly. "An' this isn't my day out. I get my day out once a month same as th' rest. Then I go home an' clean up for mother an' give her a day's rest."

Mary drank some tea and ate a little toast and some marmalade.

"You wrap up warm an' run out an' play you," said Martha. "It'll do you good and give you some stomach for your meat."

Mary went to the window. There were gardens and paths and big trees, but everything looked dull and wintry.

"Out? Why should I go out on a day like this?"

"Well, if tha' doesn't go out tha'lt have to stay in, an' what has tha' got to do?"

Mary glanced about her. There was nothing to do. When Mrs. Medlock had prepared the nursery she had not thought of amusement. Perhaps it would be better to go and see what the gardens were like.

"Who will go with me?" she inquired.

Martha stared.

"You'll go by yourself," she answered. "You'll have to learn to play like other children does when they haven't got sisters and brothers. Our Dickon goes off on th' moor by himself an' plays for hours. That's how he made friends with th' pony. He's got sheep on th' moor that knows him, an' birds as comes an' eats out of his hand. However little there is to eat, he always saves a bit o' his bread to coax his pets."

It was really this mention of Dickon which made Mary decide to go out, though she was not aware of it. There would be birds outside though there would not be ponies or sheep. They would be different from the birds in India and it might amuse her to look at them.

Martha found her coat and hat for her and a pair of stout little boots and she showed her her way downstairs.

"If tha' goes round that way tha'll come to th' gardens," she said, pointing to a gate in a wall of shrubbery. "There's lots o' flowers in summer-time, but there's nothin' bloomin' now." She seemed to hesitate a second before she added, "One of th' gardens is locked up. No one has been in it for ten years."

"Why?" asked Mary in spite of herself. Here was another locked door added to the hundred in the strange house.

"Mr. Craven had it shut when his wife died so sudden. He won't let no one go inside. It was her garden. He locked th' door an' dug a hole and buried th' key. There's Mrs. Medlock's bell ringing—I must run."

After she was gone Mary turned down the walk which led to the door in the shrubbery. She could not help thinking about the garden which no one had been into for ten years. She wondered what it would look like and whether there were any flowers still alive in it. When she had passed through the shrubbery gate she found herself in great gardens, with wide lawns and winding walks with clipped borders. There were trees, and flower-beds, and evergreens clipped into strange shapes, and a large pool with an old gray fountain in its midst. But the flower-beds were bare and wintry and the fountain was not playing. This was not the garden which was shut up. How could a garden be shut up? You could always walk into a garden.

She was just thinking this when she saw that, at the end of the path she was following, there seemed to be a long wall, with ivy growing over it. She was not familiar enough with England to know that she was coming upon the kitchen-gardens where the vegetables and fruit were growing. She went toward the wall and found that there was a green door in the ivy, and that it stood open. This was not the closed garden, evidently, and she could go into it.

She went through the door and found that it was a garden with walls all round it and that it was only one of several walled gardens which seemed to open into one another. She saw another open green door, revealing bushes and pathways between beds containing winter vegetables. Fruit-trees were trained flat against the wall, and over some of the beds there were glass frames. The place was bare and ugly enough, Mary thought, as she stood and stared about her. It might be nicer in summer when things were green, but there was nothing pretty about it now.

Presently an old man with a spade over his shoulder walked through the door leading from the second garden. He looked startled when he saw Mary, and then touched his cap. He had a surly old face, and did not seem at all pleased to see her—but then she was dis-

pleased with his garden and wore her "quite contrary" expression, and certainly did not seem at all pleased to see him.

"What is this place?" she asked.

"One o' th' kitchen-gardens," he answered.

"What is that?" said Mary, pointing through the other green door.

"Another of 'em," shortly. "There's another on t'other side o' th' wall an' there's th' orchard t'other side o' that."

"Can I go in them?" asked Mary.

"If tha' likes. But there's nowt to see."

Mary made no response. She went down the path and through the second green door. There she found more walls and winter vegetables and glass frames, but in the second wall there was another green door and it was not open. Perhaps it led into the garden which no one had seen for ten years. As she was not at all a timid child and always did what she wanted to do, Mary went to the green door and turned the handle. She hoped the door would not open because she wanted to be sure she had found the mysterious garden—but it did open quite easily and she walked through it and found herself in an orchard. There were walls all round it also and trees trained against them, and there were bare fruit-trees growing in the winter-browned grass—but there was no green door to be seen anywhere. Mary looked for it, and yet when she had entered the upper end of the garden she had noticed that the wall did not seem to end with the orchard but to extend beyond it as if it enclosed a place at the other side. She could see the tops of trees above the wall, and when she stood still she saw a bird with a bright red breast sitting on the topmost branch of one of them, and suddenly he burst into his winter song—almost as if he had caught sight of her and was calling to her.

She stopped and listened to him and somehow his cheerful, friendly little whistle gave her a pleased feeling—even a disagreeable little girl may be lonely, and the big closed house and big bare moor and big bare gardens had made this one feel as if there was no one left in the world but herself. If she had been an affectionate child, who had been used to being loved, she would have broken her heart, but even though she was "Mistress Mary Quite Contrary" she was desolate, and the bright-breasted little bird brought a look into her sour little face which was almost a smile. She listened to him until he flew away. He was not like an Indian bird and she liked him and wondered if she should ever see him again. Perhaps he lived in the mysterious garden and knew all about it.

Perhaps it was because she had nothing whatever to do that she thought so much of the deserted garden. She was curious about it and wanted to see what it was like. Why had Mr. Archibald Craven buried the key? If he had liked his wife so much why did he hate her garden? She wondered if she should ever see him, but she knew that if she did she should not like him, and he would not like her, and that she should only stand and stare at him and say nothing, though she should be wanting dreadfully to ask him why he had done such a queer thing.

"People never like me and I never like people," she thought. "And I never can talk as the Crawford children could. They were always talking and laughing and making noises."

She thought of the robin and of the way he seemed to sing his song at her, and as she remembered the tree-top he perched on she stopped rather suddenly on the path.

"I believe that tree was in the secret garden—I feel sure it was," she said. "There was a wall round the place and there was no door."

She walked back into the first kitchen-garden she had entered and found the old man digging there. She went and stood beside him and watched him a few moments in her cold little way. He took no notice of her and so at last she spoke to him.

"I have been into the other gardens," she said.

"There was nothin' to prevent thee," he answered crustily.

"I went into the orchard."

"There was no dog at th' door to bite thee," he answered.

"There was no door there into the other garden," said Mary.

"What garden?" he said in a rough voice, stopping his digging for a moment.

"The one on the other side of the wall," answered Mistress Mary. "There are trees there—I saw the tops of them. A bird with a red breast was sitting on one of them and he sang."

To her surprise the surly old weather-beaten face actually changed its expression. A slow smile spread over it and the gardener looked quite different. It made her think that it was curious how much nicer a person looked when he smiled. She had not thought of it before.

He turned about to the orchard side of his garden and began to whistle—a low soft whistle. She could not understand how such a surly man could make such a coaxing sound.

Almost the next moment a wonderful thing happened. She heard a soft little rushing flight through the air—and it was the bird with the red breast flying to them, and he actually alighted on the big clod of earth quite near to the gardener's foot.

"Here he is," chuckled the old man, and then he spoke to the bird as if he were speaking to a child.

"Where has tha' been, tha' cheeky little beggar?" he said. "I've not seen thee before today. Has tha' begun tha' courtin' this early in th' season? Tha'rt too forrad."

The bird put his tiny head on one side and looked up at him with his soft bright eye which was like a black dewdrop. He seemed quite familiar and not the least afraid. He hopped about and pecked the earth briskly, looking for seeds and insects. It actually gave Mary a queer feeling in her heart, because he was so pretty and cheerful and seemed so like a person. He had a tiny plump body and a delicate beak, and slender delicate legs.

"Will he always come when you call him?" she asked almost in a whisper.

"Aye, that he will. I've knowed him ever since he was a fledgling. He come out of th' nest in th' other garden an' when first he flew over th' wall he was too weak to fly back for a few days an' we got friendly. When he went over th' wall again th' rest of th' brood was gone an' he was lonely an' he come back to me."

"What kind of a bird is he?" Mary asked.

"Doesn't tha' know? He's a robin redbreast an' they're th' friendliest, curiousest birds alive. They're almost as friendly as dogs—if you know how to get on with 'em. Watch him peckin' about there an' lookin' round at us now an' again. He knows we're talkin' about him."

It was the queerest thing in the world to see the old fellow. He looked at the plump little scarlet-waistcoated bird as if he were both proud and fond of him.

"He's a conceited one," he chuckled. "He likes to hear folk talk about him. An' curious—bless me, there never was his like for curiosity an' meddlin'. He's always comin' to see what I'm plantin'. He knows all th' things Mester Craven never troubles hissel' to find out He's th' head gardener, he is."

The robin hopped about busily pecking the soil and now and then stopped and looked at them a little. Mary thought his black dewdrop eyes gazed at her with great curiosity. It really seemed as if he were finding out all about her. The queer feeling in her heart increased.

"Where did the rest of the brood fly to?" she asked.

"There's no knowin'. The old ones turn 'em out o' their nest an' make 'em fly an' they're scattered before you know it. This one was a knowin' one an' he knew he was lonely."

Mistress Mary went a step nearer to the robin and looked at him very hard.

"I'm lonely," she said.

She had not known before that this was one of the things which made her feel sour and cross. She seemed to find it out when the robin looked at her and she looked at the robin.

The old gardener pushed his cap back on his bald head and stared at her a minute.

"Art tha' th' little wench from India?" he asked.

Mary nodded.

"Then no wonder tha'rt lonely. Tha'lt be lonelier before tha's done," he said.

He began to dig again, driving his spade deep into the rich black garden soil while the robin hopped about very busily employed.

"What is your name?" Mary inquired.

He stood up to answer her.

"Ben Weatherstaff," he answered, and then he added with a surly chuckle, "I'm lonely mysel' except when he's with me," and he jerked his thumb toward the robin. "He's th' only friend I've got."

"I have no friends at all," said Mary. "I never had. My Ayah didn't like me and I never played with any one."

It is a Yorkshire habit to say what you think with blunt frankness, and old Ben Weatherstaff was a Yorkshire moor man.

"Tha' an' me are a good bit alike," he said. "We was wove out of th' same cloth. We're neither of us good lookin' an' we're both of us as sour as we look. We've got the same nasty tempers, both of us, I'll warrant."

This was plain speaking, and Mary Lennox had never heard the truth about herself in her life. Native servants always salaamed and submitted to you, whatever you did. She had never thought much about her looks, but she wondered if she was as unattractive as Ben Weatherstaff and she also wondered if she looked as sour as he had looked before the robin came. She actually began to wonder also if she was "nasty tempered." She felt uncomfortable.

Suddenly a clear rippling little sound broke out near her and she turned round. She was standing a few feet from a young apple-tree and the robin had flown on to one of its branches and had burst out into a scrap of a song. Ben Weatherstaff laughed outright.

"What did he do that for?" asked Mary.

"He's made up his mind to make friends with thee," replied Ben. "Dang me if he hasn't took a fancy to thee."

"To me?" said Mary, and she moved toward the little tree softly and looked up.

"Would you make friends with me?" she said to the robin just as if she was speaking to a person. "Would you?" And she did not say it either in her hard little voice or in her imperious Indian voice, but in a tone so soft and eager and coaxing that Ben Weatherstaff was as surprised as she had been when she heard him whistle.

"Why," he cried out, "tha' said that as nice an' human as if tha' was a real child instead of a sharp old woman. Tha' said it almost like Dickon talks to his wild things on th' moor."

"Do you know Dickon?" Mary asked, turning round rather in a hurry.

"Everybody knows him. Dickon's wanderin' about everywhere. Th' very blackberries an' heather-bells knows him. I warrant th' foxes shows him where their cubs lies an' th' skylarks doesn't hide their nests from him."

Mary would have liked to ask some more questions. She was almost as curious about Dickon as she was about the deserted garden. But just that moment the robin, who had ended his song, gave a little shake of his wings, spread them and flew away. He had made his visit and had other things to do.

"He has flown over the wall!" Mary cried out, watching him. "He has flown into the orchard—he has flown across the other wall—into the garden where there is no door!"

"He lives there," said old Ben. "He came out o' th' egg there. If he's courtin', he's makin' up to some young madam of a robin that lives among th' old rose-trees there."

"Rose-trees," said Mary. "Are there rose-trees?"

Ben Weatherstaff took up his spade again and began to dig.

"There was ten year' ago," he mumbled.

"I should like to see them," said Mary. "Where is the green door? There must be a door somewhere."

Ben drove his spade deep and looked as uncompanionable as he had looked when she first saw him.

"There was ten year' ago, but there isn't now," he said.

"No door!" cried Mary. "There must be."

"None as any one can find, an' none as is any one's business. Don't you be a meddlesome wench an' poke your nose where it's no cause to go. Here, I must go on with my work. Get you gone an' play you. I've no more time."

And he actually stopped digging, threw his spade over his shoulder and walked off, without even glancing at her or saying good-by.

CHAPTER 27. IN THE GARDEN

In each century since the beginning of the world wonderful things have been discovered. In the last century more amazing things were found out than in any century before. In this new century hundreds of things still more astounding will be brought to light. At first people refuse to believe that a strange new thing can be done, then they begin to hope it can be done, then they see it can be done—then it is done and all the world wonders why it was not done centuries ago. One of the new things people began to find out in the last century was that thoughts—just mere thoughts—are as powerful as electric batteries—as good for one as sunlight is, or as bad for one as poison. To let a sad thought or a bad one get into your mind is as dangerous as letting a scarlet fever germ get into your body. If you let it stay there after it has got in you may never get over it as long as you live.

So long as Mistress Mary's mind was full of disagreeable thoughts about her dislikes and sour opinions of people and her determination not to be pleased by or interested in anything, she was a yellow-faced, sickly, bored and wretched child. Circumstances, however, were very kind to her, though she was not at all aware of it. They began to push her about for her own good. When her mind gradually filled itself with robins, and moorland cottages crowded with children, with queer crabbed old gardeners and common little Yorkshire housemaids, with springtime and with secret gardens coming alive day by day, and also with a moor boy and his "creatures," there was no room left for the disagreeable thoughts which affected her liver and her digestion and made her yellow and tired.

So long as Colin shut himself up in his room and thought only of his fears and weakness and his detestation of people who looked at him and reflected hourly on humps and early death, he was a hysterical half-crazy little hypochondriac who knew nothing of the sunshine and the spring and also did not know that he could get well and could stand upon his feet if he tried to do it. When new beautiful thoughts began to push out the old hideous ones, life began to come back to him, his blood ran healthily through his veins and strength poured into him like a flood. His scientific experiment was quite practical and simple and there was nothing weird about it at all. Much more surprising things can happen to any one who, when a disagreeable or discouraged thought comes into his mind, just has the sense to remember in time and push it out by putting in an agreeable determinedly courageous one. Two things cannot be in one place.

> "Where you tend a rose, my lad,
> A thistle cannot grow."

While the secret garden was coming alive and two children were coming alive with it, there was a man wandering about certain far-away beautiful places in the Norwegian fiords and the valleys and mountains of Switzerland and he was a man who for ten years had kept his mind filled with dark and heart-broken thinking. He had not been courageous; he had never tried to put any other thoughts in the place of the dark ones. He had wandered by blue lakes and thought them; he had lain on mountainsides with sheets of deep blue gentians blooming all about him and flower breaths filling all the air and he had thought them. A terrible sorrow had fallen upon him when he had been happy and he had let his soul fill itself with blackness and had refused obstinately to allow any rift of light to pierce through. He had forgotten and deserted his home and his duties. When he traveled about, darkness so brooded over him that the sight of him was a wrong done to other people because it was as if he poisoned the air about him with gloom. Most strangers thought he must be either half mad or a man with some hidden crime on his soul. He was a tall man with a drawn face and crooked shoulders and the name he always entered on hotel registers was, "Archibald Craven, Misselthwaite Manor, Yorkshire, England."

He had traveled far and wide since the day he saw Mistress Mary in his study and told her she might have her "bit of earth." He had been in the most beautiful places in Europe, though he had remained nowhere more than a few days. He had chosen the quietest and remotest spots. He had been on the tops of mountains whose heads were in the clouds and had looked down on other mountains when the sun rose and touched them with such light as made it seem as if the world were just being born.

But the light had never seemed to touch himself until one day when he realized than for the first time in ten years a strange thing had happened. He was in a wonderful valley in the Austrian Tyrol and he had been walking alone through such beauty as might have lifted any man's soul out of shadow. He had walked a long way and it had not lifted his. But at last he had felt tired and had thrown himself down to rest on a carpet of moss by a stream. It was a clear little stream which ran quite merrily along on its narrow way through the luscious damp greenness. Sometimes it made a sound rather like very low laughter as it bubbled over and round stones. He saw birds come and dip their heads to drink in it and then flick their wings and fly away. It seemed like a thing alive and yet its tiny voice made the stillness seem deeper. The valley was very, very still.

As he sat gazing into the clear running of the water, Archibald Craven gradually felt his mind and body both grow quiet, as quiet as the valley itself. He wondered if he were going to sleep, but he was not. He sat and gazed at the sunlit water and his eyes began to see things growing at its edge. There was one lovely mass of blue forget-me-nots growing so close to the stream that its leaves were wet and at these he found himself looking as he remembered he had looked at such things years ago. He was actually thinking tenderly how lovely it was and what wonders of blue its hundreds of little blossoms were. He did not know that just that simple thought was slowly filling his mind— filling and filling it until other things were softly pushed aside. It was as if a sweet clear spring had be-

gun to rise in a stagnant pool and had risen and risen until at last it swept the dark water away. But of course he did not think of this himself. He only knew that the valley seemed to grow quieter and quieter as he sat and stared at the bright delicate blueness. He did not know how long he sat there or what was happening to him, but at last he moved as if he were awakening and he got up slowly and stood on the moss carpet, drawing a long, deep, soft breath and wondering at himself. Something seemed to have been unbound and released in him, very quietly.

"What is it?" he said, almost in a whisper, and he passed his hand over his forehead, "I almost feel as if—I were alive!"

I do not know enough about the wonderfulness of undiscovered things to be able to explain how this had happened to him. Neither does any one else yet. He did not understand at all himself—but he remembered this strange hour months afterward when he was at Misselthwaite again and he found out quite by accident that on this very day Colin had cried out as he went into the secret garden:

"I am going to live forever and ever and ever!"

The singular calmness remained with him the rest of the evening and he slept a new reposeful sleep; but it was not with him very long. He did not know that it could be kept. By the next night he had opened the doors wide to his dark thoughts and they had come trooping and rushing back. He left the valley and went on his wandering way again. But, strange as it seemed to him, there were minutes—sometimes half-hours— when, without his knowing why, the black burden seemed to lift itself again and he knew he was a living man and not a dead one. Slowly—slowly—for no reason that he knew of—he was "coming alive" with the garden.

As the golden summer changed into the deep golden autumn he went to the Lake of Como. There he found the loveliness of a dream. He spent his days upon the crystal blueness of the lake or he walked back into the soft thick verdure of the hills and tramped until he was tired so that he might sleep. But by this time he had begun to sleep better, he knew, and his dreams had ceased to be a terror to him.

"Perhaps," he thought, "my body is growing stronger."

It was growing stronger but—because of the rare peaceful hours when his thoughts were changed—his soul was slowly growing stronger, too. He began to think of Misselthwaite and wonder if he should not go home. Now and then he wondered vaguely about his boy and asked himself what he should feel when he went and stood by the carved four-posted bed again and looked down at the sharply chiseled ivory-white face while it slept and the black lashes rimmed so startlingly the close-shut eyes. He shrank from it.

One marvel of a day he had walked so far that when he returned the moon was high and full and all the world was purple shadow and silver. The stillness of lake and shore and wood was so wonderful that he did not go into the villa he lived in. He walked down to a little bowered terrace at the water's edge and sat upon a seat and breathed in all the heavenly scents of the night. He felt the strange calmness stealing over him and it grew deeper and deeper until he fell asleep.

He did not know when he fell asleep and when he began to dream; his dream was so real that he did not feel as if he were dreaming. He remembered afterward how intensely wide awake and alert he had thought he was. He thought that as he sat and breathed in the scent of the late roses and listened to the lapping of the water at his feet he heard a voice calling. It was sweet and clear and happy and far away. It seemed very far, but he heard it as distinctly as if it had been at his very side.

"Archie! Archie! Archie!" it said, and then again, sweeter and clearer than before, "Archie! Archie!"

He thought he sprang to his feet not even startled. It was such a real voice and it seemed so natural that he should hear it.

"Lilias! Lilias!" he answered. "Lilias! where are you?"

"In the garden," it came back like a sound from a golden flute. "In the garden!"

And then the dream ended. But he did not awaken. He slept soundly and sweetly all through the lovely night. When he did awake at last it was brilliant morning and a servant was standing staring at him. He was an Italian servant and was accustomed, as all the servants of the villa were, to accepting without question any strange thing his foreign master might do. No one ever knew when he would go out or come in or where he would choose to sleep or if he would roam about the garden or lie in the boat on the lake all night. The man held a salver with some letters on it and he waited quietly until Mr. Craven took them. When he had gone away Mr. Craven sat a few moments holding them in his hand and looking at the lake. His strange calm was still upon him and something more—a lightness as if the cruel thing which had been done had not happened as he thought—as if something had changed. He was remembering the dream—the real—real dream.

"In the garden!" he said, wondering at himself. "In the garden! But the door is locked and the key is buried deep."

When he glanced at the letters a few minutes later he saw that the one lying at the top of the rest was an English letter and came from Yorkshire. It was directed in a plain woman's hand but it was not a hand he knew. He opened it, scarcely thinking of the writer, but the first words attracted his attention at once.

"Dear Sir:

I am Susan Sowerby that made bold to speak to you once on the moor. It was about Miss Mary I spoke. I will make bold to speak again. Please, sir, I would come home if I was you. I think you would be glad to come and—if you will excuse me, sir—I think your lady would ask you to come if she was here.

Your obedient servant,
Susan Sowerby."

Mr. Craven read the letter twice before he put it back in its envelope. He kept thinking about the dream.

"I will go back to Misselthwaite," he said. "I'll go at once."

And he went through the garden to the villa and ordered Pitcher to prepare for his return to England.

In a few days he was in Yorkshire again, and on his long railroad journey he found himself thinking of his boy as he had never thought in all the ten years past. During those years he had only wished to forget him. Now, though he did not intend to think about him, memories of him constantly drifted into his mind. He remembered the black days when he had raved like a madman because the child was alive and the mother was dead. He had refused to see it, and when he had gone to look at it at last it had been such a weak wretched thing that everyone had been sure it would die in a few days. But to the surprise of those who took care of it the days passed and it lived and then everyone believed it would be a deformed and crippled creature.

He had not meant to be a bad father, but he had not felt like a father at all. He had supplied doctors and nurses and luxuries, but he had shrunk from the mere thought of the boy and had buried himself in his own misery. The first time after a year's absence he returned to Misselthwaite and the small miserable looking thing languidly and indifferently lifted to his face the great gray eyes with black lashes round them, so like and yet so horribly unlike the happy eyes he had adored, he could not bear the sight of them and turned away pale as death. After that he scarcely ever saw him except when he was asleep, and all he knew of him was that he was a confirmed invalid, with a vicious, hysterical, half-insane temper. He could only be kept from furies dangerous to himself by being given his own way in every detail.

All this was not an uplifting thing to recall, but as the train whirled him through mountain passes and golden plains the man who was "coming alive" began to think in a new way and he thought long and steadily and deeply.

"Perhaps I have been all wrong for ten years," he said to himself. "Ten years is a long time. It may be too late to do anything—quite too late. What have I been thinking of!"

Of course this was the wrong Magic—to begin by saying "too late." Even Colin could have told him that. But he knew nothing of Magic—either black or white. This he had yet to learn. He wondered if Susan Sowereby had taken courage and written to him only because the motherly creature had realized that the boy was much worse—was fatally ill. If he had not been under the spell of the curious calmness which had taken possession of him he would have been more wretched than ever. But the calm had brought a sort of courage and hope with it. Instead of giving way to thoughts of the worst he actually found he was trying to believe in better things.

"Could it be possible that she sees that I may be able to do him good and control him?" he thought. "I will go and see her on my way to Misselthwaite."

But when on his way across the moor he stopped the carriage at the cottage, seven or eight children who were playing about gathered in a group and bobbing

seven or eight friendly and polite curtsies told him that their mother had gone to the other side of the moor early in the morning to help a woman who had a new baby. "Our Dickon," they volunteered, was over at the Manor working in one of the gardens where he went several days each week.

Mr. Craven looked over the collection of sturdy little bodies and round red-checked faces, each one grinning in its own particular way, and he awoke to the fact that they were a healthy likable lot. He smiled at their friendly grins and took a golden sovereign from his pocket and gave it to "our 'Lizabeth Ellen" who was the oldest.

"If you divide that into eight parts there will be half a crown for each of you," he said.

Then amid grins and chuckles and bobbing of curtsies he drove away, leaving ecstasy and nudging elbows and little jumps of joy behind.

The drive across the wonderfulness of the moor was a soothing thing. Why did it seem to give him a sense of homecoming which he had been sure he could never feel again—that sense of the beauty of land and sky and purple bloom of distance and a warming of the heart at drawing nearer to the great old house which had held those of his blood for six hundred years? How he had driven away from it the last time, shuddering to think of its closed rooms and the boy lying in the four-posted bed with the brocaded hangings. Was it possible that perhaps he might find him changed a little for the better and that he might overcome his shrinking from him? How real that dream had been—how wonderful and clear the voice which called back to him, "In the garden—In the garden!"

"I will try to find the key," he said. "I will try to open the door. I must—though I don't know why."

When he arrived at the Manor the servants who received him with the usual ceremony noticed that he looked better and that he did not go to the remote rooms where he usually lived attended by Pitcher. He went into the library and sent for Mrs. Medlock. She came to him somewhat excited and curious and flustered.

"How is Master Colin, Medlock?" he inquired.

"Well, sir," Mrs. Medlock answered, "he's—he's different, in a manner of speaking."

"Worse?" he suggested.

Mrs. Medlock really was flushed.

"Well, you see, sir," she tried to explain, "neither Dr. Craven, nor the nurse, nor me can exactly make him out."

"Why is that?"

"To tell the truth, sir, Master Colin might be better and he might be changing for the worse. His appetite, sir, is past understanding—and his ways—"

"Has he become more—more peculiar?" her master asked, knitting his brows anxiously.

"That's it, sir. He's growing very peculiar—when you compare him with what he used to be. He used to eat nothing and then suddenly he began to eat something enormous—and then he stopped again all at once and the meals were sent back just as they used to be. You never knew, sir, perhaps, that out of doors he never would let himself be taken. The things we've gone through to get him to go out in his chair would leave a body trembling like a leaf. He'd throw himself into such a state that Dr. Craven said he couldn't be responsible for forcing him. Well, sir, just without warning—not long after one of his worst tantrums he suddenly insisted on being taken out every day by Miss Mary and Susan Sowerby's boy Dickon that could push his chair. He took a fancy to both Miss Mary and Dickon, and Dickon brought his tame animals, and, if you'll credit it, sir, out of doors he will stay from morning until night."

"How does he look?" was the next question.

"If he took his food natural, sir, you'd think he was putting on flesh—but we're afraid it may be a sort of bloat. He laughs sometimes in a queer way when he's alone with Miss Mary. He never used to laugh at all. Dr. Craven is coming to see you at once, if you'll allow him. He never was as puzzled in his life."

"Where is Master Colin now?" Mr. Craven asked.

"In the garden, sir. He's always in the garden—though not a human creature is allowed to go near for fear they'll look at him."

Mr. Craven scarcely heard her last words.

"In the garden," he said, and after he had sent Mrs. Medlock away he stood and repeated it again and again. "In the garden!"

He had to make an effort to bring himself back to the place he was standing in and when he felt he was on earth again he turned and went out of the room. He took his way, as Mary had done, through the door in the shrubbery and among the laurels and the fountain beds. The fountain was playing now and was encircled by beds of brilliant autumn flowers. He crossed the lawn and turned into the Long Walk by the ivied walls. He did not walk quickly, but slowly, and his eyes were on the path. He felt as if he were being drawn back to the place he had so long forsaken, and he did not know why. As he drew near to it his step became still more slow. He knew where the door was even though the ivy hung thick over it—but he did not know exactly where it lay—that buried key.

So he stopped and stood still, looking about him, and almost the moment after he had paused he started and listened—asking himself if he were walking in a dream.

The ivy hung thick over the door, the key was buried under the shrubs, no human being had passed that portal for ten lonely years—and yet inside the garden there were sounds. They were the sounds of running scuffling feet seeming to chase round and round under the trees, they were strange sounds of lowered suppressed voices—exclamations and smothered joyous cries. It seemed actually like the laughter of young things, the uncontrollable laughter of children who were trying not to be heard but who in a moment or so—as their excitement mounted—would burst forth. What in heaven's name was he dreaming of—what in, heaven's name did he hear? Was he losing his reason and thinking he heard things which were not for human ears? Was it that the far clear voice had meant?

And then the moment came, the uncontrollable moment when the sounds forgot to hush themselves. The feet ran raster and faster—they were nearing the garden door—there was quick strong young breathing and a wild outbreak of laughing shouts which could not be contained—and the door in the wall was flung wide open, the sheet of ivy swinging back, and a boy burst through it at full speed and, without seeing the outsider, dashed almost into his arms.

Mr. Craven had extended them just in time to save him from falling as a result of his unseeing dash against him, and when he held him away to look at him in amazement at his being there he truly gasped for breath.

He was a tall boy and a handsome one. He was glowing with life and his running had sent splendid color leaping to his face. He threw the thick hair back from his forehead and lifted a pair of strange gray eyes—eyes full of boyish laughter and rimmed with black lashes like a fringe. It was the eyes which made Mr. Craven gasp for breath.

"Who—What? Who!" he stammered.

This was not what Colin had expected—this was not what he had planned. He had never thought of such a meeting. And yet to come dashing out—winning a race—perhaps it was even better. He drew himself up to his very tallest. Mary, who had been running with him and had dashed through the door too, believed that he managed to make himself look taller than he had ever looked before.

"Father," he said, "I'm Colin. You can't believe it. I scarcely can myself. I'm Colin."

Like Mrs. Medlock, he did not understand what his father meant when he said hurriedly:

"In the garden! In the garden!"

"Yes," hurried on Colin. "It was the garden that did it—and Mary and Dickon and the creatures—and the Magic. No one knows. We kept it to tell you when you came. I'm well, I can beat Mary in a race. I'm going to be an athlete."

He said it all so like a healthy boy—his face flushed, his words tumbling over each other in his eagerness—that Mr. Craven's soul shook with unbelieving joy.

Colin put out his hand and laid it on his father's arm.

"Aren't you glad, Father?" he ended. "Aren't you glad? I'm going to live forever and ever and ever!"

Mr. Craven put his hands on both the boy's shoulders and held him still. He knew he dared not even try to speak for a moment.

"Take me into the garden, my boy," he said at last. "And tell me all about it."

And so they led him in.

The place was a wilderness of autumn gold and purple and violet blue and flaming scarlet and on every side were sheaves of late lilies standing together—lilies which were white or white and ruby. He remembered well when the first of them had been planted that just at this season of the year their late glories should reveal themselves. Late roses climbed and hung and clustered and the sunshine deepening the hue of the yellowing trees made one feel that one stood in an embowered temple of gold. The newcomer stood silent just as the children had done when they came into its grayness. He looked round and round.

"I thought it would be dead," he said.

"Mary thought so at first," said Colin. "But it came alive."

Then they sat down under their tree—all but Colin, who wanted to stand while he told the story.

It was the strangest thing he had ever heard, Archibald Craven thought, as it was poured forth in headlong boy fashion. Mystery and Magic and wild creatures, the weird midnight meeting—the coming of the spring—the passion of insulted pride which had dragged the young Rajah to his feet to defy old Ben Weatherstaff to his face. The odd companionship, the play acting, the great secret so carefully kept. The listener laughed until tears came into his eyes and sometimes tears came into his eyes when he was not laughing. The Athlete, the Lecturer, the Scientific Discoverer was a laughable, lovable, healthy young human thing.

"Now," he said at the end of the story, "it need not be a secret any more. I dare say it will frighten them nearly into fits when they see me—but I am never going to get into the chair again. I shall walk back with you, Father—to the house."

Ben Weatherstaff's duties rarely took him away from the gardens, but on this occasion he made an excuse to carry some vegetables to the kitchen and being invited into the servants' hall by Mrs. Medlock to drink a glass of beer he was on the spot—as he had hoped to be—when the most dramatic event Misselthwaite Manor had seen during the present generation actually took place.

One of the windows looking upon the courtyard gave also a glimpse of the lawn. Mrs. Medlock, knowing Ben had come from the gardens, hoped that he might have caught sight of his master and even by chance of his meeting with Master Colin.

"Did you see either of them, Weatherstaff?" she asked.

Ben took his beer-mug from his mouth and wiped his lips with the back of his hand. "Aye, that I did," he answered with a shrewdly significant air.

"Both of them?" suggested Mrs. Medlock.

"Both of 'em," returned Ben Weatherstaff. "Thank ye kindly, ma'am, I could sup up another mug of it."

"Together?" said Mrs. Medlock, hastily overfilling his beer-mug in her excitement.

"Together, ma'am," and Ben gulped down half of his new mug at one gulp.

"Where was Master Colin? How did he look? What did they say to each other?"

"I didna' hear that," said Ben, "along o' only bein' on th' step-ladder lookin' over th' wall. But I'll tell thee this. There's been things goin' on outside as you house people knows nowt about. An' what tha'll find out tha'll find out soon."

And it was not two minutes before he swallowed the last of his beer and waved his mug solemnly toward the window which took in through the shrubbery a piece of the lawn.

"Look there," he said, "if tha's curious. Look what's comin' across th' grass."

When Mrs. Medlock looked she threw up her hands and gave a little shriek and every man and woman servant within hearing bolted across the servants' hall and stood looking through the window with their eyes almost starting out of their heads.

Across the lawn came the Master of Misselthwaite and he looked as many of them had never seen him. And by his side with his head up in the air and his eyes full of laughter walked as strongly and steadily as any boy in Yorkshire—

Master Colin!

Elizabeth Lennox Keyser (b. 1942)

In this close reading of Burnett's classic children's novel *The Secret Garden,* Elizabeth Keyser illuminates the qualities that make Mary Lennox a vivid and memorable character. She analyzes Mary's relationships with Martha Sowerby, Colin Craven, and other people in the novel to show why Mary is the invigorating, memorable character at the center of the book, despite the fact that she is described as "contrary" and "disagreeable" and unattractive. In contrast, the narrator praises Colin's qualities, but they fail to convince some readers that Colin is actually appealing. Keyser finds the roots of this contradiction in Burnett's own psychology and inner conflicts, which are imbedded not only in her biography, but in the gender-role expectations of her time. Starting with her own experience of reading and recalling the book, Keyser provides a nuanced interpretation in this 1983 essay, showing that it is not a classless idyll, as some critics claim, but a story full of interesting tensions that reveal Burnett's ambivalences about the ways in which girls and boys were supposed to behave. Keyser is the author of *Whispers in the Dark: The Fiction of Louisa May Alcott* (1993) and *Little Women: A Family Romance* (1999).

"Quite Contrary"

Frances Hodgson Burnett's The Secret Garden

When Mary Lennox was sent to Misselthwaite Manor to live with her uncle everybody said she was the most disagreeable-looking child ever seen.[1]

Thus begins Frances Hodgson Burnett's *The Secret Garden*. Ann Thwaite, Burnett's biographer, remarks that "the most original thing about [*The Secret Garden*] was that its heroine and one of its heroes were both thoroughly unattractive children."[2] And Marghanita Laski has written, "I do not know of any children's book other than *The Secret Garden* that frankly poses this problem of the introspective unlikeable child in terms that children can understand."[3] Burnett herself describes Mary Lennox as wondering "why she had never seemed to belong to anyone even when her father and mother had been alive. Other children seemed to belong to their fathers and mothers, but she had never seemed to really be anyone's little girl. . . . She did not know that this was because she was a disagreeable child; but then, of course, she did not know she was disagreeable. She often thought that others were, but she did not know that she was so herself" (p. 12). Unattractive, unlikeable, disagreeable—these are the ways in which the critics and the author herself characterize Mary Lennox and the way in which the critics at least characterize Colin Craven. But I want to examine closely what the term "disagreeable" really means in connection with the heroine, Mary, and to distinguish between the ways in which the two children are unattractive or unlikeable.

Mary initially "disagrees" with the adult characters in the story not only because her looks and manners fail to please them but also because she refuses to accept their authority. From the outset, however, she is by no means "thoroughly unattractive" to the narrator, who, in the passage quoted above, conveys sympathy as well as antipathy for Mary by mingling the child's point of view with the omniscient. Nor is Mary "thoroughly unattractive" even to the critic who so labels her, for that critic obviously finds a powerful attraction in that very unattractiveness. As the book proceeds, Mary becomes at least moderately agreeable, both to others in the novel and to the narrator, who grants her a grudging approval. But as Mary ostensibly "improves," her role in the book diminishes, and she loses for the reader her main appeal. Instead the other "thoroughly unattractive" child, Master Colin, increasingly gains the center of the stage.

Colin, I would argue, is never as unattractive to the narrator as Mary, nor is he ever as attractive to the reader. Unlike Mary, who is never described as more than "almost pretty" even when she gains flesh and color, Colin, though far more fretful and selfish, is described from the beginning as having a "sharp, delicate face the color of ivory" and great black-fringed eyes like those of his dead mother (p. 124). The narrator tells us that Colin, having had the advantage of "wonderful books and pictures," is more imaginative than Mary, and as he recovers his health he acquires both extraordinary physical beauty and a charismatic

power. At the end of *The Secret Garden* we see Colin besting Mary in a footrace, and, indeed, he has already run away with, or been allowed to dominate, the final third of the book.

The race is not always to the swift, however. Ask an adult what he or she remembers from a childhood reading of *The Secret Garden*.[4] Memories will differ, of course. But what I remembered before I re-read it recently was Mary's first finding and awakening the garden and then, in a reversal of the "Sleeping Beauty" story, her finding and awakening Colin. I remembered Mary exploring the winding paths and gardens within gardens, and indoors the winding corridors with their many locked rooms. And I remembered Mary as stubborn and defiant in her attitude toward adult authority and even toward Colin, but also tender and nurturing. I remembered Colin, too, but always as lying in his room being comforted by Mary or being wheeled by her into the garden. And I remembered his first faltering steps, supported by Mary, but I did not remember his digging, his running, and his calisthenics. And I certainly did not remember his expounding on magic and science. In fact, if my memory serves me, the more conventionally attractive that Colin grew and the more he came to dominate the book, the less memorable both he, and it, became.

Burnett seems to have intended to evoke sympathy for both Mary and Colin while at the same time portraying them as genuinely disagreeable children—children who treat others hatefully and are hated in turn because, having never known love, they feel hatred for themselves. She then apparently meant to show their transformation from self-hating and hateful to loving and lovable through the acquisition of self-esteem. For reasons which I will suggest later, however, Burnett makes Mary too attractive in her disagreeableness and Colin too unattractive in his agreeableness. As Mary becomes less disagreeable, she becomes, after a certain point, less interesting. And Colin, as he becomes more agreeable in some ways, becomes something of a prig and a bore. But before speculating as to why Burnett allows both characters to get out of control, let us consider how Mary, despite—or rather because of—authorial severity, becomes such a compelling figure.

An early example of Mary's unpleasantness earns her the nickname "Mistress Mary Quite Contrary." As a little boy named Basil watches Mary "making heaps of earth and paths for a garden," he suggests that they make a rockery. She spurns his offer, but what strikes us is not so much Mary's ill temper at what she takes to be his interference as her attempt, literally and metaphorically, to make something grow from barren ground. Although the narrator later tells us that Mary is less imaginative than Colin, we, having witnessed her persistent efforts to bring forth life, tend to disbelieve the narrator or at least to question her use of the word *imagination*. True, Mary must overcome the distrustfulness that makes her contrary with well-meaning people like Basil. And she succeeds by admitting first Dickon and then Colin to her secret garden. After admitting Dickon, she tells him about the incident with Basil. He replies, in characteristic fashion, "There doesn't seem to be no need for no one to be contrary when there's flowers an' such like" (p. 108). But Dickon is, in some respects, more naive than Mary, who knows there is more to the world than flowers and friendly wild things. Sometimes, as it was for Mary in India, contrariness is necessary for self-preservation; and sometimes, as for Mary in England, it is even necessary for self-renewal.[5]

We can sympathize with Mary even though she is not a "nice sympathetic child" in part because of the deprivation she has endured. Her mistreatment of the Indian servants, though shocking, seems excusable, since she has been left almost entirely to their care by an apathetic, invalid father and a vain, frivolous mother. When, after her parents' death, she is passed from one reluctant guardian to another, her suspiciousness seems justified. And when, on arriving at Misselthwaite Manor, she overhears the housekeeper, Mrs. Medlock, being warned to keep her out of her uncle's sight and confined to her own two rooms, we can understand why Mary "perhaps never felt quite so contrary in all her life" (p. 23). Yet while we can see that Mary's unhappiness gives rise to her naughtiness,[6] the narrator, by saying that Mary never belonged to anyone because she was a disagreeable child, implies that the reverse is true. In fact, the narrator's refusal to intervene on behalf of Mary, as she does on behalf of Colin, forces us into the position of defending her ourselves.

If Mary's contrariness consisted of mere sullenness, we might agree with the narrator and the adult characters' assessment of her. But there is, as I have suggested, a positive side to her contrariness, which is supported by other characters in the book as well. On her first morning at Misselthwaite, Mary awakens to find the servant Martha in her room. There had been no reciprocity in Mary's relationship with her Indian servants. She could verbally, and even physically, abuse her ayah with impunity. On meeting Martha, however, Mary wonders how she would react to being slapped. Something tells her that Martha would slap her right back. Sure enough, when Mary calls her a "daughter of a pig," as she was wont to insult her ayah, Martha reproves her. The way Martha reacts to and affects Mary resembles the way in which Mary later reacts to and affects Colin. When Martha forces Mary to make at least some effort to dress herself, the narrator comments: "If Martha had been a well-trained fine young lady's maid she would have been more subservient and respectful and would have known that it was her business to brush hair, and button boots, and pick things up and lay them away. She was, however, only an untrained Yorkshire rustic" (p. 30). When Mary later tells Colin that she hates him and contradicts him when, in a bid for her pity, he says he feels a lump on his back, the narrator similarly comments: "A nice sympathetic child could neither have thought nor said such things" (p. 175). But in fact both the untrained Yorkshire rustic and "savage little Mary" have a salutary effect on those who are used to being coddled, and the ironic treatment of Mary's antitypes—the well-trained maid, the fine young lady, and the nice sympathetic child—suggests both the author's need to condemn plainspokenness and her even stronger desire to condone it.

Martha insists that the reluctant Mary play out-of-doors, where she meets another character whose contrariness matches her own. Ben Weatherstaff, the crusty gardener, "had a surly old face, and did not seem at all pleased to see her—but then she was displeased with his garden and wore her 'quite contrary' expression, and certainly did not seem at all pleased to see him" (p. 34). But when Mary mentions a robin and Ben describes how it was abandoned by its parents, she is able for the first time to recognize and admit her own loneliness. Like Martha, Ben Weatherstaff is given to plainspokenness. He says to Mary: "We was wove out of th' same cloth. We're neither of us good lookin' an' we're both of us as sour as we look. We've got the same hasty tempers, both of us, I'll warrant" (p. 40). Mary is taken aback and contrasts him, like

Martha, with the native servants who always "salaamed and submitted to you, whatever you did." But Ben's bluntness, too, helps Mary both to know herself and to see herself as others see her.

Dickon, with his intuitive understanding of nature, and his mother, with her equally wonderful understanding of human nature, not only aid Mary but also counter the asperity of the narrator toward her. But in doing justice to Dickon and his mother, one tends to forget that it is Ben who befriends the robin, whose plight was analogous to Mary's and Colin's, and that it is Ben who kept the garden alive during the ten years it was locked up. It is also Ben who, along with Martha, piques Mary's curiosity about the garden but refuses to satisfy it, thus arousing by *his* contrariness all her stubborn determination to seek it out. And during the time that Mary searches for an entrance to the garden, Ben and Martha provide her with the insights necessary to appreciate her eventual discovery. In the chapter in which Mary finds the key, Martha forces Mary to consider the possiblity that perhaps she does not really like herself. In the chapter in which Mary finds the gate, Martha, with her gift of a skipping-rope, persuades Mary that she is likeable and that she, in turn, is capable of liking others. Thus encouraged, Mary actively seeks and gains Ben's approval, so that by the time "the robin shows the way," Ben and Martha have already helped her find the key to her own heart.

Contrariness then, of the kind that Mary gradually loses, originates in sourness, irritability, an unwillingness to be interested or pleased. But the kind of contrariness that Mary retains, at least until Colin comes to dominate the book, arises from emotional honesty and reliance on one's own judgment.[7] Mary finds both the garden and Colin largely because "she was not a child who had been trained to ask permission or consult her elders about things" (p. 66). Despite repeated denials by Martha that Mary hears crying in the night, and despite repeated warnings from Mrs. Medlock against exploring the house, Mary continues to believe the evidence of her own senses and to search for the source of the cries she hears. What she finds is a boy very similar to herself. Like Mary, Colin has been rejected by his father and has become used to overhearing terrible things about himself, many of which he now believes. Even more than Mary, he has become a tyrant to those who are paid to wait on him. Given everything he ever requested, never forced to do what

he didn't wish, he is the object of pity but also of dislike and disgust. But because Mary has also played the tyrant out of misery, acting the little ranee to her ayah, and because she is not afraid to impose her will on others, she is able to do for Colin what no doctor or even Dickon can.

Mary not only encourages Colin to believe that he can live; she persuades him that he need not live as a chronic invalid. In order to do so Mary must oppose her contrariness to Colin's own and act in a way not "nice" by conventional standards. When Colin unjustly accuses Mary of neglecting him, she becomes angry but, after reflection, relents. When she awakens to hear Colin in hysterics, however, she becomes enraged at the way her emotions, and those of everyone else in the house, are being manipulated. In expressing to Colin what no nice child would say or, according to the narrator, even feel—namely, that Colin is an emotional rather than a physical cripple whose self-centeredness has made him an object of contempt and loathing—Mary is actually expressing what everyone, including the reader, is feeling or would feel in similar circumstances. Her "savagery," as the narrator calls it, her ability to set aside the civilized veneer which has thinly disguised everyone else's hostility towards Colin, has a purgative effect on the entire household. And by disclosing what the nurse and doctor have long known but feared to say, that Colin is only weak from lying in bed and indulging in self-pity, Mary relieves him of his morbid fear and sets him on the road to recovery.

Gradually, with Mary's and Dickon's help, Colin gains enough strength to enter the garden. But although Dickon plants the suggestion that Colin will one day be able to walk, it is plain-spoken Ben Weatherstaff who brings him to his feet. Like Mary, Weatherstaff will express the unmentionable thoughts in everyone's minds: on finding the children in the secret garden, he blurts out, "But tha'rt th' poor cripple" (p. 222). And he is condemned as "ignorant" and "tactless" (p. 223) just as Mary is castigated for being "savage" and not "nice." But his bluntness also has a salutary effect on Colin. "The strength which Colin usually threw into his tantrums rushed through him now in a new way. . . . His anger and insulted pride made him forget everything but this one moment and filled him with a power he had never known before, an almost unnatural strength" (p. 223). Though "magic" later enables him to run and perform calisthenics, it is his passionate desire to refute Ben that enables him to take his first steps.

After watching Colin stand and walk, and after examining his legs, Ben decides that Colin, far from being "th' poor cripple," "'lt make a mon yet" (p. 224). From that point on Colin's athletic prowess, his leadership ability, his interest in science, and his magical powers all seem meant to prove Ben right. In the early chapters the narrator often reminded us of Mary's unattractiveness and unpleasantness; now she stresses Colin's beauty and charisma. At one point the narrator intervenes to tell us that Colin "was somehow a very convincing sort of boy," and it is doubtless this convincing quality that is meant to convince *us* of Colin's ascendancy over Ben, Dickon, and even Mary. Whereas earlier Colin had been a peevish little tyrant, he now becomes a benevolent despot, a combination rajah and priest. Colin, "fired by recollections of fakirs and devotees in illustrations," arranges the group cross-legged in a circle under a tree which makes "a sort of temple" (p. 241). Later Colin heads the rajah's procession "with Dickon on one side and Mary on the other. Ben Weatherstaff walked behind, and the 'creatures' trailed after them" (p. 243). It has been argued that "in this Eden, nature dissolves class—gardner and Pan-boy share the broadly human vocation of nursing the invalid boy to straight health."[8] These doings in the garden, however, suggest a definite hierarchy, one that includes sex as well as class.

During Colin's lectures, "Mistress Mary" is described as feeling "solemnly enraptured" and listening "entranced" (pp. 241–42). Although we are doubtless meant to be as charmed by Colin as the other characters are and to see in his domination of the little group the promise of his future manhood, we are in fact disenchanted to find Mary little more than a worshipful Huck to the antics of Colin's Tom Sawyer. Yet Mary and Huck are the truly imaginative and convincing children who do not, like Colin and Tom, need the stimulus of books in order to have real adventures and solve real problems. Huck's escape from Pap and his flight down the river with Jim, Mary's discoveries of Colin and the garden, and, above all, her selfdiscoveries, make Tom's "evasion" and Colin's "magic" anticlimactic. And just as Jim loses stature because of the indignities inflicted on him by Tom, so the roles of Martha and Ben Weatherstaff, so important to

Mary's development, diminish. Martha, as remarkable in her way as Dickon and their mother, simply disappears from the final chapters; but since she is the first person for whom Mary feels anything like trust and affection, it is hard to believe that Mary would forget her. Ben, like Mrs. Sowerby a party to the secret in the garden, is treated condescendingly by Colin—and by the author. When Ben makes a joke at the expense of Colin's "scientific discoveries," Colin snubs him, a snub which Ben—acting out of character—takes humbly (p. 245). But at least at the end of Twain's book we are left with its true hero. In *The Secret Garden* Burnett shifts from Mary's to Colin's point of view shortly after the scene in which Mary confronts him with his cowardice and hypochondria. From there on Mary slips into the background until she disappears entirely from the final chapter. The novel ends with the master of Misselthwaite and his son, Master Colin, crossing the lawn before their servants' admiring eyes.

Perhaps the analogy between Mary and Huck can do more than suggest why the final third of *The Secret Garden* is so unsatisfying. Huck is a memorable, even magical, creation not only because he is a very convincing boy (so is Tom, for that matter), but because he is, at the same time, unconventional. He resists being civilized in a way that Tom, for all his infatuation with outlaws, does not. Mary, too, is a more memorable creation than Colin because she is both recognizably human and refreshingly different. Thwaite and Laski have tried to link this difference with her unpleasantness, but I believe it lies more in her freedom from sex-role stereotypes.[9] (This, of course, is why girls have always found Jo March so appealing, especially in Part 1 of *Little Women*.)

From the first Mary is an independent, selfcontained, yet self-assertive child. Unlike Colin, she discovers and enters the secret garden all by herself, and she defies adult authority in order to find, befriend, and liberate Colin. Unlike her mother, she is never vain of her appearance; she is proud when she finds herself getting plump, rosy, and glossy-haired, but only because these are signs of her growing strength. When she receives a present from Mr. Craven, she is delighted to find books rather than dolls, and she works and exercises in the garden along with Colin and Dickon. She does not wish to have a nurse or governess but seems to thrive on an active life out-ofdoors. Early in the relationship with Colin she is the leader, and even when he is able to run about, it is she who, on a rainy day, suggests that they explore his house. Colin, when we first meet him, is a hysterical invalid, and his father, as the name "Craven" signifies, is a weak and cowardly man, still mourning after ten years his dead wife and, in doing so, neglecting their living son. It is as though Burnett so generously endowed Mary at the expense of Colin and his father that she had to compensate for it by stressing Mary's disagreeable traits and exaggerating Colin's charm. And in the final chapter Colin's ascendancy suggests that if he becomes a "mon," as Ben predicts, then Mary will have to become a woman—quiet, passive, subordinate, and self-effacing. Huck at the end of *Huckleberry Finn* cannot escape civilization; Mary cannot escape the role that civilization has assigned her.

Burnett's ambivalence toward Mary and her indulgence of Colin probably reflect lifelong conflicts. As a child Burnett was encouraged by her widowed mother to cultivate genteel and ladylike manners. And as a young married woman she is described by Thwaite as "obviously trying her best . . . to appear as the nineteenth century's ideal of womanhood" (p. 52). Often, especially during these early years, Burnett regarded her writing as a necessary, even sacrificial task, performed for the sake of her husband, struggling to establish himself as an ophthalmologist, and their sons. Yet Burnett continued to write long after Dr. Swan Burnett was well able to support his family. By then, however, writing, and the fame and fortune which attended it, seems to have become a psychological necessity. Her favorite image of herself was that of a fairy godmother, and the power as well as the magnanimity of that role must have appealed to her. So like many successful women writers, including Louisa May Alcott and Burnett's prolific friend Mrs. Humphry Ward, she tried to rationalize her writing as unselfish service, and, when she could not ignore its self-assertive and self-serving role, punished herself with ill health. And finally, again like other women writers (great ones such as the Brontës and George Eliot as well as minor ones such as Alcott and Ward), she chastened her self-assertive female characters.[10]

The Secret Garden, written in 1911 toward the end of a long, successful career, seems to suggest not only self-condemnation and self-punishment in its treatment of Mary but an attempted reparation for wrongs Burnett may have felt she inflicted on the males closest to her. Most obviously, the idealized Colin seems to represent her elder son, Lionel, and his recovery a wish-fulfilling revision of what actually happened. After the extraordinary success of *Little Lord Fauntleroy* in 1886, Burnett began to spend much of each year abroad. Although she was a doting mother, able from her earnings to give her sons whatever their hearts desired, she may have felt that even these luxuries, like those Colin's father provides for him, could not compensate for her absence. And when, during one of these absences, Lionel became consumptive, her guilt must have been intensified. To assuage it she nursed Lionel devotedly and especially prided herself on protecting him from the knowledge that he was dying.[11] But in a notebook entry, written a few months after Lionel's death, she asks: "Did I do right to hide from you that you were dying? It seemed to me that I *must* not give you the terror of knowing."[12] The situation in *The Secret Garden* is significantly reversed: Colin is kept in ignorance not of his imminent death but of his capacity for life; Mary, by breaking the conspiracy of silence, enables him to live.

The figure of Colin is reminiscent not only of Lionel but also of Swan Burnett and of Mrs. Burnett's second husband, Stephen Townesend. Swan, himself crippled in his youth, became a successful eye specialist, but the marriage seems never to have been a happy one. Two years after their divorce, Burnett married Townesend, a doctor and aspiring actor ten years younger than herself. Burnett had long attempted to use her theatrical connections to further his acting career, especially after Townesend helped her to nurse Lionel through his fatal illness. As her son Vivian wrote: "This was one of the few solaces that Dearest had in her dark hours, making her feel that surely some good had come out of her wish to help her older—disappointed—Stephen boy."[13] And as Burnett wrote to her friend Kitty Hall, "If I had done no other one thing in my life but help Lionel to die as he did, I should feel as if I ought to be grateful to God for letting me live to do it—but if I can help Stephen to *live*, that will be another beautiful thing to have done."[14] As these quotations suggest, Burnett's interest in Stephen Townesend was largely maternal, a desire to play fairy godmother as she had in the lives of her sons. To use her fortune and influence to aid a struggling young man would somehow justify her possession of it. But although Stephen, unlike Lionel, survived, she never succeeded in helping either him or their marriage to "live."

Thus *The Secret Garden,* far from combining "the ideal remembered holiday in a golden age . . . with a classless, reasonable, and joyous Utopia for the future," reflects its author's ambivalence about sex roles.[15] On the one hand, she vindicates Mary's self-assertiveness and her own career by allowing Mary to bring the garden, Colin, and, eventually, Mr. Craven back to life. On the other hand, she chastens herself and Mary by permitting the narrator to intervene only to reprove her and by making her subordinate to Colin in the final chapters of the book. By idealizing Colin at the expense of Mary she seems to be affirming male supremacy, and the final vision of the master of Misselthwaite with his son, Master Colin, further suggests a defense of patriarchal authority. While Mr. Craven can be seen as the neglectful, erring parent of either sex—and thus still another means by which Burnett atones for her maternal failings—he, like the peevish invalid Colin, can also be viewed as an expression of her impatience with male weakness. And her attempts to glorify Colin are unsuccessful enough to make us wonder if even here her ambivalence—even her resentment and hostility—does not show through. For all her efforts to make Mary disagreeable and to efface her, Mary remains a moving and memorable creation, whereas Colin's "magic" never amounts to more than a mere trick. Mary, like the author herself, seems to have both gained and lost from her contrariness, and *The Secret Garden* succeeds and fails accordingly.

NOTES

1. Frances Hodgson Burnett, *The Secret Garden* (1911; rpt. New York: Dell, 1977), p. 1. All further references will be to this edition and will be cited parenthetically in the text.

2. *Waiting for the Party: The Life of Frances Hodgson Burnett 1849–1924* (New York: Charles Scribner's Sons, 1974), p. 221.

3. *Mrs. Ewing, Mrs. Molesworth, and Mrs. Hodgson Burnett* (London: Arthur Barker, 1950), p. 88. Although Laski sees Mary and Colin as original, she also places them in the tradition of Charlotte Yonge's Ethel May, the heroine of *The Daisy Chain* (1856).

4. Madelon S. Gohlke, in "Re-reading *The Secret Garden,*" *College English,* 41 (1980), 894–902, insists that *The Secret Garden* withstands the test of adult rereading. On subjecting the book to the same test, however, I find that only the part I remember most vividly from childhood—that in which Mary predominates—meets my adult criteria.

5. When the cholera epidemic strikes the Lennox compound, Mary is the only one who neither flees nor dies. In the midst of death and destruction she remains calm and self-possessed, partly out of ignorance, of course, but largely out of toughness. Burnett tells us that "as she was a self-absorbed child she gave her entire thought to herself" (p. 8). It is this self-absorption that insulates her from fear during the epidemic and from desolation on learning of her parents' death.

6. Clarissa M. Rowland, in "Bungalows and Bazaars: India in Victorian Children's Fiction," *Children's Literature,* 2 (1973), identifies the connection between naughtiness and unhappiness as a theme of Victorian children's fiction set in India (p. 194).

7. In "Little Girls without Their Curls," pp. 14–31, U. C. Knoepflmacher argues that the guise of fantasy enables Juliana Ewing, in "Amelia and the Dwarfs," and Burnett herself, in "Behind the White Brick," to indulge more fully a wish for female aggression in defiance of Victorian taboos than is possible in a realistic fiction such as *The Secret Garden.* I would argue, however, that because less "anarchic," Mary's aggressiveness or contrariness, at least that which she retains until Colin comes to dominate the book, has more social value than that of Amelia or Jem/Baby and thus her "domestication" represents a loss rather than a gain.

8. Fred Inglis, *The Promise of Happiness: Value and Meaning in Children's Fiction* (Cambridge: At the University Press, 1981), p. 112.

9. Inglis, in his chapter on sex roles in children's fiction, praises Burnett for endowing her heroines with the intelligence and independence of Elizabeth Bennet (ibid., p. 165), but this seems true of Mary only in the first two-thirds of the story.

10. Another interesting topic for exploration would be Burnett's use of the Brontë novels in her children's fiction. The Yorkshire setting of *The Secret Garden,* of course, resembles that of *Jane Eyre* and *Wuthering Heights,* but Mary has elements of Jane Eyre and both Catherines, Dickon resembles a more benign little Heathcliff, and Colin seems a blend of Rochester, Linton Heathcliff, and Hareton Earnshaw. As Inglis says, "The influence of the Brontës is felt on every page" (ibid., p. 112).

11. To a cousin she wrote: "It will perhaps seem almost incredible to you as it does to others when I tell you that he never did find out. He was ill nine months but I never allowed him to know that I was *really* anxious

about him. I never let him know he had consumption or that he was in danger." Quoted in Vivian Burnett, *The Romantick Lady* (New York: Scribner's, 1930), pp. 211–12.

12. Ibid., p. 214.
13. Ibid., p. 212.
14. Ibid., p. 222–23.
15. Inglis, p. 113.

E. Vincent Millay (1892–1950)

The writer of this poem was seventeen when "Friends" appeared in *St. Nicholas Magazine,* the leading periodical for children and young people in late nineteenth- and early twentieth-century America. She became famous as the poet Edna St. Vincent Millay, but it is interesting to note here that before she was widely known, she chose a version of her name that does not reveal her sex. The speakers of the poem are indeed friends, but they regard each other with affectionate puzzlement across the divide of gender. The poem cleverly reveals both what is different about their ways of enjoying themselves and what enables them to remain friends. It would be interesting to speculate on whether any of the behaviors that set Molly and Bob apart still endure a century later and what qualities make friendship between boys and girls possible today.

Friends

I. HE

I've sat here all the afternoon, watching her busy fingers send
That needle in and out. How soon, I wonder, will she reach the end?
Embroidery! I can't see how a girl of Molly's common sense
Can spend her time like that. Why, now—just look at that! I may be dense,
But, somehow, I don't see the fun in punching lots of holes down through
A piece of cloth; and, one by one, sewing them up. But Molly'll do
   A dozen of them, right around
   That shapeless bit of stuff she's found.
   A dozen of them! Just like that!
   And think it's sense she's working at.

But then, she's just a girl (although she's quite the best one of the lot!)
And I'll just have to let her sew, whether it's foolishness or not.

II. SHE

He's sat here all the afternoon, talking about an awful game;
One boy will not be out till June, and then he may be always lame.
Foot-ball! I'm sure I can't see why a boy like Bob—so good and kind—
Wishes to see poor fellows lie hurt on the ground. I may be blind,
But, somehow, I don't see the fun. Some one calls, "14-16-9";

You kick the ball, and then you run and try to
   reach a white chalk-line.
   And Bob would sit right there all day
   And talk like that, and never say
   A single word of sense; or so

It seems to me. I may not know.
   But Bob's a faithful friend to me. So let him talk
     that game detested,
   And I will smile and seem to be most wonderfully
     interested!

L. M. Montgomery (1874–1942)

Although she is not as well known as her predecessor, Anne of Green Gables, the orphan Emily Byrd Starr is an equally engaging and unconventional heroine of Prince Edward Island. The most autobiographical of L. M. Montgomery's characters, Emily is less awkward physically and more ethereal than Anne. Montgomery had lost her mother when very young and was left with relatives who never appreciated her writing or passionate temperament. Emily also shares characteristics with her favorite heroines of domestic romance, such as Charlotte Brontë's Jane Eyre and Elizabeth Barrett Browning's Aurora Leigh. "Sacrilege," a chapter late in *Emily of New Moon* (1923), depicts a climactic battle of wills between Emily and Aunt Elizabeth, a turning point in their relationship and in Emily's growth toward womanhood and self-reliance.

While Emily's emotions are still tempestuous and romantic in the third book, *Emily's Quest* (1927), painful experiences in her years after high school show that succeeding in both personal relationships and art requires complex skills of understanding and endurance. Like Jo March, Emily is linked romantically with a girlhood playmate and soulmate named Teddy. Also like Jo March, Emily suffers the agony of rejection from publishers and disillusionment with her writing after an older friend critiques her work. Furthermore, her impetuous actions are followed by the kind of accident that modern readers often view as an unfortunate attempt to punish or tame the heroine's aggressive and independent nature in coming-of-age novels for girls. Severe injury or illness more often symbolizes the end of childhood innocence and freedom for fictional girls than for boys (see Elizabeth Segel's essay in this section). With mixed feelings about writing sequels, Montgomery observed that female adolescence was more difficult to depict than childhood. Whether one views the novel as flawed or believes that Montgomery was struggling with ways to help Emily cope with limitations imposed by her culture as she reached womanhood, these episodes represent some typical dilemmas that are found in traditional girls' fiction. Nevertheless, Emily's self-reliant character at the beginning and end of the trilogy provided a progressive role model for girls in the 1920s. (See also the excerpt from *Anne of Green Gables* in Part 2.)

From *Emily of New Moon*

CHAPTER 29. SACRILEGE

There had been several clashes between Aunt Elizabeth and Emily that winter and spring. Generally Aunt Elizabeth came out victorious; there was that in her that would not be denied the satisfaction of having her own way even in trifling matters. But once in a while she came up against that curious streak of granite in Emily's composition which was unyielding and unbendable and unbreakable. Mary Murray, of a hundred years agone, had been, so family chronicle ran, a gentle and submissive creature generally; but she had that same streak in her, as her "Here I Stay" abundantly testified. When Aunt Elizabeth tried conclusions with that element in Emily she always got the worst of it. Yet she did not learn wisdom therefrom but pursued her policy of repression all the more rigorously; for it occasionally came home to her, as Laura let down tucks, that Emily was on the verge of beginning to grow up and that various breakers and reefs loomed ahead, ominously magnified in the mist of unseen years. Emily must not be allowed to get out of hand now, lest later on she make shipwreck as her mother had done—or as Elizabeth Murray firmly believed she had done. There were, in short, to be no more elopements from New Moon.

One of the things they fell out about was the fact that Emily, as Aunt Elizabeth discovered one day, was in the habit of using more of her egg money to buy paper than Aunt Elizabeth approved of. What did Emily do with so much paper? They had a fuss over this and eventually Aunt Elizabeth discovered that Emily was writing stories. Emily had been writing stories all winter under Aunt Elizabeth's very nose and Aunt Elizabeth had never suspected it. She had fondly supposed that Emily was writing school compositions. Aunt Elizabeth knew in a vague way that Emily wrote silly rhymes which she called "poetry" but this did not worry her especially. Jimmy made up a lot of similar trash. It was foolish but harmless and Emily would doubtless outgrow it. Jimmy had not outgrown it, to be sure, but then his accident—Elizabeth always went a little sick in soul when she remembered it—had made him more or less a child for life.

But writing stories was a very different thing and Aunt Elizabeth was horrified. Fiction of any kind was an abominable thing. Elizabeth Murray had been trained up in this belief in her youth and in her age she had not departed from it. She honestly thought that it was a wicked and sinful thing in anyone to play cards, dance, or go to the theatre, read or write novels, and in Emily's case there was a worse feature—it was the Starr coming out in her—Douglas Starr especially. No Murray of New Moon had ever been guilty of writing "stories" or of ever wanting to write them. It was an alien growth that must be pruned off ruthlessly. Aunt Elizabeth applied the pruning shears; and found no pliant, snippable root but that same underlying streak of granite. Emily was respectful and reasonable and above-board; she bought no more paper with egg money; but she told Aunt Elizabeth that she could not give up writing stories and she went right on writing them, on pieces of brown wrapping paper and the blank backs of circulars which agricultural machinery firms sent Cousin Jimmy.

"Don't you know that it is wicked to write novels?" demanded Aunt Elizabeth.

"Oh, I'm not writing novels—yet," said Emily. "I can't get enough paper. These are just short stories. And it isn't wicked—Father liked novels."

"Your father—" began Aunt Elizabeth, and stopped. She remembered that Emily had "acted up" before now when anything derogatory was said of her father. But the very fact that she felt mysteriously compelled to stop annoyed Elizabeth, who had said what seemed good to her all her life at New Moon without much regard for other people's feelings.

"You will not write any more of *this stuff*," Aunt Elizabeth contemptuously flourished "The Secret of the Castle" under Emily's nose. "I forbid you—remember, I forbid you."

"Oh, I must write, Aunt Elizabeth," said Emily gravely, folding her slender, beautiful hands on the table and looking straight into Aunt Elizabeth's angry face with the steady, unblinking gaze which Aunt Ruth called unchildlike. "You see, it's this way. It is *in* me. I can't help it. And Father said I was *always* to keep on writing. He said I would be famous some day. Wouldn't you like to have a famous niece, Aunt Elizabeth?"

"I am not going to argue the matter," said Aunt Elizabeth.

"I'm not arguing—only explaining." Emily was exasperatingly respectful. "I just want you to understand how it is that I *have* to go on writing stories, even though I am so very sorry you don't approve."

"If you don't give up this—this worse than nonsense, Emily, I'll—I'll—"

Aunt Elizabeth stopped, not knowing what to say she would do. Emily was too big now to be slapped or shut up; and it was no use to say, as she was tempted to, "I'll send you away from New Moon," because Elizabeth Murray knew perfectly well she would not send Emily away from New Moon—*could* not send her away, indeed, though this knowledge was as yet only in her feelings and had not been translated into her intellect. She only felt that she was helpless and it angered her; but Emily was mistress of the situation and calmly went on writing stories. If Aunt Elizabeth had asked her to give up crocheting lace or making molasses taffy, or eating Aunt Laura's delicious drop cookies, Emily would have done so wholly and cheerfully, though she loved these things. But to give up writing stories—why, Aunt Elizabeth might as well have asked her to give up breathing. *Why* couldn't she understand? It seemed so simple and indisputable to Emily.

"Teddy can't help making pictures and Ilse can't help reciting and I can't help writing. *Don't* you see, Aunt Elizabeth?"

"I see that you are an ungrateful and disobedient child," said Aunt Elizabeth.

This hurt Emily horribly, but she could not give in; and there continued to be a sense of soreness and disapproval between her and Aunt Elizabeth in all the little details of daily life that poisoned existence more or less for the child, who was so keenly sensitive to her environment and to the feelings with which her kindred regarded her. Emily felt it all the time—except when she was writing her stories. *Then* she forgot everything, roaming in some enchanted country between the sun and moon, where she saw wonderful beings whom she tried to describe and wonderful deeds which she tried to record, coming back to the candle-lit kitchen with a somewhat dazed sense of having been years in No-Man's Land.

She did not even have Aunt Laura to back her up in the matter. Aunt Laura thought Emily ought to yield in such an unimportant matter and please Aunt Elizabeth.

"But it's not unimportant," said Emily despairingly. "It's the most important thing in the world to me, Aunt Laura. Oh, I thought *you* would understand."

"I understand that you like to do it, dear, and I think it's a harmless enough amusement. But it seems to annoy Elizabeth some way and I do think you might give it up on that account. It is not as if it was anything that mattered much—it *is* really a waste of time."

"No—no," said distressed Emily. "Why, some day, Aunt Laura, I'll write real books—and make lots of money," she added, sensing that the businesslike Murrays measured the nature of most things on a cash basis.

Aunt Laura smiled indulgently.

"I'm afraid you'll never grow rich that way, dear. It would be wiser to employ your time preparing yourself for some useful work."

It was maddening to be condescended to like this—maddening that nobody could see that she *had* to write—maddening to have Aunt Laura so sweet and loving and stupid about it.

"Oh," thought Emily bitterly, "if that hateful *Enterprise* editor had printed my piece they'd have believed *then.*"

"At any rate," advised Aunt Laura, "don't let Elizabeth *see* you writing them."

But somehow Emily could not take this prudent advice. There *had* been occasions when she had connived with Aunt Laura to hoodwink Aunt Elizabeth on some little matter, but she found she could not do it in this. *This* had to be open and above-board. She *must* write stories—and Aunt Elizabeth *must* know it—that was the way it had to be. She could not be false to herself in this—she could not *pretend* to be false.

She wrote her father all about it—poured out her bitterness and perplexity to him in what, though she did not suspect it at the time, was the last letter she was to write him. There was a great bundle of letters by now on the old sofa shelf in the garret—for Emily had written many letters to her father besides those which have been chronicled in this history. There were a great many paragraphs about Aunt Elizabeth in them, most of them very uncomplimentary and some of them, as Emily herself would have owned when her first bitterness was past, overdrawn and exaggerated.

They had been written in moments when her hurt and angry soul demanded some outlet for its emotion and barbed her pen with venom. Emily was mistress of a subtly malicious style when she chose to be. After she had written them the hurt had ceased and she thought no more about them. But they remained.

And one spring day, Aunt Elizabeth, housecleaning in the garret while Emily played happily with Teddy at the Tansy Patch, found the bundle of letters on the sofa shelf, sat down, and read them all.

Elizabeth Murray would never have read any writing belonging to a grown person. But it never occurred to her that there was anything dishonourable in reading the letters wherein Emily, lonely and—sometimes—misunderstood, had poured out her heart to the father she had loved and been loved by, so passionately and understandingly. Aunt Elizabeth thought she had a right to know everything that this pensioner on her bounty did, said, or thought. She read the letters and she found out what Emily thought of her—of her, Elizabeth Murray, autocrat unchallenged, to whom no one had ever dared to say anything uncomplimentary. Such an experience is no pleasanter at sixty than at sixteen. As Elizabeth Murray folded up the last letter her hands trembled—with anger, and something underneath it that was not anger.

"Emily, your Aunt Elizabeth wants to see you in the parlour," said Aunt Laura, when Emily returned from the Tansy Patch, driven home by the thin grey rain that had begun to drift over the greening fields. Her tone—her sorrowful look—warned Emily that mischief was in the wind. Emily had no idea what mischief—she could not recall anything she had done recently that should bring her up before the tribunal Aunt Elizabeth occasionally held in the parlour. It must be serious when it was in the parlour. For reasons best known to herself Aunt Elizabeth held super-serious interviews like this in the parlour. Possibly it was because she felt obscurely that the photographs of the Murrays on the walls gave her a backing she needed when dealing with this hop-out-of-kin; for the same reason Emily detested a trial in the parlour. She always felt on such occasions like a very small mouse surrounded by a circle of grim cats.

Emily skipped across the big hall, pausing, in spite of her alarm, to glance at the charming red world through the crimson glass; then pushed open the parlour door. The room was dim, for only one of the slat blinds was partially raised. Aunt Elizabeth was sitting bolt upright in Grandfather Murray's black horsehair-chair. Emily looked at her stern, angry face first—and then at her lap.

Emily understood.

The first thing she did was to retrieve her precious letters. With the quickness of light she sprang to Aunt Elizabeth, snatched up the bundle and retreated to the door; there she faced Aunt Elizabeth, her face blazing with indignation and outrage. Sacrilege had been committed—the most sacred shrine of her soul had been profaned.

"How dare you?" she said. "How dare you touch *my private papers,* Aunt Elizabeth?"

Aunt Elizabeth had not expected *this.* She had looked for confusion—dismay—shame—fear—for anything but this righteous indignation, as if *she,* forsooth, were the guilty one. She rose.

"Give me those letters, Emily."

"No, I will not," said Emily, white with anger, as she clasped her hands around the bundle. "They are mine and Father's—not yours. You had no right to touch them. I will *never* forgive you!"

This was turning the tables with a vengeance. Aunt Elizabeth was so dumfounded that she hardly knew what to say or do. Worst of all, a most unpleasant doubt of her own conduct suddenly assailed her—driven home perhaps by the intensity and earnestness of Emily's accusation. For the first time in her life it occurred to Elizabeth Murray to wonder if she had done rightly. For the first time in her life she felt ashamed; and the shame made her furious. It was intolerable that *she* should be made to feel ashamed.

For the moment they faced each other, not as aunt and niece, not as child and adult, but as two human beings each with hatred for the other in her heart—Elizabeth Murray, tall and austere and thin-lipped; Emily Starr, white of face, her eyes pools of black flame, her trembling arms hugging her letters.

"*So this* is your gratitude," said Aunt Elizabeth. "You were a penniless orphan—I took you to my home—I have given you shelter and food and education and kindness—and *this* is my thanks."

As yet Emily's tempest of anger and resentment prevented her from feeling the sting of this.

"You did not *want* to take me," she said. "You made me draw lots and you took me because the lot fell to you. You knew some of you had to take me because you were the proud Murrays and couldn't let a relation go to an orphan asylum. Aunt Laura loves me now but you don't. So why should I love you?"

"Ungrateful, thankless child!"

"I'm *not* thankless. I've tried to be good—I've tried to obey you and please you—I do all the chores I can to help pay for my keep. And you had *no business* to read my letters to Father."

"They are disgraceful letters—and must be destroyed," said Aunt Elizabeth.

"No," Emily clasped them tighter. "I'd sooner burn myself. You shall not have them, Aunt Elizabeth."

She felt her brows drawing together—she felt the Murray look on her face—she knew she was conquering.

Elizabeth Murray turned paler, if that were possible. There were times when she could give the Murray look herself; it was not that which dismayed her—it was the uncanny something which seemed to peer out behind the Murray look that always broke her will. She trembled—faltered—yielded.

"Keep your letters," she said bitterly, "and scorn the old woman who opened her home to you."

She went out of the parlour. Emily was left mistress of the field. And all at once her victory turned to dust and ashes in her mouth.

She went up to her own room, hid her letters in the cupboard over the mantel, and then crept up on her bed, huddling down in a little heap with her face buried in her pillow. She was still sore with a sense of outrage—but underneath another pain was beginning to ache terribly.

Something in her was hurt because she had hurt Elizabeth—for she felt that Aunt Elizabeth, under all her anger, was *hurt*. This surprised Emily. She would have expected Aunt Elizabeth to be angry, of course, but she would never have supposed it would affect her in any other way. Yet she had seen something in Aunt Elizabeth's eyes when she had flung that last stinging sentence at her—something that spoke of bitter hurt.

"Oh! Oh!" gasped Emily. She began to cry chokingly into her pillow. She was so wretched that she could not get out of herself and watch her own suffering with a sort of enjoyment in its drama—set her mind to analyse her feelings—and when Emily was as wretched as that she was very wretched indeed and wholly comfortless. Aunt Elizabeth would not keep her at New Moon after a poisonous quarrel like this.

She would send her away, of course. Emily believed this. Nothing was too horrible to believe just then. How could she live away from dear New Moon?

"And I may have to live eighty years," Emily moaned.

But worse even than this was the remembrance of that look in Aunt Elizabeth's eyes.

Her own sense of outrage and sacrilege ebbed away under the remembrance. She thought of all the things she had written her father about Aunt Elizabeth—sharp, bitter things, some of them just, some of them unjust. She began to feel that she should not have written them. It was true enough that Aunt Elizabeth had not loved her—had not wanted to take her to New Moon. But she *had* taken her and though it had been done in duty, not in love, the fact remained. It was no use for her to tell herself that it wasn't as if the letters were written to any one living, to be seen and read by others. While she was under Aunt Elizabeth's roof—while she owed the food she ate and the clothes she wore to Aunt Elizabeth—she should not say, even to her father, harsh things of her. A Starr should not have done it.

"I must go and ask Aunt Elizabeth to forgive me," thought Emily at last, all the passion gone out of her and only regret and repentance left. "I suppose she never will—she'll hate me always now. But I must go."

She turned herself about—and then the door opened and Aunt Elizabeth entered. She came across the room and stood at the side of the bed, looking down at the grieved little face on the pillow—a face that in the dim, rainy twilight, with its tear-stains and black shadowed eyes, looked strangely mature and chiseled.

Elizabeth Murray was still austere and cold. Her voice sounded stern; but she said an amazing thing.

"Emily, I had no right to read your letters. I admit I was wrong. Will you forgive me?"

"Oh!" The word was almost a cry. Aunt Elizabeth had at last discerned the way to conquer Emily. The latter lifted herself up, flung her arms about Aunt Elizabeth, and said chokingly,

"Oh—Aunt Elizabeth—I'm sorry—I'm sorry—I shouldn't have written those things—but I wrote them when I was vexed—and I didn't mean them *all*—truly, I didn't mean the worst of them. Oh, you'll believe *that*, won't you, Aunt Elizabeth?"

"I'd like to believe it, Emily." An odd quiver passed through the tall, rigid form. "I—don't like to think you—*hate* me—my sister's child—little Juliet's child."

"I don't—oh, I don't," sobbed Emily. "And I'll *love* you, Aunt Elizabeth, if you'll let me—if you *want* me to. I didn't think you cared. *Dear* Aunt Elizabeth."

Emily gave Aunt Elizabeth a fierce hug and a passionate kiss on the white, fine-wrinkled cheek. Aunt Elizabeth kissed her gravely on the brow in return and then said, as if closing the door on the whole incident.

"You'd better wash your face and come down to supper."

But there was yet something to be cleared up.

"Aunt Elizabeth," whispered Emily. "I *can't* burn those letters, you know—they belong to Father. But I'll tell you what I will do. I'll go over them all and put a star by anything I said about you and then I'll add an explanatory footnote saying that I was mistaken."

Emily spent her spare time for several days putting in her "explanatory footnotes," and then her conscience had rest. But when she again tried to write a letter to her father she found that it no longer meant anything to her. The sense of reality—nearness—of close communion had gone. Perhaps she had been outgrowing it gradually, as childhood began to merge into girlhood—perhaps the bitter scene with Aunt Elizabeth had only shaken into dust something out of which the spirit had already departed. But, whatever the explanation, it was not possible to write such letters any more. She missed them terribly but she could not go back to them. A certain door of life was shut behind her and could not be re-opened.

From *Emily's Quest*

SIX

I

Teddy Kent and Ilse Burnley came home in the summer for a brief vacation. Teddy had won an Art Scholarship which meant two years in Paris and was to sail for Europe in two weeks. He had written the news to Emily in an offhand way and she had responded with the congratulations of a friend and sister. There was no reference in either letter to rainbow gold or Vega of the Lyre. Yet Emily looked forward to his coming with a wistful, ashamed hope that would not be denied. Perhaps—dared she hope it?—when they met again face to face, in their old haunted woods and trysts—this coldness that had grown up so inexplicably between them would vanish as a sea-fog vanishes when the sun rose over the gulf. No doubt Teddy had had his imitation love affairs as she had hers. But when he came—when they looked again into each other's eyes—when she heard his signal whistle in Lofty John's bush—

But she never heard it. On the evening of the day when she knew Teddy was expected home she walked in the garden among brocaded moths, wearing a new gown of "powder-blue" chiffon and listened for it. Every robin call brought the blood to her cheek and made her heart beat wildly. Then came Aunt Laura through the dew and dusk.

"Teddy and Ilse are here," she said.

Emily went in to the stately, stiff, dignified parlour of New Moon, pale, queenly, aloof. Ilse hurled herself upon her with all her old, tempestuous affection, but Teddy shook hands with a cool detachment that almost equalled her own. Teddy? Oh, dear, no. Frederick Kent, R.A.-to-be. What was there left of the old Teddy in this slim, elegant young man with his sophisticated air and cool, impersonal eyes, and general implication of having put off forever all childish things—including foolish visions and insignificant little country girls he had played with in his infancy?

In which conclusion Emily was horribly unjust to Teddy. But she was not in a mood to be just to anybody. Nobody is who has made a fool of herself. And Emily felt that that was just what she had done—again. Mooning romantically about in a twilight garden, specially wearing powder-blue, waiting for a lover's signal from a beau who had forgotten all about her—or only re-membered her as an old schoolmate on whom he had very properly and kindly and conscientiously come to call. Well, thank heaven, Teddy did not know how ab-surd she had been. She would take excellent care that he should never suspect it. Who could be more friendly and remote than a Murray of New Moon? Emily's man-ner, she flattered herself, was admirable. As gracious and impersonal as to an entire stranger. Renewed con-gratulations on his wonderful success, coupled with an absolute lack of all real interest in it. Carefully phrased, polite questions about *his* work on her side; carefully phrased polite questions about *her* work on his side. She had seen some of *his* pictures in the magazines. He had read some of *her* stories. So it went, with a wider gulf opening between them at every moment. Never had Emily felt herself so far away from Teddy. She recognised with a feeling that was almost terror how completely he had changed in those two years of ab-sence. It would in truth have been a ghastly interview had it not been for Ilse, who chattered with all her old breeziness and tang, planning out a two weeks of gay doings while she was home, asking hundreds of ques-tions; the same lovable old madcap of laughter and jest and dressed with all her old gorgeous violations of ac-cepted canons of taste. In an extraordinary dress—a thing of greenish-yellow. She had a big pink peony at her waist and another at her shoulder. She wore a bright green hat with a wreath of pink flowers on it. Great hoops of pearl swung in her ears. It was a weird cos-tume. No one but Ilse could have worn it successfully. And she looked like the incarnation of a thousand tropic springs in it—exotic, provocative, beautiful. So beautiful! Emily realised her friend's beauty afresh with a pang not of envy, but of bitter humiliation. Be-side Ilse's golden sheen of hair and brilliance of amber eyes and red-rose loveliness of cheeks she must look pale and dark and insignificant. Of course Teddy was in love with Ilse. He had gone to see her first—had been with her while Emily waited for him in the gar-den. Well, it made no real difference. Why should it? She would be just as friendly as ever. And was. Friendly with a vengeance. But when Teddy and Ilse had gone —together— laughing and teasing each other through the old To-morrow Road Emily went up to her room and locked the door. Nobody saw her again until the next morning.

II

The gay two weeks of Ilse's planning followed. Pic-nics, dances and jamborees galore. Shrewsbury soci-ety decided that a rising young artist was somebody to be taken notice of and took notice accordingly. It was a veritable whirl of gaiety and Emily whirled about in it with the others. No step lighter in the dance, no voice quicker in the jest, and all the time feeling like the mis-erable spirit in a ghost story she had once read who had a live coal in its breast instead of a heart. All the time, feeling, too, far down under surface pride and hidden pain, that sense of completion and fulfilment which always came to her when Teddy was near her. But she took good care never to be alone with Teddy, who certainly could not be accused of any attempt to inveigle her into twosomes. His name was freely coupled with Ilse's and they took so composedly the teasing they encountered, that the impression gained ground that "things were pretty well understood be-tween them." Emily thought Ilse might have told her if it were so. But Ilse, though she told many a tale of lovers forlorn whose agonies seemed to lie very lightly on her conscience, never mentioned Teddy's name, which Emily thought had a torturing significance of its own. She inquired after Perry Miller, wanting to know, if he were as big an oaf as ever and laughing over Emily's indignant defence.

"He will be Premier some day no doubt," agreed Ilse scornfully. "He'll work like the devil and never miss anything by lack of asking for it, but won't you always smell the herring-barrels of Stovepipe Town?"

Perry came to see Ilse, bragged a bit too much over his progress and got so snubbed and manhandled that he did not come again. Altogether the two weeks seemed a nightmare to Emily, who thought she was un-reservedly thankful when the time came for Teddy to go. He was going on a sailing vessel to Halifax, want-ing to make some nautical sketches for a magazine, and an hour before flood-tide, while the *Mira Lee* swung at anchor by the wharf at Stovepipe Town, he came to say good-bye. He did not bring Ilse with him—no doubt, thought Emily, because Ilse was visiting in Charlotte-town; but Dean Priest was there, so there was no dreaded solitude à deux. Dean was creeping back into his own, after the two weeks' junketings from which he had been barred out. Dean would not go to dances and clam-bakes, but he was always hovering in the background, as everybody concerned felt. He stood with Emily in the garden and there was a certain air of victory and possession about him that did not escape Teddy's eye. Dean, who never made the mistake of thinking gaiety was happiness, had seen more than others of the little drama that had been played out in Blair Water during those two weeks and the dropping of the curtain left him a satisfied man. The old, shadowy, childish affair between Teddy Kent of the Tansy Patch and Emily of New Moon, was finally ended. Whatever its significance or lack of significance had been, Dean no longer counted Teddy among his rivals.

Emily and Teddy parted with the hearty handshake and mutual good wishes of old schoolmates who do indeed wish each other well but have no very vital interest in the matter.

"Prosper and be hanged to you," as some old Murray had been wont to say.

Teddy got himself away very gracefully. He had the gift of making an artistic exit, but he did not once look back. Emily turned immediately to Dean and resumed the discussion which Teddy's coming had interrupted. Her lashes hid her eyes very securely. Dean with his uncanny ability to read her thoughts, should not—must not guess—what? What was there to guess? Nothing—absolutely nothing. Yet Emily kept her lashes down.

When Dean, who had some other engagement that evening, went away half an hour later she paced sedately up and down among the gold of primroses for a little while, the very incarnation, in all seeming, of maiden meditation fancy free.

"Spinning out a plot, no doubt," thought Cousin Jimmy proudly, as he glimpsed her from the kitchen window. "It beats me how she does it."

III

Perhaps Emily was spinning out a plot. But as the shadows deepened she slipped out of the garden through the dreamy peace of the old columbine orchard—along the Yesterday Road—over the green pasture field—past the Blair Water—up the hill beyond—past the Disappointed House—through the thick fir wood. There, in a clump of silver birches, one had an unbroken view of the harbour, flaming in lilac and rose-colour. Emily reached it a little breath-lessly—she had almost run at the last. Would she be too late? Oh, what if she should be too late!

The *Mira Lee* was sailing out of the harbour, a dream vessel in the glamour of sunset, past purple headlands and distant, fairylike, misty coasts. Emily stood and watched her till she had crossed the bar into the gulf beyond. Stood and watched her until she had faded from sight in the blue dimness of the falling night, conscious only of a terrible hunger to see Teddy once more—just once more. To say good-bye as it should have been said.

Teddy was gone. To another world. There was no rainbow in sight. And what was Vega of the Lyre but a whirling, flaming, incredibly distant sun?

She slipped down among the grasses at her feet and lay there sobbing in the cold moonshine that had suddenly taken the place of the friendly twilight.

Mingled with her sharp agony was incredulity. This thing could not have happened. Teddy could not have gone away with only that soulless, chilly, polite good-bye. After all their years of comradeship, if nothing else. Oh, how could she ever get herself past three o'clock this night?

"I am a hopeless fool," she whispered savagely. "He has forgotten. I am nothing to him. And I deserve it. Didn't I forget him in those crazy weeks when I was imagining myself in love with Aylmer Vincent? Of course somebody has told him all about that. I've lost my chance of real happiness through that absurd affair. Where is my pride? To cry like this over a man who has forgotten me. But—but—it's so nice to cry after having had to laugh for these hideous weeks."

IV

Emily flung herself into work feverishly after Teddy had gone. Through long summer days and nights she wrote, while the purple stains deepened under her eyes and the rose stains faded out of her cheeks. Aunt Elizabeth thought she was killing herself and for the first time was reconciled to her intimacy with Jarback Priest, since he dragged Emily away from her desk in the evenings at least for walks and talks in the fresh air. That summer Emily paid off the last of her indebtedness to Uncle Wallace and Aunt Ruth with her "pot-boilers."

But there was more than pot-boiling a-doing. In her first anguish of loneliness, as she lay awake at three o'clock, Emily had remembered a certain wild winter night when she and Ilse and Perry and Teddy had been "stormed in" in the old John House on the Derry Pond Road;* remembered all the scandal and suffering that had arisen therefrom; and remembered also that night of rapt delight "thinking out" a story that had flashed into her mind at a certain gay, significant speech of Teddy's. At least, she had thought it significant then. Well, *that* was all over. But wasn't the story somewhere? She had written the outline of that alluring, fanciful tale in a Jimmy-book the next day. Emily sprang out of bed in the still summer moonlight, lighted one of the famous candles of New Moon, and rummaged through a pile of old Jimmy-books. Yes, here it was. *A Seller of Dreams.* Emily squatted down on her haunches and read it through. It was *good.* Again it seized hold of her imagination and called forth all her creative impulse. She would write it out—she would begin that very moment. Flinging a dressing-gown over her white shoulders to protect them from the keen gulf air she sat down before her open window and began to write. Everything else was forgotten—for a time at least —in the subtle, all-embracing joy of creation. Teddy was nothing but a dim memory—love was a blown-out candle. Nothing mattered but her story. The characters came to life under her hand and swarmed through her consciousness, vivid, alluring, compelling. Wit, tears, and laughter trickled from her pen. She lived and breathed in another world and came back to New Moon only at dawn to find her lamp burned out, and her table littered with manuscript—the first four chapters of her book. Her book! What magic and delight and awe and incredulity in the thought.

For weeks Emily seemed to live really only when she was writing it. Dean found her strangely rapt and remote, absent and impersonal. Her conversation was as dull as it was possible for Emily's conversation to be, and while her body sat or walked beside him her soul was—where? In some region where he could not follow, at all events. It had escaped him.

V

Emily finished her book in six weeks—finished it at dawn one morning. She flung down her pen and went

---

*See *Emily Climbs.*

to her window, lifting her pale, weary, triumphant little face to the skies of morning.

Music was dripping through the leafy silence in Lofty John's bush. Beyond were dawn-rosy meadows and the garden of New Moon lying in an enchanted calm. The wind's dance over the hills seemed some dear response to the music and rhythm in her being. Hills, sea, shadows, all called to her with a thousand elfin voices of understanding and acclaim. The old gulf was singing. Exquisite tears were in her eyes. She had written it—oh, how happy she was! This moment atoned for everything.

Finished—complete! There it lay—*A Seller of Dreams*—her first book. Not a great book—oh, no, but *hers*—her very own. Something to which she had given birth, which would never have existed had she not brought it into being. And it was *good*. She knew it was—felt it was. A fiery, delicate tale, instinct with romance, pathos, humour. The rapture of creation still illuminated it. She turned the pages over, reading a bit here and there—wondering if she could really have written *that*. She was right under the rainbow's end. Could she not touch the magic, prismatic thing? Already her fingers were clasping the pot of gold.

Aunt Elizabeth walked in with her usual calm disregard of any useless formality such as knocking.

"Emily," she said severely, "have you been sitting up all night *again?*"

Emily came back to earth with that abominable mental jolt which can only be truly described as a thud—a "sickening thud" at that. Very sickening. She stood like a convicted schoolgirl. And *A Seller of Dreams* became instantly a mere heap of scribbled paper.

"I—I didn't realise how time was passing, Aunt Elizabeth," she stammered.

"You are old enough to have better sense," said Aunt Elizabeth. "I don't mind your writing—now. You seem to be able to earn a living by it in a very ladylike way. But you will wreck your health if you keep this sort of thing up. Have you forgotten that your mother died of consumption? At any rate, don't forget that you must pick those beans to-day. It's high time they were picked."

Emily gathered up her manuscript with all her careless rapture gone. Creation was over; remained now the sordid business of getting her book published. Emily typewrote it on the little third-hand machine

Perry had picked up for her at an auction sale—a machine that wrote only half of any capital letter and wouldn't print the "m's" at all. She put the capitals and the "m's" in afterwards with a pen and sent the MS. away to a publishing firm. The publishing firm sent it back with a type-written screed stating that "their readers had found some merit in the story but not enough to warrant an acceptance."

This "damning with faint praise" flattened Emily out as not even a printed slip could have done. Talk about three o'clock that night! No, it is an act of mercy not to talk about it—or about many successive three o'clocks.

"Ambition!" wrote Emily bitterly in her diary. "I could laugh? Where is my ambition now? What is it like to be ambitious? To feel that life is before you, a fair, unwritten white page where you may inscribe your name in letters of success? To feel that you have the wish and power to win your crown? To feel that the coming years are crowding to meet you and lay their largess at your feet? I *once* knew what it was to feel so."

All of which goes to show how very young Emily still was. But agony is none the less real because in later years when we have learned that everything passes, we wonder what we agonised about. She had a bad three weeks of it. Then she recovered enough to send her story out again. This time the publisher wrote to her that he might consider the book if she would make certain changes in it. It was too "quiet." She must "pep it up." And the ending must be changed entirely. It would never do.

Emily tore his letter savagely into bits. Mutilate and degrade her story? Never! The very suggestion was an insult.

When a third publisher sent it back with a printed slip Emily's belief in it died. She tucked it away and took up her pen grimly.

"Well, I can write short stories at least. I must continue to do that."

Nevertheless, the book haunted her. After a few weeks she took it out and reread it—coolly, critically, free alike from the delusive glamour of her first rapture and from the equally delusive depression of rejection slips. And still it seemed to her good. Not quite the wonder-tale she had fancied it, perhaps; but still a good piece of work. What then? No writer, so she had been told, was ever capable of judging his own work

correctly. If only Mr. Carpenter were alive! He would tell her the truth. Emily made a sudden terrible resolution. She would show it to Dean. She would ask for his calm, unprejudiced opinion and abide by it. It would be hard. It was always hard to show her stories to any one, most of all to Dean, who knew so much and had read everything in the world. But she must *know*. And she knew Dean would tell her the truth, good or bad. He thought nothing of her stories. But *this* was different. Would he not see something worth while in this? If not—

VI

"Dean, I want your candid opinion about this story. Will you read it carefully and tell me exactly what you think of it? I don't want flattery—or false encouragement—I want the truth—the naked truth."

"Are you sure of that?" asked Dean dryly. "Very few people can endure seeing the naked truth. It has to have a rag or two to make it presentable."

"I *do* want the truth," said Emily stubbornly. "This book has been"—she choked a little over the confession, "refused three times. If you find any good in it I'll keep on trying to find a publisher for it. If you condemn it I'll burn it."

Dean looked inscrutably at the little packet she held out to him. So *this* was what had wrapped her away from him all summer—absorbed her—possessed her. The one black drop in his vein—that Priest jealousy of being first—suddenly made its poison felt.

He looked into her cold, sweet face and starry eyes, grey-purple as a lake at dawn, and hated whatever was in the packet, but he carried it home and brought it back three nights later. Emily met him in the garden, pale and tense.

"Well," she said.

Dean looked at her, guilty. How ivory white and exquisite she was in the chill dusk!

" 'Faithful are the wounds of a friend.' I should be less than your friend if I told you falsehoods about this, Emily."

"So—it's no good."

"It's a pretty little story, Emily. Pretty and flimsy and ephemeral as a rose-tinted cloud. Cobwebs—only cobwebs. The whole conception is too far-fetched. Fairy tales are out of the fashion. And this one of yours makes overmuch of a demand on the credulity of the reader. And your characters are only puppets. How could you write a real story? You've never *lived*."

Emily clenched her hands and bit her lips. She dared not trust her voice to say a single word. She had not felt like this since the night Ellen Greene had told her her father must die. Her heart, that had beaten so tumultuously a few minutes ago, was like lead, heavy and cold. She turned and walked away from him. He limped softly after her and touched her shoulder.

"Forgive me, Star. Isn't it better to know the truth? Stop reaching for the moon. You'll never get it. Why try to write, anyway? Everything has already been written."

"Some day," said Emily, compelling herself to speak steadily, "I may be able to thank you for this. To-night I hate you."

"Is that just?" asked Dean quietly.

"No, of course it isn't just," said Emily wildly. "Can you expect me to be just when you've just killed me? Oh, I know I asked for it—I know it's good for me. Horrible things always are good for you, I suppose. After you've been killed a few times you don't mind it. But the first time one does—squirm. Go away, Dean. Don't come back for a week at least. The funeral will be over then."

"Don't you believe I know what this means to you, Star?" asked Dean pityingly.

"You can't—altogether. Oh, I know you're sympathetic. I don't want sympathy. I only want time to bury myself decently."

Dean, knowing it would be better to go, went. Emily watched him out of sight. Then she took up the little dogeared, discredited manuscript he had laid on the stone bench and went up to her room. She looked it over by her window in the fading light. Sentence after sentence leaped out at her—witty, poignant, beautiful. No, that was only her fond, foolish, material delusion. There was nothing of that sort in the book. Dean had said so. And her book people. How she loved them. How real they seemed to her. It was terrible to think of destroying them. But they were *not* real. Only "puppets." Puppets would not mind being burned. She glanced up at the starlit sky of the autumn night. Vega of the Lyre shone bluely down upon her. Oh, life was an ugly, cruel, wasteful thing!

Emily crossed over to her little fireplace and laid *A Seller of Dreams* in the grate. She struck a match, knelt down and held it to a corner with a hand that did not

tremble. The flame seized on the loose sheets eagerly, murderously. Emily clasped her hands over her heart and watched it with dilated eyes, remembering the time she had burned her old "account book" rather than let Aunt Elizabeth see it. In a few moments the manuscript was a mass of writhing fires—in a few more seconds it was a heap of crinkled ashes, with here and there an accusing ghost-word coming out whitely on a blackened fragment, as if to reproach her.

Repentance seized upon her. Oh, why had she done it? Why had she burned her book? Suppose it was no good. Still, it was hers. It was wicked to have burned it. She had destroyed something incalculably precious to her. What did the mothers of old feel when their children had passed through the fire to Moloch—when the sacrificial impulse and excitement had gone? Emily thought she knew.

Nothing of her book, her dear book that had seemed so wonderful to her, but ashes—a little, pitiful heap of black ashes. Could it be so? Where had gone all the wit and laughter and charm that had seemed to glimmer in its pages—all the dear folks who had lived in them—all the secret delight she had woven into them as moonlight is woven among pines? Nothing left but ashes. Emily sprang up in such an anguish of regret that she could not endure it. She must get out—away—anywhere. Her little room, generally so dear and beloved and cosy, seemed like a prison. Out—somewhere—into the cold, free autumn night with its grey ghost-mists—away from walls and boundaries—away from that little heap of dark flakes in the grate—away from the reproachful ghosts of her murdered book folks. She flung open the door of the room and rushed blindly to the stair.

VII

Aunt Laura never to the day of her death forgave herself for leaving that mending-basket at the head of the stair. She had never done such a thing in her life before. She had been carrying it up to her room when Elizabeth called peremptorily from the kitchen asking where something was. Laura set her basket down on the top step and ran to get it. She was away only a moment. But that moment was enough for predestination and Emily. The tear-blinded girl stumbled over the basket and fell—headlong down the long steep staircase of New Moon. There was a moment of fear—a moment of wonderment—she felt plunged into deadly cold—she felt plunged into burning heat—she felt a soaring upward—a falling into unseen depth—a fierce stab of agony in her foot—then nothing more. When Laura and Elizabeth came running in there was only a crumpled silken heap lying at the foot of the stairs with balls and stockings all around it and Aunt Laura's scissors bent and twisted under the foot they had so cruelly pierced.

SEVEN

I

From October to April Emily Starr lay in bed or on the sitting-room lounge watching the interminable windy drift of clouds over the long white hills or the passionless beauty of winter trees around quiet fields of snow, and wondering if she would ever walk again—or walk only as a pitiable cripple. There was some obscure injury to her back upon which the doctors could not agree. One said it was negligible and would right itself in time. Two others shook their heads and were afraid. But all were agreed about the foot. The scissors had made two cruel wounds—one by the ankle, one on the sole of the foot. Blood-poisoning set in. For days Emily hovered between life and death, then between the scarcely less terrible alternative of death and amputation. Aunt Elizabeth prevented that. When all the doctors agreed that it was the only way to save Emily's life she said grimly that it was not the Lord's will, as understood by the Murrays, that people's limbs should be cut off. Nor could she be removed from this position. Laura's tears and Cousin Jimmy's pleadings and Dr. Burnley's execrations and Dean Priest's agreements budged her not a jot. Emily's foot should not be cut off. Nor was it. When she recovered unmaimed Aunt Elizabeth was triumphant and Dr. Burnley confounded.

The danger of amputation was over, but the danger of lasting and bad lameness remained. Emily faced that all winter.

"If I only *knew* one way or the other," she said to Dean. "If I *knew*, I could make up my mind to bear it—perhaps. But to lie here—wondering—wondering if I'll ever be well."

"You will be well," said Dean savagely.

Emily did not know what she would have done without Dean that winter. He had given up his invari-

able winter trip and stayed in Blair Water that he might be near her. He spent the days with her, reading, talking, encouraging, sitting in the silence of perfect companionship. When he was with her Emily felt that she might even be able to face a lifetime of lameness. But in the long nights when everything was blotted out by pain she could not face it. Even when there was no pain her nights were often sleepless and very terrible when the wind wailed drearily about the old New Moon eaves or chased flying phantoms of snow over the hills. When she slept she dreamed, and in her dreams she was forever climbing stairs and could never get to the top of them, lured upward by an odd little whistle—two higher notes and a low one—that ever retreated as she climbed. It was better to lie awake than to have that terrible, recurrent dream. Oh, those bitter nights! Once Emily had not thought that the Bible verse declaring that there would be no night in heaven contained an attractive promise. No night? No soft twilight enkindled with stars? No white sacrament of moonlight? No mystery of velvet shadow and darkness? No ever-amazing miracle of dawn? Night was as beautiful as day and heaven would not be perfect without it.

But now in these dreary weeks of pain and dread she shared the hope of the Patmian seer. Night was a dreadful thing.

People said Emily Starr was very brave and patient and uncomplaining. But she did not seem so to herself. They did not know of the agonies of rebellion and despair and cowardice behind her outward calmness of Murray pride and reserve. Even Dean did not know—though perhaps he suspected.

She smiled gallantly when smiling was indicated, but she never laughed. Not even Dean could make her laugh, though he tried with all the powers of wit and humour at his command.

"My days of laughter are done," Emily said to herself. And her days of creation as well. She could never write again. The "flash" never came. No rainbow spanned the gloom of that terrible winter. People came to see her continuously. She wished they would stay away. Especially Uncle Wallace and Aunt Ruth, who were sure she would never walk again and said so every time they came. Yet they were not so bad as the callers who were cheerfully certain she would be all right in time and did not believe a word of it themselves. She had never had any intimate friends except

Dean and Ilse and Teddy. Ilse wrote weekly letters in which she rather too obviously tried to cheer Emily up. Teddy wrote once when he heard of her accident. The letter was very kind and tactful and sincerely sympathetic. Emily thought it was the letter any indifferent friendly acquaintance might have written and she did not answer it though he had asked her to let him know how she was getting on. No more letters came. There was nobody but Dean. He had never failed her —never would fail her. More and more as the interminable days of storm and gloom passed she turned to him. In that winter of pain she seemed to herself to grow so old and wise that they met on equal ground at last. Without him life was a bleak, grey desert devoid of colour or music. When he came the desert would—for a time at least—blossom like the rose of joy and a thousand flowerets of fancy and hope and illusion would fling their garlands over it.

II

When spring came Emily got well—got well so suddenly and quickly that even the most optimistic of the three doctors was amazed. True, for a few weeks she had to limp about on a crutch, but the time came when she could do without it—could walk alone in the garden and look out on the beautiful world with eyes that could not be satisfied with seeing. Oh, how good life was again! How good the green sod felt beneath her feet! She had left pain and fear behind her like a cast-off garment and felt gladness—no, not gladness exactly, but the possibility of being glad once more sometime.

It was worth while to have been ill to realise the savour of returning health and well-being on a morning like this, when a sea-wind was blowing up over the long, green fields. There was nothing on earth like a sea-wind. Life might, in some ways, be a thing of shreds and tatters, everything might be changed or gone; but pansies and sunset clouds were still fair. She felt again her old joy in mere existence.

"Truly the light is sweet and a pleasant thing it is for the eye to behold the sun," she quoted dreamily.

Old laughter came back. On the first day that Emily's laughter was heard again in New Moon Laura Murray, whose hair had turned from ash to snow that winter, went to her room and knelt down by her bed to thank God. And while she knelt there Emily was talking about God to Dean in the garden on one of the most beautiful spring twilights imaginable, with a little, growing moon in the midst of it.

"There have been times this past winter when I felt God hated me. But now again I feel sure He loves me," she said softly.

"So sure?" questioned Dean dryly. "*I* think God is interested in us but He doesn't love us. He likes to watch us to see what we'll do. Perhaps it amuses Him to see us squirm."

"What a horrible conception of God!" said Emily with a shudder. "You don't really believe that about Him, Dean."

"Why not?"

"Because He would be worse than a devil then—a God who thought only about his own amusement, without even the devil's justification of hating us."

"Who tortured you all winter with bodily pain and mental anguish?" asked Dean.

"Not God. And He—sent me *you*," said Emily steadily. She did not look at him; she lifted her face to the Three Princesses, in their Maytime beauty—a white-rose face now, pale from its winter's pain. Beside her the big spirea, which was the pride of Cousin Jimmy's heart, banked up in its June-time snow, making a beautiful background for her. "Dean, how can I ever thank you for what you've done for me—been to me—since last October? I can never put it in words. But I want you to know how I feel about it."

"I've done nothing except snatch at happiness. Do you know what happiness it was to me to do something for you, Star—help you in some way—to see you turning to me in your pain for something that only I could give—something I had learned in my own years of loneliness? And to let myself dream something that couldn't come true— that I knew ought not to come true—"

Emily trembled and shivered slightly. Yet why hesitate—why put off that which she had fully made up her mind to do?

"Are you so sure, Dean," she said in a low tone, "that your dream—can't come true?"

Franklin W. Dixon

Edward Stratemeyer (1862–1930) used the pseudonym Franklin W. Dixon to create the popular Hardy Boys series and the pseudonym Carolyn Keene for all the writers of the Nancy Drew books. Stratemeyer, the son of German immigrants, hired a "stable" of writers to flesh out plots he supplied. *The Tower Treasure* (1927), the first of the Hardy Boys series, was probably written by Leslie McFarlane, one of the Stratemeyer authors. McFarlane's introductory essay in this 1991 reprint provides interesting insights into the process of ghostwriting and the amusing effects of keeping his identity as the writer of a popular series secret. The Stratemeyer Syndicate was the most prolific and influential source of cheap juvenile literature in early twentieth-century America. In the Hardy Boys series, Frank (aged 18) and Joe (aged 17), sons of the veteran detective Fenton Hardy, are "young New Age Americans, products of a prosperous urban middle class," as Gillian Avery has observed.[1] They ride motorcycles and have friends who drive "hot rods" and "jalopies." Their dialogue is wooden, the descriptions are full of clichés, the plots are sensational and implausible—yet the series continues to find avid readers. David Baumann, a series book collector, has written, "Some of the best times in the old series book world are when nothing momentous is happening. This is what adds real flavor to the stories. We are pleased and entertained and moved when, at the end of *The Tower Treasure,* the menu of the celebratory feast is laid out for us."[2] This statement suggests that in addition to the appeal of certain wish-fulfillment fantasies, series such as the Hardy Boys books appeal to the ability to fantasize about ordinary pleasures like eating, traveling, or having adventures with friends.

NOTES

1. Gillian Avery, *Behold the Child: American Children and Their Books, 1621–1922* (London: Bodley Head, 1994) 212.
2. David Baumann, "Series Books: Their Appeal," *The X Bar X Boys: Sons of the Golden West.* 1998–99. 8 April 2005 <http://home.pacbell.net/dbaumann/series_books_their_appear.htm>.

A Little Ghostly History

LESLIE MCFARLANE

Stratemeyer wrote that detective stories had become very popular in the world of adult fiction. He instanced the works of S.S. Van Dine, which were selling in prodigious numbers as I was well aware. S.S. Van Dine was neither an ocean liner nor a living man, but the pseudonym of Willard Huntington Wright, a literary craftsman who wrote sophisticated stories for Mencken's *Smart Set.*

It had recently occurred to him, Stratemeyer continued, that the growing boys of America might welcome similar fare. Of course, he had already given them Nat Ridley, but Nat really didn't solve mysteries; he merely blundered into them and, after a given quota of hairbreadth escapes, blundered out again. What Stratemeyer had in mind was a series of detective stories on the juvenile level, involving two brothers of high-school age who would solve such mysteries as came their way. To lend credibility to their talents, they would be the sons of a professional private investigator, so big in his field that he had become a sleuth of international fame. His name— Fenton Hardy. His sons, Frank and Joe, would therefore be known as . . .

The Hardy Boys!

This would be the title of the series. My pseudonym would be Franklin W. Dixon. (I never did learn what the "W" represented. Certainly not Wealthy.)

Stratemeyer noted that the books would be cloth-bound and therefore priced a little higher than paperbacks. This in turn would justify a little higher payment for the manuscript—$125 to be exact. He had attached an information sheet for guidance and the plot outline of the initial volume, which would be called *The Tower Treasure*. In closing, he promised that if the manuscript came up to expectations—which were high—I would be asked to do the next two volumes of the series.

The background information was terse. The setting would be a small city called Bayport on Barmet Bay "somewhere on the Atlantic Coast." The boys would attend Bayport High. Their mother's name would be Laura. They would have three chums: Chet, a chubby farm boy, humorist of the group; Biff Hooper, an athletic two-fisted type who could be relied on to balance the scales in the event of a fight; and Tony Prito, who would presumably tag along to represent all ethnic minorities.

Two girls would also make occasional appearances. One of them, Iola Morton, sister of Chet, would be favorably regarded by Joe. The other, Callie Shaw, would be tolerated by Frank. It was intimated that relations between the Hardy boys and their girl friends would not go beyond the borders of wholesome friendship and discreet mutual esteem.

I skimmed through the outline. It was about a robbery in a towered mansion belonging to Hurd Applegate, an eccentric stamp collector. The Hardy Boys solved it. I greeted Frank and Joe Hardy with positive

rapture, and I wrote to Stratemeyer to accept the assignment. Then I rolled a sheet of paper into the typewriter and prepared to go to work.

It was not until sometime in the 1940s, as a matter of fact, that I discovered that Franklin W. Dixon and the Hardy Boys were conjurable names. One day my son had come into the workroom, which had never been exalted into a "study," and pointed to the bookcase with its shelf of Hardy Boys originals. "Why do you keep these books, Dad? Did you read them when you were a kid?"

"Read them? I wrote them." And then, because it doesn't do to deceive any youngster, "At least I wrote the words."

He stared. I saw incredulity. Then open-mouthed respect.

"Why didn't you tell me?"

"I suppose it never occurred to me."

This was true. The Hardy Boys were never mentioned in the household. They were never mentioned to friends. Maybe it was a holdover from Edward Stratemeyer's long past injunction to secrecy. Habit. I wasn't ashamed of them. I had done them as well as I could, at the time. They had merely provided a way of making a living.

"But they're wonderful books," he said. "I used to borrow them from the other kids all the time until I found them here."

"Other kids read them?"

"Dad, where have you been? Everybody reads them. You can buy them in Simpson's. Shelves of them."

Next day I went to the department store and damned if the lad wasn't right! They *did* have shelves of them.

I asked a clerk if the Hardy Boys books were popular.

"Most popular boys' books we carry," he said. "Matter of fact, they're supposed to be the best-selling boys' books in the world."

"Imagine that!" I said in downright wonderment.

From *The Tower Treasure*

CHAPTER 1. THE SPEED DEMON

"After the help we gave dad on that forgery case I guess he'll begin to think we *could* be detectives when we grow up."

"Why shouldn't we? Isn't he one of the most famous detectives in the country? And aren't we his sons? If the profession was good enough for him to follow it should be good enough for us."

Two bright-eyed boys on motorcycles were speeding along a shore road in the sunshine of a morning in spring. It was Saturday and they were enjoying a holiday from the Bayport high school. The day was ideal for a motorcycle trip and the lads were combining business with pleasure by going on an errand to a nearby village for their father.

The older of the two boys was a tall, dark youth, about sixteen years of age. His name was Frank Hardy. The other boy, his companion on the motorcycle trip, was his brother Joe, a year younger.

While there was a certain resemblance between the two lads, chiefly in the firm yet good-humored expression of their mouths, in some respects they differed greatly in appearance. While Frank was dark, with straight, black hair and brown eyes, his brother was pink-cheeked, with fair, curly hair and blue eyes.

These were the Hardy boys, sons of Fenton Hardy, an internationally famous detective who had made a name for himself in the years he had spent on the New York police force and who was now, at the age of forty, handling his own practice. The Hardy family lived in Bayport, a city of about fifty thousand inhabitants, located on Barmet Bay, three miles in from the Atlantic, and here the Hardy boys attended high school and dreamed of the days when they, too, should be detectives like their father.

As they sped along the narrow shore road, with the waves breaking on the rocks far below, they discussed their chances of winning over their parents to agreement with their ambition to follow in the footsteps of their father. Like most boys, they speculated frequently on the occupation they should follow when they grew up, and it had always seemed to them that nothing offered so many possibilities of adventure and excitement as the career of a detective.

"But whenever we mention it to dad he just laughs at us, " said Joe Hardy. "Tells us to wait until we're through school and then we can think about being detectives."

"Well, at least he's more encouraging than mother," remarked Frank. "She comes out plump and plain and says she wants one of us to be a doctor and the other a lawyer."

"What a fine lawyer either of us would make!" sniffed Joe. "Or a doctor, either! We were both out out to be detectives and dad knows it."

"As I was saying, the help we gave him in that forgery case proves it. He didn't say much, but I'll bet he's been thinking a lot."

"Of course we didn't actually *do* very much in that case," Joe pointed out.

"But we suggested something that led to a clue, didn't we? That's as much a part of detective work as anything else. Dad himself admitted he would never have thought of examining the city tax receipts for that forged signature. It was just a lucky idea on our part, but it proved to him that we can use our heads for something more than to hang our hats on."

"Oh, I guess he's convinced all right. Once we get out of school he'll probably give his permission. Why, this is a good sign right now, isn't it? He asked us to deliver these papers for him in Willowville. He's letting us help him."

"I'd rather get in on a real, good mystery," said Frank. "It's all right to help dad, but if there's no more excitement in it than delivering papers I'd rather start in studying to be a lawyer and be done with it."

"Never mind, Frank," comforted his brother. "We may get a mystery all of our own to solve some day."

"If we do we'll show that Fenton Hardy's sons are worthy of his name. Oh boy, but what wouldn't I give to be as famous as dad! Why, some of the biggest cases in the country are turned over to him. That forgery case, for instance. Fifty thousand dollars had been stolen right from under the noses of the city officials and all the auditors and city detectives and private detectives they called in had to admit that it was too deep for them."

"Then they called in dad and he cleared it up in three days. Once he got suspicious of that slick bookkeeper whom nobody had been suspecting at all, it was all over but the shouting. Got a confession out of him and everything."

"It was smooth work. I'm glad our suggestion helped him. The case certainly got a lot of attention in the papers."

"And here *we* are," said Joe, "plugging along the shore road on a measly little errand to deliver some legal papers at Willowville. I'd rather be on the track of some diamond thieves or smugglers—or something."

"Well, we have to be satisfied, I suppose," replied Frank, leaning farther over the handlebars. "Perhaps dad may give us a chance on a real case some time."

"Some time! I want to be on a real case *now!*"

The motorcycles roared along the narrow road that skirted the bay. An embankment of tumbled rocks and boulders sloped steeply to the water below, and on the other side of the road was a steep cliff. The roadway itself was narrow, although it was wide enough to permit two cars to meet and pass, and it wound about in frequent curves and turnings. It was a road that was not often traveled, for Willowville was only a small village and this shore road was an offshoot of the main highways to the north and the west.

The Hardy boys dropped their discussion of the probability that some day they would become detectives, and for a while they rode on in silence, occupied with the difficulties of keeping to the road. For the road at this point was dangerous, very rough and rutty, and it sloped sharply upward so that the embankment leading to the ocean far below became steeper and steeper.

"I shouldn't want to go over the edge around here," remarked Frank, as he glanced down the rugged slope.

"It's a hundred-foot drop. You'd be smashed to pieces before you ever hit the shore."

"I'll say! It's best to stay in close to the cliff. These curves are bad medicine."

The motorcycles took the next curve neatly, and then the boys confronted a long, steep slope. The rocky cliffs frowned on one side, and the embankment jutted far down to the tumbling waves below, so that the road was a mere ribbon before them.

"Once we get to the top of the hill we'll be all right. It's all smooth sailing from there to Willowville," re-

marked Frank, as the motorcycles commenced the climb.

Just then, above the sharp put-put of their own motors, they heard the high humming roar of an automobile approaching at great speed. The car was not yet in sight, but there was no mistaking the fact that it was coursing along with the cut-out open and with no regard for the speed laws.

"What idiot is driving like that on this kind of road!" exclaimed Frank. They looked back.

Even as he spoke the automobile flashed into sight.

It came around the curve behind and so swiftly did the driver take the dangerous turn that two wheels were off the ground as the car shot into view. A cloud of dust and stones arose, the car veered violently from left to right, and then it roared at headlong speed down the slope.

The boys glimpsed a tense figure at the wheel. How he kept the car on the road was a miracle, for the racing automobile swung from side to side. At one moment it would be in imminent danger of crashing over the embankment, down on the rocks below; the next instant the car would be over on the other side of the road, grazing the cliff.

"He'll run us down!" shouted Joe, in alarm. "The idiot!"

Indeed, the position of the two lads was perilous.

The roadway was narrow enough at any time, and this speeding car was taking up every inch of space. In a great cloud of dust it bore directly down on the two motorcyclists. It seemed to leap through the air. The front wheels left a rut, the rear of the car skidded violently about. By a twist of the wheel the driver pulled the car back into the roadway again just as it seemed about to plunge over the embankment. It shot over toward the cliff, swerved back again into the middle of the road-way, and then shot ahead at terrific speed.

Frank and Joe edged their motorcycles as far to the right of the road as they dared. To their horror they saw that the car was skidding again.

The driver made no attempt to slacken speed.

The automobile came hurtling toward them!

CHAPTER 2. THE STOLEN ROADSTER

The auto brakes squealed.

The driver of the oncoming car swung the wheel viciously about. For a moment it appeared that the wheels would not respond. Then they gripped the gravel and the automobile swerved, then shot past.

Bits of sand and gravel were flung about the two boys as they crouched by their motorcycles at the edge of the embankment. The car had missed them only by inches!

Frank caught a glimpse of the driver, who turned about at that moment and, in spite of the speed at which the automobile was traveling and in spite of the perils of the road, shouted something they could not catch at them and shook his first.

The car was traveling at too great a speed to enable the lad to distinguish the driver's features, but he saw that the man was hatless and that he had a shock of red hair blowing in the wind.

Then the automobile disappeared from sight around the curve ahead, roaring away in a cloud of dust.

"The road hog!" gasped Joe, as soon as he had recovered from his surprise.

"He must be crazy!" Frank exclaimed angrily. "Why, he might have pushed us both right over the embankment!"

"At the rate he was going I don't think he cared whether he ran any one down or not."

Both boys were justifiably angry. On such a narrow, treacherous road there was danger enough when an automobile passed them traveling at even a reasonable speed, but the reckless and insane driving of the red-headed motorist was nothing short of criminal.

"If we ever catch up to him I'm going to give him a piece of my mind!" declared Frank. "Not content with almost running us down he had to shake his fist at us."

"Road hog!" muttered Joe again. "Jail is too good for the likes of him. If it was only his own life he endangered it wouldn't be so bad. Good thing we only had motorcycles. If we had been in another car there would have been a smash-up, sure."

The boys resumed their journey and by the time they had reached the curve ahead that enabled them to see the village of Willowville lying in a little valley along the bay beneath them, there was no trace of the reckless motorist.

Frank delivered the legal papers his father had given to him, and then the boys had the rest of the day to themselves.

"It's too early to go back to Bayport just now," he said to Joe. "What say we go out and visit Chet Morton?"

"Good idea," agreed Joe. "He has often asked us to come out and see him."

Chet Morton was a school chum of the Hardy boys. His father was a real estate dealer with an office in Bayport, but the family lived in the country, about a mile from the city. Although Willowville was some distance away, the boys knew of a road that would take them across country to the Morton home, and from there they could return to Bayport. It would make their journey longer, but they would have the pleasure of visiting their chum. Chet was a great favorite with all the boys, not the least of the reasons for his popularity being the fact that he had a roadster of his own, in which he drove to school every day and with which he was very generous in giving rides to his friends after school hours.

The Hardy boys drove along the country roads in the spring sunlight, enjoying the freedom of their holiday as only boys can. When they had reached a culvert not far from the Morton place Frank suddenly brought his motorcycle to a stop and peered down into a clump of bushes in the deep ditch.

"Somebody's had a spill," he remarked.

Down in the bushes lay an upturned automobile. The car was a total wreck, and lay bottom upward, a mass of tangled junk.

"Must have been hitting an awful clip to crumple up like that," Joe commented. "Perhaps there's some one underneath. Let's go and see."

The boys left their motorcycles by the road and went down to the wrecked car. But there was no sign of either driver or passengers.

"If any one was hurt they've been taken away by now. Probably this wreck is a day or so old," said Frank "Let's go. We can't do any good here."

They left the wreckage and returned to the road again, resuming their journey.

"I thought at first it might be our red-headed speed fiend," said Frank. "If it was, he was sure lucky to get out of it alive."

The boys gave little further thought to the incident and before long they were in sight of the Mortons' house, a big, homelike, rambling old farmhouse with an apple orchard at the rear. When the boys drove down the lane they saw a figure awaiting them at the barnyard gate.

"That's Chet," said Frank. "I'm glad we found him at home. I thought he might have gone out in the car."

"It *is* strange," Joe agreed. "On a holiday like this he doesn't usually stay around the farm."

As they approached, they saw Chet leave the gate and come down the lane to meet them. Chet was one of the most popular boys at the Bayport high school, one reason for his popularity being his unfailing good nature and his ability to see fun in almost everything. He was full of jokes and good humor and was rarely seen without a smile on his plump, freckled face.

But to-day the Hardy boys saw that there was something wrong. Chet's face had an anxious expression, and as they brought their motorcycles to a stop they saw that their chum's usually cheery face was clouded.

"What's the matter?" asked Frank, as their friend hastened up to them.

"You're just in time," replied Chet hurriedly. "You didn't meet a fellow driving my roadster, did you?"

The brothers looked at each other blankly.

"*Your* roadster! We'd recognize it anywhere. No, we didn't see it," said Joe. "What's happened?"

"It's been stolen."

"Stolen?"

"An auto thief stole it from the garage not half an hour ago. He just went in as cool as you please and made away with the car. The hired man saw the roadster disappearing down the lane, but he supposed I was in it so he didn't think anything of it Then he saw me out in the yard a little while later, so he got suspicious—and the roadster was gone."

"Wasn't it locked?"

"That's the strange part of it. The car was locked, although the garage door was open. I can't see how he got away with it."

"A professional job," commented Frank. "These auto thieves always carry scores of keys with them. But we're losing time here. The only thing is to set out in pursuit and to notify the police. The hired man didn't see which way the fellow went, did he?"

"No."

"There is only the one road, and we didn't meet him, so he must have taken the turning to the right at the end of the lane."

"We'll chase him," said Joe. "Climb onto my bike, Chet. We'll get the thief yet."

"Wait a minute," cried Frank suddenly. "I have an idea! Joe, do you remember that car we saw wrecked in the bushes?"

"Sure."

"Perhaps the driver stole the first automobile he could lay his hands on after the wreck."

"What wreck was that?" asked Chet.

The Hardy boys told him of the wrecked car they had found by the roadside. It had occurred to Frank that perhaps the smash-up might have occurred just a short while before and that the driver of the wrecked car had resumed his interrupted journey in a stolen automobile.

"It sounds reasonable," said Chet. "Let's go and take a look at this wreck. We can get the license number and that may help us find the name of the owner."

The motorcycles roared as the three chums set out back along the road toward the place where the upturned automobile had been seen among the bushes. The boys lost no time in reaching the place, for they realized that every second was precious and that the longer they delayed the greater was the advantage to the car thief.

The car had not been disturbed and apparently no one had been near it since the boys had discovered the wreck. They parked their motorcycles by the roadside and again went down into the bushes to examine the wrecked car.

To their disappointment the car bore no license plates.

"That looks suspicious," said Frank.

"It's more than suspicious," said Joe, who had withdrawn a little to one side and was examining the automobile from the rear. "Don't you remember seeing this car before, Frank. It didn't occur to me until you mentioned the matter of license plates."

"I have been wondering if this isn't the same car that passed us on the shore road at the curve," replied Frank slowly.

"It *is* the same car. There's no doubt of it in my mind. It didn't have a license plate, I noticed at the time, for I wanted to get the fellow's number. And it was a touring car of the same make as this."

"You're right, Joe. There's no mistake. The red-headed driver came to grief in the ditch, just as we said he would, and then he went on to the nearest farmhouse, which happened to be Chet's place, and stole the first car he saw."

"The busted car was the one the fellow was running who nearly sent us over the cliff," Joe declared. "And it's ten chances to one that he's the fellow who stole

Chet's roadster. And he's red-headed. We have those clues, anyway."

"And he went on past our farmhouse instead of turning back the way he came," cried Chet. "Come on, fellows—let's get after him! There was only a little bit of gas in the roadster anyway. Perhaps he's stalled by this time."

Thrilling with the excitement of a chase, the boys clambered back onto the motorcycles and within a few moments a cloud of dust rose from the road as the Hardy boys and Chet Morton set out in swift pursuit of the red-headed automobile thief.

Carolyn Keene

Like the Hardy Boys and other popular series for children, such as the Bobbsey Twins and Tom Swift, the Nancy Drew series was created by Edward Stratemeyer, who died in 1930, the same year that *The Secret of the Old Clock* was published. The pseudonym Carolyn Keene appears on all Nancy Drew books, including dozens of new ones with contemporary settings that have been published in recent years. But it was a secret closely guarded by the Stratemeyer Syndicate that Mildred Wirt Benson (1905–2002) wrote this first Nancy Drew book and twenty-two others through 1953. Appropriately enough for a writer of mysteries, it was litigation between publishers that made her name public in 1980. Benson immediately became a world-renowned celebrity, attending a Nancy Drew conference in 1993 and receiving fan mail and autograph seekers at her columnist's desk at the Toledo *Blade* until the day she died at age 96.

An author from Iowa who wrote over 130 series books under different pen names, Benson used the plots and situations dictated by the syndicate, but her skill with characterization and style made Nancy Drew the most popular series heroine ever. She insisted on going beyond Stratemeyer's vision for Nancy's character, believing that girls needed a heroine who was more independent and adventurous, more active like a boy. Ironically, when the earlier books were updated and abridged in later decades, Nancy was not only changed from age sixteen to age eighteen, but she was depicted as more passive and less outspoken. The dust jacket on Applewood Books' 1991 reprint of the original edition says, "If you met Nancy Drew before 1959, this is *The Secret of the Old Clock* you remember." Sara Paretsky, who began her own series of novels about a woman detective in 1982, analyzes the history and continuing popularity of Nancy Drew in this 1991 preface to *The Secret of the Old Clock*.

Keeping Nancy Drew Alive

SARA PARETSKY

Mention Nancy Drew to any woman between the ages of twenty-five and seventy, and chances are her face will turn dreamy and she'll say, "Nancy Drew! I haven't thought about her for years, but I used to love her." Nancy Drew and her blue roadster have been symbols of freedom for little girls since Grosset & Dunlap first published *The Secret of the Old Clock,* in

1930. With almost two hundred titles in the series, and new adventures arriving at the rate of eighteen a year, it's clear that Nancy's appeal is as strong as ever.

Hardcover sales of Nancy Drew adventures have surpassed Agatha Christie's phenomenal record. Publications from the *Journal of Popular Culture* to the *Wall Street Journal* have pondered the series' popularity without presenting a convincing explanation. At the same time, scholars complain about the pell-mell pace of the adventures and the protected environment in which Nancy lives.

It is easy to poke fun at the girl detective—at her adeptness with Old English and modern French, her intrepidity when locked in closets or towers, buried in mudslides, or threatened by the dastardly. It's easy, too, to lampoon the conscious assumption of WASP superiority in the early books in the series. Government and social status, at least in the early books, rightly belong to "the wise, the rich, and the well," in Alexander Hamilton's phrase.

Of course Peter Wimsey could match Nancy Drew skill for skill, intrepid moment for intrepid moment, and outdoes her in keeping all grace, intelligence, and morality in upper class hands. But maybe we tolerate French, Latin, brandy tasting, professional levels of acrobatics, diving, and piano playing, expertise with swords, guns, automobiles, Scarlatti, sonnet writing, and medicine in a titled Englishman that we scoff at in a Midwestern girl.

The early books in the series were slightly rewritten to modernize them in the late fifties. The most objectionable racial stereotyping was removed. Nancy was aged from sixteen to eighteen. Perhaps in the Depression, a sixteen-year-old who didn't have to go to school and who successfully managed her father's house didn't seem as anomalous as it later became. Perhaps series editors didn't like a sixteen-year-old at the wheel of a roadster. Whatever the reason, Nancy's a little older and she dresses more casually. Her hair changed from gold to titian and back to gold again. She still solves her own problems, though without adult or male interference.

Going back to the original Nancy Drew, as Applewood Books has done, is to take a revealing journey into our nation's social history. The books we relished as children dished up some dreadful racial attitudes. Hopefully we have outgrown those views, but we shouldn't forget how pervasive a part of American culture they were for many decades.

At the same time, Nancy Drew offered girls of 1930 an amazing alternative to the career choice of secretary and milliner that other children's books provided. Her enduring popularity probably has no deeper cause than that: little girls need to see a bigger girl act competently and solve problems they keep being told belong to boys. Even though today's children can look at female spies, astronauts, doctors, and other fictional heroes, they still need the girl detective to inspire them.

> "A puncture!" Nancy murmured in disgust "If that isn't just my luck! Oh, well, I suppose I must fix it myself, because there won't be another car for an hour on this road."
>
> It was not the first time Nancy Drew had changed a tire, but she never relished the task. Rummaging under the seat, she pulled out the tools and quickly jacked up the rear axle. She loosened the lugs . . . and tugged at [the tire] . . . [T]he huge balloon tire could not be budged. Then, as she gave one mighty tug, it came off and Nancy Drew fell backwards into a sitting posture in the road.
>
> "Well it's off, anyway," she told herself with satisfaction, as she brushed the dirt from her clothing.
>
> —*The Secret of the Old Clock* (page 107)

What could be more inspiring and appealing? Here's a heroine who is undaunted by car problems, tackles a job she doesn't relish and succeeds at it, and doesn't mind landing in the dirt in her nice clothes.

Nancy Drew made a wonderful antidote to the America of my childhood. When I was four a neighbor boy and I watched a woman drive a panel truck across the University of Kansas campus. "Ladies don't drive trucks," the toddler pronounced in disgust. His mother chortled over his wisdom, repeating it for years after with all the delight of Mrs. Newton recapitulating her son's laws of gravity.

Of course ladies in the fifties did drive trucks, especially in the farm community where I grew up, but we weren't supposed to applaud them. Yet Nancy Drew handled her blue sports car on dangerous roads with unfailing expertise. She spent eight hours on a lake in a stalled boat without panicking or screaming for help, learned to fly so well she awed her instructor, and diagnosed and fixed a flawed distributor when her car misbehaved. To a nation where car mechanics still mock or brush off complaints by women Nancy remains a significant role model.

In my childhood women were supposed to be as ignorant of mathematics as of motors. It's still hard to get young girls to test their analytical powers. But Nancy Drew's thoughts turn immediately to Archimedes when she's locked in a closet; she knows if she can find a lever she can pry open the hinges. She feels some fear in that closet, and—contrary to the monolithic view scholars like to suggest—she experiences remorse. She knows she has only herself to thank that her father thinks she's having a good time at camp and won't look for her for at least a week. What makes her heroic is that she rises above fear and despair and finds herself a lever.

Nancy's lifestyle is just as appealing to girls raised with endless shibboleths. Her mother is dead. Her lawyer-father and his housekeeper treat her opinions with adult respect. They place no restrictions on her comings and goings, because they know she won't behave irresponsibly.

Early in the series Nancy acquired a boyfriend, handsome Ned Nickerson, who flexes his muscles for a college football team. She also has two enduring girlfriends, boyish George Fayne and George's ultra-feminine cousin Bess Marvin. Like Dr. Watson, none of the three is a match for the sleuth, either in ability to figure out clues or in the scope of their skills. And in a reversal of the usual male-female relations in crime fiction, Ned's function is primarily decorative. He also is more attached to Nancy than she to him. Occasionally he brings up the question of marriage, but Nancy refuses to respond; she doesn't want to give up her independent sleuthing life for domesticity.

Little girls today still grow up without a strong sense of themselves as people or of their right to play active roles in adult life. Scholarly studies show that as girls head into their teens they stop trying to succeed for fear of showing up boys. Today, girls emerge from adolescence with a much lower sense of self-esteem than boys. Nancy never minded leaving Ned Nickerson in the dirt; his adoration never flagged for all the times she proved herself smarter and quicker than he.

In parts of the country, the highpoint of a girl's life may be making the cheerleading squad: a Texas mother was charged with attempting murder to guarantee that *summum bonum* to her daughter.

Nancy Drew doesn't lead cheers. She undertakes the heroics that keep others cheering. She is expert in some traditional girlish arts—tap-dancing, for instance. She uses that skill, though, not to become a cheerleader or Miss America, but to tap out Morse code when she's imprisoned.

Nancy's adventures appeal most to girls of ten or eleven. After that they move—is it on or backwards?—to stories where romantic conflict plays a bigger role and where heroines aren't as invincible as the girl detective. They leave the fantasy world of eleven to deal with the hard reality of women's lives.

Of course, girls couldn't really imagine undertaking Nancy's detective adventures. The facts of violent assault are a strong inducement to stay close to home, even if that home has a parent as adoring and considerate as Carson Drew. But it's a wonderful dream, that a girl can get in her blue roadster, steer it down perilous roads, and come home triumphant. Instead of making little girls leave that dream, maybe it's time we changed their realty. Keeping Nancy Drew alive for them can only help.

From *The Secret of the Old Clock*

CHAPTER 1. THE LOST WILL

"It would be a shame if all that money went to the Tophams! They will fly higher than ever!"

Nancy Drew, a pretty girl of sixteen, leaned over the library table and addressed her father who sat reading a newspaper by the study lamp.

"I beg your pardon, Nancy. What were you saying about the Tophams?"

Carson Drew, a noted criminal and mystery-case lawyer, known far and wide for his work as a former district attorney, looked up from his evening paper and smiled indulgently upon his only daughter. Now, as he gave her his respectful attention, he was not particularly concerned with the Richard Topham family but rather with the rich glow of the lamp upon Nancy's curly golden bob. Not at all the sort of head which one expected to indulge in serious thoughts, he told himself.

Mischievously, Nancy reached over and tweaked his ear.

"You weren't paying a bit of attention," she accused him sternly. "I was saying I think it's mean if those snobbish Tophams fall heir to all of Josiah Crowley's fortune. Can't something be done about it?"

Removing his horn-rimmed spectacles and carefully folding the paper, Carson Drew regarded his daughter meditatively.

"I'm afraid not, Nancy. A will is a will, you know."

"But it does seem unfair that *all* the money should go to them. Especially when they never treated Josiah Crowley like a human being!"

"The Tophams were never noted for their charitable dispositions," Carson Drew observed, with a smile. "However, they did give Josiah a home."

"Yes, and everyone knows why! They wanted to work him into leaving all his money to them. And it seems that their scheme worked, too! They treated him like a prince until he made his will in their favor and then they acted as though he were dirt under their feet. Folks said he died just to be rid of their everlasting nagging."

"The Tophams aren't very well liked in our little city, are they?" Mr. Drew commented dryly.

"Who could like them, father? Richard Topham is an old skinflint who made his money by gambling on the stock exchange. And Cora, his wife, is nothing but a vapid social climber. The two girls, Isabel and Ada, are even worse. I went to school with them, and I never saw such stuck-up creatures in all my life. If they fall heir to any more money, this town won't be big enough to hold them!"

In her estimate of the Topham family, Nancy Drew did not exaggerate. Nearly everyone in River Heights shared the opinion that the Tophams were snobbish and arrogant, and the treatment they accorded old Josiah Crowley had aroused a great deal of unfavorable comment.

Nancy had never known Josiah well, but had often seen him on the street and secretly had regarded him as a rather nice but extremely queer sort of individual. His wife had died during the influenza epidemic fol-

lowing the World War, and since that time Crowley had made his home with various relatives. Although well-to-do, he preferred to "visit around."

At first, the Tophams had evidenced no interest in the old man and he had been forced to live with kindly relatives who were scarcely able to have him with them. Crowley appreciated the sacrifice and openly declared that he intended to make his will in their favor.

Then, three years before his death, the Topham family experienced a sudden change of heart. They begged Josiah Crowley to make his home with them, and at last he consented. Presently, rumor had it that the Tophams had induced him to make his will in their favor.

But as time went on and Mr. Crowley, though failing in health, maintained as firm a grip on life as ever, the Tophams treated him unkindly. Although he continued to live with them, it was whispered about that frequently he slipped away to visit his old friends and that he intended to change his will again, cutting the Tophams out entirely.

Then one day Josiah Crowley took to his bed and did not get up. Just before his death he attempted to communicate something to the doctor who attended him, but his words were unintelligible. After the funeral, only one will came to light and, to the surprise of everyone, it gave the entire fortune to the Tophams.

"Father, what do you suppose it was that Mr. Crowley tried to tell the doctor just before he died?" Nancy demanded, after a moment of thought. "Do you imagine he was trying to disclose something about his will?"

"Very likely, Nancy. Probably he intended to leave his money to more deserving relatives. But fate cheated him of the opportunity."

"But isn't it possible that he did make such a will and that he was trying to tell what he had done with it?"

"Yes, that's a possibility of course. Josiah Crowley was rather queer in many ways."

"Perhaps he hid the will somewhere," Nancy suggested thoughtfully.

"If he did, I'm afraid it will never come to light. The Tophams will see to that."

"What do you mean, father?"

"The estate is a considerable one, I understand, Nancy, and the Tophams don't intend that anyone shall get a cent of it. It's my private opinion that they will take care that a second will is never found."

"Do you mean that if they discovered the will they would destroy it?"

"Well, I'm not making any accusations, Nancy. But I do know that Richard Topham is shrewd, and he isn't noted for his honesty."

"Can't the present will be broken?"

"I doubt it. While I haven't gone into the case, I am of the opinion that the Tophams have a legal right to the fortune. It would cost considerable to contest the will, and so far as I know the other relatives are in poverty. They have filed a claim, declaring that a later will was made in their favor, but I doubt that the matter will ever go further."

"But the Tophams don't deserve the fortune, father. It doesn't seem fair."

"No, it isn't fair. But it is legal, and I'm afraid nothing can be done about it There were two girls who live somewhere on the River Road that were great pets of Crowley's when they were children. It seems to me that they should have had something. And there are a number of relatives who really deserve a portion of the fortune."

Nancy nodded thoughtfully and relapsed into silence while she digested the facts of the case. From her father she had acquired the habit of thinking things through to their logical conclusion. Frequently, Carson Drew had assured her that she went at a thing "like a detective." Certainly she had a naturally clever mind and took more than an ordinary interest in strange or baffling cases.

Carson Drew, a widower, showered a great deal of affection upon his daughter; it was his secret boast that he had taught her to think for herself and to think logically. Since he knew that Nancy could be trusted with confidential information, he frequently discussed his interesting cases with her.

A number of times Nancy had been present at interviews which her father had had with noted detectives who desired his aid in solving perplexing mysteries, and those occasions stood out as red letter days for her.

There was something about a mystery which aroused Nancy's interest, and she was never content until it was solved. More than once her father had found her suggestions, or "intuitions" as he called them, extremely helpful.

For a reason which she could not understand, the Crowley case had attracted Nancy's attention, although it had not fallen into her father's hands. She had a certain feeling that a mystery lurked behind it.

"Father, do you believe Josiah Crowley ever made a second will?" Nancy demanded suddenly.

"You're a regular lawyer, the way you cross-examine me," Carson Drew protested, but with evident enjoyment. "To tell you the truth, I don't know whether he ever made a second will or not. All I do know is that—but perhaps I shouldn't mention it since my information is not very definite."

"Go on!" Nancy commanded impatiently. "You're trying to tease me!"

"Well, I do remember that one day nearly a year ago I was standing in the First National Bank when Crowley came in with Henry Rolsted."

"Not the attorney who specializes in wills and legal documents?"

"Yes. Well, as I was saying, they came into the bank together. I had no intention of listening to their conversation, but I couldn't help but hear that they were discussing a will. Crowley made an appointment to call at Rolsted's office the following day."

"That looks as though Mr. Crowley had made up his mind to write a new will, doesn't it?"

"That was the thought which passed through my mind at the time."

"You say you overheard the conversation nearly a year ago," Nancy mused. "That was nearly two years after Mr. Crowley had made the will in favor of the Tophams, wasn't it?"

"Yes. It's likely Crowley had made up his mind to change the will. I suspect he intended to cut the Tophams out, but whether or not he did, I have no way of knowing."

"Mr. Rolsted is an old friend of yours, isn't he?"

"He is. An old friend and an old college classmate."

"Then why don't you ask him if he ever drew up a will for Mr. Crowley?"

"That's a rather delicate question to ask, young lady. He may tell me it's none of my business."

"You know he won't. You're such a noted attorney that other lawyers feel flattered when you take an interest in their cases. Will you do it? Please!"

"I can't promise to blunder into his office and demand the information. Why this sudden interest in the case, Nancy?"

"Oh, I don't know. A mystery always interests me, I

guess, and it does seem to me that someone ought to help those poor relatives."

"You take after your old dad, I am afraid. But I'm curious to know what mystery you have discovered."

"If a will is missing, isn't that a mystery?"

"If it is actually missing—yes. But it's possible that if Crowley ever wrote the will he changed his mind and destroyed it. He was subject to sudden whims, you know."

"Anyhow, I'd like to learn more about the case if I can. Will you talk with Mr. Rolsted?"

"You are persistent, Nancy," and Mr. Drew smiled. "Well, I suppose I could invite him to take luncheon with me to-morrow——"

"Oh, please do," Nancy interrupted eagerly. "That would be a splendid opportunity to find out everything he knows about the will."

"All right, I'll try to do it. But I warn you not to expect startling news." Carson Drew glanced at his watch. "Why, it's nearly midnight, Nancy. We've been discussing this case for over an hour. Better run off to bed now and forget the Tophams."

"All right," Nancy agreed somewhat reluctantly. "Don't forget your promise tomorrow at luncheon!"

Long after his daughter had retired, Carson Drew sat by the fire. At last he, too, arose.

"It wouldn't surprise me if Nancy has stumbled upon a real mystery," he told himself, as he snapped out the electric light and turned toward the stairway. "Perhaps I shouldn't encourage her to dig into it, but after all it's in a good cause!"

Isabelle Holland (1920–2002)

Known for her bold and controversial young adult novels, Isabelle Holland was the publicity director for Harper Lee's *To Kill a Mockingbird* at J. B. Lippincott in New York City and the author of Gothic novels for adults. *The Man Without a Face* (1972) was one of the first post–World War II novels for older children to address issues of sexuality, even though it does so in a rather restrained way. The novel served as the basis for Mel Gibson's directorial debut with a film by the same name but a somewhat different story in 1993. In the novel, Charles, a fatherless fourteen–year–old, experiences a transforming but problematic relationship with Justin McLeod, a sympathetic teacher whose face has been scarred in an automobile accident. Unlike the film, in which the relationship between Justin and Charles remains platonic, the novel suggests that they have a sexual encounter. Charles's older sister, Gloria, and his mother are thoroughly unsympathetic characters, while Justin provides encouragement and support during the summer when he tutors Charles. Holland stated in *The Horn Book Magazine* that she "didn't set out to write about homosexuality" in *The Man Without a Face*. "I started this book with only the idea of a fatherless boy who experiences with a man some of the forms of companionship and love that have been nonexistent in his life."[1]

NOTE

1. Isabelle Holland, "Tilting at Taboos," *The Horn Book Magazine* 49 (June 1973): 299–305.

From *The Man Without a Face*

CHAPTER 6

Meg was right. Staying up there after the actual coaching took off a lot of the strain and made everything easier. I'd leave the house shortly after seven, which was no sweat since I'm an early riser. McLeod would work with me till eleven. Then I'd have some milk and cookies and a sandwich and was usually eating those when I heard him ride past on Richard. At that point I'd have to remind myself why I was there and what I was doing and whose idea it was in the first place, because getting back to studying while I could still hear Richard's hooves galloping back over the fields was almost more than I could bear. Sometimes McLeod wouldn't return till nearly two, quitting time. Sometimes he'd come back sooner, walk in and sit down with a book, all without saying a word. But if he was in the room it was almost like he wasn't there. I mean, normally I have to be alone to concentrate, but he didn't bother me. The first day when I got up to go out at two he said I'd better have something to eat, so we went out to the kitchen.

"There's stuff in the refrigerator. Make yourself a sandwich."

Usually after that we had sandwiches and milk or coffee. At first this happened only a couple of times a week. Other days I'd have a hot dog and a milkshake as soon as I got to the village. But then I got to staying up at McLeod's three or four times a week, then every day. Sometimes I'd ask him questions about what I'd been working on, although I was afraid at first that he'd think I was trying to scrounge more coaching out of him, but he didn't seem to. Then around two thirty or a quarter to three I'd wander down to the beach. Once or twice, when he was going to the village or back into the mainland, he drove me as far as the bridge.

The work got more interesting. What I really found I liked was history and next to that, math, which really rocked me. But it made me feel a lot better about the future, because Meg always said that with my math grades the whole system would have to go back to the Wright brothers before they'd let me in the Air Force Academy.

As the days went on I sometimes stayed later and later. One afternoon we got to talking in the kitchen. I found myself looking at the kitchen clock and it was five to five.

"It's got to be wrong," I said.

"What?"

"Your clock."

He turned and looked at it. "No, it's right, I wound it this morning."

I stood up so fast I knocked my chair over. "I didn't know it was s-so late."

McLeod got up. "If you're stricken because you took so much of my valuable time, don't be. My time isn't that sacred."

That made me think of something. "Is it true that you—"

Why, I mentally kicked myself, when things were going well, did I always have to ask some question that wasn't any of my business? If McLeod had made one thing clear above all others it was that he had a highly developed sense of privacy. It spread out like a moat around him. Every so often, like this afternoon, I would find myself inside it and then, instead of leaving well enough alone, I'd shove my whole leg in my mouth and start asking pointy little questions.

He was standing, hands on the back of his chair. "Is it true that I what?"

One thing I had learned: If you start something like the wrong question with McLeod you finish it, you don't just stop in the middle and leave by the nearest exit—not if you wanted to come back. I felt sick but I went on. "That you make your living writing porno under a pseudo-whatever-it-is?"

There was a second's pause. That's done it, I thought. Then he started to laugh and went right on as he picked up the dishes and put them in the sink.

I was so relieved I felt weak.

"Is that the current story?"

"Yes. It's all those packages and what look like checks from publishers."

"You mean our dedicated postmistress has been corrupted?"

I grinned. "No. At least I don't think so. But the word's around." I told him about the mass pilgrimage to the bookstores and he laughed even harder. At that moment he was warm and funny and almost young.

He finished washing the two dishes, glasses, and the cup and saucer. I dried them and put them away.

"It's not porno," he said finally. "It would be a lot more lucrative if it were."

"Novels?" Somehow he didn't seem the novel type, at least not the kind that Meg's father, the publisher, or The Hairball left lying around the house.

"Yes. In a sense. A mixture of science fiction and mythology."

"Under your name?"

"No. Terence Blake."

I whistled. "Wow!" The Terence Blake books hadn't yet caught on like Tolkien but they were really good. "That's great! I mean—your books are super!" I was impressed. What a pity I couldn't tell everybody, although the minute I thought of that I knew I didn't want to.

He smiled. "Sweet words to any author. Which ones have you read?"

I told him. "There're two earlier ones I haven't read. Somebody stole them from the school library and the bookstores say they're out of print. But they're coming out in paperback in the fall so I'll get 'em then."

"I have them. You can borrow them."

As we went towards the living room I said, "Why Terence Blake?"

"Terence was my father's name and Blake my mother's maiden name."

"But why a pseudonym? I mean—I'd be pretty proud if I'd written them."

"But when I wrote the first I had no idea how it would go."

Somehow I knew that wasn't the real reason, but I also knew I'd better not press it. He had that remote note in his voice. We went over to the bookshelves. He pulled down two books and handed them to me.

"Are they your only copies?" I asked.

"That's all right. I trust you."

I felt pretty good when he said that. But I shook my head.

"No. If anybody saw them they'd last about five minutes. Every kid on the beach would want them, and then they'd want to know how I'd got hold of them." Reluctantly, but feeling heroic, I handed them back. "When they come out in paper I'll send them to you to autograph. Would you? I mean autograph them?"

"Of course."

He said it so abruptly I wondered if I had put my foot in my mouth again. "You don't mind?"

He was putting the books back on the shelf, but he turned and looked at me. "No, Charles. I don't mind."

I remember that summer partly as pictures that spring into my mind, knife-sharp, partly as fragments of conversation.

Once he asked me, "What do you want most? Quickly—don't think."

"To be free."

"Free from what?"

"From being crowded. To do what I want."

"Fair enough. Just don't expect to be free from the consequences of what you do, while you're doing what you want."

At the time I was disappointed in McLeod. It sounded like some typical adult double-talk.

Another time, I was copying down the poem he read me, "High Flight," so I could put it in a notebook along with the other stuff about flying that I had been keeping off and on since I was about seven. I asked him if he believed in God.

"Of course." He said it almost impatiently.

I waited for him to ask what I thought, but he didn't. Then he saw my face and laughed. "What were you expecting? That I would proselytize you?"

I grinned, feeling foolish. His ability to read me was unnerving. "Well, The Hairball always said that was the trouble with True Believers—they had to spread the word."

"In a sense, he's right. But in your case it's time you reached out for what you want—instead of waiting for people to come after you."

"How do you mean?"

"About ninety percent of your time seems to have been spent resisting things and people, so that it's now an emotional habit. It's time you reached out on your own."

"I came here."

"Yes. Did you ever stop to think—if your mother or one of your numerous stepfathers had said, 'Charles, we've arranged for you to have coaching this summer. You'll be coached for three hours five days a week and then you'll spend an equal amount of time studying while your friends are down on the beach or out in boats, and as your reward you'll get into a school that you don't much want to go to but is the lesser of two evils,' how do you think you would have felt?"

He had a point. "Lousy."

Looked at that way six hours of studying and being coached sounded like the worst nightmare of sweat labor. I must be out of my mind. But the truth of the matter was that I was enjoying myself which, since I wasn't any shakes as a student even now, meant I was enjoying McLeod. He wasn't like anybody I had ever known. I finished copying the poem and read it over. According to the footnote the author, Magee, died at nineteen—killed during the Battle of Britain—in 1941 which, as far as I was concerned, was practically back in the American Revolution. But I started doing some calculations. What I was really trying to find out was whether McLeod had gotten burned as a pilot. The idea appealed to me. Anybody who was, say, nineteen in 1941 would be—I did some figuring on the edge of my paper—about fifty now. Possible. I looked up at McLeod who was rearranging some books on a shelf. The good side of his face was turned toward me so that I could see only a swatch of the burn coming around his chin. There was a lot of gray in his hair. On the other hand, some people got gray at thirty.

"What are you trying to figure out?" he asked, without turning.

Caught short I blurted out, "I was wondering how old you are."

"The easiest method is to ask. Forty-seven."

Some more figuring. But not even McLeod was fighting the Battle of Britain at sixteen. But he could have been an American Air Force pilot at the very end of the war. My heart started to beat faster. "Were you in the Air Corps during World War II?

"No."

"You weren't in the war?"

"Yes. Infantry. A foot-slogging private soldier."

"Is that where you—" Asking about his age and asking about a burn that disfigured half his face was not exactly the same thing.

"Where I—?"

I wished I hadn't started. But I was still stinging from his comment about my tendency to run. "Where—where you got burned."

He was looking at me but his face didn't flicker. For the first time I wondered what it could be like for him. "I shouldn't have asked that," I mumbled.

"Most people do, sooner or later." He put another book on the shelf from a pile on the floor. "I got burned in a car accident." He paused and then added deliberately, "I was too drunk to know what I was doing, slid on some ice, and went over the side of the road down a ravine."

I was stunned. It sure knocked my picture of the wounded war hero to fragments. "I'm sorry," I said, not sure whether I was sorry he had lost his face or I had lost the war hero.

He was watching me. "So am I. Not just because of this—" he gestured to the burned half of his face—but because there was a boy with me, a boy about your age. He was burned to death."

A bee had somehow got in the room and was buzzing around. In the silence that followed it sounded like a 747.

Then McLeod said, "It's late, Charles. You'd better go."

The day after, I woke up before dawn, thinking about what McLeod had said. The queer part was that I expected to feel disgusted and disillusioned, and I didn't. I felt sorry. I felt sorry for the boy who was killed, but I felt more sorry for McLeod. It didn't make much sense because the boy was dead, but I was sure McLeod had been dragging around the guilt ever since, and that it had a lot to do with the way he lived and why he had never had his face fixed the way Mother and everyone in the summer community said he could—and should.

"What a lousy deal," I said to Moxie, who was lying under the sheet next to me. My voice must have waked him, because I felt suddenly the deep vibration against my ribs that meant he was purring. In a few seconds the noise followed, sounding like a bad case of bronchitis.

A while later Meg came into my room. Since I had a lot to think about I wasn't too pleased to see her.

"How is the Great Man?" she said, wiggling her backside against the footboard and crowding my feet.

"Okay." I didn't want to talk about McLeod.

"You're getting very protective about him."

"What's to talk about?"

"All right. Keep your hair on. But people are beginning to ask what you're doing all the time and where you are."

"And what do you tell them?"

"I tell the kids you're being forced to study with some teaching type on the mainland. And whenever Mother says 'Where's Chuck?' which she does sometimes in the afternoons—she's resigned to your studying in the mornings—I say wherever your gang is at the moment, except when they're right there, then I make up something else. But one of these days she won't ask me, she'll ask Pete or Sam or Tom, and then the fat will be in the fire."

"And Gloria? What's with her?"

"She's still got a clutch on Peerless Percy. But Sue Robinson's coming here from camp next week."

"Yuch!" I struggled up and sat leaning against the headboard. "That's bad news." It was. Sue is Gloria's only real competition: red hair, green eyes, and if her figure isn't quite as nymphy as our Gloria's, her personality is several light-years better.

"And," Meg went on, as though winding up for a real knockout blow, "she was the one Peerless Percy was in love with all last summer."

Things did not look good. But somehow I didn't care. It all seemed remote and unimportant. My mind slid back to what McLeod had told me.

"You don't seem interested," Meg said.

"Sure I'm interested, Meg. But I've got other things to think about. Besides, I'm tired. I haven't slept much. I'd like to catch another hour's shut-eye before I have to get up. After all," I finished virtuously, "you may be having a vacation. I have to work."

"All right." Meg was mad and I knew it.

"Don't be miffed, Megsy."

She turned. "You're different. Chuck. You've changed."

"What d'ya mean?"

"I don't know," Meg said slowly. "I can't say what I mean. But you're different. And I don't like it."

"Meg!"

But she was out of the room, and I was fairly sure she was crying. Well, I thought, getting back under the sheet, I'd make it up to her somehow. I knew she was kind of lonely because there weren't too many of her age group up here this year. Our summer community is very age-oriented. The grown-ups do their thing, which is mostly dropping in on each other for drinks or lying out at their end of the beach or back of one another's houses nursing their tans. Only the kids swim much. It's pretty rocky and the water's cold. Which is probably why I had gotten away with my double life for so long. Structure was a bad word around here and asking too many questions was showing definite signs of structure.

I comforted myself with this thought (Meg's forebodings had upset me more than I wanted to admit) and went to sleep thinking about McLeod, knowing there was something I had to say and hoping that when the moment came I'd say it properly.

He was remote and full of trick and trap questions later that morning, really grilling me as to what I had learned, not just lately, but right from the beginning. By the time the three hours were over I felt limp. He must have seen this because he brought some milk and cookies into the library immediately.

"You'd better go out and run for half an hour after you've eaten. I'd lend you Richard if he weren't so neurotic."

"How is he?" I asked, downing cookies at a great speed.

"All right."

"Look," I burst out. I was determined to have my say. "About what you told me yesterday. About the accident—" I kept my eyes on the table where I was nervously turning the cookie dish around and around. "What I want to say is—well, it was a lousy thing to happen to you, and it probably wasn't your fault."

"You're wrong. It most definitely was."

"All right. So it was. What I mean is—" I wanted so badly to tell him how I felt, but I couldn't find the words. Then a strange thing happened. Without my volition, my hand reached towards his arm and I grasped it.

He didn't move or say anything. The good half of his face was as white as paper. Then he jerked my hand off and walked out.

CHAPTER 7

I was sore as a boil. Worse—I felt like a fool.

So. He thought I ought to reach out! What a hypocrite! Here I had been thinking he was something special in grown-ups, and he turned out to be like all the rest: say one thing, do another.

I was so mad I found it hard to concentrate. Even so, I couldn't get over the feeling there was a funny side to it. If this coaching had been Mother's—or the school's—idea, what an opportunity to walk out and say screw 'em. But it was mine, so I had to stay even though McLeod had acted like my hand was a cockroach or something, like, for pete's sake, I had made a pass at him. That's what burned me up. Well—screw him! I'd take what I could from him, pass my exam, and then tell him to go to hell.

But fantasies of telling him to go shove didn't help me to concentrate. I stuck it out till around twelve thirty. At that point, having taken in about zero, I split.

As I was pelting down the path I heard Richard's hooves behind the long belt of pines on the other side of the cliff, coming at a fast clip. I didn't want to meet McLeod, so I put on a burst of speed, vaulted over the gate, and high-tailed it to the bridge and across. Then I left the main road and went down the steep hill that gave onto the back of the village. Once there I felt safe. I strolled to the outdoor counter of the malt shop and treated myself to two hamburgers and a double malt which, having paid for, I could only eat half of. This morning was really a bomb!

From where I was standing I could see inside. A whole lot of Gloria's gang were there, but I couldn't see any of mine. So when I had eaten all I could, I decided to pay the cove a visit.

Running down the pier I jumped into one of the dinghies, untied it, and rowed past the point and north along the coast until I hit the cove. One of the reasons we had picked the cove was that from the seaward side it looked more or less like any other string of big rocks

lining that part of the shore. But when you got right up to one end where there was a narrow opening, you could see the rocks were sort of a jetty running parallel with the shore, shielding a small beach in the elbow.

I turned in at the right place, rowed across the tiny cove, and tied the dinghy to a tree stump near the edge of the water. Then I ran around the curve, dodged around a big boulder, and there they all were—Pete Minton (Percy's brother), Sam Leggett, Tommy Klein, Luke and Mike Warner, and Matt Henry. They were all stretched out except Pete, who was sitting with his back against a rock. Thin spirals of smoke rose from each. Then I smelled it: pot.

That was something I certainly hadn't bargained for. There was always a lot of talk about getting some, but grass in these parts is about as easy to find as porno. But I couldn't go back now.

"Behold the grind!" Pete said dreamily.

"How's the studying going?" Mike asked

"And how's the guy without a face?" Tommy pitched in. "What's his name, fellers?"

"McLeod," they all chorused.

So they knew. "Okay." I sat down and leaned against a tree. I was really shaken but didn't want to show it. I wanted very much to know how they knew, but knew better than to ask. Pulling a grass blade from near one of the rocks I smoothed it between my thumbs and blew it a couple of times, making a thin screeching noise.

"Man, you must really want to get into that funky school," Pete said.

"Haven't you heard, he wants to be a flyboy," Sam took a long drag on his joint. "Off we go, into the wild blue yond-der. . . ." He broke off into a giggle.

"Shove it," I said.

"So solly, sir. *Achtung! Sieg heil!* Up yours!"

"I said shove it."

"My, aren't we sensitive? Who said you could come out here, anyway? You aren't one of us any more."

"Yeah? So who's gonna make me move?"

They were so bombed I felt pretty safe saying that, although even if they weren't I could take any of them on alone, even Pete, who's heavier than I am. None of them is exactly what you'd call athletic.

There were no takers, but I knew I was on very dicey territory. Somehow, I didn't know how, they knew what I was doing and they'd read me out of the club. I lay back and thought about it. It didn't take a genius to arrive at the answer: Meg had meant well but they knew I wasn't being forced to study. If this had been Mother's or the school's idea I would have been down here every afternoon griping about it. What's more, it would have been the same time every day—the second school was out. That would have made it okay. I would have been just another victim of terrible parental and school pressure to achieve. It was doing it on my own that made me a leper. But they hadn't told anybody, or Gloria would have heard it. Mother would have heard it. Meg would have heard it. And you can believe that by sundown I would have heard it. By the same logic Meg hadn't known this morning, which now seemed a year ago. Or did she? She might have been going to tell me that when she left in a huff. That made me think of McLeod, whom I'd been carefully keeping out of my mind since I'd lammed out of his house. Bastard.

"How'd you know?" I asked Pete.

"Saw you go up a couple of times and followed you."

"Fink."

"You're the fink. What's the matter with school in New York?"

"Nothing. I just want out from home."

There was silence. I waited for him to say something about Gloria and his brother, half wishing he would and half wishing he wouldn't in case I would have to clonk him over the nose. But he didn't. I also wanted to ask him if Percy knew about McLeod, just to reassure myself. But that would have been a major blunder.

"Have a drag," Pete said, holding out his joint.

This is what I was afraid of. I'd gone along with the talk about finding pot because I didn't think there was a prayer of getting any. At school I was always in training for something or other—baseball, football, basketball, hockey—which was an acceptable excuse if you were a jock. The one time I'd smoked it with some of my class in the locker room, I had gotten so stoned they were scared to let me go home. Not that the faculty cracked the whip—most of them smoked grass themselves. But any cop who saw me would know exactly what I'd been doing, and in the state I was in I'd probably tell him where and with whom. Actually, the whole thing scared me and I was glad to have the training excuse. I had a weird—but strong—feeling that

pot was not for me, not because of the law or all the crap they hand out at school, tongue in cheek. And it didn't have anything to do with what anybody else did. It was just like there was some steering gear in me that kept pointing away from it.

But now I wasn't in training and Pete didn't know what had happened at school and I was tired of being out instead of in. I said as casually as I could. "I get sick on that stuff."

"Listen to the boy scout! You're just too good for us, Chuck. Maybe you'd better run back to teacher."

"He'll probably tell teacher, anyway, all about the nasty boys smoking grass."

"I told you, shove it! Here—" I took the joint out of Pete's hand. The mention of McLeod had done it. Gingerly, so I wouldn't show what an amateur I was, I took a drag, inhaling as little as I possibly could. Nothing happened. Then I took another.

"Here," Pete said. "Have one of your own."

In the beginning, it wasn't like the last time in the locker room, probably because I went at it cautiously. I lay back against a boulder. After a drag or two I started feeling relaxed. Then I felt good, like absolutely everything was going to turn out all right. And if it didn't, it still didn't matter.

"How'd McLeod get the scar?" Pete said.

Since everything had slowed down, it took me a while to answer.

"In a car accident," I said dreamily. McLeod had really shoved me back. The memory of that morning sliced through my pleasant fog, bringing with it a muffled jab of pain and anger, so I added, "He was drunk and he had a kid with him who was burned to death."

"Wow! Hear that, you guys?"

The good feeling went. Something had gone wrong. I was afraid if I learned what it was everything would get worse, so I took another deep drag.

I can't explain what happened after that. Afterwards I figured I just passed out. Went to sleep. Had a nightmare, whatever. . . .

The sky and water seemed to swim together. Gulls were flying. After a while they seemed to be flying in formations and then I noticed they had jet engines and weren't gulls after all—they were planes. Then came a great, wonderful, floating feeling, because I was in one of the planes and sometimes I was in the sky and sometimes I was floating in the water only it was all the same. I got happier and happier. Then I landed on the water, just like one of the gulls, and got out of the plane and splashed through to the shore to my father who was standing there. I knew it was my father because the sun was blazing on his yellow hair. It was funny, though. I couldn't see his face because the sun was shining in it and it was just a blur. I said to my mother as I walked towards the shore, "But you must have another picture of him *somewhere*. How am I ever to know what he looked like?" And she said, "But that's why I threw the pictures away. I don't want you to know what he looked like, because then you might get to look like him and then you would hate me the way he did." Which is just the kind of thing you can expect from a female.

"But you were the one who hated *him*," I said. "That's why—"

I stopped because I suddenly realized I now could see Father's face very well. It had a red scar on one side, but it was getting smaller and smaller. It was odd, though, about his hair. I could have sworn it was yellow. I could see now it was black and gray. All of a sudden it was McLeod, minus scar. He was smiling and holding out his hands. I gave a shout and started running towards him. And that's where things went wrong, badly wrong. How, I don't know, but the sky was almost black. McLeod's face was as white as the stones and he was terribly angry. He was so angry I knew I would never be forgiven and that, anyway, I was going to die because I had forgotten about the undertow which was pulling me out and down, down into the water where I couldn't breathe. . . .

"Push his head down again," Pete said.

"No," I tried to say, as the water filled my mouth.

"Now you've drowned him." That was Sam.

There was a stinging slap on my face, then another. Slowly I came to. The sky wasn't black, it was its usual watery sun-and-blue effect.

"Come on, Chuck! Wake up! Do you want to get us all in trouble? If your mother sees you and squeals, we'll have the pigs all over this place."

I was standing, fully clothed, hip-deep in the water. The others, naked, were standing around. Pete gave me another slap. "Wake up!"

I tried to launch a blow that would knock his head off, but all I did was lose my footing and I had to be held up.

"I'm all right. Lemme go."

"Man! you weren't kidding, were you, when you said you got sick."

I pushed him away and staggered to the shore. I had barely gotten up onto the stony beach when I really got sick. Maybe it was the pot, maybe the sea water I had swallowed. Whatever it was, I felt like I was bringing up my breakfast of day before last.

I was shivering and my forehead was clammy with sweat, but, after a minute, I managed to crawl back to the water, wash my face and slosh some up on the beach to clean it up.

"You'd better stick to straightsville," Pete said, putting on his pants. "You're a walking menace."

"Thanks a lot."

"You can go back in the rowboat," he went on grudgingly. "One of us can row the dinghy back."

"I can row it back myself."

"Suit yourself. I don't have to tell you that if you open your big mouth about this, we'll total you."

"Don't worry," I said sarcastically. "Your secret is safe with me." I swallowed the bad taste in my mouth. "What I told you about McLeod. Keep that to yourself, too."

"Who'd I tell?" Pete said, getting into the boat.

I tried to convince myself that since McLeod was a creep he deserved anything I did to him. But I couldn't make myself quit feeling lousy, like I had started something I couldn't stop. Shakily I got into the dinghy and, keeping the other boat well in sight, rowed back around the point.

For the first time in that putrid day, fate seemed to be for me. There was no one in when I got back to the house. I got out of my wet clothes, put on a dry pair of shorts and a sweater, laid the wet ones out on the garage roof outside my window where they could get the setting sun, and passed out on the bed.

The next morning early I sneaked down to get some milk and breakfast. I was starved. But even after I had eaten a couple of bowls of cereal and four pieces of toast with butter and honey and drunk two glasses of milk I didn't feel the way I usually do—rarin' to go. I felt like my head was stuffed with cotton and what I wanted to do was go back to bed. I also didn't want to go up to McLeod's. As a matter of fact, it was the last place I wanted to go. I didn't know what to do.

I was sitting there, too zonked out even to move, when the door opened and Mother came in. What's more, she looked wide awake. If I hadn't been sitting down you could have knocked me over with one of Gloria's false eyelashes. Mother had on a silky blue robe that looked as if it had been made in Hong Kong or somewhere, and her dark hair was piled on top of her head and tied with a matching blue ribbon. She looked pretty enough to eat. If she had but known it, I was sitting there like ice cream on a dish for her to have. Luckily, I guess, she didn't know it.

"Where were you yesterday, Chuck?"

So that was the game. "With the gang."

"What were you doing?"

"What we always do. Swimming, shooting bull."

"Were you smoking marijuana?"

"No. Where would we get it around here?"

"Then why were you out like a light when we came in? Both Meg and I tried to get you up but you wouldn't stir. I'm worried about you, Chuck. Meg tells me you've found someplace to study. If that's what you were really doing, then all I can say is what I've been saying all along. You're studying too hard. You should be out with the others."

I pulled myself together. "First you grill me about what was I doing with the others, then you tell me I should be with them more." Against every inclination I stood up. "It doesn't matter what I do. It's wrong. Well, I'm going to pass that exam so I can go to St. Matthew's next year. That's why I'm studying."

"I don't want you to go to St. Matthew's. I don't want you to go to boarding school at all. You know what I think of them. I'm not sure whether I'll let you go even if you pass the exam."

It was funny. A couple of minutes ago I didn't think I ever wanted to see McLeod again and going up there to study seemed about as desirable as going to jail. The trouble with Mother was she didn't know when the odds were on her side. "I'm not going back to school in New York. If you don't let me go to St. Matthew's, then I'll drop out."

She looked frightened. "You can't—you can't drop out until you're sixteen."

"Then I'll leave home, and you can't stop me. Do you know how many kids my age are walking around the country? I'll go where you won't find me and don't think I don't have the contacts, because I do, any kid I know does."

Which was sheer bull, but Mother didn't know that. And given the way things are today, she couldn't be sure that I wouldn't get away with it.

At that moment the screen door opened and in walked Barry.

"Hi," he said. Then he did something that absolutely knocked me out. He went over and kissed Mother, right on the mouth, like he had every right to. Mother turned pink and her eyes looked bigger and browner than ever. It made me furious.

"Help yourself," I said nastily.

He turned around. Barry could lose twenty pounds, but I'll say this for him, he doesn't have a paunch and it's not flab. Square face, bluish eyes, light hair, what there is of it—Mr. Average, almost as pink as Mother, which didn't suit him the way it did her.

"Your mother has agreed to marry me, Chuck. I came by to tell you. I guess that was a tactless way of doing it."

He sounded apologetic, which turned me off. All I could think was that McLeod, if I had handed him lip like that, would have said something icily sarcastic that would have cut me down to size. Thinking about McLeod didn't make me feel any better, either, especially when I remembered that I had given him the bridegroom's role. For a second I tried to imagine him kissing Mother. I couldn't. It didn't work. I didn't know why it didn't, but it didn't.

"Congratulations," I said. "That's just what I need, another stepfather."

Barry looked at me, eyeball to eyeball. "Yes, Charles. That's what I think you need."

"Chuck!" Mother said. "Please be nice!"

I was about to say something else nasty when I remembered what we were talking about when Barry walked in.

"All right. Best wishes and all that. But I'm not going back to that school in New York."

"Is that St. Matthew's you want to go to?" Barry asked, going over to the stove and pouring himself some coffee.

"Yeah."

"It's not a bad school."

I'd been all braced for a fight and was therefore surprised.

"I thought it was supposed to be terrible," Mother said.

Barry took a swallow or two of coffee. "It went

through a bad patch. It's okay now. And they've got a
new headmaster who's beefing up the curriculum—
Evans, I think his name is."

"That's the guy that wrote to me."

Gloria walked in. The two horizontal strips of knitted nothing she had on would not have filled a tea-
cup. Other than that she looked like a free-floating
thunderstorm.

"Aren't you afraid you're going to feel constricted
in all those clothes?" Barry said.

"Gloria, go up and put on a shirt or something,"
Mother said. "You're practically naked."

"So what? It's my house." Gloria put some water in
the kettle and put it on the stove. Then she got a bowl
and poured herself some cereal.

"Please, Gloria."

"After I've had breakfast. Maybe."

Mother looked unhappy.

"Heard the news?" I said, curious as to whether that
was behind her scowl. "Mother's going to marry
Barry."

"I heard it yesterday."

"Don't overdo the delight," Barry said amiably, "it
might go to my head."

Gloria went on eating. Barry walked over and stood
beside her. "Look, I'd like us to be friends. It makes it
a lot easier for me, and, more important, for your
mother. She'd like a little moral support."

"It's not as though it were the first time."

"In view of you and Chuck and Meg, that's on the
whole rather a good thing, don't you think?"

Gloria didn't look at him. She swallowed another
mouthful of cereal. "You've got Meg." That's our
Gloria—if she's not first, she won't play.

"Yes, thank heaven," Barry said. "And here she is.
Just like the Marines."

I don't know whether Meg had heard all that or not.
She went over to Mother and gave her a smack on the
cheek. Then she went to Barry. She not only gave him
a smack. She put her arms around him. He bent and
gave her a bear hug and lifted her off the floor.

"You'll get a hernia," Gloria said.

Mother looked at her quickly. "Gloria—that's
mean!"

Barry put Meg down. "It would be well worth
it. We'll go on a diet together after the wedding,
Meg."

What I wanted to do was go back up to bed and sleep
off this cottony feeling in my head. I don't mean my
head hurt. But I felt funny, sort of unfocused. The
house was obviously no place to sack out in today.
Besides—more than ever I wanted to go to St.
Matthew's now. And, for once, it looked like I might
have some support.

I plunked my cereal bowl and the plate in the sink
and headed for the door.

"Chuck, where are you going?"

"To study."

"Where—where do you study?"

There was a short silence, then I had an inspiration.
"Up above the cove." The beauty about that was that it
was true. McLeod's cliff was above the cove—by a
couple of hundred feet. I just didn't add that it was also
several miles further along the coastline.

"Well where do you keep your books?"

"There's an abandoned shack there." Also true. I
could even shove a couple of old texts there for any
snoop.

Barry was watching me. So was Gloria. I could feel
my face beginning to get hot.

"S'long," I muttered, and started to leave.

"By the way, Chuck," Gloria said, getting up and
pouring hot water into the drip pot, "that mangy animal of yours nearly bit Percy yesterday. You know
if he ever bites anybody the vet'll have to put him
away."

"And what was Percy doing to him?" I said angrily.

"Just trying to take a woodchuck away from him—
like any humane person."

"Moxie has to hunt. Nobody feeds him around
here. You have no right to interfere and you can tell
your scrofulous boyfriend to keep his filthy hands
away from him, or I'll——"

"You'll do what—lick him? He's on every team
in his college. He'd make *mincemeat* of you,
Chuck."

I was still boiling with fury when Barry said, "No
one's going to hurt Moxie, Chuck. So keep your shirt
on. She just said that to irritate you. When will you
learn?"

Meg had got up and come to the door. "Come on. Chuck. Let's go."

As we walked down toward the road I finally said, "All right. She laid the booby trap and I walked into it. But why does she do it?"

"Does it matter?" Meg said. "Besides. You know the answer. She has to be number one, like in the commercial."

"But why me?"

"Because you're handy. Because you let her get to you. Because she's jealous of you."

"Jealous of what, for the love of Mike? You mean from when we were babies?"

"Maybe. I wasn't around. You're good-looking and people like you. Gloria's good-looking, too, but people don't like her. She tries hard to make them, but after a while they all go away. You're the opposite. People would like to get closer to you but you won't let them. Were you smoking pot yesterday?"

The abrupt switch threw me off. "Is that any business of yours? I suppose now you're going to tell Barry." That was dirty and I knew it and was ashamed right away. But I felt so all-around lousy that I had to make somebody else miserable, too.

Meg stopped dead in the road. "No, I won't tell Barry, though sometimes I think I ought to. If you're going to go and be a drug addict I don't think I'm doing you any good by not telling anybody. But I don't care as much as I used to, because you're not my friend any more. I guess you must be McLeod's friend. But I don't see why you can't be both. But you needn't bother now because I don't care any more."

"Megsy!"

"Let me go. I'm *glad* Barry is going to marry Mother. You just think I'm a nuisance now, but he *likes* me." She pulled her arm away and shot across the road towards the beach.

Joey once had his horoscope read and was really turned on because the swami or fortune-teller said Joey was going to have a great political career, except maybe he was also going to jail. But, as Joey said, today one often goes with the other, and maybe he should take up law as a preparation for politics.

I said law might also be useful if he got put in jail, and he agreed.

But what I'm getting at is I'd always looked on the whole horoscope scene as bull, but I was beginning to wonder if my moon or planet or whatever was in some undesirable place these past couple of days, because nothing was coming out right.

I was still sore at McLeod and I was thinking about this when I suddenly remembered the other thing that was bothering me: I had ratted on him.

I stopped walking. I had told Pete about McLeod's drunk driving and killing a kid. I now wished to God I hadn't. When I thought of what they could do with that—and how inevitably that would get the news to Mother about what I was doing all day—sweat broke out all over me. I'd done it because I was mad and, I suppose—I didn't like to think about this—to buy my way back into the good graces of Pete and the others. Talk about a fink!

I started walking again. The rest of the walk I tried to convince myself that in view of the way he'd acted towards me, I was justified. It didn't work too well. I still felt like a ratfink. If the whole family situation hadn't got worse instead of better, what with Barry joining the troops and adding one more body to our apartment, I might have turned back. But it had, so I went on.

CHAPTER 8

When I walked into the library McLeod was standing by the fireplace staring down into what were probably last night's ashes. It sounds loony, but up here, even in early August, fires feel pretty good at night.

He looked up.

"Sorry to be late," I muttered, and slid into my seat at the table.

"I want to talk to you," McLeod said abruptly. For one sickening minute I wondered if he had already heard about my telling on him.

"Yes?" And added, without much conviction, "Sir."

But it wasn't what I was afraid of. It was somehow worse. Typically, he went straight to the point. "I'm sorry about—about what happened yesterday. I told you once that I had lived alone too long. I accused you of always running away. Well, that's what I did. Only instead of running I built a wall. Being a writer made it easy; easy to be up here earning a living, easy to be alone and keep clear of people."

Stubborn pride made me say, "It doesn't matter."

He looked at me then. "Doesn't it, Charles? Then why did you leave so abruptly?"

I had no answer to give. Or rather, I didn't want to answer, so we didn't say anything for a bit.

"Well?"

Nothing.

"If you can make me believe that I didn't make you angry, or hurt you, then I'll stop."

It was a hand held out, but I wouldn't let myself take it. How could I after ratting on him?

"Why can't we just forget it?"

"Is that what you want?"

"Yes."

"All right. Then let's get back to Vergil."

But it wasn't. As we crawled through the whole dreary Carthage bit, what I had told Pete was there like a ghost, getting larger and larger. Words that I knew perfectly well I couldn't remember. Whole parts that I knew we had gone through might as well have been new. Finally McLeod put down his book.

"What's the matter with you? You act as though you've never seen this. We went over it a few days ago."

That strange unfocused feeling was back. Pot doesn't affect any of the other kids this way—at least not that I knew of. But then I remembered hearing in school or reading in one of those dumb pamphlets they're always giving out that some people can't take it, like some people can't drink. This made me think about my father. Why, I don't know. Then I remembered the dream I had at the cove.

"Charles!"

McLeod's voice cracked like a whip. Suddenly he was standing over me. "What did you do yesterday?" he asked. "After you left here?"

Mother had asked that, but it wasn't the same. Besides, I had left her and come here. Now there was no more place to go to, and if there had been I wasn't at all sure I could get it all together and go there, or that I wanted to. . . .

"I went to the cove where my gang hangs out."

"And?"

"Smoked some grass." So now I had ratted on Pete and the others. But it didn't feel like ratting the way it had about telling on McLeod. I waited for him to wade in.

But he didn't. Not right away, anyway. Then he said

wearily, "Oh, my God," and went and stood by the window.

"If your generation drinks, what's wrong with mine smoking grass. When you were in school didn't you ever sneak beer?"

"Yes."

"Then what's all the flak about?"

"How do you feel?"

"Fine. What's that got to do with it?"

"Because you're not concentrating very well—as you know."

"So? Did you ever have hangovers?"

"I thought marijuana wasn't supposed to give those."

"I'm not hung over. Look, Mc—Mr. McLeod. What I do when I'm not here is my own business."

The moment I said that I knew it was a mistake. This was the perfect opening for him to remind me that it was my idea being here, not his. I held my breath.

"That's true. But since trying to teach you when you're like this is like trying to get a bell tone out of cotton wadding, I'd appreciate it if you would desist while I'm coaching you. That is, if you want to pass that exam—and not waste my time and yours."

That sounded more like the old McLeod. But it was so much milder than I had expected that I felt almost let down. Besides, I had no intention anyway of smoking grass again.

He came over to the table and closed the book. "You might as well give yourself a holiday. You're not doing anything. Come back when you feel better."

I went back the next day. I still wasn't up to form, but I wasn't as zonked out as the day before. Another good night's sleep had helped a lot.

As the days passed I worked hard, harder than I had done before. After a while I realized that I was trying to get things back on the footing they'd been on before I'd made that stupid move in a burst of sympathy or something. It felt like a year since that morning, but it was only a week. I found myself thinking about it a lot, whenever I wasn't actually working. I still didn't understand it. I didn't understand McLeod. I didn't even understand me. But I saw what he meant about a wall, because he was back behind it.

In the background, I was vaguely aware that Mother and Barry were fluttering around on a kind of party circuit. Barry, who was now on vacation from his law firm, was nominally staying with some friends down the beach road, but every time I was at home he was there, amid much talk of wedding dates, apartment hunting, and what Gloria once acidly referred to as creeping *kitsch*. I tried a couple of times—but not very hard—to talk to Meg, but since she had left off visiting at her usual dawn hour and I was away from home during the day I didn't get much of a chance. What with my early rising, walking to and from McLeod's, and my six hours' work in between, I almost went to sleep with my head on the dinner table. Fortunately, Mother was too starry-eyed to ask any more leading questions about where I was going and what I was doing. Also, with Gloria the only holdout from the general rejoicing, they were concentrating on winning her over. They took her and Peerless Percy to anything they showed the faintest interest in going to—swinging parties, any summer stock in the area, a couple of music festivals with all-day picnics listening to Beethoven under the trees. Not so dumb, my sister Gloria. She was melting, but not rapidly enough so that their solicitude and desire to please should flag in any way. I could see their progress at dinner. Instead of the usual scowl, there'd be a soft smile and a sidelong glance at Barry. Whether it fooled Barry or not, I somehow doubted. But it made Mother happy which, I grudgingly had to admit, was for him the all-important thing. I finally also decided that he wasn't as dumb as I had always thought, either. In his own way he was playing Gloria's game as cannily as she was, which in his case meant sitting there as stolidly as a tree stump while she whinnied and pranced and did the siren bit, so that she couldn't know she'd gotten anywhere—and (naturally) stop trying to please. But he'd pile on the outings, so she couldn't get sour through failing to score any goals.

When Gloria wasn't around, Barry's frozen front would thaw. Meg knew, I guess, what he was doing and why, because when Gloria wasn't around he'd kid and joke with her and she'd glow like a miniature sunflower. She was so happy, in fact, that she began eating less and looking less like a tub and more like the beginnings of a female. Not that I was up to noticing that much. But both Mother and Barry commented on it, and Meg lit up some more.

Nobody paid much attention to me. I think Barry had convinced Mother that my going to St. Matthew's was not a catastrophic idea. Because other than saying once, "I don't think you get enough exercise, Chuck," she let me alone.

Curiously, McLeod one day said the same. I was in sort of a limbo these days. After what had happened down at the cove I had no desire to go there. Just thinking about Pete made me feel guilty. On the other hand the kind of open-door relationship with McLeod that had kept me up there until after five in the past seemed gone. Sometimes I felt he had slammed the door. Other times that I had. I wasn't happy. I wanted to be friends with him, but every time I tried somehow to get through to him again I'd feel like Richard balking at a jump. I couldn't account for it because I had never felt this way before. I've always been a loner. Mother—and all five school analysts— have talked to me about that *ad nauseam*. Until now, I've felt it was a good thing. It kept me loose. Now all I could think about was that I had ratted on McLeod. It made me sicker than ever. All by itself it got to be a wall around me getting higher and higher. And the higher it got the less I could do about it, and, with a real show of logic, the sorer I got at McLeod.

Then one day as I was being particularly thick-headed he said, "I think you must need more exercise."

"I get enough."

"Doing what?"

"Climbing up here and down again, for one thing."

"For a boy—and an athletic one—of your age, who are you trying to kid?" He paused. "What about swimming?"

"It's too cold."

"I didn't know you were in such bad physical shape."

I could see by the clock on the chimney piece that it was eleven twenty. "Isn't it time for your ride?"

"That can wait."

He was looking at me and I was trying to read his expression. It certainly didn't show the warmth I had once seen. Sometimes I thought I would give almost anything to see it again, but the moment I thought that, a wave of sickening guilt came over me. Then I'd be like a stalled car.

"Well, this isn't getting us anywhere." He got up and left the room. Relieved, I waited to hear Richard's hooves. But in a few minutes McLeod was back carrying a knapsack in his hand.

"Come on."

"Where?"

"Never mind. Just come." The command was given in his usual autocratic fashion and was easier to obey than argue with. Besides, I didn't have much fight.

To my surprise he led me outside across the path to his car. "Get in."

"Where—?"

"Just get in."

It vaguely occurred to me that someone might see me with him. But that didn't seem important, either. When we got to the gate, instead of turning left onto the main road, he turned right into the cliff road that grew narrower and bumpier as it climbed. But the view from the top was really spectacular. I'd never seen it.

"Wow," I said. The sea was so blue it was almost green. There wasn't a house or a soul in sight. Just dark green rocky hills at left and in front, and to the right, the high edge of the cliff and the sea.

"Okay. Out you get."

I got out. "Where're we going?"

He came round the car. "We're going to play follow the leader. I lead. You follow."

"Aye, aye, sir," I muttered. What did he think I was—a Scout troop? But man, could he move!

We went straight for the cliff edge and then to my horror he stepped down into what looked like nothing. He turned, saw my face and laughed. "Don't worry. There's a path here."

There was: rocky, winding slowly down where, for a change, the cliff bulged out instead of in. Part of the path was where the rock naturally shelved out. Part looked as though it had been hammered out.

"How's your head for heights?" McLeod asked.

"Okay."

He started down. I followed.

I said, "You must be a climber."

"Yes."

"Where'd you climb?"

"Tetons, Rockies, Alps, Dolomites."

"What's the matter with Everest?"

"Too crowded."

A few minutes later we were down onto big, flat boulders. "Here." McLeod pulled some towels and trunks out of his knapsack. "Put these on."

They fit, but they looked ancient. "Where did these come from, the Ark?"

"I suppose you'd think so. They were mine, when I was about your age."

He had put his own on underneath his jeans, so all he did was step out of them and pull off his sweater. I guess he must have ridden Richard here a lot because he was tanned a lot darker than I. But all over one side of his body and down his leg were burns, some red, some paler, the skin shiny. Like his face, the other side was good—very thin, except for the hard muscles around his shoulders and arms and thighs.

"Dive in, Charles. It looks like an armchair but isn't. There's a current underneath. I'll go first." With that, he stepped to the edge of the rock and dived in. He came up about thirty feet away. "What are you waiting for?"

I went to the edge and headed in. It had been about two weeks since that day in the cove, and the water here, on the other side of the point, was colder. The shock almost paralyzed me. I came up by instinct more than anything else.

McLeod had swum back a little to where I was. "All right, now. Swim. Straight out."

I didn't hesitate—not with that cold. I plunged out. Feeling came back and suddenly I felt much better. Taking great mouthfuls of air I cut through the water. I hadn't swum like that in a long time, because mostly at the cove and the pier and the beach we just fool around. I kept on going until I was ready to stop, McLeod about two yards to one side and keeping even. Then I started to play. I rolled over and duck-dived, then came up and rolled over some more and lay on my back, thrashing my feet, and then tried a backward dive. Coming up, I saw McLeod above me in the water and butted him gently in the stomach then shot away laughing as I came up. I felt marvelous. He turned, shaking the water out of his hair, and started after me. I knew I couldn't outswim him, so I went down again and swam underwater and looked around and there he was, so I surfaced and changed course and then went down and butted him again on the side.

I forgot he was an adult and a teacher and forty-seven years old. I even forgot what I had done to him. I forgot everything but the water and being in it and chasing and being chased, far from the shore with nothing around or moving except us. It was like flying. I thought suddenly, I'm free. And the thought was so great I poked him again on the way up. We swam some more, this time parallel with the shore, then played some more, then back to where we'd been.

"Okay. Let's go in," he said and turned towards the shore. I turned and we went together, although he took about one stroke to my three. If I hadn't seen how far one stroke carried him I would have thought he was just fooling around.

When I pulled onto the rock I realized that if I had been out any longer I would have been tired instead of just relaxed. The sun was hot and we lay on towels on a big flat rock above the one we used as a diving board.

The happy euphoric feeling should have gone on to a happy drowsy one, but even though I was physically relaxed, it didn't. It was as though by stepping out of the water I had lost that sense of freedom. It was too bad, I thought, really too bad. But that terrible weight was back.

And then McLeod, lying beside me, reached out and with his hand grasped my arm, just the way I had his two weeks ago.

"All right, Charles. Whatever it is, spill it. I'm not just prying. But you can't carry it around any longer. And I don't think I can watch any longer. It's making you sick."

I thought of getting up and going, but his hand was there, holding me. I could imagine it withdrawing when he knew what I had done. I thought about the water and the afternoon.

His hand tightened. "Come on, son."

Maybe it was the "son" that did it, although I'd never liked it before when somebody said it.

"I ratted on you. I told Pete that day we were all smoking grass how you got your scar, about being drunk and the kid with you. It wasn't even that I was stoned—I was later, a real bad trip, but not then. I just wanted—I was sore at you. You made me feel like I'd made some kind of pass at you. And they were mad at me for studying and knew I came up here because Pete

saw me come. So he asked me how you got the scar. So I told 'em. I'm sorry, McLeod. I feel like an absolute skunk. A real fink."

What I wanted to do was cry like a baby. But I couldn't do that, of course, so I put my other arm over my eyes like the sun was getting into them. Curiously, he hadn't withdrawn his hand. I waited to see if he would in a delayed reaction, but he didn't.

"It's my fault as much as yours. I knew I had . . . had hurt you, which was why I tried to talk to you about it. I should have made you listen. Then you wouldn't have been carting this load around."

But the load had rolled away. "Then we're still friends?"

"Yes, Charles. Still friends."

That great feeling I had in the water like, I guess, a sort of a high, came back. The sun was hot on my skin. The air smelled of salt and pines and grass (the real kind!) and hay. I felt super. I moved the arm he was holding and he let go instantly, but all I did was to slide my hand in his. I felt his fingers close around it.

After a while he said, "Tell me about that bad trip."

So I told him, and then about the dream. Until that moment I really hadn't thought much about it. But when I was finished I said, "I guess that means I wish you were my father."

"I wish so too."

"Did you ever have any sons?"

"No."

My mind drifted off. Then I said, "Meg asked me if I thought you'd be interested in marrying Mother."

There was a muffled laugh. "Your mother might not have cared for that arrangement."

"Maybe not. But when I think of The Hairball and Meg's father I'd think she'd be thrilled."

"Do you remember your own father?"

"A little." And then out of nowhere I said, "I have a funny feeling there was something wrong about him. Something the others know that I don't." I told him about the fracas at the beach three years ago with Gloria. "But I can't get anything out of anyone."

"Then don't try. And if some day you stumble over it, don't break your heart. We're all fallible. Like me. Like you."

I could imagine what all the kids I knew, even Joey, would say about the way I felt about McLeod. But here, lying beside him on the rock, I didn't care. I didn't care about anything. Everything else, everybody else, seemed far away, unimportant.

"I like you a lot," I said.

There was something beating in his hand or mine, I couldn't tell which. I wanted to touch him. Moving the arm that had been across my eyes I reached over and touched his side. The hot skin was tight over his ribs. I knew then that I'd never been close to anyone in my life, not like that. And I wanted to get closer.

But at that moment McLeod sat up and then stood up. He stood facing away from me for a minute. Then he jumped down onto the lower rock. In a minute he was back, dressed. He smiled down at me. "Up. You may not feel like it, but if you stay there longer you'll get cold."

"That's a lot of bull."

"Maybe. Have you forgotten you have three hours of study yet? To say nothing of eating something?"

"Couldn't we take the day off?" I asked, as winningly as I could.

"Certainly not. Get dressed. The trip back up the cliff should wake you up. I'm going ahead of you. It's easier up than down."

As the car bumped over the path, and McLeod swerved to avoid the worst potholes, muttering under his breath when we hit one, something that had been bothering me suddenly made me say, "McLeod—"

"Yes? You can call me Justin, by the way."

I was pleased. "All right."

"What were you going to ask?"

I blurted out, "Do you think I'm a queer?"

"No, I do not think you're a queer." He glanced down at me. "Because of this afternoon?"

"Yes."

"No. Everybody wants and needs affection and you don't get much. Also you're a boy who badly needs a father."

That was what Barry had said. But I didn't tell him about Barry and Mother. I didn't want to think about home at all. I felt like I was in a sort of golden cocoon and I didn't want to break out of it.

Katherine Paterson (b. 1932)

Katherine Paterson was born in Qing Jiang, Jiangsu, the daughter of American Christian missionaries. She has twice won the Newbery Award, for *Jacob Have I Loved* (1980) and for *Bridge to Terabithia* (1977). Paterson combines a vivid, at times painful, honesty about children's feelings and experiences with spiritual vision and a sense of hard-won hope.

Set in the Chesapeake Bay region in the 1940s, *Jacob Have I Loved* tells of the sibling rivalry between the talented Caroline and her sister Louise. Caroline overshadows Louise and, with their grandmother's encouragement, disparages and demoralizes her, calling her "Wheeze." The title is taken from a cruel jibe of Grandmother's, who quotes the Old Testament passage in which God says, "Jacob have I loved, but Esau have I hated," referring to the rivalry between twin brothers in which Esau, the elder brother, resented Jacob, the younger one, who bought his birthright from him. Jacob deceived their father into giving him the blessing intended for Esau. Like Jacob and Esau, Caroline and Louise have an intense and bitter sibling rivalry; like Esau, Louise feels that she has been cheated out of her birthright by Caroline.

Louise knows and loves the island and the bay, and she takes a traditionally male job, crabbing. Despite her oppressive situation, she does not despair, but gradually grows in strength and knowledge of herself and what she can do. The captain is a friend and mentor to Louise; he left the island in despair fifty years earlier after making an embarrassing mistake. Now he has returned to rebuild his life on the island. Paterson has written novels from the perspective of boys (as in *Bridge to Terabithia*—see discussion in Part 4—and *Park's Quest*) and from the point of view of girls (*Lyddie, Flip-Flop Girl,* and *The Great Gilly Hopkins*). See excerpts from *The Great Gilly Hopkins* and Paterson's reflections about "hope and happy endings" in Part 8.

From *Jacob Have I Loved*

15

I served the tea with a smile sunk in concrete pilings.

"Thank you, Louise," my mother said.

The Captain nodded at me as he took his cup off the tray. Caroline, distracted with happiness, seemed not to see me at all. I took the cup that I had prepared for her back to the kitchen, brushing past my grandmother, who was grinning at me in the doorway. After I had put down the tray, I had to squeeze past her once more to get to the protection of my room. "Jacob have I loved—" she began, but I hurried by and up the steps as quickly as I could.

I closed the door behind me. Then, without thinking, I took off my dress and hung it up and put on my nightgown. I crawled under the covers and closed my eyes. It was half-past three in the afternoon.

I suppose I meant never to get up again, but of course I did. At suppertime my mother came in to ask if I were ill, and being too slow-witted to invent an ailment, I got up and went down to the meal. No one said much at the table. Caroline was positively glowing, my mother quiet and thoughtful, my grandmother grinning. and stealing little peeks at my face.

At bedtime Caroline finally remembered that she had a sister. "Please don't mind too much, Wheeze. It means so much to me."

I just shook my head, not trusting myself to reply. Why should it matter if I minded? How would that change anything? The Captain, who I'd always believed was different, had, like everyone else, chosen her over me. Since the day we were born, twins like Jacob and Esau, the younger had ruled the older. Did anyone ever say Esau and Jacob?

"Jacob have I loved . . ." Suddenly my stomach flipped. Who was speaking? I couldn't remember the passage. Was it Isaac, the father of the twins? No, even the Bible said that Isaac had favored Esau. Rebecca, the mother, perhaps. It was her conniving that helped Jacob steal the blessing from his brother. Rebecca—I had hated her from childhood, but somehow I knew that these were not her words.

I got up, pulled the black out curtains, and turned on the table lamp between our beds.

"Wheeze?" Caroline propped herself up on one elbow and blinked at me.

"Just have to see something." I took my Bible from our little crate bookcase, and bringing it over to the light, looked up the passage Grandma had cited. Romans, the ninth chapter and the thirteenth verse. The speaker was God.

I was shaking all over as I closed the book and got back under the covers. There was, then, no use struggling or even trying. It was God himself who hated me. And without cause. "Therefore," verse eighteen had gone on to rub it in, "hath he mercy on whom he will have mercy, and whom he will he hardeneth." God had chosen to hate me. And if my heart was hard, that was his doing as well.

My mother did not hate me. The next two days part of me watched her watching me. She wanted to speak to me, I could tell, but my heart was already beginning to harden and I avoided her.

Then Friday after supper while Caroline was practicing, she followed me up to the room.

"I need to talk with you, Louise."

I grunted rudely. She flinched but didn't correct me. "I've been giving this business a lot of thought," she said.

"What business?" I was determined to be cruel.

"The offer—the idea of Caroline going to school in Baltimore."

I watched her coldly, my right hand at my mouth.

"It—it—well, it is a wonderful chance for her, you know. A chance we, your father and I, could never hope—Louise?"

"Yes?" I bit down savagely on a hang nail and ripped it so deeply that the blood started.

"Don't do that to your finger, please."

I grabbed my hand from my mouth. What did she want from me? My permission? My blessing?

"I-I was trying to think—we could never afford this school in Baltimore, but maybe Crisfield. We could borrow something on next year's earnings—"

"Why should Caroline go to Crisfield when she has a chance—"

"No, not Caroline, you. I thought we might send you—"

She did hate me. There. See. She was trying to get rid of me. "Crisfield!" I cried contemptuously. "Crisfield! I'd rather be chopped for crab bait!"

"Oh," she said. I had plainly confused her. "I really thought you might like—"

"Well, you were wrong!"

"Louise—"

"Momma, would you just get out and leave me alone!" If she refused, I would take it for a sign, not only that she cared about me but that God did. If she stayed in that room—She stood up, hesitating.

"Why don't you just go?"

"All right, Louise, if that's what you want." She closed the door quietly behind her.

My father came home as usual on Saturday. He and my mother spent most of Sunday afternoon at the Captain's. I don't know how the matter was settled in a way that satisfied my father's proud independence, but by the time they returned it was settled. Within two weeks we were on the dock to see Caroline off to Baltimore. She kissed us all, including the Captain and Call, who turned the color of steamed crab at her touch. She was back for summer vacation a few days before Call left for the navy, at which time she provided the island with another great show of kissing and carrying on. You couldn't doubt that she'd go far in grand opera judging by that performance.

After Call left, I gave up progging and took over the responsibility of my father's crab floats. I poled my skiff from float to float, fishing out the soft crabs and taking them to the crab house to pack them in boxes filled with eelgrass for shipping. I knew almost as much about blue crabs as a seasoned waterman. One look at a crab's swimming leg and I could tell almost to the hour when the critter was going to shed. The next to the last section is nearly transparent and if the crab is due to moult in less than a couple of weeks, the faint line of the new shell can be seen growing there beneath the present one. It's called a "white sign." Gradually, the shadow darkens. When a waterman catches a "pink sign," he knows the moulting will take place in about a week, so he gently breaks the crab's big claws to keep it from killing all its neighbors and brings it home to finish peeling in his floats. A "red sign" will begin to shed in a matter of hours and a "buster" has already begun.

Shedding its shell is a long and painful business for a big Jimmy, but for a she-crab, turning into a sook, it seemed somehow worse. I'd watch them there in the float, knowing once they shed that last time and turned into grown-up lady crabs there was nothing left for them. They hadn't even had a Jimmy make love to them. Poor sooks. They'd never take a trip down the Bay to lay their eggs before they died. The fact that there wasn't much future for the Jimmies once they were packed in eelgrass didn't both me so much. Males, I thought, always have a chance to live no matter how short their lives, but females, ordinary, ungifted ones, just get soft and die.

At about seven I would head home for breakfast and then back to the crab house and floats until our four-thirty supper. After supper sometimes one of my parents would go back with me, but more often I went alone. I didn't really mind. It made me feel less helpless to be a girl of fifteen doing what many regarded as a man's job. When school started in the fall, I, like every boy on Rass over twelve, was simply too busy to think of enrolling. My parents objected, but I assured them that when the crab season was over, I would go and catch up with the class. Secretly, I wasn't sure that I could stand school with neither Caroline nor Call there with me, but, of course, I didn't mention this to my parents.

We had another severe storm that September. It took no lives, in the literal sense, but since it took another six to eight feet of fast land off the southern end of the island, four families whose houses were in jeopardy moved to the mainland. They were followed within the month by two other families who had never quite recovered from the storm of '42. There was plenty of war work on the mainland for both men and women at what seemed to us to be unbelievable wages. So as the water nibbled away at our land, the war nibbled away at our souls. We were lucky, though. In the Bay we could still work without fear. Fishermen off the Atlantic coast were being stalked by submarines. Some were killed, though we like the rest of the country were kept ignorant of those bodies that washed ashore just a few miles to the east of us.

Our first war deaths did not come until the fall of 1943, but then there were three at once when three island boys who had signed aboard the same ship were lost off a tiny island in the South Pacific that none of us had ever heard of before.

I did not pray anymore. I had even stopped going to church. At first I thought my parents would put up a fight when one Sunday morning I just didn't come back from the crab house in time for church. My grandmother lit into me at suppertime, but to my surprise my father quietly took my part. I was old enough, he said, to decide for myself. When she launched into prophecies of eternal damnation, he told her that God was my judge, not they. He meant it as a kindness, for how could he know that God had judged me before I was born and had cast me out before I took my first breath? I did not miss church, but sometimes I wished I might pray. I wanted, oddly enough, to pray for Call. I was so afraid he might die in some alien ocean thousands of miles from home.

If I was being prayed for mightily at Wednesday night prayer meetings, I was not told of it. I suppose people were a little afraid of me. I must have been a strange sight, always dressed in man's work clothes, my hands as rough and weathered as the sides of the crab house where I worked.

It was the last week in November when the first northwest blow of winter sent the egg-laden sooks rushing toward Virginia and the Jimmies deep under the Chesapeake mud. My father took a few days off to shoot duck, and then put the culling board back on the *Portia Sue* and headed out for oysters. One week in school that fall had been enough for me and one week alone on the oyster beds was enough for him. We

hardly discussed it. I just got up at two Monday morning, dressed as warmly as I could with a change of clothes in a gunnysack. We ate breakfast together, my mother serving us. No one said anything about my not being a man—maybe they'd forgotten.

I suppose if I were to try to stick a pin through that most elusive spot "the happiest days of my life," that strange winter on the *Portia Sue* with my father would have to be indicated. I was not happy in any way that would make sense to most people, but I was, for the first time in my life, deeply content with what life was giving me. Part of it was the discoveries—who would have believed that my father sang while tonging? My quiet, unassuming father, whose voice could hardly be heard in church, stood there in his oilskins, his rubber-gloved hands on his tongs, and sang to the oysters. It was a wonderful sound, deep and pure. He knew the Methodist hymnbook by heart. "The crabs now, they don't crave music, but oysters," he explained shyly, "there's nothing they favor more than a purty tune." And he would serenade the oysters of Chesapeake Bay with the hymns the brothers Wesley had written to bring sinners to repentance and praise. Part of my deep contentment was due, I'm sure, to being with my father, but part, too, was that I was no longer fighting. My sister was gone, my grandmother a fleeting Sunday apparition, and God, if not dead, far removed from my concern.

It was work that did this for me. I had never had work before that sucked from me every breath, every thought, every trace of energy.

"I wish," said my father one night as we were eating our meager supper in the cabin, "I wish you could do a little studying of a night. You know, keep up your schooling."

We both glanced automatically at the kerosene lamp, which was more smell than light. "I'd be too tired," I said.

"I reckon."

It had been one of our longer conversations. Yet once again I was a member of a good team. We were averaging ten bushels of oysters a day. If it kept up, we'd have a record year. We did not compare ourselves to the skipjacks, the large sailboats with five or six crew members, that raked dredges across the bottom to harvest a heavy load of muck and trash and bottom spat along with oysters each time the mechanical winch cranked up a dredge. We tongers stood perched on the wash-boards of our tiny boats, and, just as our fathers and grandfathers had before us, used our fir wood tongs, three or four times taller than our own bodies, to reach down gently to the oyster bed, feel the bottom until we came to a patch of market-sized oysters, and then closing the rakes over the catch, bringing it up to the culling board. Of course, we could not help but bring up some spat, as every oyster clings to its bed until the culling hammer forces a separation, but compared to the dredge, we left the precious bottom virtually undisturbed to provide a bed for the oysters that would be harvested by our children's children.

At first, I was only a culler, but if we found a rich bed, I'd tong as well, and then when the culling board was loaded, I'd bring my last tong full hand over hand, dump it on the board, and cull until I'd caught up with my father.

Oysters are not the mysterious creatures that blue crabs are. You can learn about them more quickly. In a few hours, I could measure a three-inch shell with my eyes. Below three inches they have to go back. A live oyster, a good one, when it hits the culling board has a tightly closed shell. You throw away the open ones. They're dead already. I was a good oyster in those days. Not even the presence at Christmastime of a radiant, grown-up Caroline could get under my shell.

The water began to freeze in late February. I could see my culling like a trail behind us on the quickly forming ice patches. "Them slabs will grow together blessed quick," my father said. And without further discussion, he turned the boat. We stopped only long enough to sell our scanty harvest to a buy boat along the way and then headed straight for Rass. The temperature was dropping fast. By morning we were frozen in tight.

There followed two weeks of impossible weather. My father made no attempt to take the *Portia Sue* out. The first day or so I was content simply to sleep away some of the accumulated exhaustion of the winter. But the day soon came when my mother, handing me a ten o'clock cup of coffee, was suggesting mildly that I might want to take in a few days of school since the bad weather was likely to hold out for some time.

Her kindly intended words lay on me like a wet sail. I tried to appear calm, but I was caught and suffocated by the idea of returning to school. Didn't she realize that I was by now a hundred years older than anyone there, including Miss Hazel? I put my coffee down, sloshing it over the saucer onto the table. Coffee was rationed then and to waste it, inexcusable. I jumped up mumbling an apology to get a rag, but she was quicker and began sponging the brown liquid off the oilcloth before I could move, so I sat down again and let her do it.

"I worry about you, Louise," she said, mopping carefully and not looking at me. "Your father and I are grateful, indeed. I hardly know what we'd have done without you. But—" She trailed off, reluctant, I suppose, to predict what might become of me if I went on in my present manner of life. I didn't know whether to seem touched or annoyed. I was certainly irritated. If they were willing to accept the fruits of my life, they should at least spare me the burden of their guilt.

"I don't want to go back to school," I said evenly.

"But—"

"You can teach me here. You're a teacher."

"But you're so lonely."

"I'd be lonelier there. I've never belonged at that school." I was becoming, much to my own displeasure, a bit heated as I spoke. "I hate them and they hate me." There. I had overstated my case. They had never cared enough about me one way or the other to hate me. I might have from time to time served as the butt of their laughter, but I had never achieved enough status to earn their hatred.

She straightened up, sighing, and went over to the sink to wash the coffee from her cloth. "I suppose I could," she said finally. "Teach you, I mean, if Miss Hazel would lend me the books. Captain Wallace might be willing to do the math."

"Can't you do that?" Although I was no longer in love with the Captain, I did not wish to be thrown in such close company with him again—just the two of us. There was a residue of pain there.

"No," she said. "If you want to be taught at home, I'd have to ask someone else to do the math. There is no one else with the—with the time." She was always very careful not to seem to sneer at the rest of the islanders for their lack of education.

I'm not sure how my mother persuaded Miss Hazel to go along with the arrangement. The woman was very jealous of her position as the one high school teacher on Rass. Perhaps my mother argued that my irregular attendance would be disruptive, I don't know, but she came home with the books, and we began our kitchen-table school.

As for my lessons with the Captain, my mother, sensitive to the least hint of inappropriate behavior, always went with me. She would sit and knit while we had our very proper lesson, no more poker or jokes, and afterward, she and the Captain would chat across my head. He was always eager for news of Caroline, who was prospering in Baltimore as the Prophet Jeremiah claimed only the wicked do. Her letters were few and hurried but filled with details of her conquests. In turn, the Captain would share news from Call, from whom he heard nearly as often as we heard from Caroline. Between letters there was a lot of "Did I remember to tell you . . . ?" or "Did I read the part about . . . ?" Censorship kept Call from revealing very much about where he was or what was going on, but in what he didn't say there was enough to make my flesh crawl. The Captain, having been through naval battles before, seemed to regard the whole thing with more interest than fear.

There were only a few more days of oystering left that winter of '44. During the end of March and most of April, my father caught and salted alewives for crab bait, overhauled the motor on the *Portia Sue,* and converted it once more for crabbing. After he had caught and salted his crab bait, he did a little fishing to pass the days and even some house repairs. I crammed in as much schooling at home as possible, because once the crabs were moving, I'd be back on duty at the floats and in the crab house.

My mother heard the report of D day on our ancient radio and walked up to the crab house to tell me. She seemed more excited than I, to whom it signified only more war and killing. Besides, it was not the European war that concerned me.

17

Call was not discharged as soon as he had hoped, so it was the next year, the day before Christmas 1946 that he and Caroline were married. My parents went up for the ceremony in the Juilliard chapel, which, I gathered, was stark in word and dress, but rich in Bach and Mozart, thanks to Caroline's school friends.

I stayed home with Grandma. It was my choice. My parents spoke of getting a neighbor to stay with her, and each offered to remain and let me go instead. But I felt they were greatly relieved by my insistence. The way Grandma was or could be, we dreaded the thought of asking someone outside the family to endure even a few days alone with her. Besides, as they said later, it was the first trip of any length that the two of them had ever taken together. They left, with apologies to me, on the twenty-second. Perhaps my soul, now as calloused as my hands, could have borne such a wedding. I don't know. I was glad not to be put to the test.

Grandma was like a child whose parents have gone off and left her without making plain where they have gone or when they could be expected to return. "Where's Truitt?"

"He's gone to New York for Caroline's wedding, Grandma."

She looked blank, as though she were not quite sure who Caroline was but felt she shouldn't ask. She rocked quietly for a few minutes, picking a thread on her knitted shawl. "Where's Susan?"

"She went with Daddy to New York."

"New York?"

"For Caroline's wedding."

"I know," she snapped. "Why did they leave me?"

"Because you hate to ride the ferry, Grandma, especially in the wintertime."

"I hate the water." She dully observed the worn-out ritual. Suddenly she stopped rocking and cocked her head at me. "Why are you here?"

"You hate to be alone, Grandma."

"Humph." She sniffed and pulled the shawl tight about her shoulders. "I don't need to be watched like one of your old peelers."

The image of Grandma as an old sook caught in my mind. *Get it?* I wanted to say to somebody.

"What you cutting on?"

"Oh, just whittling." It was in fact a branch of almost straight driftwood, which I had decided would make a good cane for Grandma. I had spread out part of the Sunday *Sun* and was trimming the wood down before sanding it.

"I ain't seen that old heathen about," she said. "I guess he's dead like everybody else."

"No. Captain Wallace is just fine."

"He don't ever come around here." She sighed.

"Too snobby to pay attention to the likes of me, I reckon."

I stopped whittling. "I thought you didn't like him, Grandma."

"No, I don't favor him. He thinks he's the cat's pajamas. Too good for the daughter of a man who don't even own his own boat."

"What are you talking about, Grandma?"

"He never paid me no mind. Old heathen."

I felt as though I had stumbled off a narrow path right into a marsh. "Grandma, do you mean *now?*"

"You was always a ignorant child. I wouldn't have him on a silver plate *now.* I mean *then.*"

"Grandma," I was still trying to feel my way, "you were a lot younger than the Captain."

She flashed her eyes at me. "I would've growed," she said like a stubborn child. "He run off and left before I had a chance." Then she put her head down on her gnarled hands and began to cry. "I turned out purty," she said between sobs. "By the time I was thirteen I was the purtiest little thing on the island, but he was already gone. I waited for two more years before I married William, but he never come back 'til now." She wiped her eyes on her shawl and leaned her head back watching a spot on the ceiling. "He was too old for me then, and now it 'pears he's too young. After scatter-headed children like you and Caroline. Oh, my blessed, what a cruel man."

What was I to do? For all the pain she had caused me, to see her like that, still haunted by a childish passion, made me want to put my arm around her and comfort her. But she had turned on me so often, I was afraid to touch her. I tried with words.

"I think he'd be glad to be your friend," I said. "He's all alone now." At least she seemed to be listening to me. "Call and Caroline and I used to go to see him. But—they are gone now, and it isn't proper for me to go down alone."

She raised her head. For a moment I was sure she was about to hurl one of her biblical curses at me, but she didn't She just eased back and murmured something like "not proper."

So I took another bold step. "We could ask him for Christmas dinner," I said. "There'll be just the two of us. Wouldn't it seem more like Christmas to have company?"

"Would he be good?"

I wasn't sure what she meant by "good," but I said I was sure he would be.

"Can't have no yelling," she explained. "You can't have a body yelling at you when you're trying to eat."

"No," I said. "You can't have that." And added, "I'll tell him you said so."

She smiled slyly. "Yes," she said. "If he wants to come calling here, he better be good."

I wonder if I shall ever feel as old again as I did that Christmas. My grandmother with her charm, gaudy and perishable as dime-store jewelry—whoever had a more exasperating child to contend with? The Captain responded with the dignity of a young teen who is being pestered by a child whose parents he is determined to impress. While I was the aged parent, weary of the tiresome antics of the one and the studied patience of the other.

But I shouldn't complain. Our dinner went remarkably well. I had a chicken—a great treat for us in those days—stuffed with oysters, boiled potatoes, corn pudding, some of Momma's canned beans, rolls, and a hot peach cobbler.

Grandma picked the oysters out of the stuffing and pushed them to the side of her plate. "You know I don't favor oysters," she said pouting at me.

"Oh, Miss Louise," said the Captain. "Try them with a bite of the white meat. They're delicious."

"It's all right," I said quickly. "Just leave them. Doesn't matter."

"I don't want them on my plate."

I jumped up and took her plate to the kitchen, scraped off the offending oysters, and brought it back, smiling as broadly as I could manage.

"How's that now?" I asked, sitting down.

"I don't favor corn pudding neither," she said. I hesitated, not sure if I should take the pudding off her plate or not. "But I'll eat it." She flashed a proud smile at the Captain. "A lot of times I eat things I don't really favor," she told him.

"Good," he said. "Good for you." He was beginning to relax a bit and enjoy his own dinner.

"Old Trudy died," she said after a while. Neither the Captain nor I replied to this. "Everybody dies," she said sadly.

"Yes, they do," he answered.

"I fear the water will get my coffin," she said. "I hate the water."

"You got some good years to go yet, Miss Louise."

She grinned at him saucily. "Longer than you anyway. I guess you wish now you was young as me, eh, Hiram Wallace?"

He put down his fork and patted his napkin to his beard. "Well—"

"One time I was too young and too poor for you to pay me any mind."

"I was a foolish young man, but that's a long time ago, now, Miss Louise."

"You had no cause to leave, you know. There was ones who would have had you, coward or no."

"Grandma? How about some more chicken?"

She was not to be distracted. "There's others who's not favored lightning, you know."

"Lightning?"

"'Course, chopping down your daddy's mast—" She tittered.

"That's just an old story, Grandma. The Captain never—"

"But I did," he said. "Took me twenty minutes to chop it down and fifty years to set it back." He smiled at me, taking another roll from the tray I was offering. "It's so good to be old," he said. "Youth is a mortal wound."

"What's he talking about, Wheeze? I don't know what he's saying."

He put down his roll and reached over and took her gnarled hand, stroking the back of it with this thumb. "I'm trying to tell the child something only you and I can understand. How good it is to be old."

I watched her face go from being startled by his gesture to being pleased that he had somehow joined her side against me. Then she seemed to remember. She drew back her hand. "We'll die," she said.

"Yes," he said. "But we'll be ready. The young ones never are."

She would not leave us that day, even for her nap, but rocking in her chair after dinner, she fell asleep, her mouth slightly open, her head rolled awkwardly against her right soulder.

I came in from washing the dishes to find the two of them in silence, she asleep and he watching her. "I thank you," I said. He looked up at me. "This would have been a lonesome day without you."

"I thank you," he said. And then, "It's hard for you, isn't it?"

I sat down on the couch near his chair. There was no need to pretend, I knew. "I had hoped when Call came home—"

He shook his head. "Sara Louise. You were never meant to be a woman on this island. A man, perhaps. Never a woman."

"I don't even know if I wanted to marry him," I said. "But I wanted something." I looked down at my hands. "I know I have no place here. But there's no escape."

"Pish."

"What?" I couldn't believe I'd heard him correctly.

"Pish. Rubbish. You can do anything you want to. I've known that from the first day I met you—at the other end of my periscope."

"But—"

"What is it you really want to do?"

I was totally blank. What was it I really wanted to do?

"Don't know?" It was almost a taunt. I was fidgeting under his gaze. "Your sister knew what she wanted, so when the chance came, she could take it."

I opened my mouth, but he waved me quiet. "You, Sara Louise. Don't tell me no one ever gave you a chance. You don't need anything given to you. You can make your own chances. But first you have to know what you're after, my dear." His tone was softening.

"When I was younger I wanted to go to boarding school in Crisfield—"

"Too late for that now."

"I—this sounds silly—but I would like to see the mountains."

"That's easy enough. Couple of hundred miles west is all." He waited, expecting more.

"I might—" the ambition began to form along with the sentence. "I want to be a doctor."

"So?" He was leaning forward, staring warmly at me. "So what's to stop you?"

Any answer would have been an excuse to him, the one I gave, most of all. "I can't leave them," I said, knowing he wouldn't believe me.

18

Two days after my parents' return from New York, I came the closest I ever came to fighting with my mother. Children raised as I was did not fight with their parents. There was even a commandment to take care of it, number five: "The only one of the Ten Commandments with a promise attached." I can still hear the preacher's twang as he lectured us. "Honor thy father and thy mother, that thy days may be long upon the land which the Lord thy God giveth thee."

When my mother got off the ferry, there was something different about her. At first I thought it was the hat. Caroline had bought her a new hat for the wedding, and she had worn it on the trip home. It was pale blue felt with a wide rolled-up brim that went out from her face at a slant There was charm, both in the color, which exactly matched her eyes, and in the angle, which made her face look dramatic instead of simply thin. I could tell by looking at her how beautiful the hat made her feel. She was radiant My father beside her looked proud and a little awkward in his Sunday suit. The sleeves had never been quite long enough to cover his brown wrists, and his huge weathered hands stuck out rather like the pinchers on a number one Jimmy.

They seemed glad enough to see me, but I could tell that they weren't quite ready to let go of their time together. I carried one of the suitcases and lagged behind them in the narrow street. Occasionally, one or the other of them would turn and smile at me to say something like "Everything go all right?" but they walked closer together than they needed to, touching each other as they walked every few steps and then smiling into each other's faces. My teeth rattled, I was shivering so.

Grandma was standing in the doorway waiting for us. They patted her as they went in. She seemed to sense at once whatever it was going on between them. Without a word of greeting she rushed to her chair, snatched up her Bible, and pushed the pages roughly and impatiently until she found the place she wanted.

"'My son, give me thine heart, and let thine eyes observe my ways. For a whore is a deep ditch; and a strange woman is a narrow pit.'"

Momma's whole body shrank from the word "whore," but she recovered herself and went over to the umbrella stand where she carefully took the pins out of her hat. Her eyes steadily on her own image, she took off the hat, replaced the pins in the brim, and then patted her hair down with one hand. "There," she said, and taking one last look, turned from the mirror toward us. I was furious. Why didn't she scream? Grandma had no right—

"We'd best change," my father said and started up the stairs with the suitcases. She nodded and followed him up.

Grandma stood there, panting with frustration, all those words that she was bursting to say and no one but me to hear. Apparently, I would have to do. She glared at me and then began reading to herself as hastily as she could, searching, I suppose, for something she could fire at me and thus release her coiled spring.

"Here, Grandma," I said, my voice dripping molasses. "Let me help you." I'd been preparing for this moment for months. "Read it here. Proverbs twenty-five, twenty-four." I flipped over and stuck my finger on the verse that I had memorized gleefully. "'It is better,'" I recited piously, "'to live in a corner of the housetop than in a house with a contentious woman.'" I smiled as sweetly as ever I knew how.

She snatched her Bible out from under my hand, slammed it shut, and holding it in both hands whacked me on the side of the head so hard that it was all I could do to keep from crying out. But at the same time I was glad that she hit me. Even while she stood there grinning at my surprise and pain, I felt a kind of satisfaction. I was deserving of punishment. I knew that. Even if I was not quite clear what I deserved it for.

But the incident didn't help Grandma. She was at my mother all the time now, following three steps behind her as she swept or cleaned, carrying the black Bible and reading and reciting to her. My father, meanwhile, seemed less than anxious to get the *Portia Sue* out on the Bay again. He spent several precious days happily tinkering with his engine, wasting lovely, almost warm, oyster weather. Couldn't he see how badly I needed to get away from that awful house? Couldn't he see that being cooped up with Grandma when she was going full throttle was driving me to the brink of insanity?

And my mother didn't help. Every waking moment was poisoned by Grandma's hatred, but my mother, head slightly bent as though heading into the wind, kept her silent course around the house with only a murmured word or two when a reply seemed necessary and could be given without risking further rancor. It would have been easier for me if she'd screamed or wept, but she didn't.

She did, however, propose that we wash the windows, a job we had done quite thoroughly at the end of the crab season. As I opened my mouth to protest, I saw her face and realized how much she needed to be outside the house, though she would never say so. I fetched the buckets of warm water and ammonia. We scrubbed and wiped in blessed silence for nearly a half hour. Through the porch window, where I was working, I could see Grandma, poking anxiously about the living room. She wouldn't dare step out because of her arthritis, but it was clear that our peculiar behavior was disturbing to her. Watching her pinched face, I went through a spectrum of emotions. First a kind of perverted pride that my meek mother had bested the old woman, if only for an afternoon. Then a sort of nagging guilt that I should take such pleasure in my grandmother's discomfort. I could not forget that only the week before I had been touched by her childish griefs. This shifted to a growing anger that my clever, gentle, beautiful mother should be so unjustly persecuted, which was transformed, heaven knows how, into a fury against my mother for allowing herself to be so treated.

I moved my bucket and chair to the side of the house where she was standing on her chair, scrubbing and humming happily. "I don't understand it!" The words burst out unplanned.

"What, Louise?"

"You were smart. You went to college. You were goodlooking. Why did you ever come here?"

She had a way of never seeming surprised by her children's questions. She smiled, not at me, but at some memory within herself. "Oh, I don't know," she said. "I was a bit of a romantic. I wanted to get away from what I thought of as a very conventional small town and try my wings." She laughed. "My first idea was to go to France."

"France?" I might not surprise her, but she could certainly surprise me.

"Paris, to be precise." She shook her head as she wrung out her rag over the bucket beside her on the chair. "It just shows how conventional I was. Everyone in my college generation wanted to go to Paris and write a novel."

"You wanted to go to Paris and write a novel?"

"Poetry, actually. I had published a few little things in college."

"You published poetry?"

"It's not as grand as it sounds. I promise you. Anyhow, my father wouldn't consider Paris. I didn't have the heart to defy him. My mother had just died." She added the last as though it explained her renunciation of Paris.

"You came to Rass instead of going to *Paris?*"

"It seemed romantic—" She began scrubbing again as she talked. "An isolated island in need of a schoolteacher. I felt—" She was laughing at herself. "I felt like one of the pioneer women, coming here. Besides—" She turned and looked at me, smiling at my incomprehension. "I had some notion that I would find myself here, as a poet, of course, but it wasn't just that."

The anger was returning. There was no good reason for me to be angry but my body was filled with it, the way it used to be when Caroline was home. "And did you find yourself here on this little island?" The question was coated with sarcasm.

She chose to ignore my tone. "I found very quickly," she scratched at something with her fingernail as she spoke, "I found there was nothing much to find."

I exploded. It was as though she had directly insulted me by speaking so slightingly of herself. "Why? Why did you throw yourself away?" I flung my rag into the bucket, sloshing gray ammonia water all over my ankles. Then I jumped from my chair and wrung out the rag as though it were someone's neck. "You had every chance in the world and you threw it all away for that—" and I jabbed my wrenched rag toward Grandma's face watching us petulantly from behind the glass.

"Please, Louise."

I turned so that I would not see either of their faces, a sob rising from deep inside me. I pounded on the side of the house to stop the tears, smashing out each syllable. "God in heaven, what a stupid waste."

She climbed off her chair and came over to me where I stood, leaning against the clapboard, shaking with tears of anger, grief—who knew what or for whom? She came round where I could see her, her arms halfway stretched out as though she would have liked to embrace me but dared not. I jumped aside. Did I think her touch would taint me? Somehow infect me with the weakness I perceived in her? "You could have anything, been anything you wanted."

"But I am what I wanted to be," she said, letting her arms fall to her sides. "I chose. No one made me become what I am."

"That's sickening," I said.

"I'm not ashamed of what I have made of my life."

"Well, just don't try to make me like you are," I said.

She smiled. "I can promise you I won't."

"I'm not going to rot here like Grandma. I'm going to get off this island and do something." I waited for her to stop me, but she just stood there. "You're not going to stop me, either."

"I wouldn't stop you," she said. "I didn't stop Caroline, and I certainly won't stop you."

"Oh, Caroline. Caroline's different. Everything's always been for Caroline. Caroline the delicate, the gifted, the beautiful. Of course, we must all sacrifice our lives to give her greatness to the world!"

Did I see her flinch, ever so slightly? "What do you want us to do for you, Louise?"

"Let me go. Let me leave!"

"Of course you may leave. You never said before you wanted to leave."

And, oh, my blessed, she was right. All my dreams of leaving, but beneath them I was afraid to go. I had clung to them, to Rass, yes, even to my grandmother, afraid that if I loosened my fingers an iota, I would find myself once more cold and clean in a forgotten basket.

"I chose the island," she said. "I chose to leave my own people and build a life for myself somewhere else. I certainly wouldn't deny you that same choice. But," and her eyes held me if her arms did not, "oh, Louise, we will miss you, your father and I."

I wanted so to believe her. "Will you really?" I asked. "As much as you miss Caroline?"

"More," she said, reaching up and ever so lightly smoothing my hair with her fingertips.

I did not press her to explain. I was too grateful for that one word that allowed me at last to leave the island and begin to build myself as a soul, separate from the long, long shadow of my twin.

19

Every spring a waterman starts out with brand clean crab pots. Crabs are particular critters, and they won't step into your little wire house if your bait is rank or your wire rusty and clogged with sea growth. But throw down a nice shiny pot with a bait box full of alewife that's just barely short of fresh, and they'll come swimming in the downstairs door, and before they know it they're snug in the upstairs and on the way to market.

That's the way I started out that spring. Shiny as a new crab pot, all set to capture the world. At my mother's suggestion, I wrote the county supervisor who had graded my high school exams, and he was happy to recommend me for a scholarship at the University of Maryland. My first thought was to stay home and help with the crabs until September. My father brushed the offer aside. I think my parents were afraid that if I didn't go at once, I'd lose my nerve. I wasn't worried about that, but I was eager to go, so I took off for College Park in April and got a room near the campus, waiting tables to pay my way until the summer session when I was able to move into the dormitory and begin my studies.

One day in the spring of my sophomore year, I found a note in my box directing me to see my advisor. It was a crisp, blue day that made me feel as I walked across the quadrangle that out near Rass the crabs were beginning to move. The air was fresh with the smell of new growth, and I went into that building and up to that office humming with the pure joy of being alive. I had forgotten that life, like a crab pot, catches a lot of trash you haven't bargained for.

"Miss Bradshaw." He cleaned his pipe, knocking it about the ashtray until I was ready to offer to clean it for him. "Miss Bradshaw. So."

He coughed and then elaborately refilled and lit his pipe.

"Yes, sir?"

He took a puff before going on. "I see you are doing well in your courses."

"Yes, sir."

"I suppose you are considering medicine."

"Yes, sir. That's why I'm in premed."

"I see." He puffed and sucked a bit. "You're serious about this? I would think that a good-looking young woman like you—"

"Yes, sir, I'm sure."

"Have you thought about nursing?"

"No, sir. I want to be a doctor."

When he saw how determined I was, he stopped fooling with his pipe. He wished it were different, he said, but with all the returning veterans, the chances of a girl, "even a bright girl like you" getting into medical school were practically nonexistent. He urged me to switch to nursing at the end of the semester.

A sea nettle hitting me in the face couldn't have stung worse. For a few days I was desolate, but then I decided that if you can't catch crabs where you are, you move your pots. I transferred to the University of Kentucky and into the nursing school, which had a good course in midwifery. I would become a nurse-midwife, spend a few years in the mountains where doctors were scare, and then use my experience to persuade the government to send me to medical school on a public health scholarship.

When I was about ready to graduate, a list of Appalachian communities asking for nurse-midwives was posted on the student bulletin board. From the neat, doublespaced list, the name "Truitt" jumped out at me. When I was told the village was in a valley completely surrounded by mountains, the nearest hospital a two-hour drive over terrible roads, I was delighted. It seemed exactly the place for me to work for two or three years, see all the mountains I ever wanted to see, and then, armed with a bit of money and a lot of experience, to batter my way into medical school.

A mountain-locked valley is more like an island than anything else I know. Our water is green grass and often treacherous, our boats, the army surplus jeeps we count on to navigate our washboard roads and the hairpin curves across the mountains. There are a few trucks, freely loaned about in good weather to any valley farmer who must take his pigs or calves to market. The rest of us seldom leave the valley.

The school is larger than the one on Rass, not only because there are twice the number of families, but because people here, even more than islanders, tend to count their wealth in children. There is a one-room Presbyterian Church, built of native stone, to which a preacher comes every three weeks when the road is passable. And every fourth Sunday, God and the weather willing, a Catholic priest says mass in the school-house. There are no mines open in our pocket of western Virginia now, but the Polish and Lithuanian miners who were brought down from Pennsylvania

two generations ago stayed and turned their hands to digging fields and cutting pastures out of the hillsides. They are still considered outsiders by the tough Scotch-Irish who have farmed the rocks of the valley floor for nearly two hundred years.

The most pressing health problem is one never encountered on Rass. On Saturday night, five or six of the valley men get blind drunk and beat their wives and children. In the Protestant homes I am told it is a Catholic problem, and in the Catholic homes, a Protestant. The truth, of course, is that the ailment crosses denominational lines. Perhaps it is the fault of the mountains, glowering above us, delaying sunrise and hastening the night. They are as awesome and beautiful as the open water, but the valley people do not seem to notice. Nor are they grateful for the game and timber that the mountains so generously provide. Most of them only see the ungiving soil from which a man must wrestle his subsistence and the barriers that shut him out from the world. These men struggle against their mountains. On Rass men followed the water. There is a difference.

Although the valley people are slow to accept outsiders, they did not hesitate to come to me. They needed my skill.

"Nurse?" An old ruddy-faced farmer was at my door in the middle of the night. "Nurse, would you be kind enough to see to my Betsy? She's having a bad go of it."

I dressed and went with him to his farm to deliver what I thought was a baby. To my amazement, he drove straight past the house to the barn. Betsy was his cow, but neither of us would have been prouder of that out-sized calf had it been a child.

I came to wonder if every disease of man and beast had simply waited for my arrival to invade the valley. My little house, which was also the clinic, was usually jammed, and often there was a jeep waiting at the door to take me to examine a child or a cow or a woman in labor.

The first time I saw Joseph Wojtkiewicz (what my grandmother would have done to that name!), the first time I saw him to know who he was, that is, he arrived in his jeep late one night to ask me to come and treat his son, Stephen. Like most of the valley men, he seemed ill at ease with me, his only conversation during the ride was about the boy who had a severe earache and a fever of 105, which had made his father afraid to bring him out in the cold night air to the clinic.

The Wojtkiewicz house was a neatly built log cabin with four small rooms. There were three children, the six-year-old patient, and his two sisters, Mary and Anna, who were eight and five. The mother had been dead for several years.

The county had sent me an assortment of drugs including a little penicillin, so I was able to give the child a shot. Then an alcohol rubdown to bring the fever down a bit until the drug had time to do its work, a little warm oil to soothe the ear, a word or two to commend bravery, and I was ready to go.

I had repacked my bag and was heading for the door when I realized the boy's father had made coffee for me. It seemed rude not to drink it, so I sat opposite him at his kitchen table, my face set in my most professional smile, mouthing reassurance and unnecessary directions for the child's care.

I became increasingly aware that the man was staring at me, not impolite, but as though he were studying an unknown specimen. At last he said, "Where do you come from?"

"The University of Kentucky," I said. I prided myself on never letting remarks made by patients or their families surprise me.

"No, no," he said. "Not school. Where do you really come from?"

I began to tell him quite matter-of-factly about Rass, where it was, what it looked like, slipping into a picture of how it had been. I hadn't returned to the island since entering nursing school except for two funerals, my grandmother's and the Captain's. Now as I described the marsh as it was when I was a child, I could almost feel the wind on my arms and hear the geese baying like a pack of hounds as they flew over. No one on the mainland had ever invited me to talk about home before, and the longer I talked, the more I wanted to talk, churning with happiness and homesickness at the same time.

The little girls had come into the kitchen and were leaning on either side of their father's chair, listening with the same dark-eyed intensity. Joseph put an arm around each of them, absently stroking the black curls of Anna who was on his right.

At last I stopped, a little shy for having talked so much. I even apologized.

"No, no," he said. "I asked because I wanted to know. I knew there was something different about you. I kept wondering ever since you came. Why would a woman like you, who could have anything she wanted, come to a place like this? Now I understand." He left off stroking his daughter's hair and leaned forward, his big hands open as though he needed their help to explain his meaning. "God in heaven,"—I thought at first it was an oath, it had been so long since I'd heard the expression used in any other way—"God in heaven's been raising you for this valley from the day you were born."

I was furious. He didn't know anything about me or the day I was born or he'd never say such a foolish thing, sitting there so piously at his kitchen table, sounding for all the world like a Methodist preacher.

But then, oh, my blessed, he smiled. I guess from that moment I knew I was going to marry Joseph Wojtkiewicz—God, pope, three motherless children, unspellable surname and all. For when he smiled, he looked like the kind of man who would sing to the oysters.

20

It is far simpler to be married to a Catholic than anyone from my Methodist past would believe. I am quite willing for the children, his, of course, but also ours as they come along, to be raised in the Catholic faith. The priest frets about me when we meet, but he's only around once a month, and Joseph himself has never suggested that I ought to turn Catholic or even religious. My parents showed their approval by making the long trip from Rass to attend our schoolhouse wedding. I will always be glad that my father and Joseph met each other that once, because this year, on the second of October, my father went to sleep in his chair after a day of crabbing and never woke up.

Caroline called me from New York. I couldn't remember ever having heard her cry aloud before, and there she was weeping for the benefit of the entire Truitt village party line. I was unreasonably irritated. She and Call were going down at once and would stay through the funeral. It seemed wrong that she should be able to go and not me I was the child who had fished his crab floats and culled his oysters, but I was so far along in my ninth month that I knew better than anyone how crazy it would be to try such a trip; so Joseph went in my place and got back to the farm four days before our son was born.

We thought he might bring Momma back with him then, but Caroline was making her New Haven debut as Musetta in *La Bohème* on the twenty-first. Our parents had planned to go before my father's death, so Caroline and Call begged her to return with them and stay on through the opening. Since she would be coming to live with us soon, it seemed the right thing for her to do. Joseph did not plead my condition. He was already learning midwifery, and I think my mother understood that he would have been disappointed not to deliver our child himself.

I suppose every mother is reduced to idiocy when describing her firstborn, but, oh, he is a beauty—large and dark like his father, but with the bright blue eyes of the Bradshaws. I swear from his cry that he will be a singer and from his huge hands that he will follow the water, which makes his father laugh aloud and tease me about our son setting sail on the trickle of a stream that crosses our pasture.

The older children adore him, and, as for the valley people, it doesn't matter how often I explain that we named the baby for my father, they are all sure that Truitt is their namesake. Their need for me made them accept me into their lives, but now I feel that they are taking me into their hearts as well.

My work did not, could not, end with my marriage to Joseph and his children or even with the birth of Truitt. There is no one else to care for the valley. The hospital remains two hours away, and the road is impassable for much of the winter.

This year our winter came early. In November I was watching over two pregnancies, one of which I worried about. The mother is a thin, often-beaten girl of about eighteen. From the size of her, I quickly suspected twins and urged her and her husband to go to the hospital in Staunton or Harrisonburg for the delivery.

Despite his bouts of drunkenness, the young husband is well-meaning. He would have taken her, I believe, had there been any money at all. But how could I urge them to make the trip when the hospital might well reject her? And without money where could they stay in the city until the babies actually came? I counted the days and measured her progress as best I could and then sent word to a doctor in Staunton that I would need help with the births. But it snowed twenty inches the day before Essie went into labor, so when they called me, I went alone.

The first twin, a nearly six-pound boy, came fairly easily, depite Essie's slender frame, but the second did not follow as I thought it should. I had begun to fear for it, when I realized that it was very small, but in a breach position. I reached in and turned the twin so that she was delivered head first, but blue as death. Before I even cut the cord, I put my mouth down and breathed into her tiny one. Her chest, smaller than my fist, shuddered, and she gave a cry, but so weak, so like a parting, that I was near despair.

"Is it all right?" Essie asked.

"Small," I said and busied myself cutting and tying off the cord. How cold she was. It sent painful shivers up my arms. I called the grandmother, who had been taking care of the boy, to get me blankets and see to the afterbirth.

I swathed the child tightly and held her against my body. It was like cuddling a stone. I almost ran from the bedroom. What was I to do? They must give me an incubator if they expected me to care for newborn babies in this godforsaken place.

The kitchen was slightly warmer than the bedroom. I went over to the enormous iron stove. A remnant of a fire was banked in the far corner under the stove top. I put my hand on the stove and found it comfortingly warm. I grabbed an iron pot, stuffed it with all the dishrags and towels I could reach with one hand, lay the baby in it, and set it in the oven door. Then I pulled up a kitchen stool and sat there with my hand on the baby's body and watched. It may have been hours. I was too intent to keep track, but, at length, a sort of pinkness invaded the translucent blue skin of her cheek.

"Nurse?" I jumped at the sound. The young father had come into the kitchen. "Nurse, should I go for the priest?" His eyes widened at the sight of the nurse cooking his baby in the oven, but, rather than protest, he repeated his question about fetching the priest.

"How could you on these roads?" I'm sure I sounded impatient. I wanted to be left in peace to guard my baby.

"Should I do it myself?" he asked, apparently alarmed by whatever it was he was suggesting. "Or you could."

"Oh, do be quiet."

"But, Nurse, it must be baptized before it dies."

"She won't die!"

He flinched. I'm sure he found me terrifying. "But, if it did—"

"She will not die." But to keep him quiet and get rid of him, I poured water out of the cold teakettle onto my hand and reached into the oven, placing my hand on the blur of dark hair. "What is her name?"

He shook his head in bewilderment. Apparently, everything was left for me to do. Susan. Susan was the name of a saint, wasn't it? Well, if not, they could have the priest fix it later. "Essie Susan," I said, "I baptize you in the name of the Father and of the Son and of the Holy Ghost. Amen." Under my hand the tiny head stirred.

The father crossed himself, nodded a scared-rabbit kind of thank you, and hurried out to report the sacrament to his wife. Soon the grandmother was in the kitchen.

"Thank you, Nurse. We're grateful to you."

"Where is the other twin?" I asked, suddenly stricken. I had forgotten him. In my anxiety for his sister, I had completely forgotten him. "Where have you put him?"

"In the basket." She looked at me, puzzled. "He's sleeping."

"You should hold him," I said. "Hold him as much as you can. Or let his mother hold him."

She started for the door. "Nurse. Should I baptize him as well?"

"Oh, yes," I said. "Baptize him and then let Essie nurse him."

My own breasts were swollen with milk for Truitt. I knew his father would bring him to me soon, but there was plenty. I took my baby out of the oven and held her mouth to catch the milk which began to flow of its own accord. A perfect tongue, smaller than a newborn kitten's, reached out for the drops of milk on her lips. Then the little mouth rooted against my breast until she had found the nipple for herself.

Hours later, walking home, my boots crunching on the snow, I bent my head backward to drink in the crystal stars. And clearly, as though the voice came from just behind me, I heard a melody so sweet and pure that I had to hold myself to keep from shattering:

I wonder as I wander out under the sky . . .

Phyllis Reynolds Naylor (b. 1933)

Phyllis Reynolds Naylor, a prolific children's book author, is best known for her Newbery Award–winning novel *Shiloh* (1991), about the moral dilemma of a West Virginia boy who befriends and hides an abused dog. Naylor has written for a range of ages from early childhood to young adulthood. In her 1987 young adult novel *The Year of the Gopher,* seventeen-year-old George Richards has the grades to get into a good university. He just is not sure yet what he wants to do. However, his father, a lawyer, is certain that he should be going to an Ivy League school and studying law. George notices how his younger brother is singled out for criticism and his older sister is getting into trouble. But he gets himself into trouble when he decides to take a year off, in defiance of his father, and work in a nursery as a gopher (hence the title). This perceptive novel is about a young man with good sense who has to resist parental pressure in order to figure out what he really wants. Naylor is also the author of the humorous and insightful *Alice* series about a girl whose mother died and who is being raised by her father.

From *The Year of the Gopher*

FOUR

Thirty thousand feet above Lake Ontario, the stewardess gave us lunch—some kind of cold meat with a green sauce on top, and chocolate pudding. While Dad was talking to her, I slipped him all my green sauce. After I tasted the pudding, I slipped him that, too.

"College-hunting, I'll bet," the stewardess said, pouring more coffee for Dad.

He beamed. He gets this certain smile on his face when he talks to a pretty woman. Even his voice sounds different. More gentle. Chivalrous.

"I'm taking him back to my old Alma Mater," he said, hoping, I'll bet, she'd ask which one. Then, before she could get away, he told her. "Harvard," he said.

This time the stewardess smiled down at me.

"Good luck," she said, and I couldn't tell if her eyes were laughing or not.

Dad had said that we could visit three schools, and since he was paying for the trip, he ought to be able to choose two of the three—Harvard and Yale, of course—but that I could choose the third.

"University of Miami," I'd said, without even thinking.

I could tell by the look on Dad's face that the offer didn't extend to Florida.

"Northeastern United States, preferably," Dad said. "What about Brown, Columbia, Cornell, Dartmouth . . . ?"

"Swarthmore," I said. It was the first school that came to mind. I didn't even know where it was.

"Good college" said Dad, but he wasn't exactly turning handsprings. "It's Quaker, though, you know."

"I want to visit Swarthmore," I repeated. Maybe all the professors looked like the man on the oatmeal box, but I had to save face.

"Okay," said Dad. "Pennsylvania we can manage."

We'd started out the trip all right. I'd brought along a deck of cards, and Dad and I played a couple hands of Crazy Eights. You can't sit very long on a plane, though, without someone putting food in front of you, so while Dad ate the meat with the green stuff on top, I thumbed through *The Insider's Guide to Colleges* that I'd picked up at a bookstore before we left. *Written by students, for students—what the colleges are really like,* it said on the cover.

I suppose the guidebook said some good things about Harvard, but that wasn't what I was looking for. I ran my finger down the first paragraph:

. . . The Harvard insignia is associated with power, prestige, and wealth. . . . This leads us to the obvious conclusion that Harvard is an elitist university for the elite. . . .

Then I found a paragraph on the next page that really cracked me up. "Hey, Dad," I said, nudging him, "read this."

. . . But the feeling that there are basically three types of students on campus (wonks, jocks, and preppies) seems to be as accurate as ever. Wonks are the nerds who, given a choice between a night in the library and a pair of tickets to the World Series, select the former. Jocks are those who would give up eleven term credits for tickets to a game in the American Soccer League (with a few beers thrown in). Preppies are just that, the Exeter and St. Paul graduates who walk around in Brooks Brothers cords and L.L. Bean hunting boots.

The problem with all students here is that they are taught to think, talk, and act in a certain way: obnoxious, superior, and self-confident. So they do. . . .

I don't know why I thought Dad would laugh.

"Whoever wrote that is an ass," he said. "I went through Harvard Law School and never saw a wonk in my life."

After an hour or so, I reached down to put the *Insider's Guide* in my gym bag under the seat, and noticed an envelope that Mom must have stuck in.

To read on the plane, she had written on the front. I opened the envelope and pulled out a quiz she had clipped from a magazine.

You'd think that Mom, being a teacher, would be sick of tests. She's not. She loves them. She takes every quiz in sight, putting her answers on a separate sheet of paper so she can pass the tests on to Jeri and me: *The Great American Values Test; Your Leadership Potential; Your Hostility Profile; Are You a Romantic?*

. . . The do-it-yourself test Mom had chosen for me to take on the trip was called *Your Introvert-Extrovert Ratio: How It Can Affect Your Career.*

While Dad was settling back with a crossword puzzle, I looked the quiz over:

For every one of the questions below, circle the response that most often applies to you:

1. When entering a roomful of strangers, I:
   A. Single out one person and start a conversation
   B. Smile and wait until I am approached
   C. Head for the bar
   D. Find an excuse to leave
2. My idea of an enjoyable evening is:
   A. A large party with many new faces
   B. A small dinner with friends
   C. An intimate evening with one person
   D. A few hours alone doing the things I love
3. When called upon to speak in public. . . .

I crammed the test into the ashtray of my armrest and turned my attention to the window. I was remembering back to ninth grade, when I had to give a talk in Oral Communication—some dumb thing like "How to Trace Your Family Tree." The evening before the talk, I had a panic attack. I told Dad I didn't think I could do it.

"Look at it this way," Dad had said. "If you were going to address the Minnesota Bar Review, you just might have reason to shake a little. But of all the speeches being given in the city tomorrow, yours is probably the least important. Of all the speeches being given in the state of Minnesota, yours is the least significant. Of all the speeches being given in the United States, yours hardly amounts to a gurgle. . . ."

By the time Dad got to the United Nations, my speech was merely a speck of dust in the cosmos, so I'd told him it obviously didn't make any difference whether I gave it or not.

I gave the speech.

The pilot's voice came over the intercom and said we would be landing at Boston's Logan Airport in ten minutes. The stewardess came by to collect our trays, Dad straightened his tie, and I clutched the armrests as we made our descent and prepared for my interview at Harvard.

By six that evening, we were sitting in a seat on Amtrak, heading for New Haven. Dad and I were barely speaking.

"You walked in there with a chip on your shoulder," he said at last.

I'd been reading more of *The Insider's Guide,* mostly to keep from talking to Dad. *One crucial point,* it said, *keep your parents at least a thousand feet and preferably a thousand miles away from the interview session. . . .*

"How do you know?" I asked him.

"I was watching from down the hall. You walked in with your shoulders slumped and that hangdog look on your face. Might as well have worn a sign saying 'kick me.'"

"They weren't exactly friendly," I answered.

"It's all an *act!*" Dad said earnestly. "They just want to see how you respond."

"Could have fooled me," I told him.

Dad opened the pages of his *Wall Street Journal,* then closed them again. "Did you tell them that I'm an alumnus?"

"*You* told them that, Dad. How else do you think I got the interview? The man said he hardly ever conducts an interview before he's seen the application."

"So whose fault is that?" Dad countered. "We've been after you for weeks to get those applications in the mail."

"Look!" I said. "It was your idea to fly out here, not mine. I'm not *ready* for an interview. I've got a lot more thinking to do."

"So do your thinking later!" Dad said in exasperation. I could tell he was getting really sick of me. "Nobody's asking you to decide anything right this minute. All you have to do is apply, get the ball rolling." He opened the *Wall Street Journal* again, giving the pages a hard shake, cracking them into position. "Life's going to pass you by, George. Opportunity's going to take one look at you and go the other way."

We fell into silence again. I tried to picture it, me sitting in the grass somewhere and this big yellow box labeled "opportunity" stopping to look me over. I must have been smiling because Dad cracked his newspaper again, even louder, and I wiped the smile off my face, folded my hands over my stomach, and watched the lights whiz by in the growing darkness beyond the window.

The interview at Harvard hadn't gone well at all. It was one of those situations where the harder you try not to say something stupid, the more stupid it sounds when you say it. There was one awful moment, after I'd been asked how I spent last summer and what books I'd read lately, when the man just grew silent. Just sat there looking at me, and I was staring down at this thread on the sleeve of my jacket, wondering whether or not to pull it. I realized I was sitting with one foot resting on top of the other, too, like a country hick, but I knew if I moved it then he'd be sure to notice. I thought of a dozen things to say to break the silence, but they all seemed too stupid for words.

I had just taken hold of the thread and was ready to give it a yank when the man said, "What do you consider your worst faults?"

Oh, God, I'd thought. *Sitting there like a brick was one. Wearing a blue blazer with threads at the seam was another. The Insider's Guide* said that the most important thing about the interview was to give the other guy a good time. *If you can make the interviewer laugh or interest him with your unorthodox or forthright views,* it said, *you have a good chance of success.*

When he asked my worst faults, I could have looked at my watch and quipped, "How much time do you have?" and made him laugh.

I could have said, "This week or last?"

Instead, I pulled hard at the thread on my jacket, puckering the cloth along the seam, and said, "I guess I'd have to think about that one awhile." Like I'm so perfect or something.

The interview was over after that. The guy shook my hand and said he was glad to meet me and how I should remember there were a whole lot of good schools out there besides Harvard and that it wouldn't be the end of the world if I didn't get in.

I already knew that I didn't belong. It was like all the people I saw had these big brains pressing against the insides of their skulls. The professors all looked busy and brilliant, hurrying off to some international conference or something, and I just knew if I said "hello," they'd answer me in Latin.

I didn't go for an interview at Yale. In New Haven the next morning, Dad and I just walked around looking at the Gothic buildings with their turrets and spires, and the huge iron gates of the courtyards that probably clanked shut each night, like a prison. CLASS OF 1773, it read on a statue of Nathan Hale,

and engraved around the top of the pedestal were the words, "I only regret that I have but one life to lose for my country." I stood there looking at Nathan, with his wrinkled shirt and scuffed shoes. Put him in Levi's and he bore an uncanny resemblance to me. I wondered if Dad noticed.

"Fine young man," Dad murmured beside me.

I swallowed as we started off again. Part of me was furious at Dad for arranging this stupid trip. Another part was grateful that he cared. Despite the fiasco at Harvard, he was making a super effort to get along. He'd wanted this to be a good time for us both—two old buddies going off to look over the old colleges; wanted to get back some of the camaraderie we used to have. I knew it for sure when, in a coffee shop near campus that noon, Dad said, "Now there's a foxy chick."

I swallowed a bite of hamburger and hoped nobody heard. I hadn't heard anybody call a girl a "foxy chick" since fourth grade. Slowly I turned and looked where Dad was looking. A dark-haired girl sat at a table by the window pulling the toothpicks out of her club sandwich. She had on three different shirts, each one larger than the next, in shades of orange and yellow. There was a purplish scarf draped loosely around her neck, the kind of casual toss that somehow you know she spent ten minutes in front of the mirror getting right. She had a sort of ethereal look about her that told me she was reading a collection of French sonnets. I didn't belong at Yale either. That wasn't my life, it was Dad's. *I only regret that I have but one life to live for my father.* As soon as I'd finished my hamburger, I said, like a sullen ingrate, "Can we go? Are we through?"

We headed for the airport for a plane to Philadelphia, where we'd rent a car and drive to Swarthmore.

"You know," Dad said as we waited in line at the ticket counter, "it wouldn't hurt to see Princeton while we're here in the East. Wouldn't be much out of the way at all."

Something seemed to grow heavier inside my chest, pressing against my ribs. I could feel the throb of pulse in my temples.

"I don't want to see Princeton," I said darkly. "I don't even want to see Swarthmore. I didn't want to come in the first place. It was all your idea."

I never saw Dad look at me the way he did then. It was a hurt, questioning look, and I was on the verge of apologizing when it was our turn at the counter. Dad's face suddenly frosted over.

"Two tickets to Minneapolis," he said. "How do we get there from here?"

I don't think we said anything at all on the way home. Dad worked on some papers he'd brought along in a briefcase, and I sat beside him pretending to sleep, but it was only because I didn't have anything to read. *The Insider's Guide* had already caused enough trouble. I would even have taken the quiz Mom sent, just for something to do, if I'd still had it.

I knew I had been ungrateful. Dad had taken three days off work, which was a sacrifice you wouldn't believe. I felt miserable, but something told me that if I didn't stand up to him now, I'd be lost. If I let him put me on the old railroad, I'd never get off, and before you knew it, Jeri and Ollie would be on it, too. Somebody had to look out for them. Especially for Ollie.

I guess I worry about Ollie more than anyone else in our family. Jeri's smart—brain-smart, I mean—but Ollie's different. I don't think you could call him dumb, exactly—just slow. Once he catches onto something, he's got it and doesn't forget, but it takes him a while to understand.

Mom says it's his attention span. She says he lets his eyes wander when he's supposed to be reading, and if he looks up every time someone enters the room, it's bound to take him all night to read a chapter. Dad says Ollie just doesn't "apply himself." I don't know. I've watched the kid study—the way he frowns down at the book, twists a lock of hair around and around his finger, squirms, sighs. . . . He tries. He really does. But "slow" isn't a word that Mom and Dad can accept.

Dad reached up and adjusted the light above his seat, then went on working. He was holding a contract of some kind, in small print, the sort of thing that would take me a couple of hours to read. But Dad just breezed along, making checks in the margin here and there with a red pen.

I suppose the two smartest people in our family are Dad and Trish. Patricia, in fact, is about Most Perfect Everything: Most Perfect Daughter, Most Perfect Student, Most Perfect Teenager, Most Perfect Bride. . . . Especially Most Perfect Bride.

The wedding had Mom mesmerized for five months. It was scheduled for May, but the moment the engagement announcement appeared in the *Minneapolis Tribune,* the preparations went into high gear. Every few weeks Trish had to fly back from New York for another fitting or something, and Mom even commissioned Aunt Sylvia to make a needlepoint pillow for the ring-bearer. It had a satin ruffle around the edge and two satin ribbons sewn on top to tie the ring on so it wouldn't fall off. But get this: the ring was fake. The best man would keep the real ring in his pocket. Seven weeks of needlepoint just so some four-year-old cousin could walk down the aisle holding a pillow with a fake ring.

Meanwhile, Trish was trying to finish her second year of college, and we found out she'd been battling an ulcer all semester. The day after finals, she flew home, saw the doctor, got a prescription, and the following day she was married.

The stewardess came by and asked Dad if he'd like a drink.

"No, thanks," he said, and went on working. Any other time he would have turned to me and said, "How about you, George? Want a Coke or something?" This time it was like I wasn't even there. The stewardess looked at me, and I just shook my head. The plane droned on, heading back to Minnesota in the dark.

I was thinking about the champagne we drank at Trish's wedding.

"You ought to offer a toast to your sister," Dad had told me behind the stephanotis, just after he'd said how happy he was and how he wished she had waited till she'd graduated, both in the same breath. So after everyone sat down at the tables with the cream-colored roses in the center, I stood up to make a toast, but nobody noticed. I picked up my butter knife and hit it against the side of my water glass a couple times. The room grew still.

"To the happy couple," I'd said, raising my champagne glass. "I . . . uh . . . guess the traditional thing to say is that I'm not losing a sister, I'm gaining a brother-in-law." The guests laughed politely, but I felt something cold on my shoe. I moved my foot. "Well," I said, "I've known Trish ever since she was a little girl

. . ." More laughter. ". . . and I want to say that Roger couldn't be marrying a nicer person." Something cold was running down my pant leg. I looked. There was a puddle of water on the table, trickling over the edge in a steady stream. I realized I had cracked my glass with the butter knife. "To Trish and Roger," I said. "Here's wishing them the best of luck." I sat down before I realized there was water on my chair as well.

A week after the wedding, Ollie and I had sat out on the porch eating lunch and looking at Trish's wedding picture in the paper. Ollie had leaned on my shoulder, his jaws moving against my shirt as he chewed his sandwich. I was reading about how the bride's father was senior partner in the law firm of Richards, Barnes, and Marks. "She is the granddaughter of Horace L. Richards, founder of the firm," the paper said, "and grand-niece of the late Elberta Hampton, on her mother's side, who was, for seven years, the president of the Women's Historical Society of Greater Minneapolis."

The writeup had said that Trish was a student at Cornell University where her husband had graduated *summa cum laude.*

"What's that mean?" Ollie had asked, pointing to the words and leaving a trace of peanut butter on the page, for which Mom would kill him.

"It's Latin," I'd said. "With highest honors."

Ollie continued to point to the Latin words, one at a time. "With," he repeated, pointing to *summa,* "highest," pointing to *cum,* "honors," pointing to *laude.*

"No, actually it reads, 'highest with praise,'" I'd told him, "but we just call it, 'with highest honors.'"

Ollie had looked at me blankly, then wiped his hand across his mouth. "That's why I get mixed up," he said. "Words never say what they mean, do they, George?"

Dad put his papers away finally, closed his briefcase, and leaned back against the seat. I couldn't tell if his eyes were closed or not. He was very quiet, and I knew what he was thinking.

I don't care, I told myself. *I'm doing it for Ollie.*

SIX

I didn't much care what happened the last half of my senior year. I already had the credits I needed to graduate, so I just coasted. A lot of us did. Our SAT scores, along with last semester's grades, had already been forwarded to the colleges we'd applied to, and unless we really bombed out our last semester, our final grades wouldn't make much difference. It felt sort of useless going to school at all, but I went out of habit, just like I still ate meals with the family out of habit. Table conversations were usually between Mom and Dad or me and Ollie, though we all talked to Typhus when the silence got to be too much. It was as though plexiglass walls had been erected there on the table, dividing us into cubicles. We could see each other, but we didn't communicate. We knew the walls were there, but we weren't sure why or what to do about them.

Mom threw herself into her work, sponsoring her school's science fair, and Dad was representing some big firm uptown that was supposed to have filed a fraudulent tax return. Dinner conversation usually revolved around that.

Sometimes, on weekends, if Ollie wasn't being punished for another assignment he didn't do— *couldn't do,* maybe—I'd take him to a movie or bowling. Try to give the kid some fun. But I could see that, little by little, he was just giving up. He knew that should he, by some miracle, pass Introductory Spanish II, he'd only have Spanish One and Two to take in high school, followed by Spanish Three and Four, algebra, geometry, physics, and calculus. He started blinking his eyes when he talked.

"Ollie, you need a change of contacts or something?" Dad asked him. "What's wrong with your eyes?"

"I don't know," said Ollie.

"Do they hurt? Itch?"

Ollie shook his head.

"Well, try to pay attention to what you're doing. When you feel the need to blink, do something else instead."

"What do you suggest, Dad—a nervous cough?" I threw in, the first time I'd spoken to him in a month.

Dad gave me an icy look, and I returned the stare. It was as cold at our table as it was outside.

"Just hang in there, Ollie," I said later. "Something will happen."

Something did.

Around the middle of March, the seniors started hearing from colleges. Discount got accepted at Carnegie-Mellon, and the guys took a six-pack over to his house to celebrate. The first of our gang to make the break. We gave him the old handshake and the slap on the back and all, but at the same time, Pittsburgh seemed one heck of a ways away.

In the next two weeks, almost all the seniors heard from at least one of their schools, and every day someone else had an acceptance or rejection to talk about at lunchtime.

Columbia was the first college to write to me. *Dear applicant,* the form letter read, *we regret to inform you . . .* I left the letter on the coffee table where the folks would find it and went up in my room to watch Bill Cosby.

"I know you must be disappointed," Mom said later when I came down for the Keebler chocolate-covered grahams, "but it's only one school. I'm not even sure I'd want you living in New York anyway."

I murmured something and took the cookies up to my room.

Princeton's letter came a day later. *Dear Mr. Richards: After careful consideration, the admissions office is sorry to tell you that . . .*

Mom was indignant. "Well, New Jersey you can do without, too," she said. "You know where I see you, George? In one of those New England colleges, with the fall leaves and the lacrosse games, the skiing. . . . Did you know that tourists have to reserve rooms a *year* in advance if they want to stay in Vermont in the fall?"

"No," I said. "I didn't know that."

Harvard and Yale came exactly on the same day, and I'd swear they were written by the same person: *Dear Prospective Student: It is with real regret that we inform you . . .*

Dad studied the letter from Harvard for a long time. "Well," he said, "it was that interview, no doubt about it. The minute I saw you walk in there with your shoulders slumped . . ." Mom gave him a look, and he stopped.

"You can always go your first two years somewhere else and then transfer," she told me. "Students do that all the time. Once the schools know you're serious, they'll reconsider. Have you heard from Dartmouth yet?"

I shook my head.

Dartmouth came around the first of April, followed by Brown and Cornell a few days later. *Dear Mr. Richards: Dear Sir: Dear Applicant. . . .*

Mother faced me in the living room one afternoon when she got in. She was holding the latest rejection and hadn't even taken her coat off.

"George, I simply can't understand this. Your combined SAT scores were over 1300 and you're twenty-sixth in a class of three hundred fifty."

"I don't know, Mom," I said, and spread the sports section out on my lap.

She stared at me some more. "Most of them didn't even bother to answer personally. You would *think,* after all the work involved in those applications, they could at least call you something besides 'applicant.'"

"Well, some of them did, anyway," I told her.

An acceptance came from the University of Minnesota.

"I didn't even know you'd applied there," said Dad.

"My ace in the hole," I told him.

By April 15, however, the last of the Ivy Leagues had answered, a rejection by the University of Pennsylvania. It was unanimous.

"My gosh!" said Jeri at the dinner table. "If George can't get in any of the Ivy Leagues, how will I?"

"You won't have any trouble," I told her. "Your grades are better than mine."

"Not *that* much better," Jeri commented. Strangely, she and I were talking again.

"You going to college in Minneapolis, George?" Ollie asked hopefully.

"Looks that way," I told him.

Mom and Dad said nothing. The salt and pepper were passed back and forth across the table along with the Worcestershire sauce. Mom hadn't even changed out of her school clothes. Sometimes, when she's really upset, she forgets to change. Dad's face had that wired look again. His lips opened only wide enough to admit his fork, then clamped shut like a Venus fly trap.

I took Ollie with me that evening to weight-lift at Psycho's. We read in *Muscle Fitness* magazine that weight-lifting doesn't stunt your growth after all, so I was starting Ollie out on a program to build up his biceps and traps where it would be noticed the most. We'd work on the rest later. Psycho gave him an old T-shirt with the words "Live Bait" on the front, and we worked him for an hour or so. Afterward Ollie's legs were wobbly, but he smiled all the way home. Couldn't stop smiling.

When we stepped inside, though, Mom and Dad weren't smiling. They were sitting side by side on the couch with a handful of papers spread out on the coffee table. Jeri was sitting over on the stairs, as though ready to flee the room at any moment. At first I thought Jeri was in some kind of trouble. Then, when I saw the look on Dad's face, I knew it was me. Even now, I don't think I could describe that look—a mixture of disappointment and rage. Disbelief, maybe.

"Sit down," he said.

"What's wrong?"

"I said sit down!" he roared, and I sat. By the time my hands had touched my knees, however, I knew what was the matter.

"You've been in my desk," I said to Mom.

"Yes, I have," Mom said, and her voice shook. "I did something I've never done before, and I know I shouldn't have, but I had to find out."

I didn't answer.

"Find out what?" ventured Ollie.

Mother picked up a sheet of yellow tablet paper with handwriting on one side: "'How College Life Mirrors the World at Large,'" she read. "'This question amply illustrates the fact that there are as many boneheads on campus as there are off. The world is full of pretentious people, and the author of this question obviously thought that he could intimidate prospective students by requiring an essay on a subject that is as ridiculous as it is pompous.'" Mother stopped reading and looked straight at me. "Shall I go on?"

I didn't answer. I don't know why I'd kept my scribbled drafts. So I could gloat over them after I'd sent off the typed copies?

She started to read some more, then put that paper down and picked up another: "'If I could alleviate one of mankind's most pressing problems, I would put men in skirts, because the pressing problem which needs alleviating most is the ironing of men's trousers. . . .'"

"What a jerk!" Jeri murmured from the stairs.

"Did you really think this was amusing?" Mom asked me. "That you could get admitted to a prestigious college by such smart-aleck jokes? That they would admire your cleverness and originality?"

Dad couldn't control himself any longer: "Did you even *think?*" he bellowed, leaning forward, the veins on his neck standing out. I sat stiffly on the chair across from him, my knees trembling with tension, vaguely wondering if this could give him a coronary. Fear alternated with anger inside my chest. Before I could answer, Dad picked up another sheet of tablet paper and began reading: "'Why did I choose this university? I didn't. My Dad arranged for an interview I didn't want, to a school I never picked, that is full of wealthy snots I couldn't like in a million years.'" Dad's hand was shaking with rage. I'd never seen him so angry. My own anger began to travel up my body like the mercury in a thermometer—past my collar bone and up my throat. "Do you realize how deeply you've embarrassed me?" Dad said.

To tell the truth, I had forgotten exactly what I'd written on the applications, except that for the University of Minnesota, I'd played it straight. It had never occurred to me that Mom would go through my desk—that they would try to figure out *why* no Ivy League school had accepted me. If it had, I would have had my speech all ready. Now, I had to wing it; all I had to go on was feelings.

"*Why,* George?" Mom was saying. "Why did you do it?"

"Because I didn't want to go," I told her. My teeth felt as though they were clamped together, as though my jaws had locked. I actually had trouble talking. Little pains shot up the side of my cheek.

"You got on that plane with me knowing you were going to pull something like this?" Dad asked. "You went through that charade of visiting those schools, secretly sabotaging things at every turn?"

"George, if you didn't want to go, why didn't you just say so?" Mom asked.

"I said it every way I knew how, but you weren't listening," I told her, and now *I* was shouting. My voice didn't sound like mine at all, though—hollow and high, like someone in a tower. Ollie stared at me as if I were somebody else. Jeri, sitting back on the stairs, didn't move a muscle. All eyes were on me. "You don't care about me, you don't care about my education, you only care how it makes *you* look!" I said.

"That was totally uncalled for," said Mother, and there were tears in her eyes.

In order not to see the tears, to not even think about them, I went on yelling: "*Somebody* had to make the break. I'm not going to end up at an Ivy League school with a bottle of Maalox just to please you and Dad."

"George, that's unfair!"

But I was unstoppable now. The words came tumbling out: "Take a good look, Mom. Trish is having stomach problems, Ollie's got a tic. . . ."

"George!"

"Somebody had to break the chain. And you want to know something else? I'm not going to college at all next year. Not even the University of Minnesota."

Dad slowly got to his feet, as though he didn't quite trust himself not to rush me. "Okay, you've said it," he said, and his words seemed like chunks of concrete clunking to the floor. "You're my son, and I'm responsible for your food, shelter, and medical care, but beyond that, you're on your own. You want to live your life without any help from me, you've got it. Anything you want beyond the mere necessities, you buy yourself. Is that understood?"

"Yes," I said, my heart still pounding. "Understood."

"Good," Dad said. He turned and strode out of the room, his legs moving rigidly from the hip sockets as though the knees wouldn't bend.

Mom slowly straightened the papers and finally she stood up, too.

"George, how could you?" she said bitterly, and without waiting for an answer, followed Dad out of the room.

My eyes met Ollie's. They were large and scared. I wanted to say something to him about how I hoped this would make things easier for him and Jeri, but it sounded too righteous somehow. I crossed the room and started up the stairs where Jeri was still sitting in exactly the same position she'd been before. She was staring up at me, a dazed expression on her face. She drew her legs up tight to let me pass, and I went in my room and lay on my back till it was time for bed.

When the May issue of the school newspaper came out, it carried the names of all the seniors and what they planned to do after graduation:

Marshall Evans, University of Minnesota . . . David Hahn, Oberlin College . . . Bud Irving, Carnegie-Mellon . . . George Richards, work.

SEVEN

I was living at home, with meals provided, but I still felt like a pioneer. It was uncharted territory; nothing had ever happened like this in our family before.

At first I figured I could get by with working funerals at Saunders. After all, I'd been paying my expenses all along, hadn't I? Then I kept track of everything I bought for a week—T-shirt, watchband, pizza, haircut, English Leather deodorant stick, gas, Clearasil, windshield wipers, bowling. . . . I was surprised how much it came to, and I realized I couldn't use Dad's charge accounts anymore. I put off buying some new Adidas sneakers. Put off buying a record album. My old Chevy needed an oil change, so I got that, but what if it needed a tuneup? Then, when Dad handed me the bill for my car insurance instead of paying it himself, I knew I had to be able to count on more than the possibility that someone would be buried over the weekend.

I knew, too, that right now I saw it as a challenge. The old adrenaline was working overtime—me against Dad. When September came, though, and the guys went off to college, I was going to be in limbo. I'd been all set to enter the U. of M. come fall, but once I said I wouldn't, there was no backing down.

I needed a job, a nine-to-five job. I could still do funerals on weekends.

For three days the last week in May, I skipped school to go job hunting. Each morning after the others left, I circled the possibilities in the want ads and started calling.

"Experience?" they all asked. Parking cars for a funeral home didn't seem to count. I was offered a telephone solicitation job, one of those deals where you go down the numbers in the telephone book and try to finish your spiel before they hang up on you. The guy kept telling me how much I could earn and how I could do it in the comfort of my own home. I knew better. I'd hung up on a few myself.

I managed to get two interviews, one with a carpet-cleaning company and the other with a fencing contractor. The carpet man said he'd call me if he decided to take me on, not to call him. And after I'd driven clear over to St. Paul, the fencing contractor said he couldn't hire me because he knew I wouldn't stay— I'd only stick with the job till I went off to college in September.

"I'm not going to college in September," I told him.

He looked me over. "What's your dad do for a living?"

I hesitated. Then I told him.

"Yeah, you're not going to college and I'm the attorney-general," he said. And he waved me out.

By the first of June I still didn't have anything lined up and I was feeling desperate. Discount was lifeguard at the municipal pool; Psycho was working for his uncle; Dave was clerking in a hardware store; and even Jeri had a job, dipping ice cream at Bridgeman's. I told myself I'd say yes to the first place that wanted to hire me.

It was the Green Thumb Garden Center that took me on.

"Well, now, I'll tell you," said the owner. "I'm looking for someone who's willing to do just about anything we've got. A gopher, that's what I need."

I stared at him blankly.

"This is going to be a little different from standing outside a funeral parlor," Mr. Fletcher said.

I nodded.

"I'll start you out at minimum wage, and raise you fifty cents by the end of summer if you stay on. Another fifty by Christmas. You've got to dress in old enough clothes that you can haul fifty-pound sacks of fertilizer off a truck, but not so old you scare the customers if you're working the cash register."

"I'm hired?" I said, scarcely believing.

"Got you down for the day after graduation," he said. "June seventeenth."

"Got a job," I said that night at Psycho's, grinning. "Out at the Green Thumb. Minimum wage, but I get a fifty-cent raise at the end of summer."

"Doing what?" asked Discount.

I tried to remember exactly what Fletcher had told me. "He called it something crazy . . . an animal . . . a groundhog, I think."

Psycho gave me a puzzled look. "A groundhog?"

"He said I'd be doing just about anything they had to do."

"Sure it wasn't a gopher?" asked Discount.

"Yeah! That was it! How'd you know? A gopher!"

Discount and Psycho fell over the bench press, laughing.

"Go-for, you ninny!" Discount yelped. "He means 'go for this,' 'go for that.'"

I felt like a moron, but I also felt good. I was going to show Dad I could make it on my own. Well, almost on my own. From then on, however, I wasn't George anymore. "Gopher," the guys called me.

I didn't wear a 17-inch collar by the week of the prom; it was barely a 16, but I'll admit I looked pretty nice in the tux. Discount, Dave, and I were all going to pick up our dates in separate cars, meet at Murray's Restaurant for dinner, then drive to the prom from there so we'd each have his own car afterward. Psycho, of course, wasn't going. He kept saying all week he'd invited some girl from another school, and the day of the prom he said she was sick. It's a good thing, too, because I bet five dollars he wouldn't show, Dave bet that he would, and Discount bet that he'd show but bring his cousin.

Discount's tux was really awesome—all white, white shoes, the works—with a red cummerbund. Dave had rented a gray tux and a silk top hat, while I chose a midnight blue with tails.

Discount's mom whistled when she went by the door and saw us parading about Bud's room, trying them on.

"You guys are going to knock 'em dead," she told us, and checked to make sure the cuffs came where they were supposed to be, the creases perfect.

Right at that moment I wished I had a mother who would say "knock 'em dead" to me. I couldn't imagine Mom ever saying that; it wasn't in her vocabulary. Dave gave Mrs. Irving a wide smile as she left, and I wondered if he was thinking the same thing. His mom and little sister live across town, and Dave drops by every weekend, but it's not the same as having your mom in the house.

The reason I went to the prom with Maureen Kimball was that I kept comparing every girl to Karen Gunderson, and nobody measured up. There was one girl in homeroom who was a close second, but she had a boyfriend at the University and was taking him. So I asked Maureen. She didn't even act surprised—almost seemed as though she knew I'd take her.

The prom sure put a hole in my budget. The tuxedo rental, the tickets, and the corsage came to a hundred bucks right there. Dinner, another sixty. Every time I turned around, there was something else to buy. Dave said that his dad wanted to take photos of all three couples before the dance, so at least we wouldn't have the expense of photos there at the prom.

That afternoon, after Dave and I had picked up the flowers, we passed a drugstore and Dave slipped inside.

"One more stop," he said, so I ambled in after him. Dave was looking over the assortment of condoms there on a rack next to pipe tobacco.

I stared at him.

"Just want to pick up a box," he said.

I pretended I was looking at the tobacco, but my eyes kept drifting back to the condoms. On every box there was a misty photo of a couple in water. A guy and gal standing in a lake with their arms around each other, kissing. . . . A couple smiling at each other on a sailboat. . . . A man and woman walking out into the surf holding hands. . . . You'd think they were spawning or something. *For feeling in love,* it said on one box. *Golden transparent,* said another. *For her pleasure—the ribbed condom with the lubra-tip.*

I could feel my neck getting hot.

Dave chose two boxes of the golden transparent and plunked them down on the counter. The clerk rang them up without batting an eye. When we got outside, Dave handed one of the boxes to me.

"Live a little," he said.

"I don't think I need that," I told him.

"Well, keep it, just in case," he said. "You never know. Better safe than sorry."

Back in my room, I crammed two condoms behind the driver's license in my wallet. You didn't usually have a wallet with you when you went out in the water with a girl, but didn't I know what else to do with them?

It was warm that night—for Minneapolis, anyway. I was ready by seven-fifteen. Ollie had shined my shoes to such a luster they reflected the dark blue of my tails. I'd washed my car but forgotten to vacuum the inside, so I paid Ollie to do it while I dressed.

"You look very nice," Mom said as I took Maureen's corsage from the refrigerator. Dad aimed a weak smile in my direction.

"Thanks," I said.

She followed me to the door. "Are we going to see Maureen?" she asked tentatively. "Do you want us to take a picture of the two of you?"

"We've got that all arranged," I said. "See you later." I clattered down the steps, grinned at Ollie, who stood holding the car door open, the nozzle of the vacuum in his other hand, and took off.

I didn't especially enjoy driving away without waving at Mom, didn't like not sharing more with my parents. But every time guilt got the best of me and I made some small gesture to patch things up, they seemed cold and distant. Then, after they'd thought better of it and were nice to me in turn, I was mad again and not speaking. We just never seemed to connect.

Maureen was waiting for me at the door, and she didn't even look like the same person. She was wearing a silver dress with the back bare to the waist, little spaghetti straps over the shoulders.

"Wow!" I said appreciatively. Her red hair was piled on top her head except for one long curl that hung down at the side, and there were silver earrings shaped like snowflakes in her ears.

"Like it?" Maureen asked.

"You look great," I told her.

"Have fun, you two," her mother said. Just before we left, Maureen pulled a large wicker basket from the hall closet and handed it to me.

"Picnic," she said, smiling.

I looked at the basket. "I thought I was taking you to dinner."

Maureen tugged impatiently at my arm. "You are, silly. I mean afterward. My treat."

I put her basket in the trunk, and when we got to Dave's, Bud's car was already there. It didn't occur to me until we were all lined up in front of the mantel, the girls in long dresses, guys behind them, that this was the first time I had ever been in Dave Hahn's living room. First time I'd entered his house.

Mr. Hahn had the camera on a tripod.

"Dave, it's really nice of your dad to do this for us," said his date, a dark-haired girl in a red dress.

"It's his job," Dave said. "He does weddings, bar mitzvahs, commercial photography, you name it. . . ."

And then I realized that Mr. Hahn was a professional photographer. He was a man with a job, a firm, a house, a son. . . . He wasn't just a homosexual. Funny about labels.

"Now if the young lady on the end will move in just a little," Mr. Hahn said, smiling. "That's it. Now the gentleman in the middle—raise your chin just a bit. Good. Perfect!"

Mr. Hahn's male friend was standing in the doorway to the living room holding a cup of coffee, watching the proceedings. He was about the same age as my dad. It occurred to me that he had a job of some kind, too—wasn't just a label.

Mr. Hahn stepped back from the camera, holding a cable release in his hand. "Okay, now, I want you all to think about school, studying, final exams," he intoned.

We all groaned.

"Now think about *sum*-mer!" he said.

We sent up a cheer. The shutter clicked. He took another and another. A picture of the girls together, the guys together, then each couple separately.

"Could I order a print of each?" Discount asked him. "I'll be glad to pay."

"It's on the house," said Dave's father. "Glad to do it."

We had a good time at the restaurant. The girls kept teasing Discount about his white tux, insisting there was a gravy stain on the lapel, or that he had caught his sleeve in the butter. Maureen passed up the shrimp cocktail, which helped out my budget, but didn't order the least expensive thing on the menu either, and make me feel like a cheapskate. She was looking more attractive to me all the time.

When we got to the Calhoun Beach Club about ten, it seemed as though the entire senior class had come—all except Psycho, of course. Karen Gunderson was there in a pale green dress that hugged her body, outlining her hip bones, and she and Bob Ellis had eyes only for each other. During the slow numbers, I turned Maureen so I could watch Karen—drink her in with my eyes. It didn't make sense holding one girl in my arms and thinking about another, but some things don't run on logic.

About eleven o'clock, when the band took a break, we went outside and followed some of the couples down to Lake Calhoun. A guy named Wally Baisinger had his dad's boat for the evening, a thirty-two-foot cruiser, and you could look down into the cabin and see where Wally and his date ate their champagne supper before the prom. Wally was inviting some of his friends aboard for a cruise on the lake, and Dave Hahn

and his date got on. I took Maureen back to the Beach Club, and we danced a few more numbers.

It was supposed to last till one o'clock, but at midnight, Maureen looked up at me and said, "Let's go. I promised you a picnic."

"Sure you don't want to stay around a little longer?" I asked.

"I'm sure," she said. "What about you?"

"Bring on the picnic," I said.

The place she had in mind was within walking distance, she told me. I got the wicker basket out of the trunk, and we started down the path. Out on the water, we could see the lights of a few boats, and I wondered which one was Wally's.

It was a half-hour's walk, actually, to the place Maureen was going; there was a three-quarters moon that illuminated the way. Maureen held her shoes in her hand and went barefoot. When we reached the fence around Lakewood Cemetery, she said, "This is it." There was even an opening to crawl through.

"You been here before?" I asked her.

"Not with you," came her answer.

Lakewood Cemetery had everything you could want—winding paths, a pond, hilly places, and dark grottoes in the trees. We chose a secluded spot where the damp grass gave way to the crunch of dry pine needles. Maureen sat down and opened her basket.

She'd thought of everything. There was a blanket, a tiny lantern with a candle in it, matches, a bottle of wine, cheese, crackers, olives, strawberries the size of plums, and some kind of lemony cake. There was also a bottle of mosquito repellent.

"Boy, you come prepared!" I laughed. She smiled and spread a cloth on the blanket while I opened the wine.

We could see only well enough to find the food. Maureen's face was just a blur in the shadows, and we sat cross-legged on the blanket across from each other. Now and then leaves rustled somewhere above us or the distant noise of traffic on Lake Street drifted through, but mostly we listened to the sound of our own chewing. I sort of wished we had a radio. Music. Something.

"This was a great idea," I told her.

"It always seems such an anticlimax to go straight home," she said.

We fed each other the olives, then the strawberries. One slipped from my grasp and we laughed as we hunted around on the blanket for it. Sheltered in the thick pines and warmed by the wine, I began to perspire. I took off my jacket and tie. As I looked around for a place to lay them, I saw Maureen slipping out of her dress. She blew out the candle.

"Hey!" I laughed.

"Why not stretch out and be comfortable?" she asked, and lay down on the blanket beside me. I could barely see her. I couldn't even tell if she had on anything at all. I swallowed.

"Well?" she said.

"What?"

"Why not be comfortable?"

My heart began to pound. "Why not?" I said, and took off my shirt and socks. I leaned over and kissed her. She put her hands on the back of my neck and drew me down beside her. I wondered if I'd known all along what was coming. It wasn't as though she were talking me into something I didn't want to do. I reached back into my hip pocket for my wallet. Then I stroked her arms, her neck, her chest, and finally, I just let it happen—just swam with the tide. And when we walked slowly back to the car later, I knew I'd be in that cemetery again with Maureen. If not there, someplace else. I didn't feel especially proud of myself, but I didn't feel guilty either. Just different. Very adult. Easy and uneasy, both at the same time.

The way Mom found out about it was that I told her, more or less. Two weeks after the prom, Dave gave Discount and me a set of the photos his dad had taken, and I left them on our coffee table. Jeri found them after dinner and was looking them over, commenting on the girls' dresses and how I looked like a nerd, the way I was smiling. Then she passed them on to Mom.

"These look like professional photos, George," Mom said. "Who took them?"

"Mr. Hahn." I went down in the basement to get my lifting gloves and came back up, pulling on a T-shirt. Typhus danced around, thinking I was taking her out.

"Dave's father? In their house?"

"Where else?" I said.

Mom laid the photos in her lap. "I thought we had an understanding about your going over there," she told me.

I started toward the door. "If it's my sexual identity," I said, "you can stop worrying about that now."

"Meaning . . .?" Mother asked.

"Figure it out for yourself," I said, quoting Grandpa Richards, and drove on over to Psycho's.

TEN

We all turned eighteen over the summer—Dave and Marsh and I. This made us eligible, along with Bud, for the 18–20 Club, but once I knew I could go, it lost its appeal. I'd thought of taking Maureen there in hopes of pairing her off with somebody else. Then I got a better idea: Get her interested in Marshall Evans. Psycho was big, he was brawny, he was handsome—a lot better-looking than me. Both he and Maureen were going to the University of Minnesota in the fall, and they'd have a lot in common. All I had to do, I figured, was give them a chance to get acquainted. Not that I expected instant miracles. But if Maureen ever latched onto Psycho the way she latched onto me, he'd be in heaven.

Marsh was okay with guys, but around girls, he became excruciatingly shy—one big silent lump of mashed potato.

"I don't know what to talk about," he'd confessed once.

"Say *anything,* Psycho!" we told him. "Smile at the girl and say the first thing that enters your head."

"They'd arrest me," said Marsh.

"Ask questions," I suggested. "That'll get a girl talking about herself and the heat will be off you."

We tried coaching from the sidelines. We tried setting him up with friends of friends. Psycho always ducked out at the last minute. I figured that what Marsh needed was a girl who came on strong, and what better person than Maureen Kimball.

"Marsh," I said when I called him, "you busy tonight?"

"No," said Psycho.

"Meet us at Nilsson's about eight. If you get there first, grab a booth. Okay?"

"Sure," said Psycho.

He didn't ask who the "us" was, so I didn't tell him. If his mind traveled along the same old rut and he was expecting Dave and Discount, that was his problem. Nilsson's was about the last soda fountain drugstore in Minneapolis with a marble-topped counter and booths where you could get a shake, and it was a favorite place to meet on Friday nights while you were deciding where to go after.

"Where we going?" Maureen said when I picked her up. She was wearing a sort of loose sundress without any bra, and you could see little dark circles in front where her breasts brushed up against the material.

"Thought maybe we'd drop by Nilsson's and get some ice cream," I said.

"I couldn't possibly eat a thing," Maureen told me, stretching one arm across the back of the seat and draping her hand over my shoulder.

"Well, I'm starved," I said. "Split a sundae with me."

Maureen fondled my ear. "I'll feed your hungers." She laughed.

I never could figure her out. Maureen wasn't what I'd call wild. She may have slept with a guy or two before me, but if she did, she kept it to herself. I think she really liked me, and decided to do whatever it took to keep me. She never asked what I did when I wasn't with her—didn't want to scare me away, I guess. She was just always, totally available, and that was the problem. God, though, what she could do for Psycho!

I purposely got to Nilsson's late so that Marsh would be in a booth. Through the window I could see him sitting there, checking his watch, then leaning forward, his massive arms on the table, furtively eyeing a couple of girls in the next booth.

"Hey, Psycho!" I said, as though I'd never expected meeting him there. "How you doing?" I slid onto the seat across from him, and Maureen sat down beside me.

Marsh stared at us, his eyes sort of glazing over when he saw Maureen. You could hear him swallow.

"You know Maureen, don't you?" I asked.

She answered for him. "Sure. We've seen each other around school."

Psycho managed a faint smile and went on staring somewhere beyond our heads.

"You ordered yet?" I asked him. "I'm going to have the Gold Rush Sundae."

"I just ate," said Psycho. "At home, I mean."

"Well, why don't we order two sundaes, and you can split one with Maureen, since she's not very hungry either," I suggested. I knew I was pushing it.

The waitress turned in our direction and before we could discuss it further, Psycho bleated, "Coke for me." Maureen said she only wanted a glass of water and I ordered my sundae. When the waitress left, we lapsed into embarrassed silence.

"Guess what?" I said suddenly. "Both of you are going to the University this fall. Talk about coincidence!"

"Us and about eighty-five others from our graduating class," Maureen said dryly. She looked at Psycho. "Have you registered yet?"

"No," he told her.

"What date did you get for orientation?"

"August second."

"Hey! Me, too!" said Maureen.

Psycho looked down at his hands.

Come on, buddy! I pleaded under my breath. Pick up the ball! Run with it!

Marsh looked up suddenly and fastened his eyes on Maureen, his neck a strange shade of pink. "You ever do any weight-lifting?" he asked.

I could almost feel my lungs deflate. Almost feel the smile that crept across Maureen's face.

"No," she said, "I never did."

Across the table, the pink spread to Marshall's cheeks, his ears.

Our order came, and while Maureen and I passed my spoon back and forth between us, I tried to keep up a steady banter. I told Maureen about how many pounds Psycho could bench, how many squats he could do, but she just kept digging away at my caramel syrup and all the while Psycho's Coke was getting lower and lower in his glass. I had to do something.

"Wait right here," I said. "Just remembered I was supposed to call Dad and tell him something about the car."

Maureen slid her legs to one side and I inched past her and over to the phones on the other side of the store.

Wedged in the phone booth behind Dr. Sholl's foot remedies, I held the receiver against my ear and listened to the dial tone, studying the second-hand of Gramp's gold watch. I forced myself to stay in the booth for a full five minutes. All I wanted to do was give them a couple minutes together—let Psycho find out there was at least one girl he could talk to. Secretly, I was hoping that some irresistible urge would rise up in Maureen and she would see in Marsh a challenge—a mountain of muscle just waiting to be conquered.

When the five minutes were up, I put the receiver back, stepped outside the booth, and slowly raised my head above the bunion pads.

Maureen was sitting alone at the table, studying her nails, and Psycho was standing over by the magazine rack, thumbing through a copy of *Newsweek,* his face fever-red. Before I could get over there, he put the magazine back, gave Maureen a slight nod of his head, and barged on outside.

"Where's Marsh?" I asked Maureen.

"The poor guy!" she said. "He got up about ten seconds after you did, George. He's a basket case if I ever saw one. Do me a favor; if we ever come here again, don't let's sit with Marshall Evans."

Psycho was pretty sore about what happened at Nilssons'.

"What the hell was I supposed to think?" he asked. "She's your girl!"

"Hey, I told you we were all going out to a movie, didn't I?" I said. I was lying, and Marsh knew it, and that made it worse.

"No, you didn't say a thing about Maureen. You didn't say you were bringing a girl with tits showing right through her dress. There wasn't even a safe place I could look."

"Well, jeez, Marsh, she wasn't going to bite you. You're going to be seeing her around the University. What's the big deal?"

"What's the big deal is right! How come Discount and Dave didn't show? It's like you were trying to push her off on me."

"Oh, come off it, Psycho," I said, but I knew he had me. I also knew that what I'd done only made Marsh feel worse about himself—made it look as though he were so bad off he needed help.

Maybe I was trying to punish myself for it, I don't know, but when I went to work on Monday, I smashed my hand—got my fingers caught between the wheelbarrow and a cinderblock wall.

I told Shirl that the scrape wasn't as bad as it looked, but she insisted on washing my hand in soap and water and bandaging it up, her long fingers with the copper-colored nails holding my palm very gently while she patted it dry.

"Hey, Shirl, it's not amputated or anything," I protested, as she wrapped it in layer after layer of gauze. Anne passed the door of the office, and I saw her smile as she went by. I shifted impatiently.

"Hold still," Shirl said. "I'm not about to let this get infected and have you sue us or something."

"Fat chance," I told her.

"What were you laughing at?" I asked Anne later as I helped her move the perennials over to the sale table. I had to carry each plant with the palm of my right hand.

"Just the way Shirley was going about it." Anne grinned. "You've got enough gauze there to wrap a belly dancer."

I laughed, too. "I'll take it off when I get home. Got to keep the she-boss happy, though."

"Yeah, I know what you mean," said Anne.

I found myself searching Anne's fingers as she worked, trying to see if she were wearing an engagement ring or something; someone's class ring on a chain around her neck, maybe. She wasn't. She stopped once and held her hair up off the back of her neck, fanning herself with a garden brochure.

"It's so hot!" she said. "For two cents I'd sit down in the wishing well over there."

I reached in my jeans for pennies, and she laughed.

"I'm going swimming after I leave today," she said. "It'll wait."

"Want some company?"

"You can't. Your hand, remember." She walked over to the corner table to rearrange the geraniums and I followed.

"I'll take off the bandage," I said.

She just smiled and shook her head. "I'm meeting some girlfriends."

"Some other time?" I persisted.

"Maybe," she told me.

There was something different about our house that evening. It took me a minute or two to figure it out. Then I realized that there was music coming from the living room and it wasn't the stereo. It was Jeri playing the piano, which she does on rare occasions. Classical music. Like everything else Jeri did, she played well. Except that Trish had done everything well first, so what Jeri accomplished was no big deal around our house.

Mom and Dad sat waiting.

"I almost hate to call her," Mom said. "It's been so long since she's played."

"Well, let her be, then," Dad suggested. "A little dinner music might be nice."

It's strange, sometimes, the difference one person can make in a family. Jeri deciding to play the piano instead of shutting herself up in her room, for example. Even Dad's "pass the butter" seemed more mellow.

"What happened to your hand, George?" Mom asked, and because there was real concern in her voice, I answered civilly:

"Smashed it against a wall with a wheelbarrow. It's not as bad as it looks." I reached for the corn and rolled it around on my plate in a thin puddle of melting butter. Mom started to say something else, but right then Jeri flubbed a couple of notes and ran her hands disgustedly across the keys before she shuffled on into the dining room.

"Why couldn't Chopin have written everything in the key of C?" she asked plaintively, plopping down in her chair.

Mom and Dad laughed. Ollie too. Even grumpy old me managed a smile.

"Why couldn't *War and Peace* be written in half the number of pages?" said Mom, carrying the joke a step further.

It's sort of a family tradition at our house. Somebody starts something ridiculous, and the others try to carry it along. Ollie jumped in with both feet. "Why can't a basketball net be three feet lower?"

Dad was not to be outdone. "Why couldn't Form 1040 be answered true or false?" he said, and that got another burst of laughter.

I wished I had something funny to contribute, but nothing special came to mind. What I was really thinking, though, was how there *were* good times in our family. I wondered why all the faults seemed to rise up lately and smack me between the eyes—as though I had to focus on those in order to get up enough steam to break away.

I was lying on the blanket, staring up at the odd-shaped patches of sky that gleamed through the tangled silhouette of branches. The woods were still in the late afternoon except for the occasional rustle of a squirrel overhead and the faraway drone of cicadas.

Maureen rolled over and put one arm around my neck.

"Hey, lover," she said. I lifted my head and brushed my lips against her cheek, then lay back again. For a moment I felt a stirring of tenderness toward Maureen, not the nothingness I'd been feeling for the past several weeks. Maybe it all had to do with whether I was upside down or right side up, I thought. Wouldn't it be crazy if all life's problems could be solved just by lying on your back? But I knew better. This was it. Maureen had said in the car that she was thinking about going on the Pill. I couldn't let her see a doctor and get a prescription just for me—then walk out on her. It was now or never.

She probed at my ribs with one finger. I grabbed her hand and held it.

"What are you thinking right now?" she asked.

"Everything and nothing," I said finally, which was as loaded an answer as there ever was.

She must have sensed something, because she took her arm off my chest and laid back down beside me, not quite touching.

"What's wrong, George?"

"I'm not really sure," I told her, trying to figure out how to say it.

She ran one hand along my leg. "Something *I* can't cure?"

"Yep." I smiled. "Something not even you can cure." I could tell, however, that *she* wasn't smiling.

"I began to suspect that . . . when you didn't want to make love today."

I sat up. "Sometimes I even surprise myself," I said. "I've just been thinking about us, and feel we ought to start seeing other people, Maureen. You're going to be meeting new guys at the University—they'll ask you out. . . ." Big, magnanimous me.

I could tell it was a line she'd heard before. Girls had even used it on me. When you want to break up, you focus on all the potential dates your partner could get. Mr. Generous here.

Maureen just looked at me. "Maybe I don't *want* to date anyone else, George."

"You ought to be free, though, Maureen, just in case," I told her.

Maureen took the cue and stood up, so I got up too, and together we folded the blanket. She picked up the picnic basket we'd scarcely opened. The sandwiches had gone untouched.

"So who is she?" Maureen asked finally as we started back to the car. "You can tell me. There weren't any strings attached." I glanced over at her. Her lips were pressed bravely together. There was a flatness in her voice, however, that matched the way I felt. I was lower than low.

"Nobody yet. But I want to feel free to date other people, and you deserve the same. That's hard to do when . . . we're as close as we've been."

"It bothers you that you're not going to college this fall. Is that it?" she asked. "That I'll be a student again and you won't? It's *okay,* George, really! That doesn't bother me."

I knew I had to be more specific. If Maureen thought that college was the problem, she'd drop out just to make me feel better. If I wanted to end the relationship once and for all, I had to say so. Sort of.

"It's more than that, Maureen," I told her. "It's really over between us, that's all." Don't make me say anything else, I thought. Don't make me spell it out. How does a guy ever say I don't care for you as much as I should? He doesn't.

She didn't make me say it. Her eyes finally told me that she knew. She moved ahead of me where the path narrowed. Her step was a little too brisk and deliberate, and I felt a rush of guilt that rose, then receded. We didn't talk all the way back to her house. In her driveway, however, she put one hand on top of mine.

"Well, George, it's been fun," she said at last. "Maybe we both need a change. So good-bye, good luck, and all that sort of thing."

Casual to the last. Even Maureen had trouble being herself, I was thinking. But it was easier this way.

"I'll see you around," I said. And that was it.

Christopher Paul Curtis (b. 1954)

A distinguished African American children's book author, Christopher Paul Curtis was born in Flint, Michigan, where his award-winning novel *The Watsons Go to Birmingham—1963* is set. In this novel, the Watson family travels from Flint to Birmingham, where they become witnesses to the bombing of the Sixteenth Avenue Baptist Church, a racist attack in which four young girls died. The early parts of the novel are more humorous than tragic. In the chapter reprinted here, ten-year-old Kenny struggles with his outcast status at school. He finds two new friends who are treated as outcasts, too, but he realizes the worth of their friendship when he gives in to the temptation to laugh at their poor clothes. Kenny learns an important lesson about respect and loyalty. Curtis is also the author of the Newbery Award–winning novel *Bud, Not Buddy* (1999), about a boy's quest for his unknown father during the Great Depression of the 1930s.

From *The Watsons Go to Birmingham—1963*

CHAPTER 3. THE WORLD'S GREATEST DINOSAUR WAR EVER

I couldn't believe it! The door opened in the middle of math class and the principal pushed the older raggedy kid in. Mrs. Cordell said, "Boys and girls, we have a new student in our class starting today, his name is Rufus Fry. Now I know all of you will help make Rufus feel welcome, won't you?"

Someone sniggled.

"Good. Rufus, say hello to your new classmates, please."

He didn't smile or wave or anything, he just looked down and said real quiet, "Hi."

A couple of girls thought he was cute because they said, "Hi, Rufus."

"Why don't you sit next to Kenny and he can help you catch up with what we're doing," Mrs. Cordell said.

I couldn't believe it! I'd wanted my personal saver to be as far away from me as he could get. I knew when you had two people who were going to get teased a lot and they were close together people didn't choose one of them to tease, they picked on both of them, and instead of picking on them the normal amount they picked on them twice as much.

Mrs. Cordell pushed the new kid over to the empty seat next to me.

"Kenny, show Rufus where we are in the book."

I watched the new kid sideways. He said, "Kenny? I thought they said your name was Poindexter." The class cracked up, part from his country style of talking and part from laughing at me. I could tell that even Mrs. Cordell was fighting not to break out laughing.

Though he was looking friendly when he said this I kind of knew it had to be teasing, because whoever heard of anybody's momma giving them a name like Poindexter? When he sat down next to me I tried to imitate Byron's "Death Stare" but it didn't work because the kid smiled at me real big and said, "My name's Rufus, what are we doing?"

"Times tables."

"That's easy! You need some help?"

"No!" I said, and scooted around in my chair so all he could do was look at my back. This guy was real desperate for a friend because even though I wouldn't say much back to him he kept jabbering away at me all through class.

When lunchtime came he followed me outside right to the part of the playground where I sit to eat. He forgot about bringing a lunch so I gave him one of Momma's throat-choking peanut butter sandwiches and let him eat the last half of my apple. He really was a strange kid; he only ate half the sandwich and folded the rest up in the waxed paper and when I handed him the apple he even ate the spots where you could see my teeth had been, he didn't even wipe the slob off first.

And, man, this kid could really talk! He was yakking a mile a minute, saying stuff like "Your momma sure can make a good peanut butter sandwich" and "How come these kids is so darn mean?"

Then he said something that made me get all funny and nervous inside, he said, "How come your eyes ain't lookin' in the same way?" I looked to see if maybe this was the start of some teasing but he looked like he really wanted to know. He wasn't staring at me either, he was kind of looking down and kicking at the dirt with his raggedy shoes.

"It's a lazy eye."

He stopped kicking dirt and said, "Don't it hurt?"

"No."

He said, "Oh," then kicked a little more dirt and hollered out, "Ooh, boy! Look at how fat that there is!"

"What?"

"You don't see that squirrel?" he asked me, and pointed up at a tree across the street. "That sure is one fat, dumb squirrel!"

I looked at the squirrel, it didn't look fat or dumb to me, it was a regular old squirrel sitting on a branch chewing on something. "How come you think it's dumb?"

"What kind of squirrel sits out in the open like that with folks all round him? That squirrel wouldn't last two seconds in Arkansas, I'da picked him off easy as nothing." The new kid pointed at the squirrel like his finger was a gun and said, "Bang! Squirrel stew tonight!"

"You mean you shot a gun before?"

"Ain't you?"

"You mean you really ate a squirrel before?"

"You ain't?"

"A real, real gun?"

"Just a twenty-two."

"How's a squirrel taste?"

"It taste real good!"

"You mean you really shoot 'em with real bullets and then you really eat 'em?"

"Why else shoot 'em?"

"Real squirrels, like that one?"

"Not that fat and not that stupid. I guess all the fat, stupid ones been got already. Since I been born all that's left in Arkansas is skinny, sneaky ones. I think them Michigan squirrels is worth two Arkansas ones."

"You aren't lying?"

He raised his hand and said, "I swear for God. Ask Cody."

"Who?"

The little shrunk-up version of the new kid was standing by himself up against the fence that runs around Clark, watching us. The new kid waved at him and his little brother came running over.

The big one pointed over at the squirrel. "Cody, lookit there!"

Cody laughed and said, "Ooh boy! That sure is a fat squirrel!"

"Think you could pick him off from here?"

Cody pointed his finger like it was a gun and said, "Bang! Squirrel stew tonight!"

I couldn't believe this little kid had shot a gun too. "You shot a real gun?"

"Just a twenty-two."

"With real bullets?"

The little one looked at his big brother to see why I was asking all this stuff. It seemed like they were trying to be patient with me, like I was a real dummy or something. The older one said, "Tell him."

"Yeah, it was real bullets, what else you gonna shoot out a gun?"

I still didn't believe them but the bell rang and lunch was over. I know he didn't think I noticed, but the big kid gave his little brother the other half of my sandwich. I guess both of them had forgot about lunch.

This saver stuff wasn't going anything like I thought it was supposed to. Rufus started acting like I was his friend. In the morning on the bus he'd always come sit next to me, and Mrs. Cordell put his regular seat next to mine in school. Every day at lunchtime he followed me out to the playground and ate half of my second sandwich, then sneaked the other half to Cody. He even found out where we lived and started coming over every night around five-thirty.

I didn't mind him coming over to play, because both our favorite game was playing with the little plastic dinosaurs that I had and you couldn't really have any fun playing by yourself. That was because someone had to be the American dinosaurs and someone had to be the Nazi ones. Rufus didn't even mind being the Nazi dinosaurs most of the time and it was O.K. playing with him because he didn't cheat and didn't try to steal my plastic monsters.

The only other guy I used to play with was LJ Jones, but I quit playing with him when a lot of my dinosaurs started disappearing. I've got about a million of them but before LJ started coming over I had two million. It's kind of embarrassing how LJ got them from me. At first he'd steal them one or two at a time and I asked Byron what I should do to stop him.

By said, "Don't sweat it, punk. The way I figure it one or two of them stupid little monsters ain't a real high price for you to pay to get someone to play with you."

But LJ wasn't satisfied with doing one or two, I guess he wanted a raise, so one day he said to me, "You know, we should stop having these little fights all the time. We need to have one great big battle!"

"Yeah, we could call it the World's Greatest Dinosaur War Ever," I said, "but I get to be the Americans."

I should have known something was fishy when LJ said, "O.K., but I get first shot." Most of the time it always took a big fight to decide who had to be the Nazis.

I started setting up my dinosaurs and LJ said, "This ain't right. If this really is the World's Greatest Dinosaur War Ever we need more monsters. You should go get the rest of 'em."

He was right. If this was going to be a famous battle we needed more fighters. "O.K., I'll be right back," I said.

This wasn't going to be easy. I wasn't allowed to take all of my dinosaurs out at once because Momma was afraid I'd lose most of them. Especially because she didn't trust LJ. Every time he'd come over she'd tell me, "You watch out for that boy, he's a little too sneaky for my tastes." I had a plan, though. I'd go upstairs and drop the pillowcase I kept my dinosaurs in out of the window. I wasn't so stupid that I'd drop them down to LJ, I'd drop them out of the other side of the house and then run around to get them.

My plan worked perfect! After I went and picked up the pillowcase I set up my dinosaurs and LJ set up the Nazis and we started the battle.

He took first shot and killed about thirty of mine with an atomic bomb. My dinosaurs shot back and got twenty of his with a hand grenade. The battle was going great! Dinosaurs were falling right, left and center.

We had a great big pile of dead dinosaurs off to the side and had to keep shaking more and more reinforcements out of the pillowcase. Then in the middle of one big fight LJ said, "Wait a minute, Kenny, there's something we forgot about."

I was ready for a trick. I knew LJ was going to try to get me to go away for a minute so he could steal a bunch of my monsters. I said, "What?"

"These dinosaurs been droppin' atom bombs on each other. Think about how dangerous that is."

"How's it dangerous?"

LJ said, "Look." He made one of his brontosauruses run by the pile of dead dinosaurs and when it got two steps past them it started shaking and twitching and fell over on its side, dead as a donut. LJ flipped him on the dead dinosaur pile.

I said, "What happened to him?"

"It was the radioactiveness. We gotta bury the dead ones before they infect the rest of the live ones."

Maybe it was because we had such a great war going on and I was kind of nervous about who'd win, but this stupid stuff made sense, so instead of digging each one of the couple hundred dead dinosaurs a grave we dug one giant hole and buried all the radioactive ones in it, then we put a big rock on top so no radioactivity could leak out.

This really was the World's Greatest Dinosaur War Ever. We fought and killed dinosaurs for such a long time that we had to make two more graves with two more big rocks on top of them. LJ finally pulled the trick I knew he was going to but he did it so cool that I didn't even see it coming.

"Kenny, you ever been over in Banky and Larry Dunn's fort?"

LJ knew I hadn't. "Uh-uh."

"I found out where it is."

"Where?"

"You wanna come see it?"

"Are you crazy?"

"They ain't there, this is Thursday night, they're up at the community center playin' ball."

"Really?"

"Well, if you too scared . . ."

I knew this was a worm with a hook in it but I bit anyway. "I'm not scared if you aren't."

"Let's go!"

I figured the trick would come in right here so I kept a real good eye on LJ while we put my monsters back in the pillowcase. When we were done I sneaked a look at his back pockets, 'cause I knew when he stole dinosaurs he put them back there or in his socks. From the way his pockets were sticking out it looked like he had one *Tyrannosaurus rex* and one triceratops. I couldn't tell how many he had in his socks. I figured that wasn't too bad a price for as much fun as we'd had.

LJ was talking a mile a minute. "They even got some books with nekkid ladies! You ever seen a nekkid lady?"

"Yeah, lots of times!" I had too. Byron had borrowed lots of nasty magazines from Buphead's library. I knew LJ didn't believe me, though. For some reason if you were famous for being smart no one thought you'd ever looked at a dirty book.

LJ said, "You gotta be in the house by seven, don't you?"

"Yeah."

"O.K., we better hurry before it gets too late."

After I'd sneaked the dinosaurs back into the house we ran off toward Banky and Larry Dunn's secret fort.

It wasn't until nine o'clock at night when I was in bed that a bell went off in my head. I'd forgotten all about the radioactive dinosaurs!

I put on my tennis shoes, got my night-reading flashlight, climbed out the back window and went down the tree into the backyard. I got to the battleground and saw the three radioactive graves, but when I moved the rock on the first one and dug a little bit down I didn't hit one dinosaur, not one! The second grave was empty too. I didn't even move the rock from the third one, I just sat there and felt real stupid.

I couldn't help thinking about Sunday school again. I remembered the story about how a bunch of angels came down and rolled away the rock that was in front of Jesus's grave to let him go to heaven. I think it took them three days to push the rock far enough so he could squeeze out. My dinosaurs weren't even in their graves for three hours before someone rolled their rocks away. Maybe it was a lot easier for a bunch of angels to get a million dinosaurs to heaven than it was to get the saver of the whole world there, but I wished they'd given me a couple more hours.

But I was just making excuses to myself for being so stupid. I know if a detective had looked at these rocks he wouldn't have found a clue of a single angel being there, but I'd bet a million bucks that he'd have seen that those rocks were covered with a ton of LJ Jones fingerprints.

I never played with LJ again after that. So playing with Rufus got to be O.K. It was a lot better not to have to worry about getting stuff stolen when you were with your friends, and it was a lot better not spending half the time arguing about who's going to be the Nazi dinosaurs.

I was wrong when I said that me and Rufus being near each other all the time would make people tease both of us twice as much. People started leaving me alone and going right after Rufus. It was easy for them to do 'cause he was kind of like me, he had two things wrong with him too.

The first thing wrong with Rufus was the way he talked. After he said that "Hiya, y'all" stuff on the bus he got to be famous for it and no matter how much he tried to talk in a different way people wouldn't let him forget what he'd said.

The other thing wrong with him was his clothes. It didn't take people too long before they counted how many pairs of pants and shirts Rufus and Cody had. That was easy to do because Rufus only had two shirts and two pairs of pants and Cody only had three shirts and two pairs of pants. They also had one pair of blue jeans that they switched off on; some days Rufus wore them and some days Cody rolled the legs up and put them on. It's really funny how something as stupid as a pair of blue jeans can make you feel real, real bad but that's what happened to me.

We had been sort of secret friends for a couple of weeks before people really started getting on them about not having a bunch of clothes. Me and Rufus and Cody were on the bus right behind the driver one day when Larry Dunn walked up to our seat and said, "Country Corn Flake, I noticed how you and the Little Flake switch off on them pants, and I know Fridays is your day to wear 'em, but I was wonderin' if the same person who gets to wear the pants gets to wear the drawers that day too?"

Of course the whole bus started laughing and hollering. Larry Dunn went back to his seat real quick before the driver had a chance to tell anybody the secret

he knew about Larry's momma. I looked over at Cody. He had the blue jeans on today and was pulling the waist out to check out his underpants.

Maybe it was because everybody else was laughing, maybe it was because Cody had such a strange look on his face while he peeked at his underpants, maybe it was because I was glad that Larry hadn't jumped on me, but whatever the reason was I cracked up too.

Rufus shot a look at me. His face never changed but I knew right away I'd done something wrong. I tried to squeeze the rest of my laugh down.

Things got real strange. Instead of Rufus jabbering away at me a mile a minute in school he scooted around in his seat so all I could see was his back. He didn't follow me out on the playground either, and he acted like he didn't want my sandwiches anymore. Ever since Momma had met Rufus and I told her about sharing my sandwiches with him she had been giving me four sandwiches and three apples for lunch. When I saw him and Cody weren't going to come under the swing at lunchtime I set the bag with their sandwiches and apples in it on the swing set. The bag was still there when the bell rang.

They quit sitting next to me on the bus too, and Rufus didn't show up that night to play. After this junk went on for three or four days I sneaked the pillowcase full of dinosaurs out and headed over to where Rufus lived. I knocked on the door and Cody answered. I thought things might be back to being O.K. because Cody gave me a great big smile and said, "Hiya, Kenny, you wanna talk to Rufus?"

"Hi, Cody."

"Just a minute."

Cody closed the door and ran back inside. A minute later Rufus came to the door.

"Hey, Rufus, I thought you might want to play dinosaurs. It's your turn to be the Americans."

Rufus looked at the pillowcase, then back at me. "I ain't playin' with you no more, Kenny."

"How come?" I knew, though.

"I thought you was my friend. I didn't think you was like all them other people," he said. "I thought you was different." He didn't say this stuff like he was mad, he just sounded real, real sad. He pulled Cody out of the doorway and shut it.

Rufus might as well have tied me to a tree and said, "Ready, aim, fire!" I felt like someone had pulled all my teeth out with a pair of rusty pliers. I wanted to knock on his door and tell him, "I *am* different," but I was too embarrassed so I walked the dinosaurs back home.

I couldn't believe how sad I got. It's funny how things could change so much and you wouldn't notice. All of a sudden I started remembering how much I hated riding the bus, all of a sudden I started remembering how lunchtime under the swing set alone wasn't very much fun, all of a sudden I started remembering that before Rufus came to Flint my only friend was the world's biggest dinosaur thief, LJ Jones, all of a sudden I remembered that Rufus and Cody were the only two kids in the whole school (other than Byron and Joey) that I didn't automatically look at sideways.

A couple of days later Momma asked me to sit in the kitchen with her for a while.

"How's school?"

"O.K." I knew she was fishing to find what was wrong and hoped it wouldn't take her too long. I wanted to tell her what I'd done.

"Where's Rufus been? I haven't seen him lately."

It was real embarrassing but tears just exploded out of my face and even though I knew she was going to be disappointed in me I told Momma how I'd hurt Rufus's feelings.

"Did you apologize?"

"Sort of, but he wouldn't let me talk to him."

"Well, give him some time, then try again."

"Yes, Momma."

The next day after school when the bus pulled up at Rufus's stop Momma was standing there. When Rufus and Cody got off they said, "Hi, Mrs. Watson," and gave her their big smiles. The three of them walked toward Rufus's house. Momma put her hand on Rufus's head while they walked.

Momma didn't say anything when she got home and I didn't ask her but I kept my eye on the clock. At exactly five-thirty there was a knock and I knew who it was and I knew what I had to do.

Momma and Joey were in the living room and when they heard the knock everything there got real quiet. Rufus and Cody were standing on the porch smiling a mile a minute. I said, "Rufus, I'm sorry."

He said, "That's O.K."

I wasn't through, though. I really wanted him to know. "I *am* different."

He said, "Shoot, Kenny, you think I don't know? Why you think I came back? But remember, you said it's my turn to be the Americans."

People started moving around in the living room again. I guess I should have told Momma that I really appreciated her helping me get my friend back but I didn't have to. I was pretty sure she already knew.

Victor Martinez (b. 1949)

Victor Martinez was born and raised in Fresno, California, the fourth of twelve children. He attended Cal State Fresno and Stanford University and worked as a field laborer, welder, truck driver, firefighter, teacher, and office clerk. He published poetry and short stories before writing his semiautobiographical novel subtitled *mi vida: my life. Parrot in the Oven: mi vida* (1996) won the prestigious National Book Award. Manny Hernandez, the main character, has a rough life; his father likes to call him "el perico," the parrot, from a Mexican saying about a parrot who complains how hot it is in the shade while all along he is sitting in the oven and does not know it. But Manny intends to be smarter than the parrot. He has to negotiate around gangs and the temptation to join them; his father's drunken, violent rages; and his outsider status at school. His mother cleans the house obsessively, his brother "flips through more jobs than a thumb through a deck of cards," and his sister has a miscarriage. But Manny persists—and his perceptions are often shot through with poetic beauty. In this excerpt, we see the peer pressures and bonds of the various competing groups at school in action at a boxing match.

From *Parrot in the Oven: mi vida*

CHAPTER 7. THE BOXING MATCH

When summer ended, I was again at the same school. Mom's plans to get me transferred didn't work out. The administration said it was too late. There were already too many kids in that school. There was an imbalance in the student body—whatever that meant. They said lots of things, but it all ended with me not transferring.

So I was sitting with my friend Albert Sosa, eating lunch on the picnic table over by the maple trees, when all of a sudden Lencho Dominguez came and parked his big beefy shadow above us. We liked eating lunch there, because every day around twelve o'clock one of the English teachers, Miss Van der Meer, would step out of her classroom and swoon our minds with the gorgeous way she'd fluff her hair and fix the collar of her ruffly blouse. Her legs dangled from the hem of her skirt like two shapely white bowling pins, and her shoulders were straight as a geography book.

We acted like that wasn't why we ate lunch there, but it was. Anybody could see how cold it got. The wind already had glass edges to it, stiffening muscles and practically cutting through the stitches of our clothes. When it blew, the chill stabbed our teeth like icicles, and our voices jiggled every time we talked. Yet our eyes melted when Miss Van der Meer appeared at the door.

Anyway, Lencho came over and eyed us like we were hopeless. He was dressed in Big Ben pants, starched stiff as ironing-boards, and a plaid Pendleton shirt with the lap and tail out. Hardly a smile of a wrinkle showed anywhere. He cleared his throat with an exaggerated gutter.

"You *vatos* are real screwy, you know that?" he said, in his strep-throaty voice.

Rumor had it that Lencho stripped his voice by smoking cartons of Lucky Strike cigarettes and drinking Jack Daniel's whisky straight from a thermos bottle stashed in his locker. He leaned over and fingered about a dozen of Albert's fried potatoes. "That white bitch teaches a class of *gavachos,* and you guys hang around waiting to see her ass."

"Whataya mean?" Albert said, acting sore about Lencho thieving his potatoes. He knew better than to complain, though. No one complained to Lencho. I once saw him grab Mark Calavasos by the tits and squeeze until he grit his teeth and begged Lencho to please, please let him go.

"You guys ever been in that room?" Lencho mumbled, snatching and pushing another load of Albert's potatoes into his mouth.

"No," I said, pretending to not be interested Actually, I must have wondered a thousand times about what was behind that door.

Daintily flicking salt from his fingers, Lencho did a curious thing. He wet his two fingers on his tongue, and pinching the crease of his pants, ran them down to his knee. He did the same with the other pant leg. We watched him with open-mouthed fascination.

"Well, let me tell you *vatos,*" he said, finishing his grooming with a swipe of his pocket. "There's couches and sofas in there. You guys ever seen couches and sofas in a *class*room?" He laughed, a sort of half chuckle, half sneering laugh. We looked dumbly at him, and he laughed again, only louder. "You *vatos* are screwy—you know that? You're a couple of real sissies."

He didn't say it like an insult, but more a statement of fact. If he'd have asked us, we'd have agreed with him in a second. Compared to Lencho, *everybody* was a sissy. He had lumpy sacks of potatoes for shoulders, and even the weight of his breathing made you feel puny.

He put his knuckle to his mouth and cleared a big wad of phlegm and spat it out. "I want to talk to you about something, Manny," he said, seriously. "Do you think that maybe Bernardo might wanna join my boxing team?"

"I don't know," I said.

"He's a pretty tough *vato,* ain't he?"

"I guess so."

"What do you mean you *guess* so? Don't you know anything about your own brother?"

"He doesn't tell me everything!" I said, trying to toughen my voice. I must have sounded whiny, though, because Albert ducked his eyes.

It was the truth about Nardo. He mostly told me what he had done and how he felt about what he had done, but never anything about what he was planning to do or anything about what he wanted to do. If he thought about something, he'd ask me in a question, like, 'Hey, Manny, do you think I should join Lencho's boxing team?' He hadn't asked me a thing like that lately, so I didn't know.

"Well, anyway, ask your brother if he wants to join," Lencho said. He stamped his Stacy Adams shoes on the bench and walked away, eyeing his snazzy polish.

That's when Miss Van der Meer came out of her classroom. She had a load of books crooked under her arm and was mangling a cluster of keys against her hip. As usual, there were some white students pattering like puppies behind her. She fished a key out and locked the door. Lencho walked toward her, tiptoeing—with dignity—trying not to get any grass on his shoes. He hopped on the concrete walkway.

"Hey, Lench!" I yelled. "Albert says he wants to join. He says he could whip anybody in the whole school—even Boise. He says he'll even take on Boise." I got up and gave Albert's shoulders a champion's massage.

Annoyed, but not wanting to make a big commotion around a teacher, Lencho turned and shot a hidden Screw You finger at me from his hip; then, coolly deadening his face, he zipped past Miss Van der Meer, almost bumping her shoulder.

As he passed, the white students cold-stared Lencho like he'd just peed on the Queen of England. They weren't about to say anything, though. They knew his reputation. Besides, Miss Van der Meer pretended like she hadn't noticed a thing. That's the kind of teacher she was, too precious to notice anything.

That's when I yelled out, "Hi, Miss Van der Meer!" It was one of those phony-baloney hi's that always comes out sounding smoochy. She turned around and automatically started to wave back, but then recognized that she didn't know who I was. She tossed a polite hand at me anyway, and her students hurried her away.

"You jerk! What the hell you do that for?" Albert moaned after Miss Van der Meer and her pack of puppies rounded the corner. He was steamed. He snatched angrily at his hair. He stood up, grabbed his books like he was about to huff off, then changed his mind and plunked them back down on the table. "Man," he said,

in a mopey voice, "now she's gonna think we're a coupla idiots."

"We *are* a coupla idiots, you idiot," I said, defiantly, but I could see regret tightening on Albert's face. He was convinced that we'd never get another chance to moon over Miss Van der Meer on the sly. But to me, Lencho was right. It was stupid sitting out there stuffed in a mountain of double sweaters, waiting for some teacher to make a grand appearance. She paid us less mind than she would a wad of chewing gum stuck on the sidewalk. That much I could tell by the way she waved at me.

I wanted to tell Albert this, but he was looking like he just got plugged on the shoulder with an arrow. "Man, Lencho's gonna have it *in* for you!" he said finally, perking up in almost a gleeful way, like he wouldn't be *too* sorry if Lencho knocked in my teeth.

"He won't do anything," I said.

"Oh, no!?" Albert stressed, anxious to prove me wrong.

"No," I said. "He doesn't want to mess with Nardo."

"Oh, yeah."

He was glum again. He didn't have a brother, only a sister, and she'd as soon slap him in the face as smile. When you're like Albert, and you don't have protection, any day of the week, on any street corner, a guy like Lencho can kick in your rib cage and nobody would give a damn.

All in all, I thought it amazing that Lencho even *tried* to spark up the Chicano guys to join his boxing team. Not that the Chicano guys couldn't fight or anything. There were a lot of ornery *vatos* around, but they just hung around and smoked and ditched class and acted like the school was some kind of contaminated nuclear zone. They'd never join any team that wasn't a gang.

Lencho did recruit two suckers, though. One was a guy named Chico. A nice guy, but as my brother Nardo once said about him, the only shining he ever did came from his teeth. He could draw a neat picture of a naked girl and follow the numbers in a bingo game, but putting his finger on an algebra problem would probably burn him to ashes. Chico once tried out for the basketball team, but he was too short and couldn't dribble to save his life. When scratched from the roster, he blamed Coach Rogers, the basketball and boxing coach. The coach wore tortoise-shell glasses and talked in a Marine voice. He had a head that reflected the sun and a blue-black carpet of hair over his muscular arms. Where Chico got the story, I don't know, but he said the coach once caught a Mexican guy frisking around with his daughter and ever since then he didn't like Mexican guys.

The other fish Lencho hooked—and no one could believe it at first, especially me—was "Skinny Boy" Albert Sosa, my friend. I thought this was a pretty sorry thing for Lencho to do, considering Albert couldn't punch the air out of a soap bubble. Of course, it was a robustly stupid thing for Albert to do, too, since teachers lifted their eyebrows with appreciation when handing back his test papers.

But Albert wanted to show something about himself. He wanted to impress his dad maybe, who sat around watching TV all day, making fun of the white actors, or maybe he wanted to impress Miss Van der Meer, who you could tell sent fingers of ice down his neck.

I tried warning him. I tried explaining how ribs crack easy as dry twigs, and how a punch sometimes welcomes paralysis. But he wouldn't listen. He practically begged to sign up, and you could tell Lencho was disappointed at such a scrawny catch. He wanted guys like Nardo and Sammy Fuentes—dangers known to everyone.

But I think it was enough for Lencho to know that Chico and Albert would yank in whatever direction he pulled. They hung on his every word, and he could sure pump guys up with confidence. He belonged to this group called the Berets; older guys, mostly, already out of school. Actually, Lencho was only a Junior Beret, him still being in school and all. But to him, being a Junior Beret was still halfway better than a plain nobody.

The Berets believed that white people were our worst enemy, and if they had one purpose in mind, it was to keep brown people down. We, on the other hand, were descendants of Indians blessed with a color that was as necessary as dirt to the earth, as important as the sun to all the trees. We had treasures buried deep inside our blood, hidden treasures we hardly knew existed.

This is the kind of stuff I listened to from Lencho, who figured if he made me his equipment manager and

handler, then maybe Nardo might change his mind and put on the leather.

For three weeks, I hung out with the boxers. Training was held after school in the weight room, where the guys bounced around swiveling their necks, skipping rope and running in place until wet as fish. Then, with faces swelling, they'd groan out a few dozen sit-ups. (Lencho didn't let them lift iron because he said weights make muscles bulky, and they needed to be quick and springy in the exchanges.)

For equipment, we had an old, hobo-looking punching bag and one of those rubber tetherballs suspended on a bungee cord. On the first day, Albert hit the ball with a left, then came over—or *tried* to come over—with a right. The ball snapped back in a wobble and the cord gashed his fist. Between his two big knuckles, a flap of skin the size of a postage stamp opened a jagged eye.

Unwinding a jump rope in his hand, Lencho told him to skip the day's training, but to stick around for the pep talk. He didn't mean that, of course. What he really meant to say was that Albert should show his fireball commitment by toughing it out. He didn't say this, exactly; Lencho never said anything, exactly. Instead, he coolly started jumping rope and talking about how *real* fighters never let little chicken stuff like cuts put the coward's bite on them. After a long stare at the blood creeping under the Band-Aid he'd put on, Albert wrapped his hand in a T-shirt and began shuffling his feet around, jabbing at the air.

One of the fighters in Coach Rogers's stable was a black guy named Boise Johnson. During training, Lencho took particular attention to stink up his name. Clapping his hands, he'd roughen his voice and say we were going to pluck him like a chicken, crush him like a pasta shell. These put-downs were meant to lift the guys' confidence, but both Chico and Albert blessed their skinny bones they weren't going to fight Boise.

There was also a feud going on between Lencho and Coach Rogers. The coach didn't appreciate him mavericking fighters on his own. He was a former Golden Gloves boxing champion, and he considered that a big deal. I think every student at J. Edgar Hoover High knew the coach was a Golden Gloves boxing champion. Even in junior high I remember knowing, and I think even my dad knew, and my dad didn't give a rat's ass about anything that happened in my school.

Coach Rogers selected his fighters from those who

scored highest on the school's physical exams, which included climbing the high rope and squat-jumping and running windsprints until our lungs collapsed; but he depended, mostly, on who could lift the heaviest weights, or repeat the lighter weights the longest. This torture of selection dragged on for about two weeks, after which the guys who scored Excellent were given free gold trunks to wear and were invited later to join the football, basketball and boxing teams. The guys who scored Average could buy purple trunks with silver trim to announce their standing. Those who scored Poor, like me, had to wear those gray gym trunks like a flag of shame.

What mostly fired us up, though, was Lencho's inspirational talks. He spoke with braids of lightning in his voice, saying stuff he'd learned in the Berets about Mexicans and Chicanos being a special people, how power slept in our fists and we could awaken it with a simple nod of our heroic will. He piled it on about being proud, about how marvelous it was going to be after we pulverized those other guys. Lencho could really swell the chest muscles.

After a couple of weeks of watching punches pop deeper into the bag, and guys skip blurs on the jump rope—Albert actually hit the tetherball four swipes in a row!—I began to get a little swell-headed about our chances. Sure, at first I was a bit leery, since those other guys were bigger and could cross their arms when jumping rope, but they weren't any better than us, not really.

One day, while walking over by B Hall, I was surprised to hear my name called from behind. "Oh, Manuel! Manuel!"

It was Miss Van der Meer, bustling over, a pile of books shoved up against her breasts. She was walking in that cute, pigeon-toed way that used to make Albert and me do crazy rolls with our eyes.

"Do you think Leonard will win the contest?" she asked, stopping in front of me. She began to busily shuffle the order of her books on her chest.

"Yeah, I guess so," I said. "He's pretty confident."

"Yes, I noticed that about him," she said, waving her finger in the air. "He's a regular Hotspur."

"A hot what?" I asked. I thought maybe she was talking about some kind of bullsticker or thorn.

"Hotspur, in Shakespeare, you know."

I must have looked blank, because she got this disappointed frown on her face.

"Well, it's not important," she said, matter-of-factly. Her face was sprayed with sun freckles, and with her finger she delicately crooked back her bangs. She was beautiful, with swirls of glowing sunlight floating on her hair.

I was going to grab her free hand and shake it, but she started fiddling with the bindings of her books.

"Anyway," she said, "you tell Leonard for me that I wish him all the luck in the world. Will you do that, Manuel?" She made her hand straight as a Ping-Pong paddle and patted me a couple of times on the shoulder.

My heart lumped in my throat, and when I said, "Yeah, sure, Miss Van der Meer," my voice was thick as oatmeal.

Of course I didn't tell Lencho anything. He'd probably have spit at my shoes and said, *What a bitch!* He'd probably say something nasty, too, like why was a dog like me still sniffing after her tail. He talked like that sometimes when he wasn't getting all glorious about the Mexican race.

Not until Miss Van der Meer walked away did I wonder how she knew my name. I figured she must have asked someone, or looked it up in the administration files. Whichever way, I could tell by her eyes that she knew something about me. But then, I'd found out some things about her, too. For one, she wasn't one of the regular teachers, but a sort of extra teacher for the white students bussed in from Alemany High. I also found out about the couches and sofas in her classroom, because I asked the janitor, an El Salvadoran man who once worked with my dad in the onion fields. He scratched the back of his neck, and said, "*O sí, allí tienen sofás, lámparas y todo.*" He thought it was a teachers' lounge.

What all this has to do with the fight, I don't know. Usually I didn't like thoughts about teachers browsing around inside my head, but Miss Van der Meer was special. I hoped, in fact, that by some wildcard of luck they'd transfer me over from Mr. Shattler's class, where all we did was read magazines and play bingo games, to hers, where students read detective books and stuff by that Shakespeare guy. Except for Albert, the guys I hung with thought that if they even flicked through the pages of a book, ink would rub off on their hands and mark them sissies for life. I could imagine them in a classroom like Miss Van der Meer's, getting all cushy on the couches; throwing spit-wads at her butt.

The boxing tournament was announced in every home room in the school, and on flyers stapled in the hallways. Hardly a word passed across anyone's lips that didn't include the thrill they *hoped* they'd get when somebody got knocked out cold.

Being an official trainer, I got a reputation among a couple of girls, Rachel and Mary, who hung over by the baseball diamond. Their attitudes toward me couldn't have changed more completely. They said hi to me now, whereas before I would've died if just one of them had thrown me her eyes.

The day of the tournament, the basketball gym was packed from hoop to hoop. Waves of nervous anticipation washed like an ocean surf across the bleachers, and there was barely standing room by the push-open doors, where it was so pressed no one dared breathe.

The boxing ring was four brass stands taken from the school auditorium, linked by a long, furry velvet rope. They were just for show. A fighter would have to be crazy to lean against those ropes. The actual ring was a square of thick brown masking tape in the center of a huge wrestling mat.

Lencho invited his cronies from the Berets to come witness his spectacle. Decked out in khaki shirts and brown beret hats, their shoes polished to a smooth military sheen, they stood over by the exit doors intimidating anyone who happened to walk into their space. I was surprised to see Miss Van der Meer there, trying not to look excited. Old Mr. Hart, my history teacher, was there too, pacing on the sidelines and bogusly snuffling his nose with a crumpled handkerchief. Being the timekeeper and bell ringer, he was sweating diamonds.

I waited at ringside. I saw Nardo pump a fist at me as he and his friends Felix Contreras and Johnny Martinez crowded their way to a middle bleacher. He called to me, but I couldn't hear. The noise in the gym sounded warped, like a blackboard bending, about to

splinter and crack. Blood hissed along my temples and my earlobes pulsed like tiny engines, *This is the biggest moment of my life,* I thought.

I was supposed to get the ring corner organized, so I gave everything an anxious onceover; Lencho didn't want to be bothered by details. I had gym towels, water bottles, an already melting ice pack stuffed in a plastic bucket, and three mouthpieces wrapped in a clean white handkerchief. I had tape and Vaseline and those stretch wraps used for sprained ankles, although what I'd actually use them for was a mystery. The Berets paid for all the equipment, so I'd grabbed everything on the shelf.

The first fight was Albert's. He was to take on Boise's brother, Rochel Johnson, and from the look of Roach's arms, I knew somebody didn't keep an eye on the weight scales. Albert, if he breathed deep, probably weighed no more than an ounce above a hundred and nine pounds. Rochel looked, not a little, but a lot heavier.

I saw worry leaking out of Lencho's face. Unfortunately, Albert saw this too, because he stared at Rochel like he was Godzilla about to trample over Tokyo.

The fight was lopsided from the beginning, and lasted only about two minutes, although for me it was a hundred and twenty long, painfully slow seconds. Albert kept backing away and backing away until the crowd started whistling. The whistling soon turned to jeering and the jeering into sneering disgust. But that was okay, since the sneers shrunk the noise down enough for Lencho to holler, "Throw a combination! Throw a combination!" He punched his fists in the air to demonstrate, but Albert just looked at him like he'd been slapped on the face with a wet towel. "Charge, then, goddam it. Charge!" Lencho urged.

Unfortunately, Albert charged. But Rochel saw him coming from a mile away, and with his gloves up and head leaning to one side he moved smartly out of the way. Albert stumbled past him, tripped and smacked his nose on one of the auditorium stands. Everybody oohhed and awwhed and mangled their collars like it was them that got their noses smashed. Coach Mazzini mercifully waved the fight over.

Albert's face was awful with defeat; Lencho's was a torment of disappointment. He stuffed some ice in a towel and roughly pinched Albert's nose shut. The nosebleed bloomed a rose of blood in the towel, and Albert started to cry in wet, little puppy whimpers.

Lencho, with a sigh, told me to grab the towel and take him into the locker room.

That sure was a mistake. I knew it as soon as I walked into the locker room because there, dressing for his fight, was Chico—late as usual. Before I could tell him it was just a plain bloody nose, Chico took one look at the blood sopping the towel, and his face glazed over with shock.

"Hey, it's okay," I said, reassuringly. I left Albert by his locker. "It's only a bloody nose."

"Only a bloody nose!" Chico cried, clutching at his hair. He was stiff with panic. If somebody at that moment had pushed him over, he'd have landed flat on the back of his head.

I tried to grab his arm and lead him into the gym, but he shrugged me off and walked like a zombie down the locker aisle. I was afraid he'd suddenly bolt for the exit doors. *Oh no,* I said to myself. *What am I going to do?* I ran down the aisle and grabbed him by the shoulder.

"Hey, you're not *scared,* are you?" I said, trying to be peppy.

Chico stared blank at me for a while, then a little spark of embarrassment flashed in his eyes. "Hell, no, I was just, I was just going to get my towel."

"No, no," I insisted, "I got towels, I got plenty of towels! Hey man," I said with exaggerated pride, "I came *prepared!*"

This seemed to boost Chico's spirit a little, and he let me steer him through the swinging rubber doors and into the gym.

As soon as Chico and I walked in, a stampede began in the bleachers. The Mexicans, both guys and girls, began hammering the floorboards and hooting like wild Yaquis. It was a big cheer, considering the school was mostly black, with a few whites bussed in from across town.

When Chico and I reached the corner, Lencho was clapping these hard, buffeting claps, like he was a thousand times relieved to see us. He practically popped the knuckles out of my hand when he grabbed it.

I looked over and saw Nardo jamming his arm in the air, and could hear Rachel and Mary screeching Chico's and my names. The girlish pitch of their voices sliced through the noise like a paper cut. It touched down softly on my heart and opened a tiny slit that spilled sweet and aching all around inside me.

Lencho hurriedly sat Chico on the stool. "You hear that?" he said, stoking his courage. "That's for you! That's so you can show this guy who the real man is. Now, don't let your *Raza* down."

I left off listening and glanced about hoping to spot Rachel or Mary. I saw them, hair teased high and stiff, excitedly smacking their lips and rolling gum over their teeth. I saw Nardo again, too, standing on the bleachers. He was winding his shoulders as if readying to fight himself. Feeling proud and nervous at the same time, I flipped the towel over my shoulder, but it landed on the floor.

Lencho had revved Chico up. When the bell rang, he shot off his stool like a man in a desperate search for dropped money. He started punching at the guy, aiming for his stomach, but mostly hitting arms and shoulders.

The guy Chico fought was Malcolm Augustus, who was now in my biology class. He was the only one in the whole class who knew the answer to the teacher's question about how much blood spills when a girl's on her period. Guys were saying a gallon and girls were acting like they knew it already, but nobody really knew—except Malcolm, who said it was about six tablespoons. Imagine, six tablespoons!

Surprised at first by Chico's aggressiveness, Malcolm soon calmed down and stabbed him with some head jabs. When Chico ducked low to avoid getting his head snapped back, Malcolm unhinged an uppercut right under his chin. Chico stumbled back, looking like he'd stuck a fork into a light socket. I thought, *Oh no, we're doomed!* But Chico sparked up again and in a flutter of blows drove Malcolm outside the ring tape.

"You see that, did you see that uppercut!" Lencho shouted when Chico stumbled back to the corner. "That was the stupidest move the vato could've done. When he does that, just ignore it and come over the top with a left hook. You'll knock him out, I'm not kidding, you'll knock him out!" Lencho grabbed one of the bottles from my hand and splashed water on Chico's face. He fumbled when handing the bottle back and clunked me on the forehead. "Now, I want you to body punch that bastard until he squirms," he said, turning to Chico again, "and remember, remember the left hook!"

Chico didn't remember the left hook. He couldn't have remembered his name if you asked him. Halfway through the round his legs were making wobbly journeys around the ring. He did toss some slaps and chicken-wing flutters, but at the end of the second round he looked so winded you couldn't have put a baby to sleep in his arms.

In the third round Chico tried to duck a jab and come inside, but instead ran smack into Malcolm's elbow, and was knocked out cold. They had to carry him out flat on a blanket. People's eyes widened as they took him out the exit doors. His own eyes were ditched back inside his head, and he was slobbering all over one of the blanket carrier's hands. A smart aleck from the rafters yelled out, "Emergency! Emergency!" That got a big laugh from everybody, except Coach Rogers, who shoved his way up the bleachers and gave the guy the heave-ho out of the gym.

Right away talk turned to Boise and Lencho. All the excitement became sharp as a cone.

What happened first, though, was that the leader from the Berets, a guy named Miguel, wearing a cadet's starched khaki uniform, took over my job at the corner just as I was putting Lencho's gloves on. "Take a seat, Ace," he said, and without so much as an Excuse Me, he swished the towel off my shoulder and draped it over his own.

I tried to say something in Lencho's ear about uppercuts and strategy, but Miguel pushed me away. Lencho was too nervous to listen, anyway. And no wonder. Miguel right away started nudging him on the ribs, nodding up, and reminding him how many people were in the audience. Lencho's face wrung stiff as a twisted rope.

In the other corner, Coach Rogers and Boise seemed like two cozy sweet potatoes in the dirt. Boise's face was smooth from his warm-up, dark and shiny, like an icy glass of Coca-Cola. He wasn't wearing a shirt, and a tiny sapphire necklace of sweat strung across his lean belly. Just another fight to old Boise, I thought. Cool, that's what he was, cool, with nothing jumping around in his face and nobody in his corner giving him the jitters.

Lencho and Boise being about the same size, and the two guys in the school whose muscles were the most crowded together, it was natural that people would get excited about pitting them against each other. Seeing Lencho, proud and ready for action, you couldn't help but back him. And then there was Boise. He didn't strain against the threads of his clothes like Lencho, but he was what everybody in the Boys' Gym

called "ribbed." He even looked like a boxer, his nose square and puffy around the eyes, like he'd just awakened from a dream of beating up people.

The referee was Coach Mazzini. He had this big watersack gut that got in the way of everything, but otherwise he knew what to do, which was mostly to keep fighters from chickening out of the ring. When Mr. Hart clanged the bell announcing the start of the fight, everyone screwed their butts tight to their seat.

After a moment of staring at each other hard enough to shove a crowbar across a table, Lencho right away began wrenching left hooks and long winding right crosses; Boise ducked and upper-cutted to the body. It was a mean fight, a blur that even if you slowed it down by half, it would still be a blur. Even Coach Mazzini, fat belly and all, sprinted out of the ring and didn't go back in until Mr. Hart smacked the bell ending the first round.

The whole gym busted open with screams and foot stomping that almost brought the bleachers crashing down. Lencho came back to the corner, breathing huge and proud in his sweaty T-shirt, a fat grin on his face.

In the bleachers, it was a circus. Guys were dancing and girls collapsing over each other. The girls pawed over the guys and the guys pretended to hug them as they fainted on their laps. But then needling stuff, like arguing and weasely bragging, sparked between some black and brown guys. A few even began to shove each other and spit into arguments. Then the bell to the second round clanged and everybody right away sat down.

Boise was still calm, a gob of Vaseline dangling on his chin. At first he'd dip his shoulder and ease over to the side when Lencho charged. Then he began grinding punches into Lencho's belly, and suddenly, like a tidal wave, rise up to hammer him on the side of the head. A queery smile smeared across Lencho's face a couple of times.

That's when he began to shy away, stirring his gloves in the air like he was waving away flies. To show he wasn't stunned when he came back to the corner, he sunk his lips into a confident smirk. You could tell, though, that this was a sloppy excuse. In the bleachers, it was so quiet you could practically hear people breathing.

Whatever Lencho's plans were for the third round, they weren't very good. Boise began laying up for him, butting him on the jaw with jabs and swinging catapult blows against his ribs, making him grunt deep. To protect himself, Lencho crossed his arms and began stepping back, stubbornly jerking his chin from side to side to avoid blows. When Boise sledgehammered him on the side of the ear, his shoulders stiffened and his jaw squinched like a little electricity had run through it.

My heart was jerking around inside my chest, I was so nervous. My eyelashes were tiny wings beating in a fevery air, yet my face felt frozen, as if blasted by an arctic wind. I couldn't tell if my mouth was smiling or grinning.

Lencho didn't even bother coming in anymore, but just stood there gritting tighter on his mouthpiece, following Boise around the ring with beaten eyes. You could tell then that he was finished.

I pressed the sides of my cheeks to settle the nerves down, but my face kept on jumbling. Miguel, beside me, was yelling for Lencho to go forward. "Come on, Lencho! Come on! Attack! Attack! "

I felt like screaming for him to shut up. The truth was, I was afraid that Lencho would go down. If he did, I didn't know what I'd do. I had expected and wanted so much from him, that for him to disappoint me then would hurt, really hurt. I suddenly realized that the whole fight shouldn't have been given so much meaning. When pumped up with pride, something so ugly as a boxing match could only grow too cruel to maintain; it could only burst, right in everybody's faces.

When old Mr. Hart finally clanged the bell, ending the fight, I was relieved. It was obvious who had won. Coach Rogers gave Boise a big bear hug of victory. Then he rushed over and—real corny!—like he really meant it, cupped Lencho behind the neck like a proud father, staring into his eyes.

Miguel left the ringside in a hurry to talk with the Beret guys standing over by the exit doors. You could see their faces had hardened against showing what they really felt. Later, when it was all over, after they had *analyzed* it and all, they decided to kick Lencho out of the Berets. They said that he brought embarrassment to them, and worse, caused a loss of unity between them and their black brothers.

But that was later. Right then no one was around, except me, and Lencho kept searching for somebody to take off his gloves. Even when Boise came over—his own gloves off and, with his two naked hands, shook Lencho's arms—Lencho looked down at his gloves sort of funny, the way you look at a dog that has just dug up your garden, halfway angry at the dog and halfway sad about the garden. A hunk of concrete weighed on my chest and gopher teeth were gnawing at my heart, but I went over and began peeling the tape and undoing the laces—because Lencho wanted somebody to take off his gloves.

FURTHER RECOMMENDED READING

MILDRED TAYLOR (b. 1943)

THE ROAD TO MEMPHIS

Born in Jackson, Mississippi, but raised in Toledo, Ohio, Mildred Taylor drew on her family's stories of survival in the racist atmosphere of the South in her series of novels about the Logan family, which begins with *Song of the Trees* (1975) and continues with *Roll of Thunder, Hear My Cry* (1976) and further sequels and prequels. This highly acclaimed series tells the story of survival and determination in the face of racism and oppression. Cassie Logan and her family confront such problems with dignity and resourcefulness while living in rural Mississippi in the 1930s and 1940s. In *The Road to Memphis* (1990), Cassie is a high school student in Jackson. She and her brothers have to help a friend, Moe, escape to Chicago after Moe injured a white boy in a fight. The time is 1941, and the Japanese have just attacked Pearl Harbor. Cassie values her friendship with Moe, who loves her, but when she meets Solomon Bradley, an enterprising young lawyer and publisher, she discovers new feelings that create unexpected conflicts within her. The gender relationships are interesting in *The Road to Memphis* because Cassie is the only girl in a family of boys, but in this novel she grows into young adulthood sufficiently to begin to have romantic feelings for the opposite sex, and it is intriguing to see how she copes with the changes within herself as she recognizes new inner stirrings that, at times, pit friendship against romantic attraction. (See also discussion of *Roll of Thunder* in Part 2.)

PART SIX

WORDS AND PICTURES

" 'What is the use of a book,' thought Alice, 'without pictures or conversations?' "

Lewis Carroll

This idle thought sends a bored Victorian child into a dreamlike fantasy adventure, in a book famous for its combination of narration, conversation, and pictures. Although Lewis Carroll's stories in *Alice's Adventures in Wonderland* and *Through the Looking-Glass* have been reillustrated by a wide variety of artists over the years, his words are inextricably linked in the minds of generations of readers with John Tenniel's illustrations for the original editions (see excerpts in Part 1). Alice's question also suggests that by 1865, children, as well as creators of children's books, were developing high standards for books with appealing stories and illustrations. Readers today take for granted the availability of countless children's books with full-color reproductions of lavish paintings and many other types of artwork, but the photographic processes that led to this luxury were not developed until the 1880s in England. While children's books had been illustrated with woodcuts and engravings for several centuries, in Alice's day the innovative publisher Edmund Evans was just beginning to apply his new, economical techniques for color printing with wood blocks to the brilliant designs of several of England's most talented artists. Together they launched the art form that we call the modern picture book, a creation that skillfully combines the arts and crafts of writing, illustration, and book production, adding new dimensions to the ways in which words and pictures work together to create meaning.

The interplay of words and pictures in children's books is created in a variety of ways—by illustrators working closely with writers, artists working separately from the creators of the words they illustrate, or artists illustrating their own writing, in both picture books and longer illustrated books. Like Lewis Carroll and John Tenniel, Americans L. Frank Baum and W. W. Denslow developed fiction for children that was innovative in Baum's conception of an American fantasy adventure and Denslow's original style of illustration as they collaborated on *The Wonderful Wizard of Oz* and other books (see excerpts in Part 4). E. H. Shepard based his drawings of Winnie the Pooh and friends on A. A. Milne's son Christopher Robin, his toys, and their surroundings. Ever since Milne's books were first published in the 1920s, Shepard's illustrations (now labeled "classic Pooh" images on commercial products, to distinguish them from

Americanized depictions by the Disney Company) have reminded readers that the main characters are toys, while the text takes them on imaginary adventures in the woods like real animals and people. Shepard's other best-known work has shown generations of readers how woodland animals could look and act like people in his 1931 illustrations for Kenneth Grahame's *The Wind in the Willows,* although they did not appear until the twenty-first edition (see examples in Part 4). Garth Williams was influenced by E. B. White's views on natural life and animal fantasy while creating his famous images of Charlotte and Wilbur for the original edition of *Charlotte's Web,* and by visiting Laura Ingalls Wilder and places where she had lived when he illustrated later editions of her realistic Little House books (see Part 8).

Some texts seem inseparable from the art created by their author-illustrators, while others are not so strongly associated with particular sets of illustrations. The drawings by Louise Fitzhugh in Part 1, Edward Lear and Shel Silverstein in Part 3, and Louise Erdrich in Part 8 show how authors who are best known as novelists and poets sometimes illustrate their own work. Students of Victorian nonsense poetry may be interested in Lear's drawings, for example, but his poems, which have a much wider audience, are included in Part 3 because of their verbal appeal and links with the nursery rhymes and animal fantasies of the oral tradition. "The Owl and the Pussy-cat" has also been published separately with illustrations by other artists since Lear's time. Examples of more recent poems that have been illustrated as picture books are "knoxville, tennessee" by Nikki Giovanni (in Part 4) and "BOOK" by George Ella Lyon (at the front of this anthology). Occasionally the artwork in an illustrated children's book comes first and serves as an inspiration for the writer. For example, poems by Lucille Clifton (see Part 1), Maya Angelou (see Part 4), and others were written to accompany Tom Feelings' illustrations in *Soul Looks Back in Wonder.* More often the text exists long before the illustrations. As many examples in Part 3 and in this section show, rhymes and tales from the oral tradition have often been illustrated by prominent artists since the nineteenth century. Great picture-book artists, from Walter Crane and Randolph Caldecott to Maurice Sendak, have created intriguing new visual interpretations of old nursery rhymes and fairy tales.

Sendak began to have a significant influence on the art of the modern picture book when he started illustrating his own texts, such as *Where the Wild Things Are,* in the 1960s. Although an essay by Sendak in this section praises Caldecott's nursery rhyme books for uniting words and images with such "ingenious" economy and rhythm, achieving "a counterpoint that never happened before," Sendak and a host of other modern illustrators who began with training and experience as artists before they wrote their own texts are also like their predecessor Beatrix Potter in composing original stories to create magical combinations of narrative and art. An anthology such as this cannot do justice to the multifaceted wonders of modern picture books, which should be read in their entirety, with the format and colors designed by their creators. But the examples of children's book illustrations throughout this volume and this section's introductions to a variety of artists represent some landmarks in the history of book illustration and different approaches to combining words and images, which we hope will encourage readers to seek out the books mentioned here and many others.

Understanding the crosscurrents of words and pictures in children's books is related to debates that were considered in earlier sections about whether to treat literature as instruction or entertainment and whether literature privileges adult authority or the child's point of view. Since adults have often valued literacy over most forms of oral and visual communication and fine art over illustration and other types of commercial art, illustrated books that are viewed primarily as serving to educate young children have not always been highly regarded as works of art or literature. By the end of the twentieth century, however, critics were applying multidisciplinary theories to analyses of the complex relationships between words and picture in picture books, as Perry Nodelman's chapter from *Words About Pictures* demonstrates in this section. Influences that recent critics such as Nodelman have examined in detail range from the great masters and movements of art history to popular media that children enjoy and adults sometimes try to keep children away from, including comic books and animated cartoons. In an essay reprinted in this section, Maurice Sendak, one of many artists who have been influenced by cartoons and advertising from his own childhood, describes Winsor McCay's early twentieth-century comic strips as a type of children's book with an audience of all ages: "McCay and I serve the same master, our child selves." Many children's book illustrators began their careers as cartoonists, from George Cruikshank, the influential English caricaturist who illustrated novels of Charles Dickens and fairy tales, to Dr. Seuss, William Steig, and Tom Feelings in twentieth-century America (see Cruikshank and Steig in Part 3 and Feelings in this section). Cartoonists and caricaturists are also given due credit by critic David Lewis, who concludes from his research on picture books that histories of book illustration and art have overshadowed several important developments that shaped the modern picture book:

> When we look back to the origins of the picture book and to its development through the nineteenth century, I believe we can detect a number of important features that have survived to the present day and which give the picture book its unique character. There is its brevity, and its interweaving of word and image, both originally inherited from the chapbook. These are the features that give the form its flexibility, its willingness to ingest other genres and forms of representation, and its ability to hybridise—sometimes bizarrely—with games and toys. This lack of respect for genre boundaries and conventions goes hand in hand with a general air of irreverence born equally of the picture book's folkloric origins and of the shaping experience it had in the hands of the nineteenth century caricaturists. This latter body of artists and writers not only injected wit and humour and narrative energy into the form, they introduced a degree of irony by exploiting and thereby demonstrating its capacity for counterpointing word and image.[1]

When Alice complained about her sister's book having no pictures or conversations, she may have been thinking of some of these forerunners of the modern picture book. Edmund Evans published his first artfully designed "toy book" by Walter Crane in 1865, the same year that *Alice* was published, but less notable toy books had been sold by others since the 1830s. These were not actual toys like the toy theaters, fold-out designs, pop-ups, and other novelties that Lewis discusses as games and toys that combined story with play, but inexpensive mass-produced books for children that featured colored illustrations and reprints of traditional tales and rhymes. And chapbooks had been widely available since the seventeenth century, cheap booklets sold by peddlers with all kinds of writings and crude woodcuts, including illustrated alphabets, folktales, and ballads. Writers such as James Boswell and William Wordsworth declared their affection for the chapbooks of their youth, and Maurice Sendak paid tribute to the chapbook in his 1962 *Nutshell Library,* a miniature quartet of illustrated rhymes in the traditional genres of alphabet, counting rhyme, cautionary tale, and book of months.

Other developments in pre-Golden Age children's books are represented by Johan Amos Comenius and Thomas Bewick in this section. Although children would have looked at the woodcuts in early chapbooks and editions of Aesop's fables soon after the printing press was invented, the *Orbis Sensualium Pictus* by Comenius, published in Latin and vernacular languages beginning in 1658, is considered the first fully illustrated textbook for children. As such, its title is appropriately translated as "The World of Things Evident to the Senses through Pictures." Aware that children would be attracted by the woodcuts before they could read, Comenius coordinated pictures and words carefully for readers who were expanding their vocabulary in Latin and other languages. His book is the forerunner of countless illustrated dictionaries and encyclopedias, as well as contemporary word books for younger children that match basic vocabulary with objects in a series of scenes or groupings. Alphabets and other concept books in the twentieth century developed into sophisticated works of art that incorporate many kinds of wordplay, artistic styles, multicultural content, and multimedia visual effects, as the examples by Mitsumasa Anno, Tom Feelings, and Chris Van Allsburg in this section illustrate. Thomas Bewick's most popular books were also intended to expand the reader's knowledge, through his hundreds of engravings of birds and animals, in *A General History of Quadrupeds* and *A History of British Birds*. Bewick is remembered primarily for his late-eighteenth-century advances in the art of wood engraving, since his ability to include fine details, textures, and depth and to depict nature and everyday English life with affection and humor inspired his students and others to follow his methods of book illustration until photographic techniques began in the 1880s; he continues to influence illustrators who admire his style, such as Maurice Sendak.

Bewick also added narrative interest to his informational books on birds and animals by filling extra spaces with vignettes that have attracted readers as much as his primary subjects. Charlotte Brontë described her heroine Jane Eyre as a lonely child who was happy with a volume of Bewick's *History of British Birds* on her knee, imagining mysterious and dramatic scenes, as "each picture told a story."[2] Bewick's vignettes offered "readers" the same kinds of pleasure that so many wordless picture books have provided in recent times. Mercer Mayer, in the United States, and Renate Meyer, a German-born artist in Britain, are credited with launching the popularity of wordless picture books in the 1960s. As the excerpts in this section from *Frog Goes to Dinner* show, Mayer's series of wordless books about an ordinary boy and a mischievous frog uses skillful drawing of bodies, facial expressions, and background details to tell lighthearted stories with realistic and amusing characters. *The Snowman* by Raymond Briggs (1982) is one of the most popular wordless fantasies for young children, with softly painted panels that take a boy on a more magical, dreamlike fantasy adventure with a snowman than Mayer's amusing escapades of a frog and a boy in pencil drawings. Mitsumasa Anno created wordless picture books that promote a kind of cultural literacy through intricately detailed scenes full of landmarks and famous figures in different countries. The Japanese artist felt that these wordless travel books, beginning with *Anno's Journey* in 1977, could represent the hearts of people even though the languages of the Western world are difficult for him. Another artist demonstrating that wordless books could present serious subjects with emotional and intellectual appeal was Tom Feelings, whose paintings in *The Middle Passage: White Ships/Black Cargo* (1995) tell the painful story of the slave trade between Africa and America. With or without words, contemporary picture books appeal to readers of all ages, ranging widely across the spectrum of different genres and types of literature that educate and entertain readers.

Edmund Evans's groundbreaking success with Victorian picture books was not only preceded by a long history of chapbooks and toy books, but the Romantic movement had initiated a century of folklore collecting, interest in childhood, and fascination with works of fantasy and imagination. William Blake's late-eighteenth-century volumes of original poetry that he illustrated, colored by hand, and printed himself provided a model of integrated artistic design for later illustrators and printers. His *Songs of Innocence* (1789) expressed a radical new approach to childhood, although his books were not well known in his time and are not published for children with his illustrations. Evans brought books for children with a high standard of art and design to the public by uniting his new methods for engraving with wood blocks and printing large numbers of inexpensive books, with the artistic skills of the brilliant illustrators he hired, beginning with Walter Crane's bold designs for nursery rhymes and fairy tales. Evans's great triumvirate of illustrators collaborated closely with him and, at times, with each other, although their styles were different. Crane criticized Randolph Caldecott's sketchy lines and Kate Greenaway's overdressed characters, while Caldecott thought that Crane was too dependent on Italian art, rather than developing a more natural style. Crane, whose lavishly decorated scenes for fairy tales like "Beauty and the Beast" are most memorable, transformed the picture book by designing every part of it, from cover to cover, as a harmonious work of art, while Caldecott added energetic, humorous visual details and narrative twists to nursery rhymes and comic poems. Evans took a chance on Kate Greenaway by publishing her original verses in *Under the Window* in 1878, and when her delicately designed pages with charming portraits of elaborately dressed children became wildly fashionable, she also illustrated books of nursery rhymes, flowers, calendars, and legends. All these artists produced illustrated rhymes and tales that are still reprinted frequently, well over a century after Evans and Crane began.

Since the dawn of this Golden Age of imagination and high-quality art in children's books, a wide range of artists around the world have illustrated nursery rhymes and fairy tales in every possible style, attesting to the power and versatility of the oral tradition as illustrators find new ways to reinterpret and expand on the traditional forms of poetry, animal tales, and magical tales. Crane was obviously interested in playing with symbolic images, rather than helping a first-time reader follow the tale from start to finish, since his decorations for "Rapunzel" place figures of the heroine with her children, her father, the witch with her shears, and the prince in locations where the text is not describing their actions. Before and after the success of Edmund Evans's toy books, many artists in addition to Crane illustrated longer collections of fairy tales and nursery rhymes, including, among those represented in this anthology, Gustave Doré in France; Eleanor Vere Boyle from Scotland; and Englishmen George Cruikshank, John Batten, John Leech, Charles Folkard, L. Leslie Brooke, and Arthur Rackham. Rackham's silhouette for "The Emperor's New Clothes" (in Part 2), energetic line drawing for "Three Blind Mice," and elegant painting for "Little Miss Muffet" (in Part 3) demonstrate the range of styles mastered by this prolific illustrator. From the particularly rich tradition of fairy tale illustration in Russia, Ivan Bilibin's illustration for "Vasilissa the Beautiful" in Part 3 shows the influence of Art Nouveau styles in the early twentieth century, while Wanda Gág's more folksy style of retelling and illustrating Grimms' fairy tales was influenced by her Eastern European ancestry.

The last several decades of the twentieth century saw a huge outpouring of new books retelling classic fairy tales and introducing modern adaptations and lesser-known tales from the oral tradition. The dominant style, sometimes called fairy tale realism in the late twentieth century, was influenced by Renaissance realism and by the nineteenth-century narrative paintings of the British pre-Raphaelites and the American Brandywine School of painters. Just as European artists in the second half of the fifteenth century, in the transition from medieval to Renaissance art, were able to create scenes full of intricate detail, integrating supernatural themes with natural and domestic realism through new developments in oil painting and printmaking, illustrators in the second half of the twentieth century could produce lavish, detailed paintings and drawings for books, as offset lithography became the dominant method of printing and it was possible by the 1960s to reproduce full-color paintings and all kinds of artworks more accurately and inexpensively. Trina Schart Hyman and Maurice Sendak are among recent artists who have explored the dark mysteries and sensual undertones of old fairy tales in their detailed illustrations with pre-twentieth-century settings and costumes. Italian artist Roberto Innocenti took a different approach when illustrating "Cinderella," placing Perrault's seventeenth-century text within a 1920s setting through a style of photographic realism in sepia illustrations that create the illusion of looking into Cinderella's photograph album (see Part 5). As Part 4 discusses, the great writers of fantasy and illustrators of fantasy and folklore create a magical blend of reality and fantasy to make the world of the imagination real to the reader.

Although Hyman is best known for her sumptuous fairy tale paintings with medieval settings, the selection from *Jane, Wishing,* by Tobi Tobias, presented in this section shows how she created black-and-white contemporary scenes for a story in which they alternate with colored illustrations of an ordinary girl's romantic fantasies. Domestic fantasy has been just as popular in picture books of the past century as the nonsense of nursery rhymes and the high romance of fairy tales and ancient legends. Beatrix Potter led the way at the end of the Victorian period by transforming her drawings of animals that she had observed all her life and stories that she began writing in letters to child friends into small books of well-told animal tales set in the English countryside and villages that she loved. She drew and painted with the eye of a naturalist, but in the ancient tradition of fables and animal folktales (like the American Uncle Remus tales that she read), her animals dramatize the comic foibles, family bonds, and heartwarming friendships of human life. Peter Rabbit is a mischievous boy who takes the reader on a hair-raising adventure through Mr. McGregor's garden and worries his mother, suffering from fright, indigestion, and his resulting inability to have blackberries with his obedient sisters at home. Potter's stories depict cozy homes, village friendships, farms, and picturesque wild areas of the Lake District, but they also contain horrible predators, such as Samuel Whiskers, the rat who wants to eat a lost kitten, just as older nursery tales and rhymes blend appealing domestic scenes with grotesque horrors and amusing fantasies. Potter knew that choosing just the right words and realistic images would draw children into her animal fantasies, refusing to simplify her language and scoffing at Kenneth Grahame's unrealistic description of Toad combing his hair in *The Wind and the Willows.*[3]

Half a century later, Garth Williams's line drawings for *Charlotte's Web* also combined realistic animal characters, humans, and farm scenes. Writer E. B. White instructed Williams to make Charlotte look like a real spider, and Williams used farms that he knew as backdrops, but he wove fantasy into Charlotte's miraculous web writings and his drawings of some of the animals' antics and conversations. When illustrating *Bedtime for Frances* by Russell Hoban, Williams worked with an indoor story that could have been populated by humans or any small animals, and after he chose to draw badgers, Frances's family became popular bedtime companions for millions of parents who were trying to get their own children settled down in bed. Robert McCloskey's *Blueberries for Sal* is primarily a human story about a mother and daughter picking berries, but there is a touch of fantasy in his imagining that a bear mother and child could bump into the humans and have parallel feelings during their friendly mix-up. Margaret Wise Brown's *The Runaway Bunny* is much like *Peter Rabbit,* in that illustrator Clement Hurd blended realistic images of rabbits in their natural habitat with the plot's magic elements. There is an additional layer of make-believe in this story, in that the mother bunny convinces her child not to run away by matching each of his fantasies of escape with her own plans for transforming herself into something that could pursue him. Hurd's wordless double-spread color paintings dramatize these imaginary scenarios, with warm green-and-blue landscapes in most scenes. The bunny's fantasy about becoming a boy in a house appears surprisingly multilayered after the brief text that sets it up, since Hurd's painting adds the intertextual dimension of a cozy interior scene that is reminiscent of the setting of the earlier book *Goodnight Moon,* complete with a painting of a cow jumping over the moon and a small bunny in a human child's striped pajamas. For children who read both stories, the climax is not the daring adventures imagined by the little bunny, but his emotional capture in this familiar world of family and fireside, leading to his decision to stay as he is with his mother bunny in their home outdoors.

It has been recognized for several centuries that pictures can interest children in reading and that illustrations help the beginning reader master the complex skills of deciphering words and comprehending texts. Comenius's *Orbis Sensualium Pictus* and *The New-England Primer,* the Puritan textbook with its famous illustrated alphabet, show that educators had this awareness by the late seventeenth century. The discovery of Jane Johnson's handmade nursery library for her children, from the first half of the eighteenth century, has led recent scholars to reconsider the role of mothers in providing multimedia materials (oral, written, and illustrated) for the benefit of their children before there were many published children's books.[4] Jacob Abbott's nineteenth-century "Notice to Parents" emphasizes the value of "a practical lesson" with careful instructions in how to combine the pictures in his *Rollo* books with reading and talking to teach language to young children (see Part 1). By the 1950s, books such as Dr. Seuss's *The Cat in the Hat* and *Green Eggs and Ham,* as well as the Little Bear series by Else Holmelund Minarik and Maurice Sendak, were launching a new era of books for beginning readers with more engaging stories, more captivating fantasies, and more interesting art than the primers used in schools. *Bedtime for Frances* by Hoban and Williams is an I Can Read book from 1960, and these books about Frances, Little Bear, and Dr. Seuss's characters are still widely read in the twenty-first century. They followed a century-long tradition of producing high-quality children's book art that would also stimulate the imagination and develop the child's aesthetic sensibilities. As critic Leonard Marcus wrote of Ursula Nordstrom, the legendary editor at Harper's in the early days of Sendak, Hurd, and Williams, she believed in promoting books that "validated young people's complex emotional lives while providing them with aesthetic experiences of the highest order."[5]

However, picture books have too often been put away after children gain full mastery of reading words in longer books. What was not widely recognized until the late twentieth century was the value of illustrated books for readers of all ages and the complex skills involved in decoding the patterns and traditions of picture books. It became obvious through the twentieth century, as the popularity of films, comic books, television, video games, and then the Internet grew, that Alice's preference for pictures and conversation is shared by modern people of all ages, but educators and librarians often clung to their belief in the superiority of the written word. Some tried to keep these other forms of popular culture and multimedia storytelling out of the library and classroom or, at least, limit them to the fringes of the curriculum, even blaming them for declines in literacy. But by the end of the century, visual literacy (a term coined by artists and educators in the 1950s and 1960s) was widely accepted in schools as a set of skills to be developed for understanding how visual images communicate, comparable to mastering the techniques of language, and many books and articles advocated the use of picture books in teaching beyond the primary level.

Since the 1980s, studies such as William Moebius's "Introduction to Picture Book Codes" and Perry Nodelman's *Words About Pictures* have expanded our appreciation of the ways in which words and art work together in picture books.[6] Not only are there complex codes in the crosscurrents of words and pictures as they lead us through a book, supplementing and counterpointing each other in a wide variety of patterns, but contemporary artists find new ways to play with the traditional codes; they create picture books that blend familiar images or styles from the history of art and popular culture with postmodern literary and artistic techniques, sometimes reflecting on the process of reading itself and the structure of books. Morag Styles and Victor Watson write that "picture books are subversive both of narrative expectations and cultural influences. . . . they tend to be concerned with rule-breaking, mischief and challenge. They teach the rules, and at the same time they invoke laughter and subversive questioning."[7] Chris Van Allsburg's *The Z Was Zapped* makes the alphabet into a surrealistic, absurdly violent drama. *The Stinky Cheese Man and Other Fairly Stupid Tales* (1992), by Jon Scieszka and Lane Smith, not only satirizes fairy tales, but makes fun of every detail of a book's structure, from the dedication to the ISBN code. In *The Three Pigs,* by David Wiesner (2001), the pigs are drawn most realistically when they are shown flying outside the pages of their own story, traveling through pages in other artistic styles, wrinkling pages, and scattering letters of the text as they escape from the wolf and create a new story. Some adults worry that children will not comprehend artistically sophisticated illustrations and the multilayered, sometimes indeterminate, effects of picture books that use intertextuality and metafiction so brilliantly, but recent studies have shown that young children engage in complex processes of interpretation when they are "reading pictures" and that they have much to teach adults about these processes. Children are experts on imaginative play, and from Caldecott to Sendak and Van Allsburg, illustrators of children's books have shaped the interplay of words and pictures in a multitude of books that are both meaningful and fun.

NOTES

1. David Lewis, "Pop-ups and Fingle-fangles," *Talking Pictures: Pictorial Texts and Young Readers,* ed. Victor Watson and Morag Styles (London: Hodder & Stoughton, 1996) 20.
2. Charlotte Bronte, Chapter 1, *Jane Eyre* (1847).
3. Judy Taylor et al., *Beatrix Potter, 1846–1943: The Artist and her World* (London: Frederick Warne and The National Trust, 1987) 137.
4. M. Hilton, Morag Styles, and Victor Watson, ed. *Opening the Nursery Door: Reading, Writing and Childhood 1600–1900* (London: Routledge, 1997).
5. Ursula Nordstrom, *Dear Genius: The Letters of Ursula Nordstrom,* ed. Leonard S. Marcus (New York: HarperCollins, 1998).
6. William Moebius, "Introduction to Picturebook Codes," *Word & Image* 2.2 (1986): 141–58.
7. "Introduction—A Variety of Voices," *Talking Pictures: Pictorial Texts and Young Readers,* ed. Victor Watson and Morag Styles (London: Hodder & Stoughton, 1996) 2.

Perry Nodelman (b. 1942)

Perry Nodelman is a writer for children and young adults and one of the most distinguished critics of children's literature. He teaches at the University of Winnipeg and has written about a wide range of topics in over 100 articles and two highly influential books about children's literature: *The Pleasures of Children's Literature* (1992) and *Words About Pictures: The Narrative Art of Children's Picture Books* (1988). *Words About Pictures* contains one of the most extensive studies of picture book art ever undertaken. The book begins by observing that "picture books—books intended for young children which communicate information or tell stories through a series of many pictures combined with relatively slight texts or no texts at all—are unlike any other form of verbal or visual art." Nodelman's Preface also stresses the "pleasure and value" that both children and adults will find in picture books if they develop a "deeper understanding" and more precise ways to discuss art (pp. x–xi). The book's ten chapters develop new perspectives on picture books by drawing on a variety of approaches, such as theories of aesthetics and verbal narrative, cognitive theories of perception, and comparisons with narrative techniques of novels and films. Since 1988, *Words About Pictures* has influenced both picture book artists and scholars who have produced many more in-depth studies of artistic techniques used by individual artists, new theories about picture book art, and methods of analyzing and enriching children's responses to picture books. Chapter 7, "The Relationships of Pictures and Words," discusses readers' perceptions of words and pictures in relation to functions of the right and left brain. Nodelman's own experiments with readers' responses show how interdependent texts and pictures are as readers combine physical and mental faculties to experience the picture book's "total effect." Examples from illustrated editions of "Snow White" and other books show "how the relative strengths and weaknesses of words and pictures" function as the best picture books make use of their differences. (For related writings, see "Snow White" in Part 3 and Nodelman's statement on fantasy in Part 4.)

The Relationships of Pictures and Words

As we respond to picture books, the words of the texts so permeate our experience of the pictures that the two seem to mirror each other. But they do not in fact do so—as becomes obvious as soon as we separate them from each other. I have asked hundreds of different people—both children and adult students of children's literature—to record the stories that occur to them as they experience only the pictures of picture books that do have texts; they always express frustration and arrive at a surprising variety of different stories. While my audience is less frustrated when I perform the reverse procedure and read the texts of picture-book stories without the accompanying pictures, they do often seriously misunderstand the implications of the words they hear. These experiences reveal much about the different ways in which words and pictures contribute to the total effect of a picture-book narrative.

In *The Art of Art for Children's Books,* Diana Klemin asserts that Celestino Piatti's pictures for *The Happy Owls* "cast a powerful illusion of storytelling" (64). That the narrative effect is indeed illusory is made clear in the stories made up by those who view these pictures without hearing the words. As it happens, *The Happy Owls* is an ideal book for this procedure, for the pictures are not on the same page as the words and can easily be separated from them. To avoid the confusion caused by not knowing where the earlier events of a story are leading, I show all the pictures in sequence once through and then ask people to write stories as they see the pictures for a second time. The result is a wide variety of stories: descriptions of an ordinary day in the life of two owls, reports on how two owls distributed important information, attempts to solve a food shortage in a barnyard, disputes about which bird is most beautiful—and not surprisingly, stories about owls whose bafflement or frustration seems to have been transferred from their perplexed storytellers.

But the pictures in *The Happy Owls* are unlike each other both in composition and subject: some focus on a pair of owls, others on groups of other birds, others on forest landscapes; one is a close-up of a sunflower with a human face. Since that lack of consistency may make this book an unfair choice for this experiment, I have also followed the same procedure with a more cohesive series of pictures. Maurice Sendak's pictures for *Mr. Rabbit and the Lovely Present* also appear on separate pages from the text and are enough like each other in style, in subject, and in mood to imply that they might actually be telling a story. And in fact, while the details vary, people do find a series of events in these pictures that are similar to each other—and similar, too, to Charlotte Zolotow's story about a journey through the woods in search of something.

Nevertheless, and not surprisingly, no one ever guesses the fact that the object of the search is a birthday present: the person the present is intended for is prominent in the text but never appears in the pictures. That apparently small detail makes a large difference: without a specific motive for the search, the actions that most people find in these pictures are not really stories at all; they are more like plotless travelogues, in which the rabbit shows the girl a number of unrelated sights merely because they are interesting or beautiful.

That seems a just response to Sendak's pictures: as Barbara Bader quite rightly suggests, the girl and the rabbit "turn up in this dappled painting and that . . .

without there being any sense of their going from here to there, without our having any sense, in fact, of where they are or where they're going" (*American Picturebooks* 498). These pictures make the woods look so attractive and suggest so little in the way of danger or even of action that it is logical to assume that their beauty is a key factor in the story.

Interestingly, however, the stories people find in *The Happy Owls* pictures also often focus on the act of seeing and build plots around the owls' viewing of the birds or the forest. In a sense, the actual stories of both *The Happy Owls* and *Mr. Rabbit* are about seeing things; but the owls describe their forest, and the rabbit and girl inspect theirs, for reasons that relate only peripherally to the interest or beauty of appearances. Apparently, the pictures by themselves convey only the general idea of viewing, of looking at interesting or beautiful sights, as perhaps all pictures do. But they provide no suggestion of a focus, no specific idea about *why* one might be looking. Consequently, people asked to find stories in these pictures tend to transform their own interest in looking at the pictures into the interest of the characters within the pictures. Without a context of accompanying words, the visual impact of pictures as sources of sensuous pleasure is more significant than any specific narrative information they might contain.

The extent to which the meaning in pictures depends on exterior contexts is confirmed by the stories that people do and do not find in these two sets of pictures. The stories people do tell tend most often to be versions of the most conventional kinds of children's narratives, descriptions of journeys which end with the statement that home is best or disputes about beauty or talent which end with the realization that we are all beautiful in our own way. That people complete the meaning of these pictures by making use of their prior knowledge of other texts shows that the pictures themselves can imply narrative information only in relationship to a verbal context; if none is actually provided, we tend to find one in our memories. On the other hand, when I show adults Sendak's first picture of the little girl and the huge rabbit, there is always someone who giggles in a knowing way, yet no one has ever made up a sniggly story about a nymphet and a rabbit on the make; the assumption that this is a children's story narrows the range of acceptable interpretations.

Without a text to complete it, furthermore, people tend even to misinterpret the visual information in these pictures in ways that reveal how fragmentary that information is. Some people read gloom and depression into Sendak's moody pictures, and a number of people have interpreted Piatti's powerful picture of a red sunset over a snow-covered wood as a depiction of a fire. It is particularly revealing that many people create stories about Sendak's pictures in which a house figures prominently, and stories about Piatti's pictures in which a fox figures prominently. While there is a house in one of Sendak's pictures, the text says only that some roofs are red and does not even mention the house, and while there is a fox in one of Piatti's pictures, the text accompanying that picture not only does not mention the fox but actually suggests that the forest in which he appears is a peaceful place. What was simply background for the artist becomes an important fact in need of explanation for those who do not know the specific focus the words provide.

Nevertheless, when I tell people the original stories after the exercise, they are surprised by what they have missed. With the focus offered by the words, it is hard not to see that Piatti's pictures depict changes in season, something viewers probably do not notice at first because they do not expect the time that is supposed to have passed between one picture and the next to be so long; it is usually a matter of minutes or hours, not months. And with the words, it is hard not to notice that Sendak's pictures centrally focus on differences in color, a fact no one even comments on at first. With the words to guide our perception of them, these two sequences of pictures both do create a powerful illusion of storytelling. Words can make pictures into rich narrative resources—but only because they communicate so differently from pictures that they change the meanings of pictures.

For the same reason, also, pictures can change the narrative thrust of words. I hope that the earlier chapters of this book have revealed the variety and subtlety of narrative information that pictures can provide, but in those chapters, of course, I interpreted visual information in the context of the accompanying texts that I was already familiar with, and in consequence I tended to focus on elements that supported the implications of the texts. That pictures actually *change* the meanings of texts in the process of supporting them becomes particularly clear if we perform the reverse experiment of the ones described above and explore the effects on listeners of a story told to them without the accompanying pictures. When I have read the text of Sendak's *Where the Wild Things Are* to adults who have not previously heard it, without showing them the pictures, many feel it to be a terrifying story, too frightening for young children. Without Sendak's *particular* Wild Things to look at, they conjure up wild things out of their own nightmares, and those they find scary indeed. When I then tell them the story accompanied by the pictures, they always change their minds. Sendak's monsters are relatively reassuring, adorable rather than terrifying, and Sendak's Max is much more arrogant and assertive than they had imagined him. In fact, it is the pictures and not the words that tell us there is nothing to worry about, that despite our assumptions about the weakness of children and the violence of monsters, this particular child can take care of himself with these particular monsters. The illustrations in *Wild Things* communicate information that changes the effect and meaning of the story as a whole, just as the words of *The Happy Owls* and *Mr. Rabbit* communicate information that changes the effect and meaning of the story as a whole.

Those changes can occur because words and pictures communicate in ways so different that commentators tend to exaggerate the differences. It has been fashionable in recent years to suggest, on the basis of research into the activity of the human brain, that the two might even require perception by two different organs. The brain consists of two hemispheres joined only by a bundle of interconnecting fibers; studies of patients with lesions in various areas of one half or the other seem to suggest that the two halves are responsible for different kinds of thinking. In general terms, the left hemisphere seems to handle analytical, sequential thinking and thus to control language functioning; the right seems to manage holistic thinking, simultaneous rather than sequential operations, and thus to control visual and spatial capacities.

In a list he calls "The Two Modes of Consciousness: A Tentative Dichotomy," the psychologist Robert Ornstein identifies the qualities of the two hemispheres as two quite different visions of reality; among other things, he suggests that left-hemisphere consciousness is lineal, sequential, causal, focal, explicit, and verbal—typical of Western "rational" thought—and that right-hemisphere consciousness is nonlineal,

simultaneous, acausal, diffuse, tacit, and spatial—typical of the "intuitional" thought of so-called primitive societies (83).

In the light of these categories, some commentators have concluded that words communicate in ways that relate to these left-hemisphere activities and that pictures communicate in ways that relate to the right-hemisphere activities. Stories obviously occupy time, pictures space. The stories that words tell are certainly lineal, sequential, causal; a plot is a unified sequence of causes and effects, and it is the order in which events are communicated, and their temporal relationships with each other, that make them into stories. Furthermore, words easily focus our attention. If the shape of a woman's nose is important to the meaning of a story, then the words in the story about her will mention the shape of her nose; looking at a picture of her, we might be so interested by the curtains on the window behind her that we do not even notice the nose. In that way, pictures tend to be diffuse, words explicit. We first experience a picture all at once, a glance taking in the whole image, and theoretically we have no way of determining what in it might have caused what else in it. If we see a woman sitting in front of a window, we do not know if she is smiling because the curtains have been freshly laundered or if she laundered them because she is happy—or if the happy face and the clean curtains have nothing whatsoever to do with each other and that it is actually the nose that we should be paying attention to.

But further consideration reveals that words and pictures are not in fact so totally separable. As the inadequacies of patients with lesions reveal so clearly, the properly working brain requires both its hemispheres. In *The Shattered Mind*, Howard Gardner says, "it is almost unthinkable that our 'normal' minds should not utilize both halves of the brain during waking activity" (376). What research into hemispheric activity actually suggests about picture books is what my experiments in separating words from pictures reveal—not that words and pictures are quite separate from each other but, rather, that placing them into relationship with each other inevitably changes the meaning of both, so that good picture books as a whole are a richer experience than just the simple sum of their parts.

The idea that words are merely lineal and pictures merely spatial is extremely simplistic. We could not read words if we could not interpret the visual symbols that stand for them on paper; reading is itself an act of vision. Furthermore, our understanding of language demands that we find holistic shapes in the sequences of words. In coming to an end, a sentence creates an implication of finality that demands not just our understanding of the words in sequence but also our simultaneous consciousness of everything that has already happened in the sequence so that we can understand the shape of the whole. Stories extend the shaping power of individual sentences. We will not be satisfied with a story until we perceive, consciously or not, that it does indeed contain the organizational patterns that make it a story rather than a "slice of life": most literary criticism is about such patterns, about how writers weave spatial systems of opposition and variation into the lineal structures of a plot, so that stories can shape time and thus conquer time's open-endedness.

Meanwhile, the pictures in a picture book form a sequence—they can contribute to the act of story-telling because they do imply the cause-and-effect relationships of time. And as I suggested in my earlier discussions of how pictures imply meaning, even one picture on its own can organize space in ways that suggest some of the sequential ordering of time and provide some of its focus.

So perception of language requires activity in both hemispheres, and well-wrought words do in fact impose holistic patterns on the lineal; and perception of the visible world also requires activity in both hemispheres, and well-wrought pictures do in fact demand specific lineal interpretations of the visual whole. Describing how we understand words "by partly reversing the linear progress, remembering *simultaneously* what we have read consecutively," and how understanding pictures is "a process *in time,*" Joseph Schwarcz rightly concludes, "Following an illustrated text is, then, a complex activity" (*Ways of the Illustrator* 9).

The differences in the activities of the halves of the brain tell us how complex: as we respond to words and pictures which tell us about the same events in different ways, we must integrate two different sorts of information about the same events. We must gather spatial information from both pictures and words; in *Mr. Rabbit,* for instance, the pictures show us the settings, but the words of the text tell us how to see them—the colors that are significant in them. We must also gather temporal information from both words and pictures; in

Mr. Rabbit, the words imply only the specific time occupied by the words of the conversation—it takes the pictorial depiction of the girl and rabbit in different locations to imply the more extended passage of time in which they move from one part of the forest to another between various parts of the conversation. As in *Mr. Rabbit,* the temporal information in pictures is often different from that offered by words, and the spatial information in words different from that in pictures; we must integrate time and space, and two different versions of time and space, before we can understand the whole.

The whole, then, is more than the sum of its parts. Speaking of cartoons and comic strips, Roland Barthes isolates an effect he calls *relaying:* his description of it could easily apply to picture books also: "Here language . . . and image are in a complementary relation; the words are then fragments of a more general syntagm, as are the images, and the message's unity occurs on a higher level; that of the story" (*Responsibility* 30).

Furthermore, the most successful picture books seem to be those in which the "unity on a higher level" emerges from pictures and texts which are noticeably fragmentary—whose differences from each other are a significant part of the effect and meaning of the whole. In *Problems of Art,* Susanne Langer says that, although the arts are different, "the fact that they are distinct is what enables them to have all sorts of highly specialized, interesting relations to each other" (82). As a highly specialized art form that combines different arts, the picture book is distinguished by the ways in which it takes advantage of such highly specialized relationships. What follows is a discussion of how the relative strengths and weaknesses of words and pictures affect their relationships in picture books.

According to William Ivins, it is the "communication of visual information and ideas which, for the last four centuries, has been the primary function of the exactly repeatable pictorial statement" (24). He suggests that, before methods of reproducing pictures were invented, science could not advance, for people could not actually *see* how things worked. In fact, words cannot communicate descriptive information as easily as pictures can. "Common nouns and adjectives, which are the material with which a verbal description is made, are after all only the names of vaguely described classes of things of the most indefinite kind and without precise concrete meanings" (15). A careful artist with words can make them wonderfully evocative, but they merely evoke rather than offer specific visual information, so that a novelist's description of his heroine's face might communicate how we are to respond to her appearance quite exactly, without ever giving us a specific idea of how she looks. And even then, we are forced by the nature of language to follow the writer's logic as he or she guides us through the material; the novelist can make the heroine's nose the most significant aspect of her face by leaving it to the end of the description and thus making it climactic, but that means we "see" the details of her face as a verbal sequence rather than as a visual whole. She has no nose for us at all until we get to the end of the list.

If I try to describe a character's face in words, therefore, I face two problems. First, I have to use words vague in themselves, such as "nose" and "long" and "handsome," in such a way that their relationship to each other can suggest something more or less specific: "handsome long nose"—and I have to assume that those who read my description share my idea about what "long" means and what sort of nose might be considered "handsome." Second, I have to present my information about various features in a sequence to guide my readers through the details of the knowledge I wish to share; the readers must suspend understanding of each of the individual details until the whole list of such details is complete, so that they can see the relationship between "long nose" and descriptions of other features, such as "curly hair"—and the relationship of such specific details to overall impressions, such as "beautiful."

Since words are the separable parts of meaningful sentences, we can understand language only by understanding parts first, then building up to a whole that might in fact be an accurate combination of all the parts. But we see pictures all at once first and only then can begin to notice the potential relationships of their various parts. Our understanding of language starts with details and moves toward wholes; our understanding of pictures starts with wholes and breaks down into details. In terms of the halves of the brain, Jeremy Campbell suggests, "the right side tends to use a 'top-down' strategy, processing information as a whole, perceiving its full meaning rather than approaching it 'bottom-up,' using the parts to construct the whole, which is often more than the sum of its parts" (239–40). We have to approach words bottom-up—one at a time, in the sequence in which they are given us. Consequently, words are best at describing relationships of details, pictures best at giving a sense of the whole. But each can eventually do both, and they can certainly help each other to do both.

Nevertheless, picture-book artists almost always convey information about the ways things look by means of pictures. While that may seem too obvious to be worth saying, the main difficulty facing neophyte writers of texts for picture books is understanding that they must leave such visual information in the hands of their illustrators. A good picture-book text does not tell us that the girl had brown eyes or that the room was gloomy—yet practitioners of literary art use exactly such visual details to establish character, mood, and atmosphere. Writers of picture books must imply character and mood without recourse to such details—and hope that illustrators sensitive to their stories will invent the right visual details to express the appropriate information.

There are two sorts of information that pictures can convey more readily than words: what *type* of object is implied by words and which particular *one* of that type is being referred to. The pictures in alphabet books and in compendia like Richard Scarry's *The Best Word Book Ever* are meant to represent types; if the words on a page say "C is for cat," then the creature depicted on that page is meant to represent cats in general—to show what the word "cat" refers to each time it is used in reference to many different individual creatures of different colors and shapes and sizes. It is by providing us with such visual types that picture books can be informative about the world we live in; they offer us a sort of dictionary of visual ideas, a set of labeled images by which we can identify the objects we actually see. Furthermore, schematic drawings can allow us to understand the workings of things, such as the interior of the human body or the construction of a medieval cathedral.

In the preface to his book about the construction of a medieval cathedral, David Macaulay says, "the cathedral of Chutreaux is imaginary, but the methods of its construction correspond closely to the actual construction of a Gothic cathedral. . . . Although the people of Chutreaux are imaginary, their single-mindedness, their spirit, and their incredible courage are typical of the people of twelfth-, thirteenth-, and fourteenth-century Europe." In order to provide useful information, Macaulay had to normalize—create a "typical" situation rather than the actually untypical circumstances that surrounded the building of each and every actual medieval cathedral. Exactly because they are nothing but typical, because they possess nothing but the characteristics that a number of things share, usefully typical types do not actually exist in the real world. That may be why the illustrations in dictionaries tend to be drawings rather than photographs of specific objects.

Macaulay's solution to that problem is to depict the building of a "typical" cathedral as if it were an actual one; he names specific names, and invents specific dates. In fact, an artist cannot choose but to identify the typical by depicting it as if it were actual; the word "face" carries with it no image of a specific face, but we can convey the idea "face" in a picture only by showing a specific face. The cat depicted beside the words "C is for cat" may be meant to represent all cats; but it would be a bad drawing indeed if it did not in fact look like a possible, actual, unique cat—for it is exactly the way a cat does look that such a picture is attempting to convey.

On the other hand, the drawing would still not be serving its purpose if it had enough distinguishing characteristics to stop it from being typical. A cat with one leg and wearing glasses would not successfully illustrate "C is for cat" for those who did not already know enough about the appearance of cats to realize what was unusual about this one. People who assume (probably incorrectly) that Brian Wildsmith really wanted to convey information in his visually exciting but minimally informative *ABC* might rightly be upset by the fact that his horse has no legs and that his unicorn's most notable feature is its rear end.

The balance required in both capturing the typical and making the typical seem actual is the source of much of the difficulty adults have in coming to terms with picture books. Those who believe that the main purpose of pictures is typical information are upset whenever the objects shown in pictures diverge from ideally normalized types—when Wildsmith in his *ABC* uses some green paint in his depiction of a mouse and they are convinced that mice do not have green fur, or when Sendak's children do not look as blond and pink and ingenuous as conventionally typical children do. In assuming that every picture in a picture book must represent a type, however, we inevitably neglect the other sort of information pictures can convey so well—information about the uniqueness of separate objects; for a picture of a cat can and ideally always does show us not just what cats in general are but also what this particular cat looks like. In her fine discussion of the house style developed in the Golden Books series—the emphasis on caricature, the flattening of space, and so on—Barbara Bader makes an important point: "common to all the foregoing is the intent—to put across an idea or a piece of information rather than to call forth real people, a particular moment. . . . [The difference between these two styles is] generally what is meant, justly or not, by the distinction between illustration-as-communication and illustration-as-art" (*American Picturebooks* 288–89). In order to put across ideas, the Golden Book illustrators, and many-others like them, sacrifice details in order to focus on the typical; in assuming that the purpose of pictures in all children's books is to put across ideas, we tend to ignore and misunderstand details. In doing so we miss the unique qualities of the pictures we look at, and that is not only what makes them worthy of consideration as works of art but also an important source of information of a quite different sort.

We look at a picture of a young woman. She is sitting at a window and smiling, and we know a great deal about her—most of it difficult to put into words. Her hair is done in a certain way. She wears a hat that appears to be of some woven or perhaps scalelike material and a dress patterned with leaves and branches and with fur at collar and cuff. She sits in a room that appears to be filled with tapestries; we see into the room from outside, and we also see that outside it is snowing and that the building she sits in appears to be some sort of castle. She holds up a finger. This picture is Nancy Ekholm Burkert's illustration for the words "At a window with a frame of ebony a queen sat and sewed," the opening of *Snow White*. It adds at least six different kinds of information to that provided by the words.

The first is that this is indeed the specific queen the words refer to—the basic relationship between illustration and text, in which the picture confirms the message of the words. The second is that this is a queen, a type of person; and that this is what sewing is. After reading the words and perhaps wondering what a "queen" or "sewing" is, we can look at the picture and see what they look like. So far, the picture merely offers a visual equivalent to the words. But beyond these basic aspects of illustration, the picture adds other information.

Third, and perhaps most important, it communicates what words could never convey, no matter how many of them one used. It communicates in a detailed way what this particular woman looks like and what the world around her looks like. We could make up a verbal list of details that the picture shows, and we could supply them with adjectives for a long time before we would have an exhaustive catalog of all the different information this picture easily provides about how things look. But the length of that catalog would depend on our varying abilities to distinguish specific namable objects, to determine figures by separating them from grounds—it would be a list of separate facts rather than a holistic totality. Even the longest possible such catalog still would not convey all the visual information the picture conveys so effortlessly, and it would have quite a different effect: it would imply visual information rather than specify it.

Fourth, the picture communicates the appearances of objects we do not even have names for—and therefore might not have been able to describe accurately in our catalog. We may not know what a fleur-de-lis is, but we can understand what one looks like simply because there are a number of them on the tapestry behind the woman. We may not know they are called fleurs-de-lis, but that does not prevent us from being able to see them and even admire them. Similarly, we may not know the technical name for the strange hat the woman is wearing, but we can see the hat; and we can guess not just that this woman is wearing a hat but that this is the sort of hat a woman in this situation would be likely to wear. In fact, we might see a similar hat in another picture later on and conclude from the similarity that such hats were once typically worn by a certain sort of woman; we would be able to know that such hats were typical without having a word for them. It would take the technical jargon of a hairdresser to express the exact nature of the woman's upswept locks, and of a seamstress to describe the cut of her

dress or the points of her sleeves. But we can understand from the picture what even very exact words could not tell us.

A fifth kind of information: if we bring into play our knowledge of conventions of appearance and gesture, we can guess something about the character of this woman sitting at the window—something that it would take many words to convey. Her clothing and her environment suggest that she is well off. We can guess, from the delicacy of her gesture and the very nature of her activity, that she is a lady. Her gentle features suggest that she is a gentle person, probably a likable one, certainly a quiet one. The picture easily communicates information about personality that writers must work hard at expressing in words.

A more telling example of how pictures readily convey personality can be seen if we compare Burkert's portrait of Snow White, as it appears on the dust jacket of her version of the story, with Snow White as she first appears in Trina Schart Hyman's version. Both girls have a fair complexion and dark hair; a catalog of their features would have to be very specific indeed before it could distinguish between the surprisingly similar shapes of their lips and noses. Yet despite the large degree of similarity, they are clearly two quite different sorts of people. Burkert's Snow White is "pretty," gentle, innocent, well-mannered, like her mother. Hyman's Snow White is a beauty, and something of an ingenuous nymphet; she may not know it herself yet, but she is clearly a sensuous, passionate individual.

But what exactly is it that conveys these important differences? It is hard to say. Part of it is certainly the difference between an attractive girl in front of some precisely drawn leaves and another attractive girl with a malevolent hawk on her wrist in front of trees tossed by tempestuous winds. Part of it is found in the implications of stance and gesture that we usually read without even being conscious that we are aware of them. But it is also something else about the shape of lips and eyes, something literally indefinable, something words could not capture. As Ivins suggests, "When we try to describe a particular object in such a way as to communicate an idea of its personality or unique character to someone who is not actually acquainted with it, all that we can do is to pile up a selected group of . . . class names. . . . But beyond that it is impossible for us to go with words, for the ipseity, the particularity of the object, its this-and-no-other-ness, cannot be communicated by the use of class names" (52–53). Interestingly, Gardner's discussion of brain lesions provides support for this idea; Gardner suggests that "unfamiliar shapes tend to be processed by the right hemisphere, whereas shapes capable of verbalization (as well as other linguistic materials) are processed by the left hemisphere" (381). A possible conclusion is that, since language is a codification of what we already know—we would not have learned words to describe experiences we have not encountered yet—the information in pictures that we cannot yet verbalize is the information that is new to us, the information that transcends our preexisting categories or class names. Seen in this way pictures can teach us about unfamiliar visual objects, but only if we use the words of an accompanying text as cognitive maps, schemata to apply to them in order to understand exactly what is new, left over beyond the schemata. We can say "hat" in response to an image of the one on Snow White's mother, then become conscious of how the visual details of the hat in question differ from our idea of a typical hat.

In addition to conveying two quite different Snow Whites by means of the way they depict them, Burkert and Hyman also provide two quite different attitudes toward them—a sixth sort of information. Through the devices of symbol and gesture, of pictorial dynamics, of color and mood and atmosphere that I discussed earlier, Hyman makes Snow White the enticing but ingenuous victim of a lurid romantic melodrama; one must feel sympathy for her. Burkert makes her passive, the sort of girl who always does as she ought and is rightfully admired for her lack of rebelliousness; the admiration demanded implies her triumph from the beginning. Similarly, Burkert's picture of Snow White's mother provides a way of thinking about her—an attitude toward her. She depicts her as seen from outside the window as through a frame; the bright, cheerful tapestries behind her contrast strongly with the gray walls of the castle and suggest that her place is a warm and comfortable one. But it has no depth; it merely looks like a series of different intricate patterns, a highly decorated surface that she herself becomes part of. We can enjoy looking at this pretty woman surrounded by beautiful designs, but we cannot feel much involvement with her. The picture requires us to appreciate the beauty but to keep our dis-tance. Meanwhile, Hyman depicts Snow White's mother from inside the room; we look out with her, rather than at her from without. We are asked to empathize, and because we see details of the room—her maid, her religious triptych hanging on the wall, and so on—we know something about the particular interests and lifestyle of the person we are empathizing with.

These artists set out to illustrate the beginning of "Snow White," the idea that a woman sat at a window and sewed. They have each shown one version of what that might have looked like, but they have also shown much else: what *a* queen might look like, what *this* queen might have looked like, where she might have lived and how she might have dressed, what sort of person she might be, and what sort of attitude we might take toward her. While words can convey information about clothing and setting, personality, and the attitudes we should take toward what is being described, pictures do so more readily. We can enjoy looking at this complex portrait of a queen, and even have some sense of the sort of person she is and how we might feel about her, even if we did not comprehend or enjoy the complex language we would need to know in order to understand the amount and kinds of information the pictures so simply show us.

The first sort of information I learned from Burkert's picture of Snow White's mother merely showed what the words say. The second is a generalization that the picture may or may not actually allow, for perhaps all queens did not look like this. But the other four sorts of information imply exactly that—that this queen looks like herself, that she is different from other queens. That amounts to a statement about the uniqueness of this woman at this moment, the particular thing seen at the moment of seeing. To return to the paradox I suggested earlier, pictures provide both information about the world in being typical and information about the specific objects they depict in being unique. But it is uniqueness—in personality, in atmosphere, in attitude—that makes the pictures in picture books so enjoyable. If we allow ourselves to judge them only in terms of their informative typicality, we misrepresent them, and if we encourage children to look at them for such information, we deprive them not only of much pleasure but also of much significant information—information that words are often silent about.

Many picture books—indeed, possibly all of the best ones—do not just reveal that pictures show us more than words can say; they achieve what Barthes called "unity on a higher level" by making the difference between words and pictures a significant source of pleasure. That pleasure is available even in a very simple book like *Goodnight Moon.* Margaret Wise Brown's spare text is little more than a rhythmic catalog of objects, a list of details that encourages those who hear it to look for the objects mentioned in Clement Hurd's pictures. In doing so, however, they learn information the text does not mention. The old lady and the child to whom she says goodnight are both rabbits and not people. The old lady is knitting, and the kittens play with her wool. The "little house" is a playhouse, and it has its own lights; knowledgeable viewers will even realize that the picture on the bedroom wall is actually an illustration from Brown and Hurd's *The Runaway Bunny.* The delight viewers feel in discovering these things with their own eyes rather than with their ears reveals how basic and important is the difference between the information available in words and in pictures.

Anno's hiding of animals in the complex foliage of his *Anno's Animals* is another clever instance of how that delight in searching pictures for details can be evoked, but the difference between this wordless book and the similar picture in Nancy Burkert's *Snow White* of Snow White alone in the forest surrounded by animals hidden in foliage shows how illustrators can use differences between words and picture for more than the simple pleasure of puzzle solving. Finding Anno's animals is just a game, for no text accompanies these pictures to tell us that they might represent anything more significant. But once we have found Burkert's animals, we must then deal with the fact that the text does not mention them. In fact, they represent a danger to Snow White that she, in her innocence, does not notice either; our perception of them in relation to the words of the text tells us how blind and unprotected innocence may be when threatened by savagery. In seeing what she does not see, we come to interpret her situation more specifically than we would have had we not found the animals in the foliage.

That a simple game without words becomes a source of complex narrative information when accompanied by them suggests that my analysis of the kinds of information communicated by Burkert's picture of Snow White's mother was incomplete. While pictures can convey these kinds of information, they do so most subtly and most completely in the context of a text that supports and sustains them. A reconsideration makes that clear.

We can learn much about medieval Europe from Burkert's illustrations for Snow White—but only if we *know* already that the details in these pictures are characteristic of medieval Europe. And we could learn that only by being told it in words: by another person or by means of a book like this one that discusses the significance of the pictures in picture books. The pictures themselves can indeed *show* us these details in ways that words could not, but without words to explain that they are doing that, we could not know what the details represent. We need to be told what we are being shown.

Similarly, if we share knowledge of gestures and appearances, we can learn that Snow White's mother was gentle and well-mannered from Burkert's pictures and that Burkert wants us to view her from an objective distance. But unless we *know* the picture represents Snow White's mother, we will not know who it is that is so gentle and well-mannered, and we will not, therefore, have any use for the information. Without a name—that is, a word—to attach to it, the picture communicates nothing of particular interest or value to us. Even if the picture were hung in a gallery as *Portrait of a Woman* rather than as an illustration of Snow White's mother, it would be that context, that set of meaningful words, in which we viewed it and understood it: and if it were, indeed, captioned *Portrait of a Woman,* we would then read it as we have learned to read portraits and look for details that might be evocative of character.

In other words, pictures can communicate much to us, and particularly much of visual significance—but only if words focus them, tell us what it is about them that might be worth paying attention to. In a sense, trying to understand the situation a picture depicts is always an act of imposing language upon it—interpreting visual information in verbal terms; it is not accidental that we speak of "visual literacy," of the "grammar" of pictures, of "reading" pictures. Reading a picture for narrative meaning is a matter of applying our understanding of words—words like mine throughout this book; in applying such words to pictures, we are engaged in the act of turning visual information into verbal, even if we do not actually speak the words aloud. Even wordless books demand our previous knowledge of how stories operate before we can find a story in them, and so do the pictures of *The Happy Owls* and *Mr. Rabbit* divorced from their texts. Walter Ong says, "We have all heard it said that one picture is worth a thousand words. Yet, if this statement is true, why does it have to be a saying? Because a picture is worth a thousand words only under special conditions—which commonly include a context of words in which a picture is set" (7).

That is true for the same reason that pictures can show us more than words can say: in duplicating the surface appearance of objects, a picture inevitably contains more visual information than necessary for the verbal message it accompanies. An artist might want to show us a woman sitting at a window, but in order to do so, the artist *must* show us a particular woman with a particular sort of nose sitting in a particular posture. And the woman must have clothes on, unless the artist is determined to make us respond to her naked body. The characters in novels frequently do not have noses, or elbows, or clothes—or at least, these details are not mentioned—and we are left to assume that they have such features but that those features are simply not important to our understanding of the characters in question. Words can, in this way, focus on what is important, and we can read stories in the faith that, if they are good stories, every detail will be of significance in terms of our understanding of the whole. But because an illustrator has to give every character a nose whether that nose is important or not, or else draw a picture of a person remarkably odd because he has no nose, a picture contains information that might not necessarily be relevant to our understanding of the story as a whole. It takes a context of specific words, or at least a previously established idea of what to look for that was probably first expressed to us in words, to point us toward what is significant and thus lessen the number of words the picture evokes from as many as a thousand down to the few specific words actually found in the text.

In "What Novels Can Do That Films Can't," Seymour Chatman says that "the camera depicts but does not describe" (128). In other words, it shows us objects that ought to interest us, and it might even, by means of switches in camera angles and such, focus our attention on which of those objects ought to attract

our attention. But it cannot tell us what it is about these objects that we ought to notice—*why* we should be interested in them. A novelist can say, "The woman was beautiful, despite her shabby clothing." A film—or a picture in a book—can indeed show us a woman in shabby clothing. But we might not share the casting director's conviction that she is beautiful and so miss the point, and we may be more interested in the pony she sits on than in the woman herself and so miss the point altogether. What Chatman suggests of film is true of the pictures in picture books: "The dominant mode is presentational, not assertive. A film doesn't say, 'this is the state of affairs'; it merely shows you that state of affairs" (128).

But in picture books (as, often, in films), the words can focus our attention on pictures in such a way as to make them assertive. Words can provide a cognitive map, a schema that we can apply to inherently unassertive pictures in order to determine the varying significance we might find in their details. Barthes calls this effect of texts in relation to pictures *anchoring:* "Language helps identify purely and simply the elements of the scene and the scene itself. . . . the text *directs* the reader among the various signifieds of the image, causes him to avoid some and to accept others; through an often subtle dispatching, it teleguides him toward a meaning selected in advance" (*Responsibility* 28–29). An obvious example of such "teleguiding" is the caption under a picture in an art gallery—in giving us a name or an idea, it provides us with a pattern to apply to the image before our eyes and thus allows us to see that image in a specific way. We see not just a woman but *Portrait of a Woman;* we see not just a few daubs of red paint but *Composition* or *Angry Evening*—and we look at *Composition* differently from the way we would look at *Angry Evening.*

The texts of picture books often function as anchoring labels in exactly this way. Even the simple sentence "This is a cat" allows us to see the accompanying picture differently from the label "This is my friend, Peter, who is a cat," or the label "Peter was not happy that day." The first merely demands we pick up the general idea of cats, the second asks us to look for something like human personality, and the third requires our attention to a specific emotion. Similarly, Sendak's picture of Zolotow's Mr. Rabbit and little girl relaxing in the woods would look quite different if it were labeled "Have some Madeira, my dear?" That label would change the emotional implications of the visual image—tell us to interpret this visible appearance in terms of different emotions. We cannot see what goes on in the minds of the characters we see in pictures; it takes words to point out the emotional content of visible gestures.

In a slightly less obvious way, the picture in *Wild Things* of Max making mischief by chasing a dog with a fork would be changed drastically if the words accompanying it read, "The dog ran so fast trying to escape the bad boy that she nearly banged her head on the door." With these different words, the same picture is now centrally about the dog and not the boy. Or consider another possibility: "The boy and the dog rushed into the living room to attack the monster; the dog was a little frightened, and looked back to make sure the boy was with her"; now the dog and boy are no longer enemies. Or another: "Max picked up the magic fork and, just as the dog fairy had promised, he began to fly. The dog fairy got out of his way in a hurry."

In these instances, the new words I have provided imply that the same visible gestures might stand for quite different situations. If we then look at the picture and believe that it might indeed be showing us what we have been told, then we have learned something important about the relationships of words and pictures. We would not accept a text that told us that this picture of a boy and a dog showed a goat and a pig running down the stairs; we tend to believe the evidence of our eyes when it comes to appearances. But the fact that we do so easily accept even minimally plausible verbal descriptions that change the meaning of the action suggests how words predominate in our reading of pictorial information about causes and effects and about the passage of time. As I showed earlier, pictures can and do convey these things, just as words can describe faces, but in picture books the texts more significantly specify temporal information, just as the pictures convey the most significant descriptive information.

Some aspects of pictorial meaning are particularly in need of the clarifying presence of texts. A picture cannot by itself tell us that it is a flashback, and without the use of conventions like the cloudy shapes that surround dreams in cartoons, a picture cannot by itself tell us that it represents a character's fantasy. Consequently, when looking at Piatti's *Happy Owls* pictures without the accompanying words, no one guesses that

he or she is looking at representations of the visual images the owls are merely talking about. In Arnold Lobel's pictures for Judith Viorst's *I'll Fix Anthony*, similarly, while we see the same characters throughout the book, we see them in two different sorts of reality. At the beginning and end we see what they are actually doing; in the middle they appear inside the young narrator's imagination. But we can only know that the two boys are *not* actually playing bingo on one page but *are* really playing with a toy car on the facing page because of the grammatical relationships provided by the accompanying words. Stephen Roxburgh's suggestion in "A Picture Equals How Many Words" that the first and last pictures in *Outside Over There* are "almost identical images that comprise a sequence depicting an action, in fact, a baby's step" (21) reveals how Sendak takes advantage of the vagueness of the temporal information in pictures: without a text which asserts that the events of the story in between these two pictures occur instantaneously, in the time of a baby's step, we are left only with a sense of something wrong that supports the mystery this book so successfully conveys.

I said earlier that the fact that words do not describe everything that can be seen in a picture creates a game, since we can ourselves notice details that have not been mentioned. That suggests a third important effect of words on pictures. In addition to informing us of the emotional or narrative significance of visible gestures, and specifying cause-and-effect and other grammatical relationships between parts of pictures and series of pictures, words can tell us what matters and what does not. It is the text that tells us that the insignificant-looking bone that we did not even at first notice in *The Amazing Bone* is an important part of the story; on the other hand, it is the text's silence about the fox in Piatti's *The Happy Owls* that tells us not to be concerned about him or to imagine that he has a part in the story—as people believe he has when they do not know Piatti's words. Similar silences inform us that the man in eighteenth-century dress playing a musical instrument inside a cottage in the exact center of one of the pictures in Sendak's *Outside Over There* is not at all significant to the plot and tell us to ignore the goat who appears centrally in some of the pictures in *Rosie's Walk*.

If pictures show us more than words can say, then they can easily confuse us as to what is important about all the things they show. In this sense, the pictures in picture books, like all pictures, are most significantly images to put words around—most interesting, and most communicative, when we have some words to accompany them. The *Mona Lisa* on its own may or may not be an interesting image: it becomes a fascinating one when we look at it with knowledge of even a few of the vast number of words that commentators have woven around it. Even the most abstract of pictures becomes an illustration when its artist provides it with a title, and even a title like *A Canvas All Painted Blue* tells us what to see in what we look at—not night, not melancholy, just the color blue on a canvas. The pictures in picture books are most interesting when the words that accompany them tell us how to understand them.

So far in this chapter, I have suggested two paradoxical truths: first, that words without pictures can be vague and incomplete, incommunicative about important visual information, and second, that pictures without words can be vague and incomplete, lacking the focus, the temporal relationships, and the internal significance so easily communicated by words. In *Ideology and the Image,* Bill Nichols sums up the relative strengths and weaknesses of the two different media when he suggests that language, which is made up of the discrete units of individual words separated by moments of non-sense, is something like the on-off digital code of computers—capable of conveying subtle connections and relationships simply because it misrepresents the continuum of reality by dividing it into discrete parts. But pictorial representation, in which the images do in some way resemble the objects they signify, are an analog code, in which separate meanings are not discrete and tend to shade off into each other. According to Nichols, "The graded quality of analog codes may make them rich in meaning but it also renders them somewhat impoverished in syntactical complexity or semantic precision. By contrast, the discrete units of digital codes may be somewhat impoverished in meaning but capable of much greater complexity or semantic signification. . . . As a consequence of this difference between analog and digital codes we are often in the position of using the complex instrument of language to speak about the rich meaning of art where a proliferation of words can never match the gradations of meaning to which the words allude" (47–48). The words Nichols refers to

here are those used in the criticism of art; but in picture books the texts themselves allude to the pictures, and the pictures have been made in response to the texts. The situation has been designed to offer information from both digital and analogical codes at once; the unity of the whole emerges from a subtle interplay of the differing parts. In terms of the geography of the brain, Gardner says, "Since the left hemisphere operates primarily by processing elements in sequence, while the right hemisphere treats elements simultaneously ('in parallel'), activities which exploit both forms are particularly enhanced by interhemispheric collaboration" (376). Reading a picture book is clearly such an activity.

I suggested earlier that the pictures in a sequence act as schemata for each other. When a story is told in words as well as pictures, we first understand both the words and the pictures by means of the schemata we have already established for them—at first, our general expectations about stories and our general understanding about how pictures communicate. Then, the words correct and particularize our understanding of the pictures they accompany, and the pictures provide information that causes us to reinterpret and particularize the meanings of the words. Then all of that information becomes a schema for each new page of words and each new picture as we continue throughout a book.

For instance, if we looked at the first picture in *Where the Wild Things Are* before we hear the text and without knowledge of the images of Wild Things on the title page, we might say that we see a boy, meaning that the figure we see fits our schema of a young human being—and, perhaps because he does not wear a skirt, a young male human being. We might add that he looks angry and upset, his downcurved mouth fitting our schema for unhappiness, and we might be confused by his bushy tail, and conclude, perhaps, that he is not human at all, but half animal. Or we might bring into play our schema of occasions for costumes and assume that it is Halloween. Thus far, our interpretation of the picture depends on our basic models of human behavior.

But if we know the title of the book, the words "Where the Wild Things Are" might change our response—we might assume that this wild-looking child is indeed one of the Wild Things and that, perhaps, equally wild children might appear in later pictures. Or, remembering the images of wild creatures on the title page, we might assume that this child is in the process of being transformed from human to monster. Or we might alternatively bring into play our schema of children's books and toys and assume that it is the stuffed animal on the left who is the main character and that this wild half-human is out to get him. Furthermore, we might also bring into play various of our schema for pictorial conventions: the picture is dark, so it must be a sad story, and so on.

If we now add the words of the text, our perception of the pictures changes—and becomes much more specific. We now know that it is night and therefore not necessarily gloomy. We know that the creature's name is Max and that he is wearing a wolf suit; that means Max is not the dog and that it is indeed a wolf suit, a costume, so that Max is indeed a person, a human being. We know that this person, Max, and not the dog, is the main character. We also know for sure that he is a male, since it is "his" wolf suit. And we are told he is making mischief, which specifies the meaning of his downturned mouth: malevolence, not gloom. Furthermore, we have learned what matters in this picture: that it is not to be about how Max built a tent—not about the specific bad action—but merely an example of the more generalized conception, mischief.

In fact, we read both words and pictures here in relation to each other; rather than make the possible wrong assumptions I have outlined, our simultaneous or almost-simultaneous experience of both words and pictures allows us to use each to correct our understanding of the other. But what might we expect next? According to conventional patterns of human behavior—and, perhaps, of children's stories—we would most likely expect an angry, adult woman to appear in the next picture. But perhaps not; the grammatical incompleteness of the text suggests that there is more of the sentence to come and therefore more mischief to come, most likely a continuation of the same sequence of action we have seen part of already, since that is what we tend to expect in stories. So perhaps we will see Max looking through a large hole in the wall that he has made with his hammer, and his mother's angry face looking through it at him.

In fact, the next picture confirms the grammar's suggestion that there was more to come, but rather than a continuation of the same sequence, we are provided with a quite different action. So the picture tells us that the phrase "of one kind" was indeed meant to be balanced off; its meaning is changed by the words

"and another" not because we did not expect those words but because we most likely expected more words than that. But those words on their own set up a sort of repetitive pattern that we might well expect to continue—an extended series of "and anothers" depicting yet more sorts of mischief. The picture changes that expectation by setting up the beginning of a chase that we might well expect to see the end of: the most likely slapstick conclusion to this situation would be a picture of Max barreling into his mother once he gets through the door. The next page thwarts that expectation both by bringing the series to an end and by showing us a quite different sort of scene. Part of the reason this sequence of pictures and words is so interesting is that the words change the meanings of the pictures, and the pictures then change the meanings of the words—sometimes by confirming our expectations and sometimes surprising us by not confirming them.

This process of making assumptions on the basis of our previous knowledge and then correcting them is basic to perception itself. As Ulric Neisser says, "The schemata that accept information and direct the search for more of it are not visual or auditory or tactual, but perceptual. To attend an event means to seek and accept every sort of information about it, regardless of modality, and to integrate all the information as it becomes available. Having heard something, we look to see it, and what we see then determines how we locate and interpret what we hear" (29–30). That last sentence nicely sums up the picture-book experience; picture books elegantly bring into play the basic patterns of perception. Having heard about something in the words, we look to see it, and having seen it, we now interpret what we hear differently. The words change the pictures, and the pictures change the words.

Pictures do that by adding visual information to what we have been told—show us, for instance, that Max is not just making mischief in general but that he is driving a nail into the wall. For that reason many commentators say that the purpose of pictures in picture books is to "extend" the texts, but cognitive theories of perception suggest that extension may be the wrong metaphor. It would be more accurate to say that pictures *limit* the text—and to add that the text also limits the pictures.

Consider some pictures of people suspended above flights of stairs. Without words we might guess that

Sendak's Max above the stairs with a fork in his hand and Van Allsburg's Alan above the stairs in Abdul Gasazi's garden are flying or floating, or that Max is a creature that is half human and half animal and that Alan is a girl in jeans, or that both are midgets. But Sendak's words tell us Max is making mischief, and since the text does not refer to them, we discount the less plausible interpretations of the picture, like flying. Even more obviously, Van Allsburg's text tells us that Alan has, indeed, fallen down the stairs. In both cases, the words limit the range of possible responses to the picture.

Now consider the sentence "The boy fell down the stairs" unaccompanied by a picture. It clearly describes an action, but we have no way of understanding the meaning of the action. So we can imagine countless possibilities. The boy tripped. The boy was pushed. The boy was wearing a dress. He was a Norwegian. He was in a wheelchair. And so on. Any picture at all will narrow these possibilities to a very few. A picture of a boy in slacks without a wheelchair will eliminate the possibility of the dress and the wheelchair, and a picture of a boy in a kilt will eliminate the possibility of the Norwegian—and a picture of a boy above a stairway in a garden will demand a quite specific response. Furthermore, the picture might even show us a banana peel that would account for the fall. Furthermore, as I suggested earlier, the quality of the picture itself might inform us of the proper attitude to take toward it; it might be a cartoon that tells us to laugh at the boy, or it might be a broodingly realistic picture that tells us to feel sorry for him. In either case, the picture would limit not only plausible interpretations of the situation but also the range of plausible responses to it.

By limiting each other, words and pictures together take on a meaning that neither possesses without the other—perform the completion of each other that Barthes calls "relaying." The words in *The Garden of Abdul Gasazi* do not in fact tell us that it is a stairway that Alan is falling down; they merely say he slipped and fell. And the picture does not tell us that it is somebody named Alan who is doing the slipping. Each tells us of something the other is incapable of telling or that the other could tell only with difficulty; together, they mean something quite different and a lot more specific than each on its own—in this case, that this is indeed a boy, that his name is Alan, that he has indeed slipped, and that it is indeed a stairway he is falling down.

Because they communicate different kinds of information, and because they work together by limiting each other's meanings, words and pictures necessarily have a combative relationship; their complementarity is a matter of opposites completing each other by virtue of their differences. As a result, the relationships between pictures and texts in picture books tend to be ironic: each speaks about matters on which the other is silent.

WORKS CONSULTED

Bader, Barbara. *American Picturebooks from Noah's Ark to the Beast Within.* New York: Macmillan, 1976.

Barthes, Roland. *The Responsibility of Forms: Critical Essays on Music, Art, and Representation.* Trans. Richard Howard. New York: Hill and Wang-Farrar, Straus and Giroux, 1985.

Campbell, Jeremy. *Grammatical Man: Information, Entropy, Language, and Life.* New York: Simon and Schuster, 1982.

Chatman, Seymour. "What Novels Can Do That Films Can't." *Critical Inquiry* 7.1 (Autumn 1980): 121–40.

Gardner, Howard. *The Shattered Mind: The Person after Brain Damage.* New York: Vintage-Random House, 1976.

Ivins, William M., Jr. *Prints and Visual Communication.* 1953. Reprint. New York: Da Capo Press, 1969.

Klemin, Diana. *The Art of Art for Children's Books: A Contemporary Survey.* New York: Clarkson N. Potter, 1966.

Langer, Susanne K. *Problems of Art: Ten Philosophical Lectures.* New York: Scribner's, 1957.

Macaulay, David. "How to Create a Successful Children's Nonfiction Picture Book." Hearne and Kaye 97–107.

Neisser, Ulric. *Cognition and Reality: Principles and Implications of Cognitive Psychology.* San Francisco: W. H. Freeman, 1976.

Nichols, Bill. *Ideology and the Image: Social Representation in the Cinema and Other Media.* Bloomington: Indiana University Press, 1981.

Ong, Walter J. *Orality and Literacy: The Technologizing of the Word.* London: Methuen, 1982.

Ornstein, Robert E. *The Psychology of Consciousness.* 1972. New York: Penguin, 1975.

Roxburgh, Stephen. "A Picture Equals How Many Words?: Narrative Theory and Picture Books for Children." *Lion and the Unicorn* 7/8 (1983–84): 20–33.

Schwarcz, Joseph H. *Ways of the Illustrator: Visual Communication in Children's Literature.* Chicago: American Library Association, 1982.

CHILDREN'S BOOKS DISCUSSED

Anno, Mitsumasa. *Anno's Animals.* New York: Philomel, 1979.

Burkert, Nancy Ekholm. *Snow White and the Seven Dwarfs.* By the Brothers Grimm. Trans. Randall Jarrell. New York: Farrar, Straus and Giroux, 1972.

Hurd, Clement. *Goodnight Moon.* By Margaret Wise Brown. New York: Harper, 1947.

———. *The Runaway Bunny.* By Margaret Wise Brown. Rev. ed. New York: Harper and Row, 1972.

Hyman, Trina Schart. *Snow White.* By the Brothers Grimm. Trans. Paul Heins. Boston: Atlantic Monthly Press-Little, Brown, 1974.

Lobel, Arnold. *I'll Fix Anthony.* By Judith Viorst. New York: Harper and Row, 1969.

Macaulay, David. *Cathedral.* Boston: Houghton Mifflin, 1973.

Piatti, Celestino. *The Happy Owls.* New York: Atheneum, 1964.

Scarry, Richard. *The Best Word Book Ever.* Rev. ed. New York: Golden Press, 1980.

Sendak, Maurice. *Mr. Rabbit and the Lovely Present.* By Charlotte Zolotow. New York: Harper and Row, 1962.

———. *Outside Over There.* New York: Harper and Row, 1981.

———. *Where the Wild Things Are.* New York: Harper and Row, 1963.

Steig, William. *The Amazing Bone.* New York: Farrar, Straus and Giroux, 1976.

Van Allsburg, Chris. *The Garden of Abdul Gasazi.* Boston: Houghton Mifflin, 1979.

Wildsmith, Brian. *ABC.* London: Oxford University Press, 1962.

Maurice Sendak (b. 1928)

Maurice Sendak became one of the world's most influential and popular picture book artists in the second half of the twentieth century. In 1970, he was the first American to win the Hans Christian Andersen Medal for illustration. He was born in Brooklyn, New York, into a family of Jewish Polish immigrants. After he met influential New York editor Ursula Nordstrom, his success as an illustrator was established with his humorous drawings of active children in *A Hole Is to Dig* by Ruth Krauss (1952). The Little Bear series, written by Else Holmelund Minarik beginning in 1957, was among the earliest storybooks designed for beginning readers. Sendak has illustrated dozens of other books by different writers, as well as his own texts and adaptations of some lesser-known nursery rhymes and folktales. *The Nutshell Library* (1962) is a set of four tiny books spoofing the chapbooks of earlier times and classic types of concept books, with an alphabet book, cautionary tale, counting book, and rhyme about months for young children. Three original and controversial picture books dealing with the child's world of make-believe and dreams are considered his major trilogy: *Where the Wild Things Are* (1963), *In the Night Kitchen* (1970), and *Outside Over There* (1981). In these and later books, Sendak revised and departed from his earlier comic style, creating darker, more romantic explorations of strong emotions and problems such as homelessness, parental neglect, and the Holocaust. His draftsmanship and treatment of the unconscious experiences of children have been admired widely. The careful lines and use of cross hatching in his drawings show the influence of eighteenth- and nineteenth-century illustrators, including the wood engravings of Thomas Bewick. Randolph Caldecott's influence appears in the continuous flow of energy in books such as *Where the Wild Things Are,* as the short text moves the reader along rhythmically in syncopation with the illustrations (see Further Recommended Readings). Sendak's expressive illustrations for a 1973 edition of Grimms' fairy tales are discussed later in this section. Sendak has also worked for television, theater, and opera on adaptations of his own works and other theatrical designs.

Sendak often speaks and writes about his preoccupation with his own childhood, with the interactions of fantasy and reality, unconscious and conscious experiences in the child's world, and his own artistic heroes and interests, including music and art history. *Caldecott & Co.*, first published in 1988, contains thirty-two of his speeches and articles, including his acceptance speeches for the Caldecott and Hans Christian Andersen medals. Sendak writes, "Despite the fact that I don't write with children in mind, I long ago discovered that they make the best audience. They certainly make the best critics. They are more candid and to the point than professional critics" (214). His essays discuss many artists, from those who influenced him, such as Hans Christian Andersen, Randolph Caldecott, and Walt Disney, to his own student Richard Egielski and his partner Arthur Yorinks. The book's third essay, from 1978, explains why Sendak traces the beginnings of the modern picture book back to Caldecott's theatrical combinations of rhymes and images in the nineteenth century. The chapter on Winsor McCay expresses Sendak's admiration for early twentieth-century comic strips as a form of children's book appealing to audiences of all ages. He compares McKay to great British fantasists who explored the relationship between childhood and manhood, such as William Blake and George McDonald.

Winsor McCay

When Pop Art breached the walls of academic snobbery, it made possible the rediscovery of some of our best popular culture. Winsor McCay, for example, the creator of *Little Nemo in Slumberland*, has begun to receive the recognition he deserves. *Little Nemo* is a comic strip—but much more than a comic strip, especially in comparison to the debased examples of the form popular in America since the late thirties. It is an elaborate and audacious fantasy that suffers only slightly from the cramped space imposed by its form. It is, in effect, a giant children's book, though no more limited to children than *Alice in Wonderland* or the Grimm tales.

Until some months ago I had never really read *Little Nemo's* text. I had responded to its visual images and had invented my own *Nemo* by reading between these "lines" and absorbing what suited me. My *Nemo* goes back a long way (the numerous histories of the comics published in the forties and fifties showed tantalizing sample pages), but it wasn't until 1966, at a Metropolitan Museum exhibit entitled "Two Fantastic Draftsmen," that I saw the actual *Little Nemo*, in original size and full color. I realized finally what up until then I had only dimly felt: McCay and I serve the same master, our child selves. We both draw not on the lit-

eral memory of childhood but on the emotional memory of its stress and urgency. And neither of us forgot our childhood dreams.

Little Nemo is a catalogue of nightmares, a profusion of extreme fantasy images rendered with such explicit definition that the dream is captured in all its surrealistic exactitude. There are many details that I suspect only children see, and those few adults who still look with a child's intelligent curiosity. McCay's theme is the fantasy of escape to "some other place," away from confusion and pain, a flight from ambivalent parents. It is easy to deduce this without actually reading the words. For years I had devoured only the images and understood them by instinct. In a sense, I had extracted the *Nemo* Id and overlooked its Superego, for McCay's text is often a calculated front for the primal antics of his hero.

Little Nemo in Slumberland began as a full-page Sunday comic in the *New York Herald* on October 15, 1905, appeared there through July 23, 1911, and then moved to Hearst's *New York American* under the title *In the Land of Wonderful Dreams*. The strip was published in the *American* and a number of other newspapers until 1913, and McCay revived it from 1924 to 1926. Throughout this history, the formula remained the same. Nemo sleeps, dreams, and, in the last panel, wakes up. (McCay wryly suggests sardines or something else Nemo ate before bed as the reason for his dreams.) When the dreams are nightmares, which they mostly are, Nemo wakes up screaming or falls out of bed. On the few occasions when they are peaceful, he has to be roughly waked up.

The strange characters who inhabit Nemo's dreams, and the astonishing landscapes that contain them, have a ruggedness and vitality derived in part from McCay's theatrical experience. McCay was born in Michigan, the son of a lumberjack, in 1869. In adolescence he traveled with a Wild West show, doing odd jobs. He studied drawing in his home state, but his wish to continue at Chicago's Art Institute was dropped because he had to earn a living. In 1889 he joined a traveling carnival as official billboard painter and then became poster artist for the Cincinnati Dime Museum—actually, a freak show. In 1900 he became staff artist for the *Cincinnati Enquirer,* and in 1904 his genius finally found itself in a series of comic strips: *Dream of the Rarebit Fiend* for the *New York Evening Telegram;* and for the *New York Herald, The Story of Hungry Henrietta* and the superb *Little Sammy Sneeze.*

By 1905, when Nemo was born, Winsor McCay had become master of the form, a master who was self-taught: "The principal factor in my success has been an absolute desire to draw constantly. I never decided to be an artist. Simply, I couldn't stop myself from drawing. I drew for my own pleasure. I never wanted to know whether or not someone liked my drawings. I have never kept one of my drawings. I drew on walls, the school blackboard, odd bits of paper, the walls of barns. Today I'm still as fond of drawing as when I was a kid—and that's a long time ago—but, surprising as it may seem, I never thought about the money I would receive for my drawings. I simply drew them." (I am indebted to Judith O'Sullivan, research fellow at the National Collection of Fine Arts, for all the biographical data included here.)

McCay's mature style reflects the carnival poster's demand for vivid, clear shapes and showy motifs. The grandiose façades, the freaks, clowns, fancily tricked-out dancers, and comic-mirror distortions became the raw material from which he fashioned Nemo's world. All that and Art Nouveau, too.

In 1904 Alphonse Mucha had established a studio in New York and no doubt this interested McCay. "I think it would be wise for every art student to set up a certain popular artist whom he likes best and adapt his 'handling' or style. You don't have to copy his drawings, but when you are puzzled with any part of your work, see how it has been handled by your favorite and fix it up in a similar manner." McCay was as good as his word. He injected new spirit into the agitated, voluptuous line and arbitrary, flat-color patterning of Art Nouveau.

His originality is confirmed by his innovative method of visual narrative (he ignored the comic strip's traditional arrangement of panels, stretched them vertically and horizontally to get his dreamlike effects) and a radically personal iconography. McCay was a born architect with a breathtaking command of perspective; the elaborate structural decors that appear over and over in *Nemo* are reminiscent of the architectural fantasies of the stage designers of the Baroque. The power of his visionary landscapes, the strength of his draftsmanship override and mitigate the softening Art Nouveau conceits he enthusiastically took up.

Slumberland abounds in exotic birds, looped lilies, trailing flora, and asexual mermaids. Small matter. *Little Nemo* is nearly pure gold. If it falters now and again—and, at the end, repeatedly—it is impressive that McCay could sustain his creation at such an exalted level while producing a color comic page every week. But then, he loved to draw, and the promise of frequent escape into his child-hero's dreams must have been a helpful impetus.

The best of *Little Nemo* is sufficient proof that McCay was one of America's rare, great fantasists. In a country that is ambivalent, at best, toward its volatile imaginations, further proof of his power is the fact that he could hold a mass audience for so long. Miraculously, McCay re-created dreams that we all had as children but few of us remember—or care to remember. This puts him squarely in league with Lewis Carroll and George MacDonald. Nemo's dreams, like Alice's, have the unquestionable ring of truth. In Slumberland, as in Wonderland, irrational taboos, forbidden places, and terrifying creatures confront our hero at every turn. But Nemo, unlike Alice, is afraid. He has none of her nimble wit and maddening pugnaciousness. He is dubious, suspicious, very much a miniature Buster Keaton ogling a hostile universe.

Nemo has good reason for his caution. The Slumberland refrain ("This is the most beautiful place you

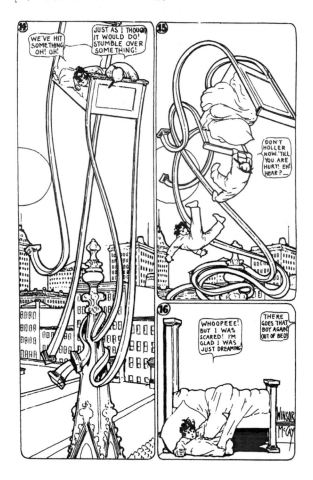

ever saw—you'll like it, Nemo!") is so much hogwash. Almost always, fun and games end in disaster. Nemo turns party pooper. He is passive, hesitates, and lets Flip, his fiery, aggressive friend-adversary, run the show. Nemo lacks savoir faire. He's as naïve and American as apple pie.

In the strip's first episodes, the basic themes are struck. The Princess of Slumberland longs for a playmate, and Nemo is her choice. He is conducted to her by a series of oddly named, lavishly costumed messengers, but, typically, it is a journey plagued with anxiety and frustration. Nemo doesn't meet the (understandably) near-crazed Princess until March 4, 1906! Besides the motive of suspense, I suspect another cause for the delay.

The Princess is almost characterless, a glossy, fortyish-looking, Klimt type; and she is often very badly drawn—something so rare for McCay it must be

significant. Slumberland, unlike Wonderland, is a male-dominated society and the Princess is its token female, the only female in the regular cast. Nemo links up here with Captain Ahab and Huck Finn in the great American flight from women. Despite all talk to the contrary, he is not altogether satisfied with his princess; he'd much rather be out with the boys.

Toward the end of 1907 the Princess is temporarily dropped, and immediately the action picks up. Nemo, Flip, and the cannibal child, Imp, have a raucous, harum-scarum time away from the restraints of Slumberland. The fantasy flowers into one of the finest *Nemo* episodes, "Befuddle Hall," and Nemo's character develops as well. At the beginning of 1908 the boys are lost—they obviously want to be lost—and the change in our hero becomes significant. An unprecedented concern with social wrongs crops up in the "Shanty Town" episode (beginning March 22, 1908), when Nemo assumes a Christ-like role and restores a dying child to life. But in spite of the Dickensian tone (sick little sister Mary), this drama is cloying.

I'd imagine that McCay was thoroughly tired of Slumberland by 1908; its rigid formalities, red tape, and stuffy social procedures were alarming, like everyday life. After that summer, Slumberland is hauled in halfheartedly now and again, and finally, in 1910, though frequently mentioned afterward, it is dropped.

The best *Little Nemo* pages, in terms of imaginative leaps, are the early ones. As time went on, *Nemo* tended to become a serial, a fantasy chopped into weekly installments. In 1909 there are some curiously sadistic episodes. McCay is in a strange mood, and out of that mood Nemo suddenly turns fierce and aggressive and physically challenges Flip. They fight and Nemo wins. A sad victory: Nemo exchanges childhood for manhood, never thinking he might have both. After that, no matter how difficult the situation, Nemo is manfully optimistic and finally a little bullheaded and domineering. McCay, I'd venture a guess, had come through a crisis. The echo of that personal battle reverberates throughout Slumberland.

Now Nemo's adventures take a new turn. On a tour of the universe, we are granted a chilling look into the future. McCay anticipates our present problems: pollution of the environment, destruction of natural resources, overpopulation. The citizens of Mars are tyrannized by large corporations, and freedom is bestowed only on those who can afford to pay for it. Over the archway to the doomed planet are the bleak words: "Abandon hope, all ye who try to enter here without the price." It is the anti-human world of today. The final adventure in this collection is a grand tour of the United States and Canada, a spectacular farewell. Here McCay indulges his lifelong interest in reportorial drawing, and the views of Yellowstone, Niagara Falls, and, best of all, the Brooklyn Bridge are dazzling.

But this is another *Nemo;* fantasy has merged with reality and is lost forever. Slumberland has vanished and so has childhood. It seems to be a particularly American equation that manhood spells the death of childhood. I wish McCay had believed in Blake's joyful vision of imagination as the child in man. Little Nemo, by the end of 1910, though still little, is nothing more than a midget Teddy Roosevelt, impeccably dressed in Rough Rider uniform and issuing orders. The Superego in full swing.

The anthology published by Nostalgia Press presents the *New York Herald Little Nemo,* with some omissions, from the beginning in 1905 through December 25, 1910. Two hundred and sixty-three pages are reproduced, over one hundred of them in color as true to the originals as the Italian printers could manage. The reproductions measure approximately ten by thirteen inches, two-thirds the original size and large enough for the finest details to be preserved. It is a magnificent book, and all the credit for its existence belongs to Woody Gelman, collector, editor, and the best friend Winsor McCay ever had. It is an ironic fact that this collection of McCay's most important work had to be published in Italy first. America, it seems, still doesn't take its great fantasists all that seriously.

Randolph Caldecott

Caldecott's work heralds the beginning of the modern picture book. He devised an ingenious juxtaposition of picture and word, a counterpoint that never happened before. Words are left out—but the picture says it. Pictures are left out—but the word says it. In short, it is the invention of the picture book.

Caldecott's *Hey Diddle Diddle* and *Baby Bunting* exemplify his rhythmic syncopation of words and images—a syncopation that is both delightful and highly musical. The characters leap across the page, loudly proclaiming their personal independence of the paper. In most versions of *Hey Diddle Diddle,* the cow literally jumps over the moon. But here the cow is merely jumping: the moon sits on the horizon in the background and, from our perspective, only gives the *appearance* of being under the cow. In this way, Caldecott is being exceedingly logical, since he obviously knows that cows can't jump over the moon. But within his logic he shows you, on the color page, two pigs dancing, the moon smiling, the hen and the rooster carrying on—all of it entirely acceptable to him and to us. Yet Caldecott won't go beyond a certain "logical" point: the cow *seems* to be jumping over the moon, but in fact it's just leaping on the ground. Still, this is bizarre enough to make the milkmaid drop her pail of milk.

When you turn the page to read "The little Dog laughed to see such fun," you might well take this line as a reference to the cow jumping over the moon. It refers, however, to the spilt milk—or whatever was in that pail—now being gobbled up by the two pigs, while the cow stares from the corner, watching it all happen, and the maid looks down, perplexed, perhaps annoyed. So Caldecott has interjected a whole new story element solely by means of the illustrations, adding and compounding image upon image.

The situation in *Baby Bunting* is a bit more conventional: the baby is being dressed, Father's going a-hunting, looking a little ridiculous as he disappears behind a wall, followed by that wonderful dog trotting after him. But Father's frantic hunting is ineffectual, and all comes to naught. So they rush off to town to buy a rabbit skin. And this, of course, is Caldecott cutting up: the father dressed in hunting regalia with his dog, unable to kill a rabbit, finally winding up in town to *buy* the skin.

Father brings the rabbit skin home to wrap the Baby Bunting in, and what follows is a scene of jollity:

Baby Bunting

So there was an end of one, two, and three,
Heigho, says ROWLEY!
The Rat, the Mouse, and the little Frog-gee!
With a rowley-powley, gammon and spinach,
Heigho, says ANTHONY ROWLEY!

the baby dressed in that silly garment, everyone rushing around, pictures on the walls from other Caldecott picture books. Then there is the lovely illustration of Mama and Baby.

And now Caldecott does the unexpected. The rhyme ends ("To wrap the Baby Bunting in"), but as you turn the page you see Baby and Mother strolling—Baby dressed in that idiotic costume with the ears poking out of her head—and up on the little hillside a group of rabbits playing. And the baby—I'd give anything to have the original drawing of that baby!—Baby is staring

with the most perplexed look at those rabbits, as though with the dawning knowledge that the lovely, cuddly, warm costume she's wrapped up in has *come* from those creatures. It's all in that baby's eye—just two lines, two mere dashes of the pen, but it's done so expertly that they absolutely express . . . well, anything you want to read into them. I read: astonishment, dismay at life. Is this where rabbit skins come from? Does something have to die to dress me?

After the comedy of what has preceded, this last scene is especially poignant. Caldecott is too careful and too elegant an artist to become melodramatic; he never forces an issue, he just touches it lightly. And you can't say it's a tragedy, but something hurts. Like a shadow quickly passing over. It is this which gives a Caldecott book—however frothy the verses and pictures—its unexpected depth.

Caldecott is an illustrator, he is a songwriter, he is a choreographer, he is a stage manager, he is a decorator, he is a theater person; he's superb, simply. He can take four lines of verse that have very little meaning in themselves and stretch them into a book that has tremendous meaning—not overloaded, no sentimentality anywhere. Everybody meets with a bad ending in *A Frog He Would A-wooing Go*. Frog gets eaten by a duck, which is very sad, and the story usually closes on that note. But, in Caldecott's version, he introduces, oddly enough, a human family. They observe the tragedy much as a Greek chorus might—one can almost hear their comments.

In the last picture, we see only Frog's hat on a rock at the stream's edge, all that remains of him. And standing on the bank are a mother, father, and two children. This is startling until you realize what Caldecott has done. It's as though the children have been watching a theatrical performance, and they are terribly upset. There are no words—I'm just inventing what I think it all means: Frog is dead, it alarms them, and, for support, they are clinging to their parents. The older child, a girl, clutches her father's arm; the younger holds fast to his coat. The mother has a quiet, forlorn expression on her face. Very gently, she points with the tip of her parasol toward the stream and the hat. The father looks resigned. They're both conveying to the children, "Yes, it is unfortunate, but such things do happen—that is the way the story ended, it can't be helped. But you have us. Hold on, everything is all right." This is impressive in a picture book for children.

Johan Amos Comenius (1592–1670)

Johan Amos Comenius, born in what is now the Czech Republic, was a visionary educator. A member of the Czech Brethren (also known as Moravians), he was an influential thinker and writer in a turbulent time in European history. He was adviser to the king of Sweden and was offered the first presidency of Harvard University but declined. A believer in universal education for boys and girls and in lifelong learning, he wrote many educational books that were influential throughout Europe and beyond. His ambition was to create an encyclopedic survey of all knowledge, from the religious to the practical. While reorganizing a grammar school in Hungary, he pioneered the use of illustrations connected with text in *Orbis Sensualium Pictus* (1658), which is widely considered to be the first picture book for children. It was published in England in 1659 and in many subsequent editions up to the nineteenth century. *Orbis Sensualium Pictus,* which can be translated as "The World of Things Evident to the Senses through Pictures," was a bi- or trilingual educational textbook. After an alphabet accompanied by animals and their noises, each entry featured a woodcut with numbered items, corresponding to the texts nearby, which were both in Latin and in one or two of the languages used by readers in everyday speech. Many pages illustrate activities and objects of everyday life, such as children's games and different adult occupations. On this page, Latin and English vocabulary identifies details in a woodcut depicting a dramatic scene at sea. The book's introduction points out that even preschool children would delight in looking at the pictures at home.

The Ship-wreck

Ship-wreck.   XCI.   Naufragium.

When a *Storm*, 1. ariseth on a sudden, they strike *Sail*, 2. lest the Ship should be dashed against *Rocks*, 3 or light upon *Shelves*, 4.

If they cannot hinder her they suffer *Ship-wreck*, 5.

And then the men, the *Wares*, and all things are miserably lost.

Nor doth the *Sheat-anchor*, 6 being cast with a *Cable*, do any good.

Some escape, either on a *Plank*, 7. and by swimming, or in the *Boat*, 8.

Part of the Wares, with the dead folks, is carried out of the *Sea*, 9. upon the Shoars.

Cum *Procella*, 1. oritur repentè contrahunt *Vela*, 2. ne Navis ad *Scopulos*, 3. allidatur, aut incidat in *Brevia* (Syrtes), 4.

Si non possunt prohibere patiuntur *Naufragium*, 5.

Tum Homines, *Merces*, omnia miserabiliter pereunt.

Neque hic *Sacra anchora*, 6. *Rudenti* jacta quidquam adjuvat.

Quidam evadunt, vel *tabula*, 7. ac enatando, vel *Scapha*, 8.

Pars Mercium cum mortuis a *Mari*, 9. in littora defertur.

Thomas Bewick (1753–1828)

Thomas Bewick revived and refined the art of wood engraving for book illustration. Raised on a farm west of Newcastle, he had no exposure to art as a child but developed a lifelong love of observing nature closely and drawing what he saw. His apprenticeship with a general engraver and talent for drawing and carving led to work for printers that appeared in chapbooks and broadsides. Since he disliked London and loved to wander in the countryside, he worked in Newcastle for fifty years after setting up shop there with his partner and his brother John. The woodblocks he produced with apprentices and associates were so skillfully detailed and so well suited for printing, with his new "white line" method of carving the blocks, that they influenced illustration and book production for the next century. A forerunner of Romantic artists, with emotional warmth in his scenes from rural life and close attention to natural details, Bewick was praised by writers such as William Wordsworth, Charlotte Brontë, and the art critic John Ruskin. *The Fables of Aesop* (1818), his last large-scale work and one of several editions of Aesop that he illustrated throughout his career, demonstrates his skill in portraying realistic animal, human, and immortal characters with detailed backgrounds (see examples in Part 3).

Bewick's first independent book, *A General History of Quadrupeds,* established his fame as a book illustrator in 1790. His autobiography explains that he was motivated by an earlier book of animals, "Having from the time that I was a school boy, been displeased with most of the cuts in children's books, and particularly with those of the 'Three hundred Animals' the figures of which even at that time I thought I could depicture much better than those in that book." He added that his work on this book of nearly 200 illustrations and descriptions of animals produced "the great pleasure I felt in imitating nature."[1] His two-volume *History of British Birds* (1797 and 1804) was even more successful; just as the quadrupeds he had drawn from life were more natural than those he copied from indirect sources, his native birds were greatly admired by readers for decades, through nine editions of the book. "The Stag" and "The Tawny Owl" show the delicacy of Bewick's detail in the textures of the animals and surrounding foliage, including romantic images of a ruined oak sprouting new branches and a woodland background with a running stag. His layered cutting technique produced variations in ink density to enhance the effects of light and dark. The miniature scenes he created for the blank spaces between sections of his books also became extremely popular. "Boys at the River," from *A History of British Birds. Volume II,* is one of many such vignettes. Charlotte Brontë's character Jane Eyre, like so many real English children, was enchanted by the narrative appeal of these scenes of everyday life and adventure.

NOTE

1. Thomas Bewick, *My Life,* ed. Iain Bain (1862; Oxford: Oxford UP, 1981).

From *A General History of Quadrupeds*

"The Stag (or Red Deer)"

From *A History of British Birds, Volume I*

"The Tawny Owl"

From *A History of British Birds, Volume II*

"Boys at the River"

Walter Crane (1845–1915)

Walter Crane was a multitalented English artist and writer of the Victorian period. With little formal art training, he absorbed influences from his father's art studio, the Devonshire country-side, an apprenticeship with one of the best wood engravers of the time, and later his European travel. He relied heavily on many styles of art and design, such as Greek pottery and architecture, Japanese prints, Renaissance art, William Blake's illustrated books, and pre-Raphaelite art of his own time. But he did not typically draw directly from nature as the pre-Raphaelite group of artists often did. As a leader of the Arts and Crafts and socialist movements, he stressed the moral significance of the craftsman in society and influenced a wide audience with his art, writing, and speeches in Europe and America. In book production, he believed that every detail should contribute to a harmonious overall design from cover to cover. He developed strong theories about shaping the intelligence and imagination of children through good pictures with bold designs, bright colors, symbolic details, and images faithful to the text. In addition to his prolific work in other media and genres, Crane illustrated a wide variety of primers, nursery rhymes, fairy tales, and other children's books with texts written by himself and others.

Crane succeeded in the growing business of children's books through close collaboration with the publisher Edmund Evans, who developed new methods for color printing with wood blocks. After hiring Crane in the 1860s, Evans recognized that his talent was better suited to the fanciful subjects of children's literature than the figures from everyday life in the mass market novels that Evans was selling successfully. Their new "toy books" were of a much higher quality than others that had been published since the 1830s. Within a decade, they created dozens of sixpenny and shilling books, elevating the quality of the illustrated children's book and influencing generations of later artists. In *Beauty and the Beast* (1874), for example, at the height of their Toybook Series' success, the full-page designs, strong black outlines, and striking decorative details in costume and setting represent Crane's mature style after his travels in Europe, with the tendency he described as his "habit of putting in all sorts of subsidiary detail that interested me."[1] These features made his designs more static and academic than those of Evans's other renowned illustrators, Randolph Caldecott and Kate Greenaway, whose styles are more spontaneous. Crane's dramatic full-page design for "The Wind and the Sun" (in *Aesop's Fables* in Part 3) integrates verses by W. J. Linton, written in calligraphy, with flowing illustrations of the contest between the wind and the sun. It appeared in *Baby's Own Aesop* (1887), which was also published under the title *Triplets* with Crane's earlier books *The Baby's Opera* and *The Baby's Bouquet.*

In the 1870s and 1880s Crane also illustrated many books in black and white, including stories by the popular Victorian children's author Mrs. Molesworth, tales by Nathaniel Hawthorne and Oscar Wilde, and the Grimms' fairy tales translated by his sister Lucy Crane in 1882. Containing some of Crane's most highly admired drawings, *Household Stories from the Collection of the Brothers Grimm* is a lavishly illustrated book with decorative initial letters, tailpieces, headpieces, and larger illustrations that highlight symbolic and dramatic images from the tales. In the full-page illustration from "Rapunzel," the influences of ancient classical arts, such as medieval illuminated manuscripts and Greek vase painting, are seen in the figures with flowing costumes, the tower arches, and the architectural frame. The witch's shears in the corner frames, also depicted in a headpiece for this tale that places profiles of the witch and prince opposite each other, foreshadow the witch's efforts to cut off Rapunzel's long hair and end her love affair with the prince. But this illustration focuses on the sensuous figures of the maiden and prince, bound together by the luxurious hair and by love that will triumph in the end. Another example from this book of fairy tales is Crane's illustration for "Snow White" in Part 3.

NOTE

1. Walter Crane quoted in Susan E. Meyer, *A Treasury of the Great Children's Book Illustrators* (New York: Abrams, 1983) 89.

Rapunzel

Randolph Caldecott (1846–86)

Maurice Sendak's essay reprinted earlier in this section describes Randolph Caldecott as the inventor of the modern picture book because of his economical method of arranging words and pictures with rhythm and theatricality. Caldecott, who was born in Chester, began sketching everything around him in childhood and later worked in a bank in Whitchurch, Shropshire. Traces of the countryside that he knew in early life appear in his famous illustrations for nursery rhymes such as *The House that Jack Built* and *The Frog Would A-Wooing Go*. After meeting artists and studying art in Manchester, Caldecott became an illustrator for periodicals in London, achieving success in 1875 with an extensive series of drawings for Washington Irving's *Old Christmas*. He was then hired by the publisher Edmund Evans, whose new methods of color printing with wood blocks could reproduce Caldecott's lively line drawings and delicate watercolors in inexpensive picture books. Beginning at Christmas 1878, they published two books of nursery rhymes and comic poems each year for eight years, continuing the series of shilling toy books begun by Caldecott's friend Walter Crane.

Evans described Caldecott's drawings as "outlines . . . racy and spontaneous."[1] Whereas Crane was inspired by formal art styles from European history and Asia, Caldecott, influenced by eighteenth-century artists such as William Hogarth, reveled in depicting energetic English life with humor and affection, combining colored scenes and smaller line drawings. He maintained spontaneity with quick drawings that he called "lightning sketches," sometimes discarding them and starting over before Evans transferred his copies to wood blocks for the formal book illustrations. His sketchy, economical style was deliberate and artful, for, as he wrote, "The art of leaving out is a science."[2] Caldecott's health was never as robust as the hearty English figures that he drew; although he sought refuge from widespread fame and overwork, he died on a trip to Florida at age thirty-nine, after working only fourteen years as an illustrator.

Caldecott is best known for innovative, humorous interpretations as he expanded on short texts. His dapper frog "with his opera-hat" dines and cavorts at Miss Mousey's Hall, where Rat asks for beer, "For Froggy and I are fond of good cheer," while a group of humans later watches the tragicomic plot unfold (see illustrations with "A Frog Went A-Courting" in Part 3 and in Sendak's essay in this section). These fully clothed animal characters were an inspiration to Beatrix Potter. In *Hey Diddle Diddle,* some pages contain only two or three words, as Caldecott draws out the brief nonsensical rhyme that combines images of farm animals, a fiddle-playing cat, and an elopement. The handsome dish and prim spoon run happily away from a roomful of rollicking dancing dishes in the colorful scene that closes the rhyme, but in the shocking wordless epilogue that Caldecott added, he sketched stern cutlery parents retrieving their daughter while the dish lies shattered on the floor among weeping saucers. In *The Three Jovial Huntsmen,* Caldecott's energetic illustrations of three foolish horsemen, who find nothing but enjoy a day of riding, complement a Lancashire dialect variation on the nursery rhyme also known as "There were three jovial Welshmen" or "There were three men of Gotham."

NOTES

1. Edmund Evans quoted in Susan E. Meyer, *A Treasury of the Great Children's Book Illustrators* (New York: Abrams, 1983) 97–98.
2. Randolph Caldecott quoted in Susan E. Meyer, *A Treasury of the Great Children's Book Illustrators* (New York: Abrams, 1983) 104.

From *Hey Diddle Diddle*

From *The Three Jovial Huntsmen*

Kate Greenaway (1846–1901)

Kate Greenaway was one of the most widely admired creators of children's picture books in Victorian England. The daughter of an engraver, she studied at art schools for twelve years beginning at age eleven and then illustrated greeting cards, calendars, books, and magazines for children. In the late 1870s, her own books of verses and drawings sold so well that her art and the old-fashioned, frilly clothing she drew in elaborate detail became enormously popular in Europe and America. Even in France, where English culture is rarely admired, avid fans imitated her styles while "Greenawisme" was in vogue. Although she preferred to work with her own texts, Greenaway also illustrated nursery rhymes, poems by Ann and Jane Taylor, *The Queen of the Pirate Isle* by Bret Harte, and Robert Browning's poem "The Pied Piper of Hamelin." *Marigold Garden* (1885) and her many almanacs also display her skillful drawings of flowers, graceful children in pastoral landscapes or formal gardens, and picturesque villages. An unmarried woman living a quiet life of hard work, Greenaway maintained that she never left behind her childhood world of the imagination and that she could be faulted for seeing everything in the world as delightful and beautiful. She was associated with the Arts and Crafts movement and corresponded for years with art critic John Ruskin, one of the mentors who admired her lovely children and urged her to perfect her craft. Like Randolph Caldecott and Walter Crane, Greenaway worked with Edmund Evans, the publisher who was in the forefront of developing color printing techniques and expanding the market for children's books that were artfully designed in all details.

Evans took a risk in 1878 by printing thousands of fairly expensive copies of *Under the Window: Pictures and Rhymes for Children,* thereby establishing Greenaway's fame, as well as the standard for her books with varied page designs, the careful use of white space and borders, and delicate watercolors with soft pastel tints. Her world is dominated by charming girls, along with some elegant ladies and boys in frilled collars, pursuing a variety of genteel activities and childhood games, while occasional mischief and tedious acts of obedience are depicted with mild humor. The opening verse reflects Greenaway's idyllic vision: "Under the window is my garden, / Where sweet, sweet flowers grow; / And in the pear-tree dwells a robin, / The dearest bird I know." The death of the bird Dickey in the middle of the book is sad, but he is honored with verbal images of nature and one of Greenaway's attractive processions of children at his burial. Both of the poems reprinted here express the child's point of view in rhythms that are reminiscent of children's songs and nursery rhymes. The poem about shuttlecocks, like the page from her alphabet book *A Apple Pie* in Part 3, shows that Greenaway's little girls are often active at play in spite of confining dresses and big caps or bonnets. With most of the shuttlecocks so high out of reach above a crowd of girls gazing up and the naive questions about their rise and fall, this page almost has the absurd feel of some old nursery rhymes. Modern critics, such as Susan E. Meyer, note that, "For all their playfulness and charm, Greenaway's girls are actually melancholy, dispirited, and strangely detached from period or place."[1] Nevertheless, *Under the Window* seemed spontaneous and captivating to Greenaway's Victorian readers.

NOTE

1. Susan E. Meyer, *A Treasury of the Great Children's Book Illustrators* (New York: Abrams, 1983) 113.

From *Under the Window*

Poor Dicky's Dead!—The bell we toll,
And lay him in the deep, dark hole.
The sun may shine, the clouds may rain,
But Dick will never pipe again!
His quilt will be as sweet as ours,—
Bright buttercups and cuckoo-flowers.

Up you go, shuttlecocks, ever so high!
Why come you down again, shuttlecocks—why?
When you have got so far, why do you fall?—
Where all are high, which is highest of all?

Beatrix Potter (1866–1943)

The Roly-Poly Pudding (1908) was the twelfth of twenty-three books in Beatrix Potter's Peter Rabbit series, which began in 1901 with one of the best-loved animal fantasies ever written for small children, *The Tale of Peter Rabbit* (see Further Recommended Reading at the end of this section). Some of her little books were based on traditional nursery rhymes and tales, but most were filled with original stories of rural life. Since they often began with picture-stories in letters to friends, Potter attributed the success of her books to their origins as stories addressed to individual children. She wrote them during a lonely life as the only daughter in a proud, well-to-do London family, educated at home and developing on her own her interests in writing and art. Potter and her younger brother indulged their passion for studying plants and animals on trips to the country, drawing all kinds of creatures and collecting many pets. Scrutinizing her animals as scientific specimens, she also described them affectionately as pets with interesting personalities and names that are now immortalized in her books, such as Peter and Benjamin Bunny, Hunca Munca (a mouse), and Mrs. Tiggy Winkle (a hedgehog).

Potter might have become a naturalist had society allowed it, but she was not permitted to read her own paper on fungi at a scientific meeting. Her father, who knew artists and took her to museums, collected works by Randolph Caldecott that Beatrix admired and tried to imitate. In her twenties, she drew illustrations for stories by Edward Lear and Lewis Carroll, and began designing Christmas cards. Aesop's fables and Joel Chandler Harris's American Uncle Remus tales influenced her own stories with animal characters depicted in realistic detail, while they also wear some clothing and have human relationships and pursuits. Potter carefully matched words and images on each page in heartwarming, amusing stories told without condescension or excessive sentimentality. The books and related products achieved such enduring international success that Potter was able to buy her own farmland in the Lake District and to preserve large tracts of land for the National Trust. After marrying at age 47, she stopped writing books during her busy, happy life as a farmer in Sawrey.

The Roly-Poly Pudding (later called *The Tale of Samuel Whiskers*) was the second book printed in a larger format with both watercolors and black-and-white drawings. It reintroduces Tom Kitten and his sisters, who get into trouble when guests come to tea in *The Tale of Tom Kitten*. With a more complicated plot alternating between events downstairs and Tom's adventure in the attic, *The Roly-Poly Pudding* begins by explaining that old Mrs. Tabitha Twitchit, "an anxious parent," knows the kittens are in mischief when they are lost, so she puts the sisters in a cupboard while she bakes, but they soon escape. Getting more frightened when Tom cannot be found and there is evidence of rat activity in the house, she sends for John Joiner, a dog who later rescues Tom and scares away the rats. Meanwhile, Tom climbs up the chimney hoping to hunt birds on the roof, but he becomes prey himself, falling into the dirty bed of Samuel Whiskers. The book's scenes inside and around Potter's Hill Top farmhouse at Sawrey (now a museum) continue to delight visitors who can see the same images today. But the attic is an unknown place of terror within Tom's own home: "he found himself in a place he had never seen before, although he had lived all his life in the house" (p. 37). Tom's futile struggles when the rats tie him up to make "a kitten dumpling roly-poly pudding" (p. 40) are described in the text, but his fears are conveyed through pictures, not words, especially the drawing presented here, in which he recoils at the sight of "an enormous rat" facing him and the subsequent scenes of his helpless position trussed up while the heartless but humorous pair of rats argue about how to make him into an edible pudding. Samuel Whiskers, named in memory of Potter's tame rat Sammy, is a fatter, grumpier version of Randolph's Caldecott's sociable rat character in "A Frog He Would A-wooing Go" (see Part 3). As noted in *Beatrix Potter 1866–1943: The Artist and Her World,* Samuel "dominates the scene, with his wife Anna Maria coming a bad second in the rat race."[1]

NOTE

1. Judy Taylor, et al. (London: Frederick Warne and the National Trust, 1987), 137.

From *The Roly-Poly Pudding*

Mrs. Tabitha Twitchit and kittens: "On baking day she determined to shut them up in a cupboard."

Tom Kitten and Samuel Whiskers: "'Please sir, the chimney wants sweeping,' said poor Tom Kitten. 'Anna Maria! Anna Maria!' squeaked the rat. There was a pattering noise and an old woman rat poked her head round a rafter."

Tom Kitten "tied with string in very hard knots"

Wanda Gág (1893–1946)

Wanda Gág, born in Minnesota, rose above the poverty and prejudice that she endured as the daughter of poor immigrant artists to achieve international acclaim as the creator of picture books and fairy tale retellings that reflect the influence of her family's Eastern European heritage. Although her parents died when she was young, their intense devotion to art motivated her to remain self-sufficient and pursue her own goals as she cared for younger siblings; attended art school; began her career as a commercial artist in New York; and exhibited wood engravings, etchings, and lithographs. Her first children's picture book, *Millions of Cats* (1928), was a huge success, establishing her distinctive style of black-and-white illustrations with strong flowing lines. A humorous tale inspired by European folktales that Gág had loved as a child, *Millions of Cats* is considered one of the first true American picture books of enduring artistic quality. Its design innovations include the use of double-page spreads, the movement of the peasant hero's journey from left to right across the pages, and a rhythmic integration of text and pictures. Gág's other books include *ABC Bunny* (1933), a popular and influential alphabet story book illustrated in large format with lithographs (prints made from drawings on a zinc surface), rather than pen-and-ink drawings.

Gág also produced several editions of Grimms' fairy tales for children, some of which were published after she died of cancer and was unable to complete all the illustrations. Like her best picture books, the tales she selected and "freely translated" were praised for their clarity and integrity. Her family's oral storytelling tradition inspired her to incorporate strong dialogue and details from related tales, while remaining true to the spirit of the Grimms' stories and challenging the attitudes of adults who thought after the world wars that modern children needed more practical literature and less fantasy.

After Walt Disney's film adaptation of *Snow White* and related publications appeared in 1937, the influential librarian and critic Anne Carroll Moore encouraged Gág to publish a more authentic version of the tale. *Snow White and the Seven Dwarfs* (1938), a Newbery Honor book, retains details from the Grimm tale, such as the stepmother's horrifying eating of a boar's heart that she thinks is Snow White's, and the tidy group of seven dwarfs with undifferentiated characters. The two largest illustrations in the book contrast the sturdy character of the child running all day to save herself, through the sheltering canopy of the forest where "many wild animals on the way . . . did not hurt her," with the wicked queen making a poison apple in her "lonely secret chamber." The proud beauty of the young queen preening in her mirror in an earlier illustration, symbolized by the peacock feather design of her skirt that is partially visible here, is obscured by the sinister effect of her face covering and swirling poisonous smoke. The three costumes against her wall represent the queen's three attempts to destroy Snow White in different disguises. While Gág's charming illustrations and texts are not as explicit in their inclusion of terrifying and violent details as Randall Jarrell's translations of Grimms' tales (see Part 3) or as dark and intense as Maurice Sendak's illustrations (presented later in this section), they remain popular for their readability and visual appeal, along with their influence in preserving authentic retellings of Grimms' fairy tales through the middle of the twentieth century.

From *Snow White and the Seven Dwarfs*

"She ran all day through woods and woods."

"There, by means of her wicked witchery, she fashioned an apple."

Clement Hurd (1908–88)

Margaret Wise Brown (1910–52) wrote many beloved picture books of the mid-twentieth century. Working as an editor as well as a writer, she encouraged Clement Hurd to illustrate children's books. A native of New York City, Hurd was a modernist painter who studied in Europe with Fernand Léger. Léger's influence can be seen in Hurd's flatly painted scenes in bright colors that blend representational images and fantasy. Hurd's best-known picture books came from two of his many collaborations with Brown, *Goodnight Moon* (1947) and *The Runaway Bunny,* originally published in 1942. Hurd's three different editions of Gertrude Stein's only children's book, *The World Is Round,* show how interpretations of a book can change over time. Among other books that Hurd illustrated later with artistic distinction is a nonfiction series on animal mothers, written by his wife Edith Thacher Hurd. Together they produced over fifty books.

These drawings are from the 1972 edition of *The Runaway Bunny,* in which Hurd reworked the illustrations after he had more experience with producing art for book reproduction. Editor Ursula Nordstrom praised his ability to retain "the warmth and love from the original . . . twenty-five years later."[1] In this imaginary hide-and-seek story, the bunny's mother assures him throughout their rhythmic, repetitive dialogue that no matter what he says about running away, she will turn herself into something that will bring him back, such as the mountain climber and fisherman depicted here. Each pair of pages like this with text and black-and-white drawings is followed by a double-page spread in watercolor that does not need words to show how the mother would carry out each promise. As Perry Nodelman points out in his chapter reprinted at the beginning of this section, discovering the relationships between words and picture and between this book and *Goodnight Moon* adds to the child's enjoyment of the picture book. Several images in this book are echoed in *Goodnight Moon,* especially a later scene when the bunnies imagine being a child and mother in a house. In the end, the mother's hug and offer of a carrot convince the bunny that, like Max in Sendak's *Where the Wild Things Are,* he is better off staying where he is loved, in the cozy warmth of their round home under a tree.

NOTE

1. Ursula Nordstrom, To Clement Hurd, 31 Jan. 1966, *Dear Genius: The Letters of Ursula Nordstrom,* ed. Leonard S. Marcus (New York: HarperCollins, 1998) 199.

From *The Runaway Bunny*

"If you become a rock on the mountain . . . , I will be a mountain climber."

"If you become a fish in a trout stream . . . , I will become a fisherman."

Robert McCloskey (1914–2003)

Robert McCloskey was an American artist who created children's picture books of enduring popularity in the middle of the twentieth century. Following the advice of an editor as he was finishing art school, he began writing stories and gave up more mythical subjects to focus on scenes in the real world. The eight books that he wrote himself grew out of his experiences in his hometown of Hamilton, Ohio, and later in Boston and Maine. *Homer Price* (1943), one of his best-loved books, and *Centerburg Tales* (1951) contain stories about the comical exploits of a boy in small-town Ohio, with satire of American popular culture and humorous allusions to classical heroes. McCloskey was the first illustrator to win the Caldecott Medal twice, for *Make Way for Ducklings* (1941) and *Time of Wonder* (1957).

Stressing the importance of good design, McCloskey advocated teaching all children to draw and to "read" pictures. The cartoonlike style in his early books captures the humor and energy of the mild adventures in his stories, while his drawings are also based on lengthy research and close observation of real people, animals, and places. The illustrations draw readers into the point of view of child and animal characters. In *Blueberries for Sal* (1948, a Caldecott Honor book), characters and details of setting were based on McCloskey's wife, his daughter, and their family homes. The text and drawings were done in an appropriate shade of dark blue. While a human mother and a bear mother look for blueberries on a Maine hill and their mixed-up daughters start following the wrong mother, the children enjoy their adventurous encounter with another species more than the confused mothers do. The expressive portraits of Sal depict a rumpled, curious, engaging little girl, thoroughly enjoying her blueberries and her outing.

From *Blueberries for Sal*

"Her mother went back to her picking, but Little Sal . . . ate blueberries."

Garth Williams (1912–96)

Garth Williams was best known for his drawings in children's books by E. B. White, Margaret Wise Brown, and Laura Ingalls Wilder. A native of New York City, with parents who were both artists, Williams spent a few childhood years on a New Jersey farm, later living and studying art in Europe. After Ursula Nordstrom, the famous editor of children's books at Harper's, asked Williams to illustrate E. B. White's *Stuart Little* (1945), the book's success convinced him to devote his career to illustrations for children. His own book, *Rabbit's Wedding* (1958), inadvertently created controversy in southern states by depicting the marriage of a black and a white rabbit. Later Williams spent six years preparing drawings for Harper's 1953 reprints of Wilder's Little House on the Prairie books, traveling to locations depicted in the books and meeting Wilder when she was eighty years old. The farm that he rented in New York state before he began these books also provided a basic backdrop for the Ingalls farms and *Charlotte's Web*.

The illustration from *Little House on the Prairie* in Part 8 and the two from *Charlotte's Web* reprinted here and in Part 4 demonstrate the expressive power of Williams's line drawings. Williams said that "the artist has to see everything with the same eyes" as the author.[1] In the early chapters of *Charlotte's Web,* Fern's nurturing and defense of Wilbur contrast with the violence of her father, intending to kill the runt, and her brother, who is introduced "heavily armed" with air rifle and wooden knife. The picture of Wilbur in Fern's doll carriage shows her ardent motherly devotion, but here, before the fantasy of talking animals begins, the text starts to focus on Wilbur's point of view. Wilbur is not tormented like some pets who are treated like dolls; he likes a carriage ride when he is tired and looks cute with his long eyelashes, sleeping next to the doll, in an idyllic childhood interlude before Fern's father sells him.

On Zuckerman's farm, the nature of White's animal fantasy is epitomized in the famous illustration of the web that says "TERRIFIC" (see Part 4). Although White sent Williams books on spiders and insisted that Charlotte not look human, the miracle of her web displaying a human word causes Wilbur to stand proud, feeling handsome and terrific. Williams wrote that "I start with the real animal, working over and over until I can get the effect of human qualities and expressions and poses. I redesign animals as it were."[2] This peaceful moment occurs between the hard work of Charlotte's web building and the excitement after humans discover it. Perry Nodelman's *Words About Pictures* notes that in *Charlotte's Web*, "the energetic line of the drawings balances the often dreamy music of the text" (p. 71).

Williams also illustrated the first Frances book by Russell Hoban, an American author of a wide variety of books for children and adults, including the animal fantasies in the novel *The Mouse and His Child* and in a series of I Can Read books about Frances's everyday childhood experiences. Frances's family is quite human, except that Hoban thought of depicting them as small animals; his editor Ursula Nordstrom agreed, with the caution that mice would be very difficult and she had tried eight artists before hiring Williams to illustrate E. B. White's *Stuart Little*.[3] After Williams also became the illustrator of *Bedtime for Frances,* she wrote to Hoban in late 1959 that Williams had "decided to make these people badgers."[4] Subsequent books in the series were illustrated by Hoban's wife Lillian Hoban. For young children and parents, the first book remains a favorite story about and for bedtime, as the badger parents reluctantly but lovingly humor the restless child through a series of fears and requests before she gets tired and falls asleep. Although the story does not incorporate details of animal life as books by E. B. White and Beatrix Potter do, Williams's illustrations are similar to Potter's in depicting realistic woodland animals with just enough clothing, props, and human expressions to inspire human readers to identify with and smile at their domestic adventures.

NOTES

1. Garth Williams, "Illustrating the Little House Books," *The Horn Book Magazine* (Dec. 1953): 413–22.
2. Garth Williams quoted in "Garth (Montgomery) Williams," *Major Authors and Illustrators for Children and Young Adults,* 2nd ed., 8 vols. (The Gale Group, 2002), *Biography Resource Center* (Thomson Gale, 2005), 16 May 2005 <http://galenet.galegroup.com/servlet/BioRC>.
3. Ursula Nordstrom, To Russell Hoban, 24 July 1959, *Dear Genius: The Letters of Ursula Nordstrom,* ed. Leonard S. Marcus (New York: HarperCollins, 1998) 119.
4. Ursula Nordstrom, To Russell Hoban, 12 November 1959, *Dear Genius: The Letters of Ursula Nordstrom,* ed. Leonard S. Marcus (New York: HarperCollins, 1998) 128.

From *Bedtime for Frances*

Frances and her parents

From *Charlotte's Web*

Chapter 2. Fern and Wilbur

Maurice Sendak (b. 1928)

Maurice Sendak's art fascinates readers of all ages as he grapples with strong emotions and experiences in original picture books as well as his illustrations for traditional rhymes and tales. After he traveled extensively in Europe to study landscape and art, his intense, flowing pen and ink drawings of Grimms' fairy tales were published in a two-volume collection called *The Juniper Tree,* which was selected as one of the Best Illustrated Children's Books of 1973 by the *New York Times Book Review.* He produced one drawing for each of the twenty-seven tales translated by Lore Segal and Randall Jarrell, recognizing the influence of earlier Grimm illustrations by Ludwig Grimm, George Cruickshank (see Jacobs's "Jack and the Beanstalk" in Part 3), and Otto Ubbelohde, as well as the Renaissance etchings of Albrecht Dürer. Sendak's drawings emphasize the uncanny and earthy qualities of the Grimm tales. Sendak uses close observation of real animals and a detailed cross-hatching style to great evocative effect, filling the picture space with texture, motion, and expressive figures, while the wide white borders enhance the psychological intensity and strangeness of the confined images. "Hans My Hedgehog" is about a hedgehog born to human peasants who reject him, but he cheerfully plays music while tending pigs and donkeys in the forest, waiting for his opportunity to marry a princess and become a human king. The illustration for another animal bridegroom tale, "The Frog King" (in Part 2), depicts one of the unnaturally large animals that Sendak drew in this book, shown at the climactic moment when he approaches the princess in her bed as she watches with a combination of fascination and repulsion. For more background on Sendak, see the introduction to his essays earlier in this section and the discussion of *Where the Wild Things Are* in Further Recommended Reading.

Hans My Hedgehog

Mercer Mayer (b. 1943)

American book illustrator Mercer Mayer was an innovator in the late-twentieth-century development of wordless picture books when his first published book appeared: *A Boy, a Dog, and a Frog* (1967). It is an autobiographical story about a boy's futile struggle to catch a frog in a net, but the frog follows him home to make friends with the boy and dog in their bathtub. In addition to five sequels about the frog and boy, Mayer has written and illustrated numerous picture books in different styles, including two extensive series of Little Monster and Little Critter stories published as Golden Books. Beginning in the 1970s, he chose the simpler format of these inexpensive mass market publications to provide families who did not frequent libraries or bookstores with stories that use humor, fantasy, and visual details to teach reassuring life lessons. Another of his most popular books is *There's a Nightmare in My Closet* (1968), with an array of frightening and amiable monsters representing a boy's nighttime fears. Later Mayer developed a rich, painterly style to illustrate fairy tales with exotic settings, such as *Everyone Knows What a Dragon Looks Like* by Jay Williams (1976) and Marianna Mayer's *Beauty and the Beast* (1978) and *East of the Sun & West of the Moon* (1980). In 1999, Mayer's experimentation with computer-generated artistic effects resulted in his first digitally illustrated book, his Japanese tale *Shibumi and the Kitemaker.*

Mayer's stories range from wild, nonsensical fantasy to contemporary realism. His wordless frog books weave lighthearted elements of animal fantasy into realistic natural and domestic settings, drawn in brown pencil within simple frames suggestive of the influence of his early cartoon work. As the boy's alter ego, the frog exhibits human behaviors, such as laughing in the same posture as the boy at the adults he has annoyed by the end of *Frog Goes to Dinner* (1974). Having ridden secretly to the "fancy restaurant" in the boy's pocket, the frog leaps from one act of mischief to another until he is caught and then retrieved from the haughty waiter. The scenes of an unwelcome frog interrupting formal dining, kissing a person on the nose, and ending the adventure in his friend's bedroom contain satiric reminders of the fairy tale "The Frog King" (see Part 2). The frog's wild escapade among shocked, angry, and bemused strangers, along with the boy's realistic family drama of public humiliation and punishment mixed with affection, demonstrates Mayer's skill at conveying a wide range of emotions through the bodies and facial expressions of his characters.

From *Frog Goes to Dinner*

Tom Feelings (1933–2003)

Tom Feelings devoted most of his career to illustrating books about Africa and African American culture, viewing himself primarily as "a storyteller—telling the black story, one that is rooted in Africa and expanded in America."[1] Born in Brooklyn, New York, he worked as a cartoonist while he also developed his interest in children and the complexities of racial identity by drawing people around him on the city streets. He was an illustrator in the air force and in freelance jobs, but his determination to focus on African American themes made work hard to find, and the art school he attended did not appreciate African art. Living in Ghana for two years, he developed a warmer, more flowing style, absorbing the impressions of bright sun and dark skin used in later picture books about Africa. When the civil rights movement produced wider interest in African American art and culture, Feelings illustrated books by distinguished African American writers, such as Julius Lester, Maya Angelou, and Nikki Grimes. For *Soul Looks Back in Wonder* (1993), a number of writers contributed poems to accompany his first full-color book illustrations (see poems by Lucille Clifton in Part 1 and Maya Angelou in Part 4). Feelings published an illustrated autobiography called *Black Pilgrimage* (1972) and turned his early comic strip into the picture book *Tommy Traveler in the World of Black History* (1991). For twenty years, he worked on the sixty-four paintings in his masterpiece, *The Middle Passage: White Ships/Black Cargo* (1995). The wordless book of compelling abstract and realistic images tells the powerful story of Africans who were taken from their homes into slavery, enduring brutal passages across the Atlantic on slave ships.

While Tom Feelings and writer Muriel Feelings were married, they collaborated on three picture books about East African culture. *Mojo Means One: Swahili Counting Book* (1971) and *Jambo Means Hello: Swahili Alphabet Book* (1974) were the first books by an African American artist to be awarded Caldecott Honors. *Jambo Means Hello* contains a map and background on the areas of Africa where Swahili is spoken, as well as detailed notes on the special technical processes that were used to draw, paint with tempera, and photograph the illustrations. Having been inspired by his African experience to breathe more life into his pictures than he could through line drawing, Feelings used tissue paper to manipulate painted shapes on a board, a method that requires careful handling of the delicate paper while allowing for spontaneity and the muted shades he preferred. He compared this technique to the resourcefulness of his African ancestors (since he began using tissue paper while he was a poor art student) and to the improvisation of jazz and blues music that he listened to while working.[2] The alphabet book depicts animals, customs, and family and community life in East Africa. Some readers now observe that, like some other books about previously marginalized cultures, *Jambo Means Hello* deals with Africa in generalities, is addressed to a narrow audience of "children of African ancestry," and does not depict modernization in Africa; nevertheless, in the early 1970s, books by Tom and Muriel Feelings that celebrate the lives of Swahili speakers with warmth and concern for culturally specific details paved the way for the publication of numerous multicultural children's books that appealed to wide audiences throughout the rest of the century and beyond.

NOTES

1. Tom Feelings quoted in *Contemporary Authors Online* (The Gale Group, 2004), 23 May 2005 <http://galenet.galegroup.com/servlet/LitRC>.
2. Rudine Sims Bishop, "Tom Feelings and 'The Middle Passage,'" *The Horn Book Magazine 72* (July–Aug. 1996): 436–42.

From *Jambo Means Hello*

R rafiki is a friend
(rah·fee·key) Children do more than play with one another. Together friends do chores like tending cattle or fetching water from the river.

Mitsumasa Anno (b. 1926)

Like many of Mitsumasa Anno's other internationally acclaimed picture books, *Anno's Alphabet* was published in both Japanese (*ABC no hon,* 1974) and English (1975). Growing up in western Japan, Anno longed to see the rest of the world that was cut off from his small village by mountains, rice fields, and ocean. As a young teacher in Tokyo, he observed that children have different perspectives from adults, and he always strives to broaden the scope of their understanding. Beginning with *Topsy-Turvies* in 1968, Anno published books that play visual tricks, incorporating his interest in mathematics, science, logic, and social studies to stimulate the imagination. As he has remarked, "Nothing is impossible to the young, not until we become caught in the problems of living and forget to make-believe. Perhaps these pictures of mine will keep all of us young a little longer, will stretch our imaginations enough to help keep us magically human."[1] A number of his books, including several that were produced in collaboration with his son, Masaichiro Anno, explore a wide range of mathematical concepts and language games.

After some years of international travel, *Anno's Journey* (1977) began a series of popular picture books that invite readers to make up their own stories as a little man journeys through different parts of Europe and the United States, where cultural landmarks and famous historical and fictional figures can be spotted among the intricate details on each page. Anno felt that these wordless books could represent the hearts of people even though the languages of the Western world are difficult for him. He later used multilayered texts and illustrations to play with the different perspectives of child and adult and of oral, written, and visual storytelling, in *Anno's Aesop: A Book of Fables by Aesop and Mr. Fox* (1987) and *Anno's Twice Told Tales: The Fisherman and His Wife and the Four Clever Brothers* (1993). Mr. Fox's interpretations of the illustrations in these books form a humorous counterpoint to the texts of traditional tales that he pretends to read to his son Freddy.

Anno's Alphabet displays Anno's typical combination of watercolor with precisely detailed pen-and-ink drawings. The letters of the alphabet on each double-page spread create optical illusions, like many works of Dutch artist M. C. Escher; in color the letters' woodgrain texture creates an effect of superrealism even though the letters are drawn in configurations that would be impossible in three dimensions or that produce illusions, such as the M that seems to be inserted through a mirror or formed with half an M reflected in a mirror. Each delicate border contains several objects beginning with the same letter, such as the mermaids and marigolds on the M pages. Among the wide variety of intriguing and humorous objects in color on the right pages, this map pays tribute to Robert Louis Stevenson's *Treasure Island* (see Part 5). Also known for his exhibits of paintings and other works of graphic art, Anno has described his artworks as maps that elicit a wide range of responses, from confusion and anger to pleasure, but readers who explore willingly will discover precise images and concepts as well as imaginative playfulness.[2]

NOTES

1. Mitsumasa Anno quoted in *Contemporary Authors Online* (The Gale Group, 2001), 6 May 2005 <http://galenet.galegroup.com/servlet/LitRC>.
2. Anno, Postscript, *The Unique World of Mitsumasa Anno: Selected Works (1968–1977)* (Tokyo: Kodansha Ltd., 1977).

From *Anno's Alphabet: An Adventure in Imagination*

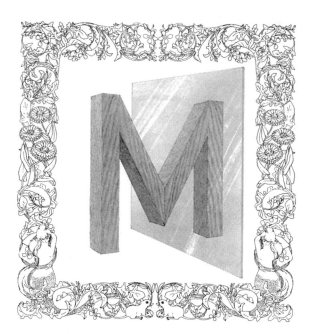

Trina Schart Hyman (1939–2004)

Trina Schart Hyman, an American illustrator and writer of numerous books, is best known for expressive paintings that blend realism and romance in her adaptations of traditional folktales and legends. A native of Philadelphia, she learned to love fairy tale illustrations and dressing up as fairy tale characters when she was a young child. After studying art in Philadelphia, Boston, and Sweden, she became the first art director of the children's magazine *Cricket* in the 1970s. Her art is often compared to that of Pennsylvania's Brandywine school of illustrators, such as Howard Pyle, N. C. Wyeth, and Jessie Willcox Smith. Among Hyman's most highly acclaimed works are her acrylic paintings for Paul Heins's 1974 translation of the Grimm Brothers' *Snow White,* her first full-color book after she illustrated many in either black and white or hand-separated colors. She won the Caldecott Medal for the vivid illustrations in Margaret Hodge's adaptation of *St. George and the Dragon* (1984). The book's detailed borders and dramatic scenes are full of symbolic details from Renaissance life.

When criticized for the sensuality of some of her characters, and for overillustrating stories, Hyman acknowledged "that I'm a compulsive filler-in of space, and also I'm basically a story-teller myself."[1] She used herself and many other people she knew as characters in her books, drawing them from memory. She commented, "The focus of my illustrations—largely because of the kinds of stories I choose to illustrate—is almost always on human beings. . . . People—and this includes monsters and other fantastic creatures—are endlessly fascinating to me as subject matter. Facial expressions, body language, gestures of both action and repose can express a wealth of information. . . . The story within the story can nearly always be found in my illustrations."[2] This devotion to details that reveal personality and setting can be seen in the black-and-white illustration reprinted here from *Jane, Wishing,* written by Tobi Tobias (1977). Scenes from Jane's ordinary life and her dream life alternate throughout the book. In her fantasy life, which Hyman illustrated in color on borderless double-page spreads, Jane is a romantic princess with flowing red hair—beautiful, poetic, and an only child. In actuality, Jane has siblings with whom she quarrels and wrangles in a series of realistic glimpses into a typical middle-class childhood, where she has to do chores and share a room with her pretty older sister. In this kitchen scene, Jane, with the brown braids she dislikes, reveals her fantasy about changing her name, and her family responds unsympathetically. Although there is no dramatic or sentimental plot twist to change her perspective in the end, Jane decides to be happy with reality. Being just herself, "plain Jane," is enough, so the last scene shows the whole down-to-earth, affectionate family in color.

NOTES

1. Trina Schart Hyman quoted in *Dictionary of Literary Biography, Vol. 61: American Writers for Children Since 1960: Poets, Illustrators, and Nonfiction Authors,* ed. Glenn E. Estes (Gale Research, 1987), *Literature Resource Center,* Hollins U Lib., 9 May 2005 <http://www.galegroup.com>.
2. Trina Schart Hyman quoted in *Children's Books and Their Creators,* ed. Anita Silvey (Boston: Houghton, 1995) 337–39.

From *Jane, Wishing*

Chris Van Allsburg (b. 1949)

Chris Van Allsburg is a master of mystery and magic in the art of picture book design. A native of Michigan, he studied sculpture and then exhibited imaginative, surreal sculptures with narrative possibilities that led him to try book illustration. *The Garden of Abdul Gasazi* (1979), his first picture book about a magic garden full of eerie topiary, won several awards. He observes in his 1982 Caldecott Medal Acceptance Speech for *Jumanji* that the illustrated book "is a unique medium that allows an artist-author to deal with the passage of time, the unfolding of events, in the same way film does. The opportunity to create a small world between two pieces of cardboard . . . is exciting and rewarding."[1] Although some of his books use color—*The Polar Express,* for example, a 1985 Christmas story of enduring popularity, and *Just a Dream* (1990), a futuristic dream fantasy about pollution, he often draws in black and white, a form that he describes as "becoming stranger and stranger—it's almost vanished from newspapers, and you never see it in broadcast anymore," but "black and white really can do it all."[2] He typically blends realistic settings and images with haunting fantasy elements because "the idea of the extraordinary happening in the context of the ordinary is what's fascinating to me. . . . I think fantasy is more provocative when it happens in the context of ordinariness, or things that you recognize. . . . I prefer surreal elements within a realistic landscape."[3] Van Allsburg helped produce film adaptations of *Jumanji* (1995) and *The Polar Express,* a 2004 Warner Brothers film created through a new method of transforming live action into computer-generated images using motion-capture technology.

The title page of Van Allsburg's intriguing 1987 alphabet book announces, "The Alphabet Theatre Proudly Presents The Z Was Zapped: A Play in Twenty-Six Acts Performed by the Caslon Players, Written and Directed by Mr. Chris Van Allsburg." Van Allsburg gave new life to the old form of the alphabet book by putting each letter on a stage in its own act of this unique drama, with the "players" drawn in a typeface named after the eighteenth-century English type designer William Caslon. The book's unusual design places each act, with a one-sentence text, on the back of the corresponding picture, so that readers see the action on stage before reading the short description of that letter. Thus, the book can become a word game if readers view a picture and guess what the next alliterative sentence will say. For example, one may guess that the S is being splashed with water, but Act 19 reads, "The S was simply Soaked." This design also contributes to the book's surreal effect because we are used to seeing text and illustrations that go together in alphabet books and other concept books; thus it is disorienting to look at the evaporating E while reading on the facing page, "The D was nearly Drowned."

This "play" is like an old-fashioned variety show with one strange act after another (especially vaudevillian when the Y is "yanked away" with a cane) or like a mystery with a new crime or catastrophe on each page: most letters are victims of actions described in passive voice (such as K being kidnapped, and Q being quartered with a knife), although some suffer without a visible cause, such as the jittery J and the warped W. Van Allsburg's website claims that the actors perform this "difficult . . . nasty" play with "great sacrifice," that the playwright's haunting work is "both poignant and painful."[4] As in *The Mysteries of Harris Burdick* (1984) and other books, Van Allsburg's pencil drawings with eerily realistic images and textures show his interest in dramatic effects of light and dark, reflections and shadows. Adult critics admire his creative, postmodern method of dramatizing the instability of language, while perhaps younger readers who are struggling to master spelling feel avenged by the violent fates that befall each letter of this alphabet.

NOTES

1. Chris Van Allsburg, Caldecott Medal Acceptance Speech, 1982, *Chris Van Allsburg,* 2004, 22 May 2005 http://www.chrisvanallsburg.com/jumanjispeech.html>.
2. Chris Van Allsburg quoted in Hilary Knight, "Return Engagements," *Publishers Weekly* 249 (14 Oct. 2002): 26+.
3. Chris Van Allsburg in Anita Silvey, "A Conversation with Chris Van Allsburg," 2000, *The Polar Express by Chris Van Allsburg,* Houghton Mifflin, 21 May 2005 <http://www.houghtonmifflinbooks .com/features/hepolarexpress/cvaconversation.shtml>.
4. *"The Z Was Zapped,"* Chris Van Allsburg, 2004, 22 May 2005 <http://www.chrisvanallsburg.com/ zwaszapped.html>.

From *The Z Was Zapped: A Play in Twenty-Six Acts*

"The A was in an Avalanche"

"The Z was finally Zapped"

FURTHER RECOMMENDED READING

BEATRIX POTTER (1866–1943)

THE TALE OF PETER RABBIT

The Tale of Peter Rabbit began as one of the picture-stories that Beatrix Potter sent in letters to the children of her former governess. Having studied plants and animals on trips to the country since childhood, Potter scrutinized them as scientific specimens, drew them as she developed her artistic skills, and wrote affectionately about the interesting personalities of her pets, giving them names now immortalized in her books, such as Peter and Benjamin Bunny. Seven years after she wrote Peter Rabbit's story in a letter, she transformed it into a little book, which she printed privately in black and white. When Frederick Warne agreed to publish it in 1902, he insisted on color illustrations, launching her series of twenty-three small books of animal tales illustrated with appealing watercolors. Following in the traditions of Aesop's fables and Joel Chandler Harris's American Uncle Remus tales, Potter created animal characters that are depicted in realistic detail while they also live and behave like humans. She skillfully matched words and images, writing heartwarming and amusing stories without condescension or excessive sentimentality.

Although Potter agreed with Warne's plan to publish *Peter Rabbit* in color, she insisted on keeping the price down, so she omitted some material that later appeared in *The Tale of Benjamin Bunny*. In addition to this sequel, in which Peter and his cousin Benjamin rescue his lost clothes but get in trouble for returning to the forbidden garden, Peter and his jacket appear in several later animal tales. *The Tale of Peter Rabbit* begins with an utterly realistic picture of his mother and several small rabbits around the roots of a tree. Only the "Once upon a time" opening and their names in the text indicate that this is a fantasy. On the second page, the mother is dressed like a Victorian housewife, with her three obedient daughters facing her to receive instructions and baskets for collecting blackberries. Peter is obviously not heeding her words, in spite of the dire warning in the reminder that their father had been eaten in a pie by the McGregors. He stands out because his blue jacket contrasts with his sisters' identical red capes; his name is more human than Flopsy, Mopsy, and Cotton-tail; and Peter is facing away from them, about to embark on an exciting escapade when Mr. McGregor chases him through the garden. His transgressions begin when he sneaks into the garden: "Peter, who was very naughty, ran straight to Mr. McGregor's garden, and squeezed under the gate!" Peter quickly brings about his own punishment by eating enough vegetables to hurt his stomach, and after his narrow escape from capture, his frustrated but loving mother puts him to bed with a dose of chamomile tea. Although generations of animal fantasies in picture books and novels have followed this one, none is more popular than Potter's lively tale of the mischievous bunny and his cozy home under the "big fir-tree." For more background on Potter and samples of her drawings, see the headnote and illustrations from *The Roly-Poly Pudding,* earlier in this section.

MAURICE SENDAK

WHERE THE WILD THINGS ARE

In the essay reprinted earlier in this section, Sendak explains why he views Randolph Caldecott as the inventor of the picture book in the Victorian period. Sendak's own *Where the Wild Things Are* is considered a masterpiece of the twentieth-century picture book. Sendak has been admired widely for his draftsmanship and his treatment of the unconscious experiences of the child, especially in the books he wrote himself. Picture book critics such as Jane Doonan have observed that the careful lines of Sendak's drawings and his use of cross hatching show the influence of eighteenth- and nineteenth-century illustrators, including the wood engravings of Thomas Bewick. Caldecott's influence shows in the story's continuous flow of energy as the short text moves the reader along rhythmically in syncopation with the illustrations. The fact that Sendak knew movies and comics but not fine art in his childhood is evident in the dramatic action of his illustrations. A friend pointed out to him that in one scene of this book, he had unconsciously imitated a moment in *King Kong* when the monster emerges from a cave.

The boy Max is one of Maurice's many child alter egos, a mischief-maker who is sent to his room for being too rowdy. Like Peter Rabbit, Max, dressed in a wolf suit, gets himself into trouble, but he knows he has a loving mother waiting for him at home. Max's mother calls him "WILD THING" in the beginning, and the book ends with assurance that she has left him some supper, "and it was still hot." Unlike Peter Rabbit, Max is shown only with a dog he chases and the "wild things," while his mother stays out of the pictures; his journey of adventure occurs in his own imagination, and the story focuses on his struggle with his emotions, rather than the external influences that Peter encounters at home and in the garden.

Alone his room, Max is angry, and then he appears nonchalant as he closes his eyes and imagines a forest growing in the room. There is a mythic quality in his ocean voyage for "almost over a year," reminiscent of the poetic sea journey of Edward Lear's owl and pussy-cat (see Part 3). Max looks unhappy when confronting the wild things, which represent his own fears and aggressions, but while the wild things have stereotypical traits of monsters, some of their childlike features, especially their big round eyes and grinning faces, provide a counterpoint to the text that describes them repeatedly as "terrible." Max tames them by staring into their eyes, until they "made him king of all the wild things" and he calls, "let the wild rumpus start." As the pictures have gradually expanded through the story to fill the book's double-page spreads, Max and the wild things now howl at the moon and romp wildly through six pages with no white borders or words.

Like many children who are sent to their room to ponder their misbehavior, Max vents his frustrations, and enjoys doing it, but then, as the pictures grow smaller again, he tires of being a king of wildness, feels lonely, and decides to go back "where someone loved him best of all." In his acceptance speech for the 1964 Caldecott medal (also reprinted in *Sendak & Co.*), Sendak described "the necessary games" of aggression, wildness, and then calm exhaustion that he had

often watched neighborhood children "conjure up to combat an awful fact of childhood: the fact of their vulnerability to fear, anger, hate, frustration—all the emotions that are an ordinary part of their lives and that they can perceive only as ungovernable and dangerous forces. To master these forces, children turn to fantasy: that imagined world where disturbing emotional situations are solved to their satisfaction."[1] Like countless folktale heroes, Max is the little guy with giant-sized adversaries to conquer. Although this book has been controversial for giving the child such strong emotions and so much autonomy, it dramatizes the wish fulfillment of both children and adults by showing that the boy can gain control of his inner monsters and choose to return peacefully to his loving home. For additional background on Sendak, see his essays and fairy tale illustrations reprinted earlier in this section and in Part 2, and Perry Nodelman's essay earlier in this section.

NOTE

1. Maurice Sendak, *Caldecott & Co: Notes on Books & Pictures* (New York: Farrar, Straus and Giroux, 1988) 150–51.

SATIRES AND SPIN-OFFS
Reworking Classic Children's Literature

The lies of Once-upon-a-Time appal.
Cinderella seeing white mice grow into horses
shrank to the wall—an event so ominous
she didn't go to the Armed Forces Ball
but phoned up Alcoholics Anonymous.

From "Pantomime Diseases" by Dannie Abse, 1979[1]

Although contemporary authors such as Dannie Abse have been especially fond of probing and mocking the fantasies of traditional tales in relation to the harsh realities of life, the practice of creating abridgements, adaptations, satires, and spin-offs of existing stories is as old as literature itself. After all, we do not know how or when human beings started making up tales, rhymes, and songs and then retelling or singing different versions of the same ones or imitating and mocking someone else's stories. As Part 3 discusses, the oral traditions that are older than written literature give us innumerable variants of popular stories, such as Cinderella tales with deserving heroines who live happily ever after, or animal fantasy folk songs that mock romantic ballads as Froggie goes a-courtin' with comic or tragic results. Since the Renaissance, the literary world has placed more and more value on the originality of the individual artist and the permanence of the printed text, especially during the mid-twentieth century when the predominant scholarly approach to literature, called New Criticism, emphasized close examination of each work of literature on its own, without much reference to the life of the author, the historical context, or the influence of oral traditions and popular culture. In the field of children's literature, however, oral traditions have always played a central role because young children are introduced to songs, rhymes, and oral stories before they learn to read, and many writers have built their work on the most popular forms known from early childhood, such as nursery rhymes and fairy tales. Modern audio-visual media make children familiar with all kinds of stories before they can read them. Their experiences may resemble those of earlier generations when family and community storytelling did not separate stories for children and adults, but children also develop new and independent perceptions about literature and life as they explore a greater variety of stories in different media than the local tales, literary classics, or series fiction that their great-grandparents knew. *Intertextuality* is a term for the network of relationships among texts, the various ways in which texts refer to other texts. Although it has become popular in recent critical theory and postmodern literature, intertextuality is not new; it was taken for granted in the crosscurrents of older storytelling traditions and is quite prominent in children's literature and multimedia popular culture.

Since the rise of the novel as a popular literary form in the eighteenth century and the growth of literacy among children and adults, abridgements and adaptations have inevitably followed the publication of almost any story that achieves enduring fame. Daniel Defoe's *Robinson Crusoe* was so successful when it appeared in 1719 that the London publisher quickly reprinted it and two sequels. But Defoe's own sequels were soon overshadowed by unauthorized abridgements that appeared immediately and continued through the twentieth century. Chapbook versions of Defoe's lengthy novel, some as short as eight pages with woodcuts, and illustrated abridgements for children from prominent publishers, such as John Newbery and Thomas Carnan, made the story of Robinson Crusoe available to poor families as well as educated children by the end of the eighteenth century. While abridgements and "spin-offs" or "rip-offs" that may be of inferior literary quality make lovers of literary classics cringe, they continue to sell in all the modern media: comic books and cartoons, as well as books and live-action films and television shows. On the other hand, original new works of high quality are often skillfully crafted as variations on the patterns established by earlier stories. Two excerpts in this volume by highly esteemed authors of boys' books in the nineteenth and twentieth centuries, respectively, *Treasure Island* by Robert Louis Stevenson and *The Island* by Gary Paulsen, represent the countless variations on the theme of island isolation that literary historians call the robinsonnade tradition in literature for children as well as adults.

Developments in technology and the arts by the late nineteenth century engendered new methods of illustrating, adapting, and reinterpreting literary texts, so that by the end of the twentieth century, there were multiple versions of most literary classics in editions that were illustrated by different artists and in adaptations for stage, film, and television. Just as oral storytelling produces variants of stories reflecting the personality and beliefs of the storyteller, any adaptation reflects the values of the people who created it and the culture in which it is produced. The context in which a book is written is different from the production of a play, ballet, opera, or film. And adaptations in different media may have interesting histories of their own that are little known to readers of the book or are separated from the work of the original writer by time or circumstance. Hans Christian Andersen loved the ballet, but the ballet based on his fairy tale "The Little Mermaid" was produced in 1909, after his death. One of the most successful productions in the history of the Royal Theatre in Copenhagen, the ballet inspired a patron of the arts to commission the bronze statue of the Little Mermaid that has drawn tourists to her Danish harbor outside Copenhagen since 1913. Adaptations in opera and ballet are often criticized by lovers of literature and praised by enthusiasts of music or dance for sacrificing so much of the plot and characterization, typically playing up the most melodramatic parts of a story, to highlight the talents of singers and dancers. Just as the Little Mermaid gave up her enchanting voice and some control over her own destiny in order to be transformed, acquiring human legs that could dance beautifully for a prince, transforming stories from one medium to another or transplanting them from one setting to another involves trade-offs for good or ill.

Some adaptations are produced in close collaboration with the book's author, but most are not, just as most writers have little or no control over the ways in which their texts are illustrated in picture books or novels. It took Walt Disney well over a decade to convince P. L. Travers to grant him the film rights to her Mary Poppins stories, and then she was dissatisfied with the 1964 musical film, although it achieved long-lasting popular and critical success. Forty years later, British producer Cameron Mackintosh, collaborating with the Disney Company and using songs from the film, believed his stage musical about Mary Poppins fulfilled the wishes that Travers conveyed while she was alive. J. K. Rowling's Harry Potter fantasies became so extraordinarily popular after the first book's publication in 1998 that Rowling retained the right to approve the film adaptations, which began to appear in late 2001 as she continued to write her planned series of seven novels. J. M. Barrie is one of many authors who worked in more than one medium himself. He published several different stories about Peter Pan, and since there have been so many adaptations for stage and screen over the past century, many people are not aware that Barrie's own play elevated the fame of his mythic boy hero in 1904, remaining a landmark in theater history through many revisions and revivals by Barrie and others. L. Frank Baum, who wrote many sequels to *The Wonderful Wizard of Oz* at the urging of enthusiastic child fans, was involved in producing both a Broadway stage musical in 1902, enjoyed by adults nationwide, and some of the later silent films based on his Oz books, all of which were eclipsed in 1939 by one of the most beloved films ever made in America; *The Wizard of Oz,* the MGM musical starring Judy Garland, also became a television phenomenon through annual holiday telecasts, until home videos and DVDs allowed repeated viewings at any time. The magic ruby slippers that glisten brilliantly in the film are a popular display at the Smithsonian Institution's National Museum of American History. Yet readers of Baum's original book, which was celebrated with 100th-anniversary reprints and special events in 2000, know that in the book, Dorothy's slippers are silver and her fantasy adventure in Oz is not a dream vision as it is in the movie.

Thus, whether adaptations achieve lasting fame or not, any successful work of literature is likely to undergo one or more transformations in another medium. Recent books and web sites reprint and analyze numerous variations on individual classic stories, such as "Little Red Riding Hood," "Cinderella," and *Alice in Wonderland.* Part 3 contains a script that Rex Stephenson wrote in 2000 for a dramatic adaptation of a folktale, "Mutsmag," and A. Waller Hastings's essay in Part 8 critiques one of the Disney Company's many animated fairy tale adaptations, *The Little Mermaid,* while Julaine Gillispie's essay in this section analyzes several live-action films based on a children's novel, *The Secret Garden.* Gillispie discusses the difficulties for filmmakers of remaining true to the spirit of a beloved classic of childhood while updating it for a contemporary medium and audience. Alcott's *Little Women* is another classic novel that has been reinterpreted in three films by major American studios from the 1930s to the 1990s, followed by Mark Adamo's successful opera in 1998 and a Broadway musical in 2005. The past century of film history, as well as the longer histories of stage adaptations and illustrated editions of classic stories, provides a wealth of insights into changing popular and critical responses to literature for children through the varying forms of different media.

Several of the texts in this section show how recent writers of fiction for children and young adults blend genres, satirizing and revising the conventions of traditional literature. Contemporary critics, such as Sandra Beckett, Jack Zipes, John Stephens, and Robyn McCallum, refer to reworkings of classic literature as recycling, reversion, or even contamination of earlier texts, or pre-texts.[2] Zipes explains that folklorists use the term *contamination* because introducing foreign elements into a pre-text that seems to come from "a pure, homogenous narrative tradition" makes it infected or impure. But, like a vaccine infecting a physical body to make it stronger, contaminating a "tale is thus to enrich it by artfully introducing extraordinary motifs, themes, words, expressions, proverbs, metaphors, and characters into its corporate body so that it will be transformed and form a new essence. Just as physical bodies constantly change, so do tales through retelling and reprinting."[3] Critic Claire Malarte-Feldman observes that " 'Recycled' tales . . . grow from old roots and gain vitality in the process."[4] *The Enchanter's Daughter,* by Antonia Barber, is more traditional than other tales in this section in its use of the forms and motifs of the literary fairy tale, like the stories by Hans Christian Andersen in this volume and Jane Yolen's "Dove Isabeau" in Part 3, yet Barber's tale is more original than some of the others in that it is not based on one particular older tale. As Joe Winston's essay observes, *The Enchanter's Daughter* shows how some writers maintain the fairy tale's traditional elements of optimistic wish fulfillment and pastoral idyll while developing modern themes. Many folk heroes return home at the end of their tales, but the return of Barber's heroine involves unconventional choices.

Another trend in adaptations and spin-offs of classic tales is transplanting them into new cultural settings. Transplantation occurs naturally in the history of oral traditions as people who move to new locations take their folklore with them. For example, although Mutsmag and Munsmeg (in Part 3) have new names in American tales, they were obviously brought to the Appalachian Mountains by settlers who knew ancient British variants of "Molly Whuppie," just as the Appalachian tale "Jack and the Bean Tree" is descended from the British "Jack and the Beanstalk." Other transplantations are created as more deliberate artistic adaptations, prompting us to rethink the thematic significance of older stories. Just as Shakespeare's plays are sometimes produced with contemporary or historical settings different from the ones that Shakespeare intended, fairy tales, often set in an undefined land "once upon a time and far away," have been reimagined in all kinds of settings. *Snow White in New York* by Fiona French, reprinted in this section, places Snow White in Jazz Age New York. *Willa: An American Snow White* is an equally ingenious film adaptation, with a heroine who escapes with three kind swindlers in a traveling medicine show until she joins a young English filmmaker on his way to Hollywood in 1915. In 1996, *Willa* concluded Virginia filmmaker Tom Davenport's series of live-action fairy tale films set in southern Appalachia at particular times in history. The film's rich intertextuality includes the transformation of Snow White's evil stepmother into Regina, a violent, bitter aging actress similar to Norma Desmond in the classic film *Sunset Boulevard.* Both French and Davenport give Snow White artistic talents (in addition to her inner and outer beauty) that will help her succeed in a specific modern cultural context. As in many tales retold in America, there is less supernatural magic than in older fairy tales, but these artists adapted "Snow White" with respect for the traditional message that love and fidelity to one's true identity will magically transform misfortune into happiness. The heroines do not acquire instant wealth by marrying princes, but we are led to expect that they will achieve the American dream and find material success through wise partnerships with loving men.

More explicit satire of traditional tales is found in most of the other texts in this section. When James Finn Garner's *Politically Correct Bedtime Stories* appeared on the bestseller list in the early 1990s, followed by several similar collections, adults roared with laughter at the way Garner ridiculed contemporary social trends through parodies of traditional fairy tales that do not convey enough respect for animal rights or feminism or dwarfs who are "vertically challenged." Many adults who are tickled by the blatant mockery in these books appear not to be aware of more subtle and clever satires throughout the annals of fairy tale literature (although they may recall the Fractured Fairy Tale segments that began appearing in 1959 in the popular television cartoon series *Rocky and Bullwinkle,* now available on videotape). While satires of many kinds became especially popular in children's books in the late twentieth century, this trend began almost as soon as written fairy tales gained widespread popularity in the nineteenth century, when writers such as Charles Dickens and William Makepeace Thackeray created their own comic versions of traditional tales.[5] As Part 1 illustrates, Lewis Carroll's groundbreaking

Alice fantasies are full of silly parodies of traditional verses and stories, satirizing Victorian education and child-rearing practices. At the end of the nineteenth century, Kenneth Grahame's "The Reluctant Dragon," one of the best-known satires of ancient legends, introduced the prototype of the modern shy and friendly dragon, with gentle parody of the carnage in traditional dragon-fighting tales, such as "St. George and the Dragon." Grahame's contemporary, E. Nesbit, published a collection of dragon tales full of light and lively parody in 1900 (*The Complete Book of Dragons*), followed in 1925 by "The Last of the Dragons," which is reprinted in this section.

Unfortunately, these early dragon parodies spawned generations of subservient, domesticated dragons begging pathetically for affection from humans and for the chance to serve their masters and contribute to social progress by functioning as furnaces, water heaters, and beasts of burden, until tame and timid dragons became predominant in picture books about dragons by the end of the twentieth century. At their worst, tame dragons in contemporary children's stories appear as stand-ins for puppy dogs and bunny rabbits, as attempts to water down the powerful legendary heritage of dragons in folklore and fantasy. But the tales of both Grahame and Nesbit contain elements that continue to amuse, as evidenced by reprints with illustrations by different artists published throughout the twentieth century. As Jon Stott explains in "'Will the Real Dragon Please Stand Up?'" children who first understand the literary traditions and conventions can learn to analyze modern satires with insight and enjoyment. And many recent children's books take dragons seriously or parody older tales as cleverly and thoughtfully as Grahame did. Jack Prelutsky's 1993 collection of poems, *The Dragons Are Singing Tonight,* offers varied perspectives on the place of dragons in the modern world, often using a dragon's or a child's voice to blend parody with belief in the magic and mystery of dragon lore.

Nesbit's princess in "The Last of the Dragons" may seem cloying or old-fashioned when she calls the dragon "dear" and Fido, prompting him to say, "Your kindness quite undragons me." She makes concessions to patriarchal tradition at the end by marrying the prince and keeping secrets from her conservative father who calls her ideas "unladylike," yet it is noteworthy that Nesbit published a satiric dragon story with an outspoken feminist heroine early in the twentieth century. By poking fun at outdated traditions, such as the helpless princess being rescued from a dragon by a valiant prince, she paved the way for independent heroines who fight or work with wise and powerful dragons in later fantasies, such as the runaway princess in Patricia Wrede's tongue-in-cheek spin-offs of fairy tale plots throughout the Enchanted Forest Chronicles; Menolly, a young misfit who breaks gender stereotypes on her planet by becoming a respected dragon hatcher and harper in Anne McCaffrey's Harper Hall Trilogy; and Aerin, a restless princess who saves her kingdom after secretly learning to fight dragons in Robin McKinley's Newbery Award–winning fantasy *The Hero and the Crown.* By the end of the twentieth century, the crosscurrents of fairy tale and fantasy traditions had produced female heroes as remarkable as their male predecessors in ancient hero tales.

Roald Dahl's poem "Little Red Riding Hood and the Wolf" spoofs another tradition that depicted girls as stereotypically passive. With his unique brand of offbeat humor, Dahl is unapologetically irreverent and shocking in his fantasies and parodies, and authors like Dahl could get away with it by the 1960s, when he began publishing children's books such as *James and the Giant Peach.* In each of the six poems in *Revolting Rhymes,* a female from the world's most popular fairy tales shows up a violent or stupid male or gets away with crime herself. Little Red Riding Hood's act of self-defense may not be especially original or subtle, but Dahl's singsong rhymes and use of details from the traditional tale are ingenious and fun. They illustrate the literary technique of metafiction, which appeared often in postmodern literature and popular culture in the late twentieth century. The girl's conversation with the wolf is comically metafictional because it draws attention to the fictional nature of the plot and its place in literary tradition, claiming that the girl can confuse the wolf by departing from the traditional sequence of remarks to the wolf disguised as her grandmother. Dahl's "revolting" plots may seem brutal, but they actually continue the age-old tradition of nursery rhymes and tales in which human and nonhuman characters fall prey to greedy, hungry, and violent adversaries. Recent picture book artists, such as Jon Scieszka and Lane Smith, have extended Dahl's satiric methods even further. *The Stinky Cheese Man and Other Fairly Stupid Tales,* published by this team in 1992, is a zany jumble of truncated, interrupted, and deconstructed tales, such as "Cinderumpelstiltskin, or, The Girl Who Really Blew It," in which Cinderella finds herself with Rumpelstiltskin instead of a fairy godmother, misses the ball, and has to keep on cleaning house. The book is a hilarious postmodern satire of both the storytelling tradition and the physical structure of a modern book.

The remaining literary texts in this section represent postmodern experiments with fairy tale forms and motifs in stories, poems, and novels for young adults, many of which rewrite specific traditional tales. Arthurian legends and other ancient classics, such as Robin Hood tales and *Beowulf,* have been similarly adapted in both short and long forms of literature for readers of different ages. Fairy tale writers such as Priscilla Galloway entice readers to discover the true story that has been hidden behind the legend (as viewers are invited to do in the 1998 Cinderella film *Ever After,* which depicts the Grimm Brothers in its frame story). In collections such as Galloway's *Truly Grim Tales,* Vivian Vande Velde's *Tales from the Brothers Grimm and Sisters Weird,* Francesca Lia Block's *The Rose and the Beast,* and Sara Henderson Hay's *Story Hour,* titles do not always give away a story's source. We become conscious of our own knowledge of traditional tales and the preconceptions they have instilled in us as we gradually recognize the reassembled parts of a familiar tale within a new context. Alternate points of view are often employed to express perspectives that were suppressed in older tales published within the mainstream of patriarchal, elitist societies. This concern with suppressed voices is especially obvious in Galloway's "The Voice of Love" in *Truly Grim Tales.* Departing from Hans Christian Andersen's original sympathetic focus on the Little Mermaid's experience, her sacrifices in pursuit of love and immortality, Galloway develops an ironic sequel revealing that the prince realizes he has married the wrong woman. The vengeful voices of the mermaid sisters and sea witch are as shocking as Miss Riding Hood's when Dahl shows her calmly shooting predatory wolves, but Galloway's cautionary tale is sinister, rather than comical in tone.

While Galloway extends an old tale to subject the well-meaning prince to the irrevocable consequences of his mistake and the misery he might suffer later in a mythic world less idealistic and Christian than the one created by Andersen, Vande Velde's "Twins" seems to begin with a prequel to a traditional tale in order to realign its dynamics of victimization and retaliation. Shifting the point of view to the stepmother generates more sympathy for her and less for the children in "Hansel and Gretel." Like Gregory Maguire's novel *Wicked* (a prequel to *The Wonderful Wizard of Oz,* adapted in a Broadway musical that won Tony awards in 2004), "Twins" reveals the earlier and inner history of female characters associated with witchcraft. In spite of significant plot revisions and unanswered questions about all the characters, many familiar details make us wonder whether we somehow got the story wrong when we heard it before.

Hay's sonnet "Juvenile Court" raises the same question by depicting the children as remorseless juvenile delinquents in a lenient modern society. Many interpretations and illustrations of "Hansel and Gretel" by other storytellers and artists merge the identities of the cannibalistic witch and the stepmother who wants to abandon the children. And many feminist critiques of traditional literature have condemned the vilification of both stepmothers and wise women or witch women. Vande Velde and Hay are not the first modern writers to suggest that children can be innately devious and even depraved and murderous, but their revisions of one of the nineteenth century's most popular folktales about young children, one that supports Romantic assumptions about youthful innocence and victimization of peasants and children, add particularly menacing twists to some of our most troubling questions about childhood.

The titles of the Galloway and Vande Velde collections, *Truly Grim Tales* and *Tales from the Brothers Grimm and Sisters Weird,* emphasize their interest in the Gothic elements of traditional tales, the psychological and sociopolitical horrors lurking beneath the surface of stories that we recognize as both antiquated and eternally irresistible. Stories for younger children more often retain the "hope and happy endings" discussed by Katherine Paterson in Part 8. But the last two young adult stories in this section also encourage a belief in hope and happiness by introducing fairy tale motifs in contemporary settings where unconventional characters deal with some of the horrors and pleasures of American society at the end of the twentieth century. Bruce Coville's "Am I Blue?" uses wish-fulfillment themes from folklore about fairy godmothers and guardian angels to develop the fantasy that homophobia could be eradicated if everyone knew how many of the people around them are gay. *Weetzie Bat* is the celebrated first novel of Francesca Lia Block, who also contributed to the anthology *Am I Blue?* in which Coville's tale is the title story. In Block's highly original short novel, Weetzie is both a contemporary troubled youth with serious, realistic problems and a fairy tale princess. Amid countless details from the landscape and subculture of Los Angeles are inserted episodes of magic realism. That is, supernatural events occur within the realistic setting, such as the gift of a genie that grants wishes in a golden vessel, the magical appearance of lovers who already have completely unrealistic names that Weetzie and her gay friend Dirk had made up, and the "witch baby" who is left on their doorstep by a woman associated with voodoo. Although love quarrels, sickness, and suicide make this unconventional household of one heterosexual and one homosexual couple question their belief in happily ever after, Weetzie keeps the family she created together and decides to accept happiness without knowing whether it is forever. In a world that seems neurotic, Block's conclusion brings together the contradictions of life and literature in a remarkably sane and satisfying way, combining the gritty realism of late twentieth-century young adult literature with the optimistic wish fulfillment of the traditional fairy tale and domestic romance.

These postmodern stories are innovative in content and in the ways in which they reshape traditional literary structures, but they are published in traditional forms—on the pages of books. The last two essays in this section discuss recent technological innovations that influence children as they experience language and narrative through new media and commercial production processes. Ellen Seiter and Marina Warner have contributed to a growing body of cultural criticism analyzing the commercialization of children's literature through spin-offs in different media and products linked with children's stories. New types of narrative are shaped by popular entertainments, such as amusement park rides, video games, Internet technologies, and series books and toys that many children collect fanatically, including the Goosebumps series (see excerpt in Part 2) and American Girl books and dolls.

Product tie-ins are not new, as John Newbery launched the modern age of the children's book market by selling balls and pincushions with *A Little Pretty Pocket-Book* in 1744. After becoming a successful writer, Beatrix Potter helped produce a doll, a game, and cards for fundraising at the beginning of the twentieth century, and the public's affection for countless products based on her beloved animal stories for young children continues today. Raggedy Ann dolls, created simultaneously with books by Johnny Gruelle in the 1910s, have remained far more popular than the stories. However, the recent development that Seiter discusses in "Toy-Based Videos for Girls: My Little Pony" is the creation of stories that are based on toys that precede them in the marketplace and the hearts of children. Like other recent critics who call for greater respect for the abilities and choices of children, Seiter cautions adults to avoid biases that are based on age and class when judging these products that may appear to be of low quality. Seiter's analysis of girls' culture in relation to My Little Pony toys and videos is complemented by "Boys Will Be Boys," Marina Warner's critique of the ways in which boys are socialized through video games and the various mythologies and cultural constructs from which they are descended.

Both Seiter and Warner provide valuable models for examining new media in relation to literary traditions and cultural developments through history. The recent stories and poems reprinted in this anthology also show that literary traditions continue to thrive and evolve. Although they can be read on computer screens as well as on paper, books will not soon be replaced by other technologies as some have feared. The overwhelming popularity of the Harry Potter novels and films has demonstrated that not only do children, teenagers, and adults enjoy reading long books that they can discuss with each other, but that quite young viewers are capable of sophisticated criticism when they compare the films in minute detail to the language of the texts and the images in their own imaginations. Half a century ago, adults began warning that television and then video games would make reading and writing obsolete, but the children's book market is bigger than ever, and Internet technology has involved many children in writing their own sequels, satires, reviews, and original literature to share with others around the world. New films and other types of adaptations and spin-offs sometimes diminish awareness of their sources, but they can also revive interest in older works of literature and folklore. As Toni Morrison commented when a television interviewer asked her about film adaptations of her novels for adults, "The book remains." Both children and adults are busily involved in reading and rereading classic books, as well as debating whether Harry Potter novels or something else will become the classics of tomorrow.

NOTES

1. Dannie Abse, "Pantomime Diseases," *Poetry* 133 (February 1979): 261.
2. Sandra Beckett, *Recycling Red Riding Hood* (New York: Routledge, 2002); John Stephens and Robyn McCallum, *Retelling Stories, Framing Culture: Traditional Story and Metanarratives in Children's Literature* (New York: Garland, 1998).
3. Jack Zipes, *Sticks and Stones: The Troublesome Success of Children's Literature from Slovenly Peter to Harry Potter* (New York: Routledge, 2001) 102–3.
4. Claire Malarte-Feldman, "Folk Materials, Re-Visions, and Narrative Images: The Intertextual Games They Play," *Children's Literature Association Quarterly* 28 (Winter 2003–2004): 210.
5. Dickens wrote the fairy tale parody "The Magic Fishbone" (1868) and Thackeray wrote the satire *The Rose and the Ring* (1855).

Julaine Gillispie (b. 1975)

Julaine Gillispie's essay appeared in a 1996 issue of *The Lion and the Unicorn* devoted to children's films. It is remarkable that Gillispie wrote the essay while she was an undergraduate at Indiana University/Purdue University at Indianapolis because her survey of three films based on *The Secret Garden* reveals extensive knowledge of twentieth-century social history and traditions in film adaptations of classic literary works for children. Although she criticizes elements in the films that do not seem true to the spirit of the novel, Gillispie's purpose is not primarily to compare the narrative strategies of the films to the book. She shows how great novels, combining a variety of themes, lend themselves to varied interpretations at different times; each American film reflects the values of the filmmakers and the decade in which it was produced. Her discussion of revisions to the ending of the story complements Elizabeth Keyser's essay (in Part 5) on Mary Lennox's treatment in the patriarchal world of the novel. Gillispie's analysis also builds on the work of Phyllis Bixler, an expert on Frances Hodgson Burnett, who has written about apparent innovations in the Broadway play and film adaptations of *The Secret Garden* that develop subtexts lying beneath the surface of the novel.

American Film Adaptations of *The Secret Garden*

Reflections of Sociological and Historical Change

The creative team behind Marsha Norman's 1991 Broadway musical of *The Secret Garden* often joked about "*The Secret Garden* club," whose members, upon mention of Frances Hodgson Burnett's children's classic, purportedly gasped, reached toward their hearts, and passionately declared, "'That was my *favorite* book'" (quoted in McGee 64). No doubt the prospect of having such ardent, die-hard fans in the musical's audience was daunting, to say the least. If asked, the filmmakers who have chosen to adapt Burnett's work (or any other perennial favorite, for that matter) probably would admit to some concerns about pleasing the legion of *Secret Garden* devotees. Douglas Street, for example, opens his introduction to *Children's Novels and the Movies* by discussing the particular problems inherent in adapting cherished childhood novels into film (xiii). He likens filming a children's classic to moving a Victorian home to a modern location. He writes, "Ultimate success is de-pendent upon the perceptive preservation of original feeling and attraction in harmony with requirements necessitated by the new, cinematic setting" (xviii). Indeed, the director's ability to remain true to the sense of the literary original and concurrently update it to reflect contemporary *mores* and cinematic techniques plays a major role in determining whether an adaptation becomes a classic or fades into obscurity.

Several scholars, including Morris Beja, George Bluestone, Judith Mayne, and Sergei Eisenstein, study adaptation, exploring the relationship between novels and films.[1] While there is, in general, concurrence among scholars about the common qualities of the two—such as narrative and point of view—novels and films are, nonetheless, different media. Morris Beja points out, "If narrative literature and film share, indeed by definition, the basic element of the story, they do not 'tell' the story in the same way or in the same 'language'" (54). Consequently, filmmakers must alter the original work to fit their cinematic medium (hence, the name adaptation).

Despite the potential difficulties of successfully condensing and converting Burnett's almost three-hundred-page novel into approximately one hundred minutes of celluloid, several directors have attempted to do so. In fact, the work's continued popularity among children and adults makes this children's classic a candidate for multiple adaptations by different media: drama, electronic multimedia, musical theater, opera, and film.[2] *The Secret Garden* (1911) inspires these multiple adaptations in part because directors aspire to stamp their unique, creative genius and society's current cultural perspectives on the text—the enchanting tale of the regeneration of two children, Mary Lennox and Colin Craven, through a garden near the moors of Yorkshire, England. Burnett's book, like all great works of literature, appeals to its audience in different ways through an ample assortment of themes: child neglect, class differences, mystical faith, the value of friendship, the healing power of positive thinking, self-reliance, healthy living, and nature. This gives *The Secret Garden* the chameleon-like ability to change to match its environment.

This dynamic quality enables box-office conscious filmmakers to tailor the story to suit a specific era. The films of the American society, in and of their time, provide a glimpse of the nation's cultural, social, and political ideologies. Traditionally, film content is a product of these shifting views and contemporary concerns. A close examination of three American live-action features of *The Secret Garden*—the 1949 Metro Goldwyn Mayer (MGM) film, the 1987 Hallmark Hall of Fame television production, and the 1993 Warner Brothers (American Zoetrope) movie—reveals that each version remains reasonably faithful to the chronology of the original and heightens the Gothic elements of the text; conversely, each adaptation's interpretation is radically different, reflecting the historical and sociological changes in American society.[3]

Just as films are often time capsules, literature, too, can function as a "'cultural reference point'" (quoted in Manna 58). Certainly *The Secret Garden* is an exemplar of this truth. As many returning-adult readers and critics note, the novel begins as Mary's book and ends as Colin's story.[4] Although scholars' opinions about the impetus for the young master's ascendancy and Mistress Mary's marginalization somewhat differ, they generally agree with feminist critic Lissa Paul's conclusion: "Burnett ends the story in accordance with the social and economic truths and values of her particular time and place" (197).

Burnett, according to her biographer, Ann Thwaite, was a woman who saw beyond the confines and customs of the Victorian and Edwardian periods. She questioned socially accepted practices at an early age, supported her family with her pen, and shocked the public with her unconventional views on marriage, smoking, and religion (5–7, 47, 226). Burnett scholar Phyllis Bixler notes that in much of the author's fiction, she "often expressed anger at male domination and suggested a more equitable balance of power between the two sexes," and "shared with late-nineteenth-century feminist novelists an exaltation of female virtue and power" (*Frances* 123, 125).

Despite her feminist stance, Burnett understandably and shrewdly (given her era, goals, and breadwinner status) masqueraded behind an "ultrafeminine romantic public image that gained her economic and social independence."[5] She built her career upon popular romances with fairy-tale endings, paralleling her romantic-with-a-capital-*R* nature and unrealistic desire for a fairy-tale life (Bixler, *Frances* 16, 121–23). Romanticism and feminism are not necessarily mutually exclusive, evident in Burnett's complex but practical personality embodied in *The Secret Garden*.

The novel begins as the story of Mary Lennox, a spoiled, sickly, unwanted, and consequently difficult child. Orphaned after a cholera epidemic in India kills her parents, she goes to live with her reclusive, hunchbacked uncle, Archibald Craven, in his great manor home on the Yorkshire moors. Largely ignored by Craven and his housekeeper, Mrs. Medlock, Miss Lennox experiences friendship with people outside the household: Ben Weatherstaff and the Sowerby family, Martha, Dickon, and their mother, Susan. The heroine subsequently discovers two intriguing secrets: a locked, walled garden and her hypochondriac, bedridden cousin and alter ego, Colin. Lord Craven keeps the garden locked and avoids his son, blaming both for the death of his wife, Lilias, who died after a tragic fall in the garden, resulting in Colin's early birth. Eventually, with some assistance from a friendly robin, Mary finds the key to the garden door. Tending the long-neglected Secret Garden ultimately brings physical and emotional healing for both Mary and Colin while Archibald is away on self-imposed exile. The book concludes with Colin's remarkable transfiguration through his newfound friends, ideas and interests, his poignant re-unification with his father, and his triumphant walk across the Misselthwaite lawn (Burnett).

Burnett's ability to elicit strong responses from her audience is one reason this classic novel, unlike many others, still sells three hundred thousand to four hundred thousand copies per year—a rate higher than current best-selling children's fiction and only comparable to other all-time children's favorites such as *Goodnight Moon, Charlotte's Web,* and *The Cat in the Hat* (McGee 64; Mullin). In fact, a *New York Times Book Review* of best-selling children's books (reflecting a recent six-week period) ranked *The Secret Garden* third among chapter books. (It was the first classic on the list.[6]) Clearly, this impressive sales record partially explains why the book has been adapted by different media and vice versa.

Already considered a classic during the Golden Age of Hollywood (1930 to 1949), *The Secret Garden* was among many established works considered financially feasible by the studio system in the postwar years. Perhaps Americans craved the entertainment that movies offer (after all, Hollywood's foundation is partially built upon the public's need for escapism) even more so after experiencing the frightening reality of World War II. Certainly viewing the reunited Cravens and idyllic landscape of *The Secret Garden* seems preferable to contemplating the horde of split families (by death or divorce) and death-ridden devastation of Europe and Asia. Over half of the approximately fifty million people who died in the global war were civilians, including the six to seven million Jews slaughtered in concentration camps. The intimidating technological innovations—aerial bombardment, guided missiles, and atomic weaponry—wreaked mass destruction in cities, such as London and Hiroshima, and begot the fear that a future war could exterminate life on Earth. The added international insecurity of the Cold War—including mainland China's conversion to Communism, the Iron Curtain across Europe, and the American military aid necessary to quell the communist aggression in Greece, Turkey, and Berlin—created a threatening atmosphere. In light of this menacing milieu, it appeared that innocent children were the hapless victims of an inferior but powerful patriarchal society.

Consequently, these factors and views permeate the 1949 MGM adaptation of *The Secret Garden.*[7] Director Fred M. Wilcox's version, perhaps more aptly titled *The Garden of Secrets,* takes on all the dimensions of a teasing thriller and embodies the multiple anxieties of the time. Just as Alfred Hitchcock does in some of his films in the forties—one thinks of *Rebecca* (1940), *Shadow of a Doubt* (1943), and *Rope* (1948)—so Wilcox's direction creates suspense immediately: the eerie music of the opening score, an unknown person opening the garden door, and vultures rapaciously circling the Lennox home. He replaces the friendly robin in the novel with a more ominous raven and relies on low-key lighting and visual details—portentous shadows, foreboding fog, and sinister glances—to emphasize the tension-filled tone. Melodramatic conventions, such as Mary (Margaret O'Brien) suddenly being frightened by her image in a mirror, a ghostly covered chair, and stern-looking Ben Weatherstaff (Reginald Owen), add mystery.

The woman's films of the forties and the family melodramas of the fifties flank Wilcox's adaptation; therefore, the MGM version predictably exaggerates, as Virginia L. Wolf notes, "the story's tendency toward melodrama" (129). Burnett's melodrama, however, was predicated on romantic sentiment and a happy ending (for example, Colin's declaration that he will live forever after visiting the Secret Garden and Archibald's joyful reunion with his son), two ingredients her largely Victorian-era audience expected. On the other hand, one type of film Wilcox's postwar audience likely anticipated is what Mary Ann Doane describes as "paranoid woman's films," which "appropriate many elements of the Gothic novel" (123–24). She specifies that one means of generating suspense in these films is "through the localization of suspense in the familiarized female space of the home in relation to a close relative" (135).[8] Furthermore, she expounds: "Quite often the female protagonist is endowed with the necessary curiosity and a desire to know but is revealed as impotent in terms of the actual ability to uncover the secret or attain the knowledge which she desires" (135). Wilcox's suspenseful strategies follow this pattern: the film's tension centers on Mary's uncle in her new home, and despite her aspiration to discover the truth about her enigmatic relative, it is Pan-like Dickon (Brian Roper) rather than "impotent" Mary who ultimately accomplishes the mission.

The movie's added Hitchcockesque subplot and the questionable circumstances surrounding Lilias Craven's death deepen the mystery by making Lord Craven (Herbert Marshall) a prime suspect. When Dickon and Mary first enter the garden together, they find an axe placed near the tree limb that fell upon Lilias, killing her. The children's conjecture of the man's innocence—Archibald surely could not have killed the woman he loved and would not have left the evidence in plain sight—plants the seed of suspicion in the already apprehensive and historically primed-for-death-and-disaster audience's mind. Distrust flourishes when Ben Weatherstaff discovers the children (ever the unfortunate casualties of a patriarchal society) in the garden and balefully warns them, "I can't tell thee what would happen if he [Archibald] finds thee here!" (*The Secret Garden,* dir. Fred M. Wilcox). Later, against the background of a terrible thunderstorm, Dickon divulges that Weatherstaff has confided in him, and Lilias' death was indeed accidental.

Despite being innocent, Archibald's character serves as the psychotic villain in this thriller. Alarming music usually foreshadows his scenes in the movie, and dramatic, low angle shots enlarge his stature. (Wilcox's treatment of Archibald is similar to Robert Stevenson's handling of Edward Rochester in Twentieth Century Fox's 1943 adaptation of *Jane Eyre,* a novel by Charlotte Brontë.[9] Always cloaked in black, the master of the house is on the brink of insanity. Seeking solace in alcohol, he vents his volatile emotions twice by deliberately destroying a decanter, which symbolizes his shattered life. Hoping to start anew in Italy, the antagonist decides, much to the dismay of the children and those faithful to the text, to sell Misselthwaite. When a prospective buyer inadvertently alerts him of the garden's transformation, he stomps to the garden in a rage, wildly threatening to kill Weatherstaff and viciously pushing his niece aside as the raven crows, signifying danger. His violent entrance prompts Colin (Dean Stockwell)—in this version's departure from the text—to walk for the first time, pitifully begging his father not to destroy the garden.

This scene, among others, depicts the common social limits repudiating father-son intimacy in both the novel's Edwardian time and the mid-twentieth-century period of this adaptation. Lord Craven's reaction in this film to Colin's pathetic pleas and first steps is telling; although Archibald is moved, he can only muster a restrained embrace for his son and a charitable hug for his niece. There are similarities between his response in the movie and his reaction in the text (remembering that in Burnett's conclusion he is not threatening to destroy the garden and Colin has been walking for some time). Burnett writes, "Mr. Craven put his hands on both the boy's shoulders and held him still. He knew he dared not even try to speak for a moment. 'Take me into the garden, my boy,' he said at last. 'And tell me all about it'" (282). There is no textual mention of an actual father-son hug, and Mary is a mere bystander. Consequently, the literary and filmic portrayal of father-son affection shows little change in the thirty-eight years spanning the publication of the novel and the premiere of the 1949 MGM film.

As equally acceptable in the postwar years as emotionally distant father-son relationships are the patriarchal ideologies typical during this era. These are evident in Wilcox's choice of props and composition. For instance, a throne-like chair emphasizes Archibald's position as king of the castle. Moreover, the director stresses Lord Craven's dominance and enigmatic personality through two over-the-shoulder shots. In his initial appearance in the movie, Archibald observes his niece walking to the gardens from a balcony; he dominates the right half of the screen as Mary seems ant-like below him. A later shot of their first meeting reinforces this image: with his back to the camera he looms large in the dark foreground while, in obvious contrast, the girl timidly and vulnerably stands facing the camera in the lighter background. Examples such as these—shots in which the male gaze predominates and the female figure seems defined for the spectator by the controlling male gaze—provide a virtual laboratory for feminist film critics, such as Doane, E. Ann Kaplan, and Laura Mulvey, who study the classical and contemporary cinema's reaffirmation of conventional gender identification.[10] These critics often examine composition that anachronistically offends many viewers but was ordinary during the classical Hollywood period.

Following another cinematic fashion of the time, the 1949 MGM adaptation promotes the developing opinion that parents were frequently responsible for their children's problems (Rhode 442). Wolf criticizes the Wilcox adaptation for its emphasis on psychology rather than magic. She points out, "As psychology replaces magic, reason replaces wonder, and nothing in the movie convinces us that the Secret Garden is the marvelous place it is in the novel."[11] Despite her assessment's validity, it is important to note how psychology, and the anxieties of parent-child relations, are deliberately explored through the medium of film. Prior to World War II, for example, Shirley Temple's *Bright Eyes* (1934) contains mise en scènes in which parents naively talk about children in the language of neo-Freudian psychology. After World War II, the publication and increasing popularity of Freud's theories on dreams, for instance, were eventually manifest in the motion picture industry as a whole and are certainly evident in the psychological theme of the 1949 MGM production of *The Secret Garden*. That is, the psychoanalytic message, only subtly implied in the novel, is overtly heard through two dialogues involving the consulting physician Dr. Fortescue (George Zucco) from London. He claims, "I diagnosed this case accurately, I believe, when I met the father. Examining the child was a formality." He explains that Colin's disease is fear and informs Lord Craven, "While you were keeping your own balance with such care, you transferred your longing to die to your son" (*The Secret Garden,* dir. Fred M. Wilcox). The subsidiary theme that children are hostages to the hopes, decisions, and fears of their parents supports the adaptation's larger criticism of adulthood.

Wilcox's production of Burnett's novel, like other films in the wake of the tragedies of World War II and the Cold War, supports the concept that childhood is superior to adulthood (Rhode 439–42). In this interpretation Mary dramatically declares, "There must be an awful lot we don't know. I don't want to know. I don't want to grow up!" (*The Secret Garden,* dir. Fred M. Wilcox). It also implies, through a story Miss Lennox tells her cousin about the Secret Garden, that only children can see the beauty in the world. A mostly black-and-white movie, *The Secret Garden* vividly illustrates the romanticization of the child-as-visionary by interpolating color sequences when the children are happily alone in the garden, highlighting the dichotomy between the innocent hopefulness of youth and the jaded cynicism of adults. Certainly, the 1949 MGM rendition is one in which the socially balanced and idealistically directed children are powerless against often emotionally enervated and passively manipulated adult authority. Similarly, Rosemont Productions' 1987 Hallmark Hall of Fame television

movie of the children's classic shows children at the mercy of grown-ups; however, rather than stressing male dominance it accentuates female power.

Recognizing the empowerment of women since the contemporary feminist movement began during the sixties and the seventies, the Hallmark Hall of Fame's version is perhaps not surprising.[12] By the mid-eighties, women, in addition to being homemakers, were visibly performing careers customarily held almost exclusively by men: engineers, doctors, lawyers, and politicians. Mounting inflation and unemployment, in part due to the energy crisis and an industrial slump, propelled even more women into the workforce. Unlike many of their mothers, who, when World War II ended, were no longer needed in the factories, and dutifully returned to the home, the women of the eighties (and nineties) were more likely to continue working when economic conditions improved: some did so because of their prevailing sense of insecurity about the economy, and others kept their jobs because they enjoyed the financial, personal, and social benefits of employment, even though much of that employment was in lower-paid, pink-collar jobs with few benefits.

Society's grudging acceptance of the burgeoning women's movement and increasing feminist influence in the entertainment industry resulted in some productions prominently featuring women as capable and valuable (for example, Sally Field's and Jessica Lange's roles in the 1984 farm films *Places in the Heart* and *Country*). Nevertheless, the mass media, the conservative Reagan-Bush White House and the fundamentalist right collectively denigrated feminism in the eighties, contributing to the defeat of the Equal Rights Amendment in 1982. Therefore, targeting a chiefly female television audience,[13] director Alan Grint tried to attract both feminists and more traditionally-minded women by conveying *The Secret Garden* as a sentimental romance updated to reflect progressive perspectives, as well.

Miss Lennox is unquestionably the controlling presence in this costume drama, evident in the added frame story: returning to Misselthwaite Manor after serving as a nurse in World War I, she (notice this adult Mary [Irina Brook] is a career woman) looks back upon her childhood memories leading up to Colin's (adult Colin—Colin Firth) mawkish proposal of marriage. (This is a deviation; in the novel they are cousins. For this interpretation, a more apropos title is *When Mary Met Colin*.) As a girl, Mary saves Colin; as a woman, she marries him. This is a romance, though, of an independent woman of the eighties who has her own terms for courtship. She refuses to respond to his written proposals while studying at Oxford and serving in France, demanding he propose in person in the Secret Garden before she answers. Just released from the hospital after being wounded by shrapnel, he arrives using a cane and limps to her. Upon her acceptance of his offer, he no longer needs the cane. Its later absence and the patient-nurse symbolism confirm her prepotency.

Besides having a career and a private life, Miss Lennox, like so many women during the eighties, takes responsibility for nurturing loved ones, too. The Hallmark Hall of Fame version credits Mary (young Mary—Gennie James), more than the magic of the garden, with almost single-handedly putting Colin (young Colin—Jadrien Steele) on his feet. Dickon (Barret Oliver) tells her, "Colin will find his way and you'll be the one who helps him find it. The way will come to you" (*The Secret Garden*, dir. Alan Grint). Later, the young man does walk, but only through her encouragement does he attain the courage to walk to his father. Afterwards, Colin tells Lord Craven (Derek Jacobi) the Secret Garden made him well and *Mary* made him walk. Her significance complements the other strong female characterizations in this adaptation.[14]

Additional gratification for the television audience comes from a designed "chain of female power"—from Mary to the late Mrs. Craven—which accentuates a woman's role as necessary caregiver and nurturer (Bixler, *Frances* 100). Grint's film characterizes Mrs. Medlock (Billie Whitelaw) as a kind but firm caregiver, unlike the novel and other productions of *The Secret Garden*. Grint's Medlock uses child psychology, redecorates Mary's room, and offers to take her shopping. She is a busy working woman who has her charge's best interests at heart; for example, the housekeeper wants to get the girl a governess because she is lonely. In the conclusion, the heroine describes Medlock as loving and compassionate. Sensitive to an ever-growing audience of working women who believe their careers do not prevent them from being successful mothers, Grint tries to appease feminists.

Nevertheless, he does not neglect the traditional viewer. He strengthens the importance of two other maternal figures, Susan Sowerby (Pat Heywood) and the late Mrs. Craven (Alison Doody). Although insightful Mrs. Sowerby appears briefly in Grint's film, her supportive presence is more keenly felt than in the other American versions. True to the text, her cogent letter to Mr. Craven hastens his return to Misselthwaite and his son. Albeit spiritual, Lilias' influence is equally medicinal, especially for her son. Colin practices walking alone at night, his mother's portrait giving him strength and willpower. By including two mothers who are essentially housewives making important contributions, Grint composes a balanced female cast that replicates the diversity in choices—professional and domestic—available to women during the eighties. (Moreover, his film seems to anticipate and voice the incipient public dissatisfaction with conservatism that facilitated the election of liberal-minded Bill Clinton.)

To attract further his largely female audience, Grint follows Burnett's example and saturates his story with romance. Rustic scenery and yards of lace underline the tender tone of his film. Soft focus backgrounds of shimmering lakes, woodland paths, and of course, the blooming Secret Garden fuel the warm ambiance. He reinforces the bucolic setting of Highclere Castle, the consummate English country house, with Victorian props: a circular, wrought-iron tree bench, a curtained canopy bed, gold-rimmed china, and ornate candelabras. Likewise, the characters' costumes emphasize a romantic motif (concurrent with the onset of the vogue to Victoriana).[15] Mary sleeps in a delicate lace bonnet while the Misselthwaite maids wear eyelet ruffled aprons and white lace caps with long satin ribbons flowing down their backs. Colin sports a gray silk bathrobe that resembles a luxurious smoking jacket. Although these cinematic devices are somewhat subtle, Grint's interpretation of Burnett's novel is direct in other respects.

Embracing the sexual undertones of the work, he initially creates an adolescent love story for Miss Mary and Master Colin. Grint incorporates pieces of girlish fantasies into his movie, making the couple's ardor apparent. Smitten young Colin (who seems even needier in this production than in the novel) begs the object of his affection to read poetry to him, wants to attend the same school to avoid the pain of separation, and gives her a heart-shaped locket. (Their costumes in this last scene—he in a formal gray suit and tie and she in a lacy white cape and matching dress—are nearly matrimonial.) She swears to wear the locket always, despite her earlier attempts to play hard-to-get while communicating her desire through sidelong glances and other flirtations. Likening them to Adam and Eve, Mary compares (as many scholars do) their Secret Garden to the Garden of Eden. The later adult love story framing Grint's interpretation is equally syrupy, the politics of romance and sentimentality clearly replacing the politics of realism and sexuality. Even so, this romantic conclusion might be an attempt to provide the women in the audience who fondly remember the book from their childhoods further sentimental satisfaction by resolving Burnett's proto-romantic triangle among an aristocratic, rich boy, an orphan girl, and a noble savage.

Although Grint's interpretation centers on romance and illustrates the dynamic cultural tenets of women, it does not exclude the corresponding change in men. In sharp contrast to the characterization of the same man in the 1949 MGM production of *The Secret Garden,* the Archibald in the Hallmark Hall of Fame version, while still a dominant and sometimes frightening figure, seems more accepting of his emotional vulnerability and nurturing capacity. He appears genuinely interested in Mary's well-being: upon meeting her he inquires about her happiness and worries that she is too thin. Visibly moved by her love of gardens (a painful reminder of his late wife), he is willing to acknowledge his feelings. Indeed, unlike the father in the 1949 MGM version, on another occasion he even relinquishes complete control, hugging his son and crying with joy when Colin demonstrates his ability to walk. Yet, Lord Craven's reaction is ephemeral: he quickly reverts to a more formal stance, as if restrained by the shackles of his patriarchal heritage.

This scene, compared to the conclusion of the novel and the 1949 MGM film, evinces a detectable change in Mary's status: Archibald seems to welcome her, taking her by the hand as he admires the garden. Her significance is evident; in a tableau of the trio, she is in the center. In spite of this improvement, Mary ultimately finds complete acceptance into the Craven family in Grint's version by agreeing to marry Colin. The budding progress, however, toward societal approval of empowerment for women and demonstrative affection from men is noticeable in this television movie.

Whilst the 1987 Hallmark Hall of Fame television adaptation validates the personal, professional, domestic, and emotional reality of many American men

The 1949 MGM film based on *The Secret Garden* starred Brian Roper as Dickon, Dean Stockwell as Colin, and Margaret O'Brien as Mary.

and women, the 1993 Warner Brothers (American Zoetrope) film of *The Secret Garden* focuses on the ecumenical, everyday existence of countless children.

In the six-year period between these two productions, the public began to worry that the increasing economic necessity and greater societal materialism requiring dual incomes in one family exacted an altogether too-costly social price upon children. Higher rates of juvenile crime and numerous stories of abandoned children, perhaps part of a larger social-control measure attempting to frighten women out of the workforce and back into the home, prompted a new Hollywood film fashion: movies concentrating on the emotional and psychological effects of child neglect. Though some of these films, including *Dennis the Menace* (1993), *The Adventures of Huckleberry Finn* (1993), *Free Willy* (1993), and *King of the Hill* (1993), deal with children's desolation in a comical manner and others handle the neglect more dolorously, the collective purpose is unmistakable—to call contemporary parents home to their children.

Likewise, director Agnieszka Holland's adaptation of Burnett's classic novel concentrates on Mary's and Colin's forlornness.[16] An expatriate Polish filmmaker known for her films about forsaken children, Holland loved *The Secret Garden* as a child.[17] She believes, "Part of the appeal of the book has to do with the child's fear of being rejected, abandoned, unloved—but also with the possibility of change" (Taubin 28). She solves the potentially complicated dilemma of how to inject her motion picture with dreaded indignity and likely transformation by utilizing a genre born of her European tradition—the fairy tale.

There are, however, more definitive elements than lost children and a happy ending establishing Holland's version as a fairy tale. She imbues her story, as the author and the genre do, with memorable magic. (More than once in Holland's film, the natural world changes the heroine's life remarkably.) Unlike the text and the other two American films, an earthquake—not a cholera epidemic—orphans Mary (Kate Maberly). The helpful robin, at Mary's polite request, dutifully shows her the door to the Secret Garden (compare the Hallmark Hall of Fame rendition, in which Mary discovers the door herself). And of course, the garden transforms not only her, but others as well. A brilliant establishing shot immediately alerts the audience to the garden's enchantment: the camera leads the viewer's eye through a brown tunnel of brush to an enticing, illuminated garden, the "light at the end of the tunnel" symbolism, obvious yet crudely effective.

Preternatural events, another attribute of fairy tales, also occur in Holland's rendition. Amidst dead, swirling leaves, the garden swing—the instrument of Lilias' (Irene Jacob) fatal fall in this interpretation—rocks mysteriously, as though her apparition watches over the sanctuary. True to the text, her spirit summons her husband to Misselthwaite and his son, but in Holland's interpretation this occurs after the children perform a bewitching druid ritual, chanting incantations to call Lord Craven (John Lynch) home. Holland's departures from the text heighten the distinctive magical elements in this adaptation.

Furthering the film's magical motif, she visually and verbally depicts Misselthwaite as an enchanted castle. Again, she communicates volumes with a brief but accomplished establishing shot of the manor implicative of a classic fairy-tale palace: huge, isolated, and mysterious.[18] She reinforces the image with voice-over narration. As Mary wanders through a cobwebbed and vine-and-pigeon invaded wing of the massive home, she tells the audience, "The house was dead, like a spell had been cast upon it" (*The Secret Garden,* dir. Agnieszka Holland). The cursed atmosphere of the mansion supports the more pervasive hex hovering over the inhabitants.

Holland elucidates immediately in the prologue the effects that the dreadful curse of parental neglect inflicts upon children with Miss Lennox's forthright, narrational confession of her inability to cry, imputable to the lack of emotional bonding with her self-absorbed, social-climbing parents. The director continues the theme of the heroine's alienation by including some incisive nonverbal images, such as Mary sleeping while pitifully clutching an ivory elephant that belonged to her mother. Her sad predicament is also evident in an emblematic dream sequence (borrowed from fairy-tale tradition): She dreams that she is a toddler again, following her mother (Irene Jacob—in this film Mary's mother and Lilias are twin sisters) through a jungle. Her mother calls to her and blithely runs away, as unreachable as ever, leaving her sobbing in the jungle. Ingeniously, Holland symbolizes what the other versions merely mention and the text states—that Mary is alone and suffering in the world.

Similarly, Holland also brings out Burnett's implications about Archibald's desertion of Colin (Heydon Prowse). Burnett insinuates that Colin's illness is a result of his embittered father's inattentiveness, and Holland verbalizes this suggestion. At one point in the movie, Colin petulantly declares to his cousin, "I'll die because he doesn't like me" (*The Secret Garden,* dir. Agnieszka Holland). Afterwards, through a dialogue between Mary and Martha (Laura Crossley), Holland announces Lord Craven's fear of intimacy since the source of his unresponsiveness to his son is the traumatic death of his wife. Rich in subtle psychology, Holland's adaptation of *The Secret Garden* employs even more cinematic devices to draw attention to the children's plight.

She adeptly uses composition to accentuate her theme of abandonment. Just as Mira Nair, in *Salaam Bombay* (1988), ends her film about street children in Bombay with a close-up of an abandoned child—here also, frequent close-ups of the two neglected youngsters accent the intensity of their situations. Likewise, high angle shots emphasize their smallness and vulnerability. Achieving a similar effect, Holland often dwarfs little Mary by placing her in a huge, ornate bed or against the background of the enormous house. Furthermore, by situating characters far apart within the frame, Holland indicates emotional distance in relationships. For instance, when Medlock (Maggie Smith—certainly the wicked stepmother) finally arrives at the station to claim "Number forty-three, Mary Lennox" (*The Secret Garden,* dir. Agnieszka Holland), the housekeeper walks ten paces ahead of the numbered orphan to their carriage—the tag prominently displaying Mary's number making her seem like a piece of goods, a commodity that might be alternatively bought and claimed, or sold and rejected.

In addition to composition, Holland relies on imagery and lighting to underscore the trauma and recovery of the two abandoned rich children. Delineating the healing effects of the garden, she shoots the first half of the film in wintry desolate imagery, followed by spring-like floral imagery as the children begin to find happiness. Similarly, the sun comes out midway through the movie as Mary and Colin enjoy nature and experience camaraderie, eradicating the dark gloominess evident in earlier scenes.

Undoubtedly one of the brightest moments in Holland's interpretation, however, is Archibald's poignant rediscovery of his son and the reunification of the expanded family. Like those of other directors before her, Holland's characterization of Archibald and her perception of the dramatic conclusion is shaped by what is permissible culturally. Although there was not an extraordinary change in society's typical father between the 1987 Hallmark Hall of Fame Production and the 1993 American Zoetrope motion picture, viewers will note distinct differences.

Unlike the other two American film adaptations, in Holland's version the children are *curious* about Lord Craven, rather than *frightened* of him. They want to know this aching man, who seems to suffer noticeably more grief than anger. His teary-eyed reaction upon seeing able-bodied Colin playing blind man's buff in the Secret Garden is anything but restrained: he hugs his son, clasps his hands, and caresses his cheeks. Upon seeing her uncle and cousin reunited, Mary's long-withheld tears tumble easily as she fears their togetherness signifies certain rejection for her. Enlightened and sensitive, Lord Craven gently reassures, thanks, and hugs her. (Appropriately, the fairy tale concludes with a thought-provoking moral.) The emotional bonding between Archibald and Colin and his affectionate acceptance of Mary into the Craven family exemplify the emergence of the sensitive man in American society and the resulting increased closeness between fathers and their children.

The history and politics of the men's and women's movements are significant social conditions that have influenced Holland's interpretation. Her different audience and cultural context provide the novel's fans something Burnett and the earlier directors, victimized by their historical moments which limited them to masculinist readings, could not—fitting closure to the story. In the literary original, Mary almost single-handedly restores the Craven family's literally crippled patriarchy but neither reaps a reward of recognition or true acceptance into the family. Wilcox's ending echoes Burnett's, and Grint's somewhat happier outcome—while highlighting Mary's independence, self-reliance and curiosity, and acknowledging her contribution to Colin's well-being—links her worth to marriage which forces her into subjugation. Holland's heroine, on the other hand, is no such dupe. Furthermore, Mary's significance does not come at the expense of the Craven men. The scenes in Holland's film of the poignant father-son reunion, and their triumphant walk free of convalescent aids to the manor with Mary, becomingly portray their emotional and physical healing.

More importantly, there is a noticeable nineties trend toward feminist interpretations of children's classics. Two new adaptations of *Little Women* (1994) and *A Little Princess* (1995) follow Holland's example (and those of other directors, such as Jane Campion, targeting an adult audience); Gillian Armstrong (who made a strong feminist statement in her 1979 film, *My Brilliant Career*) and Alfonso Cuarón invite more independent female spirit into Louisa May Alcott's (also a feminist) and Frances Hodgson Burnett's works, respectively.[19] It is logical that their texts are currently experiencing a cinematic rebirth: Hollywood seems to recognize that working women that have children do spend money on family films, and American society appears ready for movies that provide reparation for young women tired of reading about dead white men in school and dismayed by seeing so few good female role models in films: although *Dangerous Minds* (1995), starring Michelle Pfeiffer, is a problematic film, it was merely waiting for history and pedagogy to arrive.

By virtue of her time and gender, Holland bequeaths a legacy of *The Secret Garden* that seems truer to the sense of the original novel. Feminist critic Nina Baym maintains that gender-related restrictions cause male critical theorists to misinterpret texts concerning women, dismissing them as "'ubiquitous melodramas of beset womanhood'" (69). Similarly, it appears that Wilcox and Grint err in their melodramatic revisions of Burnett's work; Wilcox's mediocre melodrama mistakes it as a helpless-heroine cliffhanger even though the author is not known for writing suspense novels, and Grint's overdone romance sacrifices the fairy-tale magic of the garden for a sentimental love story and a patronizing accent on female power. Holland answers these films and the book with a classic cinematic transformation of *The Secret Garden* that captures the nuances of the text without exploiting its pathos or its characters.

NOTES

1. See, for example, Morris Beja, *Film and Literature;* George Bluestone, *Novels into Film;* Judith Mayne,

Private Novels, Public Films; and Sergei Eisenstein, "Dickens, Griffith, and the Film Today."

2. Some of the noted adaptations not discussed in this paper include the 1919 Paramount silent film; the 1975 British Broadcasting Company production; two 1991 children's operas by Nona Sheppard and Helen Glavin in England and Greg Plishka and David Ives in America; the 1991 Broadway musical by Marsha Norman; and two 1994 adaptations: American Broadcasting Corporation's televised, animated program and Sound Source International's CD-ROM computer version.

3. Film content arises out of a complicated context. Although the historical and sociological changes evident in the films discussed at length in this essay are noteworthy, these factors are by no means solely responsible for the films' complete development. Several other elements—for instance, the decline of the studio system in the case of the 1949 MGM film, the influence of the medium in the case of the 1987 television movie, and the significance of Agnieszka Holland's personal and professional background in the case of the 1993 Warner Brothers (American Zoetrope) production—contribute to the finished cinematic product, but it is beyond the scope of this paper to discuss these factors.

4. Some of the scholars who note Burnett's change of focus from Mary to Colin include: Phyllis Bixler, *Frances Hodgson Burnett,* 100–1; Elizabeth Lennox Keyser, "'Quite Contrary,'" 1–13; U. C. Knoepflmacher, "Little Girls Without Their Curls," 21–25; Claudia Marquis, "The Power of Speech," 163–87; and Lissa Paul, "Enigma Variations," 186–201.

5. Bixler, *Frances* 123. Although Bixler notes the discrepancies between Burnett's public image and her nonconformist lifestyle, she does not refer to Burnett's behavior as a masquerade. In her article, "Womanliness as a Masquerade," Joan Riviere outlines the concept of masquerade, which is applicable to Burnett (and other nineteenth-century women writers, as well). Riviere suggests that to overcompensate for achieving success in a male role, some women masquerade behind feigned femininity (90–101).

6. Eden Ross Lipson, *"New York Times* Ranks Best-selling Children's Titles," sec. I:5. The two titles ranked ahead of *The Secret Garden* were *Zlata's Diary* and *The Giver,* two current bestsellers.

7. *The Secret Garden,* dir. Fred M. Wilcox, with Margaret O'Brien, Herbert Marshall, Dean Stockwell, and Gladys Cooper, MGM, 1949. Subsequent references to the 1949 MGM film refer to this notation.

8. Mary Ann Doane, *The Desire to Desire.* Doane's chapter, "Paranoia and the Specular," defines the term com-

pletely and delineates a cycle of such films dating from 1940 to 1949.

9. *Jane Eyre,* dir. Robert Stevenson, with Orson Welles and Joan Fontaine, Twentieth Century Fox, 1943. Subsequent references to this film refer to this notation. Critics frequently compare Burnett's *The Secret Garden* to *Jane Eyre.* Two of such scholars are Ann Thwaite, *Waiting for the Party,* 220–21, and Phyllis Bixler, *Frances Hodgson Burnett,* 100.

10. The works of feminist film critics such as Doane, Kaplan, and Mulvey are important to students of children's films. For example, Mulvey's "Visual Pleasure and Narrative Cinema" explores "the way the unconscious of patriarchal society has structured film form," which is especially relevant to classical Hollywood twentieth-century adaptations of children's literature. Doane, *The Desire to Desire;* E. Ann Kaplan, *Women and Film;* and Laura Mulvey, "Visual Pleasure and Narrative Cinema," 28–40.

11. Wolf, 128. Since the film debuted in Sept. 1949, it is possible that it was a transition piece from Louis B. Mayer to Dore Schary, who took over the helm at MGM in 1948 and accented realism and social consciousness.

12. *The Secret Garden,* dir. Alan Grint, with Gennie James, Barret Oliver, Jadrien Steele, Michael Hordern, Billie Whitelaw, and Derek Jacobi, Rosemont Productions, 1987. Subsequent references to the 1987 Hallmark Hall of Fame production refer to this notation.

13. David Rosemont, telephone interview. Rosemont said that *The Secret Garden* was a "big book for today's mothers when they were young," which influenced his company's decision to adapt the novel.

14. Rosemont Productions also adapted Burnett's *Little Lord Fauntleroy* in 1980 for television, writing new material to underscore Mrs. Errol's spirit (Cf. Bixler, "Continuity and Change," 76–77, 79). Her character's lack of passivity, it seems, was a harbinger for the independent, cognizant Mary seen in Rosemont's *The Secret Garden.*

15. In the 1980s the United States, while still a dominant nation, was experiencing a change in its global status. For example, its place as a leader in per capita income and health care among Western nations was sliding as its illiteracy and infant mortality rates were climbing. Furthermore, instead of reigning as the world's largest creditor nation, it now had the dubious distinction of being the world's largest debtor nation. Consequently, many Americans looked nostalgically to their past for a world they deemed simpler and securer (as other nations did during troublesome periods, such as Germany in the 1930s and the Roman Empire in the third century). The resulting vogue to Victoriana is evident in many segments of popular culture, including fashion styles, home decor, and film. Contemporary children's films, such as *The Secret Garden* (1993), *Little Women* (1994), and *A Little Princess* (1995), demonstrate the continuing popularity of Victoriana. Stephanie Coontz explores the intrinsic myths in the American yearning for the past—whether it be for the Victorian age or the 1950s—in her book, *The Way We Never Were,* which is an asset to those studying the social history of the American family.

16. *The Secret Garden,* dir. Agnieszka Holland, with Kate Maberly, Heydon Prowse, Andrew Knott, and Maggie Smith, Warner Brothers, 1993. Subsequent references to the 1993 Warner Brothers film refer to this notation. It is interesting to note that *The Secret Garden* (1993), *Dennis the Menace* (1993), and *Free Willy* (1993) were some of the first films produced by Warner Brothers' new family entertainment line.

17. Despite Holland's Polish heritage and that *The Secret Garden* is her first American film, one must consider that she realized she must appeal to her audience's social realities and cultural values. Explaining one of the reasons why she chose to direct the American Zoetrope production, Holland said, "It seemed a way to do something I cared about but which wasn't as personal as one of my own scripts, which would have been harder to do within the Hollywood system" (Taubin 28). Most assuredly, Holland's Hollywood guinea pig was influenced by Americans on the production team, such as screenwriter Caroline Thompson and producer Francis Ford Coppola. See also note 3.

18. Other contemporary directors, such as Tim Burton in *Edward Scissorhands* (1990), Ron Howard in *Willow* (1988), and more recently, Chris Noonan in *Babe* (1995), use similar shot techniques. Coincidentally, screenwriter Caroline Thompson wrote *The Secret Garden* (1993) and *Edward Scissorhands.*

19. *Little Women,* dir. Gillian Armstrong, with Winona Ryder, Susan Sarandon, Claire Danes, Trini Alvarado, Kirsten Dunst, Samantha Mathis, Christian Bale, and Gabriel Byrne, Columbia Pictures, 1994; *A Little Princess,* dir. Alfonso Cuarón, with Liesel Matthews, Eleanor Bron, Liam Cunningham, Lomax Study, and Vanessa Lee Chester, Warner Brothers, 1995.

WORKS CITED

Babe. Dir. Chris Noonan. Prod. George Miller, Doug Mitchell, and Bill Miller. Universal Pictures, 1995. 91 min.

Baym, Nina. "Melodramas of Beset Womanhood: How Theories of American Fiction Exclude Women Authors." *The New Criticism: Essays of Women, Literature, and Theory*. Ed. Elaine Showalter. New York: Pantheon Books, 1985. 63–80.

Beja, Morris. *Film and Literature*. New York: Longman, 1979.

Bixler, Phyllis. "Continuity and Change in Popular Entertainment." *Children's Novels and the Movies*. Ed. Douglas Street. New York: Frederick Ungar, 1983. 69–80.

———. *Frances Hodgson Burnett*. Boston: Twayne Publishers, 1984.

———. "*The Secret Garden* 'Misread': The Broadway Musical as Creative Interpretation." *Annual of the Modern Language Association Division on Children's Literature and the Children's Literature Association* 22. Eds. Francelia Butler, R. H. Dillard, and Elizabeth Lennox Keyser. New Haven: Yale UP, 1994. 101–23.

Bluestone, George. *Novels into Film*. 1957. Berkeley and Los Angeles: University of California Press, 1973.

Burnett, Frances Hodgson. *The Secret Garden*. 1911. New York: Dell Publishing, 1987.

Coontz, Stephanie. *The Way We Never Were: American Families and the Nostalgia Trap*. New York: Basic Books, 1991.

David Copperfield. Dir. George Cukor. Prod. David O. Selznick. MGM, 1934. 132 min.

Dennis the Menace. Dir. Nick Castle. Prod. John Hughes and Richard Vane. Warner Brothers, 1993. 96 min.

Doane, Mary Ann. *The Desire to Desire: The Woman's Film of the 1940s*. Bloomington: Indiana University Press, 1987.

Eisenstein, Sergei, "Dickens, Griffith, and the Film Today." *Film Form: Essays in Film Theory*. Ed. Jay Leyda. New York: Harcourt Brace, 1949. 195–255.

Edward Scissorhands. Dir. Tim Burton. Prod. Denise De Novi. Fox, 1990. 98 min.

Free Willy. Dir. Simon Wincer. Prod. Jennie Lew Tugend and Lauren Shuler-Donner. Warner Brothers, 1993. 112 min.

Jane Eyre. Dir. Robert Stevenson. Prod. Robert Stevenson, John Houseman, and William Goetz. Twentieth Century Fox, 1943. 96 min.

Kaplan, E. Ann. *Women and Film: Both Sides of the Camera*. New York: Methuen, 1983.

Keyser, Elizabeth Lennox. "'Quite Contrary': Frances Hodgson Burnett's *The Secret Garden*." *Annual of the Modern Language Association Division on Children's Literature and the Children's Literature Association* 11. Eds. Francelia Butler, Compton Rees, David L. Green. New Haven: Yale University Press, 1983. 1–13.

Knoepflmacher, U. C. "Little Girls Without Their Curls: Female Aggression in Victorian Children's Literature." *Annual of the Modern Language Association Division on Children's Literature and the Children's Literature Association*, 11. Eds. Francelia Butler, Compton Rees, David L. Green. New Haven: Yale University Press, 1983. 14–31.

A Little Princess. Dir. Alfonso Cuarón. Prod. Mark Johnson. Warner Brothers, 1995. 98 min.

Little Women. Dir. Gillian Armstrong. Prod. Denise DiNovi. Columbia Pictures, 1994. 98 min.

Little Women. Dir. Mervyn LeRoy. Prod. Mervyn LeRoy. MGM, 1949. 122 min.

Lipson, Eden Ross. "*New York Times* Ranks Best-selling Children's Titles." *Indianapolis Star* August 14, 1994, sec. I: 1+.

Madame Bovary. Dir. Vincente Minnelli. Prod. Pandro S. Berman. MGM, 1949. 114 min.

Manna, Anthony. "Children's Literature and Society." *Children's Literature Association Quarterly* (Summer 1986): 58.

Marquis, Claudia. "The Power of Speech: Life in *The Secret Garden*." *AUMLA: Journal of the Australasian Universities Language and Literature Association* No. 68 (November 1987): 163–87.

Mayne, Judith. *Private Novels, Public Films*. Athens: University of Georgia Press, 1988.

McGee, Celia. "Gambling on a Garden." *New York* April 22, 1991: 64–71.

Mullin, Shirley. Personal Interview. July 27, 1994.

Mulvey, Laura. "Visual Pleasure and Narrative Cinema." *Issues in Feminist Film Criticism*. Ed. Patricia Erens. Bloomington: Indiana University Press, 1990: 28–40.

Mutiny on the Bounty. Dir. Frank Lloyd. Prod. Irving Thalberg and Albert Lewin. MGM, 1935. 135 min.

Norman, Marsha. *The Secret Garden*. New York: Theatre Communications Group, 1992.

Paul, Lissa. "Enigma Variations: What Feminist Theory Knows About Children's Literature." *Signal: Approaches to Children's Books* (Sept. 1987): 186–201.

Rhode, Eric. *A History of the Cinema from its Origins to 1970*. New York: Hill & Wang, 1976.

Riviere, Joan. "Womanliness as a Masquerade." *The Inner World and Joan Riviere*. Ed. Athol Hughes. New York: Karnac Books, 1991. 90–101.

Rosemont, David. Telephone interview. October 30, 1993.

The Secret Garden. Dir. Alan Grint. Prod. Norman Rosemont. Republic Pictures, 1987. 100 min.

The Secret Garden. Dir. Agnieszka Holland. Prod. Francis Ford Coppola. Warner Brothers, 1993. 103 min.

The Secret Garden. Dir. Fred M. Wilcox. Prod. Clarence Brown. MGM, 1949. 92 min.

Street, Douglas. "Introduction." *Children's Novels and the*

Movies. Ed. Douglas Street. New York: Frederick Ungar, 1983. xiii–xxiv.

A Tale of Two Cities. Dir. Jack Conway. Prod. David O. Selznick. MGM, 1935. 121 min.

Taubin, Amy. "Out of the Ruins." *Sight and Sound* 3 (October 1993): 26–29.

The Three Musketeers. Dir. George Sidney. Prod. Pandro S. Berman. MGM, 1948. 125 min.

Thwaite, Ann. *Waiting for the Party: The Life of Frances Hodgson Burnett.* New York: Charles Scribner's Sons, 1974.

Willow. Dir. Ron Howard. Prod. Nigel Wooll. MGM, 1988. 126 min.

Wolf, Virginia L. "Psychology and Magic: Evocative Blend or a Melodramatic Patchwork." *Children's Novels and the Movies.* Ed. Douglas Street. New York: Frederick Ungar, 1983. 121–30.

Joe Winston (b. 1953)

Joe Winston, an expert on traditional tales and drama for children, teaches at the University of Warwick's Institute of Education in England. His 1994 essay on *The Enchanter's Daughter* by Antonia Barber (with illustrations by Errol LeCain) not only demonstrates the value of a close, sensitive reading of a contemporary picture book, but it also synthesizes the psychoanalytic approach to fairy tales of critics such as Bruno Bettelheim and the "revisionist" theories of Jack Zipes. By examining carefully the way each character, image, and action in the tale uses "the emotional power" of traditional symbols to convey new meanings that reflect contemporary social values, Winston sheds light on the subtlety and beauty of literary fairy tales by recent authors such as Antonia Barber, Jane Yolen, and Robin McKinley.

Revising the Fairy Tale Through Magic

Antonia Barber's The Enchanter's Daughter

In her book *Don't Tell the Grown-ups,* Alison Lurie comments on how "highminded progressive" people have disapproved of fairy tales and folktales on educational grounds for over 200 years. Their arguments have centered around the potential lessons these tales offer children, in particular the role models that they present. In the eighteenth century, for example, a tale such as *Cinderella* was condemned for painting "some of the worst passions that can enter into the human breast . . . such as envy, jealousy . . . , vanity, a love of dress, etc." (Lurie, 1990, p. 17). The line of attack in recent decades has shifted into political and, more specifically, feminist territory. Jack Zipes succinctly summarizes these objections:

Not only are the tales considered to be too sexist, racist and authoritarian, but the general contents are said to reflect the concerns of semi-feudal, patriarchal societies. (1983, p. 170)

One of the ways writers who share this concern have responded is by finding and retelling hitherto ignored folk tales that present alternative gender role models, particularly for girls; an example is Alison Lurie's *"Clever Gretchen" and Other Forgotten Folk Tales.* More problematic responses have been to revise existing fairy stories or to write new stories that deliberately set out to challenge and reverse some of the expectations of the genre. Jay Williams' *"The Practical Princess" and Other Liberating Fairy Tales* is a well-known example of this approach, one advocated by the influential theorist, Jack Zipes. He describes these self-consciously revisionist fairy tales as "emancipatory" and "liberating" (1983, p. 191) and pinpoints *disturbance* as their aim:

They interfere with the civilising process in hope of creating change and a new awareness of social conditions.

Zipes' theory of disturbance is not dissimilar to Brecht's theory of alienation or distancing in the theater; both direct their appeal primarily at the intellect, aiming to expose what we might otherwise take for granted with empowerment for change as their ultimate goal.

The revisionist approach to fairy tales is philosophically very different from that advocated by Bruno Bettelheim. In *The Uses of Enchantment* he argues that the importance of these tales for children goes deeper than questions of role models or moral lessons.

The paramount importance of fairy tales for the growing individual resides in something other than teachings about correct ways of behaving in this world. . . . The fairy tales' concern is not useful information about the external world, but the inner processes taking place in an individual. (1976, p. 25)

For Bettelheim, these inner processes are the workings of the preconscious and subconscious as expounded by Freud. The most popular fairy tales are "purveyors of deep insights that have sustained mankind through the long vicissitudes of its existence" (p. 26). They have acquired these insights after years of retelling and refinement in response to perceived audience reaction. Thus they have come to address, in symbolic form, what Bettelheim (p. 45) calls "the eternal questions":

What is the world really like? How am I to live my life in it? How can I truly be myself?

For this reason, they should not be revised or tampered with. Moreover, the educational power of the classic fairy tale for Bettelheim resides in its very lack of didacticism; "its messages may imply solutions but it never spells them out" (p. 45). If Zipes addresses primarily the conscious, intellectual response of the reader, Bettelheim is more concerned with the hidden and the symbolic, with the reader's *emotional* response.

It is not surprising that revisionists should oppose the essentially conservative arguments of Bettelheim, and Zipes has written a very cogent and thorough attack on his theories. In particular, he criticizes his overreliance on orthodox Freudian theory, his apparent ignorance of the historical development of the fairy tale, and his ethnocentric and at times sexist definitions of what pass for universal truths. Bettelheim's strength, however, is his appreciation of the *emotional* power of the tales, a power generated and steered by their potent use of symbol; and it is here where many revisionist tales fail. *The Practical Princess,* for example, may be witty and illuminating but its self-conscious didacticism and parodic nature leave no room for the mysterious and the magical, qualities emphasized by Bettelheim and that form a substantial part of the allure of folk and fairy tales.

The revised versions of *Rumpelstiltskin* presented by Zipes at the end of his critique on Bettelheim are inspired by a similarly didactic spirit and are supposed to "point in the direction of a new humanism" (Zipes, 1979, p. 177). One ends with the miller's daughter renouncing the king and being saved by running "out into the great, wide world"; in the other, as Queen, she invites Rumpelstiltskin to come and live with her, her child, and the king "and see how much fun we can have" (p. 182). Reading them, one may sympathize with their messages or admire their purpose, but we know that they will never catch on. It is insufficient to claim, as Zipes does, that this is because children resist change due to a "conservative socialization process" (1983, p. 191); this may well be true, but teachers who blame their pupils for failing to learn might have our sympathy but they forfeit our respect.

Some feminist critics have realized the significance of this problem, which may be expressed thus: How do we create modern fairy stories that redress the problems identified in traditional tales, in particular those associated with gender, while preserving the potency and structural coherence—and hence the appeal—of the traditional fairy story? As Elizabeth Keyser has pointed out, it is not enough to expose lies and half-truths or to provide an alternative vision by writing a tale that is "polemical and thesis-ridden"; such tales "perpetrate what Charles Dickens called a 'fraud on the fairies'" (1989, p. 157). In other words, they don't work. Keyser goes on to quote Kay Stone:

Contemporary feminist scholars, instead of condemning fairy-tale heroines, are adopting a mythic approach, one sensitive to the subtler inner strength of heroines. (p. 160)

The implication here is that instead of trying to subvert the traditional archetypes of the tales, the contemporary feminist writer should appreciate and harness their qualities, creating stories far more in tune with the tradition, and hence using the allures of magic and symbolism, whose importance was stressed by Bettelheim.

The Enchanter's Daughter by Antonia Barber, with illustrations by Errol Le Cain, was published in 1987. This tale is particularly interesting as it stays true to the spirit, pattern, and structure of an archetypal fairy tale while it subtly changes or even reverses some of the meanings we have come to expect. It does this, I believe, by managing a much subtler kind of disturbance than that advocated by Zipes. In an attempt to illuminate how it achieves this, I present a detailed summary of it below, followed by an analysis of the structure, pattern, and characters of the tale, concentrating on their symbolic functions. This will hopefully provide an illustration of how the genre can be sensitively adapted from within as opposed to being bludgeoned from without.

SUMMARY OF *THE ENCHANTER'S DAUGHTER*

"In the cold white land at the top of the world there once lived an Enchanter and his daughter." The opening sentence of the story not only establishes a location and characters quite archetypal of the fairy tale genre but also an equally typical lyrical style and magical atmosphere that are sustained throughout. Every page of narrative is accompanied by a full-page illustration. These are beautifully detailed, reinforcing the atmosphere and also locating the story more precisely in a mythical Far Eastern setting, resembling Tibet. This is achieved more by an imitation of the color and style of Eastern art than by a depiction of racial stereotypes; it is quite clear from them that we are in fairy land, not China.

The first page focuses on the Enchanter himself and the extent of his magical powers, powers he has learned through study but that nonetheless leave him dissatisfied. The focus then shifts to the Daughter, where it remains for the rest of the tale. Her extreme beauty and modesty are emphasized and we see from the illustration that she has reached her adolescence. She has no name and no knowledge of any other living being apart from the Enchanter, whom she calls "Father." Sometimes at night she dreams that she once had a name, or that she is a small flying bird. Growing increasingly restless as she matures, she asks the Enchanter if she can leave the palace to see the world outside but he refuses. Instead, he transforms the valley where they live into a series of exotic places to create the illusion of travel; but each transformation makes his Daughter more restless still. Finally, in a rash moment, he gives in to a request for books, waving his hand and telling her she will find story books in her room. "She read adventure stories and fairy stories, tales of heroism and tales of romance." From them she learns not only of emotional states such as happiness, pain, and hope but also that all people have names and all children have mothers.

When she eventually returns to the Enchanter she asks him two questions: "What is my name?" and "Where is my mother?" The Enchanter, too late, realizes his mistake: "In giving her books he had given her knowledge." He tells her she never had a mother, but was conjured one day from a rose, whereupon she requests to be a rose again for a day. Her experience as a rose convinces her that the Enchanter has not told her the truth. Subsequently he transforms her into a fish, and then a fawn, neither of which, she realizes, are her true identity. Aware now that she must outwit him if she is ever to find out the truth about herself, she approaches him once again. "If I was none of these, then I must have been a bird before your magic power changed me," she says. He agrees with her but turns down her request to spend a day as a young eagle, realizing that she would escape him "if she had the power." "You were never an eagle, my daughter," he tells her, "only a pretty flying bird." And it is as a pretty flying bird that the Enchanter's Daughter makes her escape over the white mountains. This is recounted in some detail, emphasizing the pain her efforts cause her and the extent of her achievement; for her strength fails her only as she reaches the first trees beyond the white mountains and, as she falls into the snow, the spell breaks and she changes back into human form.

Lying unconscious in the snow, she is discovered by a young man who takes her to his small house, where his mother nurses her back to health. As she regains consciousness, the Daughter sees that the mother is crying. The mother explains that she reminds her of the daughter she once had, who vanished one day, years before, when a rich traveller stopped at the house and was amused by her childish play. From the accompanying illustration, we see that this man was, indeed, the Enchanter. "What was her name?" asks the Enchanter's Daughter. "We called her Thi-Phi-Yen," comes the reply, "for she was like a pretty flying bird." At this, the Daughter remembers her dreams and the words of the Enchanter and knows that she has found her mother and her true identity.

> And from that day she lived happily with her mother and her brother at the foot of the high white mountains that lie at the top of the world.

THE DYNAMIC OF THE TALE: REDEFINING THE HEROINE'S PROGRESS

It is an established pattern in many fairy tales for the central character, male or female, to start out in material poverty but to end up rich and wealthy, as a prince or princess. This is the case in *Cinderella* and *Rapunzel,* for example. Such a change of state implies a movement toward happiness and personal fulfillment and the hero or heroine does not attain it without suffering or hardship. Their material progress is, as Bettelheim points out, an outward symbol of inner growth toward maturity and independence. In *The Enchanter's Daughter,* this transition is materially reversed though its symbolic purpose remains the same; the Daughter begins the tale as a wealthy princess living in a palace and ends it as a humble peasant girl, working the land with her mother and brother. She has, however, moved to a state of happiness and fulfillment. As she tells her mother when reunited with her:

> The Enchanter gave me everything except freedom and love: now I have both. No riches can compare with freedom and no power is greater than love.

The traditional tale's tendency to equate happiness with material wealth and social status is here neatly reversed. Out of context, or as a revisionist appendage, the above quotation could smack of worthy but empty

sentimentality. In this case, however, the words are simply an expression of what the Daughter has learned through the struggle that defines the story's central theme. Essentially, this is her search for her true personal and social identity, for self-knowledge, for the answers to Bettelheim's eternal questions:

> What is the world really like? How am I to live my life in it? How can I truly be myself?

The Daughter is voicing values she has identified from engaging in a struggle to escape the isolation, powerlessness, and enforced ignorance experienced in the Enchanter's palace. The dynamic of the story still moves her from poverty to wealth but it explicitly rejects defining wealth in material terms, as this is the lesson the Daughter has learned in her journey from ignorance to knowledge.

The final full-page illustration shows the Daughter, now in simple clothing, working on the farm with her family. Behind them is a vast panorama with, towering high in the distance, the *colorless* outline of the Enchanter's palace. Without color, it has no reality and no power over the Daughter's life or imagination. She has lived the life of a fairy tale princess and found it lonely, empty, and oppressive. In its place, she has chosen to return to a life of caring—for her family and for the earth—depicted truthfully in this image, as hard work but as meaningful, worthwhile and, above all, as real.

THE PATTERN OF THE TALE: AN AFFIRMATION OF TRADITIONAL FEMALE VALUES

> The story itself is about the period of time between the hero's or heroine's leaving their family of origin and the establishment of a new family of procreation. (Lurie, 1990, p. 25)

Such is indeed the pattern of many classic fairy tales, one that focuses on the period of adolescent self-discovery and the necessary move away from the dependency of childhood to the autonomy of adulthood. However, some critics have objected to the presentation of marriage as the ultimate goal of the archetypal heroine, as though female fulfillment outside of the marriage state was impossible. Once again, *The Enchanter's Daughter* reverses the external progress of the pattern while retaining its symbolic significance; the heroine does, indeed, move from dependency to freedom but she does so not by leaving her family but by rediscovering it. When she is "rescued" by a young man, who takes her to his home, he is no handsome prince whom she will eventually marry but a simple farmer who turns out to be her brother. Unlike Rapunzel, Cinderella, or Snow White, she does not leave a life of oppression by a mother figure to begin a new life with a man but the exact reverse. Throughout the story, her search for her true identity and her reunification with her mother are seen as inseparable goals. When she is finally nursed back to life by her mother, in a scene that has many symbolic overtones of birth, her primary sensation is that of her mother's care:

> Sometimes she would feel a cool hand on her forehead and it seemed to her that it was her mother's hand.

There is a strong symbolic parallel between her recovery of consciousness and the growth into consciousness of a baby, sensually aware of the care she is receiving from her mother. Caring has, of course, been one of the traditional female roles throughout history and, although it has been seen as low status and attacked as an economic trap for women, some recent feminist writings in the field of moral education have argued that the development of one's propensity for caring should be regarded as the lynchpin of the moral life and therefore of primary concern for educators. This amounts to an argument for the importance of caring to be socially recognized and its status enhanced. The reunification of daughter and mother in the context of a fundamental caring relationship is the climax of the tale; as such, it is a strong affirmation of the traditional female caring values represented in the mother-daughter continuum and in opposition to the uncaring, patriarchal world the Enchanter's Daughter has just escaped.

Significantly, there is no father figure in her new home. This shows a positive role model of a one-parent family but the point is not labored or even made explicit in the written text. What matters for the emotional appeal of the story is not the social message conveyed by this image but its narrative and symbolic functions. In narrative terms, it focuses our attention clearly on the centrality of the mother-daughter relationship. To appreciate its symbolic function, we need to look in detail at the Enchanter himself and his relationship with the Daughter.

THE ENCHANTER: RECASTING THE WICKED STEPMOTHER

The archetypal figure of the traditional fairy tale whom the Enchanter parallels is the wicked witch/stepmother of stories such as *Rapunzel* and *Snow White*. Bettelheim contends that the wicked stepmother is essentially none other than the real mother viewed in a negative light from the perspective of the child's natural development; in Rapunzel, we have an overprotective and domineering mother; in *Snow White*, a jealous mother, with oppressive behavior intensifying as the daughter reaches sexual maturity. Indeed, the parallels between *Rapunzel* and *The Enchanter's Daughter* are striking; in each case, an overprotective stepparent keeps an adolescent daughter imprisoned so as not to lose her and in each case the parent is thwarted. However, here we have yet another instance where the symbolic function of the archetypal character is matched but its meaning is shifted. The patriarch in the traditional story is often a king, ultimately allied to the heroine; by casting him in the role of witch/stepmother he becomes structurally redefined as the oppressor. His palace, itself a prison for the Daughter, is a powerful symbol of this oppression. In the opening illustration, it is depicted in stark, phallic imagery, its soaring turrets, surrounded by icebergs and snowy mountain peaks, stretching upward within a cold, sterile landscape. As a father, the Enchanter regards his daughter as a plaything when small; but she matures, becoming less amusing in the process, and he neglects her. However, the narrative of the story implies that he embodies patriarchal oppression beyond that exercised by a father, embracing the same oppression as exercised by a husband.

The story of her origins, as revealed by the mother, is the key to this interpretation. This story resembles the pattern of such tales as *Rumplestiltskin* where the heroine is abducted by a king and taken to live with him in his castle. In material terms, she is pampered and spoiled; in exchange she forfeits her name (in other words, her identity), becoming an appendage to the man she lives with. The title of the book makes this clear, defining her only as a possession, as belonging to the Enchanter. Like a patriarchal husband, the Enchanter wants her to be his possession: passive, pretty, and compliant. To manage this, he keeps her ignorant and isolated from the outside world; meanwhile, he gets on with his work. This view of the Enchanter as both patriarch and husband is supported by the nature of their antagonism when it does surface. Unlike the traditional tales mentioned above, there is no hint that the Enchanter is trying to halt the Daughter's *sexual* development and she shows no aspiration toward finding a sexual partner; the focus is entirely on the Daughter's desire to educate herself, to liberate herself, and to *find* herself. Freedom is her aim and she gains this freedom in a way which, once again, reverses the pattern of the traditional story, not by entering a fairy tale marriage but by fleeing one. Nor does she flee from one form of patriarchy to another; in finding and returning to a family with a mother, and no father figure, she is rejecting patriarchal oppression altogether.

It is tempting to view the Enchanter as an icon of a particular type of Western patriarchy. With his white beard and piercing eyes, his image recalls such figures as Moses and the Christian Godhead. Throughout the whole story, he is poring through his books.

> He saw that age and death would rob him of all his powers and possessions unless he could unlock the one secret that had defeated all other sorcerers before him: the secret of eternal youth.

His palace and his powers are a triumph of technology, of man's control over the environment. Yet none of this is enough for him and he is obsessed with pursuing a selfish dream that is impossible even by fairy tale standards. He is the ultimate technocrat and his pursuit of and use of knowledge is in sharp contrast to that of the Daughter. His pursuit leads him into isolation and defeat; hers leads her into a fulfilling communion with her family and the earth, an image perfectly captured in the final illustration of the book.

THE DAUGHTER: ARCHETYPE AND ROLE MODEL

> The Enchanter's Daughter was very beautiful. Her hair was black and flowed over her shoulders like a waterfall; her eyes were wide and dark like the eyes of a fawn in a forest; her skin glowed like sunlight upon a ripe nectarine. She did not know she was beautiful, for she saw no-one with whom to compare herself.

Thus, from the outset, the Enchanter's Daughter is presented as the archetypal fairy tale princess, physical beauty and modesty being of paramount importance, and both being the outward expression of her inner goodness. In her behavior, however, she proves herself to be far more resourceful and proactive than Snow White, Rapunzel, Cinderella, or other such heroines. She is inquisitive, observant, and intelligent. Once she knows what she wants she is persistent and refuses to let the Enchanter deceive her or deflect her from her purpose. Her patience never leads her to respond passively or fatalistically to the challenges that she faces. She learns, from books and from experience; she shows determination and cunning in order to escape from the Enchanter and immense strength of character and physical endeavor to survive her flight. She shows as much strength of purpose in pursuit of her goal as he does in pursuit of his; but, whereas his is a selfish delusion, hers is a search for truth. At the end of the tale, she achieves wisdom and happiness through a combination of physical and moral courage—not a bad role model for a modern girl.

The symbolism associated with the character of the Daughter reinforces and deepens the meanings expressed in her behavior. Above all, its coherence and carefully chosen purpose enhance her quality as a fairy tale heroine, without which the appeal of the story would be substantially diminished. As with Snow White, the exotic imagery used to describe her beauty, quoted above, links her immediately to the world of nature and natural beauty. In a further echo of Snow White, an early illustration depicts her walking through a jungle forest surrounded by an array of wildlife, with every creature focusing its eyes upon her. This identification with the natural world is strengthened by her transformations, where she spends time living as a rose, a fish, a fawn, and a bird. It comes as no surprise that she ends the story working close to the earth, in sharp contrast to the Enchanter, whose palace we see in the final illustration symbolically far removed from the fertile ground below. Like the Tower of Babel, its colorless shell remains as a warning to men who aspire to play God.

Finally, there is the symbolism of her name, "Pretty Flying Bird." When first she realizes that she must escape from the Enchanter, the Daughter asks him to turn her into a young eagle. He refuses with the words: "You were never an eagle, my daughter, only a pretty flying bird." This not only signifies the humble nature of her origins; more importantly, it dissociates her from the aggressive, masculine eagle. Consequently, she never takes on the identity of something false to her nature in order to achieve her goal. In this case, her name, her identity, and her nature all fuse into one. She does not become a surrogate male to compete with and defeat patriarchal oppression; she does not adopt male values; she asserts her female nature, her female values, and triumphs.

CONCLUSION

Throughout this article I have attempted to show how *The Enchanter's Daughter* successfully redefines and reconstructs what Zipes calls the "fairy tale discourse" (1983, Chapter 1); and that it achieves this because its revisionist messages are implicit, dependent on the emotional power generated by its use of symbol and incorporated successfully within changes to its use of archetype, pattern, and structure. These changes alter the traditional *meanings* of these narrative devices without disrupting their traditional *functions*. Hence the story retains the atmosphere of magic and mystery we associate with the classic fairy tales, stirring the reader's imagination because it speaks primarily through the emotions.

WORKS CITED

Barber, Antonia. *The Enchanter's Daughter.* Illus. Errol Le Cain. London: Random Century Children's Books, 1987.

Bettelheim, Bruno. *The Uses of Enchantment.* London: Penguin, 1976.

Keyser, Elizabeth. "Feminist Revisions: Frauds on the Fairies?" *Children's Literature* 17 (1989): 160.

Lurie, Alison. *"Clever Gretchen" and Other Forgotten Folk Tales.* London: Heinemann, 1980.

———. *Don't Tell the Grown-ups.* London: Bloomsbury, 1990.

Williams, Jay. *"The Practical Princess," and Other Liberating Fairy Tales.* New York: Parents' Magazine Press, 1978.

Zipes, Jack. *Breaking the Magic Spell: Radical Theories of Folk and Fairy Tales.* London: Heinemann, 1979.

———. *Fairy Tales and the Art of Subversion.* New York: Wildman, 1983.

Antonia Barber (b. 1932)

Antonia Barber is the pseudonym of English author Barbara Anthony, who has retold traditional tales from a variety of oral and artistic traditions (such as stories based on classical ballets), as well as writing original stories for children. In *The Enchanter's Daughter* (1987), Barber, like American writer Jane Yolen, uses a lyrical style and evocative images to shape a new literary fairy tale that echoes the idealistic themes of many traditional tales. It deals with dreams, transformation, and self-realization as the young heroine seeks her true identity and home. Like Rapunzel (see Part 3), the daughter in this story is protected from knowledge of the world by a mysterious parent who took her from her birth parents to live in a magic secluded place. As in another popular fairy tale, "Rumpelstiltskin," a name has magical power, except that this innocent heroine needs to discover her own name and find her mother. (Her name, Thi-Phi-Yen, is the middle name of Barber's adopted daughter, a Vietnamese war orphan.) The girl's transformation into a rose in the sun, a fish, a fawn, and a bird link her with nature and the elements of fire, water, earth, and air, giving her greater freedom with each new experience. Although the optimistic wish fulfillment in this tale is not unusual because it involves home and love, the choices that this beautiful young heroine makes in order to return to her family are quite untraditional, as critic Joe Winston discusses in the essay reprinted earlier in this section. If traditional folk heroes return home at the end of a tale, especially if they return to a humble mother without a husband (as in "Jack and the Beanstalk" in Part 3), they usually bring riches or wealthy spouses with them. But this heroine's realization that love and freedom are more important than riches and power creates a most unconventional ending for a fairy tale.

The Enchanter's Daughter

In the cold white land at the top of the world there once lived an Enchanter and his daughter. So great was the power of the Enchanter that, even amid the frozen wastes, the gardens of his palace were bright with scented flowers and sweet with the music of singing birds. Beyond the walls, green fields and woods and lakes of shining water stretched right to the slopes of the icy and impassable mountains that ringed them around.

Here the Enchanter and his daughter lived alone, for they had no need of servants. Whatever they wanted, whether food or warmth or comfort, the Enchanter had only to pass his hand through the air and everything was as he desired. All his long life he had studied the books of the old magicians and necromancers until he had mastered their arts one by one. But each power once gained, whether to conjure gold out of the earth or music out of the air, left him dissatisfied. For he had no need of the gold, nor time to listen to the music.

The enchanter would not let his daughter leave the valley. When she asked to see what lay beyond the cold white mountains, he said that traveling would weary her. Instead, he transformed the valley.

First it became a tropical island with beaches of white sand and leaning palms with great feathery leaves. The shining lake became a warm lagoon where the Enchanter's daughter swam in the blue water and chased the brightly colored fish through caves of coral.

When she grew tired of this, the Enchanter turned the palace into a castle on a high crag amid pine forests where the deer roamed and the great eagles soared overhead. Watching them, his daughter began to long for freedom.

Then the Enchanter filled the valley with jungle forests where brilliant snakes and butterflies shone like jewels in the green shadows, and tribes of chattering monkeys swung through the treetops for his daughter's amusement. Watching them as they played, she began to long for company.

The enchanter's daughter was very beautiful. Her hair was black and flowed over her shoulders like a shining waterfall; her eyes were wide and dark like the eyes of a fawn in the forest; her skin glowed like sunlight upon a ripe nectarine. She did not know that she was beautiful, for she saw no one with whom to compare herself. The Enchanter knew, but he had come to take perfection for granted: so he did not praise her and she did not grow vain. Her beauty shone out from all the myriad mirrors on the palace walls, but she passed by with never a glance at them.

The Enchanter called her "Daughter" and did not give her a name. She did not think this strange, for she called him "Father" and she knew no one else. Sometimes in her dreams it seemed to her that she had once had another name, but when she awoke she could not remember it. At other times she dreamed that she was a small flying bird and did not have a name at all.

Having no one but her father, she went in search of him to the high tower where he pored over his books. But he who had once delighted in her company had now no time to talk to her. For having gained by his magic all that life could offer, he found that he was growing old. He saw that age and death would rob him of all his power and possessions unless he could unlock the one secret that had defeated all other sorcerers before him: the secret of eternal youth.

"Do not trouble me, Daughter," he said, turning the pages of a great dusty book, "for unless I unravel this last mystery I am lost."

The Enchanter's daughter saw that her father laid great store by the books. She reached to take one down to look at it more closely. Then for the first time he turned on her in anger, forbidding her to touch the books in which his power and knowledge lay.

"Then give me books of my own," she begged, "for I have no companions and time lies heavy upon my hands."

The enchanter's mind was on matters of life and death. He raised one hand and waved it distractedly. "You will find storybooks in your room," he said.

His daughter ran down all the stairs of the tower and found to her delight that the floor of her room was piled high with books. They were bound in bright leathers, tooled and edged with gold, and decorated with glowing pictures—for nothing the Enchanter did was ever done by half.

Then for a long time she did not trouble her father again. For she discovered in the books new worlds of which she had never dreamed. She read adventure stories and fairy stories, tales of heroism and tales of romance. She read of happiness and sadness, pain and courage, hope and despair, friendship and love. She learned that there were many lands beyond the mountains and that they were all full of people. She found that there were mothers as well as fathers—and brothers and sisters, cousins and friends. And all the people in the books had names, which made her wonder again about the name in her dreams she could never quite remember.

Then the enchanter's daughter went once more to her father, who could scarcely be seen amid piles of musty volumes.

"Father," she asked him, "what is my name?"

The Enchanter looked up sharply. "I call you Daughter," he said, "you do not need a name."

She tried another question. "Where is my mother?" she said.

The Enchanter turned pale. "Your mother?" he said. "What do you know of mothers?"

"I have read the books," said his daughter.

Then the Enchanter saw his mistake: for in giving her books he had given her knowledge. For a while he was silent; then he looked at her slyly.

"Daughter," he said, "you have no mother. Once when I was lonely and craved for company, I made you with a powerful spell from a rose that grew on the palace wall."

"Then let me be a rose again," said his daughter, "and I shall know if it is true."

"Very well," said the Enchanter, "but only for a day." He stirred the air with his long thin fingers and his daughter became a red rose on the south wall of the palace.

She felt the morning dew on her petals as the sun rose through the early mists. She felt the rich perfume drawn out of her by the warm rays as the day went on. She felt the many small feet of a caterpillar which passed over her in the early afternoon, and the gentle movement of the breeze which sprang up at sunset. But deep within her petals there was a strange longing which told her that she was not a rose.

Next morning, she went to the Enchanter and said, "Father, you play games with me. Tell me where my mother is."

The Enchanter saw that she was not deceived.

"You are too clever for me, Daughter," he said, "so I will tell you the truth. You were once a small bright fish in the shining lake. I caught you on my line in the old days when I had time for such sport. You pleaded for your life, so I made you into a daughter to keep me company."

"Then let me be a fish again," said his daughter, "that I may know my true self."

"For a day then," said the Enchanter, tracing a pattern in the air.

The Enchanter's daughter felt the cool water flowing like silk over her shining scales. She glided through gently swaying forests of green weed.

She leaped up into the bright air and plunged back through a circle of ripples into the mysterious depths. But all the time there were thoughts in her head which told her that she was not a fish.

On the following morning, she went to the Enchanter again and said, "Father, you tease me with your stories. Tell me, please, where my mother is?"

He frowned at her over his books.

"You grow troublesome," he said. "I wish I had not made you into my daughter but had left you a fawn in the forest. For such you were before my spell was cast, and as for your mother, she was a wild deer."

"Then let me be a fawn again," begged his daughter, "that I may run by my mother's side."

At a wave of his hand she felt the dry leaves beneath her tiny hooves and smelled the warm, comforting shelter of the doe beside her. All day, they wandered together through the shade-dappled forest, nibbling young leaves and grazing in sunlit clearings. The doe was gentle and caring and the Enchanter's daughter began to understand what it was to have a mother. And the knowledge stirred old memories deep within her which told her that she was not a fawn.

When she went to her father on the fourth day, she saw that he was growing angry. She knew that she must outwit him if ever she was to find the truth.

"Father," she said, "you have deceived me so far. It is certain that I was never a rose nor a fish nor a fawn in the forest. Why do you hide the truth from me? For surely, if I was none of these, then I must have been a bird before your magic power changed me."

The Enchanter looked at her wearily.

"Why, indeed, so you were," he said, and turned back to his book.

"Let me be a bird again," said his daughter, "for I long once more to be a young eagle on the high summer air."

"You shall be a bird if that is your wish," said the Enchanter. He raised his hand, and as he did so, a faint smile curved his mouth. "But you were never an eagle, my daughter," he said, "only a pretty flying bird." For he read her secret thoughts in her honest eyes and knew that she would escape him if she had the power.

The Enchanter's daughter stretched her tiny wings and rose high above the palace gardens. She flew out across the fields and woods and over the shining lake. She knew she must cross the high white mountains to find her mother, but for such a journey even an eagle's wings would scarcely have been strong enough. The peaks of the mountains were lost amid the clouds, and as she grew close to them, she was afraid. All day, she flew on over snow-covered wastes and pinnacles of ice and jagged rocks so steep that neither ice nor snow could cling to them.

As the mountains loomed higher, the air grew bitterly cold. Each breath was a struggle and she who had never suffered felt pain for the first time. Darkness fell and she longed to turn back, but the thought of her mother somewhere beyond the mountains put courage into her faint heart and drove her on. By moonlight she crossed the high mountain peaks, only to find more vast snowfields on the other side. Despair seized her as she felt her small strength ebbing away. For she knew that in the morning the spell would be broken and, unable to fly any farther, she would perish in that harsh and inhospitable land.

Then, just as the first light was breaking, she saw a glimpse of green on the far horizon and felt in her frozen body the sudden warmth of hope. With a last effort she flew on toward it, but even as she reached the tree line her tiny wings failed her. Down she fell, down through the branches into the soft snow, and at that very moment the spell was broken.

A young man came up through the forest with a load of firewood and saw, to his astonishment, a girl of great beauty who seemed to lie sleeping in his path. Her clothes were of silk, bright jewels hung about her neck, and her hair flowed like a dark waterfall across the snow. He threw down his load and knelt beside her, but she was stiff and cold. Swiftly he wrapped her in his cloak and carried her away down the mountainside to a small house where smoke rose from a warm fire within.

For many weeks the Enchanter's daughter lay between life and death. She tossed and turned in her fever, and as she did so, she heard a voice in the darkness and dreamed that it was her mother's voice. Sometimes she would feel a cool hand upon her forehead and it seemed to her that it was her mother's hand. The longing of the rose, the thoughts of the little fish, and the memories of the fawn in the forest all seemed to come together, and when at last she opened her eyes she knew that she looked upon her mother's face.

The woman leaning over her had gentle eyes like the doe in the forest. But the Enchanter's daughter saw that they were full of tears.

"Why do you weep?" she asked.

The woman sighed. "Forgive me," she said, "but you bring back the memory of my own daughter who was lost long ago."

"Tell me about her," begged the Enchanter's daughter, for she felt in her heart that it would be her own story.

The woman took her hand. "When I was young," she said, "my husband died, leaving me with a young son and daughter. It was hard for me to work the farm alone, for the mountain land needs a strong hand. One day when I sat weary and sad, a rich man came by on a fine horse taking the road up into the mountains. He stopped to rest and we made him welcome. My little daughter climbed upon his knee and made him laugh with her childish play. We talked and, learning of our hardship, he offered me gold if I would let him take my daughter for his own. He promised that she should live like a princess, but still I could not part with her.

"The rich man rode on into the mountains while I held my daughter in my arms and watched him go. But the next day she went out to play with her brother on the mountainside and, when night came, she was nowhere to be found. Would that I had let the rich man take her, for then I would know that she still lived somewhere beyond the mountains!"

"What was her name?" asked the Enchanter's daughter, for she knew that she had once had a name and that she would know it again.

"We called her Thi-Phi-Yen," said the woman, "for she was like a pretty flying bird."

When the Enchanter's daughter heard the name, her dreams came back to her. She remembered how the Enchanter had smiled, saying, "You were only a pretty flying bird." And she knew that it was her own name.

Then Thi-Phi-Yen put her arms around her mother's neck and wept for joy. She told her how she had lived as the Enchanter's daughter through the long years and how she had crossed the high white mountains as a small bird to find her.

Thi-Phi-Yen and her mother held each other close to wipe out the memory of the long parting. "Now I have found you and my brother too," said Thi-Phi-Yen, "and if you will have me, I will never leave you again."

"But we are not rich," said her mother. "We work the farm and live a simple life. You have grown used to jewels and clothes of silk: you have had everything you could desire. You will think our life hard and unrewarding."

"You are wrong, Mother," said Thi-Phi-Yen. "The Enchanter gave me everything except freedom and love: now I have both. No riches can compare with freedom, and no power is greater than love. Am I not your daughter? I can work as hard as you and live as simply. Please tell me that I may stay."

"With all my heart," said her mother, "for life can give me no greater gift."

So it was that the Enchanter's daughter came home again. And from that day she lived happily with her mother and brother at the foot of the high white mountains that lie at the top of the world.

Fiona French (b. 1944)

English picture book artist Fiona French has retold a number of traditional stories in original ways since the late 1960s. Most of her illustrations in the late twentieth century combined silhouettes with bold colorful designs to suit different cultural settings. In *Snow White in New York* (1986), French deftly retains the basic contours and spare verbal style of the traditional folktale while adapting it to the Jazz Age world of 1920s New York. It takes only a few old-fashioned clichés and slang phrases early in the text, such as "poor little rich girl" and "classiest dame in New York," to refashion the Snow White story as an urban American melodrama. Like other modern fairy tale satires, this one alludes to traditional images in clever and amusing ways—for example, replacing the evil stepmother's magic mirror, symbol of her ruthless vanity, with the newspaper in which she loves to read of her own fame and Snow White's demise. This is a gentle satire that does not shock us into rethinking the traditional ending, as Roald Dahl does with "Little Red Riding Hood" and both Vivian Vande Velde and Sara Henderson Hay do with "Hansel and Gretel" (all in this section). Instead, it modernizes the tale by giving Snow White less stereotypical work to do when she meets seven jazz musicians, rather than seven woodland dwarfs who want her to keep house. The traditional "happily ever after" ending is twisted only slightly so that the rich heroine can marry a handsome working man who helps promote her talent.

Snow White in New York

Once upon a time in New York there was a poor little rich girl called Snow White. Her mother was dead and for a while she lived happily with her father. But one day he married again. . . .

All the papers said that Snow White's stepmother was the classiest dame in New York. But no one knew that she was the Queen of the Underworld. She liked to see herself in the *New York Mirror.*

But one day she read something that made her very jealous. "Snow White the Belle of New York City." And she plotted to get rid of her stepdaughter.

"Take her down and shoot her," she said to one of her bodyguards. The man took Snow White deep into the dark streets, but he could not do it. He left her there, lost and alone.

Snow White wandered the streets all night, tired

Fiona French transformed Snow White into a celebrity mourned on the streets of Jazz Age New York in her picture book *Snow White in New York* (1986).

and hungry. In the early morning she heard music coming from an open door. She went inside.

The seven jazz-men were sorry for her. "Stay here if you like," they said, "but you'll have to work," "What can I do?" she asked. "Can you sing?" said one of them.

The very first night Snow White sang there was a newspaper reporter in the club. He knew at once that she would be a star.

Next day Snow White was on the front page of the *New York Mirror.* The stepmother was mad with rage. "This time I shall get rid of her myself," she said. And so she decided to hold a grand party in honour of Snow White's success . . . but . . . secretly she dropped a poisoned cherry in a cocktail and handed it to Snow White with a smile.

All New York was shocked by the death of beautiful Snow White.

Crowds of people stood in the rain and watched Snow White's coffin pass by.

The seven jazz-men, their hearts broken, carried the coffin unsteadily up the church steps. Suddenly one of them stumbled, and, to everyone's amazement, Snow White opened her eyes. The first person she saw was the reporter. He smiled at her and she smiled back. The poisoned cherry that had been stuck in her throat was gone. She was alive.

Snow White and the reporter fell in love. They had a big society wedding, and the next day cruised off on a glorious honeymoon together.

Jon C. Stott (b. 1939)

Jon C. Stott, a Canadian educator, scholar, and editor, explains modern parodies of dragon stories within the historical and theoretical context of understanding how we learn conventions of language and literature. His 1990 essay shows how parodies, such as E. Nesbit's "The Last of the Dragons," mock literary conventions and question the social values reflected in traditional stories. He then demonstrates how to teach children in Grades 4 and 5 careful analysis of parodies in relation to conventional images and stories. Stott's conclusion eloquently affirms the educational and spiritual benefits of appreciating how stories provide structure and meaning in human culture. (See also the essay by Stott in Part 8.)

"Will the Real Dragon Please Stand Up?"

Convention and Parody in Children's Stories

The most important basic element of literature is not originality or creativity, but conventionality. That is because literature makes use of language, one of the most conventional tools of those most conventional creatures, human beings. Human beings communicate linguistically by means of widely accepted word structures, and the most structured use of words occurs in literature. Until we have mastered the conventions of our native tongue—its vocabulary and, more important, its grammar—we cannot converse. Until we have mastered the conventions of a culture's literature—its symbolic vocabulary and its narrative grammar—we cannot read that literature with true perception. It is necessary for us to internalize conventions, make them our own, before we are free to engage in the interaction between author and reader which constitutes the act of reading. If we do not understand the conventions the author is using to tell the story, he or she is speaking in a tongue foreign to us even though he or she may be using words and grammatical structures that we hear in our everyday speech. But if we do understand the author's conventions, we are engaging in an act which will continue long after the initial physical act of reading; we will truly be engaged in a creative and original enterprise.

I start with these commonplaces—I'm sure that you're all thoroughly familiar with them—because they have great importance for all of us who read literature and who teach literature to children. Because the types of words and the grammatical patterns of the stories we read are those of the newspaper and the radio, we often tend to think that reading a newspaper, an encyclopedia, or a textbook involves the same processes used in reading a short story, a novel, or a play. But that is only partly so. Within the same vocabulary and sentence structure is contained a startlingly new and different language, a special code that requires training and practice to acquire and use correctly, well, and fully.

Let me give you an example. Last year, a teacher working in a remote Alaskan Inuit community told me of a special event which took place every Friday in her school. One of the elders came to her classroom to tell one of the old stories. He spoke in simple but good English and the children loved his stories, reacting strongly to them. "At first," the teacher said, "I was lost. I just couldn't understand the point of them. They didn't seem to have any meaning to me. But by the end of the year, I was looking forward to the old man's Friday visits as much as my students were, and I was reacting as strongly to his stories as they were. I loved them!" Hers was an extreme case, for she was in a distant land, in an alien culture. But the stories were in English. Essentially, she had had to learn the literary language, the vocabulary and narrative structures, which were contained within the "normal" English in which the stories were told. *Learn*—that's the key word; she had to learn the conventions of a literary language. And we all have to if we want to read stories. That's how we are able to understand them.

If we are omnivorous readers, devouring everything, good and bad, in print, hiding a flashlight under our pillows, turning, as they used to say, into bookworms, we learn this language unawares, in the same way we learn our native tongue. But if we aren't omnivorous readers—and in this day of television, video games, computers, and community-organized sports leagues, most children aren't—we come to good stories, those which make skillful (Shall we say original and creative?) use of the conventions, like foreigners learning a new language, and we must be systematically (that does not mean dully) taught the vocabulary and grammar. Unfortunately, for many of us, this instruction began in high school or even college, and often as not, we were, to shift the metaphor, thrown in at the deep end and told to sink or swim. Most of us, and I certainly was one, sank at first. Luckily I came back to the surface; but I struggled for many years before I was able to swim without too much trouble.

What I will take up now is really a practical demonstration of the theoretical material I've just summarized. What are some of the conventions of literature? How do they work? What do they mean? And more important, how can we introduce these to elementary-school children in such a way that they can become more perceptive and appreciative readers of literature? How can we guide them without making them bored and without turning them off? To answer these questions, I'd like to talk about one of the most fabulous creatures ever found in literature, a creature who is far from extinct, who is, in fact, proliferating in stories at a rate that puts rabbits to shame: the dragon.

No one has ever seen a dragon; yet everyone has a general idea of what dragons look like and what they do. Dragons do exist, but only in one place: in stories. The earliest dragon stories are shrouded in the mists of antiquity, which is just a way of saying that no one can give an accurate date for the creation of the first one. Certainly they were being told thousands of years before the birth of Christ. Stories about dragons came from two general areas: the Orient and Europe. Our focus will be on European dragons, particularly those most popular in legends and tales told from the Middle Ages onward.

If no one has ever seen a dragon, where did the details that fill the hundreds of dragon stories come from? The answer is simple: from other dragon stories. Just as children learn to speak by listening to and imitating the language they hear and by relating words to appropriate aspects of the world around them, so storytellers imitated the stories they knew and related the various conventions to their inner, imaginative lives. In fact, by the time of the Middle Ages (and probably much earlier), it wasn't necessary to borrow from a specific story. A biology of dragons existed in people's minds, and even in learned tomes. People knew what dragons looked like, their characters, habits, and habitats, even if they had never seen a

dragon. In other words, a set of literary conventions had established itself; there existed a general vocabulary and grammar of dragon lore. Just as we do not readily possess every word and grammatical combination of words, but a general structural pattern which we apply to specific linguistic situations, so, too, storytellers possessed a literary grammar and vocabulary to be used for specific dragon stories.

Everyone knows the general physical characteristics of the European dragon: generally winged, it was huge, had a virtually impenetrable body covering, long sharp claws and teeth, a lethal barbed tail, and flaming breath. It was a terrible sight to behold, even when sleeping, as J. R. R. Tolkien's hobbit, Bilbo Baggins, discovers. Physically appalling, dragons were psychologically frightening as well, for they were extremely clever and had terrible tempers. Angered, they would wreak havoc on entire villages, breathing flames over everything. Their greatest love was treasure, not their own, but stolen or usurped treasure. However, working, it would seem, on the old adage that possession is nine-tenths of the law, they jealously guarded their ill-gotten wealth. Should the tiniest part of it be stolen, they literally flew into terrible rages and set about seeking revenge.

Dragons, of course, had to eat, and their favorite delicacies were virgins. Fearful villagers, to save themselves from the resident dragon's anger, would sacrifice one of the town's virgins to the dragon at regular intervals. For the ordinary virgin, there was little to do but to submit to the inevitable. But when the supply of ordinary virgins was exhausted and a royal princess was scheduled to be the next victim, it was a different story. Then a knight in shining armour, generally riding a white (i.e., pure) steed, would perform a daring rescue, not only ridding the locale of a great menace, but also earning the right to the princess's hand. These then, were the conventions of dragon lore, the vocabulary and grammar out of which individual stories were crafted.

Why, it should be asked, were these stories so incredibly popular? Early scholars suggested that the stories arose out of attempts to find answers for mysterious natural phenomena. Far-off, rumbling, flaming volcanoes were perhaps strange giant creatures; lightning flashing and thunder rumbling over distant mountains came from these beasts. When people attempted to describe these beasts, they took elements from animals they knew (bat wings, bear claws, lizard bodies), magnified them, and created a terrifying, monstrous amalgam.

Modern scholars generally reject such interpretations and search for answers in the nature of the human mind. Stories, it is argued, are linguistic structures that give shape and, therefore, meaning to our imaginative and psychological concerns. The dragon, with its appearance, size, and personality, represents those forces which we find most fearful and threatening. The dragon is the power of evil—physical, moral, psychological, and spiritual—which threatens to overwhelm us all. In the dragon story, small, frail, and vulnerable human beings face virtually insurmountable odds with little more than their goodness, courage and intellect; and they emerge victorious. The slaying of the dragon is thus a victory for the human soul. Not surprisingly, the medieval dragon was often associated with the Devil, and its opponents were good Christians. Edmund Spenser, an ardent supporter of the Protestant queen Elizabeth I, went one step further. In *The Faerie Queene,* he identified the dragon with the Catholic Church, bent on destroying England.

Over the last hundred years, a different type of dragon story has emerged: the parody. Parody, a very sophisticated form of literature extending back at least to the days of ancient Greece, is solidly based on established literary conventions. The parodist takes the grammar and vocabulary of a well-known story type or individual story and completely inverts them. The result is usually a humorous satire. For centuries, one of the favorite kinds of parody has been the mock-heroic. The patterns of such well-known epics as the *Iliad,* the *Odyssey,* the *Aeneid,* and *Paradise Lost* and of romances of questing knights have been used to tell the stories, for example, of an oversexed barnyard rooster tricked by a sly fox, or of a society quarrel caused by the snipping of a lock of a belle's hair. Over the last century, the theories of evolution and the terrors of world wars have seriously undermined the belief in heroic human endeavor. Small wonder that dragon stories have been used for ridicule. What if the knights are wimps, the damsels pump iron, and the dragons are cream puffs? If the writer could demonstrate the ridiculousness of the conventions of dragon stories, she or he could also cast doubt on the social values they embodied.

Kenneth Grahame's "The Reluctant Dragon," Ogden Nash's "The Tale of Custard the Dragon," and Robert Munsch's *The Paper Bag Princess* are three of the best-known dragon parodies. But perhaps one of the best is, unfortunately, one of the least-known: Edith Nesbit's *The Last of the Dragons.* When a princess is informed that, at age sixteen, she will have to be tied up and rescued from a dragon by a prince, she objects: "All the princes I know are such very silly little boys. . . . Couldn't we tie up one of the silly little princes for the dragon to look at—and then I could go and kill the dragon and rescue the prince? I fence much better than any of the princes we know." When the great day arrives, she and the prince conspire to face the dragon together. However, when they enter his lair, they discover that he doesn't want to fight. He tells the couple that all such fights are fixed, that he wouldn't want to eat a princess anyway—"I wouldn't touch the horrid thing"—and that he wants to be left alone. However, when the princess calls him "dear," he begins to cry and informs them, "I *am* tame. . . . That's what nobody but you has ever found out." He attends their wedding, becomes their gentle and devoted servant, and is named Fido.

One immediately sees the parodistic elements; this isn't what we expect from a dragon story. The princess, not the prince, is the skillful and brave person; the dragon is tame and isn't slain. However, underneath the parody, the story is every bit as serious as the typical dragon story. In mocking the literary conventions, *The Last of the Dragons* criticizes social conventions which blind us to true and better realities. The prince and princess are fettered by their socially imposed roles. She is expected to be delicately and uselessly feminine; bravery and physical abilities are not encouraged. However, underneath the royal exterior, we find, as well as bravery, true concern for others and tenderness. The prince, an incompetent as far as typical princes go, genuinely loves the princess and is willing to face what he thinks will be certain death for her sake. But the greatest victim of preconceived conventional notions is the last of the dragons. Whether or not others of his species have lived up to their biological and psychological characteristics, he has not. And because people expect princes to fulfill their assigned duties, he is in danger of dying without his true nature's ever being known. Only because he meets a royal couple as unconventional as he is does he get to lead a fulfilling life.

The Last of the Dragons is a rich and satisfying story. And the reader who is fully aware of the literary conventions that the story contains and the way in which Nesbit uses them is in a position to get a great deal more out of the story than the reader who is not aware of them.

Our general overview of literary structuralism, dragon lore, and parody has all been a preamble to the important business at hand: the teaching of these elements to a good Grade 4 or an early Grade 5 class. When we have finished, the children should be able to understand the concepts and should be able to apply them to *The Last of the Dragons,* to other stories they encounter, and to their own creative writing.

Although children may think they know a lot about dragons, they can learn a great deal more by looking at a series of slides taken from dragon pictures in *Dragons,* by Peter Hogarth and Val Clery. Each slide can be used to illustrate some of the points we have noted above. After looking at them, the children are given a sheet entitled "European Dragon-Lore," on which they list as many characteristics as they can remember. A general discussion follows in which children are able to hear each other's answers and add to their own lists. We now have the conventions—the literary grammar and vocabulary—to apply to the parody we read, *The Last of the Dragons.* As we go through the story, students are asked to raise their hands when they recognize a departure from the conventions.

When we have finished reading the story, we briefly discuss it generally and then consider the deviations from the conventions, noting that nearly everything seems to be upside down or reversed when compared to what we know about usual European dragons. At this point, the term *parody* is introduced: a story which turns things upside down, or that looks at serious story conventions humorously. *The Last of the Dragons* is a parody because it reverses typical elements of a dragon story and makes fun of them. Students are surprised when they are told that, although *parody* is a new term to them, they already know quite a few parodies. To illustrate my point this year, I wrote the words "Weird Al Yankovich" on the board and asked the children why I'd done that. After a moment or two, the students recognized that he is the composer of "Eat It,"

and that "Eat It" is a parody of Michael Jackson's smash hit, "Beat It." "And that's not the only parody you know," I tell them, asking if anyone can remember the TV series "The Greatest American Hero" and who it parodied. Those who read *Mad Magazine*—and large numbers of the children do—quickly realize that *Mad* often parodies popular TV shows and movies. Finally I have a couple of *Time* magazine "Persons of the Year" covers, which I show along with a *Time* "Person of the Year" card with a polaroid snapshot of myself and a *Mad* cover in which the person of the year is Pac Man.

Appreciation of parody requires that the reader do more than see general parallels: precise parallels and reversals exist. To emphasize that point, the children are asked to review their dragon-lore sheets. They are then given a sheet with the heading "Parody" and are asked to list all of the differences between the lore they noted and the story *The Last of the Dragons.* Parody, they learn, is not a careless or casual art.

They also learn that, in addition to having fun with the conventions of story types, parody can be used to convey a serious message. As we have seen above, *The Last of the Dragons* criticizes a society which assumes that conventional notions of people and dragons represent the truth and which doesn't take the trouble to discover the true natures of individuals. After asking the students how the king, the people, and even the prince and princess expected the dragon to act, we can consider why they had these expectations and how these initially prevented them from seeing the dragon as he really was. We can also ask why the princess was expected to be the victim and the prince, the rescuer. Here we want the students to see that social roles are imposed in spite of a person's abilities or qualities. Finally, we discuss how the prince, the princess, and the dragon achieve fulfillment because they refuse to be restricted by convention and do see others as they really are.

Our lessons on dragon lore and parody, and, implicitly, on literary structuralism, do not end here. After discussing *The Last of the Dragons,* we read Ogden Nash's poem "The Tale of Custard the Dragon." The title itself suggests that the poem may be a parody, as the name and the species are in conflict. Our object in studying this poem is to decide to what extent the poem is conventional and to what extent parodistic.

Children are asked to justify their point of view with specific references to the text, and most assert, correctly, that the poem is a mixture of convention and parody.

In one school in which I work, the teacher has created an individualized learning center on dragons to help reinforce the conventions and the concept of parody. The students can listen to tapes describing famous dragons and can read dragon stories. Writing activities include entering words into a dragon dictionary kept at the center (the words are those heard on the tapes which describe the dragons), filling out dragon lore and parody sheets for the stories read at the center, and writing dragon stories. For this last activity, we have a lined sheet which supplies the title, "The Day I Met a Dragon"; the instructions, "In this story, you are to tell what you saw, what you did, and how you felt"; and this opening, "It was a cold and windy day. There were clouds covering the sky, and the wind made sad sounds. I was walking through a valley filled with large, gray boulders. I turned a corner of the path, and there it was." For the center, the teacher has also gathered several books discussing dragons and several extra dragon storybooks. She uses these as the basis for report writing, a major activity in her language arts curriculum.

Our final activities involve further reinforcement of the concepts of story structure and parody. In Grade 5 classes, the major novel we study is Jean Craighead George's *Julie of the Wolves*. Along with it, we have looked at Paul Goble's *The Friendly Wolf* and have talked about the movie *Never Cry Wolf* and European folktales relating to wolves. With our experience with dragon lore and parodies as background, we are able to reconsider these wolf stories. We first introduce the ideas that stories can be classified and that groups of stories have definite characteristics: spy stories, desert island stories, dragon stories, and wolf stories. We list as many European wolf folktales as we can, and then we list their characteristics. Then we discuss the actual qualities of wolves, the qualities that native Americans have always known about and that modern researchers are only just discovering. *Julie, Never Cry Wolf,* and *The Friendly Wolf* are used to help us compile our lists. Using *The Last of the Dragons* as our model, the class discusses how it might write a parody of wolf stories and what they might include in such a parody. Each member of the class then writes a parody. The results

have, of course, been of varying quality, but generally they have been surprisingly good—perceptive and humorous.

Now that we've looked at some aspects of literary theory and analysis and their relationship to teaching literature to children, the questions remain, "So what? Why bother? All this is interesting, but how is it important educationally? We're only dealing with stories, after all." True, we are only dealing with stories. But if, as I believe, stories represent humanity's highest use of its special skills of linguistic communication, what we are doing is very important for several reasons.

First, in studying the conventions of dragon lore and their uses in specific stories, we are helping children to comprehend more fully the implications of the actual words they read or hear. We are helping them to get more out of specific works.

Second, in examining the nature of parody, we are helping children to understand the conventional nature of literary language. We are showing them that structural patterns inform all literature, and that when we have discovered the pattern of a specific story and related it to the general structure from which it derives, we can better understand the unity of the story. Not that we just look for the skeleton of the story and ignore the flesh; but the skeleton gives shape to the flesh. The literary pattern gives a framework which provides coherence for the details.

Finally, and most important, through our approach to literature study, we are strengthening the basic human intellectual impulse, what the poet Wallace Stevens called the "blessed rage for order," that is, the need to discover and create meaningful structures out of the unshaped chaos of experience. Knowledge is not merely an accumulation of unrelated facts. Indeed, a grab bag of facts is of use only to someone who wants to appear on "Hollywood Squares" or to play "Trivial Pursuit." Only when the human mind organizes these facts into patterns—discovers, the scientist would say, laws—is knowledge achieved. Literary study is a way of introducing the children to the structural basis of all knowledge. By learning the conventions—the vocabulary (facts) and the grammar (structure)—of dragon lore, they are doing what they must do in all areas of study.

Long before there were microscopes, telescopes, or computers, people turned to the storytellers, both religious and secular, for knowledge. These linguistic structure-makers used words to explain the meaning of the spiritual, physical, and social worlds in which people find themselves.

Nowadays, we don't often listen to our storytellers, our structure makers, as closely, as carefully, as we could. There are those people who would suggest that this is one of the reasons we find so few meaningful structures to give validity to our lives. And so, for those of us who teach language arts, what we do when we bring stories and children together is of vital importance. Through the stories we share, we are bringing young readers into the presence of some very good structuralists.

Through the way we present stories, the questions we ask, and the activities we initiate, we are helping young readers to better understand the significance of the structures created by great storytellers, and most important, we are helping them to acquire the ability to create their own structures, to give or find meaningful patterns for their lives, and to give their lives richness and dignity. The poet Robert Frost, who saw metaphors as basic poetic structures, once wrote that the only lost soul was the person who got lost in his material without a gathering metaphor (that is, structure) to give it shape and order. We do not want the children we know to be like Frost's lost souls. Through helping children to become better readers of literature, we can help them to find, not only themselves, but also the wonder and glory, the structures, of the worlds they relate to.

REFERENCES

George, Jean Craighead, *Julie of the Wolves.* New York: Harper & Row, 1972.

Goble, Paul, *The Friendly Wolf.* New York: Bradbury Press, 1974.

Grahame, Kenneth, "The Reluctant Dragon," in *Dream Days.* 1898. London: Bodley Head, 1979.

Hogarth, Peter, and Val Clery, *Dragons.* New York: Penguin, 1979.

Mowat, Farley, *Never Cry Wolf.* Toronto: McClelland & Stewart, 1963.

Munsch, Robert, *The Paper Bag Princess.* Toronto: Annick, 1980.

Nash, Ogden, *Custard and Company.* Boston: Little, Brown, 1980.

Nesbit, Edith, *The Last of the Dragons.* 1925. New York: McGraw-Hill, 1980.

E. Nesbit (1858–1924)

The English author Edith Nesbit wrote many books for children and adults, as well as poetry and plays. Though she viewed writing for children as a way to support her family while she focused on her adult writing and political activism, she is best remembered today for stories and novels that represent the transition from Victorian to modern writing for children. As a founder of the Fabian Society with her husband Hubert Bland, Nesbit combined fantasy and adventure with contemporary settings and progressive socialist ideals in her children's books. Although she focused on dragons in one of her first successful collections of stories, *The Book of Dragons,* which was published in 1900 (the same year as her most highly regarded novel, *The Story of the Treasure Seekers*), "The Last of the Dragons" appeared in a 1925 book published posthumously, *Five of Us—and Madeline.* After her death, interest in her stories and novels revived as critics noted her influence on writers of fantasy for children, such as C. S. Lewis and Joan Aiken.

Through humor, magic, and lively characterization, Nesbit mocked the pretensions and injustices of British society and gave child characters more autonomy and freedom than previous writers. This is certainly evident in the outspoken, rebellious princess in "The Last of the Dragons," who seeks the gender equality that many of Nesbit's other female characters enjoy. Jon Stott's essay reprinted earlier in this section argues that this Nesbit story deserves as much fame as the other most popular dragon satires of the past century. The heroine rejects the tradition in which princesses became passive victims, "tied up and helpless," destined to be rescued from dragons by strong knights. She insists that she is best suited to fight the dragon, since she is better at fencing than are the "silly" princes she knows. Stott's assertion that the princess helps the misunderstood, peace-loving dragon find a more fulfilling life may be debatable, since his type is all too common in subsequent children's books depicting tearful, self-deprecating dragons who beg to serve humans, but in 1925, working as an airplane was a radically unconventional role for a dragon. Moreover, although today's readers may question whether the princess compromises her independence too much to please her father and prince in the end, Stott recognizes the value of Nesbit's story in showing that all individuals, human or dragon, should be free from stereotypical characterizations and rigidly imposed social roles.

The Last of the Dragons

Of course you know that dragons were once as common as motor-omnibuses are now, and almost as dangerous. But as every well-brought-up prince was expected to kill a dragon, and rescue a princess, the dragons grew fewer and fewer till it was often quite hard for a princess to find a dragon to be rescued from. And at last there were no more dragons in France and no more dragons in Germany, or Spain, or Italy, or Russia. There were some left in China, and are still, but they are cold and bronzy, and there were never any, of course, in America. But the last real live dragon left was in England, and of course that was a very long time ago, before what you call English History began. This dragon lived in Cornwall in the big caves amidst the rocks, and a very fine dragon it was, quite seventy feet long from the tip of its fearful snout to the end of its terrible tail. It breathed fire and smoke, and rattled when it walked, because its scales were made of iron. Its wings were like half-umbrellas—or like bat's wings, only several thousand times bigger. Everyone was very frightened of it, and well they might be.

Now the King of Cornwall had one daughter, and when she was sixteen, of course she would have to go and face the dragon: such tales are always told in royal nurseries at twilight, so the Princess knew what she had to expect. The dragon would not eat her, of course—because the prince would come and rescue her. But the Princess could not help thinking it would be much pleasanter to have nothing to do with the dragon at all—not even to be rescued from him. "All the princes I know are such very silly little boys," she told her father. "Why must I be rescued by a prince?"

"It's always done, my dear," said the King, taking his crown off and putting it on the grass, for they were alone in the garden, and even kings must unbend sometimes.

"Father, darling," said the Princess presently, when she had made a daisy chain and put it on the King's head, where the crown ought to have been. "Father, darling, couldn't we tie up one of the silly little princes for the dragon to look at—and then *I* could go and kill the dragon and rescue the prince? I fence much better than any of the princes we know."

"What an unladylike idea!" said the King, and put his crown on again, for he saw the Prime Minister coming with a basket of new-laid Bills for him to sign. "Dismiss the thought, my child. I rescued your mother from a dragon, and you don't want to set yourself up above her, I should hope?"

"But this is the *last* dragon. It is different from all other dragons."

"How?" asked the King.

"Because he *is* the last," said the Princess, and went off to her fencing lessons, with which she took great pains. She took great pains with all her lessons—for she could not give up the idea of fighting the dragon.

She took such pains that she became the strongest and boldest and most skilful and most sensible princess in Europe. She had always been the prettiest and nicest.

And the days and years went on, till at last the day came which was the day before the Princess was to be rescued from the dragon. The Prince who was to do this deed of valour was a pale prince, with large eyes and a head full of mathematics and philosophy, but he had unfortunately neglected his fencing lessons. He was to stay the night at the palace, and there was a banquet.

After supper the Princess sent her pet parrot to the Prince with a note. It said:

Please, Prince, come on to the terrace. I want to talk to you without anybody else hearing.

—The Princess

So, of course, he went—and he saw her gown of silver a long way off shining among the shadows of the trees like water in starlight. And when he came quite close to her he said: "Princess, at your service," and bent his cloth-of-gold-covered knee and put his hand on his cloth-of-gold-covered heart.

"Do you think," said the Princess earnestly, "that you will be able to kill the dragon?"

"I will kill the dragon," said the Prince firmly, "or perish in the attempt."

"It's no use your perishing," said the Princess.

"It's the least I can do," said the Prince.

"What I'm afraid of is that it'll be the most you can do," said the Princess.

"It's the only thing I can do," said he, "unless I kill the dragon."

"Why you should do anything for me is what I can't see," said she.

"But I want to," he said. "You must know that I love you better than anything in the world."

When he said that he looked so kind that the Princess began to like him a little.

"Look here," she said, "no one else will go out tomorrow. You know they tie me to a rock and leave me—and then everybody scurries home and puts up the shutters and keeps them shut till you ride through the town in triumph shouting that you've killed the dragon, and I ride on the horse behind you weeping for joy."

"I've heard that that is how it is done," said he.

"Well, do you love me well enough to come very quickly and set me free—and we'll fight the dragon together?"

"It wouldn't be safe for you."

"Much safer for both of us for me to be free, with a sword in my hand, than tied up and helpless. *Do* agree."

He could refuse her nothing. So he agreed. And next day everything happened as she had said.

When he had cut the cords that tied her to the rock they stood on the lonely mountainside looking at each other.

"It seems to me," said the Prince, "that this ceremony could have been arranged without the dragon."

"Yes," said the Princess, "but since it has been arranged with the dragon—"

"It seems such a pity to kill the dragon—the last in the world," said the Prince.

"Well then, don't let's," said the Princess; "let's tame it not to eat princesses but to eat out of their hands. They say everything can be tamed by kindness."

"Taming by kindness means giving them things to eat," said the Prince. "Have you got anything to eat?"

She hadn't, but the Prince owned that he had a few biscuits. "Breakfast was so very early," said he, "and I thought you might have felt faint after the fight."

"How clever," said the Princess, and they took a biscuit in each hand. And they looked here, and they looked there, but never a dragon could they see.

"But here's its trail," said the Prince, and pointed to where the rock was scarred and scratched so as to make a track leading to a dark cave. It was like cart-ruts in a Sussex road, mixed with the marks of sea-gull's feet on the sea-sand. "Look, that's where it's dragged its brass tail and planted its steel claws."

"Don't let's think how hard its tail and claws are," said the Princess, "or I shall begin to be frightened—and I know you can't tame anything, even by kindness, if you're frightened of it. Come on. Now or never."

She caught the Prince's hand in hers and they ran along the path towards the dark mouth of the cave. But they did not run into it. It really was so very *dark*.

So they stood outside, and the Prince shouted: "What ho! Dragon there! What ho within." And from the cave they heard an answering voice and great clattering and creaking. It sounded as though a rather large cotton-mill were stretching itself and waking up out of its sleep.

The Prince and the Princess trembled, but they stood firm.

"Dragon—I say, dragon!" said the Princess, "do come out and talk to us. We've brought you a present."

"Oh yes—I know your presents," growled the dragon in a huge rumbling voice. "One of those precious princesses, I suppose? And I've got to come out and fight for her. Well, I tell you straight, I'm not going to do it. A fair fight I wouldn't say no to—a fair fight and no favour—but one of those put-up fights where you've got to lose—no! So I tell you. If I wanted a princess I'd come and take her, in my own time—but I don't. What do you suppose I'd do with her, if I'd got her?"

"Eat her, wouldn't you?" said the Princess, in a voice that trembled a little.

"Eat a fiddle-stick end," said the dragon very rudely. "I wouldn't touch the horrid thing."

The Princess's voice grew firmer.

"Do you like biscuits?" she said.

"No," growled the dragon.

"Not the nice little expensive ones with sugar on the top?"

"*No,*" growled the dragon.

"Then what *do* you like?" asked the Prince.

"You go away and don't bother me," growled the dragon, and they could hear it turn over, and the clang and clatter of its turning echoed in the cave like the sound of the steam-hammers in the Arsenal at Woolwich.

The Prince and Princess looked at each other. What *were* they to do? Of course it was no use going home and telling the King that the dragon didn't want princesses—because His Majesty was very old-fashioned and would never have believed that a new-fashioned dragon could ever be at all different from an old-fashioned dragon. They could not go into the cave and kill the dragon. Indeed, unless he attacked the Princess it did not seem fair to kill him at all.

"He must like something," whispered the Princess, and she called out in a voice as sweet as honey and sugar-cane:

"Dragon! Dragon dear!"

"WHAT?" shouted the dragon. "Say that again!" and they could hear the dragon coming towards them through the darkness of the cave. The Princess shivered, and said in a very small voice:

"Dragon—Dragon dear!"

And then the dragon came out. The Prince drew his sword, and the Princess drew hers—the beautiful silver-handled one that the Prince had brought in his motor-car. But they did not attack; they moved slowly back as the dragon came out, all the vast scaly length of him, and lay along the rock—his great wings half-spread and his silvery sheen gleaming like diamonds in the sun. At last they could retreat no further—the dark rock behind them stopped their way—and with their backs to the rock they stood swords in hand and waited.

The dragon grew nearer and nearer—and now they could see that he was not breathing fire and smoke as they had expected—he came crawling slowly towards them wriggling a little as a puppy does when it wants to play and isn't quite sure whether you're not cross with it.

And then they saw that great tears were coursing down its brazen cheek.

"Whatever's the matter?" said the Prince.

"Nobody," sobbed the dragon, "ever called me 'dear' before!"

"Don't cry, dragon dear," said the Princess. "We'll call you 'dear' as often as you like. We want to tame you."

"I *am* tame," said the dragon—"that's just it. That's what nobody but you has ever found out. I'm so tame that I'd eat out of your hands."

"Eat what, dragon dear?" said the Princess. "Not biscuits?" The dragon slowly shook his heavy head.

"Not biscuits?" said the Princess tenderly. "What, then, dragon dear?"

"Your kindness quite undragons me," it said. "No one has ever asked any of us what we like to eat—always offering us princesses, and then rescuing them—and never once, 'What'll you take to drink the King's health in?' Cruel hard I call it," and it wept again.

"But what would you like to drink our health in?" said the Prince. "We're going to be married today, aren't we, Princess?"

She said that she supposed so.

"What'll I take to drink your health in?" asked the dragon. "Ah, you're something like a gentleman, you are, sir. I don't mind if I do, sir. I'll be proud to drink you and your good lady's health in a tiny drop of"—its voice faltered—"to think of you asking me so friendly like," it said. "Yes, sir, just a tiny drop of puppuppup-puppupetrol—tha-that's what does a dragon good, sir—"

"I've lots in the car," said the Prince, and was off down the mountain in a flash. He was a good judge of character and knew that with this dragon the Princess would be safe.

"If I might make so bold," said the dragon, "while the gentleman's away—p'raps just to pass the time you'd be so kind as to call me Dear again, and if you'd shake claws with a poor old dragon that's never been anybody's enemy but his own—well, the last of the dragons'll be the proudest dragon that's ever been since the first of them."

It held out an enormous paw, and the great steel hooks that were its claws closed over the Princess's hand as softly as the claws of the Himalayan bear will close over the bit of bun you hand it through the bars at the Zoo.

And so the Prince and Princess went back to the palace in triumph, the dragon following them like a pet dog. And all through the wedding festivities no one drank more earnestly to the happiness of the bride and bridegroom than the Princess's pet dragon—whom she had at once named Fido.

And when the happy pair were settled in their own kingdom, Fido came to them and begged to be allowed to make himself useful.

"There must be some little thing I can do," he said, rattling his wings and stretching his claws. "My wings and claws and so on ought to be turned to some account—to say nothing of my grateful heart."

So the Prince had a special saddle or howdah made for him—very long it was—like the tops of many tramcars fitted together. One hundred and fifty seats were fitted to this, and the dragon, whose greatest pleasure was now to give pleasure to others, delighted in taking parties of children to the seaside. It flew through the air quite easily with its hundred and fifty little passengers—and would lie on the sand patiently waiting till they were ready to return. The children were very fond of it, and used to call it Dear, a word which never failed to bring tears of affection and gratitude to its eyes. So it lived, useful and respected, till quite the other day—when someone happened to say, in his hearing, that dragons were out-of-date, now so much new machinery had come in. This so distressed him that he asked the King to change him into something less old-fashioned, and the kindly monarch at once changed him into a mechanical contrivance. The dragon, indeed, became the first aeroplane.

Jack Prelutsky (b. 1940)

Jack Prelutsky, a native of Brooklyn, New York, has written and edited many poetry collections for children that are successful in Britain as well as America. His own poems in books such as *The New Kid on the Block* (1986) reflect his belief that short, humorous poems are most relevant to contemporary children. His early experience as a singer influenced the lyrical style and easy rhythms of his poems. These selections from the seventeen poems in his popular 1993 book, *The Dragons Are Singing Tonight,* show how Prelutsky often combines fascination with mysterious, and sometimes frightening, creatures from folklore and mythology with scenes from the everyday lives of children. As a collection of lyric poems offering brief and varied glimpses of child-centered scenes, this book is comparable to Robert Louis Stevenson's *A Child's Garden of Verses* (see Part 4), except that as a whole it is more limited in length and scope, focusing on the single theme of dragons. While Prelutsky's verse is often lighthearted and comical, it is not condescending toward dragons or children like some parodies of ancient lore and stories of tame dragons. The youthful human speakers in some of these poems are filled with longing for glittering dragons of their own or wait for a dragon egg to hatch. One is "enchanted and filled with delight" to hear dragons sing once a year, while another shows off her herd of pet dragons purchased at the mall, and another worried girl feeds her sick dragon gasoline. Other dragons are created by the imaginations of a child in a bathtub, a boy plagued by his computer, and a resourceful mechanic recycling junkyard objects. The dragons who speak for themselves in other poems reveal a range of personalities, some amiable and some weary of being doubted or feared by people. There are gentle spoofs of traditional fire-breathing dragons, but the variety of details and attitudes conveyed leaves plenty of scope for the imagination to appreciate old and new perspectives on these ancient fantastical creatures.

From *The Dragons Are Singing Tonight*

A DRAGON'S LAMENT

I'm tired of being a dragon,
Ferocious and brimming with flame,
The cause of unspeakable terror
When anyone mentions my name.
I'm bored with my bad reputation
For being a miserable brute,
And being routinely expected
To brazenly pillage and loot.

I wish that I weren't repulsive,
Despicable, ruthless, and fierce,
With talons designed to dismember
And fangs finely fashioned to pierce.
I've lost my desire for doing
The deeds any dragon should do,
But since I can't alter my nature,
I guess I'll just terrify you.

MY DRAGON'S BEEN DISCONSOLATE

My dragon's been disconsolate
And cannot help but pout,
Since he defied a thunderstorm
That put his fire out.

MY DRAGON WASN'T FEELING GOOD

My dragon wasn't feeling good,
He had a nasty chill
And couldn't keep from shivering,
I saw that he was ill.

His eyes were red and watery,
His nose was running too,
His flame was but a fizzle,
And his cheeks were pallid blue.

I took him to a doctor
Just as quickly as I could,
A specialist in dragons,
And she's in our neighborhood.
She took his pulse and temperature,
Then fed him turpentine
And phosphorus and gasoline—
My dragon's doing fine.

DRAGONBRAG

Once upon a happenstance
I met a knight in armor.
I fixed my flame upon his lance—
It was a four-alarmer!

I HAVE A SECRET DRAGON

I have a secret dragon
Who is living in the tub,
It greets me when I take a bath,
And gives my back a scrub.
My parents cannot see it,
They don't suspect it's there,
They look in its direction,
And all they see is air.

My dragon's very gentle,
My dragon's very kind,

No matter how I pull its tail,
My dragon doesn't mind.
We splash around together
And play at silly things,
Then when I'm finished bathing,
It dries me with its wings.

IF YOU DON'T BELIEVE IN DRAGONS

If you don't believe in dragons,
It is curiously true
That the dragons you disparage
Choose to not believe in you.

Roald Dahl (1916–90)

Roald Dahl, one of the most popular British writers for children in the twentieth century, is best known for offbeat, humorous fantasy novels, such as *James and the Giant Peach* (1961), *Charlie and the Chocolate Factory* (1971), and *The BFG* (1982). After World War II, he became a successful writer of short stories for adults, but he suffered through injury in the military, serious illnesses in his family, and the death of a seven-year-old daughter. Although his outrageously irreverent books were criticized for vulgarity and cruelty, Dahl maintained that children have a cruder sense of humor than do adults. His novels for children blend some of the magical elements, exaggerated characters, and stark outlines of folktales with both harsh and heartwarming realities of modern life.

Roald Dahl's Revolting Rhymes (1982) is a slim volume that retells six classic fairy tales in satiric singsong couplets. The drawings by popular English illustrator Quentin Blake are as quirky and energetic as Dahl's verses. Dahl subverts the Little Red Riding Hood story (especially as it was told by Charles Perrault—see Part 1) when the focus on the wolf's greedy violence gives way to some metafictional dialogue: the girl confuses the wolf by not following the conversational formula of old tales (thereby drawing attention to the familiar structure of the tale as a storytelling tradition). The surprise ending, exchanging violence with violence, resembles the climax in a similar satire in *Fables for Our Time* (1939), where James Thurber provides the moral, "It is not so easy to fool little girls nowadays as it used to be." Dahl's fracturing of fairy tales becomes even wackier in the book's last poem, when Little Red Riding Hood reappears to shoot another wolf in "The Three Little Pigs." The book ends with a parody of the moralistic verses that Charles Perrault added to his seventeenth-century fairy tales: "Oh piglet you must never trust / Young ladies from the upper crust." Miss Riding Hood's "*two* wolfskin coats" and "PIGSKIN TRAVELING CASE" may seem shockingly brutal, but Dahl's poems actually fall within the tradition of tales published since at least the nineteenth century for young children; for example, greedy or hungry predators triumph mercilessly in Lewis Carroll's poem "The Walrus and the Carpenter" (in *Through the Looking-Glass*) and in folktales such as "Henny Penny" and "The Gingerbread Man" or "The Pancake" (see the latter in Part 3). Dahl, Thurber, and other twentieth-century satirists ridiculed classic tales about girls as passive victims, while the African American "A Wolf and Little Daughter" (by Virginia Hamilton in *The People Could Fly*) and other girl versus wolf stories that have been retold in recent decades show that some folktales in older oral traditions featured girls who could fend for themselves.

Little Red Riding Hood and the Wolf

As soon as Wolf began to feel
That he would like a decent meal,
He went and knocked on Grandma's door.
When Grandma opened it, she saw
The sharp white teeth, the horrid grin,
And Wolfie said, "May I come in?"
Poor Grandmamma was terrified,
"He's going to eat me up!" she cried.
And she was absolutely right.
He ate her up in one big bite.
But Grandmamma was small and tough,
And Wolfie wailed, "That's not enough!"
"I haven't yet begun to feel
"That I have had a decent meal!"
He ran around the kitchen yelping,
"I've *got* to have another helping!"
Then added with a frightful leer,
"I'm therefore going to wait right here
"Till Little Miss Red Riding Hood
"Comes home from walking in the wood."
He quickly put on Grandma's clothes,
(Of course he hadn't eaten those.)
He dressed himself in coat and hat.
He put on shoes and after that
He even brushed and curled his hair,
Then sat himself in Grandma's chair.
In came the little girl in red.
She stopped. She stared. And then she said,

"*What great big ears you have, Grandma.*"
"*All the better to hear you with,*" the Wolf replied.
"*What great big eyes you have, Grandma,*" said
    Little Red Riding Hood.
"*All the better to see you with,*" the Wolf replied.

He sat there watching her and smiled.
He thought, I'm going to eat this child.
Compared with her old Grandmamma
She's going to taste like caviare.

Then Little Red Riding Hood said, "*But Grandma,
    what a lovely great big furry coat you have on.*"
"That's wrong!" cried Wolf. "Have you forgot
"To tell me what BIG TEETH I've got?

"Ah well, no matter what you say,
"I'm going to eat you anyway."
The small girl smiles. One eyelid flickers.
She whips a pistol from her knickers.
She aims it at the creature's head
And *bang bang bang,* she shoots him dead.
A few weeks later, in the wood,
I came across Miss Riding Hood.
But what a change! No cloak of red,
No silly hood upon her head.
She said, "Hello, and do please note
"My lovely furry WOLFSKIN COAT."

Wolf "quickly put on Grandma's clothes (Of course he hadn't eaten those)." Quentin Blake's line-and-wash pictures enhance Roald Dahl's modern satire in "Little Red Riding Hood and the Wolf."

Vivian Vande Velde (b. 1951)

Vivian Vande Velde is an American writer of fantasies and fairy tale adaptations who has always enjoyed playing with new combinations of elements from old stories. Her 1992 novel *Dragon's Bait,* about a girl wrongly accused of witchcraft who is helped by the dragon that was supposed to eat her, shows her interest in revising traditional motifs to create sympathy for characters who are typically assumed to be the villains. A young adult vampire novel with a modern setting, *Companions of the Night,* and the story "Twins" reflect the same desire to lead the reader away from stereotypical conceptions instilled by folklore traditions and cultural biases. *The Rumpelstiltskin Problem* (2000) presents six variations on a tale that, according to this book, makes no sense in its well-known traditional form.

"Twins" was published in 1995, along with twelve other fairy tale adaptations, in *Tales from the Brothers Grimm and Sisters Weird.* Some of Vande Velde's stories are comical and lighthearted, or brutally realistic, as when a beautiful swan, the former ugly duckling, punishes his persecutors by pecking them to death. "Twins" demonstrates Vande Velde's interest in mystery and horror and in reexamining the roles of women and children. The familiar cast of characters, objects, and events make us wonder whether we misunderstood "Hansel and Gretel" when we heard it before. As in other postmodern reworkings of fairy tales, traditional motifs are twisted in ways that challenge readers to reassemble their knowledge of a familiar fairy tale and then question the assumptions about human psychology or society on which it appeared to be built. Vande Velde seems to vindicate both the stepmother and the elderly neighbor who wants the children to leave her property alone, but the story leaves many unanswered questions about the actions and fates of all the characters, including the death of the children's natural mother.

Twins

Once upon a time, before Medicare or golden-age retirement communities, there lived a beautiful young girl named Isabella, who stayed at home to take care of her parents. The boys in the village would whistle when they walked by her house and they'd call out, "Isabella, come out and play," or "Isabella, come see Clarence's new puppy," or "Isabella, will you watch us race?"

But Isabella always said no, she had to take care of her parents.

The years passed, and Isabella became a beautiful young woman. The young men of the village would carry flowers to her door and they'd say, "Isabella, come out for a picnic," or "Isabella, come to the dance," or "Isabella, will you kiss me?"

But Isabella always said no, she had to take care of her parents.

Until the day Isabella's parents died.

All the young men she had grown up with had married long ago, or they had left the village to seek their fortunes. There were new young men, of course. But—although they knew Isabella as a kind and gentle woman—they were too young to remember when Isabella had been young and beautiful, and they never came knocking at her door.

Then one day, one of her old suitors who had left the village came back. He was stooped and haggard, looking older than he was, and more wary and suspicious than Isabella remembered. The man's name was Siegfried and he was a woodcutter who lived in a small cottage in the forest. But his wife had just died and he needed help to raise his two small children.

Isabella was horrified when she learned that Siegfried had left his children alone in the cottage in the woods while he came to the village, and she immediately agreed to marry him and take care of all of them.

And beautiful children they were, Isabella thought when she and her new husband arrived back at the cottage, as beautiful as the carved marble angels over the doors of the cathedral. A boy and a girl, obviously twins, they couldn't have been older than six or seven.

"Hansel," Siegfried said to the boy, "Gretel," he said to the girl, "say hello to your new mother."

Isabella stooped down to hug the children, but Gretel said, "She's not our mother."

And Hansel said, "Our mother's dead." Then he added, "Our mother didn't love us."

And Gretel finished, "She wouldn't have died if she did."

How incredibly sad, Isabella thought. *Oh, the poor, sweet dears.* Her eyes filled with tears for the sad, sad children. "Of course your mother loved you," she said. "She didn't *want* to leave you. And I'm not here to replace her. Nobody could ever do that. But I'm here to love you and take care of you just the way your mother did."

"How can you love us . . ." Hansel started.

And Gretel finished, ". . . when you've only just met us?"

The two children looked at each other. Their expressions never changed. In fact, Isabella thought, they really *had* no expressions: not happy, nor sad, nor angry. Just . . . *there.*

She said, "But your father's told me so much about you."

Which wasn't true. All he had said was that their mother had died and that he needed help to raise them. He hadn't even said how their mother had died.

Now the children were looking at each other again, in silence. Simultaneously their gaze went back to Isabella. *They know I just lied,* she guessed. It had seemed such a kind and harmless thing to say.

"Children," Siegfried murmured as though begging them to give Isabella a chance.

Still without a word, the children turned to leave.

"Wait," Isabella called. "I have brought you gifts."

The children stopped. Turned. Waited.

Isabella went to the small bag in which she had packed all her worldly possessions. "Hansel," she called, but both children approached. "Hold out your hand."

Hansel did.

Gretel watched with large, pale, unblinking eyes.

Isabella put her father's gold pocket watch into his palm, letting the chain run through her fingers one last time. "This was my father's," she said. "His father was a famous watchmaker, and he made it."

Hansel watched her with large, pale, unblinking eyes.

"Hold it up to your ear," Isabella said, trying to get him to bend his elbow. "Listen to it tick."

Gretel said, "We're too little to know how to tell time."

"But you can learn." Isabella felt her heart sinking.

Hansel said, "There's never anyplace to go in the woods. And no special time to be there." He moved to hand the watch back to Isabella, but she wouldn't take it.

"Keep it," she told him. "You may want it when you're older." To Gretel she said, "I have something for you, too. From my mother." But now her hand shook. Isabella took Gretel's cold hand and placed her mother's wedding ring on one of the child's fingers.

"It's too big," Hansel said as his sister lifted her hand and pointed her tiny fingers down, letting the ring fall back into Isabella's hand.

"You'll grow into it," Isabella said, putting the ring back on Gretel's finger.

"It isn't something to wear in the woods," Gretel said. Again she let the ring drop from her finger.

And Hansel let the watch drop.

Isabella stopped the ring from rolling under the bed, but the glass on the watch had cracked. "I'm sorry," she said, "there was no time to buy or make . . ." But when she looked up, the children had left and she could see them walking hand in hand out the front door. "I'm sorry," she whispered after them. She looked up at Siegfried, who shrugged as though he didn't know what to say either.

The next days were not easy ones. Try as she would, Isabella could not get the two children to like her.

The first day after her arrival, Isabella spent making a dress for Gretel from the pink cloth that the children's mother had woven before she died. All day long, while the children played outside, Isabella cut and pieced and sewed. Supper was a quiet and solemn meal, with Siegfried tired—having been out since dawn chopping wood—and with Isabella's fingers sore and needle-pricked from sewing, and with the children . . . with the children sitting there saying nothing, but only watching everything with their large, pale eyes. After supper Isabella worked by candlelight, finishing the dress just in time to present it to Gretel before bedtime.

"I don't like pink," Gretel said, though she'd seen Isabella work on the pink cloth all day.

"She's never liked pink," Hansel said.

"Children," Siegfried pleaded.

But the children turned their cold eyes on him, and he ducked his head and said no more.

"I didn't know," Isabella apologized. "I'm sorry, I didn't know."

The second day after her arrival, Isabella spent making a jacket for Hansel.

"Do you like this color?" she asked before she started, holding up the green cloth.

"Yes," Hansel answered as he and his sister went out to play.

But that night, after cutting and piecing and sewing, when Isabella presented him with the jacket, Hansel said, "It's wool. I don't like wool. It itches."

"No, it doesn't," Isabella said, "not if you wear it over a shirt."

"Much too itchy," Gretel said.

Their father said nothing.

The third day after her arrival, Isabella spent baking cakes as a special supper treat. While she worked, there came a tapping at the door.

"Yes?" she said to the old woman who stood there nervously twisting her cane.

"Excuse me," the woman said, squinting nearsightedly at Isabella, "but I'm your neighbor. The baker's widow. I live on the land that borders on your woods."

Isabella was about to thank her for coming over to introduce herself, but the old woman continued speaking.

"You see, it's about them children of yours. Yesterday they come and throwed stones all over my garden. I saw them just as they was walking down the last row, dropping stones as they went. It's an awful mess, and it's going to take me the better part of a week to pick up. I hate to complain, but isn't there anything you can do?"

"I'm so sorry," Isabella gasped, feeling even worse because the woman seemed so apologetic. "I had no idea. I'll send them over to clean up—"

"No," the woman hastily interrupted her. And again, "No. No need for that. I just wanted to let you know." She kept bobbing her head, almost as though bowing, as she hobbled backward with her cane. "So sorry to bother you," she said.

At supper the children ate the cakes but said they were dry and flat and that even their mother's cakes had been better.

Isabella ignored the stinging in her eyes and said, "Our neighbor has been having a problem with stones in her garden."

Hansel said, "The soil around here is very rocky."

"Perhaps so," Isabella said, not wanting to accuse them, "but she says she saw you playing there and she thinks you might have accidentally brought some of the stones in with you."

"Our neighbor is very old," Gretel said. "She doesn't know what she sees."

"And she's never liked us," Hansel added.

Isabella looked to her husband to say something. But all he said was, "Perhaps," which said nothing.

The fourth day after her arrival, Isabella stopped the children as they went out to play. "Why don't you take this cake to our neighbor?" she asked.

The children looked at each other in that way that made Isabella almost think they were talking to each other without words.

Gretel asked, "To apologize for putting stones in her garden?"

"We already told you we didn't do that," Hansel said.

Isabella said, "And I believed you," although she didn't. "But this is simply to cheer her up about the stones, however they got there."

Hansel and Gretel looked at her with their unblinking eyes and expressionless faces. But they took the cake.

Later that morning as Isabella stood on the front stoop to shake out the dust from the rugs, she saw birds gathered on the path the children had taken. She stepped closer and saw what attracted them. It was pieces of the cake.

That evening, after the children had come home from playing and while Siegfried was still outside washing up at the water barrel by the front door, Isabella asked the children, "Did you take the cake to our neighbor as I asked you to?"

"Yes," Gretel said.

Hansel added, "She said it was dry and flat."

Isabella looked into their faces and couldn't bring herself to accuse them of lying. "Did part of the cake break off before you got there?" she asked.

"No," Hansel said.

"No," Gretel said.

Isabella had never raised children before and wasn't sure how they were supposed to act. She tried to remember when she had been a child herself and was fairly certain she had never acted like this.

The fifth day after her arrival, Isabella woke up later than usual because she'd spent a good deal of the night crying softly. Siegfried, who'd put his arms around her but said nothing, had already left to chop wood in the forest.

When Isabella opened her eyes, the first thing she saw was Gretel standing right by the side of the bed, looking at her. Isabella shivered although it wasn't cold. "Good morning," she said, but Gretel didn't say anything.

To get away from Gretel's staring eyes, Isabella turned to get her comb from the nightstand on the other side of the bed.

And there was Hansel standing right by that side of the bed, looking at her.

"What are you doing?" Isabella asked.

It was Gretel, behind her, who answered. "We made you breakfast."

Isabella turned to look at her, and Hansel—behind her—said, "We hope you like it."

Again Isabella shivered. "Why don't the two of you go out and play?" she suggested.

Without a word, without a change of expression, the two children left the house.

The breakfast that the children had made for her was porridge. They had gathered berries for it, which spread purple stains across the pale lumps of cereal in the bowl. This was the first time the children had made any effort to do anything for her, Isabella told herself. The porridge was probably meant as an apology for the night before. And yet . . . And yet it looked too ghastly to eat.

She dumped the contents of the bowl out the door and, as the day progressed, watched the grass beneath shrivel and die.

The children had lived in the woods all their lives, Isabella told herself. Surely they should know which berries were good to eat and which were not.

But she couldn't bring herself to believe they'd intentionally try to do her harm.

That evening Siegfried came home from chopping wood before the children returned from playing. Isabella set the table and kept stirring and stirring the stew so that it wouldn't overheat and stick to the pot, but still the children did not come. "Call them," she asked of Siegfried, not daring to admit to him that they never came when she called.

Siegfried stood in the doorway and called, "Hansel! Gretel! Dinner!"

Still the children did not come.

Isabella's annoyance began to turn to worry. What if something had happened to the children? What if they didn't come home because they couldn't? One moment she thought something dreadful must have happened, the next that something dreadful *better* have happened or she was going to punish those children as they had never been punished before.

Isabella walked to the end of the front walk. "Gretel!" she called. "Hansel! Come home NOW!"

The edge of the sky faded from orange to pink to gray to black, and still the children did not come.

Siegfried took a lantern out into the woods. Isabella could see the light bobbing between the trees as he walked down to the stream; she could hear him calling and calling. He didn't come back until his voice was practically gone. "No sign of them at the stream," he whispered hoarsely; no sign of them anywhere.

They left the shutters open, with candles in the windows to guide the children home, and they left the fire in the hearth to warm the children when they came home.

But the children didn't come home.

Isabella wept loudly, telling Siegfried how she had slighted Hansel and Gretel at breakfast. Now she thought of them out alone in the woods, cold and frightened and hungry, not knowing—very obviously not knowing—which berries were good to eat and which were not.

"There, there," Siegfried said, patting her back awkwardly. "There, there."

When the sixth morning after Isabella's arrival dawned, Hansel and Gretel still had not returned.

"One of us needs to be here," Isabella told Siegfried, still hoping the children might find their own way back. "But I would like to go out to search."

The first place Isabella went was to the stream behind the house. But even in the daylight there was no sign that the children had gone swimming there: no discarded shoes, no footprints in the muddy bank. Isabella went farther and farther into the woods, calling and calling, praying that no hungry animal nor desperate highwayman had come upon the helpless children.

She found nothing that even hinted the children might have passed by that way.

Once again at night they left the lights burning in hearth and windows, and once again the children did not come home.

At dawn of the seventh day after Isabella's arrival, Isabella started out once again. This time she headed in the opposite direction, toward the village. Surely in this direction there was not enough of the woods for the children to get lost in before they came upon the outlying houses, and from there they certainly would have been able to find their way back home. Still, Isabella thought she could enlist the help of the villagers in searching for the poor lost dears.

But before she got to the village, she got to the house of their neighbor, the baker's widow who had come to call about the stones in her garden. Smoke was pouring merrily from the chimney in the kitchen and also from the large, stone baker's oven in the front yard, and Isabella knocked at the door to inquire if the old woman had seen the children.

The door opened, and it was Gretel who stood there, with Hansel behind her, neither saying a word, both looking at her with large staring eyes.

"Gretel!" Isabella cried, throwing herself to her knees and flinging her arms around the young girl. "Hansel!" She tried to bring him into the hug, but he evaded her embrace, and Gretel squirmed away, too.

Isabella sat back on her heels. "We were so worried," she said. "You must have been so frightened, being lost."

They didn't look frightened. And they didn't say anything.

"You must have just found your way back here this morning," Isabella said.

"No," Hansel said.

"We've been here all the while," Gretel said.

Isabella couldn't see why the baker's widow would have let the children stay in her house for two long nights without letting anybody know. She tried to see over the heads of the children into the house. There were half-eaten ginger cakes and pastry treats all over the table, crumbs tracked on the floor, tiny jelly handprints on the walls.

The old woman couldn't be home, Isabella thought. She must have gone to the village three days ago, and the children just let themselves in. But surely the old woman wouldn't have left the oven going like that. "Where is our neighbor?" Isabella asked, feeling suddenly very small and frightened.

"Right behind you," Gretel said.

"In the front yard," Hansel said.

Isabella turned around, but there was no one there, nothing there, only the oven smoking away.

And the old woman's cane, lying on the ground before it.

Isabella scrambled to her feet, telling herself that surely there was a different explanation, surely she misunderstood everything.

The children looked at her with calm, unblinking eyes.

"What have you done?" Isabella whispered.

"She didn't like us," Hansel said.

"We didn't like her," Gretel said.

"What have you done?" Isabella cried.

"Don't yell at us," Gretel said. "She was a witch."

"She was definitely a witch," Hansel agreed. "We don't like being yelled at."

"She was just a poor old woman," Isabella shouted, "half blind and half lame."

Gretel turned in the doorway to look at Hansel. Hansel nodded. They both looked at Isabella.

Isabella took a step back.

"We don't like being yelled at," Gretel said.

Isabella took another step back. Her voice shaking, she asked, "How did your mother die?"

Once again Gretel looked over her shoulder at Hansel.

Hansel said, "We don't like you."

Isabella kept on backing up until she reached the end of the walkway, then she turned and ran. Her heart pounding wildly, she ran and ran till she spotted their own cottage in the woods. She considered stopping for Siegfried but then she ran on.

After all, he was the one who had gotten her into this.

Sara Henderson Hay (1906–87)

Sara Henderson Hay, a native of Pennsylvania, published six volumes of poetry for adults. She often wrote about nature, children, and the roles of women with ironic humor. *Story Hour* (1963) is a collection of sonnets that tease us into reinterpreting the characters and events of familiar fairy tales, often by presenting a first-person point of view not considered in the traditional tale. For example, in the title poem a child asks whether anyone felt sorry for the giant in "Jack and the Beanstalk." "One of the Seven Has Somewhat to Say" is a comical complaint by one of the seven dwarfs, wishing to marry off Snow White so the "old bachelors" can be rid of her meticulous housekeeping and go back to their messy habits. In "Interview," the stepmother tells the press that Cinderella lied about her treatment at home. A queen reveals in "The Marriage" that her daughter fabricated a story about a frog turning into a prince but it is all right that the opportunistic man isn't a prince as long as the "poor romantic daughter thinks he is," (see "The Frog King" in Part 2). Hay deftly strips away romantic illusions about women in their various roles as mothers and daughters, homemakers and lovers, good or evil influences. Our uncertainty about whether to trust her subjective narrators makes the poems more open ended than traditional tales. "Juvenile Court" uses colloquial language within the framework of the modern legal system to invert the tale of "Hansel and Gretel" and recast the witch as a murder victim. Unlike Vivian Vande Velde's more detailed, mysterious story exploring the victimization of the women in the tale, Hay's sonnet quickly builds to a humorous ending with the couplet that rhymes "provocation" and "probation." With a typical wry twist, Hay leaves us wondering whether the court's decision is based on society's long-standing belief in the innocence of children or a lax tendency to accept their excuses and let them off easily.

Juvenile Court

Deep in the oven, where the two had shoved her,
They found the Witch, burned to a crisp, of course.
And when the police had decently removed her,
They questioned the children, who showed no
    remorse.
"She threatened us," said Hansel, "with a kettle
Of boiling water, just because I threw
The cat into the well." Cried little Gretel,
"She fussed because I broke her broom in two,

And said she'd lock up Hansel in a cage
For drawing funny pictures on her fence . . ."
Wherefore the court, considering their age,
And ruling that there seemed some evidence
The pair had acted under provocation,
Released them to their parents, on probation.

Francesca Lia Block (b. 1962)

Francesca Lia Block, a native of Hollywood, California, wrote about the chaotic punk world of her own youth in her highly acclaimed and controversial first novel, *Weetzie Bat* (1989). After four sequels and prequels about the bohemian family of the young woman named Weetzie, her gay friend Dirk, their lovers, and their daughters Cherokee Bat and Witch Baby, the Weetzie books were bound together in *Dangerous Angels* (1998). Block has also published other experimental fantasies and edgy love stories for young adults and adults, including *I Was a Teenage Fairy,* as well as collections of stories, such as *The Rose and the Beast: Fairy Tales Retold.* Block's writing of poetry, short fiction, and then novels grew out of her love for modernist poetry, with its blend of classical references and concrete images. She was also influenced by Greek mythology, picture books by Maurice Sendak and Charlotte Zolotow (who became her first editor), and magic realism in the fiction of Gabriel Garcia Marquez. Her stories have been called pop fairy tales, in that images and magical events based on folklore and mythology are blended with realistic details from contemporary urban life.

This offbeat blend is illustrated in *Weetzie Bat's* prefatory introduction to the heroine and plot: "Once upon a time in a land called Shangri-L.A., a bleach-blond punk pixie named Weetzie Bat lived a life of surf and slam. But Shangri-L.A. can be Hell-A, too, and Weetzie wanted something celestial and sparkling to keep her safe. So she made three wishes and learned that love is the most beautiful and dangerous angel of all." Bursting with colorful details from the ever-changing landscape and pop culture of Los Angeles, with a few scenes in New York City, the text sometimes sounds like a jaunty American fairy tale by L. Frank Baum or Carl Sandburg: for example, when her divorced father Charlie Bat takes Weetzie to the Tick Tock Tea Room.

When a genie grants Weetzie's wishes for love and a home (with the realistic limitation that he cannot grant world peace or infinite wishes), the grandmother of her gay friend Dirk seems like a fairy godmother who leaves them "a beautiful little house for us to live in happily ever after" (p. 28). Then Dirk and Weetzie magically find lovers named Duck and My Secret Agent Lover Man. They make movies together, introducing another form of modern myth-making that enables them to express concerns about issues such as the persecution of Native Americans. In the middle of the novel, the chapter "Weetzie Wants a Baby" compares Weetzie to fairy tale princesses, such as Cinderella and Sleeping Beauty (waking up after a long ordeal to find flowers and a lover at her bedside, for example). As in other chapters in which the characters deal with death and sickness (including the beginning of the AIDS epidemic, although it is not mentioned by name), Weetzie endures conflict and suffering with her unconventional extended family, but emerges exuberant and blissful. Block has commented that her books are about the most important things in life: tolerance and the healing power of love and art. Amid a jumble of harsh realities and fairy tale magic, Weetzie's choice at the end to confront fear and accept happiness dramatizes Block's belief "[t]hat you must face the darkness, acknowledge it and still have hope."[1]

NOTE

1. "Francesca Lia Block," quoted in *Contemporary Authors Online* (The Gale Group, 2005), January 13, 2006 <http://galenet.galegroup.com/servlet/LitRC>.

From *Weetzie Bat*

WEETZIE WANTS A BABY

"What does 'happily ever after' mean anyway, Dirk?" Weetzie said. She was thinking about buildings. The Jetson-style Tiny Naylor's with the roller-skating waitresses had been torn down. In its place was a record-video store, a pizza place, a cookie place, a Wendy's, and a Penguin's Yogurt. Across the street, the old Poseur, where Weetzie and Dirk had bought kilts, was a beauty salon. They had written their names on the columns of the porch but all the graffiti had been painted over. Even Elvis Land was gone. Elvis Land had been in the front yard of an old house on Melrose. There had been a beat-up pink Cadillac, a picture of Elvis, and a giant love letter to Elvis on the lawn.

Then there were the really old places. Like the Tiki restaurant in the Valley, which had gone out of business years ago and had become overgrown with reeds so that the Tiki totems peered out of the watery-sounding darkness. Now it was gone—turned into one of the restaurants that lined Ventura Boulevard with valets in red jackets sitting out in the heat all day waiting for BMW's. And Kiddie Land, the amusement park where Weetzie's dad, Charlie, had taken her (Weetzie's pony had just dawdled, and sometimes turned around and gone back to the start, because Weetzie wouldn't use the whip, and once Weetzie was traumatized by a plastic cow that swung onto the track); Kiddie Land was now the big, brown Beverly Center that Weetzie would have painted almost any other color—at least, if they *had* to go ahead and put it up in place of Kiddie Land.

"What does happily ever after mean anyway?" Weetzie said.

She was still living in Fifi's cottage with Dirk and Duck and My Secret Agent Lover Man. They had finished their third film, called *Coyote,* with Weetzie as a rancher's daughter who falls in love with a young Indian named Coyote and ends up helping him defend his land against her father and the rest of the town. They had filmed *Coyote* on an Indian reservation in New Mexico. Weetzie grew her hair out, and she wore Levi's and snaky cowboy boots and turquoise. Dirk and Duck played her angry brothers; Valentine did the music, and Ping was wardrobe. My Secret Agent Lover Man was the director. His friend Coyote played Coyote.

The film was quite a success, and it brought Weetzie and My Secret Agent Lover Man and Dirk and Duck and their friends money for the first time. They bought a mint 1965 T-bird, and Weetzie went to Gräu and bought a jacket made out of peach and rose and gold silk antique kimonos. They had enough to go to Noshi for sushi whenever they wanted (which was a lot because Weetzie was addicted to the hamachi, which only cost $1.50 an order). They also ate guacamole tostadas at El Coyote (which had, they agreed, some of the best decorations in Hollywood, especially the painting with the real little lights right in it), putting the toppings of guacamole, canned vegetables, Thousand Island dressing, and cheese into the corn tortillas that were served between two plates to keep them warm. Weetzie also bought beads and feathers and white Christmas lights and roses that she saved and dried. She decorated everything in sight with these things until the whole house was a collage of glitter and petals.

"I feel like Cinderella," Weetzie said, driving around in the T-bird, wearing her kimono jacket, while My Secret Agent Lover Man covered her with kisses, and Dirk and Duck and Slinkster Dog crooned along with the radio.

Everything was fine except that Weetzie wanted a baby.

"How could you want one?" My Secret Agent Lover Man said. "There are way too many babies. And diseases. And nuclear accidents. And crazy psychos. We can't have a baby," he said.

They had hiked to the Hollywood sign and were eating canned smoked oysters and drinking red wine from real glasses that My Secret Agent Lover Man had packed in newspaper in his backpack.

"But we could have such a cool, beautiful baby," Weetzie said, sticking her toothpick into an oyster.

"And it would be so happy and we would love it so much."

"I don't want one, Weetz," he said. "Just forget about babies—you have enough already anyway: me and Dirk and Duck and Slinkster Dog. And you're just one yourself."

Weetzie stood up, shoved her hands into the back pockets of her Levi's, and looked out over the top of the Hollywood sign. My Secret Agent Lover Man and Weetzie had spray-painted their initials on the back of the "D" when they first met. Beneath the sign the city was only lights, safe and sparkling, like the Hollywood in "Hollywood in Miniature" on Hollywood Boulevard. It didn't look like any of the things that My Secret Agent Lover Man was talking about.

The next day, My Secret Agent Lover Man came home carrying a cardboard box that made scratching, yipping sounds. "I brought you a baby," he said to Weetzie. "This is Go-Go Girl. She is a girlfriend for Slinkster Dog. When she grows up, she and Slink can have some more babies for you. We can have as many puppy babies as you want."

Slinkster Dog wriggled with joy, and Weetzie kissed My Secret Agent Lover Man and held Go-Go Girl against her chest. The puppy's fur had a pinkish cast from her skin and she wore a rhinestone collar. She would make a perfect girlfriend for Slinkster Dog, Weetzie thought. But she was not a *real* baby.

"We'll have a baby with you," Dirk said.

He and Duck had come home to find Weetzie alone on the living room couch among the collage pillows, which were always leaving a dust of glitter and dried petals. She was crying and blowing her nose with pink Kleenex, and there were wadded up Kleenex roses all over the floor.

"Yeah," Duck said. "I saw it on that talk show once. These two gay guys and their best friend all slept together so no one would know for sure whose baby it was. And then they had this really cool little girl and they all raised her, and it was so cool, and when someone in the audience said, 'What sexual preference do you hope she has?' they all go together, they go 'Happiness.' Isn't that cool?"

"But what about My Secret Agent Lover Man?" Weetzie said.

"Nothing has to change," Dirk said. "We'll just have a baby."

"But he doesn't want one."

"It might not be his baby," Dirk said. "But I'll bet he likes it when he sees it, and we'll all go to a doctor to make sure we can make the perfect healthy baby."

Weetzie looked at Dirk's chiseled features and Duck's glossy, tan, surfer-dude face and she smiled. It would be a beautiful slinkster girl baby, or a hipster baby boy, and they would all love it more than any of their parents had ever loved them—more than any baby had ever been loved, Weetzie thought.

When My Secret Agent Lover Man came home that night he looked weary. His eyes looked like glasses of gin. Weetzie ran to kiss him, and when she put her arms around him, he felt tense and somehow smaller.

"What's wrong, honey-honey?"

"I wish I could stop listening to the news," he said.

Weetzie kissed him and ran her hands through his hair.

"Let's take a bath," she said.

They lit candles and incense, and made Kahlua and milks, and got into the bathtub in the pink-and-aqua-tiled bathroom. Weetzie felt as if she were turning into steam and milk and honey. She massaged My Secret Agent Lover Man's pale, clenched back with aloe vera oil and pikake lotion.

"If I was ever going to have a baby, it would be with you, Miss Weetzie," he said after they had made love. "You would make a great mom."

Weetzie just kissed his fingers and his throat, but she didn't say anything about the plan.

One night, while My Secret Agent Lover Man was away fishing with his friend Coyote, Weetzie and Dirk and Duck went out to celebrate. They had received their test results, and now they could have a baby. At Noshi, they ordered hamachi, anago, maguro, ebi, tako, kappa maki, and Kirin beer. They were buzzing from the beer and from the burning neon-green wasabe and the pink ginger and from the massive protein dose of sushi. ("Like, sushi is the heavy protein buzz," Duck said.)

"Here's to our baby," Dirk said. "I always wanted one, and I thought I could never get one, and now we are going to. And it will be all of ours—My (your) Secret Agent Lover Man's, too."

They drank a toast and then they all got into Dirk's car, Jerry, and drove home.

Weetzie changed into her lace negligée from Trashy Lingerie and went into Dirk and Duck's room and climbed into bed between Dirk and Duck. They all just sat there, bolt upright, listening to "I Wanna Hold Your Hand."

"I feel weird," Weetzie said.

"Me too," Dirk said.

Duck scratched his head.

"But we want a baby and we love each other," Weetzie said.

"I love you, Weetz. I love you, Dirk," Duck said.

"'I Wanna Hold Your Hand,'" the Beatles said.

And that was how Weetzie and Dirk and Duck made the baby—well, at least that was how it began, and no one could be sure if that was really the night, but that comes later on.

When My Secret Agent Lover Man came back from fishing with Coyote he looked healthier and rested. "I haven't seen the paper in three weeks," he said, sitting down at the kitchen table with the *Times*.

Weetzie took the paper away. "Honey, I have something to tell you," she said.

Weetzie was pregnant. She felt like a Christmas package. Like a cat full of kittens. Like an Easter basket of pastel chocolate-malt eggs and solid-milk-chocolate bunnies, and yellow daffodils and doll-house-sized jelly-bean eggs.

But My Secret Agent Lover Man stared at her in shock and anger. "You did what?"

"The world's a mess," My Secret Agent Lover Man said. "And there is no way I feel okay about bringing a kid into it. And for you to go and sleep with Dirk and Duck without even telling me is the worst thing you have ever done."

Weetzie could not even cry and make Kleenex roses. She remembered the day her father, Charlie, had driven away in the smashed yellow T-bird, leaving her mother Brandy-Lynn clutching her flowered robe with one hand and an empty glass in the other, and leaving Weetzie holding her arms crossed over her chest that was taking its time to develop into anything. But My Secret Agent Lover Man was not going to send Weetzie postcards of the Empire State Building, or come visit every so often to buy her turkey platters at the Tick Tock Tea Room like Charlie did. Weetzie knew by his eyes that he was going away forever. His eyes that had always been like lakes full of fishes, or waves of love, or bathtub steam and candle smoke, or at least like glasses of gin when he was sad, were now like two heavy green marbles, like the eyes of the mechanical fortune-teller on the Santa Monica pier. She hardly recognized him because she knew he didn't recognize her, not at all. Once, on a bus in New York, she had seen the man of her dreams. She was twelve and he was carrying a guitar case and roses wrapped in green paper, and there were raindrops on the roses and on his hair, and he hadn't looked at her once. He was sitting directly across from her and staring ahead and he didn't see anyone, anything there. He didn't see Weetzie even though she had known then that someday they must have babies and bring each other roses and write songs together and be rock stars. Her heart had felt as meager as her twelve-year-old chest, as if it had shriveled up because this man didn't recognize her. That was nothing compared to how her heart felt when she saw My Secret Agent Lover Man's dead marble fortune-teller eyes.

Nine months is not very long when you consider that a whole person with fingers and toes and everything is being made. But for Weetzie nine months felt like a long time to wait. It felt especially long because she was not only waiting for the baby with its fingers and toes and features that would reveal who its dad was, but she was also waiting for My Secret Agent Lover Man, even though she knew he was not going to come.

Dirk and Duck were wonderful fathers-in-waiting. Dirk read his favorite books and comic books out loud to Weetzie's stomach, and Duck made sure she ate only health food. ("None of those gnarly grease-burgers and NO OKI DOGS!" Duck said.) They cuddled with her and gave her backrubs, and tickled her when she was sad, to make sure she got enough physical affection. ("Because I heard that rats shrivel up and die if they aren't, like, able to hang out with other rats," Duck said.) Whenever Weetzie thought of My Secret Agent Lover Man and started to cry, Dirk and Duck waited patiently, hugged her, and took her to a movie on Hollywood Boulevard or for a Macro-Erotic at I Love Jucy. Valentine and Ping and Raphael came over

with fortune cookies, and pictures and poems that Raphael had made. Brandy-Lynn called and said, "I don't approve . . . but what can I get for you? I'm sure it's a girl. She'll need the right clothes. None of those feathered outfits."

Weetzie was comforted by Dirk and Duck, Valentine, Ping, Raphael, and even Brandy-Lynn, and by the baby she felt rippling inside of her like a mermaid. But the movie camera and the slouchy hat and baggy trousers and the crackly voice and the hands that soothed the jangling of her charm-bracelet nerves—all that was gone. My Secret Agent Lover Man was gone.

Weetzie had the baby at the Kaiser on Sunset Boulevard, where she had been born.

"Am I glad that's over!" Duck said, coming into Weetzie's hospital room with a pale face. "Dirk has been having labor pains out there in the waiting room."

"What about you?" Dirk said to Duck. "Duck has been moaning and sweating out there in the waiting room."

Weetzie laughed weakly. "Look what we got," she said.

It was a really little baby—almost too little.

"You can't tell who it looks like yet," Duck said. "It's too little and pink."

"No matter who it looks like, it's all of ours," Dirk said. He put his arms around Weetzie and Duck, and they sat looking at their baby girl.

"What are we going to name it?" Duck said.

They had thought about Sweet and Fifi and Duckling and Hamachi and Teddi and Lambie, but they decided to name her Cherokee.

When they left the hospital the next day, Weetzie looked down Sunset Boulevard to where Norm's coffee shop used to be. Weetzie's dad, Charlie, had waited all night in that Norm's, drinking coffee black and smoking packs until Weetzie was born. Weetzie had always thought that when she had a baby its father would wait in Norm's for her, looking like her secret agent lover. But Norm's was torn down and My Secret Agent Lover Man was gone.

Weetzie and Dirk and Duck brought Cherokee home and the house felt different, lighter and more musical now, because someone was always opening a window to let in the sun or putting on a record. The sun streamed in, making the walls glow like the inside of a rose. But even in the rosy house, Weetzie felt bittersweet; bittersweetness was like a liqueur burning in her throat and dripping down slowly into her heart.

Then one morning, Weetzie woke up feeling different, not bittersweet, but expectant the way she used to feel on the morning of her birthday. She opened her eyes and saw the flowers—there were flowers heaped on top of the quilt. Big, ruffly peonies, full-blown roses, pink-spotted lilies, pollen-dusty poppies. Weetzie blinked in the sunlight and saw My Secret Agent Lover Man standing over her and Cherokee. He looked very pale and hunched in his trench coat, and his eyes were moist.

Weetzie put out her arms, and he came and sat on the bed and held her very tight. Then he looked at Cherokee.

"Whose is she?" he asked. "She is so completely perfect."

"She looks like Dirk," Weetzie said. "Because of her cheekbones."

My Secret Agent Lover Man's mouth twitched a little.

"And she looks like Duck," Weetzie said. "Because she is blonde . . . And her nose."

My Secret Agent Lover Man wrinkled his brow.

"And she looks like me, of course, because she is so itsy-witsy and silly-looking," Weetzie said, laughing.

"But really, she absolutely has no one else's eyes but yours, and your pretty lips. I think she's all of ours," Weetzie said. "I hope that is okay with you."

Dirk and Duck came into the room.

"We missed you," Dirk said. "And we hope you stay around and help raise our kid."

My Secret Agent Lover Man smiled. Weetzie held Cherokee against her breast. Cherokee looked like a three-dad baby, like a peach, like a tiny moccasin, like a girl love-warrior who would grow up to wear feathers and run swift and silent through the L.A. canyons.

Bruce Coville (b. 1950)

"Am I Blue?" by Bruce Coville plays with widely known traditional folk motifs to develop a most controversial and contemporary theme. The title story in a 1994 collection of young adult short stories by sixteen writers, it was published at a time when there were few explicit depictions of homosexual characters in literature for young readers. As editor Marion Dane Bauer wrote in the Introduction, "The intention of this anthology is to tell challenging, honest, affecting stories that will open a window for all who seek to understand themselves or others" (p. ix). Coville's humorous story reflects his abiding interest in combining entertainment with education, and bringing archetypal and mythic images into modern settings. His many popular series of fantasy, science fiction, and horror books for children and young adults range from humorous novels, such as *My Teacher Is an Alien* (1989), to more serious ones like *Jeremy Thatcher, Dragon Hatcher* (1991), a sensitive depiction of an artistic sixth-grade boy who gets through a difficult stage of life while raising a dragon.

In "Am I Blue?" the confused teenage narrator Vincent may be an unlikely Cinderella character, but Coville wittily transferred the theme of stepsister bashing, from the world's most popular fairy tale, to the problem of gay bashing in 1990s America. Of course, a boy who is bullied for possibly being gay deserves a "fairy" godfather and guardian angel. Vincent's mentor with magic powers helps him think about an array of thorny issues that are connected with stereotyping, the language and actions of discrimination, hypocrisy at all levels of society, the consequences of centuries of secrecy, and the gay community's longing for openness and acceptance. Vincent's colorful use of his three wishes is a far-fetched and hilarious fantasy, but it also suggests that there could be a wondrously simple solution to the problem of homophobia.

Am I Blue?

It started the day Butch Carrigan decided I was interested in jumping his bones.

"You little fruit," he snarled. "I'll teach you to look at *me!*"

A moment or two later he had given me my lesson.

I was still lying facedown in the puddle into which Butch had slammed me as the culminating exercise of my learning experience when I heard a clear voice exclaim, "Oh, my dear! That *was* nasty. Are you all right, Vince?"

Turning my head to my left, I saw a pair of brown Docksiders, topped by khaki pants. Given the muddy condition of the sidewalks, pants and shoes were both ridiculously clean.

I rolled onto my side and looked up. The loafers belonged to a tall, slender man. He had dark hair, a neat mustache, and a sweater slung over his shoulders. He was kind of handsome—almost pretty. He wore a gold ring in his left ear. He looked to be about thirty.

"Who are you?" I asked suspiciously.

"Your fairy godfather. My name is Melvin. Come on, stand up and let's see if we can't do something with you."

"Are you making fun of me?" I asked. After Butch's last attack I had had about enough of people calling me a fruit for one day.

"Moi?" cried the man, arching his eyebrows and laying a hand on his chest. "Listen, honey, I have nothing but sympathy for you. I had to deal with my share of troglodytes when I was your age, and I *know* it's no fun. I'm here to help."

"What the hell are you talking about?"

"I told you, I'm your fairy godfather."

He waited for me to say something, but I just sat in the puddle, glaring at him. (It was uncomfortable, but I was already soaked right through my undershorts, so it didn't make that much difference.)

"You know," he said encouragingly. "Like in 'Cinderella'?"

"Go away and let me suffer in peace," I growled, splashing muddy water at him.

He flinched and frowned, but it was a reflex action; the water that struck his pants vanished without a trace.

I blinked, and splashed at him again, this time spattering a double handful of dirty water across his legs.

"Are you angry or just making a fashion statement?" he asked.

I felt a little chill. No spot of mud nor mark of moisture could be seen on the perfectly pressed khakis. "How did you do that?" I asked.

He just smiled and said, "Do you want your three wishes or not, Vincent?"

I climbed out of the puddle. "What's going on here?" I asked.

He made a *tsk*ing sound. "I think it's pretty obvious," he said, rolling his eyes. "Come on, let's go get a cup of coffee and talk. All your questions will be answered in good time."

The first question I thought of was "How much trouble is it going to give me to be seen with this guy?" With Butch and his crowd already calling me "faggot" and "fruit," walking around with a guy who moved the way Melvin did wasn't going to do anything to improve the situation.

The first question I actually *asked* was "Do you have to walk like that?"

"Like what?"

"You know," I said, blushing a little. "So swishy."

Melvin stopped. "Honey, I gave my life to be able to walk like this. Don't you dare try to stop me now."

"Don't call me honey!" I snapped.

He sighed and rolled his eyes toward the sky. "I can't say you didn't warn me," he said, clearly not speaking to me.

We went to a little cafe on Morton Street called Pete's. It's mostly frequented by kids from the university, but some of the high school kids hang out there as well, especially kids from the theater group.

"Not bad," said Melvin as we entered. "Brings back memories."

Things were slow, and we found a corner table where we could talk in private.

"Okay," I said, "what's going on?"

I won't relate the first part of the conversation, because you've probably read a lot of things like it before. I couldn't believe what he was saying was real, so I kept trying to figure out what this was really about—*Candid Camera,* an elaborate practical joke, that kind of thing. But after he instantly dried my puddle-soaked pants by snapping his fingers, I had to accept it: Whether or not he was actually my fairy godfather, this guy was doing real magic left and right.

"Okay, if you're real," I said, lifting my coffee (which had changed from plain coffee to Swiss double mocha *while* I was drinking it), "then tell me how come I never heard of fairy godfathers before."

"Because I'm the first."

"Care to explain that?"

"Certainly. Once you buy the farm, you get some choices on the other side. What kind of choices depends on the usual stuff—how good you've been and so on. Well, I was going up and not down, and it was pretty much expected that I would just opt to be an angel; tracking system, you know. But I said I didn't want to be anyone's guardian angel, I wanted to be a fairy godfather."

He took a sip of coffee and rolled his eyes. "Let me tell you, *that* caused a hullaballoo! But I said people had been calling me a fairy all my life, and now that I was dead, that was what I wanted to be. Then I told them that if they didn't let me be a fairy godfather, I was going to bring charges of sexism against them. So they let me in. You're my first case."

"Does that have any significance?" I asked nervously.

"What do you mean?"

"Me being your first case. Does that mean I'm gay?"

I didn't mention that I had been trying to figure out the same thing myself for about a year now.

He got that look in his eye that meant he was about to make another wisecrack. But suddenly his face got serious. Voice soft, he said, "You may be, you may not. The point is, you're getting picked on because people *think* you are—which is why I've been sent to work with you. Gaybashing is a special issue for me."

"How come?"

"It's how I met my maker, so to speak. I was walking down the street one day last year, minding my own business, when three bruisers dragged me into an alley, shouting, 'We'll teach you, faggot!' They never did explain exactly what it was they were going to teach me. Last thing I remember from life on earth was coming face to face with a tire iron. Next thing I knew, I was knocking at the Pearly Gates."

We were both silent for a moment. Then he shrugged and took another sip of his coffee.

"You're taking this awfully casually," I said, still stunned by the awfulness of what he had told me.

"Honey, I did a lot of screaming and shouting while it was happening. Afterward too, for that matter. Didn't do me a bit of good—I was still dead. Once you've been on the other side for a while, you get a little more zen about this kind of thing."

"But don't you want to go get those guys or something?"

He shook his head. "I prefer reform to vengeance. Besides, it's against the rules. Why don't we just concentrate on your case for the time being."

"Okay, do I really get three wishes?"

"Sure do. Well, two, now."

"What do you mean?"

"You used up the first one on that coffee."

"I didn't tell you to change it into Swiss double mocha!" I yelped.

"You didn't have to. You wished for it."

"I'm glad I didn't wish I was dead!" I muttered.

"Oh!" he cried. "Getting personal, are we? Don't you think that remark was a little tasteless under the circumstances?"

"Are you here to help me or to drive me nuts?"

"It hurts me that you could even ask. Anyway, the three wishes are only part of the service, even though that's what people always focus on. I'm really here to watch over you, advise you, guide you, till we get things on track."

He leaned back in his chair, glanced around the room, then winked at a nice-looking college student sitting about five tables away from us.

"Will you stop that!" I hissed.

"What's the matter, afraid of guilt by association?"

"No, I'm afraid he'll come over here and beat us up. Only he probably can't beat you up, so he'll have to settle for me."

Melvin waved his hand. "I guarantee you he wasn't offended. He's one of the gang."

"What gang?"

Melvin pursed his lips and raised his eyebrows, as if he couldn't believe I could be so dense.

I blinked. "How can you tell something like that just from looking at him?"

"Gaydar," said Melvin, stirring his coffee. "Automatic sensing system that lets you spot people of similar persuasion. A lot of gay guys have it to some degree or other. If it was more reliable, it would make life easier on us—"

I interrupted. "Speak for yourself."

Melvin sighed. "I wasn't necessarily including *you* in that particular 'us.' I was just pointing out that it's harder spotting potential partners when you're gay. If a guy asks a girl for a date, about the worst that can happen is that she laughs at him. If he asks another guy, he might get his face pounded in."

That thought had crossed my mind more than once as I was trying to figure myself out over the last year— and not only with regard to dating. I would have been happy just to have someone I felt safe *talking* to about this.

"Is this gaydar something you can learn?" I asked.

He furrowed his brow for a moment, then said, "I don't think so."

"It must be lonely," I muttered, more to myself than to him.

"It doesn't have to be," he replied sharply. "If gay people hadn't been forced to hide for so long, if we could just openly identify ourselves, there would be plenty of people you knew that you could ask for advice. Everybody knows gay people; they just think they don't."

"What do you mean?"

"Listen, honey, the world is crawling with faggots. But most of them are in hiding because they're afraid they'll get treated the way you did about an hour ago."

I took in my breath sharply. Melvin must have seen the look of shock on my face, because he looked puzzled for a moment. Then he laughed. "That word bother you?"

"I was taught that it was impolite."

"It is. But if you live in a world that keeps trying to grind you down, you either start thumbing your nose at it or end up very, very short. Taking back the language is one way to jam the grinder. My friends and I called each other 'faggot' and 'queer' for the same reason so many black folks call each other 'nigger'—to take the words away from the people who want to use them to hurt us."

His eyes went dreamy for a moment, as if he was looking at something far away, or deep inside. "I walk and talk the way I do because I'm not going to let anyone else define me. I can turn it off whenever I want, you know."

He moved in his seat. I couldn't begin to tell you exactly what changed, but he suddenly looked more masculine, less . . . swishy.

"How did you do that?" I asked.

"Protective coloration," he said with a smile. "You learn to use it to get along in the world if you want. Only I got sick of living in the box the world prescribed; it was far too small to hold me. So I knocked down a few walls."

"Yeah, and look what happened. You ended up dead."

"They do like to keep us down," he said, stirring his coffee. Suddenly he smiled and looked more like himself again. "Do you know the three great gay fantasies?" he asked.

"I don't think so," I said nervously.

He looked at me. "How old are you?"

"Sixteen."

"Skip the first two. You're too young. It was number three that I wanted to tell you about anyway. We used to imagine what it would be like if every gay person in the country turned blue for a day."

My eyes went wide. "Why?"

"So all the straights would have to stop imagining that they didn't know any gay people. They would find out that they had been surrounded by gays all the time, and survived the experience just fine, thank you. They'd have to face the fact that there are gay cops and gay farmers, gay teachers and gay soldiers, gay parents and gay kids. The hiding would finally have to stop."

He looked at me for a moment. "How would you like to have the sight?" he asked.

"What?"

"How would you like to have gaydar for a while? You might find it interesting."

"Does this count as a wish?" I asked suspiciously.

"No, it's education. Comes under a different category."

"All right," I said, feeling a little nervous.

"Close your eyes," said Melvin.

After I did as he requested, I felt him touch each of my eyelids lightly. My cheeks began to burn as I wondered if anyone else had seen.

"Okay," he said. "Open up, big boy, and see what the world is really like."

I opened my eyes and gasped.

About a third of the people in the cafe—including the guy Melvin had winked at—were blue. Some were bright blue, some were deep blue, some just had a bluish tint to them.

"Are you telling me all those people are gay?" I whispered.

"To some degree or other."

"But so many of them?"

"Well, this isn't a typical place," said Melvin. "You told me the theater crowd hangs around in here." He waved his hand grandly. "Groups like that tend to have a higher percentage of gay people, because we're so naturally artistic." He frowned. "Of course, some bozos take a fact like that and decide that *everyone* doing theater is gay. Remember, two thirds of the people you're seeing *aren't* blue."

"What about all the different shades?" I asked.

"It's an indicator of degree. The dark blues are pretty much exclusively queer, while the lighter ones are less committed—or maybe like you, trying to make up their minds. I set it up so that you'll see at least a hint of blue on anyone who has had a gay experience. Come on, let's go for a walk."

It was like seeing the world though new eyes. Most of the people looked just the same as always, of course. But Mr. Alwain, the fat guy who ran the grocery store, looked like a giant blueberry—which surprised me, be-cause he was married and had three kids. On the other hand, Ms. Thorndyke, the librarian, who everyone *knew* was a lesbian, didn't have a trace of blue on her.

"Can't tell without the spell," said Melvin. "Straights are helpless at it. They're always assuming someone is or isn't for all the wrong reasons."

We were in the library because Melvin wanted to show me some books. "Here, flip through this," he said, handing me a one-volume history of the world.

My bluevision worked on pictures, too!

"Julius Caesar?" I asked in astonishment.

"'Every woman's husband, every man's wife,'" said Melvin. "I met him at a party on the other side once. Nice guy." Flipping some more pages, he said, "Here, check this one out."

"Alexander the Great was a fairy!" I cried.

"Shhhhh!" hissed Melvin. "We're in a library!"

All right, I suppose you're wondering about me—as in, was I blue?

The answer is, slightly.

When I asked Melvin to explain, he said, "The Magic Eight Ball says, 'Signs Are Mixed.' In other words, you are one confused puppy. That's the way it is sometimes. You'll figure it out after a while."

Watching the news that night was a riot. My favorite network anchor was about the shade of a spring sky—pale blue, but very definite. So was the congressman he interviewed, who happened to be a notorious Republican homophobe.

"Hypocrite," I spat.

"What brought that on?" asked Dad.

"Oh, nothing," I said, trying to figure out whether I was relieved or appalled by the slight tint of blue that covered his features.

Don't get the idea that everyone I saw was blue. It broke down pretty much the way the studies indicate—about one person in ten solid blue, and one out of every three or four with some degree of shading.

I did get a kick out of the three blue guys I spotted in the sports feature on the team favored to win the Superbowl.

But it was that congressman who stayed on my mind. I couldn't forget his hypocritical words about "the great crime of homosexuality" and "the gay threat to American youth." I was brushing my teeth when I figured out what I wanted to do.

"No," I whispered, staring at my bluish face in the mirror. "I couldn't."

For one thing, it would probably mean another beating from Butch Carrigan.

Yet if I did it, nothing would ever be the same.

Rinsing away the toothpaste foam, I whispered Melvin's name.

"At your service!" he said, shimmering into existence behind me. "Ooooh, what a tacky bathroom. Where was your mother brought up, in a Kmart?"

"Leave my mother out of this," I snapped. "I want to make my second wish."

"And it is?"

"Gay fantasy number three, coast to coast."

He looked at me for a second, then began to smile. "How's midnight for a starting point?"

"Twenty-four hours should do the trick, don't you think?" I replied.

He rubbed his hands, chuckled, and disappeared.

I went to bed, but not to sleep. I kept thinking about what it would mean when the rest of the world could see what I had seen today.

I turned on my radio, planning to listen to the news every hour. I had figured the first reports would come in on the one-o'clock news, but I was wrong. It was about twelve thirty when special bulletins started an-

nouncing a strange phenomenon. By one o'clock every station I could pick up was on full alert. Thanks to the wonders of modern communication, it had become obvious in a matter of minutes that people were turning blue from coast to coast.

It didn't take much longer for people to start figuring out what the blue stood for. The reaction ranged from panic to hysterical denial to dancing in the streets. National Public Radio quickly summoned a panel of experts to discuss what was going to happen when people had to go to work the next day.

"Or school," I muttered to myself. Which was when I got my next idea.

"Melvin!" I shouted.

"You rang?" he asked, shimmering into sight at the foot of my bed.

"I just figured out my third wish." I took a breath. "I want you to turn Butch Carrigan blue."

He looked at me for a moment. Then his eyes went wide. "Vincent," he said, "I like the way you think. I'll be back in a flash."

When he returned he was grinning like a cat.

"You've still got one wish left, kiddo," he said with a chuckle. "Butch Carrigan was already blue as a summer sky when I got there."

If I caused you any trouble with Blueday, I'm sorry. But not much. Because things are never going to be the same now that it happened. Never.

And my third wish?

I've decided to save it for when I really need it—maybe when I meet the girl of my dreams.

Or Prince Charming.

Whichever.

Ellen Seiter (b. 1957)

While most of the selections in Part 7 deal with modern reworkings of classic works of children's literature, this essay by Ellen Seiter is different, focusing on late twentieth-century stories that are based on commercial products, such as dolls and toy animals. Seiter, an expert on mass media, gender issues, and children's popular culture, places contemporary product lines for boys and girls within the historical context of books that have been aimed at separate audiences of boys and girls since the nineteenth century. (See Elizabeth Segel's essay on boys' and girls' books in Part 5.) Seiter's books *Television and New Media Audiences* (1999) and *Sold Separately: Children and Parents in Consumer Culture* (1993) are based on close analyses of audience responses to popular stories and products. In *Sold Separately,* Seiter critiques shows for boys, such as *Ghostbusters,* in a chapter that precedes this one on toys and videos for girls. Her observations on the perpetuation of traditional depictions of masculinity in modern films and television could be applied to more recent examples, such as the hugely popular children's films *Toy Story* and *The Lion King,* which were accompanied by many product tie-ins. However, Seiter reminds adults that we should not judge children's popular culture hastily when we recoil at the apparent "kitschiness" and "low culture" tastes that are reflected in fads like collecting My Little Pony products. Her detailed analysis of the *My Little Pony* videos in relation to literary traditions, such as science fiction, fantasy, and romances for women, shows that they are complex stories, not exactly feminist, but nevertheless offering choices for girls that free them from having to identify with or measure up to masculine heroes and values. Because of their emphasis on resolving conflicts and emotional problems through "rehabilitation, reform, and reintegration into a community," Seiter believes that we should respect girls who choose these videos and toys over the other limited fare in "the commercial culture of femininity."

Toy-Based Videos for Girls

My Little Pony

When in doubt, use boys.
— Cy Schneider, *Children's Television*

Television producers, like most children's authors, cartoonists, and moviemakers, have favored male characters in action-packed adventures for boys. Male characters predominate because conventional wisdom has it that boys will not watch girls on television but girls will watch programs for boys. Until recently, little girls were not thought to constitute a large enough market to justify the cost of the programming. In the 1980s, with the rise of home video recorders and rental tapes, animated series were specifically designed for girls for the first time. The shows *Strawberry Short-cake, The Care Bears, Rainbow Brite* (1983–1987), and *My Little Pony* (1984–1986) were denigrated as the trashiest, most saccharine, most despicable products of the children's television industry. Yet these series were the first animated shows that did not require girls to cross over and identify with males. I want to take a close look in this chapter at *My Little Pony*— a limited, toy-based series of videos unmistakably coded as feminine—as representative of children's animated series and their appeal on the basis of gender.

THE BOYS' WORLD OF CHILDREN'S FICTION

The preference for male characters in children's media has its origins in popular children's books from the nineteenth century, though the marketing of children's books to the middle class began in the eighteenth century, with strongly moralistic books that were intended for boys and girls alike. As Elizabeth Segel has explained, "Neither the Puritan aim of saving the child's soul nor the characteristic Georgian aim of developing good character seemed to require the distinction between girl-child and boy-child." Instead, children's books of the late eighteenth and early nineteenth century "clearly taught obedience, submission to authority and selflessness as the cardinal virtues of both girls and boys." In the 1850s a division between adventure stories featuring male characters and domestic chronicles first appears.

> Before the boys' book appeared on the scene, fiction for children typically had been domestic in setting, heavily didactic, and morally or spiritually uplifting, and this kind of earnest family story remained the staple of younger children's fiction. The boys' book was, above all, an escape from domesticity and from the female domination of the domestic world. . . . The liberation of nineteenth-century boys into the book worlds of sailors and pirates, forests and battles, left their sisters behind in the world of childhood—that is, the world of home and family.[1]

The differentiation between boys' and girls' books coincided with the nineteenth-century expansion of the book market and the attempt to expand sales through segmentation.[2] Pulp fiction in the form of romances for girls developed later than boys' action stories. The rise of girls' popular romances coincided with the growth of the middle-class "cult of domesticity" and the notion of separate worlds for male and female. In fiction—as in ideology—boys belonged in a public world of work and adventure, girls in a domestic world of personal relationships. According to Segel, from the outset of a gendered distinction in popular children's literature, boys shied away from girls' books, while "girls were avid readers of boys' books from the start."[3]

Decades later, Walt Disney set the standard for gender representation in children's motion picture productions. In adapting fairy tales and literary sources, he handed out a few starring roles to young women: Cinderella, Sleeping Beauty, Snow White, and, more recently, Ariel in *The Little Mermaid* and Belle in *Beauty and the Beast*. In each case, however, the heroine was innocent and selfless, and the story placed her in a situation of enforced passivity whether through physical confinement, muteness, or death. (Belle was supposed to be a different kind of heroine—feisty and bookish—but her narrative function closely resembled her predecessors.) Any deviance from these characteristics immediately marks a female character as villainous in Disney's universe. Disney's best-known animated film characters—and the most fanciful—were always male: the Dwarfs, Jiminy Cricket, Bambi, Dumbo, Peter Pan. All of the popular cartoon characters, at Disney and at Warners and Hanna-Barbera, were males: Mickey Mouse, Donald Duck, Tom and Jerry, Daffy Duck, Elmer Fudd and Bugs Bunny, Coyote and Road Runner, Tweety and Sylvester. In many of the cartoons, two male characters are locked in a sadistic game of entrapment and punishment. On the relatively rare occasions when female companions were used—Minnie Mouse, Daisy Duck, Petunia Pig—they were given human breasts, heavily made-up faces, short skirts, and high heels. Sybil DelGaudio has characterized the gendered roles of the cartoons this way:

> the female as comic foil for the male is superseded by all-male rivalries in which comic incongruity is created by means other than sex differences . . . the cartoon seems to be a favorite place for the depiction of the pursuit/capture plot structure. When female characters enter the picture, they automatically take their places in line with the pursued, while the means of pursuit is changed to seduction and the end is clearly sexual.[4]

The striking difference between the female characters in the toy-based series of the 1980s involving licensed characters and in the cartoons of the classic period is that the heroines for the first time are not pursued but pursuing—the initiators and actors on a quest. Strawberry Shortcake, My Little Pony, and Rainbow Brite were not token female members of a male gang; and they are not drawn in the sexualized caricature of adult women repeated since Betty Boop.

One of the axioms of motion picture and television production (and of publishing) is that the female audience will take an interest in stories about male adventurers (the Western, the detective story, science fiction, action-adventure) but the male audience will not take an interest in stories about female adventurers (the romance, the domestic melodrama, the family saga). Thus, female characters were rare on the science fiction children's shows produced in the 1950s, and the heroes were adult men such as *Captain Video and His Video Rangers* (1949–1955), *Commando Cody, Sky Marshal of the Universe* (1955), and *Tom Corbett— Space Cadet* (1950–1955).[5] These live-action shows were forerunners of the science fiction and superhero cartoon series produced in the 1960s and 1970s. *The Adventures of Johnny Quest* (a very successful show, intermittently aired between 1964 and 1980) was based on the characters Dr. Benton Quest, anthropologist, his blond son Johnny, and his son's Asian Indian companion, Hadji. *The Fantastic Four* (1966–1970) included one female, Sue Richards, on its team of superheroes. Sports and music series with a more comical bent featured a cast of male protagonists; among these were *The Monkees* (1966–1972), *The Harlem Globetrotters* (1970–1973), and *The Jackson Five* (1971–1973). *Fat Albert and the Cosby Kids* (1969–1977)—one of the longest-running and most critically acclaimed children's television series for its depiction of African American children—counted not a single girl among its gang of seven living in the inner city. *Fat Albert* attempted to deal realistically with childhood problems and feelings—and its positive messages emphasizing self-esteem were later borrowed by shows like *My Little Pony* and *The Care Bears*.

Girls fared somewhat better in children's shows based on family situation comedies. Equal numbers of boys and girls enabled the battle-of-the-sexes theme to flourish on shows such as *The Flintstones* (1960–1966), *The Jetsons* (1962–1963), and *The Brady Kids* (1972–1974). Only as teenagers, however, were girls given primary roles—as though it was beyond the writers' ability to create story lines that included girls without some element of heterosexual flirtation. Thus animated shows followed the conventions of *Archie* comics, with their long-standing rivalry between Betty and Veronica, even though the Saturday morning television audience was in large part made up of young, preadolescent girls. Judy Jetson loved to dance and

chase her rock idol. Pebbles, born in 1963, was given a love interest in Bamm-Bamm Rubble, the boy next door, while still a toddler. When she was given her own show, *Pebbles and Bamm-Bamm* (1971–1976), the screenwriters accelerated her development so as to make her an adolescent.

Throughout the 1970s, teenage girls appeared as tokens on shows like *Hot Wheels.* Two popular series starred teen girls, notably *Josie and the Pussycats* (1970–1976), featuring the sweet redhead Josie, the brainy Black girl Valerie, and the scatterbrained blond Melody; and *Samantha the Teenage Witch,* based on an *Archie* character. *Josie* was a landmark for its establishment of the comedy adventure—or "let's get out of here"—format involving teenagers menaced by supernatural foes. *Scooby-Doo*—probably the most successful series of this type—originally featured two teenage girls—Daphne, the pretty one, and Velma, the smart one—to complement the beatnik Shaggy and the straight-laced Fred.

Designers of children's commercials and promotional campaigns have also preferred male characters. The roster of mascots is entirely male: Captain Crunch (cereal); Tony the Tiger (Frosted Flakes); the elves Snap, Crackle, and Pop (Rice Krispies); Sugar Bear (Super Golden Crisp); Ronald McDonald; Geoffrey Giraffe (Toys "R" Us). Conventional wisdom in the advertising business has it that a female trademark for a children's product will immediately turn away every boy in the audience; their belief is repeatedly proven to them by market research. Even in the world of educational programming for preschoolers, where combating sexism was explicitly placed on the agenda in the 1970s, we find ourselves in a man's world. Adult women all but disappeared in the 1960s as hosts and puppeteers—Shari Lewis with Lamb Chop, Romper Room, and Fran of Kukla, Fran, and Ollie—only Mister Rogers and Captain Kangaroo remained.[6]

Big Bird and Bert and Ernie dominate *Sesame Street.* All of the beloved monsters are male: Snuffalupagus, Honkers, Grover, Cookie Monster. The two females in residence on *Sesame Street,* Betty Lou and Prairie Dawn, are human-looking muppets rather than more fanciful creatures and tend to be strictly bound to realistic, rather than fantastic, actions and story lines, as though the celebrated creativity of *Sesame Street*'s writers and puppeteers dried up when confronted with female heroines.[7] Miss Piggy from the Muppet shows and films is an exception to this, but she is a figure bound to incite feelings of confusion and ambivalence in little girls, combining as Piggy does a flamboyant willingness to break the norms of girlish behavior with an obsessive pursuit of her romantic interest, Kermit, and an avid pursuit of beauty with a ridiculous, porcine appearance.[8]

THE CONTROVERSY OVER
TOY-BASED PROGRAMS

The girls' cartoons *Strawberry Shortcake, The Care Bears, My Little Pony,* and *Rainbow Brite* were produced in the 1980s during a boom in licensed characters in the toy industry. A firm called Those Characters from Cleveland, established in the late 1970s to create popular characters for the toy industry and its many licensees, chose as its first task the job of reaching—in some ways creating—the young girls' market, using interviews, focus groups, and storyboards of character designs to determine what girls found most appealing. Before the 1980s, Barbie and Mary Poppins had been the only successful girls' licenses. This effort was made because the market for girls' toys was underdeveloped and seen as a potential income producer. Innovations in girls' toys are relatively rare: season after season, toymakers limit their new toy lines to baby dolls that mimic human babies in different or more realistic ways (in 1990, all the major manufacturers planned dolls that soil their diapers). Perhaps this is because the industry's executives are overwhelmingly male. Whatever the reason, toy store owners consider the girls' market harder to buy for than the boys' market. For a brief period, the heyday of licensed characters portrayed on videos, there were many new toys for girls: Rainbow Brite and her friends the Color Kids (Canary Yellow, Patty O' Green, Buddy Blue—a token male character); the Care Bears, each a different color and different emotion;[9] Strawberry Shortcake and her girlfriends in lime, lemon, orange, and blueberry, and She-Ra, Princess of Power (twin sister of He-Man); and a lengthy procession of My Little Ponies.[10] Significantly, the critic Tom Engelhardt labeled the process of first designing characters using the tools of market research and then producing a cartoon the "Strawberry Shortcake Strategy," suggesting the special link between licensed characters in the eighties and the girls'

market. To a large extent these toy-based cartoons resulted from the discovery and exploitation of a marketing niche of girls aged three to seven, produced by the overwhelmingly male orientation of classic cartoons, comic books, and toys.

Many critics found these characters especially offensive because they were developed specifically for marketing purposes. Manufacturers wondered aloud why what they were doing was considered substantially different from what Disney had done since the 1930s in licensing the likenesses of cartoon characters for use by manufacturers of watches, clothes, cereal boxes, toys, and other items. But the toy-based shows offended cherished notions of creative integrity. Engelhardt charged, "[F]or the first time on such a massive scale, a 'character' has been born free of its specific structure in a myth, fairy tale, story, or even cartoon, and instead embedded from the beginning in a consortium of busy manufacturers whose goals are purely and simply to profit by multiplying the image itself in any way that conceivably will make money."[11] ACT led the protest against these programs and filed suit with the FCC to get them banned from television.

Some of the most virulent attacks on the licensed character shows were in fact diatribes against their "feminine" appeal. One of the reasons they seemed so dopey, so contrived, so schmaltzy was that they borrowed from popular women's genres—the romance, the soap opera, the family melodrama. Engelhardt complained that "a group of bossy, demanding, doll-like creatures dominate the relentlessly 'happy' realm of girls' TV." These remarks reveal a lack of familiarity with the stories, which actually concentrate to a large extent on unhappiness, suffering, and feelings of worthlessness. One reason these programs appeared so artificial to critics such as Engelhardt was that a willed, intentional act—the act of targeting the female consumer—was required to revise the dominant conventions of the twentieth-century children's story so as to center on female protagonists and the conventional concerns and play of little girls. Engelhardt noted with irritation that in the absence of the adventure plots and special effects typical of boys' cartoons there is an emphasis on prosocial, pop psychology values:

> An endless stream of these happy little beings with their magical unicorns in their syrupy cloud-cuckoo lands have paraded across the screen demanding that they be snuggled, cuddled, nuzzled, loved, and

adored, generally enticing children to lay bare their emotions so that they can be examined and made healthy.[12]

Girls' cartoons, like women's soap operas, were about emotional life. Engelhardt argued that the proliferation of characters on these shows leads to "personality fragmentation," and he worried about the effect on the audience in a tone that recalls concerns for the mental health of the soap opera viewer:[13]

> If we all have trouble with caring or hugging, if intervention is called for, and if you also have to sell lots of licensed characters, then you have to present the managing (or healing) process as a highly complicated one that needs lots of cooperation by lots of highly specialized dolls, so specialized that instead of being complex individual personalities, they are no more than carefully labeled fragments of a personality: Tenderheart Bear, Share Bear, Cheer Bear, Grumpy Bear.[14]

But personality fragmentation is not an invention of Those Characters from Cleveland. It could be found in early Disney films, such as *The Three Little Pigs,* which was praised by critics for its original "character differentiation." The single adjectives used to designate the Seven Dwarfs of *Snow White* (Grumpy, Happy, Sleepy, etc.) are probably the first examples of this trick in animation. But Disney's work was enthusiastically embraced by critics, probably in large part because of his painstaking attention to animation.[15] (Today, Disney's work is the standard for the genre.)

The difference between Disney's animation and today's television programs is above all that of style. The limited-animation techniques used to produce children's television series were pioneered by Hanna-Barbera in the late 1950s. The television series were made for a fraction of the cost and in a fraction of the time spent on film cartoons. Characters stand in one place more of the time, and the same background drawings are repeatedly used, now stored in memory with computer animation. Discussing the cartoons based on licensed characters, communications scholar Stephen Kline complains:

> The cartoon creature who acts, thinks, and feels just as humans, but is simplified in form and personality provides a perfect vehicle for children's characterizations. The drawings appear infantalized. Characters' features and expressions are reduced to the simplest

and most easily recognized by the young. Animators emphasize those features and expressions that children most quickly and easily identify with. Indeed, the characters rarely learn anything in these programs—their nature is inherent and fixed by their species-specific and immutable characteristics.[16]

Kline's criticism concerns simplification and fixed character types: he wants characters that change and grow, the individualistic, well-rounded characters of the nineteenth-century realist novel. But between the lines in these critiques one also hears a denigration of the emotional and psychological, an irritation with the actionlessness of these shows. These are precisely the same grounds on which adult women's genres have been denigrated. Engelhardt and Kline note with dismay that these cartoons submerge the child in a fantasy world unknown to the parents; they complain that they are too specific to the child's gender and age group; they ghettoize the child's viewing. But if the narrative situations and plots are as simple as Kline and Engelhardt claim, shouldn't a parent be able to catch on quickly? I read in these passages a father's irritation at the daughter's immersion in a program and a fictional world just for girls. The licensed character shows were not essentially different from other animated programs for children that had been around since the 1960s: what was new about them was that it was girls—and very young girls at that—who were being approached as a separate audience.

MY LITTLE PONY: TOYS AND VIDEOS

My Little Pony toys are popular with girls as young as two years of age and as old as eight. In 1990, most children had heard of them, seen other children with the toys, watched the programs, seen commercials for the toys, discussed them with playmates at preschool or day care by the age of three. This will not last forever; the license is already past the peak of its popularity. But in 1990, I had never met a girl between the ages of three and six who did not either already have a pony or want one.[17] Many girls collect ten, twenty, thirty ponies. According to Hasbro, 150 million ponies were sold during the 1980s.

According to Sydney Ladensohn Stern and Ted Schoenhaus, My Little Pony was the result of some "blue sky" research with little girls. "Hasbro asked the little girls, 'what do you see when you go to bed and close your eyes?' and the answer was often 'Horses.'"[18] In 1982, Hasbro was surprised when half a million brown plastic ponies sold without any advertising. The next year they changed the ponies from brown to "fantasy colors" and sold $25 million worth of them. Sales increased with advertising to $85 million in 1984 and $100 million in 1985, and with the production of the *My Little Pony* television shows and movie. Individual examples of My Little Pony are differentiated from one another based on body color, hair color, and decoration. The ponies are kitschy, anthropomorphized creatures with brightly colored, flowing manes and tails, and large blue eyes adorned with eye shadow, eyeliner, and thick lashes. Their manes and tails are made of rooted synthetic hair and can be combed, unlike those of the many molded horses that preceded them. The eyes are especially prominent because no other features are painted on the rubber body of the pony. There are two small indentations for nostrils, two rounded ears on top, and a curling, smiling line of a mouth, but except for the eyes, ponies are a solid color of molded rubber. The poses vary slightly, but the ponies always stand very solidly on four broad-based hooves caught in stride. My Little Ponies are available in a range of pastels and in more intense colors such as bright turquoise, hot pink, and deep purple. The palette of colors is based on the exclusion of brown and black (the colors of real animals) and of primary red, blue, and green (the colors of boys' clothes and boys' toys). Each pony has a different name and a different decoration painted on the haunch that stands as a totem for its name (butterflies, stars, flowers). All ponies are made in China; all come with a brush; all cost between four and ten dollars. They are sold at Kmart, Target, Toys "R" Us, Costco: never at upscale toy stores or stores that specialize in educational goods.

My Little Ponies appeal to girls as collectors, cultivating an appreciation of small differences in color and design from object to object. The toys themselves are low-tech. The principle for line extensions is based almost entirely on cosmetic changes, on distinctions of appearance and name. As with consumer goods targeted at adult women, such as clothing and home furnishings, the shopper is encouraged to buy many different products in the same category. Color or other design features (style) are the realm of diversification among objects that are essentially similar.[19] Like all fashions, conformity and individuality are involved here: choosing one's favorite pony means exercising individual taste while acquiring a toy that will look like all other ponies. This principle applies to most toys available to girls: there are relatively few successful brands or models (Barbie, Cabbage Patch), compared with boys' toys, but there are hundreds of different styles within each brand.

Ponies live in an idyllic outdoor world of flowers, birds, butterflies, bunnies, and fun. The name on the package is written across a rainbow. The packaging emphasizes that Ponyland is a world of miracles and magic, of helpful, laughing, playing ponies. Every package includes a cheerful story about the pony that emphasizes its visually dazzling qualities and its physical agility:

> "Rise and Shine," Sunspot called to the sleeping ponies, but they only yawned and snuggled deeper into their beds. "I know how to wake them!" she thought, flying into the air. She flew up to her friend, Mr. Sun, and whispered in his ear. Smiling happily, she sent sunbeams into the ponies' bedroom windows. The sunbeams filled each room and sprinkled glittering flecks of sunshine on the ponies. They awoke with smiling faces, and cheerfully tossed some of the bright flecks on Sunspot as she skipped into their bedrooms.[20]

Being ponies, rather than baby dolls to be taken care of, these toys allow for a certain kind of freedom: fantasies of galloping, flying, swimming. They are not, however, for riding. Play involves being a pony yourself, not owning one as a pet. The ponies exist outside the world of mommies, grocery stores, automobiles, schools, shopping malls. All of the ponies, like the groups of children who play with them, are girls, with the exception of the rare appearance of a baby brother. Boyfriends and the attraction of the opposite sex, which figure so prominently in other toys for girls, have no place here. Neither the human characters from the animated series nor the villains are available for purchase.

The success of My Little Pony spawned many imitations. Mattel worked vigorously to launch a competitor. Its Little Pretty line of kittens and puppies bore a strong resemblance to the ponies. Little Pretties were sold in sets: for example, the Little Pretty Polished Paws Kitty set included Catra, Peekablue Kitty, Bow

Kitty, Happy Feet Kitty, and Dixie Kitty. Mattel, whose fortune was made with Barbie, tried to combine Barbie's glamour and interest in the opposite sex with the animal motif. (The kitties are female, the puppies male.) One package reads:

> "I'm a Polished Paws Kitty and I love to look pretty" sang Catra, as she pounced on a leaf. Just then her puppy pal Dixie ran up: "Quick, we're going to have our pictures taken for the newspaper!" Catra quickly polished her paws her favorite shade of red, then purring proudly pussyfooted it to the photographer.[21]

The Little Pretty line has met with only limited success. One reason was that parents and children were resisting the obsessions with clothing and boys that characterize Barbie and her many imitations. My Little Pony has proven singular in the longevity of its success as a girls' license. I believe this was due to the relative innocence of the concept and the depth of little girls' identification with the utopian world of the ponies. Many middle-class parents are offended by the kitschiness of the ponies' design, which mirrors low-culture taste, but at least they aren't Barbie.

My Little Pony and *My Little Pony, The Movie* were never part of the Saturday morning network schedule—they were one-shot specials and limited syndication offerings—but they live on long past their original release dates (1985–1986) as rentals at the home video store.[22] *My Little Pony* is the kind of tape that girls pick out from the shelves at the video rental store; they recognize from the pink boxes and from the flowers, animals, and rainbows that this is for them. In educated middle-class families, the girls' enthusiasm for *My Little Pony* (and their satisfaction in correctly identifying the videos targeted at them) is met with parental disdain for kitsch and disapproval of sex-stereotyped entertainment. Some parents recommend substitute tapes, such as educational shows, fairy tale adaptations, or videos with more realistic settings and a mixture of male and female characters—in short, the public television-style fare favored by the college-educated middle class. Parents want more from children's videos than mere entertainment and try to inculcate this lesson through discussions at the video store. Such attempts to get children to emulate the respectable norms of television consumption meet with limited success, since young children tend to be more interested in real or imagined peer-group affiliations than in adult approval.

Parents and children recognize that, in Bourdieu's formulation, "taste classifies," but they have different systems of evaluation at stake. When middle-class parents complain of their children's bad taste in videos—judging children's selections as escapist, repetitive, trivial (out for fun rather than redeemed by a loftier educational goal, such as learning letters and numbers or zoological information)—they repeat the familiar strategy of dismissing the consumption of lower, inferior groups as merely hedonistic. Rarely do middle-class parents explicitly recognize that the conflict stems from the fact that mass-market children's toys and videos lean toward working-class aesthetics, gender representations, and popular genres. The parental position, which encourages more ambitious motivations for consumption than mere enjoyment, has been well described by Bourdieu, who argues that it "implies an affirmation of the superiority of those who can be satisfied with the sublimated, refined, disinterested, gratuitous, distinguished pleasures forever closed to the profane."[23] One of my local video stores (staffed almost entirely by college graduates in film studies) stopped carrying *Rainbow Brite* in 1990 because it received too many complaints from parents—"The children loved it but the parents hated it!" the manager told me.

My Little Pony plays its childlike and female orientation totally straight: no attempt is made to appeal to a broader audience—and this, I argue, is the reason for its success. Something was gained and lost when marketers and video producers began exploiting little girls as a separate market. Little girls found themselves in a ghettoized culture that no self-respecting boy would take an interest in; but for once girls were not required to cross over, to take on an ambiguous identification with a group of male characters.

In the following section, I offer a plot synopsis of three *My Little Pony* videos, focusing on their borrowing from women's popular culture genres, their range of character types, and their psychological themes. Doing this has taught me above all that children's cartoons have complicated narratives. It was surprisingly difficult to summarize these videos, given the many twists and turns of plot that occur within half an hour. There is an important lesson in this: adults tend to think children's videos are simple and closed to any but a single interpretation, because adults rarely watch children's videos in their entirety.

By describing each video at length, I hope to demonstrate both their complexity and their openness to a variety of interpretations. As with most television, children watch these with mixed levels of attention, focusing in on what they consider the good spots, often letting their attention waver—perhaps while they play with their miniature plastic replicas of the characters on the screen.

In "Mish Mash Melee," Windwhistler, Dizzy, and two other ponies experience an adventure that takes them to the brink of ecological disaster and back again. The episode takes place in the "mystificent" forest of the Delldroves, gnomelike male creatures who replenish their land by polishing stones and hammering acorns in an underground factory. As Windwhistler notes, "They are an orderly and well-balanced society, and they do all this work without any glory or reward." While in the factory, the ponies accidentally upset a barrel marked "Balance." Colored drops called Frazzits escape, causing the Delldroves to smash the acorns and pulverize the stones and the ponies to act out of character. The ponies celebrate the fun of "being somebody else" with a musical number, but they realize that balance must be restored. Dizzy, who is usually scatter-brained, organizes a scheme that returns the Frazzits to the barrel for good. The Delldroves gather to thank the ponies, and Windwhistler credits Dizzy with saving the day. When Dizzy, scatterbrained again, says, "I did?" the group shares a good laugh, and the screen goes to black.

This episode employs a number of narrative conventions from science fiction and fantastic literature that are frequently used in the plots of contemporary children's cartoons: the escape of a contaminating substance (the Frazzits); the existence of a parallel or lost world (the Delldroves); the placing of familiar characters in altered states induced by changes in body chemistry or sometimes by the substitution of a mechanical double (the ponies' altered personalities when the Frazzits are released). In "Mish Mash Melee," the altered-state device from science fiction provides the motivation for the cartoon's obligatory musical number. All of the girls' cartoons include musical numbers in which the characters express their true feelings of the moment. In boys' cartoons, none of the characters burst into song unless it is motivated in the story or clearly set off from the rest of the story as a music-video interlude.

The ecological themes in "Mish Mash Melee" are common to a variety of boys' and girls' cartoons produced in the 1980s: *Rainbow Brite, He-Man, Ghostbusters, Thundercats, The Care Bears.* (In 1990 the theme became the mainstay of Ted Turner's *Captain Planet* series.) Animators render pollution and toxic waste as colorful enemies that allow considerable artistic freedom in their visualization. The vaguely environmentalist themes that emerge in the cartoons are usually inoffensive to parents, prosocial and relatively nonviolent. Pollution can be seen as a contemporary interpretation of the images of blight and infertility that have typically motivated the hero's quest in the romance.[24] Often the cartoons portray the terrible effects of pollution, which temporarily transforms the cartoon's setting into a wasteland: Ponyland is frozen or stripped of color;[25] Rainbowland is turned brown; a ruined, smoking Manhattan under a sort of postnuclear holocaust sky appears repeatedly in *Ghostbusters.*

In girls' cartoons, the threat of toxicity and the turning of a homeland into a wasteland often motivates a group to act together as a team, replacing the traditional figure of the lone hero setting off on a quest. Thus, a set of cute, tiny girls (or furry female creatures) proves to be capable of nothing short of saving the world. In girls' cartoons, redemption often takes the form of a cleanup rather than a direct battle with a villain using weapons. In *Rainbow Brite, Strawberry Shortcake, The Care Bears, Fraggle Rock,* and *My Little Pony,* there is a vision of work behind the scenes that typically represents natural forces in the form of the industrial factory. The color in Rainbowland, for example, comes from "Star Sprinkles" that are produced by midget mascots called Sprites; working in an underground operation that is a cross between a factory and a bakery with a furnace and conveyor belt, the Sprites press out stars with cookie cutters. In "Mish Mash Melee," we find a typical attribution of natural processes (weathering of stones or sprouting of trees) to industrial techniques and the assembly line. Underlying the forest floor is a factory. In *Fraggle Rock,* a society of miniature workers, called Doozers, exists parallel to the Fraggles. Doozers do nothing but build. These representations serve both to relegate all natural processes to industrial ones and to form an image of a perfect society of workers: the Delldroves work all day without glory or reward. Although the workers are represented as very tiny and nonhuman, they essentially represent adulthood.

The girls' programs take cognizance of work behind the scenes, the work that adults do, and sometimes express an admiration for the discipline, order, and hard work that constantly occur. This workers-behind-the-scenes motif is exclusive to girls' cartoons. On boys' shows, magic, bravery, weaponry, and combat produce the results; no imagination is wasted on the boring, sacrificial, repetitive work that adults might do. (And the main characters are themselves often already adults, as in *Thundercats, Ghostbusters,* and *He-Man,* or nearly so, as in *Teenage Mutant Ninja Turtles.*) In the magical settings of the girls' cartoons, a less exciting, more mundane picture of adult work and responsibility is never far out of sight.

In "Baby, It's Cold Outside," the ponies again save the world, but this time by teaching a wise lesson about compassion and emotional warmth. Evil King Charlatan of the North Pole, a penguin, wants to take over the world by freezing it with his new machine. His first victim is Sunny, a little duck who is also his son's best friend. Back in Ponyland, Galaxy has noticed that the rivers and even the ever-present rainbow are freezing and sends Surprise to find Megan, the human heroine of the series, a blond, blue-eyed girl of about eight. Surprise sings a song of determination and courage ("We're not gonna freeze, no sir!") and then travels with the other ponies and Megan to the North Pole. There they find themselves trapped in a maze, chased by a gorilla, captured, and imprisoned. After applying various kinds of problem solving (can they tunnel out? bend the bars?), they escape and join forces with Prince Edward and the frozen Sunny. The group finally reaches King Charlatan, who reacts with such rage that he freezes his own son. Megan sings her argument with the king as she boldly points her finger at him: "How can you be so cold?" During the song, we see flashbacks of King Charlatan as a good father, giving the infant Edward a bottle, cradling him and playing with him. The king is moved to tears, which melt the ice around his son, and the ponies blast the evil machine with a magic ray. Megan and the ponies smile approvingly at the scene of paternal love and walk off into the sunset.

Both boys' and girls' animated series of the 1980s routinely associate villainy with technology, thus borrowing a strain of technophobia from science fiction novels. Male and female heroes use different means to wrest the technologically based power from the villains. In boys' cartoons, evil uses of technology—typically, the desire to take over the world and subordinate all others—are pitted against good uses of technology by the heroes. The audience hopes that the good guys' guns, lasers, swords, or ninja weapons—combined with cleverness—will be sufficient to put down the bad guys. In girls' cartoons, direct conflicts employing weapons or evil machines are avoided. In "Baby, It's Cold Outside," Megan tries to talk King Charlatan out of his evil, while his power is turned against himself. Megan and the ponies encounter mazes, traps, and physical barriers on their journey to confront the villain. Overcoming obstacles and extricating oneself from a trap provide the suspense, rather than direct, hand-to-hand or weapon-to-weapon battles. Once the villain is encountered, the heroines must shame him into admitting error and showing remorse. In *My Little Pony* the villains resemble those of the classic quest-romance, as described by Northrop Frye: "The antagonists of the quest are often sinister figures, giants, ogres, witches and magicians, that clearly have a parental origin."[26] The end results in the girls' cartoons are rehabilitation, reform, and reintegration into a community rather than, as in the boy's cartoons, zapping away the villain forever or locking it in a "ghost trap" or "containment chamber" as in *Ghostbusters.*

In *My Little Pony,* as in *The Care Bears* and *Rainbow Brite,* threat is founded on feeling. Typically, emotional coldness is the real evil: King Charlatan's icy stare propels the machine that could take over the world. Feelings rule the world. All of the childlike heroines, whether as teams or as individuals such as Megan and Rainbow Brite, possess the acumen of psychotherapists and the bravery of saints. They demonstrate that most courses of action can be changed through increased self-knowledge, through understanding a deed's consequences, through remembering someone you love. Emotional insight turns out to be the most powerful force in the world, and all the heroines possess it to a superior degree and in abundant quantities. The villains are usually male (even in the case of an evil queen, her henchmen are always male); the healers are female. Often the villains are incorrigible, infantile figures, like the *Rainbow Brite* villains Murky, a short, balding, middle-aged man, and his companion Lurky, a big, brown blob of a creature; or the bald Professor Coldheart of *The Care Bears*. All men are babies in this world order, and hostility and aggression can be cured by a combination of firmness and kindness.

Absent in *My Little Pony* is one of the central figures of girls' fiction: the rebellious, headstrong, egocentric preadolescent who eventually gets her comeuppance. Like Madeleine or Pollyanna, these girls end up, like many adult women in melodramatic fiction, bedridden from illness or accident. A number of series designed for a mixed audience of boys and girls, of the kind stamped with the approval of the National Education Association and shown on PBS, feature such a female as a permanent character in a predominantly male cast: Miss Piggy of *The Muppets* and Baby Piggy of *Muppet Babies* are examples of this type, as are Red of *Fraggle Rock* and Whazzat of *Zoobilee Zoo*. These female characters enjoy more latitude in their behavior than does a figure like Megan—they get to be tomboys or to be unapologetically narcissistic or selfish—but in the end there is usually punishment and remorse and an explicit moral lesson about the dangers of selfishness. On *My Little Pony,* there are only mature big sisters who already know how to act like wise, sympathetic mothers. They are ever prepared to deal with the feelings of all, to ferret out sorrow or inadequacy or coldness. There is a kind of power in Megan's position when she stands up to the penguin father and lectures him about his coldness. Though she does not break many rules of femininity, she is allowed the privilege of being always right. Unlike the more rebellious heroines who are eventually chastised for their selfishness and immaturity and lack of consideration, the ponies and their friends always possess moral rectitude. The girls are always on the side of the angels.

In "The Glass Princess," the threat to Ponyland is tied to one pony's sense of inadequacy and self-doubt. The forty-five-minute episode, planned as an hourlong special for television, opens with Shady repeatedly failing exercise drills for the pony olympics: "Everyone thinks I'm useless, and they're probably mad at me for messing things up." Meanwhile, Princess Porcina, a vain middle-aged pig who lives in a messy castle, discovers that her magic cloak is wearing thin. The cloak allows her to turn all things into glass so she can admire her own image everywhere. Her henchmen, the Raptorians, capture a group of ponies, whose hair they plan to weave into a new cloak. They tie the ponies on a conveyor belt and move them through an operation that resembles a carwash: shower heads, dryer, mechanical arms with towels, curlers, powder, combs, brushes, and makeup. Once Porcina has the new cloak in hand, she unthinkingly turns Ponyland into glass at the request of the Raptorians, who have their own evil designs for world conquest. Back in Ponyland, Megan learns of the kidnapping and begins to organize a rescue mission, while Shady blames herself for all the trouble ("If only I hadn't been so oversensitive, maybe I could have helped."). It is Shady, though, who hatches the plan that saves the day. When the characters finally confront each other, Porcina sees the error and, instead of turning the ponies to glass, turns the Raptorians into ice ("Don't worry, they never felt it. They never felt anything, not about you or me."). Porcina becomes a groomer for the Bushwoolies, a group of diminutive forest creatures who live in Ponyland and occasionally help the ponies. Megan praises Shady: "Your bravery and good thinking came through when we needed it most."

Shady's feelings of inadequacy form the backdrop for the formidable complications of plot in "The Glass Princess," as they do in several other episodes and in *My Little Pony, The Movie.* Shady's often repetitive recitation of her own worthlessness provides the story's only breaks from the action. Many girls' cartoons focus on a character's wounded or resentful feelings, and often these feelings function as a catalyst in the plot by leaving a character sufficiently vulnerable and isolated that she is easily taken advantage of by the villain. Males such as Murky and Lurky in *Rainbow Brite* and the Raptorians in *My Little Pony* prey on the female feelings of inadequacy. One of the most common character flaws in girls' cartoons is being too sensitive and self-critical. While there is always a cheery ending, characters often suffer from an underlying depression. But Shady is also ambitious in a way; she wants to stand out from the crowd, to make a unique contribution, to gain some credit and recognition. Porcina has obviously gone too far in this direction; her narcissistic ambition has left her ridiculous and vulnerable.

Shady's voice is especially grating to adults: a high-pitched, singsong, nasal whine. Early in the episode, Maureen, Megan's younger sister, comforts Shady as she sings, "All wrong, all wrong, all my plans always go all wrong . . . I'm a klutz and I don't belong." Each of the ponies has one personality attribute that is primary: Shady's is feeling insecure and inadequate. She is unable to distinguish herself with a special talent; she is inept at sports; she inadvertently does the wrong thing; she causes trouble for her friends. If Shady represents a masochistic response to the problem of being a little girl, she at least represents an acknowledgment of that identity as problematic. The drama of the girls' cartoons regularly revolves around feelings of worthlessness, a narrative motivation unheard of—perhaps logically impossible—in the boys' cartoons.

Why is there this difference from boys' cartoons? Valerie Walkerdine has analyzed the precarious position of girls in a world where the official word as handed down by liberal teachers is that gender is unimportant. To succeed in the classroom, girls must present themselves as active learners; but our culture symbolizes activity as male, passivity as female. There may be an irreconcilable conflict between identifying with the female, and with the mother, and identifying with the part of the good student. Walkerdine argues that the failure to acknowledge the conflicts inherent in the role of the little girl, and these split identifications, can be especially harmful:

> Our education system in its most liberal form treats girls "as if" they were boys. Equal opportunities and much work on sex-role stereotyping deny difference in a most punitive and harmful way. . . . A denial of the reality of difference means that the girl must bear the burden of her anxiety herself. It is literally not spoken. She is told that she can be successful and yet the painful recognition that is likely to result from the fear of loss of one or the other (her femininity, her success, or both) is a failure to be either, producing neurotic anxiety, depression or worse. . . . In a sense, then, rather than perpetuating the denial operating in the spurious circulation of needs, fulfillment and happiness, a recognition of struggle, conflict, difficulty and pain might actually serve to aid such girls.[27]

Shady's feeling "all wrong" seems to represent the very struggle Walkerdine suggests: Shady feels inadequate, and then she feels ashamed for feeling dejected. Male peers are not around to compete with; traditional femininity is validated. Megan's skills and achievements are those of the good mother. But the ponies, unlike the girls, are allowed to feel negative, sad, listless, and insecure.

Most obviously, girls' cartoons present an unambiguous, segregated world of the feminine. Segregation by gender (within the audience and among the characters), the display of traditional feminine behaviors, and the use of kitschy aesthetic codes (pink and furry) in the girls' cartoons have offended many television critics and child educators, whose position is usually implicitly informed by a liberal feminist political agenda and middle-class norms for cultural consumption. Adults prefer their children's consumption to be rational and politically correct and associate certain political beliefs (equality of the sexes) with the selection of clothing, toys. books, and videos that gravitate toward "gender-neutral" styles: primary colors, coeducational groups of characters (boys and girls together), and more abstract decorative motifs, such as those based on alphabets, numbers, or geometric shapes. My Little Pony violates these adult-oriented and upper middle-class taste codes and offers instead representations that historically belong to "low culture": flamboyant colors and hairstyles; wide-eyed, babyish animal figures; and a baroque flair for decorative detail. Thus some adults perceive their child's interest in My Little Pony as a consumption error, driven by peer-group identification but inappropriate to their familial class membership. Parents are disturbed by children's lack of individuality, their herd instinct for loving My Little Pony and other mass-culture fads (while often failing to recognize the large measure of conformity that generally governs adults' seemingly more individualistic and "unique" selections among "higher-class" consumer goods). Children's taste for My Little Pony embarrasses educated middle-class parents because it represents an emulation of working-class aesthetics and a blatant marking of gender difference that seems incompatible with liberal feminist ideals.

In *Feminist Politics and Human Nature*, Allison Jaggar has argued that rationality and individualism are the cornerstones of political rights in liberal political philosophy, so liberal feminism must assert the female capacity for both of these. Liberal feminists minimize gender differences. Liberal feminism looks forward to a future in which psychological differences between men and women, boys and girls will be much less pronounced and education, once it is truly providing equal opportunities, will further enhance the female capacity for the development of reason. But female gender socialization, as well as the work women are expected to do as adults, poses special problems for the liberal conception of individualism and rationality. As Jaggar explains:

> The instrumentalist strand within the liberal conception of rationality equates rational behavior with the efficient maximization of individual utility. To be rational in this sense it is necessary, although not sufficient, for an individual to be egoistic. As we saw earlier, liberal theorists assume that all individuals tend toward egoism, even though they may be capable of a greater or lesser degree of limited altruism. While this model may provide a plausible approximation for the behavior of contemporary males, it is obvious immediately that it is much less appropriate to the behavior of women, who often find their own fulfillment in serving others.[28]

Megan and Maureen encourage the ponies to voice their emotions, so they can be cured of the negative ones. It is easy to see this aspect of the plot as simply parroting a therapeutic, self-help strategy made popular through television talk shows, talk radio, self-help groups, and popular advice literature, as Stephen Kline has done. But rather than reinforcing the need for individual solutions to problems, *My Little Pony* emphasizes the importance of the loyal community of females. "I tried to be so helpful," sings Shady. Maureen assures her: "Shady, it's not your fault." The self-deprecating pony makes herself or others vulnerable to the more powerful forces of evil, but in the world of *My Little Pony* there is safety in numbers. Shady's sulking might cause some ponies to be captured, but another group will come to their rescue. As Tania Modleski has said about the seemingly powerless heroines of the romance, "victims endure." In the end, the group rallies around to affirm the importance of each member. Like the members of a good family, Megan, Maureen, and the ponies learn to respect individual differences and to be vigilantly attentive to one another's feelings. The commitment to and sense of belonging in a group surpass the individual's needs. This is the moral of the story.

"The Glass Princess" expresses a deep ambivalence toward those aspects of girls' socialization having to do with physical appearance. The most traumatic moment in the cartoon is when the ponies are tied down to have their hair washed and curled, a routine familiar to little girls in many different cultures.

Porcina verbally directs this torturous exercise, but it is the sinister Raptorians who carry out the dirty work and seem to relish the ponies' distress. Hair care is such a traumatic and difficult aspect of gender socialization that a host of consumer products have been developed and marketed that promise to make it a happier experience for parents and children: no-tears shampoo; headbands and neck rests to help keep soap out of eyes; cream rinses to take the pain out of combing wet hair. Feminists have seen hair grooming as the first lesson in submission for the sake of appearance. It is a long and troubled one, especially for African American girls. The success of the My Little Pony toys may largely be due to the fact that they double as bath toys. Girls' play with ponies often involves doing to the ponies what mothers have done to them, washing hair, combing and brushing it, fixing it with ribbons and barrettes.[29]

Girls' animated series in the 1980s borrowed from popular genres for adult women. In *My Little Pony,* the ethos of the soap opera—that feelings are all important—is combined with some conventions of the paperback romance, which, as Tania Modleski and Janice Radway have argued in their powerful work on the subject, are worthy of serious consideration by critics interested in the possibilities for producing popular feminist narratives. Like the soap opera, there is an emphasis on understanding the often mysterious codes of feelings. Unlike the soap opera, the characters never appear in the domestic sphere. In *My Little Pony,* Megan is transported away from her real home to straighten out the world. Adventure comes with her departure from her home (when the ponies come to pick her up, she is usually already out in the yard of her house). Megan's position is similar to that of the sympathetic heroines of soap opera: the mothers who worry over all their children's (read ponies') competing desires.[30] In the animated series, there is a somewhat more affirmative order, a greater effectivity of female action than on soap opera. The axioms of popular psychology *work* here: revelations change evildoers instantaneously, and males can be quickly set right.

These cartoons dramatize the thrill of vulnerability found in the paperback romance, minus the romantic love. The ponies often find themselves wandering through a maze, similar to the heroine's search through the mansion in the gothic romance. (Feminist critics have argued that the house represents the mother's body.[31]) The good characters on girls' cartoons resemble the heroine of the romance: modest, unassuming, average, flawed. In the end the heroine in the romance is loved for just who she is: so on the girls' cartoon the individuals in the group are accepted no matter what their feelings, no matter what mistakes they have made.

Tania Modleski has argued that a utopian strain exists in the traditional women's genres of popular culture, the soap opera, gothic novel, and romance. A utopian element also exists in the girls' animated series. The animals live in a happy playful world of love and friendship. When in danger, a coterie of friends always arrives to back them up; the word is more powerful than the sword. The viewer can shift between identifications with the humans Megan or Maureen, or with the ponies themselves, and thereby acquire a long list of magical physical abilities, such as flying or disappearing. These are the pleasures to be gained by an identification with the universe of the girls' series.

The criticism of the toy-based shows as a practice made it harder to notice what was most unusual about many of the shows: that they were reaching out to the audience of little girls, and that this necessitated changing and adapting the conventions of the cartoon in significant ways. Of course, not all of the toy-based shows catered to the audience of girls in the same way or to the same extent. *The Smurfs,* for example, counted a lone female called Smurfette among its dozens of characters, and *The Smurfs* television series relied on standard male-adventure plots. *The Pound Puppies* used roughly equal numbers of male and female dogs and mixed melodrama and detective fiction in its stories about locating dog owners or lost puppies. But marketing for girls brought about some interesting innovations in many of the animated television series: however crassly commercial the toy tie-in, shows like *My Little Pony* and *Rainbow Brite* created fictional worlds in which females were dominant. It was hardly feminist, and it starred blond, blue-eyed girls, but it offered much more than the literary and media fare in which girls are nearly always required to identify with boys and men. In that respect, *My Little Pony* achieved something rarely accomplished in educational public television—the television fare most palatable to the intellectual middle class. Parents should understand that for the little girl at the video or toy store to choose *My Little Pony,* then, is to make a quite rational choice among the limited offerings of children's consumer culture. The choice is not made out of identification with an insipid and powerless femininity but out of identification with the limited sources of power and fantasy that are available in the commercial culture of femininity.

NOTES

1. Elizabeth Segel, "'As the Twig Is Bent . . .': Gender and Childhood Reading," in *Gender and Reading: Essays on Readers, Texts, and Contexts,* ed. Elizabeth A. Flynn and Patrocinio P. Schweickart (Baltimore: Johns Hopkins University Press, 1986), 171.

2. Increasing sales through segmentation is tricky, but with children's goods it works on a per family basis when brothers and sisters can no longer share the same clothes, books, and toys.

3. Segel, "'As the Twig Is Bent . . . ,'" 175.

4. Sybil DelGaudio, "Seduced and Reduced: Female Animal Characters in Some Warner's Cartoons," in *The American Animated Cartoon,* ed. Danny Peary and Gerald Peary (New York: E. P. Dutton, 1980), 212.

5. My sources for this survey of female characters on children's television are Stuart Fischer, *Kid's TV: The First Twenty-Five Years* (New York: Facts On File Publications, 1983), George Woolery, *Children's Television: The First Thirty-five Years, 1946–1981* (Metuchen, N.J.: Scarecrow, 1983), and Hal Erickson, *Syndicated Television: The First Forty Years, 1947–1987* (Jefferson, N.C.: McFarland, 1989).

6. It is interesting to note that when Fred Rogers first appeared in 1955 on a show called *Children's Corner,* he worked behind the scenes as a puppeteer and a woman named Josie Carey hosted the show; see Fischer, *Kids' TV,* 68–70.

7. *Eureeka's Castle,* a program for preschoolers on Nickelodeon, which was introduced in 1990 with the deliberate intention of snagging the *Sesame Street* audience, clearly redresses this situation. The presence of a female lead both offers the possibility of some segmentation—getting the girls' and mothers' attention—and lends an air of nonsexism to the show. Eureeka, however, remains more of a figurehead than a developed personality.

As of the 1991 schedule, Nickelodeon seemed to be orienting itself to girls in its daytime programming with some animated series, *The Little Bits,* and *The Koalas,* and the situation comedy *Clarissa Explains It All.* This mimics the way the cable network Lifetime specializes in adult women viewers.

8. Miss Piggy has been read more positively by feminists Judith Williamson and Kathleen Rowe; I agree with these interpretations but do not find them pertinent to the experience of young girls.

9. The Care Bears were reintroduced in 1991 with a new, explicitly ecological bent to their characters; now they were interested in such things as kindness to animals and keeping the environment clean.

10. The girls' toys that were part of this phase outnumber the boys' toys: He-Man and the Masters of the Universe, the Transformers, the Thundercats. He-Man was merely a "swords and sorcery" version of superheroes who were long familiar to the boys' toy and media market such as Superman, Batman, and Spiderman. There was certainly nothing new about producing an animated series for boys whose licensed characters were "tied in" with toy merchandising.

11. Tom Engelhardt, "Children's Television: The Strawberry Shortcake Strategy," in *Watching Television: A Pantheon Guide to Popular Culture,* ed. Todd Gitlin (New York: Pantheon, 1987), 84.

12. Ibid., 97.

13. See Robert C. Allen, *Speaking of Soap Operas* (Chapel Hill: University of North Carolina Press, 1985), and Ellen Seiter, " 'To Teach and to Sell': Irna Phillips and Her Sponsors, 1930–1954," *Journal of Film and Video* 41 (1989): 150–163.

14. Engelhardt, "Children's Television," 97.

15. For a comprehensive discussion of the critical reception of Disney's work and the elaborate care that went into the drawing of the characters' movement, see Richard Schickel, *The Disney Version* (New York: Simon & Schuster, 1968). Ariel Dorfman attacks the content of Disney on ideological grounds in "Of Elephants and Ducks," *The Empire's Old Clothes* (New York: Pantheon, 1983), 17–63, and *How to Read Donald Duck: Imperialist Ideology in the Disney Comic* (London: International General, 1975).

16. Stephen Kline, "Limits to the Imagination: Marketing and Children's Culture," in *Cultural Politics in Contemporary America,* ed. Ian Angus and Sut Jhally (New York: Routledge, 1989), 299–316.

17. My informal survey ranges from the children of university faculty to the children of low-income, unemployed families served by a free day-care program I worked at in 1988–1989.

18. Stern and Schoenhaus, *Toyland,* 117.

19. Roland Marchand has noted that introducing a choice of colors became a standard advertising technique in the 1920s. Marketers began to suggest changes in color scheme for bathroom fixtures, towels, sheets, fountain pens, and kitchen cabinets and appliances once the market had become saturated. Colors going in and out of fashion helps to drive the market for many consumer goods bought by adult women; see Marchand, *Advertising,* 120–127.

20. Hasbro, United Kingdom, 1988.

21. Mattel, 1989.

22. For an animated series to be considered for a network series, at least sixty-five episodes must be made.

23. Bourdieu, *Distinction,* 7.

24. "Translated into ritual terms, the quest-romance is the victory of fertility over the waste land." Northrop Frye, *Anatomy of Criticism* (Princeton, N.J.: Princeton University Press, 1957), 193.

25. The frozen blight is reminiscent of the winter Demeter causes while she grieves over the separation from her daughter Persephone; in cartoons the blight appears, but the mother is always already absent.

26. Frye, *Anatomy,* 93.

27. Valerie Walkerdine, "On the Regulation of Speaking and Silence: Subjectivity, Class, and Gender in Contemporary Schooling," in *Language, Gender, and Childhood,* ed. Carolyn Steedman, Cathy Urwin, and Valerie Walkerdine (London: Routledge & Kegan Paul, 1985), 224–225.

28. Allison M. Jaggar, *Feminist Politics and Human Nature* (Totowa, N.J.: Rowan & Allanheld, 1983), 45.

29. In this respect it is very similar to a lot of somewhat older girls' play with Barbie dolls. Part of the success of the pony line may have been the way that it extended this possibility to younger girls, who may not have had the rather formidable hand-eye coordination required to style a Barbie doll's hair—and to dress her. It also places the hair care issue at some remove from its meaning in heterosexual romance.

30. See Tania Modleski's description of the "ideal mother" as the soap opera viewer's position in "The Search for Tomorrow on Today's Soap Opera," *Film Quarterly* 33, no. 1 (Fall 1979): 3–18. Modleski discusses both romance and soap opera in *Loving with a Vengeance: Mass-produced Fantasies for Women* (New York: Methuen, 1982).

31. See Janice Radway, *Reading the Romance: Women, Patriarchy and Popular Literature* (Chapel Hill: University of North Carolina Press, 1984).

Marina Warner (b. 1946)

"Boys Will Be Boys" is another chapter from Marina Warner's 1994 book *Six Myths of Our Time*" (see "Little Angels, Little Monsters: Keeping Childhood Innocent" in Part 2). In this essay, Warner explains how she discovered that video games are "a man's world." The predominant images of warriors conquering monsters, made vividly realistic and accessible to the senses through new video technology, represent a theme that Warner sees in many forms throughout the world. She compares recent variations on this theme to the portrayal of man and monster in Mary Shelley's *Frankenstein*. While C. W. Sullivan III examines Shelley's novel as it influenced modern fantasy fiction (see "Fantasy" in Part 4), Warner's discussion ranges widely, from ancient depictions of warriors by Homer and other classical mythmakers to modern movies and initiation rituals for boys in remote and dominant cultures today. For Warner, Shelley's novel provides "the crucial knowledge that monsters are made, not given." Although contemporary media perpetuate attitudes that are less optimistic than Shelley's, reinforcing the assumption that male aggression and violence are innate, rather than learned, Warner's analysis raises the hope that our culture could reject "the warrior ethic" in favor of narratives and actions that would encourage males to value positive, lasting relationships, diplomacy, and "cunning intelligence" more than physical power. Warner provides an intriguing example of criticism that shows how classic literary texts can influence culture and how social attitudes, which may be flawed and detrimental, control the socialization of children as they are spread through modern media.

Boys Will Be Boys

The Making of the Male

As I was going to the Future Entertainment Show, held in Olympia last year, I soon found I was the only woman waiting for the tube. The station was unusually full for the middle of the morning, with scattered young men in jeans and sneakers, gaggles of young boys, one or two fathers. When the train came and the carriage doors opened, a rather dazed-looking London pigeon fluttered out. A man near me laughed. "Don't worry," he said, "it's only a virtual reality pigeon."

I streamed into the show with the crowd, clutching my razzle-dazzle, high-tech, impossible-to-forge ticket, and plunged into the roaring hall. The video games industry has grown in value from almost nothing to $1 billion over the last four years. On multiple screens the season's new offerings in interactive play and 3D simulation were being triggered by the very latest in ergonomic joypads to keep bleeping, scrolling, beaming up, blasting, crashing, bursting into flames and starting up again. I wasn't the only woman any longer: there were one or two grannies, one or two mums. And the marketing staff on the stalls were almost all women—"skirt power" to the trade—and they were selling and busking in green bug costumes as Zools or Zoozes or other technical gremlins. But we were interlopers. It was a man's world: the customers and players were almost all boys.

In the "chill out zone" in the gallery, at stands and on platforms, the players at the banked consoles of games were busy zapping and slicing and chopping and headbutting and dragon punching. Popular culture teems with monsters, with robots, cyborgs and aliens, fiends, mutants, vampires and replicants. Millennial turmoil, the disintegration of so many familiar political blocs and the appearance of new national borders, ferocious civil wars, global catastrophes from famine to AIDS, threats of ecological disasters—of another Chernobyl, of larger holes in the ozone—all these dangers feed fantasies of the monstrous. At the same time, scientific achievements in genetics, reproduction, cosmetic surgery, and transplants have also raised tough and unresolved ethical anxieties about the manufacture of new beings. These are reflected in myths at every level of our culture: in the plots of books, in films, advertisements, song lyrics—and games.

Film's realism, enhanced by the whole revolutionary gamut of illusory techniques, from camera-shot live animation to computer-generated texture mapping, places phantoms within grasp of the sensations. These monsters are made actual, they seem to surround us. The manuals accompanying the role-playing game of "Dungeons and Dragons" illustrate the Ghast or the Ghoul, the Flail Snail or the Dimensional Shambler with diagrams of their thumb-grip and their bite, and provide maps of where they roam. And in games like "Streets of Rage," "Mortal Kombat," "Instruments of Chaos," "Night Trap," "Cannon Fodder," "Street Fighter," "Legacy of Sorasil," "The Rise of the Robots," "Zombie Apocalypse," "Psycho Santa," "Splatterhouse"—the hero slays monsters. Just as Jason and his Argonauts did or Hercules and his Twelve Labours—indeed some of the games quote classical adventures and their pantheons.

Sometimes rescuing a maiden offers a pretext for the exploits, sometimes control or domination of the imaginary horror leads to treasure, as it did to the Golden Fleece or to the Golden Apple of the Hesperides. But the computer's capacity to proliferate means that in video games there be many many dragons, many monsters, many enemies, many aliens, one after another, and they have to be shot'n'blasted, hacked'n'slashed, one by one, level by level as the player works through the stacked platforms of the plot. Some maze puzzles, some role-playing games require strategy, but mostly, the hero busts his way through. A review described "Rivet," a contest between Robocop and Terminator: "It's total cyberpunk ultraviolence.

The kind of game where you just kill everything. It's great." The treasure and the wisdom attained at the end of the slaughter—the pause before it begins again—confer authority, in other words, power.

Myths and monsters have been interspliced since the earliest extant poetry from Sumer: the one often features the other. The word "myth," from the Greek, means a form of speech, while the word "monster" is derived, in the opinion of one Latin grammarian, from *monstrum,* via *moneo,* and encloses the notions of advising, of reminding, above all of warning. But *moneo,* in the word *monstrum,* has come under the influence of Latin *monstrare,* to show, and the combination neatly characterises the form of speech myth often takes: a myth shows something, it's a story spoken to a purpose, it issues a warning, it gives an account which advises and tells often by bringing into play showings of fantastical shape and invention—monsters. Myths define enemies and aliens and in conjuring them up they say who we are and what we want, they tell stories to impose structure and order. Like fiction, they can tell the truth even while they're making it all up.

The appearance of monsters is intrinsic to at least one kind of fundamental mythological story—the story of origins. Dragons, serpents and beasts multiply in the genealogies of the gods and the origins of the created world. Even the Bible's monotheism allows a glimpse or two of Leviathan and Behemoth—dragons lingering on from the cosmologies of the Babylonians and Assyrians. The presence of monsters also marks the beginning of nations, of cities—think of St. George and the Dragon, and of Cadmus who sowed the Dragon's teeth to build and people Thebes. In Antwerp, in the sixteenth century, the city fathers were still showing distinguished visitors the bones of Druon Antigoon, the giant who had been slain by the first king of the region, Brabo, friend and relation of Julius Caesar. The gargantuan shoulder blade and magnificent rib actually belonged to a sperm whale, but they served very well to represent the vanquishing of the brute—and the coming of civilisation to Antwerp.

Chaos threatens in various forms: the she-monster Chimaera spat fire from three heads but the hero Bellerophon, flying down on the winged horse Pegasus, pierced her in her fiery gullet—the flames melted his speartip and she choked to death as the lead cooled inside her. Chimaera's name came to mean illusion: the ultimate monster of monsters, who is both frighteningly there and yet a spectre, who shows something real that at the same time only exists in the mind.

Reason can be awake and beget monsters. Extreme, fantastical, and insubstantial as they are, they materialise real desires and fears, they embody meaning at a deep, psychic level. We're living in a new age of faith of sorts, of myth-making, of monsters, of chimaeras. And these chimaeras define human identity—especially the role of men.

In Mary Shelley's novel, *Frankenstein,* published in 1818, one of the dominant myths today finds its most powerful and tragic expression; the book's central figures have leaped the boundaries of the novel itself into all kinds of retellings, parodic and straight—it's no accident that it's being remade yet again for the screen this year with Kenneth Branagh and Robert de Niro. *Frankenstein* has become *the* contemporary parable of perverted science, but this reading overlooks the author's much more urgent message. Mary Shelley grasped the likelihood that a man might make a monster in his own image and then prove incapable of taking responsibility for him. When the creature at last confronts Victor Frankenstein, the creator who shuns him, he pleads with him, using "thou," the archaic address of intimacy:

I am thy creature, and I will be even mild and docile to my natural lord and king if thou wilt also perform thy part, the which thou owest me. Oh, Frankenstein, be not equitable to every other and trample upon me alone, to whom thy justice, and even thy clemency and affection, is most due. Remember that I am thy creature; I ought to be thy Adam, but I am rather the fallen angel, whom thou drivest from joy for no misdeed. Everywhere I see bliss, from which I alone am irrevocably excluded. I was benevolent and good; misery made me a fiend. Make me happy and I shall again be virtuous."

"Begone! I will not hear you. There can be no community between you and me; we are enemies. Begone, or let us try our strength in a fight, in which one must fall."

Victor Frankenstein rejects and wants to destroy the being he's generated from his own intelligence and imagination; he can only flee, and then, when confronted, offer mortal combat—in the desire to be the victor, as his name suggests. The book *Frankenstein* offers a dazzling allegory of monsters' double presence: at one level they're emanations of ourselves, but at another, they're perceived as alien, abominable and separate so that we can deny them, and zap them into oblivion at the touch of a button.

But monsters in the new, nightmare pandemonium of popular culture have something in common which distinguishes them in a crucial way from the ancient Hydra or Medusa or Chimaera: they don't emanate from nature, but they're either men—or manmade. Frankenstein's creature is their immediate ancestor in this too—but Shelley doesn't set up a superior warrior figure to vanquish her monster; her novel pleads on the creature's behalf: he's capable of goodness if Frankenstein would only love him and teach him and include him, not abandon him to his pariah state. The remedy for Frankenstein's hubris doesn't lie in destroying the monster; Shelley writes explicitly against dealing with evil by heroic, lethal exploits. Implicitly, she's recasting the monstrous in the image of its creator: the creature issues from Frankenstein as his brainchild who's also his double, who acts to define him. Here, the beast is the one who knows this, and presses his maker to accept it. Frankenstein's instant, murderous hostility to his creation may resonate with some of Mary Shelley's own disillusion with her father and her husband and their revolutionary ambitions. It may reflect her feelings about male and female antagonism. But its mainspring is located in her hero's self-loathing: her extraordinary and brilliant book inaugurates a new breed of monster, one who isn't ultimately alien, but my brother, my self.

When popular myth places characters like Slugathon or Robocop centre stage, and then annihilates them until the next avatar appears, they're conjuring the perverted products of human intelligence. Unlike Mary Shelley's book, these plotlines almost invariably reject the offspring of science and propose the enemy monster's defeat through force. Nobody in this kind of story sits down to learn to talk, as Frankenstein's creature does so poignantly and so elaborately when he eavesdrops on the English lessons given in the woodland cottage by the old man and his family to the beautiful Arabian fugitive, Safie. Current tales of conflict and extermination never hear the monster say: "I am malicious, because I am miserable." Or, "Make me happy, and I shall again be virtuous." The phrases sound absurd, because we're so accustomed to expect the hero to have no other way of managing the monsters than slaying them.

Monsters who manifest their nature, like Frankenstein's creature, clearly present easier targets than those in disguise. Deception is a theme that runs through the history of fantasy art, which itself constitutes an attempt to deceive. It achieves a brilliant apotheosis with the replicants of *Blade Runner,* Ridley Scott's cult movie. Replicants are androids, impervious, almost invulnerable; but they look like humans and have been artificially provided with memories of childhood and they don't know that they're monsters. As the word *android* implies, they're men—and yet not men at the same time. Philip K. Dick's book, on which *Blade Runner* is based, puts the dilemma succinctly in its witty title, *Do Androids Dream of Electric Sheep?* This is the ultimate, representative nightmare of this fin de siècle. A hundred and fifty odd years ago, Frankenstien's creature suffered because he knew his own deformity. Jekyll and Hyde knew each other well, though the evil Hyde, as his name tells us, was already concealed within Jekyll. This is still optimistic stuff compared to *Blade Runner.* The film—and the book—touch a live contemporary nerve when they imagine that the robotic monsters look just like humans, that their nature isn't apparent—neither to us, nor to them.

The acute, painful problem today is that these manufactured monsters are ourselves; and ourselves especially as the male of the species. A recent shift in the telling of an old, widely distributed legend illustrates rather well the new fascination and unease surrounding men: in this urban myth, a woman living alone hears a strange sound coming from her kitchen, and going in, sees a hand working its way through an opening that's just been sawn in the door. So she takes a poker, lays it in the fire and when it's glowing attacks the hand, which instantly withdraws, with a howl of pain.

The next day, the woman bumps into the child who lives next door, who tells her by the way that her father has gone to hospital—with a terrible burn on his hand.

In the old, familiar version, the intruder was a witch, a recurrent monster in such creepy tales; but she's turned into a man—an ordinary family man, a neighbour who—and this is crucial—doesn't *look* dangerous.

Fear of men has grown alongside belief that aggression—including sexual violence—inevitably defines the character of the young male. Another myth shadows the contemporary concept of male nature: that intruder could be a rapist. Alongside the warrior, the figure of the sex criminal has dug deep roots in the cultural formation of masculinity. The kids who kill a series of ghouls or aliens can tell themselves they are not like the monsters they are killing. But the serial killer—the very term is of recent coinage—has a human face like theirs. He's dominated contemporary folklore, a figure of thrill and dread, for a hundred years. The terror of Jack the Ripper gripped the Victorians, and present-day murderers are now interviewed on television from prison. The part work magazine, *Real-Life Crimes,* giving details and methods, sells around 60,000 copies an issue.

Films—and the books they're based on—often mete out punishment to sexual women, in the same way as spectators of the Ripper's victims in the London Dungeon enjoy the horror even as they shudder at it. But video games are more scrupulous about current taboos: most of their heroes can't be seen to attack and murder women as such—with the result that women have pretty much disappeared from the plots altogether. There's the occasional dewy-eyed girl hoodlum or pixie-haired hellraiser or "salacious spider woman" and there are some female streetfighters—all active, assertive types and good examples of how positive imaging can backfire. And, as I said, the stock motive of the damsel in distress recurs. But the effect of the almost total absence of women from this all-engulfing imaginary world of boys is to intensify the sense of apartness, of alienation, of the deep oppositeness of the female sex.

Modern myths still approach the enigma of sexual difference using very old simple formulae—and if the girls are getting tough, the tough get tougher. In this emphasis on warrior strength, the new stories conform to very ancient ones, stories which were grounded in the different social circumstances of a military or pastoral, archaic society—the heroes of Greece, the samurai of Japan. Slaying monsters, controlling women, still offers a warrant for the emerging hero's heroic character; this feeds the definition of him as a man. But this narrative is so threadbare, it has come away from the studs that held it to the inner stuff of experience: warrior fantasies today offer a quick rush of compensatory power, but pass on no survival skills—either for a working or a family life.

When the young Achilles is hidden by his mother in women's clothes, because she knows from an oracle that he's to die in the Trojan War, it proves child's play to winkle him out. Odysseus the crafty one disguises himself as a merchant and goes to the court of Lycomedes, among whose daughters Achilles has been concealed. Odysseus devises a kind of Trojan Horse: a chestful of gifts, overflowing with jewels and trinkets and textiles—and precious weapons.

The king's daughters bedeck themselves, of course, but Achilles girds himself over his frock with sword and buckler and is unmasked by a triumphant Odysseus and carried off to win the war for the Greeks. Piquant baroque paintings also exist of the warrior revealed, grasping his weapon while the girls primp, and the subject inspired a baroque tragicomic opera by Metastasio, as well as a broader English version, called *Achilles in Petticoats*.

But the mighty Greek heroes aren't the only models of the male. Achilles might choose a mighty sword and buckler, and Hercules use muscle power and a big stick, but in the fairy-tale tradition, by contrast, heroes develop other skills. In *The Arabian Nights* a poor fisherman finds a bottle in his nets, and when he opens it, a huge angry ogre of a genie rises up and threatens the fisherman with instant death. The fisherman responds that he can't believe that anyone so awesome and so magnificent could ever have fitted into such a little bottle—and begs the genie to show him how he did it. The genie obliges, and gradually winds himself into the vessel. The fisherman jumps on it, stoppers it up in a trice. He then refuses to let the genie out until he's granted him fabulous riches.

"Cunning and high spirits" are the mark of those hopeful myths which imagine a different world, which hold out a promise of happiness—and transformation. The story ends, "The fisherman became the richest man of his day, and his daughters were the wives of kings till the end of their lives." Some sceptics might object that the cunning hero or the lucky simpleton doesn't belong in epic or tragedy, where the ideals of manliness are forged; but fairy-tale elements are impossible to keep separate from the grandest of myths: when Oedipus, too, meets the Sphinx, it's a battle of wits. No bloodshed accompanies his defeat of her reign of terror—after solving her riddle, he just leaves her, whereupon, her mystery undone, she hurls herself from a precipice.

In Homer, Odysseus tells the Cyclops that his name is Nobody. So, when Odysseus blinds the Cyclops in his one eye, the giant howls for help to his father the god of the sea and the other Olympians. But all the gods hear is his cry, "Nobody has blinded me." And so they do nothing.

This trick from the *Odyssey* is literally one of the oldest in the book. The hero who lives by his wits survives in countless hard-luck, Puss in Boots-style stories. The prankster or riddler who—fool though he might be—makes good against the odds, flourishes in the folklore of people all over the world; he travelled from West Africa to the Caribbean, for example, in the figure of Anansi, the spider, and features in the stories told there since the seventeenth century.

Charlie Chaplin, and even Woody Allen, have worked this groove, the heroic pathetic. But a gleeful use of cunning and high spirits against brute force, a reliance on subterfuge have almost faded from heroic myth today. In the prevailing popular concept of masculinity, as reflected in comics, rock bands, street fashion, Clint Eastwood or Arnold Schwarzenegger movies, the little man, the riddler or trickster, has yielded before the type of warrior hero, the paradigm of the fittest survivor.

It's striking to see, from old footage of the Olympic Games, how skinny and scrawny athletes used to be: the bigness of men—body-building, muscle-toning—has never been so important to gender definition as it is today.

This contemporary belief that fitness is literally embodied in physical size neglects to pay attention to the rather more important question: what kind of way of life are the survivors defending, what society are they making? It's interesting that the doctrine of the survival of the fittest has become conventional wisdom—opposing theories have pointed out that the animal cooperation and respect for resources are rather more necessary for survival than dog eats dog. But ideas which stress thoughtful and mutual divisions and exchanges in nature sound like marginal, utopian, New Age crankery. Cunning intelligence—in Greek, the goddess Metis—has been superseded by force as the wellspring of male authority, of power; in today's morality, force even feels somehow cleaner, purer, more upright. The very word "wily," the very idea of subterfuge, carry a stain of dishonour. Boys are not raised to be cozeners or tricksters—it'd be unthinkable to train the future man in lures and wiles and masks and tricks; they're brought up to play with Action

Man, and his heavy-duty, futuristic Star Wars arsenal; they're taught to identify with Ninja Turtles, as crusaders, vigilantes, warriors on behalf of the planet, to flick a transformer toy from a flash car into a heavy-duty fighting exoskeleton, bristling with weapons, a monster of technological innovation—the Terminator, Robocop. There are even games with a create-your-own-deity option, in which, having chosen "which god you want to be," you then acquire nearly thirty ways "of smiting your enemy." The army recognises the link between such narratives and their recruitment needs: they take prominent advertisements in the specialist advanced computer games magazines.

I'm not advancing the con man over the soldier, or the cozener over the honest gentleman—that would be absurd; I'm observing a trend towards defining male identity and gender through visible, physical, sexualised signs of potency rather than verbal, mental agility.

Such signs course through the hardening capillaries of the social system with unprecedented fluidity, carried by a thousand different conduits in a million images and sound bites. It's so obvious, but it bears repeating: no participant in the mysteries celebrating the exploits of Hercules, no member of the audience at the tragedy of Agamemnon or Jason had the story recapitulated and reproduced and beamed at him—or her—again and again in a frenzied proliferation of echoes. This use of repetition combines with another new and very popular form of storytelling: the advertisement. The principal task of an ad—to persuade—has altered response to the myths advertising often absorbs and reinterprets. Sometimes ads do give warnings—as in public safety campaigns. But these are recognised to be ambiguous, and warnings against drugs can be taken all too easily as glamorising invitations to sample them. Almost always, ads trigger desire and excite imitation and identification.

The mythic heroes of the Greek story cycles, like Oedipus, like Jason, like Orestes, served as tragic warnings; their pride, their knowing and unknowing crimes, the matricides and infanticides, self-blindings and suicides, all the strife and horror they undergo and perpetrate didn't make them exemplary, but cautionary: they provoked terror and pity, not emulation. The tragedies they inspired offered their heroes as objects of debate, not models. No one coming out of *Oedipus at Colonus* would feel he wanted to be Oedipus in the way that a spaghetti Western excites hero-worship for Clint Eastwood.

But in the arenas of contemporary culture—the TV channel, the computer game, the toy shop, the street—traditional mythic figures of masculinity like the warrior and the rapist circulate and recirculate every day, setting up models, not counter examples, and the forms which convey them do not contain argument or counter-argument, as in a Greek tragedy, but reiterate the message, as in an advertisement. They're appealing to the group's purchasing power, shaping tastes, playing on rivalry and vulnerability. They don't cry, "Beware," but rather "Aspire!"

Boys will be boys, people say when they mean aggression, violence, noise, guns. But does the warrior ethic, which exposed Achilles in the women's quarters, fit the needs of our civil society? Why does an age which believes in medical and scientific intervention on a heroic scale, which works for change—and delivers it—coexist with a determinist philosophy about human nature and gender? The point about Frankenstein assembling the monster from body parts haunts contemporary consciousness, but the book's main philosophical argument, that his viciousness is learned, not innate, is somehow overlooked. The biological and genetic revolution already upon us can alter and save bodies, but stories which feature such bodies assume that their natures are static, determined, doomed—rare is the character in a video game or comic strip who develops or learns to be different. Yet anthropology has shown that, in the territory of sexuality as well as other human areas, social expectation affects character. Masculinity varies from group to group, place to place, and its varieties are inculcated, not naturally so.

Societies who expect boys to be unflinching warriors subject them to rituals of traumatic severity in order to harden them. Among the Sambia in New Guinea, a tribe in which men are warriors and hunters and women are feared and despised, boys are removed into exclusive male control around the age of six, and begin a series of violent initiations which will turn them into men like their fathers. Proper, cultural masculinity doesn't come naturally, it seems, to a New Guinea Highlander. Why should it to a child living in Kentish Town or Aberdeen?

Among other, rather less remote people, living today in the Balkans, in the mountains of Montenegro, the birth of a daughter inspires routine, ritual lamentation. Blood feuds are handed down from generation to generation, and if there's no son surviving in a family to carry on the feud, a daughter can be raised in his place and become a "sworn virgin," a warrior in disguise to defend her family like a man. Her true sex will never again, on pain of death, be alluded to either in her presence or out of it.

When the Serbian-Montenegrin forces in the current war in the Balkans cursed the women they raped that they would bear children who would forever be their enemies and fight against their mother and her people, they were behaving according to a particular complex of inherited social beliefs, they were speaking out of commitment to military values, paternal lineage and a cult of male heroism.

I'm not offering an excuse, a rationale, or adequate explanation of men's capacity to rape and kill. But I am rejecting the universalising argument about male nature that the rapes committed in former Yugoslavia are committed simply because men are rapists. This argument goes, in the words of one prominent American rights lawyer, Catharine MacKinnon: "men do in war what they do in peace, only more so" and also that "similar acts are common everywhere in peacetime and are widely understood as sex." These sweeping assertions work against mobilising change; they present as sovereign truth beyond history, beyond society, the idea that the swagger and the cudgel come naturally to men, due to their testosterone, a hormone that according to this view, is always in excess. The Serbian rapist becomes the summation of male nature.

The problem, how to make a man of men without turning out killers and rapists, has inspired a men's movement in America, which is enjoying a huge international success, led by its guru, the poet Robert Bly, and his personal growth best-seller, *Iron John*. Bly rightly notices that women are unhappy about men, that this does not make men happy either, and that the absence of fathers is keenly mourned. Feminism has taught women vibrancy and knowledge, he argues, masculinism must follow its example. Bly advocates the appointment of surrogate fathers—men who take younger men under their protection, and writes admiringly of tribal rites of passage in which men are socialised in this way, alluding to shared blood-letting among the Kikuyu, and other symbolic woundings (so called—the wounds are real enough). Though Bly

doesn't actually argue for direct bodily assault, the men's movement has adapted many of the socialising methods used by warrior tribes like the New Guinea Sambia, such as separation from women in male bonding weekends and homoerotic physical contact—though so far none of the men's groups have started practising ritual fellatio of men by boys, as do the Sambia in order to transmit the necessary semen for manhood from generation to generation.

Bullying a boy to become one of the boys has taken physical form, in places rather closer than New Guinea. Today, in the hazings, or initiations practised among college fraternities in America, the idea of entering into a bond with other men also requires submission to secret, physical rituals. The popularity of horror, of blood'n'guts stories, arises from a similar urge to test oneself to the limits: the pleasure may lie in surviving the ordeal. Certainly ads for games like to make jokes about players shitting on themselves: for example, a row of men's briefs on the washing line, and the message, Nincontinent, Nintimidating, Nintendo.

It seems to me that Bly has framed his cure the wrong way round: the monsters of machismo are created in societies where men and women are already too far separated by sexual fear and loathing, segregated by contempt for the prescribed domestic realm of the female, and above all by exaggerated insistence on aggression as the defining characteristic of heroism and power.

The presence of fathers will only reduce the threatening character of maleness flourishing around us if sexual polarities are lessened, not increased. Delinquency among young men has provoked acute alarm recently—one man in three in Britain will have been convicted of a crime by the age of 30. And it's carelessly repeated that single mothers are specially to blame.

But it's interesting to look at the problem of fatherless boys from another angle. The popular argument goes that boys brought up by their mothers alone compensate through violence for the lack of a strong male role model in their lives, that they express the anger they feel at the sole female authority at home. This could be put the other way round: the culture that produces irresponsible fathers openly extols a form of masculinity that is opposed to continuity, care, negotiation, and even cunning—qualities necessary to make lasting attachments between men and children, men and women.

These boys aren't deprived of strong masculine role models, they aren't in rebellion, but are suffering from the compulsion of conforming. They're exposed to blanket saturation in a myth of masterful, individualist independence; they're bit players training to be heroes in a narrative which can proceed only by conflict to rupture. Men have been abandoning their families, and almost half never see their children again after two years.

In Mary Shelley's later, apocalyptic novel, significantly called *The Last Man,* the hero exclaims, "'This,

I thought, is Power! Not to be strong of limb, hard of heart, ferocious and daring; but kind, compassionate and soft.'"

It's a measure of the depths of our present failure of nerve that these words sound ridiculous, embarrassing, inappropriate, that Verney's cry strikes one as a heap of hooey—a foolish dream, a chimaera. Mary Shelley's utopianism is too ardent for our cynical times. But we can take away from her work the crucial knowledge that monsters are made, not given. And if monsters are made, not given, they can be unmade, too.

FURTHER RECOMMENDED READING

PRISCILLA GALLOWAY (b. 1930)

TRULY GRIM TALES

Priscilla Galloway, a Canadian educator and scholar who began writing stories for younger children in the late 1970s, has since produced both nonfictional and fantastical books for young adults based on history, myth, and folklore. Like many such collections of tales that were published in the late twentieth century, Galloway's *Truly Grim Tales* (1995) develops startling new points of view on eight classic fairy tales (all of which appear in this volume except "Rumpelstiltskin"). Galloway claims she had "always known" that the storytellers who preceded her "left out a lot," so she continued to look for the truth and "gradually the stories behind the stories have come clear" (p. ix). "The Woodcutter's Wife" focuses on the stepmother in "Hansel and Gretel," like Vivian Vande Velde's "Twins," except that Galloway depicts the woman defending herself in the first person from charges of cannibalism and acknowledging that she is a witch over 300 years old.

Without mentioning Hans Christian Andersen or the title of "The Little Mermaid," a dispassionate third-person narrator begins "The Voice of Love" by observing that people never know the whole story. This type of contemporary fairy tale revision extends the old familiar plot and deflates its idealistic ending, exposing the story of the miserable prince who realizes after his honeymoon that he identified the

wrong woman as his savior. It then becomes a tale of punishment and revenge, with statues of the beloved that remind us of the myth of Pygmalion and echoes of dangerous ancient sirens in the mermaid sisters and the pitiless sea witch who acquired the Little Mermaid's voice. This grim rewrite of Andersen also contrasts with many modern retellings and spin-offs that allow the mermaid heroine and her lover to live happily ever after. Hollywood, with its history of sometimes adding happy endings to literary classics, lets the mermaid get her man in the Disney film discussed by A. Waller Hastings in Part 8 and in *Splash,* another romantic comedy about a mermaid that was produced in the 1980s for older audiences.

In "Blood and Bone," a modern woman living on a high cliff explains that she and her husband became giants because of a disease that is treated by consuming rare bonemeal from two-legged animals. A saucy "pygmy" named Jack interrupts her inner debate about sacrificing her own bones to extend her husband's life, since she cannot bear the idea of living without him. The tale ends with a horrifying cliffhanger as the pathetic giantess hears something crash over the cliff. These macabre stories are for readers who are familiar enough with traditional fairy tales and brave enough to follow Galloway's ominous and twisted path into the dark allusive mysteries of each tale. Another story with an open-ended conclusion is "The Prince," narrated by a homosexual prince with a foot fetish who seeks an unnamed Cinderella character, since his father has ordered him to find a wife and produce an heir. The collection also contains a science fiction variation on "Little Red Riding Hood," a story based on "Rapunzel" that is narrated by a mother who loses and strives to reclaim her daughter, and a tale of revenge about Snow White's stepmother.

JANE YOLEN (b. 1939)

BRIAR ROSE

Jane Yolen, an American writer of over 200 books for children and young adults, as well as fiction and poetry for adults, is best known as a writer of fairy tales and fantasy. (See Part 3 for one of her essays and her fairy tale "Dove Isabeau.") She writes in one of her collections of original tales, *Dream Weaver*, "The stories that touch us—child and adult—most deeply are, like our myths, crafted visions, shaped dreams . . . the larger dreams that belong to all humankind, or as the Dream Weaver says, 'The heart and soul made visible.'"[1] Two of Yolen's novels with modern settings use elements of folklore and fantasy to portray young heroines confronting the horrific experiences of their family members during World War II. In *The Devil's Arithmetic* (1988), a time-travel episode transports a Jewish twelve-year-old from a family Seder to a Polish concentration camp in the 1940s, where she loses her indifference to family history as she participates in "the quiet heroism in the camps" and learns the importance of remembering the past.

Briar Rose (1992), which was published in the Fairy Tale Series of fiction for adults, edited by Terri Windling, won awards as a fantasy novel and a compelling modern story that appeals to young adults. Linking fairy tale symbols of evil with the atrocities of the Holocaust, the novel explores the emotional power of old tales in relation to the life of a Jewish family in America several decades after World War II. It tells three interwoven stories, all interlaced with fairy tale motifs: the adventures of the contemporary American heroine Rebecca; her grandmother's frequent retellings of "Briar Rose"; and the testimony of a Holocaust survivor, a wealthy homosexual man who had loved Rebecca's grandfather and helped her grandmother escape from Poland. Becca, a young writer in Massachusetts, is the youngest of three sisters and the one most interested in exploring their family history after their grandmother dies and leaves Becca a secret box of treasures with a carved rose and a briar on its top. Becca's search for clues to Gemma's past makes the novel an exciting mystery story, while the novel's division into sections called "Home," "Castle," and "Home Again" reinforces the archetypal structure of her quest. The clues Gemma leaves behind take Becca to Poland and the site of a concentration camp at Chelmno.

Flashbacks throughout Becca's story contain fragments of the "decidedly odd" version of "Briar Rose" that Gemma has told her grandchildren repeatedly since they were babies. Readers realize gradually that the unusual details in her version of the Sleeping Beauty tale reflect experiences in the Holocaust that she could not speak of directly: the barbed wire in place of the fairy-tale thorns, the castle where Briar Rose's whole family was cursed, the bad fairy in black with big boots, the resuscitation of the sleeping princess and her love for a prince who disappears from the end of Gemma's tale. Yolen learned from the documentary *Shoah* that Chelmno was a concentration camp in a ruined castle, but there is no record of any women escaping from the gas chambers there, so her novel is a wish-fulfillment fantasy of one victim's miraculous survival. The flashbacks reveal how children respond to fairy tales at different ages and how powerful their imagery is when it is fused with the adult's unspeakable memories.

Becca learns about some of these memories when she finds Gemma's friend, Josef Potocki, in Poland, and he tells his nightmare story of Holocaust horrors. The novel has been criticized and banned in some places—even burned on the steps of the Kansas City Board of Education—because this sympathetic character is homosexual, although many readers appreciate the novel's valuable contribution in exploring the little-known history of the persecution of homosexuals during the Holocaust.[2] Josef Potocki's story also reinforces the novel's emphasis on the timeless blend of truth and fiction lying beneath the surface of fairy tales, the parallels between sleep and death that "Briar Rose" dramatizes.

Becca's grandmother recognized that Becca had the imagination, love, and courage needed to confront the tale's hidden meaning. Becca comprehends Gemma's tale as her sisters do not, because of her intuitive, loving acceptance of the teller's devotion and the tale's magic—its horrors and sadness as well as its joys. Thus, she inherits the privilege and the responsibility of reclaiming her family's lost heritage, like the generations of daring young folk heroes before her who returned from their adventures to tell their own tale of the past, present, and future.

NOTES

1. Jane Yolen, Introduction, *Dream Weaver* (New York: Philomel, 1979).
2. Stone, Rose Etta. "A Book Review and a Discussion with Jane Yolen, Author," 2001, *Writing, Illustrating, and Publishing Children's Books: The Purple Crayon*, ed. Harold D. Underdown, 20 Jan. 2006 <http://www.underdown.org/yolen.htm>.

PART EIGHT

VALUES AND CENSORSHIP

The fact is that censorship always defeats its own purpose, for it creates, in the end, the kind of society that is incapable of exercising real discretion.

Henry Steele Commager, *Freedom, Loyalty, and Dissent* (1954)[1]

In earlier sections of this anthology, we have examined some of the current polarities in children's literature, from the control of reading and behavior by adults versus children to the interaction of words and pictures and of oral and written forms. As we have shown, there are heated debates about the values conveyed through children's literature in such issues as who should determine children's behavior: children themselves or adults. But perhaps the most contentious area of disagreement in contemporary studies of children's literature is the debate over values and censorship.

Most people, when asked, will say that they oppose censorship. However, the issue is not simple, especially when it comes to censorship of children's books. It is not merely a question of whether offensive books should be suppressed or controversial ideas should be given a hearing. It is ultimately a question about what kind of society we want. And how to achieve the kind of society we desire is a complicated matter. Democratic constitutions generally contain statements about the importance of freedom of speech. In practice, however, all societies limit freedom of expression in some ways, whether through laws against pornography, hate speech, incitement to violence, or political sedition. Furthermore, as Mark West points out in his essay on censorship, many writers and editors perform some kind of self-censorship, which may be the choice not to write about certain issues, not to write about them in provocative ways, or not to submit a manuscript that the writer knows will get her or him into trouble in one way or another. Censorship of children's literature is a special problem because adults choose literature for children and parents have the right to control their children's experiences, yet there are different views on whether parents can and should limit their children's reading, as well as whether community members should be able to limit what other people's children have access to.

There are many different forms of censorship, and if we consider censorship a negative thing, we sometimes just relabel the act in question to make it more acceptable. For instance, is putting a controversial book on a special reserve shelf instead of out in the open stacks censorship or appropriate classification? What if the book contains information about how to make a bomb or how to commit a crime? Should young children have access to violent comic books or books that are likely to give them nightmares? Conversely, is it censorship if someone wants to opt out of reading a certain book that he or she considers offensive or immoral? Should a teacher have the right to assign any book in a literature class as required reading, regardless of the sensibilities of the students or parents? Is maintaining a library collection or forming a curriculum always implicitly an act (or a series of acts) of censorship because it involves the exclusion of all the things that are not going to be purchased or retained or taught?

One can approach this issue from a positive angle as well and ask, What are the values and ideas that we want to teach or convey through children's books? Perhaps efforts to censor certain books are testimony to the power that we ascribe to books. This idea is contradicted, however, by the circumstance that people who seek to censor certain books have frequently not read the books in question. They are reacting to the idea of what the book represents to them, rather than to the book itself. However, they still see the printed word as having power—even if they have not read it! In any case, there may be broad areas in which most people agree on the values that are worth transmitting to the next generation, such as courage, honesty, and persistence in the face of adversity.

Nonetheless, areas of disagreement quickly emerge. For instance, the Little House on the Prairie books admirably represent the virtues of the pioneer families who settled the West: ingenuity, resourcefulness, self-reliance, bravery, and family loyalty. However, as Michael Dorris recounts in his essay on reading the Laura Ingalls Wilder books, when he came to read the Little House books to his own daughters, he realized with a shock that although he had enjoyed the books as a boy and admired the author's ability, the stories implied that his own ancestors were nonexistent, when, in fact, they and other Native Americans inhabited the regions of Wisconsin where the Ingalls family began its journey westward. Even more problematic is the representation of the Native Americans as either primitive enemies (one of the white settlers expresses the view that "the only good Indian is a dead Indian") or noble savages. Pa Ingalls has sympathy for the Native Americans, whom he treats with respect—but he has no apparent qualms about the fact that they are being driven off their land by the federal government and that he and others like him will ultimately profit from their removal.

Thus, for Dorris, the Little House books pose a fundamental problem. The stories are well told, illustrate historical circumstances of an important period of American history, and show the admirable qualities of the main characters. But they also represent a skewed or partial point of view, one that favors the white settlers who participated in and benefited from the process of expropriating the land from those who had lived there for centuries and ignores or diminishes the significance of the lives of the people who were there first. Laura Ingalls Wilder's books do not celebrate or even recognize the dignity and complexity of the cultures of the Native Americans, who are Dorris and his daughters' ancestors. Should Dorris read them these stories or quietly censor them? Louise Erdrich wrote a children's book, *The Birchbark House* (excerpted here), that corresponds in some ways to Wilder's Little House books but expands the vision of Native American life and serves as a corrective to Wilder's perspective. Neither Erdrich nor Dorris nor the literary scholar Jon Stott, in his essay on children's novels by Native American writers, advocates censorship; rather, they all advocate providing a more accurate portrayal of what has been misrepresented. Part of what has been missing is an explicit acknowledgment of what has been there all along: the racist assumptions that have gone unquestioned. As Erdrich put it, in talking about Ma Ingalls in *The Little House* series, "I love their humor and warmth, but am disturbed by Ma's racism. Given their widespread use in the schools, I do not think it would be wrong to annotate some of her more insulting remarks."[2]

Political issues furnish a large source of controversy in the discussion of children's books. As Hazel Rochman, Masha Rudman, and Diane Stanley make clear in "Is That Book Politically Correct?" politics are central to historical children's books. The term *political correctness* was coined to mock the effort to adhere to certain values—values that the person using the phrase considers trivial or conformist. What the phrase often disguises is the attempt to substitute other values in place of whatever principles the person or piece being attacked represents. Thus, the term is used as a rhetorical weapon, rather than as a rational argument. It needs to be examined in its context: what is meant by *political correctness,* and why is *political correctness* a negative thing, in the mind of the person using the phrase?

"History is written by the victors" is a common, if cynical, claim. If that is so, some skepticism is needed to evaluate historical fiction properly: whose perspective is represented? How selective or exclusive is the point of view of the story? Whose interest is served by telling the story in the way in which it is told? While authors such as Langston Hughes began in the first few decades of the twentieth century to write eloquent, powerful children's literature from inside minority cultures (see Part 1), the reality remains that much literature about minority or "parallel cultures" (to use the term preferred by Virginia Hamilton) has been written by those outside the cultures. Rochman believes that any reader can imaginatively grasp what it means to be an "immigrant," a person on the margins of society, someone who has been dispossessed in one way or another. Rudman argues that all children should have their ancestry and culture represented respectfully and accurately in children's historical fiction. Diane Stanley, who has written and illustrated historical and biographical books, demonstrates how political correctness can be both a positive and a negative concept, whether you support it or attack it.

From the influential antislavery novel *Uncle Tom's Cabin* by Harriet Beecher Stowe onward, race relations and the history of slavery have been crucial issues in American children's literature. May Justus, who lived in the Smoky Mountains all her life and wrote books for children over five decades of the twentieth century, probably never heard the term *political correctness,* although she was influenced by *Uncle Tom's Cabin* and the civil rights activists she met at the Highlander Folk School in Tennessee. She was compelled to expand her literary settings from mountain cabins and schoolrooms to the city of Nashville after witnessing the effects of discrimination on her friends and hearing of bombings at desegregated schools. Her chapter book *New Boy in School* (1963), illustrated by Joan Balfour Payne, was most likely the first book for early readers about school desegregation. It offered an alternative to violence by depicting a seven-year-old African American boy overcoming his discomfort at a new school, where he is the only nonwhite child in his class, with the help of a kind teacher, friendly classmates, and supportive parents. George Loveland observes that Justus's book "did not lecture or moralize about the need for revolutionary social change. It simply showed how some white folks in Nashville, the kind of folks she had lived around all her life, might choose to act when their schools were integrated and how much better life might be if they would simply respond to the positive and constructive values of their culture."[3] Justus adopted a gentle, optimistic approach to social justice issues that were controversial at the time she was writing, while later authors, such as Mildred Taylor and Virginia Hamilton, as well as picture book artists like Tom Feelings (see Part 6), would produce more painfully realistic books about slavery and racism of the past, always mindful of the need to balance horrifying realities with positive depictions of the human spirit. Marilyn Nelson brilliantly adds to our understanding of historical events by showing us Emmett Till and the circumstances of his 1955 murder from many different angles, reflecting on it with wisdom and outrage in her 2005 sonnets in *A Wreath for Emmett Till.*

The most famous modern controversy over the issue of race in literature is the ongoing debate about *Adventures of Huckleberry Finn,* both because of its use of the word *nigger* and because of its portrayal of the slave Jim. "Was Mark Twain racist?" is one form in which the issue surfaces, but the answer may be irrelevant to teachers or parents who are concerned about the effect of reading a book in a twenty-first-century classroom in which nineteenth-century southern concepts of race are ironically fictionalized. It may take a certain level of sophistication as a reader to recognize the antiracist sentiments in Huck's story. White author E. L. Doctorow discusses the book as a partial artistic failure; as many critics have observed (and others have contested), the ending of *Huckleberry Finn* is a descent into repetitive comedy, comedy that demeans the dignity Jim has achieved and Huck has acknowledged at crucial moments earlier in the novel. African American novelist David Bradley recounts the impact that Twain's novel has had in his own life and contrasts it with the experience of racism encountered firsthand. Bradley defends the novel, arguing that how and in what context the "n" word is used makes all the difference. Katherine Paterson alludes to its power in her story of the nasty girl Gilly Hopkins, who tries to exploit the explosive power of the "n" word to infuriate her teacher—only to discover that her teacher is not so easily controlled. Paterson's books are frequently censored, no doubt partly because she understands the fault lines of tension in American culture so well. Paula Fox's *The Slave Dancer,* one of the first children's novels to address the horrors of slavery, was controversial, in part, because although it portrayed the nightmare of the middle passage—the shipping of slaves across the Atlantic under brutal conditions—its main character was a white boy, and the white characters were far more developed than the African ones.

At least equally controversial is the topic of sexuality in children's books. Should children learn about sex from fiction, and, if so, at what age and in what ways? Should children's books that address sexuality be subject to special rules about what is portrayed because the topic is such a sensitive and influential one—or should children's book authors have the same freedom to entertain and interest their readers as in any other area? Some parents and teachers think that children's books should not address the subject of sex at all. This was, in fact, the consensus in the children's book world for decades. However, that silence began to be broken in the 1970s, most notably by Judy Blume, whose books for children and young adults have become synonymous with frank discussion of sexual topics, such as masturbation, menstruation, and even sexual intercourse and birth control.

Banning books, such as Blume's *Forever . . .* , has the interesting effect of making them all the more appealing to the young readers who are not supposed to read them. What could be more desirable than a book that you are forbidden to read? Censors often fail to take into account this consequence of making a book the subject of heated debate and prohibition. Nonetheless, it does matter how adults treat the subject of what children read about sex—whether they neglect to pay attention to the subject, or whether they try too hard to control access to information about this natural subject of intense curiosity.

A more effective enemy of honest portrayals of life in fiction than censorship may be the homogenizing and "prettifying" effects of popular media, as embodied by the Walt Disney company. As A. Waller Hastings shows in his thorough critique of Disney's version of "The Little Mermaid," adaptations and reworkings of classic tales may have serious sociopolitical implications when they simplify conflicts between good and evil. The popular film contradicts and undercuts the bittersweet melancholy of Hans Christian Andersen's original literary fairy tale so thoroughly as to present opposite meanings. The expectation of a happy ending may be one of the most powerful forces working against truthfulness and complexity in children's books, an expectation that Katherine Paterson argues against in her persuasive essay "Hope and Happy Endings." In a culture that expects the resolution of fictional problems in its prime-time episodes and major box office draws, the idea of children's books that present difficult problems without resolution seems heretical and against the grain.

Yet many writers of books for children and young adults are doing precisely that: arguing, against the grain of mass culture, for greater depth and complexity in the portrayals of life and its difficult issues, with greater faith in the capacity of young readers to make their own judgments and form their own values, discerning among the welter of choices what is useful and constructive for themselves. Australian writer Lee Harding's "Night of Passage" presents a story of a quest that is both a vision of a future, possibly post-nuclear-holocaust, and a rite of passage, in which the relation between indigenous and Western culture has been inverted: the powerful, enduring society is the aboriginal one. Stories such as Harding's allow children to question the fundamental assumptions of dominant culture and, in the process, become critical readers themselves.

NOTES

1. Henry Steele Commager, *Freedom, Loyalty, Dissent* (New York: Oxford UP, 1954).
2. "Louise Erdrich Bio," *Kidsreads.com,* Hyperion Books for Children, 1999, 28 March 2005 <http://www.kidsreads.com/authors/au-erdrich-louise.asp>.
3. George Loveland, "A Greater Fairness: May Justus as Popular Educator," *Journal of Research in Rural Education* 17 (Fall 2001): 102–11, *AppLit,* ed. Tina L. Hanlon, 2002, Ferrum College, 12 April 2005 <http://www.Ferrum.edu/AppLit/articles/JustusArt.htm>.

Mark I. West (b. 1955)

The desire to protect children from certain kinds of experience and knowledge leads some people to prevent young readers from encountering books that they consider unsuitable. Censorship can take many other forms besides the effort to ban books. Knowing that some topics will be controversial can also lead writers, editors, and teachers to refrain from introducing them in the first place, as University of North Carolina–Charlotte English professor Mark West points out in his discussion. West provides a valuable, brief history of censorship in the United States and offers some good advice about steps to take in countering censorship efforts. He gives an insightful explanation for why some of the books by writers who are the most popular with young readers, such as Judy Blume or Norma Klein, are also most frequently the target of censorship efforts: adults tend to read children's books in search of their remembered innocence, while children often read to obtain knowledge about the adult world, including controversial subjects such as sexuality. Thus, what shocks adults may be exactly the same thing that delights and attracts young readers. Censorship of children's books has continued to kindle heated debates since West's essay was published in 1992. Since the late 1990s, for example, the Harry Potter series of fantasy books and films have attracted worldwide attention for topping many bestseller lists and for the disapproval voiced by adults who oppose their treatment of magic and witchcraft.

Teaching Banned Children's Books

HISTORY OF CENSORSHIP CASES

Censorship is generally equated with the banning of books from libraries, but this is only one form of censorship. Restrictions are often imposed on books long before they ever reach library shelves. Such restrictions have strongly influenced the history of children's literature. As early as the late seventeenth century, distinctions were drawn between subjects that could be dealt with in children's books and those that could be addressed only in books for adults. In 1693, for example, the English philosopher John Locke argued that ghosts and goblins should not appear in stories for children (MacDonald 105). Once the idea of childhood innocence took root, restrictions of this sort greatly increased.

To ensure that children's books conformed to the idea of childhood innocence, publishers sometimes engaged in blatant censorship. Many nineteenth-century publishers, for example, decided that some of the bawdy passages from Jonathan Swift's *Gulliver's Travels* were inappropriate for children and excised them from juvenile editions of the book. The most frequently censored passage, according to a survey conducted by Sarah Smedman, was the one in which Gulliver extinguishes a fire in the Lilliputians' palace by urinating on it. This incident was deleted or rewritten in nearly every children's edition published during the second half of the nineteenth century (84–85).

For the most part, however, nineteenth-century publishers had no need to engage in such overt forms of censorship. Children's authors generally censored their own books; they were well aware of the taboos and automatically observed them. This tradition of self-censorship continued well into the twentieth century. Until quite recently, children's authors simply assumed that they could not refer to sexuality, graphically describe violent acts, portray adults in a negative light, use curse words, or address controversial social problems. If, for some reason, they deliberately or unwittingly violated one of these taboos, their editors would strongly recommend that they revise the offending passage. Once in a while, of course, books intended for young readers were published that did

break taboos, and some of these became the focus of censorship attempts. For example, Mark Twain's *Adventures of Tom Sawyer* was banned from many public libraries during the 1870s and 1880s largely because the child characters are seldom punished for misbehaving (Jordan 34–35). In the 1950s and 1960s, J. D. Salinger's *Catcher in the Rye* attracted the attention of censors who disapproved of its profanity (Nelson and Roberts 182–83). Still, most children's books published before the 1960s sparked little controversy.

The only children's authors who systematically violated taboos before the 1960s were writers for publications that children generally purchased on their own, such as dime novels, series books, and comic books. Since they were more concerned with meeting the demands of children than with winning approval of parents, they tended to write about subjects that children found interesting even if the result was the breaking of certain taboos. For instance, the creators of both dime novels and comic books frequently portrayed violence, while series books tended to ignore accepted norms concerning adult-child relationships. In many series books, children were described as being equal or even superior to adult characters. Because these forms of popular culture broke so many taboos, they often came under attack by self-appointed censors.

Anthony Comstock (1844–1915) had led the campaign against dime novels. As head of the New York Society for the Suppression of Vice, he frequently called for the banning of all these works, especially those that dealt with violent crimes. Such stories, he argued in *Traps for the Young* (1883), were a primary cause of juvenile delinquency. When children started to buy more series books than dime novels, librarians mounted their own censorship campaign, which began in the 1880s and continued until the 1920s. In addition to attacking series books in their professional journals, they published lengthy lists of books that were "not to be circulated" in respectable libraries (West, *Children* 20–30). The movement to ban comic books was led by Fredric Wertham, a prominent New York psychiatrist. In his book *Seduction of the Innocent* (1954), Wertham argued that comic book reading could lead otherwise normal children to become criminals, sadists, or homosexuals. He lobbied for the enactment of anti-comic book laws and nearly succeeded in getting such legislation passed in New York State.

For the most part, the campaigns against dime novels, series books, and comic books focused on genres rather than on particular titles or authors. It was not until the 1970s that censors began waging major battles against individual children's books.

MODERN CENSORED BOOKS

The tradition of self-censorship continued to exert a strong influence on children's literature until the late 1960s. However, the social changes that occurred during that decade gradually helped break down the practice. As Americans became more accepting of sexuality and less confident in the infallibility of authority figures, a number of authors and editors questioned the legitimacy of the taboos that had encumbered children's literature for so many years. As a result, the early 1970s saw the emergence of a new breed of children's books. The works of Judy Blume, Norma Klein, and Maurice Sendak dealt with the issue of sexuality, while other authors, such as Louise Fitzhugh, Paul Zindel, and Robert Cormier, depicted adult characters unflatteringly. At the same time, S. E. Hinton, Alice Childress, Isabelle Holland, and several others wrote about controversial social issues, such as gang violence, drug abuse, and homosexuality. Scholars and critics began referring to these types of books as the new realism in children's literature.

While several works of new realism raised eyebrows when they first appeared, few were censored during the first half of the 1970s. This situation started to change as the Moral Majority and other conservative religious and political groups gained power and influence. As the leaders of these organizations urged their followers to speak out against sex education, the teaching of evolution, and "sinful" children's books, the new realism in children's literature came under serious attack. Parents demanded that numerous children's books be banned from libraries and not be taught in public schools. This trend accelerated dramatically in the early 1980s, and it shows no signs of abating.

The most frequently censored children's author is Judy Blume. The censors have focused their attacks on five of her books: *Are You There God? It's Me, Margaret; Then Again, Maybe I Won't; Deenie; Blubber;* and *Forever.* During the first half of the 1980s, over sixty attempts to ban these works were reported to the *Newsletter on Intellectual Freedom,* and it is estimated that many more went unreported. With the exception of *Blubber,* the censorship of Blume's books is the result of their sexual content. The censors dislike *Are You There, God?* because it discusses menstruation and breast development. *Then Again, Maybe I Won't* and *Deenie* are vilified for mentioning wet dreams and masturbation, and *Forever* gets in trouble because it deals with sexual intercourse and describes the use of birth control devices.

Norma Klein, the second most frequently censored children's author, also comes under fire for including sexually related material in her books. Klein's first children's book, *Mom, the Wolf Man, and Me,* is sometimes censored because it contains a single mother who remains sexually active. A number of her other books are targeted for similar reasons. Critics attack *It's Not What You Expect* for including a character who has an abortion, *Naomi in the Middle* for explaining how conception occurs, and *It's Okay If You Don't Love Me* for portraying a teenage girl who initiates a sexual relationship.

Blume's and Klein's stories are certainly not the only children's books that have been declared taboo. Maurice Sendak's *In the Night Kitchen* is often censored because it contains pictures of a nude boy. *My Darling, My Hamburger* and *The Pigman,* by Paul Zindel, are sometimes attacked by people who dislike Zindel's disparaging comments about parents and teachers. Robert Cormier's *Chocolate War* and *I Am the Cheese* come under pressure from those who feel that they undermine parental, institutional, and governmental authority. Another book that is frequently censored is *A Hero Ain't Nothin' but a Sandwich,* by Alice Childress. Censors do not approve of this book's discussion of drug abuse or its use of street language. While these titles are favorite targets, a complete list of censored children's books would run on for pages.

In addition to attacking individual books, contemporary Comstocks frequently condemn textbooks. This practice has attracted attention in recent years in part because of three prominent court cases involving disputes over the use of textbooks in the public schools. The first case surfaced in Louisiana, where, in

1981, religious fundamentalists pushed through a state law requiring public school science courses in which evolution is taught to use textbooks that discuss creationism. In June 1987, however, the Supreme Court struck down the law on the grounds that it introduced religious dogma into the public school curriculum. The second case originated in eastern Tennessee, where fundamentalists argued against the use of a standard set of reading textbooks that they deemed "anti-Christian." In August 1987, the United States Circuit Court of Appeals for the Sixth District ruled that the school board had not infringed on the religious freedom of these parents by requiring the use of the textbooks. The third case took place in Alabama, where several hundred fundamentalists argued that dozens of commonly used textbooks should be banned for promoting the "religion" of "secular humanism." In August 1987, a few days after the Tennessee decision, the Circuit Court of Appeals for the Eleventh District declared that secular humanism is not a religion and that therefore the textbooks could not be banned. Although the outcome of these cases has weakened the current censorship movement, there is no indication that it is coming to an end.

TREATING CENSORED BOOKS IN THE CLASSROOM

Because censorship has become such a serious problem in children's literature, a number of teachers of children's literature are now including discussions of censorship in their classes. Such discussions, however, are most helpful when students read some of the targeted books. While it would be impossible to acquaint students with every controversial children's book, it is certainly feasible to have them read a few of Blume's or Klein's censored works. Without firsthand knowledge of at least a few censored titles, students may find it difficult to make sense of the intense rhetoric that is often used by those who wish to ban these books from libraries and classrooms. Several censors, for example, have proclaimed that *Deenie* is a how-to manual about masturbation when in reality the subject is mentioned on only two or three pages.

Requiring students to read a few of these books can also help them understand some of the reasons for a seldom discussed but omnipresent tension within the field of children's literature. It is not simply a coincidence that the two most controversial children's authors are also two of the most popular among children and teenagers. Throughout the history of children's literature, the books that children have selected on their own have often met with disapproval from adults. Conversely, children's books that have won praise from adults have often been ignored by children (Norby). Students of children's literature should be aware of this pattern and ask themselves why it exists.

If students research this question, they would soon find that the most common explanation is that children's literary tastes are underdeveloped. However, an examination of the controversy surrounding Blume's and Klein's books indicates that this idea is something of a ruse. In the end, it is not the books' literary qualities that trouble adults; it is their contents. Even among adults who disapprove of censorship there is a tendency to frown on the inclusion of sexuality in children's books (Rees 173–84). Most scholars specializing in children's literature, for example, do not advocate the banning of Blume's books, but few actively defend her right to discuss sexuality.

Students who probed deeper might arrive at another explanation for why adults and children tend to like different children's books. Students might discover that some grownups enjoy children's literature because it allows them to escape the complexities of adult life and relive the perceived pleasures of childhood. For these readers, children's literature has a nostalgic appeal. Many children, by contrast, are anxious to grow up and thus seek books that help explain the mysterious worlds of adolescence and adulthood. Consequently, while children often appreciate Blume's and Klein's willingness to write openly about menstruation, masturbation, and other taboo subjects, adults who want to read about childhood innocence may feel repulsed or even betrayed by the writers' frankness. In a sense, children and adults have conflicting tastes because they approach children's literature with different expectations. This is an important point for students to think about, for it might help them come to a clearer understanding of their own expectations of children's literature.

The insights that students can gain through reading controversial children's books are greatly enhanced if they also do some writing on the subject of censorship. One possible assignment is to ask students to write a personal response paper about a censored children's book. In their papers, they should address such questions as the following: Why is the book controversial? Do you think it is objectionable? Would you have been interested in reading this book as a child? Would you allow your own children to read it? Do you think the book should be banned?

In addition to describing their reactions to a book, students could be asked to include research findings in their papers. A simple project is to require students to look through a number of issues of the *Newsletter on Intellectual Freedom* and read about the censorship cases involving the book they have chosen. At the beginning of each issue of the *Newsletter* there is a guide for finding information about particular titles. Another fairly simple research project is for students to interview a local children's librarian about censorship. Many librarians have had to deal with censorship pressures, and some are quite willing to talk about their experiences. Both of these research projects provide students with concrete information they can go on to interpret in their papers.

SUPPLEMENTARY READINGS ON CENSORSHIP

Students who take a serious interest in the censorship of children's literature should be encouraged to do some outside readings on the subject. *Dealing with Censorship,* an NCTE publication edited by James E. Davis, is a good place for students to start. The fact that the book came out in 1979 makes it a bit dated, but most of the book's eighteen chapters remain stimulating and useful. *Protecting the Freedom to Learn,* by Barbara Parker and Stefanie Weiss, is another good source of information about censorship trends. It also provides material on how to prevent censorship from occurring. This book, published by People for the American Way, can be purchased only through the organization's office. The address is 1424 16th Street, NW, Suite 601, Washington, DC 20036. One other book students might find helpful is Nicholas Tucker's *Suitable for Children.* Although this book was published in 1976, many of its essays raise issues that pertain to ongoing controversies.

Numerous articles about censorship have been published in recent years. The *Newsletter on Intellectual Freedom* occasionally publishes full-length articles about censored children's books; one of these articles deals specifically with the censorship of Blume's books (Goldberger). The *Children's Literature Association Quarterly* has published a number of articles on censorship, including two excellent overviews by Amy McClure entitled "Limiting the Right to Choose" and "Intellectual Freedom and the Young Child." For a discussion of recent censorship involving books for young adults, students should turn to Ken Donelson's "Almost 13 Years of Book Protests." Students should also read about censorship from the perspective of an author whose works have been banned. A helpful source in this area is *Trust Your Children* (West). This book contains interviews with Judy Blume, Norma Klein, Robert Cormier, Betty Miles, Harry Mazer, Nat Hentoff, Roald Dahl, Daniel Keyes, Maurice Sendak, and John Steptoe. It also includes interviews with children's book publishers and anticensorship activists.

There are two children's novels about censorship that students might find especially interesting. Nat Hentoff's *The Day They Came to Arrest the Book* is aimed at teenagers. The story revolves around an attempt to ban *Adventures of Huckleberry Finn* because it contains the word *nigger.* The major proponents of censorship in this story are a black student, this student's father, and a young feminist. Hentoff is well aware that these characters are not typical book censors, but he uses them to show that the urge to ban books is not limited to the Moral Majority crowd. Although Hentoff's plot is a bit contrived, the book provides a thoughtful introduction to the meaning of the First Amendment. *Maudie and Me and the Dirty Book,* by Betty Miles, is intended for a somewhat younger audience than Hentoff's book, but it is the stronger of the two novels. The major characters in the story, two eleven-year-old girls, begin working as aides in a first-grade class. Their job is to select picture books and read them aloud to the class. One of the girls chooses a book that deals with the birth of a puppy. After hearing the story, a first-grade boy asks how the puppy got inside the mother dog, and the girl gives him a simple but honest answer. A few parents hear about this incident and demand that the book never be used again. In addition to providing an accurate description of how censorship cases typically develop, Miles does an excellent job of capturing the children's reactions to the whole affair. She makes it clear that the children feel much more confused and threatened by the parents' near hysteria than they do by the contested book.

These various books and articles on censorship can supply students with valuable background information and help them realize what a severe problem censorship has become. If, however, students read only secondary sources, their understanding would be superficial. In the end, the best way to teach students about censorship is to have them read the banned books along with the related material. This approach prevents students from viewing censorship as an abstract problem and helps prepare them to resist future censorship efforts.

WORKS CITED

Comstock, Anthony. *Traps for the Young.* New York: Funk, 1883.

Davis, James E., ed. *Dealing with Censorship.* Urbana, IL: NCTE, 1979.

Donelson, Ken. "Almost Thirteen Years of Book Protests . . . Now What?" *School Library Journal* Mar. 1985: 93–98.

Goldberger, Judith M. "Judy Blume: Target of the Censor." *Newsletter on Intellectual Freedom* May 1981: 57.

Hentoff, Nat. *The Day They Came to Arrest the Book.* New York: Delacorte, 1982.

Jordan, Alice M. *From Rollo to Tom Sawyer and Other Papers.* Boston: Horn, 1948.

McClure, Amy. "Intellectual Freedom and the Young Child." *Children's Literature Association Quarterly* 8.3 (1983): 41–43.

———. "Limiting the Right to Choose: Censorship of Children's Reading." *Children's Literature Association Quarterly* 7.1 (1982): 39–42.

MacDonald, Ruth K. *Literature for Children in England and America from 1646–1774.* Troy: Whitston, 1982.

Miles, Betty. *Maudie and Me and the Dirty Book.* New York: Knopf, 1980.

Nelson, Jack, and Gene Roberts, Jr. *The Censors and the Schools.* Boston: Little, 1963.

Norby, Shirley. "Kids as Book Critics." *Proceedings of the Eighth Annual Conference of the Children's Literature Association.* Ed. Priscilla A. Ord. 27 March 1981. Boston, 1982. 136–40.

Parker, Barbara, and Stefanie Weiss. *Protecting the Freedom to Learn: A Citizen's Guide.* Washington: People for the American Way, 1983.

Rees, David. *The Marble in the Water.* Boston: Horn, 1980.

Smedman, Sarah. "Like Me, Like Me Not: *Gulliver's Travels* as Children's Book." *The Genres of Gulliver's Travels.* Ed. Frederik N. Smith. Newark: U of Delaware P, 1990. 75–100.

Tucker, Nicholas, ed. *Suitable for Children: Controversies in Children's Literature.* Berkeley: U of California P, 1976.

Wertham, Fredric. *Seduction of the Innocent.* New York: Rinehart, 1954.

West, Mark I. *Children, Culture, and Controversy.* Hamden: Archon, 1988.

———. *Trust Your Children: Voices against Censorship in Children's Literature.* New York: Neal-Schuman, 1988.

Judy Blume (b. 1938)

The irony of the title of *Forever . . .* is that the love that Kath feels for Michael, her first lover, turns out not to be eternal. This 1975 novel has been passionately and furtively read by thousands of young readers who have been anxious to find out what sexual intercourse is actually like. Judy Blume's fictional account is frank and explicit, which has caused it to be the subject of many censorship efforts, but it also seeks to promote what we now call "safe sex" by including realistic information about contraceptives and birth control; thus, it is definitely conceived as an educational book. Perhaps most important, Blume captures the emotional tone of young lovers' exchanges—impulsive, passionate, worried, and inexperienced. Judy Blume's books were among the first books for children and young adults to deal openly with the subjects of masturbation and first menstruation (in *Deenie,* 1973, and in *Are You There, God? It's Me, Margaret,* 1970). Those books were for middle school-age readers, but *Forever* . . . is a young adult novel. However, because of Blume's popularity and her reputation for dealing with taboo subjects, many children read *Forever* . . . prior to adolescence, a matter of further concern to her detractors. Despite the efforts of her critics, Blume has a well-deserved reputation for writing fiction that validates children's feelings about difficult, sometimes painful subjects. In 2004 Blume was the first author of young adult literature (and the fifth woman) to receive a medal for Distinguished Contribution to American Letters from the National Book Foundation, which recognized her literary achievements, as well as her years of activism in opposition to censorship and in defense of the intellectual freedom of young people.

From *Forever* . . .

12

Sharon and Ike live in a garden apartment in Springfield. All the outside doors are painted green. "I hope nobody thinks we're trying to break in," I said, as Michael put the key in the lock, "because there's an old lady watching us." I pointed to a window.

"Don't worry about her." Michael pushed the door open. "That's Mrs. Cornick . . . she lives downstairs she's always in the window." He waved at her and she dropped her shade. "Come on . . . their place is upstairs."

The stairs led into the living room. "It's nice," I said, looking around. There wasn't much furniture but they had a fantastic Persian rug and three posters of chimpanzees riding bicycles. I walked over to a plant and held up a leaf. "Too much water . . . that's why the edges are turning brown."

"I'll tell Sharon you said so."

"No, don't . . . then she'll know I've been here."

"So?"

"So, I just don't want her to know . . . okay?"

"I don't see why . . . but okay. You want something to eat?"

"Maybe . . ." We went to the kitchen which was small and narrow with no outside window.

Michael opened the refrigerator. "How about an apple . . . or a grapefruit? That's about all I see."

"I'll have an apple."

He polished it off on his shirt, then tossed it to me. "I'll show you around the place," he said.

Since I'd already seen the living room and the kitchen we started with the bathroom. "Notice the indoor plumbing." Michael demonstrated how to flush the toilet.

"Very interesting," I told him.

"And hot and cold running water." He turned on both faucets.

"Luxurious."

"Also, a genuine bathtub." He stepped into it and I pulled the curtain around him. While he was in there I wrapped the apple core in some toilet paper and hid it in my pocketbook. Michael jumped out of the tub, grabbed my hand and said, "Onward . . ."

We both knew there was just one room left to see. "Presenting . . ." Michael said, and he bowed, "the bedroom."

There was a brass bed, covered with a patchwork quilt and a LOVE poster hanging on the wall, above it. There were also two small chests, piled high with books.

Michael jumped up and down on the bed while I watched from the doorway. "Good mattress . . ." he said, "nice and firm . . . in case you're interested."

"For jumping, you mean?"

"For whatever . . ." He lay down and looked at the ceiling. "Kath . . ."

"Hmmm . . ."

"Come here . . ."

"I thought we were just going to talk."

"We are . . . but you're so far away . . . don't want to shout."

"I can hear you fine."

"Cut it out . . . will you?"

I went to the bed and sat on the edge. "There's one thing I'd really like to know . . ."

"What's that?"

"Have you brought any other girls up here?"

"Your jealous streak is showing."

"I admit it . . . but I still want to know."

"Never," he said. "I've never brought a girl up here."

"Good."

"Because I just got my own key."

"You rat!" I yelled, grabbing a pillow and swatting him with it.

"Hey . . ." He knocked the pillow out of my hands and pinned me down on the bed. Then he kissed me.

"Let me go, Michael . . . please."

"I can't . . . you're too dangerous."

"I'll be good . . . I promise."

He let go of my arms and I wrapped them around him and we kissed again.

"You're beautiful," he said, looking down at me.

"Don't say things like that . . ."

"Why, do they embarrass you?"

"Yes."

"Okay . . . you're ugly! You're so ugly you make me want to puke." He turned away and leaned over the side of the bed making this terrible retching noise.

"Michael . . . you're crazy . . . stop it . . . I can't stand that!"

"Okay."

We lay next to each other kissing, and soon Michael unbuttoned my sweater and I sat up and unhooked my bra for him. While I slipped out of both, Michael pulled his sweater over his head. Then he held me. "You feel so good," he said, kissing me everywhere. "I love to feel you next to me. You're as soft as Tasha."

I started to laugh.

"What?" Michael asked.

"Nothing . . ."

"I love you, Kath."

"And I love you," I said, "even though you're an *outsy*."

"What's an *outsy?*"

"Your belly button sticks out," I said, tracing it with my fingers.

"That's not the only thing that sticks out."

"Michael . . . we're talking about belly buttons."

"You are . . ."

"I was explaining that you're an *outsy* and I'm an *insy* . . . you see how mine goes in?"

"Umm . . ." he said, kissing it.

"Do belly buttons have a taste?" I asked.

"Yours does . . . it's delicious . . . like the rest of you." He unbuckled my jeans, then his own.

"Michael . . . I'm not sure . . . please . . ."

"Shush . . . don't say anything."

"But Michael . . ."

"Like always, Kath . . . that's all . . ."

We both left on our underpants but after a minute Michael was easing mine down and then his fingers began exploring me. I let my hands wander across his stomach and down his legs and finally I began to stroke Ralph.

"Oh, yes . . . yes . . ." I said, as Michael made me come. And he came too.

We covered up with the patchwork quilt and rested. Michael fell asleep for a while and I watched him, thinking the better you know a person the more you can love him. Do two people ever reach the point where they know absolutely everything there is to know about each other? I leaned over and touched his hair. He didn't move.

The next night Michael picked me up at 7:30 and we headed straight for the apartment. I knew we would. Neither one of us could wait to be alone together. And when we were naked, in each other's arms, I wanted to do everything—I wanted to feel him inside me. I don't know if he sensed that or not but when he whispered, "Please, Kath . . . please let's keep going . . ." I told him, "Yes, Michael . . . yes . . . but not here . . . not on the bed."

"Yes . . . here . . ." he said, moving over me.

"No, we can't . . . I might bleed."

He rolled away from me. "You're right . . . I forgot about that . . . I'll get something."

He came back with a beach towel. "Down here," I called, because he couldn't find me in the dark.

"On the floor?" he asked.

"Yes."

"The floor's too hard."

"I don't mind . . . and we won't have to worry about stains."

"This is crazy."

"Please, Michael . . . just give me the towel . . . I hope it's not a good one."

He lay down next to me. "It's freezing down here," he said.

"I know . . ."

He jumped up and grabbed the quilt off the bed. We snuggled under it. "That's better." He put his arms around me.

"Look," I said, "you might as well know . . . I'm scared out of my mind."

"Me too."

"But you've at least had some experience."

"Not with anyone I love."

"Thank you," I said, kissing the side of his face.

He ran his hands up and down my body but nothing happened. I guess I was too nervous. "Michael . . . do you have something?" I asked.

"What for?" he said, nibbling my neck.

"You know . . ."

"Didn't you finish your period?"

"Last week . . . but I'm not taking any chances."

"If you're thinking about VD I promise I'm fine."

"I'm thinking about getting pregnant. Every woman has a different cycle."

"Okay . . . okay . . ." He stood up. "I've got a rubber in my wallet . . . if I can just find it." He looked around for his pants, found them on the floor next to the bed, then had to put on the light to find the rubber. When he did he held it up. "Satisfied?" he asked, turning the light off again.

"I will be when you put it on."

He kneeled beside me and rolled on the rubber. "Anything else?"

"Don't be funny now . . . please . . ."

"I won't . . . I won't . . ." he said and we kissed. Then he was on top of me and I felt Ralph, hard, against my thigh. Just when I thought, Oh God . . . we're really and truly going to do it, Michael groaned and said, "Oh no . . . no . . . I'm sorry . . . I'm so sorry . . ."

"What's wrong?"

"I came . . . I don't know what to say. I came before I even got in. I ruined it . . . I ruined everything."

"It's all right," I told him. "It's okay . . . really."

"No, it's not."

"It doesn't matter."

"Maybe not to you . . ."

"It could have been all that talking. We shouldn't have talked so much."

"Next time it'll be better," Michael said. "I promise . . . Ralph won't fail me twice."

"Okay." I took his hand and kissed it.

"Let's just sleep for a while, then we can try again."

"I'm not tired," I said, "but I'm very hungry."

"There's nothing to eat here."

"We could go out."

"Get dressed and go out?"

"Why not?"

"Yeah . . . I suppose we could," he said.

We went to Stanley's for hamburgers and on the way back to the apartment we stopped at a drugstore so Michael could buy some more rubbers. I stayed in the car.

"Let's try the living room," Michael said when we got back.

"I couldn't . . . not on that beautiful rug."

"Oh, hell . . . it's got so many colors nothing would show on it anyway . . . and it's softer than the wood floor."

"I don't know . . ." I said, looking at the rug.

"I'll double up the towel." He spread it out. "There . . . that should take care of it."

This time I tried to relax and think of nothing—nothing but how my body felt—and then Ralph was pushing against me and I whispered, "Are you in . . . are we doing it?"

"Not yet," Michael said, pushing harder. "I don't want to hurt you."

"Don't worry . . . just do it!"

"I'm trying, Kath . . . but it's very tight in there."

"What should I do?"

"Can you spread your legs some more . . . and maybe raise them a little?"

"Like this?"

"That's better . . . much better."

I could feel him halfway inside me and then Michael whispered, "Kath . . ."

"What?"

"I think I'm going to come again."

I felt a big thrust, followed by a quick sharp pain that made me suck in my breath. "Oh . . . oh," Michael cried, but, but I didn't come. I wasn't even close. "I'm sorry," he said, "I couldn't hold off." He stopped moving. "It wasn't any good for you, was it?"

"Everybody says the first time is no good for a virgin. I'm not disappointed." But I was. I'd wanted it to be perfect.

"Maybe it was the rubber," Michael said. "I should have bought the more expensive kind." He kissed my cheek and took my hand. "I love you, Kath. I wanted it to be good for you too."

"I know."

"Next time it'll be better . . . we've got to work on it. Did you bleed?"

"I don't feel anything." I wrapped the beach towel around my middle and went to the bathroom. When I wiped myself with tissues I saw a few spots of blood, but nothing like what I'd expected.

On the way home I thought, I am no longer a virgin. I'll never have to go through the first-time business again and I'm glad—I'm so glad it's over! Still, I can't help feeling let down. Everybody makes such a big thing out of actually doing it. But Michael is probably right—this takes practice. I can't imagine what the first time would be like with someone you didn't love.

Hazel Rochman (b. 1938), Masha Kabakow Rudman (b. 1933), and Diane Stanley (b. 1943)

In these three talks, Hazel Rochman, Masha Kabakow Rudman, and Diane Stanley discuss historical fiction for children and young adults and how political considerations have influenced the writing and reading of history for young people. Rochman, an editor who grew up in apartheid South Africa and thus views America from the perspective of an immigrant, advocates presenting a range of books with gripping stories on any given historical topic, so that readers can imaginatively become "immigrants" themselves and understand the issues in a complex way. Rudman, an educator, argues that all children should have accurate and respectfully conveyed information about their own history, whether they are Jewish (as in her case) or African American (as in the case of her grandson) and that the term *political correctness* is manipulative and itself political: an insulting put-down. She examines stereotypes and the power of language to demean or celebrate. So much depends on the point of view of the one who is telling the story, as her examples of books about Columbus and Native Americans show. "We want multiple perspectives," Rudman states. Finally, writer Stanley celebrates political correctness as a positive concept, although she shows some of its drawbacks, too, and her account of her self-censorship in writing historical books for young people can be seen as admirable or regrettable, depending on your point of view. These talks were presented at the American Library Association Conference in 1993 and published in 1994.

Is That Book Politically Correct?

Truth and Trends in Historical Literature for Young People

AN EDITOR SPEAKS . . .

HAZEL ROCHMAN

I didn't grow up and go to school in this country, so I come fresh to American history, its myths like Manifest Destiny or whatever, and the way you tell them and revise them. But it's interesting that as a white child in apartheid South Africa I heard many of the same myths, only they were more crudely stated. The social critic Robert Hughes calls these sorts of myths "patriotic correctness."[1]

- First, there was the story of "discovery." The history of the country began with the coming of the whites. Before that there may have been "natives" there, but there were no people. I once heard the comedian Dick Gregory talk about that kind of discovery: "I think I'll discover this Cadillac," he said.[2]
- After discovery came the pioneer story of "expansion." The phrase they used was "opening up." In the Great Trek some brave whites trekked into the interior in covered wagons and opened up the country to Christianity and "civilization." Whites battled the savage hordes; and when the blacks won, it was a massacre; and when the whites won, it was because God was on their side in a brave victory against desperate odds. With that version of history, and with guns on their side, the whites took the land.
- We heard lots of stories about immigration from Europe, about desperate people like my own grandfather, who came to South Africa to escape anti-Semitism and forced servitude in the tsar's army. Whites who came there from all over Europe made up the melting pot, the uneasy mainstream, the culture, even though they were a minority, one-fifth of the population. Blacks were called "non-Europeans," outsiders, foreigners in their own land. The law said they were inferior: couldn't vote, couldn't learn what whites did,

couldn't live in white areas except as migrant workers without their families.

And under the apartheid military dictatorship alternative versions of history were fiercely censored. Other than a chief, like Moshesh or Shaka, or a whole nation, like the Zulus, we never read about a black person and couldn't begin to imagine her or his story, past or present.

We always heard about the heroic leaders of the Great Trek. I never thought what it must have been like to be an ordinary pioneer woman in one of those covered wagons, struggling over the mountains, far from home. I was against apartheid, but I never imagined the life of a black Xhosa child forced to move to a barren reservation and see his or her father leave to work in the mines for eleven months of the year. As a white privileged child, I didn't know the history of the people all around me, and because of that, I didn't know who I was or where I fit in. I was as much a stranger there, as I am an immigrant here.

I've just reviewed Allen Say's stunning new picture book *Grandfather's Journey,*[3] which brings a new dimension to the immigrant story. Here's a version of the American Dream that's in some ways like my own: it includes adventure and discovery but no sense of arrival. Say's Japanese grandfather made a life in California and he loved America but he also longed to return to Japan. And as soon as he was in one country, he was "homesick for the other." With the particulars of his own family history, Say universalizes everyone's quest for home, and his paintings show that he finds not one place but many, connection and also discontent. This is history that revitalizes the myth of the American Dream and takes it far beyond any kind of "correct" message.

Say captures what the Jewish American writer Irving Howe calls our "eager restlessness."[4] Whether the travelers come across the border or across the sea or from farm to factory, there are so many voices missing from the official history books. And what happened to them affects us. As we begin to open up to the histories of "foreigners" everywhere, our view of the world and of the mainstream is changed and enriched and complicated. The gay writer Christopher Gram says that we get to see around corners we didn't even know were there.[5]

But it's no use going to the other extreme and inventing new lies. Those who were left out of the history books were not all brave, strong, wise, and noble. They were people, like us. Things didn't get solved by what the critic John Leonard calls a formula of "goodwill, coincidence, and pluck."[6]

Sometimes the historical truth is grim, and it's hard to confront it. Do we give children books about racial oppression and mass suffering? How do we evaluate such books? Young people want to know about these things and it's important that they know. A recent survey showed 22 percent of Americans either don't know what the Holocaust was or don't believe it happened.[7] So the fact that the Holocaust history is now a required part of the curriculum in many states is a good thing. And with the opening of the Holocaust Museum, the question of how to present the Holocaust to young people has been widely debated. I've reviewed a flood of new books, fiction and nonfiction. But they're not all good. You can't harangue kids into reading just because the message is important.

The best books don't exploit the violence; they don't grab attention by dwelling on sensational detail. And they don't offer slick comfort and kitsch entertainment; the Holocaust did not have a happy ending. Stories about the death camps can't make you feel good.

One of the best of the recent books is Isabella Leitner's *The Big Lie*.[8] In the barest prose she tells what happened to her. Only the facts. In 1944 the Nazis came to her small Hungarian town and rounded up all the Jews, first into crowded ghettos and then into cattle trains bound for Auschwitz. On their arrival at the death camp, Dr. Joseph Mengele was there in white gloves, pointing either to the left or to the right. Isabella, her three sisters, and her brother went to the right. Her mother and baby sister went to the left, where they died in the gas chambers and then were burned in the crematoriums. Immediately Isabella lost her clothes, her name, her hair. "At Auschwitz between ten and twenty thousand people were killed every day in the summer of 1944," Leitner says. There's no rhetoric about "atrocity" and "horror," no

tears, no hand-wringing. Just facts. The telling has the elemental power of the best children's literature, in which the simplicity is poetic and speaks volumes.

Or there is Ida Vos' book *Anna Is Still Here*,[9] which tells with unsparing honesty about survival after the Holocaust. When you've had to lie in order to survive, how do you tell the truth? How do you live as a family again, when so many are dead? When you haven't talked to anyone for three years, how do you learn to shout?

There's no sentimentality in the Batchelder Award winner, *The Man from the Other Side* by Uri Orlev.[10] The teenager in Warsaw bears witness to the way hunger and fear affected individual behavior. The Jews weren't an amorphous group of victims and heroes. Some were brave, some weren't; there were traitors among them. That, too, is a part of history.

As a Jew, an awareness of the Holocaust is part of my identity. I've been haunted by it since childhood. But I also connect that history with other accounts of what racism can do, from slavery to apartheid to ethnic cleansing. Extreme as the Nazi genocide was, it was not a thing apart; it was human experience. The camp survivor Bruno Bettelheim said it was what ordinary people did to ordinary people.

M. E. Kerr dramatizes the issue in another way in her classic YA novel *Gentlehands*.[11] Teenager Buddy in Seaville, New York, discovers that his grandfather hides a secret—he had once been a Nazi commander in a death camp. That book still raises a lot of controversy. It's not easy to see savagery in people like "us."

Let me tell you about a mistake I made when I reviewed *Prairie Songs* by Pam Conrad,[12] about a loving pioneer family on the Nebraskan Prairie. This is a lyrical piece of historical fiction, telling a story of women much neglected in frontier history, and I praised it in the review. But I also said something that I regret. I was worried about the scenes where the pioneers see the Indians as unwashed savages, so I warned librarians that they might want to warn kids about the false stereotypes.[13] I think my mistake reveals some common pitfalls in the PC debate:

- First, I take what the narrator says or what one character sees as the view of the author. If you judge every character to be the author, then you can never allow debate in a book, never have a protagonist who has an ugly or erroneous thought, never have a narrator who is less than perfect—perfect, that is, according to the prevailing fashion.

- Second, I ask for anachronism, historical inaccuracy, demanding that a nineteenth-century pioneer child have contemporary PC attitudes. Doesn't this kid know that Indians aren't scary and strange, that they're really noble mystics who can teach her about conserving the environment?
- Third, I cannot allow an oppressed ethnic group to appear anything but beautiful, wise, proud, and strong.

I was wrong. And I'll try not to do it again—even though I know those passages are still very difficult for me to read.

Michael Dorris confronts another kind of complexity in a wry, honest essay about Laura Ingalls Wilder in a recent issue of *Booklist*.[14] His argument is as full of surprise as his children's book *Morning Girl*,[15] which won the Scott O'Dell Award for historical fiction. What makes the article so wonderful is that Dorris writes as a reader. He remembers reading the Little House books as a child and loving them. Then he talks about reading them today to his own daughters. On the first page of *Little House in the Big Woods*, he hears his own voice reading, "'As far as a man could go to the north in a day, or a week, or a whole month, there was nothing but woods. There were no houses. There were no roads. There were no people' . . . Say what? Excuse me, but weren't we forgetting the Chippewa branch of my daughters' immediate ancestry, not to mention the thousands of resident Menominees, Potawatomis, Sauks, Foxes, Winnebagos, Ottawas who inhabited mid-nineteenth-century Wisconsin, as they had for many hundreds of years."[16]

So what do you do about the omissions, the lies, the stereotypes? Do you throw away the books? Do you discuss the issues while you're reading the story? What does that do to the story?

Underlying much of the debate is the demand that each book must do it all. If you think that the book you're reviewing is the only one kids are ever going to read on a subject—about the pioneers or about Columbus or about the suffragettes—then there's intense pressure to choose the "right" book with the "right" message; to scrutinize it so that there's nothing in it that might give the wrong impression, to make sure that it doesn't leave out anything that will give the right impression. If we don't watch out, reading becomes medicine, therapy. We start to recommend books because they give us the right role models, depending on what's considered "right" in the current political climate.

The poet Katha Pollitt[17] says that it's because young people read so little that there's such furious debate about the canon. If they read all kinds of books all the time, particular books wouldn't matter so much. The paradox is that if we give young people didactic tracts about history, or books so bland that they offend nobody, we're going to make them read even less. For stories to give pleasure there has to be tension and personality and passionate conflict, if you're going to grab kids and touch them deeply. If you want them to read.

The apartheid government with its rigorous censorship was right about one thing: a good story challenges stereotype. The history we read affects our view of who we are and how we live now. Books matter.

Reading is a private experience, but it makes immigrants of us all. That's why the best books break down apartheid. They surprise us—not with reverential role models and literal recipes, not with consciousness-raising messages, but with enthralling stories that make us imagine the lives of others.

NOTES

1. Robert Hughes, *The Culture of Complaint* (New York: Oxford, 1993), 28.
2. Dick Gregory, in performance at the University of Chicago in the mid-1970s.
3. Allen Say, *Grandfather's Journey* (Boston: Houghton, 1993), discussed in *Booklist* "Focus" review by H. Rochman, July 1993.
4. Irving Howe, *World of Our Fathers* (New York: Harcourt, 1976), 646.
5. Christopher Gram, "Part of the Family: Gay and Lesbian Literature in the Mainstream," *Booklist* 89, no. 18 (May 15, 1993): 1657.
6. John Leonard, "Machine Dreams," *Nation* 256, no. 19 (May 17, 1993): 668.
7. *New York Times*, Apr. 20, 1993.
8. Isabella Leitner, *The Big Lie: A True Story* (New York: Scholastic, 1992).

9. Ida Vos, *Anna is Still Here,* trans. Terese Edelstein and Inez Smidt (Boston: Houghton, 1993).

10. Uri Orlev, *The Man from the Other Side,* trans. Hillel Halkin (Boston: Houghton, 1991).

11. M. E. Kerr, *Gentlehands* (New York: HarperCollins, 1978).

12. Pam Conrad, *Prairie Songs* (New York: HarperCollins, 1985).

13. Reviewed in *Booklist* 82, no. 1 (Sept. 1, 1985): 56.

14. Michael Dorris, "Trusting the Words," *Booklist* 89, nos. 19–20 (June 1 & 15, 1993): 1820–22.

15. Michael Dorris, *Morning Girl* (New York: Hyperion, 1992).

16. Dorris, "Trusting the Words," 1820.

17. Katha Pollitt, "Why We Read: Canon to the Right of Me . . ." *Nation* 253, no. 9 (Sept. 23, 1991): 328–32.

AN EDUCATOR SPEAKS . . .

Masha Kabakow Rudman

My six-year-old grandson is biracial and I worry about how the world will treat him. Fortunately he goes to a local public school where they care very much about affirming diversity and helping children feel proud of their heritage. Recently the school held a read-in of African American authors' works, and illustrators' works, too, and I was invited to do some of the reading. In the kindergarten class that my grandson attended, I read one of Ashley Bryan's books—*Turtle Knows My Name*. Afterward, Sam came to me and said, "Grandma, you should have read one of the books I've written because I'm an African American author." So of course, I read his book aloud too. He's learning that he is valued and competent, and that his rich heritage is something he can draw on. Every child has a right to that. It's important for us to provide children with information about their history that is accurate and respectful.

Children deserve to be told the truth. They also need to be taught to search for it. *Truth* is defined in *Webster's New Collegiate Dictionary* as "the body of real things, events, and facts." But of course it doesn't stop there. The dictionary goes on to say that truth is "fidelity to an original or to a standard." So the question becomes Whose reality? Whose standard? Whose truth?

Let's go a little further in looking at today's topic. Political Correctness. What an insulting term, cleverly coined in order to make a manipulative political statement and to provide an automatic put-down. I looked up the word *political* in the *Oxford English Dictionary*. One of its meanings is "in a sinister sense: scheming, crafty, cunning"; it involves "having regard for the interests of politics rather than questions of principle." And I think therein lies the definition of political correctness. Whenever, and I hate the term by the way, somebody says it's "politically correct," the indication or accusation is that principle doesn't exist and that something is being done purely for political reasons.

Let's think of an example of vocabulary that might be labeled "PC". . . how about the use of the term *woman* instead of *girl* for a mature female? Language is very powerful, and relegating a woman to the status of a girl, while some people might consider it flattering ("You look so young"), in actuality is demeaning and disempowering. In some cases, such as the use of the term *African American* to replace *black* or *Afro-American,* which effectively replaced *Negro,* which replaced *colored,* words are used in an attempt to build a certain kind of self-image and stance toward the world. It almost always turns out that this kind of changeover is controversial, with some members of the group itself disliking the new terminology, and others advocating strongly for it. Admittedly, part of the pressure comes from groups who are attempting to establish a certain kind of power base. But certainly some of the push is a result of a people's reclaiming a heritage, and, therefore, affirming an identity. What to one group is a demonstration of respect, referring to people in the way they want to be called, to others is "political correctness."

Some of the people doing this labeling are disturbed by any attempt to modify language. Some are uncomfortable with anything beyond a Eurocentric outlook; others genuinely underestimate the effect of language and semantics on popular understanding and attitude. On the other hand, there are some people who are honestly afraid that the use of new language and ways of thinking about people can turn into censorship. They worry that only the new terminology will be accepted by publishers and other people in power. They are rightly concerned about cutting off debate and mindlessly conform to vocabulary without the commitment of principle.

What I would like to encourage is the assembling of a library collection of all sorts of viewpoints, vocabulary, and political, moral, and intellectual stances. I'd like us to get deeper into the issues of truth and values and investigate how we can bring to children the challenge of examining different attitudes and positions without fear of being stigmatized as racist or sexist or accused of caring only about political correctness.

That is not to say that all language and ideas have equal value. I firmly believe that we must help young readers to identify cliché and stereotype in order to help them make astute judgments about the quality of the information and literature they are being exposed to. Let's look at typecasting and its effect on us. Please take a minute to turn to a neighbor and exchange with him or her what your heritage is. Then I'd like you to name one or two stereotypes that bother you, that you know people have about your heritage. If you can't think of any about your group, ask your neighbor what he or she has heard about your group's characteristics.

For most of you that was an easy thing to do. Some of you identify with more than one heritage, and that's fine, and some of you are fortunate enough not to have been marked by stereotypic thinking. But most of us have felt, if not victimized, then perhaps wounded, or at least annoyed by some of the automatic assumptions people make about us strictly because of our heritage. And it doesn't even have to be negative! I'm Jewish. And I don't like to cook. I feel even less competent than I might if I were not Jewish and therefore not expected to enjoy cooking. But there it is. Sometimes when I tell people I don't cook, they don't believe me, because, after all, I'm Jewish. Ascribing characteristics to an individual solely because of membership in a group is unfair and dehumanizing, even if the intention is to be complimentary (all Irish people are poetic; all Africans have rhythm; all Asians are good at math).

Literature can go a long way toward cementing or dispelling stereotypes. We need to be careful to discern when characters and situations in books are affirming negative and typecast images and then to talk about it with young readers. Let's do a little demonstration of the power of stereotypes, in this case literary ones, and the necessity to go beyond them. What does a princess look like? (Answers are almost always: blonde, blue-eyed, petite, passive.) How about a prince? (Tall, dark, and handsome, of course.) Now let's describe stepmothers. (Ugly, mean, abusive, wicked.) Do you really believe that? Maybe not intel-

lectually, but you surely do viscerally. My mother died when I was seventeen. She was my best friend and I missed her sorely. About two years later my father married a woman who was funny and feisty and bright and competent. I have never been able to refer to her as my stepmother. I'm an adult, and I know the difference between fantasy and reality. I also recognize the legitimacy of the term *stepmother.* But that image of the wicked stepmother is so strong inside me that I can't get beyond it. I call her my second mother, or, when I don't want to go into any lengthy explanations, simply, my mother. Terminology represents how we feel and what our attitudes are.

How do we help children go beyond these literary templates and hurtful societal stigmas? One way is to amass a collection of books that challenge assumptions. There are many Cinderellas from all over the world; for example, *Yeh-Shen: A Cinderella Story from China, Rough-Face Girl* (from Algonquin Native American lore), "Askenbasken, Who Became Queen" (from Denmark),[1] "Cenerentola" (from Italy),[2] and *Korean Cinderella* are a few of the hundreds of variants that can help us in terms of what Cinderella looks like and how she behaves. Ed Young, who did the gorgeous illustrations for *Yeh-Shen,* went to great lengths to research the origins of the story. His work always represents accuracy and authentic depth of understanding of the culture he's portraying. Rich examples of different sorts of beauty, like the daughters in *Mufaro's Beautiful Daughters,* or the young girl in *Honey I Love,* are also useful to blast any one-sided conventional notion of beauty.

Becoming immersed in a variety of literature prepares young people to become open to differing ideas and ways of looking at the world. Whether it's fantasy, fiction, or nonfiction, it's essential to acknowledge that multiple viewpoints exist. Furthermore, documentation and honesty are needed in presenting any story to make it work even when it's not labeled "history."

Now let's examine the word *history.* The *Oxford English Dictionary* defines it primarily as "narrative of past events, tale, story. A learning or knowing by inquiry . . ." and goes on to explain that in early use the term meant "the relating of incidents either true or imaginary"; only later did it become "the relating solely of what was professed to be true." It evolved to be "that branch of knowledge which deals with past events, as recorded in writings or otherwise ascertained; the formal record of the past, especially of human affairs or actions; the study of the formation and growth of communities and nations." This was particularly interesting to me because much of my history instruction had to do with wars. We "did" the American Revolution, the Civil War, and World War II. It's as if as a country we had lurched along from war to war, ignoring our growth as a community and as a nation and the roles different groups in the United States had in contributing to our development.

In a letter to the editor of one of our local newspapers recently, a woman faculty member in the History Department at Harvard wrote in because a history teacher at Amherst Regional High School had died. She paid tribute to a history teacher she had had in high school. She said, "I liked history before I met Mr. Heffley, but I loved it after he had shown me the drama that infused the study of history. Suddenly the dates, names, and places seemed worth knowing because they were set within a context of rich and complex experience. In Mr. Heffley's class the Industrial Revolution wasn't just an event about which to memorize details. It was a puzzle to be solved, a mystery to unravel, a phenomenon that mattered even now, well over 100 years after the fact. I learned from him that historians disagreed, that they made use of fact but relied on interpretation, that they constructed their tales of the past from a mass of tangled evidence. I came to see that past generations spoke to us all and offered the wisdom and pain of their experience through history. Most of all, I began to understand that human beings, once every bit as alive as we, lived again through the study of history."[3]

So what are some "trends" now in historical fiction? "Story" figures importantly in history. And it is very much through story and literature that we transmit important values, philosophy, and information to young people. One of the dramatic instances of how the current approach to history has incensed some people and delighted others is the revisiting and rethinking of Columbus and his voyages. Children have been invited to see many sides of this milestone in history.

For example, Michael Dorris's *Morning Girl* introduces us to a close and loving Taino family on the eve of Columbus's landing, helping us to see how important to their culture their hospitable and courteous values were, and hitting us hard with the realization that once those strangers' ships landed, it literally meant the end of life for this family and their entire community. Milton Meltzer's *Columbus and the World around Him* and Charlotte and David Yue's *Christopher Columbus: How He Did It* reflect careful research and evenhanded looks at the specifics of the voyages and the talents as well as deficiencies of this shadowy man.

The February 1992 edition of *Language Arts* included an article by William Bigelow called "Once upon a Genocide: Christopher Columbus in Children's Literature," containing fifteen titles of books about Columbus, all of which he sharply criticizes for their lack of historical accuracy.[4] That wonderful periodical *Book Links* in September 1991 featured forty-six books at all levels about several aspects of the Columbus voyages and with varying views.[5] The cornucopia of titles published during the quincentennial went a long way to help adults as well as children rethink the whole era of fifteenth- and sixteenth-century exploration and the way it has been presented to us as history.

The *New Yorker* had a cartoon last year that captured the sense of the new thinking: it depicts a young man apprehended by police officers, protesting loudly, "ARREST ME? WHAT DO YOU MEAN ARREST ME? I DISCOVERED THIS APARTMENT, AND I CLAIM ITS CONTENTS FOR MYSELF AND MY FAMILY!" The analogy is not exactly perfect, but it will do. Children need to learn that there were civilizations in existence in this so-called New World and that to "claim" someone else's land was, in a sense, to steal from the indigenous inhabitants of that land.

On the other hand, we learn all the time about conquering armies and the taking of land by invasion and force. After all, that's how we got Texas, New Mexico, and Puerto Rico. However, Columbus wasn't billed in the past as a conqueror or invader. He was thought of as an explorer and discoverer, a valiant and even noble man who changed the world. Well, in a sense he did. Again, the *New Yorker* had a cartoon depicting some native people on the shore, watching Columbus sail in with his three ships. One turns to the other and says,"This marks the end of Western Civilization as we know it." And he was right.

But I suspect you've been "Columbused" to distraction this past year, so I'd like to look at some other aspects of history to aid in my quest for truth and how to present it. In the recent book *The Story of Ourselves: Teaching History through Children's Literature,* edited by Michael Tunnel and Richard Ammon, Terrie Epstein points out that what some people call the "western migration" to others was the "eastern invasion."[6]

James Lincoln and Christopher Collier's *My Brother Sam Is Dead* changed forever the way many people look at the Revolutionary War by giving readers a picture of an ordinary family caught in the everyday ugliness of the war. In this book no one dies valiantly, and justice is not served. *Across Five Aprils* by Irene Hunt did the same for the Civil War and demonstrated that just because people were on the "right" side of the war, they weren't necessarily good people. Conversely, not everyone fighting for the South was a villain. In both of these authentic and forceful books the causes of war and its consequences are not oversimplified. The complexity of the human involvement as well as the political questions are explored with craft and elegance.

Jean Fritz has enlivened history with her profiles of famous Americans, and has helped young readers to see that history contains passion and humor through everyday events pertinent to their own young lives. Milton Meltzer and Russell Freedman are among the talented authors of nonfiction who disseminate history through a combination of narrative and documentation and introduce issues that invite thought and investigation. Julius Lester's body of work about slavery represents a point of view not often included in the classroom. *To Be a Slave, Long Journey Home,* and *This Strange New Feeling* strongly affect readers' understanding of what the institution of slavery was about. Ann Turner's work captures a sense of history poetically, and generally from a very intimate perspective. *Dakota Dugout* and *Grass Songs* represent the voices of pioneer women. Mildred Taylor's saga of the Logan family presents us with history of the Depression era in Mississippi as nothing else can.

Katherine Paterson re-creates twelfth-century Japan in *Of Nightingales That Weep,* focusing through the eyes of a young woman on the civil war raging at the time—and also incidentally helping us to understand transformations of what one considers to be beauty. Mid-nineteenth-century Lowell, Massachusetts, comes alive in the book *Lyddie,* and we feel the tension and sorrow evoked by the war in Vietnam when we follow Park on his quest to find his father and himself at the Vietnam Veterans Memorial in *Park's Quest.* Walter Dean Myers has offered an on-the-spot

raw look at that war in *Fallen Angels* through Richie Perry's experiences with his group of fellow soldiers.

One aspect of history that I am particularly absorbed with is the Holocaust. For a long time it was characterized mainly by its representation in one autobiography: *The Diary of Anne Frank.* It was interesting for me to read recently that Otto Frank tried in vain for a long time to get it into print. He was turned down by numerous publishers who told him that no one would be interested in an ordinary girl's diary, and besides that, the topic was terribly depressing. It is our good fortune that he persevered.

Now there are hundreds of books on the Holocaust, aimed at different age levels, and providing many perspectives, upsetting stereotypes, and telling a variety of stories. In addition to those that describe the years of Hitler's domination, the mass murders, and the concentration camp era, some of the books include information about the pre-Nazi time, and several tell of what happened after the war. Some are terribly explicit about atrocities, the fight for survival, and the cruelty of neighbors and former friends. Many, on the other hand, detail incidents of courage and compassion. In a number of the stories the characters survive, often against all odds, and several books powerfully deal with the survivors' dilemma. Some of the books are hopeful, others are bitter and angry. The main characters are Germans, Danes, other Europeans, and Americans. Jews and Gentiles are represented.

There is even one book, *Gentlehands* by M. E. Kerr, that introduces readers to a character who seems sensitive, refined, and loving—he's even a grandfather—who turns out to have been a torturer in the concentration camps. The illustrations can be photographs, drawings by professional artists, and paintings by children. The genres include poetry, novels, autobiographies, nonfiction, time travel, and allegory.

The time travel book is Jane Yolen's *The Devil's Arithmetic,* which starts from the premise of an assimilated, modern Jewish American child who hasn't wanted to think about the Holocaust. She is transported back to the midst of the horror, and the reader experiences the event with her. The comfortable contemporary setting makes the drama even more potent through the contrast with the journey into the past.

The Newbery Award winner *Number the Stars,* by Lois Lowry, is told very much from the perspective of Annemarie, a Danish child who takes part in the harboring and eventual transfer to Sweden of her Jewish friend, Ellen. It is Annemarie's story, so it makes sense that she is the active one whose feelings and thoughts the reader is most in tune with.

Lisa's War, by Carol Matas, tells of the same circumstances, the Danes' assistance of about 6,500 Danish Jews in their escape to Sweden. This time, however, the protagonist is a Jewish girl. The story is told in the first person, and includes much that the Jews themselves did to aid in their own rescue. Both stories are valid and truthful and provide a kind of balancing effect for the reader.

But a balanced view is not enough. Anti-Semitism, like any racism, doesn't die; it just sleeps. It can too easily be awakened. Depth and breadth of understanding occur only when children are invited and challenged to question, explore, discuss, and confront how authors handle the issues and events making up any historical era.

If we want children to gain an understanding of any period of history, we can't be satisfied with one or two books. We have to communicate that we only get at the truth if we are comprehensive and wide-ranging in our search for it. That's how we can avoid a party line or a romance with the trivial. That's how we avoid censorship, too: we don't want "mind-control" from any faction. We need to sort through as many points of view as we can possibly find. We want high-quality well-researched literature with stellar characterization and plot. We want multiple perspectives. We want the richness of story.

With that combination our young people can value differences, appreciate literature, and learn from history so that it can affect current and future behavior. They will want to search out what is respectful, honest, principled, and truthful. Then their statements about past and current events and their understanding of issues in today's society will not contain even a tinge of conforming to political pressure or paying surface lip-service to matters of deep concern.

The allegory *Terrible Things,* by Eve Bunting, thankfully brought back into print by the Jewish Publication Society, dramatically brings home many points I've tried to convey. It is part of the wealth of books now available on the Holocaust. It is aimed at every age level and urges readers to learn from history. Its implications form the conclusion to my comments.

The story tells of a group of woodland creatures living in harmony until the day the "Terrible Things" invade. These "Things" are formless and nameless. They systematically remove each species from the forest, with none of the others offering resistance, and the white rabbits, in particular, assiduously avoiding any sort of protest or confrontation. In the end, even the white rabbits, who have considered themselves impervious to harm, are eliminated. Only the littlest of the rabbits escapes and he sadly concludes that if he and the others had banded together, perhaps they all could have survived. He leaves his home, vowing to spread the word about what he has learned. He hopes someone will listen.

Thank you for listening.

NOTES

1. "Askenbasken, Who Became Queen," in *The Cinderella Story,* ed. Philip Neil (New York: Viking, 1989), 52–57.
2. Rose Laura Mincielli, "Cenerentola," in *Old Neapolitan Fairy Tales* (New York: Knopf, 1963), 24–34.
3. Ellen Fitzpatrick, letter to the editor, *Amherst Bulletin* (June 11, 1993): 1.
4. William Bigelow, "Once upon a Genocide: Christopher Columbus in Children's Literature," *Language Arts* 69 (Feb. 1992): 112–20.
5. Barbara Elleman, "The Columbus Encounter," *Book Links* 1 (Sept. 1991): 6–13.
6. Michael Tunnel and Richard Ammon, eds., *The Story of Ourselves: Teaching History through Children's Literature* (Portsmouth, N.H.: Heinemann, 1993).

WORKS CITED

Adams, Edward B. *Korean Cinderella.* Soeul, Korea: Seoul International Tourist Pub. Co., 1982.

Bunting, Eve. *Terrible Things: An Allegory of the Holocaust.* Philadelphia: Jewish Publication Society, 1989.

Collier, James Lincoln, and Christopher Collier. *My Brother Sam Is Dead.* New York: Scholastic, 1974.

Dorris, Michael. *Morning Girl.* New York: Hyperion, 1992.

Frank, Otto. *The Diary of Anne Frank.* New York: Simon & Schuster, 1953.

Greenfield, Eloise. *Honey I Love: And Other Love Poems.* New York: HarperCollins, 1978.

Hunt, Irene. *Across Five Aprils.* New York: Pacer, 1989.

Kerr, M. E. *Gentlehands.* New York: HarperCollins, 1978.

Lester, Julius. *Long Journey Home*. New York: Scholastic, 1972.

———. *This Strange New Feeling*. New York: Dial Bks., 1982.

———. *To Be a Slave*. New York: Scholastic, 1968.

Louie, Ai-Ling. *Yeh-Shen: A Cinderella Story from China*. New York: Putnam, 1990.

Lowry, Lois. *Number the Stars*. New York: Houghton, 1989.

Martin, Rafe. *Rough-Face Girl*. New York: Putnam, 1992.

Matas, Carol. *Lisa's War*. New York: Macmillan, 1989.

Meltzer, Milton. *Columbus and the World around Him*. New York: Watts, 1990.

Myers, Walter Dean. *Fallen Angels*. New York: Scholastic, 1988.

Paterson, Katherine. *Lyddie*. New York: Viking Penguin, 1991.

———. *Of Nightingales That Weep*. New York: Harper & Row, 1974.

———. *Park's Quest*. New York: Lodestar, 1988.

Steptoe, John. *Mufaro's Beautiful Daughters: An African Tale*. New York: Lothrop, 1987.

Turner, Ann. *Dakota Dugout*. New York: Macmillan, 1985.

———. *Grass Songs*. New York: HBJ, 1993.

Yolen, Jane. *The Devil's Arithmetic*. New York: Viking, 1988.

Yue, Charlotte, and David Yue. *Christopher Columbus: How He Did It*. New York: Houghton, 1992.

A WRITER SPEAKS . . .

DIANE STANLEY

I think there is no question that the doctrine of political correctness has had a significant impact on the publishing industry, especially with regard to children's books. While virtually anything goes in adult books, as long as it is reasonably well written and someone thinks there is a market for it, those of us who write and publish books for children recognize our obligation not only to entertain them but to help them develop socially desirable values. Since those values shift from time to time, so do the messages we send our children.

The doctrine of political correctness is one of the most influential, and also perhaps controversial, social movements of the day. It seeks to bring about a more tolerant, inclusive, and earth-friendly society, a universal goal of great value that we all embrace. It has raised the consciousness of America in amazing and wonderful ways and has had a real and positive effect on society as a whole. The publishing industry has played a large part in this new awareness, and the result over the past ten or fifteen years has been the production of better, more thoughtful books that reflect the diversity of our country. But in any sweeping social movement, there are bound to be excesses, and there is no question that political correctness is thick in the air these days. Authors and publishers, already sensitive to the nuances of language and concerned about these issues because of their own beliefs, are doubly careful for fear of being somehow misunderstood. And so we censor ourselves.

I would like to explore some thoughts about writing history in the age of political correctness and some of the ways this self-censorship has affected me personally in the writing of historical books for children.

First, let me say I think political correctness has brought about some very important changes in the way history is written. It asks us to take a second look at the record, not only at what has long been accepted as fact, but also at the traditional interpretation of those facts, and to try to correct the record for bias. History has always been written from the point of view of the authors, who unconsciously select from the record those facts that support their beliefs while ignoring those that contradict them. This has usually meant that the history of any country was at the mercy of the dominant group. Today historians are more likely to search out parts of the story that were never told because they were not considered important at the time, to reevaluate the contributions of minorities and women which were ignored by a society that did not value them. However, we must be careful not to create new myths and falsifications in our zeal to get rid of old stereotypes and bias. It is the job of the historian to demythologize the record, and though history and biography can never be as pure as science, we must set our standards high in the hope of at least coming close to the truth.

There is a strong feeling today that, whenever possible, books about people belonging to a certain culture should be written by members of that culture. Certainly we all know our own group best, and trying to step into the mind of a character whose life is very different from our own can result in a bad book. We may impose stereotypes on the character, or make mistakes, or miss some important part of their worldview, which will make the book ring false. Because of this, I felt I was treading on dangerous ground when I decided to write a book about Shaka, king of the Zulus. Did I have the right to tell his story? I wanted to very much. There are few books on African history available for American children, and Shaka was an important and fascinating figure. Since he lived two hundred years ago and in Africa, I felt that any other American writer would have to approach his story just as I did— through research. I decided to risk it.

As always, I tried to present the story in as balanced and honest a manner as I could. But there was now an added pressure to present Shaka in as positive a light as possible for fear that someone would think I was disparaging him out of ignorance or prejudice. Shaka, like many other great national leaders, accomplished his goals through making war on his neighbors and taking their land. While this is out of keeping with our current sense of morality, facts are facts, and those facts should only be judged by the standards of the times in which the character lived. For much of history, including Shaka's time, such conquest was the road to glory.

Looking back on the many decisions I made in the course of writing the book, I remember one in particular that was influenced by political correctness. I chose not to include an anecdote that, while not central to the story, shed light on Shaka's emotional life in a most poignant way. If I had found the same story in my research on Peter the Great, I would have used it.

Shaka had heard from some Englishmen about a certain Rowland's Macassar Oil. It was because of Macassar Oil that Victorian ladies draped little lacy "antimacassars" over the backs of their chairs to protect the upholstery. Some of this hair oil contained a dye that darkened gray hair. Shaka believed that anything that could turn gray hair black again must have magical rejuvenating properties and he became obsessed with obtaining some for his beloved mother, who was old and frail. He sent ambassadors to the king of England asking for some. Alas, the Englishmen of Cape Town did not take his request seriously. The ambassadors never got to England and, to Shaka's despair, returned with no Macassar Oil.

This story would have been a perfect lead-in to the subsequent death of his mother and his reaction to it by sliding into madness. But I was afraid that this story made Shaka look foolish and reinforced ancient stereotypes. Both from an artistic and historical point

of view the story fit, but because I was reaching out of my own experience to explore another culture, I did not feel comfortable using that story.

To generalize from that specific incident, the writing of a book involves a series of tiny decisions, one after the other, some as small as the choice of a single word, others more important, such as which slant to take, what to tell, and what to leave out. It is very difficult not to let political correctness join the forces of intellectual honesty and artistic judgment in making those decisions.

I am currently at work on a biography of Cleopatra. Because she was the enemy of Rome, much valuable source material was destroyed shortly after her death. The most intimate and complete source that remains was written by Plutarch, and it presents her primarily in relation to the two men in her life, Julius Caesar and Mark Antony. Cleopatra has been much maligned as a sexpot and I have certainly set the record straight: she was an intellectual, a most forceful woman, and not beautiful at all. Nevertheless, as far as we can know the details of her life, the big events are unquestionably connected to her unions with the two most important men of her day. So I have to tell it as it was—I cannot put a feminist agenda on the story.

An interesting sidelight is the *Newsweek* article of some years back focusing on Afrocentrism, and particularly the book *Black Athena*. Looking for a catchy headline, the editors of *Newsweek* came up with "Was Cleopatra black?" Anyone who read past the cover would have discovered that those same editors did in fact realize that not only was Cleopatra not black, she wasn't Egyptian either: she was Greek. Now the issues raised in *Black Athena* have nothing to do with Cleopatra, though some of the more extreme proponents of Afrocentric views claim she was black. No single source I have encountered has indicated anything besides the historically accepted view of her origins, and we can trace her parentage back more than three hundred years. In the end, you just have to trust your research.

My next book after *Cleopatra* is about a whaling voyage. Both the editor and I were somewhat worried about the subject, because we obviously regret the fact that whales were hunted to the brink of extinction. We feared that in even approaching the subject we might seem insensitive to the whole issue of endangered species.

Nevertheless, it is a vivid piece of American history and one worth knowing about. It will be mentioned in the text that these voyages often took as long as two to four years, the reason being that they had to go all the way around Cape Horn into the Pacific Ocean. Why? Because there were scarcely any whales left in the Atlantic. Would I have made a point of mentioning this if it weren't for political correctness? Probably I would, because it is part of the big picture, but in the politically correct nineties, it *had* to be there.

In preparation for this book, I have been reading a number of true narrative accounts of whaling voyages, and it has been fascinating to observe that in the nineteenth century, whales were perceived as fierce and malicious creatures, whereas today they are sentimentalized as "gentle giants of the deep." The truth lies somewhere between these two extremes, and it is a fitting analogy for the challenge facing anyone writing history today. We must always try to find that middle ground. We must approach our work within an agenda, politically correct or otherwise. We must attempt to write a reliable account well supported by fact, to consider it in the light of its context, and, we hope, to tell it well.

Herbert R. Kohl (b. 1937)

A gifted educator, Kohl examines his own history of reading the childhood classic *Babar* by Jean de Brunhoff, the story of an orphaned elephant and his adventures in the land of human beings and, later, as the king in his own country. As an adult, Kohl finds in this charming picture book (and its sequels) a disturbing history of colonialism, racism, and sexism. What to do with the book? Kohl's title is intentionally provocative because he is about as far from being a conventional censor of books as it is possible to get. However, Kohl's thoughtful 1995 essay probes the values implicit in de Brunhoff's stories and asks how one ought to deal with them: Should we ignore stories from the past that no longer reflect our values (or actively contradict them), or should we incorporate them into our reading and discussion and balance them with other stories that counteract the unquestioned assumptions that they represent? A first step, of course, is to become conscious that seemingly innocent children's books can, in fact, convey damaging assumptions about how the world works or ought to work.

Should We Burn *Babar*?

Questioning Power in Children's Literature

THE CHARMING *BABAR*

When I was about five or six my mother or aunt bought a copy of *Babar the Elephant* along with a recording of the book on three 78 rpm records. They read me the book over and over, and I listened to the records endlessly. I remember crying when Babar's mother was killed, being delighted that the Rich Lady was willing to take Babar in and civilize him, feeling happy for Babar when he returned home and was made king, and wishing him the most wonderful time when he and Celeste got married and flew off in an air balloon to have adventures. I loved the book, identified with Babar, and found an abiding affectionate place for him in my heart. The illustrations made Babar seem friendly, socialized—a child-adult. I remembered him leaning on the fireplace, dressed in a three-piece suit and conversing with the Rich Lady's friends, telling them about his life in the wilds, and also him holding a piece of chalk in his trunk doing arithmetic at a chalkboard. The thought of *Babar* evoked memories of moments in my childhood when my aunts and my mother cared for me and indulged my wishes the way the Rich Lady did for the errant elephant.

Recently I decided to reread *Babar* and other children's books that had been part of my growing up. I had revisited some of these books in the early 1970s when my children were very young. My wife and I read to them every night and occasionally shared books we loved as children with our children. My current concern with *Babar* and other classics has derived from work I have been doing in California with Native American children and their parents, and in New York City with high school students. One youngster I work with at home in California is currently engaged in a battle over *The Little House on the Prairie* series. As moving as that "classic" might seem to European American readers, it is offensive to Native American people who are portrayed in the books as barely human savages. The subtext of the books is the conquest of the prairies, and, though the series' personal tales of White settlers are beautifully rendered, its dehumanization of the Native Peoples whose lands are being stolen makes it painful reading. This is especially so for Daniel and a few of his friends who live on a reservation and whose families have experienced similar thievery within living memory of the tribal elders. Daniel is being punished in school for rejecting the book and refusing to answer questions about it. He is also being supported in this resistance by the tacit approval of older people in the community who correctly believe that the local schools do not serve their children well.

In New York a number of high school students I have had occasion to talk with have expressed passionate pleas for exposure to literature they can relate to as well as equally strong objections to the literature they were exposed to as children. Their vehement anger at books and tales such as *Dr. Doolittle, Snow White and the Seven Dwarves,* and *The Little Prince* surprised me. They were not merely asking for the inclusion of texts that represented the stories of African Americans and Latinos, but for the wholesale reconsideration of what is considered appropriate reading for young people.

My inclination was to sympathize with these young people, yet I felt uneasy about throwing out all the books that I read or that were read to me as a child. Hence the question of dear *Babar*. Was *Babar* so offensive that it should be eliminated? Or so powerful an influence that it was dangerous to young children? More generally, if literature has an influence on children's behavior, then the classics may present a problem for parents and teachers if their content portrays, sanctions, and even models inequity. What to do about kings and princesses? About the triumph of the strong and the mocking of the weak? About the glorification of wealth and the sanction of "deserved" poverty? About the portrayal of some people as civilized and others as savage? Should books that represent these antidemocratic sentiments be a major part of our children's earliest repertoire of stories and tales, or should we avoid purchasing them and sharing them with our children? Should we burn books like *Babar*?

I decided to take another, closer, look at *Babar* and ask myself whether I thought burning *Babar* could in any way be in the interest of young people. In particular, I decided to analyze the way in which power is represented in that story, since power relationships in literature reveal the politics of both the story and, frequently, the author. Power relationships also provide examples and models for children of social and moral behavior. I chose *Babar* as my exemplar because I liked the book and want to believe that its charm overrides any offensive attitudes it embodies. In addition, the book reaches tens, if not hundreds, of thousands of children every year. It has been continuously in print in English since 1933, and has reached such a level of popularity that there are dolls, cups, mugs, T-shirts, bibs, sheets, and pillowcases all displaying and celebrating the elephant king. In addition there is an innocence to *Babar* that must be seductive for young children.

Jean de Brunhoff, the creator of *Babar*, is a master narrator. His text ignores transitions. One event happens after another with no explanations; no motives or causes are revealed, no actions justified or excused—

events are just told. The reader is swept along without questioning any of the premises of the story. Babar's mother is killed. The Rich Lady gives Babar her purse. Celeste and Arthur run away and immediately find Babar. That's it—scene after scene, so that the book reads almost like an animated cartoon in which events follow so quickly after each other that there is no time for reflection or examination. *Babar* is compelling that way, and effective because it draws the reader on, or, more accurately, it draws the listener on. It is a book that begs a lap or a small circle of children looking up at the illustrations. The book is a perfect model of the genre of illustrated children's books meant to be read aloud. And, if offensive, it is a masterpiece of propaganda, since it is easy to accept the whole of it unquestioned and even to internalize some of the attitudes and ideas it presents.

I want to question the text of *Babar* in a way that children don't, and speculate on the potential effects of this apparently innocent and charming tale. The first and simplest question I'd like to ask is: Who has the power in *Babar?* Who makes the decisions in the story? Who is obeyed and tells the other characters what to do? And how is power distributed among the characters in the text?

In *Babar* the power is with people and not animals. The story begins when a hunter shoots Babar's mother and tries to trap Babar. Next we find Babar lost in a city, where a Rich Lady takes him under her wing.

The hunter is dressed in full colonial regalia, pith helmet and all. He has a double-barreled shotgun and is faceless. All we see of him is his heavy, imposing body, the back of his head, and the side of his face. He is an impersonal force, and his hidden face makes it impossible for children to identify him with the other, more benevolent, humans in the book. In particular the contrast between him and the "very rich Rich Lady," who has a kind though slightly imperious face and elaborate and elegant clothes, is enormous. She is personal—she even does setting-up exercises with Babar in the morning—whereas the hunter and his bullet are one, anonymous and indifferent to the fate of elephants.

Babar flees the hunter but is putty in the hands of the Rich Lady. Resistance to the temptations to lose his elephant nature seems foreign to him. The Rich Lady dresses Babar like a person, teaches him human eating and bathing habits, and educates him like a per-

son. Babar seems to welcome all of this. At the same time the reader is never told what motivates the hunter, the Rich Lady, or Babar. People power works mysteriously and unambiguously in the story.

The Rich Lady has money, lots of it. The source of her wealth is unclear. (Maybe it has to do with hiring hunters to trap and kill elephants?) It is clear that in the book the use of money and the earning of it are two totally different matters, and that it is perfectly normal and in fact delightful that some people have wealth they do not have to work for. Babar becomes one of them.

Babar is impressed both by the ways of the city (especially by the clothes of two elegant men) and with the fact that the Rich Lady feels perfectly comfortable giving him her purse to buy himself some proper clothes. I remember loving the scene where Babar goes into a department store and rides up and down on the elevator until he is chased out and told that he must do his shopping. I always wanted to do that, but my mother was always too busy to ride the elevator just for the fun of it. I also remember giggling at Babar trying his clothes on and can still remember the part on my records where the narrator describes Babar's buying clothes. The whole business of Babar's getting peopleized was an intriguing idea to me as a child, and though we didn't have any pets I could imagine dressing up a dog or cat and pretending that I was the Rich Lady and my pet was Babar. At the same time, rereading the book, I remember being tired as a child of being dressed up by adults and admired for doing what they wanted me to do rather than what I wanted to do. I loved Babar and must have hated him a bit too. However, as an adult I am bothered by his malleability and the good humor with which he jumps into becoming a well-dressed rich person-like elephant. I know if I read *Babar* with a class of young children I would certainly bring up that issue.

In the story there seem to be no limits to the Rich Lady's generosity. "She gives him whatever he wants," including an automobile. She also has a learned professor give Babar lessons, and she shows Babar off to her distinguished friends, whom Babar tells "all about life in the great forest." The only thing she does not give him is a map and food for the journey home, even though we see Babar looking forlornly out the window and thinking of the elephants he left behind.

The Rich Lady has no husband in the story. She does have distinguished friends and is clearly of a better class than the floorwalker and the other shopkeepers Babar encounters. The source of her power is her money—we know little else about her.

The role of money in the story points up the powerlessness of Babar. He does what he is told, is as passive as a paper doll and as uncomplaining. It is hard to imagine Babar opposing the Rich Lady or hurting her feelings. Whenever there is a question of Babar's doing something that might be disagreeable to her, he agonizes over it. And when he finally decides to return to the world of elephants for a temporary visit, he does it with her consent. Is all of this because of her money and its power over Babar?

In *Babar* the reader learns that there are different classes of people and the Rich Lady is of the better (that is richer) class and that elephants are not as good as people, but might be if they imitate people. Was I aware of those distinctions as a child? Did I learn to admire the rich from reading the book? Did I also learn about the inferiority of creatures from the jungle (people included)? I can't be sure, but I do think that from my early reading I got the impression that people who served the rich weren't as good as the rich.

Yet I got the opposite impression from my neighborhood and home. In fact my grandparents were deeply involved in union activities and talked about the rich and the bosses as if they were morally, intellectually, and otherwise evil and deficient. My reading contradicted my family's attitudes, and, since I never met a rich person, I was left with a certain puzzlement. I believe my reading made me feel that my grandparents might not have been telling the full truth about the rich; nevertheless, I didn't believe everything I read. *Babar,* as a story, was just that: one tale to weigh against both the other stories I heard and read, and my own experience. And my experiences with people, even as a six-, seven-, and eight-year-old, told me that people just aren't as generous as the Rich Lady was without ultimately wanting something back. I suspected the Rich Lady and still do. But I didn't dislike her and wouldn't mind running into someone like her who would take a fancy to me on my own terms.

I believe *Babar* set me to musing on trust and wealth but don't believe any conclusions resulted from those thoughts. The book showed me one way things might work. Other books and the world showed me other ways. The Rich Lady didn't do me any harm. However, the image of transforming one's life and fundamentally changing, which I knew from other fairy tales as well, did stay with me. Perhaps what I held dearest about Babar was his ability to recover from his mother's death and go on to make a life for himself. The loss of a mother, which I had not experienced, was, in the charged atmosphere of my growing up at the end of the Depression and during World War II, symptomatic of all the losses people were experiencing in my neighborhood. One appeal of that cute little elephant story was that it began with a loss and then went on to show that life was still possible.

Babar's story centers on the tension between his elephant world and the world to which the Rich Lady introduces him. There are many questions that can be raised about her and her wealth. For example, how does the Rich Lady maintain her fortune? Is she safe from thieves and selfish relatives? What might she do if Babar turned out to be dishonest? Had Babar ever thought about taking her money and running?

There are several ways to look at the Rich Lady's generosity with her money. One is as a way to buy power, protection, and an amusing life. From this view she is seen as an extension of the patriarchy, a product of capitalism and colonialism who maintains power by buying it. A totally different way of looking at the Rich Lady's role is as a caring and sympathetic woman who is providing an alternative to the patriarchy. She introduces generosity and kindness into a male-dominated world, as represented by the hunter and the image of the city as a difficult place to know without friends. There are elements in the story that support this view. She does nothing to exploit Babar (except perhaps to show him off to her friends), and she lets him go home when he wants. Perhaps she can even be interpreted as the Jane Addams of her time, a social worker who welcomes immigrant elephants and helps them settle into their new land.

Both ways of looking at the Rich Lady can be supported by the text, and in fact there is no contradiction in her being a kind person who, while benefiting from her family's exploitation of others, does not herself exploit others. Under this interpretation, the Rich Lady maintains her power through money, but builds other, more humane and affectionate relationships through the generous use of that wealth. This lesson on the use of wealth can even be appealed to in support of having children read the book.

However, there is a third interpretation of the Rich Lady's generosity that has been suggested to me. Under that view, the Rich Lady is very insecure in the world of people and immediately finds herself through contact with the innocence and purity of Babar. They are kindred souls, and so she takes him in as a member of the family, perhaps as a foster son. In that way, her relationship with Babar helps her maintain power over her feelings and acquire strength to overcome the alienation she feels in the world of people. This suggestion is intriguing, though we do meet four of the Rich Lady's people friends in the book.

Toward the middle of the story Babar finds his cousins Celeste and Arthur, who have run away from the forest. It is not clear whether they had Babar in mind when they set out on their adventure, but it is pretty clear that life in the wild was not enough for them. The attractions of civilization were becoming seductive for the young generation of the elephant world.

Babar promptly takes to civilizing his cousins. Through acquiring the accoutrements of civilization and access to the Rich Lady's purse, he has assumed power over other, less fortunate elephants. After kissing his cousins hello, the first thing Babar does is introduce them to the benefits of wealth. He takes them to the department store and buys them expensive clothes. He has learned his lessons thoroughly and presumably still has access to the Rich Lady's purse, for he treats his cousins quite well. They seem delighted to be transformed into imitations of people. The three of them even go to a pastry shop and have some sweets.

The story moves on relentlessly from Babar's civilizing Arthur and Celeste. Babar has been so taken in by people-ways that he does the job of recruiting for them. This is one form of colonization: seducing some members of the group into letting them proselytize for you.

Arthur's and Celeste's mothers come to fetch them from the city, and Babar decides to take them all back to the forest. Before he leaves he packs his trunk with all of his possessions—his hat and tie and walking cane and toiletries and box of bonbons. He has no desire to revert to kind and be just an elephant again. As they leave, the Rich Lady stands on the balcony of her house and sadly wonders, "When shall I see *my* little Babar again?" (italics mine). She has it right: by the time she is done civilizing him, she owns him.

I've always been troubled by the picture de Brunhoff drew of that parting scene. Babar, Celeste, and Arthur, dressed to kill, drive off in Babar's automobile, while Celeste's and Arthur's mothers, naked as elephants, follow along behind the car with their trunks lifted up "to avoid breathing the dust." Babar, the male, drives, and the mothers, both uncivilized, trot along behind. The parents are made to follow their remade children while they are, at the same time, losing them. Power has been transferred to the young Europeanized generation.

In de Brunhoff's illustrations the civilized elephants have personal identity and distinction; the natural elephants are portrayed as indistinguishable from each other. Here we see where the power is when the wild and the civilized make contact. Every time I looked at the book as a child, I felt there was something here that wasn't right. The mothers weren't being treated fairly. They should have been the ones in the car and the children should have been running behind, or they should all have been together in the car. Yet that wouldn't work either, since the idea of dressed and naked elephants riding together seemed embarrassing to me. That illustration was and is painful for me to look at.

The concept of nakedness is introduced here in a dramatic way. In the first page of the book, when we see Babar being rocked to sleep in a hammock by his mother, the elephants seem natural. Of course they have no clothes since elephants don't wear clothes. When Babar becomes dressed, there are no elephants around, so there is no thought of naked elephants. But as soon as the civilized Babar encounters naked elephants the question of deficiency arises. Babar is normal where he is living and the other elephants are deficient. Civilization creates desires which turn into necessities. If Celeste and Arthur are to associate with Babar, they must be dressed. Their mothers' natural state now becomes "nakedness" by contrast. Once Babar and his cousins reach home, the mother elephants merge into the crowd, indistinguishable from all the other elephants. We never see them again, and they cannot even be made out at Babar's marriage to Celeste; Celeste's mother is lost in the crowd of no-face elephants, her power completely obliterated.

Babar returns to his jungle home to find a crisis in the elephant patriarchy; the old king has died, and a new king is selected. The reader is presented with the dominance of males in the elephant world, and that's that.

The elephants see Babar, Arthur, and Celeste and exclaim, "What beautiful clothes! What a beautiful car!" and, at the suggestion of the oldest elephant, Cornelius, choose Babar as their new king since he has "learned so much living among men." All we are shown of his learning is that he knows how to choose clothes, order a meal at a restaurant, and add 2+2. He knows how to buy things and, once again, we see that power lies with money.

Before accepting his crown Babar (not Celeste) lets everyone know that he and Celeste have become engaged and they must accept Celeste as queen if they are to have him as king. There is no indication that Celeste has had much of a say in their engagement or anything else for that matter.

The elephants accept Babar's condition and shout in unison: "Long Live Queen Celeste! Long Live King Babar!"

After Babar's coronation King Babar praises the wise old Cornelius for having good ideas (the only one we hear about in the book is the idea that Babar should be king) and says, ". . . therefore I will make you general, and when I get my crown, I will give you my hat."—a touch of civilization for the general who is to rule when Babar and Celeste go on a honeymoon in a beautiful yellow balloon (another result of the Rich Lady's largesse, one has to presume). Thus power is given to the male military by the Europeanized king who goes off to new adventures.

What might children learn from this? I asked friends of mine who also read *Babar* as children if they remembered this scene, and without exception they did. In fact they remembered thinking it was a wonderful triumph for poor Babar who had lost his mother. One of these friends told me that she now hates the scene that shows Babar with his arm resting on Celeste's shoulder, Celeste with her head bowed, and the oldest elephant, Cornelius, with his glasses on, handing to Babar power over all the elephants. What had appeared magical to her as a child now represented the triumph of the Europeanized male. Did it harm her to have loved this scene as a child? Perhaps. It was one of many children's books that showed her

that women's happiness derives from being chosen by the right male. Should she have been given a copy of *Babar* to read when she was six? Perhaps not.

She had this insight while reading the book to her oldest child in the early 1980s and vowed never to read it to any other child. It wasn't just *Babar* that she rejected but all children's books that presented women in subservient roles. She brought up the issue of having *Babar* and books like it in the library at the co-op nursery school that her children attended. This led the parents in the school to reread these books with a critical sensibility. Up to that time the parent group had simply accepted without comment the books they'd found in the library.

This critical reading came up with statistics that surprised the parents. Almost all the books were popular children's books found in most nurseries those days, though there were a few with an emphasis on co-operation instead of competition, and several on peace and racial harmony. Nevertheless, almost without exception, females were portrayed in the books as passive, dependent, and best when most domesticated. This was completely contrary to the values of most of the parents, so the questions arose: How much influence do these books have on children? Should they throw out all the old books that portrayed values contrary to theirs? And where were they to find new books with different values that were still as charming and compelling as much of traditional literature?

The parent group never reached a consensus. Some parents read books like *Babar* and discussed them with the children, others made up their own stories, and some had children make up stories and share them with the group. Friends of a few of the parents actually formed a number of small presses and published books of their own that were explicitly feminist and anti-racist. The question of what to do with *Babar,* however, was never directly faced.

It is troubling for people who believe in a strong free press and want to trust their children's judgment to face the issue of censorship. Despite the desire to have their children exposed to the widest range of books, and especially the classics of children's literature, they also want their children to be free of sexist and racist attitudes. Yet in our society it is just about impossible to protect children from a barrage of sexist and racist books, videos, and comics aimed directly at them. The temptation to control children's reading and exposure to television and movies is not surprising, and for many parents it exists in uneasy tension with the desire to let children have free access to books and media.

SHOULD WE PROTECT OUR CHILDREN FROM *BABAR* AND BARBIE?

This raises the issue of how pure a book has to be for it to benefit children. Should there be no princes or kings, no princesses or queens, no portrayal of the benefits of wealth or the nature of male-centered families? Should children be protected from many of the classics of children's literature if these works seem to celebrate oppression, embody racism, or provide images of women as subordinate to men?

Two stories come to mind. A friend of mine who has two sons decided to prohibit them from playing with toy guns. One of the boys seemed to have a passion to play rough with guns. My perception of him was that he was gentle, not particularly violent or troubled. His friends had toy guns, and the fact that he was prohibited from having one made them very desirable. I expect he was nudged along by his friends, who might have humiliated him and accused him of letting his parents get away with too much. (Unfortunately, in our culture many middle-class kids become critical of their parents for depriving them of what they see as the necessary trappings of their class status. Certain toys become "necessities" for children bombarded by ads, comics, and TV.) In this case the boy, Steven, reached the limits of his frustration and screamed at his mother, "If you don't let me play with toy guns now, when I'm grown up I'm going to get real guns, and then you won't be able to stop me from using them."

Steven's mother was stunned, and we talked a lot about the situation. She decided not to respond to his threat immediately, but let him buy a toy pistol with money he had saved up a few weeks later. I remember he played with toy violence for a few weeks and then moved on to other things. Now he is a gourmet chef who looks back on the incident with amusement.

In a more personal case, my daughters passionately wanted Barbie dolls when they were six and seven. My wife and I had some serious doubts, and in my case, though I love and collect toys, I found Barbie and her entourage repugnant. We were both concerned about the effect Barbie would have on the girls' images of themselves as women if Barbie got too deep into their souls. However, their nagging and their argument that Barbie was just a toy and they knew the difference between dolls and people persuaded us to give in. I convinced myself that since I had overcome a heavy dose of World War II games of violence, casual and everyday sexism on the part of the older males in my home environment as a child, and a passion for reading boys' and girls' adventure books and fairy tales, my daughters could recover from Barbie. I believed this would be especially true if Barbie was used creatively and if Barbie was not their whole life.

I suggested that the girls make their own costumes for Barbie and use the dolls in games where Barbie and her friends did everything from building skyscrapers to flying planes. They did some of what I suggested and seemed to enjoy it, but sometimes they played with Barbies in ways that Barbie's manufacturer intended. Did it harm them? I asked my daughters, who are now in their mid-twenties and are both confirmed feminists. Their response was that playing with Barbies was fun, and Erica reminded me that she and Tonia always knew they were toys and not reality. She also reminded me that they loved Barbie's Dune Buggy and used to build sand cities and develop complex scenarios for their fantasy adventures, which also included stuffed animals, some of my toys and figurines, and other artistic creations of their own. They had felt free to play the Barbie script or change it; once they even had a long game that they called S&M Barbie, in which they tied up Barbie and Ken.

One of their friends, who is African American, also had a Barbie collection. She, as well as my daughters, had African American Barbies as well as White ones, and they played out all the ranges and varieties of sexual unions possible with the palette at their command. Interracial love, gay and lesbian love, the love of people dolls for stuffed animals, all figured in their fantasy play.

Both Tonia and Erica pointed out that they knew Barbie's body was silly and perverse, that Barbie was nothing like their mom, Judy, and that the thought of my being like Ken was absolutely hilarious. However, they did say that they have met young women in their lives for whom Barbie was a more serious matter. It is Erica's analysis that the damaging effects of Barbie arise with children whose fathers act as if women were dolls and whose mothers buy into the idea that Barbie-like styling is "the" model of beauty. In these cases the problem is more complex than the toys children use, and the Barbies are part of a complex that can lead to bulimia and anorexia at worst, or to other problems with one's body and sexuality. For Erica the problem is the context in which Barbie is set rather than Barbie itself.

Besides, Tonia pointed out, there was no avoiding knowing about Barbies and there was no avoiding the danger they held of socializing young girls to become sex objects. If you were prevented from playing with them, they became more attractive. I know several people in their twenties who collect old Barbies with a vengeance, having been prohibited from playing with them as children. However, this doesn't seem to interfere with their commitment to feminism or their rejection of the oppression of women. It is a benign contradiction in their lives of the sort people have when they grow up at cross-purposes to the society they live in.

More generally, there is no way to avoid having your children exposed to many objectionable or problematic aspects of our culture. Guns and Barbies, and *Babar* too, are part of cultural life in the United States, and children have to develop critical attitudes toward them. These attitudes will not develop through prohibition. On the contrary, what will more likely develop is a distaste for parental authority and a heightened critical scrutiny of adult life. The challenge parents face is how to integrate encounters with stereotypes into their children's sensibility and help their children become critical of aspects of the culture that denigrate or humiliate them or anyone else. The challenge is also how to let children feel free to develop their own evaluation of cultural practices. Instead of prohibiting things that tempt children, this means allowing them the freedom to explore things while trusting them to make sensible and humane judgments. It also means being explicitly critical of books and TV and encouraging children to discuss questions of judgment and values. This might seem a bit abstract, but I have found that watching TV and questioning what one sees, that visiting a toy store and suggesting which behaviors certain dolls and toys are designed to influence, can begin as early as children can talk. Nor need it be a grim exercise.

One of the places where I drew a hard line with my children was with G.I. Joe war toys, which socialize all children to accept war as play. I tried as much as possible to explain to my children how they represented the worst in people, glorified killing, and made war seem a casual matter of play. I even refused to buy them for my children, though I didn't prohibit them from using allowances or birthday or Christmas money to buy them. At the time, our three children (Josh the youngest as well as his two sisters) were exposed to G.I. Joe, my wife and I were actively engaged in protesting the Vietnam War. We took the children on marches when it was safe, explained to them what we were protesting, why we were doing it, and what risks we decided to take. The whole experience of the anti-war movement must have had a profound influence on them, for there was never any question of their buying the dolls or playing with them with friends. My son, Josh, became a pacifist at a very early age and still is one, and my daughters are profoundly antiwar. I suppose if they had bought G.I. Joe and played at making war I would have found a way to tolerate it, but I am sure it would have upset me deeply. Still, I don't believe it would have been my business to do more than try to influence them with reason and with the force of my example in the adult world.

Children will not come to a healthy critical stance without adult help. It is not developmentally inevitable that children will learn how to evaluate with sensitivity and intelligence what the adult world presents them. It is our responsibility, as critical and sensitive adults, to nurture the development of this sensibility in our children. This may require letting them play with Barbies, putting our foot down when it comes to G.I. Joe, and still keeping the door open for them to disagree with us without our rejecting them. In my experience, children quickly come to understand that critical sensibility strengthens them. It allows them to stand their ground, to develop opinions that are consistent with deeply held values, and, when conscience requires it, to act against consensus or the crowd. It is a source of pleasure as well—of the joy that comes from feeling that one is living according to conviction and understanding rather than being subject to the pressures and seductions of others.

Babar, my token for what is objectionable in children's literature, is a cultural phenomenon, an established children's classic that most children are likely to encounter. Often the question is not *whether* they encounter Babar, but *how.* Are they aware of colonialism? Do they understand that civilizing the elephants is symbolic of destroying the culture of colonized people? Or that the beneficent free-flowing money of the Rich Lady is a form of glorifying the ruling class? And does it matter? At this point I can imagine a reader wondering whether all this analysis is more than a book like *Babar* merits, but more people in the United States have probably read *Babar* than have read most best-sellers and classics. They buy the book for their children and read it together, and that's reason enough to take the text seriously; it becomes part of people's cultural heritage or cultural baggage, depending upon how you look at it. And we all have an abiding soft spot for *Babar*. We put aside the colonialism, the implied racism and sexism of the tale that are apparent upon rereading it. The image of the poor young elephant who has no father and whose mother is killed is powerful. What else could he do but fall into any temptation, and who among us could say they would resist the Rich Lady?

Recently I heard a speech given by Laurent de Brunhoff, the son of Jean de Brunhoff, the creator of Babar. The son is writing new sequels to *Babar* (there are many old sequels written by Jean de Brunhoff himself). Laurent said explicitly that he's trying to update Babar's image and indicated that he was very aware of the power relationships represented in the book and the way in which they imply support of sexism, racism, and colonialism. Thus, the analysis here is not unique. Analysis of the content of *Babar* and many other children's books is fairly common practice in commercial publishing houses, particularly those that sell to a school market increasingly sensitive about stereotyping. The publishers show little reluctance to censor or change original texts, so it is important to develop textual analysis of one's own and examine whether publishers, in the name of cleaning up old textbooks, aren't in fact introducing other equally distressing biases. For example, in an article published in the Teachers and Writers Collaborative Newsletter in the fall of 1989, Nancy Kricorian described a twelve-page editor's taboo list she was given by a textbook publisher that hired her to find poems for a reading series they were developing. She says the list "forbade the mention of ghosts, magic, religion, tobacco, cheating, sugar and candy. Birthday cake, death, divorce, negative emotions, and religious holidays were to be avoided." In their attempt to root out every possible

bias and please everybody, the publishers extinguished life in all its complexity and variability, and in doing so routed much of good poetry from the series. The hunt for hidden bias should not create an image of life that corresponds to no lived experience. Racism, sexism, and colonialism, as well as suicide, divorce, and cheating, figure in life and literature, and should certainly be read about and discussed at home and in the classroom. It's when books explicitly propagandize for inequality and misery that one has to be careful about how and whether they are used with young children who are not explicitly aware of their biases.

IS *BABAR* PROPAGANDA?

Does *Babar* explicitly propagandize children through the way power works in the story? So far I have discussed several questions about the nature of power in *Babar*. Some other questions are, Who wants power, and Who takes others' power from them? Are there any power struggles in the book? And if so, how are they dealt with?

Babar doesn't covet power. In fact, he seems to throw it away or at least delegate it to old Cornelius so he and Celeste can go on adventures. The Rich Lady provides a model of life without working, and Babar embraces it. Not for him the weight of kingship. He heads off in his balloon and ventures among the world of people. The military establishment will take care of things.

There are no apparent power struggles in the book, but let's imagine what might happen when Babar and Celeste leave the jungle. What we have left behind is Cornelius, the general, who wears Babar's hat, and cousin Arthur, who is dressed in people clothes. All the other elephants are naked, including Arthur's own mother. Do we have an incipient class structure developing? Will Arthur join with Cornelius, or will he try to displace him? Will other elephants join with Arthur, or develop their own type of clothes made from indigenous materials and raise a rebellion for local control and against the foreign influences Babar imported to the jungle? Will there be a purist rebellion of elephants who believe that it is in the nature of elephanthood to be naked and will try to purge all signs of foreign influence? Will the female elephants claim power? And will they be purists, local developers, or imitators? Or will the military mobilize itself and establish and maintain order in the name of the absent king? Or maybe even throw off monarchy and develop an elephant oligarchy or military dictatorship? One thing is for sure; things will never be the same after Babar's return.

In *Babar* the symbols, signs, and rituals of power and of loyalty work throughout the story and become unspoken ways of getting children to acknowledge the validity of the power relations portrayed. Babar's power, for example, is represented by his clothes, his hat, and his car. The two naked mother elephants stand out in the city. Their nakedness is not a sign merely of their innocence but of their naiveté, their ignorance, and their vulnerability (to the hunter as well as the city). A dressed and educated elephant is something else, the kind of creature who can stand by the fireplace, recounting wild tales to amuse the civilized. Babar's standing in front of the fireplace, telling the Rich Lady's friends tales of the jungle, reminds me of another children's story about Pocahontas, the Native American woman who saved John Smith in the Virginia colony and was taken back to England by him. The story tells how she amused the people in the court of King James in London, where she lived the rest of her life. According to the myth constructed by European American authors, she told tales of her own people, about their quaint habits and culture. One wonders what she thought of these strangers, and whether it occurred to her that they considered her people savages and her tales justification for considering Native Peoples less than fully human. Or, more likely, was the story of the benign and friendly Pocahontas a tale invented to soothe the consciences of White people whose ancestors had practiced genocide?

Many of the rituals of power in *Babar* reinforce some of the least functional habits in our society. The first ritual, one that might certainly interest many children in our society, is going shopping. Not only does Babar shop; he can get anything he wants. What a dream for young children whose lives are full of "I want" and "buy me." This ritual makes Babar similar to, but luckier than, most children, and may account for much of the book's popularity in the capitalist world. I know I often imagined as a kid what it would be like to be able to get anything I wanted, and my cousin Marlyn and friends Bobby and Ronny used to make up imaginary shopping lists and compare them.

Wanting things is serious business in our society, and I feel uncomfortable with books that reinforce that obsession.

Marriage is another ritual, and Babar's marriage is an interesting one. He marries his cousin, Celeste, perhaps keeping the royal line within the family. Cousin marriages are not well regarded in our society, and teachers I've spoken with get very nervous about this aspect of the Babar story. They try to skip over it in class, redirect discussion, or tie the issue up by saying that elephants have a different sense of family than people do. However, the relationship between Celeste and Babar is not based on their mutual elephantness at all. It's based on his being able to dress and thereby civilize her. Their mutual distance from the community of their origin is a defining part of their relationship, a fact that might cause some people in immigrant communities in the United States some pause.

There is another place in *Babar* where the maintenance of power raises some interesting questions. Babar gives his derby hat to Cornelius as a symbol of the transference of power. Yet how is a hat enough to ensure that Cornelius can maintain authority over the other elephants? This raises the question of the power of symbols and the role of vested authority in children's literature. I am convinced that children believe in the power of objects such as scepters, wands, and crowns, all of which have a symbolic relation to authority. These objects, when used in tales and stories, reinforce ideas of how authority is legitimized and transferred. Babar becomes king because he is better than the other elephants, and his power is transferred through his hat to Cornelius, who is thereby deemed qualified to rule. Therefore Cornelius becomes qualified to rule. That's not dissimilar to a teacher making a child a monitor in a classroom and giving her or him a badge or a pencil and pad to write down the names of miscreants regardless of whether the role is a suitable one for the child or whether the other children will recognize that authority.

The use of symbols and possessions to legitimize authority is dangerous and antidemocratic. It suggests to children that blind acceptance of authority is good behavior. The question of whether one encourages a child to accept or question authority is a major one in childrearing. It is generally assumed that children should not question adult authority. Yet, in a world where there is so much illegitimate authority, or legitimized authority that acts in illegitimate ways, knowing how to question authority is very healthy. Books that slip in, as a characteristic of reality, the acceptance and transference of kingly authority give little credit to democratic citizenship and could conceivably set up young people for obediently fighting in other people's wars and believing that their vote and voice does not count for much in the world. One compelling reason for not reading *Babar* is that it makes a thoroughly undemocratic way of governance seem natural and unquestioned.

The establishment and maintenance of power is presented as a major theme at the very beginning of the story. The hunter kills Babar's mother. He who owns the gun has the power over life and death. Babar knows this, and when he stumbles into a human world and gets seduced into adopting its ways, does he forget his mother's killer? Or does he always keep, somewhere in the recesses of his mind, the fact that if he crosses the Rich Lady or does something really wrong in the world of people, his mother's fate awaits him? This reading makes *Babar* a much sadder story than it is usually taken to be, one colored at every point by guns, death, and the cruelty of people. Babar in this reading is a frightened, obedient slave who is allowed to go home, but not without wearing the mark of oppression.

I have recently discovered that pointing this out to children can have a devastating effect on their reaction to the story. I visited a third-grade class and gave them a talk on the making of this essay. I told them that my motivation was to examine the different meanings that could be found in *Babar.* Then I defined colonialism and pointed out that the costume of the hunter gave him away as a colonist. Next I gave them some history of French colonialism in Africa, and we discussed the meaning of clothes in the story. There is no reason why a discussion like this shouldn't be part of the critical literature program as early as the third grade, if not earlier. Not surprisingly, one of the questions that arose in our discussion was what Babar felt about the death of his mother. Why didn't he stomp on some of the people he encountered? And why did the author never mention anything about bringing the hunter to justice? Finally the issue of what Babar learned from people came up, and to the group it seemed that he no longer liked being an elephant. Thus, not only was he not trying to avenge the death of his mother; in a way he became the friend of his mother's murderers. Frantz

Fanon described this internalization of the colonists' culture as one of the deepest forms of dehumanization experienced by the victims of colonialism, one which, according to him, can only be overcome through bloody revolution. The third-graders must have sensed some of this, because most of them expressed anger at the hunter and no longer thought the story was cute or charming.

Do children who have not had an opportunity to analyze the text see this sinister aspect of the Babar story? Most youngsters I've questioned seem to acknowledge its existence and then forget it. They just want that man with the gun out of the story, never to come back and haunt Babar's life. However, one summer, during the year I was teaching at a school for severely disturbed children, I lived with a seven-year-old boy who had been classified as childhood schizophrenic. Mark was a brilliant reader and often memorized books that he'd read. At night, when he was alone in his bedroom, I could hear him talking to characters in his favorite books. *Babar* was one of them. Mark was obsessed with the death scene at the beginning of the book and had made up a name for the hunter, creating a whole scenario for the hunt, which ended in Babar's mother's death. For him, death hung over the book. He wondered whether the clerks in the store knew the hunter, speculated that one of the Rich Lady's friends was the hunter, and told Babar over and over again in imaginary conversation that he would be killed just like his mother was killed, even by the same hunter.

Mark's case was extreme, but the murder at the beginning of the story is remembered by everyone who reads the book. It is what bonds the reader to Babar and makes one want him to be treated well. Yet the death is awful and arbitrary, and reminds one of the importance of current attempts to ban the sale of ivory and eliminate elephant poaching. So, is it good or bad that children read about the cold-blooded murder of a mother in front of her child, even if they are elephants in a fantasy tale? Especially when there is no revenge or justice in the story? What if some children identify with the hunter and not Babar or his mother? Is that reason enough to ban or burn the book? Or can children bear the unpleasant along with the pleasant, and do they even need it as a way to help them face the fact that life ends in death?

These seem like profound and complex questions to raise in the context of thinking about a short children's classic. Yet critical reading consists of questioning a text, challenging it, and speculating on ways in which the world it creates can illuminate the one we live in. A book is a wonderful tutor for the imagination which thrives on being challenging as much as it does on being challenged. Part of the experience of reading *Babar* for a child is raising questions, like Did Babar forget his mother when he met the Rich Lady? Did he ever talk to her about his mother? What happened between Celeste and Arthur in that car ride back to the jungle that led to getting married? Why is wearing clothes so important in this story? And what would I do if I met the Rich Lady?

For a more experienced and older reader, the challenges can go beyond the text itself to inquiries about the author's politics, social class, and family background, and to speculation about the emotional impact of books in general that show children losing their parents. In all of these cases, reading becomes dialogue. The text can be reimagined and invested with multiple meanings. For the active reader, there is no need for one authoritative interpretation, and even absurd fights over the meaning of the text are part of the whole experience of reading. However, read uncritically, there is always the possibility that a book like *Babar* can contribute to the formation of stereotypes and attitudes that might be reinforced by other reading, by TV, and by the nature and shape of the toys manufactured for children's use. Children's books contribute to the formation of culture, and some books can even transform the way children look at and relate to the world. Therefore the question of reading *Babar*, for me, can be reduced to the question of whether uncritical reading of the book is so potentially damaging that it should be withheld from children when possible.

There is even more to the case of *Babar*. Thinking about the death of Babar's mother leads to another question related to power: How does a story define and deal with good and evil? In *Babar* the hunter is evil, but if there is any other evil present it is hidden from obvious view. The elephants are simple and good. In fact they trust and admire people so much that they're willing to give up their elephant nature for some clothes and a car. The Rich Lady, who is "very rich," is also portrayed as good and generous. And Babar, when all dressed up, is also good. It's important to note that he is not dressed like a taxicab driver in Paris or a salesman or factory worker; he's dressed like an

entrepreneur with a little derby hat and spats on his shoes. These are symbols of the upper class, but in this book they are also symbols of goodness. The rich are good, money is good, simple elephants who believe those things are also good. Babar's mother is good, but isn't the hunter who "is wicked" also dressed in a way that identifies him as upper class? Could there be a relationship between hunting and money? Is the hunter's evil also to be found in the city? We are never told. The story sweeps evil under the rug. The hunter disappears. With him also goes what might have created wrenching tension in the story. I can, however, imagine an adult version of *Babar* that centers around Babar, dressed to kill, hunting down the killer of his mother, and killing him in an elephant way in the midst of his family somewhere in Paris. However, *Babar* isn't an adult thriller or a psychological novel about revenge and the myths of primitivity and civilization. It's a story for little children, and its main tension comes from Babar's loneliness for his elephant friends and his life in the jungle.

Studying how tension and dissonance are dealt with in a plot is another way of discovering the role of power relations in a story. Babar is drawn home and has to leave the Rich Lady. However, she has made a lasting change in his life, one that affects the way he returns home and his subsequent need to leave and travel in the world outside the jungle. In the gentlest and most seductive way, Babar has given up his elephant power and become a bit of a dandy. One way of reading this central theme in the story is that Babar has been marginalized in both the human and animal worlds by his contact with the Rich Lady. The ruling class has made him dependent on money and things without giving him any independent way to earn them. It has also taken away his identity as an elephant among elephants. He is an exile, a stranger in a strange land and in his own land at the same time.

A less political reader might find all of this farfetched. She or he might see the book as a way of getting children to overcome fear of large wild animals. Of course this is just speculation, playing around with reading. Children most likely see Babar as a kid elephant with all four feet in two worlds simultaneously. And they see him as part of a story, one take on many imaginary worlds, not as a character in a cautionary tale about identity. It's easy to take children's literature more seriously than children take it, and it's sensible, in the midst of critical musings, to remember that sometimes an elephant in a green suit is just an elephant in a green suit.

WHAT'S MISSING FROM *BABAR*?

So far I've been looking at power relationships within the text of *Babar.* Another way to examine the book is to step outside of it and consider what is not in the text. This is a bit like trying to understand the nature of a private political meeting from a list of people who weren't invited. Who has been uninvited to Babar's world? Among others, working-class people who don't work in stores and serve the rich; poor people; human children; and humans Babar's age. The people in Paris don't all live like the Rich Lady, her friends, and the people that serve them. Providing young children with a steady diet of the untroubled lives of the rich (there is no friction in the Rich Lady's world and no apparent pain) is one way to equate wealth with well-being. Though most books for young children don't portray a world of the rich and their servants, and are much more middle class in character, they still tie well-being to money and portray lives full of comfort and joy. By implication they provide an ideal type of life, one worth aspiring to. However, it is possible to live a full and decent life without great wealth, and it may be that the acquisition of great wealth always comes at the cost of other peoples' impoverishment. These possibilities are rarely if ever raised in children's literature.

I mentioned this once to a group of parents who are friends of ours, mostly middle-class academics, whose response in part was: Why not let children remain innocent for a while and be given stories about people who live well and enjoy life? My response is that there are many ways to live well, and it's important to show children that you don't have to be rich to live well, that living well is not simply a matter of being able to buy things and have other people take care of your everyday needs. Of course, there's probably nothing wrong with allowing an occasional elephant with a green jacket who can buy everything he wants into children's lives if there are other visions for them to ponder as well.

There is another major absence in the tale of Babar, one that I remember worrying about. Where is Babar's father? There is no mention that Babar has a father in the entire story. Was his father also killed by a hunter? Did he leave home and abandon Babar and his mother? Did de Brunhoff consciously leave him out or simply forget to put him in? Or did he intend Babar to be born, like Jesus, without a father? Was Babar illegitimate or was he meant to be symbolically special so that when his mother is killed he becomes orphaned and can't be claimed by any family in the society? Is that a presage of his coming coronation and special relationship with the world of civilization? Or, to negate all of my idle chatter, my wife suggested that there was a much simpler interpretation. Elephants are polygamous, with the major males the only ones mating with all of the bearing female elephants. The analogy between the human nuclear family and the elephant herd completely breaks down here. In addition, polygamy was illegal and considered sinful in de Brunhoff's world. Perhaps, rather than bring up the issue of anthropomorphism, he simply skirted the question of Babar's paternity.

These days publishers of children's books resist stories that personalize animals because the analogy between human and animal life is never exact. There is more concern than in the past about providing accurate descriptions of animal life. It's possible that if de Brunhoff were to submit *Babar* for publication these days it would be rejected for scientific inaccuracy as well as for its portrayal of colonialism and gender, and its implications of racism. Yet this too is an interesting issue with respect to children's book classics: How many of them would be accepted for publication today given the current increased sensitivity to issues of gender, race, and homophobia?

SHOULD WE BURN *BABAR*?

So, finally, what are we to do with this charming elephant in a green suit who, despite all of these complaints, attracts and amuses many children? What are we to do about the "universal" experiences of fun and fantasy the book can provide to all children? Are we to deprive children of them? Or do they even exist?

Universal is a big word. Is it true that children in South Africa or any of the former French colonies in Africa will find *Babar* amusing? Do young children there need to read such a remnant of colonialism?

Don't they have other things to be concerned with and other delightful stories and tales to be regaled with? I would find it sensible in that context to consign *Babar* to the children's literature research library or use it as a text to be studied in a class on the instruments of colonialism, or on critical thinking and the development of child intelligence.

I recently faced a situation similar to this one. During the quincentenary celebration of Columbus's invasion of the Americas I received over a dozen children's books on Columbus for review. While cleaning out my library I came upon the books and had to decide what to do with them. Usually I loan review copies of books to teachers at our local schools or give them to the town library. However, I found all of these books objectionable, glorifying Columbus as they did. In most cases Native Peoples were either totally absent or represented as grateful for the arrival of civilization. It was astonishing to me, given the amount of attention supposedly paid to the sensitivities of Native Americans in current publishing, how like the old books even the newest and most elegant Columbus books were. I read some of them with parents of a few of the Native American youngsters I worked with, and they were offended and wouldn't show them to their young children, who already knew enough about being stereotyped by White culture. So, should I burn these books? There seemed few other options. I refused to donate them to the library or the school since I agreed that children needed a truthful and compassionate view of the European colonization of the Americas. My decision was to save two of the books for our library as examples to critique and to take the rest to the dump and bury them. It was hard for me to make this decision as I love books and have no fear myself of reading anything. But in our school most of the teachers are not sensitive to the insults these books contain, and I didn't want to contribute to this insensitivity.

This has to do with the question of what children learn from "good" literature written for their consumption. This last question assumes that all children have some common traits that lie at the core of their appreciation of "good" literature. However, using the word "children" masks the differences in experience and culture that shapes appreciation and pleasure. It opens up seemingly logical and coherent arguments to bias and misunderstanding. I remember talking about *Babar* with a friend of mine who is a Black South African from Capetown. I showed him the book, and he stopped at the second page, the one where the hunter is shooting Babar's mother. He told me that if children in his community saw that hunter, dressed in safari clothes with his white pith helmet, their response would not be sympathy with Babar and sadness over the death of his mother so much as hatred of the colonial with a gun. There are innumerable fables and stories in southern Africa that educate young Black children about the dangers of the White oppressors, some funny and some grim. Many have explicitly to do with a man dressed just as the hunter in *Babar* who tries to kill monkeys, elephants, or some other animals. According to my friend, who had been a school teacher before being sent into exile for his political activity, the fact that the hunter disappears after killing Babar's mother would puzzle and anger children he taught. To them, the hunter would be the antagonist in the story. Dressing up an elephant in a suit and putting a happy face on the story was an insult to them, and he couldn't imagine them finding anything amusing or edifying or charming about the whole thing.

In addition, he said that the analogy between the naked elephants and African people was so transparent and insulting as to make the book overtly racist and without redeeming factors from his perspective.

On the other hand, I remember my own children liking the books, mostly the drawings, which are charming. My wife, Judy, and I got the books for the children because we remembered loving them as children. Judy and I were not damaged for life by liking the books, but I do believe that they contributed to my not questioning many aspects of patriarchy earlier in life, and to a misunderstanding of the intensity of the horrors of colonialist attitudes. How much they contributed is hard to say. It's very difficult to sort out childhood influences and specify exactly how much one particular experience related to all of the other influences in one's environment.

I am pretty sure that my children would think carefully about whether to buy *Babar* for their own (not yet born) children. They are much more aware of stereotyping and bias in children's books than I was in my early twenties, and much more concerned about their damaging effect. In addition, there is a whole new literature for children that has emerged over the past twenty-five years, one that is built upon a sensitivity to bias and a vision of equality that was thoroughly absent in almost all the books written for children in the past. It is to this literature, I am confident, that they will turn to provide growing-up stories for their children. Certainly it is what I will draw upon if and when I become a grandparent.

I wouldn't ban or burn *Babar,* or pull it from libraries. But buy it? No. I see no reason to go out of one's way to make *Babar* available to children, primarily because I don't see much critical reading going on in the schools, and children don't need to be propagandized about colonialism, sexism, or racism. There are many other cute and well-illustrated, less offensive animal tales for young people. I believe *Babar* would best be relegated to the role of collector's item, an item in a museum of stereotypes. My wife disagrees. She has much more confidence than I do in children's ability to develop critical sensitivity unaided; she might buy it for our grandchildren after all.

Beyond her disagreement, there still is something else that makes me uncomfortable about my own conclusions. *Babar* has some appealing aspects. De Brun-

hoff's drawings and the story of his elephant in a green suit who has all the money and resources to do anything he cares to do can be looked at as a parable of freedom. The free unencumbered adventurer has its appeal, and I might dig out my old copy and share it with my grandchildren as an example of what us older people were reading almost fifty years ago. We'd discuss the limitations of de Brunhoff's vision, and maybe even reconceive the story as it might be told if it assumed a more equitable world as background for the action. I might do the same thing in my teaching. But, in both cases, I'd use *Babar* only if the children had been surrounded by a wealth of books and stories and tales, and had the opportunity to talk about the relationships of stories to people's dreams.

If there were only a few books a child had access to, it would be foolish to select any that have racial, class, or sexual bias woven into their content and imagery as positive things, no matter how charming or "classic" they are. *Babar's* time as a central experience in childhood must pass. In this case I use the word "childhood" as a universally applicable noun.

Hans Christian Andersen (1805–75)

One of the most beloved fairy tales in world literature, "The Little Mermaid" deals with dreams deferred, rather than wishes fulfilled. Hans Christian Andersen's romantic descriptions of the natural beauties of sea, earth, and land; his vision of a fantastical kingdom under the sea; and his close attention to the little mermaid's emotions through each stage of her quest for love and immortality illustrate the differences between the spare narrative style of most oral folktales and the stylistic embellishments created by masters of the literary fairy tale. Andersen crafted this original tale, first published in 1837, about a mysterious, beautiful creature taken from ancient mythology and folklore, one who reflected his own frustrations with unrequited love and psychological isolation. His seafaring Danish nation has always had ships in its navy called *Mermaid,* and Andersen's mermaid does bring good luck to at least one shipwrecked man, but loving him destroys her own life. Subverting legendary images of ruthless sirens whose songs lured sailors to their deaths, Andersen created a tenderhearted heroine who saves the prince of her dreams and willingly endures great suffering—ironically giving up her alluring voice in order to obtain a human body and immortal soul. Andersen's sentimental heroine has attracted so much earthly sympathy that a bronze statue of the little mermaid, placed in a Copenhagen harbor in 1913, remains one of Denmark's most treasured landmarks.

Critic Maria Tatar wrote that Andersen "promotes . . . a cult of suffering, death and transcendence for children rivaled only by what passed for the spiritual edification of children in Puritan cultures."[1] Along with writers such as P. L. Travers and Maurice Sendak, Tatar is repelled by the violence and self-denial in Andersen's tales, yet A. Waller Hastings, in the essay reprinted here, argues that it is more pernicious for the Disney film to give the little mermaid simplified moral choices and a conventional happy ending. While the tale's pervasive Christian morality may seem heavy-handed and outdated to some modern readers, Andersen eloquently symbolizes the struggles of adolescence in the little mermaid's intense longing to grow up and visit unknown lands alone, her inability to fit in and conform to the expectations of undersea or earthly kingdoms, her self-inflicted isolation and pain, and her passionate devotion to her risky and unconventional goals. (For more information on Andersen and "The Emperor's New Clothes," see Part 2.)

NOTE

1. Maria Tatar, *The Classic Fairy Tales,* Norton Critical Edition (New York: Norton, 1999) 212. See also Maurice Sendak, *Caldecott & Co.* (New York: Farrar, Straus & Giroux, 1990) 33–34.

The Little Mermaid

TRANSLATED BY H. P. PAULL (1872)

Far out in the ocean, where the water is as blue as the prettiest cornflower, and as clear as crystal, it is very, very deep; so deep, indeed, that no cable could fathom it: many church steeples, piled one upon another, would not reach from the ground beneath to the surface of the water above.

There dwell the Sea King and his subjects. We must not imagine that there is nothing at the bottom of the sea but bare yellow sand. No, indeed; the most singular flowers and plants grow there; the leaves and stems of which are so pliant, that the slightest agitation of the water causes them to stir as if they had life. Fishes, both large and small, glide between the branches, as birds fly among the trees here upon land. In the deepest spot of all, stands the castle of the Sea King. Its walls are built of coral, and the long, gothic windows are of the clearest amber. The roof is formed of shells, that open and close as the water flows over them. Their appearance is very beautiful, for in each lies a glittering pearl, which would be fit for the diadem of a queen.

The Sea King had been a widower for many years, and his aged mother kept house for him. She was a very wise woman, and exceedingly proud of her high birth; on that account she wore twelve oysters on her tail; while others, also of high rank, were only allowed to wear six. She was, however, deserving of very great praise, especially for her care of the little sea-princesses, her granddaughters. They were six beautiful children; but the youngest was the prettiest of them all; her skin was as clear and delicate as a rose-leaf, and her eyes as blue as the deepest sea; but, like all the others, she had no feet, and her body ended in a fish's tail. All day long they played in the great halls of the castle, or among the living flowers that grew out of the walls. The large amber windows were open, and the fish swam in, just as the swallows fly into our houses when we open the windows, excepting that the fishes swam up to the princesses, ate out of their hands, and allowed themselves to be stroked. Outside the castle there was a beautiful garden, in which grew bright red and dark blue flowers, and blossoms like flames of fire; the fruit glittered like gold, and the leaves and stems waved to and fro continually. The earth itself was the finest sand, but blue as the flame of burning sulphur. Over everything lay a peculiar blue radiance, as if it were surrounded by the air from above, through which the blue sky shone, instead of the dark depths of the sea. In calm weather the sun could be seen, looking like a purple flower, with the light streaming from the calyx. Each of the young princesses had a little plot of ground in the garden, where she might dig and plant as she pleased. One arranged her flower-bed into the form of a whale; another thought it better to make hers like the figure of a little mermaid; but that of the youngest was round like the sun, and contained flowers as red as his rays at sunset. She was a strange child, quiet and thoughtful; and while her sisters would be delighted with the wonderful things which they obtained from the wrecks of vessels, she cared for nothing but her pretty red flowers, like the sun, excepting a beautiful marble statue. It was the representation of a handsome boy, carved out of pure white stone, which had fallen to the bottom of the sea from a wreck. She planted by the statue a rose-colored weeping willow. It grew splendidly, and very soon hung its fresh branches over the statue, almost down to the blue sands. The shadow had a violet tint, and waved to and fro like the branches; it seemed as if the crown of the tree and the root were at play, and trying to kiss each other. Nothing gave her so much pleasure as to hear about the world above the sea. She made her old grandmother tell her all she knew of the ships and of the towns, the people and the animals. To her it seemed most wonderful and beautiful to hear that the flowers of the land should have fragrance, and not those below the sea; that the trees of the forest should be green; and that the fishes among the trees could sing so sweetly, that it was quite a pleasure to hear them. Her grandmother called the little birds fishes, or she would not have understood her; for she had never seen birds.

"When you have reached your fifteenth year," said the grandmother, "you will have permission to rise up out of the sea, to sit on the rocks in the moonlight, while the great ships are sailing by; and then you will see both forests and towns."

In the following year, one of the sisters would be fifteen: but as each was a year younger than the other,

the youngest would have to wait five years before her turn came to rise up from the bottom of the ocean, and see the earth as we do. However, each promised to tell the others what she saw on her first visit, and what she thought the most beautiful; for their grandmother could not tell them enough; there were so many things on which they wanted information. None of them longed so much for her turn to come as the youngest, she who had the longest time to wait, and who was so quiet and thoughtful. Many nights she stood by the open window, looking up through the dark blue water, and watching the fish as they splashed about with their fins and tails. She could see the moon and stars shining faintly; but through the water they looked larger than they do to our eyes. When something like a black cloud passed between her and them, she knew that it was either a whale swimming over her head, or a ship full of human beings, who never imagined that a pretty little mermaid was standing beneath them, holding out her white hands towards the keel of their ship.

As soon as the eldest was fifteen, she was allowed to rise to the surface of the ocean. When she came back, she had hundreds of things to talk about; but the most beautiful, she said, was to lie in the moonlight, on a sandbank, in the quiet sea, near the coast, and to gaze on a large town nearby, where the lights were twinkling like hundreds of stars; to listen to the sounds of the music, the noise of carriages, and the voices of human beings, and then to hear the merry bells peal out from the church steeples; and because she could not go near to all those wonderful things, she longed for them more than ever. Oh, did not the youngest sister listen eagerly to all these descriptions? and afterwards, when she stood at the open window looking up through the dark blue water, she thought of the great city, with all its bustle and noise, and even fancied she could hear the sound of the church bells, down in the depths of the sea.

In another year the second sister received permission to rise to the surface of the water, and to swim about where she pleased. She rose just as the sun was setting, and this, she said, was the most beautiful sight of all. The whole sky looked like gold, while violet and rose-colored clouds, which she could not describe, floated over her; and, still more rapidly than the clouds, flew a large flock of wild swans towards the setting sun, looking like a long white veil across the sea. She also swam towards the sun; but it sunk into the waves, and the rosy tints faded from the clouds and from the sea.

The third sister's turn followed; she was the boldest of them all, and she swam up a broad river that emptied itself into the sea. On the banks she saw green hills covered with beautiful vines; palaces and castles peeped out from amid the proud trees of the forest; she heard the birds singing, and the rays of the sun were so powerful that she was obliged often to dive down under the water to cool her burning face. In a narrow creek she found a whole troop of little human children, quite naked, and sporting about in the water; she wanted to play with them, but they fled in a great fright; and then a little black animal came to the water; it was a dog, but she did not know that, for she had never before seen one. This animal barked at her so terribly that she became frightened, and rushed back to the open sea. But she said she should never forget the beautiful forest, the green hills, and the pretty little children who could swim in the water, although they had not fish's tails.

The fourth sister was more timid; she remained in the midst of the sea, but she said it was quite as beautiful there as nearer the land. She could see for so many miles around her, and the sky above looked like a bell of glass. She had seen the ships, but at such a great distance that they looked like sea-gulls. The dolphins sported in the waves, and the great whales spouted water from their nostrils till it seemed as if a hundred fountains were playing in every direction.

The fifth sister's birthday occurred in the winter; so when her turn came, she saw what the others had not seen the first time they went up. The sea looked quite green, and large icebergs were floating about, each like a pearl, she said, but larger and loftier than the churches built by men. They were of the most singular shapes, and glittered like diamonds. She had seated herself upon one of the largest, and let the wind play with her long hair, and she remarked that all the ships sailed by rapidly, and steered as far away as they could from the iceberg, as if they were afraid of it. Towards evening, as the sun went down, dark clouds covered

the sky, the thunder rolled and the lightning flashed, and the red light glowed on the icebergs as they rocked and tossed on the heaving sea. On all the ships the sails were reefed with fear and trembling, while she sat calmly on the floating iceberg, watching the blue lightning, as it darted its forked flashes into the sea.

When first the sisters had permission to rise to the surface, they were each delighted with the new and beautiful sights they saw; but now, as grown-up girls, they could go when they pleased, and they had become indifferent about it. They wished themselves back again in the water, and after a month had passed they said it was much more beautiful down below, and pleasanter to be at home. Yet often, in the evening hours, the five sisters would twine their arms round each other, and rise to the surface, in a row. They had more beautiful voices than any human being could have; and before the approach of a storm, and when they expected a ship would be lost, they swam before the vessel, and sang sweetly of the delights to be found in the depths of the sea, and begging the sailors not to fear if they sank to the bottom. But the sailors could not understand the song, they took it for the howling of the storm. And these things were never to be beautiful for them; for if the ship sank, the men were drowned, and their dead bodies alone reached the palace of the Sea King.

When the sisters rose, arm-in-arm, through the water in this way, their youngest sister would stand quite alone, looking after them, ready to cry, only that the mermaids have no tears, and therefore they suffer more. "Oh, were I but fifteen years old," said she: "I know that I shall love the world up there, and all the people who live in it."

At last she reached her fifteenth year. "Well, now, you are grown up," said the old dowager, her grandmother; "so you must let me adorn you like your other sisters;" and she placed a wreath of white lilies in her hair, and every flower leaf was half a pearl. Then the old lady ordered eight great oysters to attach themselves to the tail of the princess to show her high rank.

"But they hurt me so," said the little mermaid.

"Pride must suffer pain," replied the old lady. Oh, how gladly she would have shaken off all this grandeur, and laid aside the heavy wreath! The red flowers in her own garden would have suited her much better, but she could not help herself: so she said, "Farewell," and rose as lightly as a bubble to the surface of the water. The sun had just set as she raised her head above the waves; but the clouds were tinted with crimson and gold, and through the glimmering twilight beamed the evening star in all its beauty. The sea was calm, and the air mild and fresh. A large ship, with three masts, lay becalmed on the water, with only one sail set; for not a breeze stirred, and the sailors sat idle on deck or amongst the rigging. There was music and song on board; and, as darkness came on, a hundred colored lanterns were lighted, as if the flags of all nations waved in the air. The little mermaid swam close to the cabin windows; and now and then, as the waves lifted her up, she could look in through clear glass window-panes, and see a number of well-dressed people within. Among them was a young prince, the most beautiful of all, with large black eyes; he was sixteen years of age, and his birthday was being kept with much rejoicing. The sailors were dancing on deck, but when the prince came out of the cabin, more than a hundred rockets rose in the air, making it as bright as day. The little mermaid was so startled that she dived under water; and when she again stretched out her head, it appeared as if all the stars of heaven were falling around her, she had never seen such fireworks before. Great suns spurted fire about, splendid fireflies flew into the blue air, and everything was reflected in the clear, calm sea beneath. The ship itself was so brightly illuminated that all the people, and even the smallest rope, could be distinctly and plainly seen. And how handsome the young prince looked, as he pressed the hands of all present and smiled at them, while the music resounded through the clear night air.

It was very late; yet the little mermaid could not take her eyes from the ship, or from the beautiful prince. The colored lanterns had been extinguished, no more rockets rose in the air, and the cannon had ceased firing; but the sea became restless, and a moaning, grumbling sound could be heard beneath the waves: still the little mermaid remained by the cabin window, rocking

up and down on the water, which enabled her to look in. After a while, the sails were quickly unfurled, and the noble ship continued her passage; but soon the waves rose higher, heavy clouds darkened the sky, and lightning appeared in the distance. A dreadful storm was approaching; once more the sails were reefed, and the great ship pursued her flying course over the raging sea. The waves rose mountains high, as if they would have overtopped the mast; but the ship dived like a swan between them, and then rose again on their lofty, foaming crests. To the little mermaid this appeared pleasant sport; not so to the sailors. At length the ship groaned and creaked; the thick planks gave way under the lashing of the sea as it broke over the deck; the mainmast snapped asunder like a reed; the ship lay over on her side; and the water rushed in. The little mermaid now perceived that the crew were in danger; even she herself was obliged to be careful to avoid the beams and planks of the wreck which lay scattered on the water. At one moment it was so pitch dark that she could not see a single object, but a flash of lightning revealed the whole scene; she could see every one who had been on board excepting the prince; when the ship parted, she had seen him sink into the deep waves, and she was glad, for she thought he would now be with her; and then she remembered that human beings could not live in the water, so that when he got down to her father's palace he would be quite dead. But he must not die. So she swam about among the beams and planks which strewed the surface of the sea, forgetting that they could crush her to pieces. Then she dived deeply under the dark waters, rising and falling with the waves, till at length she managed to reach the young prince, who was fast losing the power of swimming in that stormy sea. His limbs were failing him, his beautiful eyes were closed, and he would have died had not the little mermaid come to his assistance. She held his head above the water, and let the waves drift them where they would.

In the morning the storm had ceased; but of the ship not a single fragment could be seen. The sun rose up red and glowing from the water, and its beams brought back the hue of health to the prince's cheeks; but his eyes remained closed. The mermaid kissed his high, smooth forehead, and stroked back his wet hair; he seemed to her like the marble statue in her little garden, and she kissed him again, and wished that he might live. Presently they came in sight of land; she saw lofty blue mountains, on which the white snow rested as if a flock of swans were lying upon them. Near the coast were beautiful green forests, and close by stood a large building, whether a church or a convent she could not tell. Orange and citron trees grew in the garden, and before the door stood lofty palms. The sea here formed a little bay, in which the water was quite still, but very deep; so she swam with the handsome prince to the beach, which was covered with fine, white sand, and there she laid him in the warm sunshine, taking care to raise his head higher than his body. Then bells sounded in the large white building, and a number of young girls came into the garden. The little mermaid swam out farther from the shore and placed herself between some high rocks that rose out of the water; then she covered her head and neck with the foam of the sea so that her little face might not be seen, and watched to see what would become of the poor prince. She did not wait long before she saw a young girl approach the spot where he lay. She seemed frightened at first, but only for a moment; then she fetched a number of people, and the mermaid saw that the prince came to life again, and smiled upon those who stood round him. But to her he sent no smile; he knew not that she had saved him. This made her very unhappy, and when he was led away into the great building, she dived down sorrowfully into the water, and returned to her father's castle. She had always been silent and thoughtful, and now she was more so than ever. Her sisters asked her what she had seen during her first visit to the surface of the water; but she would tell them nothing. Many an evening and morning did she rise to the place where she had left the prince. She saw the fruits in the garden ripen till they were gathered, the snow on the tops of the mountains melt away; but she never saw the prince, and therefore she returned home, always more sorrowful than before. It was her only comfort to sit in her own little garden, and fling her arm round the beautiful marble statue which was like the prince; but she gave up tending her flowers, and they grew in wild confusion over the paths, twining their long leaves and stems round the branches of the trees, so that the whole place became dark and gloomy. At length she could bear it no longer, and told one of her sisters all about it. Then the others heard the secret, and very soon it became known to two mermaids whose intimate friend happened to know who the prince was. She had also seen the festival on board ship, and she told them where the prince came from, and where his palace stood.

"Come, little sister," said the other princesses; then they entwined their arms and rose up in a long row to the surface of the water, close by the spot where they knew the prince's palace stood. It was built of bright yellow shining stone, with long flights of marble steps, one of which reached quite down to the sea. Splendid gilded cupolas rose over the roof, and between the pillars that surrounded the whole building stood life-like statues of marble. Through the clear crystal of the lofty windows could be seen noble rooms, with costly silk curtains and hangings of tapestry; while the walls were covered with beautiful paintings which were a pleasure to look at. In the centre of the largest saloon a fountain threw its sparkling jets high up into the glass cupola of the ceiling, through which the sun shone down upon the water and upon the beautiful plants growing round the basin of the fountain. Now that she knew where he lived, she spent many an evening and many a night on the water near the palace. She would swim much nearer the shore than any of the others ventured to do; indeed once she went quite up the narrow channel under the marble balcony, which threw a broad shadow on the water. Here she would sit and watch the young prince, who thought himself quite alone in the bright moonlight. She saw him many times of an evening sailing in a pleasant boat, with music playing and flags waving. She peeped out from among the green rushes, and if the wind caught her long silvery-white veil, those who saw it believed it to be a swan, spreading out its wings. On many a night, too, when the fishermen, with their torches, were out at sea, she heard them relate so many good things about the doings of the young prince, that she was glad she had saved his life when he had been tossed about half-dead on the waves. And she remembered that his head had rested on her bosom, and how heartily she had kissed him; but he knew nothing of all this, and could not even dream of her. She grew more and more fond of human beings, and wished more and more to be able to wander about with those whose world seemed to be so much larger than her own. They could fly over the sea in ships, and mount the high hills which were far above the clouds; and the lands they possessed, their woods and their fields, stretched far away beyond the reach of her sight. There was so much that she wished to know, and her sisters were unable to answer all her questions. Then she applied to her old grandmother, who knew all about the upper world, which she very rightly called the lands above the sea.

"If human beings are not drowned," asked the little mermaid, "can they live forever? do they never die as we do here in the sea?"

"Yes," replied the old lady, "they must also die, and their term of life is even shorter than ours. We sometimes live to three hundred years, but when we cease to exist here we only become the foam on the surface of the water, and we have not even a grave down here of those we love. We have not immortal souls, we shall never live again; but, like the green sea-weed, when once it has been cut off, we can never flourish more. Human beings, on the contrary, have a soul which lives forever, lives after the body has been turned to dust. It rises up through the clear, pure air beyond the glittering stars. As we rise out of the water, and behold all the land of the earth, so do they rise to unknown and glorious regions which we shall never see."

"Why have not we an immortal soul?" asked the little mermaid mournfully; "I would give gladly all the hundreds of years that I have to live, to be a human being only for one day, and to have the hope of knowing the happiness of that glorious world above the stars."

"You must not think of that," said the old woman; "we feel ourselves to be much happier and much better off than human beings."

"So I shall die," said the little mermaid, "and as the foam of the sea I shall be driven about never again to hear the music of the waves, or to see the pretty flowers nor the red sun. Is there anything I can do to win an immortal soul?"

"No," said the old woman, "unless a man were to love you so much that you were more to him than his father or mother; and if all his thoughts and all his love were fixed upon you, and the priest placed his right hand in yours, and he promised to be true to you here and hereafter, then his soul would glide into your body and you would obtain a share in the future happiness of mankind. He would give a soul to you and retain his own as well; but this can never happen. Your fish's tail, which amongst us is considered so beautiful, is thought on earth to be quite ugly; they do not know any better,

and they think it necessary to have two stout props, which they call legs, in order to be handsome."

Then the little mermaid sighed, and looked sorrowfully at her fish's tail. "Let us be happy," said the old lady, "and dart and spring about during the three hundred years that we have to live, which is really quite long enough; after that we can rest ourselves all the better. This evening we are going to have a court ball."

It is one of those splendid sights which we can never see on earth. The walls and the ceiling of the large ballroom were of thick, but transparent crystal. Many hundreds of colossal shells, some of a deep red, others of a grass green, stood on each side in rows, with blue fire in them, which lighted up the whole saloon, and shone through the walls, so that the sea was also illuminated. Innumerable fishes, great and small, swam past the crystal walls; on some of them the scales glowed with a purple brilliancy, and on others they shone like silver and gold. Through the halls flowed a broad stream, and in it danced the mermen and the mermaids to the music of their own sweet singing. No one on earth has such a lovely voice as theirs. The little mermaid sang more sweetly than them all. The whole court applauded her with hands and tails; and for a moment her heart felt quite gay, for she knew she had the loveliest voice of any on earth or in the sea. But she soon thought again of the world above her, for she could not forget the charming prince, nor her sorrow that she had not an immortal soul like his; therefore she crept away silently out of her father's palace, and while everything within was gladness and song, she sat in her own little garden sorrowful and alone. Then she heard the bugle sounding through the water, and thought—"He is certainly sailing above, he on whom my wishes depend, and in whose hands I should like to place the happiness of my life. I will venture all for him, and to win an immortal soul, while my sisters are dancing in my father's palace, I will go to the sea witch, of whom I have always been so much afraid, but she can give me counsel and help."

And then the little mermaid went out from her garden, and took the road to the foaming whirlpools, behind which the sorceress lived. She had never been that way before: neither flowers nor grass grew there; nothing but bare, gray, sandy ground stretched out to the whirlpool, where the water, like foaming mill-wheels, whirled round everything that it seized, and cast it into the fathomless deep. Through the midst of these crushing whirlpools the little mermaid was obliged to pass, to reach the dominions of the sea witch; and also for a long distance the only road lay right across a quantity of warm, bubbling mire, called by the witch her turf-moor. Beyond this stood her house, in the centre of a strange forest, in which all the trees and flowers were polypi, half animals and half plants; they looked like serpents with a hundred heads growing out of the ground. The branches were long slimy arms, with fingers like flexible worms, moving limb after limb from the root to the top. All that could be reached in the sea they seized upon, and held fast, so that it never escaped from their clutches. The little mermaid was so alarmed at what she saw, that she stood still, and her heart beat with fear, and she was very nearly turning back; but she thought of the prince, and of the human soul for which she longed, and her courage returned. She fastened her long flowing hair round her head, so that the polypi might not seize hold of it. She laid her hands together across her bosom, and then she darted forward as a fish shoots through the water, between the supple arms and fingers of the ugly polypi, which were stretched out on each side of her. She saw that each held in its grasp something it had seized with its numerous little arms, as if they were iron bands. The white skeletons of human beings who had perished at sea, and had sunk down into the deep waters, skeletons of land animals, oars, rudders, and chests of ships were lying tightly grasped by their clinging arms; even a little mermaid, whom they had caught and strangled; and this seemed the most shocking of all to the little princess.

She now came to a space of marshy ground in the wood, where large, fat water-snakes were rolling in the mire, and showing their ugly, drab-colored bodies. In the midst of this spot stood a house, built with the bones of shipwrecked human beings. There sat the sea witch, allowing a toad to eat from her mouth, just as people sometimes feed a canary with a piece of sugar. She called the ugly water-snakes her little chickens, and allowed them to crawl all over her bosom.

"I know what you want," said the sea witch; "it is very stupid of you, but you shall have your way, and it will bring you to sorrow, my pretty princess. You want to get rid of your fish's tail, and to have two supports instead of it, like human beings on earth, so that the young prince may fall in love with you, and that you may have an immortal soul." And then the witch laughed so loud and disgustingly, that the toad and the snakes fell to the ground, and lay there wriggling about. "You are but just in time," said the witch; "for after sunrise tomorrow I should not be able to help you till the end of another year. I will prepare a draught for you, with which you must swim to land tomorrow before sunrise, and sit down on the shore and drink it. Your tail will then disappear, and shrink up into what mankind calls legs, and you will feel great pain, as if a sword were passing through you. But all who see you will say that you are the prettiest little human being they ever saw. You will still have the same floating gracefulness of movement, and no dancer will ever tread so lightly; but at every step you take it will feel as if you were treading upon sharp knives, and that the blood must flow. If you will bear all this, I will help you."

"Yes, I will," said the little princess in a trembling voice, as she thought of the prince and the immortal soul.

"But think again," said the witch; "for when once your shape has become like a human being, you can no more be a mermaid. You will never return through the water to your sisters, or to your father's palace again; and if you do not win the love of the prince, so that he is willing to forget his father and mother for your sake, and to love you with his whole soul, and allow the priest to join your hands that you may be man and wife, then you will never have an immortal soul. The first morning after he marries another your heart will break, and you will become foam on the crest of the waves."

"I will do it," said the little mermaid, and she became pale as death.

"But I must be paid also," said the witch, "and it is not a trifle that I ask. You have the sweetest voice of any who dwell here in the depths of the sea, and you believe that you will be able to charm the prince with it also, but this voice you must give to me; the best thing you possess will I have for the price of my draught. My own blood must be mixed with it, that it may be as sharp as a two-edged sword."

"The Little Mermaid visits the Old Witch of the Sea." John Leech's illustration for Hans Christian Andersen's "The Little Mermaid" appeared in the London periodical *Bentley's Miscellany* in 1846.

"But if you take away my voice," said the little mermaid, "what is left for me?"

"Your beautiful form, your graceful walk, and your expressive eyes; surely with these you can enchain a man's heart. Well, have you lost your courage? Put out your little tongue that I may cut it off as my payment; then you shall have the powerful draught."

"It shall be," said the little mermaid.

Then the witch placed her cauldron on the fire, to prepare the magic draught.

"Cleanliness is a good thing," said she, scouring the vessel with snakes, which she had tied together in a large knot; then she pricked herself in the breast, and let the black blood drop into it. The steam that rose formed itself into such horrible shapes that no one could look at them without fear. Every moment the witch threw something else into the vessel, and when it began to boil, the sound was like the weeping of a crocodile.

When at last the magic draught was ready, it looked like the clearest water. "There it is for you," said the witch. Then she cut off the mermaid's tongue, so that she became dumb, and would never again speak or sing. "If the polypi should seize hold of you as you return through the wood," said the witch, "throw over them a few drops of the potion, and their fingers will be torn into a thousand pieces." But the little mermaid had no occasion to do this, for the polypi sprang back in terror when they caught sight of the glittering draught, which shone in her hand like a twinkling star.

So she passed quickly through the wood and the marsh, and between the rushing whirlpools. She saw that in her father's palace the torches in the ballroom were extinguished, and all within asleep; but she did not venture to go in to them, for now she was dumb and going to leave them forever, she felt as if her heart would break. She stole into the garden, took a flower from the flower-beds of each of her sisters, kissed her hand a thousand times towards the palace, and then rose up through the dark blue waters. The sun had not risen when she came in sight of the prince's palace, and approached the beautiful marble steps, but the moon shone clear and bright. Then the little mermaid drank the magic draught, and it seemed as if a two-edged sword went through her delicate body: she fell into a swoon, and lay like one dead. When the sun arose and shone over the sea, she recovered, and felt a sharp pain; but just before her stood the handsome young prince. He fixed his coal-black eyes upon her so earnestly that she cast down her own, and then became aware that her fish's tail was gone, and that she had as pretty a pair of white legs and tiny feet as any little maiden could have; but she had no clothes, so she wrapped herself in her long, thick hair. The prince asked her who she was, and where she came from, and she looked at him mildly and sorrowfully with her deep blue eyes; but she could not speak. Every step she took was as the witch had said it would be, she felt as if treading upon the points of needles or sharp knives; but she bore it willingly, and stepped as lightly by the prince's side as a soap-bubble, so that he and all who saw her wondered at her graceful-swaying movements. She was very soon arrayed in costly robes of silk and muslin, and was the most beautiful creature in the palace; but she was dumb, and could neither speak nor sing.

Beautiful female slaves, dressed in silk and gold, stepped forward and sang before the prince and his royal parents: one sang better than all the others, and the prince clapped his hands and smiled at her. This was great sorrow to the little mermaid; she knew how much more sweetly she herself could sing once, and she thought, "Oh if he could only know that! I have given away my voice forever, to be with him."

The slaves next performed some pretty fairy-like dances, to the sound of beautiful music. Then the little mermaid raised her lovely white arms, stood on the tips of her toes, and glided over the floor, and danced as no one yet had been able to dance. At each moment her beauty became more revealed, and her expressive eyes appealed more directly to the heart than the songs of the slaves. Every one was enchanted, especially the prince, who called her his little foundling; and she danced again quite readily, to please him, though each time her foot touched the floor it seemed as if she trod on sharp knives.

The prince said she should remain with him always, and she received permission to sleep at his door, on a velvet cushion. He had a page's dress made for her, that she might accompany him on horseback. They rode together through the sweet-scented woods, where the green boughs touched their shoulders, and the little birds sang among the fresh leaves. She climbed with the prince to the tops of high mountains; and although her tender feet bled so that even her steps were marked, she only laughed, and followed him till they could see the clouds beneath them looking like a flock of birds travelling to distant lands. While at the prince's palace, and when all the household were asleep, she would go and sit on the broad marble steps; for it eased her burning feet to bathe them in the cold sea-water; and then she thought of all those below in the deep.

Once during the night her sisters came up arm-in-arm, singing sorrowfully, as they floated on the water. She beckoned to them, and then they recognized her, and told her how she had grieved them. After that, they came to the same place every night; and once she saw in the distance her old grandmother, who had not been to the surface of the sea for many years, and the old Sea King, her father, with his crown on his head. They stretched out their hands towards her, but they did not venture so near the land as her sisters did.

As the days passed, she loved the prince more fondly, and he loved her as he would love a little child, but it never came into his head to make her his wife; yet, unless he married her, she could not receive an immortal soul; and, on the morning after his marriage with another, she would dissolve into the foam of the sea.

"Do you not love me the best of them all?" the eyes of the little mermaid seemed to say, when he took her in his arms, and kissed her fair forehead.

"Yes, you are dear to me," said the prince; "for you have the best heart, and you are the most devoted to me; you are like a young maiden whom I once saw, but whom I shall never meet again. I was in a ship that was wrecked, and the waves cast me ashore near a holy temple, where several young maidens performed the service. The youngest of them found me on the shore, and saved my life. I saw her but twice, and she is the only one in the world whom I could love; but you are like her, and you have almost driven her image out of my mind. She belongs to the holy temple, and my good fortune has sent you to me instead of her; and we will never part."

"Ah, he knows not that it was I who saved his life," thought the little mermaid. "I carried him over the sea to the wood where the temple stands: I sat beneath the foam, and watched till the human beings came to help him. I saw the pretty maiden that he loves better than he loves me;" and the mermaid sighed deeply, but she could not shed tears. "He says the maiden belongs to the holy temple, therefore she will never return to the world. They will meet no more: while I am by his side, and see him every day. I will take care of him, and love him, and give up my life for his sake."

Very soon it was said that the prince must marry, and that the beautiful daughter of a neighboring king would be his wife, for a fine ship was being fitted out. Although the prince gave out that he merely intended to pay a visit to the king, it was generally supposed that he really went to see his daughter. A great company were to go with him. The little mermaid smiled, and shook her head. She knew the prince's thoughts better than any of the others.

"I must travel," he had said to her; "I must see this beautiful princess; my parents desire it; but they will not oblige me to bring her home as my bride. I cannot love her; she is not like the beautiful maiden in the temple, whom you resemble. If I were forced to choose a bride, I would rather choose you, my dumb foundling, with those expressive eyes." And then he kissed her rosy mouth, played with her long waving hair, and laid his head on her heart, while she dreamed of human happiness and an immortal soul. "You are not afraid of the sea, my dumb child," said he, as they stood on the deck of the noble ship which was to carry them to the country of the neighboring king. And then he told her of storm and of calm, of strange fishes in the deep beneath them, and of what the divers had seen there; and she smiled at his descriptions, for she knew better than any one what wonders were at the bottom of the sea.

In the moonlight, when all on board were asleep, excepting the man at the helm, who was steering, she sat on the deck, gazing down through the clear water. She thought she could distinguish her father's castle, and upon it her aged grandmother, with the silver crown on her head, looking through the rushing tide at the keel of the vessel. Then her sisters came up on the waves, and gazed at her mournfully, wringing their white hands. She beckoned to them, and smiled, and wanted to tell them how happy and well off she was; but the cabin-boy approached, and when her sisters dived down he thought it was only the foam of the sea which he saw.

The next morning the ship sailed into the harbor of a beautiful town belonging to the king whom the prince was going to visit. The church bells were ringing, and from the high towers sounded a flourish of trumpets; and soldiers, with flying colors and glittering bayonets, lined the rocks through which they passed. Every day was a festival; balls and entertainments followed one another.

But the princess had not yet appeared. People said that she was being brought up and educated in a religious house, where she was learning every royal virtue. At last she came. Then the little mermaid, who was very anxious to see whether she was really beautiful, was obliged to acknowledge that she had never seen a more perfect vision of beauty. Her skin was delicately fair, and beneath her long dark eye-lashes her laughing blue eyes shone with truth and purity.

"It was you," said the prince, "who saved my life when I lay dead on the beach," and he folded his blushing bride in his arms. "Oh, I am too happy," said he to the little mermaid; "my fondest hopes are all fulfilled. You will rejoice at my happiness; for your devotion to me is great and sincere."

The little mermaid kissed his hand, and felt as if her heart were already broken. His wedding morning would bring death to her, and she would change into the foam of the sea. All the church bells rung, and the heralds rode about the town proclaiming the betrothal. Perfumed oil was burning in costly silver lamps on every altar. The priests waved the censers, while the bride and bridegroom joined their hands and received the blessing of the bishop. The little mermaid, dressed in silk and gold, held up the bride's train; but her ears heard nothing of the festive music, and her eyes saw not the holy ceremony; she thought of the night of death which was coming to her, and of all she had lost in the world. On the same evening the bride and bridegroom went on board ship; cannons were roaring, flags waving, and in the centre of the ship a costly tent of purple and gold had been erected. It contained elegant couches, for the reception of the bridal pair during the night. The ship, with swelling sails and a favorable wind, glided away smoothly and lightly over the calm sea. When it grew dark a number of colored lamps were lit, and the sailors danced merrily on the deck. The little mermaid could not help thinking of her first rising out of the sea, when she had seen similar festivities and joys; and she joined in the dance, poised herself in the air as a swallow when he pursues his prey, and all present cheered her with wonder. She had never danced so elegantly before. Her tender feet felt as if cut with sharp knives, but she cared not for it; a sharper pang had pierced through her heart. She knew this was the last evening she should ever see the prince, for whom she had forsaken her kindred and her home; she had given up her beautiful voice, and suffered unheard-of pain daily for him, while he knew nothing of it. This was the last evening that she would breathe the same air with him, or gaze on the starry sky and the deep sea; an eternal night, without a thought or a dream, awaited her: she had no soul and now she could never win one. All was joy and gayety on board ship till long after midnight; she laughed and danced with the rest, while the thoughts of death were in her heart. The prince kissed his beautiful bride, while she played with his raven hair, till they went arm-in-arm to rest in the splendid tent. Then all became still on board the ship; the helmsman, alone awake, stood at the helm. The little mermaid leaned her white arms on the edge of the vessel, and looked towards the east for the first blush of morning, for that first ray of dawn that would bring her death. She saw her sisters rising out of the flood: they were as pale as herself; but their long beautiful hair waved no more in the wind, and had been cut off.

"We have given our hair to the witch," said they, "to obtain help for you, that you may not die to-night. She has given us a knife: here it is, see it is very sharp. Before the sun rises you must plunge it into the heart of the prince; when the warm blood falls upon your feet they will grow together again, and form into a fish's tail, and you will be once more a mermaid, and return to us to live out your three hundred years before you die and change into the salt sea foam. Haste, then; he or you must die before sunrise. Our old grandmother moans so for you, that her white hair is falling off from sorrow, as ours fell under the witch's scissors. Kill the prince and come back; hasten: do you not see the first red streaks in the sky? In a few minutes the sun will rise, and you must die." And then they sighed deeply and mournfully, and sank down beneath the waves.

The little mermaid drew back the crimson curtain of the tent, and beheld the fair bride with her head resting on the prince's breast. She bent down and kissed his fair brow, then looked at the sky on which the rosy dawn grew brighter and brighter; then she glanced at the sharp knife, and again fixed her eyes on the prince, who whispered the name of his bride in his dreams. She was in his thoughts, and the knife trembled in the hand of the little mermaid: then she flung it far away from her into the waves; the water turned red where it fell, and the drops that spurted up looked like blood. She cast one more lingering, half-fainting glance at the prince, and then threw herself from the ship into the sea, and thought her body was dissolving into foam. The sun rose above the waves, and his warm rays fell on the cold foam of the little mermaid, who did not feel as if she were dying. She saw the bright sun, and all around her floated hundreds of transparent beautiful beings; she could see through them the white sails of the ship, and the red clouds in the sky; their speech was melodious, but too ethereal to be heard by mortal ears, as they were also unseen by mortal eyes. The little mermaid perceived that she had a body like theirs, and that she continued to rise higher and higher out of the foam. "Where am I?" asked she, and her voice sounded ethereal, as the voice of those who were with her; no earthly music could imitate it.

"Among the daughters of the air," answered one of them. "A mermaid has not an immortal soul, nor can she obtain one unless she wins the love of a human being. On the power of another hangs her eternal destiny. But the daughters of the air, although they do not possess an immortal soul, can, by their good deeds, procure one for themselves. We fly to warm countries, and cool the sultry air that destroys mankind with the pestilence. We carry the perfume of the flowers to spread health and restoration. After we have striven for three hundred years to do all the good in our power, we receive an immortal soul and take part in the happiness of mankind. You, poor little mermaid, have tried with your whole heart to do as we are doing; you have suffered and endured and raised yourself to the spirit-world by your good deeds; and now, by striving for three hundred years in the same way, you may obtain an immortal soul."

The little mermaid lifted her glorified eyes towards the sun, and felt them, for the first time, filling with tears. On the ship, in which she had left the prince, there were life and noise; she saw him and his beautiful bride searching for her; sorrowfully they gazed at the pearly foam, as if they knew she had thrown herself into the waves. Unseen she kissed the forehead of the bride, and fanned the prince, and then mounted with the other children of the air to a rosy cloud that floated through the aether.

"After three hundred years, thus shall we float into the kingdom of heaven," said she. "And we may even get there sooner," whispered one of her companions. "Unseen we can enter the houses of men, where there are children, and for every day on which we find a good child, who is the joy of his parents and deserves their love, our time of probation is shortened. The child does not know, when we fly through the room, that we smile with joy at his good conduct, for we can count one year less of our three hundred years. But when we see a naughty or a wicked child, we shed tears of sorrow, and for every tear a day is added to our time of trial!"

A. Waller Hastings (b. 1952)

A. Waller Hastings's 1993 article on the Disney film *The Little Mermaid* appeared in a fascinating special issue of the journal *The Lion and the Unicorn* (volume 17.1) devoted to "the dumbing down of children's literature." Hastings, a literary critic who teaches at Northern State University in South Dakota, places the film of the late 1980s within the context of earlier criticism of Disney versions of popular stories, especially the "Disneyfication" of classic children's literature. Critiquing changes in *The Little Mermaid* that eliminate the moral and psychological complexities of the mermaid's choices and desires, Hastings focuses on the relationship between the little mermaid and the sea witch with whom she bargains for the chance to obtain human love and immortality. Hastings's assessment of the film's socioeconomic and political effects addresses the mass market in which the Disney Company and its plethora of products related to each film wield tremendous power. He also deals with the larger ideological implications of presenting children with simplified views of conflicts between good and evil. Comments at the end of this article about the Manichean world portrayed in the Disney film have particular resonance in the early twenty-first-century world of global conflict, as political powers increasingly vilify distant enemies and blame suffering not on the complexities of shared human fallibility, but on the absolute evil of enemies who must be utterly destroyed, as the Disney film destroys its satanic figure of the sea witch.

Moral Simplification in Disney's *The Little Mermaid*

While generally praising Walt Disney's technical contributions to animated film, critics have been troubled by the studio's treatment of classic children's literature and fairy tales. In a famous attack over 25 years ago, Sayers blasted Disney for showing "scant respect for the integrity of the original creations of authors" and treating folk texts "without regard for [their] anthropological, spiritual, or psychological truths. Every story is sacrificed to the 'gimmick' [of animation]" (602). Her complaint specifically addressed a tendency to "dummy down" source material by eliminating psychological conflict: "Disney falsifies life by pretending that everything is so sweet, so saccharine, so without any conflict except the obvious conflict of violence" (609).

More recently, this pattern, which Schickel calls "Disneyfication" (225),[1] has been criticized on ideological grounds for reinforcing and/or contributing to dominant patriarchal and capitalist systems. For instance, Stone charges that Disney's adaptations of *Snow White* and other "classic" fairy tales "amplify . . . the stereotype of good versus bad women" already present in the source material, offering heroines who "seem barely alive" and villains who are invariably female (44). Dorfman observes a neocolonial plundering of folklore and children's literature in the service of Disney's "average North American image" (24). So pervasive is Disneyfication that, as Zipes has noted, the Disney method has become the prototype for most film adaptations of fairy tales (and one might extend this to children's literature in general) made by other studios, all mass-mediated vehicles which co-opt fairy tales' subversive potential and convert it to the service of corporate capitalism (113–14).

Much Disneyfication, at least in the era of Walt himself, was evidently conscious; the filmmaker admitted that he sought out simple stories and simplified them further to create "nice" children's films. In *Pinocchio,* for instance, Disney intentionally narrowed the story to create a more cohesive plot and altered Pinocchio's character from that of a delinquent to "a well-meaning boy who was consistently led astray by conniving characters" (Thomas 26); this sanitized hero was judged more acceptable for children. Disney himself acknowledged his preference for the morally simple over the complex:

> I look for a story with heart. . . . It should be a simple story with characters the audience can really care about. They've got to have a rooting interest.
>   That was the trouble with *Alice.* There we had a classic we couldn't tamper with; I resolved never to do another one. The picture was filled with weird characters you couldn't get with. (Thomas 22)

The conscious effort to produce children's movies with no alarming moral ambiguities contributed to such well-known Disney signatures as the ubiquitous cute animals, either as adjuncts to the film's main characters (*Snow White, Cinderella*) or as anthropomorphized protagonists (*Robin Hood, Oliver!*). Less noted signature traits of Disneyfication include the use of dogs and cats as moral compasses[2] and the imposition of generational conflict, absent from the original, which is always satisfactorily resolved, restoring family order (*Sleeping Beauty*).

Walt Disney is dead but his successors have followed and magnified the pattern he created for animated film. All of the characteristics described above are present in the studio's adaptation of *The Little Mermaid;* as one film critic noted, "we have seen before . . . funny animal friends, a handsome prince, a grotesque villainess and *her* less funny animal friends" (Lloyd). Peter Schneider, Disney animation chief during the production of *The Little Mermaid,* says that "people have been trying to figure out what Walt would have done and to hold on to his tradition" (Solomon 273), and in *Mermaid,* as successful a commercial product as any of Disney's early triumphs, the studio appears to have identified "what Walt would have done." Schneider attempts to argue that Disney tradition was to innovate constantly; in effect, he denies any sameness to Disney products under Walt. But

a Disney studio style for animated features was noted as early as *Dumbo* in 1941 (McReynolds 788) and Disney animator Ron Clements, who originated the Little Mermaid project in 1985, acknowledged that he tried to make the melancholy original more upbeat (Flower 177), just as Disney himself had done.

Disney's *Little Mermaid* thus appears to be a classic example of the corporate appropriation of an originally creative work of art. According to Zipes, the culture industry transforms works of imagination into "commodities within a capitalist social-economic system . . . [so that] cultural objects appear to possess a life of their own beyond the control of the actual creators" (96–97). This co-opting of image and narrative is not value-neutral, but encodes ideological messages that may create a false picture of reality (Zipes 102).[3] It is thus advisable to consider the ideological basis and effect of alterations made between Andersen's tale and the Disney film.

In the Disney adaptation, the elements of the fairy tale remain recognizable, but superimposed are typical elements of Disneyfication and a happy ending that contravenes the moral intention of the original tale. McReynolds, faulting Disney for playing a Pollyanna-ish "glad game," has argued that the typical ending of a Disney film denies evil's reality: all wicked characters are banished, leaving a world "in which kindness and sympathy always prevail" (787–88). However, Disney's animated films do not so much deny the reality of evil as present a Manichean world of moral absolutes in eternal warfare, from which—in the Disney version—good always emerges triumphant. This is especially true of *The Little Mermaid.*

Andersen's mermaid is driven to the surface world by two complementary but separable impulses: a romantic/erotic desire for the handsome prince whom she rescues from drowning in a shipwreck and a moral desire, privileged in Andersen's telling, to attain a soul with the promise of an afterlife. Romantic desire is frustrated when the prince marries a human whom he wrongly believes to have been his savior, but the mermaid has a chance to resume her original form if she will abandon both erotic and moral quests and slay the prince. She rejects this opportunity, however, throwing the knife with which she was to stab the prince into the sea as the sun, which will bring her death, rises. Rather than dying, the little mermaid miraculously becomes an ethereal spirit and is told by fellow spirits:

"If for three hundred years we earnestly try to do what is good, we obtain an immortal soul and can take part in the eternal happiness of man. You, little mermaid, have tried with all your heart to do the same. You have suffered and borne your suffering bravely; and that is why you are now among us, the spirits of the air." (76)

Her willingness to sacrifice the happiness she has pursued through excruciating pain and very real dangers provides a second chance at immortality. Even though the romantic/erotic narrative is frustrated, the higher narrative of moral progress remains a possibility—is, in fact, enhanced by the mermaid's refusal to destroy another life.

Andersen, too, has been accused of saccharine sentimentality, as this synopsis of the fairy tale's Christian moral may suggest. But the Disney version accentuates the most sentimental and romantic aspects of the story at the expense of its moral and psychological complexity. Like previous Disney adaptations, *The Little Mermaid* provides wish fulfillment without true sacrifice and neatly encapsulates all "bad" desires within a figure of female evil.[4]

The Manichean world view requires an active principle—in the original heresy, Satan—who is responsible for all evil effects. In Disney's film, this principle is embodied in the sea witch Ursula, a repulsive half-woman/half-octopus who parodies the adult sexuality denied to Ariel herself. Ursula's character allows a streamlining of plot and characterization such as commonly occurs when texts are converted into film, defensible on the basis of generic convention. This defense, however, ignores the manner in which the character absolves Ariel of all responsibility for her own actions, simplifying the psychological and moral problem of desire and reconfirming the pattern of female stereotyping that Stone observed in early Disney products.

Ursula's ancestor, the sea hag, appears only once in Andersen's fairy tale; while she is undeniably evil, she acts only upon direct petition. His mermaid, having conceived her dual desires for human form, seeks transformation on her own volition; the sea hag grants it "for it will bring . . . misery" but warns her that it will involve great pain:

"Your tail will divide and shrink, until it becomes what human beings call 'pretty legs.' It will hurt; it will feel as if a sword were going through your body. . . . [E]very time your foot touches the ground it

will feel as though you were walking on knives so sharp that your blood must flow. If you are willing to suffer all this, then I can help you." (68)

The other conditions of transformation also involve suffering. In becoming human, Andersen's little mermaid takes an irrevocable step; whatever the outcome of her romantic quest, she cannot return to the sea and her family. If she fails to win the prince's love, she will die, thereby failing also to gain a human soul, which can only be received through that love. Her death will then be permanent. Finally, she must give up her voice to the sea hag by having her tongue cut out.

The Disney version purges these elements of pain. There is no physical pain associated with Ariel's transformation, as there is in Andersen; she experiences momentary hesitation at leaving her father and sisters, but separation anxiety is quickly overcome when Ursula conjures the image of handsome Prince Erik. While the price of transformation remains the loss of her voice, Ariel does not suffer physical mutilation; the voice is transferred to a shell from which it can later be released and returned to its rightful owner.

The most marked change, however, comes through a reversal of the active center of the mermaid's relationship to the sea hag. Andersen's mermaid conceives of the transformation herself and must pass through deadly obstacles to reach the sea hag; the hag tells her of all the drawbacks to the scheme, then—at the mermaid's insistence—gives her a potion to be taken only when safely on land. The dangers and pain are all generated by the mermaid's own desire; the sea hag assists, but does not actively plan for evil to befall the mermaid.

Ariel's desire in the Disney film is more innocent, in itself carrying little risk. Ursula's plotting brings on everything. The sea witch is introduced as she observes Ariel watching the human world and plots how to use the mermaid's fascination with humans to revenge herself on Triton. Ariel only comes to Ursula at the instigation of the witch's servants, the moray eels Flotsam and Jetsam, and it is Ursula who proposes that she win her prince by becoming human. Ariel lives in a fantasy land that ignores the incompatability between species; not until the sea witch plants the idea in her head does she imagine a literalization of her girlish infatuation. Ariel, not the witch, brings up the separation from family that will accompany the transformation, and Ursula's temptation is needed to overcome her hesitation. They sign a contract that is clearly reminiscent of a pact with the devil, a comparison driven home by Ursula's display of her collection of damned souls, each one shrunken into misery after failing to fulfill his or her bargain with her.

If Andersen's sea hag is evil, she also sticks by a bargain. She leaves it to the mermaid to win her prince or to fail in the attempt. While Andersen's mermaid undergoes transformation when she has safely reached shore, Disney's Ursula effects Ariel's transformation while the mermaid is still at the bottom of the sea, putting her at risk of a drowning that would quickly negate the deal—immediate evidence that the sea witch has been bargaining in bad faith. A quick end to the mermaid's quest is only prevented when Ariel's sidekicks Flounder and Sebastian rush her to the surface.

Andersen's prince never imagines that he has been rescued by the mysterious, mute girl who appears soon after he escapes the shipwreck. In the film, Erik immediately suspects Ariel's identity and is thrown off track only by her inability to speak, which means she cannot be the one who sang so beautifully after pulling him from the sea. Nevertheless, Erik seems about to fall for Ariel and is prevented from bestowing the magic kiss only by Ursula's eels, who overturn the boat in which the prince and the mermaid are sitting. When Erik is about to abandon his imaginary savior for life with Ariel, the sea witch again intervenes, disguising herself as a beautiful woman and using Ariel's stolen voice to convince the prince that she is his destined lover. Despite her evident beauty and the conclusive evidence of the voice, Ursula must hypnotize Erik to keep him from Ariel, so strong is the former mermaid's attraction.

Contrast this to Andersen's tale, in which the mermaid's erotic prospects never have a chance of fulfillment and the prince weds a mortal woman. The romantic failure of Andersen's mermaid may be seen as the inevitable heartache of human love, a heartache Andersen knew firsthand: she is destined not simply to be rejected, but to be ignored by the object of her desire. In Andersen's tale, there is no external agent to blame; the mermaid seems, before her final transfiguration, to be the tragic victim only of her own desires.

Ariel never has to face the consequences of her choices. As in Disney's *Sleeping Beauty,* even the conflict between parent and child proves illusory; order is restored through the discovery that parent's and child's wishes are the same. Triton himself makes Ariel human so that she may marry Erik, who has destroyed the sea witch, the source of her real troubles.[5] The marriage takes place aboard a ship, an intermediate locale that negotiates between the land world of humans and the undersea world of the merfolk; father and daughter are not really separated, as the newlyweds sail off under Triton's rainbow, escorted by merfolk. The evil principle has been purged through the joint courage of human and merfolk.

One might ask, "What is wrong with Disney's transformation?" It could be argued that Andersen's subtle moral tale is too complex to be grasped by most children, that children in fact need the reassurance of the conventional happy ending that Disney imposes. Niels and Faith Ingwersen have argued that the film's focus on the conflict between good and evil, while sacrificing the transcendent theme of the original, is "nevertheless truer to the folktale struggle between good and evil than Andersen's tale is" (415). They do, however, find the introduction of a strongly evil female power "troubling" and note a shift from a predominantly matriarchal world in Andersen's tale to a strong patriarchy in the film. Cravens, whose difficulties with the Disney film in some ways parallel mine, describes how she was "troubled" by aspects of the original tale when she first encountered it at age four or five. But this was counteracted by a sense of connection:

> even though her trials seemed intolerable, I felt as though the deepest part of my nature were being addressed by a sincere friend, and I was satisfied and uplifted by the ending without understanding the reason. (638)

This dimly understood sense of connection, I submit, is what the Disneyfied story, with its insistence on a "happily ever after" marriage plot, inevitably sacrifices.

Disney's conclusion certainly offers a more conventional happy ending than Andersen's original, reflecting a narrative and psychological urge to create apparent harmony that Bausinger has named "*Märchendenken*" or "fairy-tale thinking" (17). As an individual tendency of mind, *Märchendenken* has certain risks, but it also serves the useful psychological purpose of instilling hope. When embodied in the mass-mediated Disney form, however, the *Märchendenken* of *The Little Mermaid* poses social hazards.

Disney's manipulation of original material is a matter of special concern because of the studio's marketing machine, which enables Disney products to command consumer attention through interlocking movie, TV, book, record, and toy products.[6] Thus Disney versions of "standard" fairy tales tend to usurp the originals. The version of Cinderella most familiar to adults of my generation is Disney's adaptation of Perrault;[7] the image of Snow White is likely to be Disney's cartoon heroine. As "classic" texts are Disneyfied, more of children's literary legacy becomes endangered. In popular consciousness, *Alice in Wonderland* is a Disney creation, (though Disney himself thought the film a creative failure). In toy stores today, you can find many teddy bears that look like Disney's *Winnie-the-Pooh* but will search fruitlessly for one resembling the original Shepard illustrations for Milne's books.

The merchandisers' work on *The Little Mermaid* should be self-evident to anyone who has visited a toy store recently. The film itself grossed $76 million in its initial release, at the time establishing a record for an animated film (Flower 229). In an unprecedented move for Disney, *The Little Mermaid* was released on videotape within a year of its theatrical release, as the company's increasingly savvy marketing people responded to comments of those leaving the theater after seeing the film (Flower 292) Even after the releases of *Beauty and the Beast* and *Aladdin,* which promise to eclipse the earlier film in profits and spin-offs, shelves remain filled with Little Mermaid dolls, clothing, books, tapes, records, bath toys, etc. Product spin-offs continue to be introduced to an as-yet-unsaturated market.

The ideological content of children's films, like that of children's literature in general, should have a particular interest for us because it both reflects the pervasive world view of its producers and contributes to the formation of its viewers' own world view more strongly than does adult literature, thus influencing the ideology of the next generation. It is the perception of this ideologic influence that accounts for so much of the didacticism that pervades children's literature.

Faced with the near-certainty that the Disney derivative will replace the Andersen tale in popular consciousness, then, it is important to understand the moral ideology that shapes the film. The elimination of moral complexities reflects both Walt Disney's original moral vision, formed in the Depression and

World War II and continued today by successors who imbibed "the Disney version" in their own childhood, and the conservative American ideology of the 1980s, when *The Little Mermaid* was developed and released. The film encourages a pervasive world view that sees malignant evil, not human fallibility, as the chief source of conflict; a similar world view can be seen in former President Reagan's characterization of the (pre-*glasnost*) Soviet Union as the "Evil Empire" or President Bush's more recent transformation of the Gulf War from a geopolitical conflict into a crusade against the person of Saddam Hussein.

In a Manichean world, one party to any conflict must always be "bad," the other "good"; insofar as we are conditioned to see ourselves as good, this perspective encourages conflict, since we can always justify our own actions, however terrible they may seem when deprived of the moral conviction that ends justify means. Those who oppose us become figures of evil, each "another Hitler," rather than normal human beings who, like us, pursue national or personal self-interests. In this Disneyfied world, there is no reason for diplomacy; the proper way to deal with an Ursula is to destroy her, not to negotiate.

As my brief discussion of *The Little Mermaid* should indicate, Disneyfication not only homogenizes individual creations into a simplistic narrative sameness, but eliminates the moral complexities of the original text. The child who reads Andersen's fairy tale has experienced a world in which desires have consequences that may be painful, where wanting something badly enough to suffer for it need not make it happen; the child who views the Disney film experiences a world in which bad things only happen because of bad people, where desire is always fulfilled. Such moral simplification increases the likelihood that these children will become adults who find the causes of their unhappiness in personalized, "evil" antagonists—a sure formula for continued conflict.

NOTES

1. However, Schickel warns of "the folly of overinterpreting essentially innocent popular culture material in the light of any ideology—political, psychological, religious, or even literary" (166). Such criticism will rebound on the critic and leave the popular culture unaffected. Forewarned of my folly, I will yet proceed.

2. I am not aware that this aspect has been observed before, but almost inevitably, "good" characters in Disney cartoons are either dogs or dog-lovers. Cats, on the other hand, tend to be vicious, and cat-lovers are evil or morally obtuse, like the aunt in *Lady and the Tramp* who locks Lady outside and fails to recognize when Tramp saves the baby. There are some exceptions to this latter characteristic (*The Aristocats,* the eponymous hero of *Oliver!*), but none that I can think of for the positive moral value of dogs. Ursula's villainy in *The Little Mermaid* includes kicking Prince Erik's loyal dog, and Erik's goodness is shown when he risks his life to rescue the dog.

3. In my analysis of *The Little Mermaid,* I am probably guilty of what Rollin calls "the classic elitist position: a distrust of anything mass marketed for children and a confidence that one's educated personal judgment can decide what is best for others" (91). But she acknowledges that much of the Left's critique of Disney is on target, calling Disney's fairy tales "opiates . . . that tell us just what we want to hear"; the elitism lies in deciding this is wrong, she says (91).

4. "It's a film about sacrifice in which nobody has to sacrifice anything they weren't all ready to. All misfortune finally accrues to the villainess. . . .Ariel herself remains absolutely static except for having changed her place of residence. She leaves the film the same wacky, willful kid as when she entered. Nobody learns a thing" (Lloyd).

5. Note that while the resolution of Andersen's tale requires that the Little Mermaid refrain from the taking of life, Disney's version can only reach closure through the violent deaths of Ursula and her henchmen, the eels. In Andersen's story, the sea hag disappears from the tale after her transformative function has been accomplished.

6. "As capitalism, it is a work of genius; as culture, it is mostly a horror" (Schickel 18).

7. An illustration: I recently used Anne Sexton's "Cinderella," which is based on the Grimms' version of the story, in my introduction to literature class and asked students to identify changes the poet had made in the fairy tale. All of the students pointed to details like the stepsisters' cutting off parts of their feet and the birds' pecking the stepsisters' eyes out as authorial inventions, even though these details appear in Grimm. Their conception of the true Cinderella corresponded exactly to the Disney version.

WORKS CITED

Andersen, Hans Christian. "The Little Mermaid." *The Complete Fairy Tales and Stories.* Tr. Erik Christian Haugaard. Garden City: Doubleday, 1974. 57–76.

Bausinger, Hermann. "Möglichkeiten des Märchens in der Gegenwart." *Märchen, Mythos, Dichtung: Festschrift zum 90. Geburtstag Friedrich von der Levens am 19. August 1963.* Ed. Hugo Kuhn and Kurt Schier. Munich: Verlag C. H. Beck, 1963. 15–30.

Cravens, Gwyneth. "Past Present." *The Nation* 11 May 1992. 638–40.

Dorfman, Ariel. *The Emperor's Old Clothes: What the Lone Ranger, Babar, and Other Innocent Heroes Do to Our Minds.* New York: Pantheon, 1983.

Flower, Joe. *Prince of the Magic Kingdom: Michael Eisner and the Re-Making of Disney.* New York: Wiley, 1991.

Ingwersen, Niels, and Faith Ingwersen. "A Folktale/Disney Approach." *Scandinavian Studies* 62 (1990): 412–15.

Lloyd, Robert. "Trouble in Toontown." *American Film* 15 (December 1989): 17.

McReynolds, William. "Disney Plays 'The Glad Game.'" *Journal of Popular Culture* 7 (1974): 787–96.

Rollin, Lucy. "Fear of Faerie: Disney and the Elitist Critics." *Children's Literature Association Quarterly* 12 (1987): 90–93.

Sayers, Frances Clarke. "Walt Disney Accused." *Horn Book* 41 (1965): 602–11.

Schickel, Richard. *The Disney Version: The Life, Times, Art and Commerce of Walt Disney.* Rev. ed. New York: Simon and Schuster/Touchstone, 1985.

Solomon, Charles. *Enchanted Drawings: The History of Animation.* New York: Knopf, 1989.

Stone, Kay. "Things Walt Disney Never Told Us." *Women and Folklore.* Ed. Claire R. Farrer. Austin: U of Texas P, 1975.

Thomas, Bob. *Walt Disney: The Art of Animation.* New York: Simon/Disney, 1958.

Zipes, Jack. "The Instrumentalization of Fantasy: Fairy Tales, the Culture Industry, and the Mass Media." *Breaking the Magic Spell: Radical Theories of Folk and Fairy Tales.* New York: Methuen, 1979. 93–128.

Mark Twain (1835–1910)

Mark Twain was the pen name of Samuel Langhorne Clemens, a self-educated printer and river pilot who wrote his way into American literary history and popular culture with his stories of humor and frontier adventure, most importantly *Adventures of Huckleberry Finn* (1884). His versions of American boyhood in *The Adventures of Tom Sawyer* (see Parts 1 and 5), *Huck Finn,* and other books have shaped our consciousness of what it was like to be young in nineteenth-century America.

A month after its publication, *Adventures of Huckleberry Finn* was banned by the public library in Concord, Massachusetts, because of Huck's irreverence and commonness. As Myra Jehlen put it, "Jo March would not be allowed to play with Huck."[1] Yet Huck's inimitable voice and way of seeing things are the reason for his enduring fame. Perhaps the most contested book in American literature, *Huck Finn* has been praised and reviled in extreme terms. For Ernest Hemingway, it is the book from which all American literature stems.[2] For other critics, it is a book of great achievement—and notable failure: in the last portion of the book, Tom Sawyer's hijinks dominate, and Jim and Huck are reduced to comic stagehands. The great moments of the book have to do with Huck's struggle between his "deformed conscience" and his sound heart. His heart tells him to help the runaway slave Jim gain his freedom, while his conscience (with the force of all his upbringing behind it) tells him that aiding a slave to escape is theft and sin. John Wallace, a public school administrator in Fairfax, Virginia, argues that the "assignment and reading aloud of *Huckleberry Finn* in our classrooms is humiliating and insulting to black students. It contributes to their feelings of low self esteem and to the white students' disrespect for black people. It constitutes mental cruelty, harassment, and outright racial intimidation to force black students to sit in the classroom with their white peers and read *Huckleberry Finn.*"[3] On the other hand, novelist Ralph Ellison argued that "Huckleberry Finn knew, as did Mark Twain, that Jim was not only a slave but a human being . . . who expressed his essential humanity in his desire for freedom, his will to possess his own labor, in his loyalty and capacity for friendship and in his love for his wife and child"[4]—and, one might add, for Huck. The book is potent because it exposes the fault lines of American racial tension and division—and it will probably remain controversial as long as it does so. The chapters excerpted here show the evolution of Huck's relationship with Jim.

NOTES

1. Myra Jehlen, "Banned in Concord: *Adventures of Huckleberry Finn* and Classic American Literature," *The Cambridge Companion to Mark Twain,* ed. Forrest G. Robinson (New York: Cambridge University Press, 1995) 93.
2. Ernest Hemingway, *Green Hills of Africa* (New York: Scribner's, 1935) 22.
3. John H. Wallace, "The Case Against *Huck Finn," Satire or Evasion? Black Perspectives on "Huckleberry Finn,"* ed. James S. Leonard, Thomas A. Tenney, and Thadious M. Davis (Durham, NC: Duke UP, 1992) 103–120.
4. Ralph Ellison, *Shadow and Act* (New York: Vintage, 1972) 31–32.

From *Adventures of Huckleberry Finn*

XV

We judged that three nights more would fetch us to Cairo, at the bottom of Illinois, where the Ohio River comes in, and that was what we was after. We would sell the raft and get on a steamboat and go way up the Ohio amongst the free States, and then be out of trouble.

Well, the second night a fog begun to come on, and we made for a tow-head to tie to, for it wouldn't do to try to run in fog; but when I paddled ahead in the canoe, with the line, to make fast, there warn't anything but little saplings to tie to. I passed the line around one of them right on the edge of the cut bank, but there was a stiff current, and the raft come booming down so lively she tore it out by the roots and away she went. I see the fog closing down, and it made me so sick and scared I couldn't budge for most a half a minute it seemed to me—and then there warn't no raft in sight; you couldn't see twenty yards. I jumped into the canoe and run back to the stern and grabbed the paddle and set her back a stroke. But she didn't come. I was in such a hurry I hadn't untied her. I got up and tried to untie her, but I was so excited my hands shook so I couldn't hardly do anything with them.

As soon as I got started I took out after the raft, hot and heavy, right down the tow-head. That was all right as far as it went, but the tow-head warn't sixty yards long, and the minute I flew by the foot of it I shot out into the solid white fog, and hadn't no more idea which way I was going than a dead man.

Thinks I, it won't do to paddle; first I know I'll run into the bank or a tow-head or something; I got to set still and float, and yet it's mighty fidgety business to have to hold your hands still at such a time. I whooped and listened. Away down there, somewheres, I hears a small whoop, and up comes my spirits. I went tearing after it, listening sharp to hear it again. The next time it come, I see I warn't heading for it but heading away to the right of it. And the next time, I was heading away to the left of it—and not gaining on it much, either, for I was flying around, this way and that and 'tother, but it was going straight ahead all the time.

I did wish the fool would think to beat a tin pan, and beat it all the time, but he never did, and it was the still places between the whoops that was making the trouble for me. Well, I fought along, and directly I hears the whoop *behind* me. I was tangled good, now. That was somebody else's whoop, or else I was turned around.

I throwed the paddle down. I heard the whoop again; it was behind me yet, but in a different place; it kept coming, and kept changing its place, and I kept answering, till by-and-by it was in front of me again and I knowed the current had swung the canoe's head down stream and I was all right, if that was Jim and not some other raftsman hollering. I couldn't tell nothing about voices in a fog, for nothing don't look natural nor sound natural in a fog.

The whooping went on, and in about a minute I come a booming down on a cut bank with smoky ghosts of big trees on it, and the current throwed me off to the left and shot by, amongst a lot of snags that fairly roared, the current was tearing by them so swift.

In another second or two it was solid white and still again. I set perfectly still, then, listening to my heart thump, and I reckon I didn't draw a breath while it thumped a hundred.

I just give up, then. I knowed what the matter was. That cut bank was an island, and Jim had gone down 'tother side of it. It warn't no tow-head, that you could float by in ten minutes. It had the big timber of a regular island; it might be five or six mile long and more than a half a mile wide.

I kept quiet, with my ears cocked, about fifteen minutes, I reckon. I was floating along, of course, four or five mile an hour; but you don't ever think of that. No, you *feel* like you are laying dead still on the water; and if a little glimpse of a snag slips by, you don't think to yourself how fast *you're* going, but you catch your breath and think, my! how that snag's tearing along. If you think it ain't dismal and lonesome out in a fog that way, by yourself, in the night, you try it once—you'll see.

Next, for about a half an hour, I whoops now and then; at last I hears the answer a long ways off, and tries to follow it, but I couldn't do it, and directly I judged I'd got into a nest of tow-heads, for I had little dim glimpses of them on both sides of me, sometimes just a narrow channel between; and some that I couldn't see, I knowed was there, because I'd hear the wash of the current against the old dead brush and trash that hung over the banks. Well, I warn't long losing the whoops, down amongst the tow-heads; and I only tried to chase them a little while, anyway, because it was worse than chasing a Jack-o-lantern. You never knowed a sound dodge around so, and swap places so quick and so much.

I had to claw away from the bank pretty lively, four or five times, to keep from knocking the islands out of the river; and so I judged the raft must be butting into the bank every now and then, or else it would get further ahead and clear out of hearing—it was floating a little faster than what I was.

Well, I seemed to be in the open river again, by-and-by, but I couldn't hear no sign of a whoop nowheres. I reckoned Jim had fetched up on a snag, maybe, and it was all up with him. I was good and tired, so I laid down in the canoe and said I wouldn't bother no more. I didn't want to go to sleep, of course; but I was so sleepy I couldn't help it; so I thought I would take just one little cat-nap.

But I reckon it was more than a cat-nap, for when I waked up the stars was shining bright, the fog was all gone, and I was spinning down a big bend stern first. First I didn't know where I was; I thought I was dreaming; and when things begun to come back to me, they seemed to come up dim out of last week.

It was a monstrous big river here, with the tallest and the thickest kind of timber on both banks; just a solid wall, as well as I could see, by the stars. I looked away down stream, and seen a black speck on the water. I took out after it; but when I got to it it warn't nothing but a couple of saw-logs made fast together. Then I see another speck, and chased that; then another, and this time I was right. It was the raft.

When I got to it Jim was setting there with his head down between his knees, asleep, with his right arm hanging over the steering oar. The other oar was smashed off, and the raft was littered up with leaves and branches and dirt. So she'd had a rough time.

I made fast and laid down under Jim's nose on the raft, and begun to gap, and stretch my fists out against Jim, and says:

"Hello, Jim, have I been asleep? Why didn't you stir me up?"

"Goodness gracious, is dat you, Huck? En you ain' dead—you ain' drownded—you's back agin? It's too good for true, honey, it's too good for true. Lemme look at you, chile, lemme feel o' you. No, you ain' dead! you's back agin, 'live en soun', jis de same ole Huck—de same ole Huck, thanks to goodness!"

"What's the matter with you, Jim? You been a drinking?"

"Drinkin'? Has I ben a drinkin'? Has I had a chance to be a drinkin'?"

"Well, then, what makes you talk so wild?

"How does I talk wild?"

"*How?* why, hain't you been talking about my coming back, and all that stuff, as if I'd been gone away?"

"Huck—Huck Finn, you look me in de eye; look me in de eye. *Hain't* you ben gone away?"

"Gone away? Why, what in the nation do you mean? *I* hain't been gone anywheres. Where would I go to?"

"Well, looky here, boss, dey's sumf'n wrong, dey is. Is I *me*, or who *is* I? Is I heah, or whah *is* I? Now dat's what I wants to know?"

"Well, I think you're here, plain enough, but I think you're a tangle-headed old fool, Jim."

"I is, is I? Well you answer me dis. Didn't you tote out de line in de canoe, fer to make fas' to de tow-head?"

"No, I didn't. What tow-head? I hain't seen no tow-head."

"You hain't seen no tow-head? Looky here—didn't de line pull loose en de raf' go a hummin' down de river, en leave you en de canoe behine in de fog?"

"What fog?"

"Why *de* fog. De fog dat's ben aroun' all night. En didn't you whoop, en didn't I whoop, tell we got mix' up in de islands en one un us got los' en 'tother one was jis' as good as los', 'kase he didn' know whah he wuz? En didn't I bust up agin a lot er dem islands en have a turrible time en mos' git drownded? Now ain' dat so, boss—ain't it so? You answer me dat."

"Well, this is too many for me, Jim. I hain't seen no fog, nor no islands, nor no troubles, nor nothing. I been setting here talking with you all night till you went to sleep about ten minutes ago, and I reckon I done the same. You couldn't a got drunk in that time, so of course you've been dreaming."

"Dad fetch it, how is I gwyne to dream all dat in ten minutes?"

"Well, hang it all, you did dream it, because there didn't any of it happen."

"But Huck, it's all jis' as plain to me as—"

"It don't make no difference how plain it is, there ain't nothing in it. I know, because I've been here all the time."

Jim didn't say nothing for about five minutes, but set there studying over it. Then he says:

"Well, den, I reck'n I did dream it, Huck; but dog my cats ef it ain't de powerfullest dream I ever see. En I hain't ever had no dream b'fo' dat's tired me like dis one."

"Oh, well, that's all right, because a dream does tire a body like everything, sometimes. But this one was a staving dream—tell me all about it, Jim."

So Jim went to work and told me the whole thing right through, just as it happened, only he painted it up considerable. Then he said he must start in and "'terpret" it, because it was sent for a warning. He said the first tow-head stood for a man that would try to do us some good, but the current was another man that would get us away from him. The whoops was warnings that would come to us every now and then, and if we didn't try hard to make out to understand them they'd just take us into bad luck, 'stead of keeping us out of it. The lot of tow-heads was troubles we was going to get into with quarrelsome people and all kinds of mean folks, but if we minded our business and didn't talk back and aggravate them, we would pull through and get out of the fog and into the big clear river, which was the free States, and wouldn't have no more trouble.

It had clouded up pretty dark just after I got onto the raft, but it was clearing up again, now.

"Oh, well, that's all interpreted well enough, as far as it goes, Jim," I says; "but what does *these* things stand for?"

It was the leaves and rubbish on the raft, and the smashed oar. You could see them first rate, now.

Jim looked at the trash, and then looked at me, and back at the trash again. He had got the dream fixed so strong in his head that he couldn't seem to shake it loose and get the facts back into its place again, right away. But when he did get the thing straightened around, he looked at me steady, without ever smiling, and says:

"What do dey stan' for? I's gwyne to tell you. When I got all wore out wid work, en wid de callin' for you, en went to sleep, my heart wuz mos' broke bekase you wuz los', en I didn' k'yer no mo' what become er me en de raf'. En when I wake up en fine you back agin', all safe en soun', de tears come en I could a got down on my knees en kiss' yo' foot I's so thankful. En all you wuz thinkin 'bout wuz how you could make a fool uv ole Jim wid a lie. Dat truck dah is *trash;* en trash is what people is dat puts dirt on de head er dey fren's en makes 'em ashamed."

Then he got up slow, and walked to the wigwam, and went in there, without saying anything but that. But that was enough. It made me feel so mean I could almost kissed *his* foot to get him to take it back.

It was fifteen minutes before I could work myself up to go and humble myself to a nigger—but I done it, and I warn't ever sorry for it afterwards, neither. I didn't do him no more mean tricks, and I wouldn't done that one if I'd a knowed it would make him feel that way.

XVI

We slept most all day, and started out at night, a little ways behind a monstrous long raft that was as long going by as a procession. She had four long sweeps at each end, so we judged she carried as many as thirty men, likely. She had five big wigwams aboard, wide apart, and an open camp fire in the middle, and a tall flag-pole at each end. There was a power of style about her. It *amounted* to something being a raftsman on such a craft as that.

We went drifting down into a big bend, and the night clouded up and got hot. The river was very wide, and was walled with solid timber on both sides; you couldn't see a break in it hardly ever, or a light. We talked about Cairo, and wondered whether we would know it when we got to it. I said likely we wouldn't, because I had heard say there warn't but about a dozen houses there, and if they didn't happen to have them lit up, how was we going to know we was passing a town? Jim said if the two big rivers joined together there, that would show. But I said maybe we might think we was passing the foot of an island and coming into the same old river again. That disturbed Jim—and me too. So the question was, what to do? I said, paddle ashore the first time a light showed, and tell them pap was behind, coming along with a trading-scow, and was a green hand at the business, and wanted to know how far it was to Cairo. Jim thought it was a good idea, so we took a smoke on it and waited.

There warn't nothing to do, now, but to look out sharp for the town, and not pass it without seeing it. He said he'd be mighty sure to see it, because he'd be a free man the minute he seen it, but if he missed it he'd be in the slave country again and no more show for freedom. Every little while he jumps up and says:

"Dah she is!"

But it warn't. It was Jack-o-lanterns, or lightning-bugs; so he set down again, and went to watching, same as before. Jim said it made him all over trembly and feverish to be so close to freedom. Well, I can tell you it made me all over trembly and feverish, too, to hear him, because I begun to get it through my head that he *was* most free— and who was to blame for it? Why, *me*. I couldn't get that out of my conscience, no how nor no way. It got to troubling me so I couldn't rest; I couldn't stay still in one place. It hadn't ever come home to me before, what this thing was that I was doing. But now it did; and it staid with me, and scorched me more and more. I tried to make out to myself that *I* warn't to blame, because *I* didn't run Jim off from his rightful owner; but it warn't no use, conscience up and says, every time, "But you knowed he was running for his freedom, and you could a paddled ashore and told somebody." That was so—I couldn't get around that, noway. That was where it pinched. Conscience says to me, "What had poor Miss Watson done to you, that you could see her nigger go off right under your eyes and never say one single word? What did that poor old woman do to you, that you could treat her so mean? Why, she tried to learn you your book, she tried to learn you your manners, she tried to be good to you every way she knowed how. *That's* what she done."

I got to feeling so mean and so miserable I most wished I was dead. I fidgeted up and down the raft, abusing myself to myself, and Jim was fidgeting up and down past me. We neither of us could keep still. Every time he danced around and says, "Dah's Cairo!" it went through me like a shot, and I thought if it *was* Cairo I reckoned I would die of miserableness.

Jim talked out loud all the time while I was talking to myself. He was saying how the first thing he would do when he got to a free State he would go to saving up money and never spend a single cent, and when he got enough he would buy his wife, which was owned on a farm close to where Miss Watson lived; and then they would both work to buy the two children, and if their master wouldn't sell them, they'd get an Ab'litionist to go and steal them.

It most froze me to hear such talk. He wouldn't ever dared to talk such talk in his life before. Just see what a difference it made in him the minute he judged he was about free. It was according to the old saying, "give a nigger an inch and he'll take an ell." Thinks I, this is what comes of my not thinking. Here was this nigger which I had as good as helped to run away, coming right out flat-footed and saying he would steal his children—children that belonged to a man I didn't even know; a man that hadn't ever done me no harm.

I was sorry to hear Jim say that, it was such a lowering of him. My conscience got to stirring me up hotter than ever, until at last I says to it, "Let up on me— it ain't too late, yet—I'll paddle ashore at the first light, and tell." I felt easy, and happy, and light as a feather, right off. All my troubles was gone. I went to looking out sharp for a light, and sort of singing to myself. By-and-by one showed. Jim sings out:

"We's safe, Huck, we's safe! Jump up and crack yo' heels, dat's de good ole Cairo at las', I jis knows it!"

I says:

"I'll take the canoe and go see, Jim. It mightn't be, you know."

He jumped and got the canoe ready, and put his old coat in the bottom for me to set on, and give me the paddle; and as I shoved off, he says:

"Pooty soon I'll be a-shout'n for joy, en I'll say, it's all on accounts o' Huck; I's a free man, en I couldn't ever ben free ef it hadn' ben for Huck; Huck done it. Jim won't ever forgit you, Huck; you's de bes' fren' Jim's ever had; en you's de *only* fren' ole Jim's got now."

I was paddling off, all in a sweat to tell on him; but when he says this, it seemed to kind of take the tuck all out of me. I went along slow then, and I warn't right down certain whether I was glad I started or whether I warn't. When I was fifty yards off, Jim says:

"Dah you goes, de ole true Huck; de on'y white genlman dat ever kep' his promise to ole Jim."

Well, I just felt sick. But I says, I *got* to do it—I can't get *out* of it. Right then, along comes a skiff with two men in it, with guns, and they stopped and I stopped. One of them says:

"What's that, yonder?"

"A piece of a raft," I says.

"Do you belong on it?"

"Yes, sir."

"Any men on it?"

"Only one, sir."

"Well, there's five niggers run off to-night, up yonder above the head of the bend. Is your man white or black?"

I didn't answer up prompt. I tried to, but the words wouldn't come. I tried, for a second or two, to brace up and out with it, but I warn't man enough—hadn't the spunk of a rabbit. I see I was weakening; so I just give up trying, and up and says—

"He's white."

"I reckon we'll go and see for ourselves."

"I wish you would," says I, "because it's pap that's there, and maybe you'd help me tow the raft ashore where the light is. He's sick—and so is mam and Mary Ann."

"Oh, the devil! we're in a hurry, boy. But I s'pose we've got to. Come—buckle to your paddle, and let's get along."

I buckled to my paddle and they laid to their oars. When we had made a stroke or two, I says:

"Pap'll be mighty much obleeged to you, I can tell you. Everybody goes away when I want them to help me tow the raft ashore, and I can't do it by myself."

"Well, that's infernal mean. Odd, too. Say, boy, what's the matter with your father?"

"It's the—a—the—well, it ain't anything, much."

They stopped pulling. It warn't but a mighty little ways to the raft, now. One says:

"Boy, that's a lie. What *is* the matter with your pap? Answer up square, now, and it'll be the better for you."

"I will, sir, I will, honest—but don't leave us, please. It's the—the—gentlemen, if you'll only pull ahead, and let me heave you the head-line, you won't have to come a-near the raft—please do."

"Set her back, John, set her back!" says one. They backed water. "Keep away, boy—keep to looard. Confound it, I just expect the wind has blowed it to us. Your pap's got the small-pox, and you know it precious well. Why didn't you come out and say so? Do you want to spread it all over?"

"Well," says I, a-blubbering, "I've told everybody before, and then they just went away and left us."

"Poor devil, there's something in that. We are right down sorry for you, but we—well, hang it, we don't want the small-pox, you see. Look here, I'll tell you what to do. Don't you try to land by yourself, or you'll smash everything to pieces. You float along down about twenty miles and you'll come to a town on the left-hand side of the river. It will be long after sun-up, then, and when you ask for help, you tell them your folks are all down with chills and fever. Don't be a fool again, and let people guess what is the matter. Now we're trying to do you a kindness; so you just put twenty miles between us, that's a good boy. It wouldn't do any good to land yonder where the light is—it's only a wood-yard. Say—I reckon your father's poor, and I'm bound to say he's in pretty hard luck. Here—I'll put a twenty dollar gold piece on this board, and you get it when it floats by. I feel mighty mean to leave you, but my kingdom! it won't do to fool with small-pox, don't you see?"

"Hold on, Parker," says the other man, "here's a twenty to put on the board for me. Good-bye, boy, you do as Mr. Parker told you, and you'll be all right."

"That's so, my boy—good-bye, good-bye. If you see any runaway niggers, you get help and nab them, and you can make some money by it."

"Good-bye, sir," says I, "I won't let no runaway niggers get by me if I can help it."

They went off, and I got aboard the raft, feeling bad and low, because I knowed very well I had done wrong, and I see it warn't no use for me to try to learn to do right; a body that don't get *started* right when he's little, ain't got no show—when the pinch comes there ain't nothing to back him up and keep him to his work, and so he gets beat. Then I thought a minute, and says to myself, hold on,—s'pose you'd a done right and give Jim up; would you felt better than what you do now? No, says I, I'd feel bad—I'd feel just the same way I do now. Well, then, says I, what's the use you learning to do right, when it's troublesome to do right and ain't no trouble to do wrong, and the wages is just the same? I was stuck. I couldn't answer that. So I reckoned I wouldn't bother no more about it, but after this always do whichever come handiest at the time.

I went into the wigwam; Jim warn't there. I looked all around; he warn't anywhere. I says:

"Jim!"

"Here I is, Huck. Is dey out o' sight yit? Don't talk loud."

He was in the river, under the stern oar, with just his nose out. I told him they was out of sight, so he come aboard. He says:

"I was a-listenin' to all de talk, en I slips into de river en was gwyne to shove for sho' if dey come aboard. Den I was gwyne to swim to de raf' agin when dey was gone. But lawsy, how you did fool 'em, Huck! Dat *wuz* de smartes' dodge! I tell you, chile, I 'speck it save' ole Jim—ole Jim ain't gwyne to forgit you for dat, honey."

Then we talked about the money. It was a pretty good raise, twenty dollars apiece. Jim said we could take deck passage on a steamboat now, and the money would last us as far as we wanted to go in the free States. He said twenty mile more warn't far for the raft to go, but he wished we was already there.

Towards daybreak we tied up, and Jim was mighty particular about hiding the raft good. Then he worked all day fixing things in bundles, and getting all ready to quit rafting.

That night about ten we hove in sight of the lights of a town away down in a left-hand bend.

I went off in the canoe, to ask about it. Pretty soon I found a man out in the river with a skiff, setting a trot-line. I ranged up and says.

"Mister, is that town Cairo?"

"Cairo? no. You must be a blame' fool."

"What town is it, mister?"

"If you want to know, go and find out. If you stay here botherin' around me for about a half a minute longer, you'll get something you won't want."

I paddled to the raft. Jim was awful disappointed, but I said never mind, Cairo would be the next place, I reckoned.

We passed another town before daylight, and I was going out again; but it was high ground, so I didn't go. No high ground about Cairo, Jim said. I had forgot it. We laid up for the day, on a tow-head tolerable close to the left-hand bank. I begun to suspicion something. So did Jim. I says:

"Maybe we went by Cairo in the fog that night."

He says:

"Doan' less' talk about it, Huck. Po' niggers can't have no luck. I awluz 'spected dat rattle-snake skin warn't done wid it's work."

"I wish I'd never seen that snake-skin, Jim—I do wish I'd never laid eyes on it."

"It ain't yo' fault, Huck; you didn' know. Don't you blame yo'self 'bout it."

When it was daylight, here was the clear Ohio water in shore, sure enough, and outside was the old regular Muddy! So it was all up with Cairo.

We talked it all over. It wouldn't do to take to the shore; we couldn't take the raft up the stream, of course. There warn't no way but to wait for dark, and start back in the canoe and take the chances. So we slept all day amongst the cotton-wood thicket, so as to be fresh for the work, and when we went back to the raft about dark the canoe was gone!

We didn't say a word for a good while. There warn't anything to say. We both knowed well enough it was some more work of the rattle-snake skin; so what was the use to talk about it? It would only look like we was finding fault, and that would be bound to fetch more bad luck—and keep on fetching it, too, till we knowed enough to keep still.

By-and-by we talked about what we better do, and found there warn't no way but just to go along down with the raft till we got a chance to buy a canoe to go back in. We warn't going to borrow it when there warn't anybody around, the way pap would do, for that might set people after us.

So we shoved out, after dark, on the raft.

Anybody that don't believe yet, that it's foolishness to handle a snake-skin, after all that that snake-skin done for us, will believe it now, if they read on and see what more it done for us.

The place to buy canoes is off of rafts laying up at shore. But we didn't see no rafts laying up; so we went along during three hours and more. Well, the night got gray, and ruther thick, which is the next meanest thing to fog. You can't tell the shape of the river, and you can't see no distance. It got to be very late and still, and then along comes a steamboat up the river. We lit the lantern, and judged she would see it. Upstream boats didn't generly come close to us; they go out and follow the bars and hunt for easy water under the reefs; but nights like this they bull right up the channel against the whole river.

We could hear her pounding along, but we didn't see her good till she was close. She aimed right for us. Often they do that and try to see how close they can come without touching; sometimes the wheel bites off a sweep, and then the pilot sticks his head out and laughs, and thinks he's mighty smart. Well, here she comes, and we said she was going to try to shave us; but she didn't seem to be sheering off a bit. She was a big one, and she was coming in a hurry, too, looking like a black cloud with rows of glow-worms around it; but all of a sudden she bulged out, big and scary, with a long row of wide-open furnace doors shining like red-hot teeth, and her monstrous bows and guards hanging right over us. There was a yell at us, and a jingling of bells to stop the engines, a pow-wow of cussing, and whistling of steam—and as Jim went overboard on one side and I on the other, she come smashing straight through the raft.

I dived—and I aimed to find the bottom, too, for a thirty-foot wheel had got to go over me, and I wanted it to have plenty of room. I could always stay under water a minute; this time I reckon I staid under water a minute and a half. Then I bounced for the top in a hurry, for I was nearly busting. I popped out to my arm-pits and blowed the water out of my nose, and

puffed a bit. Of course there was a booming current; and of course that boat started her engines again ten seconds after she stopped them, for they never cared much for raftsmen; so now she was churning along up the river, out of sight in the thick weather, though I could hear her.

I sung out for Jim about a dozen times, but I didn't get any answer; so I grabbed a plank that touched me while I was "treading water," and struck out for shore, shoving it ahead of me. But I made out to see that the drift of the current was towards the left-hand shore, which meant that I was in a crossing; so I changed off and went that way.

It was one of these long, slanting, two-mile crossings; so I was a good long time in getting over. I made a safe landing, and clum up the bank. I couldn't see but a little ways, but I went poking along over rough ground for a quarter of a mile or more, and then I run across a big old-fashioned double log house before I noticed it. I was going to rush by and get away, but a lot of dogs jumped out and went to howling and barking at me, and I knowed better than to move another peg.

E. L. Doctorow (b. 1931) and David Bradley (b. 1950)

We often think of Tom Sawyer and Huckleberry Finn as a pair, like Don Quixote and Sancho Panza, and they do indeed belong together, but they are different in important ways. As novelist E. L. Doctorow points out in this 1995 forum in *The New Yorker,* their books are different, too, and the failed ending of the novel, as some critics see it, is due to the dominance of Tom in the latter part of *Huckleberry Finn.* David Bradley provides a firsthand account of the experience of racism through his history of reading the novel, and he puts the issue of the novel's racist language in a personal and historical perspective. Whether *Huck Finn* is read as a simple adventure story, an ironic commentary on the destructive effects of racism and bigotry, or a document about the pre–Civil War South, it remains one of the most provocative and engaging books written in the voice of a child.

Huck, Continued

You can't know about Huck Finn without you have read a book by the name of "The Adventures of Tom Sawyer." In that earlier rendition of a remembered past, Twain recalls Hannibal, Missouri, in the eighteen-forties as a perpetual summer in which distinct and sweetly irreconcilable life forms, the Child and the Adult, play out their comedic fates. Tom's adventures end in triumph, and the young reader is given the subtextual assurance that finally there is a bond that unites young and old in one moral world, in which truth can be realized and forgiveness is always possible.

The young reader? Twain had to be told that he'd written a book for children—he had intended an adult novel. He wrote by whim, without plan, giving himself totally to the pleasures of improvisation and the music he heard in speech. He was a stage humorist long before he became a literary figure. He was a colleague of Petroleum V. Nasby and Artemus Ward before he became a neighbor of Harriet Beecher Stowe of Hartford, and a guest at the New England domiciles of Emerson and Oliver Wendell Holmes.

But Twain had to have understood, finally, that, in its celebratory comedy, his book was too sentimental, too forgiving of the racist backwater that had nurtured him. He had ignored slavery as if it hadn't existed. And after all was said and done his Tom Sawyer character was a centrist, a play rebel, who, like Twain himself, had been welcomed into the bosom of a ruling society he sallied against.

Then came the great moment in American literary history, when his eye turned to the kid on Tom's left.

In "Huckleberry Finn," Twain releases himself from the tyranny of his stage voice, the voice of amused tolerance with which he has written everything heretofore, and gives the narration to Tom Sawyer's unwashed, unredeemable sidekick, Huck. He speaks as a child—and forgoes childish things. And in this rendition of his past his vision of the antebellum South is anything but celebratory. We find not loving adults enduring the mischief of their youngsters but killers, con men, drunks, and thieves. Where Tom Sawyer hid out on Jackson's Island because his little girlfriend Becky Thatcher rejected him, Huck flees

there, in desperation, to escape the abuses of his alcoholic father, who has threatened to kill him.

Huck links up with Miss Watson's escaped slave Jim, and their adventures rafting down the Mississippi are a variant of the slave narrative. Here the thrown voice of the child comes to genius: Huck, making the socially immoral choice to assist the escape of a slave—someone's rightful property, he thinks—creates in himself an ethically superior morality that he defines as outlaw, and appropriate to such a worthless tramp as he. And Twain can deal with the monstrous national catastrophe of slaveholding, not head on, in righteousness, in the manner of Harriet Beecher Stowe, but with the sharper stick, the deeper thrust, of irony.

Huck and Jim are survivalists, rafting downstream at night, hiding in the cottonwood banks by day, braving storms, fogs, and steamboat collisions to get Jim to freedom. Civilization here is not, as it is in "Tom Sawyer," a matter of having your neck washed by a prim maiden aunt. Civilization is buying and selling people, and working them to death. Civilization is a vicious confidence game played on a field of provincial ignorance. Huck, smart and resourceful, is a master of Sawyeresque deception and tale-telling as he confronts the treacherous adults who populate the towns along the river.

And then something terrible happens—terrible for Huck, terrible for American literature. The narrative moves inland, Jim is captured, and Twain brings back Tom Sawyer. Though the moral mind of the book is Huck's—as Jim's protector, he has been the one to suffer the crisis of his country's conscience—it is given to Tom Sawyer to stage Jim's ultimate escape from the Phelps plantation. Huck, who has been until now our eyes our voice, moves back to the sidekick role, and the book wallows in foolishness, playing out, long past credibility, Tom's nonsensical, overcomplicated, boy's-book fantasy escape plan. And to render everything completely pointless it turns out that Jim has been freed legally in the late Miss Watson's will, as Tom has known all along.

The greatest picaresque since Cervantes and Diderot is thrown away in doddering shtick. Twain, in his habitual practice of letting a book write itself, stopped work on "Huckleberry Finn," resumed a couple of years later, put the manuscript away in the drawer again for a few more years, eventually finishing and publishing it eight years, and several other books, after he began. And somewhere along the line he lost his resolve or his way, counting, misguidedly, on the old props of his stagecraft—the mischievous boy and his pranks—to rescue him. They are tawdry here in the real world of Huck and Jim; with the life of Jim at stake, they are cruelly inappropriate.

As a reconstructed Southerner, Twain was a repository of all the contradictions in his society. Tom's book and Huck's book are conflicting visions of the same past, and at the end one vision prevails, and it is the wrong one. The same thing that made Twain blow his greatest work generates its troublesome moral conundrum—the depiction of Jim. Twain loved dialect; he had an ear for it and it came easily to him, so it is Huck Finn who struggles against the white mores of his time to help the black man, Jim, escape from slavery, but it is Huck's progenitor who portrays Jim, in minstrelese, as a gullible black child-man led by white children.

The irony may not be redemptive.

—E. L. Doctorow

The first time I was called a nigger was on the playground on my first day of school in Bedford, Pennsylvania—in a region some have called God's country, because of an abundance of both nature and churches. There was also an abundance of bigots, and a shortage of blacks; epithets were uncommon. When a little boy of Irish extraction confronted me with "nigger," I had never before heard the word. If he hadn't bloodied my nose, I'd not have known to cry.

I kept this, and similar incidents, secret until a pair of bullies stripped me and whipped me with briars, to the usual soundtrack. Then I consulted my elders. My grandmother told me to ignore "poor white trash," and taught me to keep my face impassive "to deny them satisfaction." My mother advised me to walk away with dignity. My father said that I should turn the other cheek. Fortunately, my uncle taught me combat skills; I escaped elementary school alive.

My first encounter with "nigger" in a book came several years later, when I read "The Adventures of Tom Sawyer," which I liked, though I did not like Tom. In fact, I loathed that lazy, lying hooky player,

but I pitied "the juvenile pariah of the village," Huckleberry Finn, until he says, "Jim told Ben Rogers, and Ben told a nigger, and the nigger told me." Tom replies, "They'll all lie. Leastways all but the nigger. I don't know *him*. But I never see a nigger that *wouldn't* lie."

I almost put the book down. Suddenly, however, I saw a difference: both boys called the Negro "nigger," but Tom decided he was a liar, not because he knew he had lied, as with the white boys, but because *all* Negroes lied. Huck, on the other hand, considered the Negro as reliable as the white boys. When Huck said "nigger," he meant Negro. When Tom said "nigger," he meant liar. Tom was a bigot. Huck might not be. Hooked, I followed him to his own book.

There he says "nigger" often but means nothing by it—and Jim uses it as frequently. Huck first identifies Jim as "Miss Watson's big nigger," but afterward calls him Jim. Tom wants to tie Jim up and play tricks on him; Huck not only refuses but turns to Jim for advice, and argues with him. In town, Huck tells Tom he wouldn't want to eat with a Negro "as a steady thing"; on Jackson's Island, he just says, "Pass me along another hunk of fish and some hot cornbread."

Huck does treat Jim like a nigger once, in Chapter 15. After the two have been separated in a fog, they are reunited, but instead of expressing his relief Huck mocks Jim with an outlandish tale and calls him "a tangle-headed old fool." Jim's response is something my grandmother might have said: "Trash is what people is dat puts dirt on de head er dey fren's en makes 'em ashamed." I expected Huck to bristle at this, but he tells us, "It was fifteen minutes before I could work myself up to go and humble myself to a nigger—but I done it, and I warn't ever sorry for it afterwards, neither." So, I thought, not all poor white trash are bigots. My responses may have been unsophisticated, but, reading "Huckleberry Finn," I began to distinguish connotation from denotation, to judge intent by action rather than rhetoric.

"Huckleberry Finn" is the most frequently taught novel in the United States, and probably the most frequently attacked. In previous decades, the attacks came from whites worried about what has come to be known as "family values." Now the attacks come from blacks disturbed by the word "nigger." I understand parents' desire to protect children from the word's hurtful connotations, but I believe that "Tom Sawyer" and "Huckleberry Finn" brought valuable lessons home to me, not despite the word "nigger" but because of it. I also understand the impulse to attack "offensive" expressions. The pervasiveness of American racism often makes me feel not offended so much as overwhelmed. And "nigger" is offensive not because it was said by literary characters in 1845 but because it is *meant* by literal Americans in 1995. W. E. B. Du Bois wrote that the problem of the color line is the problem of the twentieth century. What is offensive is that it will be the problem of the twenty-first. America ought to be a place where "nigger" has only historical meaning. Until that happens, the safest place for a child to learn about the word is in a book. From there, it cannot bloody any child's nose.

—David Bradley

May Justus (1898–1989)

New Boy in School (1963) was probably the first book for early readers about school desegregation in the United States. Its author, May Justus, wrote books for children and young adults for nearly fifty years. Most of her picture books, poems, realistic fiction, and folktales were set in Smoky Mountain cabins and communities like the ones where she grew up and later taught school in Tennessee. She remarked that, like Henry David Thoreau in Concord, she traveled widely at home, receiving letters and visits from her readers around the world. As she and her brother read extensively in childhood, Jo March in Alcott's *Little Women* and Harriet Beecher Stowe's *Uncle Tom's Cabin* had important influences on her career. Later she said, "I live in a little pocket here in Summerfield, but the books, of course, have gone out all over the world."[1]

Justus became involved with labor organizing and civil rights issues as a volunteer at the Highlander Folk School, where social radicals in the South organized and trained from the 1930s until the state forced it to move in 1959. Believing that people of different races could change their prejudices by getting to know each other, Justus was motivated to speak out after witnessing the discrimination suffered by her own friends and colleagues, such as African American activist Septimus Clark, who was not allowed to use the white elevator when they visited Nashville together. Justus said, "There's nothing in the world like personal contact. Nothing. Nothing. And the people who influence you most in your life are not the people who preach to you, but the people who live with you and the people you see in their daily lives." She was also horrified about bombings at schools in Nashville and elsewhere. She said, "I wanted to do something. . . .to show that I disapprove of the school being bombed, . . . about violence happening that way. So I thought and thought about it, and I decided I'd write a book." Then she wrote two chapter books set in Nashville, *New Boy in School* and *A New Home for Billy* (1966). The second story deals more explicitly with discrimination, since Billy's family has trouble renting a house and then gaining acceptance when they move from the city to an all-white suburb, but they make friends when the neighbors realize that they simply need help fixing up their run-down house.

New Boy in School focuses primarily on Lennie's discomfort when his family moves from Louisiana to Nashville and he is the only nonwhite child in his class. The song that helps him make friends is one of many folk songs and traditional tales that Justus collected and incorporated into her fiction. It is remarkable that a writer who never joined political parties or lost the trust of her conservative neighbors wrote books for children about desegregation while it was still a violently contested social change. Justus adopted a gentler approach to problems of race than later writers did in books for older children, such as Mildred Taylor's look back at Depression-era racism in her books about the Logan family and Marilyn Nelson's twenty-first-century sonnets about the murder of Emmett Till in 1955 (presented later in this section). According to librarian George Loveland, *New Boy in School* depicts "Southern white folks acting with compassion instead of confrontation. It shows a faith in the capacity of people to seek out common humanity when confronted with people who at first seem different, rather than focusing on the differences. May Justus invites the children reading the book (and the adults who might be reading it to the children) to practice the Golden Rule. How do you think it would feel, she asks, to be Lennie?"[2] Joan Balfour Payne, an author and illustrator from Mississippi, provided realistic drawings for each double-page spread of this chapter book and illustrated several other books by Justus as well.

NOTES

1. May Justus quotations from interview with Eliot Wigginton (1980s, typescript archived at Harry Lasker Library, Highlander Research and Education Center, New Market, TN).
2. George Loveland, "A Greater Fairness: May Justus as Popular Educator," *Journal of Research in Rural Education* 17 (Fall 2001): 102–11, *AppLit,* ed. Tina L. Hanlon, 2002, Ferrum College, 12 April 2005 <http://www.Ferrum.edu/AppLit/articles/JustusArt.htm>.

New Boy in School

1

Lennie Lane's family moved from Newton, Louisiana, to Nashville, Tennessee in the middle of the school year. The day that they arrived in their new home was Lennie's birthday. He was seven years old.

He wasn't very happy on this birthday. In the hurry and scurry of moving there had been no time for a birthday party like the one he had last year. His mother had even been too busy to bake a cake for Lennie. All he had to be happy about was a pair of new shoes that he hadn't been allowed to wear yet. He would put them on tomorrow when he started to school.

Lennie didn't like the idea of going to school among strangers. He wished his folks had stayed on in Newton where he knew all the boys and girls in first grade, and Miss Ellen, the teacher.

His father explained over and over why it was best to move.

"In Nashville we'll have a nicer house in a good neighborhood," he told Lennie. "I'll have a better job

with more pay. You'll have a better school. The boss has promised me all this. It's a step up for me—a big one. That's why we are moving."

Lennie's father belonged to a crew of workmen who built houses for a large construction company. He went from place to place with them. They worked on one job, finished it, and then went on to another.

The Lanes had never lived more than a year in any town or city. They didn't mind this, but they always hoped that their next home would be better than the last.

As Lennie's father talked about the reasons for moving, Lennie was ashamed to grumble, even though he felt grumbly inside. He thought about his birthday shoes, shiny brown with golden stitching. He would wear them tomorrow when he started to the new school. This made Lennie feel a little more cheerful, even though he didn't want to face all those strange children.

Lennie was glad to have new shoes on that first morning when his father and mother took him to Miss

Joan Balfour Payne's sensitive drawing of the two boys who overcome racial differences to become friends appeared on the half-title page of *New Boy in School* by May Justus (1963).

Baker's room. It wasn't a bit like his old school. It had been an unpainted house which had only one room and one teacher for the whole school. The walls had many cracks and only a few windows. Miss Baker's room had clean, bright walls, with gay pictures, and so many windows that it seemed almost like having school outdoors. In the back of the room there was a play corner full of toys, a shelf of picture books, a bird in a yellow cage, and a fish bowl.

"A wonderful school," Lennie's mother said as Miss Baker showed them about the new place.

"A good school," Lennie's father said. "I am glad our boy can come here."

Lennie said nothing. Somehow he was a little afraid in this fine new school. It all seemed so strange to him. Most of the faces about him were friendly—Miss Baker's and those of the children—but they were white faces.

"There are so many of them," said Lennie, "and only one of me." Yes, Lennie was the only Negro boy in the room.

"This," Lennie's father explained, "is an integrated school."

"What does integrated mean?" Lennie asked.

"That means it is a school where Negro children and white children study and play together," the father explained.

"Yes," said the teacher. "There are other Negro children in the school, but you are the only one in this room."

Lennie felt too shy to say what he was thinking. He was wishing that at least half the children in that room had brown faces instead of white.

"You'll feel more at home with us later," Miss Baker said, smiling down at him as if she understood.

When his father and mother told him good-by and started to leave him, Lennie clung to them and nearly burst into tears.

"Be a good boy," his father whispered. His mother said nothing, but she gave him a quick hug.

Then his parents were gone. Lennie heard a door close. He heard the voice of the teacher say: "Come, sit here by Terry. He is making something out of clay he might like to show you."

Lennie sat down, but he wouldn't even look at Terry or what he was doing. He still wanted to cry. So he picked up a big book that was lying nearby and hid behind it for a long time. Sometimes he peeped around the book at the other children. Once he saw two boys whispering as they looked at him.

"They are talking about me," Lennie thought.

One of the boys was smiling.

"He is laughing at me," Lennie said to himself. "I am the only Negro boy here. That's why they are laughing."

This thought made Lennie very sad. He wished he were not in this school with so many white faces all around him. He wished he was back in the old tumble-down school where all the children were friendly. Here he had no friends at all.

Lennie thought of slipping out the door and running home to his mother. He would tell her how he hated this new school. He would beg her to let him stay at home. Perhaps he could talk his father into moving back to the old home.

Just then he felt a hand on his shoulder. Lennie looked up. It was Terry, with a grin on his face.

"Come over here," he said. "I'll show you what I've been making—a little horse."

But Lennie felt too shy to follow Terry. He only shook his head and settled farther down in his chair behind the big book.

When it was time for reading class, Lennie paid no attention. He just sat there behind his book. When it was time for recess, and all the children ran outside, Lennie stayed in the schoolroom.

Finally Miss Baker took him by the hand, and tried to get him to join in a singing game. As soon as she turned him loose, though, Lennie ran off. When the children laughed at him, he hid behind a big bush that grew in a corner of the schoolyard.

It wasn't a happy day for Lennie. When it was over he was glad to find his father and mother waiting to take him home.

"How was school today?" his father asked as they started off.

Lennie drew a deep breath. He might as well get it over. "I don't like that school, and I don't want to go back tomorrow."

"Oh, you'd better try it another day, at least once more," said his father. "You may like it better by this time tomorrow. I'd try it another day if I were you."

"That's a good idea," said his mother. "Your father is a smart man. You had better do what he says."

Lennie's father nodded.

"One reason we moved here," he said, "was so that you could go to such a fine school. It's one of the very best in the city—the first to be integrated."

"In-te-grated." Lennie said the word slowly. He remembered that word and his father's explanation: "An integrated school is a place where Negro children and white children study and play together."

Lennie shook his head. "They don't like me because I'm a Negro and I don't like them," he added, "because they don't like me." He sounded all mixed up, but this was the way he felt inside.

"When they get used to you they'll be friendly," said his father, "but you must be friendly, too. That's how to make friends—on a job—or going to school."

Lennie remembered Terry who had wanted to show him his horse. Terry had tried to be friendly. He had looked surprised when Lennie wouldn't go with him to see his work.

As Lennie remembered Terry, he thought of what he might do tomorrow. "I guess I could stand that new school for just *one* more day," he said.

2

Lennie was early at school next day. Miss Baker seemed glad to see him. She took him over to the worktable and gave him a big lump of clay.

"See what you can make out of this," she said.

All around the big table were things that the other children had made. Lennie saw a little horse and guessed that this might belong to Terry. It was a fine little horse. It looked almost alive, as if it were ready to run. "It is good, but it ought to have a rider," thought Lennie.

All at once he had an idea. Quickly he began to work with the clay. He was so busy that he paid no attention to what was going on around him. Soon he had made a little man.

"That looks like a cowboy." It was Terry who had come up behind him.

Lennie nodded. "I made him for you. He is to ride on your horse," he said. Terry took the cowboy and set him in place.

"Yes, they look fine together, don't they? Thank you, Lennie," Terry said with a smile.

"You're welcome," Lennie answered, smiling back.

That day when Lennie got home from school his father and mother were waiting to ask him, "How did you get along in school today?"

"I got along okay," Lennie replied. "I like school a little better on account of Terry." And he went on to explain. "Terry and I are friends. We do things together." He told them about what Terry and he had made.

Lennie's mother smiled happily. "I am glad to hear this."

Lennie's father nodded. "I am glad, too," he said. "Now you have found one friend. Soon you will have others. Just remember what I told you. Act in a friendly way to all your schoolmates. This is the way to make them like you."

Lennie thought of Jack and Joe, the two boys who had laughed at him. He didn't feel friendly toward them. He didn't like them at all, and he didn't think they would ever be his friends.

Lennie started to tell his thoughts, but he stopped because his father had just pulled something from his pocket. It was a round package tied with string.

"Here's something you might like to take to school tomorrow," he said with a smile.

Lennie's eager fingers fumbled with the string. Even before it was untied, he had guessed what was in the package.

A moment later he was bouncing it up and down on the floor. It was a beautiful red-white-and-blue ball.

"Thank you, Daddy!" cried Lennie. "This is the prettiest ball I ever saw. Tomorrow I'll take it to school and show it to Terry. I'll let him play with it, too, because he is my friend."

The next day at morning recess Lennie and Terry went off to a corner of the playground to play all by themselves.

"Let's play bounce ball," Terry said. "This ball is made of rubber and is just the right kind."

Lennie had never played bounce ball, but he listened while Terry explained.

"When I bounce the ball on the ground, you must try to catch it," Terry said. "You have to catch it on the bounce—not when it's rolling. When you miss, it's my turn."

Lennie thought this was a very fine game.

While he and Terry were playing, some of the other children came over to watch them. Among them were Jack and Joe, but Lennie paid no attention to them. He kept on playing with Terry.

"What a dandy ball!" he heard Jack say.

"It's better than the one we lost," said Joe.

"I wonder if we could join this game," Jack said to Joe.

Lennie looked up quickly to see if these boys were joking, but they weren't laughing at him. They weren't making fun of him.

"Do you think they really want to play with us?" Lennie asked Terry in a low tone. "Is it all right to let them into the game?"

"I think it would be more fun," Terry said, "to have more boys playing. That is, if you are willing," he added. "It's your ball."

Lennie bounced the ball toward Jack and Joe.

"Catch, *anybody!*" he cried.

Jack and Joe ran forward and bumped into each other. Jack fell down and it was Joe who got hold of the ball.

"Whoop-ee!" he yelled, but he was so excited that he dropped the ball before he could bounce it even once.

Now Lennie had it again.

"Here! Here!" someone shouted. He looked up and saw that the nearest boy was Joe.

"Here!" he answered, and threw it to him.

Just then Miss Baker came out to watch the game. She had an idea.

"Why not have two teams and play for the highest score?" she suggested.

All of the boys thought this a fine plan. They elected Lennie and Terry for captains. Miss Baker kept score. Sometimes Lennie's side was ahead. Sometimes it was Terry's. At the end of playtime there was a tie.

"We'll break the tie later," said Miss Baker, "at the next play period."

As they started back to the schoolroom Lennie put the ball in his pocket and went with Terry and Jack and Joe to the front of the line.

That night when Lennie got home his folks asked the usual question:

"Do you like school any better?"

"How did you get along today?"

Lennie was ready to answer: "I like school a little better. We had a big ball game today. We played with my new ball, and I was captain of our side. I was elected," he said with pride.

His father smiled. "I'm glad," he said, "but I'm not too surprised. A friendly boy is bound to make friends. Now you know these boys better, and they know you better, too. You'll probably get along fairly well now."

Lennie nodded. "First, I didn't have *any* friends in school. Then I had Terry. He's my best friend. Now there's Jack and Joe who like to play ball with me." Lennie smiled at his father and mother.

"I like school better every day, a *little* better, anyway," he said.

3

For some weeks everything went all right for Lennie. He liked the new school better all the time. He did make more and more friends. It did not seem to matter any more that he was the only Negro boy in Miss Baker's room. Indeed, the color of his skin seemed of no more importance now than the color of his clothes. Lennie was happy. His parents were happy.

Then he ran into trouble again.

It was all on account of something called a "Parents' Day Program."

One morning Miss Baker had a great piece of news for her pupils.

"Our room," she said, "has been asked to give a program. It will be the first Parents' Day Program of the year."

Lennie pricked up his ears. He had never heard of a Parents' Day Program at the old school.

Miss Baker went on: "We give a Parents' Day Program every year. It's to help the parents get acquainted with one another and with our new school. We shall give a little play. The Rhythm Band will have a number. We shall learn a few songs. It will be lots of fun."

It didn't sound like fun to Lennie. He had never been in a school program. He didn't want a part in this one. He was sure that he couldn't do as well as the others. He hoped Miss Baker wouldn't ask him to play in the Rhythm Band, or be in a play, or sing a song. He liked Miss Baker very much, and he would like to please her, but he didn't want any part in the program. The very thought of it scared him till his legs felt wobbly.

One thing he could do, and that was to write a copy of the invitation which the teacher put on the blackboard. This was the writing lesson for the day. Then, of course, he must take it home to his father and mother. It was addressed to them.

When his father and mother read it, they smiled at each other and at Lennie, too.

"Of course, we'll be glad to come," they told him.

Lennie was ashamed to tell them that he wouldn't have a part in the program, that he didn't want to be in the play, and that he didn't want to help sing. He still had a scary feeling inside himself whenever he thought about standing up with the other children.

Lennie went off in the living room. He sat by himself in a corner with a book on his lap, but he wasn't reading. He was having worry thoughts all to himself.

At supper he hardly ate a thing, though his mother had baked his favorite cake. It was chocolate with white icing at least an inch thick.

"Lennie, have you a pain in your middle?" his mother asked.

Lennie shook his head quickly. "No, ma'am!" He answered her in a hurry, because when he had a pain in his middle his mother gave him a big dose of bitter medicine.

His father looked at him keenly. "Maybe Lennie's got the mulli-grubs. That is a mighty bad thing to have. Have you got the mulli-grubs, son?"

Now mulli-grubs are gloomy, sad feelings, and Lennie felt bound to tell the truth.

"Yes, I guess I've got the mulli-grubs," he said, but still he didn't want to talk about the reason for his gloomy, sad feelings. He was glad that his folks didn't ask him questions. He didn't want to explain.

Lennie's mother looked at him anxiously. "There's *something* the matter with the boy. Maybe it's not a pain in the middle, maybe it's mulli-grubs, but bed's a good place for it anyway. So right to bed you're going to go, young man!"

Lennie felt sorry that he hadn't hidden his mulli-grubs better. He hated to go to bed so early. It wasn't even dark yet!

After Lennie was in bed, his father brought his banjo and sat by him. He didn't ask a question. He just leaned back in his chair and began to twang the strings and hum a tune Lennie knew and liked—"The Wishing Song."

"Sing it, Daddy!" Lennie begged.

Lennie's father sang:

"I wish I was an apple,
    An apple on a tree,
I'd hang so high nobody
    Could climb up after me."

"Sing on, Daddy," Lennie begged.

His father went on singing. Before the song was done, Lennie was fast asleep.

"Bed's a good cure for bad feelings, mulli-grubs, especially," his mother said when his father tiptoed out of Lennie's room and closed the door.

His father nodded and hung the banjo back in place on its peg.

The next morning Lennie got up feeling much better and hungrier, too. He proved it by eating three pancakes with honey before he left for school.

Once in school, though, he didn't feel so well. In fact, when they began to talk about the program Lennie began to feel worse and worse. It was strange.

All of a sudden he said before everyone, "I don't want to be in the program!" He didn't mean to be rude or let his voice ring out so loud, but some of the children giggled.

Miss Baker said, "Very well, Lennie, we will talk about it later on."

Lennie went to the back of the room and played at the sand table. Nobody paid any attention to him. Lennie started to hum the song his father had sung to him last night.

Soon he began singing in a low tone that was almost a whisper:

I wish I was an apple,
    An apple on a tree.
I'd hang so high nobody
    Could climb up after me.

Soon he was singing aloud as he made a house in the sand.

"I like that song," said Terry, coming up. "It has a pretty tune. Is that all there is to it?"

Lennie shook his head.

"You mean there is *more,* then? Sing the rest of it!" Terry begged. "I'd like to hear it."

Lennie glanced around. Nobody else was paying any attention to him and Terry. They were busy about their own play, and talking among themselves. Lennie went on with the song.

By this time Terry was whistling the tune. All of a sudden, Lennie noticed that the whole room was clapping. Then he knew that they had overheard his song, and were cheering him.

"Lennie must be in the program!" they cried. "Lennie must sing that song."

Everyone was smiling at him, including Miss Baker.

The friendly feeling all about him was warmer than the sunshine that filled the corner of the room. Lennie tried to smile back.

"But—but what if I get scared at the last minute when I get up before everybody, all by myself? I might forget, or make a mistake," he muttered.

The very thought made him wince.

"I know how you feel," said Terry. "When we had our first program this year I felt a little scared, too. You see I was a new boy, too, when school began. It was hard for me to stand up with the others that time. I was afraid I'd forget that bird call that I had to whistle. But I didn't. I remembered all right. I bet you will, too."

"Go ahead!" came the shout. "Go ahead, Lennie, Terry. Do the song together. Terry can whistle it. Lennie can sing."

Lennie found it no trouble at all to throw back his head and open his mouth as Terry stepped up beside him and puckered his lips to whistle the merry tune.

After that Lennie and Terry went off to practice. Both boys felt bound to do their best in this very special song. That's what Miss Baker had called it.

That night he told his parents, "I have a part on the program."

"Good for you!" his father said, looking very pleased.

"Tell us about it," his mother begged.

Lennie looked from one to the other. "If you don't mind," he told them, "I'd like to keep it for a surprise."

4

Finally Parents' Day came. All that morning Miss Baker's room practiced the program for the afternoon. The play was rehearsed three times. The Rhythm Band wiggled and giggled as they tried over and over to keep up with the tune as Miss Baker played it on the piano.

Lennie and his partner Terry tried not to worry. They had practiced their song over and over so that they wouldn't forget a word or a note. Still, the boys couldn't help feeling just a little bit frightened for fear they might forget anyway.

Finally program time came. The schoolroom was crowded with fathers and mothers. Miss Baker welcomed everyone. She seemed glad to see Lennie's father and mother and gave them a front seat where they could see all that went on.

The play was given without a hitch. The Rhythm

Band performed with only one or two small mistakes nobody seemed to mind.

Then Miss Baker made an announcement:

"The last number on our program is a special song by our newest pupil, Lennie Lane. It is called 'The Wishing Song,' and Terry Cole whistles the accompaniment."

Lennie found himself by Terry's side, standing up before all the people. Right there in the front row he saw his parents. He saw the anxious look on his mother's face and the encouraging nod his father gave him. He mustn't disappoint them now. Lennie got ready to start "The Wishing Song" by drawing a great, long breath. At the same moment Terry puckered up his lips and started to whistle the tune that rang out as sweetly as the notes of some wild bird.

The applause followed them back to their seat.

"Just listen, will you?" whispered Terry. "They are cheering louder and longer for us than for anyone else."

Lennie nodded. "And I know why. I can tell you the reason for all that cheering. You remember the teacher said ours was a *very special* song."

"That's important, I guess," Terry whispered.

But Lennie hardly heard what Terry said. He was looking at his father and mother—the happy smile on his mother's lips, the proud look on his father's face. He knew they were glad because he wasn't any longer a new boy in school. Now he belonged to the school just like everybody else.

Almost before the song was done the people started cheering. Lennie was so excited he nearly forgot to bow, but then he remembered his manners. A good thing he did, because Terry had nearly forgotten, too! When Lennie bowed, Terry bowed. Then they both bowed together.

> I wish I was a redbird,
>   A redbird in a tree.
> I'd fly so high nobody
>   Could throw a rock at me.
>
> I wish I was a squirrel,
>   A squirrel in a tree.
> I'd hide so quick no hunter
>   Could take a shot at me.

"Now he belonged to the school just like everybody else." Joan Balfour Payne's pencil drawings throughout the book help tell May Justus's story of school desegregation.

Louise Fitzhugh (1928–74)

Famous for *Harriet the Spy* (1964; see Recommended Reading, Part 1), Louise Fitzhugh portrayed children with a new freshness and radicalism in the style often called New Realism. In *Nobody's Family Is Going to Change* (1974), Emma (Emancipation) Sheridan wants to be a lawyer like her father—but he thinks that is not an appropriate choice for a girl. Her younger brother, Willie, wants to be a dancer, but her father opposes that ambition just as vehemently because he thinks that an African American boy should set his sights higher. Emma joins a Children's Liberation Army dedicated to defending children's rights because, as she has experienced in her own family, children are oppressed by adults. Emma does not want to be a submissive housewife like her mother. Her father's chauvinism appears to be the main obstacle to her progress—but she discovers that even the Children's Liberation Army has its flaws: it replicates the sexist prejudices of adult society. Ultimately, she can rely only on herself. Her family will not change, she concludes, but she can change herself. Rudine Sims, in her book *Shadow and Substance: Afro-American Experience in Contemporary Children's Fiction* (1982), criticized *Nobody's Family Is Going to Change* for being written unconvincingly from an outsider's perspective.[1]

NOTE

1. Rudine Sims, *Shadow and Substance: Afro-American Experience in Contemporary Children's Fiction* (Urbana, IL: National Council of Teachers of English, 1982).

From *Nobody's Family Is Going to Change*

By the time Martha had cleaned the kitchen and left, Emma had finished her homework. She devoted her time thereafter to the refrigerator, dividing her attention between pastrami, corned beef, bagels, hard rolls, cream cheese, olives, pickles, and a recent book on children's rights.

She was trying to write a paper for presentation to the Legal Committee of the Children's Army. She had already finished her Children's Bill of Rights, which she planned to present as well. If no other Bill of Rights had been introduced, she planned to push for adoption of hers. The paper she was working on now concerned an idea that had come to her somewhere in the back of her mind when she was having the discussion in the park with Saunders, Goldin, and Ketchum. It had come to her when she realized that she and Saunders were suffering more from a wrong attitude on the part of their respective parents than from anything their parents actually did to them.

She was trying to devise a psychological test to determine parental attitude. She had no idea how the Army would induce parents to take the test, but she reasoned that once they took it, they could be called to account for their attitudes if they were not up to par—in short, if they flunked the test.

She found the book on children's rights, which she had discovered in the library on Saturday, difficult to read. It seemed to go on and on about how there weren't any. Of course, if children didn't have any rights, then naturally it would be hard to write a book about those rights. All you could write about was the absence of them.

She figured that if her test was successful, she would trap her father. He would be exposed as having a rotten attitude. She ate and wrote, ate and wrote, until she had written fifteen pages and eaten three sandwiches, drunk six glasses of chocolate milk, and had four pickles, big ones.

When the door opened, admitting Mrs. Sheridan and Willie, they were talking. She realized that they didn't know she was in the kitchen.

She knew she should call to them, but for some reason, caught as she was with her mouth full and the fridge empty, she chose to say nothing. She didn't move, for fear of making a noise.

"Willie, sit down here a minute." Mrs. Sheridan was almost whispering.

"I know you want to tell your father tonight, but I honestly don't think it would be a good idea."

"I don't want to tell him. I just said I wasn't scared

to tell him. You and Dipsey seemed so scared. I don't know why he has to be told, and I don't know why you can't tell him, or you and me tell him together."

Emma sat in the kitchen, not moving, her hand holding a pastrami sandwich, her mouth full, afraid to chew.

"Darling, what I would like to hear you say is that you don't want to go ahead with this. I would like to hear you say that you've given up this whole thing and that you don't care about it any more and that you don't want to have this job in a musical."

Emma dropped the sandwich. She was so shocked that she tried to gasp with her mouth full, and only succeeded in choking. The kitchen was quickly filled with gasping, coughing, wheezing, dropping of books, and other signs of her imminent demise.

Mrs. Sheridan and Willie came running. "It's Emma, she's choking to death!" yelled Willie.

"Look!" he yelled again. "She's turning dark!"

Emma was pushing everybody away, arms flailing. She knew that, although it sounded bad, she was just about to catch her breath. The wheezes died down and she began to breathe again.

"My heavens, darling, what happened?" asked Mrs. Sheridan.

"She was choking, Mama," said Willie.

"Willie!" gasped Emma. "Willie has a job in a musical?"

Too late they heard, as one, the door to the study slam. Mr. Sheridan was already in the kitchen.

"What do you mean, Willie has a job? What is all this yelling about?" He looked like a tornado.

They were too stunned to speak.

"Well, what is it? Don't just stare at me like a bunch of fish. What are you talking about?"

Mrs. Sheridan burst out laughing. "Well, the cat's out of the bag now!" She slapped her hand down on the counter. "It's really funny!"

"What's funny?"

"I'd like to know too," said Emma.

"Emma almost choked to death," said Willie.

"And that's funny?" asked Mr. Sheridan.

"We have a big surprise for you," said Mrs. Sheridan. "Come into the living room. Willie has something to tell you."

She led him away. Willie whispered, "Emma, listen, could you help me?" He was shaking.

"With what?" Emma felt bleary-eyed after her fit.

"I got this job in a Broadway musical. It don't interfere with school. When he hits the ceiling, could you—would you talk good about me?"

Emma stared at him. He had a job in a musical? How good was this kid? "How did you get it?"

"Willie, come in here," called Mrs. Sheridan.

"I walked up on the stage and I danced and they took me."

This kid has guts, thought Emma, before she realized she was thinking about her brother.

"Would you help me, Emma?" His eyes were pleading as he turned to go toward the living room.

"Come on, Willie!"

Willie walked out of the kitchen. Emma sat, picking remnants of pastrami and coleslaw off her book. She slammed the book shut. "How can you get any work done in this family?" she asked the air. She thumped into the living room.

Her father and mother were seated on the couch. Willie was sitting across from them in one of the two armchairs. Emma hovered a bit at the edges of the room, until she finally chose an impartial straight chair against the wall.

"Willie has something to tell us!" said Mrs. Sheridan brightly.

"Mom!" said Willie in an agonized voice.

"Tell what happened this afternoon, dear," said Mrs. Sheridan, unperturbed. She was holding on to Mr. Sheridan's arm. Mr. Sheridan looked fairly sleepy and exceedingly grumpy.

Willie swallowed. "I went to the Winter Garden Theater, where Dipsey was in rehearsals—"

"You did what?" Mr. Sheridan sat up straight, untangling himself from his wife and putting a hand on each knee.

Willie swallowed again. "I went over to the Winter Garden Theater—"

"And just where is this Winter Garden?"

"Broadway and Fiftieth." Willie said this so low he could barely be heard.

"You mean to tell me that you went all the way from your school—I presume you went to school, did you not?"

Willie nodded, petrified.

"You went all the way from your school to Fiftieth and Broadway, even after having been told that you were not to go across town by yourself, were not, in fact, to go anywhere but school and then straight home?"

Willie nodded again.

Emma looked at Willie's legs. He was shaking so hard he seemed to be dancing with his knees.

"In other words, you performed an act of deliberate disobedience?"

Mrs. Sheridan said, "Let him tell the story."

Mr. Sheridan obviously didn't take to the idea, but he went along with it. "What did you do there?"

Something's missing, thought Emma, something important.

"I went in the theater. It was dark. I sat in one of the back rows."

"Speak up. You can't be heard!" said Mr. Sheridan.

Emma mentally finished his sentence, "You can't be heard in the courtroom," and realized, suddenly, what was missing. Of course! Here was a prosecutor in the form of her father, here was a suspected criminal in Willie, here was even a judge in the shape of her mother, but where was the defense lawyer? Willie had no one defending him!

"I sat in one of the back rows. These men were talking down front, and they were saying some boys were going to audition with Dipsey."

"Oh, they did, did they? And I suppose you thought you'd show them what you could do with some fancy stepping, right?" Mr. Sheridan was sneering.

"Objection!" said Emma. Every head turned in her direction. "Prosecutor is badgering the witness."

Her father looked as though the chair had spoken. "What is this? What do we have to hear from this one for? Isn't one rotten apple enough?"

"Pay no attention, dear," said Mrs. Sheridan, grabbing his arm again and making him lean back on the couch. "Come on, Willie, tell us about it. Don't be afraid."

"Dipsey came out and he did the number I've been practicing—"

"Oh-ho! So you've been working up a number, have you? Well, fine, that's just fine. You don't pay a damned bit of attention to what your father says, do you?"

"Let him tell it, dear."

Willie was so rattled he kept bobbing up and down in his chair like a swimmer coming up for air. "This kid comes out and dances with Dipsey—"

"Fine. So they have somebody. Why didn't you come home?"

"This kid was terrible, Dad!" This was the first display of temper on Willie's part.

"So what! Let his family worry about what happens to him in ten years. You get your ass home after school!"

"Objection!" said Emma. "The District Attorney is leading the witness."

"Leading him where?" asked Mr. Sheridan.

"Home from school," said Emma.

"Leading the witness doesn't mean that. When you don't know what you're talking about, you'd better keep your mouth shut!"

"May I remind the District Attorney that if he would question the witness fairly, he might find out what he was talking about."

"Get her out of here!" Mr. Sheridan stood up. Mrs. Sheridan grabbed at his arm.

"Sit down, William. I want Willie to tell you what happened."

Willie looked queasily at Emma. He wasn't sure what she was talking about, so he wasn't sure if she was on his side or not.

"What is this nonsense?" Mr. Sheridan looked at his wife in desperation. "Can't you handle these kids any better than this? One of them running all over town all the time, and the other one running off at the mouth!"

Emma's mind was racing ahead. How could she prepare a case for the defense when she hadn't heard the whole story? Before she knew it, she was on her feet. "May it please the court, I would like a few minutes to confer with my client."

"That does it!" said Mr. Sheridan, standing again. "What in the name of God is going on here?"

"I am simply begging the indulgence of the court for a few minutes of time to confer with my client on matters pertinent to this case."

"It takes your breath away," said Mr. Sheridan. He sat down, muttering, "If I'd ever talked to my father that way, he'd have slit my throat."

Emma ignored him. She marched over to Willie, who thought she was going to beat him up. She grabbed his arm. "Into the kitchen a minute," she said. He went with her.

"Now, I'm going to try to help you," she whispered. "But you have to tell me the truth."

"This is the truth," said Willie.

"What is the truth? What happened?"

"I went in there like I said. This nutsy kid comes out and does the number real bad. I mean, Emma, it was *bad*. So, next time Dipsey starts, I know some other kid is going to run out, because it's the same music, so I run up on the stage instead, even before Dipsey knows I'm there, and I do the number with him!"

"Why didn't you tell anyone you had been practicing something?"

"He would have stopped it, you know that. What a dumb question."

"Is that why you didn't tell anyone your whereabouts on the afternoon in question?"

"My where-a-who?"

"Is that why you didn't tell anyone where you were going when you went to the theater?"

"Sure. He wouldn't have let me!" Willie began to doubt that Emma was sane.

"After you did your dance, what happened?"

"I got the job!" said Willie, breaking into an enormous grin.

"And you want, naturally, to be able to do it."

She was definitely insane, Willie concluded. Of course he wanted the job.

"Will you have to leave school?"

"Listen, in there. Stop getting your stories straight. I don't have all night, and I have to get up early." Mr. Sheridan sounded a bit more jovial.

Willie shook his head. "Rehearsals are after school, and I'll be out for the summer before the show starts."

Emma took him back into the living room and sat him down on his chair.

"May it please the court," said Emma, standing in the middle of the room and facing her father and mother. "I would like to plead a mistrial on the basis of the fact that in this case the complainant, Mr. William Sheridan, Sr., happens also to be the District Attorney."

"Listen, smart-ass." Mr. Sheridan pointed a finger at her. "You think you know so much. I'll have you in contempt of court in three minutes."

"—and is also the judge. My client, William Sheridan, Jr., has, therefore, no possibility of a fair trial."

"But you have a very good possibility of getting your ass whacked," said Mr. Sheridan. "Now, sit down and shut up."

"I'll stand."

"All right, Willie. Since you have a loyal sister who seems to feel your rights to a fair trial are being prejudiced, I will begin again, calmly, to try to find out what you did on the afternoon of the second; that is, today."

Willie had his thumb in his mouth, having fled back into his youth.

"Sit up," said Emma. "Make a more pleasing appearance for the jury." Willie looked around for the jury.

"Finish your story, Willie," said his father.

"I watched this boy dance with Dipsey and he was real bad. He couldn't do it half as good as I could. So when Dipsey come to start again, I went up on the stage and did it with him."

"Son, you must have practiced this many times. You must therefore have disobeyed me many times. Did you not know that you were being bad?"

"Objection. My client could not be honest about this situation because he would have been incarcerated."

"Emma, get out of the way!" Mr. Sheridan bellowed.

"Willie, dear, what your father wants to know is whether you knew you were being disobedient. Did you, dear?"

"My client takes the Fifth Amendment," said Emma quickly.

"Will you tell your daughter to shut up?" asked Mr. Sheridan patiently.

"Emma, please, wait a minute until we are finished with Willie."

Emma didn't even hear her mother, so lost was she in her courtroom activities. All she heard was a sort of buzz running through the crowd filling the courtroom at Foley Square, in the middle of which she stood in a Bella Abzug hat.

"This boy is innocent until proven guilty by due process!" she fired back at her father.

"I knew I was bad, but I had to do it!" said Willie.

Emma hit her forehead with her hand. "Shut up, you nincompoop! How can I defend you when you insist on hanging yourself? May it please the court, I request a recess."

"Well now, son, if you knew you were bad, why did you do it?"

"Objection! Counsel is intimidating the witness!"

"I had to because I had to get that job," said Willie.

"Job?" Mr. Sheridan looked thoroughly confused.

"I got it, Daddy! I got the job!" Willie was grinning again.

"Don't volunteer information!" said Emma, clearly at the end of her tether.

"Let me get this straight. You say, son, that you have a job?"

"Yeah!" Willie was beaming. "I got a job in a musical!"

"You do, really?" asked Emma.

"He really does!" said Mrs. Sheridan, smiling, to Mr. Sheridan.

"Where is that Dipsey?" Mr. Sheridan got up. "He'll never see the light of day when I get through with him!"

"Dipsey didn't do it!" said Willie loudly. "I did! I did it all by myself!"

"Stop saying that," said Emma. "You could plead undue influence."

"This will all be over by tomorrow afternoon," said Mr. Sheridan. "I'll get in touch with whoever is producing this musical and tell him that a mistake has been made." He stood over Willie. "A very big mistake," he said slowly.

"Under the Constitution," said Emma, clearing her throat, "he has a right to the pursuit of happiness."

"I'll constitution you right out of this room," said Mr. Sheridan, looking steadily at Emma. Then he said, "Sit down, Emma."

It was the way he said it. Emma herself couldn't figure out how he had said it, how anybody could say anything that would make her sit down instantly, but whatever he had done, it worked. She sat down.

There was a change in everyone. Everyone waited for Mr. Sheridan to speak. Willie stopped wiggling his feet and sat still, looking up timorously at his father.

"I want to speak frankly to you people. I want to pretend, and to have you pretend, for the moment, that I am not a father and a husband, that I am just a man." He looked around at them. He took a stance that Emma recognized as the one he took when addressing the jury (the one and only time she had even seen him in a courtroom), one hand resting on his hip, the other gesturing with his glasses.

"What kind of man is this in front of you? Let me tell you a little bit about him." He rocked back on his heels, then forward again. "He grew up on the toughest street in Bedford-Stuyvesant. He worked from the time he

was nine years old, but he didn't bring his money home to his mother because he didn't have any mother at home. He didn't have any father at home either."

Oh, God, thought Emma, it's choke-up time. Now we're going to hear how sad his life was and how wonderful ours is and how wonderful he is as a father.

"The money he earned went to feed himself and his younger brother. His father appeared every now and then and stole whatever this boy could manage to save after the room rent and some food. This man standing before you went to the library every day and he read. This man made straight A's in school. He graduated from high school. This man worked while he went through City College, while he went through law school. This man has worked every day of his life since he was nine years old. This man was spit on every day of his life in one way or the other for being black." Mr. Sheridan seemed to lose control of himself. He sputtered. "I was treated like an animal." The words seemed to rip from his mouth, hurting him as they came through. "What you can't understand, you two kids who have always been clean and fed, is that I *felt* like an animal."

Emma's sympathy careened toward her father. She had felt like an animal, sometimes at school like a strange animal and always, upon looking in the mirror, like a fat animal. She had never thought of her father as *feeling* anything and she searched his face for signs of more. She watched him shake himself and get control. He resumed his speech.

"This man meets and rescues, yes, rescues, this woman, your mother, from a life of hardship and pain, heartbreak and sorrow because she was the daughter of a"—he sneered the word, looking straight at Willie—"dancer. This so-called dancer was a man who didn't want to work for a living. I supported this so-called dancer for the rest of his life, until he died a broken-down drunk." He paused to let this sink in.

"This man you see in front of you is now in middle age. This man fought to get his brother out of a slum, this man fought to rescue his wife from insecurity, this man is fighting today to keep all three of you living here in a clean place, going to private schools, wearing nice clothes, having a nice warm home to come back to at night with a good hot meal at the end of the day." He stopped and looked at them all.

"This man is not going to stop doing this. This man is not going to let anyone else stop him from doing this." He pointed to Willie. "This boy is going to continue to go to school, to come home to a nice home, to grow up straight with nobody laughing at him and calling him names. He will go to college. He will have a profession which is worthy of the name 'profession.' Nobody is going to stop me from seeing that this boy gets what he deserves in this world." He stopped and looked at Willie a long time.

"Son," he said finally. "We do not understand each other very well at this moment, but in the future I know that will change. I want you to listen to what I have to tell you now."

Willie's eyes were huge. Mr. Sheridan regarded him steadily.

"You will do what I say now, even though you don't agree with it and even though you don't understand it, because you will have faith that I can see further into your future than you can. You will continue to go to school and you will stop all this ridiculous talk about musicals. I will straighten out this situation you've gotten yourself into. By tomorrow it will be all over. There is to be no recurrence of this, do you understand?"

Willie stared, his mouth hanging open. Mr. Sheridan turned and walked heavily out of the room.

Swell, thought Emma. She had a vision of her father wearing the headdress of a gypsy fortune-teller and looking further into their futures than they could, into Willie's future, anyway. He hadn't mentioned any future for her. She didn't have a future.

"Don't feel too badly, Willie," purred Mrs. Sheridan.

Looking at Willie, Emma could see that it was not a question of feeling badly. It was not a question of feeling at all. Willie was totally defeated. He was a limp doll. He didn't sit in the chair, he hung in it, his head rolled to one side as though he didn't have the strength or the amount of caring it took to hold it up. He looked as though he would never care about anything in the whole world again.

"You mustn't be so sad about it," Mrs. Sheridan went on. "You'll understand when you're older, and perhaps not that much older either. Perhaps when you're fifteen or sixteen you'll be old enough and your father will feel differently. It's not as though this were the only job in a musical you'll ever be offered."

Something about this last remark created a change in Willie. He sat up straight. "I'm going to do it," he said. He stood up. "I don't care what you say, I'm going to do it!"

He ran toward the front door. Mrs. Sheridan gasped. He ran out into the hall.

Only Emma realized what was happening. She ran after him. She grabbed him just as the elevator door was opening.

"Oh, no, you don't," she said, holding him as he struggled.

"Leggo me! I got to go! I got to get out of here!" Willie was yelling. Emma dragged him back toward the apartment. Mrs. Sheridan was coming down the hall.

Willie was hysterical, screaming and crying at the top of his lungs. "Leggo! Leggo! You all hate me. Nobody cares what happens to me! I got to do it myself! Leggo me, *let go*, Emma!"

Mr. Sheridan appeared in the doorway. Emma was almost up to the door, dragging Willie.

"Give him to me," said Mr. Sheridan.

"No, Emma, don't let him!" Willie was a mess, bawling, crying, and drooling.

Mr. Sheridan pulled Emma's arms away and picked Willie up like a handkerchief. He was back inside the apartment before Emma or Mrs. Sheridan moved.

Emma ran back into the apartment. Mrs. Sheridan followed and closed the door.

Willie was still screaming. He was furious and miserable, punching out at his father's face as his father held him at arm's length.

"You bastid!" Willie shouted. "You don't understand anything. You never think about nobody but yourself. I'll kill you!"

Mrs. Sheridan looked terrified. Mr. Sheridan looked angry and puzzled at the same time. He still held Willie away from him, as one would hold an angry alley cat determined to scratch.

Willie landed his fist next to Mr. Sheridan's nose. Mr. Sheridan said, "You're hysterical," and gave Willie a slap across the face.

Willie dissolved into a bath of tears.

"Stop that!" yelled Emma. "Stop hitting him! You can go to jail for that, and besides, he's right. You never think about anybody else." God knows, you don't think about me, she thought. God knows.

Willie fell down into a little pile next to the couch.

"You never think about anybody, but just how you think they should live. You don't even know us! You don't know what we think!" Emma was livid. She didn't even know what she was saying, she was so angry.

Mr. Sheridan was looking at her in surprise.

"You just stand up here and tell us what your life was like! Who cares? You don't care what our lives are like!"

"Emma! Stop it," Mrs. Sheridan said anxiously. "You don't know what you're saying!"

"I do too know what I'm saying! And as for you, what are you but a fink? You go right along with whatever he says, and you think everything he does is wonderful, even all his dumb talking about what kind of hard time he had as a kid. What about the hard time we have? Just because we aren't starving doesn't mean everything is great. That's what *he* thinks. We get a nice hot meal at night. Is that it? Is that all we get? Is that all life is about?"

"When you don't have it," said Mr. Sheridan steadily, "you're damned right, that's what life is all about. You're so fat and spoiled you wouldn't know what life is about if it came up and hit you in the face!"

The word *fat* went through Emma like an ice pick. "Spoiled! That's a word you made up to make yourself feel better. What am I spoiled for? You mean because I don't think you're wonderful, because I don't wallow all over the floor after your stupid speech about your life and say, 'Daddy, Daddy, you're wonderful.' Well, you know why, don't you? Because I've heard that damn speech five thousand times, and I'm sick of hearing it."

"Shut up," said Mr. Sheridan.

Emma couldn't believe the hatred she saw in his eyes. He's looking at me like that, she said to herself, that hate is for me.

Her knees began to shake and all courage deserted her. "It doesn't make any difference anyway, your speech, because what has that got to do with us? You never even look at us!" She tried, but her voice shook and she knew she was finished. She knew the look of hatred would be forever in her mind, that nothing would ever take it away. She knew that it was all proven now, all the thoughts she'd had, all the guesses she had guessed about his hating her. It was true. He hated her.

"Shut up and go to your room," he said, his eyes the same.

"Don't leave, Emma!" screamed Willie. "Don't leave me here!"

"I'm not going to leave my brother," said Emma, looking at her father with the same hatred he'd given her.

A memory came over Emma, suddenly, of her father the way he had been before Willie was born. In those days he had taken her downtown with him, sometimes, way downtown to his office. He'd held her up to let her look out the big windows at the people, small as toys, and at the boats on the river. That was before he talked about nothing but *my boy* this and *my boy* that, after Willie was born.

"I don't know what's wrong with you, little girl," her father said heavily, "but you got a lot of problems. Look at her," he said to Mrs. Sheridan. "Look at the way she's looking at me."

Emma turned her back on him.

Willie thought she was leaving. "Emma!" he screamed.

She stood there with her back to her parents. "I'm not going anywhere. Come to my room with me."

Willie scrambled toward her across the floor.

"Hold it," said Mr. Sheridan. "This family is going to talk. We are going to sit right down here in this room and I don't care if it takes all night. We are going to understand what is going on here."

"I'll tell you what's going on," said Willie, clinging to Emma's leg, "you being a bastid, that's what's going on."

"Stop using that word, right now!" said Mrs. Sheridan.

"Mama, go make me a pot of coffee, will you, and see if there's some ice cream in there for the kids." Mr. Sheridan spoke gently to his wife. She hurried to the kitchen.

He sat back on the couch and put his legs up on the footstool. He looked tired. He examined the ceiling thoughtfully, then brought his gaze down slowly, very slowly, until it fastened on Willie and Emma. They watched.

"You kids sit down over there."

"Willie," said Emma, "you don't have to answer anything and you have the right to have a lawyer present."

Mrs. Sheridan came back in. "I put the coffee on." She handed a dish of ice cream to each child.

"Now that you've informed Willie of his rights," said Mr. Sheridan to Emma, "I want to remind you that I am not arresting him. I want all four of us to sit down here and have a conversation, that's all."

Emma and Willie ate ice cream, saying nothing, not looking at him.

"You sit down too," he said to Mrs. Sheridan.

"Now," he said, unbuttoning his vest, "this family seems to have quite a few misunderstandings going on here."

Quite a word to describe hatred, thought Emma. I know hatred when I see it, and nothing he's going to say is going to make any difference.

"First of all, I gather I've been boring Emma with stories of my life."

"Oh, she didn't mean that!" said Mrs. Sheridan.

"Oh, yes, she did."

I'll give him that, thought Emma, he's right on that one.

"She meant it. She doesn't like hearing that her father had a hard life."

Willie and Emma sat eating dutifully, looking down into their bowls.

"Second, she thinks her life is just as hard, maybe even harder, right, Emma?"

Emma didn't answer, didn't look up.

"And I gather my son here thinks I'm ruining his life."

Willie said nothing, just kept eating ice cream.

He doesn't even *like* ice cream, thought Emma. He's just doing that to have something to do so he won't have to look at Dad. I told him to keep his mouth shut and he is.

She took courage from this. She decided to keep her mouth shut too. What would their father do confronted by silence? What could he do?

Unless he puts us on a rack, she thought, and tears out our toenails, there's no way he can make us talk. She decided to let him rave on.

"I gather," he continued, "that I am regarded, by this family, as the worst excuse for a father the world has ever seen."

Emma recognized, and noted, the lawyer's technique of exaggeration.

"I gather that you two, at least, would like to have nothing more to do with this poor excuse for a father."

Emma realized what he was doing. He wanted to be corrected. He wanted somebody to jump up and say, "Oh, no, Daddy, we love you."

"Oh, no, dear," said Mrs. Sheridan, "I don't think they mean that at all."

There she goes, the jack-in-the-box. Emma watched her mother with contempt. How could she fall for such a stupid thing? How could she constantly reassure this man that he was an okay person, when he wasn't, he wasn't at all. He didn't know what he was talking about half the time, yet up she'd pop, still agreeing with him. Could it be that she was dumb?

She'd never thought about this. She'd never thought about either of her parents being dumb or smart, but just there in some way, like the sun was there, or a rock, or the sky. Her father couldn't be that dumb, she reasoned, because he was a lawyer. But what about her mother?

It was hard to think about her mother at all. Something hurt inside her when she tried to think about her mother. There were things she never wanted to ask her mother. There were answers she never wanted to hear. It was one thing to think about her father hating her. She hated him too, but she never wanted to know what her mother thought of her. She'd just as soon never find out about that.

"All right," said Mr. Sheridan. "You've finished that ice cream. You can stop looking in those bowls. You can look up here at me and tell me what all this is about."

Willie and Emma kept looking down.

"Got that coffee ready, Mama?"

"Yes, dear."

Mrs. Sheridan came back into the room with a mug from which steam rose. "It's past Willie's bedtime, dear."

To hear her, thought Emma, you'd think there was nothing happening at all.

Mr. Sheridan took a sip of coffee. "Mmm, that's good, good hot strong coffee. You always did make great coffee." He smiled at his wife and she smiled back at him.

Emma sneered. Look at that, she said to herself, look at them smiling at each other. Look at my mother, happy for a pat, like a good dog. Look at my father, thinking about coffee at a time like this, always thinking about his stomach.

"You can stop staring at your feet now, both of you." Mr. Sheridan sounded almost cheery now. "The big bad wolf isn't going to eat you up."

Emma groaned. She couldn't help herself.

"What's that for?" he asked. "Am I boring you again?"

Now she was in for it. She never should have uttered a sound. She decided she would make her speech on Willie's behalf, then get up and go to bed. Tomorrow she would organize a committee to come and talk to her father.

"I don't think you understand," she began, calmly, "that Willie cares a great deal about this musical and about dancing in general. I mean that he is going to be a dancer and that nothing you can do or say is going to change that. You can't stop him. If he has to wait until he's grown, he'll still do it. I don't think you see that."

Mr. Sheridan had obviously not seen it. He blinked his eyes. "I don't think, Emma, that you know very much about seven-year-olds. They don't always want to do what they think they want to do at seven. For instance, when you were seven, you wanted to be a shoplifter."

Emma's eyebrows flew up. "What?"

"You sat down and told me very seriously that you had seen a shoplifter on television and that you didn't understand what was wrong with that because all those things were out there for people to take and so why was this lady arrested when she took something. Furthermore, you thought you'd be a shoplifter when you grew up, because the lady had gotten a lot of nice things."

Emma was mortified. Her mother and father were laughing. Willie was looking up at her with sleepy, surprised eyes. She sat, her hands holding her ice-cream bowl, watching her mother and father laugh. It was not only not funny, it wasn't fair, bringing up something one had done when one was seven. She didn't think he'd proved his point, either.

"I may yet be a shoplifter," said Emma, and stood up. She loved watching their faces fall. "I'm going to bed now and Willie is going with me." She took Willie's hand and together they left the room and marched down the hall. There, she thought, see how they like being talked to the way they talk to us, see how they like a taste of their own medicine.

At Willie's door, she stopped. "Willie, go to sleep. If either one of them comes in and tries to talk to you

alone, then you yell for me and come into my room and get me if I'm asleep. Tomorrow I'm going to do something. You're going to keep that job, so go to sleep and don't think about anything."

Willie smiled. "Thanks," he said simply. "What are you going to do?"

"Don't worry. Just believe me. It's going to work out."

"Okay. Good night."

"Good night."

He went into his room. Emma walked down the hall. She could hear her mother and father muttering to each other in the living room, but she didn't even care what they were saying.

Emma lurked around the front of the luncheonette for five minutes, peering through the foggy window at Harrison Carter's Adam's apple making swift movements up and down as he drank his Coke.

She finally propelled herself through the door, feeling like the lead in a spy movie.

His greeting, a brief nod, did nothing to dispel this illusion.

"Sheridan, isn't it?" He nodded, jerking his long red head convulsively. He did look like a flamingo. His acne was fierce. His eyes, behind his glasses, looked like raisins.

It took her less time to explain the situation than she had thought it would. What seemed so complicated to her was evidently second nature to him. All the small details which seemed so interesting to her were dismissed by him. He got the point quickly. Emma was, evidently, not the first one to bring it up.

"We can't help you," he said shortly.

"Why? I thought that's what this Children's Army was for!"

"No." He sighed. "I seem to spend half my time explaining this. Unless a child is actually being damaged for life, we can't intervene."

"But ... can't you see that this attitude toward Willie would be damaging to him?"

"Yes. Of course, I can see that. Look at it this way: if your father were planning to have his feet amputated, we'd do something."

"Oh, swell."

"Or even if he were kicking Willie around. But he's not. He's simply saying he doesn't think it's a good idea for his son to be taking dancing lessons. And"—Harrison Carter took a deep breath—"I'm not sure I don't agree with him."

Emma's mouth fell open.

"Now, before you call me a male chauvinist pig, let me explain. I don't know how it happened, but it seems as though your brother is off on the wrong foot. He seems to be identifying with his mother, not his father. I can understand, therefore, that his father might want to stop this and get him back on the right track."

"You'd have to know Willie," said Emma. She felt tired. This wasn't getting anywhere at all. She was, in fact, beginning to dislike Harrison Carter. He seemed to have everything wrapped up.

"What do you do?" she asked. "Just take nice safe cases you know you can win?"

He frowned, looking down into his Coke. "You know, Sheridan, we've handled some very difficult situations. You haven't been with us long—"

"So far, nothing applies," Emma interrupted.

"What do you mean?"

"So far, nothing that's bothering me or my friends can be handled by the Army, that's what."

"The Army is always open to complaints, I'm always ready to listen to grievances." Harrison Carter's glasses seemed to grow thicker.

"Everything that's bothering us has to do with parental attitudes toward us. I mean, nobody is actually doing anything to us, but they're just ruining us, that's all."

"How?"

"By the way they think about us. It's the way they *see* us. After a while you can't help it, you start to see yourself that way."

"Oh. You mean, if your father keeps acting like you're a thief, you finally steal?"

"Sort of." Emma felt that, in some subtle way, she was losing ground. She found herself wishing her father had belted her once, then it would be simple.

Harrison Carter nodded shortly, as though now he understood the problem. This seemed to please him, reinforce him in some way.

"I'm afraid you've misunderstood the purpose, the most valid purpose of the Children's Army, and that is the question of children's rights. The Army is devoted, primarily, to the study of children's rights. The purpose of the complaints being filed and committees handling those complaints is primarily for the education of the membership. Naturally, pressing cases, which are the only kind we handle, are also helped, but the main purpose is not so much to help individuals as it is to impress upon the membership that children have no rights under our legal system. I mean, you understand, don't you, that your father actually owns you, like a slave?"

Emma nodded. She had thought of that, but not in exactly those terms. "He can't sell me, though. Remember that dope addict that tried to sell his baby on the subway?"

"Yes. As a matter of fact, we're looking into that. I think we may move on that. Now, there is a serious case."

Humiliating, thought Emma. My case isn't serious enough. I guess I sound like one of those kids who wants her wallpaper changed. "What does Willie have to do? Come out in a dress for you to see this is serious?" she snapped back at him.

Harrison Carter looked shocked, but recovered quickly. "If, for example, your father were dressing him or forcing him to dress in girl's clothes, we would handle that."

Emma felt totally frustrated. As usual when she felt like that, she attacked. "By the way, I have a serious complaint about the name of this organization."

"Oh?"

"Yes. I see no reason for it to be called an army. We have no guns, we have no plans to attack anyone—"

"We don't?"

"Do we?" She wondered, suddenly, how much of this group was submerged like an iceberg. Was all that she had seen only the tip?

"You see your reaction?" asked Harrison Carter. "That's exactly why we are called the Children's Army, because, if and when we are ever discovered by adults, or by the police, then at least we have the advantage of instilling fear into their hearts. People will be afraid of something called the Children's Army."

"What good will that do? If they get afraid, they'll really squash us!"

Harrison Carter smiled. "I don't think you need to worry about that." He smiled again.

She realized that it was a condescending smile. "Why not?"

"Well, first of all, you're a girl."

"So?" Emma felt a sinking feeling. Here it comes. They're all alike.

"If we're attacked, we'll mobilize. That is, the boys—"

"Oh, I see. You guys will handle the situation."

"Something like that." He seemed to want to change the subject.

"Where are you training all these midget John Waynes?" Emma was furious. They had lied. They had said there was no violence involved. Training for future violence was certainly violence.

"Listen, Sheridan, we've gotten off the subject here. I'd like you to understand that we would like to help your brother, but at the moment we can't. If things get worse, we can discuss it again. You see, if we went in there now, your father would throw us out, and he'd be right. He's just raising his kid the way he sees fit, and that's his legal right. Besides, he's a lawyer, he'd get suspicious, he might even investigate, he might find out things. He might blow everything up in our faces."

"You're chicken, aren't you?"

"If that's all you want to talk about, Sheridan, I think we'll break up this meeting now." Harrison Carter took a loud slurp of his Coke and got up. He pulled his jacket around him and went out the door, never looking back.

Emma ordered a hamburger. When it was put down in front of her, she ordered another. She ate steadily through the first and through the second.

The situation, she said to herself, is impossible. My father controls my life. He controls Willie's life. I am only fighting for Willie because I want to fight for myself.

She let this last thought fly through her mind like a southbound goose, not really hearing herself think it.

When it gets right down to it, the Children's Army is no different from any adult organization. Males were in control and would depend upon force. Did they really think they were going to have a war with adults? She had a vision of Harrison Carter in a uniform on a salt flat in Jersey somewhere, saluting and goose-stepping in front of a bunch of three-year-olds.

"Ridiculous," she said aloud, then remembered where she was. She ordered another chocolate milk.

Whatever the Children's Army was or wasn't, it was not going to help her now. That was clear.

Where did things stand?

This afternoon Willie was being allowed to go to rehearsal. He had told Emma at breakfast that their mother had told Dipsey to pick him up after school. Emma had gotten Willie out of the house before Mrs. Sheridan could change her mind.

My father will find out about it tonight. It's a good thing I ate something, she said to herself as she got up to leave. God knows what dinner will be like.

Katherine Paterson (b. 1932)

Born in China to American missionary parents, Katherine Paterson has an intuitive and experiential understanding of children who feel out of place and not at home. In *The Great Gilly Hopkins* (1978), Galadriel Hopkins—known as Gilly—is a foster child who has been shunted from one family to another as long as she can remember. Until she meets Maime Trotter, a huge, ungainly foster mother, no one has really cared about her. She yearns with all her heart for her real mother, Courtney, who lives in California. Gilly is smart—very smart—and she has been hurt and disappointed so often that she has built a tough shell to protect herself. She manipulates her teachers and classmates and, in fact, everyone she meets, to keep from revealing her vulnerability. In the chapter "Harassing Miss Harris," she tries to get her African American math teacher,

Miss Harris, to blow her cool, only to discover that Miss Harris is more than a match for her—and more like herself than Gilly recognizes.

In "Homecoming," the concluding chapter of the book, after a desperate attempt to run away and find her mother, Gilly finally gets to meet her. She finds out, however, that Courtney is not the ideal mother she always dreamed of. Instead, she realizes that Trotter, whom she ran away from but now cannot return to because she has been reunited with her grandmother, is the one person who has most genuinely loved her. Humble Trotter, despite her unprepossessing exterior, is a profoundly loving and wise person, and her advice to Gilly encapsulates Paterson's spiritual insights: Life is tough, but the struggle is worth it. As in many of her novels, Paterson touches on sensitive spots in our social consciousness: subtle undercurrents of racism, the controversial subject of religious belief, and the inadequacies of our institutions (such as family, church, school, or government agencies) to meet our needs. *The Great Gilly Hopkins* has been criticized both by religious fundamentalists who object to Gilly's language ("go to hell," "dammit") and by secularists who dislike Paterson's religious message: Trotter is a kind of incarnation of God.

"Hope and Happy Endings" is from Paterson's acceptance speech for the 1988 Regina Medal (awarded by the Catholic Library Association for her distinguished contributions to children's literature). Literary awards and medals, so much hoopla as they involve, may be justified by the fact that they elicit speeches from their recipients, speeches in which authors reflect on their practice as writers. Award speeches are frequently published and reprinted as valuable essays in which authors discuss the meanings of literature. Certainly this is the case for Katherine Paterson, who has won her share—or more—of distinguished awards. Here she examines her "body of work" with the question in mind of what it means to provide child readers with hope. For Paterson, it does not mean tacked-on happy endings. What it does mean, it emerges, is something mythic, something religious or spiritual, having to do with the difficulty and pain of life (the weight of reality), but also with the yearning and seeking for something comforting and transcendent—or, to be more accurate, for Someone greater than ourselves. She responds to her critics, and in the process clarifies and explains her own position that "children do not go to novels looking for role models. . . . When they go to a serious novel they expect to find truth, and everyone knows that role models are ideals, not realities. They want hope rooted in reality, not wishful thinking." One's response to Paterson's often-bittersweet endings may depend, in part, on whether one thinks Paterson's brand of hope is real or imaginary. (See other discussions of Paterson's novels in Parts 4 and 5.)

From *The Great Gilly Hopkins*

HARASSING MISS HARRIS

By the third week in October, Gilly had caught up with her class and gone on ahead. She tried to tell herself that she had forced Miss Harris into a corner from which the woman could give her nothing but A's. Surely, it must kill old priss face to have to put rave notices—"Excellent" "Good, clear thinking" "Nice Work"—on the papers of someone who so obviously disliked her.

But Miss Harris was a cool customer. If she knew that Gilly despised her, she never let on. So at this point Gilly was not ready to pull her time-honored trick of stopping work just when the teacher had become convinced that she had a bloody genius on her hands. That had worked so beautifully at Hollywood

Gardens—the whole staff had gone totally ape when suddenly one day she began turning in blank sheets of paper. It was the day after Gilly had overheard the principal telling her teacher that Gilly had made the highest score in the entire school's history on her national aptitude tests, but, of course, no one knew that she knew, so an army of school psychologists had been called in to try to figure her out. Since no one at school would take the blame for Gilly's sudden refusal to achieve, they decided to blame her foster parents, which made Mrs. Nevins so furious that she demanded that Miss Ellis remove Gilly at once instead of waiting out the year—the year Mrs. Nevins had reluctantly agreed to, after her first complaints about Gilly's sassy and underhanded ways.

But something warned Gilly that Miss Harris was not likely to crumble at the sight of a blank sheet of paper. She was more likely simply to ignore it. She was different from the other teachers Gilly had known. She did not appear to be dependent on her students. There was no evidence that they fed either her anxieties or her satisfactions. In Gilly's social-studies book there was a picture of a Muslim woman of Saudi Arabia, with her body totally covered except for her eyes. It reminded Gilly somehow of Miss Harris, who had wrapped herself up in invisible robes. Once or twice a flash in the eyes seemed to reveal something to Gilly of the person underneath the protective garments, but such flashes were so rare that Gilly hesitated to say even to herself what they might mean.

Some days it didn't matter to Gilly what Miss Harris was thinking or not thinking. It was rather comfortable to go to school with no one yelling or cajoling—to know that your work was judged on its merits and was not affected by the teacher's personal opinion of the person doing the work. It was a little like throwing a basketball. If you aimed right, you got it through the hoop; it was absolutely just and absolutely impersonal.

But other days, Miss Harris's indifference grated on Gilly. She was not used to being treated like everyone else. Ever since the first grade, she had forced her teachers to make a special case of her. She had been in charge of her own education. She had learned what and when it pleased her. Teachers had courted her and cursed her, but no one before had simply melted her into the mass.

As long as she had been behind the mass, she tolerated this failure to treat her in a special manner, but

now, even the good-morning smile seemed to echo the math computer's "Hello, Gilly number 58706, today we will continue our study of fractions." *Crossing threshold of classroom causes auto-teacher to light up and say "Good morning." For three thousand dollars additional, get the personalized electric-eye model that calls each student by name.*

For several days she concentrated on the vision of a computer-activated Miss Harris. It seemed to fit. Brilliant, cold, totally, absolutely, and maddeningly fair, all her inner workings shinily encased and hidden from view. Not a Muslim but a flawless tamperproof machine.

The more Gilly thought about it, the madder she got. No one had a right to cut herself off from other people like that. Just once, before she left this dump, she'd like to pull a wire inside that machine. Just once she'd like to see Harris-6 scream in anger—fall apart—break down.

But Miss Harris wasn't like Trotter. You didn't have to be around Trotter five minutes before you knew the direct route to her insides—William Ernest Teague. Miss Harris wasn't hooked up to other people. It was like old *Mission Impossible* reruns on TV: *Your mission, if you decide to accept it, is to get inside this computerized robot, discover how it operates, and neutralize its effectiveness.* The self-destructing tape never told the mission-impossible team how to complete their impossible mission, but the team always seemed to know. Gilly, on the other hand, hadn't a clue.

It was TV that gave her the clue. She hadn't been thinking about Miss Harris at all. She'd been thinking, actually, of how to get the rest of Mr. Randolph's money and hadn't been listening to the news broadcast. Then somehow it began sending a message into her brain. A high government official had told a joke on an airplane that had gotten him fired. Not just any joke, mind you. A dirty joke. But that wasn't what got him fired. The dirty joke had been somehow insulting to blacks. Apparently all the black people in the country and even some whites were jumping up and down with rage. Unfortunately the commentator didn't repeat the joke. She could have used it. But at least she knew now something that might be a key to Harris-6.

She borrowed some money from Trotter for "school supplies," and bought a pack of heavy white construction paper and magic markers. Behind the closed door of her bedroom she began to make a greeting card, fashioning it as closely as she could to the tall, thin, "comic" cards on the special whirlaround stand in the drugstore.

At first she tried to draw a picture on the front, wasting five or six precious sheets of paper in the attempt. Cursing her incompetence, she stole one of Trotter's magazines and cut from it a picture of a tall, beautiful black woman in an Afro. Her skin was a little darker than Miss Harris's, but it was close enough.

Above the picture of the woman she lettered these words carefully (She could print well, even if her drawing stank):

They're saying "Black is beautiful!"

Then below the picture:

But the best that I can figger
Is everyone who's saying so
Looks mighty like a

And inside in tiny letters:

person with a vested interest in
maintaining this point of view.

She had to admit it. It was about the funniest card she'd ever seen in her life. Gifted Gilly—a funny female of the first rank. If her bedroom had been large enough, she'd have rolled on the floor. As it was, she lay on the bed hugging herself and laughing until she was practically hysterical. Her only regret was that the card was to be anonymous. She would have enjoyed taking credit for this masterpiece.

She got to school very early the next morning and sneaked up the smelly stairs to Harris-6 before the janitor had even turned on the hall lights. For a moment she feared that the door might be locked, but it opened easily under her hand. She slipped the card into the math book that lay in the middle of Miss Harris's otherwise absolutely neat desk. She wanted to be sure that no one else would discover it and ruin everything.

All day long, but especially during math, Gilly kept stealing glances at Miss Harris. Surely at any minute, she would pick up the book. Surely she could see the end of the card sticking out and would be curious. But Miss Harris left the book exactly where it was. She borrowed a book from a student when she needed to refer to one. It was as though she sensed her own was booby-trapped.

By lunchtime Gilly's heart, which had started the day jumping with happy anticipation, was kicking angrily at her stomach. By midafternoon she was so mad that nothing had happened that she missed three spelling words, all of which she knew perfectly well. At the three o'clock bell, she slammed her chair upside down on her desk and headed for the door.

"Gilly."

Her heart skipped as she turned toward Miss Harris.

"Will you wait a minute, please?"

They both waited, staring quietly at each other until the room emptied. Then Miss Harris got up from her desk and closed the door. She took a chair from one of the front desks and put it down a little distance from her own. "Sit down for a minute, won't you?"

Gilly sat. The math book lay apparently undisturbed, the edge of the card peeping out at either end.

"You may find this hard to believe, Gilly, but you and I are very much alike."

Gilly snapped to attention despite herself.

"I don't mean in intelligence, although that is true, too. Both of us are smart, and we know it. But the thing that brings us closer than intelligence is anger. You and I are two of the angriest people I know." She said all this in a cool voice that cut each word in a thin slice from the next and then waited, as if to give Gilly a chance to challenge her. But Gilly was fascinated, like the guys in the movies watching the approach of a cobra. She wasn't about to make a false move.

"We do different things with our anger, of course. I was always taught to deny mine, which I did and still do. And that makes me envy you. Your anger is still up here on the surface where you can look it in the face, make friends with it if you want to."

She might have been talking Swahili for all Gilly could understand.

"But I didn't ask you to stay after school to tell you how intelligent you are or how much I envy you, but to thank you for your card."

It had to be sarcasm, but Harris-6 was smiling almost like a human being. When did the cobra strike?

"I took it to the teachers' room at noon and cursed

creatively for twenty minutes. I haven't felt so good in years."

She'd gone mad like the computer in *2001*. Gilly got up and started backing toward the door. Miss Harris just smiled and made no effort to stop her. As soon as she got to the stairs, Gilly began to run and, cursing creatively, ran all the way home.

HOMECOMING

The plane was late. It seemed to Gilly that everything in this world that you can't stand to wait one extra minute for is always late. Her stomach was pretzeled with eagerness and anxiety. She stood sweating in the chill of the huge waiting room, the perspiration pouring down the sleeves of her new blouse. She'd probably ruin it and stink besides.

Then, suddenly, when she'd almost stopped straining her eyes with looking at it, the door opened, and people began to come off the motor lounge into the airport. All kinds of people, all sizes, all colors, all of them rushing. Many looking about for family or friends, finding them with little cries of joy and hugs. Tired fussy babies, children dragging on their mothers. Businessmen, heads down, swinging neat thin leather briefcases. Grandparents laden with shopping bags of Christmas presents. But no Courtney.

The pretzel turned to stone. It was all a lie. She would never come. The door blurred. Gilly wanted to leave. She didn't want to cry in the stupid airport, but just at that moment she heard Nonnie say in a quavering voice, "Courtney."

"Hello, Nonnie."

But this person wasn't Courtney. It couldn't be Courtney! Courtney was tall and willowy and gorgeous. The woman who stood before them was no taller than Nonnie and just as plump, although she wore a long cape, so it was hard to make out her real shape. Her hair was long, but it was dull and stringy— a dark version of Agnes Stokes's, which had always needed washing. A flower child gone to seed. Gilly immediately pushed aside the disloyal thought.

Nonnie had sort of put her hand on the younger woman's arm in a timid embrace, but there was a huge embroidered shoulder bag between the two of them. "This is Galadriel, Courtney."

For a second, the smile, the one engraved on Gilly's soul, flashed out. The teeth were perfect. She was face to face with Courtney Rutherford Hopkins. She could no longer doubt it. "Hi." The word almost didn't come out. She wondered what she was supposed to do. Should she try to kiss Courtney or something?

At this point Courtney hugged her, pressing the huge bag into Gilly's chest and stomach and saying across her shoulder to Nonnie, "She's as tall as I am," sounding a little as though Gilly weren't there.

"She's a lovely girl," said Nonnie.

"Well, of course, she is," Courtney stepped back and smiled her gorgeous heart-shattering smile. "She's mine, isn't she?"

Nonnie smiled back, rather more weakly than her daughter had. "Maybe we should get your luggage."

"I've got it," said Courtney, slapping her shoulder bag. "It's all right here."

Nonnie looked a little as though she'd been smacked in the face. "But—" she began and stopped.

"How many clothes can you wear in two days?"

Two days? Then Courtney had come to get her after all.

"I told you on the phone that I'd come for Christmas and see for myself how the kid was doing. . . ."

"But when I sent you the money, . . ."

Courtney's face was hard and set with lines between the brows. "Look. I came, didn't I? Don't start pushing me before I'm hardly off the plane. My god, I've been gone thirteen years, and you still think you can tell me what to do." She slung the bag behind her back. "Let's get out of here."

Nonnie shot Gilly a look of pain. "Courtney—"

She hadn't come because she wanted to. She'd come because Nonnie had paid her to. And she wasn't going to stay. And she wasn't going to take Gilly back with her. "I will always love you." It was a lie. Gilly had thrown away her whole life for a stinking lie.

"I gotta go to the bathroom," Gilly said to Nonnie. She prayed they wouldn't follow her there, because the first thing she was going to do was vomit, and the second was run away.

She tried to vomit, but nothing happened. She was still shaking from the effort when she dropped her coins in the pay telephone beside the restroom and dialed. It rang four times.

"Hello."

"Trotter, it's me, Gilly." God, don't let me break down like a baby.

"Gilly, honey. Where are you?"

"Nowhere. It doesn't matter. I'm coming home."

She could hear Trotter's heavy breathing at the other end of the line. "What's the matter, baby? Your mom didn't show?"

"No, she came."

"Oh, my poor baby."

Gilly was crying now. She couldn't help herself. "Trotter, it's all wrong. Nothing turned out the way it's supposed to."

"How you mean supposed to? Life ain't supposed to be nothing, 'cept maybe tough."

"But I always thought that when my mother came. . . ."

"My sweet baby, ain't no one ever told you yet? I reckon I thought you had that all figured out."

"What?"

"That all that stuff about happy endings is lies. The only ending in this world is death. Now that might or might not be happy, but either way, you ain't ready to die, are you?"

"Trotter, I'm not talking about dying. I'm talking about coming home."

But Trotter seemed to ignore her. "Sometimes in this world things come easy, and you tend to lean back and say, 'Well, finally, happy ending. This is the way things is supposed to be.' Like life owed you good things."

"Trotter—"

"And there is lots of good things, baby. Like you coming to be with us here this fall. That was a mighty good thing for me and William Ernest. But you just fool yourself if you expect good things all the time.

They ain't what's regular—don't nobody owe 'em to you."

"If life is so bad, how come you're so happy?"

"Did I say bad? I said it was tough. Nothing to make you happy like doing good on a tough job, now is there?"

"Trotter, stop preaching at me. I want to come home."

"You're home, baby. Your grandma is home."

"I want to be with you and William Ernest and Mr. Randolph."

"And leave her all alone? Could you do that?"

"Dammit, Trotter. Don't try to make a stinking Christian out of me."

"I wouldn't try to make nothing out of you." There was a quiet at the other end of the line. "Me and William Ernest and Mr. Randolph kinda like you the way you are."

"Go to hell, Trotter," Gilly said softly.

A sigh. "Well, I don't know about that. I had planned on settling permanently somewheres else."

"Trotter"—She couldn't push the word hard enough to keep the squeak out—"I love you."

"I know, baby. I love you, too."

She put the phone gently on the hook and went back into the bathroom. There she blew her nose on toilet tissue and washed her face.

By the time she got back to an impatient Courtney and a stricken Nonnie, she had herself well under control.

"Sorry to make you wait," Gilly said. "I'm ready to go home now." No clouds of glory, perhaps, but Trotter would be proud.

Hope and Happy Endings

I am very glad to be here today. I am honored to be the thirtieth recipient of this distinguished award, especially when I read the names that have preceded mine. Today is one of those occasions when I wish my Grandmother Goetchius were still alive. Grandmother would be amazed to know that I turned out something other than trifling. She used to make sweeping pronouncements that all of her children and grandchildren were "*far* above the average," but when it came down to specific children—perhaps I should say, this specific child—she despaired daily.

There was a time when I would come home from school with a book in my hand, push open the front door, and without removing my overcoat fall prone upon the living room floor, where I lay reading until suppertime. I remember one particular afternoon, my mother was quietly sweeping the rug around me. My infuriated grandmother tolerated this scene as long as she could, then came and stood over my inert body and announced to my mother in a voice tremulous with disappointment, "I'm afraid Katherine is a lover of luxury."

Usually I couldn't hear anything when I was reading, but I remember hearing that judgment and swelling up with self-righteous indignation. I was reading *A Tale of Two Cities,* for Pete's sake, Dickens—a classic. Anybody else's grandmother would be proud to have such an intellectual grandchild, thought I. But I didn't say it. We didn't argue with my grandmother. I had graduated from a church college, earned a master's degree in English Bible, become a missionary, and married a Presbyterian minister before she died, but by the time I started straightening out, she was having to be introduced to me every time we met, so I don't think she ever gave me any credit.

Actually if she were alive and in her right mind today, she'd be a hundred and twenty-one and probably fretting that this lovely medal was being presented to me in New York City by Roman Catholics. I grew up among people for whom there was something sinister, if not slightly scandalous, about consorting with Yankees and/or Catholics. The Goetchius family of Georgia traced their Calvinist roots to the Netherlands of the sixteenth century.

There's a rather bizarre legend about that first Protestant Goetchius. He was examined, condemned, and beheaded during the Inquisition. This in itself was pretty heavy stuff for me to listen to as a child, but Aunt Helen, who was telling me the story, couldn't leave it at that. "And after the ax fell," she told me, "your ancestor rose to his feet and walked three steps before he dropped dead. That," she said, "proves that a Goetchius cannot be easily defeated."

What it proved to me at twelve was that I should take my Aunt Helen's stories with a grain of salt. She was, after all, sort of the black sheep of the family— the only one of us who smoked cigarettes, played cards, and recanted the faith to live out her life as an Episcopalian.

There is another reason it is probably fortunate that my grandmother didn't live to see this day. She was a foremost proponent of the "Be sweet, my child, and let who will be clever" Southern school of raising female children. I'm sure she would have felt that for me to see my name included in the list of winners of this award would be perilous for my soul. My mother would have handled the threat with more equanimity. After I was awarded a Newbery Medal on the heels of a National Book Award, friends and family asked my mother in alarm: "What will happen to Katherine? What will all this notoriety do to her?" My mother replied, "You don't need to worry about Katherine. She has *plenty* to keep her humble."

I'm keeping in mind all those things today as you are honoring the body of my work. I love that phrase, "body of work." Actually, to be honest, I love my books. All of them. It is similar to the way I feel about my four grown children. There they are, all different, none perfect, but I look at them—bright, funny, beautiful, loving people—and I'm very grateful to have had a part in their lives. Similarly, I look at the books and they are all different, none perfect, but I reread them with affection and a sort of surprised admiration. Knowing myself as well as I do, I am always a bit amazed that I could have written them, and grateful— believe me, very grateful.

I tell myself it's all right if my books are not universally loved and admired, but of course I don't mean that, not in my heart of hearts. I want everyone to love them as I do, faults and all. Which makes this award especially welcome. It says to me that you love them all—not just one of them. But the truth of the matter is there are people who are not as kind as the Catholic Library Association—those who fail to love my books— and I have to learn to deal with that or find another line of work.

One of my coping mechanisms over the years has involved the designing of an imaginary book jacket— the jacket for the one-volume complete works of Katherine Paterson. I don't know yet what will be on the front, but the back will consist of blurbs from reviews and articles. You know those stock paperback blurbs: "Believable and moving . . ." "So and so is a breathtakingly brilliant writer." "You emerge from this marvelous novel as if from a dream, the mind on fire. . . ."

No writer I know believes those blurbs—especially the ones that have three dots preceding or following the adjectives. It is nice to have compliments in a review that make for good blurbs on your paperback, but those are not what a writer remembers. The reviews that stick tighter than a burr are the negative ones.

Those are the ones that you need to learn how to deal with. So I am going to put them, or some of the choicest ones, on my dream jacket. Let me give you a sampling: "Gilly Hopkins is a robot constructed for the purpose of instructing the young." "Pompous, pretentious, and one wonders indeed why it was ever published." ". . . exceedingly irksome." ". . . a clutter of clinched metaphors . . ." "[dot dot dot] trivial [dot dot dot]." "Sara Louise's bright new beginning moves with astonishing haste to a final dead end."

That one really smarts. Particularly, I think, because I get a lot of questions about the endings of my books. Not long ago a child asked me, "Why are your endings all so sad?" I was a bit thrown. I know sad things happen in my books, but I certainly don't perceive of them as all having sad endings. I was forced to take another look at the body of my work, or at least at the endings of my novels, and I must confess that none of them has what might be conventionally called a happy ending. But does that make them sad? Or, as one troubled mother complained to me when speaking of *Gilly Hopkins,* "totally without hope"?

Surely not. I couldn't write a book "totally without hope." I wouldn't know how. "But what do you mean by hope?" Sarah Smedman, a children's literature scholar and a nun, asked me that question last fall, and I have been mulling it over ever since. Have you noticed that about questions? The really good ones can never be answered on the spot. The better the question, the longer it will take to answer. Which makes me wonder why we expect children immediately to raise their hands and spout forth instant wisdom. Perhaps it is because we are realistic about the quality of our questions.

Anyhow, the question Sarah asked me was perfectly legitimate. What did I mean by hope? I have from time to time made sweeping pronouncements about hope as it has to do with fiction, particularly children's fiction. Sarah had every right to think, therefore, that I had already carefully thought through my own definition of the word *hope.*

I was somewhat embarrassed to hear myself defining in negatives—what I didn't mean by hope, certainly as I thought of hope in my books. I didn't mean wishful thinking. I didn't mean happily ever after, or even conventional happy endings. Certainly in the scope of a juvenile novel I didn't mean hope of heaven or the Second Coming. So what did I mean?

When some readers—especially adult readers, in my experience—define hope in children's books, they do seem to mean wishful thinking. One critic asks:

> Must Paterson's capable, imaginative protagonist-narrator in *Jacob Have I Loved,* Sara Louise Bradshaw, be forced, in the name of historical accuracy, into the same kind of quietistic and blatantly antifeminist womanhood as her mother before her? Why must we witness "Wheeze" Bradshaw cheerfully trading her hopes of medical school for marriage to a widowed farmer in an Appalachian community no less isolated by the mountains than Rass Island was by the sea, while her gifted but pusillanimous twin sister Caroline, having stolen Wheeze's old friend Call Purnell for her husband, pursues wealth and fame as an opera singer in New York? Could Paterson provide no more equitable conclusion than this to her often powerful tale of sibling jealousy and rage—for the sake not only of her narrator's aspirations but those of her teenaged female readers as well?

My temptation here is to start yelling at the critic. What did you want for an ending? I want to say. Would you have been satisfied if Louise had ended up a feminist radiologist in Baltimore? Would that have made her worthy in your eyes? Or, Screebies! Can't you see that Louise is more a doctor than any M.D. you or I are ever likely to meet, limited as our doctors are to specialties and technology and frightened as they are by lawsuits? This woman is out there really doing it. She doesn't need a diploma on the wall to prove to her patients that she's qualified. She proves that every day in actual practice. And what's this about her mother? What have you got against women who make the conscious choice to be homemakers? This woman had a fine husband who loved her. She raised two terrific daughters. Which reminds me. Wherever did you get the idea that Caroline was pusillanimous? Don't you know better than to take as gospel the adolescent Louise's description of her sister? The whole portrait is done in green, for heaven's sake!

You'll be relieved to know that I haven't even written a letter to the editor of that scholarly journal. I've just quietly seethed that an intelligent scholar should so malign these people that I care for so deeply.

And as for those teenage female readers for whom he is concerned, none of them has ever complained to me about my antifeminism or indeed despised the ending that so many adult critics love to hate. I think we are dealing here with a fundamental disagreement between the young reader and the adult teacher, parent, or critic. Children do not go to novels looking for role models. They may go for adventure, for escape, for laughter, or for more serious concerns—to understand themselves, to understand others, to rehearse the experiences that someday they may live out in the flesh. But they don't go for role models. When they go to a serious novel they expect to find truth, and everyone knows that role models are ideals, not realities. They want hope rooted in reality, not wishful thinking.

The child who asked about my sad endings was asking for something different. I think she was expressing a wistful yearning we all share for happily ever after, and I am the last person to denigrate happily ever after. There is a stage in a child's development when his basic psychic diet should consist of large servings of fairy tales.

We owe Bruno Bettelheim a great debt. Most of us have known in our guts that we needed fairy tales, but Bettelheim has articulated the important role they play in children's lives. Children, he reminds us, think in sweeping extremes: "I'll never learn how to tie my shoes." "It'll kill me if I eat this squash." "I'm always going to hate Susie." "Mom, you're the most beautiful woman in the world!"—There's one four-year-old's sweeping declaration I hated to let go. "No one will ever like me ever again." "I hate you! I hate you! I hate you! I hope you die and never come back here again!" The child's fears and feelings are enormous and unrealistic, and thus he needs hopes that are enormous and unrealistic.

Nothing less than happily ever after will satisfy children who see themselves helpless and hedged in by huge and powerful persons. And so the fairy tale becomes a great source of comfort for them. By the time a child is reading fairy tales, she knows the difference between fantasy and reality. But the fairy tale gives the child hope. You are a nobody now, poor little Cinderella, but just you wait. You will show them all someday. It won't be easy, but you will grow up. You have a wicked stepmother who will try to stop you, but you also have a fairy godmother who will come to your aid. You must discipline yourself, obey the limitations that her magic lays upon you, and then someday, your prince will come and you will truly be somebody.

The hope that the fairy tale provides is a limited hope. It is, according to Bettelheim, simply the hope that the child will grow up. Realistic stories can't give a child this same hope, Bettelheim says, because "his unrealistic fears require unrealistic hopes. By comparison with the child's wishes, realistic and limited promises are experienced as deep disappointment, not as consolation. But they are all that a relatively realistic story can offer."

I have to admit that I think there is a great deal of truth in this view of both realistic fiction and fairy stories. And I say this as I remember that my youngest read *Cinderella* over and over again. I know perfectly well who the wicked stepmother was, and I hope like mad that the fairy godmother is the same person in this scenario. But if I say that Bettelheim is right, then don't I have to stop writing? Even if I made a switch to fairy tales, they couldn't be the old ones, the ones buried in our primitive psyches, the ones that have the power to move a child from his infantile fears and fixations toward the relative integration and self-empowerment of adulthood.

It is no use to pretend that I read *The Uses of Enchantment* before I began writing realistic fiction for children, figured out the fallacy in Bettelheim's argument, and then proceeded to write my own books on the basis of a well-thought-out philosophy. In the first place, I started writing my first novel in 1968, and *The Uses of Enchantment* wasn't published until after I had written five of my now nine novels. Even after I had read it, and found myself in essential agreement with its premises, I went right ahead and wrote the same old thing for four more novels.

I do, you see, what most writers do. I write what I can. And I never think about what I'm doing until afterward. I philosophize when questions come after the book is published. Someone asks: "Why did you do such and such?" and I wonder, "Why *did* I do such and such?" and I begin to write a speech that essentially speculates on why I did something that at the time was done totally subconsciously. This is one of those speeches.

Last month our public television station broadcast the film musical *Oliver*. *Oliver Twist* is a good example of *peripeteia* or reversal of fortune, which is as popular a theme in fairy tales as it is in Greek drama, and a favorite plot with Dickens. Oliver starts out as a foundling in an orphanage and ends up as the heir to the kindly Mr. Brownlow. Dickens loves to make things work out happily in the end. Sometimes, as in

Nicholas Nickleby, he makes us positively dizzy as he whirls about tying up all the loose ends and making all the good guys delirious with newfound joy.

I first saw the film *Oliver* years ago, so I'd frankly forgotten exactly how it ended. I remembered, of course, Nancy's tragic sacrifice and Bill Sykes's horrible end. I even remembered that wonderful non-Dickensian duet that sends our beloved rogues, Fagin and the Artful Dodger, skipping out of town together to work their villainy elsewhere.

But I'd forgotten the actual ending. What would the writer do with this devastated child, who has seen his beloved Nancy savagely murdered and then been taken hostage by the killer, dragged through the slums of London, only to end up high above the narrow street on a rotting scaffold that is rocking back and forth, back and forth, as the heavy body of Bill Sykes swings below in a grotesque parody of a public hanging?

Dickens himself has no trouble turning Oliver's trauma into an almost fairy-tale happy ending. Of course it takes three chapters and twenty-eight closely printed pages to do it, but as always, Dickens manages to tie every stray thread into a splendiferous macramé of justice and joy. The evil are punished, the good are bountifully rewarded, and those in the middle repent and reap such benefits as befit their middling estate. I've often wished that Dickens could have had Virginia Buckley for an editor. The ending of *Oliver Twist* is a dramatic example of what travesties can befall a good writer with a bad editor, or, as I darkly suspect, no editor at all.

But would the writer of a modern musical handle the ending any better? Would he insist on a reprise of "Who Will Buy?" with all of London singing lustily while clicking their heels in dazzling sunlight—which would come as a blinding surprise to anyone who has ever lived in the actual gray and drizzly city?

No. The writer of the film turned away from both the excesses of Dickens and the conventions of the musical comedy form. As you may remember, the carriage draws up in front of Mr. Brownlow's house. Mr. Brownlow and an exhausted Oliver get out and walk up the front steps. The kindly housekeeper comes out to greet them and, without a word spoken, much less sung, Oliver puts his arms around her and weeps.

What a lovely ending. I wish Dickens could have seen it. No singing, no dancing, no words. Any of them would have diminished Oliver's pain. We know

from the way Mr. Brownlow puts his arm lightly across the boy's shoulder as they walk up the steps and the way the housekeeper's warm arms enfold him, that Oliver will be cared for. But his pain is not trivialized, much less erased. He will grow up to be a wise and compassionate gentleman, but deep in his heart, he will bear the hunger of the workhouse and the grief of Jacob's Island to his grave.

This, I maintain, is a proper ending. Perhaps I should amend that. It is a proper ending for me. It is not, strictly speaking, a happy ending. It is certainly not happily ever after. But it is a positive demonstration of what I mean when I speak of hope in stories for children.

In order to make this clearer, I want to take you back to the Bible—to the call of Moses. You remember that God first speaks to Moses from a burning bush on the mountainside. The reason Moses is wandering around that mountain in the first place is that he's a fugitive from justice. He killed a man and then had to run before the law got him. He's living in the desert, most likely under an assumed name, working as a shepherd for his father-in-law, when God speaks to him out of a burning bush and tells him to do something totally crazy: Go back to Egypt where your picture is on the post office wanted posters, go straight to Pharoah's palace and tell him you've come to organize the free labor he has slaving away on those treasure cities he's building. Pharoah's workers are going to stage a permanent walkout because I've chosen you to march this unruly mob across the trackless desert to the country your ancestors left four hundred years ago, which is now inhabited by fierce nations who live in walled cities.

Moses is understandably reluctant. He offers a number of objections to this plan. Nothing much has been heard from God for the last four hundred years. God isn't exactly in the forefront of everybody's mind these days. If Moses starts talking to the average Israelite about God, the fellow's likely to reply, "God who?" So Moses says, "If I come to the people of Israel and say to them, 'The God of your fathers has sent me to you,' and they ask me, 'What is his name?' what shall I say to them?"

All of us know enough about ancient thought to know the power of the name. If the people of Israel know God's true name, they will in a sense have power over God. But at this point in the story, something wonderful happens. God does indeed give Moses a name, but it proves to be unpronounceable and a verb to boot. "Say this to the people of Israel," God says, "'I am who I am and I will be who I will be has sent me to you.'" Here is a God of the present time—of the world as it is and also the God of what will be. Nothing will ever be the same again. Being human, we will have to pronounce something to take the place of the name of this reality. We will assign nouns and pronouns, but we won't have hold of God thereby. The One whose true name is a verb is the One in whom we live and move and have our being. It is he who has hold of us. The story also assures us that the One who is and will be hears the cries of those in distress and acts to deliver them.

As a spiritual descendant of Moses, and of the prophets and apostles who followed him, I have to think of hope in this context. We are not really optimists as the common definition goes, because we, like Moses, must be absolute realists about the world in which we find ourselves. And this world looked at squarely does not allow optimism to flourish. Hope for us cannot simply be wishful thinking, nor can it be only the desire to grow up to and take control of our own lives. Hope is a yearning rooted in reality that pulls us toward the radical biblical vision of the world remade.

Those of us who worship a God whose name is an unpronounceable verb that can be translated both "I am" and "I will be," we know that what is reality for us at this moment is not the sum total of truth. We are always being pulled toward an ultimate vision of a world where truth and justice and peace do prevail in a time when the knowledge of God will cover the earth as the waters cover the sea. It is a scene that finds humanity living in harmony with nature, and all nations beating their swords into plowshares and walking together in the light of God's glory. Now there's a happy ending for you—the only purely happy ending I know of. The Book of Revelation calls it a beginning, but that's another story.

Paul tells us all creation is standing on tiptoe waiting for the ushering in of this vision. Or, we could say, the pull of that vision draws all creation toward itself. And the movement from where we are today on this dark and shadowed planet to that cosmic burst of glory—that movement is the hope by which we live.

If we think of hope in this way, there is no way that we can tack it on the end of a story like pinning the tail on the donkey. A story for children should at least have a happy ending, some say, as though happy endings are an adequate definition of hope—as though a story for children, as distinct from a story told to adults, is incomplete without a bit of cheer pasted to the end.

So what counts as an ending in a story for children by a writer who lives by hope? In the middle of writing my latest book, *Park's Quest,* I found myself once again engaged in a search for the lost parent. I was horrified. What's with you? I asked myself. Why are you always looking for a lost parent? You had two perfectly good parents of your own who loved you and did the best they could for you under often difficult circumstances. Why this constant theme of searching or yearning for the absent parent?

I think I know at last the answer to that question. I'm not sure, as I'm never sure about these things, but I think the fact that this theme keeps coming up in my books reveals a longing—not so much for my own parents—but a yearning for the One whose name is unpronounceable but whom Jesus taught us to call Father.

So the hope of my books is the hope of yearning. It is always incomplete, as all true hope must be. It is always in tension, rooted in this fallen earth but growing, yearning, stretching toward the new creation. I am sure that it does not satisfy children in the sense that Cinderella or Jack the Giant Killer will satisfy them. I know children need and deserve the kind of satisfaction they they may get only from the old fairy tales. For children who are still hungry for happily ever after, my endings will be invariably disappointing. Children need all kinds of stories. Other people will write the stories they can write, and I will write the stories I can write.

When I write realistic novels, I will be true as best I am able to what is. But I am, as Zechariah says, a prisoner of hope. My stories will lean toward hope as a sunflower toward the sun. The roots will be firmly in the world as I know it, but the face will turn inevitably toward the peaceable kingdom, the heavenly city, the loving parent watching and waiting for the prodigal's return. Because, by the grace of God, that is truth for me and all who share this hope.

Come to think of it, and I must confess, I didn't think of it when I was writing the book, Parkington Waddell Broughton the Fifth is a kind of prisoner to hope. He sets out on a quest to find his father who was killed in Vietnam. Neither Park nor most of my readers will know that as he pursues his quest he is living out the medieval legend of Parzival the Grail knight. In the legend as Wolfram von Eschenbach tells it, the Grail knight is brought by enchantment to the castle of the Grail king. The king is suffering from a wound that will not heal, and he will only be healed on the day that the Grail knight appears and asks the question.

The young Parzival, however, is the prototype of the innocent fool. He has no idea that he is the Grail knight. When he finds himself in the mysterious castle of the Grail, he's not about to ask any questions, because he has been told by those wiser than he that a man who keeps asking questions appears to be even more of a fool than he is.

So he does not ask the question. The king is not healed. And Parzival is thrown out of the castle on his ear. In his subsequent wanderings our innocent fool becomes sadder and, if not wiser, certainly less gullible, and increasingly world-weary. Try as he will he cannot find his way back to the Grail castle. He refuses to return to Camelot, convinced that he is no longer worthy to take his seat at the Round Table.

Brought back from despair by a wise hermit, Parzival comes a second time to the Grail castle, and this time he asks the suffering king the question. "Dear Uncle," Parzival asks, "what aileth thee?" And hearing these compassionate words, the king is healed.

Thus God brings both Parzival and the wounded king to wholeness. But Wolfram, like Dickens, is not content. Teller of romances that he is, he not only proceeds to restore Parzival to his kingdom and to his beloved queen, he also baptizes all in need of baptism, marries all who need marrying, and gets them "lovely children." It is truly happily ever after for Parzival and all his kin.

Park Broughton, in my story, is also an innocent fool and a bumbling knight with no notion of what his real quest is. If you read both stories, you will see that *Park's Quest* shares many elements of Wolfram's tale—the mother who tries to keep her son from the quest, the shooting of the bird, the battle with the stranger who turns out to be a brother, the king with a wound that will not heal, the failure of the knight to ask the compassionate question, and the consequences of his failure. But I did not take the happily-ever-after ending of the old romance. I tried to give it a proper ending.

And, as you tell the children, if you want to know how it comes out you'll have to read the book yourself. Actually, I thought of reading the last two pages to you, but my husband talked me out of it. And he is right. If it is indeed a proper ending, it belongs flesh, bone, and sinew to the rest of the story. If I cut it off, it will lose its life.

So to demonstrate to Sarah Smedman and to you all what I mean by hope in my books, I want to go back to a novel I wrote more than ten years ago, to a story that I think many of you already know. A book that has been called both a "story of redemption" and a story "totally without hope."

Gilly and her grandmother have gone to meet Courtney. In five minutes, or in less than two pages, her mother manages to bring Gilly's lifetime dreams crashing to the ground. Gilly flees—first to the bathroom and then to the telephone to call Trotter and tell her she's coming home because nothing has turned out the way it's supposed to. Whereupon Trotter explains to her that happy endings are a lie, and that life "ain't supposed to be nothing, 'cept maybe tough."

"If life is so bad [Gilly asks], how come you're so happy?"

"Did I say bad? I said it was tough. Nothing to make you happy like doing good on a tough job, now is there?"

"Trotter, stop preaching at me. I want to come home."

"You're home, baby. Your grandma is home."

"I want to be with you and William Ernest and Mr. Randolph."

"And leave her all alone? Could you do that?"

"Dammit, Trotter. Don't try to make a stinking Christian out of me."

"I wouldn't try to make nothing out of you." There was a quiet at the other end of the line. "Me and William Ernest and Mr. Randolph kinda like you the way you are."

"Go to hell, Trotter," Gilly said softly.

A sigh. "Well, I don't know about that. I had planned on settling permanently somewheres else."

"Trotter"—She couldn't push the word hard enough to keep the squeak out—"I love you."

"I know, baby. I love you, too."

She put the phone gently on the hook and went back into the bathroom. There she blew her nose on toilet tissue and washed her face.

By the time she got back to an impatient Courtney and a stricken Nonnie, she had herself well under control.

"Sorry to make you wait," Gilly said. "I'm ready to go home now." No clouds of glory, perhaps, but Trotter would be proud.

No happily ever after, not really a happy ending, certainly not the heavenly city, but an ending rooted in this earth and leaning in the direction of the New Jerusalem. Not perfect, but I do love it. A proper ending—at least a proper ending for me, just one more in a long line of prisoners of hope.

Lee Harding (b. 1937)

Lee Harding, born in Victoria, Australia, is a noted science fiction author. He is best known for his award-winning psychological sci-fi/young adult book *Displaced Person* (1978), described by Walter McVitty as "a dark, intriguing and suspenseful novel."[1] He has also published *Heartsease* (1997), another young adult novel. In the 1975 story "Night of Passage," he envisions a future Australian society in which urban life has collapsed and the tribe living in the outback requires its youth, here represented by a brave girl, to enter the ruins of the city and return, after a night in the savage metropolis, with a trophy of her ordeal. This rite of passage inverts the Western image of urban civilization as superior and enduring, if not progressive. It suggests that children's books can be ways of envisioning alternate futures as well as reassessing the past.

NOTE

1. Walter McVitty, quoted on book cover, Lee Harding, *Displaced Person* (Melbourne: Hyland House, 1978).

Night of Passage

When they came in sight of the city, Brin left the rest of the party behind and continued on alone.

The Elders settled down to wait. They prayed for her safe return, then drank wine and smoked ceremonial pipes and chanted the old songs. This also was part of the ritual, and they would keep it up without pause until she returned.

Brin made good time across the open ground, her natural environment. Crouching low so her dark skin merged with the sunburned grass, she moved with a lithe step. Later, the going would not be so easy.

The time was late afternoon and she planned to reach the outskirts of the city before dusk. She had no desire to enter this unknown labyrinth until daylight waned, and would bide her time until twilight, when the gathering darkness would afford her cover.

When she considered the dangers that lay ahead her fear returned, but if she survived this long night of Passage tomorrow she would be a woman, and privy to the mysteries of her clan. Such was the nature of her trial.

She paused to take stock of her surroundings. Choosing a suitable tree, she quickly scaled it and settled down high up among the sweet-scented branches to await the dusk.

Nothing moved on the landscape. A swollen orange sun dipped slowly out of sight behind the ramparts of the distant city, the gaunt buildings silhouetted against the sunset like the escarpment of some forbidding mountain range. In the distance she imagined she could hear the ritual chanting of the Elders, wafted to her on the shoulders of the night-wind. She felt lonely and isolated, but she had no wish to turn back. Not when she had come so far.

The world gradually darkened. When the first wan stars appeared overhead she clasped both hands together and whispered the Prayer of Passage, remembering home and family and brother Mark, who would make his run next summer. What tales they would share when he became a man! This done, she climbed down from her perch and set off at a brisk pace on the next stage of her journey.

As she moved closer to the city, the fields became hazardous underfoot. They were littered with relics of the Old Ones and avoiding them made for slow progress. Brin angled towards the old road, confident this would lead her to the heart of the city, yet unwilling to betray herself by stepping onto it. Instead she followed the road at a discreet distance, crouching low so her fingers brushed the ground. Her senses ranged far ahead, alert for the slightest sound that would signal the presence of predators on this no-man's-land between the city and the open country. Occasionally the ruins of an ancient wheeled vehicle loomed before her and she gave these a wide berth. It was known that wild dogs and other dangerous animals used these hulks for shelter, and she had no desire to arouse their curiosity.

Her right hand never strayed far from the knife sheathed at her waist and her left hand clutched the small bag of stones jostling against her thigh. Her body was covered with a rime of sweat, but she had no inkling of fatigue. She was no stranger to long treks, although this was the most hazardous she had undertaken. But despite her fears she drew courage from knowing that this night would conclude her quest for womanhood and provide a bridge between her childhood and the person she was destined to become. It was a long-established ritual of her people.

Tonight the sky was clear and there would be a full moon to guide her. These were auspicious omens. The city would be a maze of darkness and the light of heaven her only ally; and when she arrived at the outskirts of the city several hours would remain before she reached the centre. This road would lead her there, to be sure, but for safety she would hug the shadows and side-streets and use the darkness to conceal her presence. If she made good time she hoped to reach her goal before midnight, then find somewhere safe to remain until morning. When dawn arrived she would select her trophy—this, too, was part of the ritual—and depart in haste before the daylight betrayed her.

She paused when she reached the outskirts of the city. The stark contours of the squat buildings were a jangling discord in her mind. They were so different from the homes of her people, which everywhere blended harmoniously with their surroundings. She felt a twinge of dread standing so close to strangeness but steeled herself to move closer, for she had need of the protective shadows.

In this devious way did she enter the abandoned city, a slender figure moving deeper into darkness, her senses alert for any sign of danger. Even now, so long after The Fall, it was known that the city was not entirely deserted. Strange stories had been told by previous initiates, although one could never be sure how much was fact and how much was mere fancy, intensified by fear and anxiety. But it was sobering to recall the youngsters who had failed to return from their night of Passage. Surely this was proof that the dangers still lurked in the city.

Much of what Brin knew about the city was either legend or hearsay, from which some useful facts could be gleaned. It seemed likely that wild dogs prowled the concrete canyons and it was assumed they would be more dangerous than their counterparts in the open country. Some experts insisted that animals of the plain would not dare venture inside the city, for fear of what they might find there. Brin was not prepared to take chances. She was determined to survive her night of Passage and attain her majority, although she wished for a companion to shore up her courage. It was customary for groups of two or three to make their run together, but this summer she was the only youngster to celebrate her fifteenth birthday and, as a consequence, was expected to make her run alone.

She hurried along the crumbling footpaths, nimbly avoiding a variety of obstructions. The silence was strained and unnatural, unlike the silence of the open country, where small sounds were always present. But as her senses grew more attuned to these unfamiliar surroundings she realised that the silence was not as absolute as she had first thought. Far off, near the centre of the city, she heard faintly the sorrowful howl of some melancholy animal. Her scalp prickled with apprehension. She was too far from the source of the sound to be sure, but it reminded her of some disconsolate beast baying its loneliness to the night sky. She unsheathed her knife in preparedness as she moved deeper into the labyrinth.

The city stank. She had expected this, yet even so she was unprepared for the way the rank odour clung like a shroud. A great many people had perished here in Olden Times and the air was heavy with the burden of their passing. Perhaps in the patience of time this odour would be banished from the city by tireless winds and cleansing rains, but for now it remained trapped by the tall buildings, and this made her task even more unpleasant. The streets had a deep layer of dust that soon covered her skin and worked its way into her eyes and down her throat. She was afraid she might cough and several times had to stifle a sneeze, knowing the sound would reverberate catastrophically in these surroundings and betray her presence.

Brin watched the moon rise, transforming the road into a ribbon of light cutting a broad swathe through the darkness. This encouraged her to move faster, but it also made her more vulnerable. As she approached the centre of the city the forlorn baying grew more pronounced. There seemed to be more than one animal, spread over a wide area, tossing their loneliness back and forth across the rooftops. The doleful sound honed her fear and made her wonder how effective her knife would be against a determined predator. Bad luck for her if the dogs roamed in packs . . .

The buildings around her looked different now. They were no longer simple dwellings but resembled storage silos. Yet even so, the tallest was no more than five storeys. She checked the levels carefully, the shattered windows gaping like rows of broken teeth, and found five less than the ten required by the rules of Passage. There was no question of cheating and choosing a hideout some distance from the centre, because guilt would betray her when she faced the Elders. Disgrace would follow and the mysteries of her clan would remain closed to her. She could not and would not evade her responsibilities. The only way out was forward.

The moon rose higher, drawing a soft silver shawl over the city. Brin thought about the moon, how people had lived there long ago in their marvellous domed cities, before The Fall cut them off from Earth like divers deprived of air. Were they still there, she wondered, their dead eyes focused forever on the slowly turning Earth?

She stopped and rubbed sweaty hands on her thighs. What if the dust underfoot was all that remained of the people who had lived here long ago, a grim residue tossed and spread around by the gale-force winds that had scoured these streets for centuries?

The idea was disturbing. She scolded herself and thought, "This is mere fancy." Then she looked nervously around as though expecting some grey old ghost to sneak up from behind and tap her on the shoulder. But no such phantom appeared to mock her progress. There was only the doleful cry of lonely animals baying at the moon to sharpen her wits.

The road rose unexpectedly from ground level to become an elevated highway. Tempting though this was, Brin chose to scurry from shadow to deeper shadow between the crumbling pillars that still supported the structure. The road stretched above her like an enormous arm outflung against the stars. Further on, when the road sloped back to level ground again, she moved away from its protective shadows and hugged the flat sides of buildings. She was tiring now, but the end of her journey was in sight. The buildings either side were higher now, and the animal howling was louder.

The streets of the city were choked with derelict vehicles left behind by the Old Ones, some lying overturned and others with wheels buried in the pervasive dust like insects trapped in honey. Their diversity astonished her. Never before had she seen so many ancient artefacts crowded together, and this alone made her trek worthwhile. Legend maintained that The Fall happened so quickly people scarcely had time to save themselves, the Old World collapsing so completely that hardly anyone survived. Afterwards, great plagues had ravaged the world and left only a few precious havens untouched. But this was hearsay. Who could say with certainty what had caused The Fall and changed the face of the Earth for ever?

Brin skidded to a stop. Her pulse was racing and she was breathing heavily, but there were no other signs of strain after her long run. Grey buildings soared all around her, their topmost levels lost in darkness. She had reached the centre at last, where she must make her stand and await the dawn. But which building offered the best cover?

The doleful baying seemed everywhere now. Were the dogs closing in? she wondered. Or had anxiety overtaken her senses? She counted the rows of gaping windows on the building opposite and saw it would suffice. It was a good deal higher than the ten storeys demanded by the rules of Passage.

She crossed the street, weaving her way through a tangle of derelict vehicles. On the other side she paused, confronted by a shattered wall of glass. Great shards littered the footpath, where two wheeled vehicles had plunged their blunt snouts through the shopfront. Bodies were strewn around inside the building and this seemed odd. How could bodies be so remarkably well preserved after so long?

She took a step closer and peered into the store, sighing with relief when she realised these were not real people. They were toppled statues. The moonlight had deceived her into thinking them human. Some stood in frozen tableaux with arms extended in a parody of human gesture, their painted eyes devoid of feeling; others were sprawled on the floor in awkward postures. Scraps of fibre that might once have been cloth clung to their limbs, reminding her of the dolls she had kept as a child.

She stepped cautiously through the shattered window. Inside the huge store the darkness was almost palpable and she paused to allow time for her senses to adjust to these new surroundings. Row after row of deep shelves stretched away from her and disappeared into the deeper darkness at the back of the store. The nearest were still filled with merchandise, glass and metal containers with faded labels displaying familiar fruit or vegetables.

Brin was fascinated. What an abundance of trophies to choose from! She remembered the silver case Tony had brought back from his run, the fascia decorated with numerals and the panel that gaped open when a switch was pressed like a mouth demanding to be fed. The Elders had regarded this suspiciously at first, before they chanted the Song of Internment and buried the artefact in the ground. She was determined to select something that would astound The Elders and impress her family and friends. But this could wait until morning. Her priority was to find a safe place for the night.

She hunkered down in a far corner of the store, her back to the wall and with a clear view of the street outside. The baying had moved to another part of the city and this made her feel easier; perhaps the pack would move even further away. But just as she allowed herself to relax the silence was broken by the most mournful howl she had ever heard. This seemed very close indeed. She fingered her knife nervously—dawn seemed far away—and untied the pouch cinched to her belt. She opened this and drew out her stones, arranging them on the floor within easy reach. Knife-work could be messy and was often unnecessary. A stone could fell even the largest adversary if the thrower's aim was sure.

Fortunately, the sound was not repeated, and after a while she allowed herself to relax again. The tension ebbed from her body and she at last succumbed to weariness. Eventually she slept, secure with a hunter's knowledge that her senses would alert her to any danger. And while she slept she dreamed of home, of family and friends and the valley she loved. She dreamed how the sun illuminated every corner of their lives, how it charmed the seeds from the soil and nourished the crops. How the river sparkled on long summer afternoons . . .

She woke when the first faint light of dawn crept in through the shattered windows of the store . . . and realised she was not alone.

She was instantly on guard, senses alert for any sound. She clasped the knife in her right hand while her left gripped a throwing stone, ready to defend herself.

What sound had disturbed her? What danger had crept into her dreams and nudged her awake? Her keen eyes probed the surrounding darkness, looking for some clue. Her heart hammered in her breast like a frightened bird beating wildly at its cage. She waited, and after a while heard a faint creeping sound. Something moved on her right. She could make out a dark shape lurking there, shuffling about the store with a furtiveness unlike any animal she knew.

"Lord Sun, protect me," she whispered.

So far the creature was unaware of her presence, but when it did sense her she would face the supreme test of Passage. If she survived, her majority was assured. If she did not, her people would mourn her, as they had mourned others who had not returned from the city.

She could hear the creature groping around in the darkness, its muffled breathing moving closer to her hideaway as it shuffled past the shelves. Was it searching for food? she wondered. But what sort of animal grubbed around in the ruins of this store? Her fear gave way to curiosity. Brin had faith in her knife and her skill with the stones and she edged forward slightly, hoping for a better glimpse of the intruder. She saw a dim shape hovering around a pyramid of food cans. She drew her breath in sharply. The creature was hunched over with its back to her and was much bigger than she had anticipated.

Brin hesitated. Now was the time to make good her escape. She didn't fancy staying crouched in her corner, waiting for the creature to discover her and block her escape route. She had no idea how fast it could move, but she was the fastest runner in the valley and was confident she could outdistance any pursuer—except a marauding dog-pack.

She calculated the distance between herself and the intruder, then the distance between herself and the street. There was no sense delaying her break a moment longer. The time to make her move was *now,* while the creature was occupied. But what about her trophy? She couldn't leave empty-handed.

At this precise moment she sneezed. Afterwards, she would never be sure what had provoked the sudden paroxysm, whether it was a consequence of the dust she had inhaled or if subconsciously she had wished to challenge the intruder. Whatever the reason, the result was spectacular.

The creature let out a roar and swung around as though it had been struck, its huge arms toppling merchandise from the shelves as they spread wide in a defiant gesture of aggression. When it saw her crouched in the half-light it let loose a cry so terrifying that Brin promptly jumped to her feet, legs braced firmly as she assumed a defensive stance. For she recognised in the creature's cry the same disturbing howl she had heard during the night. *This* was the creature she had sought to avoid. No wild dog after all, but something else . . .

The creature confronting her was *huge* and vaguely manlike. Coarse white hair stood out from his head like wire and a grizzled beard straggled down past his waist. The man was naked, save for a small garment loosely tied around his loins, and under the grime his skin was the same pallid colour as the belly of a fish. There was a crazed look in his wild eyes and more menace in his emaciated frame than Brin had ever seen.

Twenty paces separated them. The creature gave another dreadful cry and launched itself towards her; enormous hands clawing the air and eyes blazing with an unreasonable hatred. Brin did not hesitate. The creature presented an easy target. She faced the charge coolly, eyeing the man with shrewd calculation. She waited until he had closed half the distance between them, then with a grim smile raised her left hand in a blur of speed. The stone flew from her fingers and struck the wild white man hard in the centre of the forehead. The creature staggered to a stop, eyes rolling heavenwards while it clawed at its head with both hands. She had another stone ready, but this was not necessary. The creature coughed once and collapsed to the floor without making another sound.

Brin waited a few moments, out of caution, but the creature did not stir. Her aim had been true and the stone had knocked him unconscious. She moved closer and looked down in wonder at the body, embedding the image in her memory for future reference. Wild white hair framed the creature's head like a crinkled halo, his chest rose and fell steadily from his breathing and she suspected it would be some time before he regained consciousness. By then she would be well clear of the city and on her way home.

Early morning sunlight filtered into the store. This was no time for musing. She remembered her trophy and wavered for a moment, uncertain. She looked again at the unconscious wild man and making her decision, leaned forward and struck swiftly with her knife. And in one lithe movement she was away and heading for the street.

She fled from the city as though all the wild dogs in the world were snapping at her heels, hugging the shadows and praying she would not be seen by other predators, detouring down side streets and alleyways when the open spaces made her conspicuous and choking back the rising clouds of dust. Several times she imagined the dreadful baying sound behind her and quickened her pace. But no predators approached her, and if any followed she out-distanced them easily.

She was surprised when the return journey was accomplished without incident. She grew light-headed and flushed with her success and found time to marvel at the enormous size of the city and the great distances separating the wild white people who lived there, subsisting on the left-overs of their ancestors and ignorant of their former glory.

Her trophy swung lightly from her belt and did not impede her progress. She ran until she was exhausted, until the outskirts of the city were far behind and the green of the open country was spread before her. Only then did she feel secure enough to ease her pace.

The Elders were waiting. Ritual required them to welcome her solemnly, yet their expressions betrayed how delighted they were to see her return safe and sound. She approached their camp with a jaunty step, proud of her accomplishment and only now appreciating the audacity of her adventure. Her long night was over and her Passage had been successful.

They acknowledged her safe return with customary dignity, which also was part of the ritual. Then they carefully examined her body for wounds and abrasions and were relieved when they found none. They inspected the crust of dried sweat and dust that covered her from head to foot and murmured their approval.

Brin smiled triumphantly as she held out her trophy. The Eldest accepted it nervously and examined the long strands of white hair in wonderment. The others crowded closer to examine her prize, their faces filled with awe. Then they each in turn examined the thatch of hair she had severed from the unconscious wild man and nodded their approval. The inspection complete, they regarded her with admiration and a new respect. No initiate had ever returned from the city with such a bizarre prize.

The trophy was returned to the Eldest, who proceeded to wrap it in a ceremonial cloth and tuck it away in the special basket designed for the purpose. Then he motioned for the group to move off. They began the slow, measured trek that would take them back to the valley, where three days hence they would celebrate her safe return and declare her Passage complete.

And from their proud and dignified expressions Brin knew she had at last achieved her majority.

Laura Ingalls Wilder (1867–1957)

For decades, Laura Ingalls Wilder's books were regarded as the most authentic recreation of the American pioneer experience in children's literature. When she was in her fifties, Wilder wrote an autobiography titled *Pioneer Girl,* recounting her childhood on the frontier. Her daughter Rose, who was a nationally known journalist, urged her to rewrite the story in greater detail. The result of their collaboration was the series of Little House books that have become representative of a period of westward expansion in American history. The popularity of a television series based on the books (and then based on the characters of the books but freely inventing further material in its eleven-year run beginning in 1974) added to the fame of the series.

Laura Ingalls Wilder was born in the woods of Wisconsin in 1867. When she was one year old, her parents decided to move West as homesteaders, a story she retells vividly in *The Little House in the Big Woods* (1932). With great clarity and detail, she re-creates a child's perspective of the experience of settling on the prairie, building a log cabin, and moving on again. The beauty of the open prairie is evoked in *Little House on the Prairie* (1935) in spare prose worthy of Willa Cather, and the terror and threat of events such as prairie fires or encircling wolves are presented with equal force. The Ingalls family moved to an emergent town, Walnut Grove, Minnesota, and continued to move, even more often than the novels or television series indicate. Laura and her husband, Almanzo Wilder, eventually settled in Missouri, where she wrote her family history in the series of books that remain American classics of frontier life.

Critics have both praised and attacked the books' portrayals of Native Americans. Elizabeth Segel showed the subtle connections between Ma's antagonism toward Indians and the feminine ideals of leisure implied in the value placed on light-toned skin for white women and girls in the Little House on the Prairie series (an ironic value, since Ma's hard labor is indispensable to the family's survival). She further illuminated the settlers' prejudice against people who do not farm the land, a prejudice that, according to Segel, Laura questions and Pa does not hold as vehemently as does Mr. Scott, who believes that "The only good Indian is a dead Indian."[1] Michael Dorris, a Native American/German American writer, recalls loving the Little House books as a boy, but being brought up short when, as a parent, he tried to read the books to his daughters and discovered that the portrayal of Native Americans in the series (and their omission in the consciousness of the pioneers) was too painful for him to reproduce without question (see Dorris's essay in this section). Louise Erdrich's *The Birchbark House* (excerpted in this section) can be read as a reply to the Little House books.

NOTE

1. Elizabeth Segel, "Laura Ingalls Wilder's America: An Unflinching Assessment," *Children's Literature in Education* 8 (Summer 1977): 63–70.

From *Little House on the Prairie*

CHAPTER 11. INDIANS IN THE HOUSE

Early one morning Pa took his gun and went hunting.

He had meant to make the bedstead that day. He had brought in the slabs, when Ma said she had no meat for dinner. So he stood the slabs against the wall and took down his gun.

Jack wanted to go hunting, too. His eyes begged Pa to take him, and whines came up from his chest and quivered in his throat till Laura almost cried with him. But Pa chained him to the stable.

"No, Jack," Pa said. "You must stay here and guard the place." Then he said to Mary and Laura, "Don't let him loose, girls."

Poor Jack lay down. It was a disgrace to be chained, and he felt it deeply. He turned his head from Pa and would not watch him going away with the gun on his shoulder. Pa went farther and farther away, till the prairies swallowed him and he was gone.

Laura tried to comfort Jack, but he would not be comforted. The more he thought about the chain, the worse he felt. Laura tried to cheer him up to frisk and play, but he only grew more sullen.

Both Mary and Laura felt that they could not leave Jack while he was so unhappy. So all that morning they stayed by the stable. They stroked Jack's smooth, brindled head and scratched around his ears, and told him how sorry they were that he must be chained. He lapped their hands a little bit, but he was very sad and angry.

His head was on Laura's knee and she was talking to him, when suddenly he stood up and growled a fierce, deep growl. The hair on his neck stood straight up and his eyes glared red.

Laura was frightened. Jack had never growled at her before. Then she looked over her shoulder, where Jack was looking, and she saw two naked, wild men coming, one behind the other, on the Indian trail.

"Mary! Look!" she cried. Mary looked and saw them, too.

They were tall, thin, fierce-looking men. Their skin was brownish-red. Their heads seemed to go up to a peak, and the peak was a tuft of hair that stood straight up and ended in feathers. Their eyes were black and still and glittering, like snake's eyes.

They came closer and closer. Then they went out of sight, on the other side of the house.

Laura's head turned and so did Mary's, and they looked at the place where those terrible men would appear when they came past the house.

"Indians!" Mary whispered. Laura was shivery; there was a queer feeling in her middle and the bones in her legs felt weak. She wanted to sit down. But she stood and looked and waited for those Indians to come out from beyond the house. The Indians did not do that.

All this time Jack had been growling. Now he stopped growling and was lunging against the chain. His eyes were red and his lips curled back and all the hair on his back was bristling. He bounded and bounded, clear off the ground, trying to get loose from the chain. Laura was glad that the chain kept him right there with her.

"Jack's here," she whispered to Mary. "Jack won't let them hurt us. We'll be safe if we stay close to Jack."

"They are in the house," Mary whispered. "They are in the house with Ma and Carrie."

Then Laura began to shake all over. She knew she must do something. She did not know what those Indians were doing to Ma and Baby Carrie. There was no sound at all from the house.

"Oh, what are they doing to Ma!" she screamed, in a whisper.

"Oh, I don't know!" Mary whispered.

"I'm going to let Jack loose," Laura whispered, hoarsely. "Jack will kill them."

"Pa said not to," Mary answered. They were too scared to speak out loud. They put their heads together and watched the house and whispered.

"He didn't know Indians would come," Laura said.

"He said not to let Jack loose." Mary was almost crying.

Laura thought of little Baby Carrie and Ma, shut in the house with those Indians. She said, "I'm going in to help Ma!"

She ran two steps, and walked a step, then she turned and flew back to Jack. She clutched him wildly and hung on to his strong, panting neck. Jack wouldn't let anything hurt her.

"We mustn't leave Ma in there alone," Mary whispered. She stood still and trembled. Mary never could move when she was frightened.

Laura hid her face against Jack and held on to him tightly.

Then she made her arms let go. Her hands balled into fists and her eyes shut tight and she ran toward the house as fast as she could run.

She stumbled and fell down and her eyes popped open. She was up again and running before she could think. Mary was close behind her. They came to the door. It was open, and they slipped into the house without a sound.

The naked wild men stood by the fireplace. Ma was bending over the fire, cooking something. Carrie clung to Ma's skirts with both hands and her head was hidden in the folds.

Laura ran toward Ma, but just as she reached the hearth she smelled a horribly bad smell and she looked up at the Indians. Quick as a flash, she ducked behind the long, narrow slab that leaned against the wall.

The slab was just wide enough to cover both her eyes. If she held her head perfectly still and pressed her nose against the slab, she couldn't see the Indians. And she felt safer. But she couldn't help moving her head just a little, so that one eye peeped out and she could see the wild men.

First she saw their leather moccasins. Then their stringy, bare, red-brown legs, all the way up. Around their waists each of the Indians wore a leather thong, and the furry skin of a small animal hung down in front. The fur was striped black and white, and now Laura knew what made that smell. The skins were fresh skunk skins.

A knife like Pa's hunting-knife, and a hatchet like Pa's hatchet, were stuck into each skunk skin.

The Indians' ribs made little ridges up their bare sides. Their arms were folded on their chests. At last Laura looked again at their faces, and she dodged quickly behind the slab.

Their faces were bold and fierce and terrible. Their black eyes glittered. High on their foreheads and above their ears where hair grows, these wild men had no hair. But on top of their heads a tuft of hair stood straight up. It was wound around with string, and feathers were stuck in it.

When Laura peeked out from behind the slab again, both Indians were looking straight at her. Her heart jumped into her throat and choked her with its pounding. Two black eyes glittered down into her eyes. The Indian did not move, not one muscle of his face moved. Only his eyes shone and sparkled at her. Laura didn't move, either. She didn't even breathe.

The Indian made two short, harsh sounds in his throat. The other Indian made one sound, like "Hah!" Laura hid her eyes behind the slab again.

She heard Ma take the cover off the bake-oven. She heard the Indians squat down on the hearth. After a while she heard them eating.

Laura peeked, and hid, and peeked again, while the Indians ate the cornbread that Ma had baked. They ate every morsel of it, and even picked up the crumbs from the hearth. Ma stood and watched them and stroked Baby Carrie's head. Mary stood close behind Ma and held on to her sleeve.

Faintly Laura heard Jack's chain rattling. Jack was still trying to get loose.

When every crumb of the cornbread was gone, the Indians rose up. The skunk smell was stronger when they moved. One of them made harsh sounds in his throat again. Ma looked at him with big eyes; she did not say anything. The Indian turned around, the other Indian turned, too, and they walked across the floor and out through the door. Their feet made no sound at all.

Ma sighed a long, long sigh. She hugged Laura tight in one arm and Mary tight in the other arm, and through the window they watched those Indians going away, one behind the other, on the dim trail toward the west. Then Ma sat down on the bed and hugged Laura and Mary tighter, and trembled. She looked sick.

"Do you feel sick, Ma?" Mary asked her.

"No," said Ma. "I'm just thankful they're gone."

Laura wrinkled her nose and said, "They smell awful."

"That was the skunk skins they wore," Ma said.

Then they told her how they had left Jack and had come into the house because they were afraid the Indi-

ans would hurt her and Baby Carrie. Ma said they were her brave little girls.

"Now we must get dinner," she said. "Pa will be here soon and we must have dinner ready for him. Mary, bring me some wood. Laura, you may set the table."

Ma rolled up her sleeves and washed her hands and mixed cornbread, while Mary brought the wood and Laura set the table. She set a tin plate and knife and fork and cup for Pa, and the same for Ma, with Carrie's little tin cup beside Ma's. And she set tin plates and knives and forks for her and Mary, but only their one cup between the plates.

Ma made the cornmeal and water into two thin loaves, each shaped in a half circle. She laid the loaves with their straight sides together in the bake-oven, and she pressed her hand flat on top of each loaf. Pa always said he did not ask any other sweetening, when Ma put the prints of her hands on the loaves.

Laura had hardly set the table when Pa was there. He left a big rabbit and two prairie hens outside the door, and stepped in and laid his gun on its pegs. Laura and Mary ran and clutched him, both talking at once.

"What's all this? What's all this?" he said, rumpling their hair. "Indians? So you've seen Indians at last, have you, Laura? I noticed they have a camp in a little valley west of here. Did Indians come to the house, Caroline?"

"Yes, Charles, two of them," Ma said. "I'm sorry, but they took all your tobacco, and they ate a lot of cornbread. They pointed to the cornmeal and made signs for me to cook some. I was afraid not to. Oh Charles! I was afraid!"

"You did the right thing," Pa told her. "We don't want to make enemies of any Indians." Then he said, "Whew! what a smell."

"They wore fresh skunk skins," said Ma. "And that was all they wore."

"Must have been thick while they were here," Pa said.

"It was, Charles. We were short of cornmeal, too."

"Oh well. We have enough to hold out awhile yet. And our meat is running all over the country. Don't worry, Caroline."

"But they took all your tobacco."

"Never mind," Pa said. "I'll get along without tobacco till I can make that trip to Independence. The main thing is to be on good terms with the Indians. We don't want to wake up some night with a band of the screeching dev—"

He stopped. Laura dreadfully wanted to know what he had been going to say. But Ma's lips were pressed together and she shook a little shake of her head at Pa.

"Come on, Mary and Laura!" Pa said. "We'll skin that rabbit and dress the prairie hens while that cornbread bakes. Hurry! I'm hungry as a wolf!"

They sat on the woodpile in the wind and sunshine and watched Pa work with his hunting-knife. The big rabbit was shot through the eye, and the prairie hens' heads were shot clean away. They never knew what hit them, Pa said.

Laura held the edge of the rabbit skin while Pa's keen knife ripped it off the rabbit meat. "I'll salt this skin and peg it out on the house wall to dry," he said. "It will make a warm fur cap for some little girl to wear next winter."

But Laura could not forget the Indians. She said to Pa that if they had turned Jack loose, he would have eaten those Indians right up.

Pa laid down the knife. "Did you girls even think of turning Jack loose?" he asked, in a dreadful voice.

Laura's head bowed down and she whispered, "Yes, Pa."

"After I told you not to?" Pa said, in a more dreadful voice.

Laura couldn't speak, but Mary choked, "Yes, Pa."

For a moment Pa was silent. He sighed a long sigh like Ma's sigh after the Indians went away.

"After this," he said, in a terrible voice, "you girls remember always to do as you're told. Don't you even think of disobeying me. Do you hear?"

"Yes, Pa," Laura and Mary whispered.

"Do you know what would have happened if you had turned Jack loose?" Pa asked.

"No, Pa," they whispered.

"He would have bitten those Indians," said Pa. "Then there would have been trouble. Bad trouble. Do you understand?"

"Yes, Pa," they said. But they did not understand.

"Would they have killed Jack?" Laura asked.

"Yes. And that's not all. You girls remember this: you do as you're told, no matter what happens."

"Yes, Pa," Laura said, and Mary said, "Yes, Pa." They were glad they had not turned Jack loose.

"Do as you're told," said Pa, "and no harm will come to you."

CHAPTER 21. INDIAN JAMBOREE

Winter ended at last. There was a softer note in the sound of the wind, and the bitter cold was gone. One day Pa said he had seen a flock of wild geese flying north. It was time to take his furs to Independence.

Ma said, "The Indians are so near!"

"They are perfectly friendly," said Pa. He often met Indians in the woods where he was hunting. There was nothing to fear from Indians.

"No," Ma said. But Laura knew that Ma was afraid of Indians. "You must go, Charles," she said. "We must have a plow and seeds. And you will soon be back again."

Before dawn next morning Pa hitched Pet and Patty to the wagon, loaded his furs into it, and drove away.

Laura and Mary counted the long, empty days. One, two, three, four, and still Pa had not come home. In the morning of the fifth day they began earnestly to watch for him.

It was a sunny day. There was still a little chill in the wind, but it smelled of spring. The vast blue sky resounded to the quacks of wild ducks and the honk-honk-honking of wild geese. The long, black-dotted lines of them were all flying north.

Laura and Mary played outdoors in the wild, sweet weather. And poor Jack watched them and sighed. He couldn't run and play any more, because he was chained. Laura and Mary tried to comfort him, but he didn't want petting. He wanted to be free again, as he used to be.

Pa didn't come that morning; he didn't come that afternoon. Ma said it must have taken him a long time to trade his furs.

That afternoon Laura and Mary were playing hop-scotch. They marked the lines with a stick in the muddy yard. Mary really didn't want to hop; she was almost eight years old and she didn't think that hop-scotch was a ladylike play. But Laura teased and coaxed, and said that if they stayed outdoors they would be sure to see Pa the minute he came from the creek bottoms. So Mary was hopping.

Suddenly she stopped on one foot and said, "What's that?"

Laura had already heard the queer sound and she was listening to it. She said, "It's the Indians."

Mary's other foot dropped and she stood frozen still. She was scared. Laura was not exactly scared, but that sound made her feel funny. It was the sound of quite a lot of Indians, chopping with their voices. It was something like the sound of an ax chopping, and something like a dog barking, and it was something like a song, but not like any song that Laura had ever heard. It was a wild, fierce sound, but it didn't seem angry.

Laura tried to hear it more clearly. She couldn't hear it very well, because hills and trees and the wind were in the way, and Jack was savagely growling.

Ma came outdoors and listened a minute. Then she told Mary and Laura to come into the house. Ma took Jack inside, too, and pulled in the latch-string.

They didn't play any more. They watched at the window, and listened to that sound. It was harder to hear, in the house. Sometimes they couldn't hear it; then they heard it again. It hadn't stopped.

Ma and Laura did the chores earlier than usual. They locked Bunny and the cow and calf in the stable, and took the milk to the house. Ma strained it and set it away. She drew a bucket of fresh water from the well, while Laura and Mary carried in wood. All the time that sound went on; it was louder, now, and faster. It made Laura's heart beat fast.

They all went into the house and Ma barred the door. The latch-string was already in. They wouldn't go out of the house till morning.

The sun slowly sank. All around the edge of the prairie the edge of the sky flushed pink. Firelight flickered in the dusky house and Ma was getting supper, but Laura and Mary silently watched from the window. They saw the colors fade from everything. The land was shadowy and the sky was clear, pale gray. All the time that sound came from the creek bottoms, louder and louder, faster and faster. And Laura's heart beat faster and louder.

How she shouted when she heard the wagon! She ran to the door and jumped up and down, but she couldn't unbar it. Ma wouldn't let her go out. Ma went out, to help Pa bring in the bundles.

He came in with his arms full, and Laura and Mary clung to his sleeves and jumped on his feet. Pa laughed his jolly big laugh. "Hey! hey! don't upset me!" he laughed. "What do you think I am? A tree to climb?"

He dropped the bundles on the table, he hugged Laura in a big bear hug, and tossed her and hugged her again. Then he hugged Mary snugly in his other arm.

"Listen, Pa," Laura said. "Listen to the Indians. Why are they making that funny noise?"

"Oh, they're having some kind of jamboree," Pa said. "I heard them when I crossed the creek bottoms."

Then he went out to unhitch the horses and bring in the rest of the bundles. He had got the plow; he left it in the stable, but he brought all the seeds into the house for safety. He had sugar, not any white sugar this time, but brown. White sugar cost too much. But he had brought a little white flour. There were cornmeal and salt and coffee and all the seeds they needed. Pa had even got seed potatoes. Laura wished they might eat the potatoes but they must be saved to plant.

Then Pa's face beamed and he opened a small paper sack. It was full of crackers. He set it on the table, and he unwrapped and set beside it a glass jar full of little green cucumber pickles.

"I thought we'd all have a treat," he said.

Laura's mouth watered, and Ma's eyes shone softly at Pa. He had remembered how she longed for pickles.

That wasn't all. He gave Ma a package and watched her unwrap it and in it was enough pretty calico to make her a dress.

"Oh, Charles, you shouldn't! It's too much!" she said. But her face and Pa's were two beams of joy.

Now he hung up his cap and his plaid coat on their pegs. His eyes looked sidewise at Laura and Mary, but that was all. He sat down and stretched out his legs to the fire.

Mary sat down, too, and folded her hands in her lap. But Laura climbed onto Pa's knee and beat him with her fists. "Where is it? Where is it? Where's my present?" she said, beating him.

Pa laughed his big laugh, like great bells ringing, and he said, "Why, I do believe there is something in my blouse pocket."

He took out an oddly shaped package, and very, very slowly he opened it.

"You first, Mary," he said, "because you are so patient." And he gave Mary a comb for her hair. "And here, flutterbudget! this is for you," he said to Laura.

The combs were exactly alike. They were made of black rubber and curved to fit over the top of a little girl's head. And over the top of the comb lay a flat piece of black rubber, with curving slits cut in it, and in the very middle of it a little five-pointed star was cut out. A bright colored ribbon was drawn underneath, and the color showed through.

The ribbon in Mary's comb was blue, and the ribbon in Laura's comb was red.

Ma smoothed back their hair and slid the combs into it, and there in the golden hair, exactly over the middle of Mary's forehead, was a little blue star. And in Laura's brown hair, over the middle of her forehead, was a little red star.

Laura looked at Mary's star, and Mary looked at Laura's, and they laughed with joy. They had never had anything so pretty.

Ma said, "But, Charles, you didn't get yourself a thing!"

"Oh, I got myself a plow," said Pa. "Warm weather'll be here soon now, and I'll be plowing."

That was the happiest supper they had had for a long time. Pa was safely home again. The fried salt pork was very good, after so many months of eating ducks and geese and turkeys and venison. And nothing had ever tasted so good as those crackers and the little green sour pickles.

Pa told them about all the seeds. He had got seeds of turnips and carrots and onions and cabbage. He had got peas and beans. And corn and wheat and tobacco and the seed potatoes. And watermelon seeds. He said to Ma, "I tell you, Caroline, when we begin getting crops off this rich land of ours, we'll be living like kings!"

They had almost forgotten the noise from the Indian camp. The window shutters were closed now, and the wind was moaning in the chimney and whining around the house. They were so used to the wind that they did not hear it. But when the wind was silent an instant, Laura heard again that wild, shrill, fast-beating sound from the Indian camps.

Then Pa said something to Ma that made Laura sit very still and listen carefully. He said that folks in Independence said that the government was going to put the white settlers out of the Indian territory. He said the Indians had been complaining and they had got that answer from Washington.

"Oh, Charles, no!" Ma said. "Not when we have done so much."

Pa said he didn't believe it. He said, "They always have let settlers keep the land. They'll make the Indians move on again. Didn't I get word straight from Washington that this country's going to be opened for settlement any time now?"

"I wish they'd settle it and stop talking about it," Ma said.

After Laura was in bed she lay awake a long time, and so did Mary. Pa and Ma sat in the firelight and can-dlelight, reading. Pa had brought a newspaper from Kansas, and he read it to Ma. It proved that he was right, the government would not do anything to the white settlers.

Whenever the sound of the wind died away, Laura could faintly hear the noise of that wild jamboree in the Indian camp. Sometimes even above the howling of the wind she thought she still heard those fierce yells of jubilation. Faster, faster, faster they made her heart beat. "Hi! Hi! Hi-yi! Hah! Hi! Hah!"

CHAPTER 23. INDIAN WAR-CRY

Next morning Pa went whistling to his plowing. He came in at noon black with soot from the burned prairie, but he was pleased. The tall grass didn't bother him any more.

But there was an uneasiness about the Indians. More and more Indians were in the creek bottoms. Mary and Laura saw the smoke from their fires by day, and at night they heard the savage voices shouting.

Pa came early from the field. He did the chores early, and shut Pet and Patty, Bunny and the cow and calf, into the stable. They could not stay out in the yard to graze in the cool moonlight.

When shadows began to gather on the prairie and the wind was quiet, the noises from the Indian camps grew louder and wilder. Pa brought Jack into the house. The door was shut and the latch-string pulled in. No one could go outdoors till morning.

Night crept toward the little house, and the darkness was frightening. It yelped with Indian yells, and one night it began to throb with Indian drums.

In her sleep Laura heard all the time that savage yipping and the wild, throbbing drums. She heard Jack's claws clicking, and his low growl. Sometimes Pa sat up in bed, listening.

One evening he took his bullet-mold from the box under the bed. He sat for a long time on the hearth, melting lead and making bullets. He did not stop till he had used the last bit of lead.

Laura and Mary lay awake and watched him. He had never made so many bullets at one time before. Mary asked, "What makes you do that, Pa?"

"Oh, I haven't anything else to do," Pa said, and he began to whistle cheerfully. But he had been plowing all day. He was too tired to play the fiddle. He might have gone to bed, instead of sitting up so late, making bullets.

No more Indians came to the house. For days, Mary and Laura had not seen a single Indian. Mary did not like to go out of the house any more. Laura had to play outdoors by herself, and she had a queer feeling about the prairie. It didn't feel safe. It seemed to be hiding something. Sometimes Laura had a feeling that something was watching her, something was creeping up behind her. She turned around quickly, and nothing was there.

Mr. Scott and Mr. Edwards, with their guns, came and talked to Pa in the field. They talked quite a while, then they went away together. Laura was disappointed because Mr. Edwards did not come to the house.

At dinner Pa said to Ma that some of the settlers were talking about a stockade. Laura didn't know what a stockade was. Pa had told Mr. Scott and Mr. Edwards that it was a foolish notion. He told Ma, "If we need one, we'd need it before we could get it built. And the last thing we want to do is to act like we're afraid."

Mary and Laura looked at each other. They knew it was no use to ask questions. They would only be told again that children must not speak at table until they were spoken to. Or that children should be seen and not heard.

That afternoon Laura asked Ma what a stockade was. Ma said it was something to make little girls ask questions. That meant that grown-ups would not tell you what it was. And Mary looked a look at Laura that said, "I told you so."

Laura didn't know why Pa said he must not act as if he were afraid. Pa was never afraid. Laura didn't want to act as if she were afraid, but she was. She was afraid of the Indians.

Jack never laid back his ears and smiled at Laura any more. Even while she petted him, his ears were lifted, his neck bristled, and his lips twitched back from his teeth. His eyes were angry. Every night he growled more fiercely, and every night the Indian drums beat faster, faster, and the wild yipping rose higher and higher, faster, wilder.

In the middle of the night Laura sat straight up and screamed. Some terrible sound had made cold sweat come out all over her.

Ma came to her quickly and said in her gentle way: "Be quiet, Laura. You mustn't frighten Carrie."

Laura clung to Ma, and Ma was wearing her dress.

The fire was covered with ashes and the house was dark, but Ma had not gone to bed. Moonlight came through the window. The shutter was open, and Pa stood in the dark by the window, looking out. He had his gun.

Out in the night the drums were beating and the Indians were wildly yelling.

Then that terrible sound came again. Laura felt as if she were falling; she couldn't hold on to anything; there was nothing solid anywhere. It seemed a long time before she could see or think or speak.

She screamed: "What is it? What is it? Oh, Pa, what is it?"

She was shaking all over and she felt sick in her middle. She heard the drums pounding and the wild yipping yells and she felt Ma holding her safe. Pa said, "It's the Indian war-cry, Laura."

Ma made a soft sound, and he said to her, "They might as well know, Caroline."

He explained to Laura that that was the Indian way of talking about war. The Indians were only talking about it, and dancing around their fires. Mary and Laura must not be afraid, because Pa was there, and Jack was there, and soldiers were at Fort Gibson and Fort Dodge.

"So don't be afraid, Mary and Laura," he said again.

Laura gasped and said, "No, Pa." But she was horribly afraid. Mary couldn't say anything; she lay shivering under the covers.

Then Carrie began to cry, so Ma carried her to the rocking-chair and gently rocked her. Laura crept out of bed and huddled against Ma's knee. And Mary, left all alone, crept after her and huddled close, too. Pa stayed by the window, watching.

The drums seemed to beat in Laura's head. They seemed to beat deep inside her. The wild, fast yipping yells were worse than wolves. Something worse was coming, Laura knew it. Then it came—the Indian war-cry.

A nightmare is not so terrible as that night was. A nightmare is only a dream, and when it is worst you wake up. But this was real and Laura could not wake up. She could not get away from it.

When the war-cry was over, Laura knew it had not got her yet. She was still in the dark house and she was pressed close against Ma. Ma was trembling all over. Jack's howling ended in a sobbing growl. Carrie began to scream again, and Pa wiped his forehead and said, "Whew!"

"I never heard anything like it," Pa said. He asked, "How do you suppose they learned to do it?" but nobody answered that.

"They don't need guns. That yell's enough to scare anybody to death," he said. "My mouth's so dry I couldn't whistle a tune to save my life. Bring me some water, Laura."

That made Laura feel better. She carried a dipper full of water to Pa at the window. He took it and smiled at her, and that made her feel very much better. He drank a little and smiled again and said, "There! now I can whistle!"

He whistled a few notes to show her that he could.

Then he listened. And Laura, too, heard far away the soft pitter-pat, pat-pat, pitter-pat pat, of a pony's galloping. It came nearer.

From one side of the house came the drum-throbbing and the fast, shrill, yapping yells, and from the other side came the lonely sound of the rider's galloping.

Nearer and nearer it came. Now the hoofs clattered loudly and suddenly they were going by. The galloping went by and grew fainter, down the creek road.

In the moonlight Laura saw the behind of a little black Indian pony, and an Indian on its back. She saw a huddle of blanket and a naked head and a flutter of feathers above it, and moonlight on a gun barrel and then it was all gone. Nothing was there but empty prairie.

Pa said he was durned if he knew what to make of it. He said that was the Osage who had tried to talk French to him.

He asked, "What's he doing, out at this hour, riding hell bent for leather?"

Nobody answered because nobody knew.

The drums throbbed and the Indians went on yelling. The terrible war-cry came again and again.

Little by little, after a long time, the yells grew fainter and fewer. At last Carrie cried herself to sleep. Ma sent Mary and Laura back to bed.

Next day they could not go out of the house. Pa stayed close by. There was not one sound from the Indian camps. The whole vast prairie was still. Only the wind blew over the blackened earth where there was no grass to rustle. The wind blew past the house with a rushing sound like running water.

That night the noise in the Indian camps was worse than the night before. Again the war-cries were more terrible than the most dreadful nightmare. Laura and Mary huddled close against Ma, poor little Baby Carrie cried, Pa watched at the window with his gun. And all night long Jack paced and growled, and screamed when the war-cries came.

The next night, and the next night, and the next night, were worse and worse. Mary and Laura were so tired that they fell asleep while the drums pounded and the Indians yelled. But a war-cry always jerked them wide awake in terror.

And the silent days were even worse than the nights. Pa watched and listened all the time. The plow was in the field where he had left it; Pet and Patty and the colt and the cow and calf stayed in the barn. Mary and Laura could not go out of the house. And Pa never stopped looking at the prairie all around, and turning his head quickly toward the smallest noise. He ate hardly any dinner; he kept getting up and going outdoors to look all around at the prairie.

One day his head nodded down to the table and he slept there. Ma and Mary and Laura were still to let him sleep. He was so tired. But in a minute he woke up with a jump and said, sharply, to Ma, "Don't let me do that again!"

"Jack was on guard," Ma said, gently.

That night was worst of all. The drums were faster and the yells were louder and fiercer. All up and down the creek war-cries answered war-cries and the bluffs echoed. There was no rest. Laura ached all over and there was a terrible ache in her very middle.

At the window Pa said, "Caroline, they are quarreling among themselves. Maybe they will fight each other."

"Oh, Charles, if they only will!" Ma said.

All night there was not a minute's rest. Just before dawn a last war-cry ended and Laura slept against Ma's knee.

She woke up in bed. Mary was sleeping beside her. The door was open, and by the sunshine on the floor Laura knew it was almost noon. Ma was cooking dinner. Pa sat on the doorstep.

He said to Ma, "There's another big party, going off to the south."

Laura went to the door in her nightgown, and she saw a long line of Indians far away. The line came up out of the black prairie and it went farther away southward. The Indians on their ponies were so small in the distance that they looked not much bigger than ants.

Pa said that two big parties of Indians had gone west that morning. Now this one was going south. It meant that the Indians had quarreled among themselves. They were going away from their camps in the creek bottoms. They would not go all together to their big buffalo-hunt.

That night the darkness came quietly. There was no sound except the rushing of the wind.

"Tonight we'll sleep!" Pa said, and they did. All night long they did not even dream. And in the morning Jack was still sleeping limp and flat on the same spot where he had been sleeping when Laura went to bed.

The next night was still, too, and again they all slept soundly. That morning Pa said he felt as fresh as a daisy, and he was going to do a little scouting along the creek.

He chained Jack to the ring in the house wall, and he took his gun and went out of sight down the creek road.

Laura and Mary and Ma could not do anything but wait until he came back. They stayed in the house and wished he would come. The sunshine had never moved so slowly on the floor as it did that day.

But he did come back. Late in the afternoon he came. And everything was all right. He had gone far up and down the creek and had seen many deserted Indian camps. All the Indians had gone away, except a tribe called the Osages.

In the woods Pa had met an Osage who could talk to him. This Indian told him that all the tribes except the Osages had made up their minds to kill the white people who had come into the Indian country. And they were getting ready to do it when the lone Indian came riding into their big pow-wow.

That Indian had come riding so far and fast because he did not want them to kill the white people. He was an Osage, and they called him a name that meant he was a great soldier.

"Soldat du Chêne," Pa said his name was.

"He kept arguing with them day and night," Pa said, "till all the other Osages agreed with him. Then he stood up and told the other tribes that if they started to massacre us, the Osages would fight them."

That was what had made so much noise, that last terrible night. The other tribes were howling at the

Osages, and the Osages were howling back at them. The other tribes did not dare fight Soldat du Chêne and all his Osages, so next day they went away.

"That's one good Indian!" Pa said. No matter what Mr. Scott said, Pa did not believe that the only good Indian was a dead Indian.

CHAPTER 24. INDIANS RIDE AWAY

There was another long night of sleep. It was so good to lie down and sleep soundly. Everything was safe and quiet. Only the owls called "Who-oo? Who-oo?" in the woods along the creek, while the great moon sailed slowly over the curve of the sky above the endless prairie.

In the morning the sun shone warmly. Down by the creek the frogs were croaking. "Garrump! Garrump!" they cried by the edge of the pools. "Knee deep! Knee deep! Better go 'round."

Ever since Ma had told them what the frogs were saying, Mary and Laura could hear the words plainly.

The door was open to let in the warm spring air. After breakfast Pa went out, whistling merrily. He was going to hitch Pet and Patty to the plow again. But his whistling suddenly stopped. He stood on the doorstep, looking toward the east, and he said, "Come here, Caroline. And you, Mary and Laura."

Laura ran out first, and she was surprised. The Indians were coming.

They did not come on the creek road. They came riding up out of the creek bottoms far to the east.

First came the tall Indian who had gone riding by the house in the moonlight. Jack was growling and Laura's heart beat fast. She was glad to be close to Pa. But she knew this was the good Indian, the Osage chief who had stopped the terrible war-cries.

His black pony came trotting willingly, sniffing the wind that blew its mane and tail like fluttering banners. The pony's nose and head were free; it wore no bridle. Not even one strap was on it anywhere. There was nothing to make it do anything it didn't want to do. Willingly it came trotting along the old Indian trail as if it liked to carry the Indian on its back.

Jack growled savagely, trying to get loose from his chain. He remembered this Indian who had pointed a gun at him. Pa said, "Be still, Jack." Jack growled again, and for the first time in their lives Pa struck him.

"Indians ride away" as settlers like the Ingalls family establish their homes on the American prairie in the late nineteenth century. Garth Williams illustrated a new edition of the Little House series in the last decade of Laura Ingalls Wilder's life (1953).

"Lie down! Be still!" Pa said. Jack cowered down and was still.

The pony was very near now, and Laura's heart beat faster and faster. She looked at the Indian's beaded moccasin, she looked up along the fringed legging that clung to the pony's bare side. A bright-colored blanket was wrapped around the Indian. One bare brown-red arm carried a rifle lightly across the pony's naked shoulders. Then Laura looked up at the Indian's fierce, still, brown face.

It was a proud, still face. No matter what happened, it would always be like that. Nothing would change it. Only the eyes were alive in that face, and they gazed steadily far away to the west. They did not move. Nothing moved or changed, except the eagle feathers standing straight up from the scalplock on the shaved head. The long feathers swayed and dipped, waving and spinning in the wind as the tall Indian on the black pony passed on into the distance.

"Du Chêne himself," Pa said, under his breath, and he lifted his hand in salute.

But the happy pony and the motionless Indian went by. They went by as if the house and stable and Pa and Ma and Mary and Laura were not there at all.

Pa and Ma and Mary and Laura slowly turned and looked at that Indian's proud straight back. Then other ponies and other blankets and shaved heads and eagle feathers came between. One by one on the path, more and more savage warriors were riding behind Du Chêne. Brown face after brown face went by. Ponies' manes and tails blew in the wind, beads glittered, fringe flapped, eagle feathers were waving on all the naked heads. Rifles lying on the ponies' shoulders bristled all along the line.

Laura was excited about the ponies. There were black ponies, bay ponies, gray and brown and spotted ponies. Their little feet went trippety-trip-trip, trip-pety-trip, pat-patter, pat-patter, trippety pat-patter, all along the Indian trail. Their nostrils widened at Jack and their bodies shied away from him, but they came on bravely, looking with their bright eyes at Laura.

"Oh, the pretty ponies! See the pretty ponies!" she cried, clapping her hands. "Look at the spotted one."

She thought she would never be tired of watching those ponies coming by, but after a while she began to look at the women and children on their backs. The women and children came riding behind the Indian men. Little naked brown Indians, no bigger than Mary and Laura, were riding the pretty ponies. The ponies did not have to wear bridles or saddles, and the little Indians did not have to wear clothes. All their skin was out in the fresh air and the sunshine. Their straight black hair blew in the wind and their black eyes sparkled with joy. They sat on their ponies stiff and still like grown-up Indians.

Laura looked and looked at the Indian children, and they looked at her. She had a naughty wish to be a little Indian girl. Of course she did not really mean it. She only wanted to be bare naked in the wind and the sunshine, and riding one of those gay little ponies.

The Indian children's mothers were riding ponies, too. Leather fringe dangled about their legs and blankets were wrapped around their bodies, but the only thing on their heads was their black, smooth hair. Their faces were brown and placid. Some had narrow bundles tied on their backs, and tiny babies' heads stuck out of the top of the bundles. And some babies and some small children rode in baskets hanging at the ponies' sides, beside their mothers.

More and more and more ponies passed, and more children, and more babies on their mothers' backs, and more babies in baskets on the ponies' sides. Then came a mother riding, with a baby in a basket on each side of her pony.

Laura looked straight into the bright eyes of the little baby nearer her. Only its small head showed above the basket's rim. Its hair was as black as a crow and its eyes were black as a night when no stars shine.

Those black eyes looked deep into Laura's eyes and she looked deep down into the blackness of that little baby's eyes, and she wanted that one little baby.

"Pa," she said, "get me that little Indian baby!"

"Hush, Laura!" Pa told her sternly.

The little baby was going by. Its head turned and its eyes kept looking into Laura's eyes.

"Oh, I want it! I want it!" Laura begged. The baby was going farther and farther away, but it did not stop looking back at Laura. "It wants to stay with me," Laura begged. "Please, Pa, please!"

"Hush, Laura," Pa said. "The Indian woman wants to keep her baby."

"Oh, Pa!" Laura pleaded, and then she began to cry. It was shameful to cry, but she couldn't help it. The little Indian baby was gone. She knew she would never see it any more.

Ma said she had never heard of such a thing. "For shame, Laura," she said, but Laura could not stop crying. "Why on earth do you want an Indian baby, of all things!" Ma asked her.

"Its eyes are so black," Laura sobbed. She could not say what she meant.

"Why, Laura," Ma said, "you don't want another baby. We have a baby, our own baby."

"I want the other one, too!" Laura sobbed, loudly.

"Well, I declare!" Ma exclaimed.

"Look at the Indians, Laura," said Pa. "Look west, and then look east, and see what you see."

Laura could hardly see at first. Her eyes were full of tears and sobs kept jerking out of her throat. But she obeyed Pa as best she could, and in a moment she was still. As far as she could see to the west and as far as she could see to the east there were Indians. There was no end to that long, long line.

"That's an awful lot of Indians," Pa said.

More and more and more Indians came riding by. Baby Carrie grew tired of looking at Indians and played by herself on the floor. But Laura sat on the doorstep, Pa stood close beside her, and Ma and Mary stood in the doorway. They looked and looked and looked at Indians riding by.

It was dinner-time, and no one thought of dinner. Indian ponies were still going by, carrying bundles of skins and tent-poles and dangling baskets and cooking pots. There were a few more women and a few more naked Indian children. Then the very last pony went by. But Pa and Ma and Laura and Mary still stayed in the doorway, looking, till that long line of Indians slowly pulled itself over the western edge of the world. And nothing was left but silence and emptiness. All the world seemed very quiet and lonely.

Ma said she didn't feel like doing anything, she was so let down. Pa told her not to do anything but rest.

"You must eat something, Charles," Ma said.

"No," said Pa. "I don't feel hungry." He went soberly to hitch up Pet and Patty, and he began again to break the tough sod with the plow.

Laura could not eat anything, either. She sat a long time on the doorstep, looking into the empty west where the Indians had gone. She seemed still to see waving feathers and black eyes and to hear the sound of ponies' feet.

Michael Dorris (1945–97)

Part German American, part Native American (Modoc), Michael Dorris was an eloquent writer of essays and novels reflecting on Native American experience. He earned an M.A. in anthropology from Yale University and founded the Native American Studies program at Dartmouth. He wrote *The Broken Cord: Fetal Alcohol Syndrome and the Loss of the Future,* an account of his adopted son's struggle with the damage inflicted by prenatal alcohol abuse. His novel *A Yel-*

low Raft in Blue Water (1987) has been widely acclaimed. He was married to Native American writer Louise Erdrich, with whom he collaborated for many years. He committed suicide in 1997. In this 1993 essay, he explores his poignantly ambivalent experience with reading Laura Ingalls Wilder's Little House books—first as a boy, then as a parent. His perspective shifts as he rereads the books as an adult, and he asks searching questions about how to deal with the resulting discomfort.

Trusting the Words

On the Banks of Plum Creek was the first brand-new hardback book I ever owned. It was not a casual or impulse purchase—such a luxury was beyond a family of our economic level—but a considered acquisition. Two summers before, during my daily browse in the small neighborhood library a short walk from where I lived, I had stumbled upon the shelf of Laura Ingalls Wilder novels. With their pastel covers, gentle illustrations, large type, and homey titles, they were appealing, inviting, but which one to try first? In the manner of Goldilocks, I decided that *Farmer Boy* looked too long, *Little House in the Big Woods* too short. *Plum Creek,* though, was just right. More than just right: by an amazing coincidence, I had just consumed a plum for lunch!

Naturally, like thousands of other readers over the past 50 years, I was hooked from page one. The snug little dwelling dug into the side of a creek bank was as irresistible to me at age eight as Bilbo Baggins' similar den proved to be some 10 years later. The ever-mobile Ingalls family—adaptable, affectionate Pa; conventional, resourceful Ma; pretty, good-girl Mary; baby Carrie—were the Swiss Family Robinson next door, the us-against-the-world American ideal of underdogs who, through grit and wit and optimism, prevailed over every natural disaster and took advantage of every available resource in their inexorable path toward increased creature comforts and status. As linchpin and leading protagonist, second-child Laura was full-swing into the adventure of growing up, and as such she was not just *me,* but me the way I *aspired* to be: plucky and brave, composed of equal parts good will and self-interest. Her life was a constantly unfolding tapestry, its events intricately connected and stitched with affectionate detail. The cast of human and animal players auxiliary to the central family was limited and manageable enough for a reader to grasp as distinct individuals, and within the balanced, safe context of ultimate parental protection, even a week-long blizzard was the occasion for a chapter titled "A Day of Games."

I doubt if one of today's powerful publishing marketing committees would project the young me as a likely target audience for the Wilder books. Superficially, Laura and I had so little in common, so few intersections of experience with which I should logically have been able to identify. As the mixed-blood, male, only child of a single-parent, mostly urban, fixed-income family, I would have been expected by the experts to prefer novels more reflective of myself. True, I wasn't immune to "boy books." I dutifully followed every scrape that Frank and Joe Hardy fell into, worked my way through James Fenimore Cooper, Charles Dickens, and Alexander Dumas, and had a stack of D.C. Comics in which both Superman and Batman figured prominently. But when the time came to own a real book, to receive the first volume in what has become an extensive personal collection of literature, I didn't hesitate: *On the Banks of Plum Creek* was an old friend I knew I'd want to read many more times in the years to come, as indeed I have.

The nine Little House books—*Little House in the Big Woods, Little House on the Prairie, Farmer Boy, On the Banks of Plum Creek, By the Shores of Silver Lake, The Long Winter, Little Town on the Prairie, These Happy Golden Years,* and *The First Four Years*—chronicle and particularize like no other source the mythic American frontier journey from precarious adversity into middle-class security. If, as it appears from *The Ghost in the Little House,* William Holtz's new and convincing life of Rose Wilder Lane—Laura's only child who grew up to be a thoroughly modern woman and one of the most far-flung and daring journalists of the 1920s and 1930s—the novels are more collaborative biography than homespun autobiography, their power is in no way diminished. That the characters arc shaped and crafted verisimilitudes rather than drawn, word-for-word, upon fact only contributes to the readability of the series. The belated discovery that a generous, self-taught, talented, and complicated daughter shaped the rough yet keenly precise recollections of her farmer mother into art is an intriguing surprise—but certainly does not undermine either the historical or the humanistic value of a saga that at its heart depicts the universal struggle of a child growing to adulthood and independence.

Far more problematic, at least for me, were the issues raised when, with the enthusiasm of a father who had long looked forward to sharing a favorite tale, I sat down last year to begin reading the books to my two daughters, ages seven and eight. Not one page into *Little House in the Big Woods,* I heard my own voice saying, "As far as a man could go to the north in a day, or a week, or a whole month, there was nothing but woods. There were no houses. There were no roads. There were no people. There were only trees and the wild animals who had their homes among them."

Say what? Excuse me, but weren't we forgetting the Chippewa branch of my daughters' immediate ancestry, not to mention the thousands of resident Menominees, Potawatomis, Sauks, Foxes, Winnebagos, Ottawas who inhabited mid-nineteenth-century Wisconsin, as they had for many hundreds of years. Exactly upon whose indigenous land was Grandma and Grandpa's snug little house constructed? Had they paid for the bountiful property, teaming with wild game and fish? This cozy, fun-filled world of extended Ingallses was curiously empty, a pristine wilderness in which only white folks toiled and cavorted, ate and harvested, celebrated and were kind to each other.

My dilemma, as raconteur, was clear. My little girls looked up to me with trusting eyes, eager to hear me continue with the first of these books I had approached with such anticipation. I had made "an event" out of their reading, an intergenerational gift, and now, in the cold light of an adult perspective, I realized that I was, in my reluctance to dilute the pleasure of a good story with the sober stuff of history, in the process of perpet-

uating a Eurocentric myth that was still very much alive. One had only to peruse newspaper accounts of contemporary Wisconsin controversies over tribal fishing rights, bingo emporia, and legal and tax jurisdiction to realize that many of Grandpa and Grandma's descendants remained determined that there could be "no people" except those who were just like them.

Okay, I admit it. I closed the book rather than be politically correct at 8 p.m. in my daughters' bedroom. I'd save the cold water of reality for the light of day, and anyway, I seemed to remember that once Ma and Pa pushed west they had encountered native people.

"Let's start instead tomorrow with *Little House on the Prairie,*" I suggested. This idea went over well, since it evoked in my girls the visual image of the pretty, if often saccharine, TV series of the same name.

Fast forward to the next evening, paragraph two: "They were going to the Indian country."

Good sign! The packing up and the journey west were lovingly and evocatively related. The sense of space and sky found on the Plains was gloriously rendered. The pages turned; my daughters eyes stayed bright long past their usual bedtime; the book was everything I remembered—realistic, lyrical, exciting in all the right ways.

And then page 46:

Laura chewed and swallowed, and she said, "I want to see a papoose." "Mercy on us!" Ma said, "Whatever makes you want to see Indians? We will see enough of them. More than we want to, I wouldn't wonder."

"They wouldn't hurt us, would they?" Mary asked. Mary was always good; she never spoke with her mouth full.

"Why don't you like Indians, Ma?" Laura asked, and she caught a drip of molasses with her tongue.

"I just don't like them, and don't lick your fingers, Laura," said Ma.

"This is Indian country, isn't it?" Laura said. "What did we come to their country for, if you don't like them?"

Ma said she didn't know whether this was Indian country or not. She didn't know where the Kansas line was. But whether or no, the Indians would not be here long. Pa had word from a man in Washington that the Indian Territory would be open to settlement soon.

What was a responsible father to do? Stop the narrative, explain that Ma is a know-nothing racist? Describe the bitter injustice of unilateral treaty abridgment? Break into a chorus of "Oklahoma" and then point out how American popular culture has long covered up the shame of the Dawes Act by glossing it over with Sooner folklore? This time, I simply created a line of dialogue.

"That's awful, Ma," I had Laura say. "I'm ashamed to hear such a thing."

But the fantasy of the 1990s-enlightened Laura evaporated not 10 pages later.

> That night by the fire Laura asked again when she would see a papoose, but Pa didn't know. He said you never saw Indians unless they wanted you to see them. He had seen Indians when he was a boy in New York State, but Laura never had. She knew they were wild men with red skins, and their hatchets were called tomahawks.
>
> Pa knew all about wild animals, so he must know about wild men, too. Laura thought he would show her a papoose, someday, just as he had shown her fawns, and little bears, and wolves.

That part, I confess, I simply skipped, edited right out, blipped. In no time flat, Pa was back to his fiddle, and Ma was doing something deft and culinary with cornmeal. Nature was Nature: "Only the wind rustled in the prairie grasses. The big, yellow moon was sailing high overhead. The sky was so full of light that not one star twinkled in it, and all the prairie was a shadowy mellowness."

And there were no Indians, no cholera-ridden, starving reservations, no prohibitions to the practice of native religion, no Wounded Knee a few hundred miles to the north, no Sand Creek an equal distance to the west. Manifest Destiny protected its own, and family values prevailed, staunchly Calvinist and oblivious to any ethical messiness that might interfere with the romance.

The next chapter, "Moving In," was heralded by a drawing of tipis. I closed the book and kissed the girls good night, then retreated to my office to continue reading on my own. For a while, beyond Ma's passing disparaging comments about not wanting to "live like Indians," the Ingalls family contented itself with building a house and fending off a wolf pack. Good clean fun, character-building hard work, the grist that made this country great.

Until . . .

Suddenly (Jack, the bulldog) stood up and growled a fierce, deep growl. The hair on his neck stood straight up and his eyes glared red.

Laura was frightened. Jack had never growled at her before. Then she looked over her shoulder where Jack was looking, and she saw two naked wild men coming, one behind the other, on the Indian trail.

"Mary! Look!" she cried. Mary looked and saw them, too.

They were tall thin, fierce-looking men. Their skin was brownish-red. Their heads seemed to go up to a peak, and the peak was a tuft of hair that stood straight up and ended in feathers. Their eyes were black and still and glittering, like snake's eyes.

The Indians went into the new house and Laura worried for the safety of Ma and baby Carrie. "I'm going to let Jack loose." Laura whispered, hoarsely. "Jack will kill them."

But no, the Indians only wanted some of Ma's cornbread and Pa's tobacco. They were wearing skunk skins, which didn't smell good, and their eyes glittered some more, but otherwise they were perfectly benign. When Pa came home, he at first dealt with news of the visit with laudable equanimity, but then went on, before stopping himself, to add, "The main thing is to be on good terms with the Indians. We don't want to wake up some night with a band of the screeching dev—"

The concluding chapters of *Little House on the Prairie* were full of Indians—some threatening, some noble. The settlers worried over the possibility of being attacked and driven out, but it didn't transpire. Instead, inevitably, the Indians were forced to evacuate in an endless line that trailed past the family home. Pa took this as a given.

> "When white settlers come into a country, the Indians have to move on. The government is going to move these Indians farther west, any time now. That's why we're here, Laura. White people are going to settle all this country, and we get the best land because we get here first and take our pick. Now do you understand?"
>
> "Yes, Pa," Laura said. "But, Pa, I thought this was Indian Territory. Won't it make the Indians mad to have to—"
>
> "No more questions Laura," Pa said firmly. "Go to sleep."

Pa never felt as guilty as I would have liked him to, though he did disagree with his friend Mr. Scott, who maintained that "the only good Indian is a dead Indian." Ma, on the other hand, remained an unreconstructed bigot—as late as *The Long Winter*, three novels and many years later, the very mention of even friendly, helpful Indians set her off.

> "'What Indian?' Ma asked [Pa]. She looked as if she were smelling the smell of an Indian whenever she said the word. Ma despised Indians. She was afraid of them, too."

For her part, Laura seemed typically open-minded, wanting at one point to adopt an Indian baby. "'Its eyes are so black,' Laura sobbed. She could not say what she meant."

At last, the Ingalls family, emblematic of all those like them who went west with the blithe assumption that resident American Indians had no title rights to the country they had occupied from time immemorial, witnessed the realization of their dream: a vanishing native population. Surprisingly, it was not a jubilant moment.

> It was dinner-time, and no one thought of dinner. Indian ponies were still going by, carrying bunches of skins and tent-poles and dangling baskets and cooking pots. There were a few more women and a few more naked Indian children and Laura and Mary still stayed in the doorway, looking, till that long line of Indians slowly pulled itself over the western edge of the world. And nothing was left but silence and emptiness. All the world seemed very quiet and lonely.

As it turned out, I *didn't* read aloud the Little House books to my daughters because, quite frankly, I realized I couldn't have kept my mouth shut at the objectionable parts. I would have felt compelled to interrupt the story constantly with editorial asides, history lessons, thought questions, critiques of the racism or sexism buried in the text. I would have studiously purified those novels, treated them as sociology or fixed them up to suit a contemporary and, I firmly believe, more enlightened sensibility.

Certainly they could be used that way, but, I wonder, would my daughters then grow up with the selective fond memories of each volume that I myself carried? Or, would they learn from me that every page of a book had to pass a test in order for the whole to entertain? Would reading with me become a chore, a "learning experience," a source of tension, and not the pleasure I wished it to be?

Laura Ingalls Wilder and her daughter Rose Wilder Lane created a series peopled by characters who were, for better or worse, true to the prevailing attitudes of their day. Resisting the temptation to stereotype or sensationalize beyond the often ill-informed opinions of both adults and children, they portray the actual incidents that involve Indians as invariably anticlimactic—more ordinary and less dramatic than anyone, even Pa, expects them to be. Distilled from the aura of mystery and danger, the Indians on the periphery of the Ingalls family's vision are thin, unfortunate, and determinedly honest. Their journey is the sad underside of the bright pioneer coin, and their defeat and banishment brings no one any glory. Ma and Pa's self-serving lack of compassion was probably no worse than most and better than some of those who filed claims west of the Mississippi 150 years ago; to create them otherwise and still present them as "typical" would be, however politically correct, false.

Thinking back on my own various interactions with the Little House books, I remembered that I had never much cared for Ma—even when I was a young boy she had struck me as prudish and cautious and uptight, with untested prejudices and unexamined rules that fairly cried out for rebellion. I remembered that I had Ma to thank, possibly more than anyone else in real life or in literature, for my first startling awareness that an adult authority figure could actually be wrong and narrow-minded. I remembered that those nagging, unanswered questions about what *did* happen to Indians in the nineteenth century, and *why,* had sent me to the history section of the library, which had led me in turn to school research projects and maps, activism in the 1960s, support of the American Indian Movement, and ultimately, no doubt, contributed heavily to my founding of the Native American Studies Program at Dartmouth College in 1972, and teaching there for the next 15 years. Take that, Ma!

Books, important as they can and should be, are after all but part of the much larger context that informs them. They illuminate our experience, but at the same time our experience sheds light back upon their ideas and theories. A book less converts than it reaffirms what we otherwise already sense or believe. Stories in which characters are distasteful or complicated merely reflect the world as it is and as such are no more threatening than, and perhaps equally as enlightening as, texts that encourage their readers toward a wider tolerance of human diversity—like the ones that apparently so terrified certain members of the New York City School Board.

I placed the Little House novels on the top shelf of the bookcase and told my daughters I thought it would be better if they read them, when and if they wanted to, to themselves. I trust that they will not be corrupted into Indianophobes even as they thrill to the description of a runaway buggy or warm to the first blush of young love when Laura and Almanzo go courting. I trust that they will be able to differentiate courage from pettiness, justice from exploitation. I'll bide my time, and when, eventually, each of my girls bursts through a door, eyes ablaze with indignation, waving a book in her hand . . . then we'll talk about it.

Louise Erdrich (b. 1954)

The author of highly acclaimed novels for adults, such as *Love Medicine* (1984), *The Beet Queen* (1986), and *The Antelope Wife* (1998), Louise Erdrich is one of the most accomplished and recognized Native American writers of her generation. Together with her husband Michael Dorris (see his essay in this section), she has created complex and subtle portrayals of American society, focusing on Native American themes. In an important essay about the task facing Native American writers, she wrote, "In the light of enormous loss, they must tell the stories of contemporary survivors while protecting and celebrating the cores of cultures left in the wake of the catastrophe."[1] Of Turtle Mountain Chippewa and European American ancestry, Erdrich has raised six children, three of whom are adopted. She describes *The Birchbark House* (1999) as "an attempt to retrace my own family's history."[2] In their research, she and her mother and her sister found ancestors on both sides who lived on Madeline Island in Lake Superior, the setting of this novel, in the 1840s, when the events described took place. At the beginning of the novel, in a brief passage entitled "The Girl from Spirit Island," which appears before the chapters reprinted here, we get a haunting glimpse of a baby girl who is the only surviving human being on an island after a smallpox epidemic. Later in the novel, we learn her identity and who rescued her.

When asked whether she regards *The Birchbark House* as a kind of answer to the Little House books, Erdrich replied, "I read the Little House books as a child and so have my children. I love their humor and warmth, but am disturbed by Ma's racism. Given their widespread use in the schools, I do not think it would be wrong to annotate some of her more insulting remarks. Perhaps their publisher will do that in time. I didn't write this book as an answer but hope it will be perceived as an enlargement of the view encompassed in Laura's world."[3] In her preface to the book, Erdrich writes, "The name Omakayas appears on a Turtle Mountain census. I am using it in the original translation because I've been told those old names should be given life. The name is pronounced Oh-MAH-kay-ahs. Dear reader, when you speak this name out loud you will be honoring the life of an Ojibwa girl who lived long ago."

NOTES

1. Louise Erdrich, "Where I Ought to Be: A Writer's Sense of Place," *New York Times Book Review* 28 July 1985: 23.
2. Louise Erdrich, "Thanks and Acknowledgments," *The Birchbark House* (New York: Hyperion, 1999).
3. Louise Erdrich Bio, *Kidsreads.com,* Hyperion Books for Children, 1999, 28 March 2005 <http://www.kidsreads.com/authors/au-erdrich-louise.asp>.

From *The Birchbark House*

CHAPTER 1. THE BIRCHBARK HOUSE

She was named Omakayas, or Little Frog, because her first step was a hop. She grew into a nimble young girl of seven winters, a thoughtful girl with shining brown eyes and a wide grin, only missing her two top front teeth. She touched her upper lip. She still wasn't used to those teeth gone, and was impatient for new, grown-up teeth to complete her smile. Just like her namesake, Omakayas now stared long at the silky patch of bog before she gathered herself and jumped. One hummock. Safety. Omakayas sprang wide again. This time she landed on the very tip-top of a pointed old stump. She balanced there, looking all around. The lagoon water moved in sparkling crescents. Thick swales of swamp grass rippled. Mud turtles napped in the sun. The world was so calm that Omakayas could hear herself blink. Only the sweet call of a solitary white-throated sparrow pierced the cool of the woods beyond.

All of a sudden Grandma yelled.

"I found it!"

Startled, Omakayas slipped and spun her arms in wheels. She teetered, but somehow kept her balance. Two big, skipping hops, another leap, and she was on dry land. She stepped over spongy leaves and moss, into the woods where the sparrows sang nesting songs in delicate relays.

"Where are you?" Nokomis yelled again. "I found the tree!"

"I'm coming," Omakayas called back to her grandmother.

It was spring, time to cut the birchbark.

All winter long Omakayas's family lived in a cabin of sweet-scented cedar at the edge of the village of La-Pointe, on an island in Lake Superior that her people called Moningwanaykaning, Island of the Golden-Breasted Woodpecker. As soon as the earth warmed, the birchbark house always took shape under Nokomis's swift hands. Now the dappled light of tiny new leaves moved on Grandma's beautiful, softly lined face. In one hand she waved her sharp knife, taken from the beaded pouch on her hip. In the other hand she held tobacco. Nokomis was ready to make an offering to the spirits, or manitous. They loved tobacco. Omakayas banged the tree her grandmother had found.

"Yes, here, here it is! This one!"

Omakayas was skinny, wiry, and tough for seven winters. She slammed the trunk of the birch with a big rotten stick. Splinters of soft wood flew.

"Booni!" Nokomis scolded. "Leave it alone!"

She walked up to the tree and put her leathery paw-like hands on the smooth bark, feeling for flaws. "Yes," she decided, her eyes sparkling at her grand-daughter. "A good one."

"Is it ready?"

"Geget," said Nokomis. "Surely."

Nokomis's tobacco pouch was decorated with blue and white beads in the shape of a pipe. She had owned this tobacco bag ever since Omakayas could remember. When she talked to the manitous, Nokomis dipped out a pinch of tobacco.

"Old Sister," she said to the birchbark tree, "we need your skin for our shelter."

At the base of the tree, Nokomis left her offering, sweet and fragrant. Then she peered closely, deciding just where to make the first cut. Suddenly, she pressed her razor-sharp knife into the bark. Omakayas stepped back. Light filtered golden and green onto their faces. Tiny white flowers poked out of dead leaves. There were still traces of grainy old snowbanks in the shadiest spots, but in places the sun was actually hot. Pow! As soon as Grandma made the proper cuts, the birchbark, filled with spring water, nearly burst from the tree!

Omakayas helped her grandmother carefully push the bark aside, then the two peeled it away strip by strip. She and Omakayas carried the light papery pink-brown rolls out of the woods, down a trail to a special place near the water.

Here, they set up the birchbark house.

Damp ground made Nokomis's old bones ache, so she spread out her brown cattail mat and sat down there to sew those pieces of bark together. Omakayas helped her, threading the tough basswood strands through holes punched by Grandma's awl. Meanwhile, Mama and Omakayas's older sister tied together a frame of bent willow poles. Finally, as the light faded, they fastened the mats of bark onto the willow frame, a half skeleton of pliable saplings. The bark mats overlapped like shingles, to shed the rain. Each one was secured to the next, so as not to blow off in a storm. When the house was swept out, smoothed, fussily arranged, and admired, they moved in. The children—Omakayas's brother Little Pinch, baby Neewo, Omakayas's older sister, pretty Angeline, and Omakayas herself—spread their blankets around the stone fire pit. Mama and Nokomis hung the smoky woven bags of rice and tools and medicines from the willow poles above.

Omakayas's family were Anishinabeg and this was their island. Her father, her Deydey, was in the fur trade business, which meant that he was often gone, paddling the great canoes for the fur company or sometimes trapping animals himself. Yellow Kettle, her mother, was quick-tempered but always laughing, and her eyes shrewdly took in the world. Yellow Kettle was a strong-looking woman, and beautiful. Her smile was generous, enigmatic, slightly crooked, and kind. She missed nothing when it came to her children—it was impossible to hide a half-done job, ridiculous even to think of sneaking away in the morning before gathering wood for the fire and water for her cooking pot. And if Mama didn't notice the younger children's whereabouts, Omakayas's older sister, Angeline, surely would.

Angeline was smart and so pretty people turned in their tracks to stare at her. Her hair was thick, her hands clever. The beads in her designs were laid down in strict rows. Her stitches never faltered. Her steps, when she walked or danced, were clear and graceful. She was so perfect that Omakayas despaired. Still, she hoped that she herself would turn out like Angeline, and was sometimes embarrassed to find herself following at Angeline's heels like a puppy. Most of the time Angeline was kind to Omakayas, and let her tag along and admire, from a distance. But there were also times her words were sharp as bee stings, and at those times Omakayas shed tears her sister never knew or probably even cared about, for as very beautiful people sometimes are, Angeline could be just a little cold-hearted at times.

Omakayas's little brother Pinch was the only really big problem in her life. The sad truth was, and she couldn't tell this to a single person, Omakayas didn't like Little Pinch. She thought there was something wrong with him—so greedy, so loud! But although his ways were mischievous and bold, Pinch loved his mother deeply, and he clung to her side. In fact, he took up all her attention, even more than the baby! He clutched Mama's skirts with fat, tough little fingers. He yelled at Omakayas if she was slow in giving up her willow doll, her little rock people, or anything else for that matter, including food, special pieces of driftwood she found, even her favorite sleeping place, near Grandma. He thought he deserved *everything*.

At least when it came to Neewo there was nothing to complain about. He was so sweet that Omakayas often pretended that he was her very own baby. Of course, she hardly ever got to hold him, for he was still very young. Still, she was sure he preferred her to Angeline, and certainly to Pinch. Sometimes he even held his arms out to her when Mama was holding him, and yelled with delight when Omakayas picked him up.

As it grew dark, the family ate makuks of moose stew and fresh greens and berries, licked their fingers and bowls clean, and at last rolled themselves into warm, fluffy rabbit-skin blankets that still smelled of the cedary smoke of their winter cabin. They were glad to be close to fire, sleeping on soft grassy earth, under leafy sky, and best of all, near water. They fell asleep to the peaceful, curious, continual lapping sound of waves. The fresh wind across the big lake blew away the smoke of cooking fires and vanquished the mosquitoes that came out in whining droves and had plagued them in town. It was good to sleep where the village dogs didn't bark all night and where the only sound to disturb their dreams was the pine trees sifting wind in a lulling roar.

Unless, of course, it stormed.

The moon went down to a fingernail's sliver and the corn popped from the ground. The leaves of the birch grew big enough to flutter in the wind. And then, one night, the first storm of the summer struck the island and startled everybody from their dreams.

The fire was down to red winking eyes when Omakayas woke with an uneasy feeling. Something approached. She'd felt a footstep. Omakayas was always the one to sleep near Grandma and now she rolled close. There was a lonely insistance to the sound of the wind, and then everything went still. Far off, she heard one huge footstep. There was a long silence. Then another step fell. The earth shook slightly beneath her, vibrated as though she lay on the head of a vast drum.

A drum! She remembered that Grandma had said the island was the drum of the thunder beings. Closer and closer they came, shaking earth with their footsteps. Omakayas's lonely feeling became fright. She hid her face and tried not to think of balls of witch fire or the hooting of Grandfather Owl. She tried to keep herself from picturing pakuks, the skeletons of little children, flying through the woods, or the icy breath of giant windigos striding over the ground, cracking trees off with every foot crunch. Another step. Another and another fell and then the wind howled to life. Rain slashed against the tightly sewn walls. A breath of air stirred up the slumbering coals and cast shadows leaping and fighting on the inside walls of the little birch-bark house.

The willow poles trembled, bouncing with the force of the gusts of wind. The birchbark scraped and flapped but was held on with tight stitches. Omakayas

hid her face as thunder rolled, smacking onto the lakeshore, waking everything and everyone with its quick violence. The storm punished the ground and then passed over, dying off in softer mumbles. The dull thuds of thunder falling in the distance now felt comforting, and before the sounds entirely faded, Omakayas was asleep.

Moningwanaykaning, Island of the Golden-Breasted Woodpecker, sparkled innocently after that night of raw thunder and lightning. Omakayas woke and immediately began wondering. What had the storm done to the trees? What had the waves washed onto the beach? What interesting bits of wood that she could use for pretend dolls? What kind of day would it be? Were the little berries on the edge of the path ripe yet? An unpleasant piece of wondering came to her, too. Had her mother finished scraping and tanning that ugly moose hide or would she have to help her? Oh, she hoped not. How she hoped! There was a saying she hated. Grandma said it all too often. "Each animal," she would say, "has just enough brains to tan its own hide." Mama tanned the moose hide with the very brains of the moose and Omakayas hated the oozy feel of them on her hands, not to mention the boring, endless scraping and rubbing that went into making a hide soft enough for makazins.

From a fire in the center of the bark house a thin curl of smoke rose, then vanished through a crescent of sunlight in the roof. If only she could escape with the smoke! She could already hear Mama and Grandma outside at the cooking fires. They were planning the day's work. In no time at all, that soaking moose hide would be stretched on a branch frame and she would be required to scrape at it with the sharpened deer's shoulder bone that her mother kept in a bundle of useful things near the door. Her arms would tire; they would feel like falling off. Her fingers would go numb. Her back would hurt. The awful smell would get into her skin. And meanwhile, all the little birds would find the luscious patch of berries she alone knew about. By the time she got that stupid old moose hide softened up, they would have eaten every last berry. She must act. Quickly!

The air was fresh, delicious, smelling of new leaves in the woods, just-popped-out mushrooms, the pelts of young deer. The air flowed in, rainwashed, under the strips of birchbark walls she had helped sew together yesterday. Like a small, striped snake, like a salamander, or a squirrel maybe, or a raccoon, something quick, little, harmless, and desperate, she slid, crept, wiggled underneath the sides of the summer house. The seam of bark caught her in the small of the back, stuck tight. If only she hadn't done such a good job of sewing it up! If only, too, Angeline didn't have such quick ears and sure knowledge of her whereabouts at all times. There was a firm pressure suddenly at the small of her back, still caught on the inside. Her sister's foot. Her sister's gloating voice.

"Neshemay! Baby sister! Little Frog, don't go jumping off!"

Then there was her mother, rounding the back of the house, one side of her hair still flowing down, unbraided. She glanced in surprise at Omakayas, trapped, and then unable to hide her amusement, a big grin spread over Mama's face. Her admired big sister, her beloved mother, laughing! There was Omakayas—laughter from the front and laughter from behind—and suddenly, all of last night's thunder in her heart.

Omakayas sat near the cooking fire and slowly, with deep inner fury, ate a bowl of cold stew. She dragged out time waiting for her hateful job to start. Mama was wrestling that hide out of the stream now, where it had been soaking for days and nights, gathering up its scummy, woolly slime. Mama had already set up the dreaded frame of branches and there were strings of hide nearby that she would use to tie the skin up tight so that it could be worked. Omakayas knew how important it was to tan the skin, how her mother would cut up the soft smoked hide and sew on the winter's makazins all summer. She pictured her mother finishing them with lovely, soft toe puckers so the girls' feet could twitch and dance. She could imagine Yellow Kettle beading them, lining them inside with the silkiest rabbit fur and pieces of an old wool blanket. Yes, it was an important task, but Omakayas still didn't want it. She finished her stew, cleaned the bowl out with

sand at the shore of the lake, and waited with a sigh for her mother to ask her to fetch the deer-bone scraper.

Her mother said something else, though.

"I need my scissors!"

Omakayas sat up, suddenly full of energy.

Omakayas's mother was well known for owning a pair of scissors, and other women were always borrowing them. Omakayas's first job ever since she could walk was to fetch her mother's scissors, kept safe from her small fingers in a beaded woolen case, and bring them home. She had never failed, for it was a job she liked not only because she was sometimes given a handful of manomin, rice, or a little chunk of maple sugar by the borrowing lady, but because there were things to see on the way there and back.

Right now her sister, Angeline, was digging at the ground near spruce trees and cutting lengths of the roots, used to secure the house better and to finish baskets. She was cheerful, humming at her work, glad to have gotten the better of Omakayas. She'd show Angeline! Let her work until her hands fell off! Omakayas had a fun job to do!

"Go fetch me the scissors from Old Tallow," said Omakayas's mother. Without a moment's hesitation, before Mama changed her mind and remembered about the help she needed with the stinky hide, Omakayas ran off.

CHAPTER 2. OLD TALLOW

Although she lived in town, Old Tallow was so isolated by the force and strangeness of her personality that she could have been surrounded by a huge dark forest. She had never had any children, and each of her three husbands had slunk off in turn during the night, never to be seen again. Nobody knew exactly what it was that Tallow, in her younger days, had done to drive them off. It had probably been something terrible. After the last husband left, her face seemed to have gotten old suddenly, though the rest of her hadn't weakened. She was a rangy woman over six feet in height. She was powerful, lean, and lived surrounded by ferocious animals more wolf than dog and fiercely devoted to her. Old Tallow could bring down a bear with her pack of dogs, her gun, or even the razor-sharp spear that she practiced throwing into the splintered base of a tree. The dogs were bull-tough and the yellow one, particularly, showed its wolf origins in the springy length of its legs.

For some reason, Old Tallow seemed to treat her, Omakayas, somewhat differently than other children. She didn't scream at her, or heap distain on her, order her away from her cabin or set her dogs on her. Omakayas thought perhaps it was because Old Tallow respected her mama and grandma. Old Tallow respected almost nobody else, so this was extra-meaningful. The three women often sat together, talking in the dusk. Also, Old Tallow, who loved to hunt and was very skilled, shared her catch with them when Deydey was gone. They would sometimes wake to find a haunch of venison just inside the door, or bear meat, a fish or two. In fact, she now remembered that Old Tallow was responsible for the hide of the moose, which she had shared. Old Tallow liked to make her deliveries at night, which was another thing. Most other people hated to go about in the dark when Grandfather Owl was calling *kokoko, kokoko,* and anything could happen.

But of course, Old Tallow was afraid of nothing.

Omakayas approached Tallow's cabin warily because of the dogs. She stood for a moment at the end of the trail, gathering her confidence before she rounded the corner. One dog in particular seemed to hate her—the big yellow one. Omakayas was careful not to startle him or gaze too long into his mean, clouded eyes. Once, he had snapped at her and worried the sleeve of her dress. There he stood now, to bar her way to Tallow's door. Omakayas screwed up her courage, breathed calmly. She walked forward, shoving him aside as though she had not a care for his dripping teeth. She got ready to deliver a hard kick if he lunged, and walked past him without showing her fear. The dog bristled at her, baring its teeth in an ugly snarl, but let her pass by. The other dogs—the black, the brown with the lopped-off tail, the small whitish one, and the droopy orange runt—merely looked alert and regarded her with neutral interest.

Old Tallow's cabin was small, neat, thickly mudded between logs. There was a log bench beside the door. Sure enough, Old Tallow sat upon it smoking her pipe. A fragrant curl of sweet kinnikinnick smoke stirred from the red stone bowl.

As though she had known Omakayas was coming for the precious scissors, Old Tallow had them on her lap, safe in the bead-decorated pouch of red trade wool that Mama had made specially to hold them.

"Ahneen, little skinny one," she growled.

Old Tallow's legs stuck out like poles, tattered makazins flapped on her wagging feet as she drew impatiently upon her pipe. She tamped the bowl of the pipe with huge hands; her arms were long and sinewy. The old blue dress she wore was trimmed with the teeth of fox at the collar, beaded halfway around the scraggly, ripped hem. Tallow, in her galloping hunts through the woods, was hard on clothes and wore out her makazins one pair right after the next. Even now, a toe stuck out from the ripped front seam. She tucked her braids up underneath a man's hat, a white man's hat with a heavy brim. She was hardly seen without it, even in her own house. In the band of the hat she always wore a little gold-shafted feather. This was the feather of the golden-breasted woodpecker, the bird that gave its name and chattering cry to this island.

"You want the scissors!" Her voice was abrupt, but not unkind.

"Yes," said Omakayas, glad that Old Tallow was outside. The yellow dog knew it was wrong to intimidate Omakayas. Sure enough, Old Tallow scolded him.

"You," she shrieked at the snarling dog, "booni! Leave her alone. This is your last warning! Touch her and you die!"

The yellow dog turned aside, shrugging and cringing mean-spiritedly, eyeing Omakayas. She imagined she heard the yellow dog say, *I'll get you next time! Wait until there's just the two of us. You'll see!*

Relieved, Omakayas walked past the other dogs straight up to the old woman and stood before her.

"Ahneen, my auntie," she said. "Mino aya sana."

She wished the old woman good health, and called her "Auntie" because it was a sign of affection, though Omakayas was really not sure exactly what she felt. After she'd spoken, she stood politely, waiting. Old Tallow smiled, nodded, and blew a blast of smoke out her nostrils. Then she put her hand into the pouch at her waist. She rummaged around for a bit, then suddenly drew forth a small, grime-covered lump of maple sugar, rock-hard and wonderful.

"You take this," she said, her voice cracked and dry, as though salted. "And this, too." She handed Omakayas the scissors, waved her back onto the trail, and as this was as friendly as Old Tallow ever got, Omakayas went away satisfied.

Before she went back on the trail, Omakayas rinsed off the old candy lump in the lake. It came out beautifully, creamy-golden, translucent and grainy-dark. And sweet. She started walking, her treasure now wrapped in a leaf. As she walked, Omakayas thought. There was no way to share such a tough nut of sweetness. How would she divide it? Omakayas decided she did not want to cause trouble at home. Furthermore, it suddenly made sense to her that at least one person in the family should get the full effect of the maple sugar. She would pop the whole thing into her mouth. All at once! This would save problems. Aaaaah. The lump was delicious, tasting of spring sweetness and the inside of trees. Besides, Omakayas reasoned, as she walked contentedly along, the taste of the sugar would save her from eating every one of the berries she was sure she would find on the path.

Omakayas's feet moved slower and even slower yet. For one thing, the moose hide waited. For another, she was still angry with her older sister, and didn't want to see Angeline. She could still feel that sister foot pressing hateful on her back. If only there were some way to impress Angeline, cause her envy, make her say, "Can I have some of those berries, please, please, please?" You can be sure, Omakayas thought, her face taking on a faraway, haughty expression, she would be slow in answering! Yet the worst of it was this: her sister was usually on her side, helping her plan tricks on the other children in the village or gathering new ferns or snaring rabbits, visiting the grave houses looking for sugar or food left for the spirits, tossing off her clothes to swim with her. And to have her older sister laugh at her hurt Omakayas so much inside that she both wanted Angeline to smile in surprise, to be proud, to envy her, and to feel rotten and be sorry forever. So Omakayas took the slow way back looking for odaemin, little red heartberries, in the sunny margins of the woods near the ground.

She carefully removed the hard lump of sweetness from her mouth, stuck it back in its leaf just inside the pocket of her dress. Just as the taste of maple sugar faded along her tongue, she bent over, pushed back delicate leaves, and found masses of plump red little berries. Ah! One, two, three. She'd eaten a huge handful. Another. She grinned, thinking that she'd allow her sister to return with her to plunder them, but only if Angeline changed her ways.

All of a sudden, a rustle and then a thump in a bush ahead made Omakayas freeze. A long moment passed as she stared through the dark leaves. Suddenly, *crash!* Two bear cubs burst from the bush and rushed pell-mell, tumbling head over heels straight for her. They came on in such a hurry that they didn't see Omakayas until they were nearly in her lap, and then, with comical looks of shock, they tried to stop themselves. One flew flat on its face, bumping its nose and squealing. The other twisted in midair and landed in a heap on the ground, shaking its head in confusion at Omakayas.

The bear boys looked at her. Slowly, she put out her open hand filled with heartberries. Curious, the cubs jumped forward, lost their nerve. They scampered backward, and then crept forward shyly again. The smaller cub seemed slightly bolder and sniffed at Omakayas's hand.

The bear cub took one berry, then jumped away in seeming fright at its own bold act. But the taste of the berry seemed to banish fear. The two now tumbled at her, growling, mock-ferocious. Their long pink tongues touched up every berry from her hands, eagerly flicking them from her fingers as fast as she could pick. They seemed to like the game. It could have gone on for hours, that is, until she stood upright. Then they tumbled backward in alarm. Their chubby bottoms rolled them over like playing balls, and she laughed out loud. She realized they had thought Omakayas was their own size. They were astonished the same way Omakayas had been the first time she saw the trader Cadotte unfold a seeing glass, something he called a telescope, a long, shiny tube that grew in his hands.

She bent down again.

"Ahneen, little brothers," she said to them kindly, and they came forward.

She looked around. No mother bear. Omakayas was well aware that she shouldn't stay so close to these cubs, but after all, they seemed deserted. She looked around again. They were orphans! Perhaps the mother bear's skin was now draped across Old Tallow's bed, although she hadn't heard about a recent kill. But still,

Omakayas makes friends with little bears. Louise Erdrich's writings and drawings provide a sympathetic view of life for a Native American child of the nineteenth century, as the Little House series did for white children.

no mother bear in sight. And these little ones so hungry. Wouldn't her big sister be thrilled when Omakayas returned with these two new brothers! Eagerly, Omakayas began to plan out her triumphant walk back to the house. She would enter the little clearing with the cubs, one at her heels and one before her. Everyone would make way, impressed. She would lead the bear cubs around the fire four times before she presented one of them to Angeline, who would look at her with new respect.

There was no warning. One moment Omakayas was wiggling a leafy stick, making it move on the ground so the cubs would jump on it, biting fiercely. The next moment, she found herself flipped over on her back and pinned underneath a huge, powerful, heavy thing that sent down a horrible stink. It was the sow bear, the mother. Breathing on her a stale breath of decayed old deer-hides and skunk cabbages and dead mushrooms. Owah! The surprising thing was, Omakayas realized later, that although she had no memory of doing so, she had the scissors out of their case and open, the sharp ends pointing at the bear's heart. But she didn't

use them as a knife. She knew for certain that *she should not move.* If the bear began to bite and claw, she would have to plunge the tip of the scissors straight in between the bear's strong ribs, use all of her strength, sink the blade all the way in to the rounded hilt and then jump clear, if she could, while the bear went through its death agony. If she couldn't get clear, Omakayas knew she would have to roll up in a ball and endure the bear's fury. She would probably be clawed from head to foot, bitten to pieces, scattered all over the ground.

Until the mother bear made the first move, Omakayas knew she should stay still, or as still as possible, given the terrified jumping of her heart.

For long moments, the bear tested her with every sense, staring down with her weak eyes, listening, and most of all smelling her. The bear smelled the morning's moose meat stew Omakayas had eaten, the wild onion seasoning and the dusty bit of maple sugar from Old Tallow stuck to the inside of her pocket. How she hoped the bear did not smell the bear-killing dogs or the bear claw that swung on a silver hoop from Old Tallow's earlobe. Perhaps the bear smelled the kind touch of Grandma and Mama's bone-and-sprucewood comb, her baby brother's cuddling body, the skins and mats she had slept in, and Little Pinch, who had whined and sobbed the night before. The bear smelled on Omakayas's skin the smell of its own cousin's bear grease used to ward off mosquitoes. Fish from the night before last night. The berries she was eating. The bear smelled all.

Omakayas couldn't help but smell her back. Bears eat anything and this one had just eaten something ancient and foul. Hiyn! Omakayas took shallow breaths. Perhaps it was to take her mind off the scent of dead things on the bear's breath that she accidentally closed the scissors, shearing off a tiny clip of bear fur, and then to cover her horror at this mistake, started to talk.

"Nokomis," she said to the bear, calling her grandmother. "I didn't mean any harm. I was only playing with your children. Gaween onjidah. Please forgive me."

The bear cuffed at Omakayas, but in a warning manner, not savagely, to hurt. Then the bear leaned back, nose working, as though she could scent the meaning of the human words. Encouraged, Omakayas continued.

"I fed them some berries. I wanted to bring them home, to adopt them, have them live with me at my house as my little brothers. But now that you're here, Grandmother, I will leave quietly. These scissors in my hands are not for killing, just for sewing. They are nothing compared to your teeth and claws."

And indeed, Omakayas's voice trembled slightly as the bear made a gurgling sound deep in her throat and bared her long, curved yellowish teeth, so good at ripping and tearing. But having totaled up all of the smells and sifted them for information, the bear seemed to have decided that Omakayas was no threat. She sat back on her haunches like a huge dog. Swinging her head around, she gave a short, quick slap at one of the cubs that sent it reeling away from Omakayas. It was as though she were telling them they had done wrong to approach this human animal, and should now stay away from her. Omakayas's heart squeezed painfully. Even though it was clear her life was to be spared, she felt the loss of her new brothers.

"I wouldn't ever hurt them," she said again.

The little cubs piled against their mother, clung to her. For a long moment the great bear sat calmly with them, deciding where to go. Then, in no hurry, they rose in one piece of dark fur. One bear boy broke away, again tried to get near Omakayas. The other looked longingly at her, but the big bear mother abruptly nosed them down the trail.

CHAPTER 3. THE RETURN

After she returned with the scissors, Omakayas quietly took up the deer bone from her mother's skin bag and began working on the moose hide without being asked. Her mother looked at her in some surprise, but said nothing. Angeline said that she had meant to do the work, but Omakayas merely shook her head.

"Go for a swim," she told her sister, "see what the waves brought to the shore last night. Catch some crayfish, ashaageshinh, watch out for their claws. I don't mind helping."

Angeline and Mama looked at Omakayas as though they couldn't have heard right. But when Omakayas nodded to signal that she meant what she said, and Mama nodded, Angeline started with delight. She had to do grown-up work now every day, and she rarely had free time to play. Angeline looked hopefully at her mother, who waved her out toward the lakeshore. Off she ran, skipping and bounding in her thin summer makazins, her soft old tradecloth dress fluttering.

Baby Neewo was sleeping in his tikinagun. Little brother Pinch was killing his willow doll men over and over with a rock. Omakayas concentrated now on the work beneath her hands. She needed to think about what had just happened to her. Boring work was just what she wanted. Her mind could wander. She sighed, irritated by the smell and buzzing flies. At least there was some breeze that day to blow away the smell. While scraping the hide, she let her thoughts roam.

The longer she thought about her encounter with the mother bear, the more Omakayas was convinced that something she did not understand had passed between the two of them. Not words. Perhaps they had communicated in smells. Or maybe in a language of feelings. Her terror, the bear's pity. Perhaps it was her own grandmother's advice that had saved her life. Nokomis had told her that the bear must be addressed with the greatest respect, as a treasured relative, that the bear had human qualities and nobody quite understood the bear. But that bears understood humans quite well.

When a bear was killed and its skin was off, Omakayas knew it looked fearfully like a person. She'd also heard that bears laugh and cry, just as humans do. Grandma had once seen a bear rocking its young in her arms just as a human mother rocks its young. Nobody on the island ever tossed the bones of a bear aside. Every bear bone was gathered respectfully and buried, all together. At a bear feast, the bear's skull was ribboned and set out on a good red cloth, spoken to, honored.

Yes, there was something about what had happened that made Omakayas very quiet. As she scraped at the hide, nicking bits of meat and gristle from the surface, she began to get all empty and peculiar and faint inside. A thought was coming. A voice approached. This happened to her sometimes. A dizzy feeling would pass over her. If she attended to it closely, once it was gone she would know something a little extra, as though she'd overheard two spirits talking.

She kept scraping, gritting her teeth, and held on to her thoughts, for once again she could feel the presence of the powerful mother bear at her shoulder. Although there were no words and although there was no odor of her presence, no bear sounds, no tracks, Omakayas's heart lightened. Turning from her work, she knew the bear had visited her. She knew the bear had followed her home. She knew that when she needed the bear she would be able to call on the bear. The bear had understood something she had said and she had understood something the bear had thought, and although she couldn't tell exactly what, Omakayas turned back to her task with her head clear and her hands cheerful.

She worked so hard, all through that afternoon, that her grandma, watching her keenly, made a great fuss over the work Omakayas had done on the hide. She said Omakayas had done as well as a full-grown woman. Her mother promised her a very special pair of winter makazins and Angeline even braided her hair with one of her own red ribbons.

Neewo means "fourth" and that was what they called the baby, but soon, Grandma said, the baby would have to have a name. The tiny boy was a spirit, so far, who had come to live here and was deciding whether or not to stay. Grandma told Omakayas to be careful with him, little baby Neewo, because he might decide to go back to the other place if he thought his big sister was mean. So Omakayas was very gentle with the baby. She rocked him in the branch-held tikinagun

with great consideration. She gathered spongy moss and old oak punk to stuff into the cradle board and use as a diaper. She twirled and dangled the little web of sinew and the tobacco ties and bitten birchbark pretties that Grandma tied onto the head guard of the tikinagun. She fed Neewo tiny bits of the best food when Mama wasn't looking. She felt, in her heart, streams of love for the baby pouring through and she begged her mother to let her take Neewo out and cart him to the lake on her hip.

But her mother smiled and touched Omakayas's hair gently and shook her head. Gaween. No. She was too young. Grandma gave her the willow doll instead, told her to let the baby sleep, directed her to play with Little Pinch. But she knew what that would mean! Pinch would jump on her back and yell, "N'dai, get moving!" He would pull her braids. He would use her as a practice bow and arrow target. He would tip over the rock children and rock people she made of specially piled lake pebbles. He would destroy her rock people village down by the beach. No, she didn't want to play with him! Little Pinch? Never!

Half the summer went by quickly after the visit from the bear. Omakayas stayed thoughtful. She helped hoe the corn patch almost every day, and never complained. She was kind, hardworking, patient. But she was also lost in her own thoughts. She startled when spoken to, went to sleep early and slept long, dreamed hard but couldn't remember the night's adventures. And she also had those dizzy moments that, her grandma said, meant she was special to the spirits. One day, her mother said to her grandmother, "If she wasn't so young, I'd give her the charcoal."

Grandma's deep and far-seeing eyes took in Omakayas. She seemed to see her granddaughter from the inside out. She watched Omakayas for a long time, then shook her head. No. Not yet. When a mother put charcoal on her child's face, it was a sign that the child was ready to starve for a vision, for power. A child with a blackened face didn't eat for days, and sometimes lived out in the woods alone until the spirits took pity on him or her and helped out with a special vision, a special visit, some information. But Omakayas was too young, according to Grandma, so Mama stirred the fire and worried. She had a lot to think about anyway, including a name for Baby Neewo, who was getting restless, trying to crawl out of the cradle board, acting as though he were anxious to have that name.

There were seven or eight people on the island who possessed the right to give names. Auntie Muskrat was one. Day Thunder, Swan, Old Man Migwans, and an ancient lady named Waubanikway knew how to dream names. Mama had asked, and each of them had tried. But not one of them had yet dreamed about a name for Neewo.

"For some reason," said Auntie Muskrat, "that dream won't come." She even slept and fasted in the woods for a name, but the spirits were stubborn.

Old Waubanikway, who dreamed many names, had no name for the baby either, but she said that she would give no other name until she found one for the boy. She searched her dreams. Meantime, Baby Neewo grew! Omakayas decided in secret that the naming was up to her. In play, when just the two of them were together, she gave her little brother names. Bird names. Chickadee, she called him. Apitchi. Robin. Little Junco. Sparrow. Grouse Chick. He seemed to like all of his bird names and when he heard them he grinned and waved his chubby arms in delight.

Omakayas could hardly resist Neewo, and played with him as often as she was allowed. There was something about the way he looked at her so sadly with big, soft eyes that made her want to cuddle him tight in her arms. There was something about the way he smiled when she made a face, surprised, so grateful, that made her kiss and touch his hair with great passion and indignation in her heart. He should have a name! And clearly, he wanted out of his tikinagun.

Omakayas wanted to help him to freedom.

Her chance came. One morning later on in the summer, Omakayas's mother, sister, grandma, and Little Pinch all wanted to go into the village and see the big canoes that had arrived to unload furs at the trader Cadotte's. Omakayas's father, Mikwam, wasn't with these voyageurs, but Mama hoped that they might have news of him. The thought itself made Mama so

anxious that she got ready to go off in haste, though Baby Neewo was still sleeping.

"Why don't you leave Neewo with me," Omakayas asked at the last moment. "I don't want to go. I can take care of him! You'll get there faster!"

She saw Mama's thoughts falter.

"You don't want to go?"

"I don't!"

Angeline and Grandma were already halfway down the path. Little Pinch was tugging on Mama's legging, whining for something to eat.

"All right," Mama decided. "We'll be right back. Now don't do anything. Just rock him, Omakayas, and play with him if he wakes up. Don't *do* anything!"

"Of course not," said Omakayas, trying hard not to show how excited she was to have her baby brother, Neewo, all to herself. She made herself tall and acted as grown-up as possible. Rocked him with one hand, gently, while she waved good-bye to Mama, and kept rocking long after her mother rounded the corner and disappeared into the ferny forest growth. He didn't wake. She quit rocking, just stared at his slumbering face. His lashes were so long and stiff, his little chin so chubby she wanted to stroke it, the skin on his cheeks so fine and delicate and soft she could hardly keep from brushing her lips across them. Tufts of silken hair stood out all over his head and his breath was still sweet with milk.

She touched him, very gently. Baby Neewo. Chickadee. The name popped into her mind. "Today, I'll call you Chickadee," she said.

His eyes opened, as though he understood. His look was bright and filled with secret jokes. He gazed up into her face. For a long time they looked at one another. It was perfect. It was love. And then his face crumpled, one fat tear squeezed from his eye, his lower lip shook. Suddenly, his mouth flew open and he bawled. Omakayas was so close, so dreamy and happy, that the force of it nearly flipped her back head over heels. His squall was like a whirlwind, like a sudden wash of freezing spray, like a harsh wind, weather like a hot wall of sound.

"Shuh, shuh, shuh . . ." Omakayas rocked and muttered, shushed, hummed and sang an old lullaby her mother used. Nothing worked. Baby Neewo screamed louder, with increasing force. Omakayas was alarmed. She'd never heard him scream like this, had she? What was wrong? Was something—a biting fly, spider, tick, bee—something stinging or biting him inside the tight binding of his tikinagun? Only one way to find out—unbind him—and that was forbidden. Still, as Neewo's miserable and now hysterical sobbing continued and even got stronger, she decided to make a grown-up decision and take Neewo from his cradle board. And so she did. She undid the twist of vine that held him inside the beaded velvet wrapping. She carefully untied and spread the embroidered wrapping, then took out his diaper moss and brushed him off like a root pulled from the ground. He was naked, of course, but it was a warm day and so she lifted him immediately into her arms, still weeping, and brought him to a sunny place just beyond the house, behind the trees, out near the water.

Omakayas suddenly realized that Neewo had quieted. Her ears were still ringing with the sounds of his cries. Seagulls wailed, a skinny shorebird ran up and down the sand, busily pecking. Neewo brandished his chubby fists, blithered at the water, blasted spit excitedly at the sparkling waves, and turned his melting and mischief-filled eyes upon his sister to tell her that she was the most wonderful human on earth.

She settled him beside her on a warm stretch of rock. Put a stick in his hand. He looked at the stick, tested it between his gums. He had one pitiful little tooth he was very proud of, and he tried to use it to bite the stick. The stick was too strong for Neewo. He banged it purposefully at little circles of green lichen scattered on the stone's surface. When the stick broke in two, he yelled in sheer joy and continued beating the rock with the short end of it. Omakayas was so happy that she laughed out loud.

"You'll be a drummer, a singer. I'll dance for you," she said. Although it was wrong of her to have set Neewo free, it was very obvious that he had always wanted to be banging a stick on a rock and feeling the warm sun on his face. They sat together for a good while longer. Omakayas tossed stones in the water, sending up splashes to surprise her little brother, and he in turn seemed to try and talk to her in serious burps and babbles about what it was like to be a baby packed into a carrier, hanging on a branch all day long, never allowed to throw rocks or stuff leaves in his mouth.

Omakayas thought she heard him tell her this was the best day of his life so far. She thought she heard him tell her that she was his very favorite sister and he liked her much, much better than Angeline. He definitely said to her that he would never forget this, and that when they were very old he would stare at her the way he was doing now, and laugh, and they'd both be toothless then.

"But I have to put you back now, or else I'll get in trouble," Omakayas said. Regretfully, she lifted him into her arms, a delicious baby weight, and carried him jouncing back to the clearing and the house. As she laid him back into his wrappings and began to lace him in, his face crumpled in betrayal and he opened his mouth. Quickly, Omakayas reached into her pocket. The remains of the treat from Old Tallow was still there. She popped the last little bit of the lump of maple sugar onto his tongue. His mouth closed. A look of blissful surprise came over his face. His body relaxed. By the time Omakayas had him laced back into the tikinagun his eyelids were drooping, and by the time her mother came home with no news of her father, but with a bit of brilliant red cloth, four brass buttons, and six thimbles for which she'd traded a load of dried fish, Omakayas was rocking Neewo as though she'd been doing so all along, and her little brother was smiling in his sleep.

The month of picking heartberries went by. Little Pinch jumped off a low branch and made a huge gash just over his eye. Blood came pouring down and he seemed both proud of himself and sorry for himself, and he selfishly hogged attention for his injury to the point where Omakayas could hardly bear it. Mama was constantly preoccupied with him. Of course, that left Neewo more and more to Omakayas's hands, and she didn't mind that. After the hours they'd spent in freedom, it always seemed to Omakayas that she and her little brother exchanged a secret knowledge in their smiles.

Grandma began to call Little Pinch by a new name, Big Pinch, because he grabbed handfuls of food and tried to stuff his face. He was very slow learning manners. It was hard to teach him. He had an eager, greedy, pushing nature. Omakayas liked him less with every day that passed, and wished desperately that someone, Old Tallow or her Auntie Muskrat, perhaps, would ask Mama if they could keep him. When he got on her nerves the worst, she imagined and dreamed. Maybe someone who'd lost a son would ask for Pinch. Or maybe their father, Mikwam, would arrive and say he needed an always-hungry little boy of five winters to accompany him on his next long trip. The missionaries. They might want to use Pinch as an example—but of what? Things *not* to do? He could live underneath the church. Something, anything, just a little relief! He was so annoying to Omakayas that she found herself occasionally wishing a dreadful wish—that an eagle or old Grandfather Owl might snatch him up and carry him to a high nest. She always stopped herself when her heart grew dark, but oh, these wishes were satisfying!

It was a cool dark summer night in the first days of blueberry picking time, and Omakayas had just fallen asleep when something made her awaken, a dream or a sound. She lay quiet with her eyes just a tiny bit open, staring confusedly at the soft flames that occasionally flickered up among the coals that glowed in the fire pit. Omakayas raised her head, drowsy. Grandma was wedged into a thick bearskin beside the door, snoring lightly, and Big Pinch was tumbled at her feet. Angeline was tucked neatly into her blanket on the other side of the door.

Suddenly, a shiver of happiness and excitement ran down through Omakayas so strongly she feared she might cry out and wake everyone. Her heart jumped. She nearly threw off her robes to dance. Deydey, her father, was home! There, at the entrance, just barely lighted, her father's makazins were heaped with Mama's. His were worn through, dirty, beaten up, although not missing a single bead of Mama's tight beadwork. Mama's, on either side, were spruce and neat. They were her fancy ones, trimmed at the ankle with a specially prepared ruff of white rabbit fur.

Her mother's and father's makazins always had a certain way of turning toward each other, Omakayas thought. Deydey's makazins were carefully made by Mama, and sometimes worn to shreds before he got home. Soft and open, they seemed relieved to flop inside the door and nestle into the safe embrace of Mama's pair. Her makazins protected Deydey's used-up ones, nuzzled them together, and seemed to be watching over and soothing away the many dangers of his footsteps.

Drifting back into sleep, Omakayas knew that by the time she woke her mother would be cutting out a new pair of makazins from the special moose hide she herself had tanned and smoked when the heartberries were first ripening. That thought brought her back to the memory of the bear mother. As she fell back into her dreams, she wondered.

Would she tell her father what had happened? Would she ever tell anyone? Once more, she decided that she would keep the encounter to herself. Not only would she be scolded, maybe even laughed at, for playing with the bear cubs, but she was quite certain that no one else would understand.

Omakayas curled even deeper into her blanket. Smiling in delight, she buried her face in the warm fur, and fell at last into a heavy, dreamless sleep knowing when she woke there would be Father, tall, bold, strong, and joking, to swing her high in the air. Mama would laugh even more than usual. Angeline, too, shy and excited. There would be gifts, new things, special food. Grandma would cook mightily for a feast. Mama would sew on her father's makazins. Uncles would come visiting, cousins, relatives to feast and listen to stories and tease endlessly. Baby Neewo would beg with his eyes for Deydey's songs, and Big Pinch would have to be good.

Jon Stott (b. 1939)

Jon Stott is a Professor Emeritus at the University of Alberta, Edmonton. He has published widely on multicultural children's literature, with particular emphasis on Native American literature for children. In the 1995 book from which this excerpt is taken and in other essays and speeches, he has been critical of misrepresentations of Native American stories, often taken out of context or distorted to fit non–Native American ideas. However, in this essay, he argues in favor of several recent Native American stories that contradict stereotypes and expand our sense of the reality of the lives of the Americans who were on this continent before Europeans arrived. In general, he opposes censorship of books that promote stereotypes and misconceptions; instead, he advocates promoting books that are authentic and that represent the experience of Native Americans with respect and understanding. Finding such books is not always easy, however.

The "homing-in" plot he refers to in Native American literature is a concept advanced by critic William Bevis, who argues that "in Native American novels, coming home, staying put, contracting, even what we call 'regressing' to a place, a past where one has been before, is not only the primary story, it is a primary mode of knowledge and a primary good."[1] (See also the essay by Stott in Part 7.)

NOTE

1. William Bevis, "Native American Novels: Homing In," *Recovering the Word,* ed. Brian Swann and Arnold Krupat (Berkeley: U of California P, 1987) 582.

Discovery and Recovery in Children's Novels by Native Writers

As Scott O'Dell did in his books, Michael Dorris, in *Morning Girl,* portrays his young protagonists encountering newly arrived Europeans. Like Jean George, Beatrice Culleton, in *In Search of April Raintree,* portrays her heroine recovering her cultural heritage. However, there are significant differences arising from the fact that both Dorris and Culleton are members of Native cultures. Viewing historical and contemporary events from their Modoc and Métis backgrounds, respectively, they understand the events of the novels in relation to their own cultures' traditional world views and with a cynicism and irony born of having had to define themselves and their peoples in opposition to the perceptions of the dominant and dominating white culture. Both novelists use the first-person point of view, giving voices to members of cultures long rendered silent because of controls exercised by the ruling majority (Fee 1990, 168). In *Morning Girl,* Dorris presents a brother and sister's responses to events in their lives just before the arrival of Christopher Columbus in 1492. Culleton's *In Search of April Raintree* is the coming-of-age novel of a Canadian Métis who faces her inner prejudices and those of modern Canadian society in general.

Until page 69 of *Morning Girl,* readers appear to be listening to the thoughts of a typical Caribbean boy and girl reacting to their own growing pains, their family and the rest of their village, and the natural world around them. Morning Girl, so named because of her love of getting up before the rest of her family, is the more social of the siblings. She frequently thinks of gifts for her parents and brother, looks forward to having a new sister, acts in a motherly way toward her brother, is ashamed for uttering "unsisterly words" (Dorris 1992, 67), and is anxious to know what her face looks like to other people. When, at the novel's conclusion, strangers arrive, she eagerly greets them, rushes home to summon the other villagers, and anticipates a festive, social welcome. By contrast, Star Boy is happiest alone, in the night, studying the stars. He frequently quarrels with his friends and family and often stays out all night by himself. There are hints that he has the potential to be some kind of shaman. He imagines himself experiencing the world as a rock and, during a hurricane, has a conversation with the spirit of his long-dead grandfather. Brother and sister are different from each other, but they complement each other, just as each member in the village is unique but forms an integral part of the social unit. Though the events and emotions the boy and girl experience are special to each of them, they are represented as being fairly typical for their people.

Until page 69, then, *Morning Girl* appears to be a simple, clearly and crisply written account of what it was probably like to be a young member of this Caribbean settlement in some unspecified precontact time. Up to this point, a reader could not be blamed for thinking: "Interesting, yes; but exciting, no! Not much of a story." However, the final six pages provide a specific historical context for the preceding events, a context that causes the reader to reconsider the significance of the earlier parts of the narrative. Morning Girl's description of a canoe of strangers she sees coming toward shore makes it obvious that they are European. They are fully clothed, have beards, wear metal helmets, and their "canoe" is a rowboat or ship's launch. Just who they are is made explicit in the first and last lines of the "Epilogue," a journal entry dated "October 11, 1492" (Dorris 1992, 73) and signed "Christopher Columbus" (Dorris 1992, 74). Morning Girl has been the first person to witness the arrival of Europeans in the Caribbean, Christopher Columbus' "discovery of the New World."

With this knowledge, the rereader of the short, apparently simple text discovers a great number of new meanings. Dorris' story is short because he and other Native peoples understand so much about the impact of Columbus's arrival. Published in 1992, the quadracentennial of the famous journey, this novel, along with *The Crown of Columbus* (an adult novel cowritten by Dorris with his wife Louise Erdrich) and many other writings by Native peoples, presents an alternate view of the historical event widely celebrated by so many Americans. For Native Americans, Columbus Day does not honor a wonderful new beginning, but a tragic end. If it was a beginning, it was the beginning of the destruction of centuries' old ways of life. The words of Morning Girl and Star Boy show life as it is to them and as their people always expect it will be. The silent text, what is not stated, is ironic and filled with ominous foreshadowings. Without direct statement, Dorris presents readers with a revisionist interpretation of the first major event in the history of European-Native relations.

The lives of Morning Girl's people, their adaptability to the rhythmic patterns of the seasons, including the devastation of a hurricane, suggest a pattern that has existed for centuries and that none of them have any idea will soon end. Just as her mother and uncle quarreled and her grandfather rescued her father, so she and Star Boy quarrel, and he is saved by his grandfather's spirit during the storm. After the hurricane passes, the people celebrate their deliverance and begin rebuilding as they have done after previous natural disasters. However, with a knowledge that this is the autumn of 1492 and an awareness of the major and destructive changes that Columbus' arrival brought for America's indigenous peoples, readers retrospectively understand that this is not just another typical October but the final typical October. The ingenuousness of the child narrators and the unspoiled purity of the lives they recount are rendered poignant because of the unstated fact that this is the last time these types of events will occur and be experienced in this way.

However, there are events that, in retrospect, seem to foreshadow the disastrous events that follow Columbus' arrival. Just before the storm, Star Boy notices that "there was a worry on . . . [father's] face I had only seen there once before—the time when the bad visitors, their bodies painted white for death, were spotted in three big rafts to the south of the nearest island" (Dorris 1992, 38). Later, the white explorers from Columbus' three ships will bring their own forms of death—physical and cultural—to the people. The day before the Europeans' arrival, Star Boy quarrels with his friend and each member of his family, and Morning Girl displeases her mother and father by speaking unkindly about her brother. The closely knit family experiences tensions on the eve of an experience that will lead to a shattering of the larger cultural unit of which they are members.

There is an even more ominous undercurrent. In the epilogue, Columbus writes that "it seems to me that they have no religion" (Dorris 1992, 74) and notes his plans to take six of the islanders back to Spain so that they can be clothed, can "learn to speak" (Dorris 1992, 74), and can be converted to Christianity—in a word, be "civilized." As the novel reveals, in their environment, they do not need clothing, they do speak a language, and they do have spiritual experiences. They are neither heathen savages nor nature's children. But by including these remarks of Columbus, Dorris not only reveals the invaders' ignorance about the nature of the people they are soon to conquer but also implicitly raises the question, "Could Morning Girl or Star Boy be one of the half-dozen about to be abducted?" Three times during the novel Star Boy spends the night alone, away from his village. One time, his mother states that she does not think he would go from home without saying goodbye. Later, his father remarks, "nothing can replace a son" (Dorris 1992, 28). Each of these incidents appears to be an ominous hint that Star Boy may be taken. If so, having him as one of the narrators of the story is highly ironic. He may be sensitively describing his attempts to understand himself in relation to his people just before he is to be parted from them forever.

Finally, read in the light of Columbus' remarks about the people and his intentions (and by implicit extension those of Europeans generally), Morning Girl's response to the arrivals is ironic. When she sees that the visitors do not wear hostile paint markings, she assumes that they are friendly and that, in spite of their odd clothing and behavior, they will get along with her people. She anticipates "a memorable day, a day full and new" (Dorris 1992, 71). She is not the hostile savage, the primitive and unregenerate heathen

so many Europeans expected they would encounter. In fact, as her story has revealed, she is kind and social and is anxious to meet them, and she is a member of a highly functional social organization. Dorris, through Morning Girl's voice, presents a vastly different view of the initial contacts between the two cultures from that presented by European writers of children's adventure novels. He also gives the meeting an ironic twist by implying that the girl's openhearted welcome of the Spaniards is the unwitting first step in the destruction of her culture, a destruction that may well include the loss of her brother.

Dorris, then, presents a simple, short text with a complex, invisible subtext. Beneath the simple narrative and description is a devastating portrayal of the beginning of the end of a culture. At a time when Columbus was being celebrated, the author used his Native point of view to reveal a situation vastly different from the one commonly accepted. It is one that can be perceived only by those readers who can interpret not only what the words say directly but what they silently imply.

Beatrice Culleton, a Canadian Métis of European-Native background, uses events from her own life to portray a young woman's rejection and recovery of her heritage. The author was raised in foster homes and two of her sisters committed suicide. She grew up with little knowledge of Métis history. The picture of "the drunken, poverty-stricken, irresponsible person remained like a truth with me until I began to write *In Search of April Raintree*" (Culleton 1989, 120). The title hero spends her school years in foster homes, and she, too, harbors a stereotypical view of her people, whom she wishes to deny. Her sister Cheryl represents another side of the author: through studying and writing, she tries to discover and recover her Métis heritage.

As the title suggests, the novel is the study of a search for identity, a coming-of-age story in which the heroine comes to live up to the sense of new beginnings inherent in her spring-time name. However, even though the narrator refers to herself as a Cinderella and the man to whom she is briefly married as Prince Charming, it is not the rags-to-riches story of European folktales, the escape from a dreary life in one place to a wonderful new one in another. Instead, it is a "Homing In Novel," typical of so many novels written by Native authors. April, whose narrative begins when she is a five-year-old in the Canadian city of Winnipeg, returns there at the novel's conclusion, a sadder and wiser person who believes that "there would be a tomorrow. And it would be better" (Culleton 1983, 228).

Culleton portrays April's life up to the time of the breakup of her marriage in ways that parallel the fairytale of the poor girl who marries the prince, the Harlequin-type story of a glorious romance leading to wealth and happiness, and the saga of the growth to maturity of a hardworking, disadvantaged individual who overcomes obstacles through determination and courage and achieves success. In drawing parallels to these popular story types, the author is showing the falseness of her heroine's expectations and the shallowness of her character. Ashamed of her Métis background, April envies white children, dreams of a beautiful home, rejects her sister's attempts to interest her in their people's past, and tries to pass as a white person. At one point, she portrays herself as a literal orphan, telling schoolmates that she lost her parents in an airplane crash; and she does not want her friends to meet her sister, who looks more Native than she does. She makes attempts to find her alcoholic parents, from whom she and her sister had been taken when she was five, but when she fails in the search she is relieved: "That part of my life was now finished for good" (Culleton 1983, 100). Shortly after, she marries a wealthy businessman and moves to his family estate in Toronto. She has escaped from her heritage and seems to have achieved the kind of life portrayed in popular literature written by white people. However, unlike the heroines of fairytales and romance novels, she has not become successful through hard work or virtuous actions. She has denied much and has succeeded only because of luck and good looks. The first half of the novel can thus be seen as a parody of the popular narratives, a criticism of the values they espouse, and a condemnation of April for having embraced these values.

The second half of the novel traces April's fall from her ill-deserved "good fortune." Her husband has married her to displease his domineering mother, who despises April for being Métis and he is having an affair with his mother's tacit approval. April returns to Winnipeg to discover that her sister, a Native rights advocate and brilliant student, has dropped out of university and developed a severe drinking problem. April is brutally raped by white men who mistake her for her sister, on whom they seek revenge. At their trial, she learns that her sister had become a prostitute. Shortly after, Cheryl commits suicide as her mother had done years earlier. April cannot escape from her past or from the heritage she denied. The rape, literally a case of mistaken identity, proves this. In spite of her non-Native appearance, the men, who think that she is Cheryl, refer to her as a "squaw" (Culleton 1983, 140) and "savage" (Culleton 1983, 142). She is forcibly subjected to the violation and degradation that, in one form or another, are inflicted on large numbers of her people.

Gradually these painful confrontations with the Native part of herself that she had attempted to deny lead her to accept and later to honor it. She suggests that she and her sister attend a Pow Wow, and at it she experiences "stirrings of pride" (Culleton 1983, 166). At the Native Friendship Centre she meets a respected elder who sees in her "something that was deserving of her respect" (Culleton 1983, 175). And to her friend Roger, she haltingly admits that she is Métis. Her greatest breakthrough occurs on the novel's final page when she meets her sister's young son, Henry Liberty Raintree. His middle name is symbolic of the new freedom April finds in joyously accepting her birthright. Together, the woman and child will form a new family, a new beginning repairing the shattering of family units that had occurred throughout the novel. She has completed her search; she has found herself in finding her roots, her past, and in hoping for a future for her nephew and "For my people" (Culleton 1983, 228). Like the central characters in Scott Momaday's *House Made of Dawn* and *The Ancient Child,* she has replaced denial with acceptance and has returned home. And, as in *House Made of Dawn* and *Sing Down the Moon,* a gentle morning rain falls, symbolizing the new life ahead.

Dorris and Culleton both deal with themes presented by non-Native writers. However, they present inside views, writing as members of Native cultures that had been "discovered" and nearly destroyed by Europeans and that are now rediscovering their own pasts and using a recovered pride to give impetus to new beginnings. As the existence of these and other children's books by Native American authors indicates, an important part of the Native Renaissance is literary. Native writers are helping Native readers use the power of story to recover a past, define a present, and envision a future.

Marilyn Nelson (b. 1946)

Marilyn Nelson, a prize-winning poet who teaches at the University of Connecticut, wrote the sonnets in *A Wreath for Emmett Till* (2005) about a fourteen-year-old African American boy from Chicago who was lynched in Money, Mississippi, on August 24, 1955, because a white woman said that he whistled at her. We learn in the notes to the sonnets that Emmett Till was a stutterer, and "his mother had encouraged him to whistle when he could not get a word out."[1] The white men who shot, beat, and mutilated Emmett Till were tried by an all-white jury and acquitted of murder. Till's mother insisted on an open-casket viewing to show the world what had been done to her son; the photos of him caused national outrage and helped to spark the Civil Rights movement. The Justice Department reopened the murder case in 2004 after several books and documentary films brought it renewed attention.

Nelson's brilliant poem is a sonnet cycle. The sonnet reprinted here is one of fifteen. The book is a heroic crown of sonnets, which means that the last line of each poem, sometimes slightly changed, becomes the first line of the next sonnet. The final sonnet is composed of variations of all of the first lines put together, and the first letters of the lines spell the acrostic "RIP EMMETT TILL." The poem is a profound meditation on injustice, evil, racial hatred, and American history.

NOTE

1. Marilyn Nelson, "Sonnet Notes, IV," *A Wreath for Emmett Till* (Boston: Houghton Mifflin, 2005).

From *A Wreath for Emmett Till*

Emmett Till's name still catches in my throat
like syllables waylaid in a stutterer's mouth.
A fourteen-year-old stutterer, in the South
to visit relatives and to be taught
the family's ways. His mother had finally bought
that White Sox cap; she'd made him swear an oath
to be careful around white folks. She'd told him
   the truth
of many a Mississippi anecdote:
Some white folks have blind souls. In his
   suitcase
she'd packed dungarees, T-shirts, underwear,
and comic books. She'd given him a note
for the conductor, waved to his chubby face,
wondered if he'd remember to brush his hair.
Her only child. A body left to bloat.

FURTHER RECOMMENDED READING

PAULA FOX (b. 1923)

THE SLAVE DANCER

Paula Fox was raised by a kindly Presbyterian minister who took her in while her parents, ostensibly too busy with their own lives, pursued their careers, a story absorbingly told in *Borrowed Finery,* her memoir. Fox began writing in her late thirties and is an accomplished writer of fiction for children and adults. Her novel *The Slave Dancer* (1973) was both acclaimed and controversial: it won the Newbery Medal, but it was also criticized for what some believed was racism. It tells the story of the thirteen-year-old boy Jessie Boller, who was kidnapped from his home in New Orleans in 1840. Boller was forced to play his fife on a slave ship to provide the music while the slaves were ordered to exercise, or "dance." Not only are some of the characters in the story racist, but the slaves are not individualized as the white characters are. Nevertheless, Fox addressed a subject previously thought unfit for children, and her novel evokes in many readers a sense of outrage at the injustice and cruelty of the slave trade.

E. L. KONIGSBURG (b. 1930)

THE VIEW FROM SATURDAY

Critic Kirk H. Beetz thinks that *The View from Saturday* criticizes what he calls "the academic concept of diversity," which Konigsburg is exposing as fashionable and hollow, in his view. "Konigsburg points out that the theory of diversity in practice excludes Jews (perhaps even discriminates against them) and other unfashionable ethnic groups, such as East Indians, and would appear to exclude handicapped peo-

ple, such as Mrs. Olinski," he states.[1] However, one can also read *The View from Saturday* as a celebration of diversity, fashionable or not.

Konigsburg won the Newbery Medal twice: for *The View from Saturday* (1996) and for *From the Mixed-up Files of Mrs. Basil E. Frankweiler* (1967), which established her fame. *From the Mixed-up Files of Mrs. Basil E. Frankweiler* tells the story of two siblings who decide to run away from home and live in the Metropolitan Museum of Art. Konigsburg's main characters are typically smart and independent minded. *The View from Saturday* tells the story of a group of friends. It is narrated by Ethan Potter (who came along before J. K. Rowling associated the name Potter with her wizard Harry worldwide). Ethan is a New Yorker (from the state, not the city) with a long family history and a strong sense of family identity. He encounters different kinds of prejudice. One type is against strangers, such as Julian Singh, an Indian American born on the high seas, whose father is a Sikh and a chef, and who speaks with a British accent and dresses like an English schoolboy. And there is prejudice against the handicapped: Mrs. Olinski, their teacher at Epiphany, is a paraplegic and teaches from her wheelchair. Julian and Ethan's classmates make life hard for Julian and for Mrs. Olinski, but Ethan has the sense and the compassion to see past the cultural and physical differences, and, as a result, he gains friendship and precious knowledge himself.

NOTE

1. Kirk H. Beetz, "The View from Saturday: Social Sensitivity," *Beacham's Encyclopedia of Popular Fiction,* ed. Kirk H. Beetz, vol. 9. (Washington, D. C.: Beacham Publishing, 1996).

Selected Bibliography: History and Criticism of Children's Literature

Alberghene, Janice M., and Beverly Lyon Clark, eds. *Little Women and the Feminist Imagination: Criticism, Controversy, Personal Essays.* New York: Garland, 1999.

Allen, Marjorie N. *One Hundred Years of Children's Books in America: Decade by Decade.* New York: Facts on File, 1996.

Altman, Anna E., and Gail de Vos. *Tales, Then and Now: More Folktales as Literary Fictions for Young Adults.* Englewood, CO: Libraries Unlimited, 2001.

Anderson, Celia Catlett, and Marilyn Apseloff. *Nonsense Literature for Children: Aesop to Seuss.* Hamden, CT: Library Professional, 1989.

Ariés, Phillipe. *Centuries of Childhood: A Social History of Family Life.* Trans. Robert Baldick. New York: Vintage Random, 1962.

Arizpe, Evelyn, and Morag Styles. *Children Reading Pictures: Interpreting Visual Texts.* London: Routledge, 2003.

Attebery, Brian. *Strategies of Fantasy.* Bloomington: Indiana UP, 1992.

Avery, Gillian. *Behold the Child: American Children and Their Books, 1621–1922.* Baltimore, MD: Johns Hopkins UP, 1994.

———. *Childhood's Pattern: A Study of Heroes and Heroines in Children's Fiction, 1770–1950.* London: Hodder & Stoughton, 1965.

Beckett, Sandra L. *Recycling Red Riding Hood.* New York: Routledge, 2002.

———, ed. *Reflections of Change: Children's Literature Since 1945.* Westport, CT: Greenwood, 1997.

———. *Transcending Boundaries: Writing for a Dual Audience of Children and Adults.* New York: Garland, 1999.

Bell, Elizabeth, Lynda Haas, and Laura Sells, eds. *From Mouse to Mermaid: The Politics of Film, Gender, and Culture.* Bloomington: Indiana UP, 1995.

Bettelheim, Bruno. *The Uses of Enchantment: The Meaning and Importance of Fairy Tales.* New York: Knopf, 1976.

Blackford, Holly. *Out of This World: Why Literature Matters to Girls.* New York: Teachers College P, 2004.

Bloom, Harold. *Women Writers of Children's Literature.* Philadelphia: Chelsea House, 1998.

Blount, Margaret. *Animal Land: The Creatures of Children's Fiction.* New York: W. Morrow, 1974.

Boone, Troy. *The Youth of Darkest England: Working-Class Children at the Heart of Victorian Empire.* New York: Routledge, 2005.

Bosmajian, Hamida. *Sparing the Child: Grief and the Unspeakable in Youth Literature about Nazism and the Holocaust.* New York: Routledge, 2002.

Bottigheimer, Ruth B. *The Bible for Children: From the Age of Gutenberg to the Present.* New Haven, CT: Yale UP, 1996.

———, ed. *Fairy Tales and Society: Illusion, Allusion, and Paradigm.* Philadelphia: Pennsylvania UP, 1986.

———. *Grimms' Bad Girls and Bold Boys: The Moral and Social Vision of the Tales.* New Haven CT: Yale UP, 1987.

Bradford, Clare. *Reading Race: Aboriginality in Australian Children's Literature.* Melbourne: Melbourne UP, 2001.

Brown, Joanne, and Nancy St. Clair. *The Distant Mirror: Reflections on Young Adult Historical Fiction.* Lanham, MD: Scarecrow, 2005.

Butts, Dennis, ed. *Stories and Society: Children's Literature in Its Social Context.* New York: St. Martin's, 1992.

Cadogan, Mary, and Patricia Craig. *You're a Brick, Angela! The Girls' Story 1839–1985.* London: V. Gollancz, 1986.

Cameron, Eleanor. *The Green and Burning Tree: On the Writing and Enjoyment of Children's Books.* Boston: Little, Brown, 1969.

Carpenter, Humphrey. *Secret Gardens: A Study of the Golden Age of Children's Literature.* Boston: Houghton Mifflin, 1985.

Cech, John. *Angels and Wild Things: The Archetypal Poetics of Maurice Sendak.* University Park: Pennsylvania State UP, 1996.

Clark, Beverly Lyon. *Kiddie Lit: The Cultural Construction of Children's Literature in America.* Baltimore: Johns Hopkins UP, 2003.

———. *Regendering the School Story: Sassy Sissies and Tattling Tomboys.* New York: Garland, 1996.

Clark, Beverly Lyon, and Margaret R. Higgonet, eds. *Girls, Boys, Books, Toys: Gender in Children's Literature.* Baltimore: John Hopkins UP, 1999.

Crouch, Marcus. *Treasure Seekers and Borrowers: Children's Books in Britain 1900–1960.* London: Library Assn., 1962.

Darling, Harold, and Peter Neumeyer, eds. *Image & Maker: An Annual Dedicated to the Consideration of Book Illustration.* La Jolla, CA: Green Tiger, 1984.

Darton, F. J. Harvey. *Children's Books in England: Five Centuries of Social Life.* 1932. 3rd ed. Rev. Brian Alderson. Cambridge: Cambridge UP, 1982.

de Vos, Gail, and Anna E. Altmann. *New Tales for Old: Folktales as Literary Fictions for Young Adults.* Englewood, CO: Libraries Unlimited, 1999.

Demers, Patricia, and Gordon Moyles, eds. *From Instruction to Delight: An Anthology of Children's Literature to 1850.* Toronto: Oxford UP, 1982.

Dobrin, Sidney I., and Kenneth B. Kidd, eds. *Wild Things: Children's Literature and Ecocriticism.* Detroit: Wayne State UP, 2004.

Driscoll, Catherine. *Girls: Feminine Adolescence in Popular Culture and Cultural Theory.* New York: Columbia UP, 2002.

Dundes, Alan, ed. *Cinderella: A Folklore Casebook.* New York: Garland, 1982.

Dusinberre, Juliet. *Alice to the Lighthouse: Children's Books and Radical Experiments in Art.* New York: St. Martin's, 1987.

Dyer, Carolyn Stewart, and Nancy Tillman Romalov, eds. *Rediscovering Nancy Drew.* Iowa City: U of Iowa P, 1995.

Egoff, Sheila, ed. *Only Connect: Readings on Children's Literature.* Toronto: Oxford UP, 1969; 2nd ed. 1980; 3rd ed. 1996.

———. *The Republic of Childhood: A Critical Guide to Canadian Children's Literature in English.* Toronto: Oxford UP, 1967. Rev. ed. Sheila Egoff and Judith Saltman, *The New Republic of Childhood: A Critical Guide to Canadian Children's Literature in English.* Toronto: Oxford UP, 1990.

———. *Worlds Within: Children's Fantasy from the Middle Ages to Today.* Chicago: American Library Assn., 1988.

Foster, Shirley, and Judy Simons. *What Katy Read: Feminist Re-Readings of "Classic" Stories for Girls.* Iowa City: U of Iowa P, 1995.

Fox, Geoff. *Celebrating* Children's Literature in Education: *A Selection.* New York: Teachers College P, 1995.

Gavin, Adrienne E., and Christopher Routledge, eds. *Mystery in Children's Literature: From the Rational to the Supernatural.* New York: Palgrave/St. Martin's, 2001.

Goldthwaite, John. *The Natural History of Make-Believe: A Guide to the Principal Works of Britain, Europe, and America.* New York: Oxford UP, 1996.

Goodenough, Elizabeth, Mark A. Heberle, and Naomi B. Sokoloff, eds. *Infant Tongues: The Voice of the Child in Literature.* Detroit: Wayne State UP, 1994.

Griswold, Jerome. *Audacious Kids: Coming of Age in America's Classic Children's Books* (also published as *The Classic American Children's Story: Novels of the Golden Age*). New York: Oxford UP, 1992.

Haase, Donald, ed. *The Reception of the Grimms' Fairy Tales: Responses, Reactions, Revisions.* Detroit: Wayne State UP, 1993.

Harries, Elizabeth Wanning. *Twice Upon a Time: Women Writers and the History of the Fairy Tale.* Princeton, NJ: Princeton UP, 2001.

Harrison, Barbara, and Gregory Maguire, eds. *Innocence & Experience: Essays & Conversations on Children's Literature.* New York: Lothrop, 1987.

———, eds. *Origins of Story: On Writing for Children.* New York: McElderry Books, 1999.

Hearn, Michael Patrick, Trinkett Clark, and H. Nichols B. Clark. *Myth, Magic and Mystery: 100 Years of American Children's Book Illustration.* Boulder, CO: Roberts Rinehart, 1996.

Hearne, Betsy. *Beauty and the Beast: Visions and Revisions of an Old Tale.* Chicago: U of Chicago P, 1989.

———, ed. *The Zena Sutherland Lectures, 1983–1991.* New York: Clarion, 1992.

Helbig, Alethea K., and Agness Regan Perkins. *This Land Is Our Land: A Guide to Multicultural Literature for Children and Young Adults.* Westport, CT: Greenwood P, 1994.

Hilton, Mary, Victor Watson, and Morag Styles, eds. *Opening the Nursery Door: Reading, Writing and Childhood 1600–1900.* London: Routledge, 1997.

Hintz, Carrie, and Elaine Ostry, eds. *Utopian and Dystopian Writing for Children and Young Adults.* New York: Routledge, 2003.

Hodges, Gabrielle Cliff, Mary Jane Drummond, and Morag Styles, eds. *Tales, Tellers and Texts.* London: Cassell, 2000.

Hollindale, Peter. *Signs of Childness in Children's Books.* Stroud, Gloucs.: Thimble, 1997.

Hourihan, Margery. *Deconstructing the Hero: Literary Theory and Children's Literature.* New York: Routledge, 1997.

Hunt, Peter, ed. *Children's Literature: An Illustrated History.* Oxford: Oxford UP, 1995; rev. ed., 2006.

———. *Criticism, Theory and Children's Literature.* Cambridge, MA: B. Blackwell, 1991.

Inglis, Fred. *The Promise of Happiness: Value and Meaning in Children's Fiction.* New York: Cambridge UP, 1981.

Jackson, Mary V. *Engines of Instruction, Mischief, and Magic: Children's Literature in England from Its Beginnings to 1839.* Lincoln: U of Nebraska P, 1989.

Jenkins, Henry, ed. *The Children's Culture Reader.* New York: New York UP, 1998.

Johnson, Dianne. *Telling Tales: The Pedagogy and Promise of African American Literature for Youth.* New York: Greenwood P, 1990.

Jones, Dudley, and Tony Watkins, eds. *A Necessary Fantasy? The Heroic in Children's Popular Culture.* Children's Literature and Culture Series. New York: Garland, 2000.

Jones, Steven Swann. *The Fairy Tale: The Magic Mirror of Imagination.* New York: Twayne, 1995.

Keenan, Celia, and Mary Shine Thompson, eds. *Studies in Children's Literature, 1500–2000.* Dublin: Four Courts, 2004.

Kertzer, Adrienne. *My Mother's Voice: Children, Literature, and the Holocaust.* Peterborough, ON: Broadview P, 2002.

Keyser, Elizabeth Lennox. *Whispers in the Dark: The Fiction of Louisa May Alcott.* Knoxville: U of Tennessee P, 1993.

Khorana, Meena, ed. *Critical Perspectives on Postcolonial African Children's and Young Adult Literature.* Westport, CT: Greenwood, 1998.

Kidd, Kenneth B. *Making American Boys: Boyology and the Feral Tale.* Minneapolis: U of Minnesota P, 2004.

Kiefer, Barbara Z. *The Potential of Picturebooks: From Visual Literacy to Aesthetic Understanding.* Englewood Cliffs, NJ: Merrill, 1995.

Kincaid, James R. *Child-Loving: The Erotic Child and Victorian Culture.* New York: Routledge, 1992.

Knoepflmacher, U. C. *Ventures into Childland: Victorians, Fairy Tales, and Femininity.* Chicago: U of Chicago P, 1998.

Kohl, Herbert. *Should We Burn Babar? Essays on Children's Literature and the Power of Stories.* New York: New Press/Norton, 1995.

Krips, Valerie. *The Presence of the Past: Memory, Heritage, and Childhood in Postwar Britain.* New York: Garland, 2000.

Kuznets, Lois. *When Toys Come Alive: Narratives of Animation, Metamorphosis, and Development.* New Haven, CT: Yale UP, 1994.

Lanes, Selma G. *Through the Looking Glass: Further Adventures and Misadventures in the Realm of Children's Literature.* Boston: D. R. Godine, 2004.

Le Guin, Ursula K. *The Language of the Night: Essays on Fantasy and Science Fiction.* New York: Putnam, 1979.

Lehr, Susan, ed. *Beauty, Brains, and Brawn: The Construction of Gender in Children's Literature.* Portsmouth, NH: Heinemann, 2001.

Lesnik-Oberstein, Karin, ed. *Children's Literature: New Approaches.* New York: Palgrave Macmillan, 2004.

Lewis, David. *Reading Contemporary Picturebooks: Picturing Text.* New York: Routledge, 2001.

Lucas, Ann Lawson, ed. *The Presence of the Past in Children's Literature.* Westport, CT: Praeger, 2003.

Lukens, Rebecca J. *A Critical Handbook of Children's Literature.* 8th ed. Boston: Allyn & Bacon, 2006.

Lukens, Rebecca J., and Ruth K. J. Cline. *A Critical Handbook of Literature for Young Adults.* New York: Longman, 1995.

Lundin, Anne H. *Constructing the Canon of Children's Literature: Beyond Library Walls and Ivory Towers.* New York: Routledge, 2004.

Lurie, Alison. *Don't Tell the Grown-Ups: Subversive Children's Literature.* Boston: Little, Brown, 1990.

Lüthi, Max. *Once Upon a Time: On the Nature of Fairy Tales.* New York: F. Ungar, 1970.

MacCann, Donnarae. *White Supremacy in Children's Literature: Characterizations of African Americans, 1830–1900.* New York: Garland, 1998.

Mackey, Margaret. *The Case of Peter Rabbit: Changing Conditions of Literature for Children.* London: Garland, 1998.

MacLeod, Anne Scott. *American Childhood: Essays on Children's Literature of the Nineteenth and Twentieth Centuries.* Athens: U of Georgia P, 1994.

———. *A Moral Tale: Children's Fiction and American Culture, 1820–1860.* Hamden, CT: Archon, 1970.

Manna, Anthony L., and Carolyn S. Brodie, eds. *Many Faces, Many Voices: Multicultural Literary Experiences for Youth: The Virginia Hamilton Conference.* Fort Atkinson, WI: Highsmith, 1992.

Marcus, Leonard. *Margaret Wise Brown: Awakened by the Moon.* Boston: Beacon, 1992.

———. *Ways of Telling: Conversations on the Art of the Picture Book.* New York: Dutton, 2002.

Martin, Michelle. *Brown Gold: Milestones of African American Children's Picture Books, 1845–2002.* New York: Routledge, 2004.

Mason, Bobbie Ann. *The Girl Sleuth.* Athens: U of Georgia P, 1995.

May, Jill P., ed. *Children and Their Literature: A Readings Book.* West Lafayette, IN: Children's Literature Assn., 1983.

———. *Children's Literature and Critical Theory: Reading and Writing for Understanding.* New York: Oxford UP, 1995.

McCallum, Robyn. *Ideologies of Identity in Adolescent Fiction: The Dialogic Construction of Subjectivity.* New York: Garland, 1999.

McCaslin, Nellie, ed. *Children and Drama.* 4th ed. Studio City, CA: Players Press, 1999.

McGillis, Roderick, ed. *Children's Literature and the Fin de Siècle.* Westport, CT: Greenwood, 2003.

———, ed. *Voices of the Other: Children's Literature and the Postcolonial Context.* New York: Garland, 1999.

———. *The Nimble Reader: Literary Theory and Children's Literature.* New York: Twayne, 1996.

Meyer, Susan E. *A Treasury of the Great Children's Book Illustrators.* New York: Abrams, 1983.

Mickenberg, Julia L. *Learning from the Left: Children's Literature, the Cold War, and Radical Politics in the United States.* New York: Oxford UP, 2005.

Mikkelsen, Nina. *Words and Pictures: Lessons in Children's Literature and Literacies.* Boston: McGraw-Hill, 2000.

Morris, Tim. *You're Only Young Twice: Children's Literature and Film.* Urbana: U of Illinois P, 2000.

Natov, Roni. *The Poetics of Childhood.* New York: Routledge, 2003.

Nelson, Claudia. *Boys Will Be Girls: The Feminine Ethic and British Children's Fiction, 1857–1917.* New Brunswick, NJ: Rutgers UP, 1991.

Nikolajeva, Maria. *Aesthetic Approaches to Children's Literature: An Introduction.* Lanham, MD: Scarecrow, 2005.

———, ed. *Aspects and Issues in the History of Children's Literature.* Westport, CT: Greenwood, 1995.

———. *Children's Literature Comes of Age: Toward a New Aesthetic.* New York: Garland, 1996.

Nodelman, Perry, ed. *Touchstones: Reflections on the Best in Children's Literature.* 3 vols. West Lafayette, IN: Children's Literature Assn., 1985, 1987, 1989.

———. *Words About Pictures: The Narrative Art of Children's Picture Books.* Athens: U of Georgia P, 1988.

Nodelman, Perry, and Mavis Reimer. *The Pleasures of Children's Literature.* 3rd ed. Boston: Allyn and Bacon, 2003.

Nordstrom, Ursula. *Dear Genius: The Letters of Ursula Nordstrom.* Ed. Leonard S. Marcus. New York: HarperCollins, 1998.

Ong, Walter. *Orality and Literacy: The Technologizing of the Word.* New York: Methuen, 1982.

Opie, Iona and Peter Opie, eds. *The Classic Fairy Tales.* New York: Oxford UP, 1974.

———, eds. *The Oxford Dictionary of Nursery Rhymes.* 2nd ed. Oxford: Oxford UP, 1997.

Opie, Iona, Robert Opie, and Brian Alderson. *The Treasures of Childhood: Books, Toys, and Games from the Opie Collection.* New York: Arcade/Little Brown, 1989.

O'Sullivan, Emer. *Comparative Children's Literature.* New York: Routledge, 2005.

Paterson, Katherine. *The Invisible Child: On Reading and Writing Books for Children.* New York: Dutton, 2001.

———. *The Spying Heart: More Thoughts on Reading and Writing Books for Children.* New York: Lodestar, 1989.

Paul, Lissa. *Reading Otherways.* Stroud, Gloucs.: Thimble, 1997.

Pellowski, Anne. *The World of Storytelling.* 2nd ed. Bronx, NY: H. W. Wilson, 1990.

Phillips, Robert S., ed. *Aspects of Alice: Lewis Carroll's Dreamchild as Seen Through the Critics' Looking-Glasses, 1865–1971.* New York: Vanguard, 1971.

Pickering, Samuel Jr. *John Locke and Children's Books in the 18th Century.* Knoxville: U of Tennessee P, 1981.

———. *Moral Instruction and Fiction for Children, 1749–1820.* Athens: U of Georgia P, 1993.

Rees, David, ed. *Marble in the Water: Essays on Contemporary Writers of Fiction for Children and Young Adults.* Boston: Horn Book, 1980.

Roberts, Chris. *Heavy Words Lightly Thrown: The Reason Behind the Rhyme.* New York: Gotham Books, 2005.

Rochman, Hazel. *Against Borders: Promoting Books for a Multicultural World.* Chicago: American Library Assn., 1993.

Rollin, Lucy, ed. *Antic Art: Enhancing Children's Literary Experiences Through Films and Video.* Fort Atkinson, WI: Highsmith, 1993.

Rollin, Lucy. *Cradle and All: A Cultural and Psychoanalytic Study of Nursery Rhymes.* Jackson: U of Mississippi P, 1992.

Rollin, Lucy, and Mark I. West, eds. *Psychoanalytic Responses to Children's Literature.* Jefferson, NC: McFarland, 1999.

Rose, Jacqueline. *The Case of Peter Pan, or The Impossibility of Children's Fiction.* London: Macmillan, 1984.

Rudman, Masha Kabakow. *Children's Literature: An Issues Approach.* 3rd ed. White Plains, NY: Longman, 1995.

Russell, David L. *Literature for Children: A Short Introduction.* 5th ed. Boston: Pearson/Allyn & Bacon, 2005.

Ruwe, Donelle Rae, ed. *Culturing the Child, 1690–1914: Essays in Memory of Mitzi Myers.* Lanham, MD: Children's Literature Assn. and Scarecrow, 2005.

Sale, Roger. *Fairy Tales and After: From Snow White to E. B. White.* Cambridge, MA: Harvard UP, 1978.

Sands, Karen, and Marietta Frank. *Back in the Spaceship Again: Juvenile Science Fiction Series Since 1945.* Westport, CT: Greenwood, 1999.

Schmidt, Gary D., and Donald R. Hettinga, eds. *Sitting at the Feet of the Past: Retelling the North American Folktale for Children.* Westport, CT: Greenwood, 1992.

Schwarcz, Joseph H., and Chava Schwarcz. *The Picture Book Comes of Age: Looking at Childhood Through the Art of Illustration.* Chicago: American Library Assn., 1991.

Seale, Doris, and Beverly Slapin, eds. *A Broken Flute: The Native Experience in Books for Children.* Berkeley, CA: Oyate, 2005.

Seelye, John D. *Jane Eyre's Daughters: From the Wide, Wide World to Anne of Green Gables: A Study of Marginalized Maidens and What They Mean.* Newark: U of Delaware P, 2005.

Sendak, Maurice. *Caldecott & Co.: Notes on Books and Pictures.* New York: Farrar, Straus & Giroux, 1988.

Shavit, Zohar. *Poetics of Children's Literature.* Athens: U of Georgia P, 1986.

Silvey, Anita, ed. *Children's Books and Their Creators.* Boston: Houghton Mifflin, 1995.

Sims, Rudine. *Shadow and Substance: Afro-American Experience in Contemporary Children's Fiction.* Urbana, IL: National Council of Teachers of English, 1982.

Singh, Rashna, ed. *Goodly Is Our Heritage: Children's Literature, Empire, and the Certitude of Character.* Lanham, MD: Scarecrow, 2004.

Slapin, Beverly, and Doris Seale. *Through Indian Eyes: The Native Experience in Books for Children.* 4th ed. Los Angeles: American Indian Studies Center, U of California, 1992.

Smedman, M. Sarah, and Joel Chaston, eds. *Bridges for the Young: The Fiction of Katherine Paterson.* Lanham, MD: Children's Literature Assn. and Scarecrow, 2003.

Smith, Joseph H., and William Kerrigan, eds. *Opening Texts: Psychoanalysis and the Culture of the Child.* Baltimore: Johns Hopkins UP, 1985.

Smith, Karen Patricia. *The Fabulous Realm: A Literary-Historical Approach to British Fantasy, 1780–1990.* Metuchen, NJ: Scarecrow, 1993.

Sommerville, C. John. *The Discovery of Childhood in Puritan England.* Athens: U of Georgia P, 1992.

———. *The Rise and Fall of Childhood.* Beverly Hills, CA: Sage, 1982.

Soter, Anna O., ed. *Young Adult Literature and the New Literary Theories: Developing Critical Readers in Middle School.* New York: Teachers College P, 1999.

Spitz, Ellen Handler. *Inside Picture Books.* New Haven CT: Yale UP, 1999.

Stephens, John. *Language and Ideology in Children's Fiction.* New York: Longman, 1992.

———, ed. *Ways of Being Male: Representing Masculinities in Children's Literature and Film.* New York: Routledge, 2002.

Stephens, John, and Robyn McCallum. *Retelling Stories, Framing Culture: Traditional Story and Metanarratives in Children's Literature.* New York: Garland, 1998.

Stone, Kay F. *Burning Brightly: New Light on Old Tales Retold Today.* Orchard Park, NY: Broadview P, 1998.

Stott, Jon C. *Native Americans in Children's Literature.* Phoenix, AZ: Oryx P, 1995.

Street, Douglas, ed. *Children's Novels and the Movies.* New York: Ungar, 1983.

Styles, Morag. *From the Garden to the Street: 300 Years of Poetry for Children.* London: Cassell, 1998.

Styles, Morag, and Eve Bearne, eds. *Art, Narrative and Childhood.* Sterling, VA: Trentham Books, 2003.

Sullivan, C. W. III. *Science Fiction for Young Readers.* Westport, CT: Greenwood, 1993.

———. *Welsh Celtic Myth in Modern Fantasy.* New York: Greenwood, 1989.

———. *Young Adult Science Fiction.* Westport, CT: Greenwood, 1999.

Sutherland, Zena, ed. *Children and Books.* 9th ed. New York: Addison-Wesley, 1996.

Tatar, Maria. *Off with Their Heads! Fairy Tales and the Culture of Childhood.* Princeton, NJ: Princeton UP, 1992. Rev. ed., 2004.

———. *The Hard Facts of the Grimms' Fairy Tales.* Princeton, NJ: Princeton UP, 1987.

Thacker, Deborah Cogan, and Jean Webb. *Introducing Children's Literature: From Romanticism to Postmodernism.* London: Routledge, 2002.

Townsend, John Rowe. *Written for Children: An Outline of En-*

glish Language Children's Literature. Philadelphia: Lippincott, 1975.

Trites, Roberta Seelinger. Disturbing the Universe: Power and Repression in Adolescent Literature. Iowa City: Iowa UP, 2000.

———. Waking Sleeping Beauty: Feminist Voices in Children's Novels. Iowa City: Iowa UP, 1997.

Tucker, Nicholas. The Child and the Book: A Psychological and Literary Exploration. New York: Cambridge UP, 1981.

Vandergrift, Kay E., ed. Ways of Knowing: Literature and the Intellectual Life of Children. Lanham, MD: Scarecrow, 1996.

Van der Walt, Thomas, ed. Change and Renewal in Children's Literature. Westport, CT: Praeger, 2004.

Warner, Marina. From the Beast to the Blonde: On Fairy Tales and Their Tellers. New York: Farrar, Straus & Giroux, 1995.

———. Six Myths for Our Time: Little Angels, Little Monsters, Beautiful Beasts, and More. New York: Vintage, 1995.

Watson, Victor. Reading Series Fiction from Arthur Ransome to Gene Kemp. New York: Routledge, 2000.

Watson, Victor, and Morag Styles, eds. Talking Pictures: Pictorial Texts and Young Readers. London: Hodder & Stoughton, 1996.

West, Mark I. Trust Your Children: Voices Against Censorship in Children's Literature. 2nd ed. New York: Neal-Schuman, 1997.

Whited, Lana, ed. The Ivory Tower and Harry Potter: Perspectives on a Literary Phenomenon. Columbia: U of Missouri P, 2002.

Wojcik-Andrews, Ian. Children's Films: History, Ideology, Pedagogy, Theory. New York: Garland, 2000.

Wullschlager, Jackie. Inventing Wonderland: The Lives and Fantasies of Lewis Carroll, Edward Lear, J. M. Barrie, Kenneth Grahame and A. A. Milne. New York: Free Press, 1995.

Yolen, Jane. Touch Magic: Fantasy, Faerie, and Folklore in the Literature of Childhood. 2nd ed. Little Rock, AK: August House, 2000.

Zipes, Jack. Breaking the Magic Spell: Radical Theories of Folk and Fairy Tales. Austin: U of Texas P, 1979.

———, ed. Don't Bet on the Prince: Contemporary Feminist Fairy Tales in North America and England. New York: Methuen, 1986.

———. Fairy Tales and the Art of Subversion: The Classical Genre for Children and the Process of Civilization. 2nd ed. New York: Routledge, 2006.

———. Happily Ever After: Fairy Tales, Children, and the Culture Industry. New York: Routledge, 1997.

———. Sticks and Stones: The Troublesome Success of Children's Literature from Slovenly Peter to Harry Potter. New York: Routledge, 2001.

———. When Dreams Came True: Classical Fairy Tales and Their Tradition. New York: Routledge, 1999.

CRITICAL JOURNALS

ALAN Review, Assembly on Literature for Adolescents, National Council of Teachers of English

Bookbird: A Journal of International Children's Literature, International Board on Books for Young People (IBBY)

Book Links

Booklist

Bulletin of the Center for Children's Books (Chicago)

Canadian Children's Literature/Littérature canadienne pour la jeunesse

Children's Literature (Johns Hopkins UP)

Children's Literature Association Quarterly

Children's Literature in Education

The Horn Book Magazine

Journal of African American Children's Literature

Journal of Children's Literature, Children's Literature Assembly, National Council of Teachers of English

Journal of Youth Services in Libraries, American Library Association

The Lion and the Unicorn

Magpies: Talking about Books for Children (Australia)

Marvels and Tales: Journal of Fairy-Tale Studies

New Advocate

Papers: Explorations into Children's Literature (Australia)

School Library Journal

Signal: Approaches to Children's Books (British; ceased publication in Sept. 2003)

Through the Looking Glass: An On-line Children's Literature Journal (http://www.the-looking-glass.net)

Timeline of Children's Literature

R hymes, tales, and songs from the oral tradition date back to prehistoric times, having been composed and recited from generation to generation. The originals of the tales that were collected and retold by Charles Perrault and by the Brothers Grimm belong to this tradition. We can trace versions of them back to earlier writers such as Giambattista Basile (c. 1575–1632), but they vary widely and recur in distinctive variations across the centuries. Folktales were originally told for audiences of adults and children alike.

C. 1000 ~ 1744

c. 1000 Aelfric, *Colloquy:* a dramatic dialogue, written in Latin, for the instruction of pupils in a monastery school.

c. 1580s Beginning of chapbooks, inexpensive pamphlets sold to circulate many types of popular, religious, and political literature into the nineteenth century, including folklore, ballads, and adventure stories.

1500s–1700s widespread use of hornbooks: small paddles with sheets of horn protecting papers used to teach reading, first recorded in Shakespeare but probably used much earlier.

1658 John Amos Comenius, *Orbis Sensualium Pictus:* an encyclopedic school text, combining words and pictures, often referred to as the first children's picture book; the text was in two languages (or more): Latin and the language of everyday speech in the country of its use—German, Czech, English.

1678 John Bunyan, *The Pilgrim's Progress:* a Christian allegory that influenced many later children's writers, including Louisa May Alcott in *Little Women.*

c. 1689 *The New England Primer:* instructional texts developed by the Puritans for religious training and reading, used in America, with revisions, into the nineteenth century.

1693 John Locke, *Some Thoughts Concerning Education:* an influential philosophical rationale of modern education.

1697 Charles Perrault, *Contes de ma mère l'oye* (Tales of Mother Goose), published by an aristocrat at the court of Louis XIV.

c. 1708 *The Arabian Nights* translated into English, also known as *The Thousand and One Nights* in Arabic: a collection with tales of Aladdin, Ali Baba, and Sinbad and many other popular stories.

1715 Isaac Watts, *Divine Songs:* a collection of poems, many of them written for children.

1719 Daniel Defoe, *Robinson Crusoe:* an archetypal castaway story, not written for children, but later frequently adapted for children and influential in children's adventure literature.

1726 Jonathan Swift, *Gulliver's Travels:* a political satire for adults; its imaginative juxtaposition of large and small beings has stimulated imitations for centuries.

1729 *Tales of Mother Goose,* the English translation of Charles Perrault's fairy tales that became popular in England.

1744 John Newbery, *A Little Pretty Pocket-book,* published in London, the first book explicitly published to instruct and delight child readers. The Newbery Award, given annually by the American Library Association, is named after this savvy, enterprising publisher.

1744 Jane Johnson, *A Very Pretty Story to Tell Children When They Are About Five or Six Years of Age:* the earliest known English fairy tale for children. Johnson's papers, including instructional cards for learning the alphabet, syllables, and sentences, reveal an early tradition of unpublished writing for children in private homes.

1749 Sarah Fielding, *The Governess; or, The Little Female Academy:* the first English novel written specifically for girls.

1762 Jean Jacques Rousseau, *Émile ou de l'éducation* (Emile or Of Education): Rousseau's revolutionary philosophy of education.

1765 John Newbery publishes *The Renowned History of Little Goody Two Shoes.*

1777–79 *Lessons for Children* by Anna Laetitia Barbauld, a Protestant dissenter and influential educator who mistrusted imaginative storytelling but wrote appealing educational books for children.

1780s Robert Raikes, an English industrialist, founds the Sunday School Movement, which results in an enormous demand for religious literature written for children.

1789 William Blake's *Songs of Innocence* published with Blake's colored engravings integrated with his poems, one of the first books of poetry for and about children. Blake's Romantic and visionary concepts in *Songs of Innocence and Experience* continue to influence writers and critics of children's books.

1796 Maria Edgeworth, *The Parent's Assistant;* 1801, *Early Lessons:* an Irish novelist, seeking to put John Locke's educational theories into practice, creates lively, believable child characters such as Rosamond in "The Purple Jar."

1806 Jane Taylor and Anne Taylor Gilbert, *Rhymes for the Nursery:* children's poems, including "Twinkle, Twinkle, Little Star."

1807 William Wordsworth, "Ode: Intimations of Immortality from Recollections of Early Childhood," *Lyrical Ballads:* an influential Romantic statement of the beauty and sanctity of the child's imagination and kinship with nature.

1812 Jakob and Wilhelm Grimm, German folklorists, publish their first collection of *Kinder- und Hausmärchen* (Children's and Household Fairy Tales) in their efforts to preserve German tradition and national identity.

1823 English translation of the Grimm Brothers' tales by Edgar Taylor, with illustrations by George Cruikshank, popularizes the tales in England.

1834 Mary Howitt, "The Spider and the Fly," *Sketches of Natural History:* an enduring cautionary poem.

1841 John Ruskin, *The King of the Golden River:* a literary fairy tale closely related to the Grimm Brothers' tales; an early ecological fable.

1843 Peter Parley (Samuel Griswold), *Make the Best of It; or Cheerful Cherry, and Other Tales,* by an optimistic and prolific American children's author.

1844 Heinrich Hoffmann, a physician in Frankfurt, Germany, publishes *Struwwelpeter* (Slovenly Peter), an illustrated series of moralistic tales, based on sketches drawn to amuse and instruct his child patients; some of the episodes appear gruesome to modern readers, but were intended as humorously didactic tales.

1846 Hans Christian Andersen's Danish literary fairy tales first appear in English editions.

1846 Edward Lear, *A Book of Nonsense:* a pioneering book of nonsense verse and pictures.

1851 Nathaniel Hawthorne, *A Wonder Book for Boys and Girls:* retellings of classical myths for children.

1854 Charles Dickens, *Hard Times:* a satiric novel attacking the cruelty of unimaginative teachers to poor, hapless children, by the author of the perennial favorite *A Christmas Carol* (1843).

1855 Jacob Abbott, *Rollo Learning to Talk* and *Rollo Learning to Read:* a gentle New England writer's series of stories aimed at motivating children to learn.

Approximately 1865–1910 Golden Age of Children's Literature: an era of popular, imaginative children's books, many of which are still frequently read.

1865 Lewis Carroll (pseudonym for Charles Lutwidge Dodgson) publishes his classic children's fantasy, *Alice's Adventures in Wonderland;* the novel is an emphatic rejection of moralistic literature for children, with strong undercurrents of anxiety and chaos as well as nonsensical humor.

1865 Wilhelm Busch, *Max and Moritz:* a German satiric cartoon-style story, pioneer of the comic book-style of storytelling.

1868–69 Louisa May Alcott, *Little Women:* enormously popular story of New England family life set during the Civil War, followed by the sequels *Little Men* and *Jo's Boys.*

1869 Thomas Bailey Aldrich, *The Story of a Bad Boy:* not a genuinely bad boy but, rather, an appealingly mischievous boy whose escapades the book celebrates.

1871 George MacDonald, *At the Back of the North Wind,* allegorical fantasy about death and the life of the spirit that influenced twentieth-century writers such as J. R. R. Tolkien and C. S. Lewis; MacDonald also wrote *The Princess and the Goblin.*

1873 *St. Nicholas Magazine* begins publishing; Mary Mapes Dodge, author of *Hans Brinker, or the Silver Skates,* is its first editor and enlists some of the best writers and illustrators of her day to publish in *St. Nicholas.*

1874 *Walter Crane's New Toy Book, Containing Sixty-four Pages of Pictures* published by the innovative London printer Edmund Evans, helping to establish Crane's reputation as one of the finest and most prolific of children's book illustrators.

1876 Mark Twain (Samuel Langhorne Clemens), *The Adventures of Tom Sawyer:* "simply a hymn, put into prose form to give it a worldly air," romanticizing boyhood adventures and imagination.

1877 Randolph Caldecott begins his distinguished career as a children's book illustrator with *The House that Jack Built* and *The Diverting History of John Gilpin,* published by Edmund Evans. The American Library Association gives the modern Caldecott Medal annually to a picture book artist.

1878 Kate Greenaway, *Under the Window:* a collection of idyllic poems about childhood in natural settings; Greenaway's illustrations established a distinctive style of children's clothing.

1880 Joel Chandler Harris, *Uncle Remus, His Songs and His Sayings:* the first of several volumes of African American folktales collected on Southern plantations by a white journalist; the lively tales of Brer Rabbit and other animal tricksters, although criticized for racial bias as Harris presented them and as Walt Disney filmed them in the twentieth century, have been retold by countless storytellers and rewritten by contemporary authors such as Julius Lester.

1880 Johanna Spyri, *Heidi:* beloved novel about an orphan in the Swiss Alps.

1883 Robert Louis Stevenson, *Treasure Island:* an unsurpassed adventure story, featuring pirates, mutiny, hidden treasure, and deadly battles—but also the education of Jim Hawkins; Stevenson also wrote the classic adventure story *Kidnapped* (1886).

1883 *The Merry Adventures of Robin Hood* establishes Howard Pyle's success as a reteller and illustrator of beautifully designed editions of traditional literature. Founder of the "Brandywine School" of illustration, Pyle developed high standards of art and design that influenced his students Jesse Willcox Smith and N. C. Wyeth.

1883 Carlo Collodi (Italian; Collodi is a pseudonym), *The Adventures of Pinocchio:* the story of a wooden puppet whose impulses continually prevent him from acting wisely; his foolish actions perpetually get him into trouble.

1884 Mark Twain (Samuel Langhorne Clemens), *Adventures of Huckleberry Finn:* a scathing critique of Southern antebellum society, told by the outcast ragamuffin, Huck Finn, himself, in his inimitable vernacular voice.

1885 Robert Louis Stevenson's enduring collection *A Child's Garden of Verses:* perceptive and evocative poems about the world as seen from a child's perspective.

1888 Frances Hodgson Burnett, *Little Lord Fauntleroy:* a popular stage play based on the **1886** novel of the same title, starting a fashion of elaborate boys' clothes and hairstyles, much loathed by later generations.

1890 Joseph Jacobs, *English Fairy Tales:* many of the famous English tales, vividly and colloquially retold by the talented cosmopolitan scholar born in Australia.

1894 Rudyard Kipling, *The Jungle Book:* classic colonialist stories about Mowgli, a boy raised by wolves in India, and adventures of his animals friends.

1898 "The Reluctant Dragon" appears in the second volume of Kenneth Grahame's *Dream Days;* the story of a mock battle between St. George and a peace-loving dragon influences later parodies of traditional tales and stories about tame dragons.

1898 Ernest Thompson Seton, *Wild Animals I Have Known:* the fascination of wild animals, as told by one of the founders of the Boy Scout movement.

1899 E. Nesbit, *The Story of the Treasure Seekers:* a children's adventure novel, the first in a series about the Bastable children by this prolific and popular author.

1900 L. Frank Baum, *The Wonderful Wizard of Oz:* a pioneering American work of fantasy.

1902 Beatrix Potter's *The Tale of Peter Rabbit* published by Frederick Warne with color illustrations; Potter, a gifted naturalist and artist, mixes keen observation of animals with humorous and wise portrayals of human traits.

1904 J. M. Barrie, *Peter Pan:* the fantasy of the boy who would not grow up became the most successful children's play ever.

1905 Frances Hodgson Burnett, *A Little Princess:* Sara Crewe, once a wealthy orphan, is exiled to the attic in this story of riches to rags to riches again.

1908 Kenneth Grahame, *The Wind in the Willows:* an arcadian celebration of male bonding in the metaphorical disguise of a group of animal friends: Mole, Toad, Badger, and the consummately civilized Water Rat.

1908 Lucy Maud Montgomery, *Anne of Green Gables:* The famous red-haired orphan seeks to please her adoptive family but keeps making hilarious, entertaining mistakes.

1911 Frances Hodgson Burnett, *The Secret Garden:* a story of healing through nature and the power of the mind over the body; Mary Lennox travels from India to Yorkshire and discovers herself and others in a hidden garden.

1914–18 World War I

1920–21 W. E. B. Dubois and Jessie Fauset edit *The Brownies' Book,* the first African American children's magazine; short-lived but influential.

1922 The Newbery Medal established by Frederick Melcher: the annual award for the best children's book as selected by the American Library Association.

1923 Lucy Maud Montgomery, *Emily of New Moon:* the education of a female artist; orphan Emily discovers and develops her talents as a writer.

1927 Franklin Dixon (pseudonym), *The Tower Treasure:* the first of a long series of Hardy Boys adventures published by the Stratemeyer Syndicate.

1927 A. A. Milne, *Winnie-the-Pooh:* the friendships and silly misadventures of a lovable stuffed bear in the English countryside, who stars in two books by Milne long before he is Americanized in Walt Disney cartoons.

1928 Wanda Gág, *Millions of Cats:* one of the first American picture books of enduring artistic quality, with innovative design features that set a high standard for the rhythmic integration of words and illustrations in modern picture books.

1930 Carolyn Keene (pseudonym), *The Secret of the Old Clock:* the first of the many Nancy Drew mysteries produced by the Stratemeyer Syndicate; a role model to generations of independent-minded girls.

1930 *Swallows and Amazons:* the first of Arthur Ransome's popular, enduring series of novels about families of English children enjoying independent, imaginative adventures outdoors.

1934 P. L. Travers, *Mary Poppins:* the first book in a series about the indomitable English nanny and the Banks children, her London charges.

1935 Laura Ingalls Wilder, *Little House on the Prairie:* a classic description of life on the American frontier, told in beautiful, clear prose; part of an extensive series of Little House books.

1936 Ruth Sawyer, *Roller Skates:* a novel about a remarkably independent ten-year-old girl who skates around New York City making friends with a variety of people while her parents are away.

1937 J. R. R. Tolkien, *The Hobbit or There and Back Again:* the adventures of the inhabitants of Middle Earth, the children's book predecessor of *Lord of the Rings,* high fantasy novels.

1937 *Snow White and the Seven Dwarfs:* the first feature-length animated film is followed by many other adaptations that earn Walt Disney praise for reviving the public's interest in fairy tales and criticism for distorting traditional stories.

1938 Caldecott Medal established, the award for best picture book of the year in the United States, given by the American Library Association.

1939–45 World War II

1941 Elizabeth Enright, *The Saturdays:* the Melendy children take turns exploring New York City in a series of absorbing adventures.

1941 Robert McCloskey, *Make Way for Ducklings:* the adventure of a family of ducks in Boston, drawn in simple, expressive lines.

1941 Hilaire Belloc, *Cautionary Verses:* mordantly humorous tales of children who come to bad ends.

1942 Maureen Daly, *Seventeenth Summer,* one of the earliest young adult novels.

1943 Antoine de Saint-Exupéry, *Le Petit Prince* (The Little Prince): a philosophical classic about friendship, love, and death.

1943 Richard Chase, *The Jack Tales;* 1848 *Grandfather Tales:* collections of Appalachian folktales told in the mountains of North Carolina and Virginia by descendants of European immigrants.

1944 Astrid Lindgren, *Pippi Longstocking:* published in an English translation by Florence Lamborn in 1950; Pippi is an early superhero and feminist heroine: stronger than policemen, able to lift a horse, Pippi does not let anyone tell her what to do.

1944 Esther Forbes, *Johnny Tremain:* a historical novel about a boy in Boston who becomes a spy for the American revolutionaries.

1947 Margaret Wise Brown, *Goodnight Moon:* the soothing bedtime classic in which each double-page spread darkens toward night.

1947 Dr. Frederick Wertham, a psychiatrist, launches a crusade to censor comic books.

1950 C. S. Lewis, *The Lion, the Witch and the Wardrobe,* the first of seven Narnia books: an eclectic mix of classical myth, fantasy, and modern invention, the series conveys Christian themes in a fashion that Lewis insisted was not strictly allegorical.

1950 Ursula Nordstrom, gifted editor at Harper, discovers Maurice Sendak; Nordstrom edited the works of Louise Fitzhugh, E. B. White, Shel Silverstein, Margaret Wise Brown, and many other distinguished writers.

1951 J. D. Salinger, *Catcher in the Rye,* articulates the sense of alienation of the postwar generation in a novel that appealed to young adults and remained controversial for decades.

1952 Iona and Peter Opie, *The Oxford Dictionary of Nursery Rhymes:* a wide-ranging compilation and history of traditional rhymes and verses by influential English collectors of children's books and folklore.

1952 E. B. White, *Charlotte's Web,* with illustrations by Garth Williams; rescuing a runt pig occupies first Fern, the farm girl, and then Charlotte, the wise spider, in a novel celebrating the seasons and the fleet passage of life.

1952 Anne Frank, *The Diary of a Young Girl:* translated from the Dutch; Anne Frank's incisive and unsparingly honest record of her life in hiding came to symbolize to the postwar generation the horror and cost of anti-Semitism in Nazi-dominated Europe.

1957 Dr. Seuss, *The Cat in the Hat:* a celebration of the anarchy that ensues when Mother leaves her children alone at home and a trouble-making cat appears; Dr. Seuss's first attempt to write exciting stories with a limited vocabulary for beginning readers, in response to a *Life* magazine article about boring basal readers used in schools.

1958 Philippa Pearce, *Tom's Midnight Garden:* a compelling time-travel fantasy about friendship between children from two different eras in southeastern England.

1961 Roald Dahl, *James and the Giant Peach:* an extravagant fantasy about an English boy for whom everything possible goes wrong—yet who triumphs nonetheless.

1961 Scott O'Dell, *Island of the Blue Dolphins:* the editors wanted O'Dell to change his heroine into a boy, but this story of a heroic Native American girl's survival on her own has won the hearts of generations of readers.

1962 Madeleine L'Engle, *A Wrinkle in Time:* a fantasy of travel through time and space (tesseracting) to a planet of evil conformity; rescue comes in the form of three wise witches.

1963 Maurice Sendak, *Where the Wild Things Are:* a mischievous boy, sent to bed without his supper, travels to the land of the Wild Things in this graphically innovative and enduring picture book.

1964 Louise Fitzhugh, *Harriet the Spy:* a milestone and a masterpiece of New Realism, heralding a new honesty and candor in children's literature that began to emerge in the 1960s.

1964 Lloyd Alexander, *The Book of Three:* the humorous adventures of an assistant pig keeper setting out on an unlikely quest.

1964 Roald Dahl, *Charlie and the Chocolate Factory:* a sometimes controversial, provocatively brash and moralistic fantasy of oral gratification.

1966 Irene Hunt, *Up a Road Slowly:* the memorable story of Julie, who comes to live with an aunt whose "integrity, compassion, and strength of character" instruct her.

1967 E. L. Konigsburg, *From the Mixed-Up Files of Mrs. Basil E. Frankweiler:* a famous running-away-from-home story; when two children go to live in the Metropolitan Museum of Art, their deliberate planning and spirit of independence pay off.

1967 S. E. Hinton, *The Outsiders,* a classic young adult novel of gang rivalry and teenage angst and isolation.

1968 Beverly Cleary, *Ramona the Pest:* humorous tales of a very young girl's relationships in her home, school, and neighborhood; she becomes the center of a series of books.

1968 Ted Hughes, *The Iron Giant:* English poet laureate Hughes weaves a mythic tale of a robot-like iron giant, the boy who befriends him, and the phenomenal space creature he battles.

1968 Ursula K. LeGuin, *A Wizard of Earthsea:* part of a fantasy series of dark adventure.

1970 Maurice Sendak, *In the Night Kitchen:* the second in Sendak's trilogy of imaginative picture books, this one inspired by cartoons of the 1930s.

1970 Judy Blume, *Are You There, God? It's Me, Margaret:* unprecedented frankness about menstruation and religious questions made this book a favorite with young readers.

1972 Isabelle Holland, *The Man Without a Face:* a sympathetic novelistic treatment of male bonding and a somewhat disguised (or idealized) homosexual encounter.

1973 Founding of the Children's Literature Association by Anne Deveraux Jordan and Francelia Butler.

1973 *Julie of the Wolves* by Jean Craighead George, one of George's many stories about survival and the natural environment: a girl in Alaska, fleeing from conflicts between Eskimo and American culture, lives with a family of wolves while stranded in the Arctic wilderness.

1973 Paula Fox, *The Slave Dancer:* a controversial early effort, by a white author, to portray the horrors of the Middle Passage of the transport of slaves from Africa to America.

1974 *Where the Sidewalk Ends* establishes Shel Silverstein's widespread popularity as an American writer and illustrator of humorous poetry collections for children.

1974 *M. C. Higgins the Great* by Virginia Hamilton, a novel about an African American boy and his family living on an Appalachian mountain ravaged by strip mining, becomes the only book ever to have been awarded the Newbery Medal (the first awarded to an African American writer), the Boston Globe-Horn Book Award, and the National Book Award.

1974 Trina Schart Hyman's illustrations for Paul Heins's retelling of *Snow White* blend realism and romance in intense, sensuous paintings with expressive and symbolic details, a style of fairy tale illustration developed by Hyman and other artists throughout the late twentieth century.

1975 Judy Blume, *Forever . . . : A Novel:* although intended for a young adult audience, this novel provided the first glimpse of the stark facts of sex for many preadolescents, all the more appealing for being forbidden by teachers and parents.

1976 Mildred Taylor, *Roll of Thunder, Hear My Cry:* the struggle of an African American family to maintain its dignity and economic independence in Jim Crow Mississippi in the 1930s; the first in a series about Logan family history.

1976 Bruno Bettelheim's *The Uses of Enchantment*, an influential defense of fairy tales as material suitable for young children, makes a Freudian argument that the symbolic traditional tales are psychologically healthier than happy modern stories for children.

1976 Susan Cooper, *The Grey King:* the crowning work in the Dark Is Rising series of fantasies about struggles with friendship, destiny, and loss.

1977 Katherine Paterson, *Bridge to Terabithia:* a keenly observant story of friendship between a boy and a girl in rural Virginia who create their own imaginary kingdom and the terrible tragedy that strikes.

1977 Robert Cormier, *I Am the Cheese:* a postmodern tale of disorientation and mind control in a world of conspiracy and brutality.

1978 Katherine Paterson, *The Great Gilly Hopkins:* a foster child with an attitude finally meets a foster mother who truly loves her, but she gambles on the idealized, unreachable biological mother she has never met—and has to pay the cost.

1979 Ellen Raskin, *The Westing Game:* a masterful mystery story about a game to discover who the legitimate heir to the Westing inheritance is.

1980 Diane Wolkstein, *The Magic Orange Tree:* a captivating book of Jamaican folktales, collected from native storytellers by a skilled teller of tales, the onetime official storyteller of Central Park.

1980 Monica Hughes, *The Keeper of the Isis Light:* raised by a nurturing robot, a girl has happily adapted to life on a distant planet—until humans arrive from their overcrowded planet, bringing their prejudices with them.

1980 Katherine Paterson, *Jacob Have I Loved:* an incisive characterization of the intricacies and injuries of sibling rivalry; the heroine, living on an island in the Chesapeake Bay, has to overcome her favored twin sister's apparent superiority.

1981 Maurice Sendak, *Outside Over There:* the third in an influential picture book trilogy, this mystical, poetic tale evokes the baroque world of Mozart's time.

1982 Roald Dahl, *Dahl's Revolting Rhymes:* humorous, sarcastic fairy tale satires in verse from the master of insult, exaggeration, and invective.

1984 Cynthia Voigt, *A Solitary Blue:* a tale of psychological struggle to come to terms with a mother who first abandons and then woos and manipulates her son.

1985 Virginia Hamilton, *The People Could Fly: American Black Folktales:* an important collection of tales retold from the oral tradition, stressing the indomitable desire for freedom in African American storytelling since slavery times.

1986 Fiona French, *Snow White in New York:* an urban picture book retelling in the Jazz Age idiom, one of many modern spin-offs of traditional tales in the late twentieth century.

1986 Patricia MacLachlan, *Sarah, Plain and Tall:* told in graceful, concise prose, a historical American story of yearning for a stepmother who proves to be all her potential stepchildren yearn for her to be—and more.

1988 Grace Nichols, *Come On Into My Tropical Garden:* a Guyanan writer weaves together Guyanan folklore and Amerindian legends into powerful Caribbean poetry.

1989 James Berry, *Spiderman Anancy:* a Jamaican author retells West African trickster tales of Anansy with humor, verve, and contemporary immediacy.

1989 Francesca Lia Block, *Weetzie Bat:* the first of Block's edgy young adult novels about the unconventional Los Angeles family of a young woman, her friend Dirk, and his lover Duck, who adopt a baby named "Cherokee."

1989 Mette Newth, *The Abduction:* a novel that attempts to recover the perspective of the Inuit people of the far north in the era of European exploration and colonialism; an unflinching depiction of the Europeans' rape, plunder, and murder of the Inuit, told in part from the point of view of an Inuit girl who, with her brother, is abducted and taken to Norway.

1989 Jane Yolen, *Dove Isabeau:* one of Yolen's lyrical stories that reshape traditional lore, illustrated by Dennis Nolan; it tells of a heroic young woman who is transformed into a dragon by an evil stepmother and the love and wisdom that enable her to recover human form.

1990 *Black and White,* a highly innovative, multilayered picture book that illustrator David Macaulay presents as containing "a number of stories" or possibly "only one," challenging the reader to explore four threads of playful, ironic narrative with images in color as well as black and white.

1991 Faith Ringgold, *Tar Beach:* an artistic celebration of life in an oasis in the sky on the rooftops above New York City by a distinguished African American artist.

1992 R. L. Stine, *Welcome to Dead House,* an early entry in the Goosebumps series, a popular gothic fantasy series specializing in the macabre; unpopular with many adult critics.

1992 Jon Scieszka and Lane Smith, *The Stinky Cheese Man and Other Fairly Stupid Tales:* an offbeat postmodern picture book that satirizes classic fairy tales and mocks traditional elements of book design.

1992 Phyllis Reynolds Naylor, *Shiloh:* the tale of the love of a boy for an abused dog; a skillful evocation of rural West Virginia culture, and a book that asks readers to think through difficult moral issues without easy answers.

1993 Lois Lowry, *The Giver:* an antiutopian fantasy of an alternate (future?) world in which social evils, such as poverty and crime, are eliminated—in fact, all kinds of suffering—but at what cost? The boy who is chosen as "Giver" in this world is destined to learn what suffering is and to keep the memory of it for the community—but he revolts.

1994 *Am I Blue? Coming Out of the Silence,* an anthology of stories edited by Marion Dane Bauer, about the lives of young gay people, containing Bruce Coville's "Am I Blue?," a metaphorical story that captures the anguished dilemmas of being gay in a straight world.

1995–2000 Philip Pullman, *His Dark Materials trilogy (The Golden Compass, The Subtle Knife, The Amber Spyglass),* an anti–C. S. Lewis fantasy, masterfully imagining an alternate Oxford and its child heroine and hero, who discover that the adults in their lives are up to no good.

1997 J. K. Rowling, *Harry Potter and the Philosopher's Stone* (British title): the first in the phenomenally popular series about a boy wizard at Hogwarts Academy.

1997 Karen Hesse, *Out of the Dust:* a Depression-era story told in free-verse diary entries; a tale of hardship shot through with beauty.

1998 Louis Sachar, *Holes:* prison camp life for an unjustly convicted boy leads to a quest for his ancestors and a mythic past that has determined his harsh present.

1998 James Still, *An Appalachian Mother Goose:* humorous traditional rhymes reshaped by generations of mountain families and a revered Kentucky author; one of many late twentieth-century collections of folklore from previously marginalized cultures.

1999 Louise Erdrich, *The Birchbark House:* the story of an Ojibwa girl in the 1840s on an island in what is now called Lake Superior; a Native American perspective on the contact between the Ojibwa and white settlers, providing a counterpoint to Wilder's Little House series.

2000 Christopher Paul Curtis, *Bud, Not Buddy:* ten-year old orphan Bud travels through Depression-era landscape hoping to find his lost father: a masterful characterization in this African American novel.

2001 Julius Lester, *When Dad Killed Mom:* a starkly realistic young adult novel narrated in the alternating voices of a brother and sister as they deal with murder in their own family.

2005 Marilyn Nelson, *A Wreath for Emmett Till:* a powerful poetic memorial to the fourteen-year-old African American boy who was murdered in 1955, allegedly for whistling at a white woman; it evokes the tragic cost of racism with quasi-Shakespearean grandeur.

CREDITS

TEXT

Lyon, George Ella. *BOOK*. Illus. Peter Catalanotto. New York: DK Ink, 1999.

PART 1. TO TEACH OR TO ENTERTAIN?

"On Three Ways of Writing for Children" from *Of Other Worlds: Essays and Stories* by C.S. Lewis, copyright © 1966 by the Executors of the Estate of C.S. Lewis and renewed 1994 by C.S. Lewis Pte. Ltd., reprinted by permission of Harcourt, Inc.

Egoff, Sheila. "Precepts, Pleasures, and Portents." *Only Connect: Readings on Children's Literature.* 2nd ed. Eds. Sheila Egoff, G. T. Stubbs and L. F. Ashley. Toronto: Oxford UP, 1980. 405–416.

"Didacticism in Modern Dress" by John Rowe Townsend from *The Horn Book Magazine,* April 1967. Reprinted by permission of The Horn Book, Inc., Boston, MA, www.hbook.com.

Aelfric. "Carius est nobis flagellari pro doctrina quam nescire." *Colloquy. From Instruction to Delight: An Anthology of Children's Literature to 1850.* Eds. Patricia Demers and Gordon Moyles. Toronto: Oxford UP, 1982. 4–9.

Perrault, Charles. "Little Red Riding-Hood," "The Master Cat, or Puss in Boots," "Blue Beard." 1697. *The Tales of Mother Goose.* Trans. Charles Welsh. Boston: Heath, 1901.

Trimmer, Sarah. "On the Care Which Is Requisite in the Choice of Books for Children." Review of *The History of Little Goody Two Shoes* and Review of *Nursery Tales. Guardian of Education* 2 (1803): 407–410; 1 (1802): 430–431; and 4 (1805): 74–75.

Watts, Isaac. "Against Idleness and Mischief," "Obedience to Parents." *Divine Songs.* London: M. Lawrence, 1715; "The Sluggard" added as one of "Moral Songs" in 1740 ed.

Southey, Robert. "The Old Man's Comforts and How He Gained Them." *Metrical Tales and Other Poems.* London: Longman, Hurst, Rees, and Orme, 1805.

Edgeworth, Maria. "The Purple Jar," "The Birthday Present." *Early Lessons.* London: J. Johnson, 1801.

Taylor, Jane. "The Little Fisherman." *Original Poems for Infant Minds.* London: Darton & Harvey, 1804–05.

Taylor, Jane, and Ann Taylor Gilbert. "Twinkle, Twinkle, Little Star." *Rhymes for the Nursery.* London: Darton & Harvey, 1806.

Howitt, Mary Botham. "The Spider and the Fly." *Sketches of Natural History.* London: E. Wilson, 1834.

Parley, Peter (Samuel Griswold). "The Pleasure Boat: or, The Broken Promise." *Make the Best of It; or Cheerful Cherry, and Other Tales.* New York: Putnam, 1843.

Hawthorne, Nathaniel. "The Tanglewood Play-room" and "The Paradise of Children." *A Wonder Book for Boys and Girls.* 1851. New York: Quality Paperback Book Club, 2000.

Abbott, Jacob. "Notice to Parents," From *Rollo Learning to Talk and Rollo Learning to Read.* 1835. New York: T. Y. Crowell, 1855.

Carroll, Lewis. From *Alice's Adventures in Wonderland.* London: Macmillan, 1865.

Carroll, Lewis. From *Through the Looking Glass.* London: Macmillan, 1872.

Alcott, Louisa May. From *Little Women.* 1868–69. Illus. Frank T. Merrill. Boston: Roberts Brothers, 1880.

Twain, Mark. From *The Adventures of Tom Sawyer.* Hartford, CT: American Publishing, 1876.

"Saturday Two" from *The Saturdays* by Elizabeth Enright. Copyright © 1941 by Elizabeth Enright Gillham. Copyright renewed © 1969 by Robert M. Gillham. Reprinted by permission of Henry Holt and Company, LLC.

"Ramona's Great Day" from *Ramona the Pest* by Beverly Cleary. Text copyright © by Beverly Cleary. Used by permission of HarperCollins Publishers. 1968.

Paulsen, Gary. From *The Island.* New York: Dell, 1988.

Chapters 1–6 from *Goosebumps: Be Careful What You Wish For* by R. L. Stine. Copyright © 1993 by Parachute Press. Reprinted by permission of Scholastic Inc.

Entire text from *Coming Home: From the Life of Langston Hughes* by Floyd Cooper, copyright © 1994 by Floyd Cooper. Used by permission of Philomel Books, A Division of Penguin Young Readers Group, A Member of Penguin Group (USA) Inc., 345 Hudson Street, New York, NY 10014. All rights reserved.

"Aunt Sue's Stories" and "Mother to Son" from *The Collected Poems of Langston Hughes* by Langston Hughes, copyright © 1994 by The Estate of Langston Hughes. Used by permission of Alfred A. Knopf, a division of Random House, Inc.

Clifton, Lucille. "Elevator." *Home.* Ed. Michael J. Rosen. New York: Charlotte Zolotow/HarperCollins, 1992. N. p.

"Under the Rainbow" by Lucille Clifton, copyright © 1993 by Lucille Clifton, from *Soul Looks Back in Wonder* by Tom Feelings. Used by permission of Dial Books for Young Readers, A

Division of Penguin Young Readers Group, A Member of Penguin Group (USA) Inc., 345 Hudson Street, New York, NY 10014. All rights reserved.

PART 2. SUBJECTION OF THE CHILD OR SUBVERSION OF ADULT AUTHORITY?

"A Child's Garden of Subversion" by Alison Lurie. Copyright © 1990 by Alison Lurie. First appeared in the *New York Times Book Review*. Reprinted by permission of Melanie Jasckon Agency L.L.C.

"Little Angels, Little Monsters: Keeping Childhood Innocent." From *Six Myths of Our Time* by Marina Warner, copyright © 1994 by Marina Warner. Used by permission of Vintage Books, a division of Random House, Inc.

Wynne, John Huddlestone. "Of the Danger of Pleasure." *Choice Emblems, natural, historical, fabulous, moral, and divine; for the improvement and pastime of youth; displaying the beauties and morals of the ancient fabulists: the whole calculated to convey the golden lessons of instruction under a new and more delightful dress. For the use of schools. Written for the amusement of a young nobleman.* 6th ed. London: J. Chapman, 1788.

Wordsworth, William. "Ode: Intimations of Immortality from Recollections of Early Childhood." *Lyrical Ballads*. London: Longman, 1807.

Segal, Lore, and Maurice Sendak, eds. "The Frog King, or Iron Henry," "Hansel and Gretel." *The Juniper Tree and Other Tales from Grimm*. Illus. Maurice Sendak. New York: Farrar, Straus, 1973.

Grimm, Jacob and Wilhelm. "Mother Holle." *Grimms' Tales for Young and Old: The Complete Stories*. Trans. Ralph Manheim. New York: Doubleday, 1977.

Andersen, Hans Christian. "The Emperor's New Clothes." *Danish Fairy Tales and Legends*. London: W. Pickering, 1846.

Hoffmann, Heinrich. "The Sad Tale of the Match-box." *Struwwelpeter OR Happy Tales and Funny Pictures, Freely Translated*. Trans. Mark Twain. New York: Marchbanks Press, 1935.

Aldrich, Thomas Bailey. From *The Story of a Bad Boy*. Boston: Fields, Osgood, 1870.

Montgomery, Lucy Maud. From *Anne of Green Gables*. Boston: L. C. Page, 1908.

"Pippi Plays Tag with Some Policemen," from *Pippi Longstocking* by Astrid Lindgren, translated by Florence Lamborn. Copyright © 1950 by the Viking Press, Inc. Copyright © renewed 1978 by Viking Penguin Inc. Copyright © Viking Penguin, Inc. 1985. Used by permission of Viking Penguin, an imprint of Penguin Putnam Books for Young Readers, a division of Penguin Putnam Inc.

Mikkelsen, Nina. "Insiders, Outsiders, and the Question of Authenticity: Who Shall Write for African American Children?" *African American Review* 32, no. 1 (Spring 1998): 33–50.

Excerpt from *The Abduction* by Mette Newth, translated by Tina Nunnally and Steven Murray. Translation copyright © 1989 by Farrar, Straus & Giroux, Inc. Reprinted by permission of Farrar, Straus and Giroux, LLC.

"On Writing the Abduction" by Mette Newth from *Book Links*, 1993. Used by permission of Mette Newth.

Approximately 5,200 words (chap's. 21–23) from *The Final Journey* by Gudrun Pausewang and translated by Patricia Crompton (First published in Germany as *Reise Im August* by Ravensburger Buchverlag Otto Meier GmbH 1992, Viking 1996, Puffin 1998). Copyright © Ravensburger Buchverlag Otto Meier GmbH, 1992. Translation copyright © Patricia Crompton, 1996. Reproduced by permission of Penguin Books Ltd.

"Up Taree Way" by Libby Hathorn from *Dream Time*, edited by Toss Gascoigne, Jo Goodman and Margot Tyrrell. Copyright © 1989 by Libby Hathorn. Collection copyright © 1989 by the Children's Book Council of Australia. Reprinted by permission of Houghton Mifflin Company. All rights reserved.

PART 3. ORAL AND WRITTEN LITERARY TRADITIONS

"How Spider Obtained the Sky-God's Stories." *Akan-Ashanti Folk Tales*. Trans. R. S. Rattray. 1930. *Best-Loved Folktales of the World*. Ed. Joanna Coles. New York: Anchor Doubleday, 1982. 620–23.

"History and Definition of Storytelling," "Folk Storytelling," "Visuality, Orality, Literacy." From *The World of Storytelling: Expanded and Revised Edition* by Anne Pellowski. Copyright © 1990 by The H. W. Wilson Company. Reprinted with permission.

"Oral Narration in Contemporary North America" by Kay F. Stone in *Fairy Tales and Society: Illusion, Allusion, and Paradigm* edited by Ruth B. Bottigheimer. Copyright © 1986 by University of Pennsylvania Press. Reprinted with permission.

"Reflections: The Uses of Enchantment." From *The Uses of Enchantment* by Bruno Bettelheim, copyright © 1975, 1976 by Bruno Bettelheim. Used by permission of Alfred A. Knopf, a division of Random House, Inc. Originally published in *The New Yorker*.

"Reading Fairy Tales" by Maria Tatar from *Teaching Children's Literature*. Copyright © 1992 by the Modern Language Association of America. Reprinted by permission of the Modern Language Association of America. Revised by author, 2005.

Langstaff, John. "The Oral Tradition: Alive, Alive-oh." *Innocence and Experience: Essays & Conversations on Children's Literature*. Eds. Barbara Harrison and Gregory Maguire. New York: Lothrop, Lee and Shepard, 1987. 427–32.

Opie, Iona and Peter. From *The Oxford Dictionary of Nursery Rhymes*. Oxford: Clarendon, 1952.

Greenaway, Kate. *A Apple Pie*. London: Frederick Warne, 1886.

"The Tree in the Wood." *A Book of Nursery Songs and Rhymes*. Ed. S. Baring-Gould. 1895. Detroit: Singing Tree Press, 1969. 33–34.

Still, James. From *An Appalachian Mother Goose*. Illus. Paul Brett Johnson. Lexington: UP of Kentucky, 1998.

"A Frog Went A-Courting." Sung by Miss Alpha Combs at Hindman School, Knott Co., KY, 1917. *English Folk Songs from the Southern Appalachians Collected by Cecil J. Sharp*. Ed. Maud Karpeles. Vol. II. London: Oxford UP, 1932. 317–18.

Lear, Edward. "The Owl and the Pussy-cat." 1871. *The Oxford Treasury of Children's Poems*. Eds. Michael Harrison and Christopher Stuart-Clark. New York: Oxford UP, 1988.

Lear, Edward. "The Broom, the Shovel, the Poker, and the Tongs." 1871. *Nonsense Poems*. New York: Dover, 1994.

Lear, Edward. "There was an old man with a beard," "There was an old man of Bohemia," "There was a young lady whose nose." *A Book of Nonsense*. 1861. New York: Routledge, 2002.

"Sarah Cynthia Stout Would Not Take the Garbage Out" from *Where the Sidewalk Ends* by Shel Silverstein. Copyright © 2004 by Evil Eye Music, Inc. Used by permission of HarperCollins Publishers.

"Zebra Question" from *A Light in the Attic* by Shel Silverstein. Copyright © 2004 by Evil Eye Music, Inc. Used by permission of HarperCollins Publishers.

"Worrywart" by Jeanne Steig from *Alpha Beta Chowder*. Copyright © 1992 by Pippin Properties, Inc. Used by permission of Pippin Properties, Inc.

Nichols, Grace. "Poor Grandma," "Riddle," "Wha Me Mudder Do," "I Like to Stay Up," "Moon Gazer," "The Sun," "They Were My People," "Sky," "I Am the Rain," "For Forest," "Sea Timeless." *Come On into My Tropical Garden*. London: HarperCollins, 1988.

"Creation," "Grandmother" and "In My Mother's Kitchen" from *Navajo: Visions and Voices Across the Mesa* by Shonto Begay. Copyright © 1995 by Shonto Begay. Reprinted by permission of Scholastic Inc.

From *The Story of the Milky Way* by Joseph Bruchac and Gayle Ross, copyright © 1995 by Joseph Bruchac and Gayle Ross. Used by permission of Dial Books for Young Readers, A Division of Penguin Young Readers Group, A Member of Penguin Group (USA) Inc., 345 Hudson Street, New York, NY 10014. All rights reserved.

Dancing Drum: A Cherokee Legend by Terri Cohlene. Copyright © 1990 by Rourke Publishing LLC. Used by permission of Rourke Publishing LLC.

Ovid. "Daedalus and Icarus." Trans. Rolfe Humphries. *Metamorphoses*. 1955. *World Masterpieces*. Englewood Cliffs, NJ: Prentice Hall, 1991.

From *Aesop's Fables*. Trans. George Fyler Townsend. 1880. Electronic Text Center. University of Virginia Library, Charlottesville, VA. July 1993. <http://etext.lib.virginia.edu>.

"How Tortoise Cracked His Shell" from *Things Fall Apart* by Chinua Achebe. Reprinted by permission of Harcourt Education. 1958.

Asbjørnsen, Peter Christen. "The Pancake." *Round the Yule Log: Norwegian Folk and Fairy Tales*. Trans. H. L. Brækstad. Philadelphia: J. B. Lippincott, n.d.

"John Henry." Traditional ballad.

"Anancy and the Making of the Bro Title" from *Spiderman Anancy*. Reprinted by permission of The Peters Fraser and Dunlop Group Limited on behalf of: James Berry. Copyright © James Berry. 1988.

Wolkstein, Diane. Introduction, "The Magic Orange Tree," "Mother of the Waters." *The Magic Orange Tree*. Illus. Elisa Henriquez. New York: Knopf, 1978.

"Vasilissa the Fair." *Strange Things Sometimes Still Happen*. Ed. Angela Carter. Boston: Faber and Faber, 1993. 78–86.

Okuhara, Rieko, trans. "Hachi-kazuki-hime: The Princess Who Wore a Hachi." 2000.

de Beaumont, Marie Le Prince. "Beauty and the Beast." Trans. Dinah M. Craik. 1863. *Classics of Children's Literature*. 4th ed. Eds. John W. Griffith and Charles H. Frey. Upper Saddle River, NJ: Prentice Hall, 1996. 24–31.

Segal, Lore, and Maurice Sendak, eds. "Snow-White and the Seven Dwarfs," "Rapunzel." Trans. Lore Segal. *The Juniper Tree and Other Tales from Grimm*. Illus. Maurice Sendak. New York: Farrar, Straus, 1973.

Grimm, Jacob and Wilhelm. "The Water of Life." Trans. Ralph Manheim. *Grimms' Tales for Young and Old: The Complete Stories*. New York: Doubleday, 1977.

"Kemp Owyne." Child 34, Version A. *English and Scottish Popular Ballads*. Ed. Francis James Child. Boston: Little, Brown, 1864.

"The Brothers Grimm and Sister Jane." Copyright © 1993 by Jane Yolen. First Appeared *The Reception of Grimm's Fairy Tales: Responses, Reactions, Revisions* published by Wayne State University Press. Reprinted by permission of Curtis Brown, Ltd.

Dove Isabeau, text copyright © 1989 by Jane Yolen, illustrations © 1989 by Dennis Nolan, reprinted by permission of Harcourt, Inc.

Jacobs, Joseph. "Jack and the Beanstalk." *English Fairy Tales*. 3rd. ed. 1898. New York: Dover, 1967.

"Munsmeg." JTA-3068, ts. Folktale collected by Richard Chase. James Taylor Adams Collection, Blue Ridge Institute, Ferrum College, Ferrum, VA, n.d.

Stephenson, R. Rex. "Mutsmag," unpublished script. Ferrum College, Ferrum, VA, 2000–05.

PART 4. REALISM AND FANTASY

"Realism and Children's Literature: Notes for a Historical Perspective" by Elizabeth Segel from *Children's Literature Association Quarterly* 5.3 (Fall 1980): 15–18. Reprinted by permission of the Children's Literature Association.

C. W. Sullivan III / Dennis Butts Ed., "Fantasy" from *Stories and Society: Children's Literature in its Social Context*, 1992, St. Martin's, reproduced with permission of Palgrave Macmillan.

"Why Are Americans Afraid of Dragons?" Copyright © 1974, 2002 by Ursula K. Le Guin; first appeared in *PNLA Quarterly* 38; from *The Language of the Night*; reprinted by permission of the author and the author's agents, the Virginia Kidd Agency, Inc.

Nodelman, Perry. "Liking and not liking fantasy." Online posting. 15 Nov. 1997. Childlit. <http://www.rci.rutgers.edu/~mjoseph/childlit/about.html>.

Dickens, Charles. From *Hard Times for these Times*. London: Bradbury & Evans, 1854.

Lorenzini, Carlo (Carlo Collodi). From *The Adventures of Pinocchio*. Trans. Nicolas J. Perella. Illus. Enrico Mazzanti. Berkeley: U of CA Press, 1986.

Stevenson, Robert Louis. "The Land of Counterpane," "My Shadow," "Foreign Children," "Foreign Lands," "The Unseen Playmate," "My Kingdom," "The Land of Story-Books," "The Flowers," "The Dumb Soldier." *A Child's Garden of Verses*. Illus. Jessie Willcox Smith. London: Longmans Green, 1885.

Baum, L. Frank. From *Father Goose, His Book*. Illus. W. W. Denslow. 1899. *A Treasury of the Great Children's Book Illustrators* by Susan E. Meyer. 1983. New York: Abrams, 1997. 256.

Baum, L. Frank. From *The Wonderful Wizard of Oz*. Illus. W. W. Denslow. New York: G. M. Hill, 1900.

Grahame, Kenneth. From *The Wind in the Willows*. London: Methuen, 1908.

Pages 92–112, unabridged from *Charlotte's Web* by E. B. White. Copyright © 1952 by E. B. White. Text copyright renewed 1980 by E. B. White. Used by permission of HarperCollins Publishers.

Extract from *Tom's Midnight Garden* by Philippa Pearce, by permission of Oxford University Press. 1958.

"Mrs. Whatsit," "Mrs. Who," and "Mrs. Which" from *A Wrinkle in Time* by Madeleine L'Engle. Copyright © 1962, renewed 1990 by Madeleine L'Engle. Reprinted by permission of Farrar, Straus and Giroux, LLC.

knoxville, tennessee by Nikki Giovanni. New York: Scholastic Inc. reprint edition copyright © 1994, by permission of author, Nikki Giovanni.

"Dolphin Dreaming" by Gillian Rubinstein from *Dream Time,* edited by Toss Gascoigne, Jo Goodman and Margot Tyrrell. Copyright © 1989 by Gillian Rubinstein. Collection Copyright © 1989 by the Children's Book Council of Australia. Reprinted by permission of Houghton Mifflin Company. All rights reserved.

Angelou, Maya. "I Love the Look of Words." *Soul Looks Back in Wonder.* Illus. Tom Feelings. New York: Dial, 1993. N.p.

PART 5. BOYS' BOOKS AND GIRLS' BOOKS: GENDER ISSUES

Segel, Elizabeth. "'As the Twig is Bent . . .': Gender and Childhood Reading." *Gender and Reading.* Eds. Elizabeth A. Flynn and Patrocinio P. Schweickart. Baltimore: Johns Hopkins UP, 1986. 165–86.

Bernikow, Louise. "Cinderella: Saturday Afternoon at the Movies." *Among Women.* New York: Harmony Books, 1980. 18–38.

Perrault, Charles. "Cinderella, or the Little Glass Slipper." 1697. Trans. Charles Welsh. Illus. D. J. Munro. Boston: Heath, 1901.

Grimm, Jacob and Wilhelm. "Ashputtle." Trans. Ralph Manheim. *Grimms' Tales for Young and Old: The Complete Stories.* New York: Doubleday, 1977.

"The Indian Cinderella." Retold by Cyrus MacMillan. *Canadian Wonder Tales.* 1920. *Best-Loved Folktales of the World.* Ed. Joanna Coles. New York: Anchor Doubleday, 1982. 694–96.

Hughes, Thomas. From *Tom Brown's School Days.* Cambridge, England: Macmillan, 1857.

Alcott, Louisa May. From *Little Women.* 1868–69. Illus. Frank T. Merrill. Boston: Roberts Brothers, 1880.

Twain, Mark. From *The Adventures of Tom Sawyer.* Hartford, CT: American Publishing Company, 1876.

Howells, William Dean. Rev. of *The Adventures of Tom Sawyer.* *Atlantic Monthly* May 1876. *My Mark Twain: Reminiscences and Criticisms.* Ed. Marilyn Austin Baldwin. Baton Rouge: Louisiana State UP, 1967.

Stevenson, Robert Louis. From *Treasure Island.* London: Cassell, 1883.

Burnett, Frances Hodgson. From *The Secret Garden.* New York: Grosset & Dunlap, 1911.

"'Quite Contrary': Frances Hodgson Burnett's *The Secret Garden*" by Elizabeth Lennox Keyser, from *Children's Literature* vol. 11 (1983), Francelia Butler, ed. Reprint permission granted by Yale University Press.

Millay, E. Vincent. "Friends." *St. Nicholas Magazine* May 1910: 660.

Montgomery, Lucy Maud. From *Emily of New Moon.* New York: Frederick A. Stokes, 1923.

Montgomery, Lucy Maud. From *Emily's Quest.* New York: Frederick A. Stokes, 1927.

McFarlane, Leslie. "A Little Ghostly History." *The Tower Treasure* by Franklin W. Dixon. New York: Penguin Putnam Books for Young Readers, 1991.

Chapter 1, "The Speed Demon" and chapter 2, "The Stolen Roadster" from *The Tower Treasure* by Franklin W. Dixon. Reprinted with the permission of Pocket Books, a Division of Simon & Schuster, Inc. from *The Tower Treasure* by Franklin W. Dixon. Copyright © 1927, 1959 by Simon & Schuster. The *Hardy Boys* is a registered trademark of Simon & Schuster Inc.

Paretsky, Sara. "Keeping Nancy Drew Alive." *The Secret of the Old Clock.* New York: Penguin Putnam Books for Young Readers, 1991.

Keene, Carolyn. From *The Secret of the Old Clock.* 1930. New York: Penguin Putnam Books for Young Readers, 1991.

Text from chapters 6, 7, and 8 from *The Man Without a Face* by Isabelle Holland. Copyright © 1972 by Isabelle Holland. Used by permission of HarperCollins Publishers.

Paterson, Katherine. From *Jacob Have I Loved.* New York: Avon, 1980.

Naylor, Phyllis Reynolds. From *The Year of the Gopher.* New York: Atheneum, 1987.

"The World's Greatest Dinosaur War Ever." From *The Watsons Go to Birmingham—1963* by Christopher Paul Curtis, copyright © 1995 by Christopher Paul Curtis. Used by permission of Random House Children's Books, a division of Random House, Inc.

Chapter 7: "The Boxing Match" from *Parrot in the Oven* by Victor Martinez. Text copyright 1996 by Victor Martinez. Used by permission of HarperCollins Publishers.

PART 6. WORDS AND PICTURES

Chapter 7: "The Relationship of Pictures and Words" from *Words about Pictures: The Narrative Art of Children's Picture Books* by Perry Nodelman, copyright © 1988 by the University of Georgia Press. Used by permission of the University of Georgia Press.

Sendak, Maurice. "Winsor McCay," "Randolph Caldecott." Caldecott & Co.: Notes on Books & Pictures. New York: Farrar, Straus & Giroux, 1990. 21–25, 77–85.

PART 7. SATIRES AND SPIN-OFFS: REWORKING CLASSIC CHILDREN'S LITERATURE

Gillispie, Julaine. "American Film Adaptations of *The Secret Garden.*" *The Lion and the Unicorn* 20:1 (1996), 132–152. © The Johns Hopkins University Press. Reprinted with permission of The Johns Hopkins University Press.

Winston, Joe. "Revising the Fairy Tale Through Magic: Antonia Barber's *The Enchanter's Daughter.*" *Children's Literature in Education* 25 (1994): 101–11.

The Enchanter's Daughter by Antonia Barber, pictures by Errol le Cain. Text copyright © 1987 by Antonia Barber. Reprinted by permission of Farrar, Straus and Giroux, LLC.

Snow White in New York by Fiona French (OUP, 1995), text and illustrations copyright © Fiona French 1986, reprinted by permission of Oxford University Press.

"'Will the Real Dragon Please Stand Up?' Convention & Parody in

Children's Stories," pp. 219–228 by Jon Stott. From *Children's Literature in Education* 21 (1990). Copyright © 1990 by Plenum Publishers. Used by permission of Plenum Publishers.

Nesbit, E. "The Last of the Dragons." *Five of Us—and Madeline.* London: E. Benn, 1925.

Prelutsky, Jack. "A Dragon's Lament," "My Dragon's Been Disconsolate," "My Dragon Wasn't Feeling Good," "Dragonbrag," "I Have a Secret Dragon," "If You Don't Believe in Dragons." *The Dragons Are Singing Tonight.* Illus. Peter Sis. New York: Greenwillow, 1993.

"Little Red Riding Hood." From *Roald Dahl's Revolting Rhymes* by Roald Dahl and Quentin Blake, illustrator, copyright © 1982 by Roald Dahl Nominee Limited. Illustrations copyright © 1982 by Quentin Blake. Used by permission of Alfred A. Knopf, an imprint of Random House Children's Books, a division of Random House, Inc.

"Twins" from *Tales from the Brothers Grimm and the Sisters Weird,* copyright © 1995 by Vivian Vande Velde, reprinted by permission of Harcourt, Inc.

"Juvenile Court" from *Story Hour* by Sarah Henderson Hay. Reprinted by permission of the University of Arkansas Press. Copyright © 1998 by Sarah Henderson Hay.

Block, Francesca Lia. "Weetzie Wants a Baby." *Weetzie Bat.* New York: Harper & Row, 1989.

Coville, Bruce. "Am I Blue?" *Am I Blue? Coming Out from the Silence.* Ed. Marion Dane Bauer. New York: HarperCollins, 1994.

"Toy-Based Videos for Girls: My Little Pony" from *Sold Separately: Parents and Children in Consumer Culture,* by Ellen Seiter, copyright © 1993 by Ellen Seiter. Reprinted by permission of Rutgers University Press.

"Boys Will Be Boys." From *Six Myths of Our Time* by Marina Warner, copyright © 1994 by Marina Warner. Used by permission of Vintage Books, a division of Random House, Inc.

PART 8. VALUES AND CENSORSHIP

"Teaching Banned Children's Books" by Mark I. West, from *Teaching Children's Literature* 51–58. Reprinted by permission of the Modern Language Association of America. Copyright © 1992 by the Modern Language Association of America.

Text from Chapter 12 (pp. 93–102) from *Forever* by Judy Blume. Reprinted with the permission of Atheneum Books for Young Readers, an imprint of Simon & Schuster Children's Publishing Division. Copyright © 1975 Judy Blume.

Rochman, Hazel, Masha Kabakow Rudman, and Diane Stanley. "Is That Book Politically Correct? Truth and Trends in Historical Literature for Young People." *Journal of Youth Services in Libraries* 7.2 (Winter 1994): 159–175.

Pp. 3–27 from *Should We Burn Babar? Essays on Children's Literature and the Power of Stories.* Copyright © 1995 *Should We Burn Babar? Essays on Children's Literature and the Power of Stories* by Herbert Kohl. Reprinted by permission of The New Press. <www.thenewpress.com>

Andersen, Hans Christian. "The Little Mermaid." *Hans Andersen's Fairy Tales.* Trans. H. P. Paull, 1872.

Hastings, A. Waller. Moral Simplification in Disney's *The Little Mermaid. The Lion and the Unicorn* 17:1 (1993), 83–92. © The Johns Hopkins University Press.

Twain, Mark. From *Adventures of Huckleberry Finn.* New York: Century Co., 1884.

Doctorow, E. L., and David Bradley. "Huck, Continued." *The New Yorker* 26 June and 3 July, 1995. 132–133.

Justus, May. *New Boy in School.* Illus. Joan Balfour Payne. New York: Hastings House, 1963.

Excerpt from *Nobody's Family Is Going to Change* by Louise Fitzhugh. Copyright © 1974 by Louise Fitzhugh. Reprinted by permission of Farrar, Straus and Giroux, LLC.

"Harassing Miss Harris" & "Homecoming" from *The Great Gilly Hopkins* by Katherine Paterson. Copyright © 1978 by Katherine Paterson. Used by permission of HarperCollins Publishers.

"Hope and Happy Endings," from *The Spying Heart* by Katherine Paterson, copyright © 1989 by Katherine Paterson. Used by permission of Lodestar Books, an affiliate of Dutton Children's Books, a division of Penguin Putnam, Inc.

"Night Passage" by Lee Harding, from *Dream Time,* edited by Toss Gascoigne, Jo Goodman and Margot Tyrrell. Copyright © 1989 by Lee Harding. Collection copyright © 1989 by the Children's Book Council of Australia. Reprinted by permission of Houghton Mifflin Company. All rights reserved.

Pages 132–46, 263–73 and 286–311; unabridged from *Little House on the Prairie* by Laura Ingalls Wilder. Text copyright © 1935, 1963, Little House Heritage Trust. Used by permission of HarperCollins Publishers.

Dorris, Michael. "Trusting the Words." *Booklist* 89.19/20 (1 & 15 June 1993): 1820–1822.

Erdrich, Louise. From *The Birchbark House.* New York: Hyperion, 1999. 5–50.

"Discovery and Recovery in Children's Novels by Native Writers" from *Native Americans in Children's Literature* by Jon Stott. Copyright © 1995 by Oryx Press. Reproduced with permission of Greenwood Publishing Group, Inc., Westport, CT.

"Emmett Till's Name Still Catches in My Throat" from *A Wreath for Emmett Till* by Marilyn Nelson. Text copyright © 2005 by Marilyn Nelson. Reprinted by permission of Houghton Mifflin Company. All rights reserved.

ART

PART 1. TO TEACH OR TO ENTERTAIN?

Gustave Doré. "Little Red Riding Hood." *Les Contes de Perrault, dessins par Gustave Dore.* Paris: J. Hetzel, 1867.

Abbott, Jacob *Rollo Learning to Talk.* New York: Sheldon, 1872. Illustrator unknown.

Carroll, Lewis. *Alice's Adventures in Wonderland.* Illus. John Tenniel. London: Macmillan, 1865.

Carroll, Lewis. *Through the Looking Glass.* Illus. John Tenniel. London: Macmillan, 1872.

Copyright © 1968 By Louis Darling. Used by permission of HarperCollins Publishers From *Ramona the Pest* by Beverly Cleary.

Hughes, Langston "Aunt Sue's Stories." *The Dream Keeper and Other Poems.* 1932. Illus. Brian Pinkney. New York: Knopf, 1994. 69.

Fitzhugh, Louise. *Harriet the Spy.* New York: Harper & Row, 1964.

PART 2. SUBJECTION OF THE CHILD OR SUBVERSION OF ADULT AUTHORITY?

Illustrations from *The Juniper Tree and Other Tales from Grimm* translated by Lore Segal and Randal Jarrell, pictures by Maurice Sendak. Translation copyright © 1973 by Lore Segal. Pictures copyright © by Maurice Sendak. Reprinted by permission of Farrar, Straus and Giroux, LLC. "The Frog King"

Andersen, Hans Christian. "The Emperor's New Clothes." *Fairy Tales by Hans Andersen.* Illus. Arthur Rackham. London: George G. Harrap, 1932.

Hoffmann, Heinrich. "The Sad Tale of the Match-Box." *Struwwelpeter OR Happy Tales and Funny Pictures, Freely Translated.* Trans. Mark Twain. New York: Marchbanks Press, 1935.

Aldrich, Thomas Bailey. From The *Story of a Bad Boy.* Illus. Edwin John Prittie. Philadelphia: John C. Winston, 1927.

Lindgren, Astrid. *Pippi Longstocking.* Trans. Florence Lamborn. Illus. Louis Glanzman. New York: Viking, 1950.

PART 3. ORAL AND WRITTEN LITERARY TRADITIONS

Rackham, Arthur. "Three Blind Mice." *Mother Goose Nursery Rhymes.* 1913. New York: Viking, 1975. 47.

Folkard, Charles. "Humpty Dumpty." *Illustrated Treasury of Children's Literature.* Ed. Margaret E. Martignoni. New York: Grossett and Dunlap, 1955. 27.

Rackham, Arthur. "Little Miss Muffet." *Mother Goose Nursery Rhymes.* 1913. New York: Viking, 1975. Facing p. 27.

Brooke, L. Leslie. "Wee Willie Winkie." *Ring O' Roses: A Nursery Rhyme Picture Book.* 1922. New York: Clarion, 1992. 89.

Greenaway, Kate. *A Apple Pie.* Engraved and printed by Edmund Evans. New York: Frederick Warne, [1886].

Illustration of cow on back legs, from *An Appalachian Mother Goose* by James Still, used by permission of Paul Brett Johnson. 1998.

Illustration of Jack and Jill, from *An Appalachian Mother Goose* by James Still, used by permission of Paul Brett Johnson. 1998.

Randolph Caldecott. *A Frog He Would A-Wooing Go.* Ed. Edmund Evans. London: Frederick Warne, n. d. Project Gutenberg EBook #14077.17 Nov. 2004. <http://www.gutenberg.org/dirs/1/4/0/7/14077/14077-h/14077-h.htm>.

Lear, Edward. "The Owl and the Pussy-cat." 1871. *The Oxford Treasury of Children's Poems.* Eds. Michael Harrison and Christopher Stuart-Clark. Oxford UP, 1988.

Lear, Edward. "The Broom, the Shovel, the Poker, and the Tongs." 1871. *Nonsense Poems.* New York: Dover, 1994.

Lear, Edward. "There Was an Old Man with a Beard," "There Was an Old Man of Bohemia," "There was a Young Lady Whose Nose." *A Book of Nonsense.* 1861. New York: Routledge, 2002.

Silverstein, Shel. "Zebra Question." *A Light in the Attic.* New York: HarperCollins, 1981. 125. Copyright © 2004 By Evil Eye Music, Inc. Used by permission of HarperCollins Publishers.

"Worrywart" illustration by William Steig from *Alpha Beta Chowder,* used by permission of Pippin Properties, Inc. 1992.

Geurber, H. A. "Daedalus and Icarus." *The Story of the Greeks.* Illus. Charles Stanley Reinhart. New York: American Book Company, 1896.

"The Crow and the Pitcher," "The Fox and the Grapes," "Hercules and the Carter." *The Fables of Aesop, and Others.* Illus. Thomas Bewick. Newcastle: E. Walker, 1818.

Crane, Walter. "The Wind and the Sun." *The Baby's Own Aesop, Being the Fables Condensed in Rhyme: With Portable Morals Pictorially Pointed.* Engraved and printed by Edmund Evans. London: Frederick Warne, 1887. London: Orion, 1996.

Jacobs, Joseph, ed. "Johnny-Cake." *English Fairy Tales.* Illus. John D. Batten. 1890. New York: Dover, 1967. 155.

Wolkstein, Diane. *The Magic Orange Tree.* Illus. Elsa Henriquez. New York: Knopf, 1978. 19.

Bilibin, Ivan. *Vasilissa the Beautiful.* Moscow: Dept. for the Production of State Documents, 1900.

Boyle, Eleanor Vere. *Beauty and the Beast: An Old Tale New-Told.* London: Sampson Low, Marston, Low, and Searle, 1875.

Grimm, Jakob and Wilhelm. "Snow-White and the Seven Dwarfs." *Household Stories from the Collection of the Brothers Grimm.* Trans. Lucy Crane. Illus. Walter Crane. London: Macmillan, 1882.

Jacobs, Joseph, ed. "The Laidly Worm of Spindleston Heugh." *English Fairy Tales.* Illus. John D. Batten. 1890. New York: Dover, 1967. 182.

Cruikshank, George, ed. and illus. *The History of Jack & the Bean-Stalk.* London: David Bogue, [1854].

McCreedy, Ken. Photograph. Jack Tale Players performing "Mutsmag" by R. Rex Stephenson. Ferrum College, Ferrum, VA. 17 May 2000.

PART 4. REALISM AND FANTASY

Dickens, Charles, *Hard Times for These Times* (British Household Edition). Illus. Harry French. London: Chapman and Hall, 1870.

Lorenzini, Carlo (Carlo Collodi). *The Adventures of Pinocchio.* Trans. Nicolas J. Perella. Illus. Enrico Mazzanti. Berkeley: U of CA Press, 1986.

Robert Louis Stevenson. "My Shadow." *A Child's Garden of Verses.* Illus. Jessie Willcox Smith. 1905. New York: Peter Possum Paperback/Mulberry, n. d. 18.

Baum, L. Frank. *Father Goose, His Book.* Illus. W. W. Denslow. 1899. *A Treasury of the Great Children's Book Illustrators* by Susan E. Meyer. 1983. New York: Abrams, 1997. 256.

Baum, L. Frank. *The Wonderful Wizard of Oz.* Illus. W. W. Denslow. 1900. Critical Heritage Series. New York: Schocken Books, 1983. 31, 26.

Grahame, Kenneth. *The Wind in the Willows.* Illus. E. H. Shepard. London: Methuen, 1931.

White, E. B. *Charlotte's Web,* 1952. Illus. Garth Williams. New York: Harper & Row, 1952. Illustrations copyright © renewed 1980 by Estate of Garth Williams. Used by permission of HarperCollins Publishers.

PART 5. BOYS' BOOKS AND GIRLS' BOOKS: GENDER ISSUES

Perrault, Charles. *Cinderella.* Illus. Roberto Innocenti. Mankato, MN: Creative Education, 1983.

Hughes, Thomas. *Tom Brown's School Days.* Illus. Arthur Hughes. Cambridge, England: Macmillan, 1857.

Alcott, Louisa May. *Little Women* Illus. Shirley Hughes. London: Puffin, 1953.

PART 6. WORDS AND PICTURES

McCay, Winsor. *Little Nemo in Slumberland. Caldecott & Co.: Notes on Books & Pictures* by Maurice Sendak. New York: Farrar, Straus & Giroux, 1988. 21–25.

Caldecott, Randolph. "Baby Bunting," "A Frog He Would A-Wooing Go." *Caldecott & Co.: Notes on Books & Pictures* by Maurice Sendak. New York: Farrar, Straus & Giroux, 1988.

Comenius, Johan Amos. "The Ship-wreck." *Orbis Sensualium Pictus.* London: John and Benj. Sprint, 1727.

Bewick, Thomas. "The Stag (or Red Deer)." *A General History of Quadrupeds.* Newcastle, 1790. "The Tawny Owl." *A History of British Birds, Volume I (On Land Birds).* Newcastle, 1797. "Boys at the River." *A History of British Birds. Volume II.* Newcastle, 1804.

Grimm, Jakob and Wilhelm. "Rapunzel." *Household Stories from the Collection of the Brothers Grimm.* Trans. Lucy Crane. Illus. Walter Crane. London: Macmillan, 1882.

Caldecott, Randolph. *Hey Diddle Diddle.* London: Routledge, 1882.

Caldecott, Randolph. *The Three Jovial Huntsmen.* London: Routledge, 1880.

Greenaway, Kate. "Poor Dickey's dead!," "Up you go, shuttlecocks, ever so high!" *Under the Window.* London, 1878.

Potter, Beatrix. *The Roly-Poly Pudding.* London: Frederic Warne, 1908.

Wanda Gág, *Snow White and the Seven Dwarfs* (University of Minnesota Press, 2004) 2 illustrations (p. 13: "She ran all day through woods and woods" and p. 32: "... witchery, she fashioned an apple . . . A very beautiful apple . . .")

Brown, Margaret Wise. *The Runaway Bunny.* Illus. Clement Hurd. 1942. Rev. ed. New York: Harper & Row, 1972. Illustrations copyright © 1972. By Edith T. Hurd, Clement Hurd, John Thacher Hurd, and George Hellyer. Used by permission of HarperCollins Publishers.

From *Blueberries for Sal* by Robert McCloskey, copyright 1948, renewed © 1976 by Robert McCloskey. Used by permission of Viking Penguin, A Division of Penguin Young Readers Group, A Member of Penguin Group (USA) Inc., 345 Hudson Street, New York, NY 10014. All rights reserved.

Hoban, Russell. *Bedtime for Frances.* Illus. Garth Williams. New York: Harper & Row, 1960. Illustrations Copyright © renewed 1980 by Estate of Garth Williams. Used by permission of HarperCollins Publishers.

White, E. B. *Charlotte's Web,* 1952. Illus. Garth Williams. New York: Harper & Row, 1952. Illustrations Copyright © renewed 1980 by Estate of Garth Williams. Used by permission of HarperCollins Publishers.

Illustrations from *The Juniper Tree and Other Tales from Grimm* translated by Lore Segal and Randall Jarrell, pictures by Maurice Sendak. Translation copyright © 1973 by Lore Segal. Pictures copyright © by Maurice Sendak. Reprinted by permission of Farrar, Straus and Giroux, LLC. "Hans My Hedgehog."

From *Frog Goes to Dinner* by Mercer Mayer, copyright © 1974 by Mercer Mayer. Used by permission of Dial Books for Young Readers, A Division of Penguin Young Readers Group, A Member of Penguin Group (USA) Inc., 345 Hudson Street, New York, NY 10014. All rights reserved.

From *Jambo Means Hello* by Muriel Feelings, illustrated by Tom Feelings, copyright © 1974 by Tom Feelings, illustrations. Used by permission of Dial Books for Young Readers, A Division of Penguin Young Readers Group, A Member of Penguin Group (USA) Inc., 345 Hudson Street, New York, NY 10014. All rights reserved.

Illustrations by Mitsumasa Anno. Copyright © 1974 by Fukuinkan-Shoten. Used by permission of HarperCollins Publishers. *Anno's Alphabet.*

From *Jane Wishing* by Tobi Tobias, illustrated by Trina Schart Hyman, copyright © 1977 by Trina Schart Hyman, illustrations. Used by permission of Viking Children's Books, A Division of Penguin Young Readers Group, A Member of Penguin Group (USA) Inc., 345 Hudson Street, New York, NY 10014. All rights reserved.

Illustrations from *The Z Was Zapped* by Chris Van Allsburg. Copyright © 1987 by Chris Van Allsburg. Reprinted by permission of Houghton Mifflin Company. All rights reserved.

PART 7. SATIRES AND SPIN-OFFS: REWORKING CLASSIC CHILDREN'S LITERATURE

Wilcox, Fred, dir. *The Secret Garden.* Screenplay by Frances Hodgson Burnett (novel) and Robert Ardrey. Perf. Margaret O'Brien, Dean Stockwell, Brian Roper. MGM, 1949.

Snow White in New York by Fiona French (OUP, 1995), text and illustrations copyright © Fiona French 1986, reprinted by permission of Oxford University Press.

"Little Red Riding Hood and the Wolf" by Quentin Blake, copyright © 1982 by Quentin Blake, from *Roald Dahl's Revolting Rhymes* by Roald Dahl and Quentin Blake, illustrator. Used by permission of Alfred A. Knopf, an imprint of Random House Children's Books, a division of Random House, Inc.

PART 8. VALUES AND CENSORSHIP

Leech, John. "The Little Mermaid" by Hans Christian Andersen. *Bentley's Miscellany,* Vol. XIX, January–June issues. London: Richard Bentley, 1846.

Justus, May. *New Boy in School.* Illus. Joan Balfour Payne. New York: Hastings House, 1963.

Wilder, Laura Ingalls. *Little House on the Prairie.* Illus. Garth Williams New York: HarperCollins, 1953.

Erdrich, Louise. *The Birchbark House.* New York: Hyperion, 1999.

INDEX

CPSIA information can be obtained at www.ICGtesting.com
Printed in the USA
BVOW060030180413

318394BV00004B/11/P